DogFriendly.com's

United States and Canada Dog Travel Guide
4th Edition

by
Tara Kain and Len Kain
DogFriendly.com, Inc.

DogFriendly.com's United States and Canada Dog Travel Guide
by Tara Kain and Len Kain

DogFriendly.com, Inc.
685 Placerville Drive, Ste 309
Placerville, CA 95667
1-877-475-2275
email: email@dogfriendly.com
http://www.dogfriendly.com

PLEASE NOTE
Although the authors and publisher have tried to make the information as accurate as possible, they do not
assume, and hereby disclaim, any liability for any loss or damage caused by errors, omissions, misleading
information or potential travel problems caused by this book, even if such errors or omissions result from
negligence, accident or any other cause.

CHECK AHEAD
We remind you, as always, to call ahead and confirm that the applicable establishment is still "dog-friendly" and that
it will accommodate your pet.

DOGS OF ALL SIZES
If your dog is over 75-80 pounds, then please call the individual establishment to make sure that they allow your
dog. Please be aware that establishments and local governments may also not allow particular breeds.

OTHER PARTIES DESCRIPTIONS
Some of the descriptions have been provided to us by our web site advertisers, paid researchers or other parties.

ISBN 13 - 978-0979555107
ISBN 10 - 0979555108

Printed in the United States of America

Photographs taken by Len Kain, Tara Kain and Jodi Kain

Cover Photographs (top to bottom, left to right):
Dog Park - Ontario, Canada
Fairmont Empress Hotel - Victoria, BC, Canada
Park Bench Cafe – Huntington Beach, CA
Oatman, AZ

Back Cover Photographs (top to bottom):
Grand Canyon, AZ
Beach – St Augustine, FL
Boston T Subway Station - Boston, MA
Welcome to Alaska Sign on the Alaska Highway

TABLE OF CONTENTS

2. Dog-Friendly Beaches 597
Beaches that allow dogs, most require leashes, some are off-leash, some have restricted hours or seasons.

3. Transportation 630
Policies for subways, buses, local air service, ferries and other transportation for you and your dog.

4. United States National Parks 648
What to see with your dogs and dog policies at the National Parks.

5. Dog-Friendly Attractions 656
Tourist sites, museums, boat tours, city tours, historical sites, amusement parks, cross-country skiing, shopping centers, wineries and other places that allow your dog.

6. Dog-Friendly Outdoor Dining 695
Restaurants and coffee shops with outdoor patios or tables that allow your dog to accompany you. In some establishments you pick up your own food and in others they serve you outdoors.

7. Off-Leash Dog Parks 734
Areas in parks that are authorized for off-leash playtime for your dog. Some are fenced, some are not fenced. Some may have restricted hours or other restrictions.

8. Emergency Veterinarians 752
Where to find emergency and off-hours pet medical care while traveling.

Introduction

DogFriendly.com's guides have helped millions of dog lovers plan vacations and trips with their dogs. The ultimate in Dog Travel Guides, our United States and Canada Dog Travel Guide includes dog-friendly lodging and attractions such as tours, historical places and more. Also included are restaurants with outdoor patio dining where your dog is welcome, national parks, information about the airlines, subways, buses and other transportation systems that permit dogs and emergency veterinarians just in case. Coupled with DogFriendly.com's Campground and Park Guide, which offers dog-friendly camping, parks, beaches and off-leash guides these two guides include everything you need to explore the entire U.S. and Canada with your dogs. The guide gives detailed pet policies for most places, including how many dogs may be allowed per room, weight limits, fees and other useful information. In many cases, toll-free numbers and websites are given. Also very importantly, our lodging guide focuses on those places that allow dogs of all sizes and do not restrict dogs to smoking rooms only. Not included in this guide are places that allow, for example, only dogs up to ten pounds or require that your dog be carried or in a carrier while on the premises. Also, we do not think that places that require dog owners to stay in smoking rooms are dog-friendly and we do not include them. Accommodations in this book have been called by DogFriendly.com to verify pet policies although these policies do change often. Thank you for selecting our pet travel guide and we hope you spend less time researching and more time actually going places with your dog. Enjoy your dog-friendly travels!

Coupled with DogFriendly.com's Campground and Park Guide, which offers dog-friendly camping, parks, beaches and off-leash area guides these two guide books include everything you need to explore the entire U.S. and Canada with your dogs. Both books are available at http://www.dogfriendly.com.

About Author Tara Kain

Tara Kain grew up with dogs and has always loved dogs. When she moved away from home, she discovered a whole new world through traveling. But whenever she traveled, the last thing she wanted was to leave her best friend behind. Tara often spent the whole time worrying about her pooch. So she began taking her dog. It was much tougher than she originally thought. Tara would spend several days researching and planning where her dog would be accepted and what else there was to do with her dog, aside from staying in a hotel room. Unfortunately, many places did not allow dogs, especially a large dog like her standard poodle. Many times when she found a supposedly "dog-friendly" hotel or motel, they would allow pets only in smoking rooms. In her opinion, because one travels with a dog should not limit them to a smoking room. So in June of 1998, she began to compile a list of dog-friendly places, notes and photos and began posting them on a web site called DogFriendly.com. This allowed her to easily keep track of the research and also help other dog lovers know about dog-friendly places. Today she still travels with her family, including the family dog. She is devoted to finding the best pet-friendly places and letting others know about them.

Tara has traveled over 200,000 miles across the United States and Canada with her dog. She serves as DogFriendly.com's President and editor-in-chief. She has written a number of magazine articles. Tara has been interviewed by numerous reporters about dog travel, dogs in the workplace and other issues concerning dogs in public places. Tara and her family reside in California, in the Sierra Nevada foothills near Sacramento.

About Author Len Kain

Len Kain began traveling with his dog when he was young. His family traveled with a camping trailer and brought along their standard poodle, Ricky. On trips, he found places and attractions that welcomed his best friend. When Len grew up and got his own dog, he continued the tradition of bringing his dog on trips with him. Len and his family have traveled over 200,000 miles across the country on road trips. Today he continues to travel and find fun and exciting dog-friendly places.

Currently, Len serves as DogFriendly.com's Vice President of Sales and Marketing. Len has been quoted numerous times in print, on radio and television about issues relating to traveling with dogs. Prior to joining DogFriendly.com Len served in various executive and management positions in several Silicon Valley and Internet Companies. Len holds a Bachelor of Engineering degree from Stevens Tech in New Jersey, a Master of Science degree from Stanford University and an MBA from the University of Phoenix. Len resides with his family in the Sierra Nevada foothills of California.

Your Comments and Feedback

We value and appreciate your feedback and comments. If you want to recommend a dog-friendly place or establishment, let us know. If you find a place that is no longer dog-friendly, allows small dogs only or allows dogs in smoking rooms only, please let us know. You can contact us using the following information.

Mailing Address and Contact Information:
DogFriendly.com, Inc.
685 Placerville Drive, Ste 309
Placerville, CA 95667 USA
Toll free phone: 1-877-475-2275
email: email@ dogfriendly.com
http://www.dogfriendly.com

How To Use This Guide

General Guidelines

1. Please only travel with a well-behaved dog that is comfortable around other people and especially children. Dogs should also be potty trained and not bark excessively.

2. Always keep your dog leashed unless management specifically tells you otherwise.

3. Establishments listed in this book should allow well-behaved dogs of ALL sizes (at least up to 75 pounds) and in non-smoking rooms. If your dog is over 75-80 pounds, then please call the individual establishment to make sure they will allow your dog. We have listed some establishments which only allow dogs up to 50 pounds, but we try our best to make a note in the comments about the restrictions. All restaurants and attractions we list should allow dogs of all sizes.

4. Accommodations listed do not allow dogs to be left alone in the room unless specified by hotel management. If the establishment does not allow pets to be left alone, try hiring a local pet sitter to watch your dog in the room.

5. All restaurants listed as dog-friendly refer to outdoor seating only. While dogs are not permitted to sit in a chair at a restaurant's outdoor dining table, they should be allowed to sit or lay next to your table. We do not list outdoor restaurants that require your dog to be tied outside of a fenced area (with you at the dining table on one side and your dog on the other side of the fence). In our opinion, those are not truly dog-friendly restaurants. Restaurants listed may have seasonal outdoor seating.

6. Pet policies and management change often, especially within the lodging and restaurant industries. Please always call ahead to make sure an establishment still exists and is still dog-friendly.

7. After purchasing your book, please visit http://www.dogfriendly.com/updates for FREE book updates. We will do our best to let you know which places may no longer be dog-friendly.

Preparation for a Road Trip

A Month Before

If you don't already have one, get a pet identification tag for your dog. It should have your dog's name, your name and phone number. Consider using a cell phone number, a home number and, if possible, the number of where you will be staying.

Get a first aid kit for your dog. It comes in very handy if you need to remove any ticks. The kits are usually available at a pet store, a veterinary office or on the Internet.

If you do not already have a dog harness for riding the car, consider purchasing one for your dog's and your own safety. A loose dog in the car can fly into the windshield, out of the car, or into you and injure you or cause you to lose control of the car. Dog harnesses are usually sold at pet stores or on the Internet.

Make a trip to the vet if necessary for the following:

- A current rabies tag for your dog's collar. Also get paperwork with proof of the rabies vaccine.
- Dogs can possibly get heartworm from mosquitoes in the mountains, rural areas or on hikes. Research or talk to your vet and ask him or her if the area you are traveling to has a high risk of heartworm disease. The vet may suggest placing your dog on a monthly heartworm preventative medicine.
- Consider using some type of flea preventative for your dog, preferably a natural remedy. This is out of courtesy for the dog-friendly hotels plus for the comfort of your pooch.
- Make sure your dog is in good health.

Several Days Before

Make sure you have enough dog food for the duration of the trip.

If your dog is on any medication, remember to bring it along.

Some dog owners will also purchase bottled water for the trip, because some dogs can get sick from drinking water they are not used to. Talk to your vet for more information.

The Day Before

Do not forget to review DogFriendly.com's Etiquette for the Traveling Dog!

Road Trip Day

Remember to pack all of your dog's necessities: food, water, dog dishes, leash, snacks and goodies, several favorite toys, brush, towels for dirty paws, plastic bags for cleaning up after your dog, doggie first aid kit, possibly dog booties if you are venturing to an especially cold or hot region, and bring any medicine your dog might be taking.

Before you head out, put on that doggie seat belt harness.

On The Road

Keep it cool and well ventilated in the car for your dog.

Stop at least every 2-3 hours so your dog can relieve him or herself. Also offer him or her water during the stops.

Never leave your pet alone in a parked car - even in the shade with the window cracked open. According to the Los Angeles SPCA, on a hot day, a car can heat up to 160 degrees in minutes, potentially causing your pet (or child) heat stroke, brain damage, and even death.

If your dog needs medical attention during your trip, check the yellow pages phone book in the area and look under Veterinarians. If you do not see an emergency vet listed, call any local vet even   during the evening hours and they can usually inform you of the closest emergency vet.

Etiquette for the Traveling Dog

So you have found the perfect getaway spot that allows dogs, but maybe you have never traveled with your dog. Or maybe you are a seasoned dog traveler. But do you know all of your doggie etiquette? Basic courtesy rules, like your dog should be leashed unless a place specifically allows your dog to be leash-free. And do you ask for a paper bowl or cup for your thirsty pooch at an outdoor restaurant instead of letting him or her drink from your water glass?

There are many do's and don'ts when traveling with your best friend. We encourage all dog owners to follow a basic code of doggie etiquette, so places will continue to allow and welcome our best friends. Unfortunately all it takes is one bad experience for an establishment to stop allowing dogs. Let's all try to be on our best behavior to keep and, heck, even encourage new places to allow our pooches.

Everywhere...

- Well-Behaved Dogs. Only travel or go around town with a well-behaved dog that is friendly to people and especially children. If your dog is not comfortable around other people, you might consider taking your dog to obedience classes or hiring a professional trainer. Your well-behaved dog should also be potty trained and not bark excessively in a hotel or other lodging room. We believe that dogs should be kept on leash. If a dog is on leash, he or she is easier to bring under control. Also, many establishments require that dogs be on leash and many people around you will feel more comfortable as well. And last, please never leave your dog alone in a hotel or other lodging room unless you have the approval from the establishment's management.

- Leashed Dogs. Please always keep your dog leashed, unless management specifically states otherwise. Most establishments (including lodging, outdoor restaurants, attractions, parks, beaches, stores and festivals) require that your dog be on leash. Plus most cities and counties have an official leash law that requires pets to be leashed at all times when not on your property. Keeping your dog on leash will also prevent any unwanted contact with other people that are afraid of dogs, people that do not appreciate strange dogs coming up to them, and even other dog owners who have a leashed dog. Even when on leash, do not let your pooch visit with other people or dogs unless welcomed. Keeping dogs on leash will also protect them from running into traffic, running away, or getting injured by wildlife or other dogs. Even the most well-behaved and trained dogs can be startled by something, especially in a new environment.

- Be Considerate. Always clean up after your dog. Pet stores sell pooper scooper bags. You can also buy sandwich bags from your local grocery store. They work quite well and are cheap!

At Hotels or Other Types of Lodging...

- Unless it is obvious, ask the hotel clerk if dogs are allowed in the hotel lobby. Also, because of health codes, dogs are usually not allowed into a lobby area while it is being used for serving food like continental breakfast. Dogs may be allowed into the area once there is no food being served, but check with management first.

- Never leave your dog alone in the hotel room without the permission of management. The number one reason hotel management does not allow dogs is because some people leave them in the room alone. Some dogs, no matter how well-trained, can cause damage, bark continuously or scare the housekeepers. Unless the hotel management allows it, please make sure your dog is never left alone in the room. If you need to leave your dog in the room, consider hiring a local pet sitter.

- While you are in the room with your dog, place the Do Not Disturb sign on the door or keep the deadbolt locked. Many housekeepers have been surprised or scared by dogs when entering a room.

- In general, do not let your pet on the bed or chairs, especially if your dog sheds easily and might leave pet hair on the furniture. Some very pet-friendly accommodations will actually give you a sheet to lay over the bed so your pet can join you. If your pet cannot resist coming hopping onto the furniture with you, bring your own sheet.

- When your dog needs to go to the bathroom, take him or her away from the hotel rooms and the bushes located right next to the rooms. Try to find some dirt or bushes near the parking lot. Some hotels have a designated pet walk area.

At Outdoor Restaurants...

- Tie your dog to your chair, not the table (unless the table is secured to the ground). If your dog decides to get up and move away from the table, he or she will not take the entire table.

- If you want to give your dog some water, please ask the waiter/waitress to bring a paper cup or bowl of water for your dog. Do not use your own water glass. Many restaurants and even other guests frown upon this.

- Your pooch should lay or sit next to your table. At restaurants, dogs are not allowed to sit on the chairs or tables, or eat off the tables. This type of activity could make a restaurant owner or manager ban dogs. And do not let your pooch beg from other customers. Unfortunately, not everyone loves dogs!

- About Restaurant Laws regarding dogs at restaurants
State health codes in the United States prohibit all animals except for service animals inside indoor sections of restaurants. In recent years some health departments have begun banning dogs from some outdoor restaurant areas. It is complicated to determine where dogs are and are not allowed outdoors because most State laws are vague. They state something such as "Animals are not allowed on the premises of a food establishment". These laws also define animals to include "birds, vermin and insects" which are always present at outdoor restaurants. Various health departments have various interpretations of where the premises start and stop. Some allow dogs at outdoor areas where food is served, some allow dogs at outdoor areas only where you bring your own food to the table. Some will allow special pet-friendly areas or will allow dogs on the outside of the outer most tables. Any city or county can issue a variance to State law if it wants to allow dogs into outdoor (or indoor) restaurants. This can be done in two ways, directly by the local health department or through a vote of the local government. If a restaurant that you are visiting with your dog cites some curious requirement it is probably due to the health code. Please also understand that in all places the owner of a restaurant has the choice to not allow dogs with the exception of service dogs. Nationally, Austin, Dallas, Orlando, Chicago, Denver and Alexandria forced law changes to allow dogs at outdoor restaurants when their health departments went too far in banning dogs from outdoor seats. Dogs are now allowed in outdoor areas in these cities through variances (or in Orlando's case) changing Florida state law. For up to date information please see http://www.dogfriendly.com/dining . The laws are in a state of flux at the moment so please understand that they may change.

At Retail Stores...

- Keep a close eye on your dog and make sure he or she does not go to the bathroom in the store. Store owners that allow dogs inside assume that responsible dog owners will be entering their store. Before entering a dog-friendly store, visit your local pet store first. They are by far the most forgiving. If your dog does not go to the bathroom there, then you are off to a great start! If your dog does make a mistake in any store, clean it up. Ask the store clerk for paper towels or something similar so you can clean up any mess.

- In most states dogs are allowed in stores, shops and other private buildings with the exception of grocery stores and restaurants. The decision to allow dogs is the business owner's and you can always ask if you may bring your dog inside. Also in most states packaged foods (bottled sodas, waters, bags of cookies or boxes of snacks) does not cause a store to be classified as a grocery. Even pet stores do sell these items . In many states, drinks such as coffee, tea and water are also allowed. You can order food from a restaurant to a pet-friendly establishment (so long as the establishment is not also the restaurant with the kitchen) in most areas.

At Festivals and Outdoor Events...

Make sure your dog has relieved himself or herself before entering a festival or event area. The number one reason that most festival coordinators do not allow dogs is because some dogs go to the bathroom on a vendor's booth or in areas where people might sit.

Breed Specific Laws and the Effect of These Laws on Travel With Dogs

There has been a trend in cities, counties, states and provinces towards what is known as Breed-Specific Laws (BSL) in which a municipality bans or restricts the freedoms of dog owners with specific breeds of dogs. These laws vary from place to place and are effecting a greater number of dog owners every year. Most people may think that these laws effect only the "Pit Bull" but this is not always the case. Although the majority of dogs effected are pit-bulls other breeds of dogs as well as mixed breeds that include targeted breeds are also named in the various laws in North America. These laws range from registration requirements and leash or muzzle requirements to extreme laws in which the breed is banned from the municipality outright. Some places may even be permitted to confiscate a visitor's dog who unknowingly enters the region with a banned breed.

As of August 29, 2005 the province of Ontario, Canada (including Toronto, Niagara Falls, and Ottawa) passed a very broad breed-specific law banning Pit Bulls and "similar" dogs from the province. The law allows for confiscation of visiting dogs as well as dogs living in Ontario. It is extremely important that people visiting Ontario make sure that they are able to prove that their dog is not a Pit Bull with other documentation. Various cities throughout the U.S. and Canada have muzzle requirements for Pit Bulls and other restrictions on targeted breeds as well. Breed-specific laws do get repealed as well. In October, 2005 the city of Vancouver, BC removed its requirement that Pit Bulls be muzzled in public and now only requires dogs with a known history of aggressiveness to be muzzled.

The breed specific laws usually effect pit bull type dogs but are often vaguely written and may also effect mixed breed dogs that resemble the targeted breeds. These laws are always changing and can be passed by cities, counties and even states and provinces. We recommend that travelers with dogs check into whether they are effected by such laws. You may check www.DogFriendly.com/bsl for links to further information on BSL.

DogFriendly.com does not support breed-specific laws. Most people who take their dogs out in public are responsible and those that choose to train a dog to be viscous will simply choose another breed, causing other breeds to be banned or regulated in the future.

Customs Information for Traveling Between the United States and Canada

If you will be traveling between the United States and Canada, identification for Customs and Immigration is required. U.S. and Canadian citizens traveling across the border need the following:

People

- A passport or passport card is now required to move between the U.S. and Canada. This is a new policy so be sure to have your passport with you. Children also need a passport of their own now.

Dogs

- Dogs must be free of evidence of diseases communicable to humans when possibly examined at the port of entry.

- Valid rabies vaccination certificate (including an expiration date usually up to 3 years from the actual vaccine date and a veterinarian's signature). If no expiration date is specified on the certificate, then the certificate is acceptable if the date of the vaccination is not more than 12 months before the date of arrival. The certificate must show that the dog had the rabies vaccine at least 30 days prior to entry.

- Young puppies must be confined at a place of the owner's choosing until they are three months old, then they must be vaccinated. They must remain in confinement for 30 days after the vaccination.

Chain Hotel Websites

Best Western: bestwestern.com	Candlewood Suites: ichotelsgroup.com	Clarion: choicehotels.com
Comfort Inn: choicehotels.com	Days Inn: daysinn.com	Drury Inn: druryhotels.com
Extended Stay: extendedstayhotels.com	Hilton: hilton.com	Holiday Inn: ichotelsgroup.com
Howard Johnson: hojo.com	Kimpton Group: kimptonhotels.com	La Quinta: lq.com
Loews Hotels: loewshotels.com	Marriott: marriott.com	Motel 6: motel6.com
Quality Inn: www.choicehotels.com	Red Roof Inn: redroof.com	Residence Inn: residenceinn.com
Sheraton: starwoodhotels.com	Sleep Inn: choicehotels.com	Staybridge Suites: ichotelsgroup.com
Super 8: super8.com	Townplace Suites: towneplaceSuites.com	Westin: starwoodhotels.com

Traveling with a Dog By Air

Many commercial airlines allow dogs to be transported with the traveling public. Small dogs, usually no more than 15 pounds and with shorter legs, may travel in a carrier in the cabin with you. They must usually be kept under the seat. Any larger dogs must travel in a kennel in the cargo hold. It can be difficult for dogs to travel in the cargo hold of airplanes. Most airlines restrict cargo hold pet transportation during very hot and cold periods. Most require that you notify them when making reservations about the pet as they limit the number of pets allowed on each plane and the size of the carriers may vary depending on what type of plane is being used. There are no commercial airlines that we are aware of today that will allow dogs larger than those that fit in a carrier under a seat to fly in the cabin. Service animals are allowed in the cabin and are harnessed during takeoff and landing. The FAA is now tracking pet injury and death information from airline cargo section pet travel. Their monthly reports are at the website airconsumer.ost.dot.gov/reports. In the past few years, a couple of options have emerged for those people who want to transport dogs in the cabin that can't fit in the small carriers required to fit under airline seats.

Pet Airways:

Pet Airways, which began flying in July, 2009 is a pet-only airline with service to a number of North American destinations. You drop you dog off at their lounge in one city and pick them up in another. Dogs fly in the cabin, regardless of their size, and there is a veterinarian assistant on each flight as an attendent. You need to fly on another airline and meet your dog in the destination city. At the time this book went to print the cities served are Los Angeles, Denver, Phoenix, Chicago, Omaha, Atlanta, Washington, New York and Fort Lauderdale. More cities are being added. Phone: 888-738-2479 Website: petairways.com

Charters and Shared Charters:

A charter airline flight is a flight reserved by an individual, a company or a small party or club to transport in smaller jets or other small aircraft their group on a schedule and route selected by them. This option is always available to people traveling with dogs but is very expensive. A charter is a flight reserved by you. A shared charter is when you "hitch" a ride on a charter set up by another party. This is still quite expensive, but less so than a solo charter. Many charter aircraft will allow your dog of all sizes on board.

Commercial Airlines:

Airline	Cabin – Small Dogs Allowed	Cargo – Dogs Allowed	Phone	Fees (US) (each way)	General Information (For more updated information see: dogfriendly.com/airlines)
Air Canada	Yes	Yes	888-247-2262 (US)	$50 each way (cabin) - $105 each way (cargo) - North America $270 Elsewhere	Pets are again allowed on domestic Canadian/North American flights; Health Cert rqd plus some shots
Alaska Air / Horizon Air	Yes	Yes	800-252-7522	$100 each way (cabin), $100 each way (cargo)	Pets not allowed as Chked Bags during winter months; Health Cert within 30 days; Not allowed to Hawaii, or in cargo to Reno,NV.
America West/ US Airways	Yes	No	800-428-4322	$80.00	The in-cabin weight limit is 20 pounds including the kennel that must be able to fit under the seat. Only 3 pets can be on board at one time, so advance reservations are advised. They are not allowed as cargo on certain International flights.
American	Yes	Yes	800-433-7300	$100 each way (cabin), $150 each way (cargo)	Dogs, including the kennel, can weigh no more than 100 pounds for the cargo area. Dogs are not allowed in the cabin for International flights. Dogs are not allowed to be flown to the UK , and there are no dogs allowed in the cabin on flights to Hawaii .
Continental	Yes	Yes	Live animal desk - 800-575-3335 reserv 800-525-0280	$125 each way (cabin), from $149 - $369 (cargo)	Live animal desk - 800-575-3335 ; Up to 10 lbs in cabin
Delta	Yes	Yes	800-221-1212	$100 each way (cabin), $175 each way domestic $230 each way Int'l (cargo)	Only a limited # of pets allowed per flight, so check ahead. There is no cert required for domestic flights.
Frontier	No	Yes	800-432-1359	$100 each way small/ medium kennels, $200 each way larger kennels	Dogs may not be transported in the cabins, and some weather restrictions still apply to some cities as there is a certain amount of waiting time where they must be out in the open.
Jet Blue	Yes	No	800-538-2583	$100 each way (cabin only)	4 pets allowed per flight; 20 lbs or less (with kennel) in cabin
Northwest	Yes	Yes	800-225-2525	$80 Cabin $139+ Cargo	No pets to Hawaii, or the UK; A 10 day health certificate is required for International Flights; there is no cert required for domestic flights. The weight limit is 15 pounds including the kennel.
Southwest	Yes	No	800-IFLY-SWA	$75 each way (cabin only)	Dogs in cabin must fit in a carrier under the seat. Reservations with pets must be made by phone.
United	Yes	Yes	800-241-6522	$250 each way (cabin), $207 to 1,291 each way (cargo)	800-825-3788 to ship unaccompanied pets; Pets must be booked within 7 days of flight; 30 day health certificate; Short nosed dogs not allowed in summer

* We do not recommend that dogs travel in the cargo hold of airplanes unless it is absolutely necessary. Temperatures can range from freezing to sweltering and there can be delays on the runways, at the gates and elsewhere. These varying conditions can cause injury or even death to a pet.

Chapter 1

Dog-Friendly Lodging

United States

Alabama

Candlewood Suites Alabaster
1004 Balmoral Drive
Alabaster, AL
205-620-0188 (877-270-6405)
Dogs up to 80 pounds are allowed.
Pets allowed with an additional pet
fee. Up to $75 for 1-6 nights and up
to $150 for 7+ nights. A pet
agreement must be signed at check-
in.

Comfort Inn
2945 Hwy 280
Alexander City, AL
256-234-5900 (877-424-6423)
Dogs of all sizes are allowed. Dogs
are allowed for a pet fee of $15.00
per pet per night.

Days Inn Andalusia
1604 Dr.MLK Jr.Exprsway Hwy84E
Andalusia, AL
334-427-0050 (800-329-7466)
Dogs of all sizes are allowed. Dogs
are allowed for a pet fee.

Econo Lodge
1421 MLK Jr. Expressway
Andalusia, AL
334-222-7511 (877-424-6423)
Dogs of all sizes are allowed. Dogs
are allowed for a pet fee of $10.00
per pet per night.

Best Western Athens Inn
1329 US Highway 72 E
Athens, AL
256-233-4030 (800-780-7234)
Dogs of all sizes are allowed. Dogs
are allowed for a nightly pet fee.

Comfort Inn
1218 Kelli Dr.
Athens, AL
256-232-2704 (877-424-6423)
Dogs of all sizes are allowed. Dogs
are allowed for a pet fee of $30.00
per pet per night. Three or more
dogs may be allowed.

Sleep Inn
1115 Audubon Lane
Athens, AL
256-232-4700 (877-424-6423)
Dogs of all sizes are allowed. Dogs
are allowed for a pet fee of $10.00
per pet per night.

Super 8 Athens
1325 Hwy 72 East
Athens, AL

256-233-1446 (800-800-8000)
Dogs are welcome at this hotel.

Days Inn Attalla
801 Cleveland Avenue
Attalla, AL
256-538-7861 (800-329-7466)
Dogs are welcome at this hotel.

Econo Lodge
915 E 5th Avenue
Attalla, AL
256-570-0117 (877-424-6423)
Dogs of all sizes are allowed. Dogs
are allowed for a pet fee of $10.00
per pet per night.

Travelodge Attalla
901 Cleveland Avenue
Attalla, AL
256-538-4003 (800-578-7878)
Dogs of all sizes are allowed. Dogs
are allowed for a pet fee of $15.00
per pet per night.

Econo Lodge
2145 South College St.
Auburn, AL
334-826-8900 (877-424-6423)
Dogs of all sizes are allowed.

The Hotel at Auburn University
241 South College Street
Auburn, AL
334-821-8200 (800-228-2876)
Dogs of all sizes are allowed at this
luxury campus hotel at Auburn
University. There is a $250 fully
refundable deposit for pets.

Best Western Hotel & Suites
5041 Academy Ln
Bessemer, AL
205-481-1950 (800-780-7234)
Dogs of all sizes are allowed. Dogs
are allowed for a pet fee of $15.00
per pet per night.

Motel 6 - Birmingham Bessemer
1000 Shiloh Ln
Bessemer, AL
205-426-9646 (800-466-8356)
This motel welcomes your pets to
stay with you.

Baymont Inn & Suites /Vestavia
Birmingham
1466 Montgomery Highway
Birmingham, AL
205-822-2224 (877-229-6668)
Dogs are welcome at this hotel.

Best Western Mountain Brook
4627 Highway 280 S
Birmingham, AL
205-991-9977 (800-780-7234)
Dogs of all sizes are allowed. Dogs

are allowed for a pet fee of $20.00
per pet per night.

Candlewood Suites Birmingham
600 Corporate Ridge Drive
Birmingham, AL
205-991-0272 (877-270-6405)
Dogs up to 80 pounds are allowed.
Pets allowed with an additional pet
fee. Up to $75 for 1-6 nights and up
to $150 for 7+ nights. A pet
agreement must be signed at check-
in.

Days Inn AL Birmingham
905 11th Court W
Birmingham, AL
205-324-4510 (800-329-7466)
Dogs are welcome at this hotel.

Days Inn Galleria- Birmingham
1800 Riverchase Drive
Birmingham, AL
205-985-7500 (800-329-7466)
Dogs of all sizes are allowed. Dogs
are allowed for a pet fee of $25.00
per pet per stay.

Embassy Suites
2300 Woodcrest Place
Birmingham, AL
205-879-7400 (800-EMBASSY (362-
2779))
A luxury, full service, all suite hotel;
they offer a number of on site
amenities for business and leisure
travelers, plus a convenient location
to business, shopping, dining, and
entertainment districts. They also
offer a complimentary cooked-to-
order breakfast and a Manager's
reception every evening. Dogs are
allowed for an additional fee of $35
per night per pet. Multiple dogs may
be allowed.

Homestead Studio Suites
Birmingham - Perimeter Park South
12 Perimeter Park S.
Birmingham, AL
205-967-3800 (800-804-3724)
One dog is allowed per suite. There
is a $25 per night additional pet fee
up to $150 for an entire stay.

La Quinta Inn Birmingham
513 Cahaba Park Circle
Birmingham, AL
205-995-9990 (800-531-5900)
Dogs of all sizes are allowed. There
are no additional pet fees. Dogs may
not be left unattended, and they must
be leashed and cleaned up after.
Dogs are not allowed in the food
areas. Multiple dogs may be allowed.

Motel 6 - Birmingham

151 Vulcan Rd
Birmingham, AL
205-942-9414 (800-466-8356)
This motel welcomes your pets to
stay with you.

Quality Inn
1485 Montgomery Hwy.
Birmingham, AL
205-823-4300 (877-424-6423)
Dogs up to 50 pounds are allowed.
Dogs are allowed for a pet fee of
$15 per pet per night. Two dogs are
allowed per room.

Residence Inn Birmingham
Homewood
50 State Farm Parkway
Birmingham, AL
205-943-0044 (800-331-3131)
Some of the amenities at this all-
suite inn include a close location to
downtown, a daily buffet breakfast
and Manager's reception Monday
through Thursday, a swimming pool,
and a complimentary grocery
shopping service. Dogs are allowed
for an additional one time pet fee of
$75 per room. Multiple dogs may be
allowed.

Residence Inn Birmingham
Inverness
3 Greenhill Parkway
Birmingham, AL
205-991-8686 (800-331-3131)
Some of the amenities at this all-
suite inn include a daily buffet
breakfast, a Manager's reception
Monday through Thursday, a heated
swimming pool, and complimentary
grocery shopping. Dogs are allowed
for an additional one time pet fee of
$100 per room. Multiple dogs may
be allowed.

Sheraton Birmingham Hotel
2101 Richard Arrington Jr. Blvd.
North
Birmingham, AL
205-324-5000 (888-625-5144)
Dogs up to 70 pounds are allowed.
There are no additional pet fees.
Dogs are not allowed to be left alone
in the room.

TownePlace Suites Birmingham
Homewood
500 Wildwood Circle
Birmingham, AL
205-943-0114 (800-257-3000)
Situated near the University of
Alabama, the Broodwood Mall,
Discovery 2000, and numerous other
sites of interest, shopping, dining,
and entertainment areas, this all
suite inn also offers a number of in-
house amenities for all level of

travelers. Dogs are allowed for an
additional one time fee of $75 per
room. Multiple dogs may be allowed.

Days Inn Calera
11691 Hwy 25
Calera, AL
205-668-0560 (800-329-7466)
Dogs are welcome at this hotel.

Holiday Inn Express Calera-I-65 Exit
231
357 Hwy 304
Calera, AL
205-668-3641 (877-270-6405)
Dogs of all sizes are allowed. Dogs
are allowed for a pet fee of $20.00
per pet per night.

Days Inn Of Centre
1585 West Main Street
Centre, AL
256-927-1090 (800-329-7466)
Dogs of all sizes are allowed. Dogs
are allowed for a nightly pet fee.

Days Inn Childersburg
33669 US Hwy 280
Childersburg, AL
256-378-6007 (800-329-7466)
Dogs of all sizes are allowed. Dogs
are allowed for a pet fee.

Best Western Inn
801 Bradberry Ln
Clanton, AL
205-280-1006 (800-780-7234)
Dogs of all sizes are allowed. Dogs
are allowed for a nightly pet fee.

Days Inn
2000 Big M Blvd
Clanton, AL
205-755-2420 (800-329-7466)
Dogs are welcome at this hotel.

Howard Johnson Inn - Collinsville
5370 Alabama Hwy 68
Collinsville, AL
256-524-2114 (800-446-4656)
Dogs are welcome at this hotel.
There is a $10 daily pet fee.

Days Inn Cullman
1841 4th St SW
Cullman, AL
256-739-3800 (800-329-7466)
Dogs are welcome at this hotel.

Econo Lodge
1655 County Road 437
Cullman, AL
256-734-2691 (877-424-6423)
Dogs of all sizes are allowed. Dogs
are allowed for a pet fee of $10.00
per pet per night.

Sleep Inn & Suites
2050 Old Hwy 157
Cullman, AL
256-734-6166 (877-424-6423)
Dogs of all sizes are allowed.

Super 8 Cullman
6349 Al Hwy 157
Cullman, AL
256-734-8854 (800-800-8000)
Dogs are welcome at this hotel.

Econo Lodge Inn & Suites Fort
Rucker
444 N. Daleville Ave.
Daleville, AL
334-598-6304 (877-424-6423)
Dogs of all sizes are allowed. Dogs
are allowed for a pet fee of $25.00
per pet per stay. Two dogs are
allowed per room.

Best Western River City Hotel
1305 Front Avenue SW
Decatur, AL
256-301-1388 (800-780-7234)
Dogs of all sizes are allowed. Dogs
are allowed for a pet fee.

Comfort Inn & Suites
2212 Danville Road SW
Decatur, AL
256-355-1999 (877-424-6423)
Dogs of all sizes are allowed. Dogs
are allowed for a pet fee of $10.00
per pet per night.

Holiday Inn Hotel & Suites Decatur
1101 6th Ave Northeast
Decatur, AL
256-355-3150 (877-270-6405)
Dogs of all sizes are allowed. Dogs
are allowed for a pet fee of $15.00
per pet per stay.

La Quinta Inn Decatur
918 Beltline Road SW
Decatur, AL
356-355-9977 (800-531-5900)
Dogs of all sizes are allowed. There
are no additional pet fees. Dogs
must be leashed, cleaned up after,
and crated when left alone in the
room. Multiple dogs may be allowed.

Motel 6 - Decatur
810 6th Ave Ne
Decatur, AL
256-308-0312 (800-466-8356)
This motel welcomes your pets to
stay with you.

Super 8 Priceville Decatur
70 Marco Drive
Decatur, AL
256-355-2525 (800-800-8000)
Dogs of all sizes are allowed. Dogs

are allowed for a pet fee of $5.00 per pet per stay.

Days Inn Demopolis
1005 US Hwy 80 East
Demopolis, AL
334-289-2500 (800-329-7466)
Dogs of all sizes are allowed. Dogs are allowed for a pet fee.

Days Inn Dothan
3071 Ross Clark Circle
Dothan, AL
334-671-3700 (800-329-7466)
Dogs are welcome at this hotel.

Howard Johnson Inn Dothan
2244 Ross Clark Circle
Dothan, AL
334-792-3339 (800-446-4656)
Dogs are welcome at this hotel.

Knights Inn Dothan
2841 Ross Clark Circle SW
Dothan, AL
334-793-2550 (800-843-5644)
Dogs of all sizes are allowed. Dogs are allowed for a pet fee of $10.00 per pet per night.

Motel 6 - Dothan
2907 Ross Clark Cir Sw
Dothan, AL
334-793-6013 (800-466-8356)
This motel welcomes your pets to stay with you.

Residence Inn Dothan
186 Hospitality Lane
Dothan, AL
334-793-1030 (800-331-3131)
Offering a central location to all that southern Alabama and the Panhandle area of Florida has to present, this all suite inn also offers a daily buffet breakfast, free evening socials, and occasional barbecues - plus they are in walking distance to the new Dothan Pavilion Plaza and all the shopping, dining, and entertainment venues there. Dogs are allowed for an additional one time pet fee of $100 per room. 2 dogs may be allowed.

Comfort Inn
615 Boll Weevil Circle
Enterprise, AL
334-393-2304 (877-424-6423)
Dogs up to 75 pounds are allowed. Dogs are allowed for a pet fee of $25.00 per pet per stay.

Days Inn Enterprise
714 Boll Weevil Circle
Enterprise, AL
334-393-3297 (800-329-7466)

Dogs are welcome at this hotel.

Comfort Suites
12 Paul Lee Pkwy
Eufaula, AL
334-616-0114 (877-424-6423)
Dogs of all sizes are allowed. Dogs are allowed for a pet fee of $25.00 per pet per night.

Days Inn AL Eufaula
1521 South Eufaula Avenue
Eufaula, AL
334-687-1000 (800-329-7466)
Dogs are welcome at this hotel.

Quality Inn & Suites
631 East Barbour Street
Eufaula, AL
334-687-4414 (877-424-6423)
Dogs of all sizes are allowed. Dogs are allowed for a pet fee of $10.00 per pet per night. Three or more dogs may be allowed.

Comfort Inn
1571 Ted Bates Road
Evergreen, AL
251-578-4701 (877-424-6423)
Dogs of all sizes are allowed. Dogs are allowed for a pet fee of $10.00/ per pet per stay.

Days Inn Evergreen
215 Highway 83
Evergreen, AL
251-578-2100 (800-329-7466)
Dogs of all sizes are allowed. Dogs are allowed for a nightly pet fee.

Comfort Inn
6400 Kelco Place
Fairfield, AL
205-780-5155 (877-424-6423)
Dogs of all sizes are allowed. Dogs are allowed for a pet fee of $25.00 per pet per stay. Two dogs are allowed per room.

Holiday Inn Express Fairhope-Point Clear
19751 Greeno Rd.
Fairhope, AL
251-928-9191 (877-270-6405)
Dogs of all sizes are allowed. Dogs are allowed for a pet fee.

Oak Haven Cottages
355 S Mobile Street
Fairhope, AL
251-928-5431
oakhavencottages.net/
The Municipal Pier, a public beach, and downtown are only blocks from this motel resort. They offer 16 cottages and motel units and picnic areas. One dog is allowed per room

with advance reservations; there is an addition pet fee of $15 (plus tax) per night.

Knights Inn Florence
1915 Florence Blvd
Florence, AL
256-766-2620 (800-843-5644)
Dogs are welcome at this hotel.

Marriott Shoals Hotel & Spa
800 Cox Creek Parkway S
Florence, AL
256-246-3600 (800-593-6450)
This luxury resort hotel and golf refuge sits central to numerous businesses, shopping, dining, and day/night entertainment areas, plus they also offer a number of in-house amenities for business and leisure travelers. Dogs are allowed for an additional one time fee of $75 per room for 1 pet; there is an additional one time fee of $50 for each additional pet. Dogs must be crated when left alone in the room. Multiple dogs may be allowed.

Super 8 Florence
Hwy 72 and 43E
Florence, AL
256-757-2167 (800-800-8000)
Dogs of all sizes are allowed. Dogs are allowed for a pet fee of $10.00 per pet per stay.

Adam's Outdoors Cherokee Camp
6110 Cherokee County Road #103
Fort Payne, AL
256-845-2988
Dogs of all sizes are allowed. There are no additional pet fees.

Rodeway Inn
102 Drinkard Drive NW
Fort Payne, AL
256-845-2950 (877-424-6423)
Dogs of all sizes are allowed. Dogs are allowed for a pet fee of $10.00 per pet per night.

Days Inn Fultondale
616 Decatur Hwy
Fultondale, AL
205-849-0111 (800-329-7466)
Dogs of all sizes are allowed. Dogs are allowed for a pet fee of $6.00 per pet per night.

Holiday Inn Express Hotel & Suites Fultondale
1733 Fulton Rd
Fultondale, AL
205-439-6300 (877-270-6405)
Dogs up to 50 pounds are allowed. Dogs are allowed for a pet fee of $50.00 per pet per stay. Two dogs

are allowed per room.

Super 8 Birmingham Fultondale
North I-65 Ex 266 Hwy 31
Fultondale, AL
205-841-2200 (800-800-8000)
Dogs are welcome at this hotel.

Comfort Suites
96 Walker Street
Gadsden, AL
256-538-5770 (877-424-6423)
Dogs of all sizes are allowed.

Days Inn Gadsden
1612 West Grand Avenue
Gadsden, AL
256-442-7913 (800-329-7466)
Dogs of all sizes are allowed. Dogs
are allowed for a nightly pet fee.

Motel 6 - Gadsden
1600 Rainbow Dr
Gadsden, AL
256-543-1105 (800-466-8356)
Your pets are welcome to stay here
with you.

Rodeway Inn
3909 West Meighan Blvd
Gadsden, AL
256-543-0323 (877-424-6423)
Dogs of all sizes are allowed. Dogs
are allowed for a pet fee of $8.00/
per pet per night.

Comfort Inn
1029 Fort Dale Rd
Greenville, AL
334-383-9595 (877-424-6423)
Dogs of all sizes are allowed. Dogs
are allowed for a pet fee of $10.00/
per pet per night.

Days Inn Greenville
946 Fort Dale Rd
Greenville, AL
334-382-3118 (800-329-7466)
Dogs of all sizes are allowed. Dogs
are allowed for a pet fee.

Days Inn Gulf Shores
3049 W 1st Street
Gulf Shores, AL
251-968-8604 (800-329-7466)
Dogs of all sizes are allowed. Dogs
are allowed for a pet fee of $50 per
pet per stay.

Staybridge Suites Gulf Shores
3947 State Highway 59
Gulf Shores, AL
251-975-1030 (877-270-6405)
Dogs up to 80 pounds are allowed.
Pets allowed with an additional pet
fee. Up to $75 for 1-6 nights and up
to $150 for 7+ nights. A pet

agreement must be signed at
check-in.

Days Inn Guntersville
14040 US 431 South
Guntersville, AL
256-582-3200 (800-329-7466)
Dogs of all sizes are allowed. Dogs
are allowed for a nightly pet fee.

Holiday Inn Lake Guntersville
2140 Gunter Ave
Guntersville, AL
256-582-2220 (877-270-6405)
Dogs of all sizes are allowed. Dogs
are allowed for a pet fee of $50.00
per pet per stay.

Lake Guntersville State Park
Cottages and Chalets
7966 H 227
Guntersville, AL
256-571-5440 (800-548-4553)
Nestled along the shores of the
Tennessee River, this 6,000 acre
resort offers various
accommodations and a variety of
recreational amenities including a
large beach complex, hiking trails, a
day use area, an 18-hole
championship golf course, a fishing
center, nature programs, and more.
Dogs are allowed in 2 of the
lakeside cottages and 2 of the
chalets for an additional fee of $25
per day per pet; they are also
allowed in the campground for no
additional fee. Pets must be
declared at the time of reservations,
and they are not allowed in any
buildings or on the beaches. Dogs
must be kept leashed and cleaned
up after promptly. 2 dogs may be
allowed.

Days Inn Hamilton
1849 Military Street S.
Hamilton, AL
205-921-1790 (800-329-7466)
Dogs are welcome at this hotel.

Econo Lodge Inn & Suites
2031 Military Street South
Hamilton, AL
205-921-7831 (877-424-6423)
Dogs of all sizes are allowed. Dogs
are allowed for a pet fee of $10.00
per pet per night.

Super 8 Birmingham Area
Homewood
140 Vulcan Rd
Homewood, AL
205-945-9888 (800-800-8000)
Dogs of all sizes are allowed. Dogs
are allowed for a pet fee of $5.00
per pet per night.

Residence Inn Birmingham Hoover
2725 John Hawkins Parkway
Hoover, AL
205-733-1655 (800-331-3131)
Besides offering a convenient
location to business, shopping,
dining, and entertainment areas, this
hotel also provides a number of in-
house amenities, including a daily
buffet breakfast, and complementary
evening receptions. Dogs are
allowed for an additional one time
pet fee of $100 per room. Multiple
dogs may be allowed.

Candlewood Suites Huntsville
201 Exchange Place
Huntsville, AL
256-830-8222 (877-270-6405)
Dogs up to 80 pounds are allowed.
Pets allowed with an additional pet
fee. Up to $75 for 1-6 nights and up
to $150 for 7+ nights. A pet
agreement must be signed at check-
in.

Extended Stay America Huntsville -
U.S. Space and Rocket Center
4751 Governor's House Dr.
Huntsville, AL
256-830-9110 (800-804-3724)
One dog is allowed per suite. There
is a $25 per night additional pet fee
up to $150 for an entire stay.

Holiday Inn Huntsville Downtown
401 Williams Avenue
Huntsville, AL
256-533-1400 (877-270-6405)
Dogs of all sizes are allowed. Dogs
are allowed for a pet fee of $25.00
per pet per stay.

La Quinta Inn Huntsville Madison
Square Mall
4890 University Drive Nw
Huntsville, AL
256-830-8999 (800-531-5900)
Dogs of all sizes are allowed. There
are no additional pet fees. Please put
the "Do Not Disturb" sign on the door
when you are out and a dog is in the
room uncrated. Dogs must be
leashed at all times. Multiple dogs
may be allowed.

La Quinta Inn Huntsville Research
Park
4870 University Drive N.W.
Huntsville, AL
256-830-2070 (800-531-5900)
Dogs of all sizes are allowed. There
are no additional pet fees. Dogs
must be leashed and cleaned up
after. Arrangements need to be
made with housekeeping if more

than one day's stay. 2 dogs may be allowed.

La Quinta Inn Huntsville Space Center
3141 University Dr. N.W.
Huntsville, AL
256-533-0756 (800-531-5900)
Dogs of all sizes are allowed. There are no additional pet fees. Dogs must be quiet, well behaved, leashed, and cleaned up after. Multiple dogs may be allowed.

TownePlace Suites Huntsville
1125 McMurtrie Drive
Huntsville, AL
256-971-5277 (800-257-3000)
This all suite hotel sits central to a number of sites of interest for both business and leisure travelers; plus they also offer a number of on-site amenities to ensure comfort. Dogs are allowed for an additional one time fee of $100 per room. 2 dogs may be allowed.

Days Inn Lanett
2314 South Broad Ave.
Lanett, AL
334-644-2181 (800-329-7466)
Dogs are welcome at this hotel.

Days Inn Leeds
1838 Asheville Road
Leeds, AL
205-699-9833 (800-329-7466)
Dogs are welcome at this hotel.

Days Inn /Huntsville Airport/Space Center West Madison
102 Arlington Drive
Madison, AL
256-772-9550 (800-329-7466)
Dogs of all sizes are allowed. Dogs are allowed for a pet fee of $10 per pet per night.

Motel 6 - Huntsville Madison
8995 Madison Blvd
Madison, AL
256-772-7479 (800-466-8356)
Your pets are welcome to stay here with you.

Adam's Outdoors; Cherokee Camp and Yellow River Cottage
6110 H 103
Mentone, AL
256-845-2988
adamsoutdoors.com/cherokee.php
There are 2 separate seasonal camp areas for guests to explore: The Cherokee Camp area features 30 scenic acres, stunning views of the Shinbone Valley, a variety of recreational pursuits, and a large

solar powered lodge that can take up to 14 guests. The 2nd camp area-Yellow River, has a cottage that sits on 14 acres with a private dock at the confluence of the Yellow and Blackwater Rivers and the Blackwater Bay; it can sleep up to 6. Dogs are allowed at both sites for no additional fee. Dogs must be well behaved and under their owner's control at all times. 2 dogs may be allowed.

Best Western Battleship Inn
2701 Battleship Pkwy
Mobile, AL
251-432-2703 (800-780-7234)
Dogs are welcome at this hotel.

Extended Stay America Mobile - Spring Hill
508 Spring Hill Plaza Ct.
Mobile, AL
251-344-2514 (800-804-3724)
One dog is allowed per suite. There is a $25 per night additional pet fee up to $150 for an entire stay.

Howard Johnson Inn AL Mobile
3132 Government Blvd
Mobile, AL
251-471-2402 (800-446-4656)
Dogs of all sizes are allowed. Dogs are allowed for a pet fee.

La Quinta Inn Mobile
816 West I-65 Service Road South
Mobile, AL
251-343-4051 (800-531-5900)
Dogs of all sizes are allowed. There are no additional pet fees. Dogs must be leashed and cleaned up after. Please inform the front desk when leaving a dog alone in the room. Multiple dogs may be allowed.

Motel 6 - Mobile North
400 Beltline Hwy
Mobile, AL
251-343-8448 (800-466-8356)
This motel welcomes your pets to stay with you.

Motel 6 - Mobile West Tillmans Corner
5488 Inn Rd
Mobile, AL
251-660-1483 (800-466-8356)
This motel welcomes your pets to stay with you.

Red Roof Inn Mobile North
33 I-65 Service Road East
Mobile, AL
251-476-2004 (800-RED-ROOF)
One well-behaved family pet per

room. Guest must notify front desk upon arrival. Guest is liable for any damages. In consideration of all guests, pets must never be left unattended in the guest rooms.

Red Roof Inn Mobile South
5450 Coca Cola Road
Mobile, AL
251-666-1044 (800-RED-ROOF)
One well-behaved family pet per room. Guest must notify front desk upon arrival. Guest is liable for any damages. In consideration of all guests, pets must never be left unattended in the guest rooms.

Renaissance Battle House Hotel
26 N Royal Street
Mobile, AL
251-338-2000 (866-316-5957)
Located in the heart of downtown in one of the city's most historic buildings, this elegant hotel sits central to numerous businesses, shopping, dining, and day/night entertainment areas, plus they also offer a number of in-house amenities for business and leisure travelers. Dogs are allowed for an additional one time fee of $50 per room. 2 dogs may be allowed.

Residence Inn Mobile
950 West I 65 Service Road S
Mobile, AL
251-304-0570 (800-331-3131)
Offering a convenient location to business, historic, shopping, dining, and entertainment areas, this all suite hotel also offers a number of in-house amenities, including a daily buffet breakfast and evening socials Monday through Thursday. Dogs are allowed for an additional one time pet fee of $75 per room. Multiple dogs may be allowed.

TownePlace Suites Mobile
1075 Montlimar Drive
Mobile, AL
251-345-9588 (800-257-3000)
In addition to being rich in historical sites and only 30 minutes to the beaches, this all suite inn also sits near a number of shopping and dining areas, plus they offer several in-house amenities. Dogs up to 75 pounds are allowed for an additional one time fee of $75 per room. Multiple dogs may be allowed.

Wingate by Wyndham AL Mobile
516 Springhill Plaza Ct
Mobile, AL
251-441-1979 (800-228-1000)
Dogs are welcome at this hotel.

Days Inn Monroeville
4389 South Alabama Ave
Monroeville, AL
251-743-3297 (800-329-7466)
Dogs of all sizes are allowed. Dogs
are allowed for a pet fee.

Baymont Inn & Suites Montgomery
5837 Monticello Drive
Montgomery, AL
334-277-4442 (877-229-6668)
Dogs of all sizes are allowed. Dogs
are allowed for a pet fee of $10.00
per pet per night.

Days Inn Midtown Montgomery
2625 Zelda Road
Montgomery, AL
334-269-9611 (800-329-7466)
Dogs of all sizes are allowed. Dogs
are allowed for a pet fee.

Embassy Suites
300 Tallapoosa Street
Montgomery, AL
334-269-5055 (800-EMBASSY (362-
2779))
A full service, atrium-style hotel, they
offer a number of on site amenities
for business and leisure travelers,
plus a convenient location to
business, shopping, dining, historic,
and recreation areas. They also offer
a complimentary cooked-to-order
breakfast and a Manager's reception
every evening. Dogs are allowed for
an additional one time fee of $35 per
pet. 2 dogs may be allowed.

Extended Stay America Montgomery
- Eastern Blvd.
2491 Eastern Blvd.
Montgomery, AL
334-279-1204 (800-804-3724)
One dog is allowed per suite. There
is a $25 per night additional pet fee
up to $150 for an entire stay.

La Quinta Inn Montgomery
1280 East Blvd.
Montgomery, AL
334-271-1620 (800-531-5900)
Dogs of all sizes are allowed. There
are no additional pet fees. Dogs
must be leashed and cleaned up
after. Crate or be with pet when the
room is being serviced. Multiple dogs
may be allowed.

Motel 6 - Montgomery
1051 Eastern Blvd
Montgomery, AL
334-277-6748 (800-466-8356)
Your pets are welcome to stay here
with you.

Motel 6 - Montgomery Hope Hull
7760 Slade Plaza Blvd
Montgomery, AL
334-280-1866 (800-466-8356)
Your pets are welcome to stay here
with you.

Quality Inn & Suites Convention
Center
2705 E. South Boulevard
Montgomery, AL
334-288-2800 (877-424-6423)
Dogs of all sizes are allowed. Dogs
are allowed for a pet fee of $10.00
per pet per night.

Ramada Montgomery
1185 Eastern Blvd
Montgomery, AL
334-356-3335 (800-272-6232)
Dogs of all sizes are allowed. Dogs
are allowed for a pet fee of $3 per
pet per night.

Red Roof Inn Montgomery
5601 Carmichael Road
Montgomery, AL
334-270-0007 (800-RED-ROOF)
One well-behaved family pet per
room. Guest must notify front desk
upon arrival. Guest is liable for any
damages. In consideration of all
guests, pets must never be left
unattended in the guest rooms.

Residence Inn Montgomery
1200 Hilmar Court
Montgomery, AL
334-270-3300 (800-331-3131)
This all suite inn features a
convenient location to business,
shopping, dining, and entertainment
areas, plus they also offer a number
of in-house amenities, including a
daily buffet breakfast and evening
socials Monday to Thursday with
refreshments. Dogs are allowed for
an additional one time pet fee of
$75 per room. Multiple dogs may be
allowed.

Staybridge Suites Montgomery-
Eastchase
7800 Eastchase Parkway
Montgomery, AL
334-277-9383 (877-270-6405)
Dogs up to 80 pounds are allowed.
Pets allowed with an additional pet
fee. Up to $75 for 1-6 nights and up
to $150 for 7+ nights. A pet
agreement must be signed at
check-in.

Super 8 Montgomery
2707 East South Blvd
Montgomery, AL
334-281-4884 (800-800-8000)

Dogs are welcome at this hotel.

TownePlace Suites Montgomery
5047 TownePlace Drive
Montgomery, AL
334-396-5505 (800-257-3000)
This all suite hotel sits central to a
number of sites of interest for both
business and leisure travelers; plus
they also offer a number of on-site
amenities to ensure comfort. Dogs
are allowed for an additional one
time fee of $100 per room. Multiple
dogs may be allowed.

Super 8 Moody
2451 Moody Parkway
Moody, AL
205-640-7091 (800-800-8000)
Dogs are welcome at this hotel.

Days Inn Opelika
1014 Anand Ave
Opelika, AL
334-749-5080 (800-329-7466)
Dogs of all sizes are allowed. Dogs
are allowed for a pet fee of $20.00
per pet per night.

Motel 6 - Opelika
1015 Columbus Pkwy
Opelika, AL
334-745-0988 (800-466-8356)
This motel welcomes your pets to
stay with you.

Travelodge Opelika
1002 Columbus Parkway
Opelika, AL
334-749-1461 (800-578-7878)
Dogs of all sizes are allowed. Dogs
are allowed for a pet fee of $10 per
pet per night.

Baymont Inn & Suites Oxford
1600 Hwy 21 S
Oxford, AL
256-835-1492 (877-229-6668)
Dogs are welcome at this hotel.

Comfort Inn
138 Elm St.
Oxford, AL
256-831-0860 (877-424-6423)
Dogs of all sizes are allowed. Dogs
are allowed for a pet fee of $25.00
per pet per stay. Three or more dogs
may be allowed.

Days Inn Oxford
1 Recreation Drive
Oxford, AL
256-835-0300 (800-329-7466)
Dogs of all sizes are allowed. Dogs
are allowed for a pet fee of $10 per
pet per stay.

Econo Lodge
25 Elm St.
Oxford, AL
256-831-9480 (877-424-6423)
Dogs up to 50 pounds are allowed.
Dogs are allowed for a pet fee of
$10.00 per pet per night. Two dogs
are allowed per room.

Holiday Inn Express Hotel & Suites
Anniston/Oxford
160 Colonial Drive
Oxford, AL
256-835-8768 (877-270-6405)
Dogs of all sizes are allowed. Dogs
are allowed for a pet fee of $25.00
per pet per night.

Motel 6 - Anniston Oxford/talladega
Speedway
202 Grace St
Oxford, AL
256-831-5463 (800-466-8356)
This motel welcomes your pets to
stay with you.

Sleep Inn
88 Colonial Drive
Oxford, AL
256-831-2191 (877-424-6423)
Dogs of all sizes are allowed. Dogs
are allowed for a pet fee of $10.00
per pet per stay.

Quality Inn & Suites
858 US Hwy. 231 South
Ozark, AL
334-774-7300 (877-424-6423)
Dogs up to 75 pounds are allowed.
Dogs are allowed for a pet fee of
$15.00 per pet per night. Two dogs
are allowed per room.

Quality Inn
797 Business Park Drive
Prattville, AL
334-365-6003 (877-424-6423)
Dogs up to 100 pounds are allowed.
Dogs are allowed for a pet fee of $10
per pet per stay. Two dogs are
allowed per room.

Comfort Inn
3239 Point Mallard Pkwy
Priceville, AL
256-355-1037 (877-424-6423)
Dogs of all sizes are allowed. Dogs
are allowed for a pet fee of $10.00
per pet per night.

Days Inn - Decatur Priceville
63 Marco Dr
Priceville, AL
256-355-3297 (800-329-7466)
Dogs of all sizes are allowed. Dogs
are allowed for a pet fee.

Joe Wheeler State Park
201 McLean Drive
Rogersville, AL
256-685-2656 (800-ALAPARK (1-
800-252-7275))
alapark.com/JoeWheeler/
Set alongside the Tennessee River
near Wheeler Dam, this camp area
has cabins with TVs and basic
supplies that will house 4 to 15
guests; plus, there is a boat ramp
for Wheeler Lake in the cabin area.
Well mannered dogs are allowed in
the cabins for an additional $10 per
night per pet; they must be declared
at the time of check in, and a credit
card must be on file. Dogs must be
crated if left alone in the room, and
they must be kept on no more than
a 6 foot leash and cleaned up after
promptly. Dogs are not allowed in
any other park buildings, at the
beach, or at the swimming pool. All
pets must have proof of current tags
and vaccinations. 2 dogs may be
allowed.

Comfort Inn
23518 John T. Reid Pkwy.
Scottsboro, AL
256-574-6740 (877-424-6423)
Dogs of all sizes are allowed. Dogs
are allowed for a pet fee of $10.00
per pet per night.

Days Inn Scottsboro
23945 John T Reid Parkway
Scottsboro, AL
256-574-1212 (800-329-7466)
Dogs of all sizes are allowed. Dogs
are allowed for a nightly pet fee.

Ramada
1710 W Highland Ave
Selma, AL
334-872-0461 (800-272-6232)
Dogs are welcome at this hotel.

Days Inn Shorter
450 Main Street
Shorter, AL
334-727-6034 (800-329-7466)
Dogs of all sizes are allowed. Dogs
are allowed for a pet fee.

Super 8 Sylacauga
40770 Hwy 280
Sylacauga, AL
256-249-4321 (800-800-8000)
Dogs are welcome at this hotel.

Super 8 AL Talladega
220 Haynes Street
Talladega, AL
256-315-9511 (800-800-8000)
Dogs are welcome at this hotel.

Days Inn Troy
1260 Hwy 231 South
Troy, AL
334-566-1630 (800-329-7466)
Dogs are welcome at this hotel.

Candlewood Suites Tuscaloosa
651 Skyland Blvd East
Tuscaloosa, AL
205-722-0999 (877-270-6405)
Dogs up to 80 pounds are allowed.
Pets allowed with an additional pet
fee. Up to $75 for 1-6 nights and up
to $150 for 7+ nights. A pet
agreement must be signed at check-
in.

Jameson Inn
5021 Oscar Baxter Drive
Tuscaloosa, AL
205-345-5024 (800-JAMESON (526-
3766))
homesteadhotels.com/
This inn will allow dogs for an
additional $10 per night per room.
Dogs must be quiet, well behaved,
leashed, and cleaned up after on
site. Multiple dogs may be allowed.

La Quinta Inn Tuscaloosa
4122 McFarland Blvd. E.
Tuscaloosa, AL
205-349-3270 (800-531-5900)
Dogs of all sizes are allowed. There
are no additional pet fees. Dogs
must be leashed and cleaned up
after. Dogs may not be left
unattended unless they will be quiet
and well behaved. 2 dogs may be
allowed.

Motel 6 - Tuscaloosa
4700 Mcfarland Blvd
Tuscaloosa, AL
205-759-4942 (800-466-8356)
This motel welcomes your pets to
stay with you.

Wingate by Wyndham Tuscaloosa
4918 Skyland Blvd. E.
Tuscaloosa, AL
205-553-5400 (800-228-1000)
Dogs are welcome at this hotel.

Days Inn York
17700 Hwy 17
York, AL
205-392-9675 (800-329-7466)
Dogs of all sizes are allowed. Dogs
are allowed for a pet fee of $10.00
per pet per stay.

Alaska

America's Best Suites
4110 Spenard Road

Anchorage, AK
907-243-3433 (800-237-8466)
Dogs of all sizes are allowed for a
$100 fee, $50 of which is refundable
for 1 dog, and a $150 fee, $50 of
which is refundable for 2 dogs. Dogs
must be declared at the time of
reservations, and they must be well
mannered, leashed, and cleaned up
after. 2 dogs may be allowed.

Days Inn Downtown Anchorage
321 East 5th Avenue
Anchorage, AK
907-276-7226 (800-329-7466)
Dogs of all sizes are allowed. Dogs
are allowed for a pet fee of $10.00
per pet per night.

Hawthorn Suites
1110 W 8th Avenue
Anchorage, AK
907-222-5005 (888-469-6575)
In addition to providing a convenient
location to many local sites and
activities, this all-suite hotel offers a
number of amenities for business
and leisure travelers, including their
signature breakfast buffet and
beautifully appointed rooms. Dogs
are allowed for an additional one
time fee of $150 per room. There
may be 2 small dogs 10 pounds and
under or 1 average size dog per
room.

Howard Johnson Plaza Anchorage
239 W. 4th Avenue
Anchorage, AK
907-793-5500 (800-446-4656)
Dogs are welcome at this hotel.

Knights Inn AK Anchorage
441 E. 15th Ave
Anchorage, AK
907-276-3114 (800-843-5644)
Dogs are welcome at this hotel.

Long House Alaskan Hotel
4335 Wisconsin Street
Anchorage, AK
907-243-2133 (888-243-2133)
longhousehotel.com/
Rich in Alaskan character décor and
able to accommodate the business
or leisure traveler, this inn also sits
across from Lake Hood and provides
a large walk-in freezer for "catches".
Dogs of all sizes are allowed for an
additional fee of $10 per night per
pet, and they have been known to
keep doggy treats at the front desk.
Dogs must be leashed and cleaned
up after. 2 dogs may be allowed.

Merrill Field Inn
420 Sitka Street

Anchorage, AK
907-276-4547 (800-898-4547)
merrillfieldinn.com/
This inn is centrally located to a
number of activities, shopping, and
eateries, plus they also have an
onsite restaurant specializing in
American and Chinese cuisine.
Dogs of all sizes are allowed for an
additional fee of $7 per night per
pet. Dogs must be leashed and
cleaned up after. 2 dogs may be
allowed.

Millennium Alaskan Hotel
4800 Spenard Rd
Anchorage, AK
907-243-2300
This 248-room hotel is located on
the eastern shore of Lake Spenard.
There is a $20 per night per pet
additional fee. Multiple dogs may be
allowed.

Motel 6 - Anchorage Midtown
5000 Street
Anchorage, AK
907-677-8000 (800-466-8356)
This motel welcomes your pets to
stay with you.

Parkwood Inn
4455 Juneau St
Anchorage, AK
907-563-3590
There is a $5 per night per pet
additional fee. The fee may be less
for very small dogs. Multiple dogs
may be allowed.

Puffin Inn
4400 Spenard Road
Anchorage, AK
907-243-4044 (800-478-3346)
puffininn.net/
Offering many conveniences for the
business or leisure traveler, they
are also central to many other
notable services and attractions.
Dogs of all sizes are allowed for an
additional fee of $3 per night per
pet, unless the Pet Friendly Lodging
package is purchased which
includes a collapsible food/water
bin, treats, a toy, sanitary bags, and
a foldable dog food mat. Dogs must
be leashed and cleaned up after. 2
dogs may be allowed.

Red Roof Inn Anchorage
1104 East 5th Avenue
Anchorage, AK
907-274-1650 (800-RED-ROOF)
One well-behaved family pet per
room. Guest must notify front desk
upon arrival. Guest is liable for any
damages. In consideration of all
guests, pets must never be left

unattended in the guest rooms.

Residence Inn Anchorage Midtown
1025 35th Avenue
Anchorage, AK
907-563-9844 (888-236-2427)
Some of the amenities of this inn
include a daily buffet breakfast, a
Manager's reception Monday through
Thursday, a heated swimming pool,
and complimentary grocery
shopping. Dogs are allowed for an
additional one time pet fee of $100
per room. Multiple dogs may be
allowed.

Sourdough Visitors Lodge
801 E Erikson St
Anchorage, AK
907-279-4148 (800-777-3716)
There is a $100 refundable deposit
and a $50 one time pet fee.

Super 8 Anchorage
3501 Minnesota Dr
Anchorage, AK
907-276-8884 (800-800-8000)
Dogs of all sizes are allowed. Dogs
are allowed for a pet fee of $20.00
per pet per night.

Long House Bethel Hotel
751 3rd Avenue
Bethel, AK
907-486-4300 (866-543-4613)
longhousebethelinn.com/
This guest house can accommodate
large or small groups comfortably,
and they make a good starting point
for exploring the beauty of the area.
Dogs of all sizes are allowed for an
additional fee of $50 per pet per stay
plus a $50 refundable deposit. Dogs
must be leashed and cleaned up
after. 2 dogs may be allowed.

Border City Motel & RV Park
Mile 1225 Alaska Hwy
Border City, AK
907-774-2205
There is one pet room in this hotel.
There is a $50 additional refundable
pet deposit.

Backwoods Lodge
At George Parks Hwy, Milepost 210
Cantwell, AK
907-768-2232
This motel's log building offers nine
large comfortable rooms with satellite
TVs, microwaves, refrigerators and
barbecues. The property has a view
of Mt. McKinley. They have hiking
trails and a canoe which guests can
use on a nearby small pond. Call
ahead for reservations because they
do tend to book up early, especially

during the summer. The nice folks here give out pet blankets to put over the furniture if your dog is going to be on the bed or chairs. They are located about 30 miles from Denali National Park. Pets must be on leash when outside of the rooms and may not be left unattended at any time. Dogs under 705pounds are allowed for no additional fee. 2 dogs may be allowed.

Chena Hot Springs
56.5 Chena Hot Springs Road
Chena Hot Springs, AK
907-451-8104 (800-478-4681)
chenahotsprings.com/
This resort is a great place to view the Aurora Borealis due to it's location in the northern region and it's distance from the city lights. They offer hotel rooms, cabins, RV parking and camping. There are lots of outdoor activities to do on this 440 acre resort. They are located approximately 60 miles east of Fairbanks. Dogs are allowed in a number of the rooms that are designated as pet rooms. There is a one time $350 pet deposit--$300 is refundable. 2 dogs may be allowed.

Alaska 7 Motel
Mile 270 Richardson Hwy
Delta Junction, AK
907-895-4848
Small to medium sized dogs are allowed in a few pet rooms in this motel.

Alaskan Steak House & Motel
265 Richardson Hwy
Delta Junction, AK
907-895-5175
wildak.net/~akstkhse/
Dogs of all sizes are allowed. There is a $50 one time additional pet fee.

Clearwater Lodge
7028 Remington Rd
Delta Junction, AK
907-895-5152
This is not actually a hotel but they have a number of camping cabins. Showers and bathrooms are in a separate building and you need to bring your own sleeping bags. There are no additional pet fees.

McKinley Chalet Resort
Milepost 238 George Parks H
Denali, AK
907-267-7234 (800-423-7846)
Nestled among tree on the shores of the Nenana River only a half mile from the Denali National Park, this resort sits close to a variety of recreational pursuits, and has on site

a restaurant, a bar/lounge, and numerous amenities. They are open from mid-May to mid-September, weather permitting. Dogs of all sizes are allowed for no additional fee. Dogs must be leashed and cleaned up after. 2 dogs may be allowed.

McKinley Village Lodge
Mile 231 Alaska H3
Denali, AK
907-683-8900 (800-276-7234)
In addition to a number of amenities and close proximity to the Denali National Park, this lodge also has a full service restaurant, saloon, coffee stand, and a gift shop on site. Dogs of all sizes are allowed for no additional fee. Dogs must be leashed and cleaned up after. Multiple dogs may be allowed.

Comfort Inn
1908 Chena Landings Loop
Fairbanks, AK
907-479-8080 (877-424-6423)
Dogs of all sizes are allowed. Dogs are allowed for a pet fee of $10.00 per pet per night.

Golden North Motel
4888 Old Airport Way
Fairbanks, AK
907-479-6201 (800-447-1910)
goldennorthmotel.com/
Dogs, but not cats, are allowed at this motel. There are no additional pet fees but a credit card is required for a refundable pet deposit.

Pike's Waterfront Lodge
1850 Hoselton Rd
Fairbanks, AK
907-456-4500 (877-774-2400)
pikeslodge.com
Dogs of all sizes are allowed. There is a $10 additional pet fee.

The New Caribou Hotel
Box 329
Glennallen, AK
907-822-3302 (800-478-3302)
alaskan.com/caribouhotel/
Rooms are in a log cabin style building. There is a $10 per day per pet fee. Multiple dogs may be allowed.

Glacier Bay Lodge and Tours
179 Bartlett Cove
Gustavus, AK
888-BAY-TOUR
Offering the only accommodations in the Glacier Bay National Park amid some of the most pristine wilderness and majestic scenery in

the world, this rustic lodge offers modern amenities and a good starting point for a number of activities and recreation. Dogs of all sizes are allowed for no additional fee. Dogs must be under their owner's control, leashed, and cleaned up after. Dogs are not allowed on public tours, at food service areas, or the gift shop. 2 dogs may be allowed.

Captain's Choice
108 2nd Avenue North
Haines, AK
907-766-3111 (800-478-2345)
capchoice.com/
Get panoramic views of the water from the Captain's Choice Motel. Dogs of all sizes are allowed. There is a $15 one time additional pet fee.

Eagle's Nest Motel
1069 Haines Hwy
Haines, AK
907-766-2891
Dogs of all sizes are allowed. There is a $10 one time additional pet fee.

Fort Seward Lodge
39 Mud Bay Rd
Haines, AK
907-766-2009 (877-617-3418)
ftsewardlodge.com/
Dogs of all sizes are allowed. There is a $10 per night pet fee and a $50 credit card pet deposit that will only be charged if there is damage to the room. The hotel is closed in November and December each year.

Hotel Halsingland
13 Fort Seward Dr
Haines, AK
907-766-2000
hotelhalsingland.com
Dogs of all sizes are allowed. There is a $10 per night additional pet fee.

Thunderbird Motel
216 Dalton Street
Haines, AK
907-766-2131 (800-327-2556)
thunderbird-motel.com
Dogs of all sizes are allowed. There are no additional pet fees.

Denail Park Hotel
Otto Lake Road and Parks Highway
Healy, AK
907-683-1800 (866-683-1800)
denaliparkhotel.com/
In addition to a convenient location to some of the areas best attractions, activities, and dining sites, this hotel offers a peaceful setting and a number of in-house amenities. Dogs

declared in advance are allowed for an additional one time pet fee of $20 per room. Multiple dogs may be allowed.

Heritage Hotel
147 E Pioneer Ave
Homer, AK
907-235-7787
There is a $10 per day pet fee. They usually place pets in smoking rooms but will give you a non-smoking room if requested.

Homer Seaside Cottages
58901 East End Road
Homer, AK
907-235-2716 (877-374-2716)
Only a block from the ocean and sandy beaches, this spacious cottage will sleep six and allow dogs for an additional fee of $5 per night per pet with a $15 minimum fee. Dogs may not be left unattended, and they must be leashed and cleaned up after at all times. 2 dogs may be allowed.

Jenny Lane Cottage
353 D Jenny Lane
Homer, AK
907-235-5434
akms.com/jennyln/
This cozy get-a-way is only a short walk to town and sits overlooking Kachemak Bay offering great views of area's landscapes, and it's variety of marine, bird, and wildlife. Dogs of all sizes are allowed (on approval) for an additional fee of $15 per night per room. Aggressive breed dogs are not allowed, and dogs must be quiet, well behaved, leashed, and cleaned up after. 2 dogs may be allowed.

Lakewood Inn Bed and Breakfast
984 Ocean Dr #1
Homer, AK
907-235-6144
There is a $10 (+ tax) per day per pet fee. 2 dogs may be allowed.

Otter Cove Resort
PO Box 2543
Homer, AK
907-235-7770 (800-426-6212)
ottercoveresort.com/
Accessed by water taxi or biplane, this lodging area offers a private beach and sets in a lush maritime forest with miles of scenic hiking trails. Dogs of all sizes are allowed for no additional fee, although having limited pet friendly facilities, they suggest calling ahead. Dogs must be quiet, well behaved, leashed, and cleaned up after at all times. Dogs are not allowed at the restaurant. 2

dogs may be allowed.

Extended Stay Deluxe
1800 Shell Simmons Drive
Juneau, AK
907-790-6435 (800-804-3724)
extendedstaydeluxe.com/
Dogs of all sizes are allowed for an additional fee of $25 per night per pet (maximum $75 each). Dogs must be well behaved, leashed, and cleaned up after. 2 dogs may be allowed.

Juneau Hotel
1250 W 9th Street
Juneau, AK
907-586-5666
juneauhotels.net/
Dogs up to 50 pounds or 18 inches high to the shoulder are allowed for an additional fee of a one time fee of $50 for a 1 to 3 day stay, and a $150 one time fee for over 3 days. Dogs must be declared at the time of reservation, and they must be quiet, leashed, and cleaned up after.

Prospector Hotel
375 Whittier Street
Juneau, AK
907-586-3737 (800-331-2711 (US & Hawaii))
prospectorhotel.com/
Business and leisure travelers will both enjoy the variety of amenities and recreational opportunities at this hotel. Dogs of all sizes are allowed for an additional $10 per night per pet. Dogs must be very friendly, well behaved, leashed, cleaned up after, and kenneled when left alone in the room. Dogs are not allowed in food service areas. 2 dogs may be allowed.

Super 8 Juneau
2295 Trout St
Juneau, AK
907-789-4858 (800-800-8000)
Dogs are welcome at this hotel.

The Driftwood Lodge
435 Willoughby Ave
Juneau, AK
907-586-2280 (800-544-2239)
alaskan.com/driftwoodlodge/
There is a $10 per day per pet fee. Dogs are not allowed for extended stays. Multiple dogs may be allowed.

Black Bear Inn
5528 N Tongass H/H 7
Ketchikan, AK
907-225-4343

stayinalaska.com/
This premier waterfront inn offers elegant surroundings, great views, and many amenities. One dog is allowed in the Bunk House cabin for an additional pet fee of $10 per night. Dogs must be well behaved, leashed, and cleaned up after at all times. Dogs are not allowed on the furniture or beds, and if pets have a propensity to get on the furnishings, they request they be kenneled at night.

Super 8 Ketchikan
2151 Sea Level Dr.
Ketchikan, AK
907-225-9088 (800-800-8000)
Dogs are welcome at this hotel.

The Narrows Inn, Restaurant and Marina
4871 N Tongass H/H 7
Ketchikan, AK
907-247-2600 (888-686-2600)
narrowsinn.com/
This beautiful waterfront inn offer ocean front rooms, a restaurant and lounge, and numerous amenities. Dogs of all sizes are allowed for an additional fee of $10 per night per pet. Dogs must be well mannered, leashed, and cleaned up after at all times. 2 dogs may be allowed.

Best Western Kodiak Inn
236 W Rezanof Drive
Kodiak, AK
907-486-5712 (800-780-7234)
Dogs of all sizes are allowed. Dogs are allowed for a pet fee.

Comfort Inn
1395 Airport Way
Kodiak, AK
907-487-2700 (877-424-6423)
Dogs up to 50 pounds are allowed. Dogs are allowed for a pet fee of $15 per pet per night.

Shelikof Lodge
211 Thorsheim Street
Kodiak, AK
907-486-4141
ptialaska.net/~kyle/index2.htm
This hotel offers a restaurant, lounge, and a number of amenities and services, as well as providing a good starting point for exploring the variety of activities and recreation in the area. One medium to large dog or 2 small dogs are allowed per room for no additional fee. Dogs are not allowed on the furniture and must be kenneled when left alone in the room. Dogs must be leashed and cleaned up after at all times.

A Cottage on the Bay
13710 Beach Drive
Lowell Point, AK
907-224-8237 (888-334-8237)
onthebayak.com/
This seasonal cottage sits on the shores of the scenic Resurrection Bay and offers a number of amenities, including freezer storage for any "catches" from the bay. Dogs of all sizes are allowed for no additional fee. Dogs must be well behaved, under their owner's control, and cleaned up after at all times. Multiple dogs may be allowed.

Gold Miner's Hotel
918 S Colony Way
Palmer, AK
907-745-6160 (800-7ALASKA)
goldminershotel.com/
In addition to providing spacious accommodations, a restaurant, and a bar/lounge, they are also central to a variety of activities and recreational pursuits. Dogs of all sizes are allowed for a $50 to $100 refundable deposit with prior approval. Aggressive breed dogs are not allowed. Dogs must be quiet, well behaved, leashed, and cleaned up after at all times. 2 dogs may be allowed.

Paxson Inn and Lodge
Mile 185 Richardson H
Paxson, AK
907-822-3330
Sitting central to several fishing lakes and hiking trails, this inn also provides a restaurant and bar on site, and there is a camp area with hook-ups that allows dogs for no additional fee. One dog is allowed per room at the lodge for an additional pet fee of $20 per night. Dogs must be leashed and cleaned up after.

Scandia House
110 N Nordic Drive
Petersburg, AK
907-772-4281 (800-722-5006)
scandiahousehotel.com/
Great views, convenient location, Jacuzzi rooms, and fresh muffins in the morning are some of the amenities offered here. Dogs of all sizes are allowed for an additional fee of $10 per night per pet. Dogs must be leashed and cleaned up after.

Seward Cabins
31730 Bronze Avenue
Seward, AK
907-224-4891
sewardcabins.com/
Newly constructed with modern heated concrete floors, these creek-side cabins offer year round recreational opportunities. Dogs of all sizes are allowed for no additional fee. Dogs must be under owner's control, leashed, and cleaned up after at all times. Multiple dogs may be allowed.

Super 8 Sitka
404 Sawmill Creek Rd.
Sitka, AK
907-747-8804 (800-800-8000)
Dogs of all sizes are allowed. Dogs are allowed for a nightly pet fee.

Sgt Preston's Lodge
370 6th Ave
Skagway, AK
907-983-2521
Dogs of all sizes are allowed. There is a $15 one time additional pet fee. The entire hotel is non-smoking.

Talkeetna Inn
25 Coffee Lane
Talkeetna, AK
907-733-7530 (888-582-4890)
talkeetna-bandb.com/index.html
This lakeside inn sits only a short distance from the confluence of the Talkeetna, Susitna and Chulitna rivers, offering visitors spectacular scenery, and a great starting point for year round recreation. Dogs of all sizes are allowed for no additional fee; puppies are not allowed. Dogs must be well behaved, leashed, and cleaned up after at all times. 2 dogs may be allowed.

Burnt Paw Cabins
Box 7
Tok, AK
907-883-4121
burntpawcabins.com
There is one pet-friendly cabin. Dogs of all sizes are allowed. There is a $25 refundable additional cash deposit for pets.

Cleft on the Rock Bed and Breakfast
Mile 0.5 Sundog Trail
Tok, AK
907-883-4219
tokalaska.com/cleftroc.shtml
Pets are not allowed on the furniture. The owner has a cat and your dog needs to be ok around cats. There is a $15 per night per pet fee. Dogs are not allowed during their winter season when they only have lodging in the main house. 2 dogs may be allowed.

Showshoe Motel
Mile 1314 Alaska Hwy
Tok, AK
907-883-4511
alaska-snowshoemotel.com
Dogs of all sizes are allowed. There is a $25 damage deposit required that can be handled with a credit card. Dogs must always be leashed when outside of your room and they may not be left unattended in the room.

Westmark Tok Hotel
Alaska Hwy & Glenn Hwy
Tok, AK
907-883-5174
The hotel has a couple of pet rooms. Dogs of all sizes are allowed. There is no additional pet fee.

Young's Motel
Box 482
Tok, AK
907-883-4411
Dogs of all sizes are allowed. There are no additional pet fees.

Totem Inn
144 E Egan Drive
Valdez, AK
907-835-4443
toteminn.com/
Only a few steps from the harbor, this inn also offers cottages for rent, an eatery open from 5 am to 11 pm during the summer, and a gift shop that carries hand made native art. The cottages are non-smoking; however rooms at the inn are smoking-optional. Dogs of all sizes are allowed for an additional fee of $10 per night per pet. Dogs must be well behaved, leashed, and cleaned up after. Multiple dogs may be allowed.

Best Western Lake Lucille Inn
1300 W Lake Lucille Drive
Wasilla, AK
907-373-1776 (800-780-7234)
Dogs are welcome at this hotel.

Stikine Inn
107 Front Street
Wrangell, AK
907-874-3388 (888-874-3388)
stikineinn.com/
Set in a lush environment rich in marine, bird, and wild life as well as natural and Native American history, this oceanside hotel offers a great starting point for exploring the area. Dogs of all sizes are allowed for a refundable deposit of $75 per room. Dogs must be leashed, cleaned up

after, and crated when left alone in the room. 2 dogs may be allowed.

Arizona

Super 8 Apache Junction
251 East 29th Avenue
Apache Junction, AZ
480-288-8888 (800-800-8000)
Dogs are welcome at this hotel.

Motel 6 - Bellemont, Az
12380 I-40
Bellemont, AZ
928-556-9599 (800-466-8356)
This motel welcomes your pets to stay with you.

Motel 6 - Benson
637 Whetstone Commerce
Benson, AZ
520-586-0066 (800-466-8356)
This motel welcomes your pets to stay with you.

Super 8 Benson
855 North Ocotillo Rd
Benson, AZ
520-586-1530 (800-800-8000)
Dogs of all sizes are allowed. Dogs are allowed for a pet fee.

The Gardens at Mile High Ranch
901 Tombstone Canyon Road
Bisbee, AZ
520-432-3866
gardensatmilehighranch.com
Stately 150+ year old cottonwood trees sitting among lush gardens create a protected, peaceful ambiance at this beautiful 3 acre retreat. They also offer healing and spa treatments, a healthy continental breakfast in your apartment, cable TV, and spacious units with private baths and furnished kitchens. Well behaved pets are welcome for no additional fee. 2 dogs may be allowed.

The Sleepy Dog Guest House
212A Opera Drive
Bisbee, AZ
520-432-3057
sleepydogguesthouse.com/
This unique retreat sits nestled in a natural setting with lots of hiking and off leash trails just out the door. Artist owned, with his studio only a few steps from the house, guests can enjoy the colorful Southwestern art décor, lush surroundings, and privacy. Simple makings for breakfast, coffee, and tea are provided. Dogs are allowed for no additional fee; they must be well

mannered, housebroken, quiet, and cat and dog friendly. There is also a fenced-in yard for off leash time. Dogs are not allowed on the furniture or beds. 2 dogs may be allowed.

Days Inn Buckeye
25205 W Yuma Rd
Buckeye, AZ
623-386-5400 (800-329-7466)
Dogs of all sizes are allowed. Dogs are allowed for a pet fee.

Best Western Bullhead City Inn
1126 Highway 95
Bullhead City, AZ
928-754-3000 (800-780-7234)
Dogs of all sizes are allowed. Dogs are allowed for a pet fee.

El Rio Waterfront Resort & RV Park
1641 H 95
Bullhead City, AZ
928-763-4385
Dogs are allowed for no additional pet fee. Aggressive breeds are not allowed. 2 dogs may be allowed.

Comfort Inn
340 North Goswick Way
Camp Verde, AZ
928-567-9000 (877-424-6423)
Dogs of all sizes are allowed. Two dogs are allowed per room.

Days Inn
1640 West Highway 260
Camp Verde, AZ
928-567 3700 (000-329-7466)
Dogs of all sizes are allowed. Dogs are allowed for a pet fee.

Super 8 AZ Camp Verde
1550 W Hwy 260
Camp Verde, AZ
928-567-2622 (800-800-8000)
Dogs are welcome at this hotel.

Boulders Resort
34631 N Tom Darlington Rd
Carefree, AZ
480-488-9009
wyndham.com/Boulders/
There is a one-time $100 dog fee. Two dogs are allowed if their combined weight does not exceed 80 pounds. 2 dogs may be allowed.

Carefree Resort & Villas
37220 Mule Train Road
Carefree, AZ
888-667-6690
Pets are allowed in the standard rooms and villas. There is a a $50 pet fee for a standard room and higher pet fees for the villas.

Super 8 Casa Grande
2066 E Florence
Casa Grande, AZ
520-836-8800 (800-800-8000)
Dogs of all sizes are allowed. Dogs are allowed for a pet fee of $10.00 per pet per night.

Comfort Inn Chandler
255 N. Kyrene Road
Chandler, AZ
480-705-8882 (877-424-6423)
tristarhotels.com/ci-chandler
This hotel offers a free full hot breakfast daily, wireless high speed internet access,a heated outdoor pool, cable TV with expanded HBO and laundry facilities. There are no additional pet fees.

Hawthorn Suites
5858 W Chandler Blvd
Chandler, AZ
480-705-8881 (800-527-1133)
In addition to providing a convenient location to many local sites and activities, this all-suite hotel offers a number of amenities for business and leisure travelers, including their signature breakfast buffet and beautifully appointed rooms. Dogs are allowed for an additional one time fee of $125 per pet, plus $25 per night per pet. 2 dogs may be allowed.

Motel 6 - Chandler, Az
7445 Chandler Blvd
Chandler, AZ
480-940-0308 (800-466-8356)
This motel welcomes your pets to stay with you.

Red Roof Inn Phoenix - Chandler
7400 West Boston Street
Chandler, AZ
480-857-4969 (800-RED-ROOF)
One well-behaved family pet per room. Guest must notify front desk upon arrival. Guest is liable for any damages. In consideration of all guests, pets must never be left unattended in the guest rooms.

Sheraton Wild Horse Pass Resort & Spa
5594 W. Wild Horse Pass Blvd.
Chandler, AZ
602-225-0100 (888-625-5144)
Dogs up to 80 pounds are allowed. Dogs are restricted to rooms on the first floor only. There are no additional pet fees. Dogs are not allowed to be left alone in the room.

Super 8 Phoenix Chandler

7171 W Chandler Blvd
Chandler, AZ
480-961-3888 (800-800-8000)
Dogs of all sizes are allowed. Dogs
are allowed for a pet fee.

Windmill Inn of Chandler
3535 W Chandler Blvd
Chandler, AZ
480-812-9600
There is no additional pet fee. There
is a special pet section of the hotel.
Multiple dogs may be allowed.

Motel 6 - Douglas
111 16th St
Douglas, AZ
520-364-2457 (800-466-8356)
This motel welcomes your pets to
stay with you.

Best Western Sunrise Inn
128 N Main Street
Eagar, AZ
928-333-2540 (800-780-7234)
Dogs are welcome at this hotel for a
$10 pet fee.

Best Western Desert Oasis
I-10 Exit 1 S Frontage RD
Ehrenberg, AZ
928-923-9711 (800-780-7234)
Dogs of all sizes are allowed. Dogs
are allowed for a pet fee of $20.00
per pet per stay.

Days Inn Casa Grande
5300 S Sunland Gin Rd
Eloy, AZ
520-426-9240 (800-329-7466)
Dogs of all sizes are allowed. Dogs
are allowed for a pet fee.

Motel 6 - Casa Grande
4965 Sunland Gin Rd
Eloy, AZ
520-836-3323 (800-466-8356)
This motel welcomes your pets to
stay with you.

Red Roof Inn Eloy - Casa Grande
4015 West Outer Drive
Eloy, AZ
520-466-2522 (800-RED-ROOF)
One well-behaved family pet per
room. Guest must notify front desk
upon arrival. Guest is liable for any
damages. In consideration of all
guests, pets must never be left
unattended in the guest rooms.

Travelodge Casa Grande
7190 South Sunland Gin Road
Eloy, AZ
520-836-5000 (800-578-7878)
Dogs are welcome at this hotel.

Best Western Pony Soldier Inn &
Suites
3030 E Route 66
Flagstaff, AZ
928-526-2388 (800-780-7234)
Dogs of all sizes are allowed. Dogs
are allowed for a pet fee of $15.00
per pet per stay.

Comfort Inn I-17 & I-40
2355 S. Beulah Blvd.
Flagstaff, AZ
928-774-2225 (877-424-6423)
Dogs of all sizes are allowed. Dogs
are allowed for a pet fee of $10.00
per pet per night.

Days Inn - West Route 66 Flagstaff
1000 West Hwy 66/I-40
Flagstaff, AZ
928-774-5221 (800-329-7466)
Dogs of all sizes are allowed. Dogs
are allowed for a pet fee.

Days Inn And Suites East Flagstaff
3601 E. Lockett Rd
Flagstaff, AZ
928-527-1477 (800-329-7466)
Dogs of all sizes are allowed. Dogs
are allowed for a pet fee.

Econo Lodge University
914 S. Milton Rd.
Flagstaff, AZ
928-774-7326 (877-424-6423)
Dogs of all sizes are allowed. Dogs
are allowed for a pet fee of $10.00
per pet per night.

Howard Johnson I-40 Exit 198 E.
Lucky Lane Flagstaff
2520 E. Lucky Lane
Flagstaff, AZ
928-779-5121 (800-446-4656)
Dogs of all sizes are allowed. Dogs
are allowed for a nightly pet fee.

Howard Johnson Inn - Flagstaff
3300 East Rt 66/I-40
Flagstaff, AZ
928-526-1826 (800-446-4656)
Dogs are welcome at this hotel.

Kings House Hotel
1560 East Route 66
Flagstaff, AZ
928-774-7186 (888-577-7186)
kingshousehotel.com
Dogs are allowed for no additional
fee. There are some breed
restrictions.

Knights Inn Flagstaff
224 S. Mikes Pike
Flagstaff, AZ
928-774-8888 (800-843-5644)
Dogs of all sizes are allowed. Dogs

are allowed for a pet fee of $10.00
per pet per night.

La Quinta Inn & Suites Flagstaff
2015 South Beulah Blvd.
Flagstaff, AZ
928-556-8666 (800-531-5900)
Dogs of all sizes are allowed. Dogs
must be well behaved, leashed, and
cleaned up after. 2 dogs may be
allowed.

Motel 6 - Flagstaff Butler Avenue
2010 Butler Ave
Flagstaff, AZ
928-774-1801 (800-466-8356)
This motel welcomes your pets to
stay with you.

Motel 6 - Flagstaff East Lucky Lane
2440 Lucky Ln
Flagstaff, AZ
928-774-8756 (800-466-8356)
This motel welcomes your pets to
stay with you.

Motel 6 - Flagstaff West Woodland
Village
2745 Woodlands Village
Flagstaff, AZ
928-779-3757 (800-466-8356)
This motel welcomes your pets to
stay with you.

Quality Inn
2500 East Lucky Lane
Flagstaff, AZ
928-226-7111 (877-424-6423)
Dogs of all sizes are allowed. Dogs
are allowed for a pet fee of $15.00
per pet per stay. Two dogs are
allowed per room.

Quality Inn I-40 & I-17
2000 S. Milton Rd.
Flagstaff, AZ
928-774-8771 (877-424-6423)
Dogs of all sizes are allowed.

Ramada East Flagstaff
2350 E Lucky Lane
Flagstaff, AZ
928-779-3614 (800-272-6232)
Dogs of all sizes are allowed. Dogs
are allowed for a pet fee of $10.00
per pet per night.

Residence Inn Flagstaff
3440 N Country Club Drive
Flagstaff, AZ
928-526-5555 (800-331-3131)
Besides offering a convenient
location to the Northern Arizona
State University, and to business,
shopping, dining, and recreation
areas, this hotel also provides a
number of in-house amenities,

including a daily buffet breakfast and complementary evening social hours with light fare. Dogs are allowed for an additional one time pet fee of $100 per room. Multiple dogs may be allowed.

S8 Downtown NAU Conference Center Flagstaff
602 W. Route 66
Flagstaff, AZ
928-774-4581 (800-800-8000)
Dogs of all sizes are allowed. Dogs are allowed for a pet fee.

Super 8 I-40 Ex 198 Lucky Lane Flagstaff
2540 E. Lucky Lane
Flagstaff, AZ
928-773-4888 (800-800-8000)
Dogs of all sizes are allowed. Dogs are allowed for a pet fee of $15.00 per pet per night.

Super 8 I-40 Mall Flagstaff
3725 Kasper Avenue
Flagstaff, AZ
928-526-0818 (800-800-8000)
Dogs of all sizes are allowed. Dogs are allowed for a pet fee of $15 per pet per night.

Travelodge - NAU Conference Center Flagstaff
990 West Route 66
Flagstaff, AZ
928-213-5800 (800-578-7878)
Dogs are welcome at this hotel.

Travelodge Grand Canyon Flagstaff
2610 East Route 66
Flagstaff, AZ
928-526-1399 (800-578-7878)
Dogs of all sizes are allowed. Dogs are allowed for a pet fee.

Travelodge Flagstaff
2200 East Butler Ave
Flagstaff, AZ
928-779-6944 (800-578-7878)
Dogs of all sizes are allowed. Dogs are allowed for a pet fee.

Holiday Inn Hotel & Suites Fountain Hills - N. Scottsdale
12800 N Saguaro Blvd.
Fountain Hills, AZ
480-837-6565 (877-270-6405)
Dogs of all sizes are allowed. Dogs are allowed for a pet fee of $25.00 per pet per stay.

Best Western Space Age Lodge
401 E Pima
Gila Bend, AZ
928-683-2273 (800-780-7234)
Dogs are welcome at this hotel.

Knights Inn Gila Bend
1046 East Pima Street
Gila Bend, AZ
928-683-6303 (800-843-5644)
Dogs are welcome at this hotel.

Comfort Suites
9824 W Camelback Rd
Glendale, AZ
623-271-9005 (877-424-6423)
Dogs up to 60 pounds are allowed. Dogs are allowed for a pet fee of $25.00 per pet per stay.

Residence Inn Phoenix Glendale
7350 N Zanjero Boulevard
Glendale, AZ
623-772-8900 (800-331-3131)
This all suite inn features a convenient location to business, historic, shopping, dining, and entertainment areas, plus they also offer a number of in-house amenities, including a daily buffet breakfast and evening socials. Dogs are allowed for an additional one time pet fee of $100 per room. Multiple dogs may be allowed.

Staybridge Suites Phoenix-Glendale
9340 West Cabela Drive
Glendale, AZ
623-842-0000 (877-270-6405)
Dogs up to 80 pounds are allowed. Pets allowed with an additional pet fee. Up to $75 for 1-6 nights and up to $150 for 7+ nights. A pet agreement must be signed at check-in.

Motel 6 - Globe
1699 Ash St
Globe, AZ
928-425-5741 (800-466-8356)
This motel welcomes your pets to stay with you.

Quality Inn
1565 East South Street
Globe, AZ
928-425-7575 (877-424-6423)
Dogs up to 50 pounds are allowed. Dogs are allowed for a pet fee of $10.00 per pet per night. Two dogs are allowed per room.

Best Western Phoenix Goodyear Inn
55 N Litchfield Road
Goodyear, AZ
623-932-3210 (800-780-7234)
Dogs up to 100 pounds are allowed. Dogs are allowed for a pet fee of $15.00 per pet per night.

Comfort Suites

15575 W. Roosevelt St
Goodyear, AZ
623-266-2884 (877-424-6423)
Dogs up to 60 pounds are allowed. Dogs are allowed for a pet fee of $50.00 per pet per stay.

Holiday Inn Hotel & Suites Goodyear - West Phoenix Area
1188 N Dysart Road
Goodyear, AZ
623-547-1313 (877-270-6405)
Dogs of all sizes are allowed. Dogs are allowed for a pet fee of $35.00 per pet per stay.

Residence Inn Phoenix Goodyear
2020 N Litchfield Road
Goodyear, AZ
623-866-1313 (800-331-3131)
Located on the lush Palm Valley Golf Course just west of Phoenix, this all suite inn offers a perfect starting point to many of the area's sports complexes/fields, the Phoenix International Raceway, and the World Wildlife Zoo. They also offer a number of in-house amenities, including a daily buffet breakfast and evening socials Monday through Thursday with light dinner fare. Dogs are allowed for an additional one time pet fee of $100 per room. Multiple dogs may be allowed.

Super 8 /Phoenix Area Goodyear
840 N. Dysart
Goodyear, AZ
623-932-9622 (800-800-8000)
Dogs are welcome at this hotel.

Red Feather Lodge
Highway 64
Grand Canyon, AZ
800-538-2345
redfeatherlodge.com
This motel is located just one mile south of the south entrance to the Grand Canyon National Park. Pets are welcome, but they must not be left unattended in the room. There is a $50 refundable pet deposit and a $10 pet fee per night per pet. Multiple dogs may be allowed.

Big Ten Resort Cabins
45 Main Street
Greer, AZ
928-735-7578
bigtencabins.com
These are rustic Cabins located in the cozy town of Greer in the center of the White Mountains in AZ. They are located 13 Miles from Sunrise Ski Resort & many other outdoor activities. Some amenities include Satellite TV/VCR/DVD, fireplaces and bar-b-cues. Well behaved dogs

are welcome for $15 each per night.

Best Western Sawmill Inn
1877 Highway 260
Heber, AZ
928-535-5053 (800-780-7234)
Dogs are welcome at this hotel.

Best Western Adobe Inn
615 W Hopi Drive
Holbrook, AZ
928-524-3948 (800-780-7234)
Dogs of all sizes are allowed. Dogs
are allowed for a pet fee.

Best Western Arizonian Inn
2508 Navajo Boulevard
Holbrook, AZ
928-524-2611 (800-780-7234)
Dogs are welcome at this hotel.

Comfort Inn
2602 E. Navajo Blvd.
Holbrook, AZ
928-524-6131 (877-424-6423)
Dogs of all sizes are allowed. Dogs
are allowed for a pet fee of $10.00
per pet per night.

Econo Lodge
2596 Navajo Blvd.
Holbrook, AZ
928-524-1448 (877-424-6423)
Dogs of all sizes are allowed. Dogs
are allowed for a pet fee of $25.00
per pet per stay. Two dogs are
allowed per room.

Holiday Inn Express Holbrook-
Navajo Blvd
1308 E. Navajo Blvd.
Holbrook, AZ
928-524-1466 (877-270-6405)
Dogs of all sizes are allowed. Dogs
are allowed for a pet fee of $20.00
per pet per night.

Knights Inn Holbrook
602 Navajo Blvd
Holbrook, AZ
928-524-6263 (800-843-5644)
Dogs are welcome at this hotel.
There is a $5 per visit additional pet
fee.

Motel 6 - Holbrook
2514 Navajo Blvd
Holbrook, AZ
928-524-6101 (800-466-8356)
This motel welcomes your pets to
stay with you.

Ramada Limited Holbrook
2608 E. Navajo Blvd
Holbrook, AZ
928-524-2566 (800-272-6232)
Dogs are welcome at this hotel.

Ghost City Inn
541 Main Street
Jerome, AZ
928-634-4678
One dog is allowed in the Miner's
Suite for a one time $20 pet fee.

Best Western A Wayfarer's Inn and
Suites
2815 E Andy Devine Avenue
Kingman, AZ
928-753-6271 (800-780-7234)
Dogs of all sizes are allowed. Dogs
are allowed for a pet fee of $10 per
pet per stay. Two dogs are allowed
per room.

Comfort Inn
3129 E Andy Devine
Kingman, AZ
928-718-1717 (877-424-6423)
Dogs of all sizes are allowed. Dogs
are allowed for a pet fee of $20.00
per pet per stay.

Days Inn East Kingman
3381 East Andy Devine
Kingman, AZ
928-757-7337 (800-329-7466)
Dogs of all sizes are allowed. Dogs
are allowed for a pet fee of $15.00
per pet per night.

Days Inn West Kingman
3023 East Andy Devine
Kingman, AZ
928-753-7500 (800-329-7466)
Dogs of all sizes are allowed. Dogs
are allowed for a pet fee of $10 per
pet per night.

Econo Lodge
3421 E. Andy Devine Ave.
Kingman, AZ
928-757-7878 (877-424-6423)
Dogs of all sizes are allowed. Dogs
are allowed for a pet fee of $10.00
per pet per night.

I-40 Travelodge Kingman
3275 East Andy Devine
Kingman, AZ
928-757-1188 (800-578-7878)
Dogs are welcome at this hotel.

Motel 6 - Kingman East
3351 Andy Devine Ave
Kingman, AZ
928-757-7151 (800-466-8356)
This motel welcomes your pets to
stay with you.

Motel 6 - Kingman West
424 Beale St
Kingman, AZ
928-753-9222 (800-466-8356)

This motel welcomes your pets to
stay with you.

Quality Inn
1400 E. Andy Devine Ave.
Kingman, AZ
928-753-4747 (877-424-6423)
Dogs of all sizes are allowed. Dogs
are allowed for a pet fee of $20.00
per pet per stay.

Rodeway Inn
3016 East Andy Devine Avenue
Kingman, AZ
928-753-9555 (877-424-6423)
Dogs up to 50 pounds are allowed.
Dogs are allowed for a pet fee of
$10.00 per pet per night. Two dogs
are allowed per room.

Super 8
3401 E Andy Devine Ave.
Kingman, AZ
928-757-4808 (800-800-8000)
Dogs of all sizes are allowed. Dogs
are allowed for a pet fee of $15 per
pet per night.

Days Inn Lake Havasu
1700 McCulloch Blvd North
Lake Havasu City, AZ
928-855-7841 (800-329-7466)
Dogs are welcome at this hotel.

Island Inn Hotel
1300 W McCulloch Blvd
Lake Havasu City, AZ
928-680-0606 (800-243-9955)
rentor.com/hotels/islanlin.htm
There is a $10 one time fee per pet.
Multiple dogs may be allowed.

Lake Havasu Travelodge
480 London Bridge Road
Lake Havasu City, AZ
928-680-9202 (800-578-7878)
Dogs of all sizes are allowed. Dogs
are allowed for a pet fee of $10.00
per pet per night.

Motel 6 - Lake Havasu City Lake
View
2176 Birch Square
Lake Havasu City, AZ
928-855-5566 (800-466-8356)
This motel welcomes your pets to
stay with you.

Motel 6 - Lake Havasu City Lakeside
111 London Bridge Rd
Lake Havasu City, AZ
928-855-3200 (800-466-8356)
Your pets are welcome to stay here
with you.

Quality Inn & Suites
271 S. Lake Havasu Ave

Lake Havasu City, AZ
928-855-1111 (877-424-6423)
Dogs of all sizes are allowed. Two
dogs are allowed per room.

Super 8 Lake Havasu City
305 London Bridge Rd.
Lake Havasu City, AZ
928-855-8844 (800-800-8000)
Dogs of all sizes are allowed. Dogs
are allowed for a pet fee of $10 per
pet per night.

The Wigwam Golf Resort & Spa
300 Wigwam Blvd.
Litchfield Park, AZ
623-935-3811
Dogs up to 80 pounds are allowed
for no additional pet fees. Dogs must
be crated when left alone in the
room.

Motel 6 - Tucson North
4630 Ina Rd
Marana, AZ
520-744-9300 (800-466-8356)
This motel welcomes your pets to
stay with you.

Arizona Golf Resort
425 S Power Road
Mesa, AZ
480-832-3202
azgolfresort.com/
There is an additional one time pet
fee of $25 per room. 2 dogs may be
allowed.

Best Western Mesa Inn
1625 E Main Street
Mesa, AZ
480-964-8000 (800-780-7234)
Dogs of all sizes are allowed. Dogs
are allowed for a pet fee of $20.00
per pet per stay.

Best Western Mezona Inn
250 W Main Street
Mesa, AZ
480-834-9233 (800-780-7234)
Dogs of all sizes are allowed. Dogs
are allowed for a pet fee.

Days Hotel Country Club Mesa
333 W Juanita Ave
Mesa, AZ
480-844-8900 (800-329-7466)
Dogs of all sizes are allowed. Dogs
are allowed for a nightly pet fee.

Extended Stay America Phoenix
Mesa
455 W. Baseline Rd.
Mesa, AZ
480-632-0201 (800-804-3724)
One dog is allowed per suite. There
is a $25 per night additional pet fee

up to $150 for an entire stay.

Hilton Phoenix East/Mesa
1011 West Holmes Avenue
Mesa, AZ
480-833-5555
An oasis in the desert, this luxury
hotel offers a number of on site
amenities for business and leisure
travelers, plus a convenient location
to business, shopping, dining,
recreation, and entertainment
areas. Dogs up to 75 pounds are
allowed for an additional one time
pet fee of $75 per room. Dogs must
be crated or removed for
housekeeping. The front desk must
be informed and the Pet in Room
sign put on the door if there is a pet
in the room alone.

Homestead Studio Suites Phoenix -
Mesa
1920 W. Isabella
Mesa, AZ
480-752-2266 (800-804-3724)
One dog is allowed per suite. There
is a $25 per night additional pet fee
up to $150 for an entire stay.

Motel 6 - Mesa North
336 Hampton Ave
Mesa, AZ
480-844-8899 (800-466-8356)
This motel welcomes your pets to
stay with you.

Motel 6 - Mesa South
1511 Country Club Dr
Mesa, AZ
480-834-0066 (800-466-8356)
This motel welcomes your pets to
stay with you.

Motel 6 - Phoenix Mesa Main St
630 Main St
Mesa, AZ
480-969-8111 (800-466-8356)
This motel welcomes your pets to
stay with you.

Phoenix/ Travelodge Suites Mesa
4244 East Main Street
Mesa, AZ
480-832-5961 (800-578-7878)
Dogs of all sizes are allowed. Dogs
are allowed for a pet fee.

Residence Inn Phoenix Mesa
941 W Grove Avenue
Mesa, AZ
480-610-0100 (800-331-3131)
Some of the amenities at this all-
suite inn include a daily buffet
breakfast, evening socials Monday
through Wednesday with
refreshments, a heated swimming

pool, and a complimentary grocery
shopping service. Dogs up to 80
pounds are allowed for an additional
one time pet fee of $100 per room. 2
dogs may be allowed.

Sleep Inn
6347 E. Southern Ave.
Mesa, AZ
480-807-7760 (877-424-6423)
Dogs of all sizes are allowed.

Super 8 /Phoenix Power and Main
Mesa
6733 E Main St
Mesa, AZ
480-981-6181 (800-800-8000)
Dogs are welcome at this hotel.

Super 8 Phoenix//Gilbert Road Mesa
1550 S. Gilbert Rd
Mesa, AZ
480-545-0888 (800-800-8000)
Dogs of all sizes are allowed. Dogs
are allowed for a pet fee of $5.00 per
pet per night.

Candlewood Suites Nogales
875 North Frank Reed Rd
Nogales, AZ
520-281-1111 (877-270-6405)
Dogs up to 80 pounds are allowed.
Pets allowed with an additional pet
fee. Up to $75 for 1-6 nights and up
to $150 for 7+ nights. A pet
agreement must be signed at check-
in.

Motel 6 - Nogales
141 Mariposa Rd
Nogales, AZ
520-281-2951 (800-466-8356)
This motel welcomes your pets to
stay with you.

Super 8 Nogales
547 W Mariposa Rd
Nogales, AZ
520-281-2242 (800-800-8000)
Dogs of all sizes are allowed. Dogs
are allowed for a pet fee.

Days Inn and Suites / Lake Powell
Page
961 N Hwy 89
Page, AZ
928-645-2800 (800-329-7466)
Dogs of all sizes are allowed. Dogs
are allowed for a pet fee.

Motel 6 - Page
637 Lake Powell Blvd
Page, AZ
928-645-5888 (800-466-8356)
This motel welcomes your pets to
stay with you.

Quality Inn at Lake Powell
287 N. Lake Powell Blvd.
Page, AZ
928-645-8851 (877-424-6423)
Dogs of all sizes are allowed.

Rodeway Inn
107 South Lake Powell Blvd
Page, AZ
928-645-2406 (877-424-6423)
Dogs of all sizes are allowed. Dogs are allowed for a pet fee of $10.00 per pet per night. Two dogs are allowed per room.

Super 8 /Lake Powell Page
649 South Lake Powell
Page, AZ
928-645-5858 (800-800-8000)
Dogs are welcome at this hotel.

Travelodge AZ Page
207 North Lake Powell Blvd
Page, AZ
928-645-2451 (800-578-7878)
Dogs of all sizes are allowed. Dogs are allowed for a pet fee.

Wahweap Lodge and Marina
100 Lakeshore Drive
Page, AZ
928-645-2433
The lodge offers a fine dining restaurant, gift shop, pool, lounge, and spectacular views of Lake Powell. Pets are allowed for an additional fee of $20 per night per per. Pets must be on a leash at all times when outside the room, and they are not to be left unattended or tied up outside on the patio or balcony. Dogs must be attended to or removed for housekeeping. If your pet is accustomed to being on the bed, they request you ask for a sheet to put over the bedspread. There is also a marina on site where they rent watercraft. Your pet may join you on a boat ride if you rent an 18' or 19' personal craft, as they are not allowed on the tour boats. 2 dogs may be allowed.

Hermosa Inn
5532 N Palo Cristi Rd
Paradise Valley, AZ
602-955-8614
hermosainn.com/home.asp
Dogs up to 50 pounds are allowed for an additional one time fee of $100 per pet. 2 dogs may be allowed.

Best Western Parker Inn
1012 Geronimo Avenue
Parker, AZ
928-669-6060 (800-780-7234)
Dogs are welcome at this hotel.

Motel 6 - Parker
604 California Ave
Parker, AZ
928-669-2133 (800-466-8356)
This motel welcomes your pets to stay with you.

Best Western Payson Inn
801 N Beeline Highway
Payson, AZ
928-474-3241 (800-780-7234)
Dogs of all sizes are allowed. Dogs are allowed for a pet fee of $25.00 per pet per stay.

Motel 6 - Payson
101 Phoenix St
Payson, AZ
928-474-4526 (800-466-8356)
This motel welcomes your pets to stay with you.

Comfort Suites Peoria Sports Complex
8473 West Paradise Ln.
Peoria, AZ
623-334-3993 (877-424-6423)
Dogs up to 50 pounds are allowed. Dogs are allowed for a pet fee of $25.00 per pet per stay.

Extended Stay America Phoenix - Peoria
7345 W. Bell Rd.
Peoria, AZ
623-487-0020 (800-804-3724)
One dog is allowed per suite. There is a $25 per night additional pet fee up to $150 for an entire stay.

La Quinta Inn & Suites Phoenix West Peoria
16321 North 83rd Ave.
Peoria, AZ
623-487-1900 (800-531-5900)
Dogs of all sizes are allowed. There are no additional pet fees. Dogs must be leashed and cleaned up after. Multiple dogs may be allowed.

Ramada /Glendale Convention Center Peoria
8955 W Grand Avenue
Peoria, AZ
623-979-7200 (800-272-6232)
Dogs of all sizes are allowed. Dogs are allowed for a pet fee of $10.00 per pet per night.

Arizona Biltmore Resort and Spa
2400 E Missouri Avenue
Phoenix, AZ
602-955-6600 (800-950-0086)
A magnificent oasis in the desert, this gone-green world renowned resort and spa covers 39 lush, landscaped acres; features a championship 18 hole putting course, and offers a wellness spa that uses only natural and organic products and practices. They also offer several dining and party options, 8 swimming pools, life-size lawn chess, and a number of other planned activities. Dogs up to 50 pounds are allowed in the cottages only for a $100 deposit per pet; $50 for each is refundable. Dogs are not allowed in food service areas. 2 dogs may be allowed.

Best Western InnSuites Hotel & Suites
1615 E Northern Avenue
Phoenix, AZ
602-997-6285 (800-780-7234)
Dogs of all sizes are allowed. Dogs are allowed for a pet fee.

Best Western Phoenix I-17 MetroCenter Inn
8101 N Black Canyon Highway
Phoenix, AZ
602-864-6233 (800-780-7234)
Dogs of all sizes are allowed. Dogs are allowed for a pet fee.

Candlewood Suites Phoenix
11411 N. Black Canyon Hwy
Phoenix, AZ
602-861-4900 (877-270-6405)
Dogs up to 80 pounds are allowed. Pets allowed with an additional pet fee. Up to $75 for 1-6 nights and up to $150 for 7+ nights. A pet agreement must be signed at check-in.

Clarion Hotel Phoenix Tech Center
5121 E. La Puente Ave.
Phoenix, AZ
480-893-3900 (877-424-6423)
Dogs of all sizes are allowed. Dogs are allowed for a pet fee of $25.00 per pet per stay. Two dogs are allowed per room.

Comfort Inn
2641 W. Union Hills Drive
Phoenix, AZ
602-978-2222 (877-424-6423)
Dogs up to 50 pounds are allowed. Dogs are allowed for a pet fee of $10.00 per pet per night. Two dogs are allowed per room.

Comfort Inn
5050 N. Black Canyon Hwy.
Phoenix, AZ
602-242-8011 (877-424-6423)
Dogs of all sizes are allowed. Dogs are allowed for a pet fee of $35.00 per pet per stay.

Comfort Suites at Metro Center
10210 N. 26th Dr.
Phoenix, AZ
602-861-3900 (877-424-6423)
Dogs up to 50 pounds are allowed.
Dogs are allowed for a pet fee of
$25.00 per pet per stay. Two dogs
are allowed per room.

Crowne Plaza Hotel Phoenix
2532 W. Peoria Ave
Phoenix, AZ
602-943-2341 (877-270-6405)
Dogs of all sizes are allowed. Dogs
are allowed for a pet fee of $25 per
pet per stay.

Crowne Plaza Hotel Phoenix-Airport
4300 East Washington
Phoenix, AZ
602-273-7778 (877-270-6405)
Dogs up to 50 pounds are allowed.
Dogs are allowed for a pet fee.

Days Inn - I 17 and Thomas Phoenix
2420 West Thomas
Phoenix, AZ
602-257-0801 (800-329-7466)
Dogs are welcome at this hotel.

Days Inn and Conference Center
Phoenix
502 Camelback Rd.
Phoenix, AZ
602-264-9290 (800-329-7466)
Dogs are welcome at this hotel.

Embassy Suites
2630 E Camelback Road
Phoenix, AZ
602-955-3992 (800-EMBASSY (362-
2779))
Only minutes from downtown and the
Phoenix Sky Harbor Airport, this
upscale hotel offers a number of on
site amenities for business and
leisure travelers, plus a convenient
location to numerous business,
shopping, dining, and entertainment
areas. They also offer a
complimentary cooked-to-order
breakfast and a Manager's reception
every evening. Dogs up to 50 pounds
are allowed for an additional one
time fee of $40 per pet. 2 dogs may
be allowed.

Embassy Suites
2577 W Greenway Road
Phoenix, AZ
602-375-1777 (800-EMBASSY (362-
2779))
Set on 17 beautifully landscaped
acres, this full service, upscale hotel
offers a number of on site amenities
for business and leisure travelers,

plus a convenient location to
numerous business, shopping,
dining, and entertainment areas.
They also offer a complimentary
cooked-to-order breakfast and a
Manager's reception every evening.
Dogs are allowed for an additional
one time pet fee of $50 per room.
Multiple dogs may be allowed.

Embassy Suites
2333 East Thomas Road
Phoenix, AZ
602-957-1910 (800-EMBASSY
(362-2779))
Located only a couple of miles from
the Sky Harbor International Airport
and downtown, this full service,
upscale hotel offers a number of on
site amenities for business and
leisure travelers, plus a convenient
location to numerous business,
shopping, dining, and entertainment
areas. They also offer a
complimentary cooked-to-order
breakfast and a Manager's
reception every evening. Dogs are
allowed for an additional fee of $20
per night per pet. 2 dogs may be
allowed.

Extended Stay America Phoenix -
Airport
3421 E. Elwood St.
Phoenix, AZ
602-438-2900 (800-804-3724)
One dog is allowed per suite. There
is a $25 per night additional pet fee
up to $150 for an entire stay.

Extended Stay America Phoenix -
Airport - E. Oak St.
4357 East Oak Street
Phoenix, AZ
602-225-2998 (800-804-3724)
One dog is allowed per suite. There
is a $25 per night additional pet fee
up to $150 for an entire stay.

Extended Stay America Phoenix -
Chandler
14245 S. 50th St.
Phoenix, AZ
480-785-0464 (800-804-3724)
One dog is allowed per suite. There
is a $25 per night additional pet fee
up to $150 for an entire stay.

Extended Stay America Phoenix -
Deer Valley
20827 N. 27th Ave.
Phoenix, AZ
623-879-6609 (800-804-3724)
One dog is allowed per suite. There
is a $25 per night additional pet fee
up to $150 for an entire stay.

Extended Stay America Phoenix - E.
Chandler Blvd.
5035 E. Chandler Blvd.
Phoenix, AZ
480-753-6700 (800-804-3724)
One dog is allowed per suite. There
is a $25 per night additional pet fee
up to $150 for an entire stay.

Extended Stay America Phoenix -
Metro Center
11211 N. Black Canyon Hwy
Phoenix, AZ
602-870-2999 (800-804-3724)
One dog is allowed per suite. There
is a $25 per night additional pet fee
up to $150 for an entire stay.

Hilton Hotel
10 E Thomas Road
Phoenix, AZ
602-222-1111 (800-HILTONS (445-
8667))
This luxury, all suite hotel offers a
long list of on site amenities for
business and leisure travelers, plus a
convenient location to business,
shopping, dining, recreation areas,
and numerous sites of interest. Dogs
up to 50 pounds are allowed for an
additional one time fee of $50 per
pet. Multiple dogs may be allowed.

Homestead Studio Suites Phoenix -
North Metro
2102 W. Dunlap Ave.
Phoenix, AZ
602-944-7828 (800-804-3724)
One dog is allowed per suite. There
is a $25 per night additional pet fee
up to $150 for an entire stay.

Knights Inn Airport Phoenix
3101 North 32nd Street
Phoenix, AZ
602-956-4900 (800-843-5644)
Dogs of all sizes are allowed. Dogs
are allowed for a nightly pet fee.

Knights Inn Fairground - Phoenix
1624 N. Black Canyon Highway
Phoenix, AZ
602-269-6281 (800-843-5644)
Dogs of all sizes are allowed. Dogs
are allowed for a pet fee of $11.21
per pet per night.

La Quinta Inn Phoenix Sky Harbor
Airport North
4727 E Thomas Rd
Phoenix, AZ
602-956-6500 (800-531-5900)
Dogs of all sizes are allowed. There
are no additional pet fees. Dogs
must be leashed and cleaned up
after. Please put the "Do Not Disturb"
sign on the door if there is a dog

alone in the room uncrated. Multiple dogs may be allowed.

La Quinta Inn Phoenix Thomas Road
2725 N. Black Canyon Hwy.
Phoenix, AZ
602-258-6271 (800-531-5900)
Dogs of all sizes are allowed. Dogs must be well behaved, leashed, and cleaned up after. Multiple dogs may be allowed.

Motel 6 - Phoenix Black Canyon
4130 Black Canyon Hwy
Phoenix, AZ
602-277-5501 (800-466-8356)
This motel welcomes your pets to stay with you.

Motel 6 - Phoenix Northern Avenue
8152 Black Canyon Hwy
Phoenix, AZ
602-995-7592 (800-466-8356)
This motel welcomes your pets to stay with you.

Motel 6 - Phoenix Sweetwater
2735 Sweetwater Ave.
Phoenix, AZ
602-942-5030 (800-466-8356)
This motel welcomes your pets to stay with you.

Motel 6 - Phoenix Airport 24th Street
214 24th St
Phoenix, AZ
602-244-1155 (800-466-8356)
This motel welcomes your pets to stay with you.

Motel 6 - Phoenix East
5315 Van Buren St
Phoenix, AZ
602-267-8555 (800-466-8356)
This motel welcomes your pets to stay with you.

Motel 6 - Phoenix North Bell Road
2330 Bell Rd
Phoenix, AZ
602-993-2353 (800-466-8356)
This motel welcomes your pets to stay with you.

Motel 6 - Phoenix West
1530 52nd Dr
Phoenix, AZ
602-272-0220 (800-466-8356)
This motel welcomes your pets to stay with you.

Pointe Hilton Squaw Peak Resort
7677 N 16th Street
Phoenix, AZ
602-997-2626 (800-947-9784)
pointehilton.com/
Offering the best in luxury

accommodations, this award-winning resort features a variety of fun activities and amenities for the business and leisure travelers. The amenities include 563 well appointed suites, 48,000 square feet of meeting space, 3 restaurants, a putting course, gaming courts, and a 9-acre waterpark. Dogs of all sizes are welcome. There is a $75 one time additional pet fee per room. Dogs must be leashed and cleaned up after at all times, and they must be removed or crated for housekeeping. There are some breed restrictions. 2 dogs may be allowed.

Pointe Hilton Tapatio Cliffs
11111 N 7th Street
Phoenix, AZ
602-866-7500 (800-947-9784)
pointehilton.com/
Nestled atop a desert mountain preserve with miles of scenic trails, this award winning resort features variety of fun activities and amenities for the business and leisure travelers, and is also home to the Lookout Mountain Golf Club. Some of the amenities include 547 elegantly appointed suites, 65,000 square feet of meeting space, 5 restaurants, a golf instruction academy, and a 3 1/2 acre water wonderland village. Dogs up to 70 pounds are allowed for a one time additional pet fee of $75. Dogs must be leashed, cleaned up after, removed or crated for housekeeping, and they may not be left alone in the room.

Red Roof Inn Phoenix - Bell Road
17222 North Black Canyon Highway
Phoenix, AZ
602-866-1049 (800-RED-ROOF)
One well-behaved family pet per room. Guest must notify front desk upon arrival. Guest is liable for any damages. In consideration of all guests, pets must never be left unattended in the guest rooms.

Red Roof Inn Phoenix West
5215 West Willeta Street
Phoenix, AZ
602-233-8004 (800-RED-ROOF)
One well-behaved family pet per room. Guest must notify front desk upon arrival. Guest is liable for any damages. In consideration of all guests, pets must never be left unattended in the guest rooms.

Residence Inn Phoenix Airport
801 N 44th Street

Phoenix, AZ
602-273-9220 (800-331-3131)
This all suite hotel sits close to the airport and central to many of the city's star attractions, shopping, dining, and business areas, plus they offer a number of in-house amenities that include a daily buffet breakfast, nightly social hours with light dinner fare, and Wednesday night barbecues. Dogs are allowed for an additional one time pet fee of $100 per room. Multiple dogs may be allowed.

Residence Inn Phoenix North/Happy Valley
2035 W Whispering Wind Drive
Phoenix, AZ
623-580-8833 (800-331-3131)
Although near a number of major corporations, attractions, and activities, this all suite inn also provides a central location to several sports related sites, a daily buffet breakfast, a resort sized pool, and evening socials. Dogs are allowed for an additional one time pet fee of $100 per room. 2 dogs may be allowed.

Sheraton Crescent Hotel
2620 West Dunlop Avenue
Phoenix, AZ
602-943-8200 (888-625-5144)
Dogs up tp 60 pounds are allowed. There are no additional pet fees. Dogs are not allowed to be left alone in the room.

Sleep Inn Airport
2621 S. 47th Pl.
Phoenix, AZ
480-967-7100 (877-424-6423)
Dogs of all sizes are allowed.

Studio 6 - Phoenix Deer Valley
18405 27th Ave
Phoenix, AZ
602-843-1151 (800-466-8356)
Your pets are welcome to stay here with you for a pet fee of $10 per day up to $50 for an entire stay.

Super 8 West I-10 Phoenix
1242 North 53rd Avenue
Phoenix, AZ
602-415-0888 (800-800-8000)
Dogs of all sizes are allowed. Dogs are allowed for a pet fee of $25 per pet per night.

TownePlace Suites Phoenix Metrocenter Mall/I-17
9425 N. Black Canyon Freeway
Phoenix, AZ
602-943-9510 (800-257-3000)

This all suite hotel sits within walking distance to a number of sites of interest for both business and leisure travelers; plus they also offer a number of on-site amenities - including a deluxe continental breakfast. Dogs are allowed for an additional one time fee of $75 per room. Multiple dogs may be allowed.

Best Western Inn of Pinetop
404 E White Mountain Boulevard
Pinetop, AZ
928-367-6667 (800-780-7234)
Dogs of all sizes are allowed. Dogs are allowed for a nightly pet fee.

Buck Springs Resort
6126 Buck Springs Road
Pinetop, AZ
928-369-3554 (800-339-1909)
bucksspringsresort.com/
Sitting on 20 acres of tall pines offering lots of hiking trails, this scenic resort features 20 one bedroom cottages and 4 three bedroom townhouses around a wonderful courtyard area with benches and a small raised pavilion. There are barbecues available, and all units have a covered front porch, cable TV, a wood burning stove, and are fully equipped with all the essentials, including the kitchen. Dogs of all sizes are allowed for an additional fee of $10 per night per pet, and they must be declared at the time of reservations. Dogs may not be left alone in the room, and they must be leashed and cleaned up after at all times. 2 dogs may be allowed.

Apple Creek Cottages
1001 White Spar
Prescott, AZ
928-445-7321 (888-455-8003)
applecreekcottages.com
These pet-friendly cottages are one, two or three bedrooms. Pets are allowed with a refundable $35.00 deposit.

Best Western Prescottonian
1317 E Gurley Street
Prescott, AZ
928-445-3096 (800-780-7234)
Dogs of all sizes are allowed. Dogs are allowed for a pet fee of $10 per pet per night.

Comfort Inn at Ponderosa Pines
1290 White Spar Rd.
Prescott, AZ
928-778-5770 (877-424-6423)
Dogs up to 50 pounds are allowed. Dogs are allowed for a pet fee of $20.00 per pet per night.

Motel 6 - Prescott
1111 Sheldon Street
Prescott, AZ
928-776-0160 (800-466-8356)
This motel welcomes your pets to stay with you.

Prescott Cabin Rentals
SR69 and Onyx Rd
Prescott, AZ
928-778-9573
prescottcabinrentals.com/
There is an additional $10 per day or $50 per week per pet fee. Pets may not be left in the room unattended. Multiple dogs may be allowed.

Residence Inn Prescott
3599 Lee Circle
Prescott, AZ
928-775-2232 (800-331-3131)
In addition to offering a central location to business, shopping, dining, and several entertainment venues, this hotel also provides a number of in-house amenities, including a daily buffet breakfast and an evening social hour. Dogs are allowed for an additional one time pet fee of $10 per room for the 1st week; $25 for the 2nd week; $50 for the 3rd week, and $100 for 4 weeks or more. Multiple dogs may be allowed.

Comfort Suites
2601 N. Crownpointe Drive
Prescott Valley, AZ
928-771-2100 (877-424-6423)
Dogs up to 60 pounds are allowed.

Days Inn Prescott Valley
7875 East Hwy-69
Prescott Valley, AZ
928-772-8600 (800-329-7466)
Dogs are welcome at this hotel.

Super 8
2050 Dome Rock Rd
Quartzsite, AZ
928-927-8080 (800-800-8000)
Dogs of all sizes are allowed. Dogs are allowed for a pet fee of $10 per pet per night.

Esplendor Resort at Rio Rico
1069 Camino Caralampi
Rio Rico, AZ
520-281-1901 (800-288-4746)
Dogs of all sizes are allowed. There is a $25 one time additional pet fee.

Days Inn Safford
520 East Highway 70
Safford, AZ

928-428-5000 (800-329-7466)
Dogs of all sizes are allowed. Dogs are allowed for a pet fee.

Quality Inn & Suites
420 E. Hwy 70
Safford, AZ
928-428-3200 (877-424-6423)
Dogs of all sizes are allowed. Dogs are allowed for a pet fee of $room/ per pet per night.

3 Palms Resort Oasis Scottsdale
7707 E. McDowell Rd
Scottsdale, AZ
800-450-6013
scottsdale-resort-hotels.com
The hotel is located directly on El Dorado Park with miles of lakes and lawns. The hotel is near Old Town Scottsdale. Hotel provides rooms and suites, some with full kitchens.

Best Western Sundial
7320 E Camelback Road
Scottsdale, AZ
480-994-4170 (800-780-7234)
Dogs of all sizes are allowed. Dogs are allowed for a nightly pet fee.

Comfort Inn
7350 E. Gold Dust Ave.
Scottsdale, AZ
480-596-6559 (877-424-6423)
Dogs of all sizes are allowed. Dogs are allowed for a pet fee of $15.00 per pet per night up to a maximum of $75.

Comfort Suites
3275 N. Drinkwater Blvd.
Scottsdale, AZ
480-946-1111 (877-424-6423)
Dogs of all sizes are allowed. Dogs are allowed for a pet fee of $25.00 per pet per stay.

Doubletree Hotel
5401 N Scottsdale Road
Scottsdale, AZ
480-947-5400 (800-222-TREE (8733))
This resort style hotel sits on 22 lush acres and offers a number of on site amenities for all level of travelers - including their signature chocolate chip cookies at check in, plus a convenient location to business, shopping, dining, and recreation areas. Dogs up to 75 pounds are allowed for an additional one time pet fee of $50 per room. 2 dogs may be allowed.

Extended Stay America Phoenix - Scottsdale
15501 N. Scottsdale Rd.

Scottsdale, AZ
480-607-3767 (800-804-3724)
One dog is allowed per suite. There is a $25 per night additional pet fee up to $150 for an entire stay.

Fairmont Scottsdale Princess
7575 E Princess Drive
Scottsdale, AZ
480-585-4848
Dogs are allowed for an additional pet fee of $25 per night per room.

Firesky Resort and Spa
4925 North Scottsdale Rd
Scottsdale, AZ
480-945-7666
This Kimpton boutique hotel allows dogs of all sizes. It is located in the heart of Old Towne. There are no additional pet fees.

Homestead Studio Suites Phoenix - Scottsdale
3560 N. Marshall Way
Scottsdale, AZ
480-994-0297 (800-804-3724)
One dog is allowed per suite. There is a $25 per night additional pet fee up to $150 for an entire stay.

Hotel Indigo Scottsdale
4415 N. Civic Center Plaza
Scottsdale, AZ
480-941-9400
ScottsdaleHipHotel.com
This pet-friendly luxury hotel has no weight limit and no additional pet fees. Guest rooms have hardwood floors and there are a number of amenities, a lounge and a restaurant.

La Quinta Inn & Suites Phoenix Scottsdale
8888 E. Shea Blvd.
Scottsdale, AZ
480-614-5300 (800-531-5900)
Dogs of all sizes are allowed. There are no additional pet fees. Dogs may not be left unattended, and they must be leashed and cleaned up after. Multiple dogs may be allowed.

Marriott Scottsdale McDowell Mountain
16770 N Perimeter Drive
Scottsdale, AZ
480-502-3836 (800-228-9290)
Besides offering a number of in-house amenities for all level of travelers, this all suite luxury hotel also provides a convenient location to world class shopping, dining, golfing, and entertainment areas. Dogs are allowed for an additional one time fee of $50 per pet; there is a pet policy to sign at check in. 2

dogs may be allowed.

Motel 6 - Scottsdale
6848 Camelback Rd
Scottsdale, AZ
480-946-2280 (800-466-8356)
This motel welcomes your pets to stay with you.

Ramada Limited Scottsdale
6935 East 5th Avenue
Scottsdale, AZ
480-994-9461 (800-272-6232)
Dogs of all sizes are allowed. Dogs are allowed for a pet fee of $15 per pet per night.

Residence Inn Scottsdale North
17011 N Scottsdale Road
Scottsdale, AZ
480-563-4120 (800-331-3131)
Some of the amenities at this all-suite inn include a great location for a variety of pursuits for the business or leisure traveler, a daily buffet breakfast, evening social hours, a heated swimming pool, and a complimentary grocery shopping service. Dogs are allowed for an additional one time pet fee of $100 per room. Multiple dogs may be allowed.

Residence Inn Scottsdale Paradise Valley
6040 N Scottsdale Road
Scottsdale, AZ
480-948-8666 (800-331-3131)
Over 200 golf courses, a variety of night clubs, numerous fine dining options, world class shopping, and more than 125 unique art galleries are all within a few miles of this all suite inn. Additionally, they offer a daily buffet breakfast, evening social hours Monday to Thursday, and Wednesday night barbecues. Dogs are allowed for an additional one time pet fee of $100 per room. Multiple dogs may be allowed.

Sleep Inn at North Scottsdale Road
16630 N. Scottsdale Road
Scottsdale, AZ
480-998-9211 (877-424-6423)
Dogs of all sizes are allowed. Dogs are allowed for a pet fee of $15.00/ per pet per night.

The Inn at Pima
7330 N Pima Rd
Scottsdale, AZ
480-948-3800
There is a $10 per night per pet additional pet fee. Dogs are not allowed in the lobby. Multiple dogs may be allowed.

TownePlace Suites Scottsdale
10740 N 90th Street
Scottsdale, AZ
480-551-1100 (800-257-3000)
In addition to offering a number of in-house amenities for all level of travelers, this all suite inn also offers a convenient location to historic, business, shopping, dining, and day/night entertainment areas. Dogs are allowed for an additional one time fee of $100 per room. Multiple dogs may be allowed.

Best Western Inn of Sedona
1200 W Highway 89A
Sedona, AZ
928-282-3072 (800-780-7234)
Dogs of all sizes are allowed. Dogs are allowed for a pet fee of $20.00 per pet per stay.

El Portal - Sedona's Luxury Hacienda
95 Portal Lane
Sedona, AZ
928-203-9405 (800-313-0017)
elPortalsedona.com
There are five pet rooms at this 1910 adobe hacienda located in the center of Sedona. Pets are allowed for a $35 non-refundable cleaning fee.

Hilton Sedona Resort & Spa
90 Ridge Trail Dr
Sedona, AZ
928-284-4040 (877-273-3762)
hiltonsedonaresort.com
The Hilton Sedona Resort & Spa allows dogs up to 75 pounds. Dogs are welcome at the outdoor patio dining area as well.

Kings Ransom Sedona Hotel
771 H 179
Sedona, AZ
928-282-7151 (800-846-6164)
kingsransomsedona.com/
a 3rd dog would be an additional $15 per night. Dogs must be well mannered, leashed and cleaned up after at all times, and they must be removed or crated for housekeeping. Directly adjacent to the property, the hotel created a Doggy Park complete with plastic bags and a receptacle for disposal. They ask that dogs are not walked in the courtyard, rather at the Doggy Park or on the trails behind the hotel.

Matterhorn Motor Lodge
230 Apple Ave
Sedona, AZ
928-282-7176
sedona.net/hotel/matterhorn/
This inn is located in the center of

uptown Sedona. Dogs are allowed for an additional pet fee of $10 per night per room. 2 dogs may be allowed.

Oak Creek Terrace Resort
4548 N. Hwy. 89A
Sedona, AZ
928-282-3562 (800-224-2229)
oakcreekterrace.com
Relax by the creek or in one of the Jacuzzi rooms. Dogs are welcome with a $35 non-refundable pet fee. Amenities include in-room fireplaces, barbecue and picnic areas, air conditioning and cable TV.

Red Agave Resort
120 Canyon Circle Dr
Sedona, AZ
928-284-9327
redagaveresort.com/
Dogs are allowed for an additional pet fee of $40 for the 1st night and $15 each night thereafter per room. 2 dogs may be allowed.

Sedona Real Inn & Suites
95 Arroyo Pinon Drive
Sedona, AZ
928-282-1414
sedonareal.com
The Sedona Real Inn & Suites allows dogs up to 55 pounds. They have designated pet-friendly rooms. There is a $30 one time additional pet fee.

Sedona Rouge Hotel & Spa
2250 West Hwy 89A
Sedona, AZ
928-203-4111 (866-312-4111)
sedonarouge.com
Dogs up to 50 pounds are allowed at this chic hotel in West Sedona. There is a $100 refundable damage deposit and a $50 non-refundable cleaning fee. The hotel offers the Rouge & Pooch Package for each pet.

Sky Ranch Lodge
Airport Rd
Sedona, AZ
928-282-6400 (888-708-6400)
skyranchlodge.com/
There is a $10 per day per pet fee, dogs up to 65 pounds are ok. 2 dogs may be allowed.

Super 8 Sedona
2545 West Highway 89A
Sedona, AZ
928-282-1533 (800-800-8000)
Dogs of all sizes are allowed. Dogs are allowed for a pet fee of $25.00 per pet per stay.

The Red Agave Resort
120 Canyon Circle Drive
Sedona, AZ
928-284-9327 (877-284-9237)
redagaveresort.com
The Red Agave Resort is located at the base of Sedona's famous red rocks. There is a $40 pet fee for the first night and a $15 pet fee for each additional night.

Days Inn Show Low
480 West Deuce Of Clubs
Show Low, AZ
928-537-4356 (800-329-7466)
Dogs are welcome at this hotel.

Sleep Inn
1751 W. Deuce of Clubs
Show Low, AZ
928-532-7323 (877-424-6423)
Dogs of all sizes are allowed. Dogs are allowed for a pet fee of $15.00usd per pet per night.

Best Western Mission Inn
3460 E Fry Boulevard
Sierra Vista, AZ
520-458-8500 (800-780-7234)
Dogs up to 50 pounds are allowed. Dogs are allowed for a pet fee of $10.00 per pet per night.

Candlewood Suites Sierra Vista
1904 S. Highway 92
Sierra Vista, AZ
520-439-8200 (877-270-6405)
Dogs up to 80 pounds are allowed. Pets allowed with an additional pet fee. Up to $75 for 1-6 nights and up to $150 for 7+ nights. A pet agreement must be signed at check-in.

Holiday Inn Express Sierra Vista
1902 S. Hwy 92
Sierra Vista, AZ
520-439-8800 (877-270-6405)
Dogs of all sizes are allowed. Dogs are allowed for a pet fee of $7 per pet per night.

Motel 6 - Sierra Vista Fort Huachuca
1551 Fry Blvd
Sierra Vista, AZ
520-459-5035 (800-466-8356)
This motel welcomes your pets to stay with you.

Quality Inn
1631 South Highway 92
Sierra Vista, AZ
520-458-7900 (877-424-6423)
Dogs up to 50 pounds are allowed. Dogs are allowed for a pet fee of $10.00 per pet per night.

Super 8 Sierra Vista
201 W Fry Blvd
Sierra Vista, AZ
520-458-6711 (800-800-8000)
Dogs of all sizes are allowed. Dogs are allowed for a pet fee.

TownePlace Suites Sierra Vista
3399 Rodeo Drive
Sierra Vista, AZ
520-515-9900 (800-257-3000)
Besides offering a number of in-house amenities for all level of travelers, this all suite inn also offers a convenient location to historic, business, shopping, dining, and entertainment areas. Dogs are allowed for an additional one time fee of $100 per room. 2 dogs may be allowed.

Comfort Inn
2055 S. Main St.
Snowflake, AZ
928-536-3888 (877-424-6423)
Dogs of all sizes are allowed. Dogs are allowed for a pet fee of $15.00 per pet per night. Two dogs are allowed per room.

Days Inn St. Johns
125 E Commercial St.
St Johns, AZ
928-337-4422 (800-329-7466)
Dogs are welcome at this hotel.

Best Western Inn & Suites of Sun City
11201 Grand Avenue
Sun City, AZ
623-933-8211 (800-780-7234)
Dogs are welcome at this hotel.

Days Inn & Suites AZ Surprise
12477 West Bell Road
Surprise, AZ
623-933-4000 (800-329-7466)
Dogs of all sizes are allowed. Dogs are allowed for a pet fee.

Quality Inn & Suites of the Sun Cities
16741 N. Greasewood Street
Surprise, AZ
623-583-3500 (877-424-6423)
Dogs of all sizes are allowed. Dogs are allowed for a pet fee of $20.00 per pet per night.

Rodeway Inn Silver Creek Inn
825 North Main St.
Taylor, AZ
928-536-2600 (877-424-6423)
Dogs of all sizes are allowed. Dogs are allowed for a pet fee of $.00 per pet per night. Two dogs are allowed per room.

Candlewood Suites Phoenix/Tempe
1335 W. Baseline Rd
Tempe, AZ
480-777-0440 (877-270-6405)
Dogs up to 80 pounds are allowed. Pets allowed with an additional pet fee. Up to $75 for 1-6 nights and up to $150 for 7+ nights. A pet agreement must be signed at check-in.

Country Inns & Suites by Carlson
1660 W Elliot Rd
Tempe, AZ
480-345-8585
Dogs of all sizes are allowed. There is a $25 per night per pet additional fee. There is a $250 pet fee for stays over two weeks.

Homestead Studio Suites Phoenix - Tempe
2165 W. 15th
Tempe, AZ
480-557-8880 (800-804-3724)
One dog is allowed per suite. There is a $25 per night additional pet fee up to $150 for an entire stay.

Motel 6 - Phoenix Tempe Arizona State Univ
1612 Scottsdale Rd
Tempe, AZ
480-945-9506 (800-466-8356)
This motel welcomes your pets to stay with you.

Motel 6 - Phoenix Tempe Broadway Asu
513 Broadway Rd
Tempe, AZ
480-967-8696 (800-466-8356)
This motel welcomes your pets to stay with you.

Motel 6 - Phoenix Tempe Priest Dr Asu
1720 Priest Dr
Tempe, AZ
480-968-4401 (800-466-8356)
Your pets are welcome to stay here with you.

Quality Inn Aiport East
1550 S. 52nd St.
Tempe, AZ
480-967-3000 (877-424-6423)
Dogs of all sizes are allowed. Dogs are allowed for a pet fee of $25.00 per pet per stay.

Quality Suites near Old Town Scottsdale
1635 N Scottsdale Rd.
Tempe, AZ
480-947-3711 (877-424-6423)

Dogs up to 75 pounds are allowed. Dogs are allowed for a pet fee of $10.00 per pet per night. Two dogs are allowed per room.

Ramada at Arizona Mills Mall Tempe
1701 W Baseline Road
Tempe, AZ
480-413-1188 (800-272-6232)
Dogs of all sizes are allowed. Dogs are allowed for a pet fee.

Ramada Limited University Tempe
1915 East Apache Blvd
Tempe, AZ
480-736-1700 (800-272-6232)
Dogs are welcome at this hotel.

Red Roof Inn Phoenix Airport
2135 West 15th Street
Tempe, AZ
480-449-3205 (800-RED-ROOF)
One well-behaved family pet per room. Guest must notify front desk upon arrival. Guest is liable for any damages. In consideration of all guests, pets must never be left unattended in the guest rooms.

Residence Inn Tempe
5075 South Priest Drive
Tempe, AZ
480-756-2122 (800-331-3131)
This upscale, all suite hotel sits central to a plethora of activities and attractions, plus they offer a number of on-site amenities, including a daily buffet breakfast and evening socials with light dinner fare. Dogs are allowed for an additional one time pet fee of $100 per room. 2 dogs may be allowed.

Sheraton Phoenix Airport Hotel Tempe
1600 South 52nd St.
Tempe, AZ
480-967-6600 (888-625-5144)
Dogs up to 75 pounds are allowed. There is a $75 one time refundable pet fee per visit. Dogs are not allowed to be left alone in the room.

Studio 6 - Tempe
4909 Wendler Dr
Tempe, AZ
602-414-4470 (800-466-8356)
Your pets are welcome to stay here with you for a pet fee of $10 per day up to $50 for an entire stay.

Super 8 /ASU/Airport Tempe
1020 E Apache Blvd
Tempe, AZ
480-967-8891 (800-800-8000)
Dogs are welcome at this hotel.

TownePlace Suites Tempe
5223 S Priest Drive
Tempe, AZ
480-345-7889 (800-257-3000)
In addition to offering a convenient location to business, shopping, dining, and entertainment areas, this hotel also provides a number of in-house amenities, including a daily buffet breakfast and an evening social hour Monday to Wednesday. Dogs are allowed for an additional one time fee of $75 per room. Multiple dogs may be allowed.

Econo Lodge
1520 N. 84th Dr.
Tolleson, AZ
623-936-4667 (877-424-6423)
Dogs of all sizes are allowed. Dogs are allowed for a pet fee of $non-refundable per pet per night. Two dogs are allowed per room.

Best Western Lookout Lodge
781 N Highway 80
Tombstone, AZ
520-457-2223 (800-780-7234)
Dogs of all sizes are allowed. Dogs are allowed for a pet fee of $20 per pet per night.

Trail Rider's Inn
13 N. 7th Street
Tombstone, AZ
520-457-3573 (800-574-0417)
trailridersinn.com
You and your pup can walk to the historic Tombstone district from this inn. They offer large, clean, quiet rooms and cable TV. There is a $5 per day per pet fee. Multiple dogs may be allowed.

Quality Inn Navajo Nation
10 North Main Street
Tuba City, AZ
928-283-4545 (877-424-6423)
Dogs up to 50 pounds are allowed. Dogs are allowed for a pet fee of $10.00. per pet per night. Two dogs are allowed per room.

Best Western InnSuites Tucson Foothills Hotel & Suites
6201 N Oracle Road
Tucson, AZ
520-297-8111 (800-780-7234)
Dogs of all sizes are allowed. Dogs are allowed for a pet fee.

Comfort Suites
7007 E Tanque Verde Rd
Tucson, AZ
520-298-2300 (877-424-6423)
comfortsuites.com/

There is a $25 per night per pet additional fee. Dogs up to 80 pounds are allowed. 2 dogs may be allowed.

Comfort Suites Airport
6935 S. Tucson Blvd.
Tucson, AZ
520-295-4400 (877-424-6423)
Dogs of all sizes are allowed. Dogs are allowed for a pet fee of $25.00 per pet per night.

Comfort Suites at Sabino Canyon
7007 E. Tanque Verde
Tucson, AZ
520-298-2300 (877-424-6423)
Dogs of all sizes are allowed. Dogs are allowed for a pet fee of $25.00 per pet per night.

Comfort Suites at Tucson Mall
515 West Automall Dr
Tucson, AZ
520-888-6676 (877-424-6423)
Dogs of all sizes are allowed. Dogs are allowed for a pet fee of $10.00 per pet per stay. Two dogs are allowed per room.

Country Inns & Suites by Carlson
7411 N Oracle Rd
Tucson, AZ
520-575-9255
Dogs of all sizes are allowed. There is a $50 one time additional pet fee.

Doubletree Hotel
445 S Alvernon Way
Tucson, AZ
520-881-4200 (800-222-TREE (8733))
This upscale, resort-style hotel offers a number of on site amenities for all level of travelers - including their signature chocolate chip cookies at check in, plus a convenient location to business, shopping, dining, and entertainment areas. Dogs are allowed for an additional one time pet fee of $25 per room. 2 dogs may be allowed.

Econo Lodge
1136 N. Stone Ave.
Tucson, AZ
520-622-6714 (877-424-6423)
Dogs of all sizes are allowed.

Extended Stay America Tucson - Grant Road
5050 E. Grant Rd.
Tucson, AZ
520-795-9510 (800-804-3724)
One dog is allowed per suite. There is a $25 per night additional pet fee up to $150 for an entire stay.

Hilton El Conquistador Golf & Tennis Resort
10000 N Oracle Road
Tucson, AZ
520-544-5000 (800-HILTONS (445-8667))
A full-service resort, this upscale hotel offers outstanding scenery and numerous on site amenities for business and leisure travelers, plus a convenient location to business, shopping, dining, and recreation areas. Dogs up to 50 pounds are allowed for an additional one time pet fee of $50 per room with prior arrangements only. 2 dogs may be allowed.

Hilton Hotel
7600 East Broadway
Tucson, AZ
520-721-5600 (800-HILTONS (445-8667))
Located in the heart of the city, this upscale hotel offers a number on site amenities for business and leisure travelers, plus a convenient location to the airport, business, shopping, dining, and recreation areas. Dogs up to 75 pounds are allowed for an additional one time pet fee of $75 per room. There may be one dog up to 75 pounds or 2 dogs that total 75 pounds per room.

Holiday Inn Express Tucson-Airport
2548 E. Medina Road
Tucson, AZ
520-889-6600 (877-270-6405)
Dogs are welcome at this hotel.

La Quinta Inn & Suites Tucson Airport
7001 South Tucson Blvd.
Tucson, AZ
520-573-3333 (800-531-5900)
Dogs of all sizes are allowed. There are no additional pet fees. Dogs must be leashed and cleaned up after. Multiple dogs may be allowed.

La Quinta Inn Tucson Downtown
750 West Starr Pass Blvd
Tucson, AZ
520-624-4455 (800-531-5900)
Dogs of all sizes are allowed. There are no additional pet fees; however, there is a pet waiver to sign at check in. Dogs may not be left unattended, and they must be leashed and cleaned up after. Multiple dogs may be allowed.

La Quinta Inn Tucson East
6404 E. Broadway
Tucson, AZ
520-747-1414 (800-531-5900)
Dogs of all sizes are allowed. There

are no additional pet fees. Dogs must be leashed and cleaned up after. Multiple dogs may be allowed.

Lodge on the Desert
306 North Alvernon Way
Tucson, AZ
520-325-3366
lodgeonthedesert.com/
This lodge offers hacienda-style rooms and many have tile covered patios and fireplaces. Amenities include garden pathways, a pool and a restaurant with an outdoor patio where your pooch can join you. Room rates range from $79 to $269 depending on the season or type of room. Rates are subject to change. Dogs up to 40 pounds are welcome for an additional $25 per day per pet fee and a $50 refundable pet deposit. All 35 rooms and suites are non-smoking and dogs are allowed in any of the rooms. Multiple dogs may be allowed.

Loews Ventana Canyon Resort
7000 North Resort Drive
Tucson, AZ
520-299-2020
All well-behaved dogs of any size are welcome. This upscale hotel offers their "Loews Loves Pets" program which includes special pet treats, local dog walking routes, and a list of nearby pet-friendly places to visit. There is an additional one time pet cleaning fee of $25 per room.

Motel 6 - Tucson 22nd Street
1222 Freeway
Tucson, AZ
520-624-2516 (800-466-8356)
Your pets are welcome to stay here with you.

Motel 6 - Tucson Congress Street
960 Freeway
Tucson, AZ
520-628-1339 (800-466-8356)
Your pets are welcome to stay here with you.

Motel 6 - Tucson Airport
1031 Benson Hwy
Tucson, AZ
520-628-1264 (800-466-8356)
Your pets are welcome to stay here with you.

Quality Inn
1025 E. Benson Highway
Tucson, AZ
520-623-7792 (877-424-6423)
Dogs of all sizes are allowed. Dogs are allowed for a pet fee of $15.00 per pet per stay.

Quality Inn Airport
2803 E. Valencia Rd
Tucson, AZ
520-294-2500 (877-424-6423)
Dogs up to 50 pounds are allowed.
Dogs are allowed for a pet fee of
$10.00 per pet per night. Dogs are
allowed for a pet fee of $night per pet
per stay.

Red Roof Inn Tucson North
4940 West Ina Road
Tucson, AZ
520-744-8199 (800-RED-ROOF)
One well-behaved family pet per
room. Guest must notify front desk
upon arrival. Guest is liable for any
damages. In consideration of all
guests, pets must never be left
unattended in the guest rooms.

Red Roof Inn Tucson South
3704 East Irvington Road
Tucson, AZ
520-571-1400 (800-RED-ROOF)
One well-behaved family pet per
room. Guest must notify front desk
upon arrival. Guest is liable for any
damages. In consideration of all
guests, pets must never be left
unattended in the guest rooms.

Residence Inn Tucson
6477 E Speedway
Tucson, AZ
520-721-0991 (800-331-3131)
In addition to offering a convenient
location to numerous activities and
attractions for all level of travelers,
this all suite hotel also offers a
number of in-house amenities,
including a daily buffet breakfast and
complimentary evening socials
Monday to Thursday. Dogs are
allowed for an additional one time
pet fee of $100 per room. 2 dogs
may be allowed.

Residence Inn Tucson Airport
2660 East Medina Road
Tucson, AZ
520-294-5522 (800-331-3131)
In addition to offering a convenient
location to numerous sites of
interest, activities, and attractions for
all level of travelers, this all suite
hotel also offers a number of in-
house amenities, including a daily
buffet breakfast and evening socials.
Dogs up to 50 pounds are allowed
for an additional one time pet fee of
$100 per room. 2 dogs may be
allowed.

Residence Inn Tucson Williams
Centre

5400 E Williams Circle
Tucson, AZ
520-790-6100 (800-331-3131)
In addition to offering a convenient
location to numerous sites of
interest, year around recreation,
and attractions for all level of
travelers, this all suite hotel also
offers a number of in-house
amenities, including a daily buffet
breakfast and evening socials.
Dogs are allowed for an additional
one time pet fee of $100 per room.
Multiple dogs may be allowed.

Sheraton Tucson Hotel & Suites
5151 East Grant Rd.
Tucson, AZ
520-323-6262 (888-625-5144)
Dogs of all sizes are allowed. There
are no additional pet fees. Dogs are
not allowed to be left alone in the
room.

Studio 6 - Tucson Irvington Rd
4950 Outlet Center Dr
Tucson, AZ
520-746-0030 (800-466-8356)
Your pets are welcome to stay here
with you for a pet fee of $10 per day
up to $50 for an entire stay.

The Hotel Congress
311 E Congress Street
Tucson, AZ
520-622-8848 (800-722-8848)
This historic, landmark 1919 hotel
sits in the heart of the downtown
area and features a comfortable
vintage decor and atmosphere of
the 1930's. Additionally, they offer a
lively night club, fine dining, and a
number of other on-site amenities.
Quiet, well mannered dogs are
allowed for an additional fee of $10
per night per room. Leashed dogs
are also allowed at the outer tables
of the hotel's cafe. 2 dogs may be
allowed.

TownePlace Suites Tucson
405 W Rudasill Road
Tucson, AZ
520-292-9697 (800-257-3000)
This all suite hotel sits central to a
number of sites of interest for both
business and leisure travelers; plus
they also offer a number of on-site
amenities to ensure comfort. Dogs
are allowed for an additional one
time fee of $75 per room. Multiple
dogs may be allowed.

Westward Look Resort
245 East Ina Road
Tucson, AZ
520-297-1151 (800-722-2500)
westwardlook.com

This resort comes highly
recommended from one of our
readers. They said it was the most
pet-friendly resort around and they
can't say enough good things about
it. This former 1912 guest ranch, now
a desert resort hideaway, is nestled
in the foothills of Tucson's
picturesque Santa Catalina
Mountains. It offers guests a
Southwestern experience on 80
desert acres. They have walking
trails at the resort, tennis, swimming
pools and much more. Special room
rates can be as low as $69 during
certain times and seasons. There is
a $75 one time additional pet fee.

Windmill Suites
4250 N Campbell Avenue
Tucson, AZ
623-583-0133
Dogs of all sizes are allowed. There
are no additional pet fees. 2 dogs
may be allowed.

Best Western Rancho Grande
293 E Wickenburg Way
Wickenburg, AZ
928-684-5445 (800-780-7234)
Dogs of all sizes are allowed. Dogs
are allowed for a nightly pet fee.

Super 8 AZ Wickenburg
1021 North Tegner
Wickenburg, AZ
928-684-0808 (800-800-8000)
Dogs of all sizes are allowed. Dogs
are allowed for a pet fee of $10.00
per pet per night.

Days Inn Willcox
724 N Bisbee Avenue
Willcox, AZ
520-384-4222 (800-329-7466)
Dogs of all sizes are allowed. Dogs
are allowed for a pet fee of $7.00 per
pet per night.

Super 8 Willcox
1500 West Fort Grant Road
Willcox, AZ
520-384-0888 (800-800-8000)
Dogs of all sizes are allowed. Dogs
are allowed for a pet fee of $6.00 per
pet per night.

Best Western Inn of Williams
2600 W Route 66
Williams, AZ
928-635-4400 (800-780-7234)
Dogs of all sizes are allowed. Dogs
are allowed for a pet fee of $25 per
pet per stay.

Days Inn Williams
2488 W Route 66

Williams, AZ
928-635-4051 (800-329-7466)
Dogs are welcome at this hotel.

Grand Canyon Travelodge Williams
430 E. Route 66
Williams, AZ
928-635-2651 (800-578-7878)
Dogs of all sizes are allowed. Dogs
are allowed for a pet fee of $10.00
per pet per stay.

Holiday Inn Williams
950 N. Grand Canyon Blvd
Williams, AZ
928-635-4114 (877-270-6405)
Dogs are welcome at this hotel.

Motel 6 - Williams East Grand
Canyon
710 Route 66
Williams, AZ
928-635-4464 (800-466-8356)
This motel welcomes your pets to
stay with you.

Motel 6 - Williams West Grand
Canyon
831 Route 66
Williams, AZ
928-635-9000 (800-466-8356)
This motel welcomes your pets to
stay with you.

Quality Inn Mountain Ranch & Resort
6701 E. Mountain Ranch Rd.
Williams, AZ
928-635-2693 (877-424-6423)
Dogs up to 50 pounds are allowed.
Dogs are allowed for a pet fee of
$45.00 per pet per stay. Two dogs
are allowed per room.

Quality Inn Navajo Nation Capital
48 West Highway 264
Window Rock, AZ
928-871-4108 (877-424-6423)
Dogs of all sizes are allowed.

Econo Lodge at I-40
1706 N. Park Dr.
Winslow, AZ
928-289-4687 (877-424-6423)
Dogs of all sizes are allowed.

Holiday Inn Express Winslow
816 Transcon Lane
Winslow, AZ
928-289-2960 (877-270-6405)
Dogs of all sizes are allowed. Dogs
are allowed for a nightly pet fee.

La Posada
303 E 2nd Street
Winslow, AZ
928-289-4366
Dogs of all sizes are allowed. There

is a $10 one time fee per room and
a pet policy to sign at check in.

Motel 6 - Winslow
520 Desmond St
Winslow, AZ
928-289-9581 (800-466-8356)
This motel welcomes your pets to
stay with you.

Super 8 AZ Winslow
1916 W 3rd St.
Winslow, AZ
928-289-4606 (800-800-8000)
Dogs of all sizes are allowed. Dogs
are allowed for a pet fee of $10.00
per pet per stay.

Motel 6 - Phoenix Sun City
Youngtown
11133 Grand Ave
Youngtown, AZ
623-977-1318 (800-466-8356)
This motel welcomes your pets to
stay with you.

Best Western Coronado Motor
Hotel
233 S 4th Avenue
Yuma, AZ
928-783-4453 (800-780-7234)
Dogs up to 50 pounds are allowed.

Best Western InnSuites Yuma Mall
Hotel & Suites
1450 S Castle Dome Avenue
Yuma, AZ
928-783-8341 (800-780-7234)
Dogs of all sizes are allowed. Dogs
are allowed for a pet fee.

Candlewood Suites Yuma
2036 S. Ave 3e
Yuma, AZ
928-726-2800 (877-270-6405)
Dogs up to 80 pounds are allowed.
Pets allowed with an additional pet
fee. Up to $75 for 1-6 nights and up
to $150 for 7+ nights. A pet
agreement must be signed at
check-in.

Comfort Inn
1691 S. Riley Ave.
Yuma, AZ
928-782-1200 (877-424-6423)
Dogs up to 70 pounds are allowed.
Dogs are allowed for a pet fee of
$USD per pet per night.

Howard Johnson Inn Yuma
3181 South 4th Avenue
Yuma, AZ
928-344-1420 (800-446-4656)
Dogs are welcome at this hotel.

Motel 6 - Yuma Oldtown

1640 Arizona Ave
Yuma, AZ
928-782-6561 (800-466-8356)
This motel welcomes your pets to
stay with you.

Motel 6 - Yuma East
1445 16th St
Yuma, AZ
928-782-9521 (800-466-8356)
This motel welcomes your pets to
stay with you.

Ramada Chilton Conference Center
Yuma
300 East 32nd Street
Yuma, AZ
928-344-1050 (800-272-6232)
Dogs of all sizes are allowed. Dogs
are allowed for a pet fee.

Shilo Inn- Conference Center &
Resort Hotel
1550 S Castle Dome Road
Yuma, AZ
928-782-9511
Dogs of all sizes are allowed. There
is an additional one time pet fee of
$25 per room. 2 dogs may be
allowed.

Super 8 Yuma
1688 S Riley Ave
Yuma, AZ
928-782-2000 (800-800-8000)
Dogs of all sizes are allowed. Dogs
are allowed for a pet fee of $15.00
per pet per night.

TownePlace Suites Yuma
1726 S Sunridge Drive
Yuma, AZ
928-783-6900 (800-257-3000)
This all suite hotel sits central to a
number of sites of interest for
business, government, military, and
leisure travelers; plus they also offer
a number of on-site amenities to
ensure a comfortable stay. Dogs are
allowed for an additional one time
fee of $100 per room. Multiple dogs
may be allowed.

Arkansas

Days Inn Alma
250 North U.S. Hwy 71
Alma, AR
479-632-4595 (800-329-7466)
Dogs of all sizes are allowed. Dogs
are allowed for a nightly pet fee.

Best Western Continental Inn
136 Valley Street
Arkadelphia, AR
870-246-5592 (800-780-7234)

Dogs of all sizes are allowed. Dogs are allowed for a pet fee of $9.00 per pet per night.

Comfort Inn
100 Crystal Palace
Arkadelphia, AR
870-246-3800 (877-424-6423)
Dogs of all sizes are allowed. Dogs are allowed for a pet fee of $35.00 per pet per night. Three or more dogs may be allowed.

Days Inn Arkadelphia
137 Valley Drive
Arkadelphia, AR
870-246-3031 (800-329-7466)
Dogs of all sizes are allowed. Dogs are allowed for a nightly pet fee.

Motel 6 - Arkadelphia, Ar
106 Crystal Palace Dr
Arkadelphia, AR
870-246-6333 (800-466-8356)
This motel welcomes your pets to stay with you.

Super 8 Caddo Valley Area
Arkadelphia
118 Valley
Arkadelphia, AR
870-246-8585 (800-800-8000)
Dogs are welcome at this hotel.

Ramada Arkansas Batesville
1325 N. St. Louis
Batesville, AR
870-698-1800 (800-272-6232)
Dogs are welcome at this hotel.

Super 8 Batesville
1287 N Saint Louis St.
Batesville, AR
870-793-5888 (800-800-8000)
Dogs are welcome at this hotel.

Days Inn Beebe
100 Tammy Lane
Beebe, AR
501-882-2008 (800-329-7466)
Dogs of all sizes are allowed. Dogs are allowed for a nightly pet fee.

Days Inn Benton
17701 I-30
Benton, AR
501-776-3200 (800-329-7466)
Dogs of all sizes are allowed. Dogs are allowed for a pet fee of $5 per pet per night.

Econo Lodge
16732 I - 30
Benton, AR
501-776-1900 (877-424-6423)
Dogs of all sizes are allowed. Dogs are allowed for a pet fee of $10.00

per pet per night.

Clarion Hotel & Conference Center
211 SE Walton Blvd
Bentonville, AR
479-464-4600 (877-424-6423)
Dogs of all sizes are allowed. Dogs are allowed for a pet fee of $5.00 per pet per night. Two dogs are allowed per room.

Comfort Suites
2011 S.E. Walton Blvd
Bentonville, AR
479-254-9099 (877-424-6423)
Dogs up to 50 pounds are allowed. Dogs are allowed for a pet fee of $50.00 per pet per stay. Two dogs are allowed per room.

Days Inn & Suites Bentonville
3408 S. Moberly Lane
Bentonville, AR
479-271-7900 (800-329-7466)
Dogs are welcome at this hotel.

La Quinta Inn & Suites Bentonville
1001 S.E. Walton
Bentonville, AR
479-271-7555 (800-531-5900)
Dogs of all sizes are allowed. There are no additional pet fees. Dogs may not be left unattended, and they must be leashed and cleaned up after. 2 dogs may be allowed.

Sleep Inn
215 SE Walton Blvd
Bentonville, AR
479-464-4400 (877-424-6423)
Dogs of all sizes are allowed. Dogs are allowed for a pet fee of $5.00 per pet per night. Two dogs are allowed per room.

Super 8 Bentonville
2301 South East Walton Blvd
Bentonville, AR
479-273-1818 (800-800-8000)
Dogs are welcome at this hotel.

TownePlace Suites Bentonville Rogers
3100 SE 14th Street
Bentonville, AR
479-621-0202 (800-257-3000)
In addition to offering a number of in-house amenities for all level of travelers, this all suite inn also provides a convenient location to business, shopping, dining, and entertainment areas. Dogs are allowed for an additional one time fee of $100 per room. Multiple dogs may be allowed.

Travelodge Bentonville

2307 SE Walton Blvd.
Bentonville, AR
479-273-9727 (800-578-7878)
Dogs of all sizes are allowed. Dogs are allowed for a pet fee.

Wingate by Wyndham AR Bentonville
7400 SW Old Farm Blvd
Bentonville, AR
479-418-5400 (800-228-1000)
Dogs of all sizes are allowed. Dogs are allowed for a pet fee.

AR Travelodge Blytheville
102/A South Porter Drive
Blytheville, AR
870-780-1332 (800-578-7878)
Dogs of all sizes are allowed. Dogs are allowed for a pet fee of $6.00 per pet per night.

Comfort Inn & Suites
1510 E Main St.
Blytheville, AR
870-763-0900 (877-424-6423)
Dogs up to 60 pounds are allowed. Dogs are allowed for a pet fee of $15.00 per pet per stay. Two dogs are allowed per room.

Days Inn Blytheville
102 South Porter Drive
Blytheville, AR
870-763-1241 (800-329-7466)
Dogs of all sizes are allowed. Dogs are allowed for a nightly pet fee.

Quality Inn
1520 E. Main St.
Blytheville, AR
870-763-7081 (877-424-6423)
Dogs of all sizes are allowed. Two dogs are allowed per room.

Baymont Inn & Suites Brinkley
1815 N. Main St
Brinkley, AR
870-734-4300 (877-229-6668)
Dogs of all sizes are allowed. Dogs are allowed for a pet fee of $10 per pet per night.

Days Inn and Suites Brinkley
2005-A North Main Street
Brinkley, AR
870-734-4680 (800-329-7466)
Dogs of all sizes are allowed. Dogs are allowed for a nightly pet fee.

Econo Lodge & Suites
2203 N. Main Street
Brinkley, AR
870-734-1052 (877-424-6423)
Dogs of all sizes are allowed. Dogs are allowed for a pet fee of $10.00 per pet per night.

Super 8 Little Rock Area Bryant
201 Dell Dr
Bryant, AR
501-847-7888 (800-800-8000)
Dogs are welcome at this hotel.

Days Inn and Suites - Cabot
1302 West Locust Street
Cabot, AR
501-605-1810 (800-329-7466)
Dogs of all sizes are allowed. Dogs
are allowed for a pet fee of $10 per
pet per night.

Super 8 Cabot
15 Ryeland Drive
Cabot, AR
501-941-3748 (800-800-8000)
Dogs are welcome at this hotel.

Super 8
942 Adams Avenue
Camden, AR
870-836-2535 (800-800-8000)
Dogs of all sizes are allowed. Dogs
are allowed for a pet fee of $10.00
per pet per night.

Days Inn Clarksville
2600 West Main Street
Clarksville, AR
479-754-8555 (800-329-7466)
Dogs of all sizes are allowed. Dogs
are allowed for a pet fee of $10.00
per pet per night.

Super 8 AR Clarksville
1238 S Rodgers
Clarksville, AR
479-754-8800 (800-800-8000)
Dogs are welcome at this hotel.

Best Western Hillside Inn
1025 Highway 65 B
Clinton, AR
501-745-4700 (800-780-7234)
Dogs are welcome at this hotel.

Best Western Conway
816 E Oak Street
Conway, AR
501-329-9855 (800-780-7234)
Dogs are welcome at this hotel.

Candlewood Suites Conway
2360 Sanders St.
Conway, AR
501-329-8551 (877-270-6405)
Dogs up to 80 pounds are allowed.
Pets allowed with an additional pet
fee. Up to $75 for 1-6 nights and up
to $150 for 7+ nights. A pet
agreement must be signed at check-
in.

Days Inn Conway

1002 East Oak Street/I-40
Conway, AR
501-450-7575 (800-329-7466)
Dogs are welcome at this hotel.

Howard Johnson Inn - Conway
1090 Skyline Dr
Conway, AR
501-329-2961 (800-446-4656)
Dogs are welcome at this hotel.

Motel 6 - Conway
1105 Skyline Dr
Conway, AR
501-327-6623 (800-466-8356)
This motel welcomes your pets to
stay with you.

Quality Inn
150 US 65 N.
Conway, AR
501-329-0300 (877-424-6423)
Dogs of all sizes are allowed. Dogs
are allowed for a pet fee of $20.00
per pet per stay.

Econo Lodge Conference Center
1920 Junction City Road
El Dorado, AR
870-862-5191 (877-424-6423)
Dogs of all sizes are allowed. Two
dogs are allowed per room.

La Quinta Inn El Dorado
2303 Junction City Road
El Dorado, AR
870-863-6677 (800-531-5900)
Dogs of all sizes are allowed. There
are no additional pet fees. There is
a pet waiver to sign at check in.
Dogs may not be left unattended,
and they must be quiet, well
behaved, leashed, and cleaned up
after. Multiple dogs may be allowed.

Super 8 El Dorado
1925 Junction City Road
El Dorado, AR
870-862-1000 (800-800-8000)
Dogs are welcome at this hotel.

5 Ojo Inn
5 Ojo Street
Eureka Springs, AR
479-253-6734 (800-656-6734)
5ojo.com/
Nestled among the trees only a
short walk from town, this historic
inn offers guests a relaxing
ambiance and beautifully
accommodated rooms. One dog up
to 60 pounds or 1 medium and 1
small dog per room is allowed for
an additional fee of $20 per night
per pet. Dogs must be leashed and
cleaned up after.

Crescent Hotel and New Moon Spa
75 Prospect Avenue
Eureka Springs, AR
479-253-9766 (877-342-9766)
crescent-hotel.com/
Registered with the Historic Hotels of
America, this grand hotel also offers
15 acres of landscaped gardens, a
wedding chapel, a lounge,
restaurant, and a wonderful venue
for special events. Dogs are allowed
for an additional fee of $10 per night
per pet. 2 dogs may be allowed.

Lazee Daze
5432 H 23 S
Eureka Springs, AR
479-253-7026 (866 534-5761)
logcabinresort.com/
These beautiful cabins nestled
among the trees offer complete
kitchens, fireplaces, barbecues, a
large covered porch with a swing and
rockers, Jacuzzis, TV/VCR, and
wonderful views. Dogs are allowed
for an additional one time pet fee of
$30 and a credit card must be on file
in case of damages. There may be 1
large dog or 2 small to medium dogs
per cabin. Dogs must be crated
when left alone, leashed, and
cleaned up after at all times.

Motel 6 - Eureka Springs
3169 East Van Buren
Eureka Springs, AR
479-253-5600 (800-466-8356)
This motel welcomes your pets to
stay with you.

Roadrunner Inn
3034 Mundell Road
Eureka Springs, AR
479-253-8166 (888-253-8166)
beaverlakeview.com/
Certified as a backyard wildlife
habitat by the National Wildlife
Federation and the Arkansas Game
and Fish Commission, this getaway
offers guests an abundance of
marine and wildlife, great lake views,
barbecue and picnic areas,
kitchenettes, gardens, and plenty of
hiking trails. Dogs are allowed for an
additional one time fee of $10 per pet
at the inn; they are not allowed in the
cabins. Dogs must be crated when
left alone, and any "pet mistakes"
must be reported as they would like
to repair or clean up as soon as
possible. 2 dogs may be allowed.

Best Western Windsor Suites
1122 S Futrall Drive
Fayetteville, AR
479-587-1400 (800-780-7234)
Dogs of all sizes are allowed. Dogs
are allowed for a pet fee of $10.00

per pet per stay.

Candlewood Suites Fayetteville
2270 W. 6th Street
Fayetteville, AR
479-856-6262 (877-270-6405)
Dogs up to 80 pounds are allowed. Pets allowed with an additional pet fee. Up to $75 for 1-6 nights and up to $150 for 7+ nights. A pet agreement must be signed at check-in.

Motel 6 - Fayetteville
2980 College Ave
Fayetteville, AR
479-443-4351 (800-466-8356)
This motel welcomes your pets to stay with you.

Red Roof Inn Fayetteville, AR
1000 S. Futrall Dr.
Fayetteville, AR
479-442-3041 (800-RED-ROOF)
One well-behaved family pet per room. Guest must notify front desk upon arrival. Guest is liable for any damages. In consideration of all guests, pets must never be left unattended in the guest rooms.

Sleep Inn
728 Millsap Rd.
Fayetteville, AR
479-587-8700 (877-424-6423)
Dogs of all sizes are allowed. Dogs are allowed for a pet fee of $25.00 per pet per stay.

Staybridge Suites Fayetteville
1577 West 15th Street
Fayetteville, AR
479-695-2400 (877-270-6405)
Dogs up to 80 pounds are allowed. Pets allowed with an additional pet fee. Up to $75 for 1-6 nights and up to $150 for 7+ nights. A pet agreement must be signed at check-in.

Holiday Inn Forrest City
200 Holiday Drive
Forrest City, AR
870-633-6300 (877-270-6405)
Dogs of all sizes are allowed. Dogs are allowed for a pet fee of $15.00 per pet per stay.

Baymont Inn & Suites Fort Smith
2123 Burnham Road
Fort Smith, AR
479-484-5770 (800-531-5900)
Dogs of all sizes are allowed. There are no additional pet fees. Dogs may not be left unattended for long periods, and they must be leashed, cleaned up after, and removed for

housekeeping. Multiple dogs may be allowed.

Candlewood Suites Fort Smith
7501 Madison Street
Fort Smith, AR
479-424-3800 (877-270-6405)
Dogs up to 80 pounds are allowed. Pets allowed with an additional pet fee. Up to $75 for 1-6 nights and up to $150 for 7+ nights. A pet agreement must be signed at check-in.

Comfort Inn
2120 Burnham Rd.
Fort Smith, AR
479-484-0227 (877-424-6423)
Dogs of all sizes are allowed.

Days Inn Fort Smith
1021 Garrison Ave
Fort Smith, AR
479-783-0548 (800-329-7466)
Dogs are welcome at this hotel.

Holiday Inn Express Fort Smith
Executive Park
6813 Phoenix Ave
Fort Smith, AR
479-452-7500 (877-270-6405)
Dogs of all sizes are allowed. Dogs are allowed for a nightly pet fee.

Howard Johnson Inn AR Fort Smith
101 North 11th St.
Fort Smith, AR
479-494-7700 (800-446-4656)
Dogs up to 75 pounds are allowed. Dogs are allowed for a nightly pet fee.

Motel 6 - Ft Smith
6001 Rogers Ave
Fort Smith, AR
479-484-0576 (800-466-8356)
This motel welcomes your pets to stay with you.

Residence Inn Fort Smith
3005 S 74th Street
Fort Smith, AR
479-478-8300 (800-331-3131)
Some of the amenities at this all-suite inn include a daily buffet breakfast, a Manager's reception Monday through Thursday with light dinner fare, a heated swimming pool, and a complimentary grocery shopping service. Dogs are allowed for an additional one time pet fee of $75 per room. 2 dogs may be allowed.

Days Inn Harrison
1425 Hwy 62-65 North
Harrison, AR

870-391-3297 (800-329-7466)
Dogs of all sizes are allowed. Dogs are allowed for a pet fee of $10.00 per pet per night.

Quality Inn
1210 US 62/65 N
Harrison, AR
870-741-7676 (877-424-6423)
Dogs of all sizes are allowed.

Super 8 Hazen
4167 Highway 63 North
Hazen, AR
870-255-2888 (800-800-8000)
Dogs are welcome at this hotel.

Super 8 /Earle Area Heth
453 Hwy 149 North
Heth, AR
870-657-2101 (800-800-8000)
Dogs of all sizes are allowed. Dogs are allowed for a pet fee of $5.00 per pet per stay.

Best Western of Hope
1800 Holiday Drive
Hope, AR
870-777-9222 (800-780-7234)
Dogs are welcome at this hotel.

Super 8 Hope
I-30 Exit 30 at Hwy 4
Hope, AR
870-777-8601 (800-800-8000)
Dogs are welcome at this hotel.

Arlington Resort Hotel and Spa
101 Park Avenue/H 7
Hot Springs, AR
501-623-5511 (800-643-1504)
arlingtonhotel.com/
This grand Old-Southern style hotel shares a long and rich history in addition to providing a number of amenities for the leisure or business traveler, a full service salon, a thermal bath house, cascading swimming pools, 3 restaurants, weekend entertainment, and a central location to many other points of interest. One dog up to 65 pounds is allowed for an additional one time pet fee of $30. Dogs must be leashed and cleaned up after.

Candlewood Suites Hot Springs
3416 Central Ave
Hot Springs, AR
501-624-4000 (877-270-6405)
Dogs up to 80 pounds are allowed. Pets allowed with an additional pet fee. Up to $75 for 1-6 nights and up to $150 for 7+ nights. A pet agreement must be signed at check-in.

Dog-Friendly Lodging - Please always call ahead to make sure an establishment is still dog-friendly.

Embassy Suites
400 Convention Blvd
Hot Springs, AR
501-624-9200
Located at what has become known as America's Spa City, this luxury inn offers a wide range of amenities and close proximity to a number of other sites of interest and recreational opportunities. Dogs are allowed for an additional one time fee of $35 per pet. Multiple dogs may be allowed.

Historic Park Hotel
211 Fountain Street
Hot Springs, AR
501-624-5323
thehistoricparkhotel.com/r
Dogs of all sizes are allowed. There is an additional one time pet fee of $28.25 per room. Dogs are not allowed to be left alone in the room except for short periods. 2 dogs may be allowed.

Howard Johnson Express Inn - Hot Springs
400 West Grand Avenue
Hot Springs, AR
501-624-4441 (800-446-4656)
Dogs of all sizes are allowed. Dogs are allowed for a pet fee.

Lake Hamilton Resort
2803 Albert Pike Road/H 270
Hot Springs, AR
501-767-8606 (866-712-8606)
lakehamiltonresort.com/
This peninsula resort offers an island feel and amenities for business, leisure, or family getaways. Dogs are allowed for an additional fee of $10 per night per pet. Multiple dogs may be allowed.

Rodeway Inn
1125 E. Grand Ave.
Hot Springs, AR
501-624-3321 (877-424-6423)
Dogs of all sizes are allowed. Dogs are allowed for a pet fee of $10.00 per pet per night. Two dogs are allowed per room.

Staybridge Suites Hot Springs
103 Lookout Circle
Hot Springs, AR
501-525-6500 (877-270-6405)
Dogs up to 80 pounds are allowed. Pets allowed with an additional pet fee. Up to $75 for 1-6 nights and up to $150 for 7+ nights. A pet agreement must be signed at check-in.

Velda Rose Resort Hotel and Spa
218 Park Avenue/H 7

Hot Springs, AR
501-623-3311 (888-624-3311)
veldarose.net/index.html
A seasonal pool, restaurant, grand ballroom, nightclub, convention space, and a central location to several sites of interest have made this hotel popular for business or leisure travelers. Dogs are allowed for an additional fee of $10 per night per pet. 2 dogs may be allowed.

Days Inn Jacksonville
1414 John Harden Drive
Jacksonville, AR
501-982-1543 (800-329-7466)
Dogs of all sizes are allowed. Dogs are allowed for a pet fee.

Comfort Suites
3404 Access Road
Jonesboro, AR
870-336-2280 (877-424-6423)
Dogs of all sizes are allowed. Dogs are allowed for a pet fee of $20.00 per pet per night. Two dogs are allowed per room.

Days Inn AR Jonesboro
2904 Phillips Drive
Jonesboro, AR
870-972-8686 (800-329-7466)
Dogs of all sizes are allowed. Dogs are allowed for a nightly pet fee.

Econo Lodge
2406 Phillips Drive
Jonesboro, AR
870-932-9339 (877-424-6423)
Dogs of all sizes are allowed. Dogs are allowed for a pet fee of $6.00 per pet per night.

Holiday Inn Jonesboro
3006 South Caraway Rd
Jonesboro, AR
870-935-2030 (877-270-6405)
Dogs of all sizes are allowed. Dogs are allowed for a pet fee of $15.00 per pet per night.

Motel 6 - Jonesboro
2300 Caraway Rd
Jonesboro, AR
870-932-1050 (800-466-8356)
This motel welcomes your pets to stay with you.

Super 8 Jonesboro
2500 S Caraway Rd
Jonesboro, AR
870-972-0849 (800-800-8000)
Dogs are welcome at this hotel.

Ramada Limited Lake Village
912 Hwy 65/82 South
Lake Village, AR

870-265-4545 (800-272-6232)
Dogs are welcome at this hotel.

Gaston's White River Resort
1777 River Rd
Lakeview, AR
870-431-5202
gastons.com/
There are no pet fees. There are no designated smoking or non-smoking cottages. Multiple dogs may be allowed.

Airport Travelodge Little Rock
7615 Fluid Drive
Little Rock, AR
501-490-2200 (800-578-7878)
Dogs are welcome at this hotel.

Baymont Inn And Suites Little Rock
6100 Mitchell Drive
Little Rock, AR
501-562-6667 (877-229-6668)
Dogs are welcome at this hotel.

Best Western Luxury Inn & Suites
8219 Interstate 30
Little Rock, AR
501-562-4448 (800-780-7234)
Dogs of all sizes are allowed. Dogs are allowed for a pet fee of $10.00 per pet per night.

Candlewood Suites West Little Rock
10520 West Markham
Little Rock, AR
501-975-3800 (877-270-6405)
Dogs up to 80 pounds are allowed. Pets allowed with an additional pet fee. Up to $75 for 1-6 nights and up to $150 for 7+ nights. A pet agreement must be signed at check-in.

Days Inn And Suites - Airport Little Rock
3200 Bankhead Drive
Little Rock, AR
501-490-2010 (800-329-7466)
Dogs of all sizes are allowed. Dogs are allowed for a pet fee.

Embassy Suites
11301 Financial Centre Parkway
Little Rock, AR
501-312-9000 (800-EMBASSY (362-2779))
Nestled among rolling hills and lush forest, this upscale hotel offers a number of on site amenities for business and leisure travelers, plus a convenient location to business, shopping, dining, and entertainment districts. They also offer a complimentary cooked-to-order breakfast and a Manager's reception every evening. Dogs are allowed for

an additional one time pet fee of $50 per room. Multiple dogs may be allowed.

Extended Stay America Little Rock - West
600 Hardin Rd.
Little Rock, AR
501-954-9199 (800-804-3724)
One dog is allowed per suite. There is a $25 per night additional pet fee up to $150 for an entire stay.

Hilton Hotel
925 S University Avenue
Little Rock, AR
501-664-5020 (800-HILTONS (445-8667))
This upscale hotel is located in the heart of the city and offers a number of on site amenities for business and leisure travelers, plus a convenient location to business, shopping, dining, and entertainment areas. Dogs are allowed for an additional one time pet fee of $50 per room. Multiple dogs may be allowed.

Holiday Inn Express Little Rock-Airport
3121 Bankhead Dr
Little Rock, AR
501-490-4000 (877-270-6405)
Dogs of all sizes are allowed. Dogs are allowed for a pet fee of $25.00 per pet per night.

Holiday Inn Little Rock-Airport-Conf Ctr
3201 Bankhead Dr.
Little Rock, AR
501-490-1000 (877-270-6405)
Dogs of all sizes are allowed. Dogs are allowed for a pet fee of $25.00 per pet per night.

La Quinta Inn Little Rock West
200 Shackleford Rd.
Little Rock, AR
501-224-0900 (800-531-5900)
Dogs of all sizes are allowed. There are no additional pet fees. Dogs may not be left unattended unless they will be quiet and well behaved, and they must be crated. Dogs must be leashed, cleaned up after, and removed for housekeeping. Multiple dogs may be allowed.

La Quinta Inn Little Rock at Rodney Parham Rd
1010 Breckeneridge Drive
Little Rock, AR
501-225-7007 (800-531-5900)
Dogs of all sizes are allowed. There are no additional pet fees. Dogs must be crated or removed for

housekeeping. Also, please put the "Do Not Disturb" sign on the door when you are out and a dog is in the room uncrated. Dogs must be leashed and cleaned up after. 2 dogs may be allowed.

La Quinta Inn North Little Rock - Landers Road
4100 E. McCain Blvd.
Little Rock, AR
501-758-8888 (800-531-5900)
Two large dogs or 3 small dogs are allowed. There are no additional pet fees. Dogs must be leashed and cleaned up after.

Motel 6 - Little Rock South
7501 I-30
Little Rock, AR
501-568-8888 (800-466-8356)
This motel welcomes your pets to stay with you.

Motel 6 - Little Rock West
10524 Markham St
Little Rock, AR
501-225-7366 (800-466-8356)
This motel welcomes your pets to stay with you.

Residence Inn Little Rock
1401 S Shackleford Road
Little Rock, AR
501-312-0200 (800-331-3131)
Besides offering a convenient location to business, shopping, dining, recreational, and historical areas, this all suite inn also provides a number of in-house amenities, including a daily buffet breakfast and complementary evening receptions Monday to Thursday. Dogs are allowed for an additional one time pet fee of $100 per room. Multiple dogs may be allowed.

Days Inn Lonoke
105 Dee Dee Lane
Lonoke, AR
501-676-5138 (800-329-7466)
Dogs of all sizes are allowed. Dogs are allowed for a pet fee of $10.00 per pet per stay.

Super 8 Lonoke
102 Dee Dee Lane
Lonoke, AR
501-676-8880 (800-800-8000)
Dogs are welcome at this hotel.

Super 8 Malvern
3445 Oliver Lancaster Blvd.
Malvern, AR
501-332-5755 (800-800-8000)
Dogs are welcome at this hotel.

Comfort Suites
14322 Frontier Drive
Maumelle, AR
501-851-8444 (877-424-6423)
Dogs of all sizes are allowed. Dogs are allowed for a pet fee of $25.00 per pet per night. Dogs are allowed for a pet fee of $25.00/night per pet per stay.

Super 8
306 Hwy 425 North
Monticello, AR
870-367-6271 (800-800-8000)
Dogs are welcome at this hotel.

Days Inn Morrilton
1506 N. Oak Street
Morrilton, AR
501-354-5101 (800-329-7466)
Dogs are welcome at this hotel.

Days Inn Mountain Home
1746 Hwy 62 East
Mountain Home, AR
870-425-1010 (800-329-7466)
Dogs are welcome at this hotel.

Ramada Arkansas Mountain Home
1127 NE Hwy 62
Mountain Home, AR
870-425-9191 (800-272-6232)
Dogs are welcome at this hotel.

Teal Point Resort
715 Teal Point Rd
Mountain Home, AR
870-492-5145
norfork.com/tealpoint/
There is a $7 per night per pet fee. Dogs are allowed in the free-standing cabins. There are no designated smoking or non-smoking cabins. 2 dogs may be allowed.

Best Western Fiddlers Inn
601 Sylamore Avenue
Mountain View, AR
870-269-2828 (800-780-7234)
Dogs of all sizes are allowed. Dogs are allowed for a pet fee of $10.00 per pet per night.

Days Inn Mountain View
703 E Main Street
Mountain View, AR
870-269-3287 (800-329-7466)
Dogs of all sizes are allowed. Dogs are allowed for a pet fee.

Country Inns & Suites by Carlson
901 Hwy 367 N
Newport, AR
870-523-5851
Dogs of all sizes are allowed. There are no additional pet fees.

Dog-Friendly Lodging - Please always call ahead to make sure an establishment is still dog-friendly.

Holiday Inn North Little Rock
120 West Pershing
North Little Rock, AR
501-758-1851 (877-270-6405)
Dogs of all sizes are allowed. Dogs are allowed for a pet fee of $25 per pet per stay.

Motel 6 - Little Rock North
400 29th St
North Little Rock, AR
501-758-5100 (800-466-8356)
This motel welcomes your pets to stay with you.

Red Roof Inn North Little Rock
5711 Pritchard Drive
North Little Rock, AR
501-945-0080 (800-RED-ROOF)
One well-behaved family pet per room. Guest must notify front desk upon arrival. Guest is liable for any damages. In consideration of all guests, pets must never be left unattended in the guest rooms.

Residence Inn Little Rock North
4110 Health Care Drive
North Little Rock, AR
501-945-7777 (800-331-3131)
Besides offering a convenient location to downtown, shopping, dining, recreational, and historical areas, this all suite inn also provides a number of in-house amenities, including a daily buffet breakfast and complementary evening receptions Monday to Thursday with light dinner fare. Dogs are allowed for an additional one time pet fee of $100 per room. Multiple dogs may be allowed.

Super 8 Little Rock/North/Airport
1 Gray Street
North Little Rock, AR
501-945-0141 (800-800-8000)
Dogs are welcome at this hotel.

Black Oak Resort
8543 Oakland Road
Oakland, AR
870-431-8363
Dogs are allowed for an additional pet fee of $8 per night or for $40 by the week. The fee is per pet or per room depending on the size/cleaning needed of the pet and the accommodations. Dogs must be kept leashed at all times when out of the room as other pets also make their home here. 2 dogs may be allowed.

Days Inn Ozark
105 Airport Road
Ozark, AR
479-667-2530 (800-329-7466)
Dogs of all sizes are allowed. Dogs are allowed for a pet fee of $10 per pet per night.

Ozark Mountain Meadows
2669 Country Road 4021
Ozark, AR
479-497-2127
Dogs of all sizes are allowed, and there is no fee if your pet is well behaved. This is a single cabin in the Ozark Mountains and it also has an outside kennel. Dogs are not allowed to be left unattended in the cabin, and they must be on a flea and tick program. 2 dogs may be allowed.

Comfort Inn
2809 Pines Mall Dr.
Pine Bluff, AR
870-535-5300 (877-424-6423)
Dogs of all sizes are allowed.

Econo Lodge
4101 West Barraque Street
Pine Bluff, AR
870-575-0400 (877-424-6423)
Dogs of all sizes are allowed. Dogs are allowed for a pet fee of $USD per pet per night.

Ramada Plaza Hotel Pine Bluff
2 Convention Center Plaza
Pine Bluff, AR
870-535-3111 (800-272-6232)
Dogs of all sizes are allowed. Dogs are allowed for a pet fee of $25 per pet per stay.

Days Inn Suites Pocahontas
2805 Hwy 67 South
Pocahontas, AR
870-892-9500 (800-329-7466)
Dogs of all sizes are allowed. Dogs are allowed for a nightly pet fee.

Candlewood Suites
Rogers/Bentonville
4601 West Rozell
Rogers, AR
479-636-2783 (877-270-6405)
Dogs up to 80 pounds are allowed. Pets allowed with an additional pet fee. Up to $75 for 1-6 nights and up to $150 for 7+ nights. A pet agreement must be signed at check-in.

Embassy Suites
3303 Pinnacle Hills Parkway
Rogers, AR
479-254-8400 (800-EMBASSY (362-2779))
In addition to being connected to the John Q Hammons Center, this up scale, atrium-style hotel offers a number of on site amenities for business and leisure travelers, plus a convenient location to business, shopping, dining, and entertainment areas. They also offer a complimentary cooked-to-order breakfast and a Manager's reception every evening. Dogs up to 50 pounds are allowed for an additional one time pet fee of $75 per room. Multiple dogs may be allowed.

Residence Inn Rogers
4611 West Locust Street
Rogers, AR
479-636-5900 (800-331-3131)
Some of the amenities at this all-suite inn include a daily buffet breakfast, evening socials, a heated indoor swimming pool, a Sport Court, and a complimentary grocery shopping service. Dogs are allowed for an additional one time pet fee of $75 per room. Multiple dogs may be allowed.

Staybridge Suites Rogers -
Bentonville
1801 South 52nd Street
Rogers, AR
479-845-5701 (877-270-6405)
Dogs up to 80 pounds are allowed. Pets allowed with an additional pet fee. Up to $75 for 1-6 nights and up to $150 for 7+ nights. A pet agreement must be signed at check-in.

Super 8 /Bentonville Area Rogers
915 South 8th Street
Rogers, AR
479-636-9600 (800-800-8000)
Dogs are welcome at this hotel.

Holiday Inn Russellville
2407 N Arkansas
Russellville, AR
479-968-4300 (877-270-6405)
Dogs of all sizes are allowed. Dogs are allowed for a pet fee of $25.00 per pet per night.

Motel 6 - Russellville
215 Birch St
Russellville, AR
479-968-3666 (800-466-8356)
This motel welcomes your pets to stay with you.

Quality Inn
3019 E. Parkway Dr.
Russellville, AR
479-967-7500 (877-424-6423)
Dogs of all sizes are allowed. Dogs are allowed for a pet fee of $10.00 per pet per night.

Dog-Friendly Lodging - Please always call ahead to make sure an establishment is still dog-friendly.

Super 8 Russellville
2404 N Arkansas Ave
Russellville, AR
479-968-8898 (800-800-8000)
Dogs of all sizes are allowed. Dogs are allowed for a pet fee of $10.00 per pet per night.

Holiday Inn Express Hotel & Suites Searcy
3660 Ferren Trail
Searcy, AR
501-279-9991 (877-270-6405)
Dogs of all sizes are allowed. Dogs are allowed for a pet fee of $50.00 per pet per night.

Extended Stay America Fayetteville - Springdale
5000 Luvene Ave.
Springdale, AR
479-872-1490 (800-804-3724)
One dog is allowed per suite. There is a $25 per night additional pet fee up to $150 for an entire stay.

La Quinta Inn & Suites Springdale
1300 S. 48th Street
Springdale, AR
479-751-2626 (800-531-5900)
Dogs of all sizes are allowed. There are no additional pet fees. Dogs may only be left in the room alone if they will be quiet and well behaved. Dogs must be leashed, cleaned up after, and crated or removed for housekeeping. Multiple dogs may be allowed.

Residence Inn Springdale
1740 South 48th Street
Springdale, AR
479-872-9100 (800-331-3131)
Some of the amenities at this all-suite inn include a daily buffet breakfast, evening social hours, a Sport Court, an indoor pool, and a complimentary grocery shopping service. Dogs are allowed for an additional one time pet fee of $75 per room. Multiple dogs may be allowed.

Travelodge Springdale
1394 West Sunset Avenue
Springdale, AR
479-751-3100 (800-578-7878)
Dogs are welcome at this hotel.

Days Inn and Suites Stuttgart
708 W Michigan
Stuttgart, AR
870-673-3616 (800-329-7466)
Dogs of all sizes are allowed. Dogs are allowed for a pet fee of $10.00 per pet per night.

Super 8 Stuttgart
701 West Michigan
Stuttgart, AR
870-673-2611 (800-800-8000)
Dogs of all sizes are allowed. Dogs are allowed for a pet fee of $10.00 per pet per night.

La Quinta Inn Texarkana
5102 N State Line Road
Texarkana, AR
870-773-1000 (800-531-5900)
Dogs of all sizes are allowed. There are no additional pet fees. Dogs may only be left alone in the room if they will be quiet and well behaved. Dogs must be leashed, cleaned up after, and crated or removed for housekeeping. Multiple dogs may be allowed.

Quality Inn
5210 N. Stateline Ave.
Texarkana, AR
870-772-0070 (877-424-6423)
Dogs up to 65 pounds are allowed. Dogs are allowed for a pet fee of $35.00 per pet per stay. Two dogs are allowed per room.

Days Inn AR Trumann
400 Commerce Drive
Trumann, AR
870-483-8383 (800-329-7466)
Dogs of all sizes are allowed. Dogs are allowed for a nightly pet fee.

Best Western Van Buren Inn
1903 N 6th Street
Van Buren, AR
479-474-8100 (800-780-7234)
Dogs of all sizes are allowed. Dogs are allowed for a pet fee of $25.00 per pet per night.

Comfort Inn
3131 Cloverleaf St.
Van Buren, AR
479-474-2223 (877-424-6423)
Dogs of all sizes are allowed. Dogs are allowed for a pet fee of $25.00 per pet per stay.

Motel 6 - Van Buren
1716 Fayetteville Rd
Van Buren, AR
479-474-8001 (800-466-8356)
This motel welcomes your pets to stay with you.

Super 8 /Ft. Smith Area Van Buren
106 N Plaza Court
Van Buren, AR
479-471-8888 (800-800-8000)
Dogs are welcome at this hotel.

Motel 6 - West Helena, Ar

1207 Us 49
West Helena, AR
870-572-7915 (800-466-8356)
This motel welcomes your pets to stay with you.

Best Western West Memphis Inn
3401 Service Loop Road
West Memphis, AR
870-735-7185 (800-780-7234)
Dogs are welcome at this hotel.

Motel 6 - West Memphis, Ar
2501 South Service Rd
West Memphis, AR
870-735-0100 (800-466-8356)
This motel welcomes your pets to stay with you.

Red Roof Inn West Memphis, AR
1401 N. Ingram Boulevard
West Memphis, AR
870-735-7100 (800-RED-ROOF)
One well-behaved family pet per room. Guest must notify front desk upon arrival. Guest is liable for any damages. In consideration of all guests, pets must never be left unattended in the guest rooms.

Super 8 West Memphis
901 Martin Luther King Jr Dr
West Memphis, AR
870-735-8818 (800-800-8000)
Dogs are welcome at this hotel.

Super 8 Wheatley
129 Lawson Rd
Wheatley, AR
870-457-2202 (800-800-8000)
Dogs of all sizes are allowed. Dogs are allowed for a pet fee of $10.00 per pet per night.

Days Inn and Suites Wynne
1011 Highway 64 East
Wynne, AR
870-261-1100 (800-329-7466)
Dogs of all sizes are allowed. Dogs are allowed for a pet fee of $7.00 per pet per night.

California

Days Inn -Victorville Adelanto
11628 Bartlett Ave
Adelanto, CA
760-246-8777 (800-329-7466)
Dogs are welcome at this hotel.

Extended Stay America Oakland - Alameda
1350 Marina Village Pkwy.
Alameda, CA
510-864-1333 (800-804-3724)
One dog is allowed per suite. There

is a $25 per night additional pet fee up to $150 for an entire stay.

The Doors
North Hwy 1
Albion, CA
707-937-9200 (800-525-0049)
This vacation home rental is dog-friendly. There is an additional one time fee of $50 per pet. Please call to make reservations. Multiple dogs may be allowed.

Best Western Trailside Inn
343 N Main Street
Alturas, CA
530-233-4111 (800-780-7234)
Dogs of all sizes are allowed. Dogs are allowed for a pet fee of $100.00 per pet per stay.

Super 8 Alturas
511 N Main St.
Alturas, CA
530-233-3545 (800-800-8000)
Dogs are welcome at this hotel.

Holiday Inn Express Hotel & Suites Napa Valley-American Canyon
5001 Main St
American Canyon, CA
707-552-8100 (877-270-6405)
Dogs of all sizes are allowed. Dogs are allowed for a pet fee.

Embassy Suites
3100 E Frontera
Anaheim, CA
714-632-1221 (800-EMBASSY (362-2779))
This upscale New Orleans atrium-style hotel offers a number of on site amenities for business and leisure travelers, and they are only minutes from Disneyland, plus they are close to numerous business, shopping, dining, and entertainment areas. They also offer a complimentary cooked-to-order breakfast and a Manager's reception every evening. Dogs up to 50 pounds are allowed for an additional fee of $50 per night per pet. 2 dogs may be allowed.

Extended Stay America Orange County - Anaheim Convention Center
1742 S. Clementine St.
Anaheim, CA
714-502-9988 (800-804-3724)
One dog is allowed per suite. There is a $25 per night additional pet fee up to $150 for an entire stay.

Extended Stay America Orange County - Anaheim Hills
1031 N.Pacificenter Dr.

Anaheim, CA
714-630-4006 (800-804-3724)
One dog is allowed per suite. There is a $25 per night additional pet fee up to $150 for an entire stay.

Motel 6 - Anaheim Fullerton East
1440 State College Blv
Anaheim, CA
714-956-9690 (800-466-8356)
This motel welcomes your pets to stay with you.

Motel 6 - Anaheim Maingate
100 West Disney Way
Anaheim, CA
714-520-9696 (800-466-8356)
This motel welcomes your pets to stay with you.

Quality Inn Maingate
2200 S. Harbor Blvd.
Anaheim, CA
714-750-5211 (877-424-6423)
Dogs of all sizes are allowed. Two dogs are allowed per room.

Residence Inn Anaheim Maingate
1700 S Clementine Street
Anaheim, CA
714-533-3555 (888-236-2427)
This resort style hotel is close to many sites of interest and only a mile from Disneyland, giving it a convenient location to a variety entertainment, shopping, and dining venues, plus they offer a number of on site amenities, including a daily buffet breakfast and a Manager's reception Monday through Thursday. Dogs are allowed for an additional one time pet fee of $100 per room. 2 dogs may be allowed.

Staybridge Suites Anaheim-Resort Area
1855 S. Manchester Avenue
Anaheim, CA
714-748-7700 (877-270-6405)
Dogs up to 80 pounds are allowed. Pets allowed with an additional pet fee. Up to $75 for 1-6 nights and up to $150 for 7+ nights. A pet agreement must be signed at check-in.

TownePlace Suites Anaheim
1730 S State College bLVD
Anaheim, CA
714-939-9700 (800-257-3000)
In addition to offering a number of in-house amenities for all level of travelers, this all suite inn also provides a convenient location to numerous sites of interest, business, shopping, dining, and entertainment areas. One dog is

allowed for an additional one time fee of $100 (+ tax) per room.

Travelodge International Inn
Anaheim
2060 South Harbor Blvd
Anaheim, CA
714-971-9393 (800-578-7878)
Dogs are welcome at this hotel.

Residence Inn Anaheim Hills Yorba Linda
125 S Festival Drive
Anaheim Hills, CA
714-974-8880 (888-236-2427)
This hotel gives a convenient location to shopping, dining, and entertainment areas, plus they offer a daily buffet breakfast and a Manager's reception Monday through Thursday. Dogs are allowed for an additional one time pet fee of $75 (plus tax) per room. 2 dogs may be allowed.

Baymont Inn & Suites Anderson
2040 Factory Outlets Drive
Anderson, CA
530-365-6100 (877-229-6668)
Dogs of all sizes are allowed. Dogs are allowed for a pet fee of $10.00 per pet per night.

Best Western Anderson Inn
2688 Gateway Drive
Anderson, CA
530-365-2753 (800-780-7234)
Dogs of all sizes are allowed. Dogs are allowed for a nightly pet fee.

Best Western Cedar Inn & Suites
444 S Main Street
Angels Camp, CA
209-736-4000 (800-780-7234)
Dogs of all sizes are allowed. Dogs are allowed for a pet fee of $15 per pet per night.

Apple Lane Inn B&B
6265 Soquel Drive
Aptos, CA
831-475-6868 (800-649-8988)
applelaneinn.com/
You and your well-behaved dog are allowed in the Wine Cellar room of this Victorian farmhouse built in the 1870s. It is situated on over 2 acres with fields, gardens, and apple orchards. There are also many farm animals such as horses, chickens, goats, ducks and geese. Room stay includes a full breakfast, and afternoon and evening refreshments. Rates are $120 per night and up. There is a $25 charge for a dog, extra person or crib. No smoking is allowed indoors. This bed and

breakfast is located on Soquel Drive, near Cabrillo Jr. College. From Hwy 17 south, exit Hwy 1 south towards Watsonville. Take the Park Avenue/New Brighton Beach exit. Turn left onto Park Ave. Turn right onto Soquel. It will be near Atherton Drive and before Cabrillo College. 2 dogs may be allowed.

The Surf House
205 Rio Del Mar Blvd
Aptos, CA
805-260-1255
lynnsbeachhouse.com
This 800 square foot vacation rental allows pets. Please mention your pet when making reservations.

Extended Stay America Los Angeles - Arcadia
401 E. Santa Clara St.
Arcadia, CA
626-446-6422 (800-804-3724)
One dog is allowed per suite. There is a $25 per night additional pet fee up to $150 for an entire stay.

Motel 6 - Los Angeles Arcadia/pasadena Area
225 Colorado Pl
Arcadia, CA
626-446-2660 (800-466-8356)
This motel welcomes your pets to stay with you.

Residence Inn Pasadena Arcadia
321 E Huntington Drive
Arcadia, CA
626-446-6500 (800-331-3131)
This all suite hotel sits central to many of the city's star attractions, shopping, dining, and business areas, plus they offer a number of in-house amenities that include a daily buffet breakfast and evening socials Monday through Thursday with light dinner fare. Dogs are allowed for an additional one time pet fee of $100 per room. Multiple dogs may be allowed.

Best Western Arcata Inn
4827 Valley West Boulevard
Arcata, CA
707-826-0313 (800-780-7234)
Dogs are welcome at this hotel. There is a pet fee of $20 a visit.

Days Inn CA Arcata
4975 Valley West Blvd
Arcata, CA
707-822-4861 (800-329-7466)
Dogs of all sizes are allowed. Dogs are allowed for a pet fee.

Motel 6 - Arcata Humboldt University

4755 Valley West Blvd
Arcata, CA
707-822-7061 (800-466-8356)
This motel welcomes your pets to stay with you.

Quality Inn
3535 Janes Rd.
Arcata, CA
707-822-0409 (877-424-6423)
Dogs of all sizes are allowed. Dogs are allowed for a pet fee of $10.00 per pet per night. Two dogs are allowed per room.

Super 8 Arcata
4887 Valley West Boulevard
Arcata, CA
707-822-8888 (800-800-8000)
Dogs are welcome at this hotel.

Ebbetts Pass Lodge
1173 Highway 4, Box 2591
Arnold, CA
209-795-1563
There is a $5 per day pet charge.

Motel 6 - Atascadero
9400 El Camino Real
Atascadero, CA
805-466-6701 (800-466-8356)
This motel welcomes your pets to stay with you.

Best Western Golden Key
13450 Lincoln Way
Auburn, CA
530-885-8611 (800-780-7234)
Dogs of all sizes are allowed. Dogs are allowed for a pet fee of $20.00 per pet per stay.

Foothills Motel
13431 Bowman Road
Auburn, CA
530-885-8444 (800-292-5694)
This motel offers microwaves, refrigerators, HBO/cable TV, and a barbecue, gazebo and picnic area next to the pool. Dogs of all sizes are allowed for an additional pet fee of $10 per night per pet. Dogs may not be left alone in the room, and they must be leashed and cleaned up after.

Motel 6 - Auburn
1819 Auburn Ravine Rd
Auburn, CA
530-888-7829 (800-466-8356)
This motel welcomes your pets to stay with you.

Super 8 Auburn
140 E Hilcrest Dr.
Auburn, CA
530-888-8808 (800-800-8000)

Dogs are welcome at this hotel.

Best Western Hill House
700 Truxtun Avenue
Bakersfield, CA
661-327-4064 (800-780-7234)
Dogs up to 50 pounds are allowed. Dogs are allowed for a pet fee of $10.00 per pet per night.

Doubletree Hotel
3100 Camino Del Rio Court
Bakersfield, CA
661-323-7111 (800-222-TREE (8733))
This upscale hotel offers a number of on site amenities for all level of travelers, plus a convenient location to a variety of business, shopping, dining, and recreation areas. Dogs are allowed for an additional one time fee of $50 per pet. Multiple dogs may be allowed.

Extended Stay America Bakersfield - California Avenue
3318 California Ave.
Bakersfield, CA
661-322-6888 (800-804-3724)
One dog is allowed per suite. There is a $25 per night additional pet fee up to $150 for an entire stay.

Howard Johnson Express Inn - Bakersfield
2700 White Lane
Bakersfield, CA
661-396-1425 (800-446-4656)
Dogs are welcome at this hotel.

La Quinta Inn Bakersfield
3232 Riverside Dr.
Bakersfield, CA
661-325-7400 (800-531-5900)
Dogs of all sizes are allowed. There are no additional pet fees. Dogs must be housebroken, well behaved, leashed, and cleaned up after. Multiple dogs may be allowed.

Motel 6 - Bakersfield Airport
5241 Olive Tree Ct
Bakersfield, CA
661-392-9700 (800-466-8356)
This motel welcomes your pets to stay with you.

Motel 6 - Bakersfield Convention Center
1350 Easton Dr
Bakersfield, CA
661-327-1686 (800-466-8356)
This motel welcomes your pets to stay with you.

Motel 6 - Bakersfield East
8223 Brundage Ln

Bakersfield, CA
661-366-7231 (800-466-8356)
This motel welcomes your pets to
stay with you.

Motel 6 - Bakersfield South
2727 White Ln
Bakersfield, CA
661-834-2828 (800-466-8356)
This motel welcomes your pets to
stay with you.

Ramada Limited Central
830 Wible Rd
Bakersfield, CA
661-831-1922 (800-272-6232)
Dogs of all sizes are allowed. Dogs
are allowed for a pet fee of $10.00
per pet per night.

Red Lion
2400 Camino Del Rio Court
Bakersfield, CA
661-327-0681
Dogs up to 80 pounds are allowed
for a $20 per night per pet additional
fee. There are no additional pet fees
for R&R members, and the R&R
program is free to sign up. 2 dogs
may be allowed.

Residence Inn Bakersfield
4241 Chester Lane
Bakersfield, CA
661-321-9800 (888-236-2427)
This hotel gives a convenient
location to business, shopping,
dining, and entertainment areas, plus
they offer a daily buffet breakfast and
a Manager's reception Monday
through Thursday. Dogs are allowed
for an additional one time pet fee of
$100 per room. Multiple dogs may be
allowed.

Rodeway Inn Near I-5
200 Trask St.
Bakersfield, CA
661-764-5221 (877-424-6423)
Dogs of all sizes are allowed. Dogs
are allowed for a pet fee of $5.00 per
pet per night.

Sleep Inn & Suites
6257 Knudsen Drive
Bakersfield, CA
661-399-2100 (877-424-6423)
Dogs of all sizes are allowed. Dogs
are allowed for a pet fee of $10.00
per pet per night.

Super 8 /Central Bakersfield
901 Real Rd.
Bakersfield, CA
661-322-1012 (800-800-8000)
Dogs are welcome at this hotel.

Travelodge Bakersfield
1011 Oak Street
Bakersfield, CA
661-325-0772 (800-578-7878)
Dogs of all sizes are allowed. Dogs
are allowed for a nightly pet fee.

Motel 6 - Los Angeles Baldwin Park
14510 Garvey Ave
Baldwin Park, CA
626-960-5011 (800-466-8356)
This motel welcomes your pets to
stay with you.

Days Inn Casino/Outlet Mall
Banning
2320 West Ramsey St/I-10
Banning, CA
951-849-0092 (800-329-7466)
Dogs of all sizes are allowed. Dogs
are allowed for a pet fee of $10.00
per pet per night.

Super 8
1690 W Ramsey St.
Banning, CA
951-849-8888 (800-800-8000)
Dogs are welcome at this hotel.

Best Western Desert Villa Inn
1984 E Main Street
Barstow, CA
760-256-1781 (800-780-7234)
Dogs of all sizes are allowed. Dogs
are allowed for a pet fee of $15.00
per pet per stay.

Days Inn Barstow
1590 Cool Water Lane
Barstow, CA
760-256-1737 (800-329-7466)
Dogs are welcome at this hotel.

Days Inn South Lenwood
2551 Commerce Parkway
Barstow, CA
760-253-2121 (800-329-7466)
Dogs are welcome at this hotel.

Econo Lodge
1230 E. Main St.
Barstow, CA
760-256-2133 (877-424-6423)
Dogs of all sizes are allowed. Dogs
are allowed for a pet fee of $10.00
per pet per night.

Holiday Inn Express Barstow-
Historic Route 66
1861 West Main Street
Barstow, CA
760-256-1300 (877-270-6405)
Dogs of all sizes are allowed. Dogs
are allowed for a pet fee of $25.00
per pet per night.

Holiday Inn Express Hotel & Suites

Barstow
2700 Lenwood Road
Barstow, CA
760-253-9200 (877-270-6405)
Dogs are welcome at this hotel.

Motel 6 - Barstow
150 Yucca Ave
Barstow, CA
760-256-1752 (800-466-8356)
This motel welcomes your pets to
stay with you.

Super 8 Barstow
170 Coolwater Lane
Barstow, CA
760-256-8443 (800-800-8000)
Dogs of all sizes are allowed. Dogs
are allowed for a pet fee of $10 per
pet per night.

Travelodge Barstow
1630 E Main St
Barstow, CA
760-256-8931 (800-578-7878)
Dogs of all sizes are allowed. Dogs
are allowed for a pet fee of $8.00 per
pet per night.

Rodeway Inn
1265 E. 6th Street
Beaumont, CA
951-845-1436 (877-424-6423)
Dogs up to 50 pounds are allowed.
Dogs are allowed for a pet fee of
$10.00 per pet per night. Two dogs
are allowed per room.

Motel 6 - Los Angeles Bellflower
17220 Downey Ave
Bellflower, CA
562-531-3933 (800-466-8356)
This motel welcomes your pets to
stay with you.

Extended Stay America San
Francisco - Belmont
120 Sem Ln.
Belmont, CA
650-654-0344 (800-804-3724)
One dog is allowed per suite. There
is a $25 per night additional pet fee
up to $150 for an entire stay.

Motel 6 - San Francisco Belmont
1101 Shoreway Rd
Belmont, CA
650-591-1471 (800-466-8356)
This motel welcomes your pets to
stay with you.

Beau Sky Hotel
2520 Durant Ave
Berkeley, CA
510-540-7688
This small hotel offers personalized
service. Some rooms have

balconies. If your room doesn't, you can sit at the chairs and tables in the patio at the front of the hotel. Your small, medium or large dog will feel welcome here because they don't discriminate against dog size. It is located close to the UC Berkeley campus and less than a block from the popular Telegraph Ave (see Attractions). There aren't too many hotels in Berkeley, especially around the campus. So if you are going, be sure to book a room in advance. To get there from Hwy 880 heading north, take the Hwy 980 exit towards Hwy 24/Walnut Creek. Then take the Hwy 24 exit on the left towards Berkeley/Walnut Creek. Exit at Claremont Ave and turn left onto Claremont Ave. Make a slight left onto College Ave. Turn left onto Haste St. Turn right onto Telegraph Ave and then right onto Durant. The hotel will be on the right. There are no additional pet fees. All rooms are non-smoking. 2 dogs may be allowed.

Doubletree Hotel and Executive Meeting Center
200 Marina Blvd
Berkeley, CA
510-548-7920 (800-222-TREE (8733))
Overlooking the San Francisco Bay, this resort style, luxury hotel offers a number of on site amenities for business or leisure travelers, plus a convenient location to all this vibrant city and surrounding areas have to offer. Dogs up to 50 pounds are allowed for an additional one time pet fee of $100 per room. 2 dogs may be allowed.

Golden Bear Motel
1620 San Pablo Ave
Berkeley, CA
510-525-6770
This motel has over 40 rooms. Eight of the rooms have two-bedroom units and there are four two-bedroom cottages with kitchens. Parking is free. To get there from Hwy 80 heading north, exit University Ave. Turn right onto University Ave, and then left on San Pablo Ave. The motel is on the left. There is a $10 per day per pet additional fee. Multiple dogs may be allowed.

Lake Oroville Bed and Breakfast
240 Sunday Drive
Berry Creek, CA
530-589-0700
lakeoroville.com/lakeoroville/
Dogs are welcome, but should be okay around other dogs. The owner

has dogs and cats on the premises. There is a $10 per day pet fee. Children are also welcome.

The Tower-Beverly Hills Hotel
1224 S Beverwil Drive
Beverly Hills, CA
310-277-2800 (800-421-3212)
This 12 story, luxury hotel offers an upscale destination for business and leisure travelers with an outstanding location to numerous activities and recreation in the Los Angeles/Hollywood areas. Specializing in making you feel at home, they offer elegant accommodations, a heated pool, 24 hour room service, a complete business center, private balconies, an award winning restaurant with patio dining service, and more. Dogs of all sizes are allowed. There is a $100 additional pet fee. Dogs must be well mannered, and leashed and cleaned up after at all times. Dogs may also join their owners at the outside dining tables. Multiple dogs may be allowed.

Access Big Bear Cabin Rentals
Call for Cabins
Big Bear Lake, CA
909-584-BEAR (800-817-3687)
inbigbear.com
These private cabins and vacation homes allow dogs. All have kitchens, TVs, barbecues and fireplaces.

Best Western/Big Bear Chateau
42200 Moonridge Rd
Big Bear Lake, CA
909-866-6666 (800-780-7234)
In addition to being less than a mile from the Snow Summit and Bear Mountain Ski resorts, this resort offers numerous in-house amenities. Dogs are allowed for an additional one time fee of $25 for the 1st dog and $5 for a 2nd dog. 2 dogs may be allowed.

Big Bear Cabins California
43630 Rainbow Lane
Big Bear Lake, CA
888-336-2891
bigbearcabinscalifornia.com
There is a $10 per day pet fee. Pets may not be left unattended in the cottages. According to a reader "4 cozy, clean and comfortable cottages on 40 acres adjoining BLM land. Very relaxed, run by nice people. Plenty of leash-free hiking right from your door."

Big Bear Cool Cabins
Book Online

Big Bear Lake, CA
909-866-7374 (800-550-8779)
coolcabins.com
Big Bear Lake vacation rentals on or near the lake and ski slopes - all with fireplace, barbecue, kitchen, and many with hot tubs, pool tables, docks, and more. Cleaning, fresh towels and linens provided. No extra pet fee for responsible pet owners.

Eagle's Nest Lodge
41675 Big Bear Blvd.
Big Bear Lake, CA
909-866-6465 (888-866-6465)
bigbear.com/enbb/
There are 5 cabins and only 1 allows dogs, but it is a pretty nice cabin. It's called the Sierra Madre and includes a kitchen, fireplace and separate bedroom. You can order breakfast delivered to the room for an additional $10 per person. Dogs are allowed for an additional fee of $10 per night per pet. 2 dogs may be allowed.

Golden Bear Cottages
39367 Big Bear Blvd/H 18
Big Bear Lake, CA
805-226-0102 (800-461-1023)
goldenbearcottages.com/
Some of the amenities of this beautiful get-a-way destination include a convenient location to some of the area's best attractions and ski resorts; a wide variety of seasonal activities; a heated pool and spa, and gaming fields/courts. The 6 acre park sits lakeside and also offers barbecue and picnic areas, a large play area for small children, and a gift shop with video rentals, karaoke machines, board-games, snacks, and beverages. Dogs are allowed for an additional fee of $10 per night per pet, and they also get their very own lockable fenced pet yard at each cottage. Pet carriers and quilts are available for rent if needed. 2 dogs may be allowed.

Majestic Moose Lodge
39328 Big Bear Blvd/H 18
Big Bear Lake, CA
909-866-9586 (877-585-5855)
majesticmooselodge.com/
This getaway offers 20 unique cabins/rooms, and is nestled on 2 acres of lush park-like grounds among tall pine trees with plenty of indoor and outdoor recreational opportunities available. Some of the amenities include fireplaces and kitchens/kitchenettes, cable TV, VCRs, and large covered porches. Housebroken dogs of all sizes are

allowed for no additional fee. Treats, a pet coverlet (to keep dog hair off the furniture), and waste bags are available at the front desk for their four-legged guests. There are several dog friendly hiking trails and eateries nearby. Dogs must be kenneled when left alone in the room, and they must be leashed and cleaned up after at all times. 2 dogs may be allowed.

Motel 6 - Big Bear
42899 Big Bear Blvd
Big Bear Lake, CA
909-585-6666 (800-466-8356)
This motel welcomes your pets to stay with you.

Pine Knot Guest Ranch
908 Pine Knot Ave.
Big Bear Lake, CA
909-866-3446 (800-866-3446)
pineknotguestranch.com
This dog-friendly guest ranch in Big Bear is in a wooded area. They have seven cabins and one guest room. There is an off-leash area for well-behaved and controlled dogs. The ranch has some llamas on the premises.

Shore Acres Lodge
40090 Lakeview Drive
Big Bear Lake, CA
909-866-8200 (800-524-6600)
bigbear.com/shorea/shorea.html
Dogs are allowed for an additional fee of $10 per night per pet. Multiple dogs may be allowed.

Timber Haven Lodge
877 Tulip Lane
Big Bear Lake, CA
909-866-7207
Dogs are welcome in designated cabins. Dogs are allowed for an additional fee of $20 per night per pet. 2 dogs may be allowed.

Timberline Lodge
39921 Big Bear Blvd.
Big Bear Lake, CA
909-866-4141 (800-803-4111)
thetimberlinelodge.com/
The 'Pets Welcome' sign at the main entrance will let you know your pup is more than welcome here. Some of the 13 cabins have fireplaces and full kitchens. There is also a playground for kids. There is a $15 per day additional pet per pet. Dogs must be crated when left alone in the room. Multiple dogs may be allowed.

Big Pine Motel
370 S Main St

Big Pine, CA
760-938-2282
There is a $10 per day per pet additional pet fee. 2 dogs may be allowed.

Bristlecone Motel
101 N. Main St.
Big Pine, CA
760-938-2067
According to one of our website readers 'Neat,inexpensive rooms with kitchens or fridge and microwave. Barbecue and fish cleaning area. Easy day trip to the ancient Bristlecone Pine Forest, which is extremely dog friendly.' There is no additional pet fee. Dogs may not be left alone in the room. 2 dogs may be allowed.

Big Sur Vacation Retreat
off Highway One
Big Sur, CA
831-624-5339 Ext 13
thawley.com/bigsur/
Rent this vacation rental by the week or longer. The home is situated on ten acres and at an elevation of 1,700 feet which is usually above the coastal fog and winds. Well-behaved dogs are welcome. No children under 10 years old allowed without the prior consent of the owner. This rental is usually available between June and mid-October. Rates are about $2300 per week. The home is located about 45 minutes south of Carmel.

Best Western Bishop Holiday Spa Lodge
1025 N Main Street
Bishop, CA
760-873-3543 (800-780-7234)
Dogs are welcome at this hotel.

Bishop Village Motel
286 W Elm Street
Bishop, CA
888-668-5546
Dogs of all sizes are allowed. There is a $10 per night per pet additional pet fee. 2 dogs may be allowed.

Comfort Inn
805 N. Main St.
Bishop, CA
760-873-4284 (877-424-6423)
Dogs of all sizes are allowed. Dogs are allowed for a pet fee of $15.00 per pet per night. Two dogs are allowed per room.

Days Inn Bishop
724 West Line Street

Bishop, CA
760-872-1095 (800-329-7466)
Dogs of all sizes are allowed. Dogs are allowed for a pet fee of $10 per pet per night.

Holiday Inn Express Hotel & Suites Bishop
636 North Main St
Bishop, CA
760-872-2423 (877-270-6405)
Dogs of all sizes are allowed. Dogs are allowed for a pet fee of $25.00 per pet per night.

Motel 6 - Bishop
1005 Main St
Bishop, CA
760-873-8426 (800-466-8356)
This motel welcomes your pets to stay with you.

Ramada Limited Bishop
155 East Elm Street
Bishop, CA
760-872-1771 (800-272-6232)
Dogs are welcome at this hotel.

Rodeway Inn
150 E Elm Street
Bishop, CA
760-873-3564
There is a $5 per day per pet fee. Dogs are allowed in certain rooms only. 2 dogs may be allowed.

Super 8 Bishop
535 S. Main St.
Bishop, CA
760-872-1386 (800-800-8000)
Dogs are welcome at this hotel.

Vagabond Inn
1030 N Main Street
Bishop, CA
760-873-6351
There is a $15 per day per pet fee. Multiple dogs may be allowed.

Best Western Sahara Motel
825 W Hobsonway
Blythe, CA
760-922-7105 (800-780-7234)
Dogs are welcome at this hotel.

Days Inn CA Blythe
9274 East Hobson Way
Blythe, CA
760-922-5101 (800-329-7466)
Dogs of all sizes are allowed. Dogs are allowed for a pet fee.

Knights Inn Blythe
9820 East Hobson Way
Blythe, CA
760-922-4126 (800-843-5644)
Dogs of all sizes are allowed. Dogs

are allowed for a pet fee of $5.00 per pet per night.

Motel 6 - Blythe
500 Donlon St
Blythe, CA
760-922-6666 (800-466-8356)
This motel welcomes your pets to stay with you.

Rodeway Inn & Suites
1725 E. Hobson Way
Blythe, CA
760-922-3334 (877-424-6423)
Dogs up to 50 pounds are allowed. Dogs are allowed for a pet fee of $10.00 per pet per night. Two dogs are allowed per room.

Super 8 Blythe
550 W Donlon St.
Blythe, CA
760-922-8881 (800-800-8000)
Dogs are welcome at this hotel.

Bodega Bay and Beyond
575 Coastal H One
Bodega Bay, CA
707-875-3942
Dogs of all sizes are allowed. There is a a $50 per room per stay fee and a pet policy to sign at check in. 2 dogs may be allowed.

Redwood Croft B&B
275 Northwest Drive
Bonny Doon, CA
831-458-1939
www2.cruzio.com/~cummings/ .
This bed and breakfast, located in the Santa Cruz Mountains, is set on a sunny hill amidst the redwood forest. It is the perfect country getaway, especially since they allow dogs. They are very dog-friendly. This B&B has two rooms each with a private bath and full amenities. The Garden Room has its own entrance, private deck with a secluded 7 foot Jacuzzi spa, full-size bed, woodburning stone fireplace and a skylighted loft with a queen futon. The West Room is sunny and spacious, has a California king bed and large bathroom with a double shower and roman tub. Room stay includes a lavish country breakfast. Room rates start at $165 per night. The dog-friendly Davenport Beach (see Parks) is only about 10-15 minutes away. Call the inn for directions or for a brochure. Dogs are allowed for no additional fee. 2 dogs may be allowed.

Boonville Hotel
Highway 128

Boonville, CA
707-895-2210
boonvillehotel.com/
This historic hotel was built in 1862. Dogs and children are allowed in the Bungalow and the Studio rooms which are separate from the main building. Both of these rooms are in the Creekside building with private entrances and yards. Room rates start at $225 per night. They have 2 pet-friendly rooms. There is an additional $25 per day per pet charge. Please note that their restaurant is closed on Tuesdays and Wednesdays. This hotel is in Anderson Valley, which is located 2 1/2 hours north of San Francisco. 2 dogs may be allowed.

Best Western Main Street Inn
1562 E Main Street
Brawley, CA
760-351-9800 (800-780-7234)
Dogs of all sizes are allowed. Dogs are allowed for a nightly pet fee.

Chase Suites
3100 E Imperial H
Brea, CA
714-579-3200
chasehotelbrea.com/
Dogs are allowed for an additional fee of $10 per night per pet, plus a $250 refundable deposit.

Homestead Studio Suites Orange County - Brea
3050 E. Imperial Hwy.
Brea, CA
714-528-2500 (800-804-3724)
One dog is allowed per suite. There is a $25 per night additional pet fee up to $150 for an entire stay.

Walker River Lodge
100 Main Street
Bridgeport, CA
760-932-7021
Well behaved dogs of all sizes are allowed. There is a pet policy to sign at check in and there are no additional pet fees. Dogs may not be left alone in the room at any time.

Marriott Santa Ynez Valley
555 McMurray Road
Buellton, CA
805-688-1000 (800-638-8882)
This luxury hotel provides a central location to a number of sites of interest for both business and leisure travelers; plus they also offer numerous on-site amenities to ensure a comfortable stay. Dogs are allowed for an additional one time fee of $75 per room. 2 dogs

may be allowed.

Motel 6 - Buellton Solvang Area
333 Mcmurray Rd
Buellton, CA
805-688-7797 (800-466-8356)
This motel welcomes your pets to stay with you.

Motel 6 - Buena Park-knotts Berry Farm/disneyland
7051 Valley View St
Buena Park, CA
714-522-1200 (800-466-8356)
This motel welcomes your pets to stay with you.

Red Roof Inn Buena Park
7121 Beach Boulevard
Buena Park, CA
714-670-9000 (800-RED-ROOF)
One well-behaved family pet per room. Guest must notify front desk upon arrival. Guest is liable for any damages. In consideration of all guests, pets must never be left unattended in the guest rooms.

Super 8 Buena Park
7800 Crescent Avenue
Buena Park, CA
714-527-2201 (800-800-8000)
Dogs of all sizes are allowed. Dogs are allowed for a pet fee of $15.00 per pet per night.

Extended Stay America Los Angeles - Burbank Airport
2200 Empire Ave.
Burbank, CA
818-567-0952 (800-804-3724)
One dog is allowed per suite. There is a $25 per night additional pet fee up to $150 for an entire stay.

Holiday Inn Burbank-Media Center
150 E. Angeleno
Burbank, CA
818-841-4770 (877-270-6405)
Dogs of all sizes are allowed. Dogs are allowed for a pet fee of $50.00 per pet per night.

Ramada Airport Burbank
2900 N San Fernando/I-5
Burbank, CA
818-843-5955 (800-272-6232)
Dogs are welcome at this hotel.

Residence Inn Burbank Downtown
321 S First Street
Burbank, CA
818-260-8787 (800-331-3131)
This all suite hotel sits central to many of the city's star attractions, the Bob Hope Airport, dining, and entertainment areas, plus they offer

a number of in-house amenities that include a daily buffet breakfast, and a complimentary weekly social hour. Dogs are allowed for an additional one time pet fee of $100 per room. Multiple dogs may be allowed.

Safari Inn
1911 Olive Avenue
Burbank, CA
818-845-8586
Dogs are allowed for a $25 one time fee per pet. Dogs may not be left alone in the room at any time. 2 dogs may be allowed.

Crowne Plaza Hotel San Francisco-Intl Airport
1177 Airport Blvd
Burlingame, CA
650-342-9200 (877-270-6405)
Dogs of all sizes are allowed. Dogs are allowed for a pet fee.

Doubletree Hotel
835 Airport Blvd
Burlingame, CA
650-344-5500 (800-222-TREE (8733))
Overlooking the beautiful San Francisco Bay, this upscale hotel offers numerous on site amenities, plus they are only 2 miles to the SF Airport, and their location gives a convenient starting point to explore an amazing choice of world class attractions, dining, and shopping arenas. Dogs are allowed for an additional one time fee of $40 per pet. 2 dogs may be allowed.

Embassy Suites
150 Anza Blvd
Burlingame, CA
650-342-4600 (800-EMBASSY (362-2779))
Only minutes from downtown and one of the city's largest hotels, they offer full service, upscale accommodations, and a number of on site amenities for business and leisure travelers, plus a convenient location to business, shopping, and dining scenes, and an amazing amount of tourist attractions. They also offer a complimentary cooked-to-order breakfast and a Manager's reception every evening. Dogs are allowed for an additional one time fee of $50 per pet. Multiple dogs may be allowed.

Red Roof Inn San Francisco Airport
777 Airport Blvd.
Burlingame, CA
650-342-7772 (800-RED-ROOF)
One well-behaved family pet per room. Guest must notify front desk

upon arrival. Guest is liable for any damages. In consideration of all guests, pets must never be left unattended in the guest rooms.

Sheraton Gateway
600 Airport Blvd.
Burlingame, CA
650-340-8500 (888-625-5144)
Dogs up to 50 pounds are allowed for no additional pet fee; there is a pet agreement to sign at check in. Dogs are allowed on the 5th floor only, and they may not be left alone in the room.

Vagabond Inn
1640 Bayshore Highway
Burlingame, CA
650-692-4040 (800-522-1555)
vagabondinn.com
This motel overlooks the San Francisco Bay. It is located just south of the airport and about 16 miles from downtown San Francisco. All rooms include coffee makers, cable television and air conditioning. Dogs are allowed for an additional fee of $10 (+ tax) per night per pet. 2 dogs may be allowed.

Motel 6 - Bakersfield Buttonwillow
20638 Tracy Ave
Buttonwillow, CA
661-764-5153 (800-466-8356)
This motel welcomes your pets to stay with you.

Red Roof Inn Buttonwillow
20645 Tracy Avenue
Buttonwillow, CA
661-764-5121 (800-RED-ROOF)
One well-behaved family pet per room. Guest must notify front desk upon arrival. Guest is liable for all damages. In consideration of all guests, pets must never be left unattended in the guest rooms.

Super 8 Buttonwillow
20681 Tracy Ave
Buttonwillow, CA
661-764-5117 (800-800-8000)
Dogs of all sizes are allowed. Dogs are allowed for a pet fee.

Best Western John Jay Inn
2421 Scaroni Road
Calexico, CA
760-768-0442 (800-780-7234)
Dogs of all sizes are allowed. Dogs are allowed for a pet fee of $10.00 per pet per night.

Quality Inn
801 Imperial Ave

Calexico, CA
760-357-3271 (877-424-6423)
Dogs of all sizes are allowed. Dogs are allowed for a pet fee of $10.00 per pet per night.

Brannan Cottage Inn
109 Wapoo Avenue
Calistoga, CA
707-942-4200
brannancottageinn.com
Two of the six rooms at this small inn are pet-friendly.

Calistoga Ranch
580 Lommel Road
Calistoga, CA
707-254-2800
calistogaranch.com/
Nestled away in a private canyon, this 157 acre luxury resort is a great getaway with oak tree covered hills, a stream and private lake, and a private restaurant. Some of the amenities include natural spring-fed mineral pools, a heated outdoor pool, miles of hiking trails, 24 hour room service, a variety of indoor and outdoor spaces so visitors get to fully enjoy the surroundings, and much more. Dogs of all sizes are allowed for a $125 one time additional pet fee per room. Dogs must be well behaved, kept leashed, and cleaned up after.

Hillcrest Country Inn
3225 Lake County Hwy
Calistoga, CA
707-942-6334
Hillcrest is a country home secluded on a hilltop with a view of vineyards and the Napa Valley. Rooms have fireplaces, balconies, some Jacuzzi tubs for 2 and HBO. There is swimming, hiking and fishing on 36 acres. Breakfast is served on weekends. There is an outdoor hot tub and a large cold water pool. Dogs of all sizes are allowed.

Meadowlark Inn
601 Petrified Forest Road
Calistoga, CA
707-942-5651 (800-942-5651)
meadowlarkinn.com/
On 20 scenic acres in the heart of wine country is this elegant Inn with gardens, hiking trails, meadows, forests, and horses grazing in pastures. Other features/amenities include a clothing optional mineral pool, hot tub, sauna, in-house massages, well appointed rooms, and a full, gourmet breakfast. Dogs of all sizes are welcome for no additional fee. Dogs must be very well behaved, leashed, and cleaned

up after at all times. 2 dogs may be allowed.

Pink Mansion Bed and Breakfast
1415 Foothill Blvd.
Calistoga, CA
707-942-0558
pinkmansion.com
This restored 1875 home offers modern amenities for wine country travelers. The Pink Mansion has been featured in The Wine Spectator, Best Places To Kiss and the New York Post. Dogs are allowed in one of their six rooms. Each room has a private bathroom. There is a $25 per day pet pet charge. 2 dogs may be allowed.

Motel 6 - Camarillo
1641 Daily Dr
Camarillo, CA
805-388-3467 (800-466-8356)
This motel welcomes your pets to stay with you.

Blue Whale Inn B&B and Vacation Rentals
6736 Moonstone Beach Drive
Cambria, CA
805-927-4647 (800-753-9000)
bluewhaleinn.com
The Blue Whale Inn has one pet-friendly room at the inn and they also manage 3 pet-friendly vacation rentals. There is a $25 per visit pet fee for rooms.

Cambria Pines Lodge
2905 Burton Drive
Cambria, CA
805-927-4200
This lodge is a 125 room retreat with accommodations ranging from rustic cabins to fireplace suites. It is nestled among 25 acres of Monterey Pines with forested paths and flower gardens. There is a $25 per night per pet additional fee.

Cambria Shores Inn
6276 Moonstone Beach Drive
Cambria, CA
805-927-8644 (800-433-9179)
cambriashores.com
Dogs are allowed for a $10.00 per night per dog fee. Pets must be leashed and never left alone. The inn offers local pet sitting services and provide treats for dogs. 2 dogs may be allowed.

Coastal Escapes Inc.
778 Main Street
Cambria, CA
805-927-3182 (800-578-2100)
calcoastvacationrentals.com/

There are a couple of hundred listings with this company and not all houses allow dogs. The properties are located in the picturesque communities of Cayucos and Cambria, and offer an impressive diversity of accommodations from secluded forest settings to oceanfront headlands, and a variety of recreational opportunities nearby. Dogs of all sizes are allowed for no additional pet fee. Dogs must be housetrained, well behaved, leashed, and cleaned up after both inside and out. 2 dogs may be allowed.

Fogcatcher Inn
6400 Moonstone Beach Drive
Cambria, CA
805-927-1400
there is also a pet policy to sign at check in. Dogs are not allowed to be left alone in the room, and they are not allowed on the bed. Treats are also offered for their canine visitors at this inn.

Pine Lodge
2905 Burton Drive
Cambria, CA
805-927-4200
Dogs of all sizes are allowed. There is a $25 per night per pet fee and a pet policy to sign at check in.

The Big Red House
370- B Chelsea Lane
Cambria, CA
805-927-1390
thebigredhouse.com
The Big Red House is located 2 blocks from the beach. These vacation rentals have an ocean view from each room. There is a $200 refundable pet deposit.

Motel 6 - Cameron Park
3444 Coach Lane
Cameron Park, CA
530-677-7177 (800-466-8356)
This motel welcomes your pets to stay with you.

Quality Inn & Suites
3361 Coach Lane
Cameron Park, CA
530-677-2203 (877-424-6423)
Dogs up to 100 pounds are allowed. Dogs are allowed for a pet fee of $15.00 per pet per night. Three or more dogs may be allowed.

Motel 6 - San Jose Campbell
1240 Camden Ave
Campbell, CA

408-371-8870 (800-466-8356)
This motel welcomes your pets to stay with you.

Residence Inn San Jose Campbell
2761 S Bascom Avenue
Campbell, CA
408-559-1551 (800-331-3131)
Sitting in the heart of the Silicon Valley, this all suite inn offers a central location to numerous major companies, several shopping and dining areas, and a variety of local attractions. Dogs are allowed for an additional one time pet fee of $100 per room. 2 dogs may be allowed.

TownePlace Suites San Jose Campbell
700 E Campbell Avenue
Campbell, CA
408-370-4510 (800-257-3000)
Located across from the scenic Campbell Park, this all suite inn sits only minutes from the airport and all that the downtown area has to offer; plus they offer a number of in-house amenities for all level of travelers. Dogs up to 75 pounds are allowed for an additional one time fee of $75 per room. 2 dogs may be allowed.

Motel 6 - Canoga Park, Ca
7132 De Soto Ave
Canoga Park, CA
818-883-6666 (800-466-8356)
This motel welcomes your pets to stay with you.

Beach House Rentals
312 Capitola Ave Suite D
Capitola, CA
800-330-2979
beach-houserentals.com
This vacation rental company specializes in rentals in Capitola, Santa Cruz and Aptos. Many of these rentals are pet friendly.

Capitola Inn
822 Bay Ave
Capitola, CA
831-462-3004
getawaylodging.com/capitolainn
This inn is located a few blocks from Capitola Village. They offer 56 rooms with either a private patio or balcony. There is a $20 one time fee per pet charge. 2 dogs may be allowed.

Extended Stay America San Diego - Carlsbad
1050 Grand Ave.
Carlsbad, CA
760-729-9380 (800-804-3724)
One dog is allowed per suite. There is a $25 per night additional pet fee

up to $150 for an entire stay.

Motel 6 - Carlsbad Downtown
1006 Carlsbad Village Dr
Carlsbad, CA
760-434-7135 (800-466-8356)
Your pets are welcome to stay here
with you.

Motel 6 - Carlsbad East, Ca
6117 Paseo Del Norte
Carlsbad, CA
760-438-1242 (800-466-8356)
Your pets are welcome to stay here
with you.

Motel 6 - Carlsbad South, Ca
750 Raintree Dr
Carlsbad, CA
760-431-0745 (800-466-8356)
Your pets are welcome to stay here
with you.

Quality Inn & Suites North Legoland
Area
751 Raintree Drive
Carlsbad, CA
760-931-1185 (877-424-6423)
Dogs up to 60 pounds are allowed.
Dogs are allowed for a pet fee of
$10.00 per pet per night. Two dogs
are allowed per room.

Ramada by the Sea Carlsbad
751 Macadamia Drive
Carlsbad, CA
760-438-2285 (800-272-6232)
Dogs are welcome at this hotel.

Ramada Carlsbad-by-the-Sea
751 Macadamia Drive
Carlsbad, CA
760-438-2285 (800-644-9394)
ramadacarlsbad.com
This hotel has pet-friendly one
bedroom suites. The hotel is 2 miles
from Legoland. Up to 2 dogs per
suite are allowed for a $25 per night
pet fee. There is a 50 pound weight
limit.

Residence Inn San Diego Carlsbad
2000 Faraday Avenue
Carlsbad, CA
760-431-9999 (800-331-3131)
Some of the amenities at this all-
suite inn include a close location to
the beach, downtown, and Legoland,
a daily buffet breakfast, evening
socials, and a complimentary grocery
shopping service. Dogs are allowed
for an additional one time pet fee of
$75 per room. Multiple dogs may be
allowed.

West Inn and Suites
4970 Avenida Encinas

Carlsbad, CA
760-208-4929 (866-375-4705)
This boutique style, 4 star hotel
offers the ultimate in luxury
surroundings and recreational
activities for both the business and
leisure traveler. Some of the
amenities include 2 fine dining
restaurants, pool and Jacuzzi, a
business center, library, and an on-
site pantry. They are also close to
the beach and several attractions.
Dogs of all sizes are allowed. There
is a $75 flat fee for 1 or 2 nights and
a $150 flat fee for 3 or more nights
per room. Dogs may not be left
alone in the room, and they must be
leashed and cleaned up after.

Briarwood Inn Bed and Breakfast
San Carlos Street between 4th and
5th Streets
Carmel, CA
831-626-9056 (800-999-8788)
briarwood-inn-carmel.com/
$40 for 2 dogs, and $55 for 3 dogs.
Dogs may not be left alone in the
rooms or in automobiles at any
time, and they must be leashed and
cleaned up after.

Carmel Country Inn
Dolores Street & Third Avenue
Carmel, CA
831-625-3263 (800-215-6343)
carmelcountryinn.com
This dog-friendly bed and breakfast
has 12 rooms and allows dogs in
several of these rooms. It's close to
many downtown outdoor dog-
friendly restaurants (see
Restaurants). A 20-25 minute walk
will take you to the dog-friendly
Carmel City Beach. There is a $20
per night per pet charge.

Carmel Fireplace Inn
San Carlos Street at 4th
Carmel, CA
831-624-4862 (800-634-1300)
fireplaceinncarmel.com/
the fee for 1 large dog is $40 per
night. If there are 2 pets the fee is
$40 per night. Aggressive breed
dogs are not allowed. Dogs may not
be left alone in the rooms, and they
must be leashed and cleaned up
after.

Casa De Carmel
Monte Verde & Ocean Ave
Carmel, CA
831-624-2429
There is an additional fee of $30 per
day for 1 pet, and $50 a day for 2
pets. 2 dogs may be allowed.

Coachman's Inn

San Carlos St. & 7th
Carmel, CA
831-624-6421 (800-336-6421)
coachmansinn.com
Located in downtown, this motel
allows dogs. It's close to many
downtown outdoor dog-friendly
restaurants (see Restaurants). A 20-
25 minute walk will take you to the
Carmel City beach which allows
dogs. There is an additional fee of
$20 per night per pet. Dogs may not
be left alone in the room at any time.
Multiple dogs may be allowed.

Cypress Inn
Lincoln & 7th
Carmel, CA
831-624-3871 (800-443-7443)
cypress-inn.com
This hotel is located within walking
distance to many dog-friendly
outdoor restaurants in the quaint
town of Carmel and walking distance
to the Carmel City Beach. This is
definitely a pet-friendly hotel. Here is
an excerpt from the Cypress Inn's
web page 'Co-owned by actress and
animal rights activist Doris Day, the
Cypress Inn welcomes pets with
open arms -- a policy which draws a
high percentage of repeat guests. It's
not unusual to see people strolling in
and out of the lobby with dogs of all
sizes. Upon arrival, animals are
greeted with dog biscuits, and other
pet pamperings.' Room rates are
about $125 - $375 per night. If you
have more than 2 people per room
(including a child or baby), you will
be required to stay in their deluxe
room which runs approximately $375
per night. One dog is allowed for an
additional fee of $30 per pet per
day,,, each additional dog is an
additional $20 with a maximum of 3
pets. 2 dogs may be allowed.

Happy Landing Inn
Monte Verde at 6th
Carmel, CA
831-624-7917 (800-297-6250)
carmelhappylanding.com
This dog-friendly B&B is located six
blocks from the Carmel leash free
beach and in the middle of Carmel-
By-The-Sea. Pets of all sizes are
allowed. There is a $20 per day pet
fee for one pet and $30 per day for
two pets. 2 dogs may be allowed.

Hofsas House Hotel
San Carlos Street
Carmel, CA
831-624-2745
There is a $15 per day additional pet
fee. The hotel is located between 3rd
Ave and 4th Ave in Carmel. Thanks

to one of our readers for recommending this hotel. Multiple dogs may be allowed.

Lamp Lighter Inn
Camino Real and Ocean Ave
Carmel, CA
831-624-4884
carmellamplighter.com/
In addition to their classic accommodations, lush gardens, and many on-site amenities, this charming vacation destination also offers a convenient location to world class beaches and to some of the area's star attractions. One dog is allowed for an additional one time fee of $30,,, the fee for 2 dogs is $50. Declare your pet at the time of registration so that food/water bowls, a doggy bed, toys, and treats will be waiting for your pooch upon arrival. 2 dogs may be allowed.

The Tradewinds at Carmel
Mission Street at 3rd Avenue
Carmel, CA
831-624-2776 (800-624-6665)
tradewindscarmel.com
This motel allows dogs in several of their rooms. They are a non-smoking inn. It's located about 3-4 blocks north of Ocean Ave and close to many outdoor dog-friendly restaurants in downtown Carmel. A 20-25 minute walk will take you to the dog-friendly Carmel City beach. There is a $25 per day pet charge.

Vagabond's House Inn B&B
PO Box 2747
Carmel, CA
831-624-7738
vagabondshouseinn.com
Beautifully landscaped grounds surrounding an English-styled Tudor dwelling await the guests of this romantic bed and breakfast inn. Dogs are allowed for an additional fee of $30 per night for 1 dog,,, $50 per night for 2 dogs, and $70 per night for 3 dogs. Multiple dogs may be allowed.

Carmel Valley Lodge
Carmel Valley Rd
Carmel Valley, CA
831-659-2261 (800-641-4646)
valleylodge.com
Your dog will feel welcome at this country retreat. Pet amenities include heart-shaped, organic homemade dog biscuits and a pawtographed picture of Lucky the Lodge Dog. Dogs must be on leash, but for your convenience, there are doggy-hitches at the front door of every unit that has a patio or deck and at the

pool. There are 31 units which range from standard rooms to two bedroom cottages. A great community park is located across the street and several restaurants with outdoor seating are within a 5 minute walk. Drive about 15 minutes from the lodge and you'll be in downtown Carmel or at one of the dog-friendly beaches. Dogs are an extra $10 per day and up to two dogs per room. There is no charge for childen under 16. The lodge is located in Carmel Valley. From Carmel, head south on Hwy 1. Turn left on Carmel Valley Rd., drive about 11-12 miles and the lodge will be located at Ford Rd. Multiple dogs may be allowed.

Los Laureles Lodge
313 W Carmel Valley Road
Carmel Valley, CA
831-659-2233
There is a $20 per night per pet fee. Dogs are not allowed to be left unattended at any time in the rooms or auto. Dogs are also allowed at the outside dining patio of the on-site restaurant. 2 dogs may be allowed.

Forest Lodge Cottages
Corner of Ocean and Torres
Carmel by the Sea, CA
831-624-7023
Dogs of all sizes are allowed. There is a $20 per night fee for one dog, a $30 per night fee for 2 dogs, and a pet policy to sign at check in. They request you exercise and relieve your pet off the grounds.

Holiday Inn Express Hotel & Suites Carpinteria
5606 Carpinteria Ave
Carpinteria, CA
805-566-9499 (877-270-6405)
Dogs of all sizes are allowed. Dogs are allowed for a pet fee of $10 per pet per night.

Motel 6 - Santa Barbara Carpinteria North
4200 Via Real
Carpinteria, CA
805-684-6921 (800-466-8356)
This motel welcomes your pets to stay with you.

Motel 6 - Santa Barbara Carpinteria South
5550 Carpinteria Ave
Carpinteria, CA
805-684-8602 (800-466-8356)
This motel welcomes your pets to stay with you.

Extended Stay America Los Angeles - Carson
401 E. Albertoni St.
Carson, CA
310-323-2080 (800-804-3724)
One dog is allowed per suite. There is a $25 per night additional pet fee up to $150 for an entire stay.

Doral Desert Princess Resort
67967 Vista Chino
Cathedral City, CA
760-322-7000 (888-FUN-IN-PS (386-4677))
doralpalmsprings.com/
This 4-star golf resort offers elegance and comprehensive services for the business or leisure traveler. Some of the features include 27 holes of championship golf, 285 luxury guestrooms and suites, conference and banquet facilities, room service, pool/Jacuzzi/sauna, a gift shop, and golf and tennis shops. Dogs up to 50 pounds are allowed for an additional $75 one time pet fee per pet room. Dogs are placed in first floor rooms, and they may only be left alone in the room if they will be quiet and well behaved. Dogs must be leashed and cleaned up after at all times. 2 dogs may be allowed.

Travelodge Cathedral City
67-495 Highway 111
Cathedral City, CA
760-328-2616 (800-578-7878)
Dogs are welcome at this hotel.

Cayucos Beach Inn
333 South Ocean Avenue
Cayucos, CA
805-995-2828
There is a $10 one time pet fee. All rooms in the inn are non-smoking. Family pets are welcome. The inn even has a dog walk and dog wash area. Thanks to one of our readers for this recommendation. 2 dogs may be allowed.

Cypress Tree Motel
125 S. Ocean Avenue
Cayucos, CA
805-995-3917
This pet-friendly 12-unit motel is located within walking distance to everything in town. Amenities include a garden area with lawn furniture and a barbecue. There is a $10 one time pet charge. 2 dogs may be allowed.

Dolphin Inn
399 S Ocean Ave
Cayucos, CA

805-995-3810
There is a $10 per day per pet charge. 2 dogs may be allowed.

Shoreline Inn
1 North Ocean Avenue
Cayucos, CA
805-995-3681 (800-549-2244)
centralcoast.com/shorelineinn
This dog-friendly motel is located on the beach (dogs are not allowed on this State Beach). Dogs are allowed in the first floor rooms which have direct access to a patio area. One dog is allowed for an additional one time fee of $15,,, there is an additional one time fee of $5 for a second dog. 2 dogs may be allowed.

Sunrise Motel & RV Park
54889 Highway 200 West
Cedarville, CA
530-279-2161
Located at the base of the dog-friendly Modoc National Forest, this motel offers all non-smoking rooms. Dogs up to 60 pounds are allowed for an additional fee of $5 per night per pet. If you are out during the day and cannot bring your pooch with you, they do have an outdoor kennel available for an extra $5. 2 dogs may be allowed.

Staybridge Suites Chatsworth
21902 Lassen Street
Chatsworth, CA
818-773-0707 (877-270-6405)
Dogs up to 80 pounds are allowed. Pets allowed with an additional pet fee. Up to $75 for 1-6 nights and up to $150 for 7+ nights. A pet agreement must be signed at check-in.

Best Western Rose Quartz Inn
306 Main Street
Chester, CA
530-258-2002 (800-780-7234)
Dogs of all sizes are allowed. Dogs are allowed for a pet fee of $30 per pet per night.

Best Western Heritage Inn - Chico
25 Heritage Ln
Chico, CA
530-894-8600 (800-780-7234)
Dogs of all sizes are allowed. Dogs are allowed for a pet fee of $30.00 per pet per stay.

Chico Oxford Suites
2035 Buisness Lane
Chico, CA
530-899-9090 (800-870-7848)
oxfordsuiteschico.com/
This hotel offers a variety of beautiful rooms, a full country breakfast buffet, an evening reception with two complimentary beverages and light hors d'ouevres. Also featured are a 24 hour gift/snack shop, business center, and an outdoor pool and Jacuzzi. Dogs up to about 75 pounds are allowed for an additional $35 one time pet fee per room. Dogs may only be left alone in the room if they will be quiet and well behaved, and a contact number is left with the front desk. Dogs must be leashed or crated, and cleaned up after. Pets must be declared at the time of reservations. 2 dogs may be allowed.

Motel 6 - Chico
665 Manzanita Ct
Chico, CA
530-345-5500 (800-466-8356)
This motel welcomes your pets to stay with you.

Music Express Inn Bed and Breakfast
1091El Monte Avenue
Chico, CA
530-891-9833
now2000.com/musicexpress/
This B&B is located near the dog-friendly Bidwell Park, the third largest municipal park in the United States. The B&B offers nine rooms all with private baths, refrigerators and microwaves. All rooms are non-smoking. A well-behaved dog is allowed, but must be leashed when outside your room. Pets must be attended at all times. There are no pet fees. Children are also allowed. 2 dogs may be allowed.

Residence Inn Chico
2485 Carmichael Drive
Chico, CA
530-894-5500 (800-331-3131)
In addition to offering a convenient location to the state university, business, historic, and entertainment areas, this hotel also provides a number of in-house amenities, including a daily buffet breakfast and an evening hospitality hour Monday to Thursday. Dogs are allowed for an additional one time pet fee of $100 per room. 2 dogs may be allowed.

Super 8 Chico
655 Manzanita Ct
Chico, CA
530-345-2533 (800-800-8000)
Dogs of all sizes are allowed. Dogs are allowed for a pet fee of $10.00 per pet per night.

Extended Stay America Los Angeles - Chino Valley
4325 Corporate Center Ave.
Chino, CA
909-597-8675 (800-804-3724)
One dog is allowed per suite. There is a $25 per night additional pet fee up to $150 for an entire stay.

Motel 6 - Chino Los Angeles Area
12266 Central Ave
Chino, CA
909-591-3877 (800-466-8356)
This motel welcomes your pets to stay with you.

Days Inn Gateway to Yosemite Chowchilla
220 East Robertson Blvd
Chowchilla, CA
559-665-4821 (800-329-7466)
Dogs are welcome at this hotel.

Motel 6 - San Diego Chula Vista
745 St
Chula Vista, CA
619-422-4200 (800-466-8356)
This motel welcomes your pets to stay with you.

Shinneyboo Creek Cabin Resort
11820 Eagle Lakes Road
Cisco, CA
530-587-5160
shinneyboocreek.com
These secluded cabins are located in the High Sierra, surrounded by the Tahoe National Forest. There is a $10 per pet per day additional pet fee. 2 dogs may be allowed.

Pacific Palms Resort and Conference Center
One Industry Hills Parkway
City of Industry, CA
626-810-4455 (800-524-4557)
pacificpalmsresort.com/main.htm
Sitting on 650 acres of meticulously landscaped grounds with 2 championship golf courses, 17 tennis courts, an Olympic-sized pool, miles of riding and hiking trails, and home to one of the most prestigious conference centers with cutting-edge technology in the US, this resort is a consummate retreat for the business or leisure traveler. Some of the amenities include 292 spacious well-appointed guestrooms and suites each with a balcony and many in-room amenities, and 2 outstanding restaurants and a lounge. Dogs of all sizes are allowed for an additional fee of $25 per night per pet. Dogs must be friendly and well behaved and removed or crated for housekeeping. Dogs must be kept on leash out of the room and cleaned up

after at all times.

Travelodge Clearlake
4775 Old Highway 53
Clearlake, CA
707-994-1499 (800-578-7878)
Dogs are welcome at this hotel.

Best Western Big Country Inn
25020 W Dorris Avenue
Coalinga, CA
559-935-0866 (800-780-7234)
Dogs up to 50 pounds are allowed.
Dogs are allowed for a pet fee of $20
per pet per stay.

Motel 6 - Coalinga East
25008 Dorris Ave
Coalinga, CA
559-935-1536 (800-466-8356)
This motel welcomes your pets to
stay with you.

Travelodge Coalinga
25278 West Dorris Ave
Coalinga, CA
559-935-2063 (800-578-7878)
Dogs of all sizes are allowed. Dogs
are allowed for a nightly pet fee.

Becker's Bounty Lodge and Cottage
HCR #2 Box 4659
Coffee Creek, CA
530-266-3277
beckersbountylodging.com/
The lodge is a secluded mountain
hideaway at the edge of the one-half
million acre Trinity Alps Wilderness.
Dogs are not allowed on the
furniture. There is a $50 one time pet
charge.

Andruss Motel
106964 Highway 395
Coleville, CA
530-495-2216
There is a $5 per night per pet
additional fee. Multiple dogs may be
allowed.

Golden Lotus Bed and Breakfast Inn
1006 Lotus Road
Coloma, CA
530-621-4562
This pre-Victorian B&B, located in
the historic town of Coloma, is
surrounded by herb gardens. Dogs
are allowed in one of their rooms.
Dogs must be well-behaved and
owners must agree to pay for any
damages. There is a $20 per day
additional pet fee.

Columbia Gem Motel
22131 Parrotts Ferry Rd
Columbia, CA
209-532-4508

columbiagem.com/business/gem/
This dog-friendly motel offers
gracious, country hospitality,
comfort and privacy. The motel is
set on a sunny park-like acre
beneath towering, majestic pines,
cedars and sequoias, which provide
a shady umbrella over their 6 cozy
log cabins and 4 motel rooms. For a
little extra, they can provide the
perfect getaway with champagne on
ice, flowers, wine, cheese, crackers,
chocolates, or bubblebath waiting
for you in your room. They can also
arrange breakfast in bed or can
help with any other ideas. The
motel is located within walking
distance (about 1 mile) from the
popular dog-friendly Columbia State
Historic Park. The Gold Mine
Winery/Micro-Brewery is located
about 1 block away from the motel.
The winery has a nice outdoor
covered patio and lawn area. They
have free wine and beer tasting and
they also make pizza from scratch,
any way you like it. The
management are of the belief that
people who travel with their 'best
friends' are responsible pet owners
and a pleasure to have as guests at
The Gem. Dog owners are not
penalized with an extra fee here.
Instead, management has a simple,
common sense pet regulation form
they have each owner read and
sign. Dogs must be crated if left
alone in the room. 2 dogs may be
allowed.

Ramada Commerce
7272 East Gage Avenue
Commerce, CA
562-806-4777 (800-272-6232)
Dogs are welcome at this hotel.

Crowne Plaza Hotel Concord
45 John Glenn Drive
Concord, CA
925-825-7700 (877-270-6405)
Dogs of all sizes are allowed. Dogs
are allowed for a pet fee.

Motel 6 - Concord, Ca
3606 Clayton Road
Concord, CA
925-682-7850 (800-466-8356)
This motel welcomes your pets to
stay with you.

Best Western Inn Corning
2165 Solano Street
Corning, CA
530-824-2468 (800-780-7234)
Complimentary continental
breakfast deluxe expanded
breakfast - waffle and hard boiled
eggs Complimentary coffee

Outdoor pool Safe deposit box
Complimentary newspaper
Ice/vending machines Cold weather
hook-ups Free parking motor coach
Truck/RV parking Fax services
Higher rates may apply for
holidays/special events Parking for
the physically challenged Exterior
corridor High-speed Internet access

Comfort Inn
910 Hwy 99 West
Corning, CA
530-824-5200 (877-424-6423)
Dogs of all sizes are allowed. Dogs
are allowed for a pet fee of $10.00-
17.00 per pet per night.

Days Inn Corning
3475 Hwy 99 West/I-5
Corning, CA
530-824-2000 (800-329-7466)
Dogs are welcome at this hotel.

Holiday Inn Express Hotel & Suites
Corning
3350 Sunrise Way
Corning, CA
530-824-6400 (877-270-6405)
Dogs of all sizes are allowed. Dogs
are allowed for a pet fee of $10.00
per pet per night.

Motel 6 - Corona
200 Lincoln Ave
Corona, CA
951-735-6408 (800-466-8356)
This motel welcomes your pets to
stay with you.

Residence Inn by Marriott Corona
Riverside
1015 Montecito Drive
Corona, CA
951-371-0107 (800-331-3131)
In addition to offering a convenient
location to a plethora of business,
shopping, dining, and entertainment
areas, this hotel also provides a
number of in-house amenities,
including a daily buffet breakfast and
an evening social hour Monday
through Thursday. Dogs are allowed
for an additional one time pet fee of
$100 per room. Multiple dogs may be
allowed.

Coronado Bay Resort
4000 Coronado Bay Road
Coronado, CA
619-424-4000
Dogs of all sizes are allowed. There
is a $25 one time fee per room and a
pet policy to sign at check in. 2 dogs
may be allowed.

Crown City Inn

520 Orange Ave
Coronado, CA
619-435-3116
crowncityinn.com/
This inn is located in beautiful Coronado which is across the harbor from downtown San Diego. Walk to several outdoor restaurants or to the Coronado Centennial Park. Room service is available. Pet charges are $8 per day for a designated pet room and $25 per day for a non-designated pet room. They have non-smoking rooms available. Pets must never be left unattended in the room. 2 dogs may be allowed.

Loews Coronado Bay Resort
4000 Coronado Bay Road
Coronado, CA
619-424-4000
All well-behaved dogs of any size are welcome. This upscale hotel offers their "Loews Loves Pets" program which includes special pet treats, local dog walking routes, and a list of nearby pet-friendly places to visit. There is an additional one time pet cleaning fee of $25 per room.

Holiday Inn Costa Mesa-Orange Co Airport
3131 South Bristol Street
Costa Mesa, CA
714-557-3000 (877-270-6405)
Dogs of all sizes are allowed. Dogs are allowed for a pet fee.

Motel 6 - Costa Mesa
1441 Gisler Ave
Costa Mesa, CA
714-957-3063 (800-466-8356)
This motel welcomes your pets to stay with you.

Ramada Inn and Suites /Newport Beach Costa Mesa
1680 Superior Ave I-405
Costa Mesa, CA
949-645-2221 (800-272-6232)
Dogs are welcome at this hotel.

Residence Inn Costa Mesa Newport Beach
881 W Baker Street
Costa Mesa, CA
714-241-8800 (800-331-3131)
This all suite hotel sits central to many of the areas star attractions, dining, and business areas, plus they offer a number of in-house amenities that includes a daily buffet breakfast and evening socials. Dogs are allowed for an additional one time pet fee of $100 per room. 2 dogs may be allowed.

The Westin South Coast Plaza
686 Anton Blvd.
Costa Mesa, CA
714-540-2500 (888-625-5144)
Dogs up to 80 pounds are allowed. There are no additional pet fees.

Travelodge Orange County Airport/ Costa Mesa
Suite A
Costa Mesa, CA
714-557-8700 (800-578-7878)
Dogs are welcome at this hotel.

Vagabond Inn
3205 Harbor Blvd
Costa Mesa, CA
714-557-8360
vagabondinn.com/
This motel offers a complimentary continental breakfast. The Bark Park dog park is located nearby. Dogs are allowed for an additional fee of $10 per night per pet. 2 dogs may be allowed.

Wyndham Orange County
3350 Avenue of the Arts
Costa Mesa, CA
714-751-5100 (877-999-3223)
wyndhamorangecounty.com
The Wyndham Orange County welcomes dogs up to 40 pounds for an additional one time pet fee of $50 per room. The outdoor patio at the Terra nova Restaurant at the hotel is also pet-friendly throughout the week. 2 dogs may be allowed.

Yosemite Gold Country Motel
10407 Highway 49
Coulterville, CA
209-878-3400
yosemitegoldcountrymotel.com
All rooms are completely furnished with a heater and air conditioner, color TV, telephones, bathroom with tub-shower and free coffee. Your dog is more than welcome here, but he or she must stay on a leash when outside and should use their Doggie Park when going to the bathroom. Also, they require that you do not leave your dog outside unattended. This motel is located about hour from Yosemite Valley (40 min. to the main gate and 20 min. to the valley). There is a $10 per night per pet fee. 2 dogs may be allowed.

Town House Motel
444 US H 101S
Crescent City, CA
707-464-4176
Well behaved and friendly dogs are allowed. There is a $10 per night per pet fee and there is only 1 pet

friendly room available. There are some breed restrictions.

Four Points by Sheraton Culver City
5990 Green Valley Circle
Culver City, CA
310-641-7740 (888-625-5144)
Dogs up to 50 pounds are allowed for an additional fee of $25 per night per pet. Dogs may not be left alone in the room.

Radisson Hotel Los Angeles Westside
6161 Centinela Avenue
Culver City, CA
310-649-1776
Dogs up to 50 pounds are allowed. Dogs are allowed in first floor rooms only. These are all non-smoking rooms. There is a $150 deposit of which $100 is refundable.

Cypress Hotel
10050 S. DeAnza Blvd.
Cupertino, CA
408-253-8900
thecypresshotel.com/
Well-behaved dogs of all sizes are welcome at this pet-friendly hotel. The boutique hotel offers both rooms and suites. Hotel amenities include complimentary evening wine service, an a 24 hour on-site fitness room. There are no pet fees, just sign a pet liability form.

Homestead Studio Suites Orange County - Cypress
5990 Corporate Ave.
Cypress, CA
714-761-2766 (800-804-3724)
One dog is allowed per suite. There is a $25 per night additional pet fee up to $150 for an entire stay.

Woodfin Suite Hotel
5905 Corporate Ave
Cypress, CA
714-828-4000
All rooms are non-smoking. All well-behaved dogs are welcome. Every room is a suite with wetbars or full kitchens. Hotel amenities include a pool, exercise facility, complimentary video movies, and a complimentary hot breakfast buffet. There is a $5 per day pet fee and you will need to sign a pet waiver.

Doubletree Guest Suites
34402 Pacific Coast H
Dana Point, CA
949-661-1100 (800-222-TREE (8733))
Only steps from the beach but still close to the big city, this upscale

hotel offers a number of on site amenities for business or leisure travelers, plus a convenient location to business, shopping, dining, and recreation areas. Dogs are allowed for an additional fee of $30 per night per pet. Multiple dogs may be allowed.

Holiday Inn Express Hotel & Suites
Dana Point-Harbor/Doheny Beach
34280 Pacific Coast Highway
Dana Point, CA
949-248-1000 (877-270-6405)
Dogs are welcome at this hotel. There is a $75 one time pet fee.

Best Western University Lodge
123 B Street
Davis, CA
530-756-7890 (800-780-7234)
Dogs are welcome at this hotel.

Econo Lodge
221 D St.
Davis, CA
530-756-1040 (877-424-6423)
Dogs of all sizes are allowed. Dogs are allowed for a pet fee of $5.00 per pet per night.

Motel 6 - Davis Sacramento Area
4835 Chiles Rd
Davis, CA
530-753-3777 (800-466-8356)
This motel welcomes your pets to stay with you.

University Inn Bed and Breakfast
340 A Street
Davis, CA
530-756-8648
All rooms are non-smoking. There are no pet fees. Children are also allowed.

University Park Inn & Suites
1111 Richards Blvd.
Davis, CA
530-756-0910
stayanight.com/upi/upimain.htm
Located within walking distance of downtown Davis. There is an additional pet fee of $10 per night per room. Multiple dogs may be allowed.

Stovepipe Wells Village Motel
H 190
Death Valley, CA
760-786-2387
The Village Motel is a short distance from some of the most photographed sand dunes in the world. They offer such amenities as comfortable ground floor guest rooms, a Restaurant and Saloon, general

store and gift shop, service station, private landing strip, and an on-site RV park. Dogs of all sizes are allowed for an additional $20 refundable deposit for the motel rooms,,, there is no fee or deposit for dogs in the RV park. Dogs may not be left unattended in motel rooms. Dogs must be leashed and cleaned up after. Dogs are allowed in public places only,,, they are not allowed on trails or in canyon areas. 2 dogs may be allowed.

Best Western Stratford Inn
710 Camino Del Mar
Del Mar, CA
858-755-1501 (800-780-7234)
Dogs of all sizes are allowed. Dogs are allowed for a pet fee of $50.00 per pet per stay.

Hilton Hotel
15575 Jimmy Durante Blvd
Del Mar, CA
858-792-5200 (800-HILTONS (445-8667))
Located in the heart of the city, this upscale hotel offers numerous on site amenities for business and leisure travelers, plus a convenient location to beaches, business districts, shopping, dining, historical, and entertainment areas. Dogs are allowed for an additional one time pet fee of $50 per room, plus a $200 refundable deposit. Multiple dogs may be allowed.

Les Artists
944 Camino Del Mar
Del Mar, CA
858-755-4646
Dogs are allowed for a $100 refundable deposit, plus an additional $30 per night for 1 dog and $40 per night if there are 2 dogs. 2 dogs may be allowed.

Coachman's Inn
2231 Girard Street
Delano, CA
661-725-7551
coachmans-inn.com/about.html
Amenities include a deluxe complimentary continental breakfast, a guest laundromat, and a seasonal outdoor pool and spa. Conveniently located between Fresno & Bakersfield off Highway 99. Dogs are allowed for an additional $7.70 per night per pet. Multiple dogs may be allowed.

Rodeway Inn
2211 Girard St.
Delano, CA
661-725-1022 (877-424-6423)

Dogs of all sizes are allowed. Dogs are allowed for a pet fee of $10.00 per pet per night.

Lilac Ridge Cabin in San Diego
Call to Arrange
Descanso, CA
619-445-1899 (888-894-4626)
lilacridgecabin.com
This pet-friendly stone cabin vacation rental is 45 minutes from San Diego and 5 minutes from Cuyamaca State Park. There are several nearby dog-friendly hikes.

San Diego Backcountry Retreat
Call to Arrange
Descanso, CA
888-894-4626
haylapa.1888twigman.com
The Haylapa House is located on a small ranch east of San Diego. The Haylapa is one large open room. It has a full kitchen and bathroom. Outside, it has a fenced area for your dog and nearby hiking.

Holiday Inn Express Hotel & Suites
Dinuba West
375 S. Alta Ave
Dinuba, CA
559-595-1500 (877-270-6405)
Dogs are welcome at this hotel. There is a $25 one time pet fee.

Best Western Inn Dixon
1345 Commercial Way
Dixon, CA
707-678-1400 (800-780-7234)
Dogs of all sizes are allowed. Dogs are allowed for a pet fee of $20.00 per pet per stay.

Embassy Suites
8425 Firestone Blvd
Downey, CA
562-861-1900 (800-EMBASSY (362-2779))
This upscale, full service, atrium-style hotel offers a number of on site amenities for business and leisure travelers, plus a convenient location to LAX and the Long Beach Airport, and to business, shopping, dining, and entertainment districts. They also offer a complimentary cooked-to-order breakfast and a Manager's reception every evening. Dogs up to 75 pounds are allowed for an additional fee of $25 per night per pet. 2 dogs may be allowed.

Downieville Carriage House Inn
110 Commercial Street
Downieville, CA
530-289-3573
This 9 room inn is located in historic

downtown Downieville and is open year round. Well-behaved dogs are allowed. Dogs should be able to get along well with other guests, as this is a house. One or two dogs up to 40 pounds are allowed, depending on the size of the room, for an additional fee of $15 per night per pet. 2 dogs may be allowed.

Downieville Loft
208 Main Street
Downieville, CA
510-501-2516
This amazing retreat along the Yuba River offers many features and amenities, some of which include 2,700 feet of retreat space on 2 levels, 8 full-size skylights, all custom made furniture, a large well equipped kitchen with river views, 2 fireplaces and bathrooms, and excellent summer swimming and fishing just steps from the loft. Dogs of all sizes are welcome for an additional fee of $10 per night per pet. Dogs are not allowed on the furnishings, and they must be leashed and cleaned up after. Dogs may not be left alone in the loft, and the must be dry before entering. 2 dogs may be allowed.

Downieville River Inn
121 River Street
Downieville, CA
530-289-3308
freewebs.com/downieville/
One dog up to 40 pounds is allowed for no additional fee with a credit card on file. There is a pet policy to sign at check in and they request you kennel your dog when out of the room.

Old Well Motel
15947 State Highway 49
Drytown, CA
209-245-6467
This motel is located near the Shenandoah Valley. There is a $5 per day additional pet fee. 2 dogs may be allowed.

Extended Stay America Dublin - Hacienda Dr.
4500 Dublin Blvd.
Dublin, CA
925-875-9556 (800-804-3724)
One dog is allowed per suite. There is a $25 per night additional pet fee up to $150 for an entire stay.

Dunsmuir Lodge
6604 Dunsmuir Avenue
Dunsmuir, CA
530-235-2884 (877-235-2884)
dunsmuirlodge.net/
Located in a mountain setting on 4

landscaped acres with a beautiful meadow and great mountain views, this lodge offers country log home decor and all rooms open out to a central courtyard. Some of the amenities include a great location for many other recreational activities, barbecues, and if you like to fish, there is a place to clean and freeze your catch. Dogs of all sizes are allowed. There is an additional one time fee of $7.50 per pet. Dogs may not be left alone in the rooms at any time, and there are designated areas to walk your pet. Dogs must be leashed, and they ask that pets are cleaned up after both inside and out.

Railroad Park Resort
100 Railroad Park Road
Dunsmuir, CA
530-235-4440
rrpark.com/
Spend a night or more inside a restored antique railroad car at this unique resort. Dogs are allowed for an additional $15 per day per pet. This resort also offers RV hookup spaces. 2 dogs may be allowed.

Four Seasons Hotel Silicon Valley
2050 University Ave.
East Palo Alto, CA
650-566-1200
Dogs of all sizes are allowed. There are no additional pet fees. Dogs are not allowed to be left alone in the room.

Motel 6 - San Diego El Cajon
550 Montrose Ct
El Cajon, CA
619-588-6100 (800-466-8356)
This motel welcomes your pets to stay with you.

Quality Inn & Suites San Diego East County
1250 El Cajon Blvd.
El Cajon, CA
619-588-8808 (877-424-6423)
Dogs of all sizes are allowed. Dogs are allowed for a pet fee of $10.00 per pet per night.

Relax Inn and Suites
1220 W Main Street
El Cajon, CA
619-442-2576
relaxinnsd.com/
Dogs of all sizes are allowed. There is a $10 per night per pet additional fee. 2 dogs may be allowed.

Super 8 San Diego Area/ El Cajon
588 N Mollison Avenue

El Cajon, CA
619-579-1144 (800-800-8000)
Dogs of all sizes are allowed. Dogs are allowed for a pet fee of $10.00 per pet per night.

Travelodge El Cajon
425 W Main St
El Cajon, CA
619-441-8250 (800-578-7878)
Dogs are welcome at this hotel.

Knights Inn El Centro
2030 Cottonwood Circle
El Centro, CA
760-353-7750 (800-843-5644)
Dogs of all sizes are allowed. Dogs are allowed for a nightly pet fee.

Motel 6 - El Centro
395 Smoketree Dr
El Centro, CA
760-353-6766 (800-466-8356)
This motel welcomes your pets to stay with you.

Motel 6 - Los Angeles El Monte
3429 Peck Rd
El Monte, CA
626-448-6660 (800-466-8356)
This motel welcomes your pets to stay with you.

Yosemite View Lodge
H 140
El Portal, CA
209-379-2681 (888-742-4371)
Just steps away from the entrance to the National Park, this lodge offers luxury accommodations and many extras. Some of the amenities include private balconies or patios, 1 indoor and 3 outdoor pools, 1 indoor and 5 outdoor spas, a cocktail lounge, gift shop, convenience store, restaurant, and a visitor and guide center. Dogs of all sizes are allowed for an additional fee of $10 per night per pet. Dogs must be leashed and cleaned up after at all times, and they may only be left alone in the room if they will be quiet, well behaved, and the Do Not Disturb sign is put on the door.

Homestead Studio Suites Los Angeles International Airport - El Segundo
1910 E. Mariposa Ave.
El Segundo, CA
310-607-4000 (800-804-3724)
One dog is allowed per suite. There is a $25 per night additional pet fee up to $150 for an entire stay.

Residence Inn Los Angeles LAX/El Segundo

2135 East El Segundo Blvd
El Segundo, CA
310-333-0888 (800-331-3131)
In addition to being located in the
heart of the city's business district
and close to a multitude of activities
and sites of interests, this all suite
inn also offers a number of in-house
amenities, including a daily buffet
breakfast and evening socials. Dogs
are allowed for an additional one
time pet fee of $100 per room.
Multiple dogs may be allowed.

The Greenwood Pier Inn
5928 S H 1
Elk, CA
707-877-9997
Dogs of all sizes are allowed. There
is a $25 one time fee per pet. 2 dogs
may be allowed.

The Griffin House Inn
5910 S H 1
Elk, CA
707-877-1820
griffinhouseinn.com/
this cottage also has a back yard.
Dogs up to 75 pounds are allowed
for an additional fee of $20 per pet
per stay. Dogs must be leashed and
cleaned up after at all times. The
reservation number is 707-877-3422.

Extended Stay America Sacramento
- Elk Grove
2201 Longport Ct.
Elk Grove, CA
916-683-3753 (800-804-3724)
One dog is allowed per suite. There
is a $25 per night additional pet fee
up to $150 for an entire stay.

Best Western Encinitas Inn & Suites
at Moonlight Beach
85 Encinitas Boulevard
Encinitas, CA
760-942-7455 (800-780-7234)
Dogs of all sizes are allowed. Dogs
are allowed for a pet fee.

Casa Leucadia
Call to Arrange
Encinitas, CA
760-633-4497
This large vacation rental in
Encinitas can sleep up to 13 people.
It consists of a main house and two
separate suites. There is a nice yard
and dogs are welcome.

Howard Johnson San Diego
Encinitas
607 Leucadia Blvd
Encinitas, CA
760-944-3800 (800-446-4656)
Dogs of all sizes are allowed. Dogs

are allowed for a pet fee of $25 per
pet per night.

Quality Inn & Suites North Coast
186 N. Hwy 101
Encinitas, CA
760-944-0301 (877-424-6423)
Dogs of all sizes are allowed. Dogs
are allowed for a pet fee of $15.00
per pet per night.

Angel Way
One block south of Santa Fe Ave
on Summit Ave
Encinitas/Cardiff, CA
760-298-9877
This 2 bedroom beach house and 1
bedroom guesthouse allow dogs to
accompany their families.

Castle Creek Inn Resort
29850 Circle R Way
Escondido, CA
760-751-8800 (800-253-5341)
Quiet, well behaved dogs are
allowed for an additional fee of $35
per night per pet. 2 dogs may be
allowed.

Motel 6 - Escondido
900 Quince St
Escondido, CA
760-745-9252 (800-466-8356)
This motel welcomes your pets to
stay with you.

Palm Tree Lodge Motel
425 W Mission Avenue
Escondido, CA
760-745-7613
This hotel offers 38 guest rooms
(some with kitchens or fireplaces),
an outdoor pool and a restaurant on
site. Dogs of all sizes are allowed
for an additional fee of $20 per night
per pet. The fee may be more for
very large dogs. Dogs may not be
left alone in the room at any time,
and they must be well behaved,
leashed, and cleaned up after. 2
dogs may be allowed.

Rodeway Inn
250 W. El Norte Pkwy
Escondido, CA
760-746-0441 (877-424-6423)
Dogs up to 50 pounds are allowed.
Dogs are allowed for a pet fee of
$30.00 per pet per night. Two dogs
are allowed per room.

Best Western Bayshore Inn
3500 Broadway Street
Eureka, CA
707-268-8005 (800-780-7234)
Dogs of all sizes are allowed. Dogs
are allowed for a pet fee.

Discovery Inn
2832 Broadway
Eureka, CA
707-441-8442
There is a $10 per day per pet
additional pet fee. 2 dogs may be
allowed.

Motel 6 - Eureka
1934 Broadway St
Eureka, CA
707-445-9631 (800-466-8356)
This motel welcomes your pets to
stay with you.

Quality Inn
1209 Fourth Street
Eureka, CA
707-443-1601 (877-424-6423)
Dogs of all sizes are allowed.

Extended Stay America
1019 Oliver Road
Fairfield, CA
707-438-0932
Dogs of all sizes are allowed. There
is a $25 per day pet fee for the 1st 3
days. The fee is per room or per pet
depending on length of stays, and
size of room and pets. A cell number
must be left with the front desk if
there is a pet alone in the room. 2
dogs may be allowed.

Motel 6 - Fairfield North, Ca
1473 Holiday Ln
Fairfield, CA
707-425-4565 (800-466-8356)
This motel welcomes your pets to
stay with you.

Staybridge Suites Fairfield Napa
Valley Area
4775 Business Center Drive
Fairfield, CA
707-863-0900 (877-270-6405)
Dogs up to 80 pounds are allowed.
Pets allowed with an additional pet
fee. Up to $75 for 1-6 nights and up
to $150 for 7+ nights. A pet
agreement must be signed at check-
in.

Pala Mesa Golf Resort
2001 Old H 395
Fallbrook, CA
760-728-5881 (800-722-4700)
palamesa.com/
There are 205 beautifully landscaped
acres at this golf resort with
amenities for all levels of travelers.
Dogs are allowed for an additional
one time pet fee of $75 per room. 2
dogs may be allowed.

Quail Cove

39117 Northshore Drive
Fawnskin, CA
800-595-2683
quailcove.com/
This lodge offers rustic and cozy cabins in a quiet wooded surrounding on Big Bear Lake. They are located within walking distance to several restaurants, markets, marinas and some of the hiking trails and fishing spots. Pets are always welcome. There is no additonal pet fee. Never leave your pet unattended in the cabin. 2 dogs may be allowed.

Narrow Gauge Inn
48571 Highway 41
Fish Camp, CA
559-683-7720
narrowgaugeinn.com/
This inn is located amidst pine trees in the Sierra Mountains. They are located about four miles from the southern entrance to Yosemite National Park (about 45 minutes to Yosemite Valley). There are some trails nearby in the dog-friendly Sierra National Forest near Bass Lake. All rooms are non-smoking. Dogs are allowed in the main level rooms and there is a $25 one time fee per pet. Dogs may not be left alone in the room. Children are also welcome. Multiple dogs may be allowed.

Tenaya Lodge at Yosemite
1122 Highway 41
Fish Camp, CA
866-487-6375
This classic resort with 244 guest rooms and suites has created an elegant retreat with all the modern services. The resort sits on 35 scenic acres only two miles from the south entrance of Yosemite National Park and offers many in-room amenities and a variety of dining choices. Dogs up to 55 pounds are allowed for a $75 one time additional pet fee per room. Dogs may not be left unattended in the room, and they are not allowed in the shops and restaurants. Dogs must be leashed and cleaned up after at all times. They also offer a canine amenity package that includes treats, disposable mitts, a plush dog bed, water bowl, and a canine concierge fact sheet of fun areas to roam. With advanced booking they can also provide a dog walking/sitting service.

Lake Natoma Inn
702 Gold Lake Drive
Folsom, CA
916-351-1500
lakenatomainn.com/

This inn offers 120 guest rooms and 12 Lakeview Suites nestled in a wooded natural environment overlooking Lake Natoma. Enjoy over 20 miles of beautiful bike and dog-friendly walking trails along the American river. This inn is also located next to Historic Folsom. There is a $45 one time per stay pet fee and a $15 per day pet charge per pet. Multiple dogs may be allowed.

Residence Inn Sacramento Folsom
2555 Iron Point Road
Folsom, CA
916-983-7289 (800-331-3131)
Folsom Lake, the historic Folsom State Prison Museum, the American River, the Palladio Lifestyle Center Mall, and the newly opened Red Hawk Casino are all just a short distance from this all suite hotel. Additionally they offer a daily buffet breakfast and evening socials Monday through Thursday with light dinner fare. Dogs are allowed for an additional one time pet fee of $50 per room. Multiple dogs may be allowed.

Motel 6 - Fontana
10195 Sierra Ave
Fontana, CA
909-823-8686 (800-466-8356)
This motel welcomes your pets to stay with you.

Beachcomber Motel
1111 N. Main Street
Fort Bragg, CA
707-964-2402 (800-400-SURF)
thebeachcombermotel.com/
This ocean front motel is next to a walking, jogging, and cycling trail that stretches for miles along the coast. Many rooms have ocean views. They allow well-behaved dogs up to about 75-80 pounds. There is an additional $20 per day per pet charge. Dogs may not be left alone in the room. Multiple dogs may be allowed.

Cleone Gardens Inn
24600 N. Hwy 1
Fort Bragg, CA
707-964-2788 (800-400-2189)
cleonelodgeinn.com/
This park-like inn is on 5 acres. One dog is allowed for an additional one time fee of $25,,, there is an additional one time fee of $6 for each additional dog. Dogs may not be left alone in any of their 3 pet-friendly rooms. Multiple dogs may be allowed.

Delamere Seaside Cottages
16821 Ocean Drive
Fort Bragg, CA
707-964-3175
delamerecottages.com
These two small pet-friendly cottages are located on the Mendocino Coast and have nice ocean views. One cottage has two decks and the other has a gazebo. Your well-behaved dog is welcome.

Harbor View Seasonal Rental
Call to arrange.
Fort Bragg, CA
760-438-2563
Watch the boats go in and out of the harbor and listen to the sea lions and fog horns from this dog-friendly vacation rental. This 3,000 square foot house is entirely furnished. The main floor has a living room, dining room, kitchen, 2 bedrooms, 1 bathroom and a deck with a view of the harbor. The upstairs has a large master suite with a deck and a view of the bridge and ocean. The yard has redwood trees and even deer wandering through. This area is popular for year-round fishing. The rental is available throughout the year. Please call to inquire about rates and available dates.

Pine Beach Inn
16801 N H 1
Fort Bragg, CA
888-987-8388
pinebeachinn.com/index.html
Located on 11 lush, tranquil acres with its own private beach and cove, this scenic inn also features easy access to several other recreational activities, shopping, and dining. Some of the amenities include a large lawn with a gazebo, 2 championship tennis courts, and a restaurant (south of the border cuisine) and full bar. Dogs of all sizes are allowed for an additional $10 per night per pet. The fee may be less for multiple nights or dogs. Dogs may not be left alone in the rooms, and they must be leashed and cleaned up after. 2 dogs may be allowed.

Quality Inn & Suites Tradewinds
400 S. Main Street
Fort Bragg, CA
707-964-4761 (877-424-6423)
Dogs of all sizes are allowed. Dogs are allowed for a pet fee of $10.00 per pet per night.

Shoreline Cottages
18725 N H 1
Fort Bragg, CA
707-964-2977

Adult dogs only are allowed, no puppies. There is an additional $10 pet fee for the 1st night and $5 for each additonal night per room.

Super 8 Fort Bragg
N. Harbor & Main St
Fort Bragg, CA
707-964-4003 (800-800-8000)
Dogs are welcome at this hotel.

Surf Motel and Gardens
1220-south main street
Fort Bragg, CA
707-964-5361 (800-339-5361)
surfmotelfortbragg.com
The Surf Hotel has pet-friendly rooms and a six person suite. There is a large enclosed pet play area and also gardens to stroll through.

The Rendezvous Inn and Restaurant
647 North Main Street
Fort Bragg, CA
707-964-8142 (800-491-8142)
rendezvousinn.com/
A romantic and elegant destination, this beautifully crafted 1897 home offers charm, relaxation, beautiful gardens, a large sunny guest parlor, and an inviting ambiance. They can also tailor your stay with a food and wine pairing. Their award-winning restaurant offers French gourmet dining in a casual but elegant atmosphere, an extensive wine list, and seasonal outdoor dining where your four-legged companion may join you. Dogs of all sizes are welcome for no additional fee. Dogs must be leashed and cleaned up after. Multiple dogs may be allowed.

Residence Inn Huntington Beach Fountain Valley
9930 Slater Avenue
Fountain Valley, CA
714-965-8000 (800-331-3131)
This all suite hotel sits central to many of the area's star attractions, mega-shopping, dining, and business areas, plus they offer a number of in-house amenities that include a daily hot breakfast and evening socials. Dogs up to 80 pounds are allowed for an additional one time pet fee of $100 per room. 2 dogs may be allowed.

Extended Stay America Fremont - Newark
5355 Farwell Pl.
Fremont, CA
510-794-8040 (800-804-3724)
One dog is allowed per suite. There is a $25 per night additional pet fee up to $150 for an entire stay.

Extended Stay America Fremont - Warm Springs
46312 Mission Blvd.
Fremont, CA
510-979-1222 (800-804-3724)
One dog is allowed per suite. There is a $25 per night additional pet fee up to $150 for an entire stay.

Homestead Studio Suites Fremont - Fremont Blvd. South
46080 Fremont Blvd.
Fremont, CA
510-353-1664 (800-804-3724)
One dog is allowed per suite. There is a $25 per night additional pet fee up to $150 for an entire stay.

La Quinta Inn & Suites Fremont
46200 Landing Pkwy.
Fremont, CA
510-445-0808 (800-531-5900)
Dogs of all sizes are allowed. There are no additional pet fees. Dogs must be quiet, well behaved, leashed and cleaned up after. Multiple dogs may be allowed.

Marriott Fremont Silicon Valley
46100 Landing Parkway
Fremont, CA
510-413-3700 (800-228-9290)
This luxury hotel sits near many of the area's star attractions, world class shopping and dining venues, and major business areas, plus they also offer a number of in-house amenities for all level of travelers. Dogs are allowed for an additional one time fee of $100 per room. Multiple dogs may be allowed.

Motel 6 - Fremont North
34047 Fremont Blvd
Fremont, CA
510-793-4848 (800-466-8356)
This motel welcomes your pets to stay with you.

Motel 6 - Fremont South
46101 Research Ave
Fremont, CA
510-490-4528 (800-466-8356)
This motel welcomes your pets to stay with you.

Residence Inn Fremont Silicon Valley
5400 Farwell Place
Fremont, CA
510-794-5900 (800-331-3131)
Besides offering a convenient location to business, shopping, dining, and entertainment areas, this hotel also provides a number of in-house amenities, including a

daily buffet breakfast and complementary evening receptions Monday to Thursday. Dogs are allowed for an additional one time pet fee of $100 per room. 2 dogs may be allowed.

Best Western Village Inn
3110 N Blackstone Avenue
Fresno, CA
559-226-2110 (800-780-7234)
Dogs are welcome at this hotel. There is a $25 one time pet fee.

Days Inn Fresno
1101 North Parkway Drive
Fresno, CA
559-268-6211 (800-329-7466)
Dogs of all sizes are allowed. Dogs are allowed for a pet fee of $10.00 per pet per night.

Days Inn South Fresno
2640 South Second St
Fresno, CA
559-237-6644 (800-329-7466)
Dogs are welcome at this hotel.

Extended Stay America Fresno - North
7135 N. Fresno St.
Fresno, CA
559-438-7105 (800-804-3724)
One dog is allowed per suite. There is a $25 per night additional pet fee up to $150 for an entire stay.

Howard Johnson Fresno
1415 W Olive Ave
Fresno, CA
559-237-2175 (800-446-4656)
Dogs are welcome at this hotel.

La Quinta Inn Fresno Yosemite
2926 Tulare
Fresno, CA
559-442-1110 (800-531-5900)
Dogs of all sizes are allowed. There are no additional pet fees, and there is a pet waiver to sign at check in. Dogs must be leashed and cleaned up after. Multiple dogs may be allowed.

Motel 6 - Fresno Blackstone North
4245 Blackstone Ave
Fresno, CA
559-221-0800 (800-466-8356)
This motel welcomes your pets to stay with you.

Motel 6 - Fresno Blackstone South
4080 Blackstone Ave
Fresno, CA
559-222-2431 (800-466-8356)
This motel welcomes your pets to stay with you.

Motel 6 - Fresno Sr-99
1240 Crystal Ave
Fresno, CA
559-237-0855 (800-466-8356)
This motel welcomes your pets to stay with you.

Motel 6 - Fresno, Ca
5021 Barcus Ave.
Fresno, CA
559-276-1910 (800-466-8356)
This motel welcomes your pets to stay with you.

Quality Inn
4278 W. Ashlan Ave
Fresno, CA
559-275-2727 (877-424-6423)
Dogs of all sizes are allowed.

Ramada Fresno
5046 North Barcus Avenue
Fresno, CA
559-277-5700 (800-272-6232)
Dogs of all sizes are allowed. Dogs are allowed for a pet fee of $20.00 per pet per stay.

Residence Inn Fresno
5322 N Diana Avenue
Fresno, CA
559-222-8900 (800-331-3131)
Located in one of the most beautiful areas of the state and central to business, shopping, dining, and recreation areas, this hotel also provides a number of in-house amenities, including a daily buffet breakfast and complementary evening social hours. Dogs are allowed for an additional one time pet fee of $100 per room. 2 dogs may be allowed.

Rodeway Inn
959 N. Parkway Drive
Fresno, CA
559-445-0322 (877-424-6423)
Dogs of all sizes are allowed. Dogs are allowed for a pet fee of $15.00 per pet per night. Two dogs are allowed per room.

Super 8 Convention Centre Area Fresno
2127 Inyo St
Fresno, CA
559-268-0621 (800-800-8000)
Dogs of all sizes are allowed. Dogs are allowed for a pet fee.

Super 8 Fresno
1087 N Parkway Drive
Fresno, CA
559-268-0741 (800-800-8000)
Dogs of all sizes are allowed. Dogs

are allowed for a pet fee of $10 per pet per stay.

TownePlace Suites Fresno
7127 N Fresno Street
Fresno, CA
559-435-4600 (800-257-3000)
This all suite inn sits central to numerous business, shopping, dining, and entertainment areas, plus they offer a number of in-house amenities for business and leisure travelers. Dogs are allowed for an additional one time fee of $100 per room. Multiple dogs may be allowed.

Marriott Fullerton at California State University
2701 East Nutwood Avenue
Fullerton, CA
714-738-7800 (800-228-9290)
In addition to being located adjacent to the California State University, this luxury hotel sits near many of the area's star attractions, world class shopping and dining venues, and major business areas, plus they also offer a number of in-house amenities for all level of travelers. Dogs up to 100 pounds are allowed for an additional fee of $35 per night per room with a $150 refundable deposit. 2 dogs may be allowed.

Best Western Humboldt House Inn
701 Redwood Drive
Garberville, CA
707-923-2771 (800-780-7234)
Dogs of all sizes are allowed. Dogs are allowed for a pet fee of $10 per pet per stay.

Candlewood Suites North Orange County
12901 Garden Grove Blvd.
Garden Grove, CA
714-539-4200 (877-270-6405)
Dogs up to 80 pounds are allowed. Pets allowed with an additional pet fee. Up to $75 for 1-6 nights and up to $150 for 7+ nights. A pet agreement must be signed at check-in.

Residence Inn Anaheim Resort Area/Garden Grove
11931 Harbor Blvd
Garden Grove, CA
714-591-4000 (888-236-2427)
Although this all suite hotel sits close to many of the area's most exciting attractions - including only blocks away from Disneyland, they offer some nice on-site amenities too, including a daily buffet breakfast, a Manager's reception Monday through Thursday, a

tropically inspired courtyard with pool, Kids Suites, and Kids Theater - featuring Disney movies. Dogs are allowed for an additional one time pet fee of $75 per room. 2 dogs may be allowed.

Extended Stay America Los Angeles - South
18602 S. Vermont Ave.
Gardena, CA
310-515-5139 (800-804-3724)
One dog is allowed per suite. There is a $25 per night additional pet fee up to $150 for an entire stay.

American River Bed and Breakfast Inn
Main and Orleans Streets
Georgetown, CA
530-333-4499
americanriverinn.com
They have certain pet rooms and you need to call in advance to make a reservation. All rooms are non-smoking. Dogs are allowed for an additional fee of $10 per night per pet. Extra large dogs can not be accommodated. Dogs must have their own bedding or crate,,, they are not allowed on the bed or the furniture. 2 dogs may be allowed.

Best Western Forest Park Inn
375 Leavesley Road
Gilroy, CA
408-848-5144 (800-780-7234)
Dogs of all sizes are allowed. Dogs are allowed for a pet fee of $30 per pet per night.

Motel 6 - Gilroy
6110 Monterey Hwy
Gilroy, CA
408-842-6061 (800-466-8356)
This motel welcomes your pets to stay with you.

Quality Inn & Suites
8430 Murray Ave
Gilroy, CA
408-847-5500 (877-424-6423)
Dogs of all sizes are allowed. Dogs are allowed for a pet fee of $10.00 per pet per night. Two dogs are allowed per room.

Super 8 Gilroy
8435 San Ysidro Ave.
Gilroy, CA
408-848-4108 (800-800-8000)
Dogs of all sizes are allowed. Dogs are allowed for a pet fee.

Homestead Studio Suites Los Angeles - Glendale
1377 W. Glenoaks Blvd.

Glendale, CA
818-956-6665 (800-804-3724)
One dog is allowed per suite. There is a $25 per night additional pet fee up to $150 for an entire stay.

Vagabond Inn
120 W. Colorado Street
Glendale, CA
818-240-1700
vagabondinn.com
This motel is located near Universal Studios. Amenities include a complimentary breakfast and during the week, a free USA Today newspaper. Dogs up to 60 pounds are allowed for an additional fee of $10 per night per pet. 2 dogs may be allowed.

Hawthorn Suites
12180 Tributary Point Drive
Gold River, CA
916-351-9192 (866-856-7044)
hawthorngr.com/
In addition to providing a convenient location to many local sites and activities, this all-suite hotel offers a number of amenities for business and leisure travelers, including their signature breakfast buffet and beautifully appointed rooms. Dogs are allowed for an additional one time fee of $50 per pet. 2 dogs may be allowed.

Motel 6 - Santa Barbara Goleta
5897 Calle Real
Goleta, CA
805-964-3596 (800-466-8356)
This motel welcomes your pets to stay with you.

Econo Lodge
49713 Gorman Post Rd.
Gorman, CA
661-248-6411 (877-424-6423)
Dogs of all sizes are allowed. Dogs are allowed for a pet fee of $10.00 per pet per night.

Gray Eagle Lodge
5000 Gold Lake Rd.
Graeagle, CA
800-635-8778 (800-635-8778)
grayeaglelodge.com/
Stay in a rustic cabin at this mountain getaway located in the Sierra Mountains, about 1.5 hours north of Truckee. There are many hiking trails within a short walk from the cabins. There are over 40 alpine lakes nearby. There is a $20 per pet, per day, fee with a maximum of 2 pets per cabin. Guests are expected to follow guidelines provided by the lodge and will sign a pet policy form upon arrival. Dogs up to 50 pounds

are allowed.

Grass Valley Courtyard Suites
210 N Auburn Street
Grass Valley, CA
530-272-7696
gvcourtyardsuites.com/
they have provided a doggy station with a scooper and receptacles.

Holiday Inn Express Hotel & Suites
Gold Miners Inn-Grass Valley
121 Bank Street
Grass Valley, CA
530-477-1700 (877-270-6405)
Dogs of all sizes are allowed. Dogs are allowed for a pet fee of $50 per pet per stay.

Swan Levine House Bed and Breakfast
328 South Church Street
Grass Valley, CA
916-272-1873
This renovated historic house was built in 1880. It was originally owned by a local merchant who made his fortune by selling mining equipment. He sold it to a doctor who converted the house into a hospital and it served as a community medical center until 1968. There are four rooms, each with a private bath. They have one room available for guests who bring a large dog. Dogs are not to be left alone in the room. There is a $15 per day pet charge. They are also kid-friendly. They do have a cat that resides in the house.

Historic Groveland Hotel
18767 Main Street
Groveland, CA
209-962-4000 (800-273-3314.)
groveland.com/
Your dog or cat is welcome at this 1849 historic inn. Country Inns Magazine rated the Groveland Hotel as one of the Top 10 Inns in the United States. The inn is located 23 miles from Yosemite's main gate. Make your reservations early as they book up quickly. This inn is located about an hour from Yosemite Valley. There is a $15 per day per pet additional pet fee. All rooms are non-smoking. Multiple dogs may be allowed.

Hotel Charlotte
18736 Main Street
Groveland, CA
209-962-6455
Dogs are allowed for an additional one time pet fee of $20 per room. 2 dogs may be allowed.

Sunset Inn
33569 Hardin Flat Rd.
Groveland, CA
209-962-4360
This inn offers three cabins near Yosemite National Park. The cabins are located on two acres and are surrounded by a dog-friendly National Forest at a 4500 foot elevation. All cabins are non-smoking and include kitchens and private bathrooms. Children are also welcome. The Sunset Inn is located just 2 miles from the west entrance to Yosemite, one mile from Highway 120. There is a $20 per day pet charge.

Mar Vista Cottages
35101 S H 1
Gualala, CA
707-884-3522 (877-855-3522)
marvistamendocino.com/
they are not permitted on the beds and furniture, and they may not be left alone in the cottage at any time. Dogs may be off lead only if they are under good voice control as there are other dogs and animals in residence. Dogs must be friendly, well behaved, and cleaned up after at all times.

Ocean View Properties
P.O. Box 1285
Gualala, CA
707-884-3538
oceanviewprop.com/
Ocean View Properties offers vacation home rentals on The Sea Ranch and Mendocino Coast. Some of their vacation homes are pet-friendly. They offer a wide variety of special vacation home rentals, located on the oceanfront, oceanside and hillside at The Sea Ranch. Each of the rental homes has a fully equipped kitchen, a fireplace or wood stove, blankets, pillows, and telephones. Most have hot tubs, televisions, VCR's, radios, CD/cassette players, and washer/dryers. Guests provide kindling, bed linens, and towels. With advance notice, linens can be rented and maid service can be hired. Please call and ask them which rentals are dog-friendly. There is an additional one time pet fee of $50. Multiple dogs may be allowed.

Sea Ranch Vacation Homes
P.O. Box 246
Gualala, CA
707-884-4235
searanchrentals.com/
Rent a vacation home for the

weekend, week or longer along the coast or on a forested hillside. Some of their 50 homes allow well-behaved dogs.There is a $40 one time pet fee per pet. 2 dogs may be allowed.

Serenisea Vacation Homes
36100 Highway 1 S.
Gualala, CA
707-884-3836
serenisea.com
Serenisea maintains and manages a number of vacation homes and cottages in this community on the Mendocino coast. Some of them allow dogs of all sizes. 2 dogs may be allowed.

Surf Motel
39170 S. Highway 1
Gualala, CA
707-884-3571
gualala.com
There is a $10 per day per pet charge. Multiple dogs may be allowed.

Creekside Inn & Resort
16180 Neeley Rd
Guerneville, CA
707-869-3623
creeksideinn.com
Dogs are allowed in one of their cottages. During the summer it books up fast, so please make an early reservation. The inn will be able to help you find some pet-friendly hiking trails and beaches nearby. Dogs are allowed for no additional pet fee, and they may not be left alone in the room. 2 dogs may be allowed.

Dawn Ranch Lodge
16467 Hwy. 116
Guerneville, CA
707-869-0656
dawnranch.com
This lodge is located minutes away from many wineries and has nearby access to the Russian River. There are a number of pet-friendly rooms equipped with doggie beds, water bowls and treats. There is a $50 one time non-refundable pet fee per room and up to two dogs are allowed. Dogs may dine on the outside patio at the restaurant.

Ferngrove Cottages
16650 H 116
Guerneville, CA
707-869-8105
This charming retreat offers cottages nestled among redwoods and colorful gardens. Some of the amenities include spa tubs, fireplaces and skylights, a delicious

extended continental breakfast, pool and sun deck, a barbecue and picnic area, individual decks or patios, and it is only a short walk to the river/beaches and town. Dogs of all sizes are allowed. There is a $25 per night per pet additional fee. Dogs may not be left alone in the room at any time, and they must be well behaved, leashed, cleaned up after, and kept off the furniture/bed. There are some breed restrictions. Dogs must be declared at the time of reservations. 2 dogs may be allowed.

River Village Resort and Spa
14880 River Road
Guerneville, CA
888-342-2624
rivervillageresort.com
This inn is located just minutes from the Russian River. At this inn, dogs are allowed in certain cottages and there is a $10 per day pet fee. Please do not walk pets on the lawn. Children are also welcome.

Russian River Getaways
14075 Mill Street, P.O. Box 1673
Guerneville, CA
707-869-4560 (800-433-6673)
rrgetaways.com
This company offers about 40 dog-friendly vacation homes in Russian River wine country with leash free beaches nearby. There are no pet fees and no size limits for dogs. There is a $75 refundable pet deposit.

Motel 6 - Santa Nella Los Banos
12733 South Hwy 33
Gustine, CA
209-826-6644 (800-466-8356)
This motel welcomes your pets to stay with you.

Motel 6 - Los Angeles Hacienda Heights
1154 7th Ave
Hacienda Heights, CA
626-968-9462 (800-466-8356)
This motel welcomes your pets to stay with you.

Comfort Inn
2930 N Cabrillo Hwy.
Half Moon Bay, CA
650-712-1999 (877-424-6423)
Dogs up to 85 pounds are allowed. Dogs are allowed for a pet fee of $10.00 per pet per night. Two dogs are allowed per room.

Days Inn Half Moon Bay
3020 N. Cabrillo Hwy

Half Moon Bay, CA
650-726-9700 (800-329-7466)
Dogs of all sizes are allowed. Dogs are allowed for a pet fee of $15 per pet per night.

Half Moon Bay Inn
401 Main Street
Half Moon Bay, CA
650-726-1177
halfmoonbayinn.com
Dogs are allowed in this 1932 inn which was renovated in 2005. There is a $25 per stay pet fee and a $100 refundable pet deposit.

The Ritz-Carlton
One Miramontes Point Road
Half Moon Bay, CA
650-712-7000 (800-241-3333)
they are not allowed in the lobby, pool area, the Club Lounge, Navio, The Conservatory, or the golf course. Dogs are allowed for an additional one time fee of $125. Dogs must be well mannered, disease free, leashed and cleaned up after at all times, and the Do Not Disturb sign put on the door if they are in the room alone.

Super 8 Hanford
918 E Lacey Blvd
Hanford, CA
559-582-1736 (800-800-8000)
Dogs of all sizes are allowed. Dogs are allowed for a pet fee of $20.00 per pet per stay.

Motel 6 - Los Angeles Harbor City
820 Sepulveda Blvd
Harbor City, CA
310-549-9560 (800-466-8356)
This motel welcomes your pets to stay with you.

Candlewood Suites Hawthorne East
4334 W. Imperial Highway
Hawthorne, CA
310-722-2707 (877-270-6405)
Dogs up to 80 pounds are allowed. Pets allowed with an additional pet fee. Up to $75 for 1-6 nights and up to $150 for 7+ nights. A pet agreement must be signed at check-in.

Comfort Inn Cockatoo
11500 Acacia Avenue
Hawthorne, CA
310-973-3335 (877-424-6423)
Dogs up to 50 pounds are allowed. Dogs are allowed for a pet fee of $10.00 per pet per night. Two dogs are allowed per room.

TownePlace Suites Los Angeles

LAX/Manhattan Beach
14400 Aviation Blvd
Hawthorne, CA
310-725-9696 (800-257-3000)
This all suite hotel sits central to a number of sites of interest for both business and leisure travelers - including Manhattan Beach and LAX; plus they also offer a number of on-site amenities to ensure comfort. Dogs are allowed for an additional one time fee of $100 per room. Multiple dogs may be allowed.

Motel 6 - Hayward
30155 Industrial Pkwy Sw
Hayward, CA
510-489-8333 (800-466-8356)
This motel welcomes your pets to stay with you.

Best Western Dry Creek Inn
198 Dry Creek Road
Healdsburg, CA
707-433-0300 (800-780-7234)
Dogs of all sizes are allowed. Dogs are allowed for a pet fee of $30.00 per pet per night. Two dogs are allowed per room.

Duchamp Hotel
421 Foss Street
Healdsburg, CA
707-431-1300
duchamphotel.com
This hotel, located in Healdsburg, allows dogs in two of their cottages. There is an an additional pet fee of $60 for 1 night and $40 dollars for each additional night per pet. Every cottage features a king bed, oversized spa shower, private terrace, fireplace, mini bar, and more. Children over 16 years old are allowed. The entire premises is non-smoking. Dogs are not allowed in the pool area and they request that you take your dog away from the cottages and hotel when they go to the bathroom. 2 dogs may be allowed.

Russian River Adventures Canoe Rentals
20 Healdsburg Ave
Healdsburg, CA
707-433-5599 (800-280-7627 (SOAR))
Take a self-guided eco-adventure with your pooch. Rent an inflatable canoe and adventure along the Russian River. The SOAR 16 is the largest model and is great for taking children and dogs. There are many refreshing swimming holes along the way. Dogs and families of all ages are welcome. Be sure to call ahead as reservations are required.

Motel 6 - Hemet
3885 Florida Ave
Hemet, CA
951-929-8900 (800-466-8356)
This motel welcomes your pets to stay with you.

Super 8 Hemet
3510 West Florida Ave
Hemet, CA
951-658-2281 (800-800-8000)
Dogs are welcome at this hotel.

Quality Inn & Suites
901 Aviation Blvd
Hermosa Beach, CA
310-374-2666 (877-424-6423)
qualityinnsts-hermosa.com
This hotel allows dogs for a pet fee of $20 per night. Pets are welcomed with a Gift Bag at check in.

Days Suites
14865 Bear Valley Rd
Hesperia, CA
760-948-0600
There is a $10 per day pet fee for 1 dog, and $15 per day for 2 dogs. 2 dogs may be allowed.

Motel 6 - Hesperia
9757 Cataba Road
Hesperia, CA
760-947-0094 (800-466-8356)
This motel welcomes your pets to stay with you.

Super 8 /Victorville Area Hesperia
12033 Oakwood Ave
Hesperia, CA
760-949-3231 (800-800-8000)
Dogs are welcome at this hotel.

Chateau Marmont Hotel
8221 Sunset Blvd
Hollywood, CA
323-656-1010
chateaumarmont.com/
Modeled after a royal residence in France, grand eloquence awaits guests to this castle on the hill. Some of the features/amenities include a full service bar, gourmet dining either indoor or in a beautiful garden patio setting, many in room amenities, a heated outdoor pool, and personalized services. Dogs up to 100 pounds are allowed. There is a $150 one time additional pet fee per room and a pet policy to sign at check in. Dogs must be well behaved, kept leashed, cleaned up after, and the Do Not Disturb sign put on the door if they are in the room alone.

Motel 6 - Los Angeles Hollywood
1738 Whitley Ave
Hollywood, CA
323-464-6006 (800-466-8356)
Well-behaved dogs are allowed. Dogs are allowed for a pet fee of $$10.00 per pet per night. One dog is allowed per room.

Ramada Near Universal Studios Hollywood
1160 North Vermont Avenue
Hollywood, CA
323-315-1800 (800-272-6232)
Dogs are welcome at this hotel.

Sorensen's Resort
14255 Highway 88
Hope Valley, CA
530-694-2203 (800-423-9949)
sorensensresort.com/
This secluded mountain resort is located in beautiful Hope Valley which is about 30 minutes south of South Lake Tahoe. Dogs are allowed in several of the cabins. The dog-friendly cabins sleep from two up to four people. Each cabin has a wood-burning stove (for heat) and kitchen. The Hope Valley Cross Country Ski Rentals are located on the premises (see Attractions). Hiking is available during the summer on the trails of the Toiyable National Forest. There are also several nearby lakes. Cabin rates start at $85 per night and go up to about $450 for a large bedroom cabin. There are no additional pet fees. 2 dogs may be allowed.

Extended Stay America Orange County - Huntington Beach
5050 Skylab West Cir.
Huntington Beach, CA
714-799-4887 (800-804-3724)
One dog is allowed per suite. There is a $25 per night additional pet fee up to $150 for an entire stay.

Hilton Waterfront Beach Resort
21100 Pacific Coast H
Huntington Beach, CA
714-845-8000 (800-HILTONS (445-8667))
This oceanfront, upscale hotel offers a number on site amenities for business and leisure travelers - including miles of white sand beaches and planned activities, plus a convenient location to business, shopping, dining, and recreation areas. Dogs up to 75 pounds are allowed for an additional fee of $75 per night per pet. 2 dogs may be allowed.

Stellar Summit Cabin
Call to arrange

Idyllwild, CA
626-482-6006
stellarsummitcabin.com
This secluded cabin is perched high on a hill in Idyllwild. There is a fenced deck, loft, Jacuzzi and views. There is a $15 pet fee per visit.

Tahquitz Inn
25840 Highway 243
Idyllwild, CA
909-659-4554 (877-659-4554)
tahquitzinn.com
This inn is located in the heart of Idyllwild and allows all well-behaved dogs. They offer one and two bedroom suites with a separate bedroom, kitchen and porches. The inn has also been a location for several Hollywood film shoots. All of their rooms accommodate dogs and there is a $10 per day pet charge.

The Fireside Inn
54540 N Circle Drive
Idyllwild, CA
877-797-FIRE (3473)
thefireside-inn.com/
Surrounded by the natural landscape of the San Jacinto Mountains, this comfortable inn offers 7 duplex cottages and a private cottage. Some of the amenities include wood-burning fireplaces in all cottages, outdoor seating, barbecue and picnic areas, and daily feeding of the birds and small animals of the area. Dogs of all sizes are allowed for an additional pet fee per room of $10 per night for the first 2 nights. Dogs may not be left alone in the room at any time, and they must be leashed and cleaned up after. 2 dogs may be allowed.

Independence Courthouse Motel
157 N Edwards Street
Independence, CA
760-878-2732
There is a $10 per day per room additional pet fee. All rooms are non-smoking. 2 dogs may be allowed.

Best Western Date Tree Hotel
81909 Indio Boulevard
Indio, CA
760-347-3421 (800-780-7234)
Dogs of all sizes are allowed. Dogs are allowed for a pet fee of $10.00 per pet per night.

Motel 6 - Indio Palm Springs Area
82195 Indio Blvd
Indio, CA
760-342-6311 (800-466-8356)
This motel welcomes your pets to stay with you.

Palm Shadow Inn
80-761 Highway 111
Indio, CA
760-347-3476
palmshadowinn.com/
A well-behaved large dog is okay. Nestled among date palm groves, there are eighteen guest rooms which overlook nearly three acres of lawns, flowers and citrus trees. There is a $5 per day per pet charge. Dogs must be crated when left alone in the room. 2 dogs may be allowed.

Royal Plaza Inn
82347 Hwy 111
Indio, CA
760-347-0911 (800-228-9559)
royalplazainn.com/
This motel offers a laundry room, whirlpool and room refrigerators. There is a $10 per day additional pet fee. 2 dogs may be allowed.

Super 8 Indio
81753 Hwy 111
Indio, CA
760-342-0264 (800-800-8000)
Dogs of all sizes are allowed. Dogs are allowed for a pet fee of $15.00 per pet per night.

Motel 6 - Los Angeles Lax
5101 Century Blvd
Inglewood, CA
310-419-1234 (800-466-8356)
This motel welcomes your pets to stay with you.

Rosemary Cottage
75 Balboa Ave
Inverness, CA
415-663-9338
rosemarybb.com/
Dogs are welcome at the Rosemary Cottage and The Ark Cottage. Families are also welcome. The Rosemary Cottage is a two room cottage with a deck and garden. It is adjacent to the Point Reyes National Seashore. The Ark Cottage is a two room cottage tucked in the forest a mile up the ridge from the village of Inverness. There is a $40 one time pet charge for one dog,,, a $50 one time pet charge for two dogs, and a $60 one time fee for 3 dogs. Multiple dogs may be allowed.

Candlewood Suites Orange County/Irvine Spectrum
16150 Sand Canyon Avenue
Irvine, CA
949-788-0500 (877-270-6405)

Dogs up to 80 pounds are allowed. Pets allowed with an additional pet fee. Up to $75 for 1-6 nights and up to $150 for 7+ nights. A pet agreement must be signed at check-in.

Embassy Suites
2120 Main Street
Irvine, CA
949-553-8332 (800-EMBASSY (362-2779))
This upscale hotel offers a number of on site amenities for business and leisure travelers, plus a convenient location to the John Wayne/Orange County Airport, and business, shopping, dining, and entertainment districts. They also offer a complimentary cooked-to-order breakfast and a Manager's reception every evening. One dog is allowed per room for a $500 pet deposit; $100 is not refundable.

Hilton Hotel
18800 MacArthur Blvd
Irvine, CA
949-833-9999 (800-HILTONS (445-8667))
Located in the heart of the city, this upscale, downtown hotel offers a number of on site amenities for business and leisure travelers, plus a convenient location to business, shopping, dining, and entertainment districts. Dogs up to 100 pounds are allowed for an additional one time fee of $50 per pet. 2 dogs may be allowed.

Hilton Irvine/Orange County Airport
18800 MacArthur Blvd
Irvine, CA
949-833-9999 (800-HILTONS (445-8667))
Dogs up to 75 pounds are allowed for an additional one time pet fee of $50 per room, and there is a pet policy to sign at check in. Canine guests also get their own doggy bed and food/water bowls. Dogs may not be left in the room alone for long periods, and a contact number must be left with the front desk when they are alone. 2 dogs may be allowed.

Homestead Studio Suites Orange County - Irvine Spectrum
30 Technology Dr.
Irvine, CA
949-727-4228 (800-804 3724)
One dog is allowed per suite. There is a $25 per night additional pet fee up to $150 for an entire stay.

Residence Inn Irvine John Wayne Airport/Orange County

2855 Main Street
Irvine, CA
949-261-2020 (800-331-3131)
In addition to offering a convenient location to business, shopping, dining, and entertainment areas, this hotel also provides a number of in-house amenities, including a daily buffet breakfast and evening social hours. Dogs are allowed for an additional one time pet fee of $100 per room. 2 dogs may be allowed.

Amador Motel
12408 Kennedy Flat Rd
Jackson, CA
209-223-0970
This motel has a large backyard, not completely enclosed, where you can walk your dog. They allow all well-behaved dogs. There are no additional pet fees. Multiple dogs may be allowed.

Best Western Amador Inn
200 S State Highway 49
Jackson, CA
209-223-0211 (800-780-7234)
Dogs of all sizes are allowed. Dogs are allowed for a pet fee.

Jackson Gold Lodge
850 N. State Hwy 49
Jackson, CA
209-223-0486
jacksongoldlodge.com/
This lodge has been dog-friendly for years. They allow dogs in the motel rooms and in the cottages. They have eight duplex cottages, each with a separate living room, kitchen, dining room, bedroom and patio. Amenities include a free continental breakfast. Dogs are an additional $15 per day. There are no designated smoking or non-smoking cottages. 2 dogs may be allowed.

The National Hotel
18183 Main Street
Jamestown, CA
209-984-3446
national-hotel.com
Established in 1859, this is one of the oldest continuously operating hotels in California. Taking a day trip or going for a hike? Just ask for a picnic basket the day before and their chef will provide you with a meal to take with you and enjoy next to a cool Sierra Nevada stream or at one of the many picnic areas throughout the dog-friendly Stanislaus National Forest. There is a $25 per day per pet charge. 2 dogs may be allowed.

Jenner Inn
10400 H 1
Jenner, CA
707-865-2377
jennerinn.com/index.html
Located where the Russian River meets the Pacific Ocean, this unique resort features rooms, suites, and cottages set in historic houses and cottages with something to fit everyone's budget. A full country breakfast is included, and cafe dining is also available. Dogs of all sizes are allowed for a $35 one time additional fee per pet. They have only four pet friendly rooms, and dogs may not be left alone in the room at any time. Dogs must be well behaved, leashed, and cleaned up after. 2 dogs may be allowed.

Joshua Tree
6426 Valley View Street
Joshua Tree, CA
760-366-2212
lazyhmhp.com/
Well behaved dogs of all sizes are allowed. There are no additional pet fees.

Apple Tree Inn
4360 Highway 78
Julian, CA
800-410-8683
julianappletreeinn.com
This is a small country motel located near the historic gold mining town of Julian. Families are always welcome. There is no additional pet fee. Dogs are not allowed on the bed, they may not be left alone in the room, and aggressive breeds are not allowed. 2 dogs may be allowed.

Pine Haven Cabin Rental
Call to Arrange.
Julian, CA
760-726-9888
pinehavencabin.com/
Enjoy this dog-friendly mountain getaway on 1.25 acres. The entire lot is securely fenced, offering your pet the freedom to run off-leash. The cabin has one bedroom plus a small loft upstairs, a bathroom with a tiled walk-in shower (no tub), and a fully equipped kitchen. The cabin sleeps 2 people and is off a small private lane, so you will have lots of privacy. No smoking allowed. For reservations call Teresa at 760-726-9888 or email to pinehavencabin@sbcglobal.net.

Big Rock Resort
Big Rock Road at Boulder Drive
June Lake, CA
760-648-7717

bigrockresort.net
Dogs of all sizes are allowed in some of these one to three bedroom cabins right on June Lake. A maximum of one dog is allowed per cabin. There is a $15 per day additional pet fee. All cabins are non-smoking.

Double Eagle Resort and Spa
5587 Highway 158
June Lake, CA
760-648-7004
doubleeagle.com
This resort on 13 acres allows dogs of all sizes in some of the cabins. Dogs must be on leash on the premises at all times. All cabins are non smoking. There is a $15 per day additional pet fee up to a maximum of $60 for a stay.

June Lake Villager Inn
Boulder Dr & Knoll Ave
June Lake, CA
760-648-7712 (800-655-6545)
junelakevillager.com
Dogs of all sizes are allowed at this inn located in the village of June Lake. The inn has been here in business since the 1920s. Dogs of all sizes are allowed and there are no additional pet fees.

Edgewater Resort and RV Park
6420 Soda Bay Road
Kelseyville, CA
707-279-0208 (800-396-6224)
edgewaterresort.net/
the fee for RV and tent sites is $5 per night per pet. (The fee could be less depending on size of dog, length of stay, and the season. Dogs may not be left unattended outside at any time, may only be left alone in cabins if they are kenneled, and they must have proof of current shots. Dogs must be quiet, well behaved, be inside at night, and leashed and cleaned up after (there is a pet station with bags at the beach). They are not allowed in park buildings or the gated swimming pool area, but they are allowed at the beach. They have provided an OK-9 Corral outside the general store with fresh water for your pet, and they offer a pet tag that says Guest at Edgewater Resort with an address and phone number of the resort for a $5 refundable deposit.

Birmingham Bed and Breakfast
8790 H 12
Kenwood, CA
707-833-6996 (800-819-1388)
birminghambb.com/
whether it's a stroll through the 2

acres of trees, berry patches, and gardens, or just resting on the big wrap around porch enjoying the amazing view. There is one pet friendly cottage that was built onto the original water tower, and is spacious with many features and amenities, including a fenced-in back yard. Dogs of all sizes are welcome for an additional fee of $10 per night per pet and a pet policy to sign at check in. Since there is a dog that lives on site, they ask that guests check in before removing pets from their car. Dogs may not be left alone in the cottage, and they must be friendly, well behaved, and leashed and cleaned up after at all times.

River View Lodge
2 Sirreta Street
Kernville, CA
760-376-6019
Dogs of all sizes are allowed. There is a $20 per night per room fee and a pet policy to sign at check in. Aggressive breeds are not allowed. 2 dogs may be allowed.

Motel 6 - King City, Ca
Broadway Circle
King City, CA
831-385-5000 (800-466-8356)
Your pets are welcome to stay here with you.

Quality Inn
401 Sierra Street
Kingsburg, CA
559-897-1022 (877-424-6423)
Dogs of all sizes are allowed. Dogs are allowed for a pet fee of $15.00 per pet per night.

Motel Trees
15495 Highway 101 South
Klamath, CA
707-482-3152
This motel is located directly across Highway 101 from the dog-friendly Trees of Mystery attraction. The motel offers pet rooms and allows all well-behaved dogs. There is a $10 per pet per night fee. Dogs may not be left alone in the room. They have a AAA 2 diamond rating. 2 dogs may be allowed.

Kyburz Resort Motel
13666 Highway 50
Kyburz, CA
530-293-3382
kyburzresort.com
Nestled among the pines along 300 feet of the South Fork of the American River, this motel is located in the heart of the El Dorado National Forest. It is located about 30 minutes

east of Placerville and about 15-20 minutes from Apple Hill. Well-behaved dogs are allowed and they must be leashed when outside your room. There is a $10 per day per pet fee. 2 dogs may be allowed.

Hilton Hotel
10950 N Torrey Pines Road
La Jolla, CA
858-558-1500 (800-HILTONS (445-8667))
Sitting on the bluffs overlooking the ocean and Torrey Pines Golf Course, this upscale hotel offers a sense of seclusion while still being only a short distance from business, shopping, dining, and entertainment opportunities. Dogs are allowed for an additional one time pet fee of $75 per room. 2 dogs may be allowed.

Hotel La Jolla at the Shores
7955 La Jolla Shores Drive
La Jolla, CA
858-551-3600 (800-666-0261)
hotellajolla.com/
This lush luxury resort is conveniently located to many other attractions and recreational opportunities, and they offer a comprehensive list of amenities. Dogs up to 60 pounds are allowed for an additional one time fee of $75 per pet. Dogs must be leashed, cleaned up after, and crated if they are in the room alone.

La Jolla Village Lodge
1141 Silverado Street
La Jolla, CA
858-551-2001
There is a $20 one time pet fee. Dogs may not be left alone in the room. Thanks to a reader for recommending this hotel. Multiple dogs may be allowed.

La Valencia Hotel
1132 Prospect Street
La Jolla, CA
858-454-0771 (800-451-0772)
lavalencia.com/
This resort hotel blends European flair and old Southern California charm and hospitality with all the modern day amenities. Dogs are allowed for an additional one time pet fee of $25. Dogs must be quiet, well mannered, leashed, cleaned up after, and the Do Not Disturb sign put on the door if they are in the room alone.

Marriott San Diego La Jolla
4240 La Jolla Village Drive
La Jolla, CA

858-587-1414 (800-228-9290)
This luxury hotel sits central to a number of sites of interest for both business and leisure travelers, and they are only a skywalk away from University Town Shopping Center with more than 140 shops, services, and entertainment; plus they also offer numerous on-site amenities for all level of travelers. Dogs are allowed for an additional one time fee of $75 per room. 2 dogs may be allowed.

Residence Inn San Diego La Jolla
8901 Gilman Drive
La Jolla, CA
858-587-1770 (800-876-1778)
This all suite hotel sits central to many of the city's star attractions, shopping, dining, and business areas, plus they offer a number of in-house amenities that include a daily buffet breakfast and a Manager's reception Monday through Thursday. Dogs are allowed for an additional one time pet fee of $100 per room. Multiple dogs may be allowed.

Motel 6 - San Diego La Mesa
7621 Alvarado Rd
La Mesa, CA
619-464-7151 (800-466-8356)
This motel welcomes your pets to stay with you.

Extended Stay America Los Angeles - La Mirada
14775 Firestone Blvd.
La Mirada, CA
714-670-8579 (800-804-3724)
One dog is allowed per suite. There is a $25 per night additional pet fee up to $150 for an entire stay.

Residence Inn La Mirada Buena Park
14419 Firestone Blvd
La Mirada, CA
714-523-2800 (800-331-3131)
This all suite hotel sits central to many of the area's star attractions, shopping, dining, and business areas, plus they offer a number of in-house amenities that include a daily buffet breakfast and evening socials. Well mannered dogs up to 60 pounds are allowed for an additional one time pet fee of $100 per room. 2 dogs may be allowed.

La Quinta Inn & Suites Buena Park
3 Centerpointe Drive
La Palma, CA
714-670-1400 (800-531-5900)
Dogs of all sizes are allowed. There are no additional pet fees. Dogs must be quiet, well behaved, leashed

and cleaned up after. Multiple dogs may be allowed.

La Porte Cabin Rentals
Main Street and Pike Road/P. O. Box 225
La Porte, CA
530-675-0850
laportecabins.com/index.html
all with complete kitchens so just bring your own cuisine. There is satellite TV available, and the cabins have private porches. Dogs of all sizes are allowed for no additional fee. Dogs may only be left alone in the rooms if they will be quiet and well mannered, and they must be leashed and cleaned up after.

Casa Laguna Inn & Spa
2510 S Coast Highway
Laguna Beach, CA
949-494-2996 (800-233-0449)
casalaguna.com
This Spanish-style bed and breakfast sits on a hillside with views of the ocean. It was voted Orange County's Best B&B four years in a row. The rooms are decorated with a blend of antique and contemporary furnishings. There are 15 guest rooms plus several guest suites and cottages. While in Laguna Beach, browse the variety of speciality shops or dine at one of the dog-friendly restaurants. Interested in a stroll on the beach - Main Beach (certain dog hours) is a short drive from the inn. There is a $25 per day additional pet fee.CATEGORY: Accommodation

Holiday Inn Laguna Beach
696 South Coast Highway
Laguna Beach, CA
949-494-1001 (877-270-6405)
Dogs of all sizes are allowed. Dogs are allowed for a pet fee of $75.00 per pet per night.

Pacific Edge Hotel
647 South Coast Hwy
Laguna Beach, CA
866-932-2896
pacificedgehotel.com
Dogs of all sizes are allowed. There is a $50 non-refundable additional pet fee.

Holiday Inn Laguna Hills (Mission Viejo)
25205 Lapaz Rd
Laguna Hills, CA
949-586-5000 (877-270-6405)
Dogs of all sizes are allowed. Dogs are allowed for a nightly pet fee.

Arrowhead Saddleback Inn
PO Box 1890
Lake Arrowhead, CA
800-858-3334 (800-358-8733)
lakeArrowhead.com/saddleback/
This historic inn was originally constructed in 1917 as the Raven Hotel. It is now totally restored and a historical landmark. The inn is located at the entrance of the Lake Arrowhead Village. Dogs are allowed in some of the cottages. The cottages feature stone fireplaces, double whirlpool baths, heated towel racks and refrigerators. There is no additional pet fee. Dog owners also need to sign a pet agreement. Multiple dogs may be allowed.

Prophet's Paradise B&B
26845 Modoc Lane
Lake Arrowhead, CA
909-336-1969
This bed and breakfast has five stories which cascade down its alpine hillside. This provides guests with privacy and intimate decks. All rooms have private baths. Amenities include a gym, a pool room, ping-pong, and darts, a horseshoe pit and a nearby hiking trail. Room rates start at $100 per night and include a gourmet breakfast. Your well-behaved dog is welcome. The owners also have pets. There are no additional pet fees.

Arrowhead Pine Rose Cabins
25994 State Highway I89
Lake Arrowhead - Twin Peaks, CA
909-337-2341
pinerose.com
Dogs are allowed in the cabins for a $100 refundable deposit and a $10 per day pet fee. per pet.

Candlewood Suites Orange County/Irvine East
3 South Pointe Dr
Lake Forest, CA
949-598-9105 (877-270-6405)
Dogs up to 80 pounds are allowed. Pets allowed with an additional pet fee. Up to $75 for 1-6 nights and up to $150 for 7+ nights. A pet agreement must be signed at check-in.

Extended Stay America Orange County - Lake Forest
20251 Lake Forest Dr.
Lake Forest, CA
949-598-1898 (800-804-3724)
One dog is allowed per suite. There is a $25 per night additional pet fee up to $150 for an entire stay.

Quality Inn & Suites
23702 Rockfield Boulevard
Lake Forest, CA
949-458-1900 (877-424-6423)
Dogs of all sizes are allowed. Dogs are allowed for a pet fee of $fee per pet per night.

Staybridge Suites Irvine East/Lake Forest
2 Orchard
Lake Forest, CA
949-462-9500 (877-270-6405)
Dogs up to 80 pounds are allowed. Pets allowed with an additional pet fee. Up to $75 for 1-6 nights and up to $150 for 7+ nights. A pet agreement must be signed at check-in.

Lake San Marcos Resort
1025 La Bonita Drive
Lake San Marcos, CA
760-744-0120
lakesanmarcosresort.com/
This beautiful resort destination will allow well mannered dogs for an additional one time fee of $75 per pet. 2 dogs may be allowed.

Sugarloaf Cottages Resort
19667 Lakeshore Drive
Lakehead, CA
800-953-4432
shastacabins.com/
These cottages are located near the shore of Lake Shasta and have air conditioning, heating, bathrooms, linens and complete kitchens, but no phones, televisions or maid service. They charge a $10 per night pet fee and allow only one pet per unit.

Tsasdi Resort Cabins
19990 Lakeshore Dr.
Lakehead, CA
530-238-2575
shastalakecabins.com/Cabins.html
All cabins have private baths, linens, cable TV, air conditioning, heating, outdoor barbecue and private decks, most of which overlook Shasta Lake. There is a $12 per day pet fee. In order for them to continuing being pet-friendly, they ask that all pets be kept on a leash and not be left unattended in the cabins or on the decks. Please clean up after your pets. Multiple dogs may be allowed.

Holiday Inn Express Lancaster
43719 17th Street West
Lancaster, CA
661-951-8848 (877-270-6405)
Dogs of all sizes are allowed. Dogs are allowed for a pet fee of $10.00 per pet per night.

Motel 6 - Lancaster
43540 17th St
Lancaster, CA
661-948-0435 (800-466-8356)
This motel welcomes your pets to
stay with you.

Days Inn Lathrop
14750 S. Harlan Road
Lathrop, CA
209-982-1959 (800-329-7466)
Dogs are welcome at this hotel.

Ramada Limited -
9000 Countryside Ct
Lebec, CA
661-248-1530 (800-272-6232)
Dogs are welcome at this hotel.

Murphey's Hotel
51493 Hwy 395
Lee Vining, CA
760-647-6316
There is a $5 per day per pet
additional fee. Dogs are not to be left
alone in rooms. 2 dogs may be
allowed.

Days Inn Lemoore
877 East D Street
Lemoore, CA
559-924-1261 (800-329-7466)
Dogs of all sizes are allowed. Dogs
are allowed for a pet fee of $25.00
per pet per night.

Motel 6 - Lemoore
1290 Sierra Circle
Lemoore, CA
559-925-6100 (800-466-8356)
This motel welcomes your pets to
stay with you.

Lewiston Valley RV Park
4789 Trinity Dam Blvd.
Lewiston, CA
530-778-3942
lewistonca.com/lewvally.htm
This motel and RV park is on 8 acres
and offers 7 pull through sites and 2
back-in sites. The sites have 50 amp
service. Amenities include a
seasonal heated pool. Within walking
distance is a family style restaurant,
gas station and mini-mart. Well-
behaved leashed dogs are allowed.
There is a $5 per night per pet for
dogs in the motel,,, there is no
additional pet fee for the RV park.
Dogs must be declared at the time of
reservations, and aggressive breeds
are not allowed. 2 dogs may be
allowed.

S. S. Seafoam Lodge
6751 N H 1

Littleriver, CA
707-937-1827
seafoamlodge.com/
This lodge comprises a total of 8
separate buildings with 24 guest
accommodations and a conference
center. Located on 6 acres of
coastal gardens and pines, there
are spectacular ocean views and a
private cove and beach access.
Some of the amenities include a
Continental breakfast delivered to
your room, private baths and decks,
a hot tub, and conference facilities.
Dogs of all sizes are allowed for an
additional one time fee of $10 per
pet. Dogs may not be left alone in
the room at any time, and they must
be well mannered, leashed, and
cleaned up after.

Extended Stay America Livermore -
Airway Blvd.
2380 Nissen Dr.
Livermore, CA
925-373-1700 (800-804-3724)
One dog is allowed per suite. There
is a $25 per night additional pet fee
up to $150 for an entire stay.

Motel 6 - Livermore
4673 Lassen Rd
Livermore, CA
925-443-5300 (800-466-8356)
Your pets are welcome to stay here
with you.

Residence Inn Livermore
Pleasanton
1000 Airway Blvd
Livermore, CA
925-373-1800 (800-331-3131)
Some of the amenities at this all-
suite inn include a daily buffet
breakfast, evening socials Monday
through Thursday, a heated
swimming pool, and a
complimentary grocery shopping
service. Dogs are allowed for an
additional one time pet fee of $75
per room. Multiple dogs may be
allowed.

Best Western Royal Host Inn
710 S Cherokee Ln
Lodi, CA
209-369-8484 (800-780-7234)
Dogs of all sizes are allowed. Dogs
are allowed for a nightly pet fee.

Days Inn CA Lompoc
1122 North H Street
Lompoc, CA
805-735-7744 (800-329-7466)
Dogs are welcome at this hotel.

Motel 6 - Lompoc

1521 St
Lompoc, CA
805-735-7631 (800-466-8356)
This motel welcomes your pets to
stay with you.

Quality Inn & Suites
1621 N. H St.
Lompoc, CA
805-735-8555 (877-424-6423)
Dogs of all sizes are allowed.

Travelodge California Lompoc
1415 E Ocean Avenue
Lompoc, CA
805-736-6514 (800-578-7878)
Dogs of all sizes are allowed. Dogs
are allowed for a pet fee of $15.00
per pet per night.

Hilton Hotel
300 King Street
London, CA
519-439-1661 (800-HILTONS (445-
8667))
This upscale hotel is located in the
heart of downtown and offers a
number of on site amenities for
business and leisure travelers, plus a
convenient location to business,
shopping, dining, and entertainment
areas. One dog up to 79 pounds or 2
dogs that total 70 pounds are
allowed for an additional one time
fee of $65 per pet. 2 dogs may be
allowed.

Best Western Frontier Motel
1008 S Main Street
Lone Pine, CA
760-876-5571 (800-780-7234)
Dogs are welcome at this hotel.

Comfort Inn
1920 South Main Street
Lone Pine, CA
760-876-8700 (877-424-6423)
Dogs of all sizes are allowed. Dogs
are allowed for a pet fee of $20.00
per pet per night. Two dogs are
allowed per room.

Extended Stay America Los Angeles
- Long Beach Airport
4105 E. Willow St.
Long Beach, CA
562-989-4601 (800-804-3724)
One dog is allowed per suite. There
is a $25 per night additional pet fee
up to $150 for an entire stay.

Guesthouse International Hotel
5325 E Pacific Coast Highway
Long Beach, CA
562-597-1341
guesthouselb.com/
Located by several other attractions

and recreational activities, this hotel offers a courtesy shuttle service to the attractions within a 5 mile radius. Some of the features/amenities include 142 spacious, stylish rooms with conveniences for leisure and business travelers, gardens, a complimentary continental breakfast, and a heated, tropically landscaped pool complete with cascading waterfall. Dogs of all sizes are allowed for an additional $10 per night per pet. Dogs may only be left for short periods, and they must be crated and a contact number left with the front desk. Dogs must be leashed and cleaned up after at all times. Multiple dogs may be allowed.

Hilton Hotel
701 W Ocean Blvd
Long Beach, CA
562-983-3400 (800-HILTONS (445-8667))
This luxury hotel offers a number of on site amenities for business and leisure travelers, plus a convenient location to the World Trade Center, LAX and the Long Beach Airport, and it is located only 1 mile from the beach. Dogs are allowed for an additional fee of $25 per night per pet. Multiple dogs may be allowed.

Motel 6 - Long Beach International City
1121 Pacific Coast Hwy
Long Beach, CA
562-591-3321 (800-466-8356)
This motel welcomes your pets to stay with you.

Motel 6 - Los Angeles Long Beach
5665 7th St
Long Beach, CA
562-597-1311 (800-466-8356)
This motel welcomes your pets to stay with you.

Renaissance Long Beach Hotel
111 East Ocean Blvd
Long Beach, CA
562-437-5900 (800-HOTELS-1 (468-3571))
Located downtown in the heart of the entertainment district, this luxury hotel sits central to numerous businesses, shopping, dining, and day/night entertainment areas, plus they also offer a number of in-house amenities for business and leisure travelers. Dogs are allowed for an additional one time fee of $75 per room. Multiple dogs may be allowed.

Residence Inn Long Beach
4111 E Willow Street
Long Beach, CA

562-595-0909 (800-331-3131)
In addition to offering a convenient location to business, shopping, dining, and entertainment areas, this all suite hotel also provides a number of in-house amenities, including a daily buffet breakfast and evening social hours with light dinner fare. Dogs are allowed for an additional one time pet fee of $100 per room. 2 dogs may be allowed.

Residence Inn Palo Alto Los Altos
4460 El Camino Real
Los Altos, CA
650-559-7890 (800-331-3131)
This all suite inn is located in the heart of Silicon Valley near a number of major corporations, Stanford University, and Great America. Additionally, they also offer a number of in-house amenities, including a daily buffet breakfast and evening socials Monday to Thursday. Dogs are allowed for an additional one time fee of 100 per pet. Multiple dogs may be allowed.

Beverly Laurel Hotel
8018 Beverly Blvd
Los Angeles, CA
323-651-2441
There is a $25 per day per pet fee. Thanks to one of our readers who wrote 'Our large German Shepherd was welcome.' 2 dogs may be allowed.

Extended Stay America Los Angeles - LAX Airport
6531 S. Sepulveda Blvd.
Los Angeles, CA
310-568-9337 (800-804-3724)
One dog is allowed per suite. There is a $25 per night additional pet fee up to $150 for an entire stay.

Hilton Hotel
5711 W Century Blvd
Los Angeles, CA
310-410-4000 (800-HILTONS (445-8667))
This luxury hotel offers a number of on site amenities for business and leisure travelers, plus a convenient location to LAX, business, shopping, dining, and entertainment areas. Dogs up to 50 pounds are allowed for an additional fee of $25 per night per pet. 2 dogs may be allowed.

La Quinta Inn & Suites LAX
5249 West Century Blvd
Los Angeles, CA
310-645-2200 (800-531-5900)
Dogs of all sizes are allowed. There

are no additional pet fees, but they request to meet your pet, and to know that you have a pet so as to inform housekeeping. Dogs must be leashed and cleaned up after. Multiple dogs may be allowed.

Le Meridien Hotel
465 South La Cienega Blvd.
Los Angeles, CA
310-247-0400
Dogs up to 50 pounds are allowed. This luxury class hotel is located in one of the most prestigious areas in Los Angeles. They welcome both business and leisure travelers, as well as your dog of any size. Room rates at this first class hotel start at the low $300s per night. They sometimes offer special weekend rates. Dogs up to 40 pounds are allowed for an additional one time fee of $120 per pet. Dogs may not be left alone in the room at any time. 2 dogs may be allowed.

Residence Inn Beverly Hills
1177 S Beverly Drive
Los Angeles, CA
310-228-4100 (866-440-5370)
A boutique style hotel, they offer 186 luxury suites, a close location to the famous Rodeo Drive, and a number of on-site amenities including a daily breakfast buffet and evening receptions. Dogs up to 50 pounds are allowed for an additional one time pet fee of $100 plus $10 per night per pet. 2 dogs may be allowed.

Super 8 /Alhambra Los Angeles
5350 S Huntington Drive
Los Angeles, CA
323-225-2310 (800-800-8000)
Dogs of all sizes are allowed. Dogs are allowed for a pet fee of $20 per pet per night.

Travelodge Hotel at LAX Airport
5547 W Century Blvd.
Los Angeles, CA
310-649-4000 (800-578-7878)
Dogs of all sizes are allowed. Dogs are allowed for a nightly pet fee.

W Los Angeles Westwood
930 Hilgard Ave.
Los Angeles, CA
310-208-8765
Dogs up to 50 pounds are allowed for an additional cleaning fee of $100 plus $25 per night per pet with a credit card on file. Dogs must be declared at the time of registration. Pets receive a special welcome with a pet amenity kit that includes a custom pet bed, food and water

dishes with a floor mat, a Pet-in-Room sign, treats, pet tag, a toy, and more. The concierge can also offer additional services such as dog-walking and information about local dog services and parks. Dogs must be removed or crated for housekeeping or for any in-room services.

Best Western Executive Inn
301 W Pacheco Boulevard
Los Banos, CA
209-827-0954 (800-780-7234)
Dogs of all sizes are allowed. Dogs are allowed for a pet fee.

Days Inn Los Banos
2169 E Pacheco Blvd
Los Banos, CA
209-826-9690 (800-329-7466)
Dogs of all sizes are allowed. Dogs are allowed for a pet fee of $10.00 per pet per night.

Knights Inn Los Banos
1621 East Pacheco Blvd.
Los Banos, CA
209-827-4600 (800-843-5644)
Dogs of all sizes are allowed. Dogs are allowed for a pet fee of $10.00 per pet per night.

Sunstar Inn
839 W. Pacheco Blvd
Los Banos, CA
209-826-3805
There is a $10 per day additional pet fee. Multiple dogs may be allowed.

Days Inn Lost Hills
14684 Aloma Street
Lost Hills, CA
661-797-2371 (800-329-7466)
Dogs of all sizes are allowed. Dogs are allowed for a pet fee of $10 per pet per night.

Motel 6 - Lost Hills
14685 Warren St
Lost Hills, CA
661-797-2346 (800-466-8356)
This motel welcomes your pets to stay with you.

Days Inn Madera
25327 Avenue 16
Madera, CA
559-674-8817 (800-329-7466)
Dogs are welcome at this hotel.

Motel 6 - Madera, Ca
22683 Ave 18 1/2
Madera, CA
559-675-8697 (800-466-8356)
This motel welcomes your pets to stay with you.

Super 8 Madera
1855 West Cleveland Ave
Madera, CA
559-661-1131 (800-800-8000)
Dogs of all sizes are allowed. Dogs are allowed for a pet fee.

Convict Lake Resort
2000 Convict Lake Road
Mammoth Lakes, CA
760-934-3800 (800-992-2260)
convictlake.com/index.php
In addition to providing a wide range of recreational activities, a restaurant, marina, and a store, this scenic park also shares a long cultural and natural history. Dogs are allowed in the cabins for an additional one time $20 pet fee. Dogs are not allowed to be left alone in cabins or vehicles. Dogs must be kept leashed and cleaned up after; there are doggy sanitary stations throughout the park. There are no additional pet fees for RV or tent camping. 2 dogs may be allowed.

Crystal Crag Lodge
P.O. Box 88
Mammoth Lakes, CA
760-934-2436
This lodge offers cabins at 9,000 feet elevation on beautiful Lake Mary in the dog-friendly Inyo National Forest. Lake Mary is known as one of the best fishing spots in the Eastern Sierra, regularly producing trophy size trout. You will find a number of other lakes, most of the best hiking trailheads, Lake Mary Store, and some of the best scenery that the Eastern Sierra has to offer within walking distance of your cabin. The cabins, all non-smoking, have full kitchens and baths. Most cabins have living rooms with fireplaces. The lodge also offers 14-foot aluminum boats with or without a motor. Dogs are allowed on the boats as well. Please note that the lodge is only open during the summer season, from about late May to early October. Dogs are allowed for an additional fee of $10 per night for 1 dog and $5 per night for each additional dog. Pets must never be left unattended in the cabins. Multiple dogs may be allowed.

Econo Lodge Wildwood Inn
3626 Main St. (SR 203)
Mammoth Lakes, CA
760-934-6855 (877-424-6423)
Dogs of all sizes are allowed.

Edelweiss Lodge
1872 Old Mammoth Road
Mammoth Lakes, CA
760-934-2445 (877-2Edelweiss)
Edelweiss-Lodge.com
Cabins on a 1 acre wooded site near hiking trails, lakes and streams. Dogs of all sizes are allowed. There is a $15 per day per pet fee. All rooms are non-smoking. Multiple dogs may be allowed.

Mammoth Creek Inn
663 Old Mammoth Road
Mammoth Lakes, CA
760-934-6162
There is a $29 per day fee for one dog and a $25 per day per pet fee for 2 dogs. Well-behaved pets are welcome. Just make sure you mention you will be bringing a pet as they have specific 'pet-friendly' rooms. Pets may not be left alone in the rooms unless they are trained to stay in a crate. This inn is located within walking distance to grocery and boutique shopping, restaurants, cross country skiing, snowshoe area and Mammoth's biking and running path. Amenities include in room high speed Internet access, limited in room dining, indoor dry sauna, hot tub, and a game, movie and book library. 2 dogs may be allowed.

Motel 6 - Mammoth Lakes
3372 Main St
Mammoth Lakes, CA
760-934-6660 (800-466-8356)
This motel welcomes your pets to stay with you.

Shilo Inn
2963 Main Street
Mammoth Lakes, CA
760-934-4500 (800-222-2244)
Your dog is welcome here. Each room in this motel is a mini-suite complete with microwaves, refrigerators and more. This motel is located across the street from the Visitors Center which has trails that border up to the Shady Rest Park where there are many hiking trails. If you are there in the winter, try some cross-country skiing with your pup. The cross country ski rental store is very close to this motel (see Attractions.) Dogs are allowed for an additional one time fee of $25 per room for 2 pets. Dogs may not be left alone in the room at any time. 2 dogs may be allowed.

Sierra Lodge
3540 Main Street
Mammoth Lakes, CA

760-934-8881
There is a $10 per night per pet fee.
Amenities include continental
breakfast and kitchenettes in the
rooms. All rooms are non-smoking. 2
dogs may be allowed.

Swiss Chalet
3776 Viewpoint Road
Mammoth Lakes, CA
760-934-2403
This inn offers a few pet rooms. All
rooms are non-smoking. Dogs must
be one year or older and only one
pet per room. Pets cannot be left
unattended in the room. There is up
to a $14 per night per pet fee
depending on the size. 2 dogs may
be allowed.

Tamarack Lodge
P.O. Box 69/Lake Mary Road
Mammoth Lakes, CA
760-934-2442 (800-MAMMOTH
(626-6684))
tamaracklodge.com/
This historic lodge has been in
operation since 1924 with their
cabins and lodge rooms ranging from
simple and rustic to deluxe
accommodations. On site is the
Lakefront Restaurant specializing in
blending classic French cuisine with
regional influences of the eastern
Sierra (Dogs not allowed). Watercraft
rentals, fishing, easy to strenuous
hiking trails, and other recreational
pursuits are available throughout the
summer. Their cabins have private
bathrooms, porches, and telephones.
Dogs are allowed in the summer and
in the cabins only. There is an
additional fee of $30 per night per
pet. Dogs must be well behaved,
under owner's control at all times,
and be leashed and cleaned up after.
2 dogs may be allowed.

Travelodge Mammoth Lakes
54 Sierra Blvd
Mammoth Lakes, CA
760-934-8892 (800-578-7878)
Dogs are welcome at this hotel.

Villa De Los Pinos #3
3252 Chateau Rd
Mammoth Lakes, CA
760-722-5369
mammoth-lakes-condo.com
This is a year-round vacation rental
townhouse-style condominium in
Mammoth Lakes. The amenities
include two downstairs bedrooms,
two bathrooms, a large living room,
dining room, and kitchen. The condo
is fronted by a large deck
overlooking the development
courtyard (where dogs are allowed

off-leash), swimming pool, and
Jacuzzi building. All dogs are
welcome. The $25 per visit pet fee
helps with the cleaning.

Marriott Manhattan Beach
1400 Parkview Avenue
Manhattan Beach, CA
310-546-7511 (800-228-9290)
Only a couple of miles to LAX and
the beach, this luxury hotel sits
central to many of the city's star
attractions, world class shopping
and dining venues, and major
business areas, plus they also offer
a number of in-house amenities for
all level of travelers.. Dogs are
allowed for an additional one time
fee of $200 per room, and there is a
pet policy to sign at check in. 2
dogs may be allowed.

Motel 6 - Monterey Marina
100 Reservation Rd
Marina, CA
831-384-1000 (800-466-8356)
Your pets are welcome to stay here
with you.

Indian Peak Ranch MountainTop
Hideaway
Call to arrange
Mariposa, CA
209-966-5259
indianpeakranch.com
This mountaintop vacation rental is
located on 122 acres. To make
reservations or for more information
see www.indianpeakranch.com or
call.

The Mariposa Lodge
5052 Hwy 140
Mariposa, CA
209-966-3607 (800-341-8000)
mariposalodge.com
Thanks to one of our readers for
recommending this hotel. Here is
what they said about it: 'We stayed
here after a clogged 4 hour drive
from San Jose, CA. Mia at the front
desk was courteous and friendly --
not what you always get when you
are traveling with a 90 lb dog (black
lab). The room was large, new and
very nice. Lovely pool and Jacuzzi.
A little sitting area under a patch of
trees with benches. It was very
warm and Mia recommended a
restaurant where we could sit
outside and take our dog. Castillos
on 5th Street. Our extra nice
waitress brought him water and us
an excellent Mexican dinner.
Couldn't have been nicer. All in all
Mariposa and the hotel was an A+
experience.' If you take Highway
140, this motel is located about 50

minutes from Yosemite Valley (45
min. to the main gate and about 10
min. to the valley). Pets are an
additional $10 per pet per night.
Dogs may not be left unattended at
any time. Multiple dogs may be
allowed.

Yosemite's Little Lodge
Please call to arrange
Mariposa, CA
209-966-4945
yosemitevacations.biz
This 1500 square food cabin allows
well-behaved dogs.

Best Western John Muir Inn
445 Muir Station Road
Martinez, CA
925-229-1010 (800-780-7234)
Dogs of all sizes are allowed. Dogs
are allowed for a pet fee.

Super 8 Martinez
4015 Alhambra Avenue
Martinez, CA
925-372-5500 (800-800-8000)
Dogs are welcome at this hotel.

Comfort Suites
1034 North Beale Rd.
Marysville, CA
530-742-9200 (877-424-6423)
Dogs up to 50 pounds are allowed.
Dogs are allowed for a pet fee of
$10.00 per pet per night. Two dogs
are allowed per room.

Motel 6 - Marysville, Ca
803 Street
Marysville, CA
530-743-5465 (800-466-8356)
This motel welcomes your pets to
stay with you.

Century House Inn
433 Lawndale Court
McCloud, CA
530-964-2206
mccloudcenturyhouse.com/
for 2 dogs or more there is an
additional fee of $10 per night per
pet. Dogs must be leashed and
cleaned up after at all times, and be
removed or crated for housekeeping.

Stoney Brook Inn
309 W Colombero Road
McCloud, CA
800-369-6118
1 dog is allowed for a $17 one time
additional pet fee.

Blackberry Inn
44951 Larkin Road
Mendocino, CA
707-937-5281 (800-950-7806)

blackberryinn.biz/
Located at one of California's most beautiful locations overlooking the Mendocino Bay, this country inn offers ocean views, finely appointed rooms with fresh cut flowers daily from their garden, and a Continental breakfast. There are 2 pet-friendly rooms available, and dogs must be friendly as there are other animals (wild and domestic) on the property. Dogs up to 40 pounds are allowed for an additional fee of $10 per night for 1 dog and $15 per night for 2 dogs. Dogs may not be left alone in the rooms or in cars on the property at any time, and they must be leashed and cleaned up after. 2 dogs may be allowed.

Coastal Getaways
10501 Ford Street POB1355
Mendocino, CA
707-937-9200 (800-525-0049)
coastgetaways.com
Coastal Getaways has over 5 vacation homes that allow dogs. Most of the homes have ocean front views and one is located in the quaint village of Mendocino. The rates range from $140 to $250 and up per night. They also have weekly rates. The usual pet fee is an additional one time $50 fee per pet. 2 dogs may be allowed.

Cottages at Little River Cove
7533 N. Highway 1
Mendocino, CA
707 937 5339
cottagesatlittlerivercove.com
These nine stand alone cottages welcome your pet with pet beds, treats, water bowls and a pet package.

Inn at Schoolhouse Creek
7051 N. Highway 1
Mendocino, CA
707-937-5525
schoolhousecreek.com
With 8+ acres of ocean view gardens, meadows, forest, hiking trails and a secluded beach cove you and your pets will truly feel like you've gotten away from it all. To help your pets get in the vacation mood they will be welcomed with their own pet basket that includes a bed, towel, blanket and a treat. At the end of your day, relax in the ocean view hot tub.

Little River Inn
7901 Highway One
Mendocino, CA
707-937-5942
littleriverinn.com

This coastal resort has oceanview rooms, some with fireplaces and Jacuzzis. There are gardens to walk through and breakfast and dinner are available in the restaurant. Pets are $25 per night, per pet.

MacCallum House
45020 Albion Street
Mendocino, CA
707-937-0289
maccallumhouse.com
Pets of all varieties are welcomed at the MacCallum House Inn, located in the heart of the Mendocino Village. Pets are allowed in the cottages and Barn and are provided with blankets and sheets. The original Victorian mansion, built in 1882 by William H. Kelley, was a wedding gift to his daughter, Daisy MacCallum, and is a historic landmark. Rooms include a full breakfast and a complimentary wine hour is served in the Grey Whale Bar featuring wines from throughout the California wine country. Children are also welcome.

Mendocino Preferred Vacation Rentals
Call to Arrange
Mendocino, CA
707-937-1456 (800-942-6300)
mendocinopreferred.com
Dogs are allowed in some of the Mendocino vacation home rentals. Contact them to check on availability.

Mendocino Seaside Cottages
10940 Lansing St
Mendocino, CA
707-485-0239
romancebythesea.com/
Accommodations have Jacuzzi spas, wet bars,& fireplaces. It is located within easy walking distance of Mendocino. Dogs are allowed for an additional one time fee of $25 per pet. 2 dogs may be allowed.

Stanford Inn by the Sea and Spa
44850 Comptche Ukiah Rd and Highway One
Mendocino, CA
707-937-5615
stanfordinn.com
This resort is specially designed to accommodate travelers with pets. The inn is rustic and elegant. Amenities include feather beds, wood burning fireplaces, antiques, sofas, televisions with VCRs and DVDs. The resort offers complimentary breakfast featuring a choice from organic selections of

omelets, waffles, burritos, and more. A large pool, sauna and Jacuzzi are protected from the fog by a solarium. Massage in the Forest provides massage and body work and yoga. The Inn's Catch A Canoe & Bicycles, too! offers kayaking and canoeing on Big River Estuary as well as mountain biking and. Special canoes are set-up to provide secure footing for your dog as well as a bowl of fresh water (Big River is tidal and for eight miles and therefore salty). The Ravens vegetarian/vegan restaurant serves organic cuisine. Well behaved pets may join you at breakfast or dinner in a dining area created especially for them. Feed and water dishes, covers to protect bedding and furniture, sleeping beds and treats are provided in the rooms. There is a $25 pet fee per stay.

Sweetwater Spa & Inn
44840 Main Street
Mendocino, CA
707-937-4076 (800-300-4140)
sweetwaterspa.com/
Sweetwater Spa & Inn offers a unique variety of accommodations, including cabin and vacation home rentals. They give dog treats at check-in as well as sheets for the guests to cover furniture and towels for wet paws in the rainy season. Some of the rentals are located in the village of Mendocino. The other rentals are located around the Mendocino area. There is a two night minimum on weekends and three night minimum on most holidays. All units are non-smoking. Your well-behaved dog is welcome. Room rates start at the low $100s and up. There is a $20 per day per pet additional fee. Multiple dogs may be allowed.

The Andiron - Seaside Inn & Cabins
6051 Highway One
Mendocino, CA
707-937-1543 (800-955-6478)
TheAndiron.com
These cabins and inn allow dogs. The cabins have kitchenettes and there is a spa.

The Blair House Inn
45110 Little Lake Street
Mendocino, CA
707-937-1800 (800-699-9296)
blairhouse.com/
Although built in 1888, this home has been called a Victorian Treasure , and it still offers luxury surroundings, beautifully appointed rooms, gardens and ocean vistas. Room rates include breakfast and a

complimentary bottle of wine. They have one pet-friendly cottage, and dogs of all sizes are allowed for an additional pet fee of $10 per night per room. Dogs may not be left alone in the cottage at any time, and they must be well mannered, leashed, and cleaned up after. 2 dogs may be allowed.

Whitegate Inn
Heart Of the Historical Village
Mendocino, CA
800-962-0934
whitegateinn.com/abigails.php
Pets are welcome in the Whitegate Inn cottage. They are not allowed in the main house. The cottage has 4 bedrooms and 3 baths. Stroll with your dog in beautiful Mendocino and nearby state parks.

Comfort Inn
730 Motel Dr.
Merced, CA
209-383-0333 (877-424-6423)
Dogs of all sizes are allowed.

Motel 6 - Merced North
1410 St
Merced, CA
209-384-2181 (800-466-8356)
This motel welcomes your pets to stay with you.

Quality Inn
1213 V Street
Merced, CA
209-723-3711 (877-424-6423)
Dogs of all sizes are allowed. Dogs are allowed for a pet fee of $10.00 per pet per night.

Ramada Merced
2010 E Childs Ave
Merced, CA
209-723-3121 (800-272-6232)
Dogs are welcome at this hotel.

Super 8 Merced
1983 E Childes Avenue
Merced, CA
209-384-1303 (800-800-8000)
Dogs of all sizes are allowed. Dogs are allowed for a pet fee.

Travelodge Yosemite Merced
1260 Yosemite Parkway
Merced, CA
209-722-6224 (800-578-7878)
Dogs are welcome at this hotel.

Child's Meadow Resort
41500 Highway 36E
Mill Creek, CA
530-595-3383
Dogs are allowed in this all season

resort. Located between the towns of Susanville and Red Bluff, this quiet resort is on 18 acres of picturesque meadows and streams at the end of the Shasta/Cascade Mountain Range. The resort is just 9 miles from the southwest entrance to Lassen Volcanic National Park. RV hookups are available at the resort. There is no pet charge for the campground,,, there is an additional fee of $10 per night per pet for the motel. Aggressive breeds are not allowed. 2 dogs may be allowed.

Holiday Inn Express Mill Valley-Sausalito
160 Shoreline Highway
Mill Valley, CA
415-332-5700 (877-270-6405)
Dogs of all sizes are allowed. Dogs are allowed for a pet fee of $75.00 per pet per stay.

Clarion Hotel San Francisco Airport
401 E. Millbrae Ave.
Millbrae, CA
650-692-6363 (877-424-6423)
Dogs of all sizes are allowed.

Embassy Suites
901 E Calaveras Blvd
Milpitas, CA
408-942-0400 (800-EMBASSY (362-2779))
Located in the Silicon Valley, this full service, atrium-style hotel offers a number of on site amenities for business and leisure travelers, plus a convenient location to an international airport, and to business, shopping, dining, and entertainment districts. They also offer a complimentary cooked-to-order breakfast and a Manager's reception every evening. Dogs up to 50 pounds are allowed for an additional one time fee of $50 per room. 2 dogs may be allowed.

Extended Stay America San Jose - Milpitas
1000 Hillview Ct.
Milpitas, CA
408-941-9977 (800-804-3724)
One dog is allowed per suite. There is a $25 per night additional pet fee up to $150 for an entire stay.

Homestead Studio Suites San Jose - Milpitas
330 Cypress Dr.
Milpitas, CA
408-433-9700 (800-804-3724)
One dog is allowed per suite. There is a $25 per night additional pet fee up to $150 for an entire stay.

Residence Inn Milpitas Silicon Valley
1501 California Circle
Milpitas, CA
408-941-9222 (800-331-3131)
Some of the amenities at this all-suite inn include a daily buffet breakfast, a hospitality hour Monday through Thursday, a heated swimming pool, Sport Court, and a complimentary grocery shopping service. Dogs are allowed for an additional one time pet fee of $100 per room. Multiple dogs may be allowed.

Sheraton San Jose Hotel
1801 Barber Lane
Milpitas, CA
408-943-0600 (888-625-5144)
Dogs of all sizes are allowed. You must sign a pet policy. Dogs are not to be left alone in the rooms.

Staybridge Suites Silicon Valley-Milpitas
321 Cypress Drive
Milpitas, CA
408-383-9500 (877-270-6405)
Dogs up to 80 pounds are allowed. Pets allowed with an additional pet fee. Up to $75 for 1-6 nights and up to $150 for 7+ nights. A pet agreement must be signed at check-in.

TownePlace Suites Milpitas
1428 Falcon Drive
Milpitas, CA
408-719-1959 (800-257-3000)
This all suite hotel sits central to many of the area's star attractions and to numerous other sites of interest for both business and leisure travelers; plus they also offer a number of on-site amenities. Dogs are allowed for an additional one time fee of $100 per room. 2 dogs may be allowed.

Miranda Gardens Resort
6766 Avenue of the Giants
Miranda, CA
707-943-3011
mirandagardens.com/
The cottages are surrounded by flowering gardens and surrounded by ancient redwoods. From this resort, you can take day trips to the Avenue of the Giants or the Lost Coast. All cottages are non-smoking. Children are welcome and the resort has a children's play area.Well trained pets are allowed in certain cabins for an additional fee of $15 per night per pet. Dogs may not be left alone in the units. Multiple dogs may be allowed.

Days Inn Modesto
1312 McHenry Avenue
Modesto, CA
209-527-1010 (800-329-7466)
Dogs are welcome at this hotel.

Motel 6 - Modesto
1920 Orangeburg Ave
Modesto, CA
209-522-7271 (800-466-8356)
This motel welcomes your pets to
stay with you.

Super 8 Modesto
4100 Salida Blvd
Modesto, CA
209-543-9000 (800-800-8000)
Dogs of all sizes are allowed. Dogs
are allowed for a pet fee.

Days Inn CA Mojave
16100 Sierra Highway
Mojave, CA
661-824-2421 (800-329-7466)
Dogs of all sizes are allowed. Dogs
are allowed for a nightly pet fee.

Econo Lodge
2145 SR 58(Business)
Mojave, CA
661-824-2463 (877-424-6423)
Dogs of all sizes are allowed. Dogs
are allowed for a pet fee of $5.00 per
pet per night. Two dogs are allowed
per room.

Motel 6 - Mojave
16958 Sr 58
Mojave, CA
661-824-4571 (800-466-8356)
This motel welcomes your pets to
stay with you.

Homestead Studio Suites Los
Angeles - Monrovia
930 S. 5th Ave.
Monrovia, CA
626-256-6999 (800-804-3724)
One dog is allowed per suite. There
is a $25 per night additional pet fee
up to $150 for an entire stay.

Grandma's House Bed and Breakfast
20280 River Blvd
Monte Rio, CA
707-865-1865
This dog-friendly bed and breakfast
inn is located on the Russian River.
The inn offers three rooms, all with
private bathrooms. Each room also
includes a private phone line, TV and
VCR, refrigerator, microwave, and
more. One of the rooms is
handicapped accessible. Clean, well-
behaved dogs may accompany their
owners, with advance notice, for $10

per dog per day. There is a $75
damage and cleaning deposit,
refundable (if not needed) at
departure. Owners are expected to
clean up behind their dog on the
grounds. Pooper-scooper bags are
available for this purpose. Dogs
must not be left unattended in the
room for long periods. Owners are
responsible for not letting their dog
disturb other guests and making
sure their dog is not destructive to
the property.

San Ysidro Ranch
900 San Ysidro Lane
Montecito, CA
805-969-5046
Dogs are allowed in the free
standing cottages for an additional
one time fee of $100 per pet. Dogs
may not be left unattended.

Bay Park Hotel
1425 Munras Avenue
Monterey, CA
831-649-1020
Dogs of all sizes are allowed. There
is a $20 per night per pet additional
fee. Dogs are not allowed to be left
alone in the room.

Bay Travelodge Monterey
2030 North Fremont Street
Monterey, CA
831-373-3381 (800-578-7878)
Dogs are welcome at this hotel.

Best Western Beach Resort
Monterey
2600 Sand Dunes Drive
Monterey, CA
831-394-3321 (800-780-7234)
Dogs are welcome at this hotel.
There is a pet fee of $25 a day.

Best Western Victorian Inn
487 Foam Street
Monterey, CA
831-373-8000 (800-780-7234)
victorianinn.com
Dogs are allowed for an additional
pet fee of $30 per night per room. 2
dogs may be allowed.

Comfort Inn Monterey Bay -
Monterey
2050 North Fremont Street
Monterey, CA
888-990-7666 (877-424-6423)
montereygetaway.com
This hotel allows pets in a number
of it's rooms.

Comfort Inn Monterey by the Sea -
Cannery Row Hotel
1252 Munras Avenue

Monterey, CA
831-372-2908 (877-424-6423)
stayatmonterey.com
Dogs are allowed in a number of pet
rooms in the hotel.

El Adobe Inn
936 Munras Ave.
Monterey, CA
831-372-5409
This inn is located on Munras Ave.
about 1/2 mile east of Hwy 1. Dogs
are allowed for an additional fee of
$15 per night per pet. Dogs may not
be left alone in the room at any time.
2 dogs may be allowed.

Hyatt Regency Monterey
1 Old Golf Course Road
Monterey, CA
831-372-1234
The warm colors and fireplaces
throughout this resort offer a relaxed
atmosphere for the business or
leisure traveler. Amenities include
spacious guestrooms, room service,
pools, a golf course, tennis courts,
massage therapy, dining and
entertainment, an award winning
sports bar, and a 24 hour fully
automated business center. Dogs of
all sizes are allowed. There is a $50
one time additional pet fee per room.
Dogs must be crated when left alone
in the room, and they must be
leashed and cleaned up after. 2 dogs
may be allowed.

Monterey Bay Lodge
55 Camino Aguaiito/H 1
Monterey, CA
831-372-8057 (800-558-1900)
This lush garden hotel offers nicely
appointed rooms, courtyard settings,
an on-site restaurant, outdoor heated
pool with spa, and many in-room
extras. Small to medium sized dogs
are allowed for an additional pet fee
of $15 per night per room with a
$100 refundable deposit required if
paying by cash. Since there are only
certain pet-specific rooms available,
dogs must be declared at time of the
reservation. Dogs must be quiet,
leashed, and cleaned up after. Dogs
may not be left alone in the room
unless you are on the premises or in
the restaurant, and a cell number is
left at the front desk. They may not
be left in the room if you leave the
property. 2 dogs may be allowed.

Monterey Fireside Lodge
1131 10th Street
Monterey, CA
831-373-4172 (800-722-2624)
montereyfireside.com/
All 28 rooms have gas fireplaces.

Dogs are allowed for an additional fee of $10 per night per pet for dogs 20 pounds and under, and a fee of $20 per night per pet for dogs over 20 pounds. Dogs may not be left alone in the room at any time and they are not allowed on the bed. 2 dogs may be allowed.

Motel 6 - Monterey
2124 N. Fremont St.
Monterey, CA
831-646-8585 (800-466-8356)
Your pets are welcome to stay here with you.

Comfort Inn
23330 Sunnymead Blvd.
Moreno Valley, CA
951-242-0699 (877-424-6423)
Dogs up to 50 pounds are allowed. Dogs are allowed for a pet fee of $10.00 per pet per night. Two dogs are allowed per room.

Extended Stay America San Jose - Morgan Hill
605 Jarvis Dr.
Morgan Hill, CA
408-779-9660 (800-804-3724)
One dog is allowed per suite. There is a $25 per night additional pet fee up to $150 for an entire stay.

Quality Inn
16525 Condit Road
Morgan Hill, CA
408-779-0447 (877-424-6423)
Dogs of all sizes are allowed. Dogs are allowed for a pet fee of $15.00 per pet per night.

Residence Inn San Jose South/Morgan Hill
18620 Madrone Parkway
Morgan Hill, CA
408-782-8311 (800-331-3131)
This Silicon Valley all suite inn offers a central location to numerous major companies, shopping and dining areas, and world class attractions. Additionally they offer a daily buffet breakfast and evening social hours Monday through Thursday. Dogs up to 50 pounds are allowed for an additional one time pet fee of $100 per room. 2 dogs may be allowed.

Bayfront Inn
1150 Embarcadero
Morro Bay, CA
805-772-5607
bayfront-inn.com
There is a pet fee per room of $12.50 every 3rd day. 2 dogs may be allowed.

Best Western El Rancho
2460 Main Street
Morro Bay, CA
805-772-2212 (800-780-7234)
Dogs are allowed in this Best Western in Morro Bay. There is a $15 pet fee for one night and a $25 pet fee for two or more nights.

Days Inn Morro Bay
1095 Main Street
Morro Bay, CA
805-772-2711 (800-329-7466)
Dogs of all sizes are allowed. Dogs are allowed for a nightly pet fee.

Motel 6 - Morro Bay
298 Atascadero Rd
Morro Bay, CA
805-772-5641 (800-466-8356)
This motel welcomes your pets to stay with you.

Pleasant Inn Motel
235 Harbor Street
Morro Bay, CA
805-772-8521
pleasantinnmotel.com/
This motel, family owned and operated, is just one block east of the beautiful Morro Bay waterfront and one block west of old downtown. All rooms are non-smoking. Dogs and cats are welcome for an extra $10 per day. Multiple dogs may be allowed.

Rodeway Inn
540 Main Street
Morro Bay, CA
805-772-7503 (877-424-6423)
Dogs up to 60 pounds are allowed. Dogs are allowed for a pet fee of $25.00 per pet per night. Two dogs are allowed per room.

Sunset Travelodge Morro Bay
1080 Market Avenue
Morro Bay, CA
805-772-1259 (800-578-7878)
Dogs are welcome at this hotel.

Best Western Tree House Motor Inn
111 Morgan Way
Mount Shasta, CA
530-926-3101 (800-780-7234)
Dogs of all sizes are allowed. Dogs are allowed for a nightly pet fee.

Dream Inn Bed and Breakfast
326 Chestnut Street
Mount Shasta, CA
530-926-1536
home.att.net/~dreaminn
Dogs (and children) are welcome at this bed and breakfast inn. The Victorian home, built in 1904 and

completely restored, is located at 3,500 ft. in downtown Mount Shasta. Lying at the base of 14,162 ft. Mount Shasta, they are surrounded by National Forest. The inn offers 4 bedrooms with shared bathrooms. The owners also have a dog on the premises. There are no pet fees. Multiple dogs may be allowed.

Mount Shasta Ranch Bed and Breakfast
1008 W. A. Barr Rd.
Mount Shasta, CA
530-926-3870
stayinshasta.com
Dogs are allowed at this ranch style house bed and breakfast built in 1923. This B&B offers 12 bedrooms including a cottage. Five of the rooms have private bathrooms. There is a $10 one time per stay, per pet fee. Children are also welcome. 2 dogs may be allowed.

Swiss Holiday Lodge
2400 S. Mt. Shasta Blvd.
Mount Shasta, CA
530-926-3446
There is an additional $10 per day per pet charge. Multiple dogs may be allowed.

The Woodsman Hotel and Lodge
1121 S Mount Shasta Blvd
Mount Shasta, CA
530-926-3411
There is an additional one time pet fee of $15 per room. Multiple dogs may be allowed.

Homestead Studio Suites San Jose - Mountain View
190 E. El Camino Real
Mountain View, CA
650-962-1500 (800-804-3724)
One dog is allowed per suite. There is a $25 per night additional pet fee up to $150 for an entire stay.

Residence Inn Palo Alto Mountain View
1854 El Camino Real W
Mountain View, CA
650-940-1300 (800-331-3131 i)
In addition to offering a convenient location to Silicon Valley businesses, and local shopping, dining, and major entertainment areas, this hotel also provides a number of in-house amenities, including a daily buffet breakfast and evening social hours. Dogs are allowed for an additional one time pet fee of $75 per room. Multiple dogs may be allowed.

Tropicana Lodge

1720 El Camino Real
Mountain View, CA
650-961-0220
Pets may not be left alone in the rooms,,, there are no additional pet fees. 2 dogs may be allowed.

Beazley House Bed & Breakfast Inn
1910 First Street
Napa, CA
707-257-1649
beazleyhouse.com
This Bed and Breakfast is located in a residential area in historic downtown Napa. There is a $30 per day per dog charge, with a maximum of 2 dogs.

Embassy Suites
1075 California Blvd
Napa, CA
707-253-9540 (800-EMBASSY (362-2779))
A full service, atrium-style hotel, they offer a number of on site amenities for business and leisure travelers, plus a convenient location to business, shopping, dining, and recreation areas. They also offer a complimentary cooked-to-order breakfast and a Manager's reception every evening. Dogs up to 50 pounds are allowed for an additional one time pet fee of $75 per room. 2 dogs may be allowed.

Napa River Inn
500 Main Street
Napa, CA
707-251-8500
napariverinn.com/
This beautiful inn sits on 2.5 picturesque acres along the Napa River, is on the National Registry of Historic Places, and offer top amenities to visitors and their pets. They participate in a pet VIP program which gives your pooch their own in-house care package too. It includes a blanket, feeding mat with stainless steel bowls, a Cab-Bone-Nay dog biscuit made with real wine, and a supply of doggy clean up bags. Dogs are allowed for an additional pet fee of $25 per night per room. Dogs must be well mannered, leashed, and cleaned up after. Dogs may only be left alone in the room if they will be quiet and they are in a kennel.

The Chablis Inn
3360 Solono Ave
Napa, CA
707-257-1944 (800-443-3490)
chablisinn.com
There is a 150 pound limit for dogs. There is a $10 per day per pet

additional fee. All rooms are non-smoking. Multiple dogs may be allowed.

The Inn On First
1938 First Street
Napa, CA
707-253-1331 (866-253-1331)
theinnonfirst.com
This circa 1900 B&B is located in downtown Napa. There is a $25 per day per dog pet fee. Up to two dogs are allowed per room. Your dog will receive a dog basket upon arrival.

The Napa Inn Bed and Breakfast
1137 Warren Street
Napa, CA
707-257-1444
napainn.com
Located on a quiet street in historic, downtown Napa, this inn is within an easy walking distance of shops and restaurants. Dogs are allowed in one room, the garden cottage. This private cottage is decorated in French Provincial prints. It has a queen size bed, sofa, fireplace, French doors overlooking a private flower garden, skylight, wet bar with refrigerator and microwave, and an outdoor spa. It sleeps up to four people. There is a $20 one time pet fee per room if the dogs are small,,, there is a one time fee of $20 per pet if the dogs are large. 2 dogs may be allowed.

Best Western Marina Gateway Hotel
800 Bay Marina Drive
National City, CA
619-259-2800 (800-780-7234)
Dogs are welcome at this hotel.

Best Western Colorado River Inn
2371 W Broadway
Needles, CA
760-326-4552 (800-780-7234)
Dogs of all sizes are allowed. Dogs are allowed for a nightly pet fee.

Days Inn and Suites Needles
1215 Hospitality Lane
Needles, CA
760-326-5836 (800-329-7466)
Dogs of all sizes are allowed. Dogs are allowed for a pet fee.

Motel 6 - Needles
1420 St
Needles, CA
760-326-3399 (800-466-8356)
This motel welcomes your pets to stay with you.

Travelers Inn

1195 3rd Street Hill
Needles, CA
760-326-4900
Dogs are allowed for an additional one time pet fee of $10 per room. 2 dogs may be allowed.

The Outside Inn
575 E. Broad Street
Nevada City, CA
530-265-2233
outsideinn.com/
This inn is located in a quiet residential neighborhood two blocks from downtown Nevada City. This completely renovated 1940's era motor court features never smoked in rooms under tall pines. Children and pets are welcome. There is a $20 per night per pet charge. Multiple dogs may be allowed.

Motel 6 - Newark
5600 Cedar Ct
Newark, CA
510-791-5900 (800-466-8356)
This motel welcomes your pets to stay with you.

Residence Inn Newark Silicon Valley
35466 Dumbarton Court
Newark, CA
510-739-6000 (800-455-8038)
This all suite, townhouse-style inn features a convenient location to business, shopping, dining, and recreation areas, plus they also offer a number of in-house amenities, including a daily buffet breakfast and evening socials. Dogs are allowed for an additional one time pet fee of $100 per room. Multiple dogs may be allowed.

Woodfin Suite Hotel
39150 Cedar Blvd.
Newark, CA
510-795-1200
All well-behaved dogs are welcome. Every room is a suite with a full kitchen. Hotel amenities include free video movies and a complimentary hot breakfast buffet. There is a $50 one time per stay pet fee.

Motel 6 - Thousand Oaks South
1516 Newbury Rd
Newbury Park, CA
805-499-0711 (800-466-8356)
This motel welcomes your pets to stay with you.

Best Western Newport Beach Inn
6208 W Coast Highway
Newport Beach, CA
949-642-8252 (800-780-7234)
Dogs of all sizes are allowed. Dogs

are allowed for a pet fee.

Extended Stay America Orange
County - John Wayne Airport
4881 Birch St.
Newport Beach, CA
949-851-2711 (800-804-3724)
One dog is allowed per suite. There
is a $25 per night additional pet fee
up to $150 for an entire stay.

Fairmont Newport Beach
4500 MacArthur Blvd
Newport Beach, CA
949-476-2001 (800-257-7544)
fairmont.com/newportbeach/
A $32 million renovation was
undergone at this hotel to ensure
visitors a true luxury hotel experience
with all the conveniences and
services. Some of the
features/amenities include 440
elegant guest rooms and 54 suites, a
restaurant and lounge with 24 hour
room service, a state of the art
business center, a heated sky pool
and deck, and tennis courts. Dogs up
to 40 pounds are allowed for an
additional one time pet fee of $25 per
pet, and there is a pet policy to sign
at check in. Dogs must be leashed,
cleaned up after, and the Do Not
Disturb sign put on the door if they
are in the room alone.

Motel 6 - Sacramento North
Highlands
4600 Watt Ave
North Highlands, CA
916-973-8637 (800-466-8356)
Your pets are welcome to stay here
with you.

Motel 6 - Los Angeles Van
Nuys/sepulveda
15711 Roscoe Blvd
North Hills, CA
818-894-9341 (800-466-8356)
This motel welcomes your pets to
stay with you.

Agate Bay Realty Lake Tahoe
Call to Arrange
North Lake Tahoe, CA
530-546-4256 (800-550-6740)
agatebay.com
These vacation rentals are located in
North Tahoe. Many of the homes are
dog-friendly, and some offer lake
views or easy access to beaches.

Enchanted Vacation Properties
Call to Arrange
North Lake Tahoe, CA
530-546-2066
enchantedvacationproperties.com
These vacation rentals are located

on the north side of Lake Tahoe.
Dogs of all sizes are welcome. Pet
amenities include dog beds, dog
bowls and treats, dog toys and a
doggie guest book. There are no
pet fees.

Motel 6 - Palm Springs North
63950 20th Ave
North Palm Springs, CA
760-251-1425 (800-466-8356)
This motel welcomes your pets to
stay with you.

Tahoe Time Vacation Rentals
Visit Website to Review
North and West Lake Tahoe, CA
530-583-5522 (888-583-5520)
tahoetvr.com
Centered in Tahoe City, this
vacation rental company has a
number of dog-friendly homes in
North and West Tahoe.

Extended Stay America Los
Angeles - Northridge
19325 Londelius St.
Northridge, CA
818-734-1787 (800-804-3724)
One dog is allowed per suite. There
is a $25 per night additional pet fee
up to $150 for an entire stay.

Motel 6 - Los Angeles Norwalk
10646 Rosecrans Ave
Norwalk, CA
562-864-2567 (800-466-8356)
This motel welcomes your pets to
stay with you.

Days Inn /San Francisco Novato
8141 Redwood Blvd
Novato, CA
415-897-7111 (800-329-7466)
Dogs are welcome at this hotel.

Inn Marin
250 Entrada Drive
Novato, CA
415-883-5952 (800-652-6565)
innmarin.com/
Inn Marin invites both business and
leisure travelers. Nestled in a
beautiful resort setting and richly
restored, this inn welcomes your
best friend. Amenities include a
large outdoor heated pool and spa,
garden patio area with barbecue,
exercise facility, guest laundry
facility and a continental breakfast.
Rooms include data ports, voice
mail and two line speaker phone,
iron and ironing board, and
handicapped rooms/facilities are
available. They are located just off
Highway 101, perfect for the
business or tourist traveler. Dogs

are allowed for an additional fee of
$20 every 7 days per pet. Dogs may
not be left alone in the room. Multiple
dogs may be allowed.

Oakridge Inn
780 Ventura Avenue
Oak View, CA
805-649-4018
oakridgeinn.com/
This great getaway offers 33
spacious, clean, nicely appointed
rooms. Some of the
features/amenities include a heated
pool and spa, complimentary
continental breakfast, and a
convenient location to several other
attractions and activities. Dogs up to
50 pounds are allowed for an
additional pet fee of $15 per night
per pet. They may require an
additional pet deposit for very hairy
dogs. Dogs must be quiet, leashed,
cleaned up after, and they may not
be left alone in the room at any time.
Multiple dogs may be allowed.

A Bed of Roses
43547 Whispering Pines Drive
Oakhurst, CA
559-642-6975 (877-624-7673)
abedofrosesbandb.com/
Individually, beautifully decorated
rooms with private baths, a freshly
prepared hearty breakfast, 24 hour
cookie jar and snacks, an outdoor
swimming pool and hot tub with
lighted waterfalls, a petting zoo, and
spectacular views are just a few of
the features of this inn. Rooms with
Jacuzzi tubs, skylights, private
outdoor decks, and wood burning
stoves, are also available. Although
pet rooms are limited, dogs of all
sizes are welcome for an additional
fee of $20 per night per pet, and
advanced reservations are required
with a valid credit card. Reservations
may be made toll free at 877-624-
7673. A throw blanket, extra towels,
a comfortable sleeping pad, water
bowl, and treats are provided for
canine guests. Dogs must be
leashed or crated when in common
areas, and be cleaned up after at all
times. Dogs are not allowed on the
furniture in the room or the common
use areas, and they are not allowed
in the dining room. 2 dogs may be
allowed.

Comfort Inn Yosemite Area
40489 Highway 41
Oakhurst, CA
559-683-8282 (877-424-6423)
Dogs of all sizes are allowed. Dogs
are allowed for a pet fee of $20.00
per pet per night.

High Sierra RV & Mobile Park
40389 H 41
Oakhurst, CA
559-683-7662
Friendly dogs of all sizes are allowed for no additional fee. Dogs may not be left unattended at any time. There is a large field for dogs to run and play and a swimming hole as well. 2 dogs may be allowed.

Pine Rose Inn Bed and Breakfast
41703 Road 222
Oakhurst, CA
559-642-2800 (866-642-2800)
pineroseinn.com/
The inn is located 13 miles from the south gate of Yosemite National Park, 2 miles from Bass Lake and surrounded by the Sierra National Forest. The entire inn is non-smoking, except for outside. There is a $10 per day pet charge. Dogs and other pets are welcome.

Extended Stay America Oakland - Emeryville
3650 Mandela Pkwy.
Oakland, CA
510-923-1481 (800-804-3724)
One dog is allowed per suite. There is a $25 per night additional pet fee up to $150 for an entire stay.

La Quinta Inn Oakland Airport/Coliseum
8465 Enterprise Way
Oakland, CA
510-632-8900 (800-531-5900)
Dogs of all sizes are allowed. There are no additional pet fees. Dogs must be leashed and cleaned up after. Multiple dogs may be allowed.

Motel 6 - Oakland Embarcadero
1801 Embarcadero
Oakland, CA
510-436-0103 (800-466-8356)
Well-behaved dogs are allowed. Dogs are allowed for a pet fee of $additional per pet per night. One dog is allowed per room.

Motel 6 - Oakland Airport
8480 Edes Ave
Oakland, CA
510-638-1180 (800-466-8356)
This motel welcomes your pets to stay with you.

Inn at Occidental
3657 Church Street
Occidental, CA
707-874-1047 (800-522-6324)
innatoccidental.com/
Set among towering redwoods, this completely restored Victorian inn offers world class comfort and elegance in a country setting. Some of the amenities/features include a welcoming verandah, antiques, a complimentary Sonoma-harvest gourmet breakfast, an afternoon hors d'oeuvre and wine reception, private baths, fireplaces, and spa tubs. They offer a spacious cottage for guests with pets. Dogs of all sizes are allowed for an additional pet fee of $35 per night per room. Dogs must be kenneled when left unattended in the cottage, and they must be well behaved, leashed, and cleaned up after. Dogs are not allowed on the furnishings. 2 dogs may be allowed.

Occidental Hotel
3610 Bohemian Hwy
Occidental, CA
707-874-3623
There is an $10 per day per pet fee. Dogs must be on leash and may not be left alone in the rooms. 2 dogs may be allowed.

Best Western Marty's Valley Inn
3240 Mission Avenue
Oceanside, CA
760-757-7700 (800-780-7234)
Dogs up to 50 pounds are allowed. Dogs are allowed for a pet fee of $10.00 per pet per night.

Extended Stay America San Diego - Oceanside
3190 Vista Way
Oceanside, CA
760-439-1499 (800-804-3724)
One dog is allowed per suite. There is a $25 per night additional pet fee up to $150 for an entire stay.

La Quinta Inn San Diego - Oceanside
937 N. Coast Highway
Oceanside, CA
760-450-0730 (800-531-5900)
Dogs of all sizes are allowed. There are no additional pet fees. Dogs may not be left unattended, and they must be leashed and cleaned up after. Multiple dogs may be allowed.

Motel 6 - Oceanside
3708 Plaza Dr
Oceanside, CA
760-941-1011 (800-466-8356)
This motel welcomes your pets to stay with you.

Motel 6 - Oceanside Downtown
909 Coast Hwy

Oceanside, CA
760-721-1543 (800-466-8356)
This motel welcomes your pets to stay with you.

Ramada Oceanside
1440 Mission Avenue
Oceanside, CA
760-967-4100 (800-272-6232)
Dogs are welcome at this hotel.

Residence Inn San Diego Oceanside
3603 Ocean Ranch Blvd
Oceanside, CA
760-722-9600 (800-331-3131)
This upscale, all suite hotel sits central to many of the city's star attractions, shopping, dining, and business areas, plus they offer a number of in-house amenities that include a daily buffet breakfast and evening social hours. Dogs are allowed for an additional one time pet fee of $100 per room. 2 dogs may be allowed.

Best Western Casa Ojai
1302 E Ojai Avenue
Ojai, CA
805-646-8175 (800-780-7234)
Dogs of all sizes are allowed. Dogs are allowed for a pet fee of $25.00 per pet per night.

Blue Iguana
11794 N Ventura Avenue
Ojai, CA
805-646-5277
blueiguanainn.com/
Dogs up to 40 pounds are allowed. Built in the style of the old California/Mexican missions, guests will find unique and authentic details throughout this Southwestern villa inn. There is a large open lawn framed by big oaks and comfy benches, lushly landscaped grounds, an outdoor pool and spa, and spacious worldly-decorated rooms with many amenities. One dog is allowed in a standard room, and up to 2 dogs are allowed in the one bedroom suites for an additional pet fee of $20 per night per pet,,, there is also a pet policy to sign at check in and a credit card must be on file. Dogs may not be left alone in the room at any time, and they must be leashed and cleaned up after. Dogs are not allowed in the pool area. 2 dogs may be allowed.

Lavender Inn
210 E Matilija Street
Ojai, CA
805-646-6635
lavenderinn.com/
This tranquil retreat offers 7 rooms

and an attached cottage, each with its own unique décor of bold colors and detail, and it is conveniently located to several other attractions and activities. The private gardens and fountains are breathtaking complete with tall oaks, mountain views, and a wonderful variety of lavenders. A separate building on the property houses an intimate day spa that offer a variety of massages. Dogs up to 50 pounds is allowed for an additional one time fee of $25. They may accept a slightly larger dog in the cottage only. There is also a large fenced yard for off-leash fun. Dogs must be quiet, well behaved, leashed and cleaned up after. 2 dogs may be allowed.

Ojai Valley Inn and Spa
905 Country Club Road
Ojai, CA
805-646-2420 (888-697-8780)
ojairesort.com/
This award-winning historic resort is elegance inside and out with 220 tree-shaded acres that include luxury accommodations, a premier championship golf course, a comprehensive 31,000 square foot spa village, and a first-of-its-kind artist cottage where local artists inspire and help guests to create in a variety of medias. In addition to several amenities, they also offer in room dining, handcrafted picnics, a cocktail lounge, and several dining options featuring California Central Coast cuisine prepared with locally harvested, seasonal foods and herbs. Dogs of all sizes are allowed but they must be acknowledged at the time of reservations. There is a $50 per night additional fee per pet for the first 3 nights for a total of no more than $150. Dogs must be quiet, leashed, cleaned up after, and crated when left alone in the room. 2 dogs may be allowed.

Ranch Motel
2051 S Highway 395
Olancha, CA
760-764-2387
Dogs are allowed for no additional pet fee. (There may be a small charge for long haired dogs if extra cleaning is required.) 2 dogs may be allowed.

Olema Inn
10,000 Sir Francis Drake Blvd
Olema, CA
415-663-9559
theolemainn.com/index.html
Only moments from beautiful coastline, this restored inn offers

elegant rooms, exceptional fine dining from a mostly organic menu, a splendid outdoor patio, lush gardens, and more. One dog is allowed for no additional fee. Dogs must be well mannered, leashed, and cleaned up after. Additionally, there is a restaurant on-site with seasonal patio dining where your pet may dine with you from noon until 4 pm.

Best Western InnSuites Hotel & Suites Ontario
3400 Shelby Street
Ontario, CA
909-466-9600 (800-780-7234)
Dogs of all sizes are allowed. Dogs are allowed for a pet fee.

Doubletree Hotel
222 N Vineyard Avenue
Ontario, CA
909-937-0900 (800-222-TREE (8733))
Located adjacent to the Ontario Convention Center and only 3 minutes away from the international airport, this upscale hotel offers a number of on site amenities for business and leisure travelers, plus a convenient location to shopping, dining, and recreation areas. Dogs are allowed for an additional one time fee of $50 per pet. Multiple dogs may be allowed.

Extended Stay America Los Angeles - Ontario Airport
3990 E. Inland Empire Blvd.
Ontario, CA
909-944-8900 (800-804-3724)
One dog is allowed per suite. There is a $25 per night additional pet fee up to $150 for an entire stay.

Knights Inn Ontario
1120 East Holt Blvd
Ontario, CA
909-984-9655 (800-843-5644)
Dogs are welcome at this hotel.

La Quinta Inn & Suites Ontario Airport
3555 Inland Empire Blvd
Ontario, CA
909-476-1112 (800-531-5900)
Dogs of all sizes are allowed. There are no additional pet fees, but a credit card must be on file. Dogs must be crated if left alone in the room, and be leashed and cleaned up after. Multiple dogs may be allowed.

Motel 6 - Ontario Airport
1560 4th St

Ontario, CA
909-984-2424 (800-466-8356)
This motel welcomes your pets to stay with you.

Red Roof Inn Ontario Airport
1818 East Holt Boulevard
Ontario, CA
909-988-8466 (800-RED-ROOF)
One well-behaved family pet per room. Guest must notify front desk upon arrival. Guest is liable for any damages. In consideration of all guests, pets must never be left unattended in the guest rooms.

Residence Inn Ontario Airport
2025 Convention Center Way
Ontario, CA
909-937-6788 (800-736-0554)
Offering apartment style suites, this inn sits adjacent to the Ontario Convention Center, and near the Ontario International Airport, the Citizen's Business Bank Arena, and Ontario Mills-the area's largest entertainment and shopping complex. Additionally, they offer a number of in-house amenities, including a daily buffet breakfast, social hours Monday through Thursday, a heated swimming pool, and a Sport Court. Dogs are allowed for an additional one time pet fee of $100 per room. Multiple dogs may be allowed.

Doubletree Hotel
100 The City Drive
Orange, CA
714-634-4500 (800-222-TREE (8733))
Only a few minutes from Disneyland and the Anaheim Convention Center, this upscale hotel offers a number of on site amenities for all level of travelers, plus a convenient location to business, shopping, dining, and recreation areas. Dogs up to 75 pounds are allowed for an additional one time pet fee of $75 per room. 2 dogs may be allowed.

Extended Stay America Orange County - Katella Ave.
1635 W. Katella Ave.
Orange, CA
714-639-8608 (800-804-3724)
One dog is allowed per suite. There is a $25 per night additional pet fee up to $150 for an entire stay.

Motel 6 - Anaheim Stadium Orange
2920 Chapman Ave
Orange, CA
714-634-2441 (800-466-8356)
This motel welcomes your pets to stay with you.

Days Inn Oroville
1745 Feather River Blvd
Oroville, CA
530-533-3297 (800-329-7466)
Dogs of all sizes are allowed. Dogs
are allowed for a pet fee of $10 per
pet per night.

Motel 6 - Oroville
505 Montgomery St
Oroville, CA
530-532-9400 (800-466-8356)
This motel welcomes your pets to
stay with you.

Residence Inn Oxnard River Ridge
2101 W Vineyard Avenue
Oxnard, CA
805-278-2200 (800-331-3131)
Besides offering a convenient
location to business, shopping,
dining, and entertainment areas, this
hotel also provides a number of in-
house amenities, including a daily
buffet breakfast and complementary
evening receptions. Dogs are
allowed for an additional one time
pet fee of $100 per room. 2 dogs
may be allowed.

Vagabond Inn
1245 N. Oxnard Blvd.
Oxnard, CA
805-983-0251
vagabondinn.com
Amenities at this motel include a free
continental breakfast and weekday
newspaper. They also have an on-
site coffee shop, which might be
helpful in getting food to go for the
room. Dogs are allowed for an
additional one time fee of $10 per
night per pet. 2 dogs may be
allowed.

Andril Fireplace Cottages
569 Asilomar Blvd
Pacific Grove, CA
831-375-0994
There is an additional fee of $14 per
day per pet. Well-behaved, quiet
dogs are allowed.

Lighthouse Lodge and Suites
1249 Lighthouse Ave
Pacific Grove, CA
831-655-2111
Dogs are allowed for an additional
fee of $25 per night per pet. Multiple
dogs may be allowed.

Pacific Palisades Guest Studio
Beach
643 Baylor Street
Pacific Palisades, CA
310-741-8276

This vacation rental has a $50 non-
refundable cleaning fee for dogs
and a $50 refundable deposit. It is
1/2 mile to the ocean.

Best Western Palm Desert Resort
74695 Highway 111
Palm Desert, CA
760-340-4441 (800-780-7234)
Dogs of all sizes are allowed. Dogs
are allowed for a nightly pet fee.

Embassy Suites
74-700 H 111
Palm Desert, CA
760-340-6600 (800-EMBASSY
(362-2779))
Located near the Dallas Fort Worth
International Airport, this upscale,
all suite hotel offers a number of on
site amenities for business and
leisure travelers, plus a convenient
location to numerous shopping,
dining, and business areas, and a
long list of attractions. They also
offer a complimentary cooked-to-
order breakfast and a Manager's
reception every evening. Dogs are
allowed for an additional one time
fee of $50 per pet. 2 dogs may be
allowed.

Motel 6 - Palm Desert Palm Springs
Area
78100 Varner Rd
Palm Desert, CA
760-345-0550 (800-466-8356)
This motel welcomes your pets to
stay with you.

Residence Inn Palm Desert
38305 Cook Street
Palm Desert, CA
760-776-0050 (800-331-3131)
A beautiful oasis in the desert, this
all suite, resort-style hotel is central
to a number of recreational pursuits
and the Palm Springs Aerial
Tramway that visitors on a
breathtaking journey up Mt. San
Jacinto; plus they also offer a
number of in-house amenities,
including a daily buffet breakfast
and evening socials. Dogs are
allowed for an additional one time
pet fee of $75 per room. Multiple
dogs may be allowed.

The Inn at Deep Canyon
74470 Abronia Trail
Palm Desert, CA
760-346-8061 (800-253-0004)
inn-adc.com/
This hotel features a palm garden,
pool and fully-equipped
kitchenettes. They have pet-friendly
rooms available. There is an
additional fee of $10 per night per

pet.

7 Springs Resort and Hotel Palm
Springs
950 N. Indian Canyon Dr.
Palm Springs, CA
800-585-3578
palm-springs-hotels.cc
7 Springs Inn and Suites offers a
variety of accommodations in the
heart of Palm Springs. Enjoy fully
furnished suites with Kitchens, free
daily Continental Breakfast, Heated
Pool, Jacuzzi, barbecue area,
Remote control T.V., direct dial
telephones, free parking. Close to
area shopping, restaurants, casinos,
golf, tennis, and indian canyons.
Pets are welcome for a $15 per night
fee. Pets cannot be left unattended
and must be kept on a leash when
out of the room.

Ace Hotel & Swim Club
701 E Palm Canyon Drive
Palm Springs, CA
760-325-9900
acehotel.com/palmsprings
Chic, organic, and hip have all been
used to describe this get-a-way
destination. In addition to
implementing eco-friendly elements
throughout the hotel, their restaurant
also features a local, organic, and
seasonally inspired menu; the bar -
fresh signature cocktails, and
medicinal spa services. An off-leash
dog park is also on site. One dog is
$25 per night and each dog
thereafter is an additional $10 per
night. Dogs are not allowed in food
or drink service areas; however they
are allowed out by the pool where
guests may be served food and
drinks. Multiple dogs may be
allowed.

Best Western Palm Springs
1633 South Palm Canyon
Palm Springs, CA
800-222-4678 (800-780-7234)
bwpalmsprings.com
Best Western Inn at Palm Springs is
a Southern California resort hotel
with updated guestroom
accommodations near dozens of
Palm Desert attractions including
theater, golfing, shopping, Joshua
Tree hiking and rock climbing.

Casa Cody Country Inn
175 S. Cahuilla Rd.
Palm Springs, CA
760-320-9346
casacody.com
This is a quaint romantic historic inn
that was founded in the 1920s. The
founder, Harriet Cody, was a cousin

of Buffalo Bill. The inn is nestled against the mountains and has adobe buildings. The rooms have fireplaces, kitchens and private patios. Dogs are allowed for an additional fee of $15 per night per pet. 2 dogs may be allowed.

Extended Stay America Palm Springs - Airport
1400 E. Tahquitz Canyon Way
Palm Springs, CA
760-416-0084 (800-804-3724)
One dog is allowed per suite. There is a $25 per night additional pet fee up to $150 for an entire stay.

Hilton Hotel
400 E Tahquitz Canyon Way
Palm Springs, CA
760-320-6868 (800-HILTONS (445-8667))
Sitting on seven lushly landscaped acres, this upscale hotel offers a number of on site amenities for business and leisure travelers, plus a convenient location to business, shopping, dining, and entertainment areas. Dogs are allowed for an additional fee of $25 per night per pet. Multiple dogs may be allowed.

Motel 6 - Palm Springs Downtown
660 Palm Canyon Dr
Palm Springs, CA
760-327-4200 (800-466-8356)
This motel welcomes your pets to stay with you.

Motel 6 - Palm Springs East East Palm Canyon
595 Palm Canyon Dr
Palm Springs, CA
760-325-6129 (800-466-8356)
This motel welcomes your pets to stay with you.

Musicland Hotel
1342 S Palm Canyon Drive
Palm Springs, CA
760-325-1326
This budget hotel offers garden landscaped grounds against a modern white stucco 2 story building. Amenities include a game room, refrigerators, cable, and kitchenettes. Dogs of all sizes are allowed for an additional $5 per night per pet. Dogs may not be left alone in the room at any time, and they must be leashed and cleaned up after. 2 dogs may be allowed.

Orchid Tree Inn
261 South Belardo Road
Palm Springs, CA
760-325-2791

This inn has two pet rooms. Dogs must be attended at all times and leashed when outside the room. There is a $250 refundable pet deposit.

Palm Springs Hotels Caliente Tropics Resort
411 E. Palm Canyon Drive
Palm Springs, CA
800-658-5975
calientetropics.com
Well-behaved dogs up to 60 pounds are allowed. Leashed pets are allowed in the lawn and pool areas. Pets may not be left alone in the rooms. There is no smoking indoors at the Caliente Tropics Resort.

Quality Inn
1269 E. Palm Canyon Dr.
Palm Springs, CA
760-323-2775 (877-424-6423)
Dogs of all sizes are allowed.

The Rental Connection
190 E Palm Canyon Dr
Palm Springs, CA
760-320-7336 (800-462-7256)
therentalconnection.com
This rental home company has dozens of pet-friendly Palm Springs area properties. Pet deposits are required for the rentals.

Vacation Palm Springs
1401 N Palm Canyon Drive, Suite 201
Palm Springs, CA
760-778-7832
Dogs are allowed for a $75 one time fee per pet. 2 dogs may be allowed.

Motel 6 - Palmdale
407 Palmdale Blvd
Palmdale, CA
661-272-0660 (800-466-8356)
This motel welcomes your pets to stay with you.

Residence Inn Palmdale Lancaster
514 West Avenue P/Rancho Vista Blvd
Palmdale, CA
661-947-4204 (800-331-3131)
Because of their close location to air/spacecraft companies, this all suite inn has become a popular destination among aerospace travelers; however, there are sites and activities for all level of travelers to explore. They also offer a number of in-house amenities, including a daily buffet breakfast and evening socials. Dogs are allowed for an additional one time

pet fee of $75 per room. Multiple dogs may be allowed.

Staybridge Suites Palmdale
420 West Park Drive
Palmdale, CA
661-9479300 (877-270-6405)
Dogs up to 80 pounds are allowed. Pets allowed with an additional pet fee. Up to $75 for 1-6 nights and up to $150 for 7+ nights. A pet agreement must be signed at check-in.

Super 8 Palmdale
200 W Palmdale Blvd.
Palmdale, CA
661-273-8000 (800-800-8000)
Dogs of all sizes are allowed. Dogs are allowed for a pet fee.

Motel 6 - Palo Alto
4301 El Camino Real
Palo Alto, CA
650-949-0833 (800-466-8356)
This motel welcomes your pets to stay with you.

Sheraton Palo Alto Hotel
625 El Camino Real
Palo Alto, CA
650-328-2800 (888-625-5144)
Dogs of all sizes are allowed. You must sign a pet policy. Dogs are not allowed to be left alone in the room.

The Westin Palo Alto
675 El Camino Real
Palo Alto, CA
650-321-4422 (888-625-5144)
Dogs up to 80 pounds are allowed. There are no additional pet fees. Dogs are not allowed to be left alone in the room.

Panamint Springs Resort
Highway 190
Panamint Springs, CA
775-482-7680
deathvalley.com/
There is a $5 per day per pet additional fee for dogs in the motel, and a one time $5 fee per pet for the campground. The resort is located on Highway 190, 48 miles east of Lone Pine and 31 miles west of Stovepipe Wells. Multiple dogs may be allowed.

Comfort Inn Central
5475 Clark Road
Paradise, CA
530-876-0191 (877-424-6423)
Dogs of all sizes are allowed. Dogs are allowed for a pet fee of $10.00/ per pet per night.

Ponderosa Gardens Motel
7010 The Skyway
Paradise, CA
530-872-9094
True to its name, this motel features a garden like setting, a pool and Jacuzzi, gift shop, picnic grounds, and a continental breakfast. Dogs of all sizes are allowed for an additional fee of $10 per night per pet. Dogs may not be left alone in the room at any time, and they must be leashed and cleaned up after.

Quality Inn
3321 E. Colorado Blvd
Pasadena, CA
626-796-9291 (877-424-6423)
Dogs of all sizes are allowed. Dogs are allowed for a pet fee of $20.00 per pet per night.

Holiday Inn Express Hotel & Suites
Paso Robles
2455 Riverside Ave
Paso Robles, CA
805-238-6500 (877-270-6405)
Dogs of all sizes are allowed. Dogs are allowed for a pet fee.

Motel 6 - Paso Robles
1134 Black Oak Dr
Paso Robles, CA
805-239-9090 (800-466-8356)
This motel welcomes your pets to stay with you.

Travelodge Paso Robles
2701 Spring Street
Paso Robles, CA
805-238-0078 (800-578-7878)
Dogs are welcome at this hotel.

The Lodge at Pebble Beach
1700 17 Mile Drive
Pebble Beach, CA
831-624-3811 (800-654-9300)
they are not allowed on the golf courses.

The Nomad House
16764 Nomad Way
Penn Valley, CA
415-759-5073
thenomadhouse.com
This 3 bedroom pet-friendly vacation home is located 20 minutes from Grass Valley and Nevada City. It can sleep up to seven.

Motel 6 - Petaluma
1368 Mcdowell Blvd
Petaluma, CA
707-765-0333 (800-466-8356)
This motel welcomes your pets to stay with you.

Quality Inn
5100 Montero Way
Petaluma, CA
707-664-1155 (877-424-6423)
Dogs of all sizes are allowed. Dogs are allowed for a pet fee of $15.00 per pet per night. Two dogs are allowed per room.

Sheraton Sonoma County - Petaluma
745 Baywood Dr.
Petaluma, CA
707-283-2888 (888-625-5144)
Dogs of all sizes are allowed. Pet rooms are available on the first floor only. You must sign a pet policy when checking in with a dog. Dogs are not allowed to be left alone in the room. 2 dogs may be allowed.

Anderson Valley Inn
8480 H 128
Philo, CA
707-895-3325
Dogs only, and of all sizes are allowed in the suites only. There is a $30 one time fee for 1 dog and a 2nd dog would be an additional $15 one time fee. No pit bulls are allowed, and dogs must be on a leash at all times. Dogs may not be left alone at any time. 2 dogs may be allowed.

Highland Ranch
18941 Philo Greenwood Rd.
Philo, CA
707-895-3600
highlandranch.com/home.html
This 125 year old ranch house sits on 300 acres along the mountainside among majestic trees with 8 individually decorated cabins nestled around it. At this country resort you can take in a wide variety of land and water recreation and activities, a massage, a yoga class, trek a hundred miles of multi-use trails, or take part in a myriad of other events. They also feature good home-cooked meals served family-style in the main house. Dogs of all sizes are welcome for no additional fee. They are greeted with treats, and some towels and blankets that they'll need after a day of enjoying country life. Dogs must be well mannered, leashed, and cleaned up after. Dogs may also run off leash in certain areas if they are under good voice control. 2 dogs may be allowed.

Motel 6 - Pinole
1501 Fitzgerald Dr
Pinole, CA
510-222-8174 (800-466-8356)

This motel welcomes your pets to stay with you.

Pioneer Town Motel
5040 Curtis Road
Pioneertown, CA
760-365-4879
All of this rustic motel's 20 rooms are decorated with the authentic charm of an era past, but updated with Satellite TV, HBO, a kitchen area, microwave, a refrigerator, and shaded seating areas where you can enjoy the views. Because the town was built also as a movie set to be a complete old west town, many Western stars and movie star greats of the past have slept in these rooms while shooting films here. Dogs of all sizes are allowed. There is a $15 per night per pet additional fee. Dogs may not be left alone in the rooms, and they must be leashed and cleaned up after. 2 dogs may be allowed.

Cottage Inn by the Sea
2351 Price Street
Pismo Beach, CA
805-773-4617
There is a $20 per night per room additional pet fee and a pet policy to sign at check in. Dogs must be crated if left alone in the room. 2 dogs may be allowed.

Motel 6 - Pismo Beach
860 4th St
Pismo Beach, CA
805-773-2665 (800-466-8356)
This motel welcomes your pets to stay with you.

Oxford Suites
651 Five Cities Drive
Pismo Beach, CA
805-773-3773 (800-982-SUITE)
oxfordsuites.com
This motel is located within a short drive of the dog-friendly Pismo State Beach. Amenities include a year-round pool & spa, complimentary full breakfast buffet, an evening reception with beverages & light hor d'oeuvres. Room amenities for the guest suites include a work table, sofa, microwave oven, refrigerator, TV/VCR, and wheelchair accessibility. Dogs up to 50 pounds are allowed for an additional fee of $10 per day per pet. Dogs must never be left unattended in the room, even if they are in a crate. 2 dogs may be allowed.

Sancastle Inn
300 Stinson Avenue
Pismo Beach, CA

805-773-2422
Dogs are allowed for an additional pet fee of $20 per night per room.

Sea Gypsy Motel
1020 Cypress Street
Pismo Beach, CA
805-773-1801
seagypsymotel.com/
This motel is located on the beach and they allow dogs of any size. One dog is allowed for an additional $15 per night fee.

Spyglass Inn
2703 Spyglass Drive
Pismo Beach, CA
805-773-4855 (800-824-2612)
spyglassinn.com/
In addition to offering a number of on site amenities - including a restaurant, pool, and spa, this luxury, ocean-side resort also offers a convenient location to some of the areas best tourist attractions. Dogs are allowed in the 1st floor rooms for an additional fee of $20 per night per pet. Dogs may not be left alone in the room, and they must be quiet, leashed, and cleaned up after at all times. Well mannered pooches are also welcome at the outside tables of the restaurant. 2 dogs may be allowed.

Motel 6 - Pittsburg
2101 Loveridge Rd
Pittsburg, CA
925-427-1600 (800-466-8356)
This motel welcomes your pets to stay with you.

Residence Inn Anaheim Placentia/Fullerton
700 W Kimberly Avenue
Placentia, CA
714-996-0555 (888-236-2427)
This all suite hotel is close to many of the area's most exciting attractions, plus they offer a number of on site amenities, including a daily buffet breakfast, a Manager's reception Monday through Thursday, and an outdoor picnic and barbecue area. Dogs are allowed for an additional one time pet fee of $100 per room. Multiple dogs may be allowed.

Best Western Placerville Inn
6850 Green Leaf Drive
Placerville, CA
530-622-9100 (800-780-7234)
Dogs of all sizes are allowed. Dogs are allowed for a pet fee of $25.00 per pet per night.

Fleming Jones Homestead B&B
3170 Newtown Road
Placerville, CA
530-344-0943
robinsnestranch.com
This historic homestead is a B&B at a working miniature horse ranch. It is located 5 minutes from Placerville and near the Apple Hill farms that are open to the public each fall. Well-behaved dogs are welcome in the Woodshed and Bunkhouse rooms of the B&B. There is a $10 per day per dog. Dogs may not be left unattended and guests are responsible for any damages caused by their pets.

Extended Stay America Pleasant Hill - Buskirk Ave.
3220 Buskirk Ave.
Pleasant Hill, CA
925-945-6788 (800-804-3724)
One dog is allowed per suite. There is a $25 per night additional pet fee up to $150 for an entire stay.

Residence Inn Pleasant Hill Concord
700 Ellinwood Way
Pleasant Hill, CA
925-689-1010 (800-331-3131)
This all suite hotel sits central to many of the area's star attractions, shopping, dining, and business areas, plus they offer a number of in-house amenities that include a daily buffet breakfast and evening socials. Dogs are allowed for an additional one time pet fee of $100 per room. Multiple dogs may be allowed.

Best Western Pleasanton Inn
5375 Owens Ct
Pleasanton, CA
925-463-1300 (800-780-7234)
Dogs of all sizes are allowed. Dogs are allowed for a pet fee of $35 per pet per night.

Motel 6 - Pleasanton
5102 Hopyard Rd
Pleasanton, CA
925-463-2626 (800-466-8356)
Your pets are welcome to stay here with you.

Residence Inn Pleasanton
11920 Dublin Canyon Road
Pleasanton, CA
925-227-0500 (800-331-3131)
In addition to offering a convenient location to business, shopping, dining, and entertainment areas, this hotel also provides a number of in-house amenities, including a daily buffet breakfast, summer barbecues, and evening socials Monday through Thursday with light dinner fare. Well mannered dogs are allowed for an additional one time pet fee of $100 per room. Multiple dogs may be allowed.

Point Reyes Station Inn Bed and Breakfast
11591 Highway One, Box 824
Point Reyes Station, CA
415-663-9372
pointreyesstationinn.com/
They offer private, romantic rooms with thirteen foot vaulted ceilings, whirlpool baths, fireplaces and views of rolling hills. This inn is located at the gateway of the Point Reyes National Seashore. Well-behaved dogs are welcome and there is no extra pet charge. Children are also welcome. 2 dogs may be allowed.

Tree House Bed and Breakfast Inn
73 Drake Summit, P.O. Box 1075
Point Reyes Station, CA
415-663-8720
treehousebnb.com/
This inn offers a secluded and peaceful getaway in West Marin. It is located on the tip of Inverness Ridge with a view of Point Reyes Station. The Point Reyes National Seashore is nearby. All three rooms have a private bathroom. Pets and children are always welcome. Smoking is allowed outdoors. There are no pet fees.

Motel 6 - Los Angeles Pomona
2470 Garey Ave
Pomona, CA
909-591-1871 (800-466-8356)
This motel welcomes your pets to stay with you.

Sheraton Suites Fairplex
601 West McKinley Ave.
Pomona, CA
909-622-2220 (888-625-5144)
Dogs of all sizes are allowed. Pet rooms are available on the second floor only. You must sign a pet policy when checking in with a dog. Dogs are not allowed to be left alone in the room.

Shilo Inn
3200 Temple Ave
Pomona, CA
909-598-0073 (800-222-2244)
shiloinns.com
Amenities include a complimentary breakfast buffet, outdoor pool & spa, guest laundromat, fitness center and fresh fruit, popcorn & coffee. Rooms include microwaves, refrigerators, hair dryers, iron/ironing boards and

more. Dogs are allowed for an additional one time fee of $25 per pet. 2 dogs may be allowed.

Best Western Porterville Inn
350 W Montgomery Avenue
Porterville, CA
559-781-7411 (800-780-7234)
Dogs of all sizes are allowed. Dogs are allowed for a pet fee.

Motel 6 - Porterville
935 Morton Ave
Porterville, CA
559-781-7600 (800-466-8356)
This motel welcomes your pets to stay with you.

Ramada San Diego North Poway
12448 Poway Rd
Poway, CA
858-748-7311 (800-272-6232)
Dogs of all sizes are allowed. Dogs are allowed for a pet fee of $15.00 per pet per night.

Bucks Lake Lodge
23685 Bucks Lake
Quincy, CA
530-283-2262
There is a $10 per day additional pet fee. Dogs are allowed in the cabins, but not the motel section. The cabins are not designated as smoking or non-smoking. Thanks to one of our readers for this recommendation. 2 dogs may be allowed.

Comfort Inn & Suites
12249 Folsom Blvd
Rancho Cordova, CA
916-351-1213 (877-424-6423)
Dogs of all sizes are allowed.

Days Inn and Suites Rancho Cordova
3240 Mather Field Rd
Rancho Cordova, CA
916-363-3344 (800-329-7466)
Dogs of all sizes are allowed. Dogs are allowed for a pet fee of $20.00 per pet per night.

Extended Stay America Sacramento - Rancho Cordova
10721 White Rock Rd.
Rancho Cordova, CA
916-635-2363 (800-804-3724)
One dog is allowed per suite. There is a $25 per night additional pet fee up to $150 for an entire stay.

Holiday Inn Sacramento Rancho Cordova
11269 Point East Drive
Rancho Cordova, CA
916-635-4040 (877-270-6405)

Dogs of all sizes are allowed. Dogs are allowed for a pet fee of $25 per pet per stay. Two dogs are allowed per room.

Inns of America
12249 Folsom Blvd
Rancho Cordova, CA
916-351-1213 (800-826-0778)
innsofamerica.com/sac12.htm
This motel offers a complimentary continental breakfast. To get there from Sacramento, take Hwy 50 and exit Hazel Ave. Turn right onto Hazel. Then turn right onto Folsom Blvd. The hotel will be on the right. Friendly dogs are allowed for an additional pet fee of $10 per night per room. 2 dogs may be allowed.

Motel 6 - Sacramento Rancho Cordova East
10694 Olson Dr
Rancho Cordova, CA
916-635-8784 (800-466-8356)
Your pets are welcome to stay here with you.

Red Roof Inn Rancho Cordova - Sacramento
10800 Olson Drive
Rancho Cordova, CA
916-638-2500 (800-RED-ROOF)
One well-behaved family pet per room. Guest must notify front desk upon arrival. Guest is liable for any damages. In consideration of all guests, pets must never be left unattended in the guest rooms.

Residence Inn Sacramento Rancho Cordova
2779 Prospect Park Drive
Rancho Cordova, CA
916-851-1550 (800-331-3131)
Folsom Outlets, the American River Parkway, Red Hawk Casino, the Natomas Aquatic Center, and the Mather golf Course are all just a short distance from this all suite hotel. Additionally they offer a daily buffet breakfast and evening socials Monday through Thursday. Dogs are allowed for an additional one time pet fee of $100 per room. 2 dogs may be allowed.

TownePlace Suites Ontario Airport
9625 Milliken Avenue
Rancho Cucamonga, CA
909-466-1100 (800-257-3000)
This all suite inn sits close to numerous business, shopping, dining, and entertainment areas, plus they offer a number of in-house amenities for business and leisure travelers. Dogs up to 80 pounds are allowed for an additional one time

fee of $100 per room. 2 dogs may be allowed.

Motel 6 - Palm Springs Rancho Mirage
69570 Sr 111
Rancho Mirage, CA
760-324-8475 (800-466-8356)
This motel welcomes your pets to stay with you.

Comfort Inn
90 Sale Lane
Red Bluff, CA
530-529-7060 (877-424-6423)
Dogs of all sizes are allowed. Dogs are allowed for a pet fee of $15.00/ per pet per night.

Days Inn Red Bluff
5 Sutter Street
Red Bluff, CA
530-527-6130 (800-329-7466)
Dogs are welcome at this hotel.

Motel 6 - Red Bluff
20 Williams Ave
Red Bluff, CA
530-527-9200 (800-466-8356)
This motel welcomes your pets to stay with you.

Sportsman's Lodge
768 Antelope Blvd
Red Bluff, CA
530-527-2888
rbsportsmanlodge.com/
Some of the amenities at this lodge include refrigerators in all the rooms and a swimming pool. Dogs are allowed for an additional pet fee of $7 per night for 1 dog and $10 per night for 2 dogs. The fee may be higher for larger or heavily-haired dogs. Dogs may not be left unattended in the rooms at any time, and they must be well behaved, leashed, and cleaned up after. 2 dogs may be allowed.

Super 8 Red Bluff
30 Gilmore Road
Red Bluff, CA
530-529-2028 (800-800-8000)
Dogs of all sizes are allowed. Dogs are allowed for a pet fee.

Travelodge Inn CA Red Bluff
38 Antelope Boulevard
Red Bluff, CA
530-527-6020 (800-578-7878)
Dogs of all sizes are allowed. Dogs are allowed for a nightly pet fee.

Bridge Bay Resort
10300 Bridge Bay Road
Redding, CA

530-275-3021 (800-752-9669)
This is a complete resort that offers a full-service marina with tackle and bait, small boats and houseboat rentals, dining, a lounge, gift shop, convenience store, banquet rooms, a pool, and lakeside accommodations. Dogs of all sizes are welcome for an additional fee of $10 per night per pet, plus a $50 deposit if paying by cash. There is no additional pet fee for the dogs on the boats. Dogs may be left alone in the rooms for a short time if they are house-trained and they will be quiet and well behaved. Dogs must be leashed and cleaned up after at all times.

Fawndale Lodge and RV Resort
15215 Fawndale Road
Redding, CA
800-338-0941
members.aol.com/fawnresort/
Nestled in the pines, this lodge offers acres of lawn, a pool and easy access to many recreational activities. All rooms are non-smoking. There is a $10 per day pet charge per room. Multiple dogs may be allowed.

Holiday Inn Redding
1900 Hilltop Drive
Redding, CA
530-221-7500 (877-270-6405)
Dogs of all sizes are allowed. Dogs are allowed for a pet fee of $10.00 per pet per night.

La Quinta Inn Redding
2180 Hilltop Drive
Redding, CA
530-221-8200 (800-531-5900)
Dogs of all sizes are allowed. There are no additional pet fees. Dogs may not be left unattended at any time, and they must be leashed and cleaned up after. Multiple dogs may be allowed.

Motel 6 - Redding Central
1640 Hilltop Dr
Redding, CA
530-221-1800 (800-466-8356)
This motel welcomes your pets to stay with you.

Motel 6 - Redding North
1250 Twin View Blvd
Redding, CA
530-246-4470 (800-466-8356)
This motel welcomes your pets to stay with you.

Motel 6 - Redding South
2385 Bechelli Ln
Redding, CA

530-221-0562 (800-466-8356)
This motel welcomes your pets to stay with you.

Ramada Limited Redding
1286 Twin View Blvd
Redding, CA
530-246-2222 (800-272-6232)
Dogs are welcome at this hotel.

Red Lion
1830 Hilltop Drive
Redding, CA
530-221-8700
There is a $20 per night per pet additional fee. There are no additional pet fees for R&R members, and the R&R program is free to sign up. Multiple dogs may be allowed.

River Inn
1835 Park Marina Drive
Redding, CA
530-241-9500 (800-995-4341)
redding-online.com/riverinn.htm
This inn is adjacent to the Sacramento River and has a private grass area next to their lake. There is a $6 per day per pet charge. Thanks to one of our readers for recommending this inn. 2 dogs may be allowed.

Rodeway Inn
532 N. Market Street
Redding, CA
530-241-6464 (877-424-6423)
Dogs of all sizes are allowed. Dogs are allowed for a pet fee of $20.00 per pet per night.

Shasta Lodge
1245 Pine Street
Redding, CA
530-243-6133
One dog is allowed for an additonal fee of $10 per night.

Howard Johnson Redlands
1120 W. Colton Avenue
Redlands, CA
909-793-2001 (800-446-4656)
Dogs of all sizes are allowed. Dogs are allowed for a pet fee.

Dean Creek Resort Motel
4112 Redwood Drive
Redway, CA
707-923-2555 (877-923-2555)
Located along the Eel River in Giant Redwood country, and only three miles from the famous 'Avenue of the Giants', this resort offers a long list of amenities and recreation. Dogs up to 75 pounds are allowed for an additional fee of $10 per night

per pet. Dogs may not be left unattended at any time, either in the motel or in the RV park. Dogs are allowed on the trails and on the beach. Dogs must be leashed and cleaned up after. Please check with the resort for breed restrictions. 2 dogs may be allowed.

Days Inn Redwood City
2650 El Camino Real
Redwood City, CA
650-369-9200 (800-329-7466)
Dogs are welcome at this hotel.

TownePlace Suites Redwood Shores
1000 Twin Dolphin Drive
Redwood City, CA
650-593-4100 (800-257-3000)
In addition to offering a number of in-house amenities for all level of travelers, this all suite inn also provides a convenient location to major companies, shopping, dining, and entertainment areas. Dogs up to 50 pounds are allowed for an additional one time fee of $75 per room. 2 dogs may be allowed.

Days Inn Point Richmond
915 W Cutting Blvd
Richmond, CA
510-237-3000 (800-329-7466)
Dogs of all sizes are allowed. Dogs are allowed for a nightly pet fee.

Extended Stay America Richmond - Hilltop Mall
3170 Garrity Way
Richmond, CA
510-222-7383 (800-804-3724)
One dog is allowed per suite. There is a $25 per night additional pet fee up to $150 for an entire stay.

Best Western China Lake Inn
400 S China Lake Boulevard
Ridgecrest, CA
760-371-2300 (800-780-7234)
Dogs of all sizes are allowed. Dogs are allowed for a nightly pet fee.

Econo Lodge Inn & Suites
201 W. Inyokern Rd.
Ridgecrest, CA
760-446-2551 (877-424-6423)
Dogs of all sizes are allowed.

Motel 6 - Ridgecrest
535 China Lake Blvd
Ridgecrest, CA
760-375-6866 (800-466-8356)
This motel welcomes your pets to stay with you.

La Quinta Inn Ripon
1524 Colony Road

Ripon, CA
209-599-8999 (800-531-5900)
Dogs of all sizes are allowed. There
are no additional pet fees. Dogs
must be leashed and cleaned up
after. Multiple dogs may be allowed.

Econo Lodge
10705 Magnolia Ave.
Riverside, CA
951-351-2424 (877-424-6423)
Dogs of all sizes are allowed. Dogs
are allowed for a pet fee of $10.00
per pet per night.

Motel 6 - Riverside East
1260 University Ave
Riverside, CA
951-784-2131 (800-466-8356)
This motel welcomes your pets to
stay with you.

Motel 6 - Riverside South
3663 La Sierra Ave
Riverside, CA
951-351-0764 (800-466-8356)
This motel welcomes your pets to
stay with you.

Rodeway Inn
10518 Magnolia Ave
Riverside, CA
951-359-0770 (877-424-6423)
Dogs up to 60 pounds are allowed.
Dogs are allowed for a pet fee of
$20.00 per pet per night. Two dogs
are allowed per room.

Howard Johnson O'Cairns Inn and
Suites
4420 Rocklin Raod
Rocklin, CA
916-624-4500 (800-446-4656)
Dogs are welcome at this hotel.

Staybridge Suites Rocklin
6664 Lonetree Blvd.
Rocklin, CA
916-781-7500 (877-270-6405)
Dogs up to 80 pounds are allowed.
Pets allowed with an additional pet
fee. Up to $75 for 1-6 nights and up
to $150 for 7+ nights. A pet
agreement must be signed at check-
in.

Doubletree Hotel
One Doubletree Drive
Rohnert Park, CA
707-584-5466 (800-222-TREE
(8733))
Located in the heart of the state's
central wine country, this luxury hotel
offers a number of on site amenities
for all level of travelers - including
their signature chocolate chip
cookies at check in, plus a

convenient location to hundreds of
wineries, and shopping, dining, and
recreation areas. Dogs up to about
50 pounds (exceptions may be
made for show dogs) are allowed
for an additional pet fee of $35 per
night per room. Multiple dogs may
be allowed.

Motel 6 - Rohnert Park
6145 Commerce Blvd
Rohnert Park, CA
707-585-8888 (800-466-8356)
This motel welcomes your pets to
stay with you.

Motel 6 - Los Angeles Rosemead
1001 San Gabriel Blvd
Rosemead, CA
626-572-6076 (800-466-8356)
This motel welcomes your pets to
stay with you.

Extended Stay America
Sacramento - Roseville
1000 Lead Hill Blvd.
Roseville, CA
916-781-9001 (800-804-3724)
One dog is allowed per suite. There
is a $25 per night additional pet fee
up to $150 for an entire stay.

Residence Inn Roseville
1930 Taylor Road
Roseville, CA
916-772-5500 (800-331-3131)
In addition to offering a convenient
location to local major corporations,
and shopping, dining, and
entertainment areas, this hotel also
provides a number of in-house
amenities, including a daily buffet
breakfast and an evening social
hour. Dogs are allowed for an
additional one time pet fee of $100
per room. Multiple dogs may be
allowed.

Motel 6 - Los Angeles-rowland
Heights/pomona
18970 Labin Ct
Rowland Heights, CA
626-964-5333 (800-466-8356)
This motel welcomes your pets to
stay with you.

Motel 6 - Riverside West
6830 Valley Way
Rubidoux, CA
951-681-6666 (800-466-8356)
This motel welcomes your pets to
stay with you.

Best Western Expo Inn & Suites
1413 Howe Avenue
Sacramento, CA
916-922-9833 (800-780-7234)

Dogs of all sizes are allowed. Dogs
are allowed for a pet fee of $25.00
per pet per night.

Best Western Sandman Motel
236 Jibboom Street
Sacramento, CA
916-443-6515 (800-780-7234)
Dogs of all sizes are allowed. Dogs
are allowed for a pet fee.

Canterbury Inn Hotel
1900 Canterbury Rd
Sacramento, CA
916-927-0927
This inn is located about a 5-10
minute drive from Old Sacramento.
Guest laundry services are available.
To get there from Hwy 160, take the
Leisure Lane ramp towards
Canterbury Rd. Turn right onto
Canterbury Rd. Two small dogs or 1
large dog are allowed for an
additional fee of $10 per night per
pct. 2 dogs may be allowed.

Clarion Hotel Mansion Inn
700 16th St.
Sacramento, CA
916-444-8000 (877-424-6423)
Dogs up to 50 pounds are allowed.
Dogs are allowed for a pet fee of
$50.00 per pet per stay. Two dogs
are allowed per room.

Days Inn Downtown Sacramento
228 Jibboom Street
Sacramento, CA
916-443-4811 (800-329-7466)
Dogs of all sizes are allowed. Dogs
are allowed for a pet fee of $10 per
pet per night.

Days Inn /North Highlands
Sacramento
3425 Orange Grove Ave
Sacramento, CA
916-488-4100 (800-329-7466)
Dogs are welcome at this hotel.

Doubletree Hotel
2001 Point West Way
Sacramento, CA
916-929-8855 (800-222-TREE
(8733))
Although conveniently located across
the street from the Arden Mall
Shopping Center; only 20 minutes to
the Sacramento International Airport,
just a couple of blocks to Cal Expo,
and only minutes to the State
Capitol, this full service hotel also
offers a number of on site amenities
for business and leisure travelers.
Dogs are allowed for an additional
one time pet fee of $50 per room. 2
dogs may be allowed.

Econo Lodge
711 16th St.
Sacramento, CA
916-443-6631 (877-424-6423)
Dogs of all sizes are allowed. Dogs are allowed for a pet fee of $6.00 per pet per night.

Extended Stay America Sacramento - Arden Way
2100 Harvard St.
Sacramento, CA
916-921-9942 (800-804-3724)
One dog is allowed per suite. There is a $25 per night additional pet fee up to $150 for an entire stay.

Extended Stay America Sacramento - Northgate
3825 Rosin Ct.
Sacramento, CA
916-920-8199 (800-804-3724)
One dog is allowed per suite. There is a $25 per night additional pet fee up to $150 for an entire stay.

Hawthorn Suites
321 Bercut Drive
Sacramento, CA
916-441-1200 (800-527-1133)
sacramentohawthorn.com/
In addition to providing a convenient location to many local sites and activities, this all-suite hotel offers a number of amenities for business and leisure travelers, including their signature breakfast buffet and beautifully appointed rooms. Dogs are allowed for an additional one time fee of $50 per pet. 2 dogs may be allowed.

Holiday Inn Express Sacramento Convention Center
728 Sixteenth Street
Sacramento, CA
916-444-4436 (877-270-6405)
Dogs of all sizes are allowed. Dogs are allowed for a pet fee of $50.00 per pet per night.

Homestead Studio Suites Sacramento - South Natomas
2810 Gateway Oaks Dr.
Sacramento, CA
916-564-7500 (800-804-3724)
One dog is allowed per suite. There is a $25 per night additional pet fee up to $150 for an entire stay.

La Quinta Inn Sacramento Downtown
200 Jibboom St.
Sacramento, CA
916-448-8100 (800-531-5900)
Dogs of all sizes are allowed. There

are no additional pet fees. Dogs must be leashed and cleaned up after. Multiple dogs may be allowed.

Motel 6 - Cal Expo Sacramento
2030 Arden Way
Sacramento, CA
916-929-5600 (800-466-8356)
This motel welcomes your pets to stay with you.

Motel 6 - Sacramento Old Sacramento North
227 Jibboom St
Sacramento, CA
916-441-0733 (800-466-8356)
Your pets are welcome to stay here with you.

Motel 6 - Sacramento Central
7850 College Town Dr
Sacramento, CA
916-383-8110 (800-466-8356)
Your pets are welcome to stay here with you.

Motel 6 - Sacramento Downtown
1415 30th St
Sacramento, CA
916-457-0777 (800-466-8356)
Your pets are welcome to stay here with you.

Motel 6 - Sacramento North
5110 Interstate Ave
Sacramento, CA
916-331-8100 (800-466-8356)
Your pets are welcome to stay here with you.

Motel 6 - Sacramento South
7407 Elsie Ave
Sacramento, CA
916-689-6555 (800-466-8356)
Your pets are welcome to stay here with you.

Motel 6 - Sacramento Southwest
7780 Stockton Blvd
Sacramento, CA
916-689-9141 (800-466-8356)
Your pets are welcome to stay here with you.

Quality Inn Natomas-Sacramento
3796 Northgate Blvd
Sacramento, CA
916-927-7117 (877-424-6423)
Dogs up to 50 pounds are allowed.

Radisson Hotel Sacramento
500 Leisure Lane
Sacramento, CA
916-922-2020 (800-395-7046)
radissonsac.com
Dogs of all sizes are allowed. There is a $50 one time additional pet fee.

Ramada Limited CA Sacramento
350 Bercut Drive
Sacramento, CA
916-442-6971 (800-272-6232)
Dogs of all sizes are allowed. Dogs are allowed for a pet fee of $20 per pet per night.

Red Lion
1401 Arden Way
Sacramento, CA
916-922-8041
There is a $25 one time pet fee per room. There are no additional pet fees for R&R members, and the R&R program is free to sign up. Multiple dogs may be allowed.

Residence Inn Sacramento Airport Natomas
2410 W El Camino Avenue
Sacramento, CA
916-649-1300 (800-331-3131)
In addition to offering a convenient location to the Sacramento Airport, and shopping, dining, and entertainment areas, this hotel also provides a number of in-house amenities, including a daily buffet breakfast and an evening social hour. Dogs are allowed for an additional one time pet fee of $100 per room. Multiple dogs may be allowed.

Residence Inn Sacramento Cal Expo
1530 Howe Avenue
Sacramento, CA
916-920-9111 (800-218-7214)
Sitting only a short walk from the Cal Expo State Fairgrounds, and numerous shopping, dining, and entertainment venues, this all suite, upscale hotel also offers a number of in-house amenities including a daily buffet breakfast and evening receptions. Dogs are allowed for an additional one time pet fee of $100 per room. Multiple dogs may be allowed.

Residence Inn Sacramento Downtown at Capitol Park
1121 15th Street
Sacramento, CA
916-443-0500 (800-331-3131)
Sitting only a short walk from the State Capitol, the Convention Center, and numerous world class dining, and entertainment venues, this all suite, upscale hotel also offers a number of in-house amenities including a daily buffet breakfast and Manager Receptions. Dogs are allowed for an additional one time fee of $100 per pet. Multiple dogs may be allowed.

Sheraton Grand Sacramento Hotel
1230 J St. (13th & J St)
Sacramento, CA
916-447-1700 (888-625-5144)
The dog-friendly Sheraton Grand
Sacramento Hotel is located directly
across the street from the Capitol
Park and within easy walking
distance of Downtown Plaza and Old
Sacramento. Dogs are allowed for a
$100 refundable pet deposit. Dogs
are allowed on the 6th floor only, and
they may not be left alone in the
room. 2 dogs may be allowed.

Staybridge Suites Sacramento
Natomas
140 Promenade Circle
Sacramento, CA
916-575-7907 (877-270-6405)
Dogs up to 80 pounds are allowed.
Pets allowed with an additional pet
fee. Up to $75 for 1-6 nights and up
to $150 for 7+ nights. A pet
agreement must be signed at check-
in.

TownePlace Suites Sacramento Cal
Expo
1784 Tribute Road
Sacramento, CA
916-920-5400 (800-257-3000)
This all suite inn offers a central
location to all the major areas of the
city and surrounding towns, plus they
sit only a short distance from Arden
Mall and the California State
Fairgrounds and Exposition Center.
Dogs are allowed for an additional
one time fee of $100 per room. 2
dogs may be allowed.

Travelodge / Rancho Cordova
Sacramento
9646 Micron Avenue
Sacramento, CA
916-361-3131 (800-578-7878)
Dogs of all sizes are allowed. Dogs
are allowed for a nightly pet fee.

Motel 6 - Salinas North Monterey
Area
140 Kern St
Salinas, CA
831-753-1711 (800-466-8356)
Your pets are welcome to stay here
with you.

Motel 6 - Salinas South Monterey
Area
1257 De La Torre Blvd
Salinas, CA
831-757-3077 (800-466-8356)
Your pets are welcome to stay here
with you.

Residence Inn Salinas Monterey
17215 El Rancho Way
Salinas, CA
831-775-0410 (800-331-3131)
Only about 20 minutes from scenic
Monterey and Carmel-by-the-Sea
and to a number of top agricultural
firms and world class attractions,
this all suite inn also provides a
number of in-house amenities,
including a daily buffet and evening
social hours. Dogs are allowed for
an additional one time pet fee of
$100 per room. Multiple dogs may
be allowed.

Super 8 Salinas
131 Kern Street
Salinas, CA
831-758-4693 (800-800-8000)
Dogs of all sizes are allowed. Dogs
are allowed for a pet fee of $15 per
pet per stay.

Best Western Hospitality Lane
294 E Hospitality Ln
San Bernardino, CA
909-381-1681 (800-780-7234)
Dogs up to 50 pounds are allowed.
Dogs are allowed for a nightly pet
fee.

Days Inn -University Parkway San
Bernardino
2000 Ostrems Way
San Bernardino, CA
909-880-8425 (800-329-7466)
Dogs of all sizes are allowed. Dogs
are allowed for a pet fee.

Days Inn /Redlands San Bernardino
1909 Business Center Dr.
San Bernardino, CA
909-889-0090 (800-329-7466)
Dogs are welcome at this hotel.

Hilton Hotel
285 E Hospitality Lane
San Bernardino, CA
909-889-0133 (800-HILTONS (445-
8667))
Located in the heart of the city, this
upscale hotel offers numerous on
site amenities for business and
leisure travelers, plus a convenient
location to an international airport,
business, shopping, dining, and
entertainment areas. Dogs up to 65
pounds are allowed for an
additional one time fee of $75 per
pet. 2 dogs may be allowed.

Motel 6 - San Bernardino North
1960 Ostrems Way
San Bernardino, CA
909-887-8191 (800-466-8356)
This motel welcomes your pets to

stay with you.

Motel 6 - San Bernardino South
111 Redlands Blvd
San Bernardino, CA
909-825-6666 (800-466-8356)
This motel welcomes your pets to
stay with you.

Residence Inn San Bernardino
1040 E Harriman Place
San Bernardino, CA
909-382-4564 (800-331-3131)
This all suite inn features a
convenient location to major
corporations, shopping, dining, and
entertainment areas, plus they also
offer a number of in-house
amenities, including a daily buffet
breakfast and evening socials
Monday to Thursday. Dogs are
allowed for an additional one time
pet fee of $75 per room. Multiple
dogs may be allowed.

Super 8 /Hospitality Lane San
Bernardino
225 E Hospitality Lane
San Bernardino, CA
909-888-6777 (800-800-8000)
Dogs are welcome at this hotel.

Staybridge Suites San Francisco
Airport
1350 Huntington Ave.
San Bruno, CA
650-588-0770 (877-270-6405)
Dogs up to 80 pounds are allowed.
Pets allowed with an additional pet
fee. Up to $75 for 1-6 nights and up
to $150 for 7+ nights. A pet
agreement must be signed at check-
in.

Homestead Studio Suites San
Francisco - San Carlos
3 Circle Star Way
San Carlos, CA
650-368-2600 (800-804-3724)
One dog is allowed per suite. There
is a $25 per night additional pet fee
up to $150 for an entire stay.

Best Western Casablanca Inn
1601 N El Camino Real
San Clemente, CA
949-361-1644 (800-780-7234)
Dogs of all sizes are allowed. Dogs
are allowed for a pet fee of $25.00
per pet per night.

Holiday Inn San Clemente (Camp
Pendleton)
111 S. Ave. De La Estrella
San Clemente, CA
949-361-3000 (877-270-6405)
Dogs of all sizes are allowed. Dogs

are allowed for a nightly pet fee.

Best Western Lamplighter Inn & Suites
6474 El Cajon Boulevard
San Diego, CA
619-582-3088 (800-780-7234)
Dogs of all sizes are allowed. Dogs are allowed for a pet fee of $15.00 per pet per night.

Doubletree Hotel
7450 Hazard Center Drive
San Diego, CA
619-297-5466 (800-222-TREE (8733))
This stylish, upscale hotel offers a number of on site amenities for business and leisure travelers, plus a convenient location to world class shopping, dining, and entertainment areas. Dogs are allowed for an additional one time pet fee of $75 per room. Multiple dogs may be allowed.

Doubletree Hotel San Diego/Del Mar
11915 El Camino Real
San Diego, CA
858-481-5900 (800-222-TREE (8733))
Sitting central to world class beaches, tourist/animal attractions, championship golf courses, and outstanding dining and shopping areas, this resort style hotel also offers a number of on site amenities for all level of travelers. Dogs up to 50 pounds are allowed for an additional one time pet fee of $50 per room. 2 dogs may be allowed.

Extended Stay America San Diego - Hotel Circle
2087 Hotel Cir. S.
San Diego, CA
619-296-5570 (800-804-3724)
One dog is allowed per suite. There is a $25 per night additional pet fee up to $150 for an entire stay.

Extended Stay America San Diego - Mission Valley - Stadium
3860 Murphy Canyon Rd.
San Diego, CA
858-292-8927 (800-804-3724)
One dog is allowed per suite. There is a $25 per night additional pet fee up to $150 for an entire stay.

Four Points by Sheraton San Diego
8110 Aero Drive
San Diego, CA
858-277-8888 (888-625-5144)
Dogs are allowed for a $100 deposit; $25 is non-refundable. Dogs may not be left alone in the room.

Harborview Inn and Suites
550 W Grape Street
San Diego, CA
619-233-7799
This 3 story hotel is only minutes from a variety of attractions and recreational opportunities. Some of the amenities include a free continental breakfast, room service, and accommodations for both the business and leisure traveler. Dogs of all sizes are welcome for a $10 per night per pet additional fee. Dogs may not be left unattended in the room at any time, and they must be quiet, leashed, and cleaned up after.

Hawthorn Suites
1335 Hotel Circle S
San Diego, CA
619-299-3501 (800-527-1133)
In addition to providing a convenient location to many local sites and activities, this all-suite hotel offers a number of amenities for business and leisure travelers, including their signature breakfast buffet and beautifully appointed rooms. Dogs are allowed for an additional one time pet fee of $75 per room. Multiple dogs may be allowed.

Heritage Inn/Sea World San Diego Hotel
3333 Channel Way
San Diego, CA
619-223-9500 (877-300-9126)
In addition to numerous on-site amenities and its location in the Sea World Sports Arena area, this hotel also offers a convenient location to many of the areas star attractions, shopping, dining, and commerce areas. Dogs up to 50 pounds are allowed for an additional fee of $10 per night per pet. 2 dogs may be allowed.

Hilton Hotel
901 Camino del Rio S
San Diego, CA
619-543-9000 (800-HILTONS (445-8667))
Located in the heart of the city, this upscale hotel offers numerous on site amenities for business and leisure travelers, plus a convenient location to business, shopping, dining, historical, and entertainment areas. Dogs are allowed for an additional pet fee of $50 per room. Multiple dogs may be allowed.

Holiday Inn San Diego-On The Bay
1355 North Harbor Drive
San Diego, CA
619-232-3861 (877-270-6405)

Dogs of all sizes are allowed. Dogs are allowed for a pet fee of $25.00 per pet per night. Two dogs are allowed per room.

Holiday Inn San Diego-Rancho Bernardo
17065 W. Bernardo Dr.
San Diego, CA
858-485-6530 (877-270-6405)
Dogs are welcome at this hotel. There is a $50 one time additional pet fee.

Homestead Studio Suites San Diego - Mission Valley
7444 Mission Valley Rd.
San Diego, CA
619-299-2292 (800-804-3724)
One dog is allowed per suite. There is a $25 per night additional pet fee up to $150 for an entire stay.

Homestead Studio Suites San Diego - Sorrento Mesa
9880 Pacific Heights Blvd.
San Diego, CA
858-623-0100 (800-804-3724)
One dog is allowed per suite. There is a $25 per night additional pet fee up to $150 for an entire stay.

Hotel Indigo San Diego CA Hotel
509 9th Avenue
San Diego, CA
619-727-4000
hotelsandiegodowntown.com
Dogs of all sizes are allowed. There are no additional pet fees.

Hotel Solamar
453 6th Avenue
San Diego, CA
619-531-8740 (877-230-0300)
hotelsolamar.com/
This hip luxury boutique hotel features a vibrant décor, a great location to the area's best shopping, dinning, and entertainment, and a full list of amenities for the business or leisure traveler. They feature elegantly appointed rooms, an evening wine hour, 24 hour room service from the adjacent J6Restaurant and J6Bar, a pool and spa, and several in-room amenities. Dogs of all sizes are welcome for no additional pet fee. Dogs must be friendly, quiet, leashed and cleaned up after, and the Dog in Room sign put on the door if they are in the room alone. 2 dogs may be allowed.

La Quinta Inn San Diego Rancho Penasquitos
10185 Paseo Montril
San Diego, CA

858-484-8800 (800-531-5900)
Dogs up to 60 pounds are allowed.
There are no additional pet fees, but
a credit card must be on file. Dogs
must be crated when left alone in the
room or place the Do Not Disturb
sign on the door. Dogs must be
leashed and cleaned up after. 2 dogs
may be allowed.

Marriott San Diego Hotel & Marina
333 W Harbor Drive
San Diego, CA
619-234-1500 (800-228-9290)
Located on the waterfront with a 446
slip marina, this luxury hotel sits
close to a number of the city's star
attractions, world class shopping and
dining venues, and major
corporations; plus they offer a
number of in-house amenities for all
level of travelers. Dogs are allowed
for an additional one time fee of $75
per room. Multiple dogs may be
allowed.

Marriott San Diego Mission Valley
8757 Rio San Diego Drive
San Diego, CA
619-692-3800 (800-842-5329)
Besides offering a number of in-
house amenities for all level of
travelers, this luxury hotel also
provides a convenient location to a
number of premier attractions,
businesses, shopping, dining, and
entertainment areas. Dogs are
allowed for an additional one time
fee of $75 per room. 2 dogs may be
allowed.

Motel 6 - San Diego Hotel Circle
2424 Hotel Circle
San Diego, CA
619-296-1612 (800-466-8356)
This motel welcomes your pets to
stay with you.

Motel 6 - San Diego Airport/harbor
2353 Pacific Hwy
San Diego, CA
619-232-8931 (800-466-8356)
This motel welcomes your pets to
stay with you.

Motel 6 - San Diego Downtown
1546 2nd Ave
San Diego, CA
619-236-9292 (800-466-8356)
This motel welcomes your pets to
stay with you.

Motel 6 - San Diego North
5592 Clairemont Mesa Blv
San Diego, CA
858-268-9758 (800-466-8356)
This motel welcomes your pets to

stay with you.

Ocean Villa Inn
5142 West Point Loma Blvd
San Diego, CA
619-224-3481 (800-759-0012)
oceanvillainn.com
Ocean Villa Inn is in the Ocean
Beach district near the Dog Beach.
They allow pets in all of their
downstairs rooms with a $100.00
refundable deposit and a one time
per stay fee of $25.00.

Old Town Inn
4444 Pacific H
San Diego, CA
619-260-8024 (800-643-3025)
oldtown-inn.com/oldtown.htm
This scenic inn offers deluxe and
economy units, a complimentary
continental breakfast, heated
swimming pool, close proximity to
several attractions and recreational
opportunities, and beautiful well-
kept grounds. Dogs are allowed for
an additional fee of $15 per night
per pet. Dogs may not be left alone
in the room, and they must be
leashed and cleaned up after.

Pacific Inn Hotel & Suites
1655 Pacific Hwy
San Diego, CA
619-232-6391
There is a $20 per day per pet
additional pet fee. Dogs must be
crated and a contact number left
with the front desk if there is a dog
alone in the room. Multiple dogs
may be allowed.

Premier Inn
2484 Hotel Circle Place
San Diego, CA
619-291-8252
premierinns.com
Dogs up to 40 pounds are allowed
for no additional fee. Aggressive
breeds are not allowed. Dogs may
not be left alone in the room. 2 dogs
may be allowed.

Ramada Limited Airport San Diego
1403 Rosecrans St
San Diego, CA
619-225-9461 (800-272-6232)
Dogs are welcome at this hotel.

Residence Inn San Diego Central
5400 Kearny Mesa Road
San Diego, CA
858-278-2100 (800-331-3131)
Centrally located in the heart of the
county's inland area with easy
access to 3 interstates, this all suite
hotel gives a great starting point to

many world class attractions and
activities. They also offer a daily
buffet breakfast and evening socials
Monday through Thursday with light
dinner fare. Dogs up to 75 pounds
are allowed for an additional one
time pet fee of $75 per room. 2 dogs
may be allowed.

Residence Inn San Diego Downtown
1747 Pacific Highway
San Diego, CA
619-338-8200 (800-331-3131)
Overlooking the bay in the heart of
downtown, this upscale, all suite
hotel is surrounded by a number of
attractions and activities for the
business or leisure travelers; plus
they also offer a daily buffet
breakfast and evening social hours.
Dogs up to 65 pounds are allowed
for an additional one time pet fee of
$75 per room. 2 dogs may be
allowed.

Residence Inn San Diego Mission
Valley
1865 Hotel Circle S
San Diego, CA
619-881-3600 (800-331-3131)
Besides offering a convenient
location to universities, businesses,
historical sites, and shopping, dining,
and entertainment areas, this hotel
also provides a number of in-house
amenities, including a daily buffet
breakfast and complementary
evening receptions Monday to
Thursday. Dogs are allowed for an
additional one time pet fee of $75
(plus tax) per room. Multiple dogs
may be allowed.

Residence Inn San Diego Rancho
Bernardo/Carmel Mountain Ranch
11002 Rancho Carmel Drive
San Diego, CA
858-673-1900 (800-331-3131)
In addition to offering a convenient
location to business, shopping,
dining, and entertainment areas, this
hotel also provides a number of in-
house amenities, including a daily
buffet breakfast and an evening
social hour. Dogs are allowed for an
additional one time pet fee of $100
per room. Multiple dogs may be
allowed.

Residence Inn San Diego Rancho
Bernardo/Scripps Poway
12011 Scripps Highland Drive
San Diego, CA
858-635-5724 (800-331-3131)
Some of the amenities at this all-
suite inn include a daily buffet
breakfast, evening socials Monday
through Thursday with light dinner

fare, weekly barbecues, and a complimentary grocery shopping service. Dogs are allowed for an additional one time pet fee of $75 per room. Multiple dogs may be allowed.

Residence Inn San Diego Sorrento Mesa/Sorrento Valley
5995 Pacific Mesa Court
San Diego, CA
858-552-9100 (800-331-3131)
This ENERGY STAR®, all suite hotel sits central to numerous business, historic, shopping, dining, and entertainment areas; plus they offer a number of in-house amenities, including a daily buffet breakfast and evening socials. Dogs are allowed for an additional one time pet fee of $100 per room. Multiple dogs may be allowed.

Sheraton San Diego Hotel and Marina
1380 Harbor Island Drive
San Diego, CA
619-291-2900 (888-625-5144)
Dogs up to 80 pounds are allowed. There are no additional pet fees. Multiple dogs may be allowed.

Sheraton Suites San Diego
701 A. Street
San Diego, CA
619-696-9800 (888-625-5144)
Dogs up to 80 pounds are allowed. There are no additional pet fees.

Staybridge Suites San Diego Rancho Bernardo Area
11855 Avenue Of Industry
San Diego, CA
858-487-0900 (877-270-6405)
Dogs up to 80 pounds are allowed. Pets allowed with an additional pet fee. Up to $75 for 1-6 nights and up to $150 for 7+ nights. A pet agreement must be signed at check-in.

Staybridge Suites San Diego-Sorrento Mesa
6639 Mira Mesa Boulevard
San Diego, CA
858-453-5343 (877-270-6405)
Dogs up to 80 pounds are allowed. Pets allowed with an additional pet fee. Up to $75 for 1-6 nights and up to $150 for 7+ nights. A pet agreement must be signed at check-in.

The Hohe's Beach House
4905 Dixie Drive
San Diego, CA
858-273-0324
The Hohe House is a non-smoking 2

bedroom/2 bath, Ocean View, vacation rental in the Pacific Beach neighborhood. The Hohe House sleeps 6 and is fully furnished with all linens provided. There is a 4 night minimum during the low season, $200 nightly, (Mid-Sept to Mid-June), and rates vary for low to high season, from $1275 to $1875 weekly. A $350 refundable, security deposit is required to reserve a week's stay. There is a $10 per night pet fee. Well-behaved dogs over 18 months and under 80 pounds are welcome.

The Sofia Hotel
150 West Broadway
San Diego, CA
619-234-9200 (800-826-0009)
TheSofiaHotel.com
Dogs of all sizes are allowed. There is a $50 one time additional pet fee.

U. S. Grant Hotel
326 Broadway
San Diego, CA
619-232-3121 (800-237-5029)
usgrant.net/
Listed in the National Registrar of Historic Places, this world class hotel has been a luxury landmark since 1910, and a recent $52 million dollar renovation has refined its level of elegance and sophistication. There are 270 lavish guest rooms and 47 suites, gourmet dining, a lounge, business center, gift store, thousands of square feet of event space, a romantic roof-top terrace, and many in-room amenities. Dogs up to 75 pounds are welcome for an additional one time pet fee of $150 per room. Dogs may not be left alone in the room at any time, and they must be quiet, well mannered, leashed, and cleaned up after. 2 dogs may be allowed.

Vagabond Inn-Point Loma
1325 Scott St.
San Diego, CA
619-224-3371 (800-522-1555)
vagabondinn.com
This motel is located less than five miles from downtown San Diego and Sea World. It is close to the popular Dog Beach in Ocean Beach. The motel features an outdoor swimming pool, family unit rooms, cable television and more hotel amenities. Dogs up to about 70-75 pounds are allowed and there is an additional $10 per day pet fee. Multiple dogs may be allowed.

W San Diego

421 West B. Street
San Diego, CA
619-231-8220
Dogs up to 65 pounds are allowed for an additional cleaning fee of $100 plus $25 per night per pet with a credit card on file. Dogs must be declared at the time of registration. Pets receive a special welcome with a pet amenity kit that includes a custom pet bed, food and water dishes with a floor mat, a doggy menu, Pet-in-Room sign, treats, pet tag, a toy, and more. The concierge can also offer additional services such as dog-walking and information about local dog services and parks. Dogs must be removed or crated for housekeeping or for any in-room services.

Extended Stay America Los Angeles - San Dimas
601 W. Bonita Ave.
San Dimas, CA
909-394-1022 (800-804-3724)
One dog is allowed per suite. There is a $25 per night additional pet fee up to $150 for an entire stay.

Motel 6 - Los Angeles San Dimas
502 Arrow Hwy
San Dimas, CA
909-592-5631 (800-466-8356)
This motel welcomes your pets to stay with you.

Red Roof Inn San Dimas
204 North Village Court
San Dimas, CA
909-599-2362 (800-RED-ROOF)
One well-behaved family pet per room. Guest must notify front desk upon arrival. Guest is liable for any damages. In consideration of all guests, pets must never be left unattended in the guest rooms.

Argonaut Hotel Fisherman's Wharf
495 Jefferson Street
San Francisco, CA
415-563-0800 (866-415-0704)
argonauthotel.com
This Kimpton boutique hotel allows dogs of all sizes. The hotel is an entirely non-smoking hotel and is located near Fisherman's Wharf. There are no additional pet fees.

Best Western Americania
121 7th Street
San Francisco, CA
415-626-0200 (800-780-7234)
Dogs up to 50 pounds are allowed.

Best Western The Hotel California
580 Geary Street

San Francisco, CA
415-441-2700 (800-780-7234)
Dogs of all sizes are allowed. Dogs are allowed for a pet fee of $50.00 per pet per stay.

Best Western Tuscan Inn
425 N. Point Street
San Francisco, CA
800-648-4626 (800-780-7234)
tuscaninn.com
Well behaved dogs are allowed for no additional pet fee.

Campton Place Hotel
340 Stockton Street
San Francisco, CA
415-781-5555
camptonplace.com
This dog-friendly hotel holds many awards including 'Top 100 Hotels in the World' by Conde Nast Traveler. Room rates are approximately $230 to $345 a night. Dogs are allowed for an additional one time fee of $100 (+ tax) per pet. 2 dogs may be allowed.

Fairmont Heritage Place, Ghirardelli Square
900 N Point, Suite D100
San Francisco, CA
415-268-5706 (888-991-4300)
fairmont.com/ghirardelli
Located in the landmark setting of Ghirardelli Square and overlooking the bay, this luxury, full-service hotel offers numerous in-house amenities and services as well as a central location to many of the city's star attractions and activities. They offer 1, 2, and 3 bedroom suites. Well mannered dogs are allowed for an additional fee of $20 to $45 per night per pet - it depending on 1 or 2 dogs and the size of the suite. Aggressive breeds are not allowed. 2 dogs may be allowed.

Four Seasons Hotel San Francisco
757 Market St.
San Francisco, CA
415-633-3000
Dogs are allowed for no additional pet fee. Dogs may not be left alone in the room. Pet sitting services are available.

Grand Hyatt San Francisco
345 Stockton Street
San Francisco, CA
415-398-1234
Located on Union Square, this luxury hotel offers dining, nightlife and is pet-friendly. Well-behaved dogs of all sizes are allowed and there is a $75 per stay additional pet fee.

Harbor Court Hotel
165 Steuart Street
San Francisco, CA
415-882-1300
harborcourthotel.com/
Well-behaved dogs of all sizes are welcome at this pet-friendly hotel. Amenities include a complimentary evening wine reception, and an adjacent fitness room. There are no pet fees, just sign a pet liability form. 2 dogs may be allowed.

Hilton Hotel
333 O'Farrell Street
San Francisco, CA
415-771-1400 (800-HILTONS (445-8667))
Located in the heart of the city, this upscale hotel offers numerous on site amenities for business and leisure travelers, plus a convenient location to numerous beaches, business districts, shopping, dining, historical, and entertainment areas. Dogs up to 75 pounds are allowed for an additional one time pet fee of $75 per room. 2 dogs may be allowed.

Holiday Inn San Francisco-Fishermans Wharf
1300 Columbus Avenue
San Francisco, CA
415-771-9000 (877-270-6405)
Dogs up to 50 pounds are allowed. Dogs are allowed for a pet fee.

Hotel Beresford Arms
701 Post Street
San Francisco, CA
415-673-2600 (800-533-6533)
beresford.com/arms/default.htm
they must be declared at the time of reservations. Dogs may not be left alone in the room, and they must be leashed and cleaned up after at all times.

Hotel Diva
440 Geary Street
San Francisco, CA
800-553-1900
hoteldiva.com/
At the hub of Union Square, this ultra modern hotel offers exceptional personalized service for the leisure or business traveler, and a convenient location for a wide variety of shopping, entertainment, and dining opportunities. One dog up to 40 pounds is allowed for an additional one time pet fee of $25. Dogs must be leashed, cleaned up after, and crated if left alone in the room.

Hotel Metropolis

25 Mason Street
San Francisco, CA
800-553-9100
hotelmetropolis.com/
This 1930, 105 room hotel will indulge your senses with a bit of paradise featuring rich fabrics, bright colors, custom furnishings, and each floor of this 10 story hotel gives reflection to the elements of earth, wind, fire, or water. They feature many in room amenities, exceptional personalized service for the leisure or business traveler, and a convenient location for a wide variety of shopping, entertainment, and dining opportunities. One dog up to 40 pounds is allowed for an additional one time pet fee of $25. Dogs must be leashed, cleaned up after, and crated if left alone in the room.

Hotel Monaco
501 Geary Street
San Francisco, CA
415-292-0100 (866-622-5284)
monaco-sf.com
This Kimpton boutique hotel allows dogs of all sizes. There are no additional pet fees.

Hotel Palomar
12 Fourth Street
San Francisco, CA
415-348-1111
hotelpalomar.com/
Well-behaved dogs of all sizes are welcome at this pet-friendly hotel. The boutique hotel offers both rooms and suites. Hotel amenities include room service, an on-site 24 hour fitness room and complimentary high speed Internet access. There are no pet fees, just sign a pet liability form. Pets cannot be left alone in the room.

Hotel Triton
342 Grant Avenue
San Francisco, CA
415-394-0500
hoteltriton.com
Well-behaved dogs of all sizes are welcome at this pet-friendly hotel. The boutique hotel offers both rooms and suites. Hotel amenities include a complimentary evening wine reception, room service, and a 24 hour on-site fitness room. There are no pet fees, just sign a pet liability form.

Hotel Union Square
114 Powell Street
San Francisco, CA
800-553-1900
hotelunionsquare.com/

Known as the city's original boutique-style hotel, and graced with a great location in Union Square right on the cable car line, this striking 1913 hotel offers 131 stylish guest rooms with full private baths, a 1930's Art Deco lobby, beautiful jewel toned décor, and many in-room amenities. One dog up to 40 pounds is allowed for an additional one time pet fee of $25. Dogs must be leashed, cleaned up after, and crated if left alone in the room.

Kensington Park Hotel
450 Post Street
San Francisco, CA
800-553-9100
kensingtonparkhotel.com/
This stylish hotel offers luxury, modern day conveniences, 92 richly detailed-finely appointed rooms, exceptional personalized service for the leisure or business traveler, and a convenient location for a wide variety of shopping, entertainment, and dining opportunities. They are also home to the Farallon Restaurant,,, an attraction in and of itself. One dog up to 40 pounds is allowed for an additional one time pet fee of $25. Dogs must be leashed, cleaned up after, and crated if left alone in the room.

Marina Motel - on Lombard Street
2576 Lombard St.
San Francisco, CA
415-921-9406 (800-346-6118)
marinamotel.com/
All friendly dogs are welcome regardless of size. Walk to the Golden Gate Bridge along Crissy Field beach five blocks away. Miles of hiking trails in the historical Presidio Park are nearby. All rooms have refrigerators, coffee makers, irons and hair dryers. There is no pet fee for stays of one week or longer otherwise there is a $10/night pet fee. Dogs may not be left unattended in the room at any time. There is free garage parking for overnight guests of the hotel.

Marriott San Francisco Fisherman's Wharf
1250 Columbus Avenue
San Francisco, CA
415-775-7555 (800-228-9290)
Located at Fisherman's Wharf near Pier 39, this luxury hotel sits close to a number of the city's star attractions, world class shopping and dining venues, entertainment areas, and major corporations; plus they offer a number of in-house amenities for all level of travelers. Dogs up to

50 pounds are allowed for an additional one time fee of $100 per room. 2 dogs may be allowed.

Monticello Inn
127 Ellis Street
San Francisco, CA
415-392-8800
monticelloinn.com
Well-behaved dogs of all sizes are welcome at this pet-friendly hotel. The boutique hotel offers both rooms and suites. Hotel amenities include complimentary evening wine service, evening room service, hotel library with magazines, newspapers and books, and a Borders Books and Music room service. There are no pet fees, just sign a pet liability form.

Motel 6 - San Francisco, Ca
895 Geary Street
San Francisco, CA
415-441-8220 (800-466-8356)
This motel welcomes your pets to stay with you.

Palace Hotel
2 New Montgomery Street
San Francisco, CA
415-512-1111
Dogs are allowed for an additional one time pet fee of $100 per room. Declare your pet at the time of registration and food/water bowls, a doggy bed, and treats will be waiting for your pooch upon arrival. This is a Sheraton Hotel. 2 dogs may be allowed.

Prescott Hotel
545 Post Street
San Francisco, CA
415-563-0303
prescotthotel.com/
Well-behaved dogs of all sizes are allowed at this pet-friendly hotel. The luxury boutique hotel is located in Union Square and offers both rooms and suites. Hotel amenities include room service and an on-site 24 hour fitness room. There are no pet fees, just sign a pet liability form.

San Francisco Lofts
1501 Mariposa, Suite 328
San Francisco, CA
415-355-1018
One to 2 dogs are allowed for an additional fee ranging from $50 to $100 depending on the unit. 2 dogs may be allowed.

Serrano Hotel
405 Taylor Street

San Francisco, CA
415-885-2500
serranohotel.com
Well-behaved dogs of all sizes are welcome at this pet-friendly hotel. The luxury boutique hotel offers both rooms and suites. Hotel amenities include an evening hospitality hour, and a 24 hour on-site fitness room. There are no pet fees, just sign a pet liability form. Multiple dogs may be allowed.

Sheraton Fisherman's Wharf Hotel
2500 Mason St.
San Francisco, CA
415-362-5500 (888-625-5144)
Dogs up to 80 pounds are allowed. Only 5 rooms are available in the hotel for dogs. You must sign a pet policy. Dogs are not allowed to be left alone in the room.

Sir Francis Drake Hotel
450 Powell Street
San Francisco, CA
415-392-7755 (800-795-7129)
The Sir Francis Drake is a Kimpton Hotel in downtown San Francisco. Since 1928, this elegant hotel offers accommodations in Union Square. Shopping, tourist sites and more are nearby. The Sir Francis Drake Hotel is pet-friendly and has a VIP (Very Important Pet Program). Pet sitting, pet grooming, pet walking and pet massage are available through the concierge.

Super 8 /Union Square Area San Francisco
415 OFarrell St
San Francisco, CA
415-928-6800 (800-800-8000)
Dogs are welcome at this hotel.

The Inn San Francisco
943 S Van Ness Avenue
San Francisco, CA
415-641-0188
Well behaved, friendly, dogs of all sizes are allowed. There are no additional pet fees. Dogs may not be left alone at any time and they are not allowed in the gardens. 2 dogs may be allowed.

The Laurel Inn
444 Presidio Ave.
San Francisco, CA
415-567-8467
thelaurelinn.com/
This pet-friendly hotel is a boutique hotel in San Francisco's atmospheric Pacific Heights neighborhood. This newly renovated hotel includes a classic 1960's modern architectural design. Amenities include a

complimentary continental breakfast served daily in the lobby, free indoor parking, laundry and valet service, room service from Dine-One-One and more. Dogs are allowed for no additional pet fee with a credit card on file. Dogs may not be left alone in the room. 2 dogs may be allowed.

The W San Francisco
181 3rd St.
San Francisco, CA
415-777-5300
Dogs are allowed for an additional cleaning fee of $100 with a credit card on file. Dogs must be declared at the time of registration. Pets receive a special welcome with a pet amenity kit that includes a custom pet bed, food and water dishes with a floor mat, a doggy menu, Pet-in-Room sign, treats, pet tag, a toy, and more. The concierge can also offer additional services such as dog-walking and information about local dog services and parks. Dogs must be removed or crated for housekeeping or for any in-room services.

Travelodge at the Presidio San Francisco
2755 Lombard Street
San Francisco, CA
415-931-8581 (800-578-7878)
Dogs of all sizes are allowed. Dogs are allowed for a nightly pet fee.

Travelodge by the Bay
1450 Lombard Street
San Francisco, CA
415-673-0691 (800-578-7878)
Dogs of all sizes are allowed. Dogs are allowed for a nightly pet fee.

Villa Florence Boutique Hotel
225 Powell Street
San Francisco, CA
866-823-4669
villaflorence.com/
Guests are immersed in an Italian Renaissance through the art, décor, and hospitality of this historic, boutique hotel. Some of the features here include an Italian restaurant, a classic Italian sidewalk café, a comprehensive business center, and a hosted daily evening wine hour. Dogs up to 50 pounds are allowed for no additional fee. There is a pet policy to sign at check in, and pet rooms are located on the 2nd floor. Dogs must be quiet, well behaved, leashed, cleaned up after, and a contact number left with the front desk if they are in the room alone.

Hilton Hotel

225 W Valley Blvd
San Gabriel, CA
626-270-2700 (800-HILTONS (445-8667))
This luxury hotel offers a number of on site amenities for business and leisure travelers, plus a convenient location to historical, business, shopping, dining, and entertainment areas. Dogs up to 75 pounds are allowed for a $75 refundable deposit plus an additional one time pet fee of $25 per room. 2 dogs may be allowed.

Crowne Plaza Hotel San Jose-Downtown
282 Almaden Blvd
San Jose, CA
408-998-0400 (877-270-6405)
Dogs of all sizes are allowed. Dogs are allowed for a pet fee.

Days Inn Airport San Jose
1280 N Fourth Street
San Jose, CA
408-437-9100 (800-329-7466)
Dogs are welcome at this hotel.

Doubletree Hotel
2050 Gateway Place
San Jose, CA
408-453-4000 (800-222-TREE (8733))
This upscale hotel has a number of on site amenities for all level of travelers - including their signature chocolate chip cookies at check in, plus a convenient location to business, shopping, dining, historical, and entertainment areas. Dogs are allowed for an additional one time fee of $50 per pet. Dogs must be crated when left alone in the room. Multiple dogs may be allowed.

Extended Stay America San Jose - Santa Clara
2131 Gold St.
San Jose, CA
408-262-0401 (800-804-3724)
One dog is allowed per suite. There is a $25 per night additional pet fee up to $150 for an entire stay.

Extended Stay America San Jose - South - Edenvale
6199 San Ignacio Ave.
San Jose, CA
408-226-4499 (800-804-3724)
One dog is allowed per suite. There is a $25 per night additional pet fee up to $150 for an entire stay.

Fairmont Hotel
170 S Market Street

San Jose, CA
408-998-1900 (800-257-7544)
fairmont.com/sanjose/
This luxury hotel offers 731 beautifully appointed guest rooms and 74 suites, and being set in the high-tech Silicon Valley, they are fully equipped for the business traveler. Vacationers can enjoy the historic grandeur of the inn and its close proximity to several recreational activities. Some of the features include several dining options, a lounge, pool and spa, and many in room amenities. Dogs up to 70 pounds are allowed for an additional one time fee of $75 per pet. Dogs may not be left alone in the room at any time, and they must be leashed and cleaned up after.

Hilton Hotel
300 Almaden Blvd
San Jose, CA
408-287-2100 (800-HILTONS (445-8667))
Located in the heart of Silicon Valley and only 3 miles to an international airport, this upscale hotel also offers a convenient location to shopping, dining, and entertainment areas. One dog is allowed per room for no additional fee and there is a pet policy to sign at check in.

Holiday Inn San Jose
1740 North First Street
San Jose, CA
408-793-3300 (877-270-6405)
Dogs up to 50 pounds are allowed. Dogs are allowed for a pet fee of $50.00 per pet per stay.

Homestead Studio Suites San Jose - Downtown
1560 N. 1st St.
San Jose, CA
408-573-0648 (800-804-3724)
One dog is allowed per suite. There is a $25 per night additional pet fee up to $150 for an entire stay.

Howard Johnson Express Inn San Jose
1215 S First Street
San Jose, CA
408-280-5300 (800-446-4656)
Dogs of all sizes are allowed. Dogs are allowed for a pet fee of $10.00 per pet per night.

Motel 6 - San Jose Airport
2081 1st St
San Jose, CA
408-436-8180 (800-466-8356)
This motel welcomes your pets to stay with you.

Motel 6 - San Jose Airport Central
1440 1st Street
San Jose, CA
408-453-7750 (800-466-8356)
This motel welcomes your pets to
stay with you.

Motel 6 - San Jose Convention
Center
1041 The Alameda
San Jose, CA
408-295-0159 (800-466-8356)
This motel welcomes your pets to
stay with you.

Motel 6 - San Jose South
2560 Fontaine Rd
San Jose, CA
408-270-3131 (800-466-8356)
Your pets are welcome to stay here
with you.

Red Roof Inn San Jose
1440 North 1st Street
San Jose, CA
408-453-7750 (800-RED-ROOF)
One well-behaved family pet per
room. Guest must notify front desk
upon arrival. Guest is liable for any
damages. In consideration of all
guests, pets must never be left
unattended in the guest rooms.

Residence Inn San Jose South
6111 San Ignacio Avenue
San Jose, CA
408-226-7676 (800-331-3131)
This Silicon Valley all suite inn offers
a central location to numerous major
companies, shopping and dining
areas, and world class attractions.
Dogs are allowed for an additional
one time pet fee of $75 per room. 2
dogs may be allowed.

Staybridge Suites San Jose
1602 Crane Court
San Jose, CA
408-436-1600 (877-270-6405)
Dogs up to 80 pounds are allowed.
Pets allowed with an additional pet
fee. Up to $75 for 1-6 nights and up
to $150 for 7+ nights. A pet
agreement must be signed at check-
in.

San Juan Inn
410 The Alameda #156
San Juan Bautista, CA
831-623-4380
Located near the center of Monterey
Peninsula, you'll enjoy excellent
nearby hiking trails at this inn. Dogs
are allowed for a $10 per night per
pet additional fee. Dogs may not be
left alone in the room, and they must

be leashed and cleaned up after. 2
dogs may be allowed.

Best Western Royal Oak Hotel
214 Madonna Road
San Luis Obispo, CA
805-544-4410 (800-780-7234)
royaloakhotel.com
Dogs of all sizes are allowed. There
is a $15 pet fee every 5th day.

Days Inn San Luis Obispo
2050 Garfield St
San Luis Obispo, CA
805-549-9911 (800-329-7466)
Dogs of all sizes are allowed. Dogs
are allowed for a pet fee of $12.00
per pet per night.

Motel 6 - San Luis Obispo North
1433 Calle Joaquin
San Luis Obispo, CA
805-549-9595 (800-466-8356)
This motel welcomes your pets to
stay with you.

Motel 6 - San Luis Obispo South
1625 Calle Joaquin
San Luis Obispo, CA
805-541-6992 (800-466-8356)
This motel welcomes your pets to
stay with you.

Sands Suites & Motel
1930 Monterey Street
San Luis Obispo, CA
805-544-0500 (800-441-4657)
sandssuites.com/
This motel is close to Cal Poly.
Amenities include a heated pool
and spa, free continental breakfast,
self serve laundry facilities and
wheelchair accessibility. There is a
$25 one time per pet fee. Multiple
dogs may be allowed.

Super 8 San Luis Obispo
1951 Monterey St
San Luis Obispo, CA
805-544-6888 (800-800-8000)
Dogs of all sizes are allowed. Dogs
are allowed for a pet fee.

Vagabond Inn
210 Madonna Rd.
San Luis Obispo, CA
805-544-4710 (800-522-1555)
vagabondinn.com
This motel is located near Cal Poly.
Amenities include a heated pool
and whirlpool, complimentary
continental breakfast, dry
cleaning/laundry service and more.
There is a $10 per day per pet
charge. Multiple dogs may be
allowed.

Ramada Limited San Marcos
517 San Marcos Blvd
San Marcos, CA
760-471-2800 (800-272-6232)
Dogs are welcome at this hotel.

Comfort Inn Airport South
350 North Bayshore Blvd
San Mateo, CA
650-344-6376 (877-424-6423)
Dogs of all sizes are allowed. Dogs
are allowed for a pet fee of $35.00
per pet per stay.

Homestead Studio Suites San
Francisco - San Mateo - SFO
1830 Gateway Dr.
San Mateo, CA
650-574-1744 (800-804-3724)
One dog is allowed per suite. There
is a $25 per night additional pet fee
up to $150 for an entire stay.

Residence Inn San Francisco
Airport/San Mateo
2000 Winward Way
San Mateo, CA
650-574-4700 (800-331-3131)
Besides offering a convenient
location to business, shopping,
dining, and entertainment areas, this
hotel also provides a number of in-
house amenities, including a daily
buffet breakfast and evening socials
Monday through Thursday with light
dinner fare. Dogs are allowed for an
additional one time pet fee of $75 per
room. Multiple dogs may be allowed.

Motel 6 - San Rafael, Ca
737 Francisco Blvd
San Rafael, CA
415-453-3450 (800-466-8356)
This motel welcomes your pets to
stay with you.

Villa Inn
1600 Lincoln Avenue
San Rafael, CA
415-456-4975
Dogs up to 50 pounds is allowed.
There are no additional pet fees. 2
dogs may be allowed.

Extended Stay America San Ramon
- Bishop Ranch
2100 Camino Ramon
San Ramon, CA
925-242-0991 (800-804-3724)
One dog is allowed per suite. There
is a $25 per night additional pet fee
up to $150 for an entire stay.

Homestead Studio Suites San
Ramon - Bishop Ranch
18000 San Ramon Valley Blvd.
San Ramon, CA

925-277-0833 (800-804-3724)
One dog is allowed per suite. There is a $25 per night additional pet fee up to $150 for an entire stay.

Marriott San Ramon
2600 Bishop Drive
San Ramon, CA
925-867-9200 (800-228-9290)
This luxury hotel provides a great location to a number of sites of interest for both business and leisure travelers; plus they also offer numerous on-site amenities to ensure a comfortable stay - including free breakfast weekends and beautifully landscaped grounds. Dogs are allowed for an additional one time fee of $75 per room Multiple dogs may be allowed.

Residence Inn San Ramon
1071 Market Place
San Ramon, CA
925-277-9292 (800-331-3131)
In addition to offering a convenient location to business, shopping, dining, and entertainment areas, this hotel also provides a number of in-house amenities, including a daily buffet breakfast and evening social hours with light dinner fare. Dogs are allowed for an additional one time pet fee of $100 per room. Multiple dogs may be allowed.

Best Western Cavalier Oceanfront Resort
9415 Hearst Drive
San Simeon, CA
805-927-4688 (800-780-7234)
Dogs are welcome at this hotel.

Motel 6 - San Simeon Hearst Castle Area
9070 Castillo Dr
San Simeon, CA
805-927-8691 (800-466-8356)
This motel welcomes your pets to stay with you.

Silver Surf Motel
9390 Castillo Drive
San Simeon, CA
805-927-4661 (800-621-3999)
silversurfmotel.com/
This coastal motel is situated around a courtyard in a park like setting. There are beautiful flower gardens, majestic pine trees, and scenic ocean views. Some rooms offer private balconies, fireplaces or ocean views. Amenities include an indoor pool & spa, and guest laundry facility. There is a $10 per day per pet charge. Multiple dogs may be allowed.

Motel 6 - San Ysidro San Diego/border
160 Calle Primera
San Ysidro, CA
619-690-6663 (800-466-8356)
This motel welcomes your pets to stay with you.

Candlewood Suites Oc Airport-Irvine West
2600 S. Red Hill Ave
Santa Ana, CA
949-250-0404 (877-270-6405)
Dogs up to 80 pounds are allowed. Pets allowed with an additional pet fee. Up to $75 for 1-6 nights and up to $150 for 7+ nights. A pet agreement must be signed at check-in.

La Quinta Inn Santa Ana
2721 Hotel Terrace
Santa Ana, CA
714-540-1111 (800-531-5900)
Dogs up to 75 pounds are allowed. There are no additional pet fees. Dogs must be leashed, cleaned up after, and removed for housekeeping. 2 dogs may be allowed.

Motel 6 - Irvine Orange County Airport
1717 East Dyer Road
Santa Ana, CA
949-261-1515 (800-466-8356)
This motel welcomes your pets to stay with you.

Motel 6 - Santa Ana
1623 1st St
Santa Ana, CA
714-558-0500 (800-466-8356)
This motel welcomes your pets to stay with you.

Red Roof Inn Santa Ana
2600 North Main Street
Santa Ana, CA
714-542-0311 (800-RED-ROOF)
One well-behaved family pet per room. Guest must notify front desk upon arrival. Guest is liable for any damages. In consideration of all guests, pets must never be left unattended in the guest rooms.

Blue Sands Motel
421 South Milpas Street
Santa Barbara, CA
805-965-1624
bluesandsmotel.com
Dogs are allowed at this 11 room motel.

Casa Del Mar Hotel

18 Bath Street
Santa Barbara, CA
805-963-4418 (800-433-3097)
casadelmar.com
This popular Mediterranean-style inn is within walking distance of several restaurants, shops and parks. Amenities include a relaxing courtyard Jacuzzi and sun deck surrounded by lush gardens year round. All rooms are non-smoking and equipped with a writing desk and chair or table, telephone, color TV with remote control, and private bathroom. There is a 2 or 3 night minimum stay on the weekends. Pets are welcome. They allow up to two pets per room and there is a $15 per pet per night charge. Pets must never be left alone or unattended, especially in the rooms. Children under 12 are free and there is no charge for a crib. State Street, a popular shopping area, is within walking distance. Multiple dogs may be allowed.

Extended Stay America Santa Barbara - Calle Real
4870 Calle Real
Santa Barbara, CA
805-692-1882 (800-804-3724)
One dog is allowed per suite. There is a $25 per night additional pet fee up to $150 for an entire stay.

Four Seasons Resort
1260 Channel Dr.
Santa Barbara, CA
805-969-2261
Dogs up to 50 pounds are allowed for no additional pet fee. Dogs may not be left alone in the room. Pet sitting services are available.

Motel 6 - Santa Barbara Beach
443 Corona Del Mar
Santa Barbara, CA
805-564-1392 (800-466-8356)
This motel welcomes your pets to stay with you.

Motel 6 - Santa Barbara State Street
3505 State St
Santa Barbara, CA
805-687-5400 (800-466-8356)
This motel welcomes your pets to stay with you.

San Ysidro Ranch
900 San Ysidro Lane
Santa Barbara, CA
805-969-5046
sanysidroranch.com
This is an especially dog-friendly upscale resort located in Santa Barbara. They offer many dog amenities including a Privileged Pet

Program doggie turn down and several miles of trails and exercise areas. Pet Massage Service is available. Choose from the Slow & Gentle Massage or the Authentic Reiki massage for your dog. Dogs are allowed in the freestanding cottages and prices start around $600 and up per night. There is a one time cleaning fee of $100 (+ 10.1% tax) per pet. Multiple dogs may be allowed.

Secret Garden Inn and Cottages
1908 Bath Street
Santa Barbara, CA
805-687-2300
secretgarden.com
Dogs are allowed in six of the cottages. There is a $50 refundable pet deposit. Dogs are not allowed in the main house.

Candlewood Suites Silicon Valley/San Jose
481 El Camino Real
Santa Clara, CA
408-241-9305 (877-270-6405)
Dogs up to 80 pounds are allowed. Pets allowed with an additional pet fee. Up to $75 for 1-6 nights and up to $150 for 7+ nights. A pet agreement must be signed at check-in.

Madison Street Inn
1390 Madison Street
Santa Clara, CA
408-249-5541
madisonstreetinn.com/
This attractive inn sits on one third acre of lush greens and gardens and features a pool and spa, fine dining, a house with a parlor and six guest rooms. Dogs up to 40 pounds are allowed for no additional fee. Dogs must be quiet, well mannered, and leashed and cleaned up after. 2 dogs may be allowed.

Marriott Santa Clara
2700 Mission College Blvd
Santa Clara, CA
408-988-1500 (800-228-9290)
Located in the heart of the Silicon Valley, this luxury hotel provides a central location to a number of sites of interest for both business and leisure travelers; plus they also offer numerous on-site amenities to ensure a comfortable stay. Dogs are allowed for an additional one time fee of $75 per room. Pets must be crated when left alone in the room. 2 dogs may be allowed.

Motel 6 - Santa Clara
3208 El Camino Real

Santa Clara, CA
408-241-0200 (800-466-8356)
This motel welcomes your pets to stay with you.

Vagabond Inns
3580 El Camino Real
Santa Clara, CA
408-241-0771
Dogs up to 70 pounds are allowed. There is a $20 per night per pet additional fee.

Residence Inn Santa Clarita Valencia
25320 The Old Road
Santa Clarita, CA
661-290-2800 (800-331-3131)
In addition to offering a convenient location to business, shopping, dining, and entertainment areas, this hotel also provides a number of in-house amenities, including a daily buffet breakfast and evening social hours Monday to Thursday. Dogs are allowed for an additional one time pet fee of $75 per room. Multiple dogs may be allowed.

Buck's Beach Bungalow
341 35th Avenue
Santa Cruz, CA
831-476-0170
Dogs of all sizes are allowed. There is a pet policy to sign at check in and there are no additional pet fees.

Edgewater Beach Motel
525 Second Street
Santa Cruz, CA
831-423-0440 (888-809-6767)
edgewaterbeachmotel.com/
This motel has ocean views, beach views, and 17 uniquely designed suites (for one to eight people). Some of the rooms have ocean views, microwaves, refrigerators. A couple of the rooms have fireplaces, private lawns and full kitchens. Non-smoking rooms are available. While dogs are not allowed on the Boardwalk or on the nearby beach, they are allowed on the West Cliff Drive Walkway. Walk to the waterfront, then go north (away from the Boardwalk) along the sidewalk on the street closest to the ocean. It will become a walkway that is used by walkers, joggers and bicyclists. If you walk about 1 1/2 - 2 miles, you'll reach several dog beaches (see Parks). To get to the motel, take Hwy 17 south. Take the Hwy 1 North exit. Then take the Ocean St exit on the left towards the beaches. Head towards the beach on Ocean St and then turn right on San Lorenzo Blvd. Turn left

on Riverside Ave and then right on 2nd St. The motel will be on the left. Ample parking is available in their parking lot. There is a $30 one time additional pet fee. Aggressive know breeds are not allowed. 2 dogs may be allowed.

Guesthouse International
330 Ocean Street
Santa Cruz, CA
831-425-3722
There is a $15 per day per pet fee. Only dogs are allowed. Multiple dogs may be allowed.

Hilton Hotel
6001 La Madrona Drive
Santa Cruz, CA
831-440-1000 (800-HILTONS (445-8667))
Centrally located between Silicon Valley and Monterey Bay, this upscale hotel offers numerous on site amenities for business and leisure travelers, plus a convenient location to business districts, beaches, shopping, dining, and entertainment areas. Dogs are allowed for an additional one time pet fee of $50 per room. Multiple dogs may be allowed.

Redtail Ranch by the Sea
Call to Arrange.
Santa Cruz, CA
831-429-1322
redtailranch.com/
This 3 bedroom, 1 1/2 bath ranch house is located on a 72 acre horse ranch, the Redtail Ranch. The house features a 180 degree ocean view of the Monterey Bay and views of the coastal hills. The house sleeps 1 to 8 people and comes with a complete full kitchen. The home is located about a 5 minute drive to local beaches, a 1 hour drive to Monterey, Carmel and Big Sur, and a 1 1/2 hour scenic coastal drive to San Francisco. The rental is available year-round for nightly, weekly, and extended vacation rentals.

Motel 6 - Los Angeles Santa Fe Springs
13412 Excelsior Dr
Santa Fe Springs, CA
562-921-0596 (800-466-8356)
This motel welcomes your pets to stay with you.

Holiday Inn Hotel & Suites Santa Maria
2100 N. Broadway
Santa Maria, CA
805-928-6000 (877-270-6405)
Dogs of all sizes are allowed. Dogs

are allowed for a pet fee of $25.00 per pet per night.

Motel 6 - Santa Maria
2040 Preisker Ln
Santa Maria, CA
805-928-8111 (800-466-8356)
This motel welcomes your pets to stay with you.

Quality Inn & Suites
210 South Nicholson
Santa Maria, CA
805-922-5891 (877-424-6423)
Dogs of all sizes are allowed. Dogs are allowed for a pet fee of $usd per pet per stay. Two dogs are allowed per room.

JW Marriott Le Merigot Beach Hotel & Spa Santa Monica
1740 Ocean Avenue
Santa Monica, CA
310-395-9700 (877-MER-IGOT (637-4468))
Located near the beach and the Santa Monica Pier, this luxury hotel sits central to numerous businesses, shopping, dining, and day/night entertainment areas, plus they also offer a number of in-house amenities for business and leisure travelers. Dogs are allowed for a $250 pet deposit per room - $150 is refundable. Multiple dogs may be allowed.

Loews Santa Monica Beach Hotel
1700 Ocean Avenue
Santa Monica, CA
310-458-6700
All well-behaved dogs of any size are welcome. This upscale hotel offers their "Loews Loves Pets" program which includes special pet treats, local dog walking routes, and a list of nearby pet-friendly places to visit. There is an additional one time pet cleaning fee of $25 per room.

Sheraton Delfina Santa Monica Hotel
530 West Pico Blvd.
Santa Monica, CA
310-399-9344 (888-625-5144)
Dogs of all sizes are allowed. There is a $50 additional pet fee. Pet rooms are limited to ground floor cabanas. You must sign a pet policy when checking in with a dog. Dogs are not allowed to be left alone in the room. 2 dogs may be allowed.

The Fairmont Miramar Hotel Santa Monica
101 Wilshire Blvd
Santa Monica, CA
310-576-7777 (800-257-7544)

fairmont.com/santamonica/
Nestled atop the scenic bluffs of Santa Monica beach, this hotel features historic elegance with all the modern-day conveniences and services. Some of the features/amenities include 302 stylish guest rooms, 32 secluded garden bungalows, casual elegant indoor and outdoor dining, and 24 hour room service. There can be up to 3 dogs in one room if they are all small, otherwise there are only 2 dogs allowed per room. There are no additional pet fees and there is a pet policy to sign at check in. Dogs may not be left alone in the room at any time.

Viceroy Hotel
1819 Ocean Avenue
Santa Monica, CA
310-260-7500
Well behaved dogs up to 100 pounds are allowed. There is a $100 non-refundable one time additional pet fee per pet.

Best Western Andersen's Inn
12367 S Highway 33
Santa Nella, CA
209-826-5534 (800-780-7234)
Dogs of all sizes are allowed. Dogs are allowed for a pet fee.

Motel 6 - Santa Nella Los Banos, Ca
28821 Gonzaga Rd.
Santa Nella, CA
209-827-8700 (800-466-8356)
This motel welcomes your pets to stay with you.

Best Value Inn
1800 Santa Rosa Ave
Santa Rosa, CA
707-523-3480
In addition to offering a number of on-site amenities, this inn also provides a convenient location to local attractions, entertainment and commerce areas, and shopping and dining sites. Dogs up to 50 pounds are allowed for an additional fee of $10 per night per pet. 2 dogs may be allowed.

Best Western Garden Inn - Santa Rosa
1500 Santa Rosa Avenue
Santa Rosa, CA
707-546-4031 (800-780-7234)
thegardeninn.com
Dogs up to 50 pounds are allowed at this hotel in the heart of the Sonoma Valley wine region. A maximum of two dogs per room are allowed with a $15 per night pet fee.

Comfort Inn
2632 Cleveland Avenue
Santa Rosa, CA
707-542-5544 (877-424-6423)
Dogs of all sizes are allowed. Dogs are allowed for a pet fee of $15.00 per pet per night.

Days Inn Santa Rosa
3345 Santa Rosa Ave
Santa Rosa, CA
707-568-1011 (800-329-7466)
Dogs of all sizes are allowed. Dogs are allowed for a pet fee of $10.00 per pet per night.

Extended Stay America Santa Rosa - North
100 Fountain Grove Pkwy.
Santa Rosa, CA
707-541-0959 (800-804-3724)
One dog is allowed per suite. There is a $25 per night additional pet fee up to $150 for an entire stay.

Extended Stay America Santa Rosa - South
2600 Corby Ave.
Santa Rosa, CA
707-546-4808 (800-804-3724)
One dog is allowed per suite. There is a $25 per night additional pet fee up to $150 for an entire stay.

Hilton Hotel
3555 Round Barn Blvd
Santa Rosa, CA
707-523-7555 (800-HILTONS (445-8667))
This upscale hotel sits on 13 meticulously landscaped grounds overlooking the Santa Rosa Valley, and offers numerous on site amenities for business and leisure travelers, plus a convenient location for exploring the Sonoma County wine country. Dogs up to 80 pounds are allowed for an additional one time pet fee of $50 per room. 2 dogs may be allowed.

Motel 6 - Santa Rosa North, Ca
3145 Cleveland Ave
Santa Rosa, CA
707-525-9010 (800-466-8356)
This motel welcomes your pets to stay with you.

Motel 6 - Santa Rosa South, Ca
2760 Cleveland Ave
Santa Rosa, CA
707-546-1500 (800-466-8356)
This motel welcomes your pets to stay with you.

Travelodge Downtown Santa Rosa

635 Healdsburg Ave
Santa Rosa, CA
707-544-4141 (800-578-7878)
Dogs of all sizes are allowed. Dogs are allowed for a pet fee of $10.00 per pet per night.

Travelodge Santa Rosa
1815 Santa Rosa Avenue
Santa Rosa, CA
707-542-3472 (800-578-7878)
Dogs of all sizes are allowed. Dogs are allowed for a pet fee of $20.00 per pet per night.

Best Western
6020 Scott's Valley Drive
Scotts Valley, CA
831-438-6666 (800-780-7234)
Dogs of all sizes are allowed. There can be 1 large dog or 2 small dogs per room. There is a $100 refundable pet deposit per room. Dogs must be leashed, cleaned up after, and the front desk informed if they are in the room alone. 2 dogs may be allowed.

Sea Ranch Lodge
60 Sea Walk Drive
Sea Ranch, CA
707-785-2371 (800-SEA-RANCH (732-7262))
searanchlodge.com/
Shinning with a natural rustic elegance along a dramatic ocean side location, this award-winning 20 room lodge is an idyllic retreat for special events, and the business or leisure traveler. Some the features/amenities include miles of scenic hiking trails, a full breakfast, exquisite wining and dining with the freshest ingredients available and ocean views, and Concierge Services. Friendly dogs of all sizes are allowed for an additional one time fee of $50 per pet. Dogs must be leashed and cleaned up after at all times, and pet rooms are located on the 1st floor only. Canine guests receive a welcome package that includes a welcome note with suggestions for activities, a cookie, bottled water, a cushy bed, a furniture cover, food/water bowls, and a place mat. 2 dogs may be allowed.

Super 8 /Fresno Area Selma
3142 S Highland Ave
Selma, CA
559-896-2800 (800-800-8000)
Dogs are welcome at this hotel.

The Cliffs Resort
2757 Shell Beach Road
Shell Beach, CA
805-773-5000 (800-826-7827)

cliffsresort.com/hotel/
With a multi-million dollar renovation and a visually stunning location, this award winning resort features a private oceanfront cliff setting with access to the beach, indoor or outdoor dining and many in room amenities. Dogs are welcome on the 1st floor only, and there is a $50 one time additional pet fee per room. Normally one dog is allowed per room, but they may allow 2 dogs if they are 10 pounds or under. Canine guests are greeted with an amenity kit that includes a comfy bed, a clip ID tag, a treat, water, and food and water bowls. Dogs may be left alone in the room only if they will be quiet and well behaved, and they must be removed or crated for housekeeping. Dogs must be leashed and cleaned up after at all times. 2 dogs may be allowed.

Best Western Carriage Inn
5525 Sepulveda Boulevard
Sherman Oaks, CA
818-787-2300 (800-780-7234)
Dogs are welcome at this hotel.

Extended Stay America Los Angeles - Simi Valley
2498 Stearns St.
Simi Valley, CA
805-584-8880 (800-804-3724)
One dog is allowed per suite. There is a $25 per night additional pet fee up to $150 for an entire stay.

Motel 6 - Simi Valley
2566 Erringer Rd
Simi Valley, CA
805-526-3533 (800-466-8356)
This motel welcomes your pets to stay with you.

Royal Copenhagen Inn
1579 Mission Drive
Solvang, CA
800-624-6604
This inn is located in the heart of the Solvang village. Walk to dog-friendly restaurants, stores and parks. Well-behaved dogs are allowed. There is an additional fee of $15 per night per pet. Dogs may not be left alone in the room. Multiple dogs may be allowed.

Wine Valley Inn
1554 Copenhagen Drive
Solvang, CA
805-688-2111 (800-824-6444)
winevalleyinn.com/
A luxurious blend of old world ambiance and modern day comforts, this chateau-style retreat

offers accommodations for all tastes and budgets. Set among beautifully landscaped courtyards complete with koi ponds, a stone fireplace, and private gardens are individually decorated guest rooms, cottages, and a grand suite, all with many in-room amenities. Dogs of all sizes are allowed for an additional pet fee of $25 per night per pet. Dogs may not be left alone in the room at any time, and they must be leashed and cleaned up after at all times. Multiple dogs may be allowed.

Best Western Sonoma Valley Inn & Krug Event Center
550 2nd Street W
Sonoma, CA
707-938-9200 (800-780-7234)
Dogs of all sizes are allowed. Dogs are allowed for a pet fee of $35 per pet per night.

Renaissance - The Lodge at Sonoma Resort and Spa
1325 Broadway
Sonoma, CA
707-935-6600 (866-263-0758)
This luxury hotel provides a great location to a number of sites of interest for both business and leisure travelers; plus they also offer numerous on-site amenities to ensure a comfortable stay. Dogs are allowed for an additional one time fee of $75 per room. 2 dogs may be allowed.

Best Western Sonora Oaks
19551 Hess Avenue
Sonora, CA
209-533-4400 (800-780-7234)
Dogs are welcome at this hotel. There is a $25 daily pet fee.

Days Inn Sonora
160 S Washington St
Sonora, CA
209-532-2400 (800-329-7466)
Dogs are welcome at this hotel.

Sonora Aladdin Motor Inn
14260 Mono Way (Hwy 108)
Sonora, CA
209-533-4971
aladdininn.com
This motel's rooms offer Southwest decor with king or queen sized beds, table & chairs, refrigerators, coffee makers, climate control, cable TV & HBO, and direct dial phones with free local & credit card calls. They also feature a guest laundry. Dogs are welcome with a $15 one time charge. The motel is about an hour and a half from Yosemite. Multiple dogs may be allowed.

Ramada El Monte
1089 Santa Anita/I-605
South El Monte, CA
626-350-9588 (800-272-6232)
Dogs are welcome at this hotel.

3 Peaks Resort and Beach Club -
South Lake Tahoe Hotel
931 Park Avenue
South Lake Tahoe, CA
800-957-5088
lake-tahoe-california-hotels.com
The 3 Peaks Resort and Beach Club
is a family resort near the center of
South Lake Tahoe. All pets are
welcome for a $15 per night fee.
Pets cannot be left unattended and
must be kept on a leash when out of
the room.

7 Bedroom Deluxe Rental
1572 Black Bart Ave
South Lake Tahoe, CA
415-505-2525
tahoehouse.net
This large 7 bedroom, 4 bath
vacation rental in South Lake Tahoe
welcomes your dog.

Alder Inn
1072 Ski Run Blvd
South Lake Tahoe, CA
530-544-4485 (800-544-0056)
alderinntahoe.com
Minutes from Heavenly Valley Ski
Resort and the casinos. All rooms
have a small refrigerator and
microwave. There is a $10.00 per
night pet fee.

Best Western Timber Cove Lodge
3411 Lake Tahoe Boulevard
South Lake Tahoe, CA
530-541-6722 (800-780-7234)
Dogs of all sizes are allowed. Dogs
are allowed for a pet fee of $25 per
pet per night.

Big Pines Mountain House
4083 Cedar Ave
South Lake Tahoe, CA
530-541-5155 (800-288-4083)
thebigpines.com
Dogs are welcome at this motel
located near Heavenly Village and
the center of South Lake Tahoe.

Colony Inn at South Lake Tahoe
3794 Montreal Road
South Lake Tahoe, CA
530-544-6481
gototahoe.com/rooms/colony.html
The Colony Inn at South Lake Tahoe
is located just 1.5 blocks from
Harrah's and the other casinos and
just down the street from Heavenly

Ski Resort. Want to experience the
beautiful outdoors? The Colony
Inn's backyard is National Forest
Land, featuring dog-friendly hiking,
mountain biking, and peace and
quiet. There is a $25 refundable pet
deposit, and pets cannot be left
unattended in the rooms.

Fireside Lodge
515 Emerald Bay Rd.
South Lake Tahoe, CA
530-544-5515 (800-My-Cabin)
tahoefiresidelodge.com/
This inn offers log cabin style
suites. The rooms have a unique
'Country Mountain' theme decor
with crafted fireplaces, and custom
woodwork. Each room offers a
microwave, refrigerator and coffee-
maker, private bath w/shower, cable
TV and VCR with numerous free
videos available in their Gathering
Room. Full kitchen units are
available as well as private 1 to 4
bedroom cabins, off the property.
There is a $20 per day pet fee for 1
dog and an additional $10 per day
fee for a 2nd dog. 2 dogs may be
allowed.

Hollys Place
1201 Rufus Allen Blvd.
South Lake Tahoe, CA
530-544-7040 (800-745-7041)
hollysplace.com/
This resort and retreat has 5 cabins
on 2.5 fenced acres near South
Lake Tahoe. There is a pet fee of
$15 per night per dog. Multiple dogs
may be allowed.

Inn at Heavenly B&B
1261 Ski Run Boulevard
South Lake Tahoe, CA
530-544-4244 (800-692-2246)
innatheavenly.com/
You and your dog are welcome at
this log-cabin style bed and
breakfast lodge. The property is all
dog-friendly and dogs are allowed
everywhere but their Gathering
Room. They offer 14 individual
rooms each with a private bath and
shower. Room conveniences
include refrigerators, microwaves
and VCRs. Some rooms have a
fireplace. Three to four bedroom
cabins are also available. The lodge
is located on a 2-acre wooded park
complete with picnic areas,
barbecues and log swings.
Continental breakfast is served and
snacks are available throughout the
day. One large dog is allowed per
room and pet charges apply. Room
rates range from the low to mid
$100s per night. Call for cabin

prices. The owners have friendly
dogs on the premises. The lodge is
located in South Lake Tahoe. There
is a $20 per day pet fee per pet.

Motel 6 - South Lake Tahoe
2375 Lake Tahoe Blvd
South Lake Tahoe, CA
530-542-1400 (800-466-8356)
Your pets are welcome to stay here
with you.

Rodeway Inn Casino Center
4127 Pine Blvd.
South Lake Tahoe, CA
530-541-7150 (877-424-6423)
Dogs of all sizes are allowed. Dogs
are allowed for a pet fee of $15.00
per pet per stay.

Spruce Grove Cabins & Suites
P.O. Box 16390
South Lake Tahoe, CA
530-544-0549 (800-777-0914)
sprucegrovetahoe.com
Spruce Grove Cabins puts you
amidst a mountain resort off of Ski
Run Blvd. at the foot of Heavenly Ski
Area and within walking distance to
the center of Lake Tahoe. Children
and well-behaved dogs are welcome.
This dog friendly retreat offers a fully
fenced acre of land that is next to an
open field of pine trees.

Stonehenge Vacation Properties
Call to Arrange.
South Lake Tahoe, CA
800-822-1460 (800-822-1460)
tahoestonehenge.com/
This vacation rental company offers
several elegant and unique dog-
friendly vacation homes located
around South Lake Tahoe.

Super 8 Lake Tahoe South
3600 Lake Tahoe Blvd
South Lake Tahoe, CA
530-544-3476 (800-800-8000)
Dogs of all sizes are allowed. Dogs
are allowed for a pet fee of $10 per
pet per stay.

Tahoe Keys Resort
599 Tahoe Keys Blvd
South Lake Tahoe, CA
530-544-5397 (800-698-2463)
petslovetahoe.com
They feature approximately 50 pet
friendly cabins, condos and homes in
South Lake Tahoe. All dogs receive
treats upon check-in. A $25.00 pet
fee is taken per reservation. There is
also a $100.00 refundable security
deposit upon check in.

TahoeWoods Lodging

See Website or Call
South Lake Tahoe, CA
415-444-0777
These three vacation homes in
South Lake Tahoe feature at least 5
bedrooms and access to the Tahoe
National Forest.

The Nash Cabin
3595 Betty Ray
South Lake Tahoe, CA
415-759-6583
Dogs of all sizes are allowed in the
RV area for no additional pet fee.

Embassy Suites SF Airport
250 Gateway Blvd
South San Francisco, CA
650-589-3400 (800-EMBASSY (362-
2779))
This upscale hotel offers a number of
on site amenities for business and
leisure travelers, plus a convenient
location to business, shopping,
dining, and entertainment districts.
They also offer a complimentary
cooked-to-order breakfast and a
Manager's reception every evening.
Dogs are allowed for an additional
one time fee of $50 per pet. 2 dogs
may be allowed.

Howard Johnson Express Inn
222 S. Airport Blvd
South San Francisco, CA
650-589-9055 (800-446-4656)
hojosfo.com/
Besides offering a full line-up of on-
site amenities, this inn also provides
a convenient location to a number of
the city's star attractions, commerce
areas, and world-class shopping and
dining sites. Dogs are allowed for an
additional fee of $20 per night per
pet. 2 dogs may be allowed.

La Quinta Inn San Francisco Airport
20 Airport Blvd.
South San Francisco, CA
650-583-2223 (800-531-5900)
Dogs of all sizes are allowed. There
are no additional pet fees. Dogs
must be leashed and cleaned up
after. Be sure to inform the front desk
you have a pet, and put the Do Not
Disturb sign on the door if the dog is
alone in the room. Multiple dogs may
be allowed.

Motel 6 - San Francisco Airport
111 Mitchell Ave
South San Francisco, CA
650-877-0770 (800-466-8356)
Your pets are welcome to stay here
with you.

Residence Inn San Francisco

Airport/Oyster Point Waterfront
1350 Veterans Blvd
South San Francisco, CA
650-837-9000 (800-331-3131)
Overlooking the beautiful San
Francisco Bay and offering a
convenient location to numerous
business, historic, shopping, dining,
and entertainment areas, this all
suite hotel also offers a number of
in-house amenities, including a
daily buffet breakfast, evening
socials, and weekly barbecues.
Dogs are allowed for an additional
one time pet fee of $100 (+ $9 tax)
per room. Multiple dogs may be
allowed.

El Bonita Motel
195 Main Street
St Helena, CA
707-963-3216 (800-541-3284)
elbonita.com/
Amenities at this motel include a
continental breakfast, pool,
whirlpool, sauna, and over two
acres of peaceful gardens. Room
amenities include microwaves,
refrigerators, and more. Room rates
start at about $130 per night and
up. Dogs are allowed for an
additional fee of $15 per night per
pet. 2 dogs may be allowed.

Harvest Inn
One Main Street
St Helena, CA
707-963-9463 (800-950-8466)
harvestinn.com/
This inn is nestled among 8-acres
of award winning landscape. Most
guest rooms feature wet bars,
unique brick fireplaces and private
terraces. Amenities include two
outdoor heated pools and whirlpool
spas and jogging and bike trails
bordering the grounds. Dogs are
allowed in the standard rooms.
There is a $75 one time pet charge.
2 dogs may be allowed.

Motel 6 - Stanton
7450 Katella Ave
Stanton, CA
714-891-0717 (800-466-8356)
This motel welcomes your pets to
stay with you.

Comfort Suites Near Six Flags
Magic Mountain
25380 N. The Old Road
Stevenson Ranch, CA
661-254-7700 (877-424-6423)
Dogs up to 50 pounds are allowed.
Dogs are allowed for a pet fee of
$25.00 per pet per stay. Three or
more dogs may be allowed.

Extended Stay America Los Angeles
- Valencia
24940 W. Pico Canyon Rd.
Stevenson Ranch, CA
661-255-1044 (800-804-3724)
One dog is allowed per suite. There
is a $25 per night additional pet fee
up to $150 for an entire stay.

Beach Front Retreat
90 Calle Del Ribera
Stinson Beach, CA
415-383-7870
beachtime.org
This vacation home rental offers 3
bedrooms, 2 baths, a fireplace and a
beach deck with barbecue. You can
view the ocean from the balcony
located next to the master bedroom.
There is an additional $50 one time
per stay pet charge

Redwoods Haus Beach
1 Belvedere
Stinson Beach, CA
415-868-9828
Dogs are allowed for no additional
pet fee. 2 dogs may be allowed.

Comfort Inn
2654 West March Lane
Stockton, CA
209-478-4300 (877-424-6423)
Dogs of all sizes are allowed.

Days Inn Stockton
550 West Charter Way
Stockton, CA
209-948-0321 (800-329-7466)
Dogs are welcome at this hotel.

Extended Stay America Stockton -
March Lane
2844 W. March Ln.
Stockton, CA
209-472-7588 (800-804-3724)
One dog is allowed per suite. There
is a $25 per night additional pet fee
up to $150 for an entire stay.

Howard Johnson Express Inn CA
Stockton
33 N. Center Street
Stockton, CA
209-948-6151 (800-446-4656)
Dogs of all sizes are allowed. Dogs
are allowed for a pet fee of $10.00
per pet per night.

Knights Inn Stockton
4540 N El Dorado St
Stockton, CA
209-478-2944 (800-843-5644)
Dogs are welcome at this hotel.

La Quinta Inn Stockton
2710 W. March Ln.

Stockton, CA
209-952-7800 (800-531-5900)
Dogs of all sizes are allowed. There
are no additional pet fees. Dogs
must be leashed and cleaned up
after. The Do Not Disturb sign must
be placed on the door if there is a pet
alone in the room. Multiple dogs may
be allowed.

Motel 6 - Stockton Charter Way West
817 Navy Dr
Stockton, CA
209-946-0923 (800-466-8356)
This motel welcomes your pets to
stay with you.

Motel 6 - Stockton I-5 Southeast
1625 French Camp Tpke Rd
Stockton, CA
209-467-3600 (800-466-8356)
This motel welcomes your pets to
stay with you.

Motel 6 - Stockton North
6717 Plymouth Rd
Stockton, CA
209-951-8120 (800-466-8356)
This motel welcomes your pets to
stay with you.

Ramada Plaza Stockton
111 East March Lane
Stockton, CA
209-474-3301 (800-272-6232)
Dogs are welcome at this hotel.

Red Roof Inn Stockton
1707 W Freemont St
Stockton, CA
209-466-7777 (800-RED-ROOF)
One well-behaved family pet per
room. Guest must notify front desk
upon arrival. Guest is liable for any
damages. In consideration of all
guests, pets must never be left
unattended in the guest rooms.

Residence Inn Stockton
3240 March Lane
Stockton, CA
209-472-9800 (800-331-3131)
Some of the amenities at this all-
suite inn include a daily buffet
breakfast, Manager's receptions, a
heated swimming pool, and a
complimentary grocery shopping
service. Dogs are allowed for an
additional one time pet fee of $100
per room. Multiple dogs may be
allowed.

Homestead Studio Suites San Jose
-Sunnyvale
1255 Orleans Dr.
Sunnyvale, CA
408-734-3431 (800-804-3724)

One dog is allowed per suite. There
is a $25 per night additional pet fee
up to $150 for an entire stay.

Motel 6 - Sunnyvale North
775 Mathilda Ave
Sunnyvale, CA
408-736-4595 (800-466-8356)
This motel welcomes your pets to
stay with you.

Motel 6 - Sunnyvale South
806 Ahwanee Ave
Sunnyvale, CA
408-720-1222 (800-466-8356)
This motel welcomes your pets to
stay with you.

Quality Inn
1280 Persian Dr.
Sunnyvale, CA
408-744-1100 (877-424-6423)
Dogs of all sizes are allowed. Dogs
are allowed for a pet fee of $10.00
per pet per night.

Residence Inn Sunnyvale Silicon
Valley I
750 Lakeway Drive
Sunnyvale, CA
408-720-1000 (800-228-9290)
This all suite hotel sits central to
many of the city's star attractions,
shopping, dining, and business
areas, plus they offer a number of
in-house amenities that include a
daily buffet breakfast and evening
socials Monday through Thursday
with light dinner fare. Dogs are
allowed for an additional one time
pet fee of $100 per room. Multiple
dogs may be allowed.

Residence Inn Sunnyvale Silicon
Valley II
1080 Stewart Drive
Sunnyvale, CA
408-720-8893 (800-331-3131)
This all suite hotel sits central to
many of the area's star attractions,
shopping, dining, and business
areas, plus they offer a number of
in-house amenities that include a
daily buffet breakfast and evening
socials. Dogs are allowed for an
additional one time pet fee of $75
per room. Multiple dogs may be
allowed.

Sheraton Sunnyvale Hotel
1100 North Mathilda Ave.
Sunnyvale, CA
408-745-6000 (888-625-5144)
Dogs up to 80 pounds are allowed.
You must sign pet policy. Dogs are
not allowed to be left alone in the
room.

Staybridge Suites Sunnyvale
900 Hamlin Court
Sunnyvale, CA
408-745-1515 (877-270-6405)
Dogs up to 80 pounds are allowed.
Pets allowed with an additional pet
fee. Up to $75 for 1-6 nights and up
to $150 for 7+ nights. A pet
agreement must be signed at check-
in.

TownePlace Suites Sunnyvale
Mountain View
606 S Bernardo Avenue
Sunnyvale, CA
408-733-4200 (800-257-3000)
This all suite hotel sits central to a
number of sites of interest for both
business and leisure travelers; plus
they also offer a number of on-site
amenities to ensure comfort. Dogs
are allowed for an additional one
time fee of $75 per room. 2 dogs
may be allowed.

Woodfin Suite Hotel
635 E. El Camino Real
Sunnyvale, CA
408-738-1700
All well-behaved dogs are welcome.
All rooms are suites with full
kitchens. Hotel amenities include a
heated pool. There is a $5 per day
pet fee.

Budget Host Frontier Inn
2685 Main St
Susanville, CA
530-257-4141
There is a one time additonal pet fee
of $10 per room. 2 dogs may be
allowed.

River Inn
1710 Main St
Susanville, CA
530-257-6051
There is an $11 per day per pet
additional pet fee. 2 dogs may be
allowed.

Super 8 Susanville
2975 Johnstonville Road
Susanville, CA
530-257-2782 (800-800-8000)
Dogs are welcome at this hotel.

Days Inn Sutter Creek
271 Hanford Street
Sutter Creek, CA
209-267-9177 (800-329-7466)
Dogs of all sizes are allowed. Dogs
are allowed for a nightly pet fee.

Motel 6 - Los Angeles Sylmar
12775 Encinitas Ave

Sylmar, CA
818-362-9491 (800-466-8356)
This motel welcomes your pets to stay with you.

Percy's Place
Email or call to arrange
Tahoe City, CA
415-215-6575
percysplace.com
Percy's Place is a 3-bedroom, 2-bath home just outside Tahoe City. The rental is a short walk to a US Forest Service trail. Dogs of all sizes are allowed. Please email percy@percysplace.com to make reservations.

Tahoe Moon Properties
P.O. Box 7521
Tahoe City, CA
530-581-2771 (866-581-2771)
tahoemoonproperties.com
They have over 15 beautiful homes that allow well-behaved dogs. All of the houses are close to Tahoe City or ski areas. Bath and bed linens are provided. There are a few dog rules; no dogs on the furniture, dogs are not to be left alone in the house, you must clean up after your dog and pet owners are responsible for any damages. Rates start at $150 per night with a 2 night minimum. There is a $30 per dog charge.

Knights Inn Cedar Glen Lodge Lake Tahoe
6589 North Lake Blvd
Tahoe Vista, CA
800-500-8246 (800-843-5644)
Dogs are welcome at this hotel.

Rustic Cottages
7449 N Lake Blvd
Tahoe Vista, CA
530-546-3523
Dogs of all sizes are allowed. There is a $20 per night per pet fee and dogs may not be left unattended. They request to clean up after your pet, keep it leashed, and they are not allowed on the furniture.

Waters of Tahoe Vacation Properties
PO Box 312
Tahoe Vista, CA
530-546-8904 (800-215-8904)
watersoftahoe.com
These vacation homes are near the Tahoe National Forest and the lake. They provide pet amenities such as a dog basket with treats, toys, an extra leash, dog bowls and other miscellaneous goodies.

Norfolk Woods Inn

6941 West Lake Blvd.
Tahoma, CA
530-525-5000
norfolkwoods.com/
Up to 2 dogs are allowed in the cabins and 1 dog in the lodge for no additional pet fee. They only have 4 cozy kitchen cabins, so call ahead. Also note that the entire premises are smoke free. Located directly in front of this inn is the Tahoe bike trail where you and your pup can walk or run for several miles. The trail is mostly paved except for a small dirt path section. The inn is located approx. 8-9 miles south of Tahoe City on Hwy 89. Dogs may not be left alone in the cabins or in the lodge rooms at any time. Cabins are usually rented by the month. 2 dogs may be allowed.

Tahoma Lodge
7018 West Lake Blvd
Tahoma, CA
530-525-7721
Dogs are allowed for an additional pet fee of $10 per night per room. Dogs must be crated when left alone in the room. There are some breed restrictions. 2 dogs may be allowed.

Tahoma Meadows Bed and Breakfast
6821 W. Lake Blvd.
Tahoma, CA
530-525-1553
tahomameadows.com/
A well-behaved dog is allowed only if you let them know in advance that you are bringing your dog. Pets are allowed in one of their cabins, the Mountain Hideaway (previously known as Dogwood). There is an extra $25 one time pet charge per stay, plus a security deposit.

Summit Travelodge Tehachapi
500 Steuber Road
Tehachapi, CA
661-823-8000 (800-578-7878)
Dogs of all sizes are allowed. Dogs are allowed for a nightly pet fee.

Extended Stay America Temecula - Wine Country
27622 Jefferson Ave.
Temecula, CA
951-587-8881 (800-804-3724)
One dog is allowed per suite. There is a $25 per night additional pet fee up to $150 for an entire stay.

Motel 6 - Temecula Rancho California
41900 Moreno Dr
Temecula, CA

951-676-7199 (800-466-8356)
This motel welcomes your pets to stay with you.

TownePlace Suites Thousand Oaks Ventura County
1712 Newbury Road
Thousand Oaks, CA
805-499-3111 (800-257-3000)
Besides offering a number of in-house amenities for all level of travelers, this all suite inn also provides a convenient location to many of the area's star attractions, major businesses, shopping, dining, and day/night entertainment areas. Dogs are allowed for an additional one time fee of $75 per room. Multiple dogs may be allowed.

Red Roof Inn Palm Springs - Thousand Palms
72215 Varner Road
Thousand Palms, CA
760-343-1381 (800-RED-ROOF)
One well-behaved family pet per room. Guest must notify front desk upon arrival. Guest is liable for any damages. In consideration of all guests, pets must never be left unattended in the guest rooms.

Buckeye Tree Lodge
46,000 Sierra Drive/H 198
Three Rivers, CA
559-561-5900
buckeyetree.com/
This lodge sits in the Kaweah River Canyon along the banks of the Kaweah River. The beautiful grounds offer a grassy lawn, a picnic area on the river surrounded by Sycamore trees, an outdoor pool, and miles of multi-use trails to explore. Dogs of all sizes are allowed for an additional fee of $10 per night per pet. Dogs may not be left alone in the rooms at any time, and they must be well behaved, leashed, and cleaned up after.

Sequoia Village Inn
45971 Sierra Drive/H 198
Three Rivers, CA
559-561-3652
sequoiavillageinn.com/
Neighboring the Sequoia National Park, this inn features spectacular mountain and river scenery, 1.3 acres of native oak trees, grasses, an abundance of wildflowers, and 8 private chalet and/or cottages. Some of the amenities include a seasonal swimming pool and spa, satellite TV, kitchens with basic needs/utilities, and beautiful hand-crafted accommodations. Dogs of all sizes are allowed for an additional fee of

$10 per night per pet. Dogs may not be left alone in the rooms at any time, and they must be well behaved, leashed, and cleaned up after.

Days Inn Redondo Beach Torrance
4111 Pacific Coast Hwy
Torrance, CA
310-378-8511 (800-329-7466)
Dogs of all sizes are allowed. Dogs are allowed for a pet fee of $10 per pet per night.

Extended Stay America Los Angeles - Torrance
3525 Torrance Blvd.
Torrance, CA
310-540-5442 (800-804-3724)
One dog is allowed per suite. There is a $25 per night additional pet fee up to $150 for an entire stay.

Extended Stay America Los Angeles - Torrance Harbor Gateway
19200 Harbor Gateway
Torrance, CA
310-328-6000 (800-804-3724)
One dog is allowed per suite. There is a $25 per night additional pet fee up to $150 for an entire stay.

Holiday Inn Torrance
19800 S Vermont
Torrance, CA
310-781-9100 (877-270-6405)
Dogs of all sizes are allowed. Dogs are allowed for a pet fee of $50.00 per pet per stay.

Homestead Studio Suites Los Angeles - Torrance
3995 Carson St.
Torrance, CA
310-543-0048 (800-804-3724)
One dog is allowed per suite. There is a $25 per night additional pet fee up to $150 for an entire stay.

Residence Inn Los Angeles Torrance/Redondo Beach
3701 Torrance Blvd
Torrance, CA
310-543-4566 (800-331-3131)
Offering a convenient location to business, shopping, dining, and entertainment areas, this all suite hotel also offers a number of in-house amenities, including a daily buffet breakfast and weekday socials. Dogs are allowed for an additional one time pet fee of $100 per room. 2 dogs may be allowed.

Staybridge Suites Torrance/Redondo Beach
19901 Prairie Avenue
Torrance, CA

310-371-8525 (877-270-6405)
Dogs up to 80 pounds are allowed. Pets allowed with an additional pet fee. Up to $75 for 1-6 nights and up to $150 for 7+ nights. A pet agreement must be signed at check-in.

Super 8 LAX Airport Area Torrance
2360 Sepulveda Blvd
Torrance, CA
310-534-4900 (800-800-8000)
Dogs are welcome at this hotel.

Extended Stay America Stockton - Tracy
2526 Pavilion Pkwy.
Tracy, CA
209-832-4700 (800-804-3724)
One dog is allowed per suite. There is a $25 per night additional pet fee up to $150 for an entire stay.

Motel 6 - Tracy
3810 Tracy Blvd
Tracy, CA
209-836-4900 (800-466-8356)
This motel welcomes your pets to stay with you.

Quality Inn
3511 North Tracy Blvd
Tracy, CA
209-835-1335 (877-424-6423)
Dogs of all sizes are allowed. Dogs are allowed for a pet fee of $10.00 per pet per night.

Beautiful Tahoe Donner Home - Sleeps 12!
Visit Website to Book
Truckee, CA
408-354-5779
dogfriendlyrentalsllc.com
This non-smoking vacation rental is located across the street from the Tahoe National Forest in Truckee. The pet-friendly house sleeps up to 12 people and guests have access to the recreation facilities available in the community.

Best Western Truckee Tahoe Inn
11331 Brockway Road
Truckee, CA
530-587-4525 (800-780-7234)
Dogs of all sizes are allowed. Dogs are allowed for a pet fee.

Surry Cottage
Call to Arrange
Truckee, CA
530-414-3866
We are a 3 bedroom 2 bath house located in Truckee Ca. Located close to the Truckee River in a quiet subdivision. You can go to the

website to look at the property at...tahoecabinrentals.com/surrycottage. It states prices etc for one's visit.

Best Western Town & Country Lodge
1051 N Blackstone Street
Tulare, CA
559-688-7537 (800-780-7234)
Dogs of all sizes are allowed. Dogs are allowed for a pet fee of $20.00 per pet per stay.

Days Inn Tulare
1183 North Blackstone St
Tulare, CA
559-686-0985 (800-329-7466)
Dogs are welcome at this hotel.

Motel 6 - Tulare
1111 Blackstone Dr
Tulare, CA
559-686-1611 (800-466-8356)
This motel welcomes your pets to stay with you.

Best Western Orchard Inn
5025 N Golden State Boulevard
Turlock, CA
209-667-2827 (800-780-7234)
Dogs are welcome at this hotel.

Candlewood Suites Turlock
1000 Powers Court
Turlock, CA
209-250-1501 (877-270-6405)
Dogs up to 80 pounds are allowed. Pets allowed with an additional pet fee. Up to $75 for 1-6 nights and up to $150 for 7+ nights. A pet agreement must be signed at check-in.

Days Inn Turlock
185 N Tully Road
Turlock, CA
209-634-2944 (800-329-7466)
Dogs of all sizes are allowed. Dogs are allowed for a pet fee of $10.00 per pet per night.

Motel 6 - Turlock
250 Walnut Ave
Turlock, CA
209-667-4100 (800-466-8356)
This motel welcomes your pets to stay with you.

Travelodge Turlock
201 W Glenwood Ave
Turlock, CA
209-668-3400 (800-578-7878)
Dogs are welcome at this hotel.

29 Palms Inn
73950 Inn Avenue
Twentynine Palms, CA
760-367-3505

29palmsinn.com/
A natural high mountain desert oasis, this wonderful retreat is located on 30 acres of natural preserve and offers a variety of well- appointed accommodations and amenities. They also have a great garden to supply their seasonally influenced restaurant with fresh new tastes of the seasons, and there is dining inside or at the poolside tables. Dogs of all sizes are allowed for an additional one time fee of $35 per pet. Dogs may only be left alone if they will be well behaved, and they must be leashed and cleaned up after.

Harmony Hotel
71161 29 Palms H/H 62
Twentynine Palms, CA
760-367-3351
harmonymotel.com/
per pet for 2 dogs in the cabin, and a credit card must be on file. Dogs must be tick and flea free, housetrained, and friendly. Dogs may not be left alone in the room, and they must be leashed and cleaned up after at all times.

Motel 6 - Twentynine Palms
72562 Twentynine Palms
Twentynine Palms, CA
760-367-2833 (800-466-8356)
This motel welcomes your pets to stay with you.

Days Inn /Gateway to Redwoods Wine Country Ukiah
950 North State Street
Ukiah, CA
707-462-7584 (800-329-7466)
Dogs of all sizes are allowed. Dogs are allowed for a nightly pet fee.

Motel 6 - Ukiah
1208 State St
Ukiah, CA
707-468-5404 (800-466-8356)
This motel welcomes your pets to stay with you.

Quality Inn
1050 South State St.
Ukiah, CA
707-462-2906 (877-424-6423)
Dogs of all sizes are allowed.

Super 8 Ukiah
693 South Orchard Ave
Ukiah, CA
707-468-8181 (800-800-8000)
Dogs of all sizes are allowed. Dogs are allowed for a pet fee.

Extended Stay America Union City -

Dyer St.
31950 Dyer St.
Union City, CA
510-441-9616 (800-804-3724)
One dog is allowed per suite. There is a $25 per night additional pet fee up to $150 for an entire stay.

Sheraton Universal Hotel
333 Universal Hollywood Drive
Universal City, CA
818-980-1212 (888-625-5144)
Dogs up to 70 pounds are allowed at this luxury hotel near Universal Studios. There are no additional pet fees. Pet Sitting can be arranged by the hotel.

Super 8 Upper Lake
450 E Hwy 20
Upper Lake, CA
707-275-0888 (800-800-8000)
Dogs of all sizes are allowed. Dogs are allowed for a nightly pet fee.

Extended Stay America
Sacramento - Vacaville
799 Orange Dr.
Vacaville, CA
707-469-1371 (800-804-3724)
One dog is allowed per suite. There is a $25 per night additional pet fee up to $150 for an entire stay.

Motel 6 - Vacaville
107 Lawrence Dr
Vacaville, CA
707-447-5550 (800-466-8356)
This motel welcomes your pets to stay with you.

Residence Inn Vacaville
360 Orange Drive
Vacaville, CA
707-469-0300 (800-331-3131)
In addition to offering a convenient location to numerous sites of interest, activities, and world class attractions for business or pleasure travelers, this all suite hotel also offers a number of in-house amenities, including a daily buffet breakfast and evening socials Monday through Thursday with light dinner fare. Dogs are allowed for an additional one time pet fee of $100 per room. Multiple dogs may be allowed.

Super 8 Vacaville
101 Allison Court
Vacaville, CA
707-449-8884 (800-800-8000)
Dogs are welcome at this hotel.

Best Western Valencia Inn
27413 Wayne Mills Place

Valencia, CA
661-255-0555 (800-780-7234)
Dogs of all sizes are allowed. Dogs are allowed for a pet fee of $10.00 per pet per night.

Best Western Inn & Suites at Discovery Kingdom
1596 Fairgrounds Drive
Vallejo, CA
707-554-9655 (800-780-7234)
Dogs of all sizes are allowed. Dogs are allowed for a pet fee.

Motel 6 - Vallejo Maritime North
597 Sandy Beach Rd
Vallejo, CA
707-552-2912 (800-466-8356)
Your pets are welcome to stay here with you.

Motel 6 - Vallejo Six Flags East/fairgrounds
458 Fairgrounds Dr
Vallejo, CA
707-642-7781 (800-466-8356)
Your pets are welcome to stay here with you.

Motel 6 - Vallejo Six Flags West
1455 Enterprise St
Vallejo, CA
707-643-7611 (800-466-8356)
Your pets are welcome to stay here with you.

Ramada /Napa Valley Area Vallejo
1000 Admiral Callaghan Lane
Vallejo, CA
707-643-2700 (800-272-6232)
Dogs are welcome at this hotel.

Crowne Plaza Hotel Ventura Beach
450 E Harbor Blvd
Ventura, CA
805-648-2100 (877-270-6405)
Dogs of all sizes are allowed. Dogs are allowed for a pet fee of $50.00 per pet per night.

La Quinta Inn Ventura
5818 Valentine Rd.
Ventura, CA
805-658-6200 (800-531-5900)
Dogs of all sizes are allowed. There are no additional pet fees. Dogs must be leashed and cleaned up after. Dogs must be crated or attended to for housekeeping. Multiple dogs may be allowed.

Marriott Ventura Beach
2055 E Harbor Blvd
Ventura, CA
805-643-6000 (800-228-9290)
This luxury, beachfront hotel sits central to numerous businesses,

shopping, dining, and day/night entertainment areas, plus they also offer a number of in-house amenities for business and leisure travelers. Dogs are allowed for an additional one time fee of $75 per room. 2 dogs may be allowed.

Motel 6 - Ventura Beach
2145 Harbor Blvd
Ventura, CA
805-643-5100 (800-466-8356)
This motel welcomes your pets to stay with you.

Motel 6 - Ventura South
3075 Johnson Dr
Ventura, CA
805-650-0080 (800-466-8356)
This motel welcomes your pets to stay with you.

Vagabond Inn
756 E. Thompson Blvd.
Ventura, CA
805-648-5371
vagabondinn.com
Amenities at this motel include a free continental breakfast, weekday newspaper, and heated Jacuzzi. They also have an on-site coffee shop, which might be helpful in getting food to go for the room. There is a $10 per day per pet fee. Dogs may not be left alone in the rooms. 2 dogs may be allowed.

Days Inn Victorville
15401 Park Ave East
Victorville, CA
760-241-7516 (800-329-7466)
Dogs are welcome at this hotel.

Hawthorn Suites
11750 Dunia Road
Victorville, CA
760-949-4700 (800527-1133)
In addition to providing a convenient location to many local sites and activities, this all-suite hotel offers a number of amenities for business and leisure travelers, including their signature breakfast buffet and beautifully appointed rooms. Dogs are allowed for a $100 refundable deposit, plus an additional fee of $5 per night per pet. Multiple dogs may be allowed.

Howard Johnson Inn Victorville
16868 Stoddard Wells Road
Victorville, CA
760-243-7700 (800-446-4656)
Dogs of all sizes are allowed. Dogs are allowed for a pet fee of $15.00 per pet per night.

Motel 6 - Victorville
16901 Stoddard Wells Rd
Victorville, CA
760-243-0666 (800-466-8356)
This motel welcomes your pets to stay with you.

Red Roof Inns Victorville
13409 Mariposa Road
Victorville, CA
760-241-1577 (800-RED-ROOF)
One well-behaved family pet per room. Guest must notify front desk upon arrival. Guest is liable for any damages. In consideration of all guests, pets must never be left unattended in the guest rooms.

Travelodge Victorville
12175 Mariposa Rd
Victorville, CA
760-241-7200 (800-578-7878)
Dogs of all sizes are allowed. Dogs are allowed for a pet fee of $6.00 per pet per stay.

Holiday Inn Visalia-Hotel & Conf Center
9000 W Airport Dr
Visalia, CA
559-651-5000 (877-270-6405)
Dogs of all sizes are allowed. Dogs are allowed for a nightly pet fee.

Motel 6 - Visalia, Ca
4645 Noble Ave.
Visalia, CA
559-732-5611 (800-466-8356)
This motel welcomes your pets to stay with you.

Super 8 Visalia
4801 West Noble Ave
Visalia, CA
559-627-2885 (800-800-8000)
Dogs of all sizes are allowed. Dogs are allowed for a pet fee.

La Quinta Inn San Diego Vista
630 Sycamore Ave.
Vista, CA
760-727-8180 (800-531-5900)
Dogs of all sizes are allowed. There are no additional pet fees. Dogs may not be left unattended, and they must be leashed and cleaned up after. Multiple dogs may be allowed.

The St. George Hotel
16104 Main Street
Volcano, CA
209-296-4458
stgeorgehotel.com/
A well-behaved large dog, or 2 small dogs are allowed in one of the bungalow rooms. The non-smoking

pet-friendly room has hardwood floors, a queen bed, a private bath and garden views. There is an additional fee of $10 per night per pet. 2 dogs may be allowed.

Holiday Inn Express Walnut Creek
2730 No Main St
Walnut Creek, CA
925-932-3332 (877-270-6405)
Dogs up to 50 pounds are allowed. Dogs are allowed for a pet fee.

Motel 6 - Walnut Creek
2389 Main St
Walnut Creek, CA
925-935-4010 (800-466-8356)
This motel welcomes your pets to stay with you.

Best Western Rose Garden Inn
740 Freedom Boulevard
Watsonville, CA
831-724-3367 (800-780-7234)
Dogs of all sizes are allowed. Dogs are allowed for a pet fee of $15.00 per pet per night.

Comfort Inn
112 Airport Blvd.
Watsonville, CA
831-728-2300 (877-424-6423)
Dogs up to 50 pounds are allowed. Dogs are allowed for a pet fee of $15.00 per pet per night. Two dogs are allowed per room.

Motel 6 - Watsonville Monterey Area
125 Silver Leaf Dr
Watsonville, CA
831-728-4144 (800-466-8356)
This motel welcomes your pets to stay with you.

Red Roof Inn Watsonville
1620 West Beach Street
Watsonville, CA
831-740-4520 (800-RED-ROOF)
One well-behaved family pet per room. Guest must notify front desk upon arrival. Guest is liable for any damages. In consideration of all guests, pets must never be left unattended in the guest rooms.

Comfort Inn Central
1844 Shastina Drive
Weed, CA
530-938-1982 (877-424-6423)
Dogs of all sizes are allowed.

Lake Shastina Golf Resort
5925 Country Club Drive
Weed, CA
530-938-3201
lakeshastinagolfresort.net/
Dogs are allowed in some of the

condos at this 18 hole golf course resort. There is a $25 one time pet charge. 2 dogs may be allowed.

Motel 6 - Weed Mount Shasta
466 Weed Blvd
Weed, CA
530-938-4101 (800-466-8356)
This motel welcomes your pets to stay with you.

Quality Inn & Suites
1830 Black Butte Drive
Weed, CA
530-938-1308 (877-424-6423)
Dogs up to 90 pounds are allowed. Dogs are allowed for a pet fee of $15.00 per pet per night. Two dogs are allowed per room.

Le Montrose Suites
900 Hammond Street
West Hollywood, CA
310-855-1115 (800- 776-0666)
lemontrose.com/
A multi-million dollar renovation transformed this hotel into an elegant, stylish urban retreat with many conveniences for the business or leisure traveler. Some of the features include personalized services, several in-room amenities, a business center, and a beautiful outdoor pool and sunning area. Dogs are allowed for an additional $100 one time pet fee per room. Dogs may only be left alone in the room if they will be quiet, well behaved, and a contact number is left with the front desk. They also request that the sliding glass door be kept closed if a pet is in the room alone. Dogs must be leashed and cleaned up after at all times. Dogs are not allowed in food service areas or on the roof.

Extended Stay America Sacramento - West Sacramento
795 Stillwater Rd.
West Sacramento, CA
916-371-1270 (800-804-3724)
One dog is allowed per suite. There is a $25 per night additional pet fee up to $150 for an entire stay.

Motel 6 - Sacramento West
1254 Halyard Dr
West Sacramento, CA
916-372-3624 (800-466-8356)
This motel welcomes your pets to stay with you.

Residence Inn Los Angeles Westlake Village
30950 Russell Ranch Road
Westlake Village, CA
818-707-4411 (800-331-3131)

Besides offering a convenient location to universities, businesses, shopping, dining, and recreation areas, this all suite hotel also offers a number of in-house amenities, including a daily buffet breakfast and evening socials Monday through Thursday. Dogs are allowed for an additional one time pet fee of $75 per room. 2 dogs may be allowed.

Days Inn Westley
7144 McCracken Rd
Westley, CA
209-894-5500 (800-329-7466)
Dogs are welcome at this hotel.

Holiday Inn Express Westley
4525 Howard Rd / Po Box 307
Westley, CA
209-894-8940 (877-270-6405)
Dogs of all sizes are allowed. Dogs are allowed for a pet fee of $25.00 per pet per night.

Motel 6 - Westminster North
13100 Goldenwest St
Westminster, CA
714-895-0042 (800-466-8356)
This motel welcomes your pets to stay with you.

Motel 6 - Westminster South Long Beach Area
6266 Westminster Blvd
Westminster, CA
714-891-5366 (800-466-8356)
This motel welcomes your pets to stay with you.

Howard Creek Ranch Inn B&B
40501 N. Highway 1
Westport, CA
707-964-6725
howardcreekranch.com/
Howard Creek Ranch is a historic, 40 acre ocean front farm located about 5-6 hours north of San Francisco. Accommodations include cabins, suites and rooms. It is bordered by miles of beach and mountains. They offer award winning gardens, fireplaces or wood stoves, farm animals, a hot tub, and a sauna. Dog-friendly beaches nearby include Westport Union Landing State Beach in Westport, MacKerricher State Park 3-4 miles north of Fort Bragg and the 60 mile Sinkyone Wilderness Area (Lost Coast). Outdoor restaurants nearby are Jenny's Giant Burgers and Sea Pal (in Fort Bragg). Room rates are $80 and up (includes a full hearty ranch breakfast). There is a $15 (+ tax) per day pet charge. Certain dog rules apply: don't leave your dog

alone in the room, dogs must be supervised and attended at all times, bring towels to clean up your pooch if he/she gets dirty from outside, clean up after your dog, and if your dog will be on the bed, please use a sheet to cover the quilt (sheets can be provided). Dogs must not harrass the local animal population in any way. The inn is located 3 miles north of Westport. 2 dogs may be allowed.

Motel 6 - Los Angeles Whittier
8221 Pioneer Blvd
Whittier, CA
562-692-9101 (800-466-8356)
This motel welcomes your pets to stay with you.

Granzella's Inn
391 6th Street
Williams, CA
530-473-3310 (800-643-8614)
granzellasinn.com
This pet-friendly hotel offers a central location near the Sacramento Wildlife Refuge and the Colusa Casino.

Motel 6 - Williams, Ca
455 4th St
Williams, CA
530-473-5337 (800-466-8356)
This motel welcomes your pets to stay with you.

Quality Inn
400 C St.
Williams, CA
530-473-2381 (877-424-6423)
Dogs of all sizes are allowed. Dogs are allowed for a pet fee of $10.00usd per pet per night.

Ramada Williams
374 Ruggieri Way
Williams, CA
530-473-5120 (800-272-6232)
Dogs of all sizes are allowed. Dogs are allowed for a pet fee of $25.00 per pet per stay.

Days Inn CA Willows
475 N Humboldt Ave/I-5
Willows, CA
530-934-4444 (800-329-7466)
Dogs are welcome at this hotel.

Motel 6 - Willows
452 Humboldt Ave
Willows, CA
530-934-7026 (800-466-8356)
This motel welcomes your pets to stay with you.

Super 8 Willows
457 Humboldt Avenue

Willows, CA
530-934-2871 (800-800-8000)
Dogs of all sizes are allowed. Dogs are allowed for a pet fee.

Travelodge Willows
249 North Humboldt Ave
Willows, CA
530-934-4603 (800-578-7878)
Dogs of all sizes are allowed. Dogs are allowed for a pet fee.

Wickyup Bed and Breakfast Cottage
22702 Avenue 344
Woodlake, CA
559-564-8898
wickyup.com/
Dogs are allowed in the Calico Room Cottage. It offers bunk beds, a half-bath, and a discrete, enclosed outdoor shower. The cottage is located in the garden and has a private entrance. There is a $30 one time pet fee.

Days Inn Woodland
1524 E. Main Street
Woodland, CA
530-666-3800 (800-329-7466)
Dogs of all sizes are allowed. Dogs are allowed for a pet fee of $10 per pet per stay.

Holiday Inn Express Woodland
2070 Freeway Drive
Woodland, CA
530-662-7750 (877-270-6405)
Dogs of all sizes are allowed. Dogs are allowed for a nightly pet fee. Two dogs are allowed per room.

Motel 6 - Woodland Sacramento Area
1564 Main St
Woodland, CA
530-666-6777 (800-466-8356)
This motel welcomes your pets to stay with you.

Extended Stay America Los Angeles - Woodland Hills
20205 Ventura Blvd.
Woodland Hills, CA
818-710-1170 (800-804-3724)
One dog is allowed per suite. There is a $25 per night additional pet fee up to $150 for an entire stay.

Hilton Hotel
6360 Canoga Avenue
Woodland Hills, CA
818-595-1000 (800-HILTONS (445-8667))
This upscale hotel offers numerous on site amenities for business and leisure travelers, plus a convenient location to business, shopping,

dining, and entertainment areas. Dogs are allowed for an additional one time pet fee of $75 per room. 2 dogs may be allowed.

Warner Center Marriott
21850 Oxnard Street
Woodland Hills, CA
818-887-4800
warnercentermarriott.com
You and your dog are welcome at this Marriott hotel in the heart of the west San Fernando Valley. The hotel is located just off Highway 101 near Topanga Plaza and the Promenade Mall. There is a one time non-refundable $50 pet fee.

Extended Stay America Orange County -Yorba Linda
22711 Oakcrest Cir.
Yorba Linda, CA
714-998-9060 (800-804-3724)
One dog is allowed per suite. There is a $25 per night additional pet fee up to $150 for an entire stay.

The Other Place and the Long Valley Ranch
P.O. Box 49
Yorkville, CA
707-894-5322
Dogs of all sizes are allowed. There is no additional pet fee for 2 pets. If there are more than 2 pets the fee is $25 per night per pet

The Redwoods In Yosemite
PO Box 2085; Wawona Station
Yosemite National Park, CA
209-375-6666 (888-225-6666)
redwoodsinyosemite.com
Dog-friendly vacation rentals inside Yosemite National Park offer year-round vacation rentals that range in size from one to six bedrooms. Some of the rentals allow pets, but not all, so please specify your need for a pet unit when you make your reservation. There is a $10/night pet fee (per pet). Please abide by Yosemite's pet regulations, which require that pets be leashed at all times and are not permitted on many Park trails (a couple of exceptions are paved paths in the Valley Floor and a couple of short trails in the south Yosemite area). The rentals are located approximately 10 minutes inside the southern entrance of Yosemite National Park and offer 120 privately owned vacation rentals.

Vintage Inn
6541 Washington St.
Yountville, CA
707-944-1112 (800-351-1133)

vintageinn.com
This motel is located less than five miles from downtown San Diego and Sea World. It is close to the popular Dog Beach in Ocean Beach. The motel features an outdoor swimming pool, family unit rooms, cable television and more hotel amenities. Dogs are allowed for an additional one time pet fee of $40 per room. Dogs may not be left alone in the room at any time. Multiple dogs may be allowed.

Comfort Inn
1804 B Fort Jones Rd
Yreka, CA
530-842-1612 (877-424-6423)
Dogs of all sizes are allowed. Dogs are allowed for a pet fee of $10.00 per pet per night. Two dogs are allowed per room.

Econo Lodge Inn & Suites
526 S Main Street
Yreka, CA
530-842-4404 (877-424-6423)
Dogs up to 50 pounds are allowed. Dogs are allowed for a pet fee of $7.00/ per pet per night. Two dogs are allowed per room.

Motel 6 - Yreka
1785 Main St
Yreka, CA
530-842-4111 (800-466-8356)
This motel welcomes your pets to stay with you.

Relax Inn
1210 S Main Street
Yreka, CA
530-842-2791
Dogs of all sizes are allowed. There is a $5 per night per pet additional fee. 2 dogs may be allowed.

Rodeway Inn
1235 South Main Street
Yreka, CA
530-842-4412 (877-424-6423)
Dogs of all sizes are allowed. Dogs are allowed for a pet fee of $5.00 per pet per night. Two dogs are allowed per room.

Super 8 Yreka
136 Montague Rd
Yreka, CA
530-842-5781 (800-800-8000)
Dogs of all sizes are allowed. Dogs are allowed for a nightly pet fee.

Days Inn Yuba City
700 N. Palora Ave
Yuba City, CA
530-674-1711 (800-329-7466)

Dogs of all sizes are allowed. Dogs are allowed for a pet fee of $10 per pet per night.

Econo Lodge Inn & Suites
730 Palora Ave.
Yuba City, CA
530-674-1592 (877-424-6423)
Dogs up to 60 pounds are allowed. Dogs are allowed for a pet fee of $10.00 per pet per night.

Super 8 Yucca Val/Joshua Tree Nat Pk Area
57096 29 Palms Highway
Yucca Valley, CA
760-228-1773 (800-800-8000)
Dogs of all sizes are allowed. Dogs are allowed for a pet fee.

Colorado

Comfort Inn
6301 US 160
Alamosa, CO
719-587-9000 (877-424-6423)
Dogs of all sizes are allowed. Dogs are allowed for a pet fee of $20.00 per pet per night.

Days Inn Alamosa
224 O'Keefe Parkway
Alamosa, CO
719-589-9037 (800-329-7466)
Dogs are welcome at this hotel.

Super 8 Alamosa
2505 W Main
Alamosa, CO
719-589-6447 (800-800-8000)
Dogs are welcome at this hotel.

Harmel's Ranch Resort
P.O. Box 399
Almont, CO
970-641-1740 (800-235-3402)
harmels.com
Harmel's offers an exciting dude ranch experience for the entire family, including pets. They are located in the middle of Gunnison National Forest. They offer horseback riding, flyfishing, whitewater rafting, great dining, barbecue's, hayrides, square-dances, and numerous activities. The resort is located near Crested Butte and Gunnison.

Hotel Aspen
110 W. Main Street
Aspen, CO
970-925-3441 (800-527-7369)
hotelaspen.com
This dog-friendly hotel is located right on Main Street in Aspen.

Rooms are large and beautifully appointed and they come equipped with a wet bar, small refrigerator, coffee maker, microwave, iron, ironing board, hairdryer, humidifier, VCR, and air conditioning. Most rooms open onto terraces or balconies and some have private Jacuzzis. Dogs are allowed for an additional one time fee of $20 per pet. Multiple dogs may be allowed.

Hotel Jerome
330 E Main Street/H 82
Aspen, CO
970-920-1000 (800-331-7213)
This luxury hotel has been in service for more than a hundred years in the magnificent setting of the Rocky Mountains. Amenities include elegant accommodations, world class cuisine with 2 fine dining restaurants and outdoor dining in summer, 2 taverns, heated outdoor pool/Jacuzzi, underground parking, and much more. Dogs of all sizes are allowed. There is a $75 one time additional pet fee per room, and this includes a bed, bowls, and a doggy menu for canine companions. Dogs must be leashed and cleaned up after at all times, and they may only be left alone in the room for short periods. 2 dogs may be allowed.

Little Nell
675 E Durant Street
Aspen, CO
970-920-4600
There is a $125 one time pet fee, plus an additional $25 per night per room. Dogs are not allowed to be left unattended.

St. Regis Resort Aspen
315 East Dean St.
Aspen, CO
970-920-3300
Dogs of all sizes are allowed. There is a $100 per dog one time nonrefundable fee due at check in time. Dogs are not allowed to be left alone in the room.

The Sky Hotel
709 East Durant Avenue
Aspen, CO
970-925-6760
Well-behaved dogs of all kinds and sizes are welcome at this pet-friendly hotel. The luxury boutique hotel offers both rooms and suites. Hotel amenities include a heated outdoor pool, and a fitness room. There are no pet fees, just sign a pet waiver.

Best Western Gateway Inn & Suites
800 S Abilene Street
Aurora, CO
720-748-4800 (800-780-7234)
Dogs of all sizes are allowed. Dogs are allowed for a nightly pet fee.

Comfort Inn Denver International Airport
16921 E. 32nd Ave.
Aurora, CO
303-367-5000 (877-424-6423)
Dogs of all sizes are allowed. Dogs are allowed for a pet fee of $10.00 per pet per night.

Homestead Studio Suites Denver - Aurora
13941 E. Harvard Ave.
Aurora, CO
303-750-9116 (800-804-3724)
One dog is allowed per suite. There is a $25 per night additional pet fee up to $150 for an entire stay.

La Quinta Inn Denver Aurora
1011 S. Abilene St.
Aurora, CO
303-337-0206 (800-531-5900)
Dogs of all sizes are allowed. There are no additional pet fees. Dogs must be crated when left alone in the room, and they must be leashed and cleaned up after. 2 dogs may be allowed.

Motel 6 - Denver East Aurora
14031 Iliff Ave
Aurora, CO
303-873-0286 (800-466-8356)
This motel welcomes your pets to stay with you.

Residence Inn Denver Airport
16490 E 40th Circle
Aurora, CO
303-459-8000 (800-331-3131)
This all suite hotel sits central to several sites and institutes of interest, the airport, and major businesses, plus they offer a number of in-house amenities that include a daily buffet breakfast and evening socials Monday through Thursday. Dogs are allowed for an additional one time pet fee of $75 per room. Multiple dogs may be allowed.

Sleep Inn Denver International Airport
15900 E. 40th Ave
Aurora, CO
303-373-1616 (877-424-6423)
Dogs of all sizes are allowed. Dogs are allowed for a pet fee of $2.00 per pet per night. Two dogs are allowed per room.

Comfort Inn
0161 W. Beaver Creek Blvd.
Avon, CO
970-949-5511 (877-424-6423)
Dogs up to 50 pounds are allowed.
Dogs are allowed for a pet fee of
$50.00 per pet per stay.

Glen Isle Resort
Highway 285 (near milepost marker
221)
Bailey, CO
303-838-5461
Dogs are welcome in the cabins (no
designated smoking or non-smoking
cabins). All cabins contain fully
equipped kitchens, private baths,
easy chairs, bedding and linens,
fireplaces (wood provided) and gas
heat. Resort amenities include a
children's playground, games and
game room and a library. The resort
is within walking distance of the Pike
National Forest and the Platte River.
There you will find hours of dog-
friendly hiking trails. There is a $5
per day per pet charge. There are no
designated smoking or non-smoking
cabins. The resort is located 45 miles
southwest of Denver. 2 dogs may be
allowed.

Boulder Outlook Motel and Suites
800 28th Street
Boulder, CO
303-443-3322 (800-542-0304)
This luxury hotel offers a wide variety
of amenities and services, some of
which include a chlorine-free heated
indoor pool, a hot tub, a bouldering
wall for climbing, an Adventure guide
onsite to book outdoor activities,
complimentary continental breakfast,
restaurants, a bar, concierge level
service, and a lot more. They
welcome dogs and have a fully
fenced in dog run complete with
disposal amenities located adjacent
to the designated pet rooms. Dogs
are allowed for no additional fee.
Dogs may be left alone in the room
only if they will be quiet, and they
must be leashed and cleaned up
after. 2 dogs may be allowed.

Foot of the Mountain Motel
200 Arapahoe Ave.
Boulder, CO
303-442-5688
Pets are welcome at this log cabin
motel. There is an additional $5 per
day pet charge and a $50 refundable
deposit. There are no designated
smoking or non-smoking cabins.
Multiple dogs may be allowed.

Holiday Inn Express Boulder

4777 North Broadway
Boulder, CO
303-442-6600 (877-270-6405)
Dogs of all sizes are allowed. Dogs
are allowed for a pet fee of $25.00
per pet per night.

Homewood Suites
4950 Baseline Rd.
Boulder, CO
303-499-9922
There are no additional pet fees. 2
dogs may be allowed.

Quality Inn & Suites Boulder Creek
2020 Arapahoe Ave
Boulder, CO
303-449-7550 (877-424-6423)
Dogs up to 65 pounds are allowed.
Dogs are allowed for a pet fee of
$15.00 per pet per night.

Residence Inn Boulder
3030 Center Green Drive
Boulder, CO
303-449-5545 (800-331-3131)
There are a number of amenities
offered at this upscale hotel besides
having a great location to the areas
premier attractions - including a hot
continental breakfast, a
complimentary light dinner at a
nightly social hour, and in the
summer they have Wednesday
poolside barbecues. Dogs are
allowed for an additional one time
pet fee of $75 per room. Multiple
dogs may be allowed.

Great Divide Lodge
550 Village Road
Breckenridge, CO
970-547-5550 (888-906-5698)
This full-service, slope side hotel
features 208 spacious, luxury
guestrooms rich with amenities, 24
hour guest service, indoor and
outdoor pools and hot tubs, a large
sun deck, in room dining, a
restaurant and lounge, expansive
mountain views, and heated
underground parking. Although pet
friendly rooms are limited, dogs are
allowed for an additional pet fee of
$30 per night per room with
advance reservations. Dogs must
be well behaved, leashed, and
cleaned up after. 2 dogs may be
allowed.

Super 8 Brighton
15040 Brighton Rd
Brighton, CO
303-659-6063 (800-800-8000)
Dogs are welcome at this hotel.

TownePlace Suites Boulder

Broomfield
480 FlatIron Blvd
Broomfield, CO
303-466-2200 (800-257-3000)
This all suite inn sits central to
numerous business, shopping,
dining, and entertainment venues,
plus they offer a number of in-house
amenities for business and leisure
travelers. Dogs are allowed for an
additional one time fee of $100 per
room. Multiple dogs may be allowed.

Econo Lodge
1208 N. Colorado Ave
Brush, CO
970-842-5146 (877-424-6423)
Dogs of all sizes are allowed. Dogs
are allowed for a pet fee of $10.00
per pet per night. Two dogs are
allowed per room.

Comfort Inn
282 S. Lincoln
Burlington, CO
719-346-7676 (877-424-6423)
Dogs up to 70 pounds are allowed.
Dogs are allowed for a pet fee of
$15.00 per pet per night. Two dogs
are allowed per room.

Econo Lodge
15 5th Street
Calhan, CO
719-347-9589 (877-424-6423)
Dogs up to 50 pounds are allowed.
Dogs are allowed for a pet fee of
$15.00 per pet per night. Two dogs
are allowed per room.

Comfort Inn
311 Royal Gorge Blvd
Canon City, CO
719-276-6900 (877-424-6423)
Dogs of all sizes are allowed. Dogs
are allowed for a pet fee of $10.00
per pet per night.

Holiday Inn Express Canon City
110 Latigo Lane
Canon City, CO
719-275-2400 (877-270-6405)
Dogs of all sizes are allowed. Dogs
are allowed for a pet fee of $15.00
per pet per night. Two dogs are
allowed per room.

Quality Inn & Suites
3075 E. US 50
Canon City, CO
719-275-8676 (877-424-6423)
Dogs of all sizes are allowed.

Comfort Inn & Suites
920 Cowen Dr
Carbondale, CO
970-963-8880 (877-424-6423)

Beautiful property nestled in the Roaring Fork Valley, 30 minutes to Aspen. Ski, Golf, Fishing, Hiking, and Biking

Days Inn Carbondale
950 Cowen Drive
Carbondale, CO
970-963-9111 (800-329-7466)
Dogs of all sizes are allowed. Dogs are allowed for a pet fee of $10.00 per pet per night.

Best Western Inn & Suites of Castle Rock
595 Genoa Way
Castle Rock, CO
303-814-8800 (800-780-7234)
Dogs of all sizes are allowed. Dogs are allowed for a pet fee.

Comfort Suites
4755 Castleton Way
Castle Rock, CO
303-814-9999 (877-424-6423)
Dogs of all sizes are allowed. Dogs are allowed for a pet fee of $10.00 per pet per night.

Days Inn & Suites Castle Rock
4691 Castleton Way
Castle Rock, CO
303-814-5825 (800-329-7466)
Dogs of all sizes are allowed. Dogs are allowed for a pet fee.

Super 8 Colorado Castle Rock
1020 Park Street
Castle Rock, CO
303-688-0880 (800-800-8000)
Dogs are welcome at this hotel.

Howard Johnson Express - Cedaredge
530 South Grand Mesa Drive
Cedaredge, CO
970-856-7824 (800-446-4656)
Dogs are welcome at this hotel. There is a $10 one time pet fee.

Candlewood Suites Denver/Dtc
6780 South Galena Street
Centennial, CO
303-792-5393 (877-270-6405)
Dogs up to 80 pounds are allowed. Pets allowed with an additional pet fee. Up to $75 for 1-6 nights and up to $150 for 7+ nights. A pet agreement must be signed at check-in.

Staybridge Suites Denver Tech Center
7150 South Clinton Street
Centennial, CO
303-858-9990 (877-270-6405)
Dogs up to 80 pounds are allowed.

Pets allowed with an additional pet fee. Up to $75 for 1-6 nights and up to $150 for 7+ nights. A pet agreement must be signed at check-in.

Steamboat Lake Marina Camper Cabins
P. O. Box 867/H 62
Clark, CO
970-879-7019
Located in the scenic Steamboat Lake State Park at 8,100 feet on a beautiful 1,100 acre lake, this marina is now offering rental cabins for year around campers. Nestled in the pines and of log construction, the cabins each have a small refrigerator/freezer, coffee maker, some with table and chairs, and all have electric heat and fire pits. There is a convenience store at the marina, coin operated showers, flush toilets, and running water close to sites. Boat rentals are also available, and your dog is allowed to join you. Dogs of all sizes are allowed in the cabins. There is a $5 per night per pet additional fee. Dogs must be leashed and cleaned up after, and under owner's control at all times. A park pass is also required in addition to cabin fees.

Best Western Grande River Inn & Suites
3228 I-70 Business Loop
Clifton, CO
970-434-3400 (800-780-7234)
Dogs of all sizes are allowed. Dogs are allowed for a pet fee.

Days Inn Colorado
6670 W. Hwy 165
Colorado City, CO
719-676-2340 (800-329-7466)
Dogs of all sizes are allowed. Dogs are allowed for a pet fee.

Best Western The Academy Hotel
8110 N Academy Boulevard
Colorado Springs, CO
719-598-5770 (800-780-7234)
Dogs are welcome at this hotel.

Candlewood Suites Colorado Springs
6450 North Academy Boulevard
Colorado Springs, CO
719-590-1111 (877-270-6405)
Dogs up to 80 pounds are allowed. Pets allowed with an additional pet fee. Up to $75 for 1-6 nights and up to $150 for 7+ nights. A pet agreement must be signed at check-in.

Comfort Inn North
6450 Corporate Center Dr.
Colorado Springs, CO
719-262-9000 (877-424-6423)
Dogs of all sizes are allowed. Dogs are allowed for a pet fee of $10.00 per pet per night.

Comfort Inn South
1410 Harrison Rd
Colorado Springs, CO
719-579-6900 (877-424-6423)
Dogs of all sizes are allowed. Dogs are allowed for a pet fee of $25.00 per pet per stay.

Crowne Plaza Hotel Colorado Springs
2886 South Circle Drive
Colorado Springs, CO
719-576-5900 (877-270-6405)
Dogs up to 50 pounds are allowed. Dogs are allowed for a pet fee of $50.00 per pet per stay.

Days Inn Colorado Springs
2409 East Pikes Peak Ave
Colorado Springs, CO
719-471-0990 (800-329-7466)
Dogs are welcome at this hotel.

Days Inn Colorado Springs
2850 South Circle Dr/I-25
Colorado Springs, CO
719-527-0800 (800-329-7466)
Dogs of all sizes are allowed. Dogs are allowed for a pet fee.

Doubletree Hotel
1775 E Cheyenne Mountain Blvd.
Colorado Springs, CO
719-576-8900 (800-222-TREE (8733))
This upscale hotel offers a number of on site amenities for business or leisure travelers, plus a convenient location to historical, business, shopping, dining, and year around recreation areas. Dogs are allowed for an additional fee of $10 per night per pet. Multiple dogs may be allowed.

Econo Lodge Inn and Suites World Arena
1623 South Nevada
Colorado Springs, CO
719-632-6651
choicehotels.com/hotel/co725
This hotel has a large wooded park on site. They also have a staff veterinarian. There is no size restrictions for dogs. There is a playground for children on site. Pets and their owners may select either smoking or non smoking rooms. There is a $20 refundable pet

deposit. Pets must be crated if left in rooms and are not allowed to stay if they engage in persistent or periodic barking. Pets must be leashed while on the hotel property outside of the guest room.

Extended Stay America Colorado Springs - West
5855 Corporate Dr.
Colorado Springs, CO
719-266-4206 (800-804-3724)
One dog is allowed per suite. There is a $25 per night additional pet fee up to $150 for an entire stay.

Holiday Inn Express Hotel & Suites Co Springs-Air Force Academy
7110 Commerce Center Dr
Colorado Springs, CO
719-592-9800 (877-270-6405)
Dogs of all sizes are allowed. Dogs are allowed for a pet fee of $25.00 per pet per night.

Howard Johnson Colorado Springs
8280 Highway 83
Colorado Springs, CO
719-598-6700 (800-446-4656)
Dogs are welcome at this hotel.

La Quinta Inn & Suites Colorado Springs South AP
2750 Geyser Dr.
Colorado Springs, CO
719-527-4788 (800-531-5900)
Dogs up to 80 pounds are allowed. There are no additional fees. Leave a cell number with the front desk if your dog is alone in the room, and make arrangements with housekeeping if staying more than one day. Dogs may not be left unattended, and they must be leashed and cleaned up after. Multiple dogs may be allowed.

La Quinta Inn Colorado Springs Garden of the Gods
4385 Sinton Rd.
Colorado Springs, CO
719-528-5060 (800-531-5900)
Dogs of all sizes are allowed. There are no additional pet fees. Dogs may not be left unattended, and they must be leashed and cleaned up after. Multiple dogs may be allowed.

Motel 6 - Colorado Springs
3228 Chestnut St
Colorado Springs, CO
719-520-5400 (800-466-8356)
This motel welcomes your pets to stay with you.

Radisson Inn & Suites Colorado Springs Airport

1645 N. Newport Road
Colorado Springs, CO
719-597-7000
Up to 2 dogs per room are allowed. Each dog must not be larger than 50 pounds. There is a $100 refundable pet deposit and a $25 (+ tax) non-refundable one time fee per pet.

Ramada Limited East
520 N Murray Blvd
Colorado Springs, CO
719-596-7660 (800-272-6232)
Dogs of all sizes are allowed. Dogs are allowed for a pet fee.

Residence Inn Colorado Springs Central
3880 North Academy Blvd
Colorado Springs, CO
719-574-0370 (800-331-3131)
Located near many of the city's star attractions, universities, shopping, entertainment, and business areas, this all suite inn also offers a number of in-house amenities that include a daily buffet breakfast, evening socials Monday through Thursday, a children's playground, and a pet play area. Dogs are allowed for an additional one time pet fee of $75 per room. Multiple dogs may be allowed.

Residence Inn Colorado Springs North at Interquest
9805 Federal Drive
Colorado Springs, CO
719-388-9300 (800-331-3131)
Located in one of the area's budding communities, this upscale inn offers a convenient location to business, shopping, dining, and entertainment areas; plus, they also provide a number of in-house amenities - including a daily buffet breakfast and an evening social hour Monday to Wednesday with light dinner fare. Dogs are allowed for an additional one time pet fee of $75 per room. Multiple dogs may be allowed.

Residence Inn Colorado Springs South
2765 Geyser Drive
Colorado Springs, CO
719-576-0101 (800-331-3131)
This all suite hotel sits central to many of the city's star attractions, dining, shopping, and business areas, plus they offer a number of in-house amenities that include a daily buffet breakfast and evening socials Monday through Wednesday with light dinner fare. Dogs up to 75 pounds are allowed

for an additional one time pet fee of $75 per room. 2 dogs may be allowed.

Rodeway Inn & Suites
1623 S. Nevada Ave.
Colorado Springs, CO
719-623-2300 (877-424-6423)
Dogs of all sizes are allowed. Dogs are allowed for a pet fee of $10.00 per pet per stay. Two dogs are allowed per room.

Rodeway Inn Central
2409 E Pikes Peak
Colorado Springs, CO
719-471-0990
Dogs are allowed for an additional fee of $5 per night per pet.

Super 8
605 Peterson Rd
Colorado Springs, CO
719-597-4100 (800-800-8000)
Dogs are welcome at this hotel.

Staybridge Suites Co Springs-Air Force Academy
7130 Commerce Center Drive
Colorado Springs, CO
719-590-7829 (877-270-6405)
Dogs up to 80 pounds are allowed. Pets allowed with an additional pet fee. Up to $75 for 1-6 nights and up to $150 for 7+ nights. A pet agreement must be signed at check-in.

Super 8 Airport Colorado Springs
1790 Aeroplaza Dr.
Colorado Springs, CO
719-570-0505 (800-800-8000)
Dogs are welcome at this hotel.

Super 8 /Afa Area Colorado Springs
8135 N Academy Blvd (5)
Colorado Springs, CO
719-528-7100 (800-800-8000)
Dogs of all sizes are allowed. Dogs are allowed for a pet fee of $10.00 per pet per night.

TownePlace Suites Colorado Springs
4760 Centennial Blvd
Colorado Springs, CO
719-594-4447 (800-257-3000)
This all suite hotel offers a number of in-house amenities for all level of travelers, plus a convenient location to many of the area's star attractions, and business, shopping, and dining areas. Dogs are allowed for an additional one time pet fee of $100 per room. Multiple dogs may be allowed.

TownePlace Suites Colorado Springs

South
1530 N Newport Road
Colorado Springs, CO
719-638-0800 (800-257-3000)
This all suite inn sits central to numerous local attractions as well as business, shopping, and dining areas; plus, they also offer a number of in-house amenities for business and leisure travelers. Dogs are allowed for an additional one time pet fee of $75 per room. Multiple dogs may be allowed.

Travelodge Colorado Springs
2625 Ore Mill Rd.
Colorado Springs, CO
719-632-4600 (800-578-7878)
Dogs are welcome at this hotel.

Travelodge South Colorado Springs
1703 South Nevada Ave
Colorado Springs, CO
719-632-7077 (800-578-7878)
Dogs are welcome at this hotel.

Baymont Inn and Suites Cortez
2321 East Main Street
Cortez, CO
970-565-3400 (877-229-6668)
Dogs are welcome at this hotel.

Best Western Turquoise Inn & Suites
535 E Main Street
Cortez, CO
970-565-3778 (800-780-7234)
Dogs of all sizes are allowed. Dogs are allowed for a pet fee.

Days Inn Cortez
430 N State Hwy 145
Cortez, CO
970-565-8577 (800-329-7466)
Dogs are welcome at this hotel.

Econo Lodge
2020 E. Main St.
Cortez, CO
970-565-3474 (877-424-6423)
Dogs of all sizes are allowed. Dogs are allowed for a pet fee of $10.00 per pet per night.

Mesa Verde Inn
640 S. Broadway
Cortez, CO
970-565-3773 (800-972-6232)
cortezmesaverdeinn.com/
Dogs are allowed for an additional fee of $6 per night per pet. Multiple dogs may be allowed.

Rodeway Inn
1120 East Main
Cortez, CO
970-565-3761 (877-424-6423)
Dogs of all sizes are allowed. Dogs

are allowed for a pet fee of $10.00 per pet per night.

Super 8 /Mesa Verde Area Cortez
505 E Main St
Cortez, CO
970-565-8888 (800-800-8000)
Dogs are welcome at this hotel.

Best Western Deer Park Inn & Suites
262 Commerce Street (Hwy 13)
Craig, CO
970-824-9282 (800-780-7234)
Dogs are welcome at this hotel. There is a $10 pet fee.

Candlewood Suites Craig-Northwest
92 Commerce Street
Craig, CO
970-824-8400 (877-270-6405)
Dogs up to 80 pounds are allowed. Pets allowed with an additional pet fee. Up to $75 for 1-6 nights and up to $150 for 7+ nights. A pet agreement must be signed at check-in.

Holiday Inn Hotel & Suites Craig
300 S. Colorado Hwy 13
Craig, CO
970-824-4000 (877-270-6405)
Dogs are welcome at this hotel.

San Moritz Condos
18 Hunter Hill Rd.
Crested Butte, CO
970-349-5150 (800-443-7459)
petfriendlycrestedbutte.com
These 2, 3 and 4 bedroom condos allow dogs of all sizes for $10 per night for one dog or $15 per night for two dogs. Puppies are not allowed.

The Ruby of Crested Butte
624 Gothic Avenue
Crested Butte, CO
970-349-1338
Dogs of all sizes are allowed. There is a pet policy to sign at check in and there are no additional fees. 2 dogs may be allowed.

Comfort Inn
180 Gunnison River Dr.
Delta, CO
970-874-1000 (877-424-6423)
Dogs of all sizes are allowed. Dogs are allowed for a pet fee of $10.00 per pet per night.

Brown Palace Hotel & Spa
321 17th Street
Denver, CO
303-297-3111 (800-321-2599)

Dogs are allowed for an additional pet fee of $19 per day.

Cameron Motel
4500 E Evans
Denver, CO
303-757-2100
Dogs up to 50 pounds are allowed for a $5 per night per pet additional fee. Dogs must be well behaved, leashed, and cleaned up after. 2 dogs may be allowed.

Comfort Inn Central
401 E. 58th Ave.
Denver, CO
303-297-1717 (877-424-6423)
Dogs up to 50 pounds are allowed. Dogs are allowed for a pet fee of $10.00 per pet per night. Two dogs are allowed per room.

Comfort Inn Downtown
401 17th St.
Denver, CO
303-296-0400 (877-424-6423)
Dogs up to 75 pounds are allowed. Dogs are allowed for a pet fee of $50.00 per pet per night.

Crowne Plaza Hotel Denver - Intl Airport
15500 East 40th Ave
Denver, CO
303-371-9494 (877-270-6405)
Dogs of all sizes are allowed. Dogs are allowed for a pet fee.

Days Inn Central CO Denver
620 Federal Blvd
Denver, CO
303-571-1715 (800-329-7466)
Dogs are welcome at this hotel.

Denver East Drury Inn
4380 Peoria Street
Denver, CO
303-373-1983 (800-378-7946)
Dogs of all sizes are allowed for no additional pet fee with a credit card on file, and there is a pet agreement to sign at check in. There may be up to 3 dogs if they are small.

Econo Lodge Downtown
930 E. Colfax Ave
Denver, CO
303-813-8000 (877-424-6423)
Dogs of all sizes are allowed. Dogs are allowed for a pet fee of $25.00 per pet per night. Two dogs are allowed per room.

Embassy Suites
7525 E Hampden Avenue
Denver, CO
303-696-6644 (800-EMBASSY (362-

2779))

Offering a number of on site amenities for business and leisure travelers, this hotel sits in the city's tech center, and close to the downtown area where there are plenty of business, shopping, dining, and entertainment opportunities. They also offer a complimentary cooked-to-order breakfast and a Manager's reception every evening. The dog friendly rooms have an extra charge included in the room rate, so there is no additional fee. There is an additional pet fee of $100 per day per room for non-pet friendly rooms. Multiple dogs may be allowed.

Embassy Suites
4444 N Havana Street
Denver, CO
303-375-0400 (800-EMBASSY (362-2779))
This luxury, all suite hotel offers a number of on site amenities for all level of travelers, plus a convenient location to business, shopping, dining, and entertainment districts. They also offer a complimentary cooked-to-order breakfast and a Manager's reception every evening. Dogs are allowed for a $50 cash refundable deposit per room or a credit card on file. Multiple dogs may be allowed.

Four Points by Sheraton Denver South East
6363 East Hampden Ave.
Denver, CO
303-758-7000 (888-625-5144)
Dogs of all sizes are allowed. There are no additional pet fees. Dogs are not allowed to be left alone in the room.

Homestead Studio Suites Denver - Tech Center - North
4885 S. Quebec St.
Denver, CO
303-689-9443 (800-804-3724)
One dog is allowed per suite. There is a $25 per night additional pet fee up to $150 for an entire stay.

Hotel 3737
3737 Quebec St.
Denver, CO
303-388-6161 (800-2-RAMADA)
Pets are allowed for $25 per pet per visit. Multiple dogs may be allowed.

Hotel Monaco Denver
1717 Champa Street at 17th
Denver, CO
303-296-1717
monaco-denver.com/
Well-behaved dogs of all sizes are

welcome at this pet-friendly hotel. The luxury boutique hotel offers both rooms and suites. Hotel amenities include complimentary evening wine service, a 24 hour on-site fitness room, and a gift shop. There are no pet fees, just sign a pet liability form. Pit Bulls are not allowed in the city of Denver.

Hotel Teatro
1100 Fourteenth Street
Denver, CO
303-228-1100
hotelteatro.com/
Dogs are allowed at this luxury boutique hotel. There is no extra pet charge. Multiple dogs may be allowed.

Howard Johnson Inn - Denver
4765 Federal Boulevard
Denver, CO
303-433-8441 (800-446-4656)
Dogs of all sizes are allowed. Dogs are allowed for a pet fee.

Hyatt Regency Denver Tech Center
7800 East Tufts Avenue
Denver, CO
303-779-1234
This luxury hotel in the Denver Tech Center is an ideal location for access to the Tech Center and it is also close to downtown. There is a full business center, restaurant, snack bar and a sports bar in the hotel. Dogs up to 40 pounds are welcome. There is a $25 one time additional pet fee.

Inn at Cherry Creek
233 Clayton Street
Denver, CO
303-377-8577
innatcherrycreek.com/
Located in the heart of the Cherry Creek North shopping and restaurant district, this unique hotel features 35 cozy quest rooms and 2 corporate residences with an outdoor roof-top terrace that is perfect for open air parties. There are many in-room amenities, and a full service restaurant/bar that puts focus on a fresh seasonally influenced menu. Dogs of all sizes are allowed for an additional pet fee. Dogs may only be left alone in the room if they will be quiet and well behaved. Dogs must be leashed and cleaned up after at all times. 2 dogs may be allowed.

JW Marriott Denver at Cherry Creek
150 Clayton Lane
Denver, CO
303-316-2700 (800-228-9290)

In addition to offering a number of in-house amenities for all level of travelers, this luxury hotel also provides a convenient location to business, shopping, dining, and day/night entertainment areas. Dogs are allowed for no additional pet fee. Canine companions get their own sheepskin bed, a personalized engraved biscuit from Three Dog Bakery, and a designer food bowl. Multiple dogs may be allowed.

Knights Inn - Gateway to Downtown Denver
2601 Zuni B Street
Denver, CO
303-433-8586 (800-843-5644)
Dogs are welcome at this hotel.

La Quinta Inn Denver Central
3500 Park Ave. West
Denver, CO
303-458-1222 (800-531-5900)
Dogs of all sizes are allowed. There are no additional pet fees. Dogs must be crated with the "Do Not Disturb" sign on the door when left alone in the room, and crated or removed for housekeeping. Dogs must be leashed and cleaned up after. Multiple dogs may be allowed.

La Quinta Inn Denver Cherry Creek
1975 S. Colorado Blvd.
Denver, CO
303-758-8886 (800-531-5900)
Dogs of all sizes are allowed. There are no additional pet fees. Dogs may not be left unattended, and they must be leashed and cleaned up after. Multiple dogs may be allowed.

Loews Denver Hotel
4150 East Mississippi Ave.
Denver, CO
303-782-9300
All well-behaved dogs of any size are welcome. This upscale hotel offers their "Loews Loves Pets" program which includes special pet treats, local dog walking routes, and a list of nearby pet-friendly places to visit. There is an additional one time pet cleaning fee of $25 per room.

Marriott TownePlace Suites - Downtown
685 Speer Blvd
Denver, CO
303-722-2322 (800-257-3000)
towneplacesuites.com/dencb
Marriott TownePlace Suites is an all suite hotel designed for the extended stay traveler. All studio, one, and two-bedroom suites offer full kitchens and weekly housekeeping. Pets are welcome for a non-refundable fee of

$20 a day up to $200.00. On-site amenities include a guest laundry, business center, fitness room and free parking.

Motel 6 - Denver Airport
12020 39th Ave
Denver, CO
303-371-1980 (800-466-8356)
This motel welcomes your pets to stay with you.

Motel 6 - Denver Central Federal Boulevard
3050 49th Ave
Denver, CO
303-455-8888 (800-466-8356)
This motel welcomes your pets to stay with you.

Oxford Hotel
1600 17th St
Denver, CO
303-628-5400 (800-228-5838)
theoxfordhotel.com
This hotel is located in Denver's trendy LoDo District. Please mention that you are bringing a pet when making reservations.

Ramada Midtown Denver
2601 Zuni Street
Denver, CO
303-433-6677 (800-272-6232)
Dogs of all sizes are allowed. Dogs are allowed for a pet fee.

Ramada Inn Downtown Denver
1150 E. Colfax Ave
Denver, CO
303-831-7700 (800-272-6232)
Dogs are welcome at this hotel.

Renaissance Denver
3801 Quebec Street
Denver, CO
303-399-7500 (800-HOTELS-1 (468-3571))
In addition to offering a number of in-house amenities for all level of travelers, this luxury hotel also provides a convenient location to business, shopping, dining, and day/night entertainment areas. Dogs are allowed for an additional one time fee of $35 per pet. 2 dogs may be allowed.

Residence Inn Denver City Center
1725 Champa Street
Denver, CO
303-296-3444 (800-593-2809)
Besides being in easy walking distance to the Convention Center and all that downtown has to offer, this all suite inn also offers a number of in-house amenities including a

daily buffet breakfast and evening socials Monday through Thursday with light dinner fare. Dogs are allowed for an additional one time fee of $75 per pet. 2 dogs may be allowed.

Residence Inn Denver Downtown
2777 Zuni Street
Denver, CO
303-458-5318 (888-526-7135)
In addition to offering a convenient location to business, shopping, dining, and entertainment areas, this hotel also provides a number of in-house amenities, including a daily buffet breakfast and a happy hour Monday to Thursday. Dogs are allowed for an additional one time pet fee of $75 per room. Multiple dogs may be allowed.

Staybridge Suites Denver International Airport
6951 Tower Road
Denver, CO
303-574-0888 (877-270-6405)
Dogs up to 80 pounds are allowed. Pets allowed with an additional pet fee. Up to $75 for 1-6 nights and up to $150 for 7+ nights. A pet agreement must be signed at check-in.

Super 8 Stapleton Denver
7201 E 36th Ave
Denver, CO
303-393-7666 (800-800-8000)
Dogs are welcome at this hotel.

Super 8 /I-25 & 58th Ave. Denver
5888 N Broadway
Denver, CO
303-296-3100 (800-800-8000)
Dogs are welcome at this hotel.

The Curtis Hotel
1405 Curtis Street
Denver, CO
800-525-6651
There is an additional pet fee of $15 per night per room. 2 dogs may be allowed.

The Timbers
4411 Peoria Street
Denver, CO
303-373-1444
Dogs of all sizes are allowed. There is a $50 per stay per room fee and a pet policy to sign at check in.

The Westin Tabor Center
1672 Lawrence St.
Denver, CO
303-572-9100 (888-625-5144)
Dogs up to 50 pounds are allowed.

There are no additional pet fees. Dogs are not allowed to be left alone in the room.

TownePlace Suites Denver Downtown
685 Speer Blvd
Denver, CO
303-722-2322 (800-257-3000)
Situated along scenic Cherry Creek only a few blocks from the State Capitol and Civic Center Park, this all suite hotel also offers travelers a number of in-house amenities - including being located in the historic 1947 A.B. Hirschfeld Press Building. Dogs are allowed for an additional one time fee of $100 per room. Multiple dogs may be allowed.

TownePlace Suites Denver Southeast
3699 S Monaco Parkway
Denver, CO
303-759-9393 (800-257-3000)
This all suite inn sits adjacent to the light rail giving easy access to the university, convention center and the downtown area, plus they also offer travelers a number of in-house amenities. Dogs are allowed for an additional one time fee of $100 per room. 2 dogs may be allowed.

Ramada Plaza Denver North
10 East 120th Avenue
Denver (Northglenn), CO
303-452-4100 (800-272-6232)
Dogs of all sizes are allowed. Dogs are allowed for a nightly pet fee.

Best Western Ptarmigan Lodge
652 Lake Dillon Drive
Dillon, CO
970-468-2341 (800-780-7234)
Dogs of all sizes are allowed. Dogs are allowed for a pet fee of $15.00 per pet per stay.

Best Western Durango Inn & Suites
21382 US Highway 160 W
Durango, CO
970-247-3251 (800-780-7234)
Dogs of all sizes are allowed. Dogs are allowed for a nightly pet fee.

Doubletree Hotel
501 Camino Del Rio
Durango, CO
970-259-6580 (800-222-TREE (8733))
Set overlooking the Animas River, this downtown, upscale hotel offers a number of on site amenities for all level of travelers, plus a convenient location to business, shopping, dining, and year around recreation

areas. Dogs are allowed for an additional pet fee of $15 per night per room. Multiple dogs may be allowed.

Holiday Inn Durango
800 Camino Del Rio
Durango, CO
970-247-5393 (877-270-6405)
Dogs of all sizes are allowed. Dogs are allowed for a nightly pet fee.

Quality Inn
2930 N. Main Ave.
Durango, CO
970-259-5373 (877-424-6423)
Dogs of all sizes are allowed. Dogs are allowed for a pet fee of $15.00 per pet per night.

Residence Inn Durango
21691 H 160 W
Durango, CO
970-259-6200 (800-331-3131)
This all suite inn sits central to several year around recreational pursuits and a variety of interesting sites, plus they offer a number of in-house amenities - including a daily buffet breakfast and an evening hospitality hour Monday to Thursday from 5 to 7 pm. Dogs are allowed for an additional one time pet fee of $75 per room. 2 dogs may be allowed.

Rochester Hotel
726 E. Second Ave.
Durango, CO
970-385-1920 (800-664-1920)
rochesterhotel.com/
This beautifully renovated hotel offers fifteen spacious rooms with high ceilings, king or queen beds, and private baths, and is decorated in an Old West motif. This hotel, located in downtown Durango, was designated as 'The Flagship Hotel of Colorado' by Conde' Nast Traveler. They are very pet-friendly and offer two pet rooms, with a $20 per day per pet charge. The fee may be less depending on length of stay and size of dog. 2 dogs may be allowed.

Super 8 /Purgatory Durango
20 Stewart Drive
Durango, CO
970-259-0590 (800-800-8000)
Dogs are welcome at this hotel.

Travelodge Durango
2970 Main Avenue
Durango, CO
970-247-1741 (800-578-7878)
Dogs of all sizes are allowed. Dogs are allowed for a pet fee of $15 per pet per stay.

Best Western Eagle Lodge
200 Loren Ln
Eagle, CO
970-328-6316 (800-780-7234)
Dogs of all sizes are allowed. Dogs are allowed for a pet fee of $10 per pet per night.

Holiday Inn Express Eagle
0075 Pond Road
Eagle, CO
970-328-8088 (877-270-6405)
Dogs of all sizes are allowed. Dogs are allowed for a pet fee of $50.00 per pet per stay.

Candlewood Suites Meridian Business Park
10535 El Diente Ct
Englewood, CO
303-858-9900 (877-270-6405)
Dogs up to 80 pounds are allowed. Pets allowed with an additional pet fee. Up to $75 for 1-6 nights and up to $150 for 7+ nights. A pet agreement must be signed at check-in.

Days Inn Denver Tech Center Englewood
9719 E Geddes
Englewood, CO
303-768-9400 (800-329-7466)
Dogs are welcome at this hotel.

Embassy Suites
10250 E Costilla Avenue
Englewood, CO
303-792-0433 (800-EMBASSY (362-2779))
Located in the heart of the city's Tech Center, this luxury, all suite hotel offers a number of on site amenities for all level of travelers, plus a convenient location to business, shopping, dining, and entertainment districts. They also offer a complimentary cooked-to-order breakfast and a Manager's reception every evening. Dogs are allowed for no additional fee. Multiple dogs may be allowed.

Holiday Inn Express Hotel & Suites Englewood
7380 South Clinton Street
Englewood, CO
303-662-0777 (877-270-6405)
Dogs of all sizes are allowed. Dogs are allowed for a pet fee of $50.00 per pet per stay.

Homestead Studio Suites Denver - Tech South - Inverness
9650 E. Geddes Ave.
Englewood, CO

303-708-8888 (800-804-3724)
One dog is allowed per suite. There is a $25 per night additional pet fee up to $150 for an entire stay.

Residence Inn Denver South/Park Meadows Mall
8322 South Valley Highway
Englewood, CO
720-895-0200 (800-331-3131)
Located in the Inverness and Meridian Business Parks, this hotel offers a convenient location to several businesses, plus they offer a number of in-house amenities, including a daily buffet breakfast and evening socials Monday through Thursday with light dinner fare from 5 to 7 pm. Dogs are allowed for an additional one time pet fee of $100 per room. 2 dogs may be allowed.

Residence Inn Denver Tech Center
6565 S Yosemite
Englewood, CO
303-740-7177 (800-331-3131)
Besides being located at the Denver Tech Center and only 15 miles from downtown, this all suite hotel offers a number of in-house amenities including a daily buffet breakfast and evening socials Monday through Thursday. Dogs are allowed for an additional one time pet fee of $75 per room. Multiple dogs may be allowed.

Sheraton Denver Technical Center Hotel
7007 South Clinton St.
Englewood, CO
303-799-6200 (888-625-5144)
Dogs up to 80 pounds are allowed for no additional pet fee. Dogs may not be left alone in the room.

TownePlace Suites Denver Tech Center
7877 S Chester Street
Englewood, CO
720-875-1113 (800-257-3000)
Besides offering a number of in-house amenities, this all suite inn, located in the Denver Tech Center, gives a convenient location to major businesses and the Park Meadows Mall is only a mile away. Dogs are allowed for an additional one time fee of $100 per room. Multiple dogs may be allowed.

Cliffside Cottages
2445 H 66
Estes Park, CO
970-586-4839
cliffsidecottages.com/
Set among tall pines and lush grass and foliage, this get-a-way destination offers a variety of

completely furnished cottages (except food/clothing) with cable TV; a fenced in dog exercise area with night lighting, and WiFi access. Well mannered dogs are welcome for no additional fee. Multiple dogs may be allowed.

Econo Lodge Inn & Suites
1650 Big Thompson Avenue
Estes Park, CO
970-586-3386 (877-424-6423)
Dogs up to 75 pounds are allowed. Dogs are allowed for a pet fee of $20.00 per pet per night. Two dogs are allowed per room.

Rodeway Inn
1701 North Lake Ave
Estes Park, CO
970-586-5363 (877-424-6423)
Dogs of all sizes are allowed. Dogs are allowed for a pet fee of $10.00 per pet per night.

Motel 6 - Greeley Evans
3015 8th Avenue
Evans, CO
970-351-6481 (800-466-8356)
This motel welcomes your pets to stay with you.

Quality Suites at Evergreen Parkway
29300 US Highway 40
Evergreen, CO
303-526-2000 (877-424-6423)
Dogs up to 80 pounds are allowed. Dogs are allowed for a pet fee of $10.00 per pet per night. Two dogs are allowed per room.

Super 8 Canon City A Florence
4540 State Hwy 67
Florence, CO
719-784-4800 (800-800-8000)
Dogs are welcome at this hotel.

Best Western Kiva Inn
1638 E Mulberry Street
Fort Collins, CO
970-484-2444 (800-780-7234)
Dogs of all sizes are allowed. Dogs are allowed for a pet fee of $10 per pet per night.

Best Western University Inn
914 S College Avenue
Fort Collins, CO
970-484-1984 (800-780-7234)
Dogs of all sizes are allowed. Dogs are allowed for a pet fee of $15 per pet per night.

Comfort Suites
1415 Oakridge Drive
Fort Collins, CO
970-206-4597 (877-424-6423)

Dogs up to 50 pounds are allowed. Dogs are allowed for a pet fee of $15.00 per pet per night.

Days Inn Fort Collins
3625 East Mulberry/I-25
Fort Collins, CO
970-221-5490 (800-329-7466)
Dogs of all sizes are allowed. Dogs are allowed for a pet fee.

Holiday Inn Express Hotel & Suites Ft. Collins
1426 Oakridge Drive
Fort Collins, CO
970-225-2200 (877-270-6405)
Dogs of all sizes are allowed. Dogs are allowed for a pet fee of $30.00 per pet per night.

Motel 6 - Fort Collins
3900 Mulberry St
Fort Collins, CO
970-482-6466 (800-466-8356)
This motel welcomes your pets to stay with you.

Residence Inn Fort Collins
1127 Oakridge Drive
Fort Collins, CO
970-223-5700 (800-548-2635)
Offering a convenient location to business, historic, shopping, dining, and recreation areas, this all suite hotel also offers a number of in-house amenities, including a daily buffet breakfast and evening social hours. Dogs are allowed for an additional one time pet fee of $100 per room. 2 dogs may be allowed.

Sleep Inn
3808 E. Mulberry St.
Fort Collins, CO
970-484-5515 (877-424-6423)
Dogs of all sizes are allowed. Dogs are allowed for a pet fee of $10.00 per pet per stay.

Super 8 Fort Collins
409 Centro Way
Fort Collins, CO
970-493-7701 (800-800-8000)
Dogs of all sizes are allowed. Dogs are allowed for a nightly pet fee.

Motel 6 - Fort Lupton
65 Grand Ave
Fort Lupton, CO
303-857-1800 (800-466-8356)
This motel welcomes your pets to stay with you.

Rodeway Inn
1409 Barlow Rd.
Fort Morgan, CO
970-867-9481 (877-424-6423)

Dogs up to 65 pounds are allowed. Dogs are allowed for a pet fee of $10.00 per pet per night.

Super 8 Fountain
6120 East Champlain Drive
Fountain, CO
719-382-4610 (800-800-8000)
Dogs are welcome at this hotel.

Best Western Lake Dillon Lodge
1202 Summit Boulevard
Frisco, CO
970-668-5094 (800-780-7234)
Dogs of all sizes are allowed. Dogs are allowed for a pet fee of $20 per pet per stay.

Holiday Inn Summit County-Frisco
1129 N. Summit Blvd.
Frisco, CO
970-668-5000 (877-270-6405)
Dogs of all sizes are allowed. Dogs are allowed for a pet fee of $50.00 per pet per stay.

Hotel Frisco
308 Main Street
Frisco, CO
970-668-5009 (800-262-1002)
Dogs are welcome at this classic Rocky Mountain lodge which is located on Frisco's historic Main Street. The hotel offers two dog-friendly rooms with access to the back porch and to the doggie run. Enjoy hiking and swimming with your dog right from the hotel's front door! Dog amenities include dog beds and treats. Dog sitting and walking services are also available. There is a $10 per day pet fee.

Ramada Limited Frisco
990 Lakepoint Dr
Frisco, CO
970-668-8783 (800-272-6232)
Dogs of all sizes are allowed. Dogs are allowed for a pet fee of $10.00 per pet per night.

Comfort Inn
400 Jurassic Ave
Fruita, CO
970-858-1333 (877-424-6423)
Dogs of all sizes are allowed.

La Quinta Inn & Suites Fruita
570 Raptor Road
Fruita, CO
970-858-8850 (800-531-5900)
Dogs of all sizes are allowed. There are no additional pet fees. Dogs must be crated when left alone in the room, and they may not be left unattended at all between the hours or 8 pm and 9 am. Dogs must be

kept leashed. Multiple dogs may be allowed.

Super 8 Fruita
I-70 Exit 19
Fruita, CO
970-858-0808 (800-800-8000)
Dogs of all sizes are allowed. Dogs are allowed for a pet fee of $5 per pet per night.

Super 8 Georgetown
1600 Argentine St
Georgetown, CO
303-569-3211 (800-800-8000)
Dogs are welcome at this hotel.

Homestead Studio Suites Denver - Cherry Creek
4444 Leetsdale Dr.
Glendale, CO
303-388-3880 (800-804-3724)
One dog is allowed per suite. There is a $25 per night additional pet fee up to $150 for an entire stay.

Staybridge Suites Denver-Cherry Creek
4220 E. Virginia Avenue
Glendale, CO
303-321-5757 (877-270-6405)
Dogs up to 80 pounds are allowed. Pets allowed with an additional pet fee. Up to $75 for 1-6 nights and up to $150 for 7+ nights. A pet agreement must be signed at check-in.

Hotel Colorado
526 Pine Street
Glenwood Springs, CO
970-945-6511 (800-544-3998)
This elegant hotel offers a superior setting and a great location near a wide variety of recreational opportunities. Dogs of all sizes are allowed. There is a $25 per night per pet additional fee. Dogs must be declared at check in, and they prefer that dogs are not left alone in the room because the hotel is also registered as a haunted hotel . If it is necessary for a short time, a Do Not Disturb sign can be put on the door. If there is a chance they may become uncomfortable and/or bark, they request you leave a contact number at the front desk, and they must be crated unless they will be relaxed and quiet. Dogs must be well behaved, leashed, and cleaned up after.

Quality Inn & Suites On The River
2650 Gilstrap Court
Glenwood Springs, CO
970-945-5995 (877-424-6423)

Dogs of all sizes are allowed. Dogs are allowed for a pet fee of $10.00 per pet per night.

Ramada Inn and Suites
124 West 6th Street
Glenwood Springs, CO
970-945-2500 (800-272-6232)
Dogs of all sizes are allowed. Dogs are allowed for a nightly pet fee.

Red Mountain Inn
51637 H 6/24
Glenwood Springs, CO
970-945-6353 (800-748-2565)
Dogs of all sizes are allowed. There is a $10 per night per pet additional fee. Dogs may only be left alone in the room if they will be well behaved and quiet, and the Do Not Disturb sign is put on the door. Dogs must be leashed and cleaned up after.

Candlewood Suites Denver/Lakewood
895 Tabor Street
Golden, CO
303-232-7171 (877-270-6405)
Dogs up to 80 pounds are allowed. Pets allowed with an additional pet fee. Up to $75 for 1-6 nights and up to $150 for 7+ nights. A pet agreement must be signed at check-in.

Comfort Suites Denver West/Federal Center
11909 W. 6th Ave.
Golden, CO
303-231-9929 (877-424-6423)
Dogs of all sizes are allowed. Dogs are allowed for a pet fee of $10.00 per pet per night.

Holiday Inn Denver-W(Across From Co Mills)
14707 W. Colfax Ave.
Golden, CO
303-279-7611 (877-270-6405)
Dogs are welcome at this hotel.

La Quinta Inn Denver Golden
3301 Youngfield Service Rd.
Golden, CO
303-279-5565 (800-531-5900)
Dogs of all sizes are allowed. There are no additional pet fees. Dogs may only be left unattended in the room if they will be quiet and well behaved. Multiple dogs may be allowed.

Residence Inn Denver West/Golden
14600 W 6th Avenue
Golden, CO
303-271-0909 (800-283-1084)
In addition to offering a convenient

location to business, shopping, dining, and entertainment areas, this all suite hotel offers a number of in-house amenities including a daily buffet breakfast and evening socials Monday through Thursday. Dogs up to 50 pounds are allowed for an additional pet fee of $25 per night per room for the 1st one to three days, and the fee is $100 for 4 or more days. 2 dogs may be allowed.

The Golden Hotel, an Ascend Collection hotel
800 11th Street
Golden, CO
303-279-0100 (877-424-6423)
Dogs up to 75 pounds are allowed. Dogs are allowed for a pet fee of $15.00 per pet per night.

TownePlace Suites Denver West/Federal Center
800 Tabor Street
Golden, CO
303-232-7790 (800-257-3000)
This all suite inn features Green and Gluten-Free accommodations, plus they also provide a number of other in-house amenities. Dogs are allowed for an additional one time fee of $100 per room. Multiple dogs may be allowed.

Best Western Sandman Motel
708 Horizon Drive
Grand Junction, CO
970-243-4150 (800-780-7234)
Dogs of all sizes are allowed. Dogs are allowed for a pet fee of $25.00 per pet per stay.

Clarion Inn
755 Horizon Drive
Grand Junction, CO
970-243-6790 (877-424-6423)
Dogs of all sizes are allowed. Two dogs are allowed per room.

Hawthorn Suites
225 Main Street
Grand Junction, CO
970-242-2525 (800-527-1133)
In addition to providing a convenient location to many local sites and activities, this all-suite hotel offers a number of amenities for business and leisure travelers, including their signature breakfast buffet and beautifully appointed rooms. Dogs are allowed for an additional fee of $25 per night per pet up to 5 nights; then there is no further charge. 2 dogs may be allowed.

La Quinta Inn & Suites Grand Junction

2761 Crossroads Blvd.
Grand Junction, CO
970-241-2929 (800-531-5900)
Dogs of all sizes are allowed. There are no additional pet fees. Dogs may not be left unattended, and they must be leashed and cleaned up after. Dogs must be crated or removed for housekeeping. Multiple dogs may be allowed.

Motel 6 - Grand Junction
776 Horizon Dr
Grand Junction, CO
970-243-2628 (800-466-8356)
This motel welcomes your pets to stay with you.

Ramada Inn Grand Junction
752 Horizon Drive
Grand Junction, CO
970-243-5150 (800-272-6232)
Dogs are welcome at this hotel.

Residence Inn Grand Junction
767 Horizon Drive
Grand Junction, CO
970-263-4004 (800-936-1903)
Besides offering a convenient location to the airport and business, shopping, dining, and recreation areas, this hotel also provides a number of in-house amenities, including a daily buffet breakfast and evening social hours Monday and Wednesday and every other Tuesday. Dogs are allowed for an additional one time pet fee of $100 per room. Multiple dogs may be allowed.

Rodeway Inn
141 N First Street
Grand Junction, CO
970-245-8585 (877-424-6423)
Dogs of all sizes are allowed. Dogs are allowed for a pet fee of $15.00 per pet per night. Two dogs are allowed per room.

Super 8 Colorado Grand Junction
728 Horizon Drive
Grand Junction, CO
970-248-8080 (800-800-8000)
Dogs are welcome at this hotel.

Mountain Lakes Lodge
10480 H 34
Grand Lake, CO
970-627-8448
There is a $25 one time pet fee per room on the 1st visit to this lodge, but the pet fee is reduced to only $10 for every stay thereafter.

Clarion Hotel and Conference Center
701 8th Street

Greeley, CO
970-353-8444 (877-424-6423)
Dogs up to 50 pounds are allowed. Dogs are allowed for a pet fee of $25.00 per pet per stay. Two dogs are allowed per room.

Comfort Inn
2467 W. 29th Street
Greeley, CO
970-330-6380 (877-424-6423)
Dogs of all sizes are allowed. Dogs are allowed for a pet fee of $15.00 per pet per night. Two dogs are allowed per room.

Days Inn Greeley
5630 W. 10th St.
Greeley, CO
970-392-1530 (800-329-7466)
Dogs of all sizes are allowed. Dogs are allowed for a pet fee.

Super 8 Greeley
2423 W 29th St
Greeley, CO
970-330-8880 (800-800-8000)
Dogs of all sizes are allowed. Dogs are allowed for a pet fee of $15.00 per pet per night.

Extended Stay America Denver - Tech Center - North
5200 S. Quebec St.
Greenwood Village, CO
303-220-8448 (800-804-3724)
One dog is allowed per suite. There is a $25 per night additional pet fee up to $150 for an entire stay.

La Quinta Inn & Suites Denver Englewood/Tech Ctr
9009 E. Arapahoe Road
Greenwood Village, CO
303-799-4555 (800-531-5900)
Dogs of all sizes are allowed. There are no additional pet fees. Dogs must be leashed, cleaned up after, removed for housekeeping, and the front desk notified if there is a pet in the room alone. 2 dogs may be allowed.

Motel 6 - Denver South South Tech Center
9201 E. Arapahoe Road
Greenwood Village, CO
303-790-8220 (800-466-8356)
This motel welcomes your pets to stay with you.

Homestead Studio Suites Denver - Tech South - Greenwood Village
9253 E. Costilla Ave.
Greenwood Villiage, CO
303-858-1669 (800-804-3724)
One dog is allowed per suite. There

is a $25 per night additional pet fee up to $150 for an entire stay.

Days Inn Gunnison
701 West Highway 50
Gunnison, CO
970-641-0608 (800-329-7466)
Dogs are welcome at this hotel.

Quality Inn
400 E. Tomichi Avenue
Gunnison, CO
970-641-1237 (877-424-6423)
Dogs up to 65 pounds are allowed. Dogs are allowed for a pet fee of $15.00 per pet per night.

Super 8 /Crested Butte Area
Gunnison
411 E Tomichi Ave
Gunnison, CO
970-641-3068 (800-800-8000)
Dogs of all sizes are allowed. Dogs are allowed for a pet fee of $10.00 per pet per night.

Comfort Suites Denver South
7060 E. County Line Rd.
Highlands Ranch, CO
303-770-5400 (877-424-6423)
Dogs up to 50 pounds are allowed. Dogs are allowed for a pet fee of $15.00 per pet per night.

Residence Inn Denver Highlands Ranch
93 West Centennial Blvd
Highlands Ranch, CO
303-683-5500 (800-331-3131)
Located in an elite residential and business community with a number of shopping districts and attractions close by, this all suite inn offers a great location plus a number of in-house amenities including a daily buffet breakfast and evening socials. Dogs are allowed for an additional one time pet fee of $100 per room. 2 dogs may be allowed.

Best Western Denver Southwest
3440 S Vance Street
Lakewood, CO
303-989-5500 (800-780-7234)
Dogs are welcome at this hotel.

Comfort Suites Southwest
7260 W. Jefferson
Lakewood, CO
303-988-8600 (877-424-6423)
Dogs of all sizes are allowed. Dogs are allowed for a pet fee of $15.00 per pet per night.

Extended Stay America Denver - Lakewood South
7393 W. Jefferson Ave.

Lakewood, CO
303-986-8300 (800-804-3724)
One dog is allowed per suite. There is a $25 per night additional pet fee up to $150 for an entire stay.

Extended Stay America Denver - Lakewood West
715 Kipling St.
Lakewood, CO
303-275-0840 (800-804-3724)
One dog is allowed per suite. There is a $25 per night additional pet fee up to $150 for an entire stay.

La Quinta Inn & Suites Denver Southwest Lakewood
7190 West Hampden Ave.
Lakewood, CO
303-969-9700 (800-531-5900)
Dogs of most sizes are allowed; no extra large dogs. There are no additional pet fees. Dogs may only be left unattended in the room if they will be very quiet and well behaved, and leave the "Do Not Disturb" sign on the door. Dogs must be leashed. 2 dogs may be allowed.

Motel 6 - Denver Lakewood
480 Wadsworth Blvd
Lakewood, CO
303-232-4924 (800-466-8356)
This motel welcomes your pets to stay with you.

Residence Inn Denver Southwest/Lakewood
7050 W Hampden Avenue
Lakewood, CO
303-985-7676 (800-331-3131)
Offering a convenient location to business, shopping, dining, and entertainment areas, this all suite hotel also offers a number of in-house amenities including a daily buffet breakfast and evening socials Monday through Thursday. Dogs are allowed for an additional one time pet fee of $100 per room. 2 dogs may be allowed.

Sheraton Denver West Hotel
360 Union Blvd.
Lakewood, CO
303-987-2000 (888-625-5144)
Dogs are allowed for no additional pet fee. Dogs are restricted to rooms on the 4th floor only, and they may only be left alone in the room for very short periods. 2 dogs may be allowed.

Super 8 /Denver Area Lakewood
7240 West Jefferson Avenue
Lakewood, CO
303-989-4600 (800-800-8000)

Dogs of all sizes are allowed. Dogs are allowed for a nightly pet fee.

Super 8 Lamar
1202 N Main St
Lamar, CO
719-336-3427 (800-800-8000)
Dogs are welcome at this hotel.

Best Western Bent's Fort Inn
E US 50
Las Animas, CO
719-456-0011 (800-780-7234)
Dogs of all sizes are allowed. Dogs are allowed for a pet fee of $10.00 per pet per night.

Econo Lodge
985 Hwy. 24
Limon, CO
719-775-2867 (877-424-6423)
Dogs of all sizes are allowed. Dogs are allowed for a pet fee of $12.50 per pet per night.

Super 8 Limon
I-70 Hwy 24
Limon, CO
719-775-2889 (800-800-8000)
Dogs of all sizes are allowed. Dogs are allowed for a pet fee.

Holiday Inn Express Hotel & Suites Littleton
12683 West Indore Place
Littleton, CO
720-981-1000 (877-270-6405)
Dogs are welcome at this hotel.

Staybridge Suites Denver South-Park Meadows
7820 Park Meadows Dr
Littleton, CO
303-649-1010 (877-270-6405)
Dogs up to 80 pounds are allowed. Pets allowed with an additional pet fee. Up to $75 for 1-6 nights and up to $150 for 7+ nights. A pet agreement must be signed at check-in.

TownePlace Suites Denver Southwest
10902 W Toller Drive
Littleton, CO
303-972-0555 (800-257-3000)
This all suite hotel gives a convenient location to local major companies, shopping, dining, and recreation areas, plus they also offer a number of in-house amenities for all level of travelers. Dogs are allowed for an additional one time fee of $100 per room. 2 dogs may be allowed.

Extended Stay America Denver -

Park Meadows
8752 S. Yosemite St.
Lone Tree, CO
303-662-1511 (800-804-3724)
One dog is allowed per suite. There is a $25 per night additional pet fee up to $150 for an entire stay.

Days Inn Longmont
3820 Hwy 119
Longmont, CO
303-651-6999 (800-329-7466)
Dogs are welcome at this hotel.

Hawthorn Suites
2000 Sunset Way
Longmont, CO
303-774-7100 (800-527-1133)
In addition to providing a convenient location to many local sites and activities, this all-suite hotel offers a number of amenities for business and leisure travelers, including their signature breakfast buffet and beautifully appointed rooms. Dogs are allowed for a $50 refundable deposit for 1 week, and a $100 refundable deposit if over 1 week. Multiple dogs may be allowed.

Holiday Inn Express Hotel & Suites Longmont
1355 Dry Creek Drive
Longmont, CO
303-684-0404 (877-270-6405)
Dogs of all sizes are allowed. Dogs are allowed for a pet fee of $30.00 per pet per night.

Residence Inn Boulder Longmont
1450 Dry Creek Drive
Longmont, CO
303-702-9933 (800-331-3131)
This all suite inn features a convenient location to business, shopping, dining, and entertainment areas, plus they also offer a number of in-house amenities, including a daily buffet breakfast and evening socials Monday to Wednesday. Dogs are allowed for an additional one time pet fee of $100 per room. 2 dogs may be allowed.

Super 8 /Twin Peaks Longmont
2446 N Main St
Longmont, CO
303-772-8106 (800-800-8000)
Dogs are welcome at this hotel.

Super 8/Del Camino Longmont
10805 Turner Blvd
Longmont, CO
303-772-0888 (800-800-8000)
Dogs are welcome at this hotel.

Comfort Inn

1196 Dillon Rd.
Louisville, CO
303-604-0181 (877-424-6423)
Dogs up to 100 pounds are allowed.
Dogs are allowed for a pet fee of
$15.00 per pet per night. Two dogs
are allowed per room.

La Quinta Inn & Suites Denver
Louisville Boulder
902 Dillon Rd.
Louisville, CO
303-664-0100 (800-531-5900)
Dogs of all sizes are allowed. There
are no additional pet fees. There is a
pet waiver to sign at check in, and a
cell number needs to be left with the
front desk if your pet is left alone in
the room. Also, place the "Do Not
Disturb" sign on the door so
housekeeping does not enter. There
is a specified pet area where dogs
are to be taken, and they must be
leashed and cleaned up after.
Multiple dogs may be allowed.

Quality Inn & Suites
960 W. Dillon Road
Louisville, CO
303-327-1215 (877-424-6423)
Dogs of all sizes are allowed. Dogs
are allowed for a pet fee of $15.00
per pet per night.

Residence Inn Boulder Louisville
845 Coal Creek Circle
Louisville, CO
303-665-2661 (800-331-3131)
Offering a convenient location to
business, shopping, dining, and
entertainment areas, this all suite
hotel also offers a number of in-
house amenities, including a daily
buffet breakfast, and an evening
hospitality hour Monday through
Thursday. Dogs are allowed for an
additional one time pet fee of $100
per room. 2 dogs may be allowed.

Best Western Crossroads Inn &
Conference Center
5542 E US Highway 34
Loveland, CO
970-667-7810 (800-780-7234)
Dogs of all sizes are allowed. Dogs
are allowed for a nightly pet fee.

Candlewood Suites Loveland
6046 East Crossroads Blvd
Loveland, CO
970-667-5444 (877-270-6405)
Dogs up to 80 pounds are allowed.
Pets allowed with an additional pet
fee. Up to $75 for 1-6 nights and up
to $150 for 7+ nights. A pet
agreement must be signed at check-
in.

Residence Inn Loveland
5450 McWhinney Blvd
Loveland, CO
970-622-7000 (800-331-3131)
In addition to offering a convenient
location to business, shopping,
dining, and recreation areas, this
hotel also provides a number of in-
house amenities, including a daily
buffet breakfast and an evening
social hour Monday to Thursday
with adult beverages and
appetizers. Dogs are allowed for an
additional one time pet fee of $75
per room. 2 dogs may be allowed.

Super 8 /Fort Collins Area Loveland
1655 E Eisenhower Blvd
Loveland, CO
970-663-7000 (800-800-8000)
Dogs of all sizes are allowed. Dogs
are allowed for a nightly pet fee.

Far View Lodge
Mesa Verde National Park
Mancos, CO
970-529-4421
Far View Lodge sits on a high
shoulder of the Mesa Verde,
offering panoramic vistas into three
states. There is a $50 refundable
pet deposit, plus an additional pet
fee of $10 per night per pet in the
lodge. Dogs are allowed in standard
rooms only. There is no additional
fee for dogs in the campground.
Dogs are not allowed on the trails,
at archeological sites, in buildings,
or on tours. Multiple dogs may be
allowed.

Morefield Lodge and Campground
34879 H 160
Mancos, CO
800-449-2288
Dogs of all sizes are allowed. There
is a $50 refundable deposit plus an
additional $10 per night per pet fee.
Dogs may not be left unattended,
and they must be leashed and
cleaned up after at all times. There
is an RV and campground on site
where dogs are allowed at no extra
fee. Dogs may not be on the trails
or in the camp buildings. 2 dogs
may be allowed.

Super 8 Cos Area/Pikes P Manitou
Springs
229 Manitou Ave
Manitou Springs, CO
719-685-5898 (800-800-8000)
Dogs are welcome at this hotel.

Best Western Red Arrow
1702 E Main Street

Montrose, CO
970-249-9641 (800-780-7234)
Dogs of all sizes are allowed. Dogs
are allowed for a nightly pet fee.

Black Canyon Motel
1605 E. Main Street
Montrose, CO
970-249-3495 (800-348-3495)
innfinders.com/blackcyn/
There is a $5 per day per pet
additional fee. Multiple dogs may be
allowed.

Days Inn Montrose
1417 E Main St
Montrose, CO
970-249-4507 (800-329-7466)
Dogs of all sizes are allowed. Dogs
are allowed for a pet fee of $10.00
per pet per stay.

Holiday Inn Express Hotel & Suites
Montrose-Townsend
1391 S Townsend Ave
Montrose, CO
970-240-1800 (877-270-6405)
Dogs are welcome at this hotel.

Quality Inn & Suites
2751 Commercial Way
Montrose, CO
970-249-1011 (877-424-6423)
Dogs of all sizes are allowed. Dogs
are allowed for a pet fee of $10.00
per pet per night.

Rodeway Inn
1705 E. Main St.
Montrose, CO
970-249-9294 (877-424-6423)
Dogs of all sizes are allowed. Dogs
are allowed for a pet fee of $10.00
per pet per stay. Two dogs are
allowed per room.

Best Western Lodge at Nederland
55 Lakeview Drive
Nederland, CO
303-258-9463 (800-780-7234)
Dogs of all sizes are allowed. Dogs
are allowed for a pet fee of $10.00
per pet per night.

Rodeway Inn
781 Burning Mountain Avenue
New Castle, CO
970-984-2363 (877-424-6423)
Dogs of all sizes are allowed. Dogs
are allowed for a pet fee of $10.00
per pet per night.

Comfort Inn
191 5th Ave
Ouray, CO
970-325-7203 (877-424-6423)
Dogs of all sizes are allowed. Dogs

are allowed for a pet fee of $15.00 per pet per night.

Rivers Edge Motel
110 7th Avenue
Ouray, CO
970-325-4621
There is a $10 per day pet charge. Multiple dogs may be allowed.

Econo Lodge
315 Navajo Trail Drive
Pagosa Springs, CO
970-731-2701 (877-424-6423)
Dogs of all sizes are allowed. Dogs are allowed for a pet fee of $10.00 per pet per night.

Fireside Inn
1600 E Hwy 160
Pagosa Springs, CO
970-264-9204 (888-264-9204)
They offer modern one and two bedroom cabins (built in 1996) with fireplaces, hot tubs, kitchens and more. The cabins are located on seven acres on the San Juan River. Dogs and horses are welcome. There is a $8.50 per day per pet additional fee. 2 dogs may be allowed.

High Country Lodge
3821 E Hwy 160
Pagosa Springs, CO
970-264-4181 (800-862-3707)
Dogs are allowed in the cabins. There is a $10 per night per pet additional fee. All cabins are non-smoking. Multiple dogs may be allowed.

Candlewood Suites Parachute
233 Grand Valley Way
Parachute, CO
970-285-9880 (877-270-6405)
Dogs up to 80 pounds are allowed. Pets allowed with an additional pet fee. Up to $75 for 1-6 nights and up to $150 for 7+ nights. A pet agreement must be signed at check-in.

Holiday Inn Select Denver-Parker-E470/Parker Rd
19308 Cottonwood Drive
Parker, CO
303-248-2147 (877-270-6405)
Dogs of all sizes are allowed. Dogs are allowed for a pet fee.

Super 8 /SE Denver Area Parker
6230 East Pine Lane
Parker, CO
720-851-2644 (800-800-8000)
Dogs of all sizes are allowed. Dogs are allowed for a pet fee.

Best Western Eagleridge Inn & Suites
4727 N Elizabeth Street
Pueblo, CO
719-543-4644 (800-780-7234)
Dogs of all sizes are allowed. Dogs are allowed for a nightly pet fee.

Holiday Inn Hotel & Suites Pueblo
4530 Dillon Drive
Pueblo, CO
719-542-8888 (877-270-6405)
Dogs of all sizes are allowed. Dogs are allowed for a pet fee.

Howard Johnson Pueblo
4005 N. Elizabeth Street
Pueblo, CO
719-543-1278 (800-446-4656)
Dogs of all sizes are allowed. Dogs are allowed for a pet fee of $10.00 per pet per stay.

Motel 6 - Pueblo I-25
4103 Elizabeth St
Pueblo, CO
719-543-6221 (800-466-8356)
This motel welcomes your pets to stay with you.

Ramada Pueblo
4703 North Freeway
Pueblo, CO
719-544-4700 (800-272-6232)
Dogs are welcome at this hotel.

Sleep Inn
3626 North Freeway
Pueblo, CO
719-583-4000 (877-424-6423)
Dogs of all sizes are allowed. Dogs are allowed for a pet fee of $15.00/pet, per pet per night.

Super 8 Pueblo
1100 Hwy 50 W
Pueblo, CO
719-545-4104 (800-800-8000)
Dogs of all sizes are allowed. Dogs are allowed for a nightly pet fee.

Sundance Trail Guest Ranch
17931 Red Feather Lakes Road
Red Feather Lakes, CO
970-224-1222
Dogs of all sizes are allowed. There are no additional pet fees.

Buckskin Inn
101 Ray Avenue
Rifle, CO
970-625-1741 (877-282-5754)
buckskininn.com/
Amenities include Satellite TV, multiple HBO, microwaves, refrigerators, and free local calls.

There is no charge for a pet, but please let staff know when reserving a room. Pets cannot be left unattended in the rooms. Multiple dogs may be allowed.

Super 8 Rifle
301 S. 7th Street
Rifle, CO
970-625-9912 (800-800-8000)
Dogs are welcome at this hotel.

Super 8 Salida
525 W Rainbow Blvd
Salida, CO
719-539-6689 (800-800-8000)
Dogs are welcome at this hotel.

Travelodge Salida
7310 West US Hwy 50
Salida, CO
719-539-2528 (800-578-7878)
Dogs of all sizes are allowed. Dogs are allowed for a pet fee.

Woodland Motel
903 W 1st Street
Salida, CO
719-539-4980
Dogs are allowed for no additional pet fees. 2 dogs may be allowed.

Days Inn Silverthorne
580 Silverthorne Lane
Silverthorne, CO
970-468-8661 (800-329-7466)
Dogs of all sizes are allowed. Dogs are allowed for a pet fee of $5 per pet per night.

Quality Inn & Suites Summit County
530 Silverthorne Lane
Silverthorne, CO
970-513-1222 (877-424-6423)
Dogs of all sizes are allowed. Dogs are allowed for a pet fee of $10.00 per pet per night.

Canyon View Motel
661 Greene Street
Silverton, CO
970-387-5400
Every room really does have a canyon view here. Dogs are allowed for no additional fee. Dogs may not be left alone in the room, and they must be leashed and cleaned up after.

The Wyman Hotel & Inn
1371 Greene Street
Silverton, CO
970-387-5372 (800-609-7845)
This hotel and inn, the recipient of several accolades for food and service and listed on the National Register of Historic Places, offer the

ambiance of a bed and breakfast, and personal service for any special occasion. They feature a full gourmet breakfast each morning, and a 3-course candlelight diner each evening. Friendly dogs of all sizes are allowed. There is a $25 one time additional pet fee per room, and a pet policy to sign at check in. Dogs may not be left alone in the room, and they must be leashed and cleaned up after. 2 dogs may be allowed.

Alpiner Lodge
424 Lincoln Ave.
Steamboat Springs, CO
970-879-1430 (800-538-7519)
toski.com/sli/2s.html
There is an $10 one time pet fee. Multiple dogs may be allowed.

Comfort Inn
1055 Walton Creek Rd.
Steamboat Springs, CO
970-879-6669 (877-424-6423)
Dogs of all sizes are allowed. Dogs are allowed for a pet fee of $20.00 per pet per night.

Holiday Inn Steamboat Springs
3190 South Lincoln Ave
Steamboat Springs, CO
970-879-2250 (877-270-6405)
Dogs of all sizes are allowed. Dogs are allowed for a nightly pet fee.

La Quinta Inn Steamboat Springs
3155 Ingles Lane
Steamboat Springs, CO
970-871-1219 (800-531-5900)
Dogs of all sizes are allowed. There is a $10 per night per stay additional fee. Dogs may not be left unattended unless they will be quiet, well behaved, and a contact number left with the front desk. Dogs must be leashed and cleaned up after. Multiple dogs may be allowed.

Rabbit Ears Motel
201 Lincoln Avenue /H 40
Steamboat Springs, CO
970-879-1150
This motel is located across from the famous Steamboat Health and Recreation Association and their natural hot spring pools as well as several other worthy local attractions. Some of the amenities offered are a free full continental breakfast, discounted Hot Springs Pool passes, and a large gathering room. Dogs of all sizes are allowed. There is a $15 one time additional pet fee per room. Dogs may not be left alone in the room, and they must be leashed and cleaned up after.

Sheraton Steamboat Resort & Conference Center
2200 Village Inn Court
Steamboat Springs, CO
970-879-2220 (888-625-5144)
Dogs up to 80 pounds are allowed for an additional one time pet fee of $35 per room. Dogs may not be left alone in the room.

Best Western Sundowner
125 Overland Trl
Sterling, CO
970-522-6265 (800-780-7234)
Dogs of all sizes are allowed. Dogs are allowed for a pet fee of $10.00 per pet per night.

Ramada Sterling
22140 East Highway 6
Sterling, CO
970-522-2625 (800-272-6232)
Dogs are welcome at this hotel.

Super 8 CO Sterling
12883 Hwy 61
Sterling, CO
970-522-0300 (800-800-8000)
Dogs of all sizes are allowed. Dogs are allowed for a pet fee of $10.00 per pet per night.

Travelodge
12881 Highway 61
Sterling, CO
970-522-2300 (800-578-7878)
Dogs of all sizes are allowed. Dogs are allowed for a pet fee of $10 per pet per night.

Best Western Golden Prairie Inn
700 Colorado Avenue
Stratton, CO
719-348-5311 (800-780-7234)
Dogs are welcome at this hotel. There is a $10 pet fee.

Hotel Columbia Telluride
300 W. San Juan Ave.
Telluride, CO
970-728-0660 (800-201-9505)
columbiatelluride.com/
This full service resort hotel welcomes your best friend. They are located just two blocks from the downtown shops and restaurants. There is a $15 per day pet charge. All rooms are non-smoking.

Mountain Lodge Telluride
457 Mountain Village Blvd.
Telluride, CO
866-368-6867
This rustic pet-friendly lodge is located in Telluride's Mountain Village Resort community with

views of the San Juan Mountains. There are 125 dog-friendly rooms in the lodge. There is a $50 per day pet fee up to a maximum of $150 per stay. The lodge offers pet beds, bowls and treats to their dog visitors and have pet pick-up stations around the property.

The Peaks Resort and Spa
136 Country Club Drive
Telluride, CO
970-728-6800 (800-789-2220)
thepeaksresort.com/
There is a $75 one time fee for 1 dog, and a $100 one time fee for 2 dogs. 2 dogs may be allowed.

Motel 6 - Denver Thornton
83rd Pl
Thornton, CO
303-429-1550 (800-466-8356)
This motel welcomes your pets to stay with you.

Sleep Inn
12101 Grant Street
Thornton, CO
303-280-9818 (877-424-6423)
Dogs of all sizes are allowed. Dogs are allowed for a pet fee of $10.00 per pet per stay.

Holiday Inn Hotel & Suites Trinidad
3130 Santa Fe Trail Dr.
Trinidad, CO
719-845-8400 (877-270-6405)
Dogs of all sizes are allowed. Dogs are allowed for a pet fee of $20.00 per pet per night.

Super 8 Trinidad
1924 Freedom Rd
Trinidad, CO
719-846-8280 (800-800-8000)
Dogs are welcome at this hotel.

Antlers at Vail
680 W. Lionshead Place
Vail, CO
970-476-2471 (800-843-8245)
antlersvail.com/
This hotel and condo complex is definitely dog-friendly. They have had large doggie guests like a 250 pound mastiff. They have several pet rooms and there is a $15 per day pet charge. There are no designated smoking or non-smoking units. Multiple dogs may be allowed.

Holiday Inn Vail
2211 N. Frontage Road
Vail, CO
970-476-2739 (877-270-6405)
Dogs up to 50 pounds are allowed. Dogs are allowed for a nightly pet

fee.

Lifthouse Condominiums
555 E Lionshead Circle
Vail, CO
970-476-2340 (800-654-0635)
lifthousevail.com/index.cfm
Looking out upon Vail's ski runs, the Lifthouse has a great location for many other activities, and offer several in-house amenities. Dogs of all sizes are allowed for an additional fee of $25 per night per pet. Dogs must be crated or removed for housekeeping, and they must be leashed and cleaned up after at all times. 2 dogs may be allowed.

Sonnenalp Resort of Vail
20 Vail Road
Vail, CO
970-479-5441 (866-284-4411)
sonnenalp.com
One dog is allowed at this European Style resort in Vail for an additional $100 fee per room.

Best Western Rambler
457 US Highway 85 87
Walsenburg, CO
719-738-1121 (800-780-7234)
Dogs of all sizes are allowed. Dogs are allowed for a nightly pet fee.

Days Inn Wellington
7860 6th St
Wellington, CO
970-568-0444 (800-329-7466)
Dogs are welcome at this hotel.

Jack's Cabin
30 County Road 388
Wentmore, CO
719-784-3160
Dogs of all sizes are allowed. There are no additional pet fees and they request you kennel your pet when out. Dogs may not be left alone outside at night at any time. 2 dogs may be allowed.

Comfort Inn Northwest
8500 Turnpike Dr.
Westminster, CO
303-428-3333 (877-424-6423)
Dogs of all sizes are allowed. Dogs are allowed for a pet fee of $10.00 per pet per night. Two dogs are allowed per room.

Comfort Suites
12085 Delaware St.
Westminster, CO
303-429-5500 (877-424-6423)
Dogs of all sizes are allowed. Dogs are allowed for a pet fee of $15.00 per pet per stay.

Doubletree Hotel
8773 Yates Drive
Westminster, CO
303-427-4000 (800-222-TREE (8733))
This upscale hotel offers a number of on site amenities for business or leisure travelers, plus a convenient location to airports, business, shopping, dining, and year around recreation areas. Dogs are allowed for an additional one time fee of $25 per pet. 2 dogs may be allowed.

Extended Stay America Denver - Westminster
1291 W. 120th Ave.
Westminster, CO
303-280-0111 (800-804-3724)
One dog is allowed per suite. There is a $25 per night additional pet fee up to $150 for an entire stay.

La Quinta Inn & Suites Westminster Promenade
10179 Church Ranch Way
Westminster, CO
303-438-5800 (800-531-5900)
Dogs of all sizes are allowed. There are no additional pet fees. Dogs must be leashed and cleaned up after. Multiple dogs may be allowed.

La Quinta Inn Denver Northglenn
345 West 120th Ave.
Westminster, CO
303-252-9800 (800-531-5900)
Dogs of all sizes are allowed. There are no additional pet fees. Dogs must be crated when left alone in the room. Dogs must be leashed and cleaned up after. Multiple dogs may be allowed.

La Quinta Inn Denver Westminster Mall
8701 Turnpike Dr.
Westminster, CO
303-425-9099 (800-531-5900)
One large dog or 2 small to medium dogs are allowed. There are no additional pet fees. Dogs must be leashed.

Residence Inn Denver North/Westminster
5010 W 88th Place
Westminster, CO
303-427-9500 (800-331-3131)
In addition to offering a convenient location to business, shopping, dining, and entertainment areas, this hotel also provides a number of in-house amenities, including a daily buffet breakfast and an evening social hour. Dogs are

allowed for an additional one time pet fee of $75 per room. 2 dogs may be allowed.

Super 8 Westminister Denver North
12055 Melody Dr
Westminster, CO
303-451-7200 (800-800-8000)
Dogs of all sizes are allowed. Dogs are allowed for a nightly pet fee.

The Westin Westminster
10600 Westminster Blvd.
Westminster, CO
303-410-5000 (888-625-5144)
Dogs of all sizes are allowed. There are no additional pet fees. Dogs are not allowed to be left alone in the room.

Holiday Inn Express Hotel & Suites Wheat Ridge-Denver West
10101 South I-70 Service Road
Wheat Ridge, CO
303-424-8300 (877-270-6405)
Dogs of all sizes are allowed. Dogs are allowed for a nightly pet fee.

Motel 6 - Denver West Wheat Ridge North
9920 49th Ave
Wheat Ridge, CO
303-424-0658 (800-466-8356)
This motel welcomes your pets to stay with you.

Ramada Denver West
4700 Kipling Street
Wheat Ridge, CO
303-423-4000 (800-272-6232)
Dogs of all sizes are allowed. Dogs are allowed for a pet fee.

Howard Johnson Denver West
12100 W 44th Ave
Wheatridge, CO
303-467-2400 (800-446-4656)
Dogs of all sizes are allowed. Dogs are allowed for a pet fee of $10.00 per pet per stay.

Super 8 Windsor
1265 Main Street
Windsor, CO
970-686-5996 (800-800-8000)
Dogs are welcome at this hotel.

Beaver Village Lodge
79303 H 40
Winter Park, CO
970-726-5741
Dogs of all sizes are allowed in the main lodge only. There is a $20 one time pet fee. 2 dogs may be allowed.

Best Western Alpenglo Lodge
78665 US Highway 40

Winter Park, CO
970-726-8088 (800-780-7234)
Dogs of all sizes are allowed. Dogs are allowed for a pet fee of $10.00 per pet per night.

Winter Park Resort
85 Parsenn Road
Winter Park, CO
970-726-5514 (800-979-0332)
skiwinterpark.com/index.htm
There is an abundance of year around recreation at this mountain resort; they have planned events and fun activities for all ages to enjoy, a free daytime lift for easy get-a-around, and the resort is home to the state's longest alpine slide. Additionally, there are shopping, dining, and various entertainment opportunities, and besides being the only major ski resort with regular AMTRAK service, they are also the closest major recreation resort to the Denver International Airport. Dogs are allowed at the Vintage Hotel and Winter Park Mountain Lodge for an additional one time pet fee of $25 for 1 dog and an additional one time pet fee of $10 for a 2nd dog. Dogs are also allowed on the Village Cabriolet lift and the resort usually runs summer specials for canines and their human companions. 2 dogs may be allowed.

BackCountry Estate in Vail Valley
Call to Arrange
Wolcott, CO
970-949-0229 (800-525-2076)
vailvalleylodging.com
About 20 Minutes from Vail and Beaver Creek, this home sits on 35 acres and is over 4000 square feet. Dogs of all sizes are allowed.

Connecticut

Residence Inn Hartford Avon
55 Simsbury Road
Avon, CT
860-678-1666 (800-331-3131)
In addition to being within walking distance to shopping, dining, and recreation areas - including a walking trail less than a block away, this hotel also provides a number of in-house amenities, including a daily buffet breakfast and evening social hours. Dogs are allowed for an additional one time pet fee of $100 per room. Multiple dogs may be allowed.

Days Inn CT Berlin
2387 Berlin Turnpike
Berlin, CT

860-828-4181 (800-329-7466)
Dogs are welcome at this hotel.

Days Inn - Danbury Bethel
18 Stony Hill Road
Bethel, CT
203-743-5990 (800-329-7466)
Dogs of all sizes are allowed. Dogs are allowed for a pet fee.

Baymont Inn & Suites /New Haven Branford
3 Business Park Drive
Branford, CT
203-488-4991 (877-229-6668)
Dogs are welcome at this hotel.

Motel 6 - New Haven Branford
320 East Main Street
Branford, CT
203-483-5828 (800-466-8356)
This motel welcomes your pets to stay with you.

Holiday Inn Bridgeport
1070 Main Street
Bridgeport, CT
203-334-1234 (877-270-6405)
Dogs of all sizes are allowed. Dogs are allowed for a nightly pet fee.

Twin Tree Inn
1030 Federal Rd
Brookfield, CT
203-775-0220
There is a $10 per night per pet additional fee. 2 dogs may be allowed.

Comfort Inn
111 Berlin Rd.
Cromwell, CT
860-635-4100 (877-424-6423)
Dogs of all sizes are allowed. Dogs are allowed for a pet fee of $15.00 per pet per night. Dogs are allowed for a pet fee of $60.00 per pet per stay. Two dogs are allowed per room.

Holiday Inn Danbury-Bethel @ I-84
80 Newtown Rd
Danbury, CT
203-792-4000 (877-270-6405)
Dogs of all sizes are allowed. Dogs are allowed for a nightly pet fee. Two dogs are allowed per room.

Residence Inn Danbury
22 Segar Street
Danbury, CT
203-797-1256 (800-331-3131)
Besides offering a convenient location to business, shopping, dining, and entertainment areas, this hotel also provides a number of in-house amenities, including a

daily buffet breakfast and complementary evening socials Monday through Thursday with light dinner fare. Dogs are allowed for an additional one time pet fee of $100 per room. Multiple dogs may be allowed.

Sheraton Danbury Hotel
18 Old Ridgebury Road
Danbury, CT
203-794-0600 (888-625-5144)
Dogs up to 80 pounds are allowed. There are no additional pet fees. Dogs are not allowed to be left alone in the room.

Comfort Inn & Suites
16 Tracy Road
Dayville, CT
860-779-3200 (877-424-6423)
Dogs of all sizes are allowed. Dogs are allowed for a pet fee of $15.00 per pet per night.

Econo Lodge
490 Main Street
East Hartford, CT
860-569-1100 (877-424-6423)
Dogs of all sizes are allowed. Dogs are allowed for a pet fee of $10.00 per pet per night.

Holiday Inn East Hartford
363 Roberts St
East Hartford, CT
860-528-9611 (877-270-6405)
Dogs of all sizes are allowed. Dogs are allowed for a pet fee.

Sheraton Hartford Hotel
100 East River Drive
East Hartford, CT
860-528-9703 (888-625-5144)
Dogs of all sizes are allowed. There are no additional pet fees. Dogs are not allowed to be left alone in the room. 2 dogs may be allowed.

Quality Inn East Haven
30 Frontage Road
East Haven, CT
203-469-5321 (877-424-6423)
Dogs of all sizes are allowed. Two dogs are allowed per room.

Clarion Inn & Suites
161 Bridge Street
East Windsor, CT
860-623-9411 (877-424-6423)
Dogs up to 50 pounds are allowed. Two dogs are allowed per room.

Holiday Inn Express East Windsor
260 Main Street
East Windsor, CT
860-627-6585 (877-270-6405)

Dogs of all sizes are allowed. Dogs are allowed for a pet fee of $40.00 per pet per night.

Motel 6 - Hartford Enfield
11 Hazard Avenue
Enfield, CT
860-741-3685 (800-466-8356)
This motel welcomes your pets to stay with you.

Red Roof Inn Enfield
5 Hazard Avenue
Enfield, CT
860-741-2571 (800-RED-ROOF)
One well-behaved family pet per room. Guest must notify front desk upon arrival. Guest is liable for any damages. In consideration of all guests, pets must never be left unattended in the guest rooms.

Super 8 Windsor Locks Airport Enfield
1543 King St
Enfield, CT
860-741-3636 (800-800-8000)
Dogs of all sizes are allowed. Dogs are allowed for a pet fee of $10.00 per pet per night.

Centennial Inn Hotel
5 Spring Lane
Farmington, CT
860-677-4647 (800-852-2052)
centennialinn.com
Centennial Suites is located 13 miles west of Hartford and 5 miles off I-84. They offer one and Two Bedroom Suites with fully equipped kitchens, cable television with remote, videocassette player and fireplaces. There is an on-site exercise facility. It is located on 10 wooded acres with plenty of space to walk your dog. There is a $15 per day pet fee, per pet. Dogs of all sizes are welcome.

Delmar Greenwich Harbor Hotel
500 Steamboat Road
Greenwich, CT
203-661-9800 (866-335-2627)
thedelamar.com/index2.html
This luxury waterfront inn has mooring on its own private dock (yachts up to 160'), sits near a cornucopia of eateries and shops, offers indoor or outdoor dining, and most of the room have spacious balconies that overlook the harbor. Dogs up to 45 pounds are allowed for an additional fee of $25 per night per pet. Dogs get their own special welcome package; some items included are a cushy doggie bed, personalized ID tag, a bottle of Figi water, and a food and water bowl. Dogs must be quiet, well mannered,

leashed, and cleaned up after. 2 dogs may be allowed.

Homespun Farm Bed and Breakfast
306 Preston Road/H 164
Griswold, CT
860-376-5178 (888-889-6673)
homespunfarm.com/
This colonial farmhouse inn is listed on the National Register of Historic Places as well as being a certified National Wildlife Federation Backyard Wildlife Habitat. Dogs of all sizes are allowed for an additional pet fee of $15 per night per room, and they only allow one guest with a pet to stay at a time. Dogs must be leashed, cleaned up after, and securely crated and the front desk informed when they are alone in the room. Please use a mat under their water/food dishes or feed pets outside, wipe dogs off before entering if they are wet (towel provided), and place your own throw on any furniture pets may want to be on. Dogs must be declared at the time of registration, and be quiet and friendly as there are other pets in residence. Multiple dogs may be allowed.

Ramada /Mystic Area Groton
156 Kings Hwy
Groton, CT
860-446-0660 (800-272-6232)
Dogs of all sizes are allowed. Dogs are allowed for a pet fee of $15.00 per pet per stay.

Days Inn /Closest Downtown Hartford
207 Brainard Road
Hartford, CT
860-247-3297 (800-329-7466)
Dogs are welcome at this hotel.

Hilton Hotel
315 Trumbull Street
Hartford, CT
860-728-5151 (800-HILTONS (445-8667))
Offering a number of on-site amenities for all levels of guests, this hotel also offers a coffee shop, a cocktail lounge, and a skywalk, to the XL Center (formally the Hartford Civic Center). Dogs up to 60 pounds are allowed for an additional one time fee of $75 per pet. 2 dogs may be allowed.

Holiday Inn Express Hartford - Downtown
440 Asylum Street
Hartford, CT
860-246-9900 (877-270-6405)
Dogs of all sizes are allowed. Dogs

are allowed for a pet fee of $50.00 per pet per stay.

Holiday Inn Express Hotel & Suites Hartford Convention Ctr Area
185 Brainard Road
Hartford, CT
860-525-1000 (877-270-6405)
Dogs of all sizes are allowed. Dogs are allowed for a pet fee of $25 per pet per night.

Residence Inn Hartford Downtown
942 Main Street
Hartford, CT
860-524-5550 (800-960-5045)
Located in the heart of downtown and near numerous business, shopping, dining, and entertainment areas, this hotel also provides a number of in-house amenities, including a daily buffet breakfast and evening socials Monday through Thursday with light dinner fare. Dogs are allowed for an additional one time pet fee of $100 per room. 2 dogs may be allowed.

Copper Beach Inn
46 Main Street
Ivoryton, CT
860-767-0330 (888-809-2056)
copperbeechinn.com/
This 1890 inn rests in a beautiful garden setting, has been the recipient of several awards for the inn itself, for their 4-diamond restaurant, and for their 5,000+ bottle wine cellar. Dogs of all sizes are welcome on the 1st floor of the Carriage House for an additional fee of $35 per night for 1 dog, and there is an additional fee of $10 per night if there is a 2nd dog. Dogs must be leashed, cleaned up after, and may only be left alone in the room if they are crated and will be quiet and well behaved. 2 dogs may be allowed.

Interlaken Inn
74 Interlaken Road
Lakeville, CT
860-435-9878
interlakeninn.com/
Charming resort with lakes to swim in, trails to walk and a PUPS amenity package. In the heart of the cultural Berkshires! The hotel offers 30 open acres, a great property with lake frontage to frolic on and off-leash play areas too! There are miles of pet-friendly walking and hiking trails nearby. There is a $15 per day pet fee.

Abbey's Lantern Hill Inn
780 Lantern Hill Road
Ledyard, CT

860-572-0483
abbeyslanternhill.com/
Nestled among the trees and rolling countryside, this contemporary inn features fireplaces, Jacuzzis, 6 outer decks, and it is also close to other activities, recreation, and a couple of casinos. Dogs of all sizes are allowed in the private bungalow. There is no fee for one dog. There is an additional $15 one time fee for a second dog. Dogs must be leashed, cleaned up after, and may only be left alone in the room if they will be quiet and well behaved. 2 dogs may be allowed.

Litchfield Hills B&B
548 Bantam Road/H 202
Litchfield, CT
860-567-2057
litchfieldhillsbnb.com/
This 1735 colonial inn is surrounded by untouched woodlands, beautiful gardens, stone patios and pathways, and they are located within a short distance to many other attractions, activities, and recreation. Dogs of all sizes are allowed for no additional pet fee. Dogs must be quiet, well behaved, leashed, and cleaned up after. 2 dogs may be allowed.

Clarion Suites Inn
191 Spencer St.
Manchester, CT
860-643-5811 (877-424-6423)
Dogs of all sizes are allowed. Dogs are allowed for a pet fee of $10.00 per pet per night.

Extended Stay America Hartford - Manchester
340 Tolland Tpke.
Manchester, CT
860-643-5140 (800-804-3724)
One dog is allowed per suite. There is a $25 per night additional pet fee up to $150 for an entire stay.

Residence Inn Hartford Manchester
201 Hale Road
Manchester, CT
860-432-4242 (800-331-3131)
Besides being located in the heart of downtown and near numerous business, shopping, dining, and entertainment areas, this hotel also provides a number of in-house amenities, including a daily buffet breakfast and evening socials Monday through Thursday. Dogs are allowed for an additional one time pet fee of $75 per room. Multiple dogs may be allowed.

Candlewood Suites Hartford/Meriden
1151 East Main Street

Meriden, CT
203-379-5048 (877-270-6405)
Dogs up to 80 pounds are allowed. Pets allowed with an additional pet fee. Up to $75 for 1-6 nights and up to $150 for 7+ nights. A pet agreement must be signed at check-in.

Extended Stay America Hartford - Meriden
366 Bee St.
Meriden, CT
203-630-1927 (800-804-3724)
One dog is allowed per suite. There is a $25 per night additional pet fee up to $150 for an entire stay.

Residence Inn Meriden
390 Bee Street
Meriden, CT
203-634-7770 (800-331-3131)
Offering a convenient location to business, shopping, dining, and entertainment areas, this all suite hotel also offers a number of in-house amenities, including a daily buffet breakfast, nightly social events, and summer barbecues. Dogs are allowed for an additional one time pet fee of $100 per room. Multiple dogs may be allowed.

Red Roof Inn Milford
10 Rowe Avenue
Milford, CT
203-877-6060 (800-RED-ROOF)
One well-behaved family pet per room. Guest must notify front desk upon arrival. Guest is liable for any damages. In consideration of all guests, pets must never be left unattended in the guest rooms.

Residence Inn Milford
62 Rowe Avenue
Milford, CT
203-283-2100 (800-331-3131)
Located only 15 minutes from Yale University and to a number of local businesses and attractions, this all suite inn provides a number of in-house amenities, including a daily buffet breakfast and evening socials Monday to Thursday. Dogs are allowed for an additional one time pet fee of $112 per room. 2 dogs may be allowed.

Comfort Inn
48 Whitehall Ave.
Mystic, CT
860-572-8531 (877-424-6423)
Dogs up to 50 pounds are allowed. Dogs are allowed for a pet fee of $25.00 per pet per stay.

Econo Lodge
251 Greenmanville Avenue
Mystic, CT
860-536-9666 (877-424-6423)
Dogs up to 50 pounds are allowed. Dogs are allowed for a pet fee of $10.00 per pet per night. Two dogs are allowed per room.

Harbour Inne & Cottage
15 Edgemont Street
Mystic, CT
860-572-9253
harbourinne-cottage.com/
The Harbour Inne & Cottage B&B is an easy walk to all the shops, restaurants and sights of downtown Mystic. The inn has a social area with a fireplace and piano. The four bedrooms each have a private bath, kitchen privileges, cable television and are air conditioned. Pets are welcome for $10 per night.

Hilton Hotel
20 Coogan Blvd
Mystic, CT
860-772-0731 (800-HILTONS (445-8667))
Located in the heart of the city, this upscale hotel offers a number of on site amenities for business and leisure travelers, plus a convenient location to business, shopping, dining, and entertainment areas. Dogs up to 75 pounds are allowed for an additional one time pet fee of $75 per room and there is a pet waiver to sign at check in. Dogs must be crated when left alone in the room. 2 dogs may be allowed.

Residence Inn Mystic Groton
40 Whitehall Avenue
Mystic, CT
860-536-5150 (800-331-3131)
This all suite hotel sits central to many of the city's star attractions, historical sites, shopping, dining, and entertainment areas, plus they offer a number of in-house amenities that include a daily buffet breakfast and evening socials. Dogs are allowed for an additional one time pet fee of $100 per room. Multiple dogs may be allowed.

Econo Lodge Conference Center
100 Pond Lily Ave.
New Haven, CT
203-387-6651 (877-424-6423)
Dogs of all sizes are allowed. Dogs are allowed for a pet fee of $10.00 per pet per night.

Premiere Hotel and Suites
3 Long Wharf Drive
New Haven, CT

203-777-5337
newhavensuites.com
Pets of all sizes are allowed. There is a $75 one time fee per room and a pet policy to sign at check in. 2 dogs may be allowed.

Red Roof Inn Mystic - New London
707 Colman Street
New London, CT
860-444-0001 (800-RED-ROOF)
One well-behaved family pet per room. Guest must notify front desk upon arrival. Guest is liable for any damages. In consideration of all guests, pets must never be left unattended in the guest rooms.

Motel 6 - New London Niantic
269 Flanders Road
Niantic, CT
860-739-6991 (800-466-8356)
This motel welcomes your pets to stay with you.

Holiday Inn North Haven
201 Washington Ave
North Haven, CT
203-239-6700 (877-270-6405)
Dogs of all sizes are allowed. Dogs are allowed for a pet fee of $50.00 per pet per stay.

High Acres
222 NW Corner Road
North Stonington, CT
860-887-4355 (888-680-7829 (STAY))
highacresbb.com/
This 150 acre, groomed hilltop 18th century estate is a delight of green meadows, wildflowers, gardens, woodlands, and country charm, with horses in the fields, numerous hiking trails, and many other activities and recreation only a few minutes away. They have 1 pet friendly room, and dogs of all sizes are allowed for no additional fee. Dogs must be quiet, well behaved, cleaned up after, and they must have their own bedding as they are not allowed on the furnishings. Dogs may be off lead on the estate only if they are under firm voice control. 2 dogs may be allowed.

Homestead Studio Suites Norwalk - Stamford
400 Main Ave.
Norwalk, CT
203-847-6888 (800-804-3724)
One dog is allowed per suite. There is a $25 per night additional pet fee up to $150 for an entire stay.

Old Lyme Inn

85 Lyme Street
Old Lyme, CT
860-434-2600 (800-434-5352)
oldlymeinn.com/
This small, but elegant inn is just minutes from the beach and two large outlet malls. Dogs of all sizes are allowed for a $50 refundable deposit per stay. Dogs may not be left alone in the room, and they must be leashed and cleaned up after at all times. 2 dogs may be allowed.

Days Inn Old Saybrook
1430 Boston Post Rd/I-95
Old Saybrook, CT
860-388-3453 (800-329-7466)
Dogs are welcome at this hotel.

Liberty Inn
55 Springbrook Road
Old Saybrook, CT
860-388-1777
Well mannered pooches that are declared at the time of reservations are welcome for an additional fee of $15 per night per pet. Dogs may not be left unattended at any time, and they must be leashed and cleaned up after. 2 dogs may be allowed.

Econo Lodge
1845 Meriden Waterbury Road
Plantsville, CT
860-621-9181 (877-424-6423)
Dogs up to 50 pounds are allowed. Dogs are allowed for a pet fee of $25.00 per pet per night. Two dogs are allowed per room.

King's Inn
5 Heritage Rd
Putnam, CT
860-928-7961
There is a $5 per night per pet additional fee. 2 dogs may be allowed.

Days Inn Ridgefield
296 Ethan Allen Hwy
Ridgefield, CT
203-438-3781 (800-329-7466)
Dogs are welcome at this hotel.

Residence Inn Hartford Rocky Hill
680 Cromwell Avenue
Rocky Hill, CT
860-257-7500 (800-331-3131)
In addition to being located only a few minutes to downtown and numerous shopping, dining, and year around recreation areas, this hotel also provides a number of in-house amenities, including a daily buffet breakfast and evening social hours. Dogs are allowed for an

additional one time pet fee of $100 per room. 2 dogs may be allowed.

Super 8 Hartford South Area/ Rocky Hill
1499 Silas Deane Highway
Rocky Hill, CT
860-372-4636 (800-800-8000)
Dogs are welcome at this hotel.

Homestead Studio Suites Shelton - Fairfield County
945 Bridgeport Ave.
Shelton, CT
203-926-6868 (800-804-3724)
One dog is allowed per suite. There is a $25 per night additional pet fee up to $150 for an entire stay.

Residence Inn Shelton Fairfield County
1001 Bridgeport Avenue
Shelton, CT
203-926-9000 (800-331-3131)
This all suite inn features a convenient location to universities, businesses, shopping, dining, and entertainment areas, plus they also offer a number of in-house amenities, including a daily buffet breakfast and evening socials Monday through Thursday with light dinner fare. Dogs are allowed for an additional one time pet fee of $100 per room. 2 dogs may be allowed.

Iron Horse Inn
969 Hopmeadow St
Simsbury, CT
860-658-2216 (800245-9938)
One dog up to 60 pounds is allowed for $15 per night.

Crowne Plaza Hotel Southbury
1284 Strongtown Road
Southbury, CT
203-598-7600 (877-270-6405)
Dogs of all sizes are allowed. Dogs are allowed for a pet fee of $25.00 per pet per night.

Knights Inn Southington
462 Queen Street
Southington, CT
860-621-0181 (800-843-5644)
Dogs of all sizes are allowed. Dogs are allowed for a pet fee of $10.00 per pet per night.

Motel 6 - Hartford Southington
625 Queen St
Southington, CT
860-621-7351 (800-466-8356)
This motel welcomes your pets to stay with you.

Residence Inn Southington

778 West Street
Southington, CT
860-621-4440 (800-331-3131)
Besides offering a convenient location to business, shopping, dining, and entertainment areas, this hotel also provides a number of in-house amenities, including a daily buffet breakfast, weekly barbecues, and weekday evening socials. Dogs up to 80 pounds are allowed for an additional one time pet fee of $100 per room. 2 dogs may be allowed.

Marriott Stamford Hotel & Spa
243 Tresser Blvd
Stamford, CT
203-357-9555 (800-732-9689)
This luxury hotel and spa provides a great location to a number of sites of interest for both business and leisure travelers; plus they also offer numerous on-site amenities to ensure a comfortable stay. Dogs are allowed for an additional one time fee of $49 per pet. There may be a reduced rate for 3 small pets. Canine guests also get a cozy mat to lay on and a tasty bone.

Sheraton Stamford Hotel
2701 Summer Street
Stamford, CT
203-359-1300 (888-625-5144)
Dogs up to 50 pounds are allowed. There are no additional pet fees. Dogs are not allowed to be left alone in the room.

Super 8 /New York City Area Stamford
32 Grenhart Rd
Stamford, CT
203-324-8887 (800-800-8000)
Dogs are welcome at this hotel.

Howard Johnson Express Inn - Vernon
451 Hartford Trnpk/I-84
Vernon, CT
860-875-0781 (800-446-4656)
Dogs are welcome at this hotel.

Rodeway Inn
211 Parkway North
Waterford, CT
860-442-7227 (877-424-6423)
Dogs of all sizes are allowed. Dogs are allowed for a pet fee of $25.00 per pet per night. Two dogs are allowed per room.

Motel 6 - Hartford Wethersfield
1341 Silas Deane Highway
Wethersfield, CT
860-563-5900 (800-466-8356)
This motel welcomes your pets to

stay with you.

Residence Inn Hartford Windsor
100 Dunfey Lane
Windsor, CT
860-688-7474 (800-331-3131)
This all suite hotel sits central to many of the city's star attractions, shopping, dining, and business areas, plus they offer a number of in-house amenities that include a daily buffet breakfast and evening socials Monday through Thursday with light dinner fare. Dogs are allowed for an additional one time pet fee of $75 per room. 2 dogs may be allowed.

Candlewood Suites Windsor Locks Bradley Arpt
149 Ella Grasso Turnpike
Windsor Locks, CT
860-623-2000 (877-270-6405)
Dogs up to 80 pounds are allowed. Pets allowed with an additional pet fee. Up to $75 for 1-6 nights and up to $150 for 7+ nights. A pet agreement must be signed at check-in.

Econo Lodge Inn & Suites Airport
34 Old County Road
Windsor Locks, CT
860-623-2533 (877-424-6423)
Dogs of all sizes are allowed. Dogs are allowed for a pet fee of $20.00 per pet per night. Two dogs are allowed per room.

Motel 6 - Hartford Windsor Locks
National Drive
Windsor Locks, CT
860-292-6200 (800-466-8356)
This motel welcomes your pets to stay with you.

Ramada - Bradley Airport
5 Ella Grasso Turnpike
Windsor Locks, CT
860-623-9494 (800-272-6232)
Dogs of all sizes are allowed. Dogs are allowed for a pet fee.

Sheraton Bradley Airport Hotel
1 Bradley International Airport
Windsor Locks, CT
860-627-5311 (888-625-5144)
Dogs of all sizes are allowed. There are no additional pet fees. Dogs are not allowed to be left alone in the room.

Elias Child House
50 Perrin Road
Woodstock, CT
860-974-9836 (877-974-9836)
eliaschildhouse.com/

Rich in colonial craftsmanship, this inn sits on 47 acres of woodlands and pastures with an in-ground pool, walking trails, great shopping opportunities close by, and they even offer hearth cooking demonstrations; there are 2 walk-in cooking hearths. Dogs of all sizes are allowed for an additional fee of $20 per night per pet. Dogs must go with the owners when they leave the premises, but can be crated in the room if they are on the property. Dogs must be well mannered, leashed, cleaned up after, and be friendly to other animals as there is another dog there who likes to greet the canine visitors. 2 dogs may be allowed.

D.C.

Crowne Plaza Hotel The Hamilton - Washington Dc
14th And K Streets, NW
Washington, DC
202-682-0111 (877-270-6405)
Dogs of all sizes are allowed. Dogs are allowed for a pet fee of $250.00 per pet per stay.

Doubletree Guest Suites
801 New Hampshire Avenue NW
Washington, DC
202-785-2000 (800-222-TREE (8733))
Set in one of the finest historic neighborhoods in DC, this upscale hotel offers a number of on site amenities for business or leisure travelers, plus a convenient location to business, shopping, dining, historical, and entertainment areas. Dogs are allowed for an additional one time fee of $20 per pet. 2 dogs may be allowed.

Hilton Hotel
1919 Connecticut Avenue NW
Washington, DC
202-483-3000 (800-HILTONS (445-8667))
Set in a splendid garden setting overlooking the skyline of the capitol city, this upscale hotel offers a number of on site amenities for business and leisure travelers, plus a convenient location to business, shopping, and dining areas, and numerous sites of interest. One dog up to 70 pounds is allowed for no additional fee.

Hotel George
15 E Street, NW
Washington, DC
202-347-4200

hotelgeorge.com
This Kimpton boutique hotel allows dogs of all sizes. There are no additional pet fees.

Hotel Harrington
436 11th Street NW
Washington, DC
202-628-8140
Dogs are allowed for no additional pet fee. Dogs are not allowed to be left unattended.

Hotel Helix
1430 Rhode Island Ave
Washington, DC
202-462-9001
hotelhelix.com/
Well-behaved dogs of all sizes are welcome at this hotel; they must be declared at the time of reservations. The boutique hotel offers both rooms and suites. Amenities include room service, and a 24 hour on-site exercise room. There are no pet fees.

Hotel Madera
1310 New Hampshire Ave
Washington, DC
202-296-7600
hotelmadera.com/
Well-behaved dogs up to 200 pounds are welcome at this boutique hotel. Amenities include an evening wine hour, and room service. There are no pet fees.

Hotel Monaco
700 F Street NW
Washington, DC
202-628-7177
monaco-dc.com/
Well-behaved dogs of all sizes are welcome. There is no pet fee.

Hotel Palomar
2121 P Street NW
Washington, DC
202-448-1800 (877-866-3070)
hotelpalomar-dc.com
This Kimpton boutique hotel allows dogs of all sizes. There are no additional pet fees.

Hotel Rouge
1315 16th Street NW
Washington, DC
202-232-8000
rougehotel.com/
Well-behaved dogs of all sizes are welcome at this luxury boutique hotel. Amenities include complimentary high speed Internet access in the rooms, 24 hour room service, and a 24 hour on-site fitness room. There are no pet fees.

Howard Johnson Express Inn - Washington
600 New York Avenue NE
Washington, DC
202-546-9200 (800-446-4656)
Dogs are welcome at this hotel. There is a $7 one time pet fee.

Marriott Wardman Park Hotel
2660 Woodley Road NW
Washington, DC
202-328-2000 (800-228-9290)
Nestled among 16 acres of meticulously landscaped grounds, this luxury hotel sits central to numerous businesses, shopping, dining, historical, and day/night entertainment areas, plus they also offer a number of in-house amenities for business and leisure travelers. Dogs up to 50 pounds are allowed for an additional one time fee of $50 per room. Three pets may be allowed if they are all very small.

Motel 6 - Washington Dc Convention Center
1345 4th Street Ne
Washington, DC
202-544-2000 (800-466-8356)
This motel welcomes your pets to stay with you.

Motel 6 - Washington, Dc
6711 Georgia Ave Nw
Washington, DC
202-722-1600 (800-466-8356)
This motel welcomes your pets to stay with you.

Park Hyatt Washington
1201 24th St NW
Washington, DC
202-789-1234
There is an additional one time pet fee of $150 per room. Multiple dogs may be allowed.

Red Roof Inn Washington, DC - Downtown
500 H Street Northwest
Washington, DC
202-289-5959 (800-RED-ROOF)
One well-behaved family pet per room. Guest must notify front desk upon arrival. Guest is liable for any damages. In consideration of all guests, pets must never be left unattended in the guest rooms.

Renaissance Mayflower Hotel
1127 Connecticut Avenue NW
Washington, DC
202-347-3000 (800-228-7697)
A member of the Historic Hotels of America and still the largest luxury hotel in DC, guests will find numerous on-site amenities and services for a comfortable stay, plus they sit central to some of the areas most exciting attractions. Dogs are allowed for an additional one time fee of $100 per pet. 2 dogs may be allowed.

Residence Inn Washington, DC / Capitol
333 E Street SW
Washington, DC
202-484-8280 (800-331-3131)
Located in the heart of the nation's capitol, this all suite hotel offers a great location for exploring all this dynamic city has to offer; plus they offer a daily buffet breakfast and evening socials Monday to Wednesday with light dinner fare. Dogs are allowed for an additional one time pet fee of $200 per room plus an additional nightly fee of $10. 2 dogs may be allowed.

Residence Inn Washington, DC/Dupont Circle
2120 P Street NW
Washington, DC
202-466-6800 (800-331-3131)
Located downtown in an elite, upscale area, this all suite hotel offers a great location to governmental sites and for exploring all this dynamic city has to offer; plus they offer a daily buffet breakfast and evening socials. Dogs are allowed for an additional one time pet fee of $100 per room plus an additional nightly fee of $10. For 3 dogs the fee is $200 plus $20 per night. 2 dogs may be allowed.

Residence Inn Washington, DC/Vermont Avenue
1199 Vermont Avenue NW
Washington, DC
202-898-1100 (800-331-3131)
Located in the heart of the nation's capitol, this striking high-rise, all suite hotel offers a great location for exploring all this dynamic city has to offer; plus they offer a daily buffet breakfast and evening socials Monday to Wednesday. Dogs are allowed for an additional one time pet fee of $100 per room plus an additional nightly fee of $8. 2 dogs may be allowed.

Sofitel Lafayette Square
806 15th Street N.W.
Washington, DC
202-730-8441
sofitel.com
Dogs up to 50 pounds are allowed

for no additional fee. Dogs must be declared at the time of reservations. 2 dogs may be allowed.

The Jefferson Hotel
1200 16th St. NW
Washington, DC
202-347-2200
Well-behaved dogs of any size are welcome. There is a $25 per day additional pet fee.

The Madison, A Loews Hotel
1177 Fifteenth St. NW
Washington, DC
202-862-1600
All well-behaved dogs of any size are welcome. This upscale hotel offers their "Loews Loves Pets" program which includes special pet treats, local dog walking routes, and a list of nearby pet-friendly places to visit. There is an additional one time $25 fee per pet.

Topaz Hotel
1733 N Street NW
Washington, DC
202-393-3000 (800-775-1202)
topazhotel.com
This Kimpton boutique hotel allows dogs of all sizes. There are no additional pet fees.

Delaware

Bethany Beach House
Off Central Avenue
Bethany Beach, DE
443-621-6649
quietresortbeachhouse.com/
This spacious home puts visitors within minutes of over a dozen golf courses, the beach, the boardwalk, and a number of eateries, attractions, and recreation. Dogs of all sizes are welcome for a refundable deposit of $75 per pet, and there is also a large fenced yard for them to enjoy. A visit to their website shows a number of pets who have enjoyed their visits here. The city enforces a leash and pooper-scooper law, and dogs are not allowed on the beach or boardwalk from May 15th to September 30th. At all other times dogs must be leashed and cleaned up after. Multiple dogs may be allowed.

Lagoon Front/#125307
217 Belle Road
Bethany Beach, DE
954-782-8277
This vacation house sits facing the lagoon for great crabbing right off the

deck, is just 3 blocks from the beach, is large enough to accommodate family reunions and group retreats, and is also close to many other interests and activities. Dogs of all sizes are allowed for no additional pet fee, and they must be house trained and cleaned up after at all times. Dogs are allowed on the lower level of the house and on the fenced-in back deck only. Dogs are allowed on the beach on no more than a 6 foot leash, and are not to be walked where people are sunbathing. 2 dogs may be allowed.

Atlantic Oceanside Hotel
1700 Coastal H
Dewey Beach, DE
302-227-8811 (800-422-0481)
atlanticoceanside.com/
Dogs of all sizes are allowed for an additional fee of $5 per night per pet, and a credit card must be on file. Dogs are not allowed in the motel rooms from Memorial Day through Labor Day; however, they are allowed at their Suites property year round. Pets may only be left alone in rooms for a short time if they will be quiet and well behaved. Dogs must be leashed, cleaned up after, and removed for housekeeping. Multiple dogs may be allowed.

Ocean Block #47227
given at time of reservations
Dewey Beach, DE
302-542-3570
vrbo.com/47227
This duplex vacation rental is only a few steps from the Atlantic Ocean and great bay views, sleeps up to 12 people, is only a short distance from town, and offers a fenced in dog run. Dogs of all sizes are allowed for a one time additional pet fee of $200. Dogs must be housebroken, leashed, and cleaned up after. 2 dogs may be allowed.

Sea-Esta Motel I
2306 Hwy 1
Dewey Beach, DE
302-227-7666
seaesta.com/
There is a $8.00 charge per pet per night. There are no designated smoking or non-smoking rooms. Multiple dogs may be allowed.

Comfort Inn
222 S. DuPont Hwy.
Dover, DE
302-674-3300 (877-424-6423)
Dogs up to 100 pounds are allowed. Dogs are allowed for a pet fee of

$35.00 per pet per stay.

Days Inn Downtown Dover
272 North Dupont Hwy
Dover, DE
302-674-8002 (800-329-7466)
Dogs up to 100 pounds are allowed. Dogs are allowed for a pet fee of $25.00 per pet per night. Two dogs are allowed per room.

Holiday Inn Express Hotel & Suites Dover
1780 N. Dupont Hwy
Dover, DE
302-678-0600 (877-270-6405)
Dogs are welcome at this hotel.

Red Roof Inn Dover
652 North Dupont Highway
Dover, DE
302-730-8009 (800-RED-ROOF)
One well-behaved family pet per room. Guest must notify front desk upon arrival. Guest is liable for any damages. In consideration of all guests, pets must never be left unattended in the guest rooms.

Sheraton Dover Hotel
1570 North DuPont Highway
Dover, DE
302-678-8500 (888-625-5144)
Dogs of all sizes are allowed. There is a $50 one time nonrefundable pet fee per visit. Dogs are not allowed to be left alone in the room.

Sleep Inn & Suites
1784 N. Dupont Hwy
Dover, DE
302-735-7770 (877-424-6423)
Dogs up to 70 pounds are allowed. Dogs are allowed for a pet fee of $10.00 per pet per night. Two dogs are allowed per room.

Rodeway Inn
111 S Dupont Hwy
Dutch Inn, DE
302-328-6246
dutchinnde.net/
There is a $10 per day pet fee. 2 dogs may be allowed.

Comfort Inn & Suites
20530 DuPont Blvd
Georgetown, DE
302-854-9400 (877-424-6423)
Dogs of all sizes are allowed. Dogs are allowed for a pet fee of $15.00 per pet per night.

Lazy L at Willow Creek - A B&B Resort
16061 Willow Creek Road
Lewes, DE

302-644-7220
lazyl.net
Located on 8 secluded acres overlooking a marsh and creek, the Lazy L offers creature comforts for pets and pet owners. They offer 5 large rooms with Queen sized beds, a swimming pool, hot tub, pool table, guest kitchen and a barbecue. The dogs have a fenced in 1 acre run area, are allowed to sleep in the guest rooms and stay by themselves while you shop or go to dinner.

Sleep Inn & Suites
18451 Coastal Hwy
Lewes, DE
302-645-6464 (877-424-6423)
Dogs up to 50 pounds are allowed. Dogs are allowed for a pet fee of $35.00 per pet per night.

Clarion Hotel The Belle
1612 North DuPont Highway
New Castle, DE
302-428-1000 (877-424-6423)
Dogs up to 50 pounds are allowed. Dogs are allowed for a pet fee of $10.00 per pet per night. Two dogs are allowed per room.

Motel 6 - Wilmington, De
1200 West Ave
New Castle, DE
302-571-1200 (800-466-8356)
This motel welcomes your pets to stay with you.

Quality Inn & Suites Skyways
147 N. Dupont Hwy.
New Castle, DE
302-328-6666 (877-424-6423)
Dogs of all sizes are allowed. Dogs are allowed for a pet fee of $10.00 per pet per night.

Super 8 New Castle
215 S Dupont Hwy
New Castle, DE
302-322-9480 (800-800-8000)
Dogs of all sizes are allowed. Dogs are allowed for a pet fee.

Days Inn Wilmington Newark
900 Churchmans Road
Newark, DE
302-368-2400 (800-329-7466)
Dogs of all sizes are allowed. Dogs are allowed for a pet fee of $10.00 per pet per night.

Hilton Hotel
100 Continental Drive
Newark, DE
302-454-1500 (800-HILTONS (445-8667))
Set in a suburban setting on just over 10 acres, this upscale hotel offers numerous on site amenities for business and leisure travelers - including planned activities such as the Royal Swan feeding that happens daily at 5:30, plus they are convenient to business, tax-free shopping, dining, historical, and entertainment areas. Dog up to 50 pounds are allowed for an additional one time pet fee of $45 per room. 2 dogs may be allowed.

Homestead Studio Suites Newark - Christiana
333 Continental Dr.
Newark, DE
302-283-0800 (800-804-3724)
One dog is allowed per suite. There is a $25 per night additional pet fee up to $150 for an entire stay.

Howard Johnson Inn and Suites and Conference Center
1119 S College Ave/I-95
Newark, DE
302-368-8521 (800-446-4656)
Dogs of all sizes are allowed. Dogs are allowed for a pet fee.

Quality Inn University
1120 S. College Ave.
Newark, DE
302-731-3131 (877-424-6423)
Dogs of all sizes are allowed. Dogs are allowed for a pet fee of $10.00 per pet per night.

Red Roof Inn Wilmington, DE
415 Stanton Christiana Road
Newark, DE
302-292-2870 (800-RED-ROOF)
One well-behaved family pet per room. Guest must notify front desk upon arrival. Guest is liable for any damages. In consideration of all guests, pets must never be left unattended in the guest rooms.

Residence Inn Wilmington Newark
240 Chapman Road
Newark, DE
302-453-9200 (800-331-3131)
This all suite hotel sits central to a number of sites of interest and activities for all level of travelers; plus they offer a daily buffet breakfast, nightly socials, summer barbecues, and a 24 hour market. Dogs are allowed for an additional pet fee of $50 per night not to exceed $200 per room. Multiple dogs may be allowed.

Staybridge Suites Wilmington-Newark
270 Chapman Road

Newark, DE
302-366-8097 (877-270-6405)
Dogs up to 80 pounds are allowed. Pets allowed with an additional pet fee. Up to $75 for 1-6 nights and up to $150 for 7+ nights. A pet agreement must be signed at check-in.

TownePlace Suites Wilmington
410 Eagle Run Road
Newark, DE
302-369-6212 (800-257-3000)
This all suite hotel sits central to a number of sites of interest for both business and leisure travelers; plus they also offer a number of on-site amenities to ensure a comfortable stay. One dog up to 50 pounds is allowed for an additional one time fee of $100.

American Hotel
329 ∠ Airport Road
Rehoboth, DE
302-226-0700
Dogs of all sizes are allowed. There is a $20 per night per pet fee and a pet policy to sign at check in.

Sea Esta Motel III
1409 DE 1
Rehoboth Beach, DE
302-227-4343 (800-436-6591)
seaesta.com/
There is a $0 per day per pet additional fee. Multiple dogs may be allowed.

The Homestead at Rehoboth
35060 Warrington Road
Rehoboth Beach, DE
302-226-7625
homesteadatrehoboth.com/
This charming country inn sits on 2 acres by the ocean and is only a short walk to the beach and the boardwalk; they are also a short distance from tax-free shopping. Dogs of all sizes are welcome, but if they are over 80 pounds, prior arrangements must be made. There is an additional fee of $15 per night per pet. Dogs must be cleaned up after inside and out; clean-up bags and a towel (if wet or sandy from the beach) are provided. They ask that you cover the bed if your pet will be on it, and they may only be left for short periods alone in the room. Dogs may be off lead if they respond well to voice command. 2 dogs may be allowed.

Holiday Inn Express Seaford-Route 13
24058 Sussex Highway
Seaford, DE

302-629-2000 (877-270-6405)
Dogs are welcome at this hotel.

Quality Inn
225 N. Dual Hwy
Seaford, DE
302-629-8385 (877-424-6423)
Dogs up to 50 pounds are allowed.
Dogs are allowed for a pet fee of
$30.00 per pet per night.

Best Western Brandywine Valley Inn
1807 Concord Pike
Wilmington, DE
302-656-9436 (800-780-7234)
Dogs of all sizes are allowed. Dogs
are allowed for a pet fee of $25.00
per pet per stay.

Quality Inn & Suites
4000 Concord Pike
Wilmington, DE
302-478-2222 (877-424-6423)
Dogs of all sizes are allowed.

Sheraton Suites Wilmington
422 Delaware Ave.
Wilmington, DE
302-654-8300 (888-625-5144)
Dogs up to 80 pounds are allowed.
There are no additional pet fees.
Dogs are not allowed to be left alone
in the room.

Florida

Econo Lodge
15920 Northwest US Hwy 441
Alachua, FL
386-462-2414 (877-424-6423)
Dogs of all sizes are allowed. Dogs
are allowed for a pet fee of $10.00
per pet per night.

Quality Inn
15960 NW US Hwy 441
Alachua, FL
386-462-2244 (877-424-6423)
Dogs of all sizes are allowed. Dogs
are allowed for a pet fee of $15.00
per pet per night.

Candlewood Suites Orlando
644 Raymond Avenue
Altamonte Springs, FL
407-767-5757 (877-270-6405)
Dogs up to 80 pounds are allowed.
Pets allowed with an additional pet
fee. Up to $75 for 1-6 nights and up
to $150 for 7+ nights. A pet
agreement must be signed at check-
in.

Clarion Inn and Conference Center
230 W State Road 436
Altamonte Springs, FL

407-862-4455 (877-424-6423)
Dogs up to 50 pounds are allowed.
Dogs are allowed for a pet fee of
$40.00 per pet per stay. Two dogs
are allowed per room.

Days Inn and Suites Altamonte
Springs
150 South Westmonte Drive
Altamonte Springs, FL
407-788-1411 (800-329-7466)
Dogs are welcome at this hotel.

Embassy Suites
225 Shorecrest Drive
Altamonte Springs, FL
407-834-2400 (800-EMBASSY
(362-2779))
Located waterside, this upscale, all
suite hotel offers a number of on
site amenities for business and
leisure travelers, plus a convenient
location to beaches, shopping,
dining, and entertainment areas.
They also offer a complimentary
cooked-to-order breakfast and a
Manager's reception every evening.
Dogs up to 55 pounds are allowed
for an additional fee of $20 per night
per pet. 2 dogs may be allowed.

Homestead Studio Suites Orlando -
Altamonte Springs
302 Northlake Blvd.
Altamonte Springs, FL
407-332-9300 (800-804-3724)
One dog is allowed per suite. There
is a $25 per night additional pet fee
up to $150 for an entire stay.

Residence Inn Orlando Altamonte
Springs/Maitland
270 Douglas Avenue
Altamonte Springs, FL
407-788-7991 (800-331-3131)
Although close to all the world class
attractions of Orlando, this upscale,
all suite hotel also sits central to
many great local attractions and
sports sites, business districts, and
shopping and dining areas.
Additionally, they also offer a buffet
breakfast and evening socials
Monday to Thursday. Dogs are
allowed for an additional one time
pet fee of $75 per room. Multiple
dogs may be allowed.

Amelia Island Oceanfront Condo
1323 Beach Walker Road
Amelia Island, FL
904-642-5563
ameliaislandcondo.blogspot.com
This pet-friendly condo with 1500
square feet is located on the ocean
and a few miles from Fernandina
Beach.

Days Inn And Suites Amelia Island
2707 Sadler Road
Amelia Island, FL
904-277-2300 (800-329-7466)
Dogs of all sizes are allowed. Dogs
are allowed for a nightly pet fee.

Florida House Inn
22 South 3rd Street
Amelia Island, FL
800-258-3301 (800-258-3301)
floridahouseinn.com/
Built in 1857, this registered historic
inn/bed & breakfast is located in
the heart of the Fernandina Beach
Historic District. This dog-friendly inn
offers nine comfortable bedrooms
and two suites, all with private baths.
Six rooms have working fireplaces,
two have old fashioned claw-footed
tubs and two have large Jacuzzi
tubs. All accommodations are air-
conditioned and offer access to their
spacious porches, perfect for rocking
and relaxing. They are located near
the Victorian seaport village. Walk
through the 30 block historic district.
Browse a variety of quaint stores,
antique shops and restaurants along
Centre Street, the main
thoroughfare. There is a $15 per day
pet fee. Dogs must be on a flea
program. 2 dogs may be allowed.

Rancho Inn
240 Hwy 98
Apalachicola, FL
850-653-9435
There is a $10 per day per pet
charge. Multiple dogs may be
allowed.

The Gibson Inn
Market St and Avenue C
Apalachicola, FL
850-653-2191
gibsoninn.com/
The fee for dogs less than 15 pounds
is $15 (+ tax) per night per pet,,,
there is a $25 (+ tax) per night per
pet fee for dogs 15 pounds and over.
The fee tops out after 3 days. 2 dogs
may be allowed.

Howard Johnson Express Inn -
Orlando FL Apopka
1317 S Orange Blossom
Apopka, FL
407-886-1010 (800-446-4656)
Dogs of all sizes are allowed. Dogs
are allowed for a pet fee of $20 per
pet per night.

Knights Inn Arcadia
504 S Brevard Ave
Arcadia, FL

863-494-4884 (800-843-5644)
Dogs of all sizes are allowed. Dogs are allowed for a pet fee of $15.00 per pet per night.

Residence Inn Miami Aventura Mall
19900 W Country Club Drive
Aventura, FL
786-528-1001 (888-236-2427)
This all suite inn offers amenities for all level of travelers, including a convenient location to a number of area attractions, the beach, shopping, and dining areas, plus they offer a daily buffet breakfast, a grocery shopping service, and an evening hospitality hour. Dogs are allowed for an additional one time pet fee of $100 per room. Known aggressive breed dogs are not allowed. A total of only 4 occupants are allowed per room - including pets. 2 dogs may be allowed.

Turnberry Isle Resort and Club
19999 W Country Club Drive
Aventura, FL
305-932-6200 (800-257-7544)
fairmont.com/turnberryisle/
This stunning Mediterranean-style resort sits secluded on 300 tropical acres with 392 ultra-luxurious spacious rooms, numerous upscale amenities, an international staff, meticulously manicured grounds, and the award-winning Willow Stream Spa. Some other features include 2 swimming pools, a jogging path, 3 restaurants and 4 lounges, 24-hour in-room dining, shops and boutiques, tennis courts, a lush, tropical golf course with waterfalls/golf shop/driving range, and a spectacular koi pond. Dogs up to 25 pounds are welcome for an additional fee of $25 per night per pet, and they must be declared at the time of reservations. Dogs must be well mannered, and leashed and cleaned up after at all times.

Econo Lodge Sebring
2511 US 27 S
Avon Park, FL
863-453-2000 (877-424-6423)
Dogs of all sizes are allowed. Dogs are allowed for a pet fee of $10.00 per pet per night.

Sandcastles by the Sea
229 Blue Mountain Road
Blue Mountain Beach, FL
985-845-8126
Dogs of all sizes are allowed. There are no additional pet fees. There is smoking inside, however they say there are no curtains or carpets inside to hold the smoke.

Hilton Hotel
7920 Glades Road
Boca Raton, FL
561-483-3600 (800-HILTONS (445-8667))
Located in a 6 acre lakeside complex, this luxury, all suite hotel is located in the heart of the city and offers a number of on site amenities for business and leisure travelers, plus a convenient location to business, shopping, dining, and recreation areas. Dogs up to 75 pounds are allowed for an additional one time pet fee of $75 per room. 2 dogs may be allowed.

Homestead Studio Suites Boca
Raton - Commerce
501 N.W. 77th St.
Boca Raton, FL
561-994-2599 (800-804-3724)
One dog is allowed per suite. There is a $25 per night additional pet fee up to $150 for an entire stay.

Quality Inn
2899 N. Federal Hwy.
Boca Raton, FL
561-395-7172 (877-424-6423)
Dogs up to 50 pounds are allowed. Dogs are allowed for a pet fee of $25.00 per pet per stay.

Residence Inn Boca Raton
525 NW 77th Street
Boca Raton, FL
561-994-3222 (800-331-3131)
Some of the amenities at this inn include a daily buffet breakfast, weekly social hours, a swimming pool and spa, a Sport Court, and a complimentary grocery shopping service. Up to 3 dogs are allowed (depending on size) for an additional one time pet fee of $75 per room.

TownePlace Suites Boca Raton
5110 NW 8th Avenue
Boca Raton, FL
561-994-7232 (800-257-3000)
Located between 2 International airports, this all suite inn also sits central to numerous business, shopping, dining, and recreation areas. Dogs are allowed for an additional one time fee of $100 per room. Multiple dogs may be allowed.

Holiday Inn Express Hotel & Suites
Bonita Springs
27891 Crown Lake Blvd
Bonita Springs, FL
239-948-0699 (877-270-6405)

Dogs of all sizes are allowed. Dogs are allowed for a pet fee of $25.00 per pet per night. Two dogs are allowed per room.

Hyatt Regency Coconut Point Resort & Spa
5001 Coconut Road
Bonita Springs, FL
239-444-1234
Stay at this pet-friendly resort along the south Florida western Gulf Coast. The resort is situated on 26 acres and has a championship golf course, tennis course and numerous swimming pools, bars and restaurants. Dogs up to 50 pounds are welcome to accompany you. There is a $100 reservation fee for pets and a $50 per day additional pet fee. You must provide proof of your dogs rabies, distemper and parvo vaccinations.

Days Inn - Near the Gulf Bradenton
3506 1St Street West
Bradenton, FL
941-746-1141 (800-329-7466)
Dogs of all sizes are allowed. Dogs are allowed for a pet fee of $10.00 per pet per night.

Howard Johnson Inn -Sarasota
Airport Bradenton
6511 14th Street W
Bradenton, FL
941-756-8399 (800-446-4656)
Dogs are welcome at this hotel.

Motel 6 - Bradenton
660 67th St Circle
Bradenton, FL
941-747-6005 (800-466-8356)
This motel welcomes your pets to stay with you.

Super 8 Sarasota Area Bradenton
6516 14th Street West
Bradenton, FL
941-756-6656 (800-800-8000)
Dogs are welcome at this hotel.

Homestead Studio Suites Tampa - Brandon
330 Grand Regency Blvd.
Brandon, FL
813-643-5900 (800-804-3724)
One dog is allowed per suite. There is a $25 per night additional pet fee up to $150 for an entire stay.

La Quinta Inn & Suites Tampa Bay
Brandon
310 Grand Regency Blvd.
Brandon, FL
813-643-0574 (800-531-5900)
Dogs of all sizes are allowed. There

are no additional pet fees. There is a pet policy to sign at check in. Dogs must be house trained, and a cell number left with the front desk if the dog is in the room alone. Please put the Do Not Disturb sign on the door. Dogs must be leashed and cleaned up after. Multiple dogs may be allowed.

Days Inn Brooksville
6320 Windmere Road
Brooksville, FL
352-796-9486 (800-329-7466)
Dogs are welcome at this hotel.

Holiday Inn Express Hotel & Suites Brooksville-I-75
30455 Cortez Boulevard
Brooksville, FL
352-796-0455 (877-270-6405)
Dogs of all sizes are allowed. Dogs are allowed for a pet fee of $25 per pet per stay.

Residence Inn Cape Canaveral Cocoa Beach
8959 Astronaut Blvd/H A1A
Cape Canaveral, FL
321-323-1100 (800-331-3131)
Located in Belden Village in the city's leading shopping and entertainment district and only a short distance from the Pro Football Hall of Fame, this upscale, all suite inn offers guests a variety of amenities, including a daily breakfast buffet and evening socials during the week. Dogs are allowed for an additional one time pet fee of $75 per room. Multiple dogs may be allowed.

Bayview B&B
PO Box 35, 12251 Shoreview Dr
Cape Coral, FL
941-283-7510
webbwiz.com/bayviewbb
The bed and breakfast has one room that allows pets. There is a $100 refundable pet deposit.

Holiday Inn Express Cape Coral S-Ft. Myers Area
1538 Cape Coral Parkway East
Cape Coral, FL
239-542-2121 (877-270-6405)
Dogs of all sizes are allowed. Dogs are allowed for a pet fee of $15.00 per pet per night.

Cape San Blas - Uncrowded, Pet Friendly Beach & Rentals.
Barrier Dunes: Gulf Front, Gated Neighborhood.
Cape San Blas, FL
770-569-9215
TheCapeEscape.com

These six vacation rentals are located on a dog-friendly white sandy beach. The vacation rentals are in the gated Barier Dunes with access to pools, tennis courts and fishing ponds.

Pristine Properties Pet Friendly Vacation Rentals on Cape San Blas
Call to Arrange
Cape San Blas, FL
877-378-1273
This vacation rental company has nearly 100 pet-friendly properties. Pets are allowed by prior arrangement.

Sunset Reflections Vacation Rentals
Call to Arrange
Cape San Blas, FL
850-227-5432 (877-265-4252)
sunsetreflections.com
This vacation rental company has a number of pet-friendly vacation rentals in the Cap San Blas area.

Pirate's Cove Bayside Cottages
12633 State Road 24
Cedar Keys, FL
352-543-5141
Dogs only are allowed and up to 50 pounds. There is a $5 per night per pet additional fee. 2 dogs may be allowed.

Best Western Suwannee Valley Inn
1125 N Young Boulevard
Chiefland, FL
352-493-0663 (800-780-7234)
Dogs of all sizes are allowed. Dogs are allowed for a pet fee.

Super 8 Chipley
1150 Motel Drive
Chipley, FL
850-638-8530 (800-800-8000)
Dogs are welcome at this hotel.

Best Western St. Petersburg/Clearwater Int'l Airport Hotel
3655 Hospitality Ln
Clearwater, FL
727-577-9200 (800-780-7234)
Dogs of all sizes are allowed. Dogs are allowed for a pet fee.

Candlewood Suites Clearwater
13231 49th Steet North
Clearwater, FL
727-573-3344 (877-270-6405)
Dogs up to 80 pounds are allowed. Pets allowed with an additional pet fee. Up to $75 for 1-6 nights and up to $150 for 7+ nights. A pet agreement must be signed at

check-in.

Days Inn and Suites St.Pete/Clearwater
11333 US Hwy 19
Clearwater, FL
727-572-4929 (800-329-7466)
Dogs of all sizes are allowed. Dogs are allowed for a pet fee.

Extended Stay America St. Petersburg - Clearwater
3089 Executive Dr.
Clearwater, FL
727-561-9032 (800-804-3724)
One dog is allowed per suite. There is a $25 per night additional pet fee up to $150 for an entire stay.

Holiday Inn Express Clearwater-Gateway Area
13625 Icot Blvd (Ulmerton Rd)
Clearwater, FL
727-536-7275 (877-270-6405)
Dogs up to 50 pounds are allowed. Dogs are allowed for a pet fee. Two dogs are allowed per room.

Homestead Studio Suites St. Petersburg - Clearwater
2311 Ulmerton Rd.
Clearwater, FL
727-572-4800 (800-804-3724)
One dog is allowed per suite. There is a $25 per night additional pet fee up to $150 for an entire stay.

Howard Johnson Inn and Suites FL Clearwater
27988 US 19 North
Clearwater, FL
727-796-0135 (800-446-4656)
Dogs are welcome at this hotel.

Residence Inn Clearwater Downtown
940 Court Street
Clearwater, FL
727-562-5400 (877-562-5422)
This all suite hotel sits central to many of the city's star attractions, dining, entertainment, and commerce areas, plus they offer a number of in-house amenities that include a daily buffet breakfast and a cocktail reception each night. Dogs are allowed for an additional one time pet fee of $100 per room. 2 dogs may be allowed.

Residence Inn St. Petersburg Clearwater
5050 Ulmerton Road
Clearwater, FL
727-573-4444 (800-331-3131)
In addition to offering a central location to world class beaches, businesses, shopping, dining, and

entertainment areas, this hotel also provides a number of in-house amenities, including a daily buffet breakfast and evening social hours Monday to Thursday. Dogs are allowed for an additional one time pet fee of $75 per room. Multiple dogs may be allowed.

Rodeway Inn
16405 US Highway 19 North
Clearwater, FL
727-535-0505 (877-424-6423)
Dogs of all sizes are allowed. Dogs are allowed for a pet fee of $1.00 per pet per night. Two dogs are allowed per room.

Super 8 /US Hwy 19 N Clearwater
22950 US Hwy 19 North
Clearwater, FL
727-799-2678 (800-800-8000)
Dogs of all sizes are allowed. Dogs are allowed for a pet fee of $15.00 per pet per night.

Sea Spray Inn
331 Coronado Drive
Clearwater Beach, FL
727-442-0432
clearwaterbeach.com/seaspray/
Sea Spray Inn is just a one minute walk to the Gulf of Mexico. There are 6 rooms, 4 with full kitchens, 2 rooms have refrigerators. There are microwaves in rooms, cable TV and a swimming pool.

Days Inn and Suites Clermont
20390 North US Highway 27
Clermont, FL
352-429-0483 (800-329-7466)
Dogs of all sizes are allowed. Dogs are allowed for a nightly pet fee.

Holiday Inn Express Clermont
1810 South Hwy 27
Clermont, FL
352-243-7878 (877-270-6405)
Dogs of all sizes are allowed. Dogs are allowed for a pet fee of $50.00 per pet per stay.

Howard Johnson Express Inn FL Clermont
20329 US Hwy 27 North
Clermont, FL
352-429-9033 (800-446-4656)
Dogs of all sizes are allowed. Dogs are allowed for a pet fee of $25.00 per pet per night.

Secluded Sunsets
10616 South Phillips Road
Clermont, FL
352-429-0512 (866-839-2180)
secludedsunsets.com

This is a pet friendly duplex on Pine Island Lake. It has a two bedroom unit sleeping up to 6 adults and 3 pets and a one bedroom unit sleeping up to 4 adults and 2 pets overlooking a central Florida spring fed lake. Pet fees are $5 per pet per night. Amenities include a Hot tub, 4 person paddle boat, 2 person canoe, gas and charcoal grills, fire pit area for evening campfires, swimming, fishing, satellite TV and fully furnished kitchens.

Days Inn Expo Cocoa
5600 State Road 524/I-95
Cocoa, FL
321 636-6500 (800-329-7466)
Dogs are welcome at this hotel.

Econo Lodge Space Center
3220 N. Cocoa Blvd. (US 1)
Cocoa, FL
321-632-4561 (877-424-6423)
Dogs of all sizes are allowed.

Motel 6 - Cocoa, Fl
4150 King Street
Cocoa, FL
321-632-5721 (800-466-8356)
This motel welcomes your pets to stay with you.

Ramada Beach Area Cocoa
900 Friday Rd
Cocoa, FL
321-631-1210 (800-272-6232)
Dogs are welcome at this hotel.

Days Inn Cocoa Beach
5500 North Atlantic Ave
Cocoa Beach, FL
321-784-2550 (800-329-7466)
Dogs of all sizes are allowed. Dogs are allowed for a pet fee.

La Quinta Inn Cocoa Beach
1275 N. Atlantic Avenue
Cocoa Beach, FL
321-783-2252 (800-531-5900)
Dogs of all sizes are allowed. There are no additional pet fees. There is a pet waiver to sign at check in. Dogs must be leashed and cleaned up after. Dogs may not be left unattended unless they will be quiet and well behaved. Multiple dogs may be allowed.

Motel 6 - Cocoa Beach
3701 Atlantic Ave
Cocoa Beach, FL
321-783-3103 (800-466-8356)
This motel welcomes your pets to stay with you.

Quality Suites

3655 N. Atlantic Ave.
Cocoa Beach, FL
321-783-6868 (877-424-6423)
Dogs up to 50 pounds are allowed.

South Beach Inn
1701 S Orlando Avenue
Cocoa Beach, FL
321-784-3333 (877-546-6835)
Set in a tropical paradise with an ocean front setting, this inn offers a quiet getaway but still gives a convenient location to some of the areas best shopping, dining, and tourist attractions. Well mannered, quiet dogs are allowed for an additional fee of $15 per night per pet. Dogs must be leashed and cleaned up after at all times; they request that guests bring their own waste disposal bags. Dogs are not allowed on the beach. Multiple dogs may be allowed.

Surf Studio Beach Resort
1801 S. Atlantic Ave.
Cocoa Beach, FL
321-783-7100
There is a $15 per day per pet charge. There are no designated smoking or non-smoking rooms, but they keep the rooms very clean. 2 dogs may be allowed.

Residence Inn Miami Coconut Grove
2835 Tigertail Avenue
Coconut Grove, FL
305-285-9303 (800-331-3131)
Some of the amenities at this all-suite, tropically-inspired inn include a daily buffet breakfast, evening social hours with adult beverages and light dinner fare, a swimming pool, and a complimentary grocery shopping service. Dogs are allowed for an additional one time pet fee of $100 per room. Multiple dogs may be allowed.

La Quinta Inn Ft. Lauderdale Coral Springs
3701 University Dr.
Coral Springs, FL
954-753-9000 (800-531-5900)
Dogs of all sizes are allowed. There are no additional pet fees. Dogs may not be left unattended unless they will be quiet and well behaved. Dogs must be leashed and cleaned up after. 2 dogs may be allowed.

Studio 6 - Ft Lauderdale Coral Springs
5645 University Dr
Coral Springs, FL
954-796-0011 (800-466-8356)
Your pets are welcome to stay here with you for a pet fee of $10 per day

up to $50 for an entire stay.

Wellesley Inn Coral Springs
3100 N. University Drive
Coral Springs, FL
954-344-2200 (800-531-5900)
Dogs of all sizes are allowed. There
are no additional pet fees. Dogs
must be leashed and cleaned up
after. Multiple dogs may be allowed.

Best Western Crestview Inn
900 Southcrest Drive
Crestview, FL
850-682-1481 (800-780-7234)
Dogs up to 50 pounds are allowed.
Dogs are allowed for a pet fee of $25
per pet per night.

Days Inn Crestview
4255 South Ferdon Blvd
Crestview, FL
850-682-8842 (800-329-7466)
Dogs of all sizes are allowed. Dogs
are allowed for a pet fee of $15 per
pet per night.

Quality Inn
4050 South Ferdon Blvd
Crestview, FL
850-682-6111 (877-424-6423)
Dogs up to 60 pounds are allowed.
Dogs are allowed for a pet fee of
$10.00 per pet per night. Three or
more dogs may be allowed.

Super 8 Crestview
3925 S Ferdon Blvd
Crestview, FL
850-682-9649 (800-800-8000)
Dogs are welcome at this hotel.

Days Inn Crystal River
2380 NW Hwy 19
Crystal River, FL
352-795-2111 (800-329-7466)
Dogs of all sizes are allowed. Dogs
are allowed for a nightly pet fee.

Motel 6 - Cutler Bay
10775 Caribbean Blvd
Cutler Bay, FL
305-253-9960 (800-466-8356)
This motel welcomes your pets to
stay with you.

Motel 6 - Dania Beach
825 Dania Beach Blvd
Dania, FL
954-921-5505 (800-466-8356)
This motel welcomes your pets to
stay with you.

Sheraton Fort Lauderdale Airport
Hotel
1825 Griffin Rd.
Dania, FL

954-920-3500 (888-625-5144)
Dogs up to 75 pounds are allowed
for no additional fees; there is a pet
agreement to sign at check in. Dogs
may not be left alone in the room.

Super 8 /Fort Lauderdale Arpt
Dania
333 South Federal Highway
Dania, FL
954-921-6500 (800-800-8000)
Dogs are welcome at this hotel.

Super 8 / Maingate South
Davenport
I-4 exit 55
Davenport, FL
863-420-8888 (800-800-8000)
Dogs of all sizes are allowed. Dogs
are allowed for a nightly pet fee.

Homestead Studio Suites Fort
Lauderdale - Plantation
7550 State Rd. 84
Davie, FL
954-476-1211 (800-804-3724)
One dog is allowed per suite. There
is a $25 per night additional pet fee
up to $150 for an entire stay.

Days Inn -Speedway Daytona
Beach
2900 Int'l Speedway/I-95
Daytona Beach, FL
386-255-0541 (800-329-7466)
Dogs of all sizes are allowed. Dogs
are allowed for a nightly pet fee.

La Quinta Inn Daytona Beach
2725 International Speedway
Daytona Beach, FL
386-255-7412 (800-531-5900)
Dogs of all sizes are allowed. There
are no additional pet fees. Dogs
must be leashed and cleaned up
after. Multiple dogs may be allowed.

Ramada Speedway Daytona
1798 W. Int'l Speedway
Daytona Beach, FL
386-255-2422 (800-272-6232)
Dogs are welcome at this hotel.

Residence Inn Daytona Beach
1725 Richard Petty Blvd
Daytona Beach, FL
386-252-3949 (800-331-3131)
This all suite hotel sits central to
dozens of great local attractions -
like the famous Daytona Beach and
the Daytona International
Speedway, plus they offer a number
of in-house amenities that include a
daily buffet breakfast and a
Manager's reception Monday
through Wednesday. Dogs are
allowed for an additional one time

pet fee of $75 per room. 2 dogs may
be allowed.

Super 8 Oceanfront Daytona Beach
133 South Ocean Ave
Daytona Beach, FL
386-253-0666 (800-800-8000)
Dogs are welcome at this hotel.

Super 8 /Speedway Area Daytona
Beach
2992 W Intl Speedway Blvd
Daytona Beach, FL
386-253-0643 (800-800-8000)
Dogs of all sizes are allowed. Dogs
are allowed for a pet fee of $10 per
pet per night.

Best Western Crossroads Inn
2343 US Highway 331 S
De Funiak Springs, FL
850-892-5111 (800-780-7234)
Dogs of all sizes are allowed. Dogs
are allowed for a pet fee of $20.00
per pet per stay.

Comfort Inn
326 Coy Burgess Loop
DeFuniak Springs, FL
850-951-2225 (877-424-6423)
Dogs up to 50 pounds are allowed.
Dogs are allowed for a pet fee of
$25.00 per pet per night.

Comfort Suites
1040 E. Newport Center Dr.
Deerfield Beach, FL
954-570-8887 (877-424-6423)
Dogs of all sizes are allowed. Dogs
are allowed for a pet fee of $50.00
per pet per stay. Two dogs are
allowed per room.

Embassy Suites Resort and Spa
950 S Ocean Drive
Deerfield Beach, FL
954-426-0478 (800-EMBASSY (362-
2779))
This luxury, all suite, GREEN,
oceanfront hotel offers a number of
on site amenities for all level of
travelers, plus a convenient location
to shopping, dining, and
entertainment districts. They also
offer a complimentary cooked-to-
order breakfast and a Manager's
reception every evening. Dogs are
allowed for an additional fee of $35
per night per pet. Multiple dogs may
be allowed.

Extended Stay America Fort
Lauderdale - Deerfield Beach
1200 F.A.U. Research Park Blvd.
Deerfield Beach, FL
954-428-5997 (800-804-3724)
One dog is allowed per suite. There

is a $25 per night additional pet fee up to $150 for an entire stay.

La Quinta Inn Ft. Lauderdale Deerfield Beach
351 W Hillsboro Blvd.
Deerfield Beach, FL
954-421-1004 (800-531-5900)
Dogs of all sizes are allowed. There are no additional pet fees. Dogs must be leashed and cleaned up after. Dogs must be attended to or crated for housekeeping. Multiple dogs may be allowed.

Travelodge Defuniak Springs
472 Hugh Adams Road
Defuniak Springs, FL
850-892-6115 (800-578-7878)
Dogs of all sizes are allowed. Dogs are allowed for a pet fee.

Howard Johnson Inn Daytona Beach/ FL Deland
2801 East New York Ave
Deland, FL
386-736-3440 (800-446-4656)
Dogs of all sizes are allowed. Dogs are allowed for a pet fee of $10 per pet per night.

Residence Inn Delray Beach
1111 E Atlantic Avenue
Delray Beach, FL
561-276-7441 (800-331-3131)
Located in the heart of downtown and only a short walk to beautiful sandy beaches, this all suite inn also offers a variety of on-site amenities for all level of travelers including a daily buffet breakfast and complementary evening receptions. Dogs are allowed for an additional one time pet fee of $100 per room. 2 dogs may be allowed.

The Colony Hotel
525 E. Atlantic Ave.
Delray Beach, FL
561-276-4123 (800-552-2363)
thecolonyhotel.com
This dog-friendly hotel in Delray Beach is a historic hotel with 69 rooms.

Candlewood Suites Destin-Miramar Beach
11396 US 98 West
Destin, FL
850-337-3770 (877-270-6405)
Dogs up to 80 pounds are allowed. Pets allowed with an additional pet fee. Up to $75 for 1-6 nights and up to $150 for 7+ nights. A pet agreement must be signed at check-in.

Days Inn Destin
1029 Hwy 98 East
Destin, FL
850-837-2599 (800-329-7466)
Dogs of all sizes are allowed. Dogs are allowed for a nightly pet fee.

DestinFLRentals.com
Call to Arrange
Destin, FL
850-650-5524 (800-998-1035accesscode42)
destinflrentals.com
These pet-friendly condos are located along the Gulf of Mexico.

Extended Stay America Destin - US 98 - Emerald Coast Pkwy.
4615 Opa Locka Lane
Destin, FL
850-837-9830 (800-804-3724)
One dog is allowed per suite. There is a $25 per night additional pet fee up to $150 for an entire stay.

Motel 6 - Destin
405 Highway 98e #a
Destin, FL
850-837-0007 (800-466-8356)
This motel welcomes your pets to stay with you.

Ocean Reef Resorts
10221 Emerald Coast Parkway
Destin, FL
800-782-8736
oceanreefresorts.com
This vacation rental company has over 400 homes and condominiums along the Gulf Coast of Florida. Dogs are allowed in some of them. Please mention that you will be bringing a pet when discussing properties.

Residence Inn Sandestin at Grand Boulevard
300 Grand Boulevard
Destin, FL
850-650-7811 (800-331-3131)
A beautiful coastal location next to a 2400 acre golf and beach resort, a complimentary tram service, near exciting nightlife venues, a daily buffet breakfast and evening socials during the week are just a few of the amenities of this all suite inn. Dogs up to 75 pounds are allowed for an additional one time pet fee of $100 per room. 2 dogs may be allowed.

Quality Inn
2625 SR 207
Elkton, FL
904-829-3435 (877-424-6423)
Dogs of all sizes are allowed. Dogs

are allowed for a pet fee of $15.00 per pet per night.

GuestHouse International
4915 17th Street East
Ellenton, FL
941-729-0600 (866-891-1801)
guesthouseintl.com/
There is a $10 one time pet charge per room. 2 dogs may be allowed.

Ramada Limited /Bradenton Area Ellenton
5218 17th Street East
Ellenton, FL
941-729-8505 (800-272-6232)
Dogs are welcome at this hotel.

Sleep Inn & Suites Riverfront
5605 18TH Street E.
Ellenton, FL
941-721-4933 (877-424-6423)
Dogs up to 70 pounds are allowed. Dogs are allowed for a pet fee of $20.00 per pet per night. Two dogs are allowed per room.

Florida House Inn and Restaurant
20-22 South 3rd Street
Fernandina Beach, FL
904-261-3300 (800-258-3301)
floridahouseinn.com/
Located on the National Register of Historic Places, this hotel is the oldest operating guest house in the state. They offer timeless, romantic accommodations, a weekly variety of music and entertainment, complimentary scooters for checking out the local neighborhood, and an on-site restaurant and pub. Dogs are allowed for no additional fee at the inn, and they are allowed at the outside dining area of the restaurant. Dogs must be well mannered, leashed and under their owner's control. 2 dogs may be allowed.

Hampton Inn
2549 Sadler Road
Fernandina Beach, FL
904-321-1111 (800-HAMPTON (426-7866))
ameliaislandhamptoninn.com/
Nestled among stately oak trees, this inn offers a great location and amenities for the business or leisure traveler, but pooches get to feel pampered here too. They receive a welcome pack with a stuffed dog toy, a floating ball for the beach, a doggy bowl, and "people crackers". Dogs up to 50 pounds are allowed for an additional one time fee of $25 per pet. 2 dogs may be allowed.

Si Como No Inn

2480 N Oceanshore Blvd
Flagler Beach, FL
386-864-1430
sicomonoinn.com
This inn is located on 1.5 acres of land between Daytona Beach and St Augustine.

Topaz Motel
1224 S Oceanshore Blvd
Flagler Beach, FL
386-439-3301
Dogs are allowed for a $15 per stay per room additional pet fee. 2 dogs may be allowed.

Ramada Florida City
124 East Palm Drive
Florida City, FL
305-247-8833 (800-272-6232)
hotelfloridacity.com
Dogs up to 50 pounds are allowed.

Super 8 /Homestead Florida City
1202 N Krome Ave
Florida City, FL
305-245-0311 (800-800-8000)
Dogs are welcome at this hotel.

Travelodge /Homestead/Everglades Florida City
409 Southeast First Ave
Florida City, FL
305-248-9777 (800-578-7878)
Dogs of all sizes are allowed. Dogs are allowed for a pet fee of $10 per pet per night.

Candlewood Suites Ft. Lauderdale Airport/Cruise
1120 W. State Road 84
Fort Lauderdale, FL
954-522-8822 (877-270-6405)
Dogs up to 80 pounds are allowed. Pets allowed with an additional pet fee. Up to $75 for 1-6 nights and up to $150 for 7+ nights. A pet agreement must be signed at check-in.

Embassy Suites
1100 SE 17th Street
Fort Lauderdale, FL
954-527-2700 (800-EMBASSY (362-2779))
Certified under the Florida Green Lodging Program, this beautiful all suite hotel offers a number of on site amenities for business and leisure travelers, plus a convenient location to the Intra-coastal Waterway, the Water-taxi, and to many of the other activities/sites of interest that this area has to offer. They also offer a complimentary cooked-to-order breakfast and a Manager's reception every evening. Dogs up to 75 pounds

are allowed. There is a $25 per night additional pet fee per pet. Multiple dogs may be allowed.

Extended Stay America Fort Lauderdale - Convention Center - Marina
1450 SE 17th Street Cswy.
Fort Lauderdale, FL
954-761-9055 (800-804-3724)
One dog is allowed per suite. There is a $25 per night additional pet fee up to $150 for an entire stay.

Extended Stay America Fort Lauderdale - Cypress Creek
5851 N. Andrews Ave. Ext.
Fort Lauderdale, FL
954-776-9447 (800-804-3724)
One dog is allowed per suite. There is a $25 per night additional pet fee up to $150 for an entire stay.

Extended Stay America Fort Lauderdale - Plantation
7755 SW 6th St.
Fort Lauderdale, FL
954-382-8888 (800-804-3724)
One dog is allowed per suite. There is a $25 per night additional pet fee up to $150 for an entire stay.

La Quinta Inn Ft. Lauderdale Cypress Creek I-95
999 West Cypress Creek Rd.
Fort Lauderdale, FL
954-491-7666 (800-531-5900)
Dogs of all sizes are allowed. There are no additional pet fees. Dogs must be leashed and cleaned up after. Dogs must be attended to or crated for housekeeping. Multiple dogs may be allowed.

La Quinta Inn Ft. Lauderdale Tamarac East
3800 W. Commercial Boulevard
Fort Lauderdale, FL
954-485-7900 (800-531-5900)
Dogs of all sizes are allowed. There are no additional pet fees. Dogs may not be left unattended, and they must be leashed and cleaned up after. 2 dogs may be allowed.

Motel 6 - Ft Lauderdale
1801 Sr 84
Fort Lauderdale, FL
954-760-7999 (800-466-8356)
This motel welcomes your pets to stay with you.

Ramada Plaza Fort Lauderdale
5100 N. State Road 7
Fort Lauderdale, FL
954-739-4000 (800-272-6232)
Dogs of all sizes are allowed. Dogs

are allowed for a pet fee of $15.00 per pet per night.

Red Roof Inn Ft Lauderdale
4800 Powerline Road
Fort Lauderdale, FL
954-776-6333 (800-RED-ROOF)
One well-behaved family pet per room. Guest must notify front desk upon arrival. Guest is liable for any damages. In consideration of all guests, pets must never be left unattended in the guest rooms.

Renaissance Fort Lauderdale Hotel
1617 SE 17th Street
Fort Lauderdale, FL
954-626-1700 (800-HOTELS-1 (468-3571))
Besides offering a number of in-house amenities for all level of travelers, this luxury hotel also provides a convenient location to beaches, businesses, shopping, dining, and day/night entertainment areas. Dogs are allowed for no additional fee with a credit card on file. Multiple dogs may be allowed.

Rodeway Inn & Suites Airport/Cruise Port
2440 West State Road 84
Fort Lauderdale, FL
954-792-8181 (877-424-6423)
Dogs up to 50 pounds are allowed. Dogs are allowed for a pet fee of $tax per pet per night.

Sheraton Yankee Clipper Hotel
1140 Seabreeze Blvd.
Fort Lauderdale, FL
954-524-5551 (888-625-5144)
Dogs up to 70 pounds are allowed for no additional pet fee. Dogs may not be left alone in the room.

TownePlace Suites Fort Lauderdale West
3100 Prospect Road
Fort Lauderdale, FL
954-484-2214 (800-257-3000)
This all suite inn sits central to beaches, businesses, shopping, dining, and entertainment areas, plus they offer a number of in-house amenities for business and leisure travelers. Dogs are allowed for an additional one time fee of $100 per room. Multiple dogs may be allowed.

Candlewood Suites Fort Myers Northwest
9740 Commerce Center Ct
Fort Myers, FL
239-210-7777 (877-270-6405)
Dogs up to 80 pounds are allowed. Pets allowed with an additional pet

fee. Up to $75 for 1-6 nights and up to $150 for 7+ nights. A pet agreement must be signed at check-in.

Candlewood Suites Ft Myers I-75
3626 Colonial Court
Fort Myers, FL
239-344-4400 (877-270-6405)
Dogs up to 80 pounds are allowed. Pets allowed with an additional pet fee. Up to $75 for 1-6 nights and up to $150 for 7+ nights. A pet agreement must be signed at check-in.

Comfort Suites Airport
13651-A Indian Paint Ln.
Fort Myers, FL
239-768-0005 (877-424-6423)
Dogs of all sizes are allowed. Dogs are allowed for a pet fee of $10.00 per pet per night.

Country Inns & Suites by Carlson
13901 Shell Point Plaza
Fort Myers, FL
239-454-9292
Dogs up to 80 pounds are allowed. There is an additional fee of $20 per night per pet.

Days Inn Fort Myers North
13353 N Cleveland Avenue
Fort Myers, FL
239-995-0535 (800-329-7466)
Dogs are welcome at this hotel.

Econo Lodge North
13301 N. Cleveland
Fort Myers, FL
239-995-0571 (877-424-6423)
Dogs up to 60 pounds are allowed. Dogs are allowed for a pet fee of $10.00 per pet per night.

Hotel Indigo Ft Myers-River District
1520 Broadway
Fort Myers, FL
239-337-3446 (877-865-6578)
Dogs are welcome at this hotel. There is a $75 one time pet fee.

Howard Johnson Inn - Ft. Myers FL
4811 Cleveland Ave.
Fort Myers, FL
239-936-3229 (800-446-4656)
Dogs are welcome at this hotel.

La Quinta Inn Fort Myers
4850 S. Cleveland Ave.
Fort Myers, FL
239-275-3300 (800-531-5900)
One dog of any size is allowed. There are no additional pet fees. Dogs may not be left unattended, and they must be leashed and

cleaned up after.

Motel 6 - Ft Myers
3350 Marinatown Ln
Fort Myers, FL
239-656-5544 (800-466-8356)
This motel welcomes your pets to stay with you.

Residence Inn Fort Myers
2960 Colonial Blvd
Fort Myers, FL
239-936-0110 (800-331-3131)
This all suite hotel sits central to many of the city's star attractions, beaches, shopping, dining, and business areas, plus they offer a number of in-house amenities that include a daily buffet breakfast, and evening socials Monday through Thursday with light dinner fare. Dogs are allowed for an additional one time pet fee of $100 per room. Multiple dogs may be allowed.

Suburban Extended Stay Hotel
10150 Metro Parkway
Fort Myers, FL
239-938-0100 (877-424-6423)
Dogs up to 50 pounds are allowed. Dogs are allowed for a pet fee of $15.00/ per pet per night.

Days Inn Fort Pierce
6651 Darter Court/I-95
Fort Pierce, FL
772-466-4066 (800-329-7466)
Dogs are welcome at this hotel.

Motel 6 - Ft Pierce
2500 Peters Rd
Fort Pierce, FL
772-461-9937 (800-466-8356)
This motel welcomes your pets to stay with you.

Royal Inn
222 Hernando Street
Fort Pierce, FL
772-672-8888
royalinnbeach.com
There is a $25 one time pet fee per pet. Pets must be well-behaved. The hotel has limited pet rooms. Please call ahead to reserve a pet room. 2 dogs may be allowed.

Bayside Inn
314 Miracle Strip Parkway
Fort Walton Beach, FL
850-243-6162
baysideinn.com/
Dogs of all sizes are allowed. There is a $10 plus tax per night additional fee. The pet fee may be less for long stays. 2 dogs may be allowed.

Days Inn - Fort Walton Beach
135 Miracle Strip Pkwy SW
Fort Walton Beach, FL
850-244-6184 (800-329-7466)
Dogs of all sizes are allowed. Dogs are allowed for a pet fee.

Econo Lodge
203 Southwest Miracle Strip Pk
Fort Walton Beach, FL
850-244-8663 (877-424-6423)
Dogs up to 50 pounds are allowed. Dogs are allowed for a pet fee of $15.00 per pet per night. Three or more dogs may be allowed.

Super 8 Ft Walton Beach
333 Miracle Strip Parkway SW
Fort Walton Beach, FL
850-244-4999 (800-800-8000)
Dogs of all sizes are allowed. Dogs are allowed for a pet fee of $20.00 per pet per night.

Best Western Gateway Grand
4200 NW 97th Boulevard
Gainesville, FL
352-331-3336 (800-780-7234)
Dogs of all sizes are allowed. Dogs are allowed for a nightly pet fee.

Comfort Inn University
2435 SW 13th St.
Gainesville, FL
352-373-6500 (877-424-6423)
Dogs up to 50 pounds are allowed. Dogs are allowed for a pet fee of $10.00 per pet per night.

Comfort Inn West
3440 Southwest 40th Blvd.
Gainesville, FL
352-264-1771 (877-424-6423)
Dogs of all sizes are allowed. Dogs are allowed for a pet fee of $10.00 per pet per night.

Days Inn University Gainesville
1901 SW 13th Street
Gainesville, FL
352-376-2222 (800-329-7466)
Dogs of all sizes are allowed. Dogs are allowed for a pet fee of $10.00 per pet per night.

Econo Lodge West
700 N.W. 75th St.
Gainesville, FL
352-332-2346 (877-424-6423)
Dogs up to 50 pounds are allowed. Dogs are allowed for a pet fee of $10.00 per pet per night. Two dogs are allowed per room.

Extended Stay America Gainesville - I-75
3600 SW 42nd St.

Gainesville, FL
352-375-0073 (800-804-3724)
One dog is allowed per suite. There is a $25 per night additional pet fee up to $150 for an entire stay.

Hilton Hotel
1714 SW 34th Street
Gainesville, FL
352-371-3600 (800-HILTONS (445-8667))
Located on the University of Florida campus, this upscale hotel is an approved IACC conference center and they offer numerous on site amenities for business and leisure travelers, plus a convenient location to business, shopping, dining, and recreation areas. Dogs up to 75 pounds are allowed for an additional one time pet fee of $50 per room. 2 dogs may be allowed.

La Quinta Inn Gainesville
920 N.W. 69th Terrace
Gainesville, FL
352-332-6466 (800-531-5900)
Dogs of all sizes are allowed. There are no additional pet fees. Dogs must be leashed and cleaned up after. Dogs must be crated or removed for housekeeping. Multiple dogs may be allowed.

Magnolia Plantation Bed and Breakfast
305 SE 7th Street
Gainesville, FL
352-375-6653 (800-201-2379)
magnoliabnb.com
The Magnolia Plantation has 6 private historic cottages located within walking distance of downtown Gainesville. It is surrounded by 1.5 acres of lush gardens. They have no pet fees or weight restrictions, and only require that pets be kept on a leash while wandering around the property. Pets are not permitted in the main house but are allowed in one of the six cottages.

Motel 6 - Gainesville University Of Florida
4000 Sw 40th Blvd
Gainesville, FL
352-373-1604 (800-466-8356)
This motel welcomes your pets to stay with you.

Red Roof Inn Gainesville
3500 Southwest 42nd Street
Gainesville, FL
352-336-3311 (800-RED-ROOF)
One well-behaved family pet per room. Guest must notify front desk upon arrival. Guest is liable for any damages. In consideration of all

guests, pets must never be left unattended in the guest rooms.

Travelodge FL Gainesville
3461 S. W. Williston Road
Gainesville, FL
352-335-6355 (800-578-7878)
Dogs of all sizes are allowed. Dogs are allowed for a pet fee of $10.00 per pet per night.

Hibiscus Coffee Guest House
85 Defuniak St
Grayton Beach, FL
850-231-2733
hibiscusflorida.com
There are no additional pet fees. There is one room available for pets.

Howard Johnson Inn -
33224 Hwy. 27 South
Haines City, FL
863-422-8621 (800-446-4656)
Dogs of all sizes are allowed. Dogs are allowed for a nightly pet fee.

Rodeway Inn & Suites
605 B Moore Road
Haines City, FL
863-421-6929 (877-424-6423)
Dogs of all sizes are allowed. Dogs are allowed for a pet fee of $10.00 per pet per night.

Days Inn Fort Lauderdale /Airport South Hollywood
2601 N 29th Avenue/I-95
Hollywood, FL
954-923-7300 (800-329-7466)
Dogs of all sizes are allowed. Dogs are allowed for a pet fee of $10 per pet per night.

Quality Inn & Suites Hollywood Boulevard
4900 Hollywood Blvd
Hollywood, FL
954-981-1800 (877-424-6423)
Dogs of all sizes are allowed. Dogs are allowed for a pet fee of $15.00/ per pet per night.

Sun Cruz Inn
340 Desoto St.
Hollywood, FL
954-925-7272
suncruzinn.com
This 17 unite motel and apartment building has studios and efficiencies. Pet walking is available for a fee. There is a deposit and other pet fees. Call the hotel for more information.

Hollywood - Ft. Lauderdale Oceanfront Rental

South Ocean Drive
Hollywood Beach, FL
786-208-7004
AptTherapist.com
This two bedroom, two bathroom condo near the beach allows dogs up to 80 pounds.

Swan/Mermaid Motel
319 Pierce Street (office)
Hollywood Beach, FL
954-921-4097
Dogs are only allowed with guests that are staying for a week or more. One dog up to 50 pounds is allowed for no additional fee.

Barrett Beach Bungalows
19646 Gulf Blvd
Indian Shores, FL
727-455-2832
barrettbeachbungalows.com
Beachfront bungalows plus a cottage in the heart of picturesque Indian Shores. One, two and three bedroom bungalows and a pool. Any number and size of pets welcome. Private dog runs with each bungalow. Enjoy sunsets, volleyball and barbecues in your own backyard.

Candlewood Suites Jacksonville
4990 Belfort Road
Jacksonville, FL
904-296-7785 (877-270-6405)
Dogs up to 80 pounds are allowed. Pets allowed with an additional pet fee. Up to $75 for 1-6 nights and up to $150 for 7+ nights. A pet agreement must be signed at check-in.

Candlewood Suites Jacksonville East
Merril Road
2700 Jane Street
Jacksonville, FL
904-342-6099 (877-270-6405)
Dogs up to 80 pounds are allowed. Pets allowed with an additional pet fee. Up to $75 for 1-6 nights and up to $150 for 7+ nights. A pet agreement must be signed at check-in.

Embassy Suites
9300 Baymeadows Road
Jacksonville, FL
904-731-3555 (800-EMBASSY (362-2779))
This upscale, full service hotel offers a number of on site amenities for business and leisure travelers, plus a convenient location to beaches, business, shopping, dining, and entertainment districts. They also offer a complimentary cooked-to-order breakfast and a Manager's reception every evening. Dogs up to

50 pounds are allowed for an additional one time pet fee of $75 per room. 2 dogs may be allowed.

Extended Stay America Jacksonville - Butler Blvd.
6961 Lenoir Ave.
Jacksonville, FL
904-296-0181 (800-804-3724)
One dog is allowed per suite. There is a $25 per night additional pet fee up to $150 for an entire stay.

Extended Stay America Jacksonville - Riverwalk
1413 Prudential Dr.
Jacksonville, FL
904-396-1777 (800-804-3724)
One dog is allowed per suite. There is a $25 per night additional pet fee up to $150 for an entire stay.

Holiday Inn Express Hotel & Suites Jacksonville - Blount Island
10148 New Berlin Road
Jacksonville, FL
904-696-3333 (877-270-6405)
Dogs of all sizes are allowed. Dogs are allowed for a pet fee of $30.00 per pet per stay.

Homestead Studio Suites Jacksonville - Baymeadows
8300 Western Way
Jacksonville, FL
904-739-1881 (800-804-3724)
One dog is allowed per suite. There is a $25 per night additional pet fee up to $150 for an entire stay.

Homestead Studio Suites Jacksonville - Salisbury Rd. - Southpoint
4693 Salisbury Rd.
Jacksonville, FL
904-296-0661 (800-804-3724)
One dog is allowed per suite. There is a $25 per night additional pet fee up to $150 for an entire stay.

Homestead Studio Suites Jacksonville - Southside - St. Johns Towne Center
10020 Skinner Lake Dr.
Jacksonville, FL
904-642-9911 (800-804-3724)
One dog is allowed per suite. There is a $25 per night additional pet fee up to $150 for an entire stay.

Hotel Indigo Jacksonville-Deerwood Park
9840 Tapestry Park Circle
Jacksonville, FL
019-049-9671 (877-865-6578)
Dogs up to 80 pounds are allowed. Dogs are allowed for a nightly pet

fee.

Howard Johnson Inn and Suites FL Jacksonville
4300 Salisbury Rd North
Jacksonville, FL
904-281-0198 (800-446-4656)
Dogs of all sizes are allowed. Dogs are allowed for a pet fee of $15 per pet per night.

La Quinta Inn Jacksonville Airport North
812 Dunn Ave.
Jacksonville, FL
904-751-6960 (800-531-5900)
Dogs of all sizes are allowed. There are no additional pet fees. Dogs are not allowed to go through the lobby during food service hours. Dogs may only be left unattended if they are crated and will be quiet. Dogs must be leashed and cleaned up after. Multiple dogs may be allowed.

La Quinta Inn Jacksonville Baymeadows
8255 Dix Ellis Trail
Jacksonville, FL
904-731-9940 (800-531-5900)
Dogs of all sizes are allowed. There are no additional pet fees. Dogs must be leashed and cleaned up after. Multiple dogs may be allowed.

La Quinta Inn Jacksonville Orange Park
8555 Blanding Blvd
Jacksonville, FL
904-778-9539 (800-531-5900)
Dogs of all sizes are allowed. There are no additional pet fees. Dogs must be leashed and cleaned up after, and removed or crated for housekeeping. Multiple dogs may be allowed.

Motel 6 - Jacksonville Orange Park
6107 Youngerman Circle
Jacksonville, FL
904-777-6100 (800-466-8356)
This motel welcomes your pets to stay with you.

Motel 6 - Jacksonville Airport
10885 Harts Rd
Jacksonville, FL
904-757-8600 (800-466-8356)
This motel welcomes your pets to stay with you.

Motel 6 - Jacksonville Southeast
8285 Dix Ellis Trail
Jacksonville, FL
904-731-8400 (800-466-8356)
This motel welcomes your pets to stay with you.

Quality Inn & Suites Baymeadows
8333 Dix Ellis Trail
Jacksonville, FL
904-739-1155 (877-424-6423)
Dogs of all sizes are allowed. Dogs are allowed for a pet fee of $10.00 per pet per night.

Ramada Conference Center Mandarin
3130 Hartley Rd
Jacksonville, FL
904-268-8080 (800-272-6232)
Dogs of all sizes are allowed. Dogs are allowed for a pet fee of $30.00 per pet per stay.

Red Roof Inn Jacksonville - Orange Park
6099 Youngerman Circle
Jacksonville, FL
904-777-1000 (800-RED ROOF)
One well-behaved family pet per room. Guest must notify front desk upon arrival. Guest is liable for any damages. In consideration of all guests, pets must never be left unattended in the guest rooms.

Red Roof Inn Jacksonville - Southpoint
6969 Lenoir Avenue East
Jacksonville, FL
904-296-1006 (800-RED-ROOF)
One well-behaved family pet per room. Guest must notify front desk upon arrival. Guest is liable for any damages. In consideration of all guests, pets must never be left unattended in the guest rooms.

Red Roof Inn Jacksonville Airport
14701 Airport Entrance Road
Jacksonville, FL
904-741-4488 (800-RED-ROOF)
One well-behaved family pet per room. Guest must notify front desk upon arrival. Guest is liable for any damages. In consideration of all guests, pets must never be left unattended in the guest rooms.

Residence Inn Jacksonville Airport
1310 Airport Road
Jacksonville, FL
904-741-6550 (800-331-3131)
Located only a few minutes from the airport and to all that the downtown areas has to offer, this all suite inn also offers a number of in-house amenities, including a daily buffet breakfast and a complimentary evening social Monday to Thursday with a full meal offered on Wednesdays. Dogs are allowed for an additional one time pet fee of $75

per room. Multiple dogs may be allowed.

Residence Inn Jacksonville Baymeadows
8365 Dix Ellis Trail
Jacksonville, FL
904-733-8088 (800-331-3131)
Besides offering a convenient location to business, shopping, dining, recreation, and entertainment areas, this hotel also provides a number of in-house amenities, including a daily buffet breakfast, complementary evening receptions with light dinner fare, and Wednesday barbecues. Dogs up to 50 pounds are allowed for an additional one time pet fee of $75 per room. 2 dogs may be allowed.

Residence Inn Jacksonville Butler Boulevard
10551 Deerwood Park Blvd
Jacksonville, FL
904-996-8900 (800-331-3131)
Besides offering a convenient location to business, shopping, dining, recreation, and entertainment areas, this hotel also provides a number of in-house amenities, including a daily buffet breakfast, complementary evening receptions with light fare, and Wednesday barbecues. Dogs up to 60 pounds are allowed for an additional one time pet fee of $100 (+ tax) per room. 2 dogs may be allowed.

Staybridge Suites Jacksonville
8511 Touchton Rd
Jacksonville, FL
904-253-7120 (877-270-6405)
Dogs up to 80 pounds are allowed. Pets allowed with a valid pet fee. Up to $75 for 1-6 nights and up to $150 for 7+ nights. A pet agreement must be signed at check-in.

Studio 6 - Jacksonville Baymeadows
8765 Baymeadows Rd
Jacksonville, FL
904-731-7317 (800-466-8356)
Your pets are welcome to stay here with you for a pet fee of $10 per day up to $50 for an entire stay.

TownePlace Suites Jacksonville Butler Boulevard
4801 Lenoir Avenue
Jacksonville, FL
904-296-1661 (800-257-3000)
This all suite hotel sits central to a number of sites of interest for both business and leisure travelers; plus they also offer a number of on-site amenities to ensure comfort. Dogs

are allowed for an additional one time fee of $75 per room. 2 dogs may be allowed.

Travelodge Inn And Suites Airport Jacksonville
1153 Airport Road
Jacksonville, FL
904-741-4600 (800-578-7878)
Dogs of all sizes are allowed. Dogs are allowed for a pet fee of $15.00 per pet per night.

Days Inn Jasper
8182 State Road 6 West
Jasper, FL
386-792-1987 (800-329-7466)
Dogs of all sizes are allowed. Dogs are allowed for a pet fee.

Holiday Inn Express North Palm Beach-Oceanview
13950 U.S. Hwy 1
Juno Beach, FL
561-622-4366 (877-270-6405)
Dogs of all sizes are allowed. Dogs are allowed for a pet fee of $10.00 per pet per night.

Ambrosia House Tropical Lodging
622 Fleming Street
Key West, FL
305-296-9838 (800-535-9838)
ambrosiakeywest.com/
This inn, located on almost two private acres, offers a variety of rooms, suites, town houses and a cottage, all with private baths. The inn is located in the heart of historic Old Town. There is a one time non-refundable pet fee of $25. There is no weight limit or limit to the number of pets.

Avalon
1317 Duval Street
Key West, FL
305-294-8233
Dogs are allowed for a $20 one time additional pet fee, and there is a pet policy to sign at check in. There are only 2 pet-friendly rooms.

Banana Bay Resort and Marina
2319 N. Roosevelt Blvd/H 1
Key West, FL
305-296-6925 (866-566-6688)
bananabayresortkeywest.com/
Offering a paradisiacal setting, this elite adult oceanfront resort offers a number of amenities, plus is sits only minutes from all that the Keys have to offer. Well mannered dogs are allowed for no additional pet fee. (Children and spring breakers are not allowed.) 2 dogs may be allowed.

Bone Island Vacation Rentals
219 Simonton Street
Key West, FL
305-293-9953 (888-820-9953)
Pets and kids can stay at these vacation rentals in Key West which are available for daily, weekly or monthly rental.

Casa 325
325 Duval Street
Key West, FL
305-292-0011 (866-CASA325 (227-2325))
casa325.com/
In addition to offering a beautiful setting and a number of in-house amenities, this inn also offers a central location to a number of the areas best attractions, shopping, dining, and nightlife. Dogs are allowed for an additional fee of $25 every 3 days per room. 2 dogs may be allowed.

Chelsea House
707 Truman Avenue
Key West, FL
305-296-2211 (800-845-8859)
There is a $20 per day pet charge. 2 dogs may be allowed.

Courtney's Place
720 Whitmarsh Lane
Key West, FL
305-294-3480 (800-869-4639)
keywest.com/courtney.html
This inn has historic guest cottages. There are no designated smoking or non-smoking cottages. Dogs are allowed for an additional one time pet fee of $25. 2 dogs may be allowed.

Douglas House and Cuban Club Suites
419 Amelia St
Key West, FL
305-294-5269 (800-833-0372)
cubanclub.com
Small dogs are welcome at the Douglas House. Large dogs are welcome at the Cuban Club Suites. There is a $10 per day pet fee. There are no designated smoking or non-smoking rooms.

Francis Street Bottle Inn
535 Francis Street
Key West, FL
305-294-8530 (800-294-8530)
bottleinn.com/aboutus.htm
Dogs are allowed, including well-behaved large dogs. There is a $25 one time pet fee per room. 2 dogs may be allowed.

Dog-Friendly Lodging - Please always call ahead to make sure an establishment is still dog-friendly.

Key West's Travelers Palm - Inn and Cottages
915 Center Street
Key West, FL
800-294-9560
travelerspalm.com/
Special dog treats upon check-in. Dogs are welcome in the suites and cottages. Amenities include premier Old Town locations and 3 heated pools. Dogs of all sizes and breeds are welcome.

Pelican Landing Resort and Marina
915 Eisenhower Drive
Key West, FL
305-296-9976
keywestpelican.com
Waterfront condos each with 2 bedrooms and 2 baths. A boat slip comes with each condo. The Subtropic Dive Center is located next door. There is a heated swimming pool and all well-behaved dogs and cats are welcome.

Seascape Tropical Inn
420 Olivia St
Key West, FL
305-296-7776 (800-765-6438)
seascapetropicalinn.com
Pets are allowed in all of the cottages and two rooms in the main guesthouse. There is a $25 one time pet fee. All rooms are non-smoking. Children are allowed in the cottages. The owner has two dogs on the premises.

Sheraton Suites Key West
2001 S. Roosevelt Blvd.
Key West, FL
305-292-9800 (888-625-5144)
Dogs of all sizes are allowed. There are no additional pet fees. Dogs are not allowed to be left alone in the room.

Whispers
409 William St
Key West, FL
305-294-5969 (800-856-7444)
whispersbb.com
Dogs are allowed, but no puppies please. There is a $25 one time pet fee. Children over 10 years old are allowed.

Baymont Inn and Suites Kissimmee
4156 West Vine Street
Kissimmee, FL
407-994-1900 (877-229-6668)
Dogs are welcome at this hotel.

Caribbean Villas Privately Owned Condo near Disney

Call to Arrange
Kissimmee, FL
407-973-8924
myfloridacondorental.com
This 2 bedroom, 2 bath condominium vacation rental is located in Carribbean Villas in Kissimmee. There are no additional pet fees.

Clarion Resort Waterpark
2261 E. Irlo Bronson Hwy.
Kissimmee, FL
407-846-2221 (877-424-6423)
Dogs up to 50 pounds are allowed. Dogs are allowed for a pet fee of $15.00 per pet per night. Two dogs are allowed per room.

Days Inn - Orlando-Maingate East of Walt Disney Wor Kissimmee
5840 W Irlo Bronson Hwy
Kissimmee, FL
407-396-7969 (800-329-7466)
Dogs of all sizes are allowed. Dogs are allowed for a pet fee of $10.00 per pet per night.

House at Disney
Call to Arrange
Kissimmee, FL
978-562-4132
houseatdisney.com
Pets are allowed in these vacation rentals by special arrangement only. Up to 3 or 4 small to medium sized dogs are allowed.

Howard Johnson Enchantedland Hotel FL Kissimmee
4985 W. Irlo Bronson Hwy.
Kissimmee, FL
407-396-4343 (800-446-4656)
Dogs of all sizes are allowed. Dogs are allowed for a pet fee of $10.00 per pet per night.

Indian Wells Villas
Call to Arrange
Kissimmee, FL
407-350-3289
indianwellsvillas.com
Dogs are allowed at many of these vacation rentals. There is a $30 weekly pet fee and a $300 security deposit that is refundable if there is no damage.

La Quinta Inn & Suites Orlando/Maingate
3484 Polynesian Isle Blvd
Kissimmee, FL
407-997-1700 (800-531-5900)
Dogs of all sizes are allowed. There are no additional pet fees. Dogs must be leashed and cleaned up after. A call number must be left

with the front desk, and the Do Not Disturb sign placed on the door if there is a pet inside alone. Make arrangements with housekeeping if you need your room serviced. 2 dogs may be allowed.

Motel 6 - Orlando Kissimmee (main Gate East)
5731 Irlo Bronson Hwy
Kissimmee, FL
407-396-6333 (800-466-8356)
This motel welcomes your pets to stay with you.

Motel 6 - Orlando Kissimmee (main Gate West)
7455 Irlo Bronson Hwy
Kissimmee, FL
407-396-6422 (800-466-8356)
This motel welcomes your pets to stay with you.

Palms Hotel and Villas
3100 Parkway Blvd.
Kissimmee, FL
407-396-2229
thepalmshotelandvillas.com/
Dogs up to 60 pounds are allowed for an additional one time pet fee of $100 per room. Multiple dogs may be allowed.

Ramada Gateway Kissimmee
7470 W Hwy 192
Kissimmee, FL
407-396-4400 (800-272-6232)
Dogs are welcome at this hotel.

Ramada Maingate West Kissimmee
7491 West Hwy 192
Kissimmee, FL
407-396-6000 (800-272-6232)
Dogs of all sizes are allowed. Dogs are allowed for a nightly pet fee.

Ramada Orlando Celebration Resort and Convention Center
6375 W Irlo Bronson Mem Hwy
Kissimmee, FL
407-390-5800 (800-272-6232)
Dogs are welcome at this hotel.

Red Roof Inn Kissimmee
4970 Kyng's Heath Road
Kissimmee, FL
407-396-0065 (800-RED-ROOF)
One well-behaved family pet per room. Guest must notify front desk upon arrival. Guest is liable for any damages. In consideration of all guests, pets must never be left unattended in the guest rooms.

Rodeway Inn Maingate
5995 W. Irlo Bronson Hwy.
Kissimmee, FL

407-396-4300 (877-424-6423)
Dogs up to 50 pounds are allowed.
Dogs are allowed for a pet fee of
$1.69 per pet per night.

Studio 6 - Orlando Kissimmee
5733 Irlo Bronson Mem
Kissimmee, FL
407-390-1869 (800-466-8356)
Your pets are welcome to stay here
with you for a pet fee of $10 per day
up to $50 for an entire stay.

Sun N Fun Vacation Homes
Bear Path
Kissimmee, FL
407-932-4079 (800-874-3660)
sunnfunusa.com/page2/index.html
These vacation Homes are located
just 5 minutes to Disney and very
close to other area attractions. All
homes have private screened pools
and fenced yards. Most homes
welcome well-behaved pets and their
families. There is a pet fee of $30 per
pet, per week plus a $300 security
deposit, which is refundable
assuming there is no damage.

Super 8 Orlando//Lakeside
Kissimmee
4880 W. Irlo Bronson Hwy
Kissimmee, FL
407-396-1144 (800-800-8000)
Dogs are welcome at this hotel.

The Idyll Mouse One
8092 Roaring Creek
Kissimmee, FL
603-524-4000
theidyllmouse.com/one/index.html
2 Vacation Home Rentals near
Disney World. Each house has many
luxuries. One house is a 7 bedroom ,
four bath. The other is a 4 bedroom,
3 bath.

Comfort Inn Lake Buena Vista
8442 Palm Pkwy.
Lake Buena Vista, FL
407-996-7300 (877-424-6423)
Dogs of all sizes are allowed. Dogs
are allowed for a pet fee of $10.00
per pet per night.

Best Western Lake City Inn
3598 US 90 W
Lake City, FL
386-752-3801 (800-780-7234)
Dogs of all sizes are allowed. Dogs
are allowed for a pet fee of $10.00
per pet per stay.

Days Inn I-10 Lake City
3430 North U.S. Highway 441
Lake City, FL
386-758-4224 (800-329-7466)

Dogs are welcome at this hotel.

Knights Inn Lake City
117 North West Knights Avenue
Lake City, FL
386-752-7720 (800-843-5644)
Dogs of all sizes are allowed. Dogs
are allowed for a nightly pet fee.

Motel 6 - Lake City, Fl
3835 Us 90
Lake City, FL
386-755-4664 (800-466-8356)
This motel welcomes your pets to
stay with you.

Oaks 'N Pines RV/Campground
3864 N H 441
Lake City, FL
386-752-0830
Dogs must be leashed when out of
the room at all other times.

Ramada Limited Lake City
3340 W. US HWY 90
Lake City, FL
386-752-6262 (800-272-6232)
Dogs of all sizes are allowed. Dogs
are allowed for a pet fee.

Red Roof Inn Lake City
414 Southwest Florida Gateway
Blvd.
Lake City, FL
386-752-6693 (800-RED-ROOF)
One well-behaved family pet per
room. Guest must notify front desk
upon arrival. Guest is liable for any
damages. In consideration of all
guests, pets must never be left
unattended in the guest rooms.

Rodeway Inn
205 SW Commerce Dr.
Lake City, FL
386-755-5203 (877-424-6423)
Dogs of all sizes are allowed. Dogs
are allowed for a pet fee of $5.00
per pet per night.

Super 8 Lake City
3954 S.W. State Road 47
Lake City, FL
386-752-6450 (800-800-8000)
Dogs of all sizes are allowed. Dogs
are allowed for a pet fee of $10 per
pet per stay.

Travelodge High Springs Lake City
13771 South US Hwy 441
Lake City, FL
386-752-7582 (800-578-7878)
Dogs of all sizes are allowed. Dogs
are allowed for a pet fee of $10 per
pet per night.

Travelodge Lake City

3711 West Hwy 90
Lake City, FL
386-755-9306 (800-578-7878)
Dogs of all sizes are allowed. Dogs
are allowed for a pet fee of $8.00 per
pet per night.

Candlewood Suites Lake Mary
1130 Greenwood Blvd
Lake Mary, FL
407-585-3000 (877-270-6405)
Dogs up to 80 pounds are allowed.
Pets allowed with an additional
fee. Up to $75 for 1-6 nights and up
to $150 for 7+ nights. A pet
agreement must be signed at check-
in.

Extended Stay America Lake Mary -
Heathrow
1036 Greenwood Blvd
Lake Mary, FL
407-833-0011 (800-804-3724)
One dog is allowed per suite. There
is a $25 per night additional pet fee
up to $150 for an entire stay.

Homestead Studio Suites Lake Mary
- Heathrow
1040 Greenwood Blvd.
Lake Mary, FL
407-829-2332 (800-804-3724)
One dog is allowed per suite. There
is a $25 per night additional pet fee
up to $150 for an entire stay.

La Quinta Inn & Suites Orlando Lake
Mary
1060 Greenwood Blvd.
Lake Mary, FL
407-805-9901 (800-531-5900)
Dogs of all sizes are allowed. There
are no additional pet fees. Dogs
must be leashed and cleaned up
after. A cell number must be left with
the front desk and the Do Not Disturb
sign on the door, if pets are in the
room alone. Multiple dogs may be
allowed.

Super 8 Lake Wales
541 West Central Ave
Lake Wales, FL
863-676-7925 (800-800-8000)
Dogs are welcome at this hotel.

Holiday Inn Lakeland I-4 Hotel &
Conf Ctr
3260 US Highway 98n
Lakeland, FL
863-688-8080 (877-270-6405)
Dogs of all sizes are allowed. Dogs
are allowed for a pet fee.

La Quinta Inn & Suites Lakeland
1024 Crevasse St.
Lakeland, FL

863-859-2866 (800-531-5900)
Dogs of all sizes are allowed. There are no additional pet fees. Dogs must be leashed and cleaned up after. Dogs may not be left unattended unless they will be quiet and well behaved. Multiple dogs may be allowed.

Motel 6 - Lakeland
3120 Us 98
Lakeland, FL
863-682-0643 (800-466-8356)
This motel welcomes your pets to stay with you.

Residence Inn Lakeland
3701 Harden Blvd
Lakeland, FL
863-680-2323 (800-331-3131)
In addition to offering a convenient location to some local major corporations and attractions, as well as some great shopping and dining areas, this all suite hotel also provides a number of in-house amenities, including a daily buffet breakfast and evening social hours Monday to Thursday with appetizers and beverages. Dogs are allowed for an additional one time pet fee of $100 per room. Multiple dogs may be allowed.

Motel 6 - Lantana
1310 Lantana Rd
Lantana, FL
561-585-5833 (800-466-8356)
This motel welcomes your pets to stay with you.

Days Inn Leesburg
1115 W. North Blvd
Leesburg, FL
352-787-3131 (800-329-7466)
Dogs of all sizes are allowed. Dogs are allowed for a pet fee of $12.50 per pet per night.

Econo Lodge
1308 North 14th Street
Leesburg, FL
352-787-1210 (877-424-6423)
Dogs of all sizes are allowed. Dogs are allowed for a pet fee of $15.00 per pet per stay.

Super 8 Leesburg
1392 N Blvd W
Leesburg, FL
352-787-6363 (800-800-8000)
Dogs of all sizes are allowed. Dogs are allowed for a pet fee of $10.00 per pet per night.

Econo Lodge
6811 N. US 129 & I-10

Live Oak, FL
386-362-7459 (877-424-6423)
Dogs of all sizes are allowed. Dogs are allowed for a pet fee of $10.00 per pet per stay.

Residence Inn Tampa Suncoast Parkway at NorthPointe Village
2101 Northpointe Parkway
Lutz, FL
813-792-8400 (800-331-3131)
This all suite inn features a convenient location to business, shopping, dining, and entertainment areas, plus they also offer a number of in-house amenities, including a daily buffet breakfast and complimentary manager's receptions Tuesday, Wednesday, and Thursday. Dogs are allowed for an additional one time pet fee of $100 per room. Multiple dogs may be allowed.

Travelodge Suites MacClenny
1651 S 6th Street
MacClenny, FL
904-259-6408 (800-578-7878)
Dogs are welcome at this hotel.

Econo Lodge
151 Woodlawn Rd.
Macclenny, FL
904-259-3000 (877-424-6423)
Dogs of all sizes are allowed. Dogs are allowed for a pet fee of $10.00 (per pet per stay.

Changing Tides Cottages
225 Boca Ciega Dr
Madeira Beach, FL
727-397-7706
changingtidescottages.com
These one and two bedroom cottages are located near Boca Ciega Bay. They are fully equipped. There are no cleaning fees but there is a pet fee of $5 per day or $25 per week.

Island Paradise Cottages & Apartments of Madeira Beach
13215 2nd Street East
Madeira Beach, FL
727-395-9751
islandparadise.com
Some of these vacation rentals allow dogs with prior approvals. Call them to make reservations.

Snug Harbor Inn Waterfront Bed and Breakfast
13655 Gulf Blvd
Madeira Beach, FL
727-395-9256 (866-395-9256)
snugharborflorida.com
This bed and breakfast offers a

location on the waterfront, continental breakfast, and a boat slip. Pets are welcome with prior approval.

Days Inn- Madison
6160 South State Road 53
Madison, FL
850-973-3330 (800-329-7466)
Dogs of all sizes are allowed. Dogs are allowed for a pet fee.

Super 8 Madison
6246 State Rd. 53 South
Madison, FL
850-973-6267 (800-800-8000)
Dogs of all sizes are allowed. Dogs are allowed for a pet fee.

Knights Inn Marianna
4655 Highway 90 East
Marianna, FL
850-526-3251 (800-843-5644)
Dogs of all sizes are allowed. Dogs are allowed for a pet fee of $10.00 per pet per night.

Quality Inn
2175 Hwy 71 South
Marianna, FL
850-526-5600 (877-424-6423)
Dogs of all sizes are allowed. Dogs are allowed for a pet fee of $12.00 per pet per night.

Crane Creek Inn
909 E Melbourne Ave
Melbourne, FL
321-768-6416
cranecreekinn.com
The inn is at 909 and 907 E. Melbourne Ave. There are no additional pet fees. Children are not allowed at the inn.

Days Inn Melbourne
4500 West New Haven Avenue
Melbourne, FL
321-724-2051 (800-329-7466)
Dogs of all sizes are allowed. Dogs are allowed for a nightly pet fee.

Hilton Hotel
3003 N H A1A
Melbourne, FL
321-777-5000 (800-HILTONS (445-8667))
A beach front hotel with private balconies and an atrium, offers a number of on site amenities for business and leisure travelers, plus a convenient location to shopping, dining, and recreational areas. Dogs up to 75 pounds are allowed for an additional one time pet fee of $50 per room. Multiple dogs may be allowed.

Hilton Hotel
200 Rialto Place
Melbourne, FL
321-768-0200 (800-HILTONS (445-8667))
This coastal luxury hotel offers a number of on site amenities for business and leisure travelers, plus a convenient location to business, shopping, dining, and recreational areas. Dogs up to 70 pounds are allowed for an additional one time pet fee of $50 per room. 2 dogs may be allowed.

La Quinta Inn & Suites Melbourne
7200 George T. Edwards Drive
Melbourne, FL
321-242-9400 (800-531-5900)
Dogs of all sizes are allowed. There are no additional pet fees. Dogs must be leashed and cleaned up after. Multiple dogs may be allowed.

Residence Inn Melbourne
1430 S Babcock Street
Melbourne, FL
321-723-5740 (800-331-3131)
In addition to being only a mile from the airport, near the Kennedy Space Center, beaches, and a variety of business and recreation areas, this all suite inn also offers a number of in-house amenities, including a daily buffet breakfast and evening socials. Dogs are allowed for an additional one time pet fee of $100 per room. 2 dogs may be allowed.

Super 8 Melbourne
1515 S Harbour City Blvd
Melbourne, FL
321-723-4430 (800-800-8000)
Dogs of all sizes are allowed. Dogs are allowed for a pet fee of $10.00 per pet per night.

Beach Bungalow
Call to Arrange
Melbourne Beach, FL
321-984-1330 (888-414-5314)
1stbeach.com
The Beach Bungalow is 3 large, luxurious 2 bedroom oceanfront villas with private gardens in a small beach town. Dogs of any size are allowed with a $50 cleaning fee. The private gardens are entirely fenced and the floors are tile and hardwood.

Candlewood Suites Miami Airport West
8855 NW 27th Street
Miami, FL
305-591-9099 (877-270-6405)
Dogs up to 80 pounds are allowed. Pets allowed with an additional pet fee. Up to $75 for 1-6 nights and up to $150 for 7+ nights. A pet agreement must be signed at check-in.

Epic Hotel
270 Biscayne Blvd Way/H 1/5/41
Miami, FL
305-424-5226 (866-760-3742)
epichotel.com
This beautiful luxury hotel and spa is located on the bay, and more than 50 earth-friendly practices and products have been implemented here since this Kimpton Hotel formally launched their EarthCare program in 2005. Some of these include an in-house water purification system, all organic and sustainable foods coffee/tea, organic/biodynamic and sustainable wines, and sustainable seafood. Additionally, with a commitment to social responsibility, there is emphasis on waste reduction, energy and water management, and supporting like-minded sources and organizations. Dogs are allowed for no additional fee; plus they receive a pet amenity package upon arrival. Multiple dogs may be allowed.

Extended Stay America Miami - Airport - Doral
8655 NW 21 Terrace
Miami, FL
786-331-7717 (800-804-3724)
One dog is allowed per suite. There is a $25 per night additional pet fee up to $150 for an entire stay.

Extended Stay America Miami - Brickell - Port of Miami
298 SW 15th Rd.
Miami, FL
305-856-3700 (800-804-3724)
One dog is allowed per suite. There is a $25 per night additional pet fee up to $150 for an entire stay.

Extended Stay America Miami - Coral Gables
3640 SW 22nd Street
Miami, FL
305-443-7444 (800-804-3724)
One dog is allowed per suite. There is a $25 per night additional pet fee up to $150 for an entire stay.

Hilton Hotel
5101 Blue Lagoon Drive
Miami, FL
305-262-1000 (800-HILTONS (445-8667))
This coastal, luxury hotel offers a number of on site amenities for business and leisure travelers, plus a convenient location to the Miami International Airport, business, shopping, dining, and recreational areas. Dogs are allowed for an additional one time pet fee of $75 per room. Multiple dogs may be allowed.

Homestead Studio Suites Miami - Airport - Blue Lagoon
6605 NW 7th St.
Miami, FL
305-260-0085 (800-804-3724)
One dog is allowed per suite. There is a $25 per night additional pet fee up to $150 for an entire stay.

Homestead Studio Suites Miami - Airport - Doral
8720 NW 33rd St.
Miami, FL
305-436-1811 (800-804-3724)
One dog is allowed per suite. There is a $25 per night additional pet fee up to $150 for an entire stay.

Homestead Studio Suites Miami - Airport - Miami Springs
101 Fairway Dr.
Miami, FL
305-870-0448 (800-804-3724)
One dog is allowed per suite. There is a $25 per night additional pet fee up to $150 for an entire stay.

Homestead Village-Miami Airport
8720 NW 33rd Street
Miami, FL
305-436-1811 (888-782-9473)
Well mannered dogs are welcome for an additional pet fee of $25 per night per room, not to total more than $150. 2 dogs may be allowed.

La Quinta Inn & Suites Miami Airport West
8730 NW 27th St.
Miami, FL
305-436-0830 (800-531-5900)
One large dog (over 50 pounds) or two medium to small dogs are allowed. There are no additional pet fees. Dogs must be leashed and cleaned up after.

Red Roof Inn Miami Airport
3401 Northwest LeJeune Road
Miami, FL
305-871-4221 (800-RED-ROOF)
One well-behaved family pet per room. Guest must notify front desk upon arrival. Guest is liable for any damages. In consideration of all guests, pets must never be left unattended in the guest rooms.

Residence Inn Miami Airport West/Doral Area
1212 NW 82nd Avenue
Miami, FL

305-591-2211 (800-331-3131)
Some of the amenities at this all-suite inn include a daily buffet breakfast, evening social hours, a swimming pool, Sport Court, and a complimentary grocery shopping service. Dogs are allowed for an additional one time pet fee of $100 per room. 2 dogs may be allowed.

Staybridge Suites Miami Doral Area
3265 NW 87th Ave
Miami, FL
305-500-9100 (877-270-6405)
Dogs up to 80 pounds are allowed. Pets allowed with an additional pet fee. Up to $75 for 1-6 nights and up to $150 for 7+ nights. A pet agreement must be signed at check-in.

TownePlace Suites Miami Airport West/Doral Area
10505 NW 36th Street
Miami, FL
305-718-4144 (800-257-3000)
In addition to offering a number of in-house amenities for all level of travelers, this all suite inn also provides a convenient location to several corporate parks, shopping, dining, and entertainment areas. Dogs are allowed for an additional one time fee of $100 per room. Multiple dogs may be allowed.

Wellesley Inn Miami Lakes
7925 NW 154th Street
Miami, FL
305-821-8274 (800-531-5900)
Dogs of all sizes are allowed. There is a $10 per night per room additional pet fee. Dogs must be leashed, cleaned up after, and crated when left alone in the room. Multiple dogs may be allowed.

Brigham Gardens Guesthouse
1411 Collins Avenue
Miami Beach, FL
305-531-1331
brighamgardens.com
This guesthouse offers hotel Rooms, Studios and one Bedroom Apartments. Pets are welcome for a nightly fee of $6.00.

Hotel Indigo Miami Beach
1050 Washington Avenue
Miami Beach, FL
305-674-1930 (877-865-6578)
Dogs of all sizes are allowed. Dogs are allowed for a pet fee.

Hotel Leon
841 Collins Avenue
Miami Beach, FL

305-673-3767
hotelleon.com/
This hotel is a stone's throw from the beach and in the heart of the Art Deco District of Miami Beach.

Hotel Ocean
1230 Ocean Drive
Miami Beach, FL
800-783-1725
hotelocean.com
Pets are welcome in this Miami Beach boutique hotel. They have created a special package that includes a bed, treats, and walking service for only $19.95 per pet per day. The regular pet fee is $15.00 per pet per day.

Loews Miami Beach Hotel
1601 Collins Avenue
Miami Beach, FL
305-604-1601
All well-behaved dogs of any size are welcome. This upscale hotel offers their "Loews Loves Pets" program which includes special pet treats, local dog walking routes, and a list of nearby pet-friendly places to visit. While pets are not allowed in the pool, they are welcome to join you at the side of the pool or at the pool bar. There is an additional one time pet cleaning fee of $25 per room.

Marriott South Beach
161 Ocean Drive
Miami Beach, FL
305-536-7700 (800-228-9290)
Located in what is known as 'America's Riviera', this luxury hotel sits central to numerous world class shopping, dining, and day/night entertainment areas, plus they also offer a number of in-house amenities for business and leisure travelers. Dogs up to 100 pounds are allowed for an additional one time fee of $150 per pet. 2 dogs may be allowed.

TownePlace Suites Miami Lakes
8079 NW 154 Street
Miami Lakes, FL
305-512-9191 (800-257-3000)
Besides being nestled among several world class shopping, dining, nightlife, beaches, and entertainment venues, this all suite inn also provides a number of in-house amenities for level of travelers. Dogs are allowed for an additional one time fee of $100 per room. Multiple dogs may be allowed.

Howard Johnson Express Inn

Tallahassee Midway
56 Fortune Boulevard
Midway, FL
850-574-8888 (800-446-4656)
Dogs of all sizes are allowed. Dogs are allowed for a pet fee of $10.00 per pet per night.

Red Roof Inn Pensacola East - Milton
2672 Avalon Blvd.
Milton, FL
850-995-6100 (800-RED-ROOF)
One well-behaved family pet per room. Guest must notify front desk upon arrival. Guest is liable for any damages. In consideration of all guests, pets must never be left unattended in the guest rooms.

Residence Inn Fort Lauderdale SW/Miramar
14700 Hotel Road
Miramar, FL
954-450-2717 (800-331-3131)
Besides offering a convenient location to the beaches, business, shopping, dining, and entertainment areas, this hotel also provides a number of in-house amenities, including a daily buffet breakfast and complementary evening receptions Monday to Thursday from 5 to 7 pm. Dogs are allowed for an additional one time fee pet of $100 per room. 2 dogs may be allowed.

Beach Condos in Destin
2606 Scenic Gulf Drive
Miramar Beach, FL
850-269-3342 (888-251-5214)
beachcondosindestin.com
These condos along the Gulf of Mexico allow pets in some of their rentals.

Super 8 Monticello
140 Pafford Rd
Monticello, FL
850-997-8888 (800-800-8000)
Dogs of all sizes are allowed. Dogs are allowed for a pet fee of $10 per pet per night.

Ramada Plaza Marco Polo Beach Resort
19201 Collins Ave
N Miami Beach, FL
305-932-2233 (800-272-6232)
Dogs of all sizes are allowed. Dogs are allowed for a nightly pet fee.

Hilton Hotel
5111 Tamiami Trail N
Naples, FL
239-430-4900 (800-HILTONS (445-8667))

This upscale hotel offers a number of on site amenities for business and leisure travelers, plus a convenient location to the beach, shopping, dining, and entertainment areas. Dogs up to 65 pounds are allowed for a $200 refundable deposit, plus an additional one time pet fee of $75 per room, and they must be declared at the time of reservations. 2 dogs may be allowed.

La Quinta Inn Naples Airport
185 Bedzel Circle
Naples, FL
239-352-8400 (800-531-5900)
Dogs of all sizes are allowed. There are no additional pet fees. Dogs may not be left unattended in the rooms except for a short time, and they must be well behaved and kept on leash. Multiple dogs may be allowed.

Naples Red Roof Inn & Suites
1925 Davis Boulevard
Naples, FL
239-774-3117 (800-RED-ROOF)
One well-behaved family pet per room. Guest must notify front desk upon arrival. Guest is liable for any damages. In consideration of all guests, pets must never be left unattended in the guest rooms.

Ramada Of Naples
1100 Tamiami Trail North
Naples, FL
239-263-3434 (800-272-6232)
Dogs of all sizes are allowed. Dogs are allowed for a pet fee of $25 per pet per night.

Residence Inn Naples
4075 Tamiami Trail N
Naples, FL
239-659-1300 (800-331-3131)
Besides offering a convenient location to beaches, shopping, dining, commerce, and entertainment areas, this all suite inn also offers a number of in-house amenities, including a daily buffet breakfast and evening socials Monday to Wednesday with light dinner fare. Dogs are allowed for an additional one time pet fee of $75 per room. Multiple dogs may be allowed.

Staybridge Suites Naples-Gulf Coast
4805 Tamiami Trail North
Naples, FL
239-643-8002 (877-270-6405)
Dogs up to 80 pounds are allowed. Pets allowed with an additional pet fee. Up to $75 for 1-6 nights and up to $150 for 7+ nights. A pet agreement must be signed at check-in.

Days Inn Neptune Beach
1401 Atlantic Blvd.
Neptune Beach, FL
904-249-2777 (800-329-7466)
Dogs are welcome at this hotel.

Ramada Bayside New Port Richey
5015 US Hwy 19 North
New Port Richey, FL
727-849-8551 (800-272-6232)
Dogs are welcome at this hotel.

EastWind Villas
New Smyrna Beach, FL
386-428-1387
newsmyrnabeachvillas.com
Five pet-friendly vacation rentals are available near the beach . High Speed Internet access is available in the rentals. There are no weight restrictions for dogs and each vacation rental allows up to two pets. Dogs must be on a flea program.

Best Western Ocala Park Centre
3701 SW 38th Avenue
Ocala, FL
352-237-4848 (800-780-7234)
Dogs of all sizes are allowed. Dogs are allowed for a pet fee of $10.00 per pet per night.

Days Inn Ocala
3811 NW Bonnie Heath Blvd
Ocala, FL
352-629-7041 (800-329-7466)
Dogs are welcome at this hotel.

Days Inn West Ocala
3620 W Silver Springs Blvd
Ocala, FL
352-629-0091 (800-329-7466)
Dogs are welcome at this hotel.

Hilton Hotel
3600 SW 36th Avenue
Ocala, FL
352-854-1400 (800-HILTONS (445-8667))
Located in the heart of horse country, this resort style hotel sits on six acres and offers a number of on site amenities for business and leisure travelers, plus a convenient location to the areas best attractions. Dogs are allowed for an additional one time pet fee of $49 per room, and there is a pet policy to sign at check in. 2 dogs may be allowed.

Howard Johnson Inn - FL Ocala
3951 NW Blitchton Road
Ocala, FL
352-629-7021 (800-446-4656)

Dogs are welcome at this hotel.

La Quinta Inn & Suites Ocala
3530 S.W. 36th Ave.
Ocala, FL
352-861-1137 (800-531-5900)
Dogs of all sizes are allowed. There are no additional pet fees. Dogs must be leashed, cleaned up after, and removed or attend to the pet for housekeeping. Dogs must be leashed and cleaned up after. Multiple dogs may be allowed.

Ocala Red Roof Inn & Suites
120 Northwest 40th Ave
Ocala, FL
352-732-4590 (800-RED-ROOF)
One well-behaved family pet per room. Guest must notify front desk upon arrival. Guest is liable for any damages. In consideration of all guests, pets must never be left unattended in the guest rooms.

Ramada Conference Center Ocala
3810 NW Bonnie Heath Blvd
Ocala, FL
352-732-3131 (800-272-6232)
Dogs up to 50 pounds are allowed. Dogs are allowed for a pet fee.

Residence Inn Ocala
3610 SW 38th Avenue
Ocala, FL
352-547-1600 (800-331-3131)
In addition to being a member of the Florida Green Lodging Program, this upscale, all suite inn offers guests a community ambiance, a daily buffet breakfast, evening socials, a putting green, and a Sport Court. Dogs are allowed for an additional one time pet fee of $75 per room. 2 dogs may be allowed.

Super 8 Ocala
I-75 Exit 352
Ocala, FL
352-629-8794 (800-800-8000)
Dogs are welcome at this hotel.

Red Roof Inn Orlando West
11241 West Colonial Drive
Ocoee, FL
407-347-0140 (800-RED-ROOF)
One well-behaved family pet per room. Guest must notify front desk upon arrival. Guest is liable for any damages. In consideration of all guests, pets must never be left unattended in the guest rooms.

Residence Inn Tampa Oldsmar
4012 Tampa Road
Oldsmar, FL
813-818-9400 (800-331-3131)

In addition to being located in Telecom Park Business Center and only a short distance from numerous sites of interest for business and leisure travelers, this all suite hotel also offers a number of on-site amenities, including a daily buffet breakfast and evening socials Monday to Thursday with light dinner fare. Dogs are allowed for an additional one time pet fee of $100 per room. Multiple dogs may be allowed.

Comfort Inn
445 S. Volusia Ave.
Orange City, FL
386-775-7444 (877-424-6423)
Dogs of all sizes are allowed. Dogs are allowed for a pet fee of $10.00 per pet per night.

Days Inn /Deland Orange City
2501 North Volusia Avenue
Orange City, FL
386-775-4522 (800-329-7466)
Dogs of all sizes are allowed. Dogs are allowed for a pet fee of $10.00 per pet per night.

Comfort Inn
341 Park Ave.
Orange Park, FL
904-644-4444 (877-424-6423)
Dogs of all sizes are allowed.

Howard Johnson Inn Orange Park
150 Park Avenue
Orange Park, FL
904-264-9513 (800-446-4656)
Dogs of all sizes are allowed. Dogs are allowed for a pet fee of $30.00 per pet per stay.

Rodeway Inn & Conference Center
300 Park Avenue
Orange Park, FL
904-264-1211 (877-424-6423)
Dogs of all sizes are allowed. Dogs are allowed for a pet fee of $20.00 per pet per night. One dog is allowed per room.

Suburban Extended Stay South
1656 Wells Road
Orange Park, FL
904-264-4616 (877-424-6423)
Dogs of all sizes are allowed. Dogs are allowed for a pet fee of $2.00 per pet per night.

Baymont Inn & Suites Florida Mall/ Orlando
8820 S Orange Blossom Trail
Orlando, FL
407-851-8200 (877-229-6668)
Dogs of all sizes are allowed. Dogs

are allowed for a pet fee.

Best Western Orlando Gateway Hotel
7299 Universal Boulevard
Orlando, FL
407-351-5009 (800-780-7234)
Dogs of all sizes are allowed. Dogs are allowed for a pet fee of $10.00 per pet per night.

Celebration World Resort
7503 Atlantis Way
Orlando, FL
407-997-7421
Dogs up to 30 pounds are allowed as long as they have proof of up to date shots. There is a $75 (+ tax) one time fee per pet.

Comfort Suites Universal South
9350 Turkey Lake Rd.
Orlando, FL
407-351-5050 (877-424-6423)
Dogs up to 50 pounds are allowed. Dogs are allowed for a pet fee of $49.00 per pet per stay. Two dogs are allowed per room.

Country Inns & Suites by Carlson
5440 Forbes Place
Orlando, FL
407-856-8896
Dogs are allowed for an additional $75 one time pet fee per room.

Days Inn Midtown Orlando
3300 S Orange Blossom Trl
Orlando, FL
407-422-4521 (800-329-7466)
Dogs of all sizes are allowed. Dogs are allowed for a pet fee of $10.00 per pet per night.

Days Inn Universal Maingate Orlando
5827 Caravan Ct
Orlando, FL
407-351-3800 (800-329-7466)
Dogs are welcome at this hotel.

Days Inn -North Of Universal Studios Orlando
2500 West 33rd Street
Orlando, FL
407-841-3731 (800-329-7466)
Dogs of all sizes are allowed. Dogs are allowed for a pet fee of $10 per pet per night.

Days Inn /International Drive Orlando
5858 International Drive
Orlando, FL
407-351-4410 (800-329-7466)
Dogs of all sizes are allowed. Dogs are allowed for a pet fee of $15.00

per pet per night.

Days Inn and Suites /UCF Research Park Orlando
11639 East Colonial Drive
Orlando, FL
407-282-2777 (800-329-7466)
Dogs of all sizes are allowed. Dogs are allowed for a pet fee of $15.00 per pet per night.

Doubletree Castle Hotel
8629 International Drive
Orlando, FL
407-345-1511 (800-222-TREE (8733))
Sitting central to an amazing array of attractions - including several theme parks, and shopping and dining hot spots, this enchanting, castle-themed, luxury hotel also offers guests a number of on-site amenities. Dogs up to 50 pounds are allowed for an additional one time pet fee of $100 per room. Multiple dogs may be allowed.

Extended Stay America Orlando - Convention Center - Westwood Blvd.
6451 Westwood Blvd.
Orlando, FL
407-352-3454 (800-804-3724)
One dog is allowed per suite. There is a $25 per night additional pet fee up to $150 for an entire stay.

Extended Stay America Orlando - Maitland
1760 Pembrook Drive
Orlando, FL
407-667-0474 (800-804-3724)
One dog is allowed per suite. There is a $25 per night additional pet fee up to $150 for an entire stay.

Extended Stay America Orlando - Universal Studios
5620 Major Blvd.
Orlando, FL
407-351-1788 (800-804-3724)
One dog is allowed per suite. There is a $25 per night additional pet fee up to $150 for an entire stay.

Hard Rock Hotel
5800 Universal Blvd
Orlando, FL
407-503-2000 (800-BEASTAR (232-7827))
This full service resort has many extras such as a 12,000 square foot pool with a sand beach, an underwater sound system, interactive fountains, and a water slide, a variety of planned activities and recreation, and express access and transportation to the Universal

Orlando Theme Park. Dogs of all sizes are welcome for an additional one time pet fee of $25 per room. Guests must have a health certificate for each pet obtained within 10 days prior to arrival. Dogs must be quiet, well behaved, leashed, cleaned up after, and removed for housekeeping. Dogs must be walked in designated areas only, and they are not allowed in pool/lounge, or restaurant areas. Dogs are not allowed in Club rooms. 2 dogs may be allowed.

Hawthorn Suites Orlando Airport
7450 Augusta National Drive
Orlando, FL
407-438-2121 (800-527-1133)
In addition to providing a convenient location to many local sites and activities, this all-suite hotel offers a number of amenities for business and leisure travelers, including their signature breakfast buffet and beautifully appointed rooms. Dogs up to 50 pounds are allowed for an additional pet fee of $20 per night per room. Dogs must be crated or removed for housekeeping. 2 dogs may be allowed.

Holiday Inn Orlando-Intl Drive Resort
6515 International Dr
Orlando, FL
407-351-3500 (877-270-6405)
Dogs up to 75 pounds are allowed. Dogs are allowed for a pet fee of $15.00 per pet per night.

Homestead Studio Suites Orlando - John Young Parkway
4101 Equity Row
Orlando, FL
407-352-5577 (800-804-3724)
One dog is allowed per suite. There is a $25 per night additional pet fee up to $150 for an entire stay.

Howard Johnson Inn International Drive Orlando
6603 International Dr/I-4
Orlando, FL
407-351-2900 (800-446-4656)
Dogs of all sizes are allowed. Dogs are allowed for a nightly pet fee.

Howard Johnson Inn near Int'l. Airport Orlando
9393 S. Orange Blossom Trail
Orlando, FL
407-851-1050 (800-446-4656)
Dogs of all sizes are allowed. Dogs are allowed for a nightly pet fee.

La Quinta Inn
5825 International Drive

Orlando, FL
407-351-4100
Dogs up to 50 pounds are allowed for no additional face. 2 dogs may be allowed.

La Quinta Inn & Suites Orlando Airport North
7160 N. Frontage Rd.
Orlando, FL
407-240-5000 (800-531-5900)
Dogs of all sizes are allowed. There are no additional pet fees. Dogs may not be left unattended, and they must be leashed and cleaned up after. Dogs must be removed or crated for housekeeping. Multiple dogs may be allowed.

La Quinta Inn & Suites Orlando Convention Center
8504 Universal Blvd.
Orlando, FL
407-345-1365 (800-531-5900)
Dogs of all sizes are allowed. There are no additional pet fees. Dogs must be leashed and cleaned up after. Dogs must be crated if left alone in the room. Multiple dogs may be allowed.

La Quinta Inn & Suites Orlando UCF
11805 Research Pkwy.
Orlando, FL
407-737-6075 (800-531-5900)
Dogs of all sizes are allowed. There are no additional pet fees. Dogs must be leashed and cleaned up after. A call number must be left at the front desk, and the Do Not Disturb sign left on the door, if there is a pet alone inside. 2 dogs may be allowed.

La Quinta Inn Orlando Airport West
7931 Daetwyler Dr.
Orlando, FL
407-857-9215 (800-531-5900)
Dogs of all sizes are allowed. There are no additional pet fees. Dogs must be leashed and cleaned up after. Dogs may not be left unattended unless they will be quiet and well behaved. Multiple dogs may be allowed.

La Quinta Inn Orlando International Dr
8300 Jamaican Court
Orlando, FL
407-351-1660 (800-531-5900)
Dogs of all sizes are allowed. There are no additional pet fees. Dogs must be leashed and cleaned up after. Dogs must be well behaved, and the Do Not Disturb must be on the door if there is a pet alone

inside. Multiple dogs may be allowed.

La Quinta Inn Orlando South
2051 Consulate Drive
Orlando, FL
407-240-0500 (800-531-5900)
Dogs of all sizes are allowed. There are no additional pet fees. Dogs may not be left unattended, and they must be leashed and cleaned up after. Multiple dogs may be allowed.

Motel 6 - Orlando International Dr
5909 American Way
Orlando, FL
407-351-6500 (800-466-8356)
This motel welcomes your pets to stay with you.

Motel 6 - Orlando Winter Park
5300 Adanson Rd
Orlando, FL
407-647-1444 (800-466-8356)
This motel welcomes your pets to stay with you.

Portofino Bay Hotel
5601 Universal Blvd
Orlando, FL
407-503-1000 (800-BEASTAR (232-7827))
Built to resemble an Italian Riviera seaside village, this beautiful bay hotel features 3 themed swimming pools, special privileges to the areas best golf courses, and express access and transportation to the Universal Orlando Theme Park. This upscale hotel offers their "Loews Loves Pets" program which includes special pet treats, local dog walking routes, and a list of nearby pet-friendly places to visit. Dogs of all sizes are welcome for an additional one time pet fee of $25 per room. Guests must have a health certificate for each pet obtained within 10 days prior to arrival. Dogs must be quiet, well behaved, leashed and cleaned up after, and removed for housekeeping. Dogs must be walked in designated areas only, and they are not allowed in pool/lounge, or restaurant areas. Dogs are not allowed in Club rooms. 2 dogs may be allowed.

Quality Inn At International Drive
7600 International Dr.
Orlando, FL
407-996-1600 (877-424-6423)
Dogs of all sizes are allowed. Dogs are allowed for a pet fee of $10.00 per pet per night.

Quality Inn Plaza
9000 International Dr.

Orlando, FL
407-996-8585 (877-424-6423)
Dogs up to 50 pounds are allowed.
Dogs are allowed for a pet fee of
$10.00 per pet per night.

Red Roof Inn Orlando Convention
Center
9922 Hawaiian Court
Orlando, FL
407-352-1507 (800-RED-ROOF)
One well-behaved family pet per
room. Guest must notify front desk
upon arrival. Guest is liable for any
damages. In consideration of all
guests, pets must never be left
unattended in the guest rooms.

Residence Inn Orlando Airport
7024 Augusta National Drive
Orlando, FL
407-856-2444 (800-331-3131)
Located in the heart of the Lee Vista
Office Park only minutes from the
airport and the newly developing
Lake Nona Medical City, this all suite
inn also provides a great location to
world class attractions, a daily buffet
breakfast, and evening socials. Dogs
up to 50 pounds are allowed for an
additional pet fee of $75 per room. 2
dogs may be allowed.

Residence Inn Orlando International
Drive
7975 Canada Avenue
Orlando, FL
407-352-2689 (800-380-6761)
This all suite hotel sits central to
several world class attractions, The
Orlando Convention Center, and to
some great shopping areas; plus
they offer a number of in-house
amenities that include a daily buffet
breakfast and weekday social hours.
Dogs are allowed for an additional
one time pet fee of $79 per room.
Multiple dogs may be allowed.

Residence Inn Orlando Lake Buena
Vista
11450 Marbella Palm Court
Orlando, FL
407-465-0075 (800-331-3131)
This all suite hotel sits central to
several world class attractions, The
Orlando Convention Center, and to
the Orlando Premium Outlets; plus
they offer a number of in-house
amenities that include a daily buffet
breakfast and a manager's reception
Monday to Thursday. Dogs are
allowed for an additional one time
pet fee of $100 per room. Multiple
dogs may be allowed.

Residence Inn SeaWorld
11000 Westwood Blvd.

Orlando, FL
407-313-3600 (800-331-3131)
residenceinnseaworld.com/
There is a $150 one time pet fee.

Rodeway Inn
6119 S Orange Blossom Trail
Orlando, FL
407-545-6465 (877-424-6423)
Dogs of all sizes are allowed. Dogs
are allowed for a pet fee of $25.00
per pet per stay.

Rodeway Inn International
6327 International Dr.
Orlando, FL
407-996-4444 (877-424-6423)
Dogs of all sizes are allowed. Dogs
are allowed for a pet fee of $10.00
per pet per night.

Royal Pacific Resort
6300 Hollywood Way
Orlando, FL
407-503-3000 (800-BEASTAR
(232-7827))
Nestled in a lush lagoon setting, this
full service family resort features
such extras as authentic luaus with
entertainment, a large pool with a
sandy beach and interactive water
play area, and express access and
transportation to the Universal
Orlando Theme Park. Dogs of all
sizes are welcome for an additional
one time pet fee of $25 per room.
Guests must have a health
certificate for each pet obtained
within 10 days prior to arrival. Dogs
must be quiet, well behaved,
leashed and cleaned up after, and
removed for housekeeping. Dogs
must be walked in designated areas
only, and they are not allowed in
pool/lounge, or restaurant areas.
Dogs are not allowed in Club
rooms. Multiple dogs may be
allowed.

The Safari Hotel & Suites Lake
Buena Vista
12205 S. Apopka Vineland Road
Orlando, FL
407-239-0444
Dogs up to 80 pounds are allowed.
There are no additional pet fees.
Dogs are not allowed to be left
alone in the room.

TownePlace Suites Orlando
East/UCF
11801 High Tech Avenue
Orlando, FL
407-243-6100 (800-257-3000)
This all suite inn sits close to
numerous business, shopping,
dining, and entertainment areas,
plus they offer a number of in-house

amenities for business and leisure
travelers. Dogs are allowed for an
additional fee of $25 per night per
room for a maximum total of $100
per stay. Multiple dogs may be
allowed.

Travelodge Intl Drive Universal
Studios Orlando
5859 American Way
Orlando, FL
407-345-8880 (800-578-7878)
Dogs of all sizes are allowed. Dogs
are allowed for a pet fee of $10.00
per pet per night.

Travelodge Inn and Suites Airport
Orlando
1853 McCoy Road
Orlando, FL
407-851-1113 (800-578-7878)
Dogs of all sizes are allowed. Dogs
are allowed for a pet fee of $15.00
per pet per stay.

Super 8 Ormond Beach
1634 North US 1 & I-95
Ormond Beach, FL
386-672-6222 (800-800-8000)
Dogs are welcome at this hotel.

Days Inn Space Coast Riverside
Palm Bay
4700 Dixie Hwy NE
Palm Bay, FL
321-951-0350 (800-329-7466)
Dogs are welcome at this hotel.

Motel 6 - Palm Bay
1170 Malabar Rd Se
Palm Bay, FL
321-951-8222 (800-466-8356)
This motel welcomes your pets to
stay with you.

Plaza Inn
215 Brazilian Avenue
Palm Beach, FL
561-832-8666 (800-233-2632)
plazainnpalmbeach.com/
This pet friendly hotel has
accommodated dogs up to 100 lbs.
This inn, located on the Island of
Palm Beach, is a historic 50 room
hotel which has been fully renovated
with warm textures of lace, polished
wood, antiques and quality
reproductions. Take a look at their
website for pictures of this elegant
inn. There are no pet fees.

The Chesterfield Hotel
363 Cocoanut Row
Palm Beach, FL
561-659-5800
Dogs are allowed for an additional
one time fee of $75 per pet. 2 dogs

may be allowed.

400 Avenue of Champions
400 Avenue of Champions
Palm Beach Gardens, FL
800-633-9150
pgaresort.com/
A luxury, waterside golf resort, there
are 339 richly decorated guest rooms
and suites, meticulously manicure
landscaping, and a number of
recreational activities available. Dogs
up to 30 pounds are allowed for an
additional fee of $150 per pet. Pets
may only be left for a maximum of 2
hours in the room and they must be
kenneled. Proof of current
vaccinations/rabies is required. Dogs
must be leashed or crated at all
times when not in the room. 2 dogs
may be allowed.

Doubletree Palm Beach Gardens
4431 PGA Boulevard
Palm Beach Gardens, FL
561-622-2260
This hotel provides a lush garden,
heated outdoor pool, complimentary
wireless Internet and a fitness room.
There is an open lounge and
veranda as well. The hotel hosts a
full service restaurant and bar. Dogs
up to 50 pounds are allowed. There
is a $75 one time additional pet fee.

Best Western Palm Coast
5 Kingswood Drive
Palm Coast, FL
386-446-4457 (800-780-7234)
Dogs of all sizes are allowed. Dogs
are allowed for a pet fee.

Red Roof Inn Clearwater - Palm
Harbor
32000 US Rt 19 North
Palm Harbor, FL
727-786-2529 (800-RED-ROOF)
One well-behaved family pet per
room. Guest must notify front desk
upon arrival. Guest is liable for any
damages. In consideration of all
guests, pets must never be left
unattended in the guest rooms.

Candlewood Suites Melbourne/Viera
2930 Pineda Causeway
Palm Shores, FL
321-821-9009 (877-270-6405)
Dogs up to 80 pounds are allowed.
Pets allowed with an additional pet
fee. Up to $75 for 1-6 nights and up
to $150 for 7+ nights. A pet
agreement must be signed at check-
in.

Comfort Inn & Conference Center
1013 E. 23rd St.

Panama City, FL
850-769-6969 (877-424-6423)
Dogs of all sizes are allowed. Dogs
are allowed for a pet fee of $10.00
per pet per night.

La Quinta Inn & Suites Panama City
1030 East 23rd Street
Panama City, FL
850-914-0022 (800-531-5900)
Dogs of all sizes are allowed. There
are no additional pet fees. Dogs
must be quiet, well behaved,
leashed and cleaned up after. A call
number must be left at the front
desk, and the Do Not Disturb sign
left on the door, if there is a pet
alone inside. Multiple dogs may be
allowed.

Red Roof Inn Panama City
217 US Rt. 231
Panama City, FL
850-215-2727 (800-RED-ROOF)
One well-behaved family pet per
room. Guest must notify front desk
upon arrival. Guest is liable for any
damages. In consideration of all
guests, pets must never be left
unattended in the guest rooms.

Pineapple Villas on Laguna Beach
19979 Front Beach Rd
Panama City Beach, FL
850-234-1788 (800-234-1788)
PineappleVillasOnLagunaBeach.co
m
Pets are allowed in some of these
Caribbean style villas in a boutique
hotel format.

Sleep Inn & Suites
9201 Front Beach Road
Panama City Beach, FL
850-249-2501 (877-424-6423)
Dogs of all sizes are allowed. Dogs
are allowed for a pet fee of $10.00
per pet per night. Two dogs are
allowed per room.

Days Inn - Historic Downtown
Pensacola
710 North Palafox Street
Pensacola, FL
850-438-4922 (800-329-7466)
Dogs of all sizes are allowed. Dogs
are allowed for a pet fee.

Extended Stay America Pensacola -
University Mall
809 Bloodworth Ln.
Pensacola, FL
850-473-9323 (800-804-3724)
One dog is allowed per suite. There
is a $25 per night additional pet fee
up to $150 for an entire stay.

Howard Johnson Inn FL Pensacola
6919 Pensacola Blvd
Pensacola, FL
850-478-4499 (800-446-4656)
Dogs are welcome at this hotel.
There is a $25 one time pet fee.

La Quinta Inn Pensacola
7750 North Davis Hwy.
Pensacola, FL
850-474-0411 (800-531-5900)
Dogs up to 50 pounds are allowed.
There are no additional pet fees.
Dogs must be leashed and cleaned
up after. Multiple dogs may be
allowed.

Motel 6 - Pensacola East
7226 Plantation Rd
Pensacola, FL
850-474-1060 (800-466-8356)
This motel welcomes your pets to
stay with you.

Motel 6 - Pensacola North
7827 Davis Hwy
Pensacola, FL
850-476-5386 (800-466-8356)
This motel welcomes your pets to
stay with you.

Motel 6 - Pensacola West
5829 Pensacola Blvd
Pensacola, FL
877-770-9801 (800-466-8356)
This motel welcomes your pets to
stay with you.

Quality Inn N.A.S.-Corry
3 New Warrington Rd.
Pensacola, FL
850-455-3233 (877-424-6423)
Dogs of all sizes are allowed. Dogs
are allowed for a pet fee of $25.00
per pet per stay. Two dogs are
allowed per room.

Red Roof Inn Pensacola University
Mall
7340 Plantation Road
Pensacola, FL
850-476-7960 (800-RED-ROOF)
One well-behaved family pet per
room. Guest must notify front desk
upon arrival. Guest is liable for any
damages. In consideration of all
guests, pets must never be left
unattended in the guest rooms.

Residence Inn Pensacola Downtown
601 E Chase Street
Pensacola, FL
850-432-0202 (800-331-3131)
Some of the amenities at this all-
suite inn include a daily buffet
breakfast, evening social hours
Monday through Thursday, a heated

swimming pool, and a complimentary grocery shopping service. Dogs are allowed for an additional one time pet fee of $100 per room. 2 dogs may be allowed.

TownePlace Suites Pensacola
481 Creighton Road
Pensacola, FL
850-484-7022 (800-257-3000)
This all suite inn sits close to historical, cultural, business, shopping, dining, and recreation areas, plus they also offer a number of in-house amenities for business and leisure travelers. Dogs are allowed for an additional one time fee of $100 per room. Multiple dogs may be allowed.

Travelodge Inn and Suites Pensacola
6950 Pensacola Blvd.
Pensacola, FL
850-473-0222 (800-578-7878)
Dogs of all sizes are allowed. Dogs are allowed for a pet fee.

Days Inn Perry
2277 So Byron Butler Pkwy
Perry, FL
850-584-5311 (800-329-7466)
Dogs of all sizes are allowed. Dogs are allowed for a pet fee of $10.00 per pet per night.

Howard Johnson Gateway
9359 US Highway 19 North
Pinellas Park, FL
727-577-3838 (800-446-4656)
Dogs of all sizes are allowed. Dogs are allowed for a pet fee of $10.00 per pet per night.

La Quinta Inn Tampa Bay Pinellas Park Clearwater
7500 Hwy 19 North
Pinellas Park, FL
727-545-5611 (800-531-5900)
Dogs of all sizes are allowed. There are no additional pet fees. Dogs must be leashed and cleaned up after. Dogs must be healthy; tick and flea free, and be removed for housekeeping. 2 dogs may be allowed.

Comfort Inn
2003 South Frontage Rd
Plant City, FL
813-707-6000 (877-424-6423)
Dogs up to 50 pounds are allowed. Two dogs are allowed per room.

Days Inn Plant City
301 South Frontage Road
Plant City, FL

813-752-0570 (800-329-7466)
Dogs are welcome at this hotel.

Holiday Inn Express Hotel & Suites Ft. Lauderdale-Plantation
1701 N University Dr
Plantation, FL
954-472-5600 (877-270-6405)
Dogs of all sizes are allowed. Dogs are allowed for a pet fee.

Residence Inn Fort Lauderdale Plantation
130 N University Drive
Plantation, FL
954-723-0300 (954-723-0300)
Some of the amenities at this all-suite inn include a daily buffet breakfast, evening socials with light fare and drinks, a heated swimming pool, a Sport Court, and a complimentary grocery shopping service. Dogs are allowed for an additional one time pet fee of $100 per room. 2 dogs may be allowed.

Staybridge Suites Ft. Lauderdale-Plantation
410 North Pine Island Road
Plantation, FL
954-577-9696 (877-270-6405)
Dogs up to 80 pounds are allowed. Pets allowed with an additional pet fee. Up to $75 for 1-6 nights and up to $150 for 7+ nights. A pet agreement must be signed at check-in.

Motel 6 - Pompano Beach
1201 Nw 31st Ave
Pompano Beach, FL
954-977-8011 (800-466-8356)
This motel welcomes your pets to stay with you.

Days Inn Port Charlotte
1941 Tamiami Trail
Port Charlotte, FL
941-627-8900 (800-329-7466)
Dogs are welcome at this hotel.

Knights Inn Port Charlotte
4100 Tamiami Trail
Port Charlotte, FL
941-743-2442 (800-843-5644)
Dogs of all sizes are allowed. Dogs are allowed for a pet fee of $10.00 per pet per night.

Comfort Inn
11810 US 19
Port Richey, FL
727-863-3336 (877-424-6423)
Dogs of all sizes are allowed. Dogs are allowed for a pet fee of $10.00 per pet per night. Three or more dogs may be allowed.

Travelodge Port Richey
11736 US 19 North
Port Richey, FL
727-863-1502 (800-578-7878)
Dogs of all sizes are allowed. Dogs are allowed for a pet fee of $10 per pet per night.

Motel 6 - Punta Gorda
9300 Knights Dr
Punta Gorda, FL
941-639-9585 (800-466-8356)
This motel welcomes your pets to stay with you.

Holiday Inn Express Tampa-Sun City Center
3113 College Ave East
Ruskin, FL
813-641-3437 (877-270-6405)
Dogs of all sizes are allowed. Dogs are allowed for a pet fee of $25.00 per pet per night.

Quality Inn
2310 State Road 16
Saint Augustine, FL
904-823-8636 (877-424-6423)
Dogs of all sizes are allowed. Dogs are allowed for a pet fee of $10.00 per pet per night.

Rodeway Inn
2800 N Ponce De Leon Blvd
Saint Augustine, FL
904-829-6581 (877-424-6423)
Dogs up to 50 pounds are allowed. Dogs are allowed for a pet fee of $10.00 per pet per night. Two dogs are allowed per room.

Hilton Hotel
333 First Street S
Saint Petersburg, FL
727-894-5000 (800-HILTONS (445-8667))
This bayfront hotel offer numerous on site amenities for business and leisure travelers, plus a convenient location to business, shopping, dining, and recreational areas. Dogs are allowed for an additional one time pet fee of $75 per room for up to 2 dogs; a 3rd dog would require a $100 one time fee. A pet amenity kit is also available that includes a bed and bowls. Multiple dogs may be allowed.

Hilton Hotel
950 Lake Carillon Drive
Saint Petersburg, FL
727-540-0050 (800-HILTONS (445-8667))
This luxury hotel offers a number on site amenities for business and

leisure travelers, plus a convenient location to an international airport, and business, shopping, dining, and recreation areas. Dogs up to 75 pounds are allowed for an additional fee of $75 per pet. 2 dogs may be allowed.

Days Inn Sanford
4650 West State Rd.46
Sanford, FL
407-323-6500 (800-329-7466)
Dogs of all sizes are allowed. Dogs are allowed for a pet fee of $20.00 per pet per night.

Holiday Inn Express Sanford (Lake Mary Area)
3401 S. Orlando Dr (Us17-92)
Sanford, FL
407-320-0845 (877-270-6405)
Dogs are welcome at this hotel.

Rose Cottage Inn & Tea Room
1301 S Park Ave
Sanford, FL
407-323-9448
rosecottageinn.com
There is a $10 per day additional dog fee. Dogs are not allowed on the furniture.

Super 8 Sanford
4750 State Rd. 46 W.
Sanford, FL
407-323-3445 (800-800-8000)
Dogs of all sizes are allowed. Dogs are allowed for a nightly pet fee.

Signal Inn
1811 Olde Middle Gulf Drive
Sanibel, FL
800-992-4690
signalinn.com
Signal Inn, situated in a quiet, peaceful and casual atmosphere on the Gulf, consists of 19 furnished elevated beach houses. The pet fee (per pet) is $80 per week or $55 for 3 nights. Only particular units allow pets so please inquire about pets when contacting the inn.

Tropical Winds Motel & Cottages
4819 Tradewinds Drive
Sanibel Island, FL
239-472-1765
for a 2nd dog there is a $15 per night additional charge. Puppies are not allowed to be left alone in the room, and adult dogs for short periods.

Sandcastles By the Sea
229 Blue Mountain Road #101
Santa Rosa Beach, FL
985-845-8126
addieagogo.com

Dogs are allowed in the this condo off of Hwy 30-A near the beaches of South Walton.

Best Western Midtown
1425 S Tamiami Trl
Sarasota, FL
941-955-9841 (800-780-7234)
Dogs of all sizes are allowed. Dogs are allowed for a pet fee.

Coquina On the Beach Resort
1008 Ben Franklin Drive
Sarasota, FL
941-388-2141 (800-833-2141)
coquinaonthebeach.com/
There is a $35 one time pet charge. There are no designated smoking or non-smoking rooms. 2 dogs may be allowed.

Residence Inn Sarasota Bradenton
1040 University Parkway
Sarasota, FL
941-358-1468 (800-331-3131)
Located across from the Sarasota Bradenton International Airport, this all suite inn sits central to many of the areas star attractions and activities; plus they offer a daily buffet breakfast and evening socials. Dogs are allowed for an additional one time pet fee of $75 per room. Multiple dogs may be allowed.

Super 8 FL Sarasota
4309 North Tamiami Trail
Sarasota, FL
941-355-9326 (800-800-8000)
Dogs of all sizes are allowed. Dogs are allowed for a pet fee.

Days Inn /Space Coast Satellite Beach
180 Hwy A1A
Satellite Beach, FL
321-777-3552 (800-329-7466)
Dogs of all sizes are allowed. Dogs are allowed for a pet fee of $10.00 per pet per stay.

The Little Pink House
152 Seacrest Drive
Seagrove, FL
877-868-4659
thelittlepinkhouse.org
Dogs are welcome at this vacation rental a few steps from the beach.

Pelican's Landing RV Resort
11330 Indian River Drive
Sebastian, FL
772-589-5188
pelicanslandingresort.com
Dogs up to 75 pounds are allowed. There are some breed restrictions.

Dogs are allowed in cottages for a $65 pet fee per stay.

Quality Inn & Suites
6525 US 27 North
Sebring, FL
863-385-4500 (877-424-6423)
Dogs of all sizes are allowed. Dogs are allowed for a pet fee of $10.00 per pet per night.

Residence Inn Sebring
3221 Tubbs Road
Sebring, FL
863-314-9100 (800-331-3131)
This all suite hotel sits central to many of the area's star attractions, festivals, shopping, dining, and business areas, plus they offer a number of in-house amenities that include a daily buffet breakfast and evening social hours. Dogs are allowed for no additional fee with a credit card on file. 2 dogs may be allowed.

Dog-Friendly Fenced Vacation Home near Tampa/Disney.
1 mile East of I-75, 1/4 mile off of I-4
Seffner, FL
866-980-1234
This pet-friendly vacation rental sits on one fenced acre near I-75 and I-4.

Banana Bay Club
8254 Midnight Pass Road
Siesta Key, FL
941-346-0113
Dogs of all sizes are allowed. There is a $50 one time additional pet fee per room.

Cottages at Turtle Beach Resort
9049 Midnight Pass Road
Siesta Key, FL
941-349-4554
turtlebeachresort.com
This resort was featured in the Florida Living Magazine as one of the best romantic escapes in Florida. There is a pet charge added, which is about 10% of the daily room rate.

Siesta Holiday House
1011-1015 Cresent Street
Siesta Key, FL
941-312-9882
Dogs of all sizes are allowed. There is a $100 refundable deposit. Small non-hairy dogs are free, otherwise there is a maximum fee of $50 per room per stay. The fee also depends on the breed, how much hair and how large the dog is. 2 dogs may be allowed.

Days Inn FL Silver Springs

5751 E Silver Springs Blvd
Silver Springs, FL
352-236-2575 (800-329-7466)
Dogs of all sizes are allowed. Dogs are allowed for a pet fee of $10.00 per pet per night.

Hilton Hotel
3700 N Ocean Drive
Singer Island, FL
561-848-3888 (800-HILTONS (445-8667))
This luxury hotel offers a number of on site amenities for all level of travelers including balcony rooms with ocean or island views and an oceanfront restaurant, plus they are conveniently located to business, shopping, dining, and entertainment areas. Dogs up to 75 pounds are allowed for an additional one time pet fee of $75 per room. 2 dogs may be allowed.

Quality Inn Weeki Wachee
6172 Commercial Way
Spring Hill, FL
352-596-2007 (877-424-6423)
Dogs of all sizes are allowed. Dogs are allowed for a pet fee of $15.00 per pet per night.

Days Inn /Historic Downtown St Augustine
1300 N Ponce de Leon Blvd
St Augustine, FL
904-824-3383 (800-329-7466)
Dogs of all sizes are allowed. Dogs are allowed for a pet fee.

Days Inn St. Augustine West
SR 16/I-95 2560 SR 16
St Augustine, FL
904-824-4341 (800-329-7466)
Dogs of all sizes are allowed. Dogs are allowed for a pet fee of $10.00 per pet per night.

Inn at Camachee Harbor
201 Yacht Club Dr.
St Augustine, FL
904-825-0003 (800-688-5379)
camacheeinn.com
Fourteen of the nineteen rooms at this inn are pet friendly. The inn is located at the Camachee Harbor only about five minutes from historic St Augustine. You will need to get special permission from management to leave a pet alone in the room.

Ocean Blue Motel
10 Vilano Road
St Augustine, FL
904-829-5939
Dogs of all sizes are allowed. There

is a $10 per night per pet additional fee, and a credit card needs to be on file. 2 dogs may be allowed.

Ramada Historic Downtown St. Augustine
116 San Marco Avenue
St Augustine, FL
904-824-4352 (800-272-6232)
Dogs of all sizes are allowed. Dogs are allowed for a pet fee.

Ramada Limited St. Augustine
2535 State Road 16
St Augustine, FL
904-829-5643 (800-272-6232)
Dogs of all sizes are allowed. Dogs are allowed for a pet fee of $10.00 per pet per night.

St Francis Inn
279 St George Street
St Augustine, Fl.
904-824-6068 (800-824-6062)
stfrancisinn.com/
A gourmet breakfast buffet, private balconies, an evening social hour (5:30 - 6:30 pm daily), homemade desserts each evening from 7:30 to 9 pm, and an espresso/coffee drink bar each morning from 7:30 am until noon are just some of the amenities at this bed and breakfast. They also offer pet friendly accommodations at the Comanche Love Yacht Harbor and 2 pet friendly apartments at the beach. Dogs up to 50 pound are allowed for an additional fee of $15 per night per pet. Dogs must be housetrained and under their owner's control at all times. 2 dogs may be allowed.

Super 8 St. Augustine
2550 State Road 16
St Augustine, FL
904-829-5686 (800-800-8000)
Dogs are welcome at this hotel.

Comfort Inn
901 A1A Beach Blvd.
St Augustine Beach, FL
904-471-1474 (877-424-6423)
Dogs of all sizes are allowed. Dogs are allowed for a pet fee of $20.00 per pet per night.

An Angel's Dream
2008 E Pelican Court
St George Island, FL
850-927-3520
Dogs of all sizes are allowed. There are no additional pet fees.

Collins Vacation Rentals
60 E Gulf Beach Drive
St George Island, FL

850-927-2900
Dogs of all sizes are allowed. There is a pet policy to sign at check in and there are no additional pet fees. 2 dogs may be allowed.

Resort Vacation Properties of St. George Island
123 W. Gulf Beach Drive
St George Island, FL
850-927-2322 (866-976-7287)
resortvacationproperties.com/df
Pets are allowed at these vacation properties on the beach at St. George Island.

TradeWinds Island Grand
5500 Gulf Blvd
St Pete Beach, FL
727-367-6461 (800-360-4016)
This award-winning resort offers water sports, paddleboats, water trykes, WiFi connections and business center computers. There are five restaurants on site, five swimming pools, two whirlpools, concierge service and a kids activity center. Up to 2 pets are allowed per room up to 80 pounds each. There is a $30 per pet per day additional pet fee.

Hotel Indigo St. Petersburg Downtown-North
234 Third Ave North
St Petersburg, FL
727-822-4814 (877-865-6578)
Dogs up to 50 pounds are allowed. Dogs are allowed for a pet fee of $50.00 per pet per stay.

La Quinta Inn Tampa Bay St. Petersburg
4999 34th Street North
St Petersburg, FL
727-527-8421 (800-531-5900)
Dogs of all sizes are allowed. There are no additional pet fees. Dogs must be leashed and cleaned up after, and they request that you use the dog walk area. Dogs may not be left unattended unless they will be quiet and well behaved. They do not allow aggressive breeds. Multiple dogs may be allowed.

Ramada St. Petersburg
5005 34th Street North
St Petersburg, FL
727-525-1181 (800-272-6232)
Dogs are welcome at this hotel.

Valley Forge Motel
6825 Central Avenue
St Petersburg, FL
727-345-0135
Well behaved dogs are allowed for

an additional one time pet fee of $12 per room. They also provide a fenced, off-leash play area. 2 dogs may be allowed.

Days Inn Starke
1101 N Temple Ave
Starke, FL
904-964-7600 (800-329-7466)
Dogs of all sizes are allowed. Dogs are allowed for a nightly pet fee.

Pirates Cove Resort and Marina
4307 S.E. Bayview Street
Stuart, FL
772-287-2500
Pets must be well-mannered and quiet,,, there is a $20 per night per pet additional fee. The hotel has limited pet rooms. Please call ahead to reserve a pet room. Multiple dogs may be allowed.

Days Inn Of Sun City Center
809 N Pebble Beach Blvd
Sun City Center, FL
813-634-3331 (800-329-7466)
Dogs of all sizes are allowed. Dogs are allowed for a pet fee.

Holiday Inn Hotel & Suites Ft Lauderdale-Univ Dr. Sunrise
3003 North University Dr.
Sunrise, FL
954-748-7000 (877-270-6405)
Dogs up to 50 pounds are allowed. Dogs are allowed for a pet fee of $25.00 per pet per night.

La Quinta Inn Sunrise/Sawgrass Mills
13651 N.W. 2nd Street
Sunrise, FL
954-846-1200 (800-531-5900)
Dogs may not be left unattended, and they must be leashed and cleaned up after. Dogs must be well behaved and housebroken. Dogs may not be left unattended, and they must be leashed and cleaned up after. Multiple dogs may be allowed.

Wellesley Inn Sunrise at Sawgrass Mills
13600 Northwest 2nd Street
Sunrise, FL
954-845-9929 (800-531-5900)
A dog up to 60 pounds is allowed. There is a $10 per night additional pet fee. Dogs may not be left unattended, and they must be leashed and cleaned up after.

Super 8 Tallahassee FL
2801 N Monroe Street
Tallahasee, FL
850-386-8286 (800-800-8000)

Dogs of all sizes are allowed. Dogs are allowed for a nightly pet fee.

Days Inn University Center Tallahassee
1350 W.Tennessee St/US 90
Tallahassee, FL
850-222-3219 (800-329-7466)
Dogs are welcome at this hotel.

Days Inn -Government Center Tallahassee
3100 Apalachee Parkway
Tallahassee, FL
850-877-6121 (800-329-7466)
Dogs of all sizes are allowed. Dogs are allowed for a pet fee of $12.00 per pet per night.

Holiday Inn Tallahassee-Capitol-East
1355 Apalachee Parkway
Tallahassee, FL
850-877-3171 (877-270-6405)
Dogs up to 50 pounds are allowed. Dogs are allowed for a pet fee.

La Quinta Inn Tallahassee North
2905 North Monroe
Tallahassee, FL
850-385-7172 (800-531-5900)
Dogs of all sizes are allowed. There are no additional pet fees. Dogs must be leashed and cleaned up after. Dogs may not be left unattended unless they will be quiet and well behaved. Multiple dogs may be allowed.

La Quinta Inn Tallahassee South
2850 Apalachee Pkwy.
Tallahassee, FL
850-878-5099 (800-531-5900)
Dogs of all sizes are allowed. There are no additional pet fees. Dogs must be leashed and cleaned up after. Dogs may not be left unattended unless they will be quiet and well behaved, and they need to be attended to or removed for housekeeping. Multiple dogs may be allowed.

Motel 6 - Tallahassee Downtown
1027 Apalachee Pkwy
Tallahassee, FL
850-877-6171 (800-466-8356)
This motel welcomes your pets to stay with you.

Motel 6 - Tallahassee North
1481 Timberlane Rd
Tallahassee, FL
850-668-2600 (800-466-8356)
This motel welcomes your pets to stay with you.

Motel 6 - Tallahassee West
2738 Monroe St
Tallahassee, FL
850-386-7878 (800-466-8356)
This motel welcomes your pets to stay with you.

Quality Inn & Suites
2020 Apalachee Pkwy.
Tallahassee, FL
850-877-4437 (877-424-6423)
Dogs up to 50 pounds are allowed.

Ramada Conference Center Tallahassee
2900 N. Monroe St.
Tallahassee, FL
850-386-1027 (800-272-6232)
Dogs of all sizes are allowed. Dogs are allowed for a nightly pet fee.

Red Roof Inn Tallahassee
2930 Hospitality Street
Tallahassee, FL
850-385-7884 (800-RED-ROOF)
One well-behaved family pet per room. Guest must notify front desk upon arrival. Guest is liable for any damages. In consideration of all guests, pets must never be left unattended in the guest rooms.

Residence Inn Tallahassee North/I-10 Capital Circle
1880 Raymond Diehl Road
Tallahassee, FL
850-422-0093 (800-331-3131)
This all suite inn features a convenient location to the State Capitol, Florida State and A&M Universities, and numerous shopping, dining, and entertainment areas. They also offer a number of in-house amenities, including a daily buffet breakfast and evening socials Monday to Thursday. Dogs are allowed for an additional one time pet fee of $100 per room. Multiple dogs may be allowed.

Residence Inn Tallahassee Universities at the Capitol
600 W Gaines Street
Tallahassee, FL
850-329-9080 (800-922-3291)
This all suite inn sits in the downtown capitol complex with Florida State and A&M Universities only a short distance away as well as numerous sites of interest for both business and leisure travelers. They also offer a daily buffet breakfast and evening socials. Dogs are allowed for an additional one time pet fee of $100 per room. Multiple dogs may be allowed.

Sleep Inn
1695 Capital Circle N.W.
Tallahassee, FL
850-575-5885 (877-424-6423)
Dogs up to 50 pounds are allowed.
Dogs are allowed for a pet fee of
$25.00 per pet per stay. Two dogs
are allowed per room.

Staybridge Suites Tallahassee I-10
East
1600 Summit Lake Drive
Tallahassee, FL
850-219-7000 (877-270-6405)
Dogs up to 80 pounds are allowed.
Pets allowed with an additional pet
fee. Up to $75 for 1-6 nights and up
to $150 for 7+ nights. A pet
agreement must be signed at check-
in.

Suburban Extended Stay Hotel
522 Silver Slipper Lane
Tallahassee, FL
850-386-2121 (877-424-6423)
Dogs up to 50 pounds are allowed.

TownePlace Suites Tallahassee
North/Capital Circle
1876 Capital Circle NE
Tallahassee, FL
850-219-0122 (800-257-3000)
Besides offering a number of in-
house amenities for all level of
travelers, this all suite inn also
provides a convenient location to
universities, businesses, shopping,
dining, and recreation areas. Dogs
are allowed for an additional one
time fee of $100 per room. Multiple
dogs may be allowed.

Homestead Studio Suites Fort
Lauderdale - Tamarac
3873 W. Commercial Blvd.
Tamarac, FL
954-733-6644 (800-804-3724)
One dog is allowed per suite. There
is a $25 per night additional pet fee
up to $150 for an entire stay.

Wellesley Inn Fort Lauderdale-
Tamarac
5070 North State Road 7
Tamarac, FL
954-484-6909 (800-531-5900)
Dogs of all sizes are allowed. There
are no additional pet fees. Dogs
must be leashed and cleaned up
after. Multiple dogs may be allowed.

Baymont Inn and Suites Sabal Park
Tampa
10007 Princess Palm Ave
Tampa, FL
813-622-8557 (877-229-6668)
Dogs of all sizes are allowed. Dogs

are allowed for a pet fee of $20 per
pet per night.

Best Western Brandon Hotel &
Conference Center
9331 Adamo Drive
Tampa, FL
813-621-5555 (800-780-7234)
Dogs up to 50 pounds are allowed.
Dogs are allowed for a pet fee of
$25 per pet per stay.

Best Western Tampa Airport Inn &
Suites
3826 W Waters Avenue
Tampa, FL
813-490-9090 (800-780-7234)
Dogs are welcome at this hotel.

Comfort Inn Airport at RJ Stadium
4732 N. Dale Mabry
Tampa, FL
813-874-6700 (877-424-6423)
Dogs of all sizes are allowed. Dogs
are allowed for a pet fee of $5.00
per pet per night. Dogs are allowed
for a pet fee of $25.00 per pet per
stay. Two dogs are allowed per
room.

Comfort Inn Conference Center
820 East Busch Blvd.
Tampa, FL
813-933-4011 (877-424-6423)
Dogs of all sizes are allowed. Dogs
are allowed for a pet fee of $25.00
per pet per stay.

Days Inn -North of Busch Gardens
Tampa
701 East Fletcher Ave
Tampa, FL
813-977-1550 (800-329-7466)
Dogs are welcome at this hotel.

Days Inn Airport Stadium Tampa
2522 North Dale Mabry
Tampa, FL
813-877-6181 (800-329-7466)
Dogs of all sizes are allowed. Dogs
are allowed for a pet fee of $3 per
pet per night.

Days Inn / West of Busch Gardens
Tampa
2901 E Busch Blvd
Tampa, FL
813-933-6471 (800-329-7466)
Dogs are welcome at this hotel.

Extended Stay America Tampa -
Airport - Westshore Blvd.
4312 W. Spruce St.
Tampa, FL
813-873-2850 (800-804-3724)
One dog is allowed per suite. There
is a $25 per night additional pet fee

up to $150 for an entire stay.

Holiday Inn Express Hotel & Suites
Tampa-Anderson Rd/Veterans Exp
9402 Corporate Lake Dr.
Tampa, FL
813-885-3700 (877-270-6405)
Dogs are welcome at this hotel.

Holiday Inn Express Hotel & Suites
Tampa-Fairgrounds-Casino
8610 Elm Fair Boulevard
Tampa, FL
813-490-1000 (877-270-6405)
Dogs of all sizes are allowed. Dogs
are allowed for a pet fee of $10 per
pet per night.

Homestead Studio Suites Tampa -
North Airport
5401 Beaumont Center Blvd. E.
Tampa, FL
813-243-1913 (800-804-3724)
One dog is allowed per suite. There
is a $25 per night additional pet fee
up to $150 for an entire stay.

Howard Johnson Express Inn -
North/Busch Gardens Tampa
720 E Fowler Ave/I-275
Tampa, FL
813-971-5150 (800-446-4656)
Dogs of all sizes are allowed. Dogs
are allowed for a pet fee of $10 per
pet per night.

Howard Johnson Hotel -
Airport/Stadium Tampa
2055 N Dale Mabry
Tampa, FL
813-875-8818 (800-446-4656)
Dogs of all sizes are allowed. Dogs
are allowed for a pet fee of $25.00
per pet per night.

Howard Johnson Plaza -Downtown
Tampa
111 W Fortune St
Tampa, FL
813-223-1351 (800-446-4656)
Dogs of all sizes are allowed. Dogs
are allowed for a pet fee.

La Quinta Inn & Suites USF (Near
Busch Gardens)
3701 East Fowler Ave.
Tampa, FL
813-910-7500 (800-531-5900)
Dogs of all sizes are allowed. There
are no additional pet fees. Dogs may
be alone in the room if they will be
quiet, well behaved, a contact
number is left with the front desk,
and the Do Not Disturb sign is left on
the door. Dogs must be leashed and
cleaned up after. Multiple dogs may
be allowed.

La Quinta Inn Tampa Brandon West
602 S. Falkenburg Road
Tampa, FL
813-684-4007 (800-531-5900)
Dogs of all sizes are allowed. There are no additional pet fees. Dogs may not be left unattended at any time, and they must be quiet, well behaved, leashed, and cleaned up after. Multiple dogs may be allowed.

La Quinta Inn Tampa East-Fairgrounds
4811 U.S. Highway 301 N.
Tampa, FL
813-626-0885 (800-531-5900)
Dogs of all sizes are allowed. There are no additional pet fees. There is a pet waiver to sign at check in. Dogs may not be left unattended, and they must be leashed and cleaned up after. Multiple dogs may be allowed.

Motel 6 - Tampa Downtown
333 Fowler Ave
Tampa, FL
813-932-4948 (800-466-8356)
This motel welcomes your pets to stay with you.

Motel 6 - Tampa East Fairgrounds
6510 Us 301
Tampa, FL
813-628-0888 (800-466-8356)
This motel welcomes your pets to stay with you.

Quality Inn & Suites
2708 N. 50th Street
Tampa, FL
813-623-6000 (877-424-6423)
Dogs of all sizes are allowed. Dogs are allowed for a pet fee of $25.00 per pet per night. Two dogs are allowed per room.

Red Roof Inn Tampa - Brandon
10121 Horace Avenue
Tampa, FL
813-681-8484 (800-RED-ROOF)
One well-behaved family pet per room. Guest must notify front desk upon arrival. Guest is liable for any damages. In consideration of all guests, pets must never be left unattended in the guest rooms.

Red Roof Inn Tampa - Busch
2307 East Busch Boulevard
Tampa, FL
813-932-0073 (800-RED-ROOF)
One well-behaved family pet per room. Guest must notify front desk upon arrival. Guest is liable for any damages. In consideration of all guests, pets must never be left unattended in the guest rooms.

Red Roof Inn Tampa Fairgrounds
5001 North US Route 301
Tampa, FL
813-623-5245 (800-RED-ROOF)
One well-behaved family pet per room. Guest must notify front desk upon arrival. Guest is liable for any damages. In consideration of all guests, pets must never be left unattended in the guest rooms.

Residence Inn Tampa Downtown
101 East Tyler Street
Tampa, FL
813-221-4224 (800-331-3131)
Located in the heart of downtown and close to all this lively city has to offer, this all suite inn offers a great location and amenities for all level of travelers. They also provide a daily buffet breakfast and evening socials. Dogs are allowed for an additional one time pet fee of $100 per room. Multiple dogs may be allowed.

Residence Inn Tampa North/I-75 Fletcher
13420 N Telecom Parkway
Tampa, FL
813-972-4400 (800-331-3131)
In addition to being located in Telecom Park Business Center and only a short distance from numerous sites of interest to business and leisure travelers, this all suite hotel also offers a number of on-site amenities, including a daily buffet breakfast and evening socials Monday to Thursday. Dogs are allowed for an additional one time pet fee of $100 per room. Multiple dogs may be allowed.

Residence Inn Tampa Sabal Park/Brandon
9719 Princess Palm Avenue
Tampa, FL
813-627-8855 (800-331-3131)
In addition to being located in Sabal Park Business Center and only a short distance from numerous sites of interest for business and leisure travelers, this all suite hotel also offers a number of on-site amenities, including a daily buffet breakfast and evening socials Monday to Thursday. Dogs are allowed for an additional one time pet fee of $100 per room. Multiple dogs may be allowed.

Residence Inn Tampa Westshore/Airport
4312 W Boy Scout Blvd
Tampa, FL
813-877-7988 (800-331-3131)
This all suite inn features a convenient location to business, upscale shopping, fine dining, and entertainment areas, plus they also offer a number of in-house amenities, including a daily buffet breakfast and evening socials Monday to Thursday. Dogs are allowed for an additional one time fee of $100 per pet. 2 dogs may be allowed.

Rodeway Inn
210 E. Fowler Ave.
Tampa, FL
813-933-7275 (877-424-6423)
Dogs up to 50 pounds are allowed. Dogs are allowed for a pet fee of $15.00 per pet per night. Two dogs are allowed per room.

Sheraton Riverwalk Hotel
200 North Ashley Dr.
Tampa, FL
813-223-2222 (888-625-5144)
Dogs up to 80 pounds are allowed. There are no additional pet fees. Dogs are not allowed to be left alone in the room.

Sheraton Suites Tampa Airport
4400 West Cypress St.
Tampa, FL
813-873-8675 (888-625-5144)
Dogs up to 50 pounds are allowed. There are no additional pet fees. Dogs are not allowed to be left alone in the room.

Staybridge Suites Tampa Sabal Park
3624 North Falkenburg Road
Tampa, FL
813-227-4000 (877-270-6405)
Dogs up to 80 pounds are allowed. Pets allowed with an additional pet fee. Up to $75 for 1-6 nights and up to $150 for 7+ nights. A pet agreement must be signed at check-in.

Super 8 U.S.F. Near Busch Gardens Downtown Tampa
321 E Fletcher Ave
Tampa, FL
813-933-4545 (800-800-8000)
Dogs of all sizes are allowed. Dogs are allowed for a pet fee of $10 per pet per night.

TownePlace Suites Tampa North/I-75 Fletcher
6800 Woodstork Road
Tampa, FL
813-975-9777 (800-257-3000)
Besides offering a number of in-house amenities for all level of

travelers, this all suite inn also provides a convenient location to some of the area's star attractions, universities, businesses, and entertainment areas. Dogs are allowed for an additional one time fee of $100 per room. Multiple dogs may be allowed.

TownePlace Suites Tampa Westshore
5302 Avion Park Drive
Tampa, FL
813-282-1081 (800-257-3000)
Located in one of the area's prime business districts and near several world-class attractions, this all suite hotel offers a great location plus a number of in-house amenities for all level of travelers. Dogs are allowed for an additional one time fee of $100 per room. Multiple dogs may be allowed.

Wingate by Wyndham - USF Tampa
3751 E. Fowler Ave
Tampa, FL
813-979-2828 (800-228-1000)
Dogs are welcome at this hotel.

Wingate by Wyndham New Tampa
17301 Dona Michelle Drive
Tampa, FL
813-971-7676 (800-228-1000)
Dogs of all sizes are allowed. Dogs are allowed for a pet fee of $50.00 per pet per stay.

Extended Stay America Tampa - North - USF - Attractions
12242 Morris Bridge Rd.
Temple Terrace, FL
813-989-2264 (800-804-3724)
One dog is allowed per suite. There is a $25 per night additional pet fee up to $150 for an entire stay.

Comfort Suites
1202 Avenida Central
The Villages, FL
352-259-6578 (877-424-6423)
Dogs of all sizes are allowed.

Holiday Inn Express Hotel & Suites The Villages
1205 Avenida Central North
The Villages, FL
352-750-3888 (877-270-6405)
Dogs of all sizes are allowed. There is a $35.00 one time additional pet fee.

TownePlace Suites The Villages
1141 Alonzo Avenue
The Villages, FL
352-753-8686 (800-257-3000)
In addition to offering a number of in-

house amenities for all level of travelers, this all suite inn also provides a convenient location to business, shopping, dining, and day/night entertainment areas. Dogs up to 50 pounds are allowed for an additional one time fee of $100 per room. 2 dogs may be allowed.

Clarion Inn Kennedy Space Center
4951 S. Washington Avenue
Titusville, FL
321-269-2121 (877-424-6423)
Dogs up to 50 pounds are allowed. Dogs are allowed for a pet fee of $35.00 per pet per stay.

Comfort Inn Kennedy Space Center
3655 Cheney Hwy.
Titusville, FL
321-269-7110 (877-424-6423)
Dogs up to 50 pounds are allowed. Dogs are allowed for a pet fee of $10.00 per pet per night. Two dogs are allowed per room.

Ramada Kennedy Space Center
3500 Cheney Highway
Titusville, FL
321-269-5510 (800-272-6232)
Dogs are welcome at this hotel.

Riverside Inn
1829 Riverside Drive
Titusville, FL
321-267-7900
This inn was formerly the Howard Johnson Lodge. There is a $10 one time pet fee per room. 2 dogs may be allowed.

Super 8 Kennedy Space Center Area Titusville
3480 Garden St.
Titusville, FL
321-269-9310 (800-800-8000)
Dogs of all sizes are allowed. Dogs are allowed for a pet fee.

Lorelei Resort Motel
10273 Gulf Blvd
Treasure Island, FL
727-360-4351
Dogs of all sizes are allowed. There is no additional fee for up to 2 pets. 2 dogs may be allowed.

Holiday Inn Express Venice
380 Commercial Court
Venice, FL
941-584-6800 (877-270-6405)
Dogs are welcome at this hotel.

Motel 6 - Venice, Fl
281 Us 41 Bypass North
Venice, FL

941-485-8255 (800-466-8356)
This motel welcomes your pets to stay with you.

Howard Johnson Inn - FL Vero Beach
1985 90th Ave/I-95
Vero Beach, FL
772-778-1985 (800-446-4656)
Dogs of all sizes are allowed. Dogs are allowed for a pet fee of $15 per pet per night.

South Beach Motel & Resort
1705 South Ocean Drive
Vero Beach, FL
772-231-5366
The rooms can accomodate 1 medium size dog or 2 small dogs. There is no additional pet fee. Dogs must have records of up to date shots and good health. There are some breed restrictions. 2 dogs may be allowed.

Best Western Nature Coast
9373 Cortez Boulevard
Weeki Wachee, FL
352-596-9000 (800-780-7234)
Dogs are welcome at this hotel.

Days Inn West Palm Beach
2300 45th Street
West Palm Beach, FL
561-689-0450 (800-329-7466)
Dogs of all sizes are allowed. Dogs are allowed for a pet fee.

Hibiscus House Bed & Breakfast
501 30th Street
West Palm Beach, FL
561-863-5633 (800-203-4927)
hibiscushouse.com/
This bed and breakfast was ranked by the Miami Herald as one of the ten best in Florida. The owner has a dog, and there are no pet charges. Large dogs usually stay in the cottage. 2 dogs may be allowed.

La Quinta Inn & Suites West Palm Beach
1910 Palm Beach Lakes Boulevard
West Palm Beach, FL
561-689-8540 (800-531-5900)
Dogs of all sizes are allowed. There are no additional pet fees. Dogs must be leashed, cleaned up after, and a contact number left with the front desk if there is a pet in the room alone. Multiple dogs may be allowed.

La Quinta Inn West Palm Beach
5981 Okeechobee Blvd
West Palm Beach, FL
561-697-3388 (800-531-5900)
Dogs of all sizes are allowed. There

are no additional pet fees. Dogs must be leashed and cleaned up after. Dogs must be crated if left alone in the room. Multiple dogs may be allowed.

Red Roof Inn West Palm Beach
2421 Metrocentre Boulevard East
West Palm Beach, FL
561-697-7710 (800-RED-ROOF)
One well-behaved family pet per room. Guest must notify front desk upon arrival. Guest is liable for any damages. In consideration of all guests, pets must never be left unattended in the guest rooms.

Residence Inn West Palm Beach
2461 Metrocentre Boulevard E
West Palm Beach, FL
561-687-4747 (800-331-3131)
This all suite hotel gives a convenient location to a number of sites of interest and activities for all level of travelers, plus they also offer a number of in-house amenities, including a daily buffet breakfast and evening socials Monday to Thursday with light dinner fare. Dogs are allowed for an additional one time pet fee of $100 per room. 2 dogs may be allowed.

Studio 6 - West Palm Beach
1535 Centrepark Dr North
West Palm Beach, FL
561-640-3335 (800-466-8356)
Your pets are welcome to stay here with you for a pet fee of $10 per day up to $50 for an entire stay.

Hyatt Regency Bonaventure
250 Racquet Club Road
Weston, FL
954-616-1234
Dogs up to 50 pounds are allowed. There is a $50 one time additional pet fee and up to 2 dogs are allowed per room.

Residence Inn Fort Lauderdale Weston
2605 Weston Road
Weston, FL
954-659-8585 (800-331-3131)
Besides offering a convenient location to business, shopping, dining, and entertainment areas, this hotel also provides a number of in-house amenities, including a daily buffet breakfast and complementary evening receptions. Dogs are allowed for an additional one time pet fee of $100 per room. Multiple dogs may be allowed.

TownePlace Suites Fort Lauderdale

Weston
1545 Three Village Road
Weston, FL
954-659-2234 (800-257-3000)
This all suite inn sits central to beaches, businesses, shopping, dining, and entertainment areas, plus they offer a number of in-house amenities for business and leisure travelers. Dogs are allowed for an additional one time fee of $100 per room. Multiple dogs may be allowed.

Days Inn Wildwood
551 East State Rt 44/I-75
Wildwood, FL
352-748-7766 (800-329-7466)
Dogs of all sizes are allowed. Dogs are allowed for a pet fee of $10.00 per pet per night.

Super 8 Wildwood
I-75 exit 329
Wildwood, FL
352-748-3783 (800-800-8000)
Dogs of all sizes are allowed. Dogs are allowed for a pet fee.

Howard Johnson Inn - FL Winter Haven
1300 3rd Street SW
Winter Haven, FL
863-294-7321 (800-446-4656)
Dogs of all sizes are allowed. Dogs are allowed for a pet fee of $10 per pet per night.

Ramada Winter Haven
1150 3rd Street SW
Winter Haven, FL
863-294-4451 (800-272-6232)
Dogs of all sizes are allowed. Dogs are allowed for a pet fee.

Comfort Inn
76043 Sidney Place
Yulee, FL
904-225-2600 (877-424-6423)
Dogs of all sizes are allowed.

Days Inn Yulee
852374 US Hwy 17 North
Yulee, FL
904-225-2011 (800-329-7466)
Dogs are welcome at this hotel.

Georgia

Best Western Acworth Inn
5155 Cowan Road
Acworth, GA
770-974-0116 (800-780-7234)
Dogs of all sizes are allowed. Dogs are allowed for a nightly pet fee.

Econo Lodge
4980 Cowan Rd.
Acworth, GA
770-974-1922 (877-424-6423)
Dogs of all sizes are allowed. Dogs are allowed for a pet fee of $7.00 per pet per night.

Motel 6 - Acworth, Ga
5035 Cowan Rd
Acworth, GA
770-974-1700 (800-466-8356)
This motel welcomes your pets to stay with you.

Super 8 /Atlanta Area Acworth
4970 Cowan Rd
Acworth, GA
770-966-9700 (800-800-8000)
Dogs of all sizes are allowed. Dogs are allowed for a pet fee of $7.00 per pet per night.

Ramada Limited Adairsville
500 Georgia North Circle
Adairsville, GA
770-769-9726 (800-272-6232)
Dogs of all sizes are allowed. Dogs are allowed for a pet fee of $10.00 per pet per stay.

Days Inn--South Georgia-Motorsports Park Adel
1204 West Fourth Street
Adel, GA
229-896-4574 (800-329-7466)
Dogs of all sizes are allowed. Dogs are allowed for a nightly pet fee.

Days Inn Albany
422 W. Oglethorpe Blvd.
Albany, GA
229-888-2632 (800-329-7466)
Dogs of all sizes are allowed. Dogs are allowed for a pet fee of $10.00 per pet per night.

Knights Inn GA Albany
1201 Schley Avenue
Albany, GA
229-888-9600 (800-843-5644)
Dogs of all sizes are allowed. Dogs are allowed for a pet fee of $10.00 per pet per night.

Motel 6 - Albany, Ga
201 Thornton Dr
Albany, GA
229-439-0078 (800-466-8356)
This motel welcomes your pets to stay with you.

Super 8 Albany
2444 N Slappy Blvd
Albany, GA
229-888-8388 (800-800-8000)
Dogs of all sizes are allowed. Dogs

are allowed for a nightly pet fee.

Wingate by Wyndham - Albany
2735 Dawson Road
Albany, GA
229-883-9800 (800-228-1000)
Dogs of all sizes are allowed. Dogs are allowed for a pet fee.

Days Inn Alma
930 S. Pierce Street
Alma, GA
912-632-7000 (800-329-7466)
Dogs of all sizes are allowed. Dogs are allowed for a pet fee of $10.00 per pet per night.

Extended Stay America Atlanta - Alpharetta - Rock Mill Rd.
1950 Rock Mill Rd.
Alpharetta, GA
770-475-2676 (800-804-3724)
One dog is allowed per suite. There is a $25 per night additional pet fee up to $150 for an entire stay.

La Quinta Inn & Suites Atlanta Alpharetta
1350 North Point Dr.
Alpharetta, GA
770-754-7800 (800-531-5900)
Dogs of all sizes are allowed. There are no additional pet fees. Dogs must be leashed and cleaned up after, and removed or crated for housekeeping. Multiple dogs may be allowed.

Residence Inn Atlanta Alpharetta/North Point Mall
1325 North Point Drive
Alpharetta, GA
770-587-1151 (888-236-2427)
Located in one of the city's most prominent shopping, dining, and entertainment areas, this hotel also offers a number of in-house amenities, including a daily buffet breakfast, a Manager's reception Monday through Thursday, a complimentary grocery shopping service, and summer barbecues. Dogs are allowed for an additional one time pet fee of $100 per room. Multiple dogs may be allowed.

Residence Inn Atlanta Alpharetta/Windward
5465 Windward Pkwy West
Alpharetta, GA
770-664-0664 (888-236-2427)
In addition to offering a convenient location to business, shopping, dining, and entertainment areas, this hotel also provides a number of in-house amenities, including a daily buffet breakfast, and a Manager's

reception Monday through Thursday. Dogs are allowed for an additional one time pet fee of $100 per room. Multiple dogs may be allowed.

Staybridge Suites Alpharetta-North Point
3980 North Point Pkwy
Alpharetta, GA
770-569-7200 (877-270-6405)
Dogs up to 80 pounds are allowed. Pets allowed with an additional pet fee. Up to $75 for 1-6 nights and up to $150 for 7+ nights. A pet agreement must be signed at check-in.

TownePlace Suites Alpharetta
7925 Westside Parkway
Alpharetta, GA
770-664-1300 (800-257-3000)
In addition to offering a number of in-house amenities for all level of travelers, they also provide a convenient location to numerous business, shopping, dining, and entertainment areas. Dogs are allowed for an additional one time fee of $75 per room. 2 dogs may be allowed.

Wingate by Wyndham GA Alpharetta
1005 Kingswood Place
Alpharetta, GA
770-649-0955 (800-228-1000)
Dogs up to 50 pounds are allowed.

Days Inn Americus
1007 Martin Luther King
Americus, GA
229-924-3613 (800-329-7466)
Dogs are welcome at this hotel.

Holiday Inn Express Americus
1611 E. Lamar St.
Americus, GA
229-928-5400 (877-270-6405)
Dogs of all sizes are allowed. Dogs are allowed for a pet fee.

Best Western Ashburn Inn
820 Shoney's Drive
Ashburn, GA
229-567-0080 (800-780-7234)
Dogs of all sizes are allowed. Dogs are allowed for a pet fee of $10 per pet per night.

Days Inn Ashburn
823 E. Washington Ave.
Ashburn, GA
229-567-3346 (800-329-7466)
Dogs of all sizes are allowed. Dogs are allowed for a nightly pet fee.

Super 8 Ashburn
749 E Washington Ave
Ashburn, GA
229-567-4688 (800-800-8000)
Dogs are welcome at this hotel.

Travelodge Downtown Athens
898 West Broad Street
Athens, GA
706-549-5400 (800-578-7878)
Dogs are welcome at this hotel.

Airport Drury Inn & Suites
1270 Virginia Avenue
Atlanta, GA
404-761-4900 (800-378-7946)
Dogs of all sizes are allowed for no additional pet fee with a credit card on file, and there is a pet agreement to sign at check in.

Crowne Plaza Hotel Atlanta-Airport
1325 Virginia Ave
Atlanta, GA
404-768-6660 (877-270-6405)
Dogs are welcome at this hotel.

Days Inn Northwest Atlanta
1701 Northside Drive NW
Atlanta, GA
404-351-6500 (800-329-7466)
Dogs of all sizes are allowed. Dogs are allowed for a pet fee of $20.00 per pet per stay.

Doubletree Hotel
2055 S Park Place
Atlanta, GA
770-272-9441 (800-222-TREE (8733))
This upscale hotel offers a number of on site amenities for all level of travelers, plus a convenient location to an international airport, and business, shopping, dining, and recreation areas. Dogs are allowed for an additional one time pet fee of $100 per room. 2 dogs may be allowed.

Extended Stay America Atlanta - Clairmont
3115 Clairmont Rd.
Atlanta, GA
404-679-4333 (800-804-3724)
One dog is allowed per suite. There is a $25 per night additional pet fee up to $150 for an entire stay.

Extended Stay America Atlanta - Perimeter
905 Crestline Pkwy.
Atlanta, GA
770-396-5600 (800-804-3724)
One dog is allowed per suite. There is a $25 per night additional pet fee up to $150 for an entire stay.

Grand Hyatt Atlanta
3300 Peachtree Road NE
Atlanta, GA
404-237-1234
Dogs up to 70 pounds are welcome.
There is a $100 one time pet fee.

Hawthorn Suites
1500 Parkwood Circle SE
Atlanta, GA
770-952-9595 (800-527-1133)
In addition to providing a convenient
location to many local sites and
activities, this all-suite hotel offers a
number of amenities for business
and leisure travelers, including their
signature breakfast buffet and
beautifully appointed rooms. Dogs up
to 50 pounds are allowed for an
additional one time pet fee of $125
per room. Multiple dogs may be
allowed.

Holiday Inn Atlanta Northeast
2001 Clearview Ave.
Atlanta, GA
770-455-3700 (877-270-6405)
Dogs up to 50 pounds are allowed.

Holiday Inn Select Atlanta-
Perimeter/Dunwoody
4386 Chamblee-Dunwoody Rd.
Atlanta, GA
770-457-6363 (877-270-6405)
Dogs of all sizes are allowed. Dogs
are allowed for a pet fee of $75.00
per pet per stay.

Homestead Studio Suites Atlanta -
North Druid Hills
1339 Executive Park Dr.
Atlanta, GA
404-325-1223 (800-804-3724)
One dog is allowed per suite. There
is a $25 per night additional pet fee
up to $150 for an entire stay.

Homestead Studio Suites Atlanta -
Perimeter
1050 Hammond Dr.
Atlanta, GA
770-522-0025 (800-804-3724)
One dog is allowed per suite. There
is a $25 per night additional pet fee
up to $150 for an entire stay.

Hotel Indigo Atlanta Midtown
683 Peachtree St. NE
Atlanta, GA
404-874-9200 (877-865-6578)
Dogs of all sizes are allowed. Dogs
are allowed for a pet fee.

La Quinta Inn & Suites Atlanta
Perimeter Medical
6260 Peachtree Dunwoody

Atlanta, GA
770-350-6177 (800-531-5900)
Dogs of all sizes are allowed. There
are no additional pet fees. Dogs
must be well behaved, leashed, and
cleaned up after. Dogs must be
crated if left unattended in the room.
Multiple dogs may be allowed.

Marriott Perimeter Center
246 Perimeter Center Parkway NE
Atlanta, GA
770-394-6500 (888-858-2451)
Located adjacent to the Perimeter
Mall and only 15 minutes from
downtown, this luxury hotel gives
convenient access to numerous
businesses, shopping, dining, and
day/night entertainment areas, plus
they also offer a number of in-house
amenities for business and leisure
travelers. Dogs are allowed for an
additional one time fee of $75 per
pet. Multiple dogs may be allowed.

Motel 6 - Atlanta Downtown
311 Courtland Street N.e
Atlanta, GA
404-659-4545 (800-466-8356)
This motel welcomes your pets to
stay with you.

Motel 6 - Atlanta, Ga
2820 Chamblee-tucker Rd
Atlanta, GA
770-458-6626 (800-466-8356)
This motel welcomes your pets to
stay with you.

Ramada Airport Conference Center
Atlanta
1380 Virginia Avenue
Atlanta, GA
404-762-8411 (800-272-6232)
Dogs of all sizes are allowed. Dogs
are allowed for a pet fee of $20.00
per pet per stay.

Red Roof Inn Atlanta - Airport North
1200 Virginia Avenue
Atlanta, GA
404-209-1800 (800-RED-ROOF)
One well-behaved family pet per
room. Guest must notify front desk
upon arrival. Guest is liable for any
damages. In consideration of all
guests, pets must never be left
unattended in the guest rooms.

Red Roof Inn Atlanta - Buckhead
1960 North Druid Hills Road
Atlanta, GA
404-321-1653 (800-RED-ROOF)
One well-behaved family pet per
room. Guest must notify front desk
upon arrival. Guest is liable for any
damages. In consideration of all

guests, pets must never be left
unattended in the guest rooms.

Red Roof Inn Atlanta Downtown
311 Courtland St Northeast
Atlanta, GA
404-659-4545 (800-RED-ROOF)
One well-behaved family pet per
room. Guest must notify front desk
upon arrival. Guest is liable for any
damages. In consideration of all
guests, pets must never be left
unattended in the guest rooms.

Residence Inn Atlanta Buckhead
2960 Piedmont Road NE
Atlanta, GA
404-239-0677 (888-236-2427)
Located in one of the city's most
exciting neighborhoods, this all suite
hotel offers a convenient location to
business, shopping, dining, and
entertainment areas, plus they have
a number of in-house amenities that
include a daily buffet breakfast, a 24
hour market, and an evening
reception Monday through Thursday.
Dogs are allowed for an additional
one time pet fee of $100 per room.
Multiple dogs may be allowed.

Residence Inn Atlanta
Buckhead/Lenox Park
2220 Lake Blvd
Atlanta, GA
404-467-1660 (888-236-2427)
In addition to offering a convenient
location to business, dining,
entertainment, and world class
shopping areas, this hotel also
provides a number of in-house
amenities, including a daily buffet
breakfast, and evening socials. Dogs
are allowed for an additional one
time pet fee of $75 per room.
Multiple dogs may be allowed.

Residence Inn Atlanta Downtown
134 Peachtree Street NW
Atlanta, GA
404-522-0950 (800-331-3131)
In addition to offering a convenient
location to business, shopping,
dining, and entertainment areas, this
hotel also provides a number of in-
house amenities, including a daily
buffet breakfast, and a Manager's
reception Monday through Thursday.
Dogs up to 50 pounds are allowed
for an additional one time pet fee of
$75 per room. Multiple dogs may be
allowed.

Residence Inn Atlanta Midtown/17th
Street
1365 Peachtree Street
Atlanta, GA
404-745-1000

Offering boutique loft style lodging, this inn sits in the heart of the city's art district and offers a convenient location to Atlantic Station, the arts center, and museums, plus they have a number of in-house amenities that include a daily buffet breakfast, and a weekday hospitality hour. Dogs are allowed for an additional one time pet fee of $100. 2 dogs may be allowed.

Residence Inn Atlanta
Midtown/Historic
1041 W Peachtree Street
Atlanta, GA
404-872-8885 (888-236-2427)
This all suite hotel sits central to many of the city's star attractions, dining, and entertainment areas, plus they offer a number of in-house amenities that include a daily buffet breakfast, and an evening reception Monday through Thursday. Dogs are allowed for an additional one time pet fee of $100. Multiple dogs may be allowed.

Residence Inn Atlanta Perimeter
Center
6096 Barfield Road
Atlanta, GA
404-252-5066 (888-236-2427)
Located in the heart of the business district, this inn offers a convenient location to business, shopping, dining, and entertainment areas, plus they have a number of in-house amenities that include a daily buffet breakfast, and a Manager's reception Monday through Thursday. Dogs up to 50 pounds are allowed for an additional one time pet fee of $100 per room. 2 dogs may be allowed.

Sheraton Atlanta Hotel
165 Courtland Street at International Blvd.
Atlanta, GA
404-659-6500 (888-625-5144)
Dogs up to 80 pounds are allowed. There are no additional pet fees. Dogs are not allowed to be left alone in the room.

Sheraton Buckhead Hotel Atlanta
3405 Lenox Road NE
Atlanta, GA
404-261-9250 (888-625-5144)
Dogs up to 80 pounds are allowed. There are no additional pet fees. Dogs are not allowed to be left alone in the room.

Sheraton Gateway Hotel Atlanta
Airport
1900 Sullivan Road
Atlanta, GA

770-997-1100 (888-625-5144)
Dogs up to 80 pounds are allowed for no additional pet fee. There is a pet agreement to sign at check in, and dogs may not be left alone in the room.

Staybridge Suites Atlanta Perimeter
Center West
760 Mt. Vernon Hwy
Atlanta, GA
404-250-0110 (877-270-6405)
Dogs up to 80 pounds are allowed. Pets allowed with an additional pet fee. Up to $75 for 1-6 nights and up to $150 for 7+ nights. A pet agreement must be signed at check-in.

Staybridge Suites Atlanta Perimeter
Ctr East
4601 Ridgeview Road
Atlanta, GA
678-320-0111 (877-270-6405)
Dogs up to 80 pounds are allowed. Pets allowed with an additional pet fee. Up to $75 for 1-6 nights and up to $150 for 7+ nights. A pet agreement must be signed at check-in.

Stonehurst Place
923 Piedmont Avenue NE
Atlanta, GA
404-881-0722
stonehurstplace.com
Listed on the National Register of Historic Mansions, this 1896 home went through an earth friendly conversion that won them the EarthCraft Home and Southface 2008 Renovation Project of the Year award. Some of the conversions included solar paneling, a whole-house Icynene insulation system, an in-house six step city-water purification system, solar heated water tanks, stored/recycled rainwater for the gardens, and a Brac Greywater Recycling System. Dogs up to about 50 pounds are allowed for a $150 refundable deposit. 2 dogs may be allowed.

Super 8 Northeast GA Atlanta
2822 Chamblee Tucker Road
Atlanta, GA
770-458-2671 (800-800-8000)
Dogs are welcome at this hotel.

Super 8 /Jonesboro Road Atlanta
3701 Jonesboro Road
Atlanta, GA
404-361-1111 (800-800-8000)
Dogs of all sizes are allowed. Dogs are allowed for a pet fee of $10 per pet per night.

Super 8 /Midtown Atlanta
1641 Peachtree Street NE
Atlanta, GA
404-873-5731 (800-800-8000)
Dogs are welcome at this hotel.

The Westin Atlanta Perimeter North
7 Concourse Pkwy
Atlanta, GA
770-395-3900 (888-625-5144)
Dogs of all sizes are allowed for a $25 refundable deposit, and there is a pet agreement to sign at check in. Dogs may not be left alone in the room.

TownePlace Suites Atlanta Northlake
3300 Northlake Parkway
Atlanta, GA
770-938-0408 (800-257-3000)
Besides offering a number of in-house amenities for all level of travelers, this all suite inn also provides a convenient location to Emory University, major corporations, shopping, dining, and entertainment areas. Dogs are allowed for an additional one time pet fee of $75 per room. Multiple dogs may be allowed.

Travelodge Airport Atlanta
2788 Forrest Hills Drive SW
Atlanta, GA
404-768-7750 (800-578-7870)
Dogs are welcome at this hotel.

Augusta Red Roof Inn & Suites
4328 Frontage Road
Augusta, GA
706-228-3031 (800-RED-ROOF)
One well-behaved family pet per room. Guest must notify front desk upon arrival. Guest is liable for any damages. In consideration of all guests, pets must never be left unattended in the guest rooms.

Candlewood Suites Augusta
1080 Claussen Road
Augusta, GA
706-733-3300 (877-270-6405)
Dogs up to 80 pounds are allowed. Pets allowed with an additional pet fee. Up to $75 for 1-6 nights and up to $150 for 7+ nights. A pet agreement must be signed at check-in.

Country Inns & Suites Riverwalk
Three Ninth Street
Augusta, GA
706-774-1400
Dogs up to 50 pounds are allowed. There is an additional one time fee of $25 per pet.

Days Inn Augusta
906 Molly Pond Rd
Augusta, GA
706-722-4545 (800-329-7466)
Dogs are welcome at this hotel.

Econo Lodge Fort Gordon
2051 Gordon Hwy.
Augusta, GA
706-738-6565 (877-424-6423)
Dogs up to 50 pounds are allowed.
Dogs are allowed for a pet fee of
$.00 per pet per night. Three or more
dogs may be allowed.

Hawthorn Suites
4049 Jimmie Dyess Parkway
Augusta, GA
706-228-1990 (800-527-1133)
In addition to providing a convenient
location to many local sites and
activities, this all-suite hotel offers a
number of amenities for business
and leisure travelers, including their
signature breakfast buffet and
beautifully appointed rooms. Dogs
are allowed for an additional one
time pet fee of $150 per room. Dogs
must be crated or removed for
housekeeping. 2 dogs may be
allowed.

La Quinta Inn Augusta
3020 Washington Rd.
Augusta, GA
706-733-2660 (800-531-5900)
Dogs of all sizes are allowed. There
are no additional pet fees. Dogs
must be crated if left alone in the
room, be leashed at all times, and
cleaned up after. Multiple dogs may
be allowed.

Marriott Augusta Hotel & Suites
Two Tenth Street
Augusta, GA
706-722-8900 (800-868-5354)
This luxury riverfront hotel sits central
to numerous business, shopping,
dining, and entertainment areas, plus
they also offer a number of in-house
amenities for business and leisure
travelers. Dogs are allowed for an
additional one time fee of $25 per
room. 2 dogs may be allowed.

Quality Inn Medical Center Area
1455 Walton Way
Augusta, GA
706-722-2224 (877-424-6423)
Dogs up to 100 pounds are allowed.
Dogs are allowed for a pet fee of
$25.00 per pet per stay. Three or
more dogs may be allowed.

Staybridge Suites Augusta

2540 Center West Pkwy
Augusta, GA
706-733-0000 (877-270-6405)
Dogs up to 80 pounds are allowed.
Pets allowed with an additional pet
fee. Up to $75 for 1-6 nights and up
to $150 for 7+ nights. A pet
agreement must be signed at
check-in.

Super 8 Ft Gordon Belair Augusta
456 Parkwest Drive
Augusta, GA
706-396-1600 (800-800-8000)
Dogs are welcome at this hotel.

The Partridge Inn
2110 Walton Way
Augusta, GA
706-737-8888 (800-476-6888)
Designated a Historic Hotel of
America, this has been a full service
hotel for business and leisure
travelers for more than a hundred
years. They have added a full
complement of state of the art
renovations to blend its rich past
with all the modern comforts and
amenities you would expect of a
luxury retreat. Some of the
amenities/features include the
award winning Verandah Grill and
the Bamboo Room and Piano Bar
with live music, large meeting
rooms, event planners/caterers for
conferences or social affairs, a
great Sunday brunch, richly
furnished rooms/studios/suites, a
secluded courtyard pool, room
service, and more than a ¼ mile of
verandahs and balconies. Dogs of
all sizes are allowed. There is a $25
one time fee for one dog, and a
second dog would be an additional
$10 one time fee. Dogs may not be
left alone in the room at any time,
and they must be leashed and
cleaned up after. 2 dogs may be
allowed.

Travelodge Augusta
3039 Washington Road
Augusta, GA
706-868-6930 (800-578-7878)
Dogs of all sizes are allowed. Dogs
are allowed for a pet fee of $10.00
per pet per night.

Baymont Inn & Suites Atlanta West/
Austell
7377 Six Flags Dr.
Austell, GA
770-944-2110 (877-229-6668)
Dogs are welcome at this hotel.

Howard Johnson Inn at Six Flags
95 South Service Road
Austell, GA

770-941-1400 (800-446-4656)
Dogs of all sizes are allowed. Dogs
are allowed for a pet fee of $10.00
per pet per night.

Quality Inn & Suites at Six Flags
1100 North Blairs Bridge Road
Austell, GA
770-941-1499 (877-424-6423)
Dogs of all sizes are allowed. Dogs
are allowed for a pet fee of $15.00
per pet per night.

Days Inn Bainbridge
1407 Tallahassee Hwy
Bainbridge, GA
229-248-6300 (800-329-7466)
Dogs of all sizes are allowed. Dogs
are allowed for a nightly pet fee.

A Toccoa Riverfront Cabin Vacation
Call to Arrange.
Blairsville, GA
478-862-9733
toccoa-riverfront-cabin.com
A North Georgia mountain cabin on
the Toccoa River. Located near Blue
Ridge/Blairsville/Dahlonega. Very
private. Sleeps 6. Central heat/AC,
fireplace, satellite TV, barbecue grill,
swings, screened porch, catfish pond
and river fishing year-round. Fenced
acreage and barn for horses. Pets
are welcome.

Misty Mountain Inn
4376 Town Creek Road
Blairsville, GA
706-745-4786 (888-MISTY MN (647-
8966))
jwww.com/misty/
Although dogs are not allowed in the
Victorian farmhouse, they are
allowed in any of the 6 cottages that
are nestled in the woods along the
mountainside. There is a $20 one
time fee per pet. Dogs must be well
behaved, leashed, and under
owner's care. 2 dogs may be
allowed.

1 My Mountain Cabin Rentals
P.O. Box 388
Blue Ridge, GA
800-844-4939
1MyMountain.com
These are rental cabins in the
beautiful Blue Ridge area of North
Georgia. Pets are allowed in most of
the cabins for a $10 per night fee per
pet and a $150 refundable damage
deposit. Please notify the
management that you are bringing a
pet when making reservations.

Avenair Mtn Cabin Rentals North
Georgia

1862 Old Highway 76
Blue Ridge, GA
706-632-0318 (800-MTN-CABINS)
avenairmtncabins.com
These cabin rentals are located in
Georgia's Blue Ridge Mountains
about 1 1/2 hours from Atlanta.
Many, but not all, of the cabins are
pet-friendly.

Black Bear Cabin Rentals
21 High Park Drive Ste 7
Blue Ridge, GA
706-632-4794 (888-902-2246)
blackbearcabinrentals.com
Black Bear Cabin Rentals are
available with mountain views, water
access and forests all around. Pets
are allowed with a pet fee.

Comfort Inn & Suites
83 Blue Ridge Overlook
Blue Ridge, GA
706-946-3333 (877-424-6423)
Dogs up to 50 pounds are allowed.

Douglas Inn and Suites
1192 Windy Ridge Road
Blue Ridge, GA
706-258-3600 (877-416-3664)
douglasinn.com/blueridge.html
There are 1 and 2 bedroom suites
offered at this inn. Dogs are allowed
for an additional fee of $10 for the
1st night per pet, and $5 per night
per pet after. Dogs must be leashed
and under owner's care. 2 dogs may
be allowed.

Tica Cabin Rentals Inc.
699 East Main Street
Blue Ridge, GA
706-632-4448 (800-871-8422)
ticacabins.com
There are a number of pet-friendly
vacation rentals some with excellent
views and various amenities. From
one to five bedrooms are available.
Call for more information or to
reserve the cabins.

Holiday Inn Express Chateau Elan
Lodge
2069 Highway 211
Braselton, GA
770-867-8100 (877-270-6405)
Dogs of all sizes are allowed. Dogs
are allowed for a pet fee of $50.00
per pet per night.

Days Inn GA Bremen
35 Price Creek Rd.
Bremen, GA
770-537-4646 (800-329-7466)
Dogs of all sizes are allowed. Dogs
are allowed for a pet fee of $10.00
per pet per night.

Brunswick I-95 Red Roof Inn &
Suites
25 Tourist Drive
Brunswick, GA
912-264-4720 (800-RED-ROOF)
One well-behaved family pet per
room. Guest must notify front desk
upon arrival. Guest is liable for any
damages. In consideration of all
guests, pets must never be left
unattended in the guest rooms.

Knights Inn Brunswick
450 Warren Mason Blvd
Brunswick, GA
912-267-6500 (800-843-5644)
Dogs are welcome at this hotel.
There is a $5 per day pet fee.

La Quinta Inn & Suites Brunswick
165 Warren Mason Blvd
Brunswick, GA
912-265-7725 (800-531-5900)
A dog up to 60 pounds is allowed.
There are no additional pet fees.
Dogs may not be left unattended,
and they must be leashed at all
times, and cleaned up after. 2 dogs
may be allowed.

Motel 6 - Brunswick, Ga
403 Butler Dr
Brunswick, GA
912-264-8582 (800-466-8356)
This motel welcomes your pets to
stay with you.

Super 8 /St Simons Island Area
Brunswick
I-95 exit 36B
Brunswick, GA
912-264-8800 (800-800-8000)
Dogs of all sizes are allowed. Dogs
are allowed for a pet fee of $10 per
pet per night.

Best Western Inn & Suites
101 Dunbar Road
Byron, GA
478-956-3056 (800-780-7234)
Dogs of all sizes are allowed. Dogs
are allowed for a pet fee of $10.00
per pet per night.

Knights Inn Byron
12009 Watson Blvd
Byron, GA
478-956-5300 (800-843-5644)
Dogs are welcome at this hotel.
There is a $15 one time additional
pet fee.

Quality Inn
115 Chapman Rd.
Byron, GA
478-956-1600 (877-424-6423)

Dogs of all sizes are allowed. Dogs
are allowed for a pet fee of $10.00
per pet per night.

Days Inn Calhoun
915 Hwy 53 East SE
Calhoun, GA
706-629-9501 (800-329-7466)
Dogs of all sizes are allowed. Dogs
are allowed for a pet fee of $10.00
per pet per stay.

Motel 6 - Calhoun, Ga
742 Highway 53 East S.e.
Calhoun, GA
706-629-8271 (800-466-8356)
This motel welcomes your pets to
stay with you.

Ramada Limited
1204 Red Bud Rd, N.E.
Calhoun, GA
706-629-9207 (800-272-6232)
Dogs of all sizes are allowed. Dogs
are allowed for a pet fee.

Super 8 Calhoun
1446 US Hwy 41 N
Calhoun, GA
706-602-1400 (800-800-8000)
Dogs are welcome at this hotel.

Comfort Inn
138 Keith Dr
Canton, GA
770-345-1994 (877-424-6423)
Dogs of all sizes are allowed.

Days Inn Cartersville
5618 Hwy 20 Southeast
Cartersville, GA
770-382-1824 (800-329-7466)
Dogs of all sizes are allowed. Dogs
are allowed for a nightly pet fee.

Econo Lodge
26 SR 20 Spur SE
Cartersville, GA
770-386-3303 (877-424-6423)
Dogs of all sizes are allowed. Dogs
are allowed for a pet fee of $5.00 per
pet per night.

Howard Johnson Express Inn
Cartersville
25 Carson Loop NW
Cartersville, GA
770-386-0700 (800-446-4656)
Dogs of all sizes are allowed. Dogs
are allowed for a pet fee of $5.00 per
pet per night.

Motel 6 - Cartersville, Ga
5657 Hwy 20 Ne
Cartersville, GA
770-386-1449 (800-466-8356)
This motel welcomes your pets to

stay with you.

Super 8 Cartersville
41 SR 20 Spur SE
Cartersville, GA
770-382-8881 (800-800-8000)
Dogs are welcome at this hotel.

Holiday Inn Express Hotel & Suites
Cedartown
100 E John Hand Rd
Cedartown, GA
770-749-0006 (877-270-6405)
Dogs of all sizes are allowed. Dogs
are allowed for a pet fee of $25.00
per pet per stay.

Residence Inn Atlanta
Perimeter/Dunwoody
1901 Savoy Drive
Chamblee, GA
770-455-4446 (888-236-2427)
In addition to offering a convenient
location to shopping, dining, and
entertainment areas, this hotel also
provides a number of in-house
amenities, including a daily buffet
breakfast, and a Manager's reception
Monday through Thursday. Dogs are
allowed for an additional one time
pet fee of $100 per room. 2 dogs
may be allowed.

Econo Lodge
118 General Bushrod Johnson Av
Chickamauga, GA
706-375-7007 (877-424-6423)
Dogs of all sizes are allowed. Dogs
are allowed for a pet fee of $10.00
per pet per night. Two dogs are
allowed per room.

Days Inn
4505 Best Rd
College Park, GA
404-767-1224 (800-329-7466)
Dogs of all sizes are allowed. Dogs
are allowed for a pet fee of $10.00
per pet per night.

Motel 6 - Atlanta Airport South
2471 Old National Pkwy
College Park, GA
404-761-9701 (800-466-8356)
This motel welcomes your pets to
stay with you.

Super 8 Atlanta Hartsfield-Jackson
Arpt
2010 Sullivan Road
College Park, GA
770-991-8985 (800-800-8000)
Dogs are welcome at this hotel.

Days Inn -Fort Benning Columbus
3170 Victory Drive
Columbus, GA

706-689-6181 (800-329-7466)
Dogs are welcome at this hotel.

Extended Stay America Columbus -
Airport
5020 Armour Rd.
Columbus, GA
706-653-0131 (800-804-3724)
One dog is allowed per suite. There
is a $25 per night additional pet fee
up to $150 for an entire stay.

Extended Stay America Columbus -
Bradley Park
1721 Rollins Way
Columbus, GA
706-653-9938 (800-804-3724)
One dog is allowed per suite. There
is a $25 per night additional pet fee
up to $150 for an entire stay.

Holiday Inn Columbus-North I-185
2800 Manchester Expressway
Columbus, GA
706-324-0231 (877-270-6405)
Dogs of all sizes are allowed. Dogs
are allowed for a pet fee of $25.00
per pet per stay.

Howard Johnson Inn and Suites GA
Columbus
1011 Veterans Parkway
Columbus, GA
706-322-6641 (800-446-4656)
Dogs are welcome at this hotel.
There is a $15 one time pet fee.

La Quinta Inn Columbus
3201 Macon Rd, Suite 200
Columbus, GA
706-568-1740 (800-531-5900)
Dogs of all sizes are allowed. There
are no additional pet fees. Dogs
must be crated if left alone in the
room, be leashed, and cleaned up
after. Multiple dogs may be allowed.

La Quinta Inn Columbus State
University
2919 Warm Springs Road
Columbus, GA
706-323-4344 (800-531-5900)
Dogs of all sizes are allowed. There
are no additional pet fees. There is
a pet waiver to sign at check in, and
they request dogs be taken to the
designated pet area to due their
business. Dogs may not be left
unattended, and they must be
leashed and cleaned up after.
Multiple dogs may be allowed.

Motel 6 - Columbus, Ga
3050 Victory Dr
Columbus, GA
706-687-7214 (800-466-8356)
This motel welcomes your pets to

stay with you.

Residence Inn Columbus
2670 Adams Farm Drive
Columbus, GA
706-494-0050 (800-331-3131)
This hotel offers a central location to
business, shopping, dining, and
entertainment areas, plus they offer
a number of in-house amenities,
including a daily buffet breakfast and
weekday evening socials with
complimentary light fare. Dogs are
allowed for an additional one time
pet fee of $100 per room. 2 dogs
may be allowed.

Staybridge Suites Columbus Ft.
Benning
1694 Whittlesey Road
Columbus, GA
706-507-7700 (877-270-6405)
Dogs up to 80 pounds are allowed.
Pets allowed with an additional pet
fee. Up to $75 for 1-6 nights and up
to $150 for 7+ nights. A pet
agreement must be signed at check-
in.

Super 8 Airport Columbus
2935 Warm Springs Rd
Columbus, GA
706-322-6580 (800-800-8000)
Dogs are welcome at this hotel.

TownePlace Suites Columbus
4534 E Armour Road
Columbus, GA
706-322-3001 (800-257-3000)
This all suite inn sits central to major
medical centers as well as a number
of businesses, shopping, dining, and
entertainment areas, plus they offer
a number of in-house amenities for
business and leisure travelers. Dogs
are allowed for an additional one
time pet fee of $75 per room.
Multiple dogs may be allowed.

Admiral Benbow Inn
30747 Hwy 441 S.
Commerce, GA
706-335-5183
There is a $15 pet fee for the 1st
night and a $5 pet fee for each
additional night per room. 2 dogs
may be allowed.

Best Western Commerce Inn
157 Eisenhower Drive
Commerce, GA
706-335-3640 (800-780-7234)
Dogs of all sizes are allowed. Dogs
are allowed for a pet fee of $20 per
pet per stay.

Howard Johnson Inn GA Commerce

148 Eisenhower Dr.
Commerce, GA
706-335-5581 (800-446-4656)
Dogs of all sizes are allowed. Dogs
are allowed for a pet fee of $10 per
pet per stay.

Motel 6 - Commerce, Ga
128 Frontage Rd
Commerce, GA
706-335-5561 (800-466-8356)
This motel welcomes your pets to
stay with you.

Quality Inn
165 Eisenhower Dr.
Commerce, GA
706-335-9001 (877-424-6423)
Dogs of all sizes are allowed. Dogs
are allowed for a pet fee of $10.00
per pet per night.

Super 8 Commerce
152 Eisenhower Drive
Commerce, GA
706-336-8008 (800-800-8000)
Dogs are welcome at this hotel.

Hawthorn Suites Golf Resort
1659 Centennial Olympic Parkway
Conyers, GA
770-228-1990 (800-527-1133)
In addition to providing a convenient
location to many local sites and
activities, this all-suite hotel offers a
number of amenities for business
and leisure travelers, including their
signature breakfast buffet and
beautifully appointed rooms. Dogs
are allowed for an additional one
time pet fee of $75 per room for 2
dogs; there is an additional one time
$75 fee for a 3rd pet. 2 dogs may be
allowed.

La Quinta Inn & Suites Atlanta
Conyers
1184 Dogwood Dr.
Conyers, GA
770-918-0092 (800-531-5900)
Dogs of all sizes are allowed. There
are no additional pet fees. Dogs may
not be left unattended, and they must
be well behaved, leashed, and
cleaned up after. Multiple dogs may
be allowed.

Ramada Conyers
1351 Dogwood Drive
Conyers, GA
770-483-3220 (800-272-6232)
Dogs of all sizes are allowed. Dogs
are allowed for a pet fee.

Suburban Extended Stay Hotel
1385 Old McDonough Hwy
Conyers, GA

770-918-0618 (877-424-6423)
Dogs up to 80 pounds are allowed.

Super 8 Conyers
1070 Dogwood Dr
Conyers, GA
770-760-0777 (800-800-8000)
Dogs are welcome at this hotel.

Best Western Colonial Inn
1706 E 16th Avenue
Cordele, GA
229-273-5420 (800-780-7234)
Dogs up to 50 pounds are allowed.
Dogs are allowed for a pet fee.

Days Inn Cordele
2109 E. 16th Ave
Cordele, GA
229-273-7366 (800-329-7466)
Dogs of all sizes are allowed. Dogs
are allowed for a nightly pet fee.

Ramada Cordele
2016 16th Avenue East
Cordele, GA
229-273-5000 (800-272-6232)
Dogs are welcome at this hotel.

Travelodge Cordele
1618 East 16th Avenue
Cordele, GA
229-273-2456 (800-578-7878)
Dogs of all sizes are allowed. Dogs
are allowed for a pet fee of $5.00
per pet per stay.

Best Western Cornelia Inn
1105 Highway 441 Business
Cornelia, GA
706-778-3600 (800-780-7234)
Dogs of all sizes are allowed. Dogs
are allowed for a pet fee of $10.00
per pet per night.

Baymont Inn & Suites Covington
10111 Alcovy Road
Covington, GA
770-787-4900 (877-229-6668)
Dogs are welcome at this hotel.

Super 8 GA Covington
10130 Alcovy Road
Covington, GA
770-786-5800 (800-800-8000)
Dogs are welcome at this hotel.

Comfort Suites
905 Buford Rd.
Cumming, GA
770-889-4141 (877-424-6423)
Dogs of all sizes are allowed. Dogs
are allowed for a pet fee of $25.00
per pet per night.

Bend of the River Cabins and
Chalets

319 Horseshoe Lane
Dahlonega, GA
706-219-2040
Dogs of all sizes are allowed. There
is a $10 per night per pet additional
fee. The fee may be less for small
dogs and longer stays. Dogs are not
allowed on the beds and must be
kept leashed when out.

Hidden River Cabin
1104 Horseshoe Bend Rd.
Dahlonega, GA
770-518-9942
georgiacabins.tripod.com
Cabin with fenced yards. There is a
$50 weekly pet fee.

Days Inn Dallas
1007 Old Harris Road
Dallas, GA
770-505-4567 (800-329-7466)
Dogs of all sizes are allowed. Dogs
are allowed for a nightly pet fee.

Comfort Inn & Suites
905 West Bridge Road
Dalton, GA
706-259-2583 (877-424-6423)
Dogs up to 50 pounds are allowed.
Dogs are allowed for a pet fee of
$15.00 per pet per night. Two dogs
are allowed per room.

Days Inn Dalton
1518 West Walnut Ave
Dalton, GA
706-278-0850 (800-329-7466)
Dogs of all sizes are allowed. Dogs
are allowed for a pet fee.

Motel 6 - Dalton
2200 Chattanooga Rd
Dalton, GA
706-278-5522 (800-466-8356)
This motel welcomes your pets to
stay with you.

Quality Inn
875 College Dr.
Dalton, GA
706-278-0500 (877-424-6423)
Dogs of all sizes are allowed. Dogs
are allowed for a pet fee of $10.00
per pet per night.

Super 8 /Convention Center Area
Dalton
2107 Chattanooga Road
Dalton, GA
706-226-9579 (800-800-8000)
Dogs of all sizes are allowed. Dogs
are allowed for a pet fee.

Travelodge Convention Center Area
Dalton
911 Market Street

Dalton, GA
706-275-0100 (800-578-7878)
Dogs are welcome at this hotel.

Comfort Inn
12924 GA HWY 251
Darien, GA
912-437-4200 (877-424-6423)
Dogs of all sizes are allowed. Dogs
are allowed for a pet fee of $15.00
per pet per night.

Quality Inn
Highway 251 I-95 Exit 49
Darien, GA
912-437-5373 (877-424-6423)
Dogs of all sizes are allowed. Dogs
are allowed for a pet fee of $10.00
per pet per night. Two dogs are
allowed per room.

Super 8 Darien
I-95 exit 49
Darien, GA
912-437-6660 (800-800-8000)
Dogs of all sizes are allowed. Dogs
are allowed for a nightly pet fee.

Econo Lodge
938 Forrester Dr. SE
Dawson, GA
229-995-5725 (877-424-6423)
Dogs of all sizes are allowed. Dogs
are allowed for a pet fee of $7.00 per
pet per night. Two dogs are allowed
per room.

Comfort Inn
127 Beartooth Pkwy
Dawsonville, GA
706-216-1900 (877-424-6423)
Dogs up to 100 pounds are allowed.
Dogs are allowed for a pet fee of
$15.00 per pet per night. Two dogs
are allowed per room.

Super 8 Dawsonville
GA 400 & Hwy 53
Dawsonville, GA
706-216-6801 (800-800-8000)
Dogs are welcome at this hotel.

Motel 6 - Decatur, Ga
2572 Candler Rd
Decatur, GA
404-243-6679 (800-466-8356)
This motel welcomes your pets to
stay with you.

Knights Inn Dillard
3 Best Inn Way
Dillard, GA
706-746-5321 (800-843-5644)
Dogs are welcome at this hotel.

Days Inn Donalsonville
208 West 3rd Street

Donalsonville, GA
229-524-2185 (800-329-7466)
Dogs of all sizes are allowed. Dogs
are allowed for a nightly pet fee.

Super 8 Donalsonville
415 W 3rd Street
Donalsonville, GA
229-524-8695 (800-800-8000)
Dogs are welcome at this hotel.

Days Inn -Atlanta-Fairburn Road
Douglasville
5489 Westmoreland Plaza
Douglasville, GA
770-949-1499 (800-329-7466)
Dogs of all sizes are allowed. Dogs
are allowed for a pet fee.

Ramada Limited Douglasville
8315 Cherokee Blvd
Douglasville, GA
770-949-3090 (800-272-6232)
Dogs of all sizes are allowed. Dogs
are allowed for a pet fee.

Days Inn GA Dublin
2111 US Hwy 441 S
Dublin, GA
478-275-7637 (800-329-7466)
Dogs of all sizes are allowed. Dogs
are allowed for a pet fee of $15.00
per pet per night.

Travelodge Suites and Conference
Center GA Dublin
2121 Highway 441 S
Dublin, GA
478-275-2650 (800-578-7878)
Dogs of all sizes are allowed. Dogs
are allowed for a pet fee of $15.00
per pet per night.

Candlewood Suites Atlanta
3665 Shackleford Road
Duluth, GA
678-380-0414 (877-270-6405)
Dogs up to 80 pounds are allowed.
Pets allowed with an additional pet
fee. Up to $75 for 1-6 nights and up
to $150 for 7+ nights. A pet
agreement must be signed at
check-in.

Holiday Inn Express Atlanta-
Gwinnett Place
3670 Shackleford Rd.
Duluth, GA
770-935-7171 (877-270-6405)
Dogs of all sizes are allowed. Dogs
are allowed for a pet fee of $50.00
per pet per stay.

Holiday Inn Gwinnett Center
6310 Sugarloaf Parkway
Duluth, GA
770-476-2022 (877-270-6405)

Dogs of all sizes are allowed. Dogs
are allowed for a pet fee of $25 per
pet per stay.

Quality Inn
3500 Venture Parkway
Duluth, GA
770-623-9300 (877-424-6423)
Dogs of all sizes are allowed. Dogs
are allowed for a pet fee of $10.00
per pet per night.

Residence Inn Atlanta Gwinnett
Place
1760 Pineland Road
Duluth, GA
770-921-2202 (888-236-2427)
In addition to offering a convenient
location to business, dining,
entertainment, areas, this hotel also
provides a number of in-house
amenities, including a daily buffet
breakfast, a Sports Court, and
weekly barbecues. Dogs up to about
50 pounds are allowed for an
additional one time pet fee of $100
per room. Dogs must be crated or
removed for housekeeping. 2 dogs
may be allowed.

Studio 6 - Atlanta Gwinnett Place
3525 Breckinridge Blvd
Duluth, GA
770-931-3113 (800-466-8356)
Your pets are welcome to stay here
with you for a pet fee of $10 per day
up to $50 for an entire stay.

Econo Lodge
970 Elbert Street
Elberton, GA
706-283-8811 (877-424-6423)
Dogs of all sizes are allowed. Dogs
are allowed for a pet fee of $10.00
per pet per night.

Days Inn Atlanta//Airport East Forest
Park
5116 GA Hwy 85
Forest Park, GA
404-768-6400 (800-329-7466)
Dogs are welcome at this hotel.

Econo Lodge
5060 Frontage Rd.
Forest Park, GA
404-363-6429 (877-424-6423)
Dogs of all sizes are allowed. Dogs
are allowed for a pet fee of $15.00
per pet per night. Two dogs are
allowed per room.

Super 8 Forest Park
410 Old Dixie Way
Forest Park, GA
404-363-8811 (800-800-8000)
Dogs of all sizes are allowed. Dogs

are allowed for a pet fee of $7.00 per pet per stay.

Travelodge Atlanta South Forest Park
6025 Old Dixie Road
Forest Park, GA
404-361-3600 (800-578-7878)
Dogs of all sizes are allowed. Dogs are allowed for a pet fee of $10 per pet per night.

Best Western Hilltop Inn
951 GA Highway 42 N
Forsyth, GA
478-994-9260 (800-780-7234)
Dogs of all sizes are allowed. Dogs are allowed for a nightly pet fee.

Comfort Inn
333 Harold G. Clark Pkwy
Forsyth, GA
478-994-3400 (877-424-6423)
Dogs up to 50 pounds are allowed. Dogs are allowed for a pet fee of $15.00 per pet per night.

Days Inn Forsyth
343 North Lee Street
Forsyth, GA
478-994-2900 (800-329-7466)
Dogs of all sizes are allowed. Dogs are allowed for a pet fee of $10.00 per pet per night.

Econo Lodge
320 Cabiness Road
Forsyth, GA
478-994-5603 (877-424-6423)
Dogs of all sizes are allowed. Dogs are allowed for a pet fee of $6.00/pet, per pet per night.

Holiday Inn Forsyth-I-75 (Exit 186)
Juliette Road & I-75
Forsyth, GA
478-994-5691 (877-270-6405)
Dogs of all sizes are allowed. Dogs are allowed for a pet fee of $10.00 per pet per night.

Best Western Battlefield Inn
2120 Lafayette Road
Fort Oglethorpe, GA
706-866-0222 (800-780-7234)
Dogs of all sizes are allowed. Dogs are allowed for a pet fee of $.$10 per pet per night.

Days Inn Gainesville
520 Queen City Parkway S.W.
Gainesville, GA
770-535-8100 (800-329-7466)
Dogs of all sizes are allowed. Dogs are allowed for a pet fee.

Motel 6 - Gainesville, Ga

1585 Monroe Dr
Gainesville, GA
770-532-7531 (800-466-8356)
This motel welcomes your pets to stay with you.

Howard Johnson Inn & Suites Griffin
1690 North Expressway
Griffin, GA
770-227-1516 (800-446-4656)
Dogs of all sizes are allowed. Dogs are allowed for a pet fee of $25.00 per pet per stay.

Motel 6 - Grovetown Augusta, Ga
459 Park West Dr
Grovetown, GA
706-651-8300 (800-466-8356)
This motel welcomes your pets to stay with you.

Knights Inn - /Valdosta Area Hahira
1300 GA Hwy 122 West
Hahira, GA
229-794-8000 (800-843-5644)
Dogs are welcome at this hotel. There is a $7 per night additional pet fee.

Residence Inn Atlanta Airport North/Virginia Avenue
3401 International Blvd
Hapeville, GA
404-761-0511 (888-236-2427)
This hotel offers a number of in-house amenities, including a daily buffet breakfast, a Manager's reception Monday through Thursday, a complimentary grocery shopping service, a Sport Court, and summer barbecues. Dogs are allowed for an additional one time pet fee of $75 per room. 2 dogs may be allowed.

Motel 6 - Helen, Ga
8171 Sr 75
Helen, GA
706-878-8888 (800-466-8356)
This motel welcomes your pets to stay with you.

Ramada Lake Chatuge Lodge of Hiawassee
653 US Hwy 76
Hiawassee, GA
706-896-5253 (800-272-6232)
Dogs are welcome at this hotel.

Knights Inn Hinesville
738 East Oglethorpe Highway
Hinesville, GA
912-368-4146 (800-843-5644)
Dogs are welcome at this hotel. There is a $20 one time additional pet fee.

The 74 Ranch
9205 H 53 W
Jasper, GA
706-692-0123
seventyfourranch.com/contact.htm
This unique B&B is a working ranch offering an authentic Old West ranch experience for the whole family. There are numerous activities from cookouts to trail rides, special events like the Civil War Reenactments, and historic lodging with period antiques. Dogs are allowed for no additional fee but they must be declared prior to arrival. All the gates at the ranch use pet-proof safety locks; plus there are 3 fenced acres for them to run leash free. Dogs are not allowed on the beds. 2 dogs may be allowed.

Oceanside Inn and Suites
711 Beachview Dr.
Jekyll Island, GA
912-635-2211 (800-228-5150)
This beachfront motel's amenities include a playground and room service. There is a $10 per day per pet charge. Multiple dogs may be allowed.

Quality Inn & Suites
700 North Beachview Drive
Jekyll Island, GA
912-635-2202 (877-424-6423)
Dogs of all sizes are allowed. Dogs are allowed for a pet fee of $10.00 per pet per night. Two dogs are allowed per room.

Villas by the Sea
1175 N Beachview Drive
Jekyll Island, GA
866-920-1263
jekyllislandga.com
This beautiful vacation spot on the ocean features a lush tropical landscape with scenic nature trails, unspoiled beaches, gourmet dining, and a number of recreational opportunities. The villas come in various sizes; plus they offer a solar heated pool and a bistro. Dogs are allowed for an additional one time fee that depends on the size of the villa. Multiple dogs may be allowed.

Clarion Hotel Atlanta Airport South
6288 Old Dixie Rd
Jonesboro, GA
770-968-4300 (877-424-6423)
Dogs of all sizes are allowed. Dogs are allowed for a pet fee of $20.00 per pet per night.

Howard Johnson Inn and Suites Jonesboro

701 Southside Commercial Pkwy
Jonesboro, GA
678-610-2528 (800-446-4656)
Dogs of all sizes are allowed. Dogs
are allowed for a pet fee of $20 per
pet per night.

Motel 6 - Jonesboro, Ga
6370 Old Dixie Highway
Jonesboro, GA
770-961-6336 (800-466-8356)
This motel welcomes your pets to
stay with you.

Best Western Kennesaw Inn
3375 Busbee Drive NW
Kennesaw, GA
770-424-7666 (800-780-7234)
Dogs up to 50 pounds are allowed.
Dogs are allowed for a nightly pet
fee.

Days Inn /Atlanta Kennesaw
760 Cobb Place Blvd.
Kennesaw, GA
770-419-1576 (800-329-7466)
Dogs of all sizes are allowed. Dogs
are allowed for a nightly pet fee.

Extended Stay America Atlanta -
Kennesaw
3000 George Busbee Pkwy.
Kennesaw, GA
770-422-1403 (800-804-3724)
One dog is allowed per suite. There
is a $25 per night additional pet fee
up to $150 for an entire stay.

La Quinta Inn Kennesaw
2625 George Busbee Parkway NW
Kennesaw, GA
770-426-0045 (800-531-5900)
Dogs of all sizes are allowed. There
are no additional pet fees. There is a
pet waiver to sign at check in. Dogs
must be leashed and cleaned up
after. Multiple dogs may be allowed.

Quality Inn
750 Cobb Place
Kennesaw, GA
770-419-1530 (877-424-6423)
Dogs of all sizes are allowed. Dogs
are allowed for a pet fee of $15.00
per pet per night. Two dogs are
allowed per room.

Red Roof Inn Atlanta - Kennesaw
520 Roberts Court Northwest
Kennesaw, GA
770-429-0323 (800-RED-ROOF)
One well-behaved family pet per
room. Guest must notify front desk
upon arrival. Guest is liable for any
damages. In consideration of all
guests, pets must never be left
unattended in the guest rooms.

Residence Inn Atlanta
Kennesaw/Town Center
3443 George Busbee Drive NW
Kennesaw, GA
770-218-1018 (888-236-2427)
Located only a few miles to
downtown, this inn offers a
convenient location to business,
shopping, dining, and entertainment
areas, plus they have a number of
in-house amenities that include a
daily buffet breakfast, and an
outdoor pool and spa. Dogs are
allowed for an additional one time
pet fee of $100. 2 dogs may be
allowed.

TownePlace Suites Atlanta
Kennesaw
1074 Cobb Place Blvd NW
Kennesaw, GA
770-794-8282 (800-257-3000)
Besides offering a number of in-
house amenities for all level of
travelers, this all suite inn also
offers a convenient location to
business, shopping, dining,
entertainment areas, and
Kennesaw State University. Dogs
up to 50 pounds are allowed for an
additional one time fee of $75 per
room. 2 dogs may be allowed.

Travelodge Atlanta North Kennesaw
1460 George Busbee Parkway NW
Kennesaw, GA
770-590-0519 (800-578-7878)
Dogs of all sizes are allowed. Dogs
are allowed for a pet fee.

Comfort Inn Kingsland
111 Robert L. Edenfield Dr.
Kingsland, GA
912-729-6979 (877-424-6423)
Dogs of all sizes are allowed. Dogs
are allowed for a pet fee of
$10.00/pet per pet per night.

Days Inn Kingsland
1224 Boone Ave Ext
Kingsland, GA
912-576-7958 (800-329-7466)
Dogs of all sizes are allowed. Dogs
are allowed for a nightly pet fee.

Econo Lodge Cumberland
1135 E. King Ave.
Kingsland, GA
912-673-7336 (877-424-6423)
Dogs of all sizes are allowed. Dogs
are allowed for a pet fee of $5.00
per pet per night.

Quality Inn & Suites
1311 E. King Ave
Kingsland, GA

912-729-5454 (877-424-6423)
Dogs of all sizes are allowed. Dogs
are allowed for a pet fee of $10.00
per pet per night.

Red Roof Inn
1363 Hwy. 40 E
Kingsland, GA
912-729-1130
redroof.com
Dogs of all sizes are allowed. There
are no additional pet fees.

Super 8 Kingsland
120 Robert L Edenfield Dr
Kingsland, GA
912-729-6888 (800-800-8000)
Dogs of all sizes are allowed. Dogs
are allowed for a pet fee of $10.00
per pet per night.

Days Inn La Grange
2606 Whitesville Rd
La Grange, GA
706-882-8881 (800-329-7466)
Dogs of all sizes are allowed. Dogs
are allowed for a pet fee.

Days Inn La Fayette
2209 North Main Street
LaFayette, GA
706-639-9362 (800-329-7466)
Dogs of all sizes are allowed. Dogs
are allowed for a pet fee.

Baymont Inn & Suites Lagrange
107 Hoffman Drive
Lagrange, GA
706-885-9002 (877-229-6668)
Dogs of all sizes are allowed. Dogs
are allowed for a pet fee of $10.00
per pet per night.

Days Inn /Valdosta Lake Park
4913 Timber Drive
Lake Park, GA
229-559-0229 (800-329-7466)
Dogs are welcome at this hotel.

Quality Inn
1198 Lakes Blvd
Lake Park, GA
229-559-5181 (877-424-6423)
Dogs of all sizes are allowed.

Super 8 Valdosta Area Lake Park
4907 Timber Drive
Lake Park, GA
229-559-8111 (800-800-8000)
Dogs are welcome at this hotel.

Best Western Regency Inn & Suites
13705 Jones Street
Lavonia, GA
706-356-4000 (800-780-7234)
Dogs are welcome at this hotel.

Dog-Friendly Lodging - Please always call ahead to make sure an establishment is still dog-friendly.

Super 8 Lavonia
14227 Jones St.
Lavonia, GA
706-356-8848 (800-800-8000)
Dogs of all sizes are allowed. Dogs are allowed for a pet fee of $15.00 per pet per night.

Days Inn Lawrenceville
731 Duluth Hwy
Lawrenceville, GA
770-995-7782 (800-329-7466)
Dogs of all sizes are allowed. Dogs are allowed for a pet fee.

Extended Stay America Atlanta - Lawrenceville
474 W. Pike St.
Lawrenceville, GA
770-962-5660 (800-804-3724)
One dog is allowed per suite. There is a $25 per night additional pet fee up to $150 for an entire stay.

Knights Inn Lenox
33 Kinard Bridge Rd
Lenox, GA
229-546-4223 (800-843-5644)
Dogs are welcome at this hotel. There is an additional pet fee per stay.

Motel 6 - Atlanta Lithia Springs
920 Bob Arnold Blvd
Lithia Springs, GA
678-945-0606 (800-466 8356)
This motel welcomes your pets to stay with you.

Motel 6 - Atlanta East Panola Rd
2859 Panola Rd
Lithonia, GA
 (800-466-8356)
This motel welcomes your pets to stay with you.

Red Roof Inn Lithonia
5400 Fairington Rd
Lithonia, GA
770-322-1400 (800-RED-ROOF)
One well-behaved family pet per room. Guest must notify front desk upon arrival. Guest is liable for any damages. In consideration of all guests, pets must never be left unattended in the guest rooms.

Locust Grove Red Roof Inn & Suites
4840 Bill Gardner Parkway
Locust Grove, GA
678-583-0004 (800-RED-ROOF)
One well-behaved family pet per room. Guest must notify front desk upon arrival. Guest is liable for any damages. In consideration of all guests, pets must never be left unattended in the guest rooms.

Super 8 Locust Grove
4605 Bill Gardners Pkwy I-75 E
Locust Grove, GA
770-957-2936 (800-800-8000)
Dogs are welcome at this hotel.

Baymont Inn And Suites / Plantation Dr Macon
At Zebulon Road
Macon, GA
478-474-8004 (877-229-6668)
Dogs of all sizes are allowed. Dogs are allowed for a pet fee of $15.00 per pet per night.

Baymont Inn And Suites / Riverside Drive Macon
3680 Riverside Drive
Macon, GA
478-474-4989 (877-229-6668)
Dogs are welcome at this hotel.

Best Western Riverside Inn
2400 Riverside Drive
Macon, GA
478-743-6311 (800-780-7234)
Dogs of all sizes are allowed. Dogs are allowed for a pet fee.

Candlewood Suites Macon
3957 Riverplace Dr
Macon, GA
478-254-3530 (877-270-6405)
Dogs up to 80 pounds are allowed. Pets allowed with an additional pet fee. Up to $75 for 1-6 nights and up to $150 for 7+ nights. A pet agreement must be signed at check-in.

Days Inn West Macon
6000 Harrison Road
Macon, GA
478-784-1000 (800-329-7466)
Dogs of all sizes are allowed. Dogs are allowed for a nightly pet fee.

Days Inn East Macon
2856 Jeffersonville Road
Macon, GA
478-755-9091 (800-329-7466)
Dogs of all sizes are allowed. Dogs are allowed for a pet fee of $10.00 per pet per night.

Econo Lodge
4951 Romeiser Dr.
Macon, GA
478-474-1661 (877-424-6423)
Dogs of all sizes are allowed. Dogs are allowed for a pet fee of $5.00 per pet per night.

Howard Johnson Inn Macon
4173 Cavalier Drive
Macon, GA

478-474-8800 (800-446-4656)
Dogs are welcome at this hotel.

La Quinta Inn & Suites Macon
3944 River Place Dr.
Macon, GA
478-475-0206 (800-531-5900)
Housetrained dogs of all sizes are allowed. There are no additional pet fees. A contact number must be left with the front desk if your pet is in the room alone. Dogs must be leashed, cleaned up after, and crated or removed for housekeeping. Multiple dogs may be allowed.

Motel 6 - Macon I-475
4991 Harrison Rd
Macon, GA
478-474-2870 (800-466-8356)
This motel welcomes your pets to stay with you.

Motel 6 - Macon I-75
2690 Riverside Dr
Macon, GA
478-746-8855 (800-466-8356)
This motel welcomes your pets to stay with you.

Quality Inn
4630 Chambers Rd.
Macon, GA
478-781-7000 (877-424-6423)
Dogs of all sizes are allowed. Dogs are allowed for a pet fee of $10.00 per pet per night.

Ramada Macon
4755 Chambers Rd
Macon, GA
478-788-0120 (800-272-6232)
Dogs are welcome at this hotel.

Ramada Plaza Macon
108 First Street
Macon, GA
478-746-1461 (800-272-6232)
Dogs of all sizes are allowed. Dogs are allowed for a pet fee.

Red Roof Inn Macon
3950 River Place Drive
Macon, GA
478-477-7477 (800-RED-ROOF)
One well-behaved family pet per room. Guest must notify front desk upon arrival. Guest is liable for any damages. In consideration of all guests, pets must never be left unattended in the guest rooms.

Residence Inn Macon
3900 Sheraton Drive
Macon, GA
478-475-4280 (800-331-3131)
Located in what has become known

as the Cherry Blossom Capitol of the World, this hotel provides a convenient location to historical, cultural, and entertainment districts, plus they also offer a number of in-house amenities, including a daily buffet breakfast and complementary evening receptions Monday to Thursday. Dogs are allowed for an additional one time pet fee of $100 per room. Multiple dogs may be allowed.

Rodeway Inn
4999 Eisenhower Pkwy.
Macon, GA
478-781-4343 (877-424-6423)
Dogs of all sizes are allowed. Dogs are allowed for a pet fee of $5.00 per pet per stay.

Super 8 Macon
107 Holiday Drive N
Macon, GA
478-471-8660 (800-800-8000)
Dogs of all sizes are allowed. Dogs are allowed for a pet fee.

Super 8 West Macon
6009 Harrison Rd
Macon, GA
478-788-8800 (800-800-8000)
Dogs are welcome at this hotel.

Travelodge I-475 Macon
5000 Harrison Road
Macon, GA
478-471-6116 (800-578-7878)
Dogs are welcome at this hotel.

Red Roof Inn Madison, GA
2080 Eatonton Road
Madison, GA
706-342-3433 (800-RED-ROOF)
One well-behaved family pet per room. Guest must notify front desk upon arrival. Guest is liable for any damages. In consideration of all guests, pets must never be left unattended in the guest rooms.

Days Inn Warm Spring Manchester
2546 Roosevelt Hwy
Manchester, GA
706-846-1247 (800-329-7466)
Dogs are welcome at this hotel.

Comfort Inn
2100 Northwest Pkwy.
Marietta, GA
770-952-3000 (877-424-6423)
Dogs of all sizes are allowed.

Crowne Plaza Hotel Atlanta-Marietta
1775 Parkway Place SE
Marietta, GA
770-428-4400 (877-270-6405)

Dogs are welcome at this hotel.

Days Inn Marietta
753 N. Marietta Parkway
Marietta, GA
678-797-0233 (800-329-7466)
Dogs of all sizes are allowed. Dogs are allowed for a pet fee of $15.00 per pet per night.

Extended Stay America Atlanta - Marietta - Windy Hill
1967 Leland Dr.
Marietta, GA
770-690-9477 (800-804-3724)
One dog is allowed per suite. There is a $25 per night additional pet fee up to $150 for an entire stay.

Homestead Studio Suites Atlanta - Marietta - Powers Ferry
2239 Powers Ferry Rd.
Marietta, GA
770-303-0043 (800-804-3724)
One dog is allowed per suite. There is a $25 per night additional pet fee up to $150 for an entire stay.

Howard Johnson Inn Marietta
2375 Delk Road
Marietta, GA
770-951-1144 (800-446-4656)
Dogs of all sizes are allowed. Dogs are allowed for a pet fee of $10.00 per pet per night.

La Quinta Inn Atlanta Marietta
2170 Delk Rd.
Marietta, GA
770-951-0026 (800-531-5900)
Dogs of all sizes are allowed. There are no additional pet fees. Dogs must be leashed and cleaned up after. Multiple dogs may be allowed.

Motel 6 - Atlanta Northwest Marietta
2360 Delk Rd
Marietta, GA
770-952-8161 (800-466-8356)
This motel welcomes your pets to stay with you.

Ramada Limited Suites - Marietta
630 Franklin Rd
Marietta, GA
770-919-7878 (800-272-6232)
Dogs of all sizes are allowed. Dogs are allowed for a pet fee.

Studio 6 - Atlanta Marietta
2360 Delk Rd
Marietta, GA
770-952-2395 (800-466-8356)
Your pets are welcome to stay here with you for a pet fee of $10 per day up to $50 for an entire stay.

Super 8 /West/Atl Area Marietta
610 Franklin Rd
Marietta, GA
770-919-2340 (800-800-8000)
Dogs are welcome at this hotel.

Comfort Inn
80 SR 81 W.
McDonough, GA
770-954-9110 (877-424-6423)
Dogs of all sizes are allowed. Dogs are allowed for a pet fee of $10.00 per pet per night.

Days Inn McDonough
744 Hwy 155 S
McDonough, GA
770-957-5261 (800-329-7466)
Dogs of all sizes are allowed. Dogs are allowed for a nightly pet fee.

Econo Lodge
1279 Hwy. 20 W.
McDonough, GA
770-957-2651 (877-424-6423)
Dogs of all sizes are allowed. Dogs are allowed for a pet fee of $10.00 per pet per night.

Quality Inn & Suites Conference Center
930 Highway 155 South
McDonough, GA
770-957-5291 (877-424-6423)
Dogs of all sizes are allowed. Dogs are allowed for a pet fee of $10.00 per pet per night.

Motel 6 - Mcdonough, Ga
1170 Hampton Road
Mcdonough, GA
770-957-2458 (800-466-8356)
This motel welcomes your pets to stay with you.

Days Inn Milledgeville
2551 N Columbia Street
Milledgeville, GA
478-453-8471 (800-329-7466)
Dogs of all sizes are allowed. Dogs are allowed for a nightly pet fee.

Traveler's Rest
318 N Dody Street
Montezuma, GA
478-472-0085
Well behaved dogs are allowed for a $10 one time fee. There can be up to 2 small to medium dogs or 1 large dog per room. 2 dogs may be allowed.

Best Western Southlake Inn
6437 Jonesboro Road
Morrow, GA
770-961-6300 (800-780-7234)
Dogs of all sizes are allowed. Dogs

are allowed for a pet fee of $10 per pet per night.

Extended Stay America Atlanta - Morrow
2265 Mt. Zion Pkwy.
Morrow, GA
770-472-0727 (800-804-3724)
One dog is allowed per suite. There is a $25 per night additional pet fee up to $150 for an entire stay.

Quality Inn & Suites Southlake
6597 Jonesboro Rd.
Morrow, GA
770-960-1957 (877-424-6423)
Dogs of all sizes are allowed. Dogs are allowed for a pet fee of $10.00 per pet per night.

Red Roof Inn Atlanta South
1348 Southlake Plaza Drive
Morrow, GA
770-968-1483 (800-RED-ROOF)
One well-behaved family pet per room. Guest must notify front desk upon arrival. Guest is liable for any damages. In consideration of all guests, pets must never be left unattended in the guest rooms.

Sleep Inn
2185 Mt. Zion Pkwy.
Morrow, GA
770-472-9800 (877-424-6423)
Dogs of all sizes are allowed. Dogs are allowed for a pet fee of $10.00 per pet per night.

South Drury Inn & Suites
6520 S. Lee Street
Morrow, GA
770-960-0500 (800-378-7946)
Dogs of all sizes are allowed for no additional pet fee with a credit card on file, and there is a pet agreement to sign at check in.

Days Inn Newnan
1344 South Hwy 29
Newnan, GA
770-253-8550 (800-329-7466)
Dogs of all sizes are allowed. Dogs are allowed for a nightly pet fee.

Howard Johnson Inn GA Newnan
1310 Hwy 29 South
Newnan, GA
770-683-1499 (800-446-4656)
Dogs of all sizes are allowed. Dogs are allowed for a pet fee of $15.00 per pet per night.

La Quinta Inn Newnan
600 Bullsboro Drive
Newnan, GA
770-502-8430 (800-531-5900)

Dogs of all sizes are allowed. There are no additional pet fees. There is a pet waiver to sign at check in. Dogs are not allowed in dining areas, and they may not be left unattended in the room. Dogs must be leashed and cleaned up after. Multiple dogs may be allowed.

Motel 6 - Newnan, Ga
40 Parkway North
Newnan, GA
770-251-4580 (800-466-8356)
This motel welcomes your pets to stay with you.

Travelodge Newnan
1344 Hwy 29 South Suite B
Newnan, GA
678-854-0501 (800-578-7878)
Dogs of all sizes are allowed. Dogs are allowed for a pet fee.

Extended Stay America Atlanta - Jimmy Carter Blvd.
6295 Jimmy Carter Blvd.
Norcross, GA
770-446-9245 (800-804-3724)
One dog is allowed per suite. There is a $25 per night additional pet fee up to $150 for an entire stay.

Extended Stay America Atlanta - Norcross
200 Lawrenceville St.
Norcross, GA
770-729-8100 (800-804-3724)
One dog is allowed per suite. There is a $25 per night additional pet fee up to $150 for an entire stay.

Homestead Studio Suites Atlanta - Peachtree Corners
7049 Jimmy Carter Blvd.
Norcross, GA
770-449-9966 (800-804-3724)
One dog is allowed per suite. There is a $25 per night additional pet fee up to $150 for an entire stay.

Knights Inn Norcross
5122 Brook Hollow Parkway
Norcross, GA
770-446-5490 (800-843-5644)
Dogs are welcome at this hotel.

La Quinta Inn Norcross
5945 Oakbrook Parkway
Norcross, GA
770-368-9400 (800-531-5900)
Dogs of all sizes are allowed. There is a $10 refundable deposit per room. There is a pet waiver to sign at check in. Dogs may not be left unattended, and they must be quiet, well behaved, leashed, and cleaned up after. Multiple dogs may be

allowed.

Motel 6 - Atlanta Northeast Norcross
6015 Oakbrook Parkway
Norcross, GA
770-446-2311 (800-466-8356)
This motel welcomes your pets to stay with you.

Motel 6 - Norcross
5395 Peachtree In Bvd Nw
Norcross, GA
770-446-2882 (800-466-8356)
This motel welcomes your pets to stay with you.

Northeast Drury Inn & Suites
5655 Jimmy Carter Blvd
Norcross, GA
770-729-0060 (800-378-7946)
Dogs up to 70 pounds are allowed for no additional pet fee with a credit card on file, and there is a pet agreement to sign at check in.

Red Roof Inn Atlanta - Indian Trail
5171 Brook Hallow Parkway
Norcross, GA
770-448-8944 (800-RED-ROOF)
One well-behaved family pet per room. Guest must notify front desk upon arrival. Guest is liable for any damages. In consideration of all guests, pets must never be left unattended in the guest rooms.

Residence Inn Atlanta Norcross/Peachtree Corners
5500 Triangle Drive
Norcross, GA
770-447-1714 (888-236-2427)
This all suite inn offers amenities for all level of travelers, including a convenient location to a number of area attractions, a daily buffet breakfast, an evening reception, and a grocery shopping service. Dogs are allowed for an additional one time pet fee of $100. Known aggressive breed dogs are not allowed. 2 dogs may be allowed.

Super 8 /I-85 Atlanta Norcross
5150 Willow Oak Trail
Norcross, GA
770-931-5353 (800-800-8000)
Dogs of all sizes are allowed. Dogs are allowed for a pet fee of $15.00 per pet per night.

TownePlace Suites Atlanta Norcross/Peachtree Corners
6640 Bay Circle
Norcross, GA
770-447-8446 (800-257-3000)
Located in a quiet residential neighborhood near downtown, this all

suite inn offers a number of on-site amenities plus a convenient location to business, shopping, dining, and entertainment areas. Dogs are allowed for an additional one time fee of $75 per room. 2 dogs may be allowed.

Wingate by Wyndham Atlanta GA Norcross
5800 Peachtree Industrial Blvd
Norcross, GA
770-263-2020 (800-228-1000)
Dogs are welcome at this hotel.

Country Inns & Suites by Carlson
4535 Oakwood Road
Oakwood, GA
770-535-8080
Dogs of all sizes are allowed. There is a $20 per night per room additional pet fee.

Best Western Peachtree City Inn/Suites
976 Crosstown Road
Peachtree City, GA
770-632-9700 (800-780-7234)
Dogs of all sizes are allowed. Dogs are allowed for a pet fee of $25.00 per pet per night.

Holiday Inn Hotel & Suites Peachtree City
203 Newgate Road
Peachtree City, GA
770-487-4646 (877-270-6405)
Dogs of all sizes are allowed. Dogs are allowed for a pet fee of $20 per pet per night.

America's Best Inn - Perry
110 Perimeter Road
Perry, GA
478-987-4454
americasbestinnperry.com
There is a $10 per night additional pet fee for one pet and $15 per night for two pets.

Holiday Inn Perry
200 Valley Dr
Perry, GA
478-987-3313 (877-270-6405)
Dogs are welcome at this hotel.

Howard Johnson Inn GA Perry
100 Marketplace Drive
Perry, GA
478-987-8400 (800-446-4656)
Dogs of all sizes are allowed. Dogs are allowed for a pet fee of $10.00 per pet per night.

Knights Inn Perry
704 Mason Terrace
Perry, GA

478-987-1515 (800-843-5644)
Dogs are welcome at this hotel.

New Perry Hotel & Motel
800 Main Street
Perry, GA
478-987-1000
Dogs are allowed for a $10 per night per pet fee for small dogs, and a $15 per night per pet fee for large dogs. There is a pet policy to sign at check in. 2 dogs may be allowed.

Rodeway Inn
1504 Sam Nunn Boulevard
Perry, GA
478-987-1345 (877-424-6423)
Dogs of all sizes are allowed.

Super 8 GA Perry
102 Plaza Drive
Perry, GA
478-987-0999 (800-800-8000)
Dogs of all sizes are allowed. Dogs are allowed for a pet fee of $10.00 per pet per night.

White Columns Motel
524 S Main Avenue/Hwy 27
Pine Mountain, GA
706-663-2312 (800-722-5083)
whitecolumnsmotel.com/
Offering meticulously landscaped grounds and a number of amenities, this motel is also in a central location to a number of restaurants, shops, historic sites, and several recreational activities. Small dogs are allowed for an additional fee of $5 per night per pet, and large dogs are $10 per night per pet. Dogs must be leashed and under their owner's control at all times. 2 dogs may be allowed.

Best Western Bradbury Suites
155 Bourne Avenue
Pooler, GA
912-330-0330 (800-780-7234)
Dogs are welcome at this hotel.

Econo Lodge
500 E. US 80
Pooler, GA
912-748-4124 (888-econo-50)
econolodge-savannah.com
There is a $10 additional pet fee. Pets are allowed in the pet rooms on the ground floor. The hotel offers free cable w/HBO, a continental breakfast, free local calls, an outdoor pool, and in-room coffee. The hotel is located 11 miles from downtown Savannah near Interstate 95.

Econo Lodge

500 E. US 80
Pooler, GA
912-748-4124 (877-424-6423)
Dogs of all sizes are allowed. Dogs are allowed for a pet fee of $20.00 per pet per night. Two dogs are allowed per room.

Holiday Inn Hotel & Suites Savannah-Pooler
103 San Drive
Pooler, GA
912-330-5100 (877-270-6405)
Dogs up to 50 pounds are allowed. Dogs are allowed for a pet fee.

Ramada Limited - Savannah Airport
1016 E. Hwy 80
Pooler, GA
912-748-5242 (800-272-6232)
Dogs are welcome at this hotel.

Savannah Airport Red Roof Inn & Suites
20 Mill Creek Circle
Pooler, GA
912-748-4050 (800-RED-ROOF)
One well-behaved family pet per room. Guest must notify front desk upon arrival. Guest is liable for any damages. In consideration of all guests, pets must never be left unattended in the guest rooms.

Travelodge Suites Savannah Pooler
130 Continental Blvd
Pooler, GA
912-748-6363 (800-578-7878)
Dogs are welcome at this hotel.

Comfort Suites Savannah North
115 Traveler's Way
Port Wentworth, GA
912-965-1445 (877-424-6423)
Dogs of all sizes are allowed. Dogs are allowed for a pet fee of $20.00 per pet per stay.

Ramada Limited /Savannah Area
Port Wentworth
110 Traveler's Way
Port Wentworth, GA
912-964-6060 (800-272-6232)
Dogs of all sizes are allowed. Dogs are allowed for a pet fee of $10.00 per pet per night.

Super 8 Savannah Area Port Wentworth
7200 Hwy 21 North
Port Wentworth, GA
912-965-9393 (800-800-8000)
Dogs are welcome at this hotel.

Comfort Suites Savannah South
4601 US Highway 17
Richmond Hill, GA

912-756-6668 (877-424-6423)
Dogs up to 50 pounds are allowed.
Dogs are allowed for a pet fee of
$10.00 per pet per night.

Days Inn /Savannah Richmond Hill
3926 Hwy 17
Richmond Hill, GA
912-756-3371 (800-329-7466)
Dogs of all sizes are allowed. Dogs
are allowed for a nightly pet fee.

Motel 6 - Savannah Richmond Hill
4071 Us 17
Richmond Hill, GA
912-756-3543 (800-466-8356)
This motel welcomes your pets to
stay with you.

Quality Inn
4300 Coastal Hwy US 17 South
Richmond Hill, GA
912-756-3351 (877-424-6423)
Dogs of all sizes are allowed. Dogs
are allowed for a pet fee of $20 per
pet per night.

Travelodge Richmond Hill
4120 Highway 17
Richmond Hill, GA
912-756-3325 (800-578-7878)
Dogs are welcome at this hotel.

Days Inn Rincon
582 Columbia Avenue
Rincon, GA
912-826-6966 (800-329-7466)
Dogs are welcome at this hotel.

Days Inn Chattanooga- GA Ringgold
5435 Alabama Highway
Ringgold, GA
706-965-5730 (800-329-7466)
Dogs are welcome at this hotel.

Red Roof Inn Ringgold
5437 Alabama Highway
Ringgold, GA
706-965-4100 (800-RED-ROOF)
One well-behaved family pet per
room. Guest must notify front desk
upon arrival. Guest is liable for any
damages. In consideration of all
guests, pets must never be left
unattended in the guest rooms.

Super 8 Ringgold
5400 Alabama Hwy
Ringgold, GA
706-965-7080 (800-800-8000)
Dogs of all sizes are allowed. Dogs
are allowed for a pet fee of $12.00
per pet per night.

Sleep Inn & Suites
6286 Georgia Hwy 85
Riverdale, GA

678-216-1300 (877-424-6423)
Dogs up to 75 pounds are allowed.
Dogs are allowed for a pet fee of
$25.00 per pet per stay. Two dogs
are allowed per room.

Day Inn Rockmart
105 G T M Parkway
Rockmart, GA
770-684-9955 (800-329-7466)
Dogs are welcome at this hotel.

Howard Johnson Express Inn Rome
1610 Martha Berry Blvd NW
Rome, GA
706-291-1994 (800-446-4656)
Dogs of all sizes are allowed. Dogs
are allowed for a pet fee of $10.00
per pet per night.

Motel 6 - Rome, Ga
390 Dodd Blvd Se
Rome, GA
706-234-8182 (800-466-8356)
This motel welcomes your pets to
stay with you.

Doubletree Hotel
1075 Holcomb Bridge Road
Roswell, GA
770-992-9600 (800-222-TREE
(8733))
This upscale hotel offers a number
of on site amenities for all level of
travelers, plus a convenient location
to historical, business, shopping,
dining, and recreation areas. Dogs
are allowed for an additional one
time pet fee of $75 per room.
Multiple dogs may be allowed.

Studio 6 - Atlanta Roswell
9955 Old Dogwood Rd
Roswell, GA
770-992-9449 (800-466-8356)
Your pets are welcome to stay here
with you for a pet fee of $10 per day
up to $50 for an entire stay.

Days Inn Sandersville
128 Commerce St
Sandersville, GA
478-553-0393 (800-329-7466)
Dogs are welcome at this hotel.

Best Western Promenade Hotel in
the Historic District
412 W Bay Street
Savannah, GA
912-233-1011 (800-780-7234)
Dogs of all sizes are allowed. Dogs
are allowed for a pet fee.

Candlewood Suites Savannah
Airport
50 Stephen S Green Dr.
Savannah, GA

912-966-9644 (877-270-6405)
Dogs up to 80 pounds are allowed.
Pets allowed with an additional pet
fee. Up to $75 for 1-6 nights and up
to $150 for 7+ nights. A pet
agreement must be signed at check-
in.

Clubhouse Inn and Suites
6800 Abercorn/H 204
Savannah, GA
912-356-1234 (800-CLUB-INN (258-
2466))
clubhouseinn.com
Convenient location, a free breakfast
buffet, and a seasonal pool are just
some of the popularities of this inn.
Dogs are allowed for an additional
fee of $10 per night per pet. Dogs
must be leashed and under owner's
care. 2 dogs may be allowed.

Days Inn - Abercorn Southside
Savannah
11750 Abercorn Street
Savannah, GA
912-927-7720 (800-329-7466)
Dogs are welcome at this hotel.

Days Inn Airport Savannah
2500 Dean Forest Road
Savannah, GA
912-966-5000 (800-329-7466)
Dogs are welcome at this hotel.

Days Inn and Suites Gateway/I-95
And 204 Savannah
6 Gateway Boulevard East
Savannah, GA
912-925-6666 (800-329-7466)
Dogs of all sizes are allowed. Dogs
are allowed for a pet fee of $10.00
per pet per night.

East Bay Inn
225 E Bay Street/H 25
Savannah, GA
912-0238-1225 (800-500-1225)
eastbayinn.com/
Offering a blend of old and new
world, this beautiful inn also has a
restaurant on site, a wine and hors d'
oeuvres reception each evening, and
a number of comforts for the
business or leisure traveler. Dogs
are allowed for an additional one
time pet fee of $35 per room. Dogs
are not allowed in the common
areas, and a contact number must
be left with the front desk if there is a
pet alone in the room. Dogs must be
leashed and under owner's care.
Multiple dogs may be allowed.

Econo Lodge Savannah South
3 Gateway Blvd S
Savannah, GA

912-925-2770 (877-424-6423)
Dogs up to 50 pounds are allowed.
Dogs are allowed for a pet fee of
$10.00/ per pet per night.

Extended Stay America Savannah -
Midtown
5511 Abercorn St.
Savannah, GA
912-692-0076 (800-804-3724)
One dog is allowed per suite. There
is a $25 per night additional pet fee
up to $150 for an entire stay.

Hilton Hotel
15 E Liberty Street
Savannah, GA
912-232-9000 (800-HILTONS (445-
8667))
This upscale hotel offers numerous
on site amenities for business and
leisure travelers, plus a convenient
location to historic, shopping, dining,
and entertainment areas. Dogs up to
75 pounds are allowed for an
additional one time pet fee of $50 per
room. 2 dogs may be allowed.

Joan's on Joan
17 W Jones Street
Savannah, GA
912-234-3863 (888-989-9806)
This stately Victorian inn gives the
feel of a different era, but with all the
modern conveniences. One medium
to large dog or 2 very little dogs are
allowed per room for an additional
one time pet fee of $50 per room.
Dogs must be quiet, well mannered,
leashed and under owners care.

Knights Inn Savannah
1 Fort Argyle Road
Savannah, GA
912-925-2640 (800-843-5644)
Dogs of all sizes are allowed. Dogs
are allowed for a nightly pet fee.

La Quinta Inn Savannah I-95
6 Gateway Blvd. South
Savannah, GA
912-925-9505 (800-531-5900)
Dogs of all sizes are allowed. There
are no additional pet fees. Dogs
must be well behaved, leashed, and
cleaned up after. Multiple dogs may
be allowed.

La Quinta Inn Savannah Midtown
6805 Abercorn St.
Savannah, GA
912-355-3004 (800-531-5900)
Dogs of all sizes are allowed. There
are no additional pet fees; however,
a credit card must be on file. Dogs
must be leashed and cleaned up
after. A contact number must be left

with the front desk if the pet is in the
room alone. Multiple dogs may be
allowed.

La Quinta Inn Savannah Southside
8484 Abercorn Street
Savannah, GA
912-927-7660 (800-531-5900)
Dogs of all sizes are allowed. There
are no additional pet fees. Dogs
may only be left in the room alone if
they will be quiet, well behaved, and
you have informed the front desk.
Dogs must be kept leashed.
Multiple dogs may be allowed.

Olde Harbour Inn
508 E Factors Walk
Savannah, GA
912-234-4100 (800-553-6533)
oldeharbourinn.com/
In addition to being a beautiful
riverfront inn with large suites that
overlook the river and plenty of
modern conveniences, they are
also centrally located to numerous
recreational activities, a monthly
arts/crafts festival each month and
various annual celebrations on the
waterfront, shopping, and dining.
One medium to large dog or 2 very
little dogs are allowed per room for
an additional one time pet fee of
$35 per room; they must be
declared at the time of reservations.
Dogs must be quiet, well mannered,
leashed and under owners care.

Quality Inn Midtown
7100 Abercorn Street
Savannah, GA
912-352-7100 (877-424-6423)
Dogs up to 50 pounds are allowed.
Dogs are allowed for a pet fee of
$50.00 per pet per stay. Two dogs
are allowed per room.

Ramada I 95 Gateway Savannah
17007 Abercorn Street
Savannah, GA
912-925-1212 (800-272-6232)
Dogs of all sizes are allowed. Dogs
are allowed for a pet fee.

Red Roof Inn Savannah - Midtown
201 Stephenson Avenue
Savannah, GA
912-355-4100 (800-RED-ROOF)
One well-behaved family pet per
room. Guest must notify front desk
upon arrival. Guest is liable for any
damages. In consideration of all
guests, pets must never be left
unattended in the guest rooms.

Residence Inn Savannah Midtown
5710 White Bluff Road

Savannah, GA
912-356-3266 (800-331-3131)
Offering a convenient location to
business, historic, shopping, dining,
and entertainment areas, this all
suite hotel also offers a number of in-
house amenities, including a daily
buffet breakfast and evening socials
Monday to Thursday. Dogs are
allowed for an additional one time
pet fee of $100 per room. 2 dogs
may be allowed.

Rodeway Inn
3 Gateway Blvd South
Savannah, GA
912-920-1900 (877-424-6423)
Dogs of all sizes are allowed. Dogs
are allowed for a pet fee of $5.00 per
pet per night. Two dogs are allowed
per room.

Savannah Red Roof Inn & Suites
405 Al Henderson Boulevard
Savannah, GA
912-920-3535 (800-RED-ROOF)
One well-behaved family pet per
room. Guest must notify front desk
upon arrival. Guest is liable for any
damages. In consideration of all
guests, pets must never be left
unattended in the guest rooms.

Staybridge Suites Savannah Airport
One Clyde E. Martin Dr.
Savannah, GA
912-965-1551 (877-270-6405)
Dogs up to 80 pounds are allowed.
Pets allowed with an additional pet
fee. Up to $75 for 1-6 nights and up
to $150 for 7+ nights. A pet
agreement must be signed at check-
in.

Staybridge Suites Savannah Historic
District
301 East Bay Street
Savannah, GA
912-721-9000 (877-270-6405)
Dogs up to 80 pounds are allowed.
Pets allowed with an additional pet
fee. Up to $75 for 1-6 nights and up
to $150 for 7+ nights. A pet
agreement must be signed at check-
in.

Suites on Lafayette
201 East Charlton Street
Savannah, GA
912-233-7815
suitesonlafayette.com
Dogs of all sizes are allowed in these
three restored historic buildings.
There is a $45 pet fee per dog.

Super 8 Savannah
387 Canebrake Rd

Savannah, GA
912-925-6996 (800-800-8000)
Dogs of all sizes are allowed. Dogs are allowed for a pet fee of $10 per pet per night.

TownePlace Suites Savannah Airport
4 Jay R Turner Drive
Savannah, GA
912-629-7775 (800-257-3000)
This all suite inn sits central to historic, business, shopping, dining, and day/night entertainment areas, plus they also offer a number of in-house amenities for business and leisure travelers. Dogs are allowed for an additional fee of $25 per night per room up to a maximum fee of $75 per stay. 2 dogs may be allowed.

TownePlace Suites Savannah Midtown
11309 Abercorn Street
Savannah, GA
912-920-9080 (800-257-3000)
Besides offering a number of in-house amenities for all level of travelers, this all suite inn also offers a convenient location to historic, business, shopping, dining, and day/night entertainment areas. Dogs are allowed for an additional one time fee of $100 per room. Multiple dogs may be allowed.

Travelodge Savannah
7 Gateway Blvd W
Savannah, GA
912-925-2280 (800-578-7878)
Dogs of all sizes are allowed. Dogs are allowed for a pet fee of $10.00 per pet per night.

Baymont Inn & Suites Smyrna
5130 South Cobb Drive
Smyrna, GA
404-794-1600 (877-229-6668)
Dogs are welcome at this hotel.

Holiday Inn Express Atlanta/Smyrna-Cobb Galleria
2855 Spring Hill Parkway
Smyrna, GA
770-435-4990 (877-270-6405)
Dogs of all sizes are allowed. Dogs are allowed for a nightly pet fee.

Homestead Studio Suites Atlanta - Cumberland Mall
3103 Sports Ave.
Smyrna, GA
770-432-4000 (800-804-3724)
One dog is allowed per suite. There is a $25 per night additional pet fee up to $150 for an entire stay.

Knights Inn Atlanta Northwest

5230 South Cobb Drive
Smyrna, GA
404-794-3000 (800-843-5644)
Dogs are welcome at this hotel.

Red Roof Inn Atlanta - Smyrna
2200 Corporate Plaza
Smyrna, GA
770-952-6966 (800-RED-ROOF)
One well-behaved family pet per room. Guest must notify front desk upon arrival. Guest is liable for any damages. In consideration of all guests, pets must never be left unattended in the guest rooms.

Residence Inn Atlanta Cumberland
2771 Cumberland Blvd
Smyrna, GA
770-433-8877 (888-236-2427)
Located in the city's business district by the Air Force base and Lockheed-Martin, this all suite hotel offers a convenient location to business, shopping, dining, and entertainment areas, plus they have a number of in-house amenities that include a daily buffet breakfast, a 24 hour market, and evening socials. Dogs are allowed for an additional one time pet fee of $100 per room. Multiple dogs may be allowed.

Beachview House
537 Beachview Drive
St Simons Island, GA
603-524-4000
beachviewhouse.com/
This historic 1892 House on Cumberland Island offers a fully fenced in yard, 3 bedrooms, 4 baths and sleeps up to 9. Pets welcome with prior approval.

Days Inn Statesboro
461 South Main Street
Statesboro, GA
912-764-5666 (800-329-7466)
Dogs of all sizes are allowed. Dogs are allowed for a pet fee of $10.00 per pet per night.

Howard Johnson Inn - GA Statesboro
316 South Main Street
Statesboro, GA
912-489-2626 (800-446-4656)
Dogs of all sizes are allowed. Dogs are allowed for a pet fee of $10.00 per pet per night.

Atlanta Southeast
637 St Rt 138 West
Stockbridge, GA
678-782-4100 (800-RED-ROOF)
One well-behaved family pet per room. Guest must notify front desk

upon arrival. Guest is liable for any damages. In consideration of all guests, pets must never be left unattended in the guest rooms.

Baymont Inn & Suites Stockbridge
100 North Park Court
Stockbridge, GA
770-507-6500 (877-229-6668)
Dogs of all sizes are allowed. Dogs are allowed for a pet fee of $10 per pet per night.

Motel 6 - Atlanta South Stockbridge
7233 Davidson Pkwy
Stockbridge, GA
770-389-1142 (800-466-8356)
This motel welcomes your pets to stay with you.

Best Western Stone Mountain
1595 E Park Place Boulevard
Stone Mountain, GA
770-465-1022 (800-780-7234)
Dogs of all sizes are allowed. Dogs are allowed for a pet fee of $25.00 per pet per night.

Best Western Gwinnett Inn
77 Gwinco Boulevard
Suwanee, GA
770-271-5559 (800-780-7234)
Dogs of all sizes are allowed. Dogs are allowed for a pet fee of $15.00 per pet per night.

Comfort Inn
2945-A Lawrenceville Suwanee
Suwanee, GA
770-945-1608 (877-424-6423)
Dogs of all sizes are allowed. Dogs are allowed for a pet fee of $25.00 per pet per stay.

Motel 6 - Suwanee
3103 Lawrenceville Suwan
Suwanee, GA
770-945-8372 (800-466-8356)
This motel welcomes your pets to stay with you.

Days Inn Sylvester
909 Franklin St
Sylvester, GA
229-776-9700 (800-329-7466)
Dogs are welcome at this hotel.

Days Inn Thomaston
1211 Hwy 19 N.
Thomaston, GA
706-648-9260 (800-329-7466)
Dogs of all sizes are allowed. Dogs are allowed for a nightly pet fee.

Econo Lodge
1207 Highway 19 North
Thomaston, GA

706-648-2900 (877-424-6423)
Dogs of all sizes are allowed. Dogs are allowed for a pet fee of $10.00 per pet per night.

Comfort Inn
14866 US HWY 19 South
Thomasville, GA
229-228-5555 (877-424-6423)
Dogs of all sizes are allowed.

Days Inn Thomasville
15375 US-19
Thomasville, GA
229-226-6025 (800-329-7466)
Dogs are welcome at this hotel.

Knights Inn Thomson
2658 Cobbham Road I-20
Thomson, GA
706-595-2262 (800-843-5644)
Dogs are welcome at this hotel.

Days Inn Tifton
1199 Hwy 82 West
Tifton, GA
229-382-8505 (800-329-7466)
Dogs of all sizes are allowed. Dogs are allowed for a pet fee of $10.00 per pet per night.

Econo Lodge
1025 West 2nd St
Tifton, GA
229-382-0280 (877-424-6423)
Dogs up to 65 pounds are allowed. Dogs are allowed for a pet fee of $10.00 per pet per night. Two dogs are allowed per room.

Motel 6 - Tifton, Ga
579 Old Omega Rd
Tifton, GA
229-388-8777 (800-466-8356)
This motel welcomes your pets to stay with you.

Ramada Limited and Conference Center
1211 Highway 82 West
Tifton, GA
229-382-8500 (800-272-6232)
Dogs of all sizes are allowed. Dogs are allowed for a pet fee of $10 per pet per stay.

Super 8 Tifton
1022 W 2nd St
Tifton, GA
229-382-9500 (800-800-8000)
Dogs of all sizes are allowed. Dogs are allowed for a pet fee of $7.00 per pet per night.

Travelodge GA Tifton
1103 King Road
Tifton, GA

229-382-0395 (800-578-7878)
Dogs are welcome at this hotel.

Days Inn Townsend
RR4
Townsend, GA
912-832-4411 (800-329-7466)
Dogs are welcome at this hotel.

Knights Inn Townsend
Route 2 Box 2848
Townsend, GA
912-832-4444 (800-843-5644)
Dogs are welcome at this hotel. There is a $10 one time additional pet fee.

Days Inn Trenton
95 Killian Avenue
Trenton, GA
706-657-2550 (800-329-7466)
Dogs of all sizes are allowed. Dogs are allowed for a pet fee of 10 per pet per night.

Motel 6 - Atlanta Tucker Northeast
2810 Lawrenceville Hwy
Tucker, GA
770-496-1311 (800-466-8356)
This motel welcomes your pets to stay with you.

Studio 6 - Atlanta Northlake
1795 Crescent Centre Blv
Tucker, GA
770-934-4040 (800-466-8356)
Your pets are welcome to stay here with you for a pet fee of $10 per day up to $50 for an entire stay.

Tybee Island Bed and Breakfast Inn
24 Van Horne Ave
Tybee Island, GA
912-786-9255 (866-892-4667)
tybeeislandinn.com
Dogs are allowed at this B&B 5 minutes from the Tybee Island Beach. Dogs are not allowed on the beach.

Days Inn /Atlanta SW/Arpt Union City
6840 Shannon Parkway South
Union City, GA
770-306-6067 (800-329-7466)
Dogs of all sizes are allowed. Dogs are allowed for a nightly pet fee.

Econo Lodge
7410 Oakley Rd.
Union City, GA
770-964-9999 (877-424-6423)
Dogs of all sizes are allowed. Dogs are allowed for a pet fee of $5.00 per pet per night. Two dogs are allowed per room.

Motel 6 - Atlanta Airport Union City
3860 Flatshoals Rd
Union City, GA
770-969-0110 (800-466-8356)
This motel welcomes your pets to stay with you.

Days Inn North Valdosta
4598 North Valdosta Road
Valdosta, GA
229-244-4460 (800-329-7466)
Dogs are welcome at this hotel.

Days Inn--Conference Center Valdosta
1827 W Hill Ave
Valdosta, GA
229-249-8800 (800-329-7466)
Dogs of all sizes are allowed. Dogs are allowed for a pet fee of $10.00 per pet per night.

Econo Lodge
3022 James Rd.
Valdosta, GA
229-671-1511 (877-424-6423)
Dogs up to 50 pounds are allowed. Dogs are allowed for a pet fee of $25.00 per pet per stay.

Knights Inn
2110 W. Hill Ave
Valdosta, GA
229-247-2440 (800-843-5644)
Dogs of all sizes are allowed. Dogs are allowed for a pet fee of $10.00 per pet per night.

La Quinta Inn & Suites Valdosta
1800 Clubhouse Drive
Valdosta, GA
229-247-7755 (800-531-5900)
Dogs of all sizes are allowed. There are no additional pet fees. Dogs must be quiet, well behaved, leashed and cleaned up after. Dogs may not be left unattended in the room for long periods, and they are not allowed in the lobby or pool area. Multiple dogs may be allowed.

Motel 6 - Valdosta University
2003 Hill Ave
Valdosta, GA
229-333-0047 (800-466-8356)
This motel welcomes your pets to stay with you.

Quality Inn South
1902 W. Hill Ave.
Valdosta, GA
229-244-4520 (877-424-6423)
Dogs up to 50 pounds are allowed. Dogs are allowed for a pet fee of $8.00 per pet per night.

Super 8 /Conf Center Area Valdosta

1825 West Hill Avenue
Valdosta, GA
229-249-8000 (800-800-8000)
Dogs of all sizes are allowed. Dogs are allowed for a pet fee of $10 per pet per stay.

Wingate by Wyndham - Moody AFB Valdosta
2010 West Hill Avenue
Valdosta, GA
229-242-1225 (800-228-1000)
Dogs are welcome at this hotel.

Days Inn Vidalia
1503 Lyons Hwy 280 E
Vidalia, GA
912-537-9251 (800-329-7466)
Dogs of all sizes are allowed. Dogs are allowed for a pet fee of $5.00 per pet per night.

Holiday Inn Express Vidalia-Lyons Hwy
2619 E. First Street(Hwy 280 E)
Vidalia, GA
912-537-9000 (877-270-6405)
Dogs of all sizes are allowed. Dogs are allowed for a nightly pet fee.

Days Inn Villa Rica
195 Hwy 61 Connector
Villa Rica, GA
770-459-8888 (800-329-7466)
Dogs of all sizes are allowed. Dogs are allowed for a nightly pet fee.

Super 8 Villa Rica
128 HWY 61 Connector
Villa Rica, GA
770-459-8000 (800-800-8000)
Dogs are welcome at this hotel.

Best Western White House Inn
2526 White House Pkwy
Warm Springs, GA
706-655-2750 (800-780-7234)
Dogs of all sizes are allowed. Dogs are allowed for a pet fee.

Best Western Peach Inn
2739 Watson Boulevard
Warner Robins, GA
478-953-3800 (800-780-7234)
Dogs of all sizes are allowed. Dogs are allowed for a pet fee of $7.00 per pet per night.

Candlewood Suites Warner Robins/Robins Afb
110 Willie Lee Pkwy
Warner Robins, GA
478-333-6850 (877-270-6405)
Dogs up to 80 pounds are allowed. Pets allowed with an additional pet fee. Up to $75 for 1-6 nights and up to $150 for 7+ nights. A pet

agreement must be signed at check-in.

Suburban Extended Stay
2727 Watson Blvd
Warner Robins, GA
478-953-5100 (877-424-6423)
Dogs of all sizes are allowed.

Super 8 Warner Robins
105 Woodcrest Blvd.
Warner Robins, GA
478-923-8600 (800-800-8000)
Dogs of all sizes are allowed. Dogs are allowed for a pet fee of $10 per pet per night.

Lake Blackshear Resort and Golf Club
2459 H 280
West Cordele, GA
229-276-1004
Dogs of all sizes are allowed. There is a $50 (+ tax) one time fee per room and a pet policy to sign at check in. 2 dogs may be allowed.

Travelodge West Point
1870 State Route 18
West Point, GA
706-643-9922 (800-578-7878)
Dogs of all sizes are allowed. Dogs are allowed for a pet fee of $10 per pet per night.

Best Western Winder Hotel
177 W Athens Street
Winder, GA
770-868-5303 (800-780-7234)
Dogs of all sizes are allowed. Dogs are allowed for a nightly pet fee.

Hawaii

Haiku Private Home Rental
Call to Arrange.
Haiku, HI
808-575-9610
This 3 bedroom, 3 bathroom house rental is on 4 acres of landscaped grounds. Well-behaved dogs up to 50 pounds are allowed for no additional fee,,, however, there may be a higher security deposit required. Dogs must be well behaved and they are not allowed on the beds or furniture. 2 dogs may be allowed.

North Shore Vacation Rental
Call to Arrange.
Haiku, HI
307-733-3903
This 3 bedroom, 2 bathroom vacation home allows well-behaved dogs.

Bjornen's Mac Nut Farm and Vacation Rental
805 Kauhi Ula Road
Hilo, HI
808-969-7753
This large room with a king bed, a kitchenette and a private entrance is located on a 25 acre fenced property within 1 1/2 miles of Hilo. It also has a swimming pool and hot tub. Rates are $100 per day with a two day minimum. Well behaved dogs are allowed for no additional fee. Owners may be willing to pet-sit for you. Dogs must be up to date on their vaccines, be flea and tick free, and hound and human friendly. You can also contact them via email at e.bjornen@hawaiiantel.net. 2 dogs may be allowed.

Hilo Seaside Retreat Rentals
Call to Arrange.
Hilo, HI
808-961-6178
hilo-inns.com
This private home offers two private suites available for rent. The rentals are located about 10 minutes from the Hilo Airport. Well-behaved dogs are allowed.

Hilo Vacation Rental
Call to Arrange.
Hllo, HI
707-865-1200
This 3 bedroom, 2 bathroom summer vacation home rental allows well-behaved dogs for no additional pet fee.

Best Western The Plaza Hotel
3253 N Nimitz Highway
Honolulu, HI
808-836-3636 (800-780-7234)
Dogs of all sizes are allowed. Dogs are allowed for a pet fee of $10 per pet per night.

Doubletree Alana Hotel Waikiki
1956 Ala Moana Blvd
Honolulu, HI
808-941-7275 (800-222-TREE (8733))
In addition to sitting just steps from the famous Waikiki Beach, the Hawaii Convention Center, and to all that this amazing city has to offer, this hotel also offers guests a number of on-site amenities. Dogs are allowed for an additional one time pet fee of $75 per room. 2 dogs may be allowed.

The Kahala Hotel and Resort
5000 Kahala Avenue

Honolulu, HI
808-739-8888 (800-367-2525)
kahalaresort.com/
Located on a secluded beach only minuets from all that Waikiki has to offer, this luxury resort also provides a long list of amenities and on-site activities. One dog up to 40 pounds is allowed for an additional $150 one time pet fee. There is a pet agreement to sign at check in, and dogs must be up to date on all vaccinations.

W Honolulu - Diamond Head
2885 Kalakaua Avenue
Honolulu, HI
808-922-1700
In addition to a wide range of amenities and on-site activities, this beautiful luxury resort offers a great starting point for exploring many local sites of interest and activities. Dogs up to 40 pounds are allowed for an additional cleaning fee of $100 plus $25 per night per pet with a credit card on file. Dogs must be declared at the time of registration. Pets receive a special welcome with a pet amenity kit that includes a custom pet bed, food and water dishes with a floor mat, a Pet-in-Room sign, treats, pet tag, a toy, and more. The concierge can also offer additional services such as dog-walking and information about local dog services and parks. Dogs must be removed or crated for housekeeping or for any in-room services. 2 dogs may be allowed.

Paradise Cottage Vacation Rental
Call to Arrange.
Kaihua, HI
808-254-3332
This private cottage rental sleeps six people, and has air-conditioning. Well-behaved dogs are allowed for an extra charge.

Kailua Beach Vacation Home
Call to Arrange.
Kailua, HI
808-230-2176
This 5 bedroom, 2 bathroom vacation home allows well-behaved dogs. It is located about 30 minutes from the Honolulu Airport.

Garden Island Inn
3445 Wilcox Road
Kalapaki Beach - Lihue, HI
808-245-7227 (800 648 0154)
gardenislandinn.com/
Located in the heart of the city's harbor area, this lush garden retreat offers numerous activities and recreational opportunities, and a

great location for exploring the island. One dog is allowed for no additional pet fee.

Makaleha Mountain Retreat
Call to Arrange.
Kapaa, HI
808-822-5131
This vacation rental home has 2 bedroom and 1 bathroom, plus a studio. Well-behaved dogs are allowed.

The Westin Maui Resort and Spa
2365 Kaanapali Parkway
Lahaina, HI
808-667-2525 (888-625-5144)
An elegant getaway, this resort sits along white sandy beaches and offers guests a long list of amenities and recreational opportunities. Dogs up to 40 pounds are allowed for no additional pet fee with advance registration; they must be current on shots, and they may not be left alone in the room at any time. Dogs are allowed on the beach here on leash. 2 dogs may be allowed.

Coco's Kauai B&B Rental
Call to Arrange.
Makaweli, HI
808-338-0722
cocoskauai.com
This 2 bedroom, 1 bathroom vacation rental allows well-behaved dogs. The rental is about five minutes from historic Waimea.

Hilton Hotel
69-425 Waikoloa Beach Drive
Waikoloa, HI
808-886-1234 (800-HILTONS (445-8667))
This oceanfront, upscale hotel offers a long list of on site amenities for business and leisure travelers - including planned activities, programs for children, and an outstanding island atmosphere, plus a convenient location to business, shopping, dining, and entertainment areas. Dogs up to 75 pounds are allowed for an additional one time pet fee of $75 per room and there is a pet policy to sign at check in. 2 dogs may be allowed.

Idaho

High Country Inn
4232 Old Ahsahka Grade
Ahsahka, ID
208-476-7570
thehighcountryinn.com/

Pets of all sizes are allowed for an additional $25 per pet per stay. Dogs must be well-trained, have their own bed and/or crate, be cleaned up after at all times, and friendly as there is another dog and other pets in residence. Dogs are not allowed on the beds or furniture, and they must be crated if they are shedders. Dogs may not be left alone in the room, so there is an outdoor kennel available for guests free of charge.

Best Western Blackfoot Inn
750 Jensen Grove Drive
Blackfoot, ID
208-785-4144 (800-780-7234)
Dogs are welcome at this hotel.

Super 8 Blackfoot
1279 Parkway Drive
Blackfoot, ID
208-785-9333 (800-800-8000)
Dogs of all sizes are allowed. Dogs are allowed for a pet fee.

Candlewood Suites Boise towne Square
700 North Cole Road
Boise, ID
208-322-4300 (877-270-6405)
Dogs up to 80 pounds are allowed. Pets allowed with an additional pet fee. Up to $75 for 1-6 nights and up to $150 for 7+ nights. A pet agreement must be signed at check-in.

Doubletree Club Hotel
475 W Parkcenter Blvd
Boise, ID
208-345-2002 (800-222-TREE (8733))
In addition to offering a number of on site amenities for all level of travelers, this hotel sits only minutes from the state capitol, the university, the Boqus Basin Ski Area, the Boise Airport, and to many other sites of interest. Dogs are allowed for an additional fee of $10 per night per pet. Multiple dogs may be allowed.

Doubletree Hotel
2900 Chinden Blvd
Boise, ID
208-343-1871 (800-222-TREE (8733))
Sitting on 14 lush, green acres on the shores of the Boise River, this upscale hotel gives direct access to the 26 mile Greenbelt trail; plus, it is only a short distance from the downtown area and a variety of attractions, business areas, and recreational opportunities. Dogs up to 50 pounds are allowed for an additional one time pet fee of $25 per

room. 2 dogs may be allowed.

Extended Stay America Boise - Airport
2500 S. Vista Avenue
Boise, ID
208-363-9040 (800-804-3724)
One dog is allowed per suite. There is a $25 per night additional pet fee up to $150 for an entire stay.

Holiday Inn Express Boise
2613 S. Vista Ave.
Boise, ID
208-388-0800 (877-270-6405)
Dogs of all sizes are allowed. Dogs are allowed for a pet fee of $20.00 per pet per night.

Motel 6 - Boise Airport
2323 Airport Way
Boise, ID
208-344-3506 (800-466-8356)
This motel welcomes your pets to stay with you.

Red Lion
1800 Fairview Avenue
Boise, ID
208-344-7691
There is a $20 one time fee per pet. There are no additional pet fees for R&R members, and the R&R program is free to sign up. Multiple dogs may be allowed.

Residence Inn Boise Central/Capitol Boulevard
1401 Lusk Avenue
Boise, ID
208-344-1200 (800-331-3131)
Only a short distance from the heart of downtown, the state capitol, and the state university, this all suite, upscale hotel offers a number of amenities for all level of travelers - including a daily buffet breakfast and complementary evening receptions. Dogs are allowed for an additional one time pet fee of $75. Multiple dogs may be allowed.

Residence Inn Boise West
7303 West Denton Street
Boise, ID
208-385-9000 (800-331-3131)
Besides offering a convenient location to business, shopping, dining, and entertainment areas, this hotel also provides a number of in-house amenities, including a daily buffet breakfast, and weekly complementary evening receptions. Dogs are allowed for an additional one time pet fee of $100. Multiple dogs may be allowed.

Rodeway Inn
1115 N Curtis Road
Boise, ID
208-376-2700
Dogs of all sizes are allowed. There is a $10 one time fee for 1 dog and an additional $5 one time fee for a 2nd dog. 2 dogs may be allowed.

Super 8 Boise
I-84 Exit 53 at Vista Ave
Boise, ID
208-344-8871 (800-800-8000)
Dogs of all sizes are allowed. Dogs are allowed for a pet fee.

TownePlace Suites Boise Downtown
1455 S Capitol Blvd
Boise, ID
208-429-8881 (800-257-3000)
Besides being located across the street from the Boise State University and only a half mile from downtown, this all suite hotel also offers a number of in-house amenities for all level of travelers. Dogs are allowed for an additional one time fee of $100 per room. Multiple dogs may be allowed.

Super 8 Heyburn Area Burley
Interstate 84 Exit 208
Burley, ID
208-678-7000 (800-800-8000)
Dogs of all sizes are allowed. Dogs are allowed for a pet fee.

Best Western Caldwell Inn & Suites
908 Specht Avenue
Caldwell, ID
208-454-7225 (800-780-7234)
Dogs of all sizes are allowed. Dogs are allowed for a pet fee of $5.00 per pet per night.

La Quinta Inn Caldwell
901 Specht Ave
Caldwell, ID
208-454-2222 (800-531-5900)
Dogs of all sizes are allowed. There are no additional pet fees. Dogs must be quiet, well-behaved, leashed, and they request dogs be taken to the dog run out back. Multiple dogs may be allowed.

Days Inn Coeur D Alene
2200 Northwest Blvd
Coeur D Alene, ID
208-667-8668 (800-329-7466)
Dogs of all sizes are allowed. Dogs are allowed for a pet fee of $5 per pet per night.

Super 8 Coeur D Alene
Interstate 90 Exit 12

Coeur D Alene, ID
208-765-8880 (800-800-8000)
Dogs of all sizes are allowed. Dogs are allowed for a pet fee of $10.00 per pet per stay.

Best Western Coeur d'Alene Inn
506 W Appleway Avenue
Coeur D'Alene, ID
208-765-3200 (800-780-7234)
Dogs of all sizes are allowed. Dogs are allowed for a pet fee of $25.00 per pet per stay.

La Quinta Inn & Suites Coeur D Alene East
2209 E Sherman Ave
Coeur D'Alene, ID
208-667-6777 (800-531-5900)
Dogs of all sizes are allowed. There are no additional pet fees. Please leash and clean up after your pet. Multiple dogs may be allowed.

La Quinta Inn Coeur D Alene Appleway
280 W Appleway
Coeur D'Alene, ID
208-765-5500 (800-531-5900)
Dogs of all sizes are allowed. There are no additional pet fees. Please leash and clean up after your pet. Multiple dogs may be allowed.

Shilo Inn
702 W. Appleway
Coeur D'Alene, ID
208-664-2300 (800-222-2244)
There is a $25 per stay pet charge for up to two pets. 2 dogs may be allowed.

Motel 6 - Coeur D'alene
610 West Appleway Ave
Coeur D'alene, ID
208-664-6600 (800-466-8356)
This motel welcomes your pets to stay with you.

Coeur d'Alene Resort
115 S 2nd Street
Coeur d'Alene, ID
208-765-4000
There is an additional $75 one time fee per pet.

Comfort Inn
2303 North 4th Street
Coeur d'Alene, ID
208-664-1649 (877-424-6423)
Dogs up to 50 pounds are allowed.

Dog Bark Park Inn
2421 H 95
Cottonwood, ID
208-962-3647
dogbarkparkinn.com/index.htm

Definitely a unique traveling experience! The inn is built into the shape of a 30 foot tall Beagle and its 12 foot tall puppy . They offer a 2nd floor private deck with sleeping accommodations for four, a cozy reading nook in the dog's nose, and an extended continental breakfast. The owners' obvious love of dogs shows in the folk-art style wooden canine carvings (over 60 different breeds) that are offered in their gift store. Carvings from real or still life (like pictures), and tours of the studio where they are made are also available. They are open seasonally and at times close when business may take them away, so call ahead. Dogs of all sizes are welcome for an additional $10 per night per pet. Dogs may not be left alone in the room at any time, or on the beds, and they must be well behaved, leashed and cleaned up after. 2 dogs may be allowed.

Pine Motel Guest House
105 S MainH33
Driggs, ID
208-354-2774 (800-354-2778)
This guest house is surrounded by an acre of tree covered lawn, and a big country breakfast is an option they also offer. One large dog or 2 small dogs are allowed per room. There is a $10 per night per room additional pet fee. Dogs may not be left alone in the room at any time. Dogs must be leashed and cleaned up after. 2 dogs may be allowed.

Super 8 Grangeville
801 S.W. 1st Street
Grangeville, ID
208-983-1002 (800-800-8000)
Dogs of all sizes are allowed. Dogs are allowed for a pet fee of $10.00 per pet per night.

Woods River Inn
601 Main Street/H 75
Hailey, ID
208-578-0600 (877-542-0600)
woodriverinn.com/
Located in the Sun Valley area of Idaho, this motel offers oversized, well-appointed guest rooms, and conveniences for both the vacation or business traveler. Some of the amenities include Jacuzzi, fireplace, and full kitchen suites, an indoor heated pool and hot tub, and a complimentary expanded Continental breakfast. Dogs of all sizes are welcome. There is a $25 one time additional pet fee per room, and a damage waiver to sign at check in. Dogs must be quiet, well behaved,

leashed, and cleaned up after. Dogs may not be left alone in the room at any time. 2 dogs may be allowed.

Holiday Inn Express Hotel & Suites Hayden-Coeur D'Alene North
151 W. Orchard St.
Hayden, ID
208-772-7900 (877-270-6405)
Dogs up to 60 pounds are allowed. Dogs are allowed for a pet fee of $10.00 per pet per night.

Candlewood Suites Idaho Falls
665 Pancheri Dr.
Idaho Falls, ID
208-525-9800 (877-270-6405)
Dogs up to 80 pounds are allowed. Pets allowed with an additional pet fee. Up to $75 for 1-6 nights and up to $150 for 7+ nights. A pet agreement must be signed at check-in.

Comfort Inn
195 S. Colorado Ave.
Idaho Falls, ID
208-528-2804 (877-424-6423)
Dogs of all sizes are allowed. Dogs are allowed for a pet fee of $10.00 per pet per night.

Motel 6 - Idaho Falls
1448 Broadway St
Idaho Falls, ID
208-522-0112 (800-466-8356)
This motel welcomes your pets to stay with you.

Red Lion
475 River Parkway
Idaho Falls, ID
208-523-8000
Dogs up to 50 pounds are allowed. There is a $20 one time pet fee per room. There are no additional pet fees for R&R members, and the R&R program is free to sign up. 2 dogs may be allowed.

Shilo Conference Hotel
780 Lindsay Blvd
Idaho Falls, ID
208-523-0088 (800-222-2244)
There is an additional one time pet fee of $25 per room. Pet rooms are located on the ground floor on the river side of the inn. 2 dogs may be allowed.

Super 8 Idaho Falls
705 Lindsay Blvd
Idaho Falls, ID
208-522-8880 (800-800-8000)
Dogs are welcome at this hotel.

Best Western Sawtooth Inn & Suites
2653 S Lincoln Avenue
Jerome, ID
208-324-9200 (800-780-7234)
Dogs are welcome at this hotel.

Morning Star Lodge
602 Bunker Avenue
Kellogg, ID
208-783-1111 (866-344-2675)
This premier condominium lodge sits in the heart of the Silver Mountain Resort's new Gondola Village just steps from shopping, dinning, and a variety of recreational activities. Some of the amenities include fully furnished kitchenettes, a large community room with a big-screen TV, and rooftop hot tubs. Dogs are allowed for an additional $30 one time pet fee per room. Dogs may only be left alone in the room if they will be quiet, well behaved, checked on regularly, and a contact number is left with the front desk. Dogs must be leashed and cleaned up after at all times. Dogs are also allowed on the 3.1 mile long gondola to the top of the mountain during the summer season. 2 dogs may be allowed.

Silverhorn Motor Lodge
699 W Cameron Avenue
Kellogg, ID
208-783-1151
silverhornmotorinn.com/
This motor lodge is just 6 blocks from Gondola Village, and a 3.1 mile long gondola (the longest single stage people carrier in the world) to the top of the mountain and spectacular views. In the summer, your pet may join you on this journey. The lodge offers an in-house restaurant, the largest hot tub in town, and spacious rooms with private baths. Dogs of all sizes are allowed for no additional fee. Dogs may not be left alone in the room unless you are somewhere in the lodge where they can reach you, and then only if they will be quiet and well mannered. Dogs must be leashed and cleaned up after at all times.

Best Western Tyrolean Lodge
260 Cottonwood Street
Ketchum, ID
208-726-5336 (800-780-7234)
Dogs of all sizes are allowed. Dogs are allowed for a pet fee of $10.00 per pet per night.

Comfort Inn
2128 8th Ave
Lewiston, ID
208-798-8090 (877-424-6423)
Dogs of all sizes are allowed. Dogs

are allowed for a pet fee of $10.00 per pet per night.

Econo Lodge
1021 Main Street
Lewiston, ID
208-743-0899 (877-424-6423)
Dogs of all sizes are allowed. Dogs are allowed for a pet fee of $15.00 per pet per night. Two dogs are allowed per room.

Guest House Inn and Suites
1325 Main Street
Lewiston, ID
208-746-1393
This inn is located only 1 block from the Snake River and the Clearwater Rivers, and some of the amenities they offer include a complimentary continental breakfast, a cocktail lounge, seasonal outdoor pool, and a hot tub. Dogs of all sizes are welcome for an additional fee of $10 per night per pet. Dogs may not be left alone in the room at any time, and they must be leashed and cleaned up after. 2 dogs may be allowed.

Holiday Inn Express Lewiston
2425 Nez Perce Drive
Lewiston, ID
208-750-1600 (877-270-6405)
Dogs of all sizes are allowed. Dogs are allowed for a pet fee of $20 per pet per stay.

Red Lion
621 21st Street
Lewiston, ID
208-799-1000
There is a $20 one time pet fee per room. There are no additional pet fees for R&R members, and the R&R program is free to sign up. 2 dogs may be allowed.

Super 8 Lewiston
3120 North South Hwy.
Lewiston, ID
208-743-8808 (800-800-8000)
Dogs of all sizes are allowed. Dogs are allowed for a pet fee of $10.00 per pet per night.

Brundage Inn
1005 W Lake Street/H 55
McCall, ID
208-634-2344 (800-643-2009)
This inn is an enchanting family style lodge only a few blocks from Payette Lake, and is also a perfect launching spot for bikers, hikers, and skiers. Some of the amenities include TV/VCRs with cable, kitchens, family suites, some rooms with fireplaces,

outside barbecue grills and tables, and all rooms include a microwave and refrigerator. Dogs are allowed for a $20 per night per pet additional fee. Dogs must be well mannered, leashed, and cleaned up after at all times. Dogs are not allowed on the furniture or beds.

Super 8 McCall
303 South 3rd St
McCall, ID
208-634-4637 (800-800-8000)
Dogs of all sizes are allowed. Dogs are allowed for a pet fee of $10.00 per pet per stay.

Candlewood Suites Boise-Meridian
1855 S. Silverstone Way
Meridian, ID
208-888-5121 (877-270-6405)
Dogs up to 80 pounds are allowed. Pets allowed with an additional pet fee. Up to $75 for 1-6 nights and up to $150 for 7+ nights. A pet agreement must be signed at check-in.

Motel 6 - Meridian, Id
1047 South Progress Ave
Meridian, ID
208-888-1212 (800-466-8356)
This motel welcomes your pets to stay with you.

Hillcrest Motel
706 North Main Street
Moscow, ID
208-882-7579 (800-368-6564)
There is a $5 per day per pet charge. Dogs up to 60 pounds are allowed, and there can be 1 large or 2 small dogs per room. 2 dogs may be allowed.

La Quinta Inn Moscow-Pullman
185 Warbonnet Drive
Moscow, ID
208-882-5365 (800-531-5900)
Dogs of all sizes are allowed. There are no additional pet fees. Dogs may not be left unattended at any time, and they must be leashed and cleaned up after. Multiple dogs may be allowed.

Palouse Inn
101 Baker Street
Moscow, ID
208-882-5511
2 of which are non-smoking. There is a $9 per night per pet additional fee.

Super 8 Moscow
175 Peterson Dr
Moscow, ID

208-883-1503 (800-800-8000)
Dogs of all sizes are allowed. Dogs are allowed for a pet fee of $10.00 per pet per night.

Best Western Foothills Motor Inn
1080 Highway 20
Mountain Home, ID
208-587-8477 (800-780-7234)
Dogs of all sizes are allowed. Dogs are allowed for a pet fee of $10.00 per pet per night.

Sleep Inn
1180 US 20
Mountain Home, ID
208-587-9743 (877-424-6423)
Dogs of all sizes are allowed. Dogs are allowed for a pet fee of $10.00 per pet per night.

Super 8 Nampa
Interstate 84 Exit 35
Nampa, ID
208-467-2888 (800-800-8000)
Dogs are welcome at this hotel.

Elkin's Resort on Priest Lake
404 Elkins Road
Nordman, ID
208-443-2432
elkinsresort.com/
There is a $15 per day per pet charge and there are no designated smoking or non-smoking cabins. Multiple dogs may be allowed.

Helgeson Place Hotel Suites
125 Johnson Avenue
Orofino, ID
208-476-5729 (800-404-5729)
helgesonhotel.com/
This hotel is situated right on the Lewis and Clark trail, and they offer a great location for activities and recreation and serve a continental breakfast. Dogs of all sizes are allowed for an additional one time fee of $20 per night per pet. Dogs must be quiet, well behaved, leashed, and cleaned up after. 2 dogs may be allowed.

Best Western CottonTree Inn
1415 Bench Road
Pocatello, ID
208-237-7650 (800-780-7234)
Dogs are welcome at this hotel.

Comfort Inn
1333 Bench Rd.
Pocatello, ID
208-237-8155 (877-424-6423)
Dogs of all sizes are allowed. Dogs are allowed for a pet fee of $10.00 per pet per night.

Motel 6 - Pocatello Chubbuck
291 Burnside Ave
Pocatello, ID
208-237-7880 (800-466-8356)
This motel welcomes your pets to
stay with you.

Ramada Pocatello
133 West Burnside
Pocatello, ID
208-237-0020 (800-272-6232)
Dogs are welcome at this hotel.

Red Lion
1555 Pocatello Creek Road
Pocatello, ID
208-233-2200
There is a $20 one time pet fee per
room. There are no additional fees
for R&R members, and the R&R
program is free to sign up. 2 dogs
may be allowed.

Rodeway Inn University
835 South 5th Ave.
Pocatello, ID
208-233-0451 (877-424-6423)
Dogs of all sizes are allowed. Dogs
are allowed for a pet fee of $10.00
per pet per night. Two dogs are
allowed per room.

Super 8 Pocatello
1330 Bench Rd
Pocatello, ID
208-234-0888 (800-800-8000)
Dogs of all sizes are allowed. Dogs
are allowed for a pet fee.

TownePlace Suites Pocatello
2376 Via Caporatti
Pocatello, ID
208-478-7000 (800-257-3000)
Located in the heart of the city, this
all suite inn site central to a number
of sites of interest for both business
and leisure travelers; plus they also
offer a number of on-site amenities -
including a deluxe continental
breakfast. Quiet, well mannered
dogs are allowed for an additional
one time fee of $100 per room. Dogs
may not be left alone in the room
without prior arrangements and a
contact number left with the front
desk. Multiple dogs may be allowed.

Days Inn Sandpoint
363 Bonner Mall Way
Ponderay, ID
208-263-1222 (800-329-7466)
Dogs of all sizes are allowed. Dogs
are allowed for a pet fee of $10.00
per pet per night.

Comfort Inn
3175 E. Seltice Way

Post Falls, ID
208-773-8900 (877-424-6423)
Dogs of all sizes are allowed. Dogs
are allowed for a pet fee of $20.00
per pet per stay.

Red Lion
414 E First Avenue
Post Falls, ID
208-773-1611
There is a $20 per night per pet
additional fee. There are no
additional pet fees for R&R
members, and the R&R program is
free to sign up. 2 dogs may be
allowed.

Sleep Inn
157 S. Pleasant View Road
Post Falls, ID
208-777-9394 (877-424-6423)
Dogs of all sizes are allowed. Dogs
are allowed for a pet fee of $15.00/
per pet per stay.

Hill's Resort
4777 W. Lakeshore Rd.
Priest Lake, ID
208-443-2551
hillsresort.com/
There is a $10 per night per pet
additional fee. Dogs are also
allowed on the beaches. Multiple
dogs may be allowed.

Best Western Mountain View Inn
450 W 4th S
Rexburg, ID
208-356-4646 (800-780-7234)
Dogs of all sizes are allowed. Dogs
are allowed for a pet fee of $10.00
per pet per night.

Comfort Inn
885 W. Main St.
Rexburg, ID
208-359-1311 (877-424-6423)
Dogs of all sizes are allowed.

Days Inn- Rexburg
271 South 2nd West
Rexburg, ID
208-356-9222 (800-329-7466)
Dogs are welcome at this hotel.

Best Western Salmon Rapids
Lodge
1010 S Main Street
Riggins, ID
208-628-2743 (800-780-7234)
Dogs of all sizes are allowed. Dogs
are allowed for a pet fee of $15. per
pet per stay.

Salmon River Motel
1203 S H 95
Riggins, ID

208-628-3231
salmonrivermotel.com/
This motel is situated in a deep
canyon at the confluence of the
Salmon River and the Little Salmon
Rivers, and fishing is a favorite
pastime. Amenities include clean,
spacious rooms, cable TV, and a
convenient location for hunters,
hikers, and sightseers. Dogs are
allowed for no additional fee with a
credit card on file. Dogs are not
allowed on the beds or furnishings,
and they must be leashed and
cleaned up after at all times. 2 dogs
may be allowed.

Syringa Lodge
13 Gott Lane
Salmon, ID
208-756-4424 (877-580-6482)
syringalodge.com/
Made of large spruce logs, this
beautiful lodge is located on a bluff
on 19 acres of an old homestead
which offers great views of the river
and mountains. Some of the
features/amenities include a home-
cooked breakfast served in the
dining room or on the sun porch, six
porches, a great room with an ornate
fireplace, and private baths. Dogs up
to 50 pounds are allowed for an
additional $10 one time fee per
room. Dogs must be quiet, well
mannered, leashed, cleaned up
after, and hound and human friendly.
2 dogs may be allowed.

Best Western Edgewater Resort
56 Bridge Street
Sandpoint, ID
208-263-3194 (800-780-7234)
Dogs of all sizes are allowed. Dogs
are allowed for a pet fee.

Motel 6 - Sandpoint
477255 Us 95
Sandpoint, ID
208-263-5383 (800-466-8356)
This motel welcomes your pets to
stay with you.

Quality Inn
807 N. 5th Ave.
Sandpoint, ID
208-263-2111 (877-424-6423)
Dogs of all sizes are allowed. Dogs
are allowed for a pet fee of $10.00
per pet per night.

Super 8 Sandpoint
476841 Hwy 95 N
Sandpoint, ID
208-263-2210 (800-800-8000)
Dogs are welcome at this hotel.

Mountain Village Resort
P. O. Box 150/ @ H 75/21
Stanley, ID
208-774-3661 (800-843-5475)
mountainvillage.com/
This 61 room lodge offers a warm, inviting decor, a natural hot springs for guests, and satellite television. Dogs of all sizes are allowed for an additional fee of $8 (+ tax) per night per pet. Dogs must be well behaved, leashed, cleaned up after, and the Do Not Disturb sign put on the door if they are in the room alone.

Best Western Twin Falls Hotel
1377 Blue Lakes Boulevard
Twin Falls, ID
208-736-8000 (800-780-7234)
Dogs of all sizes are allowed. Dogs are allowed for a nightly pet fee.

Comfort Inn & Suites
1910 Fillmore Avenue North
Twin Falls, ID
208-734-7494 (877-424-6423)
Dogs up to 75 pounds are allowed. Dogs are allowed for a pet fee of $20.00 per pet per night. Two dogs are allowed per room.

Motel 6 - Twin Falls
1472 Blue Lakes Blvd
Twin Falls, ID
208-734-3993 (800-466-8356)
This motel welcomes your pets to stay with you.

Red Lion
1357 Blue Lakes Blvd N
Twin Falls, ID
208-734-5000
Dogs up to 50 pounds are allowed for a $20 per night per room additional pet fee. There are no additional pet fees for R&R members, and the R&R program is free to sign up. Multiple dogs may be allowed.

Super 8 Twin Falls
1260 Blue Lakes Blvd. N
Twin Falls, ID
208-734-5801 (800-800-8000)
Dogs are welcome at this hotel.

Hells Canyon Jet Boat Trips and Lodging
1 mile S of White Bird on Old H 95
White Bird, ID
800-469-8757
Dogs of all sizes are allowed for an additional one time pet fee of $15 per room. There is one pet-friendly room available, and dogs may not be left unattended in the room at any time. Dogs must be leashed and cleaned

up after. 2 dogs may be allowed.

Coeur d' Alene Casino Resort Hotel
27068 S H 95
Worley, ID
800-523-2464
cdacasino.com/
This luxury gaming resort offers over 200 finely appointed rooms, over 100,000 square feet of gaming space, several eateries, a heated swimming pool and Jacuzzi, top-name entertainment, and they have a world class golf course adjacent to the hotel. Dogs of all sizes are allowed in standard rooms for an additional $15 per night per pet. Dogs must be well mannered, leashed, and cleaned up after.

Illinois

Howard Johnson OHare Airport Addison
600 E Lake Street
Addison, IL
630-834-8800 (800-446-4656)
Dogs are welcome at this hotel. There is a 10 one time pet fee.

Baymont Inn & Suites Chicago/ Alsip
12801 South Cicero
Alsip, IL
708-597-3900 (877-229-6668)
Dogs are welcome at this hotel.

Days Inn Alsip
5150 West 127th Street
Alsip, IL
708-371-5600 (800-329-7466)
Dogs of all sizes are allowed. Dogs are allowed for a nightly pet fee.

Knights Inn Altamont
1304 South Main
Altamont, IL
618-483-6101 (800-843-5644)
Dogs are welcome at this hotel. There is a $5 one time additional pet fee.

Super 8 Altamont
3091 E. Mill Rd.
Altamont, IL
618-483-6300 (800-800-8000)
Dogs of all sizes are allowed. Dogs are allowed for a pet fee of $10 per pet per night.

Comfort Inn
11 Crossroads Ct.
Alton, IL
618-465-9999 (877-424-6423)
Dogs of all sizes are allowed. Two dogs are allowed per room.

Holiday Inn Alton (Lewis&Clark Trail Site)
3800 Homer Adams Parkway
Alton, IL
618-462-1220 (877-270-6405)
Dogs of all sizes are allowed. Dogs are allowed for a pet fee of $25.00 per pet per night.

Super 8 Alton
1800 Homer Adams Parkway
Alton, IL
618-465-8885 (800-800-8000)
Dogs are welcome at this hotel.

Best Western Annawan Inn
315 Canal Street
Annawan, IL
309-935-6565 (800-780-7234)
Dogs are welcome at this hotel.

Comfort Inn
610 East Springfield
Arcola, IL
217-268-4000 (877-424-6423)
Dogs of all sizes are allowed.

Doubletree Hotel
75 W Algonquin Road
Arlington Heights, IL
847-364-7600 (800-222-TREE (8733))
This upscale hotel offers a number of on site amenities for business or leisure travelers, plus a convenient location to historical, business, shopping, dining, and year around recreation areas. Quiet, well mannered dogs are allowed for a $100 refundable pet deposit per room. 2 dogs may be allowed.

La Quinta Inn Chicago Arlington Heights
1415 W. Dundee Rd.
Arlington Heights, IL
847-253-8777 (800-531-5900)
Dogs of all sizes are allowed. There are no additional pet fees. Dogs must be leashed and cleaned up after. Dogs must be crated or removed for housekeeping. Multiple dogs may be allowed.

Motel 6 - Chicago North Central Arlington Hgts
441 Algonquin Rd
Arlington Heights, IL
847-806-1230 (800-466-8356)
This motel welcomes your pets to stay with you.

Red Roof Inn Chicago - O'Hare Airport
22 West Algonquin Road
Arlington Heights, IL

847-228-6650 (800-RED-ROOF)
One well-behaved family pet per room. Guest must notify front desk upon arrival. Guest is liable for any damages. In consideration of all guests, pets must never be left unattended in the guest rooms.

Sheraton Chicago Northwest
3400 West Euclid Ave.
Arlington Heights, IL
847-394-2000 (888-625-5144)
Dogs up to 70 pounds are allowed for no additional pet fee with a credit card on file. Dogs may not be left alone in the room.

Candlewood Suites Chicago/Aurora
2625 West Sullivan Rd
Aurora, IL
630-907-9977 (877-270-6405)
Dogs up to 80 pounds are allowed. Pets allowed with an additional pet fee. Up to $75 for 1-6 nights and up to $150 for 7+ nights. A pet agreement must be signed at check-in.

Motel 6 - Chicago Southwest Aurora
2380 Farnsworth Ave
Aurora, IL
630-851-3600 (800-466-8356)
This motel welcomes your pets to stay with you.

Staybridge Suites Aurora/Naperville
Sr 59 & 4320 Meridian Parkway
Aurora, IL
630-978-2222 (877-270-6405)
Dogs up to 80 pounds are allowed. Pets allowed with an additional pet fee. Up to $75 for 1-6 nights and up to $150 for 7+ nights. A pet agreement must be signed at check-in.

La Quinta Inn & Suites Chicago North Shore
2000 Lakeside Drive
Bannockburn, IL
847-317-7300 (800-531-5900)
Dogs of all sizes are allowed. There are no additional pet fees. Dogs may not be left unattended unless they will be quiet, well behaved, and a contact number is left with the front desk. Dogs must be leashed and cleaned up after. Multiple dogs may be allowed.

Days Inn - Chicago Barrington
405 W. Northwest Hwy
Barrington, IL
847-381-2640 (800-329-7466)
Dogs of all sizes are allowed. Dogs are allowed for a pet fee.

Super 8 IL Beardstown
9918 Grand Avenue
Beardstown, IL
217-323-5858 (800-800-8000)
Dogs are welcome at this hotel.

Extended Stay America Chicago - Midway
7524 State Rd.
Bedford Park, IL
708-496-8211 (800-804-3724)
One dog is allowed per suite. There is a $25 per night additional pet fee up to $150 for an entire stay.

Residence Inn Chicago Midway Airport
6638 S Cicero Avenue
Bedford Park, IL
708-458-7790 (800-331-3131)
This all suite hotel sits only 8 miles to all the city of Chicago has to offer, plus they offer a number of in-house amenities that include a daily buffet breakfast and evening socials during the week. Only 2 dogs are allowed per room unless they are toy size then up to 3 dogs are allowed for an additional one time pet fee of $100 per room.

Super 8 Belleville
600 East Main Street
Belleville, IL
618-234-9670 (800-800-8000)
Dogs of all sizes are allowed. Dogs are allowed for a pet fee of $10.00 per pet per night.

Days Inn Benton
711 West Main St.
Benton, IL
618-439-3183 (800-329-7466)
Dogs of all sizes are allowed. Dogs are allowed for a pet fee of $10.00 per pet per night.

Super 8 /West City Area Benton
I-57, Exit 71
Benton, IL
618-438-8205 (800-800-8000)
Dogs of all sizes are allowed. Dogs are allowed for a nightly pet fee.

Residence Inn Chicago Bloomingdale
295 Knollwood Drive
Bloomingdale, IL
630-893-9200 (800-331-3131)
There are numerous shopping, dining, and entertainment venues only a short walk from this all suite hotel, plus they are only a few miles from other major attractions and business districts. Dogs are allowed for an additional one time pet fee of $100 per room. 2 dogs may be

allowed.

Baymont Inn & Suites Bloomington
604 1/2 I.A.A. Drive
Bloomington, IL
309-662-2800 (877-229-6668)
Dogs are welcome at this hotel.

Days Inn - Normal Bloomington
1707 West Market Street
Bloomington, IL
309-829-6292 (800-329-7466)
Dogs of all sizes are allowed. Dogs are allowed for a pet fee.

Doubletree Hotel
10 Brickyard Drive
Bloomington, IL
309-664-6446 (800-222-TREE (8733))
Located only minutes from the state university, the airport, and train station, this upscale hotel also offers a number of on site amenities for all level of travelers, plus a convenient location to a variety of business, shopping, dining, and recreation areas. Dogs up to 50 pounds are allowed for an additional one time pet fee of $50 per room. 2 dogs may be allowed.

Econo Lodge
403 Brock Dr
Bloomington, IL
309-829-3100 (877-424-6423)
Dogs of all sizes are allowed. Dogs are allowed for a pet fee of $10.00 per pet per night.

Extended Stay America Bloomington - Normal
1805 S. Veterans Pkwy.
Bloomington, IL
309-662-8533 (800-804-3724)
One dog is allowed per suite. There is a $25 per night additional pet fee up to $150 for an entire stay.

Quality Inn & Suites
1803 East Empire St.
Bloomington, IL
309-662-7100 (877-424-6423)
Dogs of all sizes are allowed. Dogs are allowed for a pet fee of $10.00 per pet per night.

Ramada Limited and Suites Bloomington
919 Maple Hill Rd
Bloomington, IL
309-828-0900 (800-272-6232)
Dogs are welcome at this hotel.

Super 8 Bloomington
818 IAA Dr
Bloomington, IL

309-663-2388 (800-800-8000)
Dogs are welcome at this hotel.

La Quinta Inn Bolingbrook
225 W. South Frontage Road
Bolingbrook, IL
630-226-0000 (800-531-5900)
Dogs of all sizes are allowed. There
are no additional pet fees. Dogs
must be crated, and the front desk
notified, when left alone in the room,
and they must be leashed and
cleaned up after. Multiple dogs may
be allowed.

Motel 6 - Kankakee Bourbonnais
1311 Il Sr 50
Bourbonnais, IL
815-933-2300 (800-466-8356)
This motel welcomes your pets to
stay with you.

Days Inn Bridgeview
9625 South 76th Ave
Bridgeview, IL
708-430-1818 (800-329-7466)
Dogs are welcome at this hotel.

Extended Stay America Chicago -
Buffalo Grove - Deerfield
1525 Busch Pkwy.
Buffalo Grove, IL
847-215-0641 (800-804-3724)
One dog is allowed per suite. There
is a $25 per night additional pet fee
up to $150 for an entire stay.

Extended Stay America Chicago -
Burr Ridge
15 W. 122nd S. Frontage Rd.
Burr Ridge, IL
630-323-6630 (800-804-3724)
One dog is allowed per suite. There
is a $25 per night additional pet fee
up to $150 for an entire stay.

Days Inn Cairo
13201 Kessler Rd
Cairo, IL
618-734-0215 (800-329-7466)
Dogs of all sizes are allowed. Dogs
are allowed for a nightly pet fee.

Motel 6 - Calumet Park, Il
12800 S. Ashland Avenue
Calumet Park, IL
708-389-2600 (800 466 8356)
This motel welcomes your pets to
stay with you.

Super 8 IL Canton
2110 Main St
Canton, IL
309-647-1888 (800-800-8000)
Dogs are welcome at this hotel.

Motel 6 - Carbondale

700 East Main Street
Carbondale, IL
618-457-5566 (800-466-8356)
This motel welcomes your pets to
stay with you.

Super 8 Carbondale
1180 E Main
Carbondale, IL
618-457-8822 (800-800-8000)
Dogs are welcome at this hotel.

Best Western Carlinville Inn
I-55 & IL Route 108
Carlinville, IL
217-324-2100 (800-780-7234)
Dogs up to 50 pounds are allowed.
Dogs are allowed for a pet fee of
$10.00 per pet per night.

Super 8 Carlyle
1371 William Rd.
Carlyle, IL
618-594-8888 (800-800-8000)
Dogs of all sizes are allowed. Dogs
are allowed for a pet fee of $10 per
pet per night.

Comfort Inn
933 SR 49
Casey, IL
217-932-2212 (877-424-6423)
Dogs of all sizes are allowed. Dogs
are allowed for a pet fee of $10.00
per pet per night. Three or more
dogs may be allowed.

Econo Lodge Inn & Suites
2423 Old Country Inn Drive
Caseyville, IL
618-397-3300 (877-424-6423)
Dogs up to 80 pounds are allowed.
Dogs are allowed for a pet fee of
$USD per pet per night.

Motel 6 - St Louis East Caseyville, Il
2431 Old Country Inn Rd
Caseyville, IL
618-397-8867 (800-466-8356)
Your pets are welcome to stay here
with you.

Baymont Inn And Suites
Champaign
302 West Anthony Drive
Champaign, IL
217-356-8900 (877-229-6668)
Dogs of all sizes are allowed. Dogs
are allowed for a pet fee.

Drury Inn & Suites
905 W. Anthony Drive
Champaign, IL
217-398-0030 (800-378-7946)
Dogs of all sizes are allowed for no
additional pet fee with a credit card
on file, and there is a pet agreement

to sign at check in.

Econo Lodge Inn & Suites
914 W. Bloomington Rd.
Champaign, IL
217-356-6000 (877-424-6423)
Dogs of all sizes are allowed. Dogs
are allowed for a pet fee of $10.00
per pet per stay.

Extended Stay America Champaign -
Urbana
610 W. Marketview Dr.
Champaign, IL
217-351-8899 (800-804-3724)
One dog is allowed per suite. There
is a $25 per night additional pet fee
up to $150 for an entire stay.

Hawthorn Suites
101 Trade Centre Drive
Champaign, IL
217-398-3400 (800-527-1133)
In addition to providing a convenient
location to many local sites and
activities, this all-suite hotel offers a
number of amenities for business
and leisure travelers, including their
signature breakfast buffet and
beautifully appointed rooms. Dogs
are allowed for an additional one
time pet fee of $25 per room.
Multiple dogs may be allowed.

Red Roof Inn Champaign
212 West Anthony Drive
Champaign, IL
217-352-0101 (800-RED-ROOF)
One well-behaved family pet per
room. Guest must notify front desk
upon arrival. Guest is liable for any
damages. In consideration of all
guests, pets must never be left
unattended in the guest rooms.

Super 8 Champaign
202 Marketview Dr.
Champaign, IL
217-359-2388 (800-800-8000)
Dogs are welcome at this hotel.

Super 8 Chenoa
505 Hoselton Drive
Chenoa, IL
815-945-5900 (800 800 8000)
Dogs are welcome at this hotel.

China Doll Guest House
738 W Schubert
Chicago, IL
773-525-4967 (866-361-1819)
chinadollguesthouse.com
Located in the Lincoln Park
neighborhood this pet-friendly
vacation rental has three self-
contained apartment suites.

Conrad Chicago
521 North Rush Street
Chicago, IL
312-327-0664
Located in the heart of Chicago's
Magnificent Mile shopping district,
this luxury hotel offers top amenities
to visitors and their pets. Some of the
amenities include 3 restaurants, a
lounge, room service, an inviting
decor, and for an additional $20 you
can have a welcome kit for your
canine companion. It includes clean-
up supplies, a dog walking map, food
and water bowls, a personal name
tag, a canine menu, bed, toys, and a
leash. Dogs up to 75 pounds are
allowed for no additional fee with a
credit card on file, and there is a pet
agreement to sign at check in. Dogs
must be quiet, well behaved, leashed
and cleaned up after at all times, and
a contact number left with the front
desk if they are in the room alone. 2
dogs may be allowed.

Holiday Inn Chicago O'Hare Area
5615 North Cumberland Ave.
Chicago, IL
773-693-5800 (877-270-6405)
Dogs up to 50 pounds are allowed.
Dogs are allowed for a pet fee of
$25.00 per pet per night.

Hotel Allegro
171 West Randolph Street
Chicago, IL
312-236-0123
allegrochicago.com/
Well-behaved dogs of all sizes are
welcome at this pet-friendly hotel.
The luxury boutique hotel offers both
rooms and suites. Hotel amenities
include complimentary evening wine
served in the living room, a gift shop,
and an on-site fitness center. There
are no pet fees.

Hotel Burnham
1 West Washington
Chicago, IL
312-782-1111
burnhamhotel.com
Dogs of all kinds and sizes are
welcome at this pet-friendly hotel.
The luxury boutique hotel offers both
rooms and suites. Hotel amenities
include a fully equipped fitness room,
and complimentary evening wine in
the lobby. There are no pet fees, just
sign a pet liability form, and dogs
must be declared at the time of
reservations.

Hotel Indigo
1244 North Dearborn Parkway
Chicago, IL
312-787-4980 (866-521-6950)

goldcoastchicagohotel.com/
One dog up to 40 pounds is allowed
for an additional one time fee of
$75.

Hotel Monaco Chicago
225 North Wabash
Chicago, IL
312-960-8500
monaco-chicago.com/
Well-behaved dogs of all sizes are
welcome at this pet-friendly hotel.
The luxury boutique hotel offers
both rooms and suites. Hotel
amenities include complimentary
evening wine service, 24 hour room
service, and an on-site fitness
room. There are no pet fees, just
sign a pet liability form.

House of Blues Hotel
333 North Dearborn
Chicago, IL
312-245-0333
All well-behaved dogs of any size
are welcome at this downtown
hotel. There are no pet fees. Dogs
are not allowed in the Bar or
Restaurant.

Howard Johnson Inn Downtown
Chicago
720 North LaSalle Street
Chicago, IL
312-664-8100 (800-446-4656)
Dogs are welcome at this hotel.

Red Roof Inn Chicago Downtown
162 E Ontario St.
Chicago, IL
312-787-3580 (800-RED-ROOF)
One well-behaved family pet per
room. Guest must notify front desk
upon arrival. Guest is liable for any
damages. In consideration of all
guests, pets must never be left
unattended in the guest rooms.

Residence Inn Chicago
Downtown/Magnificent Mile
201 E Walton Place
Chicago, IL
312-943-9800 (800-331-3131)
Located along the city's Magnificent
Mile, this hotel offers a convenient
location to business, shopping,
dining, and entertainment areas,
plus they offer a number of in-house
amenities, including a daily buffet
breakfast, weekly evening socials,
and a complimentary full dinner
buffet on Wednesdays. Dogs are
allowed for an additional one time
pet fee of $100 per room. 2 dogs
may be allowed.

Sheraton Chicago Hotel and

Towers
301 E. North Water St.
Chicago, IL
312-464-1000 (888-625-5144)
Dog up to 75 pounds are allowed for
no additional pet fee. A credit card
must be on file and there is a pet
agreement to sign. Dogs may not be
left alone in the room.

The James Chicago
55 East Ontario
Chicago, IL
877-526-3755
lenoxsuites.com/index.php
This very dog-friendly luxury boutique
hotel rolls out the red carpet for your
dog. There is a $75 one time pet fee
per room. The hotel provides in-room
bowls and snacks for your dog and
has additional options for massages
or room service bones from the
hotel's steakhouse. Multiple dogs
may be allowed.

W Chicago City Center
172 West Adams St.
Chicago, IL
312-332-1200
Dogs up to 50 pounds are allowed
for an additional cleaning fee of $100
plus $25 per night per pet with a
credit card on file. Dogs must be
declared at the time of registration.
Pets receive a special welcome with
a pet amenity kit that includes a
custom pet bed, food and water
dishes with a floor mat, a doggy
menu, Pet-in-Room sign, treats, pet
tag, a toy, and more. The concierge
can also offer additional services
such as dog-walking and information
about local dog services and parks.
Dogs must be removed or crated for
housekeeping or for any in-room
services.

W Chicago Lakeshore
644 N. Lakeshore Dr.
Chicago, IL
312-943-9200
Dogs up to 80 pounds are allowed
for an additional cleaning fee of $100
plus $25 per night per pet with a
credit card on file. Dogs must be
declared at the time of registration.
Pets receive a special welcome with
a pet amenity kit that includes a
custom pet bed, food and water
dishes with a floor mat, a doggy
menu, Pet-in-Room sign, treats, pet
tag, a toy, and more. The concierge
can also offer additional services
such as dog-walking and information
about local dog services and parks.

Super 8 Chillicothe
615 South 4th St

Dog-Friendly Lodging - Please always call ahead to make sure an establishment is still dog-friendly.

Chillicothe, IL
309-274-2568 (800-800-8000)
Dogs are welcome at this hotel.

Collinsville Drury Inn
602 N. Bluff
Collinsville, IL
618-345-7700 (800-378-7946)
Dogs of all sizes are allowed for no additional pet fee with a credit card on file, and there is a pet agreement to sign at check in.

Motel 6 - Collinsville, Il
552 Ramada Blvd
Collinsville, IL
618-345-9500 (800-466-8356)
This motel welcomes your pets to stay with you.

Super 8 St. Louis Collinsville
2 Gateway Dr.
Collinsville, IL
618-345-8008 (800-800-8000)
Dogs of all sizes are allowed. Dogs are allowed for a pet fee of $15 per pet per stay.

Super 8 Crystal Lake
577 Crystal Point Dr
Crystal Lake, IL
815-788-8888 (800-800-8000)
Dogs of all sizes are allowed. Dogs are allowed for a nightly pet fee.

Comfort Inn
383 Lynch Dr.
Danville, IL
217-443-8004 (877-424-6423)
Dogs of all sizes are allowed.

Sleep Inn & Suites
361 Lynch Drive
Danville, IL
217-442-6600 (877-424-6423)
Dogs of all sizes are allowed. Dogs are allowed for a pet fee of $15.00 per pet per night.

Super 8 Danville
377 Lynch Dr
Danville, IL
217-443-4499 (800-800-8000)
Dogs of all sizes are allowed. Dogs are allowed for a pet fee.

Extended Stay America Chicago - Darien
2345 Sokol Court
Darien, IL
630-985-4708 (800-804-3724)
One dog is allowed per suite. There is a $25 per night additional pet fee up to $150 for an entire stay.

Travelodge IL De Kalb
1116 West Lincoln Highway

De Kalb, IL
815-756-3398 (800-578-7878)
Dogs are welcome at this hotel.

Super 8 IL DeKalb
800 W. Fairview Dr
DeKalb, IL
815-748-4688 (800-800-8000)
Dogs of all sizes are allowed. Dogs are allowed for a pet fee.

Baymont Inn Decatur
5100 Hickory Point Frontage RD
Decatur, IL
217-875-5800 (800-531-5900)
Dogs of all sizes are allowed. There are no additional pet fees. Dogs may not be left unattended, and they must be quiet and kept leashed. Multiple dogs may be allowed.

Days Inn Decatur
333 North Wyckles Rd/I-72
Decatur, IL
217-422-5900 (800-329-7466)
Dogs of all sizes are allowed. Dogs are allowed for a pet fee.

Ramada Limited IL Decatur
355 E Hickory Point Rd.
Decatur, IL
217-876-8011 (800-272-6232)
Dogs are welcome at this hotel.

Sleep Inn
3920 E. Hospitality Lane
Decatur, IL
217-872-7700 (877-424-6423)
Dogs of all sizes are allowed.

Marriott Chicago Deerfield Suites
2 Parkway North
Deerfield, IL
847-405-9666 (800-228-9290)
This luxury boutique hotel sits central to many of the area's star attractions, major businesses, world class shopping and dining, and day/night entertainment areas, plus they also offer a number of in-house amenities for business and leisure travelers. Dogs are allowed for an additional fee of $75 per pet for 1 to 6 nights; the fee is $10 per night per pet for 7 or more nights. 2 dogs may be allowed.

Red Roof Inn Chicago - Northbrook/Deerfield
340 South Waukegan Road
Deerfield, IL
847-205-1755 (800-RED-ROOF)
One well-behaved family pet per room. Guest must notify front desk upon arrival. Guest is liable for any damages. In consideration of all

guests, pets must never be left unattended in the guest rooms.

Residence Inn Chicago Deerfield
530 Lake Cook Road
Deerfield, IL
847-940-4644 (800-331-3131)
Some of the amenities at this all-suite inn include a daily buffet breakfast, a complimentary evening social Monday through Thursday, a heated swimming pool, and complimentary grocery shopping. Dogs are allowed for an additional one time pet fee of $75 per room; they must be removed for housekeeping. 2 dogs may be allowed.

Comfort Inn O'Hare
2175 E. Touhy Ave.
Des Plaines, IL
847-635-1300 (877-424-6423)
Dogs of all sizes are allowed. Dogs are allowed for a pet fee of $20.00 per pet per night. Two dogs are allowed per room.

Extended Stay America Chicago - O'Hare
1201 E. Touhy Ave.
Des Plaines, IL
847-294-9693 (800-804-3724)
One dog is allowed per suite. There is a $25 per night additional pet fee up to $150 for an entire stay.

Comfort Inn
136 Plaza Dr
Dixon, IL
815-284-0500 (877-424-6423)
Dogs up to 50 pounds are allowed. Dogs are allowed for a pet fee of $15.00 per pet per night.

Quality Inn & Suites
154 Plaza Drive
Dixon, IL
815-288-2001 (877-424-6423)
Dogs up to 50 pounds are allowed. Dogs are allowed for a pet fee of $15.00 per pet per night.

Comfort Inn
3010 Finley Rd.
Downers Grove, IL
630-515-1500 (877-424-6423)
Dogs of all sizes are allowed. Dogs are allowed for a pet fee of $35.00 per pet per stay. Two dogs are allowed per room.

Extended Stay America Chicago - Downers Grove
3150 Finley Rd.
Downers Grove, IL
630-810-4124 (800-804-3724)

One dog is allowed per suite. There is a $25 per night additional pet fee up to $150 for an entire stay.

Red Roof Inn Chicago - Downers Grove
1113 Butterfield Road
Downers Grove, IL
630-963-4205 (800-RED-ROOF)
One well-behaved family pet per room. Guest must notify front desk upon arrival. Guest is liable for any damages. In consideration of all guests, pets must never be left unattended in the guest rooms.

Super 8 Du Quoin
1010 South Jefferson
Du Quoin, IL
618-542-4335 (800-800-8000)
Dogs of all sizes are allowed. Dogs are allowed for a nightly pet fee.

Super 8 Dwight
14 E. Northbrook Dr
Dwight, IL
815-584-1888 (800-800-8000)
Dogs are welcome at this hotel.

Super 8 East Moline
2201 John Deere Road
East Moline, IL
309-796-1999 (800-800-8000)
Dogs of all sizes are allowed. Dogs are allowed for a pet fee.

Motel 6 - Peoria East
104 Camp St
East Peoria, IL
309-699-7281 (800-466-8356)
This motel welcomes your pets to stay with you.

Super 8 Peoria East
725 Taylor St
East Peoria, IL
309-698-8889 (800-800-8000)
Dogs are welcome at this hotel.

Comfort Inn
1304 W. Evergreen Drive
Effingham, IL
217-347-5050 (877-424-6423)
Dogs of all sizes are allowed. Dogs are allowed for a pet fee of $5.00 per pet per stay.

Comfort Suites
1310 W. Fayette Rd
Effingham, IL
217-342-3151 (877-424-6423)
Dogs of all sizes are allowed. Dogs are allowed for a pet fee of $fee per pet per stay.

Days Inn Effingham
1205 North Keller Drive

Effingham, IL
217-347-7131 (800-329-7466)
Dogs of all sizes are allowed. Dogs are allowed for a pet fee of $10.00 per pet per night.

Econo Lodge
1412 W. Fayette Ave
Effingham, IL
217-342-9271 (877-424-6423)
Dogs up to 75 pounds are allowed. Dogs are allowed for a pet fee of $5.00 per pet per night. Three or more dogs may be allowed.

Motel 6 - Effingham, Il
1305 Keller Dr
Effingham, IL
217-347-5141 (800-466-8356)
This motel welcomes your pets to stay with you.

Rodeway Inn
1205 North Keller Drive
Effingham, IL
217-347-7515 (877-424-6423)
Dogs of all sizes are allowed. Dogs are allowed for a pet fee of $10.00 per pet per night. Three or more dogs may be allowed.

Super 8 Effingham
1400 Thelma Keller Ave
Effingham, IL
217-342-6888 (800-800-8000)
Dogs are welcome at this hotel.

Days Inn El Paso
630 West Main Street
El Paso, IL
309-527-7070 (800-329-7466)
Dogs of all sizes are allowed. Dogs are allowed for a pet fee.

Super 8 IL El Paso
25 Linco Dr.
El Paso, IL
309-527-4949 (800-800-8000)
Dogs are welcome at this hotel.

Candlewood Suites Elgin NW -Chicago
1780 Capital Street
Elgin, IL
847-888-0600 (877-270-6405)
Dogs up to 80 pounds are allowed. Pets allowed with an additional pet fee. Up to $75 for 1-6 nights and up to $150 for 7+ nights. A pet agreement must be signed at check-in.

Days Inn Elgin
1585 Dundee Avenue/I-90
Elgin, IL
847-695-2100 (800-329-7466)
Dogs of all sizes are allowed. Dogs

are allowed for a pet fee.

Quality Inn
500 Tollgate Road
Elgin, IL
847-608-7300 (877-424-6423)
Dogs of all sizes are allowed. Dogs are allowed for a pet fee of $10.00 per pet per night.

Rim Rock's Dogwood Cabins
Karbers Ridge/Pounds Hollow blacktop
Elizabethtown, IL
618-264-6036
rimrocksdogwoodcabins.com/
Surrounded by The Shawnee National Forest, these new rustic cabins offer modern comforts (like screened porches, showers, and supplied kitchens), close proximity to a wide variety of land and water recreation, and some fantastic scenery. Dogs of all sizes are allowed for no additional fee. Dogs may not be left unattended, and they must be leashed and cleaned up after. 2 dogs may be allowed.

Baymont Inn & Suites OHare/ Elk Grove Village
2881 Touhy Ave
Elk Grove Village, IL
847-803-9400 (877-229-6668)
Dogs are welcome at this hotel.

Comfort Inn O'Hare Int'l Airport
2550 Landmeier Rd.
Elk Grove Village, IL
847-364-6200 (877-424-6423)
Dogs of all sizes are allowed. Dogs are allowed for a pet fee of $25.00 per pet per night. Two dogs are allowed per room.

Days Inn /Chicago/OHare Airport West Elk Grove Village
1920 East Higgins Road
Elk Grove Village, IL
847-437-1650 (800-329-7466)
Dogs are welcome at this hotel.

Days Inn Schaumburg/Elk Grove
1000 West Devon Ave
Elk Grove Village, IL
847-895-2085 (800-329-7466)
Dogs are welcome at this hotel.

Motel 6 - Chicago Elk Grove
1601 Oakton St
Elk Grove Village, IL
847-981-9766 (800-466-8356)
This motel welcomes your pets to stay with you.

Sheraton Suites Elk Grove Village
121 Northwest Point Blvd.

Elk Grove Village, IL
847-290-1600 (888-625-5144)
Dogs up to 75 pounds are allowed
for no additional pet fee with a credit
card on file. Dogs may not be left
alone in the room.

Super 8 Chicago OHare Airport
2951 Touhy Avenue
Elk Grove Village, IL
847-827-3133 (800-800-8000)
Dogs of all sizes are allowed. Dogs
are allowed for a pet fee of $20.00
per pet per night.

Extended Stay America Chicago -
Elmhurst
550 West Grand Ave.
Elmhurst, IL
630-530-4353 (800-804-3724)
One dog is allowed per suite. There
is a $25 per night additional pet fee
up to $150 for an entire stay.

Quality Inn
933 S. Riverside Drive
Elmhurst, IL
630-279-0700 (877-424-6423)
Dogs of all sizes are allowed. Dogs
are allowed for a pet fee of $25.00
per pet per stay.

Comfort Suites
137 Ludwig Drive
Fairview Heights, IL
618-394-0202 (877-424-6423)
Dogs up to 50 pounds are allowed.
Dogs are allowed for a pet fee of
$10.00 per pet per night. Two dogs
are allowed per room.

Fairview Heights Drury Inn & Suites
12 Ludwig Drive
Fairview Heights, IL
618-398-8530 (800-378-7946)
Dogs of all sizes are allowed for no
additional pet fee with a credit card
on file, and there is a pet agreement
to sign at check in.

Ramada Fairview Heights
6900 N Illinois St./I-64
Fairview Heights, IL
618-632-4747 (800-272-6232)
Dogs of all sizes are allowed. Dogs
are allowed for a pet fee of $25 per
pet per stay.

Super 8 -St. Louis Fairview Heights
45 Ludwig Dr.
Fairview Heights, IL
618-398-8338 (800-800-8000)
Dogs are welcome at this hotel.

Days Inn Farmer City
975 E Clinton Ave
Farmer City, IL

309-928-9434 (800-329-7466)
Dogs of all sizes are allowed. Dogs
are allowed for a pet fee of $5.00
per pet per night.

Best Western Lorson Inn
201 Hagen Drive
Flora, IL
618-662-3054 (800-780-7234)
Dogs of all sizes are allowed. Dogs
are allowed for a pet fee of $8.00
per pet per stay.

Comfort Inn O'Hare
3001 N. Mannheim Road
Franklin Park, IL
847-233-9292 (877-424-6423)
Dogs of all sizes are allowed. Dogs
are allowed for a pet fee of $15.00
per pet per night.

Baymont Inn & Suites Freeport
1060 Route 26
Freeport, IL
815-599-8510 (877-229-6668)
Dogs of all sizes are allowed. Dogs
are allowed for a pet fee.

Best Western Quiet House & Suites
9923 W US Route 20
Galena, IL
815-777-2577 (800-780-7234)
Dogs are welcome at this hotel.

Cloran Mansion
1237 Franklin Street
Galena, IL
815-777-0583 (866-234-0583)
cloranmansion.com/
Sitting on 1½ acres of landscaped
lawns and gardens, this 1880
Italianate Victorian mansion
provides guests a venue for a
romantic getaway, plus they offer a
number of in-house amenities, a
pond with 2 waterfalls, and a
beautiful cottage that is pet friendly;
dogs are not allowed in the
mansion. Breakfast is still served in
the main house for cottage guests.
Dogs are allowed for a one time pet
fee of $25. Dogs must be well
behaved, leashed or crated, and
cleaned up after. 2 dogs may be
allowed.

Galena Rentals
95 Heatherdowns Lane
Galena, IL
773-631-5253
Located near the General Golf
Course and the Shenandoah Riding
Center, this 2 bedroom, 2 bathroom
home offers a number of amenities
and access to the owner's club and
outdoor pool. Dogs of all sizes are
allowed for no additional fee. Dogs

may not be left unattended, and they
must be leashed and cleaned up
after. 2 dogs may be allowed.

Goldmoor Inn and Gardens
9001 Sand Hill Road
Galena, IL
815-777-3925 (800-255-3925)
goldmoor.com/Inn
Located only 6 miles from town, this
beautiful estate offers a variety of
accommodations, amenities,
services, and lush landscaped
grounds and gardens. Dogs of all
sizes are allowed for no additional
fee in the cabins. Dogs must be well
behaved, leashed, cleaned up after,
and crated when left alone in the
room. 2 dogs may be allowed.

Comfort Inn
907 W. Carl Sandburg Dr.
Galesburg, IL
309-344-5445 (877-424-6423)
Dogs of all sizes are allowed. Dogs
are allowed for a pet fee of $20.00
per pet per stay.

Holiday Inn Express Galesburg
2285 Washington Street
Galesburg, IL
309-343-7100 (877-270-6405)
Dogs of all sizes are allowed. Dogs
are allowed for a pet fee of $25 per
pet per stay.

Super 8 IL Galesburg
737 Knox HWY 10
Galesburg, IL
309-289-2100 (800-800-8000)
Dogs of all sizes are allowed. Dogs
are allowed for a pet fee.

Super 8 Geneseo
Hwy 6 & W Main Street
Geneseo, IL
309-945-1898 (800-800-8000)
Dogs of all sizes are allowed. Dogs
are allowed for a pet fee of $10.00
per pet per night.

Super 8 Gilman
1301 S. Crescent St.
Gilman, IL
815-265-7000 (800-800-8000)
Dogs are welcome at this hotel.

Crowne Plaza Hotel Glen
Ellyn/Lombard
1250 Roosevelt Road
Glen Ellyn, IL
630-629-6000 (877-270-6405)
Dogs are welcome at this hotel.

Baymont Inn & Suites Glenview
1625 Milwaukee Avenue
Glenview, IL

847-635-8300 (877-229-6668)
Dogs are welcome at this hotel.

Motel 6 - Chicago North Glenview
1535 Milwaukee Ave
Glenview, IL
847-390-7200 (800-466-8356)
This motel welcomes your pets to
stay with you.

Staybridge Suites Glenview
2600 Lehigh Avenue
Glenview, IL
847-657-0002 (877-270-6405)
Dogs up to 80 pounds are allowed.
Pets allowed with an additional pet
fee. Up to $75 for 1-6 nights and up
to $150 for 7+ nights. A pet
agreement must be signed at check-
in.

Comfort Suites
1775 East Belvidere Road
Grayslake, IL
847-223-5050 (877-424-6423)
Dogs of all sizes are allowed. Dogs
are allowed for a pet fee of $USD per
pet per stay. Two dogs are allowed
per room.

Super 8 Grayville
2060 County Road 2450 North
Grayville, IL
618-375-7288 (800-800-8000)
Dogs are welcome at this hotel.

Econo Lodge & Suites
1731 South SR-127
Greenville, IL
618-664-3030 (877-424-6423)
Dogs of all sizes are allowed. Dogs
are allowed for a pet fee of $10.00
per pet per night. Two dogs are
allowed per room.

Best Western Gurnee Hotel & Suites
5430 Grand Avenue
Gurnee, IL
847-782-0890 (800-780-7234)
Dogs are welcome at this hotel.
There is a $50 one time pet fee.

Comfort Inn
6080 Gurnee Mills Circle E.
Gurnee, IL
847-855-8866 (877-424-6423)
Dogs of all sizes are allowed. Dogs
are allowed for a pet fee of $30.00
per pet per stay.

Extended Stay America Chicago -
Gurnee
5724 Northridge Dr.
Gurnee, IL
847-662-3060 (800-804-3724)
One dog is allowed per suite. There
is a $25 per night additional pet fee

up to $150 for an entire stay.

La Quinta Inn Chicago/Gurnee
5688 N. Ridge Road
Gurnee, IL
847-662-7600 (800-531-5900)
Dogs up to 100 pounds are allowed.
There are no additional pet fees.
Dogs may not be left unattended,
and they must be well behaved,
leashed, and cleaned up after. They
are not allowed in the pool area. 2
dogs may be allowed.

Super 8 Motel -
115 Arrowhead Dr
Hampshire, IL
847-683-0888 (800-800-8000)
Dogs of all sizes are allowed. Dogs
are allowed for a pet fee.

Extended Stay America Chicago -
Hanover Park
1075 Lake St.
Hanover Park, IL
630-893-4823 (800-804-3724)
One dog is allowed per suite. There
is a $25 per night additional pet fee
up to $150 for an entire stay.

Comfort Inn & Suites
16900 S. Halsted Street
Harvey, IL
708-331-0700 (877-424-6423)
Dogs up to 50 pounds are allowed.
Dogs are allowed for a pet fee of
$10.00 per pet per night.

Best Western Chicago Hillside
4400 Frontage Road
Hillside, IL
708-544-9300 (800-780-7234)
Dogs of all sizes are allowed. Dogs
are allowed for a pet fee of $5 per
pet per night.

Extended Stay America Chicago -
Hillside
4575 Frontage Rd.
Hillside, IL
708-544-4409 (800-804-3724)
One dog is allowed per suite. There
is a $25 per night additional pet fee
up to $150 for an entire stay.

Candlewood Suites
Chicago/Hoffman Estates
2875 Greenspoint Parkway
Hoffman Estates, IL
847-490-1686 (877-270-6405)
Dogs up to 80 pounds are allowed.
Pets allowed with an additional pet
fee. Up to $75 for 1-6 nights and up
to $150 for 7+ nights. A pet
agreement must be signed at
check-in.

La Quinta Inn Chicago Hoffman
Estates
2280 Barrington Rd.
Hoffman Estates, IL
847-882-3312 (800-531-5900)
Dogs of all sizes are allowed. There
are no additional pet fees. Dogs
must be leashed and cleaned up
after. Dogs must be removed or
crated for housekeeping. Multiple
dogs may be allowed.

Red Roof Inn Chicago - Hoffman
Estates
2500 Hassell Road
Hoffman Estates, IL
847-885-7877 (800-RED-ROOF)
One well-behaved family pet per
room. Guest must notify front desk
upon arrival. Guest is liable for any
damages. In consideration of all
guests, pets must never be left
unattended in the guest rooms.

Extended Stay America Chicago -
Itasca
1181 N. Rohlwing Rd.
Itasca, IL
630-250-1111 (800-804-3724)
One dog is allowed per suite. There
is a $25 per night additional pet fee
up to $150 for an entire stay.

Econo Lodge Inn & Suites
1914 Southbrooke Road
Jacksonville, IL
217-245-9575 (877-424-6423)
Dogs of all sizes are allowed.

Holiday Inn Express Hotel & Suites
Jacksonville
2501 Holliday Lane
Jacksonville, IL
217-245-6500 (877-270-6405)
Dogs of all sizes are allowed. Dogs
are allowed for a pet fee of $10.00
per pet per night.

Super 8 Jacksonville
1003 W Morton Ave
Jacksonville, IL
217-479-0303 (800-800-8000)
Dogs are welcome at this hotel.

Super 8 Jerseyville
1303 State Highway 109
Jerseyville, IL
618-498-7888 (800-800-8000)
Dogs are welcome at this hotel.

Holiday Inn Joliet - Conference
Center
411 South Larkin Ave
Joliet, IL
815-729-2000 (877-270-6405)
Dogs of all sizes are allowed. Dogs
are allowed for a pet fee.

Dog-Friendly Lodging - Please always call ahead to make sure an establishment is still dog-friendly.

Motel 6 - Chicago Joliet I-55
3551 Mall Loop Drive
Joliet, IL
815-439-1332 (800-466-8356)
This motel welcomes your pets to stay with you.

Motel 6 - Joliet I-80
1850 Mcdonough Road
Joliet, IL
815-729-2800 (800-466-8356)
This motel welcomes your pets to stay with you.

Red Roof Inn Joliet
1750 McDonough Street
Joliet, IL
815-741-2304 (800-RED-ROOF)
One well-behaved family pet per room. Guest must notify front desk upon arrival. Guest is liable for any damages. In consideration of all guests, pets must never be left unattended in the guest rooms.

TownePlace Suites Joliet South
1515 Riverboat Center Drive
Joliet, IL
815-741-2400 (800-257-3000)
This all suite hotel sits central to a number of sites of interest for both business and leisure travelers; plus they also offer a number of on-site amenities to ensure comfort. Dogs are allowed for an additional one time fee of $100 per room. Multiple dogs may be allowed.

Super 8 IL Kewanee
901 S Tenney St
Kewanee, IL
309-853-8800 (800-800-8000)
Dogs of all sizes are allowed. Dogs are allowed for a pet fee.

Extended Stay America Chicago - Lansing
2520 173rd St.
Lansing, IL
708-895-6402 (800-804-3724)
One dog is allowed per suite. There is a $25 per night additional pet fee up to $150 for an entire stay.

Howard Johnson IL Lansing
17301 Oak Ave
Lansing, IL
708-474-6900 (800-446-4656)
Dogs are welcome at this hotel.

Red Roof Inn Chicago - Lansing
2450 East 173rd Street
Lansing, IL
708-895-9570 (800-RED-ROOF)
One well-behaved family pet per room. Guest must notify front desk

upon arrival. Guest is liable for any damages. In consideration of all guests, pets must never be left unattended in the guest rooms.

Super 8 Le Roy
1 Demma Dr
Le Roy, IL
309-962-4700 (800-800-8000)
Dogs are welcome at this hotel.

Candlewood Suites
Chicago/Libertyville
1100 N US Highway 45
Libertyville, IL
847-247-9900 (877-270-6405)
Dogs up to 80 pounds are allowed. Pets allowed with an additional pet fee. Up to $75 for 1-6 nights and up to $150 for 7+ nights. A pet agreement must be signed at check-in.

Days Inn Six Flag Libertyville
1809 N Milwaukee Ave
Libertyville, IL
847-816-8006 (800-329-7466)
Dogs of all sizes are allowed. Dogs are allowed for a pet fee.

Best Western Lincoln Inn
1750 5th Street
Lincoln, IL
217-732-9641 (800-780-7234)
Dogs of all sizes are allowed. Dogs are allowed for a pet fee of $15.00 per pet per night.

Staybridge Suites Lincolnshire
100 Barclay Blvd
Lincolnshire, IL
847-821-0002 (877-270-6405)
Dogs up to 80 pounds are allowed. Pets allowed with an additional pet fee. Up to $75 for 1-6 nights and up to $150 for 7+ nights. A pet agreement must be signed at check-in.

Extended Stay America Chicago - Lisle
445 Warrenville Rd.
Lisle, IL
630-434-7710 (800-804-3724)
One dog is allowed per suite. There is a $25 per night additional pet fee up to $150 for an entire stay.

Hilton Hotel
3003 Corporate West Drive
Lisle, IL
630-505-0900 (800-HILTONS (445-8667))
This luxury hotel offers a number of on site amenities for business and leisure travelers, plus a convenient location to business, shopping,

dining, and entertainment areas. Dogs are allowed for an additional one time pet fee of $75 per room. 2 dogs may be allowed.

Holiday Inn Express Litchfield
1405 W. Hudson Drive
Litchfield, IL
217-324-4556 (877-270-6405)
Dogs are welcome at this hotel.

Super 8 Litchfield
I-55, Exit 52
Litchfield, IL
217-324-7788 (800-800-8000)
Dogs are welcome at this hotel.

Embassy Suites
707 East Butterfield Road/H 56
Lombard, IL
630-969-7500 (800-EMBASSY (362-2779))
A luxury, full service, atrium-style, all suite hotel; they offer a number of on site amenities for business and leisure travelers, plus a convenient location to business, shopping, dining, and entertainment districts. They also offer a complimentary cooked-to-order breakfast and a Manager's reception every evening. Dogs up to 70 pounds are allowed for an additional fee of $50 per night per pet. Dogs must be quiet, leashed, and removed or crated for housekeeping. Dogs may not be left alone in the room at any time. 2 dogs may be allowed.

Homestead Studio Suites Chicago - Lombard - Oak Brook
2701 Technology Dr.
Lombard, IL
630-928-0202 (800-804-3724)
One dog is allowed per suite. There is a $25 per night additional pet fee up to $150 for an entire stay.

Residence Inn Chicago Lombard
2001 S Highland Avenue
Lombard, IL
630-629-7800 (866-792-9185)
In addition to offering a convenient location to business, shopping, dining, and recreation areas, this hotel also provides a number of in-house amenities, including a daily buffet breakfast and an evening social hour. Dogs are allowed for an additional one time pet fee of $75 per room. Multiple dogs may be allowed.

TownePlace Suites Chicago Lombard
455 E 22nd Street
Lombard, IL
630-932-4400 (800-228-9290)

This all suite inn offers a number of in-house amenities for all level of travelers - including a deluxe continental breakfast and barbecue/picnic areas. Dogs are allowed for an additional one time fee of 75 per room. Multiple dogs may be allowed.

Super 8 Macomb
313 University Ave
Macomb, IL
309-836-8888 (800-800-8000)
Dogs of all sizes are allowed. Dogs are allowed for a pet fee.

Days Inn Marion
1802 Bittle Place
Marion, IL
618-997-1351 (800-329-7466)
Dogs of all sizes are allowed. Dogs are allowed for a nightly pet fee.

Drury Inn
2706 W. DeYoung
Marion, IL
618-997-9600 (800-378-7946)
Dogs of all sizes are allowed for no additional pet fee with a credit card on file, and there is a pet agreement to sign at check in.

Econo Lodge
1806 Bittle Place
Marion, IL
618-993-1644 (877-424-6423)
Dogs of all sizes are allowed. Dogs are allowed for a pet fee of $20.00 per pet per night. Two dogs are allowed per room.

Motel 6 - Marion
1008 Halfway Road
Marion, IL
618-993-2631 (800-466-8356)
This motel welcomes your pets to stay with you.

OldSquat Inn
14160 Liberty School Road
Marion, IL
618-982-2916
they can't take extra large dogs. There is a $20 per night additional pet fee.

Super 8 Marion
2601 West De Young
Marion, IL
618-993-5577 (800-800-8000)
Dogs are welcome at this hotel.

Super 8 Marshall
106 E Trefz Drive
Marshall, IL
217-826-8043 (800-800-8000)
Dogs of all sizes are allowed. Dogs

are allowed for a pet fee of $20 per pet per night.

Econo Lodge
2701 Maryville Rd.
Maryville, IL
618-345-5720 (877-424-6423)
Dogs up to 50 pounds are allowed. Two dogs are allowed per room.

La Quinta Inn Chicago/Matteson
5210 W. Southwick Drive
Matteson, IL
708-503-0999 (800-531-5900)
Dogs of all sizes are allowed. There are no additional pet fees. There is a pet waiver to sign at check in, and dogs must be leashed and cleaned up after. Multiple dogs may be allowed.

Holiday Inn Express Hotel & Suites Mattoon
121 Swords Drive
Mattoon, IL
217-235-2060 (877-270-6405)
Dogs of all sizes are allowed. Dogs are allowed for a pet fee of $25.00 per pet per night.

Super 8 Mattoon
205 McFall Road
Mattoon, IL
217-235-8888 (800-800-8000)
Dogs of all sizes are allowed. Dogs are allowed for a nightly pet fee.

Super 8 McLean
500 East South Street
McLean, IL
309-874-2366 (800-800-8000)
Dogs are welcome at this hotel.

Comfort Inn
1307 Kailash Drive
Mendota, IL
815-538-3355 (877-424-6423)
Dogs of all sizes are allowed.

Super 8 Mendota
508 Hwy 34 East & I-39
Mendota, IL
815-539-7429 (800-800-8000)
Dogs of all sizes are allowed. Dogs are allowed for a pet fee.

Day Plaza Inn
1415 E 5th Street/H 45
Metropolis, IL
618-524-9341 (800-329-7466)
daysinn.com
Dogs of all sizes are allowed for an additional fee of $7 per night per pet. Dogs must be leashed when out of the room, and cleaned up after at all times. 2 dogs may be allowed.

Residence Inn Chicago Lake Forest/Mettawa
26325 N Riverwoods Blvd
Mettawa, IL
847-615-2701 (800-331-3131)
This all suite hotel sits central to many of the city's star attractions, dining, shopping, and business areas, plus they offer a number of in-house amenities that include a daily buffet breakfast and evening socials during the week. Dogs up to 75 pounds are allowed for an additional one time pet fee of $100 per room. 2 dogs may be allowed.

Motel 6 - Minonk, Il
1312 Carolyn Dr
Minonk, IL
309-432-3663 (800-466-8356)
This motel welcomes your pets to stay with you.

Super 8 /Frankfort /I-80 Mokena
9485 West 191st Street
Mokena, IL
708-479-7808 (800-800-8000)
Dogs are welcome at this hotel.

Comfort Inn
2600 52nd Ave.
Moline, IL
309-762-7000 (877-424-6423)
Dogs of all sizes are allowed. Dogs are allowed for a pet fee of $10.00/ per pet per night.

Days Inn And Suites Airport Moline
6910 27th St
Moline, IL
309-762-8300 (800-329-7466)
Dogs of all sizes are allowed. Dogs are allowed for a pet fee.

Econo Lodge
6920 27th St.
Moline, IL
309-762-1548 (877-424-6423)
Dogs of all sizes are allowed. Dogs are allowed for a pet fee of $10.00 per pet per night.

La Quinta Inn Moline Airport
5450 27th St.
Moline, IL
309-762-9008 (800-531-5900)
Dogs of all sizes are allowed. There are no additional pet fees. Dogs must be quiet, leashed, and cleaned up after. A cell number must be left with the front desk if your dog is alone in the room. Multiple dogs may be allowed.

Ramada Airport Conference Center IL Moline

6902 27th Street
Moline, IL
309-762-8811 (800-272-6232)
Dogs are welcome at this hotel.

Residence Inn Moline Quad Cities
4600 53rd Street
Moline, IL
309-796-4244 (800-331-3131)
Located in the heart of the city, this all suite inn gives a convenient location to a plethora of year around interests, recreation, and activities for either the business or leisure traveler. Additionally, they offer a number of in-house amenities, including a daily buffet breakfast and evening socials Monday through Thursday. Dogs are allowed for an additional one time pet fee of $100 per room. 2 dogs may be allowed.

Super 8 Moline
2501 52nd Ave
Moline, IL
309-797-5580 (800-800-8000)
Dogs are welcome at this hotel.

Best Western Monticello Gateway Inn
805 Iron Horse Place
Monticello, IL
217-762-9436 (800-780-7234)
Dogs of all sizes are allowed. Dogs are allowed for a pet fee of $10 per pet per night.

Comfort Inn
70 Gore Rd. W.
Morris, IL
815-942-1433 (877-424-6423)
Dogs of all sizes are allowed. Dogs are allowed for a pet fee of $25.00 per pet per stay.

Days Inn and Suites of Morris
80 Hampton Road
Morris, IL
815-942-9000 (800-329-7466)
Dogs of all sizes are allowed. Dogs are allowed for a pet fee of $10.00 per pet per night.

Quality Inn
200 Gore Road
Morris, IL
815-942-6600 (877-424-6423)
Dogs of all sizes are allowed. Dogs are allowed for a pet fee of $25.00 per pet per stay. Two dogs are allowed per room.

Super 8 Morris
70 Green Acres Dr
Morris, IL
815-942-3200 (800-800-8000)
Dogs of all sizes are allowed. Dogs

are allowed for a pet fee of $10 per pet per night.

Baymont Inn & Suites Morton
210 East Ashland St
Morton, IL
309-266-8888 (877-229-6668)
Dogs of all sizes are allowed. Dogs are allowed for a nightly pet fee.

Best Western Ashland House & Conference Center
201 E Ashland Street
Morton, IL
309-263-5116 (800-780-7234)
Dogs of all sizes are allowed. Dogs are allowed for a pet fee of $15.00 per pet per stay.

Days Inn Peoria Area Morton
150 West Ashland Street
Morton, IL
309-266-9933 (800-329-7466)
Dogs are welcome at this hotel.

Best Western Morton Grove Inn
9424 Waukegan Road
Morton Grove, IL
847-965-6400 (800-780-7234)
Dogs of all sizes are allowed. Dogs are allowed for a pet fee of $10.00 per pet per night.

Comfort Suites
404 South 44th Street
Mount Vernon, IL
618-244-2700 (877-424-6423)
Dogs of all sizes are allowed.

Drury Inn
145 N 44th Street
Mount Vernon, IL
618-244-4550 (800-378-7946)
Dogs up to 60 pounds are allowed for no additional pet fee with a credit card on file, and there is a pet agreement to sign at check in.

Holiday Inn Mount Vernon
222 Potomac Blvd
Mount Vernon, IL
618-244-7100 (877-270-6405)
Dogs up to 60 pounds are allowed. Dogs are allowed for a pet fee of $10.00 per pet per night.

Motel 6 - Mt Vernon
333 44th St
Mount Vernon, IL
618-244-2383 (800-466-8356)
Your pets are welcome to stay here with you.

Red Roof Inn Mt Vernon
220 South 44th Street
Mount Vernon, IL
618-242-1200 (800-RED-ROOF)

One well-behaved family pet per room. Guest must notify front desk upon arrival. Guest is liable for any damages. In consideration of all guests, pets must never be left unattended in the guest rooms.

Super 8 Mt. Vernon
401 S. 44th St.
Mount Vernon, IL
618-242-8800 (800-800-8000)
Dogs are welcome at this hotel.

Thrifty Inn
100 North 44th Street
Mount Vernon, IL
618-244-7750 (800-378-7946)
Dogs of all sizes are allowed for no additional pet fee with a credit card on file, and there is a pet agreement to sign at check in.

Crowne Plaza Hotel Chicago-North Shore
510 E. Rt. 83
Mundelein, IL
847-949-5100 (877-270-6405)
Dogs are welcome at this hotel.

Super 8 /Libertyville Area Mundelein
1950 S. Lake St.
Mundelein, IL
847-949-8842 (800-800-8000)
Dogs of all sizes are allowed. Dogs are allowed for a pet fee of $10.00 per pet per night.

Baymont Inn & Suites Naperville
1585 Naperville Wheaton Road
Naperville, IL
630-357-0022 (877-229-6668)
Dogs are welcome at this hotel.

Best Western Naperville Inn
1617 N Naperville Road
Naperville, IL
630-505-0200 (800-780-7234)
Dogs of all sizes are allowed. Dogs are allowed for a pet fee of $10.00 per pet per stay.

Extended Stay America Chicago - Naperville
1575 Bond St.
Naperville, IL
630-983-0000 (800-804-3724)
One dog is allowed per suite. There is a $25 per night additional pet fee up to $150 for an entire stay.

Homestead Studio Suites Chicago - Naperville
1827 Centre Point Cir.
Naperville, IL
630-577-0200 (800-804-3724)
One dog is allowed per suite. There is a $25 per night additional pet fee

up to $150 for an entire stay.

Red Roof Inn Chicago - Naperville
1698 West Diehl Road
Naperville, IL
630-369-2500 (800-RED-ROOF)
One well-behaved family pet per
room. Guest must notify front desk
upon arrival. Guest is liable for any
damages. In consideration of all
guests, pets must never be left
unattended in the guest rooms.

TownePlace Suites Chicago
Naperville
1843 W Diehl Road
Naperville, IL
630-548-0881 (800-257-3000)
Besides offering a number of in-
house amenities for all level of
travelers, this all suite inn also offers
a convenient location to business,
shopping, dining, and entertainment
areas. Dogs are allowed for an
additional one time fee of $100 per
room. Multiple dogs may be allowed.

Best Western University Inn
6 Traders Circle
Normal, IL
309-454-4070 (800-780-7234)
Dogs of all sizes are allowed. Dogs
are allowed for a nightly pet fee.

Candlewood Suites Bloomington-
Normal
203 Susan Drive
Normal, IL
309-862-4100 (877-270-6405)
Dogs up to 80 pounds are allowed.
Pets allowed with an additional pet
fee. Up to $75 for 1-6 nights and up
to $150 for 7+ nights. A pet
agreement must be signed at check-
in.

Days Inn and Suites Normal
202 Landmark Drive
Normal, IL
309-454-6600 (800-329-7466)
Dogs of all sizes are allowed. Dogs
are allowed for a pet fee of $7.00 per
pet per night.

Motel 6 - Normal Bloomington Area
1600 Main St
Normal, IL
309-452-0422 (800-466-8356)
This motel welcomes your pets to
stay with you.

Super 8 Bloomington Normal
Two Traders Circle
Normal, IL
309-454-5858 (800-800-8000)
Dogs are welcome at this hotel.

Baymont Inn And Suites
Chicago/Aurora
308 South Lincolnway
North Aurora, IL
630-897-7695 (877-229-6668)
Dogs are welcome at this hotel.

Knights Inn North Chicago
2315 N Green Bay Rd.
North Chicago, IL
847-689-4500 (800-843-5644)
Dogs of all sizes are allowed. Dogs
are allowed for a pet fee of $10.00
per pet per night.

Hilton Hotel
2855 N Milwaukee Avenue
Northbrook, IL
847-480-7500 (800-HILTONS (445-
8667))
This upscale hotel offers a number
of on site amenities for business
and leisure travelers, including a
riverfront restaurant presenting
world class cuisine, a free 5 mile
radius shuttle service, and it's close
to the O'Hare International Airport.
One dog up to 75 pounds is allowed
for an additional one time pet fee of
$75.

Renaissance Chicago North Shore
Hotel
933 Skokie Blvd
Northbrook, IL
847-498-6500 (800-HOTELS-1
(468-3571))
Located in the city's esteemed
North Shore area, this luxury hotel
sits central to many of the city's star
attractions, world class shopping
and dining venues, entertainment
areas, and major business areas,
plus they also offer a number of in-
house amenities for all level of
travelers. Dogs are allowed for an
additional one time fee of $75 per
room. 2 dogs may be allowed.

Extended Stay America St. Louis -
O' Fallon, Il
154 Regency Park
O'Fallon, IL
618-624-1757 (800-804-3724)
One dog is allowed per suite. There
is a $25 per night additional pet fee
up to $150 for an entire stay.

Quality Inn
1409 W US 50
O'Fallon, IL
618-628-8895 (877-424-6423)
Dogs of all sizes are allowed. Dogs
are allowed for a pet fee of $10.00
per pet per night. Two dogs are
allowed per room.

Days Inn O'Fallon
1320 Park Plaza Drive
OFallon, IL
618-628-9700 (800-329-7466)
Dogs are welcome at this hotel.

Residence Inn Chicago Oak Brook
790 Jorie Blvd
Oak Brook, IL
630-571-1200 (800-331-3131)
In addition to offering a convenient
location to business, shopping,
dining, and entertainment areas, this
hotel also provides a number of in-
house amenities, including a daily
buffet breakfast and an evening
social hour Monday to Wednesday.
One dog up to 100 pounds is allowed
for an additional one time pet fee of
$100 per room.

Staybridge Suites Chicago-Oakbrook
Terrace
200 Royce Blvd
Oakbrook Terrace, IL
630-953-9393 (877-270-6405)
Dogs up to 80 pounds are allowed.
Pets allowed with an additional pet
fee. Up to $75 for 1-6 nights and up
to $150 for 7+ nights. A pet
agreement must be signed at check-
in.

Candlewood Suites Ofallon
1332 Park Plaza Drive
Ofallon, IL
618-622-9555 (877-270-6405)
Dogs up to 80 pounds are allowed.
Pets allowed with an additional pet
fee. Up to $75 for 1-6 nights and up
to $150 for 7+ nights. A pet
agreement must be signed at check-
in.

Days Inn / Starved Rock Oglesby
120 North Lewis Ave
Oglesby, IL
815-883-9600 (800-329-7466)
Dogs of all sizes are allowed. Dogs
are allowed for a pet fee of $15.00
per pet per stay.

Holiday Inn Express Oglesby (La
Salle/Peru Area)
900 Holiday St
Oglesby, IL
815-883-3535 (877-270-6405)
Dogs of all sizes are allowed. Dogs
are allowed for a pet fee of $35.00
per pet per stay.

Super 8 Okawville
812 North Hen House Road
Okawville, IL
618-243-6525 (800-800-8000)
Dogs are welcome at this hotel.

Super 8 Olney
425 SW Route 130
Olney, IL
618-392-7888 (800-800-8000)
Dogs of all sizes are allowed. Dogs are allowed for a pet fee of $8 per pet per night.

Motel 6 - Chicago Northwest Palatine
1450 Dundee Rd
Palatine, IL
847-359-0046 (800-466-8356)
This motel welcomes your pets to stay with you.

Super 8 IL Paris
11642 IL Hwy 1
Paris, IL
217-463-8888 (800-800-8000)
Dogs of all sizes are allowed. Dogs are allowed for a pet fee.

Econo Lodge & Suites
3240 N. Vandever Ave.
Pekin, IL
309-353-4047 (877-424-6423)
Dogs of all sizes are allowed. Dogs are allowed for a pet fee of $10.00 per pet per night.

Candlewood Suites Peoria At Grand Prairie
5300 W. Landens Way
Peoria, IL
309-691-1690 (877-270-6405)
Dogs up to 80 pounds are allowed. Pets allowed with an additional pet fee. Up to $75 for 1-6 nights and up to $150 for 7+ nights. A pet agreement must be signed at check-in.

Comfort Suites
1812 W. War Memorial Dr.
Peoria, IL
309-688-3800 (877-424-6423)
Dogs of all sizes are allowed. Dogs are allowed for a pet fee of $25.00USD per pet per stay.

Extended Stay America Peoria - North
4306 North Brandywine Dr.
Peoria, IL
309-688-3110 (800-804-3724)
One dog is allowed per suite. There is a $25 per night additional pet fee up to $150 for an entire stay.

Jameson Inn and Suites
4112 N Brandywine
Peoria, IL
309-685-2556 (800-JAMESON (526-3766))
This inn offers a number of amenities including a swimming pool. Dogs are allowed for an additional one time

fee of $15 per pet. Dogs must be leashed and cleaned up after at all times. 2 dogs may be allowed.

Mark Twain Hotel
225 NE Adams Street
Peoria, IL
309-676-3600 (866-325-6351)
marktwainhotel.com/
Warmly and richly decorated, this 110 room hotel has undergone extensive renovations-turning it from ordinary to extra-ordinary with many comforts and amenities; there is also a restaurant and cyber-cafe on site. Dogs of all sizes are allowed for a $50 refundable deposit per pet. Dogs must be leashed, cleaned up after, and crated when left alone in the room. 2 dogs may be allowed.

Red Roof Inn Peoria
1822 W War rive
Peoria, IL
309-685-3911 (800-RED-ROOF)
One well-behaved family pet per room. Guest must notify front desk upon arrival. Guest is liable for any damages. In consideration of all guests, pets must never be left unattended in the guest rooms.

Residence Inn Peoria
2000 W War Memorial Drive
Peoria, IL
309-681-9000 (800-331-3131)
This all suite hotel, near NorthWoods Mall, sits central to many of the city's star attractions, universities, and business areas, plus they offer a number of in-house amenities that include a daily buffet breakfast and evening social hours. Dogs are allowed for an additional one time pet fee of $25 for 1 to 2 nights; $50 for 4 to 7 nights; $75 for 8 to 14 nights, and $100 for 15 nights or more per room (plus tax on all fees). Multiple dogs may be allowed.

Super 8 Peoria
1816 West War Memorial Drive
Peoria, IL
309-688-8074 (800-800-8000)
Dogs are welcome at this hotel.

La Quinta Inn Peru
4389 Venture Drive
Peru, IL
815-224-9000 (800-531-5900)
Dogs of all sizes are allowed. There are no additional pet fees. There is a pet waiver to sign at check in. Dogs may not be left unattended in the room unless they will be very quiet and well behaved. Dogs must

be leashed and cleaned up after. 2 dogs may be allowed.

Super 8 Peru
1851 May Rd.
Peru, IL
815-223-1848 (800-800-8000)
Dogs of all sizes are allowed. Dogs are allowed for a pet fee.

Super 8 Pinckneyville
5700 State Route 154
Pinckneyville, IL
618-357-5600 (800-800-8000)
Dogs of all sizes are allowed. Dogs are allowed for a nightly pet fee.

Comfort Inn
1821 W. Reynolds St.
Pontiac, IL
815-842-2777 (877-424-6423)
Dogs of all sizes are allowed. Dogs are allowed for a pet fee of $10.00 per pet per night.

Super 8 Pontiac
601 S Deerfield Rd
Pontiac, IL
815-844-6888 (800-800-8000)
Dogs of all sizes are allowed. Dogs are allowed for a pet fee.

Three Roses Bed and Breakfast
209 E. Howard Street/H 116
Pontiac, IL
815-844-3404
threerosesbedandbreakfast.com/
Victorian décor creates a warm, romantic ambiance for guests, and in addition to personalized breakfasts, they also offer an optional extensive dinner menu. Housebroken dogs of all sizes are allowed for no additional fee. Dogs must be leashed when not in the house, and cleaned up after at all times. 2 dogs may be allowed.

Super 8
4141 Timberlake Drive
Pontoon Beach, IL
618-931-8808 (800-800-8000)
Dogs are welcome at this hotel.

Days Inn Princeton
2238 North Main Street
Princeton, IL
815-875-3371 (800-329-7466)
Dogs of all sizes are allowed. Dogs are allowed for a pet fee of $6.00 per pet per night.

Econo Lodge
2200 N. Main St.
Princeton, IL
815-872-3300 (877-424-6423)
Dogs of all sizes are allowed. Dogs are allowed for a pet fee of $20.00

per pet per night. Two dogs are allowed per room.

Super 8 /Northbrook Prospect Heights
540 Milwaukee Ave
Prospect Heights, IL
847-459-0545 (800-800-8000)
Dogs are welcome at this hotel.

Wingate by Wyndham - Northbrook/ Prospect Heights
600 Milwaukee Ave
Prospect Heights, IL
847-419-3600 (800-228-1000)
Dogs of all sizes are allowed. Dogs are allowed for a pet fee.

Comfort Inn
4122 Broadway
Quincy, IL
217-228-2700 (877-424-6423)
Dogs of all sizes are allowed. Dogs are allowed for a pet fee of $10.00 per pet per night.

Days Inn Quincy
200 Maine Street
Quincy, IL
217-223-6610 (800-329-7466)
Dogs of all sizes are allowed. Dogs are allowed for a pet fee.

Super 8 Quincy
224 N. 36th St.
Quincy, IL
217-228-8808 (800-800-8000)
Dogs of all sizes are allowed. Dogs are allowed for a pet fee.

Best Western Heritage Inn
420 S Murray Road
Rantoul, IL
217-892-9292 (800-780-7234)
Dogs are welcome at this hotel.

Days Inn Rantoul
801 W Champaign Ave
Rantoul, IL
217-893-0700 (800-329-7466)
Dogs are welcome at this hotel.

Super 8 Rantoul
207 S. Murray Rd.
Rantoul, IL
217-893-8888 (800-800-8000)
Dogs are welcome at this hotel.

Baymont Inn & Suites Rochelle
567 E Hwy 38
Rochelle, IL
815-562-9530 (877-229-6668)
Dogs are welcome at this hotel.

Comfort Inn & Suites
1133 N. 7th St.
Rochelle, IL

815-562-5551 (877-424-6423)
Dogs up to 50 pounds are allowed. Dogs are allowed for a pet fee of $15.00/ per pet per night. Two dogs are allowed per room.

Holiday Inn Rock Island - Quad Cities
226 17th St.
Rock Island, IL
309-794-1212 (877-270-6405)
Dogs are welcome at this hotel.

Baymont Inn & Suites Rockford
662 North Lyford Road
Rockford, IL
815-229-8200 (877-229-6668)
Dogs are welcome at this hotel.

Candlewood Suites Rockford
7555 Walton Street
Rockford, IL
815-229-9300 (877-270-6405)
Dogs up to 80 pounds are allowed. Pets allowed with an additional pet fee. Up to $75 for 1-6 nights and up to $150 for 7+ nights. A pet agreement must be signed at check-in.

Comfort Inn
7392 Argus Dr.
Rockford, IL
815-398-7061 (877-424-6423)
Dogs of all sizes are allowed. Dogs are allowed for a pet fee of $25 per pet per stay.

Days Inn Rockford
220 S Lyford Rd
Rockford, IL
815-332-4915 (800-329-7466)
Dogs are welcome at this hotel.

Extended Stay America Rockford - East
653 Clark Dr.
Rockford, IL
815-226-8969 (800-804-3724)
One dog is allowed per suite. There is a $25 per night additional pet fee up to $150 for an entire stay.

Motel 6 - Rockford, Il
7712 Potawatomi Trail
Rockford, IL
815-397-8000 (800-466-8356)
This motel welcomes your pets to stay with you.

Red Roof Inn Rockford
7434 East State St
Rockford, IL
815-398-9750 (800-RED-ROOF)
One well-behaved family pet per room. Guest must notify front desk upon arrival. Guest is liable for any

damages. In consideration of all guests, pets must never be left unattended in the guest rooms.

Residence Inn Rockford
7542 Colosseum Drive
Rockford, IL
815-227-0013 (800-331-3131)
This all suite inn features a convenient location to business, shopping, dining, and entertainment areas, plus they also offer a number of in-house amenities, including a daily buffet breakfast and evening socials. Dogs are allowed for an additional one time pet fee of $100 per room. Multiple dogs may be allowed.

Sleep Inn
725 Clark Drive
Rockford, IL
815-398-8900 (877-424-6423)
Dogs up to 50 pounds are allowed. Dogs are allowed for a pet fee of $15.00 per pet per night. Two dogs are allowed per room.

Staybridge Suites Rockford
633 North Bell School Road
Rockford, IL
815-397-0200 (877-270-6405)
Dogs up to 80 pounds are allowed. Pets allowed with an additional pet fee. Up to $75 for 1-6 nights and up to $150 for 7+ nights. A pet agreement must be signed at check-in.

Super 8 Rockford
7646 Colosseum Dr.
Rockford, IL
815-229-5522 (800-800-8000)
Dogs of all sizes are allowed. Dogs are allowed for a pet fee.

Travelodge - Rockford
4850 East State Street
Rockford, IL
815-398-5050 (800-578-7878)
Dogs of all sizes are allowed. Dogs are allowed for a pet fee of $10.00 per pet per night.

Extended Stay America Chicago - Rolling Meadows - Schaumburg Convention Center
2400 Golf Rd.
Rolling Meadows, IL
847-357-1000 (800-804-3724)
One dog is allowed per suite. There is a $25 per night additional pet fee up to $150 for an entire stay.

Motel 6 - Chicago Northwest Rolling Meadows
1800 Winnetka Circle

Rolling Meadows, IL
847-818-8088 (800-466-8356)
This motel welcomes your pets to
stay with you.

Best Western Romeoville Inn
1280 W Normantown Road
Romeoville, IL
815-372-1000 (800-780-7234)
Dogs of all sizes are allowed. Dogs
are allowed for a pet fee of $25.00
per pet per stay.

Extended Stay America Chicago -
Romeoville
1225 Lakeview Dr.
Romeoville, IL
630-226-8966 (800-804-3724)
One dog is allowed per suite. There
is a $25 per night additional pet fee
up to $150 for an entire stay.

Super 8 Bolingbrook Romeoville
1301 Marquette Dr.
Romeoville, IL
630-759-8880 (800-800-8000)
Dogs are welcome at this hotel.

Crowne Plaza Hotel Chicago Ohare
Hotel & Conf Ctr
5440 North River Road
Rosemont, IL
847-671-6350 (877-270-6405)
Dogs of all sizes are allowed. Dogs
are allowed for a pet fee.

Doubletree Hotel
5460 N River Road
Rosemont, IL
847-292-9100 (800-222-TREE
(8733))
This full service, upscale hotel offers
a number of on site amenities for
business or leisure travelers, plus a
convenient location to the O'Hare
International Airport, and business,
shopping, dining, and recreation
areas. Dogs up to 50 pounds are
allowed for an additional one time
pet fee of $25 per room. 2 dogs may
be allowed.

Embassy Suites
5500 N River Road
Rosemont, IL
847-678-4000 (800-EMBASSY (362-
2779))
A luxury, full service, all suite hotel;
they offer a number of on site
amenities for all level of travelers,
plus a convenient location to
business, shopping, dining, and
entertainment districts. They also
offer a complimentary cooked-to-
order breakfast and a Manager's
reception every evening. Dogs up to
50 pounds are allowed for a $100

deposit--$75 is refundable per pet.
2 dogs may be allowed.

Residence Inn Chicago O'Hare
7101 Chestnut Street
Rosemont, IL
847-375-9000 (800-331-3131)
Located only 3 miles from the
Chicago O'Hare Airport and near
the CTA rail system for easy access
to all the city has to offer, this hotel
presents a convenient location to
business, shopping, dining, and
entertainment areas, plus they offer
a number of in-house amenities,
including a daily buffet breakfast
and a complimentary full dinner
buffet Monday to Thursday. Dogs
are allowed for an additional one
time pet fee of $100 per room.
Multiple dogs may be allowed.

Sheraton Gateway Suites Chicago
O'Hare
6501 North Mannheim Road
Rosemont, IL
847-699-6300 (888-625-5144)
Offering luxury accommodations,
this hotel also has a restaurant,
lounge, and bakery café, and they
sit central to many of the city's
services, recreational pursuits, and
sites of interest. Dogs of all sizes
are allowed for no additional fee.
Dogs must be quiet, leashed or
crated, and cleaned up after at all
times. 2 dogs may be allowed.

The Westin O'Hare
6100 North River Road
Rosemont, IL
847-698-6000 (888-625-5144)
westinohare.com
Offering luxury accommodations,
this hotel has a restaurant, lounge,
and bakery café, and they also sit
central to many of the city's
services, recreational pursuits, and
sites of interest. Dogs of all sizes
are allowed for no additional fee.
Dogs must be quiet, leashed or
crated, and cleaned up after at all
times. 2 dogs may be allowed.

Best Western Inn of St. Charles
1635 E Main Street
Saint Charles, IL
630-584-4550 (800-780-7234)
Dogs of all sizes are allowed. Dogs
are allowed for a pet fee of $10 per
pet per night.

Super 8 Salem
118 Woods Lane
Salem, IL
618-548-5882 (800-800-8000)
Dogs are welcome at this hotel.

L & M Motel
2000 N Oakton Road
Savanna, IL
815-273-7728
Medium-sized dogs are $20, and
large dogs are $30.

Super 8 IL Savanna
101 Valley View Drive
Savanna, IL
815-273-2288 (800-800-8000)
Dogs of all sizes are allowed. Dogs
are allowed for a pet fee.

The Oscar Swan Country Inn
3315 Elizabeth-Scales Road
Scales Mound, IL
815-541-0653
oscarswangalena.com/
Located on 30 acres of green rolling
hills, this full restored inn offers a
good venue for business or leisure
travelers with indoor and outdoor
meeting spaces and catering
services. Dogs of all sizes are
allowed for no additional fee. Dogs
must be well behaved, leashed, and
cleaned up after. 2 dogs may be
allowed.

Candlewood Suites Chicago/
Schaumburg
1200 East Bank Drive
Schaumburg, IL
847-517-7644 (877-270-6405)
Dogs up to 80 pounds are allowed.
Pets allowed with an additional pet
fee. Up to $75 for 1-6 nights and up
to $150 for 7+ nights. A pet
agreement must be signed at check-
in.

Extended Stay America Chicago -
Schaumburg - Convention Center
2000 N. Roselle Rd.
Schaumburg, IL
847-882-7011 (800-804-3724)
One dog is allowed per suite. There
is a $25 per night additional pet fee
up to $150 for an entire stay.

Extended Stay America Chicago -
Woodfield Mall - Schaumburg
Convention Center
1200 American Ln.
Schaumburg, IL
847-517-7255 (800-804-3724)
One dog is allowed per suite. There
is a $25 per night additional pet fee
up to $150 for an entire stay.

Hawthorn Suites Schaumburg
1251 E. American Lane
Schaumburg, IL
847-706-9007 (800-527-1133)
hawthornschaumburg.com

The hotel has 135 Suites. Studio, One and Two-bedroom Suites are available. They offer all guests a complimentary hot breakfast buffet daily, evening reception Monday thru Thursday, and Dinner on Wednesday evenings. They have an indoor pool and fitness center, and passes to both Lifetime Fitness and Bally Total Fitness for guests to use. They offer full kitchens in each guestroom, high speed internet access, and a daily paper. Pets are welcome. There is a one time fee of $50-$100.00 depending on the size of the dog.

Homestead Studio Suites Chicago - Schaumburg - Convention Center
51 E. State Pkwy.
Schaumburg, IL
847-882-6900 (800-804-3724)
One dog is allowed per suite. There is a $25 per night additional pet fee up to $150 for an entire stay.

La Quinta Inn Chicago Schaumburg
1730 E. Higgins Rd.
Schaumburg, IL
847-517-8484 (800-531-5900)
Dogs of all sizes are allowed. There are no additional pet fees. Dogs may not be left unattended, and they must be leashed and cleaned up after. Dogs are not allowed in the lobby. Multiple dogs may be allowed.

Residence Inn Chicago Schaumburg
1610 McConnor Parkway
Schaumburg, IL
847-517-9200 (800-331-3131)
In addition to offering a convenient location to business, shopping, dining, and entertainment areas, this hotel also provides a number of in-house amenities, including a daily buffet breakfast and a complimentary manager's reception Monday to Thursday. Dogs up to 50 pounds are allowed for an additional one time pet fee of $100 per room. 2 dogs may be allowed.

Staybridge Suites Schaumburg
901 East Woodfield Office Ct
Schaumburg, IL
847-619-6677 (877-270-6405)
Dogs up to 80 pounds are allowed. Pets allowed with an additional pet fee. Up to $75 for 1-6 nights and up to $150 for 7+ nights. A pet agreement must be signed at check-in.

Candlewood Suites Chicago-O`hare
4021 North Mannheim Road
Schiller Park, IL
847-671-4663 (877-270-6405)
Dogs up to 80 pounds are allowed.

Pets allowed with an additional pet fee. Up to $75 for 1-6 nights and up to $150 for 7+ nights. A pet agreement must be signed at check-in.

Comfort Suites O'Hare Arprt
4200 N. River Road
Schiller Park, IL
847-233-9000 (877-424-6423)
Dogs up to 50 pounds are allowed.

Motel 6 - Chicago O'hare Schiller Park
9408 Lawrence Ave
Schiller Park, IL
847-671-4282 (800-466-8356)
This motel welcomes your pets to stay with you.

Comfort Inn
9333 Skokie Boulevard
Skokie, IL
847-679-4200 (877-424-6423)
Dogs of all sizes are allowed. Two dogs are allowed per room.

Extended Stay America Chicago - Skokie
5211 Old Orchard Rd.
Skokie, IL
847-663-9031 (800-804-3724)
One dog is allowed per suite. There is a $25 per night additional pet fee up to $150 for an entire stay.

Holiday Inn Chicago North Shore (Skokie)
5300 West Touhy Ave
Skokie, IL
847-679-8900 (877-270-6405)
Dogs are welcome at this hotel. There is a $50 one time pet fee.

Best Western Legacy Inn & Suites
5910 Technology Drive
South Beloit, IL
815-389-4211 (800-780-7234)
Dogs of all sizes are allowed. Dogs are allowed for a pet fee.

Comfort Inn
200 Comfort Drive
South Jacksonville, IL
217-245-8372 (877-424-6423)
Dogs of all sizes are allowed. Dogs are allowed for a pet fee of $15.00USD/ per pet per night. Two dogs are allowed per room.

Baymont Inn & Suites Springfield
5871 South 6TH ST.
Springfield, IL
217-529-6655 (877-229-6668)
Dogs are welcome at this hotel.

Best Western Clearlake Plaza

3440 E Clearlake Avenue
Springfield, IL
217-525-7420 (800-780-7234)
Dogs of all sizes are allowed. Dogs are allowed for a pet fee of $35 per pet per stay.

Candlewood Suites Springfield
2501 Sunrise Drive
Springfield, IL
217-522-5100 (877-270-6405)
Dogs up to 80 pounds are allowed. Pets allowed with an additional pet fee. Up to $75 for 1-6 nights and up to $150 for 7+ nights. A pet agreement must be signed at check-in.

Drury Inn & Suites
3180 S. Dirksen Parkway
Springfield, IL
217-529-3900 (800-378-7946)
Dogs of all sizes are allowed for no additional pet fee with a credit card on file, and there is a pet agreement to sign at check in. There may be up to 3 dogs if they are small.

Hilton Hotel
700 East Adams Street
Springfield, IL
217-789-1530 (800-HILTONS (445-8667))
Located downtown across from the Prairie Capital Convention Center, this luxury hotel offers numerous on site amenities for business and leisure travelers, plus a convenient location to historic sites, and shopping, dining, and recreational areas. Dogs are allowed for an additional one time pet fee of $75 per room. (Pet friendly rooms are limited.) 2 dogs may be allowed.

Holiday Inn Express Hotel & Suites Springfield
3050 S. Dirksen Pkwy
Springfield, IL
217-529-7771 (877-270-6405)
Dogs of all sizes are allowed. Dogs are allowed for a pet fee of $25.00 per pet per stay.

Howard Johnson Inn - Suites Springfield
1701 J. David Jones Parkway
Springfield, IL
217-541-8762 (800-446-4656)
Dogs of all sizes are allowed. Dogs are allowed for a pet fee of $10.00 per pet per night.

Mansion View Inn and Suites
529 S 4th Street
Springfield, IL
800-252-1083

mansionview.com/index.php
In addition to providing a variety of accommodations, this inn sits across the street from the Governor's Mansion and central to a number of local attractions, activities, and other sites of interest. Dogs are allowed for an additional one time pet fee of $25 per room. 2 dogs may be allowed.

Motel 6 - Springfield, Il
6011 6th St Rd
Springfield, IL
217-529-1633 (800-466-8356)
This motel welcomes your pets to stay with you.

Pear Tree Inn by Drury Hotel
3190 S Dirksen Parkway
Springfield, IL
217-529-9100 (800-DRURYINN (378-7946))
Dogs of all sizes are allowed for no additional pet fee with a credit card on file, and there is a pet agreement to sign at check in.

Ramada Limited South Springfield
5970 South 6th Street
Springfield, IL
217-529-1410 (800-272-6232)
Dogs of all sizes are allowed. Dogs are allowed for a nightly pet fee.

Red Roof Inn Springfield, IL
3200 Singer Avenue
Springfield, IL
217-753-4302 (800-RED-ROOF)
One well-behaved family pet per room. Guest must notify front desk upon arrival. Guest is liable for any damages. In consideration of all guests, pets must never be left unattended in the guest rooms.

Signature Inn
3090 Stevenson Drive
Springfield, IL
217-529-6611 (800-JAMESON (526-3766))
This inn offers a number of amenities including an indoor swimming pool. Dogs are allowed for an additional fee of $10 per night per pet. Dogs may not be left alone in the room, and they must be leashed and cleaned up after at all times. Dogs are not allowed in food service areas. 2 dogs may be allowed.

Sleep Inn
3470 Freedom Dr.
Springfield, IL
217-787-6200 (877-424-6423)
Dogs of all sizes are allowed. Dogs are allowed for a pet fee of $25.00 per pet per stay. Three or more dogs

may be allowed.

Staybridge Suites Springfield-South
4231 Schooner Drive
Springfield, IL
217-793-6700 (877-270-6405)
Dogs up to 80 pounds are allowed. Pets allowed with an additional pet fee. Up to $75 for 1-6 nights and up to $150 for 7+ nights. A pet agreement must be signed at check-in.

Super 8 South Springfield
3675 S 6th St.
Springfield, IL
217-529-8898 (800-800-8000)
Dogs of all sizes are allowed. Dogs are allowed for a pet fee of $10 per pet per night.

Days Inn St Charles
100 S Tyler Road
St Charles, IL
630-513-6500 (800-329-7466)
Dogs of all sizes are allowed. Dogs are allowed for a pet fee of $10 per pet per night.

Super 8 St. Charles
1520 E. Main
St Charles, IL
630-377-8388 (800-800-8000)
Dogs of all sizes are allowed. Dogs are allowed for a pet fee of $15 per pet per night.

The Courtyard Chicago St. Charles
700 Courtyard Drive
St Charles, IL
630-377-6370 (888-236-2427)
Featuring a quiet setting only a mile from all the downtown area has to offer, this hotel also has a number of in house amenities, including a breakfast buffet with cooked to order items. One dog up to 75 pounds or 2 dogs totaling no more than 100 pounds are allowed for an additional one time pet fee of $75 per room. 2 dogs may be allowed.

Super 8 Motel - Staunton
1527 Herman Road
Staunton, IL
618-635-5353 (800-800-8000)
Dogs are welcome at this hotel.

La Quinta Inn Chicago/Tinley Park
7255 W. 183rd Street
Tinley Park, IL
708-633-1200 (800-531-5900)
Dogs of all sizes are allowed. There are no additional fees. If pets are left in the room, please hang the "Do Not Disturb" sign. Dogs must be removed from the room for

housekeeping, be leashed, and cleaned up after. Multiple dogs may be allowed.

Red Roof Inn Troy
2030 Formosa Road
Troy, IL
618-667-2222 (800-RED-ROOF)
One well-behaved family pet per room. Guest must notify front desk upon arrival. Guest is liable for any damages. In consideration of all guests, pets must never be left unattended in the guest rooms.

Super 8
910 Edwardsville Rd
Troy, IL
618-667-8888 (800-800-8000)
Dogs of all sizes are allowed. Dogs are allowed for a nightly pet fee.

Baymont Inn & Suites Tuscola
1006 Southline Road
Tuscola, IL
217-253-3500 (877-229-6668)
Dogs are welcome at this hotel.

Super 8 Tuscola
1007 E. Southline Drive
Tuscola, IL
217-253-5488 (800-800-8000)
Dogs are welcome at this hotel.

Motel 6 - Urbana, Il
1906 N. Cunningham Ave.
Urbana, IL
217-344-1085 (800-466-8356)
This motel welcomes your pets to stay with you.

Ramada Urbana
902 West Killarney Street
Urbana, IL
217-328-4400 (800-272-6232)
Dogs are welcome at this hotel.

Sleep Inn
1908 N. Lincoln Ave.
Urbana, IL
217-367-6000 (877-424-6423)
Dogs of all sizes are allowed. Dogs are allowed for a pet fee of $10.00 per pet per night.

Days Inn Vandalia
1920 Kennedy Boulevard
Vandalia, IL
618-283-4400 (800-329-7466)
Dogs are welcome at this hotel.

Holiday Inn Express Hotel & Suites Vandalia
21 Mattes Avenue
Vandalia, IL
618-283-0010 (877-270-6405)
Dogs of all sizes are allowed. Dogs

are allowed for a pet fee of $20 per pet per stay.

Ramada Vandalia
2707 Veterans Ave.
Vandalia, IL
618-283-1400 (800-272-6232)
Dogs of all sizes are allowed. Dogs are allowed for a pet fee of $10.00 per pet per night.

Travelodge Vandalia
1500 North 6th Street
Vandalia, IL
618-283-2363 (800-578-7878)
Dogs are welcome at this hotel.

Extended Stay America Chicago - Vernon Hills - Lake Forest
215 N. Milwaukee Ave.
Vernon Hills, IL
847-821-7101 (800-804-3724)
One dog is allowed per suite. There is a $25 per night additional pet fee up to $150 for an entire stay.

Homestead Studio Suites Chicago - Vernon Hills - Lincolnshire
675 Woodlands Pkwy.
Vernon Hills, IL
847-955-1111 (800-804-3724)
One dog is allowed per suite. There is a $25 per night additional pet fee up to $150 for an entire stay.

Hotel Indigo Chicago-Vernon Hills
450 North Milwaukee Avenue
Vernon Hills, IL
847-918-1400 (877-865-6578)
Dogs are welcome at this hotel.

Motel 6 - Chicago West Villa Park
10 Roosevelt Rd
Villa Park, IL
630-941-9100 (800-466-8356)
This motel welcomes your pets to stay with you.

Candlewood Suites Chicago/Naperville
27 W. 300 Warrenville Road
Warrenville, IL
630-836-1650 (877-270-6405)
Dogs up to 80 pounds are allowed. Pets allowed with an additional pet fee. Up to $75 for 1-6 nights and up to $150 for 7+ nights. A pet agreement must be signed at check-in.

Residence Inn Chicago Naperville/Warrenville
28500 Bella Vista Parkway
Warrenville, IL
630-393-3444 (800-331-3131)
In addition to offering a convenient location to business, shopping,

dining, and entertainment areas, this hotel also provides a number of in-house amenities, including a daily buffet breakfast and an evening reception Monday to Thursday. Dogs are allowed for an additional one time pet fee of $100 per room. 2 dogs may be allowed.

Super 8 /Peoria Area Washington
1884 Washington Rd
Washington, IL
309-444-8881 (800-800-8000)
Dogs of all sizes are allowed. Dogs are allowed for a pet fee of $8.00 per pet per night.

Super 8 Watseka
710 West Walnut St
Watseka, IL
815-432-6000 (800-800-8000)
Dogs are welcome at this hotel.

Candlewood Suites Chicago-Waukegan
1151 South Waukegan Rd
Waukegan, IL
847-578-5250 (877-270-6405)
Dogs up to 80 pounds are allowed. Pets allowed with an additional pet fee. Up to $75 for 1-6 nights and up to $150 for 7+ nights. A pet agreement must be signed at check-in.

Days Inn of Waukegan
3633 N Lewis Ave
Waukegan, IL
847-249-7778 (800-329-7466)
Dogs are welcome at this hotel.

Motel 6 - Waukegan, Il
31 Green Bay Rd
Waukegan, IL
847-336-9000 (800-466-8356)
This motel welcomes your pets to stay with you.

Super 8 Chicago//I-94 N. Waukegan
630 N. Green Bay Rd.
Waukegan, IL
847-249-2388 (800-800-8000)
Dogs are welcome at this hotel.

Super 8 Wenona
5 Cavalry Drive
Wenona, IL
815-853-4371 (800-800-8000)
Dogs of all sizes are allowed. Dogs are allowed for a pet fee of $5 per pet per night.

TownePlace Suites Chicago Elgin/West Dundee
2185 Marriott Drive
West Dundee, IL

847-608-6320 (800-257-3000)
In addition to offering a number of in-house amenities for all level of travelers, this all suite inn also provides a convenient location to businesses, shopping, dining, and entertainment areas. Dogs are allowed for an additional one time fee of $75 per pet. Multiple dogs may be allowed.

Homestead Studio Suites Chicago - Westmont - Oak Brook
855 Pasquinelli Dr.
Westmont, IL
630-323-9292 (800-804-3724)
One dog is allowed per suite. There is a $25 per night additional pet fee up to $150 for an entire stay.

Candlewood Suites Chicago-Wheeling
8000 Capitol Drive
Wheeling, IL
847-520-1684 (877-270-6405)
Dogs up to 80 pounds are allowed. Pets allowed with an additional pet fee. Up to $75 for 1-6 nights and up to $150 for 7+ nights. A pet agreement must be signed at check-in.

The Executive Plaza Hotel & Conference Center
1090 S. Milwaukee Ave
Wheeling, IL
847-537-9100
stayplazahotel.com
Dogs of all sizes are allowed. There is a $25 per night pet fee.

Red Roof Inn Chicago - Willowbrook
7535 Kingery Highway/State Route 83
Willowbrook, IL
630-323-8811 (800-RED-ROOF)
One well-behaved family pet per room. Guest must notify front desk upon arrival. Guest is liable for any damages. In consideration of all guests, pets must never be left unattended in the guest rooms.

Super 8 Willowbrook
820 West 79th Street
Willowbrook, IL
630-789-6300 (800-800-8000)
Dogs are welcome at this hotel.

Super 8 Woodstock
1220 Davis Rd
Woodstock, IL
815-337-8808 (800-800-8000)
Dogs of all sizes are allowed. Dogs are allowed for a pet fee.

Indiana

Lees Inn
2114 East 59th Street
Anderson, IN
765-649-2500 (800-SEE-LEES (733-5337))
leesinn.com/
In addition to a number of on-site amenities - including a hot breakfast buffet, they offer a convenient location to a number of local attractions, shopping, and dining areas. Dogs are allowed for no additional fee with a credit card on file; there is a pet policy to sign at check in. Dogs must be declared at the time of reservations. 2 dogs may be allowed.

Motel 6 - Anderson
5810 Scatterfield Rd
Anderson, IN
765-642-9023 (800-466-8356)
This motel welcomes your pets to stay with you.

Super 8 Anderson
2215 East 59th St
Anderson, IN
765-642-2222 (800-800-8000)
Dogs of all sizes are allowed. Dogs are allowed for a pet fee of $10.00 per pet per night.

Ramada of /Fremont
3855 N State Road 127
Angola, IN
260-665-9471 (800-272-6232)
Dogs of all sizes are allowed. Dogs are allowed for a pet fee.

Days Inn Auburn
1115 7th St
Auburn, IN
260-925-1316 (800-329-7466)
Dogs of all sizes are allowed. Dogs are allowed for a pet fee of $10.00 per pet per night.

Holiday Inn Express Auburn-Touring Dr
404 Touring Drive
Auburn, IN
260-925-1900 (877-270-6405)
Dogs are welcome at this hotel.

La Quinta Inn & Conference Center Auburn
306 Touring Drive
Auburn, IN
260-920-1900 (800-531-5900)
Dogs of all sizes are allowed. There are no additional pet fees, however no discounts/coupons can be applied to the room. There is a pet waiver to

sign at check in. Dogs must be leashed and cleaned up after. Multiple dogs may be allowed.

Super 8 Auburn
503 Ley Drive
Auburn, IN
260-927-8800 (800-800-8000)
Dogs are welcome at this hotel.

Super 8 Raceway Park/Indianapolis Airport Area Avon
8229 East US Hwy 36
Avon, IN
317-272-8789 (800-800-8000)
Dogs are welcome at this hotel.

Super 8 Bedford
501 Bell Back Road
Bedford, IN
812-275-8881 (800-800-8000)
Dogs are welcome at this hotel.

A Summerhouse Inn
4501 E 3rd Street/H 46
Bloomington, IN
812-332-2141 (800-371-0934)
asummerhouseinn.com/
This popular inn offers 96 rooms, an outdoor pool, a sunken boat sand box, a picnicking areas with tables, grills, an open fire pit, and gaming areas. Dogs up to 85 pounds are allowed for an additional fee of $10 per night per pet. Dogs must be kept leashed and picked up after. 2 dogs may be allowed.

Country Hearth Inn
1722 N Walnut Street
Bloomington, IN
812-339-1919 (888-4HEARTH (443-2784))
countryhearthbloomington.com/
This family friendly inn and hotel offers a number of amenities and a good location to numerous other attractions and activities. Dogs are allowed for an additional fee of $10 per night per pet. Dogs must be well behaved, leashed, and under owner's care. Multiple dogs may be allowed.

Crowne Plaza Hotel Bloomington
1710 N. Kinser Pike
Bloomington, IN
812-334-3252 (877-270-6405)
Dogs of all sizes are allowed. Dogs are allowed for a pet fee of $75.00 per pet per night.

Motel 6 - Bloomington Indiana University
1800 Walnut St
Bloomington, IN
812-332-0820 (800-466-8356)

This motel welcomes your pets to stay with you.

TownePlace Suites Bloomington
105 S Franklin
Bloomington, IN
812-334-1234 (800-257-3000)
This all suite inn sits near many of the area's star attractions and event venues, the Indiana University, and the vibrant downtown area with numerous shopping, dining, and nightlife activities. Dogs are allowed for an additional one time fee of $75 per room. Multiple dogs may be allowed.

Travelodge Bloomington
2615 East Third Street
Bloomington, IN
812-339-6191 (800-578-7878)
Dogs are welcome at this hotel.

Holiday Inn Express Indianpolis-Brownsburg(I-74 W)
31 Maplehurst Drive
Brownsburg, IN
317-852-5353 (877-270-6405)
Dogs of all sizes are allowed. Dogs are allowed for a pet fee.

Super 8 /Indianapolis Area Brownsburg
1100 N Green Street
Brownsburg, IN
317-852-5211 (800-000-8000)
Dogs are welcome at this hotel.

Super 8 -Richmond Centerville
2407 N. Centerville Rd
Centerville, IN
765-855-5461 (800-800-8000)
Dogs are welcome at this hotel.

Econo Lodge
713 Plaza Dr.
Chesterton, IN
219-929-4416 (877-424-6423)
Dogs of all sizes are allowed. Two dogs are allowed per room.

Super 8 Indiana Dunes Area Chesterton
I-94 Exit 26A Trnkpk Exit 31
Chesterton, IN
219-929-5549 (800-800-8000)
Dogs are welcome at this hotel.

Knights Inn IN Clarks Hill
11425 US 52 South
Clarks Hill, IN
765-523-2111 (800-843-5644)
Dogs of all sizes are allowed. Dogs are allowed for a pet fee of $7.00 per pet per night.

Best Western Green Tree Inn

1425 Broadway Street
Clarksville, IN
812-288-9281 (800-780-7234)
Dogs of all sizes are allowed. Dogs
are allowed for a pet fee.

Candlewood Suites Louisville-North
1419 Bales Lane
Clarksville, IN
812-284-6113 (877-270-6405)
Dogs up to 80 pounds are allowed.
Pets allowed with an additional pet
fee. Up to $75 for 1-6 nights and up
to $150 for 7+ nights. A pet
agreement must be signed at check-
in.

Holiday Inn Louisville-North
(Clarksville)
505 Marriott Drive
Clarksville, IN
812-283-4411 (877-270-6405)
Dogs of all sizes are allowed. Dogs
are allowed for a pet fee of $35.00
per pet per night.

Suburban Extended Stay Hotel
1620 Leisure Way
Clarksville, IN
812-283-9696 (877-424-6423)
Dogs up to 80 pounds are allowed.
Two dogs are allowed per room.

Days Inn
1031 N. Main St.
Cloverdale, IN
765-795-6400 (800-329-7466)
Dogs of all sizes are allowed. Dogs
are allowed for a pet fee.

Motel 6 - Cloverdale
924 Main St
Cloverdale, IN
765-795-3000 (800-466-8356)
This motel welcomes your pets to
stay with you.

Super 8 Cloverdale
1020 N Main St
Cloverdale, IN
765-795-7373 (800-800-8000)
Dogs are welcome at this hotel.

Days Inn - Columbus
3445 Jonathon Moore Pike
Columbus, IN
812-376-9951 (800-329-7466)
Dogs of all sizes are allowed. Dogs
are allowed for a pet fee.

Holiday Inn Columbus
2480 Jonathan Moore Pike
Columbus, IN
812-372-1541 (877-270-6405)
Dogs are welcome at this hotel. Pets
may stay in exterior entrance rooms
only.

Hotel Indigo Columbus Architectural
Center
400 Brown Street
Columbus, IN
812-375-9100 (877-865-6578)
Dogs up to 80 pounds are allowed.
Dogs are allowed for a nightly pet
fee.

Motel 6 - Columbus, In
161 Carrie Lane
Columbus, IN
812-372-6888 (800-466-8356)
This motel welcomes your pets to
stay with you.

Baymont Inn & Suites Corydon
2495 Landmark Avenue NE
Corydon, IN
812-738-1500 (877-229-6668)
Dogs of all sizes are allowed. Dogs
are allowed for a pet fee of $10.00
per pet per night.

Super 8
168 Pacer Drive
Corydon, IN
812-738-8887 (800-800-8000)
Dogs are welcome at this hotel.

Comfort Inn
2991 N. Gandhi St.
Crawfordsville, IN
765-361-0665 (877-424-6423)
Dogs of all sizes are allowed. Dogs
are allowed for a pet fee of $15.00
per pet per night.

Motel 6 - Crawfordsville, In
1040 Corey Boulevard
Crawfordsville, IN
765-362-0300 (800-466-8356)
This motel welcomes your pets to
stay with you.

Best Western Lincoln Land Inn
1339 N Washington Street
Dale, IN
812-937-7000 (800-780-7234)
Dogs up to 50 pounds are allowed.
Dogs are allowed for a pet fee of
$10 per pet per night.

Motel 6 - Dale
1334 Washington St
Dale, IN
812-937-2294 (800-466-8356)
This motel welcomes your pets to
stay with you.

Baymont Inn & Suites Decatur
1201 South 13th Street
Decatur, IN
260-728-4600 (877-229-6668)
Dogs are welcome at this hotel.

Ohio River Cabins
13445 N H 66
Derby, IN
812-836-2289
Dogs of all sizes are allowed. There
is a $15 per night per pet additional
fee. 2 dogs may be allowed.

Candlewood Suites Elkhart
300 North Pointe Blvd.
Elkhart, IN
574-262-8600 (877-270-6405)
Dogs up to 80 pounds are allowed.
Pets allowed with an additional pet
fee. Up to $75 for 1-6 nights and up
to $150 for 7+ nights. A pet
agreement must be signed at check-
in.

Econo Lodge
3440 Cassopolis St.
Elkhart, IN
574-262-0540 (877-424-6423)
Dogs of all sizes are allowed. Dogs
are allowed for a pet fee of $5.00 per
pet per night. Two dogs are allowed
per room.

Knights Inn Elkhart
3254 Cassopolis Street
Elkhart, IN
574-970-0361 (800-843-5644)
Dogs of all sizes are allowed. Dogs
are allowed for a pet fee of $5.00 per
pet per night.

Ramada Elkhart
I-80/90 exit 92
Elkhart, IN
574-262-1581 (800-272-6232)
Dogs of all sizes are allowed. Dogs
are allowed for a pet fee.

Red Roof Inn Elkhart
2902 Cassopolis Street
Elkhart, IN
574-262-3691 (800-RED-ROOF)
One well-behaved family pet per
room. Guest must notify front desk
upon arrival. Guest is liable for any
damages. In consideration of all
guests, pets must never be left
unattended in the guest rooms.

Super 8 Elkhart
345 East Windsor Ave
Elkhart, IN
574-262-0000 (800-800-8000)
Dogs of all sizes are allowed. Dogs
are allowed for a pet fee.

Baymont Inn and Suites East
Evansville
8005 East Division Street
Evansville, IN
812-477-2677 (877-229-6668)
Dogs are welcome at this hotel.

Best Western Gateway Inn & Suites
324 Rusher Crk
Evansville, IN
812-868-8000 (800-780-7234)
Dogs of all sizes are allowed. Dogs are allowed for a pet fee.

Days Inn East Evansville
4819 Tecumseh Lane/I-164
Evansville, IN
812-473-7944 (800-329-7466)
Dogs are welcome at this hotel.

Econo Lodge
2508 Hwy 41 North
Evansville, IN
812-425-1092 (877-424-6423)
Dogs of all sizes are allowed. Dogs are allowed for a pet fee of $10.00 per pet per night.

Econo Lodge East
5006 E. Morgan Ave.
Evansville, IN
812-477-2211 (877-424-6423)
Dogs up to 50 pounds are allowed. Dogs are allowed for a pet fee of $10.00 per pet per night. Two dogs are allowed per room.

Holiday Inn Express Evansville - West
5737 Pearl Dr.
Evansville, IN
812-421-9773 (877-270-6405)
Dogs of all sizes are allowed. Dogs are allowed for a pet fee.

Motel 6 - Evansville
4321 Us 41
Evansville, IN
812-424-6431 (800-466-8356)
This motel welcomes your pets to stay with you.

North Drury Inn
3901 US 41 North
Evansville, IN
812-423-5818 (800-378-7946)
Dogs of all sizes are allowed for no additional pet fee with a credit card on file, and there is a pet agreement to sign at check in.

Residence Inn Evansville East
8283 East Walnut Street
Evansville, IN
812-471-7191 (800-331-3131)
In addition to offering a convenient location to business, shopping, dining, and entertainment areas, this hotel also provides a number of in-house amenities, including a daily buffet breakfast and an evening social hour Monday to Thursday. Dogs are allowed for an additional

one time pet fee of $100 per room. Multiple dogs may be allowed.

Super 8 East Evansville
4600 E Morgan
Evansville, IN
812-476-4008 (800-800-8000)
Dogs of all sizes are allowed. Dogs are allowed for a pet fee of $10 per pet per night.

Super 8 North Evansville
19601 Elpers Rd
Evansville, IN
812-867-8500 (800-800-8000)
Dogs are welcome at this hotel.

Baymont Inn & Suites Ft. Wayne
1005 W. Washington Center RD
FT. Wayne, IN
260-489-2220 (877-229-6668)
Dogs are welcome at this hotel.

Comfort Inn
440 South Main Street
Ferdinand, IN
812-367-1122 (877-424-6423)
Dogs up to 50 pounds are allowed. Dogs are allowed for a pet fee of $usd per pet per night. Two dogs are allowed per room.

Holiday Inn Express Indianapolis-Fishers (Ne Blvd)
9790 North By Northeast Boulevard
Fishers, IN
317-578-2000 (877-270-6405)
Dogs of all sizes are allowed. Dogs are allowed for a pet fee of $45.00 per pet per night.

Hotel Indigo Fishers-Indy'S Uptown
9791 North By Northeast Blvd
Fishers, IN
317-558-4100 (877-865-6578)
Dogs of all sizes are allowed. Dogs are allowed for a pet fee of $20.00 per pet per night.

Studio 6 - Indianapolis Fishers
8250 By Northeast Blvd
Fishers, IN
317-913-1920 (800-466-8356)
Your pets are welcome to stay here with you for a pet fee of $10 per day up to $50 for an entire stay.

Best Western Luxbury Inn Fort Wayne
5501 Coventry Ln
Fort Wayne, IN
260-436-0242 (800-780-7234)
Dogs of all sizes are allowed. Dogs are allowed for a pet fee of $15.00 per pet per night.

Candlewood Suites Fort Wayne -

NW
5251 Distribution Drive
Fort Wayne, IN
260-484-1400 (877-270-6405)
Dogs up to 80 pounds are allowed. Pets allowed with an additional pet fee. Up to $75 for 1-6 nights and up to $150 for 7+ nights. A pet agreement must be signed at check-in.

Extended Stay America Fort Wayne - South
8309 W. Jefferson Blvd.
Fort Wayne, IN
260-432-1916 (800-804-3724)
One dog is allowed per suite. There is a $25 per night additional pet fee up to $150 for an entire stay.

Knights Inn Ft. Wayne
2901 Goshen Rd
Fort Wayne, IN
260-484-2669 (800-843-5644)
Dogs of all sizes are allowed. Dogs are allowed for a pet fee of $5.00 per pet per night.

Motel 6 - Ft Wayne
3003 Coliseum Blvd
Fort Wayne, IN
260-482-3972 (800-466-8356)
This motel welcomes your pets to stay with you.

Red Roof Inn Ft Wayne
2920 Goshen Road
Fort Wayne, IN
260-484-8641 (800-RED-ROOF)
One well-behaved family pet per room. Guest must notify front desk upon arrival. Guest is liable for any damages. In consideration of all guests, pets must never be left unattended in the guest rooms.

Residence Inn Fort Wayne
4919 Lima Road
Fort Wayne, IN
260-484-4700 (800-331-3131)
In addition to offering a convenient location to business, shopping, dining, and entertainment areas, this hotel also provides a number of in-house amenities, including a daily buffet breakfast, an evening social hour Monday to Wednesday, and a Sport Court. Dogs are allowed for an additional one time pet fee of $100 per room. Multiple dogs may be allowed.

Residence Inn Fort Wayne Southwest
7811 West Jefferson Blvd
Fort Wayne, IN
260-432-8000 (800-331-3131)

Some of the amenities at this all-suite inn include a daily buffet breakfast, a Manager's reception Monday through Thursday with light dinner fare, an indoor swimming pool, and complimentary grocery shopping. Dogs are allowed for an additional one time pet fee of $100 per room. 2 dogs may be allowed.

Staybridge Suites Fort Wayne
5925 Ellison Road
Fort Wayne, IN
260-432-2427 (877-270-6405)
Dogs up to 80 pounds are allowed. Pets allowed with an additional pet fee. Up to $75 for 1-6 nights and up to $150 for 7+ nights. A pet agreement must be signed at check-in.

Super 8 Fort Wayne
5710 Challenger Pkwy
Fort Wayne, IN
260-489-0050 (800-800-8000)
Dogs are welcome at this hotel.

Holiday Inn Express Frankfort
592 South County Rd 200
Frankfort, IN
765-659-4400 (877-270-6405)
Dogs of all sizes are allowed. Dogs are allowed for a pet fee of $25 per pet per stay.

Holiday Inn Express Fremont
(Angola Area)
6245 North Old 27, Suite 400
Fremont, IN
260-833-6464 (877-270-6405)
Dogs of all sizes are allowed. Dogs are allowed for a pet fee of $35.00 per pet per night.

Comfort Suites
9530 West State Road 56
French Lick, IN
812-936-5300 (877-424-6423)
Dogs of all sizes are allowed. Dogs are allowed for a pet fee of $35.00 per pet per night.

Super 8 Marion Area Gas City
5172 Kaybee Dr
Gas City, IN
765-998-6800 (800-800-8000)
Dogs are welcome at this hotel.

Motel 6 - Louisville Georgetown, In
1079 Luther Rd
Georgetown, IN
812-923-0441 (800-466-8356)
This motel welcomes your pets to stay with you.

Best Western Inn
900 Lincolnway E

Goshen, IN
574-533-0408 (800-780-7234)
Dogs are welcome at this hotel.

Red Roof Inn Mishawaka - Notre Dame
1325 E. University Drive Court
Granger, IN
574-271-4800 (800-RED-ROOF)
One well-behaved family pet per room. Guest must notify front desk upon arrival. Guest is liable for any damages. In consideration of all guests, pets must never be left unattended in the guest rooms.

Quality Inn & Suites
2270 N. State Street
Greenfield, IN
317-462-7112 (877-424-6423)
Dogs up to 100 pounds are allowed. Dogs are allowed for a pet fee of $15.00 per pet per night. Two dogs are allowed per room.

Holiday Inn Express Greensburg
915 Ann Blvd.
Greensburg, IN
812-663-5500 (877-270-6405)
Dogs are welcome at this hotel.

Baymont Inn Greenwood
1281 South Park Drive
Greenwood, IN
317-865-0100 (877-229-6668)
Dogs of all sizes are allowed. Dogs are allowed for a nightly pet fee.

Candlewood Suites Greenwood
1190 N. Graham Road
Greenwood, IN
317-882-4300 (877-270-6405)
Dogs up to 80 pounds are allowed. Pets allowed with an additional pet fee. Up to $75 for 1-6 nights and up to $150 for 7+ nights. A pet agreement must be signed at check-in.

Red Roof Inn Greenwood
110 Sheek Rd
Greenwood, IN
317-887-1515 (800-RED-ROOF)
One well-behaved family pet per room. Guest must notify front desk upon arrival. Guest is liable for any damages. In consideration of all guests, pets must never be left unattended in the guest rooms.

Motel 6 - Hammond Chicago Area
3840 179th St
Hammond, IN
219-845-0330 (800-466-8356)
This motel welcomes your pets to stay with you.

Quality Inn North
12798 Access 1250 South
Haubstadt, IN
812-768-5878 (877-424-6423)
Dogs of all sizes are allowed.

Holiday Inn Express Howe (Sturgis
45 W. 750 N.
Howe, IN
260-562-3660 (877-270-6405)
Dogs of all sizes are allowed. Dogs are allowed for a pet fee of $35.00 per pet per stay.

Super 8 Huntington
2801 Guilford Street
Huntington, IN
260-358-8888 (800-800-8000)
Dogs of all sizes are allowed. Dogs are allowed for a pet fee.

Baymont Inn and Suites Indianapolis
1540 Brookville Crossing Way
Indianapolis, IN
317-322-2000 (877-229-6668)
Dogs are welcome at this hotel.

Candlewood Suites Indianapolis
8111 Bash St
Indianapolis, IN
317-595-9292 (877-270-6405)
Dogs up to 80 pounds are allowed. Pets allowed with an additional pet fee. Up to $75 for 1-6 nights and up to $150 for 7+ nights. A pet agreement must be signed at check-in.

Candlewood Suites Indianapolis Airport
5250 W. Bradbury Street
Indianapolis, IN
317-241-9595 (877-270-6405)
Dogs up to 80 pounds are allowed. Pets allowed with an additional pet fee. Up to $75 for 1-6 nights and up to $150 for 7+ nights. A pet agreement must be signed at check-in.

Candlewood Suites Indianapolis City Centre
1152 N White River Pkwy, West Drive
Indianapolis, IN
317-536-7700 (877-270-6405)
Dogs up to 80 pounds are allowed. Pets allowed with an additional pet fee. Up to $75 for 1-6 nights and up to $150 for 7+ nights. A pet agreement must be signed at check-in.

Candlewood Suites Indianapolis Northwest
7455 Woodland Drive
Indianapolis, IN

317-298-8000 (877-270-6405)
Dogs up to 80 pounds are allowed.
Pets allowed with an additional pet
fee. Up to $75 for 1-6 nights and up
to $150 for 7+ nights. A pet
agreement must be signed at check-
in.

Comfort Inn & Suites
5755 N. German Church Rd.
Indianapolis, IN
317-823-7700 (877-424-6423)
Dogs up to 75 pounds are allowed.
Dogs are allowed for a pet fee of
$10.00 per pet per night. Two dogs
are allowed per room.

Comfort Inn East
2295 N. Shadeland
Indianapolis, IN
317-359-9999 (877-424-6423)
Dogs of all sizes are allowed. Dogs
are allowed for a pet fee of $$25.00
per pet per night.

Comfort Suites-Fishers
9760 Crosspoint Blvd
Indianapolis, IN
317-578-1200 (877-424-6423)
Dogs of all sizes are allowed. There
is a $10 per night per pet additional
fee.

Days Inn Indianapolis
2150 North Post Road
Indianapolis, IN
317-899-2100 (800-329-7466)
Dogs of all sizes are allowed. Dogs
are allowed for a pet fee.

Days Inn and Suites
8275 Craig St.
Indianapolis, IN
317-841-9700 (800-329-7466)
Dogs of all sizes are allowed. Dogs
are allowed for a pet fee of $10 per
pet per night.

Drury Inn
9320 N. Michigan Road
Indianapolis, IN
317-876-9777 (800-378-7946)
Dogs of all sizes are allowed for no
additional pet fee with a credit card
on file, and there is a pet agreement
to sign at check in.

Econo Lodge
5241 West Bradbury
Indianapolis, IN
317-248-1231 (877-424-6423)
Dogs of all sizes are allowed. Dogs
are allowed for a pet fee of $10.00
per pet per night. Two dogs are
allowed per room.

Extended Stay America Indianapolis

- Airport
2730 Fortune Cir. W.
Indianapolis, IN
317-248-0465 (800-804-3724)
One dog is allowed per suite. There
is a $25 per night additional pet fee
up to $150 for an entire stay.

Extended Stay America Indianapolis
- Castleton
7940 N. Shadeland Ave.
Indianapolis, IN
317-596-1288 (800-804-3724)
One dog is allowed per suite. There
is a $25 per night additional pet fee
up to $150 for an entire stay.

Extended Stay America Indianapolis
- North
9750 Lakeshore Dr.
Indianapolis, IN
317-843-1181 (800-804-3724)
One dog is allowed per suite. There
is a $25 per night additional pet fee
up to $150 for an entire stay.

Extended Stay America Indianapolis
- Northwest
9030 Wesleyan Rd.
Indianapolis, IN
317-872-3090 (800-804-3724)
One dog is allowed per suite. There
is a $25 per night additional pet fee
up to $150 for an entire stay.

Holiday Inn Indianapolis-East
6990 East 21st Street
Indianapolis, IN
317-359-5341 (877-270-6405)
Dogs up to 50 pounds are allowed.
Dogs are allowed for a pet fee.

Homestead Studio Suites
Indianapolis - Northwest
8520 N.W. Blvd.
Indianapolis, IN
317-334-7829 (800-804-3724)
One dog is allowed per suite. There
is a $25 per night additional pet fee
up to $150 for an entire stay.

Knights Inn Airport South
Indianapolis
4909 Knights Way
Indianapolis, IN
317-788-0125 (800-843-5644)
Dogs are welcome at this hotel.
There is a $10 per night additional
pet fee.

La Quinta Inn Indianapolis East
7304 East 21st Street
Indianapolis, IN
317-359-1021 (800-531-5900)
Dogs of all sizes are allowed. There
are no additional pet fees. Dogs
may not be left unattended, and

they must be leashed and cleaned
up after. Multiple dogs may be
allowed.

La Quinta Inn Indianapolis East -
Post Drive
2349 Post Drive
Indianapolis, IN
317-897-2300 (800-531-5900)
Dogs of all sizes are allowed. There
are no additional pet fees. Dogs may
only be left alone in the room if they
will be quiet and well behaved. Also,
please put the "Do Not Disturb" sign
on the door when you are out and a
dog is in the room uncrated. Dogs
must be kept leashed. Multiple dogs
may be allowed.

La Quinta Inn Indianapolis North at
Pyramids
3880 W. 92nd St
Indianapolis, IN
317-872-3100 (800-531-5900)
Dogs of all sizes are allowed. There
is a $10 one time pet fee. Dogs may
not be left unattended unless they
will be quiet and well behaved. Dogs
must be crated or removed for
housekeeping. 2 dogs may be
allowed.

Marriott Indianapolis East
7202 E 21st Street
Indianapolis, IN
317-352-1231 (800-228-9290)
Only a short distance from
downtown, this luxury hotel provides
a great location to a number of sites
of interest and activities for both
business and leisure travelers; plus
they also offer numerous on-site
amenities to ensure a comfortable
stay. Dogs are allowed for an
additional one time fee of $75 per
room. 2 dogs may be allowed.

Motel 6 - Indianapolis East
2851 Shadeland Ave
Indianapolis, IN
317-546-5864 (800-466-8356)
This motel welcomes your pets to
stay with you.

Motel 6 - Indianapolis South
5151 Elmwood Ave
Indianapolis, IN
317-783-5555 (800-466-8356)
This motel welcomes your pets to
stay with you.

Quality Inn & Suites
4345 Southport Crossing Way
Indianapolis, IN
317-859-8888 (877-424-6423)
Dogs of all sizes are allowed. Dogs
are allowed for a pet fee of $10.00

per pet per night. Two dogs are allowed per room.

Quality Inn & Suites Airport
2631 S. Lynhurst Drive
Indianapolis, IN
317-381-1000 (877-424-6423)
Dogs of all sizes are allowed. Dogs are allowed for a pet fee of $10.00 per pet per night.

Ramada Conference Center South
520 E Thompson Road
Indianapolis, IN
317-787-8341 (800-272-6232)
Dogs of all sizes are allowed. Dogs are allowed for a pet fee.

Ramada Limited West Indianapolis
West 38th and I 465 Exit 17
Indianapolis, IN
317-297-1848 (800-272-6232)
Dogs are welcome at this hotel.

Red Roof Inn Indianapolis - Speedway
6415 Debonair Lane
Indianapolis, IN
317-293-6881 (800-RED-ROOF)
One well-behaved family pet per room. Guest must notify front desk upon arrival. Guest is liable for any damages. In consideration of all guests, pets must never be left unattended in the guest rooms.

Red Roof Inn Indianapolis North
9520 Valparaiso Court
Indianapolis, IN
317-872-3030 (800-RED-ROOF)
One well-behaved family pet per room. Guest must notify front desk upon arrival. Guest is liable for any damages. In consideration of all guests, pets must never be left unattended in the guest rooms.

Red Roof Inn Indianapolis South
5221 Victory Drive
Indianapolis, IN
317-788-9551 (800-RED-ROOF)
One well-behaved family pet per room. Guest must notify front desk upon arrival. Guest is liable for any damages. In consideration of all guests, pets must never be left unattended in the guest rooms.

Residence Inn Indianapolis Airport
5224 W Southern Avenue
Indianapolis, IN
317-244-1500 (800-331-3131)
Only a ½ mile from the Indianapolis International Airport and near many of the area's star attractions and activities, this all suite inn also offers a number of in-house amenities

including a daily buffet breakfast and evening socials Monday to Wednesday. Dogs up to 50 pounds are allowed for an additional one time pet fee of $100 per room. 2 dogs may be allowed.

Residence Inn Indianapolis Downtown on the Canal
350 W New York Street
Indianapolis, IN
317-822-0840 (800-331-3131)
Located on the popular canal walk downtown, this all suite inn is also centrally located to a number of local attractions, shopping, dining, and business districts and offer a number of amenities - including a daily buffet breakfast and evening socials. Dogs up to 100 pounds are allowed for an additional one time pet fee of $100 per room. Aggressive known breeds are not allowed. Multiple dogs may be allowed.

Residence Inn Indianapolis Fishers
9765 Crosspoint Blvd
Indianapolis, IN
317-842-1111 (800-331-3131)
This all suite hotel sits central to many of the city's star attractions, shopping, dining, and business areas, plus they offer a number of in-house amenities that include a daily buffet breakfast and evening socials Monday through Thursday with light dinner fare. Dogs are allowed for an additional one time pet fee of $100 per room. 2 dogs may be allowed.

Residence Inn Indianapolis North
3553 Founders Road
Indianapolis, IN
317-872-0462 (800-331-3131)
This all suite hotel sits central to many of the city's star attractions, shopping, dining, and business areas, plus they offer a number of in-house amenities that include a daily buffet breakfast and evening socials Monday through Thursday. Dogs are allowed for an additional one time pet fee of $100 per room. 2 dogs may be allowed.

Residence Inn Indianapolis Northwest
6220 Digital Way
Indianapolis, IN
317-275-6000 (800-331-3131)
Some of the amenities at this all-suite inn include a daily buffet breakfast, evening hospitality hours, weekly barbecues, a heated swimming pool, and a complimentary grocery shopping

service. Dogs are allowed for an additional one time pet fee of $100 per room. Multiple dogs may be allowed.

Sheraton Indianapolis Hotel & Suites
8787 Keyston Crossing
Indianapolis, IN
317-846-2700 (888-625-5144)
Dogs up to 80 pounds are allowed. There are no additional pet fees. Dogs are not allowed to be left alone in the room.

Staybridge Suites Indianapolis Dwtn City Centre
535 S. West Street
Indianapolis, IN
317-536-7500 (877-270-6405)
Dogs up to 80 pounds are allowed. Pets allowed with an additional pet fee. Up to $75 for 1-6 nights and up to $150 for 7+ nights. A pet agreement must be signed at check-in.

Staybridge Suites Indianapolis-Fishers
9780 Crosspoint Blvd
Indianapolis, IN
317-577-9500 (877-270-6405)
Dogs up to 80 pounds are allowed. Pets allowed with an additional pet fee. Up to $75 for 1-6 nights and up to $150 for 7+ nights. A pet agreement must be signed at check-in.

Suburban Extended Stay Northeast
8055 Bash Street
Indianapolis, IN
317-598-1914 (877-424-6423)
Dogs up to 100 pounds are allowed. Dogs are allowed for a pet fee of $25.00 per pet per stay. Two dogs are allowed per room.

Super 8 Indianapolis
4530 S Emerson Ave
Indianapolis, IN
317-788-0955 (800-800-8000)
Dogs of all sizes are allowed. Dogs are allowed for a pet fee.

Super 8 South Indianapolis
450 Bixler Road
Indianapolis, IN
317-788-0811 (800-800-8000)
Dogs are welcome at this hotel.

Super 8 /NE/Castleton Area
Indianapolis
7202 East 82nd Street
Indianapolis, IN
317-841-8585 (800-800-8000)
Dogs of all sizes are allowed. Dogs are allowed for a pet fee of $10.00

per pet per night.

Super 8 Indpls/NW/College Park Area
9251 Wesleyan Road
Indianapolis, IN
317-879-9100 (800-800-8000)
Dogs are welcome at this hotel.

TownePlace Suites Indianapolis Park 100
5802 W 71st Street
Indianapolis, IN
317-290-8900 (800-257-3000)
This all suite hotel sits central to a number of sites of interest for both business and leisure travelers; plus they also offer a number of on-site amenities to ensure comfort. Dogs are allowed for an additional one time fee of $50 per room. 2 dogs may be allowed.

TownePlace Suites Indy Keystone
8468 Union Chapel Road
Indianapolis, IN
317-255-3700 (800-257-3000)
This all suite hotel sits close to a number of sites of interest for both business and leisure travelers; plus they also offer a number of on-site amenities to ensure comfort. Dogs are allowed for an additional one time fee of $50 per room. 2 dogs may be allowed.

Wingate by Wyndham - Airport East Indianapolis
5797 Rockville Road
Indianapolis, IN
317-243-8310 (800-228-1000)
Dogs are welcome at this hotel.

Comfort Suites
360 Eastern Blvd
Jeffersonville, IN
812-282-2100 (877-424-6423)
Dogs up to 50 pounds are allowed. Dogs are allowed for a pet fee of $10.00 per pet per night.

Days Inn And Suites IN Jeffersonville
354 Eastern Boulevard
Jeffersonville, IN
812-288-7100 (800-329-7466)
Dogs are welcome at this hotel.

Knights Inn Jeffersonville
350 Eastern Blvd
Jeffersonville, IN
812-288-9331 (800-843-5644)
Dogs of all sizes are allowed. Dogs are allowed for a nightly pet fee.

Motel 6 - Louisville North
Jeffersonville, In
2016 Old Us 31

Jeffersonville, IN
812-283-7703 (800-466-8356)
This motel welcomes your pets to stay with you.

TownePlace Suites Louisville North
703 N Shore Drive
Jeffersonville, IN
812-280-8200 (800-853-6113)
This all suite hotel sits central to a number of sites of interest for both business and leisure travelers; plus they also offer a number of on-site amenities to ensure comfort. Dogs are allowed for an additional one time fee of $100 per room. 2 dogs may be allowed.

Best Western Kendallville Inn
621 Professional Way
Kendallville, IN
260-347-5263 (800-780-7234)
Dogs are welcome at this hotel. There is a $25 one time pet fee.

Comfort Inn
522 Essex Dr.
Kokomo, IN
765-452-5050 (877-424-6423)
Dogs up to 50 pounds are allowed. Dogs are allowed for a pet fee of $15.00 per pet per stay.

Days Inn and Suites Kokomo
US 31 & Albany Ave
Kokomo, IN
765-453-7100 (800-329-7466)
Dogs are welcome at this hotel.

Motel 6 - Kokomo
2808 Reed Rd
Kokomo, IN
765-457-8211 (800-466-8356)
This motel welcomes your pets to stay with you.

Super 8 Kokomo
5110 Clinton Ave
Kokomo, IN
765-455-3288 (800-800-8000)
Dogs of all sizes are allowed. Dogs are allowed for a pet fee.

Candlewood Suites Lafayette
240 Meijer Drive
Lafayette, IN
765-807-5735 (877-270-6405)
Dogs up to 80 pounds are allowed. Pets allowed with an additional pet fee. Up to $75 for 1-6 nights and up to $150 for 7+ nights. A pet agreement must be signed at check-in.

Comfort Suites
31 Frontage Rd.
Lafayette, IN

765-447-0016 (877-424-6423)
Dogs of all sizes are allowed. Dogs are allowed for a pet fee of $10.00 per pet per stay.

Days Inn And Suites
151 Frontage Road
Lafayette, IN
765-446-8558 (800-329-7466)
Dogs are welcome at this hotel.

Holiday Inn Express Lafayette
201 Frontage Road
Lafayette, IN
765-449-4808 (877-270-6405)
Dogs of all sizes are allowed. Dogs are allowed for a pet fee of $10.00 per pet per night.

Knights Inn Midwest Lafayette
4110 SR 26 E
Lafayette, IN
765-447-5611 (800-843-5644)
Dogs of all sizes are allowed. Dogs are allowed for a pet fee.

Motel 6 - Lafayette, In
139 Frontage Rd
Lafayette, IN
765-447-7566 (800-466-8356)
This motel welcomes your pets to stay with you.

Red Roof Inn Lafayette, IN
4201 State Route 26 East
Lafayette, IN
765-448-4671 (800-RED-ROOF)
One well-behaved family pet per room. Guest must notify front desk upon arrival. Guest is liable for any damages. In consideration of all guests, pets must never be left unattended in the guest rooms.

Super 8 Lafayette
4301 State Rd 26
Lafayette, IN
765-447-5551 (800-800-8000)
Dogs are welcome at this hotel.

TownePlace Suites Lafayette
163 Frontage Road
Lafayette, IN
765-446-8668 (800-257-3000)
This all suite hotel sits central to a number of sites of interest for both business and leisure travelers; plus they also offer a number of on-site amenities to ensure comfort - including a complimentary deluxe continental breakfast. Dogs up to 50 pounds are allowed for an additional one time fee of $45 per room. 2 dogs may be allowed.

Best Western LaPorte Hotel & Conference Center

444 Pine Lake Avenue
Laporte, IN
219-362-4585 (800-780-7234)
Dogs of all sizes are allowed. Dogs
are allowed for a pet fee.

Quality Inn & Suites
1000 Eads Parkway
Lawrenceburg, IN
812-539-4770 (877-424-6423)
Dogs of all sizes are allowed. Dogs
are allowed for a pet fee of $20.00
per pet per night.

Comfort Inn
210 Sam Ralston Rd.
Lebanon, IN
765-482-4800 (877-424-6423)
Dogs of all sizes are allowed. Dogs
are allowed for a pet fee of $15.00
per pet per night. Two dogs are
allowed per room.

Econo Lodge
1245 W. State Rd 32
Lebanon, IN
765-482-9611 (877-424-6423)
Dogs up to 80 pounds are allowed.
Dogs are allowed for a pet fee of
$20.00 per pet per night. Two dogs
are allowed per room.

Holiday Inn Express Lebanon
335 North Mt Zion Rd
Lebanon, IN
765-483-4100 (877-270-6405)
Dogs of all sizes are allowed. Dogs
are allowed for a pet fee of $10.00
per pet per night.

Motel 6 - Lebanon, In
1280 S.r. 32 West
Lebanon, IN
765-482-9190 (800-466-8356)
This motel welcomes your pets to
stay with you.

Super 8 Lebanon
405 Mt. Zion Road
Lebanon, IN
765-482-9999 (800-800-8000)
Dogs of all sizes are allowed. Dogs
are allowed for a pet fee.

Ramada Conference Center of
Logansport
3550 E. Market St.
Logansport, IN
574-753-6351 (800-272-6232)
Dogs are welcome at this hotel.

Super 8 Logansport
3801 E Market
Logansport, IN
574-722-1273 (800-800-8000)
Dogs are welcome at this hotel.

Comfort Suites
1345 N. Baldwin Ave.
Marion, IN
765-651-1006 (877-424-6423)
Dogs of all sizes are allowed. Dogs
are allowed for a pet fee of $10 per
pet per stay.

Super 8 IN Marion
1615 N Baldwin Avenue
Marion, IN
765-664-9100 (800-800-8000)
Dogs are welcome at this hotel.

Super 8 Markle
610 Annette Drive
Markle, IN
260-758-8888 (800-800-8000)
Dogs of all sizes are allowed. Dogs
are allowed for a pet fee of $10.00
per pet per night.

Best Western Martinsville Inn
50 Bill's Boulevard
Martinsville, IN
765-342-1842 (800-780-7234)
Dogs up to 50 pounds are allowed.
Dogs are allowed for a pet fee of
$10 per pet per night.

Holiday Inn Express Hotel & Suites
Martinsville
2233 Burton Lane
Martinsville, IN
765-813-3999 (877-270-6405)
Dogs of all sizes are allowed. Dogs
are allowed for a pet fee of $25.00
per pet per night.

Super 8 Martinsville
55 Bills Boulevard
Martinsville, IN
765-349-2222 (800-800-8000)
Dogs are welcome at this hotel.

Candlewood Suites Merrillville
8339 Ohio Street
Merrillville, IN
219-791-9100 (877-270-6405)
Dogs up to 80 pounds are allowed.
Pets allowed with an additional pet
fee. Up to $75 for 1-6 nights and up
to $150 for 7+ nights. A pet
agreement must be signed at
check-in.

Extended Stay America Merrillville -
Us Rte. 30
1355 E. 83rd Ave.
Merrillville, IN
219-769-4740 (800-804-3724)
One dog is allowed per suite. There
is a $25 per night additional pet fee
up to $150 for an entire stay.

La Quinta Inn Merrillville
8210 Louisiana St.

Merrillville, IN
219-738-2870 (800-531-5900)
Dogs of all sizes are allowed. There
are no additional pet fees. Dogs
must be leashed and cleaned up
after. Multiple dogs may be allowed.

Motel 6 - Merrillville
8290 Louisiana St
Merrillville, IN
219-738-2701 (800-466-8356)
This motel welcomes your pets to
stay with you.

Red Roof Inn Merrillville
8290 Georgia Street
Merrillville, IN
219-738-2430 (800-RED-ROOF)
One well-behaved family pet per
room. Guest must notify front desk
upon arrival. Guest is liable for any
damages. In consideration of all
guests, pets must never be left
unattended in the guest rooms.

Super 8 /Gary Area Merrillville
8300 Louisiana St.
Merrillville, IN
219-736-8383 (800-800-8000)
Dogs are welcome at this hotel.

Knights Inn Michigan City
201 W. Kieffer Rd
Michigan City, IN
219-878-8100 (800-843-5644)
Dogs are welcome at this hotel.
There is a $10 per day pet fee per
pet.

Red Roof Inn Michigan City
110 W Kieffer Rd
Michigan City, IN
219-874-5251 (800-RED-ROOF)
One well-behaved family pet per
room. Guest must notify front desk
upon arrival. Guest is liable for any
damages. In consideration of all
guests, pets must never be left
unattended in the guest rooms.

Troy Farm Guest House
1400 Tryon Road
Michigan City, IN
219-879-3618
tryonfarmguesthouse.com/
There are 170 pastoral acres to
explore around this beautiful 1896
Victorian farmhouse inn. Dogs are
allowed at the inn; there is an
additional one time fee of $25 for one
dog, and an additional one time fee
of $35 for two dogs. Pets must be
hound and human friendly, leashed,
and under their owner's control. For
a small additional fee a pet amenity
kit can be included, and there is also
a partially fenced yard where dogs

under good voice control may run without a leash. 2 dogs may be allowed.

Extended Stay America South Bend - Mishawaka
5305 N. Main St.
Mishawaka, IN
574-277-9912 (800-804-3724)
One dog is allowed per suite. There is a $25 per night additional pet fee up to $150 for an entire stay.

Holiday Inn Express Mishawaka (South Bend Area)
420 West University Drive
Mishawaka, IN
574-277-2520 (877-270-6405)
Dogs of all sizes are allowed. Dogs are allowed for a pet fee of $50.00 per pet per stay.

Motel 6 - Mishawaka, In
2754 Lincolnway East
Mishawaka, IN
574-256-2300 (800-466-8356)
This motel welcomes your pets to stay with you.

Residence Inn South Bend Mishawaka
231 Park Place
Mishawaka, IN
574-271-9283 (800-331-3131)
This all suite hotel sits central to many of the city's star attractions, the University of Notre Dame, major companies, and shopping and dining areas, plus they offer a number of in-house amenities that include a daily buffet breakfast and evening socials. Dogs are allowed for an additional one time pet fee of $100 per room. 2 dogs may be allowed.

Super 8 /South Bend Area Mishawaka
535 W. University Drive
Mishawaka, IN
574-247-0888 (800-800-8000)
Dogs of all sizes are allowed. Dogs are allowed for a pet fee.

Days Inn -Ball State University Muncie
3509 N. Everbrook Lane
Muncie, IN
765-288-2311 (800-329-7466)
Dogs of all sizes are allowed. Dogs are allowed for a pet fee.

Super 8 /Ball St. College Area Muncie
3601 W. Foxridge Lane
Muncie, IN
765-286-4333 (800-800-8000)
Dogs of all sizes are allowed. Dogs

are allowed for a pet fee.

Quality Inn & Suites
16025 Prosperity Drive
Noblesville, IN
317-770-6772 (877-424-6423)
Dogs of all sizes are allowed. Dogs are allowed for a pet fee of $10.00 per pet per night. Two dogs are allowed per room.

Super 8 Indianapolis Noblesville
17070 Dragonfly Lane
Noblesville, IN
317-776-7088 (800-800-8000)
Dogs of all sizes are allowed. Dogs are allowed for a pet fee.

Comfort Inn
150 FDR Drive
North Vernon, IN
812-352-9999 (877-424-6423)
Dogs up to 60 pounds are allowed. Dogs are allowed for a pet fee of $usd per pet per night. Two dogs are allowed per room.

Knights Inn Peru
2661 South Business 31
Peru, IN
765-472-3971 (800-843-5644)
Dogs are welcome at this hotel. There is a $10 one time pet fee per pet.

Baymont Inn & Suites Indianapolis Airport/ Plainfield
6010 Gateway Drive
Plainfield, IN
317-837-9000 (877-229-6668)
Dogs of all sizes are allowed. Dogs are allowed for a pet fee of $10.00 per pet per stay.

Days Inn Plainfield
2245 East Perry Road
Plainfield, IN
317-839-5000 (800-329-7466)
Dogs of all sizes are allowed. Dogs are allowed for a pet fee.

Motel 6 - Indianapolis Airport Plainfield
6105 Cambridge Way
Plainfield, IN
317-838-9300 (800-466-8356)
This motel welcomes your pets to stay with you.

Staybridge Suites Indianapolis-Airport
6295 Cambridge Way
Plainfield, IN
317-839-2700 (877-270-6405)
Dogs up to 80 pounds are allowed. Pets allowed with an additional pet fee. Up to $75 for 1-6 nights and up

to $150 for 7+ nights. A pet agreement must be signed at check-in.

Days Inn Plymouth
2229 North Michigan St.
Plymouth, IN
574-935-4276 (800-329-7466)
Dogs of all sizes are allowed. Dogs are allowed for a nightly pet fee.

Comfort Inn
2300 Willowcreek Rd
Portage, IN
219-763-7177 (877-424-6423)
Dogs of all sizes are allowed. Dogs are allowed for a pet fee of $20.00 per pet per stay.

Super 8 Portage
6118 Melton Rd
Portage, IN
219-762-8857 (800-800-8000)
Dogs are welcome at this hotel.

Days Inn Richmond
5775 National Rd East
Richmond, IN
765-966-4900 (800-329-7466)
Dogs are welcome at this hotel.

Holiday Inn Richmond
5501 National Road East
Richmond, IN
765-966-7511 (877-270-6405)
Dogs of all sizes are allowed. Dogs are allowed for a pet fee of $20.00 per pet per night.

Knights Inn IN Richmond
3020 East Main Street
Richmond, IN
765-966-1505 (800-843-5644)
Dogs of all sizes are allowed. Dogs are allowed for a nightly pet fee.

Lee's Inn
6030 National Rd. E.
Richmond, IN
765-966-6559
Dogs are allowed for no additional pet fee. Multiple dogs may be allowed.

Motel 6 - Richmond, In
419 Commerce Dr
Richmond, IN
765-966-6682 (800-466-8356)
This motel welcomes your pets to stay with you.

Super 8 Richmond
2525 Chester Blvd
Richmond, IN
765-962-7576 (800-800-8000)
Dogs of all sizes are allowed. Dogs are allowed for a pet fee.

Billie Creek Inn
1659 H 36E
Rockville, IN
765-569-3430
billiecreekvillage.org/
Although dogs are not allowed in the living history village here, they are allowed at this inn for an additional fee of $10 per night per pet. The inn offers a seasonal outdoor pool and picnic areas with grills. Dogs must be well mannered and leashed when out of the room. 2 dogs may be allowed.

Comfort Inn
320 Conrad Harcourt Way
Rushville, IN
765-932-2999 (877-424-6423)
Dogs up to 100 pounds are allowed. Dogs are allowed for a pet fee of $50.00 per pet per stay. Two dogs are allowed per room.

Holiday Inn Express Hotel & Suites Scottsburg
200 Beechwood Drive
Scottsburg, IN
812-752-0000 (877-270-6405)
Dogs of all sizes are allowed. Dogs are allowed for a pet fee of $25.00 per pet per stay.

Super 8 Scottsburg
1522 West Mcclain Avenue
Scottsburg, IN
812-752-2122 (800-800-8000)
Dogs are welcome at this hotel.

Days Inn - Louisville Sellersburg
7618 Old State Road 60
Sellersburg, IN
812-246-4451 (800-329-7466)
Dogs of all sizes are allowed. Dogs are allowed for a pet fee of $10 per pet per night.

Ramada /Louisville North Sellersburg
360 Triangle Dr
Sellersburg, IN
812-246-3131 (800-272-6232)
Dogs are welcome at this hotel.

Days Inn Seymour
302 South Commerce Drive
Seymour, IN
812-522-3678 (800-329-7466)
Dogs are welcome at this hotel.

Econo Lodge
220 Commerce Dr.
Seymour, IN
812-522-8000 (877-424-6423)
Dogs of all sizes are allowed.

Knights Inn Seymour
207 N.Sandy Creek Drive

Seymour, IN
812-522-3523 (800-843-5644)
Dogs of all sizes are allowed. Dogs are allowed for a pet fee of $5.00 per pet per night.

Motel 6 - Seymour North
365 Tanger Blvd
Seymour, IN
812-524-7443 (800-466-8356)
This motel welcomes your pets to stay with you.

Quality Inn
2025 E. Tipton Street
Seymour, IN
812-522-6767 (877-424-6423)
Dogs of all sizes are allowed.

Super 8 Seymour
401 Outlet Blvd
Seymour, IN
812-524-2000 (800-800-8000)
Dogs of all sizes are allowed. Dogs are allowed for a pet fee.

Travelodge Seymour
306 S Commerce Dr
Seymour, IN
812-519-2578 (800-578-7878)
Dogs are welcome at this hotel.

Comfort Inn
36 W Rampart Road
Shelbyville, IN
317-398-8044 (877-424-6423)
Dogs up to 60 pounds are allowed. There is a $15 per night per pet additional fee.

Super 8 Shipshewana
740 South VanBuren Street
Shipshewana, IN
260-768-4004 (800-800-8000)
Dogs of all sizes are allowed. Dogs are allowed for a pet fee.

Candlewood Suites South Bend Airport
3916 Lincolnway West
South Bend, IN
574-968-1072 (877-270-6405)
Dogs up to 80 pounds are allowed. Pets allowed with an additional pet fee. Up to $75 for 1-6 nights and up to $150 for 7+ nights. A pet agreement must be signed at check-in.

Comfort Suites
52939 US 933 North
South Bend, IN
574-272-1500 (877-424-6423)
Dogs up to 85 pounds are allowed. Dogs are allowed for a pet fee of $20.00 per pet per stay.

Cushing Manor Inn
508 West Washington
South Bend, IN
574-288-1990
cushingmanorinn.com
The state's oldest Bed and Breakfast is considered a prime example of Second Empire architecture. This 1872 inn offers a number of modern amenities, beautifully landscaped grounds, private baths, a gift shop, and more. One well mannered dog is allowed per room for no additional fee (unless damage). Dogs must be leashed, under their owner's control, and crated when left alone in the room.

Econo Lodge Airport
3233 Lincoln Way W.
South Bend, IN
574-232-9019 (877-424-6423)
Dogs up to 50 pounds are allowed. Dogs are allowed for a pet fee of $20.00 per pet per stay. Two dogs are allowed per room.

Knights Inn South Bend
236 N Dixie Hwy
South Bend, IN
574-277-2960 (800-843-5644)
Dogs are welcome at this hotel.

Motel 6 - South Bend
52624 Us 31
South Bend, IN
574-272-7072 (800-466-8356)
This motel welcomes your pets to stay with you.

Oliver Inn
630 W Washington Street
South Bend, IN
574-232-4545 (888-697-4466)
oliverinn.com/
A beautiful Victorian home with luxury accommodations, gourmet breakfasts with live piano music, lush grounds, and more all greet visitors at this inn. Dogs are allowed for an additional $10 per night per pet. Dogs must be well mannered, leashed, and under their owner's control. 2 dogs may be allowed.

Quality Inn University
515 North Dixieway
South Bend, IN
574-272-6600 (877-424-6423)
Dogs of all sizes are allowed. Dogs are allowed for a pet fee of $25.00 per pet per night.

Residence Inn South Bend
716 N Niles Avenue
South Bend, IN
574-289-5555 (800-331-3131)

Only a mile from the University of Notre Dame and near a number of attractions and activities for all level of travelers, this all suite hotel also offers a daily buffet breakfast and evening socials. Dogs are allowed for an additional one time pet fee of $100 per room. Multiple dogs may be allowed.

Sleep Inn
4134 Lincolnway West
South Bend, IN
574-232-3200 (877-424-6423)
Dogs up to 50 pounds are allowed. Dogs are allowed for a pet fee of $10.00 per pet per night. Two dogs are allowed per room.

Suburban Extended Stay Hotel
52825 Indiana Route 933 N
South Bend, IN
574-968-4737 (877 424-6423)
Dogs up to 100 pounds are allowed. Dogs are allowed for a pet fee of $25.00 per pet per stay.

Super 8 South Bend
4124 Ameritech Drive
South Bend, IN
574-243-0200 (800-800-8000)
Dogs of all sizes are allowed. Dogs are allowed for a pet fee.

Motel 6 - Indianapolis West Speedway
6330 Debonair Ln
Speedway, IN
317-293-3220 (800-466-8356)
This motel welcomes your pets to stay with you.

Days Inn Sullivan
907 West SR 154
Sullivan, IN
812-268-6391 (800-329-7466)
Dogs are welcome at this hotel.

Red Roof Inn Taylorsville
10330 N. US Rt 31
Taylorsville, IN
812-526-9747 (800-RED-ROOF)
One well-behaved family pet per room. Guest must notify front desk upon arrival. Guest is liable for any damages. In consideration of all guests, pets must never be left unattended in the guest rooms.

Days Inn Tell City
17 Highway 66 East
Tell City, IN
812-547-3474 (800-329-7466)
Dogs are welcome at this hotel.

Holiday Inn Express Hotel & Suites
Tell City

310 Orchard Hill Dr
Tell City, IN
812-547-0800 (877-270-6405)
Dogs are welcome at this hotel. There is a pet fee.

Ramada Limited Indiana Tell City
235 Orchard Hill Drive
Tell City, IN
812-547-3234 (800-272-6232)
Dogs of all sizes are allowed. Dogs are allowed for a pet fee of $10 per pet per night.

Candlewood Suites Terre Haute
721 Wabash Avenue
Terre Haute, IN
018-122-3434 (877-270-6405)
Dogs up to 80 pounds are allowed. Pets allowed with an additional pet fee. Up to $75 for 1-6 nights and up to $150 for 7+ nights. A pet agreement must be signed at check-in.

Days Inn And Suites Terre Haute
101 East Margaret Ave
Terre Haute, IN
812-232-8006 (800-329-7466)
Dogs of all sizes are allowed. Dogs are allowed for a pet fee.

Drury Inn
3040 South US Hwy 41
Terre Haute, IN
812-238-1206 (800-378-7946)
Dogs of all sizes are allowed for no additional pet fee with a credit card on file, and there is a pet agreement to sign at check in.

Econo Lodge
401 East Margaret Ave.
Terre Haute, IN
812-234-9931 (877-424-6423)
Dogs of all sizes are allowed. Dogs are allowed for a pet fee of $10.00 per pet per stay.

Knights Inn Terre Haute
1 West Honey Creek Drive
Terre Haute, IN
812-238-1586 (800-843-5644)
Dogs are welcome at this hotel.

Pear Tree Inn
3050 South US Hwy 41
Terre Haute, IN
812-234-4268 (800-378-7946)
Dogs of all sizes are allowed for no additional pet fee with a credit card on file, and there is a pet agreement to sign at check in. There may be up to 3 dogs if they are small.

Super 8 Terre Haute
3089 S. 1st St

Terre Haute, IN
812-232-4890 (800-800-8000)
Dogs of all sizes are allowed. Dogs are allowed for a pet fee.

Terre Haut Travelodge
530 South 3rd Street
Terre Haute, IN
812-232-7075 (800-578-7878)
Dogs are welcome at this hotel.

Rosemont Inn
806 W Market Street
Vevay, IN
812-427-3050 (800-705-0376)
rosemont-inn.com/
A magnificently restored 1881 Victorian mansion, this inn offers a number of amenities and a great location for exploring other sites of interest in the area. The beautifully landscaped grounds that overlook the Ohio River (where the American Queen Paddle-wheeler is often seen) also has a wood-burning fire pit to cozy around and a hot tub. Dogs are allowed for an additional fee of $5 per night per pet. Dogs must be hound and human friendly, leashed, and picked up after at all times. 2 dogs may be allowed.

Econo Lodge
600 Old Wheatland Rd.
Vincennes, IN
812-882-1479 (877-424-6423)
Dogs of all sizes are allowed. Dogs are allowed for a pet fee of $5.00 per pet per night.

Comfort Inn
7275 S. County Rd 75 East
Warren, IN
260-375-4800 (877-424-6423)
Dogs up to 50 pounds are allowed. Dogs are allowed for a pet fee of $15.00 per pet per night.

Motel 6 - Warren, In
7281 South 75 East
Warren, IN
260-375-4688 (800-466-8356)
This motel welcomes your pets to stay with you.

Comfort Inn & Suites
3328 E. Center Street
Warsaw, IN
574-269-6655 (877-424-6423)
Dogs up to 50 pounds are allowed. Dogs are allowed for a pet fee of $10.00 per pet per night. Two dogs are allowed per room.

Holiday Inn Express Hotel & Suites Warsaw
3825 Lake City Hwy

Warsaw, IN
574-268-1600 (877-270-6405)
Dogs up to 50 pounds are allowed.
Dogs are allowed for a pet fee of
$50.00 per pet per stay.

Ramada Plaza Warsaw
2519 E Center Street
Warsaw, IN
574-269-2323 (800-272-6232)
Dogs are welcome at this hotel.

Baymont Inn And Suites Washington
7 Cumberland Drive
Washington, IN
812-254-7000 (877-229-6668)
Dogs of all sizes are allowed. Dogs
are allowed for a pet fee.

Econo Lodge
2030 Northgate Drive
West Lafayette, IN
765-567-7100 (877-424-6423)
Dogs up to 50 pounds are allowed.
Dogs are allowed for a pet fee of
$15.00 per pet per night.

Iowa

Super 8 IA Adair
111 S 5th Street
Adair, IA
641-742-5251 (800-800-8000)
Dogs of all sizes are allowed. Dogs
are allowed for a pet fee.

Super 8 Algona
210 E Norwood Dr
Algona, IA
515-295-7225 (800-800-8000)
Dogs are welcome at this hotel.

Motel 6 - Des Moines East Altoona
3225 Adventureland Dr
Altoona, IA
515-967-5252 (800-466-8356)
This motel welcomes your pets to
stay with you.

Best Western University Park Inn &
Suites
2500 University Boulevard
Ames, IA
515-296-2500 (800-780-7234)
Dogs of all sizes are allowed. Dogs
are allowed for a pet fee of $5.00 per
pet per night.

Comfort Inn
1605 S. Dayton Ave.
Ames, IA
515-232-0689 (877-424-6423)
Dogs of all sizes are allowed. Dogs
are allowed for a pet fee of $10.00
per pet per night.

Quality Inn & Suites Starlite Village
Conference Center
2601 East 13th Street
Ames, IA
515-232-9260 (877-424-6423)
Dogs of all sizes are allowed. Dogs
are allowed for a pet fee of $10.00
per pet per stay.

Super 8 Ames
1418 S Dayton Ave
Ames, IA
515-232-6510 (800-800-8000)
Dogs of all sizes are allowed. Dogs
are allowed for a pet fee.

Super 8 IA Anamosa
100 Grant Wood Dr
Anamosa, IA
319-462-3888 (800-800-8000)
Dogs are welcome at this hotel.

Days Inn - Des Moines Ankeny
105 NE Delaware Ave
Ankeny, IA
515-965-1995 (800-329-7466)
Dogs of all sizes are allowed. Dogs
are allowed for a pet fee of $5.00
per pet per stay.

Super 8 /Des Moines Area Ankeny
206 SE Delware Street
Ankeny, IA
515-964-4503 (800-800-8000)
Dogs of all sizes are allowed. Dogs
are allowed for a pet fee.

Super 8 Atlantic
1902 East 7th Street
Atlantic, IA
712-243-4723 (800-800-8000)
Dogs of all sizes are allowed. Dogs
are allowed for a pet fee.

Motel 6 - Avoca
211 Marty Dr
Avoca, IA
712-343-6507 (800-466-8356)
This motel welcomes your pets to
stay with you.

Ramada /Davenport Bettendorf
3020 Utica Ridge Road
Bettendorf, IA
563-355-7575 (800-272-6232)
Dogs are welcome at this hotel.

Super 8 Bettendorf
890 Golden Valley Drive
Bettendorf, IA
563-355-7341 (800-800-8000)
Dogs are welcome at this hotel.

Super 8 Boone
1715 S. Story Street
Boone, IA

515-432-8890 (800-800-8000)
Dogs are welcome at this hotel.

Comfort Suites
1780 Stonegate Center Drive
Burlington, IA
319-753-1300 (877-424-6423)
Dogs of all sizes are allowed. Dogs
are allowed for a pet fee of
$Charge:15.00 per pet per night.
Two dogs are allowed per room.

Quality Inn
3051 Kirkwood
Burlington, IA
319-753-0000 (877-424-6423)
Dogs of all sizes are allowed. Two
dogs are allowed per room.

Super 8 Burlington
3001 Kirkwood
Burlington, IA
319-752-9806 (800-800-8000)
Dogs of all sizes are allowed. Dogs
are allowed for a pet fee of $10 per
pet per night.

Super 8 Carroll
1757 Hwy 71 North
Carroll, IA
712-792-4753 (800-800-8000)
Dogs of all sizes are allowed. Dogs
are allowed for a pet fee.

Holiday Inn Express Hotel & Suites
Omaha Airport
2510 Abbott Plaza
Carter Lake, IA
402-505-4900 (877-270-6405)
Dogs up to 50 pounds are allowed.
Dogs are allowed for a pet fee of
$10.00 per pet per night.

Super 8 /Eppley Arpt. Carter Lake
3000 Airport (Eppley) Drive
Carter Lake, IA
712-347-5588 (800-800-8000)
Dogs of all sizes are allowed. Dogs
are allowed for a pet fee.

Days Inn - University Plaza Cedar
Falls
5826 University Ave Bldg 2
Cedar Falls, IA
319-266-1222 (800-329-7466)
Dogs are welcome at this hotel.

Baymont Inn & Suites Cedar Rapids
1220 Park Place NE
Cedar Rapids, IA
319-378-8000 (877-229-6668)
Dogs are welcome at this hotel.

Best Western Cooper's Mill Hotel
100 F Avenue NW
Cedar Rapids, IA
319-366-5323 (800-780-7234)

Dogs up to 50 pounds are allowed. Dogs are allowed for a nightly pet fee.

Best Western Longbranch Hotel & Convention Center
90 Twixt Town Road NE
Cedar Rapids, IA
319-377-6386 (800-780-7234)
Dogs of all sizes are allowed. Dogs are allowed for a nightly pet fee.

Clarion Hotel & Convention Center
525 33rd Avenue SW
Cedar Rapids, IA
319-366-8671 (877-424-6423)
Dogs of all sizes are allowed. Dogs are allowed for a pet fee of $15.00 per pet per night.

Comfort Inn South
390 33rd Ave. S.W.
Cedar Rapids, IA
319-363-7934 (877-424-6423)
Dogs of all sizes are allowed.

Econo Lodge
622 33rd Ave. S.W.
Cedar Rapids, IA
319-363-8888 (877-424-6423)
Dogs of all sizes are allowed. Dogs are allowed for a pet fee of $10.00 per pet per night. Two dogs are allowed per room.

Hawthorn Suites
4444 Czech Lane NE
Cedar Rapids, IA
319-294-8700 (800-527-1133)
In addition to providing a convenient location to many local sites and activities, this all-suite hotel offers a number of amenities for business and leisure travelers, including their signature breakfast buffet and beautifully appointed rooms. Dogs are allowed for no additional pet fee. Multiple dogs may be allowed.

Howard Johnson Inn Cedar Rapids
616 33rd Ave S.W.
Cedar Rapids, IA
319-366-2475 (800-446-4656)
Dogs are welcome at this hotel.

MainStay Suites
5145 Rockwell Drive NE
Cedar Rapids, IA
319-363-7829 (877-424-6423)
Dogs up to 80 pounds are allowed. Dogs are allowed for a pet fee of $25.00 per pet per stay. Two dogs are allowed per room.

Motel 6 - Cedar Rapids
3325 Southgate Ct Sw
Cedar Rapids, IA

319-366-7523 (800-466-8356)
This motel welcomes your pets to stay with you.

Quality Inn
4747 1st Avenue SE
Cedar Rapids, IA
319-393-8800 (877-424-6423)
Dogs up to 50 pounds are allowed. Dogs are allowed for a pet fee of $10.00 per pet per night.

Red Roof Inn Cedar Rapids, IA
Cedar Rapids, IA
3642000 (800-RED-ROOF)
One well-behaved family pet per room. Guest must notify front desk upon arrival. Guest is liable for any damages. In consideration of all guests, pets must never be left unattended in the guest rooms.

Residence Inn Cedar Rapids
1900 Dodge Road NE
Cedar Rapids, IA
319-395-0111 (800-331-3131)
Offering a convenient location to business, shopping, dining, and entertainment areas, this all suite hotel also offers a number of in-house amenities, including a daily buffet breakfast and evening socials. Dogs are allowed for an additional one time pet fee of $75 per room. Multiple dogs may be allowed.

Super 8 Cedar Rapids
720 33rd Ave SW
Cedar Rapids, IA
319-362-6002 (800-800-8000)
Dogs of all sizes are allowed. Dogs are allowed for a pet fee.

Super 8 East Cedar Rapids
400 33rd Ave SW
Cedar Rapids, IA
319-363-1755 (800-800-8000)
Dogs of all sizes are allowed. Dogs are allowed for a pet fee.

Sleep Inn & Suites
1416 South Grand Avenue
Charles City, IA
641-257-6700 (877-424-6423)
Dogs of all sizes are allowed. Dogs are allowed for a pet fee of $usd per pet per night.

Super 8 Charles City
Highway 218, Exit 218
Charles City, IA
641-228-2888 (800-800-8000)
Dogs of all sizes are allowed. Dogs are allowed for a pet fee.

Best Western La Grande Hacienda

1401 N 2nd Street
Cherokee, IA
712-225-5701 (800-780-7234)
Dogs are welcome at this hotel.

Super 8 Cherokee
1400 N 2nd St
Cherokee, IA
712-225-4278 (800-800-8000)
Dogs are welcome at this hotel.

Super 8 Clarinda
1203 S 12th Street
Clarinda, IA
712-542-6333 (800-800-8000)
Dogs are welcome at this hotel.

Best Western Holiday Lodge
I-35 & Highway 18 Exit 194
Clear Lake, IA
641-357-5253 (800-780-7234)
Dogs of all sizes are allowed. Dogs are allowed for a nightly pet fee.

Super 8 Clear Lake
2809 4th Ave. South
Clear Lake, IA
641-357-7521 (800-800-8000)
Dogs are welcome at this hotel.

Best Western Frontier Inn
2300 Lincoln Way
Clinton, IA
563-242-7112 (800-780-7234)
Dogs are welcome at this hotel. There is a $10 daily pet fee.

Country Inns & Suites by Carlson
2224 Lincoln Way
Clinton, IA
563-244-9922
Dogs of all sizes are allowed. There is a $10 (+ tax) per day per pet additional fee.

Motel 6 - Clinton, Ia
1522 Lincoln Way
Clinton, IA
563-243-8841 (800-466-8356)
This motel welcomes your pets to stay with you.

Super 8 Clinton
1711 Lincoln Way
Clinton, IA
563-242-8870 (800-800-8000)
Dogs are welcome at this hotel.

Best Western Des Moines West Inn & Suites
1450 NW 118th Street
Clive, IA
515-221-2345 (800-780-7234)
Dogs of all sizes are allowed. Dogs are allowed for a nightly pet fee.

Chase Suite Hotel by Woodfin

11 428 Forest Ave.
Clive, IA
515-223-7700
All well-behaved dogs are welcome.
Every room is a suite with a full
kitchen. Hotel amenities include a
pool, exercise facility, and a
complimentary breakfast buffet.
There is a $5 per day pet fee and a
$50 refundable pet deposit.

Comfort Inn
1402 North Walnut Street
Colfax, IA
515-674-4455 (877-424-6423)
Dogs of all sizes are allowed. Dogs
are allowed for a pet fee of $12.50
per pet per night. Three or more
dogs may be allowed.

Baymont Inn & Suites Iowa City/
Coralville
200 6th Street
Coralville, IA
319-337-9797 (877-229-6668)
Dogs are welcome at this hotel.

Days Inn - Iowa City Coralville
205 2nd Street (HWY 6)
Coralville, IA
319-354-4400 (800-329-7466)
Dogs are welcome at this hotel.

Holiday Inn Coralville
1220 First Avenue
Coralville, IA
319-351-5049 (877-270-6405)
Dogs of all sizes are allowed. Dogs
are allowed for a pet fee of $20.00
per pet per night.

Motel 6 - Iowa City
810 1st Ave
Coralville, IA
319-354-0030 (800-466-8356)
This motel welcomes your pets to
stay with you.

Super 8 Iowa City/ Coralville
611 1st Avenue
Coralville, IA
319-337-8388 (800-800-8000)
Dogs of all sizes are allowed. Dogs
are allowed for a pet fee.

Days Inn -Lake Manawa Council
Bluffs
3208 South 7th Street
Council Bluffs, IA
712-366-9699 (800-329-7466)
Dogs are welcome at this hotel.

Days Inn /9th Ave Council Bluffs
3619 9th Ave
Council Bluffs, IA
712-323-2200 (800-329-7466)
Dogs of all sizes are allowed. Dogs

are allowed for a pet fee of $10.00
per pet per night.

Motel 6 - Council Bluffs
3032 Expressway St
Council Bluffs, IA
712-366-2405 (800-466-8356)
This motel welcomes your pets to
stay with you.

Quality Inn & Suites
3537 W. Broadway
Council Bluffs, IA
712-328-3171 (877-424-6423)
Dogs of all sizes are allowed. Dogs
are allowed for a pet fee of $15.00/
per pet per night. Two dogs are
allowed per room.

Cresco Motel
620 2nd Avenue SE/H 9E
Cresco, IA
563-547-2240
crescomotel.com/
Located in a quiet residential area,
this motel will allow pets for no
additional fee. Dogs must be
leashed when out of the room. 2
dogs may be allowed.

Super 8 IA Cresco
511 Second Ave SE
Cresco, IA
563-547-9988 (800-800-8000)
Dogs of all sizes are allowed. Dogs
are allowed for a pet fee.

Super 8 Creston
Intersection of Hwy. 34 & 25
Creston, IA
641-782-6541 (800-800-8000)
Dogs are welcome at this hotel.

Baymont Inn & Suites Davenport
400 Jason Way Court
Davenport, IA
563-386-1600 (800-531-5900)
Dogs of all sizes are allowed. There
are no additional pet fees. Dogs
may only be left alone in the room if
they will be quiet and well behaved.
Dogs must be leashed and cleaned
up after, and they are not allowed in
the pool or breakfast area. Multiple
dogs may be allowed.

Clarion Hotel Conference Center
5202 Brady Street
Davenport, IA
563-391-1230 (877-424-6423)
Dogs up to 50 pounds are allowed.
Dogs are allowed for a pet fee of
$10.00 per pet per night. Two dogs
are allowed per room.

Country Inns & Suites by Carlson
140 East 55th Street

Davenport, IA
563-388-6444
Dogs up to 75 pounds are allowed.
There is a $25 one time additional
pet fee. If a non-smoking room is
desired, please specifically request
one. The hotel has complimentary
high-speed Internet access.

Days Inn East Davenport
3202 E. Kimberly Rd/I-74
Davenport, IA
563-359-7165 (800-329-7466)
Dogs are welcome at this hotel.

La Quinta Inn Davenport
3330 E. Kimberly Rd
Davenport, IA
563-359-3921 (800-531-5900)
Dogs of all sizes are allowed. There
are no additional pet fees. There is a
pet waiver to sign at check in. Dogs
must be leashed and cleaned up
after. Multiple dogs may be allowed.

Motel 6 - Davenport
6111 Brady St
Davenport, IA
563-391-8997 (800-466-8356)
This motel welcomes your pets to
stay with you.

Residence Inn Davenport
120 E 55th Street
Davenport, IA
563-391-8877 (800-331-3131)
This all suite hotel sits central to
many of the city's star attractions,
shopping, dining, and business
areas, plus they offer a number of in-
house amenities that include a daily
buffet breakfast and evening social
hours. Dogs are allowed for an
additional one time pet fee of $100
per room. Multiple dogs may be
allowed.

Staybridge Suites Davenport
4729 Progress Drive
Davenport, IA
563-359-7829 (877-270-6405)
Dogs up to 80 pounds are allowed.
Pets allowed with an additional pet
fee. Up to $75 for 1-6 nights and up
to $150 for 7+ nights. A pet
agreement must be signed at check-
in.

Super 8 - Davenport
410 E 65th Street
Davenport, IA
563-388-9810 (800-800-8000)
Dogs of all sizes are allowed. Dogs
are allowed for a pet fee.

Travelodge Davenport
6310 N Brady St

Davenport, IA
563-386-6350 (800-578-7878)
Dogs are welcome at this hotel.

Super 8 Decorah
810 Hwy 9 East
Decorah, IA
563-382-8771 (800-800-8000)
Dogs of all sizes are allowed. Dogs
are allowed for a pet fee.

Days Inn Denison
315 Chamberlin Drive
Denison, IA
712-263-2500 (800-329-7466)
Dogs are welcome at this hotel.

Super 8 Denison
502 Boyer Valley Rd
Denison, IA
712-263-5081 (800-800-8000)
Dogs of all sizes are allowed. Dogs
are allowed for a pet fee.

Best Western Des Moines Airport
Hotel
1810 Army Post Road
Des Moines, IA
515-287-6464 (800-780-7234)
Dogs of all sizes are allowed. Dogs
are allowed for a pet fee.

Candlewood Suites Des Moines
7625 Office Plaza Drive North
Des Moines, IA
515-221-0001 (877-270-6405)
Dogs up to 80 pounds are allowed.
Pets allowed with an additional pet
fee. Up to $75 for 1-6 nights and up
to $150 for 7+ nights. A pet
agreement must be signed at check-
in.

Comfort Inn
5231 Fleur Dr.
Des Moines, IA
515-287-3434 (877-424-6423)
Dogs of all sizes are allowed. Dogs
are allowed for a pet fee of $10.00
per pet per night.

Des Moines Red Roof Inn & Suites
4950 Northeast 14th Street
Des Moines, IA
515-266-6800 (800-RED-ROOF)
One well-behaved family pet per
room. Guest must notify front desk
upon arrival. Guest is liable for any
damages. In consideration of all
guests, pets must never be left
unattended in the guest rooms.

Econo Lodge Inn & Suites
4755 Merle Hay Rd.
Des Moines, IA
515-278-8858 (877-424-6423)
Dogs of all sizes are allowed. Dogs

are allowed for a pet fee of $10.00
per pet per night. One dog is
allowed per room.

Econo Lodge Inn & Suites
Fairgrounds
410 E. 30th Street
Des Moines, IA
515-262-2525 (877-424-6423)
Dogs of all sizes are allowed. Dogs
are allowed for a pet fee of $15.00
per pet per night.

Holiday Inn Des Moines-
Airport/Conf Center
6111 Fleur Drive
Des Moines, IA
515-287-2400 (877-270-6405)
Dogs up to 50 pounds are allowed.
Dogs are allowed for a pet fee of
$50.00 per pet per night.

La Quinta Inn Des Moines/West-
Clive
1390 N.W. 118th Street
Des Moines, IA
515-221-9200 (800-531-5900)
Dogs of all sizes are allowed. There
are no additional pet fees. Dogs
may not be left unattended, and
they must be leashed and cleaned
up after. Multiple dogs may be
allowed.

Motel 6 - Des Moines North
4940 Ne 14th St
Des Moines, IA
515-266-5456 (800-466-8356)
This motel welcomes your pets to
stay with you.

Motel 6 - Des Moines South Airport
4817 Fleur Dr
Des Moines, IA
515-287-6364 (800-466-8356)
This motel welcomes your pets to
stay with you.

Quality Inn & Suites Event Center
929 3rd Street
Des Moines, IA
515-282-5251 (877-424-6423)
Dogs of all sizes are allowed. Dogs
are allowed for a pet fee of $10.00
per pet per night.

Ramada West/Clive Des Moines
1600 NW 114th Street
Des Moines, IA
515-226-1600 (800-272-6232)
Dogs are welcome at this hotel.

Ramada Northwest - Des Moines
5000 Merle Hay Road
Des Moines, IA
515-278-0271 (800-272-6232)
Dogs are welcome at this hotel.

Rodeway Inn
5020 N.E. 14th Street
Des Moines, IA
515-265-7511 (877-424-6423)
Dogs of all sizes are allowed. Dogs
are allowed for a pet fee of $10.00
per pet per night.

Comfort Inn
4055 McDonald Dr.
Dubuque, IA
563-556-3006 (877-424-6423)
Dogs of all sizes are allowed.

Days Inn Dubuque
1111 Dodge Street
Dubuque, IA
563-583-3297 (800-329-7466)
Dogs of all sizes are allowed. Dogs
are allowed for a pet fee of $10.00
per pet per night.

Holiday Inn Dubuque/Galena
450 Main Street
Dubuque, IA
563-556-2000 (877-270-6405)
Dogs of all sizes are allowed. Dogs
are allowed for a pet fee of $25 per
pet per stay.

Motel 6 - Dubuque, Ia
2670 Dodge Street
Dubuque, IA
563-556-0880 (800-466-8356)
This motel welcomes your pets to
stay with you.

Super 8 /Galena Area Dubuque
2730 Dodge Street
Dubuque, IA
563-582-8898 (800-800-8000)
Dogs of all sizes are allowed. Dogs
are allowed for a pet fee.

Super 8 Dyersville
925 15th Ave SE
Dyersville, IA
563-875-8885 (800-800-8000)
Dogs of all sizes are allowed. Dogs
are allowed for a pet fee.

Super 8 Emmetsburg
3501 Main Street
Emmetsburg, IA
712-852-2667 (800-800-8000)
Dogs are welcome at this hotel.

Sleep Inn
2008 Central Ave.
Estherville, IA
712-362-5522 (877-424-6423)
Dogs of all sizes are allowed.

Super 8 Estherville
1919 Central Ave
Estherville, IA

712-362-2400 (800-800-8000)
Dogs are welcome at this hotel.

Days Inn Waterloo Evansdale
450 Evansdale Drive
Evansdale, IA
319-235-1111 (800-329-7466)
Dogs of all sizes are allowed. Dogs
are allowed for a pet fee of $10.00
per pet per night.

Best Western Fairfield Inn
2200 W Burlington Avenue
Fairfield, IA
641-472-2200 (800-780-7234)
Dogs of all sizes are allowed. Dogs
are allowed for a pet fee of $25 per
pet per stay.

Super 8 Fairfield
3001 W Burlington Ave
Fairfield, IA
641-469-2000 (800-800-8000)
Dogs are welcome at this hotel.

Comfort Inn
2938 5th Ave. S.
Fort Dodge, IA
515-573-5000 (877-424-6423)
Dogs up to 50 pounds are allowed.

Comfort Inn & Suites
6169 Reve Court
Fort Madison, IA
319-372-6800 (877-424-6423)
Dogs of all sizes are allowed. Two
dogs are allowed per room.

Knights Inn Fort Madison
3440 Avenue L
Fort Madison, IA
319-372-7740 (800-843-5644)
Dogs are welcome at this hotel.

Super 8 Fort Madison
5107 Avenue O
Fort Madison, IA
319-372-8500 (800-800-8000)
Dogs of all sizes are allowed. Dogs
are allowed for a nightly pet fee.

Travelodge - Fort Madison
5001 Ave O
Fort Madison, IA
319-372-7510 (800-578-7878)
Dogs are welcome at this hotel.

Best Western Pioneer Inn
2210 West Street S
Grinnell, IA
641-236-6116 (800-780-7234)
Dogs of all sizes are allowed. Dogs
are allowed for a pet fee of $10 per
pet per night.

Comfort Inn & Suites
1630 West Street South

Grinnell, IA
641-236-5236 (877-424-6423)
Dogs of all sizes are allowed. Dogs
are allowed for a pet fee of $25.00
per pet per night. Two dogs are
allowed per room.

Days Inn and Suites Grinnell
1902 West Street South
Grinnell, IA
641-236-6710 (800-329-7466)
Dogs are welcome at this hotel.

Super 8 IA Grinnell
2111 West Street S
Grinnell, IA
641-236-7888 (800-800-8000)
Dogs of all sizes are allowed. Dogs
are allowed for a pet fee.

Super 8 Ida Grove
90 East Highway 175
Ida Grove, IA
712-364-3988 (800-800-8000)
Dogs are welcome at this hotel.

Super 8 Independence
2000 1st Street West
Independence, IA
319-334-7041 (800-800-8000)
Dogs of all sizes are allowed. Dogs
are allowed for a pet fee.

Super 8 Des Moines Indianola
1701 N Jefferson
Indianola, IA
515-961-0058 (800-800-8000)
Dogs of all sizes are allowed. Dogs
are allowed for a pet fee.

Alexis Park Inn and Suites
1165 S Riverside Drive
Iowa City, IA
319 337-8665 (888-9ALEXIS (925-
3947))
This unique all suite inn features
aviation-themed suites-most with
Jacuzzis, breakfast personally
delivered, a full sized pool, an
aviation library, and an HD theater
with 35 seats. However, what really
sets them apart is their full-sized
flight simulator-available to guests
free, and they offer airplane and
biplane rides. Dogs are allowed for
an additional one time fee of $10
per pet. Dogs must be leashed and
under their owner's control. Multiple
dogs may be allowed.

Sheraton Iowa City Hotel
210 S. Dubuque St.
Iowa City, IA
319-337-4058 (888-625-5144)
Dogs up to 80 pounds are allowed.
There are no additional pet fees.
Dogs are not allowed to be left

alone in the room.

Travelodge Iowa City
2216 North Dodge St
Iowa City, IA
319-351-1010 (800-578-7878)
Dogs of all sizes are allowed. Dogs
are allowed for a pet fee of $10.00
per pet per night.

Super 8 Iowa Falls
839 S Oak Hwy 65 S
Iowa Falls, IA
641-648-4618 (800-800-8000)
Dogs of all sizes are allowed. Dogs
are allowed for a pet fee.

Inn At Merle Hay
5055 Merle Hay Rd
Johnston, IA
515-270-1111
There is an additional fee of $10 per
night per pet. 2 dogs may be
allowed.

TownePlace Suites Des Moines
Urbandale
8800 NorthPark Drive
Johnston, IA
515-727-4066 (800-257-3000)
Some of the amenities of this all
suite inn include neighborhood style
accommodations, a complimentary
continental breakfast, and a central
location to a number of activities and
sites. Dogs are allowed for an
additional one time fee of $100 per
room. The fee may be adjusted when
there is only 1 pet. Multiple dogs may
be allowed.

Super 8 Keokuk
3511 Main St
Keokuk, IA
319-524-3888 (800-800-8000)
Dogs of all sizes are allowed. Dogs
are allowed for a pet fee of $10.00
per pet per night.

Comfort Inn & Suites Riverview
902 Mississippi View Court
Le Claire, IA
563-289-4747 (877-424-6423)
Dogs of all sizes are allowed. Dogs
are allowed for a pet fee of $10.00
per pet per night.

Holiday Inn Express Le Claire
Riverfront-Davenport
1201 Canal Shore Drive
Le Claire, IA
563-289-9978 (877-270-6405)
Dogs of all sizes are allowed. Dogs
are allowed for a pet fee of $25.00
per pet per night.

Super 8 /Quad Cities Le Claire

1552 Welcome Center Drive
Le Claire, IA
563-289-5888 (800-800-8000)
Dogs of all sizes are allowed. Dogs
are allowed for a pet fee of $10.00
per pet per night.

Baymont Inn & Suites LeMars
1314 12th Street SW
Le Mars, IA
712-548-4910 (877-229-6668)
Dogs of all sizes are allowed. Dogs
are allowed for a pet fee.

Super 8
South Hwy 75
Le Mars, IA
712-546-8800 (800-800-8000)
Dogs of all sizes are allowed. Dogs
are allowed for a pet fee of $10.00
per pet per night.

Super 8 Manchester
1020 W Main
Manchester, IA
563-927-2533 (800-800-8000)
Dogs are welcome at this hotel.

Best Western Regency Inn
3303 S Center Street
Marshalltown, IA
641-752-6321 (800-780-7234)
Dogs of all sizes are allowed. Dogs
are allowed for a nightly pet fee.

Comfort Inn
2613 S. Center St.
Marshalltown, IA
641-752-6000 (877-424-6423)
Dogs of all sizes are allowed. Dogs
are allowed for a pet fee of $10.00
per pet per night.

Super 8 IA Marshalltown
3315 South Center Street
Marshalltown, IA
641-753-3333 (800-800-8000)
Dogs of all sizes are allowed. Dogs
are allowed for a pet fee.

Days Inn Mason City
2301 Fourth Street SW
Mason City, IA
641-424-0210 (800-329-7466)
Dogs are welcome at this hotel.

Holiday Inn Mason City
2101 4th St SW
Mason City, IA
641-423-1640 (877-270-6405)
Dogs of all sizes are allowed. Dogs
are allowed for a pet fee.

Super 8 Mason City
3010 4th Street SW
Mason City, IA
641-423-8855 (800-800-8000)

Dogs are welcome at this hotel.

Days Inn Missouri Valley
1967 Hwy 30
Missouri Valley, IA
712-642-4003 (800-329-7466)
Dogs of all sizes are allowed. Dogs
are allowed for a nightly pet fee.

Super 8 Missouri Valley
3167 Joliet Ave
Missouri Valley, IA
712-642-4788 (800-800-8000)
Dogs are welcome at this hotel.

Ramada Limited
1200 East Baker St.
Mount Pleasant, IA
319-385-0571
innovativehotels.com
The hotel offers King and Queen
Rooms, 18 Suites, hot and cold
Breakfast, an Indoor Pool and Hot
Tubs. There is plenty of open space
to walk your pet. The pet fee is a
one time $8.00 charge.

Super 8 Mt Pleasant
1000 N. Grand Avenue
Mount Pleasant, IA
319-385-8888 (800-800-8000)
Dogs of all sizes are allowed. Dogs
are allowed for a pet fee of $10 per
pet per night.

Sleep Inn & Suites
310 Virgil Avenue
Mount Vernon, IA
319-895-0055 (877-424-6423)
Dogs up to 100 pounds are allowed.
Dogs are allowed for a pet fee of
$12.50 per pet per night.

Econo Lodge
2402 Park Ave.
Muscatine, IA
563-264-3337 (877-424-6423)
Dogs of all sizes are allowed.

Holiday Inn Muscatine
2915 N. Hwy. 61
Muscatine, IA
563-264-5550 (877-270-6405)
Dogs up to 50 pounds are allowed.
Dogs are allowed for a nightly pet
fee.

Super 8 Muscatine
2900 North Highway 61
Muscatine, IA
563-263-9100 (800-800-8000)
Dogs of all sizes are allowed. Dogs
are allowed for a pet fee of $5 per
pet per night.

Super 8 New Hampton
825 S Linn St

New Hampton, IA
641-394-3838 (800-800-8000)
Dogs of all sizes are allowed. Dogs
are allowed for a pet fee.

Days Inn Newton
1605 West 19th Street South
Newton, IA
641-792-2330 (800-329-7466)
Dogs are welcome at this hotel.

Econo Lodge Inn & Suites
1405 W. 19th Street South
Newton, IA
641-792-8100 (877-424-6423)
Dogs up to 100 pounds are allowed.

Super 8 Oelwein
210 10th Street
Oelwein, IA
319-283-2888 (800-800-8000)
Dogs of all sizes are allowed. Dogs
are allowed for a pet fee.

Super 8 Onawa
2835 Iowa Avenue
Onawa, IA
712-423-2101 (800-800-8000)
Dogs of all sizes are allowed. Dogs
are allowed for a pet fee.

Super 8 Orange City
810 Lincoln Place
Orange City, IA
712-737-2600 (800-800-8000)
Dogs of all sizes are allowed. Dogs
are allowed for a pet fee of $10.00
per pet per stay.

Super 8 Osage
1530 E Main Street
Osage, IA
641-732-1800 (800-800-8000)
Dogs of all sizes are allowed. Dogs
are allowed for a pet fee.

Days Inn Osceola
710 Warren Ave
Osceola, IA
641-342-6666 (800-329-7466)
Dogs are welcome at this hotel.

Super 8 IA Osceola
720 Warren Ave
Osceola, IA
641-342-6594 (800-800-8000)
Dogs of all sizes are allowed. Dogs
are allowed for a pet fee.

Terribles Lakeside Casino Resort
777 Casino Drive
Osceola, IA
641-342-9511 (877-477-5253)
Dogs of all sizes are allowed. There
are no additional pet fees. Dogs may
not be left unattended in the rooms
unless they are crated, and they

must be quiet, well behaved, leashed, and cleaned up after. There is an RV camping area on site where dogs are also allowed. 2 dogs may be allowed.

Comfort Inn
2401 A Ave West
Oskaloosa, IA
641-676-6000 (877-424-6423)
Dogs up to 50 pounds are allowed.

Super 8 IA Oskaloosa
306 S 17th Street
Oskaloosa, IA
641-673-8481 (800-800-8000)
Dogs of all sizes are allowed. Dogs are allowed for a pet fee.

Super 8 Pella
105 E Oskaloosa St
Pella, IA
641-628-8181 (800-800-8000)
Dogs of all sizes are allowed. Dogs are allowed for a pet fee of $10 per pet per night.

Super 8 Nebraska City
2103 249th Street
Percival, IA
712-382-2828 (800-800-8000)
Dogs are welcome at this hotel.

Sleep Inn & Suites
5850 Morning Star Court
Pleasant Hill, IA
515-299-9922 (877-424-6423)
Dogs of all sizes are allowed. Dogs are allowed for a pet fee of $12.50 per pet per night. Two dogs are allowed per room.

Super 8 Red Oak
800 Senate Ave
Red Oak, IA
712-623-6919 (800-800-8000)
Dogs of all sizes are allowed. Dogs are allowed for a pet fee.

Econo Lodge
103 Sergeant Square
Sergeant Bluff, IA
712-943-5079 (877-424-6423)
Dogs of all sizes are allowed.

Holiday Inn Express Hotel & Suites Sheldon
201 34th Ave.
Sheldon, IA
712-324-3000 (877-270-6405)
Dogs of all sizes are allowed. Dogs are allowed for a pet fee of $25.00 per pet per night.

Super 8 Sheldon
210 North 2nd Ave
Sheldon, IA

712-324-8400 (800-800-8000)
Dogs of all sizes are allowed. Dogs are allowed for a pet fee.

Super 8 Sibley
1108 2nd Ave
Sibley, IA
712-754-3603 (800-800-8000)
Dogs are welcome at this hotel.

Econo Lodge
86 9th St. Cir. N.E.
Sioux Center, IA
712-722-4000 (877-424-6423)
Dogs of all sizes are allowed. Dogs are allowed for a pet fee of $10.00 per pet per night.

Holiday Inn Express Hotel & Suites Sioux Center
100 Saint Andrews Way
Sioux Center, IA
712-722-3500 (877-270-6405)
Dogs of all sizes are allowed. Dogs are allowed for a pet fee of $25.00 per pet per night.

Baymont Inn And Suites Airport Sioux City
3101 Singing Hills Boulevard
Sioux City, IA
712-233-2302 (877-229-6668)
Dogs of all sizes are allowed. Dogs are allowed for a pet fee.

Comfort Inn
4202 S. Lakeport St.
Sioux City, IA
712-274-1300 (877-424-6423)
Dogs of all sizes are allowed. Dogs are allowed for a pet fee of $25.00 per pet per stay.

Days Inn Sioux City
3000 Singing Hills Blvd
Sioux City, IA
712-258-8000 (800-329-7466)
Dogs of all sizes are allowed. Dogs are allowed for a pet fee.

Motel 6 - Sioux City
6166 Harbor Dr
Sioux City, IA
712-277-3131 (800-466-8356)
This motel welcomes your pets to stay with you.

Ramada City Centre
130 Nebraska Street
Sioux City, IA
712-277-1550 (800-272-6232)
Dogs of all sizes are allowed. Dogs are allowed for a pet fee of $10 per pet per night.

Rodeway Inn & Conference Center
1401 Zenith Dr.

Sioux City, IA
712-277-3211 (877-424-6423)
Dogs up to 50 pounds are allowed. Two dogs are allowed per room.

Econo Lodge Inn & Suites
14 11th Street SE
Spencer, IA
712-262-9123 (877-424-6423)
Dogs up to 80 pounds are allowed. Dogs are allowed for a pet fee of $10.00 per pet per night. Two dogs are allowed per room.

Ramada /Okoboji Spirit Lake
2704 17th Street
Spirit Lake, IA
712-336-3984 (800-272-6232)
Dogs of all sizes are allowed. Dogs are allowed for a pet fee of $50.00 per pet per stay.

Super 8 /Okoboji Spirit Lake
2203 Circle Drive West
Spirit Lake, IA
712-336-4901 (800-800-8000)
Dogs are welcome at this hotel.

Comfort Inn
425 Timberland Dr.
Story City, IA
515-733-6363 (877-424-6423)
Dogs of all sizes are allowed. Dogs are allowed for a pet fee of $12.50 per pet per night. Two dogs are allowed per room.

Super 8 Story City
515 Factory Outlet Dr.
Story City, IA
515-733-5281 (800-800-8000)
Dogs of all sizes are allowed. Dogs are allowed for a pet fee.

Super 8 Stuart
203 SE 7th Street
Stuart, IA
515-523-2888 (800-800-8000)
Dogs of all sizes are allowed. Dogs are allowed for a pet fee.

Super 8 Toledo
207 Hwy 30 W
Toledo, IA
641-484-5888 (800-800-8000)
Dogs of all sizes are allowed. Dogs are allowed for a pet fee.

Extended Stay America Des Moines - Urbandale
3940 114th St.
Urbandale, IA
515-276-1929 (800-804-3724)
One dog is allowed per suite. There is a $25 per night additional pet fee up to $150 for an entire stay.

Sleep Inn
11211 Hickman Rd
Urbandale, IA
515-270-2424 (877-424-6423)
Dogs of all sizes are allowed. Dogs are allowed for a pet fee of $10.00 per pet per night.

Super 8 /Des Moines Area Urbandale
5900 Sutton Drive
Urbandale, IA
515-270-1037 (800-800-8000)
Dogs of all sizes are allowed. Dogs are allowed for a pet fee.

Marriott West Des Moines
1250 Jordan Creek Parkway
W Des Moines, IA
515-267-1500 (800-228-9290)
This luxury hotel provides a great location to a number of sites of interest for both business and leisure travelers; plus they also offer numerous on-site amenities to ensure a comfortable stay. Dogs are allowed for an additional one time fee of $75 per room. Multiple dogs may be allowed.

Days Inn Davenport Walcott
2889 N Plainview RD
Walcott, IA
563-284-6600 (800-329-7466)
Dogs of all sizes are allowed. Dogs are allowed for a pet fee.

Econo Lodge
241 Interstate Street
Walcott, IA
563-284-5083 (877-424-6423)
Dogs of all sizes are allowed. Dogs are allowed for a pet fee of $5.00 per pet per stay.

Super 8 Walnut
2109 Antique City Dr
Walnut, IA
712-784-2221 (800-800-8000)
Dogs of all sizes are allowed. Dogs are allowed for a pet fee.

Super 8 Washington
119 Westview Drive
Washington, IA
319-653-6621 (800-800-8000)
Dogs of all sizes are allowed. Dogs are allowed for a pet fee.

Baymont Inn & Suites Waterloo
2141 La Porte Road
Waterloo, IA
319-233-9191 (877-229-6668)
Dogs of all sizes are allowed. Dogs are allowed for a pet fee of $10 per pet per night.

Candlewood Suites Waterloo-Cedar Falls
2056 La Porte Rd.
Waterloo, IA
319-235-7000 (877-270-6405)
Dogs up to 80 pounds are allowed. Pets allowed with an additional pet fee. Up to $75 for 1-6 nights and up to $150 for 7+ nights. A pet agreement must be signed at check-in.

Comfort Inn
1945 LaPorte Rd.
Waterloo, IA
319-234-7411 (877-424-6423)
Dogs of all sizes are allowed.

Motel 6 - Waterloo
2343 Logan Ave
Waterloo, IA
319-236-3238 (800-466-8356)
This motel welcomes your pets to stay with you.

Quality Inn & Suites
226 W. 5th St.
Waterloo, IA
319-235-0301 (877-424-6423)
Dogs up to 50 pounds are allowed. Dogs are allowed for a pet fee of $10.00 per pet per night.

Ramada Hotel & Convention Center
205 W 4th Street
Waterloo, IA
319-233-7560 (800-272-6232)
Dogs are welcome at this hotel.

Super 8 Waterloo
1825 LaPorte Rd
Waterloo, IA
319-233-1800 (800-800-8000)
Dogs of all sizes are allowed. Dogs are allowed for a pet fee.

Comfort Inn
404 29th Avenue SW
Waverly, IA
319-352-0399 (877-424-6423)
Dogs up to 50 pounds are allowed. Dogs are allowed for a pet fee of $10.00 per pet per night. Two dogs are allowed per room.

Super 8 Waverly
301 13th Ave
Waverly, IA
319-352-0888 (800-800-8000)
Dogs of all sizes are allowed. Dogs are allowed for a pet fee.

Super 8 IA Webster City
I-20 & Hwy 17
Webster City, IA
515-832-2000 (800-800-8000)
Dogs are welcome at this hotel.

Motel 6 - Des Moines West
7655 Office Plaza Dr
West Des Moines, IA
515-267-8885 (800-466-8356)
This motel welcomes your pets to stay with you.

Residence Inn Des Moines West at Jordan Creek Town Center
160 S Jordan Creek Parkway
West Des Moines, IA
515-267-0338 (800-331-3131)
In addition to offering a convenient location to business, shopping, dining, and entertainment areas, this hotel also provides a number of in-house amenities, including a daily buffet breakfast and an evening social hour. Dogs are allowed for an additional one time pet fee of $100 per room. Multiple dogs may be allowed.

Sheraton West Des Moines Hotel
1800 50th St.
West Des Moines, IA
515-223-1800 (888-625-5144)
A dog up to 50 pounds is allowed for an additional one time pet fee of $75. Dogs may not be left alone in the room.

Staybridge Suites West Des Moines
6905 Lake Dr.
West Des Moines, IA
515-223-0000 (877-270-6405)
Dogs up to 80 pounds are allowed. Pets allowed with an additional pet fee. Up to $75 for 1-6 nights and up to $150 for 7+ nights. A pet agreement must be signed at check-in.

Econo Lodge
1943 Garfield Ave.
West Liberty, IA
319-627-2171 (877-424-6423)
Dogs of all sizes are allowed.

Super 8 West Union
108 South Hwy 150
West Union, IA
563-422-3537 (800-800-8000)
Dogs are welcome at this hotel.

Best Western Norseman Inn
3086 220th Street
Williams, IA
515-854-2281 (800-780-7234)
Dogs are welcome at this hotel. No cats are allowed.

Best Western Cozy House & Suites
1708 N Highland Street
Williamsburg, IA
319-668-9777 (800-780-7234)

Dogs are welcome at this hotel. There is a $16.80 one time pet fee.

Super 8 /Amana Colonies Area
Williamsburg
I-80, Exit 220
Williamsburg, IA
319-668-9718 (800-800-8000)
Dogs of all sizes are allowed. Dogs are allowed for a pet fee.

Super 8 Motel - /Amana Areas
Williamsburg
2228 U Avenue
Williamsburg, IA
319-668-2800 (800-800-8000)
Dogs of all sizes are allowed. Dogs are allowed for a nightly pet fee.

Super 8 Winterset
1312 Cedar Bridge Road
Winterset, IA
515-462-4888 (800-800-8000)
Dogs of all sizes are allowed. Dogs are allowed for a pet fee.

Kansas

Holiday Inn Express Hotel & Suites
Abilene
110 E. Lafayette
Abilene, KS
785-263-4049 (877-270-6405)
Dogs of all sizes are allowed. Dogs are allowed for a pet fee of $20.00 per pet per night.

Super 8 KS Abilene
2207 N. Buckeye Ave
Abilene, KS
785-263-4545 (800-800-8000)
Dogs are welcome at this hotel.

Best Western Atrium Gardens
3232 N Summit Street
Arkansas City, KS
620-442-7700 (800-780-7234)
Dogs are welcome at this hotel.

Super 8 KS Arkansas City
3228 N. Summit
Arkansas City, KS
620-442-8880 (800-800-8000)
Dogs are welcome at this hotel.

The Inn on Oak Street
1003 L Street
Atchison, KS
913-367-1515
Well behaved dogs are allowed for no additional pet fees. 2 dogs may be allowed.

Super 8 Belleville
Hwy 36

Belleville, KS
785-527-2112 (800-800-8000)
Dogs are welcome at this hotel.

Super 8 Beloit
3018 West Highway 24
Beloit, KS
785-738-4300 (800-800-8000)
Dogs are welcome at this hotel.

Super 8 Bonner Springs
13041 Ridge Avenue
Bonner Springs, KS
913-721-3877 (800-800-8000)
Dogs of all sizes are allowed. Dogs are allowed for a nightly pet fee.

Comfort Inn
2225 S. Range Ave.
Colby, KS
785-462-3833 (877-424-6423)
Dogs of all sizes are allowed. Dogs are allowed for a pet fee of $5.00 per pet per night.

Days Inn Colby
1925 South Range/I-70,
Colby, KS
785-462-8691 (800-329-7466)
Dogs of all sizes are allowed. Dogs are allowed for a pet fee.

Motel 6 - Colby
1985 Range Ave
Colby, KS
785-462-8201 (800-466-8356)
This motel welcomes your pets to stay with you.

Quality Inn
1950 South Range Avenue
Colby, KS
785-462-3933 (877-424-6423)
Dogs of all sizes are allowed. Dogs are allowed for a pet fee of $10.00 per pet per night.

Super 8 Concordia
1320 Lincoln St
Concordia, KS
785-243-4200 (800-800-8000)
Dogs are welcome at this hotel.

The Cottage House Hotel
25 North Neosho
Council Grove, KS
620-767-6828 (800-727-7903)
cottagehousehotel.com/
This wonderfully restored Victorian Prairie home gives visitors a sense of the old west with a touch of luxury. Dogs are allowed for an additional fee of $15 per night per pet. Multiple dogs may be allowed.

Super 8 De Soto
34085 Commerce Drive

De Soto, KS
913-583-3880 (800-800-8000)
Dogs are welcome at this hotel.

Best Western Country Inn & Suites
506 N 14th Avenue
Dodge City, KS
620-225-7378 (800-780-7234)
Dogs are welcome at this hotel.

Boot Hill Bed and Breakfast
603 W Spruce
Dodge City, KS
620-225-0111
boothilldodgecity.com/
Relive a bit of the old west at this great old house at the top of Boot Hill. Dogs are allowed for no additional pet fee, but they must be declared at the time of reservations at all times. Dogs must be quiet and well mannered. 2 dogs may be allowed.

Holiday Inn Express Dodge City
2320 W. Wyatt Earp
Dodge City, KS
620-227-5000 (877-270-6405)
Dogs of all sizes are allowed. Dogs are allowed for a pet fee of $25.00 per pet per stay.

Super 8 Dodge City
1708 W Wyatt Earp Blvd
Dodge City, KS
620-225-3924 (800-800-8000)
Dogs are welcome at this hotel.

Travelodge Dodge City
1510 W. Wyatt Earp
Dodge City, KS
620-227-2125 (800-578-7878)
Dogs are welcome at this hotel.

Kuhrt Prairie Castle Guest House and Lodge
2735 Road 75
Edson, KS
785-899-5306
kuhrtranch.com/
Noted as a bird-lovers paradise, this beautiful estate retreat sits along the south fork of the Beaver River in a lush green setting. Although dogs are not allowed in the Castle rooms, they are allowed in the lodge for no additional pet fees. 2 dogs may be allowed.

Super 8 El Dorado
2530 W Central
El Dorado, KS
316-321-4888 (800-800-8000)
Dogs are welcome at this hotel.

Best Western Hospitality House
3021 W Highway 50

Emporia, KS
620-342-7587 (800-780-7234)
Dogs are welcome at this hotel.

Candlewood Suites Emporia
2602 Candlewood Drive
Emporia, KS
620-343-7756 (877-270-6405)
Dogs up to 80 pounds are allowed.
Pets allowed with an additional pet
fee. Up to $75 for 1-6 nights and up
to $150 for 7+ nights. A pet
agreement must be signed at check-
in.

Comfort Inn
2836 W. 18th Ave.
Emporia, KS
620-342-9700 (877-424-6423)
Small dogs are allowed. Dogs are
allowed for a pet fee of $15.00 per
pet per night. Two dogs are allowed
per room.

Days Inn Emporia
3032 West Hwy 50
Emporia, KS
620-342-1787 (800-329-7466)
Dogs are welcome at this hotel.

Econo Lodge
2511 W. 18th Street
Emporia, KS
620-343-7750 (877-424-6423)
Dogs up to 50 pounds are allowed.
Two dogs are allowed per room.

Motel 6 - Emporia
2630 18th Ave
Emporia, KS
620-343-1240 (800-466-8356)
This motel welcomes your pets to
stay with you.

Rodeway Inn & Suites
3181 West Hwy. 50
Emporia, KS
620-342-7820 (877-424-6423)
Dogs of all sizes are allowed. Dogs
are allowed for a pet fee of $5.00 per
pet per night.

Clarion Inn
1911 E Kansas Ave
Garden City, KS
620-275-7471 (877-424-6423)
Dogs of all sizes are allowed. Dogs
are allowed for a pet fee of $20.00
per pet per stay. Two dogs are
allowed per room.

Comfort Inn
2608 East Kansas Ave
Garden City, KS
620-275-5800 (877-424-6423)
Dogs of all sizes are allowed. Dogs
are allowed for a pet fee of $10.00

per pet per night. Two dogs are
allowed per room.

Super 8 Gardner
2001 East Santa Fe
Gardner, KS
913-856-8887 (800-800-8000)
Dogs are welcome at this hotel.

Comfort Inn
2519 Enterprise Rd
Goodland, KS
785-899-7181 (877-424-6423)
Dogs of all sizes are allowed. Dogs
are allowed for a pet fee of $15.00
per pet per night.

Days Inn Goodland
2218 Commerce Rd
Goodland, KS
785-890-3644 (800-329-7466)
Dogs of all sizes are allowed. Dogs
are allowed for a pet fee of $10.00
per pet per night.

Motel 6 - Goodland, Ks
2420 Commerce Rd.
Goodland, KS
785-899-5672 (800-466-8356)
This motel welcomes your pets to
stay with you.

Super 8 Goodland
2520 Commerce Road
Goodland, KS
785-890-7566 (800-800-8000)
Dogs are welcome at this hotel.

Days Inn Great Bend
4701 10th Street
Great Bend, KS
620-792-8235 (800-329-7466)
Dogs of all sizes are allowed. Dogs
are allowed for a pet fee.

Travelodge Great Bend
3200 10th Street
Great Bend, KS
620-792-7219 (800-578-7878)
Dogs are welcome at this hotel.

Baymont Inn & Suites Hays
3801 North Vine Street
Hays, KS
785-625-8103 (877-229-6668)
Dogs are welcome at this hotel.

Days Inn Hays
3205 Vine/I-70
Hays, KS
785-628-8261 (800-329-7466)
Dogs are welcome at this hotel.

Motel 6 - Hays
3404 Vine St
Hays, KS
785-625-4282 (800-466-8356)

This motel welcomes your pets to
stay with you.

Quality Inn
2810 Vine St.
Hays, KS
785-628-8008 (877-424-6423)
Dogs of all sizes are allowed. Dogs
are allowed for a pet fee of
$15.00/pet per pet per night. Two
dogs are allowed per room.

Ramada Convention Center Hays
3603 Vine St
Hays, KS
785-625-7371 (800-272-6232)
Dogs are welcome at this hotel.

Red Roof Inn Holton
151 S. Arizona - Hwy. 75 South
Holton, KS
785-364-3172 (800-RED-ROOF)
One well-behaved family pet per
room. Guest must notify front desk
upon arrival. Guest is liable for any
damages. In consideration of all
guests, pets must never be left
unattended in the guest rooms.

Days Inn And Suites Hutchinson
1420 N Lorraine Street
Hutchinson, KS
620-665-3700 (800-329-7466)
Dogs are welcome at this hotel.

Knights Inn Independence
3222 West Main Street
Independence, KS
620-331-7300 (800-843-5644)
Dogs of all sizes are allowed. Dogs
are allowed for a pet fee of $10.00
per pet per stay.

Log Cabin Retreat
250 Xavier Road
Jamestown, KS
620-241-2981 (800-324-8052)
retreatlogcabin.com/
Located on 10 pastoral acres
overlooking Sportsman Lake and the
Jamestown Wildlife Refuge, this
retreat will allow dogs for no
additional pet fees with advance
reservations. Dogs must be house
trained and well mannered. 2 dogs
may be allowed.

Best Western J. C. Inn
604 E Chestnut Street
Junction City, KS
785-210-1212 (800-780-7234)
Dogs of all sizes are allowed. Dogs
are allowed for a pet fee of $20.00
per pet per night.

Candlewood Suites Junction City/Ft.
Riley

100 S. Hammons Dr.
Junction City, KS
785-238-1454 (877-270-6405)
Dogs up to 80 pounds are allowed.
Pets allowed with an additional pet
fee. Up to $75 for 1-6 nights and up
to $150 for 7+ nights. A pet
agreement must be signed at check-
in.

Days Inn Junction City
1024 S Washington St
Junction City, KS
785-762-2727 (800-329-7466)
Dogs are welcome at this hotel.

Holiday Inn Express Junction City
120 East Street
Junction City, KS
785-762-4200 (877-270-6405)
Dogs of all sizes are allowed. Dogs
are allowed for a pet fee of $5.00 per
pet per night.

Motel 6 - Junction City
1931 Lacy Dr
Junction City, KS
785-762-2215 (800-466-8356)
This motel welcomes your pets to
stay with you.

Ramada Limited Junction City
1133 S Washington Street
Junction City, KS
785-238-1141 (800-272-6232)
Dogs are welcome at this hotel.

Best Western Inn & Conference
Center
501 Southwest Boulevard
Kansas City, KS
913-677-3060 (800-780-7234)
Dogs of all sizes are allowed. Dogs
are allowed for a pet fee of $25.00
per pet per stay.

Candlewood Suites Kansas City
10920 Parallel Parkway
Kansas City, KS
913-788-9929 (877-270-6405)
Dogs up to 80 pounds are allowed.
Pets allowed with an additional pet
fee. Up to $75 for 1-6 nights and up
to $150 for 7+ nights. A pet
agreement must be signed at check-
in.

Days Inn - near Kansas Speedway
7721 Elizabeth Ave
Kansas City, KS
913-334-3028 (800-329-7466)
Dogs are welcome at this hotel.

Windy Heights Inn
607 Country Heights Road
Lakin, KS
620-355-7699

windyheightsbandb.com/
This inn offers a variety of indoor
and outdoor activities for guests.
Well mannered dogs are allowed for
no additional pet fees. 2 dogs may
be allowed.

Econo Lodge
504 N. Main St.
Lansing, KS
913-727-2777 (877-424-6423)
Dogs of all sizes are allowed. Dogs
are allowed for a pet fee of $10.00
per pet per night.

Rodeway Inn
802 E. 14th
Larned, KS
620-285-2300 (877-424-6423)
Dogs up to 50 pounds are allowed.
Dogs are allowed for a pet fee of
$10.00 per pet per night. Two dogs
are allowed per room.

Best Western Lawrence
2309 Iowa Street
Lawrence, KS
785-843-9100 (800-780-7234)
Dogs of all sizes are allowed. Dogs
are allowed for a pet fee.

Days Inn KU Lawrence
730 S Iowa Street
Lawrence, KS
785-841-6500 (800-329-7466)
Dogs are welcome at this hotel.

Econo Lodge
2222 W. 6th St.
Lawrence, KS
785-842-7030 (877-424-6423)
Dogs of all sizes are allowed. Dogs
are allowed for a pet fee of $10.00
per pet per night.

Holiday Inn Express Hotel & Suites
Lawrence
3411 Iowa St
Lawrence, KS
785-749-7555 (877-270-6405)
Dogs of all sizes are allowed. Dogs
are allowed for a pet fee of $20.00
per pet per night.

Holiday Inn Lawrence
200 Mc Donald Drive
Lawrence, KS
785-841-7077 (877-270-6405)
Dogs of all sizes are allowed. Dogs
are allowed for a pet fee of $25 per
pet per stay.

Motel 6 - Lawrence, Ks
1130 3rd St
Lawrence, KS
785-749-4040 (800-466-8356)
This motel welcomes your pets to

stay with you.

Quality Inn
801 Iowa Street
Lawrence, KS
785-842-5100 (877-424-6423)
Dogs of all sizes are allowed. Dogs
are allowed for a pet fee of $10.00
per pet per night.

Days Inn Leavenworth
3211 South 4th Street
Leavenworth, KS
913-651-6000 (800-329-7466)
Dogs of all sizes are allowed. Dogs
are allowed for a pet fee of $10 per
pet per night.

Super 8 Leavenworth
303 Montana Court
Leavenworth, KS
913-682-0744 (800-800-8000)
Dogs of all sizes are allowed. Dogs
are allowed for a nightly pet fee.

Extended Stay America Kansas City
- Lenexa
8015 Lenexa Drive
Lenexa, KS
913-894-5550 (800-804-3724)
One dog is allowed per suite. There
is a $25 per night additional pet fee
up to $150 for an entire stay.

Extended Stay America Kansas City
- Lenexa - 95th St.
9775 Lenexa Dr.
Lenexa, KS
913-541-4000 (800-804-3724)
One dog is allowed per suite. There
is a $25 per night additional pet fee
up to $150 for an entire stay.

Motel 6 - Kansas City Southwest
Lenexa
9725 Lenexa Dr
Lenexa, KS
913-541-8558 (800-466-8356)
This motel welcomes your pets to
stay with you.

Super 8 Overland Park Area Lenexa
9601 Westgate
Lenexa, KS
913-888-8899 (800-800-8000)
Dogs of all sizes are allowed. Dogs
are allowed for a pet fee.

Days Inn KS Liberal
405 E Pancake
Liberal, KS
620-626-7377 (800-329-7466)
Dogs of all sizes are allowed. Dogs
are allowed for a pet fee.

Gateway Inn
720 E H 74

Dog-Friendly Lodging - Please always call ahead to make sure an establishment is still dog-friendly.

Liberal, KS
620-624-0242
Dogs are allowed for an additional fee of $10 per night per pet. 2 dogs may be allowed.

Rodeway Inn
488 East Pancake Blvd
Liberal, KS
620-624-5642 (877-424-6423)
Dogs of all sizes are allowed. Dogs are allowed for a pet fee of $7.00 per pet per stay.

Super 8 KS Liberal
747 E Pancake Blvd
Liberal, KS
620-624-8880 (800-800-8000)
Dogs of all sizes are allowed. Dogs are allowed for a pet fee of $5.00 per pet per night.

Best Western Manhattan Inn
601 E Poyntz Avenue
Manhattan, KS
785-537-8300 (800-780-7234)
Dogs of all sizes are allowed. Dogs are allowed for a pet fee of $10.00 per pet per night.

Clarion Hotel
530 Richards Drive
Manhattan, KS
785-539-5311 (877-424-6423)
Dogs of all sizes are allowed. Dogs are allowed for a pet fee of $10.00 per pet per night.

Motel 6 - Manhattan, Ks
510 Tuttle Creek Blvd
Manhattan, KS
785-537-1022 (800-466-8356)
This motel welcomes your pets to stay with you.

Quality Inn
150 E. Poyntz Ave.
Manhattan, KS
785-770-8000 (877-424-6423)
Dogs of all sizes are allowed.

Econo Lodge
2111 E Kansas Ave
McPherson, KS
620-241-6960 (877-424-6423)
Dogs of all sizes are allowed. Dogs are allowed for a pet fee of $10.00 per pet per night. Two dogs are allowed per room.

Comfort Inn I-35 at Shawnee Mission Parkway
6401 E. Frontage Rd.
Merriam, KS
913-262-2622 (877-424-6423)
Dogs of all sizes are allowed. Dogs are allowed for a pet fee of $10.00

per pet per night.

Homestead Studio Suites Kansas City - Shawnee Mission
6451 E. Frontage Rd.
Merriam, KS
913-236-6006 (800-804-3724)
One dog is allowed per suite. There is a $25 per night additional pet fee up to $150 for an entire stay.

Best Western Red Coach Inn
1301 E 1st
Newton, KS
316-283-9120 (800-780-7234)
Dogs of all sizes are allowed. Dogs are allowed for a pet fee of $15.00 per pet per night.

Days Inn - Newton
105 Manchester/I-135
Newton, KS
316-283-3330 (800-329-7466)
Dogs of all sizes are allowed. Dogs are allowed for a pet fee.

Econo Lodge
3506 US Highway 40
Oakley, KS
785-672-3254 (877-424-6423)
Dogs up to 50 pounds are allowed. Dogs are allowed for a pet fee of $room per pet per night. Two dogs are allowed per room.

Sleep Inn & Suites
3768 East Hwy 40
Oakley, KS
785-671-1111 (877-424-6423)
Dogs up to 50 pounds are allowed. Dogs are allowed for a pet fee of $10.00 per pet per night. Two dogs are allowed per room.

Best Western Olathe Hotel & Suites
1580 S Hamilton Circle
Olathe, KS
913-440-9762 (800-780-7234)
Dogs of all sizes are allowed. Dogs are allowed for a pet fee.

Candlewood Suites Candlewood Suites Olathe
15490 South Rogers Road
Olathe, KS
913-768-8888 (877-270-6405)
Dogs up to 80 pounds are allowed. Pets allowed with an additional pet fee. Up to $75 for 1-6 nights and up to $150 for 7+ nights. A pet agreement must be signed at check-in.

Comfort Inn
15475 S. Rogers Rd
Olathe, KS
913-948-9000 (877-424-6423)

Dogs up to 75 pounds are allowed. Dogs are allowed for a pet fee of $25.00 per pet per night.

Days Inn Kansas City Olathe
211 Rawhide Drive
Olathe, KS
913-782-4343 (800-329-7466)
Dogs of all sizes are allowed. Dogs are allowed for a pet fee of $20.00 per pet per stay.

Econo Lodge South
209 E. Flaming Rd.
Olathe, KS
913-829-1312 (877-424-6423)
Dogs of all sizes are allowed. Dogs are allowed for a pet fee of $10.00 per pet per night.

Holiday Inn Olathe Medical Center
101 W. 151st St
Olathe, KS
913-829-4000 (877-270-6405)
Dogs of all sizes are allowed. Dogs are allowed for a pet fee of $30.00 per pet per night.

Sleep Inn
20662 W 151st St
Olathe, KS
913-390-9500 (877-424-6423)
Dogs of all sizes are allowed.

Days Inn Ottawa
1641 S Main Street
Ottawa, KS
785-242-4842 (800-329-7466)
Dogs are welcome at this hotel.

Econo Lodge
2331 South Cedar
Ottawa, KS
785-242-3400 (877-424-6423)
Dogs of all sizes are allowed. Dogs are allowed for a pet fee of $10.00 per pet per night.

Travelodge KS Ottawa
2209 S Princeton Rd
Ottawa, KS
785-242-7000 (800-578-7878)
Dogs are welcome at this hotel.

Candlewood Suites Kansas City- Overland Park
11001 Oakmont
Overland Park, KS
913-469-5557 (877-270-6405)
Dogs up to 80 pounds are allowed. Pets allowed with an additional pet fee. Up to $75 for 1-6 nights and up to $150 for 7+ nights. A pet agreement must be signed at check-in.

Chase Suite Hotel

6300 W 110th Street
Overland Park, KS
913-491-3333
woodfinsuitehotels.com/
Dogs are allowed for an additional fee of $10 per night per pet. Multiple dogs may be allowed.

Comfort Inn & Suites
7200 West 107th Street
Overland Park, KS
913-648-7858 (877-424-6423)
Dogs of all sizes are allowed. Dogs are allowed for a pet fee of $10.00 per pet per night. Two dogs are allowed per room.

Econo Lodge Inn & Suites
7508 Shawnee Mission Pkwy
Overland Park, KS
913-262-9600 (877-424-6423)
Dogs of all sizes are allowed. Dogs are allowed for a pet fee of $10.00 per pet per night.

Extended Stay America Kansas City - Overland Park
10750 Quivira Rd.
Overland Park, KS
913-661-9299 (800-804-3724)
One dog is allowed per suite. There is a $25 per night additional pet fee up to $150 for an entire stay.

Homestead Studio Suites Kansas City - Overland Park
5401 W. 110th St.
Overland Park, KS
913-661-7111 (800-804-3724)
One dog is allowed per suite. There is a $25 per night additional pet fee up to $150 for an entire stay.

Knights Inn Overland Park
7240 B Shawnee Mission Parkway
Overland Park, KS
913-262-9100 (800-843-5644)
Dogs of all sizes are allowed. Dogs are allowed for a pet fee of $25.00 per pet per night.

Ramada Overland Park
7240 Shawnee Mission Parkway
Overland Park, KS
913-262-3010 (800-272-6232)
Dogs are welcome at this hotel.

Red Roof Inn Kansas City Overland Park
6800 West 108th Street
Overland Park, KS
913-341-0100 (800-RED-ROOF)
One well-behaved family pet per room. Guest must notify front desk upon arrival. Guest is liable for any damages. In consideration of all guests, pets must never be left

unattended in the guest rooms.

Residence Inn Kansas City Overland Park
12010 Blue Valley Pkwy
Overland Park, KS
913-491-4444 (800-331-3131)
Some of the amenities at this all-suite inn include a daily buffet breakfast, evening socials Monday through Thursday with light dinner fare, an indoor pool, and 2 putting greens. Dogs are allowed for an additional one time pet fee of $75 per room. Multiple dogs may be allowed.

Sheraton Overland Park Hotel at the Convention Center
6100 College Blvd.
Overland Park, KS
913-234-2100 (888-625-5144)
Dogs up to 40 pounds are allowed. There are no additional pet fees. Dogs are not allowed to be left alone in the room.

Super 8 KC Area Near Convention Center Overland Park
10750 Barkley Street
Overland Park, KS
913-341-4440 (800-800-8000)
Dogs of all sizes are allowed. Dogs are allowed for a pet fee of $10 per pet per night.

TownePlace Suites Kansas City Overland Park
7020 W 133rd Street
Overland Park, KS
913-851-3100 (800-257-3000)
In addition to offering a number of in-house amenities for all level of travelers, this all suite inn also provides a convenient location to some of the areas star attractions, businesses, shopping, and dining areas. Dogs are allowed for an additional one time fee of $100 per room. 2 dogs may be allowed.

Best Western Paola
1600 Hedge Lane Ct
Paola, KS
913-294-3700 (800-780-7234)
Dogs of all sizes are allowed. Dogs are allowed for a nightly pet fee.

Super 8 /North Wichita Area Park City
I-135 Exit 14
Park City, KS
316-744-2071 (800-800-8000)
Dogs of all sizes are allowed. Dogs are allowed for a pet fee of $15.00 per pet per night.

Super 8 Parsons
229 East Main St.
Parsons, KS
620-421-8000 (800-800-8000)
Dogs are welcome at this hotel.

Super 8 KS Pittsburg
3108 N Broadway
Pittsburg, KS
620-232-1881 (800-800-8000)
Dogs are welcome at this hotel.

Comfort Suites
704 Allison
Pratt, KS
620-672-9999 (877-424-6423)
Dogs of all sizes are allowed. Dogs are allowed for a pet fee of $25.00 per pet per night. Two dogs are allowed per room.

Days Inn Pratt
1901 E First Street
Pratt, KS
620-672-9465 (800-329-7466)
Dogs of all sizes are allowed. Dogs are allowed for a pet fee.

Econo Lodge
1336 East First Street
Pratt, KS
620-672-6407 (877-424-6423)
Dogs of all sizes are allowed. Dogs are allowed for a pet fee of $USD, per pet per night.

Super 8
1906 East 1st Street
Pratt, KS
620-672-5945 (800-800-8000)
Dogs of all sizes are allowed. Dogs are allowed for a pet fee of $10.00 per pet per stay.

Days Inn Russell
1225 South Fossil Street
Russell, KS
785-483-6660 (800-329-7466)
Dogs of all sizes are allowed. Dogs are allowed for a nightly pet fee.

Best Western Heart of America Inn
632 Westport Boulevard
Salina, KS
785-827-9315 (800-780-7234)
Dogs of all sizes are allowed. Dogs are allowed for a pet fee of $10 per pet per stay.

Candlewood Suites Salina
2650 Planet Avenue
Salina, KS
785-823-6939 (877-270-6405)
Dogs up to 80 pounds are allowed. Pets allowed with an additional pet fee. Up to $75 for 1-6 nights and up to $150 for 7+ nights. A pet

agreement must be signed at check-in.

Comfort Inn
1820 W. Crawford St.
Salina, KS
785-826-1711 (877-424-6423)
Dogs of all sizes are allowed. Dogs are allowed for a pet fee of $20.00 per pet per stay.

Econo Lodge
1949 North 9th Street
Salina, KS
785-825-8211 (877-424-6423)
Dogs of all sizes are allowed. Dogs are allowed for a pet fee of $10.00 per pet per night. Three or more dogs may be allowed.

Holiday Inn Express Hotel & Suites Salina-I-70
201 East Diamond Drive
Salina, KS
785-827-9000 (877-270-6405)
Dogs of all sizes are allowed. Dogs are allowed for a pet fee of $10.70 per pet per stay.

Hunters Leigh
4109 E North Street
Salina, KS
785-823-6750 (800-889-6750)
huntersleighbandb.com/
This grand country English Manor estate features a tranquil setting along the scenic Smoky Hill River. Well mannered dogs are allowed for no additional fee. 2 dogs may be allowed.

Motel 6 - Salina
635 Diamond Dr
Salina, KS
785-827-8397 (800-466-8356)
This motel welcomes your pets to stay with you.

Quality Inn & Suites
2110 W. Crawford St.
Salina, KS
785-825-2111 (877-424-6423)
Dogs up to 50 pounds are allowed. Dogs are allowed for a pet fee of $15.00 per pet per stay. Two dogs are allowed per room.

Ramada Conference Center Salina
1616 W Crawford St
Salina, KS
785-823-1739 (800-272-6232)
Dogs of all sizes are allowed. Dogs are allowed for a pet fee.

Sleep Inn & Suites
3932 South 9th Street
Salina, KS

785-404-6777 (877-424-6423)
Dogs of all sizes are allowed. Dogs are allowed for a pet fee of $25.00 per pet per stay.

Super 8 I-70 Salina
120 E Diamond Dr
Salina, KS
785-823-8808 (800-800-8000)
Dogs are welcome at this hotel.

Candlewood Suites Topeka
914 South West Henderson
Topeka, KS
785-271-7822 (877-270-6405)
Dogs up to 80 pounds are allowed. Pets allowed with an additional pet fee. Up to $75 for 1-6 nights and up to $150 for 7+ nights. A pet agreement must be signed at check-in.

Comfort Inn
1518 S.W. Wanamaker Rd.
Topeka, KS
785-273-5365 (877-424-6423)
Dogs of all sizes are allowed. Dogs are allowed for a pet fee of $50.00 per pet per night.

Days Inn Topeka
1510 SW Wanamaker Rd
Topeka, KS
785-272-8538 (800-329-7466)
Dogs are welcome at this hotel.

Econo Lodge
2950 SW Topeka Blvd
Topeka, KS
785-267-1681 (877-424-6423)
Dogs of all sizes are allowed. Dogs are allowed for a pet fee of $8.00 per pet per night. Two dogs are allowed per room.

Motel 6 - Topeka Northwest
709 Fairlawn Rd
Topeka, KS
785-272-8283 (800-466-8356)
This motel welcomes your pets to stay with you.

Motel 6 - Topeka West
1224 Wanamaker Rd Sw
Topeka, KS
785-273-9888 (800-466-8356)
This motel welcomes your pets to stay with you.

Quality Inn
1240 S. W. Wanamaker Rd.
Topeka, KS
785-273-6969 (877-424-6423)
Dogs of all sizes are allowed. Dogs are allowed for a pet fee of $5.00/ per pet per night.

Ramada Downtown Topeka
420 Southeast 6th Ave
Topeka, KS
785-234-5400 (800-272-6232)
Dogs of all sizes are allowed. Dogs are allowed for a pet fee.

Residence Inn Topeka
1620 SW Westport Drive
Topeka, KS
785-271-8903 (800-331-3131)
In addition to offering a convenient location to business, shopping, dining, and entertainment areas, this hotel also provides a number of in-house amenities, including a daily buffet breakfast, evening social hours. Dogs are allowed for an additional one time pet fee of $100 per room. Multiple dogs may be allowed.

Sleep Inn & Suites
1024 SW Wanamaker Rd.
Topeka, KS
785-228-2500 (877-424-6423)
Dogs up to 50 pounds are allowed. Dogs are allowed for a pet fee of $10.00 per pet per night.

Super 8 at Forbes Landing Topeka
5922 Southwest Topeka Blvd
Topeka, KS
785-862-2222 (800-800-8000)
Dogs of all sizes are allowed. Dogs are allowed for a pet fee of $20.00 per pet per stay.

Super 8 /Wanamaker RD/I-70
Topeka
5968 S.W. 10th Ave.
Topeka, KS
785-273-5100 (800-800-8000)
Dogs are welcome at this hotel.

Butterfield Trail Bunkhouse
RR 2 Box 86, 23033 T Road
WaKeeney, KS
785-743-2322
butterfieldtrailbunkhouse.com/
This is a popular destination for nature or history fans and fishing/hunting enthusiast. Dogs are allowed for an additional pet fee of $10 per night per room. Dogs are not allowed on the furnishings or the bed. Multiple dogs may be allowed.

Econo Lodge
705 South 2nd Street
WaKeeney, KS
785-743-5505 (877-424-6423)
Dogs of all sizes are allowed. Dogs are allowed for a pet fee of $5.00 per pet per stay. Two dogs are allowed per room.

Best Western Wakeeney Inn & Suites
525 S 1st Street
Wakeeney, KS
785-743-2700 (800-780-7234)
Dogs of all sizes are allowed. Dogs are allowed for a pet fee of $10 per pet per night.

Super 8 Wakeeney
709 S 13th Street
Wakeeney, KS
785-743-6442 (800-800-8000)
Dogs are welcome at this hotel.

Simmer Motel
1215 W H 24
Wamego, KS
785-456-2304
the fee is per room or per pet depending on the number and size of the dogs and the accommodations.

Best Western Wichita North Hotel & Suites
915 E 53rd Street N
Wichita, KS
316-832-9387 (800-780-7234)
Dogs of all sizes are allowed. Dogs are allowed for a pet fee.

Candlewood Suites Wichita-Airport
570 South Julia
Wichita, KS
316-942-0400 (877-270-6405)
Dogs up to 80 pounds are allowed. Pets allowed with an additional pet fee. Up to $75 for 1-6 nights and up to $150 for 7+ nights. A pet agreement must be signed at check-in.

Candlewood Suites Wichita-Northeast
3141 North Webb Rd
Wichita, KS
316-634-6070 (877-270-6405)
Dogs up to 80 pounds are allowed. Pets allowed with an additional pet fee. Up to $75 for 1-6 nights and up to $150 for 7+ nights. A pet agreement must be signed at check-in.

Comfort Inn East
9525 E. Corporate Hills
Wichita, KS
316-686-2844 (877-424-6423)
Dogs of all sizes are allowed. Dogs are allowed for a pet fee of $15.00 per pet per stay.

Comfort Inn South
4849 S. Laura
Wichita, KS
316-522-1800 (877-424-6423)
Dogs of all sizes are allowed. Dogs

are allowed for a pet fee of $10.00 per pet per night.

Econo Lodge Inn & Suites Airport
600 South Holland
Wichita, KS
316-722-8730 (877-424-6423)
Dogs of all sizes are allowed.

Hawthorn Suites
411 South Webb Road
Wichita, KS
316-686-7331 (800-527-1133)
In addition to providing a convenient location to many local sites and activities, this all-suite hotel offers a number of amenities for business and leisure travelers, including their signature breakfast buffet and beautifully appointed rooms. Dogs are allowed for an additional one time pet fee of $125 per room. Multiple dogs may be allowed.

Holiday Inn Hotel & Suites Wichita Dwtn-Convention Center
221 East Kellogg
Wichita, KS
316-269-2090 (877-270-6405)
Dogs are welcome at this hotel.

Howard Johnson Express Inn - Wichita
6575 West Kellogg
Wichita, KS
316-943-8165 (800-446-4656)
Dogs are welcome at this hotel.

Motel 6 - Wichita
465 Webb Rd
Wichita, KS
316-684-6363 (800-466-8356)
This motel welcomes your pets to stay with you.

Motel 6 - Wichita Airport
5736 West Kellogg Dr
Wichita, KS
316-945-8440 (800-466-8356)
This motel welcomes your pets to stay with you.

Residence Inn Wichita East at Plazzio
1212 N Greenwich
Wichita, KS
316-682-7300 (800-331-3131)
This all suite hotel sits central to a number of sites of interest and activities for all level of travelers, plus they offer a daily buffet breakfast, evening socials, and a Sport Court. Dogs are allowed for an additional one time pet fee of $75 per room. Multiple dogs may be allowed.

Super 8 East Kellogg Wichita
527 S Webb Road
Wichita, KS
316-686-3888 (800-800-8000)
Dogs are welcome at this hotel.

TownePlace Suites Wichita East
9444 E 29th Street N
Wichita, KS
316-631-3773 (800-257-3000)
Located in what is known as the 'Aviation Capitol of the World', this all suite inn provides a great location to a number of sites of interest for all level of travelers, plus they also offer a number of in-house amenities. Dogs are allowed for an additional one time fee of $75 per room. Multiple dogs may be allowed.

Comfort Inn
US 77 at Quail Ridge
Winfield, KS
620-221-7529 (877-424-6423)
Dogs of all sizes are allowed. Dogs are allowed for a pet fee of $10.00 per pet per night.

Econo Lodge
1710 Main Street
Winfield, KS
620-221-9050 (877-424-6423)
Dogs of all sizes are allowed. Dogs are allowed for a pet fee of $10.00 per pet per night.

Super 8 /Quail Ridge Area Winfield
Hwy 77 & Pike Rd
Winfield, KS
620-229-8888 (800-800-8000)
Dogs are welcome at this hotel.

Kentucky

Days Inn Ashland
12700 Route 180
Ashland, KY
606-928-3600 (800-329-7466)
Dogs of all sizes are allowed. Dogs are allowed for a nightly pet fee.

Holiday Inn Express Hotel & Suites Ashland
13131 Slone Court
Ashland, KY
606-929-1720 (877-270-6405)
Dogs of all sizes are allowed. Dogs are allowed for a pet fee of $25 per pet per night.

Knights Inn Ashland
7216 US 60
Ashland, KY
606-928-9501 (800-843-5644)
Dogs of all sizes are allowed. Dogs are allowed for a pet fee of $5 per

pet per night.

Quality Inn
4708 Winchester Ave.
Ashland, KY
606-325-8989 (877-424-6423)
Dogs up to 50 pounds are allowed.
Dogs are allowed for a pet fee of
$15.00 per pet per night. Two dogs
are allowed per room.

Days Inn Bardstown
523 N Third Street
Bardstown, KY
502-349-0363 (800-329-7466)
Dogs of all sizes are allowed. Dogs
are allowed for a pet fee of $20 per
pet per night.

Comfort Inn & Suites
173 Carroll Road
Benton, KY
270-527-5300 (877-424-6423)
Dogs of all sizes are allowed. Dogs
are allowed for a pet fee of $10.00
per pet per night.

Boone Tavern Hotel
100 Main Street
Berea, KY
606-986-9358 (800-366-9358)
4berea.com/tavern/
This hotel is one of the registered
Historic Hotels of America. It is
owned by Berea College and is
staffed by students. Dogs are
allowed for an additional $50 per
night per pet fee. In the summer
there is outside dining where your
canine companion may join you.
Multiple dogs may be allowed.

Comfort Inn & Suites
219 Paint Lick Road
Berea, KY
859-985-5500 (877-424-6423)
Dogs of all sizes are allowed. Dogs
are allowed for a pet fee of $10.00
per pet per night. Two dogs are
allowed per room.

Days Inn Berea
Hwy 595 & I-75 Exit 77
Berea, KY
859-986-7373 (800-329-7466)
Dogs are welcome at this hotel.

Econo Lodge
254 Paint Lick Road
Berea, KY
859-986-9324 (877-424-6423)
Dogs of all sizes are allowed. Dogs
are allowed for a pet fee of $6.00 per
pet per night.

Super 8 Berea
196 Prince Royal Drive

Berea, KY
859-986-8426 (800-800-8000)
Dogs are welcome at this hotel.

Candlewood Suites Bowling Green
540 Wall Street
Bowling Green, KY
270-843-5505 (877-270-6405)
Dogs up to 80 pounds are allowed.
Pets allowed with an additional pet
fee. Up to $75 for 1-6 nights and up
to $150 for 7+ nights. A pet
agreement must be signed at
check-in.

Drury Inn
3250 Scottsville Road
Bowling Green, KY
270-842-7100 (800-378-7946)
Dogs of all sizes are allowed for no
additional pet fee with a credit card
on file, and there is a pet agreement
to sign at check in.

Econo Lodge
181 Cumberland Trace
Bowling Green, KY
270-842-6730 (877-424-6423)
Dogs of all sizes are allowed. Dogs
are allowed for a pet fee of $10.00
per pet per night.

Motel 6 - Bowling Green, Ky
3139 Scottsville Rd
Bowling Green, KY
270-843-0140 (800-466-8356)
This motel welcomes your pets to
stay with you.

Red Roof Inn Bowling Green
3140 Scottsville Road
Bowling Green, KY
270-781-6550 (800-RED-ROOF)
One well-behaved family pet per
room. Guest must notify front desk
upon arrival. Guest is liable for any
damages. In consideration of all
guests, pets must never be left
unattended in the guest rooms.

Super 8 Brandenburg
1900 Armory Place
Brandenburg, KY
270-422-1700 (800-800-8000)
Dogs are welcome at this hotel.

Baymont Inn & Suites Louisville
South I 65
149 Willabrook Drive
Brooks, KY
502-957-6900 (877-229-6668)
Dogs of all sizes are allowed. Dogs
are allowed for a pet fee of $10.00
per pet per stay.

Super 8 Cadiz
154 Hospitality Lane

Cadiz, KY
270-522-7007 (800-800-8000)
Dogs are welcome at this hotel.

Days Inn Calvert City
75 Campbell Drive
Calvert City, KY
270-395-7162 (800-329-7466)
Dogs of all sizes are allowed. Dogs
are allowed for a pet fee.

Holiday Inn Express Campbellsville
102 Plantation Drive
Campbellsville, KY
270-465-2727 (877-270-6405)
Dogs of all sizes are allowed. Dogs
are allowed for a pet fee of $20.00
per pet per night.

Super 8 KY Campbellsville
100 Albion Way
Campbellsville, KY
270-789-0808 (800-800-8000)
Dogs are welcome at this hotel.

Best Western Executive Inn
10 Slumber Ln
Carrollton, KY
502-732-8444 (800-780-7234)
Dogs of all sizes are allowed. Dogs
are allowed for a pet fee of $10 per
pet per night.

Super 8 Carrollton
130 Slumber Lane
Carrollton, KY
502-732-0252 (800-800-8000)
Dogs are welcome at this hotel.

Ramada Limited Ashland/
Catlettsburg
6000 Crider Drive US 23
Catlettsburg, KY
606-739-5700 (800-272-6232)
Dogs of all sizes are allowed. Dogs
are allowed for a pet fee of $10.00
per pet per night.

Super 8 Cave City
799 Mammoth Cave St
Cave City, KY
270-773-2500 (800-800-8000)
Dogs of all sizes are allowed. Dogs
are allowed for a nightly pet fee.

Best Western Corbin Inn
2630 Cumberland Falls Highway
Corbin, KY
606-528-2100 (800-780-7234)
Dogs of all sizes are allowed. Dogs
are allowed for a pet fee of $15 per
pet per night.

Days Inn Corbin
1860 Cumberland Falls Rd.
Corbin, KY
606-528-8150 (800-329-7466)

Dogs of all sizes are allowed. Dogs are allowed for a pet fee of $10 per pet per night.

Knights Inn Corbin
37 Highway 770
Corbin, KY
606-523-1500 (800-843-5644)
Dogs of all sizes are allowed. Dogs are allowed for a pet fee of $5.00 per pet per night.

Super 8 /London KY Corbin
171 W. Cumberland Gap Parkway
Corbin, KY
606-528-8888 (800-800-8000)
Dogs of all sizes are allowed. Dogs are allowed for a pet fee of $5.00 per pet per night.

Embassy Suites
10 East Rivercenter Blvd
Covington, KY
859-261-8400 (800-EMBASSY (362-2779))
Located on the shores of the Ohio River, this luxury, full service, all suite hotel offers a number of on site amenities for all level of travelers, plus a convenient location to business, shopping, dining, and entertainment districts. They also offer a complimentary cooked-to-order breakfast and a Manager's reception every evening. Dogs are allowed for an additional one time fee of $25 per pet. Multiple dogs may be allowed.

Extended Stay America Cincinnati - Covington
650 West 3rd St.
Covington, KY
859-581-3000 (800-804-3724)
One dog is allowed per suite. There is a $25 per night additional pet fee up to $150 for an entire stay.

Holiday Inn Express Danville
96 Daniel Drive
Danville, KY
859-236-8600 (877-270-6405)
Dogs of all sizes are allowed. Dogs are allowed for a pet fee of $25.00 per pet per stay.

Super 8 Danville
3663 Hwy 150/127 Bypass
Danville, KY
859-236-8881 (800-800-8000)
Dogs are welcome at this hotel.

Holiday Inn Express Dry Ridge
1050 Fashion Ridge Rd
Dry Ridge, KY
859-824-7121 (877-270-6405)
Dogs of all sizes are allowed. Dogs

are allowed for a pet fee of $10.00 per pet per night.

Super 8 Dry Ridge
88 Blackburn Lane
Dry Ridge, KY
859-824-3700 (800-800-8000)
Dogs of all sizes are allowed. Dogs are allowed for a pet fee.

Eddy Creek Marina Resort
7612 H 93S
Eddyville, KY
270-388-2271
Dogs of all sizes are allowed. There is a $100 refundable pet deposit. Dogs must be leashed and cleaned up after. This lodge is seasonal, as is the RV park also on site. The RV park allows pets for no additional fee or deposit. Dogs are allowed on the trails.

Best Western Atrium Gardens
1043 Executive Drive
Elizabethtown, KY
270-769-3030 (800-780-7234)
Dogs of all sizes are allowed. Dogs are allowed for a pet fee of $25.00 per pet per stay.

Comfort Inn
2009 N. Mulberry St.
Elizabethtown, KY
270-765-4166 (877-424-6423)
Dogs of all sizes are allowed. Dogs are allowed for a pet fee of $10.00 per pet per night.

Days Inn Elizabethtown
2010 North Mulberry/I-65
Elizabethtown, KY
270-769-5522 (800-329-7466)
Dogs of all sizes are allowed. Dogs are allowed for a pet fee.

Motel 6 - Elizabethtown
1042 Mulberry St
Elizabethtown, KY
270-769-3102 (800-466-8356)
This motel welcomes your pets to stay with you.

Super 8 Elizabethtown
2028 N Mulberry St
Elizabethtown, KY
270-737-1088 (800-800-8000)
Dogs of all sizes are allowed. Dogs are allowed for a pet fee of $10 per pet per night.

Comfort Inn Greater Cincinnati Airport
630 Donaldson Rd.
Erlanger, KY
859-727-3400 (877-424-6423)
Dogs of all sizes are allowed. Dogs

are allowed for a pet fee of $10.00 per pet per night.

Days Inn Cincinnati Airport Erlanger
599 Donaldson Road/I-75
Erlanger, KY
859-342-7111 (800-329-7466)
Dogs of all sizes are allowed. Dogs are allowed for a pet fee.

Econo Lodge
633 Donaldson Rd.
Erlanger, KY
859-342-5500 (877-424-6423)
Dogs of all sizes are allowed. Dogs are allowed for a pet fee of $5.00 per pet per night.

Residence Inn Cincinnati Airport
2811 Circleport Drive
Erlanger, KY
859-282-7400 (800-331-3131)
Some of the amenities at this all-suite inn include a daily buffet breakfast, weekly hospitality hours, a Sport Court, and complimentary grocery shopping plus they are only 2 miles from the Cincinnati Airport. Dogs are allowed for an additional one time pet fee of $100 per room. 2 dogs may be allowed.

Best Western Inn Florence
7821 Commerce Drive
Florence, KY
859-525-0090 (800-780-7234)
Dogs of all sizes are allowed. Dogs are allowed for a nightly pet fee.

Clarion Inn & Suites
30 Cavalier Court
Florence, KY
859-371-0081 (877-424-6423)
Dogs up to 50 pounds are allowed. Dogs are allowed for a pet fee of $10.00 per pet per night. Two dogs are allowed per room.

Extended Stay America Cincinnati - Florence
7350 Turfway Rd.
Florence, KY
859-282-7829 (800-804-3724)
One dog is allowed per suite. There is a $25 per night additional pet fee up to $150 for an entire stay.

Knights Inn /Cincinnati South Florence
8049 Dream St
Florence, KY
859-371-9711 (800-843-5644)
Dogs are welcome at this hotel.

La Quinta Inn & Suites Cincinnati Airport/Florence
350 Meijer Drive

Florence, KY
859-282-8212 (800-531-5900)
Dogs of all sizes are allowed. There are no additional pet fees. Dogs may only be left alone in the room if they will be quiet and well behaved. Dogs must be leashed and cleaned up after. Multiple dogs may be allowed.

Motel 6 - Cincinnati South Florence, Ky
7937 Dream St
Florence, KY
859-283-0909 (800-466-8356)
This motel welcomes your pets to stay with you.

Quality Inn & Suites
7915 US Highway 42
Florence, KY
859-371-4700 (877-424-6423)
Dogs of all sizes are allowed. Dogs are allowed for a pet fee of $10.00 per pet per night.

Ramada Florence
8050 Holiday Place
Florence, KY
859-371-2700 (800-272-6232)
Dogs of all sizes are allowed. Dogs are allowed for a pet fee.

Red Roof Inn Cincinnati Airport - Florence, KY
7454 Turfway Road
Florence, KY
859-647-2700 (800-RED-ROOF)
One well-behaved family pet per room. Guest must notify front desk upon arrival. Guest is liable for any damages. In consideration of all guests, pets must never be left unattended in the guest rooms.

Rodeway Inn
50 Cavalier Blvd
Florence, KY
859-371-4800 (877-424-6423)
Dogs up to 100 pounds are allowed. Dogs are allowed for a pet fee of $10.00/ per pet per night.

Super 8 Florence
7928 Dream St
Florence, KY
859-283-1221 (800-800-8000)
Dogs of all sizes are allowed. Dogs are allowed for a pet fee.

Super 8 /Cinci OH Downtown Fort Mitchell
2350 Royal Drive
Fort Mitchell, KY
859-341-2090 (800-800-8000)
Dogs of all sizes are allowed. Dogs are allowed for a pet fee.

Rodeway Inn
1937 Dixie Highway
Fort Wright, KY
859-331-1400 (877-424-6423)
Dogs of all sizes are allowed. Dogs are allowed for a pet fee of $25.00 per pet per night.

Days Inn Frankfort
1051 US 127 South/I-64
Frankfort, KY
502-875-2200 (800-329-7466)
Dogs are welcome at this hotel.

Days Inn Franklin
103 Trotter Lane
Franklin, KY
270-598-0163 (800-329-7466)
Dogs of all sizes are allowed. Dogs are allowed for a pet fee.

Super 8 Hwy 31 Franklin
3811 Nashville Rd.
Franklin, KY
270-586-5090 (800-800-8000)
Dogs up to 50 pounds are allowed. Dogs are allowed for a pet fee of $15.00 per pet per night.

Best Western Georgetown
Corporate Center Hotel
132 Darby Drive
Georgetown, KY
502-868-0055 (800-780-7234)
Dogs are welcome at this hotel.

Days Inn -North Of Lexington
Georgetown
385 Cherry Blossom Way
Georgetown, KY
502-863-5000 (800-329-7466)
Dogs of all sizes are allowed. Dogs are allowed for a nightly pet fee.

Econo Lodge
3075 Paris Pike
Georgetown, KY
502-863-2240 (877-424-6423)
Dogs of all sizes are allowed. Dogs are allowed for a pet fee of $7.00 per pet per night.

Motel 6 - Lexington North
Georgetown
401 Cherry Blossom Way
Georgetown, KY
502-863-1166 (800-466-8356)
This motel welcomes your pets to stay with you.

Quality Inn
250 Outlet Center Drive
Georgetown, KY
502-867-1648 (877-424-6423)
Dogs of all sizes are allowed. Dogs are allowed for a pet fee of $10.00 per pet per night.

Comfort Inn
210 Calvary Dr
Glasgow, KY
270-651-9099 (877-424-6423)
Dogs of all sizes are allowed. Dogs are allowed for a pet fee of $10.00 per pet per night. Two dogs are allowed per room.

Days Inn Grayson
650 CW Stevens Blvd
Grayson, KY
606-475-3224 (800-329-7466)
Dogs of all sizes are allowed. Dogs are allowed for a nightly pet fee.

Quality Inn
205 State Highway 1947
Grayson, KY
606-474-7854 (877-424-6423)
Dogs of all sizes are allowed. Dogs are allowed for a pet fee of $15.00 per pet per night.

Super 8 Grayson
125 Super Eight Lane
Grayson, KY
606-474-8811 (800-800-8000)
Dogs of all sizes are allowed. Dogs are allowed for a pet fee of $10.00 per pet per night.

Days Inn Harrodsburg
1680 Danville Rd
Harrodsburg, KY
859-734-9431 (800-329-7466)
Dogs are welcome at this hotel.

Super 8 KY Hazard
125 Village Lane
Hazard, KY
606-436-8888 (800-800-8000)
Dogs of all sizes are allowed. Dogs are allowed for a nightly pet fee.

Ramada KY Henderson
2044 US 41 North
Henderson, KY
270-826-6600 (800-272-6232)
Dogs are welcome at this hotel.

Super 8 -Evansville Henderson
2030 Highway 41
Henderson, KY
270-827-5611 (800-800-8000)
Dogs of all sizes are allowed. Dogs are allowed for a pet fee of $10 per pet per night.

First Farm Inn
2510 Stevens Road
Idlewild, KY
859-586-0199
firstfarminn.com/
This riverside inn features beautifully landscaped grounds, a convenient

location to many other sites of interest, special events, and other year around activities. There are also all kinds of farm and family critters that visitors can view or visit with. Dogs are allowed for an additional fee of $18 per night per pet. Dogs must be well trained and get along well with other animals and people. They request that dogs be cleaned up before coming inside. 2 dogs may be allowed.

Super 8 Inez
Rt 40 Blacklog Rd
Inez, KY
606-298-7800 (800-800-8000)
Dogs of all sizes are allowed. Dogs are allowed for a pet fee of $10.00 per pet per night.

Days Inn Kuttawa
139 Days Inn Drive
Kuttawa, KY
270-388-4060 (800-329-7466)
Dogs of all sizes are allowed. Dogs are allowed for a pet fee.

Comfort Suites
1500 E Crystal Dr.
La Grange, KY
502-225-4125 (877-424-6423)
Dogs up to 75 pounds are allowed. Dogs are allowed for a pet fee of $10.00 per pet per night. Two dogs are allowed per room.

Holiday Inn Express La Grange
1001 Paige Place
La Grange, KY
502-222-5678 (877-270-6405)
Dogs of all sizes are allowed. Dogs are allowed for a pet fee of $20.00 per pet per night.

Candlewood Suites Lexington
601 Ad Color Dr
Lexington, KY
859-967-1940 (877-270-6405)
Dogs up to 80 pounds are allowed. Pets allowed with an additional pet fee. Up to $75 for 1-6 nights and up to $150 for 7+ nights. A pet agreement must be signed at check-in.

Comfort Suites
3060 Fieldstone Way
Lexington, KY
859-296-4446 (877-424-6423)
Dogs of all sizes are allowed. Dogs are allowed for a pet fee of $40.00 per pet per stay.

Days Inn South Lexington
5575 Athens Boonesboro Rd
Lexington, KY

859-263-3100 (800-329-7466)
Dogs of all sizes are allowed. Dogs are allowed for a pet fee of $10.00 per pet per night.

Days Inn and Suites Lexington
1987 N. Broadway
Lexington, KY
859-299-1202 (800-329-7466)
Dogs of all sizes are allowed. Dogs are allowed for a pet fee.

Econo Lodge
5527 Athens-Boonesboro Rd.
Lexington, KY
859-263-5101 (877-424-6423)
Dogs of all sizes are allowed. Dogs are allowed for a pet fee of $10.00 per pet per night.

Extended Stay America Lexington - Nicholasville Road
2650 Wilhite Dr.
Lexington, KY
859-278-9600 (800-804-3724)
One dog is allowed per suite. There is a $25 per night additional pet fee up to $150 for an entire stay.

Extended Stay America Lexington - Patchen Village
2750 Gribbin Dr.
Lexington, KY
859-266-4800 (800-804-3724)
One dog is allowed per suite. There is a $25 per night additional pet fee up to $150 for an entire stay.

Extended Stay America Lexington - Tates Creek
3575 Tates Creek Rd.
Lexington, KY
859-271-6160 (800-804-3724)
One dog is allowed per suite. There is a $25 per night additional pet fee up to $150 for an entire stay.

Four Points by Sheraton Lexington
1538 Stanton Way
Lexington, KY
859-259-1311 (888-625-5144)
Dogs of all sizes are allowed. There is a $100 nonrefundable one time pet fee per visit. Dogs are not allowed to be left alone in the room.

Hilton Hotel
245 Lexington Green Circle
Lexington, KY
859-271-4000 (800-HILTONS (445-8667))
This luxury, all suite hotel offers a number on site amenities for business and leisure travelers, plus a convenient location to business, shopping, dining, recreation areas, and sites of interest for horse

enthusiasts. Dogs up to 75 pounds are allowed for an additional one time fee of $50 per pet. 2 dogs may be allowed.

Holiday Inn Express Hotel & Suites Lexington-Downtown/University
1000 Export Street
Lexington, KY
859-389-6800 (877-270-6405)
Dogs of all sizes are allowed. Dogs are allowed for a pet fee of $25.00 per pet per stay.

Marriott Griffin Gate Resort & Spa
1800 Newtown Pike
Lexington, KY
859-231-5100 (800-228-9290)
In addition to offering a number of in-house amenities for all level of travelers, this luxury hotel also provides a convenient location to business, shopping, dining, and day/night entertainment areas. Dogs up to 100 pounds are allowed for an additional one time fee of $100 per room. 2 dogs may be allowed.

Motel 6 - Lexington East
2260 Elkhorn Rd
Lexington, KY
859-293-1431 (800-466-8356)
This motel welcomes your pets to stay with you.

Ramada Conference Center of Lexington
2143 N Broadway
Lexington, KY
859-299-1261 (800-272-6232)
Dogs of all sizes are allowed. Dogs are allowed for a pet fee.

Red Roof Inn Lexington
1980 Haggard Court
Lexington, KY
859-293-2626 (800-RED-ROOF)
One well-behaved family pet per room. Guest must notify front desk upon arrival. Guest is liable for any damages. In consideration of all guests, pets must never be left unattended in the guest rooms.

Red Roof Inn Lexington South
2651 Wilhite Drive
Lexington, KY
606-277-9400 (800-RED-ROOF)
One well-behaved family pet per room. Guest must notify front desk upon arrival. Guest is liable for any damages. In consideration of all guests, pets must never be left unattended in the guest rooms.

Red Roof Inn Lexington Southeast
100 Canebrake Drive

Lexington, KY
859-543-1877 (800-RED-ROOF)
One well-behaved family pet per room. Guest must notify front desk upon arrival. Guest is liable for any damages. In consideration of all guests, pets must never be left unattended in the guest rooms.

Residence Inn Lexington North
1080 Newtown Pike
Lexington, KY
859-231-6191 (800-331-3131)
In addition to being central to a number of world class attractions and activities, this all suite, upscale inn also offers a number of in-house amenities, including a daily buffet breakfast and evening socials. Dogs are allowed for an additional one time pet fee of $75 per room. 2 dogs may be allowed.

Residence Inn Lexington South/Hamburg Place
2688 Pink Pigeon Parkway
Lexington, KY
859-263-9979 (800-331-3131)
Besides offering a convenient location to business, shopping, dining, and entertainment areas, this all suite inn also provides a number of in-house amenities, including a daily hot American and Japanese breakfast, and complementary evening receptions Monday to Thursday. Dogs are allowed for an additional one time pet fee of $75 per room. Multiple dogs may be allowed.

Rodeway Inn
5556 Versailles Road
Lexington, KY
859-254-6699
There is a $10 per night per pet additional fee.

Sleep Inn
1920 Plaudit Pl.
Lexington, KY
859-543-8400 (877-424-6423)
Dogs of all sizes are allowed. Dogs are allowed for a pet fee of $25.00 per pet per night.

Super 8 Winchester Rd Lexington
2351 Buena Vista Rd
Lexington, KY
859-299-6241 (800-800-8000)
Dogs are welcome at this hotel.

Days Inn London
207 Hwy 80 West
London, KY
606-864-2222 (800-329-7466)
Dogs are welcome at this hotel.

Econo Lodge
105 Melcon Lane
London, KY
606-877-9700 (877-424-6423)
Dogs up to 60 pounds are allowed. Dogs are allowed for a pet fee of $8.00 per pet per night. Three or more dogs may be allowed.

Red Roof Inn London I-75
110 Melcon Lane
London, KY
606-862-8844 (800-RED-ROOF)
One well-behaved family pet per room. Guest must notify front desk upon arrival. Guest is liable for any damages. In consideration of all guests, pets must never be left unattended in the guest rooms.

Super 8 London
285 W Hwy 80
London, KY
606-878-9800 (800-800-8000)
Dogs of all sizes are allowed. Dogs are allowed for a pet fee of $10 per pet per stay.

Super 8 Louisa
191 Falls Creek Dr
Louisa, KY
606-638-7888 (800-800-8000)
Dogs of all sizes are allowed. Dogs are allowed for a pet fee.

Aleksander House Bed and Breakfast
1213 South First Street
Louisville, KY
502-637-4985 (866-637-4985)
aleksanderhouse.com/
Stay at an 1882 Victorian bed and breakfast located in historic Old Louisville. Near downtown and Churchill Downs. There is a fenced in yard. Well-behaved dogs of all sizes are permitted. Dogs must be quiet and friendly and recently bathed. There is a $25 pet fee.

Baymont Inn & Suites Louisville
9400 Blairwood Road
Louisville, KY
502-339-1900 (877-229-6668)
Dogs of all sizes are allowed. Dogs are allowed for a pet fee of $10.00 per pet per night.

Best Western Airport East/Expo Center
1921 Bishop Ln
Louisville, KY
502-456-4411 (800-780-7234)
Dogs of all sizes are allowed. Dogs are allowed for a pet fee.

Breckinridge Inn

2800 Breckinridge Lane
Louisville, KY
502-456-5050
There is a $25 one time pet charge per room. Multiple dogs may be allowed.

Candlewood Suites Louisville Airport
1367 Gardiner Lane
Louisville, KY
502-357-3577 (877-270-6405)
Dogs up to 80 pounds are allowed. Pets allowed with an additional pet fee. Up to $75 for 1-6 nights and up to $150 for 7+ nights. A pet agreement must be signed at check-in.

Candlewood Suites Louisville-East
11762 Commonwealth Drive
Louisville, KY
502-261-0085 (877-270-6405)
Dogs up to 80 pounds are allowed. Pets allowed with an additional pet fee. Up to $75 for 1-6 nights and up to $150 for 7+ nights. A pet agreement must be signed at check-in.

Comfort Suites
1850 Resource Way
Louisville, KY
502-266-6509 (877-424-6423)
Dogs of all sizes are allowed. Dogs are allowed for a pet fee of $10.00 per pet per night.

Days Inn Airport Fair and Expo Center Louisville
2905 Fern Valley Road
Louisville, KY
502-968-8124 (800-329-7466)
Dogs of all sizes are allowed. Dogs are allowed for a pet fee of $15 per pet per night.

Days Inn Central University & Expo Center Louisville
1620 Arthur St
Louisville, KY
502-636-3781 (800-329-7466)
Dogs of all sizes are allowed. Dogs are allowed for a pet fee.

Days Inn Hurstbourne
9340 Blairwood Road
Louisville, KY
502-425-8010 (800-329-7466)
Dogs are welcome at this hotel.

Drury Inn & Suites
9501 Blairwood Road
Louisville, KY
502-326-4170 (800-378-7946)
Dogs of all sizes are allowed for no additional pet fee with a credit card on file, and there is a pet agreement

to sign at check in.

Extended Stay America Louisville - Dutchman
6101 Dutchmans Ln.
Louisville, KY
502-895-7707 (800-804-3724)
One dog is allowed per suite. There is a $25 per night additional pet fee up to $150 for an entire stay.

Extended Stay America Louisville - Hurstbourne
9801 Bunsen Way
Louisville, KY
502-499-6215 (800-804-3724)
One dog is allowed per suite. There is a $25 per night additional pet fee up to $150 for an entire stay.

Extended Stay America Louisville - St. Matthews
1401 Browns Ln.
Louisville, KY
502-897-2559 (800-804-3724)
One dog is allowed per suite. There is a $25 per night additional pet fee up to $150 for an entire stay.

Holiday Inn Hurstbourne I-64 East
1325 S Hurstbourne Pkwy
Louisville, KY
502-426-2600 (877-270-6405)
Dogs of all sizes are allowed. Dogs are allowed for a nightly pet fee.

Holiday Inn Louisville-Sw(Fair & Expo Ctr)
4110 Dixie Hwy, Box 16280
Louisville, KY
502-448-2020 (877-270-6405)
Dogs of all sizes are allowed. Dogs are allowed for a pet fee of $25.00 per pet per night.

Homestead Studio Suites Louisville - Alliant Drive
1650 Alliant Dr.
Louisville, KY
502-267-4454 (800-804-3724)
One dog is allowed per suite. There is a $25 per night additional pet fee up to $150 for an entire stay.

La Quinta Inn & Suites Louisville
4125 Preston Highway
Louisville, KY
502-368-0007 (800-531-5900)
Dogs up to 60 pounds are allowed. There are no additional pet fees. There is a pet waiver to sign at check in. Dogs are not to use the front entrance; they are to be brought in the side doors. Dogs must be leashed and cleaned up after. Multiple dogs may be allowed.

Motel 6 - Louisville Airport
3200 Kemmons Dr
Louisville, KY
502-473-0000 (800-466-8356)
This motel welcomes your pets to stay with you.

Quality Inn & Suites
3255 Bardstown Rd.
Louisville, KY
502-454-0451 (877-424-6423)
Dogs of all sizes are allowed. Dogs are allowed for a pet fee of $10.00 per pet per night. Two dogs are allowed per room.

Ramada Downtown North
1041 Zorn Avenue
Louisville, KY
502-897-5101 (800-272-6232)
Dogs are welcome at this hotel.

Ramada Limited and Suites Airport/Fair/Expo Center
2912 Crittenden Dr
Louisville, KY
502-637-6336 (800-272-6232)
Dogs of all sizes are allowed. Dogs are allowed for a pet fee of $15.00 per pet per stay.

Red Roof Inn Louisville East - Hurstbourne
9330 Blairwood Road
Louisville, KY
502-426-7621 (800-RED-ROOF)
One well-behaved family pet per room. Guest must notify front desk upon arrival. Guest is liable for any damages. In consideration of all guests, pets must never be left unattended in the guest rooms.

Red Roof Inn Louisville Expo Airport
4704 Preston Highway
Louisville, KY
502-968-0151 (800-RED-ROOF)
One well-behaved family pet per room. Guest must notify front desk upon arrival. Guest is liable for any damages. In consideration of all guests, pets must never be left unattended in the guest rooms.

Red Roof Inn Louisville Fair And Expo
3322 Red Roof Inn Place
Louisville, KY
502-456-2993 (800-RED-ROOF)
One well-behaved family pet per room. Guest must notify front desk upon arrival. Guest is liable for any damages. In consideration of all guests, pets must never be left unattended in the guest rooms.

Residence Inn Louisville Airport

700 Phillips Lane
Louisville, KY
502-363-8800 (800-331-3131)
The Louisville International Airport, the state fair and exposition center, Six Flags, and the Churchill Downs Race Track are all within a few minutes of this all suite, upscale inn. They also offer a number of in-house amenities, including a daily buffet breakfast and evening socials Monday through Thursday. Dogs are allowed for an additional one time pet fee of $100 per room. Multiple dogs may be allowed.

Residence Inn Louisville Downtown
333 E Market Street
Louisville, KY
502-589-8998 (800-331-3131)
Located in the heart of the medical district with several hospitals only a short walk away - plus a central location to a number of sites/activities of interest, this all suite, upscale inn offers a number of in-house amenities, including a daily buffet breakfast and evening socials. Dogs are allowed for an additional one time pet fee of $100 per room. 2 dogs may be allowed.

Residence Inn Louisville East
120 N Hurstbourne Parkway
Louisville, KY
502-425-1821 (800-331-3131)
Located across from the University of Louisville Shelby and near a number of the area's star attractions and commerce areas, this all suite, upscale inn offers a number of in-house amenities, including a daily buffet breakfast and evening socials. Dogs are allowed for an additional one time pet fee of $100 per room. Multiple dogs may be allowed.

Residence Inn Louisville Northeast
3500 Springhurst Commons Drive
Louisville, KY
502-412-1311 (800-331-3131)
This all suite hotel sits central to many of the city's star attractions, shopping, dining, and business areas, plus they offer a number of in-house amenities that include a daily buffet breakfast and evening socials Monday to Thursday. Dogs are allowed for an additional one time pet fee of $100 per room. Multiple dogs may be allowed.

Sleep Inn
1850 Priority Way
Louisville, KY
502-266-6776 (877-424-6423)
Dogs of all sizes are allowed. Dogs are allowed for a pet fee of $10.00/

per pet per night.

Sleep Inn & Suites Airport
3330 Preston Hwy Gate #6
Louisville, KY
502-368-9597 (877-424-6423)
Dogs of all sizes are allowed. Dogs
are allowed for a pet fee of $35.00
per pet per stay.

Staybridge Suites Louisville-East
11711 Gateworth Way
Louisville, KY
502-244-9511 (877-270-6405)
Dogs up to 80 pounds are allowed.
Pets allowed with an additional pet
fee. Up to $75 for 1-6 nights and up
to $150 for 7+ nights. A pet
agreement must be signed at check-
in.

Super 8 Airport Louisville
4800 Preston Hwy
Louisville, KY
502-968-0088 (800-800-8000)
Dogs of all sizes are allowed. Dogs
are allowed for a pet fee.

Super 8 Near Conv Expo Ctr
Louisville
1501 Alliant Ave
Louisville, KY
502-267-8889 (800-800-8000)
Dogs of all sizes are allowed. Dogs
are allowed for a pet fee.

Days Inn Madisonville
1900 Lantaff Blvd
Madisonville, KY
270-821-8620 (800-329-7466)
Dogs are welcome at this hotel.

Days Inn Mayfield
1101 W. Housman Street
Mayfield, KY
270-247-3700 (800-329-7466)
Dogs of all sizes are allowed. Dogs
are allowed for a nightly pet fee.

Days Inn Maysville
484 Moody Drive
Maysville, KY
606-564-6793 (800-329-7466)
Dogs are welcome at this hotel.

Super 8 KY Maysville
US Hwy 68
Maysville, KY
606-759-8888 (800-800-8000)
Dogs are welcome at this hotel.

Comfort Inn & Suites
2650 KY 801 North
Morehead, KY
606-780-7378 (877-424-6423)
Dogs of all sizes are allowed. Dogs
are allowed for a pet fee of $10.00

per pet per night.

Quality Inn
175 Toms Road
Morehead, KY
606-784-2220 (877-424-6423)
Dogs of all sizes are allowed. Dogs
are allowed for a pet fee of $USD
per pet per stay. Two dogs are
allowed per room.

Super 8
602 Fraley Drive
Morehead, KY
606-784-8882 (800-800-8000)
Dogs are welcome at this hotel.

Motel 6 - Morgantown
1460 Main St
Morgantown, KY
270-526-9481 (800-466-8356)
This motel welcomes your pets to
stay with you.

Ramada Limited/Conference
Center-Mt. Sterling
115 Stone Trace Drive
Mount Sterling, KY
859-497-9400 (800-272-6232)
Dogs are welcome at this hotel.

Days Inn Renfro Valley Mount
Vernon
1630 Richmond Street
Mount Vernon, KY
606-256-3300 (800-329-7466)
Dogs are welcome at this hotel.

Super 8 KY Munfordville
88 Bull Run Road
Munfordville, KY
270-524-4888 (800-800-8000)
Dogs are welcome at this hotel.

Days Inn Murray
517 South 12th Street
Murray, KY
270-753-6706 (800-329-7466)
Dogs of all sizes are allowed. Dogs
are allowed for a nightly pet fee.

Days Inn Owensboro
3720 New Hartford Road
Owensboro, KY
270-684-9621 (800-329-7466)
Dogs of all sizes are allowed. Dogs
are allowed for a pet fee of $20.00
per pet per night.

Motel 6 - Owensboro
4585 Frederica St
Owensboro, KY
270-686-8606 (800-466-8356)
This motel welcomes your pets to
stay with you.

Baymont Inn & Suites Paducah

5300 Old Cairo Rd.
Paducah, KY
270-443-4343 (877-229-6668)
Dogs of all sizes are allowed. Dogs
are allowed for a pet fee of $5.00 per
pet per night.

Candlewood Suites Paducah
3940 Coleman Crossing Circle
Paducah, KY
270-442-3969 (877-270-6405)
Dogs up to 80 pounds are allowed.
Pets allowed with an additional pet
fee. Up to $75 for 1-6 nights and up
to $150 for 7+ nights. A pet
agreement must be signed at check-
in.

Days Inn Paducah
3901 Hinkleville Road
Paducah, KY
270-442-7500 (800-329-7466)
Dogs are welcome at this hotel.

Drury Inn
3975 Hinkleville Road
Paducah, KY
270-443-3313 (800-378-7946)
Dogs of all sizes are allowed for no
additional pet fee with a credit card
on file, and there is a pet agreement
to sign at check in.

Drury Suites
2930 James-Sanders Blvd
Paducah, KY
270-441-0024 (800-378-7946)
Dogs of all sizes are allowed for no
additional pet fee with a credit card
on file, and there is a pet agreement
to sign at check in.

Econo Lodge
5106 Old Cairo Rd.
Paducah, KY
270-442-1616 (877-424-6423)
Dogs of all sizes are allowed. Dogs
are allowed for a pet fee of $10.00
per pet per night.

Motel 6 - Paducah
5120 Hinkleville Rd
Paducah, KY
270-443-3672 (800-466-8356)
This motel welcomes your pets to
stay with you.

Pear Tree Inn
5002 Hinkleville Road
Paducah, KY
270-444-7200 (800-378-7946)
Dogs of all sizes are allowed for no
additional pet fee with a credit card
on file, and there is a pet agreement
to sign at check in.

Residence Inn Paducah

3900 Coleman Crossing Circle
Paducah, KY
270-444-3966 (800-331-3131)
In addition to offering a convenient location to local attractions, businesses, shopping, dining, and entertainment areas, this hotel also provides a number of in-house amenities, including a daily buffet breakfast and evening social hours Monday to Thursday. Dogs are allowed for an additional one time pet fee of $75 per room. 2 dogs may be allowed.

Super 8 Paducah
5001 Hinkleville Rd
Paducah, KY
270-442-3334 (800-800-8000)
Dogs are welcome at this hotel.

Super 8 Prestonsburg
550 S US 23
Prestonsburg, KY
606-886-3355 (800-800-8000)
Dogs of all sizes are allowed. Dogs are allowed for a nightly pet fee.

Comfort Suites
2007 Colby Taylor Dr.
Richmond, KY
859-624-0770 (877-424-6423)
Dogs of all sizes are allowed. Dogs are allowed for a pet fee of $USD per pet per night.

Days Inn Richmond
2109 Belmont Drive
Richmond, KY
859-624-5769 (800-329-7466)
Dogs are welcome at this hotel.

Knights Inn KY Richmond
1688 Northgate Drive
Richmond, KY
859-624-2612 (800-843-5644)
Dogs are welcome at this hotel.

La Quinta Inn Richmond
1751 Lexington Rd.
Richmond, KY
859-623-9121 (800-531-5900)
Dogs of all sizes are allowed. There are no additional pet fees. Dogs must be leashed and cleaned up after. Multiple dogs may be allowed.

Red Roof Inn Lexington - Richmond
111 Bahama Court
Richmond, KY
859-625-0084 (800-RED-ROOF)
One well-behaved family pet per room. Guest must notify front desk upon arrival. Guest is liable for any damages. In consideration of all guests, pets must never be left unattended in the guest rooms.

Super 8 Richmond
107 N Keeneland
Richmond, KY
859-624-1550 (800-800-8000)
Dogs are welcome at this hotel.

Econo Lodge
11165 Frontage Rd.
Richwood, KY
859-485-4123 (877-424-6423)
Dogs of all sizes are allowed. Dogs are allowed for a pet fee of $10.00 per pet per night.

Best Western Shelbyville Lodge
115 Isaac Shelby Drive
Shelbyville, KY
502-633-4400 (800-780-7234)
Dogs are welcome at this hotel.

Days Inn - Louisville Shelbyville
101 Howard Drive
Shelbyville, KY
502-633-4005 (800-329-7466)
Dogs are welcome at this hotel.

Ramada Louisville East
251 Breighton Circle
Shelbyville, KY
502-633-9933 (800-272-6232)
Dogs of all sizes are allowed. Dogs are allowed for a pet fee of $25 per pet per stay.

Motel 6 - Louisville South Shepherdsville
144 Paroquet Springs Dr
Shepherdsville, KY
502-543-4400 (800-466-8356)
This motel welcomes your pets to stay with you.

Ramada /Louisville South Shepherdsville
191 Brenton Way
Shepherdsville, KY
502-955-5566 (800-272-6232)
Dogs of all sizes are allowed. Dogs are allowed for a nightly pet fee.

Sleep Inn & Suites
130 Spring Pointe Drive
Shepherdsville, KY
502-921-1001 (877-424-6423)
Dogs up to 50 pounds are allowed. Dogs are allowed for a pet fee of $25.00 per pet per night. One dog is allowed per room.

Days Inn Somerset
125 North Highway 27
Somerset, KY
606-678-2052 (800-329-7466)
Dogs are welcome at this hotel.

Red Roof Inn Somerset

1201 Highway 27 South
Somerset, KY
606-678-8115 (800-RED-ROOF)
One well-behaved family pet per room. Guest must notify front desk upon arrival. Guest is liable for any damages. In consideration of all guests, pets must never be left unattended in the guest rooms.

Super 8 /Goody Area South Williamson
28668 US Highway 119N
South Williamson, KY
606-237-5898 (800-800-8000)
Dogs are welcome at this hotel.

Ramada KY Sparta
525 Dale Drive
Sparta, KY
859-567-7223 (800-272-6232)
Dogs of all sizes are allowed. Dogs are allowed for a pet fee of $25 per pet per stay.

Barthell Coal Mining Camp Lodging
552 Barthell Road
Sterns, KY
606-376-8749 (888-550-5748)
barthellcoalcamp.com/lodging.htm
There are numerous points of interest to explore at this 1902 mining camp. The camp offers tours 300 feet into the mine, various events throughout the year, an eatery, and 12 modernized company houses for lodging. The mine opens April 1st. Dogs are allowed throughout the site, on the tours, and in the camp houses for no additional pet fee. Dogs must be leashed and under their owner's control at all times. 2 dogs may be allowed.

Rose Hill Inn
233 Rose Hill Avenue
Versailles, KY
859-873-5957 (800-307-0460)
rosehillinn.com/index.htm
This inn has been beautifully restored while maintaining its original features-allowing visitors a personal feel for the era of this 1823 home. There is a front veranda to relax on or 3 landscaped grounds to explore. Dogs are allowed for an additional one time pet fee of $15 per room. Dogs must be leashed when out of the room - except for free play in the fenced yard. Guests must pick up after their pets, and they must be cleaned up before entering during bad weather (towels are provided). Dogs must be hound and human friendly, be healthy, free of fleas, and well behaved. They are not allowed on furniture or beds, in the main house, or dining areas. Dogs may

not be left unattended in the room if they are prone to anxiety or barking.

Days Inn West Liberty
1613 West Main
West Liberty, KY
606-743-4206 (800-329-7466)
Dogs of all sizes are allowed. Dogs are allowed for a pet fee of $10.00 per pet per stay.

Super 8 Whiteburg KY
377A Hazard Rd & Rt 15
Whitesburg, KY
606-633-8888 (800-800-8000)
Dogs are welcome at this hotel.

Super 8 Williamsburg
30 West Highway 92
Williamsburg, KY
606-549-3450 (800-800-8000)
Dogs of all sizes are allowed. Dogs are allowed for a pet fee of $10 per pet per night.

Days Inn Williamstown
211 Kentucky Avenue 36 West
Williamstown, KY
859-824-5025 (800-329-7466)
Dogs of all sizes are allowed. Dogs are allowed for a nightly pet fee.

Best Western Country Squire
1307 W Lexington Avenue
Winchester, KY
859-744-7210 (800-780-7234)
Dogs of all sizes are allowed. Dogs are allowed for a nightly pet fee.

Quality Inn & Suites
960 Interstate Drive
Winchester, KY
859-737-3990 (877-424-6423)
Dogs of all sizes are allowed. Dogs are allowed for a pet fee of $20.00 per pet per stay. Two dogs are allowed per room.

Louisiana

La Quinta Inn & Suites Alexandria
6116 West Calhoun Dr.
Alexandria, LA
318-442-3700 (800-531-5900)
Dogs of all sizes are allowed. There are no additional pet fees. Dogs must be leashed and cleaned up after. The Do Not Disturb sign must be on the door if a pet is in the room alone. Multiple dogs may be allowed.

Motel 6 - Alexandria
546 Macarthur Dr
Alexandria, LA
318-445-2336 (800-466-8356)
This motel welcomes your pets to

stay with you.

Ramada Alexandria
742 MacArthur Drive
Alexandria, LA
318-448-1611 (800-272-6232)
Dogs are welcome at this hotel.

Super 8 Alexandria
700 Mac Arthur Drive
Alexandria, LA
318-445-6541 (800-800-8000)
Dogs are welcome at this hotel.

Best Western Richmond Suites
Hotel-Baton Rouge
5668 Hilton Avenue
Baton Rouge, LA
225-924-6500 (800-780-7234)
Dogs are welcome at this hotel. There is a $75 one time pet fee.

Chase Suites By Woodfin
5522 Corporate Blvd
Baton Rouge, LA
225-927-5630 (888-433-9669)
This all-suite upscale hotel offers numerous amenities which also includes an evening social hour and a clubhouse. Dogs are allowed for a $250 refundable deposit plus $10 per night per pet. Dogs must be well mannered and leashed when out of the room. 2 dogs may be allowed.

Crossland Baton Rouge Sherwood
Forest
11140 Boardwalk Drive
Baton Rouge, LA
225-274-8997 (800-804-3724 650)
crosslandstudios.com/
This extended stay, economy studio inn offers guests the comforts of home with a fully equipped kitchen and plenty of work space. Dogs are allowed for an additional fee of $25 per pet for 1 or 2 days, and 3 days or more is $75 per pet. Dogs must be well behaved, leashed, cleaned up after, and crated when left alone in the room or for housekeeping. 2 dogs may be allowed.

Days Inn Baton Rouge
9919 Gwenadele Ave
Baton Rouge, LA
225-925-8399 (800-329-7466)
Dogs of all sizes are allowed. Dogs are allowed for a pet fee of $15 per pet per stay.

Extended Stay America Baton
Rouge - Citiplace
6250 Corporate Blvd.
Baton Rouge, LA
225-201-0330 (800-804-3724)
One dog is allowed per suite. There

is a $25 per night additional pet fee up to $150 for an entire stay.

Knights Inn Baton Rouge
9919 Ste 4 Gwenadele Ave
Baton Rouge, LA
225-364-3520 (800-843-5644)
Dogs of all sizes are allowed. Dogs are allowed for a pet fee.

La Quinta Inn Baton Rouge
2333 S. Acadian Thruway
Baton Rouge, LA
225-924-9600 (800-531-5900)
Dogs of all sizes are allowed. There are no additional pet fees. Dogs must be leashed and cleaned up after. The Do Not Disturb sign must be on the door if a pet is in the room alone. Multiple dogs may be allowed.

Motel 6 - Baton Rouge East
9901 Gwen Adele Ave
Baton Rouge, LA
225-924-2130 (800-466-8356)
This motel welcomes your pets to stay with you.

Motel 6 - Baton Rouge Southeast
10445 Reiger Rd
Baton Rouge, LA
225-291-4912 (800-466-8356)
This motel welcomes your pets to stay with you.

Radisson Hotel
2445 S. Acadian Thruway
Baton Rouge, LA
225-236-4000 (888-368-7578)
radisson.com/
Dogs are allowed for an additional one time $20 pet fee per room. Dogs must be well behaved, leashed, and cleaned up after. They may be left alone in the room, but if there is a chance they could bark, they request you leave a contact number at the front desk. There is an outdoor pet lawn area for daily walks. 2 dogs may be allowed.

Red Roof Inn Baton Rouge
11314 Boardwalk Drive
Baton Rouge, LA
225-275-6600 (800-RED-ROOF)
One well-behaved family pet per room. Guest must notify front desk upon arrival. Guest is liable for any damages. In consideration of all guests, pets must never be left unattended in the guest rooms.

Residence Inn Baton Rouge Siegen
Lane
10333 North Mall Drive
Baton Rouge, LA
225-293-8700 (800-331-3131)

This all suite hotel sits central to many of the city's star attractions, dining, and entertainment areas, plus they offer a number of in-house amenities that include a daily buffet breakfast, and a Manager's reception Monday through Wednesday. Dogs are allowed for an additional one time pet fee of $100 (+ $9 tax) per room. Multiple dogs may be allowed.

Residence Inn Baton Rouge Towne Center at Cedar Lodge
7061 Commerce Circle
Baton Rouge, LA
225-925-9100 (800-331-3131)
In addition to offering a convenient location to business, shopping, dining, and entertainment areas, this hotel also provides a number of in-house amenities, including a daily buffet breakfast, and an evening social hour. Dogs are allowed for an additional one time pet fee of $75 per room. Multiple dogs may be allowed.

Sheraton Baton Rouge Convention Center Hotel
102 France St.
Baton Rouge, LA
225-242-2600 (888-625-5144)
Dogs of all sizes are allowed. There are no additional pet fees. Dogs are not allowed to be left alone in the room

TownePlace Suites Baton Rouge South
8735 Summa Blvd
Baton Rouge, LA
225-819-2112 (866-816-8699)
This all suite inn offers neighborhood-style accommodations with only 1 mile to the Interstate, plus they offer a number of in-house amenities. Dogs are allowed for an additional one time fee of $75 per room. Multiple dogs may be allowed.

Howard Johnson Bossier
1984 Airline Drive
Bossier, LA
318-742-6000 (800-446-4656)
Dogs are welcome at this hotel. There is a $10 one time pet fee.

Days Inn Bossier City
200 John Wesly Blvd
Bossier City, LA
318-742-9200 (800-329-7466)
Dogs of all sizes are allowed. Dogs are allowed for a pet fee of $10.00 per pet per night.

Motel 6 - Shreveport
210 John Wesley Blvd
Bossier City, LA

318-742-3472 (800-466-8356)
This motel welcomes your pets to stay with you.

Residence Inn Shreveport-Bossier City
1001 Gould Drive
Bossier City, LA
318-747-6220 (800-331-3131)
Only 2 miles from the riverfront and the downtown area, this all suite hotel offers a convenient location to all the city has to offer, plus they also provides a number of in-house amenities, including a daily buffet breakfast, evening socials, and weekly barbecues. Dogs are allowed for an additional one time pet fee of $100 per room. Multiple dogs may be allowed.

Best Western Northpark Inn
625 N Highway 190
Covington, LA
985-892-2681 (800-780-7234)
Dogs of all sizes are allowed. Dogs are allowed for a pet fee of $25.00 per pet per night.

Creole Gardens
1415 Prytania Street
Creole Gardens, LA
504-897-0540
creolegardens.com/
Dogs of all sizes are allowed for no additional fee with a credit card on file. 2 dogs may be allowed.

Days Inn Crowley
9571 Egan Highway
Crowley, LA
337-783-2378 (800-329-7466)
Dogs of all sizes are allowed. Dogs are allowed for a pet fee of $10 per pet per night.

La Quinta Inn Crowley
9565 Egan Highway
Crowley, LA
337-783-6500 (800-531-5900)
Dogs of all sizes are allowed. There are no additional pet fees. There is a pet waiver to sign at check in. Dogs must be leashed, cleaned up after, and crated if left in the room alone. Multiple dogs may be allowed.

Best Western Delhi Inn
135 Snider Road
Delhi, LA
318-878-5126 (800-780-7234)
Dogs of all sizes are allowed. Dogs are allowed for a pet fee of $10.00 per pet per stay.

Best Western Hammond Inn &

Suites
107 Duo Drive
Hammond, LA
985-419-2001 (800-780-7234)
Dogs of all sizes are allowed. Dogs are allowed for a pet fee.

Motel 6 - Hammond, La
2010 South Morrison Blvd
Hammond, LA
985-542-9425 (800-466-8356)
This motel welcomes your pets to stay with you.

Quality Inn & Conference Center
2000 South Morrison Boulevard
Hammond, LA
985-345-0556 (877-424-6423)
Dogs up to 50 pounds are allowed. Dogs are allowed for a pet fee of $50.00 per pet per stay. Two dogs are allowed per room.

TownePlace Suites New Orleans Metairie
5424 Citrus Blvd
Harahan, LA
504-818-2400 (800-257-3000)
This all suite hotel sits central to a number of sites of interest for both business and leisure travelers; plus they also offer a number of on-site amenities-including a hot continental breakfast. Dogs are allowed for an additional one time fee of $75 per room. Multiple dogs may be allowed.

Crochet House
301 Midland Drive
Houma, LA
985-879-3033 (888-483-3033)
crochethouse.com/
Located down in the bayou country, this beautiful inn is rich in Cajun culture, foods, and French influence. One dog is allowed per room for no additional fee. Dogs must be quiet and well mannered.

Days Inn LA Houma
125 Dixie Ave
Houma, LA
985-223-4788 (800-329-7466)
Dogs are welcome at this hotel.

Ramada Inn Houma
1400 West Tunnel Blvd
Houma, LA
985-879-4871 (800-272-6232)
Dogs are welcome at this hotel.

Extended Stay America New Orleans - Kenner
2300 Veterans Blvd.
Kenner, LA
504-465-8300 (800-804-3724)
One dog is allowed per suite. There

is a $25 per night additional pet fee up to $150 for an entire stay.

Hilton Hotel
901 Airline Drive
Kenner, LA
504-469-5000 (800-HILTONS (445-8667))
Located at the Louis Armstrong International Airport, this upscale hotel offers a number of on site amenities for business and leisure travelers. Dogs up to 50 pounds are allowed an additional one time pet fee of $50 per room. 2 dogs may be allowed.

La Quinta Inn New Orleans Airport
2610 Williams Blvd.
Kenner, LA
504-466-1401 (800-531-5900)
Dogs of all sizes are allowed. There are no additional pet fees. Dogs must be crated when left alone in the room, and they may not be left in the room for long periods. Dogs must be quiet, well behaved, leashed, and cleaned up after. Multiple dogs may be allowed.

Motel 6 - New Orleans Airport
2830 Loyola Dr
Kenner, LA
504-466-9666 (800-466-8356)
This motel welcomes your pets to stay with you.

Days Inn Kinder
13894 Highway 165
Kinder, LA
337-738-3240 (800-329-7466)
Dogs of all sizes are allowed. Dogs are allowed for a nightly pet fee.

Best Western La Place Inn
4289 Main Street
La Place, LA
985-651-4000 (800-780-7234)
Dogs are welcome at this hotel. There is a $10 one time pet fee.

Candlewood Suites Lafayette
2105 Kaliste Saloom Road
Lafayette, LA
337-984-6900 (877-270-6405)
Dogs up to 80 pounds are allowed. Pets allowed with an additional pet fee. Up to $75 for 1-6 nights and up to $150 for 7+ nights. A pet agreement must be signed at check-in.

Comfort Inn
1421 S.E. Evangeline Thruway
Lafayette, LA
337-232-9000 (877-424-6423)
Dogs up to 50 pounds are allowed.

Days Inn /Airport Lafayette
2501 SE Evangeline Thruway
Lafayette, LA
337-769-8000 (800-329-7466)
Dogs of all sizes are allowed. Dogs are allowed for a pet fee of $15.00 per pet per night.

Days Inn /University Lafayette
1620 N. University Ave
Lafayette, LA
337-237-8880 (800-329-7466)
Dogs of all sizes are allowed. Dogs are allowed for a pet fee.

Extended Stay America Lafayette - Airport
807 S. Hugh Wallis Rd.
Lafayette, LA
337-232-8313 (800-804-3724)
One dog is allowed per suite. There is a $25 per night additional pet fee up to $150 for an entire stay.

Holiday Inn Lafayette-Us167
2032 NE Evangeline Thruway
Lafayette, LA
337-233-6815 (877-270-6405)
Dogs of all sizes are allowed. Dogs are allowed for a pet fee of $50.00 per pet per night.

Knights Inn Lafayette
2810 NE Evangeline Thruway
Lafayette, LA
337-232-7285 (800-843-5644)
Dogs are welcome at this hotel. There is a $10 one time additional pet fee.

La Quinta Inn & Suites Lafayette
1015 West Pinhook Road
Lafayette, LA
337-291-1088 (800-531-5900)
Dogs up to 60 pounds are allowed. There are no additional pet fees. Dogs must be leashed and cleaned up after. No aggressive breeds are allowed. Multiple dogs may be allowed.

La Quinta Inn Lafayette
2100 NE Evangeline Thruway
Lafayette, LA
337-233-5610 (800-531-5900)
Dogs up to 100 pounds are allowed. There are no additional pet fees. Dogs must be leashed and cleaned up after. 2 dogs may be allowed.

Motel 6 - Lafayette
2724 Ne Evangeline Thrwy
Lafayette, LA
337-233-2055 (800-466-8356)
This motel welcomes your pets to stay with you.

Ramada Lafayette
120 E Kaliste Saloom Rd
Lafayette, LA
337-235-0858 (800-272-6232)
Dogs of all sizes are allowed. Dogs are allowed for a pet fee.

Red Roof Inn Lafayette, LA
1718 North University Avenue
Lafayette, LA
337-233-3339 (800-RED-ROOF)
One well-behaved family pet per room. Guest must notify front desk upon arrival. Guest is liable for any damages. In consideration of all guests, pets must never be left unattended in the guest rooms.

Residence Inn Lafayette Airport
128 James Comeaux Road
Lafayette, LA
337-232-3341 (800-331-3131)
In addition to offering a convenient location to business, shopping, dining, and entertainment areas, this all suite hotel also provides a number of in-house amenities, including a daily buffet breakfast and evening social hours. Dogs are allowed for an additional one time pet fee of $100 per room. Multiple dogs may be allowed.

Staybridge Suites Lafayette-Airport
129 E. Kaliste Saloom Road
Lafayette, LA
337-267-4666 (877-270-6405)
Dogs up to 80 pounds are allowed. Pets allowed with an additional pet fee. Up to $75 for 1-6 nights and up to $150 for 7+ nights. A pet agreement must be signed at check-in.

Studio 6 - Lafayette, La
1441 S.e. Evangeline Trw
Lafayette, LA
337-706-7644 (800-466-8356)
Your pets are welcome to stay here with you for a pet fee of $10 per day up to $50 for an entire stay.

Baymont Inn & Suites Lake Charles
1004 Hwy 171 North
Lake Charles, LA
337-310-7666 (877-229-6668)
Dogs are welcome at this hotel.

C.A.'s House
624 Ford Street
Lake Charles, LA
337-439-6672 (866-439-6672)
cas-house.com/
Beautifully restored, this early 1900's, 3 story Colonial home offers luxury accommodations, numerous

amenities, and is only minutes from all that Lake Charles has to offer. Dogs are allowed for no additional fee; they must be leashed and cleaned up after at all times. 2 dogs may be allowed.

La Quinta Inn Lake Charles
1320 MLK Hwy 171 N
Lake Charles, LA
337-436-5998 (800-531-5900)
Dogs of all sizes are allowed. There are no additional pet fees. There is a pet waiver to sign at check in. Dogs may not be left unattended, and they must be leashed and cleaned up after. Multiple dogs may be allowed.

Motel 6 - Lake Charles
335 Hwy 171
Lake Charles, LA
337-433-1773 (800-466-8356)
This motel welcomes your pets to stay with you.

Red Roof Inn Lake Charles
269 Highway 397
Lake Charles, LA
337-990-0165 (800-RED-ROOF)
One well-behaved family pet per room. Guest must notify front desk upon arrival. Guest is liable for any damages. In consideration of all guests, pets must never be left unattended in the guest rooms.

Super 8 /Sulphur Lake Charles
1350 East Prien Lake Road
Lake Charles, LA
337-477-1606 (800-800-8000)
Dogs are welcome at this hotel.

Extended Stay America New Orleans - Metairie
3300 I-10 S. Service Rd. W.
Metairie, LA
504-837-5599 (800-804-3724)
One dog is allowed per suite. There is a $25 per night additional pet fee up to $150 for an entire stay.

La Quinta Inn New Orleans Causeway
3100 I-10 Service Rd.
Metairie, LA
504-835-8511 (800-531-5900)
Dogs of all sizes are allowed. There are no additional pet fees. Dogs must be leashed and cleaned up after. Dogs must be removed for housekeeping. Multiple dogs may be allowed.

La Quinta Inn New Orleans Veterans
5900 Veterans Memorial Blvd
Metairie, LA
504-456-0003 (800-531-5900)

Dogs of all sizes are allowed. There are no additional pet fees. Dogs must be well behaved, leashed, and cleaned up after. Multiple dogs may be allowed.

Residence Inn New Orleans Metairie
Three Galleria Blvd
Metairie, LA
504-832-0888 (800-331-3131)
This all suite, upscale hotel gives a convenient location to local universities, major attractions and corporations, and to downtown New Orleans. Additionally, they offer a daily breakfast buffet and evening socials Monday through Thursday with light dinner fare. Dogs up to 50 pounds are allowed for an additional one time pet fee of $100 per room. 2 dogs may be allowed.

Super 8 Metairie
2421 Clearview Parkway
Metairie, LA
504-456-9081 (800-800-8000)
Dogs of all sizes are allowed. Dogs are allowed for a pet fee.

Holiday Inn Hotel & Suites Conference Center-Monroe
I-20 & 1051 US 165 Bypass
Monroe, LA
318-387-5100 (877-270-6405)
Dogs are welcome at this hotel. There is a $20 one time additional pet fee.

Motel 6 - Monroe, La
1501 Martin King Dr
Monroe, LA
318-322-5430 (800-466-8356)
This motel welcomes your pets to stay with you.

Ramada Limited
1601 Martin Luther King Drive
Monroe, LA
318-323-1600 (800-272-6232)
Dogs are welcome at this hotel.

Residence Inn Monroe
4960 Millhaven Road
Monroe, LA
318-387-0210 (800-331-3131)
This all suite hotel sits central to many of the city's star attractions, shopping, dining, and business areas, plus they offer a number of in-house amenities that include a daily buffet breakfast and evening social hours. Dogs are allowed for an additional one time pet fee of $75 per room. Multiple dogs may be allowed.

Holiday Inn Morgan City
520 Roderick St
Morgan City, LA
985-385-2200 (877-270-6405)
Dogs up to 50 pounds are allowed. Dogs are allowed for a pet fee of $50.00 per pet per stay.

Best Western Natchitoches Inn
5131 University Pkwy
Natchitoches, LA
318-352-6655 (800-780-7234)
Dogs of all sizes are allowed. Dogs are allowed for a pet fee of $25 per pet per stay.

Super 8 Natchitoches
5821 Highway 1 Bypass
Natchitoches, LA
318-352-1700 (800-800-8000)
Dogs are welcome at this hotel.

Travelodge Natchitoches
7624 Highway 1 Bypass
Natchitoches, LA
318-357-8281 (800-578-7878)
Dogs are welcome at this hotel.

Madewood Plantation
4250 H 308
Nepolianville, LA
985-369-7151 (800-375-7151)
madewood.com/index.html
This stunning Greek-Revival 1846 mansion is listed as a National Historical Landmark. In addition to the meticulously landscaped grounds and gardens, this site also shares a long and rich cultural and agricultural history. Dogs are allowed on the grounds. One dog up to 50 pounds is allowed per room at the Charlet House for an additional fee of $35 per night. Dogs must be human and hound friendly, leashed, and under their owner's control at all times.

Best Western Inn & Suites
2714 Highway 14
New Iberia, LA
337-364-3030 (800-780-7234)
Dogs are welcome at this hotel. There is a $25 one time pet fee.

Ramada Conference Center New Iberia
Intersection of Hwy. 90 & LA14
New Iberia, LA
337-367-1201 (800-272-6232)
Dogs of all sizes are allowed. Dogs are allowed for a pet fee of $100 per pet per stay.

Best Western Patio Downtown Motel
2820 Tulane Avenue
New Orleans, LA
504-822-0200 (800-780-7234)

Centrally located, The Best Western Patio is located just minutes from destinations such as The French Quarter, Harrah's Casino, The Riverwalk and the historic Garden District. There is a $35.00 pet fee per stay.

Chimes Bed and Breakfast
Constantinople St & Coliseum St
New Orleans, LA
504-899-2621 (800-729-4640)
Dogs that stay here need to like children and cats. Please clean up after your pet. One dog is allowed per room for an additional pet fee of $10 per night. Pets are not to be left alone in the room. Young dogs are not allowed and large dogs must be 3 years or older.

Creole Gardens Guesthouse
1415 Prytania Street
New Orleans, LA
504-569-8700 (866-569-8700)
creolegardens.com/
Authentic as the city itself, this inn offers a fun atmosphere, unique accommodations, a lush banana courtyard, and a great location to all local hotspots. It is also close to the pooch hotspots, such as the dog friendly Mississippi River levee at the end of Magazine Street and the off-lead dog park around the corner at Coliseum Square Park. Dogs are welcome here for no additional fee; they must be housebroken and hound and human friendly. Dogs must be leashed and under their owner's control at all times. Multiple dogs may be allowed.

Cresent City Guest House
612 Marigny Street
New Orleans, LA
504-944-8722
Dogs up to 50 pounds are allowed. There are no additional pet fees. 2 dogs may be allowed.

Drury Inn & Suites
820 Poydras Street
New Orleans, LA
504-529-7800 (800-378-7946)
Dogs of all sizes are allowed for no additional pet fee with a credit card on file, and there is a pet agreement to sign at check in.

Elysian Fields Inn
930 Elysian Fields
New Orleans, LA
504-948-9420
elysianguesthouse.com/
This beautiful guest home offers visitors a number of luxuries, plus they have a great location only steps

from the Mississippi River, the famed French Quarter, and all the local highlights. Well mannered dogs are allowed for a $25 per day additional pet fee. Dogs must be leashed and under their owner's control. 2 dogs may be allowed.

French Quarter Courtyard
1101 N Rampart
New Orleans, LA
504-522-7333 (800-290-4233)
neworleans.com/fqch/main.html
There is a $15 per night per pet additional fee. Multiple dogs may be allowed.

Hotel Monteleone
214 Royal Street
New Orleans, LA
504-523-3341
Located in the historic French Quarter, this renowned and recently restored luxury hotel will allow well mannered dogs accommodations for an additional one time fee of $100 plus $25 per night per pet. Multiple dogs may be allowed.

Lions Inn
2517 Chartres Street
New Orleans, LA
504-945-2339
they can't accept extra large dogs. There is no additional pet fees. Dogs must be hound and human friendly. There is also an enclosed garden for some off leash fun for the pooch.

Motel 6 - New Orleans
12330 I-10 Service Road
New Orleans, LA
504-240-2862 (800-466-8356)
Your pets are welcome to stay here with you.

Pontchartrain Hotel
2031 St. Charles Avenue
New Orleans, LA
504-524-0581
pontchartrainhotel.com
Located in the historic Garden District of New Orleans, The Pontchartrain Hotel has been open to guests since the 1920's. There are 118 rooms and suites, each individually designed. There is a $50 non-refundable pet fee, $10 each additional pet over 2 pets.

Quality Inn & Suites
8400 I-10 Service Road
New Orleans, LA
504-302-7300 (877-424-6423)
Dogs of all sizes are allowed. Dogs are allowed for a pet fee of $25.00

per pet per stay. Two dogs are allowed per room.

Rathbone Mansion
1244 Esplanade Avenue
New Orleans, LA
504-309-4479 (866-724-8140)
rathbonemansions.com/
In addition to providing an elegant and nostalgic ambiance, this inn also offers a great location only steps from the French Quarter, Bourbon Street, and all the local hotspots. Quiet, well mannered dogs are welcome for no additional fee with a credit card on file. There can be 1 large or 2 small to medium dogs per room. Dogs must be leashed and under owner's care at all times.

Residence Inn New Orleans Convention Center
345 St Joseph Street
New Orleans, LA
504-522-1300 (800-331-3131)
Located in the Warehouse/Arts district of the city near the convention center, the French Quarter, and to a number of area attractions, this all suite, upscale hotel also offers a number of in-house amenities, including a daily buffet breakfast, evening socials, and a 24 convenience market. Dogs are allowed for an additional one time pet fee of $100 per room. Multiple dogs may be allowed.

Sheraton New Orleans Hotel
500 Canal St.
New Orleans, LA
504-525-2500 (888-625-5144)
Dogs up to 80 pounds are allowed. There are no additional pet fees. Dogs are not allowed to be left alone in the room.

Staybridge Suites New Orleans
501 Tchoupitoulas At Poydras
New Orleans, LA
504-571-1818 (877-270-6405)
Dogs up to 80 pounds are allowed. Pets allowed with an additional pet fee. Up to $75 for 1-6 nights and up to $150 for 7+ nights. A pet agreement must be signed at check-in.

Studio 6 - New Orleans
12330 I-10 Service Road
New Orleans, LA
504-240-9778 (800-466-8356)
Your pets are welcome to stay here with you for a pet fee of $10 per day up to $50 for an entire stay.

W New Orleans

333 Poydras St.
New Orleans, LA
504-525-9444
Dogs up to 40 pounds are allowed for an additional one time pet fee of $100 per room with a credit card on file. Dogs must be declared at the time of registration. Pets receive a special welcome with a pet amenity kit that includes a custom pet bed, food and water dishes with a floor mat, a doggy menu, Pet-in-Room sign, treats, pet tag, a toy, and more. The concierge can also offer additional services such as dog-walking and information about local dog services and parks. Dogs must be removed or crated for housekeeping or for any in-room services.

Windsor Court Hotel
300 Gravier Street
New Orleans, LA
504-523-6000 (888-596-0955)
This luxury hotel offers all the comforts of a full service resort styled with a beautiful traditional English décor. It provides numerous amenities, a full service lounge, the popular New Orleans Grill, and a great location near several sites of interest. Dogs are allowed for an additional one time fee of $250 per room; they must be well mannered and kept leashed when not in the room. Dogs are not allowed in the food service areas. 2 dogs may be allowed.

Days Inn and Suites Opelousas
5761 I-49 South Service Road
Opelousas, LA
337-407-0004 (800-329-7466)
Dogs are welcome at this hotel.

Super 8 Opelousas
5791 I-49 S Service Road
Opelousas, LA
337-942-6250 (800-800-8000)
Dogs of all sizes are allowed. Dogs are allowed for a pet fee of $10.00 per pet per night.

Motel 6 - Baton Rouge Port Allen
2800 I-10 Frontage Rd
Port Allen, LA
225-343-5945 (800-466-8356)
This motel welcomes your pets to stay with you.

Days Inn Rayne
1125 Church Point Hwy
Rayne, LA
337-334-0000 (800-329-7466)
Dogs are welcome at this hotel.

Howard Johnson Inn Lafayette West
103 Harold Gauthe Drive
Scott, LA
337-593-0849 (800-446-4656)
Dogs are welcome at this hotel. There is a $10 daily pet fee.

Candlewood Suites Shreveport
5020 Hollywood Ave.
Shreveport, LA
013-186-3580 (877-270-6405)
Dogs up to 80 pounds are allowed. Pets allowed with an additional pet fee. Up to $75 for 1-6 nights and up to $150 for 7+ nights. A pet agreement must be signed at check-in.

Days Inn Airport Shreveport
4935 West Monkhouse Drive
Shreveport, LA
318-636-0080 (800-329-7466)
Dogs of all sizes are allowed. Dogs are allowed for a pet fee of $10 per pet per night.

Fairfield Place Inn
2221 Fairfield Avenue
Shreveport, LA
866-432-2632 (866-432-2632)
fairfieldbandb.com/
This inn offers the amenities of a modern hotel while keeping all the country charm of home with lush landscaping, verandah, and the aromas of freshly cooked and baked foods. One medium sized or 2 small dogs are allowed per room for an additional fee of $10 per night per room. Dogs must be quiet, well mannered, and leashed.

Jameson Inn Shreveport
6715 Rasberry Lane
Shreveport, LA
318-671-0731 (800-JAMESON (526-3766))
This contemporary hotel offers guests a number of amenities and is only minutes from several sites of interests and recreational opportunities. Quiet, well mannered dogs are allowed for an additional pet fee of $15 per night per room. Dogs must be leashed when out of the room. Multiple dogs may be allowed.

La Quinta Inn & Suites Shreveport Airport
6700 Financial Circle
Shreveport, LA
318-671-1100 (800-531-5900)
Dogs up to 100 pounds are allowed. There are no additional pet fees. Dogs must be leashed, cleaned up after, and a contact number must

be left with the front desk if there is a pet in the room alone. Multiple dogs may be allowed.

Motel 6 - Shreveport
7296 Greenwood Rd
Shreveport, LA
318-938-5342 (800-466-8356)
This motel welcomes your pets to stay with you.

Ramada Shreveport
5101 Westwood Park Dr
Shreveport, LA
318-631-2000 (800-272-6232)
Dogs are welcome at this hotel.

Residence Inn Shreveport Airport
4910 W Monkhouse Drive
Shreveport, LA
318-635-8000 (800-331-3131)
Besides offering a convenient location to businesses, casinos, shopping, dining, and recreation areas, this all suite hotel also provides a number of in-house amenities, including a daily buffet breakfast and complementary evening receptions Monday to Thursday. Dogs are allowed for an additional one time pet fee of $100 per room. Multiple dogs may be allowed.

Super 8 Shreveport
4911 Monkhouse Drive
Shreveport, LA
318-636-0771 (800-800-8000)
Dogs of all sizes are allowed. Dogs are allowed for a pet fee of $10.00 per pet per stay.

Travelodge LA Shreveport
2134 Greenwood Road
Shreveport, LA
318-425-7467 (800-578-7878)
Dogs are welcome at this hotel.

Motel 6 - New Orleans Slidell
136 Taos St
Slidell, LA
985-649-7925 (800-466-8356)
Your pets are welcome to stay here with you.

Butler Greenwood Plantation
8345 H 61
St Francisville, LA
225-635-6312
butlergreenwood.com/
This estate is considered one of the state's most impressive antebellum plantations in that it is still inhabited by members from the original family. Family members still personally conduct tours of the home, and visitors will find many wonders

around the more than 50 acres of landscaped grounds. Dogs are allowed for no additional pet fee. Dogs must be well behaved, stay off the furniture and beds, be leashed on the grounds, and cleaned up after at all times. 2 dogs may be allowed.

Lake Rosemound Inn
10473 Lindsey Lane
St Francisville, LA
504-899-0701
This lakeside inn sits in one of the most picturesque areas in plantation country, and they offer a number of amenities, and land and water recreation. Well mannered dogs are allowed for no additional fee. 2 dogs may be allowed.

Candlewood Suites Lake Charles-Sulphur
320 Arena Road
Sulphur, LA
337-528-5777 (877-270-6405)
Dogs up to 80 pounds are allowed. Pets allowed with an additional pet fee. Up to $75 for 1-6 nights and up to $150 for 7+ nights. A pet agreement must be signed at check-in.

Days Inn LA Sulphur
108 Dennis Ave
Sulphur, LA
337-312-0108 (800-329-7466)
Dogs of all sizes are allowed. Dogs are allowed for a nightly pet fee.

La Quinta Inn Sulphur
2600 South Ruth
Sulphur, LA
337-527-8303 (800-531-5900)
Dogs of all sizes are allowed. There are no additional pet fees. Dogs must be quiet, leashed, and cleaned up after. Multiple dogs may be allowed.

Super 8 LA Tallulah
I-20 Exit 171 & Hwy 65
Tallulah, LA
318-574-2000 (800-800-8000)
Dogs are welcome at this hotel.

Howard Johnson Hotel Thibodaux
203 N. Canal Blvd
Thibodaux, LA
985-447-9071 (800-446-4656)
Dogs of all sizes are allowed. Dogs are allowed for a pet fee of $10 per pet per stay

Motel 6 - West Monroe, La
401 Constitution Drive
West Monroe, LA
318-388-3810 (800-466-8356)

This motel welcomes your pets to stay with you.

Red Roof Inn West Monroe
102 Constitution Drive
West Monroe, LA
318-388-2420 (800-RED-ROOF)
One well-behaved family pet per room. Guest must notify front desk upon arrival. Guest is liable for any damages. In consideration of all guests, pets must never be left unattended in the guest rooms.

Best Western Zachary Inn
4030 Highway 19
Zachary, LA
225-658-2550 (800-780-7234)
Dogs of all sizes are allowed. Dogs are allowed for a pet fee.

Maine

Oceanside Meadows Inn
Prospect Harbor Road
Acadia Schoodic, ME
207-963-5557
oceaninn.com/
In addition to being a working inn since 1860, it is also a 200 acre preserve of numerous, carefully maintained habitats and eco-systems, and home to the Oceanside Meadows Institute for the Arts and Sciences' located in a restored barn between the inn's two guest buildings where they have a variety of events, classes, and musical performances. There are also gardens, a private beach, hiking trails, and many local recreational pursuits. Dogs of all sizes are allowed for an additional fee of $8 per night per pet. There is only one party with a pet allowed at a time in each of the two buildings. Dogs may not be left unattended at any time, and they must be very well behaved, leashed, and cleaned up after. 2 dogs may be allowed.

Arundel Meadows Inn
1024 Portland Road
Arundel, ME
207-985-3770
arundelmeadowsinn.com
From the months of April through December, this 1800's farm house (renovated in the 1990's) offers it's ambiance to guests and their four-legged companions. Dogs of all sizes are welcome for no additional pet fee, unless extra cleaning is required. Dogs must be well behaved, leashed, and cleaned up after. 2 dogs may be allowed.

Econo Lodge
170 Center Street
Auburn, ME
207-784-1331 (877-424-6423)
Dogs up to 60 pounds are allowed. Two dogs are allowed per room.

Comfort Inn Civic Center
281 Civic Center Dr.
Augusta, ME
207-623-1000 (877-424-6423)
Dogs of all sizes are allowed. Dogs are allowed for a pet fee of $10.00 per pet per night.

Econo Lodge Inn & Suites
390 Western Avenue
Augusta, ME
207-622-6371 (877-424-6423)
Dogs of all sizes are allowed.

Holiday Inn Augusta-Civic Center
110 Community Drive
Augusta, ME
207-622-4751 (877-270-6405)
Dogs are welcome at this hotel.

Motel 6 - Augusta, Me
18 Edison Drive
Augusta, ME
207-622-0000 (800-466-8356)
This motel welcomes your pets to stay with you.

Senator Inn & Spa
284 Western Avenue @ Turnpike 95
Augusta, ME
207-622-5804
Dogs of all sizes are allowed. Dogs are allowed for a pet fee.

Best Western White House Inn
155 Littlefield Avenue
Bangor, ME
207-862-3737 (800-780-7234)
Dogs are welcome at this hotel.

Comfort Inn
750 Hogan Rd.
Bangor, ME
207-942-7899 (877-424-6423)
Dogs of all sizes are allowed. Dogs are allowed for a pet fee of $10.00 per pet per stay.

Days Inn Bangor
250 Odlin Rd
Bangor, ME
207-942-8272 (800-329-7466)
Dogs of all sizes are allowed. Dogs are allowed for a nightly pet fee.

Econo Lodge Inn & Suites
327 Odlin Rd.
Bangor, ME
207-945-0111 (877-424-6423)

Dogs of all sizes are allowed.

Holiday Inn Bangor
404 Odlin Rd & 395 At Hermon
Bangor, ME
207-947-0101 (877-270-6405)
Dogs are welcome at this hotel.

Howard Johnson Inn - Bangor
336 Odlin Road/I-95
Bangor, ME
207-942-5251 (800-446-4656)
Dogs are welcome at this hotel.

Motel 6 - Bangor
1100 Hammond Street
Bangor, ME
207-947-6921 (800-466-8356)
This motel welcomes your pets to
stay with you.

Ramada Bangor
357 Odlin Rd
Bangor, ME
207-947-6961 (800-272-6232)
Dogs are welcome at this hotel.

Acadia Acres
205 Knox Road
Bar Harbor, ME
207-288-5055
acadiaacres.net/
There are now 2 pet friendly, fully
equipped homes available here; the
Knox House in Bar Harbor that offers
its own 150+ yard golf practice area,
with 6 acres of open fields for your
pup to run, and the Jordan Point
House on 23 acres in Lamoine that
overlooks the Bar Harbor Golf
Course and the water. This house
also has a 20' x 50' foot fenced
shaded yard with a doggy door so
pups can be comfortable inside or
out if the owners are away. Dogs of
all sizes are allowed for an additional
fee of $25 per dog. Dogs must be
house trained, well behaved, and
cleaned up after inside and out. The
phone listed is the daytime number;
for calls after 4 pm (to 9 pm) EST the
number is 207-288-4065. 2 dogs
may be allowed.

Balance Rock Inn
21 Albert Meadow
Bar Harbor, ME
207-288-2610 (800-753-0494)
balancerockinn.com
The oceanfront inn is within walking
distance of many restaurants and
shops in downtown Bar Harbor.
Choose from fourteen individually
decorated rooms at the inn, many of
which offer an ocean view and
private balcony. They also offer a
heated outdoor pool and fitness

room. Room rates for this inn
average $200 to $300 per night but
can start at $95 and go up to almost
$600 per night. There is also a $40
per day per pet fee. 2 dogs may be
allowed.

Bar Harbor Acadia Cottage Rentals
P.O. Box 265
Bar Harbor, ME
207-288-0307
These cottage rentals within up to
30 minutes of Bar Harbor and
Acadia allow dogs in most of the
cabins.

Days Inn Bar Harbor
120 Eden Street
Bar Harbor, ME
207-288-3321 (800-329-7466)
Dogs of all sizes are allowed. Dogs
are allowed for a pet fee of $10 per
pet per stay.

Gale's Gardens Guesthouses
Daylily Lane
Bar Harbor, ME
207-733-8811
galesgardensguesthouse.com
There are two vacation rentals
available that can be rented
separately or together. The dog-
friendly properties are located one
mile from the Acadia National Park
Entrance and four miles to the
center of Bar Harbor.

Hanscom's Motel and Cottages
273 H 3
Bar Harbor, ME
207-288-3744
hanscomsmotel.com/
This vintage motor court is only a 5
minute walk to a private rocky
beach, sits among giant oaks, white
pines, and landscaped
grounds/gardens, has shady picnic
areas with barbecues, and an
outdoor heated pool with a roomy
sundeck. Dogs of all sizes are
allowed for an additional fee of $8
per night per pet. Dogs may be left
alone only for short periods and
only if they will be quiet and well
behaved. Dogs must be leashed
and cleaned up after at all times. 2
dogs may be allowed.

Hutchins Mountain View Cottages
286 H 3
Bar Harbor, ME
207-288-4833 (800-775-4833)
hutchinscottages.com/
Trees and grazing fields grace this
20 acre country retreat that is only a
mile from the Acadia National
Park's visitor center. Dogs of all
sizes are welcome for no additional

pet fee. Dogs must be quiet, well
behaved, leashed, and cleaned up
after in common areas. 2 dogs may
be allowed.

Rose Eden Cottages
864 State Highway 3
Bar Harbor, ME
207-288-3038
roseeden.com
This small cottage complex offers ten
non-smoking cottages and some of
them have kitchenettes. They are
located just 4 miles to the entrance
of Acadia National Park and about
10 minutes from downtown Bar
Harbor. Harbor Point Beach, which
allows leashed dogs, is located
within walking distance. Dogs are
allowed for an additional fee of $10
per night per pet. 2 dogs may be
allowed.

Ryan Estate Rentals
Eagle Lake - Road Route #233
Bar Harbor, ME
207-288-5154 (Winter 520-760-
0479)
ryanestaterentals.com
These vacation rentals consist of a
pet-friendly large summer house, and
3 pet-friendly apartments on seven
acres surrounded by Acadia National
Park. You can walk right into the
park from here. There is no smoking
on the property.

Summertime Cottages
1 Bloomfield Road
Bar Harbor, ME
207-288-2893
summertimebarharbor.com/
Secluded by giant pine tress and
about a block from the ocean, these
vacation rentals offer a great starting
point for several activities and
recreation; 150 miles of hiking trails,
56 miles of carriage roads, and
proximity to the tallest summit on the
Eastern seaboard where the US gets
its first light of sun each day. Dogs of
all sizes are welcome for no
additional fee; Rottwelers and Pit
Bulls are not allowed. Dogs must be
well mannered, leashed, and cleaned
up after. Multiple dogs may be
allowed.

The Ledgelawn Inn
66 Mount Desert Street
Bar Harbor, ME
207-288-4596 (800-274-5334)
This bed and breakfast inn has a $25
per night pet charge. The B&B is
totally non-smoking and there are 8
pet rooms, each with separate
entrances.

Town and Country Cottage
230 H 3
Bar Harbor, ME
207-288-3439
townandcountrycottage.com/
Although only minutes from several other attractions and activities, this nicely appointed cottage features a large furnished deck with a barbecue grill, and a sizable lawn with a woodland meadow beyond. Dogs of all sizes are welcome for no additional pet fee. Dogs must be quiet, leashed, cleaned up after, and crated when left alone in the room. Dogs may only be left alone in the room for a short time and then only if they will be well behaved. 2 dogs may be allowed.

Holiday Inn Bath (Brunswick Area)
139 Richardson St
Bath, ME
207-443-9741 (877-270-6405)
Dogs are welcome at this hotel.

The Inn at Bath
969 Washington Street
Bath, ME
207-443-4294 (800-423-0964)
innatbath.com/
This well appointed 1800's Greek revival home sits among the trees within easy walking distance to town, and they are also close to two ocean beaches and numerous recreational opportunities. Dogs of all sizes are allowed for an additional fee of $15 per night per pet. Dogs must be quiet, leashed, and cleaned up after. Dogs may not be left alone in the room at any time. 2 dogs may be allowed.

Comfort Inn Ocean's Edge
159 Searsport Ave
Belfast, ME
207-338-2090 (877-424-6423)
Dogs of all sizes are allowed. Dogs are allowed for a pet fee of $10 per pet per night.

Day Lily Cottage
Call to Arrange
Belfast, ME
207-342-5444
landworkswaterfront.com
This vacation rental is a newly remodeled 1920 stone bungalow nestled in lovely country gardens. The cottage sits 20 feet from stairs leading to the beach. There are three bedrooms, two baths and can sleep 6. Pets welcome with $125.00 non-refundable one time fee. No Smoking. Can be rented with Tranquility Cottage next door to sleep 12.

Bethel Inn and Country Club
7 Broad Street
Bethel, ME
207-824-2175
bethelinn.com
This country resort allows dogs in some of their rooms. Pets are welcome in some of guest buildings and luxury townhouses, but not in the Chapman Building or the main inn. All well-behaved dogs up to 50 pounds are allowed. There is a $23 per day per pet fee. During the winter, dogs are also allowed on a special 2km cross-country skijoring trail. 2 dogs may be allowed.

Sudbury Inn
151 Main Street
Bethel, ME
207-824-2174
sudburyinn.com
Dogs of all sizes are allowed in the carriage house only and during selected seasons. There is a $15 per night pet fee. 2 dogs may be allowed.

The Inn at the Rostay
186 Mayville Road
Bethel, ME
888-754-0072
the fee is per room or per pet depending on the type and size of the dog. They are not allowed on the beds and dogs are not allowed to be left alone in the room. There is a pet policy to sign at check in.

Comfort Suites
45 Barra Road
Biddeford, ME
207-294-6464 (877-424-6423)
Dogs up to 100 pounds are allowed. Dogs are allowed for a pet fee of $35.00 per pet per stay. Three or more dogs may be allowed.

Rodeway Inn & Suites
287 Bath Road
Brunswick, ME
207-729-6661 (877-424-6423)
Dogs up to 50 pounds are allowed. Dogs are allowed for a pet fee of $10.00 per pet per night. Two dogs are allowed per room.

Calais Motor Inn
293 Main Street
Calais, ME
207-454-7111
There is a $10 per stay pet charge. Multiple dogs may be allowed.

International Motel
276 Main Street

Calais, ME
207-454-7515
Dogs are allowed in the older building only and not in the motel office. There are no additional pet fees. Multiple dogs may be allowed.

Blue Harbor House
67 Elm Street
Camden, ME
207-236-3196 (800-248-3196)
blueharborhouse.com/
Dogs are allowed in one of the suites in the Carriage House at this Village Inn. There is an additional one time pet fee of $25 per room. 2 dogs may be allowed.

Camden Riverhouse Hotel & Inns
11 Tannery Lane
Camden, ME
207-236-0500 (800-755-7483)
camdenmaine.com
This downtown hotel allows your dog of any size for $15 per night additional pet fee. Dogs may not be left unattended in the room.

Fisherman's Cottage
113 Bayview Street
Camden, ME
207-342-5444
landworkswaterfront.com
100-year-old fisherman cottage in a deluxe neighborhood. Ocean view from the master bedroom, living room, and kitchen. An easy walk to Camden, easy access to beach and beautiful walking and biking roads. Stone terrace across front of house for ocean harbor viewing. Available year-round. Three bedrooms, two baths, linens provided, telephone, television, cable, VCR, washer/dryer, ocean view. Sleeps six. Pets welcome with non-refundable deposit of $125.00. No Smoking. $1,800 per week.

Lord Camden Inn
24 Main Street
Camden, ME
207-236-4325 (800-336-4325)
lordcamdeninn.com
The Lord Camden Inn is located in the heart of downtown Camden. Many rooms boast ocean views, full balconies and kitchenettes. Dogs are welcome and pampered at the Lord Camden Inn with doggy biscuits and a list of activities and day care options awaiting your arrival in your room. Two well-behaved dogs are allowed per room (no size restrictions), and dogs are not to be left unattended. There is an additional $20 per pet per night fee. The hotel is open year round.

Inn By The Sea
40 Bowery Beach Road
Cape Elizabeth, ME
207-799-3134 (800-888-4287)
innbythesea.com/
Thanks to one of our readers for these comments: 'This hotel is an amazing place for dog lovers. It's a four star hotel that treats your puppy like any other hotel guest. There are two suites (bedroom, kitchen, living room) that are specifically appointed for dogs. Water dishes, biscuits, towels for paws, and outside hoses are provided. There are four nearby state parks and the hotel itself borders a feral area which my dog spent hours on end exploring. There's even a fenced-in kennel area, complete with a dog house, if you want to leave your pet for an hour and go for dinner. Wonderful place, they love dogs, great recreation, beautiful rooms, great hotel restaurant - truly a superb experience.' This hotel also offers dog walking service with 24-hour notification. They even have a special pet menu with items like gourmet chuck burgers, grilled range chicken, NY sirloin strip steak with potatoes and vegetables, and for dessert, vanilla ice cream or doggie bon bons. If you are there during Thanksgiving, Christmas or the Fourth of July, they offer a special pet holiday menu. The hotel asks that all pets be kept on a leash when not in their suite and that pets are not left alone in the suite. When making a reservation, they do require that you tell them you are bringing your pet. There is no additional pet fee. All rooms are non-smoking. Multiple dogs may be allowed.

Castine Harbor Lodge
147 Perkins Street
Castine, ME
207-326-4335
castinemaine.com/
This 1893 waterfront hotel features 250 feet of ocean-facing porches overlooking the bay, clay tennis courts, one of the country's oldest 9-hole golf courses, a steak and seafood restaurant and bar, and access to several historic walking trails. Dogs of all sizes are allowed for an additional fee of $10 per night per pet. Dogs may not be left alone in the room at any time, and they must be very well behaved, always kept leashed, and cleaned up after. 2 dogs may be allowed.

The Pilgrim's Inn

20 Main Street
Deer Isle, ME
207-348-6615 (888-778-7505)
pilgrimsinn.com/
This 1793 restored historic inn overlooks the picturesque Northwest Harbor, features a tavern restaurant, a large mill pond, and offers 3 cottages that are pet friendly. Dogs of all sizes are welcome, but there can only be 1 large or 2 small to medium dogs per room. Dogs may only be left alone in the room while dining on the property, and they must be leashed and cleaned up after at all times.

Milliken House
29 Washington Street
Eastport, ME
207-853-2955
Well behaved dogs of all sizes are allowed. There are no additional pet fees. 2 dogs may be allowed.

Sheepscot River Inn
306 Eddy Road
Edgecomb, ME
207-882-6343
Dogs of all sizes are allowed for no additional fee for their 1st visit here. There is a $15 per night per room fee thereafter.

Holiday Inn Ellsworth(Acadia Natl Pk Area)
215 High Street
Ellsworth, ME
207-667-9341 (877-270-6405)
Dogs of all sizes are allowed. Dogs are allowed for a nightly pet fee.

Best Western Freeport Inn
31 US Route 1
Freeport, ME
207-865-3106 (800-780-7234)
Dogs are welcome at this hotel.

Harraseeket Inn
162 Main Street
Freeport, ME
207-865-9377 (800-342-6423)
harraseeketinn.com/
Whether it's for the perfect vacation package, a shopping adventure (over 170 shops only 2 blocks away), or a romantic getaway, this inn also offers amenities like a live Jazz brunch on Sundays, award winning dining, and an indoor pool. Dogs of all sizes are allowed for an additional fee of $25 per night per pet, and advance notification is required. For their canine guests they place a doggy bed, a small can of dog food, water and food dishes, 4 small clean-up duty bags, and a small treat in the room. Dogs must

be kept leashed when out of the room and they must be cleaned up after at all times. Dogs are not to be left alone in the room for more than 2 hours and only then if they will be quiet and well mannered. Dogs must be removed for housekeeping, and they are not allowed in the main building. 2 dogs may be allowed.

The Main Idyll Motor Court
1411 H 1
Freeport, ME
207-865-4201
maineidyll.com/
This motor court features 20 cottages set among a grove of trees with play and barbecue/picnic areas, hiking trails, and they also provide a doggie comfort station. Dogs of all sizes are allowed for an additional $4 per night per pet. Dogs must be leased and cleaned up after. They may only be left for a short time alone in the room, and then only if they will be quiet and well behaved. 2 dogs may be allowed.

The Crocker House
967 Point Road
Hancock, ME
207-422-6808 (877-715-6017)
crockerhouse.com/
Built in 1884 (restored 1986), this seasonally operating inn sits only 300 feet from the water, offers 11 uniquely differing rooms, a restaurant and full bar, and they are within easy walking distance to several activities and attractions. Dogs of all sizes are welcome for no additional pet fee. Dogs must be under owner's control

The Hounds Tooth Inn
82 Summer Street
Kennebunk, ME
207-985-0117
houndstoothinn.biz/#
Sitting on about an acre of landscaped grounds, this 4 bedroom, 1843 farmhouse offers spacious accommodations and a large fenced-in area of the back patio where guests can watch their pooches have a good time. Dogs are allowed for an additional fee of $10 per night per pet. Dogs may not be left alone in the room, and they must be under their owner's control at all times. Dogs are allowed throughout the grounds and common areas of the house, but they are not allowed in the kitchen. Multiple dogs may be allowed.

Captain Jefferds Inn
5 Pearl St
Kennebunkport, ME

207-967-2311 (800-839-6844)
captainjefferdsinn.com
This B&B has 5 outside entrance dog-friendly rooms. There is a $30 per day per pet additional pet fee.

Lodge At Turbat's Creek
Turbats Creek Rd at Ocean Avenue
Kennebunkport, ME
207-967-8700
There is an additional one time pet fee of $25 per room. Multiple dogs may be allowed.

The Colony Hotel
140 Ocean Avenue
Kennebunkport, ME
207-967-3331
Dogs of all sizes are allowed. There is a $30 per night per pet additional fee.

The Yachtsman Lodge and Marina
Ocean Avenue
Kennebunkport, ME
207-967-2511
yachtsmanlodge.com/
Sitting right on the waterfront with all the rooms having its own patio overlooking the river, has inspired the redesign of the rooms to reflect those of a luxury yacht. This seasonal inn also provides a great starting point to several local attractions. Dogs of all sizes are allowed for an additional fee of $25 per night per pet, and they must be declared at the time of registration as pet friendly rooms are limited. Dogs may be left alone only for short periods and only if they will be quiet, well behaved, and a contact number is left with the front desk. Dogs must be leashed and cleaned up after at all times. 2 dogs may be allowed.

Enchanted Nights
29 Wentworth Street
Kittery, ME
207-439-1489
Dogs of all sizes are allowed. There are no additional pet fees. Dogs are not allowed to be left unattended. 2 dogs may be allowed.

Motel 6 - Lewiston
516 Pleasant Street
Lewiston, ME
207-782-6558 (800-466-8356)
This motel welcomes your pets to stay with you.

Travelodge Lewiston
1243 Lisbon St
Lewiston, ME
207-784-0600 (800-578-7878)
Dogs are welcome at this hotel.

Pine Grove Cottages
2076 Atlantic H
Lincolnville, ME
207-236-2929 (800-530-5265)
pinegrovemaine.com/
Offering 9 well-equipped cottages on 3 pine treed acres, all with private decks and barbecue's, this seasonal retreat is also close to several other attractions, eateries, shops, and recreation. Dogs of all sizes are welcome for no additional pet fee. Dogs may be left alone only for short periods and only if they will be quiet, well behaved, and crated. Please keep dogs off the furniture, and they must be leashed and cleaned up after at all times. They also invite your pooch in when you register for some water and a cookie, and if ok with the pet owner they would like to take a photo of the pet to go with all the other doggy guest photos. 2 dogs may be allowed.

Gateway Inn
Route 157
Medway, ME
207-746-3193
Dogs of all sizes are allowed. There are no additional pet fees.

Econo Lodge Inn & Suites
740 Central Street
Millinocket, ME
207 723-4555 (877-424-6423)
Dogs up to 110 pounds are allowed. Dogs are allowed for a pet fee of $10.00 per pet per night. Two dogs are allowed per room.

Waves Oceanfront Resort and Hotel
87 W Grand Avenue
Old Orchard Beach, ME
207-934-4949
Dogs of all sizes are allowed. There is a $10 per night per pet fee and a pet policy to sign at check in. This place will only take pets after Labor Day. 2 dogs may be allowed.

Black Bear Inn & Conference Center
4 Godfrey Drive
Orono, ME
207-866-7120
Dogs of all sizes are allowed. Dogs are allowed for a pet fee of $10.00 per pet per night.

Clarion Hotel Airport
1230 Congress St
Portland, ME
207-774-5611 (877-424-6423)

Dogs up to 50 pounds are allowed.

Embassy Suites
1050 Westbrook Street
Portland, ME
207-775-2200 (800-EMBASSY (362-2779))
This luxury, all suite hotel offers a number of on site amenities for business and leisure travelers, plus a convenient location to business, shopping, dining, and entertainment areas. They also offer a complimentary cooked-to-order breakfast and a Manager's reception every evening. Dogs up to 75 pounds are allowed for an additional one time pet fee of $50 per room. 2 dogs may be allowed.

Howard Johnson Plaza - Portland
155 Riverside Street/I-95
Portland, ME
207-774-5861 (800-446 4656)
Dogs are welcome at this hotel. There is a $50 refundable pet deposit.

Motel 6 - Portland, Me
One Riverside Street
Portland, ME
207-775-0111 (800-466-8356)
This motel welcomes your pets to stay with you.

The Eastland Park Hotel
157 High Street
Portland, ME
207-775-2872 (888-671-8008)
eastlandparkhotel.com/
There are numerous amenities for the business or leisure traveler at this upscale hotel, and being located in the heart of the downtown area brings guests only steps away from the Old Port Waterfront, and a number of business and recreational sites. Pooches can get a touch of the elegance here as well with their own welcome kit that includes an informational booklet, a doggy treat, a toy to take home, and cleaned up bags. Dogs are allowed for an additional pet fee of $25 per night per room, and there is a pet agreement to sign at check in. Dogs must be crated when left alone in the room. Multiple dogs may be allowed.

The Inn at St John
939 Congress Street
Portland, ME
207-773-6481 (800-636-9127)
innatstjohn.com/index.php
This 1897 inn, originally built to accommodate train travelers, now offers free pick up for plane, train, or bus travelers, and it has been fully

restored in European style with 3 levels of lodging offered. Dogs of all sizes are allowed for an additional fee of $10 per night per pet. Dogs may not be left alone in the room at any time, and they have a list of pet sitters if the need arises. Dogs must be well mannered, leashed, and cleaned up after. 2 dogs may be allowed.

Old Granite Inn
546 Main Street
Rockland, ME
207-594-9036
Well behaved pets of all sizes are allowed. There are no additional pet fees. Dogs are not allowed to be left alone in the room, and they must be very good around cats. 2 dogs may be allowed.

Country Inn at Camden/Rockport
8 Country Inn Way
Rockport, ME
207-236-2725 (888-707-3945)
countryinnmaine.com
This inn near Camden and Rockport allows up to two dogs per suite.

Linnel Motel
986 Prospect Avenue
Rumford, ME
207-364-4511 (800-446-9038)
Dogs of all sizes are allowed. There is a $10 per night per pet additional fee and dogs may not be left unattended. Leash at all times when on the grounds.

The Perennial Inn
141 Jed Martin Road
Rumford Point, ME
207-369-0309
There is a $20 per stay pet fee. 2 dogs may be allowed.

Super 8 Kennebunkport Area Sanford
1892 Main St.
Sanford, ME
207-324-8823 (800-800-8000)
Dogs of all sizes are allowed. Dogs are allowed for a pet fee of $15.00 per pet per night.

Extended Stay America Portland - Scarborough
2 Ashley Dr.
Scarborough, ME
207-883-0554 (800-804-3724)
One dog is allowed per suite. There is a $25 per night additional pet fee up to $150 for an entire stay.

Residence Inn Portland Scarborough
800 Roundwood Drive

Scarborough, ME
207-883-0400 (800-331-3131)
Some of the amenities at this all-suite inn include a daily buffet breakfast, evening socials with light dinner fare 4 nights a week, a Sport Court, and a complimentary grocery shopping service. Dogs are allowed for an additional one time pet fee of $75 per room, and there is a pet policy to sign at check in. Multiple dogs may be allowed.

TownePlace Suites Portland Scarborough
700 Roundwood Drive
Scarborough, ME
207-883-6800 (800-491-2268)
Besides being located only a short walk to the state's largest shopping mall and only a few minutes to Old Port, this all suite inn also offers a number of on-site amenities. Dogs are allowed for an additional one time fee of $75 per room. 2 dogs may be allowed.

Best Western Merry Manor Inn
700 Main Street
South Portland, ME
207-774-6151 (800-780-7234)
Dogs are welcome at this hotel.

Comfort Inn Airport
90 Maine Mall Rd.
South Portland, ME
207-775-0409 (877-424-6423)
Dogs of all sizes are allowed. Dogs are allowed for a pet fee of $25.00 per pet per stay.

Days Inn Airport South Portland
461 Maine Mall Road/I-95
South Portland, ME
207-772-3450 (800-329-7466)
Dogs of all sizes are allowed. Dogs are allowed for a pet fee of $10.00 per pet per night.

Holiday Inn Express Hotel & Suites South Portland
303 Sable Oaks Drive
South Portland, ME
207-775-3900 (877-270-6405)
Dogs of all sizes are allowed. Dogs are allowed for a pet fee.

Howard Johnson Hotel - South Portland
675 Main Street I-95
South Portland, ME
207-775-5343 (800-446-4656)
Dogs are welcome at this hotel.

Sheraton South Portland Hotel
363 Maines Mall Rd.
South Portland, ME

207-775-6161 (888-625-5144)
Dogs up to 80 pounds are allowed. There are no additional pet fees. Dogs are not allowed to be left alone in the room.

The Willard Beach House
14 Myrtle Avenue
South Portland, ME
207-799-9824
vacationinmaine.net/
Both of their pet friendly rentals, the Willard Beach House condo and the Carriage House with its private back yard, offer views of the ocean and Willard Beach, which has an oceanside walkway connecting a lighthouse and a fort. (Please see our Willard Beach listing for pet restrictions.) Dogs of all sizes are welcome for no additional pet fee. Dogs must be leashed and cleaned up after. 2 dogs may be allowed.

Flander's Bay Cabins
22 Harbor View Drive
Sullivan, ME
207-422-6408
Dogs of all sizes are allowed for a $35 one time fee per week. One dog is allowed during off season and up to 2 dogs are allowed during their main season months. Dogs are not allowed to be left alone in the cabins. 2 dogs may be allowed.

Harbor Watch Motel
Swans Island, ME
207-526-4563
To get to this motel on Swans Island, take the ferry from Bass Harbor in Southwest Harbor to Swans Island. Leashed dogs and cars are allowed on the Maine State Ferries. One dog is allowed for an additional $15 per day pet fee. Dogs must be quiet, well mannered, and have their own bedding.

The East Wind Inn
21 Mechanic Street
Tenants Harbor, ME
207-372-6366 (800-241-VIEW (8439))
eastwindinn.com/
This seasonal Historic Inn sits at the water's edge and has 23 spacious guest rooms, a wrap-around porch for watching all the harbor activity, and a central location to numerous other activities and recreation. One dog of any size is allowed for an additional fee of $15 per night. Dogs may not be left alone in the room at any time, and they must be leashed and cleaned up after.

Econo Lodge

455 Kennedy Memorial Dr.
Waterville, ME
207-872-5577 (877-424-6423)
Dogs of all sizes are allowed. Dogs
are allowed for a pet fee of
$10.00/pet per pet per night.

Fireside Inn & Suites
356 Main Street
Waterville, ME
207-873-3335
Dogs are welcome at this hotel.

Holiday Inn Waterville
375 Upper Main St
Waterville, ME
207-873-0111 (877-270-6405)
Dogs of all sizes are allowed. Dogs
are allowed for a pet fee.

Comfort Inn & Suites
1026 US Route 2 East
Wilton, ME
207-645-5155 (877-424-6423)
Dogs up to 50 pounds are allowed.
Dogs are allowed for a pet fee of

$35.00 per pet per night.

Maryland

Clarion Hotel
980 Hospitality Way
Aberdeen, MD
410-273-6300 (877-424-6423)
Dogs of all sizes are allowed.

Red Roof Inn Aberdeen
988 Hospitality Way
Aberdeen, MD
410-273-7800 (800-RED-ROOF)
One well-behaved family pet per
room. Guest must notify front desk
upon arrival. Guest is liable for any
damages. In consideration of all
guests, pets must never be left
unattended in the guest rooms.

Super 8 MD Aberdeen
1008 Beards Hill Rd
Aberdeen, MD
410-272-5420 (800-800-8000)
Dogs are welcome at this hotel.

The Clarion Aberdeen
980 Hospitality Way
Aberdeen, MD
410-273-6300 (877-424-6423)
clarionaberdeen.com/
This premier full service hotel allows
pets for no additional fee. Multiple
dogs may be allowed.

Travelodge Hotel Aberdeen
820 West Bel Air Ave
Aberdeen, MD

410-272-5500 (800-578-7878)
Dogs are welcome at this hotel.

Extended Stay America Annapolis -
Naval Academy
1 Womack Dr.
Annapolis, MD
410-571-9988 (800-804-3724)
One dog is allowed per suite. There
is a $25 per night additional pet fee
up to $150 for an entire stay.

Homestead Studio Suites Annapolis
- Naval Academy
120 Admiral Chochrane Dr.
Annapolis, MD
410-571-6600 (800-804-3724)
One dog is allowed per suite. There
is a $25 per night additional pet fee
up to $150 for an entire stay.

Loews Annapolis Hotel
126 West Street
Annapolis, MD
410-263-7777
All well-behaved dogs of any size
are welcome. This upscale hotel
offers their "Loews Loves Pets"
program which includes special pet
treats, local dog walking routes, and
a list of nearby pet-friendly places to
visit. There is an additional one time
pet cleaning fee of $25 per room.

Quality Inn
1542 Whitehall Rd.
Annapolis, MD
410-974-4440 (877-424-6423)
Dogs of all sizes are allowed. Two
dogs are allowed per room.

Residence Inn Annapolis
170 Admiral Cochrane Drive
Annapolis, MD
410-573-0300 (888-236-2427)
In addition to offering a convenient
location to historical, shopping,
dining, and entertainment areas,
this hotel also provides a number of
in-house amenities, including a
daily buffet breakfast, and a
Manager's reception Monday
through Thursday. Dogs are
allowed for an additional one time
pet fee of $150 per room. Multiple
dogs may be allowed.

Sheraton Annapolis Hotel
173 Jennifer Rd.
Annapolis, MD
410-266-3131 (888-625-5144)
Dogs up to 80 pounds are allowed.
There are no additional pet fees.
Dogs are not allowed to be left
alone in the room.

TownePlace Suites Baltimore/Fort

Meade
120 National Business Parkway
Annapolis Junction, MD
301-498-7477 (800-257-3000)
Besides offering a number of in-
house amenities for all level of
travelers, this all suite hotel also
offers a good location to major
corporations, shopping, dining, and
entertainment areas. Dogs are
allowed for an additional one time
fee of $100 per room. 2 dogs may be
allowed.

Brookshire Suites
120 E. Lombard Street
Baltimore, MD
410-625-1300
All well-behaved dogs are welcome
at this suites hotel. There are no pet
fees. Multiple dogs may be allowed.

Comfort Inn BWI Airport
6921 Baltimore-Annap. Blvd.
Baltimore, MD
410-789-9100 (877-424-6423)
Dogs of all sizes are allowed.

Four Points by Sheraton BWI Airport
7032 Elm Rd.
Baltimore, MD
410-859-3300 (888-625-5144)
Dogs of all sizes are allowed. There
is a $25 per night pet fee per pet.
Dogs are not allowed to be left alone
in the room.

Hilton Hotel
1726 Reisterstown Road
Baltimore, MD
410-653-1100 (800-HILTONS (445-
8667))
This luxury hotel offers a number of
on site amenities for business and
leisure travelers, including a totally
renovated hotel with many upgrades,
an attached comprehensive fitness
center, a fully equipped business
center, fine dining, and a Grand
Ballroom. Dogs up to 75 pounds are
allowed for an additional one time
pet fee of $75 per room. 2 dogs may
be allowed.

Hotel Monaco Baltimore
2 N Charles Street
Baltimore, MD
443-692-6170 (800-KIMPTON (546-
7866))
monaco-baltimore.com/
This elegant hotel is located
downtown in the landmark 1906
Baltimore & Ohio Railroad
headquarters, and there have been
more than 50 earth-friendly practices
and products implemented here
since this Kimpton Hotel formally
launched their EarthCare program in

2005. Some of these include an in-house water purification system, all organic and sustainable foods coffee/tea, organic/biodynamic and sustainable wines, and sustainable seafood. Additionally, with a commitment to social responsibility, there is an emphasis on waste reduction, energy and water management, and supporting like-minded sources and organizations. Dogs are allowed for no additional fee; plus they receive a pet amenity package upon arrival. Multiple dogs may be allowed.

Motel 6 - Baltimore West
1654 Whitehead Court
Baltimore, MD
410-265-7660 (800-466-8356)
This motel welcomes your pets to stay with you.

Pier 5 Hotel
711 Eastern Avenue
Baltimore, MD
410-539-2000
The entire hotel offers a smoke free environment. All well-behaved dogs are welcome. There are no pet fees with a credit card on file,,, a $50 refundable cash deposit is required if there is no credit card on file. Multiple dogs may be allowed.

Residence Inn Baltimore Downtown/ Inner Harbor
17 Light Street
Baltimore, MD
410-962-1220 (800-331-3131)
Sitting only a short walk from the shopping, dining, and entertainment venues of the city's Inner Harbor, this all suite, upscale hotel also offers a number of in-house amenities including a daily buffet breakfast and an evening reception. Dogs up to 100 pounds are allowed for an additional one time pet fee of $100 per room. 2 dogs may be allowed.

Residence Inn Baltimore White Marsh
4980 Mercantile Road
Baltimore, MD
410-933-9554 (888-236-2427)
This all suite hotel sits only a couple of miles to a wide variety of Baltimore's star attractions' such as the Inner Harbor, major stadiums, and shopping arenas, plus they also provide a number of in-house amenities - including a daily buffet breakfast, Manager's evening socials, and a Sport Court. Dogs are allowed for an additional one time pet fee of $75 per room. Dogs must be crated or removed for

housekeeping and a contact number left with the front desk if a pet is in the room alone. 2 dogs may be allowed.

Sheraton Baltimore City Center Hotel (formally Wyndham)
101 W Fayette Street
Baltimore, MD
410-752-1100 (888-625-5144)
Dogs up to 80 pounds are allowed for no additional fee. There is a pet waiver to sign at check in. Dogs must be well mannered, leashed or crated, and cleaned up after. Multiple dogs may be allowed.

Sheraton Baltimore North Hotel
903 Dulaney Valley Blvd.
Baltimore, MD
410-321-7400 (888-625-5144)
Dogs of all sizes are allowed. There are no additional pet fees. Dogs are not allowed to be left alone in the room.

Sheraton Inner Harbor Hotel
300 South Charles St.
Baltimore, MD
410-962-8300 (888-625-5144)
Dogs up to 50 pounds are allowed. There are no additional pet fees. Dogs are not allowed to be left alone in the room.

Sleep Inn & Suites Airport
6055 Belle Grove Rd
Baltimore, MD
410-789-7223 (877-424-6423)
Dogs of all sizes are allowed.

Super 8 /Essex Area Baltimore
98 Stemmers Run Rd
Baltimore, MD
410-780-0030 (800-800-8000)
Dogs of all sizes are allowed. Dogs are allowed for a pet fee.

The Admiral Fell Inn
888 South Broadway
Baltimore, MD
410-522-7377
harbormagic.com
The Admiral Fell Inn is a historic inn in the waterfront village of Fell's Point. All well-behaved dogs are welcome and there no additional pet fees. Multiple dogs may be allowed.

Tremont Park Hotel
8 East Pleasant Street
Baltimore, MD
410-576-1200 (800-TREMONT)
Dogs may stay in four of the one bedroom suites in this hotel. They'll provide bowls for food and water, a

treat and a Pampered Pet Placement. There is a $10 pet service fee that will be donated to the American Humane Society if there is no damage.

Candlewood Suites Bel Air
4216 Philadelphia Road
Bel Air, MD
410-914-3060 (877-270-6405)
Dogs up to 80 pounds are allowed. Pets allowed with an additional pet fee. Up to $75 for 1-6 nights and up to $150 for 7+ nights. A pet agreement must be signed at check-in.

Extended Stay America Baltimore - Bel Air
1361 James Way
Bel Air, MD
410-273-0194 (800-804-3724)
One dog is allowed per suite. There is a $25 per night additional pet fee up to $150 for an entire stay.

Comfort Inn Capital Beltway/I-95 North
4050 Powder Mill Rd.
Beltsville, MD
301-572-7100 (877-424-6423)
Dogs of all sizes are allowed. Dogs are allowed for a pet fee of $25.00 per pet per stay.

Sheraton College Park Hotel
4095 Powder Mill Rd.
Beltsville, MD
301-937-4422 (888-625-5144)
Dogs of all sizes are allowed. There are no additional pet fees. Dogs are not allowed to be left alone in the room.

Residence Inn Bethesda Downtown
7335 Wisconsin Avenue
Bethesda, MD
301-718-0200 (800-331-3131)
This all suite hotel sits central to many of the city's star attractions, the Navel Medical Center, shopping, dining, and entertainment areas, plus they offer a number of in-house amenities that include a daily buffet breakfast, and a social hour during mid-week. Dogs are allowed for an additional one time pet fee of $200 per room plus $10 per night per pet. Multiple dogs may be allowed.

TownePlace Suites Bowie Town Center
3700 Town Center Blvd
Bowie, MD
301-262-8045 (800-257-3000)
This all suite inn offers a convenient location to the university, and

business, shopping, dining, and major entertainment venues, plus they offer a number of in-house amenities for business and leisure travelers. Dogs are allowed for an additional one time fee of $100 per room. Multiple dogs may be allowed.

Super 8 Lexington Park/ Area California
22801 Three Notch Rd
California, MD
301-862-9822 (800-800-8000)
Dogs of all sizes are allowed. Dogs are allowed for a pet fee.

Hyatt Regency Chesapeake Bay Golf Resort, Spa and Marina.
100 Heron Blvd
Cambridge, MD
410-901-1234 (888) 591 1234)
This beautiful bay shore hotel has many features and amenities for the business or leisure traveler with a full service business center, a championship golf course and a 150 slip marina. Dogs up to 70 pounds are welcome for an additional fee of $50 per night per pet, and reservations must be made at least 7 days in advance or more as there are only 9 pet-friendly rooms available. Current shot records must be provided upon arrival, and dogs must be under owner's control, leashed, and cleaned up after at all times. 2 dogs may be allowed.

Super 8 s/Andrews AFB DC Area Camp Spring
5151 B Allentown Rd
Camp Spring, MD
301-702-0099 (800-800-8000)
Dogs of all sizes are allowed. Dogs are allowed for a pet fee.

Motel 6 - Washington, Dc Southeast Camp Springs
5701 Allentown Rd
Camp Springs, MD
301-702-1061 (800-466-8356)
This motel welcomes your pets to stay with you.

Quality Inn
4783 Allentown Road
Camp Springs, MD
301-420-2800 (877-424-6423)
Dogs of all sizes are allowed. Dogs are allowed for a pet fee of $25.00 per pet per stay. Two dogs are allowed per room.

Motel 6 - Washington, Dc Capitol Heights
75 Hampton Park Blvd
Capitol Heights, MD

301-499-0800 (800-466-8356)
This motel welcomes your pets to stay with you.

Brampton Inn
25227 Chestertown Road
Chestertown, MD
410-778-1860 (866-305-1860)
bramptoninn.com/
Stately and romantic, this historical estate sits on 20 wooded and landscaped acres just a short distance from river. Dogs of all sizes are allowed in one of the cottages for an additional $30 per night. Dogs must be leashed and cleaned up after. 2 dogs may be allowed.

Howard Johnson Inn Cheverly
5811 Annapolis Road
Cheverly, MD
301-779-7700 (800-446-4656)
Dogs are welcome at this hotel. There is a $35 one time pet fee.

Comfort Inn at Andrews AFB
7979 Malcolm Rd.
Clinton, MD
301-856-5200 (877-424-6423)
Dogs of all sizes are allowed. Dogs are allowed for a pet fee of $50.00 per pet per stay.

Chase Suite Hotel by Woodfin
10710 Beaver Dam Road
Cockeysville, MD
410-584-7370
All well-behaved dogs are welcome. All rooms are suites with a full kitchen. Hotel amenities include a complimentary breakfast buffet. There is a $5 per day fee.

Super 8 Wash DC Area College Park
9150 Baltimore Ave
College Park, MD
301-474-0894 (800-800-8000)
Dogs of all sizes are allowed. Dogs are allowed for a pet fee.

Extended Stay America Columbia - Columbia 100 Parkway
8870 Columbia 100 Pkwy.
Columbia, MD
410-772-8800 (800-804-3724)
One dog is allowed per suite. There is a $25 per night additional pet fee up to $150 for an entire stay.

Sheraton Columbia Hotel
10207 Wincopin Circle
Columbia, MD
410-730-3900 (888-625-5144)
Dogs up to 50 pounds are allowed. There are no additional pet fees.

Dogs are not allowed to be left alone in the room.

Staybridge Suites Baltimore-Columbia
8844 Columbia 100 Parkway
Columbia, MD
410-964-9494 (877-270-6405)
Dogs up to 80 pounds are allowed. Pets allowed with an additional pet fee. Up to $75 for 1-6 nights and up to $150 for 7+ nights. A pet agreement must be signed at check-in.

Holiday Inn Cumberland-Downtown
100 South George St
Cumberland, MD
301-724-8800 (877-270-6405)
Dogs of all sizes are allowed. Dogs are allowed for a pet fee of $25.00 per pet per night.

Railey Mountain Lake Vacations
5 Vacation Way
Deep Creek Lake, MD
301-387-2124 (800-846-RENT (7368))
deepcreek.com/
Offering a variety of property options and amenities in numerous recreational areas, this agency has about 125 pet friendly vacation rentals available in the Deep Creek Lake area. Dogs of all sizes are allowed for an additional fee of $45 for the 1st two days and $12 each night after, or $84 for the weekly rate per pet (the standard fee for any rental). Pets are not allowed in non-pet homes, and they must be pre-registered and paid for prior to arrival. Pets must be under their owner's control at all times. 2 dogs may be allowed.

Days Inn Easton
7018 Ocean Gateway
Easton, MD
410-822-4600 (800-329-7466)
Dogs are welcome at this hotel.

Eastern Shore Vacation Rentals
28282 St. Michaels Road
Easton, MD
410-770-9093 (866-398-2722)
easternshorevacations.com
Dogs are allowed in these vacation rentals. There is a $75 one time additional pet fee. Please inform them of your pet at the time of booking.

Tidewater Inn
101 E Dover Street/H 331
Easton, MD
410-822-1300 (800-237-8775)

tidewaterinn.com/
This historic inn is as rich in old world charm as it is in modern amenities and services, and it is only a short distance from Washington D.C. and Baltimore. Dogs are allowed for an additional one time fee of $25 per pet, and there is a pet agreement to sign at check in. They request that guests bring their own pet covers for the bed and furniture. A contact number must be left with the front desk when there is a pet alone in the room. Dogs must be leashed and under their owner's control at all times. 2 dogs may be allowed.

Days Inn Elkton
311 Belle Hill Road
Elkton, MD
410-392-5010 (800-329-7466)
Dogs of all sizes are allowed. Dogs are allowed for a pet fee.

Hawthorn Inn & Suites
304 Belle Hill Road
Elkton, MD
410-620-9494 (800-527-1133)
In addition to providing a convenient location to many local sites and activities, this all-suite hotel offers a number of amenities for business and leisure travelers, including their signature breakfast buffet and beautifully appointed rooms. Dogs are allowed for an additional pet fee of $25 per night per room with a $100 maximum charge. Multiple dogs may be allowed.

Motel 6 - Elkton, Md
223 Belle Hill Rd
Elkton, MD
410-392-5020 (800-466-8356)
This motel welcomes your pets to stay with you.

Residence Inn Columbia
4950 Beaver Run
Ellicott City, MD
410-997-7200 (800-331-3131)
This hotel offers a convenient location to business, shopping, dining, and entertainment areas, plus they offer a number of in-house amenities, including a daily buffet breakfast and weekly evening socials. Dogs are allowed for an additional one time pet fee of $100 per room. Multiple dogs may be allowed.

The Hotel at Turf Valley
2700 Turf Valley Road
Ellicott City, MD
410-465-1500 (888-833-8873)
turfvalleyresort.com
The Hotel at Turf Valley has over

1000 acres of land with golf, spas, meeting rooms, a children's playground, a driving range and more. Pets are allowed for a $150 one time additional pet fee.

Comfort Inn
7300 Executive Way
Frederick, MD
301-668-7272 (877-424-6423)
Dogs of all sizes are allowed.

Extended Stay America Frederick - Westview Dr.
5240 Westview Dr.
Frederick, MD
301-668-0808 (800-804-3724)
One dog is allowed per suite. There is a $25 per night additional pet fee up to $150 for an entire stay.

Holiday Inn Express Frederick-Fsk Mall(I270/Rt 85)
5579 Spectrum Drive
Frederick, MD
301-695-2881 (877-270-6405)
Dogs of all sizes are allowed. Dogs are allowed for a pet fee of $20 per pet per night.

Holiday Inn Frederick-Conf Ctr At Fsk Mall
I-270 At Route 85
Frederick, MD
301-694-7500 (877-270-6405)
Dogs of all sizes are allowed. Dogs are allowed for a pet fee of $20.00 per pet per night.

MainStay Suites
7310 Executive Way
Frederick, MD
301-668-4600 (877-424-6423)
Dogs of all sizes are allowed. Dogs are allowed for a pet fee of $10.00 per pet per night.

Motel 6 - Frederick, Md Fort Detrick
999 West Patrick Street
Frederick, MD
301-662-5141 (800-466-8356)
This motel welcomes your pets to stay with you.

Residence Inn Frederick
5230 Westview Drive
Frederick, MD
301-360-0010 (800-331-3131)
Some of the amenities at this all-suite inn include a daily buffet breakfast, a hospitality hour Monday through Thursday, an indoor pool, Sport Court, and a complimentary grocery shopping service. Dogs are allowed for an additional one time pet fee of $100 per room. Multiple dogs may be

allowed.

Travelodge Frederick
200 East Walser Drive
Frederick, MD
301-663-0500 (800-578-7878)
Dogs are welcome at this hotel.

Yough Valley Motel
138 Walnut St
Friendsville, MD
301-746-5700
Dogs of all sizes are allowed. There is a $10 per dog per night additional pet fee. 2 dogs may be allowed.

Days Inn And Suites Frostburg
11100 New Georges Creek Road
Frostburg, MD
301-689-2050 (800-329-7466)
Dogs of all sizes are allowed. Dogs are allowed for a pet fee of $15.00 per pet per night.

The Savage River Lodge
1600 Mount Aetna Rd
Frostburg, MD
301-689-3200
savageriverlodge.com/dogs.htm
This extremely pet friendly lodge has a special page on its website for visitors with pets. While there you may be greeted by Bodhi, the Lodge Dog. Visitors stay in individual non-smoking cabins. There is a $25 per night per pet fee. You must make advanced reservations with a pet. The lodge is about 30 minutes from Deep Creek Lake. 2 dogs may be allowed.

Comfort Inn at Shady Grove
16216 Frederick Rd.
Gaithersburg, MD
301-330-0023 (877-424-6423)
Dogs of all sizes are allowed.

Extended Stay America Washington, D.C. - Gaithersburg
205 Professional Dr.
Gaithersburg, MD
301-869-9814 (800-804-3724)
One dog is allowed per suite. There is a $25 per night additional pet fee up to $150 for an entire stay.

Hilton Hotel
620 Perry Parkway
Gaithersburg, MD
301-977-8900 (800-HILTONS (445-8667))
Located in the hi-tech business corridor of the DC area, this upscale hotel has a number of on site amenities for both the business or leisure traveler, plus a convenient location to business, historical,

Dog-Friendly Lodging - Please always call ahead to make sure an establishment is still dog-friendly.

shopping, dining, and recreational areas. Dogs up to 50 pounds are allowed for an additional one time fee of $50 per pet. 2 dogs may be allowed.

Holiday Inn Gaithersburg
2 Montgomery Village Ave
Gaithersburg, MD
301-948-8900 (877-270-6405)
Dogs up to 50 pounds are allowed.

Motel 6 - Washington, Dc
Gaithersburg
497 Quince Orchard Rd
Gaithersburg, MD
301-977-3311 (800-466-8356)
This motel welcomes your pets to stay with you.

Residence Inn Gaithersburg
Washingtonian Center
9721 Washingtonian Blvd
Gaithersburg, MD
301-590-3003 (800-331-3131)
Nestled in the heart of the Washingtonian Center and central to a number of world class attractions and shopping/dining areas, this all suite inn also offers a number of in-house amenities - including a daily buffet breakfast and evening social events Monday to Thursday. Dogs up to 60 pounds are allowed for an additional one time pet fee of $100 per room. 2 dogs may be allowed.

TownePlace Suites Gaithersburg
212 Perry Parkway
Gaithersburg, MD
301-590-2300 (800-257-3000)
In addition to offering a number of in-house amenities for all level of travelers, this all suite inn also provides a convenient location to business, shopping, dining, and entertainment areas. Dogs up to 50 pounds are allowed for an additional one time fee of $100 per room. 2 dogs may be allowed.

Extended Stay America Washington, D.C. - Germantown
12450 Milestone Center Dr.
Germantown, MD
301-540-9369 (800-804-3724)
One dog is allowed per suite. There is a $25 per night additional pet fee up to $150 for an entire stay.

Homestead Studio Suites
Washington, D.C. - Germantown
20141 Century Blvd.
Germantown, MD
301-515-4500 (800-804-3724)
One dog is allowed per suite. There is a $25 per night additional pet fee

up to $150 for an entire stay.

Days Inn Glen Burnie
6600 Ritchie Hwy
Glen Burnie, MD
410-761-8300 (800-329-7466)
Dogs are welcome at this hotel.

Extended Stay America Baltimore - Glen Burnie
104 Chesapeake Centre Ct.
Glen Burnie, MD
410-761-2708 (800-804-3724)
One dog is allowed per suite. There is a $25 per night additional pet fee up to $150 for an entire stay.

Residence Inn Greenbelt
6320 Golden Triangle Drive
Greenbelt, MD
301-982-1600 (800-331-3131)
Some of the amenities at this all-suite inn include a daily buffet breakfast, evening hospitality hours, weekend barbecues, a swimming pool, spa, Sport Court, and a complimentary grocery shopping service. Dogs are allowed for an additional one time pet fee of $100 per room. Multiple dogs may be allowed.

Econo Lodge Inn & Suites
1101 Dual Hwy.
Hagerstown, MD
301-733-2700 (877-424-6423)
Dogs of all sizes are allowed. Dogs are allowed for a pet fee of $10.00 per pet per night.

Motel 6 - Hagerstown
11321 Massey Blvd
Hagerstown, MD
301-582-4445 (800-466-8356)
This motel welcomes your pets to stay with you.

Super 8 Halfway/ Hagerstown
16805 Blake Rd
Hagerstown, MD
301-582-1992 (800-800-8000)
Dogs of all sizes are allowed. Dogs are allowed for a pet fee.

Sleep Inn & Suites
18216 Colonel H K Douglas Dr
Hagerstown, MD
301-766-9449 (877-424-6423)
Dogs of all sizes are allowed. Dogs are allowed for a pet fee of $10.00 per pet per night.

Super 8
118 Limestone Road
Hancock, MD
301-678-6101 (800-800-8000)
Dogs of all sizes are allowed. Dogs

are allowed for a pet fee.

Red Roof Inn Washington, DC - BW Parkway
7306 Parkway Drive
Hanover, MD
410-712-4070 (800-RED-ROOF)
One well-behaved family pet per room. Guest must notify front desk upon arrival. Guest is liable for any damages. In consideration of all guests, pets must never be left unattended in the guest rooms.

TownePlace Suites Arundel Mills
BWI Airport
7021 Arundel Mills Circle
Hanover, MD
410-379-9000 (800-257-3000)
Besides offering a number of in-house amenities for all level of travelers, this all suite inn - located near Baltimore's Inner Harbor, also provides a convenient location to professional sports arenas, business, shopping, dining, and entertainment areas. Dogs are allowed for an additional one time fee of $100 per room. Multiple dogs may be allowed.

Super 8 Aberdeen Area Havre De Grace
929 Pulaski Hwy
Havre De Grace, MD
410-939-1880 (800-800-8000)
Dogs are welcome at this hotel.

Super 8 MD Indian Head
4694 Indian Head Hwy
Indian Head, MD
301-753-8100 (800-800-8000)
Dogs are welcome at this hotel.

Extended Stay America Columbia - Laurel
8550 Washington Blvd.
Jessup, MD
301-725-3877 (800-804-3724)
One dog is allowed per suite. There is a $25 per night additional pet fee up to $150 for an entire stay.

Red Roof Inn Washington, DC - Columbia/Jessup
8000 Washington Boulevard
Jessup, MD
410-796-0380 (800-RED-ROOF)
One well-behaved family pet per room. Guest must notify front desk upon arrival. Guest is liable for any damages. In consideration of all guests, pets must never be left unattended in the guest rooms.

Best Western Braddock Motor Inn
1268 National Highway
La Vale, MD

301-729-3300 (800-780-7234)
Dogs are welcome at this hotel.

Super 8 /Cumberland Area La Vale
I-68 at Rt 53
La Vale, MD
301-729-6265 (800-800-8000)
Dogs are welcome at this hotel.

Red Roof Inn LaVale - Cumberland
12310 Winchester Road Southwest
LaVale, MD
301-729-6700 (800-RED-ROOF)
One well-behaved family pet per
room. Guest must notify front desk
upon arrival. Guest is liable for any
damages. In consideration of all
guests, pets must never be left
unattended in the guest rooms.

Extended Stay America Washington,
D.C. - Landover
9401 Largo Dr. W.
Landover, MD
301-333-9139 (800-804-3724)
One dog is allowed per suite. There
is a $25 per night additional pet fee
up to $150 for an entire stay.

Red Roof Inn Washington, DC -
Lanham
9050 Lanham Severn Road
Lanham, MD
301-731-8830 (800-RED-ROOF)
One well-behaved family pet per
room. Guest must notify front desk
upon arrival. Guest is liable for any
damages. In consideration of all
guests, pets must never be left
unattended in the guest rooms.

Comfort Suites Laurel Lakes
14402 Laurel Pl.
Laurel, MD
301-206-2600 (877-424-6423)
Dogs of all sizes are allowed. Dogs
are allowed for a pet fee of $40.00
per pet per stay.

Holiday Inn Laurel West - I-95/Rt
198w
15101 Sweitzer Ln
Laurel, MD
301-776-5300 (877-270-6405)
Dogs of all sizes are allowed. Dogs
are allowed for a pet fee of $50.00
per pet per night.

Motel 6 - Washington, Dc Northeast
Laurel
3510 Old Annapolis Rd
Laurel, MD
301-497-1544 (800-466-8356)
This motel welcomes your pets to
stay with you.

Red Roof Inn Washington, DC -

Laurel
12525 Laurel Bowie Road
Laurel, MD
301-498-8811 (800-RED-ROOF)
One well-behaved family pet per
room. Guest must notify front desk
upon arrival. Guest is liable for any
damages. In consideration of all
guests, pets must never be left
unattended in the guest rooms.

Days Inn Lexington Park
21847 Three Notch Road
Lexington Park, MD
240-725-0100 (800-329-7466)
daysinn.com/DaysInn/control/home
Dogs of all sizes are allowed for an
additional $8 per night per pet.
Dogs must be leashed and cleaned
up after. Multiple dogs may be
allowed.

Extended Stay America Lexington
Park - Pax River
46565 Expedition Park Dr.
Lexington Park, MD
240-725-0100 (800-804-3724)
One dog is allowed per suite. There
is a $25 per night additional pet fee
up to $150 for an entire stay.

Candlewood Suites Baltimore-
Linthicum
1247 Winterson Rd.
Linthicum, MD
410-850-9214 (877-270-6405)
Dogs up to 80 pounds are allowed.
Pets allowed with an additional pet
fee. Up to $75 for 1-6 nights and up
to $150 for 7+ nights. A pet
agreement must be signed at
check-in.

Extended Stay America Baltimore -
BWI Airport
1500 Aero Dr.
Linthicum, MD
410-850-0400 (800-804-3724)
One dog is allowed per suite. There
is a $25 per night additional pet fee
up to $150 for an entire stay.

Residence Inn Baltimore BWI
Airport
1160 Winterson Road
Linthicum, MD
410-691-0255 (888-236-2427)
This all suite hotel sits only a couple
of miles from an international airport
and close to a wide variety of
Baltimore's star attractions -
including the Inner Harbor, plus
they also offer a daily buffet
breakfast and evening socials.
Dogs are allowed for an additional
one time pet fee of $75 per room. 2
dogs may be allowed.

Staybridge Suites Baltimore Bwi
Airport
1301 Winterson Road
Linthicum, MD
410-850-5666 (877-270-6405)
Dogs up to 80 pounds are allowed.
Pets allowed with an additional pet
fee. Up to $75 for 1-6 nights and up
to $150 for 7+ nights. A pet
agreement must be signed at check-
in.

TownePlace Suites Baltimore BWI
Airport
1171 Winterson Road
Linthicum, MD
410-694-0060 (800-257-3000)
In addition to being only minutes
from the BWI Thurgood Marshall
Airport, this all suite hotel also sits
close to the Baltimore-Washington
Corridor's plethora of activities and
sits of interest - including Baltimore's
Inner Harbor. Dogs are allowed for
an additional one time fee of $100
per room. Multiple dogs may be
allowed.

Comfort Suites BWI Airport
815 Elkridge Landing Road
Linthicum Heights, MD
410-691-1000 (877-424-6423)
Dogs of all sizes are allowed. Dogs
are allowed for a pet fee of $25.00
per pet per stay.

Homestead Studio Suites Baltimore -
BWI Airport
939 International Dr.
Linthicum Heights, MD
410-691-2500 (800-804-3724)
One dog is allowed per suite. There
is a $25 per night additional pet fee
up to $150 for an entire stay.

Motel 6 - Baltimore Bwi Airport
5179 Raynor Ave
Linthicum Heights, MD
410-636-9070 (800-466-8356)
This motel welcomes your pets to
stay with you.

Red Roof Inn Washington, DC - BWI
Airport
827 Elkridge Landing Road
Linthicum Heights, MD
410-850-7600 (800-RED-ROOF)
One well-behaved family pet per
room. Guest must notify front desk
upon arrival. Guest is liable for any
damages. In consideration of all
guests, pets must never be left
unattended in the guest rooms.

Deep Creek Lake Resort Vacation
Rentals

23789 Garrett Highway, Suite 3
McHenry, MD
301-387-5832 (800-336-7303)
deepcreekresort.com/
Every season here brings its own beauty, pleasures, and recreational pursuits, and this agency offers a variety of property options and amenities in the Deep Creek Lake area. Dogs of all sizes are allowed for an additional $65 per pet per stay. Dogs must be well trained, and under their owner's control at all times. 2 dogs may be allowed.

WISP Resort & Conference Center
296 Marsh Hill Road
McHenry, MD
301-387-4911 (800-462-9477)
wispresort.com
Dogs up to 50 pounds are allowed in this resort lodge right at WISP ski resort. There is a $50 per stay additional pet fee. The entire property is non-smoking.

Residence Inn National Harbor
Washington, DC
192 Waterfront Street
National Harbor, MD
301-749-4755 (800-331-3131)
Located along the shores of the Potomac River only a few miles from the nation's capitol, this all suite hotel gives easy access to a number of sites of interest and activities for all level of travelers, a daily buffet breakfast, and evening socials mid-week. Dogs are allowed for an additional one time pet fee of $200 per room. 2 dogs may be allowed.

Alpine Village Inn
19638 Garrett Highway
Oakland, MD
301-387-5534 (800-745-1174)
alpinevillageinn.com
Dogs of all sizes are allowed in a few pet rooms. There is a $20 per night per pet additional pet fee. 2 dogs may be allowed.

Angler's Cove
1214 Stockslager Rd
Oakland, MD
301-387-5999 (866-351-1119)
This 3 bedroom chalet is located on the lake. Up to two dogs are allowed per reservation. There is a $45 one-time pet fee for up to 4 nights and $12 per pet for each additional night.

Swallow Falls Inn
1691 Swallow Falls Rd
Oakland, MD
301-387-9348

Barefoot Mailman Motel
16 35th Street
Ocean City, MD
410-289-5343 (800-395-3668)
barefootmailman.com/
In addition to being located only about 400 feet from the beach, this hotel offers a large outdoor pool and private balconies for all units. Dogs are allowed for no additional fee. Dogs must be leashed and cleaned up after. They are allowed on the beach from October 1st through to May 1st. 2 dogs may be allowed.

Comfort Suites
12718 Ocean Gateway
Ocean City, MD
410-213-7171 (877-424-6423)
Dogs of all sizes are allowed. Dogs are allowed for a pet fee of $35.00 per pet per night.

Serene Hotel and Suites
12004 Coastal H
Ocean City, MD
410-250-4000
Dogs of all sizes are allowed. There is a pet policy to sign at check in and there are no additional pet fees.

Parrot Bay Condos
12308 Ocean Gateway
Ocean City/H 50, MD
410-289-8530 (866-641-5930)
parrotbaycondos.com/
Besides offering a number of on-site amenities, this inn also provides a great location for exploring all this area has to offer. Well mannered dogs are allowed for an additional fee per pet of $25 for 1 or 2 nights; 3 nights is $35; 4 nights is $45; 5 nights is $55; 6 nights is $65 and 7 nights is $75. Dogs must be crated when left alone in the room. Dogs must be declared at the time of reservation as only some units accept pets. 2 dogs may be allowed.

Combsberry
4837 Evergreen Road
Oxford, MD
410-226-5353
combsberry.net/
Sitting lakeside at the end of a private dirt road is this beautiful historic brick mansion surrounded by magnolias, willows, and formal gardens. Dogs of all sizes are allowed for no additional fee. Dogs must be well behaved, leashed, and cleaned up after at all times. 2 dogs may be allowed.

Ramada Perryville

61 Heather Lane
Perryville, MD
410-642-2866 (800-272-6232)
Dogs of all sizes are allowed. Dogs are allowed for a pet fee of $20.00 per pet per night.

Days Inn City Pocomoke
1540 Ocean Highway
Pocomoke, MD
410-957-3000 (800-329-7466)
Dogs are welcome at this hotel.

Quality Inn
825 Ocean Hwy.
Pocomoke City, MD
410-957-1300 (877-424-6423)
Dogs of all sizes are allowed.

Econo Lodge
10936 Market Lane
Princess Anne, MD
410-651-9400 (877-424-6423)
Dogs of all sizes are allowed. Dogs are allowed for a pet fee of $10.00 per pet per night. Two dogs are allowed per room.

Huntingfield Manor Bed & Breakfast
4928 Eastern Neck Rd
Rock Hall, MD
410-639-7779
travelassist.com/reg/md104s.html
This B&B is located on a 70 acre working farm. Pets are allowed in the cottage which is not designated as smoking or non-smoking. There is a $25 per night per room pet fee. 2 dogs may be allowed.

Homestead Studio Suites
Washington, D.C. - Gaithersburg - Rockville
2621 Research Blvd.
Rockville, MD
301-987-9100 (800-804-3724)
One dog is allowed per suite. There is a $25 per night additional pet fee up to $150 for an entire stay.

Red Roof Inn Washington, DC - Rockville
16001 Shady Grove Road
Rockville, MD
301-987-0965 (800-RED-ROOF)
One well-behaved family pet per room. Guest must notify front desk upon arrival. Guest is liable for any damages. In consideration of all guests, pets must never be left unattended in the guest rooms.

Woodfin Suite Hotel
1380 Piccard Drive
Rockville, MD
301-590-9880
All well-behaved dogs are welcome.

Every room is a suite with either a wet bar or full kitchen. Hotel amenities includes a pool, free video movies and a complimentary hot breakfast buffet. There is a $5 per day pet fee per pet. If you are staying for one month, the pet fee is $50 for the month.

Comfort Inn
2701 N. Salisbury Blvd.
Salisbury, MD
410-543-4666 (877-424-6423)
Dogs of all sizes are allowed.

Days Inn Salisbury
2525 N Salisbury Blvd
Salisbury, MD
410-749-6200 (800-329-7466)
Dogs of all sizes are allowed. Dogs are allowed for a nightly pet fee.

Holiday Inn Salisbury Downtown Area
300 South Salisbury Boulevard
Salisbury, MD
410-546-4400 (877-270-6405)
Dogs of all sizes are allowed. Dogs are allowed for a nightly pet fee.

Residence Inn Salisbury
140 Centre Road
Salisbury, MD
410-543-0033 (800-331-3131)
Located along the scenic eastern shores of the state, this all suite inn sits only minutes from the airport, universities, major corporations, and a number of shopping and dining areas. Additionally, they offer a daily buffet breakfast and mid-week evening socials. Dogs are allowed for an additional one time pet fee of $100 per room. 2 dogs may be allowed.

Residence Inn Silver Spring
12000 Plum Orchard Drive
Silver Spring, MD
301-572-2322 (800-331-3131)
In addition to offering a convenient location to business, historical, shopping, dining, and entertainment areas, this hotel also provides a number of in-house amenities, including a daily buffet breakfast and evening social hours mid-week. Dogs are allowed for an additional one time pet fee of $100 per room. Multiple dogs may be allowed.

River House Inn Bed and Breakfast
201 E Market St
Snow Hill, MD
410-632-2722
riverhouseinn.com/
This B&B is a National Register

Victorian home located on the Pocomoke River on Maryland's Eastern Shore. Dogs are allowed for an additional $10 per night per pet. Multiple dogs may be allowed.

Five Gables Inn and Spa
209 North Talbot Street
St Michaels, MD
410-745-0100 (877-466-0100)
fivegables.com/
This inn offers 19th century ambiance, an indoor pool and spa, numerous amenities, and there is also an upscale pet boutique among the shops. One dog up to 75 pounds is allowed for an additional $35 one time fee. Dogs must be leashed or crated and cleaned up after.

The Inn at Perry Cabin
308 Watkins Lane
St Michaels, MD
410-745-2200 (866-278-9601)
Rich in colonial history, this grand manor house resort now features numerous amenities, a horizon-edged swimming pool, a spa, docking facilities, and a lot more. Dogs up to 75 pounds are allowed with advance notification for an additional fee of $75 per pet per stay. Dogs must be well mannered, leashed, and cleaned up after. 2 dogs may be allowed.

Super 8 Thurmont
300 Tippin Drive
Thurmont, MD
301-271-7888 (800-800-8000)
Dogs of all sizes are allowed. Dogs are allowed for a pet fee.

The Tilghman Island Inn
21384 Coopertown Road
Tilghman Island, MD
401-886-2141 (800-866-2141)
In addition to providing a scenic and magical setting, this waterside inn hosts several special events through the season, and also provides a venue for special occasions. Dogs are allowed for an additional $20 per night per pet in the 1st floor rooms. Dogs must be well behaved, leashed, and cleaned up after. 2 dogs may be allowed.

Extended Stay America Baltimore - Timonium
9704 Beaver Dam Rd.
Timonium, MD
410-628-1088 (800-804-3724)
One dog is allowed per suite. There is a $25 per night additional pet fee up to $150 for an entire stay.

Red Roof Inn Baltimore North - Timonium
111 West Timonium Road
Timonium, MD
410-666-0380 (800-RED-ROOF)
One well-behaved family pet per room. Guest must notify front desk upon arrival. Guest is liable for any damages. In consideration of all guests, pets must never be left unattended in the guest rooms.

Holiday Inn Baltimore-Towson
1100 Cromwell Bridge Rd
Towson, MD
410-823-4410 (877-270-6405)
Dogs up to 50 pounds are allowed. Dogs are allowed for a pet fee of $25.00 per pet per night.

Days Inn Waldorf
11370 Days Court
Waldorf, MD
301-932-9200 (800-329-7466)
Dogs of all sizes are allowed. Dogs are allowed for a pet fee of $25.00 per pet per night.

Red Roof Inn Hagerstown - Williamsport
310 E. Potomac Street
Williamsport, MD
301-582-3500 (800-RED-ROOF)
One well-behaved family pet per room. Guest must notify front desk upon arrival. Guest is liable for any damages. In consideration of all guests, pets must never be left unattended in the guest rooms.

Massachusetts

Comfort Suites
4 Riverside Drive
Andover, MA
978-475-6000 (877-424-6423)
Dogs of all sizes are allowed. Two dogs are allowed per room.

La Quinta Inn & Suites Andover
131 River Road
Andover, MA
978-685-6200 (800-531-5900)
Dogs of all sizes are allowed. There are no additional pet fees. There is a pet waiver to sign at check in. Dogs must be leashed and cleaned up after. Multiple dogs may be allowed.

Residence Inn Boston Andover
500 Minuteman Road
Andover, MA
978-683-0382 (866-449-7391)
This all suite hotel offers a number of amenities for all level of travelers,

including a daily buffet breakfast, complimentary evening socials, a swimming pool, and complimentary grocery shopping services. Dogs are allowed for an additional one time pet fee of $100 per room. 2 dogs may be allowed.

Staybridge Suites Boston-Andover
4 Tech Drive
Andover, MA
978-686-2000 (877-270-6405)
Dogs up to 80 pounds are allowed. Pets allowed with an additional pet fee. Up to $75 for 1-6 nights and up to $150 for 7+ nights. A pet agreement must be signed at check-in.

La Quinta Inn Auburn/Worcester
446 Southbridge Street
Auburn, MA
508-832-7000 (800-531-5900)
Dogs of all sizes are allowed. There are no additional fees. There is a pet waiver to sign at check in. Dogs may not be left unattended, except for short periods. Dogs must be leashed and cleaned up after. Multiple dogs may be allowed.

Best Western Roundhouse Suites
891 Massachusetts Avenue
Boston, MA
617-989-1000 (800-780-7234)
Dogs of all sizes are allowed. Dogs are allowed for a pet fee of $20 per pet per night.

Boston Harbor Hotel
70 Rowes Wharf
Boston, MA
617-439-7000
bhh.com/
There are no additional pet fees. Pet owners must sign a pet waiver. Multiple dogs may be allowed.

Comfort Inn
900 Morrissey Boulevard
Boston, MA
617-287-9200 (877-424-6423)
Dogs of all sizes are allowed.

Doubletree Guest Suites
400 Soldiers Field Road
Boston, MA
617-783-0090 (800-222-TREE (8733))
Located adjacent to Harvard University, this upscale, all suite hotel offers a number of on-site amenities at all level of travelers, plus a convenient location to a plethora of business, shopping, dining, historical and entertainment areas. Dogs are allowed for no

additional fee; they must be declared at the time of reservation, and a cell number must be left with the front desk if a pet is in the room alone. 2 dogs may be allowed.

Fairmont Copley Plaza
138 St James Avenue
Boston, MA
617-267-5300 (800-257-7544)
fairmont.com/copleyplaza/
Just steps away from historic attractions and numerous activities, this distinguished 1912 hotel echoes the rich culture and traditions of this city. They have a Canine Ambassador in residence named Catie Copley who may be present to greet guests or also go for a walk. Dogs are allowed for an additional pet fee of $25 per stay. Dogs must be well behaved, leashed and cleaned up after. Dogs may be left alone in the room for a short time only if they will be quiet and a contact number is left with the front desk. Guests with pets also like to take the nice walking path from the property that leads to the south end of town.

Howard Johnson Inn Fenway Park
Boston
1271 Boylston Street
Boston, MA
617-267-8300 (800-446-4656)
Dogs are welcome at this hotel.

Hyatt Regency Boston
One Ave de Lafayette
Boston, MA
617-451-2600
Pet owners must sign a pet waiver. Dogs up to 85 pounds are allowed for no additional fee. You need to specifically request a non-smoking pet room if you want one. Dogs need to stay in the first through fourth floors only. Pets may not be left alone in the rooms. The hotel can recommend pet sitters if needed. 2 dogs may be allowed.

Nine Zero Hotel
90 Tremont Street
Boston, MA
617-772-5800 (866-906-9090)
This boutique hotel located in downtown Boston, has all the amenities for the business and leisure traveler, and they are located across the street from Boston Common, a pet-friendly 50 acre public park. Dogs of all sizes are welcome for no additional pet fee. They offer a pet bed, bowls, and a special treat for all their canine guests. Dogs may only be

left alone in the room if assured they will be quiet, well behaved, and the "Dog in Room" sign is put on the door. Dogs must be leashed and cleaned up after at all times. Multiple dogs may be allowed.

Onyx Hotel
155 Portland Street
Boston, MA
617-557-9955 (866-660-6699)
onyxhotel.com
This Kimpton boutique hotel allows dogs of all sizes. There are no additional pet fees. Pet sitting is available for $20 per hour.

Ramada Boston
800 Morrissey Boulevard
Boston, MA
617-287-9100 (800-272-6232)
Dogs are welcome at this hotel.

Residence Inn Boston Harbor on Tudor Wharf
34-44 Charles River Avenue
Boston, MA
617-242-9000 (866-296-2297)
Located only a mile from downtown, this hotel offers a convenient location to business, shopping, dining, and entertainment areas, plus they offer a number of in-house amenities, including a daily buffet breakfast and weekly evening socials. Dogs are allowed for an additional one time pet fee of $100 per room. 2 dogs may be allowed.

Sheraton Boston Hotel
39 Dalton St.
Boston, MA
617-236-2000 (888-625-5144)
Dogs up to 50 pounds are allowed for no additional pet fee. Dogs may not be left alone in the room.

Taj Boston
15 Arlington Street
Boston, MA
617-536-5700 (800-223-6800)
This landmark luxury hotel is only a short walk from the financial and theater districts, and sits along side Boston's grand public garden. Dogs of all sizes are allowed for an additional one time pet fee of $125 per room. Dogs may not be left alone in the room, and they must be leashed and cleaned up after at all times. 2 dogs may be allowed.

The Eliot Suite Hotel
370 Commonwealth Ave
Boston, MA
617-267-1607
There are no additional pet fees.

Pets may not be left alone in the rooms, and they must be removed or crated for housekeeping. Multiple dogs may be allowed.

The Ritz-Carlton, Boston Common
10 Avery Street
Boston, MA
617-574-7100 (800-241-3333)
This hotel of contemporary luxury and design with 193 guestrooms, offers dramatic city views, in-house gourmet dining, and is conveniently located between the financial and theater districts. Dogs of all sizes are welcome for an additional $125 one time fee per room, and there is a pet policy to sign at check in. Dogs may not be left alone in the room, and they must be leashed and cleaned up after at all times. 2 dogs may be allowed.

Holiday Inn Boxborough (I-495 Exit 28)
242 Adams Place
Boxborough, MA
978-263-8701 (877-270-6405)
Dogs are welcome at this hotel. There is a $25 one time pet fee.

Candlewood Suites Boston-Braintree
235 Wood Rd.
Braintree, MA
781-849-7450 (877-270-6405)
Dogs up to 80 pounds are allowed. Pets allowed with an additional pet fee. Up to $75 for 1-6 nights and up to $150 for 7+ nights. A pet agreement must be signed at check-in.

Extended Stay America Boston - Braintree
20 Rockdale St.
Braintree, MA
781-356-8333 (800-804-3724)
One dog is allowed per suite. There is a $25 per night additional pet fee up to $150 for an entire stay.

Motel 6 - Boston South Braintree
125 Union Street
Braintree, MA
781-848-7890 (800-466-8356)
This motel welcomes your pets to stay with you.

Sheraton Braintree Hotel
37 Forbes Rd.
Braintree, MA
781-848-0600 (888-625-5144)
Dogs up to 60 pounds are allowed for no additional pet fee. Dogs may not be left alone in the room.

Residence Inn Boston Brockton

124 Liberty Street
Brockton, MA
508-583-3600 (800-331-3131)
This all suite hotel offers a number of amenities for all level of travelers, including a daily buffet breakfast, weekly barbecues, an evening hospitality hour, a swimming pool, Sport Court, and complimentary grocery shopping services. Dogs are allowed for an additional one time pet fee of $100 per room. 2 dogs may be allowed.

Holiday Inn Boston-Brookline
1200 Beacon St.
Brookline, MA
617-277-1200 (877-270-6405)
Dogs of all sizes are allowed. Dogs are allowed for a pet fee of $15.00 per pet per night.

Candlewood Suites Boston-Burlington
130 Middlesex Turnpike
Burlington, MA
781-229-4300 (877-270-6405)
Dogs up to 80 pounds are allowed. Pets allowed with an additional pet fee. Up to $75 for 1-6 nights and up to $150 for 7+ nights. A pet agreement must be signed at check-in.

Homestead Studio Suites Boston - Burlington
40 South Ave.
Burlington, MA
781-359-9099 (800-804-3724)
One dog is allowed per suite. There is a $25 per night additional pet fee up to $150 for an entire stay.

Staybridge Suites Boston-Burlington
11 Old Concord Rd
Burlington, MA
781-221-2233 (877-270-6405)
Dogs up to 80 pounds are allowed. Pets allowed with an additional pet fee. Up to $75 for 1-6 nights and up to $150 for 7+ nights. A pet agreement must be signed at check-in.

Bay Motor Inn
223 Main St
Buzzards Bay, MA
508-759-3989
capecodtravel.com/baymotorinn/
There is a $15 per day pet fee. The motel has no designated smoking or non-smoking rooms. Pets must be attended at all times. 2 dogs may be allowed.

Eastern Inn

6 Bourne Bridge Approach
Buzzards Bay, MA
508-759-2712
easterninncapecod.com
Dogs of all sizes are allowed, however, some breeds and cats are not permitted. There is a $15 pet fee.

Best Western Hotel Tria
220 Alewife Brook Pkwy
Cambridge, MA
617-491-8000 (800-780-7234)
Dogs of all sizes are allowed. Dogs are allowed for a pet fee of $25.00 per pet per stay.

Hotel Marlowe
25 Edwin H. Land Blvd.
Cambridge, MA
617-868-8000
Dogs of all kinds and sizes are welcome at this pet-friendly and family-friendly hotel. The luxury boutique hotel offers both rooms and suites. Hotel amenities include a fitness room and 24 hour room service. There are no pet fees, just sign a pet waiver.

Residence Inn Boston Cambridge
6 Cambridge Center
Cambridge, MA
617-349-0700 (800-331-3131)
In addition to offering a convenient location to business, shopping, dining, and entertainment areas, this hotel also provides a number of in-house amenities, including a daily buffet breakfast and evening socials 3 nights per week. Dogs are allowed for an additional one time pet fee of $150 per room. 2 dogs may be allowed.

Sheraton Commander Hotel
16 Garden St.
Cambridge, MA
617-547-4800 (888-625-5144)
Dogs up to 75 pounds are allowed for no additional pet fee. Dogs may not be left alone in the room.

The Charles Hotel in Harvard Square
1 Bennett St
Cambridge, MA
617-864-1200
boston4less.com/harvardsq.html
There is a $50 one time pet fee per room,,, dogs up to 50 pounds are allowed. Pets may not be left alone in the rooms, and pet owners must sign a pet agreement. 2 dogs may be allowed.

Brentwood Motor Inn
961 H 28
Cape Cod, MA

800-328-8812
Dogs of all sizes are allowed. There is a $10 per night per pet additional fee, and a credit card needs to be on file. Dogs are not allowed to be left alone in the room.

Centerville Corners Inn
1338 Craigville Beach Road
Centerville, MA
508-775-7223 (800-242-1137)
centervillecorners.com/
The pet-friendly Centerville Corners Inn is located a short stroll from the delightful warm water of the world-famous Craigville Beach in Nantucket Sound.

Days Inn Springfield/
450 Memorial Drive
Chicopee, MA
413-739-7311 (800-329-7466)
Dogs of all sizes are allowed. Dogs are allowed for a pet fee.

Econo Lodge
357 Burnett Rd.
Chicopee, MA
413-592-9101 (877-424-6423)
Dogs of all sizes are allowed. Dogs are allowed for a pet fee of $10.00 per pet per night.

Motel 6 - Springfield Chicopee
36 Burnett Road
Chicopee, MA
413-592-5141 (800-466-8356)
This motel welcomes your pets to stay with you.

Quality Inn
463 Memorial Drive
Chicopee, MA
413-592-6171 (877-424-6423)
Dogs of all sizes are allowed. Dogs are allowed for a pet fee of $15.00 per pet per stay. Two dogs are allowed per room.

Best Western at Historic Concord
740 Elm Street
Concord, MA
978-369-6100 (800-780-7234)
Dogs of all sizes are allowed. Dogs are allowed for a pet fee of $10.00 per pet per night.

Extended Stay America Boston - Danvers
102 Newbury St.
Danvers, MA
978-762-7414 (800-804-3724)
One dog is allowed per suite. There is a $25 per night additional pet fee up to $150 for an entire stay.

Motel 6 - Boston North Danvers

65 Newbury Street
Danvers, MA
978-774-8045 (800-466-8356)
This motel welcomes your pets to stay with you.

Residence Inn Boston North Shore/Danvers
51 Newbury Street/H 1
Danvers, MA
978-777-7171 (800-331-3131)
Offering a convenient location to business, historic, shopping, dining, and entertainment areas, this all suite hotel also offers a number of in-house amenities, including a daily buffet breakfast, and nightly social events. Dogs are allowed for an additional one time pet fee of $75 per room. Multiple dogs may be allowed.

TownePlace Suites Boston North Shore/Danvers
238 Andover Street
Danvers, MA
978-777-6222 (800-257-3000)
In addition to offering a number of in-house amenities for the business or leisure traveler, this all suite inn also provides a convenient location to beaches, businesses, shopping, dining, historic, and entertainment areas. Dogs are allowed for an additional one time fee of $75 per room. Multiple dogs may be allowed.

Residence Inn Boston Dedham
259 Elm Street
Dedham, MA
781-407-0999 (800-331-3131)
Offering a convenient location to business, shopping, dining, and entertainment areas, this all suite hotel also offers a number of in-house amenities, including an indoor heated pool, a daily buffet breakfast, and a free hospitality hour Monday through Thursday. Dogs are allowed for an additional one time pet fee of $75 per room. Multiple dogs may be allowed.

Green Harbor Waterfront
On H 28
East Falmouth, MA
508-548-4747
Well behaved dogs are allowed for an additional one time pet fee of $10 per room. Dogs are not allowed to be left alone in the room. They ask that you keep your dog leashed and cleaned up after. 2 dogs may be allowed.

Colonial Inn
38 North Water Street

Edgartown, MA
508-627-4711
colonialinnmvy.com/
This family friendly inn offers two pet-friendly suites for travelers with dogs. You can enjoy the daily complimentary continental breakfast outside in the Garden Courtyard with your pooch. There are no additional pet fees. The entire inn is non-smoking. 2 dogs may be allowed.

Martha's Vineyard Vacation Homes
Call to Arrange.
Edgartown, MA
800-544-2044
vineyardvacationhomes.com
Some of the vacation homes are pet-friendly. There is a $22 pet fee with a maximum of $100,,, this may be adjusted depending on the number and size dogs. For stays of one week or longer there is no pet fee. 2 dogs may be allowed.

Shiverick Inn
5 Pease Point Way
Edgartown, MA
508-627-3797
shiverickinn.com/
Pets up to about 75 pounds are allowed in the three bedroom suite which is located just off the library. Dogs are not allowed in the indoor common areas, just inside your room and outside. There is a $25 per night per pet fee. Pets cannot be left alone in the room. The entire inn is non-smoking. 2 dogs may be allowed.

Foley Real Estate
703 Main Street/H28
Falmouth, MA
508-548-3415
This rental company offers several pet friendly vacation houses in the Falmouth area and pet policy and/or fees may vary per rental. Aggressive breeds are not allowed, and dogs must be under their owner's control at all times.

Residence Inn Boston Foxborough
250 Foxborough Blvd
Foxborough, MA
508-698-2800 (800-331-3131)
Besides offering a convenient location to colleges, business, shopping, dining, and entertainment areas, this all suite hotel also provides a number of in-house amenities, including a daily buffet breakfast, weekday hospitality hours, and a grocery shopping service. Dogs are allowed for an additional one time pet fee of $100 per room. Multiple dogs may be allowed.

Best Western Framingham
130 Worcester Road
Framingham, MA
508-872-8811 (800-780-7234)
Dogs are welcome at this hotel.

Motel 6 - Boston West Framingham
1668 Worcester Road
Framingham, MA
508-620-0500 (800-466-8356)
This motel welcomes your pets to
stay with you.

Red Roof Inn Boston - Framingham
650 Cochituate Road
Framingham, MA
508-872-4499 (800-RED-ROOF)
One well-behaved family pet per
room. Guest must notify front desk
upon arrival. Guest is liable for any
damages. In consideration of all
guests, pets must never be left
unattended in the guest rooms.

Residence Inn Boston Framingham
400 Staples Drive
Framingham, MA
508-370-0001 (800-331-3131)
Located near many local businesses,
this all suite hotel also offers a
number of amenities, including a hot
buffet breakfast, a 24 hour market,
an evening hospitality hour Monday
through Thursday, an indoor pool,
and complimentary grocery
shopping. Dogs are allowed for an
additional one time pet fee of $100
per room. Multiple dogs may be
allowed.

Sheraton Framingham Hotel
1657 Worcester Rd.
Framingham, MA
508-879-7200 (888-625-5144)
Dogs up to 80 pounds are allowed
for no additional pet fee. Dogs may
not be left alone in the room.

Hawthorn Suites
835 Upper Union Street
Franklin, MA
508-553-3500 (800-527-1133)
In addition to providing a convenient
location to many local sites and
activities, this all-suite hotel offers a
number of amenities for business
and leisure travelers, including their
signature breakfast buffet and
beautifully appointed rooms. Dogs
are allowed for an additional one
time pet fee of $100 per room. 2
dogs may be allowed.

Residence Inn Boston Franklin
4 Forge Parkway
Franklin, MA
508-541-8188 (800-331-3131)

This all suite hotel sits central to
many of the area's star attractions,
dining, and entertainment areas,
plus they offer a number of in-house
amenities that include a daily buffet
breakfast, and an evening reception
Monday through Thursday. Dogs
are allowed for an additional one
time pet fee of $100 per room.
Multiple dogs may be allowed.

Super 8 Gardner
22 North Pearson Blvd
Gardner, MA
978-630-2888 (800-800-8000)
Dogs of all sizes are allowed. Dogs
are allowed for a nightly pet fee.
Two dogs are allowed per room.

Cape Ann Motor Inn
33 Rockport Road
Gloucester, MA
978-281-2900
Well behaved and quiet dogs of all
sizes are allowed. There are no
additional pet fees.

Quality Inn
125 Mohawk Trail
Greenfield, MA
413-774-2211 (877-424-6423)
Dogs of all sizes are allowed. Dogs
are allowed for a pet fee of $10.00
per pet per night.

Comfort Inn
237 Russell St.
Hadley, MA
413-584-9816 (877-424-6423)
Dogs of all sizes are allowed. Dogs
are allowed for a pet fee of $25.00
per pet per night. Two dogs are
allowed per room.

Knights Inn Hadley
208 Russell Street
Hadley, MA
413-585-1552 (800-843-5644)
Dogs are welcome at this hotel.
There is a $10 per visit additional
pet fee.

Best Western Merrimack Valley
401 Lowell Avenue
Haverhill, MA
978-373-1511 (800-780-7234)
Dogs of all sizes are allowed. Dogs
are allowed for a pet fee of $20.00
per pet per night.

Comfort Suites
106 Bank Rd.
Haverhill, MA
978-374-7755 (877-424-6423)
Dogs of all sizes are allowed.

Cape Cod Harbor House Inn

119 Ocean St
Hyannis, MA
508-771-1880
This inn has 19 non-smoking mini-
suites located near the center of
Hyannis. Pets are welcome, please
mention your pet when making
reservations.

Comfort Inn
1470 SR 132
Hyannis, MA
508-771-4804 (877-424-6423)
Dogs of all sizes are allowed. Dogs
are allowed for a pet fee of $25.00
per pet per night.

Simmons Homestead Inn
288 Scudder Ave.
Hyannis Port, MA
800-637-1649
SimmonsHomesteadInn.com
The B & B is at an 1800 Sea
Captain's estate in Hyannis Port in
the center of Cape Cod. 14 rooms in
two buildings. Full breakfasts, wine
hour(s), free bikes, beach stuff,
billiards and a bunch more. A chance
to see the collection of over 50
classic red sports cars behind the Inn
at Toad Hall is probably worth the trip
by itself.

Holiday Inn Express Andover North-
Lawrence
224 Winthrop Ave.
Lawrence, MA
978-975-4050 (877-270-6405)
Dogs of all sizes are allowed. Dogs
are allowed for a pet fee of $25.00
per pet per night.

Sally's Place
160 Orchard Street
Lee, MA
413-243-1982
This one bedroom apartment sleeps
up to four people and is only a few
minutes from the lake. Dogs of all
sizes are welcome for no additional
fee, but they must be very friendly
with children. Dogs must be well
mannered, leashed, and cleaned up
after at all times. 2 dogs may be
allowed.

Birchwood Inn
7 Hubbard Street
Lenox, MA
413-637-2600 (800-524-1646)
birchwood-inn.com
This historic inn has 11 guestrooms
and 9 fireplaces. It is located next to
the 450 acre Kennedy Park. Dogs of
all sizes are allowed. There is a $25
per day additional pet fee.

Cranwell Resort, Spa & Golf Club
55 Lee Road
Lenox, MA
413-637-1364 (800-272-6935)
cranwell.com/
This sprawling hilltop mansion is a premier year round resort that sits on 380 groomed acres and is home to the Golf Digest School, an 18 hole championship golf course, and a glass enclosed indoor heated pool. Dogs up to 35 pounds are allowed for an additional one time fee of $100 per pet. Dogs must be leashed, cleaned up after, and crated when in the room alone. 2 dogs may be allowed.

Seven Hills Inn
40 Plunkett Street
Lenox, MA
413-637-0060 (800-869-6518)
sevenhillsinn.com
The Seven Hills Inn offers pet-friendly accommodations in the Terrace House. Thanks to one of our readers who writes: 'They are on 27 beautifully groomed acres with lots of room for pets to roam.' There is a $40 per visit pet fee. 2 dogs may be allowed.

Walker House
64 Walker Street
Lenox, MA
413-637-1271 (800-235-3098)
walkerhouse.com/
A classic in American Federal architecture, this 1804 house features 8 rooms all theme decorated of favored composers, and they also have a cinema house where plays, films, and other notable events are shown on a large 12 foot screen. Dogs of all sizes are welcome for an additional pet fee of $10 per day. Dogs must be quiet, leashed, cleaned up after at all times, and cat-friendly. Dogs may only be left alone in the room if assured they will be well behaved. 2 dogs may be allowed.

Motel 6 - Leominster
48 Commercial Road
Leominster, MA
978-537-8161 (800-466-8356)
This motel welcomes your pets to stay with you.

Super 8 /Fitchburg Area Leominster
482 N Main Street
Leominster, MA
978-537-2800 (800-800-8000)
Dogs are welcome at this hotel.

Quality Inn & Suites
440 Bedford St.

Lexington, MA
781-861-0850 (877-424-6423)
Dogs up to 50 pounds are allowed. Dogs are allowed for a pet fee of $25.00 per pet per stay.

Doubletree Hotel
50 Warren Street
Lowell, MA
978-452-1200 (800-222-TREE (8733))
Set overlooking the city canals with all of its shops, eateries, and services to explore, this hotel also has a number of on site amenities for business or leisure travelers, plus a convenient location to local business and recreation areas. One dog is allowed for no additional fee.

Red Roof Inn Boston - Mansfield/Foxboro
60 Forbes Blvd.
Mansfield, MA
508-339-2323 (800-RED-ROOF)
One well-behaved family pet per room. Guest must notify front desk upon arrival. Guest is liable for any damages. In consideration of all guests, pets must never be left unattended in the guest rooms.

Embassy Suites
123 Boston Post Road W
Marlborough, MA
508-485-5900 (800-EMBASSY (362-2779))
A luxury, full service, all suite hotel; they offer a number of on site amenities for business and leisure travelers, plus a convenient location to business, shopping, dining, and entertainment districts. They also offer a complimentary cooked-to-order breakfast and a Manager's reception every evening. Dogs are allowed for an additional fee of $25 per night per pet. 2 dogs may be allowed.

Homestead Studio Suites Boston - Marlborough
19 Northborough Rd. E.
Marlborough, MA
508-490-9911 (800-804-3724)
One dog is allowed per suite. There is a $25 per night additional pet fee up to $150 for an entire stay.

Residence Inn Boston Marlborough
112 Donald Lynch Blvd
Marlborough, MA
508-481-1500 (800-331-3131)
Located across the street from the New England Sports Center and close to business, shopping, dining, and various entertainment areas, this all suite hotel also provides a

number of in-house amenities, including a daily buffet breakfast, manager barbecue's, and evening socials. Dogs are allowed for an additional one time pet fee of $75 per room. 2 dogs may be allowed.

Days Hotel And Conference Center - MA Methuen
159 Pelham St
Methuen, MA
978-686-2971 (800-329-7466)
Dogs of all sizes are allowed. Dogs are allowed for a pet fee.

Days Inn - Plymouth Middleboro
30 East Clark Street
Middleboro, MA
508-946-4400 (800-329-7466)
Dogs are welcome at this hotel.

La Quinta Inn Milford
24 Beaver Street
Milford, MA
508-478-8243 (800-531-5900)
Dogs of all sizes are allowed. There are no additional pet fees. Dogs must be leashed and cleaned up after, and they are not allowed in the breakfast area. Multiple dogs may be allowed.

Brass Lantern Inn
11 North Water Street
Nantucket, MA
508-228-4064
brasslanternnantucket.com/
There is a $20 per day per pet fee. All rooms are non-smoking. 2 dogs may be allowed.

Quidnuck Vacation Rental
Call to Arrange.
Nantucket, MA
202-663-8439
ifb.com/quidnuck/
Dogs are allowed at this vacation rental home. They ask that you do not bring a puppy and to never leave your dog alone in the house. There is a $75 one time per stay per pet fee. Ask for Jack when calling. Multiple dogs may be allowed.

Safe Harbor Guest House
2 Harbor View Way
Nantucket, MA
508-228-3222
beesknees.net/safeharbor/
Dogs are allowed at this guest house. All rooms have private bathrooms. If your dog will be on the bed, please bring a sheet with you to place over the bedspread. There is no pet fee, they just request that you give the housekeeper a tip for extra cleaning, if necessary. Aggressive

breeds are not allowed. Multiple dogs may be allowed.

The Cottages at the Boat Basin (Woof Cottages)
24 Old South Wharf, P.O. Box 2580
Nantucket, MA
508-325-1499 (866-838-9253)
thecottagesnantucket.com
Dogs and cats are welcome in "The Woof Cottages." These cottages are one and two bedroom cottages which include special pet amenities like a welcome basket of pet treats and play toys, a pet bed, food and water bowls, and a Nantucket bandana. When you make a reservation, let them know what size your pet is, so they can have the appropriate size pet bed and bowls in the room. All cottages are non-smoking. There is a $25 one time per stay pet fee.

Crowne Plaza Hotel Boston-Natick
1360 Worcester Street
Natick, MA
508-653-8800 (877-270-6405)
Dogs of all sizes are allowed. Dogs are allowed for a pet fee.

Sheraton Needham Hotel
100 Cabot St.
Needham, MA
781-444-1110 (888-625-5144)
Dogs of all sizes are allowed. There are no additional pet fees. Dogs are not allowed to be left alone in the room.

Captain Haskell's Octagon House
347 Union Street
New Bedford, MA
508-999-3933
Dogs of all sizes are allowed. There is a pet policy to sign at check in and there are no additional pet fees. They also provide you with a map of dog friendly places in the local area.

Days Inn New Bedford
500 Hathaway Road
New Bedford, MA
508-997-1231 (800-329-7466)
Dogs are welcome at this hotel.

The Porches Inn
231 River Street
North Adams, MA
413-664-0400
porches.com/
This inn features get-away packages, a nice long porch with rockers, and a year-round outdoor lap pool with heated deck. Dogs of all sizes are allowed for an additional $50 one time pet fee per room. One large dog or 2 small to medium dogs

are allowed per room. Dogs must be well mannered, leashed and cleaned up after at all times.

Hawthorn Suites
25 Research Place
North Chelmsford, MA
978-256-5151 (800-527-1133)
In addition to providing a convenient location to many local sites and activities, this all-suite hotel offers a number of amenities for business and leisure travelers, including their signature breakfast buffet and beautifully appointed rooms. Dogs up to about 50 pounds are allowed for an additional one time pet fee per room of $25 for 1 to 5 days; over 5 days the fee is $75. Multiple dogs may be allowed.

Comfort Inn
171 Faunce Corner Rd.
North Dartmouth, MA
508-996-0800 (877-424-6423)
Dogs of all sizes are allowed. Dogs are allowed for a pet fee of $50.00 per pet per stay.

Residence Inn New Bedford Dartmouth
181 Faunce Corner Road
North Dartmouth, MA
508-984-5858 (800-331-3131)
In addition to being located near the University of MA-Dartmouth and several major attractions, this all suite inn also offers a number of in-house amenities, including a daily buffet breakfast and evening socials. Dogs are allowed for an additional one time pet fee of $75 per room. Multiple dogs may be allowed.

Outer Reach Resort
535 Route 6
North Truro, MA
508-487-9500 (800-942-5388)
outerreachresort.com
Sitting on 12 acres of the highest bluff on the Lower Cape affords great views of the ocean and Pilgrim Lake, and in addition to a pool and gaming courts, there are great trails to walk with your pet down to the beach. They open for the season in mid-May. Dogs of all sizes are welcome for an additional $15 per night per pet. Dogs must be leashed and cleaned up after. 2 dogs may be allowed.

Clarion Hotel & Conference Center
1 Atwood Dr.
Northampton, MA
413-586-1211 (877-424-6423)
Dogs of all sizes are allowed. Two

dogs are allowed per room.

Econo Lodge Inn & Suites
380 Southwest Cutoff
Northborough, MA
508-842-8941 (877-424-6423)
Dogs up to 75 pounds are allowed. Dogs are allowed for a pet fee of $10.00 per pet per night.

Extended Stay America Foxboro - Norton
280 S. Washington St.
Norton, MA
508-285-7800 (800-804-3724)
One dog is allowed per suite. There is a $25 per night additional pet fee up to $150 for an entire stay.

Residence Inn Boston Norwood
275 Norwood Park S
Norwood, MA
781-278-9595 (800-331-3131)
Located next to Siemens Diagnostics and only minutes from major corporations and some of the areas top attractions, this inn also offers a number of in-house amenities, including a daily buffet breakfast and a hospitality hour Monday through Wednesday. Dogs are allowed for an additional one time pet fee of $75 per room. Multiple dogs may be allowed.

Martha's Vineyard Surfside Hotel
7 Oak Bluffs Avenue
Oak Bluffs, MA
508-693-2500 (800-537-3007)
mvsurfside.com
Overlooking Nantucket Sound, the Surfside offers a premier location in Oak Bluffs, with Oak Bluffs Harbor and the ocean in your backyard and shopping, fine restaurants and historic sites in your front yard. A year round hotel with 39 rooms and suites just footsteps from the Oak Bluffs Ferry Dock, Inkwell Beach and the historic Flying Horses Carousel. They have no weight restrictions on dogs and offer a "doggie package" of treats and pet scooper. There is an additional $10 pet charge which may be refunded on checkout.

Rodeway Inn
48 Cranberry Hwy
Orleans, MA
508-255-1514 (877-424-6423)
Dogs of all sizes are allowed. Dogs are allowed for a pet fee of $20.00 per pet per night. Two dogs are allowed per room.

Homestead Studio Suites Boston - Peabody
200 Jubilee Dr.

Peabody, MA
978-531-6632 (800-804-3724)
One dog is allowed per suite. There
is a $25 per night additional pet fee
up to $150 for an entire stay.

BayShore on the Water
493 Commercial Street
Provincetown, MA
508-487-9133
bayshorechandler.com
This five house complex has been
converted to studios, one bedroom
and two bedroom units. There are a
few non-smoking units and the rest
are not designated as smoking or
non-smoking. There is a $20 per day
pet fee for 1 dog, or a $30 per day
pet fee for 2 dogs.

Cape Inn
698 Commercial St
Provincetown, MA
508-487-1711
There is a $15 per night additional
pet fee. Pets must be attended at all
times. Multiple dogs may be allowed.

Crowne Pointe Historic Inn & Spa
82 Bradford Street
Provincetown, MA
508-487-6767 (877-276-9631)
crownepointe.com
This 140 year old sea captain's
estate was converted into a 40 room
Provincetown hotel situated in 6
buildings. There is one pet-friendly
room that allows dogs of all sizes.

Four Gables Cottages
15 Race Road
Provincetown, MA
508-487-2427 (866-487-2427)
fourgables.com
These Provincetown cottages and
apartments welcome your pets to
visit with you. Properties have decks
and porches.

Gabriel's at the Ashbrooke Inn
102 Bradford Street/H 6A
Provincetown, MA
508-487-3232
gabriels.com/
Some of the amenities at this historic
inn include 4 beautiful buildings,
landscaped grounds of fountains,
multi-tiered decks, and gardens,
barbecue areas, walking paths to the
park, and illuminated trees at
nightfall. Canine visitors are
pampered too with a doggy bed,
treats, and bowls. Dogs are allowed
for an additional fee of $20 per night
per pet; they must be well mannered,
kept leashed, and cleaned up after
promptly. Pet waste disposal bags
are available on the side of building

102. Dogs may only be left alone in
the room if owners are sure they will
be quiet and not do damage to the
room. Please bring clean furniture
coverings if the pet is accustomed
to being on beds, chairs, etc. 2
dogs may be allowed.

The Sandpiper Beach House
165 Commercial Street
Provincetown, MA
508-487-1928 (800-354-8628)
sandpiperbeachhouse.com
There is a $25 per visit pet fee.

White Wind Inn
174 Commercial St
Provincetown, MA
508-487-1526
Dogs are allowed for an additional
fee of $15 per night per pet. 2 dogs
may be allowed.

Quality Inn
164 New State Hwy
Raynham, MA
508-824-8647 (877-424-6423)
Dogs of all sizes are allowed. Dogs
are allowed for a pet fee of $10.00
per pet per night. Two dogs are
allowed per room.

Comfort Inn & Suites Logan
International Airport
85 American Legion Hwy.
Revere, MA
781-485-3600 (877-424-6423)
Dogs up to 70 pounds are allowed.
Dogs are allowed for a pet fee of
$25.00 per pet per night.

Hawthorne Hotel
18 Washington Square
Salem, MA
978-744-4080
hawthornehotel.com/
Keeping in character with its New
England charm, this historic hotel
has tastefully appointed the rooms
with 18th style reproduction
furniture, they are within walking
distance of several other
attractions, and they are home to a
restaurant specializing in fine
seasonal cuisine and a full-service
lounge. Dogs of all sizes are
welcome for an additional fee of
$10 per night per pet plus a $100
refundable deposit. Dogs must be
leashed, cleaned up after, and a
contact number left at the desk if
they are in the room alone. 2 dogs
may be allowed.

Stephen Daniels House
1 Daniels Street
Salem, MA

978-744-5709
This 300 year old house, furnished
with antiques, offers canopy beds
and fireplaces in every room, and a
quaint English garden. Dogs of all
sizes are welcome for no additional
fee. Dogs must be quiet, well
behaved, leashed, and cleaned up
after. 2 dogs may be allowed.

Sandwich Lodge and Resort
54 Route 6A
Sandwich, MA
508-888-2275
There is a $15 per night pet fee. Pets
are allowed in standard rooms only.
2 dogs may be allowed.

The Earl of Sandwich Motor Manor
378 Rt 6A
Sandwich, MA
508-888-1415
There are no additional pet fees.
Dogs must be quiet and well trained.
2 dogs may be allowed.

Red Roof Inn Boston - Saugus
920 Broadway
Saugus, MA
781-941-1400 (800-RED-ROOF)
One well-behaved family pet per
room. Guest must notify front desk
upon arrival. Guest is liable for any
damages. In consideration of all
guests, pets must never be left
unattended in the guest rooms.

Motel 6 - Providence East
821 Fall River Avenue
Seekonk, MA
508-336-7800 (800-466-8356)
This motel welcomes your pets to
stay with you.

Ramada Conference Center
Seekonk
940 Fall River Avenue
Seekonk, MA
508-336-7300 (800-272-6232)
Dogs of all sizes are allowed. Dogs
are allowed for a pet fee of $10 per
pet per night.

Birch Hill Bed and Breakfast
254 S Undermountain Road/H 41
Sheffield, MA
413-229-2143 (800-359-3969)
birchhillbb.com/
This grand 1780 bed and breakfast
filled with period antique furnishings,
sits on 20 acres at the foot of Mt
Everett, and offer a good variety of
activities and recreation. Dogs of all
sizes are allowed for no additional
fee. Dogs may not be left alone in
the room at any time; they are not
allowed on the bed or furniture, and

they must be walked away from the lawn, flowers, and pool areas. Dogs must be leashed and cleaned up after at all times. 2 dogs may be allowed.

Staveleigh House
59 Main Street
Sheffield, MA
413-229-2129 (800-980-2129)
staveleigh.com/
This stately 1817 colonial home provides comfort and a convenient location to several attractions and activities. One dog of any size is welcome for a one time pet fee of $20. Dogs must be well mannered, leashed, and cleaned up after at all times.

Quality Inn
1878 Wilbur Ave.
Somerset, MA
508-678-4545 (877-424-6423)
Dogs of all sizes are allowed. Two dogs are allowed per room.

La Quinta Inn & Suites Boston Somerville
23 Cummings Street
Somerville, MA
617-625-5300 (800-531-5900)
One dog of any size is allowed. There are no additional pet fees. Dogs must be leashed, cleaned up after, and crated if left alone in the room.

Red Roof Inn South Deerfield
9 Greenfield Road
South Deerfield, MA
413-665-7161 (800-RED-ROOF)
One well-behaved family pet per room. Guest must notify front desk upon arrival. Guest is liable for any damages. In consideration of all guests, pets must never be left unattended in the guest rooms.

Best Western Blue Water on the Ocean
291 S Shore Drive
South Yarmouth, MA
508-398-2288 (800-780-7234)
Dogs of all sizes are allowed. Dogs are allowed for a pet fee of $25 per pet per night.

Red Roof Inn Boston - Southborough
367 Turnpike Road
Southborough, MA
508-481-3904 (800-RED-ROOF)
One well-behaved family pet per room. Guest must notify front desk upon arrival. Guest is liable for any damages. In consideration of all guests, pets must never be left

unattended in the guest rooms.

Vienna Restaurant and Historic Inn
14 South Street
Southbridge, MA
508-764-0700 (866-2-VIENNA (284-3662))
Rich in European ambiance, this 1812 inn is on the National Historic Register, and they offer spacious accommodations, fine dining, music, a venue for special events, a veranda, and a lovely patio. One dog is allowed per room for an additional one time pet fee of $25. Dogs must be quiet, well behaved, non-shedding, and friendly to people and other pets. They are not allowed on the furniture or beds. Dogs are allowed at the outer tables of the restaurant; they must be leashed and under their owner's control at all times.

Sheraton Springfield Monarch Place Hotel
One Monarch Place
Springfield, MA
413-781-1010 (888-625-5144)
One dog of any size is allowed for an additional one time pet fee of $50 per room. Dogs may not be left alone in the room.

The Red Lion Inn
30 Main Street
Stockbridge, MA
413-298-5545
redlioninn.com/home.html
The surroundings and décor of this historic inn offer visitors a look into the past, but they have also provided many modern niceties, including an outdoor heated pool and hot tub surrounded by a heated stone patio. Dogs up to 80 pounds are allowed for an additional fee of $40 per night per pet, and they must be declared at the time of reservations. Pooches also get a special treat upon arrival. Dogs must be quiet, well trained, leashed, cleaned up after, and crated when left alone in the room. 2 dogs may be allowed.

Comfort Inn & Suites Colonial
215 Charlton Rd. (US 20)
Sturbridge, MA
508-347-3306 (877-424-6423)
Dogs up to 100 pounds are allowed. Dogs are allowed for a pet fee of $15.00 per pet per night. Two dogs are allowed per room.

Days Inn Sturbridge
66-68 Haynes Street
Sturbridge, MA

508-347-3391 (800-329-7466)
Dogs are welcome at this hotel.

Motel 6 - Sturbridge, Ma
408 Main Street
Sturbridge, MA
508-347-7327 (800-466-8356)
This motel welcomes your pets to stay with you.

Publick House Historic Inn
On the Common, Route 131
Sturbridge, MA
508-347-3313 (800-PUBLICK)
publickhouse.com/
There is a $15 (+ tax) per day per pet additional fee. 2 dogs may be allowed.

Sturbridge Host Hotel
366 Main Street
Sturbridge, MA
508-347-7393
Dogs of all sizes are allowed. There is a $25 per night per pet additional fee.

Super 8 Sturbridge
358 Main St
Sturbridge, MA
508-347-9000 (800-800-8000)
Dogs of all sizes are allowed. Dogs are allowed for a pet fee of $20.00 per pet per stay.

Travelodge Sturbridge
400 Route 15
Sturbridge, MA
508-347-1978 (800-578-7878)
Dogs of all sizes are allowed. Dogs are allowed for a pet fee of $10.00 per pet per stay.

Clarion Inn
738 Boston Post Rd.
Sudbury, MA
978-443-2223 (877-424-6423)
Dogs of all sizes are allowed. Dogs are allowed for a pet fee of $10.00 per pet per night. Two dogs are allowed per room.

Econo Lodge
200 Worcester Providence
Sutton, MA
508-865-5222 (877-424-6423)
Dogs of all sizes are allowed.

Extended Stay America Boston - Tewksbury
1910 Andover St.
Tewksbury, MA
978-863-9888 (800-804-3724)
One dog is allowed per suite. There is a $25 per night additional pet fee up to $150 for an entire stay.

Holiday Inn Tewksbury-Andover
4 Highwood Drive
Tewksbury, MA
978-640-9000 (877-270-6405)
Dogs of all sizes are allowed. Dogs
are allowed for a pet fee of $50.00
per pet per night.

Motel 6 - Boston Tewksbury
95 Main Street
Tewksbury, MA
978-851-8677 (800-466-8356)
This motel welcomes your pets to
stay with you.

Residence Inn Boston
Tewksbury/Andover
1775 Andover Street
Tewksbury, MA
978-640-1003 (800-331-3131)
Some of the amenities at this inn
include a daily buffet breakfast, an
evening social hour Monday through
Thursday, summer barbecues, an
outdoor heated pool, and
complimentary grocery shopping.
Dogs are allowed for an additional
one time pet fee of $100 per room. 2
dogs may be allowed.

TownePlace Suites Boston
Tewksbury
20 International Place
Tewksbury, MA
978-863-9800 (800-257-3000)
In addition to offering a number of in-
house amenities for the business or
leisure traveler, this all suite inn also
provides a convenient location to
business, shopping, dining, and
entertainment areas. Dogs are
allowed for an additional fee of $25
per day for the 1st 3 days to a
maximum of $75 per stay per room.
Multiple dogs may be allowed.

Martha's Vineyard Rental Houses
Call to Arrange.
Vineyard Haven, MA
508-693-6222
Select from a variety of pet-friendly
rental homes. Pet fees may vary per
property.

Sheraton Colonial Hotel & Golf Club
Boston North
One Audubon Rd.
Wakefield, MA
781-245-9300 (888-625-5144)
Dogs up to 80 pounds are allowed.
There are no additional pet fees.
Dogs are not allowed to be left alone
in the room.

Holiday Inn Express Boston-Waltham
385 Winter Street
Waltham, MA

781-890-2800 (877-270-6405)
Dogs of all sizes are allowed. Dogs
are allowed for a pet fee of $50 per
pet per stay.

Homestead Studio Suites Boston -
Waltham
52 4th Ave.
Waltham, MA
781-890-1333 (800-804-3724)
One dog is allowed per suite. There
is a $25 per night additional pet fee
up to $150 for an entire stay.

The Westin-Waltham Boston
70 Third Ave.
Waltham, MA
781-290-5600 (888-625-5144)
Dogs up to 50 pounds are allowed
for no additional pet fee. Dogs may
not be left alone in the room.

Candlewood Suites West
Springfield
572 Riverdale St.
West Springfield, MA
413-739-1122 (877-270-6405)
Dogs up to 80 pounds are allowed.
Pets allowed with an additional pet
fee. Up to $75 for 1-6 nights and up
to $150 for 7+ nights. A pet
agreement must be signed at
check-in.

Econo Lodge
1533 Elm St.
West Springfield, MA
413-734-8278 (877-424-6423)
Dogs of all sizes are allowed. Dogs
are allowed for a pet fee of $25.00
per pet per night.

Red Roof Inn West Springfield
1254 Riverdale Street
West Springfield, MA
413-731-1010 (800-RED-ROOF)
One well-behaved family pet per
room. Guest must notify front desk
upon arrival. Guest is liable for any
damages. In consideration of all
guests, pets must never be left
unattended in the guest rooms.

Residence Inn West Springfield
64 Border Way
West Springfield, MA
413-732-9543 (800-331-3131)
This all suite hotel gives a
convenient location to numerous
sites of interest and activities for all
level of travelers, plus they also
offer a number of in-house
amenities, including a daily buffet
breakfast and evening receptions.
Dogs are allowed for an additional
one time pet fee of $75 per room.
Multiple dogs may be allowed.

Econo Lodge
59 East Main St.
West Yarmouth, MA
508-771-0699 (877-424-6423)
Dogs up to 50 pounds are allowed.
Dogs are allowed for a pet fee of
$10.00 per pet per night. Two dogs
are allowed per room.

Extended Stay America Boston -
Westborough
19 Connector Rd.
Westborough, MA
508-616-0155 (800-804-3724)
One dog is allowed per suite. There
is a $25 per night additional pet fee
up to $150 for an entire stay.

Motel 6 - Westborough, Ma
399 Turnpike Road
Westborough, MA
508-366-0202 (800-466-8356)
This motel welcomes your pets to
stay with you.

Residence Inn Boston Westborough
25 Connector Road
Westborough, MA
508-366-7700 (800-331-3131)
Located in a quiet suburban setting
with easy I 495 access, this all suite
hotel offers a number of amenities at
this inn include a daily buffet
breakfast, complimentary evening
socials, a swimming pool, and
complimentary grocery shopping
services. Dogs up to 100 pounds are
allowed for an additional one time
pet fee of $100 per room. 2 dogs
may be allowed.

Econo Lodge Inn & Suites
2 Southampton Road
Westfield, MA
413-568-2821 (877-424-6423)
Dogs of all sizes are allowed. Two
dogs are allowed per room.

Residence Inn Boston Westford
7 Lan Drive
Westford, MA
978-392-1407 (800-331-3131)
Some of the amenities at this inn
include a hot continental breakfast,
weekly barbecues, evening
hospitality hours, an indoor pool, and
complimentary grocery shopping.
Dogs are allowed for an additional
one time pet fee of $75 per room.
Multiple dogs may be allowed.

Rodeway Inn
183 Main Street
Westminster, MA
978-874-5951 (877-424-6423)
Dogs of all sizes are allowed. Dogs

are allowed for a pet fee of $5.00 per pet per night.

Clover Hill Farm
249 Adams Rd
Williamstown, MA
413-458-3376
cloverhillfarm.net
This B&B at the farm offers pet-friendly and horse-friendly accommodations in the Berkshires. Horse riding lessons can be arranged.

Cozy Corner Motel
284 Sand Springs Rd
Williamstown, MA
413-458-8006
There is a $10 per day per pet additional fee. Multiple dogs may be allowed.

Best Western New Englander
1 Rainin Road
Woburn, MA
781-935-8160 (800-780-7234)
Dogs of all sizes are allowed. Dogs are allowed for a pet fee.

Red Roof Inn Boston - Woburn
19 Commerce Way
Woburn, MA
781-935-7110 (800-RED-ROOF)
One well-behaved family pet per room. Guest must notify front desk upon arrival. Guest is liable for any damages. In consideration of all guests, pets must never be left unattended in the guest rooms.

Residence Inn Boston Woburn
300 Presidential Way
Woburn, MA
781-376-4000 (800-331-3131)
This all suite hotel offers a number of amenities for all level of travelers, including a daily buffet breakfast, complimentary evening socials, a swimming pool, and complimentary grocery shopping services. Dogs are allowed for an additional one time pet fee of $75 per room. Multiple dogs may be allowed.

Crowne Plaza Hotel Worcester-Downtown
10 Lincoln Square
Worcester, MA
508-791-1600 (877-270-6405)
Dogs up to 50 pounds are allowed. Dogs are allowed for a pet fee of $20.00 per pet per night.

Quality Inn & Suites
50 Oriol Dr.
Worcester, MA
508-852-2800 (877-424-6423)

Dogs up to 70 pounds are allowed. Dogs are allowed for a pet fee of $10.00 per pet per night.

Residence Inn Worcester
503 Plantation Street
Worcester, MA
508-753-6300 (800-331-3131)
A close location to major universities, businesses, hospitals, and recreational areas, a daily buffet breakfast, weekday evening socials, weekly barbecues, a 24 hour market, and a complimentary grocery shopping service are just some of the amenities of this all suite hotel. Dogs are allowed for an additional one time pet fee of $100 per room. Multiple dogs may be allowed.

Colonial House
Old Kings Hwy
Yarmouth Port, MA
508-362-4348 (800-999-3416)
colonialhousecapecod.com/
There is a $5 per day pet charge. Multiple dogs may be allowed.

Michigan

Motel 6 - Adrian, Mi
1575 West Maumee Street
Adrian, MI
517-263-5741 (800-466-8356)
This motel welcomes your pets to stay with you.

Linda's Lighthouse Inn
5965 Pointe Tremble Road/H 29
Algonac, MI
810-794-2992
lindasbnb.com/
Rich in history from its prohibition days, this waterside inn on the St Clair River offers guests boat docking, a 300 foot dock, great views, and any help needed for special occasions, finding points of interest, or sightseeing. Dogs of all sizes are allowed for an additional fee of $15 per night per pet with prior arrangements. Dogs must be well behaved, leashed, and cleaned up after. When the weather permits, owners may dine with their pet on the balcony overlooking the river. 2 dogs may be allowed.

Castle in the Country
340 H 40S
Allegan, MI
269-673-8054 (888-673-8054)
castleinthecountry.com/
A popular romantic haven, this inn and spa sits in a beautiful pastoral

and wooded setting, and offers all the amenities for special occasions or a much needed getaway. One dog is allowed per room for an additional $20 per stay. Dogs must be quiet, well behaved, leashed, and cleaned up after.

Sleep Inn & Suites
4869 Becker Dr.
Allendale, MI
616-892-8000 (877-424-6423)
Dogs of all sizes are allowed. Dogs are allowed for a pet fee of $1.50 per pet per night.

Petticoat Inn
2454 W Monroe Road/H 46
Alma, MI
989-681-5728
This inn allows pets for no additional pet fee. Dogs may not be left unattended at any time, and they must be leashed and cleaned up after. Aggressive dogs are not allowed. 2 dogs may be allowed.

Days Inn Alpena
1496 M-32 West
Alpena, MI
989-356-6118 (800-329-7466)
Dogs of all sizes are allowed. Dogs are allowed for a pet fee of $10 per pet per night.

Holiday Inn Alpena
1000 US 23 North
Alpena, MI
989-356-2151 (877-270-6405)
Dogs are welcome at this hotel.

Comfort Inn & Suites
2376 Carpenter Road
Ann Arbor, MI
734-477-9977 (877-424-6423)
Dogs of all sizes are allowed. Dogs are allowed for a pet fee of $15.00 per pet per night. Three or more dogs may be allowed.

Days Inn Ann Arbor
2380 Carpenter Road
Ann Arbor, MI
734-971-0700 (800-329-7466)
Dogs are welcome at this hotel.

Extended Stay America Detroit - Ann Arbor
1501 Briarwood Cir. Dr.
Ann Arbor, MI
734-332-1980 (800-804-3724)
One dog is allowed per suite. There is a $25 per night additional pet fee up to $150 for an entire stay.

Holiday Inn Ann Arbor-Near The Univ. Of Mi

3600 Plymouth Road
Ann Arbor, MI
734-769-9800 (877-270-6405)
Dogs of all sizes are allowed. Dogs are allowed for a pet fee of $25.00 per pet per night.

Motel 6 - Ann Arbor
3764 State St
Ann Arbor, MI
734-665-9900 (800-466-8356)
This motel welcomes your pets to stay with you.

Red Roof Inn Ann Arbor - University North
3621 Plymouth Road
Ann Arbor, MI
734-996-5800 (800-RED-ROOF)
One well-behaved family pet per room. Guest must notify front desk upon arrival. Guest is liable for any damages. In consideration of all guests, pets must never be left unattended in the guest rooms.

Red Roof Inn Ann Arbor - University South
3505 South State Street
Ann Arbor, MI
734-665-3500 (800-RED-ROOF)
One well-behaved family pet per room. Guest must notify front desk upon arrival. Guest is liable for any damages. In consideration of all guests, pets must never be left unattended in the guest rooms.

Residence Inn Ann Arbor
800 Victors Way
Ann Arbor, MI
734-996-5666 (888-236-2427)
This all suite inn offers amenities for all level of travelers, including a convenient location to a number of area attractions, a daily buffet breakfast, and a Manager's reception Monday through Thursday. Dogs are allowed for an additional pet fee of $25 per night for the first 3 nights - to a total of $75 per stay per room. Multiple dogs may be allowed.

Econo Lodge Inn & Suites
510 W. Huron (US 23)
Au Gres, MI
989-876-4060 (877-424-6423)
Dogs of all sizes are allowed. Dogs are allowed for a pet fee of $10.00 per pet per stay. Three or more dogs may be allowed.

Days Inn and Suites MI Auburn
4955 South Garfield Road
Auburn, MI
989-662-7888 (800-329-7466)
Dogs of all sizes are allowed. Dogs

are allowed for a pet fee of $10.00 per pet per stay.

Candlewood Suites Detroit-Auburn Hills
1650 Opdyke Rd.
Auburn Hills, MI
248-373-3342 (877-270-6405)
Dogs up to 80 pounds are allowed. Pets allowed with an additional pet fee. Up to $75 for 1-6 nights and up to $150 for 7+ nights. A pet agreement must be signed at check-in.

Extended Stay America Detroit - Auburn Hills
1180 Doris Rd.
Auburn Hills, MI
248-373-1355 (800-804-3724)
One dog is allowed per suite. There is a $25 per night additional pet fee up to $150 for an entire stay.

Hilton Suites Hotel
2300 Featherstone Road
Auburn Hills, MI
248-334-2222 (800-HILTONS (445-8667))
This luxury, all suite hotel offers a number on site amenities for business and leisure travelers, plus a convenient location to business, shopping, dining, and recreation areas. Dogs are allowed with prior reservation for an additional one time pet fee of $75 per room. 2 dogs may be allowed.

Homestead Studio Suites Detroit - Auburn Hills
3315 University Dr.
Auburn Hills, MI
248-340-8888 (800-804-3724)
One dog is allowed per suite. There is a $25 per night additional pet fee up to $150 for an entire stay.

Motel 6 - Detroit North Auburn Hills
1471 Opdyke Rd
Auburn Hills, MI
248-373-8440 (800-466-8356)
This motel welcomes your pets to stay with you.

Staybridge Suites Detroit-Auburn Hills
2050 Featherstone Road
Auburn Hills, MI
248-322-4600 (877-270-6405)
Dogs up to 80 pounds are allowed. Pets allowed with an additional pet fee. Up to $75 for 1-6 nights and up to $150 for 7+ nights. A pet agreement must be signed at check-in.

Baymont Inn and Suites /I-94 Battle Creek
4725 Beckley Road
Battle Creek, MI
269-979-5400 (877-229-6668)
Dogs of all sizes are allowed. Dogs are allowed for a pet fee of $10.00 per pet per night.

Days Inn Battle Creek
4786 Beckley Road
Battle Creek, MI
269-979-3561 (800-329-7466)
Dogs of all sizes are allowed. Dogs are allowed for a pet fee of $25 per pet per night.

Econo Lodge
165 Capital Ave. S.W.
Battle Creek, MI
269-965-3976 (877-424-6423)
Dogs up to 50 pounds are allowed. Dogs are allowed for a pet fee of $10.00 per pet per night.

Knights Inn Battle Creek
2595 Capital Avenue S.W.
Battle Creek, MI
269-964-2600 (800-843-5644)
Dogs are welcome at this hotel.

Motel 6 - Battle Creek
4775 Beckley Rd
Battle Creek, MI
269-979-1141 (800-466-8356)
This motel welcomes your pets to stay with you.

Ramada Battle Creek
5050 Beckley Road
Battle Creek, MI
269-979-1100 (800-272-6232)
Dogs are welcome at this hotel.

Super 8 Battle Creek
5395 Beckley Rd
Battle Creek, MI
269-979-1828 (800-800-8000)
Dogs are welcome at this hotel.

Americinn of Bay City
3915 Three Mile Rd
Bay City, MI
989-671-0071
There is an additional pet fee of $10 per night per room. Multiple dogs may be allowed.

Applesauce Inn
7296 H 88S
Bellaire, MI
231-533-6448
applesauceinn.com/
This wonderfully restored 100 year old country home is now a great getaway with numerous amenities, and it offers a good central location

to many other sites of interest and recreation. There is one pet friendly room, and dogs of all sizes are allowed for an additional fee of $15 per night which is donated to Boxer rescue. Dogs may not be left alone in the room or unsupervised at any time, they are not allowed on beds or furniture, and request guests bring their pet's bedding. Dogs must be housebroken, quiet, well mannered, sociable with other pets and people, leashed, and cleaned up after at all times. Dogs must be healthy and have all their shots. 2 dogs may be allowed.

Comfort Inn
45945 S. I-94 Service Drive
Belleville, MI
734-697-8556 (877-424-6423)
Dogs of all sizes are allowed. Dogs are allowed for a pet fee of $10.00 per pet per night.

Red Roof Inn Detroit Metro Airport - Belleville
45501 North I-94 Service Dr
Belleville, MI
734-697-2244 (800-RED-ROOF)
One well-behaved family pet per room. Guest must notify front desk upon arrival. Guest is liable for any damages. In consideration of all guests, pets must never be left unattended in the guest rooms.

Super 8 Belleville
45707 S I-94 Service Rd
Belleville, MI
734-699-1888 (800-800-8000)
Dogs are welcome at this hotel.

Motel 6 - Benton Harbor
2063 Pipestone Road
Benton Harbor, MI
269-925-5100 (800-466-8356)
This motel welcomes your pets to stay with you.

Red Roof Inn Benton Harbor - St Joseph
1630 Mall Drive
Benton Harbor, MI
269-927-2484 (800-RED-ROOF)
One well-behaved family pet per room. Guest must notify front desk upon arrival. Guest is liable for any damages. In consideration of all guests, pets must never be left unattended in the guest rooms.

Howard Johnson Benton Harbor
798 Ferguson Drive
Benton Harbor/St Joseph, MI
269-927-1172 (800-446-4656)
Dogs are welcome at this hotel.

Bluffs View Motel
707 W Lead Street
Bessemer, MI
906-667-0311
Dogs only are allowed, and in all sizes. There is a $5 per night per pet additional fee. 2 dogs may be allowed.

Best Western Scenic Hill Resort
1400 US Highway 31
Beulah, MI
231-882-7754 (800-780-7234)
Dogs up to 60 pounds are allowed. Dogs are allowed for a nightly pet fee.

Holiday Inn Big Rapids
1005 Perry Ave.
Big Rapids, MI
231-796-4400 (877-270-6405)
Dogs of all sizes are allowed. Dogs are allowed for a pet fee of $15.00 per pet per night.

Quality Inn & Suites
1705 S. State Street
Big Rapids, MI
231-592-5150 (877-424-6423)
Dogs up to 50 pounds are allowed. Dogs are allowed for a pet fee of $10.00/pet per pet per night. One dog is allowed per room.

Best Western of Birch Run/Frankenmuth
9087 E Birch Run Road
Birch Run, MI
989-624-9395 (800-780-7234)
Dogs of all sizes are allowed. Dogs are allowed for a pet fee of $25.00 per pet per stay.

Holiday Inn Express Birch Run (Frankenmuth Area)
12150 Dixie Hwy
Birch Run, MI
989-624-9300 (877-270-6405)
Dogs of all sizes are allowed. Dogs are allowed for a pet fee of $50.00 per pet per stay.

Super 8 / Frankenmuth Area Birch Run
9235 E Birch Run Rd
Birch Run, MI
989-624-4440 (800-800-8000)
Dogs are welcome at this hotel.

Insel Haus
HCR 1, Box 157
Bois Blanc Island, MI
231-634-7393 (888-634-7393)
inselhausbandb.com/
A world class retreat, visitors arrive here by ferry, plane, or helicopter,

and are welcomed to a home rich in colors and history, warm with antiques, bright with stained glass, and offering wonderful views of the Straits of Mackinac. One dog is allowed for an additional fee of $20 per night. Dogs must be quiet, well behaved, leashed, and cleaned up after. Dogs may not be left unattended at any time, and they must be friendly to other pets and people; there is an older dog on site.

Baymont Inn & Suites /Frankenmuth Bridgeport
6460 Dixie Hwy
Bridgeport, MI
989-777-3000 (877-229-6668)
Dogs are welcome at this hotel.

Dewey Lake Manor
11811 Laird Road
Brooklyn, MI
517-467-7122
deweylakemanor.com/
There 18 acres to explore at this lakeside inn. Outdoor amenities include grills, picnic tables, gaming areas, and use of the paddleboat and canoe. Dogs of all sizes are allowed for an additional $10 per night per pet; there can be 1 large dog or 2 small dogs per room. They request that owners bring their pets bedding. Dogs are not allowed in the dining area, but guests are welcome to dine on the veranda with their pet. Dogs must be well mannered, leashed, and cleaned up after.

Super 8 Brooklyn
M-50 and Wamplers Lake Road
Brooklyn, MI
517-592-0888 (800-800-8000)
Dogs are welcome at this hotel.

Comfort Inn
1650 S Mitchell Street
Cadillac, MI
231-779-2900 (877-424-6423)
Dogs up to 75 pounds are allowed. Dogs are allowed for a pet fee of $20.00 per pet per night.

Econo Lodge
2501 Sunnyside Drive
Cadillac, MI
231-775-6700 (877-424-6423)
Dogs of all sizes are allowed. Dogs are allowed for a pet fee of $10.00 per pet per stay.

McGuires Resort
7880 Mackinaw Trail
Cadillac, MI
231-775-9947
mcguiresresort.com

This resort is open year round. They have on-site restaurants, gift shop, swimming pool, golf, cross-country skiing and more. All well-behaved dogs are allowed for an extra $20 every 3 days per pet. During the winter dogs are allowed on their cross-country ski trails. Pets must be leashed at the resort and on the trails. 2 dogs may be allowed.

Rodeway Inn
5676 East M-55
Cadillac, MI
231-775-2458 (877-424-6423)
Dogs of all sizes are allowed. Dogs are allowed for a pet fee of $10.00 per pet per night.

Super 8 Cadillac
6080 East M-55
Cadillac, MI
231-775-8561 (800-800-8000)
Dogs are welcome at this hotel.

Days Inn Canton
40500 Michigan Avenue
Canton, MI
734-721-5200 (800-329-7466)
Dogs of all sizes are allowed. Dogs are allowed for a pet fee of $10.00 per pet per night.

Extended Stay America Detroit - Canton
2000 Haggerty Rd.
Canton, MI
734-844-0725 (800-804-3724)
One dog is allowed per suite. There is a $25 per night additional pet fee up to $150 for an entire stay.

La Quinta Inn Detroit/Canton
41211 Ford Road
Canton, MI
734-981-1808 (800-531-5900)
One large dog or up to 3 small to medium dogs are allowed. There are no additional pet fees unless the stay is over 7 days; then there is a $25 refundable deposit required. The front desk must be informed at check in of any pets so to inform housekeeping, and they must be leashed and cleaned up after.

Super 8 /Livonia Area Canton
3933 Lotz Road
Canton, MI
734-722-8880 (800-800-8000)
Dogs of all sizes are allowed. Dogs are allowed for a pet fee.

Motel 6 - Detroit West Canton
41216 Ford Rd
Canton Township, MI
734-981-5000 (800-466-8356)

This motel welcomes your pets to stay with you.

Lodge of Charlevoix
120 Michigan Ave
Charlevoix, MI
231-547-6565
There is a $12 per day per pet fee. 2 dogs may be allowed.

Points North Inn
101 Michigan Ave
Charlevoix, MI
231-547-0055 (800-968-5433)
There is a $25 one time fee per pet. 2 dogs may be allowed.

Best Western River Terrace
847 S Main Street
Cheboygan, MI
231-627-5688 (800-780-7234)
Dogs of all sizes are allowed. Dogs are allowed for a pet fee of $10.00 per pet per night.

Comfort Inn
1645 Commerce Park Dr.
Chelsea, MI
734-433-8000 (877-424-6423)
Dogs of all sizes are allowed. Two dogs are allowed per room.

Waterloo Gardens
7600 Werkener Road
Chelsea, MI
734-433-1612 (877-433 -1612)
waterloogardensbb.com/
A master spa, solarium, lush greenery, gardens, recreation, and much more are offered guests at this lovely inn. One dog is allowed per room for no additional fee. Dogs may not be left alone in the room at any time, and they must be leashed and cleaned up after at all times. Dogs must be friendly towards both other animals and people as there are 2 Golden Retrievers who live on site.

Days Inn Clare
10100 S. Clare Ave
Clare, MI
989-802-0144 (800-329-7466)
Dogs are welcome at this hotel.

Red Roof Inn Coldwater
348 S. Willowbrook Rd
Coldwater, MI
517-279-1199 (800-RED-ROOF)
One well-behaved family pet per room. Guest must notify front desk upon arrival. Guest is liable for any damages. In consideration of all guests, pets must never be left unattended in the guest rooms.

Super 8 Coldwater
600 Orleans Blvd
Coldwater, MI
517-278-8833 (800-800-8000)
Dogs of all sizes are allowed. Dogs are allowed for a pet fee of $10.00 per pet per stay.

Extended Stay America Detroit - Dearborn
260 Town Center Dr.
Dearborn, MI
313-336-0021 (800-804-3724)
One dog is allowed per suite. There is a $25 per night additional pet fee up to $150 for an entire stay.

Red Roof Inn Detroit - Dearborn
24130 Michigan Avenue
Dearborn, MI
313-278-9732 (800-RED-ROOF)
One well-behaved family pet per room. Guest must notify front desk upon arrival. Guest is liable for any damages. In consideration of all guests, pets must never be left unattended in the guest rooms.

Ritz-Carlton
300 Town Center Drive
Dearborn, MI
313-441-2000
There is a $75 one time pet fee per room. Dogs up to 50 pounds are allowed. 2 dogs may be allowed.

TownePlace Suites Detroit Dearborn
6141 Mercury Drive
Dearborn, MI
313-271-0200 (800-257-3000)
Besides offering a number of in-house amenities for all level of travelers, this all suite inn also offers a convenient location to business, shopping, dining, and entertainment areas. Dogs are allowed for an additional one time fee of $100 per room. 2 dogs may be allowed.

Residence Inn Detroit Dearborn
5777 Southfield Service Drive
Detroit, MI
313-441-1700 (800-331-3131)
Besides offering a convenient location to business, shopping, dining, and entertainment areas, this hotel also provides a number of in-house amenities, including a daily buffet breakfast and complementary evening receptions Monday to Thursday. Dogs are allowed for an additional one time pet fee of $100 per room. Multiple dogs may be allowed.

Baymont Inn & Suites Dowagiac
29291 Amerihost Drive

Dowagiac, MI
269-782-4270 (877-229-6668)
Dogs are welcome at this hotel.

Drummond Island Resort & Conference Center
33494 S Maxton Road
Drummond Island, MI
906-493-1000 (800-999-6343)
drummondisland.com/
Resting on the shores of the US's largest freshwater island on 2000 lush acres filled with wildlife, this resort has all the amenities for business, relaxation, or recreation-including an 18-hole golf course and an ORV park. Dogs are allowed for an additional fee of $50 per pet per stay. Dogs must be well behaved, leashed, and cleaned up after. 2 dogs may be allowed.

H & H Resort
33185 S Water Street
Drummond Island, MI
800-543-4743
This beautiful oceanside park offers cabins and camping options. Dogs are allowed at either for no additional fee. They also have watercraft rentals that dogs are allowed on. Dogs must be well behaved, leashed, and cleaned up after. 2 dogs may be allowed.

Days Inn and Suites Dundee
130 Outer Dr US 23 & M-50
Dundee, MI
734-529-5505 (800-329-7466)
Dogs of all sizes are allowed. Dogs are allowed for a pet fee of $10 per pet per night.

Quality Inn
111 Waterstradt Commerce Drive
Dundee, MI
734-529-5240 (877-424-6423)
Dogs up to 50 pounds are allowed. Dogs are allowed for a pet fee of $20.00 per pet per night. Three or more dogs may be allowed.

Residence Inn East Lansing
1600 E Grand River Avenue/H 43
East Lansing, MI
517-332-7711 (800-331-3131)
Sitting only a short walk from all the exciting venues of the state university, this all suite, upscale hotel also offers a number of in-house amenities including a daily buffet breakfast and evening receptions. Dogs are allowed for an additional one time pet fee of $75 per room. Multiple dogs may be allowed.

TownePlace Suites East Lansing

2855 Hannah Blvd
East Lansing, MI
517-203-1000 (800-257-3000)
Besides being located within walking distance to the state university and central to a number of other of sites of interest, businesses, shopping, and dining areas, this all suite hotel also offers a number of on-site amenities for business or leisure travelers. Dogs are allowed for an additional one time fee of $75 per room. 2 dogs may be allowed.

Candlewood Suites Detroit-Farmington Hills
37555 Hills Tech Drive
Farmington Hills, MI
248-324-0540 (877-270-6405)
Dogs up to 80 pounds are allowed. Pets allowed with an additional pet fee. Up to $75 for 1-6 nights and up to $150 for 7+ nights. A pet agreement must be signed at check-in.

Extended Stay America Detroit - Farmington Hills
27775 Stansbury Blvd.
Farmington Hills, MI
248-473-4000 (800-804-3724)
One dog is allowed per suite. There is a $25 per night additional pet fee up to $150 for an entire stay.

Motel 6 - Detroit Northwest Farmington Hills
38300 Grand River Ave
Farmington Hills, MI
248-471-0590 (800-466-8356)
This motel welcomes your pets to stay with you.

Red Roof Inn Detroit - Farmington Hills
24300 Sinacola Court Northeast
Farmington Hills, MI
248-478-8640 (800-RED-ROOF)
One well-behaved family pet per room. Guest must notify front desk upon arrival. Guest is liable for any damages. In consideration of all guests, pets must never be left unattended in the guest rooms.

Glenn Country Inn
1286 64th Street
Fennville, MI
888-237-3009
glenncountryinn.com/
A quiet country inn located on 10 scenic farmland acres, this retreat features brightly colored gardens, walking trails, lush lawns, and special getaway packages. Dogs of all sizes are allowed for an additional $20 per pet per stay.

Your pooch is welcomed with a plush doggy bed, yummy treats, a food bowl, and water dispenser. There is also a large, fenced area for a safe off-lead area. Dogs may not be left alone in the room at any time, and they are not allowed on the bed or furnishings. Dogs must be under owner's control, leashed, and cleaned up after. Dogs must be friendly and get along well with other animals and people. The dining room is pet friendly, and your pet may join you there for any of the meals. 2 dogs may be allowed.

Sleep Inn
29101 Commerce Dr.
Flat Rock, MI
734-782-9898 (877-424-6423)
Dogs of all sizes are allowed. Dogs are allowed for a pet fee of $10.00 per pet per night.

Baymont Inn & Suites Flint
4160 Pier North Boulevard
Flint, MI
810-732-2300 (877-229-6668)
Dogs of all sizes are allowed. Dogs are allowed for a pet fee of $25.00 per pet per stay.

Holiday Inn Express Flint-Campus Area
1150 Robert T. Longway Blvd
Flint, MI
810-238-7744 (877-270-6405)
Dogs of all sizes are allowed. Dogs are allowed for a nightly pet fee.

Motel 6 - Flint
2324 Austin Pkwy
Flint, MI
810-767-7100 (800-466-8356)
This motel welcomes your pets to stay with you.

Red Roof Inn Flint - Bishop Airport
G-3219 Miller Road
Flint, MI
810-733-1660 (800-RED-ROOF)
One well-behaved family pet per room. Guest must notify front desk upon arrival. Guest is liable for any damages. In consideration of all guests, pets must never be left unattended in the guest rooms.

Residence Inn Flint
2202 W Hill Road
Flint, MI
810-424-7000 (800-331-3131)
Some of the amenities at this all-suite inn include a daily buffet breakfast, evening social hours, an indoor pool, and complimentary grocery shopping. Dogs are allowed

for an additional one time pet fee of $100 per room. Multiple dogs may be allowed.

Super 8 /Burton Area Flint
1343 South Center Rd
Flint, MI
810-743-8850 (800-800-8000)
Dogs of all sizes are allowed. Dogs are allowed for a pet fee.

Best Western Fowlerville
950 S Grand Avenue
Fowlerville, MI
517-223-9165 (800-780-7234)
Dogs of all sizes are allowed. Dogs are allowed for a pet fee.

Drury Inn & Suites
260 South Main
Frankenmuth, MI
989-652-2800 (800-378-7946)
Dogs of all sizes are allowed for no additional pet fee with a credit card on file, and there is a pet agreement to sign at check in.

Valentine's Bay Lodge
8191 H 183
Garden, MI
906-644-5012
uprentalhome.com/
Warmly inviting, this mountain lodge style getaway is located on the scenic Garden Peninsula with beautiful lakefront views, lush greenery, and tree-lined paths. Dogs of all sizes are allowed for no additional fee. Dogs may not be left unattended; they must be quiet, well behaved, leashed, and cleaned up after at all times. 2 dogs may be allowed.

Baymont Inn and Suites Gaylord
510 South Wisconsin Avenue
Gaylord, MI
989-731-6331 (877-229-6668)
Dogs of all sizes are allowed. Dogs are allowed for a pet fee of $20.00 per pet per stay.

Quality Inn
137 West St.
Gaylord, MI
989-732-7541 (877-424-6423)
Dogs of all sizes are allowed. Dogs are allowed for a pet fee of $fee per pet per night.

Norway Pines Motel
7111 US 2, 41 and M-35
Gladstone, MI
906-786-5119
baydenoc.com/norway/
There are no additional pet fees. 2 dogs may be allowed.

Grand Haven
Grand Haven, MI
616-638-1262
There are a couple of pet friendly properties offered by this agency. Dogs of all sizes are allowed for an additional pet fee of $25 per stay per house plus a $100 refundable deposit. Dogs must be housetrained, well behaved, leashed, and cleaned up after at all times. 2 dogs may be allowed.

Baymont Inn and Suites Airport
Grand Rapids
2873 Kraft Avenue SE
Grand Rapids, MI
616-956-3300 (877-229-6668)
Dogs are welcome at this hotel.

Best Western Hospitality Hotel & Suites
5500 28th Street SE
Grand Rapids, MI
616-949-8400 (800-780-7234)
Dogs up to 50 pounds are allowed. Dogs are allowed for a pet fee of $10.00 per pet per stay.

Clarion Inn & Suites Airport
4981 28th Street SE
Grand Rapids, MI
616-956-9304 (877-424-6423)
Dogs of all sizes are allowed. Dogs are allowed for a pet fee of $10.00 per pet per night. Two dogs are allowed per room.

Comfort Inn Airport
4155 28th St. S.E.
Grand Rapids, MI
616-957-2080 (877-424-6423)
Dogs of all sizes are allowed.

Comfort Suites South
7644 Caterpillar Court
Grand Rapids, MI
616-301-2255 (877-424-6423)
Dogs of all sizes are allowed. Dogs are allowed for a pet fee of $50.00 per pet per stay. Two dogs are allowed per room.

Crowne Plaza Hotel Grand Rapids - Airport
5700 28th Street S.E.
Grand Rapids, MI
616-957-1770 (877-270-6405)
Dogs of all sizes are allowed. Dogs are allowed for a pet fee of $10.00 per pet per night.

Days Hotel Downtown Grand Rapids
310 Pearl Street NW/I-196
Grand Rapids, MI

616-235-7611 (800-329-7466)
Dogs of all sizes are allowed. Dogs are allowed for a nightly pet fee.

Econo Lodge & Suites
2985 Kraft Avenue Southeast
Grand Rapids, MI
616-940-1777 (877-424-6423)
Dogs of all sizes are allowed. Dogs are allowed for a pet fee of $10.00 per pet per night. Two dogs are allowed per room.

Holiday Inn Express Hotel & Suites
Grand Rapids Airport
5401 28th Street Court S.E.
Grand Rapids, MI
616-940-8100 (877-270-6405)
Dogs are welcome at this hotel.

La Quinta Inn & Suites Grand Rapids
5500 28th Street
Grand Rapids, MI
616-949-8400 (800-531-5900)
Dogs of all sizes are allowed. There is a $10 per night per pet additional fee. Dogs may not be left unattended, and they must be leashed and cleaned up after. Multiple dogs may be allowed.

Motel 6 - Grand Rapids East Airport
3524 28th St Se
Grand Rapids, MI
616-957-3511 (800-466-8356)
This motel welcomes your pets to stay with you.

Motel 6 - Grand Rapids, Mi
7625 Caterpillar Court
Grand Rapids, MI
616-827-9900 (800-466-8356)
This motel welcomes your pets to stay with you.

Radisson Hotel Grand Rapids North
270 Ann Street NW
Grand Rapids, MI
616-363-9001
Dogs of all sizes are allowed. There is an additional one time fee of $20 per pet.

Red Roof Inn Grand Rapids
5131 East 28th Street
Grand Rapids, MI
616-942-0800 (800-RED-ROOF)
One well-behaved family pet per room. Guest must notify front desk upon arrival. Guest is liable for any damages. In consideration of all guests, pets must never be left unattended in the guest rooms.

Residence Inn Grand Rapids
2701 E Beltline Avenue SE
Grand Rapids, MI

616-957-8111 (800-331-3131)
Offering a casual, sophisticated ambiance and a convenient location to business, shopping, dining, and recreation areas, this all suite inn also provides a number of in-house amenities, including a daily buffet breakfast and evening hospitality events. Dogs are allowed for an additional one time pet fee of $100 per room. 2 dogs may be allowed.

Sleep Inn & Suites
4284 29th Street SE
Grand Rapids, MI
616-975-9000 (877-424-6423)
Dogs of all sizes are allowed. Dogs are allowed for a pet fee of $10.00 per pet per night.

Super 8 Grand Rapids
4855 28th Street SE
Grand Rapids, MI
616-957-3000 (800-800-8000)
Dogs are welcome at this hotel.

Days Inn Grayling
2556 Business Loop South
Grayling, MI
989-344-0204 (800-329-7466)
Dogs are welcome at this hotel.

Ramada Conference Center Grayling
2650 I-75 Business Loop
Grayling, MI
989-348-7611 (800-272-6232)
Dogs are welcome at this hotel.

Super 8 Grayling
5828 N A Miles Pkwy
Grayling, MI
989-348-8888 (800-800-8000)
Dogs of all sizes are allowed. Dogs are allowed for a pet fee of $7.50 per pet per night.

Best Western Copper Crown Motel
235 Hancock Street
Hancock, MI
906-482-6111 (800-780-7234)
Dogs are welcome at this hotel.

Birchwood Inn
7077 S. Lake Shore Dr.
Harbor Springs, MI
231-526-2151 (800-530-9955)
birchwoodinn.com
Dogs are allowed for a pet fee of $10 per night which includes a "Puppy Pak" for your four legged friend.

Comfort Inn
2248 N. Comfort Dr.
Hart, MI
231-873-3456 (877-424-6423)
Dogs of all sizes are allowed. Dogs are allowed for a pet fee of $10.00

per pet per night.

Days Inn Holland
717 Hastings Ave
Holland, MI
616-392-7001 (800-329-7466)
Dogs are welcome at this hotel.

Knights Inn Holland
465 US 31 Highway
Holland, MI
616-392-8521 (800-843-5644)
Dogs are welcome at this hotel. There is a $10 one time additional pet fee.

Residence Inn Holland
631 Southpointe Ridge Road
Holland, MI
616-393-6900 (800-331-3131)
Located only a few minutes from all that the downtown area has to offer, this all suite inn features a number of in-house amenities, including a daily buffet breakfast and evening socials Monday to Thursday. Dogs are allowed for an additional one time pet fee of $75 per room. Multiple dogs may be allowed.

Best Western Franklin Square Inn
820 Shelden Avenue
Houghton, MI
906-487-1700 (800-780-7234)
Dogs of all sizes are allowed. Dogs are allowed for a pet fee of $20.00 per pet per night.

Holiday Inn Express Houghton-Keweenaw
1110 Century Way
Houghton, MI
906-482-1066 (877-270-6405)
Dogs are welcome at this hotel.

Travelodge Houghton
215 Shelden Ave
Houghton, MI
906-482-1400 (800-578-7878)
Dogs are welcome at this hotel.

Baymont Inn And Suites Howell
4120 Lambert Drive
Howell, MI
517-546-0712 (877-229-6668)
Dogs of all sizes are allowed. Dogs are allowed for a pet fee of $10.00 per pet per night.

Quality Inn
3301 Highland Drive
Hudsonville, MI
616-662-4000 (877-424-6423)
Dogs of all sizes are allowed. Dogs are allowed for a pet fee of $10.00 per pet per night.

Super 8 Hudsonville
3005 Corporate Grove Drive
Hudsonville, MI
616-896-6710 (800-800-8000)
Dogs of all sizes are allowed. Dogs are allowed for a pet fee of $10 per pet per stay.

Days Inn Imlay City
6692 Newark Rd
Imlay City, MI
810-724-8005 (800-329-7466)
Dogs of all sizes are allowed. Dogs are allowed for a nightly pet fee.

Super 8 Imlay City
6951 Newark Road
Imlay City, MI
810-724-8700 (800-800-8000)
Dogs of all sizes are allowed. Dogs are allowed for a pet fee of $10.00 per pet per stay.

Super 8 MI Ionia
7245 S State Rd
Ionia, MI
616-527-2828 (800-800-8000)
Dogs are welcome at this hotel.

Days Inn Iron Mountain
2001 S Stephenson Ave
Iron Mountain, MI
906-774-2181 (800-329-7466)
Dogs are welcome at this hotel.

Motel 6 - Iron Mountain, Mi
1518 S. Stephenson Ave.
Iron Mountain, MI
906-774-7400 (800-466-8356)
This motel welcomes your pets to stay with you.

Super 8 MI Iron Mountain
US Hwys 2/141
Iron Mountain, MI
906-774-3400 (800-800-8000)
Dogs are welcome at this hotel.

Baymont Inn & Suites Jackson
2035 Holiday Inn Drive
Jackson, MI
517-789-6000 (877-229-6668)
Dogs of all sizes are allowed. Dogs are allowed for a pet fee of $10.00 per pet per night.

Econo Lodge
2001 Shirley Drive
Jackson, MI
517-788-8780 (877-424-6423)
Dogs of all sizes are allowed. Dogs are allowed for a pet fee of $10.00 per pet per night. Two dogs are allowed per room.

Motel 6 - Jackson, Mi
830 Royal Dr

Jackson, MI
517-789-7186 (800-466-8356)
This motel welcomes your pets to
stay with you.

Travelodge Jackson
901 Rosehill Drive
Jackson, MI
517-787-1111 (800-578-7878)
Dogs are welcome at this hotel.

Baymont Inn & Suites Kalamazoo
2203 South 11th Street
Kalamazoo, MI
269-372-7999 (877-229-6668)
Dogs of all sizes are allowed. Dogs
are allowed for a pet fee of $10.00
per pet per night.

Best Western Hospitality Inn
3640 E Cork Street
Kalamazoo, MI
269-381-1900 (800-780-7234)
Dogs of all sizes are allowed. Dogs
are allowed for a pet fee of $15.00
per pet per stay.

Econo Lodge
3750 Easy St.
Kalamazoo, MI
269-388-3551 (877-424-6423)
Dogs of all sizes are allowed. Dogs
are allowed for a pet fee of $10.00
per pet per night.

Holiday Inn Kalamazoo-W (W
Michigan Univ)
2747 S. 11th St
Kalamazoo, MI
269-375-6000 (877-270-6405)
Dogs up to 50 pounds are allowed.
Dogs are allowed for a pet fee.

Motel 6 - Kalamazoo
3704 Vanrick Dr
Kalamazoo, MI
269-344-9255 (800-466-8356)
This motel welcomes your pets to
stay with you.

Quality Inn
3820 Sprinkle Rd.
Kalamazoo, MI
269-381-7000 (877-424-6423)
Dogs of all sizes are allowed. Dogs
are allowed for a pet fee of $15.00
per pet per night. Two dogs are
allowed per room.

Red Roof Inn Kalamazoo East
3701 East Cork Street
Kalamazoo, MI
382635O (800-RED-ROOF)
One well-behaved family pet per
room. Guest must notify front desk
upon arrival. Guest is liable for any
damages. In consideration of all

guests, pets must never be left
unattended in the guest rooms.

Red Roof Inn Western Michigan
University
5425 West Michigan Avenue
Kalamazoo, MI
269-375-7400 (800-RED-ROOF)
One well-behaved family pet per
room. Guest must notify front desk
upon arrival. Guest is liable for any
damages. In consideration of all
guests, pets must never be left
unattended in the guest rooms.

Residence Inn Kalamazoo East
1500 E Kilgore Road
Kalamazoo, MI
269-349-0855 (800-697-1489)
Some of the amenities at this all-
suite inn include a convenient
location to the airport, daily buffet
breakfast, a Manager's reception
Monday through Thursday with light
dinner fare, a heated swimming
pool, Sport Court, and a
complimentary grocery shopping
service. Dogs are allowed for an
additional one time pet fee of $75
per room. 2 dogs may be allowed.

Staybridge Suites Kalamazoo
2001 Seneca Lane
Kalamazoo, MI
269-372-8000 (877-270-6405)
Dogs up to 80 pounds are allowed.
Pets allowed with an additional pet
fee. Up to $75 for 1-6 nights and up
to $150 for 7+ nights. A pet
agreement must be signed at
check-in.

Super 8 Kalamazoo
618 Maple Hill Dr
Kalamazoo, MI
269-345-0146 (800-800-8000)
Dogs of all sizes are allowed. Dogs
are allowed for a nightly pet fee.

TownePlace Suites Kalamazoo
5683 S 9th Street
Kalamazoo, MI
269-353-1500 (800-257-3000)
This all suite hotel sits central to a
number of sites of interest for both
business and leisure travelers; plus
they also offer a number of on-site
amenities to ensure comfort. Dogs
are allowed for an additional one
time fee of $100 per room. 2 dogs
may be allowed.

Extended Stay America Grand
Rapids - Kentwood
3747 29th St. S.E.
Kentwood, MI
616-977-6750 (800-804-3724)

One dog is allowed per suite. There
is a $25 per night additional pet fee
up to $150 for an entire stay.

Staybridge Suites Grand Rapids-
Kentwood
3000 Lake Eastbrook Blvd SE
Kentwood, MI
616-464-3200 (877-270-6405)
Dogs up to 80 pounds are allowed.
Pets allowed with an additional pet
fee. Up to $75 for 1-6 nights and up
to $150 for 7+ nights. A pet
agreement must be signed at check-
in.

Crooked Lake Resort and Bait Shop
8071 Mystic Lake Drive
Lake, MI
989-544-2383
Dogs of all sizes are allowed. There
is a $25 one time additional pet fee
per room.

The White Rabbit Inn
14634 Red Arrow H
Lakeside, MI
269-469-4620 (800-967-2224)
whiterabbitinn.com/
Popular as a relaxing, romantic
getaway, this lovely inn is also only a
short distance from a variety of other
attractions and recreation. Dogs of
all sizes are allowed in 2 of their
cabins for no additional pet fee as
long as there is advance notice that
a dog will be coming. Dogs must be
quiet, well mannered, leashed,
cleaned up after at all times, and
friendly towards people and other
animals as there are 4 other resident
dogs. Owners are responsible for
any pet damage, so they suggest
kenneling pets if they will be in the
room alone, and they may only be
left for very short periods. Multiple
dogs may be allowed.

Candlewood Suites East Lansing
3545 Forest Road
Lansing, MI
517-351-8181 (877-270-6405)
Dogs up to 80 pounds are allowed.
Pets allowed with an additional pet
fee. Up to $75 for 1-6 nights and up
to $150 for 7+ nights. A pet
agreement must be signed at check-
in.

Days Inn Lansing
7711 West Saginaw Highway
Lansing, MI
517-627-8471 (800-329-7466)
Dogs are welcome at this hotel.

Motel 6 - Lansing
7326 Saginaw Hwy

Lansing, MI
517-321-1444 (800-466-8356)
This motel welcomes your pets to stay with you.

Quality Suites
901 Delta Commerce Dr.
Lansing, MI
517-886-0600 (877-424-6423)
Dogs of all sizes are allowed. Dogs are allowed for a pet fee of $25.00 per pet per stay.

Ramada Hotel And Conference Center Lansing
7501 West Saginaw Highway
Lansing, MI
517-627-3211 (800-272-6232)
Dogs are welcome at this hotel.

Red Roof Inn Lansing - Michigan State University
3615 Dunckel Road
Lansing, MI
517-332-2575 (800-RED-ROOF)
One well-behaved family pet per room. Guest must notify front desk upon arrival. Guest is liable for any damages. In consideration of all guests, pets must never be left unattended in the guest rooms.

Red Roof Inn Lansing West
7412 West Saginaw Highway
Lansing, MI
517-321-7246 (800-RED-ROOF)
One well-behaved family pet per room. Guest must notify front desk upon arrival. Guest is liable for any damages. In consideration of all guests, pets must never be left unattended in the guest rooms.

Residence Inn Lansing West
922 Delta Commerce Drive
Lansing, MI
517-886-5030 (800-331-3131)
Besides offering a convenient location to business, shopping, dining, and entertainment areas, this all suite hotel also provides a number of in-house amenities, including a daily buffet breakfast and evening social hours Monday to Thursday. Dogs are allowed for an additional one time pet fee of $100 per room. Multiple dogs may be allowed.

Sheraton Lansing Hotel
925 South Creyts Road
Lansing, MI
517-323-7100 (888-625-5144)
Dogs up to 80 pounds are allowed for no additional pet fee. Dogs may not be left alone in the room.

Super 8 Lansing

910 American Road
Lansing, MI
517-393-8008 (800-800-8000)
Dogs of all sizes are allowed. Dogs are allowed for a pet fee.

Residence Inn Detroit Livonia
17250 Fox Drive
Livonia, MI
734-462-4201 (800-331-3131)
In addition to offering a convenient location to business, shopping, dining, and entertainment areas, this hotel also provides a number of in-house amenities including a daily buffet breakfast, evening socials Monday to Thursday, and many Japanese specific amenities. Dogs are allowed for an additional one time pet fee of $75 per room. 2 dogs may be allowed.

Best Western Splash Park Inn
5005 W US Highway 10
Ludington, MI
231-843-2140 (800-780-7234)
Dogs of all sizes are allowed. Dogs are allowed for a nightly pet fee.

Candlelight Inn
709 E Ludington Avenue/H 10
Ludington, MI
231-845-8074 (877-997-0099)
candleliteinnludington.com/
Relaxation, romantic ambiance, historic surroundings, colorful gardens, special events and packages, and a variety of special amenities greet guests at this inn. Dogs of all sizes are allowed for an additional $10 per night per pet. Your pup is greeted with their own plush bed, food/water dishes, treats, a blanket to cover over the bed or furniture, and a doggie towel for occasional muddy paws. Dogs may not be left alone in the room except during breakfast, and they are not allowed in the dining room or other areas of the house. Dogs must be leashed and cleaned up after at all times; plastic bags are available.

Days Inn Ludington
5095 West US-10
Ludington, MI
231-843-2233 (800-329-7466)
Dogs of all sizes are allowed. Dogs are allowed for a pet fee of $10 per pet per night.

Nader's Lake Shore Motor Lodge
612 N Lakeshore Dr
Ludington, MI
231-843-8757 (800-968-0109)
Pets are allowed in the main lodge building and the poolside rooms.

They are not allowed in the Suite Building. The hotel is closed during the winter months. Pets must be leashed and attended at all times. There are no additional fees. Multiple dogs may be allowed.

Ramada Inn and Convention Center
4079 West US 10
Ludington, MI
231-845-7311 (800-272-6232)
Dogs of all sizes are allowed. Dogs are allowed for a pet fee of $10.00 per pet per night.

Super 8 /Monroe/Toledo Area Luna Pier
4163 Super 8 Drive, Industrial
Luna Pier, MI
734-848-8880 (800-800-8000)
Dogs are welcome at this hotel.

Harbor Place Studio Suites
7439 Main Street
Mackinac Island, MI
800-626-6304
harborplacestudiosuites.com/
This 8-suite inn features views overlooking the harbor or historic Main Street and sits only steps from the beach. The inn is near the ferry dock and offers a convenient location to all the island has to offer. Dogs are allowed for an additional one time pet fee of $50 per room. Multiple dogs may be allowed.

Mackinac Island Home Rentals
Call to arrange.
Mackinac Island, MI
800-473-6960
Dogs are welcome in certain rooms and condos. All accommodations offer great views of the island and are non-smoking. The patio room costs about $145 per night with a $25 per stay pet fee. The one bedroom condo suite is like a studio and has a kitchen and living area. Rates are about $185 per night with a $50 per stay pet fee. If you need more space, an extra bedroom can be added to the one bedroom condo for a total of $295 per night with a $75 per stay pet fee. Rates are subject to change. Well-behaved leashed dogs of all sizes are welcome. They just ask that if you leave your dog alone in the room that he or she be in a crate that you provide. To get there from the ferry, you can take a horse taxi to the condos.

Mission Point Resort
One Lakeshore Drive
Mackinac Island, MI
906-847-3312

missionpoint.com
Amenities at this resort include an outdoor heated pool, sauna and steam rooms, movie theater, hair salon, lawn bowling, croquet, horseshoes, hot tubs, room service and full service health club. Well-behaved leashed dogs are allowed. Pets are not allowed in the main building but are welcome in the rooms at the adjacent wing. There is a $50 per stay pet fee. Reservations can be made at 1-800-833-7711. Once you reach the ferry docks on the island, your luggage will be tagged and sent directly to the Mission Point Resort. You will receive one claim ticket per bag and you can get your luggage at the hotel's bell stand. You can walk or take the horse taxi to the hotel. 2 dogs may be allowed.

Mission Street Cottage
Mission Street
Mackinac Island, MI
231-881-3343
In addition to its scenic setting on the island, this 4 bedroom, beautifully accommodated vacation cottage features a gourmet kitchen, a media room, WiFi, 3 baths, and much more. Well mannered dogs are allowed for no additional fee. 2 dogs may be allowed.

Baymont Inn and Suites Mackinaw City
109 S. Nicolet Street
Mackinaw City, MI
231-436-7737 (877-229-6668)
Dogs are welcome at this hotel.

Econo Lodge
712 S. Huron
Mackinaw City, MI
231-436-5777 (877-424-6423)
Dogs of all sizes are allowed. Dogs are allowed for a pet fee of $15.00 per pet per night. Two dogs are allowed per room.

Econo Lodge at the Bridge
412 N. Nicolet St.
Mackinaw City, MI
231-436-5026 (877-424-6423)
Dogs up to 50 pounds are allowed. Dogs are allowed for a pet fee of $10.00 per pet per night.

Super 8 Macknaw City/Beachfront Area
Central & Huron
Mackinaw City, MI
231-436-7111 (800-800-8000)
Dogs are welcome at this hotel.

Extended Stay America Detroit - Madison Heights
32690 Stephenson Hwy.
Madison Heights, MI
248-583-5522 (800-804-3724)
One dog is allowed per suite. There is a $25 per night additional pet fee up to $150 for an entire stay.

Knights Inn Madison Heights
26091 DeQuindre Rd
Madison Heights, MI
248-545-9930 (800-843-5644)
Dogs of all sizes are allowed. Dogs are allowed for a nightly pet fee.

Motel 6 - Detroit Northeast Madison Heights
32700 Barrington Rd
Madison Heights, MI
248-583-0500 (800-466-8356)
This motel welcomes your pets to stay with you.

Red Roof Inn Detroit - Madison Heights
32511 Concord Drive
Madison Heights, MI
248-583-4700 (800-RED-ROOF)
One well-behaved family pet per room. Guest must notify front desk upon arrival. Guest is liable for any damages. In consideration of all guests, pets must never be left unattended in the guest rooms.

Residence Inn Detroit Troy/Madison Heights
32650 Stephenson Highway
Madison Heights, MI
248-583-4322 (800-331-3131)
In addition to offering a convenient location to business, shopping, dining, and entertainment areas - plus a couple of major universities, this hotel also provides a number of in-house amenities including a daily buffet breakfast and complimentary Wednesday barbecues. Dogs are allowed for an additional one time pet fee of $75 per room. Multiple dogs may be allowed.

Comfort Inn
617 E. Lakeshore Drive
Manistique, MI
906-341-6981 (877-424-6423)
Dogs of all sizes are allowed. Dogs are allowed for a pet fee of $10.00 per pet per night.

Econo Lodge Lakeside
2050 S US 41
Marquette, MI
906-225-1305 (877-424-6423)
Dogs of all sizes are allowed. Dogs are allowed for a pet fee of $10.00

per pet per night.

Ramada of Marquette
412 W Washington St
Marquette, MI
906-228-6000 (800-272-6232)
Dogs of all sizes are allowed. Dogs are allowed for a pet fee.

Arbor Inn
15435 W Michigan Avenue
Marshall, MI
269-781-7772 (800-424-0807)
arborinnmarshall.com./
Clean spacious rooms, large grassy lawns, picnic tables, barbecues grills, and an outdoor pool are some of the amenities to be found at this inn. Dogs are allowed for an additional fee of $5 per night per pet. Dogs must be well behaved, leashed, and cleaned up after. Multiple dogs may be allowed.

Days Inn -Port Huron Marysville
70 Gratiot Blvd
Marysville, MI
810-364-8400 (800-329-7466)
Dogs are welcome at this hotel.

Super 8 /Port Huron Area Marysville
1484 Gratiot
Marysville, MI
810-364-7500 (800-800-8000)
Dogs of all sizes are allowed. Dogs are allowed for a nightly pet fee.

Mendon Country Inn
440 E Main Street/H 60
Mendon, MI
269-496-8132 (800-304-3366)
mendoncountryinn.com/
This retreat offers a long and colorful history from its 1843 beginnings, 14 lush acres with trails, a putting green, gardens, an island, canoes/kayaks for guests to use during their stay, and numerous other amenities. Dogs of all sizes are welcome for no additional fee. Dogs may not be left alone in the room at any time, and they must be quiet, well mannered, leashed, and cleaned up after. 2 dogs may be allowed.

Fairview Inn
2200 W Wackerly St
Midland, MI
517-631-0070 (800-422-2744)
fairviewinnmidland.com/
There is a $10 per night per pet additional fee. Multiple dogs may be allowed.

Sleep Inn
2100 W. Wackerly St.
Midland, MI

989-837-1010 (877-424-6423)
Dogs of all sizes are allowed. Dogs
are allowed for a pet fee of $10.00
per pet per night.

Sleep Inn & Suites
1230 Dexter St.
Milan, MI
734-439-1400 (877-424-6423)
Dogs of all sizes are allowed. Dogs
are allowed for a pet fee of $25.00
per pet per night. Two dogs are
allowed per room.

Baymont Inn and Suites Monroe
14774 Laplaisance Road
Monroe, MI
734-384-1600 (877-229-6668)
Dogs are welcome at this hotel.

Knights Inn MI Monroe
1250 N. Dixie Hwy
Monroe, MI
734-243-0597 (800-843-5644)
Dogs are welcome at this hotel.
There is a $10 one time pet fee per
pet.

Motel 6 - Monroe, Mi
1440 North Dixie Highway
Monroe, MI
734-289-2000 (800-466-8356)
This motel welcomes your pets to
stay with you.

Comfort Inn & Suites University Park
2424 S. Mission St.
Mount Pleasant, MI
989-772-4000 (877-424-6423)
Dogs of all sizes are allowed. Dogs
are allowed for a pet fee of $20.00
per pet per night.

Super 8 Mt. Pleasant
2323 S Mission St
Mount Pleasant, MI
989-773-8888 (800-800-8000)
Dogs of all sizes are allowed. Dogs
are allowed for a pet fee of $20.00
per pet per night.

Comfort Inn
SR 28 (M-28) E
Munising, MI
906-387-5292 (877-424-6423)
Dogs of all sizes are allowed. Dogs
are allowed for a pet fee of $10.00
per pet per stay.

Days Inn Munising
M-28 East
Munising, MI
906-387-2493 (800-329-7466)
Dogs are welcome at this hotel.

Holiday Inn Express Munising-
Lakeview

E8890 M-28
Munising, MI
906-387-4800 (877-270-6405)
Dogs of all sizes are allowed. Dogs
are allowed for a nightly pet fee.

American Lodge and Suites
11800 H 31
N Charlevoix, MI
231-237-0988
Dogs of all sizes are allowed. There
is a $50 refundable deposit plus a
$10 per night per pet fee.

New Buffalo Inn and Spa
231 E Buffalo Street/H 12
New Buffalo, MI
269-469-1000
newbuffaloinn.com/
This scenic retreat also offers a
Women's Wellness Spa. Dogs of all
sizes are allowed for an additional
fee of $25 per night per pet in some
of their cottages. Dogs are not
allowed on the bed or furniture, and
they ask that pets prone to being on
them be placed in a crate when
they are alone in the room. Dogs
must be well mannered, leashed,
and cleaned up after. 2 dogs may
be allowed.

The Rainbow Lodge
9706 County Road 423
Newberry, MI
906-658-3357
The Rainbow Lodge also offers
watercraft rentals, and it sits at the
entrance of Big Two Hearted River
overlooking Lake Superior; the river
is considered one of the 10 best
trout streams in the US. Dogs are
allowed at the lodge and on the
watercraft rentals for no additional
fee. Dogs must be quiet, well
behaved, leashed, and cleaned up
after at all times. 2 dogs may be
allowed.

Extended Stay America Detroit -
Novi
21555 Haggerty Rd.
Novi, MI
248-305-9955 (800-804-3724)
One dog is allowed per suite. There
is a $25 per night additional pet fee
up to $150 for an entire stay.

Residence Inn Detroit Novi
27477 Cabaret Drive
Novi, MI
248-735-7400 (800-331-3131)
Some of the amenities at this all-
suite inn include a daily Asian and
European buffet breakfast, evening
socials Monday through Thursday,
an indoor swimming pool, and a
convenient location to shopping,

dining, and entertainment areas.
Dogs are allowed for an additional
one time pet fee of $100 per room. 2
dogs may be allowed.

Sheraton Detroit Novi
21111 Haggerty Road
Novi, MI
248-349-4000 (888-625-5144)
Dogs up to 80 pounds are allowed.
There are no additional pet fees.
Dogs are not allowed to be left alone
in the room.

Staybridge Suites Detroit - Novi
27000 Providence Parkway
Novi, MI
248-349-4600 (877-270-6405)
Dogs up to 80 pounds are allowed.
Pets allowed with an additional pet
fee. Up to $75 for 1-6 nights and up
to $150 for 7+ nights. A pet
agreement must be signed at check-
in.

TownePlace Suites Detroit Novi
42600 Eleven Mile Road
Novi, MI
248-305-5533 (800-257-3000)
In addition to offering a number of in-
house amenities for all level of
travelers, this all suite inn also
provides a convenient location to
business, shopping, dining, and
entertainment areas. Dogs are
allowed for an additional one time
fee of $75 per room. Multiple dogs
may be allowed.

Comfort Inn
2187 University Park Drive
Okemos, MI
517-347-6690 (877-424-6423)
Dogs of all sizes are allowed.

Holiday Inn Express Hotel & Suites
Lansing-Okemos (Msu Area)
2209 University Park Drive
Okemos, MI
517-349-8700 (877-270-6405)
Dogs up to 80 pounds are allowed.
Dogs are allowed for a pet fee of
$25.00 per pet per stay. Two dogs
are allowed per room.

Staybridge Suites Lansing-Okemos
3553 Meridian Crossings Drive
Okemos, MI
517-347-3044 (877-270-6405)
Dogs up to 80 pounds are allowed.
Pets allowed with an additional pet
fee. Up to $75 for 1-6 nights and up
to $150 for 7+ nights. A pet
agreement must be signed at check-
in.

Comfort Inn & Suites

153 Ampey Road
Paw Paw, MI
269-655-0303 (877-424-6423)
Dogs up to 50 pounds are allowed.

Econo Lodge
139 Ampey Road
Paw Paw, MI
269-657-2578 (877-424-6423)
Dogs of all sizes are allowed. Two
dogs are allowed per room.

Super 8 Paw Paw
111 Ampey Road
Paw Paw, MI
269-657-1111 (800-800-8000)
Dogs of all sizes are allowed. Dogs
are allowed for a pet fee of $15.00
per pet per stay.

Comfort Inn
1314 US 31 N.
Petoskey, MI
231-347-3220 (877-424-6423)
Dogs of all sizes are allowed. Dogs
are allowed for a pet fee of $5.00 per
pet per night.

Days Inn Petoskey
1420 Spring Street US 131
Petoskey, MI
877-207-4215 (800-329-7466)
Dogs of all sizes are allowed. Dogs
are allowed for a pet fee of $10 per
pet per night.

Econo Lodge South
1859 US 131 South
Petoskey, MI
231-348-3324 (877-424-6423)
Dogs of all sizes are allowed. Dogs
are allowed for a pet fee of $10.00
per pet per night.

Grace Grange Lodge and Stable
8000 Newson Road
Petoskey, MI
231-347-5869
gracegrange.com
Dogs of all size are allowed. There is
a $10 per night additional pet fee.
Pet sitting is available.

Red Roof Inn Detroit - Plymouth
39700 Ann Arbor Road
Plymouth, MI
734-459-3300 (800-RED-ROOF)
One well-behaved family pet per
room. Guest must notify front desk
upon arrival. Guest is liable for any
damages. In consideration of all
guests, pets must never be left
unattended in the guest rooms.

Baymont Inn & Suites Port Huron
1611 Range Road
Port Huron, MI

810-364-8000 (877-229-6668)
Dogs of all sizes are allowed. Dogs
are allowed for a pet fee of $15.00
per pet per night.

Comfort Inn
1700 Yeager St.
Port Huron, MI
810-982-5500 (877-424-6423)
Dogs of all sizes are allowed.

Days Inn Port Huron
2908 Pine Grove Ave.
Port Huron, MI
810-984-1522 (800-329-7466)
Dogs of all sizes are allowed. Dogs
are allowed for a nightly pet fee.

East Bay Lakefront Lodge
125 Twelfth Street
Prudenville, MI
989-366-5910
eastbaylodge.com/
Nestled among the pines along the
shores of Houghton Lake, this 1925
lodge has all the charm of a
mountain retreat with a wide variety
of land and water recreational
opportunities. Dogs of all sizes are
allowed for no additional fee. Dogs
must be friendly, well groomed,
leashed, and cleaned up after. 2
dogs may be allowed.

Red Roof Inn Detroit -Auburn
Hills/Rochester Hills
2580 Crooks Road
Rochester Hills, MI
248-853-6400 (800-RED-ROOF)
One well-behaved family pet per
room. Guest must notify front desk
upon arrival. Guest is liable for any
damages. In consideration of all
guests, pets must never be left
unattended in the guest rooms.

Baymont Inn & Suites
Detroit/Romulus Airport
9000 Wickham Road
Romulus, MI
734-722-6000 (800-531-5900)
A dog of any size is allowed. There
are no additional pet fees with a
credit card on file. Dogs must be
leashed and cleaned up after.

Extended Stay America Detroit -
Metropolitan Airport
30325 Flynn Dr.
Romulus, MI
734-722-7780 (800-804-3724)
One dog is allowed per suite. There
is a $25 per night additional pet fee
up to $150 for an entire stay.

Quality Inn & Suites
9555 Middlebelt Rd.

Romulus, MI
734-946-1400 (877-424-6423)
Dogs of all sizes are allowed. Dogs
are allowed for a pet fee of $20.00
per pet per night.

Ramada
31119 Flynn Dr
Romulus, MI
734-728-2322 (800-272-6232)
Dogs are welcome at this hotel.

Rodeway Inn Metro Airport
8500 Wickham Rd.
Romulus, MI
734-595-1990 (877-424-6423)
Dogs of all sizes are allowed. Dogs
are allowed for a pet fee of $10.00
per pet per night.

Baymont Inn & Suites Detroit/
Roseville
20675 13 Mile Road
Roseville, MI
586-296-6910 (877-229-6668)
Dogs are welcome at this hotel.

Best Western Georgian Inn
31327 Gratiot Avenue
Roseville, MI
586-294-0400 (800-780-7234)
Dogs of all sizes are allowed. Dogs
are allowed for a pet fee.

Extended Stay America Detroit -
Roseville
20200 Thirteen Mile Rd.
Roseville, MI
586-294-0141 (800-804-3724)
One dog is allowed per suite. There
is a $25 per night additional pet fee
up to $150 for an entire stay.

Red Roof Inn Detroit - St Clair
Shores
31800 Little Mack Road
Roseville, MI
586-296-0310 (800-RED-ROOF)
One well-behaved family pet per
room. Guest must notify front desk
upon arrival. Guest is liable for any
damages. In consideration of all
guests, pets must never be left
unattended in the guest rooms.

Comfort Suites
5180 Fashion Square Blvd
Saginaw, MI
989-797-8000 (877-424-6423)
Dogs up to 50 pounds are allowed.
Dogs are allowed for a pet fee of
$50.00USD per pet per stay.

Knights Inn Saginaw
2225 Tittabawassee
Saginaw, MI
989-791-1411 (800-843-5644)

Dogs of all sizes are allowed. Dogs are allowed for a pet fee of $15.00 per pet per night.

Motel 6 - Saginaw Frankenmuth
966 Outer Dr
Saginaw, MI
989-754-8414 (800-466-8356)
This motel welcomes your pets to stay with you.

Residence Inn Saginaw
5230 Fashion Square Blvd
Saginaw, MI
989-799-9000 (800-331-3131)
Located in the heart of town, this all suite inn sits central to the airport, entertainment centers, shopping and dining venues, and major businesses. They also provide a number of in-house amenities, including a daily buffet breakfast and evening socials with light dinner fare. Dogs up to 80 pounds are allowed for an additional one time pet fee of $100; there may be 1 dog up to 80 pounds or 2 small dogs (totaling no more than 80 pounds) per room.

Quality Inn
561 Boulevard Drive
Saint Ignace, MI
906-643-9700 (877-424-6423)
Dogs of all sizes are allowed. Dogs are allowed for a pet fee of $10.00 per pet per night.

Michigan Vacation Rentals
Call to Arrange
Saugatuck, MI
269-857-8700
saugatuckvacation.com
This lodge will be a relaxing retreat for you and your pet. Play on our twenty acre property complete with pond and waterfall. Relax in beautifully appointed rooms and houses with modern conveniences. Located close to beaches, shopping, harbor and nightlife.   Children and pets are welcome at the Inn.

Park House Inn
888 Holland Street
Saugatuck, MI
269-857-4535 (866-321-4535)
parkhouseinn.com/
Flowers, greenery, trees, and 2 levels of wrap around porches to view it all, are only a couple of the favorites at this popular, historic 1857 inn. In addition to full breakfasts and concierge services, they offer spa and fireplace suites. Dogs are allowed in the Rose Garden Cottage (with hot tub) for an additional $20 per night per pet with advance reservations. Dogs must be

well behaved, leashed, and cleaned up after at all times. 2 dogs may be allowed.

Comfort Inn
4404 I-75 Bus. Spur
Sault Sainte Marie, MI
906-635-1118 (877-424-6423)
Dogs of all sizes are allowed.

Best Value Inn
3411 I-75 Business Spur
Sault Ste Marie, MI
906-635-9190
Dogs are allowed at this inn for an additional $5 per night per pet. Dogs must be quiet, leashed, and cleaned up after at all times. 2 dogs may be allowed.

Days Inn Sault Ste Marie
3651 I-75 Business Spur
Sault Ste Marie, MI
906-635-5200 (800-329-7466)
Dogs are welcome at this hotel.

Holiday Inn Express Sault Ste. Marie
1171 Riverview Way
Sault Ste Marie, MI
906-632-3999 (877-270-6405)
Dogs of all sizes are allowed. Dogs are allowed for a nightly pet fee.

Ramada Plaza Hotel Ojibway
240 West Portage Ave
Sault Ste Marie, MI
906-632-4100 (800-272-6232)
Dogs are welcome at this hotel.

Super 8 Sault Ste Marie MI
I-75 Exit 392
Sault Ste. Marie, MI
906-632-8882 (800-800-8000)
Dogs are welcome at this hotel.

Comfort Suites
1755 Phoenix Street
South Haven, MI
269-639-2014 (877-424-6423)
Dogs of all sizes are allowed. Dogs are allowed for a pet fee of $25.00 per pet per night. Two dogs are allowed per room.

Candlewood Suites Detroit-Southfield
1 Corporate Drive
Southfield, MI
248-945-0010 (877-270-6405)
Dogs up to 80 pounds are allowed. Pets allowed with an additional pet fee. Up to $75 for 1-6 nights and up to $150 for 7+ nights. A pet agreement must be signed at check-in.

Extended Stay America Detroit - Southfield
26250 American Dr.
Southfield, MI
248-355-2115 (800-804-3724)
One dog is allowed per suite. There is a $25 per night additional pet fee up to $150 for an entire stay.

Homestead Studio Suites Detroit - Southfield
28500 Northwestern Hwy.
Southfield, MI
248-213-4500 (800-804-3724)
One dog is allowed per suite. There is a $25 per night additional pet fee up to $150 for an entire stay.

Red Roof Inn Detroit - Southfield
27660 Northwestern Highway
Southfield, MI
248-353-7200 (800-RED-ROOF)
One well-behaved family pet per room. Guest must notify front desk upon arrival. Guest is liable for any damages. In consideration of all guests, pets must never be left unattended in the guest rooms.

The Westin
1500 Town Center
Southfield, MI
248-728-6536 (888-625-5144)
This hotel offers luxury accommodations, fine dining, a long list of amenities, and a convenient location to all the attractions the city has to offer. Dogs up to 40 pounds are allowed for no addition fee unless extra pet cleaning of the room is needed; there is a pet waiver to sign at check in. They also offer pet amenities including their own bed and dishes. Dogs must be well behaved, leashed, and cleaned up after at all times. 2 dogs may be allowed.

La Quinta Inn Detroit/Southgate
12888 Reeck Road
Southgate, MI
734-374-3000 (800-531-5900)
Dogs of all sizes are allowed. There are no additional fees. There is a pet waiver to sign at check in. Dogs must be well behaved, and a cell number needs to be left with the front office when the pet is in the room alone. Dogs must be leashed and cleaned up after. Multiple dogs may be allowed.

Motel 6 - Detroit Southgate
18777 Northline Rd
Southgate, MI
734-287-8340 (800-466-8356)
This motel welcomes your pets to stay with you.

Holiday Inn Grand Haven-Spring
Lake
940 W Savidge Street
Spring Lake, MI
616-846-1000 (877-270-6405)
Dogs of all sizes are allowed. Dogs
are allowed for a pet fee of $10.00
per pet per night.

Quality Inn
913 Boulevard Dr
St Ignace, MI
906-643-9700 (877-424-6423)
There is a $10 per day per pet fee.
Dogs must be quiet and they may not
be left alone in the room. Multiple
dogs may be allowed.

Extended Stay America Detroit -
Sterling Heights
33400 Van Dyke Rd.
Sterling Heights, MI
586-983-3773 (800-804-3724)
One dog is allowed per suite. There
is a $25 per night additional pet fee
up to $150 for an entire stay.

TownePlace Suites Detroit Sterling
Heights
14800 Lakeside Circle
Sterling Heights,, MI
586-566-0900 (800-257-3000)
Set within walking distance to the
Lakeside Mall and a variety of
entertainment, a 24 hour on-site
market, and an indoor pool are just
some of the perks at this all suite inn.
Dogs are allowed for an additional
one time fee of $75 per room.
Multiple dogs may be allowed.

Baymont Inn & Suites St. Joseph/
Stevensville
2601 W. Marquette Woods Road
Stevensville, MI
269-428-9111 (877-229-6668)
Dogs of all sizes are allowed. Dogs
are allowed for a pet fee of $10 per
pet per stay.

Candlewood Suites St.
Joseph/Benton Harbor
2567 W. Marquettewood Rd
Stevensville, MI
269-428-4400 (877-270-6405)
Dogs up to 80 pounds are allowed.
Pets allowed with an additional pet
fee. Up to $75 for 1-6 nights and up
to $150 for 7+ nights. A pet
agreement must be signed at check-
in.

Tawas Motel - Resort
1124 W. Lake Street
Tawas City, MI
989-362-3822

Motel amenities include individual
heating and cooling, free local calls,
free continental breakfast, Jacuzzi,
heated outdoor pool and a picnic
area with grills. Well-behaved dogs
are welcome. There is an additional
$5 per night per pet fee. 2 dogs
may be allowed.

Red Roof Inn Detroit Metro Airport -
Taylor
21230 Eureka Road
Taylor, MI
734-374-1150 (800-RED-ROOF)
One well-behaved family pet per
room. Guest must notify front desk
upon arrival. Guest is liable for any
damages. In consideration of all
guests, pets must never be left
unattended in the guest rooms.

Super 8 /Detroit Area Taylor
15101 Huron St
Taylor, MI
734-283-8830 (800-800-8000)
Dogs are welcome at this hotel.

Crystal Mountain Resort
12500 Crystal Mountain Drive
Thompsonville, MI
800-968-7686
crystalmountain.com/lodging/
This resort offers a variety of
accommodations and recreational
pursuits both in the surrounding
area and at the resort, including an
adventure water park. They are also
home to the Michigan Legacy Art
Park, an expression of human and
nature through major works of art
on a 1.6 mile trail through hilly,
wooded terrain. One large dog or 2
small to medium dogs are allowed
per room for an additional fee of
$50 for the 1st night and $10 each
night after per pet. Dogs must be
well behaved, leashed, and cleaned
up after; they are not allowed in
other resort buildings or on the
cross-country ski trails in winter.

Super 8 Three Rivers
689 Super 8 Way
Three Rivers, MI
269-279-8888 (800-800-8000)
Dogs are welcome at this hotel.

Baymont Inn & Suites Traverse City
2326 US 31 South
Traverse City, MI
231-933-4454 (877-229-6668)
Dogs are welcome at this hotel.

Best Western Four Seasons
305 Munson Avenue (US 31)
Traverse City, MI
231-946-8424 (800-780-7234)

Dogs of all sizes are allowed. Dogs
are allowed for a pet fee of $10 per
pet per night.

Days Inn and Suites Traverse City
420 Munson Avenue
Traverse City, MI
231-941-0208 (800-329-7466)
Dogs are welcome at this hotel.

MI Travelodge Traverse City
704 Munson Ave
Traverse City, MI
231-922-9111 (800-578-7878)
Dogs of all sizes are allowed. Dogs
are allowed for a pet fee of $10.00
per pet per night.

Motel 6 - Traverse City
1582 Us 31 North
Traverse City, MI
231-938-3002 (800-466-8356)
This motel welcomes your pets to
stay with you.

Quality Inn By the Bay
1492 US 31 N.
Traverse City, MI
231-929-4423 (877-424-6423)
Dogs of all sizes are allowed. Dogs
are allowed for a pet fee of $10.60
per pet per night. Three or more
dogs may be allowed.

Super 8 MI Traverse City
1870 US Hwy 31 N
Traverse City, MI
231-938-1887 (800-800-8000)
Dogs are welcome at this hotel.

Candlewood Suites Detroit-Troy
2550 Troy Center Drive
Troy, MI
248-269-6600 (877-270-6405)
Dogs up to 80 pounds are allowed.
Pets allowed with an additional pet
fee. Up to $75 for 1-6 nights and up
to $150 for 7+ nights. A pet
agreement must be signed at check-
in.

Drury Inn
575 W. Big Beaver Road
Troy, MI
248-528-3330 (800-378-7946)
Dogs of all sizes are allowed for no
additional pet fee with a credit card
on file, and there is a pet agreement
to sign at check in.

Ramada Plaza Hotel - /Detroit Area
Troy
5500 Crooks Road
Troy, MI
248-879-2100 (800-272-6232)
Dogs are welcome at this hotel.

Red Roof Inn Detroit - Troy
2350 Rochester Road
Troy, MI
248-689-4391 (800-RED-ROOF)
One well-behaved family pet per
room. Guest must notify front desk
upon arrival. Guest is liable for any
damages. In consideration of all
guests, pets must never be left
unattended in the guest rooms.

Staybridge Suites Detroit-Utica
46155 Utica Park Blvd
Utica, MI
586-323-0101 (877-270-6405)
Dogs up to 80 pounds are allowed.
Pets allowed with an additional pet
fee. Up to $75 for 1-6 nights and up
to $150 for 7+ nights. A pet
agreement must be signed at check-
in.

Baymont Inn & Suites Grand Rapids
N/ Walker
2151 Holton Court
Walker, MI
616-735-9595 (877-229-6668)
Dogs are welcome at this hotel.

Motel 6 - Grand Rapids North Walker
777 Mile Rd
Walker, MI
616-784-9375 (800-466-8356)
This motel welcomes your pets to
stay with you.

Candlewood Suites Detroit-Warren
7010 Convention Blvd.
Warren, MI
586-978-1261 (877-270-6405)
Dogs up to 80 pounds are allowed.
Pets allowed with an additional pet
fee. Up to $75 for 1-6 nights and up
to $150 for 7+ nights. A pet
agreement must be signed at check-
in.

Hawthorn Suites
30180 North Civic Center Blvd.
Warren, MI
586-558-7870 (800-527-1133)
In addition to providing a convenient
location to many local sites and
activities, this all-suite hotel offers a
number of amenities for business
and leisure travelers, including their
signature breakfast buffet and
beautifully appointed rooms. Dogs up
to 60 pounds are allowed for an
additional one time fee of $50 per
pet. 2 dogs may be allowed.

La Quinta Inn Detroit/Warren Tech
Center
30900 Van Dyke Avenue
Warren, MI
586-574-0550 (800-531-5900)

A dog of any size is allowed. There
are no additional pet fees. Dogs
may not be left unattended, and
they must be leashed and cleaned
up after.

Motel 6 - Detroit East Warren
8300 Chicago Rd
Warren, MI
586-826-9300 (800-466-8356)
This motel welcomes your pets to
stay with you.

Red Roof Inn Detroit - Warren
26300 Dequindre Road
Warren, MI
586-573-4300 (800-RED-ROOF)
One well-behaved family pet per
room. Guest must notify front desk
upon arrival. Guest is liable for any
damages. In consideration of all
guests, pets must never be left
unattended in the guest rooms.

Residence Inn Detroit Warren
30120 Civic Center Blvd
Warren, MI
586-558-8050 (800-331-3131)
Some of the amenities at this all-
suite inn include a daily buffet
breakfast, evening socials Monday
through Thursday with light dinner
fare, a seasonal heated swimming
pool, and complimentary grocery
shopping. Dogs are allowed for an
additional one time pet fee of $75
per room. Multiple dogs may be
allowed.

Comfort Inn
7076 Highland Rd.
Waterford, MI
248-666-8555 (877-424-6423)
Dogs up to 60 pounds are allowed.
Dogs are allowed for a pet fee of
$25.00 per pet per night.

The Wren's Nest
7405 W Maple Street
West Bloomfield, MI
248-624-6874
thewrensnestbb.com/
An historic Greek Revival home
dating back to the 1840's offers
guests a country like setting with
nature trails, plenty of bird and
wildlife viewing, lush greenery, wild
flowers everywhere, and of special
interest is the Goatea Room, a
special gathering place offering
unique and rare teas from around
the world. Dogs of all sizes are
allowed for no additional pet fee.
Dogs must be quiet, well behaved,
leashed, and cleaned up after. 2
dogs may be allowed.

Best Western of Whitmore Lake
9897 Main Street
Whitmore Lake, MI
734-449-2058 (800-780-7234)
Dogs of all sizes are allowed. Dogs
are allowed for a pet fee of $25.00
per pet per night.

The Knollwood Motel
5777 H 31N
Williamsburg, MI
231-938-2040
knollwoodmotel.com/
Open from May 1st through October
31st, this small resort motel offers
180 feet of sandy beach, picnic and
barbecue areas, paddle boats, a vine
covered gazebo, and more. One dog
is allowed per room (two dogs are
allowed if they are under 5 pounds)
for an additional fee of $9 per night
per pet and there is advance notice.
Dogs may not be left alone in the
room at any time, and they must be
leashed and cleaned up after at all
times.

Best Western Woodhaven Inn
21700 West Road
Woodhaven, MI
734-676-8000 (800-780-7234)
Dogs of all sizes are allowed. Dogs
are allowed for a pet fee.

Super 8 /Grand Rapids Area
Wyoming
727 44th St SW
Wyoming, MI
616-530-8588 (800-800-8000)
Dogs of all sizes are allowed. Three
or more dogs may be allowed.

Minnesota

Comfort Inn
810 Happy Trails Ln.
Albert Lea, MN
507-377-1100 (877-424-6423)
Dogs of all sizes are allowed. Dogs
are allowed for a pet fee of $10.00
per pet per stay.

Super 8 Albert Lea
2019 E Main St
Albert Lea, MN
507-377-0591 (800-800-8000)
Dogs are welcome at this hotel.

Holiday Inn Alexandria
5637 Highway 29 South
Alexandria, MN
320-763-6577 (877-270-6405)
Dogs are welcome at this hotel.

Super 8 MN Alexandria
4620 Hwy 29 S

Alexandria, MN
320-763-6552 (800-800-8000)
Dogs of all sizes are allowed. Dogs are allowed for a nightly pet fee.

Super 8 Motel - /MPLS/St. Paul Area
Arden Hills
1125 Red Fox Rd
Arden Hills, MN
651-484-6557 (800-800-8000)
Dogs are welcome at this hotel.

Super 8 MN Austin
1401 14th St NW
Austin, MN
507-433-1801 (800-800-8000)
Dogs are welcome at this hotel.

Timber Bay Lodge and Houseboats
Babbitt, MN
218-827-3682 (800-846-6821)
timberbay.com/
There is a $15 additional per pet fee per day or $70 per week per pet for a cabin or a houseboat. The cabins and houseboats are not designated as smoking or non-smoking. 2 dogs may be allowed.

Country Inns & Suites by Carlson
15058 Dellwood Drive
Baxter, MN
218-828-2161
Dogs of all sizes are allowed. There is an additional one time $10 pet fee. Pets may not be left alone in the room.

Holiday Inn Express Hotel & Suites
Brainerd-Baxter
15739 Audubon Way, Hwy 371 N
Baxter, MN
Hol-ida-yInn (877-270-6405)
Dogs of all sizes are allowed. Dogs are allowed for a nightly pet fee.

Rodeway Inn
7836 Fairview Road
Baxter, MN
218-829-0391 (877-424-6423)
Dogs of all sizes are allowed. Dogs are allowed for a pet fee of $10.00 per pet per night. Two dogs are allowed per room.

Super 8 /Brainerd Area Baxter
14341 Edgewood Drive
Baxter, MN
218-828-4288 (800-800-8000)
Dogs are welcome at this hotel.

Sleep Inn
14435 Bank Street
Becker, MN
763-262-7700 (877-424-6423)
Dogs of all sizes are allowed. Dogs are allowed for a pet fee of $10.00

per pet per night.

Super 8 MN Becker
13804 First Street
Becker, MN
763-262-8880 (800-800-8000)
Dogs are welcome at this hotel.

Best Western Bemidji Inn
2420 Paul Bunyan Drive NW
Bemidji, MN
218-751-0390 (800-780-7234)
Dogs of all sizes are allowed. Dogs are allowed for a pet fee of $15.00 per pet per night.

Comfort Inn
3500 Moberg Dr. NW
Bemidji, MN
218-444-7700 (877-424-6423)
Dogs of all sizes are allowed. Dogs are allowed for a pet fee of $10.00 per pet per night.

Days Inn West Bloomington
7851 Normandale Blvd
Bloomington, MN
952-835-7400 (800-329-7466)
Dogs of all sizes are allowed. Dogs are allowed for a pet fee of $10.00 per pet per night.

Days Inn Minneapolis-Airport
1901 Killebrew Drive
Bloomington, MN
952-854-8400 (800-329-7466)
Dogs of all sizes are allowed. Dogs are allowed for a pet fee of $10.00 per pet per stay.

Extended Stay America Minneapolis - Bloomington
7956 Lyndale Ave. S.
Bloomington, MN
952-884-1400 (800-804-3724)
One dog is allowed per suite. There is a $25 per night additional pet fee up to $150 for an entire stay.

Hilton Hotel
3800 American Blvd E
Bloomington, MN
952-854-2100 (800-HILTONS (445-8667))
This upscale hotel offers a number of on site amenities for business and leisure travelers, plus a convenient location to an international airport, the amazing Mall of America, historic sites, dining, and recreational areas. Dogs up to 75 pounds are allowed for an additional one time pet fee of $75 per room. 2 dogs may be allowed.

La Quinta Inn Minneapolis

Airport/Bloomington
7815 Nicollet Avenue South
Bloomington, MN
952-881-7311 (800-531-5900)
Dogs of all sizes are allowed. There are no additional pet fees. Dogs must be quiet, well behaved, and leashed. Multiple dogs may be allowed.

Ramada Mall of America - Airport
2300 East American Blvd
Bloomington, MN
952-854-3411 (800-272-6232)
Dogs of all sizes are allowed. Dogs are allowed for a nightly pet fee.

Residence Inn Minneapolis Bloomington
7850 Bloomington Avenue S
Bloomington, MN
952-876-0900 (800-331-3131)
Besides offering a convenient location to business, shopping, dining, and entertainment areas, this hotel also provides a number of in-house amenities, including a daily buffet breakfast and complementary evening socials Monday to Thursday with light dinner fare. Dogs are allowed for an additional one time pet fee of $75 per room. 2 dogs may be allowed.

Staybridge Suites Minneapolis-Bloomington
5150 American Blvd West
Bloomington, MN
952-831-7900 (877-270-6405)
Dogs up to 80 pounds are allowed. Pets allowed with an additional pet fee. Up to $75 for 1-6 nights and up to $150 for 7+ nights. A pet agreement must be signed at check-in.

Super 8 /Airport Bloomington
7800 2nd Ave South
Bloomington, MN
952-888-8800 (800-800-8000)
Dogs of all sizes are allowed. Dogs are allowed for a pet fee of $10 per pet per night.

Econo Lodge
11617 Andrew St.
Brainerd, MN
218-828-0027 (877-424-6423)
Dogs of all sizes are allowed. Dogs are allowed for a pet fee of $7.00 per pet per night.

Red Roof Inn Brainerd
2115 South 6th Street
Brainerd, MN
218-829-1441 (800-RED-ROOF)
One well-behaved family pet per

room. Guest must notify front desk upon arrival. Guest is liable for any damages. In consideration of all guests, pets must never be left unattended in the guest rooms.

Comfort Inn
1600 James Circle N.
Brooklyn Center, MN
763-560-7464 (877-424-6423)
Dogs of all sizes are allowed. Dogs are allowed for a pet fee of $15.00 per pet per stay. Two dogs are allowed per room.

Days Inn and Suites / Minneapolis Brooklyn Center
6415 James Circle North
Brooklyn Center, MN
763-561-8400 (800-329-7466)
Dogs are welcome at this hotel.

Extended Stay America Minneapolis - Brooklyn Center
2701 Freeway Blvd.
Brooklyn Center, MN
763-549-5571 (800-804-3724)
One dog is allowed per suite. There is a $25 per night additional pet fee up to $150 for an entire stay.

Motel 6 - Minneapolis Brooklyn Center
2741 Freeway Blvd
Brooklyn Center, MN
763-560-9789 (800-466-8356)
This motel welcomes your pets to stay with you.

Super 8 /MPLS Brooklyn Center
6445 James Circle
Brooklyn Center, MN
763-566-9810 (800-800-8000)
Dogs are welcome at this hotel.

Super 8 Buffalo
303 10th Ave S
Buffalo, MN
763-682-5930 (800-800-8000)
Dogs are welcome at this hotel.

Days Inn Burnsville
14331 Nicollet Court
Burnsville, MN
952-892-1900 (800-329-7466)
Dogs are welcome at this hotel.

Travelodge Burnsville
12920 Aldrich Ave South
Burnsville, MN
952-890-7431 (800-578-7878)
Dogs of all sizes are allowed. Dogs are allowed for a pet fee of $10.00 per pet per night.

Quality Inn Northtown
9052 NE University

Coon Rapids, MN
763-785-4746 (877-424-6423)
Dogs up to 60 pounds are allowed. Dogs are allowed for a pet fee of $10.00 per pet per night. Two dogs are allowed per room.

Voyagaire Lodge and Houseboats
7576 Gold Coast Road
Crane Lake, MN
218-993-2266 (800-88BOATS (882-6287))
voyagaire.com/
Located in Voyageurs National Park, nestled along the beautiful Crane Lake by the Canadian border, this resort is the country's only water based national park, and in addition to some outstanding scenery on land and on water, there is dining, and houseboat and lodging accommodations Dogs are allowed at the lodge for no additional fee; there is a $50 one time pet fee for the houseboat. Dogs are allowed to explore the islands and swim in the park waters. They must be under their owner's control at all times. 2 dogs may be allowed.

Best Western Holland House
615 Highway 10 E
Detroit Lakes, MN
218-847-4483 (800-780-7234)
Dogs of all sizes are allowed. Dogs are allowed for a pet fee of $15 per pet per night.

Best Western Downtown Motel
131 W 2nd Street
Duluth, MN
218-727-6851 (800-780-7234)
Dogs are welcome at this hotel.

Days Inn MN Duluth
909 Cottonwood Ave
Duluth, MN
218-727-3110 (800-329-7466)
Dogs of all sizes are allowed. Dogs are allowed for a nightly pet fee.

Holiday Inn Hotel & Suites Duluth-Downtown Waterfront
200 West 1st Street
Duluth, MN
218-722-1202 (877-270-6405)
Dogs are welcome at this hotel.

Motel 6 - Duluth
200 27th Ave
Duluth, MN
218-723-1123 (800-466-8356)
This motel welcomes your pets to stay with you.

Red Roof Inn Duluth - Spirit

Mountain
9315 Westgate Boulevard
Duluth, MN
218-628-3691 (800-RED-ROOF)
One well-behaved family pet per room. Guest must notify front desk upon arrival. Guest is liable for any damages. In consideration of all guests, pets must never be left unattended in the guest rooms.

The Willard Munger Inn
7408 Grand Avenue
Duluth, MN
218-624-4814 (800-982-2453)
mungerinn.com
Located on the Willard Munger State Trail at the foot of the Spirit Mountain Ski Resort, this inn offers a comfortable stay while exploring or enjoying any number of recreational activities. One dog is allowed for no additional pet fee; for a 2nd dog there will be an additional pet fee of $10 per night. 2 dogs may be allowed.

Best Western Dakota Ridge
3450 Washington Drive
Eagan, MN
651-452-0100 (800-780-7234)
Dogs of all sizes are allowed. Dogs are allowed for a nightly pet fee.

Days Inn Minnesota Near Mall of America Eagan
4510 Erin Dr.
Eagan, MN
651-681-1770 (800-329-7466)
Dogs of all sizes are allowed. Dogs are allowed for a pet fee of $5.00 pet per night.

Extended Stay America Minneapolis - Airport - Eagan
3384 Norwest Ct.
Eagan, MN
651-681-9991 (800-804-3724)
One dog is allowed per suite. There is a $25 per night additional pet fee up to $150 for an entire stay.

Homestead Studio Suites Minneapolis - Airport - Eagan
3015 Denmark Ave.
Eagan, MN
651-905-1778 (800-804-3724)
One dog is allowed per suite. There is a $25 per night additional pet fee up to $150 for an entire stay.

Residence Inn Minneapolis-St. Paul Airport/Eagan
3040 Eagandale Place
Eagan, MN
651-688-0363 (800-331-3131)
This all suite inn features a

convenient location to the Mall of America, a number of major corporations, and several recreation areas; plus they also offer a number of in-house amenities, including a daily buffet breakfast, and evening socials Monday to Wednesday with light dinner fare. Dogs are allowed for an additional one time pet fee of $100 per room. Multiple dogs may be allowed.

Staybridge Suites Eagan (Mall Of America Area)
4675 Rahncliff Road
Eagan, MN
651-994-7810 (877-270-6405)
Dogs up to 80 pounds are allowed. Pets allowed with an additional pet fee. Up to $75 for 1-6 nights and up to $150 for 7+ nights. A pet agreement must be signed at check-in.

TownePlace Suites Minneapolis-St. Paul Airport/Eagan
3615 Crestridge Drive
Eagan, MN
651-994-4600 (800-257-3000)
The Mall of America, the Water Park of America, the MN/St Paul International Airport, and the downtown areas of St Paul and Minneapolis are all just a short distance from this all suite inn. Dogs up to 100 pounds are allowed for an additional one time fee of $75. 2 dogs may be allowed.

Best Western Eden Prairie Inn
11500 W 78th Street
Eden Prairie, MN
952-829-0888 (800-780-7234)
Dogs are welcome at this hotel.

Extended Stay America Minneapolis - Eden Prairie
7550 Office Ridge Cir.
Eden Prairie, MN
952-941-1113 (800-804-3724)
One dog is allowed per suite. There is a $25 per night additional pet fee up to $150 for an entire stay.

Homestead Studio Suites Minneapolis - Eden Prairie
11905 Technology Dr.
Eden Prairie, MN
952-942-6818 (800-804-3724)
One dog is allowed per suite. There is a $25 per night additional pet fee up to $150 for an entire stay.

Residence Inn Minneapolis Eden Prairie
7780 Flying Cloud Drive
Eden Prairie, MN

952-829-0033 (800-331-3131)
Some of the amenities at this all-suite inn include a daily buffet breakfast, evening socials, a seasonal heated swimming pool, and a complimentary grocery shopping service. Dogs are allowed for an additional one time pet fee of $75 per room. Multiple dogs may be allowed.

TownePlace Suites Minneapolis Eden Prairie
11588 Leona Road
Eden Prairie, MN
952-942-6001 (800-257-3000)
This all suite hotel sits central to a number of sites of interest for both business and leisure travelers; plus they also offer a number of on-site amenities. Dogs are allowed for an additional one time fee of $75 per room. Multiple dogs may be allowed.

Residence Inn Minneapolis Edina
3400 Edinborough Way
Edina, MN
952-893-9300 (800-410-9649)
In addition to being located adjacent to the Centennial Lakes Business Park and near the amazing Mall of America, this all suite inn also offers a daily buffet breakfast and a manager's reception Monday to Thursday. Dogs up to 50 pounds are allowed for an additional one time pet fee of $75 per room. 2 dogs may be allowed.

Paddle Inn
1314 E Sheridan Street
Ely, MN
218-365-6036
Dogs up to 100 pounds are allowed. There is a $10 per night per room pet fee and a pet policy to sign at check in. 2 dogs may be allowed.

Super 8 Eveleth
1080 Industrial Park Drive
Eveleth, MN
218-744-1661 (800-800-8000)
Dogs are welcome at this hotel.

Comfort Inn
2225 N. State St.
Fairmont, MN
507-238-5444 (877-424-6423)
Dogs of all sizes are allowed. Dogs are allowed for a pet fee of $12.00 per pet per night.

Holiday Inn Fairmont
1201 Torgerson Drive
Fairmont, MN
507-238-4771 (877-270-6405)

Dogs of all sizes are allowed. Dogs are allowed for a pet fee of $12.00 per pet per night.

Super 8 Fairmont
1200 Torgerson Drive
Fairmont, MN
507-238-9444 (800-800-8000)
Dogs are welcome at this hotel.

Days Inn Faribault
1920 Cardinal Lane
Faribault, MN
507-334-6835 (800-329-7466)
Dogs are welcome at this hotel.

Comfort Inn
425 Western Ave.
Fergus Falls, MN
218-736-5787 (877-424-6423)
Dogs of all sizes are allowed.

Super 8 Fergus Falls
2454 College Way
Fergus Falls, MN
218-739-3261 (800-800-8000)
Dogs of all sizes are allowed. Dogs are allowed for a pet fee of $10 per pet per stay.

Super 8 Fosston
108 S Amber
Fosston, MN
218-435-1088 (800-800-8000)
Dogs are welcome at this hotel.

Aspen Lodge
310 East U.S. Hwy. 61
Grand Marais, MN
218-387-2500 (800-247-6020)
Pets are allowed in the motel section. There are no additional pet fees. 2 dogs may be allowed.

Best Western Superior Inn & Suites
US Highway 61 E
Grand Marais, MN
218-387-2240 (800-780-7234)
Dogs of all sizes are allowed. Dogs are allowed for a pet fee of $15.00 per pet per night.

Clearwater Lodge
774 Clearwater Rd
Grand Marais, MN
218-388-2254 (800-527-0554)
canoebwca.com/
There is an additional $90 per week per pet fee. Dogs are allowed in cabins only, not in the main lodge. 2 dogs may be allowed.

East Bay Suites
21 Wisconsin Street/H 61
Grand Marais, MN
218-387-2800 (800-414-2807)
eastbaysuites.com

Although offering modern, comfortable studios and suites for cozy living inside, the beauty of the North Shore and its recreational opportunities will bring any adventurer outside. Dogs are allowed for an additional fee of $20 per night per room. Dogs may not be left alone in the room at any time, and they must be leashed and under their owner's control at all times. A pet "special" is available: for $29.95 it includes a custom EBS dog tag, yapp-atizers, chew sticks, and a specially designed water bottle for pooches. Pet sitting may be arranged at the hotel. Multiple dogs may be allowed.

Gunflint Lodge
143 S Gunflint Lake Road/H 50
Grand Marais, MN
218-388-2294 (800-328-3325)
This lodge allows well-behaved dogs of all sizes in their cabins. There is a $20 per day pet fee. They offer non-smoking cabins. Once a year, the lodge has a Dog Lovers Weekend which includes a special off-leash area, an agility course, dog treats and a special dinner for your dog delivered to your cabin. During the winter, they also have a 2 mile groomed cross-country ski trail for dogs. Pets need to be leashed. 2 dogs may be allowed.

Super 8 Grand Marais
1711 W Hwy 61
Grand Marais, MN
218-387-2448 (800-800-8000)
Dogs are welcome at this hotel.

The Outpost Motel
2935 E H 61
Grand Marais, MN
218-387-1833 (888-380-1833)
outpostmotel.com/
Nestled between the shores of Lake Superior and Superior National Forest, this motel is a good starting point for exploring all the area has to offer. Dogs are allowed for an additional fee of $10 per night per pet. 2 dogs may be allowed.

Country Inns & Suites by Carlson
2601 S Highway 169
Grand Rapids, MN
218-327-4960
Dogs of all sizes are allowed. There are no additional pet fees. Dogs may not be left alone in the rooms.

Super 8 Grand Rapids
1702 S Pokegama Ave
Grand Rapids, MN
218-327-1108 (800-800-8000)

Dogs are welcome at this hotel.

Dakota Lodge
40497 H 48
Hinckley, MN
320-384-6052
dakotalodge.com/
Nestled on 6 acres of lush, well landscaped grounds, this beautiful retreat features cozy accommodations, whirlpool tubs, wood burning fireplaces, and scenic trails through the woods to the nearby St Croix River. Well mannered dogs are welcome for an additional one time pet fee of $20 per room. Dogs are to remain off the beds and furniture, and they must be leashed, and picked up after. 2 dogs may be allowed.

Days Inn Hinckley
104 Grindstone Court/I-35
Hinckley, MN
320-384-7751 (800-329-7466)
Dogs of all sizes are allowed. Dogs are allowed for a pet fee.

Days Inn International Falls
2331 U.S. Hwy 53 South
International Falls, MN
218-283-9441 (800-329-7466)
Dogs are welcome at this hotel.

Super 8 International Falls
2326 Hwy 53 Frontage Road
International Falls, MN
218-283-8811 (800-800-8000)
Dogs are welcome at this hotel.

Econo Lodge
2007 Highway 71 North
Jackson, MN
507-847-3110 (877-424-6423)
Dogs of all sizes are allowed. Dogs are allowed for a pet fee of $10.00 per pet per night.

Super 8 MN Jackson
2025 Highway 71 North
Jackson, MN
507-847-3498 (800-800-8000)
Dogs of all sizes are allowed. Dogs are allowed for a pet fee of $10.00 per pet per night.

Motel 6 - Minneapolis South Lakeville
11274 210th St
Lakeville, MN
952-469-1900 (800-466-8356)
This motel welcomes your pets to stay with you.

Kahneetah Cottages
4210 W H 61
Lutsen, MN

218-387-2585 (800-216-2585)
kahneetah.com/
Each of the cottages are nestled among the woods with great views of Lake Superior and are available year round. This is also the site of The Gallery where over 100 local artisans show their original works. Dogs are allowed for no additional fee; they must be leashed and picked up after. 2 dogs may be allowed.

Solbakken Resort
4874 W H 61
Lutsen, MN
218-663-7566 (800-435-3950)
solbakkenresort.com/
Nestled among lush greenery on the shores of Lake Superior, this is a beautiful place to explore or take a reprieve. Dogs are allowed for an additional fee of $10 per night per pet. Dogs must be leashed and picked up after, and they may not be left alone at any time. 2 dogs may be allowed.

Super 8 Luverne
1202 South Kniss Avenue
Luverne, MN
507-283-9541 (800-800-8000)
Dogs are welcome at this hotel.

Best Western Hotel & Restaurant
1111 Range Street
Mankato, MN
507-625-9333 (800-780-7234)
Dogs of all sizes are allowed. Dogs are allowed for a pet fee.

Comfort Inn
131 Apache Pl.
Mankato, MN
507-388-5107 (877-424-6423)
Dogs of all sizes are allowed. Dogs are allowed for a pet fee of $10.00 per pet per night.

Days Inn Mankato
1285 Range Street
Mankato, MN
507-387-3332 (800-329-7466)
Dogs of all sizes are allowed. Dogs are allowed for a pet fee of $10 per pet per night.

Super 8 Mankato
51578 US Hwy 169 N
Mankato, MN
507-387-4041 (800-800-8000)
Dogs are welcome at this hotel.

Extended Stay America Minneapolis - Maple Grove
12970 63rd Ave. N.
Maple Grove, MN
763-694-9747 (800-804-3724)

One dog is allowed per suite. There is a $25 per night additional pet fee up to $150 for an entire stay.

Staybridge Suites Minneapolis-Maple Grove
7821 Elm Creek Blvd
Maple Grove, MN
763-494-8856 (877-270-6405)
Dogs up to 80 pounds are allowed. Pets allowed with an additional pet fee. Up to $75 for 1-6 nights and up to $150 for 7+ nights. A pet agreement must be signed at check-in.

Days Inn Hotel and Conference Center Maplewood
1780 East County Road
Maplewood, MN
651-288-0808 (800-329-7466)
Dogs of all sizes are allowed. Dogs are allowed for a pet fee of $10.00 per pet per night.

Best Western Marshall Inn
1500 E College Drive
Marshall, MN
507-532-3221 (800-780-7234)
Dogs of all sizes are allowed. Dogs are allowed for a nightly pet fee.

Comfort Inn
1511 E. College Dr.
Marshall, MN
507-532-3070 (877-424-6423)
Dogs of all sizes are allowed. Dogs are allowed for a pet fee of $10.00 per pet per night. Two dogs are allowed per room.

Super 8 MN Marshall
Jct Hwys 59 & 23
Marshall, MN
507-537-1461 (800-800-8000)
Dogs are welcome at this hotel.

Super 8 Melrose
231 E County Road 173
Melrose, MN
320-256-4261 (800-800-8000)
Dogs are welcome at this hotel.

Best Western The Normandy Inn & Suites
405 S 8th Street
Minneapolis, MN
612-370-1400 (800-780-7234)
Dogs of all sizes are allowed. Dogs are allowed for a pet fee.

Days Hotel - University of Minnesota Minneapolis
2407 University Ave SE
Minneapolis, MN
612-623-3999 (800-329-7466)
Dogs of all sizes are allowed. Dogs

are allowed for a pet fee.

Graves 601 Hotel
601 N 1st Avenue
Minneapolis, MN
612-677-1100 (866-523-1100)
graves601hotel.com/
Sitting at the convergence of the entertainment and theater districts, this 22 story upscale hotel also connects by a skyway path to shopping and business areas. Dogs are allowed at the hotel for an additional one time pet fee per room of $150. There may be 1 dog up to 75 pounds or 2 small dogs per room. Dogs must be quiet, well mannered, leashed, and under owners care.

Marriott Minneapolis City Center
30 S 7th Street
Minneapolis, MN
612-349-4000 (800-228-9290)
This luxury, downtown hotel sits central to many of the city's star attractions, world class shopping and dining venues, and major business areas - many of them through their famous skyway system, plus they also offer a number of in-house amenities for all level of travelers. Dogs are allowed for an additional one time fee of $100 per room; they must be declared at the time of check-in and a contact number must be left with the front desk. 2 dogs may be allowed.

Millennium Hotel
1313 Nicollet Avenue
Minneapolis, MN
612-332-6000 (612-332-6000)
In addition to a variety of amenities, fine dining, a lounge, and plenty of meeting spaces, this hotel is also in the Nicollet Mall shopping district where numerous dining, entertainment, and shopping are available. Dogs are allowed for an additional fee of $10 per night per pet. Dogs must be leashed and picked up after at all times. 2 dogs may be allowed.

Residence Inn Minneapolis Downtown at The Depot
425 S Second Street
Minneapolis, MN
612-340-1300 (800-331-3131)
This downtown, all suite inn features a convenient location to numerous business, shopping, dining, and entertainment areas, plus they also offer a number of in-house amenities, including a daily buffet breakfast, evening socials

Monday through Thursday with light dinner fare, and an indoor water-park. One dog up to 150 pounds or 2 dogs totally no more than 150 pounds are allowed per room for an additional one time pet fee of $100 per room. 2 dogs may be allowed.

Residence Inn Minneapolis Downtown/City Center
45 S Eighth Street
Minneapolis, MN
612-677-1000 (800-331-3131)
This downtown, all suite inn features a convenient location to business, shopping, dining, and entertainment areas, plus they also offer a number of in-house amenities, including a daily buffet breakfast and evening socials. Dogs are allowed for an additional one time pet fee of $100 per room. Multiple dogs may be allowed.

Sheraton Bloomington Hotel, Minneapolis South
7800 Normandale Blvd.
Minneapolis, MN
952-835-7800 (888-625-5144)
Dogs of all sizes are allowed for no additional pet fee with a credit card on file; there is a pet agreement to sign at check in. Dogs may not be left alone in the room.

Sheraton Minneapolis Midtown Hotel
2901 Chicago Ave. South
Minneapolis, MN
612-821-7600 (888-625-5144)
Dogs of all sizes are allowed. There are no additional pet fees. Dogs are not allowed to be left alone in the room.

TownePlace Suites Minneapolis Downtown
525 North 2nd Street
Minneapolis, MN
612-340-1000 (800-257-3000)
This downtown, all suite inn sits central to numerous business, shopping, dining, and day/night entertainment areas, plus they offer a number of in-house amenities for all level of travelers. Dogs up to 45 pounds are allowed for an additional one time fee of $75 per room. 2 dogs may be allowed.

Marriott Minneapolis Southwest
5801 Opus Parkway
Minnetonka, MN
952-935-5500 (888-887-1681)
This luxury hotel sits central to many of the city's star attractions, world class shopping and dining venues, and major business areas, plus they also offer a number of in-house

amenities for all level of travelers. Dogs are allowed for an additional fee of $25 per night per room. 2 dogs may be allowed.

Super 8 Moorhead
3621 S 8th St
Moorhead, MN
218-233-8880 (800-800-8000)
Dogs are welcome at this hotel.

Days Inn Twin Cities North Mounds View
2149 Program Ave
Mounds View, MN
763-786-9151 (800-329-7466)
Dogs are welcome at this hotel.

Super 8 New Ulm
1901 S. Broadway
New Ulm, MN
507-359-2400 (800-800-8000)
Dogs are welcome at this hotel.

Days Inn Nisswa
24186 North Smiley Road
Nisswa, MN
218-963-3500 (800-329-7466)
Dogs of all sizes are allowed. Dogs are allowed for a pet fee of $15.00 per pet per stay.

Super 8 Northfield
1420 Riverview Dr
Northfield, MN
507-663-0371 (800-800-8000)
Dogs are welcome at this hotel.

Best Western Regency Plaza Hotel
970 Helena Avenue N
Oakdale, MN
651-578-8466 (800-780-7234)
Dogs of all sizes are allowed. Dogs are allowed for a pet fee of $25.00 per pet per stay.

Comfort Inn
2345 43rd St NW
Owatonna, MN
507-444-0818 (877-424-6423)
Dogs of all sizes are allowed. Dogs are allowed for a pet fee of $10.00 per pet per night.

Super 8 Owatonna
1150 West Frontage Rd
Owatonna, MN
507-451-0380 (800-800-8000)
Dogs are welcome at this hotel.

Super 8 Perham
106 Jake St SE
Perham, MN
218-346-7888 (800-800-8000)
Dogs are welcome at this hotel.

Rodeway Inn

2684 State 371 SW
Pine River, MN
218-587-4499 (877-424-6423)
Dogs of all sizes are allowed. Dogs are allowed for a pet fee of $10.00 per pet per night.

Dancing Bear Resort
17025 Sitka Drive NW
Pinewood, MN
218-243-2700
There is a $25 per week per pet additional fee.

Best Western Kelly Inn
2705 Annapolis Ln N
Plymouth, MN
763-553-1600 (800-780-7234)
Dogs are welcome at this hotel.

Comfort Inn
3000 Harbor Lane
Plymouth, MN
763-559-1222 (877-424-6423)
Dogs of all sizes are allowed. Dogs are allowed for a pet fee of $10.00 per pet per night.

Days Inn West/Minneapolis Plymouth
2955 Empire Lane/I-494
Plymouth, MN
763-559-2400 (800-329-7466)
Dogs of all sizes are allowed. Dogs are allowed for a pet fee.

Red Roof Inn Minneapolis Plymouth
2600 Annapolis Lane North
Plymouth, MN
763-553-1751 (800-RED-ROOF)
One well-behaved family pet per room. Guest must notify front desk upon arrival. Guest is liable for any damages. In consideration of all guests, pets must never be left unattended in the guest rooms.

Residence Inn Minneapolis Plymouth
2750 Annapolis Circle
Plymouth, MN
763-577-1600 (800-331-3131)
In addition to offering a convenient location to business, shopping, dining, and entertainment areas, this hotel also provides a number of in-house amenities, including a daily buffet breakfast and evening social hours. Dogs are allowed for an additional one time pet fee of $100 per room. Multiple dogs may be allowed.

Star Lake Forest Rentals
14450 Bowers Drive
Ramsey, MN
866-888-8265

Dogs of all sizes are allowed. There is a pet policy to sign at check in and there are no additional pet fees. This is a monthly rental only. 2 dogs may be allowed.

Rainy Lake Inn and Suites at Tara's Wharf
2065 Spruce Street Landing
Ranier, MN
218-286-5699 (877-RAINYLK (724-6955))
taraswharf.com/welcome.htm
Well mannered dogs are allowed throughout the grounds and on the boat rentals for no additional fee as long as there is no additional clean-up required. Dogs may not be left alone in the room at any time. Dogs may be off leash if they are under strict voice control and they are friendly to humans and other animals. 2 dogs may be allowed.

Days Inn Red Wing
955 East 7th Street
Red Wing, MN
651-388-3568 (800-329-7466)
Dogs of all sizes are allowed. Dogs are allowed for a pet fee.

Super 8 Red Wing
232 Withers Harbor Dr.
Red Wing, MN
651-388-0491 (800-800-8000)
Dogs are welcome at this hotel.

Candlewood Suites Minneapolis-Richfield
351 West 77th St
Richfield, MN
612-869-7704 (877-270-6405)
Dogs up to 80 pounds are allowed. Pets allowed with an additional pet fee. Up to $75 for 1-6 nights and up to $150 for 7+ nights. A pet agreement must be signed at check-in.

Motel 6 - Minneapolis Airport Mall Of America
7640 Cedar Ave
Richfield, MN
612-861-4491 (800-466-8356)
This motel welcomes your pets to stay with you.

Comfort Inn
5708 Bandel Road NW
Rochester, MN
507-289-3344 (877-424-6423)
Dogs up to 50 pounds are allowed. Dogs are allowed for a pet fee of $35.00 per pet per stay.

Days Inn Downtown Rochester
1st Ave NW

Rochester, MN
507-282-3801 (800-329-7466)
Dogs are welcome at this hotel.

Extended Stay America Rochester - North
2814 43rd St. N.W.
Rochester, MN
507-289-7444 (800-804-3724)
One dog is allowed per suite. There is a $25 per night additional pet fee up to $150 for an entire stay.

Extended Stay America Rochester - South
55 Wood Lake Dr. S.E.
Rochester, MN
507-536-7444 (800-804-3724)
One dog is allowed per suite. There is a $25 per night additional pet fee up to $150 for an entire stay.

Holiday Inn Rochester-S (Mayo Clinic Area)
1630 South Broadway
Rochester, MN
507-288-1844 (877-270-6405)
Dogs of all sizes are allowed. Dogs are allowed for a pet fee of $15.00 per pet per night.

Marriott Rochester Mayo Clinic
101 First Avenue SW
Rochester, MN
507-280-6000 (877-623-7775)
This luxury, downtown hotel gives a convenient location to the Mayo Clinic, to several of the city's star attractions - many accessible by a climate controlled pedestrian subway and skyway, world class shopping and dining venues, and business areas, plus they also offer a number of in-house amenities for all level of travelers. Dogs are allowed for am additional one time fee of $75 per room. Multiple dogs may be allowed.

Motel 6 - Rochester, Mn
2107 Frontage Rd
Rochester, MN
507-282-6625 (800-466-8356)
This motel welcomes your pets to stay with you.

Quality Inn & Suites
1620 1st Ave. S.E.
Rochester, MN
507-282-8091 (877-424-6423)
Dogs of all sizes are allowed. Dogs are allowed for a pet fee of $10.00 per pet per night.

Residence Inn Rochester Mayo Clinic Area
441 West Center St NW
Rochester, MN

507-292-1400 (877-623-7775)
There is a climate controlled walkway connecting this all suite inn to the Mayo Clinic. Some of the other amenities include a daily buffet breakfast, a nightly social hour, and weekly barbecues. Dogs are allowed for an additional one time pet fee of $100 per room. Multiple dogs may be allowed.

Sleep Inn & Suites
7320 Airport View Dr. SW
Rochester, MN
507-536-7000 (877-424-6423)
Dogs of all sizes are allowed. Dogs are allowed for a pet fee of $10.00 per pet per night. Two dogs are allowed per room.

Staybridge Suites Rochester
1211 Second St. SW
Rochester, MN
507-289-6600 (877-270-6405)
Dogs up to 80 pounds are allowed. Pets allowed with an additional pet fee. Up to $75 for 1-6 nights and up to $150 for 7+ nights. A pet agreement must be signed at check-in.

Super 8 /Fairgrounds Area Rochester
1230 S Broadway
Rochester, MN
507-288-8288 (800-800-8000)
Dogs are welcome at this hotel.

Super 8 /South Broadway Rochester
106 SE 21st Street
Rochester, MN
507-282-1756 (800-800-8000)
Dogs of all sizes are allowed. Dogs are allowed for a pet fee.

TownePlace Suites Rochester
2829 43rd Street NW
Rochester, MN
507-281-1200 (866-814-1200)
This all suite inn sits central to numerous business, shopping, dining, and entertainment areas, plus they also offer a number of in-house amenities for business and leisure travelers. Dogs are allowed for an additional one time fee of $75 per room. Multiple dogs may be allowed.

Days Inn
2550 Cleveland Ave North
Roseville, MN
651-636-6730 (800-329-7466)
Dogs of all sizes are allowed. Dogs are allowed for a pet fee.

Motel 6 - Minneapolis North Roseville
2300 Cleveland Ave
Roseville, MN
651-639-3988 (800-466-8356)
This motel welcomes your pets to stay with you.

Residence Inn Minneapolis St. Paul/Roseville
2985 Centre Pointe Drive
Roseville, MN
651-636-0680 (800-331-3131)
This all suite inn features a central location to several downtown areas, the University of Minnesota, and the Mall of America, plus they also offer a number of in-house amenities, including a daily buffet breakfast, evening socials Monday to Wednesday, and a 2 mile walking path. Dogs are allowed for an additional one time pet fee of $100 per room. Multiple dogs may be allowed.

Super 8 Mpls St Paul Area Roseville
I-35 W & Hwy 36
Roseville, MN
651-636-8888 (800-800-8000)
Dogs of all sizes are allowed. Dogs are allowed for a pet fee.

Best Western Kelly Inn
100 4th Avenue S
Saint Cloud, MN
320-253-0606 (800-780-7234)
Dogs of all sizes are allowed. Dogs are allowed for a pet fee.

Best Western Bandana Square
1010 Bandana Boulevard W
Saint Paul, MN
651-647-1637 (800-780-7234)
Dogs of all sizes are allowed. Dogs are allowed for a pet fee of $10.00 per pet per stay.

Best Western Kelly Inn
161 Saint Anthony Avenue
Saint Paul, MN
651-227-8711 (800-780-7234)
Dogs are welcome at this hotel.

Comfort Inn
4601 W. Hwy 13
Savage, MN
952-894-6124 (877-424-6423)
Dogs up to 50 pounds are allowed. Dogs are allowed for a pet fee of $10.00 per pet per night.

Americ Inn Lodge and Suites
150 Mensing Drive
Silver Bay, MN
218-226-4300
Dogs of all sizes are allowed. There is a $10 per night per pet fee and a

pet policy to sign at check in. 2 dogs may be allowed.

Days Inn St Cloud
70 South 37th Ave.
St Cloud, MN
320-253-4444 (800-329-7466)
Dogs of all sizes are allowed. Dogs are allowed for a pet fee of $10.00 per pet per night.

Holiday Inn Express Hotel & Suites
St. Cloud
4322 Clearwater Road
St Cloud, MN
320-240-8000 (877-270-6405)
Dogs are welcome at this hotel.

St. Cloud Travelodge
3820 Roosevelt Road
St Cloud, MN
320-253-3338 (800-578-7878)
Dogs are welcome at this hotel.

Super 8 St. Cloud
50 Park Ave S
St Cloud, MN
320-253-5530 (800-800-8000)
Dogs of all sizes are allowed. Dogs are allowed for a pet fee of $10.00 per pet per stay.

Super 8 St. James
1210 Heckman Court
St James, MN
507-375-4708 (800-800-8000)
Dogs are welcome at this hotel.

TownePlace Suites Minneapolis West/St. Louis Park
1400 Zarthan Avenue S
St Louis Park, MN
952-847-6900 (800-257-3000)
This all suite hotel sits central to a number of sites of interest for both business and leisure travelers; plus they also offer a number of on-site amenities - including an on-site 24 hour market. Dogs totaling no more than 50 pounds are allowed for an additional one time fee of $100 per room. 2 dogs may be allowed.

Days Inn St. Paul-Minneapolis-Midway
1964 University Ave W
St Paul, MN
651-645-8681 (800-329-7466)
Dogs of all sizes are allowed. Dogs are allowed for a pet fee.

Super 8 /I-94 St. Paul
1739 Old Hudson Road
St Paul, MN
651-771-5566 (800-800-8000)
Dogs are welcome at this hotel.

Super 8 Staples
109 2nd Ave. NW
Staples, MN
218-894-3585 (800-800-8000)
Dogs of all sizes are allowed. Dogs are allowed for a pet fee of $7.00 per pet per night.

Super 8 /St Paul Stillwater
2190 W Frontage Rd.
Stillwater, MN
651-430-3990 (800-800-8000)
Dogs are welcome at this hotel.

The Springs Country Inn
361 Government St
Taylors Falls, MN
651-465-6565
There is no additional pet fee. Dogs are allowed on the first 2 floors. 2 dogs may be allowed.

Bluefin Bay Resort
7192 H 61W
Tofte, MN
1-800-BLUEFIN (258-3346)
bluefinbay.com/
Listed among the top resorts on Lake Superior (the largest freshwater body of water on the planet), this beautiful major recreational destination offers numerous amenities, indoor and outdoor pools, an outdoor hot tub and spa, picnic areas with grills, eateries, and a lot more. Dogs are allowed for an additional fee of $20 per night per room. Dogs must be kept leashed on the grounds, and crated when left alone in the room. 2 dogs may be allowed.

Loghouse and Homestead
44854 Fred Holm Road
Vergas, MN
218-342-2318 (800-342-2318)
loghousebb.com/
Located in a rich natural setting along beautiful Spirit Lake, this historical inn offers a 1902 Swedish style home and an 1889 log house for lodging. There are also 2 wetlands and 3 miles of hiking trails on this 115 acre property. Quiet, well behaved dogs are allowed for no additional fee; they must be hound, human, and cat friendly. Dogs must be leashed and picked up after. 2 dogs may be allowed.

Super 8 Waconia
301 East Frontage Road
Waconia, MN
952-442-5147 (800-800-8000)
Dogs are welcome at this hotel.

Motel 6 - St Cloud I-94 Waite Park

815 1st St
Waite Park, MN
320-253-7070 (800-466-8356)
This motel welcomes your pets to stay with you.

Best Western White Bear Country Inn
4940 State Highway 61
White Bear Lake, MN
651-429-5393 (800-780-7234)
Dogs up to 50 pounds are allowed. Dogs are allowed for a pet fee of $10.00 per pet per night.

Comfort Inn
2200 E. US 12
Willmar, MN
320-231-2601 (877-424-6423)
Dogs of all sizes are allowed. Dogs are allowed for a pet fee of $10.00 per pet per night.

Holiday Inn Willmar
2100 East Highway 12
Willmar, MN
320-235-6060 (877-270-6405)
Dogs of all sizes are allowed. Dogs are allowed for a pet fee of $10.00 per pet per night.

Super 8 Willmar
2655 S 1st Street
Willmar, MN
320-235-4444 (800-800-8000)
Dogs are welcome at this hotel.

Super 8 Windom
222 3rd Ave South
Windom, MN
507-831-1120 (800-800-8000)
Dogs are welcome at this hotel.

Holiday Inn Express Hotel & Suites
Winona
1128 Homer Road
Winona, MN
507-474-1700 (877-270-6405)
Dogs of all sizes are allowed. Dogs are allowed for a nightly pet fee.

Quality Inn
956 Mankato Ave.
Winona, MN
507-454-4390 (877-424-6423)
Dogs of all sizes are allowed. Dogs are allowed for a pet fee of $10.00 per pet per stay.

Extended Stay America Minneapolis - Woodbury
10020 Hudson Rd.
Woodbury, MN
651-501-1085 (800-804-3724)
One dog is allowed per suite. There is a $25 per night additional pet fee up to $150 for an entire stay.

Red Roof Inn St Paul - Woodbury
1806 Wooddale Drive
Woodbury, MN
651-738-7160 (800-RED-ROOF)
One well-behaved family pet per room. Guest must notify front desk upon arrival. Guest is liable for any damages. In consideration of all guests, pets must never be left unattended in the guest rooms.

Days Inn Worthington
207 Oxford Street
Worthington, MN
507-376-6155 (800-329-9466)
Dogs of all sizes are allowed. Dogs are allowed for a pet fee of $10.00 per pet per night.

Super 8 Minnesota Worthington
850 Lucy Drive
Worthington, MN
507-372-7755 (800-800-8000)
Dogs are welcome at this hotel.

Travelodge Worthington
2015 N. Humiston Ave
Worthington, MN
507-372-2991 (800-578-7878)
Dogs of all sizes are allowed. Dogs are allowed for a pet fee of $8.00 per pet per night.

Super 8 Zumbrota
US Hwy 52
Zumbrota, MN
507-732-7852 (800-800-8000)
Dogs are welcome at this hotel.

Mississippi

Days Inn Batesville
280 Power Drive
Batesville, MS
662-563-4999 (800-329-9466)
Dogs are welcome at this hotel.

Edgewater Inn
1936 Beach Blvd/H 90
Biloxi, MS
228-388-1100 (800-323-9676)
gcww.com/edgewaterinn/
This beachside inn sits central to many local sites of interest, eateries, casinos, recreation, and shopping. Dogs up to 50 pounds are allowed for an additional one time fee of $50 per pet. 2 dogs may be allowed.

Motel 6 - Biloxi
2476 Beach Blvd
Biloxi, MS
228-388-2601 (800-466-8356)
This motel welcomes your pets to stay with you.

Ramada Limited Ocean Springs
8015 Tucker Road
Biloxi/Ocean Springs, MS
228-872-2323 (800-272-6232)
Dogs of all sizes are allowed. Dogs are allowed for a nightly pet fee.

Best Western College Inn
805 N 2nd Street
Booneville, MS
662-728-2244 (800-780-7234)
Dogs are welcome at this hotel.

Super 8 Booneville
110 Hospitality Ave
Booneville, MS
662-720-1688 (800-800-8000)
Dogs are welcome at this hotel.

Jackson - Brandon Red Roof Inn & Suites
280 Old Hwy 80
Brandon, MS
601-824-3839 (800-RED-ROOF)
One well-behaved family pet per room. Guest must notify front desk upon arrival. Guest is liable for any damages. In consideration of all guests, pets must never be left unattended in the guest rooms.

Super 8 Brookhaven
344 Dunn Ratcliff
Brookhaven, MS
601-833-8580 (800-800-8000)
Dogs are welcome at this hotel.

Best Western Canton Inn
137 Soldier Colony Road
Canton, MS
601-859-8600 (800-780-7234)
Complimentary continental breakfast Outdoor pool Fax services Playground Ice/vending machines Free parking Truck/RV parking Photocopy services Guest laundry High-speed Internet access Interior corridor

Comfort Inn
145 Soldier Colony Road
Canton, MS
601-859-7575 (877-424-6423)
Dogs of all sizes are allowed. Dogs are allowed for a pet fee of $25.00 per pet per stay.

Best Western Ridgeland Inn
102 Clinton Loop Drive
Clinton, MS
601-926-4323 (800-780-7234)
Dogs of all sizes are allowed. Dogs are allowed for a pet fee of $15.00 per pet per night.

Motel 6 - Columbus, Ms

1203 Hwy 45
Columbus, MS
662-327-4450 (800-466-8356)
This motel welcomes your pets to stay with you.

Comfort Inn
2101 Hwy. 72 West
Corinth, MS
662-287-4421 (877-424-6423)
Dogs of all sizes are allowed.

Econo Lodge Inn & Suites
441 Yacht Club Drive
Diamondhead, MS
228-586-0210 (877-424-6423)
Dogs of all sizes are allowed. Dogs are allowed for a pet fee of $15.00 per pet per night.

Super 8 Durant
31201 Hwy 12
Durant, MS
662-653-3881 (800-800-8000)
Dogs are welcome at this hotel.

Best Value Inn
I-20 at Highway 35, PO Box 402
Forest, MS
601-469-2640
This inn offers a number of on-site amenities,,, plus they are located only a few minutes from downtown and within walking distance to shopping, dining, and entertainment. Dogs are allowed for an additional pet fee of $10 per night per pet. 2 dogs may be allowed.

Econo Lodge
3080 US 82 E.
Greenville, MS
662-378-4976 (877-424-6423)
Dogs of all sizes are allowed.

Rodeway Inn & Suites
2700 Highway 82 East
Greenville, MS
662-332-5666 (877-424-6423)
Dogs up to 50 pounds are allowed. Dogs are allowed for a pet fee of $10.00 per pet per night. Two dogs are allowed per room.

Econo Lodge Inn & Suites
401 US 82 W.
Greenwood, MS
662-453-5974 (877-424-6423)
Dogs up to 50 pounds are allowed.

Knights Inn MS Grenada
1632 Sunset Drive
Grenada, MS
662-226-8888 (800-843-5644)
Dogs of all sizes are allowed. Dogs are allowed for a pet fee of $8.00 per pet per night.

Motel 6 - Gulfport
9355 Us Hwy 49
Gulfport, MS
228-863-1890 (800-466-8356)
This motel welcomes your pets to
stay with you.

Ramada Airport Conference Center
Gulfport
9415 Highway 49
Gulfport, MS
228-868-8200 (800-272-6232)
Dogs of all sizes are allowed. Dogs
are allowed for a pet fee.

Residence Inn Gulfport-Biloxi Airport
14100 Airport Road
Gulfport, MS
228-867-1722 (800-331-3131)
Some of the amenities at this all-
suite inn include a daily buffet
breakfast, evening social hours, an
indoor swimming pool, and a
complimentary grocery shopping
service. Dogs are allowed for an
additional one time pet fee of $100
per room. 2 dogs may be allowed.

Candlewood Suites Hattiesburg
9 Gateway Drive
Hattiesburg, MS
601-264-9666 (877-270-6405)
Dogs up to 80 pounds are allowed.
Pets allowed with an additional pet
fee. Up to $75 for 1-6 nights and up
to $150 for 7+ nights. A pet
agreement must be signed at check-
in.

Comfort Inn University
6541 Highway 49
Hattiesburg, MS
601-264-1881 (877-424-6423)
Dogs up to 50 pounds are allowed.
Dogs are allowed for a pet fee of
$50.00 per pet per stay. Two dogs
are allowed per room.

Howard Johnson Express
Hattiesburg
6553 Highway 49 North
Hattiesburg, MS
601-268-1410 (800-446-4656)
Dogs are welcome at this hotel.
There is a $25 nightly pet fee.

Motel 6 - Hattiesburg University Of
Southern Ms
6508 Us Hwy 49
Hattiesburg, MS
601-544-6096 (800-466-8356)
This motel welcomes your pets to
stay with you.

Ramada Hattiesburg
6595 Hwy 49 South

Hattiesburg, MS
601-599-2001 (800-272-6232)
Dogs of all sizes are allowed. Dogs
are allowed for a pet fee of $25.00
per pet per stay.

Days Inn Hernando
943 East Commerce Street
Hernando, MS
662-429-0000 (800-329-7466)
Dogs are welcome at this hotel.

Super 8 Hernando
2425 Sloans Way
Hernando, MS
662-429-5334 (800-800-8000)
Dogs are welcome at this hotel.

Days Inn - Holly Springs
120 Heritage Drive
Holly Springs, MS
662-252-1120 (800-329-7466)
Dogs of all sizes are allowed. Dogs
are allowed for a nightly pet fee.

Best Western Goodman Inn &
Suites
6910 Wind Chase Drive
Horn Lake, MS
800-780-7234 (800-780-7234)
Dogs are welcome at this hotel.

Motel 6 - Memphis Horn Lake, Ms
701 Southwest Dr
Horn Lake, MS
662-349-4439 (800-466-8356)
This motel welcomes your pets to
stay with you.

Sleep Inn
708 Desoto Cove
Horn Lake, MS
662-349-2773 (877-424-6423)
Dogs of all sizes are allowed. Dogs
are allowed for a pet fee of $10.00
per pet per night.

Clarion Hotel The Roberts Walthall
225 East Capitol Street
Jackson, MS
601-948-6161 (877-424-6423)
Dogs of all sizes are allowed. Dogs
are allowed for a pet fee of $125.00
per pet per stay. Two dogs are
allowed per room.

Comfort Inn
5709 I-55 North
Jackson, MS
601-206-1616 (877-424-6423)
Dogs up to 80 pounds are allowed.
Dogs are allowed for a pet fee of
$20.00 per pet per stay.

Days Inn Southwest Jackson
2616 Hwy 80 West
Jackson, MS

601-969-5511 (800-329-7466)
Dogs of all sizes are allowed. Dogs
are allowed for a pet fee of $10 per
pet per stay.

Extended Stay America Jackson -
North
5354 I-55 N.
Jackson, MS
601-956-4312 (800-804-3724)
One dog is allowed per suite. There
is a $25 per night additional pet fee
up to $150 for an entire stay.

La Quinta Inn Jackson North
616 Briarwood Drive
Jackson, MS
601-957-1741 (800-531-5900)
Dogs of all sizes are allowed. There
are no additional pet fees. Dogs
must be leashed and cleaned up
after. Multiple dogs may be allowed.

Motel 6 - Jackson, Ms
6145 I-55
Jackson, MS
601-956-8848 (800-466-8356)
Your pets are welcome to stay here
with you.

Red Roof Inn Jackson Downtown -
Fairgrounds
700 Larson Street
Jackson, MS
601-969-5006 (800-RED-ROOF)
One well-behaved family pet per
room. Guest must notify front desk
upon arrival. Guest is liable for any
damages. In consideration of all
guests, pets must never be left
unattended in the guest rooms.

Residence Inn Jackson
881 E River Place
Jackson, MS
601-355-3599 (800-331-3131)
In addition to offering a convenient
location to business, shopping,
dining, and entertainment areas, this
hotel also provides a number of in-
house amenities, including a daily
buffet breakfast and an evening
social hour. Dogs are allowed for an
additional one time pet fee of $75 per
room. 2 dogs may be allowed.

Sleep Inn
2620 US 80 W.
Jackson, MS
601-354-3900 (877-424-6423)
Dogs of all sizes are allowed. Dogs
are allowed for a pet fee of $10.00
per pet per night.

Studio 6 - Jackson, Ms
5925 I-55
Jackson, MS

601-956-9988 (800-466-8356)
Your pets are welcome to stay here with you for a pet fee of $10 per day up to $50 for an entire stay.

Best Western Oak Tree Inn
12710 Highway 45 (& 14 Bypass)
Macon, MS
662-726-4334 (800-780-7234)
Dogs of all sizes are allowed. Dogs are allowed for a pet fee of $15.00 per pet per stay.

Days Inn MS McComb
2298 Delaware Avenue
McComb, MS
601-684-5566 (800-329-7466)
Dogs are welcome at this hotel.

Days Inn Meridian
145 Hwy 11 & 80E
Meridian, MS
601-483-3812 (800-329-7466)
Dogs are welcome at this hotel.

Econo Lodge
2405 S. Frontage Rd.
Meridian, MS
601-693-9393 (877-424-6423)
Dogs up to 50 pounds are allowed. Dogs are allowed for a pet fee of $10.00/ per pet per night.

La Quinta Inn Meridan
1400 Roebuck Drive
Meridian, MS
601-693-2300 (800-531-5900)
Dogs of all sizes are allowed. There are no additional fees. There is a pet waiver to sign at check in, and a credit card must be on file in case of damages. Dogs may not be left unattended, and they must be leashed and cleaned up after. Multiple dogs may be allowed.

Motel 6 - Meridian, Ms
2309 Frontage Rd
Meridian, MS
601-482-1182 (800-466-8356)
This motel welcomes your pets to stay with you.

Quality Inn
1401 Roebuck Drive
Meridian, MS
601-693-4521 (877-424-6423)
Dogs of all sizes are allowed.

La Quinta Inn Moss Point
6292 Highway 63
Moss Point, MS
228-474-4488 (800-531-5900)
Dogs of all sizes are allowed. There are no additional pet fees. Dogs must be leashed, cleaned up after, and the Do Not Disturb sign put on

the door if there is a pet in the room alone. Multiple dogs may be allowed.

Super 8 Pascagoula Moss Point
6824 Hwy 613
Moss Point, MS
228-474-1855 (800-800-8000)
Dogs are welcome at this hotel.

Days Inn Natchez
109 Hwy 61 South
Natchez, MS
601-445-8291 (800-329-7466)
Dogs up to 50 pounds are allowed. Dogs are allowed for a pet fee of $10 per pet per stay.

Devereaux Shields House
709 N Union
Natchez, MS
601-304-5378 (888-304-5378)
dshieldsusa.com/
Lush manicured grounds, period antique furnishings, full southern breakfasts, and more greet visitors at this Victorian Queen Anne home. Dogs (no puppies) are allowed in the cottage rooms for no additional fee. They must be well trained, quiet, and have their own bedding to sleep on at night. Dogs must be leashed, cleaned up after, and they are not allowed on the furniture. 2 dogs may be allowed.

Glenfield Plantation Bed and Breakfast
6 Providence Road
Natchez, MS
601-442-1002
glenfieldplantation.com/
Listed on the National Register of Historic Places, this English Gothic home dates back to 1778 and sits on 150 lush acres. It offers historic charm and modern accommodations. Dogs are allowed for an additional one time fee of $50 per night. Dogs are not allowed on the bed or furnishings, and they must be crated when left alone in the room. Dogs must be leashed and picked up after. 2 dogs may be allowed.

Days Inn s Ocean Spring
7305 Washington Ave
Ocean Spring, MS
228-872-8255 (800-329-7466)
Dogs are welcome at this hotel.

Studio 6 - Ocean Springs
2873 Bienville Blvd
Ocean Springs, MS
228-875-0123 (800-466-8356)
Your pets are welcome to stay here

with you for a pet fee of $10 per day up to $50 for an entire stay.

Super 8 Biloxi Ocean Springs
I-10 Exit 50 N.E. Crner Of Hwy
Ocean Springs, MS
228-875-2288 (800-800-8000)
Dogs are welcome at this hotel.

Candlewood Suites Olive Branch
7448 Craft Goodman Road
Olive Branch, MS
662-890-7491 (877-270-6405)
Dogs up to 80 pounds are allowed. Pets allowed with an additional pet fee. Up to $75 for 1-6 nights and up to $150 for 7+ nights. A pet agreement must be signed at check-in.

Comfort Inn
7049 Enterprise Dr.
Olive Branch, MS
662-895-0456 (877-424-6423)
Dogs up to 100 pounds are allowed. Dogs are allowed for a pet fee of $12 per pet per night.

Holiday Inn Express Hotel & Suites
Olive Branch
8900 Expressway Dr
Olive Branch, MS
662-893-8700 (877-270-6405)
Dogs of all sizes are allowed. Dogs are allowed for a pet fee of $20.00 per pet per night.

Days Inn Oxford
1101 Frontage Road
Oxford, MS
662-234-9500 (800-329-7466)
Dogs of all sizes are allowed. Dogs are allowed for a pet fee of $15.00 per pet per night.

Super 8 Oxford
2201 Jackson Avenue West
Oxford, MS
662-234-7013 (800-800-8000)
Dogs of all sizes are allowed. Dogs are allowed for a pet fee of $15.00 per pet per night.

Studio 6 - Pascagoula
4419 Denny Ave
Pascagoula, MS
228-696-9011 (800-466-8356)
Your pets are welcome to stay here with you for a pet fee of $10 per day up to $50 for an entire stay.

Candlewood Suites Pearl
632 Pearson Rd
Pearl, MS
601-936-3442 (877-270-6405)
Dogs up to 80 pounds are allowed. Pets allowed with an additional pet

fee. Up to $75 for 1-6 nights and up to $150 for 7+ nights. A pet agreement must be signed at check-in.

La Quinta Inn & Suites Jackson Airport
501 S. Pearson Rd
Pearl, MS
601-664-0065 (800-531-5900)
Dogs of all sizes are allowed. There are no additional pet fees. Dogs must be leashed and cleaned up after. Dogs may not be left unattended unless they will be quiet and well behaved. Multiple dogs may be allowed.

Motel 6 - Jackson Airport Pearl, Ms
216 Pearson Rd
Pearl, MS
601-936-9988 (800-466-8356)
This motel welcomes your pets to stay with you.

Ramada Limited Airport South Pearl
341 Airport Road
Pearl, MS
601-933-1122 (800-272-6232)
Dogs of all sizes are allowed. Dogs are allowed for a pet fee of $25.00 per pet per stay.

Days Inn Pontotoc
217 Highway 15 North
Pontotoc, MS
662-489-5200 (800-329-7466)
Dogs are welcome at this hotel.

Drury Inn & Suites
610 E. County Line Road
Ridgeland, MS
601-956-6100 (800-378-7946)
Dogs of all sizes are allowed for no additional pet fee with a credit card on file, and there is a pet agreement to sign at check in.

Econo Lodge North
839 Ridgewood Road
Ridgeland, MS
601-956-7740 (877-424-6423)
Dogs of all sizes are allowed. Dogs are allowed for a pet fee of $10.00 per pet per night.

Red Roof Inn Jackson North - Ridgeland
810 Adcock Street
Ridgeland, MS
601-956-7707 (800-RED-ROOF)
One well-behaved family pet per room. Guest must notify front desk upon arrival. Guest is liable for any damages. In consideration of all guests, pets must never be left unattended in the guest rooms.

Residence Inn Jackson Ridgeland
855 Centre Street
Ridgeland, MS
601-206-7755 (800-331-3131)
Some of the amenities at this all-suite inn include a daily buffet breakfast, evening social hours, a Sport Court, and a complimentary grocery shopping service. Dogs are allowed for an additional one time pet fee of $75 per room. 2 dogs may be allowed.

Staybridge Suites Jackson
801 Ridgewood Road
Ridgeland, MS
601-206-9190 (877-270-6405)
Dogs up to 80 pounds are allowed. Pets allowed with an additional pet fee. Up to $75 for 1-6 nights and up to $150 for 7+ nights. A pet agreement must be signed at check-in.

Motel 6 - Senatobia
501 Main St
Senatobia, MS
662-562-5241 (800-466-8356)
This motel welcomes your pets to stay with you.

Residence Inn Memphis Southaven
7165 Sleepy Hollow Drive
Southaven, MS
662-996-1500 (800-971-4738)
This all suite inn features a convenient location to business, shopping, dining, and entertainment areas, plus they also offer a number of in-house amenities, including a daily buffet breakfast and evening socials Monday to Thursday. Dogs are allowed for an additional one time pet fee of $100 per room. 2 dogs may be allowed.

Days Inn and Suites Starkville
119 Highway 12 West
Starkville, MS
662-324-5555 (800-329-7466)
Dogs of all sizes are allowed. Dogs are allowed for a pet fee.

Motel 6 - Tupelo
1500 Mccullough Blvd
Tupelo, MS
662-844-1904 (800-466-8356)
This motel welcomes your pets to stay with you.

Super 8 Airport Tupelo
3898 McCullough Blvd
Tupelo, MS
662-842-0448 (800-800-8000)
Dogs are welcome at this hotel.

Wingate by Wyndham Tupelo
186 Stone Creek Blvd
Tupelo, MS
662-680-8887 (800-228-1000)
Dogs are welcome at this hotel.

Anchuca Mansion
1010 First East Street
Vicksburg, MS
601-661-0111 (888-686-0111)
anchuca.com/
Listed on the National Register of Historic Places, this Greek Revival home is the one of the most noteworthy antebellum homes in the city. The home is surrounded by lush greenery and they have a restaurant open Thursday to Sunday offering seasonally influenced gourmet dining. One dog up to 50 pounds is allowed in the carriage house rooms for no additional fee. Dogs must be crated when left in the room alone and they are not allowed in the main house or the restaurant area. Dogs must be leashed and cleaned up after.

Battlefield Inn
4137 I-20 Frontage Rd
Vicksburg, MS
601-638-5811 (800-359-9363)
battlefieldinn.org/
There is a $10 per day per pet fee. Multiple dogs may be allowed.

Candlewood Suites
1296 South Frontage Rd
Vicksburg, MS
601-638-6900 (877-270-6405)
candlewoodsuites.com/vicksburgms
Dogs up to 80 pounds are allowed. There is a $75 one time fee for stays up to 1 week and $150 for longer stays.

Cedar Grove Inn
2200 Oak Street
Vicksburg, MS
601-636-1000 (800) 862-1300)
cedargroveinn.com/
Sitting on 5 lush acres, this is one of the areas largest inns with 33 beautifully accommodated rooms in 5 historic buildings. The inn features a swimming pool, tennis court, and an eatery and a bar that offers alfresco dining; pooches are welcome at their outer tables. Dogs are allowed in the cottages for an additional one time fee of $50 per pet. Dogs must be hound, kitty, and human friendly, and be leashed and under their owner's control. 2 dogs may be allowed.

Duff Green Mansion
1114 First East St
Vicksburg, MS

601-638-6662 (800-992-0037)
innbook.com/duff.html
There are no designated smoking or
non-smoking rooms. Dogs are
allowed for no additional fee. Multiple
dogs may be allowed.

La Quinta Inn Vicksburg
4216 Washington Street
Vicksburg, MS
601-638-5750 (800-531-5900)
Dogs up to 70 pounds are allowed.
There are no additional pet fees.
Dogs must be leashed and cleaned
up after, and they are not allowed in
the lobby. Multiple dogs may be
allowed.

Motel 6 - Vicksburg
4127 Frontage Rd
Vicksburg, MS
601-638-5077 (800-466-8356)
This motel welcomes your pets to
stay with you.

The Corners Bed and Breakfast Inn
601 Klien St
Vicksburg, MS
601-636-7421
thecorners.com/
There are no additional pet fees. 2
dogs may be allowed.

Wingate by Wyndham Vicksburg
115 Cypress Centre Blvd
Vicksburg, MS
601-630-4240 (800-228-1000)
Dogs are welcome at this hotel.

Missouri

Super 8
491 E. Hwy 76
Anderson, MO
417-845-4888 (800-800-8000)
Dogs of all sizes are allowed. Dogs
are allowed for a nightly pet fee.

Cottages on Stouts Creek
H 72
Arcadia, MO
573-546-4036
missouricottages.com/
Located along Stouts Creek in the
scenic Arcadia Valley, this resort
offers a variety of amenities in
addition to a convenient location to
numerous local activities and
recreation. Dogs are allowed for an
additional fee of $15 per night per
pet. 2 dogs may be allowed.

Ramada Limited And Suites St.
Louis/ Arnold
2121 Ridge Drive
Arnold, MO

636-282-2400 (800-272-6232)
Dogs are welcome at this hotel.

St Louis - Arnold Drury Inn
1201 Drury Lane
Arnold, MO
636-296-9600 (800-378-7946)
Dogs of all sizes are allowed for no
additional pet fee with a credit card
on file, and there is a pet agreement
to sign at check in.

Super 8 Ava
1711 South Jefferson Street
Ava, MO
417-683-1343 (800-800-8000)
Dogs of all sizes are allowed. Dogs
are allowed for a pet fee of $10 per
pet per stay.

Days Inn Belton
107 County Line Road
Belton, MO
816-268-7500 (800-329-7466)
Dogs of all sizes are allowed. Dogs
are allowed for a nightly pet fee.

Econo Lodge
222 Peculiar Dr.
Belton, MO
816-322-1222 (877-424-6423)
Dogs of all sizes are allowed. Dogs
are allowed for a pet fee of $10.00
per pet per night.

Comfort Inn
496 South 39th Street
Bethany, MO
660-425-8006 (877-424-6423)
Dogs up to 70 pounds are allowed.
Dogs are allowed for a pet fee of
$10.00 per pet per night. Three or
more dogs may be allowed.

Super 8 MO Bethany
811 South 37th Street
Bethany, MO
660-425-8881 (800-800-8000)
Dogs of all sizes are allowed. Dogs
are allowed for a pet fee.

Days Inn Blue Springs
451 NW Jefferson St
Blue Springs, MO
816-224-1199 (800-329-7466)
Dogs of all sizes are allowed. Dogs
are allowed for a pet fee of $10.00
per pet per night.

Motel 6 - Kansas City East Blue
Springs
901 Nw Jefferson St
Blue Springs, MO
816-228-9133 (800-466-8356)
This motel welcomes your pets to
stay with you.

Super 8 Bonne Terre
8 Northwood Drive
Bonne Terre, MO
573-358-5888 (800-800-8000)
Dogs are welcome at this hotel.

Days Inn Boonville
2401 Pioneer
Boonville, MO
660-882-8624 (800-329-7466)
Dogs of all sizes are allowed. Dogs
are allowed for a nightly pet fee.

Super 8 Bowling Green
1216 East Champ Clark Drive
Bowling Green, MO
573-324-6000 (800-800-8000)
Dogs of all sizes are allowed. Dogs
are allowed for a pet fee.

Branson Inn
448 MO 248
Branson, MO
417-334-5121 (800-334-5121)
There is a $10 one time pet fee. Pets
must be out of the room for maid
service. 2 dogs may be allowed.

Days Inn Branson
3524 Keeter Street
Branson, MO
417-334-5544 (800-329-7466)
Dogs of all sizes are allowed. Dogs
are allowed for a pet fee of $10.00
per pet per night.

Emory Creek Victorian Bed &
Breakfast and Gift shop
143 Arizona Drive
Branson, MO
417-334-3805 (800-362-7404)
emorycreekbnb.com/
In addition to offering an elegant
Victorian setting, their special pet
friendly room (The Dogwood Room)
has a private porch with swing and a
beautiful view over the gardens.
Dogs are allowed for an additional
pet fee per pet of $25 for 1 to 3 days,
and $20 for the next 4 to 6 days. 2
dogs may be allowed.

Hilton Hotel
3 Branson Landing Blvd
Branson, MO
417-336-5500 (800-HILTONS (445-
8667))
Although located in the heart of the
city's shopping and entertainment
district, this hotel also offers
numerous on site amenities for
business and leisure travelers. Dogs
up to 65 pounds are allowed for an
additional one time pet fee of $75 per
room. Dogs are not allowed stay at
the Promenade proper, but they are
allowed in their condos. Multiple

dogs may be allowed.

Howard Johnson Hotel - Branson
3027-A West Highway 76
Branson, MO
417-336-5151 (800-446-4656)
Dogs of all sizes are allowed. Dogs are allowed for a pet fee of $10 per pet per night.

La Quinta Inn Branson Music City Centre
1835 W Highway 76
Branson, MO
417-332-1575 (800-531-5900)
Dogs of all sizes are allowed. There are no additional pet fees. Dogs must be leashed, cleaned up after, and be crated or attended to for housekeeping. Multiple dogs may be allowed.

Quality Inn
2834 West SR 76
Branson, MO
417-334-1194 (877-424-6423)
Dogs of all sizes are allowed. Dogs are allowed for a pet fee of $10.00 per pet per night.

Ramada Limited Missouri Branson
2316 Shepherd
Branson, MO
417-337-5207 (800-272-6232)
Dogs of all sizes are allowed. Dogs are allowed for a nightly pet fee.

Ramada Resort and Conference Center
1700 W Hwy 76
Branson, MO
417-334-1000 (800-272-6232)
Dogs of all sizes are allowed. Dogs are allowed for a pet fee of $15 per pet per night.

Red Roof Inn Branson
220 South Wildwood Drive
Branson, MO
417-335-4500 (800-RED-ROOF)
One well-behaved family pet per room. Guest must notify front desk upon arrival. Guest is liable for any damages. In consideration of all guests, pets must never be left unattended in the guest rooms.

Residence Inn Branson
280 Wildwood Drive S
Branson, MO
417-336-4077 (800-331-3131)
This all suite, upscale hotel offers a central location to all the great attractions this area has to offer for both business and leisure travelers. Additionally, they offer a daily buffet breakfast and an evening social hour

Monday through Thursday. Dogs are allowed for an additional one time pet fee of $100 per room. 2 dogs may be allowed.

Stone Castle Hotel
3050 Green Mt Dr
Branson, MO
417-335-4700 (800-677-6906)
stonecastlehotel.com/
There is a $12 per day per pet fee. Pets are not allowed in theme rooms. Multiple dogs may be allowed.

Homestead Studio Suites St. Louis - Airport
11252 Lone Eagle Dr.
Bridgeton, MO
314-739-0600 (800-804-3724)
One dog is allowed per suite. There is a $25 per night additional pet fee up to $150 for an entire stay.

Motel 6 - St. Louis Bridgeton, Mo
3470 Hollenberg Drive
Bridgeton, MO
314-291-3350 (800-466-8356)
This motel welcomes your pets to stay with you.

Best Western Brookfield
28622 Highway 11
Brookfield, MO
660-258-4900 (800-780-7234)
Dogs of all sizes are allowed. Dogs are allowed for a nightly pet fee.

Days Inn Butler
100 South Fran Avenue
Butler, MO
660-679-4544 (800-329-7466)
Dogs of all sizes are allowed. Dogs are allowed for a pet fee of $10.00 per pet per night.

Super 8 Butler
1114 West Fort Scott
Butler, MO
660-679-6183 (800-800-8000)
Dogs of all sizes are allowed. Dogs are allowed for a pet fee of $7.00 per pet per night.

Comfort Inn
1803 Comfort Lane
Cameron, MO
816-632-5655 (877-424-6423)
Dogs of all sizes are allowed.

Econo Lodge
220 E. Grand
Cameron, MO
816-632-6571 (877-424-6423)
Dogs up to 50 pounds are allowed. Dogs are allowed for a pet fee of $10.00 per pet per night. Two dogs

are allowed per room.

Super 8 Cameron
1710 N Walnut Street
Cameron, MO
816-632-8888 (800-800-8000)
Dogs of all sizes are allowed. Dogs are allowed for a pet fee.

Comfort Inn
1701 Oak Street
Canton, MO
573-288-8800 (877-424-6423)
Dogs of all sizes are allowed. Dogs are allowed for a pet fee of $15.00 per pet per night. Two dogs are allowed per room.

Cape Girardeau Drury Lodge
104 S. Vantage Drive
Cape Girardeau, MO
573-334-7151 (800-378-7946)
Dogs of all sizes are allowed for no additional pet fee with a credit card on file, and there is a pet agreement to sign at check in.

Cape Girardeau Drury Suites
3303 Campster Drive
Cape Girardeau, MO
573-339-9500 (800-378-7946)
Dogs of all sizes are allowed for no additional pet fee with a credit card on file, and there is a pet agreement to sign at check in.

Cape Girardeau Pear Tree Inn
3248 William Street
Cape Girardeau, MO
573-334-3000 (800-378-7946)
Dogs of all sizes are allowed for no additional pet fee with a credit card on file, and there is a pet agreement to sign at check in.

Super 8 Cape Girardeau
2011 North Kingshighway
Cape Girardeau, MO
573-339-0808 (800-800-8000)
Dogs of all sizes are allowed. Dogs are allowed for a pet fee of $7 per pet per night.

Best Western Precious Moments Hotel
2701 Hazel Street
Carthage, MO
417-359-5900 (800-780-7234)
Dogs of all sizes are allowed. Dogs are allowed for a pet fee of $10 per pet per stay.

Econo Lodge
1441 W. Central
Carthage, MO
417-358-3900 (877-424-6423)
Dogs up to 50 pounds are allowed.

Dogs are allowed for a pet fee of $10.00 per pet per stay. Two dogs are allowed per room.

Super 8 Carthage
416 West Fir Road
Carthage, MO
417-359-9000 (800-800-8000)
Dogs of all sizes are allowed. Dogs are allowed for a pet fee of $5.00 per pet per stay.

Comfort Inn
102 Drake St.
Charleston, MO
573-683-4200 (877-424-6423)
Dogs up to 50 pounds are allowed. Dogs are allowed for a pet fee of $15.00 per pet per night.

Residence Inn St. Louis Chesterfield
15431 Conway Road
Chesterfield, MO
636-537-1444 (800-331-3131)
This all suite hotel sits central to a number of activities and attractions of interest for all level of travelers. They also offer a daily buffet breakfast, evening socials, and seasonal barbecues. Dogs are allowed for an additional one time pet fee of $100 per room. 2 dogs may be allowed.

Best Western Chillicothe Inn
1020 S Washington Street
Chillicothe, MO
660-646-0572 (800-780-7234)
Dogs of all sizes are allowed. Dogs are allowed for a pet fee of $25.00 per pet per stay.

Super 8 Chillicothe
500 Business Hwy 36 East
Chillicothe, MO
660-646-7888 (800-800-8000)
Dogs of all sizes are allowed. Dogs are allowed for a pet fee.

Baymont Inn & Suites Columbia
2500 I-70 Drive S.W.
Columbia, MO
573-445-1899 (800-531-5900)
Dogs of all sizes are allowed. There are no additional pet fees. Dogs must be leashed, cleaned up after, and be crated or removed for housekeeping Multiple dogs may be allowed.

Best Western Columbia Inn
3100 Interstate 70 Drive SE
Columbia, MO
573-474-6161 (800-780-7234)
Dogs of all sizes are allowed. Dogs are allowed for a pet fee of $10 per pet per stay.

Candlewood Suites Columbia
3100 Wingate Court
Columbia, MO
573-817-0525 (877-270-6405)
Dogs up to 80 pounds are allowed. Pets allowed with an additional pet fee. Up to $75 for 1-6 nights and up to $150 for 7+ nights. A pet agreement must be signed at check-in.

Columbia Drury Inn
1000 Knipp Street
Columbia, MO
573-445-1800 (800-378-7946)
Dogs of all sizes are allowed for no additional pet fee with a credit card on file, and there is a pet agreement to sign at check in.

Days Inn Conference Center Columbia
1900 I-70 Drive SW
Columbia, MO
573-445-8511 (800-329-7466)
Dogs of all sizes are allowed. Dogs are allowed for a nightly pet fee.

Econo Lodge
900 I-70 Dr. S.W.
Columbia, MO
573-442-1191 (877-424-6423)
Dogs up to 75 pounds are allowed. Dogs are allowed for a pet fee of $10.00 per pet per night.

Extended Stay America Columbia - Stadium Blvd.
2000 W. Business Loop 70
Columbia, MO
573-445-6800 (800-804-3724)
One dog is allowed per suite. There is a $25 per night additional pet fee up to $150 for an entire stay.

Holiday Inn Express Columbia-Reg Hosp & Med Ctr
801 Keene Street
Columbia, MO
573-449-4422 (877-270-6405)
Dogs of all sizes are allowed. Dogs are allowed for a pet fee of $25.00 per pet per stay.

Holiday Inn Select Executive Center-Columbia Mall
2200 I-70 Drive S.W.
Columbia, MO
573-445-8531 (877-270-6405)
Dogs of all sizes are allowed. Dogs are allowed for a pet fee of $25.00 per pet per stay.

La Quinta Inn Columbia
901 Conley Road
Columbia, MO

573-443-4141 (800-531-5900)
Dogs of all sizes are allowed. There are no additional pet fees. Dogs must be leashed, cleaned up after, and crated if left alone in the room. Multiple dogs may be allowed.

Motel 6 - Columbia, Mo
1800 I-70 Dr Sw
Columbia, MO
573-445-8433 (800-466-8356)
This motel welcomes your pets to stay with you.

Motel 6 - Columbia, Mo
3402 I-70 Dr Se
Columbia, MO
573-815-0123 (800-466-8356)
This motel welcomes your pets to stay with you.

Quality Inn
1612 N. Providence Road
Columbia, MO
573-449-2491 (877-424-6423)
Dogs of all sizes are allowed. Dogs are allowed for a pet fee of $20.00 per pet per night.

Red Roof Inn Columbia, MO
201 East Texas Avenue
Columbia, MO
573-442-0145 (800-RED-ROOF)
One well-behaved family pet per room. Guest must notify front desk upon arrival. Guest is liable for any damages. In consideration of all guests, pets must never be left unattended in the guest rooms.

Residence Inn Columbia
1100 Woodland Springs Court
Columbia, MO
573-442-5601 (800-331-3131)
This hotel offers a convenient location to business, shopping, dining, and entertainment areas, plus they offer a number of in-house amenities, including a daily buffet breakfast and social happy hours Monday to Thursday from 5 to 7 pm. Dogs are allowed for an additional one time pet fee of $75 per room. 2 dogs may be allowed.

Staybridge Suites Columbia-Hwy 63 & I-70
805 Keene St.
Columbia, MO
573-442-8600 (877-270-6405)
Dogs up to 80 pounds are allowed. Pets allowed with an additional pet fee. Up to $75 for 1-6 nights and up to $150 for 7+ nights. A pet agreement must be signed at check-in.

Super 8 Clark Lane Columbia
3216 Clark Lane
Columbia, MO
573-474-8488 (800-800-8000)
Dogs of all sizes are allowed. Dogs are allowed for a pet fee.

Super 8 East Columbia
5700 Freedom Drive
Columbia, MO
573-474-8307 (800-800-8000)
Dogs of all sizes are allowed. Dogs are allowed for a pet fee.

Travelodge Columbia
900 Vandiver Drive
Columbia, MO
573-449-1065 (800-578-7878)
Dogs of all sizes are allowed. Dogs are allowed for a pet fee.

Wingate by Wyndham - Columbia
3101 Wingate Court
Columbia, MO
573-817-0500 (800-228-1000)
Dogs are welcome at this hotel.

Days Inn Concordia
301 NW 3rd Street
Concordia, MO
660-463-7987 (800-329-7466)
Dogs are welcome at this hotel.

Travelodge Concordia
406 NW 2nd Street
Concordia, MO
660-463-2114 (800-578-7878)
Dogs of all sizes are allowed. Dogs are allowed for a pet fee.

St Louis - Creve Coeur Drury Inn & Suites
11980 Olive Blvd
Creve Coeur, MO
314-989-1100 (800-378-7946)
Dogs of all sizes are allowed for no additional pet fee with a credit card on file, and there is a pet agreement to sign at check in.

Best Western Cuba Inn
246 Highway P
Cuba, MO
573-885-7707 (800-780-7234)
Dogs are welcome at this hotel. There is a $10 one time pet fee.

Super 8 Cuba
28 Hwy P
Cuba, MO
573-885-2087 (800-800-8000)
Dogs of all sizes are allowed. Dogs are allowed for a pet fee.

Rock Eddy Bluff Farm
10245 Maries Road 511
Dixon, MO

573-759-6081 (800-335-5921)
rockeddy.com/
This vacation getaway is located along the Gasconade River among 150 acres of scenic Ozark forest in a country setting complete with farm animals. Dogs are allowed for no additional fee. Dogs are not allowed on the furniture or beds, and they must be crated when left alone in the units. 2 dogs may be allowed.

Candlewood Suites St. Louis
3250 Rider Trail South
Earth City, MO
314-770-2744 (877-270-6405)
Dogs up to 80 pounds are allowed. Pets allowed with an additional pet fee. Up to $75 for 1-6 nights and up to $150 for 7+ nights. A pet agreement must be signed at check-in.

Residence Inn St. Louis Airport/Earth City
3290 Rider Trail S
Earth City, MO
314-209-0995 (800-413-0906)
This all suite hotel sits central to a number of activities and attractions of interest for all level of travelers. They also offer a daily buffet breakfast and evening socials Monday to Thursday. Dogs are allowed for an additional one time pet fee of $75 per room. Multiple dogs may be allowed.

Lake Ozark Vacation Rentals
35 Kristy Road
Eldon, MO
573-365-1600
Nestled among the trees overlooking the lake, this comfortable 4 bedroom home gives guests their own private dock and a great starting point to enjoy all this beautiful area has to offer. Dogs are allowed for an additional fee of $15 per night per pet for dogs under 30 pounds, and $25 per night per pet for dogs over 30 pounds. There is a $500 refundable security deposit for guests with pets. Dogs must be leashed and under their owner's control at all times. 2 dogs may be allowed.

Econo Lodge
1725 West 5th Street
Eureka, MO
636-938-5348 (877-424-6423)
Dogs of all sizes are allowed. Dogs are allowed for a pet fee of $10.00 per pet per stay. Two dogs are allowed per room.

Holiday Inn Saint Louis West Six

Flags
4901 Six Flags Road
Eureka, MO
636-938-6661 (877-270-6405)
Dogs of all sizes are allowed. Dogs are allowed for a pet fee of $25.00 per pet per night.

Super 8 /Six Flags Nearby Eureka
1733 West 5th Street
Eureka, MO
636-938-4368 (800-800-8000)
Dogs of all sizes are allowed. Dogs are allowed for a pet fee.

Days Inn Farmington
1400 Liberty Street
Farmington, MO
573-756-8951 (800-329-7466)
Dogs of all sizes are allowed. Dogs are allowed for a nightly pet fee.

Motel 6 - St Louis Fenton Southwest
1860 Bowles Ave
Fenton, MO
636-349-1800 (800-466-8356)
This motel welcomes your pets to stay with you.

St Louis - Fenton Drury Inn & Suites
1088 South Highway Drive
Fenton, MO
636-343-7822 (800-378-7946)
Dogs of all sizes are allowed for no additional pet fee with a credit card on file, and there is a pet agreement to sign at check in.

St Louis - Fenton Pear Tree Inn
1100 S. Highway Drive
Fenton, MO
636-343-8820 (800-378-7946)
Dogs of all sizes are allowed for no additional pet fee with a credit card on file, and there is a pet agreement to sign at check in.

TownePlace Suites St. Louis Fenton
1662 Fenton Business Park Court
Fenton, MO
636-305-7000 (800-257-3000)
Besides offering a number of in-house amenities for all level of travelers, this all suite inn also offers a convenient location to major businesses, shopping, dining, and recreation areas. Dogs are allowed for an additional one time fee of $100 per room. 2 dogs may be allowed.

Red Roof Inn St Louis - Florissant
307 Dunn Road
Florissant, MO
314-831-7900 (800-RED-ROOF)
One well-behaved family pet per room. Guest must notify front desk upon arrival. Guest is liable for any

damages. In consideration of all guests, pets must never be left unattended in the guest rooms.

Best Western West 70 Inn
12 Highway W
Foristell, MO
636-673-2900 (800-780-7234)
Dogs of all sizes are allowed. Dogs are allowed for a pet fee.

Holiday Inn Express Fulton
2205 Cardinal Drive
Fulton, MO
573-642-2600 (877-270-6405)
Dogs of all sizes are allowed. Dogs are allowed for a pet fee of $10 per pet per night.

Kansas City/ Travelodge Grain Valley
105 Sunnylane Drive
Grain Valley, MO
816-224-3420 (800-578-7878)
Dogs are welcome at this hotel.

Travelodge Six Flags / Gray Summit
2875 Highway 100
Gray Summit, MO
800-782-8487 (800-578-7878)
Dogs are welcome at this hotel.

Motel 6 - Hannibal, Mo
123 Huckleberry Heights
Hannibal, MO
573-221-9988 (800-466-8356)
This motel welcomes your pets to stay with you.

Quality Inn & Suites
120 Lindsey Drive
Hannibal, MO
573-221-4001 (877-424-6423)
Dogs of all sizes are allowed. Dogs are allowed for a pet fee of $10.00 per pet per night. Two dogs are allowed per room.

Super 8 Hannibal
120 Huckleberry Heights Dr
Hannibal, MO
573-221-5863 (800-800-8000)
Dogs of all sizes are allowed. Dogs are allowed for a pet fee of $15 per pet per night.

Comfort Inn
1500 Highway 84
Hayti, MO
573-359-2200 (877-424-6423)
Dogs up to 50 pounds are allowed. Dogs are allowed for a pet fee of $20.00 per pet per stay.

Hayti Drury Inn & Suites
1317 Hwy 84
Hayti, MO

573-359-2702 (800-378-7946)
Dogs of all sizes are allowed for no additional pet fee with a credit card on file, and there is a pet agreement to sign at check in.

Extended Stay America St. Louis - Airport
6065 N. Lindbergh Blvd.
Hazelwood, MO
314-731-2991 (800-804-3724)
One dog is allowed per suite. There is a $25 per night additional pet fee up to $150 for an entire stay.

La Quinta Inn St. Louis Airport
5781 Campus Court
Hazelwood, MO
314-731-3881 (800-531-5900)
Dogs of all sizes are allowed. There are no additional pet fees. Dogs must be leashed and cleaned up after. Dogs may not be left in the room for long periods, and they must be quiet and well behaved. 2 dogs may be allowed.

La Quinta Inn St. Louis/Hazelwood
318 Taylor Road
Hazelwood, MO
314-731-4200 (800-531-5900)
Dogs of all sizes are allowed. There are no additional pet fees. Dogs may not be left unattended, and they must be well behaved, leashed, and cleaned up after. Multiple dogs may be allowed.

Ramada St. Louis Airport North
9079 Dunn Road
Hazelwood, MO
314-731-7700 (800-272-6232)
Dogs of all sizes are allowed. Dogs are allowed for a pet fee of $25 per pet per stay.

Super 8 Higginsville
I-70 and Hwy 13
Higginsville, MO
660-584-7781 (800-800-8000)
Dogs are welcome at this hotel.

Comfort Suites
19751 E. Valley View Parkway
Independence, MO
816-373-9880 (877-424-6423)
Dogs of all sizes are allowed. Dogs are allowed for a pet fee of $fee per pet per night. Three or more dogs may be allowed.

Holiday Inn Express Hotel & Suites Independence-Kansas City
19901 E Valley View Pkwy
Independence, MO
816-795-8889 (877-270-6405)
Dogs of all sizes are allowed. Dogs

are allowed for a pet fee of $25.00 per pet per stay.

Motel 6 - Independence, Mo
4200 S. Noland Road
Independence, MO
816-350-7816 (800-466-8356)
This motel welcomes your pets to stay with you.

Residence Inn Kansas City Independence
3700 S Arrowhead Avenue
Independence, MO
816-795-6466 (800-331-3131)
This all suite hotel sits central to many of the city's star attractions, shopping, dining, and business areas, plus they offer a number of in-house amenities that include a daily buffet breakfast and evening social hours. Dogs are allowed for an additional one time pet fee of $100 per room. Multiple dogs may be allowed.

Super 8 Kansas City Independence
4032 S Lynn Court Dr
Independence, MO
816-833-1888 (800-800-8000)
Dogs are welcome at this hotel.

Jackson Drury Inn & Suites
225 Drury Lane
Jackson, MO
573-243-9200 (800-378-7940)
Dogs of all sizes are allowed for no additional pet fee with a credit card on file, and there is a pet agreement to sign at check in.

Candlewood Suites Jefferson City
3514 Amazonas Drive
Jefferson City, MO
573-634-8822 (877-270-6405)
Dogs up to 80 pounds are allowed. Pets allowed with an additional pet fee. Up to $75 for 1-6 nights and up to $150 for 7+ nights. A pet agreement must be signed at check-in.

Motel 6 - Jefferson City
1624 Jefferson St
Jefferson City, MO
573-634-4220 (800-466-8356)
This motel welcomes your pets to stay with you.

Super 8 Jefferson City
1710 Jefferson Street
Jefferson City, MO
573-636-5456 (800-800-8000)
Dogs of all sizes are allowed. Dogs are allowed for a pet fee of $10.00 per pet per night.

Baymont Inn and Suites Joplin
3510 Rangeline Road
Joplin, MO
417-623-0000 (877-229-6668)
Dogs are welcome at this hotel.

Candlewood Suites Joplin
3512 South Rangeline
Joplin, MO
417-623-9595 (877-270-6405)
Dogs up to 80 pounds are allowed.
Pets allowed with an additional pet
fee. Up to $75 for 1-6 nights and up
to $150 for 7+ nights. A pet
agreement must be signed at check-
in.

Days Inn Joplin
3500 Rangeline Road
Joplin, MO
417-623-0100 (800-329-7466)
Dogs are welcome at this hotel.

Holiday Inn Joplin-I-44 & US 71
3615 Range Line Rd
Joplin, MO
417-782-1000 (877-270-6405)
Dogs of all sizes are allowed. Dogs
are allowed for a pet fee of $25.00
per pet per stay.

Joplin Drury Inn & Suites
3601 Range Line Road
Joplin, MO
417-781-8000 (800-378-7946)
Dogs of all sizes are allowed for no
additional pet fee with a credit card
on file, and there is a pet agreement
to sign at check in.

Motel 6 - Joplin
3031 Range Line Rd
Joplin, MO
417-781-6400 (800-466-8356)
This motel welcomes your pets to
stay with you.

Residence Inn Joplin
3128 East Hammons Blvd
Joplin, MO
417-782-0908 (800-331-3131)
Offering a convenient location to
business, shopping, dining,
recreation, and entertainment areas,
this all suite hotel also offers a
number of in-house amenities,
including a daily buffet breakfast and
evening socials. Dogs are allowed for
an additional one time pet fee of $75
per room. Multiple dogs may be
allowed.

Sleep Inn
I-44 & SR 43 S.
Joplin, MO
417-782-1212 (877-424-6423)
Dogs of all sizes are allowed. Dogs

are allowed for a pet fee of $15.00
per pet per stay.

Super 8 MO Joplin
I-44 & Rangeline Rd
Joplin, MO
417-782-8765 (800-800-8000)
Dogs are welcome at this hotel.

TownePlace Suites Joplin
4026 S Arizona Avenue
Joplin, MO
417-659-8111 (800-257-3000)
Besides offering a number of in-
house amenities for all level of
travelers, this all suite inn also
offers a convenient location to many
major corporations, shopping,
dining, and entertainment areas.
Dogs are allowed for an additional
one time fee of $75 per room. 2
dogs may be allowed.

Baymont Inn and Suites South
Kansas City
8601 Hillcrest Rd
Kansas City, MO
816-822-7000 (877-229-6668)
Dogs are welcome at this hotel.

Best Western Seville Plaza Hotel
4309 Main Street
Kansas City, MO
816-561-9600 (800-780-7234)
Dogs are welcome at this hotel.

Chase Suite Hotel
9900 NW Prairie View Road
Kansas City, MO
816-891-9009
This all suite hotel allows dogs for
an additional pet fee of $20 per
night per room. Multiple dogs may
be allowed.

Days Inn International Airport
Kansas City
11120 NW Ambassador Dr.
Kansas City, MO
816-746-1666 (800-329-7466)
Dogs of all sizes are allowed. Dogs
are allowed for a nightly pet fee.

Days Inn -Worlds of Fun Kansas
City
7100 NE Parvin Rd.
Kansas City, MO
816-453-3355 (800-329-7466)
Dogs of all sizes are allowed. Dogs
are allowed for a pet fee of $10 per
pet per night.

Econo Lodge Inn & Suites
Downtown
3240 Broadway
Kansas City, MO
816-531-9250 (877-424-6423)

Dogs up to 50 pounds are allowed.
Dogs are allowed for a pet fee of
$10.00 per pet per night.

Extended Stay America Kansas City
- Airport
11712 N.W. Plaza Cir.
Kansas City, MO
816-270-7829 (800-804-3724)
One dog is allowed per suite. There
is a $25 per night additional pet fee
up to $150 for an entire stay.

Extended Stay America Kansas City
- South
550 East 105th St.
Kansas City, MO
816-943-1315 (800-804-3724)
One dog is allowed per suite. There
is a $25 per night additional pet fee
up to $150 for an entire stay.

Hilton Hotel
1329 Baltimore
Kansas City, MO
816-221-9490 (800-HILTONS (445-
8667))
Located in the new Power and Light
Entertainment District, this hotel
offers numerous on site amenities for
business and leisure travelers, plus a
convenient location to business,
shopping, dining, and recreational
areas. Dogs up to 75 pounds are
allowed for an additional one time
pet fee of $75 per room. 2 dogs may
be allowed.

Hilton Hotel
8801 NW 112th Street
Kansas City, MO
816-891-8900 (800-HILTONS (445-
8667))
Offering a number of on site
amenities for business and leisure
travelers, this hotel sits only a short
distance from the airport and the
downtown area where there are
plenty of business, shopping, dining,
and entertainment opportunities.
Dogs are allowed for an additional
one time pet fee of $50 per room.
Multiple dogs may be allowed.

Holiday Inn At The Plaza
One East 45th Street
Kansas City, MO
816-753-7400 (877-270-6405)
Dogs are welcome at this hotel.
There is a $25 one time additional
pet fee.

Holiday Inn Express Kansas City-
Westport Plaza
801 Westport Road
Kansas City, MO
816-931-1000 (877-270-6405)

Dog-Friendly Lodging - Please always call ahead to make sure an establishment is still dog-friendly.

Dogs of all sizes are allowed. Dogs are allowed for a pet fee of $25.00 per pet per stay.

Holiday Inn Kansas City Airport
11728 N. Ambassador Drive
Kansas City, MO
816-801-8400 (877-270-6405)
Dogs of all sizes are allowed. Dogs are allowed for a pet fee of $30.00 per pet per night.

Holiday Inn Kansas City-Ne-I-435 North
7333 Parvin Road
Kansas City, MO
816-455-1060 (877-270-6405)
Dogs of all sizes are allowed. Dogs are allowed for a pet fee of $20.00 per pet per night.

Homestead Studio Suites Kansas City - Airport
9701 N. Shannon Ave.
Kansas City, MO
816-891-8500 (800-804-3724)
One dog is allowed per suite. There is a $25 per night additional pet fee up to $150 for an entire stay.

Homestead Studio Suites Kansas City - Country Club Plaza
4535 Main St.
Kansas City, MO
816-531-2212 (800-804-3724)
One dog is allowed per suite. There is a $25 per night additional pet fee up to $150 for an entire stay.

Howard Johnson Plaza Hotel KCI Airport
7301 Tiffany Springs Road
Kansas City, MO
816-268-1600 (800-446-4656)
Dogs are welcome at this hotel. There is a $25 one time pet fee.

Kansas City - Stadium Drury Inn & Suites
3830 Blue Ridge Cutoff
Kansas City, MO
816-923-3000 (800-378-7946)
Dogs of all sizes are allowed for no additional pet fee with a credit card on file, and there is a pet agreement to sign at check in.

La Quinta Inn Kansas City
1051 North Cambridge
Kansas City, MO
816-483-7900 (800-531-5900)
A dog of any size is allowed. There are no additional pet fees. Dogs may only be left unattended if they are housebroken, they will be quiet and well behaved, and a contact number is left at the front desk. Dogs must

be leashed and cleaned up after.

Motel 6 - Kansas City North Airport
8230 Nw Prairie View Rd
Kansas City, MO
816-741-6400 (800-466-8356)
Your pets are welcome to stay here with you.

Motel 6 - Kansas City Southeast
6400 87th St
Kansas City, MO
816-333-4468 (800-466-8356)
Your pets are welcome to stay here with you.

Red Roof Inn Kansas City North-Worlds Of Fun
3636 Northeast Randolph Road
Kansas City, MO
816-452-8585 (800-RED-ROOF)
One well-behaved family pet per room. Guest must notify front desk upon arrival. Guest is liable for any damages. In consideration of all guests, pets must never be left unattended in the guest rooms.

Residence Inn Kansas City Airport
10300 N Ambassador Drive
Kansas City, MO
816-741-2300 (800-331-3131)
In addition to offering a convenient location to business, shopping, dining, and entertainment areas, this hotel also provides a number of in-house amenities, including a daily buffet breakfast and an evening social hour Monday to Thursday. Dogs are allowed for an additional one time pet fee of $75 per room. 2 dogs may be allowed.

Residence Inn Kansas City Country Club Plaza
4601 Broadway
Kansas City, MO
816-753-0033 (800-331-3131)
Besides being located in the heart of the city's shopping and entertainment district, this all suite hotel also provides a number of in-house amenities, including a daily buffet breakfast, an evening social hour, and a Sport Court. Dogs are allowed for an additional one time pet fee of $100 per room. 2 dogs may be allowed.

Residence Inn Kansas City Downtown/Union Hill
2975 Main Street
Kansas City, MO
816-561-3000
Located downtown and central to all the city has to offer, this all suite hotel also provides a number of in-

house amenities, including a daily buffet breakfast and evening socials Monday through Thursday with light dinner fare. Dogs are allowed for an additional one time pet fee of $100 per room. Multiple dogs may be allowed.

Sheraton Suites Country Club Plaza
770 West 47th St.
Kansas City, MO
816-931-4400 (888-625-5144)
Dogs up to 60 pounds are allowed. Dogs are not allowed to be left alone in the room.

Su Casa B&B
9004 E. 92nd Street
Kansas City, MO
816-916-3444
sucasabb.com
Visit this dog-friendly ranch home with southwestern decor, situated on a five-acre lot at the outskirts of the city, but still only a 15 minute drive to Kansas City attractions. Pets must be approved in advance. There is room for dogs to run. Rates for dogs are $10 per night. Horses are $25 per night.

Econo Lodge
505 Shanks Ave.
Kearney, MO
816-628-5111 (877-424-6423)
Small dogs are allowed. Dogs are allowed for a pet fee of $12.00 per pet per night.

Super 8 /KC Area Kearney
I-35 & Hwy 92
Kearney, MO
816-628-6800 (800-800-8000)
Dogs of all sizes are allowed. Dogs are allowed for a pet fee of $10.00 per pet per stay.

Days Inn Kennett
110 Independence Ave
Kennett, MO
573-888-9860 (800-329-7466)
Dogs of all sizes are allowed. Dogs are allowed for a pet fee of $20.00 per pet per night.

Super 8 Kennett
1808 First Street
Kennett, MO
573-888-8800 (800-800-8000)
Dogs of all sizes are allowed. Dogs are allowed for a pet fee of $10 per pet per night.

Days Inn Kingdom City
3391 County Road 211
Kingdom City, MO
573-642-0050 (800-329-7466)

Dogs of all sizes are allowed. Dogs are allowed for a pet fee of $10 per pet per night.

Motel 6 - Kingdom City, Mo
5750 Jade Rd
Kingdom City, MO
573-642-1666 (800-466-8356)
This motel welcomes your pets to stay with you.

Super 8 Kingdom City
3370 Gold Avenue
Kingdom City, MO
573-642-2888 (800-800-8000)
Dogs of all sizes are allowed. Dogs are allowed for a pet fee of $5.00 per pet per night.

Budget Host Village Inn
1304 S Baltimore
Kirksville, MO
660-665-3722
There is a $10 per day per room pet fee. 2 dogs may be allowed.

Days Inn Kirksville
3805 S. Baltimore
Kirksville, MO
660-665-8244 (800-329-7466)
Dogs are welcome at this hotel.

Super 8 Kirksville
1101 Country Club Dr
Kirksville, MO
660-665-8826 (800-800-8000)
Dogs are welcome at this hotel.

Days Inn Lake Saint Louis
10600 Veterans Memorial Pkwy
Lake St Louis, MO
636-625-1711 (800-329-7466)
Dogs of all sizes are allowed. Dogs are allowed for a nightly pet fee.

Best Western Wyota Inn
1225 Millcreek Road
Lebanon, MO
417-532-6171 (800-780-7234)
Dogs of all sizes are allowed. Dogs are allowed for a nightly pet fee.

Days Inn Lebanon
2071 W Elm Street
Lebanon, MO
417-532-7111 (800-329-7466)
Dogs are welcome at this hotel.

Super 8 NE Kansas City Area Liberty
I-35 exit 16 (Hwy 152)
Liberty, MO
816-781-9400 (800-800-8000)
Dogs are welcome at this hotel.

Americas Best Value Inn
28933 Sunset Dr
Macon, MO

660-385-2125 (800-901-2125)
Dogs of all sizes are allowed. There is a $20 returnable deposit required per room. Pet must be kept in kennel when left alone. Smoking and non-smoking rooms are available for pets. Multiple dogs may be allowed.

Super 8 Macon
203 East Briggs Road
Macon, MO
660-385-5788 (800-800-8000)
Dogs of all sizes are allowed. Dogs are allowed for a nightly pet fee.

Super 8 Marshall
1355 W College Street
Marshall, MO
660-886-3359 (800-800-8000)
Dogs of all sizes are allowed. Dogs are allowed for a nightly pet fee.

Super 8 /New Madrid Marston
501 South East Outer Rd
Marston, MO
573-643-9888 (800-800-8000)
Dogs are welcome at this hotel.

Extended Stay America St. Louis - Westport
11827 Lackland Rd.
Maryland Heights, MO
314-993-6868 (800-804-3724)
One dog is allowed per suite. There is a $25 per night additional pet fee up to $150 for an entire stay.

Westport Drury Inn & Suites
12220 Dorsett Road
Maryland Heights, MO
314-576-9966 (800-378-7946)
Dogs of all sizes are allowed for no additional pet fee with a credit card on file, and there is a pet agreement to sign at check in.

Super 8 Maryville
222 Summit Drive
Maryville, MO
660-582-8088 (800-800-8000)
Dogs are welcome at this hotel.

Super 8 MO Moberly
300 Hwy. 24 E
Moberly, MO
660-263-8862 (800-800-8000)
Dogs are welcome at this hotel.

Days Inn Mountain Grove
300 19th Street/US Hwy-95
Mountain Grove, MO
417-926-5555 (800-329-7466)
Dogs of all sizes are allowed. Dogs are allowed for a pet fee of $10.00 per pet per stay.

Travelodge Mountain Grove
111 E. 17th ST.
Mountain Grove, MO
417-926-3152 (800-578-7878)
Dogs are welcome at this hotel.

Super 8 Kansas City/KCI Airport
6900 NW 83rd Terrace
N.W. Kansas City, MO
816-587-0808 (800-800-8000)
Dogs of all sizes are allowed. Dogs are allowed for a nightly pet fee.

Best Western Big Spring Lodge
1810 Southern View Drive
Neosho, MO
417-455-2300 (800-780-7234)
Dogs of all sizes are allowed. Dogs are allowed for a nightly pet fee.

Super 8 Neosho
3085 Gardner Edgewood Dr
Neosho, MO
417-455-1888 (800-800-8000)
Dogs are welcome at this hotel.

Super 8 Nevada
2301 E Austin Blvd
Nevada, MO
417-667-8888 (800-800-8000)
Dogs are welcome at this hotel.

Super 8 /Springfield Area Nixa
418 N Massey Blvd
Nixa, MO
417-725-0880 (800-800-8000)
Dogs of all sizes are allowed. Dogs are allowed for a pet fee.

La Quinta Inn Kansas City North
2214 Taney
North Kansas City, MO
816-221-1200 (800-531-5900)
Dogs of all sizes are allowed. There are no additional pet fees. Dogs may not be left unattended, and they need to be removed or crated for housekeeping. Dogs must be leashed and cleaned up after. Multiple dogs may be allowed.

Comfort Inn & Suites
100 Comfort Inn Court
O'Fallon, MO
636-696-8000 (877-424-6423)
Dogs of all sizes are allowed. Dogs are allowed for a pet fee of $10.00 per pet per night.

Residence Inn St. Louis O'Fallon
101 Progress Point Court
OFallon, MO
636-300-3535 (800-331-3131)
This all suite inn features a convenient location to major corporations, shopping, dining, and entertainment areas, plus they also

Dog-Friendly Lodging - Please always call ahead to make sure an establishment is still dog-friendly.

offer a number of in-house amenities, including a daily buffet breakfast and evening socials Monday to Thursday. Dogs are allowed for an additional one time pet fee of $100 per room. Multiple dogs may be allowed.

Days Inn Oak Grove
101 North Locust
Oak Grove, MO
816-690-8700 (800-329-7466)
Dogs are welcome at this hotel.

Econo Lodge
410 S.E. 1st. St.
Oak Grove, MO
816-690-3681 (877-424-6423)
Dogs of all sizes are allowed. Dogs are allowed for a pet fee of $10.00 per pet per night.

Holiday Inn Express Hotel & Suites
St. Louis West-O'Fallon
1175 Technology Drive
Ofallon, MO
636-300-4844 (877-270-6405)
Dogs of all sizes are allowed. Dogs are allowed for a pet fee of $15.00 per pet per night.

Staybridge Suites Ofallon Chesterfield
11 55 Technology Drive
Ofallon, MO
636-300-0999 (877-270-6405)
Dogs up to 80 pounds are allowed. Pets allowed with an additional pet fee. Up to $75 for 1-6 nights and up to $150 for 7+ nights. A pet agreement must be signed at check-in.

Country Hearth Inn Osage Beach Hotel
3518 H 54S
Osage Beach, MO
(888-4HEARTH (443-2784))
countryhearthosagebeach.com/
In addition to specializing in creating a family oriented, homelike ambiance, this inn also offers some eco-rooms, and an indoor pool. Dogs are allowed for an additional $10 per night per pet. Dogs must be well mannered, leashed, and under their owner's control. 2 dogs may be allowed.

Econo Lodge Inn & Suites Lake Of The Ozarks
5760 Hwy. 54
Osage Beach, MO
573-348-1781 (877-424-6423)
Dogs of all sizes are allowed.

Comfort Inn

1900 West Evangel Street
Ozark, MO
417-485-6688 (877-424-6423)
Dogs of all sizes are allowed. Dogs are allowed for a pet fee of $10.00 per pet per night.

Comfort Inn Near Six Flags St. Louis
1320 Thornton St.
Pacific, MO
636-257-4600 (877-424-6423)
Dogs of all sizes are allowed.

Best Western Airport Inn & Suites/KCI North
2512 NW Prairie View Road
Platte City, MO
816-858-0200 (800-780-7234)
Dogs of all sizes are allowed. Dogs are allowed for a pet fee of $25 per pet per stay.

Super 8 /KCI Airport Platte City
I-29 and Hwy 92
Platte City, MO
816-858-2888 (800-800-8000)
Dogs of all sizes are allowed. Dogs are allowed for a pet fee.

Travelodge Airport Platte City
504 Prairie View Rd
Platte City, MO
816-858-4588 (800-578-7878)
Dogs of all sizes are allowed. Dogs are allowed for a pet fee of $5.00 per pet per night.

Poplar Bluff Drury Inn
2220 Westwood Blvd North
Poplar Bluff, MO
573-686-2451 (800-378-7946)
Dogs of all sizes are allowed for no additional pet fee with a credit card on file, and there is a pet agreement to sign at check in.

Poplar Bluff Pear Tree Inn
2218 N. Westwood Blvd
Poplar Bluff, MO
573-785-7100 (800-378-7946)
Dogs of all sizes are allowed for no additional pet fee with a credit card on file, and there is a pet agreement to sign at check in.

Super 8 Missouri Poplar Bluff
Highway 67 North
Poplar Bluff, MO
573-785-0176 (800-800-8000)
Dogs are welcome at this hotel.

Super 8 Potosi
820 East High St
Potosi, MO
573-438-8888 (800-800-8000)
Dogs are welcome at this hotel.

Super 8 Richmond
888 Slumber Lane
Richmond, MO
816-776-8008 (800-800-8000)
Dogs of all sizes are allowed. Dogs are allowed for a pet fee.

Super 8 /Kansas City Riverside
800 NW Argosy Parkway
Riverside, MO
816-505-2888 (800-800-8000)
Dogs of all sizes are allowed. Dogs are allowed for a pet fee of $15.00 per pet per night.

Super 8 MO Rock Port
1301 I-29 and Hwy 136 W Ex110
Rock Port, MO
660-744-5357 (800-800-8000)
Dogs are welcome at this hotel.

Baymont Inn & Suites Rolla
1801 Martin Springs Drive
Rolla, MO
573-364-7000 (877-229-6668)
Dogs are welcome at this hotel.

Best Western Coachlight
1403 Martin Springs Drive
Rolla, MO
573-341-2511 (800-780-7234)
Dogs of all sizes are allowed. Dogs are allowed for a pet fee of $20 per pet per stay.

Budget Deluxe Motel
1908 North Bishop Ave
Rolla, MO
573-364-4488
There is a $5.00 per day pet fee.

Days Inn Rolla
1207 Kingshighway Street
Rolla, MO
573-341-3700 (800-329-7466)
Dogs are welcome at this hotel.

Econo Lodge
1417 Martin Spring Dr.
Rolla, MO
573-341-3130 (877-424-6423)
Dogs of all sizes are allowed. Dogs are allowed for a pet fee of $10.00 per pet per night.

Comfort Suites
1400 S. Fifth Street
Saint Charles, MO
636-949-0694 (877-424-6423)
Dogs of all sizes are allowed.

Best Western Kirkwood Inn
1200 S Kirkwood Road
Saint Louis, MO
314-821-3950 (800-780-7234)
Dogs of all sizes are allowed. Dogs

295

are allowed for a pet fee.

MainStay Suites
227 St. Robert Boulevard
Saint Robert, MO
573-451-2700 (877-424-6423)
Dogs up to 70 pounds are allowed.
Dogs are allowed for a pet fee of
$15.00 per pet per night. Two dogs
are allowed per room.

Best Western State Fair Inn
3120 S Limit
Sedalia, MO
660-826-6100 (800-780-7234)
Dogs are welcome at this hotel.

Hotel Bothwell
103 E 4th
Sedalia, MO
660-826-5588
Dogs up to 60 pounds are allowed.
There is a $25 one time additional
pet fee. 2 dogs may be allowed.

Super 8 MO Sedalia
3402 W. Broadway
Sedalia, MO
660-827-5890 (800-800-8000)
Dogs of all sizes are allowed. Dogs
are allowed for a pet fee of $5 per
pet per night.

Green Cocoon
On Farm Road 2212
Shell Knob, MO
417-858-8800
Dogs of all sizes are allowed. There
is a $10 per night per pet fee and a
pet policy to sign at check in.

Days Inn Sikeston
1330 South Main Street
Sikeston, MO
573-471-3930 (800-329-7466)
Dogs of all sizes are allowed. Dogs
are allowed for a nightly pet fee.

Drury Inn
2608 E Malone
Sikeston, MO
573-472-2299 (800-378-7946)
Dogs of all sizes are allowed for no
additional pet fee with a credit card
on file, and there is a pet agreement
to sign at check in.

Motel 6 - Sikeston, Mo
110 Interstate Drive
Sikeston, MO
573-471-7400 (800-466-8356)
This motel welcomes your pets to
stay with you.

Sikeston Pear Tree Inn
2602 East Malone
Sikeston, MO

573-471-4100 (800-378-7946)
Dogs of all sizes are allowed for no
additional pet fee with a credit card
on file, and there is a pet agreement
to sign at check in.

Super 8 /Miner Area Sikeston
2609 E Malone
Sikeston, MO
573-471-7944 (800-800-8000)
Dogs of all sizes are allowed. Dogs
are allowed for a pet fee of $10 per
pet per night.

Thrifty Inn
2602 Rear East Malone
Sikeston, MO
573-471-8660 (800-378-7946)
Dogs of all sizes are allowed for no
additional pet fee with a credit card
on file, and there is a pet agreement
to sign at check in.

Super 8 Lake Smithville
112 Cuttings Dr
Smithville, MO
816-532-3088 (800-800-8000)
Dogs of all sizes are allowed. Dogs
are allowed for a pet fee.

Baymont Inn and Suites Airport
Springfield
2445 North Airport Plaza Ave
Springfield, MO
417-447-4466 (877-229-6668)
Dogs of all sizes are allowed. Dogs
are allowed for a pet fee of $10 per
pet per night.

Baymont Inn and Suites South
Springfield
3776 South Glenstone
Springfield, MO
417-889-8188 (877-229-6668)
Dogs are welcome at this hotel.

Candlewood Suites Springfield
2800 N Glenstone
Springfield, MO
417-866-4242 (877-270-6405)
Dogs up to 80 pounds are allowed.
Pets allowed with an additional pet
fee. Up to $75 for 1-6 nights and up
to $150 for 7+ nights. A pet
agreement must be signed at
check-in.

Candlewood Suites Springfield
South
1035 East Republic Road
Springfield, MO
417-881-8500 (877-270-6405)
Dogs up to 80 pounds are allowed.
Pets allowed with an additional pet
fee. Up to $75 for 1-6 nights and up
to $150 for 7+ nights. A pet
agreement must be signed at

check-in.

Clarion Hotel
3333 S. Glenstone Ave.
Springfield, MO
417-883-6550 (877-424-6423)
Dogs of all sizes are allowed. Dogs
are allowed for a pet fee of $25.00
per pet per night.

Days Inn South Springfield
621 W. Sunshine
Springfield, MO
417-862-0153 (800-329-7466)
Dogs of all sizes are allowed. Dogs
are allowed for a nightly pet fee.

Days Inn Battlefield Rd/Hwy 65
3260 East Montclair Street
Springfield, MO
417-882-9484 (800-329-7466)
Dogs are welcome at this hotel.

Econo Lodge West
2808 N. Kansas Expressway
Springfield, MO
417-869-5600 (877-424-6423)
Dogs of all sizes are allowed. Dogs
are allowed for a pet fee of $20.00
per pet per stay. Three or more dogs
may be allowed.

Extended Stay America Springfield -
South
1333 E. Kingsley St.
Springfield, MO
417-823-9100 (800-804-3724)
One dog is allowed per suite. There
is a $25 per night additional pet fee
up to $150 for an entire stay.

La Quinta Inn Springfield
1610 East Evergreen
Springfield, MO
417-520-8800 (800-531-5900)
One average sized dog or 2 small
dogs are allowed. There are no
additional pet fees. Dogs must be
leashed and cleaned up after.

La Quinta Inn Springfield South
2535 S. Campbell
Springfield, MO
417-890-6060 (800-531-5900)
Dogs are allowed, but they can not
have a combined weight of over 100
pounds. There are not additional pet
fees. Dogs may not be left
unattended, and they must be
leashed, and cleaned up after.

Motel 6 - Springfield, Mo
2655 Glenstone Avenue
Springfield, MO
417-831-2100 (800-466-8356)
This motel welcomes your pets to
stay with you.

Dog-Friendly Lodging - Please always call ahead to make sure an establishment is still dog-friendly.

Motel 6 - Springfield, Mo
3404 E. Ridgeview Street
Springfield, MO
417-882-2220 (800-466-8356)
This motel welcomes your pets to
stay with you.

Quality Inn & Suites
2745 N. Glenstone Ave
Springfield, MO
417-869-0001 (877-424-6423)
Dogs of all sizes are allowed. Dogs
are allowed for a pet fee of $10.00
per pet per night.

Quality Inn South
3330 E. Battlefield Rd.
Springfield, MO
417-889-6300 (877-424-6423)
Dogs of all sizes are allowed. Dogs
are allowed for a pet fee of $10.00
per pet per night.

Ramada Limited Airport Springfield
4445 West Chestnut Expressway
Springfield, MO
417-799-2200 (800-272-6232)
Dogs of all sizes are allowed. Dogs
are allowed for a nightly pet fee.

Residence Inn Springfield
1303 E Kingsley Street
Springfield, MO
417-890-0020 (800-331-3131)
In addition to offering a central
location to local universities,
businesses, shopping, dining, and
entertainment areas, this hotel also
provides a number of in-house
amenities, including a daily buffet
breakfast, evening social hours with
hors d'oeuvres, and weekly
barbecues. Dogs are allowed for an
additional one time pet fee of $100
per room. Multiple dogs may be
allowed.

Sleep Inn Medical District
233 El Camino Alto
Springfield, MO
417-886-2464 (877-424-6423)
Dogs of all sizes are allowed.

Springfield Drury Inn & Suites
2715 N. Glenstone Avenue
Springfield, MO
417-863-8400 (800-378-7946)
Dogs of all sizes are allowed for no
additional pet fee with a credit card
on file, and there is a pet agreement
to sign at check in.

Boone's Lick Trail Inn
1000 S Main Street
St Charles, MO
636-947-7000 (888-940-0002)

booneslick.com/
Located along the Missouri River,
this 1840's Federal style inn offers
guests an experience of colonial life
with a touch of luxury. One dog is
allowed for a $75 deposit; $35 is
non-refundable. Dogs may not be
left alone in the room at any time,
and they are not allowed in the
sitting room.

Motel 6 - St Louis St Charles
3800 Harry Truman Blvd
St Charles, MO
636-925-2020 (800-466-8356)
This motel welcomes your pets to
stay with you.

Red Roof Inn St Louis -St Charles
2010 Zumbehl Road
St Charles, MO
636-947-7770 (800-RED-ROOF)
One well-behaved family pet per
room. Guest must notify front desk
upon arrival. Guest is liable for any
damages. In consideration of all
guests, pets must never be left
unattended in the guest rooms.

TownePlace Suites St. Louis St.
Charles
1800 Zumbehl Road
St Charles, MO
636-949-6800 (800-257-3000)
Besides offering a number of in-
house amenities for all level of
travelers, this all suite inn also
offers a convenient location to some
of the area's star attractions, and
numerous businesses, shopping,
dining, and recreation areas. Dogs
are allowed for an additional one
time fee of $100 per room. Multiple
dogs may be allowed.

Super 8 St. Clair MO
1010 S Outer Road
St Clair, MO
636-629-8080 (800-800-8000)
Dogs are welcome at this hotel.

Days Inn And Suites St James
110 N Outer Road
St James, MO
573-265-2900 (800-329-7466)
Dogs of all sizes are allowed. Dogs
are allowed for a pet fee of $10.00
per pet per night.

Holiday Inn St. Joseph
Riverfront/Hist.
102 South Third Street
St Joseph, MO
816-279-8000 (877-270-6405)
Dogs of all sizes are allowed. Dogs
are allowed for a pet fee of $20.00
per pet per night.

Motel 6 - St Joseph
4021 Frederick Blvd
St Joseph, MO
816-232-2311 (800-466-8356)
This motel welcomes your pets to
stay with you.

Ramada St. Joseph
4016 Frederick Blvd
St Joseph, MO
816-233-6192 (800-272-6232)
Dogs are welcome at this hotel.

St Joseph Riverfront Inn
102 S. 3rd Street
St Joseph, MO
816-279-8000
There is a $25 per night per room
additional pet fee. Multiple dogs may
be allowed.

St. Joseph Drury Inn
4213 Frederick Blvd
St Joseph, MO
816-364-4700 (800-378-7946)
Dogs of all sizes are allowed for no
additional pet fee with a credit card
on file, and there is a pet agreement
to sign at check in.

Super 8 MO St Joseph
4024 Frederick Blvd
St Joseph, MO
816-364-3031 (800-800-8000)
Dogs of all sizes are allowed. Dogs
are allowed for a pet fee.

Clayton on the Park
8025 Bonhomme Avenue
St Louis, MO
314-290-1500 (800-323-7500)
claytononthepark.com/
All-inclusive for the business or
leisure traveler, this impressive 23
story high-rise sits on 16 lush acres
of recreational opportunities making
it a worthy destination for a day or a
year. Dogs are allowed for no
additional pet fee with advance
reservations. Upon arrival a pet place
mat will be waiting with water, food,
treats, and toys. There is a pet
agreement to sign at check in. 2
dogs may be allowed.

Doubletree Hotel
1973 Craigshire Road
St Louis, MO
314-434-0100 (800-222-TREE
(8733))
A contemporary, full service hotel,
they offer a number of on site
amenities for all level of travelers -
including their signature chocolate
chip cookies at check in, plus a
convenient location to business,

shopping, dining, and recreation areas. Dogs are allowed for an additional one time pet fee of $50 per room. Multiple dogs may be allowed.

Econo Lodge River Front
1100 North 3rd Street
St Louis, MO
314-421-6556 (877-424-6423)
Dogs of all sizes are allowed. Dogs are allowed for a pet fee of $20.00 per pet per stay. Two dogs are allowed per room.

Holiday Inn St Louis-Forest Pk/Hampton Ave
5915 Wilson Avenue
St Louis, MO
314-645-0700 (877-270-6405)
Dogs of all sizes are allowed. Dogs are allowed for a pet fee of $100.00 per pet per stay.

Holiday Inn St. Louis-South (I-55)
4234 Butler Hill Road
St Louis, MO
314-894-0700 (877-270-6405)
Dogs up to 50 pounds are allowed.

Holiday Inn St. Louis-Southwest (Viking)
10709 Watson Rd.
St Louis, MO
314-821-6600 (877-270-6405)
Dogs of all sizes are allowed. Dogs are allowed for a pet fee of $25 per pet per stay.

Homestead Studio Suites St. Louis - Westport
12161 Lackland Rd.
St Louis, MO
314-878-8777 (800-804-3724)
One dog is allowed per suite. There is a $25 per night additional pet fee up to $150 for an entire stay.

Hotel Indigo St. Louis Central West End
4630 Lindell
St Louis, MO
314-361-4900 (877-865-6578)
Dogs of all sizes are allowed. Dogs are allowed for a pet fee of $50.00 per pet per stay.

Hyatt Regency St Louis at the Arch
315 Chestnut Street
St Louis, MO
314-655-1234
Dogs up to 50 pounds are allowed. There is a $50 per night additional pet fee. One dog per room is permitted.

Motel 6 - St Louis Airport
4576 Woodson Rd

St Louis, MO
314-427-1313 (800-466-8356)
This motel welcomes your pets to stay with you.

Motel 6 - St Louis North
1405 Dunn Rd
St Louis, MO
314-869-9400 (800-466-8356)
This motel welcomes your pets to stay with you.

Motel 6 - St Louis South
6500 Lindbergh Blvd
St Louis, MO
314-892-3664 (800-466-8356)
This motel welcomes your pets to stay with you.

Red Roof Inn St Louis - Forest Park
5823 Wilson Avenue
St Louis, MO
314-645-0101 (800-RED-ROOF)
One well-behaved family pet per room. Guest must notify front desk upon arrival. Guest is liable for any damages. In consideration of all guests, pets must never be left unattended in the guest rooms.

Red Roof Inn St Louis - Westport
11837 Lackland Road
St Louis, MO
314-991-4900 (800-RED-ROOF)
One well-behaved family pet per room. Guest must notify front desk upon arrival. Guest is liable for any damages. In consideration of all guests, pets must never be left unattended in the guest rooms.

Renaissance St. Louis Airport
9801 Natural Bridge Road
St Louis, MO
314-429-1100 (888-340-2594)
This luxury hotel sits central to numerous businesses, shopping, dining, and day/night entertainment areas, plus they also offer a number of in-house amenities for business and leisure travelers. Dogs are allowed for an additional pet fee of $25 per night per room. 2 dogs may be allowed.

Residence Inn St. Louis Downtown
525 S Jefferson Avenue
St Louis, MO
314-289-7500 (800-331-3131)
With its downtown location, this all suite inn sits central to a number of activities and attractions of interest for all level of travelers. They also offer a daily buffet breakfast, evening socials, and an on-site market. Dogs are allowed for an additional one time pet fee of $75

per room. Multiple dogs may be allowed.

Residence Inn St. Louis Galleria
1100 McMorrow Avenue
St Louis, MO
314-862-1900 (800-331-3131)
Only a few minutes to all the sites of interest and activities of the city, this all suite inn gives a great location and a number of on-site amenities for all level of travelers, including a daily buffet breakfast and evening social hours. Dogs are allowed for an additional one time pet fee of $100 per room. Multiple dogs may be allowed.

Residence Inn St. Louis Westport Plaza
1881 Craigshire Road
St Louis, MO
314-469-0060 (00-331-3131)
Besides offering a convenient location to business, shopping, dining, and entertainment areas, this hotel also provides a number of in-house amenities, including a daily buffet breakfast and complementary evening receptions Monday to Thursday. Dogs are allowed for an additional one time pet fee of $100 per room. 2 dogs may be allowed.

Sheraton Clayton Plaza Hotel St. Louis
7730 Bonhomme Ave.
St Louis, MO
314-863-0400 (888-625-5144)
Dogs up to 75 pounds are allowed for no additional pet fee; there is a pet agreement to sign at check in. Dogs may not be left alone in the room.

Sheraton St. Louis City Center Hotel & Suites
400 South 14th St.
St Louis, MO
314-231-5007 (888-625-5144)
Dogs up to 90 pounds are allowed for no additional pet fee. Dogs may not be left alone in the room.

Sheraton Westport Chalet Hotel St. Louis
191 Westport Plaza
St Louis, MO
314-878-1500 (888-625-5144)
Dogs of all sizes are allowed. There are no additional pet fees. Dogs are not allowed to be left alone in the room.

St Louis - Airport Drury Inn
10490 Natural Bridge Road
St Louis, MO

314-423-7700 (800-378-7946)
Dogs of all sizes are allowed for no additional pet fee with a credit card on file, and there is a pet agreement to sign at check in.

St Louis - Convention Center Drury Inn & Suites
711 North Broadway
St Louis, MO
314-231-8100 (800-378-7946)
Dogs of all sizes are allowed for no additional pet fee with a credit card on file, and there is a pet agreement to sign at check in.

St Louis - Drury Plaza Hotel
Fourth & Market Streets
St Louis, MO
314-231-3003 (800-378-7946)
Dogs of all sizes are allowed for no additional pet fee with a credit card on file, and there is a pet agreement to sign at check in.

St Louis - Union Station Drury Inn
201 South 20th Street
St Louis, MO
314-231-3900 (800-378-7946)
Dogs of all sizes are allowed for no additional pet fee with a credit card on file, and there is a pet agreement to sign at check in.

Staybridge Suites St. Louis
1855 Craigshire Road
St Louis, MO
314-878-1555 (877-270-6405)
Dogs up to 80 pounds are allowed. Pets allowed with an additional pet fee. Up to $75 for 1-6 nights and up to $150 for 7+ nights. A pet agreement must be signed at check-in.

Extended Stay America St. Louis - St. Peters
5555 Veterans Memorial Pkwy.
St Peters, MO
636-926-2800 (800-804-3724)
One dog is allowed per suite. There is a $25 per night additional pet fee up to $150 for an entire stay.

St Louis - St. Peters Drury Inn
170 Westfield Drive
St Peters, MO
636-397-9700 (800-378-7946)
Dogs of all sizes are allowed for no additional pet fee with a credit card on file, and there is a pet agreement to sign at check in.

Candlewood Suites St. Robert
140 Carmel Valley Way
St Robert, MO
573-451-2500 (877-270-6405)

Dogs up to 80 pounds are allowed. Pets allowed with an additional pet fee. Up to $75 for 1-6 nights and up to $150 for 7+ nights. A pet agreement must be signed at check-in.

Days Inn Waynesville/Ft. Leonard Wood St. Robert
14125 Hwy Z
St Robert, MO
573-336-5556 (800-329-7466)
Dogs of all sizes are allowed. Dogs are allowed for a pet fee of $10 per pet per night.

Motel 6 - St Robert, Mo
545 Highway
St Robert, MO
573-336-3610 (800-466-8356)
This motel welcomes your pets to stay with you.

Ramada Inn Fort Wood
140 Old Route 66
St Robert, MO
573-336-3121 (800-272-6232)
Dogs are welcome at this hotel.

Red Roof Inn St. Robert
129 Saint Robert Blvd.
St Robert, MO
583-336-2510 (800-RED-ROOF)
One well-behaved family pet per room. Guest must notify front desk upon arrival. Guest is liable for any damages. In consideration of all guests, pets must never be left unattended in the guest rooms.

Super 8 St Robert Ft Leonard Wood Area
I-44, Exit 159
St Robert, MO
573-451-2888 (800-800-8000)
Dogs of all sizes are allowed. Dogs are allowed for a pet fee of $10 per pet per night.

Super 8 Stafford/Springfield Area
315 Chestnut St
Strafford, MO
417-736-3883 (800-800-8000)
Dogs are welcome at this hotel.

Baymont Inn & Suites Sullivan
275 N. Service Road
Sullivan, MO
573-860-3333 (877-229-6668)
Dogs are welcome at this hotel.

Econo Lodge
307 N. Service Road
Sullivan, MO
573-468-3136 (877-424-6423)
Dogs of all sizes are allowed. Dogs are allowed for a pet fee of $5.00

per pet per night.

Super 8 Sullivan
601 N Service Road
Sullivan, MO
573-468-8076 (800-800-8000)
Dogs of all sizes are allowed. Dogs are allowed for a pet fee of $5 per pet per stay.

Knights Inn Trenton
1845 East 28th Street
Trenton, MO
660-359-2988 (800-843-5644)
Dogs are welcome at this hotel.

Days Inn Warrensburg
204 E Cleveland Street
Warrensburg, MO
660-429-2400 (800-329-7466)
Dogs of all sizes are allowed. Dogs are allowed for a nightly pet fee.

Super 8 Warrensburg
439 Russell Ave
Warrensburg, MO
660-429-2183 (800-800-8000)
Dogs of all sizes are allowed. Dogs are allowed for a pet fee of $7 per pet per night.

Days Inn Warrenton
220 Arlington Way I-70
Warrenton, MO
636-456-4301 (800-329-7466)
Dogs of all sizes are allowed. Dogs are allowed for a pet fee.

Holiday Inn Express Warrenton
1008 North Hwy 47 And I-70
Warrenton, MO
636-456-2220 (877-270-6405)
Dogs of all sizes are allowed. Dogs are allowed for a pet fee of $10 per pet per night.

Super 8 Warrenton
1429 North Service Road East
Warrenton, MO
636-456-5157 (800-800-8000)
Dogs of all sizes are allowed. Dogs are allowed for a pet fee of $10 per pet per night.

Motel 6 - Wentzville, Mo
900 Corporate Parkway
Wentzville, MO
636-327-7001 (800-466-8356)
This motel welcomes your pets to stay with you.

Super 8 West Plains
1210 Porter Wagoner Blvd
West Plains, MO
417-256-8088 (800-800-8000)
Dogs are welcome at this hotel.

Montana

River's Edge Resort
22 S Frontage Road
Alberton, MT
406-722-3375
Dogs of all sizes are allowed. There is a $10 one time pet fee per room. Dogs may not be left unattended outside, and they must be leashed and cleaned up after. There is also a camping area on site that allows dogs at no additional fee. Multiple dogs may be allowed.

Holiday Inn Express Belgrade (Bozeman Area)
6261 Jackrabbit Lane
Belgrade, MT
406-388-0800 (877-270-6405)
Dogs are welcome at this hotel.

La Quinta Inn & Suites Belgrade
6445 Jackrabbit Lane
Belgrade, MT
406-388-2222 (800-531-5900)
Dogs of all sizes are allowed. There are no additional pet fees. Dogs may not be left unattended, and they must be leashed and cleaned up after. Multiple dogs may be allowed.

Super 8 Motel - / Bozeman Airport Belgrade
6450 Jackrabbit Lane
Belgrade, MT
406-388-1493 (800-800-8000)
Dogs are welcome at this hotel.

Super 8 Big Timber
20A Big Timber Loop
Big Timber, MT
406-932-8888 (800-800-8000)
Dogs are welcome at this hotel.

Timbers Motel
8540 Hwy. 35 South
Bigfork, MT
406-837-6200 (800-821-4546)
montanaweb.com/timbers/
There is a $10.70 per day per pet fee. 2 dogs may be allowed.

Best Western ClockTower Inn
2511 1st Avenue N
Billings, MT
406-259-5511 (800-780-7234)
Dogs of all sizes are allowed. Dogs are allowed for a pet fee of $15.00 per pet per night.

Best Western Kelly Inn & Suites
4915 Southgate Drive
Billings, MT
406-256-9400 (800-780-7234)

Dogs are welcome at this hotel.

Clubhouse Inn and Suites
5610 S Frontage Road
Billings, MT
406-248-9800 (800-CLUB INN (258-2466))
clubhouseinnbillings.com/
In addition to a long list of in-house amenities, this inn also offers a central location to numerous sites of interests, institutions, shopping, and entertainment areas. Dogs are allowed for no additional fee with advance reservations; there is a pet waiver to sign at check in. Dogs must be leashed or crated when out of the room. Multiple dogs may be allowed.

Comfort Inn
2030 Overland Ave.
Billings, MT
406-652-5200 (877-424-6423)
Dogs of all sizes are allowed. Dogs are allowed for a pet fee of $15.00 per pet per stay.

Days Inn Billings
843 Parkway Lane
Billings, MT
406-252-4007 (800-329-7466)
Dogs of all sizes are allowed. Dogs are allowed for a nightly pet fee.

Dude Rancher Lodge
415 N 29th Street
Billings, MT
406-259-5561 (800-221-3302)
duderancherlodge.com/
Authentic furnishings and architecture greets guests with an "Old West" ambiance at this inn. Dogs are allowed for an additional fee of $7 per night per pet with a credit card on file. Dogs must be leashed and cleaned up after. Multiple dogs may be allowed.

Extended Stay America Billings - West End
4950 Southgate Dr.
Billings, MT
406-245-3980 (800-804-3724)
One dog is allowed per suite. There is a $25 per night additional pet fee up to $150 for an entire stay.

Hilltop Inn
1116 N 28th St
Billings, MT
406-245-5000 (800-878-9282)
There is a $7 per day pet fee. Multiple dogs may be allowed.

Holiday Inn The Grand Montana-Billings

5500 Midland Rd
Billings, MT
406-248-7701 (877-270-6405)
Dogs of all sizes are allowed. Dogs are allowed for a pet fee. One dog is allowed per room.

Kelly Inn
5425 Midland Road
Billings, MT
406-252-2700 (800-635-3559)
kellyinnbillings.com/
There is an abundance of local special events and festivals, numerous historic and other sites of interest, and educational and recreational opportunities, and this hotel sits central to most of them. Dogs are allowed for no additional fee. Dogs may not be left alone in the room, and they must be leashed and cleaned up after; they are not allowed in the lobby or food service areas. 2 dogs may be allowed.

Motel 6 - Billings
5400 Midland Rd
Billings, MT
406-252-0093 (800-466-8356)
This motel welcomes your pets to stay with you.

Quality Inn Homestead Park
2036 Overland Ave.
Billings, MT
406-652-1320 (877-424-6423)
Dogs of all sizes are allowed. Dogs are allowed for a pet fee of $5.00 per pet per night.

Red Roof Inn Billings
5353 Midland Road
Billings, MT
406-248-7551 (800-RED-ROOF)
One well-behaved family pet per room. Guest must notify front desk upon arrival. Guest is liable for any damages. In consideration of all guests, pets must never be left unattended in the guest rooms.

Residence Inn Billings
956 S 25th Street
Billings, MT
406-656-3900 (800-331-3131)
This all suite hotel sits central to many of the city's star attractions, dining, business, and entertainment areas, plus they offer a number of in-house amenities that include a daily buffet breakfast, and an evening reception Monday through Thursday. Dogs are allowed for an additional one time pet fee of $75 per room. Multiple dogs may be allowed.

Riverstone Billings Inn

880 N 29th Street
Billings, MT
406-252-6800 (800-231-7782)
riverstone-inns.com/rbi_hmpg.htm
Located only 4 blocks from
downtown and close to "just about
everything", this inn also offers
guests a long list of in-house
amenities. Dogs are allowed for an
additional fee of $7 per night per pet;
they must be leashed or crated when
out of the room. Multiple dogs may
be allowed.

Sleep Inn
4904 Southgate Dr.
Billings, MT
406-254-0013 (877-424-6423)
Dogs of all sizes are allowed. Two
dogs are allowed per room.

Super 8 Billings
I-90 Exit 447 or Exit 446
Billings, MT
406-248-8842 (800-800-8000)
Dogs of all sizes are allowed. Dogs
are allowed for a nightly pet fee.

Travelodge Hotel Billings
1345 Mullowney Lane
Billings, MT
406-252-2584 (800-578-7878)
Dogs of all sizes are allowed. Dogs
are allowed for a pet fee.

War Bonnet Inn
2612 Belknap Avenue
Billings, MT
406-248-7761
Dogs of all sizes are allowed. There
is a $10 one time pet fee per room. 2
dogs may be allowed.

Best Western GranTree Inn
1325 N 7th Avenue
Bozeman, MT
406-587-5261 (800-780-7234)
Dogs are welcome at this hotel.

Days Inn and Suites Bozeman
1321 North 7th Ave
Bozeman, MT
406-587-5251 (800-329-7466)
Dogs of all sizes are allowed. Dogs
are allowed for a nightly pet fee.

Holiday Inn Bozeman
5 East Baxter Lane
Bozeman, MT
406-587-4561 (877-270-6405)
Dogs of all sizes are allowed. There
are no additional pet fees.

Residence Inn Bozeman
6195 E Valley Center Road
Bozeman, MT
406-522-1535 (800-331-3131)

Set in the heart of the state's Rocky
Mountains, this all suite, upscale
hotel offers a central location to all
the area has to offer for both
business and leisure travelers.
Additionally, they offer a daily buffet
breakfast and an evening social
hour Monday through Thursday.
Dogs are allowed for an additional
one time pet fee of $100 per room.
Multiple dogs may be allowed.

Rodeway Inn
817 Wheat Dr.
Bozeman, MT
406-585-7888 (877-424-6423)
Dogs up to 50 pounds are allowed.
Dogs are allowed for a pet fee of
$15.00 per pet per stay. Two dogs
are allowed per room.

Super 8 Bozeman
800 Wheat Dr
Bozeman, MT
406-586-1521 (800-800-8000)
Dogs are welcome at this hotel.

Western Heritage Inn
1200 E Main St
Bozeman, MT
406-586-8534
There is an additional $5 per night
per pet fee for dogs under 50
pounds,,, $10 per night per pet for
dogs 50 pounds and over, and $15
per night per pet for dogs 100
pounds and over. . 2 dogs may be
allowed.

Best Western Butte Plaza Inn
2900 Harrison Avenue
Butte, MT
406-494-3500 (800-780-7234)
Dogs are welcome at this hotel.

Comfort Inn
2777 Harrison Ave.
Butte, MT
406-494-8850 (877-424-6423)
The newly renovated Comfort Inn is
centrally located in Butte, the
largest historical district in the West.
This

Motel 6 - Butte
122005 Nissler Rd
Butte, MT
406-782-5678 (800-466-8356)
This motel welcomes your pets to
stay with you.

Super 8 MT Butte
2929 Harrison Avenue
Butte, MT
406-494-6000 (800-800-8000)
Dogs are welcome at this hotel.

Super 8 Colstrip
Jct 39 and Castlerock Lake Rd.
Colstrip, MT
406-748-3400 (800-800-8000)
Dogs are welcome at this hotel.

Super 8 Glacier Park/ Columbia Falls
7336 Hwy 2 East
Columbia Falls, MT
406-892-0888 (800-800-8000)
Dogs are welcome at this hotel.

Super 8 Columbus
Interstate 90 Exit 408
Columbus, MT
406-322-4101 (800-800-8000)
Dogs of all sizes are allowed. Dogs
are allowed for a pet fee of $10.00
per pet per night.

Super 8 Conrad
215 N Main St
Conrad, MT
406-278-7676 (800-800-8000)
Dogs of all sizes are allowed. Dogs
are allowed for a pet fee of $10.00
per pet per night.

Super 8 Cut Bank
609 W Main St
Cut Bank, MT
406-873-5662 (800-800-8000)
Dogs of all sizes are allowed. Dogs
are allowed for a nightly pet fee.

Rodeway Inn
1150 North Main
Deer Lodge, MT
406-846-2370 (877-424-6423)
Dogs of all sizes are allowed. Dogs
are allowed for a pet fee of $10.00
per pet per stay.

Best Western Paradise Inn
650 N Montana Street
Dillon, MT
406-683-4214 (800-780-7234)
Dogs of all sizes are allowed. Dogs
are allowed for a pet fee of $10.00
per pet per night.

Comfort Inn
450 N. Interchange
Dillon, MT
406-683-6831 (877-424-6423)
Dogs of all sizes are allowed. Dogs
are allowed for a pet fee of $10.00
per pet per night.

Motel 6 - Dillon, Mt
20 Swenson Way
Dillon, MT
406-683-5555 (800-466-8356)
This motel welcomes your pets to
stay with you.

Super 8 Dillon

I-15 Exit 63 / Hwy. 41 North
Dillon, MT
406-683-4288 (800-800-8000)
Dogs of all sizes are allowed. Dogs are allowed for a pet fee of $15.00 per pet per night.

Best Western Mammoth Hot Springs
905 Scott Street West
Gardiner, MT
406-848-7311 (800-780-7234)
Dogs of all sizes are allowed. Dogs are allowed for a pet fee of $5.00 per pet per stay.

Super 8 /Yellowstone Park Area Gardiner
702 Scott St. West
Gardiner, MT
406-848-7401 (800-800-8000)
Dogs of all sizes are allowed. Dogs are allowed for a pet fee of $10.00 per pet per night.

Cottonwood Inn
45 1st Avenue NE
Glasgow, MT
800-321-8213
Dogs of all sizes are allowed. There are no additional pet fees. Dogs may not be left unattended, and they must be well behaved, leashed, and cleaned up after. There is also an RV park on site that allows dogs. Multiple dogs may be allowed.

Best Western Glendive Inn
222 N Kendrick Avenue
Glendive, MT
406-377-5555 (800-780-7234)
Dogs of all sizes are allowed. Dogs are allowed for a pet fee of $10.00 per pet per stay.

Days Inn Glendive
2000 N. Merrill Ave/I-94
Glendive, MT
406-365-6011 (800-329-7466)
Dogs of all sizes are allowed. Dogs are allowed for a nightly pet fee.

Knights Inn Glendive
1610 N. Merrill
Glendive, MT
406-377-8334 (800-843-5644)
Dogs of all sizes are allowed. Dogs are allowed for a pet fee of $15.00 per pet per night.

Super 8 Glendive
1904 N Merrill Ave
Glendive, MT
406-365-5671 (800-800-8000)
Dogs are welcome at this hotel.

Best Western Heritage Inn
1700 Fox Farm Road

Great Falls, MT
406-761-1900 (800-780-7234)
Dogs of all sizes are allowed. Dogs are allowed for a pet fee of $15.00 per pet per stay.

Comfort Inn
1120 9th St. S.
Great Falls, MT
406-454-2727 (877-424-6423)
Dogs of all sizes are allowed. Dogs are allowed for a pet fee of $room per pet per night.

Days Inn Great Falls
101 14th Avenue NW/I-15
Great Falls, MT
406-727-6565 (800-329-7466)
Dogs of all sizes are allowed. Dogs are allowed for a pet fee.

Extended Stay America Great Falls - Missouri River
800 River Dr. S.
Great Falls, MT
406-761-7524 (800-804-3724)
One dog is allowed per suite. There is a $25 per night additional pet fee up to $150 for an entire stay.

La Quinta Inn & Suites Great Falls
600 River Drive South
Great Falls, MT
406-761-2600 (800-531-5900)
Dogs of all sizes are allowed. There are no additional pet fees. There is a pet waiver to sign at check in. Dogs may not be left unattended, and they must be leashed and cleaned up after. Multiple dogs may be allowed.

Motel 6 - Great Falls, Mt
Treasure State Drive
Great Falls, MT
406-453-1602 (800-466-8356)
This motel welcomes your pets to stay with you.

Super 8 MT Great Falls
1214 13th St S
Great Falls, MT
406-727-7600 (800-800-8000)
Dogs are welcome at this hotel.

Townhouse Inn
1411 10th Avenue South
Great Falls, MT
406-761-4600
There is a $10 per day per pet charge. Dogs may not be left unattended. Multiple dogs may be allowed.

Paws Up Resort
40060 Paws Up Road
Greenough, MT

406-244-5200 (800-473-0601)
pawsup.com/resort/
Located in a beautiful pastoral countryside setting, this luxury ranch resort offers a number of on site amenities - including world class cuisine using the freshest, most natural produce/products available, in-room spa treatments, a gift store, an outfitters store, and a variety of recreation. Additionally, they provide luxury for their canine visitors with their own doggy bed, an outdoor kennel if they want to be outside for awhile, food/water dishes, doggie treats, a toy, and waste disposal bags. Dogs are allowed for an additional fee of $50 per night per pet. Dogs are not allowed in Tent City or the River Camp. 2 dogs may be allowed.

Super 8 Hardin
201 West 14th St.
Hardin, MT
406-665-1700 (800-800-8000)
Dogs are welcome at this hotel.

Super 8 Havre
1901 Hwy 2 West
Havre, MT
406-265-1411 (800-800-8000)
Dogs are welcome at this hotel.

Townhouse Inn
601 1st Street West
Havre, MT
406-265-6711
There is a $10 per day pet charge. There are no designated smoking or non-smoking rooms. Multiple dogs may be allowed.

Barrister Bed and Breakfast
416 North Ewing
Helena, MT
406-443-7330 (800-823-1148)
There are no additional pet fees. 2 dogs may be allowed.

Comfort Inn
750 Fee St.
Helena, MT
406-443-1000 (877-424-6423)
Dogs of all sizes are allowed. Dogs are allowed for a pet fee of $15.00 per pet per stay.

Howard Johnson Helena
2101 E 11th Ave
Helena, MT
406-443-2300 (800-446-4656)
Dogs are welcome at this hotel. There is a $15 one time pet fee.

Lamplighter Motel
1006 Madison Avenue

Helena, MT
406-442-9200
These cozy cottages at this motel offer a unique alternative to the usual motel rooms. Well mannered dogs are allowed for an additional pet fee of $10 per night per room. Dogs must be leashed when out of the room, cleaned up after promptly, and crated when left alone in the room. 2 dogs may be allowed.

Motel 6 - Helena
800 Oregon St
Helena, MT
406-442-9990 (800-466-8356)
This motel welcomes your pets to stay with you.

Quality Inn
2300 North Oaks
Helena, MT
406-442-3064 (877-424-6423)
Dogs up to 50 pounds are allowed. Dogs are allowed for a pet fee of $15.00 per pet per night. Two dogs are allowed per room.

Red Lion
2301 Colonial Drive
Helena, MT
406-443-2100
There is a $20 one time fee per pet. There are no additional pet fees for R&R members, and the R&R program is free to sign up. Multiple dogs may be allowed.

Shilo Inn
2020 Prospect Avenue
Helena, MT
406-442-0320 (800-222-2244)
shiloinn.com/Montana/helena.html
There is a $25 one time fee per pet. 2 dogs may be allowed.

Super 8 Helena
2200 11th Ave.
Helena, MT
406-442-2450 (800-800-8000)
Dogs of all sizes are allowed. Dogs are allowed for a pet fee.

Wingate by Wyndham - Helena
2007 North Oakes
Helena, MT
406-449-3000 (800-228-1000)
Dogs are welcome at this hotel.

Comfort Inn Big Sky
1330 US Highway 2 West
Kalispell, MT
406-755-6700 (877-424-6423)
Dogs of all sizes are allowed. Dogs are allowed for a pet fee of $20.00 per pet per stay. Two dogs are allowed per room.

Econo Lodge Inn & Suites
1680 Highway 93 South
Kalispell, MT
406-752-3467 (877-424-6423)
Dogs up to 50 pounds are allowed. Dogs are allowed for a pet fee of $10.00 per pet per night.

Holiday Inn Express Hotel & Suites Kalispell
275 Treeline Road
Kalispell, MT
406-755-7405 (877-270-6405)
Dogs of all sizes are allowed. Dogs are allowed for a pet fee of $35 per pet per stay.

Kalispell Grand Hotel
100 Main St
Kalispell, MT
406-755-8100
There are no additional pet fees. Dogs must be declared at the time of check in. 2 dogs may be allowed.

La Quinta Inn & Suites Kalispell
255 Montclair Dr
Kalispell, MT
406-257-5255 (800-531-5900)
Dogs of all sizes are allowed. There are no additional pet fees. Dogs must be well behaved, leashed, and cleaned up after. Multiple dogs may be allowed.

Motel 6 - Kalispell
1540 Us 93
Kalispell, MT
406-752-6355 (800-466-8356)
This motel welcomes your pets to stay with you.

Red Lion
North 20 Main
Kalispell, MT
406-751-5050
There is a $20 one time pet fee per room. There are no additional fees for R&R members, and the R&R program is free. 2 dogs may be allowed.

Red Lion Inn
20 N Main St
Kalispell, MT
406-752-6660
redlion.rdln.com/
There is a $20 one time pet fee per room,,, there is no additional fee for R&R members. 2 dogs may be allowed.

Super 8 Glacier Intl Arpt Area/Mt Kalispell
1341 1st Ave E
Kalispell, MT

406-755-1888 (800-800-8000)
Dogs of all sizes are allowed. Dogs are allowed for a pet fee of $10.00 per pet per night.

Travelodge Kalispell
350 North Main Street
Kalispell, MT
406-755-6123 (800-578-7878)
Dogs of all sizes are allowed. Dogs are allowed for a pet fee.

Best Western Yellowstone Crossing
205 SE 4th Street
Laurel, MT
406-628-6888 (800-780-7234)
Dogs of all sizes are allowed. Dogs are allowed for a pet fee.

Pelican Motel & RV Park
11360 S Frontage
Laurel, MT
406-628-4324
Dogs of all sizes are allowed. There is a $10 per night pet fee for the motel,,, there are no additional pet fees in the RV park section. Dogs may not be left unattended in the motel room, and they must be leashed and cleaned up after. 2 dogs may be allowed.

Rodeway Inn
448 West Highway 2
Libby, MT
406-293-2771 (877-424-6423)
Dogs of all sizes are allowed. Dogs are allowed for a pet fee of $15.00 per pet per stay.

The Caboose Motel
714 W 9th Street
Libby, MT
406-293-6201
Dogs are allowed for an additional fee of $5 per night per pet.

Best Western Yellowstone Inn
1515 W Park Street
Livingston, MT
406-222-6110 (800-780-7234)
Dogs of all sizes are allowed. Dogs are allowed for a nightly pet fee.

Quality Inn
111 Rogers Lane
Livingston, MT
406-222-0555 (877-424-6423)
Dogs of all sizes are allowed. Dogs are allowed for a pet fee of $10.00 per pet per night. Two dogs are allowed per room.

Rodeway Inn
102 Rogers Lane
Livingston, MT
406-222-6320 (877-424-6423)

Dogs up to 100 pounds are allowed. Dogs are allowed for a pet fee of $10.00 per pet per night. Two dogs are allowed per room.

Super 8 Livingston
Interstate 90 Exit 333
Livingston, MT
406-222-7711 (800-800-8000)
Dogs of all sizes are allowed. Dogs are allowed for a pet fee of $10.00 per pet per night.

Days Inn And Suites Lolo
11225 Hwy 93 South
Lolo, MT
406-273-2121 (800-329-7466)
Dogs of all sizes are allowed. Dogs are allowed for a pet fee of $10.00 per pet per night.

Best Western War Bonnet Inn
1015 S Haynes Avenue
Miles City, MT
406-234-4560 (800-780-7234)
Dogs of all sizes are allowed. Dogs are allowed for a nightly pet fee.

Econo Lodge
1209 South Haynes Ave.
Miles City, MT
406-232-8880 (877-424-6423)
Dogs of all sizes are allowed. Dogs are allowed for a pet fee of $15.00 per pet per stay.

Motel 6 - Miles City, Mt
1314 Haynes Avenue
Miles City, MT
406-232-7040 (800-466-8356)
This motel welcomes your pets to stay with you.

Super 8 Miles City
RR 2 Hwy 59 S
Miles City, MT
406-234-5261 (800-800-8000)
Dogs are welcome at this hotel.

Best Western Grant Creek Inn
5280 Grant Creek Road
Missoula, MT
406-543-0700 (800-780-7234)
Dogs of all sizes are allowed. Dogs are allowed for a pet fee of $10 per pet per stay.

Comfort Inn
4545 N. Reserve St.
Missoula, MT
406-542-0888 (877-424-6423)
Dogs of all sizes are allowed. Dogs are allowed for a pet fee of $15.00 per pet per night.

Days Inn Airport Missoula
8600 Truck Stop Road

Missoula, MT
406-721-9776 (800-329-7466)
Dogs are welcome at this hotel.

Doubletree Hotel
100 Madison
Missoula, MT
406-728-3100 (800-222-TREE (8733))
Located in the Northern Rockies on the Clark Fork River, this upscale hotel has a number of on site amenities for business or leisure travelers - including their signature chocolate chip cookies at check in, plus a convenient location to shopping, dining, and recreation areas. Dogs are allowed for an additional one time pet fee of $30 per room. 2 dogs may be allowed.

Econo Lodge
4953 North Reserve Street
Missoula, MT
406-542-7550 (877-424-6423)
Dogs up to 50 pounds are allowed. Dogs are allowed for a pet fee of $10.00 per pet per night. Two dogs are allowed per room.

Holiday Inn Missoula Downtown At The Park
200 South Pattee
Missoula, MT
406-721-8550 (877-270-6405)
Dogs of all sizes are allowed. Dogs are allowed for a pet fee of $20.00 per pet per stay.

Motel 6 - Missoula
3035 Expo Pkwy
Missoula, MT
406-549-6665 (800-466-8356)
This motel welcomes your pets to stay with you.

Motel 6 - Missoula University
630 Broadway
Missoula, MT
406-549-2387 (800-466-8356)
This motel welcomes your pets to stay with you.

Quality Inn & Conference Center
3803 Brooks Street
Missoula, MT
406-251-2665 (877-424-6423)
Dogs of all sizes are allowed. Dogs are allowed for a pet fee of $10.00 per pet per night.

Red Lion
700 W Broadway
Missoula, MT
406-728-3300
There are no additional pet fees. Multiple dogs may be allowed.

Sleep Inn
3425 Dore Lane
Missoula, MT
406-543-5883 (877-424-6423)
Dogs of all sizes are allowed. Dogs are allowed for a pet fee of $20.00 per pet per night.

Southgate Inn
3530 Brooks Street
Missoula, MT
406-252-2250 (800-247-2616)
southgateinnmissoula.com/
Some of the city's best attractions, shopping, and dining are just within walking distance of this inn. They also offer a number of on-site amenities - including freshly baked cookies every evening. Dogs are allowed for an additional fee of $10 per day for 1 dog, and $5 per day for each additional dog. Multiple dogs may be allowed.

Staybridge Suites Missoula
120 Expressway
Missoula, MT
406-830-3900 (877-270-6405)
Dogs up to 80 pounds are allowed. Pets allowed with an additional pet fee. Up to $75 for 1-6 nights and up to $150 for 7+ nights. A pet agreement must be signed at check-in.

Nevada City Hotel and Cabins
H 287
Nevada City, MT
406-843-5377 (800-829-2969)
aldergulchaccommodations.com/
Located in a historic "ghost town" that offers living history weekends, this inn offers 2 pet friendly cabins and a variety of recreational and educational activities throughout the town. Dogs are allowed for an additional one time fee of $10 per pet; they must be leashed and under their owner's control at all times. Multiple dogs may be allowed.

Best Western KwaTaqNuk Resort
49708 US Highway 93
Polson, MT
406-883-3636 (800-780-7234)
Dogs of all sizes are allowed. Dogs are allowed for a pet fee of $25 per pet per stay.

Chico Hot Springs Resort
#1 Chico Road
Pray, MT
406-333-4933 (800-HOT-WADA)
chicohotsprings.com/
This resort has a lodge and cabins which sit on 150 acres. There are

miles of hiking trails for you and your pup. They are located 30 miles from the north Yellowstone National Park entrance. There is a $20 one time additional pet fee per pet. Dogs are not allowed in Jacuzzi rooms. Multiple dogs may be allowed.

Comfort Inn
612 North Broadway
Red Lodge, MT
406-446-4469 (877-424-6423)
Dogs of all sizes are allowed.

Comfort Inn
455 McKinley
Shelby, MT
406-434-2212 (877-424-6423)
Dogs of all sizes are allowed. Dogs are allowed for a pet fee of $10.00 per pet per night.

Super 8 St. Regis
Interstate 90 Exit 33
St Regis, MT
406-649-2422 (800-800-8000)
Dogs of all sizes are allowed. Dogs are allowed for a pet fee of $10.00 per pet per night.

Best Western Desert Inn
US 20 191 & 287
West Yellowstone, MT
406-646-7376 (800-780-7234)
Dogs are welcome at this hotel.

Best Western Weston Inn
103 Gibbon Avenue
West Yellowstone, MT
406-646-7373 (800-780-7234)
Dogs of all sizes are allowed. Dogs are allowed for a pet fee of $10.00 per pet per night.

ClubHouse Inn
105 South Electric Street
West Yellowstone, MT
406-646-4892 (800-565-6803)
yellowstoneclubhouseinn.com/
In addition to a long list of in-house amenities-including an indoor swimming pool and Jacuzzi, this inn also sits close to the entrance of Yellowstone Park and numerous other sites of interest, dining, shopping, and entertainment activities. Dogs are allowed for no additional fee; they must be leashed and under their owner's control at all times. Dogs may not be left alone in the room, and they are not allowed in food service areas. Multiple dogs may be allowed.

Hibernation Station
212 Grey Wolf Avenue
West Yellowstone, MT

406-646-4200
Dogs of all sizes are allowed in the cabins. There is a $10 per night per pet fee and a pet policy to sign at check in. 2 dogs may be allowed.

Holiday Inn SunSpree Resort West Yellowstone
315 Yellowstone Avenue
West Yellowstone, MT
406-646-7365 (877-270-6405)
Dogs of all sizes are allowed. Dogs are allowed for a pet fee of $50.00 per pet per night.

Kelly Inn
104 South Canyon
West Yellowstone, MT
406-646-4544 (800-635-3559)
yellowstonekellyinn.com/
Located near the Yellowstone National Park, this hotel offers a long list of amenities and a good central location to numerous other sites of interest. Dogs are allowed for no additional fee; they may not be left alone in the room at any time. Multiple dogs may be allowed.

Pioneer Motel
515 Madison Avenue
West Yellowstone, MT
406-646-9705
There are no additional pet fees. Dogs are not allowed on the beds, must be leashed on the property, and are not allowed to be left alone in the room. 2 dogs may be allowed.

Whispering Pines Motel
321 Canyon Street
West Yellowstone, MT
406-646-1172
Dogs up to 50 pounds are allowed for no additional fee. 2 dogs may be allowed.

Best Western Rocky Mountain Lodge
6510 Highway 93 S
Whitefish, MT
406-862-2569 (800-780-7234)
Dogs of all sizes are allowed. Dogs are allowed for a pet fee of $2 per pet per stay.

Holiday Inn Express Whitefish-Glacier Park
6390 US Hwy 93 South
Whitefish, MT
406-862-4020 (877-270-6405)
Dogs of all sizes are allowed. Dogs are allowed for a pet fee of $15.00 per pet per night.

Stillwater Mountain Lodge

750 Beaver Lake Road
Whitefish, MT
406-862-7004 (888-205-7786)
stillwatermtnlodge.com/lodge.php
Nestled along the foothills of the Rocky Mountains, this lodge offers 3 beautiful suites, a well equipped community kitchen, mountain views, and year around trails for hounds and humans. Dogs are allowed for an additional fee of $10 per night per pet. They must be under good voice control when on the trails and cleaned up after promptly. There are no trail fees for guests of the lodge. 2 dogs may be allowed.

Super 8 Whitefish
Hwy 93 S 800 Spokane Ave
Whitefish, MT
406-862-8255 (800-800-8000)
Dogs of all sizes are allowed. Dogs are allowed for a pet fee of $10.00 per pet per night.

Super 8 Whitehall
515 N Whitehall St
Whitehall, MT
406-287-5588 (800-800-8000)
Dogs of all sizes are allowed. Dogs are allowed for a pet fee of $10.00 per pet per night.

The Islander Inn
39 Orchard Lane
Woods Bay, MT
406-837-5472
Dogs are allowed for an additional pet fee of $25 per night per room. 2 dogs may be allowed.

Nebraska

Days Inn Alliance
117 Cody Avenue
Alliance, NE
308-762-8000 (800-329-7466)
Dogs of all sizes are allowed. Dogs are allowed for a pet fee.

Econo Lodge
3210 N. 6th Street
Beatrice, NE
402-223-3536 (877-424-6423)
Dogs of all sizes are allowed. Dogs are allowed for a pet fee of $10.00 per pet per night. Two dogs are allowed per room.

Holiday Inn Express Hotel & Suites Beatrice
4005 N 6th Street
Beatrice, NE
402-228-7000 (877-270-6405)
Dogs are welcome at this hotel. There is no additional pet fee.

Best Western White House Inn
305 N Fort Crook Road
Bellevue, NE
402-293-1600 (800-780-7234)
Dogs of all sizes are allowed. Dogs
are allowed for a pet fee.

Candlewood Suites Bellevue
10902 E 15 St.
Bellevue, NE
402-932-8144 (877-270-6405)
Dogs up to 80 pounds are allowed.
Pets allowed with an additional pet
fee. Up to $75 for 1-6 nights and up
to $150 for 7+ nights. A pet
agreement must be signed at check-
in.

Motel 6 - Big Springs, Ne
111 Circle Rd
Big Springs, NE
308-889-3671 (800-466-8356)
This motel welcomes your pets to
stay with you.

Econo Lodge
1355 Highway 30
Blair, NE
402-426-2340 (877-424-6423)
Dogs of all sizes are allowed. Dogs
are allowed for a pet fee of $$10.00
per pet per night.

Super 8 Central City
1701 31st St.
Central City, NE
308-946-5055 (800-800-8000)
Dogs of all sizes are allowed. Dogs
are allowed for a pet fee.

Best Western West Hills Inn
1100 W 10th Street
Chadron, NE
308-432-3305 (800-780-7234)
Dogs of all sizes are allowed. Dogs
are allowed for a nightly pet fee.

Motel 6 - Chadron
755 Microtel Drive
Chadron, NE
308-432-3000 (800-466-8356)
This motel welcomes your pets to
stay with you.

Super 8 NE Chadron
840 W. HWY 20
Chadron, NE
308-432-4471 (800-800-8000)
Dogs are welcome at this hotel.

Rodeway Inn
3803 23rd St.
Columbus, NE
402-564-9955 (877-424-6423)
Dogs of all sizes are allowed. Dogs
are allowed for a pet fee of $10.00

per pet per night. Two dogs are
allowed per room.

Sleep Inn & Suites
303 23rd. St.
Columbus, NE
402-562-5200 (877-424-6423)
Dogs of all sizes are allowed. Dogs
are allowed for a pet fee of $15.00
per pet per night.

Super 8 Columbus
3324 20th St
Columbus, NE
402-563-3456 (800-800-8000)
Dogs are welcome at this hotel.

Rodeway Inn
809 S. Meridian
Cozad, NE
308-784-4900 (877-424-6423)
Dogs of all sizes are allowed.

Super 8 Crete
1880 West 12th Street
Crete, NE
402-826-3600 (800-800-8000)
Dogs of all sizes are allowed. Dogs
are allowed for a pet fee of $10.00
per pet per night.

Super 8 Gothenburg
401 Platte River Dr
Gothenburg, NE
308-537-2684 (800-800-8000)
Dogs are welcome at this hotel.

Days Inn Grand Island
2620 North Diers Ave
Grand Island, NE
308-384-8624 (800-329-7466)
Dogs of all sizes are allowed. Dogs
are allowed for a pet fee.

Holiday Inn Grand Island-I-80
7838 S Hwy 281
Grand Island, NE
308-384-7770 (877-270-6405)
Dogs of all sizes are allowed. Dogs
are allowed for a pet fee of $15.00
per pet per night.

Howard Johnson Hotel Riverside
NE Grand Island
3333 Ramada Road
Grand Island, NE
308-384-5150 (800-446-4656)
Dogs are welcome at this hotel.
There is a $10 one time pet fee. No
cats are allowed.

Motel 6 - Grand Island
7301 Bosselman Ave
Grand Island, NE
308-384-6666 (800-466-8356)
This motel welcomes your pets to
stay with you.

Rodeway Inn
3205 S. Locust St.
Grand Island, NE
308-384-1333 (877-424-6423)
Dogs of all sizes are allowed.

Super 8 Grand Island
2603 S Locust St
Grand Island, NE
308-384-4380 (800-800-8000)
Dogs are welcome at this hotel.

Travelodge Grand Island
1311 S. Locust
Grand Island, NE
308-382-5003 (800-578-7878)
Dogs are welcome at this hotel.

Quality Hotel & Convention Center
2205 Osborne Dr. East
Hastings, NE
402-463-6721 (877-424-6423)
Dogs up to 50 pounds are allowed.

Super 8 Hastings
2200 N Kansas Ave
Hastings, NE
402-463-8888 (800-800-8000)
Dogs are welcome at this hotel.

Days Inn Kearney
619 2nd Avenue East/I-80
Kearney, NE
308-234-5699 (800-329-7466)
Dogs of all sizes are allowed. Dogs
are allowed for a pet fee.

Econo Lodge
709 E. 2nd Ave
Kearney, NE
308-237-2671 (877-424-6423)
Dogs up to 100 pounds are allowed.
Dogs are allowed for a pet fee of
$10.00 per pet per night. Two dogs
are allowed per room.

Motel 6 - Kearney
101 Talmadge St
Kearney, NE
308-338-0705 (800-466-8356)
This motel welcomes your pets to
stay with you.

Quality Inn
121 3rd Ave.
Kearney, NE
308-237-0838 (877-424-6423)
Dogs up to 65 pounds are allowed.
Dogs are allowed for a pet fee of
$15.00 per pet per night. Two dogs
are allowed per room.

Rodeway Inn & Suites
411 2nd Avenue
Kearney, NE
308-698-2810 (877-424-6423)

Dogs of all sizes are allowed. Dogs are allowed for a pet fee of $10.00 per pet per night.

Super 8 Kearney
I-80 Exit 272
Kearney, NE
308-234-5513 (800-800-8000)
Dogs are welcome at this hotel.

Days Inn Kimball
611 E 3rd St
Kimball, NE
308-235-4671 (800-329-7466)
Dogs of all sizes are allowed. Dogs are allowed for a pet fee.

Super 8 NE Kimball
South Highway 71 Exit 20
Kimball, NE
308-235-4888 (800-800-8000)
Dogs of all sizes are allowed. Dogs are allowed for a nightly pet fee.

Holiday Inn Express Hotel & Suites Lexington
2605 Plum Creek Pkwy
Lexington, NE
308-324-9900 (877-270-6405)
Dogs of all sizes are allowed. Dogs are allowed for a pet fee of $10.70 per pet per night.

Candlewood Suites Lincoln
4100 Pioneer Woods Drive
Lincoln, NE
402-420-0330 (877-270-6405)
Dogs up to 80 pounds are allowed. Pets allowed with an additional pet fee. Up to $75 for 1-6 nights and up to $150 for 7+ nights. A pet agreement must be signed at check-in.

Comfort Suites
4231 Industrial Ave.
Lincoln, NE
402-476-8080 (877-424-6423)
Dogs of all sizes are allowed. Dogs are allowed for a pet fee of $10.00 per pet per night. Two dogs are allowed per room.

Country Inns & Suites by Carlson
5353 N. 27th
Lincoln, NE
402-476-5353
Dogs of all sizes are allowed. There is a $15 per day per pet additional fee. There is complimentary high-speed Internet.

Days Inn Airport Lincoln
2920 NW 12th Street
Lincoln, NE
402-475-3616 (800-329-7466)
Dogs are welcome at this hotel.

Days Inn and Suites Lincoln
2001 West O Street
Lincoln, NE
402-477-4488 (800-329-7466)
Dogs of all sizes are allowed. Dogs are allowed for a pet fee of $10.00 per pet per stay.

Holiday Inn Express Hotel & Suites Lincoln Airport
1101 West Commerce Way
Lincoln, NE
402-464-0588 (877-270-6405)
Dogs of all sizes are allowed. Dogs are allowed for a pet fee of $25 per pet per night.

Holiday Inn Express Hotel & Suites Lincoln South
8801 Amber Hill Court
Lincoln, NE
402-423-1176 (877-270-6405)
Dogs of all sizes are allowed. Dogs are allowed for a pet fee of $25.00 per pet per night.

Motel 6 - Lincoln Airport
3001 Nw 12th St
Lincoln, NE
402-475-3211 (800-466-8356)
This motel welcomes your pets to stay with you.

Ramada Airport
1101 W Bond Street
Lincoln, NE
402-475-4971 (800-272-6232)
Dogs are welcome at this hotel.

Ramada Limited South Lincoln
1511 Center Park Road
Lincoln, NE
402-423-3131 (800-272-6232)
Dogs of all sizes are allowed. Dogs are allowed for a pet fee of $5.00 per pet per stay.

Staybridge Suites Lincoln I-80
2701 Fletcher Avenue
Lincoln, NE
402-438-7829 (877-270-6405)
Dogs up to 80 pounds are allowed. Pets allowed with an additional pet fee. Up to $75 for 1-6 nights and up to $150 for 7+ nights. A pet agreement must be signed at check-in.

Suburban Extended Stay Hotel Downtown
1744 M Street
Lincoln, NE
402-475-3000 (877-424-6423)
Dogs of all sizes are allowed.

Super 8 West Lincoln

2635 West O Street
Lincoln, NE
402-476-8887 (800-800-8000)
Dogs are welcome at this hotel.

Super 8 /Cornhusker Hwy Lincoln
2545 Cornhusker Hwy
Lincoln, NE
402-467-4488 (800-800-8000)
Dogs are welcome at this hotel.

Travelodge Lincoln
2801 West O St (Not Zero)
Lincoln, NE
402-475-4921 (800-578-7878)
Dogs of all sizes are allowed. Dogs are allowed for a pet fee.

Days Inn McCook
901 North Hwy 83
McCook, NE
308-345-7115 (800-329-7466)
Dogs of all sizes are allowed. Dogs are allowed for a pet fee.

Pioneer Village Motel
224 E H 6
Minden, NE
800-445-4447
Dogs of all sizes are allowed for an additional pet fee of $10 per stay per room. Dogs may not be left unattended, and they must be leashed and cleaned up after. There is only 1 non-smoking pet friendly room available, the rest are smoking rooms. Dogs are not allowed in the museum or in any of the outer pioneer village buildings. 2 dogs may be allowed.

Rodeway Inn & Suites
2206 Market Lane
Norfolk, NE
402-371-9779 (877-424-6423)
Dogs of all sizes are allowed. Dogs are allowed for a pet fee of $10.00 per pet per night.

Super 8 Norfolk
1223 Omaha Ave
Norfolk, NE
402-379-2220 (800-800-8000)
Dogs are welcome at this hotel.

Howard Johnson Inn - North Platte
1209 S. Dewey St
North Platte, NE
308-532-0130 (800-446-4656)
Dogs are welcome at this hotel.

La Quinta Inn & Suites North Platte
2600 Eagles Wings Place
North Platte, NE
308-534-0700 (800-531-5900)
Dogs of all sizes are allowed. There are no additional pet fees. There is a

pet waiver to sign at check in. Dogs may not be left unattended, and they must be leashed and cleaned up after. Multiple dogs may be allowed.

Motel 6 - North Platte
1520 Jeffers St
North Platte, NE
308-534-6200 (800-466-8356)
This motel welcomes your pets to stay with you.

Quality Inn & Suites
2102 S Jeffers
North Platte, NE
308-532-9090 (877-424-6423)
Dogs of all sizes are allowed. Dogs are allowed for a pet fee of $10.00 per pet per night. Two dogs are allowed per room.

Ramada North Platte
3201 S. Jeffers
North Platte, NE
308-534-3120 (800-272-6232)
Dogs of all sizes are allowed. Dogs are allowed for a pet fee.

Rodeway Inn
920 North Jeffers
North Platte, NE
308-532-2313 (877-424-6423)
Dogs of all sizes are allowed. Dogs are allowed for a pet fee of $7.00 per pet per night.

Super 8 North Platte
220 Eugene Avenue
North Platte, NE
308-532-4224 (800-800-8000)
Dogs of all sizes are allowed. Dogs are allowed for a nightly pet fee.

Best Western Stagecoach Inn
201 Stagecoach Trl
Ogallala, NE
308-284-3656 (800-780-7234)
Dogs of all sizes are allowed. Dogs are allowed for a pet fee of $10.00 per pet per night.

Days Inn Ogallala
601 Stagecoach Trail
Ogallala, NE
308-284-6365 (800-329-7466)
Dogs are welcome at this hotel.

Super 8 Ogallala
500 East A St. South
Ogallala, NE
308-284-2076 (800-800-8000)
Dogs are welcome at this hotel.

Best Western Kelly Inn
4706 S 108th Street
Omaha, NE
402-339-7400 (800-780-7234)

Dogs are welcome at this hotel.

Best Western Seville Plaza Hotel
330 N 30th Street
Omaha, NE
402-345-2222 (800-780-7234)
Dogs of all sizes are allowed. Dogs are allowed for a pet fee.

Candlewood Suites Omaha
360 S. 108th Ave.
Omaha, NE
402-758-2848 (877-270-6405)
Dogs up to 80 pounds are allowed. Pets allowed with an additional pet fee. Up to $75 for 1-6 nights and up to $150 for 7+ nights. A pet agreement must be signed at check-in.

Candlewood Suites Omaha Airport
2601 Abbott Plaza
Omaha, NE
402-342-2500 (877-270-6405)
Dogs up to 80 pounds are allowed. Pets allowed with an additional pet fee. Up to $75 for 1-6 nights and up to $150 for 7+ nights. A pet agreement must be signed at check-in.

Comfort Inn & Suites West Dodge
8736 West Dodge Rd.
Omaha, NE
402-343-1000 (877-424-6423)
Dogs up to 60 pounds are allowed. Dogs are allowed for a pet fee of $30.00 per pet per night. Two dogs are allowed per room.

Comfort Inn Southwest
10728 L Street
Omaha, NE
402-593-2380 (877-424-6423)
There is a $10 per night per pet fee and a pet policy to sign at check in.

Comfort Inn West
9595 S. 145th St.
Omaha, NE
402-896-6300 (877-424-6423)
Dogs of all sizes are allowed. Dogs are allowed for a pet fee of $10.00 per pet per night.

Crowne Plaza Hotel Omaha-Old Mill
655 North 108th Avenue
Omaha, NE
402-496-0850 (877-270-6405)
Dogs of all sizes are allowed. Dogs are allowed for a pet fee of $25.00 per pet per night.

Econo Lodge
10919 J St.
Omaha, NE
402-592-2882 (877-424-6423)

Dogs of all sizes are allowed. Dogs are allowed for a pet fee of $10.00 per pet per night.

Econo Lodge West Dodge
7833 W. Dodge Rd.
Omaha, NE
402-391-7100 (877-424-6423)
Dogs of all sizes are allowed. Dogs are allowed for a pet fee of $10.00 per pet per night.

Hawthorn Suites
11025 M Street
Omaha, NE
402-331-0101 (800-527-1133)
In addition to providing a convenient location to many local sites and activities, this all-suite hotel offers a number of amenities for business and leisure travelers, including their signature breakfast buffet and beautifully appointed rooms. Dogs up to 50 pounds are allowed for an additional pet fee of $6 per night per room. 2 dogs may be allowed.

Hilton Hotel
1001 Cass Street
Omaha, NE
402-998-3400 (800-HILTONS (445-8667))
This upscale hotel offers a number of on site amenities for business and leisure travelers, plus a convenient location to business, shopping, dining, and entertainment areas. Dogs up to 50 pounds are allowed for an additional one time pet fee of $75 per room. 2 dogs may be allowed.

Holiday Inn Express Hotel & Suites Omaha West
17677 Wright St
Omaha, NE
402-333-5566 (877-270-6405)
Dogs of all sizes are allowed. Dogs are allowed for a pet fee of $25.00 per pet per stay.

Holiday Inn Omaha
11515 Miracle Hills Drive
Omaha, NE
402-496-7500 (877-270-6405)
Dogs of all sizes are allowed. Dogs are allowed for a pet fee of $10.00 per pet per night.

La Quinta Inn Omaha
3330 North 104th Ave.
Omaha, NE
402-493-1900 (800-531-5900)
Dogs of all sizes are allowed. There are no additional pet fees. There is a pet waiver to sign at check in. Dogs may not be left unattended, and they

must be leashed and cleaned up after. Multiple dogs may be allowed.

La Quinta Inn Omaha Southwest
10760 M Street
Omaha, NE
402-592-5200 (800-531-5900)
Dogs of all sizes are allowed. There are no additional pet fees. Pets may not be left unattended, and they must be leashed and cleaned up after. Multiple dogs may be allowed.

Motel 6 - Omaha
10708 St
Omaha, NE
402-331-3161 (800-466-8356)
This motel welcomes your pets to stay with you.

Motel 6 - Omaha, Ne
3511 South 84th St.
Omaha, NE
402-391-4321 (800-466-8356)
This motel welcomes your pets to stay with you.

Motel 6 - Omaha, Ne
10560 Sapp Brothers Dr.
Omaha, NE
402-896-6868 (800-466-8356)
This motel welcomes your pets to stay with you.

Ramada Omaha
3301 South 72nd Street
Omaha, NE
402-391-8129 (800-272-6232)
Dogs of all sizes are allowed. Dogs are allowed for a pet fee of $10.00 per pet per night.

Residence Inn Omaha
6990 Dodge Street
Omaha, NE
402-553-8898 (800-331-3131)
Some of the amenities at this all-suite inn include a daily buffet breakfast, a Manager's reception Monday through Wednesday with light dinner fare, a heated swimming pool, a Sport Court, and a complimentary grocery shopping service. Dogs are allowed for an additional one time pet fee of $75 per room. Multiple dogs may be allowed.

Sleep Inn & Suites Airport
2525 Abbott Dr.
Omaha, NE
402-342-2525 (877-424-6423)
Dogs of all sizes are allowed.

Super 8 NE Omaha
7111 Spring St
Omaha, NE
402-390-0700 (800-800-8000)

Dogs of all sizes are allowed. Dogs are allowed for a pet fee of $10.00 per pet per night.

Super 8 /West Dodge Omaha
11610 W Dodge Road
Omaha, NE
402-492-8845 (800-800-8000)
Dogs are welcome at this hotel.

The Hilton
1001 Cass Street
Omaha, NE
402-998-3400 (800-HILTONS (445-8667))
In addition to offering the hotel's 4-diamond property status, they also give a convenient location to the historic Old Market area, museums, entertainment, and more. Dogs up to 50 pounds are allowed for an additional one time fee of $75 per pet. 2 dogs may be allowed.

Travelodge Omaha
7101 Grover Street
Omaha, NE
402-391-5757 (800-578-7878)
Dogs of all sizes are allowed. Dogs are allowed for a nightly pet fee.

Days Inn Paxton
851 Paxton Elsie Road
Paxton, NE
308-239-4510 (800-329-7466)
Dogs of all sizes are allowed. Dogs are allowed for a pet fee.

Comfort Inn
1902 21st Ave.
Scottsbluff, NE
308-632-7510 (877-424-6423)
Dogs of all sizes are allowed. Dogs are allowed for a pet fee of $10.00 per pet per stay.

Days Inn Scottsbluff
1901 21st Ave
Scottsbluff, NE
308-635-3111 (800-329-7466)
Dogs are welcome at this hotel.

Lamplighter American Inn
606 E 27th St
Scottsbluff, NE
308-632-7108
There is a $6 per day additional pet fee. Dogs must be crated when left alone in the room. Multiple dogs may be allowed.

Super 8 Scottsbluff
2202 Delta Drive
Scottsbluff, NE
308-635-1600 (800-800-8000)
Dogs of all sizes are allowed. Dogs are allowed for a pet fee.

Super 8 NE Seward
1329 Progressive Rd
Seward, NE
402-643-3388 (800-800-8000)
Dogs are welcome at this hotel.

Holiday Inn Sidney (I-80 & Hwy 385)
664 Chase Blvd.
Sidney, NE
308-254-2000 (877-270-6405)
Dogs of all sizes are allowed. Dogs are allowed for a pet fee of $20.00 per pet per night.

Motel 6 - Sidney
3040 Silverberg Dr
Sidney, NE
308-254-5463 (800-466-8356)
This motel welcomes your pets to stay with you.

Super 8 St. Paul NE
116 Howard Avenue
St Paul, NE
308-754-4554 (800-800-8000)
Dogs are welcome at this hotel.

Sleep Inn & Suites
130 N. 30th Rd.
Syracuse, NE
402-269-2700 (877-424-6423)
Dogs of all sizes are allowed. Dogs are allowed for a pet fee of $10.00 per pet per night.

Super 8 NE Valentine
223 East Highway 20
Valentine, NE
402-376-1250 (800-800-8000)
Dogs are welcome at this hotel.

Super 8 West Point
1211 N Lincoln St
West Point, NE
402-372-3998 (800-800-8000)
Dogs are welcome at this hotel.

Wood River Motel
11774 S H 11
Wood River, NE
308-583-2256
Dogs of all sizes are allowed. There is a $5 per night per pet additional fee or $15 per pet by the week. Dogs may not be left unattended outside, and they must be leashed and cleaned up after. Multiple dogs may be allowed.

Holiday Inn York-I-80
4619 South Lincoln Ave
York, NE
402-362-6661 (877-270-6405)
Dogs of all sizes are allowed. Dogs are allowed for a pet fee of $25.00 per pet per stay.

Super 8 NE York
4112 South Lincoln Avenue
York, NE
402-362-3388 (800-800-8000)
Dogs are welcome at this hotel.

Nevada

Comfort Inn
521 E. Front St
Battle Mountain, NV
775-635-5880 (877-424-6423)
Dogs of all sizes are allowed. Dogs
are allowed for a pet fee of $10.00
per pet per night.

Super 8 Battle Mountain
825 Super 8 Dr.
Battle Mountain, NV
775-635-8808 (800-800-8000)
Dogs of all sizes are allowed. Dogs
are allowed for a pet fee.

Motel 6 - Beatty Death Valley
550 Us 95
Beatty, NV
775-553-9090 (800-466-8356)
This motel welcomes your pets to
stay with you.

Comfort Inn Central
1018 Fir Street
Carlin, NV
775-754-6110 (877-424-6423)
Dogs of all sizes are allowed. Dogs
are allowed for a pet fee of $10.00/
per pet per night.

Best Value Motel
2731 S Carson St
Carson City, NV
775-882-2007
There is a 5 per night per pet
additional fee. 2 dogs may be
allowed.

Days Inn Carson City
3103 North Carson
Carson City, NV
775-883-3343 (800-329-7466)
Dogs of all sizes are allowed. Dogs
are allowed for a pet fee.

Holiday Inn Express Hotel & Suites
Carson City
4055 N. Carson Street
Carson City, NV
775-283-4055 (877-270-6405)
Dogs up to 50 pounds are allowed.
Dogs are allowed for a pet fee of
$20.00 per pet per stay.

Motel 6 - Carson City
2749 Carson St

Carson City, NV
775-885-7710 (800-466-8356)
This motel welcomes your pets to
stay with you.

Quality Inn Trailside Inn
1300 N. Carson Street
Carson City, NV
775-883-7300 (877-424-6423)
Dogs up to 100 pounds are allowed.
Dogs are allowed for a pet fee of
$10.00 per pet per night. Two dogs
are allowed per room.

Super 8 Carson City
2829 S Carson St
Carson City, NV
775-883-7800 (800-800-8000)
Dogs of all sizes are allowed. Dogs
are allowed for a pet fee of $10.00
per pet per night.

Econo Lodge Inn & Suites
3320 East Idaho Street
Elko, NV
775-777-8000 (877-424-6423)
Dogs up to 50 pounds are allowed.

High Desert Inn
3015 Idaho Street
Elko, NV
775-738-8425
Well behaved dogs are welcome for
a $15 one time pet charge. Multiple
dogs may be allowed.

Motel 6 - Elko
3021 Idaho St
Elko, NV
775-738-4337 (800-466-8356)
This motel welcomes your pets to
stay with you.

NV Travelodge Elko
1785 Idaho Street
Elko, NV
775-753-7747 (800-578-7878)
Dogs of all sizes are allowed. Dogs
are allowed for a pet fee of $10 per
pet per night.

Red Lion
2065 Idaho Street
Elko, NV
775-738-2111
There is a $20 one time pet fee per
room. There are no additional pet
fees for R&R members, and the
R&R program is free to sign up. 2
dogs may be allowed.

Rodeway Inn
736 Idaho Street
Elko, NV
775-738-7152 (877-424-6423)
Dogs of all sizes are allowed. Dogs
are allowed for a pet fee of $15.00

per pet per night.

Shilo Inn
2401 Mountain City Highway
Elko, NV
775-738-5522 (800-222-2244)
shiloinn.com/Nevada/elko.html
There is a $28 per week pet charge.
2 dogs may be allowed.

Super 8 Elko
1755 Idaho St
Elko, NV
775-738-8488 (800-800-8000)
Dogs are welcome at this hotel.

Jailhouse Motel
211 5th Street
Ely, NV
775-289-3033
Dogs of all sizes are allowed. There
is a $10 per stay per room additional
pet fee. 2 dogs may be allowed.

Motel 6 - Ely
770 Ave
Ely, NV
775-289-6671 (800-466-8356)
This motel welcomes your pets to
stay with you.

Ramada Copper Queen Casino
805 Great Basin Boulevard
Ely, NV
775-289-4884 (800-272-6232)
Dogs are welcome at this hotel.

Best Western Eureka Inn
251 N Main Street
Eureka, NV
775-237-5247 (800-780-7234)
Dogs of all sizes are allowed. Dogs
are allowed for a pet fee of $15.00
per pet per stay.

Motel 6 - Fallon
1705 Taylor St
Fallon, NV
775-423-2277 (800-466-8356)
This motel welcomes your pets to
stay with you.

Best Western Fernley Inn
1405 Newlands Drive E
Fernley, NV
775-575-6776 (800-780-7234)
Dogs of all sizes are allowed. Dogs
are allowed for a pet fee of $10.00
per pet per night.

Super 8 /Carson City Gardnerville
1979 Hwy 395 South
Gardnerville, NV
775-266-3338 (800-800-8000)
Dogs of all sizes are allowed. Dogs
are allowed for a pet fee of $12.00
per pet per night.

Soldier Meadows Guest Ranch and Lodge
Soldier Meadows Rd
Gerlach, NV
775-849-1666
soldiermeadows.com/
Dating back to 1865 when it was known as Camp McGarry, this historic cattle ranch lies in the Black Rock Desert about three hours north of Reno. Soldier Meadows is a family owned working cattle ranch with over 500,000 acres of public and private land to enjoy. It is one of the largest and remotest guest ranches in the nation. There are no phones, faxes, or computers here. Horseback riders can work with the cowboys, take trail rides to track wild mustangs and other wildlife, or ride out to the natural hot springs for a soak. Or you may chose to go mule deer hunting, fishing, hiking, mountain biking or 4-wheeling. The lodge offers 10 guest rooms, and one suite with a private bathroom and kitchenette. The main lodge has a common living room with a large fireplace. Pets are not allowed in the kitchen area, on the furniture/bedding, and they must be animal and human friendly. There is a $10 one time fee per pet charge.

Hawthorn Inn & Suites
910 S Boulder H
Henderson, NV
702-568-7800 (800-527-1133)
In addition to providing a convenient location to many local sites and activities, this all-suite hotel offers a number of amenities for business and leisure travelers, including their signature breakfast buffet and beautifully appointed rooms. Dogs are allowed for an additional pet fee of $15 per night per room. Multiple dogs may be allowed.

Holiday Inn Henderson E Las Vegas
1553 N. Boulder Highway
Henderson, NV
702-564-9200 (877-270-6405)
Dogs up to 50 pounds are allowed. Dogs are allowed for a pet fee of $10.00 per pet per night.

Loews Lake Las Vegas Resort
101 Montelago Boulevard
Henderson, NV
702-567-6000
This upscale resort on the shores of Lake Mead offers all the luxuries. All well-behaved dogs of any size are welcome. This upscale hotel resort offers their "Loews Loves Pets" program which includes special pet treats, local dog walking routes, and a list of nearby pet-friendly places to visit. The hotel is about 30 minutes from the Las Vegas Strip. There is a $25 one time additional pet fee per room. To get to the hotel take I-215 east until it ends into Lake Mead Blvd and proceed 7 miles on Lake Mead Blvd. The hotel will be on the left and you can follow the signs.

Residence Inn Las Vegas Henderson/Green Valley
2190 Olympic Avenue
Henderson, NV
702-434-2700 (800-331-3131)
Some of the amenities at this all-suite inn include a convenient location to Las Vegas and Hoover Dam, a daily buffet breakfast, evening socials Monday through Thursday with light dinner fare, a heated swimming pool, and a complimentary grocery shopping service. Dogs are allowed for an additional one time pet fee of $100 per room. Multiple dogs may be allowed.

Best Value Inn
167 E. Tropicana Ave
Las Vegas, NV
702-795-3311
Besides offering a full line-up of on-site amenities, this inn also provides a convenient location to a number of the city's star attractions, entertainment and commerce areas, and world-class shopping and dining sites. There is a $25 one time pet fee per room. Multiple dogs may be allowed.

Best Western Main Street Inn
1000 N Main Street
Las Vegas, NV
702-382-3455 (800-780-7234)
Dogs of all sizes are allowed. Dogs are allowed for a nightly pet fee.

Best Western Nellis Motor Inn
5330 E Craig Road
Las Vegas, NV
702-643-6111 (800-780-7234)
Dogs of all sizes are allowed. Dogs are allowed for a pet fee of $10.00 per pet per stay.

Candlewood Suites Las Vegas
4034 Paradise Rd.
Las Vegas, NV
702-836-3660 (877-270-6405)
Dogs up to 80 pounds are allowed. Pets allowed with an additional pet fee. Up to $75 for 1-6 nights and up to $150 for 7+ nights. A pet agreement must be signed at check-in.

Extended Stay America Las Vegas - Boulder Highway
4240 Boulder Hwy.
Las Vegas, NV
702-433-1788 (800-804-3724)
One dog is allowed per suite. There is a $25 per night additional pet fee up to $150 for an entire stay.

Extended Stay America Las Vegas - Valley View
4270 S. Valley View Blvd.
Las Vegas, NV
702-221-7600 (800-804-3724)
One dog is allowed per suite. There is a $25 per night additional pet fee up to $150 for an entire stay.

Holiday Inn Express Las Vegas-Nellis
4035 North Nellis Blvd
Las Vegas, NV
702-644-5700 (877-270-6405)
Dogs of all sizes are allowed. Dogs are allowed for a pet fee.

Homestead Studio Suites Las Vegas - Midtown
3045 S. Maryland Pkwy.
Las Vegas, NV
702-369-1414 (800-804-3724)
One dog is allowed per suite. There is a $25 per night additional pet fee up to $150 for an entire stay.

Howard Johnson Inn Strip Las Vegas
1401 Las Vegas Blvd So.
Las Vegas, NV
702-388-0301 (800-446-4656)
Dogs of all sizes are allowed. Dogs are allowed for a pet fee of $30.00 per pet per night.

La Quinta Inn & Suites Las Vegas Summerlin Tech
7101 Cascade Valley Ct.
Las Vegas, NV
702-360-1200 (800-531-5900)
Dogs of all sizes are allowed. There are no additional pet fees. Dogs may not be left unattended, and they must be leashed and cleaned up after. Dogs are not allowed in the lounge, pool area, or the courtyard. Multiple dogs may be allowed.

La Quinta Inn & Suites Las Vegas West Lakes
9570 West Sahara
Las Vegas, NV
702-243-0356 (800-531-5900)
Dogs of all sizes are allowed. There are no additional pet fees. Dogs may not be left unattended, and they must be leashed and cleaned up after. 2 dogs may be allowed.

La Quinta Inn Las Vegas Nellis
4288 N Nellis Blvd.
Las Vegas, NV
702-632-0229 (800-531-5900)
Dogs of all sizes are allowed. There are no additional pet fees. Dogs must be crated if left alone in the room, and they must be leashed and cleaned up after. Multiple dogs may be allowed.

Motel 6 - Las Vegas Boulder Hwy
4125 Boulder Hwy
Las Vegas, NV
702-457-8051 (800-466-8356)
This motel welcomes your pets to stay with you.

Motel 6 - Las Vegas I-15
5085 Dean Martin Dr
Las Vegas, NV
702-739-6747 (800-466-8356)
This motel welcomes your pets to stay with you.

Motel 6 - Las Vegas Tropicana
195 Tropicana Ave
Las Vegas, NV
702-798-0728 (800-466-8356)
This motel welcomes your pets to stay with you.

Motel 6 - Las Vegas Downtown
707 Fremont Ave
Las Vegas, NV
702-388-1400 (800-466-8356)
This motel welcomes your pets to stay with you.

Plaza Hotel
230 Plaza
Las Vegas, NV
505-425-3591
Dogs of all sizes are allowed. There is a $10 per night per pet additional fee.

Residence Inn Las Vegas Convention Center
3225 Paradise Road
Las Vegas, NV
702-796-9300 (800-331-3131)
Although located just off The Strip and close to all this vibrant, 24 hour city has to offer; this all suite inn offers a place of quiet repose in their bungalow style guest quarters. Additionally, they offer a daily buffet breakfast and evening socials with light dinner fare. Dogs are allowed for an additional one time pet fee of $100 per room. 2 dogs may be allowed.

Residence Inn Las Vegas Hughes Center

370 Hughes Center Drive
Las Vegas, NV
702-650-0040 (800-331-3131)
Besides being located only 1 mile from the heart of the Strip and to all that this vibrant 24 hour town has to offer, this ENERGY STAR, all suite inn also provides a number of in-house amenities, including a daily buffet breakfast and evening socials. Dogs are allowed for an additional one time pet fee of $100 per room. Multiple dogs may be allowed.

Residence Inn Las Vegas South
5875 Dean Martin Drive
Las Vegas, NV
702-795-7378 (800-331-3131)
Close to the south end of town, this all suite inn gives a great location for exploring - The Strip - and the numerous sites of the area. Additionally, they offer a daily buffet breakfast and evening receptions. Dogs are allowed for an additional one time pet fee of $100 per room. Multiple dogs may be allowed.

Staybridge Suites Las Vegas
5735 Dean Martin Drive
Las Vegas, NV
702-259-2663 (877-270-6405)
Dogs up to 80 pounds are allowed. Pets allowed with an additional pet fee. Up to $75 for 1-6 nights and up to $150 for 7+ nights. A pet agreement must be signed at check-in.

Super 8 Las Vegas
4250 Koval Lane
Las Vegas, NV
702-794-0888 (800-800-8000)
Dogs of all sizes are allowed. Dogs are allowed for a nightly pet fee.

Pioneer Hotel and Gambling Hall
2200 S. Casino Drive
Laughlin, NV
702-298-2442 (800-634-3469)
This hotel allows dogs of all sizes. However, there are only ten pet rooms and these are all smoking rooms. There is a $100 cash refundable pet deposit required. We normally do not include smoking room only pet rooms but since the selection of pet friendly lodging in Laughlin is so limited we have listed this one. Multiple dogs may be allowed.

Riverside Casino Hotel
1650 S Casino Drive
Laughlin, NV
702-298-2535
Dogs up to 30 pounds are allowed

for an additional $8 per night per pet. Pet rooms are located on the 1st floor. There are some breed restrictions. 2 dogs may be allowed.

Best Western Mesquite Inn
390 N Sandhill Boulevard
Mesquite, NV
702-346-7444 (800-780-7234)
Dogs up to 50 pounds are allowed. Dogs are allowed for a nightly pet fee.

Virgin River Hotel and Casino
100 Pionner Blvd
Mesquite, NV
800-346-7721
Up to three dogs of all sizes are allowed at this hotel. There is a $10 one time pet fee per room. Dogs must be leashed and cleaned up after, and they may not be left unattended in the rooms unless crated. 2 dogs may be allowed.

Knights Inn Mill City
6000 East Frontage Rd.
Mill City, NV
775-538-7311 (800-843-5644)
Dogs are welcome at this hotel.

Best Western Minden Inn
1795 Ironwood Drive
Minden, NV
775-782-7766 (800-780-7234)
Dogs of all sizes are allowed. Dogs are allowed for a nightly pet fee.

Mount Charleston Lodge and Cabins
HCR 38 Box 325
Mount Charleston, NV
800-955-1314
mtcharlestonlodge.com/
The lodge sits at over 7,700 feet above sea level and about 35 miles from the Las Vegas Strip. There are several dog-friendly trails nearby for hikers. One dog under 25 pounds is allowed for an additional fee of $30 per night, and $50 per night for 2 dogs. The fee for 1 dog over 25 pounds is $50 per night, and $90 per night for 2 dogs over 25 pounds. 2 dogs may be allowed.

Comfort Inn North
910 E. Cheyenne Avenue
North Las Vegas, NV
702-399-1500 (877-424-6423)
Dogs of all sizes are allowed. Dogs are allowed for a pet fee of $10.00 per pet per night.

Best Western The North Shore Inn at Lake Mead
520 N Moapa Valley Boulevard
Overton, NV

Dog-Friendly Lodging - Please always call ahead to make sure an establishment is still dog-friendly.

702-397-6000 (800-780-7234)
Dogs of all sizes are allowed. Dogs
are allowed for a pet fee of $10.00
per pet per stay.

Overland Hotel
85 Main Street
Pioche, NV
775-962-5895
Well behaved dogs of all sizes are
allowed. There are no additional pet
fees. Dogs are not allowed to be left
alone in the room. 2 dogs may be
allowed.

Atlantis Casino Resort Spa
3800 S Virigina Street
Reno, NV
775-825-4700 (800-723-6500)
Dogs of all sizes are allowed in the
Motor Lodge section of this casino
hotel. There is a $25 one time fee
per pet. Dogs must be kept on leash
and cleaned up after. Please place
the Do Not Disturb sign on the door if
there is a pet alone in the room. 2
dogs may be allowed.

Baymont Inn And Suites Reno
2050 B Market Street
Reno, NV
775-786-2506 (877-229-6668)
Dogs are welcome at this hotel.

Best Western Airport Plaza Hotel
1981 Terminal Way
Reno, NV
775-348-6370 (800-780-7234)
Dogs of all sizes are allowed. Dogs
are allowed for a nightly pet fee.

Days Inn Reno
701 East 7th St.
Reno, NV
775-786-4070 (800-329-7466)
Dogs of all sizes are allowed. Dogs
are allowed for a pet fee.

Extended Stay America Reno -
South Meadows
9795 Gateway Dr.
Reno, NV
775-852-5611 (800-804-3724)
One dog is allowed per suite. There
is a $25 per night additional pet fee
up to $150 for an entire stay.

Grand Sierra Resort
2500 E Second Street
Reno, NV
775-789-2000 (800-501-2651)
World class entertainment, fine
wining and dining, family friendly
recreation, a spectacular location
nestled below the snow-capped
mountains of the Sierra Nevada, and
luxury accommodations are just

some of the offerings of this premier
resort and casino destination. Dogs
are allowed for an additional pet fee
of $30 per night per room. 2 dogs
may be allowed.

Holiday Inn Express Hotel & Suites
Reno Airport
2375 Market Street
Reno, NV
775-229-7070 (877-270-6405)
Dogs of all sizes are allowed. Dogs
are allowed for a pet fee of $20.00
per pet per night.

Knights Inn Reno
660 N Virginia St
Reno, NV
775-786-4032 (800-843-5644)
Dogs are welcome at this hotel.
There is a $10 per night additional
pet fee per pet.

La Quinta Inn Reno
4001 Market
Reno, NV
775-348-6100 (800-531-5900)
Dogs of all sizes are allowed. There
are no additional pet fees. Dogs
must be leashed, cleaned up after,
and crated or removed for
housekeeping. Multiple dogs may
be allowed.

Motel 6 - Reno Livestock Events
Center
866 Wells Ave
Reno, NV
775-786-9852 (800-466-8356)
This motel welcomes your pets to
stay with you.

Motel 6 - Reno Virginia Plumb
1901 Virginia St
Reno, NV
775-827-0255 (800-466-8356)
This motel welcomes your pets to
stay with you.

Motel 6 - Reno West
1400 Stardust St
Reno, NV
775-747-7390 (800-466-8356)
This motel welcomes your pets to
stay with you.

Ramada Hotel And Casino Reno
1000 E 6th St
Reno, NV
775-786-5151 (800-272-6232)
Dogs of all sizes are allowed. Dogs
are allowed for a pet fee of $10.00
per pet per stay.

Residence Inn Reno
9845 Gateway Drive
Reno, NV

775-853-8800 (800-331-3131)
This all suite inn sits only 20 minutes
from all the action of downtown Reno
and only 40 minutes to beautiful
Lake Tahoe - offering business and
leisure travelers a plethora of
destinations and activities to explore.
Additionally, they offer a daily buffet
breakfast, a social hour Monday to
Wednesday, and a weekly barbecue.
Dogs are allowed for an additional
one time pet fee of $100 plus tax per
room. There may be 1 dog up to 75
pounds, or up to 3 dogs that do not
total over 75 pounds per room.

Staybridge Suites Reno Nevada
10559 Professional Circle
Reno, NV
775-657-8999 (877-270-6405)
Dogs up to 80 pounds are allowed.
Pets allowed with an additional pet
fee. Up to $75 for 1-6 nights and up
to $150 for 7+ nights. A pet
agreement must be signed at check-
in.

Super 8 /University Area Reno
1651 North Virginia St
Reno, NV
775-329-3464 (800-800-8000)
Dogs are welcome at this hotel.

Vagabond Inn
3131 S. Virginia St.
Reno, NV
775-825-7134 (800-522-1555)
vagabondinn.com
This motel is located less than a
couple miles from the downtown
casinos and the Convention Center.
Amenities include a swimming pool,
24 hour cable television, air
conditioning, and more. There is a
$10 per day per pet fee. 2 dogs may
be allowed.

Holiday Inn Reno-Sparks
55 East Nugget Avenue
Sparks, NV
017-753-5869 (877-270-6405)
Dogs of all sizes are allowed. Dogs
are allowed for a nightly pet fee.

Motel 6 - Reno Airport Sparks
2405 Victorian Ave
Sparks, NV
775-358-1080 (800-466-8356)
This motel welcomes your pets to
stay with you.

Super 8 /Reno Area Sparks
1900 East Greg Street
Sparks, NV
775-358-8884 (800-800-8000)
Dogs of all sizes are allowed. Dogs
are allowed for a pet fee of $10 per

pet per night.

Best Western Hi-Desert Inn
320 Main Street Highways 6 & 95
Tonopah, NV
775-482-3511 (800-780-7234)
Dogs are welcome at this hotel.

Ramada Station Tonopah
1137 S Main Street
Tonopah, NV
775-482-9777 (800-272-6232)
Dogs are welcome at this hotel.

Motel 6 - Wells
1561 6th Street
Wells, NV
775-752-2116 (800-466-8356)
This motel welcomes your pets to
stay with you.

Super 8 Wells
Box 302
Wells, NV
775-752-3384 (800-800-8000)
Dogs of all sizes are allowed. Dogs
are allowed for a pet fee of $10.00
per pet per night.

Best Western Gold Country Inn
921 W Winnemucca Boulevard
Winnemucca, NV
775-623-6999 (800-780-7234)
Dogs of all sizes are allowed. Dogs
are allowed for a pet fee of $10.00
per pet per stay.

Days Inn Winnemucca
511 W. Winnemucca Blvd
Winnemucca, NV
775-623-3661 (800-329-7466)
Dogs are welcome at this hotel.

Holiday Inn Express Winnemucca
1987 W. Winnemucca Blvd.
Winnemucca, NV
775-625-3100 (877-270-6405)
Dogs of all sizes are allowed. Dogs
are allowed for a pet fee of $20.00
per pet per night.

Motel 6 - Winnemucca
1800 Winnemucca Blvd
Winnemucca, NV
775-623-1180 (800-466-8356)
This motel welcomes your pets to
stay with you.

Santa Fe Motel
1620 W. Winnemucca Blvd
Winnemucca, NV
775-623-1119
There are no additional pet fees.
Multiple dogs may be allowed.

Super 8 NV Winnemucca
1157 West Winnemucca Blvd

Winnemucca, NV
775-625-1818 (800-800-8000)
Dogs are welcome at this hotel.

Winnemucca Inn
741 W Winnemucca
Winnemucca, NV
775-623-2565
winnemuccainn.com/
Dogs of all sizes are allowed. There
is no fee with a credit card on file
and there is a pet policy to sign at
check in. Dogs are not allowed to
be left alone in the room. Multiple
dogs may be allowed.

New Hampshire

Comfort Inn
53 West St.
Ashland, NH
603-968-7668 (877-424-6423)
Dogs of all sizes are allowed. Dogs
are allowed for a pet fee of $20.00
per pet per night. Two dogs are
allowed per room.

The Glynn House Inn
59 Highland Street
Ashland, NH
603-968-3775 (866-686-4362)
glynnhouse.com
Pets are allowed in four of the
deluxe suites. These have direct
access from the room to the
gardens. There is a $30 pet fee per
visit per dog. There is a $250 fully
refundable damage deposit and
pets may not be left alone in the
room.

Villager Motel
I 93N at H 3
Bartlett, NH
603-374-2742
There is an $15 per night per pet
fee and a pet policy to sign at check
in. Dogs are not allowed to be left
alone in the room, and must be kept
on a leash.

Quality Inn Manchester Airport
121 South River Rd.
Bedford, NH
603-622-3766 (877-424-6423)
Dogs of all sizes are allowed. Dogs
are allowed for a pet fee of $25.00
per pet per stay.

Mountain Lake Inn
2871 Route 114
Bradford, NH
603-938-2136 (800-662-6005)
mountainlakeinn.com/
This 1760 dwelling sits on 168
acres along the shores of Lake

Massasecum and offers 9 guest
rooms with private baths, walking
trails, and a private beach equipped
with a canoe and rowboat. Dogs of
all sizes are welcome for an
additional $25 one time pet fee per
room. Dogs must be well behaved,
leashed (at times), and cleaned up
after. Dogs must be friendly and very
well mannered with children and the
other pets in residence. 2 dogs may
be allowed.

Bretton Arms Country Inn
Route 302
Bretton Woods, NH
603-278-3000 (800-258-0330)
This inn is located less than a five
minute walk from the Mount
Washington Hotel. Well-behaved
dogs of any size are allowed for an
extra $30 per dog per day pet fee, up
to two dogs per room. During the
winter the nordic center at the Mount
Washington Hotel allows dogs on a
special 8km cross-country ski trail.
Dogs need to be leashed on the
property and on the trail.

Days Inn Campton
1513 Daniel Webster Hwy
Campton, NH
603-536-3520 (800-329-7466)
Dogs are welcome at this hotel.

Lazy Dog Inn
201 White Mountain H/H 16
Chocorua Village, NH
603-323-8350 (888-323-8350)
lazydoginn.com/
This 160 year old New England
farmhouse really is a dog friendly
place (even the rooms have doggie
themed names), and there are plenty
of picturesque walking trails close by
too. Included in the rates is a fenced
in "Doggie Play Area" with agility
equipment and a climate controlled
Doggie Lodge providing doggie
daycare. They also offer a
bottomless treat jar for their canine
guests and a like jar of cookies for
their owners. Dogs must be at least
12 weeks old, and there are no
additional pet fees for one dog.
There may be an additional fee of
$25 per night per pet for 2 pets or
more depending on length of stay.
Dogs must be friendly and well
mannered with humans and the other
pets in residence. Dogs must be
leashed and cleaned up after.
Multiple dogs may be allowed.

Claremont Motor Lodge
Beauregard St, near SR 103
Claremont, NH
603-542-2540

One dog is allowed for an additional pet fee of $15 per night.

Rodeway Inn
24 Sullivan Street
Claremont, NH
603-542-9567 (877-424-6423)
Dogs up to 50 pounds are allowed. Dogs are allowed for a pet fee of $15.00 per pet per night. Two dogs are allowed per room.

Northern Comfort Motel
RR 1, Box 520
Colebrook, NH
603-237-4440
There is a $5.00 per day per pet charge. Multiple dogs may be allowed.

Best Western Concord Inn & Suites
97 Hall Street
Concord, NH
603-228-4300 (800-780-7234)
Dogs are welcome at this hotel.

Comfort Inn
71 Hall St.
Concord, NH
603-226-4100 (877-424-6423)
Dogs of all sizes are allowed. Dogs are allowed for a pet fee of $15.00 per pet per night.

Foothills Farm
P. O. Box 1368
Conway, NH
207-935-3799
foothillsfarmbedandbreakfast.com
This restored 1820 farmhouse and guest cottage sits on 50 acres of fields, forests, and streams, has close proximity to several other recreational activities and tax free shopping, and much of the food served here comes straight from their on-site organic garden. Dogs of all sizes are allowed for an additional $15 per night per pet. Dogs are usually preferred in the 2-bedroom cottage, but sometimes there may be availability in the main house. Dogs must be leashed and cleaned up after, and crated when left alone in the room. 2 dogs may be allowed.

Tanglewood Motel and Cottages
1681 H 16
Conway, NH
603-447-5932 (866-TANGLEWOOD (826-4539))
tanglewoodmotel.com/
This family recreational destination sits alongside a beautiful mountain stream and offers guests a variety of activity areas, 2 central picnic spots with barbecues, and plenty of hiking

trails are close by. Dogs are welcome in the cottages for an additional fee of $10 per night per pet. Dogs must be friendly, well mannered, and leashed and cleaned up after at all times. 2 dogs may be allowed.

Comfort Inn & Suites
10 Hotel Dr.
Dover, NH
603-750-7507 (877-424-6423)
Dogs of all sizes are allowed. Dogs are allowed for a pet fee of $35.00 per pet per night.

Days Inn Durham Downtown Dover
481 Central Avenue
Dover, NH
603-742-0400 (800-329-7466)
Dogs of all sizes are allowed. Dogs are allowed for a pet fee.

Hickory Pond Inn & Golf Course
1 Stagecoach Rd
Durham, NH
603-659-2227
There are several designated pet rooms. All rooms are non-smoking. There is a $10 one time pet fee.

Holiday Inn Express Durham - Unh
2 Main Street
Durham, NH
603-868-1234 (877-270-6405)
Dogs of all sizes are allowed. Dogs are allowed for a pet fee of $50.00 per pet per stay.

Paradise Point Cottages
Paradise Point Road
Errol, NH
603-482-3834
Dogs of all sizes are allowed. There is a pet policy to sign at check in and there are no additional pet fees. 2 dogs may be allowed.

The Inn at Crotched Mountain
534 Mountain Road
Francestown, NH
603-588-6840
This 180 year-old colonial house on 65 acres, once a stop for the Underground Railroad, has an amazing view of the Piscatagoug Valley, several hiking or winter skiing trails, food and flower gardens, an 18 hole golf course, an outdoor pool, and more. Dogs of all sizes are welcome for an additional $5 per night per pet. Dogs must be leashed, cleaned up after, and crated when left alone in the room. This inn closes for the first 3 weeks each April. Multiple dogs may be allowed.

Best Western White Mountain Resort
87 Wallace Hill Road
Franconia, NH
603-823-7422 (800-780-7234)
Dogs are welcome at this hotel.

Franconia Notch Vacations
Call or email to Arrange.
Franconia, NH
800-247-5536
franconiares.com/
Vacation rentals in Franconia and the surrounding White Mountains. Some dog-friendly rentals are available.

Horse & Hound
205 Wells Rd
Franconia, NH
603-823-5501 (800-450-5501)
Dogs are allowed for an additional $15 per day per pet. 2 dogs may be allowed.

Lovetts Inn by Lafayette Brook
SR 18
Franconia, NH
603-823-7761
There are two pet rooms, both non-smoking. There is a $25 one time additional pet fee. 2 dogs may be allowed.

Westwind Vacation Cottages
1614 Profile Road
Franconia, NH
603-823-5532
Dogs of all sizes are allowed. There is a pet policy to sign at check in and there are no additional pet fees. 2 dogs may be allowed.

Top Notch Inn
265 Main Street
Gorham, NH
603-466-5496
Dogs only are allowed and up to 50 pounds. There is a pet policy to sign at check in and there are no additional pet fees. The dogs must stay off the beds and furniture and can not have baths in the bath tub. Dogs are not allowed to be left alone in the room.

Town & Country Motor Inn
US 2
Gorham, NH
603-466-3315
townandcountryinn.com/map.html
Dogs are allowed for an additional fee of $6 per night per pet. 2 dogs may be allowed.

Best Western The Inn at Hampton
815 Lafayette Road

Hampton, NH
603-926-6771 (800-780-7234)
Dogs up to 50 pounds are allowed.
Dogs are allowed for a pet fee of
$30.00 per pet per stay.

Chieftain Motor Inn
84 Lyme Road
Hanover, NH
603-643-2550
chieftaininn.com/
Nestled along the banks of the
Connecticut River, this scenic inn
also offers an outdoor heated pool,
complimentary canoes, barbecue
areas, a gazebo, and a variety of
land and water recreation. Dogs of
all sizes are allowed for an additional
fee of $35 per night per pet. Dogs
must be quiet, well behaved,
leashed, and cleaned up after. Dogs
may only be left alone in the room if
the owner is confident in their
behavior. 2 dogs may be allowed.

Yankee Trail Motel
US 3
Holderness, NH
603-968-3535 (800-972-1492)
There are no additional pet fees.

Swiss Chalets Village Inn
Old Route 16A
Intervale, NH
603-356-2232 (800-831-2727)
swisschaletsvillage.com
Swiss Chalets Village Inn offers
comfortable lodgings, some with
fireplace Jacuzzi suites, plenty of
indoor and outdoor activities, and a
bit of Swiss charm right in the midst
of New Hampshire's White
Mountains. Pets are welcome.

Dana Place Inn
SR 16
Jackson, NH
603-383-6822 (800-537-9276)
danaplace.com/
One or 2 dogs are allowed
depending on their size. There is a
$25 per night per pet additional fee.
Dogs must be quiet and friendly. 2
dogs may be allowed.

The Village House
PO Box 359 Rt 16A
Jackson, NH
603-383-6666 (800-972-8343)
yellowsnowdoggear.com/
This bed and breakfast's rooms are
located in a 100 year old barn behind
the main house that houses the
Yellow Snow Dog Gear collar and
lead business. Rooms have
kitchenettes, balconies, Jacuzzi tubs,
and are decorated in the style of a
B&B. There are 15 guest rooms and

13 have private baths. They
welcome all well-behaved dogs and
there are no size restrictions. Rates
range from $65-140 depending on
the season. There is a $10 per day
pet fee.

Wildcat Inn & Tavern
H 16A/Village Road
Jackson Village, NH
603-356-8700 (800-637-0087)
wildcattavern.com/
Located in the heart of the White
Mountains, this inn and tavern
features a variety of comfortable
accommodations, a central location
to many of the areas best activities,
and an eatery and tavern on site
that offers various weekend
entertainment, Tuesday's 'Hoot
Night', and dancing in addition to a
full menu. Dogs are allowed at the
inn for an additional one time $30
pet fee per room. Dogs are also
allowed at the outside dining area of
the eatery. 2 dogs may be allowed.

Applebrook
110 Meadows Road/H 115A
Jefferson, NH
603-586-7713 (800-545-6504)
applebrook.com/
This large Victorian farmhouse is
only about a minutes drive away
from Santa's Village, which is also
open year round. Dogs of all sizes
are allowed for a one time
additional pet fee of $25 per pet of
which 50% is donated to the local
humane society. Dogs may only be
left alone in the room for short
periods and they must be crated.
Dogs must be under their owner's
control at all times, and please
clean up after your pet. 2 dogs may
be allowed.

Best Western Sovereign Hotel
401 Winchester Street
Keene, NH
603-357-3038 (800-780-7234)
Dogs of all sizes are allowed. Dogs
are allowed for a pet fee.

Holiday Inn Express Keene
175 Key Road
Keene, NH
603-352-7616 (877-270-6405)
Dogs up to 50 pounds are allowed.
Dogs are allowed for a pet fee of
$25.00 per pet per night.

Super 8 Keene
3 Ashbrook Road
Keene, NH
603-352-9780 (800-800-8000)
Dogs of all sizes are allowed. Dogs
are allowed for a pet fee.

The Lake Opechee Inn and Spa
62 Doris Ray Court
Laconia, NH
603-524-0111 (877-300-5253)
opecheeinn.com/
This peaceful retreat, on the shores
of Lake Opechee, is an historic
renovated mill building offering 34
luxury rooms, a steak and seafood
restaurant, a conference center, and
a full service spa. Dogs of all sizes
are allowed for an additional fee of
$20 per night per pet. Dogs must be
quiet, leashed and cleaned up after,
and crated when left alone in the
room. 2 dogs may be allowed.

Residence Inn Hanover Lebanon
32 Centerra Parkway
Lebanon, NH
603-643-4511 (800-331-3131)
Offering a convenient location to
Dartmouth College and the
Hitchcock Medical Center as well as
various business, shopping, dining,
and entertainment areas, this all
suite hotel also offers a number of in-
house amenities, including a daily
buffet breakfast and evening socials
Monday through Thursday. Dogs are
allowed for an additional one time
pet fee of $100 per room. Multiple
dogs may be allowed.

Comfort Inn & Suites
21 Railroad St.
Lincoln, NH
603-745-6700 (877-424-6423)
Dogs of all sizes are allowed. Dogs
are allowed for a pet fee of $15.00
per pet per night. Two dogs are
allowed per room.

Econo Lodge Inn & Suites
381 U.S. Route 3
Lincoln, NH
603-745-3661 (877-424-6423)
Dogs of all sizes are allowed. Dogs
are allowed for a pet fee of $15.00
per pet per night.

The Beal House Inn
2 W Main Street
Littleton, NH
603-444-2661 (888-616-BEAL
(2325))
bealhouseinn.com/
Offering fine dining, lodging, and a
full bar specializing in martinis (over
250), this inn holds special events
throughout the year, and they are
central to numerous year round
activities and recreation. Dogs of all
sizes are welcome for an additional
$25 to $35 per night per pet
depending on the room/suite, and
there may be a $150 refundable

deposit. One of the suites has a fenced private yard. Dogs must be leashed, cleaned up after, and they must be crated when left alone in the room. 2 dogs may be allowed.

Red Roof Loudon
2 Staniels Rd
Loudon, NH
603-225-8399 (800-RED-ROOF)
One well-behaved family pet per room. Guest must notify front desk upon arrival. Guest is liable for any damages. In consideration of all guests, pets must never be left unattended in the guest rooms.

Dowds County Inn
On the Common, Box 58
Lyme, NH
603-795-4712 (800-482-4712)
dowdscountryinn.com/
This country inn sits on 6 landscaped acres to explore with a natural duck pond, flower gardens, a water fountain, and historic stonework and buildings. Dogs of all sizes are welcome for an additional $10 per night per pet with a credit card on file. Dogs must be well behaved, leashed, and cleaned up after. 2 dogs may be allowed.

Loch Lyme Lodge
70 Orford Road
Lyme, NH
603-795-2141
Dog of all sizes are allowed. There are no additional pet fees, however you must have up to date vaccination information on your dog(s).

Clarion Hotel Business District
21 Front Street
Manchester, NH
603-669-2660 (877-424-6423)
Dogs up to 50 pounds are allowed. Dogs are allowed for a pet fee of $50.00 per pet per stay. Two dogs are allowed per room.

Comfort Inn Airport
298 Queen City Avenue
Manchester, NH
603-668-2600 (877-424-6423)
Dogs up to 60 pounds are allowed. Dogs are allowed for a pet fee of $50.00 per pet per stay. Two dogs are allowed per room.

Econo Lodge
75 W. Hancock St.
Manchester, NH
603-624-0111 (877-424-6423)
Dogs of all sizes are allowed. Dogs are allowed for a pet fee of $10.00 per pet per night.

Holiday Inn Express Hotel & Suites Manchester-Airport
1298 South Porter St
Manchester, NH
603-669-6800 (877-270-6405)
Dogs are welcome at this hotel.

TownePlace Suites Manchester-Boston Regional Airport
686 Huse Road
Manchester, NH
603-641-2288 (800-257-3000)
Besides offering a number of in-house amenities for all level of travelers, this all suite inn also offers a convenient location to historic, business, shopping, dining, entertainment, and recreation areas. Dogs are allowed for an additional one time fee of $100 per room. Dogs must be crated when left alone in the room. Multiple dogs may be allowed.

Residence Inn Nashua Merrimack
246 Daniel Webster H
Merrimack, NH
603-424-8100 (800-331-3131)
Besides offering a convenient location to beaches, shopping, dining, commerce, and entertainment areas, this all suite inn also offers a number of in-house amenities, including a daily buffet breakfast and evening socials. Dogs are allowed in the studio and townhouse suites for an additional one time pet fee of $75 per room. 2 dogs may be allowed.

Best Western Sunapee Lake Lodge
1403 Route 103
Mount Sunapee, NH
603-763-2010 (800-780-7234)
Dogs of all sizes are allowed. Dogs are allowed for a pet fee of $10 per pet per night.

Best Western Granite Inn
10 Saint Laurent Street
Nashua, NH
603-883-7700 (800-780-7234)
Dogs of all sizes are allowed. Dogs are allowed for a pet fee of $25 per pet per stay.

Extended Stay America Boston Nashua
2000 Southwood Dr.
Nashua, NH
603-577-9900 (800-804-3724)
One dog is allowed per suite. There is a $25 per night additional pet fee up to $150 for an entire stay.

Motel 6 - Nashua

Progress Avenue
Nashua, NH
603-889-4151 (800-466-8356)
This motel welcomes your pets to stay with you.

Red Roof Inn Nashua
77 Spitbrook Road
Nashua, NH
603-888-1893 (800-RED-ROOF)
One well-behaved family pet per room. Guest must notify front desk upon arrival. Guest is liable for any damages. In consideration of all guests, pets must never be left unattended in the guest rooms.

Sunapee Harbor Cottages (Lake Station Realty
1066 H 103
Newbury, NH
603-763-3033 (800-639-9960)
cottagesrus.com/
This multi-listing company has about a dozen of their vacation rentals in the Lake Sunapee area that allow pets and the prices and policies vary per rental. Dogs must be under their owner's control at all times, and they may not be left unattended in the rentals.

Adventure Suites
3440 White Mountain H/H16
North Conway, NH
603 356 9744 (800-N CONWAY (606-6929))
adventuresuites.com/
This inn with various themed rooms offers 16 suites with a variety of adventures from a tree house setting to a unique 2 story cave dwelling, from the penthouse to the jungle, and more, and each suite has a Jacuzzi. Dogs of all sizes are welcome for an additional $10 per night per pet, and when you reserve ahead of time there is a special treat waiting in the room for them. Dogs must be at least 1 year old, quiet, and very well behaved as there are other animals on site. Dogs must be leashed and cleaned up after at all times, and dog depots are provided. Dogs may not be left alone in the room at any time. 2 dogs may be allowed.

Best Western Red Jacket Mountain View Resort & Conf. Ctr.
Route 16
North Conway, NH
603-356-5411 (800-780-7234)
Dogs are welcome at this hotel.

Spruce Moose Lodge and Cottages
207 Seavey Street
North Conway, NH

603-356-6239 (800-600-6239)
sprucemooselodge.com/
This inn, located in the scenic Mount Washington Valley, offers both lodge and cottage accommodations and they are only a short 5 minute walk to the village. Dogs of all sizes are welcome in the cottages and in one of the lodge rooms (breakfast is not included for cottage stays) for an additional pet fee of $10 per night per pet and there may be a $100 cash refundable security deposit required. Dogs must be quiet, well behaved, leashed, and cleaned up after. Dogs may not be left alone in the lodge guest room at any time, but they may be left for a short time in the cottages if the owner is confident in the pet's behavior. 2 dogs may be allowed.

The Glen
77 The Glen Rd
Pittsburg, NH
603-538-6500
Pets are allowed in the cottages only. There are no pet fees. There are no designated smoking or non-smoking cottages. Multiple dogs may be allowed.

Plymouth Red Roof Inn & Suites
304 Main Street
Plymouth, NH
603-536-2330 (800-RED-ROOF)
One well-behaved family pet per room. Guest must notify front desk upon arrival. Guest is liable for any damages. In consideration of all guests, pets must never be left unattended in the guest rooms.

The Common Man Inn
231 Main Street
Plymouth, NH
603-536-2200 (866-THE.C.MAN (843-2626)
thecmaninn.com/
This inn is also home to the Foster's Boiler Room Lounge offering a pub-style menu and unique creations, a full service spa with many amenities including a heated waterfall Jacuzzi, and a great location to several other attractions in the area. Dogs of all sizes are welcome for no additional pet fee. Your pooch is greeted with a personalized treat with food bowls, and pet friendly rooms also provide cushy pet beds. Dogs must be leashed, cleaned up after, and crated if left alone in the room. They also provide a designated pet walking area, and a separate pet entrance. 2 dogs may be allowed.

Meadowbrook Inn

Portsmouth Traffic Circle
Portsmouth, NH
603-436-2700 (800-370-2727)
meadowbrookinn.com/
This inn offers a convenient location for exploring the seacoast and taking advantage of the tax-free shopping. Dogs of all sizes are allowed for an additional $10 per night per pet. Dogs must be leashed, cleaned up after, and they may only be left alone in the room if they will be quiet and well behaved. Dobermans and Rottweilers are not allowed. 2 dogs may be allowed.

Motel 6 - Portsmouth, Nh
Gosling Road
Portsmouth, NH
603-334-6606 (800-466-8356)
This motel welcomes your pets to stay with you.

Residence Inn Portsmouth
1 International Drive
Portsmouth, NH
603-436-8880 (877-389-0361)
Some of the benefits of this all-suite inn include easy access to the beaches and mountains, a daily buffet breakfast, evening socials, a Sport Court, an indoor pool, and a complimentary grocery shopping service. Dogs are allowed for an additional one time pet fee of $75 per room. Multiple dogs may be allowed.

Sheraton Portsmouth Harborside Hotel
250 Market St.
Portsmouth, NH
603-431-2300 (888-625-5144)
Dogs up to 80 pounds are allowed. There are no additional pet fees. Dogs are not allowed to be left alone in the room.

Anchorage Inn
80 Main St
Rochester, NH
603-332-3350
There is a $15 per day per pet additional pet fee. 2 dogs may be allowed.

Holiday Inn Express Hotel & Suites Rochester
77 Farmington Road
Rochester, NH
603-994-1175 (877-270-6405)
Dogs of all sizes are allowed. Dogs are allowed for a pet fee of $50.00 per pet per night.

Red Roof Inn Salem
15 Red Roof Lane

Salem, NH
603-898-6422 (800-RED-ROOF)
One well-behaved family pet per room. Guest must notify front desk upon arrival. Guest is liable for any damages. In consideration of all guests, pets must never be left unattended in the guest rooms.

The Hilltop Inn
9 Norton Lane
Sugar Hill, NH
603-823-5695 (800-770-5695)
hilltopinn.com/
This 1895 traditional country inn sits on 50 acres in the White Mountains with an impressive array of relaxing and recreational pursuits. There are 20 acres of un-groomed cross-country skiing here and your pooch is welcome to join you on them. They also have a large fenced in yard for pets to run free. Dogs of all sizes are welcome for an additional pet fee of $10 per night per room. They ask that you clean up after your pet if they do their business on the lawns, but it's not necessary in the fields. Dogs must be well behaved and friendly towards the other pets in residence. Dogs only need to be on lead around the house or when felt necessary by the owner, and they may only be left alone in the room if they will be quiet and the front desk is informed. 2 dogs may be allowed.

Tamworth Inn
Tamworth Village
Tamworth, NH
603-323-7721 (800-642-7352)
tamworth.com/
Offering 16 rooms and suites all with a private bath, this simple but elegant lodge offers a full country breakfast, an authentic New England Pub, and they are central to various other activities and recreation. Dogs of all sizes are allowed for an additional $15 per night per pet on a space available basis. Dogs must be quiet and well mannered, and they are welcome throughout the inn and grounds, just not in the dining room or breakfast areas. Dogs must be leashed and cleaned up after, and they may only be left alone in the room if they are crated and the owners are on the property. 2 dogs may be allowed.

Anchorage at the Lake - NH Cabin & Cottage Rentals
725 Laconia Road
Tilton, NH
603-524-3248 (800-943-6093)
anchorageatthelake.com
These cabin rentals on 35 acres are

great for you and your dog.

Rodeway Inn
788 Laconia Rd
Tilton, NH
603-524-6897 (877-424-6423)
Dogs up to 65 pounds are allowed.
Two dogs are allowed per room.

The Inn at East Hill Farm
460 Monadnock Street
Troy, NH
603-588-6495 (800-242-6495)
east-hill-farm.com/
Whether it is a winter family farm
day, a special Caribbean
night/dinner, or a special getaway,
this inn offers year round events for
just about any and every occasion,
and there also have indoor/outdoor
pools, a winter indoor skating rink,
paddle or row boating, and cross-
country ski trails. Dogs of all sizes
are allowed for an additional $10 per
night per pet. Dogs must be quiet
and well behaved, and they are not
allowed in the dining or public rooms.
Dogs must be leashed and cleaned
up after at all times. 2 dogs may be
allowed.

Johnson Motel and Cottages
364 H 3
Twin Mountain, NH
888-244-5561 (888-244-5561)
johnsonsmotel.com/
Located in the White Mountains
where there is year round activities,
this motel also include a picnic,
playground, and campfire area, in
addition to a nature trail leading to a
pond frequented by numerous birds
and wildlife. They also have direct
trail access for skiers and
snowmobilers. Dogs of all sizes are
allowed for an additional fee of $10
per night per pet, and special treats
are provided for their four-legged
guests. Aggressive dogs are not
allowed, and barkers must stay with
their owners at all times. They must
be friendly to humans and to the
other 2 dogs on site. Dogs must be
well behaved, leashed, and cleaned
up after. Dogs may only be left alone
in the room if the owner is confident
in the pet's behavior. 2 dogs may be
allowed.

Victorian Cottage
#30 Veterans Ave
Weirs Beach, NH
603-279-4583
mailto:captstus@verizon.net
Remodeled antique home located at
Weirs Beach, NH. Spectacular view
of Lake Winnipesaukee and
surrounding mountains from the

house and porch. 3
bedrooms/sleeps 6. Pets are
welcome to join you.

Chesterfield Inn
20 Cross Road
West Chesterfield, NH
603-256-3211 (800-365-5515)
chesterfieldinn.com
Dogs of all sizes are allowed - there
is even a special pet package.
There are no additional pet fees.

Baymont Inn & Suites West
Lebanon
45 Airport Road
West Lebanon, NH
603-298-8888 (877-229-6668)
Dogs are welcome at this hotel.

Fireside Inn and Suites
25 Airport Road
West Lebanon, NH
877-258-5900 (877-258-5900)
afiresideinn.com/
This inn, nestled in the beauty of
the River Valley amid numerous
educational, cultural, and
recreational opportunities, features
a garden court atrium, an indoor
heated pool and hot tub, and a full
breakfast buffet. Dogs must be well
behaved, leashed, and cleaned up
after. Dogs may not be left alone in
the room, and they must be under
their owner's control at all times. 2
dogs may be allowed.

All Seasons Motel
36 Smith St
Woodsville, NH
603-747-2157 (800-660-0644)
quikpage.com/A/allseamotel/
There is a $5 per day per pet fee.
Dogs may not be left alone in the
rooms. 2 dogs may be allowed.

New Jersey

Sheraton Atlantic City Convention
Center Hotel
Two Miss America Parkway
Atlantic City, NJ
609-344-3535 (888-625-5144)
Dogs up to 80 pounds are allowed
at this resort hotel in Atlantic City.
There are no additional pet fees.
Dogs are not allowed to be left
alone in the room.

Ramada Atlantic City West
8037 Black Horse Pike
Atlantic City West, NJ
609-646-5220 (800-272-6232)
Dogs of all sizes are allowed. Dogs
are allowed for a pet fee.

Avon Manor Inn
109 Sylvania Avenue
Avon-by-the-Sea, NJ
732-776-7770
avonmanor.com
Complete remodeled and updated,
this inn features indoor or outdoor
dining, many extras around the
property, is only 2 miles from Spring
Lake, and sits only 1 block from the
beach and boardwalk. Dogs of all
sizes are allowed in the cottages for
no additional fee. Dogs must be
quiet, well behaved, leashed,
cleaned up after, and may be left
alone in the room only if the owner is
confident in the dogs behavior. 2
dogs may be allowed.

Inn at Somerset Hills
80 Allen Road
Basking Ridge, NJ
908-580-1300 (800-688-0700)
shh.com
Located only 30 minutes from an
international airport with plenty of
recreational opportunities available,
this inn is convenient for the
business or leisure traveler. Dogs of
all sizes are allowed for an additional
pet fee of $25 per night per room.
Dogs must be leashed, cleaned up
after, and crated when left alone in
the room. Multiple dogs may be
allowed.

Engleside Inn
30 Engleside Avenue
Beach Haven, NJ
609-492-1251 (800-762-2214)
This is a nice place to go with your
pet in the off season. They are right
on the beach, have 3 in-house
restaurants, and are only minutes
from many attractions, activities, and
recreation. Dogs of all sizes are
allowed from September 10th to May
4th only (their off-season) for an
additional fee of $10 per night per
pet. Dogs must be leashed, cleaned
up after, and they may only be left
alone in the room for short periods if
they will be quiet, comfortable, and
well behaved. Multiple dogs may be
allowed.

The Sea Shell Motel, Restaurant &
Beach Club
10 S. Atlantic Ave.
Beach Haven, NJ
609-492-4611
seashellclub.com/
This premier ocean front retreat
offers 2 eateries, a pool, and live
entertainment as they are home to 2
party hotspots; the Beach Club and
Tiki Bar. This resort opens about the

1st of April and dogs are allowed up until June 21st, and then they are not allowed again until after Labor Day. Dogs of all sizes are allowed for an additional fee of $10 per night per pet. Dogs must be leashed and cleaned up after. Multiple dogs may be allowed.

Howard Johnson Express Inn - Blackwood
832 N Black Horse Pk
Blackwood, NJ
856-228-4040 (800-446-4656)
Dogs of all sizes are allowed for a pet fee of $10 per pet per night.

Candlewood Suites Bordentown-Trenton
200 Rising Sun Road
Bordentown, NJ
609-291-1010 (877-270-6405)
Dogs up to 80 pounds are allowed. Pets allowed with an additional pet fee. Up to $75 for 1-6 nights and up to $150 for 7+ nights. A pet agreement must be signed at check-in.

Somerset Hills Hotel
200 Liberty Corner Road
Bridgewater, NJ
908-647-6700 (800-688-0700)
shh.com
This premier boutique hotel is reminiscent of the hotels of Europe, and they feature indoor and outdoor dining areas, room service, an outdoor pool, live entertainment on the weekends, and much more. Dogs of all sizes are allowed for an additional fee of $25 per night per pet. Dogs may not be left unattended in the room at any time, and they must be leashed and cleaned up after. 2 dogs may be allowed.

Days Inn
801 Route 130 South
Brooklawn, NJ
856-456-6688 (800-329-7466)
Dogs of all sizes are allowed. Dogs are allowed for a pet fee.

Extended Stay America Mt. Olive - Budd Lake
71 International Dr. S.
Budd Lake, NJ
973-347-5522 (800-804-3724)
One dog is allowed per suite. There is a $25 per night additional pet fee up to $150 for an entire stay.

Residence Inn Cranbury South Brunswick
2662 H 130

Canton, NJ
609-395-9447 (888-577-7005)
Some of the amenities at this all-suite inn include a daily buffet breakfast, nightly socials, summer barbecues, a heated indoor swimming pool, and a complimentary grocery shopping service. Dogs are allowed for an additional one time pet fee of $100 per room. 2 dogs may be allowed.

Billmae Cottage
1015 Washington Street
Cape May, NJ
609-898-8558
billmae.com
Billmae Cottage offers 1 and 2 bedroom suites each with a living room, bath, and kitchen. They have occasional "Yappie Hours" on the porch. Well behaved dogs of all sizes are welcome.

Blue Fish Inn
601 Madison Avenue
Cape May, NJ
609-884-4838 (888-426-2346)
bluefishinn.com
This inn allows dogs but not cats. There is a $25.00 per night dog fee with a maximum of two dogs.

Marquis de Lafayette Hotel
501 Beach Avenue
Cape May, NJ
609-884-3500 (800-257-0432)
marquiscapemay.com/
This beach front inn affords wonderful ocean views and breezes and the inn is central to a wide variety of recreational pursuits, shops, eateries, and nightlife. Dogs of all sizes are allowed for an additional fee of $25 per night per pet, plus a $100 cash deposit (credit card not applicable), refundable upon inspection of the room. Dogs must be leashed and cleaned up after. Multiple dogs may be allowed.

Econo Lodge
395 Washington Ave.
Carlstadt, NJ
201-935-4600 (877-424-6423)
Dogs of all sizes are allowed. Dogs are allowed for a pet fee of $15.00 per pet per night.

Comfort Inn & Suites
634 Soders Road
Carneys Point, NJ
856-299-8282 (877-424-6423)
Dogs up to 50 pounds are allowed. Dogs are allowed for a pet fee of $15.00 per pet per night.

Holiday Inn Express Hotel & Suites Carneys Point Nj Trnpk Exit 1
506 Pennsville-Auburn Rd
Carneys Point, NJ
856-351-9222 (877-270-6405)
Dogs of all sizes are allowed. Dogs are allowed for a pet fee of $10.00 per pet per night.

Extended Stay America Philadelphia - Cherry Hill
1653 E. State Hwy. No. 70
Cherry Hill, NJ
856-616-1200 (800-804-3724)
One dog is allowed per suite. There is a $25 per night additional pet fee up to $150 for an entire stay.

Holiday Inn Philadelphia-Cherry Hill
2175 West Marlton Pike
Cherry Hill, NJ
856-663-5300 (877-270-6405)
Dogs are welcome at this hotel.

Wellesley Inn Clifton
265 Route 3 East
Clifton, NJ
973-778-6500 (800-531-5900)
Dogs of all sizes are allowed. There is a $10 per night per pet additional fee. Dogs may not be left unattended, and they must be leashed and cleaned up after. Multiple dogs may be allowed.

Holiday Inn Select Clinton
111 West Route 173
Clinton, NJ
908-735-5111 (877-270-6405)
Dogs of all sizes are allowed. Dogs are allowed for a pet fee of $25.00 per pet per stay.

Days Inn Columbia
I-80 and Route 94 at Exit 4
Columbia, NJ
908-496-8221 (800-329-7466)
Dogs are welcome at this hotel.

Staybridge Suites Cranbury-South Brunswick
1272 South River Road
Cranbury, NJ
609-409-7181 (877-270-6405)
Dogs up to 80 pounds are allowed. Pets allowed with an additional pet fee. Up to $75 for 1-6 nights and up to $150 for 7+ nights. A pet agreement must be signed at check-in.

Residence Inn Deptford
1154 Hurffville Road
Deptford, NJ
856-686-9188 (800-331-3131)
This all suite hotel sits central to

many of the city's star attractions, dining, shopping and business areas, plus they offer a number of in-house amenities that include a daily buffet breakfast and evening socials. Dogs are allowed for an additional one time pet fee of $75 per room. Multiple dogs may be allowed.

Motel 6 - East Brunswick
244 Sr 18
East Brunswick, NJ
732-390-4545 (800-466-8356)
This motel welcomes your pets to stay with you.

Studio 6 - East Brunswick Nyc Area
246 Sr 18
East Brunswick, NJ
732-238-3330 (800-466-8356)
Your pets are welcome to stay here with you for a pet fee of $10 per day up to $50 for an entire stay.

Homestead Studio Suites Meadowlands - East Rutherford
300 State Hwy. Rte. 3 E.
East Rutherford, NJ
201-939-8866 (800-804-3724)
One dog is allowed per suite. There is a $25 per night additional pet fee up to $150 for an entire stay.

Sheraton Meadowlands Hotel & Conference Center
2 Meadowlands Plaza
East Rutherford, NJ
201-896-0500 (888-625-5144)
Dogs up to 50 pounds are allowed. There is a $50 one time additional pet fee. Dogs are not allowed to be left alone in the room.

Quality Inn
351 Franklin Street
East Windsor, NJ
609-448-7399 (877-424-6423)
Dogs of all sizes are allowed. Dogs are allowed for a pet fee of $35.00 per pet per night. Two dogs are allowed per room.

Extended Stay America Edison - Raritan Center
1 Fieldcrest Ave.
Edison, NJ
732-346-9366 (800-804-3724)
One dog is allowed per suite. There is a $25 per night additional pet fee up to $150 for an entire stay.

Red Roof Inn Edison
860 New Durham Road
Edison, NJ
732-248-9300 (800-RED-ROOF)
One well-behaved family pet per room. Guest must notify front desk

upon arrival. Guest is liable for any damages. In consideration of all guests, pets must never be left unattended in the guest rooms.

Sheraton Edison Hotel Raritan Center
125 Raritan Center Parkway
Edison, NJ
732-225-8300 (888-625-5144)
Dogs up to 50 pounds are allowed. There are no additional pet fees but there is a $50 refundable deposit. Dogs are not allowed to be left alone in the room.

Residence Inn Atlantic City Airport Egg Harbor Township
3022 Fire Road
Egg Harbor Township, NJ
609-813-2344 (888-236-2427)
In addition to offering a convenient location to many of the areas star attractions, and business, shopping, and dining areas, this all suite hotel also provides a number of in-house amenities, including a daily buffet breakfast and an evening reception. Dogs are allowed for an additional one time pet fee of $100 per room. 2 dogs may be allowed.

Extended Stay America Elizabeth - Newark Airport
45 Glimcher RealtyWay
Elizabeth, NJ
908-355-4300 (800-804-3724)
One dog is allowed per suite. There is a $25 per night additional pet fee up to $150 for an entire stay.

Hilton Hotel
1170 Spring Street
Elizabeth, NJ
908-351-3900 (800-HILTONS (445-8667))
This upscale hotel offers a number of on site amenities for business and leisure travelers, plus a convenient location to the Newark Airport with free shuttle service to and from. Dogs up to 75 pounds are allowed for an additional one time pet fee of $75 per room. 2 dogs may be allowed.

Knights Inn Newark Airport Elizabeth
178 Spring Street
Elizabeth, NJ
908-353-3030 (800-843-5644)
Dogs are welcome at this hotel.

Residence Inn Newark Elizabeth/Liberty International Airport
83 Glimcher Realty Way

Elizabeth, NJ
908-352-4300 (800-331-3131)
This all suite inn features a convenient location to business, shopping, dining, and entertainment areas, plus they also offer a number of in-house amenities, including a daily buffet breakfast and evening socials. Dogs are allowed for an additional one time pet fee of $100 per room. 2 dogs may be allowed.

Ramada Flemington
250 Highway 202
Flemington, NJ
908-782-7472 (800-272-6232)
Dogs of all sizes are allowed. Dogs are allowed for a pet fee of $10.00 per pet per night.

Extended Stay America Somerset - Franklin
30 World's Fair Dr.
Franklin, NJ
732-469-8080 (800-804-3724)
One dog is allowed per suite. There is a $25 per night additional pet fee up to $150 for an entire stay.

The Widow McCrea House
53 Kingwood Avenue
Frenchtown, NJ
908-996-4999
widowmccrea.com/
This attractive 1878 Italiante Victorian Inn is only a 2 minute walk from all the town has to offer and the Delaware River, and they offer a cottage with an oversized Jacuzzi and a fireplace for guests with pets. Dogs of all sizes are allowed for an additional fee of $35 per night per pet with a credit card on file, and there is a pet agreement to sign at check in. Dogs must be well behaved, leashed, cleaned up after, and crated when left alone in the room. 2 dogs may be allowed.

Motel 6 - Gibbstown, Nj
299 Swedesboro Ave
Gibbstown, NJ
856-224-9182 (800-466-8356)
This motel welcomes your pets to stay with you.

Holiday Inn Hazlet
2870 Highway 35
Hazlet, NJ
732-888-2000 (877-270-6405)
Dogs are welcome at this hotel. Dogs are allowed with a $50 deposit and $25 of that is refundable upon check out.

Days Inn Hillsborough
118 US Route 206 South

Hillsborough, NJ
908-685-9000 (800-329-7466)
Dogs of all sizes are allowed. Dogs
are allowed for a pet fee of $20.00
per pet per night.

The Inn at Millrace Pond
313 Johnsonburg Road/H 519N
Hope, NJ
908-459-4884 (800-746-6467)
innatmillracepond.com/
Historic buildings, individually
decorated rooms in period
reproductions, and an active
restaurant and tavern highlight this
retreat. They offer a couple of pet-
friendly rooms, and dogs of all sizes
are allowed for no additional pet fee.
Dogs must be leashed, cleaned up
after, and they are not allowed on the
beds. They request dogs be crated
when left alone in the room unless
the owner is confident the pet will be
quiet and well mannered. 2 dogs
may be allowed.

Hilton Hotel
120 Wood Avenue S
Iselin, NJ
732-494-6200 (800-HILTONS (445-
8667))
This upscale hotel offers numerous
on site amenities for business and
leisure travelers - including an
executive health club, plus they are
convenient to business, shopping,
dining, and entertainment areas.
Dogs are allowed for an additional
one time fee of $75 per pet; there
may be 1 dog up to 75 pounds or 2
dogs that total 75 pounds per room.

Candlewood Suites Jersey City
21 Second Street
Jersey City, NJ
201-659-2500 (877-270-6405)
Dogs up to 80 pounds are allowed.
Pets allowed with an additional pet
fee. Up to $75 for 1-6 nights and up
to $150 for 7+ nights. A pet
agreement must be signed at check-
in.

Howard Johnson - Princeton/
Lawrenceville
2995 Brunswick Pike
Lawrenceville, NJ
609-896-1100 (800-446-4656)
Dogs are welcome at this hotel.

Red Roof Inn Princeton
3203 Brunswick Pike
Lawrenceville, NJ
609-896-3388 (800-RED-ROOF)
One well-behaved family pet per
room. Guest must notify front desk
upon arrival. Guest is liable for any
damages. In consideration of all

guests, pets must never be left
unattended in the guest rooms.

Ocean Place Resort and Spa
One Ocean Blvd
Long Branch, NJ
732-571-4000 (800-411-6493)
oceanplaceresort.com/
This premier ocean front resort sits
amid lush greenery and white sandy
beaches, and serves as a great
home base for a wide variety of
activities and recreation. Dogs of all
sizes are allowed for an additional
one time fee of $150 per pet. Dogs
must be well mannered, leashed,
and cleaned up after. 2 dogs may
be allowed.

Sheraton Mahwah Hotel
1 International Blvd., Route 17
North
Mahwah, NJ
201-529-1660 (888-625-5144)
Dogs of all sizes are allowed. There
are no additional pet fees. Dogs are
not allowed to be left alone in the
room.

Super 8 Mahwah
160 State Route 17 South
Mahwah, NJ
201-512-0800 (800-800-8000)
Dogs of all sizes are allowed. Dogs
are allowed for a pet fee of $10.00
per pet per night.

Motel 6 - Philadelphia Mt Laurel, Nj
2798 Sr 73 North
Maple Shade, NJ
856-235-3550 (800-466-8356)
This motel welcomes your pets to
stay with you.

Comfort Inn
750 Route 35 South
Middletown, NJ
732-671-3400 (877-424-6423)
Dogs up to 70 pounds are allowed.
Dogs are allowed for a pet fee of
$25.00 per pet per night. Dogs are
allowed for a pet fee of $maximum
per pet per stay.

Red Roof Inn Princeton North
208 New Road
Monmouth Junction, NJ
732-821-8800 (800-RED-ROOF)
One well-behaved family pet per
room. Guest must notify front desk
upon arrival. Guest is liable for any
damages. In consideration of all
guests, pets must never be left
unattended in the guest rooms.

Residence Inn Princeton-South
Brunswick

4225 US Highway 1
Monmouth Junction, NJ
732-329-9600 (800-331-3131)
Offering a convenient location to
local universities, historic, shopping,
dining, and entertainment areas, this
all suite hotel also offers a number of
in-house amenities, including a daily
buffet breakfast and evening socials
Monday to Thursday. Dogs are
allowed for an additional one time
pet fee of $100 per room. 2 dogs
may be allowed.

Candlewood Suites Parsippany-
Morris Plains
100 Candlewood Drive
Morris Plains, NJ
973-984-9960 (877-270-6405)
Dogs up to 80 pounds are allowed.
Pets allowed with an additional pet
fee. Up to $75 for 1-6 nights and up
to $150 for 7+ nights. A pet
agreement must be signed at check-
in.

Candlewood Suites Philadelphia-Mt.
Laurel
4000 Crawford Place
Mount Laurel, NJ
856-642-7567 (877-270-6405)
Dogs up to 80 pounds are allowed.
Pets allowed with an additional pet
fee. Up to $75 for 1-6 nights and up
to $150 for 7+ nights. A pet
agreement must be signed at check-
in.

Extended Stay America Philadelphia
- Mt. Laurel
101 Diemer Dr.
Mount Laurel, NJ
856-778-4100 (800-804-3724)
One dog is allowed per suite. There
is a $25 per night additional pet fee
up to $150 for an entire stay.

Red Roof Inn Mt Laurel
603 Fellowship Road
Mount Laurel, NJ
856-234-5589 (800-RED-ROOF)
One well-behaved family pet per
room. Guest must notify front desk
upon arrival. Guest is liable for any
damages. In consideration of all
guests, pets must never be left
unattended in the guest rooms.

Residence Inn Mt. Laurel at Bishop's
Gate
1001 Sunburst Lane
Mount Laurel, NJ
856-234-1025 (800-331-3131)
This all suite inn features a
convenient location to business,
shopping, dining, and entertainment
areas, plus they also offer a number
of in-house amenities, including a

daily buffet breakfast and evening socials. Dogs are allowed for an additional one time pet fee of $75 per room. 2 dogs may be allowed.

Staybridge Suites Philadelphia-Mt. Laurel
4115 Church Road
Mount Laurel, NJ
856-722-1900 (877-270-6405)
Dogs up to 80 pounds are allowed. Pets allowed with an additional pet fee. Up to $75 for 1-6 nights and up to $150 for 7+ nights. A pet agreement must be signed at check-in.

TownePlace Suites Mt. Laurel
450 Century Parkway
Mount Laurel, NJ
856-778-8221 (800-257-3000)
Besides offering a number of in-house amenities for all level of travelers, this all suite inn also offers a convenient location to historical, businesses, shopping, dining, and entertainment areas. Dogs are allowed for an additional one time fee of $100 per room. 2 dogs may be allowed.

Residence Inn Mt. Olive at International Trade Center
271 Continental Drive
Mount Olive, NJ
973-691-1720 (800-331-3131)
In addition to being in close proximity to a number of Fortune 500 companies, several entertainment areas, and a variety of shopping and dining areas, this all suite inn also offers a number of in-house amenities, including a daily buffet breakfast and evening socials. Dogs are allowed for an additional one time pet fee of $100 per room. Multiple dogs may be allowed.

Days Inn Neptune
3310 Hwy 33
Neptune, NJ
732-643-8888 (800-329-7466)
Dogs of all sizes are allowed. Dogs are allowed for a nightly pet fee.

Residence Inn Neptune at Gateway Centre
230 Jumping Brook Road
Neptune, NJ
732-643-9350 (800-331-3131)
Besides offering a convenient location to beaches, shopping, dining, commerce, and entertainment areas, this all suite inn also offers a number of in-house amenities, including a daily buffet breakfast and evening socials. Dogs are allowed for an additional one time pet fee of

$100 per room. 2 dogs may be allowed.

Sheraton Newark Airport Hotel
128 Frontage Road
Newark, NJ
973-690-5500 (888-625-5144)
Dogs up to 65 pounds are allowed. There are no additional pet fees. Dogs are not allowed to be left alone in the room.

Econo Lodge
448 Route 206 South
Newton, NJ
973-383-3922 (877-424-6423)
Dogs of all sizes are allowed. Dogs are allowed for a pet fee of $10.00 per pet per night.

Days Inn - New York City North Bergen
2750 Tonnelle Ave/I-495
North Bergen, NJ
201-348-3600 (800-329-7466)
Dogs are welcome at this hotel.

Howard Johnson North Bergen
1300 Tonnelle Avenue
North Bergen, NJ
201-863-6363 (800-446-4656)
Dogs are welcome at this hotel.

Howard Johnson Express Inn -- North Plainfield
1011 Rte 22 West
North Plainfield, NJ
908-753-6500 (800-446-4656)
Dogs of all sizes are allowed. Dogs are allowed for a pet fee.

Surf 16 Motel
1600 Surf Avenue
North Wildwood, NJ
609-522-1010
members.aol.com/surf16motl/
This motel near the beach is open during the summer only. Dogs of all sizes are accepted. They are open from May 1st through mid-October. Dogs are allowed on the beach before May 15 and after September 15. The hotel has a fenced in dog run. There is a $10 per day per pet charge. Multiple dogs may be allowed.

La Quinta Inn Paramus
393 North State Route 17
Paramus, NJ
201-265-4200 (800-531-5900)
Dogs of all sizes are allowed. There are no additional pet fees. There is a pet waiver to sign at check in. Dogs must be leashed, cleaned up after, and crated when left alone in the room. Multiple dogs may be

allowed.

Hilton Hotel
One Hilton Court
Parsippany, NJ
973-267-7373 (800-HILTONS (445-8667))
Located in the heart of Morris County's corporate district, this upscale hotel offers a number of on site amenities for business and leisure travelers, plus a convenient location to business, shopping, dining, and a variety of recreational opportunities. Dogs up to 70 pounds are allowed for no additional fee. 2 dogs may be allowed.

Ramada Limited Parsippany
949 Route 46
Parsippany, NJ
973-263-0404 (800-272-6232)
Dogs of all sizes are allowed. Dogs are allowed for a pet fee.

Red Roof Inn Parsippany
855 US Route 46
Parsippany, NJ
973-334-3737 (800-RED-ROOF)
One well-behaved family pet per room. Guest must notify front desk upon arrival. Guest is liable for any damages. In consideration of all guests, pets must never be left unattended in the guest rooms.

Residence Inn Parsippany
3 Gatehall Drive
Parsippany, NJ
973-984-3313 (800-331-3131)
Some of the amenities at this all-suite inn include a daily buffet breakfast, evening socials, summer barbecues, an indoor pool, a Sport Court, and a complimentary grocery shopping service. Dogs are allowed for an additional one time pet fee of $100 per room. Multiple dogs may be allowed.

Sheraton Parsippany Hotel
199 Smith Road
Parsippany, NJ
973-515-2000 (888-625-5144)
Dogs up to 80 pounds are allowed. There are no additional pet fees. Dogs are not allowed to be left alone in the room.

Days Inn and Suites
517 South Pennsville-Auburn Rd
Penns Grove, NJ
856-299-1996 (800-329-7466)
Dogs are welcome at this hotel.

Embassy Suites
121 Centennial Avenue

Piscataway, NJ
732-980-0500 (800-EMBASSY (362-2779))
This luxury, all suite hotel offers a number of on site amenities for business and leisure travelers, plus a convenient location to business, shopping, dining, and entertainment areas. They also offer a complimentary cooked-to-order breakfast and a Manager's reception every evening. Dogs up to 50 pounds are allowed for an additional one time fee of $50 per pet, and they must be declared at the time of reservations. There is also a pet amenity package available for an additional fee. 2 dogs may be allowed.

Motel 6 - Piscataway
1012 Stelton Road
Piscataway, NJ
732-981-9200 (800-466-8356)
This motel welcomes your pets to stay with you.

The Pillars of Plainfield
922 Central Avenue
Plainfield, NJ
908-753-0922 (888 PILLARS (745-5277))
pillars2.com/
This beautifully restored Victorian mansion is surrounded by lush greenery, gardens, and comfort, and they are central to numerous other activities, places of interest, and recreation. Dogs up to 50 pounds are allowed for no additional pet fee. Dogs are allowed on the 2nd floor only, they must be leashed and cleaned up after, and they must be crated when left alone in the room. 2 dogs may be allowed.

Best Western Regency House Hotel
140 Route 23 N
Pompton Plains, NJ
973-696-0900 (800-780-7234)
Dogs of all sizes are allowed. Dogs are allowed for a pet fee of $20.00 per pet per night.

Extended Stay America Princeton - West Windsor
3450 Brunswick Pike
Princeton, NJ
609-919-9000 (800-804-3724)
One dog is allowed per suite. There is a $25 per night additional pet fee up to $150 for an entire stay.

Holiday Inn Princeton
100 Independence Way
Princeton, NJ
609-520-1200 (877-270-6405)
Dogs of all sizes are allowed. Dogs

are allowed for a nightly pet fee.

Staybridge Suites Princeton South Brunswick
4375 US Route 1 South
Princeton, NJ
609-951-0009 (877-270-6405)
Dogs up to 80 pounds are allowed. Pets allowed with an additional pet fee. Up to $75 for 1-6 nights and up to $150 for 7+ nights. A pet agreement must be signed at check-in.

Best Western The Inn at Ramsey
1315 Route 17 S
Ramsey, NJ
201-327-6700 (800-780-7234)
Dogs of all sizes are allowed. Dogs are allowed for a pet fee of $20.00 per pet per night.

Extended Stay America Ramsey - Upper Saddle River
112 State Hwy. 17
Ramsey, NJ
201-236-9996 (800-804-3724)
One dog is allowed per suite. There is a $25 per night additional pet fee up to $150 for an entire stay.

Super 8 NJ Raritan
119 Hwy 206 South
Raritan, NJ
908-722-5400 (800-800-8000)
Dogs of all sizes are allowed. Dogs are allowed for a pet fee of $10.00 per pet per night.

Extended Stay America Red Bank - Middletown
329 Newman Springs Rd.
Red Bank, NJ
732-450-8688 (800-804-3724)
One dog is allowed per suite. There is a $25 per night additional pet fee up to $150 for an entire stay.

Best Western Rockaway Hotel
14 Green Pond Road
Rockaway, NJ
973-625-1200 (800-780-7234)
Dogs up to 50 pounds are allowed. Dogs are allowed for a pet fee of $25.00 per pet per night.

Extended Stay America Meadowlands - Rutherford
750 Edwin L. Ward Sr. Memorial Hwy.
Rutherford, NJ
201-635-0266 (800-804-3724)
One dog is allowed per suite. There is a $25 per night additional pet fee up to $150 for an entire stay.

Residence Inn Saddle River

7 Boroline Road
Saddle River, NJ
201-934-4144 (800-331-3131)
In addition to offering a convenient location to major business, shopping, dining, and world class entertainment areas, this hotel also provides a number of in-house amenities, including a daily buffet breakfast and evening socials Monday through Thursday with light dinner fare. Dogs are allowed for an additional one time pet fee of $100 per room. 2 dogs may be allowed.

Cozy Pet Friendly Townhouse
238-39th St.
Sea Isle City, NJ
215-694-4829
This vacation rental has 3 double beds and 1 queen bed. Pets are allowed with notice when booking.

Candlewood Suites Secaucus (Jersey City Area)
279 Secaucus Road
Secaucus, NJ
201-865-3900 (877-270-6405)
Dogs up to 80 pounds are allowed. Pets allowed with an additional pet fee. Up to $75 for 1-6 nights and up to $150 for 7+ nights. A pet agreement must be signed at check-in.

Extended Stay America Secaucus - Meadowlands
1 Meadowlands Pkwy.
Secaucus, NJ
201-617-1711 (800-804-3724)
One dog is allowed per suite. There is a $25 per night additional pet fee up to $150 for an entire stay.

Homestead Studio Suites Secaucus - Meadowlands
One Plaza Dr.
Secaucus, NJ
201-553-9700 (800-804-3724)
One dog is allowed per suite. There is a $25 per night additional pet fee up to $150 for an entire stay.

Red Roof Inn Meadowlands - NYC
15 Meadowlands Parkway
Secaucus, NJ
201-319-1000 (800-RED-ROOF)
One well-behaved family pet per room. Guest must notify front desk upon arrival. Guest is liable for any damages. In consideration of all guests, pets must never be left unattended in the guest rooms.

Hilton Hotel
41 John F Kennedy Parkway
Short Hills, NJ

973-379-0100 (800-HILTONS (445-8667))
This luxury hotel offers a number of on site amenities for all level of travelers plus a convenient location to business, shopping, dining, and entertainment areas. Dogs are allowed for no additional fee with a credit card on file. 2 dogs may be allowed.

Residence Inn Atlantic City Somers Point
900 Mays Landing Road
Somers Point, NJ
609-927-6400 (888-236-2427)
In addition to offering a convenient location to many world class attractions, beaches, shopping, and dining areas, this all suite hotel also provides a number of in-house amenities, including a daily buffet breakfast and a Manager's reception Monday through Thursday. Dogs are allowed for an additional one time pet fee of $100 per room. 2 dogs may be allowed.

Candlewood Suites Somerset
41 Worlds Fair Drive
Somerset, NJ
732-748-1400 (877-270-6405)
Dogs up to 80 pounds are allowed. Pets allowed with an additional pet fee. Up to $75 for 1-6 nights and up to $150 for 7+ nights. A pet agreement must be signed at check-in.

Holiday Inn Somerset-Bridgewater
195 Davidson Ave
Somerset, NJ
732-356-1700 (877-270-6405)
Dogs of all sizes are allowed. Dogs are allowed for a pet fee of $15.00 per pet per night.

Quality Inn
1850 Easton Ave.
Somerset, NJ
732-469-5050 (877-424-6423)
Dogs of all sizes are allowed. Dogs are allowed for a pet fee of $20.00 per pet per night.

Residence Inn Somerset
37 Worlds Fair Drive
Somerset, NJ
732-627-0881 (800-331-3131)
Besides a great location to a number of interests for both business and leisure travelers, some of the amenities at this all-suite inn include a daily buffet breakfast, a Manager's reception Monday through Thursday with light dinner fare, an indoor heated swimming pool, a Sport Court, and a complimentary grocery shopping service. One dog is allowed for an additional one time pet fee of $100 per room.

Staybridge Suites Somerset
260 Davidson Ave
Somerset, NJ
732-356-8000 (877-270-6405)
Dogs up to 80 pounds are allowed. Pets allowed with an additional pet fee. Up to $75 for 1-6 nights and up to $150 for 7+ nights. A pet agreement must be signed at check-in.

Extended Stay America Princeton - South Brunswick
4230 US Rte. 1
South Brunswick, NJ
732-438-5010 (800-804-3724)
One dog is allowed per suite. There is a $25 per night additional pet fee up to $150 for an entire stay.

Holiday Inn Springfield
304 Rt. 22 West
Springfield, NJ
973-376-9400 (877-270-6405)
Dogs are welcome at this hotel.

Woolverton Inn
6 Woolverton Road
Stockton, NJ
609-397-0802 (888-264-6648)
woolvertoninn.com/
Set on 300 lush, scenic acres of rolling hills and woodlands, this 1792 stone manor luxury inn offers guests indoor or outdoor garden dining, and a favorite pastime here is a walk to the Delaware River to catch the amazing sunsets over the water. Dogs of all sizes are allowed in the Garden Cottage for no additional pet fee. Dogs must be housebroken, quiet, leashed, and cleaned up after. Dogs may only be left alone in the room if owners are confident in their behavior. 2 dogs may be allowed.

Residence Inn Tinton Falls
90 Park Road
Tinton Falls, NJ
732-389-8100 (800-331-3131)
This all suite inn sits central to a plethora of activities and attractions for all level of travelers; plus they offer a number of on-site amenities, including a daily buffet breakfast and evening socials Monday to Wednesday with light dinner fare. Dogs are allowed for an additional one time pet fee of $100 per room. 2 dogs may be allowed.

Quality Inn

815 SR 37 W.
Toms River, NJ
732-341-2400 (877-424-6423)
Dogs up to 100 pounds are allowed. Dogs are allowed for a pet fee of $39.95 per pet per night. Two dogs are allowed per room.

Red Roof Inn Toms River
2 West Water Street
Toms River, NJ
732-341-6700 (800-RED-ROOF)
One well-behaved family pet per room. Guest must notify front desk upon arrival. Guest is liable for any damages. In consideration of all guests, pets must never be left unattended in the guest rooms.

Econo Lodge
998 West Landis Ave
Vineland, NJ
856-696-3030 (877-424-6423)
Dogs of all sizes are allowed. Dogs are allowed for a pet fee of $Accomodation:$15.00 per pet per night.

Residence Inn Wayne
30 Nevins Road
Wayne, NJ
973-872-7100 (800-331-3131)
This all suite inn features a convenient location to major corporations, universities, shopping, dining, and entertainment areas, plus they also offer a number of in-house amenities, including a daily buffet breakfast and evening socials Monday to Thursday. Dogs are allowed for an additional one time pet fee of $100 per room. 2 dogs may be allowed.

Sheraton Suites on the Hudson
500 Harbor Blvd.
Weehawken, NJ
201-617-5600 (888-625-5144)
Dogs of all sizes are allowed. There is a $75 one time pet fee per visit.

Quality Hotel Atlantic City West
8029 Black Horse Pike
West Atlantic City, NJ
609-641-3546 (877-424-6423)
Beach & Boardwalk 2 miles. Minutes from Casinos and Shows in Atlantic City.

The Highland House
131 N Broadway
West Cape May, NJ
609-898-1198
Dogs of all sizes are allowed. There are no additional pet fees. 2 dogs may be allowed.

Residence Inn West Orange
107 Prospect Avenue
West Orange, NJ
973-669-4700 (800-331-3131)
This all suite hotel gives a convenient location to a number of sites of interest and activities for all level of travelers, plus they also offer a number of in-house amenities, including a daily buffet breakfast and evening socials. Dogs are allowed for an additional one time pet fee of $100 per room. Multiple dogs may be allowed.

Best Western Burlington Inn
2020 Route 541 Road 1
Westampton, NJ
609-261-3800 (800-780-7234)
Dogs are welcome at this hotel.

Homestead Studio Suites Hanover - Parsippany
125 Rte. 10 E.
Whippany, NJ
973-463-1999 (800-804-3724)
One dog is allowed per suite. There is a $25 per night additional pet fee up to $150 for an entire stay.

Homestead Studio Suites Woodbridge - Newark
1 Hoover Way
Woodbridge, NJ
732-442-8333 (800-804-3724)
One dog is allowed per suite. There is a $25 per night additional pet fee up to $150 for an entire stay.

Hilton Hotel
200 Tice Blvd
Woodcliff Lake, NJ
201-391-3600 (800-HILTONS (445-8667))
This upscale hotel offers numerous on site amenities for business and leisure travelers, plus they offer a convenient location to 3 major airports, business, shopping, dining, and entertainment areas. Dogs up to 75 pounds are allowed for an additional one time pet fee of $75 per room. Dogs are allowed in standard rooms on the 1st floor only. 2 dogs may be allowed.

New Mexico

Motel 6 - Alamogordo
251 Panorama Blvd
Alamogordo, NM
575-434-5970 (800-466-8356)
This motel welcomes your pets to stay with you.

Super 8 Alamogordo

3204 N. White Sands Blvd
Alamogordo, NM
575-434-4205 (800-800-8000)
Dogs of all sizes are allowed. Dogs are allowed for a pet fee.

Albuquerque Midtown Red Roof Inn & Suites
1635 Candelaria Boulevard Northeast
Albuquerque, NM
505-344-5311 (800-RED-ROOF)
One well-behaved family pet per room. Guest must notify front desk upon arrival. Guest is liable for any damages. In consideration of all guests, pets must never be left unattended in the guest rooms.

Best Western Airport Albuquerque InnSuites Hotel & Suites
2400 Yale Boulevard SE
Albuquerque, NM
505-242-7022 (800-780-7234)
Dogs of all sizes are allowed. Dogs are allowed for a pet fee.

Best Western Rio Grande Inn
1015 Rio Grande Boulevard NW
Albuquerque, NM
505-843-9500 (800-780-7234)
Dogs of all sizes are allowed. Dogs are allowed for a pet fee of $25 per pet per stay.

Brittania and WE Mauger Estate
701 Roma Ave NW
Albuquerque, NM
505-242-8755 (800-719-9189)
bbonline.com/nm/mauger/
This bed and breakfast has one pet room. This room has a doggie door which leads to an enclosed lawn area for your dog. There is a $20 one time additional pet fee. 2 dogs may be allowed.

Candlewood Suites Albuquerque
3025 Menaul Blvd
Albuquerque, NM
505-888-3424 (877-270-6405)
Dogs up to 80 pounds are allowed. Pets allowed with an additional pet fee. Up to $75 for 1-6 nights and up to $150 for 7+ nights. A pet agreement must be signed at check-in.

Casita Chamisa
850 Chamisal Road NW
Albuquerque, NM
505-897-4644
This unique bed and breakfast features an inviting Southwestern decor. Other amenities include an indoor heated swimming pool, a country style continental breakfast,

and flower gardens and orchards to stroll through. There are also paths that lead to and along the river. Dogs of all sizes are allowed for no additional fee. Dogs may not be left alone in the room, and they must be leashed and cleaned up after at all times. 2 dogs may be allowed.

Comfort Inn & Suites North
5811 Signal Ave. N.E.
Albuquerque, NM
505-822-1090 (877-424-6423)
Dogs of all sizes are allowed. Dogs are allowed for a pet fee of $15.00 per pet per night.

Comfort Inn East
13031 Central Ave. N.E.
Albuquerque, NM
505-294-1800 (877-424-6423)
Dogs of all sizes are allowed. Dogs are allowed for a pet fee of $7.00 per pet per night. Three or more dogs may be allowed.

Comfort Inn West
5712 Iliff Rd. N.W.
Albuquerque, NM
505-836-0011 (877-424-6423)
Dogs of all sizes are allowed. Dogs are allowed for a pet fee of $15.00 per pet per night.

Days Inn Northeast Albuquerque
10321 Hotel Ave NE
Albuquerque, NM
505-275-3297 (800-329-7466)
Dogs of all sizes are allowed. Dogs are allowed for a pet fee of $10 per pet per night.

Days Inn Albuquerque
2120 Menaul NE
Albuquerque, NM
505-884-0250 (800-329-7466)
Dogs are welcome at this hotel.

Days Inn West Albuquerque
6031 Iliff Rd NW
Albuquerque, NM
505-836-3297 (800-329-7466)
Dogs of all sizes are allowed. Dogs are allowed for a pet fee.

Econo Lodge
25 1/2 Hotel Circle NE
Albuquerque, NM
505-314-2525 (877-424-6423)
Dogs of all sizes are allowed.

Econo Lodge Downtown
817 Central Ave. N.E.
Albuquerque, NM
505-243-1321 (877-424-6423)
Dogs of all sizes are allowed. Dogs are allowed for a pet fee of

$5.00/pet, per pet per night.

Econo Lodge East
13211 Central Ave. N.E.
Albuquerque, NM
505-292-7600 (877-424-6423)
Dogs of all sizes are allowed. Dogs
are allowed for a pet fee of $7.00 per
pet per night.

Econo Lodge Midtown
2412 Carlisle Blvd. N.E.
Albuquerque, NM
505-880-0080 (877-424-6423)
Dogs up to 50 pounds are allowed.
Two dogs are allowed per room.

Econo Lodge Old Town
2321 Central Ave NW
Albuquerque, NM
505-243-8475 (877-424-6423)
Dogs of all sizes are allowed. Dogs
are allowed for a pet fee of $10.00
per pet per night.

Extended Stay America Albuquerque
- Airport
2321 International Ave. S.E.
Albuquerque, NM
505-244-0414 (800-804-3724)
One dog is allowed per suite. There
is a $25 per night additional pet fee
up to $150 for an entire stay.

Holiday Inn Express Albuquerque (I-
40 Eubank)
10330 Hotel Ave NE
Albuquerque, NM
505-275-8900 (877-270-6405)
Dogs of all sizes are allowed. Dogs
are allowed for a pet fee of $25.00
per pet per stay.

Howard Johnson Express Inn -
Albuquerque
7630 Pan American Hwy NE
Albuquerque, NM
505-828-1600 (800-446-4656)
Dogs of all sizes are allowed. Dogs
are allowed for a pet fee.

La Quinta Inn & Suites Albuquerque-
Midtown
2011 Menaul Blvd NE
Albuquerque, NM
505-761-5600 (800-531-5900)
Dogs of all sizes are allowed. There
are no additional pet fees. Dogs may
only be left alone in the room if they
will be quiet and well behaved, and if
behavior is questionable, they must
be crated. Dogs must be leashed,
cleaned up after, and they are not
allowed in the back patio area.
Multiple dogs may be allowed.

La Quinta Inn Albuquerque Airport

2116 Yale Blvd. S.E.
Albuquerque, NM
505-243-5500 (800-531-5900)
Dogs of all sizes are allowed. There
are no additional pet fees. Dogs
must be leashed and cleaned up
after. Multiple dogs may be allowed.

La Quinta Inn Albuquerque I-40
East
2424 San Mateo Blvd. N.E.
Albuquerque, NM
505-884-3591 (800-531-5900)
Dogs of all sizes are allowed. There
are no additional pet fees. Dogs
must be quiet, well behaved,
leashed, and cleaned up after.
Multiple dogs may be allowed.

La Quinta Inn Albuquerque North
5241 San Antonio Dr. N.E.
Albuquerque, NM
505-821-9000 (800-531-5900)
Dogs of all sizes are allowed. There
are no additional pet fees. Dogs
must be quiet, well behaved,
leashed and cleaned up after. A
contact number must be left with
the front desk is there is a pet alone
in the room, and arrangements
need to be made with
housekeeping if staying more than
one day. Multiple dogs may be
allowed.

La Quinta Inn Albuquerque
Northwest
7439 Pan American Freeway N.E.
Albuquerque, NM
505-345-7500 (800-531-5900)
Dogs of all sizes are allowed. There
are no additional pet fees. There is
a pet waiver to sign at check in.
Dogs must be crated if left alone in
the room, and they must be leashed
and cleaned up after. 2 dogs may
be allowed.

Motel 6 - Albuquerque Carlisle
3400 Prospect Ave Ne
Albuquerque, NM
505-883-8813 (800-466-8356)
This motel welcomes your pets to
stay with you.

Motel 6 - Albuquerque Coors Road
6015 Iliff Rd Nw
Albuquerque, NM
505-831-3400 (800-466-8356)
This motel welcomes your pets to
stay with you.

Motel 6 - Albuquerque Midtown
1701 University Blvd Ne
Albuquerque, NM
505-843-9228 (800-466-8356)
This motel welcomes your pets to

stay with you.

Motel 6 - Albuquerque North
8510 Pan American Fwy Ne
Albuquerque, NM
505-821-1472 (800-466-8356)
This motel welcomes your pets to
stay with you.

Motel 6 - Albuquerque South Airport
1000 Ave Cesar Chavez Se
Albuquerque, NM
505-243-8017 (800-466-8356)
This motel welcomes your pets to
stay with you.

Motel 6 - Albuquerque West Coors
Rd
5701 Iliff Rd Nw
Albuquerque, NM
505-831-8888 (800-466-8356)
This motel welcomes your pets to
stay with you.

Plaza Inn
900 Medical Arts Ave NE
Albuquerque, NM
505-243-5693 (800-237-1307)
There is a $25 one time pet fee. 2
dogs may be allowed.

Quality Inn
6100 West Iliff Rd
Albuquerque, NM
505-836-8600 (877-424-6423)
Dogs of all sizes are allowed. Dogs
are allowed for a pet fee of $10.00
per pet per night.

Quality Inn & Suites
411 McKnight Ave NW
Albuquerque, NM
505-242-5228 (877-424-6423)
Dogs of all sizes are allowed. Dogs
are allowed for a pet fee of $10.00
per pet per night.

Quality Inn & Suites
25 Hotel Circle NE
Albuquerque, NM
505-271-1000 (877-424-6423)
Dogs of all sizes are allowed. Dogs
are allowed for a pet fee of $10.00
per pet per night.

Quality Suites
5251 San Antonio Blvd. NE
Albuquerque, NM
505-797-0850 (877-424-6423)
Dogs up to 50 pounds are allowed.
Dogs are allowed for a pet fee of
$10.00 per pet per night. Two dogs
are allowed per room.

Ramada - Midtown Albuquerque
2015 Menaul Blvd NE
Albuquerque, NM

505-881-3210 (800-272-6232)
Dogs are welcome at this hotel.

Ramada Limited Albuquerque
5601 Alameda NE/I-25
Albuquerque, NM
505-858-3297 (800-272-6232)
Dogs are welcome at this hotel.

Residence Inn Albuquerque
3300 Prospect Avenue NE
Albuquerque, NM
505-881-2661 (888-236-2427)
Located only a short distance from
the airport and the University of NM,
this all suite hotel offers a convenient
location to a wide variety of activities,
plus they offer a number of in-house
amenities, including a daily buffet
breakfast, and a Manager's reception
Monday through Thursday. Dogs are
allowed for an additional one time
pet fee of $75 per room. Multiple
dogs may be allowed.

Residence Inn Albuquerque North
4331 The Lane @25 NE
Albuquerque, NM
505-761-0200 (888-236-2427)
Offering a convenient location to
business, shopping, dining, and
entertainment areas, this all suite
hotel also offers a number of in-
house amenities, including a daily
buffet breakfast, and a Manager's
reception Monday through Thursday.
Dogs up to 50 pounds are allowed
for an additional one time pet fee of
$100 per room. 2 dogs may be
allowed.

Rodeway Inn
13141 Central Avenue NE
Albuquerque, NM
505-294-4600 (877-424-6423)
Dogs up to 75 pounds are allowed.

Rodeway Inn Midtown
2108 Menaul Blvd. N.E.
Albuquerque, NM
505-884-2480 (877-424-6423)
Dogs of all sizes are allowed. Dogs
are allowed for a pet fee of $10.00
per pet per stay.

Sheraton Albuquerque
2600 Louisiana Blvd. NE
Albuquerque, NM
505-881-0000 (888-625-5144)
Dogs up to 80 pounds are allowed
for no additional pet fee with a credit
card on file; there is a pet agreement
to sign at check in. Dogs may not be
left alone in the room.

Sleep Inn Airport
2300 International Ave SE

Albuquerque, NM
505-244-3325 (877-424-6423)
Dogs up to 65 pounds are allowed.
Dogs are allowed for a pet fee of
$10.00/pet per pet per night.

Staybridge Suites Albuquerque -
Airport
1350 Sunport Place SE
Albuquerque, NM
505-338-3900 (877-270-6405)
Dogs up to 80 pounds are allowed.
Pets allowed with an additional pet
fee. Up to $75 for 1-6 nights and up
to $150 for 7+ nights. A pet
agreement must be signed at
check-in.

Staybridge Suites Albuquerque
North
5817 Signal Avenue NE & Alameda
Albuquerque, NM
505-266-7829 (877-270-6405)
Dogs up to 80 pounds are allowed.
Pets allowed with an additional pet
fee. Up to $75 for 1-6 nights and up
to $150 for 7+ nights. A pet
agreement must be signed at
check-in.

Studio 6 - Albuquerque North
4441 Osuna Rd Ne
Albuquerque, NM
505-344-7744 (800-466-8356)
Your pets are welcome to stay here
with you for a pet fee of $10 per day
up to $50 for an entire stay.

Suburban Extended Stay
2401 Wellesley Drive
Albuquerque, NM
505-883-8888 (877-424-6423)
Dogs up to 50 pounds are allowed.
Two dogs are allowed per room.

Super 8 East Albuquerque
450 Paisano St NE
Albuquerque, NM
505-271-4807 (800-800-8000)
Dogs of all sizes are allowed. Dogs
are allowed for a pet fee of $8 per
pet per night.

Super 8 /Midtown Albuquerque
2500 University Blvd N.E.
Albuquerque, NM
505-888-4884 (800-800-8000)
Dogs are welcome at this hotel.

Super 8 /West Albuquerque
6030 Iliff NW
Albuquerque, NM
505-836-5560 (800-800-8000)
Dogs of all sizes are allowed. Dogs
are allowed for a pet fee of $8.00
per pet per night.

TownePlace Suites Albuquerque
Airport
2400 Centre Avenue SE
Albuquerque, NM
505-232-5800 (800-257-3000)
This all suite inn is located only
minutes from downtown, historic old
town, major corporations, and
numerous shopping, dining, and
entertainment areas. Dogs are
allowed for an additional one time
fee of $100 per room. Multiple dogs
may be allowed.

Travelodge Albuquerque
2500 University BL. N.E.
Albuquerque, NM
505-888-4884 (800-578-7878)
Dogs of all sizes are allowed. Dogs
are allowed for a pet fee of $8.00 per
pet per night.

Angel Fire Resort
10 Miller Lane
Angel Fire, NM
575-377-6401 (800-633-7463)
This resort offers spacious rooms, an
indoor pool, and a variety of other
amenities. Dogs are welcome to stay
in the hotel section of the resort, but
not in the condominiums. There is a
$25 one time additional fee per pet.
Dogs must be well behaved, leashed
and cleaned up after at all times.
With a summit of 10,677 feet (base-
8,600 feet), this is an active full
service ski area during their winter
season, but there are a variety of
recreational activities to do in the
summer as well with plenty of great
hiking trails. Dogs are allowed to hike
the trails, with the exception of the
ski trails during the winter season.

Super 8 NM Belen
428 S Main St
Belen, NM
505-864-8188 (800-800-8000)
Dogs of all sizes are allowed. Dogs
are allowed for a pet fee of $10.00
per pet per night.

Days Inn Bernalillo
107 N. Camino Del Pueblo Dr
Bernalillo, NM
505-771-7000 (800-329-7466)
Dogs are welcome at this hotel.

Quality Inn & Suites
210 North Hill Road
Bernalillo, NM
505-771-9500 (877-424-6423)
Dogs of all sizes are allowed. Dogs
are allowed for a pet fee of $10.00
per pet per night. Two dogs are
allowed per room.

Dog-Friendly Lodging - Please always call ahead to make sure an establishment is still dog-friendly.

Super 8 Bernalillo
265 East Hwy 550
Bernalillo, NM
505-771-4700 (800-800-8000)
Dogs of all sizes are allowed. Dogs
are allowed for a nightly pet fee.

Super 8 Bloomfield
525 W Broadway
Bloomfield, NM
505-632-8886 (800-800-8000)
Dogs are welcome at this hotel.

Days Inn Carlsbad
3910 National Park Hwy
Carlsbad, NM
575-887-7800 (800-329-7466)
Dogs of all sizes are allowed. Dogs
are allowed for a pet fee.

Motel 6 - Carlsbad
3824 National Parks Hwy
Carlsbad, NM
575-885-0011 (800-466-8356)
This motel welcomes your pets to
stay with you.

Hacienda Dona Andrea de Santa Fe
78 Vista del Oro
Cerrillos, NM
505-424-8995
hdasantafe.com
This is a large hotel on 64 acres in
the mountains overlooking Santa Fe.
Well behaved dogs are welcome.
The hotel has a resident terrier
named Daisy. There are hiking trails
in the area for you to hike with your
dog.

High Feather Ranch
29 High Feather Ranch Road
Cerrillos, NM
505-424-1333 (800-757-4410)
This award-winning, 65 acre B&B
offers plenty of privacy, and luxury
guest rooms amid the rustic
backdrop of incredible views of
thousands of acres of high mountain
desert. Just off the Turquoise Trail
National Scenic Byway, there are
also miles of hiking and wildflower
trails on the ranch, and they also
host Astronomy Adventure Star
parties. Some of the amenities
include a bountiful gourmet
breakfast, private patios, in-room
fireplaces, whirlpool baths, and
more. Friendly dogs are welcome.
There is a $15 per night per pet
additional fee. Dogs may only be left
alone in the room for short periods if
they are crated, and they must be
well behaved, quiet, kept leashed,
and cleaned up after. Dogs are not
allowed on the beds or at food areas.
2 dogs may be allowed.

Days Inn And Suites Clayton
1120 S 1st Street
Clayton, NM
575-374-0133 (800-329-7466)
Dogs are welcome at this hotel.

Super 8 Clayton
S Hwy 87
Clayton, NM
575-374-8127 (800-800-8000)
Dogs are welcome at this hotel.

The Lodge Resort
#1 Corona Place
Cloudcroft, NM
575-682-2566 (800-395-6343)
thelodgeresort.com/
they must be leashed and cleaned
up after at all times.

Days Inn and Suites Clovis
2700 Mabry Dr
Clovis, NM
575-762-4491 (800-329-7466)
Dogs are welcome at this hotel.

Econo Lodge
1400 E. Mabry Drive
Clovis, NM
575-763-3439 (877-424-6423)
Dogs of all sizes are allowed. Dogs
are allowed for a pet fee of $10.00
per pet per stay.

Howard Johnson Inn Clovis
2920 Mabry Drive
Clovis, NM
575-769-1953 (800-446-4656)
Dogs of all sizes are allowed. Dogs
are allowed for a pet fee of $10.00
per pet per night.

La Quinta Inn & Suites Clovis
4521 N. Prince St.
Clovis, NM
505-763-8777 (800-531-5900)
Dogs of all sizes are allowed. There
are no additional pet fees. Dogs
must be leashed and cleaned up
after. Dogs may not be left
unattended unless they will be quiet
and well behaved, and it is for a
short period. Multiple dogs may be
allowed.

Best Western Mimbres Valley Inn
1500 W Pine Street
Deming, NM
575-546-4544 (800-780-7234)
Dogs of all sizes are allowed. Dogs
are allowed for a pet fee of $15.00
per pet per night.

Comfort Inn & Suites
1010 West Pine Street
Deming, NM

575-544-3600 (877-424-6423)
Dogs of all sizes are allowed.

Days Inn Deming
1601 E. Pine Street
Deming, NM
575-546-8813 (800-329-7466)
Dogs are welcome at this hotel.

Holiday Inn Deming
Exit 85 & I-10
Deming, NM
575-546-2661 (877-270-6405)
Dogs are welcome at this hotel.

La Quinta Inn & Suites Deming
4300 E Pine St
Deming, NM
505-546-0600 (800-531-5900)
Dogs of all sizes are allowed. There
are no additional pet fees. Dogs
must be leashed and cleaned up
after. Multiple dogs may be allowed.

Motel 6 - Deming
I-10 Motel Dr
Deming, NM
575-546-2623 (800-466-8356)
This motel welcomes your pets to
stay with you.

Super 8 NM Deming
1217 Pine St
Deming, NM
575-546-0481 (800-800-8000)
Dogs of all sizes are allowed. Dogs
are allowed for a pet fee of $10.00
per pet per night.

Econo Lodge
715 Hwy 64 E
Eagle Nest, NM
575-377-6813 (877-424-6423)
Dogs of all sizes are allowed.

Comfort Inn
604-B S. Riverside Dr.
Espanola, NM
505-753-2419 (877-424-6423)
Dogs of all sizes are allowed. Dogs
are allowed for a pet fee of $10.00
per pet per night.

Motel 6 - Espanola, Nm
811 South Riverside Dr
Espanola, NM
505-753-5374 (800-466-8356)
This motel welcomes your pets to
stay with you.

Comfort Inn
555 Scott Ave.
Farmington, NM
505-325-2626 (877-424-6423)
Dogs up to 50 pounds are allowed.
Dogs are allowed for a pet fee of
$10.00 per pet per night. Two dogs

are allowed per room.

La Quinta Inn Farmington
675 Scott Ave.
Farmington, NM
505-327-4706 (800-531-5900)
Dogs of all sizes are allowed. There
are no additional pet fees. Dogs
must be leashed and cleaned up
after. Multiple dogs may be allowed.

Motel 6 - Farmington
1600 Bloomfield Blvd
Farmington, NM
505-326-4501 (800-466-8356)
This motel welcomes your pets to
stay with you.

Super 8 Fort Sumner
1599 E Sumner Ave
Fort Sumner, NM
575-355-7888 (800-800-8000)
Dogs of all sizes are allowed. Dogs
are allowed for a pet fee.

Days Inn East Gallup
1603 W. HWY 66
Gallup, NM
505-863-3891 (800-329-7466)
Dogs of all sizes are allowed. Dogs
are allowed for a pet fee.

Days Inn West Gallup
3201 West Hwy 66
Gallup, NM
505-863-6889 (800-329-7466)
Dogs of all sizes are allowed. Dogs
are allowed for a pet fee.

Econo Lodge
3101 W. US 66
Gallup, NM
505-722-3800 (877-424-6423)
Dogs of all sizes are allowed. Dogs
are allowed for a pet fee of $10.00
per pet per night. Two dogs are
allowed per room.

Motel 6 - Gallup
3306 Us 66
Gallup, NM
505-863-4492 (800-466-8356)
This motel welcomes your pets to
stay with you.

Red Roof Inn Gallup
3304 West Highway 66
Gallup, NM
505-722-7765 (800-RED-ROOF)
One well-behaved family pet per
room. Guest must notify front desk
upon arrival. Guest is liable for any
damages. In consideration of all
guests, pets must never be left
unattended in the guest rooms.

Rodeway Inn

1709 W. Hwy 66
Gallup, NM
505-863-9301 (877-424-6423)
Dogs up to 75 pounds are allowed.
Dogs are allowed for a pet fee of
$10.00 per pet per night. Two dogs
are allowed per room.

Sleep Inn
3820 US 66 E.
Gallup, NM
505-863-3535 (877-424-6423)
Dogs of all sizes are allowed. Dogs
are allowed for a pet fee of $15.00
per pet per night.

Travelodge Gallup
3275 W Hwy 66 Historic
Gallup, NM
505-722-2100 (800-578-7878)
Dogs of all sizes are allowed. Dogs
are allowed for a pet fee.

Best Western Inn & Suites
1501 E Sante Fe Avenue
Grants, NM
505-287-7901 (800-780-7234)
Dogs of all sizes are allowed. Dogs
are allowed for a pet fee of $10.00
per pet per stay.

Days Inn Grants
1504 East Santa Fe Avenue
Grants, NM
505-287-8883 (800-329-7466)
Dogs of all sizes are allowed. Dogs
are allowed for a pet fee.

Motel 6 - Grants
1505 Santa Fe Ave
Grants, NM
505-285-4607 (800-466-8356)
This motel welcomes your pets to
stay with you.

Travelodge Grants
1608 East Santa Fe Avenue
Grants, NM
505-287-7800 (800-578-7878)
Dogs of all sizes are allowed. Dogs
are allowed for a pet fee of $5 per
pet per stay.

Best Western Executive Inn
309 N Marland Boulevard
Hobbs, NM
575-397-7171 (800-780-7234)
Dogs of all sizes are allowed. Dogs
are allowed for a pet fee of $10.00
per pet per night.

Days Inn Hobbs
211 North Marland Blvd
Hobbs, NM
575-397-6541 (800-329-7466)
Dogs of all sizes are allowed. Dogs
are allowed for a pet fee.

Econo Lodge
619 N. Marland Blvd.
Hobbs, NM
575-397-3591 (877-424-6423)
Dogs of all sizes are allowed. Dogs
are allowed for a pet fee of $10.00
per pet per night.

Sleep Inn & Suites
4630 Lovington Hwy
Hobbs, NM
575-393-3355 (877-424-6423)
Dogs of all sizes are allowed. Dogs
are allowed for a pet fee of $10.00
per pet per night. Two dogs are
allowed per room.

Laughing Lizard Inn and Cafe
17526 H 4
Jemez Springs, NM
575-829-3108
This Inn is uniquely decorated in
Southwestern decor, and offers
spectacular views of the surrounding
mesas. Some of the amenities
include hand-painted sleeping rooms
with comfortable beds, a sitting area,
private baths, and a cafe with
outdoor dining so that your canine
companion may join you. Dogs of all
sizes are allowed for no additional
fee. Dogs may not be left alone in
the room at any time, and they must
be leashed and cleaned up after at
all times. 2 dogs may be allowed.

Comfort Suites
2101 S. Triviz
Las Cruces, NM
575-522-1300 (877-424-6423)
Dogs of all sizes are allowed. Dogs
are allowed for a pet fee of $15.00
per pet per night.

**Days Inn And Suites Mesilla Valley
Conference Center**
901 Avenida De Mesilla
Las Cruces, NM
575-524-8603 (800-329-7466)
Dogs of all sizes are allowed. Dogs
are allowed for a pet fee.

Hotel Encanto de Las Cruces
705 South Telshor Blvd.
Las Cruces, NM
575-522-4300 (866-383-0443)
Dogs of all sizes are allowed. There
is a $20 one time additional pet fee.

La Quinta Inn Las Cruces
790 Avenida de Mesilla
Las Cruces, NM
505-524-0331 (800-531-5900)
Dogs of all sizes are allowed. There
are no additional pet fees. Dogs
must be leashed and cleaned up

after. Dogs may not be left unattended at any time. Multiple dogs may be allowed.

La Quinta Inn Las Cruces Organ Mountain
1500 Hickory Drive
Las Cruces, NM
505-523-0100 (800-531-5900)
Dogs of all sizes are allowed. There are no additional pet fees. Dogs must have current shot records, not be left alone in the room, and be leashed at all times. Multiple dogs may be allowed.

Motel 6 - Las Cruces
235 La Posada Ln
Las Cruces, NM
575-525-1010 (800-466-8356)
Your pets are welcome to stay here with you.

Motel 6 - Las Cruces Telshor
2120 Summit Ct
Las Cruces, NM
575-525-2055 (800-466-8356)
Your pets are welcome to stay here with you.

Quality Inn
2200 S. Valley Dr.
Las Cruces, NM
575-524-4663 (877-424-6423)
Dogs of all sizes are allowed.

Ramada Palms de Las Cruces
201 East University Avenue
Las Cruces, NM
575-526-4411 (800-272-6232)
Dogs of all sizes are allowed. Dogs are allowed for a pet fee.

Sleep Inn
2121 S. Triviz
Las Cruces, NM
575-522-1700 (877-424-6423)
Dogs of all sizes are allowed. Dogs are allowed for a pet fee of $15.00 per pet per night.

Staybridge Suites Las Cruces
2651 Northrise Drive
Las Cruces, NM
575-521-7999 (877-270-6405)
Dogs up to 80 pounds are allowed. Pets allowed with an additional pet fee. Up to $75 for 1-6 nights and up to $150 for 7+ nights. A pet agreement must be signed at check-in.

Super 8 /La Posada Lane Las Cruces
245 La Posada Lane
Las Cruces, NM
575-523-8695 (800-800-8000)

Dogs are welcome at this hotel.

Super 8 /White Sands Area Las Cruces
3405 Bataan Memorial West
Las Cruces, NM
575-382-1490 (800-800-8000)
Dogs are welcome at this hotel.

Teakwood Inn and Suites
2600 S Valley Drive
Las Cruces, NM
575-526-4441
This inn features 130 spacious rooms, complimentary breakfasts, and an indoor pool. Dogs of all sizes are allowed for an additional $10 one time fee per pet. Dogs must be quiet, leashed, and cleaned up after at all times. 2 dogs may be allowed.

The Coachlight Inn and RV Park
301 S Motel Blvd
Las Cruces, NM
575-526-3301
Dogs of all sizes are allowed for no additional fee at the inn or in the RV only area. Dogs may not be left unattended outside, and they must be leashed and cleaned up after. Multiple dogs may be allowed.

The Lundeen Inn of the Arts
618 S Alameda
Las Cruces, NM
575-526-3326 (888-526-3326)
innofthearts.com/index.html
Named one of the top 20 inns in the country, this 100 year old restored Mexican territorial inn lends a pleasing Old World ambience in it architecture, and 20 amazing rooms, each named after, and decorated to represent a famous New Mexican or Native American artist. Amenities include healthy breakfast entrees, afternoon refreshments, a spacious art gallery, therapeutics, and the inn is also the center for many special events/activities throughout the year. Dogs up to 50 pounds are allowed for a $15 one time pet fee per room. Dogs must have their own kennels and be crated when left alone in the room. Dogs must be leashed and cleaned up after at all times. 2 dogs may be allowed.

TownePlace Suites Las Cruces
2143 Telshor Court
Las Cruces, NM
575-532-6500 (800-257-3000)
This all suite hotel sits central to a number of sites of interest for both business and leisure travelers; plus they also offer a number of on-site

amenities to ensure comfort. Dogs are allowed for an additional one time fee of $75 per room. Multiple dogs may be allowed.

Comfort Inn
2500 N. Grand Ave.
Las Vegas, NM
505-425-1100 (877-424-6423)
Dogs up to 65 pounds are allowed. Dogs are allowed for a pet fee of $USD per pet per stay. Two dogs are allowed per room.

Holiday Inn Express Hotel & Suites Las Vegas
816 South Grand Ave
Las Vegas, NM
505-426-8182 (877-270-6405)
Dogs of all sizes are allowed. Dogs are allowed for a pet fee of $15.00 per pet per night.

Plaza Hotel
230 Plaza
Las Vegas, NM
505-425-3591 (800-328-1882)
plazahotel-nm.com/amenities.htm
Although built in 1882, this hotel has been beautifully restored and offers all the 21st century amenities one would expect. It is listed on the National Register of Historic Places, and its elegance and amenities make it a premiere place for both business and vacation travelers. Amenities include a complimentary hot breakfast each morning, room service, a saloon with entertainment, a guest computer, meeting facilities, and more. Dogs of all sizes are allowed. There is a $10 per night per pet additional fee. Dogs must be crated when left alone in the room and they must be leashed and cleaned up after at all times.

Super 8 Las Vegas
2029 N Grand Ave
Las Vegas, NM
505-425-5288 (800-800-8000)
Dogs are welcome at this hotel.

Econo Lodge
1408 South Main St
Lordsburg, NM
575-542-3666 (877-424-6423)
Dogs of all sizes are allowed. Dogs are allowed for a pet fee of $10.00 per pet per night. Three or more dogs may be allowed.

Super 8 Lordsburg
110 East Maple
Lordsburg, NM
575-542-8882 (800-800-8000)
Dogs of all sizes are allowed. Dogs

are allowed for a pet fee of $10.00 per pet per night.

Best Western Hilltop House Hotel
400 Trinity Drive at Central
Los Alamos, NM
505-662-2441 (800-780-7234)
Dogs are welcome at this hotel.

Days Inn Los Lunas
1919 Main St
Los Lunas, NM
505-865-5995 (800-329-7466)
Dogs are welcome at this hotel.

Comfort Inn
119 Route 66 East
Moriarty, NM
505-832-6666 (877-424-6423)
Dogs of all sizes are allowed.

Days Inn Moriarty
1901 Main Street (Route 66)
Moriarty, NM
505-832-4451 (800-329-7466)
Dogs of all sizes are allowed. Dogs are allowed for a pet fee of $10.00 per pet per night.

Holiday Inn Express Moriarty
1507 Route 66
Moriarty, NM
505-832-5000 (877-270-6405)
Dogs of all sizes are allowed. Dogs are allowed for a nightly pet fee.

Super 8 Moriarty
1611 Old Route 66
Moriarty, NM
505-832-6730 (800-800-8000)
Dogs of all sizes are allowed. Dogs are allowed for a pet fee of $5.00 per pet per night.

Bear Creek Cabins
88 Main Street/H 15
Pinos Altos, NM
575-388-4501
bearcreekcabins.com/
These enchanting 2-story, split-level cabins are located at an elevation of 7000 feet surrounded by towering Ponderosa Pines and 3.5 million acres of the Gila National Forest. Each cabin has its own unique features, but they all have a balcony, fireplace, barbecue grill, telephone,TV, bird feeders, and coffer maker. Dogs of all sizes are allowed. There is a $10 per night per pet additional fee. Dogs may not be left alone in the room at any time, and they must be leashed and cleaned up after. 2 dogs may be allowed.

Holiday Inn Express Hotel & Suites

Raton
101 Card Avenue
Raton, NM
575-445-1500 (877-270-6405)
Dogs of all sizes are allowed. Dogs are allowed for a nightly pet fee.

Motel 6 - Raton
1600 Cedar St
Raton, NM
575-445-2777 (800-466-8356)
This motel welcomes your pets to stay with you.

Best Western Rivers Edge
301 W River Street
Red River, NM
575-754-1766 (800-780-7234)
Dogs of all sizes are allowed. Dogs are allowed for a pet fee of $10.00 per pet per stay.

Terrace Towers Lodge
712 West Main Street
Red River, NM
800-695-6343
terracetowers-lodge.com
The rooms at this lodge overlook the town of Red River and the Red River Ski Area. The lodge offers 16 two bedroom suites with a living/dining/kitchen area. Amenities include cable TV, hot tub, picnic and playground areas, guest laundry and Internet. There is a small pet fee and a limit of 2 pets per unit. There is no size or weight limit for dogs. Pets need to be leashed while on the property.

Days Inn Rio Rancho
4200 Crestview Drive
Rio Rancho, NM
505-892-8800 (800-329-7466)
Dogs of all sizes are allowed. Dogs are allowed for a pet fee of $15 per pet per stay.

Extended Stay America
Albuquerque - Rio Rancho
2608 The American Rd. N.W.
Rio Rancho, NM
505-792-1338 (800-804-3724)
One dog is allowed per suite. There is a $25 per night additional pet fee up to $150 for an entire stay.

Super 8 Rio Rancho
4100 Barbara Loop SE
Rio Rancho, NM
505-896-8888 (800-800-8000)
Dogs of all sizes are allowed. Dogs are allowed for a pet fee of $10.00 per pet per stay.

Best Western Sally Port Inn & Suites

2000 N Main Street
Roswell, NM
575-622-6430 (800-780-7234)
Dogs are welcome at this hotel.

Comfort Inn
3595 N. Main St.
Roswell, NM
575-623-4567 (877-424-6423)
Dogs of all sizes are allowed.

Cozy Cowboy Cottage Rentals
804 W 4th Street
Roswell, NM
575-624-3258
The number and size of pets depends on the size and type of unit rented. There is a $250 refundable deposit per stay per unit and a pet policy to sign at check in. Aggressive breeds are not allowed. Units also have fenced yards. 2 dogs may be allowed.

Days Inn Roswell
1310 North Main
Roswell, NM
575-623-4021 (800-329-7466)
Dogs are welcome at this hotel.

Frontier Motel
3010 N Main St
Roswell, NM
575-622-1400 (800-678-1401)
Dogs are allowed for an additional pet fee of $10 per night per pet. 2 dogs may be allowed.

Holiday Inn Express Roswell
2300 North Main Street
Roswell, NM
575-627-9900 (877-270-6405)
Dogs up to 50 pounds are allowed. Dogs are allowed for a pet fee of $10.00 per pet per night.

La Quinta Inn & Suites Roswell
200 East 19th Street
Roswell, NM
505-622-8000 (800-531-5900)
Dogs of all sizes are allowed. There are no additional pet fees. There is a pet waiver to sign at check in. Dogs may not be left unattended, and they must be leashed at all times and cleaned up after. Dogs must be crated or removed for housekeeping. Multiple dogs may be allowed.

Motel 6 - Roswell
3307 Main St
Roswell, NM
575-625-6666 (800-466-8356)
This motel welcomes your pets to stay with you.

Ramada Limited Roswell

2803 W 2nd
Roswell, NM
575-623-9440 (800-272-6232)
Dogs of all sizes are allowed. Dogs are allowed for a pet fee.

Apache Village Cabins
311 Mechem Drive
Ruidoso, NM
575-257-2435
Well behaved dogs of all sizes are allowed. There are no additional fees with a credit card on file. 2 dogs may be allowed.

Best Western Pine Springs Inn
1420 W Highway 70
Ruidoso, NM
575-378-8100 (800-780-7234)
Dogs are welcome at this hotel.

Casey's Cabins
2640 Suddereth
Ruidoso, NM
575-257-6355
Dogs of all sizes are allowed. There is a $25 refundable pet deposit. 2 dogs may be allowed.

Hawthorne Suites Conference and Golf Resort
107 Sierra Blanca Drive
Ruidoso, NM
575-258-5500 (888-323-5216)
ruidosohawthorn.com/
there is a pet policy to sign at check in. Dogs may not be left alone in the room at any time, and they must be leashed and cleaned up after at all times.

Motel 6 - Ruidoso
412 Us 70
Ruidoso, NM
575-630-1166 (800-466-8356)
This motel welcomes your pets to stay with you.

Quality Inn
307 US Highway 70 West
Ruidoso, NM
575-378-4051 (877-424-6423)
Dogs of all sizes are allowed.

Sierra Blanca Cabins
215 Country Club Drive
Ruidoso, NM
575-257-2103 (866-262-2103)
sierrablancacabins.com/
This great get-a-way place is nestled on five acres of pine forest bordering the Ruidoso River and offers a convenient location to a variety of shops, restaurants and historical sites. Each cabin has a kitchenette, cable TV, picnic areas, and a cozy rock fireplace. There is also a

playground and trails to explore. Dogs of all sizes are welcome for no additional fee. There can be 1 large dog or 2 small dogs per unit. Dogs must be well behaved, leashed, cleaned up after, and crated when left alone in the cabin. 2 dogs may be allowed.

The Lodge at Sierra Blanca
1451 Meecham Drive
Ruidoso, NM
575-258-3333 (800-47-SWISS (477-9477))
thelodgeatsierrablanca.com/
This inn sits atop the Alto Crest nestled among towering Ponderosa Pines, and in addition to luxury and stunning views, amenities also include a complimentary continental breakfast, an indoor pool, hot tub, and easy access to several recreational activities. Dogs of all sizes are allowed for a $25 one time additional pet fee per room. Dogs must be well mannered, and leashed and cleaned up after at all times.

Travelodge Ruidoso
159 West Highway 70
Ruidoso, NM
575-378-4471 (800-578-7878)
Dogs of all sizes are allowed. Dogs are allowed for a pet fee.

Whispering Pines Cabins
422 Main Road
Ruidoso, NM
575-257-4311
Well behaved dogs of all sizes are allowed. There is a $10 one time fee per pet additional fee. Dogs are not allowed to be left alone in the room.

Alexander's Inn
529 East Palace Avenue
Santa Fe, NM
505-986-1431 (888-321-5123)
This intimate inn offers their visitors privacy and a host of amenities, some of which include a welcome basket full of goodies, a lavish continental breakfast, an afternoon wine and cheese reception, luxurious authentic Southwestern decor, kiva-style fireplaces, full kitchens and patios, and a guest membership at a full-service health club. Dogs of all sizes are allowed for an additional pet fee of $20 per pet per stay, and there is a pet policy to sign at check in. They even keep a supply of doggie biscuits to treat their canine visitors. Dogs must be crated if left alone in the room, be well behaved, and

leashed and cleaned up after at all times.

Best Western Inn of Santa Fe
3650 Cerrillos Road
Santa Fe, NM
505-438-3822 (800-780-7234)
Dogs are welcome at this hotel.

Comfort Inn
4312 Cerrillos Rd.
Santa Fe, NM
505-474-7330 (877-424-6423)
Dogs of all sizes are allowed. Dogs are allowed for a pet fee of $5.00 per pet per night.

Econo Lodge
3470 Cerrillos Road
Santa Fe, NM
505-471-4000 (877-424-6423)
Dogs of all sizes are allowed. Dogs are allowed for a pet fee of $10.00 per pet per night.

El Paradero Bed and Breakfast Inn
220 W. Manhattan Ave
Santa Fe, NM
505-988-1177 (866-558-0918)
elparadero.com
This B&B is located just a few minute walk from the Plaza and the Railyard district. Dogs of all sizes are allowed. There is a $20 nightly fee for dogs.

Hacienda Nicholas
320 Marcy C
Santa Fe, NM
505-992-8385 (888-284-3170)
Behind extra thick adobe walls, this intimate, authentic hacienda offers all the amenities of a luxury hotel. It also features a beautiful, lush garden courtyard with an outdoor kiva fireplace and an afternoon wine and cheese reception. Organic and vegetarian food is available. Dogs of all sizes are allowed for an additional pet fee of $20 per pet per stay, and a pet policy to sign at check in. They even keep a supply of doggie biscuits for their canine visitors. Dogs must be crated if left alone in the room, and they must be well behaved, and leashed and cleaned up after at all times.

Hilton Hotel
100 Sandoval Street
Santa Fe, NM
505-988-2811 (800-HILTONS (445-8667))
Recently restored to reflect the ambiance of the old haciendas, this upscale hotel also offers numerous on site amenities for business and leisure travelers, plus a convenient

location to historic, shopping, dining, and entertainment areas. Dogs up to 65 pounds are allowed for an additional one time pet fee of $50 per room. Multiple dogs may be allowed.

Holiday Inn Express Santa Fe Cerrillos
3450 Cerrillos Road
Santa Fe, NM
505-474-7570 (877-270-6405)
Dogs are welcome at this hotel.

Holiday Inn Santa Fe
4048 Cerrillos Road
Santa Fe, NM
505-473-4646 (877-270-6405)
Dogs of all sizes are allowed. There is a $40 one time additional pet fee.

Hotel Plaza Real
125 Washington Avenue
Santa Fe, NM
505-988-4900
Dogs of all sizes are allowed. There is a $50 one time additional pet fee.

Hotel Santa Fe
1501 Paseo De Peralta
Santa Fe, NM
505-982-1200
Dogs of all sizes are allowed. There is a $20 (+ tax) per night per pet additional fee.

Hotel St. Francis
210 Don Gaspar Avenue
Santa Fe, NM
505-983-5700 (800-529-5700)
Dogs are welcome at this boutique hotel a short walk to historic Santa Fe Plaza.

Inn of the Five Graces
150 E. DeVargas Street
Santa Fe, NM
505-992-0957
dogs are allowed there also. Dogs are allowed for an additional one time fee of $50 per night per pet. Dogs may not be left alone in the room, and they must be well behaved, leashed, and cleaned up after.

La Posada de Santa Fe
330 E Palace Avenue
Santa Fe, NM
505-986-0000 (866-331-ROCK (7625))
Rich in Southwestern ambiance, this plush resort and spa features more than 150 adobe styled suites and guestrooms, a heated outdoor pool and whirlpool, and 6 gorgeously landscaped acres-perfect for strolls with the pooch. Dogs are allowed for

a one time fee of $75 per pet, of which a portion of the fee is donated to local shelters. Dogs are not allowed at the restaurant's outdoor patio. Multiple dogs may be allowed.

La Quinta Inn Santa Fe
4298 Cerrillos Rd.
Santa Fe, NM
505-471-1142 (800-531-5900)
Dogs of all sizes are allowed. There are no additional pet fees. Dogs may not be left unattended, and they must be leashed and cleaned up after. Multiple dogs may be allowed.

Motel 6 - Santa Fe
3007 Cerrillos Rd
Santa Fe, NM
505-473-1380 (800-466-8356)
This motel welcomes your pets to stay with you.

Motel 6 - Santa Fe Cerrillos Road South
3695 Cerrillos Road
Santa Fe, NM
505-471-4140 (800-466-8356)
This motel welcomes your pets to stay with you.

Pecos Trail Inn
2239 Old Pecos Trail
Santa Fe, NM
505-982-1943
Dogs of all sizes are allowed. There are no additional pet fees. 2 dogs may be allowed.

Red Roof Inn Santa Fe
4044 Cerrillos Road
Santa Fe, NM
505-438-8950 (800-RED-ROOF)
One well-behaved family pet per room. Guest must notify front desk upon arrival. Guest is liable for any damages. In consideration of all guests, pets must never be left unattended in the guest rooms.

Residence Inn Santa Fe
1698 Galisteo Street
Santa Fe, NM
505-988-7300 (800-331-3131)
Located at the foot of the Sangre De Cristo Mountains and near the country's 3rd largest art market, this upscale, all suite hotel sits central to a number of interests and activities for both business and leisure travelers, plus they offer a daily buffet breakfast and evening social hours. Dogs are allowed for an additional one time pet fee of $100 per room. 2 dogs may be

allowed.

Santa Fe Sage Inn
725 Cerrillos
Santa Fe, NM
505-982-5952 (866-433-0335)
This Inn offers comfortable Southwestern themed rooms, an extended continental breakfast, a swimming pool, many other amenities, and a great central location to several shopping opportunities and various attractions. Dogs of all sizes are allowed. There is a $25 per pet per stay additional fee. Dogs must be leashed and cleaned up after at all times.

Ten Thousand Waves Japanese Spa and Resort
3451 Hyde Park Road
Santa Fe, NM
505-992-5003
tenthousandwaves.com
Ten Thousand Waves is a Japanese style spa in the mountains above Santa Fe with outdoor and indoor hot tubs, facials, spa services, and many types of massage. There are 13 guest houses, most with fireplaces and either enclosed courtyards or decks. Some have full kitchens and/or separate bedrooms. The resort is about ten minutes from downtown. Pets are $22 per night for one or more.

The Lodge at Santa Fe
750 North St. Francis Drive
Santa Fe, NM
505-992-5800 (888-563-4373)
Dogs of all sizes are allowed. There is a $50 one time additional pet fee.

Comfort Inn
3343 Historic Route 66
Santa Rosa, NM
575-472-5570 (877-424-6423)
Dogs up to 85 pounds are allowed. Dogs are allowed for a pet fee of $15 to $30 per pet per stay, depending on the size of the pet.

Days Inn
1830 Historic Route 66
Santa Rosa, NM
575-472-5985 (800-329-7466)
Dogs of all sizes are allowed. Dogs are allowed for a pet fee.

Holiday Inn Express Santa Rosa
2516 Historic Route 66
Santa Rosa, NM
575-472-5411 (877-270-6405)
Dogs of all sizes are allowed. Dogs are allowed for a pet fee of $25.00 per pet per night.

La Quinta Inn Santa Rosa
1701 Will Rogers Dr.
Santa Rosa, NM
505-472-4800 (800-531-5900)
Dogs of all sizes are allowed. There are no additional pet fees as long as pets are reported at the time of registration. Dogs may not be left unattended, and they must be leashed and cleaned up after. Multiple dogs may be allowed.

Motel 6 - Santa Rosa, Nm
3400 Will Rogers Dr
Santa Rosa, NM
575-472-3045 (800-466-8356)
This motel welcomes your pets to stay with you.

Travelodge Santa Rosa
2290 Will Rogers Drive
Santa Rosa, NM
575-472-3494 (800-578-7878)
Dogs of all sizes are allowed. Dogs are allowed for a pet fee of $5.00 per pet per night.

Comfort Inn
1060 E. US Hwy 180
Silver City, NM
575-534-1883 (877-424-6423)
Dogs of all sizes are allowed. Dogs are allowed for a pet fee of $7.00 per pet per night.

Econo Lodge
1120 Hwy 180 E
Silver City, NM
575-534-1111 (877-424-6423)
Dogs of all sizes are allowed. Dogs are allowed for a pet fee of $7.00 per pet per night.

Holiday Inn Express Silver City
1103 Superior St
Silver City, NM
575-538-2525 (877-270-6405)
Dogs of all sizes are allowed. Dogs are allowed for a pet fee.

Motel 6 - Silver City
3420 Us 180
Silver City, NM
575-538-3711 (800-466-8356)
This motel welcomes your pets to stay with you.

Super 8 Silver City
1040 E Hwy 180
Silver City, NM
575-388-1983 (800-800-8000)
Dogs of all sizes are allowed. Dogs are allowed for a pet fee of $10.00 per pet per night.

Comfort Inn & Suites

1259 Frontage Rd. NW
Socorro, NM
575-838-4400 (877-424-6423)
Dogs up to 75 pounds are allowed. Dogs are allowed for a pet fee of $10.00 per pet per night.

Days Inn Socorro
507 North California Ave
Socorro, NM
575-835-0230 (800-329-7466)
Dogs of all sizes are allowed. Dogs are allowed for a pet fee of $10.00 per pet per night.

Howard Johnson Socorro
1009 California Ave
Socorro, NM
575-835-0276 (800-446-4656)
Dogs are welcome at this hotel.

Motel 6 - Socorro
807 Us 85
Socorro, NM
575-835-4300 (800-466-8356)
This motel welcomes your pets to stay with you.

Super 8 Socorro
1121 Frontage Rd NW
Socorro, NM
575-835-4626 (800-800-8000)
Dogs are welcome at this hotel.

Adobe and Pines Inn
4107 H 68
Taos, NM
575-751-0947 (800-723-8267)
adobepines.com
This luxurious, romantic hideaway is a 170+ year old adobe hacienda that has been preserved with original architecture and transformed into lush grounds with an inviting Southwestern decor. Amenities include full gourmet breakfasts, a brook with an old stone bridge, acres of country gardens, private patios, an outdoor fire ring, spa services, and more. Dogs of all sizes are welcome. There is a $25 one time additional fee per pet. Dogs may also be walked in the large yard next door, and if your dog is under good voice control, they may be off lead in that area. On the property, dogs must be leashed and cleaned up after at all times. Dogs must be crated when left alone in the room. 2 dogs may be allowed.

Alpine Village Suites
PO Box 917
Taos, NM
505-776-8540 (800-576-2666)
alpine-suites.com

Located in Taos Ski Valley, this hotel offers a completely non-smoking environment. All 24 Suites and Studios have mini-kitchens, and most have private balconies with views. Many of our suites have fireplaces, and all suites have TV/VCR's, full baths and telephones.They are located steps from the lifts, restaurants, nightlife, and shopping. The Alpine Village complex houses two full service ski shops, a restaurant and bar. They welcome kids of all ages and the family pet. There is a $20 per day per pet charge. There is also a pet agreement to sign at check in. Multiple dogs may be allowed.

American Artist Gallery House
132 Frontier Lane
Taos, NM
505-758-4446 (800-532-2041)
This B&B offers southwest hospitality in a secluded, romantic setting, and they feature luxury accommodations, gourmet breakfasts, and a stunning view of Taos Mountain. Some of the amenities include Jacuzzi suites, kiva fireplaces, private bath, an outdoor hot tub, and a guest computer. Dogs of all sizes are allowed. There is a $25 additional fee per pet for the first 1 or 2 days, and then an additional $10 per pet per day thereafter. Dogs may not be left alone in the room at any time, and they must be well mannered, leashed, and cleaned up after at all times. Dogs are not allowed on the beds or furnishings, or in the common or breakfast areas. Shots must be current. Dogs are allowed on the trails surrounding the B&B. 2 dogs may be allowed.

Casa Europa
840 Upper Ranchitos Road (HC68, Box 3F)
Taos, NM
575-758-9798 (888-758-9798)
casaeuropanm.com/
This spacious 18th century, pueblo-style estate features a warm inviting Southwestern decor with enclosed garden courtyards and water fountains. Amenities include a full gourmet breakfast, afternoon snacks, an outdoor Jacuzzi and sauna, rooms with fireplaces/private baths/whirlpool tubs, and they are close to many hiking opportunities. Dogs are allowed in the apartment suite for a $0 per night per pet additional fee. They ask that if you leave your pet in the room, that they are either crated or put in the Jacuzzi room. Dogs must be leashed and

cleaned up after.

El Monte Sagrado Living Resort and Spa
317 Kit Carson Road
Taos, NM
575-758-3502 (800-828-TAOS (8267))
This retreat, with several accolades to their name, specializes in luxury accommodations with an emphasis on environmental and ecological harmony. On site are a Biolarium, lush gardens, a spa, and a decor that reflects an array of global influences inspired by Native American culture. World class cuisine is featured on site, and although dogs are not allowed in dining areas, they have an in-suite dining menu available. Dogs up to 40 pounds are allowed for an additional one time pe fee of $75 per room. Dogs must be quiet, well behaved, leashed, and cleaned up after at all times. 2 dogs may be allowed.

La Dona Luz Inn
206 Des Georges Lane
Taos, NM
575-758-9000 (888-758-9060)
stayintaos.com
Thanks to one of our readers for recommending this dog-friendly bed and breakfast. A large dog is welcome to stay here if they are well-behaved and if the dog owner agrees to pay for room damages caused by their dog. There is a $15 per night pet fee. Dogs are not allowed to be left alone in the room. This historic B&B offers 5 rooms (up a narrow spiral stairway), all with private baths. This B&B has been recommended by both The New York Times and USA Today Weekend.

Quality Inn
1043 Paseo del Pueblo Sur
Taos, NM
575-758-2200 (877-424-6423)
Dogs of all sizes are allowed. Dogs are allowed for a pet fee of $7.00 per pet per night.

San Geronimo Lodge
1101 Witt Road
Taos, NM
575-751-3776 (800-894-4119)
sangeronimolodge.com/
however pet rooms are limited so be sure to phone ahead. There is a $15 one time fee for 1 dog, plus a $5 one time fee for each additional dog. There is a large field, and a trail from the lodge that leads to the river for some great walking areas for your canine companion. Dogs must be

well behaved and social with humans and other animals, as there are other friendly animals in residence too. Dogs must be leashed and cleaned up after.

Comfort Inn & Suites
2205 N. Date St.
Truth Or Consequences, NM
575-894-1660 (877-424-6423)
Dogs of all sizes are allowed.

Best Western Discovery Inn
200 E Estrella Avenue
Tucumcari, NM
575-461-4884 (800-780-7234)
Dogs of all sizes are allowed. Dogs are allowed for a pet fee of $10.00 per pet per stay.

Comfort Inn
2800 E. Tucumcari Blvd.
Tucumcari, NM
575-461-4094 (877-424-6423)
Dogs of all sizes are allowed. Dogs are allowed for a pet fee of $12.00 per pet per night.

Days Inn Tucumcari
2623 South 1st St./I-40
Tucumcari, NM
575-461-3158 (800-329-7466)
Dogs of all sizes are allowed. Dogs are allowed for a pet fee.

Econo Lodge
3400 E. Tucumcari Blvd.
Tucumcari, NM
575-461-4194 (877-424-6423)
Dogs of all sizes are allowed. Dogs are allowed for a pet fee of $5.00 per pet per night.

Motel 6 - Tucumcari
2900 Tucumcari Blvd
Tucumcari, NM
575-461-4791 (800-466-8356)
This motel welcomes your pets to stay with you.

Super 8 Tucumcari
4001 E Tucumcari Blvd
Tucumcari, NM
575-461-4444 (800-800-8000)
Dogs are welcome at this hotel.

Travelodge Tucumcari
1214 East Tucumcari Blvd
Tucumcari, NM
575-461-1401 (800-578-7878)
Dogs of all sizes are allowed. Dogs are allowed for a pet fee of $5.00 per pet per night.

New York

Best Western Albany Airport Inn
200 Wolf Road
Albany, NY
518-458-1000 (800-780-7234)
Dogs are welcome at this hotel. There is a $25 one time pet fee.

Best Western Sovereign Hotel - Albany
1228 Western Avenue
Albany, NY
518-489-2981 (800-780-7234)
Dogs of all sizes are allowed. Dogs are allowed for a nightly pet fee.

Clarion Hotel
3 Watervliet Ave Extension
Albany, NY
518-438-8431 (877-424-6423)
Dogs of all sizes are allowed. Dogs are allowed for a pet fee of $25.00 per pet per night. Two dogs are allowed per room.

Comfort Inn & Suites
1606 Central Ave.
Albany, NY
518-869-5327 (877-424-6423)
Dogs up to 50 pounds are allowed. Dogs are allowed for a pet fee of $15.00 per pet per night.

Cresthill Suites Hotel
1415 Washington Avenue
Albany, NY
518-454-0007 (888-723-1655)
cresthillsuites.com
In addition to offering a great starting location to many other local attractions, this hotel also has an outdoor courtyard pool with a patio and barbecue's, and lots of extras. Dogs of all sizes are allowed for an additional $75 one time fee per pet. They request that dogs be removed or crated for housekeeping. Dogs must be leashed, cleaned up after, and may only be left alone in the room if they will be quiet and well behaved. Multiple dogs may be allowed.

Days Inn SUNY Albany
1230 Western Avenue
Albany, NY
518-489-4423 (800-329-7466)
Dogs of all sizes are allowed. Dogs are allowed for a nightly pet fee.

Extended Stay America Albany - Capital
1395 Washington Ave.
Albany, NY
518-446-0680 (800-804-3724)
One dog is allowed per suite. There is a $25 per night additional pet fee

up to $150 for an entire stay.

Holiday Inn Albany
205 Wolf Rd.
Albany, NY
518-458-7250 (877-270-6405)
Dogs up to 75 pounds are allowed.
Dogs are allowed for a pet fee of
$35.00 per pet per night.

Motel 6 - Albany Airport,ny
1600 Central Avenue
Albany, NY
518-456-8982 (800-466-8356)
This motel welcomes your pets to
stay with you.

Motel 6 - Albany, Ny
100 Watervliet Avenue
Albany, NY
518-438-7447 (800-466-8356)
This motel welcomes your pets to
stay with you.

Red Roof Inn Albany Airport
188 Wolf Road
Albany, NY
518-459-1971 (800-RED-ROOF)
One well-behaved family pet per
room. Guest must notify front desk
upon arrival. Guest is liable for any
damages. In consideration of all
guests, pets must never be left
unattended in the guest rooms.

Super 8 Albany
1579 Central Ave
Albany, NY
518-869-8471 (800-800-8000)
Dogs are welcome at this hotel.

TownePlace Suites Albany SUNY
1379 Washington Avenue
Albany, NY
518-435-1900 (800-257-3000)
Centrally located in the heart of town,
this all suite inn is only a short
distance to medical centers/schools,
universities, major corporations, and
to numerous shopping, dining, and
entertainment areas. Dogs are
allowed for an additional one time
fee of $75 per room. Multiple dogs
may be allowed.

Gansett Green Manor
273 Main Street
Amagansett, NY
631-267-3133
Well behaved dogs of all sizes are
allowed. There can be up to 3 small
dogs or 2 big dogs per room. The fee
is $20 for the 1st 4 days then $5 for
each day thereafter per pet. Dogs
must be healthy and free of tics and
fleas.

Comfort Inn University
1 Flint Road
Amherst, NY
716-688-0811 (877-424-6423)
Dogs of all sizes are allowed. Dogs
are allowed for a pet fee of $20.00
per pet per night.

Extended Stay America Buffalo -
Amherst
125 Inn Keepers Ln.
Amherst, NY
716-564-0620 (800-804-3724)
One dog is allowed per suite. There
is a $25 per night additional pet fee
up to $150 for an entire stay.

Hotel Indigo Buffalo - Amherst
10 Flint Road
Amherst, NY
716-689-4414 (877-865-6578)
Dogs of all sizes are allowed. Dogs
are allowed for a pet fee of $75.00
per pet per stay.

Lord Amherst
5000 Main St
Amherst, NY
716-839-2200 (800-544-2200)
There are no additional pet fees. 2
dogs may be allowed.

Motel 6 - Buffalo Amherst
4400 Maple Road
Amherst, NY
716-834-2231 (800-466-8356)
This motel welcomes your pets to
stay with you.

Red Roof Inn University at Buffalo -
Amherst
42 Flint Road
Amherst, NY
716-689-7474 (800-RED-ROOF)
One well-behaved family pet per
room. Guest must notify front desk
upon arrival. Guest is liable for any
damages. In consideration of all
guests, pets must never be left
unattended in the guest rooms.

Quality Inn Binghamton West
7666 Route 434
Apalachin, NY
607-625-4441 (877-424-6423)
Dogs of all sizes are allowed. Dogs
are allowed for a pet fee of $10.00
per pet per night. Two dogs are
allowed per room.

Days Inn /Finger Lakes Region
Auburn
37 William St.
Auburn, NY
315-252-7567 (800-329-7466)
Dogs of all sizes are allowed. Dogs
are allowed for a pet fee.

Super 8 Auburn
19 McMaster St
Auburn, NY
315-253-8886 (800-800-8000)
Dogs of all sizes are allowed. Dogs
are allowed for a pet fee.

Caboose Motel
8620 State Route 415
Avoca, NY
607-566-2216
caboosemotel.net
Small to large dogs are allowed in
the 5 cabooses that serve as
guestrooms at this unique hotel.
There is no additional pet fee. 2 dogs
may be allowed.

Days Inn Darien Lake Theme Park
Batavia
200 Oak Street
Batavia, NY
585-343-6000 (800-329-7466)
Dogs of all sizes are allowed. Dogs
are allowed for a pet fee.

Holiday Inn Batavia-Darien Lake
Area
8250 Park Road
Batavia, NY
585-344-2100 (877-270-6405)
Dogs of all sizes are allowed. Dogs
are allowed for a pet fee of $15.00
per pet per night.

Travelodge Batavia
8204 Park Rd
Batavia, NY
585-343-1000 (800-578-7878)
Dogs are welcome at this hotel.

Days Inn Hammondsport Bath
330 West Morris Street
Bath, NY
607-776-7644 (800-329-7466)
Dogs are welcome at this hotel.

Super 8 Hammondsport Area Bath
333 W Morris
Bath, NY
607-776-2187 (800-800-8000)
Dogs of all sizes are allowed. Dogs
are allowed for a pet fee.

Extended Stay America Long Island -
Bethpage
905 S. Oyster Bay Rd.
Bethpage, NY
516-349-8759 (800-804-3724)
One dog is allowed per suite. There
is a $25 per night additional pet fee
up to $150 for an entire stay.

Big Indian Springs
74 Cruickshank Road
Big Indian, NY

845-254-5905
bigindiansprings.com/
Surrounded by lush greenery, this 37 acre waterside retreat features a large wrap-around veranda, a big swimming pool, a tennis court, an auditorium, and more. Dogs are allowed for no additional feel; they must be leashed and cleaned up after. 2 dogs may be allowed.

Comfort Inn
1000 Upper Front Street
Binghamton, NY
607-724-3297 (877-424-6423)
Dogs up to 80 pounds are allowed. Dogs are allowed for a pet fee of $5.00 per pet per night. Two dogs are allowed per room.

Econo Lodge Inn & Suites
690 Old Front Street
Binghamton, NY
607-724-1341 (877-424-6423)
Dogs of all sizes are allowed. Dogs are allowed for a pet fee of $5.00 per pet per night. Three or more dogs may be allowed.

Grand Royale Clarion Collection
80 State St.
Binghamton, NY
607-722-0000 (877-424-6423)
Dogs of all sizes are allowed. Dogs are allowed for a pet fee of $10.00 per pet per night. Two dogs are allowed per room.

Holiday Inn Binghamton-Dwtn (Hawley St)
2-8 Hawley St
Binghamton, NY
607-722-1212 (877-270-6405)
Dogs of all sizes are allowed. Dogs are allowed for a pet fee of $30.00 per pet per night.

Howard Johnson Binghamton
1156 Upper Front Street
Binghamton, NY
607-722-5353 (800-446-4656)
Dogs are welcome at this hotel. There is a $10 one time pet fee.

Motel 6 - Binghamton
1012 Front Street
Binghamton, NY
607-771-0400 (800-466-8356)
This motel welcomes your pets to stay with you.

Super 8 /Front St Binghamton
650 Old Front St
Binghamton, NY
607-773-8111 (800-800-8000)
Dogs are welcome at this hotel.

Red Roof Inn Buffalo - Niagara Airport
146 Maple Drive
Bowmansville, NY
716-633-1100 (800-RED-ROOF)
One well-behaved family pet per room. Guest must notify front desk upon arrival. Guest is liable for any damages. In consideration of all guests, pets must never be left unattended in the guest rooms.

Econo Lodge
6575 4th Section Rd.
Brockport, NY
585-637-3157 (877-424-6423)
Dogs of all sizes are allowed. Dogs are allowed for a pet fee of $10.00 per pet per night.

Holiday Inn Express Brockport
4908 South Lake Rd
Brockport, NY
585-395-1000 (877-270-6405)
Dogs are welcome at this hotel. There is a $25 one time pet fee.

Days Inn Brooklyn
437 39th Street
Brooklyn, NY
718-853-4141 (800-329-7466)
Dogs are welcome at this hotel.

Holiday Inn Express New York-Brooklyn
625 Union St.
Brooklyn, NY
718-797-1133 (877-270-6405)
Dogs of all sizes are allowed. Dogs are allowed for a pet fee of $100.00 per pet per stay.

Howard Johnson Hotel Brooklyn
599 Utica Avenue
Brooklyn, NY
718-774-0018 (800-446-4656)
Dogs are welcome at this hotel.

Best Western - On The Avenue
510 Delaware Avenue
Buffalo, NY
716-886-8333 (800-780-7234)
Dogs are welcome at this hotel.

Econo Lodge South
4344 Milestrip Rd.
Buffalo, NY
716-825-7530 (877-424-6423)
Dogs of all sizes are allowed. Dogs are allowed for a pet fee of $10.00 per pet per night.

Residence Inn Buffalo Amherst
100 Maple Road
Buffalo, NY
716-632-6622 (800-331-3131)
This all suite, upscale hotel offers a central location to all the area has to offer for both business and leisure travelers. And, among the amenities they also offer a daily buffet breakfast, an evening social hour Monday through Thursday, a seasonal outdoor pool, and a Sport Court. Dogs are allowed for an additional one time pet fee of $75 per room. Multiple dogs may be allowed.

Residence Inn Buffalo Cheektowaga
107 Anderson Road
Buffalo, NY
716-892-5410 (800-331-3131)
In addition to offering a convenient location to business, shopping, dining, and entertainment areas, this all suite, upscale inn also provides a number of in-house amenities, including a daily buffet breakfast, and a Manager's reception Monday through Thursday. Dogs are allowed for an additional one time pet fee of $100 per room. Multiple dogs may be allowed.

Cedar Terrace Resort
665 Main Street
Cairo, NY
518-622-9313
Nestled in the scenic Northern Catskill Mountains, this picturesque resort offers a relaxing atmosphere in addition to well-manicured grounds and gardens, great views, and comfortable rooms. Some of their features include gaming courts, a 9-hole miniature golf course, a multi-use sports field with bleachers, big swings, a pool, table tennis, catering for groups, and wonderful wooded hiking paths. Dogs of all sizes are allowed. There is a $15 per night per pet additional fee. Dogs may not be left alone in the room at any time, and they must be leashed and cleaned up after.

Blue Harbor House
67 Elm Street
Camden, NY
207-236-3196 (800-248-3196)
blueharborhouse.com/
This 1810 harbor house features a nice blending of old and new worlds, and is about a 4 minute walk to the harbor and a quaint coastal village. They offer one suite for guests with pets, complete with a whirlpool tub and it's own outside entrance. One dog of any size is allowed for an additional fee of $25 per night. Dogs must be leashed and cleaned up after.

The Inn at The Shaker Mill Farm
40 Cherry Lane

Canaan, NY
518-794-9345
shakermillfarminn.com/
This converted 1824 Shaker mill, complete with a brook and waterfall, features 20 uniquely different rooms with private baths, and woodland trails to explore. Dogs of all sizes are allowed for no additional fee. Dogs must be very well behaved, quiet, leashed, and cleaned up after. Multiple dogs may be allowed.

Days Inn /Syracuse Canastota
377 North Peterboro Street
Canastota, NY
315-697-3309 (800-329-7466)
Dogs are welcome at this hotel.

Knights Inn Castleton on Hudson/Schodack
1666 Columbia Turnpike
Castleton On Hudson, NY
518-477-2606 (800-843-5644)
Dogs of all sizes are allowed. Dogs are allowed for a pet fee.

Quality Inn & Conference Center
704 Rt. 23 B
Catskill, NY
518-943-5800 (877-424-6423)
Dogs of all sizes are allowed. Dogs are allowed for a pet fee of $20.00 per pet per night.

Mountain View Log Home
Hunter Mountain
Catskills, NY
212-381-2375
This fully-loaded, ready to enjoy tri-level log cabin sits on 10 elevated hilly, wooded acres and offers a sauna, a pool/gaming room, many extras-including great views of Hunter Mountain, and they are just minutes from an abundance of activities and recreation. Dogs of all sizes are welcome for no additional pet fee. They ask that dogs are kept off the furniture and the bedroom. Dogs must be leashed and cleaned up after. 2 dogs may be allowed.

Lincklaen House
79 Albany St
Cazenovia, NY
315-655-3461
cazenovia.com/lincklaen/
A landmark since 1836, this hotel was built as a luxurious stopover for colonial travelers. All rooms are non-smoking. There are no additional pet fees. Multiple dogs may be allowed.

The Brae Loch Inn
5 Albany Street
Cazenovia, NY

315-655-3431
braelochinn.com
There is a $10 one time pet fee. Prior permission for the pet must be made when making your reservation.

Comfort Inn
475 Dingens ST
Cheektowaga, NY
716-896-2800 (877-424-6423)
Dogs up to 50 pounds are allowed. Dogs are allowed for a pet fee of $20.00 per pet per night. Two dogs are allowed per room.

Holiday Inn Buffalo-Intl Airport
4600 Genesee Street
Cheektowaga, NY
716-634-6969 (877-270-6405)
Dogs of all sizes are allowed. Dogs are allowed for a pet fee.

Asa Ransom House
10529 Main Street
Clarence, NY
716-759-2315
One dog up to 50 pounds is allowed for no additional fee.

Staybridge Suites Buffalo-Airport
8005 Sheridan Drive
Clarence, NY
716-810-7829 (877-270-6405)
Dogs up to 80 pounds are allowed. Pets allowed with an additional pet fee. Up to $75 for 1-6 nights and up to $150 for 7+ nights. A pet agreement must be signed at check-in.

Best Western Inn of Cobleskill
121 Burgin Drive
Cobleskill, NY
518-234-4321 (800-780-7234)
Dogs are welcome at this hotel. There is a $15 one time pet fee.

Super 8
955 East Main Street
Cobleskill, NY
518-234-4888 (800-800-8000)
Dogs of all sizes are allowed. Dogs are allowed for a pet fee.

Howard Johnson Inn and Suites Cooperstown Hartwick
4470 State Hwy 28
Cooperstown Hartwick, NY
607-286-7600 (800-446-4656)
Dogs are welcome at this hotel.

Staybridge Suites Corning
201 Townley Avenue
Corning, NY
607-936-7800 (877-270-6405)
Dogs up to 80 pounds are allowed.

Pets allowed with an additional pet fee. Up to $75 for 1-6 nights and up to $150 for 7+ nights. A pet agreement must be signed at check-in.

Stiles Motel
9239 Victory Highway
Corning, NY
607-962-5221
There is a $3 per day pet charge.

Quality Inn
188 Clinton Ave.
Cortland, NY
607-756-5622 (877-424-6423)
Dogs of all sizes are allowed. Dogs are allowed for a pet fee of $20.00 per pet per stay.

Ramada Hotel and Conference Center Cortland
2 River Street
Cortland, NY
607-756-4431 (800-272-6232)
Dogs are welcome at this hotel.

Days Inn Cortland / Mc Graw
3775 US Rt 11
Cortland / Mc Graw, NY
607-753-7594 (800-329-7466)
Dogs of all sizes are allowed. Dogs are allowed for a pet fee.

Econo Lodge
1 North Branch Road
Cuba, NY
585-968-1992 (877-424-6423)
Dogs of all sizes are allowed. Dogs are allowed for a pet fee of $10.00 per pet per night. Two dogs are allowed per room.

Daystop Dansville
9616 Commerce Drive
Dansville, NY
585-335-6023 (800-329-7466)
Dogs are welcome at this hotel.

Econo Lodge
3400 Erie Boulevard East
DeWitt, NY
315-446-3300 (877-424-6423)
Dogs of all sizes are allowed. Dogs are allowed for a pet fee of $10.00 per pet per night.

Best Western Dunkirk & Fredonia Inn
3912 Vineyard Drive
Dunkirk, NY
716-366-7100 (800-780-7234)
Dogs are welcome at this hotel.

Comfort Inn
3925 Vineyard Dr.
Dunkirk, NY
716-672-4450 (877-424-6423)

Dogs of all sizes are allowed. Dogs are allowed for a pet fee of $10.00 per pet per night.

Residence Inn Albany East Greenbush/Tech Valley
3 Tech Valley Drive
East Greenbush, NY
518-720-3600 (888-236-2427)
Located in the Albany Capitol District, this hotel offers a convenient location to businesses and institutes of learning, plus they offer a number of in-house amenities, including a daily buffet breakfast and a Manager's reception Monday through Thursday. Dogs are allowed for an additional one time pet fee of $75 per room. Multiple dogs may be allowed.

Bend In the Road Guest House
58 Spring Close H
East Hampton, NY
631-324-4592
bendintheroadguesthouse.com/
With a convenient location to the beaches, eateries, and shops, this inn (that also functions as a pottery studio) sits on 22 acres of farmland featuring a driving range for golfers, a private jogging path great for running the pooch, a large lawn area, and a secluded garden with a large swimming pool. Dogs of all sizes are welcome for no additional pet fee. Dogs may not be left alone in the room at any time, and they must be leashed and cleaned up after in common areas. Multiple dogs may be allowed.

The Bassett House Inn
128 Montauk H
East Hampton, NY
631-324-6127
bassetthouseinn.com/
This spacious, country 1830's inn offers 12 individually adorned guest rooms, garden-style grounds, a central location to the village, walking trails, and beaches. Dogs of all sizes are welcome (with prior notice) for an additional $15 per night per pet. Dogs must be well behaved, and leashed and cleaned up after. They may only be left alone in the room for a short time if they will be quiet and the owner is confident in their behavior. 2 dogs may be allowed.

The Mill House Inn
31 N Main Street
East Hampton, NY
631-324-9766
millhouseinn.com
This inn has been recently renovated to allow guests to have a true Long Island lodging experience with great

ocean views, gas fireplaces, whirlpool baths, private decks, and the dog friendly suites have heated stone floors. Dogs of all sizes are allowed for an additional $50 per night per pet. Dogs may only be left alone in the suite if they will be quiet and owners are confident in their behavior. Dogs must be under their owner's control at all times, and please clean up after your pet. Multiple dogs may be allowed.

Extended Stay America Syracuse - Dewitt
6630 Old Collamer Rd.
East Syracuse, NY
315-463-1958 (800-804-3724)
One dog is allowed per suite. There is a $25 per night additional pet fee up to $150 for an entire stay.

Holiday Inn Syr I90 Exit 35 Carrier Circle
6555 Old Collamer Road South
East Syracuse, NY
315-437-2761 (877-270-6405)
Dogs of all sizes are allowed. Dogs are allowed for a pet fee.

Motel 6 - Syracuse
6577 Baptist Way
East Syracuse, NY
315-433-1300 (800-466-8356)
This motel welcomes your pets to stay with you.

Quality Inn
6611 Old Collamer Rd
East Syracuse, NY
315-432-9333 (877-424-6423)
Dogs up to 75 pounds are allowed. Dogs are allowed for a pet fee of $10.00 per pet per night. Two dogs are allowed per room.

The Jefferson Inn
3 Jefferson Street
Ellicottville, NY
716-699-5869 (800-577-8451)
thejeffersoninn.com/
A central location to numerous recreational activities, a wide wraparound porch, relaxed ambiance, and a village park a short distance away make this a nice destination for pets and their owners. Dogs of all sizes are allowed in the efficiency units for an additional fee of $10 per night per pet. Dogs must be leashed and cleaned up after, and they may only be left alone in the room if assured they will be quiet, relaxed, and well mannered. Multiple dogs may be allowed.

Extended Stay America White Plains - Elmsford
118 Tarrytown Rd.
Elmsford, NY
914-347-8073 (800-804-3724)
One dog is allowed per suite. There is a $25 per night additional pet fee up to $150 for an entire stay.

Rodeway Inn
749 West Main St
Endicott, NY
607-754-1533 (877-424-6423)
Dogs of all sizes are allowed. Dogs are allowed for a pet fee of $8.00 per pet per night.

Knights Inn /Binghamton Endwell
2603 East Main Street
Endwell, NY
607-754-8020 (800-843-5644)
Dogs are welcome at this hotel. There is a $7 one time additional pet fee.

Red Roof Inn Jamestown - Falconer
1980 East Main Street
Falconer, NY
716-665-3670 (800-RED-ROOF)
One well-behaved family pet per room. Guest must notify front desk upon arrival. Guest is liable for any damages. In consideration of all guests, pets must never be left unattended in the guest rooms.

TownePlace Suites Republic Airport Long Island/Farmingdale
1 Marriott Plaza
Farmingdale, NY
631-454-0080 (800-257-3000)
Besides offering a number of in-house amenities at all level of travelers, this all suite inn also offers a convenient location to major corporations, beaches, shopping, dining, and entertainment areas. Dogs are allowed for an additional one time fee of $100 per room. 2 dogs may be allowed.

Econo Lodge
6108 Loomis Road
Farmington, NY
585-924-2131 (877-424-6423)
Dogs of all sizes are allowed.

Extended Stay America Fishkill - Poughkeepsie
55 West Merritt Blvd.
Fishkill, NY
845-896-0592 (800-804-3724)
One dog is allowed per suite. There is a $25 per night additional pet fee up to $150 for an entire stay.

Homestead Studio Suites Fishkill -

Dog-Friendly Lodging - Please always call ahead to make sure an establishment is still dog-friendly.

Poughkeepsie
25 Merritt Blvd.
Fishkill, NY
845-897-2800 (800-804-3724)
One dog is allowed per suite. There is a $25 per night additional pet fee up to $150 for an entire stay.

Residence Inn Fishkill
14 Schuyler Blvd
Fishkill, NY
845-896-5210 (800-211-7302)
This all suite inn offers a number of amenities for all level of travelers, including a daily buffet breakfast, nightly social hours, summer barbecues, an outdoor pool, and a Sport Court. Dogs are allowed for an additional one time pet fee of $100 per room. Multiple dogs may be allowed.

The River Run
882 Main Street
Fleischmanns, NY
845-254-4884
riverrunbedandbreakfast.com
Located in a beautiful Queen Anne Victorian home on well landscaped grounds, this inn also offers 8 individual themed rooms of upstate mountain rivers, and a convenient location to scenic hiking trails, the Village Park and playground, shopping, and dining sites. Dogs are allowed for an additional fee of $10 per night per pet, and they must be over 1 year old. Dogs must be kept leashed and cleaned up after promptly. Multiple dogs may be allowed.

Howard Johnson LaGuardia Airport East
135-33 38th Avenue
Flushing, NY
718-461-3888 (800-446-4656)
Dogs are welcome at this hotel.

Sheraton La Guardia East Hotel
135-20 39th Ave.
Flushing, NY
718-460-6666 (888-625-5144)
Dogs up to 60 pounds are allowed. There are no additional pet fees. Dogs are not allowed to be left alone in the room.

Inn at Lake Joseph
400 Saint Joseph Road
Forestburgh, NY
845-791-9506
lakejoseph.com
The inn is a romantic 135-year-old Victorian Country Estate on a 250-acre private lake, surrounded by thousands of acres of hardwood forest and wildlife preserve. The Inn provides a variety of summer and winter recreational facilities including the use of their nearby full service health and fitness club. Breakfast is served on the screened-in Veranda allowing you to enjoy the sounds and feel of the lush green forest. When glassed in during winter, you can experience the beauty of a surrounding snowscape. Dogs are welcomed in their Carriage House and Cottage. The inn is located in Forestburgh at Lake Joseph.

Brookside Manor
3728 Route 83
Fredonia, NY
716-672-7721 (800-929-7599)
bbonline.com/ny/brookside/
Built in 1875 with over 6,000 square feet of living space, this Victorian manor sits on 5.5 partially wooded acres with its own spring-fed brook, manicured lawns and gardens, and there is beauty and activities here year round. Dogs of all sizes are welcome for no additional fee with advance registration; when doing so on line they request that you make note in the "special needs" comments that pets will be coming. Dogs must be well mannered, leashed, and cleaned up after. Multiple dogs may be allowed.

Days Inn Fredonia
10455 Bennett Road (Rt 60)
Fredonia, NY
716-673-1351 (800-329-7466)
Dogs of all sizes are allowed. Dogs are allowed for a pet fee.

Quality Inn
4242 Lakeville Road
Geneseo, NY
585-243-0500 (877-424-6423)
Dogs of all sizes are allowed. Dogs are allowed for a pet fee of $15.00 per pet per night.

Cobtree Vacation Rental Homes
440-450 Armstrong Road
Geneva, NY
315-789-1144 (866-573-6322)
cobtree.com
A number of these vacation rentals in the Finger Lakes region allow your dog. Ask them about pet-friendly properties when calling.

Motel 6 - Geneva
485 Hamilton Street
Geneva, NY
315-789-4050 (800-466-8356)
This motel welcomes your pets to stay with you.

Ramada Lakefront Geneva
41 Lakefront Dr
Geneva, NY
315-789-0400 (800-272-6232)
Dogs of all sizes are allowed. Dogs are allowed for a pet fee of $10.00 per pet per night.

Econo Lodge
15 Frontage Road
Glenmont, NY
518-449-5181 (877-424-6423)
Dogs of all sizes are allowed. Dogs are allowed for a pet fee of $5.00 per pet per night. Two dogs are allowed per room.

Econo Lodge
543 Aviation Rd.
Glens Falls, NY
518-793-3700 (877-424-6423)
Dogs of all sizes are allowed. Dogs are allowed for a pet fee of $25.00 per pet per night. Two dogs are allowed per room.

Quality Inn
547 Aviation Road
Glens Falls, NY
518-793-3800 (877-424-6423)
Dogs of all sizes are allowed. Dogs are allowed for a pet fee of $usd per pet per night. Two dogs are allowed per room.

Super 8 Queensbury/ Glens Falls
191 Corinth Road
Glens Falls, NY
518-761-9780 (800-800-8000)
Dogs are welcome at this hotel.

Chateau Motor Lodge
1810 Grand Island Blvd
Grand Island, NY
716-773-2868
There is an $15 per day pet fee for 1 dog, and an additional $20 per day for 2 pets. Non-smoking pet rooms are limited and advance reservations are suggested. 2 dogs may be allowed.

Holiday Inn Grand Island
(Buffalo/Niagara)
100 Whitehaven Rd
Grand Island, NY
716-773-1111 (877-270-6405)
Dogs of all sizes are allowed. Dogs are allowed for a pet fee of $75.00 per pet per stay.

Shorecrest Property Rentals & Bed and Breakfast
54300 County Route 48
Greenport-Southold, NY
631-765-1570

shorecrestbedandbreakfast.com
Dogs are welcome at 4 of their rental cottages. Small dogs can be accommodated in the Rose Site of the B&B.

The Trout House Village Resort
9117 Lakeshore Drive
Hague, NY
518-543-6088 (800-368-6088)
trouthouse.com/
This resort, on the shores of Lake George, offers beautiful views of the lake and surrounding Adirondack Mountains, and provides a wide array of activities and recreation, a 9-hole putting green, and rentals for bikes and watercraft. Although dogs are not allowed during the summer months between June 15th and September 15th, the beauty and activities here are year round. One dog is allowed per unit for an additional pet fee of $25 per night. Dogs are not allowed on the bed or the furniture, they must be leashed and cleaned up after, and they may not be left alone in the room. Dogs must be quiet and well mannered.

Comfort Inn & Suites
3615 Commerce Place
Hamburg, NY
716-648-2922 (877-424-6423)
Dogs of all sizes are allowed. Dogs are allowed for a pet fee of $20.00 per pet per night.

Red Roof Inn Buffalo - Hamburg
5370 Camp Road
Hamburg, NY
716-648-7222 (800-RED-ROOF)
One well-behaved family pet per room. Guest must notify front desk upon arrival. Guest is liable for any damages. In consideration of all guests, pets must never be left unattended in the guest rooms.

Bowen's by the Bays
177 West Montauk Highway
Hampton Bays, NY
631-728-1158 (800-533-3139)
gobowens.com
This lovely resort, located in the heart of the Hamptons, is very pet friendly. It offers individually decorated guest rooms and guest cottages, swimming pool, tennis court, small pond with waterfall and beautiful gardens. Pets are welcome in the guest cottages. Pet fees are $20 per pet/per day and guests are required to abide by the posted pet regulations, i.e. pets must be on leash, owners must clean up after pet, etc. Bowen's is situated on four landscaped acres, and is close to

restaurants, shopping, and the North Fork, as well as the charming towns of the Hamptons.

Residence Inn Long Island Hauppauge/Islandia
850 Veterans Memorial H
Hauppauge, NY
631-724-4188 (800-817-3301)
Offering a convenient location to business, beaches, shopping, dining, and entertainment areas, this all suite hotel also offers a number of in-house amenities, including a daily buffet breakfast and nightly social events. Dogs are allowed for an additional one time pet fee of $75 per room. 2 dogs may be allowed.

Sheraton Long Island
110 Motor Parkway
Hauppauge, NY
631-231-1100 (888-625-5144)
Dogs up to 80 pounds are allowed. There are no additional pet fees. Dogs are not allowed to be left alone in the room.

Red Roof Inn Rochester - Henrietta
4820 West Henrietta Road
Henrietta, NY
585-359-1100 (800-RED-ROOF)
One well-behaved family pet per room. Guest must notify front desk upon arrival. Guest is liable for any damages. In consideration of all guests, pets must never be left unattended in the guest rooms.

Super 8 /Rochester Area Henrietta
I90 NYS Thruway at I390
Henrietta, NY
585-359-1630 (800-800-8000)
Dogs are welcome at this hotel.

Herkimer Motel
100 Marginal Rd
Herkimer, NY
315-866-0490
Dogs are allowed for a fee of $10 per night per pet. Dogs may not be left alone in the rooms. Multiple dogs may be allowed.

Super 8 NY Highland
3423 Route 9W
Highland, NY
845-691-6888 (800-800-8000)
Dogs are welcome at this hotel.

Econo Lodge
17 Main Street
Highland Falls, NY
845-446-9400 (877-424-6423)
Dogs up to 200 pounds are allowed. Dogs are allowed for a pet fee of

$10.00 per pet per night. Three or more dogs may be allowed.

Residence Inn Long Island Holtsville
25 Middle Avenue
Holtsville, NY
631-475-9500 (800-331-3131)
Offering a convenient location to businesses, beaches, shopping, dining, and entertainment areas, this all suite hotel also offers a number of in-house amenities, including a daily buffet breakfast and evening socials Monday to Thursday. Dogs are allowed for an additional one time pet fee of $100 per room. 2 dogs may be allowed.

Days Inn NY Hornell
Route 36 and Webb Crossing
Hornell, NY
607-324-6222 (800-329-7466)
Dogs of all sizes are allowed. Dogs are allowed for a pet fee.

Econo Lodge
7462 Seneca Rd N
Hornell, NY
607-324-0800 (877-424-6423)
Dogs of all sizes are allowed. Dogs are allowed for a pet fee of $10.00 per pet per night.

Best Western Marshall Manor
3527 Watkins Road
Horseheads, NY
607-739-3891 (800-780-7234)
Dogs of all sizes are allowed. Dogs are allowed for a nightly pet fee.

Motel 6 - Elmira Horseheads
4133 Route 17
Horseheads, NY
607-739-2525 (800-466-8356)
This motel welcomes your pets to stay with you.

Finger Lakes Home
7750 County Road 153
Interlaken, NY
607-532-4770
Dogs up to 50 pounds are allowed in the cottages. There are no additional pet fees and dogs are not allowed to be left unattended. They request you brush your dog outdoors.

Best Western University Inn
1020 Ellis Hollow Road
Ithaca, NY
607-272-6100 (800-780-7234)
Dogs of all sizes are allowed. Dogs are allowed for a nightly pet fee.

Comfort Inn
356 Elmira Rd.
Ithaca, NY

607-272-0100 (877-424-6423)
Dogs of all sizes are allowed. Dogs are allowed for a pet fee of $25.00 per pet per stay.

Econo Lodge
2303 N. Triphammer Rd.
Ithaca, NY
607-257-1400 (877-424-6423)
Dogs of all sizes are allowed. Dogs are allowed for a pet fee of $15.00 per pet per night. Two dogs are allowed per room.

Holiday Inn Ithaca Downtown
222 South Cayuga Street
Ithaca, NY
607-272-1000 (877-270-6405)
Dogs of all sizes are allowed. Dogs are allowed for a pet fee of $15 per pet per stay.

Log Country Inn
South Danby and La Rue Roads
Ithaca, NY
607-589-4771 (800-274-4771)
logtv.com/inn/hispeed.html
Sitting at the edge of a vast state forest in a scenic country setting on 100 wooded acres, this spacious log home features custom made country furniture and rooms with "around the world" themes (there are even "themed" hiking trails), and they are close to wide variety of activities, recreation, and the Ithaca Falls. Dogs of all sizes are welcome for no additional pet fee. Dogs must be well behaved, leashed, and cleaned up after. Puppies must always be crated when left alone in the room, and if the owner's are confident in their dogs behavior (must be quiet), older dogs do not have to be crated. 2 dogs may be allowed.

The William Henry Miller Inn
303 N Aurora Street
Ithaca, NY
607-256-4553 (877-25-MILLER (256-4553))
millerinn.com/
Originally built in 1880 by Cornell University's 1st student of architecture, the house is rich in detail with stained glass windows and woodwork, and it is located near the Ithaca Commons area that is abundant with eateries, shops, theaters, and recreation. There is 1 pet friendly suite in the Carriage House, and dogs of all sizes are welcome for no additional pet fee. They will provide water and food dishes, but they ask that you bring your own pets bedding. Dogs must be leashed, cleaned up after, and they may not be left alone in the

room at any time. 2 dogs may be allowed.

Howard Johnson Inn JFK Airport NY Jamaica
153-95 Rockaway Boulevard
Jamaica, NY
718-723-6700 (800-446-4656)
Dogs of all sizes are allowed. Dogs are allowed for a pet fee of $50 per pet per night.

Best Western Downtown Jamestown
200 W 3rd Street
Jamestown, NY
716-484-8400 (800-780-7234)
Dogs up to 50 pounds are allowed. Dogs are allowed for a pet fee.

Comfort Inn
2800 North Main Street
Jamestown, NY
716-664-5920 (877-424-6423)
Dogs of all sizes are allowed.

Fourpeaks
Stonehouse Road
Jay, NY
518-524-6726
4peaks.com/home.htm
Fourpeaks sits secluded in a hidden valley at the end of a dirt road, and they offer a variety of accommodations, year round land and water recreation, numerous hiking trails (4 with major destinations), and cabins with full kitchens. The resident pooch here welcomes all friendly canine guests to play, go hiking, running, swimming, or just kick back at this scenic 700-acre wilderness playground of private forest land, and if they are under voice control and well behaved-no leashes are required. There are no additional pet fees. Dogs must be under their owner's control at all times. Multiple dogs may be allowed.

La Quinta Inn Johnson City
581 Harry L. Drive
Johnson City, NY
607-770-9333 (800-531-5900)
A dog of any size is allowed. There are no additional pet fees. There is a pet waiver to sign at check in. Dogs are not allowed to be left alone in the rooms, but if you have to go for a short time, a contact number must be left with the front desk.

Red Roof Inn Binghamton
590 Fairview Street
Johnson City, NY

607-729-8940 (800-RED-ROOF)
One well-behaved family pet per room. Guest must notify front desk upon arrival. Guest is liable for any damages. In consideration of all guests, pets must never be left unattended in the guest rooms.

Holiday Inn Johnstown-Gloversville
308 North Comrie Ave
Johnstown, NY
518-762-4686 (877-270-6405)
Dogs are welcome at this hotel.

Trails End Inn
62 Trails End Way
Keene Valley, NY
518-576-9860 (800-281-9860)
trailsendinn.com/
Secluded, but easily accessible, this 1902 mountain lodge offers a large front yard and porches, a barbecue and picnic area, whirlpool tubs, and it is in a great location for numerous year round recreational pursuits. Dogs of all sizes are allowed for an additional $20 per night per pet, and owners are responsible for any pet-incurred damages. There can be 1 large dog or 2 small dogs per room, and please keep them off the furniture and beds. Dogs may only be left alone in the room if assured they will be quiet and they must be crated. Dogs are not allowed in the common areas like the front porch or through the interior halls of the inn; use outer doors or stairs. Outside the inn dogs can be off lead if they are under good voice control, and "doggy towels" are provided for muddy paws. Dogs must be picked up after at all times.

Villa Rosa B&B Inn
121 Highland Street
Kings Park, NY
631-724-4872
thevillarosainn.com/
Built in 1920, this bed and breakfast inn is surrounded by spacious landscaped grounds. Some of the inn's rooms have private baths. This dog-friendly inn offers a fenced dog park area. Guests are welcome to bring their well-behaved dog, but pets must be leashed when in shared areas. There is a $20 per day pet charge. Weekly and monthly rates are available. They also have parking for larger vehicles like motorhomes and trailers.

Holiday Inn Kingston
503 Washington Ave
Kingston, NY
845-338-0400 (877-270-6405)
Dogs of all sizes are allowed. Dogs

are allowed for a nightly pet fee.

Rodeway Inn
239 Forest Hill Drive
Kingston, NY
845-331-2900 (877-424-6423)
Dogs of all sizes are allowed.

Super 8 Kingston
487 Washington Av
Kingston, NY
845-338-3078 (800-800-8000)
Dogs are welcome at this hotel.

2011 State Route 9
Lake George, NY
518-668-5421 (800-578-7878)
Dogs are welcome at this hotel.

Lake George Gardens Motel
2107 H 9N
Lake George, NY
518-668-2232
Dogs are allowed for a weekly fee of
$25 per pet Dogs may not be left
unattended for very long at a time
and must be on a leash when out. 2
dogs may be allowed.

Rodeway Inn
1449 State Route 9
Lake George, NY
518-792-5904 (877-424-6423)
Dogs of all sizes are allowed. Dogs
are allowed for a pet fee of $25.00
per pet per night.

Super 8 /Warrensburg Area Lake
George
3619 State Route 9
Lake George, NY
518-623-2811 (800-800-8000)
Dogs of all sizes are allowed. Dogs
are allowed for a pet fee.

Luzerne Court
508 Lake Ave
Lake Luzerne, NY
518-696-2734
saratoga.org/luzernecourt/
There are no additional pet fees.
Dogs must not be left alone in the
rooms. 2 dogs may be allowed.

Art Devline's Olympic
350 Main St
Lake Placid, NY
518-523-3700
artdevlins.com/
There is a $4 per night per pet fee. 2
dogs may be allowed.

Comfort Inn
2125 Saranac Ave.
Lake Placid, NY
518-523-9555 (877-424-6423)

Dogs of all sizes are allowed. Two
dogs are allowed per room.

Crowne Plaza Resort Lake Placid-
Golf Club
101 Olympic Drive
Lake Placid, NY
518-523-2556 (877-270-6405)
Dogs of all sizes are allowed. Dogs
are allowed for a pet fee of $10.00
per pet per night.

Lake Placid Lodge
Whiteface Inn Rd.
Lake Placid, NY
518-523-2700
lakeplacidlodge.com
There is a fee of $75 per night for
one dog, and a 2nd dog is an
additional $200 per night. Dogs are
allowed in the cabins,,, they are not
allowed in the main lodge. 2 dogs
may be allowed.

Rodeway Inn
6001 Big Tree Road
Lakeville, NY
585-346-2330 (877-424-6423)
Dogs of all sizes are allowed. Dogs
are allowed for a pet fee of $10.00
per pet per night. Two dogs are
allowed per room.

Century House Inn
997 New Loudon Road
Latham, NY
518-785-0931
centuryhouse.inter.net/
There is a $15 per night per pet fee.
Multiple dogs may be allowed.

Econo Lodge
622 Route 155
Latham, NY
518-785-1414 (877-424-6423)
Dogs of all sizes are allowed. Dogs
are allowed for a pet fee of $10.00
per pet per night.

Quality Inn & Suites Albany Airport
611 Troy-Schenectady Rd.
Latham, NY
518-785-5891 (877-424-6423)
Dogs of all sizes are allowed.

Ramada
946 New Loudon Road
Latham, NY
518-783-6162 (800-272-6232)
Dogs are welcome at this hotel.

Residence Inn Albany Airport
1 Residence Inn Drive
Latham, NY
518-783-0600 (888-236-2427)
This hotel offers a number of in-
house amenities, including a daily

buffet breakfast, a Manager's
reception Monday through Thursday,
a seasonal outdoor pool, a heated
spa, a Sport Court, and passes to a
local fitness facility. Dogs are
allowed for an additional one time
pet fee of $75 per room. 2 dogs may
be allowed.

The Century House Hotel
997 New Loudon Road
Latham, NY
518-785-0931 (888-674-6873)
thecenturyhouse.com/
In additional to a complimentary
country-style breakfast buffet, this
hotel also offers a full service
restaurant and bar, an outdoor pool
and tennis courts, and an historic
nature trail to walk your four legged
companion. Dogs of all sizes are
allowed for an additional fee of $15
per night per pet. Dogs may only be
left alone in the room if they will be
quiet, well behaved, and a contact
number is left with the front desk.
Dogs must be leashed and cleaned
up after. Multiple dogs may be
allowed.

Travelodge Inn and Suites Latham
831 New Loudon Rd
Latham, NY
518-785-6626 (800-578-7878)
Dogs are welcome at this hotel.

Howard Johnson Inn NY Liberty
2067 Route 52 East
Liberty, NY
845-292-7171 (800-446-4656)
Dogs are welcome at this hotel.

Knights Inn Little Falls
20 Albany Street
Little Falls, NY
315-823-4954 (800-843-5644)
Dogs of all sizes are allowed. Dogs
are allowed for a pet fee of $10.00
per pet per stay.

Best Western Liverpool Grace Inn &
Suites
136 Transistor Pkwy
Liverpool, NY
315-701-4400 (800-780-7234)
Dogs of all sizes are allowed. Dogs
are allowed for a nightly pet fee.

Knights Inn Syracuse/ Liverpool
430 Electronics Parkway
Liverpool, NY
315-453-6330 (800-843-5644)
Dogs of all sizes are allowed. Dogs
are allowed for a pet fee of $15.00
per pet per night.

Super 8 /Clay/Syracuse Area

Liverpool
7360 Oswego Rd off Ex 38
Liverpool, NY
315-451-8550 (800-800-8000)
Dogs are welcome at this hotel.

The Guest House
408 Debruce Road
Livingston Manor, NY
845-439-4000
Dogs of all sizes are allowed. There is a $10 per night per pet additional fee. 2 dogs may be allowed.

Comfort Inn
551 South Transit Street
Lockport, NY
716-434-4411 (877-424-6423)
Dogs of all sizes are allowed.

Holiday Inn Lockport
515 South Transit Street
Lockport, NY
716-434-6151 (877-270-6405)
Dogs of all sizes are allowed. Dogs are allowed for a pet fee of $10.00 per pet per night.

Econo Lodge
227 W. Main St.
Malone, NY
518-483-0500 (877-424-6423)
Dogs of all sizes are allowed. Dogs are allowed for a pet fee of $10.00 per pet per night.

Super 8 Malone
42 Finney Blvd. Jons Plaza
Malone, NY
518-483-8123 (800-800-8000)
Dogs are welcome at this hotel.

Econo Lodge
15054 State Highway 37
Massena, NY
315-764-0246 (877-424-6423)
Dogs of all sizes are allowed. Dogs are allowed for a pet fee of $10.00 per pet per night.

Extended Stay America Long Island - Melville
100 Spagnoli Rd.
Melville, NY
631-777-3999 (800-804-3724)
One dog is allowed per suite. There is a $25 per night additional pet fee up to $150 for an entire stay.

Hilton Hotel
598 Broad Hollow Road/H 110
Melville, NY
631-845-1000 (800-HILTONS (445-8667))
This luxury hotel offers a number of on site amenities for business and leisure travelers, plus a convenient location to business, shopping, dining, and entertainment areas. They offer 2 dog friendly rooms; pets are allowed for no additional fee. 2 dogs may be allowed.

Howard Johnson Hotel - Middletown
551 Rte 211 East/I-84
Middletown, NY
845-342-5822 (800-446-4656)
Dogs of all sizes are allowed. Dogs are allowed for a pet fee.

Super 8 Middletown
563 Rt 211 E
Middletown, NY
845-692-5828 (800-800-8000)
Dogs of all sizes are allowed. Dogs are allowed for a pet fee of $15 per pet per night.

Buttermilk Inn and Spa
220 North Road
Milton, NY
845-795-1310 (877-7-INN-SPA (877-746-6772))
buttermilkfallsinn.com/
This inn, set on 70 acres of meticulously landscaped acres (affording exceptional hiking), offers lush garden and river views, an extended breakfast buffet, and a number of amenities/services for business or leisure travelers and special events. Dogs of all sizes are allowed in the carriage house only for an additional one time pet fee of $25 plus a $190 refundable deposit. Pets are not allowed in the main house. Dogs must be leashed and cleaned up after, and they may only be left alone for short time periods. 2 dogs may be allowed.

Hither House Cottages
10 Lincoln Road
Montauk, NY
631-668-2714
hitherhouse.com/
This well-kept, scenic retreat offers various sized cottages, is only a mile from the ocean, and they are just minutes from numerous activities, recreation, and eateries. From Memorial Day to October 1st dogs are not allowed on the beaches between the hours of 10 am and 6 pm, but off season pooches are welcome to run off lead if they are under voice control. Dogs of all sizes are allowed for an additional fee of $15 per night, and there is a pet policy to sign at check in. Dogs are welcome in the garden and on the lawn, but it is requested that they be walked off the premises to do their business. They are not allowed on the furniture and with tiled floors they suggest bringing the pets bedding. Dogs must be well behaved, leashed, cleaned up after, and they may be left alone in the cottage only if they will be quiet and the owner is confident in their behavior. 2 dogs may be allowed.

Super 8 Maybrook Montgomery
207 Montgomery Rd.
Montgomery, NY
845-457-3143 (800-800-8000)
Dogs of all sizes are allowed. Dogs are allowed for a nightly pet fee.

Super 8 Monticello
290 East Broadway
Monticello, NY
845-791-1690 (800-800-8000)
Dogs of all sizes are allowed. Dogs are allowed for a pet fee of $10.00 per pet per night.

Glen Highland Farm
217 Pegg Road
Morris, NY
607-263-5415
glenhighlandfarm.com/
This "Canine County Getaway" sits on 175 picturesque acres complete with ponds, a stream, trails, open meadows and forests, and dogs may explore anywhere on the farm off-leash. The farm is home to several dogs but it is also a Border Collier rescue sanctuary that functions as a training/recovery and placement center, and their complete obstacle course is also available to guests and their dogs. There are several mini-activity camps and programs available to help strengthen the bond between dogs and their companions such as the "Canine Discovery" camp to learn about how smart your dog really is and the "Inner Dog" camp for a greater understanding of your dog. There is even a trainer on staff available to work one on one with guests. The getaway lodging for guests and their canine companions include cottages, cabins, rentable RVs, a few RV spaces, and a camping shelter that has all the amenities on hand for meal prep plus private showers and flush toilets are only a few feet away. There are no additional pet fees. Dogs may not be left alone, they just have to be friendly and have a great time. Multiple dogs may be allowed.

Holiday Inn Mt. Kisco (Westchester County)
1 Holiday Inn Dr
Mount Kisco, NY
914-241-2600 (877-270-6405)
Dogs of all sizes are allowed. Dogs

are allowed for a pet fee of $25.00 per pet per night.

Emerson Resort and Spa
5340 H 28
Mount Tremper, NY
845-688-2828 (877-688-2828)
emersonplace.com/
Lovingly restored, sitting among tall pines and manicured grounds alongside a stream with Mt. Tremper in the background, this resort has become a premier vacation destination for a variety of reasons. A visitor favorite is the 64 foot silo they have turned into the world's largest Kaleidoscope. Dogs are allowed for an additional fee of $25 per night per pet, and advance notification. Dogs may not be left alone in the room, and they need to be removed for housekeeping. Dogs must be quiet, well behaved, under owner's control, leashed, and cleaned up after at all times. Dogs are not allowed in the pool or food areas, or the General Store. 2 dogs may be allowed.

Candlewood Suites Nanuet-Rockland County
20 Overlook Boulevard
Nanuet, NY
845-371-4445 (877-270-6405)
Dogs up to 80 pounds are allowed. Pets allowed with an additional pet fee. Up to $75 for 1-6 nights and up to $150 for 7+ nights. A pet agreement must be signed at check-in.

Days Inn Spring Valley Nanuet
367 West Route 59
Nanuet, NY
845-623-4567 (800-329-7466)
Dogs are welcome at this hotel.

The Vagabond Inn
3300 Sliter Road
Naples, NY
585-554-6271
thevagabondinn.com/
Secluded on a mountain, this 7000 square foot inn offers great views, but they are also home to an American craft gallery, a seasonal outdoor pool, a Japanese garden, lush lawns and grounds, and many other pluses. They offer 2 pet friendly rooms, and dogs of all sizes are welcome for no additional pet fee. Dogs must be well trained, friendly, leashed, and cleaned up after. They may only be left alone in the room for a short time if they will be quiet and owners are confident in their behavior. 2 dogs may be allowed.

Days Inn Middletown

4939 Route 17M
New Hampton, NY
845-374-2411 (800-329-7466)
Dogs are welcome at this hotel.

Ramada Utica Area/ NY New Hartford
141 New Hartford Street
New Hartford, NY
315-735-3392 (800-272-6232)
Dogs of all sizes are allowed. Dogs are allowed for a pet fee of $20.00 per pet per night.

LeFevre House
14 Southside Avenue
New Paltz, NY
845-255-4747
lefevrehouse.com/
In addition to offering a spa, and tailor-made services and dining requests for one or many, this 1870's Victorian home also features an International art gallery (many items for sale), and gives access to a variety of scenic trails. Dogs of all sizes are allowed for an additional $75 one time pet fee per pet, and there is a pet waiver to sign at check in. Dogs are not allowed on the furniture and they must be crated when left alone in the room. Dogs must be leashed and cleaned up after at all times. 2 dogs may be allowed.

Residence Inn New Rochelle
35 LeCount Place
New Rochelle, NY
914-636-7888 (800-331-3131)
Being only about 20 minutes to the bustling heart of New York City and offering some outstanding views of Long Island Sound and of the Manhattan skyline are just a couple of perks of this beautiful upscale, all suite hotel. They also offer a daily breakfast buffet and evening socials. Dogs are allowed for an additional one time pet fee of $100 per room. Multiple dogs may be allowed.

Econo Lodge Near Stewart International Airport
310 Windsor Hwy.
New Windsor, NY
845-561-6620 (877-424-6423)
Dogs of all sizes are allowed. Dogs are allowed for a pet fee of $10.00 per pet per night. Two dogs are allowed per room.

70 Park Avenue Hotel
70 Park Ave
New York, NY
212-973-2400 (877-707-2752)
70parkave.com

This Kimpton boutique hotel is located at Park Avenue and 38th Street. Dogs of all sizes are allowed. There are no additional pet fees.

Candlewood Suites New York City-Times Square
339 W. 39th Street
New York, NY
212-967-2254 (877-270-6405)
Dogs up to 80 pounds are allowed. Pets allowed with an additional pet fee. Up to $75 for 1-6 nights and up to $150 for 7+ nights. A pet agreement must be signed at check-in.

Hilton Hotel
1335 Avenue of the Americas
New York, NY
212-586-7000 (800-HILTONS (445-8667))
Located in the heart of the business and media centers of the city, this upscale hotel offers a number of on site amenities for business and leisure travelers, plus a convenient location to business, shopping, dining, sites of interest, and entertainment areas. Dogs are allowed for an additional one time pet fee of $75 per room. Dogs may not be left alone in the room at any time. 2 dogs may be allowed.

Hilton Hotel
234 W 42nd Street
New York, NY
212-840-8222 (800-HILTONS (445-8667))
Located in Times Square, this modern, boutique-style hotel offers a number on site amenities for business and leisure travelers, plus a convenient location to all this exciting city has to offer. Dogs up to 50 pounds are allowed for an additional one time fee of $75 per pet. 2 dogs may be allowed.

Holiday Inn Express New York City Fifth Avenue
15 West 45th Street
New York, NY
212-302-9088 (877-270-6405)
Dogs of all sizes are allowed. Dogs are allowed for a nightly pet fee.

Holiday Inn Nyc - Manhattan 6th Ave
125 West 26th Street
New York, NY
212-430-8500 (877-270-6405)
Dogs of all sizes are allowed. Dogs are allowed for a pet fee of $25 per pet per night.

Hotel Wales

1295 Madison Avenue
New York, NY
212-876-6000 (866-WALES-HOTEL)
waleshotel.com
This recently renovated Upper East Side hotel close to Central Park offers 88 guestrooms, including 42 suites. There is a $75 per stay pet fee and dogs up to 100 pounds are allowed.

Le Parker Meridien New York
118 West 57th St.
New York, NY
212-245-5000
Dogs of all sizes are allowed. There are no additional pet fees. Dogs are not allowed to be left alone in the room.

New York's Hotel Pennsylvania
401 Seventh Avenue
New York, NY
212-736-5000 (800-223-8585)
hotelpenn.com
Pets of all sizes are welcome at this midtown hotel right next to Penn Station and Madison Square Garden. Each February, this hotel caters to the Westminster Dog Show competitors through its Very Important Pooches program. There are no additional pet fees.

Novotel - New York
226 West 52nd Street
New York, NY
212-315-0100
Novotel Hotels welcome a maximum of 2 animals (cats and dogs) per room and never require a fee. Each guest checking in with a pet will be given a Royal Canine/Novotel Pet Welcome Kit.

Ramada Plaza New Yorker Hotel
481 8th Avenue
New York, NY
212-971-0101 (800-272-6232)
Dogs are welcome at this hotel.

Regency Hotel
540 Park Avenue
New York, NY
212-759-4100
All well-behaved dogs of any size are welcome. This upscale hotel offers their "Loews Loves Pets" program which includes special pet treats, local dog walking routes, and a list of nearby pet-friendly places to visit. There is an additional one time pet cleaning fee of $25 per room.

Renaissance New York Hotel Times Square
Two Times Square, 714 Seventh

Avenue at W 48th Street
New York, NY
212-765-7676 (800-HOTELS-1 (468-3571))
This luxury hotel sits central to many of the city's star attractions, world class shopping and dining venues, day/night entertainment areas, and major business areas, plus they also offer a number of in-house amenities for all level of travelers. Dogs up to 50 pounds are allowed for an additional one time fee of $100 per pet. Dogs may not be left alone in the room at any time. 2 dogs may be allowed.

Residence Inn New York Manhattan/Times Square
1033 Avenue of the Americas
New York, NY
212-768-0007 (800-331-3131)
This upscale, all suite inn sits central to a plethora of world class sites, attractions, shopping, dining, commerce, and entertainment areas. They also offer a daily breakfast buffet and evening socials Monday to Wednesday. Dogs are allowed for an additional one time pet fee of $100 per room. Multiple dogs may be allowed.

Ritz-Carlton Central Park
50 Central Park S
New York, NY
212-308-9100
Dogs up to 70 pounds are allowed. There is a $125 one time pet fee per visit. Pet sitting, emergency veterinarian and dog walking services are available. 2 dogs may be allowed.

Soho Grand Hotel
310 West Broadway
New York, NY
212-965-3000
sohogrand.com/
This hotel is VERY pet-friendly and there are no size restrictions at all for dogs. They are owned by the Hartz Mountain Company which manufactures the 2 in 1 pet products. The hotel is located in the artistic heart of New York's cultural capital SoHo (South of Houston Street), and within an easy walking distance to the surrounding neighborhoods of Tribeca, Greenwich Village, Little Italy and Chinatown. The hotel is also just steps from Wall Street, and only minutes from Midtown Manhattan. Amenities include 24 room service and a fitness center. One of our readers has this to say about the hotel: 'This is the most incredibly

dog friendly hotel. Bellboys carry dog treats, there is a dog room service menu, doggie day care is provided. It's also one of New York's super chic hotels.' There are no pet fees. There is a pet agreement to sign at check in. Multiple dogs may be allowed.

The Marmara Manhattan
301 E 94th Street (at 2nd Avenue)
New York, NY
212-427-3100
Dogs of all sizes are allowed. There is a pet policy to sign at check in and there are no additional pet fees. 2 dogs may be allowed.

The Muse
130 West 46th Street
New York, NY
212-485-2400 (877-NYC-MUSE)
themusehotel.com
There are no additional pet fees at this pet-friendly Kimpton boutique hotel. They offer a pampered pooch package for an additional fee. 2 dogs may be allowed.

Tribeca Grand Hotel
2 Avenue of the Americas
New York, NY
212-519-6600
tribecagrand.com
This dog-friendly hotel is located just 2 blocks from it's sister hotel, the dog-friendly Soho Grand Hotel. This hotel is located within walking distance of Little Italy, Chinatown, Greenwich Village, and many department stores. Room rates begin at $399 and up. There are no pet fees. Multiple dogs may be allowed.

Trump International Hotel & Tower
1 Central Park West
New York, NY
888-448-7867
trumpintl.com/
This luxury hotel allows small dogs only up to 25 pounds are allowed. There is a $250 per visit pet fee. 2 dogs may be allowed.

W New York
541 Lexington Ave.
New York, NY
212-755-1200
One dog up to 70 pounds or dogs totaling up to 70 pounds are allowed for an additional cleaning fee of $100 plus $25 per night per room with a credit card on file. Dogs must be declared at the time of registration. Pets receive a special welcome with a pet amenity kit that includes a custom pet bed, food and water dishes with a floor mat, a doggy

menu, Pet-in-Room sign, treats, pet tag, a toy, and more. The concierge can also offer additional services such as dog-walking and information about local dog services and parks. Dogs must be removed or crated for housekeeping or for any in-room services.

W New York - The Court
130 East 39th St. between Lexington & Park Avenue
New York, NY
212-685-1100
Dogs up to 45 pounds are allowed for an additional cleaning fee of $100 plus $25 per night per pet with a credit card on file. Dogs must be declared at the time of registration. Pets receive a special welcome with a pet amenity kit that includes a custom pet bed, food and water dishes with a floor mat, a doggy menu, Pet-in-Room sign, treats, pet tag, a toy, and more. The concierge can also offer additional services such as dog-walking and information about local dog services and parks. Dogs must be removed or crated for housekeeping or for any in-room services. Dogs over 45 pounds may be allowed pending manager's approval.

W New York - The Tuscany
120 East 39th St. between Lexington and Park Ave.
New York, NY
212-686-1600
Dogs up to 45 pounds are allowed for an additional cleaning fee of $100 plus $25 per night per pet with a credit card on file. Dogs must be declared at the time of registration. Pets receive a special welcome with a pet amenity kit that includes a custom pet bed, food and water dishes with a floor mat, a doggy menu, Pet-in-Room sign, treats, pet tag, a toy, and more. The concierge can also offer additional services such as dog-walking and information about local dog services and parks. Dogs must be removed or crated for housekeeping or for any in-room services. Dogs over 45 pounds may be allowed pending manager's approval.

Quality Inn Finger Lakes Region
125 N. Main St.
Newark, NY
315-331-9500 (877-424-6423)
Dogs of all sizes are allowed. Two dogs are allowed per room.

Quality Inn
90 Route 17 K

Newburgh, NY
845-564-9020 (877-424-6423)
Dogs of all sizes are allowed. Dogs are allowed for a pet fee of $25.00 per pet per stay.

Super 8 Newburgh
1287 Route 300
Newburgh, NY
845-564-5700 (800-800-8000)
Dogs of all sizes are allowed. Dogs are allowed for a pet fee of $25.00 per pet per stay.

Howard Johnson Closest to the Falls and Casino
454 Main St/I-190
Niagara Falls, NY
716-285-5261 (800-446-4656)
Dogs of all sizes are allowed. Dogs are allowed for a pet fee of $10.00 per pet per night.

Motel 6 - Niagara Falls, Ny
9100 Niagara Falls Blvd.
Niagara Falls, NY
716-297-9902 (800-466-8356)
This motel welcomes your pets to stay with you.

Quality Hotel & Suites At The Falls
240 First Street
Niagara Falls, NY
716-282-1212 (877-424-6423)
Dogs of all sizes are allowed. Dogs are allowed for a pet fee of $30.00 per pet per night.

Best Western Syracuse Airport Inn
900 Col Eileen Collins Boulevard
North Syracuse, NY
315-455-7362 (800-780-7234)
Dogs of all sizes are allowed. Dogs are allowed for a pet fee of $25.00 per pet per stay.

Super 8 Norwich
6067 State Hwy 12
Norwich, NY
607-336-8880 (800-800-8000)
Dogs of all sizes are allowed. Dogs are allowed for a pet fee.

Quality Inn Gran-View
6765 State Hwy. 37
Ogdensburg, NY
315-393-4550 (877-424-6423)
Dogs of all sizes are allowed.

Holiday Inn Oneonta-Cooperstown Area
5206 State Highway 23
Oneonta, NY
607-433-2250 (877-270-6405)
Dogs of all sizes are allowed. Dogs are allowed for a pet fee.

Super 8 /Cooperstown Oneonta
4973 St Hwy 23
Oneonta, NY
607-432-9505 (800-800-8000)
Dogs of all sizes are allowed. Dogs are allowed for a pet fee.

Holiday Inn Orangeburg-Rockland/Bergen Co
329 Route 303
Orangeburg, NY
845-359-7000 (877-270-6405)
Dogs up to 50 pounds are allowed.

Ramada /Rome Area Oriskany
5920 Airport Road
Oriskany, NY
315-736-3377 (800-272-6232)
Dogs are welcome at this hotel.

Days Inn Oswego
101 State Route 104
Oswego, NY
315-343-3136 (800-329-7466)
Dogs are welcome at this hotel.

Travelodge Oswego
309 West Seneca Street
Oswego, NY
315-343-4900 (800-578-7878)
Dogs of all sizes are allowed. Dogs are allowed for a pet fee of $10.00 per pet per stay.

Tillinghast Manor
7246 S Main Street
Ovid, NY
716-869-3584
This historical 1873 Victorian home is located in the heart of the Finger Lakes area, and offers a central location to several other activities and recreational pursuits. Dogs of all sizes are welcome for no additional pet fee. Dogs must be quiet, well mannered, leashed, and cleaned up after. Dogs may only be left alone in the room if the owner is confident in their behavior. 2 dogs may be allowed.

Econo Lodge
200 Robert Dann Drive
Painted Post, NY
607-962-4444 (877-424-6423)
Dogs of all sizes are allowed. Dogs are allowed for a pet fee of $10.00 per pet per night.

Rodeway Inn
93 E. Grand St. (Rt 5)
Palatine Bridge, NY
518-673-3233 (877-424-6423)
Dogs of all sizes are allowed. Dogs are allowed for a pet fee of $10.00 per pet per night.

Dog-Friendly Lodging - Please always call ahead to make sure an establishment is still dog-friendly.

Hilton Hotel
500 Veterans Memorial Drive/H 20
Pearl River, NY
845-735-9000 (800-HILTONS (445-8667))
Only 20 miles from New York, this French Chateau style luxury hotel sits in a beautiful wooded area along the river and offers a number of on site amenities for business and leisure travelers, plus a convenient location to business, shopping, dining, historic, and entertainment areas. Dogs up to 75 pounds are allowed for an additional one time fee of $75 per pet. 2 dogs may be allowed.

Econo Lodge Darien Lakes
8493 SR 77
Pembroke, NY
585-599-4681 (877-424-6423)
Dogs of all sizes are allowed.

Pine Haven B&B
2781 New Prospect Rd
Pine Bush, NY
845-744-2330
pinehaven.info
Dogs are allowed at this B&B set on 10 acres with two ponds and many trees.

Rufus Tanner House
60 Sagetown Road
Pine City, NY
607-732-0213 (800-360-9259)
rufustanner.com/
Built in 1864 in Greek revival style and renovated for privacy and relaxation, this 2.5 acre farmhouse features a garden hideaway, large porches and decks, an outdoor hot tub, and is only minutes from several other activities, eateries, and plenty of recreation. Dogs of all sizes are allowed for no additional pet fees. Dogs must be leashed, cleaned up after, and crated when left alone in the room. 2 dogs may be allowed.

Residence Inn Plainview Long Island
9 Gerhard Road
Plainview, NY
516-433-6200 (800-331-3131)
Some of the amenities at this all-suite inn include a daily buffet breakfast, evening hospitality events, indoor and outdoor pools, a Sport Court, a fascinating 1,200 gallon aquarium located in the on-site eatery, and a complimentary grocery shopping service. Dogs are allowed for an additional one time pet fee of $100 per room 2 dogs may be allowed.

Best Western The Inn at Smithfield

446 Route 3
Plattsburgh, NY
518-561-7750 (800-780-7234)
Dogs of all sizes are allowed. Dogs are allowed for a pet fee of $25.00 per pet per stay.

La Quinta Inn Plattsburgh
16 Plaza Boulevard
Plattsburgh, NY
518-562-4000 (800-531-5900)
Dogs of all sizes are allowed. There are no additional fees. There is a pet waiver to sign at check in. Dogs must be attended or removed for housekeeping. Dogs must be leashed and cleaned up after. Multiple dogs may be allowed.

Super 8 Plattsburgh
7129 Rt 9 N
Plattsburgh, NY
518-562-8888 (800-800-8000)
Dogs of all sizes are allowed. Dogs are allowed for a pet fee of $10.00 per pet per night.

Days Inn Poughkeepsie
536 Haight Ave
Poughkeepsie, NY
845-454-1010 (800-329-7466)
Dogs are welcome at this hotel.

Residence Inn Poughkeepsie
2525 South Road
Poughkeepsie, NY
845-463-4343 (800-943-6717)
Besides offering a convenient location to a number of local major corporations, shopping, dining, and entertainment areas, this hotel also provides a number of in-house amenities, including a daily buffet breakfast and complementary evening receptions. Dogs are allowed for an additional one time pet fee of $100 per room. 2 dogs may be allowed.

Super 8 NY Poughkeepsie
2349 South Road/Route 9
Poughkeepsie, NY
845-462-7800 (800-800-8000)
Dogs are welcome at this hotel.

Travelodge Pulaski
3723-3724 State Route 13
Pulaski, NY
315-298-4717 (800-578-7878)
Dogs are welcome at this hotel.

America's Best Inn
24 Big Boom Road
Queensbury, NY
518-793-8891
americasbestinnqueensbury.com
There is a $25 fee per pet for the

first night and $10 per additional night fee per pet.

Red Roof Inn Glens Falls - Lake George
931 US Rt. 9
Queensbury, NY
518-745-4000 (800-RED-ROOF)
One well-behaved family pet per room. Guest must notify front desk upon arrival. Guest is liable for any damages. In consideration of all guests, pets must never be left unattended in the guest rooms.

WhistleWood Farm
52 Pells Road
Rhinebeck, NY
845-876-6838
whistlewood.com/
Guests can explore the wooded trails and wildflower gardens, sit out on large decks enjoying the views, take in the afternoon desert fare, and more at this retreat. Housebroken dogs of all sizes are allowed for an additional pet fee of $20 per night per pet. Dogs must be quiet, well behaved, leashed and cleaned up after, and crated when left alone in the room. 2 dogs may be allowed.

Best Western East End
1830 Route 25
Riverhead, NY
631-369-2200 (800-780-7234)
Dogs of all sizes are allowed. Dogs are allowed for a pet fee of $50.00 per pet per stay.

Holiday Inn Express Hotel & Suites East End
1707 Old Country Rd.
Riverhead, NY
631-548-1000 (877-270-6405)
Dogs of all sizes are allowed. Dogs are allowed for a pet fee.

Comfort Inn West
1501 W. Ridge Rd.
Rochester, NY
585-621-5700 (877-424-6423)
Dogs of all sizes are allowed. Dogs are allowed for a pet fee of $10.00 per pet per night.

Days Inn Thruway / Henrietta Rochester
4853 West Henrietta Road
Rochester, NY
585-334-9300 (800-329-7466)
Dogs are welcome at this hotel.

Extended Stay America Rochester - Greece
600 Center Place Dr.
Rochester, NY

585-663-5558 (800-804-3724)
One dog is allowed per suite. There is a $25 per night additional pet fee up to $150 for an entire stay.

Extended Stay America Rochester - Henrietta
700 Commons Way
Rochester, NY
585-427-7580 (800-804-3724)
One dog is allowed per suite. There is a $25 per night additional pet fee up to $150 for an entire stay.

Holiday Inn Express Irondequoit
2200 Goodman St. N
Rochester, NY
585-342-0430 (877-270-6405)
Dogs of all sizes are allowed. Dogs are allowed for a pet fee of $25.00 per pet per night.

Motel 6 - Rochester Airport
155 Buell Road
Rochester, NY
585-436-2170 (800-466-8356)
This motel welcomes your pets to stay with you.

Quality Inn Rochester Airport
1273 Chili Ave
Rochester, NY
585-464-8800 (877-424-6423)
Dogs up to 100 pounds are allowed. Two dogs are allowed per room.

Residence Inn Rochester
1300 Jefferson Road
Rochester, NY
585-272-8850 (800-331-3131)
Some of the amenities at this all-suite inn include a daily buffet breakfast, a weekly barbecue, a swimming pool, a Sport Court, and a complimentary grocery shopping service. Dogs are allowed for an additional one time pet fee of $90 per room. Multiple dogs may be allowed.

Residence Inn Rochester West/Greece
500 Paddy Creek Circle
Rochester, NY
585-865-2090 (866-237-5979)
Centrally located to the airport, the downtown area, and to shopping, dining, business, cultural, and historical sites, this all suite inn also offers a number of in-house amenities including a daily buffet breakfast, evening socials Monday to Thursday, and a 24 hour market on site. Dogs are allowed for an additional one time pet fee of $100 per room. Multiple dogs may be allowed.

Staybridge Suites Rochester University
1000 Genesee Street
Rochester, NY
585-527-9110 (877-270-6405)
Dogs up to 80 pounds are allowed. Pets allowed with an additional pet fee. Up to $75 for 1-6 nights and up to $150 for 7+ nights. A pet agreement must be signed at check-in.

Best Western Mill River Manor
173 Sunrise Highway
Rockville Centre, NY
516-678-1300 (800-780-7234)
Dogs of all sizes are allowed. Dogs are allowed for a pet fee of $15.00 per pet per night.

Quality Inn
200 S. James St.
Rome, NY
315-336-4300 (877-424-6423)
Dogs of all sizes are allowed. Dogs are allowed for a pet fee of $25.00 per pet per night. Two dogs are allowed per room.

Lake Flower Inn
15 Lake Flower Ave
Saranac Lake, NY
518-891-2310
Management requests that dogs are not left alone in the rooms and that guests clean up after their pets. Dogs are not allowed on the beds. There are no additional pet fees. Dogs must be on a currant flea treatment program.

Lake Side
27 Lake Flower Ave
Saranac Lake, NY
518-891-4333
There are a limited number of pets allowed in the hotel at a time. There are no additional pet fees. 2 dogs may be allowed.

Best Western Park Inn
3291 S Broadway
Saratoga Springs, NY
518-584-2350 (800-780-7234)
Dogs up to 50 pounds are allowed. Dogs are allowed for a pet fee of $15 per pet per night.

Comfort Inn & Suites
17 Old Gick Road
Saratoga Springs, NY
518-587-6244 (877-424-6423)
Dogs of all sizes are allowed. Dogs are allowed for a pet fee of $10.00 per pet per night. Two dogs are allowed per room.

Holiday Inn Saratoga Springs
232 Broadway
Saratoga Springs, NY
518-584-4550 (877-270-6405)
Dogs are welcome at this hotel.

Residence Inn Saratoga Springs
295 Excelsior Avenue
Saratoga Springs, NY
518-584-9600 (800-331-3131)
Some of the amenities at this all-suite inn include a convenient location to all that the downtown area has to offer, a daily buffet breakfast, evening social hours Monday through Thursday, a heated indoor pool, a Sport Court, and a complimentary grocery shopping service. Dogs are allowed for an additional one time pet fee of $75 per room. Multiple dogs may be allowed.

Union Gables
55 Union Avenue
Saratoga Springs, NY
518-584-1558 (800-398-1558)
uniongables.com/
This stately Queen Anne-style 100 year old plus residence complete with a large lawn area and big verandas, sits central to several attractions, recreation, eateries and shops. Dogs of all sizes are allowed for a $25 one time additional pet fee per room. Dogs must be quiet, well behaved, leashed, and cleaned up after. Multiple dogs may be allowed.

Comfort Inn
2790 RT 32
Saugerties, NY
845-246-1565 (877-424-6423)
Dogs of all sizes are allowed. Dogs are allowed for a pet fee of $10.00 per pet per night.

Fire Island Real Estate Fire Island Pines
P. O. Box 219
Sayville, NY
631-597-7575
pinesharbor.com/
This realty offers vacation homes in the Fire Island Pines area (a premiere gay community), and about 90% of the rentals allow dogs. Special conditions for the pets or deposits and fees, and the location of the rental in question are disclosed at the time of reservations. Dogs must be housetrained, well mannered, leashed, and cleaned up after. 2 dogs may be allowed.

Days Inn Schenectady
167 Nott Terrace
Schenectady, NY
518-370-3297 (800-329-7466)

Dogs are welcome at this hotel.

Super 8 Schenect/Albany Area
3083 Carman Rd
Schenectady, NY
518-355-2190 (800-800-8000)
Dogs of all sizes are allowed. Dogs are allowed for a pet fee.

Blue Ridge Motel
Route 9
Schroon Lake, NY
518-532-7521
Dogs are allowed for an additional fee of $10 per night per pet. The rate may be less for multiple days. 2 dogs may be allowed.

Starry Night Cabins
37 Fowler Avenue
Schroon Lake, NY
518-532-7907
Dogs of all sizes are allowed. There is a $8 per night per pet fee.

Bird's Nest
1601 E Genesee St
Skaneateles, NY
315-685-5641
There is a $150.00 refundable pet deposit. 2 dogs may be allowed.

Skaneateles Suites
4114 W Genesee Street
Skaneateles, NY
315-685-7568
Dogs of all sizes are allowed. There is a $35 one time fee for 1 pet and $50 for 2 pets. 2 dogs may be allowed.

The Atlantic
1655 County Road 39
Southampton, NY
631-283-6100
hrhresorts.com/atlantic.htm
This boutique motel sits on 5 groomed acres 3 miles from the ocean, is a premier vacation, special occasion, and event destination, and they offer a variety of land and water recreation on site. Dogs up to 40 pounds are allowed for an additional fee of $40 per night per pet; larger dogs may be allowed at an increased fee. Pets must have current vaccinations for rabies, distemper, and bordetella, and owners must provide documentation if needed. Dogs must be leashed and cleaned up after at all times, and plastic bags are available at the front desk if needed. Please walk your pets on the acres surrounding the property. Dogs may not be left alone in the room at any time. 2 dogs may be allowed.

Mountain House
150 Berkshire Way
Stephentown, NY
800-497-0176
berkshirebb.com/
A spring-fed pond, 50 rolling acres of meadows and woods, walking trails, and a spacious house on the hill with great views of all, make this a popular retreat. Dogs of all sizes are welcome for no additional fees. Dogs must be friendly with other dogs and well mannered. Dogs must be under owner's control and cleaned up after at all times. 2 dogs may be allowed.

Inn at Stone Ridge
Route 209
Stone Ridge, NY
845-687-0736
innatstoneridge.com/
Whether it's by the entire inn as a guest house or by individual rooms, this 18th century Dutch Colonial mansion has a lot to offer, including 150 acres of well manicured lawns and gardens, unspoiled woods, and an apple orchard. Dogs of all sizes are welcome for no additional pet fee. Dogs must be friendly, well trained, leashed and cleaned up after. Dogs may not be left alone unless owners are confident in their behavior. Multiple dogs may be allowed.

Holiday Inn Suffern
#3 Executive Blvd
Suffern, NY
845-357-4800 (877-270-6405)
Dogs of all sizes are allowed. Dogs are allowed for a pet fee.

Wellesley Inn Suffern
17 North Airmont Road
Suffern, NY
845-368-1900 (800-531-5900)
Dogs of all sizes are allowed. There is a $10 one time additional pet fee per room. Dogs may only be left alone in the room if they will be quiet and well behaved. Dogs must be leashed and cleaned up after. Multiple dogs may be allowed.

Candlewood Suites Syracuse
6550 Baptist Way
Syracuse, NY
315-432-1684 (877-270-6405)
Dogs up to 80 pounds are allowed. Pets allowed with an additional pet fee. Up to $75 for 1-6 nights and up to $150 for 7+ nights. A pet agreement must be signed at check-in.

Candlewood Suites Syracuse-Airport
5414 South Bay Road
Syracuse, NY
315-454-8999 (877-270-6405)
Dogs up to 80 pounds are allowed. Pets allowed with an additional pet fee. Up to $75 for 1-6 nights and up to $150 for 7+ nights. A pet agreement must be signed at check-in.

Comfort Inn & Suites Airport
6701 Buckley Road
Syracuse, NY
315-457-4000 (877-424-6423)
Dogs up to 70 pounds are allowed. Dogs are allowed for a pet fee of $10.00 per pet per night. Two dogs are allowed per room.

Comfort Inn Carrier Circle
6491 Thompson Rd.
Syracuse, NY
315-437-0222 (877-424-6423)
Dogs up to 50 pounds are allowed. Dogs are allowed for a pet fee of $30.00 per pet per stay.

Comfort Inn Fairgrounds
7010 Interstate Island Rd.
Syracuse, NY
315-453-0045 (877-424-6423)
Dogs of all sizes are allowed. Dogs are allowed for a pet fee of $Charge:25.00 per pet per stay.

Days Inn University Syracuse
6609 Thompson Rd
Syracuse, NY
315-437-5998 (800-329-7466)
Dogs of all sizes are allowed. Dogs are allowed for a pet fee.

Red Roof Inn Syracuse
6614 North Thompson Road
Syracuse, NY
315-437-3309 (800-RED-ROOF)
One well-behaved family pet per room. Guest must notify front desk upon arrival. Guest is liable for any damages. In consideration of all guests, pets must never be left unattended in the guest rooms.

Renaissance Syracuse Hotel
701 E Genesee Street
Syracuse, NY
315-479-7000 (877-843-6279)
Located downtown across from the Syracuse University, this luxury hotel sits central to numerous businesses, shopping, dining, and day/night entertainment areas, plus they also offer a number of in-house amenities for business and leisure travelers. Dogs are allowed for an additional

fee of $50 per night per room. 2 dogs may be allowed.

Residence Inn Syracuse
6420 Yorktown Circle
Syracuse, NY
315-432-4488 (800-331-3131)
Some of the amenities at this all-suite inn include a daily buffet breakfast, evening socials, summer barbecues, a heated swimming pool, a Sport Court, and a complimentary grocery shopping service. Dogs are allowed for an additional one time pet fee of $75 per room. Multiple dogs may be allowed.

Sheraton Syracuse University Hotel & Conference Center
801 University Ave.
Syracuse, NY
315-475-3000 (888-625-5144)
Dogs up to 80 pounds are allowed. There are no additional pet fees. Dogs are not allowed to be left alone in the room.

Super 8 Syracuse East
6620 Old Collamer Road
Syracuse East, NY
315-432-5612 (800-800-8000)
Dogs are welcome at this hotel.

Marriott Westchester Tarrytown
670 White Plains Road
Tarrytown, NY
914-631-2200 (800-882-1042)
This luxury hotel provides a great location to a number of sites of interest for both business and leisure travelers; plus they also offer numerous on-site amenities to ensure a comfortable stay. Dogs up to 75 pounds are allowed for an additional one time fee of $75 per room. Multiple dogs may be allowed.

Circle Court
440 Montcalm St
Ticonderoga, NY
518-585-7660
Dogs are allowed for no additional pet fee. (There may be a small charge for long haired dogs if extra cleaning is required.) Multiple dogs may be allowed.

Econo Lodge
2000 Niagara Falls Blvd.
Tonawanda, NY
716-694-6696 (877-424-6423)
Dogs of all sizes are allowed.

Red Roof Inn Utica
20 Weaver Street
Utica, NY
315-724-7128 (800-RED-ROOF)

One well-behaved family pet per room. Guest must notify front desk upon arrival. Guest is liable for any damages. In consideration of all guests, pets must never be left unattended in the guest rooms.

Super 8 NY Utica
309 North Genesee Street
Utica, NY
315-797-0964 (800-800-8000)
Dogs are welcome at this hotel.

Residence Inn Binghamton
4610 Vestal Parkway E
Vestal, NY
607-770-8500 (800-331-3131)
In addition to offering a convenient location to business, shopping, dining, and entertainment areas, this hotel also provides a number of in-house amenities, including a daily buffet breakfast, and a Manager's reception Monday through Thursday. Dogs are allowed for an additional one time pet fee of $75 per room. 2 dogs may be allowed.

Howard Johnson Express Inn - Binghamton/Vestal/SUNY
3601 Vestal Parkway E
Vestal/Binghamton, NY
607-729-6181 (800-446-4656)
Dogs are welcome at this hotel.

Audrey's Farmhouse
2188 Brunswyck Road
Wallkill, NY
845-895-3440 (800-501-3872)
audreysfarmhouse.com/
Sweeping manicured lawns, stately trees, an outdoor pool, Jacuzzi, and sundeck, a central location to an array of other activities, and known to be very doggy friendly, make this 1740's country inn an attractive destination for both owners and their dogs. Pets also like the many hiking trails in the area. Dogs of all sizes are allowed for no additional pet fee. Dogs must be well mannered, leashed, and cleaned up after. Multiple dogs may be allowed.

Daggett Lake Campsites & Cabins
660 Glen Athol Rd
Warrensburg, NY
518-623-2198
daggettlake.com
Well behaved, leashed pets are welcome in the RV Park and the cabins. There is no additional charge for pets in the campground and a $50 cleaning fee for cabins. Proof of rabies shots are required in the campground and fleas control in the cabins. This campground is

home of the "DOG BEACH" where dogs can go off leash if they are under voice control. There are 400 acres with hiking and mountain biking trails, canoe, kayak, and rowboat rentals, and a sandy swim beach for people.

MeadowLark Farm
180 Union Corners Road
Warwick, NY
845-651-4286
meadowlarkfarm.com/
Every season gets its full due at this scenic 1800's English style farm house and there is also a variety of local year round activities and recreational opportunities available. Dogs of all sizes are allowed for an additional fee of $10 per night per pet, but they must be friendly towards other animals as well as humans as there are other pets that live on site. Dogs may not be left alone in the room, and they must be house trained, leashed, and cleaned up after. 2 dogs may be allowed.

Best Western Carriage House Inn
300 Washington Street
Watertown, NY
315-782-8000 (800-780-7234)
Dogs of all sizes are allowed. Dogs are allowed for a pet fee of $15.00 per pet per night.

Algonquin Motel
Box 528 H 30
Wells, NY
518-924-2751
One dog up to 50 pounds is allowed. There is a $15 per night fee, and dogs are not allowed to be left alone in the room.

Staybridge Suites Buffalo
162 Slade Avenue
West Seneca, NY
716-939-3100 (877-270-6405)
Dogs up to 80 pounds are allowed. Pets allowed with an additional pet fee. Up to $75 for 1-6 nights and up to $150 for 7+ nights. A pet agreement must be signed at check-in.

Red Roof Inn Long Island
699 Dibblee Drive
Westbury, NY
516-794-2555 (800-RED-ROOF)
One well-behaved family pet per room. Guest must notify front desk upon arrival. Guest is liable for any damages. In consideration of all guests, pets must never be left unattended in the guest rooms.

Residence Inn White Plains
Westchester County
5 Barker Avenue
White Plains, NY
914-761-7700 (800-331-3131)
This all suite hotel sits central to a
number of sites of interest and
activities for all level of travelers, plus
they offer a daily buffet breakfast,
and evening socials Monday through
Thursday with light dinner fare. Dogs
are allowed for an additional one
time pet fee of $100 per room.
Multiple dogs may be allowed.

Summerfield Suites
101 Corporate Park Drive
White Plains, NY
914-251-9700
$100 for 5 to 14 days

Willkommen Hof
5367 H 86
Whiteface, NY
518-946-SNOW (7669) (800-541-
9119)
willkommenhof.com/
This comfort-minded mountain inn
features an outdoor spa and indoor
sauna, and its location allows for
numerable outdoor year round
activities. Dogs of all sizes are
allowed for an additional $10 per
night per pet plus a $50 refundable
security deposit. They must be
kenneled when left in the room
alone, or they may be put in the inn's
outdoor run; kennels can be provided
if needed. Dogs are not allowed on
the beds or furniture. Dogs must be
friendly, well behaved, leashed, and
cleaned up after at all times. 2 dogs
may be allowed.

Extended Stay America New York
City - Laguardia Airport
18-30 Whitestone Expwy.
Whitestone, NY
718-357-3661 (800-804-3724)
One dog is allowed per suite. There
is a $25 per night additional pet fee
up to $150 for an entire stay.

Motel 6 - Buffalo Airport
52 Freeman Drive
Williamsville, NY
716-626-1500 (800-466-8356)
This motel welcomes your pets to
stay with you.

Hungry Trout Resort
(on Route 86)
Wilmington, NY
518-946-2217 (800-766-9137)
hungrytrout.com
Additional $20 per day charge for a
pet.

Best Western Woodbury Inn
7940 Jericho Turnpike
Woodbury, NY
516-921-6900 (800-780-7234)
Dogs of all sizes are allowed. Dogs
are allowed for a pet fee of $50.00
per pet per night.

Days Inn Wurtsboro
21 Perron Drive
Wurtsboro, NY
845-888-2727 (800-329-7466)
Dogs are welcome at this hotel.

North Carolina

Motel 6 - Pinehurst Aberdeen, Nc
1408 Sandhills Blvd
Aberdeen, NC
910-944-5633 (800-466-8356)
This motel welcomes your pets to
stay with you.

Holiday Inn Express Hotel & Suites
High Point South
10050 North Main Street
Archdale, NC
336-861-3310 (877-270-6405)
Dogs of all sizes are allowed. Dogs
are allowed for a pet fee of $25.00
per pet per night. Two dogs are
allowed per room.

Comfort Inn Asheville Airport
15 Rockwood Rd.
Arden, NC
828-687-9199 (877-424-6423)
Dogs of all sizes are allowed. Dogs
are allowed for a pet fee of $15.00
per pet per night.

Carolina Mornings/Asheville Cabins
Call to Arrange
Asheville, NC
800-770-9055
asheville-cabins.com
This vacation rental company
centered in Asheville offers cabins
in town and out in the country. They
manage over 95 vacation properties
that are pet-friendly.

Crowne Plaza Resort Asheville
1 Resort Drive
Asheville, NC
828-254-3211 (877-270-6405)
Dogs of all sizes are allowed. Dogs
are allowed for a nightly pet fee.

Days Inn /Mall Asheville
201 Tunnel Road
Asheville, NC
828-252-4000 (800-329-7466)
Dogs are welcome at this hotel.

Days Inn Biltmore East
1435 Tunnel Road
Asheville, NC
828-298-4000 (800-329-7466)
Dogs are welcome at this hotel.

Engadine Cabins
2630 Smoky Park Highway
Asheville, NC
828-665-8325 (800-665-8868)
engadinecabins.com
The Cabins At Engadine are situated
on a hilltop overlooking the Inn. The
cabins are only 20 minutes from one
of the best known ski resorts in North
Carolina, Cataloochee Ski Resort.
Also nearby are whitewater rafting,
tubing, horse back riding, and hot air
ballooning. The cabins are 15
minutes to downtown Asheville. Both
Cabins offer privacy and are self-
contained with bedroom, kitchen,
living area, bathroom with Hot Tub,
and porches with a panoramic view
of the Blue Ridge Mountains. The
Reese Cabin is a single-bedroom
unit and the AlexAndrea is a two-
bedroom unit. Children and Pets of
any size are welcome. The cabins
are both non-smoking.

Extended Stay America Asheville -
Tunnel Rd.
6 Kenilworth Knoll
Asheville, NC
828-253-3483 (800-804-3724)
One dog is allowed per suite. There
is a $25 per night additional pet fee
up to $150 for an entire stay.

Holiday Inn - Blue Ridge Parkway
1450 Tunnel Rd
Asheville, NC
828-298-5611 (877-270-6405)
ashevilleholidayinn.com
The Holiday Inn is nestled in the Blue
Ridge Mountains and near the area's
most popular attractions. There are
mountain views and a heated
outdoor pool. They have a number of
pet friendly rooms for a pet fee of
$20 per night. They provide pet
walking areas and complimentary
treats for dogs.

Log Cabin Motor Court
330 Weaverville Highway
Asheville, NC
828-645-6546 (800-295-3392)
cabinlodging.com
There are 18 one or two bedroom log
cabins available. There is a $15 per
night additional pet fee. Dogs must
be crated if left alone in the cabin. Up
to 2 dogs are allowed in each cabin.

Motel 6 - Asheville
1415 Tunnel Rd
Asheville, NC
828-299-3040 (800-466-8356)
This motel welcomes your pets to
stay with you.

Quality Inn & Suites Biltmore East
1430 Tunnel Rd.
Asheville, NC
828-298-5519 (877-424-6423)
Dogs of all sizes are allowed. Dogs
are allowed for a pet fee of $20.00
per pet per night. Two dogs are
allowed per room.

Ramada Asheville
800 Fairview Road
Asheville, NC
828-298-9141 (800-272-6232)
Dogs of all sizes are allowed. Dogs
are allowed for a nightly pet fee.

Ramada Biltmore West
275 Smokey Park Hwy
Asheville, NC
828-667-4501 (800-272-6232)
Dogs of all sizes are allowed. Dogs
are allowed for a pet fee.

Red Roof Inn Asheville West
16 Crowell Road
Asheville, NC
828-667-9803 (800-RED-ROOF)
One well-behaved family pet per
room. Guest must notify front desk
upon arrival. Guest is liable for any
damages. In consideration of all
guests, pets must never be left
unattended in the guest rooms.

Residence Inn Asheville Biltmore
701 Biltmore Avenue
Asheville, NC
828-281-3361 (888-236-2427)
This all suite inn offers amenities for
all level of travelers, including a
convenient location to a number of
area attractions, a daily buffet
breakfast, a grocery shopping
service, and complimentary evening
socials. Dogs up to 75 pounds are
allowed for an additional one time
pet fee of $75 per room. 2 dogs may
be allowed.

Rodeway Inn
8 Crowell Road
Asheville, NC
828-667-8706 (877-424-6423)
Dogs up to 50 pounds are allowed.
Dogs are allowed for a pet fee of
$15.00 per pet per night. Two dogs
are allowed per room.

Rodeway Inn & Suites At Biltmore
Square

9 Wedgefield Drive
Asheville, NC
828-670-8800 (877-424-6423)
Dogs up to 50 pounds are allowed.
Dogs are allowed for a pet fee of
$15.00 per pet per night. Two dogs
are allowed per room.

Super 8 Asheville
180 Tunnel Road
Asheville, NC
828-505-4648 (800-800-8000)
Dogs of all sizes are allowed. Dogs
are allowed for a pet fee.

Atlantis Lodge
123 Salter Path Road
Atlantic Beach, NC
252-726-5168 (800-682-7057)
atlantislodge.com
The Atlantis has 42 units on the
ocean, most with efficiency
kitchens, dining, living and sleeping
areas. All have patios or decks
facing the surf. Use of beach chairs,
lounges and umbrellas is
complimentary. The outdoor pool is
not the normal concrete hole, but an
environment created within the
woods. Great for reading, lounging
or floating. They accept dogs for a
minimal fee, no matter the size as
long as they are well behaved. 2
dogs may be allowed.

Outer Beaches Realty
Call to Arrange
Avon, NC
866-962-0409
OuterBeachesDogFriendly.com
This vacation rental company has
over 195 pet-friendly homes on
Hatteras Island.

Best Western Mountain Lodge at
Banner Elk
1615 Tynecastle Highway -
Highway 184
Banner Elk, NC
828-898-4571 (800-780-7234)
bestwesternbannerelk.com
The Best Western is located in the
"Heart of the High Country" in a
mountain setting. The hotel offers a
full service restaurant and lounge,
conference facilities, picnic areas,
guest laundry, game room, and a
large outdoor heated pool that is
open year round. They have dog
treats and a large dog walking area.

Comfort Inn North
I-95 Exit 145
Battleboro, NC
252-972-9426 (877-424-6423)
Dogs of all sizes are allowed. Dogs
are allowed for a pet fee of $10.00
per pet per night. Two dogs are

allowed per room.

Howard Johnson Inn - Rocky Mount/
Battleboro
7568 NC Hwy 48
Battleboro, NC
252-977-9595 (800-446-4656)
Dogs of all sizes are allowed. Dogs
are allowed for a pet fee of $10 per
pet per night.

Quality Inn
7797 NC Hwy 48
Battleboro, NC
252-442-5111 (877-424-6423)
Dogs of all sizes are allowed.

Carteret Country Home
299 H 101
Beaufort, NC
252-728-4611
the fee is $25 per night for 2 dogs.

Tea House
878 Crow Hill Rd.
Beaufort, NC
252-728-7806
teahouseongoosebay.com
There is a $50 non-refundable pet
fee for your dog at this vacation
rental.

Days Inn Benson
202 N Honeycutt Street
Benson, NC
919-894-2031 (800-329-7466)
Dogs are welcome at this hotel.

Days Inn Biscoe
531 East Main Street
Biscoe, NC
910-428-2525 (800-329-7466)
Dogs of all sizes are allowed. Dogs
are allowed for a pet fee of $7.00 per
pet per night.

Super 8 Black Mountain
101 Flat Creek Road
Black Mountain, NC
828-669-8076 (800-800-8000)
Dogs are welcome at this hotel.

Holiday Inn Express Hotel & Suites
Brevard
2228 Asheville Highway
Brevard, NC
828-862-8900 (877-270-6405)
Dogs are welcome at this hotel.
There is a $25 one time pet fee.

Hidden Creek Cabins
Great Smoky Mountains
Bryson City, NC
828-507-5627 (888-333-5881)
hiddencreekcabins.com
These vacation rentals in the Smoky
Mountains of North Carolina allow

pets. There is a $50 one time additional pet fee.

Mountain Vista Log Cabins
300 Fernwood Drive
Bryson City, NC
828-508-4391 (888-508-4838)
Dogs of all sizes are allowed. There is a $45 one time additional pet fee per cabin. 2 dogs may be allowed.

Comfort Inn
2701 Kirkpatrick Rd.
Burlington, NC
336-584-4447 (877-424-6423)
Dogs of all sizes are allowed. Dogs are allowed for a pet fee of $USD per pet per stay.

Econo Lodge
2133 W. Hanford Rd.
Burlington, NC
336-227-1270 (877-424-6423)
Dogs up to 50 pounds are allowed. Dogs are allowed for a pet fee of $10.00/pet, per pet per night.

Motel 6 - Burlington, Nc
2155 Hanford Rd
Burlington, NC
336-226-1325 (800-466-8356)
This motel welcomes your pets to stay with you.

Quality Inn
2444 Maple Avenue
Burlington, NC
336-229-5203 (877-424-6423)
Dogs of all sizes are allowed. Dogs are allowed for a pet fee of $25.00 per pet per stay. Two dogs are allowed per room.

Blue Ridge Motel
204 West Blvd
Burnsville, NC
828-682-9100
Dogs of all sizes are allowed. There is a $5 per night per pet additional fee. 2 dogs may be allowed.

Outer Banks Motel
2nd Motel on left on H 12
Buxton, NC
252-995-5601 (800-995-1233)
One dog up to about 50 pounds is allowed for a $5 per night additional pet fee.

Apple Blossom Cottage
46 Drawspring Road
Candler, NC
828-255-0704
Dogs of all sizes are allowed. There is a $150 refundable pet deposit and pets must be flea protected.

Days Inn Asheville West
2551 Smoky Park Hwy
Candler, NC
866-665-2031 (800-329-7466)
Dogs of all sizes are allowed. Dogs are allowed for a pet fee.

Days Inn Canton
1963 Champion Drive
Canton, NC
828-648-0300 (800-329-7466)
Dogs are welcome at this hotel.

Beach Breeze
908 Carolina Beach Ave South
Carolina Beach, NC
888-256-4804
carolinabeachbreeze.com
This 6 bedroom, 4 bathroom cottage allows dogs for a $125 - $150 non-refundable pet fee.

United Beach Vacations
1001 North Lake Park Blvd.
Carolina Beach, NC
800-334-5806
pleasureislandholiday.com
This vacation rental company has many pet-friendly vacation rentals in the Carolina Beach area. Rentals range in size from 2 to 5 bedrooms.

Victory Beach Vacations
Visit Website or Call to Arrange
Carolina/Kure Beaches, NC
910-458-0868 (888-256-4804)
VictoryBeachVacations.com
These vacation rentals in the Carolina and Kure Beach areas have a number of dog-friendly properties.

Best Western Cary Inn & Extended Stay
1722 Walnut Street
Cary, NC
919-481-1200 (800-780-7234)
Dogs of all sizes are allowed. Dogs are allowed for a pet fee.

Extended Stay America Raleigh - Cary - Regency Parkway
1500 Regency Pkwy.
Cary, NC
919-468-5828 (800-804-3724)
One dog is allowed per suite. There is a $25 per night additional pet fee up to $150 for an entire stay.

La Quinta Inn & Suites Raleigh Cary
191 Crescent Commons
Cary, NC
919-851-2850 (800-531-5900)
Dogs of all sizes are allowed. There are no additional pet fees. Dogs must be leashed, cleaned up after,

and crated when left alone in the room. Multiple dogs may be allowed.

Red Roof Inn Raleigh Southwest - NCSU
1800 Walnut Street
Cary, NC
919-469-3400 (800-RED-ROOF)
One well-behaved family pet per room. Guest must notify front desk upon arrival. Guest is liable for any damages. In consideration of all guests, pets must never be left unattended in the guest rooms.

Residence Inn Raleigh Cary
2900 Regency Parkway
Cary, NC
919-467-4080 (800-331-3131)
This all suite inn sits central between downtown and the Research Triangle Park area and offers a great location for exploring several other points of interest in the city. Additionally, they offer a daily buffet breakfast and weekly evening socials. Dogs are allowed for an additional one time pet fee of $100 per room. Multiple dogs may be allowed.

TownePlace Suites Raleigh Cary/Weston Parkway
120 Sage Commons Way
Cary, NC
919-678-0005 (800-257-3000)
In addition to offering a number of in-house amenities for all level of travelers, this all suite inn also provides a convenient location to universities, business, shopping, dining, and entertainment areas. Dogs are allowed for an additional one time fee of $100 per room. 2 dogs may be allowed.

Holiday Inn Chapel Hill
1301 N Fordham Blvd/Hwy 15 501
Chapel Hill, NC
919-929-2171 (877-270-6405)
Dogs of all sizes are allowed. Dogs are allowed for a pet fee of $40 per pet per stay.

Residence Inn Chapel Hill
101 Erwin Road
Chapel Hill, NC
919-933-4848 (800-331-3131)
This hotel sits located near a number of esteemed institutes of learning and healing as well as other sites of interest, plus they offer a number of in-house amenities including a daily buffet breakfast and an evening reception Monday through Thursday. One dog up to 100 pounds is allowed for an additional one time pet fee of $100.

Dog-Friendly Lodging - Please always call ahead to make sure an establishment is still dog-friendly.

Candlewood Suites Charlotte-Coliseum
5840 Westpark Drive
Charlotte, NC
704-529-7500 (877-270-6405)
Dogs up to 80 pounds are allowed. Pets allowed with an additional pet fee. Up to $75 for 1-6 nights and up to $150 for 7+ nights. A pet agreement must be signed at check-in.

Candlewood Suites Charlotte-University
8812 University East Drive
Charlotte, NC
704-598-9863 (877-270-6405)
Dogs up to 80 pounds are allowed. Pets allowed with an additional pet fee. Up to $75 for 1-6 nights and up to $150 for 7+ nights. A pet agreement must be signed at check-in.

Comfort Inn Executive Park
5822 Westpark Dr.
Charlotte, NC
704-525-2626 (877-424-6423)
Dogs of all sizes are allowed. Dogs are allowed for a pet fee of $20.00 per pet per night. Two dogs are allowed per room.

Comfort Inn UNCC
5111 Equipment Drive
Charlotte, NC
704-598-0007 (877-424-6423)
Dogs of all sizes are allowed.

Comfort Suites University Area
7735 University City Blvd
Charlotte, NC
704-547-0049 (877-424-6423)
Dogs of all sizes are allowed. Dogs are allowed for a pet fee of $25.00 per pet per stay.

Crowne Plaza Hotel Charlotte
201 South Mcdowell St.
Charlotte, NC
704-372-7550 (877-270-6405)
Dogs of all sizes are allowed. Dogs are allowed for a pet fee of $25.00 per pet per stay.

Days Inn Center City Charlotte
601 North Tryon Street
Charlotte, NC
704-333-4733 (800-329-7466)
Dogs are welcome at this hotel.

Days Inn North-Speedway-UNCC-Research Park Charlotte
1408 W Sugar Creek Rd
Charlotte, NC
704-597-8110 (800-329-7466)

Dogs of all sizes are allowed. Dogs are allowed for a pet fee of $25.00 per pet per night.

Days Inn /Woodlawn Near Carowinds Charlotte
118 East Woodlawn Road
Charlotte, NC
704-525-5500 (800-329-7466)
Dogs of all sizes are allowed. Dogs are allowed for a pet fee of $20.00 per pet per stay.

Doubletree Guest Suites
6300 Morrison Boulevard
Charlotte, NC
704-364-2400 (800-222-TREE (8733))
Nestled in lushly landscaped setting and sitting adjacent to Symphony Park, this upscale hotel offers a number of on site amenities for business or leisure travelers, plus a convenient location to business, shopping, dining, and recreation areas. Dogs are allowed for a $75 one-time additional pet fee. Multiple dogs may be allowed.

Doubletree Hotel
895 W Trade Street
Charlotte, NC
704-347-0070 (800-222-TREE (8733))
In addition to offering a number of on site amenities for business or leisure travelers, they are conveniently located near the Charlotte Douglas International Airport, the Johnson and Wales University, the convention center, and to a number of other attractions. Dogs are allowed for an additional one time fee of $25 per pet. There is a pet policy to sign at check in and a credit card must be on file. 2 dogs may be allowed.

Drury Inn & Suites
415 West W.T. Harris Blvd.
Charlotte, NC
704-593-0700 (800-378-7946)
Dogs of all sizes are allowed for no additional pet fee with a credit card on file, and there is a pet agreement to sign at check in.

Econo Lodge Inn & Suites
3000 East Independence Boulevard
Charlotte, NC
704-377-1501 (877-424-6423)
Dogs up to 50 pounds are allowed. Dogs are allowed for a pet fee of $30.00 per pet per stay. Two dogs are allowed per room.

Econo Lodge Coliseum Area

575 Clanton Rd
Charlotte, NC
704-523-0633 (877-424-6423)
Dogs of all sizes are allowed. Dogs are allowed for a pet fee of $USD per pet per night.

Extended Stay America Charlotte - Pineville
10930 Park Rd.
Charlotte, NC
704-341-0929 (800-804-3724)
One dog is allowed per suite. There is a $25 per night additional pet fee up to $150 for an entire stay.

Extended Stay America Charlotte - Tyvola Rd.
6035 Nations Ford Rd.
Charlotte, NC
704-676-0569 (800-804-3724)
One dog is allowed per suite. There is a $25 per night additional pet fee up to $150 for an entire stay.

Extended Stay America Charlotte - University Place
8211 University Executive Park Dr.
Charlotte, NC
704-510-1636 (800-804-3724)
One dog is allowed per suite. There is a $25 per night additional pet fee up to $150 for an entire stay.

Holiday Inn Charlotte-Billy Graham Pkwy
321 W. Woodlawn Road
Charlotte, NC
704-523-1400 (877-270-6405)
Dogs of all sizes are allowed. Dogs are allowed for a pet fee of $35.00 per pet per stay.

Homestead Studio Suites Charlotte - Coliseum
710 Yorkmont Rd.
Charlotte, NC
704-676-0083 (800-804-3724)
One dog is allowed per suite. There is a $25 per night additional pet fee up to $150 for an entire stay.

Howard Johnson Inn - Charlotte
122 West Woodlawn Rd
Charlotte, NC
704-527-1620 (800-446-4656)
Dogs of all sizes are allowed. Dogs are allowed for a pet fee of $20.00 per pet per stay.

Knights Inn South Charlotte
7901 Nations Ford Road
Charlotte, NC
704-522-0364 (800-843-5644)
Dogs are welcome at this hotel.

La Quinta Inn & Suites Charlotte

Dog-Friendly Lodging - Please always call ahead to make sure an establishment is still dog-friendly.

Airport South
4900 S. Tryon Street
Charlotte, NC
704-523-5599 (800-531-5900)
Dogs of all sizes are allowed. There are no additional pet fees. Dogs must be leashed and cleaned up after. Dogs may not be left unattended unless they will be quiet, well behaved, and a contact number left with the front desk. Multiple dogs may be allowed.

La Quinta Inn Charlotte Airport
3100 Queen City Drive
Charlotte, NC
704-393-5306 (800-531-5900)
Dogs of all sizes are allowed. There are no additional pet fees. Dogs must be leashed, cleaned up after, and the Do Not Disturb sign left on the door if there is a pet alone in the room. Multiple dogs may be allowed.

MainStay Suites
7926 Forest Pine Drive
Charlotte, NC
704-521-3232 (877-424-6423)
Dogs of all sizes are allowed. Dogs are allowed for a pet fee of $35.00 per pet per night.

Marriott Charlotte SouthPark
2200 Rexford Road
Charlotte, NC
704-364-8220 (800-228-9290)
This luxury boutique hotel sits central to major businesses, world class shopping and dining, and day/night entertainment areas, plus they also offer a number of in-house amenities for business and leisure travelers. Dogs are allowed for an additional one time fee of $100 per room. Aggressive-known breeds are not allowed. 2 dogs may be allowed.

Motel 6 - Charlotte Coliseum
131 Red Roof Dr
Charlotte, NC
704-529-1020 (800-466-8356)
This motel welcomes your pets to stay with you.

Motel 6 - Charlotte South
3430 Saint Vardell Ln
Charlotte, NC
704-527-0144 (800-466-8356)
This motel welcomes your pets to stay with you.

Quality Inn & Suites
3100 Queen City Drive
Charlotte, NC
704-393-5306 (877-424-6423)
Dogs of all sizes are allowed.

Ramada Northeast Charlotte
5415 Equipment Drive
Charlotte, NC
704-596-2999 (800-272-6232)
Dogs are welcome at this hotel.

Ramada Airport North Charlotte
2625 Little Rock Rd
Charlotte, NC
704-394-4111 (800-272-6232)
Dogs are welcome at this hotel.

Ramada Airport South and Conference Center
212 West Woodlawn Road
Charlotte, NC
704-525-8350 (800-272-6232)
Dogs are welcome at this hotel.

Red Roof Inn Charlotte Airport - West
3300 Queen City Drive
Charlotte, NC
704-392-2316 (800-RED-ROOF)
One well-behaved family pet per room. Guest must notify front desk upon arrival. Guest is liable for any damages. In consideration of all guests, pets must never be left unattended in the guest rooms.

Residence Inn Charlotte Piper Glen
5115 Piper Station Drive
Charlotte, NC
704-319-3900 (800-331-3131)
This all suite, upscale hotel offers a central location to all the riches the area has to offer for both business and leisure travelers. And, among the amenities they also offer a daily buffet breakfast, an evening hospitality hour, a pool/spa, and a Sport Court. Dogs are allowed for an additional one time pet fee of $75 per room. Multiple dogs may be allowed.

Residence Inn Charlotte South at I-77/Tyvola Road
5816 Westpark Drive
Charlotte, NC
704-527-8110 (800-331-3131)
Besides offering a convenient location to business, shopping, dining, and entertainment areas, this hotel also provides a number of in-house amenities, including a daily hot breakfast, and complementary evening receptions Monday through Wednesday. Dogs are allowed for an additional one time pet fee of $75 per room. 2 dogs may be allowed.

Residence Inn Charlotte SouthPark
6030 Piedmont Row Drive S
Charlotte, NC

704-554-7001 (800-331-3131)
This all suite hotel sits central to many of the city's star attractions, shopping, and entertainment areas, plus they offer a number of in-house amenities that include a daily buffet breakfast and evening socials during the week. Dogs are allowed for an additional one time pet fee of $100 per room. 2 dogs may be allowed.

Residence Inn Charlotte University Research Park
8503 N Tryon Street
Charlotte, NC
704-547-1122 (800-331-3131)
Located in the University Research Park business district, this hotel also offers a central location to shopping, dining, and entertainment areas around the city, plus they offer a number of in-house amenities, including a daily buffet breakfast and weekly evening socials. Dogs are allowed for an additional one time pet fee of $100 per room. 2 dogs may be allowed.

Residence Inn Charlotte Uptown
404 S Mint Street
Charlotte, NC
704-340-4000 (800-331-3131)
This all suite hotel sits central to many of the city's star attractions, dining, and commerce areas, plus they offer a number of in-house amenities that include a daily deluxe hot breakfast and a manager's reception Monday through Thursday. Dogs are allowed for an additional one time pet fee of $75 per room. There may be one average sized dog or 2 small dogs per room.

Sheraton Charlotte Airport Hotel
3315 Scott Futkell Dr.
Charlotte, NC
704-392-1200 (888-625-5144)
Dogs of all sizes are allowed. There are no additional pet fees.

Sleep Inn North Lake
6300 Banner Elk Drive
Charlotte, NC
704-399-7778 (877-424-6423)
Dogs of all sizes are allowed. Dogs are allowed for a pet fee of $20.00 per pet per night.

Sleep Inn University Place
8525 N Tryon St.
Charlotte, NC
704-549-4544 (877-424-6423)
Dogs of all sizes are allowed. Dogs are allowed for a pet fee of $25.00 per pet per stay. Two dogs are allowed per room.

Staybridge Suites Charlotte Ballantyne
15735 John J Delaney Drive
Charlotte, NC
704-248-5000 (877-270-6405)
Dogs up to 80 pounds are allowed. Pets allowed with an additional pet fee. Up to $75 for 1-6 nights and up to $150 for 7+ nights. A pet agreement must be signed at check-in.

Staybridge Suites Charlotte-Arrowood
7924 Forest Pine Drive
Charlotte, NC
704-527-6767 (877-270-6405)
Dogs up to 80 pounds are allowed. Pets allowed with an additional pet fee. Up to $75 for 1-6 nights and up to $150 for 7+ nights. A pet agreement must be signed at check-in.

Studio 6 - Charlotte Airport
3420 Queen City Dr
Charlotte, NC
704-394-4993 (800-466-8356)
Your pets are welcome to stay here with you for a pet fee of $10 per day up to $50 for an entire stay.

Summerfield Suites
4920 S Tryon Street
Charlotte, NC
704-525-2600
One dog is allowed for a $150 one time additional pet fee. Pet rooms are located on the first floor.

The Westin Charlotte
601 South College St.
Charlotte, NC
704-375-2600 (888-625-5144)
Dogs up to 50 pounds are allowed for no additional pet fee. A contact number must be left with the front desk if a pet is in the room alone.

TownePlace Suites Charlotte Arrowood
7805 Forest Point Blvd
Charlotte, NC
704-227-2000 (800-257-3000)
Besides offering a number of in-house amenities for all level of travelers, this all suite inn also offers a convenient location to numerous business, shopping, dining, and entertainment areas. Dogs are allowed for an additional one time fee of $75 per room. Multiple dogs may be allowed.

TownePlace Suites Charlotte University Research

8710 Research Drive
Charlotte, NC
704-548-0388 (800-380-3092)
This all suite hotel sits central between Charlotte and Concord and to a plethora of activities, major recreation areas, prominent businesses, and numerous shopping and dining venues. Dogs are allowed for an additional one time fee of $75 per room. Multiple dogs may be allowed.

Best Western Great Smokies Inn
1636 Acquoni Road
Cherokee, NC
828-497-2020 (800-780-7234)
Dogs of all sizes are allowed. Dogs are allowed for a pet fee of $15.00 per pet per night.

Super 8 Chocowinity
3635 Hwy 17 South
Chocowinity, NC
252-946-8001 (800-800-8000)
Dogs are welcome at this hotel.

Days Inn Tryon Columbus
626 West Mills Street
Columbus, NC
828-894-3303 (800-329-7466)
Dogs are welcome at this hotel.

Days Inn Concord
5125 Davidson Hwy/I-85
Concord, NC
704-786-9121 (800-329-7466)
Dogs of all sizes are allowed. Dogs are allowed for a pet fee of $10.00 per pet per night.

Howard Johnson Inn /Kannapolis Concord
1601 Concord Parkway
Concord, NC
704-786-5181 (800-446-4656)
Dogs of all sizes are allowed. Dogs are allowed for a pet fee.

Sleep Inn & Suites
7821 Gateway Lane
Concord, NC
704-979-8800 (877-424-6423)
Dogs of all sizes are allowed. Dogs are allowed for a pet fee of $25.00 per pet per stay.

Suburban Extended Stay
7725 Sossaman Lane
Concord, NC
704-979-5555 (877-424-6423)
Dogs of all sizes are allowed. Two dogs are allowed per room.

Days Inn -Hickory Conover
1710 Fairgrove Church Road
Conover, NC

828-465-2378 (800-329-7466)
Dogs of all sizes are allowed. Dogs are allowed for a nightly pet fee.

Days Inn Lake Norman Cornelius
19901 Holiday Lane
Cornelius, NC
704-892-9120 (800-329-7466)
Dogs of all sizes are allowed. Dogs are allowed for a pet fee.

Econo Lodge & Suites Lake Norman
20740 Torrence Chapel Rd.
Cornelius, NC
704-892-3500 (877-424-6423)
Dogs of all sizes are allowed. Dogs are allowed for a pet fee of $15.00 per pet per night. Two dogs are allowed per room.

Twiddy & Company Realtors
Call to Arrange
Corolla, NC
252-457-1100 (866-457-1190)
twiddy.com
Over 255 pet-friendly homes are available for rent in Corolla and Duck on the North Carolina Outer Banks. There are no additional pet fees.

Paramount Destinations
Call to Arrange
Corolla and Duck, NC
866-753-3045
paramountdestinations.com
This vacation home rental management company has many dog-friendly rentals in the Corolla and Duck areas. A $100 or more non-refundable pet fee is charged. Other pets beside dogs require special homeowner approval. 2 dogs may be allowed.

Beach Vacation Rental Homes
Duck, NC
252-261-7911
weloveobx.com
Three vacation rentals, with 4 to 6 bedrooms each, are located near the beach. Dogs are welcome to join you in these rentals.

Super 8 Dunn
1125 East Broad St
Dunn, NC
910-892-1293 (800-800-8000)
Dogs of all sizes are allowed. Dogs are allowed for a pet fee of $10 per pet per night.

Budgetel Durham
3454 Hillsborough Road
Durham, NC
919-309-0037
budgeteldurham.com
There is a $10 per day additional pet

fee.

Candlewood Suites Durham-Rtp
1818 E. Highway 54
Durham, NC
919-484-9922 (877-270-6405)
Dogs up to 80 pounds are allowed.
Pets allowed with an additional pet
fee. Up to $75 for 1-6 nights and up
to $150 for 7+ nights. A pet
agreement must be signed at check-
in.

Comfort Inn
4507 NC 55/Apex Hwy
Durham, NC
919-361-2656 (877-424-6423)
Dogs of all sizes are allowed.

Comfort Inn Medical Park
1816 Hillandale Road
Durham, NC
919-471-6100 (877-424-6423)
Dogs up to 50 pounds are allowed.
Dogs are allowed for a pet fee of
$49.00 per pet per stay.

**Extended Stay America Durham -
University**
3105 Tower Blvd.
Durham, NC
919-489-8444 (800-804-3724)
One dog is allowed per suite. There
is a $25 per night additional pet fee
up to $150 for an entire stay.

Holiday Inn Express Durham
2516 Guess Road
Durham, NC
919-313-3244 (877-270-6405)
Dogs of all sizes are allowed. Dogs
are allowed for a pet fee of $10.00
per pet per night.

**Holiday Inn Express Hotel & Suites
Research Triangle Park**
4912 South Miami Blvd
Durham, NC
919-474-9800 (877-270-6405)
Dogs up to 50 pounds are allowed.
Dogs are allowed for a pet fee of
$10.00 per pet per night.

**Homestead Studio Suites Durham -
Research Triangle Park**
4515 NC Hwy. 55
Durham, NC
919-544-9991 (800-804-3724)
One dog is allowed per suite. There
is a $25 per night additional pet fee
up to $150 for an entire stay.

**Homestead Studio Suites Durham -
University**
1920 Ivy Creek Blvd.
Durham, NC
919-402-1700 (800-804-3724)

One dog is allowed per suite. There
is a $25 per night additional pet fee
up to $150 for an entire stay.

**La Quinta Inn & Suites Durham
Chapel Hill**
4414 Durham Chapel Hill Blvd.
Durham, NC
919-401-9660 (800-531-5900)
Dogs of all sizes are allowed. There
are no additional pet fees. Dogs
must be leashed and cleaned up
after. Dogs may not be left
unattended, and they are not
allowed in the lobby or the pool
area. Multiple dogs may be allowed.

Quality Inn & Suites Durham
3710 Hillsborough Road
Durham, NC
919-382-3388 (877-424-6423)
duke85.com
Dogs of all sizes are allowed. There
is a $25 per night additional pet fee.

Red Roof Inn Chapel Hill
5623 Durham-Chapel Hill Boulevard
Durham, NC
919-489-9421 (800-RED-ROOF)
One well-behaved family pet per
room. Guest must notify front desk
upon arrival. Guest is liable for any
damages. In consideration of all
guests, pets must never be left
unattended in the guest rooms.

**Red Roof Inn Durham - Duke
Medical Center**
1915 North Pointe Drive
Durham, NC
919-471-9882 (800-RED-ROOF)
One well-behaved family pet per
room. Guest must notify front desk
upon arrival. Guest is liable for any
damages. In consideration of all
guests, pets must never be left
unattended in the guest rooms.

**Red Roof Inn Durham - Triangle
Park**
4405 Highway 55 East
Durham, NC
919-361-1950 (800-RED-ROOF)
One well-behaved family pet per
room. Guest must notify front desk
upon arrival. Guest is liable for any
damages. In consideration of all
guests, pets must never be left
unattended in the guest rooms.

**Residence Inn Durham Research
Triangle Park**
201 Residence Inn Blvd
Durham, NC
919-361-1266 (800-331-3131)
In addition to being located only one
mile from the country's largest

research and development park
(over 100 companies), this hotel also
offers a number of in-house
amenities, including a daily buffet
breakfast and weekly evening
socials. Dogs are allowed for an
additional one time pet fee of $75 per
room. Dogs must be crated or
removed for housekeeping. Multiple
dogs may be allowed.

Sleep Inn
5208 Page Rd
Durham, NC
919-993-3393 (877-424-6423)
Dogs of all sizes are allowed. Dogs
are allowed for a pet fee of $40.00
per pet per stay.

**Staybridge Suites Durham-Chapel
Hill-Rtp**
3704 Mt. Moriah Road
Durham, NC
919-401-9800 (877-270-6405)
Dogs up to 80 pounds are allowed.
Pets allowed with an additional pet
fee. Up to $75 for 1-6 nights and up
to $150 for 7+ nights. A pet
agreement must be signed at check-
in.

Super 8 /University Area
2337 Guess Road
Durham, NC
919-286-7746 (800-800-8000)
Dogs of all sizes are allowed. Dogs
are allowed for a pet fee of $8.00 per
pet per night.

Econo Lodge
110 East Arbor Lane
Eden, NC
336-627-5131 (877-424-6423)
Dogs up to 50 pounds are allowed.
Dogs are allowed for a pet fee of
$10.00 per pet per night. Two dogs
are allowed per room.

Econo Lodge
522 South Hughes Boulevard B
Elizabeth City, NC
252-338-4124 (877-424-6423)
Dogs of all sizes are allowed. Two
dogs are allowed per room.

Quality Inn
522 South Hughes Blvd.
Elizabeth City, NC
252-338-3951 (877-424-6423)
Dogs of all sizes are allowed.

Bluewater GMAC Real Estate
200 Mangrove
Emerald Isle, NC
888-258-9287
bluewaterdogfriendly.com
This vacation rental company has

over 170 dog-friendly vacation homes in the Southern Outer Banks.

Baymont Inn & Suites /Ft. Bragg Fayetteville
2910 Sigman Street
Fayetteville, NC
910-485-0520 (877-229-6668)
Dogs of all sizes are allowed. Dogs are allowed for a pet fee of $10.00 per pet per night.

Comfort Inn
1957 Cedar Creek Rd
Fayetteville, NC
910-323-8333 (877-424-6423)
Dogs of all sizes are allowed. Dogs are allowed for a pet fee of $75.99 per pet per night. Dogs are allowed for a pet fee of $check-in per pet per stay.

Comfort Inn Cross Creek
1922 Skibo Rd.
Fayetteville, NC
910-867-1777 (877-424-6423)
Dogs up to 50 pounds are allowed. Dogs are allowed for a pet fee of $49.00 per pet per stay. Two dogs are allowed per room.

Econo Lodge
1952 Cedar Creek Rd.
Fayetteville, NC
910-433-2100 (877-424-6423)
Dogs of all sizes are allowed. Dogs are allowed for a pet fee of $10.00 per pet per night.

Extended Stay America Fayetteville - Owen Dr.
408 Owen Dr.
Fayetteville, NC
910-485-2747 (800-804-3724)
One dog is allowed per suite. There is a $25 per night additional pet fee up to $150 for an entire stay.

Holiday Inn Fayetteville-I-95 South
P.O. Box 2245 / I-95 & 53
Fayetteville, NC
910-323-1600 (877-270-6405)
Dogs of all sizes are allowed. Dogs are allowed for a pet fee of $25.00 per pet per night.

Knights Inn /Fort Bragg Fayetteville
2848 Bragg Blvd.
Fayetteville, NC
910-485-4163 (800-843-5644)
Dogs of all sizes are allowed. Dogs are allowed for a pet fee.

Motel 6 - Fayetteville, Nc
2076 Cedar Creek Rd
Fayetteville, NC
910-485-8122 (800-466-8356)

This motel welcomes your pets to stay with you.

Quality Inn
2035 Eastern Boulevard
Fayetteville, NC
910-485-8135 (877-424-6423)
Dogs of all sizes are allowed. Dogs are allowed for a pet fee of $20.00 per pet per stay.

Red Roof Inn Fayetteville, NC
1569 Jim Johnson Road
Fayetteville, NC
910-321-1460 (800-RED-ROOF)
One well-behaved family pet per room. Guest must notify front desk upon arrival. Guest is liable for any damages. In consideration of all guests, pets must never be left unattended in the guest rooms.

Residence Inn Fayetteville Cross Creek
1468 Skibo Road
Fayetteville, NC
910-868-9005 (800-331-3131)
Besides offering a convenient location to businesses, institutes of learning, shopping, dining, and entertainment areas, this all suite hotel also offers a number of in-house amenities, including a daily buffet breakfast and a nightly social hour Monday to Thursday with light dinner fare. Dogs are allowed for an additional one time pet fee of $100 per room. Multiple dogs may be allowed.

Super 8 Fayetteville
1875 Cedar Creek Rd
Fayetteville, NC
910-323-3826 (800-800-8000)
Dogs of all sizes are allowed. Dogs are allowed for a nightly pet fee.

Days Inn Asheville Airport
183 Underwood Road/I-26
Fletcher, NC
828-684-2281 (800-329-7466)
Dogs up to 60 pounds are allowed. Dogs are allowed for a pet fee of $15.00 per pet per night.

Holiday Inn Asheville-Airport (I-26)
550 Airport Road
Fletcher, NC
828-684-1213 (877-270-6405)
Dogs of all sizes are allowed. Dogs are allowed for a nightly pet fee.

Quality Inn
205 Commercial Dr.
Forest City, NC
828-248-3400 (877-424-6423)
Dogs of all sizes are allowed. Dogs

are allowed for a pet fee of $10.00 per pet per night. Two dogs are allowed per room.

Super 8 /Clayton/Raleigh Garner
101 Leone Court
Garner, NC
919-661-1991 (800-800-8000)
Dogs are welcome at this hotel.

Best Western Executive Inn
360 Best Western Ct
Gastonia, NC
704-868-2000 (800-780-7234)
Dogs of all sizes are allowed. Dogs are allowed for a pet fee of $25 per pet per night.

Days Inn - West of Charlotte Kings Mountain Gastonia
1700 North Chester St
Gastonia, NC
704-864-9981 (800-329-7466)
Dogs are welcome at this hotel.

Knights Inn /West of Charlotte Gastonia
1400 East Franklin Blvd
Gastonia, NC
704-864-8744 (800-843-5644)
Dogs are welcome at this hotel.

Motel 6 - Gastonia, Nc
1901 Broadcast Street
Gastonia, NC
704-810-6622 (800-466-8356)
This motel welcomes your pets to stay with you.

Super 8 Gastonia
502 Cox Road
Gastonia, NC
704-867-3846 (800-800-8000)
Dogs of all sizes are allowed. Dogs are allowed for a pet fee of $10.00 per pet per stay.

Days Inn - Rocky Mount Gold Rock
6970 Highway 4
Gold Rock, NC
252-446-0621 (800-329-7466)
Dogs of all sizes are allowed. Dogs are allowed for a pet fee of $6.00 per pet per night.

Baymont Inn & Suites /Coliseum Greensboro
2001 Veasley Street
Greensboro, NC
336-294-6220 (877-229-6668)
Dogs are welcome at this hotel.

Candlewood Suites Greensboro
7623 Thorndike Rd
Greensboro, NC
336-454-0078 (877-270-6405)
Dogs up to 80 pounds are allowed.

Pets allowed with an additional pet fee. Up to $75 for 1-6 nights and up to $150 for 7+ nights. A pet agreement must be signed at check-in.

Clarion Hotel Airport
415 Swing Road
Greensboro, NC
336-299-7650 (877-424-6423)
Dogs of all sizes are allowed. Dogs are allowed for a pet fee of $50.00 per pet per stay.

Days Inn Airport Greensboro
501 South Regional Rd
Greensboro, NC
336-668-0476 (800-329-7466)
Dogs of all sizes are allowed. Dogs are allowed for a pet fee.

Days Inn Greensboro
110 Seneca Road
Greensboro, NC
336-275-9331 (800-329-7466)
Dogs of all sizes are allowed. Dogs are allowed for a pet fee of $10.00 per pet per night.

Drury Inn & Suites
3220 High Point Road
Greensboro, NC
336-856-9696 (800-378-7946)
Dogs of all sizes are allowed for no additional pet fee with a credit card on file, and there is a pet agreement to sign at check in.

Extended Stay America Greensboro - Wendover Ave.
4317 Big Tree Way
Greensboro, NC
336-299-0200 (800-804-3724)
One dog is allowed per suite. There is a $25 per night additional pet fee up to $150 for an entire stay.

Holiday Inn Express Hotel & Suites Greensboro - Airport Area
645 S. Regional Road
Greensboro, NC
336-882-0004 (877-270-6405)
Dogs are welcome at this hotel.

Knights Inn Greensboro
110 B Seneca Road
Greensboro, NC
336-369-1075 (800-843-5644)
Dogs of all sizes are allowed. Dogs are allowed for a pet fee of $5.00 per pet per night.

La Quinta Inn & Suites Greensboro
1201 Lanada Road
Greensboro, NC
336-316-0100 (800-531-5900)
Dogs of all sizes are allowed. There

are no additional pet fees. Dogs may not be left unattended, and they must be leashed and cleaned up after. Multiple dogs may be allowed.

Motel 6 - Greensboro Airport
605 Regional Rd
Greensboro, NC
336-668-2085 (800-466-8356)
This motel welcomes your pets to stay with you.

Motel 6 - Greensboro South
831 Greenhaven Dr
Greensboro, NC
336-854-0993 (800-466-8356)
This motel welcomes your pets to stay with you.

Quality Inn & Suites Airpark East
7067 Albert Pick Road
Greensboro, NC
336-668-3638 (877-424-6423)
Dogs up to 50 pounds are allowed.

Red Roof Inn Greensboro Airport
615 Regional Road South
Greensboro, NC
336-271-2636 (800-RED-ROOF)
One well-behaved family pet per room. Guest must notify front desk upon arrival. Guest is liable for any damages. In consideration of all guests, pets must never be left unattended in the guest rooms.

Red Roof Inn Greensboro Coliseum
2101 West Meadowview Road
Greensboro, NC
336-852-6560 (800-RED-ROOF)
One well-behaved family pet per room. Guest must notify front desk upon arrival. Guest is liable for any damages. In consideration of all guests, pets must never be left unattended in the guest rooms.

Residence Inn Greensboro Airport
7616 Thorndike Road
Greensboro, NC
336-632-4666 (800-331-3131)
Besides offering a convenient location to many of the area's star attractions, this hotel also provides a number of in-house amenities, including a daily buffet breakfast and evening socials. Dogs up to 50 pounds are allowed for an additional one time pet fee of $100 per room. Multiple dogs may be allowed.

Studio 6 - Greensboro,nc
2000 Veasley Street
Greensboro, NC
336-294-8600 (800-466-8356)

Your pets are welcome to stay here with you for a pet fee of $10 per day up to $50 for an entire stay.

Candlewood Suites Greenville West
1055 Waterford Commons Drive
Greenville, NC
252-317-3000 (877-270-6405)
Dogs up to 80 pounds are allowed. Pets allowed with an additional pet fee. Up to $75 for 1-6 nights and up to $150 for 7+ nights. A pet agreement must be signed at check-in.

Motel 6 - Greenville, Nc
301 Se Greenville Blvd
Greenville, NC
252-756-2792 (800-466-8356)
This motel welcomes your pets to stay with you.

Midgett Realty
Hatteras Office: P.O. Box 250 57783
Hatteras, NC
866-976-9261
These small beach cottages and oceanfront homes are pet-friendly. Not all properties are pet-friendly so ask for a pet-friendly cottage or home when you reserve a rental.

Days Inn Henderson
1052 Ruin Creek Road
Henderson, NC
252-492-4041 (800-329-7466)
Dogs are welcome at this hotel.

Econo Lodge
112 Parham Rd.
Henderson, NC
252-438-8511 (877-424-6423)
Dogs of all sizes are allowed. Dogs are allowed for a pet fee of $10.00 per pet per night.

Sleep Inn
18 Market St.
Henderson, NC
252-433-9449 (877-424-6423)
Dogs of all sizes are allowed. Dogs are allowed for a pet fee of $15.00 per pet per night.

Comfort Inn
206 Mitchelle Dr.
Hendersonville, NC
828-693-8800 (877-424-6423)
Dogs of all sizes are allowed. Dogs are allowed for a pet fee of $10.00 per pet per night.

Days Inn Hendersonville
102 Mitchell Drive
Hendersonville, NC
828-697-5899 (800-329-7466)
Dogs of all sizes are allowed. Dogs

are allowed for a pet fee of $15 per pet per night.

Ramada Hendersonville
150 Sugarloaf Rd
Hendersonville, NC
828-697-0006 (800-272-6232)
Dogs of all sizes are allowed. Dogs are allowed for a pet fee of $15.00 per pet per night.

Red Roof Inn Hendersonville
240 Mitchelle Drive
Hendersonville, NC
828-697-1223 (800-RED-ROOF)
One well-behaved family pet per room. Guest must notify front desk upon arrival. Guest is liable for any damages. In consideration of all guests, pets must never be left unattended in the guest rooms.

Quality Inn
1725 13th Avenue Drive NW
Hickory, NC
828-431-2100 (877-424-6423)
Dogs up to 50 pounds are allowed. There is a $10 per pet per stay fee and a credit card needs to be on file. Dogs are not allowed to be left alone in the room.

Red Roof Inn Hickory
1184 Lenoir Rhyne Boulevard
Hickory, NC
828-323-1500 (800-RED-ROOF)
One well-behaved family pet per room. Guest must notify front desk upon arrival. Guest is liable for any damages. In consideration of all guests, pets must never be left unattended in the guest rooms.

Candlewood Suites Huntersville-Lake Norman Area
16530 Northcross Drive
Huntersville, NC
704-895-3434 (877-270-6405)
Dogs up to 80 pounds are allowed. Pets allowed with an additional pet fee. Up to $75 for 1-6 nights and up to $150 for 7+ nights. A pet agreement must be signed at check-in.

Charlotte - Huntersville Red Roof Inn & Suites
13830 Statesville Road
Huntersville, NC
704-875-7880 (800-RED-ROOF)
One well-behaved family pet per room. Guest must notify front desk upon arrival. Guest is liable for any damages. In consideration of all guests, pets must never be left unattended in the guest rooms.

Quality Inn
16825 Caldwell Creek Drive
Huntersville, NC
704-892-6597 (877-424-6423)
Dogs of all sizes are allowed. Dogs are allowed for a pet fee of $25.00 per pet per stay.

Residence Inn Charlotte Lake Norman
16830 Kenton Drive
Huntersville, NC
704-584-0000 (800-331-3131)
This all suite, upscale hotel offers a central location to all the riches the area has to offer for both business and leisure travelers. And, among the amenities they also offer a daily buffet breakfast, an evening hospitality hour, weekly barbecues, a pool, and a Sport Court. Dogs are allowed for an additional one time pet fee of $100 per room. 2 dogs may be allowed.

Baymont Inn and Suites Jacksonville
474 Western Blvd
Jacksonville, NC
910-347-6500 (877-229-6668)
Dogs are welcome at this hotel.

Extended Stay America Jacksonville - Camp Lejeune
20 McDaniel Dr.
Jacksonville, NC
910-347-7684 (800-804-3724)
One dog is allowed per suite. There is a $25 per night additional pet fee up to $150 for an entire stay.

TownePlace Suites Jacksonville
400 Northwest Drive
Jacksonville, NC
910-478-9795 (800-257-3000)
Besides offering a number of in-house amenities for all level of travelers, this all suite inn also offers a convenient location to beaches, businesses, shopping, dining, and day/night entertainment areas. Dogs are allowed for an additional one time fee of $75 per room. 2 dogs may be allowed.

Comfort Inn
1633 Winston Road
Jonesville, NC
336-835-9400 (877-424-6423)
Dogs of all sizes are allowed. Dogs are allowed for a pet fee of $10.00 per pet per night.

Days Inn Jonesville
1540 NC 67 Hwy
Jonesville, NC
336-526-6777 (800-329-7466)

Dogs of all sizes are allowed. Dogs are allowed for a pet fee of $10 per pet per night.

Super 8 /Elkin Area Jonesville
5601 US Hwy 21
Jonesville, NC
336-835-1461 (800-800-8000)
Dogs are welcome at this hotel.

Days Inn Kenly
1139 Johnston Parkway
Kenly, NC
919-284-3400 (800-329-7466)
Dogs are welcome at this hotel.

Econo Lodge
I-95 exit 107 & US 301
Kenly, NC
919-284-1000 (877-424-6423)
Dogs of all sizes are allowed. Dogs are allowed for a pet fee of $10.00/pet per pet per night.

Super 8 Kenly
843 Johnston Parkway
Kenly, NC
919-284-3800 (800-800-8000)
Dogs are welcome at this hotel.

Cavilier Motel
601 S Viriginia Dare Trail
Kill Devil Hills, NC
252-441-5585
Dogs of all sizes are allowed for an additional pet fee of $8 per night per room. Dogs are allowed in the cottages only.

Comfort Inn On the Ocean
1601 S Virginia Dare Trail/H 12
Kill Devil Hills, NC
252-441-6333 (877-424-6423)
In addition to a convenient location to some of the areas best attractions and activities, this inn sets beachside overlooking the Atlantic Ocean for sunrises, and overlooking the Roanoke Sound for great sunsets; plus they offer a number of on-site amenities. Dogs are allowed on the 1st floor room only for an additional fee of $20 per night per room. 2 dogs may be allowed.

Quality Inn John Yancey
2009 S. Virginia Dare Tr.
Kill Devil Hills, NC
252-441-7141 (877-424-6423)
Dogs of all sizes are allowed. Dogs are allowed for a pet fee of $20.00 per pet per night. Two dogs are allowed per room.

Travelodge Outer Banks/ Kill Devil Hills
804 North Virginia Dare Trail

Kill Devil Hills, NC
252-441-0411 (800-578-7878)
Dogs of all sizes are allowed. Dogs
are allowed for a pet fee.

Ramada Plaza Nags Head Beach
1701 S. Virginia Dare Trail
Kill Devil Hills/Nags Head, NC
252-441-2151 (800-272-6232)
Dogs of all sizes are allowed. Dogs
are allowed for a nightly pet fee.

Quality Inn
722 York Rd.
Kings Mountain, NC
704-739-7070 (877-424-6423)
Dogs up to 90 pounds are allowed.
Dogs are allowed for a pet fee of
$15.00 per pet per night. Two dogs
are allowed per room.

Joe Lamb Jr. & Associates
4607 N. Croatan Hwy
Kitty Hawk, NC
252-261-4444 (800-552-6257)
joelambjr.com
This company manages over 75 pet
friendly vacation homes ranging in
size from 3 to 7 bedrooms.

The 1927 Lake Lure Inn and Spa
2771 Memorial H/H 9/64/74
Lake Lure, NC
828-625-2525 (888-434-4970)
lakelure.com/lake_lure_inn.php
Historic charm, modern comfort,
outstanding scenery, gourmet dining,
and a variety of recreational
opportunities are only some of the
offerings of this get-a-way
destination. There are also lovely
gardens to stroll, a full service spa, a
swimming pool overlooking the lake,
2 restaurants with outdoor seating,
and a lounge that offers
complimentary hors d'oeurves daily.
Dogs are allowed at the hotel for an
additional $25 per night per pet; they
must be leashed and picked up after
at all times. Dogs are allowed at the
outdoor seating of the eateries. 2
dogs may be allowed.

Comfort Suites Magnolia Greens
1020 Grandiflora Drive
Leland, NC
910-383-3300 (877-424-6423)
Dogs up to 50 pounds are allowed.
Two dogs are allowed per room.

Days Inn Lenoir
206 Blowing Rock Blvd
Lenoir, NC
828-754-0731 (800-329-7466)
Dogs are welcome at this hotel.

Comfort Suites

1620 Cotton Grove Rd.
Lexington, NC
336-357-2333 (877-424-6423)
Dogs of all sizes are allowed.

Econo Lodge
418 Piedmont Drive
Lexington, NC
336-249-0111 (877-424-6423)
Dogs up to 50 pounds are allowed.
Dogs are allowed for a pet fee of
$25.00 per pet per stay. Two dogs
are allowed per room.

Days Inn Lincolnton
614 Clark Drive
Lincolnton, NC
704-735-8271 (800-329-7466)
Dogs of all sizes are allowed. Dogs
are allowed for a pet fee.

Best Western Inn
201 Jackson Ct
Lumberton, NC
910-618-9799 (800-780-7234)
Dogs of all sizes are allowed. Dogs
are allowed for a pet fee of $10.00
per pet per night.

Days Inn -Outlet Mall Lumberton
3030 North Roberts Ave
Lumberton, NC
910-738-6401 (800-329-7466)
Dogs are welcome at this hotel.

Motel 6 - Lumberton
2361 Lackey Rd
Lumberton, NC
 (800-466-8356)
This motel welcomes your pets to
stay with you.

Maggie Mountain
60 Twin Hickory
Maggie Valley, NC
828-926-4258
plus an additional $200 refundable
deposit will be required if there are
3 dogs.

Days Inn Marion
4248 Hwy 221 South
Marion, NC
828-659-2567 (800-329-7466)
Dogs of all sizes are allowed. Dogs
are allowed for a pet fee of $20 per
pet per night.

Super 8 NC Marion
4281 Highway 221 South
Marion, NC
828-659-7940 (800-800-8000)
Dogs are welcome at this hotel.

Country Inns & Suites by Carlson
2001 Mount Harmony Church Rd
Matthews, NC

704-846-8000
the fee is $15 per night for dogs over
50 pounds.

Comfort Inn & Suites
629 Madison Road
Mocksville, NC
336-751-5966 (877-424-6423)
Dogs of all sizes are allowed. Dogs
are allowed for a pet fee of $20.00
per pet per stay. Two dogs are
allowed per room.

Quality Inn
1500 Yadkinville Rd.
Mocksville, NC
336-751-7310 (877-424-6423)
Dogs of all sizes are allowed. Dogs
are allowed for a pet fee of $25.00
per pet per stay. Two dogs are
allowed per room.

Super 8 Monroe
608-E West Roosevelt Blvd
Monroe, NC
704-289-1555 (800-800-8000)
Dogs of all sizes are allowed. Dogs
are allowed for a pet fee of $10.00
per pet per night.

Holiday Inn Express Hotel & Suites
Morehead City
5063 Executive Dr
Morehead City, NC
252-247-5001 (877-270-6405)
Dogs of all sizes are allowed. Dogs
are allowed for a pet fee.

Days Inn And Suites
1100 Burkemont Ave
Morganton, NC
828-430-8778 (800-329-7466)
Dogs are welcome at this hotel.

Sleep Inn
2400A South Sterling Street
Morganton, NC
828-433-9000 (877-424-6423)
Dogs of all sizes are allowed. Dogs
are allowed for a pet fee of $25.00
per pet per stay.

Extended Stay America Raleigh -
RDU Airport
2700 Slater Rd.
Morrisville, NC
919-380-1499 (800-804-3724)
One dog is allowed per suite. There
is a $25 per night additional pet fee
up to $150 for an entire stay.

Residence Inn Raleigh-Durham
Airport
2020 Hospitality Court
Morrisville, NC
919-467-8689 (800-331-3131)
Only a mile from the airport and 4

miles to the country's largest research park, this all suite in offers a number of amenities for the business or leisure traveler including a daily complimentary hot breakfast and nightly social hours. Dogs are allowed for an additional one time pet fee of $75 per room. 2 dogs may be allowed.

Staybridge Suites Raleigh-Durham Apt-Morrisville
1012 Airport Blvd.
Morrisville, NC
919-468-0180 (877-270-6405)
Dogs up to 80 pounds are allowed. Pets allowed with an additional pet fee. Up to $75 for 1-6 nights and up to $150 for 7+ nights. A pet agreement must be signed at check-in.

Quality Inn
2136 Rockford St.
Mount Airy, NC
336-789-2000 (877-424-6423)
Dogs of all sizes are allowed. Dogs are allowed for a pet fee of $25.00 per pet per stay. Two dogs are allowed per room.

Best Western of Murphy
1522 Andrews Road
Murphy, NC
828-837-3060 (800-780-7234)
Dogs of all sizes are allowed. Dogs are allowed for a nightly pet fee.

Days Inn Murphy
754 Highway 64 West
Murphy, NC
828-837-8030 (800-329-7466)
Dogs of all sizes are allowed. Dogs are allowed for a pet fee of $10.00 per pet per night.

Smoky Mountain Hideaway
Mary King Mountain
Murphy, NC
727-864-0526
Dogs of all sizes are allowed for a $100 refundable pet deposit per room with advance reservations. Dogs must be current on shots and on a flea/tick prevention program. 2 dogs may be allowed.

Comfort Inn South Oceanfront
8031 Old Oregon Inlet Rd.
Nags Head, NC
252-441-6315 (877-424-6423)
Dogs of all sizes are allowed. Dogs are allowed for a pet fee of $20.00 per pet per night.

Sheraton New Bern Hotel and Marina

100 Middle Street
New Bern, NC
252-638-3585 (888-625-5144)
newbernsheraton.com
Not to mention its beautiful setting at the edge of the harbor with outstanding views, this 4 story inn features a number of amenities including a full service marina, a dockside cafe and raw bar with a bar, boat charters, a swimming pool, and a picnic area with grills. Dogs are allowed on the first floor for an additional fee of $25 per night per room; they must be kept leashed when out of the room and picked up after at all times. Dogs are allowed at the outer tables of the cafe, and on the boat rentals. Barnacle Bob's can be reached at 252-634-4100. 2 dogs may be allowed.

Idyll-by-the-Sea Two
134 Ocean View Lane
North Topsail Beach, NC
603-524-4000
This large vacation rental has 8 bedrooms and can sleep up to 18 people. It is almost 6000 square feet in size. Well behaved dogs of all sizes are welcome. You may contact the owners to make reservations at relax@idyll-by-the-sea.com or at 603-524-4000 during business hours (ET).

Oak Island Accommodations, Inc
8901 East Oak Island Drive
Oak Island, NC
910-278-6011 (800-243-8132)
rentalsatthebeach.com
This rental agency offers over 600+ resort rentals from Oceanfront to Soundside. Pets allowed in designated homes. Dogs 60 pounds and under allowed with a non-refundable $100 + tax pet fee for Cleaning and Extermination.

Blackbeard's Lodge
111 Back Road
Ocracoke Village, NC
252-928-2503 (800-892-5314)
A lodge-styled hotel, it is the oldest hotel on the island; however it lists a number of modern updates/amenities, a heated swimming pool, gaming areas, bicycles, and a great location to a number of local recreational pursuits and sites of interest. Dogs are allowed for an additional $20 per night per pet. Dogs must be leashed and cleaned up after at all times. Multiple dogs may be allowed.

The Anchorage Inn
205 Irvin Garrish H/H 12
Ocracoke Village, NC
252-928-6661
theanchorageinn.com/
In addition to the in-house amenities, this inn offers great waterfront sunsets and a convenient location to many recreational pursuits and sites of interest. Dogs are allowed for an additional $20 per night per pet. Dogs must be well behaved, under owner's control, leashed and cleaned up after at all times. Multiple dogs may be allowed.

The Island Inn
25 Lighthouse Road
Ocracoke Village, NC
252-928-4351 (877-456-3466)
ocracokeislandinn.com/
This inn has worn many faces since it's creation from shipwrecked wood in 1901 and it is also the oldest working business in the area and listed on the National Registry of Historic Places. Pets are allowed at the inn's villas for no additional fee with a credit card on file. Dogs must be well groomed and mannered, leashed and cleaned up after. 2 dogs may be allowed.

Comfort Inn & Suites
1000 Linden Avenue
Oxford, NC
919-692-1000 (877-424-6423)
Dogs up to 50 pounds are allowed. Dogs are allowed for a pet fee of $10.00 per pet per night. Two dogs are allowed per room.

Quality Inn & Suites
711 S. Key Street
Pilot Mountain, NC
336-368-2237 (877-424-6423)
Dogs of all sizes are allowed. Dogs are allowed for a pet fee of $25.00 per pet per stay.

Weddens Way, Too
231 Legra Rd
Piney Creek, NC
336-372-2985
sparta-nc.com/weddensway/
Fully furnished cabin overlooking the New River. Sleeps up to 7, rate for two is $80 plus tax per night. Pets are welcome for a $50 fee for the entire stay. Fish, canoe or enjoy the view.

Holiday Inn Express Plymouth
840 US Hwy 64 W
Plymouth, NC
252-793-4700 (877-270-6405)
Dogs of all sizes are allowed. Dogs are allowed for a pet fee of $25.00

per pet per stay.

Candlewood Suites Raleigh Crabtree
4433 Lead Mine Road
Raleigh, NC
919-789-4840 (877-270-6405)
Dogs up to 80 pounds are allowed.
Pets allowed with an additional pet
fee. Up to $75 for 1-6 nights and up
to $150 for 7+ nights. A pet
agreement must be signed at check-
in.

Candlewood Suites Raleigh-Cary
1020 Buck Jones Road
Raleigh, NC
919-468-4222 (877-270-6405)
Dogs up to 80 pounds are allowed.
Pets allowed with an additional pet
fee. Up to $75 for 1-6 nights and up
to $150 for 7+ nights. A pet
agreement must be signed at check-
in.

Comfort Suites North
4400 Capital Blvd.
Raleigh, NC
919-876-2211 (877-424-6423)
Dogs of all sizes are allowed. Dogs
are allowed for a pet fee of $1.50 per
pet per night.

Days Inn
6619 Glenwood Ave.
Raleigh, NC
919-782-8650 (800-329-7466)
Dogs of all sizes are allowed. Dogs
are allowed for a pet fee of $35.00
per pet per stay.

Days Inn Raleigh
3201 Wake Forest Road
Raleigh, NC
919-878-9310 (800-329-7466)
Dogs of all sizes are allowed. Dogs
are allowed for a pet fee of $10.00
per pet per night.

Extended Stay America Raleigh -
North Raleigh
911 Wake Towne Dr.
Raleigh, NC
919-829-7271 (800-804-3724)
One dog is allowed per suite. There
is a $25 per night additional pet fee
up to $150 for an entire stay.

Holiday Inn Raleigh-North
2805 Highwoods Blvd
Raleigh, NC
919-872-3500 (877-270-6405)
Dogs of all sizes are allowed. Dogs
are allowed for a pet fee of $35 per
pet per stay.

Homestead Studio Suites Raleigh -
Crabtree Valley

4810 Bluestone Dr.
Raleigh, NC
919-510-8551 (800-804-3724)
One dog is allowed per suite. There
is a $25 per night additional pet fee
up to $150 for an entire stay.

Homestead Studio Suites Raleigh -
North Raleigh
3531 Wake Forest Rd.
Raleigh, NC
919-981-7353 (800-804-3724)
One dog is allowed per suite. There
is a $25 per night additional pet fee
up to $150 for an entire stay.

Homestead Studio Suites Raleigh -
Northeast
2601 Appliance Ct.
Raleigh, NC
919-807-9970 (800-804-3724)
One dog is allowed per suite. There
is a $25 per night additional pet fee
up to $150 for an entire stay.

Howard Johnson Express Inn -
Raleigh
3120 New Bern Ave
Raleigh, NC
919-231-3000 (800-446-4656)
Dogs of all sizes are allowed. Dogs
are allowed for a nightly pet fee.

La Quinta Inn Raleigh
1001 Aerial Center Parkway
Raleigh, NC
919-481-3600 (800-531-5900)
Dogs of all sizes are allowed. There
are no additional pet fees. Dogs
must be well behaved, leashed, and
cleaned up after. Multiple dogs may
be allowed.

Motel 6 - Raleigh East (new Bern
Avenue)
3520 Maitland Dr
Raleigh, NC
919-231-0200 (800-466-8356)
This motel welcomes your pets to
stay with you.

Motel 6 - Raleigh Northwest
3921 Arrow Dr
Raleigh, NC
 (800-466-8356)
This motel welcomes your pets to
stay with you.

Motel 6 - Raleigh Southwest Cary
1401 Buck Jones Rd
Raleigh, NC
919-467-6171 (800-466-8356)
This motel welcomes your pets to
stay with you.

Red Roof Inn Raleigh NCSU -
Convention Center

1813 South Saunders Street
Raleigh, NC
919-833-6005 (800-RED-ROOF)
One well-behaved family pet per
room. Guest must notify front desk
upon arrival. Guest is liable for any
damages. In consideration of all
guests, pets must never be left
unattended in the guest rooms.

Residence Inn Raleigh
1000 Navaho Drive
Raleigh, NC
919-878-6100 (800-331-3131)
This all suite inn features a
convenient location to the state
university, business, shopping,
dining, and entertainment areas, plus
they also offer a number of in-house
amenities, including a daily buffet
breakfast, evening socials Monday
through Thursday with light dinner
fare, and summer barbecues. Dogs
up to 100 pounds are allowed for an
additional one time pet fee of $75 per
room. 2 dogs may be allowed.

Residence Inn Raleigh Crabtree
Valley
2200 Summit Park Lane
Raleigh, NC
919-279-3000 (800-331-3131)
Offering a central location to all that
the city has to offer, this all suite
hotel also provides a number of in-
house amenities, including a daily
buffet breakfast, evening receptions
Monday to Thursday, a putting
green, and a complementary grocery
shopping service. One dog up to 75
pounds is allowed for an additional
one time pet fee of $100 per room.

Super 8 Downtown East Raleigh
3804 New Bern Ave
Raleigh, NC
919-231-8818 (800-800-8000)
Dogs of all sizes are allowed. Dogs
are allowed for a pet fee.

Motel 6 - Roanoke Rapids, Nc
1911 Julian Alsbrook Hwy
Roanoke Rapids, NC
252-537-5252 (800-466-8356)
This motel welcomes your pets to
stay with you.

Quality Inn
1914 Julian R Allsbrook Hwy
Roanoke Rapids, NC
252-537-9927 (877-424-6423)
Dogs of all sizes are allowed. Dogs
are allowed for a pet fee of $20.00
per pet per stay.

Sleep Inn
101 Sleep Inn Dr.

Roanoke Rapids, NC
252-537-3141 (877-424-6423)
Dogs of all sizes are allowed. Dogs
are allowed for a pet fee of $20.00
per pet per stay.

Best Western Inn I-95/Goldrock
7095 Route 4
Rocky Mount, NC
252-985-1450 (800-780-7234)
Dogs of all sizes are allowed. Dogs
are allowed for a pet fee.

Best Western Rocky Mount Inn
1921 N Wesleyan Boulevard
Rocky Mount, NC
252-442-8101 (800-780-7234)
Dogs of all sizes are allowed. Dogs
are allowed for a nightly pet fee.

Candlewood Suites Rocky Mount
688 English Road
Rocky Mount, NC
252-467-2550 (877-270-6405)
Dogs up to 80 pounds are allowed.
Pets allowed with an additional pet
fee. Up to $75 for 1-6 nights and up
to $150 for 7+ nights. A pet
agreement must be signed at check-
in.

Comfort Inn
200 Gateway Blvd.
Rocky Mount, NC
252-937-7765 (877-424-6423)
Dogs of all sizes are allowed. Dogs
are allowed for a pet fee of $25.00
per pet per stay.

Days Inn Golden East Rocky Mount
1340 N Wesleyan Blvd
Rocky Mount, NC
252-977-7766 (800-329-7466)
Dogs up to 50 pounds are allowed.
Dogs are allowed for a nightly pet
fee.

Red Roof Inn Rocky Mount
1370 North Wesleyan Boulevard
Rocky Mount, NC
252-984-0907 (800-RED-ROOF)
One well-behaved family pet per
room. Guest must notify front desk
upon arrival. Guest is liable for any
damages. In consideration of all
guests, pets must never be left
unattended in the guest rooms.

Residence Inn Rocky Mount
230 Gateway Blvd
Rocky Mount, NC
252-451-5600 (800-331-3131)
This all suite inn features a
convenient location to business,
shopping, dining, and entertainment
areas, plus they also offer a number
of in-house amenities, including a

daily buffet breakfast and evening
socials. Dogs are allowed for an
additional one time pet fee of $40
per room. Multiple dogs may be
allowed.

Knights Inn Rowland
14723 US Highway 301 South
Rowland, NC
910-422-3366 (800-843-5644)
Dogs of all sizes are allowed. Dogs
are allowed for a pet fee.

Super 8 Rowland
14733 U.S. 301 South
Rowland, NC
910-422-3377 (800-800-8000)
Dogs of all sizes are allowed. Dogs
are allowed for a pet fee of $15.00
per pet per night.

Days Inn Salisbury
321 Bendix Drive
Salisbury, NC
704-633-5961 (800-329-7466)
Dogs of all sizes are allowed. Dogs
are allowed for a pet fee of $25.00
per pet per night.

Holiday Inn Salisbury
530 Jake Alexander Blvd South
Salisbury, NC
704-637-3100 (877-270-6405)
Dogs of all sizes are allowed. Dogs
are allowed for a pet fee of $15.00
per pet per night.

Travelodge Salisbury
1328 Jake Alexander Blvd South
Salisbury, NC
704-636-8910 (800-578-7878)
Dogs of all sizes are allowed. Dogs
are allowed for a pet fee of $10.00
per pet per night.

Spring Pond Cabin
640 E US Hwy 176
Saluda, NC
828-749-9824
saluda.com/springpond
This cozy cabin in the woods is
available for rent to you and your
pets. There is a covered porch with
fenced in area as well as a half mile
hiking loop on the property which is
wooded and has two spring fed
ponds. The cabin is fully equipped
and sleeps five. They ask that you
bring your own linens if your dog
sleeps on the bed.

Hummingbird Realty, Ltd.,
425 H 64W
Sapphire, NC
828-966-4737
hummingbird-realty.com
Vacation rentals are available

primarily in the Sapphire and Lake
Toxaway, NC communities through
this realty; however they also service
areas between Highlands and
Brevard, NC. They have a wide
variety of accommodations that
accept pets. Dogs must be well
trained, and there is an additional
one time fee of $75 per pet. 2 dogs
may be allowed.

Woodlands Inn of Sapphire
19259 Rosman H/64W
Sapphire, NC
828-966-4709
woodlandsinn.net
Located near the borders of 2 lush
national forests, this tranquil retreat
offers a great location for exploring
the 'Land of the Waterfall', of which
there are more than 250 of them in
the area. Dogs are allowed for an
additional fee of $10 per night per
room. Only 2 dogs are allowed in
regular rooms; there may be up to 3
dogs allowed in a suite. Dogs must
be well behaved, leashed, and
cleaned up after.

Fire Mountain Inn
On H 106
Scaley Mountain, NC
828-526-4446 (800-775-4446)
One dog up to 85 pounds is allowed,
however they may accept 2 dogs if
they are small and total no more than
85 pounds. This place takes dogs
only and they must be over a year
old and well house trained. There is
a $25 per night per pet fee plus a
$150 refundable deposit and a pet
policy to sign at check in. Dogs are
allowed in the cabins only.

Days Inn -Pine Level Selma
419 US. Highway 70 East
Selma, NC
919-965-3762 (800-329-7466)
Dogs are welcome at this hotel.

Holiday Inn Express Selma
115 US Hwy 70-A
Selma, NC
919-965-4000 (877-270-6405)
Dogs of all sizes are allowed. Dogs
are allowed for a pet fee of $25.00
per pet per night.

Quality Inn
1705 Industrial Park Drive
Selma, NC
919-965-5200 (877-424-6423)
Dogs of all sizes are allowed. Dogs
are allowed for a pet fee of $15.00
per pet per night.

Days Inn Shelby

1431 West Dixon Boulevard
Shelby, NC
704-482-1800 (800-329-7466)
Dogs of all sizes are allowed. Dogs
are allowed for a nightly pet fee.

Super 8 Shelby
I-85 to Hwy 74W Exit 10B
Shelby, NC
704-484-2101 (800-800-8000)
Dogs of all sizes are allowed. Dogs
are allowed for a pet fee of $10.00
per pet per night.

Super 8 Smithfield
735 Industrial Park Drive
Smithfield, NC
919-989-8988 (800-800-8000)
Dogs are welcome at this hotel.

Best Western Pinehurst Inn
1675 US Highway 1 S
Southern Pines, NC
910-692-0640 (800-780-7234)
Dogs of all sizes are allowed. Dogs
are allowed for a pet fee of $10.00
per pet per night.

Days Inn Conference Center
Pinehurst Southern Pines
805 South West Service Road
Southern Pines, NC
910-692-8585 (800-329-7466)
Dogs are welcome at this hotel.

Econo Lodge & Suites
408 W. Morganton Rd.
Southern Pines, NC
910-692-2063 (877-424-6423)
Dogs of all sizes are allowed. Dogs
are allowed for a pet fee of $20.00
per pet per night. Two dogs are
allowed per room.

Residence Inn Pinehurst Southern
Pines
105 Brucewood Road
Southern Pines, NC
910-693-3400 (800-331-3131)
Although there are a number of
amenities and activities for all level of
travelers, golfers will especially enjoy
staying at this all suite inn that sits
central and only 15 minutes to 40
great golf courses. Additionally, they
include a daily buffet breakfast and
evening socials Monday through
Thursday with hors d'oeuvres and
adult beverages. Dogs are allowed
for an additional one time pet fee of
$75 per room. Multiple dogs may be
allowed.

Comfort Suites
4963 Southport Supply Rd.
Southport, NC
910-454-7444 (877-424-6423)

Dogs of all sizes are allowed. Dogs
are allowed for a pet fee of $20.00
per pet per night.

Super 8 /First City Spindale
210 Reservation Dr
Spindale, NC
828-286-3681 (800-800-8000)
Dogs of all sizes are allowed. Dogs
are allowed for a pet fee of $15 per
pet per night.

Super 8 / Fort Bragg Spring Lake
256 S Main Street
Spring Lake, NC
910-436-8588 (800-800-8000)
Dogs of all sizes are allowed. Dogs
are allowed for a pet fee.

Baymont Inn & Suites Statesville
1214 Greenland Drive
Statesville, NC
704-873-2044 (877-229-6668)
Dogs are welcome at this hotel.

Motel 6 - Statesville
1137 Morland Dr
Statesville, NC
704-871-1115 (800-466-8356)
This motel welcomes your pets to
stay with you.

Quality Inn & Suites
715 Sullivan Road
Statesville, NC
704-878-2721 (877-424-6423)
Dogs of all sizes are allowed.

Red Roof Inn Statesville
1508 East Broad Street
Statesville, NC
704-878-2051 (800-RED-ROOF)
One well-behaved family pet per
room. Guest must notify front desk
upon arrival. Guest is liable for any
damages. In consideration of all
guests, pets must never be left
unattended in the guest rooms.

Super 8 Statesville
1125 Greenland Drive
Statesville, NC
704-878-9888 (800-800-8000)
Dogs are welcome at this hotel.

Carawan's Motel
510 H 94/45
Swan Quarter, NC
252-926-5861 (877-788-0764)
carawans.com/
In addition to sitting in the middle of
a sportsman's paradise, this motel
also offers guests satellite TV and
an outdoor sink for cleaning the
catch of the day. Dogs are allowed
for no additional fee; they may not
be left alone in the room. Dogs

must be leashed, cleaned up after,
and they are not allowed on the bed
or furniture. 2 dogs may be allowed.

Days Inn Thomasville
895 Lake Road.
Thomasville, NC
336-472-6600 (800-329-7466)
Dogs are welcome at this hotel.

Topsail Realty
712 S. Anderson Blvd.
Topsail Beach, NC
910-328-5241 (800-526-6432)
This realty company manages a few
dog-friendly rentals in the Topsail
Beach area. Dogs must be over 12
months old to stay in any of the
properties and each has different pet
terms.

Valle Crucis Log Cabin Rentals
P.O. Box 554
Valle Crucis, NC
828-963-7774
This company has many properties
and one large dog or 2 small dogs
are allowed. There is a $65 one time
fee per pet additional fee. They ask
you bring a blanket to cover the bed
or furniture if your pet is inclined to
get on them. 2 dogs may be allowed.

Days Inn Fayetteville/-North of Ft
Bragg I-95/Exit 58 Wade
3945 Goldsboro Road
Wade, NC
910-323-1255 (800-329-7466)
Dogs of all sizes are allowed. Dogs
are allowed for a pet fee of $12.00
per pet per night.

Days Inn Washington
916 Carolina Ave
Washington, NC
252-946-6141 (800-329-7466)
Dogs are welcome at this hotel.

Econo Lodge North
1220 W. 15th St.
Washington, NC
252-946-7781 (877-424-6423)
Dogs of all sizes are allowed. Dogs
are allowed for a pet fee of $USD,
per pet per night.

Super 8 Waynesville
79 Liner Cove Road
Waynesville, NC
828-454-9667 (800-800-8000)
Dogs are welcome at this hotel.

Days Inn Roanoke Rapids Weldon
1611 Julian R. Allsbrook Hwy
Weldon, NC
252-536-4867 (800-329-7466)
Dogs are welcome at this hotel.

Carolina Mountain Resort
8 N Jefferson Avenue
West Jefferson, NC
336-246-3010
Dogs of all sizes are allowed for an additional fee of $50 per pet with advance reservations, and there is a pet agreement to sign at check in. 2 dogs may be allowed.

Best Western Premiere Inn
503 N JK Powell Boulevard
Whiteville, NC
910-642-2378 (800-780-7234)
Dogs of all sizes are allowed for a pet fee of $20.00 per pet per night.

Baymont Inn And Suites Wilmington
306 South College Road
Wilmington, NC
910-392-6767 (877-229-6668)
Dogs of all sizes are allowed. Dogs are allowed for a nightly pet fee.

Camellia Cottage Bed and Breakfast
118 S. 4th Street
Wilmington, NC
910-763-9171
camelliacottage.net/
Well-behaved dogs are welcome in the Crane Suite at this bed and breakfast inn. There is a $15 per night per pet additional fee. Multiple dogs may be allowed.

Comfort Inn University
151 S. College Rd.
Wilmington, NC
910-791-4841 (877-424-6423)
Dogs up to 75 pounds are allowed. Dogs are allowed for a pet fee of $10.00 per pet per night. Two dogs are allowed per room.

Days Inn - Market Street Wilmington
5040 Market Street
Wilmington, NC
910-799-6300 (800-329-7466)
Dogs of all sizes are allowed. Dogs are allowed for a pet fee of $15.00 per pet per night.

Extended Stay America Wilmington - New Centre Drive
4929 New Centre Dr.
Wilmington, NC
910-793-4508 (800-804-3724)
One dog is allowed per suite. There is a $25 per night additional pet fee up to $150 for an entire stay.

Hilton Hotel
301 N Water Street
Wilmington, NC
910-763-5900 (800-HILTONS (445-

8667))
Locate in the heart of downtown along the shores of the Cape Fear River, this upscale hotel offers numerous on site amenities for business and leisure travelers, plus a convenient location to business, shopping, dining, historical, and entertainment areas. One dog up to 75 pounds is allowed for an additional one time fee of $75.

Motel 6 - Wilmington, Nc
2828 Market St
Wilmington, NC
910-762-0120 (800-466-8356)
This motel welcomes your pets to stay with you.

Residence Inn Wilmington Landfall
1200 Culbreth Drive
Wilmington, NC
910-256-0098 (800-331-3131)
In addition to offering a convenient location to business, historic, shopping, dining, and entertainment areas, this hotel also provides a number of in-house amenities, including a daily buffet breakfast and evening social hours. Dogs are allowed for an additional one time pet fee of $75 per room. Multiple dogs may be allowed.

Staybridge Suites Wilmington East
5010 New Centre Drive
Wilmington, NC
910-202-8500 (877-270-6405)
Dogs up to 80 pounds are allowed. Pets allowed with an additional pet fee. Up to $75 for 1-6 nights and up to $150 for 7+ nights. A pet agreement must be signed at check-in.

The Wilmingtonian
101 S 2nd Street
Wilmington, NC
910-343-1800 (800-525-0909)
thewilmingtonian.com/home.htm
The accommodations are spacious in this wonderfully restored 19th century home complete with balconies and formal terraced gardens; they also have a fine dining restaurant on site, catering, and venues for special events. Dogs up to 50 pounds are allowed for an additional one time fee of $25 per pet plus an additional fee $5 per night per pet, and they are allowed in the suites only. Dogs must be well behaved, leashed, and cleaned up after at all times. 2 dogs may be allowed.

TownePlace Suites Wilmington
305 Eastwood Road

Wilmington, NC
910-332-3326 (800-257-3000)
In addition to offering a number of in-house amenities for all level of travelers, this all suite inn also provides a convenient location to historic, business, shopping, dining, and entertainment areas. Dogs up to 75 pounds are allowed for an additional one time fee of $100 per room. Multiple dogs may be allowed.

Travelodge Wilmington
4118 Market Street
Wilmington, NC
910-762-4426 (800-578-7878)
Dogs of all sizes are allowed. Dogs are allowed for a pet fee.

Waterway Lodge
7246 Wrightsville Avenue
Wilmington, NC
910-256-3771 (800-677-3771)
waterwaylodge.com
The Waterway Lodge offers standard motel rooms as well as one bedroom condo units with full kitchens. It is located on the Intercoastal Waterway, and a short walk to numerous shops, restaurants, marinas and the beach.

Candlewood Suites Wilson
2915 Independence Dr W
Wilson, NC
252-291-9494 (877-270-6405)
Dogs up to 80 pounds are allowed. Pets allowed with an additional pet fee. Up to $75 for 1-6 nights and up to $150 for 7+ nights. A pet agreement must be signed at check-in.

Days Inn Wilson
1801 South Tarboro Street
Wilson, NC
252-291-2323 (800-329-7466)
Dogs are welcome at this hotel.

Holiday Inn Express Hotel & Suites New-Wilson-Downtown
2308 Montgomery Dr
Wilson, NC
252-246-1588 (877-270-6405)
Dogs of all sizes are allowed. Dogs are allowed for a pet fee of $20.00 per pet per stay.

Days Inn -Hanes Mall-Hospital-Convention Cente Winston Salem
3330 Silas Creek Pkwy
Winston Salem, NC
336-760-4770 (800-329-7466)
Dogs are welcome at this hotel.

Quality Inn University
5719 University Pkwy

Winston Salem, NC
336-767-9009 (877-424-6423)
Dogs of all sizes are allowed. Dogs are allowed for a pet fee of $25.00 per pet per stay.

Clarion Collection Hotel Sundance Plaza Hotel Spa & Wellness Ctr.
3050 University Pkwy
Winston-Salem, NC
336-723-2911 (877-424-6423)
Dogs of all sizes are allowed. Dogs are allowed for a pet fee of $25.00 per pet per stay.

Extended Stay America Winston-Salem - Hanes Mall Blvd.
1995 Hampton Inn Ct.
Winston-Salem, NC
336-768-0075 (800-804-3724)
One dog is allowed per suite. There is a $25 per night additional pet fee up to $150 for an entire stay.

La Quinta Inn & Suites Winston-Salem
2020 Griffith Road
Winston-Salem, NC
336-765-8777 (800-531-5900)
Dogs of all sizes are allowed. There are no additional pet fees. Dogs must be leashed, cleaned up after, and a contact number left with the front desk if there is a pet in the room alone. Multiple dogs may be allowed.

Residence Inn Winston-Salem
7835 North Point Blvd
Winston-Salem, NC
336-759-0777 (800-331-3131)
Besides offering a convenient location to business, shopping, dining, and entertainment areas, this hotel also provides a number of in-house amenities, including a daily buffet breakfast and complimentary evening social hours. Dogs up to 60 pounds are allowed for an additional one time pet fee of $75 (+ tax) per room. 2 dogs may be allowed.

Motel 6 - Winston Salem
3810 Patterson Ave
Winston-salem, NC
336-661-1588 (800-466-8356)
This motel welcomes your pets to stay with you.

Days Inn Yanceyville
1858 NC Hwy 86 North
Yanceyville, NC
336-694-9494 (800-329-7466)
Dogs of all sizes are allowed. Dogs are allowed for a nightly pet fee.

North Dakota

Old School
400 Vine Street
Arnegard, ND
701-586-3595
oldschoolbb.com/
Beautifully restored, this was once an old school house, and now it offers comfortable guest rooms, a game room, a small library of about 5000+ books, and a media room with a hi-def TV. Breakfasts are made to order-traditional or gourmet. Dogs are allowed for an additional pet fee of $10 per night per room; they must be well behaved, leashed, and cleaned up after at all times. Multiple dogs may be allowed.

Best Western Ramkota Hotel
800 S 3rd Street
Bismarck, ND
701-258-7700 (800-780-7234)
Dogs of all sizes are allowed. Dogs are allowed for a pet fee.

Candlewood Suites Bismarck
4400 Skyline Crossings
Bismarck, ND
701-751-8900 (877-270-6405)
Dogs up to 80 pounds are allowed. Pets allowed with an additional pet fee. Up to $75 for 1-6 nights and up to $150 for 7+ nights. A pet agreement must be signed at check-in.

Comfort Inn
1030 E. Interstate Ave.
Bismarck, ND
701-223-1911 (877-424-6423)
Dogs of all sizes are allowed.

Days Inn Bismarck
1300 E. Capitol Ave
Bismarck, ND
701-223-9151 (800-329-7466)
Dogs are welcome at this hotel.

Kelly Inn
1800 N 12th Street
Bismarck, ND
701-223-8001 (800-635-3559)
kellyinnbismarck.com/
This hotel offers a good central location to numerous sites of interest, and plenty of shopping, dining, entertainment, educational, and recreational pursuits. Dogs are allowed for no additional fee in smoking rooms; there is an additional one time fee of $20 per pet for a non-smoking room. Dogs may not be left in the room alone at any time. 2 dogs may be allowed.

Motel 6 - Bismarck
2433 State St
Bismarck, ND
701-255-6878 (800-466-8356)
This motel welcomes your pets to stay with you.

Radisson Hotel Bismarck
605 East Broadway Avenue
Bismarck, ND
701-255-6000
Dogs of all sizes are allowed. There is an additional one time pet fee of $20 per room. Dogs may not be left alone in the rooms.

Ramada Limited Suites Bismarck
3808 East Divide
Bismarck, ND
701-221-3030 (800-272-6232)
Dogs of all sizes are allowed. Dogs are allowed for a pet fee.

Select Inn
1505 Interchange Avenue
Bismarck, ND
701-223-8060
This inn will allow pets in designated rooms. There is a $25 refundable deposit plus an additional fee of $5.50 per night per pet. 2 dogs may be allowed.

Super 8 Bismarck
1124 East Capitol Avenue
Bismarck, ND
701-255-1314 (800-800-8000)
Dogs are welcome at this hotel.

Super 8 Bowman
408 3rd Ave SW
Bowman, ND
701-523-5613 (800-800-8000)
Dogs of all sizes are allowed. Dogs are allowed for a pet fee.

Days Inn Devils Lake
1109 Highway 20 S.
Devils Lake, ND
701-662-5381 (800-329-7466)
Dogs of all sizes are allowed. Dogs are allowed for a nightly pet fee.

Holiday Inn Express Devils Lake
875 Hwy#2 East
Devils Lake, ND
701-665-3200 (877-270-6405)
Dogs are welcome at this hotel.

Woodland Resort
1012 Woodland Drive
Devils Lake, ND
701-662-5996
Dogs of all sizes are allowed. There is a $10 per night per pet, additional fee for the lodge, motel, or cabins. There are no additional pet fees for

the campground on site. Dogs may not be left unattended, and they must be leashed and cleaned up after. Multiple dogs may be allowed.

Comfort Inn
493 Elk Dr.
Dickinson, ND
701-264-7300 (877-424-6423)
Dogs of all sizes are allowed. Two dogs are allowed per room.

Days Hotel Dickinson
532 15th St W
Dickinson, ND
701-483-5600 (800-329-7466)
Dogs are welcome at this hotel.

Quality Inn & Suites
71 Museum Dr.
Dickinson, ND
701-225-9510 (877-424-6423)
Dogs of all sizes are allowed. Dogs are allowed for a pet fee of $10.00 per pet per night. Two dogs are allowed per room.

Super 8 ND Dickinson
637 12th Street West
Dickinson, ND
701-227-1215 (800-800-8000)
Dogs of all sizes are allowed. Dogs are allowed for a pet fee of $10.00 per pet per stay.

AmericInn
1423 35th Street SW
Fargo, ND
701-234-9946 (800-396-5007)
americinn.com/hotels/ND/Fargo
In addition to a long list of amenities for the business or leisure traveler, this inn offers a convenient location to all the city has to offer. Dogs are allowed for an additional fee of $10 per night per pet. Multiple dogs may be allowed.

Best Western Kelly Inn & Suites
1767 S 44th Street
Fargo, ND
701-282-2143 (800-780-7234)
Dogs are welcome at this hotel.

Candlewood Suites Fargo-N. Dakota State Univ.
1831 Ndsu Research Dr.
Fargo, ND
701-235-8200 (877-270-6405)
Dogs up to 80 pounds are allowed. Pets allowed with an additional pet fee. Up to $75 for 1-6 nights and up to $150 for 7+ nights. A pet agreement must be signed at check-in.

Comfort Inn East

1407 35th St. S.
Fargo, ND
701-280-9666 (877-424-6423)
Dogs of all sizes are allowed.

Comfort Inn West
3825 9th Ave. S.W.
Fargo, ND
701-282-9596 (877-424-6423)
Dogs of all sizes are allowed.

Comfort Suites
1415 35th St. S.
Fargo, ND
701-237-5911 (877-424-6423)
Great location just blocks from the West Acres shopping area

Days Inn and Suites 19th Ave/Airport Dome Fargo
1507 19th Ave N
Fargo, ND
701-232-0000 (800-329-7466)
Dogs are welcome at this hotel.

Econo Lodge
1401 35th St. S.
Fargo, ND
701-232-3412 (877-424-6423)
Dogs of all sizes are allowed. Dogs are allowed for a pet fee of $10.00 per pet per night. Three or more dogs may be allowed.

Holiday Inn Fargo
3803 13th Ave. S
Fargo, ND
701-282-2700 (877-270-6405)
Dogs of all sizes are allowed. Dogs are allowed for a pet fee of $10.00 per pet per stay.

Howard Johnson Inn ND Fargo
301 3rd Ave North
Fargo, ND
701-232-8850 (800-446-4656)
Dogs are welcome at this hotel.

Kelly Inn
4207 13th Avenue SW
Fargo, ND
701-277-8821 (800-635-3559)
kellyinnfargo.com/
This hotel is located close to the airport, and a number of shopping, dining, entertainment, educational, and recreational areas. Dogs are allowed for no additional fee; they may not be left alone in the room at any time. Multiple dogs may be allowed.

MainStay Suites
1901 44th Street SW
Fargo, ND
701-277-4627 (877-424-6423)
Dogs of all sizes are allowed.

Motel 6 - Fargo
1202 36th St
Fargo, ND
701-232-9251 (800-466-8356)
This motel welcomes your pets to stay with you.

Rodeway Inn
2202 University Dr. S.
Fargo, ND
701-239-8022 (877-424-6423)
Dogs of all sizes are allowed. Dogs are allowed for a pet fee of $20.00 per pet per stay. Two dogs are allowed per room.

Sleep Inn
1921 44th St. S.W.
Fargo, ND
701-281-8240 (877-424-6423)
Dogs of all sizes are allowed.

Staybridge Suites Fargo
4300 20th Ave. South
Fargo, ND
701-281-4900 (877-270-6405)
Dogs up to 80 pounds are allowed. Pets allowed with an additional pet fee. Up to $75 for 1-6 nights and up to $150 for 7+ nights. A pet agreement must be signed at check-in.

Super 8 Fargo
1101 38th St NW
Fargo, ND
701-281-2109 (800-800-8000)
Dogs of all sizes are allowed. Dogs are allowed for a pet fee of $10 per pet per night.

Super 8 /I-29/West Acres Mall Fargo
3518 Interstate Blvd
Fargo, ND
701-232-9202 (800-800-8000)
Dogs of all sizes are allowed. Dogs are allowed for a pet fee of $4.00 per pet per night. Two dogs are allowed per room.

Econo Lodge
900 N. 43rd St.
Grand Forks, ND
701-746-6666 (877-424-6423)
Dogs of all sizes are allowed. Dogs are allowed for a pet fee of $7.00 per pet per night.

Ramada Grand Forks
1205 North 43rd Street
Grand Forks, ND
701-775-3951 (800-272-6232)
Dogs are welcome at this hotel.

Super 8 Grand Forks
1122 N 43rd Street

Grand Forks, ND
701-775-8138 (800-800-8000)
Dogs of all sizes are allowed. Dogs are allowed for a nightly pet fee.

Comfort Inn
811 20th St. S.W.
Jamestown, ND
701-252-7125 (877-424-6423)
Dogs of all sizes are allowed. Dogs are allowed for a pet fee of $10.00 per pet per stay.

Days Inn Jamestown
824 SW 20th Street
Jamestown, ND
701-251-9085 (800-329-7466)
Dogs of all sizes are allowed. Dogs are allowed for a pet fee of $7 per pet per night.

Super 8 Jamestown
2623 Highway 281 South
Jamestown, ND
701-252-4715 (800-800-8000)
Dogs of all sizes are allowed. Dogs are allowed for a pet fee of $10 per pet per stay.

Best Western Seven Seas Hotel & Waterpark
2611 Old Red Trl
Mandan, ND
701-663-7401 (800-780-7234)
Dogs of all sizes are allowed. Dogs are allowed for a nightly pet fee.

Days Inn Minot
2100 4th St SW
Minot, ND
701-852-3646 (800-329-7466)
Dogs of all sizes are allowed. Dogs are allowed for a pet fee of $10.00 per pet per night.

Grand International
1505 N Broadway
Minot, ND
701-852-3161 (800-735-4493)
internationalinn.com/
Formally the International Inn, it got a "Grand" remodel and offers 156 guest rooms, the largest indoor pool in town, fine dining and a lounge. Well behaved dogs are allowed for no additional fee with a credit card on file. Multiple dogs may be allowed.

Select Inn
225 22nd Ave NW
Minot, ND
701-852-3411
There is a $6 per day per pet fee. 2 dogs may be allowed.

Sleep Inn & Suites

2400 10th Street SW
Minot, ND
701-837-3100 (877-424-6423)
Dogs of all sizes are allowed. Dogs are allowed for a pet fee of $25.00 per pet per stay.

Super 8 Minot
Hwy 83 N
Minot, ND
701-852-1817 (800-800-8000)
Dogs of all sizes are allowed. Dogs are allowed for a pet fee of $10.00 per pet per night.

Four Bears Lodge
SR 23W
New Town, ND
701-627-4018
There is a $25 refundable deposit per pet. Multiple dogs may be allowed.

Econo Lodge
306 Highway 2 SE
Rugby, ND
701-776-5776 (877-424-6423)
Dogs of all sizes are allowed.

Spirit Lake Casino and Resort
7889 H 57
St Michael, ND
701-766-4747
Dogs of all sizes are allowed. There is a $10 per night per pet additional fee. Dogs may not be left unattended, and they must be leashed and cleaned up after. Multiple dogs may be allowed.

AmericInn
280 Wintershow Road SE
Valley City, ND
701-845-5551 (800-396-5007)
This inn offers a long list of amenities suitable for the business or leisure traveler. Well behaved dogs are allowed for an additional one time fee of $10 per pet. Multiple dogs may be allowed.

Super 8 Valley City
822 11th Street S.W.
Valley City, ND
701-845-1140 (800-800-8000)
Dogs of all sizes are allowed. Dogs are allowed for a pet fee of $8.00 per pet per night.

Rodeway Inn
209 13th St. S.
Wahpeton, ND
701-642-1115 (877-424-6423)
Dogs of all sizes are allowed.

Super 8 Wahpeton
995 21st Ave North

Wahpeton, ND
701-642-8731 (800-800-8000)
Dogs are welcome at this hotel.

Days Inn West Fargo
525 East Main Ave/I-94
West Fargo, ND
701-281-0000 (800-329-7466)
Dogs are welcome at this hotel.

Super 8 Main Ave ND West Fargo
825 Main Avenue
West Fargo, ND
701-282-7121 (800-800-8000)
Dogs are welcome at this hotel.

Americas Best Value Inn
213 35th Street W
Williston, ND
701-572-4242 (877-572-4242)
Located close to the airport, this inn offers a number of amenities and close proximity to several sites of interest. Dogs are allowed for an additional fee of $5 per night per pet. Dogs must be well trained, and they may not be left in the room alone at any time. Multiple dogs may be allowed.

Ohio

Motel 6 - Akron North
99 Rothrock Rd
Akron, OH
330-666-0566 (800-466-8356)
This motel welcomes your pets to stay with you.

Red Roof Inn Akron
2939 South Arlington Road
Akron, OH
330-644-7748 (800-RED-ROOF)
One well-behaved family pet per room. Guest must notify front desk upon arrival. Guest is liable for any damages. In consideration of all guests, pets must never be left unattended in the guest rooms.

Residence Inn Akron
120 Montrose West Avenue
Akron, OH
330-666-4811 (888-236-2427)
Offering a convenient location to shopping, dining, and entertainment areas, this hotel also provides a number of in-house amenities, including a daily buffet breakfast, and a Manager's reception Monday through Thursday. Dogs are allowed for an additional one time pet fee of $75 per room. Multiple dogs may be allowed.

Comfort Inn

2500 W. State St.
Alliance, OH
330-821-5555 (877-424-6423)
Dogs up to 150 pounds are allowed.
Dogs are allowed for a pet fee of
$10.00 per pet per night. Two dogs
are allowed per room.

Super 8 Alliance
2330 W State St
Alliance, OH
330-821-5688 (800-800-8000)
Dogs are welcome at this hotel.

Days Inn Amherst
934 N. Leavitt Road
Amherst, OH
440-985-1428 (800-329-7466)
Dogs are welcome at this hotel.

Motel 6 - Cleveland West Lorain
Amherst
704 Leavitt Rd
Amherst, OH
440-988-3266 (800-466-8356)
This motel welcomes your pets to
stay with you.

Days Inn Ashland
1423 County Road 1575
Ashland, OH
419-289-0101 (800-329-7466)
Dogs are welcome at this hotel.

Super 8 Ashland
736 US Hwy 250 East
Ashland, OH
419-281-0567 (800-800-8000)
Dogs are welcome at this hotel.

Super 8 Athens
2091 East State Street
Athens, OH
740-594-4900 (800-800-8000)
Dogs of all sizes are allowed. Dogs
are allowed for a pet fee of $10 per
pet per night.

Comfort Inn
1860 Austinburg Rd
Austinburg, OH
440-275-2711 (877-424-6423)
Dogs of all sizes are allowed.

Comfort Inn & Suites
5425 Clarkins Drive
Austintown, OH
330-792-9740 (877-424-6423)
Dogs up to 50 pounds are allowed.
Dogs are allowed for a pet fee of
$15.00 per pet per night.

Extended Stay America Cleveland -
Beachwood
3820 Orange Pl.
Beachwood, OH
216-595-9551 (800-804-3724)

One dog is allowed per suite. There
is a $25 per night additional pet fee
up to $150 for an entire stay.

Homestead Studio Suites Cleveland
- Beachwood
3625 Orange Pl.
Beachwood, OH
216-896-5555 (800-804-3724)
One dog is allowed per suite. There
is a $25 per night additional pet fee
up to $150 for an entire stay.

Econo Lodge
2220 Heller Drive
Beavercreek, OH
937-426-5822 (877-424-6423)
Dogs of all sizes are allowed. Dogs
are allowed for a pet fee of $10.00
per pet per night.

Residence Inn Dayton Beavercreek
2779 Fairfield Commons
Beavercreek, OH
937-427-3914 (800-331-3131)
Sitting within walking distance to a
variety of shopping, dining, and
recreation venues, this all suite,
upscale hotel also offers a number
of in-house amenities including a
daily buffet breakfast and an
evening reception Monday to
Wednesday from 6 to 7:30 pm.
Dogs are allowed for an additional
one time fee of $100 per room.
Multiple dogs may be allowed.

Suburban Extended Stay Hotel
Dayton-WP AFB
3845 Germany Lane
Beavercreek, OH
937-426-2608 (877-424-6423)
Dogs up to 50 pounds are allowed.
Dogs are allowed for a pet fee of
$75.00 per pet per stay. Two dogs
are allowed per room.

Ramada Bedford Heights
24801 Rockside Road
Bedford Heights, OH
440-439-2500 (800-272-6232)
Dogs are welcome at this hotel.

Comfort Inn
260 Northview
Bellefontaine, OH
937-599-5555 (877-424-6423)
Dogs of all sizes are allowed. Dogs
are allowed for a pet fee of $15.00
per pet per night.

Days Inn Bellville
880 State Route 97
Bellville, OH
419-886-3800 (800-329-7466)
Dogs are welcome at this hotel.

Knights Inn Mansfield OH Bellville
848 State Route 97 West
Bellville, OH
419-886-2292 (800-843-5644)
Dogs are welcome at this hotel.

Candlewood Suites Cincinnati-Blue
Ash
10665 Techwoods Circle
Blue Ash, OH
513-733-0100 (877-270-6405)
Dogs up to 80 pounds are allowed.
Pets allowed with an additional pet
fee. Up to $75 for 1-6 nights and up
to $150 for 7+ nights. A pet
agreement must be signed at check-
in.

Extended Stay America Cincinnati -
Blue Ash - North
11145 Kenwood Rd.
Blue Ash, OH
513-469-8900 (800-804-3724)
One dog is allowed per suite. There
is a $25 per night additional pet fee
up to $150 for an entire stay.

Extended Stay America Cincinnati -
Blue Ash - South
4260 Hunt Rd.
Blue Ash, OH
513-793-6750 (800-804-3724)
One dog is allowed per suite. There
is a $25 per night additional pet fee
up to $150 for an entire stay.

Homestead Studio Suites Cincinnati
- Blue Ash
4630 Creek Rd.
Blue Ash, OH
513-985-9992 (800-804-3724)
One dog is allowed per suite. There
is a $25 per night additional pet fee
up to $150 for an entire stay.

Residence Inn Cincinnati Blue Ash
11401 Reed Hartman Highway
Blue Ash, OH
513-530-5060 (800-331-3131)
This all suite inn offers a number of
amenities for all level of travelers -
including a daily breakfast buffet, an
evening hospitality hour Monday to
Thursday, a Sport Court, and a
complimentary grocery shopping
service. Dogs are allowed for an
additional one time pet fee of $75 per
room. 2 dogs may be allowed.

TownePlace Suites Cincinnati Blue
Ash
4650 Cornell Road
Blue Ash, OH
513-469-8222 (800-257-3000)
Besides offering a number of in-
house amenities for all level of
travelers, this all suite inn also offers

a convenient location to major corporations, shopping, and dining areas. Dogs are allowed for an additional one time pet fee of $75 per room 2 dogs may be allowed.

Comfort Inn
117 Commerce Lane
Bluffton, OH
419-358-6000 (877-424-6423)
Dogs of all sizes are allowed. Dogs are allowed for a pet fee of $25.00 per pet per stay.

Red Roof Inn Boardman
1051 Tiffany South
Boardman, OH
330-758-1999 (800-RED-ROOF)
One well-behaved family pet per room. Guest must notify front desk upon arrival. Guest is liable for any damages. In consideration of all guests, pets must never be left unattended in the guest rooms.

Days Inn Bowling Green
1740 East Wooster Street
Bowling Green, OH
419-352-1520 (800-329-7466)
Dogs of all sizes are allowed. Dogs are allowed for a pet fee of $10.00 per pet per stay.

Travelodge Bowling Green
1550 East Wooster Street
Bowling Green, OH
419-352-5211 (800-578-7878)
Dogs of all sizes are allowed. Dogs are allowed for a pet fee of $10.00 per pet per night.

Howard Johnson Cleveland Airport
16644 Snow Road
Brook Park, OH
216-676-5200 (800-446-4656)
Dogs of all sizes are allowed. Dogs are allowed for a pet fee.

Extended Stay America Cleveland - Brooklyn
10300 Cascade Crossing
Brooklyn, OH
216-267-7799 (800-804-3724)
One dog is allowed per suite. There is a $25 per night additional pet fee up to $150 for an entire stay.

Days Inn Brookville
100 Parkview Drive
Brookville, OH
937-833-4003 (800-329-7466)
Dogs are welcome at this hotel.

Super 8 OH Buckeye Lake
I-70 and State Route 79
Buckeye Lake, OH
740-929-1015 (800-800-8000)

Dogs are welcome at this hotel.

Knights Inn Bucyrus
1515 N Sandusky Ave
Bucyrus, OH
419-562-3737 (800-843-5644)
Dogs of all sizes are allowed. Dogs are allowed for a pet fee.

TownePlace Suites Dayton North
3642 Maxton Road
Butler Township, OH
937-898-5700 (800-257-3000)
In addition to offering a number of in-house amenities for all level of travelers, this all suite inn also provides a central location between the Dayton Airport and the downtown area. Dogs are allowed for an additional one time fee of $50 per room. 2 dogs may be allowed.

Best Western Cambridge
1945 Southgate Pkwy
Cambridge, OH
740-439-3581 (800-780-7234)
Dogs of all sizes are allowed. Dogs are allowed for a nightly pet fee.

Comfort Inn
2327 Southgate Parkway
Cambridge, OH
740-435-3200 (877-424-6423)
Dogs of all sizes are allowed. Dogs are allowed for a pet fee of $10.00/pet per pet per stay. Three or more dogs may be allowed.

Days Inn Cambridge
2328 Southgate Pkwy/I-70
Cambridge, OH
740-432-5691 (800-329-7466)
Dogs are welcome at this hotel.

Super 8 Cambridge
8779 Georgetown Rd
Cambridge, OH
740-435-8080 (800-800-8000)
Dogs of all sizes are allowed. Dogs are allowed for a pet fee.

Courtyard by Marriott
4375 Metro Circle NW
Canton, OH
330-494-6494
Dogs of all sizes are allowed for an additional one time pet fee of $49 per room.

Days Inn Canton
3970 Convenience Circle
Canton, OH
330-493-8883 (800-329-7466)
Dogs are welcome at this hotel.

Knights Inn Canton
3950 Convenience Drive NW

Canton, OH
330-492-5030 (800-843-5644)
Dogs are welcome at this hotel.

Residence Inn Canton
5280 Broadmoor Circle NW
Canton, OH
330-493-0004 (800-331-3131)
Located in Belden Village in the areas leading shopping and entertainment district and only a short distance from the Pro Football Hall of Fame, this upscale, all suite inn also offers guests a variety of amenities, including a daily breakfast buffet and evening socials during the week. Dogs are allowed for an additional one time pet fee of $75 per room. Multiple dogs may be allowed.

County Line Cabins
Call to Arrange
Carbondale, OH
740-385-1358
hockinghills.com/countyline/
Rent a cabin or a large country home in the Hocking Hills area. Both are furnished and offer a fully equipped kitchen, gas fireplace, ceiling fans, central air and heat, hot tub on the deck, catch and release pond and fire ring. Linens and towels are provided. Depending on a weekday or weekend stay (two night min. required on weekends), rates are $130 to $140 per night. There is a $15 fee for each additional person after two special allowances for children. Children under 2 years old stay free. Well-behaved pets are welcome. There is a $10 fee per pet per day and pets need to be leashed when outside your cabin. Cabins are non-smoking but you can smoke outside. Hunters are also welcome.

Days Inn Carrollton
1111 Canton Road
Carrollton, OH
330-627-9314 (800-329-7466)
Dogs of all sizes are allowed. Dogs are allowed for a pet fee of $20 per pet per stay.

Staybridge Suites
8955 Lakota Drive W
Chester, OH
513-874-1900 (877-270-6405)
there is a $75 one time pet fee per room for 7 or more nights.

Best Western Adena Inn
1250 N Bridge Street
Chillicothe, OH
740-775-7000 (800-780-7234)
Dogs of all sizes are allowed. Dogs are allowed for a nightly pet fee.

Comfort Inn
20 N. Plaza Blvd.
Chillicothe, OH
740-775-3500 (877-424-6423)
Dogs of all sizes are allowed. Dogs are allowed for a pet fee of $25.00 per pet per stay.

Baymont Inn & Suites Cincinnati
10900 Crowne Pointe Drive
Cincinnati, OH
513-771-6888 (877-229-6668)
Dogs are welcome at this hotel.

Best Western Clermont
4004 Williams Drive
Cincinnati, OH
513-528-7702 (800-780-7234)
Dogs of all sizes are allowed. Dogs are allowed for a pet fee of $20.00 per pet per stay.

Clarion Inn & Suites
8870 Governors Hill Drive
Cincinnati, OH
513-683-3086 (877-424-6423)
Dogs up to 80 pounds are allowed. Dogs are allowed for a pet fee of $10.00 per pet per night. Two dogs are allowed per room.

Days Inn East Cincinnati
4056 Mt Carmel-Tobasco Rd
Cincinnati, OH
513-528-3800 (800-329-7466)
Dogs of all sizes are allowed. Dogs are allowed for a pet fee.

Holiday Inn Cincinnati-Eastgate (I-275e)
4501 Eastgate Blvd.
Cincinnati, OH
513-752-4400 (877-270-6405)
Dogs of all sizes are allowed. Dogs are allowed for a nightly pet fee.

Holiday Inn Express Cincinnati West
5505 Rybolt Road
Cincinnati, OH
513-574-6000 (877-270-6405)
Dogs up to 50 pounds are allowed. Dogs are allowed for a pet fee of $25.00 per pet per stay.

Howard Johnson Inn - Cincinnati
400 Glensprings Drive
Cincinnati, OH
513-825-3129 (800-446-4656)
Dogs are welcome at this hotel.

Howard Johnson Inn - Cincinnati
5410 Ridge Avenue/I-71
Cincinnati, OH
513-631-8500 (800-446-4656)
Dogs are welcome at this hotel. There is a $25 one time pet fee.

La Quinta Inn & Suites Cincinnati Sharonville
11029 Dowlin Drive
Cincinnati, OH
513-771-0300 (800-531-5900)
Dogs of all sizes are allowed. There are no additional pet fees. Dogs may not be left unattended, and they must be quiet, well behaved, leashed, and cleaned up after. Multiple dogs may be allowed.

Motel 6 - Cincinnati Central-norwood
5300 Kennedy Ave
Cincinnati, OH
513-531-6589 (800-466-8356)
This motel welcomes your pets to stay with you.

Motel 6 - Cincinnati Southeast Beechmont
3960 Nine Mile Rd
Cincinnati, OH
513-752-2262 (800-466-8356)
This motel welcomes your pets to stay with you.

Red Roof Inn Cincinnati East - Beechmont
4035 Mt. Carmel - Tobasco Road
Cincinnati, OH
513-528-2741 (800-RED-ROOF)
One well-behaved family pet per room. Guest must notify front desk upon arrival. Guest is liable for any damages. In consideration of all guests, pets must never be left unattended in the guest rooms.

Red Roof Inn Cincinnati Northeast - Blue Ash
5900 Pfeiffer Road
Cincinnati, OH
513-793-8811 (800-RED-ROOF)
One well-behaved family pet per room. Guest must notify front desk upon arrival. Guest is liable for any damages. In consideration of all guests, pets must never be left unattended in the guest rooms.

Residence Inn Cincinnati North/Sharonville
11689 Chester Road
Cincinnati, OH
513-771-2525 (800-331-3131)
Located near 3 Interstates and a number of major companies, this hotel offers a central location to business, shopping, dining, and entertainment areas; plus they offer a number of in-house amenities, including a daily buffet breakfast and weekly evening socials with complimentary food and beverages

Monday to Thursday. Dogs are allowed for an additional one time pet fee of $75 per room. Multiple dogs may be allowed.

Sheraton Cincinnati North Hotel
11320 Chester Road
Cincinnati, OH
513-771-2080 (888-625-5144)
Dogs of all sizes are allowed. There are no additional pet fees. Dogs are not allowed to be left alone in the room.

Super 8 OH Cincinnati
330 Glensprings Dr
Cincinnati, OH
513-671-0556 (800-800-8000)
Dogs of all sizes are allowed. Dogs are allowed for a pet fee.

TownePlace Suites Cincinnati Northeast
9369 Waterstone Blvd
Cincinnati, OH
513-774-0610 (800-257-3000)
Located near the Kings Island Amusement Park and easily accessible to downtown, this all suite inn also offers a number of on-site amenities for all level of travelers. Dogs are allowed for an additional one time pet fee of $100 per room. 2 dogs may be allowed.

Holiday Inn Express Hotel & Suites Circleville
23911 US Rt 23 South
Circleville, OH
740-420-7711 (877-270-6405)
Dogs of all sizes are allowed. Dogs are allowed for a pet fee of $100.00 per pet per stay.

Knights Inn Circleville
23897 US Rt 23 South
Circleville, OH
740-474-6006 (800-843-5644)
Dogs are welcome at this hotel.

Comfort Inn Downtown
1800 Euclid Ave.
Cleveland, OH
216-861-0001 (877-424-6423)
Dogs of all sizes are allowed.

Days Inn Lakewood Cleveland
12019 Lake Ave
Cleveland, OH
216-226-4800 (800-329-7466)
Dogs are welcome at this hotel.

La Quinta Inn Cleveland Airport
4222 W. 150 Street
Cleveland, OH
216-251-8500 (800-531-5900)
Dogs of all sizes are allowed. There

are no additional fees. Dogs may not be left unattended, except for short periods, and a cell number must be left with the front desk. Dogs must be leashed, and removed or crated for housekeeping. Multiple dogs may be allowed.

Residence Inn Cleveland Beachwood
3628 Park East Drive
Cleveland, OH
216-831-3030 (800-331-3131)
This all suite hotel sits central to many of the city's star attractions, dining, shopping, and business areas, plus they offer a number of in-house amenities that include a daily buffet breakfast and evening socials select weeknights with free wine/beer and food. Dogs are allowed for an additional one time pet fee of $75 per room. Multiple dogs may be allowed.

Residence Inn Cleveland Downtown
527 Prospect Avenue E
Cleveland, OH
216-443-9043 (800-331-3131)
Located in the stylish Gateway District and only moments from some of the city's star attractions, this all suite hotel offers the charm of a turn-of-the century inn with a number of amenities for all level of travelers - including weekday evening socials and a daily breakfast buffet. Dogs are allowed for an additional one time pet fee of $100 per room. Multiple dogs may be allowed.

Residence Inn Cleveland Westlake
30100 Clemens Road
Cleveland, OH
440-892-2254 (800-331-3131)
Some of the amenities at this all-suite inn include a daily buffet breakfast, an evening hospitality hour 2 or 3 times a week, seasonal barbecues, a seasonal pool/spa, and a Sport Court. Dogs are allowed for an additional one time pet fee of $75 per room. Multiple dogs may be allowed.

Sheraton Cleveland Airport Hotel
5300 Riverside Drive
Cleveland, OH
216-267-1500 (888-625-5144)
Dogs up to 50 pounds are allowed for a $250 refundable pet deposit. Dogs may not be left alone in the room.

The Ritz-Carlton, Cleveland
1515 W Third Street
Cleveland, OH
216-902-5223 (800-542-8680)
Sitting in the heart of the downtown

area, this luxury, full-amenity hotel gives quick access to many of the city's sites of interest, and shopping, dining, and entertainment areas - many with indoor access from the hotel. Well mannered dogs are allowed for an additional one time fee of $75 per room. Dogs are not allowed at Club Level rooms. 2 dogs may be allowed.

Red Roof Inn Clyde
1363 W.McPherson Hwy
Clyde, OH
419-547-6660 (800-RED-ROOF)
One well-behaved family pet per room. Guest must notify front desk upon arrival. Guest is liable for any damages. In consideration of all guests, pets must never be left unattended in the guest rooms.

Baymont Inn and Suites Airport Columbus
4240 International Gateway
Columbus, OH
614-237-3403 (877-229-6668)
Dogs are welcome at this hotel.

Baymont Inn and Suites / Westerville Columbus
909 South State Street
Columbus, OH
614-890-1244 (877-229-6668)
Dogs are welcome at this hotel.

Best Western Columbus North
888 E Dublin-Granville Road
Columbus, OH
614-888-8230 (800-780-7234)
Dogs are welcome at this hotel.

Candlewood Suites Columbus Airport
590 Taylor Rd
Columbus, OH
614-863-4033 (877-270-6405)
Dogs up to 80 pounds are allowed. Pets allowed with an additional pet fee. Up to $75 for 1-6 nights and up to $150 for 7+ nights. A pet agreement must be signed at check-in.

Candlewood Suites Polaris
8515 Lyra Drive
Columbus, OH
614-436-6600 (877-270-6405)
Dogs up to 80 pounds are allowed. Pets allowed with an additional pet fee. Up to $75 for 1-6 nights and up to $150 for 7+ nights. A pet agreement must be signed at check-in.

Comfort Inn & Suites
650 South High Street

Columbus, OH
614-228-6511 (877-424-6423)
Dogs up to 80 pounds are allowed. Dogs are allowed for a pet fee of $25.00 per pet per night. Two dogs are allowed per room.

Comfort Inn North/Polaris
8400 Lyra Drive
Columbus, OH
614-791-9700 (877-424-6423)
Dogs up to 50 pounds are allowed. Dogs are allowed for a pet fee of $25.00 per pet per stay. Two dogs are allowed per room.

Comfort Suites
1690 Clara St
Columbus, OH
614-586-1001 (877-424-6423)
Dogs of all sizes are allowed. Dogs are allowed for a pet fee of $10.00 per pet per night.

Comfort Suites Airport
4270 Sawyer Rd
Columbus, OH
614-237-5847 (877-424-6423)
Dogs of all sizes are allowed.

Days Inn Fairgrounds Columbus
1700 Clara Street
Columbus, OH
614-299-4300 (800-329-7466)
Dogs are welcome at this hotel.

Days Inn North Columbus
1212 E.Dublin-Granville Rd.
Columbus, OH
614-885-9696 (800-329-7466)
Dogs of all sizes are allowed. Dogs are allowed for a nightly pet fee.

Days Inn and Suites Worthington
Worthington
7500 Vantage Dr.
Columbus, OH
614-436-0556 (800-329-7466)
Dogs of all sizes are allowed. Dogs are allowed for a nightly pet fee.

Doubletree Guest Suites
50 S Front Street
Columbus, OH
614-228-4600 (800-222-TREE (8733))
Located downtown overlooking the Scioto River and only steps away from the state capitol, this upscale hotel offers a number of on site amenities for business or leisure travelers, plus a convenient location to business, shopping, dining, and recreation areas. Dogs are allowed for an additional one time fee of $50 per pet for dogs 25 pounds and under; for dogs over 25 pounds there

is a one time fee of $100 per pet. Multiple dogs may be allowed.

Econo Lodge Brice Road
5950 Scarborough Blvd.
Columbus, OH
614-864-4670 (877-424-6423)
Dogs of all sizes are allowed. Dogs are allowed for a pet fee of $10.00 per pet per night.

Extended Stay America Columbus - East
2200 Lake Club Dr.
Columbus, OH
614-759-1451 (800-804-3724)
One dog is allowed per suite. There is a $25 per night additional pet fee up to $150 for an entire stay.

Extended Stay America Columbus - Easton
4200 Stelzer Rd.
Columbus, OH
614-428-6022 (800-804-3724)
One dog is allowed per suite. There is a $25 per night additional pet fee up to $150 for an entire stay.

Extended Stay America Columbus - North
6255 Zumstein Dr.
Columbus, OH
614-431-0033 (800-804-3724)
One dog is allowed per suite. There is a $25 per night additional pet fee up to $150 for an entire stay.

Extended Stay America Columbus - Worthington
7465 High Cross Blvd.
Columbus, OH
614-785-1006 (800-804-3724)
One dog is allowed per suite. There is a $25 per night additional pet fee up to $150 for an entire stay.

Hawthorn Suites
6191 Zumstein Drive
Columbus, OH
614-431-1819 (800-527-1133)
In addition to providing a convenient location to many local sites and activities, this all-suite hotel offers a number of amenities for business and leisure travelers, including their signature breakfast buffet and beautifully appointed rooms. Dogs up to 80 pounds are allowed for an additional one time pet fee of $125 per room. 2 dogs may be allowed.

Holiday Inn Columbus Dwtn-Capitol Square
175 East Town St.
Columbus, OH
614-221-3281 (877-270-6405)

Dogs are welcome at this hotel. There is a $50 one time pet fee.

Knights Inn Downtown West
1559 W Broad Street
Columbus, OH
614-275-0388 (800-843-5644)
Dogs of all sizes are allowed. Dogs are allowed for a nightly pet fee.

Motel 6 - Columbus Osu
750 Morse Rd
Columbus, OH
614-846-8520 (800-466-8356)
This motel welcomes your pets to stay with you.

Motel 6 - Columbus Worthington
7474 High St.
Columbus, OH
614-431-2525 (800-466-8356)
This motel welcomes your pets to stay with you.

Motel 6 - Columbus East
5910 Scarborough Blvd
Columbus, OH
614-755-2250 (800-466-8356)
This motel welcomes your pets to stay with you.

Motel 6 - Columbus North
1289 Dublin Granville
Columbus, OH
614-846-9860 (800-466-8356)
This motel welcomes your pets to stay with you.

Motel 6 - Columbus West
5500 Renner Rd
Columbus, OH
614-870-0993 (800-466-8356)
This motel welcomes your pets to stay with you.

Quality Inn & Suites North
1001 Schrock Rd
Columbus, OH
614-431-0208 (877-424-6423)
Dogs of all sizes are allowed.

Ramada North Columbus
I-270 Exit 27
Columbus, OH
614-890-8111 (800-272-6232)
Dogs of all sizes are allowed. Dogs are allowed for a pet fee.

Ramada Plaza Hotel And Conference Center
4900 Sinclair Road
Columbus, OH
614-846-0300 (800-272-6232)
Dogs of all sizes are allowed. Dogs are allowed for a pet fee.

Red Roof Inn Columbus - The Ohio

State University
441 Ackerman Road
Columbus, OH
614-267-9941 (800-RED-ROOF)
One well-behaved family pet per room. Guest must notify front desk upon arrival. Guest is liable for any damages. In consideration of all guests, pets must never be left unattended in the guest rooms.

Red Roof Inn Columbus North - Worthington
7480 North High Street
Columbus, OH
614-846-3001 (800-RED-ROOF)
One well-behaved family pet per room. Guest must notify front desk upon arrival. Guest is liable for any damages. In consideration of all guests, pets must never be left unattended in the guest rooms.

Red Roof Inn Columbus West - Hilliard
5001 Renner Road
Columbus, OH
614-878-9245 (800-RED-ROOF)
One well-behaved family pet per room. Guest must notify front desk upon arrival. Guest is liable for any damages. In consideration of all guests, pets must never be left unattended in the guest rooms.

Red Roof Inn Nationwide Arena - Columbus
111 East Nationwide Boulevard
Columbus, OH
614-224-6539 (800-RED-ROOF)
One well-behaved family pet per room. Guest must notify front desk upon arrival. Guest is liable for any damages. In consideration of all guests, pets must never be left unattended in the guest rooms.

Residence Inn Columbus Downtown
36 E Gay Street
Columbus, OH
614-222-2610 (800-331-3131)
In addition to being located in heart of the city's business district and central to some of the area's s star attractions, this all suite inn also offers a number of in-house amenities, including a daily buffet breakfast and weekday evening socials. Dogs are allowed for an additional one time pet fee of $75 per room. 2 dogs may be allowed.

Residence Inn Columbus Easton
3999 Easton Loop W
Columbus, OH
614-414-1000 (800-331-3131)
This all suite inn serves as a good central point to start exploring all the

local shopping, dining, and entertainment venues of the area; plus, they offer a daily buffet breakfast and weekday evening socials. Dogs are allowed for an additional one time pet fee of $100 per room. Multiple dogs may be allowed.

Residence Inn Columbus Worthington
7300 Huntington Park Drive
Columbus, OH
614-885-0799 (800-331-3131)
This all suite inn sits only steps to some of the best business, shopping, and dining sites in the area; plus they offer a number of in-house amenities, including a daily buffet breakfast and weekday evening socials. Dogs are allowed for an additional one time pet fee of $100 per room. Multiple dogs may be allowed.

Sheraton Suites Columbus
201 Hutchinson Avenue
Columbus, OH
614-436-0004 (888-625-5144)
Dogs up to 80 pounds are allowed. There are no additional pet fees. Dogs are not allowed to be left alone in the room.

Super 8 Columbus
1078 E Dublin-Granville Rd
Columbus, OH
614-885-1601 (800-800-8000)
Dogs are welcome at this hotel.

TownePlace Suites Columbus Gahanna
695 Taylor Road
Columbus, OH
614-861-1400 (800-257-3000)
In addition to offering a number of in-house amenities for all level of travelers, this all suite inn also provides a convenient location to business, shopping, dining, and entertainment areas. Dogs are allowed for an additional one time fee of $100 per room. Multiple dogs may be allowed.

TownePlace Suites Columbus Worthington
7272 Huntington Park Drive
Columbus, OH
614-885-1557 (800-257-3000)
Besides offering a number of in-house amenities for all level of travelers, this all suite inn also provides a convenient location to popular area attractions, businesses, shopping, and dining areas. Dogs are allowed for an additional one time fee of $100 per room. Multiple

dogs may be allowed.

Travelodge Columbus
6121 Zumstein Drive
Columbus, OH
614-846-9070 (800-578-7878)
Dogs are welcome at this hotel.

University Plaza Hotel and Conference Center
3110 Olentangy River Road
Columbus, OH
614-267-7461
There is a $20 one time pet fee per room. Multiple dogs may be allowed.

Baymont Inn And Suites /Mentor Concord
7581 Auburn Road
Concord, OH
440-579-0300 (877-229-6668)
Dogs are welcome at this hotel.

Days Inn Conneaut
600 Days Blvd
Conneaut, OH
440-593-6000 (800-329-7466)
Dogs of all sizes are allowed. Dogs are allowed for a nightly pet fee.

Extended Stay America Akron - Copley
185 Montrose West Ave.
Copley, OH
330-668-9818 (800-804-3724)
One dog is allowed per suite. There is a $25 per night additional pet fee up to $150 for an entire stay.

Roscoe Hillside Cabins
46971 County Road 495
Coshocton, OH
866-582-8146
These three cabin rentals are located on the outskirts of Historic Roscoe Village. Cabin rates are about $150 per night. Well-behaved pets are allowed. There is a $250 refundable pet deposit if paying with a check and no deposit required if paying with a credit card.

Sheraton Suites Akron/Cuyahoga Falls
1989 Front Street
Cuyahoga Falls, OH
330-929-3000 (888-625-5144)
Dogs up to 50 pounds are allowed. There are no additional pet fees. Dogs are not allowed to be left alone in the room.

Days Inn - Huber Heights - Northeast Dayton
7761 Old Country Court
Dayton, OH

937-233-1836 (800-329-7466)
Dogs are welcome at this hotel.

Econo Lodge
1944 Miamisburg Centerville
Dayton, OH
937-435-1550 (877-424-6423)
Dogs of all sizes are allowed. Dogs are allowed for a pet fee of $10.00 per pet per night.

Extended Stay America Dayton - North
6688 Miller Ln.
Dayton, OH
937-898-9221 (800-804-3724)
One dog is allowed per suite. There is a $25 per night additional pet fee up to $150 for an entire stay.

Extended Stay America Dayton - South
7851 Lois Cir.
Dayton, OH
937-439-2022 (800-804-3724)
One dog is allowed per suite. There is a $25 per night additional pet fee up to $150 for an entire stay.

Hawthorn Suites
7070 Poe Avenue
Dayton, OH
937-898-7764 (800-527-1133)
In addition to providing a convenient location to many local sites and activities, this all-suite hotel offers a number of amenities for business and leisure travelers, including their signature breakfast buffet and beautifully appointed rooms. Dogs are allowed for an additional one time pet fee of $150 per room. Multiple dogs may be allowed.

Holiday Inn Dayton-North
2301 Wagner Ford Rd
Dayton, OH
937-278-4871 (877-270-6405)
Dogs of all sizes are allowed. Dogs are allowed for a pet fee of $25.00 per pet per stay.

Marriott Dayton
1414 S Patterson Blvd
Dayton, OH
937-223-1000 (800-450-8625)
Besides offering a number of in-house amenities for all level of travelers, this luxury hotel also provides a convenient location to business, shopping, dining, and entertainment areas. Dogs are allowed for an additional one time fee of $50 per room for 1 to 3 nights, and a one time fee of $75 per room for 4 nights or more. 2 dogs may be allowed.

Motel 6 - Dayton North
7130 Miller Lane
Dayton, OH
937-898-3606 (800-466-8356)
This motel welcomes your pets to
stay with you.

Motel 6 - Dayton- Englewood
9325 North Main Street
Dayton, OH
937-836-8339 (800-466-8356)
This motel welcomes your pets to
stay with you.

Red Roof Inn Dayton North Airport
7370 Miller Lane
Dayton, OH
937-898-1054 (800-RED-ROOF)
One well-behaved family pet per
room. Guest must notify front desk
upon arrival. Guest is liable for any
damages. In consideration of all
guests, pets must never be left
unattended in the guest rooms.

Extended Stay America Columbus -
Dublin
450 Metro Pl. N.
Dublin, OH
614-760-0053 (800-804-3724)
One dog is allowed per suite. There
is a $25 per night additional pet fee
up to $150 for an entire stay.

Extended Stay America Columbus -
Sawmill Rd.
6601 Reflections Dr.
Dublin, OH
614-764-0159 (800-804-3724)
One dog is allowed per suite. There
is a $25 per night additional pet fee
up to $150 for an entire stay.

La Quinta Inn Columbus/Dublin
6145 Parkcenter Circle
Dublin, OH
614-792-8300 (800-531-5900)
Dogs of all sizes are allowed. There
are no additional pet fees, but a
credit card must be on file. Dogs may
only be left alone in the room if they
will be quiet, well behaved, and the
Do Not Disturb sign is put on the
door. Dogs must be leashed,
cleaned up after, and they are not
allowed in the breakfast area.
Multiple dogs may be allowed.

Northwest Drury Inn & Suites
6170 Parkcenter Circle
Dublin, OH
614-798-8802 (800-378-7946)
Dogs of all sizes are allowed for no
additional pet fee with a credit card
on file, and there is a pet agreement
to sign at check in. Aggressive breed

dogs are not allowed.

Quality Inn & Suites
3950 Tuller Road
Dublin, OH
614-764-0770 (877-424-6423)
Dogs of all sizes are allowed. Dogs
are allowed for a pet fee of $uds per
pet per night.

Red Roof Inn Columbus - Dublin
5125 Post Road
Dublin, OH
614-764-3993 (800-RED-ROOF)
One well-behaved family pet per
room. Guest must notify front desk
upon arrival. Guest is liable for any
damages. In consideration of all
guests, pets must never be left
unattended in the guest rooms.

Residence Inn Columbus Dublin
435 Metro Place S
Dublin, OH
614-791-0403 (614-791-0403)
Some of the amenities at this all-
suite inn include a daily buffet
breakfast, an evening social hour, a
heated outdoor pool, and a
complimentary grocery shopping
service. Dogs are allowed for an
additional one time pet fee of $100
per room. 2 dogs may be allowed.

Staybridge Suites Columbus-Dublin
6095 Emerald Parkway
Dublin, OH
614-734-9882 (877-270-6405)
Dogs up to 80 pounds are allowed.
Pets allowed with an additional pet
fee. Up to $75 for 1-6 nights and up
to $150 for 7+ nights. A pet
agreement must be signed at
check-in.

Woodfin Suite Hotel
4130 Tuller Road
Dublin, OH
614-766-7762
All well-behaved dogs are welcome.
Every room is a suite with a full
kitchen. Hotel amenities include a
pool, exercise facility,
complimentary video movies and a
complimentary hot breakfast buffet.
There is a $50 one time per stay pet
charge.

Cleveland - Elyria Red Roof Inn &
Suites
621 Midway Blvd
Elyria, OH
440-324-4444 (800-RED-ROOF)
One well-behaved family pet per
room. Guest must notify front desk
upon arrival. Guest is liable for any
damages. In consideration of all

guests, pets must never be left
unattended in the guest rooms.

Comfort Inn
739 Leona St.
Elyria, OH
440-324-7676 (877-424-6423)
Dogs of all sizes are allowed. Dogs
are allowed for a pet fee of $/pet per
pet per night. Two dogs are allowed
per room.

Holiday Inn Cleveland-Elyria/Lorain
1825 Lorain Blvd
Elyria, OH
440-324-5411 (877-270-6405)
Dogs of all sizes are allowed. Dogs
are allowed for a nightly pet fee.

Howard Johnson Inn - Elyria
1724 Lorain Blvd/I-80/90
Elyria, OH
440-323-1515 (800-446-4656)
Dogs of all sizes are allowed. Dogs
are allowed for a pet fee.

Best Western Dayton Northwest
20 Rockridge Road
Englewood, OH
937-832-2222 (800-780-7234)
Dogs are welcome at this hotel.

Holiday Inn Dayton Arpt NW
10 Rockridge Rd
Englewood, OH
937-832-1234 (877-270-6405)
Dogs of all sizes are allowed. Dogs
are allowed for a pet fee of $25.00
per pet per night.

Motel 6 - Dayton Airport Englewood
1212 Main St
Englewood, OH
937-832-3770 (800-466-8356)
This motel welcomes your pets to
stay with you.

Super 8
15 Rockridge Road
Englewood, OH
937-832-3350 (800-800-8000)
Dogs of all sizes are allowed. Dogs
are allowed for a pet fee.

Baymont Inn & Suites Wright
Patterson AFB
730 East Xenia Drive
Fairborn, OH
937-754-9109 (877-229-6668)
Dogs are welcome at this hotel.

Homewood Suites-Fairborn
2750 Presidential Drive
Fairborn, OH
937-429-0600 (800-225-5466)
There is a $100 one time pet charge
per room. Dogs must be declared at

the time of reservations. 2 dogs may be allowed.

Motel 6 - Fairborn, Oh
800 North Broad Street
Fairborn, OH
937-879-3920 (800-466-8356)
This motel welcomes your pets to stay with you.

Ramada Limited Fairborn
I-675 exits 15 or 17
Fairborn, OH
937-490-2000 (800-272-6232)
Dogs are welcome at this hotel.

Red Roof Inn Dayton - Fairborn/Nutter Center
2580 Colonel Glenn Highway
Fairborn, OH
937-426-6116 (800-RED-ROOF)
One well-behaved family pet per room. Guest must notify front desk upon arrival. Guest is liable for any damages. In consideration of all guests, pets must never be left unattended in the guest rooms.

Extended Stay America Cincinnati - Fairfield
9651 Seward Rd.
Fairfield, OH
513-860-5733 (800-804-3724)
One dog is allowed per suite. There is a $25 per night additional pet fee up to $150 for an entire stay.

Ramada Cleveland Airport West
22115 Brookpark Rd
Fairview Park, OH
440-734-4500 (800-272-6232)
Dogs are welcome at this hotel.

Quality Inn
1020 Interstate Court
Findlay, OH
419-423-4303 (877-424-6423)
Dogs of all sizes are allowed. Dogs are allowed for a pet fee of $15.00 per pet per night. Two dogs are allowed per room.

Red Roof Inn Findlay
1951 Broad Avenue
Findlay, OH
419-424-0466 (800-RED-ROOF)
One well-behaved family pet per room. Guest must notify front desk upon arrival. Guest is liable for any damages. In consideration of all guests, pets must never be left unattended in the guest rooms.

Rodeway Inn
1901 Broad Ave.
Findlay, OH
419-424-1133 (877-424-6423)

Dogs of all sizes are allowed.

Super 8 Findlay
1600 Fox St.
Findlay, OH
419-422-8863 (800-800-8000)
Dogs are welcome at this hotel.

TownePlace Suites Findlay
2501 Tiffin Avenue
Findlay, OH
419-425-9545 (800-257-3000)
This all suite inn sits central to numerous business, shopping, dining, and recreation areas, plus they offer a number of in-house amenities for business and leisure travelers. Dogs are allowed for an additional one time fee of $50 per room. Multiple dogs may be allowed.

Best Western Fostoria Inn & Suites
1690 N Countyline Street
Fostoria, OH
419-436-3600 (800-780-7234)
Dogs of all sizes are allowed. Dogs are allowed for a pet fee of $10.00 per pet per night.

Knights Inn /Middletown Franklin
8500 Claude-Thomas Road
Franklin, OH
937-746-2841 (800-843-5644)
Dogs are welcome at this hotel.

Quality Inn
2000 William C. Good Blvd.
Franklin, OH
937-743-8881 (877-424-6423)
Dogs of all sizes are allowed. Dogs are allowed for a pet fee of $10.00 per pet per night.

Ramada /Middletown Franklin
6147 West State Route 122
Franklin, OH
513-424-1201 (800-272-6232)
Dogs are welcome at this hotel.

Comfort Inn & Suites
840 Sean Dr.
Fremont, OH
419-355-9300 (877-424-6423)
Dogs of all sizes are allowed. Two dogs are allowed per room.

Days Inn Fremont
3701 N. St. Rt 53
Fremont, OH
419-334-9551 (800-329-7466)
Dogs are welcome at this hotel.

Travelodge Fremont
1750 Cedar St.
Fremont, OH
419-334-9517 (800-578-7878)

Dogs are welcome at this hotel.

Motel 6 - Geneva, Oh
1715 S. Broadway
Geneva, OH
440-466-1168 (800-466-8356)
This motel welcomes your pets to stay with you.

Days Inn And Suites Youngstown / Ohio Girard
1615 East Liberty Street
Girard, OH
330-759-9820 (800-329-7466)
Dogs of all sizes are allowed. Dogs are allowed for a nightly pet fee.

La Quinta Inn Grove City
3962 Jackpot Rd
Grove City, OH
614-539-6200 (800-531-5900)
Dogs of all sizes are allowed. There is a $25 refundable pet deposit if paying by cash. There is a pet policy to sign at check in. Dogs may not be left unattended, and they must be leashed and cleaned up after. They are not allowed in the food or pool areas. Multiple dogs may be allowed.

Motel 6 - Columbus South
1900 Stringtown Rd
Grove City, OH
614-875-8543 (800-466-8356)
This motel welcomes your pets to stay with you.

Red Roof Inn Columbus - Grove City
4055 Jackpot Road
Grove City, OH
614-871-9617 (800-RED-ROOF)
One well-behaved family pet per room. Guest must notify front desk upon arrival. Guest is liable for any damages. In consideration of all guests, pets must never be left unattended in the guest rooms.

Super 8 /Newark Heath
1177 South Hebron Road
Heath, OH
740-788-9144 (800-800-8000)
Dogs of all sizes are allowed. Dogs are allowed for a pet fee.

Red Roof Inn Columbus - Hebron
10668 Lancaster Rd. Southwest
Hebron, OH
740-467-7663 (800-RED-ROOF)
One well-behaved family pet per room. Guest must notify front desk upon arrival. Guest is liable for any damages. In consideration of all guests, pets must never be left unattended in the guest rooms.

Motel 6 - Columbus Hilliard

3950 Parkway Ln
Hilliard, OH
614-771-1500 (800-466-8356)
This motel welcomes your pets to
stay with you.

Lily Ponds Bed and Breakfast
6720 Wakefield Rd
Hiram, OH
330-569-7502
lilypondsbedandbreakfast.com
This B&B allows dogs but not cats.
Dogs have their own dishes, sheets,
towels, toys and treats.

Holiday Inn Express Hotel & Suites
Bryan-Montpelier
13399 State Hwy 15
Holiday City, OH
419-485-0008 (877-270-6405)
Dogs of all sizes are allowed. Dogs
are allowed for a pet fee of $10.00
per pet per night.

Econo Lodge
1201 East Mall Drive
Holland, OH
419-866-6565 (877-424-6423)
Dogs of all sizes are allowed. Dogs
are allowed for a pet fee of $10.00
per pet per night.

Extended Stay America Toledo -
Holland
6155 Trust Dr.
Holland, OH
419-861-1133 (800-804-3724)
One dog is allowed per suite. There
is a $25 per night additional pet fee
up to $150 for an entire stay.

Hawthorn Suites
6101 Trust Drive
Holland, OH
419-867-9555 (800-527-1133)
In addition to providing a convenient
location to many local sites and
activities, this all-suite hotel offers a
number of amenities for business
and leisure travelers, including their
signature breakfast buffet and
beautifully appointed rooms. Dogs
are allowed for an additional one
time pet fee of $50 per room.
Multiple dogs may be allowed.

Red Roof Inn Toledo - Holland
1214 Corporate Drive
Holland, OH
419-866-5512 (800-RED-ROOF)
One well-behaved family pet per
room. Guest must notify front desk
upon arrival. Guest is liable for any
damages. In consideration of all
guests, pets must never be left
unattended in the guest rooms.

Clarion Inn and Conference Center
240 East Hines Hill Road
Hudson, OH
330-653-9191 (877-424-6423)
Dogs of all sizes are allowed. Dogs
are allowed for a pet fee of $10.00
per pet per night.

Days Inn Independence
5555 Brecksville Rd
Independence, OH
216-524-3600 (800-329-7466)
Dogs are welcome at this hotel.

Red Roof Inn Cleveland -
Independence
6020 Quarry Lane
Independence, OH
216-447-0030 (800-RED-ROOF)
One well-behaved family pet per
room. Guest must notify front desk
upon arrival. Guest is liable for any
damages. In consideration of all
guests, pets must never be left
unattended in the guest rooms.

Residence Inn Cleveland
Independence
5101 West Creek Road
Independence, OH
216-520-1450 (800-331-3131)
Some of the amenities at this all-
suite inn include a daily buffet
breakfast, evening social events 2
times a week, a seasonal swimming
pool, summer barbecues, and a
complimentary grocery shopping
service. Dogs are allowed for an
additional one time pet fee of $100
per room. Multiple dogs may be
allowed.

Sheraton Independence Hotel
5300 Rockside Road
Independence, OH
216-524-0700 (888-625-5144)
Dogs up to 70 pounds are allowed.
There are no additional pet fees.
Dogs are not allowed to be left
alone in the room.

Comfort Inn
605 E. Main St.
Jackson, OH
740-286-7581 (877-424-6423)
Dogs of all sizes are allowed.

Days Inn Jackson
972 East Main Street
Jackson, OH
740-286-3464 (800-329-7466)
Dogs of all sizes are allowed. Dogs
are allowed for a pet fee of $20 per
pet per stay.

Red Roof Inn Jackson, OH
1000 Acy Avenue

Jackson, OH
740-288-1200 (800-RED-ROOF)
One well-behaved family pet per
room. Guest must notify front desk
upon arrival. Guest is liable for any
damages. In consideration of all
guests, pets must never be left
unattended in the guest rooms.

Baymont Inn & Suites Washington
Court House
11431 Allen Road N.W.
Jeffersonville, OH
740-948-2104 (877-229-6668)
Dogs of all sizes are allowed. Dogs
are allowed for a pet fee.

Econo Lodge
9060 West Lancaster Road
Jeffersonville, OH
740-948-2332 (877-424-6423)
Dogs up to 50 pounds are allowed.
Dogs are allowed for a pet fee of
$10.00 per pet per stay. Two dogs
are allowed per room.

Days Inn - Akron Kent
4422 Edson Road
Kent, OH
330-677-9400 (800-329-7466)
Dogs are welcome at this hotel.

Super 8 /Akron Area Kent
4380 Edson Rd
Kent, OH
330-678-8817 (800-800-8000)
Dogs are welcome at this hotel.

Hanna's Cottage in the Woods
Call to Arrange.
Killbuck, OH
330-377-5208
valkyrie.net/~kak/
This cottage rental is surrounded by
trees and has two bedrooms, two
bathrooms, full kitchen, living room
and porch. The cottage is handicap
accessible. Well-behaved leashed
pets are welcome. No smoking or
alchohol is allowed. The cabin costs
about $90 per night per couple and
an extra $20 per night for a child or
dog. There are trails located on the
property or you can visit the nearby
Mohican State Park which allows
leashed dogs on their 13 miles of
trails. Call ahead to make a
reservation.

Travelodge Cleveland Lakewood
11837 Edgewater Drive
Lakewood, OH
216-221-9000 (800-578-7878)
Dogs are welcome at this hotel.

Holiday Inn Express Hotel & Suites
Lancaster

Dog-Friendly Lodging - Please always call ahead to make sure an establishment is still dog-friendly.

1861 Riverway Drive
Lancaster, OH
740-654-4445 (877-270-6405)
Dogs of all sizes are allowed. Dogs
are allowed for a pet fee of $10 per
pet per night.

Knights Inn Lebanon
725 East Main Street
Lebanon, OH
513-932-3034 (800-843-5644)
Dogs are welcome at this hotel.

Days Inn Lima
1250 Neubrecht Road
Lima, OH
419-227-6515 (800-329-7466)
Dogs are welcome at this hotel.

Knights Inn Lima
2285 N Eastown Rd
Lima, OH
419-331-9215 (800-843-5644)
Dogs are welcome at this hotel in
ground floor rooms.

Motel 6 - Lima
1800 Harding Hwy
Lima, OH
419-228-0456 (800-466-8356)
This motel welcomes your pets to
stay with you.

Days Inn Lisbon
40952 State Route 154
Lisbon, OH
330-420-0111 (800-329-7466)
Dogs of all sizes are allowed. Dogs
are allowed for a pet fee of $75 per
pet per night.

Acorn Acres
14805 Berry Road
Logan, OH
740-380-1074
Acorn Acres is located on 37 acres
of trees and natural vegetation with
cleared trails and a stocked pond.
They offer two rental cabins and one
rental cottage. All rentals units are
furnished and offer air conditioning,
heating, kitchenettes, bathrooms,
towels and linens. Pets are allowed
with prior management approval.
They need to be leashed and
cleaned up after. There is a $25 fee
per pet per stay. Cabin rates range
from about $135 to $155 per night.
Prices are subject to change. The
office is open from 9am to 9pm. Call
ahead to make a reservation. Please
do not call after 9pm.

Baymont Inn And Suites Logan
12819 State Route 664 South
Logan, OH
740-385-1700 (877-229-6668)

Dogs of all sizes are allowed. Dogs
are allowed for a pet fee of $10.00
per pet per night.

Four Seasons Cabin Rentals
14435 Nickel Plate Road
Logan, OH
800-242-8453
fourseasonscabinrental.com/
These two cabin rentals are family
owned and operated and located on
55 acres along with the owner's
house. Both rental cabins are about
200 feet apart with trees in between
them. Each cabin comes with a
living room, two bedrooms, fully
equipped kitchen, heating and air
conditioning, linens, bath towels,
hot tub, wood burning fireplace,
picnic area, deck, fire ring. There
are hiking trails located on the
property. Rates are about $85 to
$165 depending on season and
weekday/weekend. Rates are for
two adults and two children. Each
additional adult or child is $15 extra,
up to a total of four adults per cabin.
Quiet well-behaved pets are
welcome. Pets need to be leashedd
when outside the cabin and cleaned
up after. There is a $10 per day pet
fee. The cabins are located one exit
south of the exit for Old Man's
Cave, Conkles Hollow and Lake
Logan. Call for details about
reservations and payment.

Motel 6 - London, Oh
870 State Route 42 Ne
London, OH
740-852-9415 (800-466-8356)
This motel welcomes your pets to
stay with you.

Bullfrog Cabin Rentals
Call to arrange.
Loudonville, OH
800-368-2791
bullfrogmountain.com/
These two cabins rentals are
located in the Amish Country. They
are furnished and have fully
equipped kitchens, bedrooms,
bathrooms, heating, ceiling fans
and sleep up to 6 people. Cabin
rates range from about $100 to
$150 per night depending on the
cabin and the day of the week.
There is no charge for children 10
and under. Well-behaved pets are
allowed and there is a $10 fee per
pet per night.

Days Inn Macedonia
275 Highland Road
Macedonia, OH
330-467-1516 (800-329-7466)
Dogs are welcome at this hotel.

Knights Inn Cleveland/ Macedonia
240 East Highland Road
Macedonia, OH
330-467-1981 (800-843-5644)
Dogs of all sizes are allowed. Dogs
are allowed for a pet fee.

Motel 6 - Cleveland East Macedonia
311 East Highland Road
Macedonia, OH
330-468-1670 (800-466-8356)
This motel welcomes your pets to
stay with you.

Best Western Richland Inn-Mansfield
180 E Hanley Road
Mansfield, OH
419-756-6670 (800-780-7234)
Dogs of all sizes are allowed. Dogs
are allowed for a nightly pet fee.

Comfort Inn North
500 N. Trimble Rd.
Mansfield, OH
419-529-1000 (877-424-6423)
Dogs of all sizes are allowed. Dogs
are allowed for a pet fee of $20.00
per pet per stay.

Econo Lodge
1017 Koogle Rd.
Mansfield, OH
419-589-3333 (877-424-6423)
Dogs of all sizes are allowed. Dogs
are allowed for a pet fee of $5.00/
per pet per night.

La Quinta Inn Mansfield
120 Stander Avenue
Mansfield, OH
419-774-0005 (800-531-5900)
Dogs of all sizes are allowed. There
are no additional fees. Dogs may not
be left unattended, and they must be
leashed and cleaned up after.
Multiple dogs may be allowed.

Motel 6 - Mansfield, Oh
555 North Trimble Road
Mansfield, OH
419-529-2100 (800-466-8356)
This motel welcomes your pets to
stay with you.

Super 8 Mansfield
2425 Interstate Circle
Mansfield, OH
419-756-8875 (800-800-8000)
Dogs are welcome at this hotel.

Travelodge Mansfield
90 West Hanley Road
Mansfield, OH
419-756-7600 (800-578-7878)
Dogs of all sizes are allowed. Dogs
are allowed for a pet fee of $10.00

per pet per night.

Majestic Motel
8629 Northshore Blvd
Marblehead, OH
419-798-4921
Dogs of all sizes are allowed. There are no additional pet fees.

Comfort Inn
700 Pike St.
Marietta, OH
740-374-8190 (877-424-6423)
Dogs of all sizes are allowed. Dogs are allowed for a pet fee of $10.00 per pet per stay.

Super 8 Marietta
46 Acme St Washington Centre
Marietta, OH
740-374-8888 (800-800-8000)
Dogs of all sizes are allowed. Dogs are allowed for a pet fee of $5.00 per pet per night.

Comfort Inn
256 Jamesway
Marion, OH
740-389-5552 (877-424-6423)
Dogs of all sizes are allowed. Dogs are allowed for a pet fee of $10.00 per pet per night.

Super 8 OH Marion
2117 Marion Mt. Gilead Road
Marion, OH
740-389-1998 (800-800-8000)
Dogs of all sizes are allowed. Dogs are allowed for a nightly pet fee.

Comfort Inn
16420 Allenby Drive
Marysville, OH
937-644-0400 (877-424-6423)
Dogs up to 80 pounds are allowed. Dogs are allowed for a pet fee of $25.00 per pet per night. One dog is allowed per room.

Super 8 Marysville
16510 Square Dr
Marysville, OH
937-644-8821 (800-800-8000)
Dogs of all sizes are allowed. Dogs are allowed for a pet fee of $10.00 per pet per night.

Motel 6 - Cincinnati Mason
5232 Bardes Road
Mason, OH
513-398-8015 (800-466-8356)
This motel welcomes your pets to stay with you.

Red Roof Inn Cincinnati NE - Mason-Kings Island
9847 Bardes Road

Mason, OH
513-398-3633 (800-RED-ROOF)
One well-behaved family pet per room. Guest must notify front desk upon arrival. Guest is liable for any damages. In consideration of all guests, pets must never be left unattended in the guest rooms.

Super 8 Mason
5589 Kings Mills Rd
Mason, OH
513-398-8075 (800-800-8000)
Dogs of all sizes are allowed. Dogs are allowed for a pet fee.

Ramada Kings Island/Mason
9665 Mason Montgomery Road
Mason (Cincinnati), OH
513-336-7911 (800-272-6232)
Dogs are welcome at this hotel.

Days Inn Toledo Maumee
1704 Tollgate Drive
Maumee, OH
419-897-6900 (800-329-7466)
Dogs of all sizes are allowed. Dogs are allowed for a pet fee.

Econo Lodge
150 Dussel Drive
Maumee, OH
419-893-9960 (877-424-6423)
Dogs of all sizes are allowed. Dogs are allowed for a pet fee of $10.00 per pet per night.

Red Roof Inn Toledo - Maumee
1570 South Reynolds Road
Maumee, OH
419-893-0292 (800-RED-ROOF)
One well-behaved family pet per room. Guest must notify front desk upon arrival. Guest is liable for any damages. In consideration of all guests, pets must never be left unattended in the guest rooms.

Residence Inn Toledo Maumee
1370 Arrowhead Drive
Maumee, OH
419-891-2233 (800-331-3131)
Some of the amenities at this all suite hotel include a daily buffet breakfast, evening socials with light dinner fare, an indoor pool, and a complimentary grocery shopping service. Dogs are allowed for an additional one time pet fee of $100 per room. Multiple dogs may be allowed.

Staybridge Suites Toledo - Maumee
2300 Village Dr. Bldg. 1800
Maumee, OH
419-878-8999 (877-270-6405)
Dogs up to 80 pounds are allowed.

Pets allowed with an additional pet fee. Up to $75 for 1-6 nights and up to $150 for 7+ nights. A pet agreement must be signed at check-in.

Baymont Inn & Suites Mayfield Heights
1421 Golden Gate Boulevard
Mayfield Heights, OH
440-442-8400 (877-229-6668)
Dogs of all sizes are allowed. Dogs are allowed for a pet fee of $10.00 per pet per night.

Staybridge Suites Cleveland East Mayfield Hts.
6103 Landerhaven Dr
Mayfield Heights, OH
440-442-9200 (877-270-6405)
Dogs up to 80 pounds are allowed. Pets allowed with an additional pet fee. Up to $75 for 1-6 nights and up to $150 for 7+ nights. A pet agreement must be signed at check-in.

Motel 6 - Cleveland Medina
3122 Eastpointe Dr
Medina, OH
330-723-3322 (800-466-8356)
This motel welcomes your pets to stay with you.

Red Roof Inn Cleveland - Medina
5021 Eastpointe Drive
Medina, OH
330-725-1395 (800-RED-ROOF)
One well-behaved family pet per room. Guest must notify front desk upon arrival. Guest is liable for any damages. In consideration of all guests, pets must never be left unattended in the guest rooms.

Rodeway Inn
2875 Medina Road
Medina, OH
330-725-4571 (877-424-6423)
Dogs of all sizes are allowed. Dogs are allowed for a pet fee of $25.00 per pet per stay. Three or more dogs may be allowed.

Super 8 Medina
5161 Montville Drive
Medina, OH
330-723-8118 (800-800-8000)
Dogs of all sizes are allowed. Dogs are allowed for a pet fee of $10 per pet per night.

Best Western Lawnfield Inn & Suites
8434 Mentor Avenue
Mentor, OH
440-205-7378 (800-780-7234)
Dogs are welcome at this hotel.

There is a $35 one time pet fee.

Residence Inn Cleveland Mentor
5560 Emeral Court
Mentor, OH
440-392-0800 (800-331-3131)
Some of the amenities at this all-suite inn include a daily buffet breakfast, weekly barbecues, an evening hospitality hour 2 or 3 times a week, a seasonal pool/spa, and a Sport Court. Dogs are allowed for an additional one time pet fee of $75 per room; they must be declared at the time of reservations. Multiple dogs may be allowed.

Studio 6 - Cleveland Mentor
7677 Reynolds Road
Mentor, OH
440-946-0749 (800-466-8356)
Your pets are welcome to stay here with you for a pet fee of $10 per day up to $50 for an entire stay.

Hawthorn Suites
155 Prestige Place
Miamisburg, OH
937-434-7881 (800-527-1133)
In addition to providing a convenient location to many local sites and activities, this all-suite hotel offers a number of amenities for business and leisure travelers, including their signature breakfast buffet and beautifully appointed rooms. Dogs are allowed for an additional one time pet fee of $100 per room. Multiple dogs may be allowed.

Holiday Inn Dayton-Mall-I-75 & Rt 725
31 Prestige Plaza Dr
Miamisburg, OH
937-434-8030 (877-270-6405)
Dogs of all sizes are allowed. Dogs are allowed for a pet fee.

Knights Inn Dayton South/
185 Byers Road
Miamisburg, OH
937-859-8797 (800-843-5644)
Dogs are welcome at this hotel for no additional pet fee.

Red Roof Inn Dayton South - I-75
Miamisburg
G-3219 Miller Road
Miamisburg, OH
937-866-0705 (800-RED-ROOF)
One well-behaved family pet per room. Guest must notify front desk upon arrival. Guest is liable for any damages. In consideration of all guests, pets must never be left unattended in the guest rooms.

Studio 6 - Dayton Miamisburg
8101 Springboro Pike
Miamisburg, OH
937-434-8750 (800-466-8356)
Your pets are welcome to stay here with you for a pet fee of $10 per day up to $50 for an entire stay.

Super 8 Dayton S Area
155 Monarch Lane
Miamisburg, OH
937-866-5500 (800-800-8000)
Dogs of all sizes are allowed. Dogs are allowed for a pet fee.

Johnston's Lakefront Cottages
1555 Diest Road
Middle Bass Island, OH
419-285-2314
ohiocottages.com
These rental cottages offer a view of the water and a large treed yard. The cottages are not designated as smoking or non-smoking. Well-behaved dogs of all sizes are allowed for a $50 refundable pet fee but need to be leashed and picked up after. To get to the cottages, you will need to take the dog-friendly Miller Ferry Boat Line. The ferry requires reservations if you plan on bringing your car. To make a reservation, call the ferry service at 1-800-500-2421 to make reservations.

Comfort Inn Cleveland Airport
17550 Rosbough Dr.
Middleburg Heights, OH
440-234-3131 (877-424-6423)
Dogs of all sizes are allowed. Dogs are allowed for a pet fee of $10.00 per pet per night. Dogs are allowed for a pet fee of $35.00 per pet per stay.

Days Inn Cleveland Airport South
7233 Engle Road
Middleburg Heights, OH
440-243-2277 (800-329-7466)
Dogs of all sizes are allowed. Dogs are allowed for a pet fee of $10.00 per pet per night.

Motel 6 - Cleveland Middleburg Heights
7219 Engle Rd
Middleburg Heights, OH
440-234-0990 (800-466-8356)
This motel welcomes your pets to stay with you.

Red Roof Inn Cleveland - Middleburg Heights
17555 Bagley Road
Middleburg Heights, OH
440-243-2441 (800-RED-ROOF)

One well-behaved family pet per room. Guest must notify front desk upon arrival. Guest is liable for any damages. In consideration of all guests, pets must never be left unattended in the guest rooms.

Residence Inn Cleveland Airport
17525 Rosbough Drive
Middleburg Heights, OH
440-234-6688 (800-331-3131)
Some of the amenities at this all-suite inn include a daily buffet breakfast, an evening hospitality hour Monday through Thursday, seasonal barbecues, an outdoor pool, spa, and a complimentary grocery shopping service. Dogs are allowed for an additional one time pet fee of $100 per room. Multiple dogs may be allowed.

TownePlace Suites Cleveland Airport
7325 Engle Road
Middleburg Heights, OH
440-816-9300 (800-257-3000)
A complimentary grab-n-go breakfast, a convenience market open 24/7, a seasonal outdoor pool, and barbecue/picnic areas are just some of the amenities of this all suite hotel. Dogs are allowed for an additional one time pet fee of $75 per room. Multiple dogs may be allowed.

Manchester Inn
1027 Manchester Avenue
Middletown, OH
513-422-5481
Dogs of all sizes are allowed. There is a $25 one time pet fee per room.

Super 8 Franklin/Middletown Area
3553 Commerce Drive
Middletown/Franklin, OH
513-422-4888 (800-800-8000)
Dogs are welcome at this hotel.

Motel 6 - Sandusky Milan
11406 Us 250 North
Milan, OH
419-499-8001 (800-466-8356)
This motel welcomes your pets to stay with you.

Red Roof Inn Milan
11303 US Rt 250 North
Milan, OH
419-499-4347 (800-RED-ROOF)
One well-behaved family pet per room. Guest must notify front desk upon arrival. Guest is liable for any damages. In consideration of all guests, pets must never be left unattended in the guest rooms.

Super 8 /Sandusky Area Milan

11313 Rt 250
Milan, OH
419-499-4671 (800-800-8000)
Dogs are welcome at this hotel.

Super 8 /Toledo Millbury
3491 Latcha Rd
Millbury, OH
419-837-6409 (800-800-8000)
Dogs of all sizes are allowed. Dogs
are allowed for a pet fee of $10 per
pet per night.

Comfort Inn
1102 Glen Drive
Millersburg, OH
330-674-7400 (877-424-6423)
Dogs of all sizes are allowed. Dogs
are allowed for a pet fee of $15.00
per pet per night. Two dogs are
allowed per room.

Econo Lodge
13-485 SR 15
Montpelier, OH
419-485-3139 (877-424-6423)
Dogs of all sizes are allowed.

Ramada Conference Center Bryan/
I-80/90 Exit 13 at St Rt 15
Montpelier, OH
419-485-5555 (800-272-6232)
Dogs are welcome at this hotel.

Super 8 /Dayton Moraine
2450 Dryden Road
Moraine, OH
937-298-0380 (800-800-8000)
Dogs of all sizes are allowed. Dogs
are allowed for a pet fee.

Knights Inn Mt. Gilead
5898 Route 95
Mount Gilead, OH
419-768-4217 (800-843-5644)
Dogs are welcome at this hotel.
There is a $10 one time pet fee per
pet.

Best Western Mt. Orab Inn
100 Leininger Street
Mount Orab, OH
937-444-6666 (800-780-7234)
Dogs of all sizes are allowed. Dogs
are allowed for a pet fee of $15.00
per pet per night.

Comfort Inn
150 Howard St.
Mount Vernon, OH
740-392-6886 (877-424-6423)
Dogs of all sizes are allowed. Dogs
are allowed for a pet fee of $10.00
per pet per night. Two dogs are
allowed per room.

Holiday Inn Express Mt. Vernon

11555 Upper Gilchrist Rd
Mount Vernon, OH
740-392-1900 (877-270-6405)
Dogs of all sizes are allowed. Dogs
are allowed for a pet fee.

Super 8 MT. Vernon
1000 Coschocton Ave.
Mount Vernon, OH
740-397-8885 (800-800-8000)
Dogs of all sizes are allowed. Dogs
are allowed for a nightly pet fee.

Best Western Napoleon Inn &
Suites
1290 Independence Drive
Napoleon, OH
419-599-0850 (800-780-7234)
Dogs are welcome at this hotel.
There is an additional pet fee.

Knights Inn Napoleon
2395 North Scott St.
Napoleon, OH
419-592-5010 (800-843-5644)
Dogs are welcome at this hotel.
There is a $10 one time additional
pet fee.

Motel 6 - New Philadelphia
181 Bluebell Drive SW
New Philadelphia, OH
330-339-6446 (800-466-8356)
This motel welcomes your pets to
stay with you.

Super 8 New Philadelphia
131 1/2 Bluebell Dr. SW
New Philadelphia, OH
330-339-6500 (800-800-8000)
Dogs of all sizes are allowed. Dogs
are allowed for a pet fee of $10 per
pet per stay.

Super 8 Newcomerstown
299 Adena Drive
Newcomerstown, OH
740-498-4116 (800-800-8000)
Dogs of all sizes are allowed. Dogs
are allowed for a pet fee.

Econo Lodge
4248 SR 5
Newton Falls, OH
330-872-0988 (877-424-6423)
Dogs of all sizes are allowed. Dogs
are allowed for a pet fee of $15.00
per pet per night.

Motel 6 - Canton
6880 Sunset Strip Ave Nw
North Canton, OH
330-494-7611 (800-466-8356)
This motel welcomes your pets to
stay with you.

Red Roof Inn Canton

5353 Inn Circle Court Northwest
North Canton, OH
330-499-1970 (800-RED-ROOF)
One well-behaved family pet per
room. Guest must notify front desk
upon arrival. Guest is liable for any
damages. In consideration of all
guests, pets must never be left
unattended in the guest rooms.

Candlewood Suites Cleveland-N.
Olmsted
24741 Country Club Blvd
North Olmsted, OH
440-716-0584 (877-270-6405)
Dogs up to 80 pounds are allowed.
Pets allowed with an additional pet
fee. Up to $75 for 1-6 nights and up
to $150 for 7+ nights. A pet
agreement must be signed at check-
in.

Homestead Studio Suites Cleveland
- Airport - North Olmsted
24851 Country Club Blvd.
North Olmsted, OH
440-777-8585 (800-804-3724)
One dog is allowed per suite. There
is a $25 per night additional pet fee
up to $150 for an entire stay.

Motel 6 - Cleveland Intl Airport
Ridgeville
32751 Lorain Road
North Ridgeville, OH
440-327-6311 (800-466-8356)
This motel welcomes your pets to
stay with you.

Baymont Inn & Suites Northwood
2600 Lauren Lane
Northwood, OH
419-662-1200 (877-229-6668)
Dogs are welcome at this hotel.

Oberlin Inn
7 N Main Street
Oberlin, OH
440-775-1111
Dogs of all sizes are allowed. There
are no additional pet fees. 2 dogs
may be allowed.

Radisson Hotel Cleveland Airport
25070 Country Club Blvd
Olmsted, OH
440-734-5060
Dogs are allowed for no additional
pet fee. Dogs may not be left alone
in the room.

Comfort Inn East
2930 Navarre Ave.
Oregon, OH
419-691-8911 (877-424-6423)
Dogs of all sizes are allowed. Dogs
are allowed for a pet fee of $10.00

per pet per stay.

Sleep Inn & Suites
1761 Meijer Circle
Oregon, OH
419-697-7800 (877-424-6423)
Dogs of all sizes are allowed.

Candlewood Suites Perrysburg
27350 Lake Vue Drive
Perrysburg, OH
419-872-6161 (877-270-6405)
Dogs up to 80 pounds are allowed.
Pets allowed with an additional pet
fee. Up to $75 for 1-6 nights and up
to $150 for 7+ nights. A pet
agreement must be signed at check-
in.

La Quinta Inn Toledo/Perrysburg
1154 Professional Drive
Perrysburg, OH
419-872-0000 (800-531-5900)
Dogs of all sizes are allowed. There
are no additional pet fees. Dogs may
not be left unattended in the rooms
except for a short time, and they
must be leashed and cleaned up
after. Multiple dogs may be allowed.

Quality Inn
27441 Helen Drive
Perrysburg, OH
419-874-9181 (877-424-6423)
Dogs of all sizes are allowed. Dogs
are allowed for a pet fee of $15.00
per pet per night. Two dogs are
allowed per room.

Comfort Inn Miami Valley Centre Mall
987 E. Ash St.
Piqua, OH
937-778-8100 (877-424-6423)
Dogs of all sizes are allowed. Dogs
are allowed for a pet fee of $25.00
per pet per night.

Knights Inn Piqua
902 Scott Drive
Piqua, OH
937-773-2314 (800-843-5644)
Dogs are welcome at this hotel.
There is a $10 additional one time
pet fee.

La Quinta Inn Piqua
950 East Ash Street
Piqua, OH
937-615-0140 (800-531-5900)
Dogs of all sizes are allowed. There
are no additional pet fees. Dogs may
not be left unattended, and they must
be leashed and cleaned up after.
Dogs are not allowed in food or pool
areas, and are not to be brought in
the front lobby entrance. Multiple
dogs may be allowed.

Residence Inn Youngstown
Boardman/Poland
7396 Tiffany S
Poland, OH
330-726-1747 (800-331-3131)
Besides offering a convenient
location to business, shopping,
dining, and entertainment areas,
this hotel also provides a number of
in-house amenities, including a
daily buffet breakfast and
complementary manager
receptions. Dogs are allowed for an
additional one time pet fee of $75
per room. Multiple dogs may be
allowed.

Comfort Inn
1723 E. Perry St.
Port Clinton, OH
419-732-2929 (877-424-6423)
Dogs of all sizes are allowed.

Holiday Village Resort
3247 N.E. Catawba Road
Port Clinton, OH
419-797-4732
holidayvillageresort.com
All rooms are not designated as
smoking or non-smoking rooms.
Pets are allowed and there is no pet
fee. Multiple dogs may be allowed.

Super 8 Port Clinton
1704 Perry Street
Port Clinton, OH
419-734-4446 (800-800-8000)
Dogs are welcome at this hotel.

Ramada Portsmouth
711 Second Street
Portsmouth, OH
740-354-7711 (800-272-6232)
Dogs of all sizes are allowed. Dogs
are allowed for a pet fee.

Super 8 Portsmouth
4266 US Route 23 N
Portsmouth, OH
740-353-8880 (800-800-8000)
Dogs are welcome at this hotel.

Bormans Cottages
Located on Monument Bay
Put-in-Bay, OH
419-285-3223
1awsm.com/BormansCottages.htm
These rental cottages are located
on Monument Bay and a ten minute
walk to downtown Put-in-Bay or a
five minute walk to Perry
Monument. All cottages
accommodate up to six people,
have lake access, a boat ramp, fully
equipped kitchens, TVs, ceiling
fans, grills and picnic tables. Pets

are allowed and there is a $25 one
time per stay pet fee. None of the
cottages are designated as smoking
or non-smoking. Make a reservation
early as the cottages usually tend to
get booked quickly.

East Point Cottages
611 Massie Lane
Put-in-Bay, OH
419-285-2204
Each of the seven cottage rentals
offer color TV with cable,
kitchenettes and air conditioning.
The cottages are not designated
smoking or non-smoking. Well-
behaved dogs are allowed with a $20
one time per stay fee. Please clean
up after your pet.

Days Inn And Suites Columbus East
Airport
2100 Brice Road
Reynoldsburg, OH
614-864-1280 (800-329-7466)
Dogs of all sizes are allowed. Dogs
are allowed for a nightly pet fee.

Red Roof Inn Columbus East -
Reynoldsburg
2449 Brice Road
Reynoldsburg, OH
614-864-3683 (800-RED-ROOF)
One well-behaved family pet per
room. Guest must notify front desk
upon arrival. Guest is liable for any
damages. In consideration of all
guests, pets must never be left
unattended in the guest rooms.

Super 8 Reynolds /East Columbus
Area
2055 Brice Road
Reynoldsburg, OH
614-864-3880 (800-800-8000)
Dogs of all sizes are allowed. Dogs
are allowed for a pet fee.

Motel 6 - Richfield, Oh
5171-b Brecksville Road
Richfield, OH
330-659-6116 (800-466-8356)
This motel welcomes your pets to
stay with you.

Super 8 Area Richfield
4845 Brecksville Rd
Richfield, OH
330-659-6888 (800-800-8000)
Dogs of all sizes are allowed. Dogs
are allowed for a pet fee.

Deer Run Manors
23095 Buena Vista Road
Rockbridge, OH
740-380-2369
Choose from the "A" Frame rental or

the Manor House rental. Both rentals are two story two bedroom furnished homes with full kitchens, ceiling fans, hot tubs. Each rental sleeps up to 6 people. Rates range from about $100 to $135 per night. Rates are based on double occupancy. There is a $25 per night fee per extra person. Rates are subject to change. Pets and children are welcome. There is a $25 pet fee. Call ahead to make a reservation.

Econo Lodge Inn & Suites
51659 National Road
Saint Clairsville, OH
740-526-0128 (877-424-6423)
Dogs of all sizes are allowed. Dogs are allowed for a pet fee of $15.00 per pet per night.

Knights Inn OH Sandusky
2405 Cleveland Road
Sandusky, OH
419-621-9000 (800-843-5644)
Dogs are welcome at this hotel.

La Quinta Inn Sandusky
3304 Milan Rd
Sandusky, OH
419-626-6766 (800-531-5900)
Dogs of all sizes are allowed. There are no additional pet fees. There is a pet policy to sign at check in. Dogs may not be left unattended, and they must be leashed and cleaned up after. Multiple dogs may be allowed.

Super 8 North Sandusky
5410 Milan Road
Sandusky, OH
419-625-7070 (800-800-8000)
Dogs of all sizes are allowed. Dogs are allowed for a pet fee of $10 per pet per night.

Comfort Inn
55 Stern Dr.
Seaman, OH
937-386-2511 (877-424-6423)
Dogs of all sizes are allowed. Dogs are allowed for a pet fee of $15.00 per pet per stay.

Hawthorn Suites
5025 Park Avenue West
Seville, OH
330-769-5025 (800-527-1133)
In addition to providing a convenient location to many local sites and activities, this all-suite hotel offers a number of amenities for business and leisure travelers, including their signature breakfast buffet and beautifully appointed rooms. Dogs are allowed for an additional one time pet fee of $75 per room.

Multiple dogs may be allowed.

Super 8 Seville
6116 Speedway Drive
Seville, OH
330-769-8880 (800-800-8000)
Dogs of all sizes are allowed. Dogs are allowed for a pet fee.

Extended Stay America Cincinnati - Sharonville
11457 Chester Rd.
Sharonville, OH
513-771-7829 (800-804-3724)
One dog is allowed per suite. There is a $25 per night additional pet fee up to $150 for an entire stay.

Motel 6 - Cincinnati North
3850 Hauck Rd
Sharonville, OH
513-563-1123 (800-466-8356)
This motel welcomes your pets to stay with you.

Red Roof Inn Cincinnati - Sharonville
2301 Sharon Road
Sharonville, OH
513-771-5552 (800-RED-ROOF)
One well-behaved family pet per room. Guest must notify front desk upon arrival. Guest is liable for any damages. In consideration of all guests, pets must never be left unattended in the guest rooms.

Days Inn Sidney
420 Folkerth Ave
Sidney, OH
937-492-1104 (800-329-7466)
Dogs of all sizes are allowed. Dogs are allowed for a nightly pet fee.

Chestnut Grove Cabins
23101 Chestnut Grove Rd
South Bloomingville, OH
740-332-7122
chestnutgrovecabins.com/
Rent a log home in the Hocking Hills area. The homes have two bedrooms, fully equipped kitchens, a hot tub, air conditioning, heating, a back porch and are wheelchair accessible. The homes are smoke free but smoking is permitted outside. Rates are about $139 to $169 per night per couple. Additional guests are $10 per person. Children 12 and under stay for free. Pets are allowed and there is a $25 one time pet fee. Pets need to be leashed when outside the rental unit and please clean up after your pet. Reservation require a 50% deposit and the balance is due upon arrival. Cancellations must be

made 7 days prior to arrival for a refund of your deposit. They accept credit cards.

Getaway Cabins in the Hocking Hills
26366 Chapel Ridge Road
South Bloomingville, OH
740-385-3734
Cabins and cottages nestled in the Hocking Hills of southeastern Ohio. Each features fireplace and hot tub, and accommodates 2-6 guests. Located close to hiking, state parks, canoeing, horseback riding, gift & antique hops, hunting, and fishing. Pets are welcome in designated cabins. The pet fee is $30/pet per stay. Up to three pets allowed.

Top O' The Caves Cabin Rentals
26780 Chapel Ridge Road
South Bloomingville, OH
800-967-2434
topothecaves.com/
This 60 acre resort offers cabins rentals as well as RV and tent sites. They are surrounded by dog-friendly state parks (dogs on leash) which you can walk to from your accommodation. The rustic cabins have two beds, a refrigerator, gas stove, picnic table inside and outside, heating, and ceiling fan. Cabin rates are about $50 to $75 per night. The resort also has two resort cabins, Hickory and Acorn, which have their own bathrooms (towels and linens provided), heating, air conditioning and full kitchens. Resort amenities include two modern shower houses with hot water, a large swimming pool, kids playground, mini golf, large game arcade, gift shop, laundry facilities and Sunday worship services. Pets are welcome for an additional one time fee of $40 per pet. Please keep your dog leashed and clean up after them. Rental rates are subject to change. Please call ahead to check pricing or to make a reservation. The resort is located on Chapel Ridge Road, near Highway 374. 2 dogs may be allowed.

Comfort Suites
2940 County Road 144
South Point, OH
740-894-1700 (877-424-6423)
Dogs of all sizes are allowed. Dogs are allowed for a pet fee of $25.00 per pet per night. Two dogs are allowed per room.

Extended Stay America Cincinnati - Springdale - North
320 Glensprings Dr.
Springdale, OH

513-671-4900 (800-804-3724)
One dog is allowed per suite. There is a $25 per night additional pet fee up to $150 for an entire stay.

Extended Stay America Cincinnati - Springdale - South
11645 Chesterdale Rd.
Springdale, OH
513-771-2457 (800-804-3724)
One dog is allowed per suite. There is a $25 per night additional pet fee up to $150 for an entire stay.

La Quinta Inn Cincinnati North
12150 Springfield Pike
Springdale, OH
513-671-2300 (800-531-5900)
Dogs of all sizes are allowed. There are no additional fees. There is a pet waiver to sign at check in. Dogs may not be left unattended, except for short periods, and a cell number must be left with the front desk. Dogs must be leashed, and removed or crated for housekeeping. Multiple dogs may be allowed.

Days Inn Springfield
11 W Leffel Lane
Springfield, OH
937-322-4942 (800-329-7466)
Dogs of all sizes are allowed. Dogs are allowed for a pet fee.

Holiday Inn Springfield-South
383 East Leffel Lane
Springfield, OH
937-323-8631 (877-270-6405)
Dogs of all sizes are allowed. Dogs are allowed for a pet fee of $20.00 per pet per night.

Knights Inn Springfield
2207 W. Main St.
Springfield, OH
937-325-8721 (800-843-5644)
Dogs of all sizes are allowed. Dogs are allowed for a pet fee of $10.00 per pet per stay.

Ramada Limited
319 E. Leffel Lane/I-70
Springfield, OH
937-328-0123 (800-272-6232)
Dogs are welcome at this hotel.

Red Roof Inn Springfield, OH
155 West Leffel Lane
Springfield, OH
937-325-5356 (800-RED-ROOF)
One well-behaved family pet per room. Guest must notify front desk upon arrival. Guest is liable for any damages. In consideration of all guests, pets must never be left unattended in the guest rooms.

Red Roof Inn St Clairsville - Wheeling West
68301 Red Roof Lane
St Clairsville, OH
740-695-4057 (800-RED-ROOF)
One well-behaved family pet per room. Guest must notify front desk upon arrival. Guest is liable for any damages. In consideration of all guests, pets must never be left unattended in the guest rooms.

Super 8 St. Clairsville OH/Wheeling WV Area
68400 Matthews Dr
St Clairsville, OH
740-695-1994 (800-800-8000)
Dogs of all sizes are allowed. Dogs are allowed for a pet fee.

Holiday Inn Steubenville
1401 University Blvd
Steubenville, OH
740-282-0901 (877-270-6405)
Dogs up to 50 pounds are allowed.

Staybridge Suites Akron-Stow-Cuyahoga Falls
4351 Steels Pointe Drive
Stow, OH
330-945-4180 (877-270-6405)
Dogs up to 80 pounds are allowed. Pets allowed with an additional pet fee. Up to $75 for 1-6 nights and up to $150 for 7+ nights. A pet agreement must be signed at check-in.

Ramada of Dover
I-77 Exit 87 at Rt. 250
Strasburg, OH
330-878-1400 (800-272-6232)
Dogs of all sizes are allowed. Dogs are allowed for a pet fee of $15 per pet per night.

TownePlace Suites Cleveland Streetsboro
795 Mondial Parkway
Streetsboro, OH
330-422-1855 (888-519-6579)
A complimentary grab-n-go breakfast, a convenience market open 24/7, a seasonal outdoor pool, and barbecue/picnic areas are just some of the amenities of this all suite hotel. Dogs are allowed for an additional pet fee of $25 per night to a maximum total of $75 for the stay per room. Multiple dogs may be allowed.

Super 8 Strongsville
15385 Royalton Rd
Strongsville, OH
440-238-0170 (800-800-8000)

Dogs of all sizes are allowed. Dogs are allowed for a pet fee.

Hide-A-Way Cabin
29043 Hide A Way Hills Road
Sugar Grove, OH
740-746-9012
This cabin rental is on 1.5 wooded acres and is located in a private gated resort in Hocking County. The cabin has two bedrooms, one bathroom, wood burning fireplace, skylights, fully equipped kitchen and cable TV with VCR/DVD player. Linens and towels are provided. The cabin is non-smoking but there are smoking areas outside. Cabin rates range from $85 to $120 per night. Children 10 and under stay for free when accompanied by an adult. Prices are subject to change. Pets are allowed but must be leashed when outside the cabin and cannot be left unattended in the cabin. The cabin is located about 45 minutes south of Columbus.

Days Inn Sunbury
7323 State Route 37 East
Sunbury, OH
740-362-6159 (800-329-7466)
Dogs are welcome at this hotel.

Days Inn Toledo Airport
10753 Airport Hwy
Swanton, OH
419-865-2002 (800-329-7466)
Dogs of all sizes are allowed. Dogs are allowed for a nightly pet fee.

Holiday Inn Express Tiffin
78 Shaffer Park Drive
Tiffin, OH
419-443-5100 (877-270-6405)
Dogs of all sizes are allowed. Dogs are allowed for a nightly pet fee.

Quality Inn
1927 S. SR 53
Tiffin, OH
419-447-6313 (877-424-6423)
Dogs of all sizes are allowed. Two dogs are allowed per room.

Comfort Inn North
445 E. Alexis Rd.
Toledo, OH
419-476-0170 (877-424-6423)
Dogs of all sizes are allowed. Dogs are allowed for a pet fee of $15.00 per pet per night.

Days Inn Toledo
1800 Miami Street
Toledo, OH
419-666-5120 (800-329-7466)
Dogs of all sizes are allowed. Dogs

are allowed for a pet fee.

Hilton Hotel
3100 Glendale Avenue
Toledo, OH
419-381-6800 (800-HILTONS (445-8667))
This upscale hotel sits on 350 landscaped acres of the Toledo Health Science Campus and offers a number on site amenities for business and leisure travelers, plus a convenient location to business, shopping, dining, and recreation areas. Dogs are allowed for an additional one time pet fee of $75 per room. 2 dogs may be allowed.

Motel 6 - Toledo
5335 Heatherdowns Blvd
Toledo, OH
419-865-2308 (800-466-8356)
This motel welcomes your pets to stay with you.

Ramada Conference Center Toledo
3536 Secor Road
Toledo, OH
419-535-7070 (800-272-6232)
Dogs are welcome at this hotel.

Red Roof Inn Toledo - University
3530 Executive Parkway
Toledo, OH
419-536-0118 (800-RED-ROOF)
One well-behaved family pet per room. Guest must notify front desk upon arrival. Guest is liable for any damages. In consideration of all guests, pets must never be left unattended in the guest rooms.

Holiday Inn Express Hotel & Suites Troy
60 Troy Town Drive
Troy, OH
937-332-1700 (877-270-6405)
Dogs up to 50 pounds are allowed. Dogs are allowed for a pet fee of $25.00 per pet per stay.

Comfort Suites
2715 Creekside Drive
Twinsburg, OH
330-963-5909 (877-424-6423)
Dogs of all sizes are allowed.

Super 8 /Cleveland Area Twinsburg
8848 Twin Hills Pkwy
Twinsburg, OH
330-425-2889 (800-800-8000)
Dogs of all sizes are allowed. Dogs are allowed for a pet fee.

Best Western Country Inn
111 W McCauley Drive
Uhrichsville, OH

740-922-0774 (800-780-7234)
Dogs of all sizes are allowed. Dogs are allowed for a nightly pet fee.

Super 8 Motel - Akron S./Green/
1605 Corporate Woods Parkway
Uniontown, OH
330-899-9888 (800-800-8000)
Dogs of all sizes are allowed. Dogs are allowed for a pet fee of $10.00 per pet per night.

Super 8 /Dayton International Airport Vandalia
550 East National Road
Vandalia, OH
937-898-7636 (800-800-8000)
Dogs of all sizes are allowed. Dogs are allowed for a pet fee.

Comfort Inn & Suites
1510 Saturn Drive
Wapakoneta, OH
419-738-8181 (877-424-6423)
Dogs of all sizes are allowed. Dogs are allowed for a pet fee of $10.00 per pet per night.

Knights Inn Wapakoneta
1659 Bellefontaine Street
Wapakoneta, OH
419-738-2184 (800-843-5644)
Dogs are welcome at this hotel.

Super 8 Wapakoneta
1011 Lunar Dr.
Wapakoneta, OH
419-738-8810 (800-800-8000)
Dogs of all sizes are allowed. Dogs are allowed for a pet fee.

Comfort Inn
136 North Park Avenue
Warren, OH
330-393-1200 (877-424-6423)
Dogs of all sizes are allowed. Dogs are allowed for a pet fee of $10.00 per pet per night.

Best Western Del Mar
8319 State Highway 108
Wauseon, OH
419-335-1565 (800-780-7234)
Dogs of all sizes are allowed. Dogs are allowed for a pet fee of $17.00 per pet per stay.

Super 8 Wauseon
8224 SH-108
Wauseon, OH
419-335-9841 (800-800-8000)
Dogs are welcome at this hotel.

Residence Inn Cincinnati North/West Chester
6240 Muhlhauser Road
West Chester, OH

513-341-4040 (888-350-3995)
Some of the amenities at this newly opened all-suite inn include a daily buffet breakfast, evening socials Monday through Thursday with light dinner fare, an indoor swimming pool, and a 24 hour food market. Dogs are allowed for no additional fee. 2 dogs may be allowed.

Staybridge Suites Cincinnati North
8955 Lakota Drive West
West Chester, OH
513-874-1900 (877-270-6405)
Dogs up to 80 pounds are allowed. Pets allowed with an additional pet fee. Up to $75 for 1-6 nights and up to $150 for 7+ nights. A pet agreement must be signed at check-in.

Knights Inn Columbus Westerville
32 Heatherdown Dr
Westerville, OH
614-794-0225 (800-843-5644)
Dogs of all sizes are allowed. Dogs are allowed for a pet fee of $10.00 per pet per night.

Holiday Inn Cleveland-West (Westlake)
1100 Crocker Rd
Westlake, OH
440-871-6000 (877-270-6405)
Dogs of all sizes are allowed. Dogs are allowed for a pet fee of $25.00 per pet per stay.

Red Roof Inn Cleveland - Westlake
29595 Clemens Road
Westlake, OH
440-892-7920 (800-RED-ROOF)
One well-behaved family pet per room. Guest must notify front desk upon arrival. Guest is liable for any damages. In consideration of all guests, pets must never be left unattended in the guest rooms.

Super 8 /Cleveland Westlake
25200 Sperry Drive
Westlake, OH
440-871-3993 (800-800-8000)
Dogs of all sizes are allowed. Dogs are allowed for a pet fee.

TownePlace Suites Cleveland Westlake
25052 Sperry Drive
Westlake, OH
440-892-4275 (800-257-3000)
Besides being located only a couple of miles from the Lake Erie beaches and near a number of sites of interest, this all suite hotel also offers a number of in-house amenities for all level of travelers. Dogs are

allowed for an additional one time pet fee of $75 per room. Multiple dogs may be allowed.

Motel 6 - Cleveland-willoughby
35110 Maplegrove Road
Willoughby, OH
440-975-9922 (800-466-8356)
This motel welcomes your pets to stay with you.

Red Roof Inn Cleveland East - Willoughby
4166 State Route 306
Willoughby, OH
440-946-9872 (800-RED-ROOF)
One well-behaved family pet per room. Guest must notify front desk upon arrival. Guest is liable for any damages. In consideration of all guests, pets must never be left unattended in the guest rooms.

Baymont Inn & Suites Wilmington
201 Carrie Drive
Wilmington, OH
937-383-3950 (877-229-6668)
Dogs are welcome at this hotel.

Holiday Inn Wilmington
123 Gano Road
Wilmington, OH
937-283-3200 (877-270-6405)
Dogs of all sizes are allowed. Dogs are allowed for a pet fee of $200.00 per pet per stay.

Super 8 Wooster
US 30 Madison Ave Exit
Wooster, OH
330-264-6211 (800-800-8000)
Dogs are welcome at this hotel.

Econo Lodge
50 E. Wilson Bridge Rd.
Worthington, OH
614-888-3666 (877-424-6423)
Dogs of all sizes are allowed. Dogs are allowed for a pet fee of $10.00 per pet per night.

Holiday Inn Xenia
300 Xenia Towne Square
Xenia, OH
937-372-9921 (877-270-6405)
Dogs of all sizes are allowed. Dogs are allowed for a pet fee of $10.00 per pet per night.

Best Western Meander Inn
870 N Canfield Niles Road
Youngstown, OH
330-544-2378 (800-780-7234)
Dogs of all sizes are allowed. Dogs are allowed for a nightly pet fee.

Econo Lodge

5431 1/2 Seventy Six Drive
Youngstown, OH
330-270-2865 (877-424-6423)
Dogs of all sizes are allowed. Dogs are allowed for a pet fee of $10.00 per pet per night.

Super 8 Airport Area Youngstown
I-80W Ex 229 I-80E Belmont Ex
Youngstown, OH
330-759-0040 (800-800-8000)
Dogs of all sizes are allowed. Dogs are allowed for a pet fee.

Super 8 /Austintown Youngstown
5280 76 Dr
Youngstown, OH
330-793-7788 (800-800-8000)
Dogs of all sizes are allowed. Dogs are allowed for a pet fee of $10.00 per pet per night.

Baymont Inn & Suites Zanesville
230 Scenic Crest Dr.
Zanesville, OH
740-454-9332 (877-229-6668)
Dogs are welcome at this hotel.

Best Western B. R. Guest
4929 East Pike
Zanesville, OH
740-453-6300 (800-780-7234)
Dogs up to 50 pounds are allowed.

Comfort Inn
500 Monroe St.
Zanesville, OH
740-454-4144 (877-424-6423)
Dogs up to 50 pounds are allowed. Dogs are allowed for a pet fee of $10.00 per pet per stay. Three or more dogs may be allowed.

Econo Lodge
135 N. 7th St.
Zanesville, OH
740-452-4511 (877-424-6423)
Dogs up to 50 pounds are allowed. Dogs are allowed for a pet fee of $10.00 per pet per night. Two dogs are allowed per room.

Super 8 Zanesville
2440 National Road
Zanesville, OH
740-455-3124 (800-800-8000)
Dogs of all sizes are allowed. Dogs are allowed for a pet fee of $10.00 per pet per night. Two dogs are allowed per room.

Travelodge of Zanesville
58 North 6th Street
Zanesville, OH
740-453-0611 (800-578-7878)
Dogs of all sizes are allowed. Dogs are allowed for a pet fee of $8.00

per pet per stay.

Oklahoma

Days Inn Altus
3202 North Main
Altus, OK
580-477-2300 (800-329-7466)
Dogs are welcome at this hotel.

Holiday Inn Express Hotel & Suites Altus
2812 East Broadway
Altus, OK
580-480-1212 (877-270-6405)
Dogs of all sizes are allowed. Dogs are allowed for a pet fee.

Motel 6 - Altus, Ok
2515 E. Broadway
Altus, OK
580-477-3000 (800-466-8356)
This motel welcomes your pets to stay with you.

Best Western Ardmore Inn
136 Holiday Drive
Ardmore, OK
580-223-7525 (800-780-7234)
Dogs are welcome at this hotel. There is an additional pet fee.

Guest Inn
2519 W H 142
Ardmore, OK
580-223-1234
Dogs of all sizes are allowed. There are no additional pet fees.

Holiday Inn Ardmore
2705 West Broadway
Ardmore, OK
580-223-7130 (877-270-6405)
Dogs of all sizes are allowed. Dogs are allowed for a pet fee of $20 per pet per stay.

La Quinta Inn Ardmore
2432 Veterans Blvd
Ardmore, OK
580-223-7976 (800-531-5900)
Dogs of all sizes are allowed. There are no additional pet fees. There is a pet waiver to sign at check in. Dogs must be leashed and cleaned up after. Dogs must be crated when left alone in the room, and the Do Not Disturb sign hung on the door. Arrangements must be made with housekeeping if stay is longer than one day. Multiple dogs may be allowed.

Motel 6 - Ardmore
120 Holiday Dr
Ardmore, OK

580-226-7666 (800-466-8356)
This motel welcomes your pets to stay with you.

Super 8 Ardmore
2120 Veterans Blvd
Ardmore, OK
580-223-2201 (800-800-8000)
Dogs of all sizes are allowed. Dogs are allowed for a pet fee of $5 per pet per night.

Comfort Inn & Suites
1502 S Mississippi Ave
Atoka, OK
580-889-8999 (877-424-6423)
Dogs of all sizes are allowed. Dogs are allowed for a pet fee of $25.00 per pet per night.

Super 8 ATOKA
1101 S Mississippi Ave
Atoka, OK
580-889-7300 (800-800-8000)
Dogs are welcome at this hotel.

Best Western Weston Inn
222 SE Washington Boulevard
Bartlesville, OK
918-335-7755 (800-780-7234)
Dogs are welcome at this hotel.

Super 8 Bartlesville
211 SE Washington Blvd
Bartlesville, OK
918-335-1122 (800-800-8000)
Dogs are welcome at this hotel.

Super 8 - Area Big Cabin/Vinita
30954 S. Hwy 69
Big Cabin/Vinita, OK
918-783-5888 (800-800-8000)
Dogs are welcome at this hotel.

Best Western Blackwell Inn
4545 W White Avenue
Blackwell, OK
580-363-1300 (800-780-7234)
Dogs of all sizes are allowed. Dogs are allowed for a nightly pet fee.

Comfort Inn
1201 N. 44th St.
Blackwell, OK
580-363-7000 (877-424-6423)
Dogs of all sizes are allowed. Dogs are allowed for a pet fee of $10.00 per pet per night.

Super 8 Blackwell
1014 West Doolin
Blackwell, OK
580-363-5945 (800-800-8000)
Dogs are welcome at this hotel.

TownePlace Suites Tulsa Broken Arrow

2251 N Stone Wood Circle
Broken Arrow, OK
918-355-9600 (800-257-3000)
This all suite inn sits central to numerous business, shopping, dining, and entertainment areas, plus they also offer a number of in-house amenities for business and leisure travelers. Dogs up to 65 pounds are allowed for an additional fee of $50 for 1 to 4 nights, per pet, and a $100 additional fee for 5 nights or more per pet. There is a pet policy to sign at check in. 2 dogs may be allowed.

Econo Lodge
600 North Price
Chandler, OK
405-258-2131 (877-424-6423)
Dogs of all sizes are allowed. Dogs are allowed for a pet fee of $5.00 per pet per night.

Lake Eufaula Inn
HC60 Box 1835
Checotah, OK
918-473-2376
Dogs of all sizes are allowed. There is an additional one time fee of $5 per pet.

Holiday Inn Express Hotel & Suites Chickasha
2610 South 4th Street
Chickasha, OK
405-224-8883 (877-270-6405)
Dogs of all sizes are allowed. Dogs are allowed for a pet fee of $10.00 per pet per night.

Super 8 Chickasha
2728 South 4th Street
Chickasha, OK
405-222-3710 (800-800-8000)
Dogs of all sizes are allowed. Dogs are allowed for a pet fee of $10 per pet per night.

Super 8
1100 East Will Roger Blvd.
Claremore, OK
918-341-2323 (800-800-8000)
Dogs are welcome at this hotel.

Days Inn Clinton
1200 South 10th
Clinton, OK
580-323-5550 (800-329-7466)
Dogs are welcome at this hotel.

Ramada - Clinton
2140 W. Gary Blvd
Clinton, OK
580-323-2010 (800-272-6232)
Dogs of all sizes are allowed. Dogs are allowed for a pet fee.

La Quinta Inn Oklahoma City Del City
5501 Tinker Diagonal
Del City, OK
405-672-0067 (800-531-5900)
Dogs of all sizes are allowed. There are no additional pet fees. Dogs must be leashed and cleaned up after. Dogs must be crated or removed for housekeeping. Multiple dogs may be allowed.

Days Inn Durant
2121 West Main St
Durant, OK
580-924-5432 (800-329-7466)
Dogs are welcome at this hotel.

Best Western Hensley's
I-40 & Country Club Road
El Reno, OK
405-262-6490 (800-780-7234)
Dogs are welcome at this hotel.

Comfort Inn
1707 SW 27th Street
El Reno, OK
405-262-3050 (877-424-6423)
Dogs of all sizes are allowed. Dogs are allowed for a pet fee of $15.00 per pet per stay. Three or more dogs may be allowed.

Days Inn El Reno
2700 S Country Club/I-40
El Reno, OK
405-262-8720 (800-329-7466)
Dogs of all sizes are allowed. Dogs are allowed for a pet fee.

Motel 6 - El Reno
1506 Domino Drive
El Reno, OK
405-262-6060 (800-466-8356)
This motel welcomes your pets to stay with you.

Super 8 El Reno
2820 S Hwy 81
El Reno, OK
405-262-8240 (800-800-8000)
Dogs are welcome at this hotel.

Econo Lodge
108 Meadow Ridge
Elk City, OK
580-225-5120 (877-424-6423)
Dogs of all sizes are allowed. Dogs are allowed for a pet fee of $5.00 per pet per night. Two dogs are allowed per room.

Motel 6 - Elk City, Ok
2604 Hwy 66
Elk City, OK
580-225-2541 (800-466-8356)

This motel welcomes your pets to stay with you.

Ramada Elk City
102 BJ Hughes Access Road
Elk City, OK
580-225-8140 (800-272-6232)
Dogs of all sizes are allowed. Dogs are allowed for a nightly pet fee.

Super 8 Elk City
2801 East Highway 66
Elk City, OK
580-225-9430 (800-800-8000)
Dogs are welcome at this hotel.

Baymont Inn and Suites Enid
3614 W Owen K. Garriott Road
Enid, OK
580-234-6800 (877-229-6668)
Dogs are welcome at this hotel.

Best Western Inn
2818 S Van Buren Street
Enid, OK
580-242-7110 (800-780-7234)
Dogs of all sizes are allowed. Dogs are allowed for a nightly pet fee.

Days Inn Enid
2901 South Van Buren
Enid, OK
580-237-6000 (800-329-7466)
Dogs of all sizes are allowed. Dogs are allowed for a pet fee.

Ramada Enid
3005 W Owen K Garriott Road
Enid, OK
580-234-0440 (800-272-6232)
Dogs of all sizes are allowed. Dogs are allowed for a pet fee of $10 per pet per night.

Comfort Inn
1001 N. Sheb Wooley Drive
Erick, OK
580-526-8124 (877-424-6423)
Dogs of all sizes are allowed. Dogs are allowed for a pet fee of $15.00 per pet per night.

Days Inn Erick
1014 North Sheb Wooley Ave
Erick, OK
580-526-3315 (800-329-7466)
Dogs of all sizes are allowed. Dogs are allowed for a pet fee.

Loyal Inn
300 Birkes Road
Eufaula, OK
918-689-9109
Dogs are allowed for an additional one time pet fee of $25 per room. Aggressive breeds are not allowed.

Best Western Glenpool/Tulsa
14831 S Casper Street
Glenpool, OK
918-322-5201 (800-780-7234)
Dogs of all sizes are allowed. Dogs are allowed for a pet fee of $20.00 per pet per stay.

Best Western TimberRidge Inn
120 W 18th Street
Grove, OK
918-786-6900 (800-780-7234)
Dogs of all sizes are allowed. Dogs are allowed for a nightly pet fee.

Ambassador Inn
1909 N Highway 64
Guymon, OK
580-338-5555
Dogs up to 60 pounds are allowed for an additional pet fee of $10 per night per room. 2 dogs may be allowed.

Best Western Guymon Hotel & Suites
1102 NE 6th Street
Guymon, OK
580-338-0800 (800-780-7234)
Dogs of all sizes are allowed. Dogs are allowed for a pet fee of $10 per pet per stay.

Holiday Inn Express Hotel & Suites Guymon
Intersection Of Hwy 3 And Hwy 54
Guymon, OK
580-338-4208 (877-270-6405)
Dogs of all sizes are allowed. Dogs are allowed for a nightly pet fee.

Super 8 Guymon
Intersection of Hwy 54 & 64
Guymon, OK
580-338-0507 (800-800-8000)
Dogs of all sizes are allowed. Dogs are allowed for a pet fee.

Gateway Inn
Hwy 75 and Trudgeon St
Henryetta, OK
918-652-4448
There is an additional pet fee of $10 per night per room. 2 dogs may be allowed.

Super 8 Henryetta
I-40 and Dewey Bartlett Ex 237
Henryetta, OK
918-652-2533 (800-800-8000)
Dogs are welcome at this hotel.

Comfort Suites
400 SE Lincoln Blvd.
Idabel, OK
580-286-9393 (877-424-6423)
Dogs of all sizes are allowed. Dogs

are allowed for a pet fee of $150.00 per pet per night.

Quality Inn
2800 NW Texas Street
Idabel, OK
580-286-6501 (877-424-6423)
Dogs up to 50 pounds are allowed. Dogs are allowed for a pet fee of $15.00 per pet per stay. Two dogs are allowed per room.

Super 8 Kiowa
901 South Garfield
Kiowa, OK
918-432-6131 (800-800-8000)
Dogs are welcome at this hotel.

Baymont Inn & Suites Lawton
1203 NW 40TH Street
Lawton, OK
580-353-5581 (877-229-6668)
Dogs are welcome at this hotel.

Best Western Lawton Hotel & Convention Center
1125 E Gore Boulevard
Lawton, OK
580-353-0200 (800-780-7234)
Dogs are welcome at this hotel. There is a $40 one time pet fee.

Motel 6 - Lawton
202 Se Lee Blvd
Lawton, OK
580-355-9765 (800-466-8356)
This motel welcomes your pets to stay with you.

Quality Inn
3110 Cache Road
Lawton, OK
580-353-3104 (877-424-6423)
Dogs up to 50 pounds are allowed. Dogs are allowed for a pet fee of $20.00 per pet per night. Two dogs are allowed per room.

Super 8 Lawton
2202 NW Hwy 277
Lawton, OK
580-353-0310 (800-800-8000)
Dogs are welcome at this hotel.

Comfort Suites
650 George Nigh Expressway
McAlester, OK
918-302-0001 (877-424-6423)
Dogs of all sizes are allowed. Two dogs are allowed per room.

Days Inn and Suites McAlester
400 S George Nigh Expressway
McAlester, OK
918-426-1111 (800-329-7466)
Dogs of all sizes are allowed. Dogs are allowed for a pet fee of $15.00

per pet per stay.

Best Western Inn of McAlester
1215 S George Nigh Expressway
Mcalester, OK
918-426-0115 (800-780-7234)
Dogs of all sizes are allowed. Dogs
are allowed for a pet fee of $25.00
per pet per stay.

Motel 6 - Mcalester, Ok
690 Bernhardt Dr
Mcalester, OK
918-429-0717 (800-466-8356)
This motel welcomes your pets to
stay with you.

Motel 6 - Oklahoma City East
Midwest City
6166 Tinker Diagonal
Midwest City, OK
405-737-6676 (800-466-8356)
This motel welcomes your pets to
stay with you.

Sheraton Midwest City Hotel at the
Reed Conference Center
5750 Will Rogers Road.
Midwest City, OK
405-455-1800 (888-625-5144)
Dogs up to 60 pounds are allowed.
There is a $25 per night pet fee per
pet. There are no additional pet fees.
Dogs are not allowed to be left alone
in the room.

Studio 6 - Oklahoma City Midwest
City
5801 Tinker Diagonal
Midwest City, OK
405-737-8851 (800-466-8356)
Your pets are welcome to stay here
with you for a pet fee of $10 per day
up to $50 for an entire stay.

Super 8 /East/Okc Area Midwest City
6821 SE 29th St
Midwest City, OK
405-737-8880 (800-800-8000)
Dogs of all sizes are allowed. Dogs
are allowed for a pet fee.

Candlewood Suites Oklahoma City-
Moore
1701 North Moore Ave.
Moore, OK
405-735-5151 (877-270-6405)
Dogs up to 80 pounds are allowed.
Pets allowed with an additional pet
fee. Up to $75 for 1-6 nights and up
to $150 for 7+ nights. A pet
agreement must be signed at check-
in.

Days Inn Muskogee
900 South 32nd Street
Muskogee, OK

918-683-3911 (800-329-7466)
Dogs of all sizes are allowed. Dogs
are allowed for a pet fee of $20.00
per pet per night.

La Quinta Inn & Suites Muskogee
3031 Military Boulevard
Muskogee, OK
918-687-9000 (800-531-5900)
Dogs of all sizes are allowed. There
are no additional pet fees. Dogs
must be leashed and cleaned up
after. There is only one dog room
available at this hotel. Multiple dogs
may be allowed.

Motel 6 - Muskogee
903 32nd St
Muskogee, OK
918-683-8369 (800-466-8356)
This motel welcomes your pets to
stay with you.

Super 8 Muskogee
2240 S 32nd
Muskogee, OK
918-683-8888 (800-800-8000)
Dogs are welcome at this hotel.

Best Western Norman Inn & Suites
2841 S Classen Boulevard
Norman, OK
405-701-4011 (800-780-7234)
Dogs of all sizes are allowed. Dogs
are allowed for a pet fee of $15.00
per pet per night.

Days Inn Norman
609 North Interstate Dr
Norman, OK
405-360-4380 (800-329-7466)
Dogs of all sizes are allowed. Dogs
are allowed for a pet fee of $10.00
per pet per night.

Holiday Inn Norman
1000 North Interstate Drive
Norman, OK
405-364-2882 (877-270-6405)
Dogs of all sizes are allowed. Dogs
are allowed for a pet fee of $20.00
per pet per stay.

Motel 6 - Norman, Ok
1016 26th Ave Nw
Norman, OK
405-701-3300 (800-466-8356)
This motel welcomes your pets to
stay with you.

Residence Inn Norman
2681 Jefferson Street
Norman, OK
405-366-0900 (800-331-3131)
Historical sites, the state university,
the Sam Noble Museum of Natural
History, and the Riverwind Casino

are all just a short distance from this
upscale all suite hotel. They also
offer a number of in-house
amenities, including a daily buffet
breakfast and evening socials. Dogs
are allowed for an additional one
time pet fee of $100 per room.
Multiple dogs may be allowed.

Super 8 Norman
2600 W Main St
Norman, OK
405-329-1624 (800-800-8000)
Dogs of all sizes are allowed. Dogs
are allowed for a pet fee of $10 per
pet per night.

Traveldoge Norman
225 N Interstate Dr
Norman, OK
405-329-7194 (800-578-7878)
Dogs are welcome at this hotel.

Days Inn Okemah
605 South Woody Guthrie St
Okemah, OK
918-623-2200 (800-329-7466)
Dogs of all sizes are allowed. Dogs
are allowed for a pet fee of $5.00 per
pet per stay.

Airport Traveldoge Oklahoma City
820 South MacArthur Blvd
Oklahoma City, OK
405-947-8651 (800-578-7878)
Dogs are welcome at this hotel.

Baymont Inn Oklahoma City South
8315 South I-35
Oklahoma City, OK
405-631-8661 (800-531-5900)
Dogs of all sizes are allowed. There
are no additional pet fees. Dogs
must be leashed, cleaned up after,
and they must be crated or removed
for housekeeping. Multiple dogs may
be allowed.

Best Western Broadway Inn & Suites
6101 N Santa Fe Avenue
Oklahoma City, OK
405-848-1919 (800-780-7234)
Dogs of all sizes are allowed. Dogs
are allowed for a pet fee.

Candlewood Suites Oklahoma City
4400 River Park Drive
Oklahoma City, OK
405-680-8770 (877-270-6405)
Dogs up to 80 pounds are allowed.
Pets allowed with an additional pet
fee. Up to $75 for 1-6 nights and up
to $150 for 7+ nights. A pet
agreement must be signed at check-
in.

Clarion Hotel Airport

737 S. Meridian Ave
Oklahoma City, OK
405-942-8511 (877-424-6423)
Dogs of all sizes are allowed.

Comfort Inn
2727 W. I-44 Service Road
Oklahoma City, OK
405-948-8000 (877-424-6423)
Dogs of all sizes are allowed.

Days Inn Northwest Oklahoma City
2801 NW 39th
Oklahoma City, OK
405-946-0741 (800-329-7466)
Dogs are welcome at this hotel.

Days Inn Oklahoma City
12013 N. I-35 Service Rd.
Oklahoma City, OK
405-478-2554 (800-329-7466)
Dogs are welcome at this hotel.

Days Inn South Oklahoma City
2616 South I-35 Service Rd.
Oklahoma City, OK
405-677-0521 (800-329-7466)
Dogs of all sizes are allowed. Dogs
are allowed for a pet fee of $15.00
per pet per night.

Days Inn West Oklahoma City
504 South Meridian
Oklahoma City, OK
405-942-8294 (800-329-7466)
Dogs are welcome at this hotel.

Econo Lodge
8200 W. I-40 Service Rd.
Oklahoma City, OK
405-787-7051 (877-424-6423)
Dogs of all sizes are allowed. Dogs
are allowed for a pet fee of $8.00 per
pet per stay.

Econo Lodge North
12001 N. I-35 Service Road
Oklahoma City, OK
405-478-0400 (877-424-6423)
Dogs of all sizes are allowed. Dogs
are allowed for a pet fee of $10.00
per pet per night.

Embassy Suites
1815 S Meridian
Oklahoma City, OK
405-682-6000 (800-EMBASSY (362-
2779))
This up scale, all suite hotel offers a
number of on site amenities for
business and leisure travelers, plus a
convenient location to business,
shopping, dining, and entertainment
areas. They also offer a
complimentary cooked-to-order
breakfast and a Manager's reception
every evening. Dogs up to 75 pounds

are allowed for an additional one
time fee of $50 per pet. 2 dogs may
be allowed.

Extended Stay America Oklahoma
City - Airport
4820 W. Reno Ave.
Oklahoma City, OK
405-948-4443 (800-804-3724)
One dog is allowed per suite. There
is a $25 per night additional pet fee
up to $150 for an entire stay.

Extended Stay America Oklahoma
City - NW Expressway
2720 N.W. Expwy.
Oklahoma City, OK
405-942-7441 (800-804-3724)
One dog is allowed per suite. There
is a $25 per night additional pet fee
up to $150 for an entire stay.

Four Points Sheraton Oklahoma
City Airport
6300 East Terminal Dr.
Oklahoma City, OK
405-681-3500 (888-625-5144)
Dogs of all sizes are allowed. There
is a $30 one time pet fee per visit.
Dogs are not allowed to be left
alone in the room.

Howard Johnson Inn Remington
Park Oklahoma City
1400 NE 63rd St
Oklahoma City, OK
405-478-5221 (800-446-4656)
Dogs of all sizes are allowed. Dogs
are allowed for a nightly pet fee.

Howard Johnson Inn - Oklahoma
City
400 S Meridian Ave
Oklahoma City, OK
405-943-9841 (800-446-4656)
Dogs of all sizes are allowed. Dogs
are allowed for a pet fee of $6.00
per pet per night.

Knights Inn Oklahoma City
11900 North I-35 Service Road
Oklahoma City, OK
405-478-2888 (800-843-5644)
Dogs of all sizes are allowed. Dogs
are allowed for a pet fee of $5.00
per pet per stay.

La Quinta Inn & Suites Oklahoma
City NW Expwy
4829 Northwest Expressway
Oklahoma City, OK
405-773-5575 (800-531-5900)
Dogs of all sizes are allowed. There
are no additional pet fees. Dogs
must be leashed, cleaned up after,
and they must be crated or
removed for housekeeping. Dogs

are not allowed to go through the
lobby during breakfast hours.
Multiple dogs may be allowed.

La Quinta Inn & Suites Oklahoma
City North
3003 W. Memorial Rd
Oklahoma City, OK
405-755-7000 (800-531-5900)
Dogs of all sizes are allowed. There
are no additional pet fees if one of
the pet friendly rooms are available.
If there is not one available, then
there is a $50 one time additional pet
fee per room. Dogs may not be left
unattended, and they must be
leashed and cleaned up after. 2 dogs
may be allowed.

La Quinta Inn Oklahoma City Airport
800 S. Meridian Avenue
Oklahoma City, OK
405-942-0040 (800-531-5900)
Dogs of all sizes are allowed. There
are no additional pet fees. Dogs
must be leashed and cleaned up
after. Multiple dogs may be allowed.

Motel 6 - Oklahoma City
1337 S.e. 44th Street
Oklahoma City, OK
405-601-3977 (800-466-8356)
This motel welcomes your pets to
stay with you.

Motel 6 - Oklahoma City Airport
820 Meridian Ave
Oklahoma City, OK
405-946-6662 (800-466-8356)
This motel welcomes your pets to
stay with you.

Motel 6 - Oklahoma City North
Frontier City
12121 I-35 Service Rd
Oklahoma City, OK
405-478-4030 (800-466-8356)
This motel welcomes your pets to
stay with you.

Motel 6 - Oklahoma City West
Fairgrounds
4200 I-40 Service Rd
Oklahoma City, OK
405-947-6550 (800-466-8356)
This motel welcomes your pets to
stay with you.

Ramada Airport North Oklahoma City
2200 S Meridian
Oklahoma City, OK
405-681-9000 (800-272-6232)
Dogs are welcome at this hotel.

Residence Inn Oklahoma City
Downtown/Bricktown
400 East Reno Avenue

Oklahoma City, OK
405-601-1700 (800-331-3131)
Located along the Bricktown Canal and near numerous great attractions, commerce, shopping, and dining areas, this luxury, all suite inn also offers guests a daily buffet breakfast, evening socials Monday to Thursday, a canal-side outdoor pool, and a Sport Court. Dogs are allowed for an additional one time pet fee of $100 per room. Multiple dogs may be allowed.

Residence Inn Oklahoma City South/Crossroads Mall
1111 East I-240 Service Road
Oklahoma City, OK
405-634-9696 (800-331-3131)
Besides offering a convenient location to business, shopping, dining, and entertainment areas, this hotel also provides a number of in-house amenities, including a daily buffet breakfast and complementary evening receptions Monday to Thursday. Dogs are allowed for an additional one time pet fee of $75 per room. Multiple dogs may be allowed.

Residence Inn Oklahoma City West
4361 W Reno Avenue
Oklahoma City, OK
405-942-4500 (800-331-3131)
Besides offering a convenient location to business, shopping, dining, and entertainment areas, this hotel also provides a number of in-house amenities, including a daily buffet breakfast and complementary evening social hours. Dogs are allowed for an additional one time pet fee of $100 per room. Multiple dogs may be allowed.

Sheraton Oklahoma City Hotel
One North Broadway
Oklahoma City, OK
405-235-2780 (888-625-5144)
Dogs up to 50 pounds are allowed for no additional pet fee. Dogs may not be left alone in the room.

Staybridge Suites Oklahoma City
4411 SW 15th
Oklahoma City, OK
405-429-4400 (877-270-6405)
Dogs up to 80 pounds are allowed. Pets allowed with an additional pet fee. Up to $75 for 1-6 nights and up to $150 for 7+ nights. A pet agreement must be signed at check-in.

Staybridge Suites Oklahoma City-Quail Springs
2740 NW 138th Street
Oklahoma City, OK

405-286-3800 (877-270-6405)
Dogs up to 80 pounds are allowed. Pets allowed with an additional pet fee. Up to $75 for 1-6 nights and up to $150 for 7+ nights. A pet agreement must be signed at check-in.

Super 8 OKC/Bricktown/I-35
3030 South I-35
Oklahoma City, OK
405-677-1000 (800-800-8000)
Dogs of all sizes are allowed. Dogs are allowed for a pet fee of $10.00 per pet per night.

Super 8 Oklahoma Fairgrounds
2821 NW 39th Street
Oklahoma City, OK
405-946-9170 (800-800-8000)
Dogs of all sizes are allowed. Dogs are allowed for a nightly pet fee.

Super 8 Oklahoma/Frontier City
11935 North I-35 Service Road
Oklahoma City, OK
405-478-8288 (800-800-8000)
Dogs of all sizes are allowed. Dogs are allowed for a nightly pet fee.

Days Inn Okmulgee
1221 S Wood Drive
Okmulgee, OK
918-758-0660 (800-329-7466)
Dogs are welcome at this hotel.

Candlewood Suites Owasso
11699 E. 96th Street North
Owasso, OK
918-272-4334 (877-270-6405)
Dogs up to 80 pounds are allowed. Pets allowed with an additional pet fee. Up to $75 for 1-6 nights and up to $150 for 7+ nights. A pet agreement must be signed at check-in.

Holiday Inn Express Hotel & Suites Perry
3002 West Fir Street
Perry, OK
580-336-5050 (877-270-6405)
Dogs are welcome at this hotel.

Super 8 Perry
2608 W Fir Street
Perry, OK
580-336-1600 (800-800-8000)
Dogs of all sizes are allowed. Dogs are allowed for a pet fee.

Motel 6 - Ponca City, Ok
1415 Bradley Ave
Ponca City, OK
580-767-1406 (800-466-8356)
This motel welcomes your pets to stay with you.

Days Inn and Suites Pryor
315 Mid America Drive
Pryor, OK
918-476-4661 (800-329-7466)
Dogs of all sizes are allowed. Dogs are allowed for a pet fee of $10.00 per pet per night.

Econo Lodge
2122 US 74 S.
Purcell, OK
405-527-5603 (877-424-6423)
Dogs of all sizes are allowed. Dogs are allowed for a pet fee of $5.00 per pet per night.

OK
900 S Paw Paw
Roland, OK
918-427-6600 (800-578-7878)
Dogs are welcome at this hotel.

Days Inn Sallisaw
710 S Kerr Blvd
Sallisaw, OK
918-774-0400 (800-329-7466)
Dogs are welcome at this hotel.

Motel 6 - Sallisaw
1300 East Cherokee Ave
Sallisaw, OK
918-775-6000 (800-466-8356)
This motel welcomes your pets to stay with you.

Super 8 Sallisaw
924 S Kerr Blvd
Sallisaw, OK
918-775-8900 (800-800-8000)
Dogs are welcome at this hotel.

Super 8 /Tulsa Area Sapulpa
1505 New Sapulpa Rd
Sapulpa, OK
918-227-3300 (800-800-8000)
Dogs are welcome at this hotel.

Motel 6 - Shawnee
4981 Harrison St
Shawnee, OK
405-275-5310 (800-466-8356)
This motel welcomes your pets to stay with you.

Super 8 Shawnee
4900 N Harrison St
Shawnee, OK
405-275-0089 (800-800-8000)
Dogs are welcome at this hotel.

Days Inn Stillwater
5010 West 6th Street
Stillwater, OK
405-743-2570 (800-329-7466)
Dogs of all sizes are allowed. Dogs are allowed for a nightly pet fee.

Motel 6 - Stillwater
5122 6th Ave
Stillwater, OK
405-624-0433 (800-466-8356)
This motel welcomes your pets to stay with you.

Quality Inn
2515 West 6th Ave
Stillwater, OK
405-372-0800 (877-424-6423)
Dogs of all sizes are allowed.

Super 8 Sulphur
2116 W Broadway Ave
Sulphur, OK
580-622-6500 (800-800-8000)
Dogs of all sizes are allowed. Dogs are allowed for a pet fee of $10 per pet per night.

Baymont Inn & Suites Tulsa
4530 E. Skelly Drive
Tulsa, OK
918-488-8777 (800-531-5900)
Dogs of all sizes are allowed. There are no additional pet fees. Dogs must be leashed, cleaned up after, and crated or removed for housekeeping. Multiple dogs may be allowed.

Best Western - Airport
222 N Garnett Road
Tulsa, OK
918-438-0780 (800-780-7234)
Dogs of all sizes are allowed. Dogs are allowed for a pet fee.

Candlewood Suites Tulsa
10008 E 73rd. Street South
Tulsa, OK
918-294-9000 (877-270-6405)
Dogs up to 80 pounds are allowed. Pets allowed with an additional pet fee. Up to $75 for 1-6 nights and up to $150 for 7+ nights. A pet agreement must be signed at check-in.

Days Inn Airport Tulsa
35 N Sheridan Road
Tulsa, OK
918-836-3931 (800-329-7466)
Dogs of all sizes are allowed. Dogs are allowed for a pet fee of $20.00 per pet per stay.

Days Inn West on I-44 Tulsa
5525 W Skelly Drive/I-44
Tulsa, OK
918-446-1561 (800-329-7466)
Dogs of all sizes are allowed. Dogs are allowed for a pet fee of $20.00 per pet per stay.

Doubletree Hotel
6110 S Yale Avenue
Tulsa, OK
918-495-1000 (800-222-TREE (8733))
Located in a park like setting, this upscale hotel offers a number of on site amenities for all level of travelers - including their signature chocolate chip cookies at check in, plus a convenient location to business, shopping, dining, and entertainment areas. Dogs are allowed for an additional one time pet fee of $50 per room. 2 dogs may be allowed.

Doubletree Hotel
616 W Seventh Street
Tulsa, OK
918-587-8000 (800-222-TREE (8733))
Set in the city's lively downtown entertainment and business district with a sky-bridge connection to the Tulsa Convention Center, this upscale hotel offers a number of on site amenities for all level of travelers - including their signature chocolate chip cookies at check in, plus a convenient location to business, shopping, dining, and recreation areas. Dogs are allowed for an additional one time fee of $50 per pet. Multiple dogs may be allowed.

Embassy Suites
3332 S 79th East Avenue
Tulsa, OK
918-622-4000 (800-EMBASSY (362-2779))
Located in the heart of the city, this up scale, all suite hotel offers a number of on site amenities for business and leisure travelers, plus a convenient location to business, shopping, dining, and entertainment areas. They also offer a complimentary cooked-to-order breakfast and a Manager's reception every evening. Dogs are allowed for a $50 pet deposit, $25 is refundable, per room. Multiple dogs may be allowed.

Extended Stay America Tulsa - Central
3414 S. 79th E. Ave.
Tulsa, OK
918-664-9494 (800-804-3724)
One dog is allowed per suite. There is a $25 per night additional pet fee up to $150 for an entire stay.

GuestHouse Suites
8181 E 41st St
Tulsa, OK

918-664-7241
guesthouseintl.com/#
Dogs up to 75 pounds are allowed for an additional fee of $10 per night per room. 2 dogs may be allowed.

Hilton Hotel
7902 S Lewis Avenue
Tulsa, OK
918-492-5000 (800-HILTONS (445-8667))
This upscale hotel offers numerous on site amenities for business and leisure travelers, plus a convenient location to 4 local universities, business, shopping, dining, and recreation areas. Dogs up to 75 pounds are allowed for an additional one time pet fee of $75 per room. 2 dogs may be allowed.

Holiday Inn Express Hotel & Suites Tulsa-Downtown Area
2316 West Cameron
Tulsa, OK
918-585-7000 (877-270-6405)
Dogs are welcome at this hotel.

Howard Johnson INN OK Tulsa
8525 East 41st Street
Tulsa, OK
918-627-0030 (800-446-4656)
Dogs are welcome at this hotel.

La Quinta Inn Tulsa Airport
35 N. Sheridan Rd.
Tulsa, OK
918-836-3931 (800-531-5900)
Dogs of all sizes are allowed. There is a $25 per pet per stay additional fee. Dogs may only be left in the room alone if they will be quiet and well behaved, and they must be leashed and cleaned up after. Multiple dogs may be allowed.

La Quinta Inn Tulsa South
12525 East 52nd Street South
Tulsa, OK
918-254-1626 (800-531-5900)
Dogs of all sizes are allowed. There are no additional pet fees. Dogs must be leashed, cleaned up after, and crated or removed for housekeeping. Multiple dogs may be allowed.

Marriott Tulsa Southern Hills
1902 E 71st Street
Tulsa, OK
918-493-7000 (866-530-3760)
This luxury hotel provides a great location to a number of sites of interest for both business and leisure travelers; plus they also offer numerous on-site amenities to ensure a comfortable stay. Dogs up

to 60 pounds are allowed for an additional one time fee of $75 per room. 2 dogs may be allowed.

Motel 6 - Tulsa East
1011 Garnett Rd
Tulsa, OK
918-234-6200 (800-466-8356)
This motel welcomes your pets to stay with you.

Motel 6 - Tulsa West
5828 Skelly Dr
Tulsa, OK
918-445-0223 (800-466-8356)
This motel welcomes your pets to stay with you.

Ramada Airport East Tulsa
1010 N Garnett Rd
Tulsa, OK
918-437-7660 (800-272-6232)
Dogs of all sizes are allowed. Dogs are allowed for a pet fee.

Red Roof Inn Tulsa
4717 South Yale Ave
Tulsa, OK
918-622-6776 (800-RED-ROOF)
One well-behaved family pet per room. Guest must notify front desk upon arrival. Guest is liable for any damages. In consideration of all guests, pets must never be left unattended in the guest rooms.

Renaissance Tulsa Hotel & Convention Center
6808 S 107th E Avenue
Tulsa, OK
918-307-2600 (800-HOTELS-1 (468-3571))
This elegant hotel sits central to numerous businesses, shopping, dining, and day/night entertainment areas, plus they also offer a number of in-house amenities for business and leisure travelers. Dogs are allowed for no additional fee with a credit card on file; there is a $50 refundable deposit if paying in cash. 2 dogs may be allowed.

Residence Inn Tulsa South
11025 E 73rd Street S
Tulsa, OK
918-250-4850 (800-331-3131)
In addition to offering a convenient location to numerous sites of interest, activities, and attractions for business or pleasure travelers, this all suite hotel also offers a number of in-house amenities, including a daily buffet breakfast and evening socials. Dogs are allowed for an additional one time pet fee of $75 per room. Multiple dogs may be allowed.

Staybridge Suites Tulsa-Woodland Hills
11111 E 73rd St South
Tulsa, OK
918-461-2100 (877-270-6405)
Dogs up to 80 pounds are allowed. Pets allowed with an additional pet fee. Up to $75 for 1-6 nights and up to $150 for 7+ nights. A pet agreement must be signed at check-in.

Super 8 /Arpt/St Fairgrounds Tulsa
6616 E Archer St
Tulsa, OK
918-836-1981 (800-800-8000)
Dogs of all sizes are allowed. Dogs are allowed for a pet fee.

Days Inn OK Woodward
1212 North West Hwy 270
Woodward, OK
580-256-1546 (800-329-7466)
Dogs of all sizes are allowed. Dogs are allowed for a pet fee.

Northwest Inn
Hwy. 270 and First St
Woodward, OK
580-256-7600 (800-727-7606)
There are only 4 occupants allowed per room including pets. There is an additional pet fee of $10 for the 1st night and $20 for 2 nights or more per room. 2 dogs may be allowed.

Super 8 Woodward
4120 Williams Ave
Woodward, OK
580-254-2964 (800-800-8000)
Dogs of all sizes are allowed. Dogs are allowed for a pet fee.

Wayfarer Inn
2901 Williams Ave
Woodward, OK
580-256-5553 (800-832-3273)
Pets are allowed for a $15 refundable pet deposit per room. Multiple dogs may be allowed.

Best Western Inn & Suites - Yukon
11440 W I-40 Service Road
Yukon, OK
405-265-2995 (800-780-7234)
Dogs are welcome at this hotel. There is a $6 pet fee.

Oregon

Comfort Suites Linn County Fairground and Expo
100 Opal Court NE
Albany, OR
541-928-2053 (877-424-6423)

Dogs of all sizes are allowed. Two dogs are allowed per room.

Econo Lodge
1212 SE Price Road
Albany, OR
541-926-0170 (877-424-6423)
Dogs of all sizes are allowed. Dogs are allowed for a pet fee of $10.00 per pet per night. Two dogs are allowed per room.

Holiday Inn Express Hotel & Suites Albany
105 Opal Court
Albany, OR
541-928-8820 (877-270-6405)
Dogs of all sizes are allowed. Dogs are allowed for a nightly pet fee.

La Quinta Inn & Suites Albany
251 Airport Rd SE
Albany, OR
541-928-0921 (800-531-5900)
Dogs of all sizes are allowed. There are no additional pet fees. There is a pet waiver to sign at check in. Dogs must be leashed and cleaned up after. Multiple dogs may be allowed.

Motel 6 - Albany, Or
2735 Pacific Blvd Se
Albany, OR
541-926-4233 (800-466-8356)
This motel welcomes your pets to stay with you.

Quality Inn
1100 Price Road SE
Albany, OR
541-928-5050 (877-424-6423)
Dogs of all sizes are allowed. Dogs are allowed for a pet fee of $10.00 per pet per night.

Super 8 Albany
315 Airport Rd SE
Albany, OR
541-928-6322 (800-800-8000)
Dogs are welcome at this hotel.

Inn Arch Cape
79340 H 101
Arch Cape, OR
503-738-7373
Dogs of all sizes are allowed. There is a $15 per night per pet fee and a pet policy to sign at check in. 2 dogs may be allowed.

Best Western Bard's Inn
132 N Main Street
Ashland, OR
541-482-0049 (800-780-7234)
Dogs are welcome at this hotel. There is a $15 one time pet fee.

Best Western Windsor Inn
2520 Ashland Street
Ashland, OR
541-488-2330 (800-780-7234)
Dogs of all sizes are allowed. Dogs
are allowed for a pet fee of $15.00
per pet per stay.

Econo Lodge
50 Lowe Road
Ashland, OR
541-482-4700 (877-424-6423)
Dogs of all sizes are allowed. Dogs
are allowed for a pet fee of $10.00
per pet per night. Two dogs are
allowed per room.

Holiday Inn Express Hotel & Suites
Ashland
565 Clover Lane
Ashland, OR
541-201-0202 (877-270-6405)
Dogs of all sizes are allowed. Dogs
are allowed for a pet fee of $15 per
pet per night.

La Quinta Inn & Suites Ashland
434 Valley View Rd
Ashland, OR
541-482-6932 (800-531-5900)
Dogs of all sizes are allowed. There
are no additional pet fees. There is a
pet waiver to sign at check in. Dogs
may not be left unattended, and they
must be leashed at all times, and
cleaned up after. Multiple dogs may
be allowed.

Windmill Inn and Suites
2525 Ashland Street
Ashland, OR
541-482-8310
Dogs of all sizes are allowed. There
is a pet policy to sign at check in and
there are no additional pet fees. 2
dogs may be allowed.

Best Western Lincoln Inn
555 Hamburg Avenue
Astoria, OR
503-325-2205 (800-780-7234)
Dogs of all sizes are allowed. Dogs
are allowed for a pet fee of $15 per
pet per stay.

Crest Motel
5366 Leif Erikson Drive
Astoria, OR
503-325-3141
Dogs of all sizes are allowed. There
are no additional pet fees. 2 dogs
may be allowed.

Holiday Inn Express Hotel & Suites
Astoria
204 West Marine Dr.
Astoria, OR

503-325-6222 (877-270-6405)
Dogs of all sizes are allowed. Dogs
are allowed for a pet fee of $15 per
pet per night.

Hotel Elliott
357 12th Street
Astoria, OR
503-325-2222
There is a one time pet fee per
room of $25 for a quest room and
$50 for a suite. 2 dogs may be
allowed.

Best Western Sunridge Inn
1 Sunridge Ln
Baker City, OR
541-523-6444 (800-780-7234)
Dogs are welcome at this hotel.

Rodeway Inn
810 Campbell St.
Baker City, OR
541-523-2242 (877-424-6423)
Dogs of all sizes are allowed. Dogs
are allowed for a pet fee of $10.00
per pet per stay.

Super 8 Baker City
250 Campbell St
Baker City, OR
541-523-8282 (800-800-8000)
Dogs of all sizes are allowed. Dogs
are allowed for a nightly pet fee.

Best Western Inn at Face Rock
3225 Beach Loop Road
Bandon, OR
541-347-9441 (800-780-7234)
Dogs of all sizes are allowed. Dogs
are allowed for a pet fee of $25.00
per pet per night.

Sunset Motel
1755 Beach Loop Rd
Bandon, OR
541-347-2453 (800-842-2407)
sunsetmotel.com/
There is a $10 per day per pet
charge. Multiple dogs may be
allowed.

Table Rock Motel
840 Beach Loop Road
Bandon, OR
541-347-2700
There is an additional $5 to $10 per
night per pet fee, depending on the
length of stay. 2 dogs may be
allowed.

Extended Stay America Portland -
Beaverton
18665 NW Eider Ct.
Beaverton, OR
503-439-1515 (800-804-3724)
One dog is allowed per suite. There

is a $25 per night additional pet fee
up to $150 for an entire stay.

Homestead Studio Suites Portland -
Beaverton
875 S.W. 158th Ave.
Beaverton, OR
503-690-3600 (800-804-3724)
One dog is allowed per suite. There
is a $25 per night additional pet fee
up to $150 for an entire stay.

Best Western Inn & Suites of Bend
721 NE 3rd Street
Bend, OR
541-382-1515 (800-780-7234)
Dogs are welcome at this hotel.

Days Inn Bend
849 NE Third St.
Bend, OR
541-383-3776 (800-329-7466)
Dogs of all sizes are allowed. Dogs
are allowed for a pet fee of $6.00 per
pet per night.

Entrada Lodge
19221 Century Dr
Bend, OR
541-382-4080
There is a $10 per day per pet fee.
Pets may not be left alone in the
room. 2 dogs may be allowed.

Holiday Inn Express Hotel & Suites
Bend
20615 Grandview Drive
Bend, OR
541-317-8500 (877-270-6405)
Dogs of all sizes are allowed. Dogs
are allowed for a nightly pet fee.

La Quinta Inn Bend
61200 S Highway 97
Bend, OR
541-388-2227 (800-531-5900)
Dogs of all sizes are allowed. There
are no additional pet fees. There is a
pet waiver to sign at check in. Dogs
must be leashed and cleaned up
after. They prefer that dogs are not
left unattended in the room, but if you
must be out for a short time, they
must be crated. Multiple dogs may
be allowed.

Motel 6 - Bend
201 Ne 3rd St
Bend, OR
541-382-8282 (800-466-8356)
This motel welcomes your pets to
stay with you.

Quality Inn
20600 Grandview Dr
Bend, OR
541-318-0848 (877-424-6423)

Dogs of all sizes are allowed. Dogs are allowed for a pet fee of $10.00 per pet per night. Two dogs are allowed per room.

Red Lion
1415 NE Third Street
Bend, OR
541-382-7011
There is a $20 per night per room additional pet fee. There are no additional pet fees for R&R members, and the R&R program is free to sign up. 2 dogs may be allowed.

Sleep Inn
600 N.E. Bellvue
Bend, OR
541-330-0050 (877-424-6423)
Dogs of all sizes are allowed. Dogs are allowed for a pet fee of $10.00 per pet per stay.

Super 8 Bend
1275 SE 3rd St. or Business 97
Bend, OR
541-388-6888 (800-800-8000)
Dogs of all sizes are allowed. Dogs are allowed for a pet fee.

The Riverhouse Resort
3075 N Hwy 97
Bend, OR
541-389-3111
You need to sign a pet policy, and dogs must be declared at the time of reservations. There are no additional pet fees. Multiple dogs may be allowed.

TownePlace Suites Bend
755 SW 13th Place
Bend, OR
541-382-5006 (800-257-3000)
This all suite hotel is only minutes to downtown, the Old Mill District and to all the recreational activities of Mt Bachelor. Dogs are allowed for an additional one time fee of $75 per room. 2 dogs may be allowed.

Westward Ho Motel
904 SE Third Street
Bend, OR
541-382-2111
There is an additional pet fee of $5 per night per room. The fee may be slightly higher for large dogs.

Rodeway Inn
105 Front Street S. W.
Boardman, OR
541-481-2375 (877-424-6423)
Dogs of all sizes are allowed.

Best Western Beachfront Inn

16008 Boat Basin Road
Brookings, OR
541-469-7779 (800-780-7234)
Dogs are welcome at this hotel.

Whaleshead Beach Resort
19921 Whaleshead Road
Brookings, OR
541-469-7446 (800-943-4325)
whalesheadresort.com/
the others will only accept 1 pet per room. Dogs must be leashed and cleaned up after, and may only be left alone in the room if they will be quiet and well behaved. There is also an RV area on site and dogs are welcome there for no additional fees or number of dog restrictions.

Silver Spur Motel
789 N Broadway Avenue
Burns, OR
541-573-2077
This motel features a breakfast buffet, HBO/cable TV and refrigerators/microwaves in all rooms. Dogs of all sizes are allowed for an additional fee of $5 per night per pet. Dogs must be well behaved, leashed, cleaned up after, and crated when left alone in the room.

Hallmark Inns
1400 S Hemlock
Cannon Beach, OR
503-436-1566
Dogs of all sizes are allowed. There is a $20 per night per pet additional fee. 2 dogs may be allowed.

Surfsand Resort
148 W. Gower
Cannon Beach, OR
503-436-2274 (1-800-547-6100)
surfsand.com/
This resort offers views of Haystack Rock and the Pacific Ocean from oceanfront and ocean-view rooms. The Surfsand is a nice vacation spot for families and couples. The hotel caters to four-legged family members and they host an annual 'For Fun' Dog Show. The resort is entirely non-smoking and it is located near a dog-friendly restaurant called The Local Scoop. There is a $15 per day per pet fee. Multiple dogs may be allowed.

The Haystack Resort
3339 S. Hemlock
Cannon Beach, OR
503-436-1577 (1-800-499-2220)
haystackresort.com/
Every room and suite at the Haystack Resort offers complete ocean views. Your pet is always

welcome. They are located near a dog-friendly restaurant called 'The Local Scoop. Dogs up to 50 pounds are allowed for an additional fee of $15 per night per pet. Multiple dogs may be allowed.

The Inn at Cannon Beach
3215 S. Hemlock
Cannon Beach, OR
503-436-9085 (800-321-6304)
There is a $10 per day per pet fee. A maximum of two pets per room is allowed. 2 dogs may be allowed.

Best Western Canyonville Inn & Suites
200 Creekside Drive
Canyonville, OR
541-839-4200 (800-780-7234)
Dogs of all sizes are allowed. Dogs are allowed for a pet fee of $10.00 per pet per night.

Junction Inn
406 Redwood Hwy
Cave Junction, OR
541-592-3106
There is a $5 one time pet fee per room. They normally put dogs in smoking rooms, but will make exceptions. 2 dogs may be allowed.

Holiday Inn Express Hotel & Suites Medford-Central Point
285 Penninger St.
Central Point, OR
541-423-1010 (877-270-6405)
Dogs of all sizes are allowed. Dogs are allowed for a pet fee of $25.00 per pet per night.

Comfort Suites
15929 SE McKinley Ave
Clackamas, OR
503-723-3450 (877-424-6423)
Dogs up to 50 pounds are allowed. Dogs are allowed for a pet fee of $10.00 per pet per night. Two dogs are allowed per room.

Best Western Holiday Motel
411 N Bayshore Drive
Coos Bay, OR
541-269-5111 (800-780-7234)
Dogs of all sizes are allowed. Dogs are allowed for a pet fee of $15.00 per pet per night.

Motel 6 - Coos Bay
1445 Bayshore Dr
Coos Bay, OR
541-267-7171 (800-466-8356)
This motel welcomes your pets to stay with you.

Red Lion

1313 N Bayshore Drive
Coos Bay, OR
541-267-4141
Dogs up to 100 pounds are allowed. There is a $20 one time fee per pet. There are no additional pet fees for R&R members, and the R&R program is free to sign up. 2 dogs may be allowed.

Super 8 /North Bend Coos Bay
1001 North Bay Shore Drive
Coos Bay, OR
541-808-0704 (800-800-8000)
Dogs are welcome at this hotel.

Best Western Grand Manor Inn
925 NW Garfield Avenue
Corvallis, OR
541-758-8571 (800-780-7234)
Dogs of all sizes are allowed. Dogs are allowed for a nightly pet fee.

Days Inn Corvallis
1113 NW 9th Street
Corvallis, OR
541-754-7474 (800-329-7466)
Dogs of all sizes are allowed. Dogs are allowed for a pet fee of $5.00 per pet per night.

Holiday Inn Express Corvallis-On The River
781 NE 2nd Street
Corvallis, OR
541-752-0800 (877-270-6405)
Dogs of all sizes are allowed. Dogs are allowed for a nightly pet fee.

Motel 6 - Corvallis
935 Nw Garfield Ave
Corvallis, OR
541-758-9125 (800-466-8356)
This motel welcomes your pets to stay with you.

Rodeway Inn Willamette River
345 N.W. 2nd St.
Corvallis, OR
541-752-9601 (877-424-6423)
Dogs of all sizes are allowed. Dogs are allowed for a pet fee of $10.00 per pet per night.

Comfort Inn
845 Gateway Blvd.
Cottage Grove, OR
541-942-9747 (877-424-6423)
Dogs of all sizes are allowed. Dogs are allowed for a pet fee of $10.00 per pet per night.

Super 8 /South Eugene Creswell
345 E. Oregon Ave
Creswell, OR
541-895-3341 (800-800-8000)
Dogs of all sizes are allowed. Dogs

are allowed for a pet fee of $15.00 per pet per stay.

Trollers Lodge
355 SW H 101
Depoe Bay, OR
541-765-2287
Dogs of all sizes are allowed. There is a $10 per night per pet additional fee, except for the ocean front homes which are $15 per night per pet.

Diamond Lake Resort
350 Resort Drive
Diamond Lake, OR
541-793-3333
diamondlake.net
This resort is located on the eastern shore of Diamond Lake. Recreation in the summer includes hiking in the nearby dog-friendly national forest, fishing and water sports. Winter recreation activities include dog-friendly cross-country skiing. Pets are allowed in the cabins and motel rooms, including non-smoking rooms. Well-behaved dogs of all sizes are welcome. There is a $10 per day per pet fee. Pets cannot be left alone in the rooms or cabins. 2 dogs may be allowed.

Barking Mad Farm Bed and Breakfast
65156 Powers Road, Enterprise, Oregon 97828
Enterprise, OR
541-426-0360
barkingmadfarm.com/
Set on 42 pastoral acres in a wonderful turn of the century farmhouse, this retreat offers a relaxing step back in time with all the modern amenities. Well mannered, hound and human friendly dogs are welcome. They even have an 8 acre fenced dog run for off leash fun. There is an additional fee of $10 per night per pet. Multiple dogs may be allowed.

Ponderosa Motel
102 E Greenwood
Enterprise, OR
541-426-3186
There is a $10 per night per pet additional fee. Dogs are not allowed to be left alone in the room.

Best Western New Oregon Motel
1655 Franklin Boulevard
Eugene, OR
541-683-3669 (800-780-7234)
Dogs are welcome at this hotel.

Days Inn Eugene

1859 Franklin Blvd
Eugene, OR
541-342-6383 (800-329-7466)
Dogs of all sizes are allowed. Dogs are allowed for a pet fee of $10.00 per pet per night.

La Quinta Inn & Suites Eugene
155 Day Island Rd
Eugene, OR
541-344-8335 (800-531-5900)
Dogs of all sizes are allowed. There are no additional pet fees, but there must be a credit card on file. Dogs may not be left unattended, and they must be leashed and cleaned up after. Multiple dogs may be allowed.

Motel 6 - Eugene South Springfield
3690 Glenwood Dr
Eugene, OR
541-687-2395 (800-466-8356)
This motel welcomes your pets to stay with you.

Red Lion
205 Coburg Road
Eugene, OR
541-342-5201
There is a $20 one time fee per pet. There are no additional pet fees for R&R members, and the R&R program is free to sign up. Multiple dogs may be allowed.

Residence Inn Eugene Springfield
25 Club Road
Eugene, OR
541-342-7171 (800-331-3131)
Located along the shores of the Willamette River, and close to the state university as well as to many local sites of interest, this all suite hotel also offers a number of in-house amenities including a daily buffet breakfast, and evening socials Monday to Thursday. Dogs are allowed for an additional one time pet fee of $75 per room.

Valley River Inn
1000 Valley River Way
Eugene, OR
541-687-0123
valleyriverinn.com/
Dogs of all sizes are allowed and pet rooms are located on the 1st floor. There are no additional pet fees and dogs are not allowed to be left alone in the room. 2 dogs may be allowed.

Best Western Pier Point Inn
85625 Highway 101
Florence, OR
541-997-7191 (800-780-7234)
Dogs of all sizes are allowed. Dogs are allowed for a pet fee of $10 per

pet per night.

Ocean Breeze Motel
85165 H 101S
Florence, OR
541-997-2642
Dogs of all sizes are accepted on an individual basis, but no cats. There is an $10 per night per pet fee and a credit card must be on file. Dogs are not allowed to be left alone in the room, and they ask you to cover the furniture.

Old Town Inn
170 Highway 101
Florence, OR
541-997-7131 (800-587-5591)
old-town-inn.com
This inn is located in the historic Old Town. There is a $10 nightly pet fee.

Best Western University Inn & Suites
3933 Pacific Avenue
Forest Grove, OR
503-992-8888 (800-780-7234)
Dogs of all sizes are allowed. Dogs are allowed for a pet fee of $15 per pet per night.

Comfort Inn
502 Garibaldi Ave.
Garibaldi, OR
503-322-3338 (877-424-6423)
Dogs up to 50 pounds are allowed. Dogs are allowed for a pet fee of $15.00/pet per pet per night. Two dogs are allowed per room.

Econo Lodge
227 Garibaldi Avenue
Garibaldi, OR
503-322-2552 (877-424-6423)
Dogs of all sizes are allowed. Dogs are allowed for a pet fee of $10.00 per pet per night.

Distinctive Beach Lodgings
67 North Cottage Ave
Gearhart, OR
503-738-7373 (800-352-8034)
distinctivebeachlodgings.com
These boutique inns are located on the North Oregon coast. There is a $15 pet fee per pet per night.

Gearhart Ocean Inn
67 N Cottage Avenue
Gearhart, OR
503-738-7373
Dogs of all sizes are allowed. There is a $15 per night per pet fee and a pet policy to sign at check in. 2 dogs may be allowed.

Jot's Resort
94360 Wedderburn Loop

Gold Beach, OR
541-247-6676 (800-FOR-JOTS)
jotsresort.com/
There is a $10 per day pet pet fee for small dogs, and a $15 pet day pet pet fee for large dogs. Pets are allowed in the deluxe rooms overlooking the river. 2 dogs may be allowed.

Motel 6 - Gold Beach
94433 Jerry's Flat Rd
Gold Beach, OR
541-247-4533 (800-466-8356)
This motel welcomes your pets to stay with you.

Mt Hood Inn
87450 E Government Camp Loop
Government Camp, OR
503-272-3205
There is a $10 per night per pet fee and a pet policy to sign at check in. Dogs may not be left alone in the room.

Best Western Grants Pass Inn
111 NE Agness Avenue
Grants Pass, OR
541-476-1117 (800-780-7234)
Dogs of all sizes are allowed. Dogs are allowed for a nightly pet fee.

Best Western Inn at the Rogue
8959 Rogue River Highway
Grants Pass, OR
541-582-2200 (800-780-7234)
Dogs are welcome at this hotel.

Comfort Inn
1889 NE 6th St.
Grants Pass, OR
541-479-8301 (877-424-6423)
Dogs of all sizes are allowed.

La Quinta Inn & Suites Grants Pass
243 NE Morgan Lane
Grants Pass, OR
541-472-1808 (800-531-5900)
Dogs of all sizes are allowed. There are no additional pet fees. Dogs must be leashed and cleaned up after. Dogs may only left for short periods, and only then if they will be quiet and well behaved. If they disturb other quests when you are away, they add a $25 fee. Multiple dogs may be allowed.

Motel 6 - Grants Pass
1800 Ne. 7th St
Grants Pass, OR
541-474-1331 (800-466-8356)
This motel welcomes your pets to stay with you.

Redwood Motel

815 NE 6th Street
Grants Pass, OR
541-476-0878
redwoodmotel.com
Dogs of all sizes are allowed for a $10 additional fee per night per pet. There are limited pet rooms so you need to tell the hotel about your pet when making reservations. 2 dogs may be allowed.

Super 8 Grants Pass
1949 NE 7th St
Grants Pass, OR
541-474-0888 (800-800-8000)
Dogs are welcome at this hotel.

Travelodge Grants Pass
1950 NW Vine Street
Grants Pass, OR
541-479-6611 (800-578-7878)
Dogs are welcome at this hotel.

Days Inn and Suites Gresham
24124 SE Stark Street
Gresham, OR
503-465-1515 (800-329-7466)
Dogs of all sizes are allowed. Dogs are allowed for a pet fee of $10.00 per pet per night.

Howard Johnson Gresham
1572 NE Burnside Road
Gresham, OR
503-666-9545 (800-446-4656)
Dogs of all sizes are allowed. Dogs are allowed for a pet fee of $20.00 per pet per stay.

Super 8 /Portland Area
121 NE 181st Ave
Gresham, OR
503-661-5100 (800-800-8000)
Dogs of all sizes are allowed. Dogs are allowed for a nightly pet fee.

Travelodge Pioneer Villa
33180 Highway 228
Halsey, OR
541-369-2804 (800-578-7878)
Dogs are welcome at this hotel.

Motel 6 - Hermiston, Or
655 North 1st St.
Hermiston, OR
541-567-7777 (800-466-8356)
This motel welcomes your pets to stay with you.

Hotel B
3500 NE Cornell Road
Hillsboro, OR
503-648-3500
hotelb-hillsboro.com/
Dogs of all sizes are allowed for an additional pet fee of $20 per night not to exceed $100 per stay. Multiple

dogs may be allowed.

Residence Inn Portland West/Hillsboro
18855 NW Tanasbourne Drive
Hillsboro, OR
503-531-3200 (800-331-3131)
Located only a few miles west of Portland in the Hillsboro high tech corridor, this all suite inn sits within walking distance to shopping, dining, and entertainment areas, offers a daily buffet breakfast, a Manager's reception Monday and Wednesdays, and a 24 hour market on site. Dogs are allowed for an additional fee of $10 per night per pet, and there is a pet policy to sign at check in. 2 dogs may be allowed.

TownePlace Suites Portland Hillsboro
6550 NE Brighton Street
Hillsboro, OR
503-268-6000 (800-257-3000)
This all suite inn site central to a number of sites of interest for both business and leisure travelers; plus they also offer a number of on-site amenities - including a complimentary continental breakfast. Dogs are allowed for an additional fee of $10 per night per pet. 2 dogs may be allowed.

Best Western Rory & Ryan Inns
534 Highway 20 N
Hines, OR
541-573-5050 (800-780-7234)
Dogs of all sizes are allowed. Dogs are allowed for a pet fee of $15.00 per pet per night.

Comfort Inn
504 N. Hwy 20
Hines, OR
541-573-3370 (877-424-6423)
Dogs of all sizes are allowed. Dogs are allowed for a pet fee of $10.00 per pet per night. Three or more dogs may be allowed.

Best Western Hood River Inn
1108 E Marina Way
Hood River, OR
541-386-2200 (800-780-7234)
Dogs of all sizes are allowed. Dogs are allowed for a pet fee of $12.00 per pet per night.

Columbia Gorge Hotel
4000 Westcliff Dr
Hood River, OR
541-386-5566 (800-345-1921)
columbiagorgehotel.com/
Dogs up to 50 pounds for an additional fee of $20 per night per

pet. 2 dogs may be allowed.

Best Western John Day Inn
315 W Main Street
John Day, OR
541-575-1700 (800-780-7234)
Dogs of all sizes are allowed. Dogs are allowed for a pet fee.

Mountain View Motel and RV Park
83450 Joseph H
Joseph, OR
541-432-2982
Dogs of all sizes are allowed. There are no additional pet fees. There are some breed restrictions.

Best Western Klamath Inn
4061 S 6th Street
Klamath Falls, OR
541-882-1200 (800-780-7234)
Dogs of all sizes are allowed. Dogs are allowed for a pet fee of $10 per pet per night.

Cimarron Motor Inn
3060 S Sixth St
Klamath Falls, OR
541-882-4601
There is a $10 per night per room additional pet fee. Multiple dogs may be allowed.

CrystalWood Lodge
38625 Westside Road
Klamath Falls, OR
541-381-2322
Located in the Southern Oregon Cascades, this lodge welcomes all well-behaved dogs. There is no pet fee. Multiple dogs may be allowed.

Days Inn Klamath Falls
3612 South Sixth
Klamath Falls, OR
541-882-8864 (800-329-7466)
Dogs are welcome at this hotel.

Econo Lodge
75 Main St.
Klamath Falls, OR
541-884-7735 (877-424-6423)
Dogs of all sizes are allowed. Dogs are allowed for a pet fee of $10.00 per pet per stay.

Motel 6 - Klamath Falls
5136 6th St
Klamath Falls, OR
541-884-2110 (800-466-8356)
This motel welcomes your pets to stay with you.

Quality Inn
100 Main St.
Klamath Falls, OR
541-882-4666 (877-424-6423)

Dogs of all sizes are allowed. Dogs are allowed for a pet fee of $10.00 per pet per night. Two dogs are allowed per room.

Shilo Suites Hotel
2500 Almond St
Klamath Falls, OR
541-885-7980
There is a $25 one time fee per pet. 2 dogs may be allowed.

Super 8 Klamath Falls
3805 Hwy 97 N
Klamath Falls, OR
541-884-8880 (800-800-8000)
Dogs are welcome at this hotel.

Rodeway Inn
402 Adams Avenue
La Grande, OR
541-962-7143 (877-424-6423)
Dogs up to 80 pounds are allowed. Dogs are allowed for a pet fee of $10.00 per pet per stay. Two dogs are allowed per room.

Crowne Plaza Hotel Portland-Lake Oswego
14811 Kruse Oaks Drive
Lake Oswego, OR
503-624-8400 (877-270-6405)
Dogs of all sizes are allowed. Dogs are allowed for a pet fee of $25.00 per pet per night.

Lakeshore Inn
210 N. State Street
Lake Oswego, OR
503-636-9679 (800-215-6431)
thelakeshoreinn.com
This downtown Lake Oswego hotel allows dogs for $10 per night per dog. Pets receive a doggy basket on arrival for us during their stay.

Residence Inn Portland South/Lake Oswego
15200 SW Bangy Road
Lake Oswego, OR
503-684-2603 (800-331-3131)
Nestled away on 7 landscaped acres only minutes from all that downtown has to offer, this all suite hotel offers a number of in-house amenities that include a daily buffet breakfast and an evening reception Monday through Wednesday. Dogs are allowed for an additional pet fee of $10 per night per room for 1 to 5 days; a $50 one time fee per room for 6 to 11 nights; a $79 one time fee per room for 12 to 29 nights, and a $100 one time fee per room for 30 nights or more. Multiple dogs may be allowed.

Chinook Winds Casino Resort Hotel
1501 NW 40th Place
Lincoln City, OR
541-996-5825 (877-4BEACH1 (423-2241))
This hotel offers ocean front property located right next to the casino. They offer an indoor heated swimming pool, sauna, spa, a full service restaurant and lounge with live entertainment on weekends, and a complimentary shuttle to the casino. Dogs of all sizes are allowed for an additional pet fee of $20 per night per room. Dogs may not be left unattended, and they must be leashed and cleaned up after. Dogs are allowed in the front lobby and around most of the grounds. There are also special dog walk areas. Dogs are not allowed in the casino, the pool, or in food service areas.

Ester Lee Motel
3803 SW H 101
Lincoln City, OR
541-996-3606
Dogs are allowed in the cottages but not the motel. There is a $9 (+ tax) per night per pet fee and a pet policy to sign at check in. 2 dogs may be allowed.

Looking Glass Inn
861 SW 51st Street
Lincoln City, OR
541-996-3996 (800-843-4940)
lookingglass-inn.com
Located only steps from the ocean and a nice sandy beach, this inn is a welcoming place to begin exploring this scenic area. They offer in-room Jacuzzis and 1 and 2 bedroom suites. Dogs are welcome here and greeted by the resident pooches and given their own basket of goodies that include 2 dog sheets, a towel, food/water bowls, waste disposal bags, and doggy treats. There is an additional fee of $10 per night per pet.

Motel 6 - Lincoln City
3517 Highway 101
Lincoln City, OR
541-996-9900 (800-466-8356)
This motel welcomes your pets to stay with you.

Comfort Inn & Suites
2520 SE Stratus Avenue
McMinnville, OR
503-472-1700 (877-424-6423)
Dogs up to 50 pounds are allowed. Dogs are allowed for a pet fee of $10.00 per pet per night. Two dogs are allowed per room.

Red Lion
2535 NE Cumulus Avenue
McMinnville, OR
503-472-1500
There is a $20 one time pet fee per room. There are no additional pet fees for R&R members, and the R&R program is free to sign up. Multiple dogs may be allowed.

Best Western Vineyard Inn Motel
2035 S Highway 99W
Mcminnville, OR
503-472-4900 (800-780-7234)
Dogs of all sizes are allowed. Dogs are allowed for a nightly pet fee.

Best Western Horizon Inn
1154 E Barnett Road
Medford, OR
541-779-5085 (800-780-7234)
Dogs of all sizes are allowed. Dogs are allowed for a nightly pet fee.

Candlewood Suites Medford
3548 Heathrow Way
Medford, OR
541-772-2800 (877-270-6405)
Dogs up to 80 pounds are allowed. Pets allowed with an additional pet fee. Up to $75 for 1-6 nights and up to $150 for 7+ nights. A pet agreement must be signed at check-in.

Howard Johnson Medford
1015 S. Riverside Avenue
Medford, OR
541-773-8266 (800-446-4656)
Dogs of all sizes are allowed. Dogs are allowed for a pet fee of $15.00 per pet per night.

Motel 6 - Medford North
2400 Biddle Rd
Medford, OR
541-779-0550 (800-466-8356)
This motel welcomes your pets to stay with you.

Motel 6 - Medford South
950 Alba Dr
Medford, OR
541-773-4290 (800-466-8356)
This motel welcomes your pets to stay with you.

Quality Inn and Suites
1950 Biddle Road
Medford, OR
541-779-0050 (877-424-6423)
Dogs of all sizes are allowed. Two dogs are allowed per room.

Ramada and Convention Center
Medford
2250 Biddle Road

Medford, OR
541-779-3141 (800-272-6232)
Dogs of all sizes are allowed. Dogs are allowed for a pet fee.

Red Lion
200 N Riverside Avenue
Medford, OR
541-779-5811
There is a $20 one time pet fee per room. There are no additional pet fees for R&R members, and the R&R program is free to sign up. Multiple dogs may be allowed.

Reston Hotel
2300 Crater Lake Hwy
Medford, OR
541-779-3141
restonhotel.com/
There is a $20 one time pet fee. Multiple dogs may be allowed.

TownePlace Suites Medford
1395 Center Drive
Medford, OR
541-842-5757 (800-257-3000)
Besides offering a number of in-house amenities for all level of travelers, this all suite inn also offers a convenient location to historic, business, shopping, dining, entertainment, and recreation areas. Dogs are allowed for an additional fee of $25 per night up to a maximum fee of $75 per room. Multiple dogs may be allowed.

Travelodge OR Medford
954 Alba Drive
Medford, OR
541-773-1579 (800-578-7878)
Dogs of all sizes are allowed. Dogs are allowed for a pet fee of $5.00 per pet per night.

Sweet Virginia's Bed and Breakfast
407 6th Street
Metolius, OR
541-546-3031
The house was built in 1915 at a time when Metolius, Oregon was a booming railroad town. The city is smaller now. Three guest rooms are available. Well-behaved dogs are welcome and the owners have two dogs on the property. They have two large fenced yards. Dog beds and other supplies are available.

Cooper Spur Mountain Resort
10755 Cooper Spur Rd
Mount Hood, OR
541-352-6692
cooperspur.com
There are only 2 pet friendly cabins available here so early reservations

are recommended. There is a $35 per night per pet fee. 2 dogs may be allowed.

Terimore Lodging by the Sea
5105 Crab Avenue
Netarts Bay, OR
503-842-4623 (800-635-1821)
oregoncoast.com/terimore/
Located off the beaten path, and in one of the most beautiful areas along the coast, this inn offers ocean views, TV with HBO/ESPN, and some of the units have kitchens and fireplaces. Dogs of all sizes are allowed for an additional fee of $7 per night for one dog and $10 per night for two dogs. Dogs may only be left for a short time if they will be quiet, well behaved, and a contact number is left with the front desk. Dogs must be leashed and cleaned up after at all times. 2 dogs may be allowed.

Travelodge Suites Newberg
2816 Portland Rd
Newberg, OR
503-537-5000 (800-578-7878)
Dogs are welcome at this hotel.

Best Western Agate Beach Inn
3019 N Coast Highway
Newport, OR
541-265-9411 (800-780-7234)
Dogs are welcome at this hotel.

Econo Lodge
606 SW Coast Hwy 101
Newport, OR
541-265-7723 (877-424-6423)
Dogs up to 200 pounds are allowed. Dogs are allowed for a pet fee of $10.00 per pet per stay.

Hallmark Resort
744 SW Elizabeth St
Newport, OR
541-265-2600
ohwy.com/or/h/hallresn.htm
There is a $20 per day per pet fee, Dogs are allowed on the first floor only. Multiple dogs may be allowed.

Hallmark Resort Newport
744 SW Elizabeth Street
Newport, OR
541-265-2600 (888-448-4449)
Although offering premium oceanside lodging with many amenities, Mother Nature supplies the best amenity here with dramatic sunrises and sunsets, a wide beautiful beach, and a view of the Yaquina Head Lighthouse to the north. Dogs are allowed for an additional fee of $15 per night per

pet, and with advance registration a special pet amenity package will await the lucky pooch. There are 2 pet walk areas; miles of pristine beach, a Dispoz-a-Scoop station at the top of the beach stairs and near the volleyball court, and a complete pet wash down station can be found at the west beach stairway. Dogs must be leashed when not romping on the beach, and they must be cleaned up after at all times. Multiple dogs may be allowed.

La Quinta Inn & Suites Newport
45 SE 32nd Street
Newport, OR
541-867-7727 (800-531-5900)
Dogs of all sizes are allowed. There are no additional pet fees. Dogs may not be left unattended, and they must be well behaved, leashed and cleaned up after. 2 dogs may be allowed.

Rogue Ales' House of Rogue
748 SW Bay Blvd
Newport, OR
541-265-3188
Dogs of all sizes are allowed. There are no additional pet fees. There are only 3 rooms available. 2 dogs may be allowed.

Shilo Oceanfront Resort
536 SW Elizabeth St
Newport, OR
541-265-7701
There is a $25 one time pet fee per room. 2 dogs may be allowed.

Holiday Inn Ontario
1249 Tapadera Ave.
Ontario, OR
541-889-8621 (877-270-6405)
Dogs of all sizes are allowed. Dogs are allowed for a pet fee.

Motel 6 - Ontario, Or
275 Ne 12th Street
Ontario, OR
541-889-6617 (800-466-8356)
This motel welcomes your pets to stay with you.

Rodeway Inn
615 East Idaho Avenue
Ontario, OR
541-889-9188 (877-424-6423)
Dogs of all sizes are allowed. Dogs are allowed for a pet fee of $5.00 per pet per night. Three or more dogs may be allowed.

Best Western Rivershore Hotel
1900 Clackamette Drive
Oregon City, OR

503-655-7141 (800-780-7234)
Dogs of all sizes are allowed. Dogs are allowed for a pet fee of $5 per pet per night.

Inn at Cape Kiwanda
33105 Cape Kiwanda Drive
Pacific City, OR
503-965-7001
There is a $20 per night per pet fee and a pet policy to sign at check in.

Best Western Pendleton Inn
400 SE Nye Avenue
Pendleton, OR
541-276-2135 (800-780-7234)
Dogs of all sizes are allowed. Dogs are allowed for a pet fee.

Econo Lodge
620 SW Tutuilla Road
Pendleton, OR
541-276-8654 (877-424-6423)
Dogs of all sizes are allowed.

Knights Inn Pendleton
105 SE Court Avenue
Pendleton, OR
541-276-3231 (800-843-5644)
Dogs of all sizes are allowed. Dogs are allowed for a nightly pet fee.

Motel 6 - Pendleton
325 Se Nye Ave
Pendleton, OR
541-276-3160 (800 466-8356)
Your pets are welcome to stay here with you.

Red Lion
304 SE Nye Avenue
Pendleton, OR
541-276-6111
There is a $20 one time pet fee per room. There are no additional pet fees for R&R members, and the R&R program is free to sign up. 2 dogs may be allowed.

Rodeway Inn
310 S E Dorion Avenue
Pendleton, OR
541-276-6231 (877-424-6423)
Dogs of all sizes are allowed. Dogs are allowed for a pet fee of $5.00 per pet per night. Two dogs are allowed per room.

Super 8 Pendleton
601 SE Nye Ave
Pendleton, OR
541-276-8881 (800-800-8000)
Dogs of all sizes are allowed. Dogs are allowed for a pet fee of $10.00 per pet per night. Three or more dogs may be allowed.

Travelodge OR Pendleton
411 Southwest Dorion Avenue
Pendleton, OR
541-276-7531 (800-578-7878)
Dogs of all sizes are allowed. Dogs
are allowed for a pet fee.

Best Western Inn at the Meadows
1215 N Hayden Meadows Drive
Portland, OR
503-286-9600 (800-780-7234)
Dogs of all sizes are allowed. Dogs
are allowed for a pet fee of $20 per
pet per night.

Best Western Pony Soldier Inn -
Airport
9901 NE Sandy Boulevard
Portland, OR
503-256-1504 (800-780-7234)
Dogs of all sizes are allowed. Dogs
are allowed for a pet fee.

Candlewood Suites Portland-Airport
11250 N.E. Holman
Portland, OR
503-255-4003 (877-270-6405)
Dogs up to 100 pounds are allowed.
Pets allowed with an additional pet
fee. Up to $75 for 1-6 nights and up
to $150 for 7+ nights. A pet
agreement must be signed at check-
in.

Days Inn /Gresham Portland
2261 NE 181ST Ave
Portland, OR
503-618-8400 (800-329-7466)
Dogs of all sizes are allowed. Dogs
are allowed for a pet fee of $15.00
per pet per night.

Extended Stay America Portland -
Gresham
17777 N.E. Sacramento St.
Portland, OR
503-661-0226 (800-804-3724)
One dog is allowed per suite. There
is a $25 per night additional pet fee
up to $150 for an entire stay.

Hilton Hotel
921 SW Sixth Avenue
Portland, OR
503-226-1611 (800-HILTONS (445-
8667))
A Green Seal Certified hotel, they
offer a number of on site amenities
for business and leisure travelers,
plus a convenient location to
business, shopping, dining, sites of
interest, and numerous
entertainment areas. Dogs up to 50
pounds are allowed for an additional
one time pet fee of $25 per room. 2
dogs may be allowed.

Holiday Inn Portland-Airport (I-205)
8439 NE Columbia Blvd.
Portland, OR
503-256-5000 (877-270-6405)
Dogs of all sizes are allowed. Dogs
are allowed for a pet fee of $25.00
per pet per stay.

Hotel Lucia
400 SW Broadway
Portland, OR
503-228-7221
There is a $45 non-refundable one
time fee per pet. There may also be
an additional pet fee per day.
Multiple dogs may be allowed.

Hotel Monaco Portland
506 S.W. Washington
Portland, OR
503-222-0001
monaco-portland.com
Well-behaved dogs of all sizes are
welcome at this pet-friendly hotel.
The luxury boutique hotel offers
both rooms and suites. Hotel
amenities include complimentary
evening wine service, and a 24 hour
on-site fitness room. There are no
pet fees, just sign a pet liability
form.

Hotel Vintage Plaza
422 SW Broadway
Portland, OR
503-228-1212
vintageplaza.com/
Well-behaved dogs of all sizes are
welcome at this pet-friendly hotel.
The luxury boutique hotel offers
both rooms and suites. Hotel
amenities include complimentary
evening wine service,
complimentary high-speed Internet
access in all guest rooms, 24 hour
room service and an on-site fitness
room. There are no pet fees, just
sign a pet liability form.

Hotel deLuxe
729 SW 15th
Portland, OR
503-223-6311 (800-228-8657)
There is a is a $45 (+ tax) one time
pet fee per room. 2 dogs may be
allowed.

Howard Johnson Airport Portland
8247 NE Sandy Blvd
Portland, OR
503-256-4111 (800-446-4656)
Dogs are welcome at this hotel.

La Quinta Inn & Suites Portland
Airport
11207 NE Holman St.
Portland, OR

503-382-3820 (800-531-5900)
Dogs of all sizes are allowed. There
are no additional pet fees, but a
credit card must be on file. Dogs
must be quiet, leashed, cleaned up
after, and crated if left alone in the
room. Dogs are not allowed in the
pool or breakfast areas. Multiple
dogs may be allowed.

La Quinta Inn & Suites Portland
Northwest
4319 NW Yeon
Portland, OR
503-497-9044 (800-531-5900)
Dogs of all sizes are allowed. There
are no additional pet fees. Dogs
must be leashed, cleaned up after,
and the Do Not Disturb sign on the
door if there is a pet alone in the
room. Multiple dogs may be allowed.

La Quinta Inn Portland Convention
Center
431 NE Multnomah
Portland, OR
503-233-7933 (800-531-5900)
Dogs of all sizes are allowed. There
are no additional pet fees. Dogs
must be leashed and cleaned up
after. Dogs must be crated if left
alone in the room. Multiple dogs may
be allowed.

Motel 6 - Portland Mall 205
9225 Se Stark St
Portland, OR
503-255-0808 (800-466-8356)
This motel welcomes your pets to
stay with you.

Motel 6 - Portland Central
3104-06 Se Powell Blvd
Portland, OR
503-238-0600 (800-466-8356)
This motel welcomes your pets to
stay with you.

Motel 6 - Portland Downtown
518 Ne Holladay St.
Portland, OR
503-234-4391 (800-466-8356)
This motel welcomes your pets to
stay with you.

Motel 6 - Portland North
1125 Schmeer Rd
Portland, OR
503-247-3700 (800-466-8356)
This motel welcomes your pets to
stay with you.

Motel 6 - Portland, Or
18323 Se Stark Street
Portland, OR
503-491-4444 (800-466-8356)
This motel welcomes your pets to

stay with you.

Red Lion
1021 NE Grand Avenue
Portland, OR
503-235-2100
There is a $20 one time pet fee per room. There are no additional pet fees for R&R members, and the R&R program is free to sign up. 2 dogs may be allowed.

Residence Inn Portland Downtown/Lloyd Center
1710 NE Multnomah Street
Portland, OR
503-288-1400 (800-331-3131)
Only a mile from downtown, this all suite hotel gives a convenient location to business, shopping, dining, and entertainment areas, plus they also offer a number of in-house amenities, including a daily buffet breakfast and evening socials with light dinner fare 4 nights a week. Dogs are allowed for an additional one time pet fee of $75 per room. The fee is $100 for 3 pets. 2 dogs may be allowed.

Residence Inn Portland Downtown/RiverPlace
2115 SW River Parkway
Portland, OR
503-552-9500 (800-331-3131)
This downtown all suite hotel gives visitors a central location to a variety of businesses, universities, shopping, dining, and entertainment areas; plus, they also provides a number of in-house amenities, including a daily buffet breakfast and an evening social hour Monday to Wednesday with adult beverages. Dogs are allowed for an additional fee of $10 per night per pet. Multiple dogs may be allowed.

Residence Inn Portland North Harbour
1250 North Anchor Way
Portland, OR
503-285-9888 (800-331-3131)
Located only a short walk to the waterfront, this all suite hotel gives visitors a central location to a variety of businesses, universities, shopping, dining, and entertainment areas; plus, they also provides a number of in-house amenities, including a daily buffet breakfast and evening socials. Dogs are allowed for an additional one time pet fee of $75 per room. Multiple dogs may be allowed.

Sheraton Airport Hotel
8235 Northeast Airport Way

Portland, OR
503-281-2500 (888-625-5144)
Dogs of all sizes are allowed for an additional one time pet fee of $25 per room. Dogs may not be left alone in the room.

Staybridge Suites Portland-Airport
11936 NE Glenn Widing Road
Portland, OR
503-262-8888 (877-270-6405)
Dogs up to 80 pounds are allowed. Pets allowed with an additional pet fee. Up to $75 for 1-6 nights and up to $150 for 7+ nights. A pet agreement must be signed at check-in.

Super 8 Airport Portland
11011 NE Holman
Portland, OR
503-257-8988 (800-800-8000)
Dogs of all sizes are allowed. Dogs are allowed for a pet fee of $10.00 per pet per night.

The Benson Hotel
309 SW Broadway
Portland, OR
503-228-2000
Dogs up to 75 pounds are allowed. There is a $25 per night per pet additional fee.

The Mark Spencer Hotel
409 SW 11th Avenue
Portland, OR
503-224-3293
Dogs of all sizes are allowed. There is a $15 per night per pet additional fee.

The Westin Portland
750 Southwest Alder St.
Portland, OR
503-294-9000 (888-625-5144)
Dogs up to 50 pounds are allowed for no additional pet fee. Dogs may not be left alone in the room.

Travelodge Airport Portland
3828 NE 82nd Avenue
Portland, OR
503-256-2550 (800-578-7878)
Dogs of all sizes are allowed. Dogs are allowed for a nightly pet fee.

Best Western Prineville Inn
1475 NE 3rd Street
Prineville, OR
541-447-8080 (800-780-7234)
Dogs of all sizes are allowed. Dogs are allowed for a pet fee of $15.00 per pet per stay.

Econo Lodge
123 NE 3rd Street

Prineville, OR
541-447-6231 (877-424-6423)
Dogs of all sizes are allowed. Dogs are allowed for a pet fee of $10.00 per pet per stay. Two dogs are allowed per room.

Comfort Suites Airport
2243 SW Yew Ave.
Redmond, OR
541-504-8900 (877-424-6423)
Dogs up to 50 pounds are allowed. Dogs are allowed for a pet fee of $25.00 per pet per stay.

Motel 6 - Redmond
2247 S. Us 97
Redmond, OR
541-923-2100 (800-466-8356)
This motel welcomes your pets to stay with you.

Sleep Inn & Suites
1847 N HWY 97
Redmond, OR
541-504-1500 (877-424-6423)
Dogs up to 50 pounds are allowed. Dogs are allowed for a pet fee of $10.00 per pet per night. Two dogs are allowed per room.

Super 8 Redmond
Hwy 97
Redmond, OR
541-548-8881 (800-800-8000)
Dogs of all sizes are allowed. Dogs are allowed for a pet fee.

Best Western Salbasgeon Inn & Suites of Reedsport
1400 Highway 101
Reedsport, OR
541-271-4831 (800-780-7234)
Dogs of all sizes are allowed. Dogs are allowed for a pet fee of $15.00 per pet per night.

Economy Inn
1593 Highway Ave 101
Reedsport, OR
541-271-3671
Dogs are allowed for an additional fee of $10 per night pet pet. 2 dogs may be allowed.

Best Western Rice Hill
621 John Long Road
Rice Hill, OR
541-849-3335 (800-780-7234)
Dogs of all sizes are allowed. Dogs are allowed for a pet fee of $10 per pet per night.

Comfort Inn
1539 Mullholland Dr.
Roseburg, OR
541-957-1100 (877-424-6423)

Dogs of all sizes are allowed. Dogs are allowed for a pet fee of $15.00 per pet per night. Two dogs are allowed per room.

Motel 6 - Roseburg
3100 Nw Aviation Dr
Roseburg, OR
541-464-8000 (800-466-8356)
This motel welcomes your pets to stay with you.

Quality Inn Central
427 NW Garden Valley Blvd.
Roseburg, OR
541-673-5561 (877-424-6423)
Dogs of all sizes are allowed. Dogs are allowed for a pet fee of $10.00 per pet per night.

Sleep Inn & Suites
2855 N.W. Edenbower Blvd.
Roseburg, OR
541-464-8338 (877-424-6423)
Dogs of all sizes are allowed.

Super 8 Roseburg
3200 North West Aviation Drive
Roseburg, OR
541-672-8880 (800-800-8000)
Dogs of all sizes are allowed. Dogs are allowed for a pet fee.

Travelodge Roseburg
315 West Harvard Ave
Roseburg, OR
541-672-4836 (800-578-7878)
Dogs of all sizes are allowed. Dogs are allowed for a pet fee of $10 per pet per stay.

Windmill Inn
1450 NW Mulholland Drive
Roseburg, OR
541-673-0901
Dogs of all sizes are allowed. There is a pet policy to sign at check in and there are no additional pet fees.

Best Western Oak Meadows Inn
585 S Columbia River Highway
Saint Helens, OR
503-397-3000 (800-780-7234)
Dogs are welcome at this hotel.

Best Western Black Bear Inn
1600 Motor Ct NE
Salem, OR
503-581-1559 (800-780-7234)
Dogs of all sizes are allowed. Dogs are allowed for a pet fee of $10.00 per pet per night.

Best Western Mill Creek Inn
3125 Ryan Drive SE
Salem, OR
503-585-3332 (800-780-7234)

Dogs of all sizes are allowed. Dogs are allowed for a pet fee.

Best Western Pacific Highway Inn
4646 Portland Road NE
Salem, OR
503-390-3200 (800-780-7234)
Dogs of all sizes are allowed. Dogs are allowed for a pet fee.

Comfort Suites Airport
630 Hawthorne SE
Salem, OR
503-585-9705 (877-424-6423)
Dogs up to 50 pounds are allowed. Dogs are allowed for a pet fee of $10.00 per pet per night. Two dogs are allowed per room.

Howard Johnson Inn OR Salem
2250 Mission St. SE
Salem, OR
503-375-7710 (800-446-4656)
Dogs of all sizes are allowed. Dogs are allowed for a pet fee of $15.00 per pet per night.

Motel 6 - Salem
1401 Hawthorne Ave Ne
Salem, OR
503-371-8024 (800-466-8356)
This motel welcomes your pets to stay with you.

Red Lion
3301 Market Street
Salem, OR
503-370-7888
There is a $20 one time pet fee per room. There are no additional pet fees for R&R members, and the R&R program is free to sign up. Multiple dogs may be allowed.

Residence Inn Salem
640 Hawthorne Avenue SE
Salem, OR
503-585-6500 (800-331-3131)
The Willamette University, the Salem Hospital, the state Fairgrounds, the Oregon National Guard Training Facility, the Willamette River and the Waterfront Park are just a few of the sites close to this all suite, upscale hotel. They also offer a daily buffet breakfast and evening socials Monday to Wednesday. Dogs are allowed for an additional one time pet fee of $100 per room. Multiple dogs may be allowed.

Super 8 Salem
1288 Hawthorne NE
Salem, OR
503-370-8888 (800-800-8000)
Dogs are welcome at this hotel.

Travelodge Salem
1555 State Street
Salem, OR
503-581-2466 (800-578-7878)
Dogs of all sizes are allowed. Dogs are allowed for a pet fee.

Best Western Sandy Inn
37465 Highway 26
Sandy, OR
503-668-7100 (800-780-7234)
Dogs of all sizes are allowed. Dogs are allowed for a nightly pet fee.

Best Western Ocean View Resort
414 N Prom
Seaside, OR
503-738-3334 (800-780-7234)
Dogs are welcome at this hotel.

Comfort Inn & Suites by Seaside Convention Center/Boardwalk
545 Broadway Ave.
Seaside, OR
503-738-3011 (877-424-6423)
Dogs up to 50 pounds are allowed. Dogs are allowed for a pet fee of $25.00 per pet per night.

Inn at Seaside
441 Second Ave
Seaside, OR
503-738-9581 (800-699-5070)
seasideccinn.com/
There is a $15 per day per pet charge. This fee includes a pet amenity basket with towels, bowls, and treats. Multiple dogs may be allowed.

Motel 6 - Seaside
2369 Roosevelt Dr
Seaside, OR
503-738-6269 (800-466-8356)
This motel welcomes your pets to stay with you.

Best Western Ponderosa Lodge
505 Highway 20 W
Sisters, OR
541-549-1234 (800-780-7234)
Dogs of all sizes are allowed. Dogs are allowed for a pet fee of $15 per pet per night.

Best Western Grand Manor Inn
971 Kruse Way
Springfield, OR
541-726-4769 (800-780-7234)
Dogs of all sizes are allowed. Dogs are allowed for a nightly pet fee.

Comfort Suites
969 Kruse Way
Springfield, OR
541-746-5359 (877-424-6423)

Dogs of all sizes are allowed. Dogs are allowed for a pet fee of $25.00 per pet per night.

Holiday Inn Express Hotel & Suites Eugene/Springfield-East (I-5)
3480 Hutton Street
Springfield, OR
541-746-8471 (877-270-6405)
Dogs of all sizes are allowed. Dogs are allowed for a nightly pet fee.

Motel 6 - Eugene North Springfield
3752 International Ct
Springfield, OR
541-741-1105 (800-466-8356)
This motel welcomes your pets to stay with you.

Quality Inn & Suites
3550 Gateway Street
Springfield, OR
541-726-9266 (877-424-6423)
Dogs of all sizes are allowed. Dogs are allowed for a pet fee of $5.00 per pet per night.

Super 8 /Eugene Springfield
3315 Gateway
Springfield, OR
541-746-1314 (800-800-8000)
Dogs of all sizes are allowed. Dogs are allowed for a pet fee of $22.00 per pet per night.

Rodeway Inn & Suites
300 Sublimity
Sublimity, OR
503-769-9579 (877-424-6423)
Dogs up to 60 pounds are allowed. Dogs are allowed for a pet fee of $10.00 per pet per night. Two dogs are allowed per room.

Bennington Properties Sunriver & Caldera Springs
56842 Venture Lane
Sunriver, OR
541-593-6300 (866-623-5202)
Dogs are welcome at over 100 dog-friendly vacation rental properties managed by this firm. The properties are in Sunriver and Caldera Springs.

Sunray Vacation Rentals
Call to Arrange
Sunriver, OR
541-593-3225 (800-531-1130)
sunrayinc.com
These vacation properties allow pets for a $25 fee per pet. Some homes have limits on the size and quantity of pets so be sure and check when making reservations.

Sunset Realty
56805 Ventura Lane

Sunriver, OR
541-593-5018 (800-541-1756)
sunriverlodging.com/
This realty company offers dozens of pet friendly, fully-furnished vacation homes and condos in the Sunriver resort area of Oregon. They feature many different amenities such as private hot tubs, pool/foos tables, barbecues, fireplaces with supplies, phones in all units, cable TV, and completely equipped kitchens. Dogs are allowed for an additional fee of $10 per night per pet. Dogs must be well mannered, leashed, and cleaned up after. 2 dogs may be allowed.

Comfort Inn Columbia Gorge
351 Lone Pine Drive
The Dalles, OR
541-298-2800 (877-424-6423)
Dogs of all sizes are allowed. Dogs are allowed for a pet fee of $10.00 per pet per night.

Motel 6 - The Dalles
2500 6th St
The Dalles, OR
541-296-1191 (800-466-8356)
This motel welcomes your pets to stay with you.

Super 8 OR The Dalles
609 Cherry Heights Road
The Dalles, OR
541-296-6888 (800-800-8000)
Dogs of all sizes are allowed. Dogs are allowed for a nightly pet fee.

The Dalles Inn
112 W 2nd Street
The Dalles, OR
541-296-9107 (888-935-2378)
thedallesinn.com
This upscale hotel is located in the downtown district of The Dalles. Dogs of all sizes are allowed. There is a $10 per night pet fee per dog. Pets may not be left uncrated alone in the rooms. 2 dogs may be allowed.

Embassy Suites
9000 SW Washington Square Road
Tigard, OR
503-644-4000 (800-EMBASSY (362-2779))
Only minutes from downtown and one of the city's largest hotels, they offer full service, upscale accommodations, and a number of on site amenities for business and leisure travelers, plus a convenient location to business, shopping, dining, and entertainment areas. They also offer a complimentary cooked-to-order breakfast and a

Manager's reception every evening. Dogs are allowed for an additional one time pet fee of $49 per night per room. 2 dogs may be allowed.

Homestead Studio Suites Portland - Tigard
13009 S.W. 68th Pkwy.
Tigard, OR
503-670-0555 (800-804-3724)
One dog is allowed per suite. There is a $25 per night additional pet fee up to $150 for an entire stay.

Motel 6 - Portland Tigard West, Or
17959 Sw Mcewan Road
Tigard, OR
503-684-0760 (800-466-8356)
This motel welcomes your pets to stay with you.

Motel 6 - Portland South Lake Oswego Tigard
17950 Sw. Mcewan Rd
Tigard, OR
503-620-2066 (800-466-8356)
This motel welcomes your pets to stay with you.

Comfort Inn & Suites-Columbia Gorge West
477 NW Phoenix Drive
Troutdale, OR
503-669-6500 (877-424-6423)
Dogs of all sizes are allowed. Dogs are allowed for a pet fee of $10.00 per pet per night. Two dogs are allowed per room.

Holiday Inn Express Portland-East (Troutdale)
1000 NW Graham Road
Troutdale, OR
503-492-2900 (877-270-6405)
Dogs up to 50 pounds are allowed. Dogs are allowed for a pet fee of $10 per pet per night.

Motel 6 - Portland East Troutdale
1610 Nw. Frontage Rd
Troutdale, OR
503-665-2254 (800-466-8356)
This motel welcomes your pets to stay with you.

Comfort Inn & Suites
7640 SW Warm Springs Street
Tualatin, OR
503-612-9952 (877-424-6423)
100 percent non-smoking hotel. Bringing you the comforts of your home away from home, the Comfort Inn and Suites delivers.

Shilo Inn
1609 E Harbor Drive
Warrenton, OR

503-861-2181 (800-222-2244)
There is a $25 one time pet fee per room. Multiple dogs may be allowed.

Days Inn And Suites Wilsonville
8855 SW Citizens Drive
Wilsonville, OR
503-682-9000 (800-329-7466)
Dogs of all sizes are allowed. Dogs are allowed for a pet fee of $15.00 per pet per stay.

Holiday Inn Portland- I-5 S (Wilsonville)
25425 SW 95th Ave
Wilsonville, OR
503-682-2211 (877-270-6405)
Dogs of all sizes are allowed. Dogs are allowed for a nightly pet fee.

La Quinta Inn Wilsonville
8815 SW Sun Place
Wilsonville, OR
503-682-3184 (800-531-5900)
Dogs of all sizes are allowed. There are no additional pet fees. Dogs must be leashed, cleaned up after, and crated for housekeeping. Multiple dogs may be allowed.

Super 8 Wilsonville
25438 SW Parkway Ave
Wilsonville, OR
503-682-2088 (800-800-8000)
Dogs are welcome at this hotel.

La Quinta Inn & Suites Woodburn
120 Arney Rd NE
Woodburn, OR
503-982-1727 (800-531-5900)
Dogs of all sizes are allowed. There are no additional pet fees. Dogs must be leashed and cleaned up after. Dogs may only be left alone in the room if they will be quiet and well behaved, and they must be crated. Multiple dogs may be allowed.

Super 8 Woodburn
821 Evergreen Road
Woodburn, OR
503-981-8881 (800-800-8000)
Dogs of all sizes are allowed. Dogs are allowed for a pet fee of $10 per pet per stay.

Adobe Resort
1555 US 101
Yachats, OR
541-547-3141
adoberesort.com/
There is a $10 per day per pet charge. Multiple dogs may be allowed.

Deane's Oceanfront Lodge
7365 Hwy 101 N

Yachats, OR
541-547-3321
deaneslodge.com
There are a number of pet-friendly rooms for a pet fee of $10 per visit.

Fireside Motel
1881 Hwy 101 North
Yachats, OR
541-547-3636 (800-336-3573)
firesidemotel.com
There is a $9 per day per pet charge. Dogs cannot be left unattended in the room. All rooms are non-smoking.

See Vue Hotel
95590 H 101
Yachats, OR
541-547-3227
Dogs of all sizes are allowed. There is an $10 per night per pet additional fee. 2 dogs may be allowed.

Puerto Rico

La Cima Hotel Carr
H 110 KM 9.2
Aguadilla, PR
787-890-2016
lacimahotel.com/
Close to all the popular activities the island has to offer, this hotel also offers a number of on-site amenities including a lounge and pool with a barbecue area. One dog is allowed for an additional fee of $10 per night

Villa Montana Beach Resort
4466 KM 1.9 Interior Barrio Bajuras
Isabela, PR
888-780-9195
This lush, eco-friendly hotel features 3 miles of secluded beaches and 35 acres of tropical paradise. Dogs up to 80 pounds are allowed for an additional fee of $20 per night per pet with advance registration. The inn provides pet sheets, towels, and pet refuse disposal bags. Dogs must be quiet and well mannered at all times. Certain aggressively known breeds are not allowed. Dogs must be leashed and under their owner's control, and not left alone in the rooms. 2 dogs may be allowed.

Hotel Melia
Cristina Street #75
Ponce, PR
787-842-0260 (800-448-8355)
hotelmeliapr.com/index.php
Located in the town's historic district, this hotel can accommodate

the business or leisure traveler, plus they offer a great location to a number of nearby attractions. Very friendly dogs are allowed for no additional fee. Dogs must be quiet and well behaved. 2 dogs may be allowed.

Sheraton Old San Juan Hotel
100 Brumbaugh Street
San Juan, PR
787-721-5100 (888-625-5144)
This beautiful waterfront hotel offers old world appeal, modern amenities, and a great location to a number of nearby attractions, eateries, shops, and entertainment. Quiet, well behaved dogs are allowed for no additional fee; there is a pet agreement to sign at check in and a credit card must be on file. Dogs may not be left alone in the room, and they must be leashed and cleaned up after at all times. 2 dogs may be allowed.

Coqui Inn
36 Calle Mar Mediterraneo
Villamar - Isla Verde, PR
787-726-4330 (800-677-8860)
coqui-inn.com/
Three hotels combined here to create the Coqui Inn offering guests a larger variety of services and amenities. Dogs are allowed for an additional fee of $15 per night per pet. 2 dogs may be allowed.

Pennsylvania

Adamstown Inn
62 W Main Street
Adamstown, PA
717-484-0800 (800-594-4808)
adamstown.com/
Located in a premier antiques and recreational destination, and only 10 minutes from an outlet shopping Mecca, this garden inn offers 1 Victorian and 2 English style pet friendly cottages. Dogs of all sizes are allowed for an additional one time pet fee of $50. Dogs must be well behaved, housebroken, and leashed and cleaned up after. Dogs may not be left alone in the cottage at any time. 2 dogs may be allowed.

Black Forest Inn
500 Lancaster Ave
Adamstown, PA
717-484-4801
Large dogs are allowed for an additional fee of $10 per night per pet,,, small dogs are $7 per night per pet. 2 dogs may be allowed.

The Barnyard Inn
2145 Old Lancaster Pike
Adamstown, PA
717-484-1111 (888-738-6624)
barnyardinn.com/
Although quite an elegant inn, there really is a barnyard of farm animals and llamas here at this 150 year old restored German schoolhouse that sits on 2½ wooded acres in the heart of a busy antiquating area, and close to the Pennsylvania Dutch attractions. Dogs of all sizes are allowed in the Carriage House and the Chicken Coop (a cute new addition) for an additional one time pet fee of $20 per room. Dogs must be friendly to humans and the other animals on site, leashed, and cleaned up after. 2 dogs may be allowed.

The Boxwood
1320 Diamond Street
Akron, PA
717-859-3466 (800-238-3466)
theboxwoodinn.net/
Surrounded by wooded and well kept grounds, this renovated colonial stone farmhouse sits on over 3 acres, and is a graceful setting for the casual or business traveler, and for special events. Dogs of all sizes are allowed in the carriage house for an additional one time pet fee of $15 (not neutered is $15 per night per pet). Dogs must be well behaved, leashed, and cleaned up after. 2 dogs may be allowed.

Red Rose Inn
243 Meckesville Road
Albrightsville, PA
570-722-3526
theredroseinn.com/
Secluded, yet central to numerous recreational activities, this B&B sits surrounded by flourishing greenery, tall trees, and some beautiful walking paths. One dog is allowed for no additional pet fee. Dogs must be quiet, leased or crated, and cleaned up after.

Allenwood Motel
1058 Hausman Rd
Allentown, PA
610-395-3707
There is a $10 per day per pet fee. 2 dogs may be allowed.

Comfort Inn Lehigh Valley West
7625 Imperial Way
Allentown, PA
610-391-0344 (877-424-6423)
Dogs of all sizes are allowed. Dogs are allowed for a pet fee of $25.00

per pet per stay. Two dogs are allowed per room.

Four Points Sheraton Hotel & Suites Allentown Jetport
3400 Airport Road, Road #4
Allentown, PA
610-266-1000 (888-625-5144)
Dogs of all sizes are allowed. There is a $49 per stay additional pet fee per pet. This includes a pet care kit with a bed, treats and toys. Pets are restricted to 1st floor rooms only. Dogs are not allowed to be left alone in the room.

Holiday Inn Allentown Center City
904 West Hamilton St
Allentown, PA
610-433-2221 (877-270-6405)
Dogs of all sizes are allowed. Dogs are allowed for a pet fee of $50.00 per pet per stay.

Holiday Inn Allentown-I-78 (Lehigh Valley)
Rt. 100 At I-78 (Rt. 22)
Allentown, PA
610-391-1000 (877-270-6405)
Dogs of all sizes are allowed. Dogs are allowed for a pet fee of $49.00 per pet per stay.

Howard Johnson Inn and Suites - Dorney Park
3220 Hamilton Blvd/I-78
Allentown, PA
610-439-4000 (800-446-4656)
Dogs of all sizes are allowed. Dogs are allowed for a pet fee of $25.00 per pet per stay.

Knights Inn And Suites Allentown
1880 Steelstone Rd
Allentown, PA
610-266-9070 (800-843-5644)
Dogs are welcome at this hotel. There is a $25 per week additional pet fee.

Quality Inn
1715 Plaza Lane
Allentown, PA
610-435-7880 (877-424-6423)
Dogs of all sizes are allowed. Dogs are allowed for a pet fee of $30.00 per pet per night. Two dogs are allowed per room.

Red Roof Inn Allentown Airport
1846 Catasauqua Road
Allentown, PA
610-264-5404 (800-RED-ROOF)
One well-behaved family pet per room. Guest must notify front desk upon arrival. Guest is liable for any damages. In consideration of all

guests, pets must never be left unattended in the guest rooms.

Rodeway Inn Conference Center
1151 Bulldog Drive
Allentown, PA
610-395-3731 (877-424-6423)
Dogs of all sizes are allowed. Dogs are allowed for a pet fee of $15.00 per pet per night. Three or more dogs may be allowed.

Staybridge Suites Allentown Airprt Lehigh Valley
1787a Airport Road
Allentown, PA
610-443-5000 (877-270-6405)
Dogs up to 80 pounds are allowed. Pets allowed with an additional pet fee. Up to $75 for 1-6 nights and up to $150 for 7+ nights. A pet agreement must be signed at check-in.

Staybridge Suites Allentown West
327 Star Road
Allentown, PA
610-841-5100 (877-270-6405)
Dogs up to 80 pounds are allowed. Pets allowed with an additional pet fee. Up to $75 for 1-6 nights and up to $150 for 7+ nights. A pet agreement must be signed at check-in.

Econo Lodge
2906 Pleasant Valley Blvd.
Altoona, PA
814-944-3555 (877-424-6423)
Dogs of all sizes are allowed.

Motel 6 - Altoona
1500 Sterling Street
Altoona, PA
814-946-7601 (800-466-8356)
This motel welcomes your pets to stay with you.

Quality Inn
2915 Pleasant Valley Blvd
Altoona, PA
814-944-4581 (877-424-6423)
Dogs of all sizes are allowed. Dogs are allowed for a pet fee of $10.00 per pet per night. Two dogs are allowed per room.

Super 8 Altoona
3535 Fairway Dr
Altoona, PA
814-942-5350 (800-800-8000)
Dogs of all sizes are allowed. Dogs are allowed for a pet fee.

Comfort Inn
137 Gibb Road
Barkeyville, PA

814-786-7901 (877-424-6423)
Dogs of all sizes are allowed. Dogs are allowed for a pet fee of $10.00 per pet per stay.

Holiday Inn Beaver Falls (Pa Tpk Exit 13)
7195 Eastwood Road
Beaver Falls, PA
724-846-3700 (877-270-6405)
Dogs up to 100 pounds are allowed. Dogs are allowed for a pet fee of $35.00 per pet per stay.

Best Western Bedford Inn
4517 Business 220 Exit 146 PA Tpk
Bedford, PA
814-623-9006 (800-780-7234)
Dogs are welcome at this hotel. There is a $10 daily pet fee.

Quality Inn Bedford
4407 Business Route 220
Bedford, PA
814-623-5188 (877-424-6423)
Dogs up to 50 pounds are allowed. Dogs are allowed for a pet fee of $15.00 per pet per night. Two dogs are allowed per room.

Extended Stay America Philadelphia - Bensalem
3216 Tillman Dr.
Bensalem, PA
215-633-6900 (800-804-3724)
One dog is allowed per suite. There is a $25 per night additional pet fee up to $150 for an entire stay.

Holiday Inn Philadelphia NE - Bensalem
3499 Street Rd
Bensalem, PA
215-638-1500 (877-270-6405)
Dogs of all sizes are allowed. Dogs are allowed for a pet fee of $100.00 per pet per stay.

Sleep Inn & Suites
3427 Street Rd.
Bensalem, PA
215-244-2300 (877-424-6423)
Dogs of all sizes are allowed. Dogs are allowed for a pet fee of $10.00 per pet per night.

Residence Inn Philadelphia Valley Forge
600 W Swedesford Road
Berwyn, PA
610-640-9494 (800-331-3131)
Some of the amenities at this all-suite inn include a daily buffet breakfast, nightly socials, a heated swimming pool, and a complimentary grocery shopping service. Dogs are allowed for an additional one time

pet fee of $100 per room. Multiple dogs may be allowed.

Comfort Inn Midway
41 Diner Road
Bethel, PA
717-933-8888 (877-424-6423)
Dogs of all sizes are allowed. Dogs are allowed for a pet fee of $10.00 per pet per night. Two dogs are allowed per room.

Best Western Lehigh Valley Hotel & Conference Center
300 Gateway Drive
Bethlehem, PA
610-866-5800 (800-780-7234)
Dogs of all sizes are allowed. Dogs are allowed for a pet fee of $10.00 per pet per stay.

Comfort Inn
3191 Highfield Drive
Bethlehem, PA
610-865-6300 (877-424-6423)
Dogs of all sizes are allowed. Dogs are allowed for a pet fee of $10.00 per pet per night.

Comfort Suites University
120 W. Third St.
Bethlehem, PA
610-882-9700 (877-424-6423)
Dogs up to 100 pounds are allowed. Dogs are allowed for a pet fee of $10.00 per pet per night. Two dogs are allowed per room.

Extended Stay America Allentown - Bethlehem
3050 Schoenersville Rd.
Bethlehem, PA
610-866-8480 (800-804-3724)
One dog is allowed per suite. There is a $25 per night additional pet fee up to $150 for an entire stay.

Residence Inn Allentown Bethlehem
2180 Motel Drive
Bethlehem, PA
610-317-2662 (888-236-2427)
Only a mile from an international airport and the sights and activities of Lehigh Valley, this hotel gives a convenient location to business, shopping, dining, and entertainment areas, plus they offer a daily buffet breakfast, and a Manager's reception Monday through Thursday. Dogs are allowed for an additional pet fee of $75 per room for 1 to 4 days; 5 days or more the fee is $150 per room. 2 dogs may be allowed.

Best Western Inn at Blakeslee-Pocono

Route 115
Blakeslee, PA
570-646-6000 (800-780-7234)
Dogs are welcome at this hotel.

Econo Lodge
189 Columbia Mall Dr.
Bloomsburg, PA
570-387-0490 (877-424-6423)
Dogs of all sizes are allowed. Dogs are allowed for a pet fee of $15.00 per pet per night. Two dogs are allowed per room.

Best Western Bradford Inn
100 Davis Street
Bradford, PA
814-362-4501 (800-780-7234)
Dogs of all sizes are allowed. Dogs are allowed for a pet fee of $10.00 per pet per night.

Comfort Inn
76 Elm Street
Bradford, PA
814-368-6772 (877-424-6423)
Dogs of all sizes are allowed. Two dogs are allowed per room.

Best Western Plaza Inn
16407 Lincoln Highway
Breezewood, PA
814-735-4352 (800-780-7234)
Dogs of all sizes are allowed. Dogs are allowed for a nightly pet fee.

Howard Johnson Breezewood
16550 Lincoln Hwy
Breezewood, PA
814-735-2200 (800-446-4656)
Dogs are welcome at this hotel.

Ramada Breezewood
16620 Lincoln Highway
Breezewood, PA
814-735-4005 (800-272-6232)
Dogs of all sizes are allowed. Dogs are allowed for a pet fee.

Quality Inn
235 Allegheny Blvd.
Brookville, PA
814-849-8381 (877-424-6423)
Dogs of all sizes are allowed. Dogs are allowed for a pet fee of $15.00 per pet per stay. Three or more dogs may be allowed.

Super 8 Brookville
251 Alleghany Blvd PA SR 28
Brookville, PA
814-849-8840 (800-800-8000)
Dogs of all sizes are allowed. Dogs are allowed for a pet fee.

Travelodge Brookville
230 Allegheny Boulevard

Brookville, PA
814-849-8001 (800-578-7878)
Dogs of all sizes are allowed. Dogs are allowed for a pet fee of $10.00 per pet per stay.

Days Inn Conference Center Butler
139 Pittsburgh Rd
Butler, PA
724-287-6761 (800-329-7466)
Dogs of all sizes are allowed. Dogs are allowed for a nightly pet fee.

Super 8 Butler
138 Pittsburgh Road
Butler, PA
724-287-8888 (800-800-8000)
Dogs of all sizes are allowed. Dogs are allowed for a pet fee.

The Merry Inn
H 390
Canadensis, PA
570-595-2011 (800-858-4182)
themerryinn.com/
Nestled amongst lush greenery and towering trees, this mountain inn offers an outdoor hot tub on an upper deck facing the woods, and they sit central to a host of other activities and year round recreational pursuits. Dogs of all sizes are allowed for a one time additional pet fee of $22 per room. Dogs must be quiet, leashed, cleaned up after, and they may be left alone in the room only if the owner is confident in the pet's behavior. 2 dogs may be allowed.

Comfort Suites
10 S. Hanover Street
Carlisle, PA
717-960-1000 (877-424-6423)
Dogs up to 50 pounds are allowed. Dogs are allowed for a pet fee of $10.00 per pet per night. Two dogs are allowed per room.

Days Inn Carlisle
101 Alexander Spring Road
Carlisle, PA
717-258-4147 (800-329-7466)
Dogs of all sizes are allowed. Dogs are allowed for a nightly pet fee.

Howard Johnson Inn
1245 Harrisburg Pike
Carlisle, PA
717-243-5411 (800-446-4656)
Dogs of all sizes are allowed. Dogs are allowed for a nightly pet fee.

Motel 6 - Harrisburg Carlisle
1153 Harrisburg Pike
Carlisle, PA
717-249-7622 (800-466-8356)
This motel welcomes your pets to stay with you.

Pheasant Field
150 Hickorytown Road
Carlisle, PA
717-258-0717 (877-258-0717)
pheasantfield.com/
Pastoral fields, wooded and nature walks, a labyrinth, gardens, and a pond are all compliment to this 200 year old restored brick farmhouse, and they are also in an area famous for collector car shows. Dogs of all sizes are welcome in the Pet-sylvania Room for an additional pet fee of $10 per night per room. Dogs must be well behaved, leashed, cleaned up after, and crated when left alone in the room. Arrangements need to be made for housekeeping, and if the owner is confident in their pets behavior and housekeeping is done, pets may be in the room without being crated, just inform the front desk they are there. Multiple dogs may be allowed.

Quality Inn
1255 Harrisburg Pike
Carlisle, PA
717-243-6000 (877-424-6423)
Dogs of all sizes are allowed. Dogs are allowed for a pet fee of $10.00 per pet per night. Two dogs are allowed per room.

Ramada Limited Carlisle
1252 Harrisburg Pike
Carlisle, PA
717-243-8585 (800-272-6232)
Dogs of all sizes are allowed. Dogs are allowed for a pet fee.

Residence Inn Harrisburg Carlisle
1164 Harrisburg Pike
Carlisle, PA
717-610-9050 (800-331-3131)
This all suite inn features a convenient location to local attractions, institutes of learning, business, shopping, dining, and entertainment areas, plus they also offer a number of in-house amenities, including a daily buffet breakfast and themed evening socials. Dogs are allowed for an additional one time pet fee of $75 per room. Multiple dogs may be allowed.

Rodeway Inn
1239 Harrisburg Pike
Carlisle, PA
717-249-2800 (877-424-6423)
Dogs of all sizes are allowed. Dogs are allowed for a pet fee of $12.00 per pet per night.

Sleep Inn
5 East Garland Drive
Carlisle, PA
717-249-8863 (877-424-6423)
Dogs of all sizes are allowed. Dogs are allowed for a pet fee of $usd per pet per night. Two dogs are allowed per room.

Super 8 North Carlisle
1800 Harrisburg pike
Carlisle, PA
717-249-7000 (800-800-8000)
Dogs of all sizes are allowed. Dogs are allowed for a pet fee of $10.00 per pet per night.

Super 8 -South Carlisle
100 Alexander Spring Rd
Carlisle, PA
717-245-9898 (800-800-8000)
Dogs of all sizes are allowed. Dogs are allowed for a pet fee.

Extended Stay America Pittsburgh - Carnegie
520 N. Bell Ave.
Carnegie, PA
412-278-4001 (800-804-3724)
One dog is allowed per suite. There is a $25 per night additional pet fee up to $150 for an entire stay.

The Pennsbury Inn
883 Baltimore Pike/H1
Chadds Ford, PA
610-388-1435
pennsburyinn.com/
Rich in colonial heritage and country charm, and listed on the National Register of Historic Places, this inn, surrounded by lush greenery and award winning gardens, serves also for a good starting point to several other activities and historic sites. Dogs of all sizes are allowed for an additional fee of $15 to $20 per pet, depending on size/hair. Dogs must be quiet, very well mannered, leashed and cleaned up after, and crated when left alone in the room. 2 dogs may be allowed.

Best Western Chambersburg
211 Walker Road
Chambersburg, PA
717-262-4994 (800-780-7234)
Dogs of all sizes are allowed. Dogs are allowed for a pet fee of $9.00 per pet per night.

Comfort Inn
3301 Black Gap Rd.
Chambersburg, PA
717-263-6655 (877-424-6423)
Dogs of all sizes are allowed. Two

dogs are allowed per room.

Days Inn Chambersburg
30 Falling Spring Road
Chambersburg, PA
717-263-1288 (800-329-7466)
Dogs are welcome at this hotel.

Econo Lodge
1110 Sheller Ave.
Chambersburg, PA
717-264-8005 (877-424-6423)
Dogs of all sizes are allowed. Dogs
are allowed for a pet fee of $10.00
per pet per night.

Travelodge Chambersburg
565 Lincoln Way East
Chambersburg, PA
717-264-4187 (800-578-7878)
Dogs are welcome at this hotel.

Hamanassett B&B and Carriage
House
Indian Springs Drive
Chester Heights, PA
610-459-3000 (877-836-8212)
hamanassett.com
Blending old world charm and
elegance with modern-day comforts,
this 1856 English country-style home
and estate offers guests exceptional
dining, landscaped grounds
complete with forested areas, green
pastures, and koi ponds, and a
convenient location to several other
local attractions. Dogs of all sizes are
welcome for an additional fee of $25
per night per pet. One dog is allowed
per room in the house area, and up
to 3 dogs are allowed in the carriage
house, which also has a yard. Dogs
must be well mannered, leashed,
and cleaned up after at all times.

Comfort Inn
129 Dolby St.
Clarion, PA
814-226-5230 (877-424-6423)
Dogs of all sizes are allowed. Dogs
are allowed for a pet fee of $10.00
per pet per night. Two dogs are
allowed per room.

Holiday Inn Clarion
45 Holiday Inn Road
Clarion, PA
814-226-8850 (877-424-6423)
Dogs of all sizes are allowed. Dogs
are allowed for a pet fee of $10.00
per pet per night.

Quality Inn & Suites
24 United Drive
Clarion, PA
814-226-8682 (877-424-6423)
Dogs of all sizes are allowed. Dogs

are allowed for a pet fee of
$5.00/pet per pet per night. Two
dogs are allowed per room.

Super 8 Clarion
135 Hotel Dr
Clarion, PA
814-226-4550 (800-800-8000)
Dogs are welcome at this hotel.

Comfort Inn
811 Northern Blvd.
Clarks Summit, PA
570-586-9100 (877-424-6423)
Dogs of all sizes are allowed. Dogs
are allowed for a pet fee of $10.00
per pet per night. Two dogs are
allowed per room.

Econo Lodge
649 Northern Blvd
Clarks Summit, PA
570-586-1211 (877-424-6423)
Dogs of all sizes are allowed. Dogs
are allowed for a pet fee of $10.00
per pet per night. Two dogs are
allowed per room.

Ramada Hotel Clarks Summit
820 Northern Blvd.
Clarks Summit, PA
570-586-2730 (800-272-6232)
Dogs are welcome at this hotel.

Days Inn Clearfield
14451 Clearfield Shawville Hwy
Clearfield, PA
814-765-5381 (800-329-7466)
Dogs of all sizes are allowed. Dogs
are allowed for a pet fee.

Super 8 Clearfield
14597 Clearfield Shawville Hwy
Clearfield, PA
814-768-7580 (800-800-8000)
Dogs of all sizes are allowed. Dogs
are allowed for a pet fee of $5.00
per pet per night.

Victorian Loft
216 S Front Street
Clearfield, PA
814-765-4805 (800-798-0456)
victorianloft.com/
This beautiful 1894 Victorian home
sits along the river just a short walk
from the town and a variety of
activities, eateries, and recreation.
Dogs of all sizes are allowed for an
additional pet fee of $10 per night
for one dog, and if there are 2 dogs,
the second dog is an additional $5
per night. Dogs may not be left
alone in the room at any time, and
they must be leashed and cleaned
up after. 2 dogs may be allowed.

Residence Inn Philadelphia
Conshohocken
191 Washington Street
Conshohocken, PA
610-828-8800 (800-331-3131)
In addition to offering a convenient
location to business, historic,
shopping, dining, and entertainment
areas, this all suite hotel also
provides a number of in-house
amenities, including a daily buffet
breakfast and evening social hours.
Dogs are allowed for an additional
one time fee of $75 per pet. Multiple
dogs may be allowed.

Crowne Plaza Hotel Pittsburgh-Intl
Airport
1160 Thorn Run Road
Coraopolis, PA
412-262-2400 (877-270-6405)
Dogs of all sizes are allowed. Dogs
are allowed for a pet fee of $25 per
pet per night.

Embassy Suites
550 Cherrington Parkway
Coraopolis, PA
412-269-9070 (800-EMBASSY (362-
2779))
This upscale hotel offers a number of
on site amenities for business and
leisure travelers, plus a convenient
location to the Pittsburgh
International Airport, business,
shopping, dining, and entertainment
districts. They also offer a
complimentary cooked-to-order
breakfast and a Manager's reception
every evening. Dogs are allowed for
an additional one time fee of $50
to $75 per room depending on the
size of the pet. 2 dogs may be
allowed.

Marriott Pittsburgh Airport
777 Aten Road
Coraopolis, PA
412-788-8800 (800-328-9297)
Besides offering a number of in-
house amenities for all level of
travelers, this luxury hotel also
provides a convenient location to the
airport (5 miles), and major
businesses, shopping, dining, and
entertainment areas. Dogs up to 60
pounds are allowed for an additional
one time fee of $50 per room. 2 dogs
may be allowed.

Motel 6 - Pittsburgh Airport
1170 Thorn Run Road
Coraopolis, PA
412-269-0990 (800-466-8356)
This motel welcomes your pets to
stay with you.

Super 8 Pittsburgh Airport/ Area

Coraopolis
8991 University Blvd.
Coraopolis, PA
412-264-7888 (800-800-8000)
Dogs are welcome at this hotel.

Residence Inn Pittsburgh Cranberry
Township
1308 Freedom Road
Cranberry Township, PA
724-779-1000 (800-331-3131)
This all suite inn is located at the
Thorn Hill Industrial Park and some
of their amenities include a daily
buffet breakfast, evening socials, an
indoor swimming pool, and a
complimentary grocery shopping
service. Dogs are allowed for an
additional one time pet fee of $75 per
room. Multiple dogs may be allowed.

Red Roof Inn Pittsburgh North -
Cranberry Township
20009 US Rt 19 and Marguerite
Road
Cranberry Twp., PA
724-776-5670 (800-RED-ROOF)
One well-behaved family pet per
room. Guest must notify front desk
upon arrival. Guest is liable for any
damages. In consideration of all
guests, pets must never be left
unattended in the guest rooms.

Best Western Danville Inn
79 Old Valley School Road
Danville, PA
570-275-5750 (800-780-7234)
Dogs of all sizes are allowed. Dogs
are allowed for a pet fee of $15.00
per pet per night.

Days Inn Conference Center Danville
50 Sheraton Rd
Danville, PA
570-275-5510 (800-329-7466)
Dogs of all sizes are allowed. Dogs
are allowed for a pet fee of $25 per
pet per stay.

Quality Inn & Suites
15 Valley West Rd.
Danville, PA
570-275-5100 (877-424-6423)
Dogs up to 50 pounds are allowed.
Dogs are allowed for a pet fee of
$25.00 per pet per stay. Two dogs
are allowed per room.

Red Roof Inn Danville
300 Red Roof Road
Danville, PA
570-275-7600 (800-RED-ROOF)
One well-behaved family pet per
room. Guest must notify front desk
upon arrival. Guest is liable for any
damages. In consideration of all

guests, pets must never be left
unattended in the guest rooms.

Super 8 Danville
35 Sheraton Road
Danville, PA
570-275-4640 (800-800-8000)
Dogs of all sizes are allowed. Dogs
are allowed for a pet fee.

Super 8 Delmont
180 Sheffield Dr
Delmont, PA
724-468-4888 (800-800-8000)
Dogs are welcome at this hotel.

Comfort Inn
2017 N. Reading Road Bldg A
Denver, PA
717-336-4649 (877-424-6423)
Dogs of all sizes are allowed. Dogs
are allowed for a pet fee of $20.00
per pet per night.

Econo Lodge Inn & Suites
2017 N. Reading Rd. Bldg B
Denver, PA
717-336-7000 (877-424-6423)
Dogs up to 50 pounds are allowed.
Dogs are allowed for a pet fee of
$20.00 per pet per night. Two dogs
are allowed per room.

Holiday Inn Lancaster County
1 Denver Road
Denver, PA
717-336-7541 (877-270-6405)
Dogs are welcome at this hotel.
There is a $15 one time pet fee.

Residence Inn Scranton
947 Viewmont Drive
Dickson City, PA
570-343-5121 (800-331-3131)
This all suite inn features a
convenient location to business,
shopping, dining, and entertainment
areas, plus they also offer a number
of in-house amenities, including a
daily buffet breakfast and evening
socials. Dogs are allowed for an
additional one time pet fee of $100
per room. 2 dogs may be allowed.

Econo Lodge
387 Ben Franklin Hwy.
Douglassville, PA
610-385-3016 (877-424-6423)
Dogs of all sizes are allowed. Dogs
are allowed for a pet fee of $12.00
per pet per night.

Best Western Inn & Conference
Center
82 N Park Place
Dubois, PA
814-371-6200 (800-780-7234)

Dogs of all sizes are allowed. Dogs
are allowed for a pet fee of $12.00
per pet per night.

Days Inn -Scranton Dunmore
1226 O'Neil Highway
Dunmore, PA
570-348-6101 (800-329-7466)
Dogs are welcome at this hotel.

Sleep Inn & Suites Scranton
Dunmore
102 Monahan Ave
Dunmore, PA
570-961-1116 (877-424-6423)
Dogs up to 75 pounds are allowed.
Dogs are allowed for a pet fee of
$15.00 per pet per night.

Budget Inn and Suites
340 Greentree Drive
East Stroudsburg, PA
570-424-5451 (888-233-8144)
poconobudgetinn.com/
Dogs of all sizes are allowed for no
additional pet fees. A credit card
must be on file and there is a pet
waiver to sign at check in. Dogs must
be quiet, leashed or crated, cleaned
up after, and crated when left alone
in the room. Multiple dogs may be
allowed.

Super 8 Stroudsburg
I-80 Exit 308
East Stroudsburg, PA
570-424-7411 (800-800-8000)
Dogs of all sizes are allowed. Dogs
are allowed for a pet fee.

The Lafayette Inn
525 W Monroe Street
Easton, PA
610-253-4500 (800-509-6990)
lafayetteinn.com
This inn has a big wrap around
porch, is surrounded by trees and
gardens with a fountain, and serves
as a great home base to a variety of
activities, recreation, and historical
sites. Dogs of all sizes are allowed
for an additional fee of $20 per night
per pet; they provide treats, mat, a
towel, and clean-up bags. Dogs must
be leashed and cleaned up after at
all times, and crated when left alone
in the room. 2 dogs may be allowed.

Comfort Inn
111 Cook Rd.
Ebensburg, PA
814-472-6100 (877-424-6423)
Dogs of all sizes are allowed. Dogs
are allowed for a pet fee of $15.00
per pet per night. Two dogs are
allowed per room.

Comfort Inn
8051 Peach St.
Erie, PA
814-866-6666 (877-424-6423)
Dogs up to 125 pounds are allowed.
Dogs are allowed for a pet fee of
$15.00 per pet per night. Two dogs
are allowed per room.

Days Inn Erie
7415 Schultz Road
Erie, PA
814-868-8521 (800-329-7466)
Dogs of all sizes are allowed. Dogs
are allowed for a pet fee of $10.00
per pet per night.

Red Roof Inn Erie
7865 Perry Highway
Erie, PA
814-868-5246 (800-RED-ROOF)
One well-behaved family pet per
room. Guest must notify front desk
upon arrival. Guest is liable for any
damages. In consideration of all
guests, pets must never be left
unattended in the guest rooms.

Residence Inn Erie
8061 Peach Street
Erie, PA
814-864-2500 (800-331-3131)
In addition to being near various
business, shopping, dining, and
entertainment areas, this all suite
hotel is also connected to the states
largest indoor water park, and offers
amenities including a daily buffet
breakfast, and evening socials. Dogs
are allowed for an additional one
time pet fee of $75 per room. 2 dogs
may be allowed.

Riviera Motel
3107 W Lake Road
Erie, PA
814-838-1997
Dogs are allowed for $10 per pet for
the 1st night and $20 per pet for 2
days or more, and there is a pet
policy to sign at check in. Dogs must
be crated if left alone in the room.
Dogs are not allowed in Jacuzzi
rooms. 2 dogs may be allowed.

TownePlace Suites Erie
2090 Interchange Road
Erie, PA
814-866-7100 (800-257-3000)
In addition to offering a number of in-
house amenities for all level of
travelers, this all suite inn also
provides a central location to the
170+ store mall adjacent to the hotel,
several major companies, and to
some of the area's star attractions.
Dogs are allowed for an additional
one time fee of $100 per room. 2

dogs may be allowed.

Wingate by Wyndham - Erie
8060 Old Oliver Road
Erie, PA
814-860-3050 (800-228-1000)
Dogs are welcome at this hotel.

Golden Pheasant Inn
763 River Road/H 32S
Erwinna, PA
610-294-9595 (800-830-4474)
goldenpheasant.com/
This inn, sitting along the Delaware
Canal, specializes in French
cuisine, and in the spring they offer
cooking classes. There is a gated
cottage suite with a porch
overlooking the canal for guests
with pets, and dogs up to 55
pounds are allowed for an
additional pet fee of $25 per night
per pet. Dogs must be well
mannered, leashed, and cleaned up
after. 2 dogs may be allowed.

Motel 6 - Philadelphia Airport
Essington
43 Industrial Highway
Essington, PA
610-521-6650 (800-466-8356)
This motel welcomes your pets to
stay with you.

Red Roof Inn Philadelphia Airport
49 Industrial Highway
Essington, PA
610-521-5090 (800-RED-ROOF)
One well-behaved family pet per
room. Guest must notify front desk
upon arrival. Guest is liable for any
damages. In consideration of all
guests, pets must never be left
unattended in the guest rooms.

Extended Stay America
Philadelphia - Exton
877 N. Pottstown Pike (Rte. 100)
Exton, PA
610-524-7185 (800-804-3724)
One dog is allowed per suite. There
is a $25 per night additional pet fee
up to $150 for an entire stay.

Residence Inn Philadelphia Great
Valley/Exton
10 N Pottstown Pike
Exton, PA
610-594-9705 (800-331-3131)
Besides offering a convenient
location to historic sites, the
pastoral lands of the Amish, and the
King of Prussia Mall, this hotel also
provides a number of in-house
amenities, including a daily buffet
breakfast and evening social hours.
Dogs are allowed for an additional

one time pet fee of $100 per room.
Multiple dogs may be allowed.

Vacation Rental by Owner
5888 Path Valley Road
Fort Loudon, PA
717-369-3235
Dogs of all sizes are allowed. There
are no additional pet fees. They say
to bring your own bed and furniture
covers if your dog will be on them.

Best Western Fort Washington Inn
285 Commerce Drive
Fort Washington, PA
215-542-7930 (800-780-7234)
Dogs are welcome at this hotel.

Holiday Inn Philadelphia N-Fort
Washington
432 Pennsylvania Avenue
Fort Washington, PA
215-643-3000 (877-270-6405)
Dogs of all sizes are allowed. Dogs
are allowed for a pet fee.

Econo Lodge
501 S. Middle St.
Frackville, PA
570-874-3838 (877-424-6423)
Dogs of all sizes are allowed. Dogs
are allowed for a pet fee of $8.00 per
pet per night.

Super 8 Franklin
847 Allegheny Blvd
Franklin, PA
814-432-2101 (800-800-8000)
Dogs of all sizes are allowed. Dogs
are allowed for a pet fee.

Sheraton Great Valley Hotel
707 East Lancaster Ave, Route 202
& 30
Frazer, PA
610-524-5500 (888-625-5144)
Dogs up to 85 pounds are allowed.
There are no additional pet fees.
Dogs are not allowed to be left alone
in the room

America Best Inn
301 Steinwehr Avenue
Gettysburg, PA
717-334-1188
Friendly dogs of all sizes are
allowed. They say they prefer to take
only 2 dogs per room, but if well
behaved, will take up to 3 dogs.
There are no additional pet fees.

Battlefield Bed & Breakfast
2264 Emmitsburg Road
Gettysburg, PA
717-334-8804
gettysburgbattlefield.com
This 30 acre Civil War farm is

located on the Gettysburg Battlefield behind Big Round Top. There are 8 guest rooms. Friday nights feature ghost stories in the parlor. Dogs of all sizes are welcome.

Comfort Inn
871 York Rd.
Gettysburg, PA
717-337-2400 (877-424-6423)
Dogs of all sizes are allowed. Dogs are allowed for a pet fee of $10.00 per pet per night.

Motel 6 - Gettysburg, Pa
606 York Street
Gettysburg, PA
717-334-4274 (800-466-8356)
This motel welcomes your pets to stay with you.

Travelodge Gettysburg
613 Baltimore Street
Gettysburg, PA
717-334-9281 (800-578-7878)
Dogs of all sizes are allowed. Dogs are allowed for a pet fee.

Comfort Inn North
5137 SR 8
Gibsonia, PA
724-444-8700 (877-424-6423)
Dogs up to 50 pounds are allowed. Dogs are allowed for a pet fee of $10.00 per pet per night. Two dogs are allowed per room.

Staybridge Suites Wilmington - Brandywine Valley
400 Evergreen Dr.
Glen Mills, PA
610-358-2560 (877-270-6405)
Dogs up to 80 pounds are allowed. Pets allowed with an additional pet fee. Up to $75 for 1-6 nights and up to $150 for 7+ nights. A pet agreement must be signed at check-in.

Sweetwater Inn
50 Sweetwater Road
Glen Mills, PA
610-459-4711 (800-SWEETWATER (793-3892))
sweetwaterfarmbb.com/
This wooded 50 acre estate of lush greenery has some great hiking trails, features a golf green, Jacuzzi and pool, indoor and outdoor dining (when weather permits), a large patio and porch, and also serves as a good starting point to explore the attractions of Brandywine Valley. Dogs of all sizes are allowed in the cottages only for an additional fee of $35 per night per pet. Dogs must be well mannered, leashed, and cleaned

up after. Multiple dogs may be allowed.

Motel 6 - Gordonville
2959 Lincoln Hwy East
Gordonville, PA
717-687-3880 (800-466-8356)
This motel welcomes your pets to stay with you.

Days Inn Grantville
252 Bow Creek Rd
Grantville, PA
717-469-0631 (800-329-7466)
Dogs are welcome at this hotel.

Holiday Inn Harrisburg (Hershey Area) I-81
604 Station Rd.
Grantville, PA
717-469-0661 (877-270-6405)
Dogs of all sizes are allowed. Dogs are allowed for a pet fee of $25.00 per pet per night.

Comfort Inn
50 Pine Dr.
Greencastle, PA
717-597-8164 (877-424-6423)
Dogs of all sizes are allowed. Dogs are allowed for a pet fee of $15.00 per pet per night.

Four Points by Sheraton Greensburg
100 Sheraton Dr., Route 30 East
Greensburg, PA
724-836-6060 (888-625-5144)
Dogs of all sizes are allowed. There is a $10 per stay pet fee per pet. Dogs are not allowed to be left alone in the room.

Knights Inn Greensburg
1215 S. Main St
Greensburg, PA
724-836-7100 (800-843-5644)
Dogs are welcome at this hotel.

Old Arbor Rose
114 W Main Street
Grove City, PA
724-458-6425 (877 596-6767)
oldarborrosebnb.com/
This 1912 rambling house offers a hint of the sea in the décor, a full gourmet breakfast, a hot tub on a private deck, and they are central to a wide variety of activities, recreation, shops, and eateries. Dogs of all sizes are allowed for an additional fee of $10 per night per pet. Dogs must be well behaved, leashed, and cleaned up after. Multiple dogs may be allowed.

Rodeway Inn

1080 Carlisle Street
Hanover, PA
717-646-1000 (877-424-6423)
Dogs up to 50 pounds are allowed. Dogs are allowed for a pet fee of $20.00 per pet per night.

Best Western Harrisburg/Hershey Hotel & Suites
300 N Mountain Road
Harrisburg, PA
717-652-7180 (800-780-7234)
Dogs of all sizes are allowed. Dogs are allowed for a pet fee of $25.00 per pet per night.

Candlewood Suites Harrisburg
504 North Mountain Rd
Harrisburg, PA
717-652-7800 (877-270-6405)
Dogs up to 80 pounds are allowed. Pets allowed with an additional pet fee. Up to $75 for 1-6 nights and up to $150 for 7+ nights. A pet agreement must be signed at check-in.

Comfort Inn
7744 Linglestown Road
Harrisburg, PA
717-540-8400 (877-424-6423)
Dogs of all sizes are allowed. Dogs are allowed for a pet fee of $10.00 per pet per night.

Holiday Inn Express Harrisburg East
4021 Union Deposit Road
Harrisburg, PA
717-561-8100 (877-270-6405)
Dogs of all sizes are allowed. Dogs are allowed for a pet fee of $10.00 per pet per night.

Holiday Inn Harrisburg-East (Airport Area)
4751 Lindle Rd
Harrisburg, PA
717-939-7841 (877-270-6405)
Dogs of all sizes are allowed. Dogs are allowed for a pet fee of $25.00 per pet per night.

Howard Johnson Inn Hershey Harrisburg
7930 Linglestown Road
Harrisburg, PA
717-540-9100 (800-446-4656)
Dogs of all sizes are allowed. Dogs are allowed for a pet fee.

La Quinta Inn Harrisburg Airport/Hershey
990 Eisenhower Boulevard
Harrisburg, PA
717-939-8000 (800-531-5900)
Dogs of all sizes are allowed. There are no additional fees. Dogs must be

leashed and cleaned up after. Dogs must be crated if left unattended in the room, and removed or crated for housekeeping. Multiple dogs may be allowed.

Motel 6 - Harrisburg- Hershey Area Pa
1006 Briarsdale Road
Harrisburg, PA
717-564-2000 (800-466-8356)
This motel welcomes your pets to stay with you.

Red Roof Inn Harrisburg - Hershey
950 Eisenhower Boulevard
Harrisburg, PA
717-939-1331 (800-RED-ROOF)
One well-behaved family pet per room. Guest must notify front desk upon arrival. Guest is liable for any damages. In consideration of all guests, pets must never be left unattended in the guest rooms.

Red Roof Inn Harrisburg North
400 Corporate Circle
Harrisburg, PA
717-657-1445 (800-RED-ROOF)
One well-behaved family pet per room. Guest must notify front desk upon arrival. Guest is liable for any damages. In consideration of all guests, pets must never be left unattended in the guest rooms.

Residence Inn Harrisburg Hershey
4480 Lewis Road
Harrisburg, PA
717-561-1900 (800-331-3131)
This all suite hotel sits central to many of the city's star attractions, shopping, dining, and business areas, plus they offer a number of in-house amenities that include a daily buffet breakfast and evening socials Monday through Thursday with light dinner fare. Dogs are allowed for an additional one time pet fee of $100 per room. 2 dogs may be allowed.

Staybridge Suites Harrisburg
920 Wildwood Park Drive
Harrisburg, PA
717-233-3304 (877-270-6405)
Dogs up to 80 pounds are allowed. Pets allowed with an additional pet fee. Up to $75 for 1-6 nights and up to $150 for 7+ nights. A pet agreement must be signed at check-in.

Super 8 North Harrisburg
4125 N Front St
Harrisburg, PA
717-233-5891 (800-800-8000)
Dogs of all sizes are allowed. Dogs

are allowed for a pet fee of $10.00 per pet per night.

TownePlace Suites Harrisburg Hershey
450 Friendship Road
Harrisburg, PA
717-558-0200 (800-257-3000)
In addition to all the attractions and activities available to visitors in the country's chocolate capital, this all suite inn also offers several in-house amenities. Dogs are allowed for an additional one time fee of $100. 2 dogs may be allowed.

Motel 6 - Barkeyville, Pa
1010 Dholu Road
Harrisville, PA
814-786-8375 (800-466-8356)
This motel welcomes your pets to stay with you.

Falls Port Inn
330 Main Ave
Hawley, PA
570-226-2600
Large dogs are allowed in the larger rooms. There are no additional pet fees. Multiple dogs may be allowed.

Best Western Genetti Inn & Suites
1341 N Church Street
Hazle Township, PA
570-454-2494 (800-780-7234)
Dogs of all sizes are allowed. Dogs are allowed for a pet fee.

Hazelton Motor Inn
615 E Broad Street
Hazleton, PA
570-459-1451
hazletonmotorinn.com/
This motor inn sits central to a variety of activities and recreational opportunities. Dogs of all sizes are allowed for an additional fee of $5 per night per pet. Dogs must be leashed, cleaned up after, and they may only be left for a short time in the room if they will be quiet and well behaved. Guests with one dog may request a non-smoking room; guests with two or more dogs are placed in a smoking room. Multiple dogs may be allowed.

Ramada Hazleton
1213 North Church Street
Hazleton, PA
570-455-2061 (800-272-6232)
Dogs of all sizes are allowed. Dogs are allowed for a nightly pet fee.

Residence Inn Hazleton
1 Station Circle
Hazleton, PA

570-455-9555 (800-331-3131)
This all suite inn sits near a number of major companies and attractions, plus they also provide a number of in-house amenities, including a daily buffet breakfast and evening socials. Dogs are allowed for an additional one time pet fee of $100 per room. 2 dogs may be allowed.

Quality Inn
3200 South Hermitage Road
Hermitage, PA
724-981-1530 (877-424-6423)
Dogs up to 50 pounds are allowed. Dogs are allowed for a pet fee of $10.00 per pet per night. Two dogs are allowed per room.

Best Western Inn Hershey
Route 422 & Sipe Avenue
Hershey, PA
717-533-5665 (800-780-7234)
Dogs of all sizes are allowed. Dogs are allowed for a pet fee of $25.00 per pet per stay.

Days Inn Hershey
350 W Chocolate Ave
Hershey, PA
717-534-2162 (800-329-7466)
Dogs of all sizes are allowed. Dogs are allowed for a pet fee of $15.00 per pet per night.

Econo Lodge
115 Lucy Ave.
Hershey, PA
717-533-2515 (877-424-6423)
Dogs of all sizes are allowed. Two dogs are allowed per room.

Motel 6 - Hershey-grantville, Pa
1518 E. Chocolate Avenue
Hershey, PA
717-533-2384 (800-466-8356)
This motel welcomes your pets to stay with you.

Barley Sheaf Farm
5281 York Road/H 202/263
Holicong, PA
215-794-5104
barleysheaf.com/
Set in the heart of a cultural and historic region, this 100+ acre luxury estate contains woodlands, pastures, gardens, 2 ponds, picturesque walking paths, a junior Olympic swimming pool, and more. One dog of any size is allowed in the "Beggar on Horseback" room for an additional fee of $50 per night with advanced reservations, and there is a pet policy to sign at check in. Dogs must be well behaved, leashed and cleaned up after at all times, and

crated when left alone in the room.

Candlewood Suites Philadelphia-
Willow Grove
250 Business Center Drive
Horsham, PA
215-328-9119 (877-270-6405)
Dogs up to 80 pounds are allowed.
Pets allowed with an additional pet
fee. Up to $75 for 1-6 nights and up
to $150 for 7+ nights. A pet
agreement must be signed at check-
in.

Days Inn Horsham
245 Easton Road
Horsham, PA
215-674-2500 (800-329-7466)
Dogs are welcome at this hotel.

Extended Stay America Philadelphia
- Horsham
114 Welsh Rd.
Horsham, PA
215-784-9045 (800-804-3724)
One dog is allowed per suite. There
is a $25 per night additional pet fee
up to $150 for an entire stay.

Homestead Studio Suites
Philadelphia - Horsham - Willow
Grove
537 Dresher Rd.
Horsham, PA
215-956-9966 (800-804-3724)
One dog is allowed per suite. There
is a $25 per night additional pet fee
up to $150 for an entire stay.

Residence Inn Philadelphia Willow
Grove
3 Walnut Grove Drive
Horsham, PA
215-443-7330 (800-331-3131)
Some of the amenities at this all-
suite inn include a daily buffet
breakfast, evening socials, a heated
swimming pool, and a complimentary
grocery shopping service. Dogs are
allowed for an additional one time
pet fee of $150 per room. Multiple
dogs may be allowed.

TownePlace Suites Philadelphia
Horsham
198 Precision Drive
Horsham, PA
215-323-9900 (800-257-3000)
This all suite hotel sits central to a
number of sites of interest for both
business and leisure travelers; plus
they also offer a number of on-site
amenities to ensure comfort. Dogs
up to 80 pounds are allowed for an
additional one time fee of $75 per
room. 2 dogs may be allowed.

Holiday Inn Indiana
1395 Wayne Ave & Rt 422
Indiana, PA
724-463-3561 (877-270-6405)
Dogs up to 65 pounds are allowed.
Dogs are allowed for a nightly pet
fee.

Comfort Inn & Suites
455 Theatre Dr.
Johnstown, PA
814-266-3678 (877-424-6423)
Dogs of all sizes are allowed. Dogs
are allowed for a pet fee of $15.00
per pet per night. Two dogs are
allowed per room.

Econo Lodge
430 Napoleon Place
Johnstown, PA
814-536-1114 (877-424-6423)
Dogs of all sizes are allowed. Dogs
are allowed for a pet fee of $10.00
per pet per night.

Holiday Inn Express Johnstown
1440 Scalp Ave
Johnstown, PA
814-266-8789 (877-270-6405)
Dogs of all sizes are allowed. Dogs
are allowed for a pet fee of $25.00
per pet per stay.

Sleep Inn
453 Theatre Dr.
Johnstown, PA
814-262-9292 (877-424-6423)
Dogs of all sizes are allowed. Dogs
are allowed for a pet fee of $15.00
per pet per night.

Quality Inn
16 Marsanna Lane
Jonestown (Lebanon), PA
717-865-6600 (877-424-6423)
Dogs up to 50 pounds are allowed.
Dogs are allowed for a pet fee of
$10.00 per pet per night. Two dogs
are allowed per room.

Motel 6 - Philadelphia King Of
Prussia
815 West Dekalb Pike
King Of Prussia, PA
610-265-7200 (800-466-8356)
This motel welcomes your pets to
stay with you.

Homestead Studio Suites
Philadelphia - King of Prussia
400 American Ave.
King of Prussia, PA
610-962-9000 (800-804-3724)
One dog is allowed per suite. There
is a $25 per night additional pet fee
up to $150 for an entire stay.

Quality Inn Royle
405 Butler Rd.
Kittanning, PA
724-543-1159 (877-424-6423)
Dogs of all sizes are allowed. Dogs
are allowed for a pet fee of $10.00
per pet per night.

Rodeway Inn
RD 6 US 422 E.
Kittanning, PA
724-543-1100 (877-424-6423)
Dogs of all sizes are allowed.

Comfort Inn Pocono Lakes Region
117 Twin Rocks Road
Lake Ariel, PA
570-689-4148 (877-424-6423)
Dogs of all sizes are allowed. Dogs
are allowed for a pet fee of $15.00
per pet per night.

Amish Country Travelodge Lancaster
2101 Columbia Ave
Lancaster, PA
717-397-4201 (800-578-7878)
Dogs of all sizes are allowed. Dogs
are allowed for a pet fee of $10.00
per pet per night.

Days Inn And Suites Conference
Center
1492 Lititz Pike
Lancaster, PA
717-293-8400 (800-329-7466)
Dogs of all sizes are allowed. Dogs
are allowed for a pet fee.

Hawthorn Inn & Suites
2045 Lincoln H E
Lancaster, PA
717-290-7100 (800-527-1133)
In addition to providing a convenient
location to many local sites and
activities, this all-suite hotel offers a
number of amenities for business
and leisure travelers, including their
signature breakfast buffet and
beautifully appointed rooms. Dogs up
to 50 pounds are allowed for an
additional pet fee of $50 per room for
each 1 to 7 days. Aggressive breed
dogs are not allowed. 2 dogs may be
allowed.

Knights Inn PA Lancaster
2151 Lincoln Highway East
Lancaster, PA
717-299-8971 (800-843-5644)
Dogs of all sizes are allowed. Dogs
are allowed for a pet fee of $10.00
per pet per stay.

Quality Inn
2250 Lincoln Hwy
Lancaster, PA
717-393-5499 (877-424-6423)

Dogs up to 50 pounds are allowed. Dogs are allowed for a pet fee of $10.00 per pet per night. Two dogs are allowed per room.

Ramada Hotel And Conference Center Lancaster
521 Greenfield Road
Lancaster, PA
717-299-2551 (800-272-6232)
Dogs are welcome at this hotel.

Red Roof Inn Lancaster
2307 Lincoln Highway East
Lancaster, PA
717-299-9700 (800-RED-ROOF)
One well-behaved family pet per room. Guest must notify front desk upon arrival. Guest is liable for any damages. In consideration of all guests, pets must never be left unattended in the guest rooms.

Super 8 PA Lancaster
2129 Lincoln Hwy East
Lancaster, PA
717-393-8888 (800-800-8000)
Dogs are welcome at this hotel.

Travel Lodge
2101 Columbia Avenue
Lancaster, PA
717-397-4201
Dogs of all sizes are allowed. There is a $10 per night per pet additional fee.

Red Roof Inn Philadelphia - Oxford Valley
3100 Cabot Boulevard West
Langhorne, PA
215-750-6200 (800-RED-ROOF)
One well-behaved family pet per room. Guest must notify front desk upon arrival. Guest is liable for any damages. In consideration of all guests, pets must never be left unattended in the guest rooms.

Residence Inn Philadelphia Langhorne
15 Cabot Blvd E
Langhorne, PA
215-946-6500 (800-331-3131)
Some of the amenities at this all-suite inn include a daily buffet breakfast, evening socials Monday to Wednesday, a heated swimming pool, a billiards room, and a complimentary grocery shopping service. Dogs up to 60 pounds are allowed for an additional one time pet fee of $100 per room. 2 dogs may be allowed.

Sheraton Bucks County Hotel
400 Oxford Valley Road.

Langhorne, PA
215-547-4100 (888-625-5144)
Dogs up to 70 pounds are allowed. There are no additional pet fees. Dogs are not allowed to be left alone in the room.

Quality Inn Lebanon Valley
625 Quentin Rd.
Lebanon, PA
717-273-6771 (877-424-6423)
Dogs of all sizes are allowed. Dogs are allowed for a pet fee of $15.00 per pet per night.

The Berry Patch
115 Moore Road
Lebanon, PA
717-865-7219
berrypatchbnb.com
Set amid lush lawns and towering trees on 20 acres, this newly built log home features large verandas with a view, the Strawberry Rose Garden, is close to hiking/biking trails, and are central to many other activities and attractions. Dogs of all sizes are allowed for an additional fee of $10 per night per pet. Dogs must be well behaved, leashed and cleaned up after, and crated when left alone in the room. 2 dogs may be allowed.

Days Inn Lebanon-Jonestown-Lickdale
3 Everest Lane
Lebanon/Jonestown, PA
717-865-4064 (800-329-7466)
Dogs of all sizes are allowed. Dogs are allowed for a pet fee.

Days Inn Lewisburg
409 North Derr Drive
Lewisburg, PA
570-523-1171 (800-329-7466)
Dogs are welcome at this hotel.

General Sutter Inn
14 E Main St
Lititz, PA
717-626-2115
generalsutterinn.com
Dogs are allowed for an additional fee of $15 per night per pet. 2 dogs may be allowed.

Best Western Lock Haven
101 E Walnut Street
Lock Haven, PA
570-748-3297 (800-780-7234)
Dogs of all sizes are allowed. Dogs are allowed for a nightly pet fee.

Extended Stay America
Philadelphia - Malvern
300 Morehall Rd. Rte. 29

Malvern, PA
610-240-0455 (800-804-3724)
One dog is allowed per suite. There is a $25 per night additional pet fee up to $150 for an entire stay.

Homestead Studio Suites
Philadelphia - Malvern
8 East Swedesford Rd.
Malvern, PA
610-695-9200 (800-804-3724)
One dog is allowed per suite. There is a $25 per night additional pet fee up to $150 for an entire stay.

Homewood Suites
12 E Swedesford Rd
Malvern, PA
610-296-3500
Dogs are allowed for a fee of $25 per pet for each five days stay. 2 dogs may be allowed.

Staybridge Suites Malvern
20 Morehall Road
Malvern, PA
610-296-4343 (877-270-6405)
Dogs up to 80 pounds are allowed. Pets allowed with an additional pet fee. Up to $75 for 1-6 nights and up to $150 for 7+ nights. A pet agreement must be signed at check-in.

Rodeway Inn Penn's Woods
2931 Lebanon Rd.
Manheim, PA
717-665-2755 (877-424-6423)
Dogs of all sizes are allowed. Dogs are allowed for a pet fee of $5.00 per pet per stay.

Comfort Inn
300 Gateway Dr.
Mansfield, PA
570-662-3000 (877-424-6423)
Dogs of all sizes are allowed. Dogs are allowed for a pet fee of $15.00 per pet per stay. Two dogs are allowed per room.

B. F. Hiestand House
722 E Market Street
Marietta, PA
717-426-8415 (877-560-8415)
bfhiestandhouse.com/
This Queen Anne style 1887 Victorian treasure sits along Susquehanna River and offers a convenient location to numerous attractions, recreational pursuits, shops, and eateries. Dogs of all sizes are allowed for an additional fee of $10 per night per pet. Dogs must be leashed at all times when out of guests' room, cleaned up after, and they may be left crated in the

room alone for short time periods only. There are other pets on site. Multiple dogs may be allowed.

Comfort Inn Cranberry Twp.
924 Sheraton Drive
Mars, PA
724-772-2700 (877-424-6423)
Dogs up to 100 pounds are allowed. Dogs are allowed for a pet fee of $10.00 per pet per stay.

Motel 6 - Pittsburgh Cranberry
19025 Perry Highway
Mars, PA
724-776-4333 (800-466-8356)
This motel welcomes your pets to stay with you.

Super 8 /Cranberry/Pittsburgh Area
Mars
929 Sheraton Dr
Mars, PA
724-776-9700 (800-800-8000)
Dogs are welcome at this hotel.

Days Inn Conference Center
Meadville
18360 Conneaut Lake Road
Meadville, PA
814-337-4264 (800-329-7466)
Dogs of all sizes are allowed. Dogs are allowed for a nightly pet fee.

Quality Inn
17259 Conneaut Lake Road
Meadville, PA
814-333-8883 (877-424-6423)
Dogs of all sizes are allowed. Dogs are allowed for a pet fee of $10.00 per pet per night. Two dogs are allowed per room.

Comfort Inn Capital City
1012 Wesley Drive
Mechanicsburg, PA
717-766-3700 (877-424-6423)
Dogs of all sizes are allowed. Dogs are allowed for a pet fee of $25.00 per pet per night. Two dogs are allowed per room.

Holiday Inn Harrisburg-West
5401 Carlisle Pike
Mechanicsburg, PA
717-697-0321 (877-270-6405)
Dogs of all sizes are allowed. Dogs are allowed for a pet fee of $25.00 per pet per stay.

Comfort Inn
835 Perry Highway
Mercer, PA
724-748-3030 (877-424-6423)
Dogs of all sizes are allowed.

Motel 6 - Mifflinville

488 West 3rd Street
Mifflinville, PA
570-752-2100 (800-466-8356)
This motel welcomes your pets to stay with you.

Super 8 Mifflinville
450 West 3rd Street
Mifflinville, PA
570-759-6778 (800-800-8000)
Dogs are welcome at this hotel.

Comfort Inn
31 Hospitality Lane
Mill Hall, PA
570-726-4901 (877-424-6423)
Dogs of all sizes are allowed.

Holiday Inn Express Hotel & Suites
Center Township
105 Stone Quarry Rd
Monaca, PA
724-728-5121 (877-270-6405)
Dogs of all sizes are allowed. Dogs are allowed for a pet fee of $20.00 per pet per night.

Days Inn Pittsburgh Monroeville
2727 Mosside Blvd
Monroeville, PA
412-856-1610 (800-329-7466)
Dogs are welcome at this hotel.

Extended Stay America Pittsburgh - Monroeville
3851 Northern Pike
Monroeville, PA
412-856-8400 (800-804-3724)
One dog is allowed per suite. There is a $25 per night additional pet fee up to $150 for an entire stay.

Red Roof Inn Pittsburgh East - Monroeville
2729 Mosside Boulevard
Monroeville, PA
412-856-4738 (800-RED-ROOF)
One well-behaved family pet per room. Guest must notify front desk upon arrival. Guest is liable for any damages. In consideration of all guests, pets must never be left unattended in the guest rooms.

Quality Inn Conference Center
969 Bethlehem Pike
Montgomeryville, PA
215-699-8800 (877-424-6423)
Dogs up to 85 pounds are allowed. Dogs are allowed for a pet fee of $25.00 per pet per night.

La Quinta Inn Pittsburgh Airport
8507 University Boulevard
Moon Township, PA
412-269-0400 (800-531-5900)
Dogs of all sizes are allowed. There

are no additional pet fees. Dogs must be quiet, well behaved, leashed and cleaned up after. Multiple dogs may be allowed.

Rodeway Inn
4130 Birney Ave.
Moosic, PA
570-457-6713 (877-424-6423)
Dogs of all sizes are allowed. Dogs are allowed for a pet fee of $10.00 per pet per night. Two dogs are allowed per room.

Holiday Inn Morgantown/Pa Turnpike Ex 298
6170 Morgantown Road
Morgantown, PA
610-286-3000 (877-270-6405)
Dogs of all sizes are allowed. Dogs are allowed for a nightly pet fee.

The Olde Square Inn
127 E Main Street
Mount Joy, PA
717-653-4525 (800-742-3533)
oldesquareinn.com/
Located near the heart of Amish country, and numerous other attractions/activities, and year round recreation, this lovely inn, surrounded by lawns and gardens, offers a full breakfast buffet with indoor or outdoor dining, and a seasonal outdoor pool. Dogs of all sizes are welcome for an additional one time pet fee of $10 per room, and are asked to come in and meet the innkeeper; there are also other dogs on site. Dogs must be leashed at all times when out of the room and be cleaned up after inside and out. Please use a mat under the pet's food and water, and a cover for the bed and/or furniture if the pet is on them. Dogs must be crated when left alone in the room and they suggest leaving on the radio or TV and having a comfort item for the pup. 2 dogs may be allowed.

MainStay Suites of Lancaster County
314 Primrose Lane
Mountville, PA
717-285-2500 (877-424-6423)
All suites hotel catering to extended stay travelers. Kitchens equipped.

Comfort Inn
330 Commerce Park
New Columbia, PA
570-568-8000 (877-424-6423)
Dogs of all sizes are allowed.

Days Inn /Harrisburg South New Cumberland
353 Lewisberry Rd

Dog-Friendly Lodging - Please always call ahead to make sure an establishment is still dog-friendly.

New Cumberland, PA
717-774-4156 (800-329-7466)
Dogs of all sizes are allowed. Dogs are allowed for a pet fee.

Motel 6 - Harrisburg
200 Commerce Drive
New Cumberland, PA
717-774-8910 (800-466-8356)
This motel welcomes your pets to stay with you.

Comfort Inn Amish Country
626 W. Main St.
New Holland, PA
717-355-9900 (877-424-6423)
Dogs up to 65 pounds are allowed. Dogs are allowed for a pet fee of $20.00 per pet per night.

The Hollander Motel
320 E Main St
New Holland, PA
717-354-4377
There is a $10 per day per pet charge. 2 dogs may be allowed.

1833 Umpleby House
111 W Bridge Street
New Hope, PA
215-862-3936
1833umplebyhouse.com/index.htm
Sitting on 2 park-like acres, this 1833 Classic Revival manor house is on the National Registry of Historic Places, is only minutes from the village center and the Delaware River, and registered guests are welcome at the inn's private mountaintop pool and tennis club. One well traveled and well behaved dog is allowed per room for an additional $20 per night. Dogs must be flee and tic free, have their own bedding, and they may not be left alone in the room. Dogs must be quiet, well mannered, leashed, and cleaned up after at all times.

Wedgwood Inn
111 W Bridge Street
New Hope, PA
215-862-2570
wedgwoodinn.com/index.htm
This historic 1870 Wedgwood-blue Victorian home features 2 acres of lush lawns and gardens, home baked goodies available all day, and is only a short walk to the eclectic, vibrant village of New Hope, and to the walking bridge to New Jersey. Dogs of all sizes are allowed for an additional fee of $20 per night per pet. Dogs may be left alone only for short periods and only if they will be quiet, well behaved, and a contact number is left with the front desk. Dogs must be leashed and cleaned

up after at all times. 2 dogs may be allowed.

Clarion Hotel
300 Tarentum Bridge Road
New Kensington, PA
724-335-9171 (877-424-6423)
Dogs of all sizes are allowed.

Days Inn PA New Stanton
127 West Byers Avenue
New Stanton, PA
724-925-3591 (800-329-7466)
Dogs are welcome at this hotel.

Howard Johnson Inn - Greensburg
New Stanton
112 West Byers Ave/I-70
New Stanton, PA
724-925-3511 (800-446-4656)
Dogs are allowed for a $7 nightly pet fee.

Quality Inn
110 North Main and Byers Ave
New Stanton, PA
724-925-6755 (877-424-6423)
Dogs up to 75 pounds are allowed. Dogs are allowed for a pet fee of $20.00 per pet per night. Two dogs are allowed per room.

Super 8 New Stanton
103 Bair Blvd
New Stanton, PA
724-925-8915 (800-800-8000)
Dogs of all sizes are allowed. Dogs are allowed for a pet fee.

Super 8 /Erie Area North East
11021 Sidehill Rd
North East, PA
814-725-4567 (800-800-8000)
Dogs are welcome at this hotel.

Comfort Inn & Suites
111 Annabel Rd
North Wales, PA
215-538-3000 (877-424-6423)
comfortinnquakertown.com
Dogs are allowed in this Comfort Inn near Philadelphia and Valley Forge.

Residence Inn Philadelphia Montgomeryville
1110 Bethlehem Pike
North Wales, PA
267-468-0111 (800-331-3131)
Offering a convenient location to business, shopping, dining, and entertainment areas, this all suite hotel also offers a number of in-house amenities for all level of travelers, including a daily buffet breakfast and evening socials. Dogs are allowed for an additional

one time pet fee of $75 per room. Multiple dogs may be allowed.

Comfort Inn Pittsburgh Airport
7011 Old Steubenville Pike
Oakdale, PA
412-787-2600 (877-424-6423)
Dogs of all sizes are allowed. Dogs are allowed for a pet fee of $10.00 per pet per night.

Arlington Hotel
1 Seneca St
Oil City, PA
814-677-1221
There is a $10 per day per pet additional fee. Multiple dogs may be allowed.

Our Farm Under the Mimosa Tree
1487 Blue School Road
Perkasie, PA
215-249-9420
mimosatreebnb.com/
This scenic 20 acre, 200 year old farmhouse surrounded by mimosa trees, has numerous farm animals, peacocks, 2 ponds, a Japanese garden complete with a koi pond, hiking trails, and many places for picnicking and exploring. Dogs of all sizes are allowed for no additional pet fee. Puppies are not allowed, and dogs must be friendly toward humans and the farm animals. Dogs must be well behaved, leashed, cleaned up after, and they are not allowed on the furnishings. 2 dogs may be allowed.

Extended Stay America Philadelphia - Airport
9000 Tinicum Blvd.
Philadelphia, PA
215-492-6766 (800-804-3724)
One dog is allowed per suite. There is a $25 per night additional pet fee up to $150 for an entire stay.

Four Points by Sheraton at Philadelphia Airport
4010 A Island Ave.
Philadelphia, PA
215-492-0400 (888-625-5144)
Dogs up to 80 pounds are allowed. There are no additional pet fees. Dogs are not allowed to be left alone in the room.

Loews Philadelphia Hotel
1200 Market Street
Philadelphia, PA
215-627-1200
All well-behaved dogs of any size are welcome. This upscale hotel offers their "Loews Loves Pets" program which includes special pet treats,

local dog walking routes, and a list of nearby pet-friendly places to visit. There is an additional one time pet cleaning fee of $25 per room.

Residence Inn Philadelphia Airport
4630 Island Avenue
Philadelphia, PA
215-492-1611 (800-331-3131)
Besides being only a ½ mile from the airport and offering a central starting point to a number of local attractions and activities, this upscale, all suite hotel also offers a number of in-house amenities, including a daily buffet breakfast and nightly social events. Dogs are allowed for an additional one time pet fee of $100 per room. Multiple dogs may be allowed.

Residence Inn Philadelphia Center City
One East Penn Square
Philadelphia, PA
215-557-0005 (800-331-3131)
Located only steps from City Hall and the Reading Terminal Market as well as being central to all this historic, vibrant city has to offer, this all suite hotel also offers a number of in-house amenities, including a daily breakfast buffet and evening social hours. Dogs are allowed for an additional one time pet fee of $75 per room. Multiple dogs may be allowed.

Sheraton Philadelphia City Center Hotel
17th & Race St.
Philadelphia, PA
215-448-2000 (888-625-5144)
Dogs up to 50 pounds are allowed. There are no additional pet fees. Dogs are not allowed to be left alone in the room.

Sheraton Society Hill Hotel
One Dock Street
Philadelphia, PA
215-238-6000 (888-625-5144)
Dogs up to 75 pounds are allowed. There are no additional pet fees. Dogs are not allowed to be left alone in the room.

Sheraton Suite Philadelphia
4101 B Island Ave.
Philadelphia, PA
215-365-6600 (888-625-5144)
Dogs up to 80 pounds are allowed. There are no additional pet fees. Dogs are not allowed to be left alone in the room.

Sheraton University City Hotel
36th and Chestnut Streets

Philadelphia, PA
215-387-8000 (888-625-5144)
Dogs up to 80 pounds are allowed. There are no additional pet fees. Dogs are not allowed to be left alone in the room.

The Conwell Inn
1331 W Berks Street
Philadelphia, PA
215-235-6200 (888-379-9737)
conwellinn.com/
This historic, landmark hotel is located in the middle of Temple University, and is close to downtown and numerous sites of interest. Dogs of all sizes are allowed for an additional fee of $20 per night per room. Dogs must be quiet, leashed, cleaned up after, and crated if left alone in the room. 2 dogs may be allowed.

The Rittenhouse
210 W Rittenhouse Square
Philadelphia, PA
215-546-9000
rittenhousehotel.com/
There is a $50 one time pet fee per room. Dogs may not be left alone in the room. The concierge can arrange in-house pet sitting for a $15 fee for one dog and $24 for 2 dogs,,, a few days notice is suggested if possible. There is a pet agreement to sign at check in. 2 dogs may be allowed.

Comfort Inn
200 Swatara Drive
Pine Grove, PA
570-345-8031 (877-424-6423)
Dogs of all sizes are allowed. Dogs are allowed for a pet fee of $10.00 per pet per night.

Econo Lodge
419 Suedberg Rd
Pine Grove, PA
570-345-4099 (877-424-6423)
Dogs of all sizes are allowed. Dogs are allowed for a pet fee of $10.00 per pet per night.

Candlewood Suites Pittsburgh-Airport
100 Chauvet Drive
Pittsburgh, PA
412-787-7770 (877-270-6405)
Dogs up to 80 pounds are allowed. Pets allowed with an additional pet fee. Up to $75 for 1-6 nights and up to $150 for 7+ nights. A pet agreement must be signed at check-in.

Comfort Inn & Suites

2898 Banksville Rd.
Pittsburgh, PA
412-343-3000 (877-424-6423)
Dogs up to 50 pounds are allowed. Dogs are allowed for a pet fee of $15.00 per pet per night.

Comfort Inn Conference Center
699 Rodi Road
Pittsburgh, PA
412-244-1600 (877-424-6423)
Dogs of all sizes are allowed. Dogs are allowed for a pet fee of $10.00 per pet per night.

Holiday Inn Pittsburgh-Intl Airport
8256 University Blvd
Pittsburgh, PA
412-262-3600 (877-270-6405)
Dogs of all sizes are allowed. Dogs are allowed for a pet fee of $49.00 per pet per night.

MainStay Suites
1000 Park Lane Drive
Pittsburgh, PA
412-490-7343 (877-424-6423)
Dogs of all sizes are allowed.

Morning Glory Inn
2119 Sarah Street
Pittsburgh, PA
412-431-1707
morningglorybedandbreakfast.com
A perfect blend of sophistication and casual comfort, this 1862 Italian style Victorian brick inn features lush greenery, a beautiful garden patio, and they are central to a host of other activities and an active nightlife. Dogs of all sizes are allowed in one suite for no additional fee. Dogs must be well mannered, they are not allowed on the furnishings, and they must be leashed and cleaned up after. Multiple dogs may be allowed.

Motel 6 - Pittsburgh Crafton
211 Beecham Drive
Pittsburgh, PA
412-922-9400 (800-466-8356)
This motel welcomes your pets to stay with you.

Radisson Hotel Pittsburgh Green Tree
101 Radisson Drive
Pittsburgh, PA
412-922-8400
Dogs of all sizes are allowed. There is a $100 refundable pet deposit. Pet owners need to sign a pet waiver.

Ramada Hotel And Conference Center Pittsburgh
401 Holiday Drive

Pittsburgh, PA
412-922-8100 (800-272-6232)
Dogs are welcome at this hotel.

Red Roof Inn Pittsburgh South - Airport
6404 Steubenville Pike
Pittsburgh, PA
412-787-7870 (800-RED-ROOF)
One well-behaved family pet per room. Guest must notify front desk upon arrival. Guest is liable for any damages. In consideration of all guests, pets must never be left unattended in the guest rooms.

Residence Inn Pittsburgh Airport Coraopolis
1500 Park Lane Drive
Pittsburgh, PA
412-787-3300 (800-331-3131)
In addition to being located in the RIDC Park West commerce area and only a mile from more than 200 shopping, dining, and entertainment opportunities, this all suite hotel also offers a number of in-house amenities, including a daily buffet breakfast and evening socials. Dogs are allowed for an additional one time pet fee of $100 per room. Multiple dogs may be allowed.

Residence Inn Pittsburgh University/Medical Center
3896 Bigelow Blvd
Pittsburgh, PA
412-621-2200 (800-513-8766)
This all suite hotel gives a good central location to local universities, research institutes, and medical centers, plus they offer a number of in-house amenities, including a daily full, hot breakfast and a Manager's reception Monday to Thursday. Dogs are allowed for an additional one time pet fee of $100 per room. 2 dogs may be allowed.

Super 8 /Monroeville Pittsburgh
1807 Golden Mile Hwy-Route 286
Pittsburgh, PA
724-733-8008 (800-800-8000)
Dogs are welcome at this hotel.

Super 8 Pittston
307 Highway 315
Pittston, PA
570-654-3301 (800-800-8000)
Dogs are welcome at this hotel.

Extended Stay America Philadelphia - Plymouth Meeting
437 Irwins Ln.
Plymouth Meeting, PA
610-260-0488 (800-804-3724)
One dog is allowed per suite. There

is a $25 per night additional pet fee up to $150 for an entire stay.

Comfort Inn & Suites
SR 100 & Shoemaker Rd.
Pottstown, PA
610-326-5000 (877-424-6423)
Dogs of all sizes are allowed. Dogs are allowed for a pet fee of $15.00 per pet per night.

Days Inn Pottstown
29 W. High Street
Pottstown, PA
610-970-1101 (800-329-7466)
Dogs are welcome at this hotel.

Motel 6 - Pottstown
78 Robinson St
Pottstown, PA
610-819-1288 (800-466-8356)
This motel welcomes your pets to stay with you.

Days Inn Pottsville
1476 Route 61 South
Pottsville, PA
570-385-3853 (800-329-7466)
Dogs are welcome at this hotel.

Ramada Pottsville
101 South Progress Avenue
Pottsville, PA
570-622-4600 (800-272-6232)
Dogs of all sizes are allowed. Dogs are allowed for a pet fee of $50.00 per pet per night.

Comfort Inn & Suites
1905 John Fries Hwy
Quakertown, PA
215-538-3000 (877-424-6423)
Dogs of all sizes are allowed. Dogs are allowed for a pet fee of $25.00 per pet per stay. Two dogs are allowed per room.

Jackson House
6 E Main Street
Railroad, PA
717-227-2022 (877-782-4672)
jacksonhousebandb.com/
This scenic inn features terraced gardens offering great views from the top, a relaxing waterfall, and they are the only state inn to sit right on the multi-use Heritage Rail Trail, a 21 mile trail that also connects to the 20 mile long Northern Central Rail Trail. They offer 1 pet friendly room with a private entrance, and there is an additional one time fee of $20 per pet. Dogs are not allowed in the common areas of the house, and they must be crated when left alone in the room. Dogs must be well

behaved, leashed, and cleaned up after at all times. 2 dogs may be allowed.

Crowne Plaza Hotel Reading
1741 Papermill Road
Reading, PA
016-103-7638 (877-270-6405)
Dogs are welcome at this hotel.

Comfort Inn
195 Comfort Lane
Saint Marys, PA
814-834-2030 (877-424-6423)
Dogs of all sizes are allowed.

Best Western Grand Victorian Inn
255 Spring Street
Sayre, PA
570-888-7711 (800-780-7234)
Dogs of all sizes are allowed. Dogs are allowed for a pet fee of $10.00 per pet per night.

Clarion Hotel
300 Meadow Avenue
Scranton, PA
570-344-9811 (877-424-6423)
Dogs of all sizes are allowed. Dogs are allowed for a pet fee of $25.00 per pet per night.

Days Inn PA Scranton
1946 Scranton-Carbondale Hwy
Scranton, PA
570-383-9979 (800-329-7466)
Dogs are welcome at this hotel.

Econo Lodge
1175 Kane St.
Scranton, PA
570-348-1000 (877-424-6423)
Dogs of all sizes are allowed. Dogs are allowed for a pet fee of $10.00 per pet per night. Two dogs are allowed per room.

Hilton Hotel
100 Adams Avenue
Scranton, PA
570-343-3000 (800-HILTONS (445-8667))
In addition to being an IACC approved conference center, this hotel offers a number of other on site amenities for business and leisure travelers, plus a convenient location to special event venues, the state university, shopping, dining, and recreation areas. Dogs up to 75 pounds are allowed for a $75 pet deposit per room. $50 is non-refundable. 2 dogs may be allowed.

Econo Lodge
2 Susquehanna Trail
Shamokin Dam, PA

570-743-1111
econolodge.com/
Dogs of all sizes are allowed. There is a $10 per night per room additional pet fee. 2 dogs may be allowed.

Super 8 West Middlesex/Sharon Area
3369 New Castle Rd
Sharon/West Middlesex, PA
724-528-3888 (800-800-8000)
Dogs of all sizes are allowed. Dogs are allowed for a nightly pet fee.

Best Western Reading Inn
2299 Lancaster Pike
Shillington, PA
610-777-7888 (800-780-7234)
Dogs of all sizes are allowed. Dogs are allowed for a nightly pet fee.

Rodeway Inn
10 Hershey Road
Shippensburg, PA
717-530-1234 (877-424-6423)
Dogs up to 50 pounds are allowed. Dogs are allowed for a pet fee of $10.00 per pet per night. Two dogs are allowed per room.

Days Inn Somerset
220 Waterworks Road
Somerset, PA
814-445-9200 (800-329-7466)
Dogs are welcome at this hotel.

Quality Inn & Conference Center
215 Ramada Road
Somerset, PA
814-443-4646 (877-424-6423)
Dogs of all sizes are allowed. Dogs are allowed for a pet fee of $25.00 per pet per stay.

Super 8 Somerset
125 Lewis Dr
Somerset, PA
814-445-8788 (800-800-8000)
Dogs are welcome at this hotel.

The Inn at Starlight Lake
2890 Starlight Lake Road
Starlight, PA
570-798-2519 (800-248-2519)
innatstarlightlake.com/
Set among lush greenery on the lakefront, this family getaway features a game room, sunroom, restaurant and bar, and they are central to a wide variety of land and water year round recreation. Dogs of all sizes are allowed in the cottages only for no additional pet fee. Dogs must be at least one year old, they are not allowed in the main house, and they may not be left unattended in the room for more than 2 hours.

Dogs must be leashed and cleaned up after at all times. 2 dogs may be allowed.

Days Inn State College
240 South Pugh Street
State College, PA
814-238-8454 (800-329-7466)
Dogs of all sizes are allowed. Dogs are allowed for a pet fee.

Quality Inn
1274 N. Atherton Street
State College, PA
814-234-1600 (877-424-6423)
Dogs up to 50 pounds are allowed. Dogs are allowed for a pet fee of $10.00 per pet per night. Two dogs are allowed per room.

Residence Inn State College
1555 University Drive
State College, PA
814-235-6960 (800-331-3131)
In addition to having a close location to Penn State and Downtown State College, there are a number of activities and sites of interest for both business and leisure travelers. Additionally, they also offer a daily buffet breakfast and a dinner buffet Monday to Thursday. Dogs are allowed for an additional one time pet fee of $75 per room. 2 dogs may be allowed.

Super 8 State College
1663 S Atherton St
State College, PA
814-237-8005 (800-800-8000)
Dogs are welcome at this hotel.

Quality Inn
1220 West Main Street
Stroudsburg, PA
570-420-1000 (877-424-6423)
Dogs up to 50 pounds are allowed.

River View Inn
103 Chestnut Street
Sunbury, PA
570-286-4800 (866-592-4800)
riverview-inn.com/
This 1870's elegant Victorian inn sits along the Susquehanna River and across from the Merle Phillips Park, and is updated with all the modern comforts. They have one pet friendly room and one dog of any size is allowed for an additional pet fee of $25 per night. Dogs must be very quiet and well behaved, leashed and cleaned up after inside and out, and shots up to date. Dogs may not be left alone in the room.

Radisson Hotel Philadelphia NE

2400 Old Lincoln Highway
Trevose, PA
215-638-8300 (800-333-3333)
Pets must stay on the first floor. Dogs up to 75 pounds are allowed. People with Pets must book the 'pet-friendly rate' when making reservations.

Red Roof Inn Philadelphia - Trevose
3100 Lincoln Highway/US Route 1
Trevose, PA
215-244-9422 (800-RED-ROOF)
One well-behaved family pet per room. Guest must notify front desk upon arrival. Guest is liable for any damages. In consideration of all guests, pets must never be left unattended in the guest rooms.

Holiday Inn Uniontown
700 West Main St, Rt 40 W
Uniontown, PA
724-437-2816 (877-270-6405)
Dogs of all sizes are allowed. Dogs are allowed for a pet fee of $10.00 per pet per night.

Days Inn - Breezewood Town Hill Warfordsburg
9648 Old Route 126
Warfordsburg, PA
814-735-3860 (800-329-7466)
Dogs of all sizes are allowed. Dogs are allowed for a pet fee of $10.00 per pet per night.

Holiday Inn Warren (Kinzua Dam-Allegheny)
210 Ludlow Street
Warren, PA
814-726-3000 (877-270-6405)
Dogs are welcome at this hotel.

Super 8 Warren
204 Struthers Street
Warren, PA
814-723-8881 (800-800-8000)
Dogs are welcome at this hotel.

Candlewood Suites Washington North
255 Meadowlands Blvd
Washington, PA
724-873-7300 (877-270-6405)
Dogs up to 80 pounds are allowed. Pets allowed with an additional pet fee. Up to $75 for 1-6 nights and up to $150 for 7+ nights. A pet agreement must be signed at check-in.

Motel 6 - Washington, Pa
1283 Motel Drive
Washington, PA
724-223-8040 (800-466-8356)
This motel welcomes your pets to

stay with you.

Ramada PA Washington
1170 W Chestnut St
Washington, PA
724-225-9750 (800-272-6232)
Dogs of all sizes are allowed. Dogs are allowed for a pet fee.

Red Roof Inn Washington, PA
1399 West Chestnut Street
Washington, PA
724-228-5750 (800-RED-ROOF)
One well-behaved family pet per room. Guest must notify front desk upon arrival. Guest is liable for any damages. In consideration of all guests, pets must never be left unattended in the guest rooms.

Happy Acres Resort Cabins and Campground
3332 Little Pine Creek Road
Waterville, PA
570-753-8000
happyacresresort.net
These dog-friendly cabins and campsites allow non-aggressive dogs. There is a one time pet fee ranging from $8 for camping to $25 for cabins.

Keen Lake Camping and Cottage Resort
155 Keen Lake
Waymart, PA
570-488-5522
Dogs of all sizes are allowed. There is a $50 one time pet fee for cottages and there is no additional pet fee for the camp sites. Dogs are not to be left alone at any time.

Days Inn Waynesboro
239 W Main St
Waynesboro, PA
717-762-9113 (800-329-7466)
Dogs of all sizes are allowed. Dogs are allowed for a pet fee of $20.00 per pet per stay.

Kaltenbachs Inn
743 Stoney Fork Road
Wellsboro, PA
570-724-4954 (800-722-4954)
kaltenbachsinn.com/
This sprawling country inn is on a 72 acre ranch with farm animals, plenty of wildlife, views, pastures and forests, picnicking areas with barbecues, and they are also only a short biking/driving distance from the newly opened 62 mile Pine Creek Rail Trail. Dogs of all sizes are allowed for an additional fee of $5 per night per pet. Dogs must be very well behaved, quiet, leashed,

cleaned up after, and crated when left alone in the room. 2 dogs may be allowed.

Comfort Inn
58 State Route 93
West Hazleton, PA
570-455-9300 (877-424-6423)
Dogs of all sizes are allowed. Dogs are allowed for a pet fee of $10.00 per pet per night.

Extended Stay America Pittsburgh - West Mifflin
1303 Lebanon Church Rd.
West Mifflin, PA
412-650-9096 (800-804-3724)
One dog is allowed per suite. There is a $25 per night additional pet fee up to $150 for an entire stay.

Holiday Inn Express Hotel & Suites Pittsburgh West Mifflin
3122 Lebanon Church Rd.
West Mifflin, PA
412-469-1900 (877-270-6405)
Dogs of all sizes are allowed. Dogs are allowed for a pet fee of $10.00 per pet per night.

Candlewood Suites Reading
55 South 3rd Ave
West Reading, PA
610-898-1910 (877-270-6405)
Dogs up to 80 pounds are allowed. Pets allowed with an additional pet fee. Up to $75 for 1-6 nights and up to $150 for 7+ nights. A pet agreement must be signed at check-in.

Comfort Inn - Pocono Mountain
Route 940 @ 1-80 and I-476
White Haven, PA
570-443-8461 (877-424-6423)
Dogs of all sizes are allowed. Dogs are allowed for a pet fee of $15.00 per pet per stay.

Knights Inn Lake Harmony/ White Haven
Box 30 Route 940
White Haven, PA
570-443-1125 (800-843-5644)
Dogs are welcome at this hotel.

Days Inn Wilkes Barre
760 Kidder Street
Wilkes Barre, PA
570-826-0111 (800-329-7466)
Dogs of all sizes are allowed. Dogs are allowed for a pet fee of $10.00 per pet per night.

Econo Lodge Arena
1075 Wilkes-Barre Twp. Blvd.
Wilkes Barre, PA

570-823-0600 (877-424-6423)
Dogs of all sizes are allowed. Dogs are allowed for a pet fee of $10.00 per pet per night. Two dogs are allowed per room.

Quality Inn & Suites Conference Center
880 Kidder Street
Wilkes Barre, PA
570-824-8901 (877-424-6423)
Dogs of all sizes are allowed. Dogs are allowed for a pet fee of $15.00 per pet per night. Two dogs are allowed per room.

Red Roof Inn Wilkes - Barre
1035 Highway 315
Wilkes-Barre, PA
570-829-6422 (800-RED-ROOF)
One well-behaved family pet per room. Guest must notify front desk upon arrival. Guest is liable for any damages. In consideration of all guests, pets must never be left unattended in the guest rooms.

Best Western Williamsport Inn
1840 E 3rd Street
Williamsport, PA
570-326-1981 (800-780-7234)
Dogs up to 50 pounds are allowed.

Candlewood Suites Williamsport
1836 East Third St.
Williamsport, PA
570-601-9100 (877-270-6405)
Dogs up to 80 pounds are allowed. Pets allowed with an additional pet fee. Up to $75 for 1-6 nights and up to $150 for 7+ nights. A pet agreement must be signed at check-in.

Econo Lodge
2019 E. Third St.
Williamsport, PA
570-326-1501 (877-424-6423)
Dogs of all sizes are allowed. Dogs are allowed for a pet fee of $10.00 per pet per night. Two dogs are allowed per room.

Econo Lodge
860 N. Front St.
Wormleysburg, PA
717-763-7086 (877-424-6423)
Dogs of all sizes are allowed. Dogs are allowed for a pet fee of $10.00 per pet per night.

Comfort Inn
RR 6 Box 6167A
Wysox, PA
570-265-5691 (877-424-6423)
Dogs of all sizes are allowed. Dogs are allowed for a pet fee of $25.00

per pet per stay. Two dogs are allowed per room.

Comfort Inn Corporate Gateway
2250 N. George St.
York, PA
717-699-1919 (877-424-6423)
Dogs of all sizes are allowed. Dogs are allowed for a pet fee of $20.00 per pet per night. Two dogs are allowed per room.

Holiday Inn Express York
140 Leader Heights Road
York, PA
717-741-1000 (877-270-6405)
Dogs of all sizes are allowed. Dogs are allowed for a pet fee of $50.00 per pet per stay.

Motel 6 - York
323 Arsenal Rd
York, PA
717-846-6260 (800-466-8356)
This motel welcomes your pets to stay with you.

Quality Inn & Suites
2600 East Market St.
York, PA
717-755-1966 (877-424-6423)
Dogs of all sizes are allowed. Dogs are allowed for a pet fee of $10.00 per pet per night. Two dogs are allowed per room.

Ramada Hotel And Conference Center York
334 Arsenal Road
York, PA
717-845-5671 (800-272-6232)
Dogs of all sizes are allowed. Dogs are allowed for a pet fee of $25.00 per pet per night.

Red Roof Inn York
125 Arsenal Road
York, PA
717-843-8181 (800-RED-ROOF)
One well-behaved family pet per room. Guest must notify front desk upon arrival. Guest is liable for any damages. In consideration of all guests, pets must never be left unattended in the guest rooms.

Rhode Island

The Blue Dory Inn
Dodge Street
Block Island, RI
401-466-2254 (800-992-7290)
blockislandinns.com/
This historic 1862 mansion sits at the head of Crescent Beach only a mile from the Atlantic Ocean on 5 rolling

acres, and every afternoon guests can meet in the parlor for wine, hors d'oevres and their specialty-Blue Dory cookies. Dogs of all sizes are welcome for an additional $25 one time fee per pet. Dogs must be leashed and cleaned up after. 2 dogs may be allowed.

The Island Home
Beach Avenue
Block Island, RI
401-466-5944
One large dog up to about 50 pounds or 2 dogs at about 10 pounds each are allowed. There is a pet policy to sign at check in and there are no additional pet fees.

Vacation Rentals by Owner
Calico Hill
Block Island, RI
401-497-0631
vrbo.com/90721
Set upon rolling hills with views of the harbor and the town only a few minutes away, this 1871 farmhouse offers all the modern amenities, and a great starting point for a wide variety of activities, and land and water recreation. Dogs of all sizes are allowed for no additional pet fees. Dogs must be house trained, well behaved, and leashed and cleaned up after at all times inside and outside. Multiple dogs may be allowed.

Days Inn /Providence Cranston
101 New London Ave
Cranston, RI
401-942-4200 (800-329-7466)
Dogs are welcome at this hotel.

Extended Stay America Providence - East Providence
1000 Warren Ave.
East Providence, RI
401-272-1661 (800-804-3724)
One dog is allowed per suite. There is a $25 per night additional pet fee up to $150 for an entire stay.

The Edith Pearl
250 W Main Road/H 77
Little Compton, RI
401-592-0053
edithpearl.com/
Located on 200 picturesque acres, this renovated colonial home is a working farm as well as a Bed and Breakfast. There are wrap-around verandas, lush lawns, perennial gardens, and a pond-plus their 2 housedogs look forward to greeting their canine guests. Pooches get their own food and water bowls, a snugly bed, and toys. Dogs are

welcome for no additional fee, but they must be freshly groomed, pest free, and picked up after. Dogs must be non-aggressive, housebroken, and pet friendly. Dogs that are not under strict voice command are to be leashed. Dog sitting and consultations are available here for an extra fee. 2 dogs may be allowed.

Bartram's
94 Kane Avenue
Middletown, RI
401-846-2259
bartramrecorders.com/bbb.html
Located near beaches and only a couple of miles from Newport, this family run inn offers comfy accommodations plus a convenient location to many other sites of interest and activities. Hound and human friendly dogs are welcome for an additional pet fee of $25 per night per room. 2 dogs may be allowed.

Bay Willows Inn
1225 Aquidneck Avenue/H 138A
Middletown, RI
401-847-8400
baywillowsinn.com/
There are 21 nice guest rooms at this inn, plus they are only a short distance from Newport and the beaches. Dogs are allowed for an additional fee of $10 per night per pet. Multiple dogs may be allowed.

Howard Johnson Inn - Newport Area/ Middletown
351 West Main Rd.
Middletown, RI
401-849-2000 (800-446-4656)
Dogs are welcome at this hotel.

Newport Whirlpool Suites and SPA
936 W Main Street
Middletown, RI
401-846-7600
newportspa.com/
This inn offers a convenient location to all the city has to offer, plus they have a seasonal shuttle service to take guests to the best of Newport attractions. Dogs are allowed for an additional fee of $15 per night per pet. Multiple dogs may be allowed.

Residence Inn by Marriott
325 W Main Road
Middletown, RI
401-845-2005 (800-331-3131)
An extended stay, all suite inn only 2 miles from downtown, there are plenty of amenities here plus a convenient location to all the sites and attractions the city has to offer. Dogs are allowed for an additional one time pet fee of $100 per room.

Multiple dogs may be allowed.

Rodeway Inn & Suites
31 W. Main Road
Middletown, RI
401-847-2735 (877-424-6423)
Dogs up to 50 pounds are allowed. Dogs are allowed for a pet fee of $10.00 per pet per night. Two dogs are allowed per room.

Seaview Inn
240 Aquidneck Avenue/H 138A
Middletown, RI
888-534-9698
seaviewinn.org/
There are 2 pet friendly rooms at this lovely inn. It sits atop a grassy knoll overlooking the ocean, Easton's Pond, and the Cliff Walk. Dogs are allowed for an additional fee of $10 per night per pet. Dogs may not be left in the room when owners leave the premises. 2 dogs may be allowed.

1 Murray House Bed & Breakfast
1 Murray Place
Newport, RI
401-846-3337 (888-848-2048)
murrayhouse.com
Pets are allowed for additional pet fees ranging from $15 to $35 per night.

Admiral Sims' White House
73 Catherine Street
Newport, RI
401-841-0009 (877-841-0009)
newportsfirstfamily.com/
Sitting atop a hill, this stately historic inn offers elegant accommodations and a convenient location to all that Newport has to offer. Dogs are allowed for an additional pet fee of $25 per night per room with a maximum of $50. 2 dogs may be allowed.

Almy Cottage
141 Coggeshall Ave
Newport, RI
401-864-0686
This vacation cottage is close to many of the attractions that draw people here such as Mansion Row on Bellevue Avenue or the exhilarating Cliff Walk, and it is only a short walk to a small private beach. Dogs of all sizes are welcome for no additional pet fee. They are allowed in the garden cottage only, and they must be leashed and cleaned up after at all times. Dogs may only be left alone in the cottage if they are comfortable being alone and will be quiet and well behaved. Multiple dogs may be allowed.

Banister Mansion
Pelham at Spring Street
Newport, RI
401-846-0059
johnbanistermansion.com/
Offering a rich colonial past, this 1751 meticulously restored mansion offers many period furnishings, 18th century artwork, fireplaces in every room, and they also provide a venue for special events. One large dog or 2 small to medium dogs are allowed per room for no additional fee. Dogs must be well mannered and housebroken.

Bannister's Wharf Guest Rooms
1 Bannister's Wharf
Newport, RI
401-846-4500
Only steps from the marina, this waterfront guest house offers a variety of accommodations, and a great location to attractions and activities. Dogs are allowed for an additional one time fee of $20 per room. 2 dogs may be allowed.

Chestnut Inn
99 3rd Street
Newport, RI
401-847-6949
members.aol.com/chstnut99/
This year round family or couples destination feature 2 oversized Victorian bedrooms, a continental breakfast, and a great location to several other attractions and recreational pursuits. Dog of all sizes are allowed for no additional fee. There can only be one dog if only 1 room is rented; however, up to 2 dogs are allowed if both rooms are taken. Dogs must be well mannered, leashed, and cleaned up after.

Cooney Cottage
87 Memorial Blvd
Newport, RI
401-849-9114
cooneycottage.com/
Set amid lush greenery flowers with a secluded backyard deck, this inn also offers a central location to a number of attractions and activities, plus they are only 1 block from the famous Cliff Walk. One dog is allowed per room for an additional fee of $25 for the 1st night, $15 for the 2nd night, and $10 for each additional night. Dogs must be crated when left alone in the room.

Dun Rovin
7 Florence Ave.
Newport, RI

401-846-2294
3 bedroom 2 bath house in the southern part of Newport. All pets are welcome. The home is near the Ocean Drive, Gooseberry Beach, Bellevue Ave. mansions,Ft. Adams, New York yacht club and Salve Regina University. All linens, dishes etc. are provided as well as cable TV, DVD, garden patio, W/D,local phone. There is a separate apt. on the premise which is occupied from time to time. There is no smoking allowed.

Hawthorne House
71 Ruggles Avenue
Newport, RI
401-847-6340
hawthornehousebb.com/
Designed for the business or leisure traveler for privacy and convenience, this guest house only rents out 1 suite, and it is available with a roomy deck, a separate entrance, private telephone, and a whirlpool bath. Dogs are allowed for no additional fee; they must be leashed, cleaned up after, and they may not be left alone in the room. 2 dogs may be allowed.

Hotel Viking
One Bellview Avenue
Newport, RI
401-847-3300 (800-556-7126)
hotelviking.com/viking_home.aspx
Although a small boutique hotel of former days and registered with Historic Hotels of America, this wonderfully updated spa hotel has numerous amenities and services for the business or leisure traveler, a convenient location to a number of sites of interest, fine dining, and more. Dogs of all sizes are allowed for an additional fee of $75 per pet per stay. Complimentary organic doggy biscuits await their canine guests, and Canine room service is only a call away. Dogs must be quiet, well behaved, leashed, cleaned up after, and crated when left alone in the room. 2 dogs may be allowed.

Hyatt Regency Newport
1 Goat Island
Newport, RI
401-851-1234 (800-233-1234)
In addition to a great waterside location, this hotel and spa offers several dining options and a long list of amenities, including an outdoor saltwater pool and lounge, an indoor pool, and live entertainment. Dogs are allowed for an additional one time pet fee of $75 per room. 2 dogs may be allowed.

Motel 6 - Newport, Ri
249 Jt Connell Highway
Newport, RI
401-848-0600 (800-466-8356)
This motel welcomes your pets to
stay with you.

Summer Cottage Guest House
21 Catherine Street
Newport, RI
401-842-7671
Dogs are allowed at this guest house
for an additional pet fee of $10 per
night per room. Dogs must be hound,
cat, and human friendly, recently
groomed and flea free. There is also
a fenced yard for some off leash
play. Multiple dogs may be allowed.

The Beech Tree Inn
34 Rhode Island Avenue
Newport, RI
401-847-9794 (800-748-6565)
beechtreeinn.com/
This modernized 1880's Victorian
home features bright, spacious
rooms, a garden, and rooftop decks.
Dogs of all sizes are welcome for an
additional fee of $25 per night per
pet. There can be 1 large dog or 2
small to medium dogs per room.
Dogs may only be left alone in the
room if they are comfortable being
alone and will be quiet and well
behaved. Dogs must be leashed,
cleaned up after, and crated with a
contact number left at the front desk
if they are in the room alone. 2 dogs
may be allowed.

The Inn at Washington Square
39 Touro Street
Newport, RI
401-847-7319 (888-847-7319)
Guests are only a stroll away from
many of the town's sites of interest
and the waterfront. There are 2 large
studio suites, a short term 3 bedroom
apartment and a long term rental as
well. Dogs up to 50 pounds are
allowed for no additional fee. 2 dogs
may be allowed.

The Poplar House
19 Poplar Avenue
Newport, RI
401-846-0976
Well behaved, clean, friendly dogs of
all sizes are allowed for no additional
pet fee. Dogs are not allowed to be
left alone in the room, and they ask
that long haired dogs be groomed
prior to arrival. 2 dogs may be
allowed.

The Sanford-Covell Villa Marina

72 Washington Street
Newport, RI
401-847-0206 (866-916-0206)
sanford-covell.com/
Once deemed the most wondrous
house ever built in city, some
believe this turn of the century
home still is. It has been
meticulously restored; offers a
piazza to enjoy the sites of the
harbor, and a romantic ambiance.
Dwell mannered, quiet dogs are
allowed for an additional fee of $10
per night per pet. 2 dogs may be
allowed.

Victorian Ladies Inn
63 Memorial Blvd
Newport, RI
401-849-9960 (888-849-9960)
victorianladies.com/
The beauty of this Victorian inn from
the outside is apparent and it only
gets better inside with period
antiques, rich vibrant colors, and a
wonderful garden with a bridge
spanning a koi pond. Dogs are
allowed for an additional fee of $25
per night per pet. Multiple dogs may
be allowed.

Marriott Providence Downtown
1 Orms Street
Providence, RI
401-272-2400 (866-807-2171)
This downtown, luxury hotel
provides a great location to a
number of sites of interest for both
business and leisure travelers; plus
they also offer numerous on-site
amenities to ensure a comfortable
stay. Dogs are allowed for no
additional fee. A contact number
must be left at the front desk if there
is a pet alone in the room. 2 dogs
may be allowed.

The Cady House
127 Power Street
Providence, RI
401-273-5398
cadyhouse.com/
Built in 1838, the Cady house offers
rooms individually decorated with
period antiques and items from
around the world, a garden patio
where guests can dine in good
weather, and a convenient location
to an array of local activities,
universities, shops, and eateries.
Dogs of all sizes are welcome for
no additional pet fee. Dogs are
allowed in the garden apartment
only, and they must be well
behaved and friendly towards the
other pets in residence. Dogs must
be leashed and cleaned up after,
and they may only be left alone in

the room if they will be calm and
comfortable. 2 dogs may be allowed.

The Kings' Rose
1747 Mooresfield Road
South Kingston, RI
401-783-5222
This colonial style home, listed on
the National Register of Historic
Places, features 16 guest rooms,
over 2 acres of gardens, and a
convenient location to several other
attractions and activities. Dogs of all
sizes are welcome for no additional
pet fees. Dogs must be leashed,
cleaned up after, and crated when
left alone in the room. 2 dogs may be
allowed.

Best Western Airport Inn
2138 Post Road
Warwick, RI
401-737-7400 (800-780-7234)
Dogs are welcome at this hotel.

Comfort Inn Airport
1940 Post Rd.
Warwick, RI
401-732-0470 (877-424-6423)
Dogs of all sizes are allowed. Dogs
are allowed for a pet fee of $50.00
per pet per stay.

Crowne Plaza Hotel Providence-
Warwick (Airport)
801 Greenwich Ave.
Warwick, RI
401-732-6000 (877-270-6405)
Dogs are welcome at this hotel.

Extended Stay America Providence -
Airport - Warwick
245 W. Natick Rd.
Warwick, RI
401-732-2547 (800-804-3724)
One dog is allowed per suite. There
is a $25 per night additional pet fee
up to $150 for an entire stay.

Holiday Inn Express Hotel & Suites
Warwick-Providence (Airport)
901 Jefferson Boulevard
Warwick, RI
401-736-5000 (877-270-6405)
Dogs are welcome at this hotel.

Homestead Studio Suites Providence
- Airport - Warwick
268 Metro Center Blvd.
Warwick, RI
401-732-6667 (800-804-3724)
One dog is allowed per suite. There
is a $25 per night additional pet fee
up to $150 for an entire stay.

Motel 6 - Providence Warwick
20 Jefferson Boulevard

Warwick, RI
401-467-9800 (800-466-8356)
This motel welcomes your pets to
stay with you.

Residence Inn Providence Warwick
500 Kilvert Street
Warwick, RI
401-737-7100 (800-331-3131)
Some of the amenities at this all-
suite inn include a daily buffet
breakfast, nightly social events,
summer barbecues, an indoor pool,
a Sport Court, and a complimentary
grocery shopping service. Dogs are
allowed for an additional one time
pet fee of $100 per room. Multiple
dogs may be allowed.

Sheraton Providence Airport Hotel
1850 Post Road
Warwick, RI
401-738-4000 (888-625-5144)
Dogs up to 80 pounds are allowed
for a $50 per stay pet fee. Dogs may
not be left alone in the room.

Residence Inn Providence Coventry
755 Center of New England Blvd
West Greenwich, RI
401-828-1170 (800-331-3131)
Located in the bustling Centre of
New England Plaza, this all suite inn
offers a great location to shopping,
dining, entertainment, local
universities, and business areas.
They also offer a number of in-house
amenities, including a daily buffet
breakfast and evening socials with
food and beverages. Dogs are
allowed for an additional one time
pet fee of $100 per room. 2 dogs
may be allowed.

Extended Stay America Providence -
Airport - West Warwick
1235 Division Rd.
West Warwick, RI
401-885-3161 (800-804-3724)
One dog is allowed per suite. There
is a $25 per night additional pet fee
up to $150 for an entire stay.

South Carolina

Days Inn - Interstate Hwy 20 Aiken
2654 Columbia Hwy N.
Aiken, SC
803-642-5692 (800-329-7466)
Dogs of all sizes are allowed. Dogs
are allowed for a pet fee.

Days Inn Downtown Aiken
1204 Richland Ave West
Aiken, SC
803-649-5524 (800-329-7466)

Dogs are welcome at this hotel.

Holiday Inn Express Aiken-Whiskey
Rd. (Dwtn)
155 Colony Parkway
Aiken, SC
803-648-0999 (877-270-6405)
Dogs of all sizes are allowed. Dogs
are allowed for a pet fee.

Howard Johnson Inn - Aiken
1936 Whiskey Rd S
Aiken, SC
803-649-5000 (800-446-4656)
Dogs of all sizes are allowed. Dogs
are allowed for a nightly pet fee.

Quality Inn & Suites
3608 Richland Ave. W.
Aiken, SC
803-641-1100 (877-424-6423)
Dogs of all sizes are allowed.

Days Inn Anderson
I-85 at Exit 19-A
Anderson, SC
864-375-0375 (800-329-7466)
Dogs are welcome at this hotel.

Holiday Inn Express Anderson-I-85
(Exit 27-Hwy 81)
410 Alliance Parkway
Anderson, SC
864-231-0231 (877-270-6405)
Dogs of all sizes are allowed. Dogs
are allowed for a pet fee of $5 per
pet per night.

La Quinta Inn Anderson
3430 Clemson Blvd.
Anderson, SC
864-225-3721 (800-531-5900)
Dogs of all sizes are allowed. There
are no additional pet fees. Dogs
may not be left unattended, and
they must be leashed and cleaned
up after. Dogs may not be left
unattended, unless they will be
quiet and well behaved. Multiple
dogs may be allowed.

Days Inn Barnwell
10747 Dunbarton Blvd
Barnwell, SC
803-541-5000 (800-329-7466)
Dogs are welcome at this hotel.

Days Inn /Parris Island Beaufort
1660 South Ribaut Rd
Beaufort, SC
843-524-1551 (800-329-7466)
Dogs of all sizes are allowed. Dogs
are allowed for a nightly pet fee.

Best Western Bennettsville Inn
213 15-401 Bypass E
Bennettsville, SC

843-479-1700 (800-780-7234)
Dogs of all sizes are allowed. Dogs
are allowed for a nightly pet fee.

Candlewood Suites Bluffton-Hilton
Head
5 Young Clyde Court
Bluffton, SC
843-705-9600 (877-270-6405)
Dogs up to 80 pounds are allowed.
Pets allowed with an additional pet
fee. Up to $75 for 1-6 nights and up
to $150 for 7+ nights. A pet
agreement must be signed at check-
in.

Holiday Inn Express
35 Bluffton Rd
Bluffton, SC
843-757-2002 (877-270-6405)
hiexpress.com/blufftonsc
Dogs up to 50 pounds are allowed.
There is a $50 per stay pet fee. 2
dogs may be allowed.

Days Inn Blythewood
114 Blythewood Rd
Blythewood, SC
803-691-1200 (800-329-7466)
Dogs are welcome at this hotel.

Best Western Charleston Downtown
146 Lockwood Drive
Charleston, SC
843-722-4000 (800-780-7234)
CharlestonBestWestern.com
Dogs of all sizes are allowed at this
downtown Charleston hotel. There is
a $25.00 nightly pet fee per pet. 2
dogs may be allowed.

Best Western Sweetgrass Inn
1540 Savannah Highway
Charleston, SC
843-571-6100 (800-780-7234)
Dogs of all sizes are allowed. Dogs
are allowed for a pet fee of $20 per
pet per night.

Charleston Cottage
Call to Arrange
Charleston, SC
207-342-5444
landworkswaterfront.com
Located on the corner of East Bay
and Tradd, this vacation rental is one
block from the waterfront park and
diagonally across the street from the
dog park. Restaurants, historic spots
of interest, fine shopping, galleries
and the Battery are all within walking
distance.

Comfort Inn Coliseum
5055 N. Arco Ln.
Charleston, SC
843-554-6485 (877-424-6423)

Dogs of all sizes are allowed. Dogs are allowed for a pet fee of $25.00 per pet per night.

Hawthorn Suites
2455 Savannah H
Charleston, SC
843-225-4411 (800-527-1133)
In addition to providing a convenient location to many local sites and activities, this all-suite hotel offers a number of amenities for business and leisure travelers, including their signature breakfast buffet and beautifully appointed rooms. Dogs are allowed for an additional one time pet fee of $50 per room. Multiple dogs may be allowed.

Indigo Inn
1 Maiden Lane
Charleston, SC
843-577-5900 (800-845-7639)
indigoinn.com
There is a $30 (+ tax) per day per pet fee. The fee may be per room for small dogs. Multiple dogs may be allowed.

La Quinta Inn Charleston Riverview
11 Ashley Pointe Drive
Charleston, SC
843-556-5200 (800-531-5900)
Dogs of all sizes are allowed. There are no additional pet fees. Dogs must be declared at the time of check in, and there is a pet waiver to sign. Dogs must be leashed, cleaned up after, and the Do Not Disturb sign put on the door if there is a pet in the room alone. Multiple dogs may be allowed.

Motel 6 - Charleston South, Sc
2058 Savannah Hwy
Charleston, SC
843-556-5144 (800-466-8356)
This motel welcomes your pets to stay with you.

Quality Suites Convention Center
5225 N. Arco Ln.
Charleston, SC
843-747-7300 (877-424-6423)
Dogs up to 50 pounds are allowed. Dogs are allowed for a pet fee of $49.00 per pet per stay.

Ramada SC Charleston
7401 Northwoods Blvd
Charleston, SC
843-572-2200 (800-272-6232)
Dogs are welcome at this hotel.

Residence Inn Charleston Downtown/Riverview
90 Ripley Point Drive

Charleston, SC
843-571-7979 (800-331-3131)
In addition to offering a convenient location to business, historic, shopping, dining, and entertainment areas, this hotel also provides a number of in-house amenities, including a daily buffet breakfast, and an evening hospitality hour Monday through Thursday. Dogs are allowed for an additional one time pet fee of $100 per room. 2 dogs may be allowed.

Days Inn Cheraw
820 Market Street
Cheraw, SC
843-537-5554 (800-329-6466)
Dogs of all sizes are allowed. Dogs are allowed for a pet fee of $10.00 per pet per night.

Comfort Inn
1305 Tiger Blvd.
Clemson, SC
864-653-3600 (877-424-6423)
Dogs of all sizes are allowed. Dogs are allowed for a pet fee of $15.00 per pet per night.

Days Inn -Presbyterian College
Clinton
Jct I-26 at Hwy 56
Clinton, SC
864 833 6600 (800-329-7466)
Dogs of all sizes are allowed. Dogs are allowed for a pet fee of $10 per pet per night.

Quality Inn
12785 Hwy 56 N.
Clinton, SC
864-833-5558 (877-424-6423)
Dogs of all sizes are allowed. Dogs are allowed for a pet fee of $10.00 per pet per night.

Best Western Fort Jackson
240 E Exchange Boulevard
Columbia, SC
803-695-0666 (800-780-7234)
Dogs of all sizes are allowed. Dogs are allowed for a pet fee of $10.00 per pet per night.

Candlewood Suites Columbia-Ft. Jackson
921 Atlas Road
Columbia, SC
803-727-1299 (877-270-6405)
Dogs up to 80 pounds are allowed. Pets allowed with an additional pet fee. Up to $75 for 1-6 nights and up to $150 for 7+ nights. A pet agreement must be signed at check-in.

Days Inn Columbia
1144 Bush River Road
Columbia, SC
803-750-7550 (800-329-7466)
Dogs of all sizes are allowed. Dogs are allowed for a pet fee of $10.00 per pet per stay.

Extended Stay America Columbia - Ft. Jackson
5430 Forest Dr.
Columbia, SC
803-782-2025 (800-804-3724)
One dog is allowed per suite. There is a $25 per night additional pet fee up to $150 for an entire stay.

Extended Stay America Columbia - West
450 Gracern Rd.
Columbia, SC
803-251-7878 (800-804-3724)
One dog is allowed per suite. There is a $25 per night additional pet fee up to $150 for an entire stay.

La Quinta Inn Columbia NE/Fort Jackson
1538 Horseshoe Drive
Columbia, SC
803-736-6400 (800-531-5900)
Dogs of all sizes are allowed. There are no additional pet fees. Dogs must be crated if left alone in the room. Dogs are not allowed in the breakfast area, and they must be leashed and cleaned up after. Multiple dogs may be allowed.

Motel 6 - Columbia East, Sc
7541 Nates Rd
Columbia, SC
803-736-3900 (800-466-8356)
This motel welcomes your pets to stay with you.

Motel 6 - Columbia West, Sc
1776 Burning Tree Rd
Columbia, SC
803-798-9210 (800-466-8356)
This motel welcomes your pets to stay with you.

Ramada
7510 Two Notch Road
Columbia, SC
803-736-3000 (800-272-6232)
There is a $10 per night per pet additional fee. Pets must be leashed when they are not in your room. Multiple dogs may be allowed.

Red Roof Inn Columbia East - Ft Jackson
7580 Two Notch Road
Columbia, SC
803-736-0850 (800-RED-ROOF)

One well-behaved family pet per room. Guest must notify front desk upon arrival. Guest is liable for any damages. In consideration of all guests, pets must never be left unattended in the guest rooms.

Red Roof Inn Columbia West, SC
10 Berryhill Road
Columbia, SC
803-798-9220 (800-RED-ROOF)
One well-behaved family pet per room. Guest must notify front desk upon arrival. Guest is liable for any damages. In consideration of all guests, pets must never be left unattended in the guest rooms.

Residence Inn Columbia
150 Stoneridge Drive
Columbia, SC
803-779-7000 (800-331-3131)
Although located in a quiet residential area, this all suite upscale hotel is only minutes from bustling downtown, the business district, major attractions, and institutes of healing and learning. Additionally, they offer a daily buffet breakfast and midweek evening socials with light fare. Dogs are allowed for an additional pet fee of $50 for the 1st day and $10 per day for each night thereafter to a maximum of $100 per room. Multiple dogs may be allowed.

Residence Inn Columbia Northeast
2320 LeGrand Road
Columbia, SC
803-788-8850 (800-331-3131)
This hotel offers a convenient location to business, shopping, dining, and entertainment areas, plus they offer a number of in-house amenities, including a daily buffet breakfast and evening socials Monday to Thursday. Dogs are allowed for an additional one time pet fee of $75 per room. 2 dogs may be allowed.

Staybridge Suites Columbia
1913 Huger St
Columbia, SC
803-451-5900 (877-270-6405)
Dogs up to 80 pounds are allowed. Pets allowed with an additional pet fee. Up to $75 for 1-6 nights and up to $150 for 7+ nights. A pet agreement must be signed at check-in.

Super 8 Columbia
5719 Fairfield Rd
Columbia, SC
803-735-0008 (800-800-8000)
Dogs of all sizes are allowed. Dogs are allowed for a pet fee of $15.00

per pet per night.

TownePlace Suites Columbia
350 Columbiana Drive
Columbia, SC
803-781-9391 (800-257-3000)
In addition to offering guests a number of in-house amenities, this all suite inn also provides a convenient location to the university, and a variety of business, shopping, dining, and entertainment areas. Dogs are allowed for an additional one time pet fee of $100 per room. Multiple dogs may be allowed.

Comfort Inn
810 Radford Blvd.
Dillon, SC
843-774-4137 (877-424-6423)
Dogs up to 50 pounds are allowed. Dogs are allowed for a pet fee of $25.00 per pet per night. Two dogs are allowed per room.

Econo Lodge
1223 Radford Blvd.
Dillon, SC
843-774-4181 (877-424-6423)
Dogs of all sizes are allowed. Dogs are allowed for a pet fee of $8.00 per pet per night.

Knights Inn Dillon
818 Radford Blvd
Dillon, SC
843-774-6041 (800-843-5644)
Dogs of all sizes are allowed. Dogs are allowed for a pet fee.

South of the Border Motor Inn
H 301/501
Dillon, SC
843-774-2411 (800-845-6011)
This South-of-the-Border themed stop offers lodging, campgrounds, shopping, dining, entertainment, and more. Dogs are allowed throughout the grounds, in the inn and at the campgrounds for no additional pet fee; they are not allowed in most of the park buildings or in food service areas. Dogs must be leashed and under their owner's control at all times. Multiple dogs may be allowed.

Holiday Inn Express Hotel & Suites Greenville-Spartanburg(Duncan)
275 Frontage Road
Duncan, SC
864-486-9191 (877-270-6405)
Dogs of all sizes are allowed. Dogs are allowed for a pet fee of $35.00 per pet per stay.

Quality Inn South
1391 E. Main St.
Duncan, SC
864-433-1333 (877-424-6423)
Dogs up to 50 pounds are allowed. Dogs are allowed for a pet fee of $15.00 per pet per stay.

Jameson Inn
901 Jackson Road
Dunn, SC
910-891-5758
There is a $15 per night per pet additional fee. The fee may vary depending on the length of stay and size/# of pets. 2 dogs may be allowed.

Days Inn West Of Greenville/Clemson Area Easley
121 Days Inn Dr.
Easley, SC
864-859-9902 (800-329-7466)
Dogs of all sizes are allowed. Dogs are allowed for a pet fee.

Comfort Inn
1920 West Lucas Street
Florence, SC
843-665-4558 (877-424-6423)
Dogs of all sizes are allowed. Dogs are allowed for a pet fee of $10.00 per pet per night.

Days Inn Florence
2111 West Lucas St/I-95
Florence, SC
843-665-4444 (800-329-7466)
Dogs are welcome at this hotel.

Days Inn Florence
3783 West Palmetto Street
Florence, SC
843-665-8550 (800-329-7466)
Dogs are welcome at this hotel.

Howard Johnson Express Inn and Suites SC Florence
3821 Bancroft Road
Florence, SC
877-665-9494 (800-446-4656)
Dogs of all sizes are allowed. Dogs are allowed for a pet fee of $10.00 per pet per stay.

Knights Inn Florence
2038 W. Lucas St
Florence, SC
843-669-4241 (800-843-5644)
Dogs are welcome at this hotel. There is a $10 additional one time pet fee.

Motel 6 - Florence, Sc
1834 Lucas St
Florence, SC
843-667-6100 (800-466-8356)

Dog-Friendly Lodging - Please always call ahead to make sure an establishment is still dog-friendly.

This motel welcomes your pets to stay with you.

Quality Inn & Suites Civic Center
150 Dunbarton Drive
Florence, SC
843-664-2400 (877-424-6423)
Dogs of all sizes are allowed. Dogs are allowed for a pet fee of $20.00 per pet per stay. Two dogs are allowed per room.

Ramada Center Florence
1819 West Lucas Street
Florence, SC
843-665-4555 (800-272-6232)
Dogs are welcome at this hotel.

Ramada SC Florence
3311 Meadors Road
Florence, SC
843-669-4171 (800-272-6232)
Dogs of all sizes are allowed. Dogs are allowed for a pet fee of $10 per pet per night.

Red Roof Inn Florence - Civic Center
2690 Davis McLeod Boulevard
Florence, SC
843-678-9000 (800-RED-ROOF)
One well-behaved family pet per room. Guest must notify front desk upon arrival. Guest is liable for any damages. In consideration of all guests, pets must never be left unattended in the guest rooms.

Super 8 Florence
1832 1/2 Lucas Street
Florence, SC
843-661-7267 (800-800-8000)
Dogs of all sizes are allowed. Dogs are allowed for a pet fee of $10.00 per pet per night.

Thunderbird Motor Inn
2004 W Lucas St
Florence, SC
843-669-1611
There are no additional pet fees. Multiple dogs may be allowed.

Travelodge SC Florence
3783A W. Palmetto St.
Florence, SC
843-673-0070 (800-578-7878)
Dogs of all sizes are allowed. Dogs are allowed for a pet fee of $5.00 per pet per night.

Young's Plantation Inn
US 76 and I-95
Florence, SC
843-669-4171
There is a $10 per day per pet fee. 2 dogs may be allowed.

Holiday Inn Folly Beach Oceanfront
One Center Street, Hwy 171 South
Folly Beach, SC
843-588-6464 (877-270-6405)
Dogs of all sizes are allowed. Dogs are allowed for a pet fee of $75.00 per pet per stay.

Comfort Inn At Carowinds
3725 Avenue Of The Carolinas
Fort Mill, SC
803-548-5200 (877-424-6423)
Dogs of all sizes are allowed.

Motel 6 - Charlotte Carowinds, Sc
255 Carowinds Blvd
Fort Mill, SC
803-548-9656 (800-466-8356)
This motel welcomes your pets to stay with you.

Days Inn Turbeville
7835 Myrtle Beach Highway
Gable, SC
843-659-8060 (800-329-7466)
Dogs of all sizes are allowed. Dogs are allowed for a nightly pet fee.

Quality Inn
143 Corona Dr.
Gaffney, SC
864-487-4200 (877-424-6423)
Dogs of all sizes are allowed. Dogs are allowed for a pet fee of $10.00 per pet per night.

Red Roof Inn Gaffney
132 New Painter Drive
Gaffney, SC
864-206-0200 (800-RED-ROOF)
One well-behaved family pet per room. Guest must notify front desk upon arrival. Guest is liable for any damages. In consideration of all guests, pets must never be left unattended in the guest rooms.

Sleep Inn
834 Windslow Ave
Gaffney, SC
864-487-5337 (877-424-6423)
Dogs up to 80 pounds are allowed. Dogs are allowed for a pet fee of $15.00 per pet per night.

Super 8 Gaffney
100 Ellis Ferry Avenue
Gaffney, SC
864-489-1699 (800-800-8000)
Dogs are welcome at this hotel.

Quality Inn
103 Red Bank Road
Goose Creek, SC
843-572-9500 (877-424-6423)
Dogs of all sizes are allowed. Dogs are allowed for a pet fee of $25.00

per pet per stay. Two dogs are allowed per room.

Best Western
5009 Pelham Rd
Greenville, SC
864-297-5353 (800-780-7234)
There is a $10 per day pet fee. 2 dogs may be allowed.

Clarion Inn & Suites
50 Orchard Park Dr.
Greenville, SC
864-254-6383 (877-424-6423)
Dogs of all sizes are allowed. Dogs are allowed for a pet fee of $15.00 per pet per stay. Two dogs are allowed per room.

Comfort Inn & Suites
831 Congaree Road
Greenville, SC
864-288-6221 (877-424-6423)
Dogs of all sizes are allowed. Dogs are allowed for a pet fee of $25.00 per pet per stay. Two dogs are allowed per room.

Extended Stay America Greenville - Airport
3715 Pelham Rd.
Greenville, SC
864-213-9698 (800-804-3724)
One dog is allowed per suite. There is a $25 per night additional pet fee up to $150 for an entire stay.

Hawthorn Suites
48 McPrice Court
Greenville, SC
864-297-0099 (800-527-1133)
In addition to providing a convenient location to many local sites and activities, this all-suite hotel offers a number of amenities for business and leisure travelers, including their signature breakfast buffet and beautifully appointed rooms. Dogs up to 75 pounds are allowed for an additional one time pet fee of $100 per room. 2 dogs may be allowed.

La Quinta Inn & Suites Greenville Haywood
65 W. Orchard Park Drive
Greenville, SC
864-233-8018 (800-531-5900)
Dogs of all sizes are allowed. There are no additional pet fees. Dogs must be leashed and cleaned up after. Multiple dogs may be allowed.

La Quinta Inn Greenville Woodruff Rd
31 Old Country Rd.
Greenville, SC
864-297-3500 (800-531-5900)

Dogs of all sizes are allowed. There are no additional pet fees. Dogs may not be left unattended, and they must be leashed and cleaned up after. Multiple dogs may be allowed.

Motel 6 - Greenville, Sc
224 Bruce Rd
Greenville, SC
864-277-8630 (800-466-8356)
This motel welcomes your pets to stay with you.

Quality Inn & Suites
1314 S. Pleasantburg Drive
Greenville, SC
864-770-3737 (877-424-6423)
Dogs of all sizes are allowed. Dogs are allowed for a pet fee of $25.00 per pet per stay.

Quality Inn Executive Center
540 N. Pleasantburg Dr.
Greenville, SC
864-271-0060 (877-424-6423)
Dogs of all sizes are allowed. Dogs are allowed for a pet fee of $15.00 per pet per stay. Two dogs are allowed per room.

Red Roof Inn Greenville
2801 Laurens Road
Greenville, SC
864-297-4458 (800-RED-ROOF)
One well-behaved family pet per room. Guest must notify front desk upon arrival. Guest is liable for any damages. In consideration of all guests, pets must never be left unattended in the guest rooms.

Residence Inn Greenville-Spartanburg Airport
120 Milestone Way
Greenville, SC
864-627-0001 (800-331-3131)
Located only a few minutes to downtown, this hotel offers a convenient location to business, shopping, dining, and recreation areas, plus they offer a number of in-house amenities including a daily buffet breakfast, and evening socials Monday through Thursday with light dinner fare. Dogs are allowed for an additional one time pet fee of $100 per room. Multiple dogs may be allowed.

Sleep Inn Carolina First Center
231 N Pleasantburg Drive
Greenville, SC
864-240-2006 (877-424-6423)
Dogs of all sizes are allowed. Dogs are allowed for a pet fee of $20.00 per pet per night. Two dogs are allowed per room.

Staybridge Suites Greenville I-85 Woodruff Road
31 Market Point Drive
Greenville, SC
864-288-4448 (877-270-6405)
Dogs up to 80 pounds are allowed. Pets allowed with an additional pet fee. Up to $75 for 1-6 nights and up to $150 for 7+ nights. A pet agreement must be signed at check-in.

TownePlace Suites Greenville Haywood Mall
75 Mall Connector Road
Greenville, SC
864-675-1670 (800-257-3000)
Besides offering a number of in-house amenities for all level of travelers, this all suite inn also offers a convenient location to business, shopping, dining, and entertainment areas. Dogs are allowed for an additional fee of $25 per night for the first 3 nights to a maximum fee of $75 per stay per room. Multiple dogs may be allowed.

Holiday Inn Express Hotel & Suites Greenville-I-85 & Pelham Rd
2681 Dry Pocket Road
Greer, SC
864-213-9331 (877-270-6405)
Dogs of all sizes are allowed. Dogs are allowed for a nightly pet fee.

MainStay Suites Pelham Road
2671 Dry Pocket Rd
Greer, SC
864-987-5566 (877-424-6423)
Dogs of all sizes are allowed. Dogs are allowed for a pet fee of $10.00 per pet per night.

Days Inn Interstate Highway 95 State Line Hardeeville
16633 Whyte Hardee Blvd
Hardeeville, SC
843-784-2281 (800-329-7466)
Dogs of all sizes are allowed. Dogs are allowed for a pet fee of $10.00 per pet per night.

Motel 6 - Hardeeville
120 Independent Blvd
Hardeeville, SC
843-784-3192 (800-466-8356)
This motel welcomes your pets to stay with you.

Quality Inn & Suites
19000 Whyte Hardee BLVD
Hardeeville, SC
843-784-7060 (877-424-6423)
Dogs of all sizes are allowed. Dogs

are allowed for a pet fee of $10.00 per pet per night. Two dogs are allowed per room.

Super 8 Hardeeville
19289 Whyte Hardee Blvd
Hardeeville, SC
843-784-2151 (800-800-8000)
Dogs of all sizes are allowed. Dogs are allowed for a pet fee of $10.00 per pet per night.

Beachwalk Hotel & Condominiums
40 Waterside Drive
Hilton Head Island, SC
843-842-8888 (888-843-4136)
hiltonheadbeachwalkhotel.com
This hotel on Hilton Head Island near the beach allows up to 2 dogs. There is a $40 non-refundable one time pet fee.

Comfort Inn - South Forest Beach
2 Tanglewood Dr.
Hilton Head Island, SC
843-842-6662 (877-424-6423)
Dogs of all sizes are allowed.

Daufuskie Island Resort & Breathe Spa
421 Squire Pope Road
Hilton Head Island, SC
800-648-6778
Daufuskie Island is a family friendly island golf and spa resort located a short ferry boat cruise from Hilton Head Island. They have a "Deluxe Doggie package" for your best friends for $35 per night per dog. They provide a Canine goodie bag at check - in, which includes doggie treats, chew toy, doggie pick-up bags, a Daufuskie Island Resort & Breathe Spa dog tag with phone number and a "Dog Guest in residence" door hanger!. Awaiting your friend in the room is a doggie bed, extra towels, food and water bowl with bottled water. The resort has two 18 hole championship golf courses.

Hilton Hotel
23 Ocean Lane
Hilton Head Island, SC
843-842-8000 (800-HILTONS (445-8667))
Located just off the east coast, this island resort-style hotel offers a number of on site amenities for business and leisure travelers, including balcony rooms with outstanding views, fine dining, and a beach bar. Dogs up to 75 pounds are allowed for an additional one time pet fee of $100 per room, and there is a pet policy to sign at check in. 2 dogs may be allowed.

Dog-Friendly Lodging - Please always call ahead to make sure an establishment is still dog-friendly.

Pet Friendly Hilton Head Rentals
Call to Arrange
Hilton Head Island, SC
843-342-5815
PetFriendlyHiltonHeadRentals.com
Dogs are allowed in a number of the
vacation rentals from this company.
Some breeds are not allowed.

Quality Inn & Suites
200 Museum Street
Hilton Head Island, SC
843-681-3655 (877-424-6423)
Dogs of all sizes are allowed.

Red Roof Inn Hilton Head Island
5 Regency Parkway
Hilton Head Island, SC
843-686-6808 (800-RED-ROOF)
One well-behaved family pet per
room. Guest must notify front desk
upon arrival. Guest is liable for any
damages. In consideration of all
guests, pets must never be left
unattended in the guest rooms.

Beautiful Dog Friendly Beach House
21 27th Avenue
Isle Of Palms, SC
843-452-6593
This 5 bedroom, 3 bath pet-friendly
vacation rental is across the street
from a dog park and recreation
center.

Days Inn Summerville Charleston
Ladson
119 Gateway Dr
Ladson, SC
843-797-1214 (800-329-7466)
Dogs of all sizes are allowed. Dogs
are allowed for a pet fee.

Days Inn Lake City
170 South Ron McNair Blvd
Lake City, SC
843-394-3269 (800-329-7466)
Dogs of all sizes are allowed. Dogs
are allowed for a nightly pet fee.

Travelodge Lancaster
1100 North Main Street
Lancaster, SC
803-286-6441 (800-578-7878)
Dogs of all sizes are allowed. Dogs
are allowed for a pet fee.

The Red Horse Inn
310 N Campbell Road
Landrum, SC
864-895-4968
There is a $25 one time fee per pet
and a pet policy to sign at check in. A
credit card must be on file. No extra-
large dogs are allowed. 2 dogs may
be allowed.

Quality Inn & Suites
328 W. Main St.
Lexington, SC
803-359-3099 (877-424-6423)
Dogs of all sizes are allowed. Dogs
are allowed for a pet fee of $40.00
per pet per night.

Holiday Inn Hotel & Suites N. Myrtle
Beach-Little River
722 Highway 17
Little River, SC
843-281-9400 (877-270-6405)
Dogs of all sizes are allowed. Dogs
are allowed for a pet fee of $20 per
pet per night.

Quality Inn & Suites
850 US HWY 1 South
Lugoff, SC
803-438-9441 (877-424-6423)
Dogs of all sizes are allowed. Dogs
are allowed for a pet fee of $25.00
per pet per stay.

Ramada Limited Lugoff
542 Hwy 601 South
Lugoff, SC
803-438-1807 (800-272-6232)
Dogs are welcome at this hotel.

Quality Inn
3031 Paxville Highway
Manning, SC
803-473-7550 (877-424-6423)
Dogs of all sizes are allowed. Dogs
are allowed for a pet fee of $12.00
per pet per stay.

Ramada of Manning
2816 Paxville Hwy
Manning, SC
803-473-5135 (800-272-6232)
Dogs of all sizes are allowed. Dogs
are allowed for a pet fee.

Super 8 Manning
1062 Cross Road
Manning, SC
803-473-4646 (800-800-8000)
Dogs of all sizes are allowed. Dogs
are allowed for a pet fee of $10 per
pet per stay.

Super 8 Greenville Area Mauldin
310 W Butler Rd
Mauldin, SC
864-751-0003 (800-800-8000)
Dogs are welcome at this hotel.

Days Inn Mount Pleasant-
Charleston-Patriots Point
261 Johnnie Dodds Blvd
Mount Pleasant, SC
843-881-1800 (800-329-7466)
Dogs of all sizes are allowed. Dogs

are allowed for a pet fee of $10 per
pet per night.

Extended Stay America Charleston -
Mt. Pleasant
304 Wingo Way
Mount Pleasant, SC
843-884-4453 (800-804-3724)
One dog is allowed per suite. There
is a $25 per night additional pet fee
up to $150 for an entire stay.

Holiday Inn Charleston-Mt. Pleasant
250 Johnnie Dodds Blvd, Hwy 17
Mount Pleasant, SC
843-884-6000 (877-270-6405)
Dogs of all sizes are allowed. Dogs
are allowed for a pet fee of $75.00
per pet per stay.

Masters Inn
300 Wingo Way
Mount Pleasant, SC
843-884-2814
There is a $10 per night fee for the
1st and 2nd nights,,, there is no
additional fee thereafter. Dogs must
be crated or removed for
housekeeping.

Red Roof Inn Mt Pleasant - Patriots
Point
301 Johnnie Dodds Boulevard
Mount Pleasant, SC
843 884-1411 (800-RED-ROOF)
One well-behaved family pet per
room. Guest must notify front desk
upon arrival. Guest is liable for any
damages. In consideration of all
guests, pets must never be left
unattended in the guest rooms.

Residence Inn Charleston Mt.
Pleasant
1116 Isle of Palms Connector
Mount Pleasant, SC
843-881-1599 (800-331-3131)
Besides offering an 'ambiance of the
islands', this all suite, upscale inn
also provides a number of in-house
amenities, including a daily buffet
breakfast and evening hospitality
hours. Dogs are allowed for an
additional one time pet fee of $100
per room. Multiple dogs may be
allowed.

Rodeway Inn
310 Highway 17 Bypass
Mount Pleasant, SC
843-884-5853 (877-424-6423)
Dogs up to 75 pounds are allowed.
Dogs are allowed for a pet fee of
$30.00 per pet per stay. Two dogs
are allowed per room.

Sleep Inn

Dog-Friendly Lodging - Please always call ahead to make sure an establishment is still dog-friendly.

299 Wingo Way
Mount Pleasant, SC
843-856-5000 (877-424-6423)
Dogs of all sizes are allowed. Dogs
are allowed for a pet fee of $15.00
per pet per night.

Booe Realty
7728 N. Kings Hwy
Myrtle Beach, SC
800-845-0647
booerealty.com
Serving the Myrtle Beach and Grand
Strand area for more than 31 years,
Booe Realty offers many properties
(condos and houses) that are pet
friendly.

Days Inn Myrtle Beach
3650 Waccamaw Blvd
Myrtle Beach, SC
843-236-9888 (800-329-7466)
Dogs of all sizes are allowed. Dogs
are allowed for a nightly pet fee.

La Quinta Inn & Suites Myrtle Beach
1561 21st Avenue North
Myrtle Beach, SC
843-916-8801 (800-531-5900)
Dogs of all sizes are allowed. There
are no additional pet fees. Dogs
must be quiet, well behaved, leashed
and cleaned up after. Dogs may not
be left alone in the room for long
periods. Multiple dogs may be
allowed.

Mariner Motel
7003 N Ocean Blvd
Myrtle Beach, SC
843-449-5281
Dogs only are allowed and of all
sizes. There is a $10 per night per
pet additional fee.

Red Roof Inn Myrtle Beach Hotel -
Market Commons
2801 South Kings Highway
Myrtle Beach, SC
843-626-4444 (800-RED-ROOF)
One well-behaved family pet per
room. Guest must notify front desk
upon arrival. Guest is liable for any
damages. In consideration of all
guests, pets must never be left
unattended in the guest rooms.

Staybridge Suites Myrtle Beach On
Hard Rock Pkwy
303 Hard Rock Parkway
Myrtle Beach, SC
843-903-4000 (877-270-6405)
Dogs up to 80 pounds are allowed.
Pets allowed with an additional pet
fee. Up to $75 for 1-6 nights and up
to $150 for 7+ nights. A pet
agreement must be signed at check-

in.

The Palm House - Dog Friendly
Vacation Rental
P O Box 51165
Myrtle Beach, SC
843-236-6623
This dog-friendly vacation rental
home offers a fenced in yard and a
central location.

The Sea Mist Resort
1200 S Ocean Blvd
Myrtle Beach, SC
843-448-1551
seamist.com/
There is a $56 fee per pet per stay.
Dogs up to 100 pounds are allowed.
2 dogs may be allowed.

Vancouver Motel
2601 S Ocean Beach Blvd
Myrtle Beach, SC
843-448-4331
Well behaved dogs up to 75 pounds
are allowed. There is a $10 per
night per room additional pet fee. 2
dogs may be allowed.

Days Inn Charleston- Airport
Coliseum
2998 West Montague Ave
N. Charleston, SC
843-747-4101 (800-329-7466)
Dogs of all sizes are allowed. Dogs
are allowed for a pet fee of $10.00
per pet per stay.

Days Inn Newberry
I-26 & Hwy 34/Winnsboro Rd
Newberry, SC
803-276-2294 (800-329-7466)
Dogs are welcome at this hotel.

Quality Inn
1147 Wilson Rd.
Newberry, SC
803-276-1600 (877-424-6423)
Dogs of all sizes are allowed. Two
dogs are allowed per room.

Candlewood Suites I-26 @
Northwoods Mall
2177 Northwoods Blvd
North Charleston, SC
843-797-3535 (877-270-6405)
Dogs up to 80 pounds are allowed.
Pets allowed with an additional pet
fee. Up to $75 for 1-6 nights and up
to $150 for 7+ nights. A pet
agreement must be signed at
check-in.

Comfort Suites
2540 North Forest Drive
North Charleston, SC
843-725-5400 (877-424-6423)

Dogs up to 100 pounds are allowed.
Dogs are allowed for a pet fee of
$10.00 per pet per night. Two dogs
are allowed per room.

Extended Stay America Charleston -
Airport - North Charleston
5059 N. Arco Ln.
North Charleston, SC
843-747-3787 (800-804-3724)
One dog is allowed per suite. There
is a $25 per night additional pet fee
up to $150 for an entire stay.

Homestead Studio Suites Charleston
- Airport - North Charleston
5045 N. Arco Ln.
North Charleston, SC
843-740-3440 (800-804-3724)
One dog is allowed per suite. There
is a $25 per night additional pet fee
up to $150 for an entire stay.

Motel 6 - Charleston North
2551 Ashley Phosphate Rd
North Charleston, SC
843-572-6590 (800-466-8356)
This motel welcomes your pets to
stay with you.

Quality Inn
7415 Northside Dr.
North Charleston, SC
843-572-6677 (877-424-6423)
Dogs of all sizes are allowed. Dogs
are allowed for a pet fee of $25.00
per pet per night.

Red Roof Inn North Charleston
Coliseum
7480 Northwoods Boulevard
North Charleston, SC
843-572-9100 (800-RED-ROOF)
One well-behaved family pet per
room. Guest must notify front desk
upon arrival. Guest is liable for any
damages. In consideration of all
guests, pets must never be left
unattended in the guest rooms.

Residence Inn Charleston
7645 Northwoods Blvd
North Charleston, SC
843-572-5757 (800-331-3131)
Some of the amenities of this inn
include a convenient location to the
historic downtown area, a daily buffet
breakfast; complimentary hospitality
hours, an outdoor pool, Sport Court,
and a grocery shopping service.
Dogs are allowed for an additional
one time pet fee of $100 per room.
Multiple dogs may be allowed.

Residence Inn Charleston Airport
5035 International Blvd
North Charleston, SC

843-266-3434 (800-331-3131)
This all suite, upscale hotel offers a central location to many of the areas numerous star attractions and sites of interest. And, among the in-house amenities they offer a daily buffet breakfast, weekday evening hospitality hours, an outdoor pool, and a Sport Court. Dogs are allowed for an additional one time pet fee of $100. 2 dogs may be allowed.

Sheraton Hotel North Charleston
Convention Center
4770 Goer Dr.
North Charleston, SC
843-747-1900 (888-625-5144)
Dogs of all sizes are allowed for an additional one time pet fee of $40 per room. Dogs may not be left alone in the room. 2 dogs may be allowed.

Sleep Inn
7435 Northside Dr.
North Charleston, SC
843-572-8400 (877-424-6423)
Dogs of all sizes are allowed. Dogs are allowed for a pet fee of $10.00 per pet per night.

Staybridge Suites North Charleston
7329 Mazyck Road
North Charleston, SC
843-377-4600 (877-270-6405)
Dogs up to 80 pounds are allowed. Pets allowed with an additional pet fee. Up to $75 for 1-6 nights and up to $150 for 7+ nights. A pet agreement must be signed at check-in.

Beautiful Barefoot Resort
6203 Catalina Drive
North Myrtle Beach, SC
845-781-6651
This 3rd floor, two bedroom, two bath villa sleeps six and is pet-friendly.

Retreat Myrtle Beach
Call to Arrange
North Myrtle Beach, SC
843-280-3015 (800-645-3618)
retreatmyrtlebeach.com
Over 65 pet friendly homes and condos on the Grand Strand. Privately owned properties include luxury oceanfront condos and private homes with pools and fences. Big and small welcome, pet fee $50 and up.

Comfort Inn & Suites
3671 Saint Matthews Rd.
Orangeburg, SC
803-531-9200 (877-424-6423)
Dogs of all sizes are allowed. Dogs are allowed for a pet fee of $10.00

per pet per night.

Days Inn South Orangeburg
3402 Five Chop Road
Orangeburg, SC
803-534-0500 (800-329-7466)
Dogs are welcome at this hotel.

Howard Johnson Express Inn - Orangeburg
3608 St Matthews Rd
Orangeburg, SC
803-531-4900 (800-446-4656)
Dogs of all sizes are allowed. Dogs are allowed for a pet fee of $10.00 per pet per night.

Quality Inn & Suites Downtown
1415 John C. Calhoun Dr.
Orangeburg, SC
803-531-4600 (877-424-6423)
Dogs of all sizes are allowed. Dogs are allowed for a pet fee of $10.00 per pet per stay.

Super 8 Greenville Area Piedmont
3104 Hwy 153
Piedmont, SC
864-220-1836 (800-800-8000)
Dogs of all sizes are allowed. Dogs are allowed for a pet fee of $10.00 per pet per stay.

Comfort Inn
3041 Lancaster Hwy
Richburg, SC
803-789-7100 (877-424-6423)
Dogs of all sizes are allowed.

Econo Lodge
3190 Lancaster Hwy
Richburg, SC
803-789-3000 (877-424-6423)
Dogs of all sizes are allowed. Dogs are allowed for a pet fee of $10.00 per pet per night.

Super 8 /Chester Area Richburg
3085 Lancaster Hwy
Richburg, SC
803-789-7888 (800-800-8000)
Dogs are welcome at this hotel.

Best Western Point South
I-95 & US 17 Exit 33
Ridgeland, SC
843-726-8101 (800-780-7234)
Dogs of all sizes are allowed. Dogs are allowed for a pet fee.

Comfort Inn
221 James Taylor Rd.
Ridgeland, SC
843-726-2121 (877-424-6423)
Dogs up to 80 pounds are allowed. Dogs are allowed for a pet fee of $10.00 per pet per night. Two dogs

are allowed per room.

Quality Inn
511 James F. Taylor Dr.
Ridgeland, SC
843-726-6213 (877-424-6423)
Dogs of all sizes are allowed. Dogs are allowed for a pet fee of $10.00 per pet per night. Two dogs are allowed per room.

Ramada Limited Ridgeway
6173 State Hwy 34
Ridgeway, SC
803-337-7575 (800-272-6232)
Dogs of all sizes are allowed. Dogs are allowed for a pet fee of $10 per pet per stay.

Baymont Inn & Suites Rock Hill
1106 N Anderson Rd
Rock Hill, SC
803-329-1330 (877-229-6668)
Dogs of all sizes are allowed. Dogs are allowed for a pet fee of $10.00 per pet per night.

Motel 6 - Rock Hill, Sc
2640 North Cherry Road
Rock Hill, SC
803-329-1122 (800-466-8356)
This motel welcomes your pets to stay with you.

Super 8 Rock Hill
888 Riverview Road
Rock Hill, SC
803-980-0400 (800-800-8000)
Dogs of all sizes are allowed. Dogs are allowed for a pet fee of $10 per pet per night.

Comfort Inn
139 Motel Dr.
Saint George, SC
843-563-4180 (877-424-6423)
Dogs of all sizes are allowed.

Quality Inn
6014 W Jim Bilton Blvd.
Saint George, SC
843-563-4581 (877-424-6423)
Dogs of all sizes are allowed. Dogs are allowed for a pet fee of $10.00/room per pet per night.

Howard Johnson Express Inn SC Santee
9112 Old # 6 Highway
Santee, SC
803-854-3870 (800-446-4656)
Dogs are welcome at this hotel. There is a $10 one time pet fee.

Motel 6 - Santee, Sc
249 Britain Street
Santee, SC

803-854-3221 (800-466-8356)
This motel welcomes your pets to stay with you.

Quality Inn & Suites
8929 Bass Drive
Santee, SC
803-854-2121 (877-424-6423)
Dogs up to 50 pounds are allowed. Dogs are allowed for a pet fee of $10.00 per pet per stay. Two dogs are allowed per room.

Super 8 Santee
I-95 Exit 98 - Hwy 6 East
Santee, SC
803-854-3456 (800-800-8000)
Dogs are welcome at this hotel.

Travelodge Santee
9091 Old Hwy 6
Santee, SC
803-854-3122 (800-578-7878)
Dogs of all sizes are allowed. Dogs are allowed for a pet fee of $10.00 per pet per night.

Days Inn Simpsonville
45 Ray E Talley CT
Simpsonville, SC
864-963-7701 (800-329-7466)
Dogs of all sizes are allowed. Dogs are allowed for a pet fee.

Motel 6 - Greenville Simpsonville
3706 Grandview Dr
Simpsonville, SC
864-962-8484 (800-466-8356)
This motel welcomes your pets to stay with you.

Quality Inn
3755 Grandview Dr.
Simpsonville, SC
864-963-2777 (877-424-6423)
Dogs of all sizes are allowed. Dogs are allowed for a pet fee of $7.00 per pet per night. Two dogs are allowed per room.

Days Inn
101 Outlet Road
Spartanburg, SC
864-576-7300 (800-329-7466)
Dogs of all sizes are allowed. Dogs are allowed for a nightly pet fee.

Days Inn Spartanburg
115 Rogers Commerce Blvd
Spartanburg, SC
864-814-0560 (800-329-7466)
Dogs are welcome at this hotel.

Econo Lodge
6765 Pottery Rd.
Spartanburg, SC
864-587-0129 (877-424-6423)

Dogs of all sizes are allowed. Dogs are allowed for a pet fee of $5.00 per pet per night.

Extended Stay America
Spartanburg - Asheville Hwy.
130 Mobile Dr.
Spartanburg, SC
864-573-5949 (800-804-3724)
One dog is allowed per suite. There is a $25 per night additional pet fee up to $150 for an entire stay.

Holiday Inn Express Hotel & Suites
I-26 & US 29 At Westgate Mall
895 Spartan Blvd
Spartanburg, SC
864-699-7777 (877-270-6405)
Dogs of all sizes are allowed. Dogs are allowed for a pet fee.

Motel 6 - Spartanburg
105 Jones Rd
Spartanburg, SC
864-573-6383 (800-466-8356)
This motel welcomes your pets to stay with you.

Super 8 /I-26 Exit 22 Spartanburg
488 South Blackstock Road
Spartanburg, SC
864-576-2488 (800-800-8000)
Dogs of all sizes are allowed. Dogs are allowed for a pet fee of $20.00 per pet per night.

Days Inn St. George
128 Interstate Drive
St George, SC
843-563-4027 (800-329-7466)
Dogs of all sizes are allowed. Dogs are allowed for a pet fee of $10.00 per pet per stay.

Super 8 St. George
114 Winningham Rd
St George, SC
843-563-5551 (800-800-8000)
Dogs of all sizes are allowed. Dogs are allowed for a pet fee of $5.00 per pet per stay.

Days Inn Summerton
400 Buff Blvd.
Summerton, SC
803-485-2865 (800-329-7466)
Dogs are welcome at this hotel.

Comfort Inn
1005 Jockey Ct.
Summerville, SC
843-851-2333 (877-424-6423)
Dogs of all sizes are allowed. Dogs are allowed for a pet fee of $35.00 per pet per stay.

Econo Lodge

110 Holiday Rd.
Summerville, SC
843-875-3022 (877-424-6423)
Dogs of all sizes are allowed. Dogs are allowed for a pet fee of $10.00 per pet per night.

Holiday Inn Express Charleston-Summerville
120 Holiday Dr.
Summerville, SC
843-875-3300 (877-270-6405)
Dogs are welcome at this hotel.

Sleep Inn
115 Holiday Dr.
Summerville, SC
843-851-9595 (877-424-6423)
Dogs of all sizes are allowed. Dogs are allowed for a pet fee of $10.00 per pet per night.

Econo Lodge
226 North Washington Street
Sumter, SC
803-775-2323 (877-424-6423)
Dogs of all sizes are allowed. Dogs are allowed for a pet fee of $10.00 per pet per night.

Quality Inn
2390 Broad Street
Sumter, SC
803-469-9001 (877-424-6423)
Dogs up to 75 pounds are allowed. Dogs are allowed for a pet fee of $25.00 per pet per stay. Two dogs are allowed per room.

Sleep Inn
110 Hawkins Rd
Travelers Rest, SC
864-834-7040 (877-424-6423)
Dogs of all sizes are allowed. Dogs are allowed for a pet fee of $15.00 per pet per night.

Microtel Inn & Suites
130 Cane Branch Road
Walterboro, SC
843-539-5656 (800-771-7171)
Pets are welcome at this dog-friendly hotel on I-95 in Walterboro.

Motel 6 - Walterboro
1288 Sniders Hwy
Walterboro, SC
843-538-6266 (800-466-8356)
This motel welcomes your pets to stay with you.

Quality Inn & Suites
1286 Sniders Highway
Walterboro, SC
843-538-5473 (877-424-6423)
Dogs up to 50 pounds are allowed. Dogs are allowed for a pet fee of

$10.00 per pet per night.

Ramada Walterboro
1245 Sniders Hwy
Walterboro, SC
843-538-5403 (800-272-6232)
Dogs of all sizes are allowed. Dogs are allowed for a pet fee of $10 per pet per night.

Rice Planters Inn
I-95 and SR 63
Walterboro, SC
843-538-8964
There is a $5 per day additional pet fee. Multiple dogs may be allowed.

Sleep Inn
3043 Hiers Corner Road
Walterboro, SC
843-539-1199 (877-424-6423)
Dogs of all sizes are allowed. Dogs are allowed for a pet fee of $10.00 per pet per night.

Super 8 Walterboro
1972 Bells Highway
Walterboro, SC
843-538-5383 (800-800-8000)
Dogs of all sizes are allowed. Dogs are allowed for a pet fee of $10.00 per pet per night.

Holiday Inn Columbia-Airport
500 Chris Drive
West Columbia, SC
803-794-9440 (877-270-6405)
Dogs of all sizes are allowed. Dogs are allowed for a pet fee of $45.00 per pet per stay.

Days Inn Winnsboro
1894 US HWY 321 Bypass
Winnsboro, SC
803-635-1447 (800-329-7466)
Dogs of all sizes are allowed. Dogs are allowed for a pet fee.

Holiday Inn Express Point South
(Yemassee Area)
138 Frampton Dr
Yemassee, SC
843-726-9400 (877-270-6405)
Dogs of all sizes are allowed. Dogs are allowed for a pet fee of $25.00 per pet per night.

KI Point South Yemassee
420 Campground Road
Yemassee, SC
843-726-8488 (800-843-5644)
Dogs of all sizes are allowed. Dogs are allowed for a nightly pet fee.

Super 8 Yemassee
409 Yemassee Hwy
Yemassee, SC

843-589-2177 (800-800-8000)
Dogs of all sizes are allowed. Dogs are allowed for a nightly pet fee.

South Dakota

Best Western Ramkota Hotel
1400 8th Avenue NW
Aberdeen, SD
605-229-4040 (800-780-7234)
Dogs are welcome at this hotel.

Comfort Inn
2923 6th Ave. S.E.
Aberdeen, SD
605-226-0097 (877-424-6423)
Dogs of all sizes are allowed.

Holiday Inn Express Hotel & Suites
Aberdeen
3310 7th Ave SE
Aberdeen, SD
605-725-4000 (877-270-6405)
Dogs of all sizes are allowed. Dogs are allowed for a pet fee of $20.00 per pet per stay.

Ramada Convention Center
Aberdeen
2727 6th Ave SE
Aberdeen, SD
605-225-3600 (800-272-6232)
Dogs of all sizes are allowed. Dogs are allowed for a pet fee of $25.00 per pet per stay.

Super 8 East Aberdeen
2405 6th Ave SE
Aberdeen, SD
605-229-5005 (800-800-8000)
Dogs of all sizes are allowed. Dogs are allowed for a pet fee of $6.00 per pet per night.

Super 8 North Aberdeen
1023 8th Ave NW
Aberdeen, SD
605-226-2288 (800-800-8000)
Dogs of all sizes are allowed. Dogs are allowed for a pet fee of $6.00 per pet per night.

Super 8 West Aberdeen
Jct Hwy 12 & 281
Aberdeen, SD
605-225-1711 (800-800-8000)
Dogs of all sizes are allowed. Dogs are allowed for a pet fee of $6.00 per pet per night.

The White House Inn
500 6th Avenue SW/H 12
Aberdeen, SD
605-225-5000 (800-225-6000)
aberdeenwhitehouseinn.com/
Dogs are allowed at this inn for an

additional pet fee of $10 per night per room. 2 dogs may be allowed.

Motel 6 - Belle Fourche
1815 5th Ave
Belle Fourche, SD
605-892-6663 (800-466-8356)
This motel welcomes your pets to stay with you.

Super 8 SD Belle Fourche
501 National Street
Belle Fourche, SD
605-892-3361 (800-800-8000)
Dogs are welcome at this hotel.

Days Inn Brookings
2500 E. 6th. St.
Brookings, SD
605-692-9471 (800-329-7466)
Dogs are welcome at this hotel.

Super 8 Brookings
3034 LeFevre Dr
Brookings, SD
605-692-6920 (800-800-8000)
Dogs are welcome at this hotel.

Super 8 SD Chamberlain
Box 36 Lakeview Heights
Chamberlain, SD
605-734-6548 (800-800-8000)
Dogs are welcome at this hotel.

Days Inn Chamberlain/Oacoma
400 East Highway 16
Chamberlain/Oacoma, SD
605-734-4100 (800-329-7466)
Dogs of all sizes are allowed. Dogs are allowed for a pet fee of $10.00 per pet per night.

Legion Lake Resort in Custer State Park
Highway 16a
Custer, SD
605-255-4521
Dogs are allowed in the cabins at the Blue Bell Lodge. There is a $10 per day per pet charge. Multiple dogs may be allowed.

State Game Lodge in Custer State Park
Highway 16
Custer, SD
605-255-4541
Dogs are allowed in the cabins only,,, they are not allowed in the historic lodge. There is a $10 per day per pet charge. This lodge was known as the Summer White House after hosting Presidents Coolidge and Eisenhower. It is open from mid-May through mid-October. All cabins are non-smoking. Multiple dogs may be allowed.

Super 8 /Crazy Horse Area Custer
535 W Mt Rushmore Rd
Custer, SD
605-673-2200 (800-800-8000)
Dogs of all sizes are allowed. Dogs
are allowed for a pet fee.

Black Hill Inn and Suites
206 Mt. Shadow Lane
Deadwood, SD
605-578-7791 (888-886-6835)
blackhillsinn.com/
Offering a beautiful mountain setting,
this creekside inn is located on the
multi-use Mickelson Trail for some
great hiking experiences. They also
provide a creekside picnic area with
grills, an indoor pool and hot tub.
Dogs are allowed for an additional
pet fee of $20 per night per room
with advance reservations. There is a
$100 refundable cash pet deposit
unless there is a credit card on file.
Dogs may not be left unattended in
the room, and they must be leashed
and cleaned up after (plastic bags
are available in the office). Dogs are
to be walked in the designated pet
areas. Multiple dogs may be allowed.

Super 8 Faulkton
700 Main St., PO Box 355
Faulkton, SD
605-598-4567 (800-800-8000)
Dogs are welcome at this hotel.

Best Western Golden Spike Inn &
Suites
601 E Main Street
Hill City, SD
605-574-2577 (800-780-7234)
Dogs of all sizes are allowed. Dogs
are allowed for a pet fee of $10.00
per pet per night.

Super 8 /Mt Rushmore/ Area Hill City
109 Main Street
Hill City, SD
605-574-4141 (800-800-8000)
Dogs are welcome at this hotel.

Anise's BnB4Pets
1 Canyon View Circle
Hot Springs, SD
605-745-7455 (800-794-4142)
bnb4pets.com/
Sitting secluded on 15 wooded
acres, this pet friendly inn even
makes homemade doggy biscuits for
their canine quests and provide a
nice off leashed fenced area. Dogs
are welcome here for no additional
fee; they must be house trained, in
good health, friendly, and crated
when left alone in the room (crates
available if needed). Dogs must be

leashed when not in the fenced
area, cleaned up after, and pets
must be current on vaccinations.
Multiple dogs may be allowed.

FlatIron Coffee Bar, Grill and Guest
Suites
745 N River Street/H 385
Hot Springs, SD
605-745-5301
flatiron.bz/
Listed on the National Historic
Register, this unique 1911 guest
house offers 4 beautiful suites, a
comfortable lounging veranda,
landscaped grounds, and a
seasonal coffee bar and grill that
roasts their coffee on-site and
grinds it fresh every day (see listing
under restaurants). Dogs are
allowed for an additional fee of $10
per night per room. They must be
leashed and cleaned up after, and
crated when left alone in the room.
Dogs are also allowed at the outer
tables of the restaurant. 2 dogs may
be allowed.

Holiday Inn Express Hotel & Suites
Hot Springs
1401 Hwy. 18 Bypass
Hot Springs, SD
605-745-4411 (877-270-6405)
Dogs are welcome at this hotel.

Motel 6 - Hot Springs, Sd
541 Indianapolis Ave
Hot Springs, SD
605-745-6666 (800-466-8356)
This motel welcomes your pets to
stay with you.

Super 8 Hot Springs
800 Mammoth Street
Hot Springs, SD
605-745-3888 (800-800-8000)
Dogs of all sizes are allowed. Dogs
are allowed for a pet fee of $10.80
per pet per night.

Best Western Of Huron
2000 Dakota Avenue S
Huron, SD
605-352-2000 (800-780-7234)
Dogs are welcome at this hotel.

Comfort Inn
100 21st Street SW
Huron, SD
605-352-6655 (877-424-6423)
Dogs up to 50 pounds are allowed.
Dogs are allowed for a pet fee of
$25.00 per pet per stay.

Dakota Plains Inn
Highway 14E
Huron, SD

605-352-1400
There are no additional pet fees.
Dogs must be crated or removed for
housekeeping. Multiple dogs may be
allowed.

Super 8 Huron
2189 Dakota Ave South
Huron, SD
605-352-0740 (800-800-8000)
Dogs of all sizes are allowed. Dogs
are allowed for a nightly pet fee.

Best Western Four Presidents Lodge
24075 Highway 16A
Keystone, SD
605-666-4472 (800-780-7234)
Dogs of all sizes are allowed. Dogs
are allowed for a pet fee of $10 per
pet per night.

Powder House Lodge
24125 H 16A
Keystone, SD
605-666-4646 (800-321-0692)
powderhouselodge.com/index.htm
Nestled among the pines, this inn
offers a number of amenities,
including offering a central location to
many other sites of interest, a heated
pool, playground, and a gift shop.
Dogs are allowed for an additional
one time fee of $15 per pet. 2 dogs
may be allowed.

Super 8 Kimball
Interstate 90-exit 284
Kimball, SD
605-778-6088 (800-800-8000)
Dogs of all sizes are allowed. Dogs
are allowed for a pet fee of $10 per
pet per stay.

Super 8 Madison
219 N Highland
Madison, SD
605-256-6931 (800-800-8000)
Dogs of all sizes are allowed. Dogs
are allowed for a pet fee of $10 per
pet per night.

Super 8 Miller
Hwy 14W and Hwy 45N
Miller, SD
605-853-2721 (800-800-8000)
Dogs of all sizes are allowed. Dogs
are allowed for a nightly pet fee.

Best Western Motor Inn
1001 S Burr Street
Mitchell, SD
605-996-5536 (800-780-7234)
Dogs are welcome at this hotel.

Days Inn SD Mitchell
1506 South Burr
Mitchell, SD

605-996-6208 (800-329-7466)
Dogs are welcome at this hotel.

Econo Lodge
1313 South Ohlman
Mitchell, SD
605-996-6647 (877-424-6423)
Dogs of all sizes are allowed. Dogs
are allowed for a pet fee of $10.00
per pet per night.

Kelly Inns
1010 Cabella Drive
Mitchell, SD
605-995-0500
Dogs of all sizes are allowed. There
is a pet policy to sign at check in and
there are no additional pet fees. 2
dogs may be allowed.

Motel 6 - Mitchell
1309 Ohlman St
Mitchell, SD
605-996-0530 (800-466-8356)
This motel welcomes your pets to
stay with you.

Ramada Inn And Suites Conference
Center
1525 West Havens Ave
Mitchell, SD
605-996-6501 (800-272-6232)
Dogs of all sizes are allowed. Dogs
are allowed for a nightly pet fee.

Siesta Motel
1210 West Havens
Mitchell, SD
605-996-5544 (800-424-0537)
siestamotel.com/
There are no additional pet fees. 2
dogs may be allowed.

Best Western Graham's
301 W 5th Street
Murdo, SD
605-669-2441 (800-780-7234)
Dogs are welcome at this hotel.

Days Inn
302 West 5th
Murdo, SD
605-669-2425 (800-329-7466)
Dogs are welcome at this hotel.

Super 8 Murdo
604 E 5th
Murdo, SD
605-669-2437 (800-800-8000)
Dogs are welcome at this hotel.

Comfort Inn
1311 River Drive
North Sioux City, SD
605-232-3366 (877-424-6423)
Dogs of all sizes are allowed. Dogs
are allowed for a pet fee of $10.00

per pet per stay.

Super 8 North Sioux City
1300 River Dr
North Sioux City, SD
605-232-4716 (800-800-8000)
Dogs are welcome at this hotel.

Howard Johnson Inn and Suites
Oacoma
203 East Highway 16
Oacoma, SD
605-234-4222 (800-446-4656)
Dogs are welcome at this hotel.
There is a $10 one time pet fee.

Oasis Inn Chamberlain
1100 E H 16
Oacoma, SD
605-734-6061 (800-635 3559)
oasisinnchamberlain.com/
In addition to being close to the
Missouri River and the Lewis and
Clark Trail, this hotel also sits
central to a number of other local
attractions. Dogs are allowed for no
additional fee; there is a pet
agreement to sign at check in. Dogs
may not be left alone in the room at
any time and they are not allowed in
food service areas. Multiple dogs
may be allowed.

Best Western Ramkota Hotel
920 W Sioux Avenue
Pierre, SD
605-224-6877 (800-780-7234)
Dogs are welcome at this hotel.

Capitol Inn & Suites
815 Wells Avenue
Pierre, SD
605-224-6387
There are no additional pet fees.
Multiple dogs may be allowed.

Comfort Inn
410 W. Sioux Ave.
Pierre, SD
605-224-0377 (877-424-6423)
Dogs of all sizes are allowed. Dogs
are allowed for a pet fee of $10.00
per pet per night.

River Lodge
713 W Sioux Avenue/H 14/83
Pierre, SD
605-224-4140 (866-457-0088)
riverlodgesd.com/
There are 47 guest rooms offered at
this hotel; they also sit close to the
Missouri River and a number of
local sites of interest. Dogs are
allowed for an additional one time
fee of $6 per pet. Dogs must be
leashed and cleaned up after.
Multiple dogs may be allowed.

Super 8 SD Pierre
320 W Sioux
Pierre, SD
605-224-1617 (800-800-8000)
Dogs are welcome at this hotel.

Best Western Town 'N Country
2505 Mount Rushmore Road S
Highway 16
Rapid City, SD
605-343-5383 (800-780-7234)
Dogs of all sizes are allowed. Dogs
are allowed for a pet fee.

Days Inn Rapid City
1570 N LaCrosse St
Rapid City, SD
605-348-8410 (800-329-7466)
Dogs are welcome at this hotel.

Econo Lodge
625 E. Disk Dr.
Rapid City, SD
605-342-6400 (877-424-6423)
Dogs of all sizes are allowed. Dogs
are allowed for a pet fee of $10.00
per pet per stay.

Hillside Country Cottages
13315 S H 16
Rapid City, SD
605-342-4121
hillsidecountrycabins.com/
Nestled in the woods of the Black
Hills, the theme here is "rustic
ambiance outside, but modern
inside". In addition to providing a
game room, small playground, and
hiking paths, they are also centrally
located to a number of local sites of
interest. Dogs are allowed for an
additional pet fee of $10 per night
per pet. Dogs may not be left
unattended in the cabins, and they
must be kept leashed (or crated),
and cleaned up after-except when in
primitive areas only. Dogs must be
well behaved, and if they are
accustomed to being on the furniture,
they request bringing a protective
cover. 2 dogs may be allowed.

Holiday Inn Express Hotel & Suites
Rapid City
645 East Disk Drive
Rapid City, SD
605-355-9090 (877-270-6405)
Dogs of all sizes are allowed. Dogs
are allowed for a nightly pet fee.

Holiday Inn Express Rapid City
750 Cathedral Drive
Rapid City, SD
605-341-9300 (877-270-6405)
Dogs are welcome at this hotel.

Dog-Friendly Lodging - Please always call ahead to make sure an establishment is still dog-friendly.

Holiday Inn Rapid City-Rushmore Plaza
505 North Fifth St
Rapid City, SD
605-348-4000 (877-270-6405)
Dogs of all sizes are allowed. Dogs are allowed for a pet fee of $15.00 per pet per night.

Motel 6 - Rapid City
620 Latrobe St
Rapid City, SD
605-343-3687 (800-466-8356)
Your pets are welcome to stay here with you.

Quality Inn
1902 LaCrosse St
Rapid City, SD
605-342-3322 (877-424-6423)
Dogs of all sizes are allowed. Dogs are allowed for a pet fee of $10.00 per pet per night.

Ramada West Rapid City
7900 Stage Stop Road
Rapid City, SD
605-787-4844 (800-272-6232)
Dogs of all sizes are allowed. Dogs are allowed for a pet fee of $10.00 per pet per night.

Rodeway Inn Mt. Rushmore Area
2208 Mt. Rushmore Rd.
Rapid City, SD
605-342-1303 (877-424-6423)
Dogs of all sizes are allowed.

Super 8 Rushmore Rd Rapid City
2520 Tower Rd
Rapid City, SD
605-342-4911 (800-800-8000)
Dogs of all sizes are allowed. Dogs are allowed for a pet fee of $5.00 per pet per stay.

Super 8 /Lacrosse St Rapid City
2124 Lacrosse St
Rapid City, SD
605-348-8070 (800-800-8000)
Dogs of all sizes are allowed. Dogs are allowed for a nightly pet fee.

Baymont Inn & Suites Sioux Falls
3200 Meadow Avenue
Sioux Falls, SD
605-362-0835 (877-229-6668)
Dogs of all sizes are allowed. Dogs are allowed for a pet fee of $15 per pet per stay.

Best Western Empire Towers
4100 W Shirley Place
Sioux Falls, SD
605-361-3118 (800-780-7234)
Dogs of all sizes are allowed. Dogs are allowed for a pet fee of $15 per

pet per night.

Best Western Ramkota Hotel
3200 W Maple Street
Sioux Falls, SD
605-336-0650 (800-780-7234)
Dogs are welcome at this hotel.

Comfort Inn South
3216 S. Carolyn Ave.
Sioux Falls, SD
605-361-2822 (877-424-6423)
Dogs of all sizes are allowed. Dogs are allowed for a pet fee of $10.00 per pet per night.

Comfort Suites
3208 S. Carolyn Ave.
Sioux Falls, SD
605-362-9711 (877-424-6423)
Dogs of all sizes are allowed. Dogs are allowed for a pet fee of $10.00 per pet per night. Two dogs are allowed per room.

Days Inn Airport Sioux Falls
5001 N Cliff Avenue/I-90
Sioux Falls, SD
605-331-5959 (800-329-7466)
Dogs of all sizes are allowed. Dogs are allowed for a nightly pet fee.

Days Inn Sioux Falls
3401 Gateway Blvd
Sioux Falls, SD
605-361-9240 (800-329-7466)
Dogs of all sizes are allowed. Dogs are allowed for a nightly pet fee.

Econo Lodge North
5100 N Cliff Ave
Sioux Falls, SD
605-331-4490 (877-424-6423)
Dogs of all sizes are allowed. Dogs are allowed for a pet fee of $10.00 per pet per stay. Two dogs are allowed per room.

Kelly Inn
3101 W. Russell Street
Sioux Falls, SD
605-338-6242
kellyinns.com/locations.html
There is no extra charge for pets, just sign a pet damage waiver. Multiple dogs may be allowed.

Knights Inn Sioux Falls
1508 W Russell St
Sioux Falls, SD
605-339-9330 (800-843-5644)
Dogs of all sizes are allowed. Dogs are allowed for a pet fee of $10 per pet per night.

Motel 6 - Sioux Falls
3009 Russell St

Sioux Falls, SD
605-336-7800 (800-466-8356)
This motel welcomes your pets to stay with you.

Quality Inn & Suites
5410 N. Granite Lane
Sioux Falls, SD
605-336-1900 (877-424-6423)
Dogs up to 50 pounds are allowed. Dogs are allowed for a pet fee of $10.00 per pet per night.

Ramada Sioux Falls
407 Lyons Avenue
Sioux Falls, SD
605-330-0000 (800-272-6232)
Dogs are welcome at this hotel.

Red Roof Inn Sioux Falls
3500 Gateway Boulevard
Sioux Falls, SD
605-361-1864 (800-RED-ROOF)
One well-behaved family pet per room. Guest must notify front desk upon arrival. Guest is liable for any damages. In consideration of all guests, pets must never be left unattended in the guest rooms.

Residence Inn Sioux Falls
4509 W Empire Place
Sioux Falls, SD
605-361-2202 (800-331-3131)
In addition to offering a convenient location to universities, businesses, shopping, dining, and entertainment areas, this hotel also provides a number of in-house amenities, including a daily buffet breakfast and evening social hours mid-week. Dogs are allowed for an additional one time pet fee of $75 per room. 2 dogs may be allowed.

Rodeway Inn
4208 West 41st St.
Sioux Falls, SD
605-361-2345 (877-424-6423)
Dogs of all sizes are allowed. Dogs are allowed for a pet fee of $15.00 per pet per stay. Two dogs are allowed per room.

Staybridge Suites Sioux Falls At Empire Mall
2505 S. Carolyn Ave.
Sioux Falls, SD
605-361-2298 (877-270-6405)
Dogs up to 80 pounds are allowed. Pets allowed with an additional pet fee. Up to $75 for 1-6 nights and up to $150 for 7+ nights. A pet agreement must be signed at check-in.

Super 8 Sioux Falls

2616 East 10th Street
Sioux Falls, SD
605-338-8881 (800-800-8000)
Dogs of all sizes are allowed. Dogs
are allowed for a pet fee of $10.00
per pet per night.

Super 8 Airport I90
4808 N Cliff
Sioux Falls, SD
605-339-9212 (800-800-8000)
Dogs are welcome at this hotel.

TownePlace Suites Sioux Falls
4545 W Homefield Drive
Sioux Falls, SD
605-361-2626 (800-257-3000)
In addition to offering a number of in-
house amenities for all level of
travelers, this all suite inn also
provides a convenient location to
business, shopping, dining, and
entertainment areas. Dogs are
allowed for an additional one time
fee of $75 per room. Multiple dogs
may be allowed.

Super 8 Sisseton
2104 SD Hwy 10
Sisseton, SD
605-742-0808 (800-800-8000)
Dogs are welcome at this hotel.

Best Western Black Hills Lodge
540 E Jackson Boulevard
Spearfish, SD
605-642-7795 (800-780-7234)
Dogs are welcome at this hotel.

Days Inn Spearfish
240 Ryan Road/I-90
Spearfish, SD
605-642-7101 (800-329-7466)
Dogs of all sizes are allowed. Dogs
are allowed for a pet fee.

Holiday Inn Spearfish-Convention
Center
305 N 27th St.
Spearfish, SD
800-999-3541 (877-270-6405)
Dogs are welcome at this hotel. The
hotel charges a $25 pet fee per room
& a refundable $100.00 fee.

Howard Johnson Express Inn-
Spearfish
323 South 27th Street
Spearfish, SD
605-642-8105 (800-446-4656)
Dogs of all sizes are allowed. Dogs
are allowed for a pet fee of $10.00
per pet per stay.

Super 8 Spearfish
440 Heritage Dr
Spearfish, SD

605-642-4721 (800-800-8000)
Dogs of all sizes are allowed. Dogs
are allowed for a pet fee.

Travelodge Spearfish
346 W Kansas ST
Spearfish, SD
605-559-3333 (800-578-7878)
Dogs are welcome at this hotel.

Days Inn Sturgis
2630 Lazelle Street
Sturgis, SD
605-347-3027 (800-329-7466)
Dogs are welcome at this hotel.

Prairie Sky Guest Ranch
44370 109th Street
Veblen, SD
605-738-2411
prairieskyranch.com/
Wide open country, a true "out
western" ambiance, ranch style
dining, and a variety of recreational
activities year around are all
available at this guest ranch. Dogs
are allowed for no additional fee;
they must be leashed and under
their owner's control. Dogs are not
allowed on the bed or furnishings,
and must be crated when left in the
room alone. 2 dogs may be allowed.

Comfort Inn
701 W. Cherry St.
Vermillion, SD
605-624-8333 (877-424-6423)
Dogs of all sizes are allowed. Dogs
are allowed for a pet fee of $10.00
per pet per night.

Super 8 SD Vermillion
1208 E Cherry St
Vermillion, SD
605-624-8005 (800-800-8000)
Dogs of all sizes are allowed. Dogs
are allowed for a pet fee of $5.40
per pet per stay.

Best Western Plains Motel
712 Glenn Street
Wall, SD
605-279-2145 (800-780-7234)
Dogs of all sizes are allowed. Dogs
are allowed for a nightly pet fee.

Econo Lodge
804 Glenn Street
Wall, SD
605-279-2121 (877-424-6423)
Dogs of all sizes are allowed.

Motel 6 - Wall
211 10th Street
Wall, SD
605-279-2133 (800-466-8356)
This motel welcomes your pets to

stay with you.

Days Inn Watertown
2900 9th Ave. SE/I-29
Watertown, SD
605-886-3500 (800-329-7466)
Dogs of all sizes are allowed. Dogs
are allowed for a pet fee.

Holiday Inn Express Hotel & Suites
Watertown
3901 9th Ave SE
Watertown, SD
605-882-3636 (877-270-6405)
Dogs of all sizes are allowed. Dogs
are allowed for a pet fee of $10.00
per pet per stay.

Quality Inn
800 35th St Cir
Watertown, SD
605-886-3010 (877-424-6423)
Dogs of all sizes are allowed. Dogs
are allowed for a pet fee of $15.00
per pet per stay.

Super 8 Watertown
3 Blks S Jct Hwys 212 & 81
Watertown, SD
605-882-1900 (800-800-8000)
Dogs are welcome at this hotel.

Iron Horse Inn
600 Whitewood Service Road
Whitewood, SD
605-722-7574 (888-888-9091)
ironhorseinnsturgis.com/
This hotel sits central to a number of
local sites of interest and activities.
Dogs are allowed for no additional
fee; they must be leashed and
cleaned up after at all times. Multiple
dogs may be allowed.

Rodeway Inn & Suites
902 Easy Highway 44
Winner, SD
605-842-0991 (877-424-6423)
Dogs of all sizes are allowed. Dogs
are allowed for a pet fee of $10.00
per pet per night.

Days Inn SD Yankton
2410 Broadway
Yankton, SD
605-665-8717 (800-329-7466)
Dogs of all sizes are allowed. Dogs
are allowed for a pet fee.

Super 8 Yankton
1603 East Highway 50
Yankton, SD
605-665-6510 (800-800-8000)
Dogs are welcome at this hotel.

Tennessee

Dog-Friendly Lodging - Please always call ahead to make sure an establishment is still dog-friendly.

Candlewood Suites Knoxville Airport-Alcoa
176 Cusick Road
Alcoa, TN
865-233-4411 (877-270-6405)
Dogs up to 80 pounds are allowed. Pets allowed with an additional pet fee. Up to $75 for 1-6 nights and up to $150 for 7+ nights. A pet agreement must be signed at check-in.

Days Inn Knoxville Airport Alcoa
2962 Alcoa Hwy
Alcoa, TN
865-970-3060 (800-329-7466)
Dogs are welcome at this hotel.

MainStay Suites
361 Fountain View Circle
Alcoa, TN
865-379-7799 (877-424-6423)
Dogs of all sizes are allowed. Dogs are allowed for a pet fee of $25.00 per pet per stay.

Super 8 Antioch
1121 Bell Rd.
Antioch, TN
615-731-8440 (800-800-8000)
Dogs are welcome at this hotel.

Econo Lodge
2620 Decatur Pike
Athens, TN
423-744-8200 (877-424-6423)
Dogs of all sizes are allowed. Dogs are allowed for a pet fee of $7.00 per pet per night. Two dogs are allowed per room.

Motel 6 - Athens
2002 Whitaker Rd
Athens, TN
423-745-4441 (800-466-8356)
This motel welcomes your pets to stay with you.

Super 8 Athens
2541 Decatur Pike
Athens, TN
423-745-4500 (800-800-8000)
Dogs of all sizes are allowed. Dogs are allowed for a pet fee of $10 per pet per stay.

Suburban Extended Stay Hotel
7380 Stage Road Highway 64
Bartlett, TN
901-388-6000 (877-424-6423)
Dogs of all sizes are allowed.

Motel 6 - Brownsville Bells
9740 Us-70 East
Bells, TN
731-772-9500 (800-466-8356)

This motel welcomes your pets to stay with you.

Lakeview RV Park
4550 Highway 11 E
Bluff City, TN
423-538-5600 (866-800-0777)
lakeviewrvpark.com
Camp at a scenic lake at the hub of the Tri-Cities area. They have no pet fees and no weight limits. Free dog treats are available at the office.

Baymont Inn and Suites Nashville/Brentwood
111 Penn Warren Drive
Brentwood, TN
615-376-4666 (877-229-6668)
Dogs of all sizes are allowed. Dogs are allowed for a nightly pet fee.

Candlewood Suites Nashville-Brentwood
5129 Virginia Way
Brentwood, TN
615-309-0600 (877-270-6405)
Dogs up to 80 pounds are allowed. Pets allowed with an additional pet fee. Up to $75 for 1-6 nights and up to $150 for 7+ nights. A pet agreement must be signed at check-in.

Extended Stay America Nashville - Brentwood
9020 Church St. E.
Brentwood, TN
615-377-7847 (800-804-3724)
One dog is allowed per suite. There is a $25 per night additional pet fee up to $150 for an entire stay.

Residence Inn Nashville Brentwood
206 Ward Circle
Brentwood, TN
615-371-0100 (800-331-3131)
Some of the amenities at this all-suite inn include a daily buffet breakfast, evening social hours during the week, a Sport Court, and a complimentary grocery shopping service. Dogs are allowed for an additional one time pet fee of $100 per room. Multiple dogs may be allowed.

Sleep Inn
1611 Galleria Blvd.
Brentwood, TN
615-376-2122 (877-424-6423)
Dogs of all sizes are allowed. Two dogs are allowed per room.

Red Roof Inn Brentwood Franklin Area
8097 Moores Lane

Brentwood (Cool Springs), TN
615-309-8860 (800-RED-ROOF)
One well-behaved family pet per room. Guest must notify front desk upon arrival. Guest is liable for any damages. In consideration of all guests, pets must never be left unattended in the guest rooms.

Days Inn Bristol
3281 W. State Street
Bristol, TN
423-968-9119 (800-329-7466)
Dogs are welcome at this hotel.

Days Inn Parkway Bristol
536 Volunteer Pkwy
Bristol, TN
423-968-2171 (800-329-7466)
Dogs of all sizes are allowed. Dogs are allowed for a pet fee of $8 per pet per night.

Days Inn Brownsville
2530 Anderson Avenue
Brownsville, TN
731-772-3297 (800-329-7466)
Dogs of all sizes are allowed. Dogs are allowed for a nightly pet fee.

Paris Landing Inn
16055 H 79N
Buchanan, TN
731-642-4311
This inn is located in the Paris Landing State Park where a variety of land and water recreation is available. Dogs of all sizes are allowed for an additional fee of $15 per night per pet. There is also a camping area where dogs are allowed at no additional fee. Dogs may not be left unattended, and they must be leashed and cleaned up after. Dogs are allowed on the trails. 2 dogs may be allowed.

Best Western Executive Inn
50 Speedway Ln
Bulls Gap, TN
423-235-9111 (800-780-7234)
Dogs of all sizes are allowed. Dogs are allowed for a pet fee of $15.00 per pet per night.

Super 8 Greeneville Area Bulls Gap
90 Speedway Lane
Bulls Gap, TN
423-235-4112 (800-800-8000)
Dogs are welcome at this hotel.

Montgomery Bell Resort and Conference Center
1020 Jackson Hill Road
Burns, TN
615-797-3101
This resort is located in the

Montgomery Bell State Park, and a variety of land and water recreation is available. Dogs of all sizes are allowed for an additional $15 per night per pet. There is also a camping area on site that allows dogs at no additional fee. Dogs may not be left unattended, and they must be leashed at all times, and cleaned up after. Dogs are not allowed in the lake or other park buildings, but they are allowed on the trails. 2 dogs may be allowed.

Iron Mountain Inn
138 Moreland Drive
Butler, TN
423-768-2446
$75 for 2 dogs, and $100 for 3 dogs. Dogs are not allowed to be left unattended.

Lakeside Cottage
1035 Piercetown Road
Butler, TN
423-768-2446
mountainlakevacation.com/
$75 for 2 dogs, and $100 for 3 dogs. Dogs are not allowed to be left unattended.

Super 8 TN Caryville
I-75 exit #134
Caryville, TN
423-562-8476 (800-800-8000)
Dogs are welcome at this hotel.

Cedar Hill Resort
2371 Cedar Hill Road
Celina, TN
931-243-3201
Dogs are allowed for an additional fee of $20 per night per pet.

Best Western Heritage Inn
7641 Lee Highway
Chattanooga, TN
423-899-3311 (800-780-7234)
Dogs are welcome at this hotel.

Comfort Inn
7620 Hamilton Park Drive
Chattanooga, TN
423-499-1993 (877-424-6423)
Dogs of all sizes are allowed.

Days Inn Lookout Mountain West Chattanooga
3801 Cummings Hwy
Chattanooga, TN
423-821-6044 (800-329-7466)
Dogs of all sizes are allowed. Dogs are allowed for a nightly pet fee.

Extended Stay America Chattanooga - Airport
6240 Airpark Dr.

Chattanooga, TN
423-892-1315 (800-804-3724)
One dog is allowed per suite. There is a $25 per night additional pet fee up to $150 for an entire stay.

Knights Inn South Chattanooga
6650 Ringgold Road
Chattanooga, TN
423-894-1860 (800-843-5644)
Dogs of all sizes are allowed. Dogs are allowed for a pet fee of $10 per pet per night.

La Quinta Inn Chattanooga
7017 Shallowford Rd.
Chattanooga, TN
423-855-0011 (800-531-5900)
Dogs of all sizes are allowed. There are no additional pet fees. Dogs must be quiet, well behaved, leashed and cleaned up after. Dogs may not be left alone in the room for long periods. Multiple dogs may be allowed.

Motel 6 - Chattanooga Downtown
2440 Williams St
Chattanooga, TN
423-265-7300 (800-466-8356)
This motel welcomes your pets to stay with you.

Motel 6 - Chattanooga East
7707 Lee Hwy
Chattanooga, TN
423-892-7707 (800-466-8356)
This motel welcomes your pets to stay with you.

Motel 6 - East Ridge, Tn
2281 Camp Jordan Parkway
Chattanooga, TN
423-894-1417 (800-466-8356)
This motel welcomes your pets to stay with you.

Quality Inn Lookout Mountain
3109 Parker Ln.
Chattanooga, TN
423-821-1499 (877-424-6423)
Dogs up to 60 pounds are allowed. Dogs are allowed for a pet fee of $15.00 per pet per night. Three or more dogs may be allowed.

Quality Suites
7324 Shallowford Rd.
Chattanooga, TN
423-892-1500 (877-424-6423)
Dogs of all sizes are allowed. Dogs are allowed for a pet fee of $10.00 per pet per night.

Ramada Limited /Lookout Mountain/I24 West Chattanooga
30 Birmingham I Iwy

Chattanooga, TN
423-821-7162 (800-272-6232)
Dogs of all sizes are allowed. Dogs are allowed for a pet fee of $10.00 per pet per night.

Red Roof Inn Chattanooga Airport
7014 Shallowford Road
Chattanooga, TN
423-899-0143 (800-RED-ROOF)
One well-behaved family pet per room. Guest must notify front desk upon arrival. Guest is liable for any damages. In consideration of all guests, pets must never be left unattended in the guest rooms.

Residence Inn Chattanooga Downtown
215 Chestnut Street
Chattanooga, TN
423-266-0600 (800-331-3131)
Besides being located only a short walk to the Tennessee River and near the areas business district, major attractions, and restaurants this all suite inn also provides numerous in-house amenities - including a daily hot breakfast buffet and evening socials Monday through Thursday. Dogs are allowed for an additional one time pet fee of $100. Multiple dogs may be allowed.

Super 8 Look Out Mtn
I-24 Exit 174
Chattanooga, TN
423-821-8880 (800-800-8000)
Dogs are welcome at this hotel.

Sheraton Read House Hotel at Chattanooga
827 Broad St.
Chattanooga, TN
423-266-4121 (888-625-5144)
Dogs of all sizes are allowed for an additional one time pet fee of $50 per room. Dogs may not be left alone in the room.

Staybridge Suites Chattanooga Dwtn - Conv Ctnr
1300 Carter Street
Chattanooga, TN
423-267-0900 (877-270-6405)
Dogs up to 80 pounds are allowed. Pets allowed with an additional pet fee. Up to $75 for 1-6 nights and up to $150 for 7+ nights. A pet agreement must be signed at check-in.

Staybridge Suites Chattanooga-Hamilton Place
7015 Shallowford Rd
Chattanooga, TN
423-826-2700 (877-270-6405)

Dogs up to 80 pounds are allowed. Pets allowed with an additional pet fee. Up to $75 for 1-6 nights and up to $150 for 7+ nights. A pet agreement must be signed at check-in.

Super 8 Chattanooga
7024 McCutcheon Road
Chattanooga, TN
423-490-8560 (800-800-8000)
Dogs of all sizes are allowed. Dogs are allowed for a pet fee of $10.00 per pet per night.

Econo Lodge
1142 Volunteer Blvd
Church Hill, TN
423-357-4121 (877-424-6423)
Dogs of all sizes are allowed. Dogs are allowed for a pet fee of $10.00 per pet per night.

Candlewood Suites Clarksville
3050 Clay Lewis Road
Clarksville, TN
931-906-0900 (877-270-6405)
Dogs up to 80 pounds are allowed. Pets allowed with an additional pet fee. Up to $75 for 1-6 nights and up to $150 for 7+ nights. A pet agreement must be signed at check-in.

Days Inn North Clarksville
130 Westfield Court
Clarksville, TN
931-552-1155 (800-329-7466)
Dogs are welcome at this hotel.

Days Inn TN Clarksville
1100 Hwy 76/I-24
Clarksville, TN
931-358-3194 (800-329-7466)
Dogs of all sizes are allowed. Dogs are allowed for a pet fee.

Quality Inn Exit 4
3095 Wilma Rudolph Blvd
Clarksville, TN
931-648-4848 (877-424-6423)
Dogs up to 50 pounds are allowed.

Quality Inn South
1112 SR 76
Clarksville, TN
931-358-2020 (877-424-6423)
Dogs of all sizes are allowed. Dogs are allowed for a pet fee of $10.00 per pet per night.

Ramada Limited
3100 Wilma Rudolph Blvd
Clarksville, TN
931-552-0098 (800-272-6232)
Dogs are welcome at this hotel.

Red Roof Inn Clarksville
197 Holiday Drive
Clarksville, TN
931-905-1555 (800-RED-ROOF)
One well-behaved family pet per room. Guest must notify front desk upon arrival. Guest is liable for any damages. In consideration of all guests, pets must never be left unattended in the guest rooms.

Super 8 Clarksville
635 Huntco Drive
Clarksville, TN
931-358-0810 (800-800-8000)
Dogs are welcome at this hotel.

Days Inn TN Cleveland
2550 Georgetown Road
Cleveland, TN
423-476-2112 (800-329-7466)
Dogs of all sizes are allowed. Dogs are allowed for a nightly pet fee.

Howard Johnson TN Cleveland
2595 Georgetown Rd.
Cleveland, TN
423-476-8511 (800-446-4656)
Dogs of all sizes are allowed. Dogs are allowed for a pet fee of $10 per pet per stay.

Ramada Limited Cleveland
156 James Asbury Drive
Cleveland, TN
423-472-5566 (800-272-6232)
Dogs of all sizes are allowed. Dogs are allowed for a pet fee.

Super 8 Cleveland
163 Berham Dr
Cleveland, TN
423-476-5555 (800-800-8000)
Dogs are welcome at this hotel.

Red Roof Inn Clinton, TN
Clinton, TN
(800-RED-ROOF)
One well-behaved family pet per room. Guest must notify front desk upon arrival. Guest is liable for any damages. In consideration of all guests, pets must never be left unattended in the guest rooms.

Super 8 Clinton
720 Park Place
Clinton, TN
865-457-2311 (800-800-8000)
Dogs are welcome at this hotel.

Days Inn and Suites Collierville
1230 W Poplar Ave
Collierville, TN
901-853-1235 (800-329-7466)
Dogs of all sizes are allowed. Dogs are allowed for a pet fee of $15 per

pet per night.

Days Inn Columbia
1504 Nashville Hwy
Columbia, TN
931-381-3297 (800-329-7466)
Dogs of all sizes are allowed. Dogs are allowed for a nightly pet fee.

Alpine Lodge & Suites
2021 E. Spring St.
Cookeville, TN
931-526-3333 (800-213-2016)
tndirectory.com/alpinelodge/
They have had Great Danes stay here before. As long as the dog is well-behaved, size does not matter. There is a $5 per day per pet charge. 2 dogs may be allowed.

Baymont Inn & Suites Cookeville
1151 South Jefferson Avenue
Cookeville, TN
931-525-6668 (877-229-6668)
Dogs are welcome at this hotel.

Best Western Thunderbird Motel
900 S Jefferson Avenue
Cookeville, TN
931-526-7115 (800-780-7234)
Dogs are welcome at this hotel. There is a $15 one time pet fee.

Clarion Inn
970 S Jefferson Ave
Cookeville, TN
931-526-7125 (877-424-6423)
Dogs of all sizes are allowed. Dogs are allowed for a pet fee of $10.00 per pet per night. Two dogs are allowed per room.

Knights Inn Cookeville
1814 Salem Road
Cookeville, TN
931-528-5411 (800-843-5644)
Dogs are welcome at this hotel.

Econo Lodge
3731 Pulaski Hwy.
Cornersville, TN
931-293-2111 (877-424-6423)
Dogs of all sizes are allowed. Dogs are allowed for a pet fee of $10.00 per pet per stay.

Days Inn Crossville
105 Executive Drive
Crossville, TN
931-484-9691 (800-329-7466)
Dogs are welcome at this hotel.

Holiday Inn Express Dandridge
119 Sharon Drive
Dandridge, TN
865-397-1910 (877-270-6405)
Dogs up to 50 pounds are allowed.

Dogs are allowed for a pet fee.

Mountain Harbor Inn
1199 H 139
Dandridge, TN
865-397-1313 (877-379-1313)
mountainharborinn.com/
This lakeside inn offers luxury in a beautiful country setting in addition to a number of recreational opportunities. Dogs of all sizes are allowed. Dogs under 25 pounds cost an additional $25 per night per pet; dogs over 25 pounds cost an additional $50 per night per pet. Dogs are not permitted on the furniture or beds, and they are not allowed in the lobby or dining areas. Pets must be leashed and cleaned up after at all times. Multiple dogs may be allowed.

Quality Inn
620 Green Valley Dr.
Dandridge, TN
865-397-2090 (877-424-6423)
Dogs of all sizes are allowed. Dogs are allowed for a pet fee of $10.00 per pet per night. Two dogs are allowed per room.

Super 8 Dandridge
I-40 Exit 417
Dandridge, TN
865-397-1200 (800-800-8000)
Dogs are welcome at this hotel.

Best Western Executive Inn
2338 Highway 46 S
Dickson, TN
615-446-0541 (800-780-7234)
Dogs of all sizes are allowed. Dogs are allowed for a pet fee.

Days Inn Dickson
2415 Highway 46 South
Dickson, TN
615-740-7475 (800-329-7466)
Dogs of all sizes are allowed. Dogs are allowed for a pet fee.

Holiday Inn Express Hotel & Suites Dickson
100 Barzani Blvd.
Dickson, TN
615-446-2781 (877-270-6405)
Dogs of all sizes are allowed. Dogs are allowed for a pet fee of $20.00 per pet per night.

Motel 6 - Dickson
2325 Sr 46
Dickson, TN
615-446-2423 (800-466-8356)
This motel welcomes your pets to stay with you.

Quality Inn
1055 E. Christi Drive
Dickson, TN
615-740-0074 (877-424-6423)
Dogs of all sizes are allowed. Dogs are allowed for a pet fee of $10.00 per pet per night. Two dogs are allowed per room.

Super 8 Dickson
150 Suzanne Dr
Dickson, TN
615-446-1923 (800-800-8000)
Dogs are welcome at this hotel.

Best Western Dyersburg Inn
770 US Highway 51 Bypass W
Dyersburg, TN
731-285-8601 (800-780-7234)
Dogs of all sizes are allowed. Dogs are allowed for a pet fee of $15.00 per pet per stay.

Super 8 Erwin
1101 North Buffalo Street
Erwin, TN
423-743-0200 (800-800-8000)
Dogs of all sizes are allowed. Dogs are allowed for a pet fee of $10.00 per pet per stay.

Days Inn Fayetteville
1651 Huntsville Hwy
Fayetteville, TN
931-433-6121 (800-329-7466)
Dogs are welcome at this hotel.

Residence Inn Fort Worth Fossil Creek
5801 Sandshell Drive
Fort Worth, TN
817-439-1300 (800-331-3131)
This all suite hotel sits central to many of the city's star attractions, dining, shopping, and business areas, plus they offer a number of in-house amenities that include a daily buffet breakfast and evening social hours. Dogs are allowed for an additional one time fee of $100 per pet. 2 dogs may be allowed.

Days Inn Nashville Franklin
3915 Carothers Parkway
Franklin, TN
615-790-1140 (800-329-7466)
Dogs of all sizes are allowed. Dogs are allowed for a nightly pet fee.

Holiday Inn Express Hotel & Suites Franklin
4202 Franklin Commons Ct.
Franklin, TN
615-591-6660 (877-270-6405)
Dogs of all sizes are allowed. Dogs are allowed for a pet fee of $30.00 per pet per night.

Homestead Studio Suites Nashville - Franklin - Cool Springs
680 Bakers Bridge Ave.
Franklin, TN
615-771-7600 (800-804-3724)
One dog is allowed per suite. There is a $25 per night additional pet fee up to $150 for an entire stay.

Quality Inn & Suites
1307 Murfreesboro Road
Franklin, TN
615-794-7591 (877-424-6423)
Dogs of all sizes are allowed. Two dogs are allowed per room.

Garden Plaza Hotel
520 Historic Nature Trail
Gatlinburg, TN
865-436-9201 (800-435-9201)
This full service hotel offers a number of on-site amenities and a variety of accommodations, plus a convenient location to shopping, dining, recreational activities, and various attractions. Dogs are allowed for an additional one time fee of $15 (plus tax) per pet. Dogs must be leashed and under their owner's care. 2 dogs may be allowed.

Greenbrier Valley Resorts
Greenbrier Valley Resorts
Gatlinburg, TN
865-436-2015 (800-546-1144)
welovegatlinburg.com
Many of these 1 to 12 bedroom log cabins and chalets are pet friendly. There is a $10 per night per pet fee as well as a $100 refundable pet security deposit. Most of the homes are in the Village of Cobbly Nob, with golf, tennis and swimming pools.

Mountain Shadows Resort
1625 Hidden Hills Road
Gatlinburg, TN
865-430-9201 (877-653-9429)
mtnshadows.com/
Nestled among the trees and lush greenery, this log cabin resort offers some great walking trails and a convenient location to food, fun and more. Visitors can step right out on their decks and enjoy stunning views of the Great Smoky Mountains Dogs are allowed for an additional one time fee of $35 per pet. Dogs must be leashed when outside at all times and crated if left alone in the cabins. Dogs may not be left alone in cars overnight at any time. 2 dogs may be allowed.

Red Roof Inn Gatlinburg
309 Ownby Street

Dog-Friendly Lodging - Please always call ahead to make sure an establishment is still dog-friendly.

Gatlinburg, TN
865-436-7813 (800-RED-ROOF)
One well-behaved family pet per
room. Guest must notify front desk
upon arrival. Guest is liable for any
damages. In consideration of all
guests, pets must never be left
unattended in the guest rooms.

Residence Inn Memphis
Germantown
9314 Poplar Pike
Germantown, TN
901-752-0900 (800-331-3131)
Some of the amenities at this new
all-suite inn include a daily buffet
breakfast, a Manager's reception
Monday through Thursday with a
manager's reception on
Wednesdays, a heated swimming
pool, and a complimentary grocery
shopping service. Dogs are allowed
for an additional one time pet fee of
$100 per room. Multiple dogs may be
allowed.

Days Inn - Goodlettsville
909 Conference Drive
Goodlettsville, TN
615-851-6600 (800-329-7466)
Dogs of all sizes are allowed. Dogs
are allowed for a nightly pet fee.

Motel 6 - Nashville Goodlettsville
323 Cartwright St
Goodlettsville, TN
615-859-9674 (800-466-8356)
Your pets are welcome to stay here
with you.

Quality Inn
925 Conference Dr.
Goodlettsville, TN
615-859-5400 (877-424-6423)
Dogs of all sizes are allowed. Dogs
are allowed for a pet fee of
$10.00usd per pet per night.

Red Roof Inn Nashville North
110 Northgate Drive
Goodlettsville, TN
615-859-2537 (800-RED-ROOF)
One well-behaved family pet per
room. Guest must notify front desk
upon arrival. Guest is liable for any
damages. In consideration of all
guests, pets must never be left
unattended in the guest rooms.

Comfort Inn
1790 E Andrew Johnson H
Greeneville, TN
423-639-4185 (877-424-6423)
Dogs of all sizes are allowed. There
is a $10 per night per room fee and a
pet policy to sign at check in. Dogs
may not be left alone in the room

unless owners are on-site. 2 dogs
may be allowed.

Best Western Harriman Inn
120 Childs Road
Harriman, TN
865-882-6200 (800-780-7234)
Dogs of all sizes are allowed. Dogs
are allowed for a pet fee of $10.00
per pet per night.

Motel 6 - Hermitage, Tn
5768 Old Hickory Blvd
Hermitage, TN
615-889-5060 (800-466-8356)
This motel welcomes your pets to
stay with you.

Super 8 Nashville Hermitage
1414 Princeton Place.
Hermitage, TN
615-871-4545 (800-800-8000)
Dogs are welcome at this hotel.

Days Inn Holladay
13845 Hwy 641 North
Holladay, TN
731-847-2278 (800-329-7466)
Dogs of all sizes are allowed. Dogs
are allowed for a pet fee of $10.00
per pet per stay.

Best Western of Hurricane Mills
15542 Highway 13 S
Hurricane Mills, TN
931-296-4251 (800-780-7234)
Dogs are welcome at this hotel.
There is a charge per pet per night
of $10.00 for small and $15.00 for
large pets.

Days Inn Hurricane Mills
15415 Hwy 13 South
Hurricane Mills, TN
931-296-7647 (800-329-7466)
Dogs of all sizes are allowed. Dogs
are allowed for a nightly pet fee.

Days Inn - North Hollywood
Jackson
2239 Hollywood
Jackson, TN
731-668-4840 (800-329-7466)
Dogs are welcome at this hotel.

Days Inn Jackson
1919 Highway-45 Bypass
Jackson, TN
731-668-3444 (800-329-7466)
Dogs of all sizes are allowed. Dogs
are allowed for a nightly pet fee.

Econo Lodge
1963 US 45 Bypass
Jackson, TN
731-668-4100 (877-424-6423)
Dogs up to 70 pounds are allowed.

Dogs are allowed for a pet fee of
$15.00 per pet per night. Two dogs
are allowed per room.

Knights Inn Jackson
2659 North Highland
Jackson, TN
731-664-8600 (800-843-5644)
Dogs are welcome at this hotel.

La Quinta Inn Jackson
2370 N. Highland
Jackson, TN
731-664-1800 (800-531-5900)
Dogs of all sizes are allowed. There
are no additional fees. Dogs may not
be left unattended, and they must be
leashed and cleaned up after.
Multiple dogs may be allowed.

Motel 6 - Jackson, Tn
1940 Us-45 Byp
Jackson, TN
731-661-0919 (800-466-8356)
This motel welcomes your pets to
stay with you.

Ramada Limited
2262 North Highland Ave
Jackson, TN
731-668-1066 (800-272-6232)
Dogs of all sizes are allowed. Dogs
are allowed for a pet fee.

Super 8 Jackson
2295 N Highland
Jackson, TN
731-668-1145 (800-800-8000)
Dogs of all sizes are allowed. Dogs
are allowed for a pet fee of $10 per
pet per night.

Econo Lodge
531 Patriot Drive
Jefferson City, TN
865-397-9437 (877-424-6423)
Dogs up to 50 pounds are allowed.
Dogs are allowed for a pet fee of
$20.00 per pet per night. Two dogs
are allowed per room.

Days Inn - Tennessee State Line
Jellico
1417 South Main Street
Jellico, TN
423-784-7281 (800-329-7466)
Dogs of all sizes are allowed. Dogs
are allowed for a pet fee of $8.00 per
pet per night.

Days Inn /Nashville Joelton
201 Gifford Place
Joelton, TN
615-876-3261 (800-329-7466)
Dogs are welcome at this hotel.

Comfort Inn

1900 S. Roan St.
Johnson City, TN
423-928-9600 (877-424-6423)
Dogs of all sizes are allowed. Dogs
are allowed for a pet fee of $15.00
per pet per night.

Holiday Inn Johnson City
101 West Springbrook Drive
Johnson City, TN
423-282-4611 (877-270-6405)
Dogs are allowed for $25 per stay.

Quality Inn & Suites
207 East Mountcastle
Johnson City, TN
423-282-3335 (877-424-6423)
Dogs of all sizes are allowed. Dogs
are allowed for a pet fee of $10.00
per pet per night. Two dogs are
allowed per room.

Red Roof Inn Johnson City
210 Broyles Drive
Johnson City, TN
423-282-3040 (800-RED-ROOF)
One well-behaved family pet per
room. Guest must notify front desk
upon arrival. Guest is liable for any
damages. In consideration of all
guests, pets must never be left
unattended in the guest rooms.

Super 8 Kimball
395 Main St.
Kimball, TN
423-837-7185 (800-800-8000)
Dogs of all sizes are allowed. Dogs
are allowed for a pet fee

Best Western Colonial Inn
I-81 Highway 36 @ Exit 59 4234 Fort
Henry Drive
Kingsport, TN
423-239-3400 (800-780-7234)
Dogs of all sizes are allowed. Dogs
are allowed for a pet fee of $10 per
pet per night.

Comfort Inn
100 Indian Center Ct.
Kingsport, TN
423-378-4418 (877-424-6423)
Dogs of all sizes are allowed. Dogs
are allowed for a pet fee of $15.00
per pet per night.

La Quinta Inn Kingsport Tri-Cities
Airport
10150 Airport Parkway
Kingsport, TN
423-323-0500 (800-531-5900)
Dogs of all sizes are allowed. There
are no additional pet fees. Dogs may
not be left unattended, and they must
be leashed and cleaned up after.
Multiple dogs may be allowed.

Super 8 Kingsport
700 Lynn Garden Drive
Kingsport, TN
423-246-5515 (800-800-8000)
Dogs are welcome at this hotel.

Knights Inn TN Kingston
1200 N. Kentucky Street
Kingston, TN
865-376-3477 (800-843-5644)
Dogs of all sizes are allowed. Dogs
are allowed for a nightly pet fee.

Motel 6 - Kingston, Tn
495 Gallaher Road
Kingston, TN
865-376-2069 (800-466-8356)
This motel welcomes your pets to
stay with you.

Best Western Harpeth Inn
116 Luyben Hills Road
Kingston Springs, TN
615-952-3961 (800-780-7234)
Dogs of all sizes are allowed. Dogs
are allowed for a pet fee of $10.00
per pet per stay.

Baymont Inn & Suites Knoxville
814 Brakebill Road
Knoxville, TN
865-246-3600 (877-229-6668)
Dogs are welcome at this hotel.

Best Western Knoxville Suites
5317 Pratt Road
Knoxville, TN
865-687-9922 (800-780-7234)
Dogs of all sizes are allowed. Dogs
are allowed for a pet fee.

Candlewood Suites Knoxville
10206 Parkside Drive
Knoxville, TN
865-777-0400 (877-270-6405)
Dogs up to 80 pounds are allowed.
Pets allowed with an additional pet
fee. Up to $75 for 1-6 nights and up
to $150 for 7+ nights. A pet
agreement must be signed at
check-in.

Crowne Plaza Hotel Knoxville
401 W Summit Hill Dr.
Knoxville, TN
865-522-2600 (877-270-6405)
Dogs up to 50 pounds are allowed.
Dogs are allowed for a pet fee of
$25 per pet per stay.

Days Inn East/Chilhowee
Park/Fairgrounds/Zoo Knoxville
5423 Asheville Hwy
Knoxville, TN
865-637-3511 (800-329-7466)
Dogs are welcome at this hotel.

Days Inn North Knoxville
5335 Central Ave Pike
Knoxville, TN
865-687-5800 (800-329-7466)
Dogs of all sizes are allowed. Dogs
are allowed for a nightly pet fee.

Days Inn West Knoxville
9240 Parkwest Blvd.
Knoxville, TN
865-693-6061 (800-329-7466)
Dogs are welcome at this hotel.

Econo Lodge Inn & Suites East
7424 Strawberry Plains Pk.
Knoxville, TN
865-932-1217 (877-424-6423)
Minutes from Gatlinburg, Pigeon
Forge, Knoxville and the Great
Smoky Mountains.

Extended Stay America Knoxville -
Cedar Bluff
214 Langley Pl.
Knoxville, TN
865-769-0822 (800-804-3724)
One dog is allowed per suite. There
is a $25 per night additional pet fee
up to $150 for an entire stay.

Extended Stay America Knoxville -
West Hills
1700 Winston Rd.
Knoxville, TN
865-694-4178 (800-804-3724)
One dog is allowed per suite. There
is a $25 per night additional pet fee
up to $150 for an entire stay.

Hilton Hotel
501 W Church Avenue
Knoxville, TN
865-523-2300 (800-HILTONS (445-
8667))
Located in the heart of the city, this
upscale hotel offer a number of on
site amenities for business and
leisure travelers, plus the hotel sits
only a short distance from business,
shopping, dining, and entertainment
opportunities. They also have a
covered sky bridge to the convention
center and are only a short walk to
the university. Dogs are allowed for
an additional one time pet fee of $50
per room. Dogs must be crated when
left alone in the room. 2 dogs may be
allowed.

Holiday Inn Express Knoxville-
Strawberry Plains
730 Rufus Graham Road
Knoxville, TN
865-525-5100 (877-270-6405)
Dogs of all sizes are allowed. Dogs
are allowed for a pet fee of $25.00

per pet per night.

Holiday Inn Knoxville Central @ Papermill
1315 Kirby Road
Knoxville, TN
865-584-3911 (877-270-6405)
Dogs of all sizes are allowed. Dogs are allowed for a pet fee of $35.00 per pet per night.

Holiday Inn Select Knoxville-West (I-40 & I-75)
304 Cedar Bluff
Knoxville, TN
865-693-1011 (877-270-6405)
Dogs of all sizes are allowed. Dogs are allowed for a pet fee of $50 per pet per stay.

Howard Johnson Plaza Hotel - Knoxville
7621 Kingston Pike
Knoxville, TN
865-693-8111 (800-446-4656)
Dogs are welcome at this hotel.

La Quinta Inn Knoxville West
258 North Peters Road
Knoxville, TN
865-690-9777 (800-531-5900)
Dogs of all sizes are allowed. There are no additional pet fees. Dogs must be leashed and cleaned up after. Dogs may not be left unattended unless they will be quiet, well behaved, and a contact number left at the front desk. Multiple dogs may be allowed.

Motel 6 - Knoxville North
5640 Merchant Cntr Blvd
Knoxville, TN
865-689-7100 (800-466-8356)
This motel welcomes your pets to stay with you.

Motel 6 - Knoxville West
402 Lovell Rd
Knoxville, TN
865-675-7200 (800-466-8356)
This motel welcomes your pets to stay with you.

Motel 6 - Knoxville, Tn
1550 Cracker Barrel Ln
Knoxville, TN
865-633-6646 (800-466-8356)
This motel welcomes your pets to stay with you.

Quality Inn East
7471 Crosswood Blvd
Knoxville, TN
865-342-0003 (877-424-6423)
Dogs of all sizes are allowed. Dogs are allowed for a pet fee of $20.00

per pet per night.

Quality Inn Merchants Drive
117 Cedar Lane
Knoxville, TN
865-342-3701 (877-424-6423)
Dogs of all sizes are allowed.

Quality Inn North
6712 Central Ave. Pike
Knoxville, TN
865-689-6600 (877-424-6423)
Dogs of all sizes are allowed. Dogs are allowed for a pet fee of $10.00 per pet per night.

Ramada Limited East
722 Brakebill Rd.
Knoxville, TN
865-546-7271 (800-272-6232)
Dogs of all sizes are allowed. Dogs are allowed for a pet fee.

Red Roof Inn Knoxville
5334 Central Avenue Pike
Knoxville, TN
865-688-1010 (800-RED-ROOF)
One well-behaved family pet per room. Guest must notify front desk upon arrival. Guest is liable for any damages. In consideration of all guests, pets must never be left unattended in the guest rooms.

Red Roof Inn Knoxville - University of Tennessee
209 Advantage Place
Knoxville, TN
865-691-1664 (800-RED-ROOF)
One well-behaved family pet per room. Guest must notify front desk upon arrival. Guest is liable for any damages. In consideration of all guests, pets must never be left unattended in the guest rooms.

Residence Inn Knoxville Cedar Bluff
215 Langley Place
Knoxville, TN
865-539-5339 (800-331-3131)
Offering a convenient location to business, historic, shopping, dining, and entertainment areas, this all suite hotel also offers a number of in-house amenities, including a daily buffet breakfast, Monday night socials, and Wednesday barbecues. Dogs are allowed for an additional one time pet fee of $75 per room. Multiple dogs may be allowed.

Sleep Inn
214 Prosperity Dr.
Knoxville, TN
865-531-5900 (877-424-6423)
Dogs up to 60 pounds are allowed.

Dogs are allowed for a pet fee of $15.00 per pet per night.

Super 8 Downtown Area Knoxville
341 Merchants Drive
Knoxville, TN
865-689-7666 (800-800-8000)
Dogs of all sizes are allowed. Dogs are allowed for a pet fee.

Super 8 Downtown/West Knoxville
6200 Paper Mill Rd
Knoxville, TN
865-584-8511 (800-800-8000)
Dogs are welcome at this hotel.

Super 8 /East Knoxville
7585 Crosswood Blvd
Knoxville, TN
865-524-0855 (800-800-8000)
Dogs of all sizes are allowed. Dogs are allowed for a pet fee of $15.00 per pet per night.

Super 8 /West Knoxville
11748 Snyder Road
Knoxville, TN
865-675-5566 (800-800-8000)
Dogs of all sizes are allowed. Dogs are allowed for a pet fee of $10.00 per pet per night.

TownePlace Suites Knoxville Cedar Bluff
205 Langley Place
Knoxville, TN
865-693-5216 (800-257-3000)
In addition to offering a number of in-house amenities for all level of travelers, this all suite inn also provides a convenient location to more than 60 historical sites, the state university, and a variety of museums. Dogs are allowed for an additional one time fee of $90 per room. Multiple dogs may be allowed.

Baymont Inn & Suites Kodak
2863 Winfield Dunn Parkway
Kodak, TN
865-933-9448 (877-229-6668)
Dogs of all sizes are allowed. Dogs are allowed for a pet fee of $10.00 per pet per night.

Days Inn - Sevierville Interstate Smokey Mountains Kodak
1 Sevierville Days Inn Interst
Kodak, TN
865-933-4500 (800-329-7466)
Dogs are welcome at this hotel.

Motel 6 - Kodak
184 Dumplin Valley Rd
Kodak, TN
865-933-8141 (800-466-8356)
This motel welcomes your pets to

stay with you.

Days Inn Lake City
221 Colonial Lane
Lake City, TN
865-426-2816 (800-329-7466)
Dogs of all sizes are allowed. Dogs
are allowed for a pet fee.

Super 8 Lakeland
9779 Huff n Puff Road
Lakeland, TN
901-372-4575 (800-800-8000)
Dogs are welcome at this hotel.

Best Western Villa Inn
2126 N Locust Avenue
Lawrenceburg, TN
931-762-4448 (800-780-7234)
Dogs are welcome at this hotel.
There is a $10 one time pet fee.

Econo Lodge
829 S. Cumberland St.
Lebanon, TN
615-444-1001 (877-424-6423)
Dogs of all sizes are allowed. Dogs
are allowed for a pet fee of $10.00
per pet per night. Two dogs are
allowed per room.

Quality Inn
641 South Cumberland St
Lebanon, TN
615-444-7020 (877-424-6423)
Dogs of all sizes are allowed. Dogs
are allowed for a pet fee of $10.00
per pet per night. Two dogs are
allowed per room.

Ramada Inn and Suites Lebanon
704 S Cumberland St
Lebanon, TN
615-444-7400 (800-272-6232)
Dogs of all sizes are allowed. Dogs
are allowed for a pet fee.

Sleep Inn & Suites
150 S. Eastgate Court
Lebanon, TN
615-449-7005 (877-424-6423)
Dogs of all sizes are allowed.

Super 8 /Nashville Area Lebanon
914 Murfreesboro Rd
Lebanon, TN
615-444-5637 (800-800-8000)
Dogs are welcome at this hotel.

Days Inn Lenoir City
1110 Hwy 321 North
Lenoir City, TN
865-986-2011 (800-329-7466)
Dogs are welcome at this hotel.

Ramada Limited Knoxville Area
400 Intrchange Park Drive

Lenoir City, TN
865-986-9000 (800-272-6232)
Dogs of all sizes are allowed. Dogs
are allowed for a pet fee.

Econo Lodge
732 West Church Street
Lexington, TN
731-968-0171 (877-424-6423)
Dogs up to 50 pounds are allowed.
Two dogs are allowed per room.

Super 8 Loudon
12452 Hwy 72 North
Loudon, TN
865-458-5669 (800-800-8000)
Dogs of all sizes are allowed. Dogs
are allowed for a pet fee of $5.00
per pet per night.

Country Inns & Suites by Carlson
126 Expressway Dr
Manchester, TN
931-728-7551
Dogs up to 40 pounds are allowed.
There are no additional pet fees.

Days Inn and Suites Manchester
2259 Hillsboro Boulevard
Manchester, TN
931-728-9530 (800-329-7466)
Dogs of all sizes are allowed. Dogs
are allowed for a nightly pet fee.

Ramada Limited TN Manchester
2314 Hillsboro Blvd
Manchester, TN
931-728-0800 (000-272-6232)
Dogs of all sizes are allowed. Dogs
are allowed for a pet fee.

Sleep Inn & Suites
84 Relco Drive
Manchester, TN
931-954-0580 (877-424-6423)
Dogs up to 50 pounds are allowed.
Dogs are allowed for a pet fee of
$15.00 per pet per night.

Super 8 Manchester
2430 Hilsboro Blvd
Manchester, TN
931-728-9720 (800-800-8000)
Dogs are welcome at this hotel.

Days Inn Martin
800 University Street
Martin, TN
731-587-9577 (800-329-7466)
Dogs of all sizes are allowed. Dogs
are allowed for a pet fee of $10.00
per pet per night.

Best Western Tree City Inn
809 Sparta Street
Mcminnville, TN
931-473-2159 (800-780-7234)

Dogs are welcome at this hotel for a
pet fee.

Baymont Inn & Suites Memphis East
6020 Shelby Oaks Drive
Memphis, TN
901-377-2233 (800-531-5900)
Dogs of all sizes are allowed. There
are no additional pet fees. Dogs
must be leashed, cleaned up after,
and crated when left alone in the
room. Multiple dogs may be allowed.

Candlewood Suites Memphis
7950 Centennial Drive
Memphis, TN
901-755-0877 (877-270-6405)
Dogs up to 80 pounds are allowed.
Pets allowed with an additional pet
fee. Up to $75 for 1-6 nights and up
to $150 for 7+ nights. A pet
agreement must be signed at check-
in.

Comfort Inn & Suites Airport
3005 Millbranch Road
Memphis, TN
901-396-5411 (877-424-6423)
Dogs up to 50 pounds are allowed.

Days Inn Memphis
2889 Austin Peay Hwy
Memphis, TN
901-386-0033 (800-329-7466)
Dogs of all sizes are allowed. Dogs
are allowed for a nightly pet fee.

Days Inn at Graceland Memphis
3839 Elvis Presley Blvd
Memphis, TN
901-346-5500 (800-329-7466)
Dogs of all sizes are allowed. Dogs
are allowed for a pet fee of $25 per
pet per stay.

East Drury Inn & Suites
1556 Sycamore View
Memphis, TN
901-373-8200 (800-378-7946)
Dogs of all sizes are allowed for no
additional pet fee with a credit card
on file, and there is a pet agreement
to sign at check in.

Extended Stay America Memphis -
Apple Tree
6085 Apple Tree Dr.
Memphis, TN
901-360-1114 (800-804-3724)
One dog is allowed per suite. There
is a $25 per night additional pet fee
up to $150 for an entire stay.

Extended Stay America Memphis -
Mt. Moriah
6520 Mt. Moriah Rd.
Memphis, TN

901-362-0338 (800-804-3724)
One dog is allowed per suite. There is a $25 per night additional pet fee up to $150 for an entire stay.

Extended Stay America Memphis - Poplar Avenue
6325 Quail Hollow
Memphis, TN
901-685-7575 (800-804-3724)
One dog is allowed per suite. There is a $25 per night additional pet fee up to $150 for an entire stay.

Extended Stay America Memphis - Sycamore View
5885 Shelby Oaks Dr.
Memphis, TN
901-386-0026 (800-804-3724)
One dog is allowed per suite. There is a $25 per night additional pet fee up to $150 for an entire stay.

Homestead Studio Suites Memphis - Airport
2541 Corporate Ave. E.
Memphis, TN
901-344-0010 (800-804-3724)
One dog is allowed per suite. There is a $25 per night additional pet fee up to $150 for an entire stay.

Homestead Studio Suites Memphis - Poplar Avenue
6500 Poplar Ave.
Memphis, TN
901-767-5522 (800-804-3724)
One dog is allowed per suite. There is a $25 per night additional pet fee up to $150 for an entire stay.

La Quinta Inn & Suites Memphis Primacy Parkway
1236 Primacy Parkway
Memphis, TN
901-374-0330 (800-531-5900)
Dogs of all sizes are allowed. There are no additional pet fees. Dogs may not be left unattended, and they must be leashed and cleaned up after. Multiple dogs may be allowed.

Motel 6 - Memphis Downtown
210 Pauline St
Memphis, TN
901-528-0650 (800-466-8356)
This motel welcomes your pets to stay with you.

Motel 6 - Memphis East
1321 Sycamore View Rd
Memphis, TN
901-382-8572 (800-466-8356)
This motel welcomes your pets to stay with you.

Quality Inn Airport/Graceland

1581 Brooks Rd.
Memphis, TN
901-345-3344 (877-424-6423)
Dogs of all sizes are allowed. Dogs are allowed for a pet fee of $25.00 per pet per night.

Ramada
1585 Sycamore Rd
Memphis, TN
901-388-6726 (800-272-6232)
Dogs of all sizes are allowed. Dogs are allowed for a pet fee.

Red Roof Inn Memphis Downtown
42 South Camilla Street
Memphis, TN
901-526-1050 (800-RED-ROOF)
One well-behaved family pet per room. Guest must notify front desk upon arrival. Guest is liable for any damages. In consideration of all guests, pets must never be left unattended in the guest rooms.

Red Roof Inn Memphis East
6055 Shelby Oaks Drive
Memphis, TN
901-388-6111 (800-RED-ROOF)
One well-behaved family pet per room. Guest must notify front desk upon arrival. Guest is liable for any damages. In consideration of all guests, pets must never be left unattended in the guest rooms.

Residence Inn Memphis Downtown
110 Monroe Avenue
Memphis, TN
901-578-3700 (800-331-3131)
This beautiful 1930s, all suite inn is registered on the National Historical Registry and guests can take the city's vintage trolley cars (located right outside the inn) to numerous places throughout the city. They also provide a daily buffet breakfast and evening socials Monday through Thursday with light dinner fare. Dogs are allowed for an additional one time pet fee of $100 per room. Multiple dogs may be allowed.

Residence Inn Memphis East
6141 Old Poplar Pike
Memphis, TN
901-685-9595 (800-331-3131)
Located in the birthplace of the Blues and Rock and Roll, there are a number of world class attractions to explore from this all suite inn. They also provide a number of in-house amenities, including a daily buffet breakfast and evening socials. Dogs up to 50 pounds are allowed for an additional one time pet fee of $100 per room. 2 dogs

may be allowed.

Rodeway Inn
1199 Linden Avenue
Memphis, TN
901-726-4171 (877-424-6423)
Dogs of all sizes are allowed. Dogs are allowed for a pet fee of $15.00 per pet per night.

Sleep Inn
2855 Old Austin Peay Hwy
Memphis, TN
901-312-7777 (877-424-6423)
Dogs of all sizes are allowed. Two dogs are allowed per room.

Staybridge Suites Memphis-Poplar Ave East
1070 Ridge Lake Blvd.
Memphis, TN
901-682-1722 (877-270-6405)
Dogs up to 80 pounds are allowed. Pets allowed with an additional pet fee. Up to $75 for 1-6 nights and up to $150 for 7+ nights. A pet agreement must be signed at check-in.

Studio 6 - Memphis
4300 American Way
Memphis, TN
901-366-9333 (800-466-8356)
Your pets are welcome to stay here with you for a pet fee of $10 per day up to $50 for an entire stay.

Super 8 /Airport/East Memphis
4060 Lamar Ave
Memphis, TN
901-362-0011 (800-800-8000)
Dogs of all sizes are allowed. Dogs are allowed for a pet fee.

Days Inn Monteagle
742 Dixie Lee Ave
Monteagle, TN
931-924-2900 (800-329-7466)
Dogs are welcome at this hotel.

Super 8 Monterey
522 East Stratton Ave
Monterey, TN
931-584-0070 (800-800-8000)
Dogs are welcome at this hotel.

Comfort Suites
3660 W. Andrew Johnson Hwy.
Morristown, TN
423-585-4000 (877-424-6423)
Dogs of all sizes are allowed. Dogs are allowed for a pet fee of $10 per pet per night.

Days Inn Morristown
2512 E Andrew Johnson Hwy
Morristown, TN

423-587-2200 (800-329-7466)
Dogs of all sizes are allowed. Dogs are allowed for a pet fee.

Holiday Inn Morristown-Conf Ctr-I-81 Ex 8
5435 S Davy Crockett Pkwy
Morristown, TN
423-587-2400 (877-270-6405)
Dogs of all sizes are allowed. Dogs are allowed for a pet fee.

Motel 6 - Morristown
5984 Andrew Johnson
Morristown, TN
423-586-8504 (800-466-8356)
This motel welcomes your pets to stay with you.

Super 8 Morristown
2430 E Andrew Johnson Hwy
Morristown, TN
423-586-8880 (800-800-8000)
Dogs are welcome at this hotel.

Super 8 /South Morristown
5400 S Davy Crockett Parkway
Morristown, TN
423-318-8888 (800-800-8000)
Dogs are welcome at this hotel.

Doubletree Hotel
1850 Old Fort Parkway
Murfreesboro, TN
615-895-5555 (800-222-TREE (8733))
This upscale hotel has a number of on site amenities for all level of travelers - including their signature chocolate chip cookies at check in, plus a convenient location to business, shopping, dining, entertainment and cultural venues. Well behaved dogs up to 50 pounds are allowed for an additional one time fee of $50 per night per pet with a credit card on file. 2 dogs may be allowed.

Baymont Inn & Suites Murfreesboro
2230 Armory Drive
Murfreesboro, TN
615-896-1172 (877-229-6668)
Dogs of all sizes are allowed. Dogs are allowed for a pet fee of $15.00 per pet per night.

Best Western Chaffin Inn
168 Chaffin Place
Murfreesboro, TN
615-895-3818 (800-780-7234)
Dogs of all sizes are allowed. Dogs are allowed for a nightly pet fee.

Howard Johnson Express Inn - Murfreesboro
2424 S Church Street/I-24

Murfreesboro, TN
615-896-5522 (800-446-4656)
Dogs of all sizes are allowed. Dogs are allowed for a pet fee of $10.00 per pet per night.

Motel 6 - Murfreesboro
148 Chaffin Pl
Murfreesboro, TN
615-890-8524 (800-466-8356)
This motel welcomes your pets to stay with you.

Quality Inn
2135 S. Church St.
Murfreesboro, TN
615-890-1006 (877-424-6423)
Dogs of all sizes are allowed. Dogs are allowed for a pet fee of $10.00 per pet per stay.

Ramada Limited Murfreesboro
1855 S Church St
Murfreesboro, TN
615-896-5080 (800-272-6232)
Dogs are welcome at this hotel.

Red Roof Inn Murfreesboro
2282 Armory Drive
Murfreesboro, TN
615-893-0104 (800-RED-ROOF)
One well-behaved family pet per room. Guest must notify front desk upon arrival. Guest is liable for any damages. In consideration of all guests, pets must never be left unattended in the guest rooms.

Baymont Inn & Suites Airport/ Briley Nashville
2350 Elm Hill Pike
Nashville, TN
615-871-0222 (877-229-6668)
Dogs are welcome at this hotel.

Baymont Inn & Suites West Nashville
5612 Lenox Avenue
Nashville, TN
615-353-0700 (877-229-6668)
Dogs up to 50 pounds are allowed. Dogs are allowed for a nightly pet fee.

Comfort Inn
2407 Brick Church Pike
Nashville, TN
615-226-3300 (877-424-6423)
Dogs of all sizes are allowed. Dogs are allowed for a pet fee of $10.00 per pet per night.

Comfort Inn
1501 Demonbreun Street
Nashville, TN
615-255-9977 (877-424-6423)
Dogs of all sizes are allowed. Dogs

are allowed for a pet fee of $10.00 per pet per night.

Days Inn At Opryland/Music Valley Dr Nashville
2460 Music Valley Drive
Nashville, TN
615-889-0090 (800-329-7466)
Dogs of all sizes are allowed. Dogs are allowed for a pet fee.

Drury Inn
341 Harding Place
Nashville, TN
615-834-7170 (800-378-7946)
Dogs of all sizes are allowed for no additional pet fee with a credit card on file, and there is a pet agreement to sign at check in.

Drury Inn & Suites
555 Donelson Pike
Nashville, TN
615-902-0400 (800-378-7946)
Dogs of all sizes are allowed for no additional pet fee with a credit card on file, and there is a pet agreement to sign at check in.

East Park Inn
822 Boscobel Street
Nashville, TN
615-226-8691 (888-484-1195)
bbonline.com/tn/eastpark/
Beautifully enriched with Victorian detailing, this 120 year old home in the city's historic district offers luxurious settings, gourmet dining, an English garden, and a great location to a number of other sites of interest. Dogs are allowed for an additional fee of $10 per night per pet. Dogs must be dog and people friendly, leashed, and under their owner's control at all times. 2 dogs may be allowed.

Econo Lodge
1412 Brick Church Pike
Nashville, TN
615-226-3230 (877-424-6423)
Dogs of all sizes are allowed. Dogs are allowed for a pet fee of $10.00 per pet per night.

Extended Stay America Nashville - Airport
2525 Elm Hill Pike
Nashville, TN
615-883-7667 (800-804-3724)
One dog is allowed per suite. There is a $25 per night additional pet fee up to $150 for an entire stay.

Extended Stay America Nashville - Vanderbilt
3311 West End Ave.

Nashville, TN
615-383-7490 (800-804-3724)
One dog is allowed per suite. There is a $25 per night additional pet fee up to $150 for an entire stay.

Holiday Inn Nashville-The Crossings
201 Crossings Place
Nashville, TN
615-731-2361 (877-270-6405)
Dogs are welcome at this hotel.

Homestead Studio Suites Nashville - Airport
727 McGavock Pike
Nashville, TN
615-316-9020 (800-804-3724)
One dog is allowed per suite. There is a $25 per night additional pet fee up to $150 for an entire stay.

Hotel Indigo Nashville-West End
1719 West End Ave.
Nashville, TN
615-329-4200 (877-865-6578)
Dogs of all sizes are allowed. Dogs are allowed for a pet fee of $75.00 per pet per night.

Hotel Preston
733 Briley Parkway
Nashville, TN
615-361-5900 (877-361-5500)
hotelpreston.com/
This luxury hotel sits central to many of the city's star attractions, world class shopping and dining venues, and major business areas, plus they also offer a number of in-house amenities for all level of travelers. Dogs are allowed for an additional one time fee of $49 per room. 2 dogs may be allowed.

La Quinta Inn Nashville Airport
2345 Atrium Way
Nashville, TN
615-885-3000 (800-531-5900)
Dogs of all sizes are allowed. There are no additional pet fees. Dogs may not be left unattended at any time, and they must be leashed and cleaned up after. Multiple dogs may be allowed.

La Quinta Inn Nashville Airport
531 Donelson Pike
Nashville, TN
615-885-3100 (800-531-5900)
Dogs of all sizes are allowed. There are no additional pet fees. Dogs may only be left unattended in the room if they will be quiet and well behaved. Dogs must be leashed and cleaned up after. Multiple dogs may be allowed.

La Quinta Inn Nashville South
4311 Sidco Drive
Nashville, TN
615-834-6900 (800-531-5900)
Dogs of all sizes are allowed. There are no additional pet fees. Dogs must be leashed and cleaned up after. Multiple dogs may be allowed.

Loews Vanderbilt Hotel
2100 West End Ave
Nashville, TN
615-320-1700
All well-behaved dogs of any size are welcome. This upscale hotel offers their "Loews Loves Pets" program which includes special pet treats, local dog walking routes, and a list of nearby pet-friendly places to visit. There is an additional one time pet cleaning fee of $25 per room.

Motel 6 - Nashville Airport
420 Metroplex Dr
Nashville, TN
615-833-8887 (800-466-8356)
Your pets are welcome to stay here with you.

Motel 6 - Nashville South
95 Wallace Rd
Nashville, TN
615-333-9933 (800-466-8356)
Your pets are welcome to stay here with you.

Red Roof Inn Nashville Airport
510 Claridge Drive
Nashville, TN
615-872-0735 (800-RED-ROOF)
One well-behaved family pet per room. Guest must notify front desk upon arrival. Guest is liable for any damages. In consideration of all guests, pets must never be left unattended in the guest rooms.

Red Roof Inn Nashville Fairgrounds
4271 Sidco Drive
Nashville, TN
615-832-0093 (800-RED-ROOF)
One well-behaved family pet per room. Guest must notify front desk upon arrival. Guest is liable for any damages. In consideration of all guests, pets must never be left unattended in the guest rooms.

Sheraton Music City Hotel
777 McGavock Pike
Nashville, TN
615-885-2200 (888-625-5144)
Dogs up to 50 pounds are allowed. Dogs are not allowed to be left alone in the room.

Sheraton Nashville Downtown Hotel

623 Union St.
Nashville, TN
615-259-2000 (888-625-5144)
Dogs of all sizes are allowed for no additional pet fee; there is a pet agreement to sign at check in. Dogs may not be left alone in the room.

Sleep Inn
3200 Dickerson Pk.
Nashville, TN
615-227-8686 (877-424-6423)
Dogs of all sizes are allowed. Dogs are allowed for a pet fee of $usd per pet per stay. Two dogs are allowed per room.

Super 8 Downtown Nashville
709 Spence Lane
Nashville, TN
615-361-0102 (800-800-8000)
Dogs of all sizes are allowed. Dogs are allowed for a pet fee of $10 per pet per night.

Super 8 West Nashville
6924 Charlotte Pike
Nashville, TN
615-356-6005 (800-800-8000)
Dogs of all sizes are allowed. Dogs are allowed for a nightly pet fee.

Thrifty Inn
343 Harding Place
Nashville, TN
615-834-4242 (800-378-7946)
Dogs of all sizes are allowed for an additional $10 to $15 pet fee with a credit card on file, and there is a pet agreement to sign at check in.

Comfort Inn
1149 Smokey Mountain Lane
Newport, TN
423-623-5355 (877-424-6423)
Dogs of all sizes are allowed. Dogs are allowed for a pet fee of $10.00 per pet per night.

Motel 6 - Newport, Tn
255 Heritage Blvd
Newport, TN
423-623-1850 (800-466-8356)
This motel welcomes your pets to stay with you.

Days Inn Knoxville Oak Ridge
206 South Illinois Avenue
Oak Ridge, TN
865-483-5615 (800-329-7466)
Dogs of all sizes are allowed. Dogs are allowed for a pet fee of $15 per pet per night.

Staybridge Suites Knoxville Oak Ridge
420 South Illinois Avenue

Oak Ridge, TN
865-298-0050 (877-270-6405)
Dogs up to 80 pounds are allowed.
Pets allowed with an additional pet
fee. Up to $75 for 1-6 nights and up
to $150 for 7+ nights. A pet
agreement must be signed at check-
in.

Super 8 Oak Ridge
1590 Oak Ridge Turnpike
Oak Ridge, TN
865-483-1200 (800-800-8000)
Dogs of all sizes are allowed. Dogs
are allowed for a pet fee of $5.00 per
pet per night.

Days Inn Oakland
6805 Hwy 64
Oakland, TN
901-465-5630 (800-329-7466)
Dogs of all sizes are allowed. Dogs
are allowed for a nightly pet fee.

Super 8 Chattanooga Ooltewah
5111 Hunter Rd
Ooltewah, TN
423-238-5951 (800-800-8000)
Dogs of all sizes are allowed. Dogs
are allowed for a pet fee of $6.00 per
pet per stay.

Super 8 Paris
1309 East Wood Street
Paris, TN
731-644-7008 (800-800-8000)
Dogs are welcome at this hotel

Americana Inn
2825 Parkway
Pigeon Forge, TN
865-428-0172 (866-858-7786)
pigeonforgeamericanainn.com
Dogs are allwoed for a $10 per night
pet fee. There are dog walk areas by
the river.

Great Outdoor Rentals
Call to Arrange
Pigeon Forge, TN
865-712-5669
greatoutdoorrentals.com
Some of these vacation rental
cabins, homes and chalets in the
Gatlinburg and Pigeon Forge are pet
friendly. There is a $50 non-
refundable fee for pets.

National Parks Resort Lodge
2385 Parkway (US 441)
Pigeon Forge, TN
865-453-4106
nprlodge.com/
There is a $20 one time pet charge
per room. Multiple dogs may be
allowed.

RiverStone Resort and Spa
212 Dollywood Lane
Pigeon Forge, TN
865-908-0660 (866-908-0660)
RiverStoneResort.com
Some of these one to four bedroom
condos are pet friendly. They offer
dog runs and pet packages.

Sunset Cottage Rentals and Realtly
3603 S River Road
Pigeon Forge, TN
865-429-8478
Dogs are allowed for an additional
one time pet fee of $50 per room,
plus a $100 refundable deposit.
Some units only allow small dogs. 2
dogs may be allowed.

Super 8 -Emert St Pigeon Forge
215 Emert Street
Pigeon Forge, TN
865-428-2300 (800-800-8000)
Dogs of all sizes are allowed. Dogs
are allowed for a pet fee.

Fall Creek Falls Inn
2536 Lakeside Drive
Pikeville, TN
423-881-5298 (800-250-8610)
This inn is located in the Fall Creek
Falls State Park and sparkling
streams, gorges, cascading
waterfalls, a variety of scenic trails,
ecosystems, and abundant
recreation are part of the package.
Dogs of all sizes are allowed for an
additional $15 (plus tax) per night
per pet. Dogs must be declared at
the time of reservation, and crated
when left alone in the room.
There is also a camping area on
site where dogs are allowed at no
additional fee. Dogs must be
leashed and cleaned up after, and
they ask that dogs do their
'business' off the trails. Dogs are
not allowed on the Overnight Trail,
but they are allowed on the other
trails in the park. Multiple dogs may
be allowed.

Super 8 /Knoxville North Powell
323 E. Emory Road
Powell, TN
865-938-5501 (800-800-8000)
Dogs are welcome at this hotel.

Super 8 /Frankewing Area Pulaski
2400 Hwy 64
Pulaski, TN
931-363-4501 (800-800-8000)
Dogs of all sizes are allowed. Dogs
are allowed for a pet fee.

Residence Inn San Antonio
North/Stone Oak

1115 N 1604 E
San Antonio, TN
210-490-1333 (800-331-3131)
Sea World Antonio, Six Flags, The
Alamo, event centers, the Riverwalk,
and several major corporations are
all only a few minutes from this all
suite inn. Additionally, they offer a
daily buffet breakfast and evening
social hours. Dogs up to 100 pounds
are allowed for an additional one
time pet fee of $75 per room. 2 dogs
may be allowed.

TownePlace Suites San Antonio
Airport
214 NE Loop 410
San Antonio, TN
210-308-5510 (800-257-3000)
In addition to being only a few
minutes from the vibrant downtown
area, an International airport, and
numerous local star attractions, this
all suite inn also offers a number of
in-house amenities for all level of
travelers. Dogs are allowed for an
additional fee of $100 per room.
Multiple dogs may be allowed.

Hidden Springs Resort Rentals
1576 Nucum Hollow Road
Sevierville, TN
865-774-2136 (888-477-8366)
hiddenspringsresort.com
These log cabins with full kitchens
and outdoor hot tubs, allow pets with
a $100 cash deposit that will be
returned within 10 days if no damage
or extra cleaning has occurred.

Little Valley Mountain Resort
2229 Little Valley Road
Sevierville, TN
865-428-8744 (800-581-7225)
littlevalleymountainresort.com
This resort on 360 acres offers
privacy and pet-friendly cabins.
There is a $65 per pet one time pet
fee. Dogs of all sizes are allowed.

Quality Inn & Suites River Suites
860 Winfield Dunn Pkwy.
Sevierville, TN
865-428-5519 (877-424-6423)
Dogs of all sizes are allowed. Dogs
are allowed for a pet fee of $10.00
per pet per night.

Sleep Inn
1020 Parkway
Sevierville, TN
865-429-0484 (877-424-6423)
Dogs up to 75 pounds are allowed.
Dogs are allowed for a pet fee of
$room per pet per night. Two dogs
are allowed per room.

Rodeway Inn & Suites
1300 Plaza Drive
Smyrna, TN
615-355-6161 (877-424-6423)
Dogs of all sizes are allowed. Dogs are allowed for a pet fee of $10.00 per pet per night. Two dogs are allowed per room.

Days Inn Sweetwater
229 Hwy 68
Sweetwater, TN
423-337-4200 (800-329-7466)
Dogs of all sizes are allowed. Dogs are allowed for a pet fee of $10 per pet per night.

Comfort Inn
340 Hester Dr.
White House, TN
615-672-8850 (877-424-6423)
Dogs of all sizes are allowed.

Days Inn Nashville White House
1009 Highway 76
White House, TN
615-672-3746 (800-329-7466)
Dogs up to 50 pounds are allowed. Dogs are allowed for a nightly pet fee.

Days Inn White Pine
3670 Roy Messer Hwy
White Pine, TN
865-674-2573 (800-329-7466)
Dogs of all sizes are allowed. Dogs are allowed for a pet fee of $6 per pet per night.

Super 8 / Nashville NW Area Whites Creek
7551 Old Hickory Blvd
Whites Creek, TN
615-876-3971 (800-800-8000)
Dogs are welcome at this hotel.

Super 8 Whiteville
2040 Highway 64
Whiteville, TN
731-254-8884 (800-800-8000)
Dogs are welcome at this hotel.

Texas

Best Western Mall South
3950 Ridgemont Drive
Abilene, TX
325-695-1262 (800-780-7234)
Dogs of all sizes are allowed. Dogs are allowed for a nightly pet fee.

Civic Plaza Hotel
505 Pine St
Abilene, TX
800-588-0222
There is a one time pet fee of $10.

Comfort Suites
3165 S. Danville Dr.
Abilene, TX
325-795-8500 (877-424-6423)
Dogs of all sizes are allowed. Dogs are allowed for a pet fee of $30.00 per pet per night. Two dogs are allowed per room.

Days Inn Abilene
1702 East I-20
Abilene, TX
325-672-6433 (800-329-7466)
Dogs of all sizes are allowed. Dogs are allowed for a pet fee.

Knights Inn Abilene
505 Pine Street
Abilene, TX
325-676-0222 (800-843-5644)
Dogs are welcome at this hotel. There is a $25 per visit additional pet fee.

La Quinta Inn Abilene
3501 West Lake Road
Abilene, TX
325-676-1676 (800-531-5900)
Dogs of all sizes are allowed. There are no additional pet fees. Although there is no set allotment for dogs, their preference is for no more than 2 large dogs or 3 small dogs per room. Dogs must be removed for housekeeping. Dogs may not be left unattended, and they must be leashed and cleaned up after.

Motel 6 - Abilene
4951 Stamford St
Abilene, TX
325-672-8462 (800-466-8356)
This motel welcomes your pets to stay with you.

Quality Inn
1758 E. I-20
Abilene, TX
325-676-0203 (877-424-6423)
Dogs of all sizes are allowed.

Super 8 North Abilene
1525 E Stamford St
Abilene, TX
325-673-5251 (800-800-8000)
Dogs of all sizes are allowed. Dogs are allowed for a pet fee of $10 per pet per stay.

Super 8 South Abilene
4397 Sayles Blvd
Abilene, TX
325-701-4779 (800-800-8000)
Dogs of all sizes are allowed. Dogs are allowed for a pet fee of $20 per pet per night.

Motel 6 - Dallas Addison
4325 Beltline Rd
Addison, TX
972-386-4577 (800-466-8356)
This motel welcomes your pets to stay with you.

Super 8 By The Galleria / North Dallas
4150 Beltway Drive
Addison, TX
972-233-2525 (800-800-8000)
Dogs of all sizes are allowed. Dogs are allowed for a pet fee.

Super 8 /Mccallen Area Alamo
714 N Alamo Road
Alamo, TX
956-787-9444 (800-800-8000)
Dogs are welcome at this hotel.

Ramada of Alpine
2800 West Highway 90
Alpine, TX
432-837-1100 (800-272-6232)
Dogs of all sizes are allowed. Dogs are allowed for a pet fee.

Days Inn Alvin
110 E. Hwy 6
Alvin, TX
281-331-5227 (800-329-7466)
Dogs of all sizes are allowed. Dogs are allowed for a pet fee of $30 per pet per stay.

Baymont Inn & Suites Amarillo
3411 I-40 West
Amarillo, TX
806-356-6800 (877-229-6668)
Dogs of all sizes are allowed. Dogs are allowed for a pet fee.

Best Western Amarillo Inn
1610 S Coulter Street
Amarillo, TX
806-358-7861 (800-780-7234)
Dogs up to 50 pounds are allowed. Dogs are allowed for a pet fee of $20.00 per pet per stay.

Best Western Santa Fe
4600 I-40 E
Amarillo, TX
806-372-1885 (800-780-7234)
Dogs of all sizes are allowed. Dogs are allowed for a pet fee.

Big Texan Steak Ranch Motel
7701 E I 40
Amarillo, TX
800-657-7177
bigtexan.com/
This 1800's themed motel offers a convenient location to food, fun, and a variety of attractions. Dogs are

allowed for an additional fee of $10 per night per pet. There is an off-leash dog area at the hotel and outdoor seats so you and your dog can enjoy food from the Big Texan Steak House. Multiple dogs may be allowed.

Days Inn - Medical Center Amarillo
2102 So Coulter Dr
Amarillo, TX
806-359-9393 (800-329-7466)
Dogs of all sizes are allowed. Dogs are allowed for a pet fee of $15 per pet per night.

Days Inn East Amarillo
1701 I-40E
Amarillo, TX
806-379-6255 (800-329-7466)
Dogs are welcome at this hotel.

Days Inn South Amarillo
8601 Canyon Drive
Amarillo, TX
806-468-7100 (800-329-7466)
Dogs are welcome at this hotel.

Extended Stay America Amarillo - West
2100 Cinema Dr.
Amarillo, TX
806-351-0117 (800-804-3724)
One dog is allowed per suite. There is a $25 per night additional pet fee up to $150 for an entire stay.

Holiday Inn Amarillo-I-40
1911 I-40 East
Amarillo, TX
806-372-8741 (877-270-6405)
Dogs of all sizes are allowed. Dogs are allowed for a pet fee of $25.00 per pet per night.

Kiva Motel
2501 Interstate Highway 40 East
Amarillo, TX
806-379-6555 (800-272-6232)
There is a $10 per night per pet additional fee. 2 dogs may be allowed.

La Quinta Inn Amarillo East/Airport Area
1708 I-40 East
Amarillo, TX
806-373-7486 (800-531-5900)
Dogs of all sizes are allowed. There are no additional pet fees. Dogs must be leashed, cleaned up after, and crated for housekeeping. Multiple dogs may be allowed.

Motel 6 - Amarillo Airport
4301 I-40 East
Amarillo, TX

806-373-3045 (800-466-8356)
This motel welcomes your pets to stay with you.

Motel 6 - Amarillo East
3930 I-40 East
Amarillo, TX
806-374-6444 (800-466-8356)
This motel welcomes your pets to stay with you.

Motel 6 - Amarillo West
6030 I-40 West
Amarillo, TX
806-359-7651 (800-466-8356)
This motel welcomes your pets to stay with you.

Ramada Amarillo
7909 I-40 East
Amarillo, TX
806-373-3303 (800-272-6232)
Dogs of all sizes are allowed. Dogs are allowed for a nightly pet fee.

Residence Inn Amarillo
6700 Interstate 40 West
Amarillo, TX
806-354-2978 (888-236-2427)
This hotel gives a convenient location to business, shopping, dining, and entertainment areas, plus they offer a daily buffet breakfast and a Manager's reception Monday through Thursday. Dogs are allowed for an additional one time pet fee of $50 per room. 2 dogs may be allowed.

Super 8 Amarillo
8701 I-40 East
Amarillo, TX
806-335-2836 (800-800-8000)
Dogs of all sizes are allowed. Dogs are allowed for a pet fee.

Super 8 Central TX Amarillo
2909 I-40 East
Amarillo, TX
806-373-3888 (800-800-8000)
Dogs of all sizes are allowed. Dogs are allowed for a nightly pet fee.

Best Western Angleton Inn
1809 N Velasco Street
Angleton, TX
979-849-5822 (800-780-7234)
Dogs of all sizes are allowed. Dogs are allowed for a pet fee of $25.00 per pet per stay.

Super 8 /El Paso Area Anthony
100 Park North Dr
Anthony, TX
915-886-2888 (800-800-8000)
Dogs are welcome at this hotel.

Best Western Cooper Inn & Suites
4024 Melear Drive
Arlington, TX
817-784-9490 (800-780-7234)
Dogs of all sizes are allowed. Dogs are allowed for a nightly pet fee.

Candlewood Suites Dallas-Arlington
2221 Brookhollow Plaza Dr
Arlington, TX
817-649-3336 (877-270-6405)
Dogs up to 80 pounds are allowed. Pets allowed with an additional pet fee. Up to $75 for 1-6 nights and up to $150 for 7+ nights. A pet agreement must be signed at check-in.

Days Inn/ Six Flags/ Ballpark/ Cowboys Stadium
910 North Collins/I-30
Arlington, TX
817-261-8444 (800-329-7466)
Dogs of all sizes are allowed. Dogs are allowed for a pet fee of $10.00 per pet per night.

Hawthorn Suites Hotel
2401 Brookhollow Plaza Drive
Arlington, TX
817-640-1188
Dogs up to 75 pounds are allowed for a $50 (+ tax) one time charge per pet. 2 dogs may be allowed.

Homestead Studio Suites Dallas - Arlington
1221 N. Watson Rd.
Arlington, TX
817-633-7588 (800-804-3724)
One dog is allowed per suite. There is a $25 per night additional pet fee up to $150 for an entire stay.

Howard Johnson Express Inn - Ballpark / Six Flags Arlington
2001 East Copeland
Arlington, TX
817-461-1122 (800-446-4656)
Dogs of all sizes are allowed. Dogs are allowed for a pet fee of $25.00 per pet per night.

Knights Inn Arlington
820 N Watson Road
Arlington, TX
817-640-5151 (800-843-5644)
Dogs are welcome at this hotel.

La Quinta Inn & Suites Dallas Arlington North
825 North Watson Rd.
Arlington, TX
817-640-4142 (800-531-5900)
Dogs of all sizes are allowed. There are no additional pet fees. Dogs must be leashed and cleaned up

after. You must inform of the pet(s) at the time of reservations, and make arrangements for housekeeping. Place the Do Not Disturb sign on the door if the pet is unattended. Multiple dogs may be allowed.

La Quinta Inn & Suites Dallas Arlington South
4001 Scot's Legacy Dr.
Arlington, TX
817-467-7756 (800-531-5900)
Dogs of all sizes are allowed. There are no additional pet fees. Dogs must be quiet, well behaved, leashed and cleaned up after. Multiple dogs may be allowed.

Residence Inn Arlington
1050 Brookhollow Plaza Drive
Arlington, TX
817-649-7300 (888-236-2427)
This all suite inn offers amenities for all level of travelers, including a convenient location to a number of area attractions, shopping, and dining areas, and a daily buffet breakfast to get you started. Dogs are allowed for an additional one time pet fee of $75 per room. 2 dogs may be allowed.

Studio 6 - Dallas South Arlington
1980 Pleasant Ridge Rd
Arlington, TX
817-465-8500 (800-466-8356)
Your pets are welcome to stay here with you for a pet fee of $10 per day up to $50 for an entire stay.

Super 8 East Arlington
1905 W Pleasant Ridge Rd
Arlington, TX
817-466-3800 (800-800-8000)
Dogs of all sizes are allowed. Dogs are allowed for a pet fee.

Super 8 /SW Arlington
2712 E Abram St
Arlington, TX
817-652-0917 (800-800-8000)
Dogs of all sizes are allowed. Dogs are allowed for a pet fee.

TownePlace Suites Arlington Near Six Flags
1709 E Lamar Blvd
Arlington, TX
817-861-8728 (800-257-3000)
In addition to offering a number of in-house amenities for all level of travelers - such as a daily buffet breakfast and evening socials Monday to Wednesday, this all suite inn also provides a convenient location to business, shopping, dining, and entertainment areas.

Dogs are allowed for an additional one time fee of $100 per room. 2 dogs may be allowed.

Super 8
205 US Hwy 175 West
Athens, TX
903-675-7511 (800-800-8000)
Dogs of all sizes are allowed. Dogs are allowed for a nightly pet fee.

Brava House
1108 Blanco Street
Austin, TX
512-478-5034
bravahouse.com/
This beautiful 1880's Victorian home offers guests a peaceful warm setting and a great location to numerous local eateries, shops, activities, and recreation. Dogs are allowed for an additional pet fee of $30 per night per room for small dogs, and per pet for large dogs. 2 dogs may be allowed.

Candlewood Suites Austin Arboretum-Northwest
9701 Stonelake Blvd.
Austin, TX
512-338-1611 (877-270-6405)
Dogs up to 80 pounds are allowed. Pets allowed with an additional pet fee. Up to $75 for 1-6 nights and up to $150 for 7+ nights. A pet agreement must be signed at check-in.

Candlewood Suites Austin-South
4320 Interstate 35 Service S
Austin, TX
512-444-8882 (877-270-6405)
Dogs up to 80 pounds are allowed. Pets allowed with an additional pet fee. Up to $75 for 1-6 nights and up to $150 for 7+ nights. A pet agreement must be signed at check-in.

Clarion Inn & Suites Conference Center
2200 S. IH-35
Austin, TX
512-444-0561 (877-424-6423)
Dogs of all sizes are allowed.

Comfort Suites Austin Airport
7501 E. Ben White Blvd.
Austin, TX
512-386-6000 (877-424-6423)
Dogs of all sizes are allowed. Dogs are allowed for a pet fee of $30.00 per pet per stay.

Days Inn Crossroads Austin
820 East Anderson Lane
Austin, TX

512-835-4311 (800-329-7466)
Dogs are welcome at this hotel.

Days Inn South Austin
4220 South IH-35
Austin, TX
512-441-9242 (800-329-7466)
Dogs of all sizes are allowed. Dogs are allowed for a pet fee of $15.00 per pet per stay.

Days Inn /University/Downtown Austin
3105 N I-35
Austin, TX
512-478-1631 (800-329-7466)
Dogs are welcome at this hotel.

Doubletree Guest Suites
303 W 15th Street
Austin, TX
512-478-7000 (800-222-TREE (8733))
Located downtown, this luxury hotel offers a number of on-site amenities for all level of travelers, plus a convenient location to shopping, dining, historical and entertainment areas. Dogs are allowed for an additional one time pet fee of $40 per room. Multiple dogs may be allowed.

Embassy Suites
300 S Congress Avenue
Austin, TX
512-469-9000
Located in the heart of the city, this all suite hotel offers a number of on site amenities for business and leisure travelers, plus a convenient location to business, shopping, dining, and entertainment districts. They also offer a complimentary cooked-to-order breakfast and a Manager's reception every evening. Dogs are allowed for an additional one time fee of $25 per pet. 2 dogs may be allowed.

Extended Stay America Austin - Arboretum
10100 N. Capital of Texas Hwy.
Austin, TX
512-231-1520 (800-804-3724)
One dog is allowed per suite. There is a $25 per night additional pet fee up to $150 for an entire stay.

Extended Stay America Austin - Downtown - 6th St.
600 Guadalupe St.
Austin, TX
512-457-9994 (800-804-3724)
One dog is allowed per suite. There is a $25 per night additional pet fee up to $150 for an entire stay.

Extended Stay America Austin - Northwest
13858 N. US Hwy. 183
Austin, TX
512-258-3365 (800-804-3724)
One dog is allowed per suite. There is a $25 per night additional pet fee up to $150 for an entire stay.

Extended Stay America Austin - Round Rock - South
16950 N. IH-35
Austin, TX
512-255-1400 (800-804-3724)
One dog is allowed per suite. There is a $25 per night additional pet fee up to $150 for an entire stay.

Extended Stay America Austin - Southwest
5100 US Hwy. 290 W.
Austin, TX
512-892-4272 (800-804-3724)
One dog is allowed per suite. There is a $25 per night additional pet fee up to $150 for an entire stay.

Hawthorn Suites
935 La Posada Drive
Austin, TX
512-459-3335 (512-459-3335)
In addition to providing a convenient location to many local sites and activities, this all-suite hotel offers a number of amenities for business and leisure travelers, including their signature breakfast buffet and beautifully appointed rooms. Dogs are allowed for an additional one time fee of $150 per pet. Multiple dogs may be allowed.

Homestead Studio Suites Austin - Arboretum
9100 Waterford Centre Blvd.
Austin, TX
512-837-6677 (800-804-3724)
One dog is allowed per suite. There is a $25 per night additional pet fee up to $150 for an entire stay.

Homestead Studio Suites Austin - Downtown -Town Lake
507 S. First St.
Austin, TX
512-476-1818 (800-804-3724)
One dog is allowed per suite. There is a $25 per night additional pet fee up to $150 for an entire stay.

Howard Johnson Inn /I-35 Austin
2711 IH 35 South
Austin, TX
512-462-9201 (800-446-4656)
Dogs are welcome at this hotel.

Hyatt Regency Austin

208 Barton Springs
Austin, TX
512-477-1234
This dog-friendly hotel is located close to many attractions, many of which are dog-friendly in this dog-friendly city. Dogs up to 70 pounds are allowed. There is a $50 per night pet fee and you must have a vaccination record for your pet.

La Quinta Inn & Suites Austin Airport
7625 E. Ben White Blvd.
Austin, TX
512-386-6800 (800-531-5900)
Dogs of all sizes are allowed. There are no additional pet fees. Dogs must be quiet, leashed, and cleaned up after. Multiple dogs may be allowed.

La Quinta Inn & Suites Round Rock South
150 Parker Drive
Austin, TX
512-246-2800 (800-531-5900)
Dogs of all sizes are allowed. There are no additional pet fees. Dogs must be leashed, cleaned up after, and a contact number left with the front desk if there is a pet alone in the room. Multiple dogs may be allowed.

La Quinta Inn Austin Capitol
300 E. 11th St.
Austin, TX
512-476-1166 (800-531-5900)
Dogs of all sizes are allowed. There are no additional pet fees. Dogs may only be left in the room if they will be quiet and well behaved, and leashed and cleaned up after. Multiple dogs may be allowed.

La Quinta Inn Austin Highland Mall
5812 I-35 North
Austin, TX
512-459-4381 (800-531-5900)
Dogs of all sizes are allowed. There are no additional pet fees. Dogs must be leashed and cleaned up after, and arrangements need to be made with housekeeping if the stay is longer than one day. Multiple dogs may be allowed.

La Quinta Inn Austin I-35 S. Ben White
4200 I-35 South
Austin, TX
512-443-1774 (800-531-5900)
Dogs of all sizes are allowed. There are no additional pet fees. Place the "Do Not Disturb" sign on the door if your pet is in the room alone. Please leash and clean up after

your pet. Multiple dogs may be allowed.

Lost Parrot Cabins Resort
15116 Storm Drive
Austin, TX
512-266-8916
austincabinrentals.com/
Located on eight wooded acres near Lake Travis, this intimate resort offers colorful themed accommodations for a truly unique visit. Dogs are allowed with prior approval for an additional fee of $15 to $30 per night per pet. There is a pet agreement to sign at check in. Multiple dogs may be allowed.

Motel 6 - Austin Central North
8010 I-35 North
Austin, TX
512-837-9890 (800-466-8356)
This motel welcomes your pets to stay with you.

Motel 6 - Austin Central South/univ Of Tx
5330 Interregional Hwy
Austin, TX
512-467-9111 (800-466-8356)
This motel welcomes your pets to stay with you.

Motel 6 - Austin North
9420 I-35
Austin, TX
512-339-6161 (800-466-8356)
This motel welcomes your pets to stay with you.

Motel 6 - Austin South Airport
2707 Interregional Hwy
Austin, TX
512-444-5882 (800-466-8356)
This motel welcomes your pets to stay with you.

Ramada - Central Austin
919 East Koenig Lane
Austin, TX
512-454-1144 (800-272-6232)
Dogs of all sizes are allowed. Dogs are allowed for a pet fee.

Red Roof Inn Austin - University of Texas
4701 South I-35
Austin, TX
512-448-0091 (800-RED-ROOF)
One well-behaved family pet per room. Guest must notify front desk upon arrival. Guest is liable for any damages. In consideration of all guests, pets must never be left unattended in the guest rooms.

Red Roof Inn Austin North

Dog-Friendly Lodging - Please always call ahead to make sure an establishment is still dog-friendly.

8210 North Interregional Hwy 35
Austin, TX
512-835-2200 (800-RED-ROOF)
One well-behaved family pet per
room. Guest must notify front desk
upon arrival. Guest is liable for any
damages. In consideration of all
guests, pets must never be left
unattended in the guest rooms.

Renaissance Austin
9721 Arboretum Blvd
Austin, TX
512-343-2626 (800-468-3571)
In addition to offering a number of in-
house amenities for all level of
travelers, this luxury, 9-story atrium-
style hotel also provides a
convenient location to business,
shopping, dining, and day/night
entertainment areas. Dogs are
allowed for an additional one time
fee of $50 per room. Multiple dogs
may be allowed.

Residence Inn Austin
Downtown/Convention Center
300 East 4th Street
Austin, TX
512-472-5553 (866-816-8694)
Besides being connected to the
Courtyard Austin Downtown and
sitting adjacent to the Austin
Convention Center, this hotel also
provides a number of in-house
amenities, including a daily buffet
breakfast and a Manager's reception
Monday through Thursday. Dogs are
allowed for an additional one time
pet fee of $100 per room. Multiple
dogs may be allowed.

Residence Inn Austin North/Parmer
Lane
12401 North Lamar Blvd
Austin, TX
512-977-0544 (88-236-2427)
This hotel gives a convenient
location to business, shopping,
dining, and recreation areas, plus
they offer a daily buffet breakfast, a
complimentary hospitality hour
Monday through Thursday, and a
Friday morning Korean breakfasts.
Dogs are allowed for an additional
one time pet fee of $100 per room. 2
dogs may be allowed.

Residence Inn Austin
Northwest/Arboretum
3713 Tudor Blvd
Austin, TX
512-502-8200 (888-236-2427)
Only minutes from downtown, this
hotel gives a convenient location to
business, shopping, dining, and
recreation areas, plus they offer a
daily buffet breakfast, and a

Manager's reception Monday
through Thursday. Dogs are
allowed for an additional one time
pet fee of $100 per room. Multiple
dogs may be allowed.

Residence Inn Austin South
4537 S IH-35
Austin, TX
512-912-1100 (888-236-2427)
Only minutes from downtown, an
international airport, and significant
shopping/dining, and recreation
areas, this up-scale hotel also
offers a number of on-site amenities
including a daily buffet breakfast
and a Manager's reception Monday
through Thursday. Dogs up to 70
pounds are allowed for an
additional one time pet fee of $100
per room. 2 dogs may be allowed.

Rodeway Inn University/Downtown
2900 N. I-35
Austin, TX
512-477-6395 (877-424-6423)
Dogs of all sizes are allowed. Dogs
are allowed for a pet fee of $10.00
per pet per night.

Staybridge Suites Austin Airport
1611 Airport Commerce Drive
Austin, TX
512-389-9767 (877-270-6405)
Dogs up to 80 pounds are allowed.
Pets allowed with an additional pet
fee. Up to $75 for 1-6 nights and up
to $150 for 7+ nights. A pet
agreement must be signed at
check-in.

Staybridge Suites Austin Arboretum
10201 Stonelake Blvd
Austin, TX
512-349-0888 (877-270-6405)
Dogs up to 80 pounds are allowed.
Pets allowed with an additional pet
fee. Up to $75 for 1-6 nights and up
to $150 for 7+ nights. A pet
agreement must be signed at
check-in.

Staybridge Suites Austin Northwest
13087 US Hwy 183 North
Austin, TX
512-336-7829 (877-270-6405)
Dogs up to 80 pounds are allowed.
Pets allowed with an additional pet
fee. Up to $75 for 1-6 nights and up
to $150 for 7+ nights. A pet
agreement must be signed at
check-in.

Studio 6 - Austin Midtown
6603 I-35
Austin, TX
512-458-5453 (800-466-8356)

Your pets are welcome to stay here
with you for a pet fee of $10 per day
up to $50 for an entire stay.

Studio 6 - Austin Northwest
11901 Pavilion Blvd
Austin, TX
512-258-3556 (800-466-8356)
Your pets are welcome to stay here
with you for a pet fee of $10 per day
up to $50 for an entire stay.

Super 8 North Austin
8128 N. Interstate 35
Austin, TX
512-339-1300 (800-800-8000)
Dogs are welcome at this hotel.

Super 8 University/Dtwn Austin
5526 N IH-35
Austin, TX
512-451-7001 (800-800-8000)
Dogs are welcome at this hotel.

TownePlace Suites Austin Northwest
10024 North Capital of TX H N
Austin, TX
512-231-9360 (800-257-3000)
Besides offering a number of in-
house amenities for all level of
travelers, this all suite inn also
provides a convenient location to
numerous business, shopping,
dining, and entertainment areas.
Dogs are allowed for an additional
one time fee of $75 per room.
Multiple dogs may be allowed.

Days Inn Bastrop
4102 Hwy 71 East
Bastrop, TX
512-321-1157 (800-329-7466)
Dogs of all sizes are allowed. Dogs
are allowed for a pet fee of $25 per
pet per night.

Pecan Street Inn
1010 Pecan Street
Bastrop, TX
512-321-3315
Well mannered dogs are allowed for
no additional pet fee. 2 dogs may be
allowed.

Best Western Matagorda Hotel &
Conference Center
407 Seventh Street
Bay City, TX
979-244-5400 (800-780-7234)
Dogs are welcome at this hotel.

Knights Inn Bay City
905 Avenue F
Bay City, TX
979-245-1751 (800-843-5644)
Dogs of all sizes are allowed. Dogs
are allowed for a pet fee.

Studio 6 - Bay City, Tx
5511 7th St
Bay City, TX
979-244-2400 (800-466-8356)
Your pets are welcome to stay here
with you for a pet fee of $10 per day
up to $50 for an entire stay.

Comfort Suites
7209 Garth Rd
Baytown, TX
281-421-9764 (877-424-6423)
Dogs of all sizes are allowed. Dogs
are allowed for a pet fee of $25.00
per pet per night.

Days Inn and Suites Baytown
3810 Decker Dr
Baytown, TX
281-424-2222 (800-329-7466)
Dogs are welcome at this hotel.

La Quinta Inn Baytown
5215 I-10 East
Baytown, TX
281-421-7300 (800-531-5900)
Dogs of all sizes are allowed. There
are no additional pet fees. Dogs may
only be left in the room alone if they
will be quiet and well behaved, and
they must be leashed and cleaned
up after. Multiple dogs may be
allowed.

Motel 6 - Houston East Baytown
8911 Sr 146
Baytown, TX
281-576-5777 (800-466-8356)
This motel welcomes your pets to
stay with you.

Sleep Inn
5222 I-10 East
Baytown, TX
281-421-7200 (877-424-6423)
Dogs of all sizes are allowed. Dogs
are allowed for a pet fee of $35.00
per pet per stay.

Super 8 Baytown
1931 East Freeway
Baytown, TX
281-843-6200 (800-800-8000)
Dogs are welcome at this hotel.

Super 8 /Mont Belvieu Baytown
9032 Highway 146 North
Baytown, TX
281-576-6521 (800-800-8000)
Dogs are welcome at this hotel.

Candlewood Suites Beaumont
5355 Clearwater Court
Beaumont, TX
409-842-9000 (877-270-6405)
Dogs up to 80 pounds are allowed.

Pets allowed with an additional pet
fee. Up to $75 for 1-6 nights and up
to $150 for 7+ nights. A pet
agreement must be signed at
check-in.

Days Inn Beaumont
2155 North 11th Street
Beaumont, TX
409-898-8150 (800-329-7466)
Dogs are welcome at this hotel.

La Quinta Inn Beaumont Midtown
220 I-10 North
Beaumont, TX
409-838-9991 (800-531-5900)
Dogs of all sizes are allowed. There
are no additional pet fees. There
needs to be a credit card on file for
damages, and dogs must be
leashed and cleaned up after.
Multiple dogs may be allowed.

Motel 6 - Beaumont, Tx
1155 I-10 South
Beaumont, TX
409-835-5913 (800-466-8356)
This motel welcomes your pets to
stay with you.

Studio 6 - Beaumont, Tx
2660 I-10 East
Beaumont, TX
409-924-0571 (800-466-8356)
Your pets are welcome to stay here
with you for a pet fee of $10 per day
up to $50 for an entire stay.

Super 8 /I-10 East Beaumont
2850 I-10 East
Beaumont, TX
409-899-3040 (800-800-8000)
Dogs are welcome at this hotel.

Baymont Inn and Suites /DFW Area
Bedford
1450 West Airport Freeway
Bedford, TX
817-267-5200 (877-229-6668)
Dogs of all sizes are allowed. Dogs
are allowed for a pet fee.

Super 8 DFW Airport West Bedford
1800 Airport Freeway
Bedford, TX
817-545-8108 (800-800-8000)
Dogs are welcome at this hotel.

TownePlace Suites Dallas DFW
Airport West/Bedford
2301 Plaza Parkway
Bedford, TX
817-283-3725 (800-257-3000)
This all suite inn sits central to
numerous aircraft related
corporations, major businesses,
shopping, dining, and entertainment

venues, plus they also offer a
number of in-house amenities for all
level of travelers. Dogs are allowed
for an additional one time fee of $100
per room. Multiple dogs may be
allowed.

Best Western Texan Inn
2001 Highway 59 E
Beeville, TX
361-358-9999 (800-780-7234)
Dogs of all sizes are allowed. Dogs
are allowed for a pet fee of $10.00
per pet per night.

Holiday Inn Express Hotel & Suites
Beeville
2199 Hwy 59
Beeville, TX
361-358-7300 (877-270-6405)
Dogs of all sizes are allowed. Dogs
are allowed for a pet fee of $20.00
per pet per night.

Motel 6 - Beeville
400 Us 181 Bypass
Beeville, TX
361-358-4000 (800-466-8356)
This motel welcomes your pets to
stay with you.

Motel 6 - Waco Bellmead
1509 Hogan Ln
Bellmead, TX
254-799-4957 (800-466-8356)
This motel welcomes your pets to
stay with you.

Motel 6 - Ft Worth Benbrook
8601 Benbrook Blvd
Benbrook, TX
817-249-8885 (800-466-8356)
This motel welcomes your pets to
stay with you.

Best Western Palace Inn & Suites
915 Lamesa Highway
Big Spring, TX
432-264-1500 (800-780-7234)
Dogs are welcome at this hotel.

Comfort Inn
2900 E. I-20
Big Spring, TX
432-267-4553 (877-424-6423)
Dogs of all sizes are allowed.

Motel 6 - Big Spring
600 I-20
Big Spring, TX
432-267-1695 (800-466-8356)
This motel welcomes your pets to
stay with you.

Quality Inn
300 Tulane Ave
Big Spring, TX

432-264-7086 (877-424-6423)
Dogs up to 50 pounds are allowed.
Dogs are allowed for a pet fee of
$20.00 per pet per night. Two dogs
are allowed per room.

Best Western Bowie Inn & Suites
900 US Highway 287 S
Bowie, TX
940-872-9595 (800-780-7234)
Dogs are welcome at this hotel.

Best Western Brady Inn
2200 S Bridge Street
Brady, TX
325-597-3997 (800-780-7234)
Dogs of all sizes are allowed. Dogs
are allowed for a nightly pet fee.

Days Inn Brady
2108 South Bridge Street
Brady, TX
325-597-0789 (800-329-7466)
Dogs are welcome at this hotel.

Knights Inn Brenham
201 Hwy 290 East
Brenham, TX
979-830-1110 (800-843-5644)
Dogs of all sizes are allowed. Dogs
are allowed for a pet fee.

Comfort Suites
2302 10th Street
Bridgeport, TX
940-683-5777 (877-424-6423)
Dogs up to 50 pounds are allowed.
Dogs are allowed for a pet fee of
$5.00 per pet per night.

Best Western Caprock Inn
321 Lubbock Road
Brownfield, TX
806-637-9471 (800-780-7234)
Dogs of all sizes are allowed. Dogs
are allowed for a pet fee of $10 per
pet per night.

Motel 6 - Brownsville
2255 North Expressway
Brownsville, TX
956-546-4699 (800-466-8356)
This motel welcomes your pets to
stay with you.

Red Roof Inn Brownsville
2377 N. Expressway 83
Brownsville, TX
956-504-2300 (800-RED-ROOF)
One well-behaved family pet per
room. Guest must notify front desk
upon arrival. Guest is liable for any
damages. In consideration of all
guests, pets must never be left
unattended in the guest rooms.

Residence Inn Brownsville

3975 N Expressway 83
Brownsville, TX
956-350-8100 (800-331-3131)
This all suite, upscale hotel offers a
central location to all the great
attractions this area has to offer for
both business and leisure travelers.
And, among the amenities they also
offer a daily buffet breakfast and an
evening social hour Monday
through Thursday. Dogs are
allowed for an additional one time
pet fee of $100 per room. Multiple
dogs may be allowed.

Staybridge Suites Brownsville
2900 Pablo Kisel Blvd
Brownsville, TX
956-504-9500 (877-270-6405)
Dogs up to 80 pounds are allowed.
Pets allowed with an additional pet
fee. Up to $75 for 1-6 nights and up
to $150 for 7+ nights. A pet
agreement must be signed at
check-in.

Knights Inn Brownwood
606 Early Boulevard
Brownwood, TX
325-643-5621 (800-843-5644)
Dogs of all sizes are allowed. Dogs
are allowed for a nightly pet fee.

Best Western Burleson Inn & Suites
516 Memorial Plaza
Burleson, TX
817-744-7747 (800-780-7234)
Dogs of all sizes are allowed. Dogs
are allowed for a pet fee of $10 per
pet per night.

Canyon of the Eagles
16942 Ranch Road
Burnett, TX
512-334-2070 (800-977-0081)
canyonoftheeagles.com/
Offering a variety of
accommodations, this country
resort offers various recreational
activities, a lights-out observatory
for the stargazers, special venue
areas, a restaurant, an
amphitheater, and 14 miles of
scenic nature trails. Dogs are
allowed in the campground for no
additional fee. There is an
additional pet fee of $10 per night
per room for the lodge. Dogs must
be leashed, cleaned up after, and
crated when left alone in the room.
Multiple dogs may be allowed.

Best Western Canton Inn
2251 N Trade Days Boulevard
Canton, TX
903-567-6591 (800-780-7234)
Dogs of all sizes are allowed. Dogs
are allowed for a pet fee of $10 per

pet per stay.

Days Inn Canton
17299 S. I-20
Canton, TX
903-567-6588 (800-329-7466)
Dogs of all sizes are allowed. Dogs
are allowed for a nightly pet fee.

Motel 6 - Canton
3001 N. Tradedays Blvd
Canton, TX
903-567-0455 (800-466-8356)
This motel welcomes your pets to
stay with you.

Super 8 Canton
17350 Interstate 20
Canton, TX
903-567-6567 (800-800-8000)
Dogs of all sizes are allowed. Dogs
are allowed for a pet fee of $10.00
per pet per night.

Best Western Palo Duro Canyon Inn
& Suites
2801 4th Avenue
Canyon, TX
806-655-1818 (800-780-7234)
Dogs of all sizes are allowed. Dogs
are allowed for a pet fee of $25.00
per pet per night.

The Mermaids Cove & Sculpture
Ranch Cabins and Lodge
Hwy 386 & Eagle Rock Rd
Canyon Lake, TX
830-885-4297
themermaidcove.com
Have your pet join you in an area
known for its outdoor adventure.
Mermaids Cove offers cabin rentals
and a 5 acre sculpture ranch.

Comfort Inn
300 E. Whitestone Blvd
Cedar Park, TX
512-259-1810 (877-424-6423)
Dogs of all sizes are allowed. Dogs
are allowed for a pet fee of $10.00
per pet per night.

Holiday Inn Express Hotel & Suites
Center
143 Express Blvd.
Center, TX
936-591-8101 (877-270-6405)
Dogs of all sizes are allowed. Dogs
are allowed for a pet fee of $25 per
pet per night.

Days Inn Centerville
I-45 and Highway 7
Centerville, TX
903-536-7175 (800-329-7466)
Dogs are welcome at this hotel.

Knights Inn Houston/ Channelview
16939 I-10 East
Channelview, TX
281-457-1640 (800-843-5644)
Dogs are welcome at this hotel.

Comfort Inn
1804 Ave. F N.W.
Childress, TX
940-937-6363 (877-424-6423)
Dogs of all sizes are allowed. Dogs
are allowed for a pet fee of $10.00
per pet per stay.

Rodeway Inn
1612 F N W US 287
Childress, TX
940-937-3695 (877-424-6423)
Dogs of all sizes are allowed.

Super 8 Childress
411 Ave F NE
Childress, TX
940-937-8825 (800-800-8000)
Dogs of all sizes are allowed. Dogs
are allowed for a pet fee of $12.50
per pet per night.

Bar H Working Dude Ranch
12064 Bar H Ranch Road
Clarendon, TX
806-874-2634 (800-627-9871)
barhduderanch.com/index.html
Whether here for a day or for a stay,
there is a full range of activities to be
enjoyed at this dude ranch. Visitors
can join in on the real working
aspects of the ranch, or just watch-
relax and enjoy all the amenities,
including a seasonal swimming pool.
Lodging includes 3 full meals a day,
horseback rides, and other ranch
activities. Dogs are allowed for no
additional fee. Dogs must be well
mannered, leashed, and cleaned up
after at all times. 2 dogs may be
allowed.

Comfort Inn
2117 N. Main
Cleburne, TX
817-641-4702 (877-424-6423)
Dogs of all sizes are allowed. Dogs
are allowed for a pet fee of $10.00
per pet per night.

Days Inn & Suites TX Cleburne
2005 North Main St
Cleburne, TX
817-645-8953 (800-329-7466)
Dogs are welcome at this hotel.

Holiday Inn Express Hotel & Suites
Cleburne
1800 West Henderson Street
Cleburne, TX
817-641-5300 (877-270-6405)

Dogs of all sizes are allowed. Dogs
are allowed for a pet fee of $25.00
per pet per night.

Super 8 TX Cleveland
427 West Southline
Cleveland, TX
281-432-8800 (800-800-8000)
Dogs of all sizes are allowed. Dogs
are allowed for a nightly pet fee.

Days Inn Clute
805 West Hwy. 332
Clute, TX
979-265-3301 (800-329-7466)
Dogs are welcome at this hotel.

La Quinta Inn Clute/Lake Jackson
1126 S. Hwy. 332 West
Clute, TX
979-265-7461 (800-531-5900)
Dogs of all sizes are allowed. There
are no additional pet fees. Dogs
must be leashed and cleaned up
after. Multiple dogs may be allowed.

MainStay Suites
1003 West Hwy. 332
Clute, TX
979-388-9300 (877-424-6423)
Dogs of all sizes are allowed. Dogs
are allowed for a pet fee of $75.00
per pet per stay.

Motel 6 - Freeport Clute
1000 Sr 332
Clute, TX
979-265-4764 (800-466-8356)
This motel welcomes your pets to
stay with you.

Hawthorn Suites
1010 University Drive East
College Station, TX
979-695-9500 (800-527-1133)
In addition to providing a convenient
location to many local sites and
activities, this all-suite hotel offers a
number of amenities for business
and leisure travelers, including their
signature breakfast buffet and
beautifully appointed rooms. Dogs
are allowed for an additional one
time pet fee of $150 per room. 2
dogs may be allowed.

Holiday Inn Express Hotel & Suites
College Station
1203 University Drive East
College Station, TX
979-846-8700 (877-270-6405)
Dogs of all sizes are allowed. Dogs
are allowed for a pet fee of $75.00
per pet per night.

Howard Johnson Express College
Station

3702 Highway 6 South
College Station, TX
979-693-6810 (800-446-4656)
Dogs of all sizes are allowed. Dogs
are allowed for a pet fee of $20.00
per pet per night.

Knights Inn College Station
104 Texas Avenue
College Station, TX
979-691-6300 (800-843-5644)
Dogs of all sizes are allowed. Dogs
are allowed for a pet fee of $15.00
per pet per night.

La Quinta Inn College Station
607 Texas Avenue
College Station, TX
979-696-7777 (800-531-5900)
A dog of any size is allowed. There
are no additional pet fees. Dogs may
not be left unattended, and they must
be leashed and cleaned up after.

Motel 6 - College Station Bryan
2327 Texas Ave
College Station, TX
979-696-3379 (800-466-8356)
This motel welcomes your pets to
stay with you.

Ramada - /Texas A&M College
Station
1502 Texas Avenue
College Station, TX
979-693-9891 (800-272-6232)
Dogs of all sizes are allowed. Dogs
are allowed for a nightly pet fee.

TownePlace Suites Bryan College
Station
1300 University Drive E
College Station, TX
979-260-8500 (800-257-3000)
An ENERGY STAR, all suite hotel,
guests will enjoy a number of in-
house amenities, plus a central
location to a number of sites of
interest for both business and leisure
travelers. Dogs are allowed for an
additional one time fee of $100 per
room. Multiple dogs may be allowed.

Days Inn Colorado City
2303 Hwy 208 North
Colorado City, TX
325-728-2638 (800-329-7466)
Dogs are welcome at this hotel.

Holiday Inn Express Hotel & Suites
Columbus
4321 Interstate 10
Columbus, TX
979-733-9300 (877-270-6405)
Dogs of all sizes are allowed. Dogs
are allowed for a pet fee of $25.00
per pet per night.

Holiday Inn Express Hotel & Suites Commerce
2207 Culver Street
Commerce, TX
903-886-4777 (877-270-6405)
Dogs of all sizes are allowed. Dogs are allowed for a pet fee of $25 per pet per stay.

River Oaks Resort
210 Encino Drive
Concan, TX
800-800-5773
frioriver.com/
This recreation destination offers comfortable homes and cabins - located on or only a short walk to the river. They all have heating and air conditioning, satellite TV/DVD, patios with barbecues, picnic tables, outside chairs, fully equipped kitchens, and some have hot tubs. Additionally, they offer miniature golf and nature trails. Dogs are allowed for no additional fee; they must be kept leashed and cleaned up after promptly. Multiple dogs may be allowed.

Baymont Inn & Suites /The Woodlands Conroe
1506 Interstate - 45 South
Conroe, TX
936-539-5100 (877-229-6668)
Dogs of all sizes are allowed. Dogs are allowed for a pet fee.

La Quinta Inn & Suites Conroe
4006 Sprayberry Lane
Conroe, TX
936-228-0790 (800-531-5900)
Dogs of all sizes are allowed. There are no additional pet fees. There is a pet policy to sign at check in. Dogs must be quiet, well behaved, leashed and cleaned up after. Multiple dogs may be allowed.

Motel 6 - Conroe
820 I-45 South
Conroe, TX
936-760-4003 (800-466-8356)
This motel welcomes your pets to stay with you.

Ramada /The Woodlands Conroe
1601 I-45 South
Conroe, TX
936-756-8941 (800-272-6232)
Dogs of all sizes are allowed. Dogs are allowed for a nightly pet fee.

Bayfront Inn
601 North Shoreline Blvd.
Corpus Christi, TX
361-883-7271

There is a $30 one time fee per pet. 2 dogs may be allowed.

Best Western Garden Inn
11217 Interstate 37
Corpus Christi, TX
361-241-6675 (800-780-7234)
Dogs of all sizes are allowed. Dogs are allowed for a nightly pet fee.

Candlewood Suites Corpus Christi-Spid
5014 Crosstown Expressway
Corpus Christi, TX
361-853-3413 (877-270-6405)
Dogs up to 80 pounds are allowed. Pets allowed with an additional pet fee. Up to $75 for 1-6 nights and up to $150 for 7+ nights. A pet agreement must be signed at check-in.

Corpus Christi Red Roof Inn & Suites
3030 Buffalo St
Corpus Christi, TX
361-888-7683 (800-RED-ROOF)
One well-behaved family pet per room. Guest must notify front desk upon arrival. Guest is liable for any damages. In consideration of all guests, pets must never be left unattended in the guest rooms.

Days Inn Airport at I 37 Corpus Christi
901 Navigation Blvd/I-37
Corpus Christi, TX
361-888-8599 (800-329-7466)
Dogs are welcome at this hotel.

Holiday Inn Corpus Christi-Emerald Beach
1102 South Shoreline
Corpus Christi, TX
361-883-5731 (877-270-6405)
Dogs of all sizes are allowed. Dogs are allowed for a pet fee of $20.00 per pet per stay.

La Quinta Inn Corpus Christi North
5155 I-37 North
Corpus Christi, TX
361-888-5721 (800-531-5900)
Dogs of all sizes are allowed. There are no additional pet fees. Dogs must be leashed and cleaned up after. Multiple dogs may be allowed.

Motel 6 - Corpus Christi East North Padre Island
8202 Padre Island Dr
Corpus Christi, TX
361-991-8858 (800-466-8356)
This motel welcomes your pets to stay with you.

Motel 6 - Corpus Christi Northwest
845 Lantana St
Corpus Christi, TX
361-289-9397 (800-466-8356)
This motel welcomes your pets to stay with you.

Residence Inn Corpus Christi
5229 Blanche Moore Drive
Corpus Christi, TX
361-985-1113 (800-331-3131)
Sitting only minutes from the Botanical Gardens, some wonderful beaches, commerce and military areas, and many other activities/sites of interest, this all suite inn also offers a number of in-house amenities - including a daily buffet breakfast and an evening social Tuesdays and Wednesdays. Dogs are allowed for an additional one time pet fee of $100 per room. Multiple dogs may be allowed.

Staybridge Suites Corpus Christi
5201 Oakhurst Dr
Corpus Christi, TX
361-857-7766 (877-270-6405)
staybridgecc.com
Dogs up to 80 pounds are allowed. Pets allowed with an additional pet fee of $25 per stay.

Surfside Condo Apartments
15005 Windward Drive
Corpus Christi, TX
361-949-8128 (800-548-4585)
surfsidecondos.com/
Dogs up to 50 pounds are allowed. There is a $18 per day per pet fee. 2 dogs may be allowed.

Motel 6 - Corsicana, Tx
2018 Hwy 287
Corsicana, TX
903-874-6300 (800-466-8356)
This motel welcomes your pets to stay with you.

Best Western Cowboy Inn
145 FM 468 W
Cotulla, TX
830-879-3100 (800-780-7234)
Dogs are allowed at this hotel subject to size and type restrictions.

Econo Lodge
123 Liberal St.
Dalhart, TX
806-244-6464 (877-424-6423)
Dogs of all sizes are allowed. Dogs are allowed for a pet fee of $10.00 per pet per night. Three or more dogs may be allowed.

Rodeway Inn
1110 Liberal Street

Dalhart, TX
806-249-8585 (877-424-6423)
Dogs of all sizes are allowed.

Super 8 Dalhart
East Hwy 54
Dalhart, TX
806-249-8526 (800-800-8000)
Dogs are welcome at this hotel.

Best Western Executive Inn
12670 E Northwest Highway
Dallas, TX
972-613-5000 (800-780-7234)
Dogs of all sizes are allowed. Dogs
are allowed for a nightly pet fee.

Candlewood Suites Dallas Park
Central
12525 Greenville Avenue
Dallas, TX
972-669-9606 (877-270-6405)
Dogs up to 80 pounds are allowed.
Pets allowed with an additional pet
fee. Up to $75 for 1-6 nights and up
to $150 for 7+ nights. A pet
agreement must be signed at check-
in.

Candlewood Suites Dallas-By The
Galleria
13939 Noel Road
Dallas, TX
972-233-6888 (877-270-6405)
Dogs up to 80 pounds are allowed.
Pets allowed with an additional pet
fee. Up to $75 for 1-6 nights and up
to $150 for 7+ nights. A pet
agreement must be signed at check-
in.

Candlewood Suites Dallas/Market
Center
7930 North Stemmons Freeway
Dallas, TX
214-631-3333 (877-270-6405)
Dogs up to 80 pounds are allowed.
Pets allowed with an additional pet
fee. Up to $75 for 1-6 nights and up
to $150 for 7+ nights. A pet
agreement must be signed at check-
in.

Comfort Inn & Suites Market Center
7138 N. Stemmons Fwy
Dallas, TX
214-461-2677 (877-424-6423)
Dogs of all sizes are allowed.

Comfort Inn by the Galleria
14975 Landmark Blvd.
Dallas, TX
972-701-0881 (877-424-6423)
Dogs up to 50 pounds are allowed.
Dogs are allowed for a pet fee of
$25.00 per pet per night. Two dogs
are allowed per room.

Crowne Plaza Hotel Dallas
Downtown
1015 Elm Street
Dallas, TX
214-742-5678 (877-270-6405)
Dogs of all sizes are allowed. Dogs
are allowed for a pet fee of $125.00
per pet per stay.

Crowne Plaza Suites Dallas-Park
Central
7800 Alpha Road
Dallas, TX
972-233-7600 (877-270-6405)
Dogs are welcome at this hotel.
There is a $100 refundable pet
deposit and a $25 non-refundable
pet fee.

Days Inn & Suites Dallas
2334 West Northwest Highway
Dallas, TX
214-350-5800 (800-329-7466)
Dogs are welcome at this hotel.

Econo Lodge Airport I-35 North
2275 Valley View Lane
Dallas, TX
972-243-5500 (877-424-6423)
Dogs of all sizes are allowed. Two
dogs are allowed per room.

Extended Stay America Dallas -
Greenville Ave.
12270 Greenville Ave.
Dallas, TX
972-238-1133 (800-804-3724)
One dog is allowed per suite. There
is a $25 per night additional pet fee
up to $150 for an entire stay.

Extended Stay America Dallas -
North - Park Central
9019 Vantage Point Road
Dallas, TX
972-671-7722 (800-804-3724)
One dog is allowed per suite. There
is a $25 per night additional pet fee
up to $150 for an entire stay.

Hawthorn Suites
7900 Brookriver Dr
Dallas, TX
214-688-1010
There is a $50 one time pet fee for
one large dog or 2 small dogs.
Dogs must be less than 75 pounds.
2 dogs may be allowed.

Homestead Studio Suites Dallas -
North - Park Central
12121 Coit Rd.
Dallas, TX
972-663-1800 (800-804-3724)
One dog is allowed per suite. There
is a $25 per night additional pet fee

up to $150 for an entire stay.

Homestead Studio Suites Dallas -
North Addison - Tollway
17425 Dallas Pkwy.
Dallas, TX
972-447-1800 (800-804-3724)
One dog is allowed per suite. There
is a $25 per night additional pet fee
up to $150 for an entire stay.

Homestead Studio Suites Dallas -
Plano
18470 N. Dallas Pkwy.
Dallas, TX
972-248-2233 (800-804-3724)
One dog is allowed per suite. There
is a $25 per night additional pet fee
up to $150 for an entire stay.

Hota Zaza
2332 Leonard Street
Dallas, TX
214-468-8399 (800-597-8399)
hotelzaza.com/dallas
This luxury boutique hotel is located
in the city's entertainment/arts and
business district offering a wide
variety of activities and recreational
opportunities. Their restaurant
Dragonfly has outside seating,
weather permitting, where your pet
may dine with you. Dogs up to 50
pounds are allowed for an additional
fee of $50 per pet for the 1st night
and $25 for each additional night. 2
dogs may be allowed.

Hotel Lawrence
302 S Houston Street
Dallas, TX
214-761-9090
Dogs up to 50 pounds are allowed.
There is a $25 one time fee per pet
and a pet policy to sign at check in.

Hotel Lumen
6101 Hillcrest Ave
Dallas, TX
214-219-2400 (800-908-1140)
hotellumen.com
This Kimpton boutique hotel allows
dogs of all sizes. There are no
additional pet fees.

Hotel Palomar Dallas
5300 E Mockingbird Lane
Dallas, TX
214-520-7969 (888-253-9030)
hotelpalomar-dallas.com/
With sophisticated modern
architecture and a rich color scheme,
this luxury boutique hotel offers 198
guestrooms and upscale suites.
Some of the highlights include 2
great restaurants (Central 214-with
an exhibition kitchen and Trader

Vic's), plenty of meeting space, an Exhale Spa, a pool, 24 hour room service and business center, and a hosted evening wine reception. Dogs of all sizes are allowed for no additional fee unless you purchase their Pet Package which includes a big comfy bed, treats, water and bowl, and a one-hour yoga-massage combo. Dogs must be quiet, leashed, and cleaned up after. Multiple dogs may be allowed.

Knights Inn Market Center
1550 Empire Central
Dallas, TX
214-638-5151 (800-843-5644)
Dogs are welcome at this hotel. There is a $5 per visit additional pet fee.

La Quinta Inn & Suites Dallas Addison-Galleria
14925 Landmark Blvd.
Dallas, TX
972-404-0004 (800-531-5900)
Dogs of all sizes are allowed. There are no additional pet fees. Dogs may not be left unattended unless they will be quiet and well behaved. Dogs must be leashed and cleaned up after. Multiple dogs may be allowed.

La Quinta Inn & Suites Dallas North Central
10001 N. Central Expressway
Dallas, TX
214-361-8200 (800-531-5900)
Dogs of all sizes are allowed. There are no additional pet fees. Dogs must be leashed and cleaned up after. Dogs may not be left unattended unless they will be quiet, well behaved, and a contact number is left with the front desk. Dogs are not allowed in the pool area. Multiple dogs may be allowed.

La Quinta Inn Dallas Cityplace
4440 North Central Expressway
Dallas, TX
214-821-4220 (800-531-5900)
Dogs of all sizes are allowed. There are no additional pet fees. Dogs must be leashed, cleaned up after, and removed for housekeeping. Multiple dogs may be allowed.

La Quinta Inn Dallas East (I-30)
8303 East R. L. Thornton Freeway
Dallas, TX
214-324-3731 (800-531-5900)
Dogs of all sizes are allowed. There are no additional pet fees. Dogs must be leashed, cleaned up after, and the front desk informed if there is a pet in the room alone. Multiple dogs may be allowed.

Marriott Suites Dallas Market Center
2493 N Stemmons Freeway
Dallas, TX
214-905-0050 (800-228-9290)
This luxury hotel provides a great location to a number of sites of interest for both business and leisure travelers; plus they also offer numerous on-site amenities to ensure a comfortable stay. Dogs are allowed for an additional one time fee of $100 per room. A contact number must be left with the front desk when a pet is left alone in the room. 2 dogs may be allowed.

Motel 6 - Dallas Forest Lane
2660 Forest Ln
Dallas, TX
972-484-9111 (800-466-8356)
This motel welcomes your pets to stay with you.

Motel 6 - Dallas Northeast
10921 Estate Lane
Dallas, TX
214-340-2299 (800-466-8356)
This motel welcomes your pets to stay with you.

Motel 6 - Dallas Southwest
4220 Independence Dr
Dallas, TX
972-296-3331 (800-466-8356)
This motel welcomes your pets to stay with you.

Quality Inn Conference Center
7815 LBJ Freeway
Dallas, TX
972-934-8668 (877-424-6423)
Dogs up to 100 pounds are allowed. Dogs are allowed for a pet fee of $25.00 per pet per stay. Two dogs are allowed per room.

Quality Suites
13636 Goldmark Dr.
Dallas, TX
972-669-0478 (877-424-6423)
Dogs up to 100 pounds are allowed. Dogs are allowed for a pet fee of $25.00 per pet per stay. Three or more dogs may be allowed.

Radisson Hotel
6060 N Central Expressway
Dallas, TX
214-750-6060
Dogs up to 80 pounds are allowed. There is a $50 one time fee per pet.

Residence Inn Dallas Addison/Quorum Drive

14975 Quorum Drive
Dallas, TX
972-866-9933 (800-331-3131)
In addition to offering a convenient location to business, shopping, dining, and entertainment areas, this hotel also provides a number of in-house amenities, including a daily buffet breakfast and evening social hours with light dinner fare. Dogs are allowed for an additional one time pet fee of $75 per room. Multiple dogs may be allowed.

Residence Inn Dallas Central Expressway
10333 N Central Expressway
Dallas, TX
214-750-8220 (800-331-3131)
In addition to being located in one of the city's largest medical districts, this all suite hotel also sits central to many of the areas star attractions, dining, shopping, and business areas; plus they offer a number of in-house amenities that includes a daily buffet breakfast, a nightly social hour, and weekly barbecues. Dogs are allowed for an additional one time pet fee of $100 per room. Multiple dogs may be allowed.

Residence Inn Dallas Market Center
6950 N Stemmons Freeway
Dallas, TX
214-631-2472
This all suite hotel sits central to many of the city's star attractions, dining, shopping, and business areas, plus they offer a number of in-house amenities that include a daily buffet breakfast and evening social hours with light dinner fare. Dogs are allowed for an additional one time pet fee of $100 per room. Multiple dogs may be allowed.

Residence Inn Dallas Park Central
7642 LBJ Freeway
Dallas, TX
972-503-1333 (800-331-3131)
Offering a convenient location to business, shopping, dining, and entertainment areas, this all suite hotel also offers a number of in-house amenities, including a daily buffet breakfast and an evening social hour Monday to Thursday. Dogs are allowed for an additional one time pet fee of $100 per room. 2 dogs may be allowed.

Sheraton Suites Market Center
2102 Stemmons Freeway
Dallas, TX
214-747-3000 (888-625-5144)
Dogs up to 80 pounds are allowed for no additional pet fee. Dogs may

not be left alone in the room.

Staybridge Suites Dallas Near The
Galleria
7880 Alpha Rd
Dallas, TX
972-391-0000 (877-270-6405)
Dogs up to 80 pounds are allowed.
Pets allowed with an additional pet
fee. Up to $75 for 1-6 nights and up
to $150 for 7+ nights. A pet
agreement must be signed at check-
in.

Staybridge Suites Dallas-Addison
16060 Dallas Parkway
Dallas, TX
972-726-9990 (877-270-6405)
Dogs up to 80 pounds are allowed.
Pets allowed with an additional pet
fee. Up to $75 for 1-6 nights and up
to $150 for 7+ nights. A pet
agreement must be signed at check-
in.

Studio 6 - Dallas Garland/ Northeast
9801 Adleta Ct
Dallas, TX
214-342-5400 (800-466-8356)
Your pets are welcome to stay here
with you for a pet fee of $10 per day
up to $50 for an entire stay.

Studio 6 - Dallas Northwest
2395 Stemmons Trail
Dallas, TX
214-904-1400 (800-466-8356)
Your pets are welcome to stay here
with you for a pet fee of $10 per day
up to $50 for an entire stay.

Studio 6 - Dallas Richardson/north
12301 North Central Expy
Dallas, TX
972-716-0600 (800-466-8356)
Your pets are welcome to stay here
with you for a pet fee of $10 per day
up to $50 for an entire stay.

Super 8 Dallas
8541 South Hampton Road
Dallas, TX
972-572-1030 (800-800-8000)
Dogs of all sizes are allowed. Dogs
are allowed for a pet fee.

Super 8 Dallas
8901 East RL Thornton Frwy
Dallas, TX
214-324-4475 (800-800-8000)
Dogs of all sizes are allowed. Dogs
are allowed for a pet fee of $15 per
pet per stay.

The Fairmont Dallas
1717 N Akard Street
Dallas, TX

214-720-2020 (800-257-7544)
fairmont.com/dallas/
The hotel is located in the city's art
district and close to many other
attractions and activities. Dogs are
allowed for an additional pet fee of
$25 per night per pet. Dogs must be
leashed and cleaned up after, and
they may not be left in the room
alone at any time.

The Mansion on Turtle Creek
2821 Turtle Creek Blvd
Dallas, TX
214-559-2100
mansiononturtlecreek.com/
There is a $100 one time pet fee
per pet. Dogs up to 50 pounds are
allowed. 2 dogs may be allowed.

Red Roof Inn Dallas South -
DeSoto
1401 North I-35E
DeSoto, TX
972-224-7100 (800-RED-ROOF)
One well-behaved family pet per
room. Guest must notify front desk
upon arrival. Guest is liable for any
damages. In consideration of all
guests, pets must never be left
unattended in the guest rooms.

Comfort Inn
1709 SR 287
Decatur, TX
940-627-6919 (877-424-6423)
Dogs of all sizes are allowed. Dogs
are allowed for a pet fee of $10.00
per pet per night.

Days Inn TX Decatur
1900 S. Trinity Street
Decatur, TX
940-627-2463 (800-329-7466)
Dogs of all sizes are allowed. Dogs
are allowed for a pet fee.

Holiday Inn Express Hotel & Suites
Decatur
1051 North Hwy 81/287
Decatur, TX
940-627-0776 (877-270-6405)
Dogs of all sizes are allowed. Dogs
are allowed for a pet fee of $150.00
per pet per stay.

Knights Inn Decatur
1600 South Highway 287
Decatur, TX
940-627-0250 (800-843-5644)
Dogs of all sizes are allowed. Dogs
are allowed for a pet fee of $10 per
pet per night.

Ramada - Texas Decatur
1507 Hwy 287 South
Decatur, TX

940-627-6262 (800-272-6232)
Dogs are welcome at this hotel.

Best Western Inn of Del Rio
810 Veterans Boulevard
Del Rio, TX
830-775-7511 (800-780-7234)
Dogs are welcome at this hotel for a
pet fee.

Days Inn and Suites Del Rio
3808 Veterans Blvd
Del Rio, TX
830-775-0585 (800-329-7466)
Dogs are welcome at this hotel.

La Quinta Inn Del Rio
2005 Veterans Blvd.
Del Rio, TX
830-775-7591 (800-531-5900)
Dogs of all sizes are allowed. There
are no additional pet fees. Dogs
must be leashed and cleaned up
after. A contact number must be left
with the front desk if there is a pet
unattended in the room. Multiple
dogs may be allowed.

Motel 6 - Del Rio
2115 Veterans Blvd
Del Rio, TX
830-774-2115 (800-466-8356)
This motel welcomes your pets to
stay with you.

Ramada - Del Rio
2101 Veterans Boulevard
Del Rio, TX
830-775-1511 (800-272-6232)
Dogs are welcome at this hotel.

Motel 6 - Denison
615 Hwy 75
Denison, TX
903-465-4446 (800-466-8356)
This motel welcomes your pets to
stay with you.

La Quinta Inn Denton
700 Ft. Worth Dr.
Denton, TX
940-387-5840 (800-531-5900)
Dogs of all sizes are allowed. There
are no additional pet fees. Dogs
must be leashed and cleaned up
after. Multiple dogs may be allowed.

Motel 6 - Denton
4125 I-35 North
Denton, TX
940-566-4798 (800-466-8356)
This motel welcomes your pets to
stay with you.

Super 8 Dallas/ Denton
620 S I-35 East
Denton, TX

Dog-Friendly Lodging - Please always call ahead to make sure an establishment is still dog-friendly.

940-380-8888 (800-800-8000)
Dogs are welcome at this hotel.

Travelodge /I-35 Denton
4211 I-35E North
Denton, TX
940-383-1471 (800-578-7878)
Dogs are welcome at this hotel.

Econo Lodge
1719 S. Dumas Ave.
Dumas, TX
806-935-9098 (877-424-6423)
Dogs up to 50 pounds are allowed.
Dogs are allowed for a pet fee of
$10.00 per pet per night. Two dogs
are allowed per room.

Super 8 TX Dumas
119 W 17th St
Dumas, TX
806-935-6222 (800-800-8000)
Dogs of all sizes are allowed. Dogs
are allowed for a pet fee of $20 per
pet per night.

Motel 6 - Dallas Duncanville
202 Jellison Blvd
Duncanville, TX
972-296-0345 (800-466-8356)
This motel welcomes your pets to
stay with you.

La Quinta Inn Eagle Pass
2525 E. Main St.
Eagle Pass, TX
830-773-7000 (800-531-5900)
Dogs of all sizes are allowed. There
are no additional pet fees. Dogs
must be well behaved, leashed, and
cleaned up after. Multiple dogs may
be allowed.

Days Inn Eastland
2501 I-20 East
Eastland, TX
254-629-2655 (800-329-7466)
Dogs are welcome at this hotel.

Super 8 Eastland
3900 I-20 East
Eastland, TX
254-629-3336 (800-800-8000)
Dogs of all sizes are allowed. Dogs
are allowed for a pet fee.

Best Western Edinburg Inn & Suites
2708 S Business Highway 281
(Closner Blvd)
Edinburg, TX
956-318-0442 (800-780-7234)
Dogs of all sizes are allowed. Dogs
are allowed for a pet fee of $15 per
pet per night.

Comfort Inn
4001 Closner

Edinburg, TX
956-318-1117 (877-424-6423)
Dogs up to 50 pounds are allowed.
Dogs are allowed for a pet fee of
$10.00 per pet per night. Two dogs
are allowed per room.

Motel 6 - Edinburg
1806 Closner Blvd
Edinburg, TX
956-383-8800 (800-466-8356)
This motel welcomes your pets to
stay with you.

Super 8 /McAllen/Central Edinburg
202 North Hwy 281
Edinburg, TX
956-381-1688 (800-800-8000)
Dogs of all sizes are allowed. Dogs
are allowed for a pet fee.

Super 8 /McAllen/South Edinburg
1210 East Canton Road
Edinburg, TX
956-381-8888 (800-800-8000)
Dogs are welcome at this hotel.

Chase Suite Hotel by Woodfin
6791 Montana Ave
El Paso, TX
915-772-8000
All well-behaved dogs are welcome.
Every room is a suite with a full
kitchen. Hotel amenities include a
complimentary breakfast buffet.
There is a $5 per day pet fee.

Comfort Inn Airport East
900 Yarbrough Dr.
El Paso, TX
915-594-9111 (877-424-6423)
Dogs of all sizes are allowed. Dogs
are allowed for a pet fee of
$20.00/pet per pet per stay.

Days Inn West El Paso
5035 South Desert Boulevard
El Paso, TX
915-845-3500 (800-329-7466)
Dogs of all sizes are allowed. Dogs
are allowed for a pet fee.

Days Inn - - East El Paso
10635 Gateway West
El Paso, TX
915-595-1913 (800-329-7466)
Dogs are welcome at this hotel.

Extended Stay America El Paso -
Airport
6580 Montana Ave.
El Paso, TX
915-772-5754 (800-804-3724)
One dog is allowed per suite. There
is a $25 per night additional pet fee
up to $150 for an entire stay.

Hawthorn Inn & Suites
6789 Boeing Drive
El Paso, TX
915-778-6789 (800-527-1133)
In addition to providing a convenient
location to many local sites and
activities, this all-suite hotel offers a
number of amenities for business
and leisure travelers, including their
signature breakfast buffet and
beautifully appointed rooms. Dogs
are allowed for an additional one
time pet fee of $116 (+ $9 tax) per
room. Multiple dogs may be allowed.

Holiday Inn El Paso-Sunland Pk Dr &
I-10 W
900 Sunland Park Drive
El Paso, TX
915-833-2900 (877-270-6405)
Dogs of all sizes are allowed. Dogs
are allowed for a pet fee of $25.00
per pet per stay.

Holiday Inn Express El Paso-Central
409 East Missouri Ave
El Paso, TX
915-544-3333 (877-270-6405)
Dogs of all sizes are allowed. Dogs
are allowed for a pet fee of $25.00
per pet per stay.

Howard Johnson Inn TX El Paso
500 Executive Center Boulevard
El Paso, TX
915-532-8981 (800-446-4656)
Dogs of all sizes are allowed. Dogs
are allowed for a pet fee.

La Quinta Inn El Paso Airport
6140 Gateway East
El Paso, TX
915-778-9321 (800-531-5900)
Dogs of all sizes are allowed. There
are no additional pet fees. Dogs
must be leashed and cleaned up
after. The front desk must be
informed when a pet is in the room
alone, and they are not allowed to be
left for long periods. 2 dogs may be
allowed.

La Quinta Inn El Paso Bartlett
7620 North Mesa
El Paso, TX
915-585-2999 (800-531-5900)
Dogs of all sizes are allowed. There
are no additional pet fees. Dogs
must be kept leashed. Multiple dogs
may be allowed.

La Quinta Inn El Paso Cielo Vista
9125 Gateway West
El Paso, TX
915-593-8400 (800-531-5900)
Dogs of all sizes are allowed. There
are no additional pet fees. Dogs

must be leashed and cleaned up after. The Do Not Disturb sign must be placed on the door if there is a pet unattended in the room. Multiple dogs may be allowed.

La Quinta Inn El Paso East
7944 Gateway East
El Paso, TX
915-591-3300 (800-531-5900)
Dogs of all sizes are allowed. There are no additional pet fees. Dogs must be leashed and cleaned up after. Multiple dogs may be allowed.

La Quinta Inn El Paso Lomaland
11033 Gateway Blvd. West
El Paso, TX
915-591-2244 (800-531-5900)
Dogs of all sizes are allowed. There are no additional pet fees. Dogs must be leashed, cleaned up after, and crated or removed for housekeeping. Multiple dogs may be allowed.

La Quinta Inn El Paso West
7550 Remcon Circle
El Paso, TX
915-833-2522 (800-531-5900)
Dogs of all sizes are allowed. There are no additional pet fees. Dogs may not be left unattended, and they must be leashed and cleaned up after. 2 dogs may be allowed.

Motel 6 - El Paso Central
4800 Gateway Blvd
El Paso, TX
915-533-7521 (800-466-8356)
This motel welcomes your pets to stay with you.

Motel 6 - El Paso East
1330 Lomaland Dr
El Paso, TX
915-592-6386 (800-466-8356)
This motel welcomes your pets to stay with you.

Motel 6 - El Paso-airport-fort Bliss
6363 Montana Ave
El Paso, TX
915-778-3311 (800-466-8356)
This motel welcomes your pets to stay with you.

Ramada El Paso
8250 Gateway Blvd East
El Paso, TX
915-591-9600 (800-272-6232)
Dogs of all sizes are allowed. Dogs are allowed for a nightly pet fee.

Red Roof Inn El Paso East
11400 Chito Samaniego Drive
El Paso, TX

915-599-8877 (800-RED-ROOF)
One well-behaved family pet per room. Guest must notify front desk upon arrival. Guest is liable for any damages. In consideration of all guests, pets must never be left unattended in the guest rooms.

Red Roof Inn El Paso West
7530 Remcon Circle
El Paso, TX
915-587-9977 (800-RED-ROOF)
One well-behaved family pet per room. Guest must notify front desk upon arrival. Guest is liable for any damages. In consideration of all guests, pets must never be left unattended in the guest rooms.

Sleep Inn
953 Sunland Park Dr.
El Paso, TX
915-585-7577 (877-424-6423)
Dogs of all sizes are allowed. Dogs are allowed for a pet fee of $usd per pet per stay.

Studio 6 - El Paso East
11049 Gateway Blvd
El Paso, TX
915-594-8533 (800-466-8356)
Your pets are welcome to stay here with you for a pet fee of $10 per day up to $50 for an entire stay.

Super 8 El Paso
450 Raynolds
El Paso, TX
915-771-8388 (800-800-8000)
Dogs of all sizes are allowed. Dogs are allowed for a pet fee of $10.00 per pet per night.

Super 8 /West El Paso
7840 N Mesa Street
El Paso, TX
915-584-4030 (800-800-8000)
Dogs of all sizes are allowed. Dogs are allowed for a pet fee of $10.00 per pet per night.

Travelodge Airport El Paso
6400 Montana Ave
El Paso, TX
800-772-4231 (800-578-7878)
Dogs of all sizes are allowed. Dogs are allowed for a pet fee.

Wingate by Wyndham El Paso
6351 Gateway West
El Paso, TX
915-772-4088 (800-228-1000)
Dogs are welcome at this hotel.

Baymont Inn & Suites Ennis
100 South I-45
Ennis, TX

972-875-3390 (877-229-6668)
Dogs are welcome at this hotel.

La Quinta Inn Dallas DFW Airport West-Euless
1001 W. Airport Freeway
Euless, TX
817-540-0233 (800-531-5900)
Dogs of all sizes are allowed. There are no additional pet fees. There is a pet waiver to sign at check in. Dogs may only be left in the room alone if they will be quiet and well behaved, and they must be leashed, cleaned up after, and crated or removed for housekeeping. Multiple dogs may be allowed.

Motel 6 - Dallas Euless
110 Airport Fwy
Euless, TX
817-545-0141 (800-466-8356)
This motel welcomes your pets to stay with you.

Quality Inn
1001 West Airport Freeway
Euless, TX
817-540-0233 (877-424-6423)
Dogs up to 50 pounds are allowed. Dogs are allowed for a pet fee of $25.00 per pet per night. Two dogs are allowed per room.

Days Inn Falfurrias
2116 Highway 281 South
Falfurrias, TX
361-325-2515 (800-329-7466)
Dogs are welcome at this hotel.

La Quinta Inn Dallas Northwest-Farmers Branch
13235 Stemmons Frwy.
Farmers Branch, TX
972-620-7333 (800-531-5900)
Dogs of all sizes are allowed. There are no additional pet fees. Dogs must be leashed, cleaned up after, and crated if left alone in the room. Multiple dogs may be allowed.

Super 8 Farmers Branch
14040 North Stemmons Freeway
Farmers Branch, TX
972-406-3030 (800-800-8000)
Dogs of all sizes are allowed. Dogs are allowed for a pet fee of $12.00 per pet per night.

Best Western Floresville Inn
1720 10th Street
Floresville, TX
830-393-0443 (800-780-7234)
Dogs of all sizes are allowed. Dogs are allowed for a pet fee.

Super 8 Forney

103 W. Highway 80
Forney, TX
972-552-3888 (800-800-8000)
Dogs of all sizes are allowed. Dogs
are allowed for a pet fee of $10 per
pet per night.

Hotel Limpia
P.O. Box 1341
Fort Davis, TX
800-662-5517 (800-662-5517)
hotellimpia.com/
This restored 1912 historic hotel
charges an additional $20 per day
per pet charge. Multiple dogs may be
allowed.

Days Inn Fort Stockton
1408 N US Hwy 285
Fort Stockton, TX
432-336-7500 (800-329-7466)
Dogs are welcome at this hotel.

Motel 6 - Ft Stockton
3001 Dickinson Blvd
Fort Stockton, TX
432-336-9737 (800-466-8356)
This motel welcomes your pets to
stay with you.

Quality Inn
1308 North US Hwy 285
Fort Stockton, TX
432-336-5955 (877-424-6423)
Dogs of all sizes are allowed.

Baymont Inn & Suites Ft. Worth
North
4681 Gemini Place
Fort Worth, TX
817-740-1099 (877-229-6668)
Dogs of all sizes are allowed. Dogs
are allowed for a nightly pet fee.

Candlewood Suites Dallas
5201 Endicott Avenue
Fort Worth, TX
817-838-8229 (877-270-6405)
Dogs up to 80 pounds are allowed.
Pets allowed with an additional pet
fee. Up to $75 for 1-6 nights and up
to $150 for 7+ nights. A pet
agreement must be signed at check-
in.

Candlewood Suites Dfw South
4200 Reggis Drive
Fort Worth, TX
817-868-1900 (877-270-6405)
Dogs up to 80 pounds are allowed.
Pets allowed with an additional pet
fee. Up to $75 for 1-6 nights and up
to $150 for 7+ nights. A pet
agreement must be signed at check-
in.

Comfort Suites North

3751 Tanacross Dr.
Fort Worth, TX
817-222-2333 (877-424-6423)
Dogs of all sizes are allowed. Dogs
are allowed for a pet fee of $25.00
per pet per night.

Days Inn West Fort Worth
8500 West Freeway
Fort Worth, TX
817-246-4961 (800-329-7466)
Dogs of all sizes are allowed. Dogs
are allowed for a pet fee of $10.00
per pet per night.

Days Inn -Stockyards Fort Worth
5370 Blue Mound Road
Fort Worth, TX
817-626-3566 (800-329-7466)
Dogs are welcome at this hotel.

Days Inn South Fort Worth
4213 I-35 W South Freeway
Fort Worth, TX
817-923-1987 (800-329-7466)
Dogs are welcome at this hotel.

Extended Stay America Fort Worth
- City View
5831 Overton Ridge Blvd.
Fort Worth, TX
817-263-9006 (800-804-3724)
One dog is allowed per suite. There
is a $25 per night additional pet fee
up to $150 for an entire stay.

Holiday Inn Express Hotel & Suites
Fort Worth-West (I-30)
2730 Cherry Lane
Fort Worth, TX
817-560-4200 (877-270-6405)
Dogs of all sizes are allowed. Dogs
are allowed for a pet fee of $15.00
per pet per night.

Homestead Studio Suites Fort
Worth - Medical Center
1601 River Run
Fort Worth, TX
817-338-4808 (800-804-3724)
One dog is allowed per suite. There
is a $25 per night additional pet fee
up to $150 for an entire stay.

Howard Johnson Fort Worth
4850 North Freeway
Fort Worth, TX
817-834-8001 (800-446-4656)
Dogs of all sizes are allowed. Dogs
are allowed for a pet fee of $15.00
per pet per stay.

La Quinta Inn & Suites Fort Worth
Southwest
4900 Bryant Irvin Rd.
Fort Worth, TX
817-370-2700 (800-531-5900)

Dogs of all sizes are allowed. There
are no additional pet fees. Dogs
must be well behaved, leashed, and
cleaned up after. A contact number
must be left with the front desk if
there is a pet alone in the room.
Multiple dogs may be allowed.

MD Resort
601 Old Base Road
Fort Worth, TX
817-489-5150
There is an additional $50 one time
fee per pet. 2 dogs may be allowed.

Motel 6 - Ft Worth East
1236 Oakland Blvd
Fort Worth, TX
817-834-7361 (800-466-8356)
This motel welcomes your pets to
stay with you.

Motel 6 - Ft Worth North
3271 I-35w
Fort Worth, TX
817-625-4359 (800-466-8356)
This motel welcomes your pets to
stay with you.

Motel 6 - Ft Worth South
6600 South Freeway
Fort Worth, TX
817-293-8595 (800-466-8356)
This motel welcomes your pets to
stay with you.

Motel 6 - Ft Worth West
8701 I-30 West
Fort Worth, TX
817-244-9740 (800-466-8356)
This motel welcomes your pets to
stay with you.

Quality Inn & Suites East
2425 Scott Ave.
Fort Worth, TX
817-535-2591 (877-424-6423)
Dogs of all sizes are allowed. Dogs
are allowed for a pet fee of $25.00
per pet per stay.

Radisson Hotel Fort Worth South
100 Alta Mesa East Boulevard
Fort Worth, TX
817-293-3088 (800-333-3333)
radisson.com/fortworthsouth
Up to 2 pets are allowed per room
and there is a $25.00 non-refundable
pet deposit.

Renaissance Worthington Hotel
200 Main Street
Fort Worth, TX
817-870-1000 (800-HOTELS-1 (468-
3571))
Located in the city's famed
Sundance Square, this luxury hotel

sits central to many of the city's star attractions, world class shopping, dining, and entertainment areas, and major businesses, plus they also offer a number of in-house amenities for all level of travelers. Dogs up to 50 pounds are allowed for a $200 refundable deposit per room, and there is a pet agreement to sign at check in. 2 dogs may be allowed.

Residence Inn Fort Worth Alliance Airport
13400 North Freeway
Fort Worth, TX
817-750-7000 (800-331-3131)
Some of the amenities at this all-suite inn include a daily buffet breakfast, an evening hospitality hour with light dinner fare, a swimming pool, Sport Court, and a complimentary grocery shopping service. Dogs are allowed for an additional one time pet fee of $75 per room. Dogs must be crated or removed for housekeeping. Multiple dogs may be allowed.

Residence Inn Fort Worth Cultural District
2500 Museum Way
Fort Worth, TX
817-885-8250 (800-331-3131)
In addition to offering a convenient location to business, shopping, dining, and entertainment areas, this hotel also provides a number of in-house amenities, including a daily buffet breakfast and an evening social hour. Dogs are allowed for an additional one time fee of $75 per pet. 2 dogs may be allowed.

Residence Inn Fort Worth Fossil Creek
5801 Sandshell Drive
Fort Worth, TX
817-439-1300 (800-331-3131)
This all suite hotel sits central to many of the city's star attractions, dining, shopping, and business areas, plus they offer a number of in-house amenities that include a daily buffet breakfast and evening social hours. Dogs are allowed for an additional one time pet fee of $100 per room. 2 dogs may be allowed.

Residence Inn Fort Worth University
1701 S University Drive
Fort Worth, TX
817-870-1011 (800-331-3131)
Located along the shores of the Trinity River with quick access to the river walking path, Forest Park, and the Fort Worth Botanic Gardens, this hotel also provides a number of in-house amenities, including a daily

buffet breakfast and an evening social hour. Dogs are allowed for an additional one time pet fee of $100 per room. Multiple dogs may be allowed.

Super 8 Fort Worth
7960 I-30 West
Fort Worth, TX
817-246-7168 (800-800-8000)
Dogs are welcome at this hotel.

The Texas White House Bed and Breakfast
1417 Eighth Avenue
Fort Worth, TX
817-923-3597 (800-279-6491)
texaswhitehouse.com/
In addition to providing spacious accommodations and various amenities, they also provide a great starting point for exploring the numerous local attractions and activities. Dogs are allowed for no additional pet fee; they must be crated when left alone in the room. 2 dogs may be allowed.

TownePlace Suites Fort Worth Southwest
4200 International Plaza
Fort Worth, TX
817-732-2224 (800-257-3000)
Set between a number of world class attractions and recreational activities, guests of this all suite hotel are also afforded a central location to numerous businesses, shopping, and dining areas as well as a number of in-house amenities. Dogs are allowed for an additional one time fee of $100 per room. There may be up to 2 dogs in the 2-bedroom suites and up to 3 dogs in the 3 bedroom suites. Multiple dogs may be allowed.

Comfort Inn & Suites
723 S. Washington Street
Fredericksburg, TX
830-990-2552 (877-424-6423)
Dogs of all sizes are allowed. Dogs are allowed for a pet fee of $40.00/ per pet per night. Two dogs are allowed per room.

Econo Lodge
810 S. Adams
Fredericksburg, TX
830-997-3437 (877-424-6423)
Dogs of all sizes are allowed.

Motel 6 - Fredericksburg, Tx
705 Washington Street
Fredericksburg, TX
830-990-1300 (800-466-8356)
This motel welcomes your pets to

stay with you.

Quality Inn
908 S. Adams St.
Fredericksburg, TX
830-997-9811 (877-424-6423)
Dogs of all sizes are allowed. Dogs are allowed for a pet fee of $20.00 per pet per night.

Super 8 Fredericksbug
514 East Main Street
Fredericksburg, TX
830-997-6568 (800-800-8000)
Dogs are welcome at this hotel.

Best Western Inn by the Bay
3902 N Highway 35
Fulton, TX
361-729-8351 (800-780-7234)
Dogs of all sizes are allowed. Dogs are allowed for a nightly pet fee.

Rodeway Inn
2103 North Interstate 35
Gainesville, TX
940-665-7737 (877-424-6423)
Dogs of all sizes are allowed. Dogs are allowed for a pet fee of $8.00 per pet per night.

Super 8
1936 N I-35
Gainesville, TX
940-665-5599 (800-800-8000)
Dogs of all sizes are allowed. Dogs are allowed for a pet fee.

Avenue O
2323 Avenue O
Galveston, TX
409-762-2868 (866-762-2868)
avenueo.com
Besides offering a central location to many of the areas best attractions and the beach, this historic Mediterranean inspired inn offers a landscaped tropical setting - perfect for a romantic getaway. One dog up to 50 pounds is allowed for no additional fee. Dogs must be well mannered, leashed, and cleaned up after promptly.

Candlewood Suites Galveston
808 61st Street
Galveston, TX
409-744-4440 (877-270-6405)
Dogs up to 80 pounds are allowed. Pets allowed with an additional pet fee. Up to $75 for 1-6 nights and up to $150 for 7+ nights. A pet agreement must be signed at check-in.

La Quinta Inn Galveston
1402 Seawall Blvd.

Dog-Friendly Lodging - Please always call ahead to make sure an establishment is still dog-friendly.

Galveston, TX
409-763-1224 (800-531-5900)
Dogs of all sizes are allowed. There are no additional pet fees. Dogs must be leashed and cleaned up after. Dogs must be crated when left unattended in the room or the Do Not Disturb sign placed on the door. Multiple dogs may be allowed.

Motel 6 - Galveston
7404 Avenue
Galveston, TX
409-740-3794 (800-466-8356)
This motel welcomes your pets to stay with you.

Sand 'N Sea Pirates Beach Vacation Rentals
13706 FM 3005
Galveston, TX
800-880-2554
They offer several pet-friendly vacation home rentals. There is a $100 one time fee per pet. 2 dogs may be allowed.

Best Western Lakeview Inn
1635 East I-30 at Bass Pro Drive
Garland, TX
972-303-1601 (800-780-7234)
Dogs of all sizes are allowed. Dogs are allowed for a pet fee of $10.00 per pet per night.

La Quinta Inn Dallas Garland
12721 I-635
Garland, TX
972-271-7581 (800-531-5900)
Dogs of all sizes are allowed. There are no additional pet fees. Dogs must be leashed, cleaned up after, and crated or removed for housekeeping. Multiple dogs may be allowed.

Motel 6 - Dallas Garland
436 I-30
Garland, TX
972-226-7140 (800-466-8356)
This motel welcomes your pets to stay with you.

Best Western George West Executive Inn
208 N Nueces ST
George West, TX
361-449-3300 (800-780-7234)
Dogs are welcome at this hotel.

La Quinta Inn Georgetown
333 North I-35
Georgetown, TX
512-869-2541 (800-531-5900)
Dogs of all sizes are allowed. There are no additional pet fees, but a credit card must be on file. Dogs

must be leashed, cleaned up after, and removed from the room for housekeeping. Multiple dogs may be allowed.

Quality Inn
1005 Leander Rd.
Georgetown, TX
512-863-7504 (877-424-6423)
Dogs of all sizes are allowed. Dogs are allowed for a pet fee of $10.00 per pet per night.

Best Western Dinosaur Valley Inn & Suites
1311 NE Big Bend Trl
Glen Rose, TX
254-897-4818 (800-780-7234)
Dogs up to 50 pounds are allowed. Dogs are allowed for a pet fee.

Country Woods Inn
420 Grand Avenue
Glen Rose, TX
817-279-3002
countrywoodsinn.com/
From the barnyard, to the swimming hole, to the scenic wildlife trails, farm and wildlife, and numerous activities, there is something for everyone at this 40 acre family vacation getaway. Dogs are allowed for an additional one time pet fee of $25 per room. 2 dogs may be allowed.

Holiday Inn Express Hotel & Suites Glen Rose
113 Paluxy Summit Boulevard
Glen Rose, TX
254-898-9900 (877-270-6405)
Dogs up to 50 pounds are allowed. Dogs are allowed for a nightly pet fee.

Paradise On the Brazos
7600 H 16 S
Graham, TX
940-549-9435 (866-549-7682)
This guest ranch offers guests a real feel of the Old West with a bit of elegance and some great home cooking thrown in. In addition to being close to several other sites of interest, there are a number of recreational opportunities at this 1000+ acre ranch. Dogs are allowed throughout the ranch, in the lodge, and in the camp area for no additional pet fee. Dogs must be under their owner's control at all times. Multiple dogs may be allowed.

Wildcatter Ranch & Resort
6062 H 16 S
Graham, TX

940-549-3555 (888 462 9277)
wildcatterranch.com/
In addition to a wide range of activities for experiencing the Lone Star State's past and present; this ranch resort also offers a full treatment spa and steakhouse restaurant on site. Dogs are allowed for an additional fee of $50 per night per pet. Dogs must be leashed, cleaned up after, and crated when left alone in the room. 2 dogs may be allowed.

Best Western Granbury Inn & Suites
1517 Plaza Drive
Granbury, TX
817-573-4239 (800-780-7234)
Dogs of all sizes are allowed. Dogs are allowed for a pet fee.

Days Inn Lake Granbury
1201 N. Plaza Dr.
Granbury, TX
817-573-2611 (800-329-7466)
Dogs of all sizes are allowed. Dogs are allowed for a pet fee of $15.00 per pet per night.

La Quinta Inn Dallas Grand Prairie
1410 N.W. 19th St.
Grand Prairie, TX
972-641-3021 (800-531-5900)
Dogs of all sizes are allowed. There are no additional pet fees. Dogs may not be left unattended for long periods, and they must be leashed and cleaned up after. Multiple dogs may be allowed.

Studio 6 - Grand Prairie, Tx
406 Palace Parkway
Grand Prairie, TX
972-642-9424 (800-466-8356)
Your pets are welcome to stay here with you for a pet fee of $10 per day up to $50 for an entire stay.

Super 8 Grand Prairie
402 East Palace Parkway
Grand Prairie, TX
972-263-4421 (800-800-8000)
Dogs of all sizes are allowed. Dogs are allowed for a pet fee of $30.00 per pet per stay.

Residence Inn DFW Airport North/Grapevine
2020 H 26
Grapevine, TX
972-539-8989 (800-331-3131)
In addition to being located only minutes from the airport, walking distance to the Grapevine Mills Shopping Mall and the Bass Pro Outdoor World, and central to many local sites of interest, this all suite inn

also offers a daily buffet breakfast and weekly evening socials. Dogs are allowed for an additional one time pet fee of $100 per room. Multiple dogs may be allowed.

Super 8 /DFW Airport Northwest Grapevine
250 E State Highway 114
Grapevine, TX
817-329-7222 (800-800-8000)
Dogs are welcome at this hotel.

Days Inn Greenville
5000 Interstate Highway 30
Greenville, TX
903-455-9600 (800-329-7466)
Dogs of all sizes are allowed. Dogs are allowed for a pet fee of $10.00 per pet per stay.

Econo Lodge Inn & Suites
1209 East I-30
Greenville, TX
903-455-7700 (877-424-6423)
Dogs of all sizes are allowed. Dogs are allowed for a pet fee of $25.00 per pet per night.

Holiday Inn Express Hotel & Suites Greenville
2901 Mustang Crossing Annex
Greenville, TX
903-454-8680 (877-270-6405)
Dogs up to 50 pounds are allowed

La Quinta Inn & Suites Greenville
3001 Mustang Crossing
Greenville, TX
903-454-3700 (800-531-5900)
Dogs of all sizes are allowed. There are no additional pet fees. There is a pet waiver to sign at check in. Dogs must be leashed, cleaned up after, and crated or removed for housekeeping. Multiple dogs may be allowed.

Motel 6 - Greenville, Tx
5109 I-30
Greenville, TX
903-455-0515 (800-466-8356)
This motel welcomes your pets to stay with you.

Super 8 Greenville
5010 Highway 69 South
Greenville, TX
903-454-3736 (800-800-8000)
Dogs are welcome at this hotel.

Days Inn and Suites Texas Hankamer
25941 I-10 Hwy 61
Hankamer, TX
409-374-2424 (800-329-7466)
Dogs are welcome at this hotel.

La Quinta Inn Harlingen
1002 S. Expwy. 83
Harlingen, TX
956-428-6888 (800-531-5900)
Dogs of all sizes are allowed; just inform them at check in that you have a pet. There are no additional pet fees. Dogs must be leashed, cleaned up after, and crated for housekeeping. Multiple dogs may be allowed.

Motel 6 - Harlingen
205 Expy 77
Harlingen, TX
956-423-9292 (800-466-8356)
This motel welcomes your pets to stay with you.

Super 8 /San Benito Area Harlingen
1115 S Expressway 83
Harlingen, TX
956-412-8873 (800-800-8000)
Dogs are welcome at this hotel.

Best Western Hebbronville Inn
37 E TX Highway 359
Hebbronville, TX
361-527-3600 (800-780-7234)
Dogs are welcome at this hotel.

Holiday Inn Express Hereford
1400 West First St
Hereford, TX
806-364-3322 (877-270-6405)
Dogs of all sizes are allowed. Dogs are allowed for a pet fee of $20.00 per pet per night.

Best Western Hillsboro Inn
307 I 35 W Service Road
Hillsboro, TX
254-582-8465 (800-780-7234)
Dogs of all sizes are allowed. Dogs are allowed for a pet fee of $12 per pet per stay.

Days Inn TX Hillsboro
307 South East I-35
Hillsboro, TX
254-582-3493 (800-329-7466)
Dogs of all sizes are allowed. Dogs are allowed for a pet fee of $8.00 per pet per night.

Motel 6 - Hillsboro
1506 Hillview Dr
Hillsboro, TX
254-580-9000 (800-466-8356)
This motel welcomes your pets to stay with you.

Super 8
1512 Hillview Drive
Hillsboro, TX
254-580-0404 (800-800-8000)

Dogs of all sizes are allowed. Dogs are allowed for a pet fee of $20.00 per pet per night.

Best Western Hondo Inn
301 US Highway 90 E
Hondo, TX
830-426-4466 (800-780-7234)
Dogs of all sizes are allowed. Dogs are allowed for a pet fee.

Marriott Horseshoe Bay Resort
200 Hi Circle N
Horseshoe Bay, TX
830-598-8600 (866-799-5384)
This luxury, waterfront hotel provides a great location to a number of sites of interest for both business and leisure travelers; plus they also offer numerous on-site amenities to ensure a comfortable stay. Dogs are allowed for an additional one time fee of $75 per room. Multiple dogs may be allowed.

Baymont Inn Houston Hobby Airport
9902 Gulf Frwy.
Houston, TX
713-941-0900 (800-531-5900)
Dogs of all sizes are allowed. There are no additional pet fees. Dogs must be leashed and cleaned up after. The Do Not Disturb sign needs to be left on the door if there is a pet alone in the room. Multiple dogs may be allowed.

Candlewood Suites Houston By The Galleria
4900 Loop Central Drive
Houston, TX
713-839-9411 (877-270-6405)
Dogs up to 80 pounds are allowed. Pets allowed with an additional pet fee. Up to $75 for 1-6 nights and up to $150 for 7+ nights. A pet agreement must be signed at check-in.

Candlewood Suites Houston Medical Center
10025 Main Street
Houston, TX
713-665-3300 (877-270-6405)
Dogs up to 80 pounds are allowed. Pets allowed with an additional pet fee. Up to $75 for 1-6 nights and up to $150 for 7+ nights. A pet agreement must be signed at check-in.

Candlewood Suites Houston NW
1500 North Sam Houston Parkway
Houston, TX
281-987-3900 (877-270-6405)
Dogs up to 80 pounds are allowed. Pets allowed with an additional pet

fee. Up to $75 for 1-6 nights and up to $150 for 7+ nights. A pet agreement must be signed at check-in.

Candlewood Suites Houston West
11280 Westheimer Road
Houston, TX
713-244-0400 (877-270-6405)
Dogs up to 80 pounds are allowed. Pets allowed with an additional pet fee. Up to $75 for 1-6 nights and up to $150 for 7+ nights. A pet agreement must be signed at check-in.

Candlewood Suites Houston-Clear Lake
2737 Bay Area Blvd
Houston, TX
281-461-3060 (877-270-6405)
Dogs up to 80 pounds are allowed. Pets allowed with an additional pet fee. Up to $75 for 1-6 nights and up to $150 for 7+ nights. A pet agreement must be signed at check-in.

Candlewood Suites Houston-Town And Country
10503 Town & Country Way
Houston, TX
713-464-2677 (877-270-6405)
Dogs up to 80 pounds are allowed. Pets allowed with an additional pet fee. Up to $75 for 1-6 nights and up to $150 for 7+ nights. A pet agreement must be signed at check-in.

Candlewood Suites Houston-Westchase
4033 West Sam Houston Parkway
Houston, TX
713-780-7881 (877-270-6405)
Dogs up to 80 pounds are allowed. Pets allowed with an additional pet fee. Up to $75 for 1-6 nights and up to $150 for 7+ nights. A pet agreement must be signed at check-in.

Comfort Inn
11230 Southwest Freeway
Houston, TX
281-498-9000 (877-424-6423)
Dogs of all sizes are allowed. Dogs are allowed for a pet fee of $50.00 per pet per night.

Comfort Suites - Near the Galleria
6221 Richmond Ave.
Houston, TX
713-787-0004 (877-424-6423)
Dogs of all sizes are allowed. Dogs are allowed for a pet fee of $50.00 per pet per stay.

Crowne Plaza Suites Houston Sugar Land
9090 Southwest Frwy
Houston, TX
713-995-0123 (877-270-6405)
Dogs are welcome at this hotel.

Days Inn West Houston
9535 Katy Freeway
Houston, TX
713-467-4411 (800-329-7466)
Dogs are welcome at this hotel.

Days Inn and Suites - Sugarland//Stafford Houston
4630 Techniplex Dr
Houston, TX
281-240-8100 (800-329-7466)
Dogs of all sizes are allowed. Dogs are allowed for a pet fee of $15.00 per pet per night.

Doubletree Guest Suites
5353 Westheimer Road
Houston, TX
713-961-9000 (800-222-TREE (8733))
Located in the heart of the city's flourishing uptown/galleria area, this upscale hotel offers a number of on site amenities for business or leisure travelers, plus a convenient location to business, shopping, dining, and entertainment areas. Dogs are allowed for an additional one time pet fee of $75 per room. Multiple dogs may be allowed.

Doubletree Hotel
400 Dallas Street
Houston, TX
713-759-0202 (800-222-TREE (8733))
Located in the heart of the city's business and financial district, this full service, luxury hotel has skywalks to the Allen Center and the Heritage Plaza, plus it is also connected to the inner-city's tunnel system. And, in addition to a number of on site amenities, they also provide a convenient location to many of the area's premier attractions and activities. Dogs up to 50 pounds are allowed for a $100 pet deposit per room; $25 is not refundable. 2 dogs may be allowed.

Extended Stay America Houston - Galleria
4701 Westheimer Rd.
Houston, TX
713-355-8500 (800-804-3724)
One dog is allowed per suite. There is a $25 per night additional pet fee up to $150 for an entire stay.

Extended Stay America Houston - Greenway Plaza
2330 Southwest Fwy.
Houston, TX
713-521-0060 (800-804-3724)
One dog is allowed per suite. There is a $25 per night additional pet fee up to $150 for an entire stay.

Extended Stay America Houston - Johnson Space Center
1410 Nasa Rd. 1
Houston, TX
281-333-9494 (800-804-3724)
One dog is allowed per suite. There is a $25 per night additional pet fee up to $150 for an entire stay.

Extended Stay America Houston - Katy Freeway
11175 Katy Fwy.
Houston, TX
713-461-6696 (800-804-3724)
One dog is allowed per suite. There is a $25 per night additional pet fee up to $150 for an entire stay.

Extended Stay America Houston - Westchase
3200 W. Sam Houston Pkwy. S.
Houston, TX
713-952-4644 (800-804-3724)
One dog is allowed per suite. There is a $25 per night additional pet fee up to $150 for an entire stay.

Extended Stay America Houston - Willowbrook
16939 Tomball Pkwy.
Houston, TX
281-970-2403 (800-804-3724)
One dog is allowed per suite. There is a $25 per night additional pet fee up to $150 for an entire stay.

Hilton Hotel
3000 NASA Road One
Houston, TX
281-333-9300 (800-HILTONS (445-8667))
This upscale, resort hotel sits overlooking the lake plus they offer a number of on site amenities for all level of guests, and a convenient location to numerous sites of interest and recreational activities. Dogs up to 75 pounds are allowed for an additional one time pet fee of $75 per room. 2 dogs may be allowed.

Hilton Hotel
6780 Southwest Freeway/H 59
Houston, TX
713-977-7911 (800-HILTONS (445-8667))
This upscale, resort hotel offers a

number of on site amenities for business and leisure travelers, plus a convenient location to business, shopping, dining, and entertainment districts. Dogs up to 50 pounds are allowed for an additional one time pet fee of $50 per room. 2 dogs may be allowed.

Holiday Inn Express Hotel & Suites Houston - Memorial Park Area
7625 Katy Freeway
Houston, TX
713-688-2800 (877-270-6405)
Dogs of all sizes are allowed. Dogs are allowed for a pet fee of $25.00 per pet per stay.

Holiday Inn Express Hotel & Suites Houston West-InterContinental
1330 N. Sam Houston Pkwy E
Houston, TX
281-372-1000 (877-270-6405)
Dogs of all sizes are allowed. Dogs are allowed for a pet fee of $50.00 per pet per stay.

Holiday Inn Houston-Astrodome @ Reliant Pk
8111 Kirby Dr.
Houston, TX
713-790-1900 (877-270-6405)
Dogs of all sizes are allowed. Dogs are allowed for a pet fee.

Holiday Inn Houston-InterContinental Arpt
15222 John F. Kennedy Blvd.
Houston, TX
281-449-2311 (877-270-6405)
Dogs of all sizes are allowed. Dogs are allowed for a pet fee of $125.00 per pet per stay.

Holiday Inn Houston-Sw-Hwy 59s@Beltwy 8
11160 Southwest Freeway
Houston, TX
281-530-1400 (877-270-6405)
Dogs of all sizes are allowed. Dogs are allowed for a pet fee of $100.00 per pet per stay.

Homestead Studio Suites Houston - Gallerla
2300 W. Loop S.
Houston, TX
713-960-9660 (800-804-3724)
One dog is allowed per suite. There is a $25 per night additional pet fee up to $150 for an entire stay.

Homestead Studio Suites Houston - Medical Center - Reliant Park
7979 Fannin St.
Houston, TX
713-797-0000 (800-804-3724)

One dog is allowed per suite. There is a $25 per night additional pet fee up to $150 for an entire stay.

Homestead Studio Suites Houston - Willowbrook
13223 Champions Centre Dr.
Houston, TX
281-397-9922 (800-804-3724)
One dog is allowed per suite. There is a $25 per night additional pet fee up to $150 for an entire stay.

Hotel Derek
2525 W Loop S
Houston, TX
713-961-3000
Dogs up to 40 pounds are allowed for an additional $50 one time fee per pet. Canine guest also receive treats upon arrival.

Hotel Indigo Houston At The Galleria
5160 Hidalgo Street
Houston, TX
713-621-8988 (877-865-6578)
Dogs are welcome at this hotel. There is a $75 one time pet fee.

Hotel ZaZa
5701 Main Street
Houston, TX
713-526-1991 (888-880-1991)
hotelzaza.com/houston/
In addition to providing luxury accommodations, fine dining, and a number of other on-site amenities, this resort hotel also provides a central location to many local areas of interest. Quiet, well mannered dogs are allowed for an additional one time fee of $75 per pet with a credit card on file. Extra large dogs are discouraged. There is pet policy to sign at check in; dogs must be crated, leashed, or removed for housekeeping, and the Pet in Room sign must be on the door when a dog is alone in the room. 2 dogs may be allowed.

Knights Inn North/IAH Houston
12500 North Freeway
Houston, TX
281-876-3888 (800-843-5644)
Dogs are welcome at this hotel. There is a $15 one time pet fee.

La Quinta Inn & Suites Houston Bush Intl Airport
15510 JFK Blvd.
Houston, TX
281-219-2000 (800-531-5900)
One dog of any size is allowed. There are no additional pet fees. Dogs must be leashed and cleaned

up after. Dogs are not allowed to go through the lobby.

La Quinta Inn & Suites Houston Park 10
15225 Katy Freeway
Houston, TX
281-646-9200 (800-531-5900)
Dogs of all sizes are allowed. There are no additional pet fees. Dogs must be leashed, cleaned up after, and crated or removed for housekeeping. Multiple dogs may be allowed.

La Quinta Inn & Suites Willowbrook
18828 HWY 249
Houston, TX
281-897-8868 (800-531-5900)
Dogs of all sizes are allowed. There is a $25 one time fee per pet. Dogs must be leashed, cleaned up after, and crated when left alone in the room. Multiple dogs may be allowed.

La Quinta Inn Houston Brookhollow
11002 Northwest Freeway
Houston, TX
713-688-2581 (800-531-5900)
Dogs of all sizes are allowed. There are no additional pet fees. Dogs must be leashed, cleaned up after, and attended to or removed for housekeeping. Dogs are not allowed in the lobby. Multiple dogs may be allowed.

La Quinta Inn Houston Cy Fair
13290 FM 1960 West
Houston, TX
281-469-4018 (800-531-5900)
Dogs of all sizes are allowed. There are no additional pet fees. Dogs must be leashed and cleaned up after. Dogs must be crated or removed for housekeeping, or place the Do Not Disturb sign on the door. Multiple dogs may be allowed.

La Quinta Inn Houston East
11999 East Freeway
Houston, TX
713-453-5425 (800-531-5900)
Dogs of all sizes are allowed. There are no additional pet fees. Dogs must be quiet, well behaved, leashed and cleaned up after. Multiple dogs may be allowed.

La Quinta Inn Houston Greenway Plaza
4015 Southwest Freeway
Houston, TX
713-623-4750 (800-531-5900)
Dogs of all sizes are allowed. There are no additional pet fees. Dogs must be leashed, cleaned up after,

and attended to for housekeeping. Multiple dogs may be allowed.

La Quinta Inn Houston I-45 North
17111 North Frwy.
Houston, TX
281-444-7500 (800-531-5900)
Dogs of all sizes are allowed. There are no additional pet fees. Dogs must be leashed and cleaned up after. Multiple dogs may be allowed.

La Quinta Inn Houston Northwest
11130 N.W. Freeway
Houston, TX
713-680-8282 (800-531-5900)
Two large dogs or 3 small dogs are allowed. There are no additional pet fees. Dogs may not be left unattended, and they must be leashed and cleaned up after.

La Quinta Inn Houston Reliant/Medical Center
9911 Buffalo Speedway
Houston, TX
713-668-8082 (800-531-5900)
Dogs of all sizes are allowed. There are no additional pet fees. Dogs must be leashed and cleaned up after. The Do Not Disturb sign needs to be left on the door if there is a pet alone in the room. Multiple dogs may be allowed.

La Quinta Inn Houston Southwest
6790 Southwest Freeway
Houston, TX
713-784-3838 (800-531-5900)
Dogs of all sizes are allowed. There are no additional pet fees. Dogs must be leashed and cleaned up after. Dogs must be crated or removed for housekeeping, or place the Do Not Disturb sign on the door. Multiple dogs may be allowed.

Lovett Inn
501 Lovett Blvd
Houston, TX
713-522-5224 (800-779-5224)
lovettinn.com/main.php
Sitting on a tree lined street near the Montrose Museum District, this beautiful colonial styled 1923 home offers a convenient location to a number of local eateries, shops, attractions, and recreation. Dogs are allowed for an additional one time pet fee of $25 per room. 2 dogs may be allowed.

Marriott Houston Hobby Airport
9100 Gulf Freeway
Houston, TX
713-943-7979 (800-228-9290)

This luxury hotel provides a great location to a number of sites of interest for both business and leisure travelers; plus they also offer numerous on-site amenities to ensure a comfortable stay. Dogs are allowed for an additional one time fee of $25 per room. Multiple dogs may be allowed.

Marriott Houston Medical Center
6580 Fannin Street
Houston, TX
713-796-0080 (800-228-9290)
Located in the heart of the Texas Medical Center, this luxury hotel provides a great location to a number of sites of interest for both business and leisure travelers; plus they also offer numerous on-site amenities to ensure a comfortable stay. Dogs are allowed for an additional one time fee of $75 per room. Multiple dogs may be allowed.

Motel 6 - Houston Hobby,tx
9005 Airport Blvd
Houston, TX
713-943-3300 (800-466-8356)
This motel welcomes your pets to stay with you.

Motel 6 - Houston Jersey Village
16884 Northwest Freeway
Houston, TX
713-937-7056 (800-466-8356)
This motel welcomes your pets to stay with you.

Motel 6 - Houston Westchase
2900 Sam Houston Pkw
Houston, TX
713-334-9188 (800-466-8356)
This motel welcomes your pets to stay with you.

Motel 6 - Houston Northwest
5555 34th St
Houston, TX
713-682-8588 (800-466-8356)
This motel welcomes your pets to stay with you.

Motel 6 - Houston Reliant Park
3223 South Loop
Houston, TX
713-664-6425 (800-466-8356)
This motel welcomes your pets to stay with you.

Motel 6 - Houston West Katy
14833 Katy Freeway
Houston, TX
281-497-5000 (800-466-8356)
This motel welcomes your pets to stay with you.

Quality Inn & Suites
9041 Westheimer Rd.
Houston, TX
713-783-1400 (877-424-6423)
Dogs of all sizes are allowed. Dogs are allowed for a pet fee of $25.00 per pet per night.

Quality Inn & Suites Reliant Park/Medical Center
2364 South Loop West
Houston, TX
713-799-2436 (877-424-6423)
Dogs up to 60 pounds are allowed. Dogs are allowed for a pet fee of $20.00 per pet per night. Two dogs are allowed per room.

Red Roof Inn Houston - Brookhollow
12929 Northwest Freeway
Houston, TX
713-939-0800 (800-RED-ROOF)
One well-behaved family pet per room. Guest must notify front desk upon arrival. Guest is liable for any damages. In consideration of all guests, pets must never be left unattended in the guest rooms.

Red Roof Inn Houston - Hobby Airport
9005 Airport Boulevard
Houston, TX
713-943-3300 (800-RED-ROOF)
One well-behaved family pet per room. Guest must notify front desk upon arrival. Guest is liable for any damages. In consideration of all guests, pets must never be left unattended in the guest rooms.

Red Roof Inn Houston - I-10 West
15701 Park Ten Place
Houston, TX
281-579-7200 (800-RED-ROOF)
One well-behaved family pet per room. Guest must notify front desk upon arrival. Guest is liable for any damages. In consideration of all guests, pets must never be left unattended in the guest rooms.

Red Roof Inn Houston - Westchase
2960 West Sam Houston Parkway South
Houston, TX
713-785-9909 (800-RED-ROOF)
One well-behaved family pet per room. Guest must notify front desk upon arrival. Guest is liable for any damages. In consideration of all guests, pets must never be left unattended in the guest rooms.

Residence Inn Houston Clear Lake
525 Bay Area Blvd

Houston, TX
281-486-2424 (800-331-3131)
This all suite hotel sits central to many of the city's star attractions - including NASA, and to a number of dining, shopping, and business areas, plus they offer a number of in-house amenities that include a daily buffet breakfast and evening social hours. Dogs are allowed for an additional one time pet fee of $100 per room. 2 dogs may be allowed.

Residence Inn Houston Intercontinental Airport at Greenspoint
655 N Sam Houston Parkway E
Houston, TX
281-820-4563 (800-331-3131)
Some of the amenities at this all-suite inn include a daily hot breakfast, complimentary evening socials Monday to Wednesday, an indoor pool, and a complimentary grocery shopping service. Dogs up to 60 pounds are allowed for an additional one time pet fee of $100 per room. 2 dogs may be allowed.

Residence Inn Houston Medical Center/Reliant Park
7710 S Main Street
Houston, TX
713-660-7993 (800-331-3131)
Some of the amenities at this all-suite inn include a daily hot breakfast, complimentary evening socials Monday through Thursday, a swimming pool, a Sport Court and a complimentary grocery shopping service. Dogs are allowed for an additional one time pet fee of $100 per room, and there may only be up to one medium to large dog or 2 small dogs per room.

Residence Inn Houston Northwest/Willowbrook
7311 W Greens Road
Houston, TX
832-237-2002 (800-331-3131)
Some of the amenities at this all-suite inn include a daily buffet breakfast, evening socials Monday through Wednesday, weekly barbecues, an indoor pool, and a complimentary grocery shopping service. Dogs are allowed for an additional one time pet fee of $100 per room. Multiple dogs may be allowed.

Residence Inn Houston West/Energy Corridor
1150 Eldridge Parkway
Houston, TX
281-293-8787 (800-331-3131)
In addition to being close to many

local Fortune 550 companies, this all suite inn also offers a number of in-house amenities, including a daily buffet breakfast and evening socials Monday through Thursday with light dinner fare and entertainment. Dogs are allowed for an additional one time pet fee of $100 per room. Multiple dogs may be allowed.

Residence Inn Houston Westchase on Westheimer
9965 Westheimer at Elmside
Houston, TX
713-974-5454 (800-331-3131)
Located in the exclusive Westchase neighborhood near a variety of eateries, shops, and various entertainments, this all suite inn also offers a daily buffet breakfast and evening social hours with refreshments. Quiet dogs are allowed for an additional one time pet fee of $100 per room. 2 dogs may be allowed.

Residence Inn Houston by The Galleria
2500 McCue Road
Houston, TX
713-840-9757 (800-331-3131)
Set in a serene residential setting, but still close to shopping, dining, attraction, and commerce areas, this all suite inn offers a number of in-house amenities that includes a daily buffet breakfast and evening socials Monday through Thursday with light dinner fare. Dogs up to 50 pounds are allowed for an additional one time pet fee of $100 per room. 2 dogs may be allowed.

Residence Inn Houston-West University
2939 Westpark Drive
Houston, TX
713-661-4660 (800-331-3131)
Besides offering a convenient location to the Texas Medical Center and to business, shopping, dining, and entertainment areas, this hotel also provides a number of in-house amenities, including a daily buffet breakfast and evening socials Monday through Thursday. Dogs are allowed for an additional one time pet fee of $100 per room. Multiple dogs may be allowed.

Robin's Nest
4104 Greeley Street
Houston, TX
713-528-5821 (800-622-8343)
therobin.com/
Located near the city's Museum District with numerous activities,

eateries, and educational institutions nearby, this guest house offers eight rooms, lush gardens and dinner mysteries. Well behaved dogs are allowed for an additional one time fee of $30 per pet. Dogs are not allowed on the furniture or bed, and they must be crated when left alone in the room. Dogs must be well groomed, have current vaccinations, and be sociable with other pets and people. 2 dogs may be allowed.

Sheraton Houston Brookhollow Hotel
3000 Northloop West Freeway
Houston, TX
713-688-0100 (888-625-5144)
Dogs up to 50 pounds are allowed for no additional pet fee. Dogs may not be left alone in the room.

Sheraton Suites Houston Near The Galleria
2400 West Loop South
Houston, TX
713-586-2444 (888-625-5144)
Dogs up to 80 pounds are allowed for no additional pet fee. Dogs may not be left alone in the room.

Staybridge Suites Houston Galleria Area
5190 Hidalgo
Houston, TX
713-355-8888 (877-270-6405)
Dogs up to 80 pounds are allowed. Pets allowed with an additional pet fee. Up to $75 for 1-6 nights and up to $150 for 7+ nights. A pet agreement must be signed at check-in.

Staybridge Suites Houston West/Energy Corridor
1225 Eldridge Parkway
Houston, TX
281-759-7829 (877-270-6405)
Dogs up to 80 pounds are allowed. Pets allowed with an additional pet fee. Up to $75 for 1-6 nights and up to $150 for 7+ nights. A pet agreement must be signed at check-in.

Staybridge Suites Houston Willowbrook
10750 N. Gessner Road
Houston, TX
281-807-3700 (877-270-6405)
Dogs up to 80 pounds are allowed. Pets allowed with an additional pet fee. Up to $75 for 1-6 nights and up to $150 for 7+ nights. A pet agreement must be signed at check-in.

Studio 6 - Houston Hobby

12700 Featherwood Dr
Houston, TX
281-929-5400 (800-466-8356)
Your pets are welcome to stay here with you for a pet fee of $10 per day up to $50 for an entire stay.

Studio 6 - Houston Spring
220 Bammel Westfield Rd
Houston, TX
281-580-2221 (800-466-8356)
Your pets are welcome to stay here with you for a pet fee of $10 per day up to $50 for an entire stay.

Studio 6 - Houston Westchase
3030 Sam Houston Pkw
Houston, TX
713-785-8550 (800-466-8356)
Your pets are welcome to stay here with you for a pet fee of $10 per day up to $50 for an entire stay.

Studio 6 - Houston Northwest
14255 Northwest Fwy
Houston, TX
713-895-2900 (800-466-8356)
Your pets are welcome to stay here with you for a pet fee of $10 per day up to $50 for an entire stay.

Studio 6 - Houston West
1255 Hwy
Houston, TX
281-579-6959 (800-466-8356)
Your pets are welcome to stay here with you for a pet fee of $10 per day up to $50 for an entire stay.

TownePlace Suites Houston
Central/Northwest Freeway
12820 Northwest Freeway
Houston, TX
713-690-4035 (800-257-3000)
This all suite inn sits central to business, shopping, dining, and day/night entertainment areas, plus they offer a number of in-house amenities for business and leisure travelers. Dogs are allowed for an additional one time fee of $75 per room. 2 dogs may be allowed.

TownePlace Suites Houston Clear Lake
1050 Bay Area Blvd
Houston, TX
281-286-2132 (800-257-3000)
This all suite inn sits close to the Johnson Space Center and to a number of other sites of interest to both business and leisure travelers; plus they offer a number of in-house amenities. Dogs are allowed for an additional one time fee of $100 per room. 2 dogs may be allowed.

TownePlace Suites Houston Northwest
11040 Louetta Road
Houston, TX
281-374-6767 (800-257-3000)
Besides offering a number of in-house amenities for all level of travelers, this all suite inn also offers a convenient location to business, shopping, dining, and entertainment areas. Dogs are allowed for an additional one time fee of $100 per room. Multiple dogs may be allowed.

TownePlace Suites Houston West
15155 Katy Freeway
Houston, TX
281-646-0058 (800-257-3000)
In addition to offering a number of in-house amenities for all level of travelers - including a hot buffet breakfast, this all suite inn also provides a convenient location to major corporations, shopping, dining, and entertainment areas. Dogs are allowed for an additional one time fee of $75 per room. 2 dogs may be allowed.

Travelodge Houston
6 N Sam Houston Parkway
Houston, TX
281-447-6888 (800-578-7878)
Dogs are welcome at this hotel.

Travelodge Near The Galleria Houston
7611 Katy Freeway
Houston, TX
713-688-2222 (800-578-7878)
Dogs are welcome at this hotel.

Motel 6 - Humble, Tx
20145 Eastway Village Dr
Humble, TX
281-446-4300 (800-466-8356)
This motel welcomes your pets to stay with you.

Motel 6 - Huntsville, Tx
122 I-45
Huntsville, TX
936-291-6927 (800-466-8356)
This motel welcomes your pets to stay with you.

Holiday Inn Express Hotel & Suites Hutto
323 Ed Schmidt Blvd
Hutto, TX
512-846-1168 (877-270-6405)
Dogs of all sizes are allowed. Dogs are allowed for a pet fee of $75.00 per pet per stay.

Best Western Naval Station Inn

2025 State Highway 361
Ingleside, TX
361-776-2767 (800-780-7234)
Dogs of all sizes are allowed. Dogs are allowed for a pet fee of $10.00 per pet per night.

Studio 6 - Ingleside
2920 Rockland Blvd
Ingleside, TX
361-775-1400 (800-466-8356)
Your pets are welcome to stay here with you for a pet fee of $10 per day up to $50 for an entire stay.

Candlewood Suites Dallas-Las Colinas
5300 Green Park Drive
Irving, TX
972-714-9990 (877-270-6405)
Dogs up to 80 pounds are allowed. Pets allowed with an additional pet fee. Up to $75 for 1-6 nights and up to $150 for 7+ nights. A pet agreement must be signed at check-in.

Dallas - Ft. Worth Airport Drury Inn & Suites
4210 W. Airport Freeway
Irving, TX
972-986-1200 (800-378-7946)
Dogs of all sizes are allowed for no additional pet fee with a credit card on file, and there is a pet agreement to sign at check in.

Days Inn Dallas/Ft. Worth Airport North Irving
4325 West John Carpenter Fwy
Irving, TX
972-621-8277 (800-329-7466)
Dogs are welcome at this hotel.

Homestead Studio Suites Dallas - DFW Airport N.
7825 Heathrow Dr.
Irving, TX
972-929-3333 (800-804-3724)
One dog is allowed per suite. There is a $25 per night additional pet fee up to $150 for an entire stay.

Homestead Studio Suites Dallas - Las Colinas
5315 Carnaby St.
Irving, TX
972-756-0458 (800-804-3724)
One dog is allowed per suite. There is a $25 per night additional pet fee up to $150 for an entire stay.

La Quinta Inn & Suites D/FW Airport South
4105 West Airport Freeway
Irving, TX
972-252-6546 (800-531-5900)

Dogs of all sizes are allowed. There are no additional pet fees. Dogs must be leashed, cleaned up after, and crated or removed for housekeeping. Multiple dogs may be allowed.

La Quinta Inn & Suites Dallas D/FW Airport North
4850 West John Carpenter Frwy
Irving, TX
972-915-4022 (800-531-5900)
Dogs of all sizes are allowed. There are no additional pet fees. Dogs must be quiet, leashed, and cleaned up after. Multiple dogs may be allowed.

MainStay Suites Irv / Mall
2323 Imperial Drive
Irving, TX
972-257-5400 (877-424-6423)
Dogs of all sizes are allowed.

Motel 6 - Dallas Dfw Airport North
7800 Heathrow Dr
Irving, TX
972-915-3993 (800-466-8356)
This motel welcomes your pets to stay with you.

Motel 6 - Dallas Dfw Airport South
2611 Airport Frwy
Irving, TX
972-570-7500 (800-466-8356)
This motel welcomes your pets to stay with you.

Motel 6 - Dallas Irving
510 South Loop 12
Irving, TX
972-438-4227 (800-466-8356)
This motel welcomes your pets to stay with you.

Quality Inn & Suites DFW North
4100 W John Carpenter Fwy
Irving, TX
972-929-4008 (877-424-6423)
Dogs of all sizes are allowed. Dogs are allowed for a pet fee of $1.00 per pet per night.

Ramada - DFW Airport North Irving
8205 Esters Blvd
Irving, TX
972-929-0066 (800-272-6232)
Dogs are welcome at this hotel.

Ramada DFW Airport South
4440 W Airport Freeway
Irving, TX
972-399-1010 (800-272-6232)
Dogs of all sizes are allowed. Dogs are allowed for a nightly pet fee.

Red Roof Inn Dallas - DFW Airport

North
8150 Esters Boulevard
Irving, TX
972-929-0020 (800-RED-ROOF)
One well-behaved family pet per room. Guest must notify front desk upon arrival. Guest is liable for any damages. In consideration of all guests, pets must never be left unattended in the guest rooms.

Residence Inn Dallas DFW Airport North/Irving
8600 Esters Blvd
Irving, TX
972-871-1331 (800-331-3131)
Some of the amenities at this all-suite inn include a daily buffet breakfast, evening social hours with light dinner fare, a deli and grocery, an outdoor pool, and a barbecue area. Dogs are allowed for an additional one time pet fee of $75 per room for the 1 bedroom suites and a fee of $100 for 2 bedroom suites. Aggressive known breeds are not allowed. Multiple dogs may be allowed.

Residence Inn Dallas Las Colinas
950 Walnut Hill Lane
Irving, TX
972-580-7773 (800-331-3131)
Besides offering a convenient location to the airport, business, shopping, dining, and entertainment areas, this hotel also provides a number of in-house amenities, including a daily buffet breakfast and complementary evening receptions with refreshments. Dogs are allowed for an additional one time pet fee of $100 per room. Multiple dogs may be allowed.

Sleep Inn DFW North
4770 Plaza Drive
Irving, TX
972-929-8888 (877-424-6423)
Dogs of all sizes are allowed. Dogs are allowed for a pet fee of $20.00 per pet per night.

Staybridge Suites Dallas-Las Colinas Area
1201 Executive Circle
Irving, TX
019-724-6594 (877-270-6405)
Dogs up to 80 pounds are allowed. Pets allowed with an additional pet fee. Up to $75 for 1-6 nights and up to $150 for 7+ nights. A pet agreement must be signed at check-in.

Staybridge Suites Dfw Airport North
2220 Market Place Blvd.
Irving, TX

972-401-4700 (877-270-6405)
Dogs up to 80 pounds are allowed. Pets allowed with an additional pet fee. Up to $75 for 1-6 nights and up to $150 for 7+ nights. A pet agreement must be signed at check-in.

TownePlace Suites Dallas Las Colinas
900 W Walnut Hill Lane
Irving, TX
972-550-7796 (800-257-3000)
This all suite inn gives a convenient location to major businesses, shopping, dining, and entertainment areas, plus they also offer a number of in-house amenities - including a daily buffet breakfast and a grocery shopping service. Dogs are allowed for an additional one time fee of $75 per room. Multiple dogs may be allowed.

Ramada - Jasper
239 E Gibson
Jasper, TX
409-384-9021 (800-272-6232)
Dogs are welcome at this hotel.

The Exotic Resort Zoo
235 Zoo Trail
Johnson City, TX
830-868-4357
zooexotics.com/
This truly unique family vacation destination allows guest to experience the natural surroundings of wild animals; a tram (dogs allowed) takes guests through the 137 acres of woods and waterways that is home to more than 500 animals and about 80 species. Very well behaved dogs are allowed for an additional fee of $10 per night per pet. Dogs must be comfortable/friendly toward other animals, and they are not allowed at the petting zoo. Dogs are to be leashed and picked up after at all times. 2 dogs may be allowed.

Days Inn Junction
111 Martinez Street
Junction, TX
325-446-3730 (800-329-7466)
Dogs are welcome at this hotel.

Motel 6 - Junction, Tx
200 Interstate 10 West
Junction, TX
325-446-3572 (800-466-8356)
This motel welcomes your pets to stay with you.

Candlewood Suites Houston Park Row

19998 Park Row Drive
Katy, TX
281-578-9993 (877-270-6405)
Dogs up to 80 pounds are allowed.
Pets allowed with an additional pet
fee. Up to $75 for 1-6 nights and up
to $150 for 7+ nights. A pet
agreement must be signed at check-
in.

Holiday Inn Express Houston-I-10 W
(Katy Area)
22105 Katy Freeway
Katy, TX
281-395-4800 (877-270-6405)
Dogs of all sizes are allowed. Dogs
are allowed for a pet fee of $50.00
per pet per night.

Days Inn Kenedy
453 N Sunset Strip
Kenedy, TX
830-583-2521 (800-329-7466)
Dogs are welcome at this hotel.

Best Western Sunday House Inn
2124 Sidney Baker Street
Kerrville, TX
830-896-1313 (800-780-7234)
Dogs of all sizes are allowed. Dogs
are allowed for a pet fee of $10.00
per pet per stay.

Days Inn Kerrville
2000 Sidney Baker St
Kerrville, TX
830-896-1000 (800-329-7466)
Dogs of all sizes are allowed. Dogs
are allowed for a pet fee of $10 per
pet per night.

La Quinta Inn & Suites Kerrville
1940 Sidney Baker Street
Kerrville, TX
830-896-9200 (800-531-5900)
Dogs of all sizes are allowed. There
are no additional pet fees. Dogs may
not be left unattended, and they must
be leashed and cleaned up after. 2
dogs may be allowed.

Motel 6 - Kerrville
1810 Sidney Baker St
Kerrville, TX
830-257-1500 (800-466-8356)
This motel welcomes your pets to
stay with you.

Best Western Inn of Kilgore
1411 US Highway 259 N
Kilgore, TX
903-986-1195 (800-780-7234)
Dogs of all sizes are allowed. Dogs
are allowed for a pet fee of $20 per
pet per stay.

Days Inn Kilgore

3505 Hwy 259 North
Kilgore, TX
903-983-2975 (800-329-7466)
Dogs of all sizes are allowed. Dogs
are allowed for a pet fee.

Ramada /Longview Kilgore
3501 Hwy 259 North
Kilgore, TX
903-983-3456 (800-272-6232)
Dogs of all sizes are allowed. Dogs
are allowed for a pet fee of $10.00
per pet per night.

Candlewood Suites Killeen
2300 Florence Rd.
Killeen, TX
254-501-3990 (877-270-6405)
Dogs up to 80 pounds are allowed.
Pets allowed with an additional pet
fee. Up to $75 for 1-6 nights and up
to $150 for 7+ nights. A pet
agreement must be signed at
check-in.

Holiday Inn Express Killeen
1602 E. Central Expressway
Killeen, TX
254-554-2727 (877-270-6405)
Dogs are welcome at this hotel.

La Quinta Inn Killeen
1112 S. Fort Hood St.
Killeen, TX
254-526-8331 (800-531-5900)
Dogs of all sizes are allowed. There
are no additional pet fees. Dogs
must be leashed, cleaned up after,
and crated when in the room
unattended. Arrangements need to
be made for housekeeping if the
stay is more than 1 day. Multiple
dogs may be allowed.

Motel 6 - Killeen
800 Central Texas Exwy
Killeen, TX
254-634-4151 (800-466-8356)
This motel welcomes your pets to
stay with you.

Residence Inn Killeen
400 E Central Texas Expressway
Killeen, TX
254-634-1020 (800-331-3131)
Located only a couple of miles from
the Ft Hood Military Base and
centrally located for business,
shopping, recreation, and culture
activities this all suite inn also
provides a number of in-house
amenities, including a daily buffet
breakfast and evening socials
Monday to Thursday. Dogs up to 50
pounds are allowed for an
additional one time fee of $100 per
pet. 2 dogs may be allowed.

Super 8 Killeen
606 E Central Texas Exprwy
Killeen, TX
254-634-6868 (800-800-8000)
Dogs are welcome at this hotel.

TownePlace Suites Killeen
2401 Florence Road
Killeen, TX
254-554-8899 (800-257-3000)
This all suite hotel sits central to a
number of sites of interest for both
business and leisure travelers; plus
they also offer a number of on-site
amenities to ensure comfort -
including a complimentary deluxe
continental breakfast. Dogs are
allowed for an additional one time
fee of $100 per room. 2 dogs may be
allowed.

Motel 6 - Kingsville
101 Us 77
Kingsville, TX
361-592-5106 (800-466-8356)
This motel welcomes your pets to
stay with you.

La Quinta Inn & Suites Kingwood
22790 US 59
Kingwood, TX
281-359-6611 (800-531-5900)
Dogs of all sizes are allowed. There
are no additional pet fees. There is a
pet waiver to sign at check in. Dogs
must be leashed, cleaned up after,
and crated or removed for
housekeeping. Multiple dogs may be
allowed.

Super 8 /Harlingen Area La Feria
1202 North Main
La Feria, TX
956-797-0200 (800-800-8000)
Dogs are welcome at this hotel.

Candlewood Suites La Porte
1250 S. 13th St
La Porte, TX
281-471-0555 (877-270-6405)
Dogs up to 80 pounds are allowed.
Pets allowed with an additional pet
fee. Up to $75 for 1-6 nights and up
to $150 for 7+ nights. A pet
agreement must be signed at check-
in.

La Quinta Inn Houston La Porte
1105 Hwy. 146 South
La Porte, TX
281-470-0760 (800-531-5900)
Dogs of all sizes are allowed. There
are no additional pet fees, but there
must be a credit card on file. Dogs
must be leashed and cleaned up
after. 2 dogs may be allowed.

Candlewood Suites Lake Jackson
506 E. Hwy 332
Lake Jackson, TX
979-297-0011 (877-270-6405)
Dogs up to 80 pounds are allowed.
Pets allowed with an additional pet
fee. Up to $75 for 1-6 nights and up
to $150 for 7+ nights. A pet
agreement must be signed at check-
in.

Motel 6 - Dallas-desoto-lancaster
1750 North I-35
Lancaster, TX
972-228-1255 (800-466-8356)
This motel welcomes your pets to
stay with you.

Super 8 /Dallas Area TX Lancaster
930 N Interstate 35 E
Lancaster, TX
972-274-3700 (800-800-8000)
Dogs are welcome at this hotel.

Comfort Suites
6551 Metro Court
Laredo, TX
956-725-5222 (877-424-6423)
Dogs up to 50 pounds are allowed.
Dogs are allowed for a pet fee of
$25.00 per pet per stay. Two dogs
are allowed per room.

Days Inn & Suites Laredo
7060 N. San Bernado Ave.
Laredo, TX
956-724-8221 (800-329-7466)
Dogs of all sizes are allowed. Dogs
are allowed for a pet fee of $10.00
per pet per night.

Extended Stay America Laredo - Del
Mar
106 W. Village
Laredo, TX
956-724-1920 (800-804-3724)
One dog is allowed per suite. There
is a $25 per night additional pet fee
up to $150 for an entire stay.

Family Gardens Inn
5830 San Bernardo
Laredo, TX
956-723-5300 (800-292-4053)
They have onsite kennels available if
you need to leave your room during
the day and can't bring your pup with
you. There is a $50 refundable pet
deposit. You have to provide your
own locks for the kennels. Multiple
dogs may be allowed.

La Quinta Inn & Suites Laredo
7220 Bob Bullock Loop
Laredo, TX
956-724-7222 (800-531-5900)

Dogs of all sizes are allowed. There
is a $50 refundable pet deposit if
paying for the room with cash; there
is no deposit required with a credit
card on file. Dogs must be leashed
and cleaned up after, and if your
room needs to be serviced, they
ask that you remove your pet.
Multiple dogs may be allowed.

La Quinta Inn Laredo
3610 Santa Ursula
Laredo, TX
956-722-0511 (800-531-5900)
Dogs of all sizes are allowed. There
are no additional pet fees. Dogs
must be leashed, cleaned up after,
and removed for housekeeping.
Multiple dogs may be allowed.

Motel 6 - Laredo North
5920 San Bernardo Ave
Laredo, TX
956-722-8133 (800-466-8356)
This motel welcomes your pets to
stay with you.

Motel 6 - Laredo South
5310 San Bernardo Ave
Laredo, TX
956-725-8187 (800-466-8356)
This motel welcomes your pets to
stay with you.

Red Roof Inn Laredo
1006 West Calton Road
Laredo, TX
956-712-0733 (800-RED-ROOF)
One well-behaved family pet per
room. Guest must notify front desk
upon arrival. Guest is liable for any
damages. In consideration of all
guests, pets must never be left
unattended in the guest rooms.

Red Roof Inn, LAREDO,TX
2010 Lomas Del Sur
Laredo, TX
956-724-7300 (800-RED-ROOF)
One well-behaved family pet per
room. Guest must notify front desk
upon arrival. Guest is liable for any
damages. In consideration of all
guests, pets must never be left
unattended in the guest rooms.

Residence Inn Laredo Del Mar
310 Lost Oaks Blvd
Laredo, TX
956-753-9700 (800-331-3131)
In addition to being located near the
International Bridge with Mexico,
numerous historical and cultural
sites, authentic Mexican food
restaurants, and to a multitude of
sporting/special events, this all suite
inn also provides a number of in-

house amenities, including a daily
buffet breakfast and evening social
hours. Dogs are allowed for an
additional one time pet fee of $100
per room. 2 dogs may be allowed.

Staybridge Suites Laredo
7010 Bob Bullock Loop
Laredo, TX
956-722-0444 (877-270-6405)
Dogs up to 80 pounds are allowed.
Pets allowed with an additional pet
fee. Up to $75 for 1-6 nights and up
to $150 for 7+ nights. A pet
agreement must be signed at check-
in.

Comfort Suites
755A Vista Ridge Mall Dr.
Lewisville, TX
972-315-6464 (877-424-6423)
Dogs of all sizes are allowed. Dogs
are allowed for a pet fee of $25.00
per pet per stay.

Country Inns & Suites by Carlson
755 B Vista Ridge Mall Drive
Lewisville, TX
972-315-6565
Dogs of all sizes are allowed. There
is a $100 per stay additional pet fee.

Extended Stay America Dallas -
Lewisville
1900 Lake Pointe Dr.
Lewisville, TX
972-315-7455 (800-804-3724)
One dog is allowed per suite. There
is a $25 per night additional pet fee
up to $150 for an entire stay.

Knights Inn Lewisville
1305 S. Stemmons Freeway
Lewisville, TX
972-221-7511 (800-843-5644)
Dogs are welcome at this hotel.
There is an additional pet fee.

La Quinta Inn Dallas Lewisville
1657 S. Stemmons Freeway
Lewisville, TX
972-221-7525 (800-531-5900)
Dogs of all sizes are allowed. There
are no additional pet fees. Dogs
must be well behaved, leashed, and
cleaned up after. Multiple dogs may
be allowed.

Motel 6 - Dallas Lewisville
1705 Lakepointe Dr
Lewisville, TX
972-436-5008 (800-466-8356)
This motel welcomes your pets to
stay with you.

Residence Inn Dallas Lewisville
755 C Vista Ridge Mall Drive

Dog-Friendly Lodging - Please always call ahead to make sure an establishment is still dog-friendly.

Lewisville, TX
972-315-3777 (800-331-3131)
In addition to offering a convenient location to business, shopping, dining, and entertainment areas, this hotel also provides a number of in-house amenities, including a daily buffet breakfast and an evening social hour. Dogs are allowed for an additional one time pet fee of $100 per room. 2 dogs may be allowed.

Super 8 Livingston
117 Highway 59 Loop South
Livingston, TX
936-327-2451 (800-800-8000)
Dogs of all sizes are allowed. Dogs are allowed for a pet fee.

Best Western Llano
901 W Young Street
Llano, TX
325-247-4101 (800-780-7234)
Dogs of all sizes are allowed. Dogs are allowed for a pet fee of $10 per pet per night.

Candlewood Suites Longview
2904 Tuttle Blvd
Longview, TX
903-663-9751 (877-270-6405)
Dogs up to 80 pounds are allowed. Pets allowed with an additional pet fee. Up to $75 for 1-6 nights and up to $150 for 7+ nights. A pet agreement must be signed at check-in.

La Quinta Inn Longview
502 S. Access Rd.
Longview, TX
903-757-3663 (800-531-5900)
Dogs of all sizes are allowed. There are no additional pet fees. Dogs must be leashed and cleaned up after. Multiple dogs may be allowed.

Motel 6 - Longview
110 Access Rd
Longview, TX
903-758-5256 (800-466-8356)
This motel welcomes your pets to stay with you.

Ramada Limited Suites - Longview
419 Spur 63
Longview, TX
903-757-0500 (800-272-6232)
Dogs of all sizes are allowed. Dogs are allowed for a pet fee of $25 per pet per night.

Hyatt Regency Lost Pines Resort and Spa
575 Hyatt Lost Pines Road
Lost Pines, TX
512-308-1234 (800-633-7313)

There are many activities and amenities available for the business or vacationing guest on this 700 acre full-service hotel resort including a comprehensive business center, a championship golf course, and live entertainment on weekends. Dogs of all sizes are welcome for an additional one time pet fee of $100 per room. Dogs may only be left alone in the room if owners are confident their pet will be quiet and well behaved, and they may either be crated or put into the bathroom. Dogs must be leashed or crated, and cleaned up after at all times. 2 dogs may be allowed.

Best Western Lubbock Windsor Inn
5410 Interstate 27
Lubbock, TX
806-762-8400 (800-780-7234)
Dogs up to 50 pounds are allowed.

Days Inn South Lubbock
6025 Ave A
Lubbock, TX
806-745-5111 (800-329-7466)
Dogs are welcome at this hotel.

Days Inn - Texas Tech University-4th Street Lubbock
2401 4th Street
Lubbock, TX
806-747-7111 (800-329-7466)
Dogs are welcome at this hotel.

Extended Stay America Lubbock - Southwest
4802 S. Loop 289
Lubbock, TX
806-785-9881 (800-804-3724)
One dog is allowed per suite. There is a $25 per night additional pet fee up to $150 for an entire stay.

La Quinta Inn Lubbock Civic Center
601 Avenue Q
Lubbock, TX
806-763-9441 (800-531-5900)
Dogs of all sizes are allowed. There is a $25 per room additional pet fee. Dogs must be leashed and cleaned up after. Multiple dogs may be allowed.

La Quinta Inn Lubbock West/Medical Center
4115 Brownfield Hwy.
Lubbock, TX
806-792-0065 (800-531-5900)
Dogs of all sizes are allowed. There are no additional pet fees. Dogs may not be left unattended, and they must be leashed and cleaned up after. 2 dogs may be allowed.

Motel 6 - Lubbock
909 66th St
Lubbock, TX
806-745-5541 (800-466-8356)
This motel welcomes your pets to stay with you.

Red Roof Inn Lubbock
6624 Interstate 27
Lubbock, TX
806-745-2208 (800-RED-ROOF)
One well-behaved family pet per room. Guest must notify front desk upon arrival. Guest is liable for any damages. In consideration of all guests, pets must never be left unattended in the guest rooms.

Staybridge Suites Lubbock
2515 19th Street
Lubbock, TX
806-765-8900 (877-270-6405)
Dogs up to 80 pounds are allowed. Pets allowed with an additional pet fee. Up to $75 for 1-6 nights and up to $150 for 7+ nights. A pet agreement must be signed at check-in.

Studio 6 - Lubbock, Tx
4521 Marsha Sharp Frwy
Lubbock, TX
806-687-6666 (800-466-8356)
Your pets are welcome to stay here with you for a pet fee of $10 per day up to $50 for an entire stay.

Super 8 Civic Center North Lubbock
501 Ave Q
Lubbock, TX
806-762-8726 (800-800-8000)
Dogs are welcome at this hotel.

TownePlace Suites Lubbock
5310 W Loop 289
Lubbock, TX
806-799-6226 (800-257-3000)
This all suite hotel sits central to a number of sites of interest for both business and leisure travelers; plus they also offer a number of on-site amenities to ensure comfort. Dogs are allowed for an additional one time fee of $100 per room. 2 dogs may be allowed.

Motel 6 - Lufkin
1110 Timberland Dr
Lufkin, TX
936-637-7850 (800-466-8356)
This motel welcomes your pets to stay with you.

Quality Inn & Suites
4306 S. 1st St.
Lufkin, TX
936-639-3333 (877-424-6423)

Dogs of all sizes are allowed. Dogs are allowed for a pet fee of $20.00 per pet per night.

Days Inn San Antonio Lytle
19525 McDonald St
Lytle, TX
830-772-4777 (800-329-7466)
Dogs are welcome at this hotel.

Super 8 McAllen
1420 East Jackson Ave
MCALLEN, TX
956-682-1190 (800-800-8000)
Dogs are welcome at this hotel.

Quality Inn & Suites
11301 Highway 290 East
Manor, TX
512-272-9373 (877-424-6423)
Dogs of all sizes are allowed. Dogs are allowed for a pet fee of $10.00 per pet per night. Two dogs are allowed per room.

Best Western Mansfield Inn & Suites
775 US 287 Highway
Mansfield, TX
817-539-0707 (800-780-7234)
Dogs of all sizes are allowed. Dogs are allowed for a nightly pet fee.

Best Western Marble Falls Inn
1403 N Highway 281
Marble Falls, TX
830-693-5122 (800-780-7234)
Dogs of all sizes are allowed. Dogs are allowed for a pet fee.

Chinati Hot Springs
1 Hot Springs Road
Marfa, TX
432-229-4165
chinatihotsprings.com/
Although this is a place for rest and relaxation or any number of recreational activities, the real attraction here are the hot mineral baths that are said to have been sharing their healing properties for thousands of years. Lodging or primitive camping under the stars is available. Dogs are welcome for lodging and camping for no additional fee. Dogs must be very dog and people friendly, leashed, and under their owner's control at all times. 2 dogs may be allowed.

Days Inn and Suites Marshall
5555 East End Blvd South
Marshall, TX
903-935-1941 (800-329-7466)
Dogs of all sizes are allowed. Dogs are allowed for a pet fee of $10 per pet per night.

La Quinta Inn Marshall
5301 E End Blvd S
Marshall, TX
903-927-0009 (800-531-5900)
Dogs of all sizes are allowed. There are no additional pet fees. There is a pet waiver to sign at check in. Dogs must be leashed, cleaned up after, and crated or removed for housekeeping. Multiple dogs may be allowed.

Motel 6 - Marshall
300 I-20 East
Marshall, TX
903-935-4393 (800-466-8356)
This motel welcomes your pets to stay with you.

La Quinta Inn McAllen
1100 South 10th St.
McAllen, TX
956-687-1101 (800-531-5900)
Two large dogs or 3 small dogs are allowed. There are not additional pet fees. There is a pet waiver to sign at check in. Dogs must be well behaved, leashed, cleaned up after, and crated or removed for housekeeping.

Posada Ana Inn
620 W. Expressway 83
McAllen, TX
956-631-6700 (800-378-7946)
Dogs of all sizes are allowed for no additional pet fee with a credit card on file, and there is a pet agreement to sign at check in.

Ramada Limited - McAllen
1505 South 9th Street
McAllen, TX
956-686-4401 (800-272-6232)
Dogs of all sizes are allowed. Dogs are allowed for a pet fee.

Residence Inn McAllen
220 W Expressway 83
McAllen, TX
956-994-8626 (800-331-3131)
Some of the amenities at this all-suite inn include a daily buffet breakfast, a Manager's reception Monday through Thursday with light dinner fare, a swimming pool, and a complimentary grocery shopping service. Dogs are allowed for an additional one time pet fee of $75 per room. Multiple dogs may be allowed.

Super 8 /Hidalgo/Mission Area McAllen
6420 South 23rd St
McAllen, TX
956-688-6666 (800-800-8000)

Dogs of all sizes are allowed. Dogs are allowed for a pet fee of $10.00 per pet per night.

Days Inn McKinney
2104 North Central Expressway
McKinney, TX
972-548-8888 (800-329-7466)
Dogs of all sizes are allowed. Dogs are allowed for a pet fee of $7.00 per pet per night.

Quality Inn
1300 N. Central Expressway
McKinney, TX
972-542-9471 (877-424-6423)
Dogs up to 100 pounds are allowed. Dogs are allowed for a pet fee of $25.00 per pet per stay. Two dogs are allowed per room.

Motel 6 - Mcallen
700 Expressway 83
Mcallen, TX
956-687-3700 (800-466-8356)
This motel welcomes your pets to stay with you.

Staybridge Suites Mcallen
620 Wichita Ave.
Mcallen, TX
956-213-7829 (877-270-6405)
Dogs up to 80 pounds are allowed. Pets allowed with an additional pet fee. Up to $75 for 1-6 nights and up to $150 for 7+ nights. A pet agreement must be signed at check-in.

Studio 6 - Mcallen
700 Savannah Ave
Mcallen, TX
956-668-7829 (800-466-8356)
Your pets are welcome to stay here with you for a pet fee of $10 per day up to $50 for an entire stay.

Motel 6 - Mckinney
2125 White Ave
Mckinney, TX
972-542-8600 (800-466-8356)
This motel welcomes your pets to stay with you.

Super 8 McKinney/Plano Area
910 N Central Expressway
Mckinney, TX
972-548-8880 (800-800-8000)
Dogs of all sizes are allowed. Dogs are allowed for a pet fee of $10 per pet per night.

Travelodge Memphis
1600 North Boykin Dr
Memphis, TX
806-259-3583 (800-578-7878)
Dogs of all sizes are allowed. Dogs

are allowed for a pet fee of $6.00 per pet per night.

Comfort Inn
923 Windbell Circle
Mesquite, TX
972-285-6300 (877-424-6423)
Dogs of all sizes are allowed. Dogs are allowed for a pet fee of $10.00 per pet per night.

Days Inn Rodeo
IH-635 And Military Parkway
Mesquite, TX
972-285-1500 (800-329-7466)
Dogs are welcome at this hotel.

La Quinta Inn & Suites Dallas/Mesquite
118 East US Highway 80
Mesquite, TX
972-216-7460 (800-531-5900)
Dogs of all sizes are allowed. There are no additional pet fees. Dogs may only be left alone in the room if they will be quiet. Dogs must be leashed and cleaned up after. Multiple dogs may be allowed.

Super 8 /Dallas Area Mesquite
121 Grand Junction
Mesquite, TX
972-289-5481 (800-800-8000)
Dogs of all sizes are allowed. Dogs are allowed for a pet fee.

Clarion Hotel & Conference Center
4300 West Wall Street
Midland, TX
432-697-3181 (877-424-6423)
Small dogs are allowed.

Comfort Suites
4706 North Garfield
Midland, TX
432-620-9191 (877-424-6423)
Dogs of all sizes are allowed. Dogs are allowed for a pet fee of $35.00 per pet per stay.

Hilton Hotel
117 W Wall Street
Midland, TX
432-683-6131 (800-HILTONS (445-8667))
This upscale hotel offers a number of on site amenities for business and leisure travelers, plus a convenient location to the Miami International Airport, shopping, dining, and recreational areas. Dogs are allowed for an additional one time pet fee of $25 per room. Multiple dogs may be allowed.

La Quinta Inn Midland
4130 West Wall Street

Midland, TX
432-697-9900 (800-531-5900)
Dogs of all sizes are allowed. There are no additional pet fees. Dogs must be well behaved, leashed, and cleaned up after. The front desk needs to be informed when there is a pet alone in the room, and the Do Not Disturb sign placed on the door. Multiple dogs may be allowed.

Residence Inn Midland
5509 Deauville Blvd
Midland, TX
432-689-3511 (800-331-3131)
This all suite inn features a convenient location to business, shopping, dining, and entertainment areas, plus they also offer a number of in-house amenities, including a daily buffet breakfast and evening socials Monday to Wednesday. Dogs are allowed for an additional one time pet fee of $75 per room 2 dogs may be allowed.

Studio 6 - Midland, Tx
1003 Midkiff Rd
Midland, TX
432-618-6660 (800-466-8356)
Your pets are welcome to stay here with you for a pet fee of $10 per day up to $50 for an entire stay.

Best Western Club House Inn & Suites
4410 Highway 180 E
Mineral Wells, TX
940-325-2270 (800-780-7234)
Dogs are welcome at this hotel. There is a $10 one time pet fee.

Hawthorn Suites
3700 Plantation Grove Blvd
Mission, TX
956-519-9696 (866-519-9696)
In addition to providing a convenient location to many local sites and activities, this all-suite hotel offers a number of amenities for business and leisure travelers, including their signature breakfast buffet and beautifully appointed rooms. Dogs are allowed for an additional one time fee of $50 per pet. Multiple dogs may be allowed.

Motel 6 - Mission, Tx
1813 Expressway 83
Mission, TX
956-581-1919 (800-466-8356)
This motel welcomes your pets to stay with you.

Best Western Mt. Pleasant Inn
102 E Burton Road
Mount Pleasant, TX

903-577-7377 (800-780-7234)
Dogs of all sizes are allowed. Dogs are allowed for a nightly pet fee.

Comfort Inn
2515 W. Ferguson Rd.
Mount Pleasant, TX
903-577-7553 (877-424-6423)
Dogs of all sizes are allowed. Dogs are allowed for a pet fee of $20.00 per pet per stay. Two dogs are allowed per room.

Super 8 Mount Vernon
401 Interstate 30 W
Mount Vernon, TX
903-588-2882 (800-800-8000)
Dogs are welcome at this hotel.

Days Inn Nacogdoches
2724 North Street
Nacogdoches, TX
936-715-0005 (800-329-7466)
Dogs are welcome at this hotel.

La Quinta Inn Nacogdoches
3215 South St.
Nacogdoches, TX
936-560-5453 (800-531-5900)
Dogs of all sizes are allowed. There are no additional pet fees. Dogs must be leashed and cleaned up after. A contact number must be left with the front desk if there is a pet left unattended in the room. Multiple dogs may be allowed.

Super 8 Nacogdoches
3909 South Street
Nacogdoches, TX
936-560-2888 (800-800-8000)
Dogs of all sizes are allowed. Dogs are allowed for a pet fee of $20 per pet per night.

Super 8 Navasota
9460 Hwy 6 Loop
Navasota, TX
936-825-7775 (800-800-8000)
Dogs of all sizes are allowed. Dogs are allowed for a pet fee of $10 per pet per night.

Candlewood Suites Nederland
2125 Hwy 69
Nederland, TX
409-729-9543 (877-270-6405)
Dogs up to 80 pounds are allowed. Pets allowed with an additional pet fee. Up to $75 for 1-6 nights and up to $150 for 7+ nights. A pet agreement must be signed at check-in.

Holiday Inn New Braunfels
1051 Ih 35 East
New Braunfels, TX

830-625-8017 (877-270-6405)
Dogs of all sizes are allowed. Dogs are allowed for a pet fee of $25.00 per pet per stay.

La Quinta Inn & Suites New Braunfels
365 Hwy 46 South
New Braunfels, TX
830-627-3333 (800-531-5900)
Dogs of all sizes are allowed. There are no additional pet fees. There is a pet waiver to sign at check in. Dogs must be leashed and cleaned up after. 2 dogs may be allowed.

Motel 6 - New Braunfels
1275 I-35
New Braunfels, TX
830-626-0600 (800-466-8356)
This motel welcomes your pets to stay with you.

Quality Inn & Suites
1533 IH-35 North
New Braunfels, TX
830-643-9300 (877-424-6423)
Dogs up to 50 pounds are allowed. Dogs are allowed for a pet fee of $25.00 per pet per stay. Two dogs are allowed per room.

Red Roof Inn New Braunfels
815 I-35 South
New Braunfels, TX
830-626-7000 (800-RED-ROOF)
One well-behaved family pet per room. Guest must notify front desk upon arrival. Guest is liable for any damages. In consideration of all guests, pets must never be left unattended in the guest rooms.

Super 8 TX New Braunfels
510 Highway 46 South
New Braunfels, TX
830-629-1155 (800-800-8000)
Dogs of all sizes are allowed. Dogs are allowed for a pet fee.

Wingate by Wyndham New Braunfels
245 FM-306
New Braunfels, TX
830-515-4701 (800-228-1000)
Dogs are welcome at this hotel.

Best Western N.E. Mall Inn & Suites
8709 Airport Freeway
North Richland Hills, TX
817-656-8881 (800-780-7234)
Dogs of all sizes are allowed. Dogs are allowed for a nightly pet fee.

Motel 6 - Ft Worth North Richland Hills
7804 Bedford Euless Rd
North Richland Hills, TX

817-485-3000 (800-466-8356)
This motel welcomes your pets to stay with you.

Studio 6 - Ft Worth North Richland Hills
7450 Ne Loop 820
North Richland Hills, TX
817-788-6000 (800-466-8356)
Your pets are welcome to stay here with you for a pet fee of $10 per day up to $50 for an entire stay.

Travelodge NE Mall
7920 Bedford Euless Road
North Richland Hills, TX
817-485-2750 (800-578-7878)
Dogs of all sizes are allowed. Dogs are allowed for a pet fee.

Best Western Garden Oasis
110 W Interstate 20
Odessa, TX
432-337-3006 (800-780-7234)
Dogs are welcome at this hotel.

La Quinta Inn Odessa
5001 E. Bus. I-20
Odessa, TX
432-333-2820 (800-531-5900)
Dogs of all sizes are allowed. There are no additional pet fees. Dogs may not be left unattended, and they must be leashed and cleaned up after. 2 dogs may be allowed.

Motel 6 - Odessa
200 I-20 Service Road
Odessa, TX
432-333-4025 (800-466-8356)
This motel welcomes your pets to stay with you.

Studio 6 - Odessa, Tx
3031 Highway 80
Odessa, TX
432-333-6660 (800-466-8356)
Your pets are welcome to stay here with you for a pet fee of $10 per day up to $50 for an entire stay.

Motel 6 - Orange
4407 27th St
Orange, TX
409-883-4891 (800-466-8356)
This motel welcomes your pets to stay with you.

Ramada TX Orange
2610 I-10 West
Orange, TX
409-883-0231 (800-272-6232)
Dogs of all sizes are allowed. Dogs are allowed for a pet fee of $10 per pet per stay.

Super 8 Orange

2710 I-10 W
Orange, TX
409-882-0888 (800-800-8000)
Dogs are welcome at this hotel.

Super 8 Ozona
3331 I 10 East
Ozona, TX
325-392-2611 (800-800-8000)
Dogs are welcome at this hotel.

Travelodge Ozona
8-11 Main Street
Ozona, TX
325-392-2656 (800-578-7878)
Dogs of all sizes are allowed. Dogs are allowed for a nightly pet fee.

Motel 6 - Pasadena,tx
3010 Pasadena Frwy
Pasadena, TX
713-472-4100 (800-466-8356)
This motel welcomes your pets to stay with you.

Cielito Guest Ranch Bed and Breakfast Cabins
1308 Clemons Switch Road
Pattison, TX
281-375-6469 (888-375-6469)
cielitoranch.com/
For a truly "back to the farm" experience, this working farm guest ranch offers 177 park-like acres, all the farm animals, miles of trails, and a variety of land and water recreational opportunities. Dogs are allowed for an additional fee of $15 per night per pet. There are kennels available when needed, and they also offer well behaved dogs extended accommodations where they have free range on the ranch (except at night) for when their owners must be away for longer periods. 2 dogs may be allowed.

Best Western Pearland Inn
1855 N Main Street (Hwy 35)
Pearland, TX
281-997-2000 (800-780-7234)
Dogs of all sizes are allowed. Dogs are allowed for a pet fee of $20.00 per pet per stay.

Best Western Pearsall Inn & Suites
1808 W Comal Street
Pearsall, TX
830-334-4900 (800-780-7234)
Dogs are welcome at this hotel.

Knights Inn Laura Lodge TX Pecos
1000 East Business 20
Pecos, TX
432-445-4924 (800-843-5644)
Dogs of all sizes are allowed. Dogs are allowed for a pet fee.

Dog-Friendly Lodging - Please always call ahead to make sure an establishment is still dog-friendly.

Motel 6 - Pecos
3002 Cedar St
Pecos, TX
432-445-9034 (800-466-8356)
This motel welcomes your pets to stay with you.

Quality Inn
4002 S. Cedar St.
Pecos, TX
432-445-5404 (877-424-6423)
Dogs up to 50 pounds are allowed. Dogs are allowed for a pet fee of $10.00 per pet per night.

Knights Inn And Suites Rio Grande Valley
2706 N. Cage Blvd.
Pharr, TX
956-783-7777 (800-843-5644)
Dogs of all sizes are allowed. Dogs are allowed for a pet fee of $10.00 per pet per stay.

La Quinta Inn & Suites Rio Grande Valley
4603 North Cage
Pharr, TX
956-787-2900 (800-531-5900)
Dogs of all sizes are allowed. There are no additional pet fees. There is a pet waiver to sign at check in. Dogs must be leashed and cleaned up after. Multiple dogs may be allowed.

Motel 6 - Pharr
4701 Cage Blvd
Pharr, TX
956-781-7202 (800-466-8356)
This motel welcomes your pets to stay with you.

Quality Inn
1301 W. Expwy. 83
Pharr, TX
956-702-4880 (877-424-6423)
Dogs up to 50 pounds are allowed. Dogs are allowed for a pet fee of $9.00 per pet per night.

Red Roof Inn Pharr
4401 North Cage Blvd.
Pharr, TX
956-782-8880 (800-RED-ROOF)
One well-behaved family pet per room. Guest must notify front desk upon arrival. Guest is liable for any damages. In consideration of all guests, pets must never be left unattended in the guest rooms.

Days Inn Plainview
3600 Olton Road
Plainview, TX
806-293-2561 (800-329-7466)
Dogs are welcome at this hotel.

Best Western Park Suites Hotel
640 E Park Boulevard
Plano, TX
972-578-2243 (800-780-7234)
Dogs of all sizes are allowed. Dogs are allowed for a pet fee.

Candlewood Suites Dallas-Plano
4701 Legacy Drive
Plano, TX
972-618-5446 (877-270-6405)
Dogs up to 80 pounds are allowed. Pets allowed with an additional pet fee. Up to $75 for 1-6 nights and up to $150 for 7+ nights. A pet agreement must be signed at check-in.

Holiday Inn Express Hotel & Suites Plano East
700 Central Parkway East
Plano, TX
972-881-1881 (877-270-6405)
Dogs of all sizes are allowed. Dogs are allowed for a pet fee.

Homestead Studio Suites Dallas - Plano - Plano Parkway
4709 West Plano Pkwy.
Plano, TX
972-596-9966 (800-804-3724)
One dog is allowed per suite. There is a $25 per night additional pet fee up to $150 for an entire stay.

La Quinta Inn & Suites Dallas Plano West
4800 West Plano Pkwy.
Plano, TX
972-599-0700 (800-531-5900)
Dogs of all sizes are allowed. There are no additional pet fees. Dogs must be leashed and cleaned up after. 2 dogs may be allowed.

La Quinta Inn Dallas Plano East
1820 North Central Expwy.
Plano, TX
972-423-1300 (800-531-5900)
Dogs of all sizes are allowed. There are no additional pet fees. Dogs must be leashed, cleaned up after, and crated or removed for housekeeping. Multiple dogs may be allowed.

Motel 6 - Dallas Plano Northeast
2550 Central Expy
Plano, TX
972-578-1626 (800-466-8356)
This motel welcomes your pets to stay with you.

Motel 6 - Plano Preston Point
4801 West Plano Pkwy
Plano, TX

972-867-1111 (800-466-8356)
This motel welcomes your pets to stay with you.

Red Roof Inn Dallas - Plano Convention Center
301 Ruisseau Drive
Plano, TX
972-881-8191 (800-RED-ROOF)
One well-behaved family pet per room. Guest must notify front desk upon arrival. Guest is liable for any damages. In consideration of all guests, pets must never be left unattended in the guest rooms.

Residence Inn Dallas Plano
5001 Whitestone Lane
Plano, TX
972-473-6761 (800-331-3131)
Located in the heart of the city's corporate district, this hotel offers a convenient location to business, shopping, dining, and entertainment areas, plus they offer a number of in-house amenities, including a daily buffet breakfast and nightly evening socials. Dogs are allowed for an additional one time pet fee of $100 per room. Multiple dogs may be allowed.

Staybridge Suites Plano - Richardson Area
301 Silverglen Drive
Plano, TX
972-612-8180 (877-270-6405)
Dogs up to 80 pounds are allowed. Pets allowed with an additional pet fee. Up to $75 for 1-6 nights and up to $150 for 7+ nights. A pet agreement must be signed at check-in.

Super 8 /Dallas Area Plano
Hwy 75 to 15th St Exit
Plano, TX
972-423-8300 (800-800-8000)
Dogs of all sizes are allowed. Dogs are allowed for a pet fee.

TownePlace Suites Dallas Plano
5005 Whitestone Lane
Plano, TX
972-943-8200 (800-257-3000)
In addition to offering a number of in-house amenities for all level of travelers, this all suite inn also provides a convenient location to business, shopping, dining, and entertainment areas. Dogs are allowed for an additional one time fee of $75 per room. 2 dogs may be allowed.

Days Inn and Suites Port Arthur
8040 Memorial Blvd

Port Arthur, TX
409-729-3434 (800-329-7466)
Dogs of all sizes are allowed. Dogs are allowed for a pet fee of $10.00 per pet per stay.

Ramada - Port Arthur
3801 Hwy 73
Port Arthur, TX
409-962-9858 (800-272-6232)
Dogs are welcome at this hotel.

Studio 6 - Port Arthur
3000 Jimmy Johnson Blvd
Port Arthur, TX
409-729-6611 (800-466-8356)
Your pets are welcome to stay here with you for a pet fee of $10 per day up to $50 for an entire stay.

Days Inn Port Lavaca
2100 State Highway 35 N
Port Lavaca, TX
361-552-4511 (800-329-7466)
Dogs are welcome at this hotel.

Motel 6 - Port Lavaca
2621 Hwy 35 North
Port Lavaca, TX
361-552-3393 (800-466-8356)
This motel welcomes your pets to stay with you.

Super 8 Porter
24085 U.S. Hwy 59
Porter, TX
281-354-7227 (800-800-8000)
Dogs of all sizes are allowed. Dogs are allowed for a pet fee of $10.00 per pet per stay.

MD Resort Bed and Breakfast Country Inn
601 Old Base Road
Rhome, TX
817-489-5150 (866-489-5150)
mdresort.com/
A real Texas guest ranch, they offer many modern amenities, an outdoor pool and spa, and a number of fun activities. Dogs are allowed for an additional one time fee of $50 per pet. 2 dogs may be allowed.

Dallas - Richardson
13685 N. Central Expressway
Richardson, TX
972-234-1016 (800-RED-ROOF)
One well-behaved family pet per room. Guest must notify front desk upon arrival. Guest is liable for any damages. In consideration of all guests, pets must never be left unattended in the guest rooms.

Hawthorn Suites
250 Municipal Drive

Richardson, TX
972-669-1000 (800-527-1133)
In addition to providing a convenient location to many local sites and activities, this all-suite hotel offers a number of amenities for business and leisure travelers, including their signature breakfast buffet, a complimentary social hour with beer/wine and a dinner buffet Monday thru Thursday, and beautifully appointed rooms. For studio suites, dogs up to 30 pounds are allowed for an additional one time $100 per room; for dogs over 30 pounds the one time fee is $150. For the penthouse suites, the fee for dogs under 30 pounds is a one time pet fee per room of $150, and for dogs over 30 pounds, the fee is $200. There is also a pet waiver to sign at check in. 2 dogs may be allowed.

Homestead Studio Suites Dallas - Richardson
901 E. Campbell Rd.
Richardson, TX
972-479-0500 (800-804-3724)
One dog is allowed per suite. There is a $25 per night additional pet fee up to $150 for an entire stay.

Renaissance Dallas Richardson Hotel
900 E Lookout Drive
Richardson, TX
972-367-2000 (800-HOTELS-1 (468-3571))
This luxury hotel provides a great location to a number of sites of interest for both business and leisure travelers; plus they also offer numerous on-site amenities to ensure a comfortable stay. Dogs are allowed for an additional one time fee of $50 per pet. Multiple dogs may be allowed.

Residence Inn Dallas Richardson
1040 Waterwood Drive
Richardson, TX
972-669-5888 (800-216-8027)
Located in the heart of the Telecom Business Park, this hotel offers a convenient location to business, universities, shopping, dining, and entertainment areas, plus they offer a number of in-house amenities, including a daily buffet breakfast and nightly evening socials. Dogs up to 50 pounds are allowed for an additional one time pet fee of $100 per room. 2 dogs may be allowed.

Summerfield Suites Dallas Richardson
2301 North Central Expressway

Richardson, TX
972-671-8080
Pets are allowed at this extended stay hotel.

Comfort Suites
801 Byron Nelson Blvd
Roanoke, TX
817-490-1455 (877-424-6423)
Dogs up to 50 pounds are allowed. Dogs are allowed for a pet fee of $10.00 per pet per night. Two dogs are allowed per room.

Motel 6 - Northlake Speedway
13601 Raceway Drive
Roanoke, TX
817-541-3625 (800-466-8356)
This motel welcomes your pets to stay with you.

Sleep Inn & Suites Speedway
13471 Raceway Dr.
Roanoke, TX
817-491-3120 (877-424-6423)
Dogs of all sizes are allowed.

Days Inn Rockport
1212 Laurel East
Rockport, TX
361-729-6379 (800-329-7466)
Dogs of all sizes are allowed. Dogs are allowed for a pet fee of $15 per pet per night.

La Quinta Inn & Suites Rockwall
689 East Interstate 30
Rockwall, TX
972-771-1685 (800-531-5900)
Dogs of all sizes are allowed. There are no additional pet fees. There is a pet waiver to sign at check in. Dogs must be leashed and cleaned up after. Multiple dogs may be allowed.

Super 8 Rockwall
1130 East I-30
Rockwall, TX
972-722-9922 (800-800-8000)
Dogs of all sizes are allowed. Dogs are allowed for a pet fee of $5 per pet per night.

Knights Inn Rosenberg
26010 Southwest Freeway
Rosenberg, TX
281-342-6671 (800-843-5644)
Dogs are welcome at this hotel.

Candlewood Suites Austin-Round Rock
521 South Ih-35
Round Rock, TX
512-828-0899 (877-270-6405)
Dogs up to 80 pounds are allowed. Pets allowed with an additional pet fee. Up to $75 for 1-6 nights and up

to $150 for 7+ nights. A pet agreement must be signed at check-in.

Extended Stay America Austin - Round Rock - North
555 S. I-35 - City Centre Business Park
Round Rock, TX
512-671-7872 (800-804-3724)
One dog is allowed per suite. There is a $25 per night additional pet fee up to $150 for an entire stay.

La Quinta Inn Austin Round Rock
2004 North I-35
Round Rock, TX
512-255-6666 (800-531-5900)
Dogs of all sizes are allowed. There are no additional pet fees. Dogs may not be left unattended, and they must be leashed and cleaned up after. Multiple dogs may be allowed.

Red Roof Inn Austin - Round Rock
1990 North I-35
Round Rock, TX
512-310-1111 (800-RED-ROOF)
One well-behaved family pet per room. Guest must notify front desk upon arrival. Guest is liable for any damages. In consideration of all guests, pets must never be left unattended in the guest rooms.

Residence Inn Austin Round Rock
2505 S I H-35
Round Rock, TX
512-733-2400 (888-236-2427)
This up-scale hotel offers a number of on-site amenities including a daily buffet breakfast, and a Manager's reception Monday through Thursday. Dogs are allowed for an additional one time pet fee of $100 per room. Multiple dogs may be allowed.

Staybridge Suites Austin-Round Rock
520 I-35 South
Round Rock, TX
512-733-0942 (877-270-6405)
Dogs up to 80 pounds are allowed. Pets allowed with an additional pet fee. Up to $75 for 1-6 nights and up to $150 for 7+ nights. A pet agreement must be signed at check-in.

Wingate by Wyndham - Round Rock
1209 N. IH 35 North
Round Rock, TX
512-341-7000 (800-228-1000)
Dogs are welcome at this hotel.

Best Western San Angelo
3017 Loop 306

San Angelo, TX
325-223-1273 (800-780-7234)
Dogs of all sizes are allowed. Dogs are allowed for a nightly pet fee.

Days Inn San Angelo
4613 South Jackson
San Angelo, TX
325-658-6594 (800-329-7466)
Dogs are welcome at this hotel.

Howard Johnson Inn - San Angelo
415 West Beauregard Ave
San Angelo, TX
325-653-2995 (800-446-4656)
Dogs are welcome at this hotel.

La Quinta Inn and Conference Center San Angelo
2307 Loop 306
San Angelo, TX
325-949-0515 (800-531-5900)
Dogs of all sizes are allowed. There are no additional pet fees. Dogs must be leashed, cleaned up after, and crated or attended to for housekeeping. Multiple dogs may be allowed.

Motel 6 - San Angelo
311 Bryant Blvd
San Angelo, TX
325-658-8061 (800-466-8356)
This motel welcomes your pets to stay with you.

Ramada Limited - San Angelo
2201 North Bryant Boulevard
San Angelo, TX
325-653-8442 (800-272-6232)
Dogs of all sizes are allowed. Dogs are allowed for a pet fee of $10.00 per pet per night.

Rodeway Inn
2502 Loop 306
San Angelo, TX
325-944-2578 (877-424-6423)
Dogs of all sizes are allowed.

Staybridge Suites San Angelo
1355 Knickerbocker Rd.
San Angelo, TX
013-256-5315 (877-270-6405)
Dogs up to 80 pounds are allowed. Pets allowed with an additional pet fee. Up to $75 for 1-6 nights and up to $150 for 7+ nights. A pet agreement must be signed at check-in.

Best Western Posada Ana Inn-Airport
8600 Jones Maltsberger Road
San Antonio, TX
210-342-1400 (800-780-7234)
Dogs are welcome at this hotel.

Brackenridge House
230 Madison
San Antonio, TX
210-271-3442 (800-221-1412)
brackenridgehouse.com/
Located in the King William historic district, this inn offers the ambience of yesteryear with the amenities of modern day, and a convenient location to numerous local attractions and activities. Dogs are allowed for no additional pet fee. 2 dogs may be allowed.

Candlewood Suites San Antonio
9350 Ih 10 West
San Antonio, TX
210-615-0550 (877-270-6405)
Dogs up to 80 pounds are allowed. Pets allowed with an additional pet fee. Up to $75 for 1-6 nights and up to $150 for 7+ nights. A pet agreement must be signed at check-in.

Days Inn /AT&T Center San Antonio
4039 East Houston Street
San Antonio, TX
210-333-9100 (800-329-7466)
Dogs are welcome at this hotel.

Days Inn /Coliseum/ATandT Center San Antonio
3443 North IH-35
San Antonio, TX
210-225-4040 (800-329-7466)
Dogs of all sizes are allowed. Dogs are allowed for a pet fee of $25 per pet per night.

Days Inn Downtown/Riverwalk Area
1500 S. IH35
San Antonio, TX
210-271-3334 (800-329-7466)
Dogs of all sizes are allowed. Dogs are allowed for a pet fee of $25 per pet per night.

Econo Lodge Central
6015 I-H 10 West
San Antonio, TX
210-737-1855 (877-424-6423)
Dogs of all sizes are allowed. Dogs are allowed for a pet fee of $15.00 per pet per night.

Econo Lodge East
218 S. W.W. White Rd.
San Antonio, TX
210-333-3346 (877-424-6423)
Dogs up to 50 pounds are allowed. Dogs are allowed for a pet fee of $5.00 per pet per night. Two dogs are allowed per room.

Econo Lodge Inn & Suites Coliseum

Dog-Friendly Lodging - Please always call ahead to make sure an establishment is still dog-friendly.

2755 Hwy 35 N
San Antonio, TX
210-229-9220 (877-424-6423)
Dogs of all sizes are allowed. Dogs are allowed for a pet fee of $10.00 per pet per night.

Grand Hyatt San Antonio
600 E. Market Street
San Antonio, TX
210-224-1234
Located near the Alamo and Riverwalk, the Grand Hyatt affords their visitors and their dogs the best in luxury. The hotel offers dining, entertainment and a 24 hour fitness center. Dogs up to 50 pounds are allowed. There is a $35 per day additional pet fee.

Hawthorn Suites
13101 E Loop 1604 N
San Antonio, TX
210-655-9491 (800-527-1133)
In addition to providing a convenient location to many local sites and activities, this all-suite hotel offers a number of amenities for business and leisure travelers, including their signature breakfast buffet and beautifully appointed rooms. Dogs are allowed for an additional one time fee of $25 per pet. Multiple dogs may be allowed.

Hilton Hotel
611 NW Loop 410
San Antonio, TX
210-340-6060 (800-HILTONS (445-8667))
Located in the heart of the city, this upscale hotel offers numerous on site amenities for business and leisure travelers, plus a convenient location to an international airport, business, shopping, dining, sites of interest, and entertainment areas. Dogs are allowed for an additional one time fee of $75 per pet. 2 dogs may be allowed.

Holiday Inn Select San Antonio- Int'l Airport
77 N. E. Loop 410
San Antonio, TX
210-349-9900 (877-270-6405)
Dogs of all sizes are allowed. Dogs are allowed for a pet fee of $25.00 per pet per stay.

Homestead Studio Suites San Antonio - Airport
1015 Central Pkwy. S.
San Antonio, TX
210-491-9009 (800-804-3724)
One dog is allowed per suite. There is a $25 per night additional pet fee up to $150 for an entire stay.

Hotel Indigo San Antonio At The Alamo
105 N. Alamo
San Antonio, TX
210-933-2000 (877-865-6578)
Dogs of all sizes are allowed. Dogs are allowed for a pet fee of $35 per pet per night.

Hotel Indigo San Antonio-Riverwalk Area
830 North Saint Mary'S
San Antonio, TX
210-527-1900 (877-865-6578)
Dogs of all sizes are allowed. Dogs are allowed for a pet fee of $50.00 per pet per night.

Howard Johnson Express Inn - 2755 North Panam Expressway
San Antonio, TX
210-229-9220 (800-446-4656)
Dogs are welcome at this hotel. There is a $25 one time pet fee.

Howard Johnson Express Inn - San Antonio
13279 West I H 10
San Antonio, TX
210-558-7152 (800-446-4656)
Dogs are welcome at this hotel.

Howard Johnson Inn And Suites -Lackland/Seaworld San Antonio
6815 Highway 90 West
San Antonio, TX
210-675-9690 (800-446-4656)
Dogs are welcome at this hotel.

Howard Johnson Inn And Suites / Balcones Heights San Antonio
6901 IH 10 West
San Antonio, TX
210-738-1100 (800-446-4656)
Dogs are welcome at this hotel.

Knights Inn /Fort Sam Houston San Antonio
1131 Austin Highway
San Antonio, TX
210-828-8881 (800-843-5644)
Dogs are welcome at this hotel. There is a $25 per visit additional pet fee.

Knights Inn /Medical Center/Fiesta Area San Antonio
9447 IH 10 West
San Antonio, TX
210-558-9070 (800-843-5644)
Dogs of all sizes are allowed. Dogs are allowed for a pet fee of $10.00 per pet per night.

Knights Inn at Lackland AFB San Antonio

6735 Highway 90 West
San Antonio, TX
210-798-0160 (800-843-5644)
Dogs are welcome at this hotel.

La Quinta Inn & Suites San Antonio Airport
850 Halm Blvd
San Antonio, TX
210-342-3738 (800-531-5900)
Dogs of all sizes are allowed. There are no additional pet fees. Dogs must be leashed, cleaned up after, the front desk informed if a pet is in the room alone, and the Do Not Disturb sign placed on the door. Multiple dogs may be allowed.

La Quinta Inn & Suites San Antonio Downtown
100 W Durango Blvd
San Antonio, TX
210-212-5400 (800-531-5900)
Dogs of all sizes are allowed. There are no additional pet fees. Dogs may only be left unattended in the rooms for a short time, and they must be quiet, well behaved, leashed, and cleaned up after. Multiple dogs may be allowed.

La Quinta Inn San Antonio I-10 East
6075 I-10 East
San Antonio, TX
210-661-4545 (800-531-5900)
Dogs of all sizes are allowed. There are no additional pet fees. There is a pet waiver to sign at check in. Dogs must be leashed and cleaned up after. 2 dogs may be allowed.

La Quinta Inn San Antonio I-35 N at Rittiman Rd
6410 I-35 North
San Antonio, TX
210-653-6619 (800-531-5900)
One dog of any size is allowed. There are no additional pet fees. Dogs must be leashed, cleaned up after, and arrangements made for housekeeping.

La Quinta Inn San Antonio I-35 N at Toepperwein
12822 I-35 North
San Antonio, TX
210-657-5500 (800-531-5900)
Dogs of all sizes are allowed. There are no additional pet fees. Dogs must be leashed, cleaned up after, and crated or removed for housekeeping. Multiple dogs may be allowed.

La Quinta Inn San Antonio Lackland
6511 Military Drive West
San Antonio, TX

210-674-3200 (800-531-5900)
Dogs of all sizes are allowed. There are no additional pet fees. Dogs must be leashed, cleaned up after, and arrangements made for. Multiple dogs may be allowed.

La Quinta Inn San Antonio Market Square
900 Dolorosa St.
San Antonio, TX
210-271-0001 (800-531-5900)
Dogs of all sizes are allowed. There are no additional pet fees. Dogs must be leashed and cleaned up after. Multiple dogs may be allowed.

La Quinta Inn San Antonio Sea World/Ingram Park
7134 N.W. Loop 410
San Antonio, TX
210-680-8883 (800-531-5900)
Dogs of all sizes are allowed. There are no additional pet fees. Dogs must be leashed, cleaned up after, and arrangements made for housekeeping. Multiple dogs may be allowed.

La Quinta Inn San Antonio South Park
7202 South Pan Am Expwy.
San Antonio, TX
210-922-2111 (800-531-5900)
Dogs of all sizes are allowed. There are no additional pet fees. Dogs must be leashed, cleaned up after, and the Do Not Disturb sign left on the door if a pet is in the room alone. Multiple dogs may be allowed.

La Quinta Inn San Antonio Vance Jackson
5922 I-10 West
San Antonio, TX
210-734-7931 (800-531-5900)
Dogs of all sizes are allowed. There are no additional pet fees. Dogs must be leashed, cleaned up after, and crated or removed for housekeeping. Multiple dogs may be allowed.

La Quinta Inn San Antonio Wurzbach
9542 I-10 West
San Antonio, TX
210-593-0338 (800-531-5900)
Dogs of all sizes are allowed. There are no additional pet fees. Dogs must be leashed, cleaned up after, and a contact number left with the front desk if there is a pet alone in the room. Multiple dogs may be allowed.

Marriott Plaza San Antonio
555 S Alamo Street

San Antonio, TX
210-229-1000 (800-421-1172)
This resort-style hotel sits central to many of the city's star attractions, world class shopping and dining venues, major business, and day/night entertainment areas, plus they also offer a number of in-house amenities for all level of travelers. Dogs up to 50 pounds are allowed for an additional one time fee of $50 per room. 2 dogs may be allowed.

Marriott San Antonio Riverwalk
889 E Market Street
San Antonio, TX
210-224-4555 (800-648-4462)
Located on the famed San Antonio Riverwalk, this luxury hotel sits close to a number of the city's star attractions, world class shopping and dining venues, and major corporations; plus they offer a number of in-house amenities for all level of travelers. Dogs up to 50 pounds are allowed for an additional one time fee of $50 per pet. 2 dogs may be allowed.

Motel 6 - San Antonio Bandera Road
11425 Loop 1604
San Antonio, TX
210-695-6616 (800-466-8356)
This motel welcomes your pets to stay with you.

Motel 6 - San Antonio Fiesta
16500 I-10 West
San Antonio, TX
210-697-0731 (800-466-8356)
This motel welcomes your pets to stay with you.

Motel 6 - San Antonio Ft Sam Houston
5522 Panam Expwy
San Antonio, TX
210-661-8791 (800-466-8356)
This motel welcomes your pets to stay with you.

Motel 6 - San Antonio Downtown Market Square
211 Pecos La Trinidad
San Antonio, TX
210-225-1111 (800-466-8356)
This motel welcomes your pets to stay with you.

Motel 6 - San Antonio Downtown/ Alamodome
748 Hot Wells Blvd
San Antonio, TX
210-533-6667 (800-466-8356)
This motel welcomes your pets to stay with you.

Motel 6 - San Antonio East
138 Ww White Rd
San Antonio, TX
210-333-1850 (800-466-8356)
This motel welcomes your pets to stay with you.

Motel 6 - San Antonio Medical Center South
7500 Louis Pasteur Dr
San Antonio, TX
210-616-0030 (800-466-8356)
This motel welcomes your pets to stay with you.

Motel 6 - San Antonio North
9503 I-35 North
San Antonio, TX
210-650-4419 (800-466-8356)
This motel welcomes your pets to stay with you.

Motel 6 - San Antonio Northeast
4621 Rittiman Rd
San Antonio, TX
210-653-8088 (800-466-8356)
This motel welcomes your pets to stay with you.

Motel 6 - San Antonio Northwest Medical Center
9400 Wurzbach Rd
San Antonio, TX
210-593-0013 (800-466-8356)
This motel welcomes your pets to stay with you.

Motel 6 - San Antonio South
7950 Pan Am Expwy
San Antonio, TX
210-928-2866 (800-466-8356)
This motel welcomes your pets to stay with you.

Motel 6 - San Antonio West Seaworld
2185 Sw Loop 410
San Antonio, TX
210-673-9020 (800-466-8356)
This motel welcomes your pets to stay with you.

Motel 6 - San Antonio, Tx
126 Kenley Place
San Antonio, TX
210-447-9000 (800-466-8356)
This motel welcomes your pets to stay with you.

Quality Inn & Suites
222 South WW White Rd
San Antonio, TX
210-359-7200 (877-424-6423)
Dogs of all sizes are allowed. Dogs are allowed for a pet fee of $USD per pet per night.

Ramada Downtown San Antonio
1122 South Laredo Street
San Antonio, TX
210-229-1133 (800-272-6232)
Dogs of all sizes are allowed. Dogs are allowed for a pet fee of $10 per pet per night.

Red Roof Inn San Antonio - Airport
333 Wolf Road
San Antonio, TX
210-340-4055 (800-RED-ROOF)
One well-behaved family pet per room. Guest must notify front desk upon arrival. Guest is liable for any damages. In consideration of all guests, pets must never be left unattended in the guest rooms.

Red Roof Inn San Antonio - I-10 East
4403 I-10 East
San Antonio, TX
210-333-9430 (800-RED-ROOF)
One well-behaved family pet per room. Guest must notify front desk upon arrival. Guest is liable for any damages. In consideration of all guests, pets must never be left unattended in the guest rooms.

Red Roof Inn San Antonio - Lackland Southwest
6861 Highway 90 West
San Antonio, TX
210-675-4120 (800-RED-ROOF)
One well-behaved family pet per room. Guest must notify front desk upon arrival. Guest is liable for any damages. In consideration of all guests, pets must never be left unattended in the guest rooms.

Red Roof Inn San Antonio Downtown - Riverwalk
1011 East Houston Street
San Antonio, TX
210-229-9973 (800-RED-ROOF)
One well-behaved family pet per room. Guest must notify front desk upon arrival. Guest is liable for any damages. In consideration of all guests, pets must never be left unattended in the guest rooms.

Red Roof Inn San Antonio West - Sea World
6880 Northwest Loop 410
San Antonio, TX
210-509-3434 (800-RED-ROOF)
One well-behaved family pet per room. Guest must notify front desk upon arrival. Guest is liable for any damages. In consideration of all guests, pets must never be left unattended in the guest rooms.

Residence Inn San Antonio Airport
1014 NE Loop 410
San Antonio, TX
210-805-8118 (800-648-4462)
This all suite hotel sits central to many of the city's star attractions, shopping, dining, and business areas, plus they offer a number of in-house amenities that include a daily buffet breakfast and nightly social hours. Dogs are allowed for an additional one time pet fee of $100 per room. 2 dogs may be allowed.

Residence Inn San Antonio Downtown/Alamo Plaza
425 Bonham Street
San Antonio, TX
210-212-5555 (800-371-6349)
Located near the Alamo and only a few steps from the San Antonio River Walk, this all suite inn offers a great location to all this vibrant city has to offer, plus a daily buffet breakfast, and evening socials with light dinner fare Monday to Thursday. Dogs are allowed for an additional one time pet fee of $100 per room. 2 dogs may be allowed.

Residence Inn San Antonio Downtown/Market Square
628 S Santa Rosa Blvd
San Antonio, TX
210-231-6000 (800-331-3131)
This all suite hotel sits central to many of the city's star attractions, major corporations, event centers, and shopping and dining areas, plus they offer a number of in-house amenities that include a daily buffet breakfast and evening socials with light dinner fare. Dogs are allowed for an additional one time pet fee of $100 per room. Multiple dogs may be allowed.

Residence Inn San Antonio Northwest
4041 Bluemel Road
San Antonio, TX
210-561-9660 (800-228-9290)
Sea World Antonio, Six Flags, The Alamo, event centers, the Riverwalk, and several major corporations are all only a few minutes from this all suite inn. Additionally, they offer a daily buffet breakfast and evening social hours. Dogs are allowed for an additional one time pet fee of $75 per room. 2 dogs may be allowed.

Residence Inn San Antonio Seaworld
2838 Cinema Ridge
San Antonio, TX

210-509-3100 (800-704-9998)
Some of the amenities at this all-suite inn include a daily buffet breakfast, an evening hospitality hour Monday through Thursday, a pool, Sport Court, and a complimentary grocery shopping service. Dogs are allowed for an additional one time pet fee of $100 per room. Multiple dogs may be allowed.

Rodeway Inn Downtown
900 N. Main Ave.
San Antonio, TX
210-223-2951 (877-424-6423)
Dogs of all sizes are allowed. Dogs are allowed for a pet fee of $20 per pet per stay.

Sheraton Gunter Hotel San Antonio
205 East Houston St.
San Antonio, TX
210-227-3241 (888-625-5144)
Dogs up to 80 pounds are allowed. Dogs are not allowed to be left alone in the room.

Staybridge Suites San Antonio La Cantera
6919 North Loop 1604 West
San Antonio, TX
210-691-3443 (877-270-6405)
Dogs up to 80 pounds are allowed. Pets allowed with an additional pet fee. Up to $75 for 1-6 nights and up to $150 for 7+ nights. A pet agreement must be signed at check-in.

Staybridge Suites San Antonio Sunset Station
123 Hoefgen
San Antonio, TX
210-444-2700 (877-270-6405)
Dogs up to 80 pounds are allowed. Pets allowed with an additional pet fee. Up to $75 for 1-6 nights and up to $150 for 7+ nights. A pet agreement must be signed at check-in.

Staybridge Suites San Antonio-Airport
66 NE Loop 410
San Antonio, TX
210-341-3220 (877-270-6405)
Dogs up to 80 pounds are allowed. Pets allowed with an additional pet fee. Up to $75 for 1-6 nights and up to $150 for 7+ nights. A pet agreement must be signed at check-in.

Staybridge Suites San Antonio-Nw Colonnade
4320 Spectrum One

San Antonio, TX
210-558-9009 (877-270-6405)
Dogs up to 80 pounds are allowed. Pets allowed with an additional pet fee. Up to $75 for 1-6 nights and up to $150 for 7+ nights. A pet agreement must be signed at check-in.

Studio 6 - San Antonio Medical Center
7719 Pasteur Ct
San Antonio, TX
210-349-3100 (800-466-8356)
Your pets are welcome to stay here with you for a pet fee of $10 per day up to $50 for an entire stay.

Studio 6 - San Antonio Six Flags
11802 I-10 West
San Antonio, TX
210-691-0121 (800-466-8356)
Your pets are welcome to stay here with you for a pet fee of $10 per day up to $50 for an entire stay.

Super 8 /Airport San Antonio
11355 San Pedro Avenue
San Antonio, TX
210-342-8488 (800-800-8000)
Dogs of all sizes are allowed. Dogs are allowed for a pet fee of $15 per pet per night.

Super 8 /Fiesta San Antonio
5319 Casa Bella Street
San Antonio, TX
210-696-6916 (800-800-8000)
Dogs are welcome at this hotel.

Super 8 /I-35 North San Antonio
11027 IH 35 North
San Antonio, TX
210-637-1033 (800-800-8000)
Dogs of all sizes are allowed. Dogs are allowed for a pet fee.

Super 8 /Riverwalk Area San Antonio
302 Roland Avenue
San Antonio, TX
210-798-5500 (800-800-8000)
Dogs are welcome at this hotel.

Super 8 Downtown Riverwalk TX
1614 N St Mary's St
San Antonio, TX
210-222-8833 (800-800-8000)
Dogs of all sizes are allowed. Dogs are allowed for a nightly pet fee.

The Emily Morgan
705 East Houston Street
San Antonio, TX
210-225-5100 (800-824-6674)
emilymorganhotel.com/
Located only a few feet from one of the state's most famous landmarks-

The Alamo, this luxury boutique hotel offers numerous amenities, including special beds and pet menus for their canine visitors. Dogs are allowed for a $75 one time additional pet fee, but they must be declared at the time of reservations. 2 dogs may be allowed.

Travelodge ATT Center / I-10 East San Antonio
3939 East Houston Street
San Antonio, TX
210-359-1111 (800-578-7878)
Dogs of all sizes are allowed. Dogs are allowed for a pet fee of $20.00 per pet per night.

Travelodge -Alamo/Riverwalk/Conv. Ctr. San Antonio
405 Broadway
San Antonio, TX
210-222-1000 (800-578-7878)
Dogs of all sizes are allowed. Dogs are allowed for a pet fee.

Travelodge Ft Sam ATT Center
3821 IH-35 North
San Antonio, TX
210-224-5114 (800-578-7878)
Dogs of all sizes are allowed. Dogs are allowed for a pet fee of $25.00 per pet per stay.

Days Inn San Juan
112 W. Expressway 83
San Juan, TX
956-782-1510 (800-329-7466)
Dogs are welcome at this hotel.

Crystal River Inn
326 West Hopkins
San Marcos, TX
512-396-3739 (888 396-3739)
crystalriverinn.com/
In addition to the beautiful gardens and wooded areas, the handcrafted foods and ambiance of this 1883 Victorian inn, they also provide a variety of fun activities and special events year round. Dogs are allowed for an additional pet fee of $50 per room. Dogs must be crated when left alone in the room. 2 dogs may be allowed.

Days Inn - San Marcos
1005 I-H 35N
San Marcos, TX
512-353-5050 (800-329-7466)
Dogs are welcome at this hotel.

La Quinta Inn San Marcos
1619 I-35 North
San Marcos, TX
512-392-8800 (800-531-5900)

Dogs of all sizes are allowed. There are no additional pet fees. Dogs may not be left unattended for long periods, and they must be leashed and cleaned up after. The Do Not Disturb sign must be on the door if a pet is in the room alone, and arrangements need to be made with housekeeping is the stay is longer than 1 day. Multiple dogs may be allowed.

Motel 6 - San Marcos
1321 I-35
San Marcos, TX
512-396-8705 (800-466-8356)
This motel welcomes your pets to stay with you.

Ramada Limited - San Marcos
1701 I-35 North
San Marcos, TX
512-395-8000 (800-272-6232)
Dogs are welcome at this hotel.

Red Roof Inn San Marcos
817 I-35 North
San Marcos, TX
512-754-8899 (800-RED-ROOF)
One well-behaved family pet per room. Guest must notify front desk upon arrival. Guest is liable for any damages. In consideration of all guests, pets must never be left unattended in the guest rooms.

Rodeway Inn
1635 Aquarena Springs Dr
San Marcos, TX
512-353-8011 (877-424-6423)
Dogs of all sizes are allowed. Dogs are allowed for a pet fee of $10.00 per pet per night. Two dogs are allowed per room.

Super 8 San Marcos
1429 I-35 North
San Marcos, TX
512-396-0400 (800-800-8000)
Dogs are welcome at this hotel.

La Quinta Inn & Suites Houston-NASA/Seabrook
3636 Nasa Road 1
Seabrook, TX
281-326-7300 (800-531-5900)
Dogs up to 60 pounds are allowed. There are no additional pet fees. Dogs must be leashed, cleaned up after, and a contact number left with the front desk if a pet is alone in the room. Multiple dogs may be allowed.

Econo Lodge
311 South Segovia Express Rd
Segovia, TX
325-446-2475 (877-424-6423)

Dog-Friendly Lodging - Please always call ahead to make sure an establishment is still dog-friendly.

Dogs of all sizes are allowed. Dogs are allowed for a pet fee of $10.00 per pet per night.

Super 8 Seguin
1525 N Hwy 46
Seguin, TX
830-379-6888 (800-800-8000)
Dogs of all sizes are allowed. Dogs are allowed for a pet fee.

Econo Lodge
1006 E. 12th St.
Shamrock, TX
806-256-2111 (877-424-6423)
Dogs of all sizes are allowed.

Days Inn & Suites /Denison Sherman
3605 Hwy 75 S
Sherman, TX
903-868-0555 (800-329-7466)
Dogs are welcome at this hotel.

Super 8 Sherman
111 E FM 1417
Sherman, TX
903-868-9325 (800-800-8000)
Dogs of all sizes are allowed. Dogs are allowed for a pet fee of $10 per pet per night.

Motel 6 - Sinton
8154 Us 77
Sinton, TX
361-364-1853 (800-466-8356)
This motel welcomes your pets to stay with you.

Knights Inn Slaton
902 Highway 84
Slaton, TX
806-828-5831 (800-843-5644)
Dogs of all sizes are allowed. Dogs are allowed for a pet fee of $10.00 per pet per stay.

Katy House
201 Ramona Street
Smithville, TX
512-237-4262 (800-843-5289)
katyhouse.com/
Rich in turn-of-the-century charm, this inn also provides a convenient location to numerous local activities, recreation, and historical sites. Dogs are allowed for no additional fee in advance registration as long as there is no additional clean-up required for the pet. 2 dogs may be allowed.

Days Inn Devils River Sonora
1312 N. Service Rd.
Sonora, TX
325-387-3516 (800-329-7466)
Dogs are welcome at this hotel.

Affordable Beach House Vacation

Rentals
PO Box 3061
South Padre Island, TX
956-761-8750
They offer pet-friendly condos and vacation home rentals. Well mannered dogs are allowed for no additional fee. Aggressive breeds are not allowed. 2 dogs may be allowed.

Best Western LaCopa Inn & Suites
350 Padre Boulevard
South Padre Island, TX
956-761-6000 (800-780-7234)
Dogs of all sizes are allowed. Dogs are allowed for a pet fee of $25.00 per pet per night.

DCH Condo Rentals
111 E Hybiscus
South Padre Island, TX
956-459-7499
Well behaved dogs up to about 60 pounds are allowed. There is a $20 one time fee by the week, and a $50 one time fee by the month, plus a $50 refundable deposit. There are some breed restrictions.

Days Inn South Padre Island
3913 Padre Blvd
South Padre Island, TX
956-761-7831 (800-329-7466)
Dogs of all sizes are allowed. Dogs are allowed for a pet fee of $10.00 per pet per night.

Howard Johnson Express Inn - Resort South Padre Island
1709 Padre Blvd
South Padre Island, TX
956-761-5658 (800-446-4656)
Dogs of all sizes are allowed. Dogs are allowed for a pet fee.

La Quinta Inn & Suites South Padre Beach Resort
7000 Padre Blvd
South Padre Island, TX
956-772-7000 (800-531-5900)
Dogs of all sizes are allowed. There are no additional pet fees. There is a pet waiver to sign at check in. Dogs must be leashed and cleaned up after, and a contact number left with the front desk if there is a pet alone in the room. Multiple dogs may be allowed.

Motel 6 - South Padre Island
4013 Padre Blvd
South Padre Island, TX
956-761-7911 (800-466-8356)
This motel welcomes your pets to stay with you.

Ramada Limited - South Padre Island
4109 Padre Boulevard
South Padre Island, TX
956-761-4097 (800-272-6232)
Dogs of all sizes are allowed. Dogs are allowed for a pet fee.

Travelodge South Padre Island
6200 South Padre Blvd
South Padre Island, TX
956-761-4744 (800-578-7878)
Dogs of all sizes are allowed. Dogs are allowed for a pet fee.

Wanna Wanna Hotel
5100 Gulf Blvd.
South Padre Island, TX
956-761-7677
wannawanna.com/
Some of the popularities of this island-themed hotel include their beach front location and a beach bar and grill (dogs allowed at the outer tables). Well behaved dogs are allowed for an additional fee of $10 per night per pet,,, plus a $50 cash refundable deposit. 2 dogs may be allowed.

Extended Stay America Houston - The Woodlands
150 Valley Wood Rd.
Spring, TX
281-296-2799 (800-804-3724)
One dog is allowed per suite. There is a $25 per night additional pet fee up to $150 for an entire stay.

Motel 6 - Houston North Spring
19606 Cypresswood Ct
Spring, TX
281-350-6400 (800-466-8356)
This motel welcomes your pets to stay with you.

Extended Stay America Houston - Stafford
4726 Sugar Grove Blvd.
Stafford, TX
281-240-0025 (800-804-3724)
One dog is allowed per suite. There is a $25 per night additional pet fee up to $150 for an entire stay.

La Quinta Inn Houston Stafford/Sugarland
12727 Southwest Freeway
Stafford, TX
281-240-2300 (800-531-5900)
Dogs of all sizes are allowed. There are no additional pet fees. Dogs must be leashed, cleaned up after, and crated or removed for housekeeping. Multiple dogs may be allowed.

Residence Inn Houston Sugar Land
12703 Southwest Freeway
Stafford, TX
281-277-0770 (800-331-3131)
This all suite inn features a convenient location to business, shopping, dining, and entertainment areas, plus they also offer a number of in-house amenities, including a daily buffet breakfast and evening socials. Dogs are allowed for an additional one time pet fee of $100 per room. Multiple dogs may be allowed.

Studio 6 - Houston Sugarland
12827 Southwest Fwy
Stafford, TX
281-240-6900 (800-466-8356)
Your pets are welcome to stay here with you for a pet fee of $10 per day up to $50 for an entire stay.

Best Western Cross Timbers
1625 W South Loop
Stephenville, TX
254-968-2114 (800-780-7234)
Dogs of all sizes are allowed. Dogs are allowed for a pet fee.

Days Inn Stephenville
701 S Loop
Stephenville, TX
254-968-3392 (800-329-7466)
Dogs are welcome at this hotel.

Econo Lodge
2925 West Washington
Stephenville, TX
254-965-7162 (877-424-6423)
Dogs of all sizes are allowed. Dogs are allowed for a pet fee of $10.00/pet, per pet per night.

Super 8 Stephenville
921 S Second Street
Stephenville, TX
254-965-0888 (800-800-8000)
Dogs of all sizes are allowed. Dogs are allowed for a pet fee of $25 per pet per stay.

Easter Egg Valley Motel
H 170 1/2 mile W of H 118
Study Butte, TX
432-371-2254
This motel is at the gateway to the Big Bend National Park. Dogs of all sizes are allowed with a one time pet fee of $20 per room. Dogs may not be left uncrated in the room. 2 dogs may be allowed.

Comfort Suites
1521 Industrial Dr. East
Sulphur Springs, TX
903-438-0918 (877-424-6423)

Dogs of all sizes are allowed. Dogs are allowed for a pet fee of $5.00 per pet per night.

Days Inn Sweetwater
701 SW Georgia
Sweetwater, TX
325-235-4853 (800-329-7466)
Dogs of all sizes are allowed. Dogs are allowed for a pet fee.

Motel 6 - Sweetwater
510 Nw Georgia Ave
Sweetwater, TX
325-235-4387 (800-466-8356)
This motel welcomes your pets to stay with you.

Days Inn Temple
1104 N General Bruce Dr
Temple, TX
254-774-9223 (800-329-7466)
Dogs of all sizes are allowed. Dogs are allowed for a pet fee of $10.00 per pet per night.

Knights Inn Temple
802 N General Bruce Drive
Temple, TX
254-771-3631 (800-843-5644)
Dogs are welcome at this hotel. There is a $15 one time pet fee per pet.

La Quinta Inn Temple
1604 W. Barton Ave.
Temple, TX
254-771-2980 (800-531-5900)
Dogs of all sizes are allowed. There are no additional pet fees. Dogs must be leashed, cleaned up after, and attended to or removed for housekeeping. Multiple dogs may be allowed.

Motel 6 - Temple
1100 General Bruce Dr
Temple, TX
254-778-0272 (800-466-8356)
This motel welcomes your pets to stay with you.

Residence Inn Temple
4301 South General Bruce Drive
Temple, TX
254-773-8400 (800-331-3131)
Conveniently located near world class medical facilities as well as major companies and attractions, this all suite hotel offers a number of on-site amenities for both business and leisure travelers, including a daily buffet breakfast and evening socials with light dinner fare. Dogs are allowed for an additional one time pet fee of $100 per room. Multiple dogs may be

allowed.

Best Western Country Inn
1604 Highway 34 S
Terrell, TX
972-563-1521 (800-780-7234)
Dogs of all sizes are allowed. Dogs are allowed for a nightly pet fee.

Days Inn Terrell
1618 Highway 34 South
Terrell, TX
972-551-1170 (800-329-7466)
Dogs of all sizes are allowed. Dogs are allowed for a pet fee of $10 per pet per night.

Motel 6 - Terrell, Tx
101 Mira Place
Terrell, TX
972-563-0300 (800-466-8356)
This motel welcomes your pets to stay with you.

Super 8 Terrell
1705 Highway 34 South
Terrell, TX
972-563-1511 (800-800-8000)
Dogs of all sizes are allowed. Dogs are allowed for a pet fee.

Candlewood Suites Texarkana
2901 S Cowhorn Creek Loop
Texarkana, TX
903-334-7418 (877-270-6405)
Dogs up to 80 pounds are allowed. Pets allowed with an additional pet fee. Up to $75 for 1-6 nights and up to $150 for 7+ nights. A pet agreement must be signed at check-in.

Howard Johnson Texarkana
5401 N State Line Ave Bldg B
Texarkana, TX
903-792-2640 (800-446-4656)
Dogs of all sizes are allowed. Dogs are allowed for a pet fee of $25 per pet per stay.

La Quinta Inn Texarkana
5201 State Line Ave.
Texarkana, TX
903-794-1900 (800-531-5900)
Dogs of all sizes are allowed. There are no additional pet fees. Dogs may not be left unattended, and they must be leashed and cleaned up after. Multiple dogs may be allowed.

Motel 6 - Texarkana
1924 Hampton Rd
Texarkana, TX
903-793-1413 (800-466-8356)
This motel welcomes your pets to stay with you.

Rodeway Inn
5105 North Stateline Ave.
Texarkana, TX
903-792-6688 (877-424-6423)
Dogs of all sizes are allowed. Dogs are allowed for a pet fee of $15.00 per pet per stay.

TownePlace Suites Texarkana
5020 N Cowhorn Creek Loop Road
Texarkana, TX
903-334-8800 (800-257-3000)
Besides offering a number of in-house amenities for all level of travelers, this all suite inn also provides a convenient location to business, shopping, dining, and entertainment areas. Dogs are allowed for an additional one time fee of $75 per room. 2 dogs may be allowed.

Comfort Suites Near Stonebriar Mall
4796 Memorial Drive
The Colony, TX
972-668-5555 (877-424-6423)
Dogs of all sizes are allowed. Dogs are allowed for a pet fee of $15.00 per pet per night.

Houston - The Woodlands Drury Inn & Suites
28099 I-45 North
The Woodlands, TX
281-362-7222 (800-378-7946)
Dogs of all sizes are allowed for no additional pet fee with a credit card on file, and there is a pet agreement to sign at check in.

La Quinta Inn & Suites Woodlands South
24868 I-45 North
The Woodlands, TX
281-681-9188 (800-531-5900)
Dogs of all sizes are allowed. There are no additional pet fees. Dogs must be leashed and cleaned up after. Dogs are not allowed in the dining area at any time. Multiple dogs may be allowed.

La Quinta Inn The Woodlands North
28673 I-45 North
The Woodlands, TX
281-367-7722 (800-531-5900)
Dogs up to 100 pounds are allowed. There are no additional pet fees. Dogs must be friendly, leashed, cleaned up after, and crated or removed for housekeeping. 2 dogs may be allowed.

Residence Inn Houston The Woodlands/Lake Front Circle
1040 Lake Front Circle
The Woodlands, TX

281-292-3252 (800-331-3131)
This all suite inn features a convenient location to many sites of interest and business, shopping, dining, and entertainment areas, plus they also offer a number of in-house amenities, including a daily buffet breakfast, evening socials Monday to Wednesday, and weekly barbecues. Dogs are allowed for an additional one time pet fee of $100 per room. Multiple dogs may be allowed.

Residence Inn Houston The Woodlands/Market Street
9333 Six Pines Drive
The Woodlands, TX
281-419-1542 (800-331-3131)
Located near some of the area's most major corporations and only a few blocks from the Memorial Herman Hospital, this all suite inn also provides a complimentary hot breakfast and evening social hours. Dogs are allowed for an additional one time pet fee of $100 per room. Multiple dogs may be allowed.

La Quinta Inn & Suites Tomball
14000 Medical Complex Drive
Tomball, TX
281-516-0400 (800-531-5900)
Dogs of all sizes are allowed. There are no additional pet fees. There is a pet waiver to sign at check in, and there must be a credit card on file. Dogs must be leashed and cleaned up after. 2 dogs may be allowed.

Super 8 Tomball
1437 Keefer Road
Tomball, TX
832-559-6600 (800-800-8000)
Dogs of all sizes are allowed. Dogs are allowed for a pet fee of $25.00 per pet per stay.

Baymont Inn & Suites Tyler
3913 Frankston Hwy
Tyler, TX
903-939-0100 (877-229-6668)
Dogs of all sizes are allowed. Dogs are allowed for a pet fee.

Candlewood Suites Tyler
315 E. Rieck Rd
Tyler, TX
903-509-4131 (877-270-6405)
Dogs up to 80 pounds are allowed. Pets allowed with an additional pet fee. Up to $75 for 1-6 nights and up to $150 for 7+ nights. A pet agreement must be signed at check-in.

Days Inn And Suites Tyler

2739 W Northwest Loop 323
Tyler, TX
903-531-9513 (800-329-7466)
Dogs of all sizes are allowed. Dogs are allowed for a pet fee of $10.00 per pet per stay.

Holiday Inn Tyler-South Broadway
5701 South Broadway
Tyler, TX
903-561-5800 (877-270-6405)
Dogs of all sizes are allowed. Dogs are allowed for a pet fee. Two dogs are allowed per room.

Motel 6 - Tyler
3236 Gentry Pkwy
Tyler, TX
903-595-6691 (800-466-8356)
This motel welcomes your pets to stay with you.

Ramada - Tyler
3310 Troup Highway
Tyler, TX
903-593-3600 (800-272-6232)
Dogs of all sizes are allowed. Dogs are allowed for a nightly pet fee.

Residence Inn Tyler
3303 Troup Highway
Tyler, TX
903-595-5188 (903-595-5188)
In addition to offering a convenient location to numerous sites of interest - like America's largest rose garden, year around activities, and a variety of attractions for business or pleasure travelers, this all suite hotel also offers a number of in-house amenities, including a daily buffet breakfast and evening socials. Dogs are allowed for an additional one time pet fee of $100 per room. 2 dogs may be allowed.

Days Inn TX Van Horn
600 East Broadway
Van Horn, TX
432-283-1007 (800-329-7466)
Dogs of all sizes are allowed. Dogs are allowed for a pet fee.

Econo Lodge
1601 W. Broadway St.
Van Horn, TX
432-283-2211 (877-424-6423)
Dogs up to 50 pounds are allowed. Dogs are allowed for a pet fee of $10.00 per pet per night. Two dogs are allowed per room.

Knights Inn Van Horn
1309 West Broadway
Van Horn, TX
432-283-2030 (800-843-5644)
Dogs are welcome at this hotel.

There is an $8 one time additional pet fee.

Motel 6 - Van Horn
1805 Broadway
Van Horn, TX
432-283-2992 (800-466-8356)
This motel welcomes your pets to stay with you.

Ramada Limited Van Horn
200 Golf Course Drive
Van Horn, TX
432-283-2800 (800-272-6232)
Dogs of all sizes are allowed. Dogs are allowed for a nightly pet fee.

Super 8 Van Horn
1807 E Service Road
Van Horn, TX
432-283-2282 (800-800-8000)
Dogs are welcome at this hotel.

Best Western Country Inn
1800 W Vega Boulevard
Vega, TX
806-267-2131 (800-780-7234)
Dogs are welcome at this hotel.

Comfort Inn
1005 South Main St
Vega, TX
806-267-0126 (877-424-6423)
Dogs of all sizes are allowed. Dogs are allowed for a pet fee of $10.00 per pet per night.

Days Inn Vernon
3110 Highway 287 West
Vernon, TX
940-552-9982 (800-329-7466)
Dogs are welcome at this hotel.

Super 8 Vernon
1829 Hwy 287
Vernon, TX
940-552-9321 (800-800-8000)
Dogs of all sizes are allowed. Dogs are allowed for a pet fee.

Best Western Victoria Inn & Suites
8106 NE Zac Lentz Pkwy
Victoria, TX
361-485-2300 (800-780-7234)
Dogs of all sizes are allowed. Dogs are allowed for a pet fee of $20.00 per pet per night.

Candlewood Suites Victoria
7103 N. Navarro Street
Victoria, TX
361-578-0236 (877-270-6405)
Dogs up to 80 pounds are allowed. Pets allowed with an additional pet fee. Up to $75 for 1-6 nights and up to $150 for 7+ nights. A pet agreement must be signed at check-in.

La Quinta Inn Victoria
7603 N. Navarro
Victoria, TX
361-572-3585 (800-531-5900)
Dogs of all sizes are allowed. There are no additional pet fees. Dogs may not be left unattended, and they must be leashed and cleaned up after. Multiple dogs may be allowed.

Motel 6 - Victoria
3716 Houston Hwy
Victoria, TX
361-573-1273 (800-466-8356)
This motel welcomes your pets to stay with you.

La Quinta Inn Vidor
165 East Courtland Street
Vidor, TX
409-783-2600 (800-531-5900)
Dogs of all sizes are allowed. There are no additional pet fees. Dogs may not be left unattended for long periods and not at all during the night. Dogs must be leashed and cleaned up after. Multiple dogs may be allowed.

Days Inn Waco
1504 I-35 North
Waco, TX
254-799-8585 (800-329-7466)
Dogs are welcome at this hotel.

Extended Stay America Waco - Woodway
5903 Woodway Dr.
Waco, TX
254-399-8836 (800-804-3724)
One dog is allowed per suite. There is a $25 per night additional pet fee up to $150 for an entire stay.

Hilton Hotel
113 S University Parks Drive
Waco, TX
254-754-8484 (800-HILTONS (445-8667))
Located downtown overlooking the Brazos River, this upscale hotel offers numerous on site amenities for business and leisure travelers, plus a convenient location to business, shopping, dining, and entertainment areas. Dogs up to 75 pounds are allowed for an additional one time fee of $75 per pet. Dogs must be declared at the time of reservations, and a contact number left with the front desk if there is a pet alone in the room. 2 dogs may be allowed.

Knights Inn South Waco
3829 Franklin Ave
Waco, TX
254-754-0363 (800-843-5644)
Dogs of all sizes are allowed. Dogs are allowed for a pet fee of $10.00 per pet per night.

La Quinta Inn Waco University
1110 S. 9th St.
Waco, TX
254-752-9741 (800-531-5900)
Dogs of all sizes are allowed. There are no additional pet fees. Dogs must be leashed, cleaned up after, and crated or removed for housekeeping. Multiple dogs may be allowed.

Motel 6 - Waco South
3120 Jack Kultgen Fwy
Waco, TX
254-662-4622 (800-466-8356)
This motel welcomes your pets to stay with you.

Residence Inn Waco
501 University Parks Drive
Waco, TX
254-714-1386 (800-331-3131)
In addition to offering a central location to numerous sites of interest, activities, and attractions for business or leisure travelers, this all suite hotel also offers a number of in-house amenities, including a daily buffet breakfast and evening socials Monday to Wednesday. Dogs are allowed for an additional one time pet fee of $100 per room. Multiple dogs may be allowed.

Super 8 /Mall area TX Waco
6624 W. Highway 84
Waco, TX
254-776-3194 (800-800-8000)
Dogs of all sizes are allowed. Dogs are allowed for a pet fee.

Travelodge Waco
7007 Waco Drive
Waco, TX
254-751-7400 (800-578-7878)
Dogs of all sizes are allowed. Dogs are allowed for a pet fee of $25.00 per pet per stay.

Knights Inn And Suites Waxahachie
803 S IH-35 E
Waxahachie, TX
972-937-8223 (800-843-5644)
Dogs are welcome at this hotel.

Super 8 TX Waxahachie
400 N I-35 East
Waxahachie, TX
972-938-9088 (800-800-8000)

Dogs of all sizes are allowed. Dogs are allowed for a pet fee.

Best Western Santa Fe Inn
1927 Santa Fe Drive
Weatherford, TX
817-594-7401 (800-780-7234)
Dogs of all sizes are allowed. Dogs are allowed for a pet fee of $10.00 per pet per stay.

Comfort Suites
210 Alford Drive
Weatherford, TX
817-599-3300 (877-424-6423)
Dogs are allowed for a $10 one time additional pet fee per room. Dogs may not be left alone in the room.

La Quinta Inn & Suites Weatherford
1915 Wall Street (c/o Adams St.)
Weatherford, TX
817-594-4481 (800-531-5900)
Dogs of all sizes are allowed. There are no additional pet fees. Dogs may not be left unattended, and they must be quiet, leashed, and cleaned up after. Multiple dogs may be allowed.

Motel 6 - Weatherford, Tx
150 Alford Dr
Weatherford, TX
817-594-1740 (800-466-8356)
This motel welcomes your pets to stay with you.

Super 8 Weatherford
720 Adams Drive
Weatherford, TX
817-598-0852 (800-800-8000)
Dogs of all sizes are allowed. Dogs are allowed for a pet fee.

Comfort Suites
16931 N. Texas Ave
Webster, TX
281-554-5400 (877-424-6423)
Dogs up to 80 pounds are allowed. Dogs are allowed for a pet fee of $50.00 per pet per stay.

La Quinta Inn & Suites Webster - Clearlake
520 West Bay Area Boulevard
Webster, TX
281-554-5290 (800-531-5900)
Dogs of all sizes are allowed. There are no additional pet fees. Dogs may not be left unattended, and they must be leashed and cleaned up after. Multiple dogs may be allowed.

Motel 6 - Houston Nasa
1001 Nasa Road
Webster, TX
281-332-4581 (800-466-8356)
This motel welcomes your pets to stay with you.

Staybridge Suites Houston- Clear Lake
501 W. Texas Ave
Webster, TX
281-338-0900 (877-270-6405)
Dogs up to 80 pounds are allowed. Pets allowed with an additional pet fee. Up to $75 for 1-6 nights and up to $150 for 7+ nights. A pet agreement must be signed at check-in.

Days Inn Weimar
102 Townsend Drive
Weimar, TX
979-725-9700 (800-329-7466)
Dogs are welcome at this hotel.

Super 8 Weslaco
1702 E Expressway 83
Weslaco, TX
956-969-9920 (800-800-8000)
Dogs are welcome at this hotel.

La Quinta Inn Fort Worth West/Medical Center
7888 I-30 West
White Settlement, TX
817-246-5511 (800-531-5900)
Dogs of all sizes are allowed. There are no additional pet fees. Dogs must be leashed, cleaned up after, and crated or removed for housekeeping. Multiple dogs may be allowed.

Baymont Inn & Suites Wichita Falls
4510 Kell Blvd
Wichita Falls, TX
940-691-7500 (877-229-6668)
Dogs are welcome at this hotel.

Best Western Northtown Inn
1317 Kenley Avenue
Wichita Falls, TX
940-766-3300 (800-780-7234)
Dogs of all sizes are allowed. Dogs are allowed for a nightly pet fee.

Best Western Wichita Falls Inn
1032 Central Freeway
Wichita Falls, TX
940-766-6881 (800-780-7234)
Dogs of all sizes are allowed. Dogs are allowed for a nightly pet fee.

Candlewood Suites Wichita Falls @ Maurine St.
1320 Central Freeway
Wichita Falls, TX
940-322-4400 (877-270-6405)
Dogs up to 80 pounds are allowed. Pets allowed with an additional pet fee. Up to $75 for 1-6 nights and up to $150 for 7+ nights. A pet

agreement must be signed at check-in.

Econo Lodge
1700 Fifth St.
Wichita Falls, TX
940-761-1889 (877-424-6423)
Dogs of all sizes are allowed. Dogs are allowed for a pet fee of $7.00 per pet per night.

Hawthorn Suites
1917 Elmwood Avenue N
Wichita Falls, TX
940-692-7900 (800-527-1133)
In addition to providing a convenient location to many local sites and activities, this all-suite hotel offers a number of amenities for business and leisure travelers, including their signature breakfast buffet and beautifully appointed rooms. Dogs are allowed in the 1st floor, main and executive building rooms for an additional one time pet fee of $50 per room. There is a fenced dog run for their dog visitors. Multiple dogs may be allowed.

Howard Johnson Plaza Wichita Falls
401 Broad Street
Wichita Falls, TX
940-766-6000 (800-446-4656)
Dogs are welcome at this hotel.

La Quinta Inn Wichita Falls Airport Area
1128 Central Frwy. North
Wichita Falls, TX
940-322-6971 (800-531-5900)
Dogs of all sizes are allowed. There are no additional pet fees. Dogs must be quiet, well behaved, leashed, cleaned up after, and crated when left alone in the room. Multiple dogs may be allowed.

Motel 6 - Wichita Falls
1812 Maurine St
Wichita Falls, TX
940-322-8817 (800-466-8356)
This motel welcomes your pets to stay with you.

Ramada Limited - /Sheppard AFB Area Wichita Falls
3209 Hwy 287
Wichita Falls, TX
940-855-0085 (800-272-6232)
Dogs are welcome at this hotel.

Days Inn and Suites Winnie
14932 FM 1663 Rd
Winnie, TX
409-296-2866 (800-329-7466)
Dogs of all sizes are allowed. Dogs are allowed for a pet fee of $20.00

per pet per stay.

Quality Inn
46318 I-10 East
Winnie, TX
409-296-9292 (877-424-6423)
Dogs of all sizes are allowed. Dogs
are allowed for a pet fee of $10.00
per pet per night. Two dogs are
allowed per room.

Studio 6 - Winnie
134 Spur
Winnie, TX
409-296-3611 (800-466-8356)
Your pets are welcome to stay here
with you for a pet fee of $10 per day
up to $50 for an entire stay.

Best Western Wylie Inn
2011 N Highway 78
Wylie, TX
972-429-1771 (800-780-7234)
Dogs are welcome at this hotel.

Best Western Inn by the Lake
1896 S US Highway 83
Zapata, TX
956-765-8403 (800-780-7234)
Dogs of all sizes are allowed. Dogs
are allowed for a pet fee of $5.00 per
pet per stay.

Utah

Best Western Butch Cassidy Inn
161 S Main
Beaver, UT
435-438-2438 (800-780-7234)
Dogs of all sizes are allowed. Dogs
are allowed for a pet fee.

Super 8 UT Beaver
626 W 1400 N
Beaver, UT
435-438-3888 (800-800-8000)
Dogs are welcome at this hotel.

Four Corners Inn
131 E Center St
Blanding, UT
435-678-3257
moabutah.com/fourcornersinn/
There are no additional pet fees.
Dogs are not allowed on the beds.
Multiple dogs may be allowed.

Howard Johnson Inn - Brigham City
1167 South Main/I-15
Brigham City, UT
435-723-8511 (800-446-4656)
Dogs are welcome at this hotel.

Best Western Ruby's Inn
Highway 63

Bryce Canyon City, UT
435-834-5341 (800-780-7234)
Dogs are welcome at this hotel.

Days Inn Cedar City
1204 South Main
Cedar City, UT
435-867-8877 (800-329-7466)
Dogs of all sizes are allowed. Dogs
are allowed for a pet fee of $10.00
per pet per night.

Motel 6 - Cedar City
1620 200
Cedar City, UT
435-586-9200 (800-466-8356)
This motel welcomes your pets to
stay with you.

Super 8 Cedar City
I-15 Exit 59.
Cedar City, UT
435-586-8880 (800-800-8000)
Dogs of all sizes are allowed. Dogs
are allowed for a pet fee of $15 per
pet per night.

Days Inn Clearfield
572 North Main St
Clearfield, UT
801-825-8000 (800-329-7466)
Dogs are welcome at this hotel.

Best Western Holiday Hills
200 South 500 West
Coalville, UT
435-336-4444 (800-780-7234)
Dogs of all sizes are allowed. Dogs
are allowed for a nightly pet fee.

Days Inn Delta
527 E. Topaz Blvd
Delta, UT
435-864-3882 (800-329-7466)
Dogs of all sizes are allowed. Dogs
are allowed for a pet fee.

Ramada Limited Salt Lake City
Draper
12605 South Minuteman Drive
Draper, UT
801-571-1122 (800-272-6232)
Dogs of all sizes are allowed. Dogs
are allowed for a pet fee of $10.00
per pet per night.

Rosebud Guest House
Call to Arrange
Fruitland, UT
435-548-2630 (866-618-7194)
rosebudguesthouse.com
This B&B is located on 40 acres. It
is pet-friendly, there are no weight
limits for dogs. You may even bring
a horse, mule, or llama and they
have stalls.

Holiday Inn Express Green River
1845 E. Main St.
Green River, UT
435-564-4439 (877-270-6405)
Dogs of all sizes are allowed. Dogs
are allowed for a pet fee of $10.00
per pet per night.

Motel 6 - Green River
1860 East Main St
Green River, UT
435-564-3436 (800-466-8356)
This motel welcomes your pets to
stay with you.

Ramada Limited Green River
1117 East Main
Green River, UT
435-564-8441 (800-272-6232)
Dogs of all sizes are allowed. Dogs
are allowed for a pet fee.

Super 8 Green River
I-70 East West Exit 164
Green River, UT
435-564-8888 (800-800-8000)
Dogs are welcome at this hotel.

Rodeway Inn
650 W State St
Hurricane, UT
435-635-4010 (877-424-6423)
Dogs of all sizes are allowed.

Super 8 Zion National Park
Hurricane
65 S 700 West
Hurricane, UT
435-635-0808 (800-800-8000)
Dogs of all sizes are allowed. Dogs
are allowed for a pet fee of $15 per
pet per night.

Red Mountain Resort and Spa
1275 E Red Mountain Circle
Ivins, UT
435-673-4905 (877-246-HIKE
(4453))
redmountainspa.com/
Set among a popular destination rich
in recreational pursuits, this inn
offers its own full calendar of
activities and special events. Some
of the offerings of this health minded
resort include dining on skillfully
prepared healthy cuisine - and
learning about it too at their Eat Well,
Feel Well Culinary School, and
enjoying world class salon and spa
services, as well as numerous
recreational pursuits. They also offer
fitness classes/workshops, wellness
education/assessment, personal
training, and weight loss and
detoxification programs. Dogs are
allowed for an additional fee of $50
per week per pet and they must be

declared at the time of reservations. Dogs must be leashed when out of the room, cleaned up after promptly, and crated when left alone in the room. Dogs are not allowed in the spa, dining, or activity areas. 2 dogs may be allowed.

Best Western Red Hills
125 W Center Street
Kanab, UT
435-644-2675 (800-780-7234)
Dogs of all sizes are allowed. Dogs are allowed for a pet fee of $10.00 per pet per stay.

Parry Lodge
89 East Center Street
Kanab, UT
435-644-2601 (800-748-4104)
infowest.com/parry/
There are 3 non-smoking pet rooms. There is a $10 per day per pet fee. 2 dogs may be allowed.

Quail Park Lodge
125 N 300 W/H 89
Kanab, UT
435-644-8700
quailparklodge.com/
Besides offering a number of on-site amenities, this inn also provides a great location for exploring all this area has to offer. Well mannered dogs are allowed for no additional fee. 2 dogs may be allowed.

Quality Hotel
815 East Highway 89
Kanab, UT
435-644-8888 (877-424-6423)
Dogs up to 75 pounds are allowed. Dogs are allowed for a pet fee of $10.00 per pet per night. Two dogs are allowed per room.

Shilo Inn
296 West 100 North
Kanab, UT
435-644-2562 (800-222-2244)
shiloinns.com/Utah/kanab.html
There is a $25 per night per room additional pet fee. 2 dogs may be allowed.

Comfort Inn
877 North 400 West
Layton, UT
801-544-5577 (877-424-6423)
Dogs of all sizes are allowed. Dogs are allowed for a pet fee of $25.00 per pet per stay. Two dogs are allowed per room.

La Quinta Inn Salt Lake City Layton
1965 North 1200 W.
Layton, UT

801-776-6700 (800-531-5900)
Dogs of all sizes are allowed. There are no additional pet fees. Dogs must be quiet, well behaved, leashed, and cleaned up after. Multiple dogs may be allowed.

TownePlace Suites Salt Lake City Layton
1743 Woodland Park Blvd
Layton, UT
801-779-2422 (800-257-3000)
This all suite hotel sits central to a number of sites of interest for both business and leisure travelers; plus they also offer a number of on-site amenities to ensure comfort. Dogs are allowed for an additional one time fee of $75 per room. Multiple dogs may be allowed.

Best Western Timpanogos Inn
195 S 850 E
Lehi, UT
801-768-1400 (800-780-7234)
Dogs of all sizes are allowed. Dogs are allowed for a pet fee of $10.00 per pet per stay.

Motel 6 - Salt Lake City South Lehi
210 1200
Lehi, UT
801-768-2668 (800-466-8356)
This motel welcomes your pets to stay with you.

Super 8 Lehi
125 South 850 East
Lehi, UT
801-766-8800 (800-800-8000)
Dogs are welcome at this hotel.

Best Western Weston Inn
250 N Main Street
Logan, UT
435-752-5700 (800-780-7234)
Dogs of all sizes are allowed. Dogs are allowed for a pet fee of $15.00 per pet per stay.

Holiday Inn Express Hotel & Suites Logan
2235 North Main Street
Logan, UT
435-752-3444 (877-270-6405)
Dogs of all sizes are allowed. Dogs are allowed for a nightly pet fee.

Super 8 Logan
865 So. Main St
Logan, UT
435-753-8883 (800-800-8000)
Dogs of all sizes are allowed. Dogs are allowed for a pet fee of $10.00 per pet per night.

Best Western Executive Inn

280 W 7200 S
Midvale, UT
801-566-4141 (800-780-7234)
Dogs of all sizes are allowed. Dogs are allowed for a nightly pet fee.

Extended Stay America Salt Lake City - Union Park
7555 S. Union Park Ave.
Midvale, UT
801-567-0404 (800-804-3724)
One dog is allowed per suite. There is a $25 per night additional pet fee up to $150 for an entire stay.

Motel 6 - Salt Lake City South Midvale
7263 Catalpa St
Midvale, UT
801-561-0058 (800-466-8356)
This motel welcomes your pets to stay with you.

Super 8 Pride /Midvalley/Salt Lake City Area Midvale
7048 S 900 E
Midvale, UT
801-255-5559 (800-800-8000)
Dogs are welcome at this hotel.

Apache Hotel
166 S 400 East
Moab, UT
435-259-5727 (800-228-6882)
moab-utah.com/apachemotel/
Dogs are allowed for no additional fee. Dogs may not be left alone in the room at any time. 2 dogs may be allowed.

Bowen Motel
169 N Main St
Moab, UT
435-259-7132
moab-utah.com/bowen/motel.html
There is a $10 per night per room additional pet fee. 2 dogs may be allowed.

Comfort Suites
800 S. Main St.
Moab, UT
435-259-5252 (877-424-6423)
Dogs of all sizes are allowed.

Days Inn Moab
426 North Main Street
Moab, UT
435-259-4468 (800-329-7466)
Dogs are welcome at this hotel.

Kokopelli Lodge and Suites
72 S 100 E
Moab, UT
435-259-7615 (888-530-3134)
kokopellilodge.com/
This charming 1950's inn offers a

quiet residential setting only a short walk from town. Dogs are allowed for an additional fee of $5 per night per pet. Canine guests get a loaner doggy rug and healthy treats, and their owners receive a list of dog hike areas. 2 dogs may be allowed.

La Quinta Inn Moab
815 S. Main St.
Moab, UT
435-259-8700 (800-531-5900)
Dogs of all sizes are allowed. There are no additional pet fees. There is a pet waiver to sign at check in. Dogs must be leashed, cleaned up after, and crated if left alone in the room. Dogs are not allowed in the food areas, and they must be walked at the designated pet walk area. Multiple dogs may be allowed.

Moab Valley Inn
711 S Main St
Moab, UT
435-259-4419 (800-831-6622)
moabvalleyinn.com/
There is a $10 per night per room additional pet fee. Dogs must be declared at the time of reservations. 2 dogs may be allowed.

Motel 6 - Moab
1089 Main St
Moab, UT
435-259-6686 (800-466-8356)
This motel welcomes your pets to stay with you.

River Canyon Lodge
71 W 200 N
Moab, UT
435-259-8838
Dogs are allowed for an additional one time fee of $20 per pet. 2 dogs may be allowed.

Sleep Inn
1051 S. Main Street
Moab, UT
435-259-4655 (877-424-6423)
Dogs of all sizes are allowed.

Super 8 Moab
889 North Main Street
Moab, UT
435-259-8868 (800-800-8000)
Dogs are welcome at this hotel.

The Gonzo Inn
100 W 200 S
Moab, UT
435-259-2515
Dogs of all sizes are allowed. There is a $30 per night per room fee and a pet policy to sign at check in.

Best Western Wayside Motor Inn
197 E Central
Monticello, UT
435-587-2261 (800-780-7234)
Dogs are welcome at this hotel.

Rodeway Inn & Suites
649 North Main St.
Monticello, UT
435-587-2489 (877-424-6423)
Dogs of all sizes are allowed. Two dogs are allowed per room.

Goulding's Lodge
1000 Main Street
Monument Valley, UT
435-727-3231
gouldings.com/
Well-behaved leashed dogs of all sizes are welcome. There is a $20 per night per pet additional pet fee. The rooms offer views of Monument Valley. The lodge is located north of the Arizona and Utah border, adjacent to the Navajo Tribal Park in Monument Valley. Thanks to one of our readers for recommending this lodging. Multiple dogs may be allowed.

Studio 6 - Salt Lake City Fort Union
975 6600
Murray, UT
801-685-2102 (800-466-8356)
Your pets are welcome to stay here with you for a pet fee of $10 per day up to $50 for an entire stay.

Motel 6 - Nephi
2195 Main St
Nephi, UT
435-623-0666 (800-466-8356)
This motel welcomes your pets to stay with you.

Super 8 Nephi
1901 S Main
Nephi, UT
435-623-0888 (800-800-8000)
Dogs of all sizes are allowed. Dogs are allowed for a pet fee of $10.00 per pet per night.

Best Western CottonTree Inn
1030 N 400 E
North Salt Lake, UT
801-292-7666 (800-780-7234)
Dogs are welcome at this hotel.

Best Western High Country Inn
1335 W 12th Street
Ogden, UT
801-394-9474 (800-780-7234)
Dogs are welcome at this hotel.

Comfort Suites
2250 S. 1200 W.

Ogden, UT
801-621-2545 (877-424-6423)
Dogs of all sizes are allowed.

Days Inn Ogden
3306 Washington Blvd
Ogden, UT
801-399-5671 (800-329-7466)
Dogs of all sizes are allowed. Dogs are allowed for a pet fee.

Motel 6 - Ogden
1455 Washington Blvd
Ogden, UT
801-627-4560 (800-466-8356)
This motel welcomes your pets to stay with you.

Motel 6 - Ogden Riverdale
1500 West Riverdale Road
Ogden, UT
801-627-2880 (800-466-8356)
This motel welcomes your pets to stay with you.

Sleep Inn
1155 S. 1700 W.
Ogden, UT
801-731-6500 (877-424-6423)
Dogs of all sizes are allowed. Dogs are allowed for a pet fee of $10.00 per pet per night.

Super 8 Ogden
I-15 Exit 343
Ogden, UT
801-731-7100 (800-800-8000)
Dogs of all sizes are allowed. Dogs are allowed for a pet fee of $10.00 per pet per night.

Comfort Inn & Suites
427 West University Parkway
Orem, UT
801-431-0405 (877-424-6423)
Dogs of all sizes are allowed. Two dogs are allowed per room.

La Quinta Inn & Suites Orem University Parkway
521 W. University Parkway
Orem, UT
801-226-0440 (800-531-5900)
Dogs of all sizes are allowed. There are no additional pet fees. Dogs must be quiet, leashed, and cleaned up after. Multiple dogs may be allowed.

La Quinta Inn Orem/Provo North
1100 West 780 North
Orem, UT
801-235-9555 (800-531-5900)
Dogs of all sizes are allowed. There are no additional pet fees. Dogs may not be left unattended, and they must be quiet, well behaved, leashed and

cleaned up after. Multiple dogs may be allowed.

Bryce Way Motel
429 N Main St
Panguitch, UT
435-676-2400
brycemotel.com
Pets are allowed for a $5 per night per pet additional fee. 2 dogs may be allowed.

Marianna Inn Motel
699 N Main St
Panguitch, UT
435-676-8844
mariannainn.com
Dogs of all sizes are allowed for a $5 per night per pet additional pet fee. The hotel is about 20 miles from Bryce. Multiple dogs may be allowed.

Best Western Landmark Inn
6560 N Landmark Drive
Park City, UT
435-649-7300 (800-780-7234)
Dogs of all sizes are allowed. Dogs are allowed for a nightly pet fee.

Holiday Inn Express Hotel & Suites Park City
1501 W. Ute Blvd.
Park City, UT
435-658-1600 (877-270-6405)
Dogs of all sizes are allowed. Dogs are allowed for a pet fee of $20 per pet per night.

The Gables Hotel
1335 Lowell Avenue, PO Box 905
Park City, UT
435-655-3315 (800-443-1045)
thegablespc.com
Pets receive a Pet Gift basket upon arrival. The Gables Hotel features 20 one bedroom condominiums and one or two bedroom penthouse suites each with a queen or king bed in the master bedroom, fully equipped kitchen, living area with a queen sofa sleeper, dining area, fireplace, balcony and bathroom with an oversized jetted tub. Property amenities include an outdoor Jacuzzi, sauna and laundry facilities. Rates start at $85.00 per night. There is a $20 per night additional pet fee. There is a $100 refundable pet deposit upon arrival.

Comfort Inn
830 N. Main St.
Payson, UT
801-465-4861 (877-424-6423)
Dogs up to 50 pounds are allowed. Dogs are allowed for a pet fee of $20.00 per pet per stay. Two dogs

are allowed per room.

National 9
641 W. Price River Drive
Price, UT
435-637-7000
There is a $10 per day per pet fee. Multiple dogs may be allowed.

Best Western CottonTree Inn
2230 N University Pkwy
Provo, UT
801-373-7044 (800-780-7234)
Dogs up to 50 pounds are allowed. Dogs are allowed for a pet fee.

Days Inn Provo
1675 North 200 West
Provo, UT
801-375-8600 (800-329-7466)
Dogs of all sizes are allowed. Dogs are allowed for a pet fee.

Econo Lodge
1625 West Center St
Provo, UT
801-373-0099 (877-424-6423)
Dogs of all sizes are allowed. Dogs are allowed for a pet fee of $10.00 per pet per night. Three or more dogs may be allowed.

Residence Inn Provo
252 W 2230 N
Provo, UT
801-374-1000 (800-331-3131)
This all suite inn features a convenient location to the Brigham Young University, business, shopping, dining, entertainment, and year around recreation areas, plus they also offer a number of in-house amenities, including a daily buffet breakfast and evening socials. Dogs are allowed for an additional one time pet fee of $100 per room. Multiple dogs may be allowed.

Sleep Inn
1505 South 40 East
Provo, UT
801-377-6597 (877-424-6423)
Dogs up to 50 pounds are allowed. Dogs are allowed for a pet fee of $10.00 per pet per night.

Super 8 BYU Orem Provo
1555 N Canyon Road
Provo, UT
801-374-6020 (800-800-8000)
Dogs of all sizes are allowed. Dogs are allowed for a pet fee of $20 per pet per night.

Days Inn Richfield
333 North Main/I-70

Richfield, UT
435-896-6476 (800-329-7466)
Dogs of all sizes are allowed. Dogs are allowed for a pet fee of $10 per pet per stay.

Holiday Inn Express Hotel & Suites Richfield
20 W. 1400 N.
Richfield, UT
435-896-8552 (877-270-6405)
Dogs of all sizes are allowed. Dogs are allowed for a pet fee of $15 per pet per night.

Super 8 UT Richfield
1377 North Main Street
Richfield, UT
435-896-9204 (800-800-8000)
Dogs are welcome at this hotel.

Travelodge Richfield
647 South Main
Richfield, UT
435-896-9271 (800-578-7878)
Dogs are welcome at this hotel.

Frontier Motel
75 S 200 E
Roosevelt, UT
435-722-2201
Dogs up to 50 pounds are allowed. There are no additional pet fees,,, dogs must be declared at the time of reservations. 2 dogs may be allowed.

St. George Travelodge
175 North 1000 East
Saint George, UT
435-673-4621 (800-578-7878)
Dogs are welcome at this hotel.

Super 8 /Scenic Hills Area Salina
375 East 1620 South
Salina, UT
435-529-7483 (800-800-8000)
Dogs are welcome at this hotel.

Best Western Garden Inn at Salt City Plaza
171 W 500 S
Salt Lake City, UT
801-325-5300 (800-780-7234)
Dogs of all sizes are allowed. Dogs are allowed for a pet fee.

Candlewood Suites Salt Lake City-Airport
2170 W North Temple
Salt Lake City, UT
801-359-7500 (877-270-6405)
Dogs up to 80 pounds are allowed. Pets allowed with an additional pet fee. Up to $75 for 1-6 nights and up to $150 for 7+ nights. A pet agreement must be signed at check-in.

Dog-Friendly Lodging - Please always call ahead to make sure an establishment is still dog-friendly.

Candlewood Suites Salt Lake City-Fort Union
6990 S Park Centre Drive
Salt Lake City, UT
801-567-0111 (877-270-6405)
Dogs up to 80 pounds are allowed. Pets allowed with an additional pet fee. Up to $75 for 1-6 nights and up to $150 for 7+ nights. A pet agreement must be signed at check-in.

Comfort Inn Airport/International Center
200 N. Admiral Byrd Rd.
Salt Lake City, UT
801-746-5200 (877-424-6423)
Dogs of all sizes are allowed. Dogs are allowed for a pet fee of $20.00 per pet per stay.

Days Inn Salt Lake City
315 West 3300 South
Salt Lake City, UT
801-486-8780 (800-329-7466)
Dogs are welcome at this hotel.

Econo Lodge Downtown
715 W. North Temple
Salt Lake City, UT
801-363-0062 (877-424-6423)
Dogs up to 100 pounds are allowed.

Hilton Hotel
255 S West Temple
Salt Lake City, UT
801-328-2000 (800-HILTONS (445-8667))
Located in the heart of the city, this upscale hotel offers numerous on site amenities for business and leisure travelers, plus a convenient location to business, shopping, dining, sites of interest, and entertainment areas. Dogs are allowed for an additional fee of $15 per night per pet. 2 dogs may be allowed.

Hilton Hotels
5151 Wiley Post Way
Salt Lake City, UT
801-539-1515 (800-HILTONS (445-8667))
Located next to a scenic 8 acre lake, this upscale hotel offers numerous on site amenities for business and leisure travelers, plus a convenient location to an international airport and many of the areas sites of interest. Dogs are allowed for an additional one time fee of $50 per pet. Multiple dogs may be allowed.

Holiday Inn Express Hotel & Suites Salt Lake City-Airport East

200 North 2100 West
Salt Lake City, UT
801-741-1500 (877-270-6405)
Dogs of all sizes are allowed. Dogs are allowed for a nightly pet fee.

Holiday Inn Express Salt Lake City
4465 Century Drive
Salt Lake City, UT
801-268-2533 (877-270-6405)
Dogs up to 50 pounds are allowed. Dogs are allowed for a pet fee of $25.00 per pet per night.

Holiday Inn Hotel & Suites Salt Lake City-Airport West
5001 West Wiley Post Way
Salt Lake City, UT
801-741-1800 (877-270-6405)
Dogs of all sizes are allowed. Dogs are allowed for a nightly pet fee.

Homestead Studio Suites Salt Lake City - Mid Valley
5683 S. Redwood Rd.
Salt Lake City, UT
801-269-9292 (800-804-3724)
One dog is allowed per suite. There is a $25 per night additional pet fee up to $150 for an entire stay.

Homestead Studio Suites Salt Lake City - Sugar House
1220 E. 2100 S.
Salt Lake City, UT
801-474-0771 (800-804-3724)
One dog is allowed per suite. There is a $25 per night additional pet fee up to $150 for an entire stay.

Hotel Monaco Salt Lake City
15 West 200 South
Salt Lake City, UT
801-595-0000
monaco-saltlakecity.com/
Well-behaved dogs of all sizes are welcome at this pet-friendly hotel. The luxury boutique hotel offers both rooms and suites. Hotel amenities include complimentary evening wine service, 24 hour room service and a 24 hour on-site fitness room. There are no pet fees, just sign a pet liability form.

Howard Johnson Express Inn - Salt Lake City
121 North 300 West
Salt Lake City, UT
801-521-3450 (800-446-4656)
Dogs of all sizes are allowed. Dogs are allowed for a pet fee.

La Quinta Inn & Suites Salt Lake City Airport
4905 W. Wiley Post Way
Salt Lake City, UT

801-366-4444 (800-531-5900)
Dogs of all sizes are allowed. There are no additional pet fees. Dogs must be leashed, cleaned up after, and crated when left alone in the room. Multiple dogs may be allowed.

Motel 6 - Salt Lake City Downtown
176 600
Salt Lake City, UT
801-531-1252 (800-466-8356)
This motel welcomes your pets to stay with you.

Motel 6 - Salt Lake City West Airport
1990 West North Temple
Salt Lake City, UT
801-364-1053 (800-466-8356)
This motel welcomes your pets to stay with you.

Quality Inn Airport
1659 West North Temple
Salt Lake City, UT
801-533-9000 (877-424-6423)
Dogs of all sizes are allowed. Dogs are allowed for a pet fee of $25.00 per pet per stay.

Ramada Airport Salt Lake City
5575 W Amelia Earhart Dr
Salt Lake City, UT
801-537-7020 (800-272-6232)
Dogs of all sizes are allowed. Dogs are allowed for a pet fee of $25.00 per pet per stay.

Ramada Limited Salt Lake City
2455 S. State Street
Salt Lake City, UT
801-486-2400 (800-272-6232)
Dogs of all sizes are allowed. Dogs are allowed for a pet fee of $10.00 per pet per night.

Red Lion
161 W 600 S
Salt Lake City, UT
801-521-7373
There is a $20 per night per pet additional fee. There are no additional pet fees for R&R members, and the R&R program is free to sign up. 2 dogs may be allowed.

Residence Inn Salt Lake City - City Center
285 W Broadway/300 S
Salt Lake City, UT
801-355-3300 (800-331-3131)
Located in the heart of the city, this all suite inn sits central to numerous sites of interest, major event centers, Temple Square, ski areas, and world class dining and shopping areas. They also offer a number of in-house

amenities, including a daily buffet breakfast and evening social hours. Dogs are allowed for an additional one time pet fee of $100 per room. 2 dogs may be allowed.

Residence Inn Salt Lake City Airport
4883 W Douglas Corrigan Way
Salt Lake City, UT
801-532-4101 (800-331-3131)
In addition to sitting adjacent to the airport, this all suite hotel sits central to many of the city's star attractions, major corporations, event centers, and shopping/dining areas; plus they offer a number of in-house amenities that include a daily buffet breakfast and a Manager's reception Monday through Thursday. Dogs are allowed for an additional one time pet fee of $100 per room. 2 dogs may be allowed.

Residence Inn Salt Lake City Cottonwood
6425 S 3000 E
Salt Lake City, UT
801-453-0430 (800-331-3131)
Guests are only minutes from all this bustling city has to offer and the recreational pursuits of the Wasatch Mountain range. Additionally, they offer a daily buffet breakfast and evening social hours. Dogs are allowed for an additional one time pet fee of $100 per room. 2 dogs may be allowed.

Sheraton City Centre Hotel, Salt Lake City
150 West 500 South
Salt Lake City, UT
801-401-2000 (888-625-5144)
Dogs up to 80 pounds are allowed. There are no additional pet fees. Dogs are not allowed to be left alone in the room.

Super 8 Airport Salt Lake City
223 Jimmy Doolittle Rd
Salt Lake City, UT
801-533-8878 (800-800-8000)
Dogs of all sizes are allowed. Dogs are allowed for a pet fee of $15.00 per pet per stay.

packURpup.com
Call to Arrange
Salt Lake City, UT
801-652-1147
These vacation rentals are located in Salt Lake and have yards, doggy doors and other pet features. Contact them for further information.

Extended Stay America Salt Lake City - Sandy

10715 Auto Mall Dr.
Sandy, UT
801-523-1331 (800-804-3724)
One dog is allowed per suite. There is a $25 per night additional pet fee up to $150 for an entire stay.

Holiday Inn Express Hotel & Suites Sandy - South Salt Lake City
10680 South Automall Dr.
Sandy, UT
801-495-1317 (877-270-6405)
Dogs of all sizes are allowed. Dogs are allowed for a pet fee of $10.00 per pet per night.

Residence Inn Salt Lake City Sandy
270 W 10000 S
Sandy, UT
801-561-5005 (800-331-3131)
In addition to being located in the heart of downtown at the bottom of the Wasatch Mountain Range and near world class ski resorts, this all suite inn also offers a number of in-house amenities, including a daily buffet breakfast and evening social hours. Dogs are allowed for an additional one time pet fee of $100 per room. Multiple dogs may be allowed.

Super 8 Scipio
230 West 400 North
Scipio, UT
435-758-9188 (800-800-8000)
Dogs are welcome at this hotel.

Sleep Inn
10676 S. 300 W.
South Jordan, UT
801-572-2020 (877-424-6423)
Dogs of all sizes are allowed. Dogs are allowed for a pet fee of $usd per pet per night.

Best Western Zion Park Inn
1215 Zion Park Boulevard
Springdale, UT
435-772-3200 (800-780-7234)
Dogs of all sizes are allowed. Dogs are allowed for a pet fee.

Canyon Ranch Motel
668 Zion Park Blvd
Springdale, UT
435-772-3357
Dogs up to about 50 pounds are allowed. There can be one dog up to 50 pounds or 2 very small dogs (about 10 pounds each) per room and there is a $10 one time fee per pet. There is a pet policy to sign at check in. Dogs may not be left unattended.

Driftwood Lodge

1515 Zion Park Blvd
Springdale, UT
435-772-3262 (888-801-8811)
driftwoodlodge.net/index.html
Dogs are allowed for an additional fee of $24 for the 1st night and $15 for each additional night per pet. The fee may be less for very small dogs. 2 dogs may be allowed.

Best Western Mountain View Inn
1455 N 1750 W
Springville, UT
801-489-3641 (800-780-7234)
Dogs of all sizes are allowed. Dogs are allowed for a pet fee of $10.00 per pet per stay.

Days Inn Springville
520 South 2000 West
Springville, UT
801-491-0300 (800-329-7466)
Dogs are welcome at this hotel.

Holiday Inn St. George
850 South Bluff St.
St George, UT
435-628-4235 (877-270-6405)
Dogs of all sizes are allowed. Dogs are allowed for a pet fee of $25 per pet per stay.

Howard Johnson Inn And Suites Saint George HWY I-15 Exit 6
1040 South Main Street
St George, UT
435-628-8000 (800-446-4656)
Dogs of all sizes are allowed. Dogs are allowed for a pet fee.

Knights Inn St George
1140 S Bluff
St George, UT
435-628-6699 (800-843-5644)
Dogs are welcome at this hotel. There is a $15 one time additional pet fee.

Motel 6 - St George
205 1000 St
St George, UT
435-628-7979 (800-466-8356)
This motel welcomes your pets to stay with you.

Ramada St George
1440 E St George Boulevard
St George, UT
435-628-2828 (800-272-6232)
Dogs are welcome at this hotel.

Super 8 UT St. George
260 East St. George Blvd.
St George, UT
435-673-6161 (800-800-8000)
Dogs of all sizes are allowed. Dogs are allowed for a pet fee of $15 per

pet per night.

TownePlace Suites St. George
251 S 1470 E
St George, UT
435-986-9955 (800-935-3129)
This all suite hotel sits central to a
number of sites of interest for both
business and leisure travelers; plus
they also offer a number of on-site
amenities to ensure comfort. Dogs
are allowed for an additional one
time fee of $100 per room. Multiple
dogs may be allowed.

**Holiday Inn Express Hotel & Suites
Tooele**
1531 North Main
Tooele, UT
435-833-0500 (877-270-6405)
Dogs of all sizes are allowed. Dogs
are allowed for a nightly pet fee.

Best Western Capitol Reef Resort
2600 E Highway 24
Torrey, UT
435-425-3761 (800-780-7234)
Dogs are welcome at this hotel.

Best Western Canyon Pines
6650 Highway 89
Uintah, UT
801-675-5534 (800-780-7234)
Dogs of all sizes are allowed. Dogs
are allowed for a pet fee of $20 per
pet per stay.

Econo Lodge Downtown
311 E. Main St.
Vernal, UT
435-789-2000 (877-424-6423)
Dogs of all sizes are allowed. Dogs
are allowed for a pet fee of $10.00
per pet per night.

Motel 6 - Vernal
1092 Hwy 40
Vernal, UT
435-789-0666 (800-466-8356)
This motel welcomes your pets to
stay with you.

Rodeway Inn
590 W. Main St.
Vernal, UT
435-789-8172 (877-424-6423)
Dogs of all sizes are allowed. Dogs
are allowed for a pet fee of $10.00
per pet per night. Two dogs are
allowed per room.

Sage Motel
54 W Main St
Vernal, UT
435-789-1442
There is an additional pet fee of $10
per night per room. 2 dogs may be

allowed.

**Holiday Inn Express Hotel & Suites
Washington-North St. George**
2450 N Town Center Drive
Washington, UT
435-986-1313 (877-270-6405)
Dogs of all sizes are allowed. Dogs
are allowed for a pet fee of $35 per
pet per stay.

Days Inn Wendover
685 E. Wendover Blvd.
Wendover, UT
435-665-2215 (800-329-7466)
Dogs of all sizes are allowed. Dogs
are allowed for a nightly pet fee.

Knights Inn Wendover
505 East Wendover Blvd
Wendover, UT
435-665-7744 (800-843-5644)
Dogs are welcome at this hotel.
There is a $5 one time additional
pet fee.

Motel 6 - Wendover
561 Wendover Blvd
Wendover, UT
435-665-2267 (800-466-8356)
This motel welcomes your pets to
stay with you.

Quality Inn Stateline
245 E. Wendover Blvd.
Wendover, UT
435-665-2226 (877-424-6423)
Dogs of all sizes are allowed. Dogs
are allowed for a pet fee of $5.00
per pet per night.

**Extended Stay America Salt Lake
City - West Valley Center**
2310 W. City Center Ct.
West Valley, UT
801-886-2400 (800-804-3724)
One dog is allowed per suite. There
is a $25 per night additional pet fee
up to $150 for an entire stay.

**Baymont Inn & Suites Salt Lake
City/West Valley**
2229 W. City Center Court
West Valley City, UT
801-886-1300 (800-531-5900)
Dogs of all sizes are allowed. There
are no additional pet fees. Dogs
must be quiet, well behaved,
leashed and cleaned up after, and
the Do Not Disturb sign put on the
door if there is a pet in the room
alone. Multiple dogs may be
allowed.

**Motel 6 - Salt Lake City North
Woods Cross**
2433 800

Woods Cross, UT
801-298-0289 (800-466-8356)
This motel welcomes your pets to
stay with you.

Vermont

Whitford House Inn
912 Grandey Road
Addison, VT
802-758-2704 (800-746-2704)
whitfordhouseinn.com/rooms.html
This restored 1790's New England
inn, sitting amid rich farm land on 37
acres of beautifully kept grounds,
offers bicycles and canoes for
guests, a bottomless cookie jar, and
a path that leads to a wildlife
preserve. One gentle dog of any size
is allowed in the guest house only.
The dog must be very friendly and
well behaved towards other animals
as there are sheep, a cat, and dogs
on site. Dogs may not be left alone at
any time, and they must be leashed
and cleaned up after.

Inn at Maplemont
2742 H 5S
Barnet, VT
802-633-4880
Dogs of all sizes are allowed. There
is a pet policy to sign at check in and
there are no additional pet fees. 2
dogs may be allowed.

Everyday Inn
593 Rockingham Road
Bellows Falls, VT
802-463-4536
everydayinn.com/
Although they are central to many
other activities, recreation, and ski
areas, each season brings its own
beauty to this inn that sits on 7 acres
of lawns and woods along the
Connecticut River. Dogs of all sizes
are allowed for an additional fee of
$10 (plus tax) per night per pet. Dogs
must be well behaved, leashed, and
cleaned up after. 2 dogs may be
allowed.

Knights Inn Bennington
693 US RT 7 South
Bennington, VT
802-442-4074 (800-843-5644)
Dogs are welcome at this hotel.
There is a $9 one time additional pet
fee.

Knotty Pine Motel
130 Northside Drive
Bennington, VT
802-442-5487
Dogs of all sizes are allowed. There

are no additional pet fees. Dogs may not be left unattended at any time and they are not allowed on the bed and furniture. 2 dogs may be allowed.

South Gate Motel
US 7S
Bennington, VT
802-447-7525
There is no additional pet fee for 1 dog, and 1 dog is perferred,,, however, they will take a 2nd dog for an additional $8 per day pet fee.

Greenhurst Inn
88 North Road
Bethel, VT
802-234-9474 (800-510-2553)
This Queen Anne Victorian mansion sits just a short distance from the White River and several other local attractions. Dogs of all sizes are welcome for no additional pet fee. Dogs must be well behaved, leashed and cleaned up after and friendly towards the other pets in residence. Dogs may not be left alone in the room at any time. Multiple dogs may be allowed.

The Black Bear Inn
4010 Bolton Access Road
Bolton Valley, VT
802-434-2126 (800-395-6335)
blackbearinn.travel/
There are miles and miles of trails to explore and enjoy at this retreat sitting on 6000 private acres, as well as tennis courts, an outdoor heated pool, a gift shop, a bar, and dinning for breakfast and dinner. They have a couple of standard rooms that are pet friendly, and there is an additional fee of $20 per night per pet. Dogs must be quiet, well mannered, and leashed and cleaned up after at all times. This inn also features the "Bone and Biscuit Inn"; a seasonal kennel with 3 private indoor/outdoor combination runs for an additional fee of $10 per day per pet. 2 dogs may be allowed.

Lilac Inn
53 Parks Street
Brandon, VT
802-247-5463 (800-221-0720)
lilacinn.com/
Whether a vacation getaway or to host your own special celebration, this beautifully restored 1900 mansion has all the amenities, 2 acres of perennial gardens, and a full service English Tavern. Dogs of all sizes are allowed for an additional one time pet fee of $30 per room. Dogs must be well behaved, leashed

and cleaned up after at all times, and crated when left alone in the room. 2 dogs may be allowed.

Molly Stark Motel
829 Marlboro Road
Brattleboro, VT
802-254-2440
Dogs up to about 50 pounds are allowed. There is an $10 per night per room additional pet fee. They will not accept cats or dogs on weekly rentals. 2 dogs may be allowed.

Motel 6 - Brattleboro
1254 Putney Road
Brattleboro, VT
802-254-6007 (800-466-8356)
This motel welcomes your pets to stay with you.

Ramada Hotel and Conference Center of Brattleboro
1380 Putney Rd
Brattleboro, VT
802-254-8701 (800-272-6232)
Dogs of all sizes are allowed. Dogs are allowed for a pet fee of $10.00 per pet per night.

Super 8 Brattleboro
1043 Putney Road
Brattleboro, VT
802-254-8889 (800-800-8000)
Dogs are welcome at this hotel

Doubletree Hotel
1117 Williston Road
Burlington, VT
802-658-0250 (800-222-TREE (8733))
In addition to scenic courtyard gardens, Sunday brunches, and a number of other on on-site amenities, this upscale hotel sits only about 5 minutes from the airport, the downtown area, and the University. Dogs are allowed for no additional fee with a credit card on file. Dogs may not be left in the room alone at any time. Multiple dogs may be allowed.

Hilton Burlington
60 Battery Street, Burlington, Vermont, 05401
Burlington, VT
802-658-6500 (800-HILTONS (800-445-8667))
In addition to its beautiful setting overlooking Lake Champlain and its central location to some the areas star attractions, this full service hotel also offers a wide array of amenities and 1st class wining and dining. Dogs are allowed for an

additional one time fee of $50 per room. 2 dogs may be allowed.

Sheraton Burlington Hotel & Conference Center
870 Williston Road
Burlington, VT
802-865-6600 (888-625-5144)
Dogs of all sizes are allowed. There are no additional pet fees. Dogs are not allowed to be left alone in the room.

Suzanne's B&B - Your Pet-Friendly Home Away From Home
218 N. Main St.
Cambridge, VT
802-644-6325
suzannesfarm.com
Dogs are allowed at this B&B for no additional pet fee.

Mountain Top Inn and Resort
196 Mountain Top Road
Chittenden, VT
802-483-2311 (800.445.2100)
mountaintopinn.com/
This year round resort sits on 350 acres above a beautiful mountain lake and a vast national forest. Dogs of all sizes are allowed in the cabins and chalets for an additional pet fee of $25 per night per pet plus a $200 security deposit. They are not allowed in the lodge area. Your pooch will feel pampered here with a doggy bed, food and water bowls, and a treat upon arrival. Dogs must be leashed, cleaned up after, and crated when left alone in the room. Pet sitters are available with a 3 day advance notice. Pets are allowed on select cross country ski trails and on all the hiking trails. Multiple dogs may be allowed.

Days Inn Burlington Colchester
124 College Parkway
Colchester, VT
802-655-0900 (800-329-7466)
Dogs are welcome at this hotel.

Motel 6 - Burlington Colchester, Vt
74 South Park Drive
Colchester, VT
802-654-6860 (800-466-8356)
This motel welcomes your pets to stay with you.

Craftsburg Outdoor Center
535 Lost Nation Road
Craftsbury Common, VT
802-586-7767
craftsbury.com
This 320 acre four season resort is located beside a secluded lake. They allow dogs in a couple of their non-

smoking cabins. There is a $80 one time pet fee per room. Well-behaved dogs of all sizes are welcome and there is limit of 2 pets per cabin. Summer activities include hiking and mountain biking. Winter activities include dog-friendly cross-country skiing on 7 kilometers of groomed trails. 2 dogs may be allowed.

Inn at Mountain View Farm
3383 Darling Hill Road
East Burke, VT
802-626-9924 (800-572-4509)
innmtnview.com/
This 440-acre historic farm estate presents visitors with breathtaking views, pastoral settings, and they are home to the Mountain View Farm Animal Sanctuary on the same property, and miles and miles of multi-use, all season trails nationally known as the Kingdom Trails. Dogs of all sizes are allowed for an additional fee of $25 per night per pet. Dogs must be quiet, well mannered, leashed, cleaned up after, and crated when left alone in the room. 2 dogs may be allowed.

The Inn at Essex
94 Poker Hill Road
Essex, VT
802-878-1100 (800-727-4295)
VTCulinaryResort.com
A luxury hotel featuring the acclaimed New England Culinary Institute. There is a $25 per night pet fee. There is a $300 fully refundable pet-damage deposit required.

The Inn at Buck Hollow Farm
2150 Buck Hollow Road
Fairfax, VT
802-849-2400 (800-849-7985)
buckhollow.com
Set in the peaceful pastoral setting of a former dairy farm, this country inn offers 400 scenic acres, period furnishings, a 40 foot heated pool, and much more. Dogs are allowed for an additional fee of $20 per night per pet. There may be up to 2 small dogs or 1 med to large dog per room. Dogs must be hound and human friendly and have proof of current vaccinations. Pets are not allowed on the beds, and they must be crated if left alone in the room. Dogs may only be left alone for short periods.

Silver Maple Lodge
520H 5 S
Fairlee, VT
802-333-4326 (800-666-1946)
silvermaplelodge.com/
In addition to being the states oldest continually running inn, they are also

central to an array of year round local attractions and activities. Dogs of all sizes are welcome for no additional fee in the cottages but not in the lodge. Dogs must be very well behaved, under owner's control at all times, and leashed and cleaned up after. 2 dogs may be allowed.

Blueberry Hill Inn
1307 Goshen Ripton Road
Goshen, VT
802-247-6735 (800-448-0707)
blueberryhillinn.com/
This early 1800's mountain inn offers traditional country ambiance, a spring fed swimming pond, gardens, gourmet dining for both breakfast and dinner (included in the rates), and plenty of skiing and hiking trails. They offer 1 pet friendly cottage and dogs of all sizes are allowed for no additional pet fee. Dogs are allowed on all the trails year round except the groomed ski trails in winter, and they are not allowed inside the inn. Dogs must be leashed and cleaned up after at all times. 2 dogs may be allowed.

Chalet Killington
2685 Killington Rd
Killington, VT
802-422-3451 (800-451-4105)
chaletkillington.com
This pet-friendly B&B allows pets for a nightly pet fee of $15.

Happy Bear Motel
1784 Killington Road
Killington, VT
802-422-3305
Dogs of all sizes are allowed. There is a $15 per night per room additional pet fee. 2 dogs may be allowed.

The Cascades Lodge
Killington Village, 58 Old Mill Rd
Killington, VT
802-422-3731 (800-345-0113)
cascadeslodge.com/contact/
This mountain ski resort offers 45 guest rooms, an indoor pool, eateries and a lounge, and year round recreation. Dogs of all sizes are allowed for an additional pet fee of $50 per night per pet with advance notice only and a credit card on file. Dogs must be current on all vaccinations, and be flea and tic free. Dogs must be leashed and cleaned up after at all times; there are waste bags in the room and more at the front desk if needed. Dogs may not be left alone in the

room at any time. 2 dogs may be allowed.

The Paw House
1376 Clarendon Avenue
Killington, VT
802-438-2738 (866-PAW-HOUSE)
pawhouse.com
The Paw House Inn is a B&B that caters exclusively to dog owners and their pets. Dog care is available on site. Before staying here with your dog you will be required to submit an application in advance.

Wise Vacations
P. O. Box 231
Killington, VT
802-422-3139 (800-639-4680)
wisevacations.com/
This vacation rental company offers pet friendly accommodations in the Killington area; there are 3 tri-level homes listed-Telefon Trail, The Meadows, and Dream Maker. The pet policy may vary some as well as the fee and number of pets allowed, but there would be no higher than a $250 one time pet fee. Dogs must be well behaved, cleaned up after inside and out, and depending on the location of the property, dogs may not have to be leashed if they are under voice control.

The Combs Family Inn
953 E Lake Road
Ludlow, VT
802-228-8799 (802-822-8799)
combesfamilyinn.com/
Located in the state's lush lake and mountain region on 50 acres of meadows and woods, this inn offers all the comforts of a cozy home, and a great location to numerous year round local activities and events. Dogs of all sizes are welcome for no additional pet fee. Dogs must be quiet, well behaved, leashed, and cleaned up after. 2 dogs may be allowed.

Econo Lodge Killington Area
51 Rt. 4
Mendon, VT
800-992-9067 (877-424-6423)
Dogs of all sizes are allowed. Dogs are allowed for a pet fee of $15.00 per pet per night.

Red Clover Inn
7 Woodward Road
Mendon, VT
802-775-2290 (800-752-0571)
redcloverinn.com/
This scenic 1840's farmhouse estate is located on 13 country acres, offers a warm and cozy atmosphere, an

intimate pub, a restaurant, and it also serves as a great starting point for a wide variety of year round activities and recreation. Dogs of all sizes are allowed in certain rooms in the Carriage House for an additional fee of $20 per night per pet. Dogs must be leashed and cleaned up after at all times, and crated when left alone in the room. Dogs are not allowed in the main inn building. 2 dogs may be allowed.

Fairhill
724 E Munger Street
Middlebury, VT
802-388-3044
midvermont.com/fairhill/
This nicely restored 1825 farmhouse is surrounded by lush lawns and gardens, and offers a great view of the mountains and valley below. Up to 2 dogs of all sizes are allowed and there is no additional pet fee; however, when they have a full house only 1 dog is allowed per room. Dogs may not be left alone in the room at any time, and they must be leashed and cleaned up after.

Middlebury Inn
14 Courthouse Square
Middlebury, VT
802-388-4961
middleburyinn.com
Dogs are allowed and will be given a treat on check-in. There are nearby dog-friendly trails to walk your dog on.

Phineas Swann Inn
195 Main Street
Montgomery Center, VT
802-326-4306
phineasswann.com/
In an area bustling with activity and recreational opportunities, this Victorian home offers guests year round lodging, antique laden and doggie accessorized surroundings, beautiful grounds, and fresh baked goodies available all day. It is evident that there is a love of dogs here as the owner has been collecting just about everything "Dog" for over 30 years; there are hundreds of dog figurines from the 1880's to the 1950's, advertising items, tins, furniture, and signs. Some of the collection is at the inn and most of the rest is at their antique store a short distance away. Since most items are for sale, they say "just ask", and your well mannered pooch is welcome inside the antique store as well. There are no addition pet fees. Dogs must be under their owner's control at all times. Multiple

dogs may be allowed.

Four Columns Inn
21 West Street
Newfane, VT
802-365-7713 (800-787-6633)
fourcolumnsinn.com/
This Federal style inn sits on a 150 acre private mountain with wooded nature trails, manicured lawns, a fine dining restaurant that is open for diner, and they are central to numerous activities and recreation. Dogs of all sizes are allowed for an additional fee of $35 per night per pet. There may be up to 2 small to medium or 1 large dog per room. Dogs must be leashed and cleaned up after at all times.

Quality Inn at Quechee Gorge
5817 Woodstock Rd. Rt. 4
Quechee, VT
802-295-7600 (877-424-6423)
Dogs of all sizes are allowed. Dogs are allowed for a pet fee of $25.00 per pet per stay. Two dogs are allowed per room.

The Parker House Inn and Restaurant
1792 Main Street
Quechee, VT
802-295-6077
theparkerhouseinn.com
This B&B allows pets with the prior permission of management. They reserve the right to limit the size of a dog to sixty pounds, but may allow larger dogs. There is horse and other large animal boarding at the owners nearby farm. There is a $30 pet fee per night, per pet.

Holiday Inn Rutland-Killington Area
476 U.S. Route 7 South
Rutland, VT
802-775-1911 (877-270-6405)
Dogs of all sizes are allowed. Dogs are allowed for a pet fee of $26.75 per pet per night.

Ramada Limited of Rutland
253 South Main Street
Rutland, VT
802-773-3361 (800-272-6232)
Dogs of all sizes are allowed. Dogs are allowed for a pet fee.

Red Roof Inn Rutland - Killington
401 US Highway 7 South
Rutland, VT
802-775-4303 (800-RED-ROOF)
One well-behaved family pet per room. Guest must notify front desk upon arrival. Guest is liable for any damages. In consideration of all

guests, pets must never be left unattended in the guest rooms.

Rodeway Inn
138 North Main Street
Rutland, VT
802-775-2575 (877-424-6423)
Dogs of all sizes are allowed. Dogs are allowed for a pet fee of $10.00/ per pet per night.

Rodeway Inn
115 Woodstock Ave
Rutland, VT
802-773-9176 (877-424-6423)
Dogs of all sizes are allowed. Dogs are allowed for a pet fee of $10.00 per pet per night.

Econo Lodge
287 S. Main St.
Saint Albans, VT
802-524-5956 (877-424-6423)
Dogs of all sizes are allowed. Dogs are allowed for a pet fee of $20.00 per pet per night.

Econo Lodge Inn & Suites
3164 Shelburne Rd.
Shelburne, VT
802-985-3377 (877-424-6423)
Dogs of all sizes are allowed. Dogs are allowed for a pet fee of $10.00 per pet per night.

Super 8 Burlington
2572 Shelburne Road
Shelburne, VT
802-985-8037 (800-800-8000)
Dogs are welcome at this hotel.

Best Western Windjammer Inn & Conference Center
1076 Williston Road
South Burlington, VT
802-863-1125 (800-780-7234)
Dogs of all sizes are allowed. Dogs are allowed for a pet fee of $10.00 per pet per night.

Hawthorn Suites
401 Dorset Street
South Burlington, VT
802-860-1212 (800-527-1133)
In addition to providing a convenient location to many local sites and activities, this all-suite hotel offers a number of amenities for business and leisure travelers, including their signature breakfast buffet and beautifully appointed rooms. Dogs are allowed for an additional pet fee of $10 per night per room. Multiple dogs may be allowed.

Rodeway Inn
1016 Shelburne Road

South Burlington, VT
802-862-6421 (877-424-6423)
Dogs of all sizes are allowed. Dogs are allowed for a pet fee of $15.00 per pet per night.

Paradise Bay
50 Light House Road
South Hero, VT
802-372-5393
This scenic inn sits by the lake, and dogs of all sizes are welcome for no additional pet fees. They request that if your pooch goes swimming to make sure they are dried off before entering the rooms. Dogs must be friendly to humans and other animals, and be quiet and well behaved. Dogs must be leashed and cleaned up after. 2 dogs may be allowed.

Kedron Valley Inn
10671 South Road
South Woodstock, VT
802-457-1473 (800-836-1193)
kedronvalleyinn.com/
This 175 year old guest house is still offering guests a variety of services and modern amenities with plenty to explore, like the spring-fed pond with 2 white sandy beaches or the many trails, and although every season brings its own beauty and activities here, it is especially convenient for a variety of winter recreation. Dogs of all sizes are allowed in the Lodge or Tavern buildings for an additional one time fee of $15 per pet. Dogs must be leashed, cleaned up after, and they may only be left alone in the room if owners are confident that the dog will be quiet and well behaved. Dogs are not allowed in the main house. Multiple dogs may be allowed.

Holiday Inn Express Springfield
818 Charlestown Road
Springfield, VT
802-885-4516 (877-270-6405)
Dogs of all sizes are allowed. Dogs are allowed for a pet fee of $25 per pet per stay.

Fairbanks Inn
401 Western Avenue
St Johnsbury, VT
802-748-5666
stjay.com
There is a $5 per day pet fee.

Commodores Inn
823 South Main St
Stowe, VT
802-253-7131
There is a $10 per day additional pet fee, and dogs must be quie and well

mannered. Multiple dogs may be allowed.

LJ's Lodge
2526 Waterbury Rd
Stowe, VT
802-253-7768 (800-989-7768)
ljslodge.com
Dogs are allowed in this lodge with mountain views of the Vermont mountains. There is a fenced in dog play area. There is a one time $5 pet fee and there are dog beds and bowls for your room.

Stowe Motel and Snowdrift
2043 Mountain Road
Stowe, VT
802-253-7629 (800-829-7629)
stowemotel.com/
This scenic mountain resort sits on 16 meticulously landscaped grounds with great mountain views, an alpine stream, year round activities and recreation, a central location to a variety shops and restaurants, and it is near the award-winning Stowe Recreation Path. Dogs of all sizes are allowed for an additional fee of $10 per night per pet. Dogs must be leashed, cleaned up after, and crated if left alone in the room. 2 dogs may be allowed.

Ten Acres Lodge
14 Barrows Rd
Stowe, VT
802-253-7638
tenacres.newnetwork.com/
Dogs are welcome in the cottages. There are no additional pet fees with a credit card on file. 2 dogs may be allowed.

The Mountain Road Resort
1007 Mountain Rd
Stowe, VT
802-253-4566
There is a $15 one time pet fee. 2 dogs may be allowed.

The Riverside Inn
1965 Mountain Road
Stowe, VT
802-253-4217 (800-966-4217)
rivinn.com
This early 1800's converted farmhouse gives visitors a comfy stay while offering a great location to several activities, shops, and eateries, and they are also backed right up to the river and Stowe's well-known recreation path. Dogs of all sizes are allowed for an additional fee of $5 per night per pet. Dogs must be quiet, well behaved, leashed, and cleaned up

after. Dogs may only be left alone in the room if the owner is confident in the pet's behavior. 2 dogs may be allowed.

Topnotch at Stowe Resort and Spa
4000 Mountain Road
Stowe, VT
802-253-8585 (800-451-8686)
topnotchresort.com
This 120-acre resort is nestled into a Vermont mountainside. There are no additional pet fees.

Basin Harbor Club
4800 Basin Harbor Road
Vergennes, VT
802-475-2311 (800-622-4000)
Lush and sitting on the shores of beautiful Lake Champlain, this 700+ acre resort offers a complete vacation experience with a variety of accommodations, land and water recreation for all age levels, miles of hiking trails, various eateries, splendid gardens, a golf course, and much more. Dogs of all sizes are allowed in the cottages only for an additional fee of $10 per night per pet; they are not allowed in any of the 4 guesthouses. Dogs must be leashed and cleaned up after at all times, and they are not allowed in the pool or waterfront areas. Multiple dogs may be allowed.

Grunberg Haus
94 Pine Street/3 miles S of Waterbury on H 100
Waterbury, VT
802-244-7726
Dogs of all sizes are allowed in the cabins. There can be one large dog or 2 small dogs per cabin. There is a $5 per night per room additional pet fee. They are open from May to late October. 2 dogs may be allowed.

Snow Goose Inn
259 H 100, Box 366
West Dover, VT
802-464-3984
Dogs of all sizes are allowed. There is a $25 per night per pet additional fee. Dogs must be leashed while on site. There are only 2 pet friendly rooms.

Super 8 White River Junction
442 North Hartland Rd
White River Jct, VT
802-295-7577 (800-800-8000)
Dogs are welcome at this hotel.

Comfort Inn
56 Ralph Lehman Dr.
White River Junction, VT

802-295-3051 (877-424-6423)
Dogs of all sizes are allowed.

Econo Lodge
91 Ballardvale Drive
White River Junction, VT
802-295-3015 (877-424-6423)
Dogs of all sizes are allowed. Dogs
are allowed for a pet fee of $10.00
per pet per night. Two dogs are
allowed per room.

Residence Inn Burlington Williston
35 Hurricane Lane
Williston, VT
802-878-2001 (800-331-3131)
Besides offering a central location to
the area's variety of business,
shopping, dining, and year around
recreation areas, this all suite hotel
also features a number of in-house
amenities that include a daily buffet
breakfast, and an evening social
hour Monday through Thursday.
Dogs are allowed for an additional
one time pet fee of $75 per room. 2
dogs may be allowed.

TownePlace Suites Burlington
Williston
66 Zephyr Road, Taft Corners
Williston, VT
802-872-5900 (800-257-3000)
This all suite hotel sits only a few
miles from the airport and the
downtown area, plus they offer a
number of in-house amenities. Dogs
are allowed for an additional pet fee
of $10 per night per room. Multiple
dogs may be allowed.

Virginia

Days Inn Abingdon
887 Empire Drive
Abingdon, VA
276-628-7131 (800-329-7466)
Dogs of all sizes are allowed. Dogs
are allowed for a pet fee.

Holiday Inn Express Abingdon
940 E. Main St
Abingdon, VA
276-676-2829 (877-270-6405)
Dogs of all sizes are allowed. Dogs
are allowed for a pet fee of $25.00
per pet per night. Two dogs are
allowed per room.

Super 8 VA Abingdon
298 Town Centre Dr
Abingdon, VA
276-676-3329 (800-800-8000)
Dogs are welcome at this hotel.

Comfort Inn

5716 S. Van Dorn St.
Alexandria, VA
703-922-9200 (877-424-6423)
Dogs up to 60 pounds are allowed.
Dogs are allowed for a pet fee of
$25.00 per pet per stay. Two dogs
are allowed per room.

Extended Stay America
Washington, D.C. - Alexandria
205 North Breckinridge Pl.
Alexandria, VA
703-941-9440 (800-804-3724)
One dog is allowed per suite. There
is a $25 per night additional pet fee
up to $150 for an entire stay.

Holiday Inn Hotel & Suites
Alexandria-Historic District
625 First Street
Alexandria, VA
703-548-6300 (877-270-6405)
Dogs of all sizes are allowed. Dogs
are allowed for a pet fee of $50.00
per pet per stay.

Homestead Studio Suites
Washington, D.C. - Alexandria
200 Blue Stone Rd.
Alexandria, VA
703-329-3399 (800-804-3724)
One dog is allowed per suite. There
is a $25 per night additional pet fee
up to $150 for an entire stay.

Hotel Monaco Alexandria
480 King St
Alexandria, VA
703-549-6080
monaco-alexandria.com
This pet-friendly Kimpton boutique
hotel allows dogs of all sizes. There
are no additional pet fees. In
addition, the Hotel Monaco in
Alexandria hosts a Doggy Happy
Hour in the spring and summer.
Dogs on leash are allowed at the
outdoor tables in the courtyard. The
happy hour is open to dogs of all
sizes between April-October on
Tuesdays and Thursdays. It runs
from 5 pm - 8 pm. You don't have to
stay at the hotel to visit the Happy
Hour. The Doggy Happy Hour was
begun at the Holiday Inn. Now it is a
pet-friendly Hotel Monaco hotel
where you can also stay with your
dog while visiting Alexandria. They
ask that dogs stay away from the
bar area and keep their paws off the
tables and chairs. Water and
gourmet biscuits are served to your
pets.

Lorien Hotel and Spa
1600 King Street/H 7
Alexandria, VA
703-894-3434 (877-9-LORIEN (877-

956-7436))
lorienhotelandspa.com
This elegant hotel is located
downtown in the landmark 1906
Baltimore & Ohio Railroad
headquarters, and there have been
more than 50 earth-friendly practices
and products implemented here
since this Kimpton Hotel formally
launched their EarthCare program in
2005. Some of these include an in-
house water purification system, all
organic and sustainable foods
coffee/tea, organic/biodynamic and
sustainable wines, and sustainable
seafood. Additionally, with a
commitment to social responsibility,
there is an emphasis on waste
reduction, energy and water
management, and supporting like-
minded sources and organizations.
Dogs are allowed for no additional
fee; plus they receive a pet amenity
package upon arrival. Multiple dogs
may be allowed.

Morrison House Hotel
116 S Alfred St
Alexandria, VA
703-838-8000
morrisonhouse.com
This Kimpton boutique hotel allows
dogs of all sizes. There are no
additional pet fees.

Quality Inn Mount Vernon
7212 Richmond Hwy.
Alexandria, VA
703-765-9000 (877-424-6423)
Dogs of all sizes are allowed. Dogs
are allowed for a pet fee of $20.00
per pet per night.

Red Roof Inn Washington, DC -
Alexandria
5975 Richmond Highway
Alexandria, VA
703-960-5200 (800-RED-ROOF)
One well-behaved family pet per
room. Guest must notify front desk
upon arrival. Guest is liable for any
damages. In consideration of all
guests, pets must never be left
unattended in the guest rooms.

Residence Inn Alexandria Old Town
1456 Duke Street
Alexandria, VA
703-548-5474 (888-236-2427)
Located in the historic Old Town
section of the city and only a short
walking distance to the King Street
DC Metro Station, this hotel offers a
convenient location to business,
shopping, dining, and entertainment
areas. Plus they offer a daily buffet
breakfast and a Manager's reception
Monday through Thursday. Dogs are

allowed for an additional one time pet fee of $150 per room. Multiple dogs may be allowed.

Sheraton Suites Old Town Alexandria
801 North Saint Asaph St.
Alexandria, VA
703-836-4700 (888-625-5144)
Dogs up to 70 pounds are allowed. There are no additional pet fees. Dogs are not allowed to be left alone in the room.

Travelodge Alexandria
700 North Washington St
Alexandria, VA
703-836-5100 (800-578-7878)
Dogs of all sizes are allowed. Dogs are allowed for a nightly pet fee.

Washington Suites
100 South Reynolds Street
Alexandria, VA
703-370-9600
washingtonsuitesalexandria.com/
Once an apartment building, this hotel offers the largest suites in the area from 500 to 1,600 square feet and is only 9 miles from Washington DC. Dogs of all sizes are allowed for an additional $20 per night per pet. Dogs must be quiet, leashed, and cleaned up after. Multiple dogs may be allowed.

Comfort Inn
1558 Main St.
Altavista, VA
434-369-4000 (877-424-6423)
Dogs of all sizes are allowed. Dogs are allowed for a pet fee of $10.00 per pet per night.

Best Western Aquia/Quantico Inn
2868 Jefferson Davis Highway
Aquia Harbour, VA
540-659-0022 (800-780-7234)
Dogs of all sizes are allowed. Dogs are allowed for a pet fee of $10 per pet per night.

Clarion Collection Hotel Arlington Court Suites
1200 N. Courthouse Rd.
Arlington, VA
703-524-4000 (877-424-6423)
Dogs up to 75 pounds are allowed. Dogs are allowed for a pet fee of $12.00 per pet per night.

Residence Inn Arlington Pentagon City
550 Army Navy Drive
Arlington, VA
703-413-6630 (888-236-2427)
In addition to offering a convenient

location to historical, shopping, dining, and entertainment areas, this hotel also provides a number of in-house amenities, including a daily buffet breakfast, and a Manager's reception Monday through Thursday. Dogs are allowed for an additional one time pet fee of $200 per room plus $8 per day. Multiple dogs may be allowed.

Residence Inn Arlington Rosslyn
1651 North Oak Street
Arlington, VA
703-812-8400 (888-236-2427)
In addition to offering a convenient location to historical, business, shopping, dining, and entertainment areas, this hotel also provides a number of in-house amenities, including a daily buffet breakfast, and a Manager's reception Monday through Thursday. Dogs are allowed for an additional one time pet fee of $100 per room. 2 dogs may be allowed.

Sheraton Crystal City Hotel
1800 Jefferson Davis Highway
Arlington, VA
703-486-1111 (888-625-5144)
Dogs of all sizes are allowed. There are no additional pet fees. Dogs are not allowed to be left alone in the room.

Days Inn Ashland
806 England Street
Ashland, VA
804-798-4262 (800-329-7466)
Dogs of all sizes are allowed. Dogs are allowed for a pet fee of $10 per pet per night.

Howard Johnson Inn And Suites-/Near Kings Dominion Ashland
107 North Carter Road
Ashland, VA
804-521-2377 (800-446-4656)
Dogs are welcome at this hotel. There is a $10 one time pet fee.

Motel 6 - Ashland
101 Cottage Green Dr
Ashland, VA
804-752-7777 (800-466-8356)
This motel welcomes your pets to stay with you.

Quality Inn & Suites
810 England Street
Ashland, VA
804-798-4231 (877-424-6423)
Dogs of all sizes are allowed. Dogs are allowed for a pet fee of $15.00 per pet per night.

Super 8 /Richmond Ashland
806 B England St
Ashland, VA
804-752-7000 (800-800-8000)
Dogs are welcome at this hotel.

Days Inn Bedford
921 Blue Ridge Ave
Bedford, VA
540-586-8286 (800-329-7466)
Dogs of all sizes are allowed. Dogs are allowed for a pet fee of $7.00 per pet per night.

The Lost Dog
211 S Church Street
Berryville, VA
540-955-1181
Well behaved pets of all sizes are allowed. There is a town leash law to obey. There are no additional pet fees, but a tip left for housekeeping is appreciated. Dogs are not allowed to be left alone in the room. There are 3 pet friendly rooms. 2 dogs may be allowed.

Clay Corner Inn B&B
401 Clay Street SW
Blacksburg, VA
540-552-4030
claycorner.com
There is a $15 per day pet fee.

Comfort Inn
3705 S. Main St.
Blacksburg, VA
540-951-1500 (877-424-6423)
Dogs of all sizes are allowed.

Days Inn Blacksburg
3503 Holiday Lane
Blacksburg, VA
540-951-1330 (800-329-7466)
Dogs of all sizes are allowed. Dogs are allowed for a pet fee.

Econo Lodge Near Motor Speedway
912 Commonwealth Ave.
Bristol, VA
276-466-2112 (877-424-6423)
Dogs of all sizes are allowed. Dogs are allowed for a pet fee of $10.00 per pet per night.

Holiday Inn Hotel & Suites Bristol Conference Ctr
3005 Linden Drive
Bristol, VA
276-466-4100 (877-270-6405)
Dogs of all sizes are allowed. Dogs are allowed for a pet fee of $50.00 per pet per night.

Knights Inn Bristol
101 Gate City Highway

Dog-Friendly Lodging - Please always call ahead to make sure an establishment is still dog-friendly.

Bristol, VA
276-591-5090 (800-843-5644)
Dogs of all sizes are allowed. Dogs are allowed for a nightly pet fee.

Motel 6 - Bristol, Va
21561 Clear Creek Rd
Bristol, VA
276-466-6060 (800-466-8356)
This motel welcomes your pets to stay with you.

Super 8 Bristol
2139 Lee Hwy
Bristol, VA
276-466-8800 (800-800-8000)
Dogs are welcome at this hotel.

Extended Stay America Washington, D.C. - Centreville - Manassas
5920 Fort Dr.
Centreville, VA
703-988-9955 (800-804-3724)
One dog is allowed per suite. There is a $25 per night additional pet fee up to $150 for an entire stay.

Extended Stay America Washington, D.C. - Dulles Airport - Chantilly
14420 Chantilly Crossing Ln.
Chantilly, VA
703-263-7173 (800-804-3724)
One dog is allowed per suite. There is a $25 per night additional pet fee up to $150 for an entire stay.

Holiday Inn Select Chantilly-Dulles-Expo (Arpt)
4335 Chantilly Shopping Center
Chantilly, VA
703-815-6060 (877-270-6405)
Dogs up to 50 pounds are allowed. Dogs are allowed for a pet fee.

Homestead Studio Suites Washington, D.C. - Chantilly
4504 Brookfield Corporate Dr.
Chantilly, VA
703-263-3361 (800-804-3724)
One dog is allowed per suite. There is a $25 per night additional pet fee up to $150 for an entire stay.

Residence Inn Chantilly Dulles South
14440 Chantilly Crossing Lane
Chantilly, VA
703-263-7900 (800-331-3131)
In addition to all the numerous in-house amenities of this all suite, upscale inn, they are also close to technology and business centers, the Washington Dulles International Airport, and the metro Washington DC area. Dogs up to 50 pounds are allowed for an additional one time pet fee of $100 per room. 2 dogs may be allowed.

Staybridge Suites Chantilly - Dulles Airport
3860 Centerview Drive
Chantilly, VA
703-435-8090 (877-270-6405)
Dogs up to 80 pounds are allowed. Pets allowed with an additional pet fee. Up to $75 for 1-6 nights and up to $150 for 7+ nights. A pet agreement must be signed at check-in.

TownePlace Suites Chantilly
14036 Thunderbolt Place
Chantilly, VA
703-709-0453 (800-257-3000)
Being located in the state's High Tech Corridor and less than a half hour to the vibrant city of Washington DC, this all suite hotel gives an optimum location to a number of world class activities and attractions for all level of travelers. Dogs are allowed for an additional one time fee of $75 per room. 2 dogs may be allowed.

Comfort Inn University
1807 Emmet St.
Charlottesville, VA
434-293-6188 (877-424-6423)
Dogs of all sizes are allowed. Dogs are allowed for a pet fee of $10.00/ per pet per night.

Days Inn /University Area
Charlottesville
1600 Emmet Street
Charlottesville, VA
434-293-9111 (800-329-7466)
Dogs of all sizes are allowed. Dogs are allowed for a pet fee of $15 per pet per night.

Doubletree Hotel
990 Hilton Heights Road
Charlottesville, VA
434-973-2121 (800-222-TREE (8733))
This upscale hotel sits overlooking the Rivanna River and offers a number of on site amenities for business or leisure travelers - including being home to the city's largest conference facility, plus a convenient location to historical, business, shopping, dining, and recreation areas. Quiet, well mannered dogs are allowed for no additional fee. Multiple dogs may be allowed.

Econo Lodge University Arena
400 Emmet St.
Charlottesville, VA
434-296-2104 (877-424-6423)

Dogs of all sizes are allowed. Dogs are allowed for a pet fee of $10.00 per pet per night.

Holiday Inn Charlottesville-Monticello
1200 5th Street Ext.
Charlottesville, VA
434-977-5100 (877-270-6405)
Dogs of all sizes are allowed. Dogs are allowed for a pet fee of $15.00 per pet per night.

Quality Inn
1600 Emmet Street
Charlottesville, VA
434-971-3746 (877-424-6423)
Dogs of all sizes are allowed. Dogs are allowed for a pet fee of $15.00 per pet per night.

Red Roof Inn Charlottesville
1309 West Main Street
Charlottesville, VA
434-295-4333 (800-RED-ROOF)
One well-behaved family pet per room. Guest must notify front desk upon arrival. Guest is liable for any damages. In consideration of all guests, pets must never be left unattended in the guest rooms.

Residence Inn Charlottesville
1111 Millmont Street
Charlottesville, VA
434-923-0300 (800-331-3131)
This all suite hotel sits central to many of the city's star attractions, dining, and shopping areas, plus they offer a number of in-house amenities that include a daily buffet breakfast, and evening socials mid-week. Dogs are allowed for an additional one time pet fee of $100 per room. Multiple dogs may be allowed.

Sleep Inn & Suites Monticello
1185 5th St. SW
Charlottesville, VA
434-244-9969 (877-424-6423)
Dogs of all sizes are allowed. Dogs are allowed for a pet fee of $15.00 per pet per night.

Super 8 Charlottesville
390 Greenbrier Drive
Charlottesville, VA
434-973-0888 (800-800-8000)
Dogs of all sizes are allowed. Dogs are allowed for a pet fee of $10 per pet per night.

Candlewood Suites Chesapeake/Suffolk
4809 Market Place
Chesapeake, VA
757-405-3030 (877-270-6405)

Dogs up to 80 pounds are allowed. Pets allowed with an additional pet fee. Up to $75 for 1-6 nights and up to $150 for 7+ nights. A pet agreement must be signed at check-in.

Extended Stay America Chesapeake - Churchland Blvd.
3214 Churchland Blvd.
Chesapeake, VA
757-483-9200 (800-804-3724)
One dog is allowed per suite. There is a $25 per night additional pet fee up to $150 for an entire stay.

Extended Stay America Chesapeake - Greenbrier - Crossways Blvd.
1540 Crossways Blvd.
Chesapeake, VA
757-424-8600 (800-804-3724)
One dog is allowed per suite. There is a $25 per night additional pet fee up to $150 for an entire stay.

Extended Stay America Chesapeake - Greenbrier Circle
809 Greenbrier Circle
Chesapeake, VA
757-523-7377 (800-804-3724)
One dog is allowed per suite. There is a $25 per night additional pet fee up to $150 for an entire stay.

Red Roof Inn Chesapeake Conference Center
724 Woodlake Drive
Chesapeake, VA
757-523-0123 (800-RED-ROOF)
One well-behaved family pet per room. Guest must notify front desk upon arrival. Guest is liable for any damages. In consideration of all guests, pets must never be left unattended in the guest rooms.

Residence Inn Chesapeake Greenbrier
1500 Crossways Blvd
Chesapeake, VA
757-502-7300 (800-331-3131)
Besides offering a convenient location to business, shopping, dining, and entertainment areas, this hotel also provides a number of in-house amenities, including a daily buffet breakfast, and complementary evening receptions. Dogs are allowed for an additional one time pet fee of $100 per room. 2 dogs may be allowed.

Staybridge Suites Chesapeake
709 Woodlake Drive
Chesapeake, VA
757-420-2525 (877-270-6405)
Dogs up to 80 pounds are allowed.

Pets allowed with an additional pet fee. Up to $75 for 1-6 nights and up to $150 for 7+ nights. A pet agreement must be signed at check-in.

Super 8 Chesapeake
3216 Churchland Blvd
Chesapeake, VA
757-686-8888 (800-800-8000)
Dogs of all sizes are allowed. Dogs are allowed for a pet fee.

Super 8 Greenbrier Chesapeake
100 Red Cedar Court
Chesapeake, VA
757-547-8880 (800-800-8000)
Dogs of all sizes are allowed. Dogs are allowed for a pet fee.

TownePlace Suites Chesapeake
2000 Old Greenbrier Road
Chesapeake, VA
757-523-5004 (800-257-3000)
In addition to offering a number of in-house amenities for all level of travelers, this all suite inn also provides a convenient location to businesses, beaches, shopping, dining, and entertainment areas. Dogs are allowed for an additional one time fee of $75 per room. 2 dogs may be allowed.

Days Inn Chester
2410 West Hundred Rd/I-95
Chester, VA
804-748-5871 (800-329-7466)
Dogs of all sizes are allowed. Dogs are allowed for a pet fee of $15.00 per pet per night.

Channel Bass Inn
6228 Church Street
Chincoteague, VA
757-336-6148 (800-249-0818)
channelbassinn.com/
This beautiful 1892, 6,800 square foot home sits surrounded by Japanese and perennial gardens with a pond, and provide a good central location for exploring the island; they also have complimentary bikes for guests. One dog of any size is welcome for an additional $10 per night, and they must be people and pet friendly as there are resident cats. Dogs must be well behaved, leashed, and cleaned up after.

Quality Inn
6273 Maddox Blvd
Chincoteague, VA
757-336-6565 (877-424-6423)
Dogs of all sizes are allowed. Dogs are allowed for a pet fee of $15.00

per pet per night.

Chincoteague Island
6378 Church Street
Chincoteague Island, VA
757-336-3100 (800-668-7836)
Offering a variety of property options and amenities in various locations around the island, this agency has more than 20 pet friendly vacation rentals available. Dogs of all sizes (depending on the rental) are allowed for an additional fee of $75 per pet per stay. Dogs must be housebroken, well behaved, leashed, and cleaned up after in and out of the unit. Dogs may not be left unattended, and they are not allowed in a "no pet" house. Dogs are not allowed anywhere on the refuge, even if they are in a car. 2 dogs may be allowed.

VIP Island Vacation Rentals
6353 Maddox Blvd
Chincoteague Island, VA
757-336-7288
This company offers several properties with various amenities at a variety of sites on this small island that is accessed from the mainland by a 4 mile long bypass. Dogs of all sizes are allowed for an additional fee of $75 per pet per stay. Dogs must be well behaved, leashed, and cleaned up after. Multiple dogs may be allowed.

Days Inn Christiansburg
2635 Roanoke Street
Christiansburg, VA
540-382-0261 (800-329-7466)
Dogs of all sizes are allowed. Dogs are allowed for a pet fee of $10.00 per pet per night.

Econo Lodge
2430 Roanoke St.
Christiansburg, VA
540-382-6161 (877-424-6423)
Dogs of all sizes are allowed. Dogs are allowed for a pet fee of $10.00 per pet per night.

Quality Inn
50 Hampton Blvd.
Christiansburg, VA
540-382-2055 (877-424-6423)
Dogs of all sizes are allowed. Dogs are allowed for a pet fee of $10.00 per pet per night.

Super 8 Christiansburg
2780 Roanoke Street
Christiansburg, VA
540-382-7421 (800-800-8000)
Dogs of all sizes are allowed. Dogs

are allowed for a pet fee of $10.00 per pet per stay.

Super 8 /Blacksburg Area Christiansburg
55 Laurel St NE
Christiansburg, VA
540-382-5813 (800-800-8000)
Dogs are welcome at this hotel.

Knights Inn Collinsville
2357 Virginia Ave
Collinsville, VA
276-647-3716 (800-843-5644)
Dogs are welcome at this hotel.

Quality Inn Dutch Inn
2360 Virginia Ave
Collinsville, VA
276-647-3721 (877-424-6423)
Dogs of all sizes are allowed. Dogs are allowed for a pet fee of $10.00 per pet per night. Two dogs are allowed per room.

Days Inn Colonial Beach
30 Colonial Ave
Colonial Beach, VA
804-224-0404 (800-329-7466)
Dogs of all sizes are allowed. Dogs are allowed for a pet fee of $15 per pet per night.

Candlewood Suites Colonial Heights-Ft Lee
15820 Woods Edge Road
Colonial Heights, VA
804-526-0111 (877-270-6405)
Dogs up to 80 pounds are allowed. Pets allowed with an additional pet fee. Up to $75 for 1-6 nights and up to $150 for 7+ nights. A pet agreement must be signed at check-in.

Econo Lodge
2310 Indian Hills Rd
Colonial Heights, VA
804-520-1010 (877-424-6423)
Dogs up to 80 pounds are allowed. Dogs are allowed for a pet fee of $10.00 per pet per night. Two dogs are allowed per room.

Best Western Mountain View
820 E Madison Street
Covington, VA
540-962-4951 (800-780-7234)
Dogs are welcome at this hotel.

Montfair Resort Farm
2500 Bezaleel Drive
Crozet, VA
434-823-5202
montfairresortfarm.com
These pet-friendly cottages and country retreat allows dogs. They are

located just 15 miles from Charlottesville. There is a $24.00 additional one time pet fee for your first pet plus $5 for any additional pets. Montfair's rustic lodge is available for a variety of pet-friendly events such as weddings, retreats or reunions.

Comfort Inn.
890 Willis Ln.
Culpeper, VA
540-825-4900 (877-424-6423)
Dogs of all sizes are allowed. Dogs are allowed for a pet fee of $15.00/pet per pet per night.

Howard Johnson Inn Roanoke
437 Roanoke Road
Daleville, VA
540-992-1234 (800-446-4656)
Dogs of all sizes are allowed. Dogs are allowed for a pet fee.

Comfort Inn & Suites
100 Tower Drive
Danville, VA
434-793-2000 (877-424-6423)
Dogs of all sizes are allowed. Dogs are allowed for a pet fee of $10.00 per pet per night. Two dogs are allowed per room.

Holiday Inn Express Danville
2121 Riverside Dr
Danville, VA
434-793-4000 (877-270-6405)
Dogs of all sizes are allowed. Dogs are allowed for a nightly pet fee.

Super 8 VA Danville
2385 Riverside Dr
Danville, VA
434-799-5845 (800-800-8000)
Dogs are welcome at this hotel.

Comfort Inn
4424 Cleburne Blvd.
Dublin, VA
540-674-1100 (877-424-6423)
Dogs of all sizes are allowed. Dogs are allowed for a pet fee of $10.00 per pet per night.

Holiday Inn Express Dublin
4428 Cleburne Blvd
Dublin, VA
540-674-1600 (877-270-6405)
Dogs of all sizes are allowed. Dogs are allowed for a pet fee of $25.00 per pet per night.

Quarterpath Inn
620 York Street
East Williamsburg, VA
757-220-0960 (800-446-9222)
quarterpathinn.com/

This inn is located only a short walk to the historical restored town of Colonial Williamsburg. Dogs of all sizes are allowed for no additional fee. Dogs must be quiet, well behaved, leashed, cleaned up after at all times, and the Do Not Disturb sign put on the door when alone in the room. 2 dogs may be allowed.

Best Western Emporia
1100 W Atlantic Street
Emporia, VA
434-634-3200 (800-780-7234)
Dogs of all sizes are allowed. Dogs are allowed for a pet fee.

Days Inn Emporia
921 West Atlantic St.
Emporia, VA
434-634-9481 (800-329-7466)
Dogs of all sizes are allowed. Dogs are allowed for a nightly pet fee.

Knights Inn Emporia
3173 Sussex Drive
Emporia, VA
434-535-8535 (800-843-5644)
Dogs are welcome at this hotel.

Quality Inn
1207 W. Atlantic Street
Emporia, VA
434-348-8888 (877-424-6423)
Dogs of all sizes are allowed. Dogs are allowed for a pet fee of $7.00 per pet per night. Two dogs are allowed per room.

Super 8
1411 Skippers Road
Emporia, VA
434-348-3282 (800-800-8000)
Dogs are welcome at this hotel.

Best Western Eastern Shore
2543 Lankford Highway
Exmore, VA
757-442-7378 (800-780-7234)
Dogs of all sizes are allowed. Dogs are allowed for a pet fee of $10.00 per pet per night.

Holiday Inn Express Hotel & Suites Exmore
3446 Lankford Highway
Exmore, VA
757-442-5522 (877-270-6405)
Dogs up to 50 pounds are allowed. Dogs are allowed for a nightly pet fee. Two dogs are allowed per room.

Candlewood Suites Washington-Fairfax
11400 Random Hills Road
Fairfax, VA
703-359-4490 (877-270-6405)

Dogs up to 80 pounds are allowed. Pets allowed with an additional pet fee. Up to $75 for 1-6 nights and up to $150 for 7+ nights. A pet agreement must be signed at check-in.

Extended Stay America Washington, D.C. - Fairfax
12055 Lee Jackson Memorial Hwy.
Fairfax, VA
703-267-6770 (800-804-3724)
One dog is allowed per suite. There is a $25 per night additional pet fee up to $150 for an entire stay.

Homestead Studio Suites Washington, D.C. - Fairfax - Fair Oaks
12104 Monument Dr.
Fairfax, VA
703-273-3444 (800-804-3724)
One dog is allowed per suite. There is a $25 per night additional pet fee up to $150 for an entire stay.

Homestead Studio Suites Washington, D.C. - Falls Church - Merrifield
8281 Willow Oaks Corporate Dr.
Fairfax, VA
703-204-0088 (800-804-3724)
One dog is allowed per suite. There is a $25 per night additional pet fee up to $150 for an entire stay.

Fox Hill Bed & Breakfast and Cottage Suites
4383 Borden Grant Trail
Fairfield, VA
540-377-9922 (800-369-8005)
foxhillbb.com
Dogs are allowed for a $15 per night pet fee.

Residence Inn Fairfax Merrifield
8125 Gatehouse Road
Falls Church, VA
703-573-5200 (800-331-3131)
Offering a convenient location to business, historic, shopping, dining, and entertainment areas, this all suite hotel also offers a number of in-house amenities, including a daily buffet breakfast and nightly social events Monday to Thursday. Dogs are allowed for an additional one time pet fee of $150 per room. 2 dogs may be allowed.

TownePlace Suites Falls Church
205 Hillwood Avenue
Falls Church, VA
703-237-6172 (800-257-3000)
A central location to world class attractions, historical sites, major businesses, only 20 minutes to

Washington DC, and an offering of a number of on-site amenities are just some of the perks of this all suite inn. Dogs are allowed for an additional one time fee of $100 per room. 2 dogs may be allowed.

Days Inn Fancy Gap
142 Kelly Road
Fancy Gap, VA
276-728-5101 (800-329-7466)
Dogs are welcome at this hotel.

Doe Run Lodging
Milepost 189 Blue Ridge Parkway
Fancy Gap, VA
276-398-4099 (866-398-4099)
doerunlodging.com/rentals/
Lush green hills against a backdrop of wooded areas, spectacular valley views from the 3000 feet altitude, and a variety of rental options make this an attractive mountain getaway. Dogs of all sizes are allowed for an additional fee of $25 per pet per stay. Dogs must be housebroken, well mannered, leashed, and cleaned up after. 2 dogs may be allowed.

Grasssy Creek Cabooses
278 Caboose Lane
Fancy Gap, VA
276-398-1100
grassycreekcabooses.com/
Sitting on grassy knolls on 33 acres along Grassy Creek, these refurbished cabooses with modern amenities (including an inside Jacuzzi) make for a unique getaway. One dog is welcome; they must be quiet, of a friendly nature, and well mannered. Dogs must be leashed and cleaned up after, and they are not allowed on the furniture.

Days Inn Farmville
2015 S. Main Street
Farmville, VA
434-392-6611 (800-329-7466)
Dogs are welcome at this hotel.

Super 8 Farmville
2012 South Main Street
Farmville, VA
434-392-8196 (800-800-8000)
Dogs are welcome at this hotel.

Miracle Farm Spa and Resort
179 Ida Rose Lane
Floyd, VA
540-789-2214
miraclefarmbnb.com/
In addition to providing guests as healthy an environment and cuisine as possible, this inn also helps to

support a non-profit animal sanctuary for injured and abandoned animals. Vegetarian food (with meat substitutes) is the fare, there are several maintained hiking paths, and for guest wanting to learn about eco-friendly living-they are encouraged to observe operations or to participate. Dogs of all sizes are allowed for an additional fee of $25 per stay for one dog, and $10 per stay for each subsequent dog. Dogs must be under owner's control, leashed, and cleaned up after at all times. Pet sitting may be available if notified in advance. Multiple dogs may be allowed.

Days Inn Franklin
1660 Armory Drive
Franklin, VA
757-562-2225 (800-329-7466)
Dogs are welcome at this hotel.

Super 8 Franklin
1599 Armory Dr
Franklin, VA
757-562-2888 (800-800-8000)
Dogs of all sizes are allowed. Dogs are allowed for a pet fee.

Best Western Central Plaza
3000 Plank Road
Fredericksburg, VA
540-786-7404 (800-780-7234)
Dogs of all sizes are allowed. Dogs are allowed for a pet fee of $10.00 per pet per night.

Best Western Fredericksburg
2205 Plank Road
Fredericksburg, VA
540-371-5050 (800-780-7234)
Dogs of all sizes are allowed. Dogs are allowed for a pet fee of $10.00 per pet per night.

Days Inn North Fredericksburg
14 Simpson Road/I-95
Fredericksburg, VA
540-373-5340 (800-329-7466)
Dogs of all sizes are allowed. Dogs are allowed for a pet fee of $10 per pet per night.

Days Inn South Fredericksburg
5316 Jefferson Davis Hwy
Fredericksburg, VA
540-898-6800 (800-329-7466)
Dogs of all sizes are allowed. Dogs are allowed for a pet fee of $25 per pet per stay.

Econo Lodge Near Fredericksburg Battlefield
5321 Jefferson Davis Hwy.
Fredericksburg, VA

540-898-5440 (877-424-6423)
Dogs of all sizes are allowed. Dogs are allowed for a pet fee of $10.00 per pet per night.

Holiday Inn Fredericksburg-North
564 Warrenton Rd
Fredericksburg, VA
540-371-5550 (877-270-6405)
Dogs are welcome at this hotel.

Motel 6 - Fredericksburg
401 Warrenton Rd
Fredericksburg, VA
540-371-5443 (800-466-8356)
This motel welcomes your pets to stay with you.

Motel 6 - Fredericksburg, Va
5308 Jefferson Davis Hwy
Fredericksburg, VA
540-898-1000 (800-466-8356)
This motel welcomes your pets to stay with you.

Quality Inn
543 Warrenton Rd
Fredericksburg, VA
540-373-0000 (877-424-6423)
Dogs of all sizes are allowed. Dogs are allowed for a pet fee of $25.00 per pet per night. Two dogs are allowed per room.

Quality Inn near Central Park
2310 Williams Street
Fredericksburg, VA
540-371-0330 (877-424-6423)
Dogs of all sizes are allowed. Dogs are allowed for a pet fee of $20.00 per pet per night.

Ramada South Fredericksburg
5324 Jefferson Davis Hwy
Fredericksburg, VA
540-898-1102 (800-272-6232)
Dogs of all sizes are allowed. Dogs are allowed for a pet fee.

Ramada Spotsylvania
2802 Plank Road
Fredericksburg, VA
540-786-8361 (800-272-6232)
Dogs are welcome at this hotel.

Residence Inn Fredericksburg
60 Towne Centre Blvd
Fredericksburg, VA
540-786-9222 (800-331-3131)
Offering a convenient location to business, historic, shopping, dining, and entertainment areas, this all suite hotel also offers a number of in-house amenities, including a daily buffet breakfast and evening social events. Dogs are allowed for an additional one time pet fee of $100

per room. 2 dogs may be allowed.

Super 8 /Central Plz Area Fredericksburg
3002 Mall Court
Fredericksburg, VA
540-786-8881 (800-800-8000)
Dogs of all sizes are allowed. Dogs are allowed for a pet fee.

TownePlace Suites Fredericksburg
4700 Market Street/H 1489
Fredericksburg, VA
540-891-0775 (800-257-3000)
Set in a scenic wooded park-like setting surrounded by historical sites, this all suite inn also offers a number of on-site amenities - including a complimentary continental breakfast. Dogs are allowed for an additional fee of $10 per night per pet. Multiple dogs may be allowed.

Bluemont Inn
1525 N. Shenandoah Ave.
Front Royal, VA
540-635-9447
They have several pet rooms. There are no additional pet fees. 2 dogs may be allowed.

Hot Tub Heaven
Off I 66 (address given with reservation)
Front Royal, VA
540-636-1522
Dogs only are allowed and of all sizes. There is a $20 additional pet fee per night. There is a pet policy to sign at check in and one of the rooms has a tall fenced in back yard. 2 dogs may be allowed.

Quality Inn Skyline Drive
10 Commerce Ave.
Front Royal, VA
540-635-3161 (877-424-6423)
Dogs up to 50 pounds are allowed. Dogs are allowed for a pet fee of $15.00 per pet per night.

Super 8 Front Royal
111 South St
Front Royal, VA
540-636-4888 (800-800-8000)
Dogs are welcome at this hotel.

Candlewood Suites Richmond North Glen Allen
10609 Telegraph Road
Glen Allen, VA
804-262-2240 (877-270-6405)
Dogs up to 80 pounds are allowed. Pets allowed with an additional pet fee. Up to $75 for 1-6 nights and up to $150 for 7+ nights. A pet

agreement must be signed at check-in.

Candlewood Suites Richmond West End Short Pump
4120 Brookriver Drive
Glen Allen, VA
804-364-2000 (877-270-6405)
Dogs up to 80 pounds are allowed. Pets allowed with an additional pet fee. Up to $75 for 1-6 nights and up to $150 for 7+ nights. A pet agreement must be signed at check-in.

Homestead Studio Suites Richmond - Innsbrook
10961 W. Broad St.
Glen Allen, VA
804-747-8898 (800-804-3724)
One dog is allowed per suite. There is a $25 per night additional pet fee up to $150 for an entire stay.

TownePlace Suites Richmond
4231 Park Place Court
Glen Allen, VA
804-747-5253 (800-257-3000)
Besides offering a number of in-house amenities for all level of travelers, this all suite inn also offers a convenient location to the state university, key businesses, shopping, dining, and entertainment areas. Dogs are allowed for an additional one time fee of $75 per room. Multiple dogs may be allowed.

Comfort Inn
6639 Forest Hill Ave.
Gloucester, VA
804-695-1900 (877-424-6423)
Dogs of all sizes are allowed. Dogs are allowed for a pet fee of $10.00/pet per pet per night.

Best Western Crossroads Inn & Suites
135 Wood Ridge Ter
Gordonsville, VA
540-832-1700 (800-780-7234)
Dogs of all sizes are allowed. Dogs are allowed for a pet fee of $15.00 per pet per night.

Arrow Inn
3361 Commander Shepard Boulevard
Hampton, VA
757-865-0300 (800-833-2520)
arrowinn.com/
This inn offers fully equipped efficiencies and kitchenettes, and a great central location to several other points of interest and recreational opportunities. Dogs are allowed for $5 per night per pet or $30 by the

month. Dogs must be well mannered, leashed, and cleaned up after at all times. 2 dogs may be allowed.

Best Western Coliseum Inn & Suites
1809 W Mercury Boulevard
Hampton, VA
757-838-5011 (800-780-7234)
Dogs of all sizes are allowed. Dogs are allowed for a pet fee.

Candlewood Suites Hampton
401 Butler Farm Road
Hampton, VA
757-766-8976 (877-270-6405)
Dogs up to 80 pounds are allowed. Pets allowed with an additional pet fee. Up to $75 for 1-6 nights and up to $150 for 7+ nights. A pet agreement must be signed at check-in.

Econo Lodge Coliseum and Convention Center
2708 W. Mercury Blvd.
Hampton, VA
757-826-8970 (877-424-6423)
Dogs of all sizes are allowed. Dogs are allowed for a pet fee of $10.00 per pet per night.

Extended Stay America Hampton - Coliseum
1915 Commerce Dr.
Hampton, VA
757-896-3600 (800-804-3724)
One dog is allowed per suite. There is a $25 per night additional pet fee up to $150 for an entire stay.

Holiday Inn Hampton-Coliseum (Conf Ctr)
1815 West Mercury Blvd
Hampton, VA
757-838-0200 (877-270-6405)
Dogs of all sizes are allowed. Dogs are allowed for a pet fee of $25.00 per pet per stay.

Red Roof Inn Hampton Coliseum Convention Center
1925 Coliseum Drive
Hampton, VA
757-838-1870 (800-RED-ROOF)
One well-behaved family pet per room. Guest must notify front desk upon arrival. Guest is liable for any damages. In consideration of all guests, pets must never be left unattended in the guest rooms.

Super 8 Hampton
1330 Thomsa St
Hampton, VA
757-723-2888 (800-800-8000)
Dogs are welcome at this hotel.

Candlewood Suites Harrisonburg
1560 Country Club Road
Harrisonburg, VA
540-437-1400 (877-270-6405)
Dogs up to 80 pounds are allowed. Pets allowed with an additional pet fee. Up to $75 for 1-6 nights and up to $150 for 7+ nights. A pet agreement must be signed at check-in.

Comfort Inn
1440 E. Market St.
Harrisonburg, VA
540-433-6066 (877-424-6423)
Dogs of all sizes are allowed. Dogs are allowed for a pet fee of $15.00 per pet per night.

Days Inn James Madison University
1131 Forest Hill Rd/I-81
Harrisonburg, VA
540-433-9353 (800-329-7466)
Dogs of all sizes are allowed. Dogs are allowed for a pet fee.

Motel 6 - Harrisonburg
10 Linda Ln
Harrisonburg, VA
540-433-6939 (800-466-8356)
This motel welcomes your pets to stay with you.

Ramada Harrisonburg
1 Pleasant Valley Rd
Harrisonburg, VA
540-434-9981 (800-272-6232)
Dogs of all sizes are allowed. Dogs are allowed for a nightly pet fee.

Sleep Inn & Suites
1891 Evelyn Byrd Ave
Harrisonburg, VA
540-433-7100 (877-424-6423)
Dogs up to 60 pounds are allowed. Dogs are allowed for a pet fee of $15.00 per pet per night.

Super 8 Harrisonburg
3330 S. Main
Harrisonburg, VA
540-433-8888 (800-800-8000)
Dogs are welcome at this hotel.

Candlewood Suites Washington-Dulles Herndon
13845 Sunrise Valley Drive
Herndon, VA
703-793-7100 (877-270-6405)
Dogs up to 80 pounds are allowed. Pets allowed with an additional pet fee. Up to $75 for 1-6 nights and up to $150 for 7+ nights. A pet agreement must be signed at check-in.

Extended Stay America

Washington, D.C. - Herndon
1021 Elden St.
Herndon, VA
703-481-5363 (800-804-3724)
One dog is allowed per suite. There is a $25 per night additional pet fee up to $150 for an entire stay.

Hilton Hotel
13869 Park Center Road
Herndon, VA
703-478-2900 (800-HILTONS (445-8667))
This luxury hotel offers a number on site amenities for business and leisure travelers, plus a convenient location to business, shopping, dining, and recreation areas, as well as numerous sites of interest. Dogs are allowed for an additional one time pet fee of $80 per room. 2 dogs may be allowed.

Residence Inn Herndon Reston
315 Elden Street
Herndon, VA
703-435-0044 (800-331-3131)
Eateries, shopping, and business areas are all only a few minutes from the inn, plus they offer a number of in-house amenities for all level of travelers, including a daily buffet breakfast, evening hospitality hours, and flat screen HD-TVs in the all the suites. One dog is allowed for an additional one time pet fee of $75 (+ tax).

Staybridge Suites Herndon-Dulles
13700 Coppermine Road
Herndon, VA
703-713-6800 (877-270-6405)
Dogs up to 80 pounds are allowed. Pets allowed with an additional pet fee. Up to $75 for 1-6 nights and up to $150 for 7+ nights. A pet agreement must be signed at check-in.

Best Western Four Seasons South
57 Airport Road
Hillsville, VA
276-728-4136 (800-780-7234)
Dogs of all sizes are allowed. Dogs are allowed for a pet fee of $15.00 per pet per stay.

Quality Inn
85 Airport Road
Hillsville, VA
276-728-2120 (877-424-6423)
Dogs up to 50 pounds are allowed. Dogs are allowed for a pet fee of $10.00/pet per pet per night. Two dogs are allowed per room.

Candlewood Suites

Petersburg/Hopewell@Fort Lee
5113 Plaza Drive
Hopewell, VA
804-541-0200 (877-270-6405)
Dogs up to 80 pounds are allowed.
Pets allowed with an additional pet
fee. Up to $75 for 1-6 nights and up
to $150 for 7+ nights. A pet
agreement must be signed at check-
in.

Hope and Glory Inn
65 Tavern Road
Irvington, VA
804-438-6053 (800-497-8228)
Wooded areas, wide open fields,
manicured lawns, and English
gardens all add to the ambiance of
this beautiful 1890's waterfront inn
that sits central to a wide range of
land and water recreational
opportunities. Dogs of all sizes are
allowed in 2 of the cottages for an
additional fee of $40 per night per
pet. Dogs must be well groomed (no
heavy shedders), well mannered,
leashed and cleaned up after. Dogs
are not allowed on the bed or any of
the furniture. There is a great lawn
across from the inn where dogs may
want to take in a good run. 2 dogs
may be allowed.

Super 8 Lebanon
711 Townview Drive
Lebanon, VA
276-889-1800 (800-800-8000)
Dogs of all sizes are allowed. Dogs
are allowed for a pet fee.

Days Inn Leesburg
721 East Market Street
Leesburg, VA
703-777-6622 (800-329-7466)
Dogs of all sizes are allowed. Dogs
are allowed for a pet fee of $6.00 per
pet per night.

Holiday Inn Leesburg At Carradoc
Hall
1500 East Market Street
Leesburg, VA
703-771-9200 (877-270-6405)
Dogs of all sizes are allowed. Dogs
are allowed for a pet fee of $25.00
per pet per stay.

1780 Stone House, rental #1350
218 S Main Street/H 11
Lexington, VA
540-463-2521
vrbo.com/1350
This 200 year old, restored stone
home has 2 foot thick walls,
guaranteeing quiet times after
exploring the areas many sites of
interests. Dogs of all sizes are
allowed for no additional fee. Dogs

must be well behaved, leashed, and
cleaned up after inside and out. 2
dogs may be allowed.

Applewood Inn
242 Tarn Beck Lane
Lexington, VA
540-463-1962 (800-463-1902)
applewoodbb.com/
Although there are a variety of
activities and sites of interest
guests can explore here and in the
vicinity, this place also makes a
good "back to nature" getaway with
plenty of wildlife, scenic views,
nature trails, seasonal gardens, and
a lot more. Dogs are allowed for an
additional fee. One dog is $20 for
the 1st night and each night after is
$10 per night. A second dog is an
additional $10 per night. Dogs must
be well mannered, leashed, and
cleaned up after.

Best Western Inn at Hunt Ridge
25 Willow Springs Road
Lexington, VA
540-464-1500 (800-780-7234)
Dogs of all sizes are allowed. Dogs
are allowed for a pet fee of $25 per
pet per stay.

Best Western Lexington Inn
850 N Lee Highway
Lexington, VA
540-458-3020 (800-780-7234)
Dogs of all sizes are allowed. Dogs
are allowed for a pet fee of $25.00
per pet per stay.

Comfort Inn Virginia Horse Center
62 Comfort Way
Lexington, VA
540-463-7311 (877-424-6423)
Dogs of all sizes are allowed. Dogs
are allowed for a pet fee of $25.00
per pet per stay.

Days Inn Lexington
325 West Midland Trail
Lexington, VA
540-463-2143 (800-329-7466)
Dogs are welcome at this hotel.

Days Inn N Lee Highway Lexington
2809 North Lee Highway
Lexington, VA
540-463-9131 (800-329-7466)
Dogs are welcome at this hotel.

Howard Johnson Inn - Virginia
Lexington
2836 North Lee Hwy
Lexington, VA
540-463-9181 (800-446-4656)
Dogs of all sizes are allowed. Dogs
are allowed for a pet fee of $12 per

pet per night.

Sleep Inn & Suites
95 Maury River Road
Lexington, VA
540-463-6000 (877-424-6423)
Dogs up to 50 pounds are allowed.

Super 8 VA Lexington
1139 N Lee Hwy
Lexington, VA
540-463-7858 (800-800-8000)
Dogs are welcome at this hotel.

Comfort Inn Gunston Corner
8180 Silverbrook Rd
Lorton, VA
703-643-3100 (877-424-6423)
Dogs of all sizes are allowed. Dogs
are allowed for a pet fee of $25.00
per pet per stay.

Inn at Meander Plantation
2333 N James Madison H
Lotus Dale, VA
540-672-4912 (800-385-4936)
meander.net/
This country inn offers visitors
everything they need to have a fun,
relaxing visit with gaming areas, trails
through woods and fields with plenty
of bird and wildlife, landscaped
grounds and gardens, and good
food. Dogs of all sizes are allowed
for an additional fee of $25 per night
per pet. Dogs must be leashed and
cleaned up after at all times. Please
take pets to the back yard; scoopers
are available. They request that the
"dog sheet" they provide be used if
pets are accustomed to being on the
bed or furniture. Dogs are not
allowed in the main house, and they
may be only left alone in the room for
short times and they must be crated.
Dogs must be quiet, well behaved,
and friendly to both people and other
animals on site. 2 dogs may be
allowed.

Accokeek Farm
170 Kibler Drive
Luray, VA
540-743-2305
shentel.net/accokeek/
Nestled at the base of a mountain
along the river, this inn offers guests
lodging in an historic restored 19th
century, 4 story bank barn, several
recreation areas, canoes, and a
great starting location for exploring
several other sites of interest. Dogs
of all sizes are allowed for an
additional fee of $50 per pet per stay.
Dogs must be well mannered,
leashed, and cleaned up after at all
times. 2 dogs may be allowed.

Adventures Await
Luray, VA
540-743-5766 (800-433-6077)
adventuresawait.com/
This company offers several properties with various amenities in the Shenandoah River valley and mountain region around Luray. Dogs of all sizes are allowed for no additional fee. Dogs must be well behaved, leashed, and cleaned up after at all times. 2 dogs may be allowed.

Allstar Lodging
21 Wallace Avenue
Luray, VA
540-843-0606 (866-780-STAR (7827))
allstarlodging.com/
This realty offers several vacation rentals with various amenities in and around Luray in the scenic Shenandoah Valley. Dogs are allowed in their cabins for an additional fee of $10 per night per pet. Dogs must be under their owner's control, leashed, and cleaned up after. 2 dogs may be allowed.

Days Inn Shenandoah Luray
138 Whispering Hill Road
Luray, VA
540-743-4521 (800-329-7466)
Dogs of all sizes are allowed. Dogs are allowed for a nightly pet fee.

Extended Stay America Lynchburg - University Blvd.
1910 University Blvd.
Lynchburg, VA
434-239-8863 (800-804-3724)
One dog is allowed per suite. There is a $25 per night additional pet fee up to $150 for an entire stay.

Holiday Inn Express Lynchburg
5600 Seminole Ave
Lynchburg, VA
434-237-7771 (877-270-6405)
Dogs are welcome at this hotel.

Super 8 VA Lynchburg
3736 Candlers Mountain Road
Lynchburg, VA
434-846-1668 (800-800-8000)
Dogs of all sizes are allowed. Dogs are allowed for a nightly pet fee.

Travelodge Lynchburg
1500 Main Street
Lynchburg, VA
434-845-5975 (800-578-7878)
Dogs are welcome at this hotel.

Knights Inn Lynchburg Madison Heights
3642 S Amherst Hwy
Madison Heights, VA
434-929-6506 (800-843-5644)
Dogs are welcome at this hotel.

Candlewood Suites Manassas
11220 Balls Ford Road
Manassas, VA
703-530-0550 (877-270-6405)
Dogs up to 80 pounds are allowed. Pets allowed with an additional pet fee. Up to $75 for 1-6 nights and up to $150 for 7+ nights. A pet agreement must be signed at check-in.

Red Roof Inn Washington, DC - Manassas
10610 Automotive Drive
Manassas, VA
703-335-9333 (800-RED-ROOF)
One well-behaved family pet per room. Guest must notify front desk upon arrival. Guest is liable for any damages. In consideration of all guests, pets must never be left unattended in the guest rooms.

Econo Lodge
1420 N. Main Street
Marion, VA
276-783-6031 (877-424-6423)
Dogs of all sizes are allowed.

Econo Lodge
1755 Virginia Avenue
Martinsville, VA
276-632-5611 (877-424-6423)
Dogs of all sizes are allowed. Dogs are allowed for a pet fee of $10.00 per pet per night.

Super 8 VA Martinsville
1044 N Memorial Blvd
Martinsville, VA
276-666-8888 (800-800-8000)
Dogs are welcome at this hotel.

Super 8 Chiswell/ Area Max Meadows
194 FT. Chiswell Rd.
Max Meadows, VA
276-637-4141 (800-800-8000)
Dogs of all sizes are allowed. Dogs are allowed for a pet fee.

Hilton Hotel
7920 Jones Branch Drive
McLean, VA
703-847-5000 (800-HILTONS (445-8667))
An atrium style hotel specializing in event venues, offers a number of on site amenities for business and leisure travelers, plus a convenient

location to Washington DC, business, shopping, dining, and entertainment areas. Dogs are allowed for no additional fee. Multiple dogs may be allowed.

Best Western Tysons Westpark
8401 Westpark Drive
Mclean, VA
703-734-2800 (800-780-7234)
Dogs of all sizes are allowed. Dogs are allowed for a pet fee of $10.00 per pet per night.

Staybridge Suites Mclean-Tysons Corner
6845 Old Dominion Drive
Mclean, VA
703-448-5400 (877-270-6405)
Dogs up to 80 pounds are allowed. Pets allowed with an additional pet fee. Up to $75 for 1-6 nights and up to $150 for 7+ nights. A pet agreement must be signed at check-in.

Super 8 Winchester Area VA Middletown
91 Reliance Road
Middletown, VA
540-868-1800 (800-800-8000)
Dogs are welcome at this hotel.

Highland Inn
68 West Main Street/H 250
Monterey, VA
540-468-2143 (888-466-4682)
highland-inn.com/
Beautiful in any season, this 1904 3-story inn is a great starting point to a number of other activities, historic sites, and recreation. Dogs are allowed for an additional $20 per night per room. Dogs must be quiet, well behaved, leashed, and cleaned up after at all times. 2 dogs may be allowed.

Super 8 Mount Jackson
250 Conicville Blvd
Mount Jackson, VA
540-477-2911 (800-800-8000)
Dogs of all sizes are allowed. Dogs are allowed for a nightly pet fee.

The Widow Kip's Country Inn
355 Orchard Drive
Mount Jackson, VA
540-477-2400 (800-478-8714)
widowkips.com/
This 1830 restored Victorian homestead features 7 rural acres overlooking the Shenandoah River with 3½ acres of landscaped grounds and a fenced 5 acre field for plenty of safe pet exercise. Dogs of all sizes are allowed in the cottages

for an additional fee of $15 per night per pet. Dogs must be well behaved, leashed (except in field) and cleaned up after at all times. 2 dogs may be allowed.

Rugby Creek Cabins and Equestrian Resort
1228 Rugby Road
Mouth of Wilson, VA
276-579-4215
rugbycreek.com
Nestled high in the Blue Ridge Mountains, this 63 acre private farm is a place you can vacation with both your horse and your pooch (or just your pooch). Dogs of all sizes are allowed in the Overlook Cabin with prior approval for an additional fee of $10 per night per pet, and they provide doggy beds, bowls, toys, and a fenced yard for their canine guests. Dogs must be leashed and cleaned up after. 2 dogs may be allowed.

1926 Caboose Vacation Rental
218 S Main Street/H 11
Natural Bridge, VA
540-463-2521
guestcaboose.com/
This interesting 1926 Caboose vacation getaway is one of two of their rentals that allow pets. Dogs of all sizes are allowed for no additional fee. Dogs must be well trained, leashed, and cleaned up after inside and outside of the units.

Natural Bridge Hotel
15 Appledore Lane
Natural Bridge, VA
540-291-2121 (800-533-1410)
naturalbridgeva.com/hotel.html
This unique getaway has been serving travelers since the late 1700's, and there are a variety of attractions here in addition to the accommodations such as the Natural Bridge and the Drama of Creation seasonal, nightly shows, Foamhenge-a styrofoam replica of Stonehenge, and much more. Dogs are allowed in the cottages for a $15 additional pet fee. Dogs must be leashed and cleaned up after at all times. Dogs are not allowed in buildings, the museums, or the caverns; they are allowed on the trails and at Natural Bridge Park. 2 dogs may be allowed.

Garden and Sea Inn
4188 Nelson Road
New Church, VA
800-824-0672
gardenandseainn.com/
With an emphasis on privacy and relaxation, this historic 1804 inn sits on 4 gorgeous landscaped acres with gardens, ponds, a seasonal pool, and they also offer gourmet dining and a convenient location to several other activities. Dogs of all sizes are allowed for no additional fee. Dogs must be quiet, leashed, and cleaned up after at all times. 2 dogs may be allowed.

Days Inn Battlefield New Market
9360 George Collins Parkway
New Market, VA
540-740-4100 (800-329-7466)
Dogs of all sizes are allowed. Dogs are allowed for a pet fee of $10.00 per pet per night.

Comfort Inn
12330 Jefferson Ave.
Newport News, VA
757-249-0200 (877-424-6423)
Dogs of all sizes are allowed. Dogs are allowed for a pet fee of $room per pet per night. Two dogs are allowed per room.

Days Inn Newport News
14747 Warwick Blvd
Newport News, VA
757-874-0201 (800-329-7466)
Dogs of all sizes are allowed. Dogs are allowed for a pet fee of $10 per pet per night.

Days Inn /Oyster Point at City Center Newport News
11829 Fishing Point Dr
Newport News, VA
757-873-6700 (800-329-7466)
Dogs are welcome at this hotel.

Extended Stay America Newport News - Oyster Point
11708 Jefferson Ave.
Newport News, VA
757-873-2266 (800-804-3724)
One dog is allowed per suite. There is a $25 per night additional pet fee up to $150 for an entire stay.

Motel 6 - Newport News
797 Clyde Morris Blvd
Newport News, VA
757-595-6336 (800-466-8356)
This motel welcomes your pets to stay with you.

Residence Inn Newport News Airport
531 St Johns Road
Newport News, VA
757-842-6214 (800-331-3131)
Located only a few minutes from major sites of interest, universities, historic districts, and the airport, this all suite inn also offers a number of in-house amenities, including a daily buffet breakfast and evening socials Monday through Wednesday with light dinner fare. Dogs are allowed for an additional one time pet fee of $100 per room. 2 dogs may be allowed.

Super 8 /Jefferson Ave. Newport News
6105 Jefferson Ave
Newport News, VA
757-825-1422 (800-800-8000)
Dogs of all sizes are allowed. Dogs are allowed for a pet fee.

Travelodge Newport News
13700 Warwick Blvd
Newport News, VA
757-874-4100 (800-578-7878)
Dogs are welcome at this hotel.

Candlewood Suites Norfolk Airport
5600 Lowery Road
Norfolk, VA
017-576-0540 (877-270-6405)
Dogs up to 80 pounds are allowed. Pets allowed with an additional pet fee. Up to $75 for 1-6 nights and up to $150 for 7+ nights. A pet agreement must be signed at check-in.

Econo Lodge near Sentara Leigh Hospital
865 N. Military Hwy.
Norfolk, VA
757-461-4865 (877-424-6423)
Dogs of all sizes are allowed. Dogs are allowed for a pet fee of $20.00 per pet per night.

Motel 6 - Norfolk
853 Military Hwy
Norfolk, VA
757-461-2380 (800-466-8356)
This motel welcomes your pets to stay with you.

Page House Inn
323 Fairfax Avenue
Norfolk, VA
757-625-5033 (800-599-7659)
pagehouseinn.com/
This stately historic mansion gives guests a glimpse of past luxury, as well as a good central location to a variety of recreation, shopping, and dining. Dogs of all sizes are allowed for an additional fee of $25 per night per pet. Dogs must be quiet, well behaved, leashed, and cleaned up after. Dogs must be crated if left alone for more than a few minutes and a cell number left at the front desk. 2 dogs may be allowed.

Quality Suites Lake Wright
6280 Northampton Blvd.
Norfolk, VA
757-461-6251 (877-424-6423)
Dogs of all sizes are allowed. Dogs are allowed for a pet fee of $35.00 per pet per stay.

Residence Inn Norfolk Airport
1590 N Military H
Norfolk, VA
757-333-3000 (800-331-3131)
This all suite inn sits only a short distance from the Norfolk International Airport, industrial parks, and to a number of sites of interest. Additionally, they offer a number of in-house amenities, including a daily buffet breakfast and evening socials. Dogs are allowed for an additional one time pet fee of $75 per room. 2 dogs may be allowed.

Sheraton Norfolk Waterside Hotel
777 Waterside Drive
Norfolk, VA
757-622-6664 (888-625-5144)
Dogs up to 60 pounds are allowed. There are no additional pet fees. Dogs are not allowed to be left alone in the room.

Sleep Inn Lake Wright
6280 Northampton Blvd
Norfolk, VA
757-461-1133 (877-424-6423)
Dogs of all sizes are allowed. Dogs are allowed for a pet fee of $25.00 per pet per stay.

Days Inn VA Norton
375 Wharton Lane
Norton, VA
276-679-5340 (800-329-7466)
Dogs of all sizes are allowed. Dogs are allowed for a pet fee.

Super 8 VA Norton
425 Wharton Lane
Norton, VA
276-679-0893 (800-800-8000)
Dogs are welcome at this hotel.

Holladay House
155 W Main Street
Orange, VA
540-672-4893 (800-358-4422)
holladayhousebandb.com/
Historically significant, this 1830's home features a rich Federal architecture, an extensive civil war and classical novel library, a variety of refreshments throughout the day, and close proximity to a number of area attractions and activities. Dogs are allowed in the Garden or Ivy rooms for an additional fee of $25

per night per pet. Dogs must be quiet, well mannered, leashed, and cleaned up after at all times. Multiple dogs may be allowed.

Days Inn - Fort Lee/South Petersburg
12208 S Crater Rd/I-95
Petersburg, VA
804-733-4400 (800-329-7466)
Dogs of all sizes are allowed. Dogs are allowed for a pet fee of $10.00 per pet per night.

Econo Lodge
900 Winfield Road
Petersburg, VA
804-861-8400 (877-424-6423)
Dogs of all sizes are allowed. Dogs are allowed for a pet fee of $15.00 per pet per night.

Econo Lodge South
16905 Parkdale Rd.
Petersburg, VA
804-862-2717 (877-424-6423)
Dogs of all sizes are allowed. Dogs are allowed for a pet fee of $10.00 per pet per night.

Howard Johnson Inn Petersburg
12205 South Crater Road
Petersburg, VA
804-733-0600 (800-446-4656)
Dogs are welcome at this hotel. There is a $10 one time pet fee.

Quality Inn
11974 S. Crater Rd.
Petersburg, VA
804-732-2900 (877-424-6423)
Dogs of all sizes are allowed. Dogs are allowed for a pet fee of $5.00/pet per pet per night.

Super 8 Petersburg
3138 South Crater Rd
Petersburg, VA
804-732-6020 (800-800-8000)
Dogs are welcome at this hotel.

Travelodge Petersburg
530 East Washington Street
Petersburg, VA
804-732-7836 (800-578-7878)
Dogs are welcome at this hotel.

Holiday Inn Express Hotel & Suites
Claypool Hill (Richlands Area)
180 Clay Dr.
Pounding Mill, VA
276-596-9880 (877-270-6405)
Dogs of all sizes are allowed. Dogs are allowed for a pet fee of $25.00 per pet per night.

Super 8 Richlands/Claypool Hill

Area
12367 Gov. G.C. Peery Hwy
Pounding Mill, VA
276-964-9888 (800-800-8000)
Dogs of all sizes are allowed. Dogs are allowed for a pet fee.

Best Western Radford Inn
1501 Tyler Avenue
Radford, VA
540-639-3000 (800-780-7234)
Dogs of all sizes are allowed. Dogs are allowed for a pet fee.

Super 8 VA Radford
1600 Tyler Ave
Radford, VA
540-731-9355 (800-800-8000)
Dogs of all sizes are allowed. Dogs are allowed for a pet fee.

Days Inn Raphine
584 Oakland Circle
Raphine, VA
540-377-2604 (800-329-7466)
Dogs of all sizes are allowed. Dogs are allowed for a pet fee of $10.00 per pet per night.

Fleeton Fields
2783 Fleeton Road
Reedville, VA
804-453-7016 (800-497-8215)
fleetonfields.com/
Set in a gorgeous park-like setting with garden benches, manicured lawns, a tidal pond, and herb and flower gardens, this beautiful colonial style, Victorian inspired retreat also offers guests complimentary bicycles, kayaks, and canoes. Dogs of all sizes are allowed for no additional fee. Dogs must be well behaved, leashed, and cleaned up after at all times. 2 dogs may be allowed.

Homestead Studio Suites
Washington, D.C. - Reston
12190 Sunset Hills Rd.
Reston, VA
703-707-9700 (800-804-3724)
One dog is allowed per suite. There is a $25 per night additional pet fee up to $150 for an entire stay.

Sheraton Reston Hotel
11810 Sunrise Valley Dr.
Reston, VA
703-620-9000 (888-625-5144)
Dogs up to 80 pounds are allowed. Dogs are not allowed to be left alone in the room.

Candlewood Suites Richmond Airport
5400 Audubon Drive

Richmond, VA
804-652-1888 (877-270-6405)
Dogs up to 80 pounds are allowed.
Pets allowed with an additional pet
fee. Up to $75 for 1-6 nights and up
to $150 for 7+ nights. A pet
agreement must be signed at check-
in.

Candlewood Suites Richmond-South
4301 Commerce Road
Richmond, VA
804-271-0016 (877-270-6405)
Dogs up to 80 pounds are allowed.
Pets allowed with an additional pet
fee. Up to $75 for 1-6 nights and up
to $150 for 7+ nights. A pet
agreement must be signed at check-
in.

Comfort Inn Conference Center
Midtown
3200 W. Broad St.
Richmond, VA
804-359-4061 (877-424-6423)
Dogs of all sizes are allowed. Dogs
are allowed for a pet fee of
$25.00/pet per pet per stay.

Days Inn Richmond
5701 Chamberlayne Road
Richmond, VA
804-266-7616 (800-329-7466)
Dogs of all sizes are allowed. Dogs
are allowed for a pet fee of $10.00
per pet per night.

Days Inn Richmond
6910 Midlothian Turnpike
Richmond, VA
804-745-7100 (800-329-7466)
Dogs of all sizes are allowed. Dogs
are allowed for a pet fee of $20.00
per pet per night.

Days Inn West Broad Richmond
2100 Dickens Road
Richmond, VA
804-282-3300 (800-329-7466)
Dogs of all sizes are allowed. Dogs
are allowed for a pet fee of $20.00
per pet per stay.

Econo Lodge
1600 Robin Hood Rd.
Richmond, VA
804-353-1287 (877-424-6423)
Dogs of all sizes are allowed. Dogs
are allowed for a pet fee of $10.00
per pet per night.

Econo Lodge Near Chippenham
Hospital
6523 Midlothian Tnpk.
Richmond, VA
804-276-8241 (877-424-6423)
Dogs of all sizes are allowed. Dogs

are allowed for a pet fee of $10.00
per pet per night.

Extended Stay America Richmond -
I-64 - West Broad Street
6811 Paragon Pl.
Richmond, VA
804-285-2065 (800-804-3724)
One dog is allowed per suite. There
is a $25 per night additional pet fee
up to $150 for an entire stay.

Homestead Studio Suites
Richmond - Midlothian
241 Arboretum Pl.
Richmond, VA
804-272-1800 (800-804-3724)
One dog is allowed per suite. There
is a $25 per night additional pet fee
up to $150 for an entire stay.

Jefferson Hotel
101 West Franklin Street
Richmond, VA
804-788-8000
Noted for its outstanding public
spaces and accommodations, this
hotel is centrally located in the
downtown historic district. Dogs of
all sizes are allowed for an
additional $40 per night per pet.
Dogs may not be left alone in the
room, and they must be leashed
and cleaned up after at all times.
There is a dog sitting and/or walking
service for an additional fee of
$7.50 per hour. 2 dogs may be
allowed.

Quality Inn West End
8008 W. Broad St.
Richmond, VA
804-346-0000 (877-424-6423)
Dogs of all sizes are allowed. Three
or more dogs may be allowed.

Ramada West Richmond
1500 Eastridge Road
Richmond, VA
804-285-9061 (800-272-6232)
Dogs of all sizes are allowed. Dogs
are allowed for a pet fee.

Red Roof Inn Richmond South
4350 Commerce Road
Richmond, VA
804-271-7240 (800-RED-ROOF)
One well-behaved family pet per
room. Guest must notify front desk
upon arrival. Guest is liable for any
damages. In consideration of all
guests, pets must never be left
unattended in the guest rooms.

Residence Inn Richmond Northwest
3940 Westerre Parkway
Richmond, VA

804-762-9852 (800-331-3131)
In addition to offering a convenient
location to universities, business,
shopping, dining, and entertainment
areas, this hotel also provides a
number of in-house amenities,
including a daily buffet breakfast and
evening socials Monday through
Thursday with light dinner fare. Dogs
are allowed for an additional one
time pet fee of $75 per room. 2 dogs
may be allowed.

Residence Inn Richmond West End
2121 Dickens Road
Richmond, VA
804-285-8200 (800-331-3131)
Besides offering a convenient
location to universities, business,
shopping, dining, and entertainment
areas, this hotel also provides a
number of in-house amenities,
including a daily buffet breakfast and
complementary evening receptions
Monday to Wednesday with light
dinner fare. Dogs are allowed for an
additional one time pet fee of $75 per
room. Multiple dogs may be allowed.

Sheraton Park South Hotel
9901 Midlothian Turnpike
Richmond, VA
804-323-1144 (888-625-5144)
Dogs up to 80 pounds are allowed.
There are no additional pet fees.
Dogs are not allowed to be left alone
in the room.

Sheraton Richmond West Hotel
6624 West Broad St.
Richmond, VA
804-285-2000 (888-625-5144)
Dogs up to 50 pounds are allowed.
There are no additional pet fees.
Dogs are not allowed to be left alone
in the room.

Super 8 Midlothian Turnpike
Richmond
8260 Midlothian Turnpike
Richmond, VA
804-320-2823 (800-800-8000)
Dogs are welcome at this hotel.

Super 8 /Chamberlayne Rd
Richmond
5615 Chamberlayne Rd
Richmond, VA
804-262-8880 (800-800-8000)
Dogs of all sizes are allowed. Dogs
are allowed for a pet fee of $10.00
per pet per night.

Days Inn Martinsville Ridgeway
3841 Greensboro Road
Ridgeway, VA
276-638-3914 (800-329-7466)

Dogs are welcome at this hotel.

Best Western Inn at Valley View
5050 Valley View Boulevard NW
Roanoke, VA
540-362-2400 (800-780-7234)
Dogs of all sizes are allowed. Dogs
are allowed for a pet fee.

Days Inn Airport Roanoke
8118 Plantation Road
Roanoke, VA
540-366-0341 (800-329-7466)
Dogs are welcome at this hotel.

Days Inn /Civic Center/ Downtown
Roanoke
535 Orange Ave NE
Roanoke, VA
540-342-4551 (800-329-7466)
Dogs of all sizes are allowed. Dogs
are allowed for a nightly pet fee.

Extended Stay America Roanoke -
Airport
2705 Frontage Rd. NW
Roanoke, VA
540-366-3216 (800-804-3724)
One dog is allowed per suite. There
is a $25 per night additional pet fee
up to $150 for an entire stay.

Holiday Inn Roanoke - Valley View
3315 Ordway Dr.
Roanoke, VA
540-362-4500 (877-270-6405)
Dogs of all sizes are allowed. Dogs
are allowed for a pet fee of $10.00
per pet per night.

Holiday Inn Roanoke-Tanglewood-Rt
419&I581
4468 Starkey Rd. SW
Roanoke, VA
540-774-4400 (877-270-6405)
Dogs of all sizes are allowed. Dogs
are allowed for a pet fee of $35.00
per pet per stay.

Knights Inn Roanoke
7120 Williamson Rd
Roanoke, VA
540-366-7681 (800-843-5644)
Dogs of all sizes are allowed. Dogs
are allowed for a pet fee of $10.00
per pet per night.

Quality Inn Tanglewood
3816 Franklin Rd. SW
Roanoke, VA
540-989-4000 (877-424-6423)
Dogs of all sizes are allowed. Dogs
are allowed for a pet fee of $15.00
per pet per night. Two dogs are
allowed per room.

Ramada Rivers Edge Conference

Center
1927 Franklin Rd SW
Roanoke, VA
540-343-0121 (800-272-6232)
Dogs of all sizes are allowed. Dogs
are allowed for a pet fee.

Residence Inn Roanoke Airport
3305 Ordway Drive
Roanoke, VA
540-265-1119 (800-331-3131)
Some of the amenities at this all-
suite inn include a daily buffet
breakfast, evening socials, a heated
swimming pool, a Sport Court, and
a complimentary grocery shopping
service. Dogs up to 50 pounds are
allowed for an additional one time
pet fee of $100 per room. 2 dogs
may be allowed.

Rodeway Inn Civic Center
526 Orange Ave. N.E.
Roanoke, VA
540-981-9341 (877-424-6423)
Dogs of all sizes are allowed. Dogs
are allowed for a pet fee of $10.00
per pet per night.

Super 8 VA Roanoke
I-81 Take I-581 Exit 2S
Roanoke, VA
540-563-8888 (800-800-8000)
Dogs of all sizes are allowed. Dogs
are allowed for a pet fee.

Comfort Inn Smith Mt. Lake
1730 N. Main St.
Rocky Mount, VA
540-489-4000 (877-424-6423)
Dogs of all sizes are allowed. Dogs
are allowed for a pet fee of $25 per
pet per stay.

Holiday Inn Express Hotel & Suites
Rocky Mount/Smith Mtn Lake
395 Old Franklin Trnpk.
Rocky Mount, VA
540-489-5001 (877-270-6405)
Dogs of all sizes are allowed. Dogs
are allowed for a pet fee of $25.00
per pet per night.

Econo Lodge
24368 Rogers Clark Blvd
Ruther Glen, VA
804-448-9694 (877-424-6423)
Dogs of all sizes are allowed. Dogs
are allowed for a pet fee of $10.00
per pet per night.

Super 8 Kings Dominion Area
Ruther Glen
24011 Ruther Glen Rd
Ruther Glen, VA
804-448-2608 (800-800-8000)
Dogs of all sizes are allowed. Dogs

are allowed for a pet fee of $15 per
pet per night.

Days Inn Salem
1535 East Main Street
Salem, VA
540-986-1000 (800-329-7466)
Dogs are welcome at this hotel.

Econo Lodge
301 Wildwood Road
Salem, VA
540-389-0280 (877-424-6423)
Dogs up to 50 pounds are allowed.
Dogs are allowed for a pet fee of
$10.00 per pet per night.

Howard Johnson Inn and Conference
Center
1671 Skyview Road
Salem, VA
540-389-7061 (800-446-4656)
Dogs of all sizes are allowed. Dogs
are allowed for a pet fee of $15.00
per pet per night.

Quality Inn
179 Sheraton Dr.
Salem, VA
540-562-1912 (877-424-6423)
Dogs of all sizes are allowed. Dogs
are allowed for a pet fee of $15.00
per pet per night.

Quality Inn
151 Wildwood Rd.
Salem, VA
540-387-1600 (877-424-6423)
Dogs up to 50 pounds are allowed.
Dogs are allowed for a pet fee of
$25.00 per pet per stay. Two dogs
are allowed per room.

Super 8 VA Salem
300 Wildwood Rd
Salem, VA
540-389-0297 (800-800-8000)
Dogs are welcome at this hotel.

Days Inn /Richmond Airport
Sandston
5500 Williamsburg Rd
Sandston, VA
804-222-2041 (800-329-7466)
Dogs are welcome at this hotel.

Econo Lodge Airport
5408 Williamsburg Rd.
Sandston, VA
804-222-1020 (877-424-6423)
Dogs of all sizes are allowed. Dogs
are allowed for a pet fee of $10.00
per pet per night.

Motel 6 - Richmond Airport
5704 Williamsburg Rd
Sandston, VA

804-222-7600 (800-466-8356)
This motel welcomes your pets to stay with you.

Red Roof Inn Richmond Airport
5209 Williamsburg Rd
Sandston, VA
804-440-5770 (800-RED-ROOF)
One well-behaved family pet per room. Guest must notify front desk upon arrival. Guest is liable for any damages. In consideration of all guests, pets must never be left unattended in the guest rooms.

Econo Lodge
1200 Moore Ferry Road
Skippers, VA
434-634-6124 (877-424-6423)
Dogs of all sizes are allowed. Dogs are allowed for a pet fee of $10.00 per pet per night.

Holiday Inn Express South Boston
1074 Bill Tuck Hwy
South Boston, VA
434-575-4000 (877-270-6405)
Dogs of all sizes are allowed. Dogs are allowed for a nightly pet fee.

Quality Inn
2001 Seymour Drive
South Boston, VA
434-572-4311 (877-424-6423)
Dogs of all sizes are allowed. Dogs are allowed for a pet fee of $15.00 per pet per night.

Super 8 VA South Boston
1040 Bill Tuck Highway
South Boston, VA
434-572-8868 (800-800-8000)
Dogs are welcome at this hotel.

Days Inn South Hill
911 East Atlantic Street
South Hill, VA
434-447-3123 (800-329-7466)
Dogs of all sizes are allowed. Dogs are allowed for a pet fee of $15.00 per pet per night.

Quality Inn
918 E. Atlantic St.
South Hill, VA
434-447-2600 (877-424-6423)
Dogs of all sizes are allowed. Dogs are allowed for a pet fee of $5.00 per pet per night.

Hopkins Ordinary
47 Main Street
Sperryville, VA
540-987-3383
hopkinsordinary.com/
Listed on the National Register of Historic Places and built around

1820 as a roadside inn and tavern, it once served the needs of the "ordinary" traveler, and now provides visitors extra-ordinary accommodations and fare, and close proximity to a number of area attractions and activities. Dogs are allowed in the garden cottage for an additional fee of $25 per night per pet (adjustable for multiple days). Dogs must be friendly (other animals on site), well mannered, leashed or crated when out of the cottage, and cleaned up after at all times. 2 dogs may be allowed.

Comfort Inn
6560 Loisdale Ct.
Springfield, VA
703-922-9000 (877-424-6423)
Dogs of all sizes are allowed. Dogs are allowed for a pet fee of $room per pet per night.

Extended Stay America
Washington, D.C. - Springfield
6800 Metropolitan Center Dr.
Springfield, VA
703-822-0992 (800-804-3724)
One dog is allowed per suite. There is a $25 per night additional pet fee up to $150 for an entire stay.

Motel 6 - Washington Dc Southwest Springfield
6868 Springfield Blvd
Springfield, VA
703-644-5311 (800-466-8356)
This motel welcomes your pets to stay with you.

TownePlace Suites Springfield
6245 Brandon Avenue
Springfield, VA
703-569-8060 (800-257-3000)
This all suite hotel sits central to a number of sites of interest for both business and leisure travelers; plus they also offer a number of on-site amenities - including a complimentary deluxe continental breakfast. Dogs are allowed for an additional one time fee of $75 per room. Multiple dogs may be allowed.

Staybridge Suites Stafford
2998 Jefferson Davis Highway
Stafford, VA
540-720-2111 (877-270-6405)
Dogs up to 80 pounds are allowed. Pets allowed with an additional pet fee. Up to $75 for 1-6 nights and up to $150 for 7+ nights. A pet agreement must be signed at check-in.

TownePlace Suites Stafford
2772 Jefferson Davis Highway
Stafford, VA
540-657-1990 (800-257-3000)
This all suite hotel sits central to a number of sites of interest for both business and leisure travelers; plus they also offer a number of on-site amenities to ensure comfort. Dogs are allowed for an additional fee of $10 per night per pet. 2 dogs may be allowed.

Best Western Staunton Inn
92 Rowe Road
Staunton, VA
540-885-1112 (800-780-7234)
Dogs are welcome at this hotel.

Comfort Inn
1302 Richmond Ave.
Staunton, VA
540-886-5000 (877-424-6423)
Dogs of all sizes are allowed. Dogs are allowed for a pet fee of $10.00 per pet per night.

Days Inn Staunton
273-D Bells Lane
Staunton, VA
540-248-0888 (800-329-7466)
Dogs are welcome at this hotel.

Days Inn / Mint Springs Staunton
372 Whitehill Road
Staunton, VA
540-337-3031 (800-329-7466)
Dogs are welcome at this hotel.

Holiday Inn Golf & Conf Ctr-Staunton
152 Fairway Lane
Staunton, VA
540-248-6020 (877-270-6405)
Dogs of all sizes are allowed. Dogs are allowed for a pet fee of $25.00 per pet per stay.

Howard Johnson Express Inn Staunton
268 N. Central Avenue
Staunton, VA
540-886-5330 (800-446-4656)
Dogs are welcome at this hotel. There is a $10 one time pet fee.

Quality Inn
96 Baker Ln
Staunton, VA
540-248-5111 (877-424-6423)
Dogs of all sizes are allowed. Dogs are allowed for a pet fee of $10.00 per pet per night.

Sleep Inn
222 Jefferson Highway
Staunton, VA
540-887-6500 (877-424-6423)

Dogs of all sizes are allowed.

Stonewall Jackson Hotel and
Conference Center
24 South Market Street
Staunton, VA
540-885-4848 (866-880-0024)
stonewalljacksonhotel.com
This pet-friendly hotel is located 1
1/2 hours from Richmond. Pets are
allowed but please mention your pet
when making a reservation.

Comfort Inn
167 Town Run Lane
Stephens City, VA
540-869-6500 (877-424-6423)
Dogs of all sizes are allowed. Dogs
are allowed for a pet fee of $10.00
per pet per night. Dogs are allowed
for a pet fee of $10.00/night., per pet
per stay. Two dogs are allowed per
room.

Candlewood Suites Sterling
45520 East Severn Way
Sterling, VA
703-674-2288 (877-270-6405)
Dogs up to 80 pounds are allowed.
Pets allowed with an additional pet
fee. Up to $75 for 1-6 nights and up
to $150 for 7+ nights. A pet
agreement must be signed at check-
in.

Extended Stay America Washington,
D.C. - Sterling
46001 Waterview Pl.
Sterling, VA
703-444-7240 (800-804-3724)
One dog is allowed per suite. There
is a $25 per night additional pet fee
up to $150 for an entire stay.

Homestead Studio Suites
Washington, D.C. - Sterling
45350 Catalina Ct.
Sterling, VA
703-904-7575 (800-804-3724)
One dog is allowed per suite. There
is a $25 per night additional pet fee
up to $150 for an entire stay.

TownePlace Suites Dulles Airport
22744 Holiday Park Drive
Sterling, VA
703-707-2017 (800-257-3000)
Besides offering a number of in-
house amenities for all level of
travelers, this all suite inn also offers
a convenient location to downtown
Washington DC, and numerous
business, shopping, dining, and
entertainment areas. Dogs up to 100
pounds are allowed for an additional
one time fee of $100 per room.
Multiple dogs may be allowed.

TownePlace Suites Sterling
21123 Whitfield Place
Sterling, VA
703-421-1090 (800-257-3000)
This all suite hotel sits central to a
number of sites of interest for both
business and leisure travelers; plus
they also offer a number of on-site
amenities to ensure comfort. Dogs
are allowed for an additional one
time fee of $100 per room. Multiple
dogs may be allowed.

Sleep Inn & Suites
11019 Blue Star Hwy.
Stony Creek, VA
434-246-5100 (877-424-6423)
Dogs up to 50 pounds are allowed.
Dogs are allowed for a pet fee of
$15.00 per pet per night. Two dogs
are allowed per room.

Days Inn Suffolk
1526 Holland Road
Suffolk, VA
757-539-5111 (800-329-7466)
Dogs of all sizes are allowed. Dogs
are allowed for a nightly pet fee.

TownePlace Suites Suffolk
Chesapeake
8050 Harbour View Blvd
Suffolk, VA
757-483-5177 (800-257-3000)
In addition to offering a number of
in-house amenities for all level of
travelers, this all suite inn also
provides a convenient location to
major corporations, shopping,
dining, and recreation areas. Dogs
are allowed for an additional one
time fee of $100 per room. Multiple
dogs may be allowed.

Days Inn Tappahannock
1414 Tappahannock Boulevard
Tappahannock, VA
804-443-9200 (800-329-7466)
Dogs of all sizes are allowed. Dogs
are allowed for a pet fee of $15 per
pet per night.

Super 8 VA Tappahannock
1800 Tappahannock Blvd.
Tappahannock, VA
804-443-3888 (800-800-8000)
Dogs of all sizes are allowed. Dogs
are allowed for a pet fee.

Comfort Inn
2545 Lee Highway
Troutville, VA
540-992-5600 (877-424-6423)
Dogs of all sizes are allowed. Dogs
are allowed for a pet fee of $25.00
per pet per stay.

Red Roof Inn Roanoke - Troutville
3231 Lee Highway South
Troutville, VA
540-992-5055 (800-RED-ROOF)
One well-behaved family pet per
room. Guest must notify front desk
upon arrival. Guest is liable for any
damages. In consideration of all
guests, pets must never be left
unattended in the guest rooms.

Knights Inn Staunton/ Verona
70 Lodge Lane
Verona, VA
540-248-8981 (800-843-5644)
Dogs of all sizes are allowed. Dogs
are allowed for a pet fee.

Homestead Studio Suites
Washington, D.C. - Tysons Corner
8201 Old Courthouse Rd.
Vienna, VA
703-356-6300 (800-804-3724)
One dog is allowed per suite. There
is a $25 per night additional pet fee
up to $150 for an entire stay.

Residence Inn Tysons Corner
8616 Westwood Center Drive
Vienna, VA
703-893-0120 (800-331-3131)
This all suite hotel sits in the heart of
one of the fast rising business
centers in America, plus they offer a
number of in-house amenities that
include a daily buffet breakfast and
evening socials Monday through
Wednesday. Dogs are allowed for an
additional one time pet fee of $70 per
room. Multiple dogs may be allowed.

Residence Inn Tysons Corner Mall
8400 Old Courthouse Road
Vienna, VA
703-917-0800 (800-331-3131)
In addition to offering a convenient
location to numerous sites of
interest, activities, and attractions for
business or pleasure travelers, this
all suite hotel also offers a number of
in-house amenities, including a daily
buffet breakfast and evening socials
Monday through Thursday with light
dinner fare. Dogs are allowed for an
additional one time pet fee of $75 per
room. Multiple dogs may be allowed.

Candlewood Suites Virginia
Beach/Norfolk
4437 Bonney Road
Virginia Beach, VA
757-213-1500 (877-270-6405)
Dogs up to 80 pounds are allowed.
Pets allowed with an additional pet
fee. Up to $75 for 1-6 nights and up
to $150 for 7+ nights. A pet

agreement must be signed at check-in.

Econo Lodge Town Center
3637 Bonney Rd.
Virginia Beach, VA
757-486-5711 (877-424-6423)
Dogs of all sizes are allowed. Dogs are allowed for a pet fee of $10.00 per pet per night.

Extended Stay America Virginia Beach - Independence Blvd.
4548 Bonney Rd.
Virginia Beach, VA
757-473-9200 (800-804-3724)
One dog is allowed per suite. There is a $25 per night additional pet fee up to $150 for an entire stay.

Holiday Inn SunSpree Resort Virginia Beach-On The Ocean
3900 Atlantic Ave
Virginia Beach, VA
757-428-1711 (877-270-6405)
Dogs of all sizes are allowed. Dogs are allowed for a pet fee of $40.00 per pet per stay.

La Quinta Inn Norfolk Virginia Beach
192 Newtown Rd.
Virginia Beach, VA
757-497-6620 (800-531-5900)
Dogs of all sizes are allowed. There are no additional pet fees. Dogs must be leashed, cleaned up after, and crated if left unattended in the room. Multiple dogs may be allowed.

Motel 6 - Virginia Beach, Va
4760 Euclid Road
Virginia Beach, VA
757-499-1935 (800-466-8356)
Well-behaved dogs are allowed. Dogs are allowed for a pet fee of $room per pet per night. One dog is allowed per room.

Red Roof Inn Virginia Beach
196 Ballard Court
Virginia Beach, VA
757-490-0225 (800-RED-ROOF)
One well-behaved family pet per room. Guest must notify front desk upon arrival. Guest is liable for any damages. In consideration of all guests, pets must never be left unattended in the guest rooms.

Red Roof Inn Virginia Beach - Norfolk Airport
5745 Northampton Blvd.
Virginia Beach, VA
757-460-3414 (800-RED-ROOF)
One well-behaved family pet per room. Guest must notify front desk upon arrival. Guest is liable for any

damages. In consideration of all guests, pets must never be left unattended in the guest rooms.

Residence Inn Virginia Beach Oceanfront
3217 Atlantic Avenue
Virginia Beach, VA
757-425-1141 (800-331-3131)
All oceanfront suites with balconies, a great location to some of the area's best attractions, shopping and dining areas, a daily buffet breakfast, and weekly barbecues are just some of the amenities of this upscale hotel. Dogs are allowed for an additional one time pet fee of $75 per room. 2 dogs may be allowed.

Sandbridge Realty
581 Sandbridge Road
Virginia Beach, VA
757-426-6262 (800-933-4800)
sandbridge.com/
This realty offers a variety of vacation rentals with various amenities in the Sandbridge Beach area. Dogs of all sizes are allowed in the house rentals (not the condos) for an additional fee of $115 per pet per stay. Dogs must be licensed, and leashed and cleaned up after at all times. Dogs are not allowed on the beach, the boardwalk, or the grassy area west of the boardwalk between Rudee Inlet and 42nd Street from the Friday before Memorial Day to Labor Day unless they are in an escape-proof container. 2 dogs may be allowed.

Sheraton Oceanfront Hotel
3501 Atlantic Ave.
Virginia Beach, VA
757-425-9000 (888-625-5144)
Dogs up to 60 pounds are allowed. Pets are restricted to first and third floor rooms only. Dogs are not allowed to be left alone in the room.

Super 8 Virginia Beach
2604 Atlantic Ave
Virginia Beach, VA
757-425-5971 (800-800-8000)
Dogs of all sizes are allowed. Dogs are allowed for a pet fee.

TownePlace Suites Virginia Beach
5757 Cleveland Street
Virginia Beach, VA
757-490-9367 (800-257-3000)
This all suite hotel sits central to a number of sites of interest for business, military, and leisure travelers; plus they also offer a number of on-site amenities to

ensure a comfortable stay. Dogs are allowed for an additional one time fee of $100 per room. Multiple dogs may be allowed.

Travelodge Bay Beach
2968 Shore Drive
Virginia Beach, VA
757-481-7992 (800-578-7878)
Dogs of all sizes are allowed. Dogs are allowed for a nightly pet fee.

Comfort Inn
7379 Comfort Inn Dr. (US 29)
Warrenton, VA
540-349-8900 (877-424-6423)
Dogs up to 50 pounds are allowed. Dogs are allowed for a pet fee of $10.00 per pet per night. Two dogs are allowed per room.

Holiday Inn Express Hotel & Suites Warrenton
410 Holiday Court
Warrenton, VA
540-341-3461 (877-270-6405)
Dogs of all sizes are allowed. Dogs are allowed for a pet fee of $10.00 per pet per night.

Howard Johnson Inn - Warrenton
6 Broadview Ave
Warrenton, VA
540-347-4141 (800-446-4656)
Dogs are welcome at this hotel.

Best Western Waynesboro Inn & Suites Conf Ctr
109 Apple Tree Ln
Waynesboro, VA
540-942-1100 (800-780-7234)
Dogs of all sizes are allowed. Dogs are allowed for a pet fee of $10 per pet per stay.

Days Inn Waynesboro
2060 Rosser Avenue/I-64
Waynesboro, VA
540-943-1101 (800-329-7466)
Dogs of all sizes are allowed. Dogs are allowed for a nightly pet fee.

Residence Inn Waynesboro
44 Windigrove Drive
Waynesboro, VA
540-943-7426 (800-331-3131)
This all suite inn features a convenient location to major corporations, shopping, dining, and entertainment areas, plus they also offer a number of in-house amenities, including a daily buffet breakfast and evening socials. Dogs up to 50 pounds are allowed for an additional one time pet fee of $100 per room. 2 dogs may be allowed.

Dog-Friendly Lodging - Please always call ahead to make sure an establishment is still dog-friendly.

Super 8 Waynesboro
2045 Rosser Ave.
Waynesboro, VA
540-943-3888 (800-800-8000)
Dogs are welcome at this hotel.

Clarion Hotel Historic District
351 York Street
Williamsburg, VA
757-229-4100 (877-424-6423)
Dogs up to 75 pounds are allowed.
Dogs are allowed for a pet fee of
$25.00 per pet per night. Three or
more dogs may be allowed.

Days Inn Colonial Area Williamsburg
902 Richmond Road/I-64
Williamsburg, VA
757-229-5060 (800-329-7466)
Dogs of all sizes are allowed. Dogs
are allowed for a nightly pet fee.

Howard Johnson Inn
505 York Street
Williamsburg, VA
757-220-3100 (800-446-4656)
Dogs of all sizes are allowed. Dogs
are allowed for a nightly pet fee.

Motel 6 - Colonial Williamsburg
824 Capitol Landing Road
Williamsburg, VA
757-259-1948 (800-466-8356)
This motel welcomes your pets to
stay with you.

Motel 6 - Williamsburg
3030 Richmond Rd
Williamsburg, VA
757-565-3433 (800-466-8356)
Your pets are welcome to stay here
with you.

Ramada 1776 Historic Williamsburg
725 Bypass Rd.
Williamsburg, VA
757-220-1776 (800-272-6232)
Dogs of all sizes are allowed. Dogs
are allowed for a pet fee.

Residence Inn Williamsburg
1648 Richmond Road
Williamsburg, VA
757-941-2000 (800-331-3131)
This all suite hotel sits nestled in the
heart of the historic district and
central to numerous sites of interest
and activities for all level of travelers.
Additionally, they offer a daily buffet
breakfast and evening receptions.
Dogs are allowed for an additional
one time pet fee of $75 per room.
Multiple dogs may be allowed.

Williamsburg Manor - An American
Inn B&B
600 Richmond Road

Williamsburg, VA
757-220-8011 (800-422-8011)
williamsburg-manor.com
This B&B three blocks from
Merchant Square and Colonial
Williamsburg allows well-behaved
pets.

Woodlands Cascades Motel
105 Visitor Center Drive
Williamsburg, VA
757-229-1000
This contemporary Motor Inn,
surrounded by landscaped grounds,
is adjacent to Colonial Williamsburg
and an abundance of activities.
Dogs up to a combined weight of 60
pounds are allowed for no
additional fee. Dogs must be well
behaved, leashed, and cleaned up
after. 2 dogs may be allowed.

Best Value Inn
2649 Valley Avenue
Winchester, VA
540-662-2521 (888-315-2378)
This inn offers a number of
amenities plus 4 meticulously
landscaped acres to explore with
your pooch. Dogs are allowed for
an additional fee of $5 per pet per
night. Dogs must be quiet, well
behaved, leashed, and cleaned up
after. 2 dogs may be allowed.

Best Western Lee-Jackson Inn &
Conference Center
711 Millwood Avenue
Winchester, VA
540-662-4154 (800-780-7234)
Dogs are welcome at this hotel.
There is a $5 pet fee.

Candlewood Suites Winchester
1135 Millwood Pike
Winchester, VA
540-667-8323 (877-270-6405)
Dogs up to 80 pounds are allowed.
Pets allowed with an additional pet
fee. Up to $75 for 1-6 nights and up
to $150 for 7+ nights. A pet
agreement must be signed at
check-in.

Comfort Inn
1601 Martinsburg Pike
Winchester, VA
540-667-8894 (877-424-6423)
Dogs up to 75 pounds are allowed.
Dogs are allowed for a pet fee of
$10.00 per pet per night.

Days Inn Winchester
2951 Valley Ave
Winchester, VA
540-667-1200 (800-329-7466)
Dogs of all sizes are allowed. Dogs

are allowed for a pet fee.

Econo Lodge North
1593 Martinsburg Pike
Winchester, VA
540-662-4700 (877-424-6423)
Dogs of all sizes are allowed.

Quality Inn
1017 Millwood Pike
Winchester, VA
540-545-8121 (877-424-6423)
Dogs up to 80 pounds are allowed.

Red Roof Inn Winchester
991 Millwood Pike
Winchester, VA
540-667-5000 (800-RED-ROOF)
One well-behaved family pet per
room. Guest must notify front desk
upon arrival. Guest is liable for any
damages. In consideration of all
guests, pets must never be left
unattended in the guest rooms.

Super 8 VA Winchester
1077 Millwood Pike
Winchester, VA
540-665-4400 (800-800-8000)
Dogs of all sizes are allowed. Dogs
are allowed for a pet fee.

Travelodge Winchester
160 Front Royal Pike
Winchester, VA
540-665-0685 (800-578-7878)
Dogs of all sizes are allowed. Dogs
are allowed for a pet fee of $10.00
per pet per stay.

Quality Inn near Potomac Mills
1109 Horner Rd.
Woodbridge, VA
703-494-0300 (877-424-6423)
Dogs of all sizes are allowed. Dogs
are allowed for a pet fee of $20.00
per pet per night. Two dogs are
allowed per room.

Residence Inn Potomac Mills
Woodbridge
14301 Crossing Place
Woodbridge, VA
703-490-4020 (800-331-3131)
This all suite inn features a
convenient location to business,
historic, shopping, dining, and
entertainment areas, plus they also
offer a number of in-house
amenities, including a daily buffet
breakfast and evening socials. Dogs
are allowed for an additional one
time pet fee of $100 per room.
Multiple dogs may be allowed.

Rodeway Inn near Potomac Mills
13964 Jefferson Davis Hwy.

Woodbridge, VA
703-494-4144 (877-424-6423)
Dogs of all sizes are allowed. Dogs are allowed for a pet fee of $10.00 per pet per night.

Comfort Inn
1011 Motel Drive
Woodstock, VA
540-459-7600 (877-424-6423)
Dogs of all sizes are allowed. Dogs are allowed for a pet fee of $10.00 per pet per night.

Best Western Wytheville Inn
355 Nye Road
Wytheville, VA
276-228-7300 (800-780-7234)
Dogs of all sizes are allowed. Dogs are allowed for a pet fee.

Comfort Inn
2594 East Lee Highway
Wytheville, VA
276-637-4281 (877-424-6423)
Dogs of all sizes are allowed. Dogs are allowed for a pet fee of $10.00 per pet per night.

Days Inn - Wytheville
150 Malin Dr
Wytheville, VA
276-228-5500 (800-329-7466)
Dogs are welcome at this hotel.

Knights Inn Wytheville
1160 E Main St.
Wytheville, VA
276-228-5517 (800-843-5644)
Dogs of all sizes are allowed. Dogs are allowed for a pet fee of $10 per pet per night.

Motel 6 - Wytheville
220 Lithia Rd
Wytheville, VA
276-228-7988 (800-466-8356)
This motel welcomes your pets to stay with you.

Super 8 Wytheville
130 Nye Circle
Wytheville, VA
276-228-6620 (800-800-8000)
Dogs are welcome at this hotel.

Travelodge Wytheville
140 Lithia Road
Wytheville, VA
276-228-3188 (800-578-7878)
Dogs are welcome at this hotel.

Wytheville Red Roof Inn & Suites
1900 E. Main Street
Wytheville, VA
276-223-1700 (800-RED-ROOF)
One well-behaved family pet per

room. Guest must notify front desk upon arrival. Guest is liable for any damages. In consideration of all guests, pets must never be left unattended in the guest rooms.

Candlewood Suites Newport News/Yorktown
329 Commonwealth Drive
Yorktown, VA
757-952-1120 (877-270-6405)
Dogs up to 80 pounds are allowed. Pets allowed with an additional pet fee. Up to $75 for 1-6 nights and up to $150 for 7+ nights. A pet agreement must be signed at check-in.

Days Inn Yorktown
4531 G Washington Memorial Hwy
Yorktown, VA
757-283-1111 (800-329-7466)
Dogs of all sizes are allowed. Dogs are allowed for a nightly pet fee.

Marl Inn
220 Church Street
Yorktown, VA
757-898-3859
marlinnbandb.com/
This colonial styled inn sits only a short distance from a number of activities, the river, historical sites, and an eclectic array of eateries and shops. Dogs of all sizes are allowed for no additional fee. Dogs must be housebroken, well behaved, leashed, cleaned up after, and friendly to the other pets on site. 2 dogs may be allowed.

Staybridge Suites Newport News-Yorktown
401 Commonwealth Drive
Yorktown, VA
757-251-6644 (877-270-6405)
Dogs up to 80 pounds are allowed. Pets allowed with an additional pet fee. Up to $75 for 1-6 nights and up to $150 for 7+ nights. A pet agreement must be signed at check-in.

TownePlace Suites Newport News Yorktown
200 Cybernetics Way
Yorktown, VA
757-874-8884 (800-257-3000)
This all suite hotel sits central to a number of sites of interest for business, government, military, and leisure travelers; plus they also offer a number of on-site amenities. Dogs are allowed for an additional one time fee of $100 per room. Multiple dogs may be allowed.

Washington

America's Best Value
521 W Wishkah
Aberdeen, WA
360-532-5210
americasbestvalueinn.com/
Dogs of all sizes are allowed. There is a $10 per night per pet fee. Multiple dogs may be allowed.

Days Inn and Suites /Spokane Airport Airway Heights
1215 South Garfield
Airway Heights, WA
509-244-0222 (800-329-7466)
Dogs of all sizes are allowed. Dogs are allowed for a nightly pet fee.

Anacortes Inn
3006 Commercial Ave
Anacortes, WA
360-293-3153
ohwy.com/wa/a/anactinn.htm
There is a $10 per night per pet fee. Multiple dogs may be allowed.

Fidalgo Country Inn
7645 St Route 20
Anacortes, WA
360-293-3494
There is a $20 per day per pet charge. There are 2 pet rooms. 2 dogs may be allowed.

Quality Inn
5200 172nd Street N.E.
Arlington, WA
360-403-7222 (877-424-6423)
Dogs up to 50 pounds are allowed. Dogs are allowed for a pet fee of $20.00 per pet per night. Two dogs are allowed per room.

Mt. Rainier Cabins at Three Bears Lodge
Call to Arrange
Ashford, WA
206-241-8080 (877-782-3277)
These four cabins near Mt Rainier National Park are pet-friendly.

Cedar's Inn
102 13th Street NE
Auburn, WA
253-833-8007
cedarsinnauburn.com/
Well behaved dogs up to 45 pounds are allowed for an additional fee of $10 per night per pet.

Days Inn Auburn
1521 D Street NE
Auburn, WA
253-939-5950 (800-329-7466)
Dogs are welcome at this hotel.

Travelodge Inn and Suites Auburn
Nine 16th St North West
Auburn, WA
253-833-7171 (800-578-7878)
Dogs of all sizes are allowed. Dogs
are allowed for a nightly pet fee.

Days Inn Seattle Bellevue
3241 156th Avenue SE
Bellevue, WA
425-643-6644 (800-329-7466)
Dogs are welcome at this hotel.

Extended Stay America Seattle -
Bellevue
11400 Main St.
Bellevue, WA
425-453-8186 (800-804-3724)
One dog is allowed per suite. There
is a $25 per night additional pet fee
up to $150 for an entire stay.

Homestead Studio Suites Seattle -
Bellevue
3700 132nd Ave. S.E.
Bellevue, WA
425-865-8680 (800-804-3724)
One dog is allowed per suite. There
is a $25 per night additional pet fee
up to $150 for an entire stay.

Homestead Studio Suites Seattle -
Redmond
15805 N.E. 28th St.
Bellevue, WA
425-885-6675 (800-804-3724)
One dog is allowed per suite. There
is a $25 per night additional pet fee
up to $150 for an entire stay.

Red Lion
11211 Main Street
Bellevue, WA
425-455-5240
There is a $20 one time pet fee per
room. There are no additional pet
fees for R&R members, and the R&R
program is free to sign up. Multiple
dogs may be allowed.

Residence Inn Seattle Bellevue
14455 NE 29th Place
Bellevue, WA
425-882-1222 (800-331-3131)
This all suite inn features a
convenient location to business,
shopping, dining, and entertainment
areas, plus they also offer a number
of in-house amenities, including a
daily buffet breakfast, grab-n-go
breakfasts, and evening socials.
Dogs up to 75 pounds are allowed
for an additional one time pet fee of
$75 per room. 2 dogs may be
allowed.

Residence Inn Seattle
Bellevue/Downtown
605 114th Ave SE
Bellevue, WA
425-637-8500 (800-331-3131)
Located next to a nature preserve,
this all suite hotel also gives a
convenient location to business,
shopping, dining, and entertainment
areas; plus they offer a number of
in-house amenities, including a
daily buffet breakfast and
complementary evening receptions
with light dinner fare. Dogs are
allowed for an additional one time
pet fee of $100 per room. 2 dogs
may be allowed.

Sheraton Bellevue Seattle East
Hotel
100 112th Avenue SE
Bellevue, WA
425-455-3330 (888-625-5144)
Dogs of all sizes are allowed. There
are no additional pet fees. Dogs are
not allowed to be left alone in the
room.

Aloha Motel
315 N Samish Way
Bellingham, WA
360-733-4900
One dog of any size is allowed.
There is an additional $5 per night
pet fee.

Best Western Heritage Inn
151 E McLeod Road
Bellingham, WA
360-647-1912 (800-780-7234)
Dogs of all sizes are allowed. Dogs
are allowed for a pet fee of $20.00
per pet per night.

Best Western Lakeway Inn
714 Lakeway Drive
Bellingham, WA
360-671-1011 (800-780-7234)
Dogs of all sizes are allowed. Dogs
are allowed for a pet fee of $25 per
pet per stay.

Motel 6 - Bellingham
3701 Byron Avenue
Bellingham, WA
360-671-4494 (800-466-8356)
This motel welcomes your pets to
stay with you.

Quality Inn Baron Suites
100 E. Kellogg Rd.
Bellingham, WA
360-647-8000 (877-424-6423)
Dogs up to 50 pounds are allowed.
Dogs are allowed for a pet fee of
$10.00 per pet per night. Two dogs
are allowed per room.

Rodeway Inn
3710 Meridian St.
Bellingham, WA
360-738-6000 (877-424-6423)
Dogs of all sizes are allowed. Dogs
are allowed for a pet fee of $10.00
per pet per night.

The Inn at Semiahmoo
9565 Semiahmoo Parkway
Blaine, WA
360-371-2000
Dogs up to 50 pounds are allowed.
There is a $50 one time additional
pet fee per room.

Comfort Inn & Suites
1414 228th St SE
Bothell, WA
425-402-0900 (877-424-6423)
Up to two pets are allowed. Pets
must be 50 pounds or less.

Extended Stay America Seattle -
Bothell
923 228th St. S.E.
Bothell, WA
425-402-4252 (800-804-3724)
One dog is allowed per suite. There
is a $25 per night additional pet fee
up to $150 for an entire stay.

Super 8 Bremerton
5068 Kitsap Way
Bremerton, WA
360-377-8881 (800-800-8000)
Dogs are welcome at this hotel.

Econo Lodge
29405 State Route 410 East
Buckley, WA
360-829-1100 (877-424-6423)
Dogs of all sizes are allowed. Dogs
are allowed for a pet fee of $10.00
per pet per stay.

Motel 6 - Centralia
1310 Belmont Ave
Centralia, WA
360-330-2057 (800-466-8356)
This motel welcomes your pets to
stay with you.

Best Western RiverTree Inn
1257 Bridge Street
Clarkston, WA
509-758-9551 (800-780-7234)
Dogs are welcome at this hotel.

Motel 6 - Clarkston, Wa
222 Bridge St
Clarkston, WA
509-758-1631 (800-466-8356)
This motel welcomes your pets to
stay with you.

Quality Inn & Suites Conference
Center
700 Port Dr.
Clarkston, WA
509-758-9500 (877-424-6423)
Dogs up to 50 pounds are allowed.
Dogs are allowed for a pet fee of
$10.00 per pet per night. Two dogs
are allowed per room.

Best Western Wheatland Inn
701 N Main Street
Colfax, WA
509-397-0397 (800-780-7234)
Dogs are welcome at this hotel.

Comfort Inn
166 N.E. Canning Dr.
Colville, WA
509-684-2010 (877-424-6423)
Dogs of all sizes are allowed. Dogs
are allowed for a pet fee of $10.00
per pct per night.

Iron Springs Ocean Beach Resort
P. O. Box 207
Copalis Beach, WA
360-276-4230
ironspringsresort.com
Iron Springs is a 100 acre resort on
the Washington Coast located
halfway between Copalis and Pacific
Beach. They offer individual cottages
with fireplaces and great ocean
views. The cottages are nestled
among the rugged spruce trees on a
low lying bluff overlooking the Pacific
Ocean. They are located near miles
of sandy beaches. There is a $16.00
per day per pet charge. There are no
designated smoking or non-smoking
cabins. They are located 130 miles
from Seattle and 160 miles from
Portland. Multiple dogs may be
allowed.

Travelodge Seattle North/ Edmonds
23825 Highway 99
Edmonds, WA
425-771-8008 (800-578-7878)
Dogs are welcome at this hotel.

Best Western Lincoln Inn & Suites
211 W Umptanum Road
Ellensburg, WA
509-925-4244 (800-780-7234)
Dogs are welcome at this hotel.

Comfort Inn
1722 Canyon Rd.
Ellensburg, WA
509-925-7037 (877-424-6423)
Dogs of all sizes are allowed. Dogs
are allowed for a pet fee of $10.00
per pet per stay.

Holiday Inn Express Ellensburg

1620 Canyon Rd.
Ellensburg, WA
509-962-9400 (877-270-6405)
Dogs of all sizes are allowed. Dogs
are allowed for a pet fee of $10.00
per pet per night.

Quality Inn & Conference Center
1700 Canyon Road
Ellensburg, WA
509-925-9800 (877-424-6423)
Dogs of all sizes are allowed. Dogs
are allowed for a pet fee of $10.00
per pet per night. Two dogs are
allowed per room.

Super 8 Ellensburg
1500 Canyon Rd
Ellensburg, WA
509-962-6888 (800-800-8000)
Dogs of all sizes are allowed. Dogs
are allowed for a pet fee of $10.00
per pet per night.

Days Inn Seattle/ Everett
1602 SE Everett Mall Way
Everett, WA
425-355-1570 (800-329-7466)
Dogs are welcome at this hotel.

Extended Stay America Seattle -
Everett
8410 Broadway
Everett, WA
425-355-1923 (800-804-3724)
One dog is allowed per suite. There
is a $25 per night additional pet fee
up to $150 for an entire stay.

Holiday Inn Downtown-Everett
3105 Pine St
Everett, WA
425-339-2000 (877-270-6405)
Dogs of all sizes are allowed. Dogs
are allowed for a pet fee.

Motel 6 - Everett North
10006 Evergreen Way
Everett, WA
425-347-2060 (800-466-8356)
This motel welcomes your pets to
stay with you.

Motel 6 - Everett South
224 128th St Sw
Everett, WA
425-353-8120 (800-466-8356)
This motel welcomes your pets to
stay with you.

Travelodge City Center Everett
3030 Broadway
Everett, WA
425-259-6141 (800-578-7878)
Dogs of all sizes are allowed. Dogs
are allowed for a nightly pet fee.

Comfort Inn
31622 Pacific Hwy South
Federal Way, WA
253-529-0101 (877-424-6423)
Dogs up to 80 pounds are allowed.
Dogs are allowed for a pet fee of
$10.00 per pet per night.

Extended Stay America Seattle -
Federal Way
1400 S. 320th St.
Federal Way, WA
253-946-0553 (800-804-3724)
One dog is allowed per suite. There
is a $25 per night additional pet fee
up to $150 for an entire stay.

Quality Inn & Suites
1400 S. 348th St.
Federal Way, WA
253-835-4141 (877-424-6423)
Dogs of all sizes are allowed. Dogs
are allowed for a pet fee of $20.00
per pet per stay.

Super 8 Motel - Federal Way
1688 S 348th St
Federal Way, WA
253-838-8808 (800-800-8000)
Dogs of all sizes are allowed. Dogs
are allowed for a pet fee.

Super 8 /Bellingham Area Ferndale
Interstate 5 Exit 262
Ferndale, WA
360 384 8881 (800-800-8000)
Dogs are welcome at this hotel.

Baymont Inn & Suites /Tacoma Fife
5805 Pacific Highway East
Fife, WA
253-922-2500 (877-229-6668)
Dogs of all sizes are allowed. Dogs
are allowed for a pet fee.

Econo Lodge Inn & Suites
3100 Pacific Highway East
Fife, WA
253-922-9520 (877-424-6423)
Dogs up to 50 pounds are allowed.
Dogs are allowed for a pet fee of
$10.00 per pet per stay. Two dogs
are allowed per room.

Extended Stay America Tacoma -
Fife
2820 Pacific Hwy. E.
Fife, WA
253-926-6316 (800-804-3724)
One dog is allowed per suite. There
is a $25 per night additional pet fee
up to $150 for an entire stay.

Howard Johnson Inn Fife
3501 Pacific Highway East
Fife, WA
253-926-1000 (800-446-4656)

Dogs of all sizes are allowed. Dogs are allowed for a pet fee of $10.00 per pet per night.

Motel 6 - Tacoma Fife
5201 20th St
Fife, WA
253-922-1270 (800-466-8356)
This motel welcomes your pets to stay with you.

Quality Inn
5601 Pacific Hwy. E.
Fife, WA
253-926-2301 (877-424-6423)
Dogs up to 50 pounds are allowed. Dogs are allowed for a pet fee of $15.00 per pet per night.

Kalaloch Ocean Lodge
157151 Hwy. 101
Forks, WA
360-962-2271
kalaloch.com
Perched on a bluff, overlooking the Pacific Ocean, sits the Kalaloch Lodge located in Olympic National Park. The Olympic National Forest is also located nearby. Dogs are not allowed in the lodge, but they are welcome in the cabins. This resort offers over 40 cabins and half of them have ocean views. There are no designated smoking or non-smoking cabins. Thanks to one of our readers who writes 'This is a great place where you can rent cabins situated on a bluff overlooking the Pacific Ocean. Great for watching storms pound the beaches and walking wide sand beaches at low tide. Near rain forest with wooded hikes and lakes throughout. Not all units allow dogs, but you can still get a good view.' There is a $15 per day per pet fee. Multiple dogs may be allowed.

The Inn at Friday Harbor
Friday Harbor, WA
360-378-4000 (800-752-5752)
earthboxmotel.com/
There is a $15 one time fee per pet. You need to take a car ferry to the island. 2 dogs may be allowed.

Best Western Wesley Inn of Gig Harbor
6575 Kimball Drive
Gig Harbor, WA
253-858-9690 (800-780-7234)
Dogs of all sizes are allowed. Dogs are allowed for a pet fee of $10 per pet per night.

Mt. Baker Lodging
7463 Mt. Baker Highway

Glacier, WA
360-599-2453 (1-800-709-7669)
mtbakerlodging.com/
Private vacation rental homes located at the gateway to Mt. Baker. There are a wide variety of rental homes to choose, from honeymoon getaways and family cabins, to accommodations for group retreats and family reunions. All properties are privately owned, unique and completely self-contained.

Econo Lodge Inn & Suites
910 Simpson Avenue
Hoquiam, WA
360-532-8161 (877-424-6423)
Dogs up to 50 pounds are allowed. Dogs are allowed for a pet fee of $10.00 per pet per night. Two dogs are allowed per room.

Motel 6 - Seattle East Issaquah
1885 15th Place Nw
Issaquah, WA
425-392-8405 (800-466-8356)
This motel welcomes your pets to stay with you.

Econo Lodge
505 N. Pacific Avenue
Kelso, WA
360-636-4610 (877-424-6423)
Dogs up to 50 pounds are allowed. Dogs are allowed for a pet fee of $15.00 per pet per night. Two dogs are allowed per room.

Motel 6 - Kelso Mt St Helens
106 Minor Rd
Kelso, WA
360-425-3229 (800-466-8356)
This motel welcomes your pets to stay with you.

Red Lion
510 Kelso Drive
Kelso, WA
360-636-4400
There is a $20 one time pet fee per room. There are no additional pet fees for R&R members, and the R&R program is free to sign up. 2 dogs may be allowed.

Super 8 Longview Area Kelso
250 Kelso Dr
Kelso, WA
360-423-8880 (800-800-8000)
Dogs of all sizes are allowed. Dogs are allowed for a pet fee of $10.00 per pet per night.

Comfort Inn
7801 W. Quinault Ave.
Kennewick, WA
509-783-8396 (877-424-6423)

Dogs of all sizes are allowed. Dogs are allowed for a pet fee of $10.00 per pet per night.

Days Inn Kennewick
2811 W. 2nd Avenue
Kennewick, WA
509-735-9511 (800-329-7466)
Dogs are welcome at this hotel.

La Quinta Inn & Suites Kennewick
4220 W 27th Place
Kennewick, WA
509-736-3326 (800-531-5900)
Dogs of all sizes are allowed. There are no additional pet fees. Dogs may not be left unattended at any time, and they must be leashed and cleaned up after. 2 dogs may be allowed.

Super 8 Kennewick
626 North Columbia Center Blvd
Kennewick, WA
509-736-6888 (800-800-8000)
Dogs of all sizes are allowed. Dogs are allowed for a nightly pet fee.

Days Inn - Meeker St. Kent
1711 West Meeker Street
Kent, WA
253-854-1950 (800-329-7466)
Dogs are welcome at this hotel.

Extended Stay America Seattle - Kent
22520 83rd Ave. S.
Kent, WA
253-872-6514 (800-804-3724)
One dog is allowed per suite. There is a $25 per night additional pet fee up to $150 for an entire stay.

Howard Johnson WA Kent
1233 North Central Avenue
Kent, WA
253-852-7224 (800-446-4656)
Dogs are welcome at this hotel.

TownePlace Suites Seattle Southcenter
18123 72nd Avenue S
Kent, WA
253-796-6000 (800-257-3000)
This all suite inn sits central to numerous business, shopping, dining, and entertainment areas, plus they also offer a number of in-house amenities for business and leisure travelers. Dogs are allowed for an additional fee of $10 per night per pet. 2 dogs may be allowed.

China Bend Bed and Breakfast and Winery
3751 Vineyard Way
Kettle Falls, WA

509-732-6123 (800-700-6123)
chinabend.com
Specializing in organic and sulfite-free wines, this winery features a variety of fine vegan wines. They also have an organic garden that provides fresh produce for the bed and breakfast, and many products are canned for sale. The tasting room and gift shop is open April 1st thru October 31st from noon until 5 pm Wednesday thru Sunday. Private events or lunches are available by reservation only, but their calendar offers a variety of other special events throughout the year. The bed and breakfast has 2 adjoining rooms and the suite is available for 1 party at a time. Pets are allowed for lodging for no additional fee with advance reservations. 2 dogs may be allowed.

Baymont Inn & Suites Kirkland
12223 NE 116th Street
Kirkland, WA
425-822-2300 (877-229-6668)
Dogs of all sizes are allowed. Dogs are allowed for a pet fee.

La Quinta Inn Seattle Bellevue Kirkland
10530 NE Northup Way
Kirkland, WA
425-828-6585 (800-531-5900)
Dogs of all sizes are allowed. There are no additional pet fees. Dogs must be leashed, cleaned up after, and the Do Not Disturb sign put on the door if there is a dog alone in the room. Multiple dogs may be allowed.

Motel 6 - Seattle North Kirkland
12010 120th Pl
Kirkland, WA
425-821-5618 (800-466-8356)
This motel welcomes your pets to stay with you.

Candlewood Suites Olympia/ Lacey
4440 3rd Avenue SE
Lacey, WA
360-491-1698 (877-270-6405)
Dogs up to 80 pounds are allowed. Pets allowed with an additional pet fee. Up to $75 for 1-6 nights and up to $150 for 7+ nights. A pet agreement must be signed at check-in.

Howard Johnson Express Inn - Leavenworth
405 Hwy 2
Leavenworth, WA
509-548-4326 (800-446-4656)
Dogs are welcome at this hotel.

Quality Inn & Suites
185 US Hwy. 2
Leavenworth, WA
509-548-7992 (877-424-6423)
Dogs up to 100 pounds are allowed. Dogs are allowed for a pet fee of $15.00 per pet per night. Two dogs are allowed per room.

Super 8 Long Beach
500 Ocean Beach Blvd
Long Beach, WA
360-642-8988 (800-800-8000)
Dogs of all sizes are allowed. Dogs are allowed for a pet fee of $10.00 per pet per night.

Quality Inn & Suites
723 7th Ave
Longview, WA
360-414-1000 (877-424-6423)
Dogs up to 80 pounds are allowed. Dogs are allowed for a pet fee of $20.00 per pet per night. Two dogs are allowed per room.

Travelodge Longview
838 15th Avenue
Longview, WA
360-423-6460 (800-578-7878)
Dogs are welcome at this hotel.

Island Vacation Rentals
1695 Seacrest Drive
Lummi Island, WA
360-758-7064
Well behaved adult dogs over a year old, and of all sizes are allowed. There is a pet policy to sign at check in and there are no additional fees.

Extended Stay America Seattle - Lynnwood
3021 196th St. S.W.
Lynnwood, WA
425-670-2520 (800-804-3724)
One dog is allowed per suite. There is a $25 per night additional pet fee up to $150 for an entire stay.

La Quinta Inn Lynnwood
4300 Alderwood Mall Blvd
Lynnwood, WA
425-775-7447 (800-531-5900)
Dogs of all sizes are allowed, and 2 dogs per room are preferred, but 3 dogs are ok if they are small dogs. There are no additional pet fees. Dogs may not be left unattended, and they must be leashed and cleaned up after. Dogs are not allowed in any of the food areas.

Residence Inn Seattle North/Lynnwood Everett
18200 Alderwood Mall Parkway

Lynnwood, WA
425-771-1100 (800-331-3131)
This all suite inn features a convenient location to business, shopping, dining, and entertainment areas, plus they also offer a number of in-house amenities, including a daily buffet breakfast and evening socials Monday to Thursday. Dogs are allowed for an additional one time pet fee of $75 per room. 2 dogs may be allowed.

Gull Wing Inn
Across the street from the Pacific Ocean
Moclips, WA
360-276-0014
gullwinginn.com
This small inn has three suites with kitchen and is directly across the street from the ocean. There is a $10 a night dog fee and rooms are about $60 to $85 per night.

Hi-Tide Ocean Beach Resort
4890 Railroad Avenue
Moclips, WA
360-276-4142 (800-MOCLIPS (WA Only))
hitideresort.com
This pet-friendly resort located right on the beach allows dogs to visit with you. There is a $12 to $15 pet fee per night depending on the season. Dogs must be leashed while on the property.

Ocean Crest Resort
4651 SR 109
Moclips, WA
360-276-4465
ohwy.com/wa/o/ocecrere.htm
There is a $18 per day per pet fee. Pets are allowed in some of the units. 2 dogs may be allowed.

Sunset Beach Cottage
40 Sunset St.
Moclips, WA
253-209-5523 (888-42BEACH)
stayatsunsetbeachcottage.com
This single level rental with a deck is across the street from the beach. Up to two dogs are welcome. There is a $10 per dog pet fee per night.

Best Western Sky Valley Inn
19233 Highway 2
Monroe, WA
360-794-3111 (800-780-7234)
Dogs of all sizes are allowed. Dogs are allowed for a nightly pet fee.

Best Western Lake Front Hotel
3000 Marina Drive
Moses Lake, WA

509-765-9211 (800-780-7234)
Dogs are welcome at this hotel.
There is a $20 one time pet fee.

Motel 6 - Moses Lake
2822 Driggs Dr
Moses Lake, WA
509-766-0250 (800-466-8356)
This motel welcomes your pets to
stay with you.

Ramada Moses Lake
1745 Kittleson Rd
Moses Lake, WA
509-766-1000 (800-272-6232)
Dogs of all sizes are allowed. Dogs
are allowed for a pet fee of $10 per
pet per stay.

Super 8 Moses Lake
I-90 & Exit 176
Moses Lake, WA
509-765-8886 (800-800-8000)
Dogs of all sizes are allowed. Dogs
are allowed for a pet fee of $10.00
per pet per night.

Best Western College Way Inn
300 W College Way
Mount Vernon, WA
360-424-4287 (800-780-7234)
Dogs of all sizes are allowed. Dogs
are allowed for a nightly pet fee.

Best Western CottonTree Inn
2300 Market Street
Mount Vernon, WA
360-428-5678 (800-780-7234)
Dogs are welcome at this hotel.

Days Inn Mt Vernon
2009 Riverside Drive
Mount Vernon, WA
360-424-4141 (800-329-7466)
Dogs of all sizes are allowed. Dogs
are allowed for a pet fee of $20.00
per pet per night.

Quality Inn
1910 Freeway Dr
Mount Vernon, WA
360-428-7020 (877-424-6423)
Dogs of all sizes are allowed. Dogs
are allowed for a pet fee of $10.00
per pet per night. Two dogs are
allowed per room.

Studio 6 - Seattle Mountlake Terrace
6017 244th St Sw
Mountlake Terrace, WA
425-771-3139 (800-466-8356)
Your pets are welcome to stay here
with you for a pet fee of $10 per day
up to $50 for an entire stay.

Extended Stay America Seattle -
Mukilteo

3917 Harbour Pointe Blvd. S.W.
Mukilteo, WA
425-493-1561 (800-804-3724)
One dog is allowed per suite. There
is a $25 per night additional pet fee
up to $150 for an entire stay.

TownePlace Suites Seattle
North/Mukilteo
8521 Mukilteo Speedway
Mukilteo, WA
425-551-5900 (800-257-3000)
This all suite hotel sits less than a
mile from Boeing's Future of Flight
Aviation Center and to many other
sites of interest for both business
and leisure travelers; plus they also
offer a number of in-house
amenities - including a daily buffet
breakfast. Dogs are allowed for an
additional fee of $10 per night per
pet. 2 dogs may be allowed.

Candlewood Suites Oak Harbor
33221 Sr 20
Oak Harbor, WA
360-279-2222 (877-270-6405)
Dogs up to 80 pounds are allowed.
Pets allowed with an additional pet
fee. Up to $75 for 1-6 nights and up
to $150 for 7+ nights. A pet
agreement must be signed at
check-in.

Coastal Cottages of Ocean Park
1511 264th Place
Ocean Park, WA
360-665-4658 (800-200-0424)
The cottages are located in a quiet
setting and have full kitchens and
fireplaces. There are no additional
pet fees. There are no designated
smoking or non-smoking rooms.
Dogs may not be left alone in the
room. 2 dogs may be allowed.

The Polynesian Condominium
Resort
615 Ocean Shores Blvd
Ocean Shores, WA
360-289-3361
There is a $15 per day per pet
additional fee. Pets are allowed on
the ground floor only. Multiple dogs
may be allowed.

Quality Inn
1211 Quince Street SE
Olympia, WA
360-943-4710 (877-424-6423)
Dogs of all sizes are allowed. Dogs
are allowed for a pet fee of $15.00
per pet per night.

Red Lion
2300 Evergreen Park Drive
Olympia, WA

360-943-4000
There is a $20 one time fee per pet.
There are no additional fees for R&R
members, and the R&R program is
free to sign up. 2 dogs may be
allowed.

Rodeway Inn & Suites
122 North Main St
Omak, WA
509-826-0400 (877-424-6423)
Dogs of all sizes are allowed. Dogs
are allowed for a pet fee of $10.00
per pet per night.

Best Western Othello Inn
1020 E Cedar Street
Othello, WA
509-488-5671 (800-780-7234)
Dogs are welcome at this hotel.

Sand Dollar Inn & Cottages
56 Central Avenue
Pacific Beach, WA
360-276-4525
sanddollarinn.net
This inn and cottages has one and
two bedroom pet friendly units. Some
of the units have kitchens. Some
have fenced yards or a dog kennel.
There is a $10 per night pet fee.

Sandpiper Ocean Beach Resort
4159 State Route 109
Pacific Beach, WA
360-276-4580
Thanks to one of our readers who
writes 'A great place on the
Washington Coast with miles of sand
beach to run.' There is a $13 per day
per pet fee. All rooms are non-
smoking. Multiple dogs may be
allowed.

King City Knights Inn/
2100 East Hillsboro Street
Pasco, WA
509-547-3475 (800-843-5644)
Dogs of all sizes are allowed. Dogs
are allowed for a pet fee.

Motel 6 - Pasco, Wa
1520 N. Oregon Ave.
Pasco, WA
509-546-2010 (800-466-8356)
Your pets are welcome to stay here
with you.

Red Lion
2525 N 20th Avenue
Pasco, WA
509-547-0701
There is a $25 one time pet fee per
room. There are no additional pet
fees for R&R members, and the R&R
program is free to sign up. Multiple
dogs may be allowed.

Sleep Inn
9930 Bedford St
Pasco, WA
509-545-9554 (877-424-6423)
Dogs of all sizes are allowed. Dogs are allowed for a pet fee of $10.00/per pet per night. Two dogs are allowed per room.

Days Inn Port Angeles
1510 E Front St
Port Angeles, WA
360-452-4015 (800-329-7466)
Dogs are welcome at this hotel.

Red Lion
221 N Lincoln
Port Angeles, WA
360-452-9215
There is a $20 one time pet fee per room. There are no additional pet fees for R&R members, and the R&R program is free to sign up. 2 dogs may be allowed.

Sol Duc Hot Springs Resort
12076 Sol Duc Hot Springs Road
Port Angeles, WA
360-327-3593 (866-875-8456)
Besides being located in a majestic mountain setting, this resort offers unique healing and relaxation opportunities with 3 natural mineral hots springs known for their therapeutic value. They also offer a swimming pool, a restaurant, cafe, grocery store, and gift shop. Dogs are allowed in the lodge or in the cabins for an additional pet fee of $15 per night per pet. Dogs must be kept on no more than a 6 foot leash and cleaned up after promptly. 2 dogs may be allowed.

Super 8 Port Angeles
2104 E 1st St
Port Angeles, WA
360-452-8401 (800-800-8000)
Dogs of all sizes are allowed. Dogs are allowed for a pet fee of $15 per pet per night.

Days Inn Port Orchard
220 Bravo Terrace
Port Orchard, WA
360-895-7818 (800-329-7466)
Dogs are welcome at this hotel.

Holiday Inn Express Poulsbo (Seattle Area)
19801 7th Avenue N.E.
Poulsbo, WA
360-697-4400 (877-270-6405)
Dogs of all sizes are allowed. Dogs are allowed for a pet fee of $30 per pet per night.

Hawthorn Inn & Suites
928 NW Olsen Street
Pullman, WA
509-332-0928 (866-333-8400)
hotelonthehill.com/
In addition to providing a convenient location to many local sites and activities, this all-suite hotel offers a number of amenities for business and leisure travelers, including their signature breakfast buffet and themed spa rooms. Dogs are allowed for an additional pet fee of $15 per night per room. Multiple dogs may be allowed.

Quality Inn Paradise Creek
S.E. 1400 Bishop Blvd.
Pullman, WA
509-332-0500 (877-424-6423)
Dogs of all sizes are allowed.

Best Western Park Plaza
620 South Hill Park Drive
Puyallup, WA
253-848-1500 (800-780-7234)
Dogs of all sizes are allowed. Dogs are allowed for a pet fee of $25.00 per pet per stay.

Holiday Inn Express Hotel & Suites Puyallup (Tacoma Area)
812 South Hill Park Drive
Puyallup, WA
253-848-4900 (077-270 6405)
Dogs of all sizes are allowed. Dogs are allowed for a pet fee of $25.00 per pet per stay.

Residence Inn Seattle East/Redmond
7575 164th Avenue NE
Redmond, WA
425-497-9226 (800-331-3131)
Located in the heart of the city with numerous activities and sites of interest for either the business or leisure traveler, this all suite hotel also provides a daily buffet breakfast and Wednesday night socials with light dinner fare. Dogs are allowed for an additional one time pet fee of $100 per room. Multiple dogs may be allowed.

TownePlace Suites Seattle South/Renton
300 SW 19th Street
Renton, WA
425-917-2000 (800-257-3000)
In addition to offering a number of in-house amenities for all level of travelers, this all suite inn also provides a convenient location to both downtown areas of Tacoma and Seattle and Super Mall - the

NW's largest outlet mall. Dogs are allowed for an additional one time fee of $100 per room. 2 dogs may be allowed.

Clarion Hotel & Conference Center
1515 George Washington Way
Richland, WA
509-946-4121 (877-424-6423)
There is an additional $10 pet fee per night per room. 2 dogs may be allowed.

Days Inn Richland
615 Jadwin
Richland, WA
509-943-4611 (800-329-7466)
Dogs of all sizes are allowed. Dogs are allowed for a nightly pet fee.

Holiday Inn Express Hotel & Suites Richland
1970 Center Parkway
Richland, WA
509-737-8000 (877-270-6405)
Dogs of all sizes are allowed. Dogs are allowed for a pet fee of $10 per pet per night.

Motel 6 - Richland Kennewick
1751 Fowler St
Richland, WA
509-783-1250 (800-466-8356)
Your pets are welcome to stay here with you.

Red Lion
802 George Washington Way
Richland, WA
509-946-7611
There is a $25 per night per room additional pet fee. There are no additional pet fees for R&R members, and the R&R program is free to sign up. Multiple dogs may be allowed.

Best Western Bronco Inn
105 Galbreath Way
Ritzville, WA
509-659-5000 (800-780-7234)
Dogs of all sizes are allowed. Dogs are allowed for a pet fee of $10 per pet per night.

La Quinta Inn Ritzville
1513 Smitty's Blvd.
Ritzville, WA
509-659-1007 (800-531-5900)
Dogs of all sizes are allowed. There are no additional pet fees. Dogs must be quiet, well behaved, leashed and cleaned up after. Dogs must be walked at the designated pet walk area, and they are not allowed in the lobby during breakfast hours. 2 dogs may be allowed.

Rodeway Inn
2930 S. 176th St.
SeaTac, WA
206-246-9300 (877-424-6423)
Dogs of all sizes are allowed. Dogs are allowed for a pet fee of $10.00 per pet per night. Two dogs are allowed per room.

Alexis Hotel
1007 First Avenue
Seattle, WA
206-624-4844
alexishotel.com/
Well-behaved dogs up to 200 pounds are welcome at this pet-friendly hotel. The luxury boutique hotel offers both rooms and suites. Hotel amenities include complimentary evening wine service, 24 hour room service and an on-site fitness room. This hotel is located near the historic Pioneer Square and Pike's Place Market. There are no pet fees, just sign a pet liability form.

Crown Plaza Downtown
1113 6th Avenue
Seattle, WA
206-464-1980 (800-2CROWNE or 800-521-2762)
One dog up to 50 pounds or 2 dogs totaling no more than 50 pounds are allowed per room. There is a $50 one time pet fee per room and a pet policy to sign at check in. 2 dogs may be allowed.

Doubletree Guest Suites
16500 Southcenter Parkway
Seattle, WA
206-575-8220 (800-222-TREE (8733))
Located only a couple of miles from the Seattle Tacoma International Airport, this upscale hotel offers a number of on site amenities for business or leisure travelers, plus a convenient location to business, shopping, dining, and entertainment areas. Dogs are allowed for an additional one time fee of $35 per pet. 2 dogs may be allowed.

Doubletree Hotel
18740 International Blvd
Seattle, WA
206-246-8600 (800-222-TREE (8733))
Located next to the SeaTac International Airport, this upscale hotel offers a number of on site amenities for all level of travelers - including their signature chocolate chip cookies at check in, plus a convenient location to business, shopping, dining, and recreation

areas. Dogs are allowed for no additional fee. 2 dogs may be allowed.

Extended Stay America Seattle - Northgate
13300 Stone Ave. N.
Seattle, WA
206-365-8100 (800-804-3724)
One dog is allowed per suite. There is a $25 per night additional pet fee up to $150 for an entire stay.

Hilton Hotel
17620 International Blvd
Seattle, WA
206-244-4800 (800-HILTONS (445-8667))
This upscale hotel sits across from the Seattle Tacoma International Airport and offers guests a number on site amenities for all level of travelers, plus a convenient location to the area's shopping, dining, and recreation areas. Dogs up to 70 pounds are allowed for an additional one time fee of $50 per pet. 2 dogs may be allowed.

Holiday Inn Express Hotel & Suites Seattle-Sea-Tac Airport
19621 International Blvd
Seattle, WA
206-824-3200 (877-270-6405)
Dogs of all sizes are allowed. Dogs are allowed for a pet fee.

Hotel Monaco Seattle
1101 4th Avenue
Seattle, WA
206-621-1770
monaco-seattle.com/
Well-behaved dogs of all sizes are welcome at this pet-friendly hotel. The luxury boutique hotel offers both rooms and suites. Hotel amenities include complimentary evening wine service, complimentary high speed Internet access in all guest rooms, 24 hour room service and a 24 hour on-site fitness room. There are no pet fees, just sign a pet liability form.

Hotel Vintage Park
1100 Fifth Avenue
Seattle, WA
206-624-8000
hotelvintagepark.com/
Well-behaved dogs of all sizes are welcome at this pet-friendly hotel. The luxury boutique hotel offers both rooms and suites. Hotel amenities include complimentary evening wine service, complimentary high speed Internet access, and 24 hour room service. There are no pet fees, just sign a

pet liability form.

Howard Johnson Sea Tac Airport
14110 Tukwila Intl Blvd So
Seattle, WA
206-244-6464 (800-446-4656)
Dogs of all sizes are allowed. Dogs are allowed for a nightly pet fee.

La Quinta Inn & Suites Seattle Downtown
2224 8th Avenue
Seattle, WA
206-624-6820 (800-531-5900)
Dogs of all sizes are allowed. There are no additional pet fees. Dogs may not be left unattended, and they must be leashed and cleaned up after. Multiple dogs may be allowed.

La Quinta Inn Seattle Sea-Tac
2824 S. 188th St.
Seattle, WA
206-241-5211 (800-531-5900)
Dogs of all sizes are allowed. There are no additional pet fees. Dogs must be leashed, cleaned up after, and attended to or removed for housekeeping. Multiple dogs may be allowed.

Motel 6 - Seattle Airport
16500 Pacific Hwy
Seattle, WA
206-246-4101 (800-466-8356)
This motel welcomes your pets to stay with you.

Motel 6 - Seattle Sea-tac Airport South
18900 47th Ave
Seattle, WA
206-241-1648 (800-466-8356)
This motel welcomes your pets to stay with you.

Motel 6 - Seattle South
20651 Military Rd
Seattle, WA
206-824-9902 (800-466-8356)
This motel welcomes your pets to stay with you.

Pensione Nichols Bed and Breakfast
1923 1st Avenue
Seattle, WA
206-441-7125 (800-440-7125)
seattle-bed-breakfast.com
Thanks to one of our readers who writes: 'A charming and very dog-friendly place to stay in downtown Seattle.' Large dogs are allowed to stay here if they are well-behaved. This B&B also requires that you do not leave your dog in the room alone. The Pensione Nichols is the only bed-and-breakfast located in the

retail and entertainment core of downtown Seattle. Housed in a remodeled, turn-of-the-century building in the historic Smith Block, Pensione Nichols overlooks the Pike Place Market. This B&B has 10 guest rooms and suites (the suites have private bathrooms). During the summer, there is a 2 night minimum. There is a $15 one time pet fee per room. 2 dogs may be allowed.

Quality Inn Sea-Tac Airport
2900 S. 192nd
Seattle, WA
206-241-9292 (877-424-6423)
Dogs of all sizes are allowed. Dogs are allowed for a pet fee of $10.00 per pet per night. Two dogs are allowed per room.

Ramada Limited Tukwila/SeaTac
13900 International Blvd
Seattle, WA
206-244-8800 (800-272-6232)
Dogs of all sizes are allowed. Dogs are allowed for a pet fee of $40 per pet per night.

Red Lion
1415 5th Avenue
Seattle, WA
206-971-8000
There is a $20 one time pet fee per room. There are no additional pet fees for R&R members, and the R&R program is free to sign up. 2 dogs may be allowed.

Red Lion
18220 International Blvd
Seattle, WA
206-246-5535
There is a $20 one time pet fee per room. There are no additional pet fees for R&R members, and the R&R program is free to sign up. Multiple dogs may be allowed.

Red Roof Inn Seattle Airport
16838 International Blvd.
Seattle, WA
206-248-0901 (800-RED-ROOF)
One well-behaved family pet per room. Guest must notify front desk upon arrival. Guest is liable for any damages. In consideration of all guests, pets must never be left unattended in the guest rooms.

Renaissance Seattle Hotel
515 Madison Street
Seattle, WA
206-583-0300 (800-546-9184)
This luxury, downtown hotel sits central to many of the city's star attractions, world class shopping and

dining venues, day/night entertainment areas, and major business areas, plus they also offer a number of in-house amenities for all level of travelers. Dogs are allowed for an additional one time fee of $100 per room. 2 dogs may be allowed.

Residence Inn Seattle
Downtown/Lake Union
800 Fairview Avenue N
Seattle, WA
206-624-6000 (800-331-3131)
Located within walking distance to the waterfront, this all suite inn also offers a convenient location to numerous businesses, shopping, dining, and entertainment areas; plus they offer a number of in-house amenities, including a daily buffet breakfast and a complimentary reception on Wednesdays that is catered by the local restaurants. Dogs are allowed for an additional fee of $10 per night per pet. 2 dogs may be allowed.

Residence Inn Seattle
South/Tukwila
16201 W Valley H
Seattle, WA
425-226-5500 (800-331-3131)
In addition to being only 4 miles from the airport and offering a convenient location to business, shopping, dining, and entertainment areas, this hotel also provides a number of in-house amenities, including a daily buffet breakfast and evening social hours. Dogs are allowed for an additional one time fee of $25 for 1 to 3 nights and $75 for 4 or more nights. Aggressive known breeds are not allowed. Multiple dogs may be allowed.

Seattle Pacific Hotel
325 Aurora Avenue N
Seattle, WA
206-441-0400 (888-451-0400)
seattlepacifichotel.com/
this hotel offers 59 nicely-appointed rooms with many in-room amenities, a free continental breakfast, and a seasonal outdoor pool and Jacuzzi. Dogs of all sizes are allowed. There is a $30 per night per pet additional fee for dogs up to 100 pounds, and a $50 per night per pet additional fee for dogs over 100 pounds. Dogs must be leashed, cleaned up after, and crated or removed for housekeeping.

Sheraton Seattle Hotel
1400 6th Ave.
Seattle, WA

206-621-9000 (888-625-5144)
Dogs up to 50 pounds are allowed for no additional pet fee. Dogs may not be left alone in the room.

Super 8 Seattle
3100 S 192nd Street
Seattle, WA
206-433-8188 (800-800-8000)
Dogs of all sizes are allowed. Dogs are allowed for a pet fee of $10.00 per pet per night.

The Fairmont Olympic Hotel
411 University Street
Seattle, WA
206-621-1700
fairmont.com/
Listed on the National Register of Historic Places, this beautiful 1924 hotel is located in the heart of downtown and offers a number of amenities including a swimming pool, restaurants, an oyster bar, and live music daily in the piano bar during cocktail hour. Dogs up to 50 pounds are allowed for no additional fee. Dogs must be well mannered, and they must be kept leashed and under their owner's control at all times. Dogs may not be left alone in the room and they are not allowed in food or beverage areas. 2 dogs may be allowed.

University Inn
4140 Roosevelt Way NE
Seattle, WA
206-632-5055
Dogs are allowed for a $20 per night per room fee and a pet policy to sign at check in. Dogs are not to be left unattended. 2 dogs may be allowed.

Vagabond Inn by the Space Needle
325 Aurora Ave N
Seattle, WA
206-441-0400
This motel is located just several blocks from the Space Needle, the waterfront and Washington St. Convention Center. The motel has a heated swimming pool and Jacuzzi, 24 hour cable television and more. Dogs up to 100 pounds are allowed for an additional fee of $30 per night per pet. 2 dogs may be allowed.

W Seattle
1112 4th Avenue
Seattle, WA
206-264-6000
Dogs are allowed for an additional fee of $25 per night per room with a credit card on file. Dogs must be declared at the time of registration. Pets receive a special welcome with a pet amenity kit that includes a

custom pet bed, food and water dishes with a floor mat, a Pet-in-Room sign, treats, pet tag, a toy, and more. The concierge can also offer additional services such as dog-walking and information about local dog services and parks. Dogs must be removed or crated for housekeeping or for any in-room services.

Bloomer Estates Vacation Rentals
1004 41st Place, P.O. Box 345
Seaview, WA
360-243-9510 (800-747-2096)
bloomerestates.com
These vacation rentals on Long Beach Peninsula welcomes dogs to many of their properties.

Sunset Marine Resort
40 Buzzard Ridge Road
Sequim, WA
206-632-5055
the fee is $15 per night per pet for dogs over 30 pounds.

Super 8 Shelton
2943 Northview Circle,
Shelton, WA
360-426-1654 (800-800-8000)
Dogs of all sizes are allowed. Dogs are allowed for a pet fee.

Silverdale Beach Hotel
3073 NW Bucklin Hill Road
Silverdale, WA
360-698-1000
silverdalebeachhotel.com/
Dogs of all sizes are allowed. There is a $25 per night per room fee and a pet policy to sign at check in. Multiple dogs may be allowed.

Howard Johnson
603 State Route 906
Snoqualmie Pass, WA
800-557-7829 (800-446-4656)
Dogs of all sizes are allowed. Dogs are allowed for a pet fee of $25.00 per pet per stay.

Pacific Beach Inn
12 First Street
South Pacific Beach, WA
360-276-4433
Dogs of all sizes are allowed. There is a $10 per night per pet additional fee. 2 dogs may be allowed.

Comfort Inn North
7111 N. Division
Spokane, WA
509-467-7111 (877-424-6423)
Dogs of all sizes are allowed. Dogs are allowed for a pet fee of $10.00 per pet per night.

Comfort Inn University District/Downtown
923 3rd Ave E.
Spokane, WA
509-535-9000 (877-424-6423)
Dogs of all sizes are allowed. Dogs are allowed for a pet fee of $10.00 per pet per night. Two dogs are allowed per room.

Days Inn Downtown Spokane
120 W. 3rd Ave
Spokane, WA
509-747-2011 (800-329-7466)
Dogs of all sizes are allowed. Dogs are allowed for a pet fee of $10.00 per pet per night.

Doubletree Hotel
322 N Spokane Falls Court
Spokane, WA
509-455-9600 (800-222-TREE (8733))
Centrally located downtown on the Spokane River, this luxury hotel offers a number of amenities for all level of travelers - including their signature chocolate chip cookies at check in and a sky bridge to the Spokane Convention Center, plus a convenient location to business, shopping, dining, and recreation areas. Dogs are allowed for an additional one time fee of $50 per pet. 2 dogs may be allowed.

Holiday Inn Spokane
1616 S. Windsor Drive
Spokane, WA
509-838-1170 (877-270-6405)
Dogs up to 70 pounds are allowed.

Howard Johnson Inn North Spokane
3033 N Division St
Spokane, WA
509-326-5500 (800-446-4656)
Dogs are welcome at this hotel.

La Quinta Inn & Suites Spokane
3808 N Sullivan Rd
Spokane, WA
509-893-0955 (800-531-5900)
Dogs of all sizes are allowed. There are no additional pet fees. Dogs must be leashed, cleaned up after, and crated when left alone in the room. Multiple dogs may be allowed.

Motel 6 - Spokane East
1919 Hutchinson Rd
Spokane, WA
509-926-5399 (800-466-8356)
Your pets are welcome to stay here with you.

Motel 6 - Spokane West Airport
1508 Rustle St
Spokane, WA
509-459-6120 (800-466-8356)
Your pets are welcome to stay here with you.

Ramada Airport and Indoor Waterpark Spokane
8909 West Airport Drive
Spokane, WA
509-838-5211 (800-272-6232)
Dogs are welcome at this hotel.

Ramada Limited Downtown Spokane
123 South Post Street
Spokane, WA
509-838-8504 (800-272-6232)
Dogs of all sizes are allowed. Dogs are allowed for a nightly pet fee.

Ramada Limited Suites Spokane
9601 N Newport Hwy
Spokane, WA
509-468-4201 (800-272-6232)
Dogs are welcome at this hotel.

Red Lion
303 W North River Drive
Spokane, WA
509-326-8000
Dogs up to 50 pounds are allowed. There is a $20 one time pet fee per room. There are no additional pet fees for R&R members, and the R&R program is free to sign up. 2 dogs may be allowed.

Red Lion
700 N Division
Spokane, WA
509-326-5577
Dogs of all sizes are allowed. There is a pet policy to sign at check and a $20 one time pet fee per room. There are no additional fees for R&R members, and the R&R program is free. 2 dogs may be allowed.

Red Lion
515 W Sprague Avenue
Spokane, WA
509-838-2711
Dogs of all sizes are allowed. There is a $100 refundable deposit per room and a pet policy to sign at check in.

Red Lion Inn
N 700 Division St
Spokane, WA
509-326-5577
redlion.rdln.com/
There is an additional one time pet fee of $20 per room. 2 dogs may be allowed.

Dog-Friendly Lodging - Please always call ahead to make sure an establishment is still dog-friendly.

Rodeway Inn & Suites
6309 East Broadway
Spokane, WA
509-535-7185 (877-424-6423)
Dogs of all sizes are allowed. Dogs are allowed for a pet fee of $10.00 per pet per night. Two dogs are allowed per room.

Super 8 Valley Spokane
2020 N Argonne Rd.
Spokane, WA
509-928-4888 (800-800-8000)
Dogs are welcome at this hotel.

Super 8 /West Spokane
11102 W Westbow Blvd
Spokane, WA
509-838-8800 (800-800-8000)
Dogs of all sizes are allowed. Dogs are allowed for a pet fee of $15.00 per pet per stay.

The Davenport Hotel
10 S Post Street
Spokane, WA
509-455-8888 (800-899-1482)
thedavenporthotel.com/#
This hotel offers a long, rich history and feature 1, 2, and 3 bedroom luxury guest rooms and suites with many in-room amenities, world class dining including a Champagne Sunday Brunch, indoor pool and Jacuzzi, and they even offer an historic walking tour. They are also home to the popular Peacock Room Lounge that showcases a giant stained-glass peacock ceiling, and provides great nightlife entertainment. Dogs of all sizes are allowed for no additional fee. Dogs may only be left alone in the room if they will be quiet and well behaved, and they must be leashed and cleaned up after at all times.

Travelodge at the Convention Center Spokane
W. 33 Spokane Falls Blvd.
Spokane, WA
509-623-9727 (800-578-7878)
Dogs of all sizes are allowed. Dogs are allowed for a pet fee of $12.00 per pet per night.

Ramada Spokane Valley
905 N Sullivan Rd
Spokane Valley, WA
509-924-3838 (800-272-6232)
Dogs of all sizes are allowed. Dogs are allowed for a pet fee of $10.00 per pet per stay.

Rodeway Inn
3209 Picard Place

Sunnyside, WA
509-837-5781 (877-424-6423)
Dogs of all sizes are allowed.

Days Inn - Tacoma Mall Tacoma
6802 Tacoma Mall Blvd
Tacoma, WA
253-475-5900 (800-329-7466)
Dogs of all sizes are allowed. Dogs are allowed for a nightly pet fee.

Days Inn /North Fife Tacoma
3021 Pacific Hwy East
Tacoma, WA
253-922-3500 (800-329-7466)
Dogs are welcome at this hotel.

Extended Stay America Tacoma - South
2120 S. 48th St.
Tacoma, WA
253-475-6565 (800-804-3724)
One dog is allowed per suite. There is a $25 per night additional pet fee up to $150 for an entire stay.

La Quinta Inn & Suites Seattle Tacoma
1425 E. 27th St.
Tacoma, WA
253-383-0146 (800-531-5900)
Dogs of all sizes are allowed. There are no additional pet fees. Dogs must be quiet, well behaved, leashed and cleaned up after. 2 dogs may be allowed.

Motel 6   Tacoma South
1811 76th St
Tacoma, WA
253-473-7100 (800-466-8356)
This motel welcomes your pets to stay with you.

Sheraton Tacoma Hotel
1320 Broadway Plaza
Tacoma, WA
253-572-3200 (888-625-5144)
Dogs of all sizes are allowed. There are no additional pet fees. Dogs are not allowed to be left alone in the room.

Best Western Toppenish Inn
515 S Elm Street
Toppenish, WA
509-865-7444 (800-780-7234)
Dogs of all sizes are allowed. Dogs are allowed for a nightly pet fee.

Quality Inn & Suites
511 S. Elm Street
Toppenish, WA
509-865-5800 (877-424-6423)
Dogs of all sizes are allowed. Dogs are allowed for a pet fee of $10.00 per pet per night.

Extended Stay America Seattle - Tukwila
15451 53rd Ave. S.
Tukwila, WA
206-244-2537 (800-804-3724)
One dog is allowed per suite. There is a $25 per night additional pet fee up to $150 for an entire stay.

Homestead Studio Suites Seattle - Southcenter
15635 W. Valley Hwy.
Tukwila, WA
425-235-7160 (800-804-3724)
One dog is allowed per suite. There is a $25 per night additional pet fee up to $150 for an entire stay.

Best Western Tumwater Inn
5188 Capitol Boulevard SE
Tumwater, WA
360-956-1235 (800-780-7234)
Dogs of all sizes are allowed. Dogs are allowed for a pet fee of $15.00 per pet per night.

Extended Stay America Olympia - Tumwater
1675 Mottman Rd. S.W.
Tumwater, WA
360-754-6063 (800-804-3724)
One dog is allowed per suite. There is a $25 per night additional pet fee up to $150 for an entire stay.

Motel 6 - Tumwater Olympia
400 Lee St Sw
Tumwater, WA
360-754-7320 (800-466-8356)
This motel welcomes your pets to stay with you.

Super 8 /Yakima Area Union Gap
2605 Rudkin Rd
Union Gap, WA
509-248-8880 (800-800-8000)
Dogs are welcome at this hotel.

Days Inn And Suites Salmon Creek Vancouver
13207 N.E. 20th Ave
Vancouver, WA
360-574-6000 (800-329-7466)
Dogs of all sizes are allowed. Dogs are allowed for a pet fee of $15 per pet per stay.

Days Inn and Suites Vancouver
9107 NE Vancouver Mall Drive
Vancouver, WA
360-253-5000 (800-329-7466)
Dogs of all sizes are allowed. Dogs are allowed for a pet fee of $20.00 per pet per night.

Econo Lodge

601 Broadway
Vancouver, WA
360-693-3668 (877-424-6423)
Dogs of all sizes are allowed. Dogs
are allowed for a pet fee of $10.00/
per pet per night. Two dogs are
allowed per room.

Extended Stay America Portland -
Vancouver
300 NE 115th Ave.
Vancouver, WA
360-604-8530 (800-804-3724)
One dog is allowed per suite. There
is a $25 per night additional pet fee
up to $150 for an entire stay.

Hilton Hotel
301 W 6th Street
Vancouver, WA
360-993-4500 (800-HILTONS (445-
8667))
Located in the heart of the city, this
upscale hotel is one of the country's
1st sustainably-designed hotels with
both LEED and Green Seal
certifications, and they offer
numerous on site amenities for
business and leisure travelers, plus a
convenient location to business,
shopping, dining, and entertainment
areas. Dogs up to 50 pounds are
allowed for an additional one time
pet fee of $35 per room. 2 dogs may
be allowed.

Motel 6 - Vancouver
221 Ne Chkalov Drive
Vancouver, WA
360-253-8900 (800-466-8356)
This motel welcomes your pets to
stay with you.

Quality Inn & Suites
7001 N.E. Highway 99
Vancouver, WA
360-696-0516 (877-424-6423)
Dogs of all sizes are allowed.

Red Lion
100 Columbia Street
Vancouver, WA
360-694-8341
There is a $20 one time pet fee per
room. There are no additional pet
fees for R&R members, and the R&R
program is free to sign up. 2 dogs
may be allowed.

Residence Inn Portland
North/Vancouver
8005 NE Parkway Drive
Vancouver, WA
360-253-4800 (800-331-3131)
Some of the amenities at this all-
suite inn include a daily buffet
breakfast, evening socials Monday

through Thursday with light dinner
fare, a Sport Court, a heated
swimming pool, and a
complimentary grocery shopping
service. Dogs are allowed for an
additional one time pet fee of $75
per room. 2 dogs may be allowed.

Rodeway Inn & Suites
9201 NE Vancouver Mall Dr.
Vancouver, WA
360-254-0900 (877-424-6423)
Dogs up to 200 pounds are allowed.
Two dogs are allowed per room.

Staybridge Suites Vancouver
7301 NE 41st Street
Vancouver, WA
360-891-8282 (877-270-6405)
Dogs up to 80 pounds are allowed.
Pets allowed with an additional pet
fee. Up to $75 for 1-6 nights and up
to $150 for 7+ nights. A pet
agreement must be signed at
check-in.

Best Western Walla Walla Suites
Inn
7 E Oak Street
Walla Walla, WA
509-525-4700 (800-780-7234)
Dogs of all sizes are allowed. Dogs
are allowed for a pet fee of $10.00
per pet per night.

Holiday Inn Express Walla Walla
1433 W Pine Street
Walla Walla, WA
509-525-6200 (877-270-6405)
Dogs of all sizes are allowed. Dogs
are allowed for a pet fee of $20.00
per pet per night.

La Quinta Inn Walla Walla
520 North 2nd Avenue
Walla Walla, WA
509-525-2522 (800-531-5900)
Dogs of all sizes are allowed. There
are no additional pet fees. Dogs
must be leashed and cleaned up
after. The Do Not Disturb sign must
be put on the door and the front
desk informed if there is a dog
alone in the room. Multiple dogs
may be allowed.

Super 8 Walla Walla
2315 Eastgate Street North
Walla Walla, WA
509-525-8800 (800-800-8000)
Dogs are welcome at this hotel.

Travelodge Walla Walla
421 East Main Street
Walla Walla, WA
509-529-4940 (800-578-7878)
Dogs are welcome at this hotel.

Econo Lodge
232 N. Wenatchee Avenue
Wenatchee, WA
509-663-7121 (877-424-6423)
Dogs of all sizes are allowed. Dogs
are allowed for a pet fee of $10.00
per pet per night. Two dogs are
allowed per room.

La Quinta Inn & Suites Wenatchee
1905 N Wenatchee Ave
Wenatchee, WA
509-664-6565 (800-531-5900)
Dogs of all sizes are allowed. There
are no additional pet fees. Dogs may
not be left unattended, and they must
be leashed and cleaned up after. 2
dogs may be allowed.

Red Lion
1225 N Wenatchee Avenue
Wenatchee, WA
509-663-0711
There is a $20 one time pet fee per
room. There are no additional pet
fees for R&R members, and the R&R
program is free to sign up. 2 dogs
may be allowed.

Super 8 Wenatchee
1401 N. Miller St.
Wenatchee, WA
509-662-3443 (800-800-8000)
Dogs of all sizes are allowed. Dogs
are allowed for a pet fee of $10 per
pet per night.

Travelodge
1004 North Wenatchee Ave
Wenatchee, WA
509-662-8165 (800-578-7878)
Dogs are welcome at this hotel.

Islander Resort
421 East Neddie Rose Dr
Westport, WA
360-268-9166 (800-322-1740)
westport-islander.com
This inn is located at the marina and
claims to make the best Bloody Mary
in Washington State. There are
standard rooms and suites available.
Dogs are allowed with a $40 pet fee
for your stay.

The Winthrop Inn
960 H 20
Winthrop, WA
509-996-2217
there can be 1 large dog or 2 small
dogs per room. They request you
bring your dog's sleeping mat and
that you keep them leashed while on
the grounds. There is a beach on the
river close by where the dogs can
run unleashed.

Willows Lodge
14580 NE 145th Street/H 202
Woodinville, WA
425-424-3900 (877-424-3930)
willowslodge.com/
In addition to a great location for
exploring many of the areas best
attractions, this resort offers 5
beautifully landscaped acres highly-
complimented by various themed
gardens, numerous on-site and in-
room amenities, and fine wining and
dining. Leashed, well mannered dogs
are allowed for an additional one
time fee of $25 per room. Dogs
must be cleaned up after promptly,
and they must be crated when left
alone in the room. 2 dogs may be
allowed.

Cedars Inn
1500 Atlantic Avenue
Woodland, WA
360-225-6548 (800-444-9667)
Frequently referred to as Woodland's
Best, this Inn has parking that will
accommodate RVs and 18-wheelers,
and they offer 60 spacious, nicely-
appointed rooms with many in-room
amenities, and a deluxe
complimentary breakfast. Dogs of all
sizes are allowed for an additional
fee of $10 per night per pet. Dogs
may not be left alone in the room at
any time, and they must be leashed
and cleaned up after. 2 dogs may be
allowed.

Days Inn Yakima
1504 N. First St.
Yakima, WA
509-248-3393 (800-329-7466)
Dogs are welcome at this hotel.

Howard Johnson Plaza
9 North 9th Street
Yakima, WA
509-452-6511 (800-446-4656)
Dogs are welcome at this hotel.

Knights Inn Yakima
818 N 1st Street
Yakima, WA
509-453-0391 (800-843-5644)
Dogs are welcome at this hotel.
There is a $15 one time additional
pet fee.

Motel 6 - Yakima
1104 1st St
Yakima, WA
509-454-0080 (800-466-8356)
Your pets are welcome to stay here
with you.

Red Lion

607 E Yakima Avenue
Yakima, WA
509-248-5900
There are no additional pet fees.
Multiple dogs may be allowed.

Comfort Inn
911 Vintage Valley Pkwy.
Zillah, WA
509-829-3399 (877-424-6423)
Dogs of all sizes are allowed. Dogs
are allowed for a pet fee of $10.00
per pet per night.

West Virginia

Comfort Inn
249 Mall Rd
Barboursville, WV
304-733-2122 (877-424-6423)
Dogs of all sizes are allowed.

Econo Lodge
1909 Harper Rd.
Beckley, WV
304-255-2161 (877-424-6423)
Dogs of all sizes are allowed.

Howard Johnson Express Inn -
Beckley
1907 Harper Road
Beckley, WV
304-255-5900 (800-446-4656)
Dogs are welcome at this hotel.

Super 8 Beckley
2014 Harper Rd
Beckley, WV
304-253-0802 (800-800-8000)
Dogs are welcome at this hotel.

Berkeley Springs Motel
468 Wilkes Street
Berkeley Springs, WV
304-258-1776
berkeleyspringsmotel.net/
Dogs are allowed for no additional
pet fee. 2 dogs may be allowed.

Hannah's House
867 Libby's Ridge Road
Berkeley Springs, WV
304-258-1718 (800-526-0807)
This antique farm home offers
seclusion and convenience to a
number of local activities and
recreation. Well behaved dogs are
allowed for an additional fee of $25
per pet for weekends, and $50 per
pet by the week. Dogs are not
allowed on the furniture, and they
must be crated when left alone in
the room. Multiple dogs may be
allowed.

Sleepy Creek Tree Farm

37 Shades Lane
Berkeley Springs, WV
304-258-4324 (866-275-8303)
maggiedot.com/sleepycreektree/
Located on 8 scenic acres of a
Christmas tree farm, this is a nature
lover's get-a-way. One dog is allowed
for no additional pet fee. Dogs must
be able to climb stairs (or be carried);
they must be friendly to cats and
other dogs, and they may not be left
unattended at any time.

Sunset Mountain Farm
Stickey Kline Road
Berkeley Springs, WV
304-258-4239
sunsetmountainfarm.com/
Great views, 40 private acres,
convenience to a number of local
activities and recreation, and more
are offered at this get-away. Dogs
are allowed for an additional one
time fee of $25 per pet. Dogs must
be well behaved, quiet, and the
furniture/beds must be covered if
pets are used to being on
furnishings. 2 dogs may be allowed.

Econo Lodge Near Bluefield College
3400 Cumberland Rd.
Bluefield, WV
304-327-8171 (877-424-6423)
Dogs of all sizes are allowed. Dogs
are allowed for a pet fee of $10.00
per pet per stay.

Knights Inn Bluefield
3144 East Cumberland Rd
Bluefield, WV
304-325-9131 (800-843-5644)
Dogs of all sizes are allowed. Dogs
are allowed for a nightly pet fee.

Holiday Inn Clarksburg-Bridgeport
100 Lodgeville Rd
Bridgeport, WV
304-842-5411 (877-270-6405)
Dogs of all sizes are allowed. Dogs
are allowed for a pet fee of $5.00 per
pet per night.

Sleep Inn
115 Tolley Rd.
Bridgeport, WV
304-842-1919 (877-424-6423)
Dogs of all sizes are allowed.

Super 8 /Clarksburg Area Bridgeport
168 Barnett Run Road
Bridgeport, WV
304-842-7381 (800-800-8000)
Dogs are welcome at this hotel.

Travelodge Of Bridgeport
1235 W Main Street
Bridgeport, WV

304-842-7115 (800-578-7878)
Dogs of all sizes are allowed. Dogs are allowed for a pet fee of $10.00 per pet per stay.

Centennial Motel
22 N Locust St
Buckhannon, WV
304-472-4100
There are no additional pet fees. 2 dogs may be allowed.

North Fork Mountain Inn
Smoke Hole Road
Cabins, WV
304-257-1108
northforkmtninn.com/
Located in a lush mountain setting, this retreat is open year round offering the best of all the seasons. Dogs are allowed at the Hideaway Cabin here but not in the inn. There is a fee of $15 per night per pet. 2 dogs may be allowed.

A Room with A View
Black Bear Woods Resort-Northside
Cortland Rd
Canaan Valley, WV
301-767-6853
This is Unit 132 in the Black Bear Woods Resort. It is a single room suite without a kitchen with a view of Canaan Valley. There are two Queen beds and a large bathroom with a Jacuzzi. Well-behaved dogs are welcome for a $30 cleaning fee per stay.

Rodeway Inn
SR 10 & US 119
Chapmanville, WV
304-855-7182 (877-424-6423)
Dogs of all sizes are allowed. Dogs are allowed for a pet fee of $10.00 per pet per night. Two dogs are allowed per room.

Country Inns & Suites by Carlson
105 Alex Lane
Charleston, WV
304-925-4300
There are no additional fees (or room discounts) if bringing 1 dog, and there is a $25 one time pet fee for a 2nd dog.

Knights Inn East Charleston
6401 MacCorkle Ave SE
Charleston, WV
304-925-0451 (800-843-5644)
Dogs are welcome at this hotel.

Motel 6 - Charleston East, Wv
6311 Maccorkle Ave Se
Charleston, WV
304-925-0471 (800-466-8356)

This motel welcomes your pets to stay with you.

Ramada Charleston
400 2nd Ave SW
Charleston, WV
304-744-4641 (800-272-6232)
Dogs are welcome at this hotel.

Residence Inn Charleston
200 Hotel Circle
Charleston, WV
304-345-4200 (800-676-6158)
This all suite hotel sit central to many of the city's star attractions and centers of industry and healing. Additionally they feature a number of in-house amenities - including a daily buffet breakfast and complimentary hospitality hours. Dogs are allowed for an additional one time pet fee of $75. 2 dogs may be allowed.

Comfort Inn West
102 Racer Dr.
Cross Lanes, WV
304-776-8070 (877-424-6423)
Dogs up to 100 pounds are allowed. Dogs are allowed for a pet fee of $25.00 per pet per stay. Two dogs are allowed per room.

Motel 6 - Charleston West Cross Lanes, Wv
330 Goff Mountain Rd
Cross Lanes, WV
304-776-5911 (800-466-8356)
This motel welcomes your pets to stay with you.

The Resort at Glade Springs
255 Resort Drive
Daniels, WV
866-562-8054 (800-634-5233)
gladesprings.com/
This resort offers year round recreational activities with a complete Leisure Center that offers a 10-lane bowling alley, an indoor poor, a small movie theater, arcade, gaming courts, and more. Dogs up to 50 pounds are welcome with advance registration for a fee per pet of $70 for the 1st night and $20 for each additional night. Dogs may not be left alone in the room at any time, and the front desk will also provide sanitary bags for pets. 2 dogs may be allowed.

Super 8 /Charleston Area Dunbar
911 Dunbar Ave
Dunbar, WV
304-768-6888 (800-800-8000)
Dogs of all sizes are allowed. Dogs are allowed for a pet fee.

Cheat River Lodge
Route 1, Box 115
Elkins, WV
304-636-2301
cheatriverlodge.com/
Dogs are allowed in the lodge and the cabins at this riverside getaway. The fee is $10 per night per pet for the lodge, and $20 per night per pet for the cabins. Dogs may be left for short periods if they are crated when left alone in the room. 2 dogs may be allowed.

Days Inn and Suites Elkins
1200 Harrison Avenue
Elkins, WV
304-637-4667 (800-329-7466)
Dogs of all sizes are allowed. Dogs are allowed for a pet fee.

Super 8 Elkins
350 Beverly Pike
Elkins, WV
304-636-6500 (800-800-8000)
Dogs of all sizes are allowed. Dogs are allowed for a pet fee.

Holiday Inn Fairmont
930 East Grafton Road
Fairmont, WV
304-366-5500 (877-270-6405)
Dogs of all sizes are allowed. Dogs are allowed for a pet fee of $25.00 per pet per stay.

Red Roof Inn Fairmont
42 Spencer Road
Fairmont, WV
304-366-6800 (800-RED-ROOF)
One well-behaved family pet per room. Guest must notify front desk upon arrival. Guest is liable for any damages. In consideration of all guests, pets must never be left unattended in the guest rooms.

Super 8 Fairmont
2208 Pleasant Valley Road
Fairmont, WV
304-363-1488 (800-800-8000)
Dogs of all sizes are allowed. Dogs are allowed for a pet fee.

Travelodge Fairmont
1117 Fairmont Avenue
Fairmont, WV
304-363-0100 (800-578-7878)
Dogs of all sizes are allowed. Dogs are allowed for a pet fee of $15 per pet per stay.

Quality Inn New River Gorge
103 Elliotts Way
Fayetteville, WV
304-574-3443 (877-424-6423)

Dogs of all sizes are allowed. Dogs are allowed for a pet fee of $10.00 per pet per night.

Hemlock Haven
P.O. Box 218
Hico, WV
304-575-1260
hemlockhavenwv.com
Dogs are allowed at these three bedroom, two bath log cabins. There is a $25 per night per pet additional pet fee.

Quality Inn
3325 US 60 E.
Huntington, WV
304-525-7001 (877-424-6423)
Dogs of all sizes are allowed. Dogs are allowed for a pet fee of $15.00 per pet per night. Two dogs are allowed per room.

Red Roof Inn Huntington
5190 US Route 60 East
Huntington, WV
304-733-3737 (800-RED-ROOF)
One well-behaved family pet per room. Guest must notify front desk upon arrival. Guest is liable for any damages. In consideration of all guests, pets must never be left unattended in the guest rooms.

Red Roof Inn Charleston West - Hurricane, WV
500 Putnam Village Drive
Hurricane, WV
304-757-6392 (800-RED-ROOF)
One well-behaved family pet per room. Guest must notify front desk upon arrival. Guest is liable for any damages. In consideration of all guests, pets must never be left unattended in the guest rooms.

Red Roof Inn Charleston - Kanawha City, WV
6305 MacCorkle Avenue Southeast
Kanawha City, WV
304-925-6953 (800-RED-ROOF)
One well-behaved family pet per room. Guest must notify front desk upon arrival. Guest is liable for any damages. In consideration of all guests, pets must never be left unattended in the guest rooms.

Holiday Inn Express Hotel & Suites Lewisburg
222 Hunter Lane
Lewisburg, WV
304-645-5750 (877-270-6405)
Dogs of all sizes are allowed. Dogs are allowed for a pet fee of $25.00 per pet per night.

Super 8 Lewisburg
550 N Jefferson St
Lewisburg, WV
304-647-3188 (800-800-8000)
Dogs are welcome at this hotel.

Super 8 Logan
316 Riverview Ave
Logan, WV
304-752-8787 (800-800-8000)
Dogs are welcome at this hotel.

Days Inn Martinsburg
209 Viking Way
Martinsburg, WV
304-263-1800 (800-329-7466)
Dogs of all sizes are allowed. Dogs are allowed for a nightly pet fee.

Econo Lodge
5595 Hammonds Mill Road
Martinsburg, WV
304-274-2181 (877-424-6423)
Dogs of all sizes are allowed.

Holiday Inn Martinsburg
301 Foxcroft Avenue
Martinsburg, WV
304-267-5500 (877-270-6405)
Dogs of all sizes are allowed. Dogs are allowed for a pet fee.

Knights Inn Martinsburg
1997 Edwin Miller Blvd
Martinsburg, WV
304-267-2211 (800-843-5644)
Dogs of all sizes are allowed. Dogs are allowed for a nightly pet fee.

Rodeway Inn
94 McMillan Court
Martinsburg, WV
304-263-8811 (877-424-6423)
Dogs of all sizes are allowed. Dogs are allowed for a pet fee of $10.00 per pet per night.

Super 8 Martinsburg
2048 Edwin Miller Blvd
Martinsburg, WV
304-263-0801 (800-800-8000)
Dogs of all sizes are allowed. Dogs are allowed for a pet fee.

Comfort Suites
167 Elizabeth Pike
Mineral Wells, WV
304-489-9600 (877-424-6423)
Dogs of all sizes are allowed. Dogs are allowed for a pet fee of $10.00 per pet per night.

Alpine Lake
700 West Alpine Drive
Morgantown, WV
304-789-2481 (800-752-7179)
alpinelake.com/

In addition to its beautiful location and numerous amenities, this resort is also a year round recreational destination. Dogs are allowed for an additional $10 per night per pet. 2 dogs may be allowed.

Comfort Inn
225 Comfort Inn Drive
Morgantown, WV
304-296-9364 (877-424-6423)
Dogs of all sizes are allowed. Dogs are allowed for a pet fee of $10.00/pet per pet per night. Two dogs are allowed per room.

Ramada Conference Center
20 Scott Avenue
Morgantown, WV
304-296-3431 (800-272-6232)
Dogs are welcome at this hotel.

Residence Inn Morgantown
1046 Willowdale Road
Morgantown, WV
304-599-0237 (800-331-3131)
Located across from the WVF Football Stadium and the Ruby Memorial Hospital, this all suite inn also offers a number of in-house amenities, including a daily buffet breakfast and evening socials. Dogs are allowed for an additional one time pet fee of $75 per room. 2 dogs may be allowed.

Super 8 Morgantown
603 Venture Dr
Morgantown, WV
304-296-4000 (800-800-8000)
Dogs of all sizes are allowed. Dogs are allowed for a pet fee.

Blennerhassett Hotel
Fourth and Market Streets
Parkersburg, WV
304-422-3131 (800-678-8946)
This 1889 hotel is listed on the National Register of Historic Hotels. There is a $50 one time pet charge for 1 dog,,, the fee is $75 for 2 dogs. 2 dogs may be allowed.

Econo Lodge
1954 E. 7th St.
Parkersburg, WV
304-428-7500 (877-424-6423)
Dogs of all sizes are allowed.

Red Carpet Inn
6333 Emerson Ave
Parkersburg, WV
304-485-1851 (800-251-1962)
bookroomsnow.com/
There is a $8 per day per pet charge. 2 dogs may be allowed.

Red Roof Inn Parkersburg
3714 East 7th Street
Parkersburg, WV
304-485-1741 (800-RED-ROOF)
One well-behaved family pet per
room. Guest must notify front desk
upon arrival. Guest is liable for any
damages. In consideration of all
guests, pets must never be left
unattended in the guest rooms.

Travelodge Parkersburg
3604 East 7th Street
Parkersburg, WV
304-424-5100 (800-578-7878)
Dogs are welcome at this hotel.

Comfort Inn
136 Ambrose Lane
Princeton, WV
304-487-6101 (877-424-6423)
Dogs of all sizes are allowed. Dogs
are allowed for a pet fee of $10.00
per pet per night.

Days Inn Princeton
347 Meadow Field Lane
Princeton, WV
304-425-8100 (800-329-7466)
Dogs of all sizes are allowed. Dogs
are allowed for a pet fee of $20.00
per pet per night.

Sleep Inn & Suites
1015 Oakvale Rd.
Princeton, WV
304-431-2800 (877-424-6423)
Dogs of all sizes are allowed.

Super 8 Princeton
901 Oakvale Rd
Princeton, WV
304-487-6161 (800-800-8000)
Dogs of all sizes are allowed. Dogs
are allowed for a pet fee.

Holiday Inn Express Ripley
One Hospitality Drive
Ripley, WV
304-372-5000 (877-270-6405)
Dogs are welcome at this hotel.

Super 8 Ripley
102 Duke Dr
Ripley, WV
304-372-8880 (800-800-8000)
Dogs are welcome at this hotel.

Comfort Inn
70 Maddex Square Drive
Shepherdstown, WV
304-876-3160 (877-424-6423)
Dogs of all sizes are allowed. Dogs
are allowed for a pet fee of $10.00
per pet per night. Two dogs are
allowed per room.

Morning Glory Inn
H 219
Snowshoe, WV
304-572-5000 (866-572-5700)
morninggloryinn.com/
Guests can relax and enjoy the
views from their 90 foot front porch
or explore a myriad of local
activities and recreation from this
retreat. One dog is allowed for no
additional pet fee. Dogs must be
quiet and well mannered.

Best Western Summersville Lake
Motor Lodge
1203 Broad Street
Summersville, WV
304-872-6900 (800-780-7234)
Dogs are welcome at this hotel.
There is a $10 additional pet fee.

Super 8 Summersville
306 Merchants Walk
Summersville, WV
304-872-4888 (800-800-8000)
Dogs of all sizes are allowed. Dogs
are allowed for a pet fee.

Comfort Inn
675 Fort Henry Road
Triadelphia, WV
304-547-0610 (877-424-6423)
Dogs of all sizes are allowed. Dogs
are allowed for a pet fee of
$accomodation:$10.00 per pet per
night. Two dogs are allowed per
room.

Comfort Inn
2906 US Highway 33 East
Weston, WV
304-269-7000 (877-424-6423)
Dogs up to 50 pounds are allowed.
Dogs are allowed for a pet fee of
$10.00 per pet per night.

Super 8 WV Weston
100 Market Place Mall Ste 12
Weston, WV
304-269-1086 (800-800-8000)
Dogs of all sizes are allowed. Dogs
are allowed for a pet fee.

Oglebay's Wilson Lodge
Route 88 North
Wheeling, WV
304-243-4000 (800-624-6988)
oglebay-resort.com/lodge.htm
Dogs are not allowed in the lodge,
but are welcome in the cottages.
There can be up to 2 large or 3
small dogs per cottage. There are
no designated smoking or non-
smoking cottages. There are no
additional pet fees. 2 dogs may be
allowed.

Super 8 Wheeling
2400 National Road
Wheeling, WV
304-243-9400 (800-800-8000)
Dogs of all sizes are allowed. Dogs
are allowed for a pet fee.

Days Inn Williamstown
1339 Highland Avenue
Williamstown, WV
304-375-3730 (800-329-7466)
Dogs are welcome at this hotel.

Wisconsin

Sleep Inn
300 East Elderberry Rd.
Abbotsford, WI
715-223-3337 (877-424-6423)
Dogs of all sizes are allowed. Dogs
are allowed for a pet fee of $10.00
per pet per night. Two dogs are
allowed per room.

Algoma Beach Motel
1500 Lake Street/H 42
Algoma, WI
920-487-2828 (888-ALGOMA1 (888-
254-6621))
algomabeach.com/
There is over 300 feet of a private
sandy beach at this motel. Dogs are
allowed for an additional fee of $15
per night per pet in the nautical units.
Dogs must be well mannered,
leashed, and under their owner's
control at all times. 2 dogs may be
allowed.

Days Inn of Antigo
525 Memory Lane
Antigo, WI
715-623-0506 (800-329-7466)
Dogs of all sizes are allowed. Dogs
are allowed for a pet fee of $10.00
per pet per stay.

Holiday Inn Express Hotel & Suites
Antigo
2407 Neva Road
Antigo, WI
715-627-7500 (877-270-6405)
Dogs of all sizes are allowed. Dogs
are allowed for a pet fee of $25.00
per pet per night.

Best Western Midway Hotel
3033 W College Avenue
Appleton, WI
920-731-4141 (800-780-7234)
Dogs of all sizes are allowed. Dogs
are allowed for a pet fee of $10.00
per pet per night.

Budgetel Inn Appleton
3920 W College Avenue

Appleton, WI
920-734-6070 (800-531-5900)
Dogs of all sizes are allowed. There are no additional pet fees, and there is a pet waiver to sign at check in. Dogs may not be left unattended, and they must be leashed and cleaned up after. 2 dogs may be allowed.

Candlewood Suites Appleton
4525 West College Avenue
Appleton, WI
920-739-8000 (877-270-6405)
Dogs up to 80 pounds are allowed. Pets allowed with an additional pet fee. Up to $75 for 1-6 nights and up to $150 for 7+ nights. A pet agreement must be signed at check-in.

Comfort Suites Appleton Airport
3809 W. Wisconsin Ave.
Appleton, WI
920-730-3800 (877-424-6423)
Dogs of all sizes are allowed. Two dogs are allowed per room.

Days Inn Appleton
210 Westhill Blvd
Appleton, WI
920-733-5551 (800-329-7466)
Dogs of all sizes are allowed. Dogs are allowed for a pet fee of $10 per pet per stay.

Extended Stay America Appleton - Fox Cities
4141 Boardwalk Ct.
Appleton, WI
920-830-9596 (800-804-3724)
One dog is allowed per suite. There is a $25 per night additional pet fee up to $150 for an entire stay.

La Quinta Inn & Suites Appleton College Avenue
3730 W. College Avenue
Appleton, WI
920-734-7777 (800-531-5900)
Dogs of all sizes are allowed. There are no additional pet fees. Dogs must be leashed, cleaned up after, and crated if they are left in the room alone. Dogs are not allowed in the common areas. Multiple dogs may be allowed.

Residence Inn Appleton
310 Metro Drive
Appleton, WI
920-954-0570 (888-236-2427)
Located only a few miles to downtown, this inn offers a convenient location to business, shopping, dining, and entertainment areas, plus they offer a number of in-

house amenities that include a daily buffet breakfast, and a Manager's reception Monday through Thursday. Dogs are allowed for an additional one time pet fee of $100 per room. Multiple dogs may be allowed.

Americinn Motel and Suites
3009 Lakeshore Drive East
Ashland, WI
715-682-9950
There is a $25 one time pet fee per designated pet room, and a $50 one time pet fee for non-designated pet rooms. Multiple dogs may be allowed.

Best Western Lake Superior Lodge
30600 US Highway 2
Ashland, WI
715-682-5235 (800-780-7234)
Dogs of all sizes are allowed. Dogs are allowed for a pet fee of $10.00 per pet per night.

Lake Aire Inn
101 E. Lake Shore Dr.
Ashland, WI
715-682-4551 (888-666-2088)
lakeaireinn.com/
There is a $10 one time per pet fee. Multiple dogs may be allowed.

Super 8 Baldwin
2110 10th Ave
Baldwin, WI
715-684-2700 (800-800-8000)
Dogs are welcome at this hotel.

Motel 6 - Lake Delton, Wi
10892 Fern Dell Rd
Baraboo, WI
608-355-0700 (800-466-8356)
This motel welcomes your pets to stay with you.

Isaac Wing House
17 South First Street/H 13
Bayfield, WI
715-779-3363 (800-382-0995)
isaac-winghouse.com/
This historic 1854 structure still holds all its charm, and in addition to the modern amenities on site, they also offer a great location for exploring all this area has to offer. Dogs are allowed for an addition one time fee of $20 per pet. 2 dogs may be allowed.

Super 8 Beaver Dam
711 Park Ave
Beaver Dam, WI
920-887-8880 (800-800-8000)
Dogs are welcome at this hotel.

Baymont Inn & Suites Platteville/ Belmont
103 W Mound View Ave
Belmont, WI
608-762-6900 (877-229-6668)
Dogs are welcome at this hotel.

Comfort Inn
2786 Milwaukee Rd.
Beloit, WI
608-362-2666 (877-424-6423)
Dogs of all sizes are allowed. Dogs are allowed for a pet fee of $10.00 per pet per night.

Rodeway Inn
2956 Milwaukee Rd.
Beloit, WI
608-364-4000 (877-424-6423)
Dogs of all sizes are allowed. Dogs are allowed for a pet fee of $10.00 per pet per night. Three or more dogs may be allowed.

The Cobblestone
319 S Main Street
Birchwood, WI
715-354-3494 (800-659-4883)
Beautifully landscaped grounds, themed rooms, and a relaxing cozy ambiance are just some of the amenities at this inn. With advance reservations, dogs are allowed for no addition fee as long as there are no damages, and they must be very well mannered and cat friendly. Dogs may not be left alone at any time, and they must be leashed and kept cleaned up after.

Days Inn Black River Falls
919 Hwy 54 East
Black River Falls, WI
715-284-4333 (800-329-7466)
Dogs of all sizes are allowed. Dogs are allowed for a pet fee of $15.00 per pet per night.

Best Western Midway Hotel
1005 S Moorland Road
Brookfield, WI
262-786-9540 (800-780-7234)
Dogs are welcome at this hotel.

Homestead Studio Suites Milwaukee - Brookfield
325 N. Brookfield Rd.
Brookfield, WI
262-782-9300 (800-804-3724)
One dog is allowed per suite. There is a $25 per night additional pet fee up to $150 for an entire stay.

La Quinta Inn Milwaukee West/Brookfield
20391 W. Bluemound Road
Brookfield, WI

262-782-9100 (800-531-5900)
Dogs of all sizes are allowed. There are no additional fees. Dogs may not be left unattended, but if they must be left in the room in case of emergency, they must be crated. 2 dogs may be allowed.

Motel 6 - Milwaukee West Brookfield
20300 Bluemound Rd
Brookfield, WI
262-786-7337 (800-466-8356)
This motel welcomes your pets to stay with you.

Residence Inn Milwaukee Brookfield
950 S Pinehurst Court
Brookfield, WI
262-782-5990 (800-331-3131)
Some of the amenities at this all-suite inn include a daily buffet breakfast, a hospitality hour Monday through Thursday, summer barbecues, a heated swimming pool, Sport Court, and a complimentary grocery shopping service. Dogs are allowed for an additional one time pet fee of $100 per room. Multiple dogs may be allowed.

Sheraton Milwaukee Brookfield Hotel
375 South Moorland Road
Brookfield, WI
262-786-1100 (888-625-5144)
Dogs up to 80 pounds are allowed. Dogs are not allowed to be left alone in the room.

TownePlace Suites Milwaukee Brookfield
600 N Calhoun Road
Brookfield, WI
262-784-8450 (800-257-3000)
This all suite hotel sits central to a number of sites of interest for both business and leisure travelers; plus they also offer a number of on-site amenities to ensure comfort. Dogs are allowed for an additional one time fee of $75 per room. 2 dogs may be allowed.

Candlewood Suites Milwaukee N-Brown Deer/Mequon
4483 West Schroeder Drive
Brown Deer, WI
414-355-3939 (877-270-6405)
Dogs up to 80 pounds are allowed. Pets allowed with an additional pet fee. Up to $75 for 1-6 nights and up to $150 for 7+ nights. A pet agreement must be signed at check-in.

Telemark Resort
4225 Telemark Road
Cable, WI

715-798-3999
Dogs of all sizes are allowed. There is a $35 one time pet fee per stay and dogs must be declared at the time of reservations. 2 dogs may be allowed.

Super 8 Chetek
1/4 Mile East on County Hwy I
Chetek, WI
715-924-4888 (800-800-8000)
Dogs are welcome at this hotel.

Americinn Motel and Suites
11 West South Avenue
Chippewa Falls, WI
715-723-5711
Dogs are allowed for an additional pet fee of $10 per night per room. They have 2 non-smoking pet rooms. Multiple dogs may be allowed.

Indianhead Motel
501 Summit Avenue
Chippewa Falls, WI
715-723-9171 (888-315-BEST (2378))
bestvalueinn.com/Lodges/W152.htm
There is a $5 per day pet charge. 2 dogs may be allowed.

Super 8 Columbus
219 Industrial Drive
Columbus, WI
920-623-8800 (800-800-8000)
Dogs are welcome at this hotel.

Kress Inn, an Ascend Collection hotel
300 Grant Street
De Pere, WI
920-403-5100 (877-424-6423)
Dogs of all sizes are allowed.

Comfort Inn & Suites
5025 County Hwy. V
DeForest, WI
608-846-9100 (877-424-6423)
Dogs of all sizes are allowed. Dogs are allowed for a pet fee of $20.00 per pet per stay.

Holiday Inn Express Deforest (Madison Area)
7184 Morrisonville Rd
Deforest, WI
608-846-8686 (877-270-6405)
Dogs of all sizes are allowed. Dogs are allowed for a pet fee.

La Quinta Inn Milwaukee-Delafield
2801 Hillside Drive
Delafield, WI
262-646-8500 (800-531-5900)
Dogs of all sizes are allowed. There

are no additional pet fees. There is a pet waiver to sign at check in. Dogs may not be left unattended, and they must be leashed and cleaned up after. Multiple dogs may be allowed.

Best Western Quiet House & Suites
1130 N Johns Street
Dodgeville, WI
608-935-7739 (800-780-7234)
Dogs of all sizes are allowed. Dogs are allowed for a pet fee of $15.00 per pet per night.

Super 8 Dodgeville
1308 Johns Street
Dodgeville, WI
608-935-3888 (800-800-8000)
Dogs are welcome at this hotel.

Best Western Derby Inn
US Highway 45 N
Eagle River, WI
715-479-1600 (800-780-7234)
Dogs are welcome at this hotel.

Days Inn Eagle River
844 Railroad Street North
Eagle River, WI
715-479-5151 (800-329-7466)
Dogs are welcome at this hotel.

Gypsy Villa Resort
950 Circle Drive
Eagle River, WI
715-479-8644
a1gypsyvilla.com/
Located on Cranberry Lake among the largest chain of lakes in the world, this resort offers a wide array of amenities including planned activities (like treasure hunts/campfire fun), fishing seminars, 200 feet of private beach with playground items, watercraft on your private dock, and much more. Dogs are allowed for an addition fee of $7 per night per pet for dogs less than 30 pounds, and $12 per night per pet for dogs over 30 pounds. This fee is reduced to half during the spring and fall months. Dogs must be well mannered, and under their owner's control at all times. 2 dogs may be allowed.

Best Western Trail Lodge Hotel & Suites
3340 Mondovi Road
Eau Claire, WI
715-838-9989 (800-780-7234)
Dogs of all sizes are allowed. Dogs are allowed for a nightly pet fee.

Comfort Inn
3117 Craig Rd.
Eau Claire, WI

715-833-9798 (877-424-6423)
Dogs of all sizes are allowed. Dogs
are allowed for a pet fee of $15.00
per pet per night.

Days Inn -Campus Eau Claire
2305 Craig Rd
Eau Claire, WI
715-834-3193 (800-329-7466)
Dogs are welcome at this hotel.

Econo Lodge Inn & Suites
4608 Royal Dr.
Eau Claire, WI
715-833-8818 (877-424-6423)
Dogs of all sizes are allowed.

Ramada Convention Center Eau
Claire
205 South Barstow Street
Eau Claire, WI
715-835-6121 (800-272-6232)
Dogs are welcome at this hotel.

Sleep Inn & Suites Conference
Center
5872 33rd Ave
Eau Claire, WI
715-874-2900 (877-424-6423)
Dogs up to 50 pounds are allowed.
Dogs are allowed for a pet fee of
$10.00 per pet per night. Two dogs
are allowed per room.

Comfort Inn
11102 Goede Road
Edgerton, WI
608-884-2118 (877-424-6423)
Dogs of all sizes are allowed. Dogs
are allowed for a pet fee of $10.00
per pet per night. Three or more
dogs may be allowed.

The Feathered Star
6202 H 42
Egg Harbor, WI
920-743-4066
Dogs of all sizes are allowed. There
is an $8 per night per room additional
pet fee.

Woofhaven Cottage
Call to Arrange
Elkhorn, WI
312-458-9549
woofhavencottage.com
The vacation cottage, with a
waterview of Lake Wandawega, is 15
minutes from Lake Geneva. Dogs of
any size are allowed. Multiple dogs
may be allowed.

Comfort Inn
77 Holiday Lane
Fond Du Lac, WI
920-921-4000 (877-424-6423)
Dogs of all sizes are allowed.

Days Inn Fond du Lac
107 North Pioneer Road
Fond Du Lac, WI
920-923-6790 (800-329-7466)
Dogs are welcome at this hotel.

Holiday Inn Fond Du Lac
625 W Rolling Meadows Drive
Fond Du Lac, WI
920-923-1440 (877-270-6405)
Dogs are welcome at this hotel.

Super 8 Fond Du Lac
391 N Pioneer Road
Fond Du Lac, WI
920-922-1088 (800-800-8000)
Dogs of all sizes are allowed. Dogs
are allowed for a pet fee of $15 per
pet per night.

Super 8 Fort Atkinson
225 S Water St East
Fort Atkinson, WI
920-563-8444 (800-800-8000)
Dogs are welcome at this hotel.

Staybridge Suites Milwaukee Airport
South
9575 South 27th Street
Franklin, WI
414-761-3800 (877-270-6405)
Dogs up to 80 pounds are allowed.
Pets allowed with an additional pet
fee. Up to $75 for 1-6 nights and up
to $150 for 7+ nights. A pet
agreement must be signed at
check-in.

Holiday Inn Express Germantown
(Nw Milwaukee)
W177n9675 Riversbend Lane
Germantown, WI
262-255-1100 (877-270-6405)
Dogs of all sizes are allowed. Dogs
are allowed for a pet fee of $50.00
per pet per stay.

Super 8 /Milwaukee Germantown
N 96 W 17490 County Line Rd
Germantown, WI
262-255-0880 (800-800-8000)
Dogs of all sizes are allowed. Dogs
are allowed for a pet fee.

Harbor House Inn
12666 H 42
Gills Rock, WI
920-854-5196 (800 853-9629)
door-county-inn.com/
Offering shelter to guests since
1904, this beautifully refurbished inn
sits on a lush scenic peninsula and
offers visitors a sauna, whirlpool, a
barbecue, gazebo, and a Great
room for gathering, gaming, or just
relaxing and watching a show. Dogs

are allowed for an additional $10 per
night per pet. Dogs are not allowed
in the main house; they may not be
left unattended, and they must be
leashed and under their owner's
control at all times. 2 dogs may be
allowed.

Baymont Inn and Suites /Milwaukee
N. Area Glendale
5485 N Port Washington Rd
Glendale, WI
414-961-7272 (877-229-6668)
Dogs are welcome at this hotel.

La Quinta Inn & Suites Milwaukee-
Glendale
5423 N. Port Washington Road
Glendale, WI
414-962-6767 (800-531-5900)
Dogs of all sizes are allowed. There
are no additional pet fees. Dogs
must be leashed, cleaned up after,
and crated or removed for
housekeeping. Multiple dogs may be
allowed.

La Quinta Inn Milwaukee
Northeast/Glendale
5110 N. Port Washington Road
Glendale, WI
414-964-8484 (800-531-5900)
Dogs up to 60 pounds are allowed.
There are no additional pet fees.
Dogs may not be left unattended,
and they must be leashed at all
times. 2 dogs may be allowed.

Baymont Inn & Suites Milwaukee/
Grafton
1415 Port Washington Road
Grafton, WI
262-387-1180 (877-229-6668)
Dogs are welcome at this hotel.

Americinn
2032 Velp Ave
Green Bay, WI
920-434-9790
inbsonline.com/americinn/
There is a $15 per day additional pet
fee. Multiple dogs may be allowed.

Best Western Midway Hotel
780 Armed Forces Drive
Green Bay, WI
920-499-3161 (800-780-7234)
Dogs are welcome at this hotel.

Candlewood Suites Green Bay
1125 East Mason Street
Green Bay, WI
920-430-7040 (877-270-6405)
Dogs up to 80 pounds are allowed.
Pets allowed with an additional pet
fee. Up to $75 for 1-6 nights and up
to $150 for 7+ nights. A pet

agreement must be signed at check-in.

Days Inn Downtown Green Bay
406 N. Washington St.
Green Bay, WI
920-435-4484 (800-329-7466)
Dogs of all sizes are allowed. Dogs are allowed for a nightly pet fee.

Days Inn Green Bay
1978 Holmgren Way
Green Bay, WI
920-498-8088 (800-329-7466)
Dogs are welcome at this hotel.

Motel 6 - Green Bay
1614 Shawano Ave
Green Bay, WI
920-494-6730 (800-466-8356)
This motel welcomes your pets to stay with you.

Quality Inn & Suites
321 S. Washington Street
Green Bay, WI
920-437-8771 (877-424-6423)
Dogs of all sizes are allowed. Dogs are allowed for a pet fee of $10.00 per pet per night. Two dogs are allowed per room.

Ramada Plaza Green Bay
2750 Ramada Way
Green Bay, WI
920-499-0631 (800-272-6232)
Dogs of all sizes are allowed. Dogs are allowed for a pet fee of $20.00 per pet per night.

Residence Inn Green Bay
335 W Saint Joseph Street
Green Bay, WI
920-435-2222 (800-331-3131)
Located only a short distance to all that the downtown area has to offer, this all suite inn also provides a number of in-house amenities, including a daily buffet breakfast and evening socials. Dogs are allowed for an additional one time pet fee of $100 per room. Multiple dogs may be allowed.

Super 8 Airport/Stadium Green Bay
2868 S Oneida St.
Green Bay, WI
920-494-2042 (800-800-8000)
Dogs are welcome at this hotel.

Super 8 I-43 Bus. Park Green Bay
2911 Voyager Dr
Green Bay, WI
920-406-8200 (800-800-8000)
Dogs are welcome at this hotel.

Travelodge /Lambeau Green Bay

2870 Ramada Way
Green Bay, WI
920-499-3599 (800-578-7878)
Dogs of all sizes are allowed. Dogs are allowed for a pet fee of $50.00 per pet per stay.

Super 8 WI Hartford
1539 E Sumner St
Hartford, WI
262-673-7431 (800-800-8000)
Dogs are welcome at this hotel.

Comfort Suites
15586 County Road B
Hayward, WI
715-634-0700 (877-424-6423)
Dogs of all sizes are allowed. Dogs are allowed for a pet fee of $12.50 per pet per night.

Ross' Teal Lake Lodge
12425 N Ross Rd
Hayward, WI
715-462-3631
teallakeresort.com/
Located along the shores of Quiet Lakes in the Chequamegon National Forest, this full service, secluded resort offers several lakeside guest houses, an abundance of land and water recreation, home cooking, and much more. Well mannered pets are very welcome to come and stay/play or take a swim in the lake and say hello to the several other happy resort dogs. The fee is $10 per day per pet; please make arrangements for housekeeping. Coverings are available for heirloom furnishings-ask if needed. Dogs must be leashed around the resort, hound and human friendly, and picked up after at all times-unless they are in the forest just across the highway. Dogs are not allowed at the swimming pool area; they are allowed on watercraft and land carts. 2 dogs may be allowed.

Super 8 Wisconsin Hayward
10444 State Hwy 27
Hayward, WI
715-634-2646 (800-800-8000)
Dogs are welcome at this hotel.

Super 8 Hudson
808 Dominion Drive
Hudson, WI
715-386-8800 (800-800-8000)
Dogs are welcome at this hotel.

Days Inn Hurley
13355N U.S. Hwy 51
Hurley, WI
715-561-3500 (800-329-7466)

Dogs of all sizes are allowed. Dogs are allowed for a pet fee.

Comfort Inn & Suites
W227 N 16890 Tillie Lake Crt
Jackson, WI
262-677-1133 (877-424-6423)
Dogs up to 50 pounds are allowed. Dogs are allowed for a pet fee of $30.00/ per pet per stay. Two dogs are allowed per room.

Baymont Inn & Suites Janesville
616 Midland Rd.
Janesville, WI
608-758-4545 (877-229-6668)
Dogs are welcome at this hotel.

Best Western Janesville
3900 Milton Avenue
Janesville, WI
608-756-4511 (800-780-7234)
Dogs of all sizes are allowed. Dogs are allowed for a pet fee.

Econo Lodge
3520 Milton Ave.
Janesville, WI
608-754-0251 (877-424-6423)
Dogs of all sizes are allowed. Dogs are allowed for a pet fee of $8.00 per pet per night. Two dogs are allowed per room.

Motel 6 - Janesville
3907 Milton Ave
Janesville, WI
608-756-1742 (800-466-8356)
This motel welcomes your pets to stay with you.

Days Inn Johnson Creek
W 4545 Linmar Lane
Johnson Creek, WI
920-699-8000 (800-329-7466)
Dogs are welcome at this hotel.

Candlewood Suites Kenosha
10200 74th Street
Kenosha, WI
262-842-5000 (877-270-6405)
Dogs up to 80 pounds are allowed. Pets allowed with an additional pet fee. Up to $75 for 1-6 nights and up to $150 for 7+ nights. A pet agreement must be signed at check-in.

Super 8 /Appleton Kimberly
761 Truman Street
Kimberly, WI
920-788-4400 (800-800-8000)
Dogs of all sizes are allowed. Dogs are allowed for a pet fee.

Best Western Midway Hotel
Riverfront Resort

1835 Rose Street
La Crosse, WI
608-781-7000 (800-780-7234)
Dogs are welcome at this hotel.

Holiday Inn Hotel & Suites La Crosse
200 Pearl Street
La Crosse, WI
608-784-4444 (877-270-6405)
Dogs of all sizes are allowed. Dogs
are allowed for a pet fee of $50.00
per pet per stay.

Howard Johnson's
2150 Rose Street
La Crosse, WI
608-781-0400 (800-446-4656)
There are no additional pet fees. 2
dogs may be allowed.

Super 8 La Crosse
I-90 at Exit 3, Hwy 53 South
La Crosse, WI
608-781-8880 (800-800-8000)
Dogs of all sizes are allowed. Dogs
are allowed for a pet fee.

Bog Lake
2848 School House Road
La Pointe, WI
715-747-2685
madelineisland.com/boglake/
In addition to providing watercraft
rentals, this company offers seasonal
lodging in town, on the lake and in
the wilderness. Dogs are allowed for
no additional fee; they must be
housetrained and under their owner's
control at all times. 2 dogs may be
allowed.

Brittany Cottages at Coole Park
351 Old Fort Road
La Pointe, WI
715-747-5023
brittanycabins.com/
Ten scenic private acres,
unsurpassed scenery, abundant
wildlife, a variety of recreation, formal
gardens, and more can be enjoyed
at this retreat that is also listed on
the National Register of Historic
Places. Dogs are allowed for an
additional one time fee of $50 per
unit. Dogs must be leashed and
cleaned up after around the cottages
and common areas, but they are
welcome to fertilize the woods at will.
Multiple dogs may be allowed.

Woods Manor
RR 1, Box 7
La Pointe, WI
715-747-3102
Dogs up to 75 pounds are allowed.
There is a $25 one time additional
fee per pet. There are some breed

restrictions.

Eleven Gables Inn on Lake Geneva
493 Wrigley Drive
Lake Geneva, WI
262-248-8393
Dogs of all sizes are allowed. There
are no additional pet fees. 2 dogs
may be allowed.

Maria's Bed & Breakfast
512 S Wells Street
Lake Geneva, WI
262-249-0632 (877-249-0632)
mariasbandb.com/
A private cozy cottage surrounded
by gardens is available here; it
offers cable TV/VHF/DVD, a private
deck with relaxation amenities plus
a small grill, and a 7 foot whirlpool.
Well mannered dogs are welcome
for no additional fee, and free pooch
disposal bags are available. 2 dogs
may be allowed.

T. C. Smith Historic Inn
834 Dodge Street
Lake Geneva, WI
262-248-1097 (800-423-0233)
tcsmithinn.com/
In addition to displaying the
historical and architectural
significance of the country's
Victorian era, this beautiful 1865
home now offers 3 bright suites with
private baths, a steam unit, and a
double whirlpool. Well mannered
dogs are allowed for no additional
fee. The must be leashed and
under their owner's control. 2 dogs
may be allowed.

Loon Call Cottage
Lake Tomahawk, WI
760-399-6308
This seasonal waterfront cottage
get-a-way sits on a private island
estate only minutes from town and
offers nature and relaxation at its
best. Amenities include a boat dock,
a great swimming area, a raft, a
rowboat with an outboard motor,
and scenic trails that take guests
and their canine companions
through a private conservation
forest. Their summer contact
number is (715) 356-3301. Dogs
are allowed for no additional fee. 2
dogs may be allowed.

Best Western Countryside Inn
W9250 Prospect Drive
Lodi, WI
608-592-1450 (800-780-7234)
Dogs of all sizes are allowed. Dogs
are allowed for a nightly pet fee.

Baymont Inn & Suites East Madison
4202 East Towne Blvd
Madison, WI
608-241-3861 (877-229-6668)
Dogs are welcome at this hotel.

Baymont Inn & Suites West Madison
8102 Excelsior Dr.
Madison, WI
608-831-7711 (877-229-6668)
Dogs are welcome at this hotel.

Best Western East Towne Suites
4801 Annamark Drive
Madison, WI
608-244-2020 (800-780-7234)
Dogs are welcome at this hotel.

Best Western West Towne Suites
650 Grand Canyon Drive
Madison, WI
608-833-4200 (800-780-7234)
Dogs of all sizes are allowed. Dogs
are allowed for a pet fee of $15.00
per pet per night.

Candlewood Suites Fitchburg
5421 Caddis Bend
Madison, WI
608-271-3400 (877-270-6405)
Dogs up to 80 pounds are allowed.
Pets allowed with an additional pet
fee. Up to $75 for 1-6 nights and up
to $150 for 7+ nights. A pet
agreement must be signed at check-
in.

Clarion Suites Central
2110 Rimrock Road
Madison, WI
608-284-1234 (877-424-6423)
Dogs of all sizes are allowed. Dogs
are allowed for a pet fee of $25.00
per pet per night.

Comfort Suites
1253 John Q. Hammons Dr.
Madison, WI
608-836-3033 (877-424-6423)
Dogs of all sizes are allowed.

Days Inn Madison
4402 E. Broadway Service Rd.
Madison, WI
608-223-1800 (800-329-7466)
Dogs of all sizes are allowed. Dogs
are allowed for a pet fee of $10.00
per pet per night.

Econo Lodge
4726 E. Washington Ave.
Madison, WI
608-241-4171 (877-424-6423)
Dogs of all sizes are allowed. Two
dogs are allowed per room.

Extended Stay America Madison -

West
55 Junction Ct.
Madison, WI
608-833-1400 (800-804-3724)
One dog is allowed per suite. There is a $25 per night additional pet fee up to $150 for an entire stay.

Hilton Hotel
9 E Wilson Street
Madison, WI
608-255-5100 (800-HILTONS (445-8667))
Located in the heart of downtown, this luxury hotel offers a number of on site amenities for business and leisure travelers, plus a convenient location to business, shopping, dining, and entertainment areas. They are also connected to the Monona Terrace Community and Convention Center via an enclosed skywalk. Dogs up to 75 pounds are allowed for an additional one time fee of $50 per pet. 2 dogs may be allowed.

Howard Johnson Madison
3841 E. Washington Avenue
Madison, WI
608-244-2481 (800-446-4656)
Dogs are welcome at this hotel. There is a $15 one time pet fee.

La Quinta Inn & Suites Madison American Center
5217 E. Terrace Drive
Madison, WI
608-245-0123 (800-531-5900)
Dogs of all sizes are allowed. There are no additional pet fees. Dogs must be leashed, cleaned up after, and crated or removed for housekeeping. Dogs are not allowed to come in through the front lobby door, or to be in the lobby area during breakfast hours. 2 dogs may be allowed.

Motel 6 - Madison North
1754 Thierer Rd
Madison, WI
608-241-8101 (800-466-8356)
This motel welcomes your pets to stay with you.

Quality Inn & Suites
2969 Cahill Main
Madison, WI
608-274-7200 (877-424-6423)
Dogs of all sizes are allowed. Dogs are allowed for a pet fee of $12.50 per pet per night. Two dogs are allowed per room.

Red Roof Inn Madison, WI
4830 Hayes Road

Madison, WI
608-241-1787 (800-RED-ROOF)
One well-behaved family pet per room. Guest must notify front desk upon arrival. Guest is liable for any damages. In consideration of all guests, pets must never be left unattended in the guest rooms.

Residence Inn Madison East
4862 Hayes Road
Madison, WI
608-244-5047 (800-331-3131)
Besides offering a convenient location to business, shopping, dining, and entertainment areas, this all suite inn also offers a number of in-house amenities, including a daily buffet breakfast and complementary evening socials Monday through Thursday with light dinner fare. Dogs are allowed for an additional one time pet fee of $100 per room. 2 dogs may be allowed.

Rodeway Inn South
4916 E. Broadway
Madison, WI
608-222-5501 (877-424-6423)
Dogs of all sizes are allowed.

Sheraton Madison Hotel
706 John Nolen Dr.
Madison, WI
608-251-2300 (888-625-5144)
Dogs up to 100 pounds are allowed for an additional one time pet fee of $25 per room.

Sleep Inn & Suites
4802 Tradewinds Parkway
Madison, WI
608-221-8100 (877-424-6423)
Dogs of all sizes are allowed. Dogs are allowed for a pet fee of $5.00 per pet per night. Two dogs are allowed per room.

Staybridge Suites Madison-East
3301 City View Dr.
Madison, WI
608-241-2300 (877-270-6405)
Dogs up to 80 pounds are allowed. Pets allowed with an additional pet fee. Up to $75 for 1-6 nights and up to $150 for 7+ nights. A pet agreement must be signed at check-in.

Super 8 East WI Madison
4765 Hayes Rd
Madison, WI
608-249-5300 (800-800-8000)
Dogs of all sizes are allowed. Dogs are allowed for a pet fee.

Super 8 South Madison

1602 W Beltline Hwy
Madison, WI
608-258-8882 (800-800-8000)
Dogs of all sizes are allowed. Dogs are allowed for a pet fee of $10.00 per pet per night.

Best Western Lakefront Hotel
101 Maritime Drive
Manitowoc, WI
920-682-7000 (800-780-7234)
Dogs of all sizes are allowed. Dogs are allowed for a pet fee of $25.00 per pet per stay.

Comfort Inn
2200 S. 44th St.
Manitowoc, WI
920-683-0220 (877-424-6423)
Dogs of all sizes are allowed. Dogs are allowed for a pet fee of $25.00usd per pet per stay.

Econo Lodge
908 Washington Street
Manitowoc, WI
920-682-8271 (877-424-6423)
Dogs of all sizes are allowed.

Holiday Inn Manitowoc
I-43 And Highway 151
Manitowoc, WI
920-682-6000 (877-270-6405)
Dogs are welcome at this hotel. There is a $100 refundable pet deposit.

Super 8 Manitowoc
4004 Calumet Avenue
Manitowoc, WI
920-684-7841 (800-800-8000)
Dogs are welcome at this hotel.

Chalet Motel
1301 Marinette Ave
Marinette, WI
715-735-6687
There is a $7 per night per pet fee. Multiple dogs may be allowed.

Super 8 Marinette
1508 Marinette Ave
Marinette, WI
715-735-7887 (800-800-8000)
Dogs are welcome at this hotel.

Baymont Inn & Suites Marshfield
2107 North Central Ave
Marshfield, WI
715-384-5240 (877-229-6668)
Dogs of all sizes are allowed. Dogs are allowed for a pet fee of $10.00 per pet per night.

Comfort Inn
114 E. Upham St.
Marshfield, WI

715-387-8691 (877-424-6423)
Dogs of all sizes are allowed. Dogs are allowed for a pet fee of $15.00 per pet per night. Two dogs are allowed per room.

Best Western Park Oasis Inn
W5641 State Road 82 E
Mauston, WI
608-847-6255 (800-780-7234)
Dogs of all sizes are allowed. Dogs are allowed for a pet fee of $5.00 per pet per night.

Super 8 Mauston
1001 A Hwy 82E
Mauston, WI
608-847-2300 (800-800-8000)
Dogs of all sizes are allowed. Dogs are allowed for a pet fee.

Motel 6 - Menomonie
2100 Stout St
Menomonie, WI
715-235-6901 (800-466-8356)
This motel welcomes your pets to stay with you.

Quality Inn & Suites
1721 Plaza Drive NE
Menomonie, WI
715-233-1500 (877-424-6423)
Dogs up to 50 pounds are allowed. Dogs are allowed for a pet fee of $15.00 per pet per night. Two dogs are allowed per room.

Super 8 WI Menomonie
1622 North Broadway
Menomonie, WI
715-235-8889 (800-800-8000)
Dogs of all sizes are allowed. Dogs are allowed for a pet fee.

Best Western Quiet House & Suites
10330 N Port Washington Road
Mequon, WI
262-241-3677 (800-780-7234)
Dogs are welcome at this hotel. There is a $15 one time pet fee.

Super 8 /City Of Parks Merrill
3209 E. Main St
Merrill, WI
715-536-6880 (800-800-8000)
Dogs of all sizes are allowed. Dogs are allowed for a pet fee.

Marriott Madison West
1313 John Q Hammons Drive
Middleton, WI
608-831-2000 (888-745-2032)
Only a short distance from downtown, this luxury hotel provides a great location to a number of sites of interest and activities for both business and leisure travelers; plus

they also offer numerous on-site amenities to ensure a comfortable stay. Dogs are allowed for an additional one time fee of $50 per room. 2 dogs may be allowed.

Residence Inn Madison West/Middleton
8400 Market Street
Middleton, WI
608-662-1100 (800-331-3131)
Besides offering a convenient location to business, shopping, dining, and entertainment areas, this all suite inn also offers a number of in-house amenities, including a daily buffet breakfast and evening social hours. Dogs are allowed for an additional one time pet fee of $75 per room. 2 dogs may be allowed.

Staybridge Suites
Middleton/Madison-West
7790 Elmwood Avenue
Middleton, WI
608-664-5888 (877-270-6405)
Dogs up to 80 pounds are allowed. Pets allowed with an additional pet fee. Up to $75 for 1-6 nights and up to $150 for 7+ nights. A pet agreement must be signed at check-in.

Acanthus Inn
3009 W Highland Blvd/H 18
Milwaukee, WI
414-342-9788 (800-361-3698)
milwaukee-bed-and-breakfast.com/
An elegant inn, this 1897 Queen Anne Mansion sits among lush landscaping and offers visitors gourmet, cooked-to-order breakfasts, stylish rooms and suites, and a great location for exploring the highlights of the area. Dogs are allowed; they must be well behaved, leashed, and cleaned up after. 2 dogs may be allowed.

Hilton Hotel
509 W Wisconsin Avenue
Milwaukee, WI
414-271-7250 (800-HILTONS (445-8667))
Located in the convention district and connected to the airport via a skywalk, this downtown hotel also offers a 20,000 foot indoor waterpark, and a number of other on site amenities for business and leisure travelers. Dogs up to 75 pounds are allowed for an additional pet fee of $75 per room.

Holiday Inn Hotel & Suites
Milwaukee Airport
545 W Layton Ave

Milwaukee, WI
414-482-4444 (877-270-6405)
Dogs up to 80 pounds are allowed. Dogs are allowed for a pet fee of $25 per pet per stay.

La Quinta Inn Milwaukee Northwest
5442 N. Lovers Lane Road
Milwaukee, WI
414-535-1300 (800-531-5900)
Dogs of all sizes are allowed. There are no additional pet fees. Dogs must be attended when housekeeping is present, and may not be left alone in the room unless they will be quiet and well behaved. Dogs must be leashed. Multiple dogs may be allowed.

Motel 6 - Milwaukee South Airport
5037 Howell Ave
Milwaukee, WI
414-482-4414 (800-466-8356)
This motel welcomes your pets to stay with you.

Rodeway Inn & Suites
4400 S. 27th Street
Milwaukee, WI
414-817-5004 (877-424-6423)
Dogs of all sizes are allowed. Dogs are allowed for a pet fee of $10.00 per pet per night. Two dogs are allowed per room.

Quality Inn
1345 Business Park Rd
Mineral Point, WI
608-987-4747 (877-424-6423)
Dogs of all sizes are allowed. Dogs are allowed for a pet fee of $10.00 per pet per night. Two dogs are allowed per room.

Best Western Concord Inn
320 Front Street
Minocqua, WI
715-356-1800 (800-780-7234)
Dogs are welcome at this hotel.

Comfort Inn
8729 US 51 N.
Minocqua, WI
715-358-2588 (877-424-6423)
Dogs of all sizes are allowed. Dogs are allowed for a pet fee of $10.00 per pet per night.

Super 8 Monroe
500 6th St and Hwy 69
Monroe, WI
608-325-1500 (800-800-8000)
Dogs of all sizes are allowed. Dogs are allowed for a pet fee.

Super 8 WI Neillsville
1000 E Division Street, Hwy 10

Neillsville, WI
715-743-8080 (800-800-8000)
Dogs are welcome at this hotel.

La Quinta Inn & Suites Milwaukee
SW/New Berlin
15300 W. Rock Ridge Rd.
New Berlin, WI
262-717-0900 (800-531-5900)
Dogs of all sizes are allowed. There
are no additional pet fees. Dogs
must be leashed, cleaned up after,
and the Do Not Disturb sign put on
the door if there is a pet in the room
alone. Multiple dogs may be allowed.

Super 8 New Richmond
1561 Dorset Lane
New Richmond, WI
715-246-7829 (800-800-8000)
Dogs are welcome at this hotel.

Comfort Suites Milwaukee Airport
6362 S. 13th Street
Oak Creek, WI
414-570-1111 (877-424-6423)
Dogs of all sizes are allowed.

La Quinta Inn Milwaukee Airport/Oak
Creek
7141 S. 13th Street
Oak Creek, WI
414-762-2266 (800-531-5900)
Dogs of all sizes are allowed. There
are no additional fees. Dogs may not
be left unattended, and they must be
leashed and cleaned up after.
Multiple dogs may be allowed.

MainStay Suites
1001 W. College Ave.
Oak Creek, WI
414-571-8800 (877-424-6423)
The MainStay Suites is conveniently
located just off Interstate 94. Deluxe
cont breakfast, airport shuttle, fitness
center.

Red Roof Inn Milwaukee Airport
6360 South 13th Street
Oak Creek, WI
414-764-3500 (800-RED-ROOF)
One well-behaved family pet per
room. Guest must notify front desk
upon arrival. Guest is liable for any
damages. In consideration of all
guests, pets must never be left
unattended in the guest rooms.

Staybridge Suites Milwaukee West-
Oconomowoc
1141 Blue Ribbon Drive
Oconomowoc, WI
262-200-2900 (877-270-6405)
Dogs up to 80 pounds are allowed.
Pets allowed with an additional pet
fee. Up to $75 for 1-6 nights and up

to $150 for 7+ nights. A pet
agreement must be signed at
check-in.

Comfort Inn
1223 Crossing Meadows Dr.
Onalaska, WI
608-781-7500 (877-424-6423)
Dogs of all sizes are allowed.

Holiday Inn Express Onalaska (La
Crosse Area)
9409 Hwy 16, Valley View Plaza
Onalaska, WI
608-783-6555 (877-270-6405)
Dogs are welcome at this hotel.

Hawthorn Inn & Suites
3105 S Washburn Street
Oshkosh, WI
920-303-1133 (800-527-1133)
In addition to providing a convenient
location to many local sites and
activities, this all-suite hotel offers a
number of amenities for business
and leisure travelers, including their
signature breakfast buffet and
beautifully appointed rooms. Dogs
are allowed for an additional pet fee
of $15 per night per room. 2 dogs
may be allowed.

Holiday Inn Express Hotel & Suites
Oshkosh-Sr 41
2251 Westowne Avenue
Oshkosh, WI
920-303-1300 (877-270-6405)
Dogs are welcome at this hotel.

La Quinta Inn Oskosh
1950 Omro Road
Oshkosh, WI
920-233-4190 (800-531-5900)
Dogs of all sizes are allowed. There
are no additional pet fees. Dogs
may not be left unattended, and
they must be leashed and cleaned
up after. Multiple dogs may be
allowed.

Super 8 Airport Oshkosh
1581 W. South Park Ave.
Oshkosh, WI
920-426-2885 (800-800-8000)
Dogs are welcome at this hotel.

Super 8 Park Falls
1212 Hwy 13 S
Park Falls, WI
715-762-3383 (800-800-8000)
Dogs are welcome at this hotel.

Best Western Waukesha Grand
2840 N Grandview Boulevard
Pewaukee, WI
262-524-9300 (800-780-7234)
Dogs of all sizes are allowed. Dogs

are allowed for a pet fee.

Super 8 Phillips
726 Lake Avenue South
Phillips, WI
715-339-2898 (800-800-8000)
Dogs of all sizes are allowed. Dogs
are allowed for a pet fee.

Governer Dodge Hotel and
Convention Center
300 Bus H 151
Platteville, WI
608-348-2301
Dogs of all sizes are allowed. There
is a $50 refundable deposit plus an
additional fee of $10 per night per
pet.

Super 8 Platteville
100 Hwy 80-81 S
Platteville, WI
608-348-8800 (800-800-8000)
Dogs of all sizes are allowed. Dogs
are allowed for a nightly pet fee.

Super 8 /Kenshoa Area Pleasant
Prairie
7601 118th Ave
Pleasant Prairie, WI
262-857-7963 (800-800-8000)
Dogs are welcome at this hotel.

Comfort Inn
1560 American Drive
Plover, WI
715-342-0400 (877-424-6423)
Dogs of all sizes are allowed. Dogs
are allowed for a pet fee of $15.00
per pet per night. Two dogs are
allowed per room.

52 Stafford Inn
52 Stafford Street
Plymouth, WI
920-893-0552 (800-421-4667)
Listed on the National Register, this
Irish Inn and Pub offers an elegant
casual ambiance, fine dining, live
music in the pub on Wednesdays,
and 19 beautifully decorated guest
rooms (15 with whirlpools). Dogs are
allowed for an additional one time
fee of $20 per pet. Dogs must be
leashed and under their owner's
control. 2 dogs may be allowed.

Comfort Suites
N 5780 Kinney Rd
Portage, WI
608-745-4717 (877-424-6423)
Dogs up to 60 pounds are allowed.
Dogs are allowed for a pet fee of
$10.00 per pet per night. Two dogs
are allowed per room.

Days Inn Portage

Dog-Friendly Lodging - Please always call ahead to make sure an establishment is still dog-friendly.

N5781 Kinney Rd
Portage, WI
608-742-1554 (800-329-7466)
Dogs of all sizes are allowed. Dogs are allowed for a pet fee.

Super 8 Portage
3000 New Pinery Rd
Portage, WI
608-742-8330 (800-800-8000)
Dogs are welcome at this hotel.

Super 8 Prairie Du Chien
1930 South Marquette Rd
Prairie Du Chien, WI
608-326-8777 (800-800-8000)
Dogs of all sizes are allowed. Dogs are allowed for a nightly pet fee.

Knights Inn Redgranite
717 E Bannerman Ave
Redgranite, WI
920-566-2111 (800-843-5644)
Dogs of all sizes are allowed. Dogs are allowed for a pet fee of $10.00 per pet per stay.

Quality Inn
2115 E. Main St.
Reedsburg, WI
608-524-8535 (877-424-6423)
Dogs of all sizes are allowed. Dogs are allowed for a pet fee of $10.00 per pet per night.

Best Western Claridge Motor Inn
70 N Stevens Street
Rhinelander, WI
715-362-7100 (800-780-7234)
Dogs up to 75 pounds are allowed.

Comfort Inn
1490 Lincoln St.
Rhinelander, WI
715-369-1100 (877-424-6423)
Dogs of all sizes are allowed. Dogs are allowed for a pet fee of $10.00 per pet per night.

Holiday Acres Resort on Lake Thompson
4060 S Shore Road
Rhinelander, WI
715-369-1500
Dogs of all sizes are allowed. There is a $18 plus tax per night per pet additional pet fee. 2 dogs may be allowed.

Quality Inn
668 West Kemp St.
Rhinelander, WI
715-369-3600 (877-424-6423)
Dogs of all sizes are allowed. Dogs are allowed for a pet fee of $10.00 per pet per stay.

Currier's Lakeview Lodge
2010 E. Sawyer Street
Rice Lake, WI
715-234-7474 (800-433-5253)
currierslakeview.com
Located on Rice Lake's scenic east side, Currier's Lakeview is the city's only all-season resort motel. The motel sits on a wooded 4-acre peninsula that is located between two beautiful bays. There are no additional pet fees. 2 dogs may be allowed.

Days Inn Rice Lake
1710 South Main Street
Rice Lake, WI
715-234-4444 (800-329-7466)
Dogs of all sizes are allowed. Dogs are allowed for a pet fee of $10.00 per pet per stay.

Super 8 Rice Lake
2401 S Main
Rice Lake, WI
715-234-6956 (800-800-8000)
Dogs are welcome at this hotel.

Comfort Suites at Royal Ridges
2 Westgate Drive
Ripon, WI
920-748-5500 (877-424-6423)
Dogs up to 50 pounds are allowed. Dogs are allowed for a pet fee of $15.00 per pet per night. Two dogs are allowed per room.

Best Western River Falls Hotel & Suites
100 Spring Street
River Falls, WI
715-425-1045 (800-780-7234)
Dogs are welcome at this hotel.

Candlewood Suites Wausau-Rib Mountain
803 Industrial Park Avenue
Rothschild, WI
715-355-8900 (877-270-6405)
Dogs up to 80 pounds are allowed. There is a $25 one time pet fee.

Comfort Inn
1510 County Road XX
Rothschild, WI
715-355-4449 (877-424-6423)
Dogs up to 50 pounds are allowed. Dogs are allowed for a pet fee of $10.00 per pet per night.

Motel 6 - Rothschild, Wi
904 Industrial Park Ave
Rothschild, WI
715-355-3030 (800-466-8356)
This motel welcomes your pets to stay with you.

Super 8 Milwaukee
Saukville/Milwaukee
180 S Foster Rd
Saukville, WI
262-284-9399 (800-800-8000)
Dogs of all sizes are allowed. Dogs are allowed for a nightly pet fee.

Super 8 Shawano
211 Waukechon St
Shawano, WI
715-526-6688 (800-800-8000)
Dogs are welcome at this hotel.

Comfort Inn
4332 N. 40th St.
Sheboygan, WI
920-457-7724 (877-424-6423)
Dogs of all sizes are allowed.

La Quinta Inn Sheboygan
2932 Kohler Memorial Drive
Sheboygan, WI
920-457-2321 (800-531-5900)
Dogs of all sizes are allowed. There are no additional pet fees. Dogs may not be left unattended unless they will be quiet and well behaved. Dogs must be leashed and cleaned up after. Multiple dogs may be allowed.

Sleep Inn & Suites
3912 Motel Road
Sheboygan, WI
920-694-0099 (877-424-6423)
Dogs of all sizes are allowed. Dogs are allowed for a pet fee of $10.00 per pet per night. Three or more dogs may be allowed.

Days Inn Sheboygan/The Falls
600 Main St. North Hwy 32
Sheboygan Falls, WI
920-467-4314 (800-329-7466)
Dogs of all sizes are allowed. Dogs are allowed for a pet fee of $10.00 per pet per stay.

Patio Motel and Restaurant
10440 Orchard Drive
Sister Bay, WI
920-854-1978
Open from late May until late October, this motel offers a number of amenities plus an eatery that will allow dogs at their outer tables. One dog up to 50 pounds is allowed per room for an additional fee of $7 per night. Dogs may not be left alone in the room, and they must be leashed and under their owner's control at all times.

Best Western Sparta Trail Lodge
4445 Theater Road
Sparta, WI
608-269-2664 (800-780-7234)

Dog-Friendly Lodging - Please always call ahead to make sure an establishment is still dog-friendly.

Dogs are welcome at this hotel. There is a $20 one time pet fee.

Country Inn by Carlson
737 Avon Rd
Sparta, WI
608-269-3110
There is a $10 per day per pet fee. 2 dogs may be allowed.

Grapevine Log Cabins
19149 Jade Road
Sparta, WI
608-269-3619
grapevinelogcabins.com/
Three lofted cabins set among the pines make for a great get-a-way here. The cabins each have picnic tables, a grill, and modern bathrooms. A tasty country breakfast is available in the main house, and there is a mile long scenic walking lane through rich foliage and a grove of Cypress trees that even the resident pooch likes to take. One dog is allowed per cabin for no additional fee. Dogs must be hound and human friendly, and leashed or under strict voice control.

Justin Trails Resort
7452 Kathryn Avenue
Sparta, WI
608-269-4522 (800-488-4521)
justintrails.com/
Specializing in the 3 R's-recreation, relaxation, and romance, this beautiful 213 acre resort offers 3 acres of formal gardens, 10 miles of trails, disc golf, and more. Pooches can also have fun here in the winter with skijoring or sledding as there is a 2 k trail groomed just for them; they are not allowed on the other trails. Dogs are allowed for an additional fee of $15 per night per pet. They must be kept leashed except in the open fields on the Westside of the Sparta cabins. Dogs are not allowed to mark territory around the buildings, and they must be cleaned-up after and waste put in the dumpster at the west end of the barn. Dogs must be well groomed, healthy, current on shots, and cat/hound/and human friendly. Also they request bringing the pet's food dishes, comfort items, and bedding. 2 dogs may be allowed.

Super 8 Sparta
716 Avon St
Sparta, WI
608-269-8489 (800-800-8000)
Dogs of all sizes are allowed. Dogs are allowed for a pet fee.

Holiday Inn Express Hotel & Suites

Stevens Point-Wisconsin Rapids
1100 Amber Avenue
Stevens Point, WI
715-344-0000 (877-270-6405)
Dogs of all sizes are allowed. Dogs are allowed for a pet fee of $25 per pet per night.

La Quinta Inn Stevens Point
4917 Main Street
Stevens Point, WI
715-344-1900 (800-531-5900)
Dogs of all sizes are allowed. There are no additional fees. Dogs may not be left unattended at any time, and they must be leashed and cleaned up after. Multiple dogs may be allowed.

Ramada Stevens Point
1501 N. Point Drive
Stevens Point, WI
715-341-1340 (800-272-6232)
Dogs are welcome at this hotel.

Beach Harbor Resort
3662 N Duluth Avenue
Sturgeon Bay, WI
920-743-3191 (800-388-8055)
beachharborresort.com/index.php
There is a variety of recreational opportunities at this lakeside resort; they also have a bar and grill on site where dogs are allowed at the outer tables. Dogs are allowed at the motel for an additional $10 per night per pet. Dogs may not be left alone in the room at any time; they must be at least 1 year old, leashed and under their owner's control at all times. 2 dogs may be allowed.

Holiday Motel
29 N Second Ave
Sturgeon Bay, WI
920-743-5571
There is a $10 per day pet fee per room. Dogs must be crated when left alone in the room. 2 dogs may be allowed.

Super 8 Sturgeon Bay
Hwy 42/57 at Sturgeon Bay Exit
Sturgeon Bay, WI
920-743-9211 (800-800-8000)
Dogs of all sizes are allowed. Dogs are allowed for a nightly pet fee.

Quality Inn & Suites
105 Business Park Drive
Sun Prairie, WI
608-834-9889 (877-424-6423)
Dogs up to 50 pounds are allowed. Dogs are allowed for a pet fee of $10.00 per pet per night. Two dogs are allowed per room.

Super 8 /Madison E Sun Prairie
1033 Emerald Terrace
Sun Prairie, WI
608-837-8889 (800-800-8000)
Dogs are welcome at this hotel.

Best Western Bay Walk Inn
1405 Susquehanna Avenue
Superior, WI
715-392-7600 (800-780-7234)
Dogs are welcome at this hotel.

Best Western Bridgeview Motor Inn
415 Hammond Avenue
Superior, WI
715-392-8174 (800-780-7234)
Dogs are welcome at this hotel.

Days Inn Bayfront Superior
110 Harborview Parkway
Superior, WI
715-392-4783 (800-329-7466)
Dogs of all sizes are allowed. Dogs are allowed for a pet fee.

Americinn
750 Vandervort St
Tomah, WI
608-372-4100
There is a $10 pet fee per room for each 1 to 3 days stay. There is one non-smoking pet room. 2 dogs may be allowed.

Comfort Inn
305 Wittig Rd.
Tomah, WI
608-372-6600 (877-424-6423)
Dogs of all sizes are allowed. Dogs are allowed for a pet fee of $10.00 per pet per stay.

Cranberry Country Lodge
319 Wittig Road
Tomah, WI
608-374-2801 (800-243-9874)
cranberrycountrylodge.com
This refreshing contemporary resort hotel offers such features as a 12,000 square foot indoor water-park, a 10,000 square foot convention center with catering facilities, a 24 hour business center, a lounge, and more. Dogs are allowed for an additional fee of $10 per night per pet with advance registration by phone only. Dogs must be leashed or under strict voice control and picked up after at all times. Multiple dogs may be allowed.

Econo Lodge
2005 N. Superior
Tomah, WI
608-372-9100 (877-424-6423)
Dogs of all sizes are allowed. Dogs are allowed for a pet fee of $10.00

per pet per night.

Lark Inn
229 N Superior Ave
Tomah, WI
608-372-5981
larkinn.com/
This inn has been sheltering
travelers since the early 1900s. It is a
comfortable retreat with country
quilts and antiques. Dogs are
allowed in the larger hotel rooms and
the log cabins. There is a $6 per day
per pet fee. Multiple dogs may be
allowed.

Super 8 Wisconsin Tomah
1008 E McCoy Blvd
Tomah, WI
608-372-3901 (800-800-8000)
Dogs of all sizes are allowed. Dogs
are allowed for a pet fee.

Rodeway Inn & Suites
1738 Comfort Drive
Tomahawk, WI
715-453-8900 (877-424-6423)
Dogs of all sizes are allowed. Dogs
are allowed for a pet fee of $25.00
per pet per stay.

Holiday Inn Express Hotel & Suites
Madison-Verona
515 W. Verona Ave
Verona, WI
608-497-4500 (877-270-6405)
Dogs of all sizes are allowed. Dogs
are allowed for a nightly pet fee.

Viking Village Motel
Main Road at Detroit Harbor, P.O.
Box 188.
Washington Island, WI
920-847-2551 (888-847-2144)
There are no designated smoking or
non-smoking rooms. There are no
additional pet fees. There is an extra
charge if you do not pick up after
your pet.

Baymont Inn & Suites Waterford
750 Fox Lane
Waterford, WI
262-534-4100 (877-229-6668)
Dogs are welcome at this hotel.

Extended Stay America Milwaukee -
Waukesha
2520 Plaza Ct.
Waukesha, WI
262-798-0217 (800-804-3724)
One dog is allowed per suite. There
is a $25 per night additional pet fee
up to $150 for an entire stay.

Ramada Limited -Milwaukee West
Waukesha

2111 East Moreland Blvd
Waukesha, WI
262-547-7770 (800-272-6232)
Dogs of all sizes are allowed. Dogs
are allowed for a pet fee of $10 per
pet per night.

Super 8 Waukesha
2510 Plaza Court
Waukesha, WI
262-786-6015 (800-800-8000)
Dogs of all sizes are allowed. Dogs
are allowed for a pet fee of $10.00
per pet per night.

Best Western Grand Seasons Hotel
110 Grand Seasons Drive
Waupaca, WI
715-258-9212 (800-780-7234)
Dogs are welcome at this hotel.

Days Inn /North/I-52 Wausau
116 S. 17th Ave
Wausau, WI
715-842-0641 (800-329-7466)
Dogs are welcome at this hotel.

La Quinta Inn Wausau
1910 Stewart Avenue
Wausau, WI
715-842-0421 (800-531-5900)
Dogs of all sizes are allowed. There
are no additional pet fees. Dogs
may not be left unattended, and
they must be leashed and cleaned
up after. Multiple dogs may be
allowed.

Stewart Inn
521 Grant Street
Wausau, WI
715-849-5858
stewartinn.com/
Richly decorated rooms and
common areas, gourmet breakfasts,
historic ambiance, modern
amenities, a large lush patio, and
more can be enjoyed at this inn.
Being located near the Wisconsin
River and several hiking paths has
made this a popular retreat for
guests with pets. Dogs are allowed
for no additional fee with advance
reservations; they must be animal
and human friendly, current on all
shots, and on a flea prevention
program. Dogs must be leashed,
kept off the furniture in the common
areas, and crated when left alone in
the room. Pet clean-up disposal
bags are available from the
innkeeper, and there is a dog
shower in the basement. 2 dogs
may be allowed.

Super 8 Wausau
2006 Stewart Ave

Wausau, WI
715-848-2888 (800-800-8000)
Dogs of all sizes are allowed. Dogs
are allowed for a pet fee of $10.00
per pet per night.

Super 8 Wautoma
W 7607 State Road 21 and 73
Wautoma, WI
920-787-4811 (800-800-8000)
Dogs of all sizes are allowed. Dogs
are allowed for a pet fee.

Extended Stay America Milwaukee -
Wauwatosa
11121 W. North Ave.
Wauwatosa, WI
414-443-1909 (800-804-3724)
One dog is allowed per suite. There
is a $25 per night additional pet fee
up to $150 for an entire stay.

Super 8 /Med Ctr/Mil West
Wauwatosa
115 N Mayfair Rd
Wauwatosa, WI
414-257-0140 (800-800-8000)
Dogs are welcome at this hotel.

Super 8 WI Whitewater
917 Milwaukee
Whitewater, WI
262-473-8818 (800-800-8000)
Dogs are welcome at this hotel.

Days Inn Madison Northeast
6311 Roslad Dr
Windsor, WI
608-846-7473 (800-329-7466)
Dogs are welcome at this hotel.

Super 8 Madison Windsor
4506 Lake Circle
Windsor, WI
608-846-3971 (800-800-8000)
Dogs are welcome at this hotel.

Baker's Sunset Bay Resort
921 Canyon Road
Wisconsin Dells, WI
608-254-8406 (800-435-6515)
sunsetbayresort.com/
Nestled along the banks of Lake
Delton on 5 scenic, wooded acres,
this resort has a number of
recreational opportunities, plus
planned activities, a free continental
breakfast, and free WiFi. Dogs are
allowed for an additional fee of $10
per night per pet, which also includes
a little treat bag. Dogs must be
friendly, leashed, and cleaned up
after; they are not allowed on the
beach. Known aggressive breed
dogs are not allowed. 2 dogs may be
allowed.

Days Inn Wisconsin Dells
944 Highway 12
Wisconsin Dells, WI
608-254-6444 (800-329-7466)
Dogs are welcome at this hotel.

Econo Lodge
350 West Munroe St
Wisconsin Dells, WI
608-253-4343 (877-424-6423)
Dogs of all sizes are allowed. Dogs are allowed for a pet fee of $15.00 per pet per night. Two dogs are allowed per room.

Kings Inn Motel
31 Whitlock Street
Wisconsin Dells, WI
608-254-2043
dellskingsinn.com/
Some of the amenities at this motel include a seasonal, indoor heated pool, a large picnic and grill area, a playground, and WiFi. Quiet, well mannered dogs are allowed for no additional fee. 2 dogs may be allowed.

Paradise Motel
1700 Wisconsin Dells Parkway/H 12/23
Wisconsin Dells, WI
608-254-7333
dellsparadise.com/
Located in the heart of the Dells on 12 landscaped acres, this resort features a variety of accommodations, WiFi, an outdoor heated pool and Jacuzzi, 2 playgrounds, picnic areas with grills, and more. Additionally, they set directly across from the Mt Olympus Water and Theme Park, and each registered guest receives a theme park pass for each day of their stay. One dog is allowed per room for an additional fee of $10 per day. Dogs must be quiet, well mannered, leashed, and cleaned up after.

Pine-Aire Motel
511 Wisconsin Dells Parkway/H 12/23
Wisconsin Dells, WI
608-254-2131 (800-635-8627)
pineaire-motel.com/
Set among tall pines, this motel offers a convenient location to many of the attractions in the area, plus they offer an adult and a kiddie indoor pool, game room, and rooms with fireplaces. Dogs are allowed for an additional fee of $5 per night per pet. Dogs need to be crated or removed for housekeeping. 2 dogs may be allowed.

Rodeway Inn

1630 Wisconsin Dells Parkway
Wisconsin Dells, WI
608-253-6500 (877-424-6423)
Dogs of all sizes are allowed. Dogs are allowed for a pet fee of $15.00 per pet per night.

Spring Brook Wisconsin Dells
242 Lake Shore Dr
Wisconsin Dells, WI
877-228-8686
springbrookwisconsindells.com/
There are more than 50 fully furnished vacation home rentals set on this 360 acre wooded resort. They offer on-site a north-woods themed clubhouse complex with indoor and outdoor pools, whirlpools, a game room, and a work-out room. Additionally there are 2 fishing lakes, scenic walking trails, a 9-hole golf course, and many planned activities. Some of the rentals allow dogs for an additional fee of about $10 per night per pet; price can vary slightly depending on the unit and size of the pets. Dogs must be kept leashed and cleaned up after on the property.

Super 8 Wisconsin Dells
800 County HWY H
Wisconsin Dells, WI
608-254-6464 (800-800-8000)
Dogs are welcome at this hotel.

Thunder Valley Inn
W15344 Waubeek Road
Wisconsin Dells, WI
608-254-4145 (877-254-4145)
thundervalleyinn.com/
Specializing in Norwegian farm family hospitality, this unique 130 year old farmstead offers all the farm animals, and a smorgasbord of food and fun "the old fashioned way" with their lively Threshing Dinner Shows. It is a popular pastime here of story-telling, singing and fiddling while homemade pot roast and all the fixings are being made and enjoyed. Dogs are allowed in the cottage: One dog is $15 per night, and a 2nd dog is allowed for a total of $25 per night. Dogs must be animal and human friendly, leashed, and cleaned up after at all times. 2 dogs may be allowed.

Motel 6 - Wisconsin Rapids, Wi
911 Huntington Ave
Wisconsin Rapids, WI
715-423-3211 (800-466-8356)
This motel welcomes your pets to stay with you.

Rodeway Inn
3300 8th St. S.
Wisconsin Rapids, WI
715-423-7000 (877-424-6423)
Dogs of all sizes are allowed. Dogs are allowed for a pet fee of $10.00 per pet per night.

Sleep Inn & Suites
4221 8th Street South
Wisconsin Rapids, WI
715-424-6800 (877-424-6423)
Dogs of all sizes are allowed.

Wyoming

Drifter's Inn Motel
210 Penland Street/H 789
Baggs, WY
307-383-2015
Dogs are allowed at this motel for a $50 refundable deposit, and a credit card must be on file. Dogs must be kept leashed, picked up after, and they are not allowed in the restaurant or bar area. Multiple dogs may be allowed.

Canyon Ranch Guest Ranch
22 Johnson Street
Big Horn, WY
307-674-6239
canyonranchbighorn.com/
Mountains, valleys, 100's of small streams and lakes, miles and miles of trails, and a true guest ranch style vacation await visitors on this 3,000 acre private reserve. There is a 3 night, 4 person minimum stay requirement and well mannered dogs are welcome for no additional fee. Dogs may be off leash if they are under good voice control; they are not allowed to pester the horses or wildlife in any way. 2 dogs may be allowed.

Best Western Crossroads Inn
75 N Bypass Road
Buffalo, WY
307-684-2256 (800-780-7234)
Dogs of all sizes are allowed. Dogs are allowed for a pet fee of $15.00 per pet per stay.

Comfort Inn
65 US Highway 16 E.
Buffalo, WY
307-684-9564 (877-424-6423)
Dogs up to 75 pounds are allowed. Two dogs are allowed per room.

Econo Lodge
333 East Hart St.
Buffalo, WY
307-684-2219 (877-424-6423)

Dog-Friendly Lodging - Please always call ahead to make sure an establishment is still dog-friendly.

Dogs of all sizes are allowed. Dogs are allowed for a pet fee of $10.00 per pet per night.

Motel 6 - Buffalo, Wy
100 Flat Iron Dr
Buffalo, WY
307-684-7000 (800-466-8356)
This motel welcomes your pets to stay with you.

Super 8 Buffalo
655 E. Hart St
Buffalo, WY
307-684-2531 (800-800-8000)
Dogs of all sizes are allowed. Dogs are allowed for a pet fee of $5.25 per pet per night.

Days Inn Casper
301 East E Street
Casper, WY
307-234-1159 (800-329-7466)
Dogs are welcome at this hotel.

Motel 6 - Casper
1150 Wilkins Circle
Casper, WY
307-234-3903 (800-466-8356)
This motel welcomes your pets to stay with you.

Quality Inn & Suites
821 North Poplar
Casper, WY
307-266-2400 (877-424-6423)
Dogs of all sizes are allowed. Dogs are allowed for a pet fee of $10.00 per pet per night.

Ramada Plaza Riverside- Wyoming Casper
300 West F Street
Casper, WY
307-235-2531 (800-272-6232)
Dogs are welcome at this hotel.

Super 8 /West Casper
3838 CY Avenue
Casper, WY
307-266-3480 (800-800-8000)
Dogs are welcome at this hotel.

Candlewood Suites Cheyenne
2335 Tura Parkway
Cheyenne, WY
307-634-6622 (877-270-6405)
Dogs up to 80 pounds are allowed. Pets allowed with an additional pet fee. Up to $75 for 1-6 nights and up to $150 for 7+ nights. A pet agreement must be signed at check-in.

Days Inn Cheyenne
2360 W Lincoln Way/I-25
Cheyenne, WY

307-778-8877 (800-329-7466)
Dogs of all sizes are allowed. Dogs are allowed for a pet fee of $5.00 per pet per night.

La Quinta Inn Cheyenne
2410 W. Lincolnway
Cheyenne, WY
307-632-7117 (800-531-5900)
Dogs of all sizes are allowed. There are no additional pet fees. Dogs may not be left unattended, and they must be leashed and cleaned up after. Multiple dogs may be allowed.

Motel 6 - Cheyenne
1735 Westland Rd
Cheyenne, WY
307-635-6806 (800-466-8356)
This motel welcomes your pets to stay with you.

Nagle-Warren Mansion
222 E 17th Street
Cheyenne, WY
307-637-3333 (800-811-2610)
naglewarrenmansion.com/welcome
This elegant Victorian Inn offers beautifully accommodated rooms; 6 in the main house, and 6 in the attached Carriage House. They also offer gourmet dining/catering, a venue for special events, and more. Dogs are allowed in the Carriage House rooms for an additional fee of $30 per night per pet with advance reservations, there is a minimum fee of $100 per pet if they are not pre-registered. Pooches will receive treats, a bandana, a "Dog Inn/Dog Gone" door sign, food and water bowls to use, and walking maps. Arrangements need to be made for housekeeping. Dogs may not be left alone in the rooms; they must be leashed and under their owner's control at all times, and they must be kitty, hound, and human friendly. 2 dogs may be allowed.

Oak Tree Inn
1625 Stillwater Avenue
Cheyenne, WY
307-778-6620 (888-456-TREE (8733))
oaktreeinn.net
In addition to a full list of on-site amenities, this inn also comps a free breakfast at Penny's Diner next door - a fun 50's style eatery; plus they are close to the Greenway for a great walk around most of the city. Dogs are allowed for an additional one time pet fee of $10 per room. Multiple dogs may be allowed.

Ramada Hitching Post Inn and Conference Center
1700 West Lincoln Way
Cheyenne, WY
307-638-3301 (800-272-6232)
Dogs of all sizes are allowed. Dogs are allowed for a pet fee of $10.00 per pet per night.

Rodeway Inn
5401 Walker Road
Cheyenne, WY
307-632-8901 (877-424-6423)
Dogs up to 150 pounds are allowed. Dogs are allowed for a pet fee of $20.00 per pet per stay. Three or more dogs may be allowed.

Super 8 WY Cheyenne
1900 W Lincolnway
Cheyenne, WY
307-635-8741 (800-800-8000)
Dogs of all sizes are allowed. Dogs are allowed for a pet fee of $11.00 per pet per night.

The Plains Hotel
1600 Central Avenue/H 85/180
Cheyenne, WY
307-638-3311 (866-2PLAINS (275-2467))
theplainshotel.com
In addition to a convenient location to shopping, dining, historic, and civic areas, this notable hotel has been offering repose to travelers since the early 1900s. Dogs are allowed for an additional one time pet fee of $25 per room. Multiple dogs may be allowed.

Windy Hills Guest House
393 Happy Jack Rd
Cheyenne, WY
307-632-6423
windyhillswyo.com/
There are no additional pet fees if there is no extra cleaning required. 2 dogs may be allowed.

The Ranch at UCross
2673 US Hwy 14 East
Clearmont, WY
307-737-2281 (800-447-0194)
This secluded resort allows one dog up to 30 pounds for an additional $100 refundable pet deposit. The dog is not allowed on the beds.

Best Western Sunset Motor Inn
1601 8th Street
Cody, WY
307-587-4265 (800-780-7234)
Dogs up to 50 pounds are allowed. Dogs are allowed for a pet fee.

Cody Lodging Company

1102 Beck Avenue
Cody, WY
307-587-6000 (800-587-6560)
Located on an organic beef ranch, the Heart Mountain cabin retreat is a secluded, sustainable get-a-way as unique in its setting as it is in its design: A Japanese styled spa cabin, some of the amenities include a Japanese cedar soaking tub, a sauna, and a wood-burning stove. Services available include private massages, a romantic catered diner, and Wednesday yoga classes onsite. Additionally, certified organic, pasture-raised all natural beef can be purchased on site. One dog is allowed at the cabin for no additional fee.

Green Creek Inn & RV Park
2908 Northfork Hwy
Cody, WY
307-587-5004 (877-587-5004)
greencreekinn.com
Dogs are allowed at teh motel and RV Park 20 miles west of Cody near the Shoshone National Forest. There is a $10 per night pet fee in the motel. There is no additional fee for pets in the RV park.

Hunter Peak Ranch
4027 Crandall Road/H 296
Cody, WY
307-587-3711
hunterpeakranch.com/
Located in the Shoshone National Forest, this 155 acre guest ranch sits at 6,700 feet elevation along the Clarksfork River and offers guests a number of recreational activities, homemade meals, and more. Dogs are allowed for an additional fee of $15 per night per pet or $45 by the week per pet. Dogs are not allowed on the beds or furnishings, and they must be well mannered, leashed, and under care of owner. 2 dogs may be allowed.

Super 8 Cody
730 Yellowstone Rd
Cody, WY
307-527-6214 (800-800-8000)
Dogs are welcome at this hotel.

Best Western Douglas Inn & Conference Center
1450 Riverbend Drive
Douglas, WY
307-358-9790 (800-780-7234)
Dogs of all sizes are allowed. Dogs are allowed for a pet fee of $10.00 per pet per night.

Holiday Inn Express Hotel & Suites
Douglas

900 West Yellowstone Highway
Douglas, WY
307-358-4500 (877-270-6405)
Dogs of all sizes are allowed. Dogs are allowed for a pet fee.

Motel 6 - Douglas, Wy
2310 E. Richards Street
Douglas, WY
307-358-4780 (800-466-8356)
This motel welcomes your pets to stay with you.

Sleep Inn & Suites
508 Cortez Drive
Douglas, WY
307-358-2777 (877-424-6423)
Dogs of all sizes are allowed. Two dogs are allowed per room.

Super 8 Douglas
314 Russell Ave
Douglas, WY
307-358-6800 (800-800-8000)
Dogs are welcome at this hotel.

Branding Iron Inn
401 W Ramshorn
Dubois, WY
307-455-2893
brandingironinn.com/
There is no additional pet fee. 2 dogs may be allowed.

Chinook Winds Mountain Lodge
640 S 1st St
Dubois, WY
307-455-2987
There is a $5 per day pet fee.

Pinnacle Buttes Lodge and Campground
3577 US Hwy 26W
Dubois, WY
307-455-2506
There is a $50 refundable pet deposit. There are no designated smoking or non-smoking rooms.

Super 8 Dubois
1412 Warm Springs Dr
Dubois, WY
307-455-3694 (800-800-8000)
Dogs are welcome at this hotel.

Lazy Acres Motel and Campground
110 Fields Avenue
Encampment, WY
307-327-5968
lazyacreswyo.com/
Nestled among the trees, this riverside park offers a number of amenities including cable TV, a laundry, picnic tables, grills, and modern bathhouses. One dog is allowed in the motel for an additional $5 per night, and 2 dogs

can be in the campground for no additional fee; they must be leashed and under their owner's control at all times.

Days Inn W Evanston
1983 Harrison Drive, Exit 3
Evanston, WY
307-789-0783 (800-329-7466)
Dogs are welcome at this hotel.

Howard Johnson Inn WY Evanston
339 Wasatch Road
Evanston, WY
307-789-2220 (800-446-4656)
Dogs of all sizes are allowed. Dogs are allowed for a pet fee.

Motel 6 - Evanston
261 Bear River Dr
Evanston, WY
307-789-0791 (800-466-8356)
This motel welcomes your pets to stay with you.

Super 8 Evanston
1710 Harrison Dr. I-80 Exit 3
Evanston, WY
307-789-2777 (800-800-8000)
Dogs of all sizes are allowed. Dogs are allowed for a pet fee of $10.00 per pet per night.

Comfort Inn
480 Lathrop
Evansville, WY
307-235-3038 (877-424-6423)
Dogs of all sizes are allowed. Dogs are allowed for a pet fee of $10.00 per pet per night.

Sleep Inn & Suites
6733 Bonanza Rd.
Evansville, WY
307-235-3100 (877-424-6423)
Dogs of all sizes are allowed. Dogs are allowed for a pet fee of $10.00 per pet per night.

Super 8 Casper East
269 Miracle Street
Evansville, WY
307-237-8100 (800-800-8000)
Dogs are welcome at this hotel.

Best Western Tower West Lodge
109 N US Highway 14-16
Gillette, WY
307-686-2210 (800-780-7234)
Dogs of all sizes are allowed. Dogs are allowed for a pet fee of $15.00 per pet per stay.

Candlewood Suites Gillette
904 Country Club Road
Gillette, WY
307-682-6100 (877-270-6405)

Dogs up to 80 pounds are allowed. Pets allowed with an additional pet fee. Up to $75 for 1-6 nights and up to $150 for 7+ nights. A pet agreement must be signed at check-in.

Clarion Inn
2009 S. Douglas Hwy.
Gillette, WY
307-686-3000 (877-424-6423)
Dogs of all sizes are allowed. Two dogs are allowed per room.

Days Inn Gillette
910 East Boxelder Road
Gillette, WY
307-682-3999 (800-329-7466)
Dogs of all sizes are allowed. Dogs are allowed for a pet fee of $15.00 per pet per night.

Holiday Inn Express Hotel & Suites Gillette
1908 Cliff Davis Dr
Gillette, WY
307-686-9576 (877-270-6405)
Dogs are welcome at this hotel.

Motel 6 - Gillette
2105 Rodgers Dr
Gillette, WY
307-686-8600 (800-466-8356)
This motel welcomes your pets to stay with you.

Super 8 Gillette
208 S Decker Court
Gillette, WY
307-682-8078 (800-800-8000)
Dogs are welcome at this hotel.

Colter Bay Cabins
Jackson Lake
Grand Teton National Park, WY
800-628-9988
gtlc.com/
There are over 200 log cabins and a number of tent cabins. Pets are allowed and there are no additional pet fees.

Jackson Lake Lodge
Jackson Lake
Grand Teton National Park, WY
800-628-9988
gtlc.com/
There is one pet-friendly room. There is a $15 per night additional pet fee.

Oak Tree Inn
1170 W Flaming Gorge Way
Green River, WY
307-875-3500 (888-456-TREE (8733))
oaktreeinn.net/
This well maintained inn will allow

pets for an additional fee of $5.40 per night per pet. Dogs must be quiet, leashed, and cleaned up after on site. Multiple dogs may be allowed.

Elk Country Inn
480 W Pearl Avenue
Jackson, WY
307-733-2364
Well behaved dogs of all sizes are allowed at the inn but not in the cabins. There are no additional pet fees. Dogs are not allowed to be left alone in the room. 2 dogs may be allowed.

Flat Creek Inn
1935 N H 89/26
Jackson, WY
307-733-5276
Dogs of all sizes are allowed. There are no additional pet fees.

Homewood Suites by Hilton
260 N Millward
Jackson, WY
307-739-0808 (800-321-3232)
There are amenities for business or leisure travelers at this Inn. Dogs are allowed for an additional one time fee of $100 per room. Multiple dogs may be allowed.

Motel 6 - Jackson, Wy
600 Hwy 89
Jackson, WY
307-733-1620 (800-466-8356)
This motel welcomes your pets to stay with you.

Pony Express Motel
1075 W Broadway/H 26/89/189/191
Jackson, WY
307-733-3835 (800-526-2658)
ponyexpresswest.com/
Specializing in old west hospitality, this motel offers a convenient location to local attractions, a seasonal heated swimming pool, and well maintained grounds. Dogs are allowed for an additional one time fee of $20 per pet. 2 dogs may be allowed.

Quality Inn & Suites 49'er
330 W. Pearl St.
Jackson, WY
307-733-7550 (877-424-6423)
Dogs of all sizes are allowed.

Jackson Hole Lodge
420 W Broadway/H 89
Jackson Hole, WY
307-733-2992 (800-604-9404)
jacksonholelodge.com/
Sitting on the edge of the Grand

Teton National Park, this lodge has been in service since 1942, and in addition to a great location to a number of activities, they also have a game room, and a 40 foot indoor heated pool with 2 spas and a sauna. Dogs are allowed in the standard motel rooms only for a $50 refundable deposit per room. Dogs must be leashed and under their owner's control. 2 dogs may be allowed.

Painted Buffalo Inn
400 West Broadway
Jackson Hole, WY
307-733-4340
paintedbuffalo.com/
There is a $10 one time pet fee per pet. 2 dogs may be allowed.

Snow King Resort
400 E Snow King Ave
Jackson Hole, WY
307-733-5200 (800-522-5464)
There is a $50 one time pet fee per room. Dogs must be quiet and well mannered. 2 dogs may be allowed.

Best Western Fossil Country Inn & Suites
760 Highway 189/30
Kemmerer, WY
307-877-3388 (800-780-7234)
Dogs of all sizes are allowed. Dogs are allowed for a pet fee.

Best Western Laramie Inn & Suites
1767 N Banner Road
Laramie, WY
307-745-5700 (800-780-7234)
Dogs of all sizes are allowed. Dogs are allowed for a pet fee of $20 per pet per night.

Holiday Inn Laramie
204 S 30th Street
Laramie, WY
307-721-9000 (877-270-6405)
Dogs are welcome at this hotel.

Motel 6 - Laramie
621 Plaza Ln
Laramie, WY
307-742-2307 (800-466-8356)
This motel welcomes your pets to stay with you.

Ramada Laramie
2313 Soldier Springs Rd
Laramie, WY
307-742-6611 (800-272-6232)
Dogs of all sizes are allowed. Dogs are allowed for a pet fee of $10.00 per pet per stay.

Travelodge Downtown Laramie

165 North Third Street
Laramie, WY
307-742-6671 (800-578-7878)
Dogs are welcome at this hotel.

Wyoming High Country Guest Ranch
H 14A, Bighorn National Forest
Lovell, WY
307-548-7820 (877-548-2301)
wyhighcountry.com/
Located in the Big Horn Mountains at
9000 feet elevation, this working
cattle ranch offers an array of
recreational activities, homemade
ranch-style meals, spectacular and
diverse scenery, miles and miles of
trails, abundant wildlife, numerous
waterways, and for the adventurous-
cattle runs. Friendly dogs are allowed
for an additional $10 per night per
pet; they must be under their owner's
control at all times. 2 dogs may be
allowed.

Rawhide Motel
805 S Main Street/H 85
Lusk, WY
307-334-2440 (888-679-2558)
rawhidemotel-lusk.com/
Dogs are allowed for no additional
pet fee; they must be kept leashed
when out of the room and under their
owner's control at all times. 2 dogs
may be allowed.

Baymont Inn and Suites Pinedale
1624 West Pine St
Pinedale, WY
307-367-8300 (877-229-6668)
Dogs are welcome at this hotel.

Best Western Pinedale Inn
864 W Pine Street
Pinedale, WY
307-367-6869 (800-780-7234)
Dogs are welcome at this hotel.

Lodge At Pinedale
1054 W Pine Ste 191
Pinedale, WY
307-367-8800 (866-WY-LODGE
(995-6343))
lodgeatpinedale.com/
Some of the amenities here include
an indoor pool and spa and a
complimentary continental breakfast.
Dogs are allowed for an additional
$10 per night per pet. Dogs must be
kept leashed and cleaned up after. 2
dogs may be allowed.

Super 8 Powell
845 E Coulter Ave
Powell, WY
307-754-7231 (800-800-8000)
Dogs of all sizes are allowed. Dogs
are allowed for a pet fee of $10.00

per pet per night.

Best Western CottonTree Inn
2221 W. Spruce
Rawlins, WY
307-324-2737 (800-780-7234)
Dogs are welcome at this hotel.
There is a $10 one time pet fee.

Days Inn Rawlins
2222 East Cedar/I-80
Rawlins, WY
307-324-6615 (800-329-7466)
Dogs are welcome at this hotel.

Econo Lodge
1500 West Spruce Street
Rawlins, WY
307-324-2905 (877-424-6423)
Dogs of all sizes are allowed. Dogs
are allowed for a pet fee of $10.00
per pet per night.

Holiday Inn Express Rawlins
201 Airport Road
Rawlins, WY
307-324-3760 (877-270-6405)
Dogs are welcome at this hotel.

Quality Inn
1801 E. Cedar St.
Rawlins, WY
307-324-2783 (877-424-6423)
Dogs of all sizes are allowed. Dogs
are allowed for a pet fee of $10.00
per pet per night.

Travelodge WY Rawlins
1617 W Spruce St
Rawlins, WY
307-328-1600 (800-578-7878)
Dogs of all sizes are allowed. Dogs
are allowed for a pet fee of $5 per
pet per night.

Comfort Inn & Suites
2020 N. Federal Blvd.
Riverton, WY
307-856-8900 (877-424-6423)
Dogs up to 100 pounds are allowed.
Dogs are allowed for a pet fee of
$10.00 per pet per night. Two dogs
are allowed per room.

Days Inn Riverton
909 West Main Street
Riverton, WY
307-856-9677 (800-329-7466)
Dogs are welcome at this hotel.

Rodeway Inn & Suites
611 West Main Street
Riverton, WY
307-856-2900 (877-424-6423)
Dogs up to 50 pounds are allowed.
Dogs are allowed for a pet fee of
$15.00 per pet per night. Two dogs

are allowed per room.

Sundowner Station
1616 N Federal Blvd
Riverton, WY
307-856-6503
There are no additional pet fees with
a credit card on file. Dogs may not
be left unattended. Multiple dogs
may be allowed.

Super 8 Riverton
1040 N Federal Blvd
Riverton, WY
307-857-2400 (800-800-8000)
Dogs of all sizes are allowed. Dogs
are allowed for a pet fee of $10.00
per pet per stay.

Best Western Outlaw Inn
1630 Elk Street
Rock Springs, WY
307-362-6623 (800-780-7234)
Dogs are welcome at this hotel.

Econo Lodge
1635 North Elk
Rock Springs, WY
307-382-4217 (877-424-6423)
Dogs of all sizes are allowed. Dogs
are allowed for a pet fee of $15.00
per pet per night.

La Quinta Inn-Rock Springs
2717 Dewar Drive
Rock Springs, WY
307-362-1770 (800-531-5900)
Dogs of all sizes are allowed. There
are no additional pet fees. Dogs may
not be left unattended at night, and
they must be leashed, cleaned up
after, and attended to or removed for
housekeeping. Multiple dogs may be
allowed.

Motel 6 - Rock Springs
2615 Commercial Way
Rock Springs, WY
307-362-1850 (800-466-8356)
This motel welcomes your pets to
stay with you.

Quality Inn
1670 Sunset Dr.
Rock Springs, WY
307-382-9490 (877-424-6423)
Dogs of all sizes are allowed.

Best Western Sheridan Center
612 N Main
Sheridan, WY
307-674-7421 (800-780-7234)
Dogs are welcome at this hotel.

Candlewood Suites Sheridan
1709 Sugarland Drive
Sheridan, WY

307-675-2100 (877-270-6405)
Dogs up to 80 pounds are allowed.
Pets allowed with an additional pet
fee. Up to $75 for 1-6 nights and up
to $150 for 7+ nights. A pet
agreement must be signed at check-
in.

Days Inn Sheridan
1104 Brundage Lane
Sheridan, WY
307-672-2888 (800-329-7466)
Dogs are welcome at this hotel.

Guest House Motel
2007 N Main St
Sheridan, WY
307-674-7496
There is a $10 per day per pet fee.
The fee may be less for small dogs.
Multiple dogs may be allowed.

Motel 6 - Sheridan
911 Sibley Circle
Sheridan, WY
307-673-9500 (800-466-8356)
This motel welcomes your pets to
stay with you.

Super 8 Sheridan
2435 N. Main St
Sheridan, WY
307-672-9725 (800-800-8000)
Dogs of all sizes are allowed. Dogs
are allowed for a pet fee of $5.00 per
pet per night.

Best Western Inn at Sundance
2719 E Cleveland
Sundance, WY
307-283-2800 (800-780-7234)
Dogs of all sizes are allowed. Dogs
are allowed for a pet fee of $10.00
per pet per night.

Days Inn Thermopolis
115 E Park Street
Thermopolis, WY
307-864-3131 (800-329-7466)
Dogs of all sizes are allowed. Dogs
are allowed for a pet fee.

Super 8 Thermopolis
166 South US Hwy 20
Thermopolis, WY
307-864-5515 (800-800-8000)
Dogs of all sizes are allowed. Dogs
are allowed for a pet fee of $10.00
per pet per night.

Days Inn Torrington
1555 S Main St
Torrington, WY
307-532-4011 (800-329-7466)
Dogs are welcome at this hotel.

Holiday Inn Express Hotel & Suites

Torrington
1700 East Valley Rd
Torrington, WY
307-532-7600 (877-270-6405)
Dogs of all sizes are allowed. Dogs
are allowed for a pet fee of $15.00
per pet per night.

Green Creek Inn
2908 Yellowstone Hwy
Wapiti, WY
307-587-5004
There is a $10 pet fee for the 1st
night and $5 for each night
thereafter for the motel,,, there is no
additional pet fee for the
campground. Dogs may not be left
in cars overnight or be left outside
unattended.. 2 dogs may be
allowed.

Best Western Torchlite Motor Inn
1809 N 16th Street
Wheatland, WY
307-322-4070 (800-780-7234)
Dogs are welcome at this hotel.

Motel 6 - Wheatland, Wy
95 16th St
Wheatland, WY
307-322-1800 (800-466-8356)
This motel welcomes your pets to
stay with you.

Vimbo's Motel
203 16th St
Wheatland, WY
307-322-3842
There are no additional pet fees. 2
dogs may be allowed.

Super 8 Worland
2500 Big Horn Ave
Worland, WY
307-347-9236 (800-800-8000)
Dogs of all sizes are allowed. Dogs
are allowed for a pet fee of $5.00
per pet per night.

Canyon Western Cabins
Yellowstone National Park, WY
307-344-7311
travelyellowstone.com
Dogs are allowed in the Cabins only
for an additional one time pet fee of
$25 per unit. The Cabins are open
seasonally from about May to
September each year.

Flagg Ranch Village
Hwy 89 Yellowstone South
Entrance
Yellowstone National Park, WY
307-543-2861 (800-443-2311)
flaggranch.com/
Dogs are allowed in cabins. This is
a seasonal hotel and is not open

year round. There is a $10 per day
per pet additional fee. 2 dogs may be
allowed.

Lake Lodge Cabins
Lake Lodge
Yellowstone National Park, WY
307-344-7311
travelyellowstone.com
Dogs are allowed in the Cabins only
for an additional one time pet fee of
$25 per unit. The Cabins are open
seasonally from about May to
September each year.

Lake Yellowstone Cabins
Lake Yellowstone
Yellowstone National Park, WY
307-344-7311
travelyellowstone.com
Dogs are allowed in the Cabins only
for an additional one time pet fee of
$25 per unit. The Cabins are open
seasonally from about May to
September each year.

Mammoth Hot Springs Cabins
Mammoth Hot Springs
Yellowstone National Park, WY
307-344-7311
travelyellowstone.com
Dogs are allowed in the Cabins only
for an additional one time pet fee of
$25 per unit. The Cabins are open
seasonally from about May to
September each year.

Old Faithful Lodge Cabins
Old Faithful
Yellowstone National Park, WY
307-344-7311
travelyellowstone.com
Dogs are allowed in the Cabins only
for an additional one time pet fee of
$25 per unit. The Cabins are open
seasonally from about May to
September each year. These cabins
are within easy walking distance of
Old Faithful.

Pioneer Cabins
Yellowstone National Park, WY
307-344-7311
travelyellowstone.com
Dogs are allowed in the Cabins only
for an additional one time pet fee of
$25 per unit. The Cabins are open
seasonally from about May to
September each year.

Canada

Alberta

Holiday Inn Express Hotel & Suites
Airdrie-Calgary North
64 East Lake Ave NE
Airdrie, AB
403-912-1952 (877-270-6405)
Dogs of all sizes are allowed. Dogs
are allowed for a nightly pet fee.

Ramada Inn and Suites Airdrie
191 East Lake Cresent
Airdrie, AB
403-945-1288 (800-272-6232)
Dogs of all sizes are allowed. Dogs
are allowed for a nightly pet fee.

Super 8 AB Airdrie
815 East Lake Blvd
Airdrie, AB
403-948-4188 (800-800-8000)
Dogs of all sizes are allowed. Dogs
are allowed for a pet fee of $15.00
per pet per stay.

Days Inn Athabasca
2805 48th Ave
Athabasca, AB
780-675-7020 (800-329-7466)
Dogs of all sizes are allowed. Dogs
are allowed for a pet fee.

Super 8 AB Athabasca
4820B Wood Heights Road
Athabasca, AB
780-675-8888 (800-800-8000)
Dogs of all sizes are allowed. Dogs
are allowed for a pet fee of $20.00
per pet per night.

Best Western Siding 29 Lodge
453 Marten Street Box 1387
Banff, AB
403-762-5575 (800-780-7234)
Dogs are welcome at this hotel.

Driftwood Inn
337 Banff Avenue
Banff, AB
403-762-4496
Dogs of all sizes are allowed. There
is a one time pet fee $20 per pet.

Beaverlodge Motor Inn
116 6A St
Beaverlodge, AB
780-354-2291
beaverlodgemotorinn.com
Dogs of all sizes are allowed. There
is a $10 per night per pet additional
pet fee.

Best Western Bonnyville Inn &
Suites
5401 43rd Street Box 4988
Bonnyville, AB
780-826-6226 (800-780-7234)
Dogs are welcome at this hotel.

Days Inn Bonnyville
5810 50th Avenue
Bonnyville, AB
780-815-4843 (800-329-7466)
Dogs of all sizes are allowed. Dogs
are allowed for a pet fee.

Ramada Brooks
1319 2nd Street West
Brooks, AB
403-362-6440 (800-272-6232)
Dogs of all sizes are allowed. Dogs
are allowed for a nightly pet fee.

Super 8 Brooks
115 15th Ave
Brooks, AB
403-363-0080 (800-800-8000)
Dogs of all sizes are allowed. Dogs
are allowed for a pet fee of $15.00
per pet per night.

5 Calgary Downtown Suites
618 - 5th Ave SW
Calgary, AB
403-451-5551 (877-890-7666)
5calgary.com/
In addition to numerous on-site
amenities, this all-suite hotel also
offers a great location to all the area
has to offer. Dogs up to 50 pounds
are allowed for an additional fee of
$10 (+ tax) per night per pet. 2 dogs
may be allowed.

Calgary Airport Hotel - Coast Plaza
Hotel & Conference Centre
1316 - 33rd Street N.E.
Calgary, AB
403-248-8888 (800-663-1144)
All Coast Hotels have on hand extra
pet amenities if you forget
something. For dogs, they have
extra doggy dishes, sleeping
cushions, nylon chew toys and dog
food. If your dog needs one of these
items, just ask the front desk. There
is a $20 one time pet fee per room.
2 dogs may be allowed.

Days Inn - South Calgary
3828 Macleod Trail S.
Calgary, AB
403-243-5531 (800-329-7466)
Dogs are welcome at this hotel.

Econo Lodge South
7505 Macleod Trail South
Calgary, AB

403-252-4401 (877-424-6423)
Dogs of all sizes are allowed.

Holiday Inn Calgary-Macleod Trail
South
4206 Macleod Trail
Calgary, AB
403-287-2700 (877-270-6405)
Dogs of all sizes are allowed. Dogs
are allowed for a pet fee.

Howard Johnson Express Inn AB
Calgary
5307 McLeod Trail S.W.
Calgary, AB
403-258-1064 (800-446-4656)
Dogs are welcome at this hotel.

Quality Hotel Airport
4804 Edmonton Trail N.E.
Calgary, AB
403-276-3391 (877-424-6423)
Dogs of all sizes are allowed. Dogs
are allowed for a pet fee of $20.00
per pet per night.

Sheraton Suites Calgary Eau Claire
255 Barclay Parade SW
Calgary, AB
403-266-7200 (888-625-5144)
Located in the heart of downtown,
this hotel is central to numerous
shopping and recreation areas. Dogs
of all sizes are allowed for no
additional pet fee. Dogs may not be
left alone in the rooms, and they
must be under their owner's control
at all times. 2 dogs may be allowed.

Staybridge Suites Calgary Airport
2825 Sunridge Way NE
Calgary, AB
403-204-7829 (877-270-6405)
Dogs up to 80 pounds are allowed.
Pets allowed with an additional pet
fee. Up to $75 for 1-6 nights and up
to $150 for 7+ nights. A pet
agreement must be signed at check-
in.

Super 8 Shawnessy Area Calgary
60 Shawville Road
Calgary, AB
403-254-8878 (800-800-8000)
Dogs of all sizes are allowed. Dogs
are allowed for a nightly pet fee.

Super 8 Village AB Calgary
1904 Crowchild Trail NW
Calgary, AB
403-289-9211 (800-800-8000)
Dogs of all sizes are allowed. Dogs
are allowed for a nightly pet fee.

The Fairmont Palliser
133 9th Avenue SW
Calgary, AB

403-262-1234 (800-257-7544)
fairmont.com/palliser/
This historical landmark hotel features 405 luxurious accommodations with amenities for the business or leisure traveler. In addition to the elegant surroundings and upscale services, they offer superb culinary adventures, numerous in room amenities, an impressive indoor pool and spa, a skywalk to other attractions, and they offer "Gold Floor" accommodations. Dogs are allowed for no additional fee, and there is a pet policy to sign at check in. Dogs must be well behaved, leashed, cleaned up after, and crated when left alone in the room.

The Westin Calgary
320 4th Avenue SW
Calgary, AB
403-266-1611 (888-625-5144)
This hotel sits along the city's pedestrian walkway that gives access to numerous eateries, shopping, and recreational activities. Dogs are allowed for no additional fee, and a Heavenly dog bed can be ready for your pooch if requested at the time of reservations. There is a pet waiver to sign at check in. Dogs must be leashed, cleaned up after, and crated when left alone in the room. 2 dogs may be allowed.

Travelodge South Calgary
7012 Macleod Trail South
Calgary, AB
403-253-1111 (800-578-7878)
Dogs are welcome at this hotel.

Travelodge University Calgary
2227 Banff Trail NW
Calgary, AB
403-289-6600 (800-578-7878)
Dogs of all sizes are allowed. Dogs are allowed for a pet fee.

Travelodge Hotel Airport Calgary
2750 Sunridge Blvd NE
Calgary, AB
403-291-1260 (800-578-7878)
Dogs of all sizes are allowed. Dogs are allowed for a pet fee of $10.00 per pet per stay.

Travelodge Hotel Macleod Trail Calgary
9206 Macleod Trail South
Calgary, AB
403-253-7070 (800-578-7878)
Dogs are welcome at this hotel.

Westways Bed and Breakfast
216 - 25 Avenue SW

Calgary, AB
403-229-1758 (866-846-7038)
westways.ab.ca/
Located within walking distance to the city, this Victorian accented heritage home offers a number of "little extras" such as jetted tubs, gas fireplaces, private restrooms, and if desired guests can be picked up in a Rolls Royce. Dogs of all sizes are allowed for an additional fee of $8 per night per pet. Dogs must be well mannered, leashed, and cleaned up after at all times. 2 dogs may be allowed.

Wingate by Wyndham AB Calgary
400 Midpark Way SE
Calgary, AB
403-514-0099 (800-228-1000)
Dogs of all sizes are allowed. Dogs are allowed for a pet fee.

Ramada Inn Camrose
4702 73rd Street
Camrose, AB
780-672-5220 (800-272-6232)
Dogs of all sizes are allowed. Dogs are allowed for a nightly pet fee.

Super 8 Camrose
4710 73rd Street
Camrose, AB
780-672-7303 (800-800-8000)
Dogs of all sizes are allowed. Dogs are allowed for a pet fee of $15.00 per pet per night.

Best Western Pocaterra Inn
1725 Mountain Avenue
Canmore, AB
403-678-4334 (800-780-7234)
Dogs are welcome at this hotel. There is a $15 one time pet fee.

Econo Lodge Canmore
1602 2nd Avenue
Canmore, AB
403-678-5488 (877-424-6423)
Dogs up to 60 pounds are allowed. Dogs are allowed for a pet fee of $15 per pet per stay. Two dogs are allowed per room.

Quality Resort Chateau Canmore
1720 Bow Valley Trail
Canmore, AB
403-678-6699 (877-424-6423)
Dogs of all sizes are allowed.

Westridge Country Inn/Canmore Rocky Mountain Inn
1719 Bow Valley Trail
Canmore, AB
403-678-5221
Dogs of all sizes are allowed. There are no additional pet fees.

Ramada Grande Prairie
7201 99th St.
Clairmont, AB
780-814-7448 (800-272-6232)
Dogs of all sizes are allowed. Dogs are allowed for a pet fee of $25 per pet per stay.

Lazy J Motel
5225 1st Street/H 2
Claresholm, AB
403-625-4949
Dogs of all sizes are allowed for an additional fee of $5 per night per pet. Dogs must be well behaved, leashed, and cleaned up after. 2 dogs may be allowed.

Motel 6 - Claresholm
11 Alberta Road
Claresholm, AB
403-625-4646 (800-466-8356)
This motel welcomes your pets to stay with you.

ThriftLodge AB Claresholm
4083 1A Street West
Claresholm, AB
403-625-3347 (800-578-7878)
Dogs of all sizes are allowed. Dogs are allowed for a nightly pet fee.

Days Inn Cochrane
5 West Side Drive
Cochrane, AB
403-932-5588 (800-329-7466)
Dogs up to 50 pounds are allowed. Dogs are allowed for a nightly pet fee.

Super 8 Cochrane
10 Westside Drive
Cochrane, AB
403-932-6355 (800-800-8000)
Dogs of all sizes are allowed. Dogs are allowed for a pet fee of $15.00 per pet per night.

Ramada Drayton Valley
2051 50th Street
Drayton Valley, AB
780-514-7861 (800-272-6232)
Dogs of all sizes are allowed. Dogs are allowed for a nightly pet fee.

Super 8 Drayton Valley
3727 50th Street
Drayton Valley, AB
780-542-9122 (800-800-8000)
Dogs of all sizes are allowed. Dogs are allowed for a pet fee of $10.00 per pet per night.

Best Western Jurassic Inn
1103 Highway 9 S P O Box 3009
Drumheller, AB

403-823-7700 (800-780-7234)
Dogs of all sizes are allowed. Dogs are allowed for a nightly pet fee.

Ramada Inn and Suites AB
Drumheller
680 2nd Street SE
Drumheller, AB
403-823-2028 (800-272-6232)
Dogs are welcome at this hotel.

Super 8 Drumheller
600-680 2nd Street SE
Drumheller, AB
403-823-8887 (800-800-8000)
Dogs of all sizes are allowed. Dogs are allowed for a pet fee of $15.00 per pet per night.

Best Western Cedar Park Inn
5116 Gateway Boulevard
Edmonton, AB
780-434-7411 (800-780-7234)
Dogs of all sizes are allowed. Dogs are allowed for a nightly pet fee.

Best Western Westwood Inn
18035 Stony Plain Road
Edmonton, AB
780-483-7770 (800-780-7234)
Dogs of all sizes are allowed. Dogs are allowed for a nightly pet fee.

Coast Edmonton Hotel
10155-105th Street
Edmonton, AB
780-423-4811 (800-663-1144)
All Coast Hotels have on hand extra pet amenities if you forget something. For dogs, they have extra doggy dishes, sleeping cushions, nylon chew toys and dog food. If your dog needs one of these items, just ask the front desk. Dogs are allowed for an additional fee of $20 per night per room to a maximum fee of $50. 2 dogs may be allowed.

Comfort Inn West
17610 100th Ave.
Edmonton, AB
780-484-4415 (877-424-6423)
Dogs of all sizes are allowed. Dogs are allowed for a pet fee of $10.00 per pet per night. Two dogs are allowed per room.

Crowne Plaza Hotel Edmonton-Chateau Lacombe
10111 Bellamy Hill
Edmonton, AB
780-428-6611 (877-270-6405)
Dogs of all sizes are allowed. Dogs are allowed for a pet fee. Two dogs are allowed per room.

Holiday Inn Express Edmonton

Downtown
10010 104th Street
Edmonton, AB
780-423-2450 (877-270-6405)
Dogs of all sizes are allowed. Dogs are allowed for a pet fee of $25 per pet per stay.

Holiday Inn Express Hotel & Suites
Edmonton South
2440 Calgary Trail
Edmonton, AB
017-804-4050 (877-270-6405)
Dogs are welcome at this hotel.

Quality Inn West Harvest
17803 Stony Plain Road
Edmonton, AB
780-484-8000 (877-424-6423)
Dogs of all sizes are allowed. Dogs are allowed for a pet fee of $15.00 per pet per night.

Ramada Hotel and Conference Centre Edmonton
11834 Kingsway
Edmonton, AB
780-454-5454 (800-272-6232)
Dogs of all sizes are allowed. Dogs are allowed for a nightly pet fee. Two dogs are allowed per room.

Ramada Inn and Water Park South Edmonton
5359 Calgary Trail
Edmonton, AB
780-434-3431 (800-272-6232)
Dogs of all sizes are allowed. Dogs are allowed for a nightly pet fee.

Super 8 South Edmonton
3610 Gateway Boulevard NW
Edmonton, AB
780-433-8688 (800-800-8000)
Dogs of all sizes are allowed. Dogs are allowed for a nightly pet fee.

The Fairmont Hotel MacDonald
10065 100th Street
Edmonton, AB
780-424-5181 (800-257-7544)
fairmont.com/macdonald/
This elegant 1915 hotel features 199 opulent guestrooms and suites (18) with state-of-the-art amenities, stunning views of the Saskatchewan River Valley, exquisite dining opportunities, a lounge, 24 hour room service, an indoor pool and spa, and wonderful gardens. Dogs of all sizes are welcome for an additional fee of $25 per night per pet (a portion of which is donated to the SPCA). Dogs must be well mannered, leashed, and cleaned up after at all times. They must be crated when

left alone in the room. Dogs are not allowed on the patio or in the gardens behind the hotel. They suggest dogs be walked at the park in front of the hotel.

The Westin Edmonton
10135 100th Street
Edmonton, AB
780-426-3636 (888-625-5144)
This hotel, connected to the Shaw Conference Center, is also central to numerous eateries, shopping, and recreational activities. Dogs are allowed for no additional fee, and a Heavenly dog bed can be ready for your pooch if requested at the time of reservations. There is a pet waiver to sign at check in. They prefer that dogs are not left unattended in the room, but if it is necessary for a short time, they must be crated. Dogs must be under their owner's control, and leashed at all times.

Travelodge East Edmonton
3414 118th Ave
Edmonton, AB
780-474-0456 (800-578-7878)
Dogs of all sizes are allowed. Dogs are allowed for a pet fee of $30 per pet per night.

Travelodge South Edmonton
10320 45th Avenue
Edmonton, AB
780-436-9770 (800-578-7878)
Dogs of all sizes are allowed. Dogs are allowed for a nightly pet fee.

Travelodge West Edmonton
18320 Stony Plain Road
Edmonton, AB
780-483-6031 (800-578-7878)
Dogs are welcome at this hotel.

Super 8 Edson
5220 2nd Avenue
Edson, AB
780-723-7373 (800-800-8000)
Dogs of all sizes are allowed. Dogs are allowed for a pet fee.

D.J. Motel
416 Main Street
Fort MacLeod, AB
403-553-4011
djmotel.com
Dogs up to around medium sized are allowed. There are no additional pet fees and there are smoking and non-smoking rooms for pet owners.

Sunset Motel
104 Highway 3 West
Fort MacLeod, AB
403-553-4448

telusplanet.net/public/sunsetmo/
Dogs of all sizes are allowed. There
is no additional pet fee.

Quality Hotel & Conference Centre
424 Gregoire Drive
Fort McMurray, AB
780-791-7200 (877-424-6423)
Dogs of all sizes are allowed. Dogs
are allowed for a pet fee of $10.00
per pet per night.

Foxwood Inn & Suites
210 Highway Avenue
Fox Creek, AB
780-622-2280 (877-723-9797)
foxwoodinnandsuites.com/
This modern inn and suite with high
speed Internet access allows dogs of
all sizes. There are no additional pet
fees and pets can stay in non-
smoking or smoking rooms.

Best Western Grande Prairie Hotel &
Suites
10745 117th Avenue
Grande Prairie, AB
780-402-2378 (800-780-7234)
Dogs are welcome at this hotel.
There is a $25 one time pet fee.

Days Inn Grande Prairie
10218 162 Avenue
Grande Prairie, AB
780-532-2773 (800-329-7466)
Dogs are welcome at this hotel.

Holiday Inn Express Grande Prairie
10226 117 Avenue
Grande Prairie, AB
780-814-9446 (877-270-6405)
Dogs of all sizes are allowed. Dogs
are allowed for a nightly pet fee.

Holiday Inn Hotel & Suites Grande
Prairie
9816 107 Street
Grande Prairie, AB
780-402-6886 (877-270-6405)
Dogs of all sizes are allowed. Dogs
are allowed for a nightly pet fee.

Motel 6 - Grande Prairie, Ab
15402-101 Street
Grande Prairie, AB
780-830-7744 (800-466-8356)
This motel welcomes your pets to
stay with you.

Quality Hotel & Conference Centre
11201 100th Avenue
Grande Prairie, AB
780-539-6000 (877-424-6423)
Dogs of all sizes are allowed. Dogs
are allowed for a pet fee of $25.00
per pet per night.

Stanford Inn
11401 100th Ave
Grande Prairie, AB
780-539-5678
grandeprairiestanfordhotel.com
Dogs of all sizes are allowed. There
is a $6.50 per night pet fee.

Super 8 Hanna
113 Palliser Trail
Hanna, AB
403-854-2400 (800-800-8000)
Dogs of all sizes are allowed. Dogs
are allowed for a pet fee.

Super 8
9502 - 114 Ave
High Level, AB
780-841-3448 (800-800-8000)
Dogs are welcome at this hotel.

Ramada High River
1512 13th Avenue S.E.
High River, AB
403-603-3183 (800-272-6232)
Dogs of all sizes are allowed. Dogs
are allowed for a pet fee of $15.00
per pet per night.

Super 8 AB High River
1601 13th Ave
High River, AB
403-652-4448 (800-800-8000)
Dogs of all sizes are allowed. Dogs
are allowed for a pet fee of $15.00
per pet per night.

Best Western White Wolf Inn
828 Carmichael Ln
Hinton, AB
780-865-7777 (800-780-7234)
Dogs of all sizes are allowed. Dogs
are allowed for a pet fee of $10 per
pet per stay.

Old Entrance Cabins
P.O. Box 6054
Hinton, AB
780-865-4760
Well behaved dogs of all sizes are
allowed. There is a $7 per night per
pet additional fee. Dogs are not
allowed on beds, but you may bring
your own cover for a chair. 2 dogs
may be allowed.

Super 8 CN Hinton
284 Smith Street
Hinton, AB
 (800-800-8000)
Dogs are welcome at this hotel.

Best Western Jasper Inn & Suites
98 Geikie Street
Jasper, AB
780-852-4461 (800-780-7234)
Dogs of all sizes are allowed. Dogs

are allowed for a nightly pet fee.

The Fairmont Jasper Park Lodge
Old Lodge Road
Jasper, AB
780-852-3301 (800-257-7544)
fairmont.com/jasper/
This resort provides visitors with a
true Grand Canadian lodge
encounter in addition to its
unparalleled views and many
recreational opportunities. Dogs of all
sizes are welcome for an additional
$50 per night per pet. Dogs may only
be left alone in the room if they will
be quiet and well behaved, and they
must be leashed and cleaned up
after at all times.

Ramada Lac La Biche
9915 83rd Avenue
Lac La Biche, AB
780-623-2250 (800-272-6232)
Dogs of all sizes are allowed. Dogs
are allowed for a nightly pet fee.

The Fairmont Chateau Lake Louise
111 Lake Louise Drive
Lake Louise, AB
403-522-3511 (800-257-7544)
fairmont.com/lakelouise/
This world-class resort sits within a
UNESCO World Heritage Site Rocky
Mountain Park, and in addition to the
spectacular surroundings there are a
variety of activities and recreational
opportunities. Dogs are allowed for
an additional fee of $25 per night per
pet, and they must have current ID
tags and shots. Dogs may not be left
alone in the room at any time, and
they must be leashed and cleaned
up after. Pet sitting services are
available for short periods.

Comfort Inn
3226 Fairway Plaza Road S
Lethbridge, AB
403-320-8874 (877-424-6423)
Dogs of all sizes are allowed. Dogs
are allowed for a pet fee

Days Inn Lethbridge
100 3rd Avenue South
Lethbridge, AB
403-327-6000 (800-329-7466)
daysinnlethbridge.com
Dogs of all sizes are allowed. There
is a $10 per night per pet additional
pet fee.

Econo Lodge Inn & Suites
1124 Mayor Magrath Dr. S.
Lethbridge, AB
403-328-5591 (877-424-6423)
Dogs of all sizes are allowed. Dogs
are allowed for a pet fee of $10.00

per pet per night.

Howard Johnson Express Inn
Lethbridge
1026 Mayor Magrath Drive South
Lethbridge, AB
403-327-4576 (800-446-4656)
Dogs of all sizes are allowed. Dogs
are allowed for a pet fee.

Lethbridge Lodge Hotel and Conf
Centre
320 Scenic Drive
Lethbridge, AB
403-328-1123 (800-661-1232)
lethbridgelodge.com/
This large and luxurious hotel is
located in downtown Lehtbridge.
Dogs of all sizes are allowed. There
is a $10 per night additional pet fee.

Quality Inn & Suites
4070 2nd Avenue South
Lethbridge, AB
403-331-6440 (877-424-6423)
Dogs of all sizes are allowed. Dogs
are allowed for a pet fee of $10.00
per pet per night.

Ramada Lethbridge
2375 Mayor Magrath Drive South
Lethbridge, AB
 (800-272-6232)
Dogs of all sizes are allowed. Dogs
are allowed for a pet fee of $5 per
pet per night.

Thriftlodge Lethbridge
2210 7th Avenue S
Lethbridge, AB
403-329-0100 (800-578-7878)
Dogs are welcome at this hotel.

Best Western Wayside Inn & Suites
5411 44th Street
Lloydminster, AB
780-875-4404 (800-780-7234)
Dogs of all sizes are allowed. Dogs
are allowed for a pet fee.

Best Western Inn
722 Redcliff Drive SW
Medicine Hat, AB
403-527-3700 (800-780-7234)
Dogs of all sizes are allowed. Dogs
are allowed for a pet fee of $10 per
pet per night.

Motel 6 - Medicine Hat
20 Strachan Ct Se
Medicine Hat, AB
403-527-1749 (800-466-8356)
This motel welcomes your pets to
stay with you.

Ramada Limited Medicine Hat
773 8th Street SW

Medicine Hat, AB
403-526-5955 (800-272-6232)
Dogs of all sizes are allowed. Dogs
are allowed for a nightly pet fee.

Super 8 AB Medicine Hat
1280 Transcanada Way SE
Medicine Hat, AB
403-528-8888 (800-800-8000)
Dogs of all sizes are allowed. Dogs
are allowed for a pet fee of $10.00
per pet per night.

Travelodge Hotel Medicine Hat
1100 Redcliff Dr. SW
Medicine Hat, AB
403-527-2275 (800-578-7878)
Dogs are welcome at this hotel.

Super 8 Oyen
Junction Hwy 9 and Hwy 41
Oyen, AB
403-664-3010 (800-800-8000)
Dogs of all sizes are allowed. Dogs
are allowed for a pet fee of $15.00
per pet per night.

Ramada Pincher Creek
1132 Table Mountain Street
Pincher Creek, AB
403-627-3777 (800-272-6232)
Dogs of all sizes are allowed. Dogs
are allowed for a pet fee of $15.00
per pet per night.

Super 8 AB Ponoka
16707 Hwy 53 West
Ponoka, AB
403-704-1177 (800-800-8000)
Dogs of all sizes are allowed. Dogs
are allowed for a pet fee of $15.00
per pet per night.

Super 8 Alberta CN Provost
3611 57th Avenue
Provost, AB
780-753-2255 (800-800-8000)
Dogs of all sizes are allowed. Dogs
are allowed for a pet fee of $15.00
per pet per night.

Best Western Red Deer Inn and
Suites
6839 66th Street
Red Deer, AB
403-346-3555 (800-780-7234)
Dogs of all sizes are allowed. There
is a $10 per pet per night fee.

Howard Johnson Inn Red Deer
37557 Hwy 2 South
Red Deer, AB
403-343-8444 (800-446-4656)
Dogs are welcome at this hotel.

Motel 6 Red Deer #5706
900-5001 19th Street

Red Deer, AB
403-340-1749
Dogs of all sizes are allowed. There
are no additional pet fees.

Ramada AB Red Deer
4217 50th Avenue
Red Deer, AB
403-358-7722 (800-272-6232)
Dogs are welcome at this hotel.

Sandman Hotel Red Deer
2818 Gaetz Ave
Red Deer, AB
403-343-7400 (800-SAN-DMAN)
Dogs of all sizes are allowed. There
are no additional pet fees. Dogs are
allowed in smoking or non-smoking
rooms.

Super 8 Red Deer
7474 Gaetz Ave
Red Deer, AB
403-343-1102 (800-800-8000)
Dogs of all sizes are allowed. Dogs
are allowed for a pet fee of $50.00
per pet per night.

Travelodge Red Deer
2807-50 Avenue
Red Deer, AB
403-346-2011 (800-578-7878)
Dogs of all sizes are allowed. Dogs
are allowed for a pet fee of $25.00
per pet per night.

Best Western Rimstone Ridge Hotel
5501 50th Avenue
Rimbey, AB
800-780-7234 (800-780-7234)
Dogs are welcome at this hotel.

Super 8 Rimbey
5702 43rd Street
Rimbey, AB
403-843-3808 (800-800-8000)
Dogs of all sizes are allowed. Dogs
are allowed for a pet fee of $15.00
per pet per night.

Best Western Rocky Mountain
House Inn & Suites
4407 41st Avenue
Rocky Mountain House, AB
403-844-3100 (800-780-7234)
Dogs are welcome at this hotel.

Holiday Inn Express Rocky Mountain
House
4715 45th St.
Rocky Mountain House, AB
403-845-2871 (877-270-6405)
Dogs of all sizes are allowed. Dogs
are allowed for a nightly pet fee.

Super 8 Rocky Mountain House
4406 41st Avenue

Rocky Mountain House, AB
403-846-0088 (800-800-8000)
Dogs of all sizes are allowed. Dogs are allowed for a pet fee of $15.00 per pet per night.

Ramada Limited Edmonton East/
Sherwood Park
30 Broadway Blvd
Sherwood Park, AB
780-467-6727 (800-272-6232)
Dogs of all sizes are allowed. Dogs are allowed for a pet fee of $15 per pet per night.

Super 8 AB Slave Lake
101 14 Avenue SW
Slave Lake, AB
780-805-3100 (800-800-8000)
Dogs of all sizes are allowed. Dogs are allowed for a pet fee of $25.00 per pet per night.

High Rigg Retreat
#3-51119 RR 255
Spruce Grove, AB
780-470-0462
highriggretreat.com/
Although providing comfort in a beautiful country setting, this inn is only a mile from the city limits and a wide variety of activities. (They usually close for a few months during the hardest part of the winter.) Dogs are allowed for no additional fee, and they need to be declared at the time of booking. Dogs may not be left unattended in the room, and they must be under their owner's control and cleaned up after at all times. There is a full kennel/run and 5 acres of fenced property for pets to have some fun times too. 2 dogs may be allowed.

Super 8 AB St Paul
5008 43rd Street
St Paul, AB
780-645-5581 (800-800-8000)
Dogs of all sizes are allowed. Dogs are allowed for a pet fee of $15.00 per pet per night.

Best Western Crusader Inn
6020 50th Avenue
Stettler, AB
403-742-3371 (800-780-7234)
Dogs of all sizes are allowed. Dogs are allowed for a nightly pet fee.

Ramada Stettler
6711 49th Avenue
Stettler, AB
403-742-6555 (800-272-6232)
Dogs of all sizes are allowed. Dogs are allowed for a nightly pet fee.

Super 8 Stettler
5720 44th Avenue
Stettler, AB
403-742-3391 (800-800-8000)
Dogs of all sizes are allowed. Dogs are allowed for a pet fee of $15.00 per pet per night.

Best Western Sunrise Inn & Suites
3101 43rd Avenue
Stony Plain, AB
780-968-1716 (800-780-7234)
Dogs are welcome at this hotel.

Motel 6 - Stony Plain
66 Boulder Blvd.
Stony Plain, AB
780-968-5123 (800-466-8356)
This motel welcomes your pets to stay with you.

Ramada Inn Stony Plain
3301 43rd Avenue
Stony Plain, AB
780-963-0222 (800-272-6232)
Dogs of all sizes are allowed. Dogs are allowed for a pet fee of $15 per pet per night.

Travelodge Stony Plain
74 Boulder Blvd
Stony Plain, AB
780-963-1161 (800-578-7878)
Dogs of all sizes are allowed. Dogs are allowed for a pet fee of $10 per pet per night.

Best Western Strathmore Inn
550 Highway #1
Strathmore, AB
403-934-5777 (800-780-7234)
Dogs are welcome at this hotel. There is a $10 one time pet fee.

Holiday Inn Express Hotel & Suites Strathmore
400 Ranch Market
Strathmore, AB
403-934-1134 (877-270-6405)
Dogs of all sizes are allowed. Dogs are allowed for a pet fee.

Super 8 Strathmore
450 Westlake Road
Strathmore, AB
403-934-1808 (800-800-8000)
Dogs of all sizes are allowed. Dogs are allowed for a nightly pet fee.

Travelodge Strathmore
350 Ridge Road
Strathmore, AB
403-901-0000 (800-578-7878)
Dogs are welcome at this hotel.

Super 8 AB Taber
5700 46th Avenue

Taber, AB
403-223-8181 (800-800-8000)
Dogs are welcome at this hotel.

Best Western Diamond Inn
351 7th Avenue NE
Three Hills, AB
403-443-7889 (800-780-7234)
Dogs are welcome at this hotel.

Super 8 AB Three Hills
208 18th Avenue North
Three Hills, AB
403-443-8888 (800-800-8000)
Dogs are welcome at this hotel.

Hi Valley Motor Inn
4001 Hwy Street
Valleyview, AB
780-524-3324
Dogs of all sizes are allowed. There is a $5 per night additional pet fee. Dogs are allowed in smoking or non-smoking rooms.

Horizon Motel & Steakhouse
5204 Highway Street
Valleyview, AB
780-524-3904

Best Western Wainwright Inn & Suites
1209 27th Street
Wainwright, AB
780-845-9934 (800-780-7234)
Dogs of all sizes are allowed. Dogs are allowed for a nightly pet fee.

Ramada Wainwright
1510 27th Street
Wainwright, AB
780-842-5010 (800-272-6232)
Dogs are welcome at this hotel.

Ramada Westlock
11311 - 100 Street
Westlock, AB
780-349-2245 (800-272-6232)
Dogs of all sizes are allowed. Dogs are allowed for a pet fee of $15 per pet per night.

Best Western Wayside Inn
4103 56th Street
Wetaskiwin, AB
780-312-7300 (800-780-7234)
Dogs are welcome at this hotel.

Alaska Highway Motel
3511 Highway St
Whitecourt, AB
780-778-4156
Dogs of all sizes are allowed. There are no additional pet fees.

Howard Johnson Whitecourt
5003 50th Street

Whitecourt, AB
780-778-2216 (800-446-4656)
Dogs are welcome at this hotel.
There is a $10 one time pet fee.

Quality Inn
5420 49th Ave.
Whitecourt, AB
780-778-5477 (877-424-6423)
Dogs of all sizes are allowed.

Super 8 Whitecourt
4121 Kepler Street
Whitecourt, AB
780-778-8908 (800-800-8000)
Dogs are welcome at this hotel.

British Columbia

Ramada Limited 100 Mile House
917 Alder Avenue
100 Mile House, BC
250-395-2777 (800-272-6232)
Dogs are welcome at this hotel.

Best Western Bakerview Inn
1821 Sumas Way
Abbotsford, BC
604-859-1341 (800-780-7234)
Dogs are welcome at this hotel.

Coast Abbotsford Hotel & Suites
2020 Sumas Way
Abbotsford, BC
604-853-1880 (800-716-6199)
Dogs of all sizes are allowed. There
is a $10 per night additional pet fee
for small dogs, and a $25 per night
pet fee for large dogs. Dogs must be
crated and a phone number left at
the desk if dogs are left alone in the
room. 2 dogs may be allowed.

Ramada Plaza And Conference
Centre
36035 N Parallel Rd
Abbotsford, BC
604-870-1050 (800-272-6232)
Dogs are welcome at this hotel.

Super 8 BC Abbotsford
1881 Sumas Way
Abbotsford, BC
604-853-1141 (800-800-8000)
Dogs of all sizes are allowed. Dogs
are allowed for a pet fee.

Nimpkish Hotel
318 Fir Street
Alert Bay, BC
250-974-2324 (888-NIMPKISH (888-
646-7547))
nimpkishhotel.com/
A 45 minute ferry trip from Port
McNeill brings visitors to this historic
inn by the sea. They offer a great

starting point for exploring the
island, and there is also a
restaurant and a pub with a large
waterfront deck on site. Two dog-
friendly rooms leading to the
outside are offered; they are
allowed for no additional fee. 2 dogs
may be allowed.

Hilton Hotel
6083 McKay Avenue
Burnaby, BC
604-438-1200 (800-HILTONS (445-
8667))
Located in the heart of the city, this
upscale hotel offers numerous on
site amenities for business and
leisure travelers, plus a convenient
location to business, shopping,
dining, and entertainment areas.
Dogs are allowed for an additional
one time pet fee of $29 per room.
Multiple dogs may be allowed.

Best Value Inn Desert Motel
1069 South Trans Canada Hwy
Cache Creek, BC
250-457-6226
This motel on the Trans-Canada
Highway and the main western
route to Alaska has three pet rooms
available. Dogs of all sizes are
allowed. There are no additional pet
fees.

Robbie's Motel
1067 Todd
Cache Creek, BC
250-457-6221
Dogs of all sizes are allowed. There
is a $10 additional pet fee for each
pet per night.

Tumbleweed Motel
1221 Quartz
Cache Creek, BC
250-457-6522
Dogs of all sizes are allowed. There
are no additional pet fees.

Coast Discovery Inn and Marina
975 Shoppers Row
Campbell River, BC
250-287-7155 (800-663-1144)
All Coast Hotels have on hand extra
pet amenities if you forget
something. For dogs, they have
extra doggy dishes, sleeping
cushions, nylon chew toys and dog
food. If your dog needs one of these
items, just ask the front desk. There
is a $20 per night per room
additional pet fee. 2 dogs may be
allowed.

Travelodge Campbell River
340 S. Island Hwy

Campbell River, BC
250-286-6622 (800-578-7878)
Dogs of all sizes are allowed. Dogs
are allowed for a pet fee of $10.00
per pet per night.

Quality Inn
1935 Columbia
Castlegar, BC
250-365-2177 (877-424-6423)
Dogs of all sizes are allowed. Dogs
are allowed for a pet fee of $10.00
per pet per night. Two dogs are
allowed per room.

Super 8 BC Castlegar
651 18th Street
Castlegar, BC
250-365-2700 (800-800-8000)
Dogs of all sizes are allowed. Dogs
are allowed for a pet fee of $10.00
per pet per night.

Best Western Chemainus Festival
Inn
9573 Chemainus Road
Chemainus, BC
250-246-4181 (800-780-7234)
Dogs of all sizes are allowed. Dogs
are allowed for a pet fee.

Chetwynd Court Motel
5104 N Access
Chetwynd, BC
250-788-2271
Dogs of all sizes are allowed. There
are no additional pet fees.

Pine Cone Motor Inn
5224 53rd Ave
Chetwynd, BC
250-788-3311
Dogs of all sizes are allowed. There
is $17 per night additional pet fee.

Stagecoach Inn
5413 S Access
Chetwynd, BC
250-788-9666
Dogs of all sizes are allowed. There
is a $20 pet deposit. $10 of this
deposit is refundable.

Comfort Inn
45405 Luckakuck Way
Chilliwack, BC
604-858-0636 (877-424-6423)
Dogs of all sizes are allowed. Dogs
are allowed for a pet fee of $5.00 per
pet per night.

Ranch Park Rentals
Off H 1
Chilliwack, BC
480-600-5114
Well behaved dogs of all sizes are
allowed, and they must be friendly to

other dogs as well. There is a $10 per night per pet fee and a pet policy to sign at check in. A credit card must also be on file. They don't want dogs on the bed unless under 10 pounds, and suggest to keep small dogs in at night. There is lots of room for the dogs to run here.

Ramada Vancouver Coquitlam
631 Lougheed Highway
Coquitlam, BC
604-931-4433 (800-272-6232)
Dogs of all sizes are allowed. Dogs are allowed for a pet fee of $10.00 per pet per night.

Best Western Westerly Hotel
1590 Cliffe Avenue
Courtenay, BC
250-338-7741 (800-780-7234)
A long list of amenities are offered at this full-service hotel. Dogs are allowed for an additional fee of $10 per night per pet. Multiple dogs may be allowed.

Kingfisher Oceanside Resort and Spa
4330 Island H S/H 19A
Courtenay, BC
250-338-1323 (800-663-7929)
kingfisherspa.com/
A spectacular natural setting on ocean shores greets guests at this resort. The resort features 64 rooms and suites all with ocean views, various dining options including a monthly seafood buffet, an outdoor pool/hot tub, and a steam cave that is open daily from 7 am until 10 pm. One dog is allowed per room for an additional fee of $25 per night.

Travelodge BC Courtenay
2605 Cliffe Avenue
Courtenay, BC
250-334-4491 (800-578-7878)
Dogs of all sizes are allowed. Dogs are allowed for a pet fee of $10 per pet per night.

Days Inn Cranbrook
600 Cranbrook Street North
Cranbrook, BC
250-426-6683 (800-329-7466)
Dogs are welcome at this hotel.

Super 8 Cranbrook
2370 Cranbrook Street North
Cranbrook, BC
250-489-8028 (800-800-8000)
Dogs are welcome at this hotel.

Airport Inn
800 120 Avenue
Dawson Creek, BC

250-782-9404
airportinn.ca
Well-behaved dogs of all sizes are allowed. There is a $10 per night additional pet fee.

Best Western Dawson Creek Inn
500 Highway 2
Dawson Creek, BC
250-782-6226 (800-780-7234)
Dogs of all sizes are allowed. Dogs are allowed for a nightly pet fee.

Days Inn Dawson Creek
640 122 Ave
Dawson Creek, BC
250-782-8887 (800-329-7466)
Dogs of all sizes are allowed. Dogs are allowed for a nightly pet fee.

Inn On The Creek
10600 8 Street
Dawson Creek, BC
250-782-8136
innonthecreek.bc.ca
Dogs of all sizes are allowed. There is a $50 refundable pet deposit. There is a $22.80 fee per dog.

Ramada Limited Dawson Creek
1748 Alaska Avenue
Dawson Creek, BC
250-782-8595 (800-272-6232)
Dogs of all sizes are allowed. Dogs are allowed for a pet fee.

Best Western Cowichan Valley Inn
6474 Trans Canada Highway
Duncan, BC
250-748-2722 (800-780-7234)
Dogs are welcome at this hotel.

Travelodge Silver Bridge Inn
140 Trans Canada Highway
Duncan, BC
250-748-4311 (800-578-7878)
Dogs of all sizes are allowed. Dogs are allowed for a nightly pet fee.

Howard Johnson Inn - Enderby
1510 George Street
Enderby, BC
250-838-6825 (800-446-4656)
Dogs are welcome at this hotel.

Blue Bell Inn
4720 50 Ave
Fort Nelson, BC
250-774-6961
bluebellinn.ca
There is one non-smoking pet room and one dog is allowed. There are no additional pet fees.

Pioneer Motel
5207-50 Ave S
Fort Nelson, BC

250-774-5800
karo-ent.com/pioneer.htm
Dogs of all sizes are allowed. There is a $5 per night pet fee for large dogs. There is also a pet-friendly RV Park on the premises. 2 dogs may be allowed.

Ramada Limited Fort Nelson
5035 - 51 Avenue West
Fort Nelson, BC
250-774-2844 (800-272-6232)
Dogs of all sizes are allowed. Dogs are allowed for a nightly pet fee.

Super 8 BC Fort Nelson
4503 50th Ave South
Fort Nelson, BC
250-233-5025 (800-800-8000)
Dogs are welcome at this hotel.

Econo Lodge
10419 Alaska Road
Fort St John, BC
250-787-8475 (877-424-6423)
Dogs of all sizes are allowed. Dogs are allowed for a pet fee of $15.00 per pet per night.

Lakeview Inn and Suites
10103 98 Avenue
Fort St John, BC
250-787-0779
lakeviewhotels.com
Dogs of all sizes are allowed. There is a $10 per night per pet additional pet fee. 2 dogs may be allowed.

Quality Inn Northern Grand
9830 100th Ave.
Fort St John, BC
250-787-0521 (877-424-6423)
Dogs of all sizes are allowed. Dogs are allowed for a pet fee of $25.00 per pet per night.

Super 8
9500 Alaska Way
Fort St John, BC
250-785-7588 (800-800-8000)
Dogs of all sizes are allowed. Dogs are allowed for a nightly pet fee.

The Shepherd's Inn
Mile 72 Alaska Highway
Fort St John, BC
250-827-3676
karo-ent.com/shepherds.htm
One dog of any size is allowed. There is only one pet room.

Super 8 Golden
1047 Trans CN Hwy 1
Golden, BC
250-344-0888 (800-800-8000)
Dogs are welcome at this hotel.

Ramada Limited Grand Forks
2729 Central Avenue
Grand Forks, BC
250-442-2127 (800-272-6232)
Dogs of all sizes are allowed. Dogs
are allowed for a pet fee of $10.00
per pet per night.

Harrison Beach Hotel
160 Esplanade Avenue
Harrison Hot Springs, BC
604-796-1111 (866-338-8111)
harrisonbeachhotel.com
Dogs of all sizes are allowed. There
is a $15 per pet per night additional
pet fee. 2 dogs may be allowed.

Harrison Hot Springs Resort
100 Esplanade Avenue
Harrison Hot Springs, BC
604-796-2244 (866-638-5075)
harrisonresort.com
This resort and spa is located
against the mountains at the south
end of Harrison Lake. Dogs of all
sizes are allowed. There is a $100
one time pet fee. Dogs must be
crated if you are out of the room. 2
dogs may be allowed.

Inn Towne Motel
510 Trans-Canada Hwy
Hope, BC
604-869-7276
2 dogs may be allowed.

Maple Leaf Motor Inn
377 Old Hope Princeton Way
Hope, BC
604-869-7107
Dogs of all sizes are allowed. There
is a $7 per night per pet additional
pet fee. 2 dogs may be allowed.

Quality Inn
350 Old Hope Princeton Way
Hope, BC
604-869-9951 (877-424-6423)
Dogs of all sizes are allowed.

Windsor Motel
778 3rd Avenue
Hope, BC
604-869-9944 (888-588-9944)
bcwindsormotel.com
Dogs of all sizes are allowed. There
is a $5 per pet per night additional
pet fee. 2 dogs may be allowed.

Houston Motor Inn
2940 H 16W
Houston, BC
250-845-7112 (800-994-8333)
This 56 room inn has a restaurant
and coffee shop, and a full hook-up
RV park on site that allows dogs for
no additional fee. Dogs are allowed

at the inn for an additional fee of
$10 per night per pet. Dogs are not
allowed on the bedding; they
request owner's bring their pet's
bedding. Dogs must be leashed and
cleaned up after. 2 dogs may be
allowed.

Best Western Invermere Inn
1310 7th Avenue
Invermere, BC
250-342-9246 (800-780-7234)
Dogs of all sizes are allowed. Dogs
are allowed for a nightly pet fee.

Accent Inn Kamloops
1325 Columbia Street W
Kamloops, BC
250-374-8877 (800-663-0298)
This inn offers a seasonal outdoor
heated pool, whirlpool, and a
sauna. Dogs of all sizes are
welcome for an additional fee of
$15 per night per pet. Dogs may not
be left alone in the room, and they
must be leashed and cleaned up
after at all times. 2 dogs may be
allowed.

Coast Canadian Inn
339 St. Paul Street
Kamloops, BC
250-372-5201 (800-663-1144)
All Coast Hotels have on hand extra
pet amenities if you forget
something. For dogs, they have
extra doggy dishes, sleeping
cushions, nylon chew toys and dog
food. If your dog needs one of these
items, just ask the front desk. There
is a $10 per day per pet additional
fee. 2 dogs may be allowed.

Econo Lodge Inn & Suites
1773 East Trans Canada Hwy
Kamloops, BC
250-372-8533 (877-424-6423)
Dogs up to 50 pounds are allowed.
Dogs are allowed for a pet fee of
$10.00 per pet per night.

Holiday Inn Express Kamloops
1550 Versatile Drive
Kamloops, BC
250-372-3474 (877-270-6405)
Dogs of all sizes are allowed. Dogs
are allowed for a pet fee of $30 per
pet per night.

Howard Johnson Downtown
530 Columbia St.
Kamloops, BC
250-372-7761 (800-446-4656)
Dogs of all sizes are allowed. Dogs
are allowed for a pet fee of $10.00
per pet per night.

Howard Johnson Inn Kamloops
610 West Columbia Street
Kamloops, BC
250-374-1515 (800-446-4656)
Dogs are welcome at this hotel.

Super 8 BC Kamloops
1521 Hugh Allan Dr
Kamloops, BC
250-374-8688 (800-800-8000)
Dogs are welcome at this hotel.

Travelodge Kamloops
430 Columbia Street
Kamloops, BC
250-372-8202 (800-578-7878)
Dogs are welcome at this hotel.

Accent Inn Kelowna
1140 Harvey Avenue
Kelowna, BC
250-862-8888 (800-663-0298)
This inn offers a seasonal outdoor
heated pool, whirlpool, and a sauna.
Dogs of all sizes are welcome for an
additional fee of $15 per night per
pet. Dogs must be leashed and
cleaned up after at all times, and
crated when left alone in the room. 2
dogs may be allowed.

Best Western Inn Kelowna
2402 Highway 97 N
Kelowna, BC
250-860-1212 (800-780-7234)
Dogs of all sizes are allowed. Dogs
are allowed for a nightly pet fee.

Coast Capri Hotel
1171 Harvey Avenue
Kelowna, BC
250-860-6060 (800-663-1144)
All Coast Hotels have on hand extra
pet amenities if you forget
something. For dogs, they have extra
doggy dishes, sleeping cushions,
nylon chew toys and dog food. If your
dog needs one of these items, just
ask the front desk. There is an
additional one time pet fee of $20 per
room. Multiple dogs may be allowed.

Days Inn Kelowna
2649 Hwy 97 North
Kelowna, BC
250-868-3297 (800-329-7466)
Dogs are welcome at this hotel.

Ramada Lodge Hotel Kelowna
2170 Harvey Ave
Kelowna, BC
250-860-9711 (800-272-6232)
Dogs of all sizes are allowed. Dogs
are allowed for a pet fee of $15 per
pet per night.

Travelodge Abbott Villa

1627 Abbott Street
Kelowna, BC
250-763-7771 (800-578-7878)
Dogs of all sizes are allowed. Dogs are allowed for a pet fee of $20 per pet per night.

Super 8 Langley
26574 Gloucester Way
Langley, BC
604-856-8288 (800-800-8000)
Dogs are welcome at this hotel.

Travelodge Langley
20470 88th Avenue
Langley, BC
604-888-4891 (800-578-7878)
Dogs of all sizes are allowed. Dogs are allowed for a pet fee of $10 per pet per night.

Liard Hot Springs Lodge
Mile 497 Alaska H
Liard River, BC
250-776-7349
In addition to offering a full service restaurant, fuel station, gift shop, and campsites, this lodge is also located across from the Liard Hot Springs. Dogs are allowed for an additional fee of $50 per pet per stay. Dogs must be leashed and cleaned up after at all times. 2 dogs may be allowed.

Travelodge Maple Ridge
21650 Lougheed Highway
Maple Ridge, BC
604-467-1511 (800-578-7878)
Dogs of all sizes are allowed. Dogs are allowed for a pet fee of $10 per pet per night.

Econo Lodge Inn & Suites
2201 Voght Street
Merritt, BC
250-378-4291 (877-424-6423)
Dogs of all sizes are allowed. Dogs are allowed for a pet fee of $5.00 per pet per night.

Knights Inn Merritt
2702 Nicola Ave
Merritt, BC
250-378-9244 (800-843-5644)
Dogs of all sizes are allowed. Dogs are allowed for a nightly pet fee.

Ramada Limited - Merritt
3571 Voght Street
Merritt, BC
 (800-272-6232)
Dogs of all sizes are allowed. Dogs are allowed for a nightly pet fee.

Super 8 BC Merritt
3561 Voght Street

Merritt, BC
250-378-9422 (800-800-8000)
Dogs of all sizes are allowed. Dogs are allowed for a nightly pet fee.

Travelodge Merritt
3581 Voght Street
Merritt, BC
250-378-8830 (800-578-7878)
Dogs of all sizes are allowed. Dogs are allowed for a nightly pet fee.

Best Western Mission City Lodge
32281 Lougheed Highway
Mission, BC
604-820-5500 (800-780-7234)
Dogs of all sizes are allowed. Dogs are allowed for a nightly pet fee.

Northern Rockies Lodge
Mile 462 Alaska Highway
Muncho Lake, BC
250-776-3481 (800-663-5269)
northernrockieslodge.com
Dogs are allowed in the rooms and the cabins. There is a $50 refundable pet deposit and a $10 per pet per night additional pet fee. 2 dogs may be allowed.

Best Western Dorchester Hotel
70 Church Street
Nanaimo, BC
250-754-6835 (800-780-7234)
Dogs are welcome at this hotel.

Best Western Northgate Inn
6450 Metral Drive
Nanaimo, BC
250-390-2222 (800-780-7234)
Dogs of all sizes are allowed. Dogs are allowed for a pet fee of $20.00 per pet per night.

Coast Bastion Inn
11 Bastion Street
Nanaimo, BC
250-753-6601 (800-780-7234)
All Coast Hotels have on hand extra pet amenities if you forget something. For dogs, they have extra doggy dishes, sleeping cushions, nylon chew toys and dog food. If your dog needs one of these items, just ask the front desk. There is a $10 per day per pet additional fee. Multiple dogs may be allowed.

Days Inn - Nanaimo
809 Island Hwy South
Nanaimo, BC
250-754-8171 (800-329-7466)
Dogs of all sizes are allowed. Dogs are allowed for a nightly pet fee.

Howard Johnson Hotel - Harbourside Nanaimo

1 Terminal Avenue
Nanaimo, BC
250-753-2241 (800-446-4656)
Dogs are welcome at this hotel.

Travelodge Nanaimo
96 Terminal Avenue North
Nanaimo, BC
250-754-6355 (800-578-7878)
Dogs of all sizes are allowed. Dogs are allowed for a pet fee of $15 per pet per stay.

Vancouver Lions Gate Travelodge
2060 Marine Drive
North Vancouver, BC
604-985-5311 (800-578-7878)
Dogs of all sizes are allowed. Dogs are allowed for a pet fee.

Best Western Sunrise Inn
5506 Main Street
Osoyoos, BC
250-495-4000 (800-780-7234)
Dogs are welcome at this hotel.

Quality Resort Bayside
240 Dogwood Street
Parksville, BC
250-248-8333 (877-424-6423)
Dogs of all sizes are allowed. Dogs are allowed for a pet fee of $15.00 per pet per night.

Tigh-Na-Mara Resort
1155 Resort Drive
Parksville, BC
250-248-2072 (800-663-7373)
tigh-na-mara.com/
Besides offering a central location to many local sites of interest and a wide choice of recreational pursuits for all ages, this seaside spa resort offers one of the best body spas in the province. They also provide all the newest equipment for working out or for having fun; plus an eatery, lounge, and a lunchtime tapas and grill. Dogs are allowed in their rustic cottages for an additional one time pet fee of $30. 2 dogs may be allowed.

Travelodge Parksville
424 West Island Highway
Parksville, BC
250-248-2232 (800-578-7878)
Dogs of all sizes are allowed. Dogs are allowed for a nightly pet fee.

Best Western Inn at Penticton
3180 Skaha Lake Road
Penticton, BC
250-493-0311 (800-780-7234)
Dogs are welcome at this hotel.

Days Inn and Conference Centre -

Dog-Friendly Lodging - Please always call ahead to make sure an establishment is still dog-friendly.

Penticton
152 Riverside Drive
Penticton, BC
250-493-6616 (800-329-7466)
Dogs of all sizes are allowed. Dogs
are allowed for a nightly pet fee.

Ramada Inn and Suites Penticton
1050 Eckhardt Ave. West
Penticton, BC
250-492-8926 (800-272-6232)
Dogs are welcome at this hotel.

Super 8 BC Penticton
1706 Main Street
Penticton, BC
250-492-3829 (800-800-8000)
Dogs are welcome at this hotel.

Travelodge Penticton
950 Westminster Avenue West
Penticton, BC
250-492-0225 (800-578-7878)
Dogs of all sizes are allowed. Dogs
are allowed for a pet fee of $10 per
pet per night.

Ramada Inn Pitt Meadows
19267 Lougheed Highway
Pitt Meadows, BC
604-460-9859 (800-272-6232)
Dogs of all sizes are allowed. Dogs
are allowed for a pet fee.

Howard Johnson Hotel Port Alberni
4850 Beaver Creek Road
Port Alberni, BC
250-724-2900 (800-446-4656)
Dogs are welcome at this hotel.
There is a $10 one time pet fee.

The Hospitality Inn
3835 Redford Street
Port Alberni, BC
250-723-8111 (877-723-8111)
hospitalityinnportalberni.com/
A long list of amenities are offered at
this full-service luxury hotel. Dogs
are allowed for an additional fee of
$10 per night per pet. Multiple dogs
may be allowed.

Pioneer Inn and RV Park
8405 Byng Road
Port Hardy, BC
250-949-7271 (800-663-8744)
vancouverisland.com/pioneerinn/
This inn sits nestled in a lush, park-
like setting only a short distance from
a variety of recreation, shopping, and
dining opportunities as well as the
ferry station, airport, and bus depot.
They also have 25 RV sites with full
hook-ups+cable and the Snuggles
Restaurant (reservations
recommended) and Lounge on site.
Dogs are allowed at the inn for an

additional pet fee of $10 per night
per room; there is no extra fee for
the RV area. Dogs must be kept
leashed and cleaned up after
promptly. 2 dogs may be allowed.

Quarterdeck Inn and Marina Resort
6555 Hardy Bay Road
Port Hardy, BC
250-902-0455 (877-902-0459)
quarterdeckresort.net/
Besides offering a convenient
location to the downtown area and
numerous recreational opportunities
(they can help arrange many of the
tours), this resort offers a full
service restaurant, lounge, pub, and
a marina on site. Dogs are allowed
for an additional one time pet fee of
$10 per room. Multiple dogs may be
allowed.

Haida-Way Motor Inn Hotel
1817 Campbell Way
Port McNeill, BC
250-956-3373 (800-956-3373)
portmcneillhotels.com/
This hotel/motel offers a central
starting point for exploring a variety
of recreational pursuits - including
lots of marine life viewing, plus a
convenient location within walking
distance to shopping, dining, the
harbor, and the ferry terminal. Dogs
are allowed in the motel rooms for
an additional fee of $10 per night
per pet. 2 dogs may be allowed.

Powell River Town Centre Hotel
4660 Joyce Avenue
Powell River, BC
604-485-3000
There is a $10 per day per room
additional pet fee. Dogs may be left
in the room for short periods only.
Multiple dogs may be allowed.

Best Western City Centre
910 Victoria Street
Prince George, BC
250-563-1267 (800-780-7234)
Dogs of all sizes are allowed. Dogs
are allowed for a nightly pet fee.

Bon Voyage Motor Inn
4222 Highway 16 West
Prince George, BC
250-964-2333
Dogs of all sizes are allowed. There
is a $15 per night additional pet fee.

Coast Inn of the North
770 Brunswick Street
Prince George, BC
250-563-0121 (800-663-1144)
All Coast Hotels have on hand extra
pet amenities if you forget

something. For dogs, they have extra
doggy dishes, sleeping cushions,
nylon chew toys and dog food. If your
dog needs one of these items, just
ask the front desk. There is a $10
per day per pet additional fee.
Multiple dogs may be allowed.

Sandman Inn and Suites
1650 Central Street
Prince George, BC
250-563-8131
sandmanhotels.com
Dogs of all sizes are allowed. There
is a $10 per night additional pet fee.

Anchor Inn
1600 Park Avenue/H 16
Prince Rupert, BC
250-627-8522 (888-627-8522)
anchor-inn.com/
In addition to having a good central
location to all modes of travel, there
is also a trailed park behind the inn
that leads to the city and its many
attractions. Dogs off all sizes are
allowed for an additional fee of $10
per night per room. Dogs must be
leashed and cleaned up after. 2 dogs
may be allowed.

Andree's Bed and Breakfast
315 4th Avenue E
Prince Rupert, BC
250-624-3666
andreesbb.com
Individually themed rooms, satellite
TV, a lounge, library, a large garden,
and a wonderful covered deck
overlooking the city and harbor are
just a few of the amenities of this inn.
One well mannered dog is allowed
for no additional fee. Aggressive
known breeds are not allowed. Dogs
may not be left unattended at any
time, and they must be kept leashed
and cleaned up after promptly.

Coast Prince Rupert Hotel
118 6th Street
Prince Rupert, BC
250-624-6711 (800-663-1144)
All Coast Hotels have on hand extra
pet amenities if you forget
something. For dogs, they have extra
doggy dishes, sleeping cushions,
nylon chew toys and dog food. If your
dog needs one of these items, just
ask the front desk. There is $10 per
night per pet additional fee. Multiple
dogs may be allowed.

Crest Hotel
222 1st Avenue West
Prince Rupert, BC
250-624-6771 (800-663-8150)
cresthotel.bc.ca/
Amenities for the business or leisure

traveler, this hotel offers great views, a convenient location to other sites of interest, a lounge, and a restaurant that specializes in BC cuisine and fresh seafood. Dogs are allowed for an additional fee of $10 per night per pet on the 1st floor only. Dogs must be quiet, leashed, and cleaned up after. 2 dogs may be allowed.

Pacific Inn
909 3rd Avenue W
Prince Rupert, BC
250-627-1711 (888-663-1999)
pacificinn.bc.ca/
In addition to the many amenities for the business or leisure traveler, they are also conveniently located to numerous attractions, shopping areas, eateries, and recreational pursuits. Dogs of all sizes are allowed. There is an additional fee of $10 per night per pet for dogs up to 25 pounds, and an additional fee of $20 per night per pet for dogs over 25 pounds. Dogs must be quiet, leashed, and cleaned up after. 2 dogs may be allowed.

Ramada Limited Quesnel
383 St Laurent Avenue
Quesnel, BC
250-992-5575 (800-272-6232)
Dogs of all sizes are allowed. Dogs are allowed for a nightly pet fee.

Super 8 BC Quesnel
2010 Valhalla Rd
Quesnel, BC
250-747-1111 (800-800-8000)
Dogs of all sizes are allowed. Dogs are allowed for a nightly pet fee.

Travelodge BC Quesnel
524 Front Street
Quesnel, BC
250-992-7071 (800-578-7878)
Dogs of all sizes are allowed. Dogs are allowed for a nightly pet fee.

Days Inn And Suites Revelstoke
301 Wright Street
Revelstoke, BC
250-837-2191 (800-329-7466)
Dogs of all sizes are allowed. Dogs are allowed for a pet fee.

The Coast Hillcrest Resort Hotel
2100 Oak Drive
Revelstoke, BC
250-837-3322
Dogs of all sizes are allowed. There is a $15 per night per room additional pet fee. Pet rooms are located on the 1st floor. 2 dogs may be allowed.

Accent Inn Vancouver-Airport

10551 St Edwards Drive
Richmond, BC
604-273-3311 (800-663-0298)
Located just minutes from the Vancouver Airport and downtown, this hotel is also home to an IHOP restaurant. Dogs of all sizes are welcome for an additional fee of $15 per night per pet, and they must be pre-registered. Dogs must be crated when left alone in the room, and they must be leashed and cleaned up after at all times. 2 dogs may be allowed.

Fairmont Vancouver Airport
3111 Gran McConachie Way
Richmond, BC
604-207-5200 (800-257-7544)
fairmont.com/vancouverairport/
This sound-proofed hotel offers a backdrop of majestic mountains and ocean views, and is located just steps up from the airport terminals. Dogs of all sizes are allowed for an additional pet fee of $25 per night per room. Dogs must be well mannered, leashed and cleaned up after.

La Quinta Inn Vancouver Airport
8640 Alexandra Road
Richmond, BC
604-276-2711 (800-531-5900)
Dogs of all sizes are allowed. There are no additional pet fees. Dogs must be leashed, cleaned up after, and crated or removed for housekeeping. The pet floor is on the 5th floor, which is a smoking floor; however, there are non-smoking rooms on that floor. Multiple dogs may be allowed.

Marriott Vancouver Airport Hotel
7571 Westminster Highway
Richmond, BC
604-276-2112 (877 323 8888)
This luxury hotel sits central to many of the city's star attractions, world class shopping and dining venues, entertainment areas, and major business areas, plus they also offer a number of in-house amenities for all level of travelers. Dogs are allowed for an additional one time fee of $60 per room. 2 dogs may be allowed.

River Rock Casino Resort
8811 River Road
Richmond, BC
604-247-8900 (866-748-3718)
riverrock.com
Featuring cascading waterfalls, entertainment, table games and slot machines, this Casino Resort is located just outside Vancouver.

They allow up to two 90 pound dogs in each suite. There is a $25 per day per dog pet fee, up to a maximum of $75 per stay. Dogs must be crated or leashed if left alone in the room.

Quality Inn Waddling Dog
2476 Mt. Newton Cross Roads
Saanichton, BC
250-652-1146 (877-424-6423)
Dogs of all sizes are allowed. Dogs are allowed for a pet fee of $15.00 per pet per night.

Super 8 Victoria Airport Saanichton
2477 Mt Newton Cross Rd
Saanichton, BC
250-652-6888 (800-800-8000)
Dogs of all sizes are allowed. Dogs are allowed for a pet fee of $15 per pet per night.

Wintercott Country House
1950 Nicholas Rd.
Saanichton, BC
250-652-2117
wintercott.com
This bed and breakfast inn is located about 15 minutes from Victoria. Well-behaved dogs of all sizes are welcome. There is no pet fee. Multiple dogs may be allowed.

Best Western Salmon Arm Inn
61 10th Street SW
Salmon Arm, BC
250-832-9793 (800-780-7234)
Dogs are welcome at this hotel.

Holiday Inn Express Hotel & Suites Salmon Arm
1090 - 22nd St NE
Salmon Arm, BC
250-832-7711 (877-270-6405)
Dogs of all sizes are allowed. Dogs are allowed for a nightly pet fee.

Travelodge BC Salmon Arm
2401 Trans Canada Highway
Salmon Arm, BC
250-832-9721 (800-578-7878)
Dogs of all sizes are allowed. Dogs are allowed for a pet fee of $10.00 per pet per stay.

Super 8 Sicamous
1120 Riverside Ave
Sicamous, BC
250-836-4988 (800-800-8000)
Dogs of all sizes are allowed. Dogs are allowed for a pet fee of $10 per pet per night.

Best Western Emerald Isle Motor Inn
2306 Beacon Avenue
Sidney, BC
250-656-4441 (800-780-7234)

Dogs of all sizes are allowed. Dogs are allowed for a pet fee.

Cedarwood Motel
9522 Lochside Dr
Sidney, BC
250-656-5551
cedrwood.com/
There is a $15 per day per pet additional fee. There can be up to 2 large dogs or 3 small dogs per room. Multiple dogs may be allowed.

Victoria Airport/ Travelodge Sidney
2280 Beacon Avenue
Sidney, BC
250-656-1176 (800-578-7878)
Dogs of all sizes are allowed. Dogs are allowed for a pet fee.

Gordon's Beach Farm Stay B&B
4530 Otter Point Road
Sooke, BC
250-642-5291
gordonsbeachbandb.com
A well-behaved dog is allowed in one of their suite rooms that has marble flooring. There is a $10 one time pet fee per stay. 2 dogs may be allowed.

Ocean Wilderness Inn
9171 W Coast Rd
Sooke, BC
250-646-2116
bestinns.net/canada/bc/ow.html
There is a $25 pet fee per visit.

Sooke Harbour House
1528 Whiffen Spit Rd
Sooke, BC
250-642-3421
There is a $40 per night pet fee for 1 dog and $20 per night for each dog thereafter. Towels, food/water bowls, a bed, walking guide, and specially made treats by their chef are also offered for canine companion guests. Multiple dogs may be allowed.

King Edward Hotel and Motel
5th Avenue/P. O. Box 86
Stewwart, BC
250-636-2244 (800-663-3126)
kingedwardhotel.com/
This rest stop has an eatery, a pub, a motel, a hotel, and they are only a short distance from the famed Grizzly Bear viewing station for spawning salmon at Fish Creek. Dogs of all sizes are allowed in the motel for no additional fee with a credit card on file; they are not allowed in the hotel. Dogs must be well behaved, leashed, and cleaned up after. 2 dogs may be allowed.

Ramada Hotel and Suites Surrey

10410 158th Street
Surrey, BC
604-930-4700 (800-272-6232)
Dogs of all sizes are allowed. Dogs are allowed for a nightly pet fee.

Super 8 Surrey
8255 166th Street
Surrey, BC
604-576-8888 (800-800-8000)
Dogs of all sizes are allowed. Dogs are allowed for a pet fee of $15.00 per pet per night.

Toad River Lodge
Mile 422 Alaska H
Toad River, BC
250-232-5401
karo-ent.com/toadriv.htm
A lot can be accomplished at this stop with a motel and RV park that accepts pets, a restaurant and bakery, showers, laundry facilities, a dump station, fuels, and a 6,000+ hat collection adorning the lodge. Dogs are allowed in the motel for $5 per night per pet, and there is no additional fee in the camp area. Dogs are also allowed at the outer tables of the restaurant-weather permitting. Dogs must be well mannered, under owner's control, leashed, and cleaned up after at all times. Multiple dogs may be allowed.

Long Beach Lodge Resort
1441 Pacific Rim Highway/H 4
Tofino, BC
250725-2442 (877-844-7873)
longbeachlodgeresort.com/
There are 40 lodge rooms and 20 cottages on 8 lush acres offered at this resort. It sits in an oceanside, forested setting with a number of comfort amenities, fine dining, and great views. Dogs are allowed for an additional one time pet fee of $50 per room with pre-registration. Provided for their canine guests are food/water dishes, a pet towel, a comfy bed, and treats. 2 dogs may be allowed.

The Inn at Tough City
350 Main Street
Tofino, BC
250-725-2021 (877-725-2021)
toughcity.com/main.php
This unique village inn sits overlooking the ocean and features a blend of antiques and modern conveniences, a popular sushi bar with outside seating, and 8 comfy rooms with hardwood floors. Dogs are allowed for an additional fee of $20 per night per pet. Dogs must be leashed, cleaned up after promptly

and be friendly to other hounds and humans. Pooches are welcome to hang out on the sushi patio and make friends with the Shepherd who also hangs out there. 2 dogs may be allowed.

Ramada Valemount
1501 5th Avenue
Valemont, BC
(800-272-6232)
Dogs of all sizes are allowed. Dogs are allowed for a nightly pet fee.

Best Western Valemount Inn & Suites
1950 Highway 5 S
Valemount, BC
250-566-0086 (800-780-7234)
Dogs of all sizes are allowed. Dogs are allowed for a pet fee.

Best Western Sands Hotel
1755 Davie Street
Vancouver, BC
604-682-1831 (800-780-7234)
rpbhotels.com
The Sands is situated in Downtown Vancouver near Stanley Park. The hotel offers 2 lounges, restaurant, room service, fitness room and a sauna. The pet fee is $10.00 per day. Pets receive a welcome doggy bag upon arrival.

Coast Plaza Suite Hotel at Stanley Park
1763 Comox Street
Vancouver, BC
604-688-7711 (800-663-1144)
All Coast Hotels have on hand extra pet amenities if you forget something. For dogs, they have extra doggy dishes, sleeping cushions, nylon chew toys and dog food. If your dog needs one of these items, just ask the front desk. There is a $20 per day per pet additional fee. 2 dogs may be allowed.

Comfort Inn Downtown
654 Nelson Street
Vancouver, BC
604-605-4333 (877-424-6423)
Dogs of all sizes are allowed. Dogs are allowed for a pet fee of $14.00 per pet per night. Dogs are allowed for a pet fee of $25.00 per pet per stay.

Fairmont Vancouver Waterfront Hotel
900 Canada Place Way
Vancouver, BC
604-691-1991 (800-257-7544)
fairmont.com/waterfront/
This hotel boosts a year around 50 foot outdoor heated pool, a

convenient enclosed walkway to the Convention/Exhibition Center and the cruise ship terminal, and they are within walking distance to Stanley Park with it's mile long seawall. Dogs are allowed for an additional one time pet fee of $35 per room. Dogs may not be left alone in the room at any time, and they must be leashed and cleaned up after.

Four Seasons Hotel Vancouver
791 West Georgia St.
Vancouver, BC
604-689-9333
Dogs of all sizes are allowed. There are no additional pet fees. Dogs are not allowed to be left alone in the room.

Granville Island Hotel
1253 Johnston St
Vancouver, BC
604-683-7373
granvilleislandhotel.com/
This hotel has a restaurant on the premises called the Dockside Restaurant. You can dine there with your pet at the outdoor tables that are closest to the grass. The hotel charges a $25 per night pet fee per room. Dogs must be crated when left alone in the room. 2 dogs may be allowed.

Howard Johnson Hotel Downtown Vancouver
1176 Granville St
Vancouver, BC
 (800 446-4656)
Dogs up to 50 pounds are allowed.

Hyatt Regency Vancouver
655 Burrard Street
Vancouver, BC
604-683-1234
The Hyatt Regency Vancouver offers stunning city views from many of the spacious rooms. The hotel offers a heated pool, health club and a central location to many of Vancouver's activities. Dogs up to 50 pounds are welcome. There is a $50 one time additional pet fee.

Metropolitan Hotel
645 Howe Street
Vancouver, BC
604-687-1122
metropolitan.com/vanc/index.htm
There are no additional pet fees. Up to 3 dogs are allowed depending on their sizes. Multiple dogs may be allowed.

Pacific Palisades Hotel
1277 Robson Street

Vancouver, BC
604-688-0461
pacificpalisadeshotel.com/
Well-behaved dogs of all sizes are welcome at this hotel which offers both rooms and suites. Amenities include workout rooms, an indoor swimming pool, and 24 hour room service.

Pacific Spirit Guest House
4080 West 35th Ave
Vancouver, BC
604-261-6837 (866-768-6837)
vanbb.com
There is a $25 per night additional pet fee at this B&B in Vancouver. Their "Very Important Pets" program includes a Three Dog Bakery gift certificate and treats.

Quality Hotel Downtown
1335 Howe St.
Vancouver, BC
604-682-0229 (877-424-6423)
Dogs up to 50 pounds are allowed.

Ramada Inn and Suites Downtown Vancouver
1221 Granville Street
Vancouver, BC
604-685-1111 (800-272-6232)
Dogs of all sizes are allowed. Dogs are allowed for a nightly pet fee.

Renaissance Vancouver Hotel Harbourside
1133 W Hastings Street
Vancouver, BC
604-689-9211 (800-905-8582)
This luxury, waterfront hotel sits central to numerous businesses, shopping, dining, and day/night entertainment areas; plus they also offer numerous on-site amenities to ensure a comfortable stay. Dogs are allowed for an additional one time fee of $75 per room. Dogs must be quiet and well mannered. Multiple dogs may be allowed.

Residence Inn Vancouver Downtown
1234 Hornby Street
Vancouver, BC
604-688-1234 (800 663 1234)
In addition to offering a central location to numerous sites of interest, activities, and attractions for business or pleasure travelers, this downtown all suite hotel also offers a number of in-house amenities, including a daily buffet breakfast and manager's receptions. Dogs are allowed for an additional one time pet fee of $75 per room. 2 dogs may be allowed.

Sheraton Vancouver Wall Centre
1088 Burrard Street
Vancouver, BC
604-331-1000 (888-625-5144)
This hotel offers numerous amenities for the business or leisure traveler, and there is a Sea Wall Walking Tour close by for some great scenery of the Pacific Ocean. One dog up to 90 pounds is allowed for an additional one time pet fee of $60, and there is a pet waiver to sign at check in. Dogs must be under their owner's control, leashed, crated when alone in the room, and removed or crated for housekeeping.

Sylvia Hotel
1154 Gilford St
Vancouver, BC
604-681-9321
sylviahotel.com/
There are no additional pet fees. Multiple dogs may be allowed.

Vancouver Marriott Pinnacle Hotel
1128 West Hastings Street
Vancouver, BC
604-684-1128 (800-207-4150)
This four star hotel is located in downtown Vancouver. The pet-friendly hotel has convention facilities and an excellent restaurant.

Best Western Vernon Lodge & Conference Center
3914 32nd Street
Vernon, BC
250-545-3385 (800-780-7234)
Dogs of all sizes are allowed. Dogs are allowed for a pet fee of $15.00 per pet per night.

Best Western Villager Motor Inn
5121 - 26th Street
Vernon, BC
250-549-2224 (800-780-7234)
Dogs of all sizes are allowed. Dogs are allowed for a pet fee of $15.00 per pet per stay.

Holiday Inn Express Hotel & Suites Vernon
4716 34th Street
Vernon, BC
250-550-7777 (877 270-6405)
Dogs of all sizes are allowed. Dogs are allowed for a pet fee of $20.00 per pet per stay.

Accent Inn Victoria
3233 Maple Street
Victoria, BC
250-475-7500 (800-663-0298)
In addition to many amenities and 118 rooms, there is also a family-

style restaurant and a 40 person theater style meeting room at this hotel. Dogs of all sizes are allowed for an additional fee of $15 per night per pet. Dogs may not be left alone in the room, and they must be leashed and cleaned up after at all times. 2 dogs may be allowed.

Best Western Carlton Plaza Hotel
642 Johnson Street
Victoria, BC
250-388-5513 (800-780-7234)
Dogs are welcome at this hotel. There is a $10 per night pet fee.

Coast Harbourside Hotel and Marina
146 Kingston Street
Victoria, BC
250-360-1211 (800-663-1144)
coasthotels.com/hotels/vic.htm
All Coast Hotels have on hand extra pet amenities if you forget something. For dogs, they have extra doggy dishes, sleeping cushions, nylon chew toys and dog food. If your dog needs one of these items, just ask the front desk. There is a $20 per day per room additional pet fee. 2 dogs may be allowed.

Comfort Inn & Suites
101 Island Hwy.
Victoria, BC
250-388-7861 (877-424-6423)
Dogs of all sizes are allowed. Dogs are allowed for a pet fee of $20.00 per pet per night.

Days Inn - On The Harbour Victoria
427 Belleville Street
Victoria, BC
250-386-3451 (800-329-7466)
Dogs are welcome at this hotel.

Executive House Hotel
777 Douglas Street
Victoria, BC
250-388-5111 (800-663-7001)
executivehouse.com
Enjoy European ambience in a downtown Victoria hotel. The hotel is directly across from the Victoria Conference Centre, one block from the magnificent Inner Harbour, Royal BC Museum, National Geographic Theater, shopping and attractions. Pets are welcome for $15 per night extra.

Fairmont Empress
721 Government Street
Victoria, BC
250-384-8111 (800-257-7544)
fairmont.com/empress/
This well manicured, chateau style resort features an 18-hole golf

course, plenty of whale watching opportunities, and an impressive array of other activities and recreational opportunities. Dogs are allowed for an additional fee of $25 per night per pet.

Harbour Towers Hotel
345 Quebec St
Victoria, BC
250-385-2405
harbourtowers.com/
There is a $20 per day additional pet fee.

Howard Johnson Hotel Victoria
310 Gorge Rd
Victoria, BC
250-382-2151 (800-446-4656)
Dogs of all sizes are allowed. Dogs are allowed for a pet fee.

Howard Johnson Hotel and Suites
4670 Elk Lake Drive
Victoria, BC
250-704-4656 (800-446-4656)
Dogs are welcome at this hotel.

Malahat Bungalows Motel, cabins, cottages
300 Trans Canada H
Victoria, BC
800-665-8066
Dogs are allowed by the night only for an $8 per night per pet additional pet fee. 2 dogs may be allowed.

Ramada Victoria
123 Gorge Road East
Victoria, BC
250-386-1422 (800-272-6232)
Dogs of all sizes are allowed. Dogs are allowed for a pet fee of $20.00 per pet per night.

Ryan's Bed and Breakfast
224 Superior St
Victoria, BC
250-389-0012
ryansbb.com
Dogs up to 50 pounds are allowed for an additional one time pet fee of $25. 2 dogs may be allowed.

Tally Ho Motor Inn
3020 Douglas St
Victoria, BC
250-386-6141
There is a $20 per night additional pet fee. 2 dogs may be allowed.

The Inn At Laurel Point
680 Montreal Street
Victoria, BC
250-386-8721 (800-663-7667)
laurelpoint.com/

Centrally located near a number of shopping, entertainment, and business areas, this inn offers conveniences and amenities for business and leisure travelers. There are 200 rooms/suites all with private balconies, a waterfront restaurant and patio, a luxuriant Japanese garden, a gift shop, and an indoor pool. Dogs are allowed in the 1st floor rooms for an additional pet fee of $50 to $75 for each 1 to 7 days depending on the room. Dogs are not allowed on the dining patio. 2 dogs may be allowed.

Travelodge Victoria
229 Gorge Road East
Victoria, BC
250-388-6611 (800-578-7878)
Dogs of all sizes are allowed. Dogs are allowed for a pet fee of $15 per pet per night.

Chateau Whistler Resort
4599 Chateau Blvd
Whistler, BC
604-938-8000
fairmonthotels.com
This is a 5 star resort. There is no weight limit for dogs. There is a $25 per night per pet additional fee. They also provide a doggy menu and a pet amenity package.

Delta Whistler Village Suites
4308 Main Street
Whistler, BC
604-905-3987 (888-299-3987)
A year round recreational destination, this all-suite hotel offers a full range of amenities, great views, a year round heated outdoor pool, a Solarice Wellness Spa, and more. Dogs of all sizes are allowed for an additional fee of $35 per pet for every 5 days. Dogs must be quiet, leashed, and cleaned up after. 2 dogs may be allowed.

Four Seasons Resort
4591 Blackcomb Way
Whistler, BC
604-935-3400 (800-819-5053)
fourseasons.com/whistler/
Only a short distance from the ski slopes of the Whistler Blackcomb Mountains (the site of the 2010 Olympic Winter Games), this world class resort offers a long list of amenities and access to a wide range of year round recreation. Dogs of all sizes are allowed for no additional pet fee. Dogs may not be left alone in the room at any time, and they must be leashed and cleaned up after at all times. 2 dogs may be allowed.

Hilton Resort and Spa
4050 Whistler Way
Whistler, BC
604-932-1982 (800-HILTONS (445-8667))
In addition to being only 22 steps to the Whistler Mountain Gondola, and located across the street from the Arnold Palmer Signature Golf Course, this upscale hotel also has a number of on site amenities for business and leisure travelers. Dogs are allowed for an additional pet fee of $25 per night per room. Multiple dogs may be allowed.

Residence Inn Whistler
4899 Painted Cliff Road
Whistler, BC
604-905-3400 (888-905-3400)
Idyllically located on the slope-side of Blackcomb Mountain and offering year around recreational activities, this resort style, all suite inn offers balconies, in-suite fireplaces, a daily buffet breakfast, and evening receptions. Dogs are allowed for an additional one time pet fee of $25 per night to a maximum total of $75 per room for one dog; a 2nd dog would be an additional $10 per night to a maximum total of $30. 2 dogs may be allowed.

The Fairmont Chateau Whistler
4599 Chateau Blvd
Whistler, BC
604-938-8000 (800-257-7544)
fairmont.com/whistler/
Nestled in a high alpine valley, this hotel sits in one of the top ranked ski areas in North America, and they are also home to a championship golf course and a golf academy. Dogs are allowed for an additional fee of $25 (plus tax) per night per pet. Dogs may not be left alone in the room at any time, and they must be leashed and cleaned up after.

Drummond Lodge
1405 Cariboo Highway South
Williams Lake, BC
250-392-5334
drummondlodge.com
Dogs of all sizes are allowed. There is a $7 per night per pet additional pet fee. Up to two small dogs or one large dog may be allowed.

Sandman Inn and Suites Williams Lake
664 Oliver Street
Williams Lake, BC
250-392-6557
sandmanhotels.com
Dogs of all sizes are allowed. There is a $10 additional pet fee. Some of the rooms have kitchenettes.

Springhouse Trails Ranch
3061 Dog Creek Road
Williams Lake, BC
250-392-4780
springhousetrails.com/
Pets are allowed in the cabins with kitchenettes. Some of the units have fireplaces. There is a $15 additional nightly pet fee. This is a functioning horse ranch and horseback rides are offered on the premises. The Springhouse Trails Ranch lodging cabins are open from May through September annually.

The Fraser Inn Hotel
285 Donald Road
Williams Lake, BC
250-398-7055 (888-311-8863 (in US))
fraserinn.com/
This lakeside inn is only a couple of minuets from downtown, has amenities for the leisure or business traveler, restaurants, and sits central to a variety of interesting sites and attractions. Dogs of all sizes are allowed in first floor rooms for no additional fee with advance notice at the time of reservations. Dogs must be well behaved, leashed, and cleaned up after. Multiple dogs may be allowed.

Manitoba

Comfort Inn
925 Middleton Ave.
Brandon, MB
204-727-6232 (877-424-6423)
Dogs of all sizes are allowed. Dogs are allowed for a pet fee of $10 per pet per night. Two dogs are allowed per room.

Days Inn - Brandon
2130 Currie Blvd
Brandon, MB
204-727-3600 (800-329-7466)
Dogs are welcome at this hotel.

Keystone Motor Inn
1050 18th Street
Brandon, MB
204-728-6620
keystonemotorinn.ca/home.html
A pizzeria, a large self-serve beer vending area, a nightclub, and a lounge are some of the extras guests will find at this inn. Quiet, very well behaved dogs are allowed for a $100 refundable deposit. Dogs are not allowed on the patio. 2 dogs may be allowed.

Super 8 MB Brandon
1570 Highland Avenue
Brandon, MB
204-729-8024 (800-800-8000)
Dogs are welcome at this hotel.

Victoria Inn
3550 Victoria Ave
Brandon, MB
204-725-1532
There is a $10 per day additional pet fee. They have 2 non-smoking pet rooms. Multiple dogs may be allowed.

Super 8 Dauphin
1457 Main Street South
Dauphin, MB
204-638-0800 (800-800-8000)
Dogs are welcome at this hotel.

Victoria Inn North
160 Hwy 10A N
Flin Flon, MB
204-687-7555
Dogs are allowed for an additional $10 per night per pet. 2 dogs may be allowed.

Solmundson Gesta Hus B&B
Hwy 8 in Hecla
Hecla, MB
204-279-2088
heclatourism.mb.ca
There is no additional pet fee,,, dogs must be leashed when outside the room. Please make sure that your dog doesn't chase the ducks. 2 dogs may be allowed.

Super 8 Morden
3010 Thornhill Street
Morden, MB
204-822-2003 (800-800-8000)
Dogs of all sizes are allowed. Dogs are allowed for a nightly pet fee.

Days Inn Portage La Prairie
Hwy 1 and Yellowquill Trail
Portage La Prairie, MB
204-857-9791 (800-329-7466)
Dogs of all sizes are allowed. Dogs are allowed for a nightly pet fee.

Super 8 MB Portage La Prairie
Hwy 1A and Saskatchewan
Portage La Prairie, MB
204-857-8883 (800-800-8000)
Dogs are welcome at this hotel.

Days Inn - Steinbach
75 PTH 12 North
Steinbach, MB
204-320-9200 (800-329-7466)

Dogs are welcome at this hotel.

Super 8 MB Swan River
115 Kelsey Trail
Swan River, MB
204-734-7888 (800-800-8000)
Dogs are welcome at this hotel.

Super 8 The Pas
1717 Gordon Avenue
The Pas, MB
204-623-1888 (800-800-8000)
Dogs are welcome at this hotel.

Best Western Pembina Inn & Suites
1714 Pembina Highway
Winnipeg, MB
204-269-8888 (800-780-7234)
Dogs of all sizes are allowed. Dogs
are allowed for a nightly pet fee.

Clarion Hotel & Suites
1445 Portage Avenue
Winnipeg, MB
204-774-5110 (877-424-6423)
Hotel is located within five minutes of
the Winnipeg International Airport
and Winnipeg's city centre,

Comfort Inn Airport
1770 Sargent Ave.
Winnipeg, MB
204-783-5627 (877-424-6423)
Dogs of all sizes are allowed. Dogs
are allowed for a pet fee of $room
per pet per night. Two dogs are
allowed per room.

Comfort Inn South
3109 Pembina Hwy.
Winnipeg, MB
204-269-7390 (877-424-6423)
Dogs up to 50 pounds are allowed.
Dogs are allowed for a pet fee of
$9.95 per pet per night.

Country Inn
730 King Edward Street
Winnipeg, MB
204-783-6900 (888-201-1746)
countryinns.com/winnipegmb
This hotel offers a number of on-site
amenities and services for the leisure
or business travelers, including a
daily full breakfast buffet. Quiet, well
behaved dogs are allowed for an
additional one time pet fee of $25 per
room. Multiple dogs may be allowed.

Days Inn - Winnipeg
550 McPhillips St
Winnipeg, MB
204-586-8525 (800-329-7466)
Dogs are welcome at this hotel.

Delta Winnipeg
350 St Mary Avenue

Winnipeg, MB
204-942-0551 (888-890-3222)
In addition to offering a number of
on-site amenities, the convenient
location of this hotel gives visitors a
great starting point to see and
experience all the city has to offer.
Dogs are allowed for an additional
fee of $35 for each 5 days stay with
a credit card must be on file; they
must be declared at the time of
reservations. Dogs must be leashed
and cleaned up after at all times. If
it is necessary to leave your pet in
the room for a short time, inform the
front desk and leave a contact
number. Dogs are not allowed in
food service areas, the pool, health
club, lounge, or any of the meeting
rooms, and they must be removed
for housekeeping. Multiple dogs
may be allowed.

Hilton Hotel
1800 Wellington Avenue
Winnipeg, MB
204-783-1700 (800-HILTONS (445-
8667))
Located at the Winnipeg Airport
Industrial Park, this luxury, all suite
hotel offers a number on site
amenities for business and leisure
travelers, plus a convenient location
to business, shopping, dining, and
recreation areas. Dogs are allowed
for no additional fee. Dogs must be
crated when left alone in the room.
2 dogs may be allowed.

Holiday Inn Winnipeg-South
1330 Pembina Hwy
Winnipeg, MB
204-452-4747 (877-270-6405)
Dogs of all sizes are allowed. Dogs
are allowed for a nightly pet fee.

Howard Johnson Airport Hotel -
Winnipeg
1740 Ellice Avenue
Winnipeg, MB
204-775-7131 (800-446-4656)
Dogs of all sizes are allowed. Dogs
are allowed for a nightly pet fee.

Place Louis Riel All-Suite Hotel
190 Smith St
Winnipeg, MB
204-947-6961
There is a $10 per night per room
pet fee. Pet owners must sign a pet
release form. 2 dogs may be
allowed.

Quality Inn & Suites
635 Pembina Hwy.
Winnipeg, MB
204-453-8247 (877-424-6423)
Dogs of all sizes are allowed. Dogs

are allowed for a pet fee of $15.00
per pet per night.

Radisson Hotel Winnipeg Downtown
288 Portage Avenue
Winnipeg, MB
204-956-0410
Dogs of all sizes are allowed. There
is a $25 one time additional pet fee.

Super 8 West Winnipeg
101 Bypass & Portage West
Winnipeg, MB
204-831-9800 (800-800-8000)
Dogs are welcome at this hotel.

The Fairmont Winnipeg
2 Lombard Place
Winnipeg, MB
204-957-1350 (800-257-7544)
fairmont.com/winnipeg/
Sitting amidst a vibrant cosmopolitan
city and one of the world's largest
historical districts, this hotel is
perfectly located for the leisure or
business traveler. Dogs up to 50
pounds are allowed for an additional
pet fee of $25 per night per room.
Your pup gets a special goody bag,
and they also provide clean up bags.
Dogs may not be left alone in the
room at any time, and they are not
allowed in food or beverage areas.

Thriftlodge Winnipeg
1400 Notre Dame Avenue
Winnipeg, MB
204-786-3471 (800-578-7878)
Dogs are welcome at this hotel.

Travelodge East Winnipeg
20 Alpine Ave
Winnipeg, MB
204-255-6000 (800-578-7878)
Dogs of all sizes are allowed. Dogs
are allowed for a pet fee of $10 per
pet per night.

New Brunswick

Comfort Inn
1170 St. Peter Ave.
Bathurst, NB
506-547-8000 (877-424-6423)
Dogs of all sizes are allowed.

Comfort Inn
111 Val D'Amour Rd
Campbellton, NB
506-753-4121 (877-424-6423)
Dogs of all sizes are allowed.

Howard Johnson Hotel Campbellton
157 Water Street
Campbellton, NB
506-753-4133 (800-446-4656)

Dogs are welcome at this hotel.

Super 8 Moncton Area NB Dieppe
370 Dieppe Blvd
Dieppe, NB
506-858-8880 (800-800-8000)
Dogs of all sizes are allowed. Dogs
are allowed for a nightly pet fee.

Best Western Edmundston Hotel
280 Boul Hebert
Edmundston, NB
506-739-0000 (800-780-7234)
Dogs are welcome at this hotel.

Days Inn Edmundston
10 Rue Mathieu
Edmundston, NB
506-263-0000 (800-329-7466)
Dogs are welcome at this hotel.

Quality Inn
919 Canada Road
Edmundston, NB
506-735-5525 (877-424-6423)
Dogs of all sizes are allowed.

Best Western Fredericton Hotel &
Suites
333 Bishop Drive
Fredericton, NB
506-455-8448 (800-780-7234)
Dogs of all sizes are allowed. Dogs
are allowed for a pet fee of $25.00
per pet per stay.

Comfort Inn
797 Prospect St.
Fredericton, NB
506-453-0800 (877-424-6423)
Dogs of all sizes are allowed.

Howard Johnson Plaza Hotel
Fredericton
958 Prospect Street
Fredericton, NB
506-462-4444 (800-446-4656)
Dogs are welcome at this hotel.

Ramada Fredericton
480 Riverside Drive
Fredericton, NB
506-460-5500 (800-272-6232)
Dogs of all sizes are allowed. Dogs
are allowed for a pet fee.

Best Western Grand Sault Hotel &
Suites
187 Ouellette Street
Grand Falls, NB
506-473-6200 (800-780-7234)
Dogs are welcome at this hotel.
There is a $25 one time pet fee.

Comfort Inn East
20 Maplewood Dr.
Moncton, NB

506-859-6868 (877-424-6423)
Dogs of all sizes are allowed.

Comfort Inn Magnetic Hill
2495 Mountain Rd.
Moncton, NB
506-384-3175 (877-424-6423)
Dogs of all sizes are allowed.

Country Inns & Suites by Carlson
2475 Mountain Road
Moncton, NB
506-852-7000
Dogs of all sizes are allowed. There
is a $25 one time additional pet fee
per room.

Crowne Plaza Hotel Moncton
Downtown
1005 Main Street
Moncton, NB
506-854-6340 (877-270-6405)
Dogs are welcome at this hotel.

Econo Lodge
1905 W. Main St.
Moncton, NB
506-382-2587 (877-424-6423)
Dogs of all sizes are allowed.

Residence Inn Moncton
600 Main Street
Moncton, NB
506-854-7100 (800-331-3131)
Located in the heart of the city, this
all suite inn gives a convenient
location to a plethora of year around
interests, recreation, and activities
for either the business or leisure
traveler. Additionally, they offer a
number of in-house amenities,
including a daily buffet breakfast,
evening socials, and a market on
site. Dogs are allowed for an
additional one time pet fee of $75
per room. Multiple dogs may be
allowed.

Days Inn and Conference Centre -
Oromocto
60 Brayson Blvd.
Oromocto, NB
506-357-5657 (800-329-7466)
Dogs of all sizes are allowed. Dogs
are allowed for a pet fee of $15.00
per pet per night.

Double Barn Ranch
566 West Galloway Road
Rexton, NB
506-523-9217
doublebarnranch.com
These log cottages are located on
293 acres of ranch land. There is a
CDN $10 per night pet fee. Dogs of
all sizes are allowed.

Best Western Saint John Hotel &
Suites
55 Majors Brook Drive
Saint John, NB
506-657-9966 (800-780-7234)
Dogs of all sizes are allowed. Dogs
are allowed for a pet fee of $15 per
pet per night.

Comfort Inn
1155 Fairville Blvd.
Saint John, NB
506-674-1873 (877-424-6423)
Dogs of all sizes are allowed.

Kingsbrae Arms Relais
219 King Street
St Andrews, NB
506-529-1897
kingsbrae.com/
This late 1800s, award winning inn
shares an interesting cultural history
of its town. Additionally, they offer
fine dining from their organically
grown foods/eggs and fresh
seafood/meats, lush lawns/greenery,
formal gardens, and scenic views of
the bay that is home to the highest
tides in the world. Well mannered
dogs are allowed for no additional
fee. Dogs must be quiet, leashed
when not in the 1 acre fenced play
area, and cleaned up after. 2 dogs
may be allowed.

The Fairmont Algonquin
184 Adolphus Street
St Andrews by the Sea, NB
506-529-8823 (800-257-7544)
fairmont.com/frontenac/
There is a stunning seaside golf
course and year around recreational
activities offered at this resort. Dogs
of all sizes are allowed for an
additional pet fee of $25 (plus tax)
per night per room. During the
summer season they have been
known to offer an amenity package
for their canine guests. A contact
number must be left with the front
desk if there is a pet alone in the
room.

Holiday Inn Express Hotel & Suites
Saint John Harbour Side
400 Main St. And Chesley Drive
St John, NB
506-642-2622 (877-270-6405)
Dogs are welcome at this hotel.

Econo Lodge
168 Route 555
Woodstock, NB
506-328-8876 (877-424-6423)
Dogs of all sizes are allowed. Dogs
are allowed for a pet fee of $10.00
per pet per night.

Dog-Friendly Lodging - Please always call ahead to make sure an establishment is still dog-friendly.

Howard Johnson Inn NB Woodstock
159 Route 555 Exit 188
Woodstock, NB
506-328-3315 (800-446-4656)
Dogs are welcome at this hotel.

Newfoundland

Comfort Inn
41 Maple Valley Rd.
Corner Brook, NF
709-639-1980 (877-424-6423)
Dogs of all sizes are allowed.

Comfort Inn
112 Trans Canada Hwy.
Gander, NF
709-256-3535 (877-424-6423)
Dogs of all sizes are allowed.

The Valhalla Lodge
Address with reservation
L'Anse aux Meadows, NF
709-754-3105 (877-623-2018)
Dogs up to 75 pounds are allowed.
There is one pet friendly cottage, and
dogs are not allowed in the lodge.
There is an additional one time $15
fee per pet. 2 dogs may be allowed.

Gros Morne Cabins
P.O. Box 151
Rocky Harbour, NF
709-458-2020 (888-603-2020)
grosmornecabins.com/
Some of the amenities of this retreat,
located in the heart of the Gros
Morne National Park, include fully
equipped cabins with great ocean
views, a modern playground for
children, and a gift/convenience
store. Dogs are allowed for an
additional pet fee of $20 per night
per room. 2 dogs may be allowed.

Comfort Inn Airport
106 Airport Road
St John's, NF
709-753-3500 (877-424-6423)
Dogs of all sizes are allowed. Dogs
are allowed for a pet fee of $35 per
pet per stay.

Fairmont Newfoundland
115 Cavendish Square
St Johns, NF
709-726-4980 (800-257-7544)
fairmont.com/newfoundland/
Located in the heart of North
America's oldest city, this hotel also
offers fantastic views of the harbor
and this historic city. Dogs of all
sizes are allowed for an additional
pet fee of $25 per night per room.
There can be one large dog over 30

pounds or 2 small dogs up to 30
pounds each per room. Dogs must
be leashed, cleaned up after, and
crated when left alone in the room.

Super 8 St Johns
175 Higgins Line
St Johns, NF
709-739-8888 (800-800-8000)
Dogs are welcome at this hotel.

The Village Inn
Cavenor Street
Trinity, NF
709-464-3269
oceancontact.com/inn/inn.html
Although restored, this inn still
imparts a wonderful nostalgic
ambiance, plus they offer an
unusual activity of expeditions for
viewing/studying the local whales,
dolphins, and porpoises with their
resident scientist that specializes in
computerized human-animal
communications. They also offer 2
dining rooms with traditional
Newfoundland foods, a pub, and
some great hiking trails. One dog is
allowed per room for no additional
pet fee.

Northwest Territories

Fraser Tower Suite Hotel
5303 52nd St
Yellowknife, NT
867-873-8700
There is a $10 per day per pet
additional fee. Pets must be crated
if left alone in the room. Multiple
dogs may be allowed.

Super 8 Yellowknife
308 Old Airport Road
Yellowknife, NT
867-669-8888 (800-800-8000)
Dogs of all sizes are allowed. Dogs
are allowed for a pet fee.

Nova Scotia

Comfort Inn
143 South Albion St.
Amherst, NS
902-667-0404 (877-424-6423)
Dogs of all sizes are allowed.

Super 8
40 Lord Amherst Drive
Amherst, NS
902-660-8888 (800-800-8000)
Dogs of all sizes are allowed. Dogs
are allowed for a pet fee.

Comfort Inn
49 North St.
Bridgewater, NS
902-543-1498 (877-424-6423)
Dogs of all sizes are allowed.

Days Inn and Conference Center -
Bridgewater
50 North Street
Bridgewater, NS
902-543-7131 (800-329-7466)
Dogs are welcome at this hotel.

Days Inn - Dartmouth
20 Highfield Park Drive
Dartmouth, NS
902-465-6555 (800-329-7466)
Dogs are welcome at this hotel.

Super 8 Dartmouth
65 King Street
Dartmouth, NS
902-463-9520 (800-800-8000)
Dogs are welcome at this hotel.

Thistle Down Country Inn
98 Montague Row
Digby, NS
902-245-4490 (800-565-8081)
thistledown.ns.ca/
Nestled along the shores of the
Annapolis Basin, this beautiful 1904
Edwardian-styled home offers an
elegant, old world elegance, fine
dining, and views of the Basin known
to have some of the highest tides in
the world. Dogs are allowed for no
additional fee. They must be quiet,
well mannered, and leashed when
out of the rooms. 2 dogs may be
allowed.

Holiday Inn Express Hotel & Suites
Halifax Airport
180 Pratt & Whitney Drive
Enfield, NS
902-576-7600 (877-270-6405)
Dogs are welcome at this hotel.

Best Western Chocolate Lake Hotel
20 Saint Margaret's Bay Road
Halifax, NS
902-477-5611 (800-780-7234)
Dogs are welcome at this hotel.

Comfort Inn
560 Bedford Hwy.
Halifax, NS
902-443-0303 (877-424-6423)
Dogs of all sizes are allowed. Dogs
are allowed for a pet fee of $10.00
per pet per stay. Two dogs are
allowed per room.

Delta Halifax
1990 Barrington Street/H 2

Halifax, NS
902-474-5150 (888-890-3222)
In addition to a number of in-house
amenities, this luxury hotel offers a
great location to some of the area's
best shopping, dining, commerce,
and entertainment areas. Dogs up to
50 pounds are allowed for an
additional pet fee of $35 per room for
each 5 day period. 2 dogs may be
allowed.

Holiday Inn Express Halifax-Bedford
133 Kearney Lake Road
Halifax, NS
902-445-1100 (877-270-6405)
Dogs of all sizes are allowed. Dogs
are allowed for a nightly pet fee. Two
dogs are allowed per room.

Lord Nelson Hotel and Suites
1515 S Park Street
Halifax, NS
902-423-6331 (800-565-2020)
lordnelsonhotel.com/
Surrounded by the Halifax public
gardens, this luxury hotel offers
warm, historic architecture,
beautifully appointed rooms, and a
convenient location to many sites of
interest, shopping and dining areas.
Dogs are allowed for no additional
pet fee. Dogs may not be left alone
in the rooms. 2 dogs may be allowed.

Residence Inn Halifax Downtown
1599 Grafton Street
Halifax, NS
902-422-0493 (866-422-0493)
Offering a convenient location to
business, historic, shopping, dining,
and entertainment areas, this all
suite hotel also offers a number of in-
house amenities, including a daily
buffet breakfast and evening socials.
Dogs are allowed for an additional
one time pet fee of $100 per room.
Multiple dogs may be allowed.

The Westin Nova Scotian
1181 Hollis Street
Halifax, NS
902-421-1000 (888-625-5144)
This hotel offers a prime location in
the heart of the city a short distance
from the harbor and numerous
activities. Dogs up to 60 pounds are
allowed for no additional pet fee;
there is a pet waiver to sign at check
in. Dogs must be leashed and
cleaned up after. 2 dogs may be
allowed.

Best Western Liverpool Hotel &
Conference Centre
63 Queens Place Drive
Liverpool, NS
902-354-2377 (800-780-7234)

Dogs are welcome at this hotel.

Comfort Inn
740 Westville Rd.
New Glasgow, NS
902-755-6450 (877-424-6423)
Dogs of all sizes are allowed. Two
dogs are allowed per room.

Country Inns & Suites by Carlson
700 Westville Road
New Glasgow, NS
902-928-1333
there is a pet policy to sign at check
in. Pets may not be left alone in the
rooms and are not allowed in the
breakfast area.

Caribou River Cottage Lodge
1308 Shore Road, RR# 3
Pictou, NS
902-485-6352
sunrise-trail.com/caribou/
One dog is allowed for an additional
pet fee of $4 per night.

Econo Lodge MacPuffin
373 Highway #4
Port Hastings, NS
902-625-0621 (877-424-6423)
Dogs of all sizes are allowed.

Holiday Inn Express Stellarton-New
Glasgow
86 Lawarence Blvd
Stellarton, NS
019-027-5510 (877-270-6405)
Dogs of all sizes are allowed. Dogs
are allowed for a pet fee.

Comfort Inn
368 Kings Rd.
Sydney, NS
902-562-0200 (877-424-6423)
Dogs of all sizes are allowed.

Days Inn Nova Scotia Sydney
480 Kings Road
Sydney, NS
902-539-6750 (800-329-7466)
Dogs are welcome at this hotel.

Quality Inn
560 Kings Road
Sydney, NS
902-539-8101 (877-424-6423)
Dogs of all sizes are allowed.

Comfort Inn
12 Meadow Dr.
Truro, NS
902-893-0330 (877-424-6423)
Dogs of all sizes are allowed.

Holiday Inn Truro
437 Prince Street
Truro, NS

019-028-9516 (877-270-6405)
Dogs of all sizes are allowed. Dogs
are allowed for a nightly pet fee.

Super 8 NS Truro
85 Treaty Trail
Truro, NS
902-895-8884 (800-800-8000)
Dogs of all sizes are allowed. Dogs
are allowed for a pet fee of $10.00
per pet per night.

Super 8 Windsor
63 Cole Drive
Windsor, NS
902-792-8888 (800-800-8000)
Dogs of all sizes are allowed. Dogs
are allowed for a pet fee.

Best Western Mermaid
545 Main Street
Yarmouth, NS
902-742-7821 (800-780-7234)
Dogs are welcome at this hotel.

Comfort Inn
96 Starrs Rd.
Yarmouth, NS
902-742-1119 (877-424-6423)
Dogs of all sizes are allowed.

Ontario

Super 8 Toronto
210 Westney Road South
Ajax, ON
905-428-6884 (800-800-8000)
Dogs are welcome at this hotel.

Quality Inn
70 Madawaska Blvd
Arnprior, ON
613-623-7991 (877-424-6423)
Dogs of all sizes are allowed. Dogs
are allowed for a pet fee of $10.00
per pet per night.

Comfort Inn
75 Hart Dr.
Barrie, ON
705-722-3600 (877-424-6423)
Dogs of all sizes are allowed.

Comfort Inn & Suites
210 Essa Rd.
Barrie, ON
705-721-1122 (877-424-6423)
Dogs of all sizes are allowed.

Days Inn - Barrie
60 Bryne Drive
Barrie, ON
705-733-8989 (800-329-7466)
Dogs of all sizes are allowed. Dogs

are allowed for a pet fee.

Holiday Inn Barrie-Hotel &
Conference Ctr
20 Fairview Road
Barrie, ON
705-722-0555 (877-270-6405)
Dogs are welcome at this hotel.

Howard Johnson Express Inn
Ontario Barrie
150 Dunlop Street West
Barrie, ON
705-728-1312 (800-446-4656)
Dogs are welcome at this hotel.

Super 8 Barrie
441 Bryne Drive
Barrie, ON
705-814-8888 (800-800-8000)
Dogs of all sizes are allowed. Dogs
are allowed for a pet fee.

Travelodge Barrie
55 Hart Drive
Barrie, ON
705-734-9500 (800-578-7878)
Dogs are welcome at this hotel.

Travelodge on Bayfield Barrie
300 Bayfield Street
Barrie, ON
705-722-4466 (800-578-7878)
Dogs are welcome at this hotel.

Best Western Belleville
387 N Front Street
Belleville, ON
613-969-1112 (800-780-7234)
Dogs are welcome at this hotel.

Comfort Inn
200 North Park St.
Belleville, ON
613-966-7703 (877-424-6423)
Dogs of all sizes are allowed.

Ramada on the Bay Conference
Resort Belleville
11 Bay Bridge Road
Belleville, ON
613-968-3411 (800-272-6232)
Dogs of all sizes are allowed. Dogs
are allowed for a pet fee.

Tyrolean Village Resort
796455 Grey Road 19
Blue Mountains, ON
705-445-1467
tyrolean.com/
This popular 4 season recreational
destination offers a convenient
location to all the town has to offer,
and on site they have their own
private beach, a fenced Pet Park,
gaming courts/fields, a children's
playground, and a barbecue area.

Dogs are allowed for no additional
fee. They are not allowed on the
bed or other furnishings, and they
must be cleaned up after promptly.
Dogs must be leashed on resort
grounds, be supervised while in the
Pet Park, leashed or under strict
voice control when on the private
beach, and they are not allowed in
the pool area. 2 dogs may be
allowed.

Howard Johnson Hotel in
Bowmanville
160 Liberty Street South
Bowmanville, ON
905-623-3373 (800-446-4656)
Dogs of all sizes are allowed. Dogs
are allowed for a pet fee of $10.00
per pet per night.

Sleep Inn
510 Muskoka Rd. 118 West
Bracebridge, ON
705-645-2519 (877-424-6423)
Dogs of all sizes are allowed.

Travelodge Bracebridge
320 Taylor Road
Bracebridge, ON
705-645-2235 (800-578-7878)
Dogs of all sizes are allowed. Dogs
are allowed for a nightly pet fee.

Comfort Inn
5 Rutherford Rd. S.
Brampton, ON
905-452-0600 (877-424-6423)
Dogs of all sizes are allowed.

Howard Johnson Express Inn and
Suites Toronto - Brampton
226 Queen Street East
Brampton, ON
905-451-6000 (800-446-4656)
Dogs of all sizes are allowed. Dogs
are allowed for a pet fee of $10.00
per pet per night.

Motel 6 - Toronto Brampton
160 Steelwell Rd
Brampton, ON
905-451-3313 (800-466-8356)
This motel welcomes your pets to
stay with you.

Comfort Inn
58 King George Rd.
Brantford, ON
519-753-3100 (877-424-6423)
Dogs of all sizes are allowed. Dogs
are allowed for a pet fee of $10.00
per pet per stay.

Days Inn - Brantford
460 Fairview Drive
Brantford, ON

519-759-2700 (800-329-7466)
Dogs are welcome at this hotel.

Comfort Inn
7777 Kent Blvd.
Brockville, ON
613-345-0042 (877-424-6423)
Dogs of all sizes are allowed. Dogs
are allowed for a pet fee of $15.00
per pet per night.

Travelodge Brockville
7789 Kent Blvd
Brockville, ON
613-345-3900 (800-578-7878)
Dogs are welcome at this hotel.

Comfort Inn
3290 South Service Rd.
Burlington, ON
905-639-1700 (877-424-6423)
Dogs of all sizes are allowed.

Motel 6 - Toronto West
Burlington/hamilton
4345 Service Rd
Burlington, ON
905-331-1955 (800-466-8356)
This motel welcomes your pets to
stay with you.

Travelodge Hotel on the Lake
Burlington
2020 Lakeshore Road
Burlington, ON
905-681-0762 (800-578-7878)
Dogs of all sizes are allowed. Dogs
are allowed for a pet fee.

/Waterloo Travelodge Hotel
Cambridge
605 Hespeler Rd
Cambridge, ON
519-622-1180 (800-578-7878)
Dogs are welcome at this hotel.

Comfort Inn
220 Holiday Inn Dr.
Cambridge, ON
519-658-1100 (877-424-6423)
Dogs of all sizes are allowed.

Langdon Hall Country House Hotel
and Spa
1 Langdon Drive
Cambridge, ON
519-740-2100 (800-268-1898)
langdonhall.ca/
Fine dining, fine accommodations,
and body pampering are some of the
specialties here. They also offer a
bar, lush gardens, and specialty
combination tours. Well mannered
dogs are allowed for no additional
fee; they must be leashed and
cleaned up after. Dogs are not
allowed in the main house rooms.

Multiple dogs may be allowed.

Comfort Inn
1100 Richmond St.
Chatham, ON
519-352-5500 (877-424-6423)
Dogs of all sizes are allowed. Two dogs are allowed per room.

Super 8 Chatham
25 Michener Road
Chatham, ON
519-354-3366 (800-800-8000)
Dogs of all sizes are allowed. Dogs are allowed for a pet fee.

Travelodge Chatham
555 Bloomfield RD
Chatham, ON
519-436-1200 (800-578-7878)
Dogs are welcome at this hotel.

Comfort Inn
121 Densmore Rd.
Cobourg, ON
905-372-7007 (877-424-6423)
Dogs of all sizes are allowed.

Thriftlodge South Cochrane
50/Highway 11 South
Cochrane, ON
705-272-4281 (800-578-7878)
Dogs are welcome at this hotel.

Comfort Inn
1625 Vincent Massey Drive
Cornwall, ON
613-937-0111 (877-424-6423)
Dogs of all sizes are allowed. Dogs are allowed for a pet fee of $20.00 per pet per stay. Two dogs are allowed per room.

Econo Lodge
1142 Brookdale Ave.
Cornwall, ON
613-936-1996 (877-424-6423)
Dogs of all sizes are allowed. Dogs are allowed for a pet fee of $10.00 per pet per night.

Best Western Motor Inn
349 Government Street
Dryden, ON
807-223-3201 (800-780-7234)
Dogs are welcome at this hotel.

Comfort Inn
522 Government St.
Dryden, ON
807-223-3893 (877-424-6423)
Dogs of all sizes are allowed.

Knights Inn Flesherton
774107 Highway 10 South
Flesherton, ON
519-924-3300 (800-843-5644)

Dogs of all sizes are allowed. Dogs are allowed for a nightly pet fee.

Holiday Inn Fort Erie/Niagara Conv Centre
1485 Garrison Road
Fort Erie, ON
888-269-5550 (877-270-6405)
Dogs of all sizes are allowed. Dogs are allowed for a nightly pet fee.

Howard Johnson Inn Fort Erie
139 Garrison Road
Fort Erie, ON
905-871-7777 (800-446-4656)
Dogs are welcome at this hotel.

Super 8 Fort Frances
810 Kings Hwy
Fort Frances, ON
807-274-4945 (800-800-8000)
Dogs of all sizes are allowed. Dogs are allowed for a pet fee of $10.00 per pet per stay.

Best Western Country Squire Resort
715 King Street E
Gananoque, ON
613-382-3511 (800-780-7234)
Dogs of all sizes are allowed. Dogs are allowed for a pet fee of $20.00 per pet per night.

Clarion Inn & Conference Centre
50 Main Street
Gananoque, ON
613-382-7272 (877-424-6423)
Dogs of all sizes are allowed. Dogs are allowed for a pet fee of $15.00 per pet per night. Two dogs are allowed per room.

Comfort Inn 1000 Islands
785 King St. E.
Gananoque, ON
613-382-4728 (877-424-6423)
Dogs of all sizes are allowed. Dogs are allowed for a pet fee of $15.00 per pet per night. Two dogs are allowed per room.

Holiday Inn Express Hotel & Suites
1000 Islands - Gananoque
777 East King Street
Gananoque, ON
613-382-8338 (877-270-6405)
Dogs of all sizes are allowed. Dogs are allowed for a nightly pet fee.

Howard Johnson Inn Gananoque
550 King St East
Gananoque, ON
613-382-3911 (800-446-4656)
Dogs are welcome at this hotel.

Quality Inn & Suites 1000 Islands

650 King St. East
Gananoque, ON
613-382-1453 (877-424-6423)
Dogs of all sizes are allowed. Dogs are allowed for a pet fee of $15.00 per pet per night. Two dogs are allowed per room.

Value Inn
2098 Montreal Road
Gloucester, ON
613-745-1531 (800-665-0306)
valueinnottawa.com/
This hotel is located only 15 minutes from the downtown area and 20 minutes to the airport. Dogs are allowed for an additional fee of $12 per night per pet. 2 dogs may be allowed.

Howard Johnson Inn - Gravenhurst
1165 Muskoka Rd South
Gravenhurst, ON
705-687-7707 (800-446-4656)
Dogs are welcome at this hotel.

Super 8 Ontario Grimsby
11 Windward Drive
Grimsby, ON
905-309-8800 (800-800-8000)
Dogs are welcome at this hotel.

Best Western Royal Brock Hotel & Conference Centre
716 Gordon Street
Guelph, ON
519-836-1240 (800-780-7234)
Dogs are welcome at this hotel.

Comfort Inn
480 Silvercreek Pkwy.
Guelph, ON
519-763-1900 (877-424-6423)
Dogs of all sizes are allowed.

Days Inn - Guelph
785 Gordon Street
Guelph, ON
519-822-9112 (800-329-7466)
Dogs are welcome at this hotel.

Holiday Inn Guelph Hotel & Conference Ctr
601 Scottsdale Dr
Guelph, ON
519-836-0231 (877-270-6405)
Dogs of all sizes are allowed. Dogs are allowed for a pet fee.

Staybridge Suites Guelph
11 Corporate Court
Guelph, ON
519-767-3300 (877-270-6405)
Dogs up to 80 pounds are allowed. Pets allowed with an additional pet fee. Up to $75 for 1-6 nights and up to $150 for 7+ nights. A pet

agreement must be signed at check-in.

Sheraton Hamilton Hotel
116 King Street W
Hamilton, ON
905-529-8266 (888-625-5144)
Although situated in the heart of the business district, there is plenty of recreational activities to be found close by. Dogs of all sizes are allowed for no additional pet fee; there is a pet waiver to sign at check in. Dogs must be well mannered, leashed, cleaned up after, and crated when left alone in the room. Multiple dogs may be allowed.

Staybridge Suites Hamilton-Downtown
118 Market Street
Hamilton, ON
905-577-9000 (877-270-6405)
Dogs up to 80 pounds are allowed. Pets allowed with an additional pet fee. Up to $75 for 1-6 nights and up to $150 for 7+ nights. A pet agreement must be signed at check-in.

Comfort Inn
86 King William St.
Huntsville, ON
705-789-1701 (877-424-6423)
Dogs of all sizes are allowed. Two dogs are allowed per room.

Holiday Inn Express Hotel & Suites Huntsville
100 Howland Drive
Huntsville, ON
705-788-9500 (877-270-6405)
Dogs are welcome at this hotel.

Motel 6 - Huntsville
70 Howland Drive
Huntsville, ON
705-787-0118 (800-466-8356)
This motel welcomes your pets to stay with you.

Travelodge Ontario Huntsville
225 Main Street West
Huntsville, ON
705-789-5504 (800-578-7878)
Dogs of all sizes are allowed. Dogs are allowed for a pet fee of $10 per pet per night.

Super 8 Kenora
240 Lakeview Drive
Kenora ON
807-468-8016 (800-800-8000)
Dogs are welcome at this hotel.

Viva Villa Vacation Rentals
497 Lakeshore Road

Kagawong, ON
705-282-2896
vivavilla.ca/
Located on Manitoulin Island, these lakefront cottages sit nestled among the trees looking out on the spring-fed Lake Kagawong. They offer numerous land and water recreational opportunities and paddle boats, bikes, and rowboats are included with rentals. One dog per cottage is allowed for no additional fee. Dogs must be leashed, cleaned up after, and under owner's control at all times. Dogs must be hound and human friendly and they may not be left unattended in the cottages.

Comfort Inn West
222 Hearst Way
Kanata, ON
613-592-2200 (877-424-6423)
Dogs of all sizes are allowed.

Comfort Inn
172 Government Rd. E.
Kapuskasing, ON
705-335-8583 (877-424-6423)
Dogs of all sizes are allowed.

Super 8 Kapuskasing
430 Government Road
Kapuskasing, ON
705-335-8887 (800-800-8000)
Dogs of all sizes are allowed. Dogs are allowed for a pet fee of $10.00 per pet per stay.

Howard Johnson Kemptville
4022 County Road 43
Kemptville, ON
613-258-5939 (800-446-4656)
Dogs are welcome at this hotel. There is a $10 one time pet fee.

Comfort Inn
1230 Hwy. 17 E.
Kenora, ON
807-468-8845 (877-424-6423)
Dogs of all sizes are allowed.

Days Inn - Kenora
920 Highway 17 East
Kenora, ON
807-468-2003 (800-329-7466)
Dogs are welcome at this hotel.

Travelodge Kenora
800 Highway 17 East
Kenora, ON
807-468-3155 (800-578-7878)
Dogs of all sizes are allowed. Dogs are allowed for a nightly pet fee.

Comfort Inn Hwy. 401
55 Warne Crescent

Kingston, ON
613-546-9500 (877-424-6423)
Dogs of all sizes are allowed.

Comfort Inn Midtown
1454 Princess St. (Hwy. 2)
Kingston, ON
613-549-5550 (877-424-6423)
Dogs of all sizes are allowed.

Confederation Place Hotel
237 Ontario Street
Kingston, ON
613-549-6300 (888-825-4656)
confederationplace.com/
Located in the heart of downtown, this hotel is close to all this vibrant city has to offer. Plus they offer waterfront dining and an outdoor pool. Dogs are allowed for an additional fee of $15 per night per room. Dogs must be leashed when out of the room, they are not allowed in the pool area, and they are only allowed to sit next to your table at the restaurant on the outside of the patio. 2 dogs may be allowed.

Days Inn and Conf Ctr Kingston
33 Benson Street
Kingston, ON
613-546-3661 (800-329-7466)
Dogs are welcome at this hotel.

Holiday Inn Kingston-Waterfront
2 Princess Street
Kingston, ON
613-549-8400 (877-270-6405)
Dogs of all sizes are allowed. Dogs are allowed for a nightly pet fee.

Comfort Inn
455 Government Rd. W.
Kirkland Lake, ON
705-567-4909 (877-424-6423)
Dogs of all sizes are allowed.

Howard Johnson - Conestoga Kitchener
1333 Weber Street East
Kitchener, ON
519-893-1234 (800-446-4656)
Dogs of all sizes are allowed. Dogs are allowed for a nightly pet fee.

Thriftlodge Kitchener
1175 Victoria Street North
Kitchener, ON
519-742-7900 (800-578-7878)
Dogs are welcome at this hotel.

Comfort Inn
279 Erie St. S.
Leamington, ON
519-326-9071 (877-424-6423)
Dogs of all sizes are allowed.

Best Western Lamplighter Inn &
Conference Centre
591 Wellington Road S
London, ON
519-681-7151 (800-780-7234)
Dogs are welcome at this hotel.
There is a $10 one time pet fee.

Comfort Inn
1156 Wellington Rd.
London, ON
519-685-9300 (877-424-6423)
Dogs of all sizes are allowed.

Days Inn - London
1100 Wellington Road South
London, ON
519-681-1240 (800-329-7466)
Dogs are welcome at this hotel.

Holiday Inn Hotel & Suites London
864 Exeter Rd.
London, ON
519-680-0077 (877-270-6405)
Dogs of all sizes are allowed. Dogs
are allowed for a nightly pet fee.

Howard Johnson Inn London
738 Exeter Road
London, ON
519-680-5151 (800-446-4656)
Dogs are welcome at this hotel.

Knights Inn South London
1170 Wellington Road
London, ON
519-681-1550 (800-843-5644)
Dogs are welcome at this hotel.

Motel 6 - London, Ontario
810 Exeter Rd
London, ON
519-680-0900 (800-466-8356)
This motel welcomes your pets to
stay with you.

Quality Suites
1120 Dearness Dr.
London, ON
519-680-1024 (877-424-6423)
Dogs of all sizes are allowed.

Residence Inn London Downtown
383 Colborne Street
London, ON
519-433-7222 (877 477 8483)
Some of the amenities at this all-
suite inn include a daily buffet
breakfast, evening socials Monday
through Thursday, and a
complimentary grocery shopping
service. Dogs are allowed for an
additional one time pet fee of $75 per
room. Multiple dogs may be allowed.

Staybridge Suites London
824 Exeter Rd.

London, ON
519-649-4500 (877-270-6405)
Dogs up to 80 pounds are allowed.
Pets allowed with an additional pet
fee. Up to $75 for 1-6 nights and up
to $150 for 7+ nights. A pet
agreement must be signed at
check-in.

Comfort Inn - Toronto Northeast
8330 Woodbine Ave.
Markham, ON
905-477-6077 (877-424-6423)
Dogs of all sizes are allowed. Dogs
are allowed for a pet fee of $15.00
per pet per night. Two dogs are
allowed per room.

Holiday Inn Hotel & Suites Toronto-
Markham
7095 Woodbine Avenue
Markham, ON
905-474-0444 (877-270-6405)
Dogs of all sizes are allowed. Dogs
are allowed for a nightly pet fee.

Howard Johnson Hotel Toronto-
Markham
555 Cochrane Drive
Markham, ON
905-479-5000 (800-446-4656)
hojomarkham.com
Dogs of all sizes are allowed.

Residence Inn Toronto Markham
55 Minthorn Blvd
Markham, ON
905-707-7933 (866 449 7395)
Offering a convenient location to a
number of activities and attractions
for all level of travelers, this all suite
hotel also offers a number of in-
house amenities, including a daily
buffet breakfast and evening socials
Monday to Thursday. One dog is
allowed for an additional one time
pet fee of $100 per room.

Staybridge Suites Toronto-Markham
355 South Park Road
Markham, ON
905-771-9333 (877-270-6405)
Dogs up to 80 pounds are allowed.
Pets allowed with an additional pet
fee. Up to $75 for 1-6 nights and up
to $150 for 7+ nights. A pet
agreement must be signed at
check-in.

Mohawk Motel
335 Sable Street
Massey, ON
705-865-2722
Dogs up to 50 pounds are allowed
for a $6 per night per room fee, and
there is a pet policy to sign at check
in. Dogs are not allowed to be left

alone in the room, and they are not
allowed on the furniture or the beds.
2 dogs may be allowed.

Comfort Inn
980 King St.
Midland, ON
705-526-2090 (877-424-6423)
Dogs of all sizes are allowed. Dogs
are allowed for a pet fee of $6 per
pet per stay. Two dogs are allowed
per room.

Howard Johnson Inn Midland
751 Yonge Street
Midland, ON
705-526-2219 (800-446-4656)
Dogs of all sizes are allowed. Dogs
are allowed for a nightly pet fee.

Super 8 Midland
1144 Hugel Avenue
Midland, ON
705-526-8288 (800-800-8000)
Dogs of all sizes are allowed. Dogs
are allowed for a pet fee.

Best Western Milton
161 Chisholm Drive
Milton, ON
905-875-3818 (800-780-7234)
Dogs of all sizes are allowed. Dogs
are allowed for a pet fee of $20.00
per pet per night.

Comfort Inn Airport West
1500 Matheson Blvd. at Dixie
Mississauga, ON
905-624-6900 (877-424-6423)
Dogs up to 50 pounds are allowed.
Two dogs are allowed per room.

Comfort Inn Meadowvale
2420 Surveyor Rd
Mississauga, ON
905-858-8600 (877-424-6423)
Dogs of all sizes are allowed. Dogs
are allowed for a pet fee of $15.00
per pet per night.

Econo Lodge Inn & Suites Toronto
Airport
6355 Airport Rd.
Mississauga, ON
905-677-7331 (877-424-6423)
Dogs up to 50 pounds are allowed.
Dogs are allowed for a pet fee of
$10/pet per pet per night.

Four Points by Sheraton
Mississauga Meadowvale
2501 Argentia Road
Mississauga, ON
905-858-2424 (888-625-5144)
This hotel is located in the heart of
the business district near several
corporate headquarters, and yet it is

still close to a variety of recreational activities. Dogs of all sizes are allowed for an additional fee of $20 per night per pet. Dogs must be leashed and cleaned up after. 2 dogs may be allowed.

Holiday Inn Toronto-Mississauga
2125 N Sheridan Way
Mississauga, ON
905-855-2000 (877-270-6405)
Dogs of all sizes are allowed. Dogs are allowed for a pet fee.

Motel 6 - Toronto Mississauga
2935 Argentia Rd
Mississauga, ON
905-814-1664 (800-466-8356)
Your pets are welcome to stay here with you.

Residence Inn Mississauga-Airport Corporate Centre West
5070 Creekbank Rd
Mississauga, ON
905-602-7777 (800-331-3131)
Besides offering a convenient location to business, shopping, dining, and entertainment areas, this hotel also offers a number of in-house amenities, including a daily buffet breakfast, and evening socials Monday to Wednesday with light dinner fare. Dogs are allowed for an additional one time pet fee of $100 per room. 2 dogs may be allowed.

Residence Inn Toronto Mississauga/Meadowvale
7005 Century Avenue
Mississauga, ON
905-567-2577 (800-331-3131)
Besides offering a convenient location to a number of activities and attractions for all level of travelers, this all suite hotel also offers a number of in-house amenities, including a daily buffet breakfast and evening socials Monday to Thursday with light dinner fare. Dogs are allowed for an additional one time pet fee of $100 per room. Multiple dogs may be allowed.

Staybridge Suites Toronto Mississauga
6791 Hurontario St.
Mississauga, ON
905-564-6892 (877-270-6405)
Dogs up to 80 pounds are allowed. Pets allowed with an additional pet fee. Up to $75 for 1-6 nights and up to $150 for 7+ nights. A pet agreement must be signed at check-in.

Studio 6 - Toronto Mississauga

60 Britannia Rd East
Mississauga, ON
905-502-8897 (800-466-8356)
Your pets are welcome to stay here with you for a pet fee of $10 per day up to $50 for an entire stay.

Days Inn - Ottawa West
350 Moodie Drive
Nepean, ON
613-726-1717 (800-329-7466)
Dogs of all sizes are allowed. Dogs are allowed for a pet fee.

Econo Lodge
998006 Hwy 11
New Liskeard, ON
705-647-6705 (877-424-6423)
Dogs of all sizes are allowed.

Quality Inn
998009 Hwy. 11
New Liskeard, ON
705-647-7357 (877-424-6423)
Dogs of all sizes are allowed.

Comfort Inn
1230 Journey's End Cir.
Newmarket, ON
905-895-3355 (877-424-6423)
Dogs of all sizes are allowed.

Best Western Fallsview
6289 Fallsview Boulevard
Niagara Falls, ON
905-356-0551 (800-780-7234)
Dogs of all sizes are allowed. Dogs are allowed for a nightly pet fee.

Howard Johnson Express Inn - Niagara Falls
8100 Lundys Lane
Niagara Falls, ON
905-358-9777 (800-446-4656)
Dogs of all sizes are allowed. Dogs are allowed for a nightly pet fee.

Howard Johnson Hotel - Niagara Falls
5905 Victoria Ave
Niagara Falls, ON
905-357-4040 (800-446-4656)
Dogs of all sizes are allowed. Dogs are allowed for a nightly pet fee.

Niagara Parkway Court Motel
3708 Main Street
Niagara Falls, ON
905-295-3331
goniagarafalls.com/npcm/
There is a $10 per day additional pet fee. The hotel only has one pet room so make your reservations early. 2 dogs may be allowed.

Super 8 North Of The Falls
4009 River Road

Niagara Falls, ON
905-356-0131 (800-800-8000)
Dogs of all sizes are allowed. Dogs are allowed for a pet fee of $10.00 per pet per night.

Best Western North Bay Hotel & Conference Centre
700 Lakeshore Drive
North Bay, ON
705-474-5800 (800-780-7234)
Dogs are welcome at this hotel.

Clarion Resort Pinewood Park
201 Pinewood Park Drive
North Bay, ON
705-472-0810 (877-424-6423)
Dogs of all sizes are allowed.

Comfort Inn
676 Lakeshore Dr.
North Bay, ON
705-494-9444 (877-424-6423)
Dogs of all sizes are allowed.

Comfort Inn Airport
1200 O'Brien St.
North Bay, ON
705-476-5400 (877-424-6423)
Dogs of all sizes are allowed.

Holiday Inn Express Hotel & Suites North Bay
1325 Seymour Street
North Bay, ON
705-476-7700 (877-270-6405)
Dogs are welcome at this hotel.

Super 8 North Bay
570 Lakeshore Drive
North Bay, ON
705-495-4551 (800-800-8000)
Dogs are welcome at this hotel.

Travelodge Lakeshore North Bay
718 Lakeshore Drive
North Bay, ON
705-472-7171 (800-578-7878)
Dogs of all sizes are allowed. Dogs are allowed for a pet fee.

Travelodge Airport North Bay
1525 Seymour Street
North Bay, ON
705-495-1133 (800-578-7878)
Dogs of all sizes are allowed. Dogs are allowed for a pet fee.

Comfort Inn Toronto North
66 Norfinch Dr.
North York, ON
416-736-4700 (877-424-6423)
Dogs of all sizes are allowed.

Holiday Inn Express Toronto-North York
30 Norfinch Drive

North York, ON
416-665-3500 (877-270-6405)
Dogs of all sizes are allowed. Dogs are allowed for a nightly pet fee.

Novotel - Toronto North York
3 Park Home Avenue
North York, ON
416-733-2929
Novotel Hotels welcome a maximum of 2 animals (cats and dogs) per room and never require a fee. Each guest checking in with a pet will be given a Royal Canine/Novotel Pet Welcome Kit.

Holiday Inn Oakville (Centre)
590 Argus Road
Oakville, ON
905-842-5000 (877-270-6405)
Dogs of all sizes are allowed. Dogs are allowed for a nightly pet fee.

Staybridge Suites Oakville-Burlington
2511 Wyecroft Road
Oakville, ON
905-847-2600 (877-270-6405)
Dogs up to 80 pounds are allowed. Pets allowed with an additional pet fee. Up to $75 for 1-6 nights and up to $150 for 7+ nights. A pet agreement must be signed at check-in.

Econo Lodge
265 Memorial Ave.
Orillia, ON
705-326-3554 (877-424-6423)
Dogs of all sizes are allowed. Dogs are allowed for a pet fee of $7.00 per pet per night. Two dogs are allowed per room.

Knights Inn Orillia
450 West St. South
Orillia, ON
705-325-7846 (800-843-5644)
Dogs of all sizes are allowed. Dogs are allowed for a pet fee of $15.00 per pet per night.

Comfort Inn
605 Bloor St. W.
Oshawa, ON
905-434-5000 (877-424-6423)
Dogs of all sizes are allowed.

Holiday Inn Oshawa Whitby Conf. Centre
1011 Bloor St. East
Oshawa, ON
905-576-5101 (877-270-6405)
Dogs of all sizes are allowed. Dogs are allowed for a nightly pet fee.

Travelodge Whitby Oshawa
940 Champlain Avenue

Oshawa, ON
905-436-9500 (800-578-7878)
Dogs of all sizes are allowed. Dogs are allowed for a pet fee.

Best Western Barons Hotel & Conference Centre
3700 Richmond Road
Ottawa, ON
613-828-2741 (800-780-7234)
Dogs of all sizes are allowed. Dogs are allowed for a nightly pet fee.

Bostonian Executive Suites
341 MacLaren Street
Ottawa, ON
613-594-5757 (866-320-4567)
thebostonian.ca/
There are a number of amenities for business and leisure travelers at this inn; plus they are only a short walk to the city's lively downtown area. Dogs are allowed for an additional fee of $50 for a 3 days stay; the fee may be up to $75 for larger or shedding dogs. Dogs may be up to about 75 pounds, and they ask that guests with pets use the stairs. 2 dogs may be allowed.

Cartier Place Suite Hotel
180 Cooper Street
Ottawa, ON
613-236-5000 (800-236-8399)
suitedreams.com/
In addition to being only a short distance from Parliament Hill, the Rideau Canal, and a popular shopping area, this hotel offers a garden patio, an indoor pool area, and a children's playground. Dogs are allowed for an additional fee of $25 per night per pet. Dogs are not allowed in the pool area, and they must be crated when left alone in the room. Multiple dogs may be allowed.

Comfort Inn
1252 Michael St.
Ottawa, ON
613-744-2900 (877-424-6423)
Dogs up to 90 pounds are allowed. Two dogs are allowed per room.

Days Inn - Ottawa
319 Rideau Street
Ottawa, ON
613-789-5555 (800-329-7466)
Dogs are welcome at this hotel.

Delta Ottawa Hotel and Suites
361 Queen Street
Ottawa, ON
613-238-6000
There is an additional $35 pet fee for each 5 days stay per room. 2

dogs may be allowed.

Downtown Bed and Breakfast
263 McLeod Street
Ottawa, ON
613-563-4399
downtownbb.com/
A day spa, vegetarian breakfasts, and close to many sites of interests and activities are some of the amenities of this inn. There are a couple of resident pooches here who likes to greet the canine guests. Dogs are allowed for an additional fee of $20 per night per pet; they must be friendly to hounds and humans. Multiple dogs may be allowed.

Holiday Inn Hotel & Suites Ottawa-Downtown
111 Cooper Street
Ottawa, ON
613-238-1331 (877-270-6405)
Dogs of all sizes are allowed. Dogs are allowed for a pet fee.

Hotel Indigo Ottawa Downtown City Centre
123 Metcalfe Street
Ottawa, ON
613-231-6555 (877-865-6578)
Dogs up to 50 pounds are allowed. Dogs are allowed for a nightly pet fee.

Les Suites Hotel
130 Besserer St
Ottawa, ON
613-232-2000
les-suites.com/english/
There is an additional $35 pet fee for each 5 days stay per room. 2 dogs may be allowed.

Novotel - Ottawa
33 Nicholas Street
Ottawa, ON
613-230-3033
Novotel Hotels welcome a maximum of 2 animals (cats and dogs) per room and never require a fee. Each guest checking in with a pet will be given a Royal Canine/Novotel Pet Welcome Kit.

Ottawa Marriott Hotel
100 Kent Street
Ottawa, ON
613 238 1122 (800 853 8463)
Located in the heart of the city, this luxury hotel sits central to many of the city's star attractions, world class shopping and dining venues, and major business areas, plus they also offer a number of in-house amenities for all level of travelers. Dogs are

allowed for no additional fee; there is a pet policy to sign at check in. A contact number must be left with the front desk when there is a pet alone in the room. 2 dogs may be allowed.

Quality Hotel Downtown
290 Rideau St.
Ottawa, ON
613-789-7511 (877-424-6423)
Dogs of all sizes are allowed.

Residence Inn Ottawa Downtown
161 Laurier Avenue West
Ottawa, ON
613-231-2020 (877 478 4838)
This upscale, all suite inn sits in the heart of downtown and only steps away from a myriad of activities, eateries, sites of interest, and services. They also offer a number of in-house amenities, including a daily buffet breakfast and evening socials a couple of nights a week. Dogs are allowed for an additional one time pet fee of $85 per room. 2 dogs may be allowed.

Sheraton Ottawa Hotel
150 Albert Street/H 42
Ottawa, ON
613-238-1500 (888-625-5144)
This hotel is central to numerous other activities and attractions, including the world's longest skating rink, a very busy Festival Plaza, and many recreational opportunities. Dogs of all sizes are allowed for no additional fee on the 3rd floor, and there is a pet waiver to sign at check in. Dogs must be well behaved, leashed, and cleaned up after at all times. 2 dogs may be allowed.

Southway Inn
2431 Bank Street
Ottawa, ON
613-737-0811
southway.com/
There is a $30 per night per pet additional fee. Multiple dogs may be allowed.

The Westin Ottawa
11 Colonel By Drive
Ottawa, ON
613-560-7000 (888-625-5144)
At the heart of city, this hotel has much to offer the business or leisure traveler. Dogs up to 80 pounds are allowed for no additional fee, and a Heavenly dog bed can be ready for your pooch if requested at the time of reservations. There is a pet waiver to sign at check in. Dogs may not be left alone in the room, and they must be well mannered, leashed, and cleaned up after at all times. 2 dogs

may be allowed.

Travelodge East Ottawa
1486 Innes Road
Ottawa, ON
613-745-1133 (800-578-7878)
Dogs of all sizes are allowed. Dogs are allowed for a pet fee.

Comfort Inn
955 9th Ave. E.
Owen Sound, ON
519-371-5500 (877-424-6423)
Dogs of all sizes are allowed.

Days Inn and Conf Centre - Owen Sound
950 Sixth St East
Owen Sound, ON
519-376-1551 (800-329-7466)
Dogs are welcome at this hotel.

Comfort Inn
120 Bowes St.
Parry Sound, ON
705-746-6221 (877-424-6423)
Dogs of all sizes are allowed.

Quality Inn & Conference Centre
1 J.R. Drive R.R. #2
Parry Sound, ON
705-378-2461 (877-424-6423)
Dogs of all sizes are allowed. Dogs are allowed for a pet fee of $10.00 per pet per night.

Comfort Inn
959 Pembroke St. E.
Pembroke, ON
613-735-1057 (877-424-6423)
Dogs of all sizes are allowed.

Comfort Hotel & Suites
1209 Lansdowne St. West
Peterborough, ON
705-740-7000 (877-424-6423)
Dogs of all sizes are allowed. Two dogs are allowed per room.

King Bethune Guest House and Spa
270 King Street
Peterborough, ON
705-743-4101 (800-574-3664)
kingbethunehouse.com
Full breakfast included. Located in the the Kawartha Lakes Cottage country. There is a $10 charge per night for pets. Pets may not be left in the rooms.

Motel 6 - Peterborough
133 Lansdowne Street
Peterborough, ON
705-748-0550 (800-466-8356)
This motel welcomes your pets to stay with you.

Quality Inn
1074 Lansdowne St.
Peterborough, ON
705-748-6801 (877-424-6423)
Dogs of all sizes are allowed. Two dogs are allowed per room.

Super 8 Peterborough
1257 Lansdowne St. W.
Peterborough, ON
705-876-8898 (800-800-8000)
Dogs of all sizes are allowed. Dogs are allowed for a pet fee.

Comfort Inn
533 Kingston Rd.
Pickering, ON
905-831-6200 (877-424-6423)
Dogs of all sizes are allowed.

Comfort Inn
Route 2211 County Road 28
Port Hope, ON
905-885-7000 (877-424-6423)
Dogs of all sizes are allowed.

Best Western Renfrew Inn & Conference Centre
760 Gibbons Road
Renfrew, ON
613-432-8109 (800-780-7234)
Dogs are welcome at this hotel. There is a $15 per night pet fee.

Holiday Inn Express Hotel & Suites Toronto - Markham
10 East Pearce Street
Richmond Hill, ON
905-695-5990 (877-270-6405)
Dogs of all sizes are allowed. Dogs are allowed for a nightly pet fee.

Sheraton Parkway Toronto North Hotel and Suites
600 H 7 E
Richmond Hill, ON
905-881-2121 (888-625-5144)
In addition to being central to many outside attractions and activities, this hotel also offers onsite social programs. One dog is allowed per room for no additional fee; there is a pet waiver to sign at check in. Pet friendly rooms are limited. Dogs must be well behaved, leashed, and cleaned up after at all times.

Travelodge Richmond Hill
10711 Yonge Street
Richmond Hill, ON
905-884-1007 (800-578-7878)
Dogs of all sizes are allowed. Dogs are allowed for a pet fee of $10 per pet per night.

Howard Johnson Ridgetown

21198 Victoria Road
Ridgetown, ON
519-674-5454 (800-446-4656)
Dogs of all sizes are allowed. Dogs
are allowed for a pet fee.

Super 8 ON Sarnia
420 N Christina St
Sarnia, ON
519-337-3767 (800-800-8000)
Dogs of all sizes are allowed. Dogs
are allowed for a pet fee.

Super 8 On Sault Ste Marie
184 Great Northern Rd
Sault Ste Marie, ON
705-254-6441 (800-800-8000)
Dogs of all sizes are allowed. Dogs
are allowed for a pet fee.

Comfort Inn
333 Great Northern Rd.
Sault Ste. Marie, ON
705-759-8000 (877-424-6423)
Dogs up to 75 pounds are allowed.
Dogs are allowed for a pet fee of
$10.00 per pet per night. Two dogs
are allowed per room.

Sleep Inn
727 Bay St.
Sault Ste. Marie, ON
705-253-7533 (877-424-6423)
Dogs of all sizes are allowed.

Howard Johnson Scarborough
4694 Kingston Rd
Scarborough, ON
416-913-7184 (800-446-4656)
Dogs are welcome at this hotel.
There is a $40 one time pet fee.

Comfort Inn
85 The Queensway E.
Simcoe, ON
519-426-2611 (877-424-6423)
Dogs of all sizes are allowed. Two
dogs are allowed per room.

Comfort Inn
2 Dunlop Dr.
St Catharines, ON
905-687-8890 (877-424-6423)
Dogs of all sizes are allowed.

Days Inn Niagara St Catharines
89 Meadowvale Dr
St Catharines, ON
905-934-5400 (800-329-7466)
Dogs of all sizes are allowed. Dogs
are allowed for a nightly pet fee.

Holiday Inn St. Catharines-Niagara
2 North Service Rd
St Catharines, ON
866-934-8004 (877-270-6405)
Dogs of all sizes are allowed. Dogs

are allowed for a nightly pet fee.

Quality Hotel Parkway Convention
Centre
327 Ontario St.
St Catharines, ON
905-688-2324 (877-424-6423)
Dogs of all sizes are allowed.

St. Catharines Travelodge
420 Ontario Street
St Catharines, ON
905-688-1646 (800-578-7878)
Dogs of all sizes are allowed. Dogs
are allowed for a pet fee of $10 per
pet per night.

Comfort Inn
100 Centennial Ave.
St Thomas, ON
519-633-4082 (877-424-6423)
Dogs up to 50 pounds are allowed.
Dogs are allowed for a pet fee of
$20.00 per pet per stay. Two dogs
are allowed per room.

Comfort Inn
11 Front Street
Sturgeon Falls, ON
877-753-5665 (877-424-6423)
Newly built 2005 three story
property. Downtown Sturgeon Falls
within walking distance.

Best Western Downtown Sudbury
Centreville
151 Larch Street
Sudbury, ON
705-673-7801 (800-780-7234)
Dogs of all sizes are allowed. Dogs
are allowed for a nightly pet fee.

Comfort Inn
2171 Regent St. S.
Sudbury, ON
705-522-1101 (877-424-6423)
Dogs of all sizes are allowed.

Comfort Inn East
440 2nd Ave. N.
Sudbury, ON
705-560-4502 (877-424-6423)
Dogs up to 50 pounds are allowed.
Dogs are allowed for a pet fee of
$15 per pet per night. Two dogs are
allowed per room.

Days Inn - Sudbury
117 Elm Street
Sudbury, ON
705-674-7517 (800-329-7466)
Dogs are welcome at this hotel.

Knights Inn
1145 Lorne St.
Sudbury, ON
705-674-4203 (800-843-5644)

Dogs are welcome at this hotel.

Quality Inn & Conference Centre
Downtown
390 Elgin Street South
Sudbury, ON
705-675-1273 (877-424-6423)
Dogs of all sizes are allowed.

Super 8 ON Sudbury
1956 Regent Street
Sudbury, ON
(800-800-8000)
Dogs are welcome at this hotel.

Travelodge Hotel Sudbury
1401 Paris Street
Sudbury, ON
705-522-1100 (800-578-7878)
Dogs of all sizes are allowed. Dogs
are allowed for a pet fee.

Kicking Mule Ranch
Gauthier Road
Tehkummah, ON
705-859-1234
There are a number of
accommodation options at this
vacation ranch and wide variety of
fun activities including wagon, trail,
and breakfast rides and jamborees
with a concession stand on site.
Dogs are allowed for an additional
fee of $5 per night per pet with
advance reservations. Dogs must be
kept leashed and cleaned up after.
They are not allowed near the horses
and mules when they are being
loaded or on the rides. 2 dogs may
be allowed.

Four Points by Sheraton St.
Catharines Niagara Suites
3530 Schmon Parkway
Thorold, ON
905-984-8484 (888-625-5144)
Located only minutes from Niagara
Falls and all the unique recreational
opportunities the area has to offer,
this hotel is also close to several
major corporate headquarters. Dogs
of all sizes are allowed an additional
fee of $10 per night per pet in the
standard rooms on the 1st or 2nd
floor. Dogs must be quiet, leashed,
cleaned up after, and crated when
left alone in the room. 2 dogs may be
allowed.

Comfort Inn
660 W. Arthur St.
Thunder Bay, ON
807-475-3155 (877-424-6423)
Dogs of all sizes are allowed. Three
or more dogs may be allowed.

Super 8 Thunder Bay

439 Memorial Ave
Thunder Bay, ON
807-344-2612 (800-800-8000)
Dogs are welcome at this hotel.

The Valhalla Inn
1 Valhalla Inn Road
Thunder Bay, ON
807-577-1121 (800-964-1121)
In addition a beautiful lush setting, this Scandinavian-inspired inn offers a variety of year around recreation, a number of in-house amenities, fine dining, and a venue for special events. Well mannered dogs are allowed in the main floor rooms for an additional fee of $20 per night per room. Dogs must be leashed and cleaned up after promptly. Multiple dogs may be allowed.

Travelodge ON Thunder Bay
450 Memorial Avenue
Thunder Bay, ON
807-345-2343 (800-578-7878)
Dogs are welcome at this hotel.

Howard Johnson CN Tillsonburg
92 Simcoe St
Tillsonburg, ON
 (800-446-4656)
Dogs are welcome at this hotel.

Comfort Inn
939 Algonquin Blvd. E.
Timmins, ON
705-264-9474 (877-424-6423)
Dogs of all sizes are allowed.

Days Inn & Conference Centre - Timmins
14 Mountjoy Street. South
Timmins, ON
705-267-6211 (800-329-7466)
Dogs are welcome at this hotel.

Howard Johnson Inn Timmins
1800 Riverside Drive
Timmins, ON
705-267-6241 (800-446-4656)
Dogs are welcome at this hotel.

Super 8 ON Timmins
730 Algonquin Blvd East
Timmins, ON
705-268-7171 (800-800-8000)
Dogs are welcome at this hotel.

Travelodge Timmins
1136 Riverside Drive
Timmins, ON
705-360-1122 (800-578-7878)
Dogs are welcome at this hotel.

Beaches Bed and Breakfast Inn
174 Waverley Road
Toronto, ON

416-699-0818
members.tripod.com/beachesbb/
This B&B, located in The Beaches neighborhood, is just 1.5 blocks from the beach. Pets and children are welcome at this bed and breakfast. Most of the rooms offer private bathrooms. The owner has cats on the premises. 2 dogs may be allowed.

Delta Toronto Airport Hotel
801 Dixon Rd West
Toronto, ON
416-675-6100
There are no additional pet fees. There can be 1 large or 2 small to medium dogs per room. Canine companions will receive a pet amenity kit with food/water bowls, a doggy bed, and treats when greeted at the front desk. 2 dogs may be allowed.

Fairmont Royal York
100 Front Street
Toronto, ON
416-368-2511 (800-257-7544)
fairmont.com/royalyork/
Located in Canada's largest city metropolis, this grand hotel is a great location to explore the numerous activities and attractions of the area. Dogs are allowed for an additional fee of $25 per night per pet. Dogs may not be left alone in the room at any time, and they must be leashed and cleaned up after.

Four Seasons Hotel Toronto
21 Avenue Road
Toronto, ON
416-964-0411
Dogs of all sizes are allowed for no additional pet fee. Dogs may not be left alone in the room; pet sitting services are available.

Holiday Inn Express Toronto-Downtown
111 Lombard Street
Toronto, ON
416-367-5555 (877-270-6405)
Dogs of all sizes are allowed. Dogs are allowed for a pet fee.

Hotel Indigo Toronto Airport
135 Carlingview Drive
Toronto, ON
416-637-7000 (877-865-6578)
Dogs of all sizes are allowed. Dogs are allowed for a nightly pet fee.

Marriott Toronto Airport Hotel
901 Dixon Road
Toronto, ON
416-674-9400 (800-905-2811)

Only a few minutes to an international airport and downtown Toronto, this luxury hotel provides a great location to a number of sites of interest for both business and leisure travelers; plus they also offer numerous on-site amenities to ensure a comfortable stay. Dogs are allowed for an additional one time fee of $30 per room. 2 dogs may be allowed.

Marriott Toronto Bloor Yorkville Hotel
90 Bloor Street E
Toronto, ON
416 961 8000 (800 859 7180)
Located in the heart of downtown, his luxury hotel sits central to many of the city's star attractions, world class shopping and dining venues, entertainment areas, and major business areas, plus they also offer a number of in-house amenities for all level of travelers. Dogs are allowed for an additional one time fee of $50 per room. 2 dogs may be allowed.

Novotel - Toronto Center
45 The Esplanade
Toronto, ON
416-367-8900
Novotel Hotels welcome a maximum of 2 animals (cats and dogs) per room and never require a fee. Each guest checking in with a pet will be given a Royal Canine/Novotel Pet Welcome Kit.

Novotel - Toronto Mississauga
3670 Hurontario Street
Toronto, ON
905-896-1000
Novotel Hotels welcome a maximum of 2 animals (cats and dogs) per room and never require a fee. Each guest checking in with a pet will be given a Royal Canine/Novotel Pet Welcome Kit.

Quality Hotel & Suites Airport East
2180 Islington Ave.
Toronto, ON
416-240-9090 (877-424-6423)
Dogs up to 50 pounds are allowed. Dogs are allowed for a pet fee of $15.00 per pet per night.

Quality Suites Toronto Airport
262 Carlingview Dr.
Toronto, ON
416-674-8442 (877-424-6423)
Dogs of all sizes are allowed. Two dogs are allowed per room.

Renaissance Toronto Hotel
Downtown
One Blue Jays Way

Toronto, ON
416-341-7100 (800-237-1512)
Located in the city's famed Entertainment District and only a short distance to the country's Financial District, this luxury hotel provides a great location to a number of sites of interest for both business and leisure travelers; plus they also offer numerous on-site amenities to ensure a comfortable stay. Dogs up to 50 pounds are allowed for an additional fee of $50 per night per room. 2 dogs may be allowed.

Residence Inn Toronto Airport
17 Reading Court
Toronto, ON
416-798-2900 (888 798 2977)
Some of the amenities at this all-suite inn include a daily buffet breakfast, evening socials weeknights, a complimentary dinner on Wednesdays, a heated swimming pool, and a complimentary grocery shopping service. Dogs are allowed for an additional one time pet fee of $100 per room. 2 dogs may be allowed.

Residence Inn Toronto Downtown/Entertainment District
255 Wellington Street W
Toronto, ON
416-581-1800 (800 960 6752)
In addition to offering a convenient location to business, shopping, dining, nightlife, and entertainment areas, this hotel also provides a number of in-house amenities, including a daily buffet breakfast and evening social hours with light fare. Dogs are allowed for an additional one time pet fee of $100 per room. 2 dogs may be allowed.

Sheraton Centre Toronto Hotel
123 Queen Street W
Toronto, ON
416-361-1000 (888-625-5144)
The centerpiece of this hotel is the 2½ acres of gardens and terraces complete with waterfalls. Dogs up to 80 pounds are allowed for no additional fee, and they are greeted with a Pet Welcome kit and a Sweet Sleeper doggy bed. There is a pet policy to sign at check in. Dogs may not be left alone in the room, and they must be leashed and cleaned up after at all times. 2 dogs may be allowed.

Sheraton Gateway Hotel in Toronto International Airport
Terminal 3, Toronto AMF
Toronto, ON
905-672-7000 (888-625-5144)

This is the only hotel located in the airport and there is a climate controlled skywalk connecting the hotel and Terminal 3. Dogs of all sizes are allowed for no additional fee. Dogs may only be left for a short time, and they request that the front desk be informed when they are alone in the room. Dogs must be well behaved, leashed, and cleaned up after. 2 dogs may be allowed.

Super 8 Downtown Toronto
222 Spadina Ave.
Toronto, ON
647-426-8118 (800-800-8000)
Dogs are welcome at this hotel.

The Westin Bristol Place Toronto Airport
950 Dixon Road
Toronto, ON
819-778-6111 (888-625-5144)
Offering comfort and a central, convenient location makes this an attractive destination for the business or leisure traveler. Dogs up to 80 pounds are allowed for no additional fee, and there is a pet waiver to sign at check in. A pet care amenity package is available when noted at the time of reservations. Dogs may not be left alone in the room, and they must be leashed and cleaned up after. Dogs may not be in food or beverage areas. 2 dogs may be allowed.

Travelodge Hotel Airport/Dixon Road Toronto
925 Dixon Road
Toronto, ON
416-674-2222 (800-578-7878)
Dogs of all sizes are allowed. Dogs are allowed for a pet fee.

Travelodge Toronto East
20 Milner Business Court
Toronto East/Scarborough, ON
416-299-9500 (800-578-7878)
Dogs are welcome at this hotel.

Toronto North/North York Travelodge
50 Norfinch Drive
Toronto/North York, ON
416-663-9500 (800-578-7878)
Dogs of all sizes are allowed. Dogs are allowed for a pet fee.

Comfort Inn
68 Monogram Pl.
Trenton, ON
613-965-6660 (877-424-6423)
Dogs of all sizes are allowed.

Holiday Inn Trenton
99 Glen Miller Road
Trenton, ON
613-394-4855 (877-270-6405)
Dogs of all sizes are allowed. Dogs are allowed for a nightly pet fee.

Travelodge Trenton
598 Old Hwy 2
Trenton, ON
613-965-6789 (800-578-7878)
Dogs are welcome at this hotel.

Holiday Inn Express Hotel & Suites Vaughan-Southwest
6100 Hwy 7
Vaughan, ON
019-058-5115 (877-270-6405)
Dogs of all sizes are allowed. Dogs are allowed for a pet fee.

Residence Inn Toronto Vaughan
11 Interchange Way
Vaughan, ON
905-695-4002 (866-630-0708)
In addition to offering a convenient location to numerous activities and attractions for all level of travelers, this all suite hotel also offers a number of in-house amenities, including a daily buffet breakfast and complimentary evening socials Monday to Wednesday. Dogs are allowed for an additional one time pet fee of $100 per room. 2 dogs may be allowed.

Days Inn Wallaceburg
76 McNaughton Ave
Wallaceburg, ON
519-627-0781 (800-329-7466)
Dogs are welcome at this hotel.

Comfort Inn
190 Weber St. N.
Waterloo, ON
519-747-9400 (877-424-6423)
Dogs of all sizes are allowed.

Comfort Inn
870 Niagara St.
Welland, ON
905-732-4811 (877-424-6423)
Dogs of all sizes are allowed. Dogs are allowed for a pet fee of $10.00 per pet per night.

Days Inn - Welland
1030 Niagara Street
Welland, ON
905-735-6666 (800-329-7466)
Dogs are welcome at this hotel.

Massey Motel
295 Sable Street
West Massey, ON
705-865-2500

Groomed dogs up to 50 pounds are allowed for no additional fee. Dogs must be quiet and they are not allowed on the bed. Heavy shedders are not allowed. 2 dogs may be allowed.

Motel 6 - Toronto East Whitby
165 Consumers Dr
Whitby, ON
905-665-8883 (800-466-8356)
This motel welcomes your pets to stay with you.

Quality Suites
1700 Champlain Ave.
Whitby, ON
905-432-8800 (877-424-6423)
Dogs of all sizes are allowed.

Residence Inn Whitby
160 Consumers Drive
Whitby, ON
905-444-9756 (866 277 9165)
Some of the amenities at this all-suite inn include a daily buffet breakfast, evening socials Monday through Thursday with light dinner fare, an indoor pool, and a complimentary grocery shopping service. Dogs are allowed for an additional one time pet fee of $75 (Canadian) per room. 2 dogs may be allowed.

Comfort Inn
2955 Dougall Ave.
Windsor, ON
519-966-7800 (877-424-6423)
Dogs of all sizes are allowed.

Comfort Inn Ambassador Bridge
2765 Huron Church Rd.
Windsor, ON
519-972-1331 (877-424-6423)
Dogs up to 75 pounds are allowed. Two dogs are allowed per room.

Comfort Suites Downtown
500 Tuscarora Rd. East
Windsor, ON
519-971-0505 (877-424-6423)
Dogs up to 50 pounds are allowed.

Hilton Hotel
277 Riverside Drive W
Windsor, ON
519-973-5555 (800-HILTONS (445-8667))
This upscale waterfront hotel offers numerous on site amenities for business and leisure travelers - including formal gardens and an extensive fitness trail, plus they are convenient to business, shopping, dining, historical, and entertainment areas. Dogs are allowed for an

additional one time fee of $50 per pet, and there is a pet amenity kit available for pooches with a bed, bowls, and more. 2 dogs may be allowed.

Holiday Inn Windsor Downtown
430 Ouellette Ave.
Windsor, ON
519-256-4656 (877-270-6405)
Dogs of all sizes are allowed. Dogs are allowed for a pet fee.

Quality Suites Downtown
250 Dougall Ave.
Windsor, ON
519-977-9707 (877-424-6423)
Dogs of all sizes are allowed.

Travelodge Ambassador Bridge Windsor
2330 Huron Church Road
Windsor, ON
519-972-1100 (800-578-7878)
Dogs are welcome at this hotel.

Travelodge Hotel Downtown Windsor
33 Riverside Drive East
Windsor, ON
519-258-7774 (800-578-7878)
Dogs are welcome at this hotel.

Quality Hotel & Suites
580 Bruin Blvd.
Woodstock, ON
519-537-5586 (877-424-6423)
Dogs of all sizes are allowed.

Super 8 Woodstock
560 Norwich Avenue
Woodstock, ON
519-421-4588 (800-800-8000)
Dogs are welcome at this hotel.

Prince Edward Island

Caernarvon Cottages and Gardens
4697 H 12
Bayside, PE
902-854-3418 (800-514-9170)
Award winning gardens, grassy fields, shade trees, a labyrinth, and a playground are just some of the amenities at this 5 acre get-away. They are also only a short walk to the beach. Dogs are allowed for no additional fee; they must be leashed and under their owner's control. Dogs must be hound and human friendly. 2 dogs may be allowed.

Shaw's Hotel
99 Apple Tree Road

Brackley Beach, PE
902-672-2022
shawshotel.ca
Located in a pastoral setting along the longest dune system in the western hemisphere, this seaside hotel offers a variety of accommodations, an extensive wine cellar, and a restaurant specializing in French country cuisine. Dogs are allowed in the cottages for an additional fee of $10 per night per pet; they are not allowed in the hotel. Dogs must be leashed when out of the cottages. Multiple dogs may be allowed.

Comfort Inn
112 Capital Drive
Charlottetown, PE
902-566-4424 (877-424-6423)
Dogs of all sizes are allowed.

Delta Prince Edward
18 Queen Street
Charlottetown, PE
902-566-2222 (866-894-1203)
In addition to having a large indoor pool, hot tub, and a kids pool, this stylish hotel also features a fine dining restaurant and a lounge. Dogs up to 50 pounds are allowed for an additional fee of $35 for each 5 days stay and a credit card must be on file. They must be declared at the time of reservations. Dogs must be leashed and cleaned up after at all times. If it is necessary to leave your pet in the room for a short time, inform the front desk and leave a contact number. Dogs are not allowed in food service areas, the pool, health club, lounge, or any of the meeting rooms, and they must be removed for housekeeping. 2 dogs may be allowed.

Econo Lodge
20 Lower Malpeque Road
Charlottetown, PE
902-368-1110 (877-424-6423)
Dogs of all sizes are allowed.

Holiday Inn Express Hotel & Suites Charlottetown
200 Capital Drive
Charlottetown, PE
902-892-1201 (877-270-6405)
Dogs are welcome at this hotel.

Howard Johnson Hotel Charlottetown
100 Trans Canada Highway
Charlottetown, PE
902-566-2211 (800-446-4656)
Dogs are welcome at this hotel.

Quality Inn on the Hill

150 Euston St.
Charlottetown, PE
902-894-8572 (877-424-6423)
Dogs of all sizes are allowed.

Super 8 PE Charlottetown
15 York Point Road
Charlottetown, PE
902-892-7900 (800-800-8000)
Dogs are welcome at this hotel.

Clarion Collection Cavendish
Gateway Resort
6596 Route 13
Mayfield, PE
902-963-2213 (877-424-6423)
Dogs of all sizes are allowed.

Quality Inn & Suites Garden of the
Gulf
618 Water St. E.
Summerside, PE
902-436-2295 (877-424-6423)
Dogs up to 50 pounds are allowed.

Doctor's Inn
32 Allen Road
Tyne Valley, PE
902-831-3057
peisland.com/doctorsinn/
Once the home of the local doctor,
this lovely home is a great example
of a traditional 1860 country home,
and there is also a certified 2 acre
organic market garden with 50
varieties of vegetables, herbs, fruits,
and flowers. Meals include fresh
from the garden salads, baked
breads/desserts, and fresh
seafood/meats-all cooked on an old-
fashioned wood stove. Dogs up to 60
pounds are allowed for no additional
fee. 2 dogs may be allowed.

Quebec

Comfort Inn
870 av du Pont Sud
Alma, PQ
418-668-9221 (877-424-6423)
Dogs of all sizes are allowed.

Comfort Inn Airport East
1255 boul. Duplessis
Ancienne Lorette, PQ
418-872-5900 (877-424-6423)
Dogs up to 50 pounds are allowed.

Quality Hotel Olympic Parc
8100 av Neuville
Anjou, PQ
514-493-6363 (877-424-6423)
Dogs up to 50 pounds are allowed.

Comfort Inn
745 Boulevard Lafleche

Baie-Comeau, PQ
418-589-8252 (877-424-6423)
Dogs up to 50 pounds are allowed.

Hotel Baie-Saint-Paul
911 boul Mgr Laval
Baie-St-Paul, PQ
418-435-3683
There is an additional fee of $10 per
night per pet. Multiple dogs may be
allowed.

Comfort Inn East
240 boul. Sainte-Anne
Beauport, PQ
418-666-1226 (877-424-6423)
Dogs up to 50 pounds are allowed.

Days Inn - Berthierville
760, Rue Gadoury
Berthierville, PQ
450-836-1621 (800-329-7466)
Dogs of all sizes are allowed. Dogs
are allowed for a nightly pet fee.

Ramada Conference Center /North
Montreal Blainville
1136 Boul Cure Labelle
Blainville, PQ
450-430-8950 (800-272-6232)
Dogs of all sizes are allowed. Dogs
are allowed for a pet fee.

Comfort Inn South
7863 boul. Taschereau
Brossard, PQ
450-678-9350 (877-424-6423)
Dogs up to 50 pounds are allowed.

Comfort Inn Aeroport
340 av Michel Jasmin
Dorval, PQ
514-636-3391 (877-424-6423)
Dogs of all sizes are allowed. Dogs
are allowed for a pet fee of $25.00
per pet per night.

Rodeway Inn Airport
580 Michel Jasmin
Dorval, PQ
514-828-5080 (877-424-6423)
Dogs of all sizes are allowed.

Comfort Inn
1055 rue Hains
Drummondville, PQ
819-477-4000 (877-424-6423)
Located in the heart of Quebec
Province. Only an hour and 15
minutes from Montreal and Quebec
City.

Comfort Inn
630 boul. la Gappe
Gatineau, PQ
819-243-6010 (877-424-6423)
Dogs of all sizes are allowed.

Four Points by Sheraton &
Conference Centre Gatineau-Ottawa
35 Rue Laurier
Gatineau, PQ
819-778-6111 (888-625-5144)
This hotel sits central to numerous
activities and recreational pursuits.
Dogs of all sizes are allowed for no
additional fee, and there is a pet
waiver to sign at check in. Dogs are
not allowed in public areas, and they
must be leashed, cleaned up after,
and crated when left alone in the
room. 2 dogs may be allowed.

Holiday Inn Gatineau-Ottawa Plz
Chaudiere
2 Montcalm Street
Gatineau, PQ
819-778-3880 (877-270-6405)
Dogs up to 100 pounds are allowed.

Hotel du Lac Carling
2255 Route #327 Nord
Grenville-sur-la-Rouge, PQ
450-533-9211 (800-661-9211)
laccarling.com
Dogs of all sizes are allowed. There
is a $25 pet fee per stay. Dogs must
be left in a crate if you are out of the
room. Up to 2 dogs are allowed per
room.

Fairmont Le Manoir Richelieu
181 rue Richelieu
La Malbaie, PQ
418-665-3703 (800-257-7544)
fairmont.com/richelieu/
This world class resort, stately
nestled amid the sea and mountains,
offers every amenity for the business
or leisure traveler and a variety of
recreational opportunities. Dogs are
allowed for an additional fee of $25
per night per pet. Dogs may not be
left alone in the room at any time,
and they must be leashed and
cleaned up after.

Mont-Tremblant Cottage Rental
Call to Arrange
Labelle, PQ
514-923-5787
One dog of any size is allowed. The
dog must be house-trained and well-
behaved. There are no additional pet
fees.

Comfort Inn
2055 Auto. des Laurentides
Laval, PQ
450-686-0600 (877-424-6423)
Dogs of all sizes are allowed.

Econo Lodge
1981 Boulevard Cure Labelle

Laval, PQ
450-681-6411 (877-424-6423)
Dogs of all sizes are allowed.

Quality Suites
2035 Auto. des Laurentides
Laval, PQ
450-686-6777 (877-424-6423)
Dogs of all sizes are allowed.

La Paysanne Motel
42 rue Queen
Lennoxville, PQ
819-569-5585
connect-quebec.com/la_paysanne/
There are no additional pet fees. 2
dogs may be allowed.

Comfort Inn
10 Du Vallon E.
Levis, PQ
418-835-5605 (877-424-6423)
Dogs up to 50 pounds are allowed.

Gite du Carrefour
11 ave St-Laurent ouest
Louiseville, PQ
819-228-4932
There are no additional pet fees.

Quality Inn
111 Bl. Paquette
Mont Laurier, PQ
819-623-3555 (877-424-6423)
Dogs of all sizes are allowed. Dogs
are allowed for a pet fee of $10.00
per pet per night. Two dogs are
allowed per room.

Le Grand Lodge Mont-Tremblant
2396 rue Labelle
Mont-Tremblant, PQ
819-425-2734 (800 567-6763)
legrandlodge.com/indexEng.html
This luxury hotel is located 5 minutes
from teh Tremblant ski resort. Dogs
up to 40 pounds are allowed. There
is a $25 per night additional pet fee.
Dogs may not be left alone in the
rooms and there are a limited
number of pet rooms.

Fairmont Le Chateau Montebello
392 Notre Dame/H148
Montebello, PQ
819-423-6341 (800-257-7574)
fairmont.com/montebello/
This red cedar log chateau offers
scenic surroundings and year-around
recreational opportunities. Dogs are
allowed for an additional $35 per
night per pet. Dogs are allowed in
the rooms only and not in other parts
of the resort. Dogs must be leashed,
cleaned up after, and crated when
left alone in the room.

Auberge du vieux-port
97 rue de la Commune Est
Montreal, PQ
514-876-0081
aubergeduvieuxport.com
The Auberge du vieux-port is
located across from the Old Port of
Montreal in Old Montreal. Dogs of
all sizes are allowed. There is a $7
per pet per night fee for small
dogs and a $14 per pet per night
pet fee for larger dogs. You need to
leave a cell phone number if you
are leaving a dog alone in the room.
One dog is allowed in the rooms but
up to two dogs may be allowed in
the studio lofts. 2 dogs may be
allowed.

Candlewood Suites Montreal
Downtown Centre Ville
191 Rene Levesque Blvd Est / East
Montreal, PQ
514-667-5002 (877-270-6405)
Dogs up to 80 pounds are allowed.
Pets allowed with an additional pet
fee. Up to $75 for 1-6 nights and up
to $150 for 7+ nights. A pet
agreement must be signed at
check-in.

Chateau Versailles
1659 Sherbrooke Street West
Montreal, PQ
514-933-8111 (888-933-8111)
This hotel is located in the
downtown area. There is a $17.25
nightly pet fee per pet. Dogs must
be leashed on the premises and
may not be left alone in the room. 2
dogs may be allowed.

Delta Montreal
475 avenue Président-Kennedy
Montreal, PQ
514-286-1986
deltamontreal.com/en/delta.html
One dog is allowed per room for an
additional $35 one time fee.

Four Points by Sheraton Montreal
Centre-Ville
475 Sherbrooke Street West/H 138
Montreal, PQ
514-842-3961 (888-625-5144)
The prime location of this hotel
gives visitors a good starting point
for numerous activities and
recreational opportunities. Dogs of
all sizes are allowed for no
additional fee. Dogs may not be left
alone in the room, and they must be
leashed and cleaned up after at all
times. Multiple dogs may be
allowed.

Hilton Hotel
900 de La Gauchetiere W

Montreal, PQ
514-878-2332 (800-HILTONS (445-
8667))
Located in the heart of the city, this
upscale hotel offers a number of on
site amenities for business and
leisure travelers, plus a convenient
location to business districts, and
numerous shopping, dining, and
recreational areas. Dogs are allowed
for no additional pet fee, but they
must be declared at the time of
reservations. Multiple dogs may be
allowed.

Holiday Inn Express Hotel & Suites
Montreal Centre-Ville Downtown
155 Blvd Rene-Levesque East
Montreal, PQ
514-448-7100 (877-270-6405)
Dogs are welcome at this hotel.

Hotel Godin
10 Sherbrooke Ouest
Montreal, PQ
514-843-6000 (866-744-6346)
hotelgodin.com
This boutique hotel allows dogs of all
sizes. There is a special doggy menu
on the room service menu and they
can provide a doggy bed if
requested. There is a $50 one time
additional pet fee.

Hotel Le Germain
2050, rue Mansfield
Montreal, PQ
514-849-2050 (877-333-2050)
hotelgermain.com
This boutique hotel is located in the
downtown district of the city. Dogs of
all sizes are allowed. There is a $30
per night additional pet fee. Dogs
may only be left in the rooms for very
short times. 2 dogs may be allowed.

Hotel Travelodge Centre Montreal
50 Boul Rene Levesque West
Montreal, PQ
514-874-9090 (800-578-7878)
Dogs are welcome at this hotel.

Le Saint-Sulpice
414 rue St-Sulpice
Montreal, PQ
514-288-1000 (877-SUL-PICE)
lesaintsulpice.com/
This Old Montreal boutique hotel
allows dogs of any size. You need to
declare pets at the time that you
make reservations. There is a $30
one time pet fee. Multiple dogs may
be allowed.

Loews Hotel Vogue
1425 Rue De La Montagne
Montreal, PQ

514-285-5555
All well-behaved dogs of any size are welcome. This upscale hotel offers their "Loews Loves Pets" program which includes special pet treats, local dog walking routes, and a list of nearby pet-friendly places to visit. There is an additional one time pet cleaning fee of $25 per room.

Novotel - Montreal Center
1180 Rue de la Montagne
Montreal, PQ
514-861-6000
Novotel Hotels welcome a maximum of 2 animals (cats and dogs) per room and never require a fee. Each guest checking in with a pet will be given a Royal Canine/Novotel Pet Welcome Kit.

Quality Hotel Dorval Aeroport
7700 Cote de Liesse
Montreal, PQ
514-731-7821 (877-424-6423)
Dogs of all sizes are allowed. Dogs are allowed for a pet fee of $15.00 per pet per night. Three or more dogs may be allowed.

Quality Hotel Downtown
3440 av du Parc
Montreal, PQ
514-849-1413 (877-424-6423)
Dogs up to 50 pounds are allowed. Dogs are allowed for a pet fee of $15.00 per pet per night. Dogs are allowed for a pet fee of $25.00 per pet per stay.

Quality Inn Downtown
1214 Crescent St.
Montreal, PQ
514-878-2711 (877-424-6423)
Dogs of all sizes are allowed.

Residence Inn Montreal Airport
6500 Place Robert-Joncas
Montreal, PQ
514-336-9333 (877-33-9334)
The only true extended stay, all suite inn in the airport district, they are near a number of major corporations and within walking distance to several entertainments; plus they also offer a number of in-house amenities, including a daily buffet breakfast and evening socials. Dogs are allowed for an additional one time pet fee of $100 per room. Multiple dogs may be allowed.

Residence Inn Montreal Downtown
2045 Peel Street
Montreal, PQ
514-982-6064 (800-331-3131)
Located in the heart of downtown,

this all suite inn features a convenient location to business, shopping, dining, and entertainment areas, plus they also offer a number of in-house amenities, including a daily buffet breakfast and evening socials. Dogs are allowed for an additional one time pet fee of $100 per room. Multiple dogs may be allowed.

Ritz-Carlton Montreal
1228 Sherbrooke Street West
Montreal, PQ
514-842-4212 (800-363-0366)
ritzmontreal.com
The Ritz-Carlton is located in the Golden Square Mile area in downtown. Dogs of all sizes are allowed. There is a $150 one time additional pet fee. The Ritz-Carlton also offers in house pet-sitting for $15 per hour. 2 dogs may be allowed.

W Montréal
901 Square Victoria
Montreal, PQ
514-395-3100 (888-625-5144)
Rich in color and ambiance, this hotel is close to many historic areas, attractions, activities, and recreation. Dogs up to 50 pounds are allowed for an additional cleaning fee of $100 plus $25 per night per pet with a credit card on file. Dogs must be declared at the time of registration. Pets receive a special welcome with a pet amenity kit that includes a custom pet bed, food and water dishes with a floor mat, a doggy menu, Pet-in-Room sign, treats, pet tag, a toy, and more. The concierge can also offer additional services such as dog-walking and information about local dog services and parks. Dogs must be removed or crated for housekeeping or for any in-room services. 2 dogs may be allowed.

Hotel Motel Manoir de Perce
212 Route 132
Perce, PQ
418-782-2022
There is a $25 one time additional pet fee per room. 2 dogs may be allowed.

Comfort Inn Montreal Aeroport
700 boul. St. Jean
Pointe Claire, PQ
514-697-6210 (877-424-6423)
Dogs of all sizes are allowed.

Quality Suites Montreal Aeroport
6300 Transcanadienne
Pointe Claire, PQ

514-426-5060 (877-424-6423)
Dogs up to 50 pounds are allowed.

Clarion Hotel
3125 Hochelaga Boulevard
Quebec, PQ
418-653-4901 (877-424-6423)
Dogs of all sizes are allowed.

Delta Quebec Hotel
690 Boul Rene-Levesque E
Quebec, PQ
418-647-1717
The Delta Quebec Hotel is located in the heart of the walled city of Quebec. There is a $35 one time additional pet fee. One large dog is allowed. Two smaller dogs may be allowed. Dogs must be well-behaved and leashed at all times.

Hotel Dominion 1912
126 St Pierre
Quebec, PQ
418-692-2224
hoteldominion.com
Dogs of any size are allowed at this boutique hotel in Quebec City. Many of the rooms have views of Old Quebec or the St Lawrence River. Up to two dogs are allowed. There is a $30 one time additional pet fee per dog. Dogs must be leashed at all times.

L'Hotel du Vieux Quebec
1190 rue St-Jean
Quebec, PQ
418-692-1850
hvq.com/
Dogs are allowed in standard rooms for an additional pet fee of $25 per night to a maximum fee of $100. 2 dogs may be allowed.

Quality Suites
1600 rue Bouvier
Quebec, PQ
418-622-4244 (877-424-6423)
Dogs up to 50 pounds are allowed.

Best Western City Centre/Centre-Ville
330 De La Couronne
Quebec City, PQ
418-649-1919 (800-780-7234)
Dogs up to 50 pounds are allowed. Dogs are allowed for a pet fee of $30 per pet per stay.

Howard Johnson Quebec City
7300 Boul Wilfrid Hamel Ouest
Quebec City, PQ
418-877-2226 (800-446-4656)
Dogs of all sizes are allowed. Dogs are allowed for a nightly pet fee.

Loews Le Concorde Hotel
1225 Cours Du General De
Montcalm
Quebec City, PQ
418-647-2222
All well-behaved dogs of any size are welcome. This upscale hotel offers their "Loews Loves Pets" program which includes room service for pets, special pet treats, local dog walking routes, and a list of nearby pet-friendly places to visit. There is an additional one time pet cleaning fee of $25 per room.

Howard Johnson Inn QU Rigaud
93 Montee Lavigne
Rigaud, PQ
450-458-7779 (800-446-4656)
Dogs of all sizes are allowed. Dogs are allowed for a pet fee of $25.00 per pet per night.

Comfort Inn
455 boul. St-Germain ouest
Rimouski, PQ
418-724-2500 (877-424-6423)
Dogs up to 50 pounds are allowed. Dogs are allowed for a pet fee of $25.00 per pet per stay.

Days Inn - Riviere-Du-Loup
182 rue Fraser
Riviere-du-loup, PQ
418-862-6354 (800-329-7466)
Dogs are welcome at this hotel.

Best Western Albert Centre-Ville
84 Principale Avenue
Rouyn-Noranda, PQ
819-762-3545 (800-780-7234)
Dogs are welcome at this hotel.

Comfort Inn
1295 av Lariviere
Rouyn-Noranda, PQ
819-797-1313 (877-424-6423)
Dogs of all sizes are allowed.

Super 8 St-Jerome
3 J F Kennedy
Saint-Jerome, PQ
450-438-4388 (800-800-8000)
Dogs are welcome at this hotel.

Super 8 Sainte Agathe Des Monts
500 Rue Leonard
Sainte-Agathe-des-Monts, PQ
819-324-8880 (800-800-8000)
Dogs of all sizes are allowed. Dogs are allowed for a nightly pet fee.

Comfort Inn & Suites
500 Boulevard du Capitaine
Shawinigan, PQ
866-400-4087 (877-424-6423)
Dogs of all sizes are allowed.

Holiday Inn Express St. Jean Sur Richelieu
700 Rue Gadbois
St Jean Sur Richelieu, PQ
450-359-4466 (877-270-6405)
Dogs are welcome at this hotel.

Howard Johnson Stastny Plaza Hotel And Golf Resort
537 Route Marie-Victorin
St Nicolas, PQ
418-836-1259 (800-446-4656)
Dogs are welcome at this hotel.

Auberge du Faubourg
280 ave de Gaspe ouest
St-Jean-Port-Joli, PQ
418-598-6455
There are no additional pet fees.

Comfort Inn Airport
7320 boul. Wilfrid-Hamel
Ste. Foy, PQ
418-872-5038 (877-424-6423)
Dogs of all sizes are allowed.

Days Inn - Ste. Helene-de-Bagot
410 rue Couture
Ste. Helene-de-Bagot, PQ
450-791-2580 (800-329-7466)
Dogs are welcome at this hotel.

Super 8 Lachenaie/ Terrebonne
1155 Yves Blais
Terrebonne, PQ
450-582-8288 (800-800-8000)
Dogs are welcome at this hotel.

Comfort Inn
123 Boul Frontenac Ouest
Thetford Mines, PQ
418-338-0171 (877-424-6423)
Dogs of all sizes are allowed. Two dogs are allowed per room.

Comfort Inn
6255 rue Corbeil
Trois-Rivieres, PQ
819-371-3566 (877-424-6423)
Dogs up to 50 pounds are allowed.

Days Inn - Trois-Rivieres
3155 Boulevard Saint Jean
Trois-Rivieres, PQ
819-377-4444 (800-329-7466)
Dogs of all sizes are allowed. Dogs are allowed for a pet fee of 10 per pet per night.

Delta Trois-Rivieres
1620 rue Notre-Dame
Trois-Rivieres, PQ
819-376-1991
There is a $35 additional pet fee for each 5 days stay. 2 dogs may be allowed.

Super 8 Trois-Rivieres
3185 Blvd. Saint-Jean
Trois-Rivieres, PQ
819-377-5881 (800-800-8000)
Dogs are welcome at this hotel.

Super 8 Montreal QC
3200 Boul. de la Gare
Vaudreuil-Montreal, PQ
450-424-8898 (800-800-8000)
Dogs of all sizes are allowed. Dogs are allowed for a pet fee.

Saskatchewan

The Pilgrim Inn
510 College Dr (Hwy 1 W)
Caronport, SK
306-756-5002
There is no additional pet fee. All rooms are non-smoking. Multiple dogs may be allowed.

Motel 6 - Estevan, Sk
88 King St. East
Estevan, SK
306-634-8666 (800-466-8356)
This motel welcomes your pets to stay with you.

Super 8 Kindersley
508 12th Ave East
Kindersley, SK
306-463-8218 (800-800-8000)
Dogs are welcome at this hotel.

Cypress Park Resort Inn
H 21
Maple Creek, SK
306-662-4477
cypressresortinn.com/
Nestled among the woods, this waterside resort offers a variety of accommodations, a large dining room, lounge, an indoor pool/hot tub, barbecues, and picnicking areas. They also host special events and provide a venue for special occasions. Dogs are allowed in the condos and cabins for an additional fee of $10 per night per pet; they are not allowed in the resort or in food service areas. Although dog may not be on the restaurant patio, there are picnic tables close by. Multiple dogs may be allowed.

Super 8 Meadow Lake
702 9th Street West
Meadow Lake, SK
306-236-1188 (800-800-8000)
Dogs of all sizes are allowed. Dogs are allowed for a pet fee of $10.00 per pet per night.

Travelodge Melfort
101 Spruce Haven Rd
Melfort, SK
306-752-5961 (800-578-7878)
Dogs are welcome at this hotel.

Comfort Inn & Suites
155 Thatcher Drive W.
Moose Jaw, SK
306-692-2100 (877-424-6423)
Dogs of all sizes are allowed. Dogs
are allowed for a pet fee of $15.00
per pet per stay.

Days Inn - Moose Jaw
1720 Main Street North
Moose Jaw, SK
306-691-5777 (800-329-7466)
Dogs of all sizes are allowed. Dogs
are allowed for a nightly pet fee.

Super 8 North Battleford
1006 Hwy 16 PO Box 1690
North Battleford, SK
306-446-8888 (800-800-8000)
Dogs of all sizes are allowed. Dogs
are allowed for a pet fee of $25.00
per pet per night.

Comfort Inn
3863 2nd Ave. W.
Prince Albert, SK
306-763-4466 (877-424-6423)
Dogs of all sizes are allowed.

Ramada Prince Albert
3245 2nd Avenue West
Prince Albert, SK
306-922-1333 (800-272-6232)
Dogs of all sizes are allowed. Dogs
are allowed for a pet fee of $10 per
pet per night.

Super 8 Prince Albert
4444 2nd Ave West
Prince Albert, SK
306-953-0088 (800-800-8000)
Dogs of all sizes are allowed. Dogs
are allowed for a pet fee of $10.00
per pet per night.

Travelodge Prince Albert
3551 2nd Avenue West
Prince Albert, SK
306-764-6441 (800-578-7878)
Dogs are welcome at this hotel.

Comfort Inn
3221 E. Eastgate Dr.
Regina, SK
306-789-5522 (877-424-6423)
Dogs of all sizes are allowed. Dogs
are allowed for a pet fee of $15.00
per pet per night.

Delta Regina Hotel
1919 Saskatchewan Drive

Regina, SK
306-525-5255 (888-890-3222)
Located in the heart of the city, this
hotel offers a number of on site
amenities-like an indoor waterpark;
it also provides a convenient
location to all the city has to offer.
Dogs up to 50 pounds are allowed
for an additional fee of $35 for each
5 days stay and a credit card must
be on file. Dogs must be leashed
and cleaned up after at all times. If
it is necessary to leave your pet in
the room for a short time, inform the
front desk and leave a contact
number. Dogs are not allowed in
food service areas, the pool, health
club, lounge, or any of the meeting
rooms, and they must be removed
for housekeeping. 2 dogs may be
allowed.

Holiday Inn Hotel & Suites Regina
1800 Prince Of Wales Drive
Regina, SK
306-789-3883 (877-270-6405)
Dogs of all sizes are allowed. Dogs
are allowed for a nightly pet fee.

Howard Johnson Regina
1110 Victoria Ave East
Regina, SK
306-565-0455 (800-446-4656)
Dogs are welcome at this hotel.
There is a $25 one time pet fee.

Quality Hotel
1717 Victoria Ave
Regina, SK
306-569-4656 (877-424-6423)
Dogs of all sizes are allowed. Dogs
are allowed for a pet fee of $7.95
per pet per stay.

Radisson Plaza Hotel
2125 Victoria Avenue
Regina, SK
306-522-7691
Dogs of all sizes are allowed. There
is a $35 one time additional pet fee.

Super 8 Regina
2730 Victoria Ave E
Regina, SK
306-789-8833 (800-800-8000)
Dogs of all sizes are allowed. Dogs
are allowed for a pet fee of $10.00
per pet per night.

Wingate by Wyndham Regina
1700 Broad Street
Regina, SK
306-584-7400 (800-228-1000)
Dogs are welcome at this hotel.

Comfort Inn
2155 Northridge Dr.

Saskatoon, SK
306-934-1122 (877-424-6423)
Dogs of all sizes are allowed. Dogs
are allowed for a pet fee of $10.00
per pet per night.

Country Inns & Suites by Carlson
617 Cynthia Street
Saskatoon, SK
306-934-3900
Dogs are allowed for a $25 one time
additional pet fee. Dogs are not
allowed in food service areas and
they must be crated or removed for
housekeeping.

Delta Bessborough
601 Spadina Crescent E
Saskatoon, SK
306-244-5521 (888-890-3222)
Although this hotel offers a
convenient location to a number of
local sites of interest, on site they
feature a large indoor atrium with a
whirlpool, swimming pool, and a
children's pool, plus 2 popular
eateries. Well behaved dogs up to 50
pounds are allowed for an additional
one time fee of $35 per pet. 2 dogs
may be allowed.

Motel 6 - Saskatoon
231 Marquis Dr
Saskatoon, SK
306-665-6688 (800-466-8356)
This motel welcomes your pets to
stay with you.

Radisson Saskatoon
405 20th Street East
Saskatoon, SK
306-665-3322
Dogs up to 50 pounds are allowed
for no additional pet fee.

Ramada Hotel and Golf Dome -
Saskatoon
806 Idylwyld Drive North
Saskatoon, SK
306-665-6500 (800-272-6232)
Dogs of all sizes are allowed. Dogs
are allowed for a pet fee.

Sheraton Cavalier Saskatoon Hotel
612 Spadina Crescent
Saskatoon, SK
306-652-6770 (888-625-5144)
This contemporary, river-front hotel
offers a water park and the city's only
rooftop ballroom. Dogs of all sizes
are allowed for no additional fee.
Dogs may not be left alone in the
room, and they must be quiet, well
behaved leashed, and cleaned up
after. Multiple dogs may be allowed.

Super 8 Saskatoon

706 Circle Drive East
Saskatoon, SK
306-384-8989 (800-800-8000)
Dogs are welcome at this hotel.

Travelodge Hotel Saskatoon
106 Circle Drive West
Saskatoon, SK
306-242-8881 (800-578-7878)
Dogs of all sizes are allowed. Dogs
are allowed for a pet fee of $10 per
pet per night.

Westgate Inn Motel
2501 22nd Street W/H 14
Saskatoon, SK
306-382-3722 (877-382-3722)
westgateinnmotel.com
This motel is located only a few
minutes to the airport, shopping,
dining, and downtown. Dogs are
allowed for an additional fee of $5
per night per pet. 2 dogs may be
allowed.

Comfort Inn
1510 South Service Rd. E.
Swift Current, SK
306-778-3994 (877-424-6423)
Dogs of all sizes are allowed.

Days Inn - Swift Current
905 North Service Road East
Swift Current, SK
306-773-4643 (800-329-7466)
Dogs are welcome at this hotel.

Howard Johnson Inn - Swift Current
1150 South Service Road East
Swift Current, SK
306-773-2033 (800-446-4656)
Dogs are welcome at this hotel.
There is a $10 one time pet fee.

Ramada Weyburn
1420 Sims Ave
Weyburn, SK
306-842-4994 (800-272-6232)
Dogs of all sizes are allowed. Dogs
are allowed for a pet fee.

Comfort Inn & Suites
22 Dracup Avenue
Yorkton, SK
306-783-0333 (877-424-6423)
Dogs of all sizes are allowed. Dogs
are allowed for a pet fee of $5.00 per
pet per night.

Ramada Yorkton
100 Broadway Street East
Yorkton, SK
306-783-9781 (800-272-6232)
Dogs of all sizes are allowed. Dogs
are allowed for a pet fee of $20.00
per pet per night.

Yukon

1202 Motor Inn and RV Park
Mile 1202 Alaska H
Beaver Creek, YU
867-862-7600 (800-661-0540)
karo-ent.com/ahytwest.htm
Offering travelers year round motel
lodging, this rest stop also has a
restaurant and bakery, lounge, a gift
shop, and fuel services. Dogs of all
sizes are allowed for no additional
fee. Dogs must be well behaved,
leashed, and cleaned up after.
There are also RV accommodations
on site that accept pets. Two dogs
are allowed at the motel and there
is no set limit on dogs in one's RV.

Westmark Inn Beaver Creek
Mile 1202 Alaska Hwy
Beaver Creek, YU
867-862-7501 (800-544-0970)
westmarkhotels.com
Dogs of all sizes are allowed. There
is a $15 per day additional pet fee.
The hotel is open from May to
September annually.

Spirit Lake Resort
MM 72.1 S Klondike H
Carcross, YU
866-739-8566
Dogs of all sizes are allowed. There
is a $5 per night per pet additional
fee. Dogs are not allowed on the
bed, and must be leashed and
cleaned up after. Dogs may not be
left unattended. There is an RV
park on site that also allows dogs.

Hotel Carmacks
On Free Gold Road
Carmacks, YU
867-863-5221
Dogs of all sizes are allowed. There
are no additional pet fees. Dogs
must be leashed and cleaned up
after. The motel is also part of an
RV park where dogs are allowed. 2
dogs may be allowed.

Bonanza Gold Motel
715.2 N Klondike H
Dawson City, YU
867-993-6789
Dogs of all sizes are allowed. There
is a $20 one time fee per pet, and
dogs must be leashed and cleaned
up after. There is a seasonal RV
park on site that also allows dogs.
Multiple dogs may be allowed.

Downtown Hotel
1026 2nd Avenue
Dawson City, YU
867-993-5346
downtownhotel.ca/
Although it has the look of the
Klondike era, this renovated hotel
has all the modern amenities and
some nice new features too. Dogs
are allowed here from mid-
September to mid-May for an
additional pet fee of $10 per room
per stay. Dogs must be well
behaved, leashed, and cleaned up
after; they are not allowed in the
dining areas. 2 dogs may be allowed.

Klondike Kate's Cabins and
Restaurant
3rd Avenue and King Street
Dawson City, YU
867-993-6527
klondikekates.ca/
Travelers stopping here will find
clean, new log cabins centrally
located to all of the town's major
attractions, and a restaurant that
specializes in Canadian and ethnic
foods; they also have espresso
coffees. They are open from Good
Friday until mid-September,
depending on weather. Dogs are
allowed in the cabins for an
additional fee of $20 per pet per stay.
Dogs must be friendly, leashed, and
cleaned up after. Dogs are not
allowed at the restaurant. 2 dogs
may be allowed.

Whitehouse Cabins
1626 Front Street/H 2
Dawson City, YU
867-993-5576
whitehousecabins.com/
Nestled among the trees just 2
blocks from the ferry landing, this
riverfront camp area offers numerous
amenities and modernized
accommodations in historic Gold
Rush era cabins. The park can also
be reached by free passage on the
George Black ferry on H 9 that
operates 24/7 during the summer
months. Dogs of all sizes are allowed
for an additional fee of $15 per night
per pet. Dogs may not be left
unattended in the rooms or on the
premises at any time, and they must
be leashed and cleaned up after;
guest rooms keep a supply of clean-
up bags. There is also a large
outdoor area nearby for giving the
pooch a good exercising. 2 dogs may
be allowed.

Destruction Bay Lodge
Mile 1083 Alaska Hwy
Destruction Bay, YU
867-841-5332
Dogs of all sizes are allowed. There

are no additional pet fees.

Talbot Arm Motel
Mile 1083 Alaska Hwy
Destruction Bay, YU
867-841-4461
Dogs of all sizes are allowed. There
are no additional pet fees.

Eagle Plains Hotel
On the Dempster H
Eagle Plains, YU
867-993-2453
Dogs of all sizes are allowed. There
are no additional pet fees. Dogs
must be well behaved, quiet, and
cleaned up after. Dogs may be off
lead if friendly and under voice
control. There is also a tent and RV
park on site that allows dogs.
Multiple dogs may be allowed.

Alcan Motor Inn
Box 5460
Haines Junction, YU
867-634-2371 (888-265-1018)
Dogs of all sizes are allowed. There
is a $10.50 per night additional pet
fee.

Kluane Park Inn
1635 Alaska Highway
Haines Junction, YU
867-634-2261
Dogs of all sizes are allowed. There
is a $5 additional pet fee. There is a
Chinese Restaurant on the premises.

Stewart Valley Bedrock Motel
Lot 99 H 11
Mayo, YU
867-996-2290
Dogs of all sizes are allowed. There
are no additional pet fees. Dogs may
not be left unattended at any time,
must be leashed, and cleaned up
after. There is a tent and RV park on
site that also allows dogs.

Continental Divide Lodge and RV
Park
Mile 721 Alaska H
Swift River, YU
867-851-6451
karo-ent.com/akhwyyt.htm
Nestled between the Mackenzie and
Yukon Rivers less than a mile from
the divide, this motel offers a
restaurant, a gift store, a pub, and a
camp area with hook-ups. Dogs are
allowed in the motel and the
campground for no additional fee.
Dogs must be well behaved,
leashed, and cleaned up after. 2
dogs may be allowed.

Dawson Peaks Resort and RV Park

KM 1232 Alaska H
Teslin, YU
867-390-2244
There is an additional $5 per night
per pet fee. Dogs must be leashed
at all times and cleaned up after.
Dogs are not allowed on the
furniture. There is a connecting tent
and RV park that do allow more
than one dog per site. 2 dogs may
be allowed.

Mukluk Annie's Salmon Bake and
Motel
Mile 784 Alaska Hwy
Teslin, YU
867-390-2600
This restaurant and lodge offers
meals of Salmon. Dogs of all sizes
are allowed in the motel and there
is a $10 per night additional pet fee.
There is also free dry camping at
the site.

Nisultin Trading Post Motel
Mile 804 Alaska Hwy
Teslin, YU
867-390-2521
Dogs of all sizes are allowed. There
are no additional pet fees.

Yukon Motel
Mile 804 Alaska Hwy
Teslin, YU
867-390-2575
yukonmotel.com
Dogs of all sizes are allowed. There
is a pet fee of $15 per room for
some rooms in the hotel.

Belvedere Motor Hotel
Box 370
Watson Lake, YU
867-536-7712
watsonlakehotels.com/Belvedere/
Dogs of all sizes are allowed. There
is a $15 per night additional pet fee.

Big Horn Hotel
Frank Trail just S of Alaska Hwy
Watson Lake, YU
867-536-2020
Dogs of all sizes are allowed. There
are no additional pet fees. A credit
card is necessary as a security
deposit for pet damage.

Gateway Motor Inn
Box 370
Watson Lake, YU
867-536-7744
watsonlakehotels.com/Gateway/
Dogs of all sizes are allowed. There
is a $20 per day additional pet fee.

Northern Beaver Post Lodge
KM 1003 Alaska H

Watson Lake, YU
867-536-2307
Dogs of all sizes are allowed. There
is a $15 per night per room additional
pet fee. Dogs must be leashed at all
times and cleaned up after. 2 dogs
may be allowed.

Racheria Lodge
MM 710 Alaska H
Watson Lake, YU
867-851-6456
Dogs of all sizes are allowed. There
is a $10 one time fee per pet. Dogs
may not be left unattended, must be
leashed, and cleaned up after.
Multiple dogs may be allowed.

Airport Chalet
91634 Alaska Hwy
Whitehorse, YU
867-668-2166
Dogs of all sizes are allowed. There
is a $10 one time additional pet fee.

Hi Country Inn
4051 4th Avenue
Whitehorse, YU
867-667-4471 (800-554-4471)
highcountryinn.yk.ca/
Dogs of all sizes are allowed for an
additional fee of $15 per night per
pet on the ground floor. Dogs must
be quiet, leashed, cleaned up after,
and they are not allowed in the bar or
restaurant area. 2 dogs may be
allowed.

Inn on the River Wilderness Resort
PO Box 10420
Whitehorse, YU
867-660-5253
This wilderness resort offers a wide
range of year round land, air, and
water activities, and great views of
the Northern Lights. They offer 2 pet
friendly cabins where dogs are
welcome for no additional fee. Dogs
must be well behaved, leashed, and
cleaned up after at all times. Dogs
are not allowed on the plane or boat
tours. 2 dogs may be allowed.

River View Hotel
102 Wood Street
Whitehorse, YU
867-667-7801
riverviewhotel.ca
Dogs of all sizes are allowed. There
are no additional pet fees.

The Yukon Inn
4220 4th Avenue
Whitehorse, YU
867-667-2527 (800-661-0454)
yukoninn.com/index2.html
Ninety-two modern rooms are

available here in addition to lounges and an eatery. Dogs are allowed at the inn for an additional pet fee of $15.90 per room per stay. Dogs must be quiet, well behaved, leashed, and cleaned up after. Multiple dogs may be allowed.

Westmark Whitehorse Hotel
201 Wood Street
Whitehorse, YU
867-393-9700 (800-544-0970)
westmarkhotels.com
Dogs of all sizes are allowed. There are no additional pet fees.

Chapter 2

Dog-Friendly Beaches

United States

Alabama

Dauphin Island Beaches
at the end of H 193
Dauphin Island, AL
251-861-3607
dauphinislandcoc.com
Considered one of the most pet-friendly beach areas on the Gulf Coast, the white sandy beaches of Dauphin Island offers several play areas for fun-loving pooches. There are large beach play areas by the Red School House and the old fishing pier; plus a few miles of undeveloped barrier beach and a campground with a beach where pets are welcome. Dogs are not allowed at the West End Beach Park on the island's far west end. Dogs must be kept leashed, cleaned up after promptly, and be hound and human friendly.

Alaska

Homer Beaches
Homer, AK
907-235-7740
Leashed dogs are allowed on the beaches of Homer Alaska. The tide in Homer varies significantly during the day and a lot of land is covered up and uncovered at various times. So keep a close eye on the tides while in Homer.

California

Rio Del Mar Beach
Rio Del Mar
Aptos, CA
831-685-6500
Dogs on leash are allowed at this beach which offers a wide strip of sand. From Highway 1, take the Rio Del Mar exit.

Mad River Beach County Park
Mad River Road
Arcata, CA
707-445-7651
Enjoy walking or jogging for several miles on this beach. Dogs on leash are allowed. The park is located about 4-5 miles north of Arcata. To get there, take Highway 101 and exit Giuntoli Lane. Then go north onto Heindon Rd. Turn left onto Miller Rd. Turn right on Mad River Road and

follow it to the park.

Avila Beach
off Avila Beach Drive
Avila Beach, CA
805-595-5400
This beach is about a 1/2 mile long. Dogs are not allowed between 10am and 5pm and must be leashed.

Olde Port Beach
off Avila Beach Drive
Avila Beach, CA
805-595-5400
This beach is about a 1/4 mile long. Dogs are not allowed between 10am and 5pm and must be leashed.

Big Bear Lake Beaches
Hwy 38
Big Bear Lake, CA
There are various beaches along the lake on Hwy 38. You can get to any of the beaches via the Alpine Pedal Path. To get there, (going away from the village), take the Stanfield Cutoff to the other side of the lake and turn left onto Hwy 38. In about 1/4 - 1/2 mile, parking will be on the left.

Pfieffer Beach
Sycamore Road
Big Sur, CA
805-968-6640
Dogs on leash are allowed at this day use beach which is located in the Los Padres National Forest. The beach is located in Big Sur, south of the Big Sur Ranger Station. From Big Sur, start heading south on Highway 1 and look carefully for Sycamore Road. Take Sycamore Road just over 2 miles to the beach. There is a $5 entrance fee per car.

Doran Regional Park
201 Doran Beach Road
Bodega Bay, CA
707-875-3540
This park offers 2 miles of sandy beach. It is a popular place to picnic, walk, surf, fish and fly kites. Dogs are allowed but must be on a 6 foot or less leash and proof of a rabies vaccination is required. There is a minimal parking fee. The park is located south of Bodega Bay.

Agate Beach
Elm Road
Bolinas, CA
415-499-6387
During low tide, this 6 acre park

provides access to almost 2 miles of shoreline. Leashed dogs are allowed.

Cardiff State Beach
Old Highway 101
Cardiff, CA
760-753-5091
This is a gently sloping sandy beach with warm water. Popular activities include swimming, surfing and beachcombing. Dogs on leash are allowed and please clean up after your pets. The beach is located on Old Highway 101, one mile south of Cardiff.

Carmel City Beach
Ocean Avenue
Carmel, CA
831-624-9423
This beach is within walking distance (about 7 blocks) from the quaint village of Carmel. There are a couple of hotels and several restaurants that are within walking distance of the beach. Your pooch is allowed to run off-leash as long as he or she is under voice control. To get there, take the Ocean Avenue exit from Hwy 1 and follow Ocean Ave to the end.

Carmel River State Beach
Carmelo Street
Carmel, CA
831-624-9423
This beach is just south of Carmel. It has approximately a mile of beach and leashes are required. It's located on Carmelo Street.

Garrapata State Park
Highway 1
Carmel, CA
831-649-2836
There are two miles of beach front at this park. Dogs are allowed but must be on a 6 foot or less leash and people need to clean up after their pets. The beach is on Highway 1, about 6 1/2 miles south of Rio Road in Carmel. It is about 18 miles north of Big Sur.

Caspar Beach
14441 Point Cabrillo Drive
Caspar, CA
707-937-5804
Dogs on leash are allowed at this sandy beach across from the Caspar Beach RV Park. The beach is located about 4 miles north of Mendocino. Please clean up after your dog.

Cayucos State Beach

Dog-Friendly Beaches - Please always call ahead to make sure an establishment is still dog-friendly.

Cayucos Drive
Cayucos, CA
805-781-5200
This state beach allows leashed dogs. The beach is located in the small town of Cayucos. To get to the beach from Hwy 1, exit Cayucos Drive and head west. There is a parking lot and parking along the street.

Cloverdale River Park
31820 McCray Road
Cloverdale, CA
707-565-2041
This park is located along the Russian River and offers seasonal fishing and river access for kayaks and canoes. There are no lifeguards at the beach area. Dogs are allowed, but must be on a 6 foot or less leash. They can wade into the water, but cannot really swim because pets must remain on leash. There is a $3 per car parking fee.

Corona Del Mar State Beach
Iris Street and Ocean Blvd.
Corona Del Mar, CA
949-644-3151
This is a popular beach for swimming, surfing and diving. The sandy beach is about a half mile long. Dogs are allowed on this beach during certain hours. They are allowed before 9am and after 5pm, year round. Pets must be on a 6 foot or less leash. Tickets will be issued if your dog is off leash.

Coronado Dog Beach
100 Ocean Blvd
Coronado, CA
619-522-7342
Coronado's Dog Beach is at the north end of Ocean Blvd. Just north of the famous Hotel del Coronado (unfortunately dogs are not allowed at the hotel)the area that is designated off leash is marked by signs. The off-leash beach is open 24 hours. Dogs must be supervised and cleaned up after. Dogs must be leashed outside of the off-leash area and fines are very steep for any violations. There are also fines for not cleaning up after your dog at the dog beach. Food and Pet Treats are not allowed at the beach.

Crescent Beach - Del Norte SP
Enderts Beach Rd
Crescent Beach, CA
707-464-6101
nps.gov/redw/home.html
Dogs are allowed on the ocean beach at Crescent Beach in the Del Norte Coast Redwoods State Park.

They are not allowed on any trails within the Redwood National or State Parks. Pets are also allowed at road accessible picnic areas and campgrounds. Dogs must be on a 6 foot or less leash and people need to pick up after their pets. To get to the beach take Enderts Beach Road South from Highway 101 just south of Crescent City.

Beachfront Park
Front Street
Crescent City, CA
707-464-9507
Dogs are allowed at park and the beach, but must be leashed. Please clean up after your pets. To get there, take Highway 101 to Front Street. Follow Front Street to the park.

Crescent Beach
Enderts Beach Road
Crescent City, CA
707-464-6101
nps.gov/redw/home.html
While dogs are not allowed on any trails in Redwood National Park, they are allowed on a couple of beaches, including Crescent Beach. Enjoy beachcombing or bird watching at this beach. Pets are also allowed at road accessible picnic areas and campgrounds. Dogs must be on a 6 foot or less leash and people need to pick up after their pets. The beach is located off Highway 101, about 3 to 4 miles south of Crescent City. Exit Enderts Beach Road and head south.

Davenport Beach
Hwy 1
Davenport, CA
831-462-8333
This beautiful beach is surrounded by high bluffs and cliff trails. Leashes are required. To get to the beach from Santa Cruz, head north on Hwy 1 for about 10 miles.

Del Mar Beach
Seventeenth Street
Del Mar, CA
858-755-1556
Dogs are allowed on the beach as follows. South of 17th Street, dogs are allowed on a 6 foot leash year-round. Between 17th Street and 29th Street, dogs are allowed on a 6 foot leash from October through May (from June through September, dogs are not allowed at all). Between 29th Street and northern city limits, dogs are allowed without a leash, but must be under voice control from October through May (from June

through September, dogs must be on a 6 foot leash). Owners must clean up after their dogs.

Rivermouth Beach
Highway 101
Del Mar, CA
This beach allows voice controlled dogs to run leash free from September 15 through June 15 (no specified hours). Leashes are required during mid-summer tourist season from mid June to mid Sept. Fans of this beach are trying to convince the Del Mar City council to extend the leash-free period to year round. The beach is located on Highway 101 just south of Border Avenue at the north end of the City of Del Mar. Thanks to one of our readers for recommending this beach

MacKerricher State Park
Highway 1
Fort Bragg, CA
707-964-9112
Dogs are allowed on the beach, but not on any park trails. Pets must be leashed and people need to clean up after their pets. Picnic areas, restrooms and campsites (including an ADA restroom and campsites), are available at this park. The park is located three miles north of Fort Bragg on Highway 1, near the town of Cleone.

Noyo Beach Off-Leash Dog Beach
North Harbor Drive
Fort Bragg, CA
frankhartzell.com/MCDOG
The dog beach is located at the north side of where the Noyo River enters the Pacific Ocean. To get to the dog beach, turn EAST (away from the ocean) on N. Harbor Drive from Highway 1. N. Harbor will go down to the river and circle under Highway 1 to the beach. The beach was organized by MCDOG (Mendocino Coast Dog Owners Group) which is now working on an off-leash dog park for the Mendocino area.

Goleta Beach County Park
5990 Sandspit Road
Goleta, CA
805-568-2460
Leashed dogs are allowed at this county beach. The beach and park are about 1/2 mile long. There are picnic tables and a children's playground at the park. It's located near the Santa Barbara Municipal Airport in Goleta, just north of Santa Barbara. To get there, take Hwy 101

to Hwy 217 and head west. Before you reach UC Santa Barbara, there will be an exit for Goleta Beach.

Kirk Creek Beach and Trailhead
Highway 1
Gorda, CA
831-385-5434
Both the Kirk Creek Beach and hiking trails allow dogs. Pets must be leashed. You can park next to the Kirk Creek Campground and either hike down to the beach or start hiking at the Kirk Creek Trailhead which leads to the Vicente Flat Trail where you can hike for miles with your dog. The beach and trailhead is part of the Los Padres National Forest and is located about 25 miles south of Big Sur.

Sand Dollar Beach
Highway 1
Gorda, CA
805-434-1996
Walk down a path to one of the longest sandy beaches on the Big Sur Coast. This national forest managed beach is popular for surfing, fishing and walking. Dogs must be on leash and people need to clean up after their pets. There is a minimal day use fee. The dog-friendly Plaskett Creek Campground is within walking distance. This beach is part of the Los Padres National Forest and is located about 5 miles south of the Kirk Creek and about 30 miles south of Big Sur.

Willow Creek Beach
Highway 1
Gorda, CA
831-385-5434
Dogs on leash are allowed at this day use beach and picnic area. The beach is part of the Los Padres National Forest and is located about 35 miles south of Big Sur.

Gualala Point Regional Park Beach
42401 Coast Highway 1
Gualala, CA
707-565-2041
This county park offers sandy beaches, hiking trails, campsites, picnic tables and restrooms. Dogs are allowed on the beach, on the trails, and in the campground, but they must be on a 6 foot or less leash. People also need to clean up after their pets. There is a $3 day use fee.

Blufftop Coastal Park
Poplar Street
Half Moon Bay, CA
650-726-8297

Leashed dogs are allowed at this beach. The beach is located on the west end of Poplar Street, off Highway 1.

Montara State Beach
Highway 1
Half Moon Bay, CA
650-726-8819
Dogs on leash are allowed at this beach. Please clean up after your pets. The beach is located 8 miles north of Half Moon Bay on Highway 1. There are two beach access points. The first access point is across from Second Street, immediately south of the Outrigger Restaurant. The second access point is about a 1/2 mile north on the ocean side of Highway 1. Both access points have steep paths down to the beach.

Surfer's Beach
Highway 1
Half Moon Bay, CA
650-726-8297
Dogs on leash are allowed on the beach. It is located at Highway 1 and Coronado Street.

Healdsburg Memorial Beach
13839 Old Redwood Highway
Healdsburg, CA
707-565-2041
This man-made swimming beach is located on the Russian River. Dogs are allowed at this park, but must be on a 6 foot or less leash. They can wade into the water, but cannot really swim because pets must remain on leash. People are urged to swim only when lifeguards are present, which is usually between Memorial Day and Labor Day. The beach area also offers picnic tables and a restroom. There is a $3 to $4 parking fee per day, depending on the season.

Huntington Dog Beach
Pacific Coast Hwy (Hwy 1)
Huntington Beach, CA
714-841-8644
dogbeach.org
This beautiful beach is about a mile long and allows dogs from 5 am to 10 pm. Dogs must be under control but may be off leash and owners must pick up after them. Dogs are only allowed on the beach between Golden West Street and Seapoint Ave. Please adhere to these rules as there are only a couple of dog-friendly beaches left in the entire Los Angeles area. The beach is located off the Pacific Coast Hwy (Hwy 1) at Golden West Street.

Please remember to pick up after your dog... the city wanted to prohibit dogs in 1997 because of the dog waste left on the beach. But thanks to The Preservation Society of Huntington Dog Beach (http://www.dogbeach.org), it continues to be dog-friendly. City ordinances require owners to pick up after their dogs. It is suggested that you bring plenty of quarters in order to feed the parking meters near the beach.

Imperial Beach
Seacoast Drive at Imperial Beach Blvd
Imperial Beach, CA
619-424-3151
Dogs on leash are allowed on the portions of the beach that are north of Palm Avenue and south of Imperial Beach Blvd. They are not allowed on the beach between Palm Avenue and Imperial Beach Blvd.

Stillwater Cove Regional Park
22455 Highway 1
Jenner, CA
707-565-2041
This 210 acre park includes a small beach, campground, picnic tables, and restrooms. The park offers a great view of the Pacific Ocean from Stillwater Cove. Dogs are allowed on the beach, and in the campground, but they must be on a 6 foot or less leash. People also need to clean up after their pets. There is a $3 day use fee. The park is located off Highway 1, about 16 miles north of Jenner.

Coon Street Beach
Coon Street
Kings Beach, CA
Located at the end of Coon Street, on the east side of Kings Beach is a small but popular dog beach. There are also picnic tables, BBQs and restrooms at this beach.

La Jolla Shores Beach
Camino Del Oro
La Jolla, CA
619-221-8900
Leashed dogs are allowed on this beach and the adjacent Kellogg Park from 6pm to 9am. The beach is about 1/2 mile long. To get there, take Hwy 5 to the La Jolla Village Drive exit heading west. Turn left onto Torrey Pines Rd. Then turn right onto La Jolla Shores Drive. Go 4-5 blocks and turn left onto Vallecitos. Go straight until you reach the beach and Kellogg Park.

Point La Jolla Beaches
Coast Blvd.
La Jolla, CA
619-221-8900
Leashed dogs are allowed on this beach and the walkway (paved and dirt trails) from 6pm to 9am. The beaches and walkway are at least a 1/2 mile long and might continue further. To get there, exit La Jolla Village Drive West from Hwy 5. Turn left onto Torrey Pines Rd. Turn right on Prospect and then park or turn right onto Coast Blvd. Parking is limited around the village area.

Main Beach
Pacific Hwy (Hwy 1)
Laguna Beach, CA
949-497-3311
Dogs are allowed on this beach between 6pm and 8am, June 1 to September 16. The rest of the year, they are allowed on the beach from dawn until dusk. Dogs must be on a leash at all times.

Long Beach Dog Beach Zone
between Roycroft and Argonne Avenues
Long Beach, CA
562-570-3100
hautedogs.org/
This 3 acre off-leash unfenced dog beach is the only off-leash dog beach in Los Angeles County. It is open daily from 6am until 8pm. It opened on August 1, 2003. The "zone" is 235 yards along the water and 60 yards deep. There is a fresh water fountain called the "Fountain of Woof" which is located near the restrooms at the end of Granada Avenue, near the Dog Zone. Only one dog is allowed per adult and dog owners are entirely responsible for their dog's actions. The beach is located between Roycroft and Argonne avenues in Belmont Shore, Long Beach. It is a few blocks east of the Belmont Pier and Olympic pool. From Ocean Blvd, enter at Bennett Avenue for the beachfront metered parking lot. The cost is 25 cents for each 15 minutes from 8am until 6pm daily. Parking is free after 5pm in the beachfront lot at the end of Granada Avenue. You can check with the website http://www.hautedogs.org for updates and additional rules about the Long Beach Dog Beach Zone.

Leo Carrillo State Beach
Hwy 1
Malibu, CA
818-880-0350
This beach is one of the very few dog-friendly beaches in the Los Angeles area. In a press release dated November 27, 2002, the California State Parks clarified the rules for dogs at Leo Carrillo State Beach. We thank the State Parks for this clear announcement of the regulations. Dogs are allowed on a maximum 6 foot leash when accompanied by a person capable of controlling the dog on all beach WEST (up coast) of lifeguard tower 3 at Leo Carrillo State Park, Staircase Beach, County Line Beach, and all Beaches within Point Mugu State Park. Dogs are NOT allowed EAST of lifeguard tower 3 at Leo Carrillo State Beach at any time. And please note that dogs are not allowed in the tide pools at Leo Carrillo. There should be signs posted. A small general store is located on the mountain side of the freeway. Here you can grab some snacks and other items. The park is located on Hwy 1, approximately 30 miles northwest of Santa Monica. We ask that all dog people closely obey these regulations so that the beach continues to be dog-friendly.

Manresa State Beach
San Andreas Road
Manresa, CA
831-761-1795
Surfing and surf fishing are both popular activities at this beach. Dogs are allowed on the beach, but must be leashed. To get there from Aptos, head south on Highway 1. Take San Andreas Road southwest for several miles until you reach Manresa. Upon reaching the coast, you will find the first beach access point.

Clam Beach County Park
Highway 101
McKinleyville, CA
707-445-7651
This beach is popular for fishing, swimming, picnicking and beachcombing. Of course, there are also plenty of clams. Dogs on leash are allowed on the beach and at the campgrounds. There are no day use fees. The park is located off Highway 101, about eight miles north of Arcata.

Big River Beach
N. Big River Road
Mendocino, CA
707-937-5804
This small beach is located just south of downtown Mendocino. There are two ways to get there. One way is to head south of town on Hwy 1 and turn left on N. Big River Rd. The beach will be on the right. The second way is to take Hwy 1 and exit Main Street/Jackson heading towards the coastline. In about 1/4-1/2 mile there will be a Chevron Gas Station and a historic church on the left. Park and then walk behind the church to the trailhead. Follow the trail, bearing left when appropriate, and there will be a wooden staircase that goes down to Big River Beach. Dogs must be on leash.

Van Damme State Beach
Highway 1
Mendocino, CA
This small beach is located in the town of Little River which is approximately 2 miles south of Mendocino. It is part of Van Damme State Park which is located across Highway 1. Most California State Parks, including this one, do not allow dogs on the hiking trails. Fortunately this one allows dogs on the beach. There is no parking fee at the beach and dogs must be on leash.

Monterey Recreation Trail
various (see comments)
Monterey, CA
monterey.org/rec/rectrl96.html
Take a walk on the Monterey Recreation Trail and experience the beautiful scenery that makes Monterey so famous. This paved trail extends for miles, starting at Fisherman's Wharf and ending in the city of Pacific Grove. Dogs must be leashed. Along the path there are a few small beaches that allow dogs such as the one south of Fisherman's Wharf and another beach behind Ghirardelli Ice Cream on Cannery Row. Along the path you'll find a few more outdoor places to eat near Cannery Row and by the Monterey Bay Aquarium. Look at the Restaurants section for more info.

Monterey State Beach
various (see comments)
Monterey, CA
831-649-2836
Take your water loving and beach loving dog to this awesome beach in Monterey. There are various starting points, but it basically stretches from Hwy 1 and the Del Rey Oaks Exit down to Fisherman's Wharf. Various beaches make up this 2 mile (each way) stretch of beach, but leashed dogs are allowed on all of them . If you want to extend your walk, you can continue on the paved Monterey Recreation Trail which goes all the

way to Pacific Grove. There are a few smaller dog-friendly beaches along the paved trail.

Muir Beach
Hwy 1
Muir Beach, CA
Dogs on leash are allowed on Muir Beach with you. Please clean up after your dog on the beach. To get to Muir Beach from Hwy 101 take Hwy 1 North from the north side of the Golden Gate Bridge.

Newport and Balboa Beaches
Balboa Blvd.
Newport Beach, CA
949-644-3211
There are several smaller beaches which run along Balboa Blvd. Dogs are only allowed before 9am and after 5pm, year round. Pets must be on a 6 foot or less leash and people are required to clean up after their pets. Tickets will be issued if your dog is off leash. The beaches are located along Balboa Blvd and ample parking is located near the Balboa and Newport Piers.

Dog Beach
Point Loma Blvd.
Ocean Beach, CA
619-221-8900
Dogs are allowed to run off leash at this beach anytime during the day. This is a very popular dog beach which attracts lots and lots of dogs on warm days. To get there, take Hwy 8 West until it ends and then it becomes Sunset Cliffs Blvd. Then make a right turn onto Point Loma Blvd and follow the signs to Ocean Beach's Dog Beach.

Ocean Beach
Point Loma Blvd.
Ocean Beach, CA
619-221-8900
Leashed dogs are allowed on this beach from 6pm to 9am. The beach is about 1/2 mile long. To get there, take Hwy 8 West until it ends and then it becomes Sunset Cliffs Blvd. Then make a right turn onto Point Loma Blvd and follow the signs to Ocean Beach Park. A separate beach called Dog Beach is at the north end of this beach which allows dogs to run off-leash.

Oceano Dunes State Vehicular Recreation Area
Highway 1
Oceano, CA
805-473-7220
This 3,600 acre off road area offers 5 1/2 miles of beach which is open for

vehicle use. Pets on leash are allowed too. Swimming, surfing, horseback riding and bird watching are all popular activities at the beach. The park is located three miles south of Pismo Beach off Highway 1.

Point Reyes National Seashore
Olema, CA
415-464-5100
nps.gov/pore/
Leashed dogs (on a 6 foot or less leash) are allowed on four beaches. The dog-friendly beaches are the Limantour Beach, Kehoe Beach, North Beach and South Beach. Dogs are not allowed on the hiking trails. However, they are allowed on some hiking trails that are adjacent to Point Reyes. For a map of dog-friendly hiking trails, please stop by the Visitor Center. Point Reyes is located about an hour north of San Francisco. From Highway 101, exit at Sir Francis Drake Highway, and continue west on Sir Francis Drake to Olema. To find the Visitor Center, turn right in Olema onto Route 1 and then make a left onto Bear Valley Road. The Visitor Center will be on the left.

Freshwater Lagoon Beach - Redwood NP
Highway 101 south end of Redwood National Park
Orick, CA
707-464-6101
nps.gov/redw/home.html
Dogs are allowed on the ocean beaches around Freshwater Lagoon, but not on any trails within Redwood National Park. Picnic tables are available at the beach. Pets are also allowed at road accessible picnic areas and campgrounds. Dogs must be on a 6 foot or less leash and people need to pick up after their pets. The beach is located off Highway 101 behind the Redwood Information Center at the south end of the Redwood National Park. The parking area for the beach is about 2 miles south of Orick. Some portions of this beach are rather rocky but there are also sandy portions as well.

Gold Bluffs Beach - Redwood NP
Davison Road
Orick, CA
707-464-6101
nps.gov/redw/home.html
Dogs are allowed on this beach, but not on any trails within this park. Picnic tables and campgrounds are

available at the beach. Pets are also allowed at road accessible picnic areas and campgrounds. Dogs must be on a 6 foot or less leash and people need to pick up after their pets. The beach is located off Highway 101. Take Highway 101 heading north. Pass Orick and drive about 3-4 miles, then exit Davison Rd. Head towards the coast on an unpaved road (trailers are not allowed on the unpaved road).

Hollywood Beach
various addresses
Oxnard, CA
This beach is located on the west side of the Channel Islands Harbor. The beach is 4 miles southwest of Oxnard. Dogs must be on leash and owners must clean up after their pets. Dogs are allowed on Hollywood Beach before 9 am and after 5 pm.

Oxnard Shores Beach
Harbor Blvd.
Oxnard, CA
This beach stretches for miles. If you enter at 5th Street and go north, there are no houses and very few people. Dogs must be on leash and owners must clean up after their pets. Thanks to one of our readers for recommending this beach.

Silverstrand Beach
various addresses
Oxnard, CA
This beach is located between the Channel Islands Harbor and the U.S. Naval Construction Battalion Center. Dogs are now only allowed on the beach after 5 pm and before 8 am. The beach is 4 miles southwest of Oxnard. Dogs must be on leash and owners must clean up after their pets.

Asilomar State Beach
Along Sunset Drive
Pacific Grove, CA
831-372-4076
Dogs are permitted on leash on the beach and the scenic walking trails. If you walk south along the beach and go across the stream that leads into the ocean, you can take your dog off-leash, but he or she must be under strict voice control and within your sight at all times.

Esplanade Beach
Esplanade
Pacifica, CA
650-738-7381
This beach offers an off-leash area for dogs. To get to the beach, take the stairs at the end of Esplanade.

Esplanade is just north of Manor Drive, off Highway 1.

Lake Nacimento Resort Day Use Area
10625 Nacimiento Lake Drive
Paso Robles, CA
805-238-3256
nacimientoresort.com/
In addition to the campgrounds and RV area, this resort also offers day use of the lake. Dogs can swim in the water, but be very careful of boats, as this is a popular lake for water-skiing. Day use fees vary by season and location, but in general rates are about $5 to $8 per person. Senior discounts are available. Dogs are an extra $5 per day. Proof of your dog's rabies vaccination is required.

Bean Hollow State Beach
Highway 1
Pescadero, CA
650-879-2170
This is a very rocky beach with not much sand. Dogs are allowed but must be on a 6 foot or less leash. Please clean up after your pets. The beach is located 3 miles south of Pescadero on Highway 1.

Pismo State Beach
Grand Ave.
Pismo Beach, CA
805-489-2684
Leashed dogs are allowed on this state beach. This beach is popular for walking, sunbathing, swimming and the annual winter migration of millions of monarch butterflies (the park has the largest over-wintering colony of monarch butterflies in the U.S.). To get there from Hwy 101, exit 4th Street and head south. In about a mile, turn right onto Grand Ave. You can park along the road.

Sonoma Coast State Beach
Highway 1
Salmon Creek, CA
707-875-3483
Dogs on leash are allowed at some of the beaches in this state park. Dogs are allowed at Shell Beach, Portuguese Beach and Schoolhouse Beach. They are not allowed at Goat Rock or Salmon Creek Beach due to the protected seals and snowy plovers. Please clean up after your pets. While dogs are allowed on some of the beaches and campgrounds, they are not allowed on any hiking trails at this park.

Samoa Dunes Recreation Area
New Navy Base Road

Samoa, CA
707-825-2300
ca.blm.gov/caso/wf-samoadun.html
The Bureau of Land Management oversees this 300 acre sand dune park. It is a popular spot for off-highway vehicles which can use about 140 of the park's acres. Dogs are allowed on leash or off-leash but under voice control. Even if your dog runs off-leash, the park service requests that you still bring a leash just in case. To get there, take Highway 255 and turn south on New Navy Base Road. Go about four miles to the parking area.

Fiesta Island
Fiesta Island Road
San Diego, CA
619-221-8900
On this island, dogs are allowed to run off-leash anywhere outside the fenced areas, anytime during the day. It is mostly sand which is perfect for those beach loving hounds. You might, however, want to stay on the north end of the island. The south end was used as the city's sludge area (mud and sediment, and possibly smelly) processing facility. The island is often used to launch jet-skis and motorboats. There is a one-way road that goes around the island and there are no fences, so please make sure your dog stays away from the road. About half way around the island, there is a completely fenced area on the beach. Please note that the fully enclosed area is not a dog park. The city of San Diego informed us that is supposed to be locked and is not intended to be used as a dog park even though there may occasionally be dogs running in this off-limits area.

Mission Beach & Promenade
Mission Blvd.
San Diego, CA
619-221-8900
Leashed dogs are allowed on this beach and promenade walkway from 6pm to 9am. It is about 3 miles long and located west of Mission Bay Park.

Baker Beach
Lincoln Blvd and Bowley St/Golden Gate Nat'l Rec Area
San Francisco, CA
415-561-4700
nps.gov/prsf/places/bakerbch.htm
This dog-friendly beach in the Golden Gate National Recreation Area has a great view of the Golden Gate Bridge. Dogs are permitted off leash under voice control on Baker Beach North of Lobos Creek; they must be leashed South of Lobos Creek. The beach is located approx. 1.5 to 2 miles south of the Golden Gate Bridge. From Lincoln Avenue, turn onto Bowley Street and head towards the ocean. There is a parking lot next to the beach. This is a clothing optional beach, so there may be the occasional sunbather.

Fort Funston/Burton Beach
Skyline Blvd./Hwy 35
San Francisco, CA
nps.gov/goga/
This is a very popular dog-friendly park and beach. In the past, dogs have been allowed off-leash. However, currently all dogs must be on leash. Fort Funston is part of the Golden Gate National Recreation Area. There are trails that run through the dunes & ice plant from the parking lot above with good access to the beach below. It overlooks the southern end of Ocean Beach, with a large parking area accessible from Skyline Boulevard. There is also a water faucet and trough at the parking lot for thirsty pups. It's located off Skyline Blvd. (also known Hwy 35) by John Muir Drive. It is south of Ocean Beach. Thanks to one of our readers for this info. Expect to see lots and lots of dogs having a great time. But not to worry, there is plenty of room for everyone.

Lands End Off Leash Dog Area
El Camino Del Mar
San Francisco, CA
415-561-4700
Owned and operated by the Golden Gate National Recreation Area, Lands End is everything west of and including the Coast Trail, and is an extraordinary combination of parkland, natural areas, and dramatic coastal cliffs. It offers great hiking, ocean and city views, a museum, the ruins of the Sutro Baths, and includes the Sutro Heights Park (dogs must be on lead in this area). This area can be accessed at Merrie Way for the cliffside paths, and at this entrance or the large lot at the end of El Camino Del Mar off Point Lobos for the Coast Trail and beaches. Dogs must be on leash on the Coast Trail, under firm voice control when in off leash areas, and they must be cleaned up after.

Ocean Beach

Great Hwy
San Francisco, CA
415-556-8642
You'll get a chance to stretch your legs at this beach which has about 4 miles of sand. The beach runs parallel to the Great Highway (north of Fort Funston). There are several access points including Sloat Blvd., Fulton Street or Lincoln Way. This beach has a mix of off-leash and leash required areas. Thanks to the San Francisco Dog Owners Group (SFDOG) for providing the following information: Dogs must be on leash on Ocean Beach between Sloat Blvd and Stairwell #21 (roughly at Fulton). North of Fulton to the Cliff House and South of Sloat for several miles are still okay for off-leash dogs, however parts of these areas may be impassible at high tide. The Golden Gate National Rec Area (GGNRA) strictly enforces the on-leash area between Sloat and Fulton. They usually give no warning tickets ($50 fine). As with all other leash required areas, we encourage dog owners to comply with the rules.

Coastal Access
off Hearst Drive
San Simeon, CA
There is parking just north of the Best Western Hotel, next to the "Coastal Access" sign. Dogs must be on leash.

Arroyo Burro Beach County Park
2981 Cliff Drive
Santa Barbara, CA
805-967-1300
Leashed dogs are allowed at this county beach and park. The beach is about 1/2 mile long and it is adjacent to a palm-lined grassy area with picnic tables. To get to the beach from Hwy 101, exit Las Positas Rd/Hwy 225. Head south (towards the ocean). When the street ends, turn right onto Cliff Drive. The beach will be on the left.

Arroyo Burro Off-Leash Beach
Cliff Drive
Santa Barbara, CA
While dogs are not allowed off-leash at the Arroyo Burro Beach County Park (both the beach and grass area), they are allowed to run leash free on the adjacent beach. The dog beach starts east of the slough at Arroyo Burro and stretches almost to the stairs at Mesa Lane. To get to the off-leash area, walk your leashed dog from the parking lot to the beach, turn left and cross the slough. At this point you can remove your

dog's leash.

Rincon Park and Beach
Bates Road
Santa Barbara, CA
This beach is at Rincon Point which has some of the best surfing waves in the world. In the winter, it is very popular with surfers. In the summer, it is a popular swimming beach. Year-round, leashed dogs are welcome. The beach is about 1/2-1 mile long. Next to the parking lot there are picnic tables, phones and restrooms. The beach is in Santa Barbara County, about 15-20 minutes south of Santa Barbara. To get there from Santa Barbara, take Hwy 101 south and go past Carpinteria. Take the Bates Rd exit towards the ocean. When the road ends, turn right into the Rincon Park and Beach parking lot.

East Cliff Coast Access Points
East Cliff Drive
Santa Cruz, CA
831-454-7900
There are many small dog-friendly beaches and coastal access points that stretch along East Cliff Drive between 12th Avenue to 41st Avenue. This is not one long beach because the water comes up to cliffs in certain areas and breaks it up into many smaller beaches. Dogs are allowed on leash. Parking is on city streets along East Cliff or the numbered avenues. To get there from Hwy 17 south, take the Hwy 1 exit south towards Watsonville. Take the exit towards Soquel Drive. Turn left onto Soquel Avenue. Turn right onto 17th Avenue. Continue straight until you reach East Cliff Drive. From here, you can head north or south on East Cliff Drive and park anywhere between 12th and 41st street to access the beaches.

Its Beach
West Cliff Drive
Santa Cruz, CA
831-429-3777
This is not a large beach, but it is big enough for your water loving dog to take a dip in the water and get lots of sand between his or her paws. Dogs must be on leash at all times. The beach is located on West Cliff Drive, just north of the Lighthouse, and south of Columbia Street.

Mitchell's Cove Beach
West Cliff Drive at Almar
Santa Cruz, CA

831-420-5270
Dogs are allowed off-leash on Mitchell's Cove Beach between sunrise and 10 am and from 4 pm to sunset. They must be on-leash during other hours. The beach is along West Cliff Drive between Woodward and Almar. While off-leash dogs must be under voice control.

Seabright Beach
Seabright Ave
Santa Cruz, CA
831-429-2850
This beach is located south of the Santa Cruz Beach Boardwalk and north of the Santa Cruz Harbor. Dogs are allowed on leash. Fire rings are available for beach bonfires. It is open from sunrise to sunset. To get there from Hwy 17 south, exit Ocean Street on the left towards the beaches. Merge onto Ocean Street. Turn left onto East Cliff Drive and stay straight to go onto Murray Street. Then turn right onto Seabright Ave. Seabright Ave will take you to the beach (near the corner of East Cliff Drive and Seabright).

Twin Lakes State Beach
East Cliff Drive
Santa Cruz, CA
831-429-2850
This beach is one of the area's warmest beaches, due to its location at the entrance of Schwann Lagoon. Dogs are allowed on leash. The beach is located just south of the Santa Cruz Harbor where Aldo's Restaurant is located. Fire rings for beach bonfires, outdoor showers and restrooms are available. It is open from sunrise to sunset. To get there from Hwy 17 south, exit Ocean Street on the left towards the beaches. Merge onto Ocean Street. Turn left onto East Cliff Drive and stay straight to go onto Murray Street. Murray Street becomes Eaton Street. Turn right onto 7th Avenue.

Sea Ranch Coastal Access Trails
Highway 1
Sea Ranch, CA
707-785-2377
Walk along coastal headlands or the beach in Sea Ranch. There are six trailhead parking areas which are located along Highway 1, south of the Sonoma Mendocino County Line. Access points include Black Point, Bluff Top Trail, Pebble Beach, Stengal Beach, Shell Beach and Walk on Beach. Dogs must be on a 6 foot or less leash. There is a $3 per car parking fee. RVs and vehicles

with trailers are not allowed to use the parking areas.

Kiva Beach
Hwy 89
South Lake Tahoe, CA
530-573-2600
This small but lovely beach is a perfect place for your pup to take a dip in Lake Tahoe. Dogs must be on leash. To get there from the intersection of Hwys 89 and 50, take Hwy 89 north approx 2-3 miles to the entrance on your right. Follow the road and towards the end, bear left to the parking lot. Then follow the path to the beach.

Upton Beach
Highway 1
Stinson Beach, CA
415-499-6387
Dogs not allowed on the National Park section of Stinson Beach but are allowed at Upton Beach which is under Marin County's jurisdiction. This beach is located north of the National Park. Dogs must be leashed on the beach.

Pebble Beach/Dog Beach
Hwy 89
Tahoe City, CA
This beach is not officially called "pebble beach" but it is an accurate description. No sand at this beach, but your water-loving dog won't mind. The water is crisp and clear and perfect for a little swimming. It's not a large area, but it is very popular with many dogs. There is also a paved bike trail that is parallel to the beach. There was no official name posted for this beach, but it's located about 1-2 miles south of Tahoe City on Hwy 89. From Tahoe City, the beach and parking will be on your left. Dogs should be on leash on the beach.

Trinidad State Beach
Highway 101
Trinidad, CA
707-677-3570
Dogs are unofficially allowed at College Cove beach, as long as they are leashed and under control. The residents in this area are trying keep this beach dog-friendly, but the rules can change at any time. Please call ahead to verify.

Harbor Cove Beach
West end of Spinnaker Drive
Ventura, CA
805-652-4550
This beach is considered the safest swimming area in Ventura because of the protection of the cove. Dogs of

all sizes are allowed at this beach as well as on the 6 miles of Ventura City Beaches and on the long wooden pier, but they are not allowed on any of the beaches south of the Ventura Pier or on any of the State beaches. Dogs must be leashed and cleaned up after at all times.

Promenade Park
Figueroa Street at the Promenade
Ventura, CA
805-652-4550
This park is a one acre oceanfront park on the site of an old Indian village near Seaside Park. Dogs of all sizes are are allowed at this beach as well as on the 6 miles of Ventura City Beaches and on the long wooden pier, but they are not allowed on any of the beaches south of the Ventura Pier or on any of the State beaches. Dogs must be leashed and cleaned up after at all times.

Surfer's Point at Seaside Park
Figueroa Street at the Promenade
Ventura, CA
800-483-6215
This park is one of the area's most popular surfing and windsurfing beaches, and it offers showers, picnic facilities and restrooms, and is connected with the Ventura Pier by a scenic landscaped Promenade walkway and the Omer Rains Bike Trail. Dogs are allowed on the 6 miles of Ventura City Beaches and on the long wooden pier, but they are not allowed on any of the beaches south of the Ventura Pier or on any of the State beaches. Dogs must be leashed and cleaned up after at all times.

Westport-Union Landing State Beach
Highway 1
Westport, CA
707-937-5804
This park offers about 2 miles of sandy beach. Dogs must be on a 6 foot or less leash at all times and people need to clean up after their pets. Picnic tables, restrooms (including an ADA restroom) and campsites are available at this park. Dogs are also allowed at the campsites, but not on any park trails. The park is located off Highway 1, about 2 miles north of Westport or 19 miles north of Fort Bragg.

North Beach at Zephyr Cove Resort
460 Highway 50

Zephyr Cove, NV
775-588-6644
Dogs are not allowed at the main beach at the Zephyr Cove Resort. They are allowed on leash, however, at the north beach at the resort. There is a $5.00 parking fee for day use. When you enter Zephyr Cover Resort head to the right (North) to the last parking area and walk the few hundred feet to the beach. The North Beach is located just into the National Forest. There usually are cleanup bags on the walkway to the beach but bring your own in case they run out. This is a nice beach that is used by a lot of people in the summer. The cabins at Zephyr Cove Resort also allow dogs.

Colorado

Union Reservoir Dog Beach
County Line Rd at E 9th Ave
Longmont, CO
303-651-8447
This is an unfenced off-leash area where dogs may swim in the Union Reservoir. Dogs may only be off-leash in the designated area and must be leashed when in the rest of the rec area. Dogs are not allowed on beaches outside of the dog beach. To get to Union Reservoir Rec Area from I-25 take Ute Hwy west to E County Line Rd and turn left (south). Turn left onto Highway 26 into the park in just over one mile.

Connecticut

Town of Fairfield Beaches
off Highway 1
Fairfield, CT
203-256-3010
Dogs are only allowed on the town beaches during the off-season. Pets are not allowed on the beaches from April 1 through October 1. Dogs must be on leash and people need to clean up after their pets.

Delaware

Bethany Beach
off Route 1
Bethany Beach, DE
302-539-8011
townofbethanybeach.com/FAQ.shtml
From May 15 to September 30, pets are not allowed on the beach or boardwalk at any time. But during the off-season, dogs are allowed but

need to be leashed and cleaned up after.

Dewey Beach
Coastal Highway/Route 1
Dewey Beach, DE
302-227-1110
Dogs are allowed on the beach year-round only with a special license and with certain hour restrictions during the summer season. A special license is required for your dog to go on the beach. You do not have to be a resident of Dewey Beach to get the license. You can obtain one from the Town of Dewey Beach during regular business hours at 105 Rodney Avenue in Dewey Beach. The cost is $15 per dog and is good for the lifetime of your dog. During the summer, from May 15 to September 15, dogs are only allowed before 9:30am and after 5:30pm. During the off-season there are no hourly restrictions. Year-round, dogs can be off-leash but need to be under your control at all times and cleaned up after.

Fenwick Island Beach
off Route 1
Fenwick Island, DE
302-539-2000
fenwickisland.org
From May 1 to September 30, dogs are not allowed on the beach at any time. The rest of the year, pets are allowed on the beach but must be leashed and cleaned up after. The beach is located of Route 1, south of Dewey Beach.

Cape Henlopen State Park
42 Cape Henlopen Drive
Lewes, DE
302-645-8983
destateparks.com/chsp/chsp.htm
This park draws thousands of visitors who enjoy sunbathing and ocean swimming. Dogs on a 6 foot or less leash are allowed on the beach, with some exceptions. Dogs are not allowed on the two swimming beaches during the summer, but they are allowed on surfing and fishing beaches, bike paths and some of the trails. Pets are not allowed on the fishing pier. During the off-season, dogs are allowed on any of the beaches, but still need to be leashed. People are required to clean up after their pets. The park is located one mile east of Lewes, 1/2 mile past the Cape May-Lewes Ferry Terminal.

Delaware Seashore State Park
Inlet 850
Rehoboth Beach, DE

302-227-2800
destateparks.com/dssp/dssp.asp
This park offers six miles of ocean and bay shoreline. Dogs on a 6 foot or less leash are allowed on the beach, with a couple of exceptions. Dogs are not allowed at the lifeguarded swimming areas. However, there are plenty of non-guarded beaches where people with dogs can walk or sunbathe. During the off-season, dogs are allowed on any of the beaches, but still need to be leashed. People are required to clean up after their pets. The park is located south of Dewey Beach, along Route 1.

Rehoboth Beach
off Route 1
Rehoboth Beach, DE
302-227-6181
cityofrehoboth.com/
From April 1 to October 31, pets are not allowed on the beach or boardwalk at any time. However, during the off-season, dogs are allowed but need to be leashed and cleaned up after. The beach is located off Route 1, north of Dewey Beach.

South Bethany Beach
off Route 1
South Bethany, DE
302-539-3653
southbethany.org/
From May 15 to October 15, dogs are not allowed on the beach at any time. The rest of the year, during the off-season, dogs are allowed on the beach. Pets must be leashed and cleaned up after. The beach is located of Route 1, south of Dewey Beach.

Florida

De Soto National Memorial Beach Area
PO Box 15390
Bradenton, FL
941-792-0458
nps.gov/deso/index.htm
Dogs must be on leash and must be cleaned up after in this park. Leashed dogs are allowed in the beach area, which is past a hut following a shell path.

Cape San Blas Barrier Dunes
Cape San Blas, FL

This is one of the nicer pet-friendly beaches in Florida. Leashed dogs are allowed year round on the

beach which has a number of stations with clean up bags. Please clean up after your dog.

Carrabelle Beach
Carrabelle Beach Rd
Carrabelle, FL
850-697-2585
Dogs are allowed on this beach, but the following rules apply. Dogs must be on leash when near sunbathers. In areas where there are no sunbathers, dogs can be off-leash, but must be under direct voice control. Picnic areas and restrooms are available. The beach is located 1.5 miles west of town.

Dog Island Park
Dog Island, FL
850-697-2585
This island is a small remote island that is accessible only by boat, ferry or airplane. Dogs are allowed on the beach, but must be on leash. There are some areas of Dog Island that are within a nature conservancy and dogs are not allowed in these areas. Dog owners will be fined in the nature conservancy. This island is south of Carrabelle.

Veteran's Memorial Park
Highway 1
Duck Key, FL
305-872-2411
Dogs on leash are allowed at this park and on the beach. People need to clean up after their pets. The park is located near mile marker 40, off Highway 1.

Honeymoon Island State Park
1 Causeway Blvd.
Dunedin, FL
727-469-5942
Dogs on a 6 foot or less leash are allowed on part of the beach. Please ask the rangers for details when you arrive at the park. The park is located at the extreme west end of SR 586, north of Dunedin.

Fernandina City Beach
14th St at the Atlantic Ocean
Fernandina Beach, FL
904-277-7305
The Fernandina City Beaches allow dogs on leash. The beach is about 2 miles long. Please make sure that you pick up after your dog.

Flagler Beach
A1A
Flagler Beach, FL
386-517-2000
Dogs are allowed north of 10th

Street and south of 10th Street. They are not allowed on or near the pier at 10th Street. Dogs must be on leash and people need to clean up after their dogs.

Canine Beach
East End of Sunrise Blvd
Fort Lauderdale, FL
954-761-5346
There is a 100 yard stretch of beach which dogs can use. Dogs must be on leash when they are not in the water. The beach is open to dogs only on Friday, Saturday and Sundays. In winter, the hours are 3 pm - 7 pm and the summer hours are 5 pm - 9 pm. A permit is required to use the Canine Beach. There are annual permits available for $25 for residents of the city or $40 for non-residents or you can get a one weekend permit for $5.65. Permits can be purchased at Parks and Recreation Department, 1350 W. Broward Boulevard. Call (954) 761-5346 for permit information.

Dog Swim at Snyder Park
3299 SW 4th Avenue
Fort Lauderdale, FL
954-828-4343
There is a $1 park admission fee for entering the park for the doggy swim area; it is available on Saturdays and Sundays from 10AM to 5PM (closed Christmas/New Years). Dogs must be sociable, current on all vaccinations and license, and under their owner's control at all times. Dogs must be leashed when not in designated off-lead areas.

Dog Beach
Estero Blvd/H 865
Fort Myers Beach, FL
239-461-7400
Located just north of the New Pass Bridge, this barrier island beach offers a perfect off-leash area for beach-lov'in pups.This beach is actually in Bonita Beach on the city line with Fort Myers Beach. Dogs are allowed in designated areas only, and they must be licensed, immunized, and non-aggressive to people, other pets, or wildlife. Dogs may not be left unattended at any time, and they must be under their owner's control at all times; clean-up stations are provided. Two healthy dogs are allowed per person over 15 years old. Dogs on Fort Myers Beach must be leashed at all times.

Fort Myers Dog Beach
3410 Palm Beach Blvd
Fort Myers Beach, FL

239-461-7400
Dogs are allowed off leash on this section of the beach. Cleanup stations are provided. Must have a copy of health records with you at all times. The beach is run by Lees County Parks and Recreation.

Lee County Off-Leash Dog Beach Park
Route 865
Fort Myers Beach, FL
Dogs are allowed off-leash at this beach. Please clean up after your dog and stay within the dog park boundaries. Dog Beach is located south of Ft. Myers Beach and north of Bonita Beach on Route 865. Parking is available near New Pass Bridge.

Walton Rocks Beach
S H A1A
Fort Pierce, FL
772-462-1517
stlucieco.gov/parks/beaches.htm
This dog friendly beach offers 24 acres of untouched beach, covered picnic tables, bathrooms with showers, a natural reef that is exposed at low tide, and plenty of parking. Dogs must be under their owner's control at all times.

Hollywood Dog Beach
North Broadwalk at Pershing St
Hollywood, FL
dboh.org
This dog beach with limited hours was approved and opened in 2008. The beach is located between Pershing Street and Custer Street along N. Broadwalk and one block from A1A. Dogs are allowed on the beach only on Fridays, Saturdays and Sundays. Please do not bring a dog to the beach on any other day. In addition during the Summer dogs are allowed on the beach only from 5 pm to 9 pm and in the Winter months they are allowed from 3 pm to 7 pm. Summer months begin when Daylight Savings time begins in March and end when Eastern Standard time is resumed in the fall. The permission to use the beach will be reviewed every six months or so it is very important that all dog owners clean up and follow the hours and other rules of the beach. For more information see the website at http://www.dboh.org. The beach is sponsored and maintained by the "Dog Beach of Hollywood" organization.

Anne's Beach
Highway 1

Islamorada, FL
Dog on leash are allowed at this beach. Please clean up after your dog. The beach is located around mile markers 72 to 74. There should be a sign.

Dogwood Park Lake Bow Wow
7407 Salisbury Rd South
Jacksonville, FL
904-296-3636
jaxdogs.com
This dog park is great for any size canine. It has 25 fenced acres in a 42 acre park. Dogs can be off leash in any part of the park. The park offers picnic tables, a pond for small dogs, a pond for large dogs (Lake Bow Wow), shower for dogs, warm water for dog baths, tennis balls and toys for play, a playground with games for your dogs, trails to walk on, and bag stations for cleanup. Locals can become members for the year for about $24.00 per month or out-of-town visitors can pay about $11 for a one time visit.

Huguenot Memorial Park
10980 Hecksher Drive
Jacksonville, FL
904-251-3335
Dogs are allowed in the park and on the beach. Dogs must be leashed and people need to clean up after their dogs. The park is located off A1A.

Katheryn Abby Hanna Park Beach
500 Wonderwood Dr
Jacksonville, FL
904-249-4700
coj.net
Dogs are allowed in this park for camping, hiking, picnics and on the dog friendly beach.

Jupiter Beach
A1A at Xanadu Road
Jupiter, FL
This is a wide, nice, white sandy beach that stretches 2 miles along the Atlantic Coast. It is one of the nicer beaches that allow dogs in South Florida. Please follow the dog rules requiring leashes and cleaning up after your dog.

Dog Beach
Vernon Ave and Waddell Ave
Key West, FL
This tiny stretch of beach is the only beach we found in Key West that a dog can go to.

Rickenbacker Causeway Beach
Rickenbacker Causeway

Miami, FL
This beach extends the length of the Rickenbacker Causeway from Downtown Miami to Key Biscayne. Dogs are allowed on the entire stretch. There are two types of beach, a Tree lined Dirt beach and a standard type of sandy beach further towards Key Biscayne. Dogs should be leashed on the beach.

Delnor-Wiggins Pass State Park
11100 Gulfshore Drive
Naples, FL
239-597-6196
Dogs are not allowed on the beaches in this park, but they can take dip in the water at the boat and canoe launch only. Dogs must be on leash. Please clean up after your dog. This park is located six miles west of Exit 17 on I-75.

Smyrna Dunes Park
Highway 1
New Smyrna Beach, FL
386-424-2935
Dogs are not allowed on the ocean beach, but are allowed almost everywhere else, including on the inlet beach and river. Bottlenosed dolphins are typically seen in the inlet as well as the ocean. Dogs must be leashed and people need to clean up after their pets. The park is located on the north end of New Smyrna Beach.

Bayview Dog Beach
In Bayou Texar off E Lloyd Street
Pensacola, FL
850-436-5511
This water park for dogs offers pets beach and water fun, and there are benches, picnic tables, trash cans, pooper scooper stations, and a washing station on site. Dogs must be sociable, current on all vaccinations, licensed, and under their owner's control at all times. Dogs must be leashed when not in designated off-lead areas.

Lighthouse Point Park
A1A
Ponce Inlet, FL
386-239-7873
You might see some dolphins along the shoreline at this park. The park is also frequented by people watching a space shuttle launch out of Cape Canaveral. If you go during a shuttle launch, be sure to hold on tight to your pooch, as the shuttles can become very, very noisy and loud. Dogs on leash are allowed at the park and on the beach. Please clean up after your dog. This park is

located at the southern point of Ponce Inlet.

Algiers Beach
Algiers Lane
Sanibel, FL
239-472-6477
This beach is located in Gulfside City Park. Dogs on leash are allowed and people need to clean up after their pets. Picnic tables and restrooms are available. There is an hourly parking fee. This beach is located about mid-way on the island. From the Sanibel causeway, turn right onto Periwinkle Way. Turn left onto Casa Ybel Rd and then left on Algiers Lane.

Bowman's Beach
Bowman Beach Road
Sanibel, FL
239-472-6477
Walk over a bridge to get to the beach. Dogs on leash are allowed and people need to clean up after their pets. Picnic tables are available. This beach is located on the west side of the island, near Captiva. From the Sanibel causeway, turn right on Periwinkle Way. Turn right on Palm Ridge Rd and then continue on Sanibel-Captiva Road. Turn left onto Bowman's Beach Rd.

Lighthouse Park Beach
Periwinkle Way
Sanibel, FL
239-472-6477
This park offers a long thin stretch of beach. Dogs on leash are allowed and people need to clean up after their pets. Picnic tables are available. This park is located on the east end of the island. From Causeway Road, turn onto Periwinkle Way.

Tarpon Bay Road Beach
Tarpon Bay Road
Sanibel, FL
239-472-6477
Take a short walk from the parking lot to the beach. Dogs on leash are allowed and people need to clean up after their pets. Picnic tables and restrooms are available. There is an hourly parking fee. This beach is located mid-way on the island. From the Sanibel causeway, turn right onto Periwinkle Way. Then turn left onto Tarpon Bay Road.

Fort Matanzas National Monument
8635 A1A South
St Augustine, FL
904-471-0116

nps.gov/foma/index.htm
Dogs on 6 ft leash are allowed in this National monument. Dogs are allowed in the park, on the beach, and on the trails. They are not allowed in the visitor center, boats, or fort.

St Augustine Lighthouse and Museum
81 Lighthouse Avenue
St Augustine, FL
904-829-0745
Dogs on leash are allowed on the grounds of the lighthouse and beach area. There are some tables for picnics or bring a blanket. There is a fee to enter the lighthouse grounds.

St Augustine Beach
Most Beaches
St Augustine Beach, FL
904-209-0655
The St. Augustine Beach allows leashed dogs. Owners must clean up after their pets. This policy extends to most of the beaches in St John's County but other rules will apply to beaches in State Parks, many of which don't allow dogs.

Public Access Beaches
Gulf Beach Drive
St George Island, FL
St. George Island beaches have been consistently ranked as one of the top 10 beaches in America. One third of the island is Florida state park land which does not allow dogs. But the rest of the island offers Franklin County public beaches, which do allow dogs on a 6 foot leash or off-leash and under direct voice control.

St George Island Beaches
St George Island, FL
850-927-2111
Dogs on leash are allowed on the beaches of St George Island. However, they are not allowed on the beaches, trails, or boardwalks in St. George State Park. Dog Owners can be fined in the state park.

Gandy Bridge Causeway
Gandy Bridge east end
St Petersburg, FL
This stretch of beach allows dogs to run and go swimming. We even saw a horse here. Dogs should be leashed on the beach.

Pinellas Causeway Beach
Pinellas Bayway
St Petersburg, FL
This stretch of beach is open to

humans and dogs. Dogs should be on leash on the beach.

Davis Island Dog Park
Severn Ave and Martinique Ave
Tampa, FL
davisislanddogs.com
This dog beach is fenced and offers a large parking area and even a doggie shower. To get there go towards Davis Island and head for the Peter Knight Airport. Loop around until you reach the water (the airport should be on the left). Thanks to one of our readers for the updated information.

Georgia

Jekyll Island Beaches and Trails
off SR 520
Jekyll Island, GA
877-453-5955
These beaches look like a Carribean island setting. It is hard to believe that you just drove here over a causeway. Dogs on leash are welcome year round on the beach and the paved and dirt trails. There are about 10 miles of beaches and 20 miles of inland paved and dirt trails. It is recommended that your pooch stay on the paved trails instead of the dirt trails during the warm summer months because there are too many ticks along the dirt trails. On warmer days you might choose a beach walk rather than the inland trails anyway because of the cooler ocean breezes.

Little St. Simons Island Beaches
off U.S. 17
St Simons Island, GA
912-554-7566
Dogs are allowed, but only during certain hours in the summer. From Memorial Day through Labor Day, dogs are allowed on the beach before 9:30am and after 4pm. During the rest of the year, dogs are allowed anytime during park hours. Dogs must be on leash and people need to clean up after their pets.

St. Simons Island Beaches
off U.S. 17
St Simons Island, GA
912-554-7566
Dogs are allowed, but only during certain hours in the summer. From Memorial Day through Labor Day, dogs are allowed on the beach before 9:30am and after 4pm. During the rest of the year, dogs are allowed anytime during park hours. Dogs

must be on leash and people need to clean up after their pets.

Hawaii

Oahu Dog-Friendly Beaches
(Leashes required)
Various
Honolulu, HI
808-946-2187
According to the Hawaiian Humane Society website in November, 2006 the following beaches on Oahu allow dogs on leash. Please check with them at:
http://www.hawaiianhumane.org/programs/dogparks/dogbeaches.html for updates. The beaches that allow well-behaved, leashed dogs are:
Aukai Beach, Jauula
Gray's Beach (Halekulani Beach), Waikiki
Haleaha Beach, Punaluu
Hanakailio Beach, Kahuku
Kaalawai Beach, Diamond Head
Kahala Beach, Kahala
Kahuku Golf Course Beach, Kahuku
Kailua Beach, Kahuku
Kaipapau Beach, Hauula
Kakela Beach, Hauula
Kaloko Beach,Kokohead
Kaluahole Beach, Diamond Head
Kanenelu Beach, Kaaawa
Kapaeloa Beach, North Shore
Kawela Bay Beach, North Shore
Kealia Beach, Mokuleia
,Kualoa Sugar Mill Beach,Kualoa
Kuilima Cove Beach, Kahuku
Laie Beach, Laie
Lanikai Beach, Kailua
Laniloa Beach, Laie
Mahakea Beach, Laie
Makao Beach, Hauula
Makua Beach, Makua
Manner's Beach, Kahe
Mokuleia Army Beach, Mokuleia
Moluleia Beach, Mokuleia
Niu Beach, Niu Valley
Oneawa Beach, Kailua
Outrigger Canoe Club Beach, Waikiki
Pahipahialua Beach, North Shore
Paiko Beach,Kuliouou
Punaluu Beach, Punaluu
Puuiki Beach, Mokuleia
Royal-Moana Beach, Waikiki
Turtle Bay Beach, North Shore.

Illinois

Belmont Harbor Dog Beach
located on Belmont Ave off Lake Shore Dr
Chicago, IL

Dogs are allowed in this small fenced beach area on-leash. The city may ticket dog owners whose dogs are off-leash even though it is often used as an off-leash area by some people.

Montrose Harbor Dog Beach
Lake Shore Drive
Chicago, IL
312-742-7529
Dogs are allowed on part of the beach near Montrose. Dogs can run leash-free on the beach. Please note that people who violate the leash law by not having their dog on a leash between the parking lot and the beach are being fined with $75 tickets, so be sure to bring your dog's leash. Beginning in September, 2005 all dogs that use the dog parks are required to have an annual permit. The permits currently cost $5 per dog. You will have to visit an approved location to get a permit. Proof of certain vaccinations are also required.

Evanston Dog Beach
Church Street
Evanston, IL
847-866-2900
Dogs are not allowed on this beach unless you first purchase a token from the city of Evanston. The cost per dog for one season is $88 for non-residents of Evanston and $44 for residents. Prices are subject to change. To purchase a token, you must have proof of your dog's current rabies vaccination and a current dog license. Dog beach is a large strip of sand located just north of the Church Street launch facility, where Church Street meets the lake. Beach hours are 7am to 8pm, May through October, weather permitting. Dog beach tokens can be purchased at the Dempster Street Beach Office from 10am to 5pm weekends only in May and after memorial day the office is open seven days a week. Tokens can also be purchased at the City Collectors Office in the Civic Center at 2100 Ridge Avenue, 8:30am to 5pm, Monday through Friday. Dog beach rules and regulations are available at the Dempster Street Beach Office.

Indiana

Indiana Dunes National Lakeshore
off Highway I-94
Porter, IN
219-926-7561x225
nps.gov/indu/

Dogs are not allowed on all of the beaches, but are allowed on two beaches which are located at the far east side of the park. One of the beaches is near Mt. Baldy and the other is near Central Avenue. Check with the visitor center when you arrive for exact locations. Pets are also allowed on some of the trails, campground and picnic area but must be leashed and cleaned up after. The park is located on Lake Michigan. To get there, take Highway 94 east and take Exit 26 Chesterton/49 North and head north.

Louisiana

Cameron Parish Beaches
433 Marshall Street (Chamber of Commerce)
Cameron, LA
337-775-5222
user.camtel.net/cameron/public/
Located in the southwestern part of the state bordering Texas, this parish offers over 25 miles of beaches on the Gulf of Mexico to be enjoyed by people and pooches. Dogs must be kept leashed and picked up after at all times.

Grand Isle State Park
Admiral Craik Drive
Grand Isle, LA
985-797-2559
lastateparks.com/
Dogs on leash are allowed at the beaches, except for some designated swimming areas. This park offers many recreational opportunities like fishing, crabbing, sunbathing, nature watching and camping. Leashed pets are also allowed at the campsites. The park is located on the east end of Grand Isle, off Highway 1 on Admiral Craik Drive. It is about 2 hours outside of New Orleans.

Maine

Hadley Point Beach
Highway 3
Bar Harbor, ME
Dogs are allowed on the beach, but must be leashed. The beach is located about 10 minutes northwest of downtown Bar Harbor, near Eden.

Kennebunk Beaches
Beach Avenue
Kennebunk, ME
Dogs are allowed with certain restrictions year round. Leashed and

off-leash dogs are allowed on the beach before 9am and after 5pm. Dogs are not allowed on the beach during the hours of 9 am to 5 pm. There are a string of beaches, including Kennebunk, Gooch's and Mother's, that make up a nice stretch of wide sandy beaches. People need to clean up after their pets. The beaches are located on Beach Avenue, off Routes 9 and 35.

Goose Rocks Beach
Dyke Street
Kennebunkport, ME
Leashed dogs are allowed, with certain restrictions. From June 15 through September 15, dogs are only allowed on the beach before 8am and after 6pm. During the rest of the year, dogs are allowed on the beach during park hours. People need to clean up after their pets. The beach is located about 3 miles east of Cape Porpoise. From Route 9, exit onto Dyke Street.

Old Orchard Beach City Beach
Old Orchard Beach, ME
207-934-0860
Leashed dogs are allowed on this beach only before 10 am and after 5 pm daily year round. People need to make sure they pick up their dog's waste with a plastic bag and throw it away in a trash can.

East End Beach
Cutter Street
Portland, ME
207-874-8793
Dogs are only allowed on this beach from the day after Labor Day to the day before Memorial Day. Dogs are not allowed on the beach from Memorial Day through Labor Day. During the months that dogs are allowed, they can be off-leash but need to be under direct voice control. People need to make sure they pick up their dog's waste with a plastic bag and throw it away in a trash can.

Old Orchard
Cutter Street
Portland, ME
207-874-8793
Dogs are only allowed on this beach from the day after Labor Day to the day before Memorial Day. Dogs are not allowed on the beach from Memorial Day through Labor Day. During the months that dogs are allowed, they can be off-leash but need to be under direct voice control. People need to make sure

they pick up their dog's waste with a plastic bag and throw it away in a trash can.

Willard Beach
South Portland, ME
207-767-7601
At Willard Beach there are restrooms, lifeguards, and parking for 75 cars. Dogs are only allowed on the beach from 6:00 a.m. to 9:00 a.m. year round. Dogs must be kept away from bird eggs and out of the dunes. There are dog bag stations at many entrances to the mile long beach. Dogs must be cleaned up after at all times. Dogs must be leashed at all times or off-leash and under excellent voice control within a limited distance of the owner.

Wells Beach
Route 1
Wells, ME
207-646-2451
Leashed dogs are allowed, with certain restrictions. During the summer, from June 16 through September 15, dogs are only allowed on the beach before 8am and after 6pm. The rest of the year, dogs are allowed on the beach during all park hours. There are seven miles of sandy beaches in Wells. People are required to clean up after their pets.

Long Sands Beach
Route 1A
York, ME
207-363-4422
Leashed dogs are allowed, with certain restrictions. During the summertime, from about Memorial Day weekend through Labor Day weekend, dogs are only allowed on the beach before 8am and after 6pm. During the off-season, dogs are allowed during all park hours. This beach offers a 1.5 mile sandy beach. Metered parking and private lots are available. The beach and bathhouse are also handicap accessible. People are required to clean up after their pets.

Short Sands Beach
Route 1A
York, ME
207-363-4422
Leashed dogs are allowed, with certain restrictions. During the summertime, from about Memorial Day weekend through Labor Day weekend, dogs are only allowed on the beach before 8am and after 6pm. During the off-season, dogs are allowed during all park hours. At the beach, there is a large parking area

and a playground. People are required to clean up after their pets.

York Harbor Beach
Route 1A
York, ME
207-363-4422
Leashed dogs are allowed, with certain restrictions. During the summertime, from about Memorial Day weekend through Labor Day weekend, dogs are only allowed on the beach before 8am and after 6pm. During the off-season, dogs are allowed during all park hours. This park offers a sandy beach nestled against a rocky shoreline. There is limited parking. People are required to clean up after their pets.

Maryland

Quiet Waters Park Dog Beach
600 Quiet Waters Park Road
Annapolis, MD
410-222-1777
friendsofquietwaterspark.org
This park is located on Chesapeake Bay, not on the ocean. Dogs are welcome to run off-leash at this dog beach and dog park. The dog park is closed every Tuesday. Leashed dogs are also allowed at Quiet Waters Park. The park offers over 6 miles of scenic paved trails, and a large multi-level children's playground. People need to clean up after their pets. To get there, take Route 665 until it ends and merges with Forrest Drive. Take Forrest Drive for 2 miles and then turn right onto Hillsmere Drive. The park entrance is about 100 yards on the right. The dog beach is located to the left of the South River overlook. Park in Lot N.

Assateague Island National Seashore
Route 611
Assateague Island, MD
410-641-1441
nps.gov/asis/
Dogs on leash are allowed on beaches, except for any lifeguarded swimming beaches (will be marked off with flags). There are plenty of beaches to enjoy at this park that are not lifeguarded swimming beaches. Dogs are not allowed on trails in the park. The park is located eight miles south of Ocean City, at the end of Route 611.

Elm's Beach Park
Bay Forest Road
Hermanville, MD

301-475-4572
The park is located on Chesapeake Bay, not on the ocean. Enjoy great views of the bay or swim at the beach. Dogs on leash are allowed at the beach. People need to clean up after their pets. Take Route 235 to Bay Forest Road and then go 3 miles. The park will be on the left.

Ocean City Beaches
Route 528
Ocean City, MD
1-800-OC-OCEAN
Dogs are only allowed during certain times of the year on this city beach. Pets are not allowed on the beach or boardwalk at any time from May 1 through September 30. The rest of the year, dogs are allowed on the beach and boardwalk, but must be on leash and people must clean up after them.

Downs Park Dog Beach
8311 John Downs Loop
Pasadena, MD
410-222-6230
This dog beach is located on Chesapeake Bay, not on the ocean. People are not permitted to go swimming, but dogs can run off-leash at this beach. The dog beach is closed every Tuesday. Dogs on leash are also allowed in Downs Park. People need to clean up after their pets. Take Route 100 until it merges with Moutain Road (Rt. 177 East). Follow Mt. Road for about 3.5 miles and the park entrance will be on your right. The dog beach is located in the northeast corner of the park.

Massachusetts

Barnstable Town Beaches
off Route 6A
Barnstable, MA
508-790-6345
Dogs are allowed only during the off-season, from September 15 to May 15. Dogs must be on leash or under voice control. People need to clean up after their pets. The town of Barnstable oversees Hyannis beaches and the following beaches: Craigville, Kalmus, and Sandy Neck. Before you go, always verify the seasonal dates and times when dogs are allowed on the beach.

Carson Beach
I-93 and William Day Blvd
Boston, MA

617-727-5114
Dogs are only allowed on the beach during the off-season. Pets are not allowed from Memorial Day weekend through Labor Day weekend. Dogs must be leashed and people are required to clean up after their pets.

Chatham Town Beaches
off Route 28
Chatham, MA
508-945-5100
Dogs are allowed only during the off-season, from mid September to end the end of May. Dogs must be leashed and people need to clean up after their pets. The town of Chatham oversees the following beaches: Hardings, Light, and Ridgevale. Before you go, always verify the seasonal dates and times when dogs are allowed on the beach.

Dennis Town Beaches
Route 6A
Dennis, MA
508-394-8300
Dogs are allowed only during the off-season, from after Labor Day up to Memorial Day. There is one exception. Dogs are allowed year-round on the four wheel drive area of Chapin Beach. Dogs must be leashed on all town beaches, and people need to clean up after their pets. The town of Dennis oversees the following beaches: Chapin, Mayflower, Howes Street and Sea Street. Before you go, always verify the seasonal dates and times when dogs are allowed on the beach.

Duxbury Beach
150 Gurnet Road
Duxbury, MA
duxburybeach.com/
This 6 mile long barrier beach reaches from Marshfield in the north to Gurnet Point and Saquish in the south. From April 1st until September 15th dogs are allowed on the beach; they must be leashed, registered at the Duxbury Town Hall if they are to be taken on the beach, and the permit acquired must be carried by the handler of the dog at all times while on beach properties. Dogs are allowed on Duxbury Beach properties from 8 am until sunset only. Dogs are not allowed on dunes, wildlife areas, or any fenced areas, and they must be cleaned up after promptly. Dogs may not be on the front beach (Resident Beach) south to the poles defining the beginning of the 4 X 4 beach or on the back beach north of the Powder Point Bridge adjacent to the resident

parking lot from April 1st until September 15th. Dogs must be under their owner's control at all times.

Joseph Sylvia State Beach
Beach Road
Edgartown, MA
508-696-3840
Dogs are allowed during the summer, only before 9am and after 5pm. You will need to keep your dog away from any bird nesting areas, which should have signs posted. During the off-season, from mid-September to mid-April, dogs are allowed all day. This beach is about 2 miles long. Dogs must be leashed and people need to clean up after their pets. Before you go, always verify the seasonal dates and times when dogs are allowed on the beach.

Norton Point Beach
end of Katama Road
Edgartown, MA
508-696-3840
Dogs are allowed during the summer, only before 9am and after 5pm. You will need to keep your dog away from any bird nesting areas, which should have signs posted. During the off-season, from mid-September to mid-April, dogs are allowed all day. This beach is about 2.5 miles long. Dogs must be leashed and people need to clean up after their pets. Before you go, always verify the seasonal dates and times when dogs are allowed on the beach.

South Beach State Park
Katama Road
Edgartown, MA
508-693-0085
Dogs are allowed during the summer, only after 5pm. During the off-season, from mid-September to mid-April, dogs are allowed all day. This 3 mile beach is located on the South Shore. Dogs must be leashed and people need to clean up after their pets. Before you go, always verify the seasonal dates and times when dogs are allowed on the beach.

Falmouth Town Beaches
off Route 28
Falmouth, MA
508-457-2567
Dogs are not allowed during the summer from May 1 through October 1. During the off-season, dogs are allowed all day. Dogs must be leashed and people need to clean up after their pets. The town of Falmouth oversees the following

beaches: Menauhant, Surf Drive, and Old Silver. Before you go, always verify the seasonal dates and times when dogs are allowed on the beach.

Harwich Town Beach
off Route 28
Harwich, MA
508-430-7514
Dogs are allowed only during the off-season, from October to mid-May. Dogs must be on leash or under voice control. People need to clean up after their pets. The town of Harwich oversees Red River Beach. Before you go, always verify the seasonal dates and times when dogs are allowed on the beach.

Singing Beach
Beach Street
Manchester, MA
978-526-2040
Dogs under excellent voice control are allowed off-leash from October 1 through May 1 on the pristine Singing Beach. Dogs are not allowed on the beach during the other months. From Manchester, take Beach Street to the water. Parking can be difficult in this area.

Brant Rock Beach
Ocean Street/H 139
Marshfield, MA
781-834-0268
Leashed dogs are allowed on the Brant Rock Beach all through the year; they must be cleaned up after promptly. Sometimes there are waste dispenser bags at the entrances.

Nantucket Island Beaches
various locations
Nantucket, MA
508-228-1700
Dogs are allowed during the summer on beaches with lifeguards only before 9am and after 5pm. On beaches that have no lifeguards, or during the winter months, dogs are allowed all day on the beach. Dogs must always be leashed. Before you go, always verify the seasonal dates and times when dogs are allowed on the beach.

Eastville Point Beach
At bridge near Vineyard Haven
Oak Bluffs, MA
508-696-3840
Dogs are allowed during the summer, only before 9am and after 5pm. You will need to keep your dog away from any bird nesting areas, which should have signs

posted. During the off-season, from mid-September to mid-April, dogs are allowed all day. Dogs must be leashed and people need to clean up after their pets. Before you go, always verify the seasonal dates and times when dogs are allowed on the beach.

Orleans Town Beaches
off Route 28
Orleans, MA
508-240-3775
Dogs are allowed only during the off-season, from after Columbus Day to the Friday before Memorial Day. Dogs are allowed off leash, but must be under voice control. People need to clean up after their pets. The town of Orleans oversees Nauset and Skaket beaches. Before you go, always verify the seasonal dates and times when dogs are allowed on the beach.

Plymouth City Beach
Route 3A
Plymouth, MA
508-747-1620
The beach in Plymouth allows dogs year round on the beach and in the water. Dogs must be leashed and cleaned up after.

Provincetown Town Beaches
off Route 6
Provincetown, MA
508-487-7000
Dogs on leash are allowed year-round. During the summer, from 6am to 9am, dogs are allowed off-leash. Before you go, always verify the seasonal dates and times when dogs are allowed on the beach.

Sandwich Town Beaches
off Route 6A
Sandwich, MA
508-888-4361
Dogs are allowed only during the off-season, from October through March. Dogs must be leashed and people need to clean up after their pets. The town of Sandwich oversees the following beaches: East Sandwich and Town Neck. Before you go, always verify the seasonal dates and times when dogs are allowed on the beach.

Truro Town Beaches
off Route 6
Truro, MA
508-487-2702
Dogs are allowed during the summer, only before 9am and after 6pm. This policy is in effect from about the third weekend in June

through Labor Day. During the off-season, dogs are allowed all day. Dogs must be leashed and people need to clean up after their pets. The town of Truro oversees the following beaches: Ballston, Corn Hill, Fisher, Great Hollow, Head of the Meadow, Longnook and Ryder. Before you go, always verify the seasonal dates and times when dogs are allowed on the beach.

Cape Cod National Seashore
Route 6
Wellfleet, MA
508-349-3785
nps.gov/caco
The park offers a 40 mile stretch of pristine sandy beaches. Dogs on leash are allowed year-round on all of the seashore beaches, except for seasonally posted nesting or lifeguarded beaches. Leashed pets are also allowed on fire roads, and the Head of the Meadow bicycle trail in Truro. Check with the visitor center or rangers for details about fire road locations. To get there from Boston, take Route 3 south to the Sagamore Bridge. Take Route 6 east towards Eastham.

Wellfleet Town Beaches
off Route 6
Wellfleet, MA
508-349-9818
Dogs are allowed during the summer, only before 9am and after 6pm. During the off-season, from after Labor Day to the end of June, dogs are allowed all day. Dogs must be leashed and people need to clean up after their pets. The town of Wellfleet oversees the following beaches: Marconi, Cahoon Hollow, and White Crest. Before you go, always verify the seasonal dates and times when dogs are allowed on the beach.

Sandy Neck Beach
425 Sandy Neck Road
West Barnstable, MA
508-362-8300
In addition to being a haven for endangered bird and wildlife, this 6 mile long coastal barrier beach also shares a unique ecology and rich cultural history. There is an off-road beach, a public beach and miles of trails here. Dogs are allowed on the trails and on the Off-Road beach area anytime (but stay on water side) throughout the year, but they are not allowed on the public beach from May 15 to September 15. Dogs are not allowed in the primitive camp area. Visitors and their pets must

remain on designated trails, off the dunes, and off the few areas of private property. Please consult trail maps. Dogs must be leashed and cleaned up after at all times.

Michigan

Young State Park Beach
C56 off 131
Boyne City, MI
231-582-7523
While dogs are not allowed on the beach, they can go into the water past the boat launch. There is a sandy and rocky area that leads to the water. Pets must be leashed and attended at all times and cleaned up after.

Burt Lake State Park Beach
Old 27 Highway
Burt Lake, MI
231-238-9392
This is not a Great Lakes beach, but is conveniently located off of I-75. While dogs are not allowed on the swimming beach, there is a special designated spot where dogs can go into the water. It is near campsite lot number 42, off Road 1, at the west end of the park. The road leads to the beach and dog run. Pets must be on a 6 foot or less leash and attended at all times.

Aloha State Park Beach
off I-75
Cheboygan, MI
231-625-2522
This is not a Great Lakes beach, but is conveniently located off of I-75. The park has a special pet swimming area which is located by the playground. Pets need to be leashed and cleaned up after. The park is located 7 miles south of Cheboygan and 25 miles from the Mackinac Bridge.

Sleeping Bear Dunes National Lakeshore Beaches
off M-72
Empire, MI
231-326-5134
nps.gov/slbe/
While pets are not allowed in certain areas of the park like the islands, Dune Climb, backcountry campsites, or inside buildings, they are allowed on some trails, campgrounds and on the following beaches. Pets are welcome on the the south side of the beach at Esch Road (south of Empire), on the south side of Peterson Beach and

on Empire Beach. Dogs must be leashed at all times and cleaned up after. To get there from Traverse City, take M-72 west to Empire.

Wilderness State Park Beach
Wilderness Park Drive
Mackinaw City, MI
231-436-5381
Dogs are not allowed at the beach but they can swim in the water on the other side of the boat launch. Pets must be a on a 6 foot or less leash and cleaned up after. The park is located 11 miles west of Mackinaw City.

Norman F. Kruse Park - Dog Beach
W Sherman Blvd and Beach Street
Muskegon, MI
231-724-6704
Although dogs are not allowed in the park area here, they are allowed at their own piece of the beach at the end of Sherman Road. Dogs must be on leash unless in the water and cleaned up after at all times. The site is open from 7 am until 11 pm.

Grand Mere State Park Beach
Thornton Drive
Stevensville, MI
269-426-4013
Dogs on leash are allowed at the beach and on the hiking trails. The one mile beach is located along the shoreline of Lake Michigan. Remember to clean up after your pet. To get there, take I-94 south of St. Joseph and take Exit 22. Go west .25 miles to Thornton Drive and head south on Thornton for .5 miles.

Mississippi

Hancock County Beaches
Beach Blvd.
Bay St Louis, MS
228-463-9222 (800-466-9048)
mswestcoast.org
Dogs on leash are allowed on Hancock County beaches. People need to clean up after their pets. The county beaches are located along the coast, between the cities of Waveland and Bay St. Louis.

Montana

Canine Beach at Bozeman Ponds
700 - 550 N. Fowler Lane
Bozeman, MT
406-582-3200
bozeman.net/parks/parks.aspx
The Canine Beach is an off-leash

dog beach on the west side of the Bozeman Pond. The park is open from 8 am to 10 pm daily. Pets must be picked up after at the beach and leashed outside of the leash-free area.

New Jersey

Barnegat Lighthouse State Park Beaches
At Broadway and the Bay
Barnegat Light, NJ
609-494-2016
Although dogs are not allowed in the lighthouse or on the beaches from April 15th to August 15, and never on the trails here, they are allowed in the park and picnic areas which provide visitors with great views of the ocean and waterway activities. Dogs are allowed on the park beaches from October 1 through April 14 each year. Dogs are welcome for no additional fee. Dogs must be under their owner's control, leashed, and cleaned up after at all times.

Higbee Beach Wildlife Management Area
County Road 641
Cape May, NJ
609-628-2103
This park offers a 1 1/2 mile stretch of beach. The beach is managed specifically to provide habitat for migratory wildlife. Dogs on leash and under control are allowed at the beach from September through April. To get there, take SR 109 west to US9. Turn left onto US9 and go to the first traffic light. Turn left onto County Road 162 (Seashore Rd.). Then turn right onto Country Road 641 (New England Rd.). Take CR641 for 2 miles to the end and the beach access parking area. Parking areas near the beach may be closed during the summer. The park is open daily from dawn to dusk.

Cape May Point State Park
Lighthouse Avenue
Cape May Point, NJ
609-884-2159
Dogs are only allowed on the beach during the off-season. Pets are not allowed from April 15 through September 15. Pets must be on a 6 foot or less leash and people need to clean up after their pets. The park is located off the southern end of the Garden State Parkway. Go over the Cape May Bridge to Lafayette Street. At the intersection, go right onto

Route 606 (Sunset Blvd.), then turn left onto Lighthouse Ave.

Brant Beach
6805 S Long Beach Blvd
Long Beach Township, NJ
609-361-1000
njlbi.com/lbidoginfo.html
Visitors will find dune fencing here giving easy access for the dogs from the beach to the water. Dogs are not allowed on the beaches from May 1st until October 1st. Owners must pick up after their pets

Fisherman's Cove Conservation Area
391 Third Avenue
Manasquan, NJ
732-922-4080
This is a 52 acre tract on the Manasquan Inlet. It is used for fishing, walking on the beach and sunbathing. Dogs must be on-leash everywhere in the park. To get to the beach take exit 98 from the Garden State Parkway and head south on Rt 34 which becomes Rt 35. Turn right on Higgins Avenue, then left onto Union Avenue (Rt 71), right on Fisk Avenue and right onto 3rd Ave.

Bayshore Waterfront Park Beach
Port Monmouth Road
Port Monmouth, NJ
732-842-4000
Located near the Monmouth Cove Marina, this 227 acre park offers a fishing pier, views of the New York City skyline, miles of beach, and access to Raritan Bay. Leashed dogs are allowed at the park; they must be leashed and cleaned up after promptly at all times.

Island Beach State Park
off Route 35
Seaside Park, NJ
732-793-0506
One of the states last significant remnants of a barrier island ecosystem, it is home to diverse wildlife and maritime plant life, and with a variety of land and water activities and 8 interesting trails. During the winter months, dogs are allowed on all of the beaches, but must be on a 6 foot or less leash. People are required to clean up after their pets. To get to the park, take Route 37 east. Then take Route 35 south to the park entrance. Dogs are not allowed on the lifeguarded swimming beaches during the summer. Dogs are not allowed on the Spizzle Creek Bird Blind Trail at any time of year.

Stone Harbor Beach
1st Avenue
Stone Harbor, NJ
609-368-6101
stoneharborbeach.com/
Stone Harbor has 'unleashed' its summer ban of dogs on the beach to allow them on the beach between 80th and 83rd Streets from dawn to 9 am and from 6 pm until dusk. Dogs must be leashed and owners must clean up after their pets.

New Mexico

Tingley Beach
1800 Tingley Drive SW
Albuquerque, NM
505-768-2000
cabq.gov/biopark/tingley/
Open from dawn to dusk daily, year around, this site offers 3 fishing lakes, a train station with a gift shop, a model boating pond, bike and watercraft rentals, walking paths, and concessionaires. This site is also home to the world's largest caught Trout; fishing licenses are available at the gift shop - open daily from 9 am until 5 pm. Dogs are allowed at Tingley; they must be leashed at all times and cleaned up after promptly; they are not allowed at the Zoo, Botanic Garden grounds, or inside the aquarium.

New York

New York City Beaches and Boardwalks
Various
Brooklyn, NY
212-NEW-YORK
From October 1 through April 30 each year, leashed dogs are allowed on the sand and the boardwalk at certain beaches. Currently, these beaches are Rockaway Beach, Coney Island, Brighton Beach, Manhattan Beach, Midland Beach and South Beach. Dogs are not allowed on the sand at any New York City beaches between May 1 and September 30. Leashed dogs are allowed year-round on the boardwalks and promenade at Coney Island, Brighton, Midland, South and Manhattan Beaches. Please check the website at http://www.nycgovparks.org for updated information and changes.

Camp Hero State Park
50 South Fairview Avenue

Montauk, NY
631-668-3781
nysparks.com/maps/
The park boasts some of the best surf fishing spots in the world. Dogs on a 6 foot or less leash are allowed on the beach areas year-round, but not in the picnic areas. To get to the park, take Route 27 (Sunrise Highway) east to the end. The park is about 130 miles from New York City.

Hither Hills State Park
50 South Fairview Avenue
Montauk, NY
631-668-2554
nysparks.com/maps/
This park offers visitors a sandy ocean beach. Dogs are allowed with certain restrictions. During the off-season, dogs are allowed on the beach. During the summer, dogs are not allowed on the beach, except for the undeveloped area on the other side of the freeway. Dogs must be on a 6 foot or less leash and people need to clean up after their pets. Dogs are not allowed in buildings or on walkways and they are not allowed in the camping, bathing and picnic areas.

Montauk Point State Park
50 South Fairview Avenue
Montauk, NY
631-668-3781
nysparks.com/maps/
This park is located on the eastern tip of Long Island. Dogs are allowed on the beach, but not near the food area. Dogs must be on a 6 foot or less leash and people need to clean up after their pets. Dogs are not allowed in buildings or on walkways and they are not allowed in the camping, bathing and picnic areas. Please note that dogs are not allowed in the adjacent Montauk Downs State Park. The park is located 132 miles from Manhattan, off Sunrise Highway (Route 27).

New York City Beaches and Boardwalks
Various
New York, NY
212-NEW-YORK
From October 1 through April 30 each year, leashed dogs are allowed on the sand and the boardwalk at certain beaches. These beaches are Rockaway Beach, Coney Island, Brighton Beach, Manhattan Beach, Midland Beach and South Beach. Dogs are not allowed on the sand at any New York City beaches between May 1 and September 30. Leashed dogs are allowed year-round on the

boardwalks and promenade at Coney Island, Brighton, Midland, South and Manhattan Beaches. Please check the website at http://www.nycgovparks.org for updated information and changes.

New York City Beaches/Boardwalks
various
New York, NY
212-NEW-YORK (639-9675)
nyc.gov/apps/311/
Dogs are not allowed on any New York beaches at any time; they are allowed on the Boardwalks from the 2nd of October until the last day of April. The Boardwalks are at Promenade Orchard Beach, Coney Island Beach, Brighton Beach, Midland Beach, South Beach, and Manhattan Beach. Dogs must be kept leashed and under their owner's control at all times.

Prospect Park Dog Beach
Prospect Park - Brooklyn
New York, NY
212-NEW-YORK
This man made, concrete beach was designed for our canine friends. It is located in Prospect Park, off 9th Street on the path leading down from the Tennis House. Dogs may only be off-leash before 9 am and after 9 pm in the summer and after 5 pm in the winter. People are not permitted to swim in the dog pool. There is a fence to keep the dogs in so you don't have to chase them across the pond.

North Carolina

Fort Macon State Park
Highway 58
Atlantic Beach, NC
252-726-3775
This park offers beach access. Dogs on a 6 foot leash or less are allowed on the beach, but not inside the Civil War fort located in the park. People need to clean up after their pets. The park is located on the eastern end of Bogue Banks, south of Morehead City.

Corolla Beaches
Ocean Trail
Corolla, NC
252-232-0719
outerbanks.com/
Dogs are allowed on the beaches in and around the Corolla area year round; they must be leashed and cleaned up after at all times.

Duck Beach
H 12
Duck, NC
252-255-1234
townofduck.com/
Dogs are welcome to romp on the beach here, and they may be off leash if they are under good voice control. Dogs must be licensed, have current rabies tags, be under their owner's control, and cleaned up after at all times. Dogs must be on no more than a 10 foot leash when off the beach.

Kill Devil Hills Beaches
N Virginia Dare Trail
Kill Devil Hills, NC
252-449-5300
kdhnc.com/
From May 15th to September 15th dogs are not allowed on the beaches between 9 AM and 6 PM. When dogs are allowed on the beach, they must be licensed, have current rabies tags, be under their owner's control, on no more than a 10 foot leash, and cleaned up after at all times.

Kitty Hawk Beaches
Virginai Dare Trail/H 12
Kitty Hawk, NC
252-261-3552
townofkittyhawk.org/
Between 10 am and 6 pm from the Friday before Memorial Day until the day after Labor Day, dogs may be on the beach on a maximum 6 foot leash; for all other times they may be on a retractable leash up to 12 feet. Well trained dogs may be off-lead from Labor Day to the Friday before Memorial Day if they are under strict voice control and never more than 30 feet from the owner. Resident dogs must display a county registration tag plus a valid rabies tags, and non-resident dogs must have a valid rabies tag. Dogs must be under their owner's control and cleaned up after at all times.

Ft. Fisher State Recreation Area
Highway 421
Kure Beach, NC
910 458-5798
Enjoy miles of beachcombing, sunbathing or hunting for shells at this beach. Dogs on leash are allowed everywhere on the beach, except for swimming areas that have lifeguards on duty. People need to clean up after their pets. The park is located on the southern tip of Pleasure Island, near Wilmington.

Cape Hatteras National Seashore
Highway 12
Manteo, NC
252-473-2111
nps.gov/caha/
This park offers long stretches of pristine beach. Dogs on a 6 foot or less leash are allowed year-round, except on any designated swimming beaches. Most of the beaches are non-designated swim beaches. People are required to clean up after their pets.

Nags Head Beaches
N Vriginia Dare Trail/H 12
Nags Head, NC
252-441-5508
townofnagshead.net/
The beaches here consist mostly of open spaces and low-density building. Dogs are allowed on the beaches year round; they must be licensed, have current rabies tags, be under their owner's control, on no more than a 10 foot leash, and cleaned up after at all times.

Oak Island Beaches
Beach Drive
Oak Island, NC
910-278-5011
oakislandnc.com/
Dogs are allowed on city beaches year round, but from mid November to about the 1st of April dogs may be off lead if they are under strict voice control. Dogs must be under their owner's control, leashed April to November, and cleaned up after at all times.

Southern Shores Beaches
H 12
Southern Shores, NC
252-261-2394
From May 15th to September 15th dogs are not allowed on the beaches. Dogs must be licensed, have current rabies tags, be under their owner's control, on no more than a 10 foot leash, and cleaned up after at all times. A parking permit is required for parking in town and can be obtained at the Town Hall, 5375 N. Virginia Dare Trail.

Topsail Beach
Ocean Blvd
Topsail Beach, NC
910-328-5841
topsailbeach.org/
There are about 20 public assesses to the beaches in this town. From May 15th to September 30th dogs must be leashed when on the beach; otherwise dogs may be off lead if they are under strict adult voice control. Dogs must be cleaned up after at all times and always be leashed when not on the beach.

Ohio

Fairport Harbor Lakefront Park Dog Swim Area.
301 Huntington Beach Drive
Fairport Harbor, OH
440-639-9972
Open May to September, this 21 acre lakefront park offers family fun recreation for all ages - even the family pooch. It has a doggy swim area where dogs can play while the park is open from dawn to dusk. Dogs must be kept leashed and are only allowed in the paved parking area and the designated dog swim area of the park.

Geneva State Park
4499 Padanarum Road
Geneva, OH
440-466-8400
While dogs are cannot go on the swim beach, they can go in the water outside of the designated swim beach. Pets must be leashed and cleaned up after. To get there from Cleveland, take Interstate 90 east to Route 534 north. The park entrance is six miles north on Route 534, on the left.

Kelleys Island State Park Beach
Division Street
Kelleys Island, OH
419-746-2546
While pets are not allowed at the small 100 foot swimming beach, they are welcome to join you at the "long beach" but you will need to keep them away from other beachgoers. Pets must be leashed and cleaned up after. To get there you will need to take a ferry to the island. Kelleys Island Ferry Boat Line operates year round, weather permitting, and offers passenger and limited vehicle service from Marblehead, Ohio to the island. Leashed pets are welcome on the ferry. Once on Kelleys Island, go west on E. Lakeshore Drive and turn right on Division Street. The park is at the end of Division Street on the right.

Maumee Bay State Park Beach
1400 State Park Road
Oregon, OH
419-836-7758
While dogs are not allowed at any beaches at this park, either on the Lake Erie shore or at the park's inland lake, dogs are permitted to take a dip in the water at the end of the inland lake which is on the south side of the road. Pets must be leashed even when in the water, and cleaned up after.

Catawba Island State Park Beach
4049 East Moores Dock Rd.
Port Clinton, OH
419-797-4530
Swimming is permitted on this small beach but there are no lifeguards. Dogs are welcome at the beach but need to be leashed when not in the water. The park is off of State Route 53.

East Harbor State Park Beach
Route 269
Port Clinton, OH
419-734-4424
While dogs are not allowed on any sandy beach at this park, they can take a dip in the pond which is located off the exit road, next to the shelter road. Pets must be leashed and cleaned up after. To get there from Cleveland, take State Route 2 West to State Route 269 North. The park is located on State Route 269. To get there from Port Clinton, go east on Route 163 to Route 269 north.

Oregon

Bullards Beach State Park
Highway 101
Bandon, OR
541-347-2209
oregonstateparks.org/park_71.php
Enjoy a walk along the beach at this park. Picnic tables, restrooms, hiking and campgrounds are available at the park. There is a minimal day use fees. Leashed dogs are allowed on the beach. Dogs are also allowed on hiking trails and campgrounds. They must be on a six foot or less leash at all times and people are required to clean up after their pets. On beaches located outside of Oregon State Park boundaries, dogs might be allowed off-leash and under direct voice control, please look for signs or postings. This park is located off U.S. Highway 101, 2 miles north of Bandon.

Seven Devils State Recreation Site
Highway 101
Bandon, OR
800-551-6949
oregonstateparks.org/park_69.php

Enjoy several miles of beach at this park. Picnic tables are available at this park. There are no day use fees. Dogs are allowed on the beach. They must be on a six foot or less leash at all times and people are required to clean up after their pets. On beaches located outside of Oregon State Park boundaries, dogs might be allowed off-leash and under direct voice control, please look for signs or postings. This park is located off U.S. Highway 101, 10 miles north of Bandon.

Harris Beach State Park
Highway 101
Brookings, OR
541-469-2021
oregonstateparks.org/park_79.php
The park offers sandy beaches for beachcombing, whale watching, and sunset viewing. Picnic tables, restrooms (including an ADA restroom) and shaded campsites are available at this park. There is a minimal day use fee. Leashed dogs are allowed on the beach. Dogs are also allowed at the campgrounds. They must be on a six foot or less leash at all times and people are required to clean up after their pets. On beaches located outside of Oregon State Park boundaries, dogs might be allowed off-leash and under direct voice control, please look for signs or postings. This park is located off U.S. Highway 101, just north of Brookings.

McVay Rock State Recreation Site
Highway 101
Brookings, OR
800-551-6949
oregonstateparks.org/park_75.php
This beach is a popular spot for clamming, whale watching and walking. Picnic tables and restrooms are available at this park. There are no day use fees. Dogs are allowed on the beach. They must be on a six foot or less leash at all times and people are required to clean up after their pets. On beaches located outside of Oregon State Park boundries, dogs might be allowed off-leash and under direct voice control, please look for signs or postings. This park is located off U.S. Highway 101, just south of Brookings.

Samuel H. Boardman State Scenic Corridor
Highway 101
Brookings, OR
800-551-6949
oregonstateparks.org/park_77.php

Steep coastline at this 12 mile long corridor is interrupted by small sandy beaches. Picnic tables, restrooms (including an ADA restroom), and a hiking trail are available at this park. There are no day use fees. Leashed dogs are allowed on the beach. Dogs are also allowed on the hiking trail. They must be on a six foot or less leash at all times and people are required to clean up after their pets. On beaches located outside of Oregon State Park boundaries, dogs might be allowed off-leash and under direct voice control, please look for signs or postings. This park is located off U.S. Highway 101, 4 miles north of Brookings.

Arcadia Beach State Recreation Site
Highway 101
Cannon Beach, OR
800-551-6949
This sandy ocean beach is just a few feet from where you can park your car. Picnic tables and restrooms are available at this park. There are no day use fees. Dogs are allowed on the beach. They must be on a six foot or less leash at all times and people are required to clean up after their pets. On beaches located outside of Oregon State Park boundaries, dogs might be allowed off-leash and under direct voice control, please look for signs or postings. This park is located off U.S. Highway 101, 3 miles south of Cannon Beach.

Ecola State Park
Highway 101
Cannon Beach, OR
503-436-2844
According to the Oregon State Parks Division, this park is one of the most photographed locations in Oregon. To reach the beach, you will need to walk down a trail. Restrooms, hiking and primitive campgrounds are available at this park. There is a $3 day use fee. Leashed dogs are allowed on the beach. Dogs are also allowed on hiking trails and campgrounds. They must be on a six foot or less leash at all times and people are required to clean up after their pets. On beaches located outside of Oregon State Park boundaries, dogs might be allowed off-leash and under direct voice control, please look for signs or postings. This park is located off U.S. Highway 101, 2 miles north of Cannon Beach.

Hug Point State Recreation Site
Highway 101
Cannon Beach, OR
800-551-6949
According to the Oregon State Parks Division, people used to travel via stagecoach along this beach before the highway was built. Today you can walk along the original trail which was carved into the point by stagecoaches. The trail is located north of the parking area. Visitors can also explore two caves around the point, but be aware of high tide. Some people have become stranded at high tide when exploring the point! This beach is easily accessible from the parking area. Picnic tables and restrooms are available at this park. There are no day use fees. Dogs are allowed on the beach. They must be on a six foot or less leash at all times and people are required to clean up after their pets. On beaches located outside of Oregon State Park boundaries, dogs might be allowed off-leash and under direct voice control, please look for signs or postings. This park is located off U.S. Highway 101, 5 miles south of Cannon Beach.

Tolovana Beach State Recreation Site
Highway 101
Cannon Beach, OR
800-551-6949
Indian Beach is popular with surfers. There is a short walk down to the beach. Picnic tables are available at this park. There are no day fees. Dogs are allowed on the beach. They must be on a six foot or less leash at all times and people are required to clean up after their pets. On beaches located outside of Oregon State Park boundaries, dogs might be allowed off-leash and under direct voice control, please look for signs or postings. This park is located off U.S. Highway 101, 1 mile south of Cannon Beach.

Sunset Bay State Park
89814 Cape Arrago H
Coos Bay, OR
541-888-4902
This scenic park's beautiful sandy beaches are protected by the towering sea cliffs surrounding them, and the day-use and picnic facilities are only a short walk from the beach allowing for easy access for beachcombing, fishing, swimming, and boating. There is a network of hiking trails that connect Sunset Bay with nearby Shore Acres and Cape Arago State Parks. These trails give

the hiker opportunities to experience the pristine coastal forests, seasonal wildflowers, and the spectacular ocean vistas of the area. There is a fully enclosed observation building that has interpretive panels describing the history of the Simpson estate along the way. From points along the trail you can see views of Gregory Point and the Cape Arago lighthouse. The park is open year round from 8 a.m. until sunset. Dogs on lead at all times are allowed, and pets must be cleaned up after. Dogs may not be left unattended at any time. There is a campground here that offer a variety of activities and recreation.

Fogarty Creek State Recreation Area
Highway 101
Depoe Bay, OR
800-551-6949
This beach and park offer some of the best birdwatching and tidepooling. Picnic tables and hiking are available at this park. There is a $3 day use fees. Leashed dogs are allowed on the beach. Dogs are also allowed on hiking trails. They must be on a six foot or less leash at all times and people are required to clean up after their pets. On beaches located outside of Oregon State Park boundaries, dogs might be allowed off-leash and under direct voice control, please look for signs or postings. This park is located off U.S. Highway 101, 2 miles north of Depoe Bay.

Carl G. Washburne Memorial State Park
Highway 101
Florence, OR
541-547-3416
This park offers five miles of sandy beach. Picnic tables, restrooms, hiking and campgrounds are available at this park. There is a day use fee. Leashed dogs are allowed on the beach. Dogs are also allowed on hiking trails and campgrounds. They must be on a six foot or less leash at all times and people are required to clean up after their pets. On beaches located outside of Oregon State Park boundaries, dogs might be allowed off-leash and under direct voice control, please look for signs or postings. This park is located off U.S. Highway 101, 14 miles north of Florence.

Heceta Head Lighthouse State Scenic Viewpoint
Highway 101
Florence, OR

800-551-6949
Go for a walk above the beach or explore the natural caves and tidepools along the beach. This is a great spot for whale watching. According to the Oregon State Parks Division, the lighthouse located on the west side of 1,000-foot-high Heceta Head (205 feet above ocean) is one of the most photographed on the Oregon coast. Picnic tables, restrooms and hiking are available at this park. There is a $3 day use fee. Leashed dogs are allowed on the beach. Dogs are also allowed on hiking trails. They must be on a six foot or less leash at all times and people are required to clean up after their pets. On beaches located outside of Oregon State Park boundaries, dogs might be allowed off-leash and under direct voice control, please look for signs or postings. This park is located off U.S. Highway 101, 13 miles north of Florence.

Pistol River State Scenic Viewpoint
Highway 101
Gold Beach, OR
800-551-6949
oregonstateparks.org/park_76.php
This beach is popular for ocean windsurfing. There has even been windsurfing national championships held at this beach. Picnic tables and restrooms are available here. There are no day use fees. Dogs are allowed on the beach. They must be on a six foot or less leash at all times and people are required to clean up after their pets. On beaches located outside of Oregon State Park boundaries, dogs might be allowed off-leash and under direct voice control, please look for signs or postings. This park is located off U.S. Highway 101, 11 miles south of Gold Beach.

D River State Recreation Site
Highway 101
Lincoln City, OR
800-551-6949
This beach, located right off the highway, is a popular and typically windy beach. According to the Oregon State Parks Division, this park is home to a pair of the world's largest kite festivals every spring and fall which gives Lincoln City the name Kite Capital of the World. Restrooms are available at the park. Dogs are allowed on the beach. They must be on a six foot or less leash at all times and people are required to clean up after their pets. On beaches located outside of

Oregon State Park boundaries, dogs might be allowed off-leash and under direct voice control, please look for signs or postings. This park is located off U.S. Highway 101 in Lincoln City.

Roads End State Recreation Site
Highway 101
Lincoln City, OR
800-551-6949
There is a short trail here that leads down to the beach. Picnic tables are available at this park. There are no day use fees. Dogs are allowed on the beach. They must be on a six foot or less leash at all times and people are required to clean up after their pets. On beaches located outside of Oregon State Park boundaries, dogs might be allowed off-leash and under direct voice control, please look for signs or postings. This park is located off U.S. Highway 101, 1 mile north of Lincoln City.

Nehalem Bay State Park
Highway 101
Manzanita, OR
503-368-5154
The beach can be reached by a short walk over the dunes. This park is a popular place for fishing and crabbing. Picnic tables, restrooms (including an ADA restroom), hiking and camping are available at this park. There is a $3 day use fee. Leashed dogs are allowed on the beach. Dogs are also allowed on hiking trails and campgrounds. They must be on a six foot or less leash at all times and people are required to clean up after their pets. On beaches located outside of Oregon State Park boundaries, dogs might be allowed off-leash and under direct voice control, please look for signs or postings. This park is located off U.S. Highway 101, 3 miles south of Manzanita Junction.

Oswald West State Park
Highway 101
Manzanita, OR
800-551-6949
The beach is located just a quarter of a mile from the parking areas. It is a popular beach that is frequented by windsurfers and boogie boarders. Picnic tables, restrooms, hiking, and campgrounds are available at this park. There are no day use fees. Leashed dogs are allowed on the beach. Dogs are also allowed on hiking trails and campgrounds. They must be on a six foot or less leash at all times and people are required to

clean up after their pets. On beaches located outside of Oregon State Park boundaries, dogs might be allowed off-leash and under direct voice control, please look for signs or postings. This park is located off U.S. Highway 101, 10 miles south of Cannon Beach.

Neskowin Beach State Recreation Site
Highway 101
Neskowin, OR
800-551-6949
Not really any facilities (picnic tables, etc.) here, but a good place to enjoy the beach. Dogs are allowed on the beach. They must be on a six foot or less leash at all times and people are required to clean up after their pets. On beaches located outside of Oregon State Park boundaries, dogs might be allowed off-leash and under direct voice control, please look for signs or postings. This park is located off U.S. Highway 101 in Neskowin.

Agate Beach State Recreation Site
Highway 101
Newport, OR
800-551-6949
This beach is popular with surfers. Walk through a tunnel to get to the beach. According to the Oregon State Parks Division, many years ago Newport farmers led cattle westward through the tunnel to the ocean salt. Picnic tables and restrooms are available at this park. There is no day use fees. Dogs are allowed on the beach. They must be on a six foot or less leash at all times and people are required to clean up after their pets. On beaches located outside of Oregon State Park boundaries, dogs might be allowed off-leash and under direct voice control, please look for signs or postings. This park is located off U.S. Highway 101, 1 mile north of Newport.

Beverly Beach State Park
Highway 101
Newport, OR
541-265-9278
To get to the beach, there is a walkway underneath the highway that leads to the ocean. Picnic tables, restrooms (including an ADA restroom), a walking trail and campgrounds are available at this park. There is a day use fee. Leashed dogs are allowed on the beach. Dogs are also allowed on the walking trail and campgrounds. They must be on a six foot or less leash at

all times and people are required to clean up after their pets. On beaches located outside of Oregon State Park boundaries, dogs might be allowed off-leash and under direct voice control, please look for signs or postings. This park is located off U.S. Highway 101, 7 miles north of Newport.

Devils Punch Bowl State Natural Area
Highway 101
Newport, OR
800-551-6949
This is a popular beach for surfing. Picnic tables, restrooms and hiking are available at this park. There are no day use fees. Leashed dogs are allowed on the beach. Dogs are also allowed on hiking trails. They must be on a six foot or less leash at all times and people are required to clean up after their pets. On beaches located outside of Oregon State Park boundaries, dogs might be allowed off-leash and under direct voice control, please look for signs or postings. This park is located off U.S. Highway 101, 8 miles north of Newport.

South Beach State Park
Highway 101
Newport, OR
541-867-4715
This beach offers many recreational opportunities like beachcombing, fishing, windsurfing and crabbing. Picnic tables, restrooms (including an ADA restroom), hiking (including an ADA hiking trail), and campgrounds are available at this park. There is a day use fee. Leashed dogs are allowed on the beach. Dogs are also allowed on hiking trails and campgrounds. They must be on a six foot or less leash at all times and people are required to clean up after their pets. On beaches located outside of Oregon State Park boundaries, dogs might be allowed off-leash and under direct voice control, please look for signs or postings. This park is located off U.S. Highway 101, 2 miles south of Newport.

Bob Straub State Park
Highway 101
Pacific City, OR
800-551-6949
This is a nice stretch of beach to walk along. Picnic tables and restrooms (including an ADA restroom) are available at this park. There are no day use fees. Dogs are allowed on the beach. They

must be on a six foot or less leash at all times and people are required to clean up after their pets. On beaches located outside of Oregon State Park boundaries, dogs might be allowed off-leash and under direct voice control, please look for signs or postings. This park is located off U.S. Highway 101 in Pacific City.

Cape Kiwanda State Natural Area
Highway 101
Pacific City, OR
800-551-6949
This beach and park is a good spot for marine mammal watching, hang gliding and kite flying. Picnic tables are available at this park. There are no day use fees. Dogs are allowed on the beach. They must be on a six foot or less leash at all times and people are required to clean up after their pets. On beaches located outside of Oregon State Park boundaries, dogs might be allowed off-leash and under direct voice control, please look for signs or postings. This park is located off U.S. Highway 101, 1 mile north of Pacific City.

Cape Blanco State Park
Highway 101
Port Orford, OR
541-332-6774
oregonstateparks.org/park_62.php
Take a stroll on the beach or hike on over eight miles of trails which offer spectacular ocean vistas. Picnic tables, restrooms, hiking and campgrounds are available at this park. There is a minimal day use fee. Leashed dogs are allowed on the beach. Dogs are also allowed on hiking trails and campgrounds. They must be on a six foot or less leash at all times and people are required to clean up after their pets. On beaches located outside of Oregon State Park boundaries, dogs might be allowed off-leash and under direct voice control, please look for signs or postings. This park is located off U.S. Highway 101, 9 miles north of Port Orford.

Humbug Mountain State Park
Highway 101
Port Orford, OR
541-332-6774
oregonstateparks.org/park_56.php
This beach is frequented by windsurfers and scuba divers. A popular activity at this park is hiking to the top of Humbug Mountain (elevation 1,756 feet) . Picnic tables, restrooms, hiking and campgrounds are available at this park. There is a

minimal day use fee. Leashed dogs are allowed on the beach. Dogs are also allowed on hiking trails and campgrounds. They must be on a six foot or less leash at all times and people are required to clean up after their pets. On beaches located outside of Oregon State Park boundaries, dogs might be allowed off-leash and under direct voice control, please look for signs or postings. This park is located off U.S. Highway 101, 6 miles south of Port Orford.

Manhattan Beach State Recreation Site
Highway 101
Rockaway Beach, OR
800-551-6949
The beach is a short walk from the parking area. Picnic tables are available at this park. There are no day use fees. Dogs are allowed on the beach. They must be on a six foot or less leash at all times and people are required to clean up after their pets. On beaches located outside of Oregon State Park boundaries, dogs might be allowed off-leash and under direct voice control, please look for signs or postings. This park is located off U.S. Highway 101, 2 miles north of Rockaway Beach.

Del Rey Beach State Recreation Site
Highway 101
Seaside, OR
800-551-6949
There is a short trail to the beach. There is no day use fee. Dogs are allowed on the beach. They must be on a six foot or less leash at all times and people are required to clean up after their pets. On beaches located outside of Oregon State Park boundaries, dogs might be allowed off-leash and under direct voice control, please look for signs or postings. This park is located off U.S. Highway 101, 2 miles north of Gearhart.

Cape Lookout State Park
Highway 101
Tillamook, OR
503-842-4981
This is a popular beach during the summer. The beach is a short distance from the parking area. It is located about an hour and half west of Portland. Picnic tables, restrooms (including an ADA restroom), hiking trails and campgrounds are available at this park. There is a $3 day use fee. Leashed dogs are allowed on the beach. Dogs are also allowed on

hiking trails and campgrounds. They must be on a six foot or less leash at all times and people are required to clean up after their pets. On beaches located outside of Oregon State Park boundaries, dogs might be allowed off-leash and under direct voice control, please look for signs or postings. This park is located off U.S. Highway 101, 12 miles southwest of Tillamook.

Cape Meares State Scenic Viewpoint
Highway 101
Tillamook, OR
800-551-6949
The beach is located south of the scenic viewpoint. The viewpoint is situated on a headland, about 200 feet above the ocean. According to the Oregon State Parks Division, bird watchers can view the largest colony of nesting common murres (this site is one of the most populous colonies of nesting sea birds on the continent). Bald eagles and a peregrine falcon have also been known to nest near here. In winter and spring, this park is an excellent location for viewing whale migrations. Picnic tables, restrooms and hiking are available at this park. There are no day use fees. Leashed dogs are allowed on the beach. Dogs are also allowed on hiking trails. They must be on a six foot or less leash at all times and people are required to clean up after their pets. On beaches located outside of Oregon State Park boundaries, dogs might be allowed off-leash and under direct voice control, please look for signs or postings. This park is located off U.S. Highway 101, 10 miles west of Tillamook.

Beachside State Recreation Site
Highway 101
Waldport, OR
541-563-3220
Enjoy miles of broad sandy beach at this park or stay at one of the campground sites that are located just seconds from the beach. Picnic tables, restrooms (including an ADA restroom), and hiking are also available at this park. There is a day use fees. Leashed dogs are allowed on the beach. Dogs are also allowed on hiking trails and campgrounds. They must be on a six foot or less leash at all times and people are required to clean up after their pets. On beaches located outside of Oregon State Park boundaries, dogs might be allowed

off-leash and under direct voice control, please look for signs or postings. This park is located off U.S. Highway 101, 4 miles south of Waldport.

Governor Patterson Memorial State Recreation Site
Highway 101
Waldport, OR
800-551-6949
This park offers miles of flat, sandy beach. It is also an excellent location for whale watching. Picnic tables and restrooms are available at this park. There are no day use fees. Dogs are allowed on the beach. They must be on a six foot or less leash at all times and people are required to clean up after their pets. On beaches located outside of Oregon State Park boundaries, dogs might be allowed off-leash and under direct voice control, please look for signs or postings. This park is located off U.S. Highway 101, 1 mile south of Waldport.

Fort Stevens State Park
Highway 101
Warrenton, OR
503-861-1671
oregonstate.org/park_179.php
There are miles of ocean beach. Picnic tables, restrooms (including an ADA restroom), hiking and campgrounds are available at this park. There is a $3 day use fee. Leashed dogs are allowed on the beach. Dogs are also allowed on hiking trails and campgrounds. They must be on a six foot or less leash at all times and people are required to clean up after their pets. On beaches located outside of Oregon State Park boundaries, dogs might be allowed off-leash and under direct voice control, please look for signs or postings. This park is located off U.S. Highway 101, 10 miles west of Astoria.

Neptune State Scenic Viewpoint
Highway 101
Yachats, OR
800-551-6949
During low tide at this beach you can walk south and visit a natural cave and tidepools. Or sit and relax at one of the picnic tables that overlooks the beach below. Restrooms (including an ADA restroom) are available at this park. There are no day use fees. Dogs are allowed on the beach. They must be on a six foot or less leash at all times and people are required to clean up after their pets. On beaches located outside of Oregon State Park

boundaries, dogs might be allowed off-leash and under direct voice control, please look for signs or postings. This park is located off U.S. Highway 101,

Yachats State Recreation Area
Highway 101
Yachats, OR
800-551-6949
This beach is a popular spot for whale watching, salmon fishing, and exploring tidepools. Picnic tables and restrooms are available at this park. There are no day use fees. Dogs are allowed on the beach. They must be on a six foot or less leash at all times and people are required to clean up after their pets. On beaches located outside of Oregon State Park boundaries, dogs might be allowed off-leash and under direct voice control, please look for signs or postings. This park is located off U.S. Highway 101 in Yachats.

Puerto Rico

El Combate Beach
Beach Road
Cabo Rojo, PR
800-866-7827
White soft sandy beaches, shade trees/palms, exquisite ocean scenery, a long dock into the water, and food close by are just some of the attractions of this popular family recreation area. Dogs are allowed throughout the park and on the beach; they must be leashed and cleaned up after promptly.

Pennsylvania

Presque Isle State Park Beach
PA Route 832
Erie, PA
814-833-7424
This state park offers beaches and almost 11 miles of hiking trails. Popular activities at the park include surfing, swimming, boating, hiking, in-line skating and bicycling. Dogs are allowed on a 6 foot or less leash at the park including on the hiking trails and only on beaches that are not guarded by lifeguard staff. Dogs can go into the water, still on leash, but people can only wade in up to their knees since there are no lifeguards in those areas. The unguarded beaches are located throughout the park, but if you want to know exact locations, please stop at the park office for details. The park

is located four miles west of downtown Erie, off Route 832.

Rhode Island

Block Island Beaches
Corn Neck Road
Block Island, RI
401-466-2982
Dogs are allowed year-round on the island beaches, but they must be leashed and people are required to clean up after their pets. To get to the beaches, take a right out of town and follow Corn Neck Road. To get to the island, you will need to take the Block Island Ferry which allows leashed dogs. The ferry from Port Judith, RI to Block Island operates daily. If you are taking the ferry from Newport, RI or New London, CT to the island, please note these ferries only operate during the summer. If you are bringing a vehicle on the ferry, reservations are required. Call the Block Island Ferry at 401-783-4613 for auto reservations.

East Beach State Beach
East Beach Road
Charlestown, RI
401-322-0450
riparks.com/misquamicut.htm
Dogs are only allowed on the beach during the off-season, from October 1 through March 31. Pets must be on leash and people are required to clean up after their pets. However, according to a representative at the Rhode Island State Parks Department, in a conversation with them July 2004, the rules may change in the future to have no dogs on the beach year round. To get there, take I-95 to Route 4 South. Then take Route 1 South to East Beach exit in Charlestown.

East Ferry
Conanicus Avenue
Jamestown, RI
401-849-2822
There is a nice green area with a memorial here, and benches placed to watch out over the busy harbor life. Leashed dogs are allowed on the wharf; they must be leashed and under their owner's control at all times. There is also dog friendly dining on the wharf.

Salty Brine State Beach
254 Great Road
Narragansett, RI
401-789-3563

riparks.com/saltybrine.htm
Dogs are only allowed on the beach during the off-season, from October 1 through March 31. Pets must be on leash and people are required to clean up after their pets. However, according to a representative at the Rhode Island State Parks Department, in a conversation with them July 2004, the rules may change in the future to have no dogs on the beach year round. To get there, take I-95 to Route 4 South. Then take Route 1 South to Route 108 South to Point Judith. If you are there during the summer, take the dog-friendly ferry at Pt. Judith to Block Island where leashed dogs are allowed year-round on the island beaches.

Easton's Beach
Memorial Blvd.
Newport, RI
401-847-6875
Dogs are only allowed on the beach during the off-season. They are not allowed on the beach from Memorial Day weekend through Labor Day weekend. Pets must be on leash and people need to clean up after their pets. The beach is located off Route 138A (Memorial Blvd.). There is a parking fee.

Sandy Point Beach
Sandy Point Avenue
Portsmouth, RI
401-683-2101
portsmouthri.com/frames.htm
Located along the Sakonnet River, this beach area offers changing rooms, restrooms, and picnic tables. There are lifeguards on duty from Memorial Day to Labor Day. Free for residents, there is a fee for non-residents; non-resident season stickers are available at the Town Clerk's office at 2200 East Main Road. Dogs are allowed on the beach after the beach has closed at 5 pm. Dogs must be leashed and cleaned up after at all times.

Teddy's Beach
Park Avenue
Portsmouth, RI
401-683-7899
portsmouthri.com/frames.htm
Although located in Island Park, this is not a staffed town beach. There are no restrooms and it is a carry in/carries out facility. Dogs are allowed; they must be leashed and cleaned up after at all times.

East Matunuck State Beach
950 Succotash Road

South Kingston, RI
401-789-8585
riparks.com/eastmatunuck.htm
Dogs are only allowed on the beach during the off-season, from October 1 through March 31. Pets must be on leash and people are required to clean up after their pets. However, according to a representative at the Rhode Island State Parks Department, in a conversation with them July 2004, the rules may change in the future to have no dogs on the beach year round. To get there, take I-95 to Route 4 South. Then take Route 1 South to East Matunuck Exit and follow the signs to the state beach.

Misquamicut State Beach
257 Atlantic Avenue
Westerly, RI
401-596-9097
riparks.com/misquamicut.htm
Dogs are only allowed on the beach during the off-season, from October 1 through March 31. Pets must be on leash and people are required to clean up after their pets. However, according to a representative at the Rhode Island State Parks Department, in a conversation with them July 2004, the rules may change in the future to have no dogs on the beach year round. To get there, take I-95 to Route 4 South. Then take Route 1 South to Westerly. Follow the signs to the state beach.

South Carolina

Edisto Beach State Park
8377 State Cabin Road
Edisto Island, SC
843-869-2756
Sunbathe, beachcomb or hunt for seashells on this 1.5 mile long beach. This park also has a 4 mile nature trail that winds through a maritime forest with great vistas that overlook the salt marsh. Dogs on a 6 foot or less leash are allowed on the beach and on the trails. People need to clean up after their pets.

Folly Beach County Park
Ashley Avenue
Folly Beach, SC
843-588-2426
beachparks.com/follybeach.htm
Dogs are only allowed during the off-season at this beach. They are not allowed from May 1 through September 30. But the rest of the year, dogs on leash are allowed on

the beach during park hours. People are required to clean up after their pets. The park is located on the west end of Folly Island. On the island, turn right at Ashley Avenue stoplight and go to the end of the road.

Alder Lane Beach Access
S. Forest Beach Drive
Hilton Head Island, SC
843-341-4600
This beach has restricted seasons and hours for dogs. During the summertime, from the Friday before Memorial Day through the Tuesday after Labor Day, dogs can only be on the beach before 10am and then after 5pm (they are not allowed from 10am to 5pm). Pets must be leashed. During the off-season and winter months, from April 1 through the Thursday before Memorial Day, dogs must be on a leash between 10am and 5pm. From the Tuesday after Labor Day through September 30, dogs again must be on a leash between 10am and 5pm. At all other times, dogs may be off-leash, but must be under direct, positive voice control. People are required to clean up after their pets. There are 22 metered spaces for beach parking. The cost is a quarter for each 15 minutes.

Coligny Beach Park
Coligny Circle
Hilton Head Island, SC
843-341-4600
This beach has restricted seasons and hours for dogs. During the summertime, from the Friday before Memorial Day through the Tuesday after Labor Day, dogs can only be on the beach before 10am and then after 5pm (they are not allowed from 10am to 5pm). Pets must be leashed. During the off-season and winter months, from April 1 through the Thursday before Memorial Day, dogs must be on a leash between 10am and 5pm. From the Tuesday after Labor Day through September 30, dogs again must be on a leash between 10am and 5pm. At all other times, dogs may be off-leash, but must be under direct, positive voice control. People are required to clean up after their pets. There are 30 metered spaces for beach parking. The cost is a quarter for each 15 minutes. A flat fee of $4 is charged at the parking lot on Fridays through Sundays and holidays.

Folly Field Beach Park

Folly Field Road
Hilton Head Island, SC
843-341-4600
This beach has restricted seasons and hours for dogs. During the summertime, from the Friday before Memorial Day through the Tuesday after Labor Day, dogs can only be on the beach before 10am and then after 5pm (they are not allowed from 10am to 5pm). Pets must be leashed. During the off-season and winter months, from April 1 through the Thursday before Memorial Day, dogs must be on a leash between 10am and 5pm. From the Tuesday after Labor Day through September 30, dogs again must be on a leash between 10am and 5pm. At all other times, dogs may be off-leash, but must be under direct, positive voice control. People are required to clean up after their pets. There are 52 metered spaces for beach parking. The cost is a quarter for each 15 minutes.

Hilton Head Island Beaches

Hilton Head Island, SC
800-523-3373
Dogs are welcome on the beaches of the island during certain times/days: They are not permitted on the beach between 10 AM and 5 PM from the Friday before Memorial Day through Labor Day; they may be on the beach between 10 AM and 5 PM from April 1st to the Thursday before Memorial Day, and between 10 AM and 5 PM the Tuesday after Labor Day through September 30th. Dogs must be leashed and picked up after at all times.

Hunting Island State Park
2555 Sea Island Parkway
Hunting Island, SC
843-838-2011
This park offers over 4 miles of beach. Dogs on a 6 foot or less leash are allowed on the beach and on the trails at this state park. People need to clean up after their pets.

Isle of Palms County Park Beach
14th Avenue
Isle of Palms, SC
843-886-3863
beachparks.com/isleofpalms.htm
Dogs on leash are allowed year-round at this beach. People are required to clean up after their pets. The park is located on the Isle of Palms, on 14th Ave., between Palm Blvd. and Ocean Blvd. Then coming to Isle of Palms from 517, continue straight at the Palm Blvd intersection

and then take the next left at the park gate.

Beachwalker County Park
Beachwalker Drive
Kiawah, SC
843-768-2395
beachparks.com/beachwalker.htm
Dogs on leash are allowed year-round at this beach. People are required to clean up after their pets. The park is located on the west end of Kiawah Island. Take Bohicket Road to the island. Just before the island security gate, turn right on Beachwalker Drive. Follow the road to the park.

Huntington Beach State Park
16148 Ocean Highway
Murrells Inlet, SC
843-234-4440
This beach is the best preserved beach on the Grand Strand. Dogs on a 6 foot or less leash are allowed on the beach. People need to clean up after their pets.

Myrtle Beach City Beaches
off Interstate 73
Myrtle Beach, SC
843-281-2662
There are certain restrictions for pets on the beach. Dogs are not allowed on the right of way of Ocean Blvd. (part of I-73), between 21st Avenue North and 13th Avenue South during March 1 through September 30. From Memorial Day weekend through Labor Day weekend, leashed dogs are allowed on Myrtle Beach city beaches before 9am and after 5pm. During off-season, leashed dogs are allowed on the city beaches anytime during park hours. People need to clean up after their pets.

Myrtle Beach State Park
4401 South Kings Highway
Myrtle Beach, SC
843-238-5325
This is one of the most popular public beaches on the South Carolina coast. It is located in the heart of the Grand Strand. During the summer time, dogs are only allowed during certain hours. From May `15 through Sept 15, dogs are only allowed on the beach after 5 pm and before 8 am. For all other months of the year, dogs are allowed on the beach anytime during park hours. Dogs must be on leash at all times. People are required to clean up after their pets.

Sullivan Island Beach

Atlantic Avenue
Sullivan's Island, SC
843-883-3198
sullivansisland-sc.com/
Dogs are allowed off leash on this barrier island beach from 5 AM to 10 AM April through October, and from 5 AM to 12 Noon November 1st to March 31st; this does not include walkways or access paths to the area where they must be leashed (no longer than 10 feet). A pet permit is required that can be obtained at the Town Hall at 1610 Middle Street-proof of vaccinations and rabies required. Dogs are NOT allowed on the beach, paths, or the adjacent waters at any time from 10 AM to 6 PM from April 1st to October 31st; however they are allowed at these areas on a leash from 6 PM to 5 AM, April 1st to October 31st, and from 12 Noon to 5 AM from November 1st to March 31st. Dogs must be under their owner's control at all times. Dogs must be leashed when not in designated off-lead areas.

Texas

Cole Park
Ocean Drive
Corpus Christi, TX
800-766-2322
Dogs on leash are allowed on the beach. People need to clean up after their pets.

Bryan Beach
Road 1495
Freeport, TX
979-233-3526
Pooches are allowed to come and frolic on this 3.5 mile long city beach or even primitive camp overnight; there are no facilities here. Dogs must be under their owner's immediate control at all times.

Big Reef Nature Park
Boddeker Drive
Galveston, TX
409-765-5023
Take a walkway to the beach which runs parallel to Bolivar Rd. Dogs on leash are allowed on the beach. People need to clean up after their pets. There are no day use fees. This park is part of East Beach which does not allow dogs on the pavilion. The beach is located on the east end of Galveston Isle, off Boddeker Drive.

Dellanera RV Park
FM 3005 at 7 Mile Rd.
Galveston, TX
409-740-0390
This RV park offers 1,000 feet of sandy beach. Dogs on leash are allowed on the beach and at the RV spaces. People need to clean up after their pets. There are over 60 full RV hookups, over 20 partial hookups and day parking. Picnic tables and restrooms are available at this park. There is a $5 day parking fee. RV spaces are about $25 and up.

Galveston Island State Park
14901 FM 3005
Galveston, TX
409-737-1222
Leashed dogs are allowed on the beach and at the campsites. There is a $3 per person (over 13 years old) day use fee. There is no charge for children 12 and under. The park can be reached from Interstate 45 by exiting right onto 61st Street and traveling south on 61st Street to its intersection with Seawall Boulevard and then right (west) on Seawall (FM 3005) 10 miles to the park entrance.

Stewart Beach
6th and Seawall Boulevard
Galveston, TX
409-765-5023
This is one of the best family beaches in Galveston. Many family-oriented events including a sandcastle competition are held at this beach. Restrooms, umbrella and chair rentals, and volleyball courts are available. There is a $7 per car admission fee. Dogs on leash are allowed on the beach. People need to clean up after their pets. The beach is located at 6th Street and Seawall Blvd.

Padre Island National Seashore
Highway 22
Padre Island, TX
361-949-8068
nps.gov/pais/
Visitors to this beach can swim, sunbathe, hunt for shells or just enjoy a walk. About 800,000 visitors per year come to this park. Dogs on leash are allowed on the beach. People need to clean up after their pets. There is a minimal day use fee. The park is located on Padre Island, southeast of Corpus Christi.

Andy Bowie Park
Park Road 100
South Padre Island, TX
956-761-3704
co.cameron.tx.us

Dogs on leash are allowed on the beach. People need to clean up after their pets. There is a minimal day use fee. This park is located on the northern end of South Padre Island.

Edwin K. Atwood Park
Park Road 100
South Padre Island, TX
956-761-3704
co.cameron.tx.us
This beach offers 20 miles of beach driving. Dogs on leash are allowed on the beach. People need to clean up after their pets. There is a minimal day use fee. This park is located almost 1.5 miles north of Andy Bowie Park.

Isla Blanca Park
Park Road 100
South Padre Island, TX
956-761-5493
This popular beach offers about a mile of clean, white beach. Picnic tables, restrooms, and RV spaces are available at this park. Dogs on leash are allowed on the beach. People need to clean up after their pets. There is a minimal day use fee. The park is located on the southern tip of South Padre Island.

Virginia

Back Bay National Wildlife Refuge
Sandpiper Road
Virginia Beach, VA
757-721-2412
backbay.fws.gov/
Dogs are only allowed on the beach during the off-season. Dogs are only allowed on the beach from October 1 through March 31. Pets must be leashed (on leashes up to 10 feet long) and people need to clean up after their pets. This park is located approximately 15 miles south of Viriginia Beach. From I-64, exit to I-264 East (towards the oceanfront). Then take Birdneck Road Exit (Exit 22), turn right onto Birdneck Road. Go about 3-4 miles and then turn right on General Booth Blvd. Go about 5 miles. After crossing the Nimmo Parkway, pay attention to road signs. Get into the left lane so you can turn left at the next traffic light. Turn left onto Princess Anne Rd. The road turns into Sandbridge Rd. Keep driving and then turn right onto Sandpiper Road just past the fire station. Follow Sandpiper Road for about 4 miles to the end of the road.

First Landing State Park
2500 Shore Drive
Virginia Beach, VA
757-412-2300
Dogs on a 6 foot or less leash are allowed year-round on the beach. People need to clean up after their pet. All pets must have a rabies tag on their collar or proof of a rabies vaccine. To get there, take I-64. Then take the Northampton Blvd/US 13 North (Exit 282). You will pass eight lights and then turn right at the Shore Drive/US 60 exit. Turn right onto Shore Drive and go about 4.5 miles to the park entrance.

Virginia Beach Public Beaches
off Highway 60
Virginia Beach, VA
757-437-4919
Dogs are only allowed during off-season on Virginia Beach public beaches. From the Friday before Memorial Day through Labor Day weekend, pets are not allowed on public sand beaches, the boardwalk or the grassy area west of the boardwalk, from Rudee Inlet to 42nd Street. People are required to clean up after their pets and dogs must be leashed.

Washington

Fay Bainbridge State Park
Sunset Drive NE
Bainbridge Island, WA
360-902-8844
This park is located on the northeast side of Bainbridge Island on Puget Sound. On a clear day, you can see Mt. Rainer and Mt. Baker from the beach. Picnic tables, restrooms and campgrounds are available at this park. Leashed dogs are allowed on the beach. Pets are not permitted on designated swimming beaches. However, there is usually a non-designated swimming beach area as well. Dogs are also allowed at the campgrounds. They must be on a eight foot or less leash at all times and people are required to clean up after their pets. To get there from From Poulsbo, take Hwy. 305 toward Bainbridge Island. Cross the Agate Pass Bridge. After three miles, come to stoplight and big brown sign with directions to park. Turn left at traffic light onto Day Rd. NE. Travel approximately two miles to a T-intersection. Turn left onto Sunrise Drive NE, and continue to

park entrance, about two miles away.

Birch Bay State Park
Grandview
Blaine, WA
360-902-8844
This beach, located near the Canadian border, offers panoramic coastal views. Picnic tables, restrooms (including an ADA restroom), and campgrounds (including ADA campsites) are available at this park. Leashed dogs are allowed on the beach. Pets are not permitted on designated swimming beaches. However, there is usually a non-designated swimming beach area as well. Dogs are also allowed in the campgrounds. They must be on a eight foot or less leash at all times and people are required to clean up after their pets. This park is located 20 miles north of Bellingham and ten miles south of Blaine. From the south take exit #266 off of I-5. Go left on Grandview for seven miles, then right on Jackson for one mile, then turn left onto Helweg. From the north take exit #266 off of I-5, and turn right onto Grandview.

Griffith-Priday State Park
State Route 109
Copalis Beach, WA
360-902-8844
This beach extends from the beach through low dunes to a river and then north to the river's mouth. Picnic tables and restrooms are available at this park. Dogs are allowed on the beach. They must be on a eight foot or less leash at all times and people are required to clean up after their pets. This park is located 21 miles northwest of Hoquiam. From Hoquiam, go north on SR 109 for 21 miles. At Copalis Beach, at the sign for Benner Rd., turn left (west).

Saltwater State Park
Marine View Drive
Des Moines, WA
360-902-8844
This state beach is located on Puget Sound, halfway between the cities of Tacoma and Seattle (near the Sea-Tac international airport). Picnic tables, restrooms and campgrounds are available at this park. Leashed dogs are allowed on the beach. Pets are not permitted on designated swimming beaches. However, there is usually a non-designated swimming beach area as well. Dogs are also allowed at the campgrounds. They must be on a eight foot or less leash at all times

and people are required to clean up after their pets. To get there from the north, take exit #149 off of I-5. Go west, then turn south on Hwy. 99 (sign missing). Follow the signs into the park. Turn right on 240th at the Midway Drive-in. Turn left on Marine View Dr. and turn right into the park.

Off-Leash Area and Beach
498 Admiral Way
Edmonds, WA
425-771-0230
olae.org
The Off-leash area and beach in Edmonds gives dogs a place to run free, swim and meet other dogs. The area is maintained and supported by O.L.A.E. and overseen by the City of Edmonds Parks and Rec Dept. From I-5 follow signs to the Edmonds Ferry until Dayton Street. Turn west on Dayton Street and then south on Admiral Way. The off-leash area is south of Marina Beach.

Howarth Park Dog Beach
1127 Olympic Blvd.
Everett, WA
425-257-8300
Most of the park and beach areas require that dogs are on-leash and there are fines for violations. There is an off-leash beach area north of the pedestrian bridge that crosses the railroad tracks. Your dog should be under excellent voice control at this beach if it is off-leash due to the nearby train tracks. In addition, the train may spook a dog. There are also some trails for leashed dogs. The park is open from 6 am to 10 pm.

Howarth Park Dog Park
1127 Olympic Blvd.
Everett, WA
425-257-8300
Most of the park and beach areas require that dogs are on-leash and there are fines for violations. There is an off-leash beach area north of the pedestrian bridge that crosses the railroad tracks. Your dog should be under excellent voice control at this beach if it is off-leash due to the nearby train tracks. In addition, the train may spook a dog. There are also some trails for leashed dogs. The park is open from 6 am to 10 pm.

Dash Point State Park
Dash Point Rd.
Federal Way, WA
360-902-8844
This beach offers great views of Puget Sound. Picnic tables,

restrooms, 11 miles of hiking trails and campgrounds are available at this park. Leashed dogs are allowed on the beach. Pets are not permitted on designated swimming beaches. However, there is usually a non-designated swimming beach area as well. Dogs are also allowed on hiking trails and campgrounds. They must be on a eight foot or less leash at all times and people are required to clean up after their pets. This park is located on the west side of Federal Way in the vicinity of Seattle. From Highway 5, exit at the 320th St. exit (exit #143). Take 320th St. west approximately four miles. When 320th St. ends at a T-intersection, make a right onto 47th St. When 47th St. ends at a T-intersection, turn left onto Hwy. 509/Dash Point Rd. Drive about two miles to the park. (West side of street is the campground side, and east side is the day-use area.)

Double Bluff Beach
6400 Double Bluff Road
Freeland, WA
360-321-4049
fetchparks.org
South of Freeland and on Whidbey Island, this unfenced off-leash area also includes a dog beach. This is one of the largest off-leash beaches in the U.S. The off-leash beach is about 2 miles long. On clear days you can see Mt Rainier, the Seattle skyline and many ships. The beach nearest the parking lot is an on-leash area and the off-leash beach starts about 500 feet from the lot. There will be steep fines for dogs that are unleashed in an inappropriate area. From WA-525 watch for a sign for Double Bluff Road and it south. The road ends at the beach.

South Beach
125 Spring Street
Friday Harbor, WA
360-378-2902
nps.gov/sajh/
Dogs on leash are allowed at South Beach, which is located at the American Camp in the San Juan Island National Historic Park.

Grayland Beach State Park
Highway 105
Grayland, WA
360-902-8844
This 412 acre park offers beautiful ocean frontage and full hookup campsites (including ADA campsites). Leashed dogs are allowed on the beach. Dogs are

also allowed at the campgrounds. They must be on a eight foot or less leash at all times and people are required to clean up after their pets. This park is located five miles south of Westport. From Aberdeen, drive 22 miles on Highway 105 south to Grayland. Traveling through the town, watch for park signs.

Cape Disappointment State Park
Highway 101
Ilwaco, WA
360-902-8844
This park offers 27 miles of ocean beach and 7 miles of hiking trails. Enjoy excellent views of the ocean, Columbia River and two lighthouses. Picnic tables, restrooms (including an ADA restroom), hiking and campgrounds (includes ADA campsites) are available at this park. Leashed dogs are allowed on the beach. Dogs are also allowed on hiking trails and campgrounds. They must be on a eight foot or less leash at all times and people are required to clean up after their pets. This park is located two miles southwest of Ilwaco.From Seattle, Take I-5 south to Olympia, SR 8 west to Montesano. From there, take U.S. Hwy. 101 south to Long Beach Peninsula.

Spencer Spit State Park
Bakerview Road
Lopez Island, WA
360-902-8844
Located in the San Juan Islands, this lagoon beach offers great crabbing, clamming and beachcombing. Picnic tables, restrooms, campgrounds and 2 miles of hiking trails are available at this park. Leashed dogs are allowed on the beach. Pets are not permitted on designated swimming beaches. However, there is usually a non-designated swimming beach area as well. Dogs are also allowed on hiking trails and campgrounds. They must be on a eight foot or less leash at all times and people are required to clean up after their pets. This park is located on Lopez Island in the San Juan Islands. It is a 45-minute Washington State Ferry ride from Anacortes. Dogs are allowed on the ferry. Once on Lopez Island, follow Ferry Rd. Go left at Center Rd., then left at Cross Rd. Turn right at Port Stanley and left at Bakerview Rd. Follow Bakerview Rd. straight into park. For ferry rates and schedules, call 206-464-6400.

Fort Ebey State Park
Hill Valley Drive
Oak Harbor, WA

360-902-8844
This 600+ acre park is popular for hiking and camping, but also offers a saltwater beach. Picnic tables and restrooms (including an ADA restroom) are available at this park. Leashed dogs are allowed on the saltwater beach. Dogs are also allowed on hiking trails and campgrounds. They must be on a eight foot or less leash at all times and people are required to clean up after their pets. To get to the park from Seattle, take exit #189 off of I-5, just south of Everett. Follow signs for the Mukilteo/ Clinton ferry. Take the ferry to Clinton on Whidbey Island. Dogs are allowed on the ferry. Once on Whidbey Island, follow Hwy. 525 north, which becomes Hwy. 20. Two miles north of Coupeville, turn left on Libbey Rd. and follow it 1.5 miles to Hill Valley Dr. Turn left and enter park.

Joseph Whidbey State Park
Swantown Rd
Oak Harbor, WA
360-902-8844
This 112 acre park offers one of the best beaches on Whidbey Island. Picnic tables, restrooms, and several miles of hiking trails (including a half mile ADA hiking trail) are available at this park. Leashed dogs are allowed on the beach. Pets are not permitted on designated swimming beaches. However, there is usually a non-designated swimming beach area as well. Dogs are also allowed on hiking trails. They must be on a eight foot or less leash at all times and people are required to clean up after their pets. To get there from the south, drive north on Hwy. 20. Just before Oak Harbor, turn left on Swantown Rd. and follow it about three miles.

Pacific Pines State Park
Highway 101
Ocean Park, WA
360-902-8844
Fishing, crabbing, clamming and beachcombing are popular activities at this beach. Picnic tables and a restroom are available at this park. Dogs are allowed on the beach. They must be on a eight foot or less leash at all times and people are required to clean up after their pets. This park is located approximately one mile north of Ocean Park. From north or south, take Hwy. 101 until you reach Ocean Park. Continue on Vernon St. until you reach 271st St.

Damon Point State Park
Point Brown Avenue

Ocean Shores, WA
360-902-8844
Located on the southeastern tip of the Ocean Shores Peninsula, this one mile long beach offers views of the Olympic Mountains, Mount Rainer, and Grays Harbor. Picnic tables are available at this park. Dogs are allowed on the beach. They must be on a eight foot or less leash at all times and people are required to clean up after their pets. To get there from From Hoquiam, take SR 109 and SR 115 to Point Brown Ave. in the town of Ocean Shores. Proceed south on Point Brown Ave. through town, approximately 4.5 miles. Just past the marina, turn left into park entrance.

Ocean City State Park
State Route 115
Ocean Shores, WA
360-902-8844
Beachcombing, clamming, surfing, bird watching, kite flying and winter storm watching are all popular activites at this beach. Picnic tables, restrooms, and campgrounds (including ADA campgrounds) are available at this park. Leashed dogs are allowed on the beach. Dogs are also allowed at the campgrounds. They must be on a eight foot or less leash at all times and people are required to clean up after their pets. This park is located on the coast one-and-a-half miles north of Ocean Shores on Hwy. 115. From Hoquiam, drive 16 miles west on SR 109, then turn south on SR 115 and drive 1.2 miles to the park.

Pacific Beach State Park
State Route 109
Pacific Beach, WA
360-902-8844
The beach is the focal point at this 10 acre state park. This sandy ocean beach is great for beachcombing, wildlife watching, windy walks and kite flying. Picnic tables, restrooms (including an ADA restroom), and campgrounds (some are ADA accessible) are available at this park. Leashed dogs are allowed on the beach. Dogs are also allowed in the campgrounds. They must be on a eight foot or less leash at all times and people are required to clean up after their pets. This park is located 15 miles north of Ocean Shores, off SR 109. From Hoquiam, follow SR 109, 30 miles northwest to the town of Pacific Beach. The park is located in town.

Kalaloch Beach
Olympic National Park
Port Angeles, WA
360-962-2283
nps.gov/olym/
Dogs are allowed on leash, during daytime hours only, on Kalaloch Beach along the Pacific Ocean and from Rialto Beach north to Ellen Creek. These beaches are in Olympic National Park, but please note that pets are not permitted on this national park's trails, meadows, beaches (except Kalaloch and Rialto beaches) or in any undeveloped area of the park. For those folks and dogs who want to hike on a trail, try the adjacent dog-friendly Olympic National Forest. Kalaloch Beach is located off Highway 101 in Olympic National Park.

Sand Point Magnuson Park Dog Off-Leash Beach and Area
7400 Sand Point Way NE
Seattle, WA
206-684-4075
This leash free dog park covers about 9 acres and is the biggest fully fenced off-leash park in Seattle. It also offers an access point to the lake where your pooch is welcome to take a dip in the fresh lake water. To find the dog park, take Sand Point Way Northeast and enter the park at Northeast 74th Street. Go straight and park near the playground and sports fields. The main gate to the off-leash area is located at the southeast corner of the main parking lot. Dogs must be leashed until you enter the off-leash area.

Twin Harbors State Park
Highway 105
Westport, WA
360-902-8844
This beach is popular for beachcombing, bird watching, and fishing. Picnic tables, restrooms (including an ADA restroom), and campgrounds (includes ADA campgrounds) are available at this park. Leashed dogs are allowed on the beach. Dogs are also allowed at the campgrounds. They must be on a eight foot or less leash at all times and people are required to clean up after their pets. This park is located three miles south of Westport on Highway 105. From Aberdeen,

Westport Light State Park
Ocean Avenue
Westport, WA
360-902-8844
Enjoy the panoramic view at this park

or take the easy access trail to the beach. Swimming in the ocean here is not advised because of variable currents or rip tides. Picnic tables, restrooms (including an ADA restroom), and a 1.3 mile paved trail (also an ADA trail) are available at this park. Leashed dogs are allowed on the beach. Dogs are also allowed on the paved trail. They must be on a eight foot or less leash at all times and people are required to clean up after their pets. This park is located on the Pacific Ocean at Westport, 22 miles southwest of Aberdeen. To get there from Westport, drive west on Ocean Ave. about one mile to park entrance.

Wisconsin

Apostle Islands National Lakeshore
Route 1
Bayfield, WI
715-779-3398
nps.gov/apis/pphtml/contact.html
You will pretty much need your own boat to access this park and beach as the boat cruise tours do not allow pets. If you do have a boat and can reach the islands, dogs are allowed on the trails, in the backcountry campgrounds and on the beaches but must be on a 6 foot or less leash at all times. People need to clean up after their pets.

Harrington Beach State Park
531 Highway D
Belgium, WI
262-285-3015
Pets are allowed only on part of South Beach. They must be leashed except while swimming in the water. But once out of the water, they need to be leashed. Pets are also allowed at one of the picnic areas and on all trails except for the nature trail. Please remember to clean up after your pet.

Kohler-Andrae State Park Beach
1020 Beach Park Lane
Sheboygan, WI
920-451-4080
Pets are not allowed on the swimming beaches but they are allowed only on the beach area north of the nature center. Pets must be on an 8 foot or less leash and cleaned up after. Pets can be off leash only in the water but if one paw hits the sand, he or she must be back on leash or you may get a citation from a park ranger. Dogs are also allowed at certain campsites and on the

regular hiking trails but not on nature trails, in the picnic areas or the playground.

Potawatomi State Park Beach
3740 Park Drive
Sturgeon Bay, WI
920-746-2890
Dogs are allowed on the beach but must be leashed except when in the water. To get there from Green Bay, take Highway 57 north. Go about 37 miles to County Highway PD. Turn north onto Highway PD and go 2.4 miles to the park entrance.

Point Beach State Forest
9400 County Highway O
Two Rivers, WI
920-794-7480
Pets are allowed only on a certain part of the beach, located south of the lighthouse. Dogs must be leashed at all times including on the beach and are not allowed in the picnic areas except for the one near the beach that allows dogs. Pets are also allowed on some of the park trails. Please remember to clean up after your pet.

Canada

British Columbia

CRAB Park at Portside Off-Leash Dog Water Access and Dog Park
101 E Waterfront Road
Vancouver, BC
604-257-8400
The CRAB Park unfenced dog off-leash area and dog beach is available for off-leash play from 6 am to 10 am and 5 pm to 10 pm. The off-leash area is the east side of the park. Dogs are not allowed in the area of the playground. Dogs must be well-behaved, have a current license, leashed outside of the off-leash areas and cleaned up after.

Fraser River Park Off-Leash Dog Water Access and Dog Park
8705 Angus Drive
Vancouver, BC
604-257-8689
The Fraser River Park unfenced dog off-leash area and dog beach is available for off-leash play from 6 am to 10 am and 5 pm to 10 pm. Please see the signs outlining the off-leash area. Dogs must be well-behaved, have a current license, leashed outside of the off-leash areas and cleaned up after. The park is located at W 75th Avenue at Angus Drive.

John Hendry Park Off-Leash Dog Water Access and Dog Park
3300 Victoria Drive
Vancouver, BC
604-257-8613
The John Hendry Park unfenced dog off-leash area and dog beach is available for off-leash play from 5 am to 10 pm. Please see the signs outlining the off-leash area. Dogs must be well-behaved, have a current license, leashed outside of the off-leash areas and cleaned up after.

New Brighton Park Off-Leash Dog Water Access and Dog Park
8705 Angus Drive
Vancouver, BC
604-257-8613
The Fraser River Park unfenced dog off-leash area and dog beach is available for off-leash play from 5 am to 10 am from May 1 to September 30 and from 5 am to 10 pm during the rest of the year. Please see the signs outlining the off-leash area.

Dogs must be well-behaved, have a current license, leashed outside of the off-leash areas and cleaned up after.

Spanish Bank Beach Park Off-Leash Dog Water Access and Dog Park
4801 NW Marine Drive
Vancouver, BC
604-257-8689
The Spanish Bank Beach Park unfenced dog off-leash area and dog beach is available for off-leash play from 6 am to 10 pm. Please see the signs outlining the off-leash area. Dogs must be well-behaved, have a current license, leashed outside of the off-leash areas and cleaned up after. The park is located on NW Marine Drive at the entrance to Pacific Spirit Park.

Sunset Beach Park Off-Leash Dog Water Access and Dog Park
1204 Beach Avenue
Vancouver, BC
604-257-8400
The Sunset Beach Park unfenced dog off-leash area and dog beach is available for off-leash play from 6 am to 10 pm. Please see the signs outlining the off-leash area. Dogs must be well-behaved, have a current license, leashed outside of the off-leash areas and cleaned up after.

Vanier Park Off-Leash Dog Water Access and Dog Park
1000 Chestnut Street
Vancouver, BC
604-257-8689
The Vanier Park unfenced dog off-leash area and dog beach is available for off-leash play from 6 am to 10 am and 5 pm to 10 pm from May 1 to September 30 and from 6 am to 10 pm during the rest of the year. Please see the signs outlining the off-leash area. Dogs must be well-behaved, have a current license, leashed outside of the off-leash areas and cleaned up after. The park is located at Chestnut Street at English Bay.

Dallas Road Off-Leash Beach
Dallas Road at Douglass St
Victoria, BC
250-385-5711
victoria.ca/dogs/
Dogs are allowed off-leash year round at the gravel beach in Beacon Hill Park. People are required to clean up after their dogs. The beach is located in downtown Victoria, along Dallas

Road, between Douglas Street and Cook Street.

Gonzales Beach Off-Leash Area
South end of Foul Bay Rd
Victoria, BC
250-361-0600
victoria.ca/dogs/
Gonzales Beach is a large beach that circles Gonzales Bay in the south-eastern section of Victoria. Dogs are allowed on Gonzales Beach 24 hours a day except from June 1 to August 31 when they are not allowed on the beach at all. Dogs must be under control at all times, must be cleaned up after and must be on-leash whenever they are outside of the off-leash area.

Ontario

Kincardine
H 21, N of H 9 beside KFC (visitor center)
Kincardine, ON
519-396-3491
sunsets.com/kincardine/
There are more than 30 km of sandy beaches here and dogs are allowed on the beaches (unless otherwise indicated) except at Station Beach. Dogs are allowed on no more than a 6 foot leash, and they must be cleaned up after promptly at all times.

Awenda Provincial Park
670 Concession 18 E
Penetanguishene, ON
705-549-2231
At this park that sits overlooking the Georgian Bay is a pet beach area where dogs are allowed; it is at the 2nd beach site and there is signage once in the park. It is a seasonal park and the gates are locked during the off season; it is a 45 minute walk to the beach from this outer parking lot. Dogs are allowed on no more than a 6 foot leash, and they must be cleaned up after promptly at all times.

Port Burwell Provincial Park Beach
Box 9
Port Burwell, ON
519-874-4691
This park provides a beach for dog frolicking fun; there is signage directing pet owners to the section of beach where dogs are allowed. Dogs must be on no more than a 6 foot leash and cleaned up after promptly at all times.

Neys Provincial Park
H 17
Thunder Bay District, ON
807-229-1624
This park provides a beach for dog frolicking fun; there is signage directing pet owners to the section of beach where they are allowed. Dogs must be on no more than a 6 foot leash and cleaned up after promptly at all times.

Wasaga Beach
Beach Drive
Wasaga Beach, ON
705-429-0412
wasagabeach.com/
This beach is home to the world's longest freshwater beach and is a prime tourist attraction. Dogs are allowed on one designated section - beach area #1. Otherwise dogs must stay on the grassy area that follows along the beach. This park closes in winter and there are no restrooms available; however, gate #1 is still left open for visitors. Dogs are allowed on no more than a 6 foot leash, and they must be cleaned up after promptly at all times.

Chapter 3

Transportation

United States

Alaska

Alaska Air Transit
2331 Merrill Field Drive #A
Anchorage, AK
907-276-5422
alaskaairtransit.com/
This air service company provides flightseeing and taxi service for the state of Alaska. Dogs are not allowed on tours; however, they are allowed for taxi service by charter. If the pet is well behaved and leashed, a kennel is not needed. Charter rates run from $700 per hour plus 7.5% tax and fuel surcharge, and up to 8 people can be transported.

Birchwood Air Services
1000 Merrill Field Drive
Anchorage, AK
907-276-0402
This air service company will transport canine companions also. The fee is $40 for a small dog, $65 for a medium dog, and $95 for a large dog each way. Dogs can ride up front with owners, and they must be under their owner's control and leashed or crated at all times.

Era Aviation
6160 Carl Brady Drive (HQ)
Anchorage, AK
800-866-8394
flyera.com/
Offering air service to a number of Alaskan areas, this company will transport dogs for an additional fee of $50 per pet each way. Kennels must be provided by owners and they may not be over a 500 series.

Grant Aviation
4451 Aircraft Dr
Anchorage, AK
907-248-7025 (888-359-4726)
flygrant.com
This commuter airline flys between Kenai, Homer and Anchorage many times a day. The flight takes under one hour. They fly 9 seat airplanes and a dog may travel with you. The dog must be in a crate and will be behind the last seats. There is a charge of about $1 per pound for the dog and crate, so a 50 pound dog with a 10 pound kennel would cost an extra $60.

Rust's Flying Service
P.O. Box 190867
Anchorage, AK

907-243-1595
flyrusts.com/
This air service company provides flightseeing and taxi service for the state of Alaska. Dogs are not allowed on tours; however, they are allowed for taxi service by charter. If the pet is well behaved and leashed, a kennel is not needed. Charter rates run from about $375 to $500 per hour.

Alaska Ferry
14 miles north of downtown Juneau
Auke Bay, AK
360-676-8445 (800-642-0066)
dot.state.ak.us/amhs
The Alaska Ferry, or Alaska Maritime Highway System connects Bellingham, Washington and Prince Rupert, BC with many Alaskan ports and also serves these Alaskan ports with Car, RV and passenger service. The ferry is essential, as many of the ports served are not accessible from the mainland by car, only by ferry or air. Dogs are allowed, but with significant restrictions. They must remain on the car deck at all times. If you have an RV or a car, this means that the dog must remain in the vehicle. If you are a foot passenger, you will have to leave your pet on the car deck in a closed kennel. You may not visit the car deck while the ferry is not in port. An exception is made for ferry segments greater than 8 hours, where they will hold occasional pet visits to the car deck to allow the dogs to relieve themselves. This is not much fun for the dogs, so we recommend that you stop often at intermediate ports with pets. In port, you may take your dog off of the ferry usually for about 20 minutes to 45 minutes. The ferry serves the Southeast area of Alaska, the Prince William Sound area, and Kodiak and points in the Aleutian Islands. The pet information is listed at http://www.dot.state.ak.us/amhs/pets.shtml.

Coyote Air
Po Box 9053/City Airport
Coldfoot, AK
907-678-5995
flycoyote.com/
In addition to providing sightseeing flights, this air service company will also help travelers with trip planning-including everything from weather conditions to the contacts needed for each leg of the journey. Customers with pets may charter

the plane individually; the fee is $725 per hour with room for 4 to 6 people depending on size of adults and pooches. Dogs must be under their owner's control and leashed or crated at all times.

Alaska Ferry
4 Blocks NE of downtown
Cordova, AK
907-424-7333 (800-642-0066)
dot.state.ak.us/amhs
For information on the Alaska Ferry, see Auke Bay (Juneau) Alaska Listing

Alaska Inter-Island Ferry
P. O. Box 495
Craig, AK
866-308-4848
interislandferry.com/
This ferry provides service between Ketchikan and Hollis, and between Coffman Cove and Wrangell. Dogs are allowed on board for no additional fee on the auto deck, either in the car or in an owner provided container.

Frontier Flying Service Inc
5245 Airport Industrial Road
Fairbanks, AK
907-450-7200
frontierflying.com/
Flying the frontiers of Alaska, this passenger and freight company will also transport dogs. The fee is $50 each way for a series 300 kennel or less, and $100 each way for a series 400 kennel or larger. Owners must supply the kennel.

Larry's Flying Service/ East Ramp International Airport
3822 University Avenue S
Fairbanks, AK
907-474-9169
larrysflying.com/
This air service company will transport dogs when the plane is chartered solely by the pet owner; the fee is $350 per hour and they can hold up to 5 to 8 passengers/pets depending on the plane. Kennels must be provided by the owner's and 400 series kennels are the largest allowed.

Alaska Ferry
5 miles north of downtown
Haines, AK
907-766-2113 (800-642-0066)
dot.state.ak.us/amhs
For information on the Alaska Ferry, see Auke Bay (Juneau) Alaska Listing

Haines-Sagway Fast Ferry
121 Beach Road
Haines, AK
907-766-2100
chilkatcruises.com/
Dogs are allowed on the ferry for an additional fee of $5 per pet per trip. They are only allowed for water taxi service and not allowed on tours or cruises. Dogs must be under their owner's control, leashed, and cleaned up after at all times.

LAB Flying Services
Main and 4th
Haines, AK
907-766-2222
labflying.com/
Dogs are allowed on regular scheduled flights; a fee for a small kennel is $30; a medium is $40; a large is $60, and an extra-large is $150. There is no additional pet fee when the plane is chartered.

Alaska Ferry
4558 Homer Spit Rd
Homer, AK
907-235-8449 (800-642-0066)
dot.state.ak.us/amhs
For information on the Alaska Ferry, see Auke Bay (Juneau) Alaska Listing

Grant Aviation
3720 FAA Road # 110
Homer, AK
907-235-2757 (888-359-4726)
flygrant.com
This commuter airline flys between Homer and Anchorage many times a day. The flight takes under one hour. They fly 9 seat airplanes and a dog may travel with you. The dog must be in a crate and will be behind the last seats. There is a charge of about $1 per pound for the dog and crate, so a 50 pound dog with a 10 pound kennel would cost an extra $60.

Kachemak Bay Flying Services
1158 Lakeshore Drive
Homer, AK
907-235-8924
alaskaseaplanes.com/
Offering flight service in Kachemak Bay area, this float plane will also take canine companions for no additional fee. The plane can be chartered for a fee of $150 per adult per hour with a 2 person minimum. They request to first meet the dog, and they must be friendly, well behaved, leashed (or kenneled), and cleaned up after at all times.

Wings of Alaska

8421 Livingston Way
Juneau, AK
907-789-0790
Serving Southeast Alaska, this air service provider offers fast freight and charter service in addition to scheduled passenger service. Dogs are allowed for transport for 1½ times normal freight rate or there can be a slightly higher fee if going as passenger luggage. Dogs must be leashed or crated when in cargo. The cargo office number is 907-790-3100.

Wings of Alaska
8421 Livingston Way
Juneau, AK
907-697-2201
Serving Southeast Alaska, this air service provider offers fast freight and charter service in addition to scheduled passenger service. Dogs are allowed for transport for 1½ times normal freight rate or there can be a slightly higher fee if going as passenger luggage. Dogs must be leashed or crated when in cargo. The cargo office number is 907-790-3100.

Wings of Alaska
8421 Livingston Way
Juneau, AK
907-766-2030
Serving Southeast Alaska, this air service provider offers fast freight and charter service in addition to scheduled passenger service. Dogs are allowed for transport for 1½ times normal freight rate or there can be a slightly higher fee if going as passenger luggage. Dogs must be leashed or crated when in cargo. The cargo office number is 907-790-3100.

Wings of Alaska
8421 Livingston Way
Juneau, AK
907-983-2442
Serving Southeast Alaska, this air service provider offers fast freight and charter service in addition to scheduled passenger service. Dogs are allowed for transport for 1½ times normal freight rate or there can be a slightly higher fee if going as passenger luggage. Dogs must be leashed or crated when in cargo. The cargo office number is 907-790-3100.

Grant Aviation
305 N Willow St
Kenai, AK
907-283-6012 (888-359-4726)
flygrant.com

This commuter airline flys between Kenai and Anchorage many times a day. The flight takes under one hour. They fly 9 seat airplanes and a dog may travel with you. The dog must be in a crate and will be behind the last seats. There is a charge of about $1 per pound for the dog and crate, so a 50 pound dog with a 10 pound kennel would cost an extra $60.

Alaska Ferry
2.5 north of Downtown
Ketchikan, AK
907-225-6181 (800-642-0066)
dot.state.ak.us/amhs
For information on the Alaska Ferry, see Auke Bay (Juneau) Alaska Listing

Island Wings Air Service
1935Tongass Avenue/H 7
Ketchikan, AK
907-225-2444
islandwings.com/
This air service offers a variety of tour and recreational options. Dogs are allowed on board if the plane is chartered by their owner for a sum of $575 per hour; the dog fee is inclusive. They are not allowed on board with other travelers. Dogs must be well behaved, under their owner's control, and leashed or kenneled at all times.

Alaska Ferry
100 Marine Way
Kodiak, AK
907-486-3800 (800-642-0066)
dot.state.ak.us/amhs
For information on the Alaska Ferry, see Auke Bay (Juneau) Alaska Listing

Sea Hawk Air Inc
505 Trident Way
Kodiak, AK
907-486-8282
seahawkair.com/
This air service company provides recreational, business, and personal flights throughout the year for Kodiak Island and the Alaskan Peninsula. Dogs are not allowed for tours, but they will provide taxi services. The fee is determined by combined weight which includes the dog. The only request the company makes is that dogs must be dry for transport. Dogs must be well behaved, under their owner's control, and leashed or crated at all times.

Bering Air
1470 Sepalla Drive
Nome, AK

907-443-5464
beringair.com/
With an exception of a couple of holiday days, this air service company is providing private charters and a number of services for visitors and 32 Western Alaska cities, with hubs in Nome, Kotzebue, and Unalakleet. They will also transport pets for a fee based on a percentage of size, weight, and destination. Owners supply the transport kennel.

Alaska Ferry
0.9 Miles South of Downtown
Petersburg, AK
907-772-3855 (800-642-0066)
dot.state.ak.us/amhs
For information on the Alaska Ferry, see Auke Bay (Juneau) Alaska Listing

Alaska Ferry
downtown
Seldovia, AK
907-234-7868 (800-642-0066)
dot.state.ak.us/amhs
For information on the Alaska Ferry, see Auke Bay (Juneau) Alaska Listing

Alaska Ferry
7.1 Miles North of Downtown
Sitka, AK
907-747-3300 (800-642-0066)
dot.state.ak.us/amhs
For information on the Alaska Ferry, see Auke Bay (Juneau) Alaska Listing

Alaska Ferry
3 Blocks South of Downtown
Skagway, AK
907-983-2229 (800-642-0066)
dot.state.ak.us/amhs
For information on the Alaska Ferry, see Auke Bay (Juneau) Alaska Listing

Alaska Ferry
West End of City Dock
Valdez, AK
907-835-4436 (800-642-0066)
dot.state.ak.us/amhs
For information on the Alaska Ferry, see Auke Bay (Juneau) Alaska Listing

Alaska Ferry
In Town
Whittier, AK
907-472-2378 (800-642-0066)
dot.state.ak.us/amhs
For information on the Alaska Ferry, see Auke Bay (Juneau) Alaska Listing

Alaska Ferry
2 Blocks North of Downtown
Wrangell, AK
907-874-3711 (800-642-0066)
dot.state.ak.us/amhs
For information on the Alaska Ferry, see Auke Bay (Juneau) Alaska Listing

Arizona

Pet Airways
4636 East Fighter Aces Dr
Mesa, AZ
623-207-9856
Pet Airways, which began flying in July, 2009 is a pet-only airline with service to a number of North American destinations. You drop you dog off at their lounge in one city and pick them up in another. Dogs fly in the cabin, regardless of their size, and there is a veterinarian assistant on each flight as an attendant. You need to fly on another airline and meet your dog in the destination city. For more information see petairways.com.

Arizona Valley Metro Bus
302 N 1st Avenue, Suite 700
Phoenix, AZ
602-262-7433
valleymetro.org/valley_metro/
Although service animals are allowed on busses without size restriction; non-service animals may only be brought on board if they can comfortably fit in a hand held carrier and do not take up a seat. Dogs must be well mannered and under owner's control at all times.

California

Pet Airways
3750 120th St
Hawthorne Airport, CA
310-756-0823
For information on Pet Airways, see Mesa (Phoenix) Arizona Listing.

Metro Transit Authority
1 Gateway Plaza
Los Angeles, CA
213-580-7500
metro.net
Small dogs in an enclosed carrier are allowed on the light rail and buses for no additional fee.

BART (Bay Area Rapid Transit)
Regional
Oakland, CA
888-968-7282

bart.gov
A small dog in an enclosed carrier is allowed on BART trains.

RT (Rapid Transit)
Regional
Sacramento, CA
916-321-2877
sacrt.com
Small dogs in carriers are allowed on the buses and light rail. The carrier must fit on the person's lap.

Metropolitan Transit System
Regional
San Diego, CA
619-233-3004
Small dogs in enclosed carriers are allowed on the buses and light rail. You must be able to transport your dog and the carrier by yourself, and you need to hold the carrier on your lap. Noise or odor may give cause for refusal to transport the animal.

BART (Bay Area Rapid Transit)
Regional
San Francisco, CA
888-968-7282
bart.gov
A small dog in an enclosed carrier is allowed on BART trains.

SF Municipal Railway (MUNI)
Throughout City
San Francisco, CA
415-673-6864
sfmuni.com
Both small and large dogs are allowed on cable cars, historic streetcars and trolley buses. People must pay the same fare for their dog that they do for themselves. Dogs are allowed to ride on Muni vehicles from 9 a.m. to 3 p.m. and from 7 p.m. to 5 a.m. on weekdays, and all day on Saturdays, Sundays, and holidays. Only one of dog may ride per vehicle. Dogs must be muzzled and on a short leash or in a small closed container.

Colorado

Pet Airways
11844 Corporate Way
Broomfield, CO
303-957-2873
For information on Pet Airways, see Mesa (Phoenix) Arizona Listing.

RTD
Regional
Denver, CO
303-299-6000
rtd-denver.com

Small dogs in hard-sided carriers are allowed on the buses and light rail.

Connecticut

The Chester - Hadlyme Ferry
Ferry Landing
Chester, CT
860-526-2743
This ferry runs between April 1st and November 30th providing a convenient link across the Connecticut River between Chester and Hadlyme. Well behaved dogs on leash are allowed on the ferry for no additional fee.

Viking Fleet
462 W Lake Drive
Montauk, NY
631-668-5700
This ferry features a triple decker, 120 foot vessel with comfort amenities on board, and service is provided between Montauk Long Island and Block Island RI, New London CT, and Martha's Vineyard, MA. Well behaved dogs are allowed on board for no additional fee. Dogs must be under their owner's control and leashed at all times. The ferries leave from the Cross Sound Ferry Dock.

Cross Sound Ferry Services
2 Ferry Street, PO Box 33
New London, CT
860-443-5281
longislandferry.com/Default.asp
This auto ferry service provides transportation between New London, CT and Orient Point on Long Island, NY. Dogs are allowed on the car ferry in dog designated areas only for no additional fee. Dogs must be well behaved, leashed or in an approved pet carrier, and cleaned up after at all times.

Fishers Island Ferry
5 Waterfront Park
New London, CT
860-442-0165
fiferry.com/
This is the connector ferry between New London, Connecticut and Fisher's Island, New York. Dogs of all sizes are allowed for no addition fee. Dogs must be well behaved, leashed, and cleaned up after at all times.

Thimble Islands Cruise & Charters
P.O. Box 3138
Stony Creek, CT
203-488-8905

thimbleislandcruise.com/
Well behaved pooches are welcome aboard the ferry for transport to the islands for no additional fee; they are not allowed on tours. Dogs must be crated or leashed, cleaned up after, and under their owner's control at all times.

D.C.

Pet Airways
1 Aaronson Dr
Glen Burnie BWI, MD
443-320-2459
For information on Pet Airways, see Mesa (Phoenix) Arizona Listing.

WMATA
Regional
Washington, DC
202-962-1234
wmata.com
Small dogs in carriers are allowed on the buses and trains. Pets must remain in the carrier, with no possibility that the pet can get out.

Delaware

Cape May-Lewes Ferry
Sandman Blvd. & Lincoln Drive
N Cape May, NJ
609-889-7200
capemaylewesferry.com/
This ferry service provides transportation for vehicles and passengers between Cape May, New Jersey and Lewes, Delaware. The ferry cuts miles off of driving along the Atlantic coast. Pets are welcome but the following rules apply. For the M.V. Cape May, M.V. Delaware and M.V. Twin Cape ferries, pets are welcome on the ferry on exterior decks and any lounge areas where food is not being made, served or eaten. Pets are not allowed in the lounge area whenever there is a private party being hosted. For the M.V. Cape Henlopen and M.V. New Jersey ferries, pets are not allowed in any interior space but are allowed on all exterior decks. For all ferries, dogs of all sizes are allowed but need to be kept under control at all times and leashed or in a carrier. People need to clean up after their pets. Pets are not allowed in the shuttles. Rates start at $20 to $25 for a vehicle and driver. For a foot passenger with no car, rates start at $6 to $8 per person. Larger vehicles

can be accommodated but there is an extra charge. The Cape May Terminal is located at Sandman Blvd. and Lincoln Drive in North Cape May, New Jersey. The Lewes Terminal is located at 43 Henlopen Drive in Lewes, Delaware. Rates are subject to change. For reservations or to check rates, call the ferry line toll free at 1-800-643-3779.

Florida

Executive Jet Charters
240 SW 34th Street
Fort Lauderdale, FL
954-359-9991 (888-355-5387)
jetscapefbo.com
This airline charter company offers charter flights from Florida to points in the Caribbean. Dogs are allowed for no additional fee unless extra cleaning is required. They are allowed in the cabin, leashed or crated, and they must be of a calm nature.

Island Air Charters
1050 Lee Wagener Boulevard Suite 102
Fort Lauderdale, FL
954-359-9942 (800-444-9904)
islandaircharters.com
Dogs are allowed on chartered aircraft for no additional fee; they are allowed in the cabin on lap or leashed on the floor. Charters run from about $650 up depending on the destination.

Pet Airways
750 SW 34th Street Suite 112
Fort Lauderdale, FL
561-491-5718
For information on Pet Airways, see Mesa (Phoenix) Arizona Listing.

Miami/Dade Transit
South of SW 216 Street
Miami, FL
305-770-3131
co.miami-dade.fl.us/transit/
A small dog in an enclosed, escape proof carrier are allowed on Metro-rail and Metro buses at no additional fee.

LYNX
Regional
Orlando, FL
407-841-5969
golynx.com
Small dogs in carriers that fit on your lap are allowed on the buses.

Broward County Transit (BCT)

3201 W Cobans Road
Pompano Beach, FL
954-357-8400
broward.org/bct
A small dog in a carrier is allowed on the trains or buses at no additional fee.

Fair Wind Air Charter
2555 S.E. Witham Field
Stuart, FL
772-288-4130 (800-989-9665)
flyfairwind.com
This airline charter company offers charter flights from Florida to points in the Caribbean. Dogs are allowed on some of their aircraft for no additional fee unless extra cleaning is required. They are allowed in the cabin crated or leashed. These charter flights use jet airplanes of various sizes.

Karl Klopman Transportation
Throughout Palm Beach and Broward Counties
West Palm Beach, FL
561-312-6117
This limo/car transportation service serves the region from Palm Beach to Ft Lauderdale with airport and port service and car services to other destinations. You may bring small or medium sized dogs up to around 30 pounds.

Georgia

MARTA
Regional
Atlanta, GA
404-848-4900
itsmarta.com
Small dogs carried in a closed pet carrier that fits on your lap are allowed on the buses and trains.

Pet Airways
2007 Flightway Dr
Atlanta, GA
404-921-9278
For information on Pet Airways, see Mesa (Phoenix) Arizona Listing.

Pet Airways
2007 Flightway Dr
Atlanta Dekalb - Peachtree Airport, GA
404-921-9278
For information on Pet Airways, see Mesa (Phoenix) Arizona Listing.

Illinois

Chicago Transit Authority (CTA)

567 W Lake Street
Chicago, IL
888-968-7282
transitchicago.com/
A small dog in an enclosed carrier is allowed on the CTA buses and on the CTA "L" trains at no additional fee.

Pet Airways
6150 S. Laramie Ave
Chicago Midway, IL
312-429-0252
For information on Pet Airways, see Mesa (Phoenix) Arizona Listing.

Brussels Free Ferry
H 100
Grafton, IL
618-786-3636
Run by the state for vehicles and passengers, this free ferry links Highway 100 in Grafton to the village of Brussels in Calhoun County, and it has become a prime bald eagle viewing route as they feed on the stunned fish from the propellers churning up the ice in winter. Dogs are allowed on the ferry for no additional fee. Dogs must be leashed, crated, or in the vehicle, and under their owner's care at all times.

Kampsville Free Ferry
H 108
Kampsville, IL
618-653-4518
Run by the state for vehicles and passengers, this free ferry crosses the Illinois River to connect Kampsville with northern Jersey County. Dogs are allowed on the ferry for no additional fee. Dogs must be leashed, crated, or in the vehicle, and under their owner's care at all times.

Indiana

Indigo Transit
209 N Delaware
Indianapolis, IN
317-635-3344
indigo.net
Small dogs in an enclosed carrier are allowed on the buses at no additional charge.

Maine

Island Explorer Buses
Bar Harbor and Acadia
Bar Harbor, ME
207-667-5796

exploreacadia.com/
Leashed dogs are allowed on the Island Explorer buses that take people between Bar Harbor, Campgrounds and hotels and Acadia National Park.

The Cat Ferry, Bar Harbor Terminal
121 Eden Street
Bar Harbor, ME
207-288-3395
catferry.com/
Quickly gaining recognition for its speed and agility on the water, this CAT carries up to 775 passengers and 240 cars (not to mention a few furry friends also) across the Gulf of Maine between Yarmouth Nova Scotia and Bar Harbor and Portland Maine from June to mid-October. Dogs of all sizes are allowed for no additional pet fee. Dogs must be well behaved, and remain in a vehicle on the auto deck or in a kennel during passage. Kennels are available on a 1st come 1st served basis.

Mohegan Boat Line
End of Port Clyde Road/H 131
Port Clyde, ME
207-372-8848
monheganboat.com/
Nature and art lovers from all over come to experience this wonderfully scenic island that provides about 17 miles of trails to explore it plus a number of shops and artists' studios. This ferry will transport dogs to the island for an additional pet fee of $5 per dog. Dogs must be well mannered, under their owner's control, leashed, and cleaned up after at all times.

Casco Bay Lines
56 Commercial Street
Portland, ME
207-774-7871
Casco Bay Lines
This year round ferry service carries vehicles, passengers, and freight from Portland to a number of off-shore islands. Dogs are allowed for an additional fee of $3.25. Dogs must be well behaved, under their owner's control, leashed, and cleaned up after at all times.

The Cat Ferry, Portland Terminal
14 Ocean Gateway Pier
Portland, ME
207-761-4228
catferry.com/
Quickly gaining recognition for its speed and agility on the water, this CAT carries up to 775 passengers and 240 cars (not to mention a few furry friends also) across the Gulf of

Maine between Yarmouth Nova Scotia and Bar Harbor and Portland Maine from June to mid-October. Dogs of all sizes are allowed for no additional pet fee. Dogs must be well behaved, and remain in a vehicle on the auto deck or in a kennel during passage. Kennels are available on a 1st come 1st served basis.

Maine State Ferry Service (Maine D.O.T.)
517A Main Street
Rockland, ME
207-596-2202
This state owned/operated year round ferry service provides a fixed route from Bass Harbor to Swans Island and Frenchboro ports. Dogs of all sizes are allowed for no additional pet fee. Dogs must be well behaved, under their owner's immediate control, securely leashed, crated, or caged, and cleaned up after at all times. There is a separate room for passengers with pets.

Maine State Ferry Service
Bass Harbor
Southwest Harbor, ME
207-596-2202
Dogs are allowed on the ferries if they are leashed, crated or caged. The ferries closest to Bar Harbor depart at the nearby Southwest Harbor and go to Swans Island. Cars can also be transported on the ferry.

Maryland

Maryland Transit Administration
Baltimore and Suburbs
Baltimore, MD
866-RIDE-MTA (743-3682)
mtamaryland.com/
MTA provides a variety of transportation options throughout Baltimore and surrounding areas with numerous pick-up and drop-off sites. A small dog is allowed to be transported in hand-held carriers for no extra fee.

Pet Airways
1 Aaronson Dr
Glen Burnie BWI, MD
443-320-2459
For information on Pet Airways, see Mesa (Phoenix) Arizona Listing.

Massachusetts

Boston T
Boston, MA

617-222-3200
mbta.com/
Both small and large dogs are allowed on the Boston T (subway) and the commuter trains run by the T from Boston. Small dogs may be transported in a carrier. Larger dogs may be taken on the T during off-peak hours and must be leashed and controlled at all times. At no time should a pet compromise safety, get in a passenger's way or occupy a seat.

Salem Ferry
New England Aquarium Dock
Boston, MA
978-741-0220
salemferry.com/
This high speed catamaran offers 45 minute service between downtown Boston and Salem. Dogs on leash are allowed. The service is open seasonally from late May through October.

Island Queen Ferry
Falmouth Heights Road
Falmouth, MA
508-548-4800
islandqueen.com/
This ferry carries passengers, bicycles and leashed dogs. It does not transport vehicles. The ferry runs between Falmouth in Cape Cod and Oak Bluffs in Martha's Vineyard (about 35 to 45 minutes).

Hy-Line Cruises Ferry Service
Ocean Street Dock
Hyannis, MA
508-778-2600
hy-linecruises.com/
This ferry service runs from Cape Cod to Nantucket Island (1 hour on the high speed ferry) or Martha's Vineyard (1.5 hours). They also offer the only Inter-Island Ferry between Nantucket and Martha's Vineyard (2.25 hours). Pets are allowed on the ferries, but not in the first class lounge. Pets need to be leashed. This ferry company provides year-round service to Nantucket and seasonal service to Martha's Vineyard. The Inter-Island Ferry is also seasonal. No vehicles are transported on these ferries. Call ahead to make reservations.

Hy-Line Cruises Ferry Service
Ocean Street Dock
Hyannis, MA
508-778-2600
hy-linecruises.com/
This ferry service runs from Cape Cod to Nantucket Island (1 hour on the high speed ferry) or Martha's

Vineyard (1.5 hours). They also offer the only Inter-Island Ferry between Nantucket and Martha's Vineyard (2.25 hours). Pets are allowed on the ferries, but not in the first class lounge. Pets need to be leashed. This ferry company provides year-round service to Nantucket and seasonal service to Martha's Vineyard. The Inter-Island Ferry is also seasonal. No vehicles are transported on these ferries. Call ahead to make reservations.

Hy-Line Cruises Ferry Service
Ocean Street Dock
Hyannis, MA
508-778-2600
hy-linecruises.com/
This ferry service runs from Cape Cod to Nantucket Island (1 hour on the high speed ferry) or Martha's Vineyard (1.5 hours). They also offer the only Inter-Island Ferry between Nantucket and Martha's Vineyard (2.25 hours). Pets are allowed on the ferries, but not in the first class lounge. Pets need to be leashed. This ferry company provides year-round service to Nantucket and seasonal service to Martha's Vineyard. The Inter-Island Ferry is also seasonal. No vehicles are transported on these ferries. Call ahead to make reservations.

Nantucket Airlines
660 Barnstable Road/North Ramp
Hyannis, MA
508-790-0300 (800-635-8787)
nantucketairlines.com
This airline offers daily flights between Hyannis and Nantucket (20 minute flight). Dogs are allowed in the cabin with you on this airline! Dogs under 35 pounds can be carried on your lap and no kennel is required. For dogs over 35 pounds, there is a "shelf" which is just a few inches off the floor, in the back of the plane where your dog can sit or lay. While you cannot sit next to your dog, you can try to get the seat directly in front of him or her. There is no reserved seating, so you'll need to arrive early to try and make special arrangements to sit in front of your pooch. Large dogs must be properly restrained with a leash, harness or similar device. No kennel is required. You will need to reserve a space for your pet in advance as the airline usually only allows one dog per flight. Their sister airline, Cape Air also allows dogs in the cabin, but most flights require your dog to be in a kennel, and they have a size limit for dogs.

Nantucket Airlines
660 Barnstable Road/North Ramp
Hyannis, MA
508-790-0300 (800-635-8787)
nantucketairlines.com
This airline offers daily flights
between Hyannis and Nantucket (20
minute flight). Dogs are allowed in
the cabin with you on this airline!
Dogs under 35 pounds can be
carried on your lap and no kennel is
required. For dogs over 35 pounds,
there is a "shelf" which is just a few
inches off the floor, in the back of the
plane where your dog can sit or lay.
While you cannot sit next to your
dog, you can try to get the seat
directly in front of him or her. There
is no reserved seating, so you'll need
to arrive early to try and make
special arrangements to sit in front of
your pooch. Large dogs must be
properly restrained with a leash,
harness or similar device. No kennel
is required. You will need to reserve
a space for your pet in advance as
the airline usually only allows one
dog per flight. Their sister airline,
Cape Air also allows dogs in the
cabin, but most flights require your
dog to be in a kennel, and they have
a size limit for dogs.

Steamship Authority Ferry Service
South Street Dock
Hyannis, MA
508-477-8600
steamshipauthority.com
This ferry services runs from Cape
Cod to Nantucket Island (2.25 hours)
or Martha's Vineyard (1.5 hours).
Pets are allowed on all ferries except
for the M/V Flying Cloud fast ferry.
Pets must be leashed or in a crate at
all times. Pets are not allowed on the
seats, tables, or in the concession
areas. The ferries transport both
passengers and cars. They provide
year-round service to Nantucket and
Martha's Vineyard. Call ahead to
make reservations.

Steamship Authority Ferry Service
South Street Dock
Hyannis, MA
508-477-8600
steamshipauthority.com
This ferry services runs from Cape
Cod to Nantucket Island (2.25 hours)
or Martha's Vineyard (1.5 hours).
Pets are allowed on all ferries except
for the M/V Flying Cloud fast ferry.
Pets must be leashed or in a crate at
all times. Pets are not allowed on the
seats, tables, or in the concession
areas. The ferries transport both
passengers and cars. They provide

year-round service to Nantucket
and Martha's Vineyard. Call ahead
to make reservations.

Steamship Authority Ferry Service
South Street Dock
Hyannis, MA
508-477-8600
steamshipauthority.com
This ferry services runs from Cape
Cod to Nantucket Island (2.25
hours) or Martha's Vineyard (1.5
hours). Pets are allowed on all
ferries except for the M/V Flying
Cloud fast ferry. Pets must be
leashed or in a crate at all times.
Pets are not allowed on the seats,
tables, or in the concession areas.
The ferries transport both
passengers and cars. They provide
year-round service to Nantucket
and Martha's Vineyard. Call ahead
to make reservations.

Viking Fleet
462 W Lake Drive
Montauk, NY
631-668-5700
This ferry features a triple decker,
120 foot vessel with comfort
amenities on board, and service is
provided between Montauk Long
Island and Block Island RI, New
London CT, and Martha's Vineyard,
MA. Well behaved dogs are allowed
on board for no additional fee. Dogs
must be under their owner's control
and leashed at all times.

Salem Ferry
Derby Street at Blaney Street
Salem, MA
978-741-0220
salemferry.com/
This high speed catamaran offers
45 minute service between
downtown Boston and Salem. Dogs
on leash are allowed. The service is
open seasonally from late May
through October.

Michigan

Arbor Limousine
2050 Commerce
Ann Arbor, MI
734-663-8898
This transport company services
Washtenaw County and further with
the area's largest variety of fleet
vehicles. Well mannered dogs are
allowed in some of the vehicles;
they must be leashed or crated and
under their owner's control at all
times.

A Dream Limousine
Canton, MI
734-542-6800
adreamlimo.com/
Serving southeastern Michigan and
the Detroit metro area, this limousine
services offers a variety of vehicles
and special pricings; they are
available for simple pick-ups to a
night on the town. Well mannered
dogs up to 60 pounds are welcome
for transport for no additional fee;
they must be under their owner's
control at all times.

Beaver Island Boat Co.
103 Bridge Park Drive
Charlevoix, MI
231-547-2311
bibco.com
This ferry line provides passenger
and vehicle service between
Charlevoix and St. James Harbor on
Beaver Island. All trips are weather
permitting and additional trips may
be possible in December. Rates start
at $20 per person one way ($35
round trip) and $10.50 per child one
way ($17 round trip). Vehicles cost
$61 and up one way ($122) round
trip. Pets are allowed but the
following rules apply. Leashed pets
are allowed on the top deck for an
extra $10 each way, but must be
kept away from other passengers.
They are not allowed inside the
passenger cabin or on any tables or
benches. You are not allowed to
groom your pet on the ferry. Dogs
barking excessively may be refused
passage. People are responsible for
cleaning up after their pets. Pets can
stay in your vehicle inside a portable
kennel away from the driver at no
charge. Or pets can stay in a
portable kennel on the car deck for
an extra $10 each way. If you do not
have a portable kennel, the ferry line
can rent one to you but reservations
in advance are required. If you have
any questions or to make a
reservation, contact the ferry line at
1-888-446-4095.

Ironton Ferry
Ferry Road
Ironton, MI
231-547-7200
This 4 car cable ferry operates from
mid-April through mid-November and
crosses a narrow point on the south
arm of Lake Charlevoix. Dogs are
allowed on the ferry for no extra fee.

Lake Michigan Car Ferry Company
701 Maritime Drive
Ludington, MI
800-841-4243

ssbadger.com
The S.S. Badger offers the largest cross-lake passenger service on the Great Lakes. The relaxing four-hour, 60-mile cruise takes passengers, and vehicles across Lake Michigan between Ludington, Michigan and Manitowoc, Wisconsin from mid-May through mid-October. Dogs may be transported in the owner's vehicle or kept in a well ventilated portable kennel on the car deck. A limited number of kennels are available free of charge on a first-come, first served basis. Owners may also bring their own kennels. (If animals are left in the vehicle, windshield sunscreens are strongly recommended during warm weather.) No pets of any kind are allowed in any passenger areas, and pets are not accessible during the cruise.

Horse Taxis
Main Street
Mackinac Island, MI
906-847-3307
mict.com/
Mackinac Island horse taxis are provided by Mackinac Island Carriage Tours Co. Rates range from $3.75 to $6.25 per person depending on the distance traveled. Baggage is allowed at no extra charge but they reserve the right to charge for excess baggage. No bicycles are allowed on the taxis, including on the luggage racks. Call about 45 minutes prior to your requested travel time and a horse taxi will be radio dispatched to your location. If arriving by ferry, also call ahead or you can also sometimes ask the ferry personnel to contact a horse taxi in advance.

Arnold Mackinac Island Ferry
various docks-see comments
Mackinaw City, MI
906-847-3351
arnoldline.com/
This passenger ferry line offers the largest ferries to Mackinac Island. They have a fleet of three triple-decked Catamaran ferries. The ride takes less than 20 minutes. Ferries depart about every hour. Round trip rates are $17 per adult, $8 per child ages 5 to 12 and free for children under 5. Bikes cost an extra $6.50. Leashed pets are allowed but you will need to show proof of current rabies vaccine (dog tag) and current license (dog tag). These large ferries offer the most room for pets versus the other ferries. Restroom and handicap facilities are available on all ferries. Parking at the dock is free for one day but overnight costs $1 to

$15 per night. To get to the docks, follow the red, green and white signs to the Arnold Line Docks in Mackinaw City or St. Ignace.

Shepler's Mackinac Island Ferry
various docks-see comments
Mackinaw City, MI
231-436-5023
This ferry line provides passenger service from Mackinaw City or St. Ignace to Mackinaw Island. The ride takes less than 20 minutes. During peak times, ferries depart every 15 minutes. Round trip rates for adults are $16 per person, $7.50 for children 5 to 12 and free for children under 5. Family pets are welcome but need to be leashed and you will need to show proof of current rabies vaccine (dog tag) and current license (dog tag). Bikes are an extra $6.50. Rates are subject to change. The ferries also have wheelchair accessible facilities. To get to the Mackinaw City dock, take exit 339 off I-75. Turn left at the stop sign and continue to Central Avenue. Turn left and into the Gateway. To get to the St. Ignace dock, take exit 344-A off I-75. Follow US 2 east through downtown to the north end of town. Free daily and overnight onsite parking are guaranteed.

Star Line Mackinac Island Ferry
various docks-see comments
Mackinaw City, MI
906-643-7635
mackinacferry.com/
This ferry line offers passenger service from St. Ignace and Mackinaw City to Mackinac Island. The ride takes less than 20 minutes. Ferries depart about every half hour during the peak season. Round trip rates are $17 per adult, $8 per child ages 5 to 12 and free for children under 5. Bikes cost an extra $6.50. Leashed dogs are allowed and you will need to show proof of current rabies vaccine (dog tag) and current license (dog tag). Secure overnight parking is available for $2 per night. The St. Ignace docks are located at 587 N. State Street in St. Ignace and the Mackinaw City Dock is located at 711 South Huron in Mackinaw City.

Tecumseh Trolley and Limousine Service
223 East Patterson Street
Tecumseh, MI
866-423-3335
michigantrolleys.com/
This transport company will allow well mannered dogs in some of the

vehicles; they must be crated and under their owner's control at all times.

Crown Limousine
3161 E 9 Mile Road
Warren, MI
313-864-3651
crownlimousine4u.com/
Serving southeastern Michigan, this limousine services offers a variety of vehicles and special pricings; they are available for simple pick-ups to a night on the town. Well mannered dogs are welcome for transport for no additional fee; they must be under their owner's control at all times.

Minnesota

Island Passenger Service
2379 Flag Island
Angle Inlet, MN
218-223-5015
This passenger only ferry will transport dogs for no additional fees. Dogs must be leashed or crated and under their owner's control at all times. Directions for visitors coming from the west or south are to go north on H 310 from Roseau to Canadian Customs to clear entry; about 1½ miles from there turn onto Canada H 12 toward Sprague; in about 32 miles take a right on H 525 at the "T" junction; go about 14 miles to the customs phone booth to reenter the US, and continue on from there to the Northwest Angle. The reporting custom's booth is located at Jim's Corner.

Metro Transit
560 N Sixth Avenue (office)
Minneapolis, MN
612-373-3333
metrotransit.org/
Metro Transit will allow a small dog that can be held in a carrier for no additional fee. Dogs must be well mannered and under their owner's control and care at all times.

Nebraska

Pet Airways
4010 Amelia Earhart Plaza
Omaha, NE
408-248-6000
For information on Pet Airways, see Mesa (Phoenix) Arizona Listing.

New Jersey

NJ Transit
Regional
Hoboken, NJ
973-762-5100
njtransit.com
Small dogs in carriers are allowed on the trains.

Cape May-Lewes Ferry
Sandman Blvd. & Lincoln Drive
North Cape May, NJ
609-889-7200
capemaylewesferry.com/
This ferry service provides transportation for vehicles and passengers between Cape May, New Jersey and Lewes, Delaware. The ferry cuts miles off of driving along the Atlantic coast. Pets are welcome but the following rules apply. For the M.V. Cape May, M.V. Delaware and M.V. Twin Cape ferries, pets are welcome on the ferry on exterior decks and any lounge areas where food is not being made, served or eaten. Pets are not allowed in the lounge area whenever there is a private party being hosted. For the M.V. Cape Henlopen and M.V. New Jersey ferries, pets are not allowed in any interior space but are allowed on the car exterior decks. For all ferries, dogs of all sizes are allowed but need to be kept under control at all times and leashed or in a carrier. People need to clean up after their pets. Pets are not allowed in the shuttles. Rates start at $20 to $25 for a vehicle and driver. For a foot passenger with no car, rates start at $6 to $8 per person. Larger vehicles can be accommodated but there is an extra charge. The Cape May Terminal is located at Sandman Blvd. and Lincoln Drive in North Cape May, New Jersey. The Lewes Terminal is located at 43 Henlopen Drive in Lewes, Delaware. Rates are subject to change. For reservations or to check rates, call the ferry line toll free at 1-800-643-3779.

New York

Fire Island Ferry
99 Maple Avenue
Bay Shore, NY
631-665-3600
fireislandferries.com/
After 4th avenue becomes Maple Avenue, the main terminal for Ocean Beach is on the left, and the Seaview/Ocean Bay Park terminal is on the right. Dogs may not go on the trips to Ocean Beach as dogs are not allowed there. Well behaved dogs

are allowed on the ferry to Seaview/Ocean Bay for an additional fee of $4 each way. Dogs must be well mannered, and leashed and cleaned up after at all times.

Pet Airways
1300 New Highway
Farmingdale, NY
312-429-0245
For information on Pet Airways, see Mesa (Phoenix) Arizona Listing.

Pet Airways
1300 New Highway
Farmingdale LI, NY
312-429-0245
For information on Pet Airways, see Mesa (Phoenix) Arizona Listing.

Long Island Railroad and Buses
Regional
Long Island, NY
718-330-1234
mta.nyc.ny.us
Small dogs in carriers are allowed on the Long Island Railroad, Long Island Bus and New York City Transit buses and subways. Small dogs in carriers or on a secure leash are allowed on the Metro-North Railroad. The pet carrier should be able to fit on your lap and should not occupy a seat. Dogs should not bother other passengers.

Long Island Railroad and Buses
Regional
Long Island, NY
718-330-1234
mta.nyc.ny.us
Small dogs in carriers are allowed on the Long Island Railroad, Long Island Bus and New York City Transit buses and subways. Small dogs in carriers or on a secure leash are allowed on the Metro-North Railroad. The pet carrier should be able to fit on your lap and should not occupy a seat. Dogs should not bother other passengers.

Viking Fleet
462 W Lake Drive
Montauk, NY
631-668-5700
This ferry features a triple decker, 120 foot vessel with comfort amenities on board, and service is provided between Montauk Long Island and Block Island RI, New London CT, and Martha's Vineyard, MA. Well behaved dogs are allowed on board for no additional fee. Dogs must be under their owner's control and leashed at all times. The ferry docks at Montauk at the Viking

Dock at 462 Westlake Drive.

Cross Sound Ferry Services
2 Ferry Street, PO Box 33
New London, CT
860-443-5281
longislandferry.com/Default.asp
This auto ferry service provides transportation between New London, CT and Orient Point on Long Island, NY. Dogs are allowed on the car ferry in dog designated areas only for no additional fee. Dogs must be well behaved, leashed or in an approved pet carrier, and cleaned up after at all times.

HoundXpress.com
Call to arrange
New York, NY
917-693-5652
houndXpress.com
This service in Manhattan provides dog walking, dog daycare in your place and a dog taxi service.

MTA
Regional
New York, NY
718-330-1234
mta.nyc.ny.us
Small dogs in carriers are allowed on the Long Island Railroad, Long Island Bus and New York City Transit buses and subways. Small dogs in carriers or on a secure leash are allowed on the Metro-North Railroad. The pet carrier should be able to fit on your lap and should not occupy a seat. Dogs should not bother other passengers.

Madison Avenue Limousine Inc.
348 East 15th Street, Suite 16
New York, NY
212-674-0060
madisonavenuelimo.com/
This Limousine company will pick you and your pup up at your front door, and there is no additional pet fee if there is no extra cleaning. They suggest bringing a large sheet or cover depending on how large or hairy the dog is. There is a 2 hour rental minimum and they suggest calling 48-72 hours in advance. Dogs must be under their owner's care/control at all times.

Metro-North Railroad
42nd Street and Park Avenue
New York, NY
212-532-4900
mta.info/mnr/index.html
Dogs up to 65 pounds are allowed on the train for no additional pet fee. Dogs are not allowed on the train when it is crowed or during peak

hours and they may not take up a seat. Dogs must be well behaved, under their owner's control at all times, and they must be securely leashed or in a carrier and cleaned up after at all times.

Pet Chauffeur
New York, NY
718-752-1767 (866-PETRIDE)
petride.com
This pet transportation service will take you and your pet (or your pet alone) just about anywhere you need or want to go. They recommend calling well in advance but you can try last minute bookings.

Pet Taxi
227 E 56th St
New York, NY
212-755-1757
When want to get around town without driving, there are numerous taxi cabs. A typical New York yellow taxi cab is supposed to pick up people with pets, however, they don't always stop if you have a pooch. Don't feel too bad, many NY cabs don't stop even for people without pets! However, with a little advance planning, you can reserve the Pet Taxi. The Pet Taxi makes runs to the vet, groomer and other pet related stuff. But they are also rented to transport you and your pooch to a park, outdoor restaurant, across town, etc. For example, if you are at a hotel near Central Park but would like to go to Little Italy and Chinatown for half a day, they will take you to your destination and then several hours later, they will pick you up and take you back to your hotel. Just be sure to reserve the Pet Taxi at least one day in advance during the weekdays. If you need the taxi on Saturday or Sunday, book your reservation by Thursday or Friday. They are open from 8am-7pm during the weekday and by reservation on the weekends. They can be reserved for $35 per hour or $25 each way for a pick up or drop off. Pet Taxi serves the Manhattan area.

Seastreak Ferry Rides
various (see below)
New York, NY
800-BOAT-RIDE
seastreakusa.com
Want to enjoy the sights of New York City from the water, including the Manhattan Skyline and the Statue of Liberty? Or maybe you want to stay at a hotel in New Jersey and visit New York City during the day. Well, the nice folks at Seastreak allow

dogs onboard their commuter ferries. Here are the rules: Dogs of all sizes must stay on the outside portion of the ferry and they need to be on a short leash. Dogs are not allowed on the inside area regardless of the weather unless you have a small dog and he or she is in a carrier. The ferries operate between Manhattan and New Jersey on a daily basis with up to 11 ferry rides during the weekday and about 4 ferry rides on the weekend. The ride lasts about 45 minutes each way and costs approximately $20 per round trip, half price for children and free for dogs! The ferries depart from Pier 11 (Wall Street) and East 34th Street in Manhattan and Atlantic Highlands and Highlands in New Jersey. Please visit their website for current ferry schedules, times and fares.

Staten Island Ferry
Whitehall Street
New York, NY
718-876-8441
siferry.com/
Small dogs in a cage or carrier are allowed on these ferries. The ferry service provides passenger transportation between St. George, Staten Island and Whitehall Street in Manhattan. The 25 minute ride provides a great view of New York Harbor, the Statue of Liberty and Ellis Island.

Lake Champlain Ferries
838-842 Cumberland Head Road
Plattsburgh, NY
802-864-9804
ferries.com/
Leashed dogs of all sizes are allowed on the Lake Champlain Ferry crossing that travels between New York and Vermont. Ferry schedules changes constantly so please confirm the time of your voyage.

Sayville Ferry Service
41 River Road
Sayville, NY
631-589-0810
sayvilleferry.com/
This ferry service offers daily schedules to a variety of stops in the South Bay area, and dogs are allowed for an additional $4 per round trip. Dogs must be under their owner's control at all times, and they must be leashed and cleaned up after.

North Ferry Company

12 Summerfield Place
Shelter Island Heights, NY
631-749-0139
northferry.com/
This ferry provides transportation service between Long Island and Shelter Island. Dogs of all sizes are allowed for no additional fee. Dogs must be under their owner's control, leashed, and cleaned up after at all times.

North Carolina

North Carolina Ferry-Bayview
229 H 306N
Bath, NC
800-BY FERRY (293-3779)
These vehicle and passenger transport ferries are run by the state and provide service every day of the year on all routes; however weather conditions can influence travel. Dogs are allowed on all ferries for no additional fee; they must be kept in the vehicle or leashed when out of the vehicle. Dogs must be under their owner's control at all times.

North Carolina Ferry-Cedar Island
H 12
Cedar Island, NC
800-BY FERRY (293-3779)
These vehicle and passenger transport ferries are run by the state and provide service every day of the year on all routes; however weather conditions can influence travel. Dogs are allowed on all ferries for no additional fee; they must be kept in the vehicle or leashed when out of the vehicle. Dogs must be under their owner's control at all times.

North Carolina Ferry-Currituck
Courthouse Road
Currituck, NC
800-BY FERRY (293-3779)
These vehicle and passenger transport ferries are run by the state and provide service every day of the year on all routes; however weather conditions can influence travel. Dogs are allowed on all ferries for no additional fee; they must be kept in the vehicle or leashed when out of the vehicle. Dogs must be under their owner's control at all times.

North Carolina Ferry-Knotts Island
S end of H 615 (on the island)
Ferry Dock Road, NC
800-BY FERRY (293-3779)
These vehicle and passenger transport ferries are run by the state and provide service every day of the

year on all routes; however weather conditions can influence travel. Dogs are allowed on all ferries for no additional fee; they must be kept in the vehicle or leashed when out of the vehicle. Dogs must be under their owner's control at all times.

Fort Fisher Ferry
Fort Fisher Blvd S
Fort Fisher, NC
800-BY FERRY (293-3779)
ncdot.org/transit/ferry/
This water taxi provides services between the outer islands and the mainland. Dogs are allowed on board for no additional fee; they must be leashed, crated, or in a vehicle for the duration of the trip. Dogs must be under their owner's control at all times.

North Carolina Ferry-Fort Fisher
Fort Fisher Road S/H 421
Fort Fisher, NC
800-BY FERRY (293-3779)
These vehicle and passenger transport ferries are run by the state and provide service every day of the year on all routes; however weather conditions can influence travel. Dogs are allowed on all ferries for no additional fee; they must be kept in the vehicle or leashed when out of the vehicle. Dogs must be under their owner's control at all times.

North Carolina Ferry-Hatteras
H 12
Hatteras, NC
800-BY FERRY (293-3779)
These vehicle and passenger transport ferries are run by the state and provide service every day of the year on all routes; however weather conditions can influence travel. Dogs are allowed on all ferries for no additional fee; they must be kept in the vehicle or leashed when out of the vehicle. Dogs must be under their owner's control at all times.

North Carolina Ferry-Cherry Branch
Ferry Road
Havelock, NC
800-BY FERRY (293-3779)
These vehicle and passenger transport ferries are run by the state and provide service every day of the year on all routes; however weather conditions can influence travel. Dogs are allowed on all ferries for no additional fee; they must be kept in the vehicle or leashed when out of the vehicle. Dogs must be under their owner's control at all times.

North Carolina Ferry-Minnesott

Beach
Point Road/H 306
Minnesott Beach, NC
800-BY FERRY (293-3779)
These vehicle and passenger transport ferries are run by the state and provide service every day of the year on all routes; however weather conditions can influence travel. Dogs are allowed on all ferries for no additional fee; they must be kept in the vehicle or leashed when out of the vehicle. Dogs must be under their owner's control at all times.

North Carolina Ferry-Ocracoke #1
H 12 N end of Island (to Hatteras)
Ocracoke, NC
800-BY FERRY (293-3779)
These vehicle and passenger transport ferries are run by the state and provide service every day of the year on all routes; however weather conditions can influence travel. Dogs are allowed on all ferries for no additional fee; they must be kept in the vehicle or leashed when out of the vehicle. Dogs must be under their owner's control at all times.

North Carolina Ferry-Ocracoke #2
H 12 S end of Island (to Cedar Island and Swan Quarter)
Ocracoke, NC
800-BY FERRY (293-3779)
These vehicle and passenger transport ferries are run by the state and provide service every day of the year on all routes; however weather conditions can influence travel. Dogs are allowed on all ferries for no additional fee; they must be kept in the vehicle or leashed when out of the vehicle. Dogs must be under their owner's control at all times.

North Carolina Ferry-Southport
Southport Ferry Road
Southport, NC
800-BY FERRY (293-3779)
These vehicle and passenger transport ferries are run by the state and provide service every day of the year on all routes; however weather conditions can influence travel. Dogs are allowed on all ferries for no additional fee; they must be kept in the vehicle or leashed when out of the vehicle. Dogs must be under their owner's control at all times.

North Carolina Ferry-Swan Quarter
Swan Quarter Ferry Road
Swan Quarter, NC
800-BY FERRY (293-3779)
These vehicle and passenger transport ferries are run by the state and provide service every day of the

year on all routes; however weather conditions can influence travel. Dogs are allowed on all ferries for no additional fee; they must be kept in the vehicle or leashed when out of the vehicle. Dogs must be under their owner's control at all times.

Ohio

Miller Boat Line
Catawba Dock
Catawba Island, OH
800-500-2421
millerferry.com/
This ferry line offers service from the town of Catawba on the Ohio mainland to the Lilm Kiln Dock on South Bay Island which is home to the town of Put-in-Bay. Travel time from dock to dock is about 18 minutes. The ferries runs year round, weather permitting, with ferries leaving every half hour during the day. Rates start at about $5 to $6 per person one way and $1 per child. The fare is free for children under 6 years old and for dogs. Leashed dogs are welcome on the ferries. Once on the island, there is a 2.5 mile walk from the ferry dock to Put-in-Bay. If you do not want to walk, you can opt to take the public Lilm Kiln Bus, a taxi or rent a golf cart. Dogs of all sizes are allowed in all of the above mentioned methods of transportation as long as they are well-behaved and leashed. The Miller Boat Line transports mainly passengers but also offers limited vehicle service. Vehicles leaving Catawba cannot be transported round trip on Saturdays, Sundays or Holiday Mondays. Drivers must show written proof of an accommodation in order to bring a vehicle to the island on the weekends. For full vehicle requirements please contact the ferry line directly by phone or check their web site at http://www.millerferry.com. This ferry line also offers passenger and vehicle service from Catawba to Middle Bass Island. To get to the Catawba Dock, take Route 2 to Route 53 which will bring you right to the dock. Free parking is provided.

SORTA Metro
1014 Vine Street, Suite 2000
Cincinnati, OH
513-632-7575
sorta.com
The Southwest Ohio Regional Transit Authority (SORTA) allows small dogs in carriers that you can

hold on your lap on their buses.

Greater Cleveland RTA
1240 West 6th Street
Cleveland, OH
216-566-5227
gcrta.org
The Greater Cleveland Regional Transit Authority (RTA) allows people to bring dogs less than 25 pounds in a carrier on their buses.

Kelleys Island Ferry Boat Line
510 West Main St. (Route 163)
Marblehead, OH
419-798-9763
kelleysislandferry.com/
This ferry line transports passengers from Marblehead to Kelleys Island which is about a 20 minute ride. It operates year round, weather permitting. They offer limited vehicle transportation. Dogs are welcome but need to be leashed.

Jet Express
off exit 163
Port Clinton, OH
800-245-1538
jet-express.com
This ferry company offers passenger service from Port Clinton on the Ohio mainland directly to downtown Put-in-Bay on South Bass Island. Their catamaran boat can travel up to 40 miles per hour making it a fast ride across the lake. Fares start at about $12 per person one way. Children 12 and under, as well as pets of all ages, ride free. Dogs are welcome but need to be leashed and well-behaved. Pets must stay on the outside deck of the ferry. To get to the Port Clinton dock, take Route 2 and take exit 163 North Port Clinton.

Commodore Perry Cab Company
various locations
Put-in-Bay, OH
This taxi cab company provides seasonal service during the summer months. They can transport you and your dog from the Lilm Kiln Dock to downtown Put-in-Bay for about $3 per person each way. There is not usually any extra charge for pets. Well-mannered leashed dogs are welcome.

Lilm Kiln Bus
Box 190
Put-in-Bay, OH
419-285-4855
put-in-bay-trans.com/lkbus.htm
Well-behaved dogs on leash are allowed on the island shuttle bus as long as there is room for them. The bus transports passengers between

the Miller Ferry Dock (Lilm Kiln Dock) and downtown Put-in-Bay. The fare is $2 per person one way.

Island Bike Rental
various island docks
South Bass Island, OH
419-285-2016
put-in-bay-trans.com/bikmini.htm
You and your pooch can rent a mini golf cart to drive from the ferry docks to the town of Put-in-Bay or around the rest of the island. Golf carts vary in size and can carry from 2 to 6 passengers. Leashed dogs are welcome on the cart rentals. The rentals are located both at the Jet Express dock in downtown Put-in-Bay and at the Miller Boat Line Ferry at the Lilm Kiln dock. Rates run about $10 to $16 per hour or $50 to $70 per day depending on the size of the golf cart.

Oregon

Tri-Met
4012 SE Center
Portland, OR
503-238-RIDE (7433)
trimet.org
A small dog in a carrier is allowed on the rail and bus lines at no additional fee.

Pennsylvania

Port Authority of Allegheny County
534 Smithfield Street
Pittsburgh, PA
412-442-2000
ridegold.com
A small dog in an enclosed carrier is allowed on both light rail and the buses at no additional fee.

the Centre Area Transportation Authority
2081 W. Whitehall Road (Main Office)
State College, PA
888-738-CATA
catabus.com/acoffice.htm
This city bus line will allow pooches to ride with their human companions for no additional fee. They may not be allowed if they are very large or aggressive. Dogs must be in a secure pet carrier, or leashed and muzzled, and they must be under their owner's control at all times.

Rhode Island

Block Island Ferry
two location-see comments
Block Island, RI
401-783-4613
This ferry line provides passenger and vehicle service from Point Judith to Block Island (one hour trip) and from Fort Adams in Newport to Block Island (two hour trip). Pets on a leash or in a carrier are allowed on the ferry. One way fares start at just under $10 per person and about $5 per child. Vehicles are transported on the ferry that leaves from Point Judith. Rates for vehicles range from about $40 to $95 or more depending on the size and type of vehicle. Call ahead to make reservations for vehicles. Only cash or travelers checks are accepted at the Newport location. At Point Judith, credit cards are also accepted. Rates are subject to change. Parking for the Point Judith ferry is located across the street from the ferry. Prices range from $5 to $10 per day. Parking for the Newport ferry is located at Fort Adams State Park at no charge.

Viking Fleet
462 W Lake Drive
Montauk, NY
631-668-5700
This ferry features a triple decker, 120 foot vessel with comfort amenities on board, and service is provided between Montauk Long Island and Block Island RI, New London CT, and Martha's Vineyard, MA. Well behaved dogs are allowed on board for no additional fee. Dogs must be under their owner's control and leashed at all times. The ferry docks on Block Island at Champlin's Marina.

Interstate Navigation/Block Island Ferry
304 Grey Island Road
Narragansett, RI
401-783-4613
blockislandferry.com
The ferry rides are about 1 hour, and they are open all year. Ther ferries leave from Newport at Fort Adams State Park and Point Judith (Galilee) just south of Narragansett. The ferries sail from Old Harbor on Block Island. Dogs are allowed, but they must be friendly, well behaved, and leashed. They request to have dogs relieve themselves before boarding, and doggie bags are required.

Interstate Navigation/Block Island

Ferry
304 Grey Island Road
Narragansett, RI
401-783-4613
blockislandferry.com
The ferry rides are about 1 hour, and they are open all year. Ther ferries leave from Newport at Fort Adams State Park and Point Judith (Galilee) just south of Narragansett. The ferries sail from Old Harbor on Block Island. Dogs are allowed, but they must be friendly, well behaved, and leashed. They request to have dogs relieve themselves before boarding, and doggie bags are required.

Texas

DART
Regional
Dallas, TX
214-979-1111
dart.org
Small dogs in carriers are allowed on the light rail and buses.

Port Bolivar Ferry - Car Only
At End of H 87
Galveston, TX
409-795-2230
This ferry goes from Galveston to Bolivar and back. The trips take about 15 minutes each way. Dogs are allowed to go on the ferry if they are in your car only. They may not go as a "walk on". The ferry runs 24 hours a day.

Metropolitan Transit Authority
1900 Main
Houston, TX
713-635-4000
ridemetro.org
Small dogs in an enclosed carrier are allowed on the bus or light rail at no additional charge.

Utah

Utah Transit Authority (MTA)
Salt Lake City, UT
801-RIDEUTA (743-3882)
rideuta.com/
This multi-modal transportation provider offers service throughout Salt Lake City and surrounding areas. At the driver's discretion, small dogs can be brought on board in a secure hand-held carrier. No aggressive breeds are allowed; and dogs may not take up an additional seat or be in the isles. Occasionally, a larger dog can be transported by making prior arrangements with the

UTA.

Virginia

Elizabeth River Ferry
6 Crawford Parkway
Portsmouth, VA
757-393-5111
Famous for being the oldest continually operating public transport in America, this ferry system can be boarded at #1 High Street or at the Parkway address, and it connects pedestrians from Olde Towne Portsmouth to Norfolk's Waterside Festival Marketplace. Dogs are allowed on board for no additional fee. Dogs must be well behaved, under their owner's control, and leashed at all times.

GRTC
Regional
Richmond, VA
804-358-GRTC
ridegrtc.com
Small dogs in carriers are allowed on the buses.

Washington

Alaska Ferry
I-5 Exit #250
Bellingham, WA
360-676-8445 (800-642-0066)
dot.state.ak.us/amhs
For information on the Alaska Ferry, see Auke Bay (Juneau) Alaska Listing

Lake Chelan Boat Company
1418 W Woodin Ave
Chelan, WA
509-682-4584
ladyofthelake.com/
Daily service passenger boats provide round-trip service between Chelan and Stehekin, with a few scheduled stops in between, from about mid-March through October 31st, and then reduced service during the winter. Dogs up to 100 pounds are allowed. Dogs must remain in a crate in the luggage area on the outside deck with the owner present at all times while underway. There is an additional fee of $13.00 round-trip in the owner's cage or $24.00 round-tip in a boat company cage.

Alaska Ferry
I-5 Exit #250
From Bellingham, WA
360-676-8445 (800-642-0066)

dot.state.ak.us/amhs
For information on the Alaska Ferry, see Auke Bay (Juneau) Alaska Listing

Leavenworth Shuttle
188 H 2
Leavenworth, WA
509-548-RIDE (7433)
leavenworthshuttle.com/
This shuttle and on-call taxi service will allow well behaved dogs transportation. Dogs must be in a carrier or leashed and under their owner's control at all times.

Black Ball Ferry Line
101 E Railroad Avenue
Port Angeles, WA
360-457-4491
cohoferry.com/main/
Offering breathtaking scenic passage for vehicles and passengers between Vancouver Island and the Olympic Peninsula is this ferry service's specialty. Dogs are also allowed for passage for no additional fee. They must have a current rabies certificate from a veterinarian, and they are allowed on the outer decks or in the vehicle only.

Victoria Express
115 Railroad Avenue
Port Angeles, WA
360-452-8088
victoriaexpress.com/welcome.html
This fast passenger ferry offers several stops between Port Angeles, Washington and Victoria, British Columbia. They have a galley on board, a currency exchange office, and duty free shopping on board. Dogs are allowed on board for no additional fee; there is a pet waiver to sign. Dogs must be leashed or in a carrier.

Sound Flight
300 Airport Way
Renton, WA
866-921-3474
soundflight.net/
This air charter offers a variety of seaplane and landplane flights throughout the northwest and beyond. Dogs are allowed in the cabin seating area for no additional fee unless clean up is required. Dogs must be well mannered and under their owner's control at all times.

King County Metro
Regional
Seattle, WA
206-553-3000
transit.metrokc.gov
Both small and large dogs are

allowed on the street cars and buses. Small dogs that fit in their owner's lap ride for free. Large dogs are charged the same fare as their owner and should not occupy a seat. One large dog per bus is allowed. Large dogs should ride on the floor of the bus, preferably under the seat. It is up to the driver as to whether or not your dog will be allowed if you have a very large dog, if there is another animal already onboard or if the bus or street car is excessively crowded. Dogs must be leashed.

Washington State Ferries
Pier 52
Seattle, WA
206-464-6400
wsdot.wa.gov/ferries/
The Washington State Ferries is the nation's largest ferry system and the state's number one tourist attraction. This ferry service offers many ferry routes, including Seattle to Bainbridge Island, Seattle to Bremerton, Edmonds to Kingston, Anacortes to Friday Harbor (San Juan Islands), and Anacortes to Sidney in British Columbia, Canada. Please see our Washington State Ferry listing in our Victoria, British Columbia, Canada City Guide for customs requirements for both people and dogs. While leashed dogs are allowed on the ferry routes mentioned above, the following pet regulations apply. On the newer ferries that have outside stairwells, dogs are allowed on the car deck and on the outdoor decks above the car deck. If the ferry has indoor stairwells, dogs are only allowed on the deck where they boarded the ferry. For example, if your dog comes onto the ferry in your car, he or she has to remain on the car deck. If you walk onto the ferry with your dog, your pooch is allowed on the outside deck where you boarded but cannot go onto other decks. In cases where your pet has to remain on the car deck, you can venture to the above decks without your pet to get food at the snack bars. However, the ferry system recommends in general that you stay with your pooch in the car. For any of the ferries, dogs are not allowed inside the ferry terminals. Ferry prices for people and autos are determined by the route and peak times, but in general tickets for people can start under $10 round trip, and more for autos. Dogs ride free!

Wisconsin

Washington Island Ferry
Northpoint Pier
Ellison Bay, WI
920-847-2546
wisferry.com
This ferry is at the north end of Highway 42 and is a 30 minute crossing to Washington Island where some of the attractions include an art and nature center, a farm museum, a park and lookout tower, shops, and ample food. The ferry runs year round. Dogs on leash are allowed on the ferry.

Madeline Island Ferry Line
Bayfield or La Pointe docks
La Pointe, WI
715-474-2051
madferry.com/
Leashed dogs are allowed on this ferry line that provides both passenger and vehicle service to Madeline Island. Round trip rates are about $8.50 per person 12 and up, $4 for children 6 to 11 and free for children 5 and under. Vehicles cost about $28 and up. They can accommodate large motorhomes. The docks are located at Bayfield and on the island at La Pointe.

Lake Michigan Car Ferry Company
701 Maritime Drive
Ludington, MI
800-841-4243
ssbadger.com
The S.S. Badger offers the largest cross-lake passenger service on the Great Lakes. The relaxing four-hour, 60-mile cruise takes passengers, and vehicles across Lake Michigan between Ludington, Michigan and Manitowoc, Wisconsin from mid-May through mid-October. Dogs may be transported in the owner's vehicle or kept in a well ventilated portable kennel on the car deck. A limited number of kennels are available free of charge on a first-come, first served basis. Owners may also bring their own kennels. (If animals are left in the vehicle, windshield sunscreens are strongly recommended during warm weather.) No pets of any kind are allowed in any passenger areas, and pets are not accessible during the cruise.

Lake Express Ferry Service
2330 S. Lincoln Memorial Drive
Milwaukee, WI
866-914-1010
lake-express.com
This ferry line provides passenger

and vehicle service between Milwaukee, Wisconsin and Muskegon, Michigan. The high speed crossing takes only 2.5 hours saving a long drive through Chicago. Pets are allowed but the following rules apply. Pets need to stay in your vehicle or in a kennel which is kept on the car deck. You cannot visit your pet during the ferry ride, but a crew person is stationed on the car deck throughout the trip. A limited supply of kennels are available to rent. Rates are $7.50 per kennel one way and $15 round trip. Reservations are required for a kennel. You can also use your own portable kennel on the car deck. Rates start at $50 per person one way ($85 round trip) and less for children and seniors. Transporting a vehicle starts a rate of $50 one way ($118 round trip). Vehicle rates do not include fares for a driver or passengers. Trailers can be accommodated for an extra fee. Rates are subject to change.

Canada

Alberta

Calgary Transit
Calgary, AB
403-262-1000
Dogs are allowed on Calgary city buses and LRT for a fee of $2.50 each way. Dogs must be well behaved, kept leashed, and under their owner's control at all times.

British Columbia

Washington State Ferries
2100 Ferry Terminal Rd
Anacortes, WA
206-464-6400
wsdot.wa.gov/ferries/
This ferry service offers many routes in Washington State, as well as a route from Sidney, near Victoria, to Anacortes in Washington. The ferry ride is about 3 hours long and the ferry carries both passengers and vehicles. You can also catch a ferry to Sidney from Friday Harbor, Washington, in the San Juan Islands. This ferry ride is about 1 hour and 15 minutes. While leashed dogs are allowed on the ferry routes mentioned above, the following pet regulations apply. On the newer ferries that have outside stairwells, dogs are allowed on the car deck and on the outdoor decks above the car deck. If the ferry has indoor stairwells, dogs are only allowed on the deck where they boarded the ferry. For example, if your dog comes onto the ferry in your car, he or she has to remain on the car deck. If you walk onto the ferry with your dog, your pooch is allowed on the outside deck where you boarded but cannot go onto other decks. In cases where your pet has to remain on the car deck, you can venture to the above decks without your pet to get food at the snack bars. However, the ferry system recommends in general that you stay with your pooch in the car. For any of the ferries, dogs are not allowed inside the ferry terminals. The ferries in Anacortes leave from 2100 Ferry Terminal Road. The ferries in Friday Harbor leave from 91 Front Street and the ferries in Sidney leave from 2499 Ocean Avenue. Reservations are recommended 48 hours or more in advance if you are bringing a vehicle. Because you will be crossing over an international border, identification for Customs and Immigration is required. U.S. and Canadian citizens traveling across the border will need proof of citizenship such as your passport or a certified copy of your birth certificate issued by the city, county or state/province where you were born. You will also need photo identification such as a current valid driver's license. People with children need to bring their child's birth certificate. Single parents, grandparents or guardians traveling with children often need proof or notarized letters from the other parent authorizing travel. Dogs traveling to Canada or returning to Canada need a certificate from their vet showing a rabies vaccination within the past 3 years. Dogs traveling to the U.S. or returning to the U.S. need to have a valid rabies vaccination certificate (including an expiration date and vet signature). The certificate must show that the dog had the rabies vaccine at least 30 days prior to entry and within the past 36 months.

BC Ferries Inside Passage Route
Bella Bella, BC
888-223-3779
bcferries.com
This ferry takes cars, RVs and passengers between Port Hardy and Prince Rupert and also to the Queen Charlotte Islands, Bella Bella and some other destinations. The principal route is between Port Hardy and Prince Rupert. This ferry is a new, large ship which appears as a small scale cruise ship. It has a number of restaurants, a bar and movies. Cabins are available for the 15 hour Inside Passage route. Dogs must remain on the car deck the entire time. They must stay in your car, RV or in a kennel. There is a separate, closed room for kenneled dogs on the car deck. There is a schedule of pet visits where people with pets are allowed to visit the car deck to walk their dogs. Each visit is about 3 hours apart. The dog will have to go on the car deck as there is a 15 hour sailing time. You can probably visit with your pet about 5 times during the 15 hour crossing. For people wanting to take the ferries to Alaska from Victoria, Vancouver or Washington we recommend this ferry from Port Hardy to Prince Rupert, then the Alaska Ferry to Juneau or Haines with intermediate stops possible on the Alaska Ferry.

BC Ferries Inside Passage Route
Port Hardy, BC
888-223-3779
bcferries.com
For information on the BC Ferries Inside Passage Route, see Bella Bella, British Columbia Listing

Alaska Ferry
Yellowhead Hwy # 16
Prince Rupert, BC
250-627-1744 (800-642-0066)
dot.state.ak.us/amhs
For information on the Alaska Ferry, see Auke Bay (Juneau) Alaska Listing

BC Ferries Inside Passage Route
Prince Rupert, BC
888-223-3779
bcferries.com
For information on the BC Ferries Inside Passage Route, see Bella Bella, British Columbia Listing

Inland Air Charters Ltd.
1 Bellas Road/Seal Cove
Prince Rupert, BC
250-624-2577
inlandair.bc.ca
Headquartered in Prince Rupert with a summer base in the Queen Charlotte Islands/Haida Gwaii, this private charter company offers a number of different services and tours. One dog up to about 50 pounds is allowed on board for no additional fee; they must be quiet, very well mannered, and under their owner's control at all times.

North Pacific Seaplanes
Seal Cove
Prince Rupert, BC
250-627-1341
northpacificseaplanes.com
Dogs are allowed on the regularly scheduled flights for an addition fee of $28 for small dogs, $45 for medium sized dogs, and up to $140 for large dogs; there is no addition pet fee if the whole plane is chartered. Dogs must be well behaved, under their owner's control, and leashed or kenneled at all times.

Translink (Ferry, Train, and Bus)
Regional
Vancouver, BC
604-953-3333
translink.bc.ca
Small dogs in hard-sided carriers are allowed on the SeaBus (ferry), SkyTrain (train) and buses.

BC Ferries
1112 Fort Street
Victoria, BC
250-386-3431
bcferries.bc.ca
Pets are allowed on most of the BC ferries, including the route from Vancouver to Victoria. This route departs from Tsawwassen which is south of Vancouver and arrives at Swartz Bay, which is north of Victoria. You will need to bring your car on the ferry in order to visit most of the dog-friendly places in Victoria. Dogs are only allowed on the open air car deck and must stay in the car or tied in a designated pet area. Owners must stay with their pets. The travel time for this route is approximately 1 hour and 35 minutes. Guide dogs and certified assistance dogs are not required to stay on the car decks.

BC Ferries
1112 Fort Street
Victoria, BC
250-386-3431
bcferries.bc.ca
Pets are allowed on most of the BC ferries, including the route from Vancouver to Victoria. These ferries depart from Tsawwassen which is south of Vancouver and arrives at Swartz Bay, which is north of Victoria. Dogs are only allowed on the open air car deck and must stay in your car or tied in a designated pet area on the car deck. Owners must stay with their pets. The travel time for this route is approximately 1 hour and 35 minutes. Guide dogs and certified assistance dogs are not required to stay on the car decks.

Black Ball Ferry Line
430 Belleville St
Victoria, BC
250-386-2202
cohoferry.com/main/
Offering breathtaking scenic passage for vehicles and passengers between Vancouver Island and the Olympic Peninsula is this ferry service's specialty. Dogs are also allowed for passage for no additional fee. They must have a current rabies certificate from a veterinarian, and they are allowed on the outer decks or in the vehicle only.

Blue Bird Cab
2659 Douglas StreetH 1
Victoria, BC
800-665-7055
taxicab.com/
In addition to providing taxi service

throughout the greater Victoria area, this cab company also offers a number of customer service amenities. Dogs are allowed for transport with prior notice for no additional fee. They must be well mannered, in a carrier or leashed, and under their owner's control at all times.

Victoria Express
Belleville Street
Victoria, BC
250-361-9144
victoriaexpress.com/
This passenger ferry service runs between Port Angeles in Washington and Victoria. Crossing time is about one hour. Dogs are allowed and must be leashed. The ferries in Port Angeles leave from the Landing Mall on Railroad Avenue. The ferries in Victoria leave from the port on Belleville Street. Currency exchange is available at the Port Angeles Reservation Office. Their toll free number in the U.S. is 1-800-633-1589. Reservations are recommended. Because you will be crossing over an international border, identification for Customs and Immigration is required. U.S. and Canadian citizens traveling across the border will need proof of citizenship such as your passport or a certified copy of your birth certificate issued by the city, county or state/province where you were born. You will also need photo identification such as a current valid driver's license. People with children need to bring their child's birth certificate. Single parents, grandparents or guardians traveling with children often need proof or notarized letters from the other parent authorizing travel. Dogs traveling to Canada or returning to Canada need a certificate from their vet showing a rabies vaccination within the past 3 years. Dogs traveling to the U.S. or returning to the U.S. need to have a valid rabies vaccination certificate (including an expiration date and vet signature). The certificate must show that your dog has had the rabies vaccine at least 30 days prior to entry and within the past 36 months.

Victoria Regional Transit System
250 Gorge Road E
Victoria, BC
250-385-2551
bctransit.com/
This regional transit system links over 50 communities throughout the

province. Dogs that can be transported in a hard-case carrier and held on the lap are allowed for no additional fee.

Nova Scotia

East Coast Ferries/ North Sydney Terminal
355 Purves Street
N Sydney, NS
800-341-7981
marineatlantic.ca/
This ferry provides year around passenger and vehicle transport between the Island of Newfoundland and Nova Scotia. Dogs are allowed on board for no additional fee; they are allowed in the vehicle or in a kennel only. Kennels are provided on a 1st come, 1st served basis.

The Cat Ferry, Yarmouth Terminal
58 Water Street
Yarmouth, NS
902-742-6800
catferry.com/
Quickly gaining recognition for its speed and agility on the water, this CAT carries up to 775 passengers and 240 cars (not to mention a few furry friends also) across the Gulf of Maine between Yarmouth Nova Scotia and Bar Harbor and Portland Maine from June to mid-October. Dogs of all sizes are allowed for no additional pet fee. Dogs must be well behaved, and remain in a vehicle on the auto deck or in a kennel during passage. Kennels are available on a 1st come 1st served basis.

Ontario

AutoShare - Car Sharing Network Inc.
26 Soho Street, Suite 203
Toronto, ON
416-340-7888
autoshare.com
A unique mode of transportation, this AutoShare program offers the largest fleet of shared cars and cargo vans in Toronto with more than 100 pick-up/drop-off locations in the city. Cars can be reserved in less than an hour and delivered to their customers location of choice 24/7; cars are insured and gas is included. Well behaved dogs are allowed in most of the autos, and there is no additional pet fee; they need to be declared at the time of reserving the vehicle.

TTC
Regional
Toronto, ON
416-393-INFO
city.toronto.on.ca/ttc
Both small and large dogs are allowed on the subway, buses, and streetcars. The driver has the discretion to decide whether or not pets are allowed if it is too crowded, there are too many pets onboard or if you have a very large dog. Pets must be on a leash or in a carrier.

Prince Edward Island

Bay Ferries Ltd
94 Water Street, Box 634
Charlottetown, PE
888-249-SAIL (7245)
nfl-bay.com/
These passenger/vehicle ships offer more than just high speed transport with amenities like onboard cafes, casinos, and movie theaters; routes cover from Maine, Nova Scotia, New Brunswick, and Prince Edward Island. Dogs are allowed on board all the ships in the vehicle or in a kennel only. The kennels are free upon request, but they are on a 1st come, 1st served basis and prior arrangements should be made or requested at the terminals. Dogs must be licensed and have proof of vaccinations.

Quebec

Atlas Taxi
Montreal, PQ
514-485-8585
Well-behaved, leashed dogs may ride in Montreal taxis with you. However, in winter you must provide a cover for the seats and you must report that you have a dog when calling for a taxi to avoid additional fees.

Metro (Subway)
Throughout the Region
Montreal, PQ
514-786-4636
stm.info
Small dogs in carriers are allowed. There is no fee for the dog but they may not take up a seat.

Unitaxi
Montreal, PQ
514-482-3000

Well-behaved, leashed dogs may ride in Montreal taxis with you. However, in winter you must provide a cover for the seats and you must report that you have a dog when calling for a taxi to avoid additional fees.

Quebec - Levis Ferry
Rue Dalhousie, Lower Town
Quebec, PQ
418-644-3704
For a fabulous view of Quebec from the river take the ferry from the Lower Town to Levis. The ferry ride takes about ten minutes each way and they leave about every 30 minutes throughout the day and evening. Well-behaved, leashed dogs are allowed for no additional fee. You can take the ferry for the views or if you need transportation to Levis.

Taxi Coop de Quebec
Throughout the city
Quebec, PQ
418-525-5191
Pets are allowed on these taxis in Quebec. They must be leashed or in a carrier at all times. People planning to take a pet on a taxi need to call ahead to get a pet-friendly cab driver.

Taxi Quebec
Throughout the city
Quebec, PQ
418-522-2001
Pets are allowed on these taxis in Quebec. They must be leashed or in a carrier at all times. People planning to take a pet on a taxi need to call ahead to get a pet-friendly driver.

Chapter 4

United States National Parks

Alaska

Wrangell-St Elias National Park and Preserve
PO Box 439
Copper Center, AK
907-822-5234
nps.gov/wrst/index.htm
Dogs on leash are allowed in the park. They are not allowed in buildings. The park features camping, hiking, auto touring, and more.

Denali National Park and Preserve
PO Box 9
Denali Park, AK
907-683-2294
nps.gov/dena/index.htm
Dogs must be on leash and must be cleaned up after in Denali National Park. Dogs are only allowed on the paved roads and dirt roads. One place to walk is on the road to Savage after mile 15, which is a dirt road and only the park buses are allowed. Access is by car depending on weather. Dogs on leash are allowed in the Denali National Park campgrounds, but they may not be left unattended in the campgrounds. The park features auto touring, camping, and scenery.

Gates of the Arctic National Park and Preserve
201 First Avenue
Fairbanks, AK
907-692-5494
nps.gov/gaar/index.htm
Dogs must be on leash and must be cleaned up after in the park. The park is accessed by plane, foot and car depending on weather. Dogs are allowed in the backcountry of the park but there are no man-made trails. It is a wilderness park. There are no campgrounds in the park and there are no facilities in the park.

Glacier Bay National Park
1 Park Road
Gustavus, AK
907-697-2230
nps.gov/glba
This national park offers coastal beaches and high mountains. The way to arrive at this park is by plane, boat, or ferry, usually from Juneau. The Glacier Bay Visitor Center is open daily from May 27 to September 11, from noon to 8:45 p.m. Dogs are not allowed to be off the road more than 100 feet, and they are not allowed on any of the trails into the back country. They are also not allowed on the Barlett Trail

or on the Forest Loop Trail, or in any of the camp buildings. The Visitor Information Station for boaters and campers, is open May through June from 8 to 5 p.m.; June, July, and August from 7 to 9 p.m., and September 8 to 5 p.m. Dogs are allowed at no additional fee, and they can be in the developed Barlett Cove area, or on any of the marked trails. Dogs may not be left unattended at any time, and they must be leashed at all times, and cleaned up after.

Katmai National Park and Preserve
PO Box 7
King Salmon, AK
907-246-3305
nps.gov/katm/index.htm
Dogs on leash are allowed only in developed areas. They are not allowed in the Brooks camping area. The park is accessed by plane or dogsled only.

Kobuk Valley National Park
PO Box 1029
Kotzebue, AK
907-442-3760
nps.gov/kova/index.htm
Dogs on leash are allowed in the park. The park is accessed by plane, foot, or dogsled only.

Western Arctic National Parklands
PO Box 1029
Kotzebue, AK
907-442-3760
nps.gov/nwak/index.htm
Pets are allowed. There is not an official pet policy. The park is accessed by plane and dogsledding.

Lake Clark National Park and Preserve
1 Park Place
Port Alsworth, AK
907-781-2218
nps.gov/lacl/index.htm
Dogs on leash are allowed in the park area. The park is accessed by plane or dogsled only. The park features boating, camping, fishing, hiking, and more.

Kenai Fjords National Park
PO Box 1727
Seward, AK
907-224-2132
nps.gov/klgo/index.htm
Dogs on leash are only allowed in the parking lot area and along roads. They are not allowed in buildings, on trails, or in the back country.

Arizona

Grand Canyon National Park
Hwy 64
Grand Canyon, AZ
928-638-7888
nps.gov/grca/
The Grand Canyon, located in the northwest corner of Arizona, is considered to be one of the most impressive natural splendors in the world. It is 277 miles long, 18 miles wide, and at its deepest point, is 6000 vertical feet (more than 1 mile) from rim to river. The Grand Canyon has several entrance areas, but the most popular is the South Rim. Dogs are not allowed in most areas of the North Rim of the Park. On the North Rim, the only trail that dogs are allowed on is the bridle trail from the lodge to the North Kaibab Trail (but not on the North Kaibab Trail). Dogs are not allowed on any trails below the rim, but leashed dogs are allowed on the paved rim trail. This dog-friendly trail is about 2.7 miles each way and offers excellent views of the Grand Canyon. Remember that the elevation at the rim is 7,000 feet, so you or your pup may need to rest more often than usual. Also, the weather can be very hot during the summer and can be snowing during the winter, so plan accordingly. And be sure you or your pup do not get too close to the edge! Feel like taking a tour? Well-behaved dogs are allowed on the Geology Walk. This is a one hour park ranger guided tour and consists of a leisurely walk along a 3/4 mile paved rim trail. They discuss how the Grand Canyon was created and more. The tour departs at 11am daily (weather permitting) from the Yavapai Observation Station. Pets are allowed in the Grand Canyon's Mather Campground in Grand Canyon Village, the Desert View Campground 26 miles east of the village, and, for RVs, the Trailer Village in Grand Canyon Village. Dogs must be leashed at all times in the campgrounds and may not be left unattended. There are kennels available at the South Rim. Its hours are 7:30 am to 5 pm. To make kennel reservations or for other kennel information call 928-638-0534. The Grand Canyon park entrance fee is currently $25.00 per private vehicle, payable upon entry to the park. Admission tickets are for 7 days.

Petrified Forest National Park
Entrances on Hwy 40 and Hwy 180
Petrified Forest National Park, AZ
928-524-6228
nps.gov/pefo/
The Petrified Forest is located in northeastern Arizona and features one of the world's largest and most colorful concentrations of petrified wood. Also included in the park's 93,533 acres are the multi-hued badlands of the Painted Desert, archeological sites and displays of 225 million year old fossils. Your leashed dog is welcome on all of the paved trails and scenic overlooks. Take a walk on the self-guided Giant Logs trail or view ancient petroglyphs from an overlook. The entrance fee is $10 per private vehicle.

Saguaro National Park
3693 South Old Spanish Trail
Tucson, AZ
520-733-5100
nps.gov/sagu/index.htm
Dogs must be on leash and must be cleaned up after on roadways and picnic areas. They are not allowed on any trails or buildings.

Arkansas

Hot Springs National Park
369 Central Avenue
Hot Springs, AR
501-624-2701
nps.gov/hosp
There are 47 hot springs here, and this reserve was established in 1832 to protect them. That makes this park our oldest national park. The park is open daily from 9:00 a.m. to 5:00 p.m., except in the summer from May 28 to August 12, when they stay open until 6:00 p.m. Dogs are allowed at no additional fee at the park and in the campground, which does not have hookups. Dogs may not be left unattended, they must be leashed, and cleaned up after. Dogs are allowed throughout the park, trails and in the camp area.

California

Death Valley National Park
Highway 190
Death Valley, CA
760-786-2331
nps.gov/deva
TDeath Valley is one of the hottest places on Earth, with summer temperatures averaging well over 100 degrees Fahrenheit. It is also the lowest point on the Western Hemisphere at 282 feet below sea level. Average rainfall here sets yet another record. With an average of only 1.96 inches per year, this valley is the driest place in North America. Because of the high summer heat, the best time to visit the park is during the winter. Even though dogs are not allowed on any trails, you will still be able to see the majority of the sights and attractions from your car. There are several scenic drives that are popular with all visitors, with or without dogs. Dante's View is a 52 mile round trip drive that takes about 2 hours or longer. Some parts of the road are graded dirt roads and no trailers or RVs are allowed. On this drive you will view scenic mudstone hills which are made of 7 to 9 million year old lakebed sediments. You will also get a great view from the top of Dantes View. Another scenic drive is called Badwater. It is located about 18 miles from the Visitor Center and can take about 1.5 to 2 hours or longer. On this drive you will view the Devil's Golf Course where there are almost pure table salt crystals from an ancient lake. You will also drive to Badwater which is the lowest point in the Western Hemisphere at 282 feet below sea level. Dogs are allowed at view points which are about 200 yards or less from roads or parking lots. Pets must be leashed and attended at all times. Please clean up after your pets. While dogs are not allowed on any trails in the park, they can walk along roads. Pets are allowed up to a few hundred yards from the paved and dirt roads. Stop at the Furnance Creek Visitor Center to pick up a brochure and more information. The visitor center is located on Highway 190, north of the lowest point..

Lassen Volcanic National Park
PO Box 100
Mineral, CA
530-595-4444
nps.gov/lavo/
This national park does not really have much to see or do if you bring your pooch, except for staying overnight at the campgrounds. However, the dog-friendly Lassen National Forest surrounds the national park. At the national forest you will be able to find dog-friendly hiking, sightseeing and camping. Pets must be leashed and attended at all times. Please clean up after your pet.

Sequoia and Kings Canyon National Park
47050 General Highway
Three Rivers, CA
559-565-3341
nps.gov/seki/
This national park does not really have much to see or do if you bring your pooch, except for driving through a giant redwood forest in your car and staying overnight at the campgrounds. However, located to the west and south of this national park is the dog-friendly Giant National Sequoia Monument. There you will be able to find dog-friendly hiking, sightseeing and camping. Pets must be leashed and attended at all times. Please clean up after your pet.

Joshua Tree National Park
74485 National Park Drive
Twentynine Palms, CA
760-367-5500
nps.gov/jotr
Dogs are not allowed on the trails, cannot be left unattended, and must be on leash. However, they are allowed on dirt and paved roads including the Geology Tour Road. This is actually a driving tour, but you'll be able to see the park's most fascinating landscapes from this road. It is an 18 mile tour with 16 stops. The park recommends taking about 2 hours for the round trip. At stop #9, about 5 miles out, there is room to turnaround if you do not want to complete the whole tour.

Channel Islands National Park
Ventura, CA
805-658-5730
nps.gov/jotr
Dogs are not allowed.

Yosemite National Park
PO Box 577
Yosemite, CA
209-372-0200
nps.gov/yose
Yosemite's geology is world famous for its granite cliffs, tall waterfalls and giant sequoia groves. As with most national parks, pets have limited access within the park. Pets are not allowed on unpaved or poorly paved trails, in wilderness areas including hiking trails, in park lodging (except for some campgrounds) and on shuttle buses. However, there are still several nice areas to walk with your pooch and you will be able to see the majority of sights and points of interest that most visitors see. Dogs are allowed in developed

areas and on fully paved trails, include Yosemite Valley which offers about 2 miles of paved trails. From these trails you can view El Capitan, Half Dome and Yosemite Falls. You can also take the .5 mile paved trail right up to the base of Bridalveil Fall which is a 620 foot year round waterfall. In general dogs are not allowed on unpaved trails, but this park does make the following exceptions. Dogs are allowed on the Meadow Loop and Four Mile fire roads in Wawona. They are also allowed on the Carlon Road and on the Old Big Oak Flat Road between Hodgdon Meadow and Hazel Green Creek. Dogs must be on a 6 foot or less leash and attended at all times. People must also clean up after their pets. There are four main entrances to the park and all four lead to the Yosemite Valley. The park entrance fees are as follows: $20 per vehicle, $40 annual pass or $10 per individual on foot. The pass is good for 7 days. Prices are subject to change. Yosemite Valley may be reached via Highway 41 from Fresno, Highway 140 from Merced, Highway 120 from Manteca and in late spring through late fall via the Tioga Road (Highway 120 East) from Lee Vining. From November through March, all park roads are subject to snow chain control .

Colorado

Rocky Mountain National Park
1000 Highway 36
Estes Park, CO
970-586-1206
nps.gov/romo/
Dogs cannot really do much in this park, but as you drive through the park, you will find some spectacular scenery and possibly some sightings of wildlife. Pets are not allowed on trails, or in the backcountry. Pets are allowed in your car, along the road, in parking lots, at picnic areas and campgrounds. Dogs must be on a 6 foot or less leash. You can still take your dog for a hike, not in the national park, but in the adjacent Arapaho-Roosevelt National Forest.

Black Canyon of the Gunnison National Park
102 Elk Creek
Gunnison, CO
970-641-2337
nps.gov/blca/index.htm
This unique canyon in the Rockies is narrow and deep. Dogs may view the Canyon with you from the Rim Rock Trail. Dogs on leash are allowed on roads, campgrounds, overlooks, the Rim Rock trail, Cedar Point Nature trail, and North Rim Chasm View Nature trail. They are not allowed on other hiking trails, inner canyon routes, or in the wilderness area within the park. Dogs on leash are permitted throughout the Curecanti National Recreation Area nearby.

Mesa Verde National Park
PO Box 8
Mesa Verde, CO
970-529-4465
nps.gov/meve/index.htm
Dogs on leash are allowed in the campgrounds and parking lots only. Dogs are not allowed on hiking trails or archaeological sites. Pets cannot be left alone or in vehicles.

Great Sand Dunes National Park and Preserve
11999 Highway 150
Mosca, CO
719-378-6300
nps.gov/grsa/index.htm
The dunes of Great Sand Dunes National Park rise over 750 feet high. Dogs are allowed throughout the park and must be on leash. You must clean up after your dog and dogs may not be left unattended in the park. Leashed dogs are also welcome in the campgrounds. The park features auto touring, camping fishing, hiking, and more.

Florida

Biscayne National Park
9700 SW 328 Street
Homestead, FL
305-230-7275
nps.gov/bisc/
In addition to providing protection for and educating visitors of the 4 primary ecosystems that this park maintains, it also shares a long cultural history with evidence of human occupation of more than 10,000 years. Guests will also find a wide variety of planned Ranger activities and plenty of land and water recreation. Dogs are allowed for no additional fee; they must be leashed and cleaned up after at all times. They are only allowed at the Elliot campground, and they are allowed on the trails unless otherwise marked. Multiple dogs may be allowed.

Everglades National Park 40001 H 9336/Main Park Road
Homestead, FL
305-242-7700 (800/365-CAMP (2267))
nps.gov/ever/
Home to many rare and endangered species, this park is also the country's largest subtropical wilderness - now designated a World Heritage Site, a Wetland of International Importance site, and an International Biosphere Reserve. Dogs are allowed for no additional fee; they may only be in the campground, picnic areas, in the parking lots and on paved roads. Dogs may not be left unattended at any time, and they must be leashed and cleaned up after. Multiple dogs may be allowed.

Dry Tortugas National Park
PO Box 6208
Key West, FL
305-242-7700
nps.gov/drto/index.htm
This set of Islands is 70 miles west of Key West in the Gulf of Mexico. Dogs must be on leash and must be cleaned up after on this island. Dogs are not allowed on the ferry but they can come over by private boat or charter from Key West. The park features picnicking, camping, fishing, swimming and more. It is open year round.

Hawaii

Haleakala National Park
It is located off Hana Highway
Hawaii, HI
808-572-4400
nps.gov/hale
Dogs are not allowed on the trails or in any wilderness area. They are allowed in the campgrounds. There are no water or bathroom facilities at this park, so be sure to bring enough for you and your pet.

Hawaii Volcanoes National Park
MM 31.5 H 11
Hawaii National Park, HI
808-985-6000
nps.gov/havo
This park covers the top of earth's most massive volcano the Mauna Loa at almost 14,000 feet. The park is open 7 days a week year round. Dogs are allowed at no additional fee, but they may only be on paved roads, the developed areas, and the campgrounds. They are not allowed on any of the trails or off the roads. Dogs may not be left unattended at

any time, and they must be leashed and cleaned up after.

Kentucky

Mammoth Cave National Park
off Interstate 65
Mammoth Cave, KY
270-758-2251
nps.gov/maca/
At this national park, leashed dogs are allowed on hiking trails and in campgrounds. There are over 70 miles of hiking trails which go through valleys, up into hills, and next to rivers, lakes and waterfalls. However, dogs are not allowed in the cave, which is the main attraction at this park. The park does offer kennels that are located near the Mammoth Cave Hotel. The kennels are outdoor and not heated or air-conditioned. If you want to try the kennels at Mammoth Cave, be sure to check them out first. You will need to make a reservation for the kennels and there is a $5 key deposit fee for the cage lock and a $2.50 fee for half a day or a $5.00 fee for the entire day. To make kennel reservations, call the Mammoth Cave Hotel directly at 270-758-2225.

Maine

Acadia National Park
Eagle Lake Road
Bar Harbor, ME
207-288-3338
nps.gov/acad/
This National Park ranks high on the tail wagging meter. Dogs are allowed on most of the hiking trails, which is unusual for a national park. There are miles and miles of both hiking trails and carriage roads. Pets are also allowed at the campgrounds, but must be attended at all times. They are not allowed on sand beaches during the summer or on the steeper hiking trails year-round. Pets must be on a 6 foot or less leash at all times. There is one exception to the leash rule. There is an area in the park that is privately owned where dogs are allowed to run leash-free. It is called Little Long Pond and is located near Seal Harbor. Don't miss the awe-inspiring view from the top of Cadillac Mountain in the park. Overall, this is a pretty popular national park for dogs and their dog-loving owners. There is a $10 entrance fee into the park, which is good for 7 days. You

can also purchase an audio tape tour of the Park Loop Road which is a self-guided auto tour. The driving tour is about 27 miles and takes 3 to 4 hours including stops. Audio tapes are available at the Hulls Cove Visitor Center.

Michigan

Isle Royale National Park
800 East Lakeshore Drive
Houghton, MI
906) 482-0984
nps.gov/isro
No dogs are allowed within the park.

Minnesota

Voyageurs National Park
3131 H 53S
International Falls, MN
218-283-9821
nps.gov/voya
Voyageurs is a water based park located on the northern edge of Minnesota, and has some of the oldest exposed rock formations in the world. The park can also be accessed on Highway 11 from the west. There is camping, but a boat is required to access the trailheads to get there. There is another camping area just outside of the park as well. Dogs are allowed in developed areas of the park, outside visitor centers, at boat ramps, picnic areas, at tent camping areas, houseboats, and day use sites on the four main lakes. There are no additional pet fees. Dogs may not be left unattended at any time, they must be on no more than a 6 foot leash, and be cleaned up after. Pets are not allowed on park trails or in the backcountry.

Montana

Glacier National Park
PO Box 128
West Glacier, MT
406-888-7800
nps.gov/glac/index.htm
Dogs must be on leash and must be cleaned up after in the park area. Dogs are not allowed on the hiking trails. They are allowed in the camping, picnic areas and along roadways and parking lots.

Nevada

Great Basin National Park
100 Great Basin
Baker, NV
775-234-7331
nps.gov/grba
The Great Basin Park rises to over 13,000 feet and hosts the Lehman Caves and an abundant variety of wildlife, plants, and waterways. They are open year round for tent and RV camping with no hook ups. There is no additional fee for dogs, but they may not be left unattended, they must be on no more than a 6 foot leash, and be cleaned up after. Dogs are not allowed on any of the trails.

New Mexico

Carlsbad Canyon National Park
727 Carlsbad Canyon H 62/180
Carlsbad, NM
505-785-2232
nps.gov/cave/
This national park was established to preserve the Carlsbad Caverns, and over 100 other caves housed within a fossil reef. It is also home to America's deepest and 4th longest limestone cave. Dogs are not allowed at the park, except in the parking lot and at the kennel that is on site, and they must be on leash and cleaned up after.

North Carolina

Great Smoky Mountains National Park
107 Park Headquarters Road
Cherokee, NC
865-436-1200
(http://www.nps.gov/grsm/)
Greate Smoky Mountains National Park is located both in Tennessee and North Carolina and is one of the most popular of the National Parks. Pets must be leashed or restrained at all times within the park and are not allowed on most of the hiking trails. They can accompany you in your car and at lookouts and stops near the road. However, there are two trails in Great Smoky Mountains National Park that will allow leashed dogs. The Gatlinburg Trail is a 1.9 mile trail from the Sugarland's Visitor Center to the outskirts of Gatlinburg; it runs along the forest with beautiful river views and it passes old homesteads along the way. It follows a creek a good portion of the way.

The Oconaluftee River Trail follows along the river for a 1.5 mile

North Dakota

Theodore Roosevelt National Park
On I 94 at Exits 25 or 27 (South Unit)
Medora, ND
701-623-4466
nps.gov/thro
This Park is located in the North Dakota Badlands. It is named after the 26th president, Theodore Roosevelt. He was a great conservationist, who, out of concern for the future of our lands, established the National Forest Service in 1906. The park is open all year although some roads close at times due to snow. The campgrounds are also open all year (no hookups). Dogs are allowed in the park and the campgrounds at no additional fee, but dogs may not be left unattended at any time, and they are not allowed in any of the buildings, or on any of the trails. However, there are trails just outside the park where dogs are allowed. One of the trails is the Maahdaahhey Trail.

Ohio

Cuyahoga Valley National Park
Canal Road
Brecksville, OH
216-524-1497
nps.gov/cuva/
This national park consists of 33,000 acres along the banks of the Cuyahoga River. Scenery and terrain varies from a rolling floodplain to steep valley walls, ravines and lush upland forests. Popular activities at this park include hiking, bicycling, birdwatching and picnicking. Dogs are allowed at the park including the hiking trails. Pets must be leashed and cleaned up after. Pets are not allowed inside any buildings. The park is open daily and can be accessed by many different highways, including I-77, I-271, I-80/Ohio Turnpike, and State Route 8. To get to Canal Visitor Center, exit I-77 at Rockside Road. Go approximately 1 mile east to Canal Road and turn right. The visitor center is about 1.5 miles on the right. To get to Happy Days Visitor Center, take State Route 8 to west State Route 303. The visitor center is about 1 mile on the left. There is no park entrance fee.

Oregon

Crater Lake National Park
PO Box 7
Crater Lake, OR
541-594-3100
nps.gov/crla/index.htm
Dogs must be on leash and must be cleaned up after in park. Dogs must remain in the developed portions of the park and are not allowed on the dirt trails or in the backcountry. They are allowed on the roads and the sidewalks. There is a road and sidewalk surrounding Crater Lake so you and your dog may view the lake and walk quite a ways around it. Dogs are not allowed in any buildings. Dogs are allowed in the campgrounds on leash in the park.

South Carolina

Congaree National Park
48 Old Bluff Road
Columbia, SC
803-776-4396
nps.gov/cosw
This 22,200-acre park protects the largest contiguous tract of old-growth bottomland hardwood forest still in the US. The park's floodplain forest has one of the highest canopies and some of the tallest trees in the eastern US. Enjoy hiking, primitive camping, birdwatching, picnicking, canoeing, kayaking, Ranger guided interpretive walks, canoe tours, nature study, and environmental education programs. Open all year; Monday to Thursday from 8:30 am to 5 pm, and Friday to Sunday from 8 am to 7 pm. To walk the trails after hours park outside the gate. Well behaved dogs on leash are allowed on the trails and the outside guided tours, but they are not allowed on the Boardwalk or in the buildings.

South Dakota

Wind Cave National Park
26611 H 385
Hot Springs, SD
605-745-4600
nps.gov/wica
This park is home to one of the world's longest and most complex caves. The park is open year round from 8 to 5 pm during summer

hours and until 4:30 pm winter hours. Dogs are allowed at the park and at the campground (no hookups) for no additional fee, but basically they can only go where your car can go. The campground is open year round except when it snows and they have to close the roads to the camping areas. Dogs are not allowed on the trails, they may not be left unattended, they must be leashed at all times, and cleaned up after.

Badlands National Park
25216 Ben Reifel Rd
Interior, SD
605-433-5361
nps.gov/badl/
This park covers 160 square acres, has America's largest mixed grass prairies, and is home to the Badlands National Monument. Highway 240 is the Badlands Loop Scenic Byway and is 31 1/2 miles long with 14 lookouts. Dogs are not allowed on any of the trails in the park. They are allowed only at the campground or the parking lots. The contact station for the Cedar Pass Campground is on Highway 240, and this campground has an amphitheater. The other campground, White River, has a visitor's center on Highway 27. The campgrounds are open year round, and there are no hook-ups at either camp. Dogs of all sizes are allowed in the campgrounds. There are no additional fees. Dogs may not be left unattended outside, and only inside if it creates no danger to the pet. Dog must be leashed and cleaned up after.

Tennessee

Great Smoky Mountains National Park
107 Park Headquarters Road
Gatlinburg, TN
865-436-1200
(http://www.nps.gov/grsm/)
Greate Smoky Mountains National Park is located both in Tennessee and North Carolina and is one of the most popular of the National Parks. Pets must be leashed or restrained at all times within the park and are not allowed on most of the hiking trails. They can accompany you in your car and at lookouts and stops near the road. However, there are two trails in Great Smoky Mountains National Park that will allow leashed dogs. The Gatlinburg Trail is a 1.9 mile trail from the Sugarland's Visitor Center to the outskirts of Gatlinburg;

it runs along the forest with beautiful river views and it passes old homesteads along the way. It follows a creek a good portion of the way. The Oconaluftee River Trail follows along the river for a 1.5 mile

Texas

Big Bend National Park
P.O. Box 129
Big Bend National Park, TX
432-477-2251
nps.gov/bibe/
This park is at the big bend of the Rio Grande, and there are 2 entrances; in the North on Highway 118, and in the West on Highway 385. Dogs are not allowed anywhere in the back country, on any of the trails, at the river, or off any of the roads.There are 3 campgrounds, and an RV park. The RV park is the only camp area with full hookups. It is concession operated, sites are on a first come/ first served basis, and full hookup capability is required. Dogs may not be left unattended at any time, they must be leashed or crated at all times, and be cleaned up after.

Guadalupe Mountains National Park
H 62/180
Pine Springs, TX
915-828-3251
nps.gov/gumo
This parks hosts an extensive Permisan Limestone fossil reef. The park is open year-round; visitor center hours are from 8:00 a.m. to 4:30 p.m., and a bit longer in summer. Dogs on lead are allowed to go to the Sitting Bull Falls and the Last Chance Canyon. Dogs are not allowed on any of the other trails, but they are allowed on the trails in the neighboring Lincoln National Forest. This forest is very rugged, and pets must be watched very closely that they do not step on the plant called Letchigia Cactus. It may even go through tires and must be removed only by surgical means. Dogs are allowed at no additional fee at either of the campgrounds, and the campsites do not have hookups. Dogs may not be left unattended, they must be leashed, and cleaned up after. This park can also be accessed from the New Mexico side on Highway 137.

Utah

Bryce Canyon National Park

PO Box 640201/ On H 63
Bryce, UT
435-834-5322
nps.gov/brca/
This park is famous for it's unique geology, creating vast and unusual limestone formations throughout the region. Dogs are not allowed on any of the trails, the shuttle, the viewpoints, or the visitor's center. The park is open 24 hours a day year round. There are 2 campgrounds; Loop A, the north campground, is open all year, and the Sunset campground is only open for the season. There are no hookups at either campground. Dogs can walk along the road in the campground. There are no additional fees for the dogs. Dogs may not be left unattended, they must be leashed at all times, and cleaned up after.

Arches National Park
PO Box 907
Moab, UT
435-719-2299
nps.gov/arch/index.htm
Pets on leash with cleanup are allowed in the campsites and paved areas of the parks. Dogs are not allowed on any trails or backcountry. They are allowed unattended if well-behaved in the Devil's Garden campground.

Canyonlands National Park
2282 SW Resource Blvd
Moab, UT
435-719-2313
nps.gov/cany/index.htm
Pets on leash are allowed in developed areas, such as campgrounds, paved roads, and the Potash/Shafer Canyon road between Moab and the Island in the Sky. They are not allowed on hiking trails or in the backcountry.

Zion National Park
State Route 9
Springdale, UT
435-772-3256
nps.gov/zion/
Dogs are allowed on one walking trail at this national park. Dogs on a 6 foot or less leash are allowed on the Pa'rus Trail which is a 1.5 mile long trail that runs from the South Campground to Canyon Junction. You and your pooch can also enjoy a 10-12 mile scenic drive on the Zion-Mount Carmel Highway which goes through the park. If you are there from November through March, you can also take your car on the Zion Canyon Scenic Drive. If

you arrive during the summer months, the Zion Canyon Scenic Drive is closed and only allows park shuttle buses. Other pet rules include no pets on shuttle buses, in the backcountry, or in public buildings. Pets are allowed in the campgrounds and along roadways.

Capitol Reef National Park
HC 70 Box 15
Torrey, UT
435-425-3791
nps.gov/care/index.htm
Dogs on leash are allowed in campsites and on paved road areas. Dogs are not allowed on hiking trails or in the backcountry.

Virgin Islands

Virgin Islands National Park
1300 Cruz Bay Creek
St John, VI
340-776-6201
nps.gov/viis
The Virgin Islands National Park is one of breathtaking beauty offering white sandy beaches, tropical forests, and coral reefs. The visitor center is open daily from 8 to 4:30pm. Park areas are open 24 hours a day year-round. Dogs are allowed in the park and on the trails. They are not allowed at the campground, or at Trunk Bay. Dogs must be leashed, cleaned up after, and under owners control at all times.

Virginia

Shenandoah National Park
3655 U.S. Highway 211 East
Luray, VA
540-999-3500
nps.gov/shen/
Shenandoah National Park is one of the most dog-friendly National Parks, with dogs allowed on most of the trails. Covering 300 mostly forested square miles of the Blue Ridge Mountains the park provides many diverse habitats for thousands of birds and wildlife. The park also provides a wide range of recreational opportunities. There are more than 500 miles of trails, including 101 miles of the Appalachian Trail, summer and fall festivals/reenactments, a rich cultural history to share, interpretive programs, and breathtaking natural beauty. There are several highlights along the 105 mile long, 35 MPH,

Skyline Drive (the only public road through the park), such as 75 scenic overlooks and Mary's Rock Tunnel at milepost 32. The 610 foot-long tunnel was considered an engineering feat in 1932; just note that the clearance for the tunnel is 12'8". Dogs of all sizes are allowed for no additional fee. Dogs must be under their owner's control, on no more than a 6 foot leash or securely crated, cleaned up after at all times, and are not to be left unattended. Dogs are not allowed in buildings or on about 14 miles of the trails; please ask the attendant at the gate for a list of the trails.

Washington

Mount Rainer National Park
Tahoma Woods State Route
Ashford, WA
360-569-2211
nps.gov/mora/index.htm
Dogs must be on leash where they are allowed. Dogs are only allowed on roads, parking lots, and campgrounds. They are not allowed on trails, snow, in buildings, or any wilderness areas. There is a small portion of Pacific Crest Trail near the park's eastern boundary that allows pets on leash.

North Cascades National Park
State Route 20
Newhalem, WA
360-856-5700
nps.gov/noca
Dogs are allowed on one of the hiking trails, the Pacific Crest Trail. This scenic hiking trail runs through the park and is rated moderate to difficult. The trail is located off Highway 20, about one mile east of Rainy Pass. At the Bridge Creek Trailhead, park on the north side of the highway and then hike north (uphill) or south (downhill). A Northwest Forest Pass is required to park at the trailhead. The cost is about $5 and can be purchased at the Visitor's Center in Newhalem. For a larger variety of trails, including a less strenuous hike, dogs are also allowed on trails at the adjacent Ross Lake National Recreation Area and the Lake Chelan National Recreation Area. Both recreation areas are managed by the national park.

Olympic National Park
600 East Park Avenue
Port Angeles, WA

360-565-3130
nps.gov/olym/
Pets are not permitted on park trails, meadows, beaches or in any undeveloped area of the park. There is one exception. Dogs are allowed on leash, during daytime hours only, on Kalaloch Beach along the Pacific Ocean and from Rialto Beach north to Ellen Creek. For those folks and dogs who want to hike on a trail, try the adjacent dog-friendly Olympic National Forest.

Wyoming

Grand Teton National Park
Moose, WY
307-739-3300
nps.gov/grte/
Grand Teton National Park offers spectacular views of the jagged Teton Range, meadows, pine trees and beautiful blue lakes. This national park limits pets mostly to where cars can go. Pets are allowed in your car, on roads and within 50 feet of any road, campgrounds, picnic areas and parking lots. Pets are not allowed on any hiking trails, in the backcountry, on swimming beaches, or in any visitor centers. However, dogs are allowed on paths in the campgrounds, and can ride in a boat on Jackson Lake only. Dogs must be on a 6 foot leash or less, caged, crated, or in your car at all times. Pets cannot be left unattended or tied to an object. An activity you can do with your pet is to take a scenic drive. There are three scenic drives in the park. Many turnouts along the road offer exhibits on park geology, wildlife and plants. The Teton Park Road follows along the base of the Teton Range from Moose to Jackson Lake Junction. The Jenny Lake Scenic Drive skirts along Jenny Lake and offers great views of the Grand Teton peaks. This drive is one-way and starts just south of String Lake. You can reach this scenic drive by driving south at the North Jenny Lake Junction. Another scenic drive is the Signal Mountain Summit Road which climbs 800 feet to offer panoramic views of the Teton Range, Jackson Hole valley and Jackson Lake. For accommodations within the park, dogs are welcome in some of the Colter Bay Cabins and in some rooms at the Jackson Lake Lodge. For hiking trails that are dog-friendly, try the nearby

Bridger-Teton National Forest.

Yellowstone National Park
various
Yellowstone National Park, WY
307-344-7381
nps.gov/yell
Yellowstone National Park was established in 1872 and is America's first national park. Most of the park is at a high altitude of 7,500 feet or greater. The park is home to a wide variety of wildlife including grizzly bears, wolves, bison, elk, deer, coyotes and more. Yellowstone is also host to many natural scenic attractions including the popular Old Faithful geyser. There are numerous other geysers, hot springs, mudpots, and fumaroles which are all evidence of ongoing volcanic activity. Included in this park is Yellowstone Lake, which is the largest high-altitude lake in North America. While the lake looks stunning with its brilliantly blue water, it does have many hot hydrothermal spots, so people are advised not to swim in most of the lake areas and pets are prohibited from swimming. Traveling to Yellowstone Park with a pet can be pretty restrictive, but you will still be able to view most of the popular sights that tourists without pets usually come to see. While pets are not allowed on the trails, in the backcountry, in thermal areas, or on the boardwalks, you will still be able to view Old Faithful from about 200 feet back. Even at that distance, Old Faithful can look pretty spectacular. And if you drive the Grand Loop Road, you will be able to view some points of interest and perhaps see some wildlife including black bears, grizzly bears, bison and elk. Dogs are allowed in parking areas, campgrounds and within 100 feet of roads. Pets must be on a 6 foot or less leash or crated or caged at all times. Pets are not allowed to be left unattended and tied to an object. However, they can remain in your car while you view attractions near roads and parking areas. The park officials do require that you provide sufficient ventilation in the car for your pet's comfort and survival. For accommodations within the park, dogs are welcome in some of the park's cabins. There are some dog-friendly cabins within easy walking distance of Old Faithful. If you are looking for some dog-friendly hiking trails, there are numerous dog-friendly trails in the nearby Shoshone National Forest, located between the Cody and Yellowstone.

Chapter 5

Dog-Friendly Attractions

United States

Alabama

Axis AL	Kirk House and Gardens	251-861-4605	11525 H 43 N
Bessemer AL	WaterMark Place Outlets	205-425-4554	4500 Katies Way
Birmingham AL	Arlington Antebellum Home and Gardens	205-780-5656	331 Cotton Avenue SW
Birmingham AL	Kelly Ingram Park (Also known as West Park)	205-254-1291	500 17th Street N
Birmingham AL	Ruffner Mountain Nature Center	205-833-8264	1214 81st Street S
Birmingham AL	Sloss Furnaces	205-324-1911	20 32nd Street North
Birmingham AL	Southern Museum of Flight	205-833-8226	4343 73rd Street N
Birmingham AL	Vulcan Park and Museum	205-739-7141	1701 Valley View Drive
Birmingham AL	Vulcan Trail	205-254-2699	21st Street S/Richard Arrington Jr Blvd S
Boaz AL	Tanger Outlet Center	256-593-9255	214 S McCleskey Street
Bridgeport AL	Russell Cave National Monument	256-495-2672	3729 County Road 98
Cullman AL	Ave Maria Grotto	256-734-4110	1600 St. Bernard Drive SE
Dauphin Island AL	Estuarium at the Dauphin Island Sea Lab	251-861-7500	101 Bienville Blvd
Dauphin Island AL	Fort Gaines Historic Site	251-861-6992	51 Bienville Blvd
Dauphin Island AL	Mobile Bay Ferry	251-861-3000	918-B Bienville Blvd
Daviston AL	Horseshoe Bend National Military Park	256-234-7111	11288 Horseshoe Bend Road
Decatur AL	Civil War Self-Guided Walking Tour	256-350-2028	Church Street
Delta AL	Chinnabee Silent Trail	256-362-2909	H 281
Dothan AL	George Washington Carver Monument	334-793-4323	5622 H 231 S
Dothan AL	Maria's Vineyard	334-702-0679	3940 Fortner Street
Fairhope AL	Downtown Fairhope	251-928-2136	Fairhope Avenue and side streets
Fairhope AL	Fairhope Municipal Pier	251-928-2136	West end of Fairhope Avenue
Foley AL	Tanger Outlet Center	251-943-8888	2601 S McKenzie Street/H 59
Fort Payne AL	Little River Canyon National Preserve	256-845-9605	2141 Gault/H 35
Gulf Shores AL	AAA Charters	251-948-2525	317 W Canal Drive
Gulf Shores AL	Fort Morgan State Historic Site	251-540-7127	110 H 180W
Haynesville AL	Selma to Montgomery National Historic Trail	334-877-1983	7001 US Highway 80
Helena AL	When it Rains, Inc.	205-874-5623	PO Box 757
Hoover AL	Moss Rock Preserve	205-739-7141	Preserve Parkway
Huntsville AL	Huntsville Botanical Garden	256-830-4447	4747 Bob Wallace Avenue SW
Huntsville AL	US Space and Rocket Center	256-837-3400	One Tranquility Base
Mobile AL	Battleship Memorial Park	251-433-2703	2703 Battleship ParkwayH 90/9998
Mobile AL	Civil War Trail - Battle for Mobile Bay	800-566-2453	Mobile Bay Visitors Bureau/P. O. Box 204
Mobile AL	Mobile Botanical Gardens	251-342-0555	5151 Museum Drive
Montgomery AL	Alabama State Capitol and Grounds	334 242-3935	600 Dexter Avenue
Moundville AL	Mound State Monument Museum	205-371-2572	1499 Mound State Parkway
Orange Beach AL	Fishing and Cruises on America II	251-981-4127	4575 Wilson Blvd
Orange Beach AL	Sailaway Charters	251-974-5055	24231 Gulf Bay Road
Orange Beach AL	Sanroc Cay Marina	251-981-5423	27267 Perdido Beach Blvd
Payneville AL	The Selma to Montgomery National Voting Rights Trail	334-877-1983	7002 H 80
Troy AL	Pike Pioneer Village	334-566-2830	138 E H 6
Troy AL	Pioneer Museum of Alabama	334-566-3597	248 H 231 N
Tuscumbia AL	Ivy Green (Helen Keller Birthplace)	256-383-4066	300 West North Commons
Tuskegee AL	Tuskegee Airman National Historic Site	334-724-0922	1616 Chappie James Avenue
Tuskegee AL	Tuskegee Institute National Historic Site	334-727-3200	1212 West Montgomery Rd

Alaska

Anchorage AK	Anchorage Market & Festival	907-272-5634	3rd & E Street
Anchorage AK	Anchorage Trolley Tours	907-276-5603	612 W 4th Ave
Anchorage AK	Balto Statue		4th Street and D Street
Anchorage AK	Planet Walk	907-258-0415	621 W 6th Ave
Cordova AK	Childs Glacier	907-743-9500	Cordova River Road H/ H10
Cordova AK	Historical Walking Tour	907-424-6665	622 1st Street
Dalton Highway AK	Dalton Highway and the Arctic Circle	907-474-2200	
Eklutna AK	Eklutna Historical Park	907-688-6026	Mile 26 Glenn H
Fairbanks AK	Alaska Outdoor Rental and Guides	907-457-2453	Peger Road/P.O. Box 82388
Fairbanks AK	Creamer's Field	907-474-1744	1300 College Road
Fairbanks AK	Pioneer Park	907-459-1059	2300 Airport Way
Girdwood AK	Portage Glacier	907-783-2326	Portage Valley Road
Haines AK	Chilkat Cruises and Tours	907-766-2100	142 Beach Road
Haines AK	Haines Self-Guided Tours	800-458-3579	122 2nd Avenue
Haines AK	Mt Riley Hike	800-458-3579	122 2nd Avenue
Homer AK	Bay Excursions	907-235-7525	PO Box 3312
Homer AK	Central Charters Booking Agency	907-235-7847	4241 Homer Spit Road
Homer AK	Mako's Water Taxi and Charters	907-235-9055	Home Spit Road (at end)
Homer AK	Nomad Shelter Yurts	907-235-0132	Sterling Highway

Homer AK	Pratt Museum	907-235-8635	3779 Bartlett St
Homer AK	Rainbow Tours and Taxi	907-235-7272	P. O. Box 1526/Homer Spit Road
Homer AK	Smokey Bay Air	907-235-1511	2100 Kachemak Drive
Homer AK	The Homer Spit	907-235-7740	Homer Spit Road
Hope AK	Hope and Sunrise Historical and Mining Museum	907-782-3740	P. O. Box 88/2nd Avenue
Juneau AK	Mendenhall Glacier and Visitor Center	907-789-0097	Glacier Spur Road
Juneau AK	Orca Eco Tours	888-SEE-ORCA (733-6722)	PO Box 35431/Franklin Street
Juneau AK	Whale Watch Company	907-463-3422	11517 Glacier Way
Ketchikan AK	Creek Street Boardwalk Shopping Area	800-770-3300	Creek Street
Ketchikan AK	Ketchikan Walking Tour	907-225-6166	131 Front Street
Ketchikan AK	Tongass Water Taxi	907-225-8294	PO Box 23143
Ketchikan AK	Totem Bright State Historical Park	907-247-8574	9883 N Tongass H/H 7
Matanuska Glacier AK	Matanuska Glacier	888-253-4480	Mile 102 Glenn Hwy
Metlakatla AK	Metlakatla Indian Community	907-886-4441	Off 5 Mile Airport Road
Nome AK	Nome Discovery Tours	907-443-2814	1st and D Street
Seward AK	Miller's Landing Water Taxi	866-541-5739	1820 Beach Drive
Sitka AK	Sitka Charters	907-747-0616	P. O. Box 556
Skagway AK	Dyea Townsite Walking Tour	907-983-2921	Broadway and 2nd Avenue
Skagway AK	White Pass and Yukon Railroad	800-343-7373	231 Second Avenue
Sutton AK	Matanuska Glacier	888-253-4480	Mile 102 Glenn H
Valdez AK	Salmon Fishing Area		
Valdez AK	Valdez Overlook		
Valdez AK	Worthington Glacier State Rec Site	907-269-8400	Mile 28.7 Richardson Highway
Whittier AK	Aquetec Water Taxi	907-362-1290	P.O. Box 643
Whittier AK	Bread N Butter Charters	907-472-2396	Harbor View Drive #7
Whittier AK	Honey Charters	907-278-2493	Harbor Traiangle #4, Port of Whittier
Whittier AK	Prince William Sound Kayak Center	907-472-2452	PO Box 622
Whittier AK	Whittier Town Center		Downtown
Wrangell AK	Mount Dewey Hiking Trails	907-874-2829	296 Campbell Drive
Wrangell AK	Rainbow Falls Hiking Trail	800-367-9745	MM 4.6 Zimovia H
Wrangell AK	Rainwalker Expeditions	907-874-2549	P.O. Box 2074

Arizona

Bisbee AZ	Bisbee Farmers' Market	520-236-8409	Vista Street
Bisbee AZ	Historic Walking Tours	520-432-3554	#2 Copper Queen Plaza/Visitor Center
Bisbee AZ	Lavender Jeep Tours	520-432-5369	#1 Copper Queen Plaza
Bisbee AZ	The Old Bisbee Ghost Tour	520-432-3308	
Bowie AZ	Fort Bowie National Historic Site	520-847-2500	3203 South Old Fort Bowie Road
Camp Verde AZ	Montezuma Castle National Monument	928-567-3322	PO Box 219
Carefree AZ	People and Pooch Pajama Party	480-497-8296	37220 Mule Train Road
Concho AZ	Concho Farmers Market		Corner of H 61 and H 180A
Coolidge AZ	Casa Grande Ruins National Monument	520-723-3172	1100 Ruins Drive
Cornville AZ	Oak Creek Vineyards and Winery	928-649-0290	1555 N Page Springs Road
Douglas AZ	Slaughter House Ranch National Historic Landmark	520-558-2474	6151 Geronimo Trail
Ganado AZ	Hubbell Trading Post National Historic Site	928-755-3475	PO Box 150
Gilbert AZ	Santan Village Shopping Center	480-282-9500	2290 S. SanTan Village Parkway
Glendale AZ	Twilight Farmers' Market	623-848-1234	59th Avenue and Utopia (Arrowhead Ranch)
Goldfield AZ	Goldfield Ghost Town	480-983-0333	4650 N Mammoth Mine Road
Kingman AZ	Powerhouse Visitor Center & Route 66 Museum	866-427-RT66	120 W. Route 66
Lake Havasu City AZ	A-1 Watercraft Rentals	928-855-8088	1435 Countryshire Ave #103
Lake Havasu City AZ	The London Bridge	928-453-8883	314 London Bridge Road (Lake Havasu City Visitor's Center)
Mesa AZ	Friends for Life Barktoberfest	480-899-5253	2048 E Baseline Road
Oatman AZ	Town of Oatman		Route 66
Page AZ	Antelope Canyon Adventures	928-645-5501	104 Lake Powell Blvd
Page AZ	Lake Powell - Glen Canyon Recreation Area	435-684-7400	
Page AZ	Navajo Village	928-660-0304	1235 Copper Mine Road
Page AZ	Wahweap Lodge and Marina Boat Rentals	928-645-2433	100 Lakeshore Drive
Phoenix AZ	Biltmore Fashion Park	602-955-8400	2502 E. Camelback Rd.
Phoenix AZ	Deer Valley Rock Art Center	623-582-8007	3711 West Deer Valley Rd.
Phoenix AZ	Pioneer Living History Village	623-465-1052	3901 West Pioneer Road
Phoenix AZ	Roadrunner Park Farmers Market	623-848-1234	3502 E Cactus Road
Scottsdale AZ	Scottsdale Downtown's Old Town Farmers' Market	623-848-1234	N Brown Avenue and 1st Street In the Old Town area
Sedona AZ	Adventure Company Jeep Tours	928-204-1973	336 H 179
Sedona AZ	Red Rock Country - Coconino National Forest	928-527-3600	various
Superior AZ	Boyce Thompson Arboretum	520-689-2723	37615 U.S. Highway 60
Tempe AZ	Walk to Save the Animals	602-273-6852	620 N Mill Avenue
Tombstone AZ	1880 Historic Tombstone	800-457-3423	70 miles from Tucson
Tombstone AZ	Charleston Ghost Town	866-275-5816	Old Charleston Road
Tombstone AZ	Gleeson Ghost Town	866-275-5816	Gleeson Road
Tombstone AZ	Old Tombstone Stagecoach Tours	520-457-3018	Allen Street (between 4th and 5th Streets)

Tombstone AZ	WF Trading Company	520-457-3664	418 Allen St
Tucson AZ	Pima Air and Space Museum	520-574-0462	6000 East Valencia Road
Tucson AZ	Trail Dust Town	520-296-4551	6541 E Tanque Verde Road
Tumacacori AZ	Tumacacori National Historical Park	520-398-2341	1891 E Frontage Rd
Valle AZ	The Planes of Fame Air Museum	928-635-1000	755 Mustang Way
Wickenburg AZ	Robson's Mining World	928-685-2609	P. O. Box 3465 (On H 71)
Williams AZ	Historic Route 66 Driving Tour		Bill Williams Avenue
Winslow AZ	Homolovi Ruins State Park	928-289-4106	State Route 87

Arkansas

Altus AR	Chateau aux Arc	800-558-WINE	8045 Highway 186
Altus AR	Post Familie Vineyards	479-468-2741	1700 St Mary's Mountain Road
Bull Shoals AR	Mountain Village 1890 and the Bull Shoals Caverns	870-445-7177	1011 C.S. Woods Blvd
Bull Shoals AR	Top O' The Ozarks	870-445-4302	Tower Road
El Dorado AR	South Arkansas Arboretum	888-AT-PARKS (287-2757)	Timberland
Eureka Springs AR	Eureka Springs Self Guided Tours	800-638-7352	516 Village Circle/H 62E
Eureka Springs AR	Eureka Springs-North Railway	479-253-6200	299 N Main Street/H 23
Eureka Springs AR	Pine Mountain Village	479-253-9156	2075 East Van Buren Street/H 62
Fort Smith AR	Fort Smith National Historic Site	479-783-3961	301 Parker Avenue
Garfield AR	Pea Ridge National Military Park	479-451-8122	15930 H 62E
Hope AR	President Bill Clinton Birthplace	870-777-4455	117 S Hervcy Street
Hot Springs AR	Belle of Hot Springs Riverboat	501-525-4438	5200 Central Avenue/H 7
Hot Springs AR	Garvan Woodland Gardens	501-262-9300	550 Arkridge Road
Little Rock AR	Big Dam Bridge	501-340-6800	7600 Rebsamen Park Road
Little Rock AR	Clinton Presidential Center and Park	501-374-4242	1200 President Clinton Ave.
Little Rock AR	MacArthur Museum of Arkansas Military History	501-376-4602	503 E. Ninth Street/MacArthur Park
Little Rock AR	River Market	501-375-2552	400 President Clinton Avenue
North Little Rock AR	Arkansas Inland Maritime Museum	501-371-8320	120 Riverfront Drive
North Little Rock AR	The Old Mill	501-791-8537	Fairway Avenue and Lakeshore Drive
Paris AR	Cowie Wine Cellars	479-963-3990	101 N Carbon City Rd
Pine Bluff AR	Arkansas Railroad Museum	870-535-8819	1700 Port Road
Prairie Grove AR	Prairie Grove Battlefield State Park	479-846-2990	506 E Douglas Street/H 45/62
Rogers AR	War Eagle Cavern	479-789-2909	21494 Cavern Road
Scott AR	Plantation Agriculture Museum	501-961-1409	4815 H 161S
Scott AR	Toltec Mounds Archeological State Park	501-961-1409	490 Toltec Mounds Road
Washington AR	Historic Washington State Park	870-983-2684	100 SW Morrison
Wiederkehr Village AR	Wiederkehr Wine Cellars	800-622-WINE	3324 Swiss Family Dr

California

Agoura Hills CA	Paramount Ranch	805-370-2301	Cornell Road
Alameda CA	Rosenblum Cellars	510-865-7007	2900 Main Street
Anaheim CA	Disneyland Kennel	714-781-4565	1313 Harbor Blvd
Arroyo Grande CA	Lake Lopez Boat Rentals	805-489-1006	6820 Lopez Drive
Barstow CA	Calico Early Man Site	760-252-6000	Minneola Road
Barstow CA	Route 66 Mother Road Museum	760-255-1890	681 North First Ave
Berkeley CA	Redwood Valley Railway	510-548-6100	Tilden Park
Berkeley CA	Telegraph Ave		Telegraph Ave
Beverly Hills CA	Beverly Hills Rodeo Drive Shopping District		Rodeo Drive
Beverly Hills CA	Hollywood Star's Homes		Self-Guided Walking Tour
Big Bear Lake CA	Bear Valley Stage Lines	909-584-2277	Village Drive and Pine Knot Avenue
Big Bear Lake CA	Belleville Ghost Town		Holcomb Valley Road
Big Bear Lake CA	Big Bear Marina	909-866-3218	500 Paine Road
Big Bear Lake CA	Holloway's Marina	909-866-5706	398 Edgemoor Road
Big Bear Lake CA	Pine Knot Landing-Boat Rentals	909-866-6463	400 Pine Knot Ave.
Big Bear Lake CA	Pleasure Point Landing	909-866-2455	603 Landlock Landing Rd
Bishop CA	Bristlecone Pine Forest	760-873-2500	White Mountain Rd
Bodega Bay CA	Bodega Bay Sportsfishing Center	707-875-3344	1500 Bay Flat Road
Boonville CA	Anderson Valley Brewing Company	707-895-BEER (895-2337)	17700 H 253
Boonville CA	Boont Berry Farm	707-895-3441	13980 H 128
Boonville CA	Foursight Wines	707-895-2889	14475 H 128
Boonville CA	Zina Hyde Cunningham Winery	707-895-9462	14077 H 128
Bridgeport CA	Bodie State Historic Park	760-647-6445	State Route 270
Burbank CA	Los Angeles Equestrian Center	818-840-9066	480 Riverside Drive
Calistoga CA	Chateau Montelena	707-942-5105	1429 Tubbs Lane
Calistoga CA	Cuvaison Winery	707-942-6266	4550 Silverado Trail
Calistoga CA	Dutch Henry Winery	707-942-5771	4300 Silverado Trail
Calistoga CA	Graeser Winery	707-942-4437	255 Petrified Forest Road
Calistoga CA	Old Faithful Geyser	707-942-6463	1299 Tubbs Lane
Calistoga CA	Petrified Forest	707-942-6667	4100 Petrified Forest Rd.
Camarillo CA	Camarillo Outlet Stores	805-445-8520	740 E. Ventura Blvd, Camarillo, CA 93010
Cambria CA	Cambria Historic Downtown		1880-2580 Main Street
Camino CA	Argyres Orchard	530-644-3862	4220 N. Canyon Rd.

Dog-Friendly Attractions - Please always call ahead to make sure an establishment is still dog-friendly.

Camino CA	Bodhaine Ranch	530-644-1686	2315 Cable Road
Camino CA	Bolster's Hilltop Ranch	530-644-2230	2000 Larsen Drive
Camino CA	Celtic Gardens Organic Farm	530-647-0689	4221 North Canyon Road
Camino CA	Denver Dan's	530-644-6881	4344 Bumblebee Ln.
Camino CA	Grandpa's Cellar	530-644-2153	2360 Cable Rd.
Camino CA	Honey Bear Ranch	530-644-3934	2826 Barkley Rd.
Camino CA	Jack Russell Brewing Company	530-644-4722	2380 Larsen Drive
Camino CA	Kids, Inc.	530-622-0084	3245 N. Canyon Rd.
Camino CA	Mother Lode Orchards	530-644-5101	4341 N. Canyon Rd.
Camino CA	O'Hallorans Apple Trail Ranch	530-644-3389	2261 Cable Rd.
Camino CA	Plubell's Family Orchard	530-647-0613	1800 Larsen Dr.
Camino CA	Stone's Throw Vineyard & Winery	530-622-5100	3541 North Canyon Rd.
Camino CA	Summerfield Berry Farm	530-647-2833	4455 Pony Express Trail
Carlsbad CA	Carlsbad Village		Carlsbad Village Drive
Carlsbad CA	Legoland Kennel	760-918-5346	One Legoland Drive
Carlsbad CA	Witch Creek Winery	760-720-7499	2906 Carlsbad Blvd/H 101
Carmel CA	Carmel Village Shopping Area		Ocean Ave
Carmel CA	Carmel Walks-Walking Tours	831-642-2700	Lincoln and Ocean Streets
Carmel CA	Seventeen Mile Drive		Seventeen Mile Drive
Carmel Valley CA	Crossroads Shopping Center		Cabrillo Hwy (Hwy 1)
Carmel-by-the-Sea CA	Carmel Plaza	831-624-1385	Ocean Avenue and Mission Street
Cedarville CA	Surprise Valley Back Country Byway	530-279-6101	Highway 299
Chula Vista CA	Otay Ranch Town Center	619-656-9100	Eastlake Pkwy At Olympic Pkwy
Coloma CA	Gold Country Carriages	530-622-6111	Hwy 49
Coloma CA	Marshall Gold Discovery State Park	530-622-3470	Hwy 49
Coloma CA	Venezio Winery & Vineyard	530-885-WINE	5821 Highway 49
Columbia CA	Columbia State Historic Park	209-532-0150	Parrotts Ferry Rd.
Corona CA	The Promenade Shops at Dos Lagos	921-277-7601	2780 Cabot Drive
Corte Madera CA	The Village at Corte Madera	415-924-8557	1618 Redwood H
Dana Point CA	Catalina Express	800-360-1212	34675 Golden Lantern
Danville CA	Eugene O'Neill National Historic Site	925-838-0249	PO Box 280
Drytown CA	Drytown Cellars	209-245-3500	16030 Highway 49
East Sonoma CA	Sebastiani Vineyards and Winery	800-888-5532	389 Fourth Street
El Centro CA	Tumco Historic Townsite	760-337-4400	Ogilby Road
Encino CA	Los Encinos State Historic Park	818-784-4849	16756 Moorpark Street
Escondido CA	Belle Marie Winery and Chateau Dragoo	760-796-7557	26312 Mesa Rock Road
Escondido CA	Orfila Vineyards	760-738-6500	13455 San Pasqual Rd
Fair Play CA	Charles B. Mitchell Vineyards	800-704-WINE	8221 Stoney Creek Road
Fair Play CA	Oakstone Winery	530-620-5303	6440 Slug Gulch Rd.
Fair Play CA	Perry Creek Vineyards	530-620-5175	7400 Perry Creek Rd.
Fawnskin CA	Captain John's Fawn Harbor and Marina	909-866-6478	39368 North Shore Drive
Felton CA	Roaring Camp & Big Trees RR	831-335-4484	P.O.Box G-1
Fish Camp CA	Yosemite Mountain Sugar Pine Railroad	559-683-7273	56001 Highway 41
Folsom CA	Old Towne Folsom		Sutter St & Riley St
Forestville CA	Joseph Swan Vineyards	707-573-3747	2916 Laguna Road
Forestville CA	Topolos Vineyards	707-887-1575	5700 Gravenstein Hwy N.
Fort Bragg CA	All Aboard Adventures	707-964-1881	32400 N Harbor Drive, Noyo Harbor
Fort Bragg CA	Anchor Charter Boats and the Lady Irma II	707-964-4550	780 N Harbor Drive
Fort Bragg CA	Mendocino Coast Botanical Gardens	707-964-4352	18220 N. Highway 1
Fortuna CA	Fortuna Depot Museum	707-725-7645	3 Park St
Garberville CA	One Log House	707-247-3717	705 US Hwy 101
Gilroy CA	Bonfante Gardens Family Theme Park Kennel	408-840-7100	3050 Hecker Pass H/H 152
Gilroy CA	Kirigin Cellars	408-847-8827	11550 Watsonville Road
Glen Ellen CA	Arrowood Vineyards and Winery	707-935-2600	14347 Sonoma H
Glen Ellen CA	Benziger Family Winery	707-935-3000	1883 London Ranch Road
Glen Ellen CA	Jack London State Historic Park	707-938-5216	2400 London Ranch Road
Glendale CA	The Americana at Brand	877-897-2097	889 Americana Way
Goleta CA	Chumash Painted Cave State Historic Park	805-733-3713	Painted Caves Road
Grass Valley CA	Empire Mine State Historic Park	530-273-8522	10791 East Empire Street
Guerneville CA	F. Korbel and Brothers Champagne Cellars	707-824-7000	13250 River Road
Half Moon Bay CA	Santa's Tree Farm	650-726-2246	78 Pilarcitos Creek Road
Healdsburg CA	Dry Creek Vineyard	707-433-1000	3770 Lambert Bridge Road
Healdsburg CA	Foppiano Vineyards	707-433-7272	12707 Old Redwood Highway
Healdsburg CA	Lambert Bridge Winery	800-975-0555	4085 W. Dry Creek Rd
Healdsburg CA	Mutt Lynch Winery	707-942-6180	1960 Dry Creek Road
Healdsburg CA	Porter Creek Vineyard and Winery	707-433-6321	8735 Westside Road
Healdsburg CA	Porter Creek Vineyard and Winery	707-433-6321	8735 Westside Road
Healdsburg CA	Quivira Vineyards	707-431-8333	4900 W Dry Creek Road
Healdsburg CA	Rodney Strong Vineyards	707-433-6511	11455 Old Redwood H
Herald CA	Blue Gum Winery	209-748-5669	13637 Borden Road
Homewood CA	Mountain High Weddings	530-525-9320	PO Box 294
Hope Valley CA	Hope Valley Outdoor Center	530-694-2266	Intersection of H 88 and H 89
Hopland CA	Brutocao Cellars and Vineyards	707-744-1664	13500 H 101
Idyllwild CA	Annual Plein Air Festival	866-439-5278	North Circle Drive
Indio CA	Oasis Date Gardens	800-827-8017	59111 Hwy 111
Irvine CA	Irvine Spectrum Center	877-ISC-4FUN	71 Fortune Drive
Jamestown CA	Railtown 1897 State Historic Park	209-984-3953	Highway 49
Julian CA	Country Carriages	760-765-1471	Washington and Main St
Julian CA	J. Jenkins Winery	760-765-3267	12555 Julian Orchards Drive

Dog-Friendly Attractions - Please always call ahead to make sure an establishment is still dog-friendly.

Julian CA	Julian Downtown and Walking Tour	760-765-1857	Main Street
Julian CA	Menghini Winery	760-765-2072	1150 Julian Orchards Drive
Klamath CA	Trees of Mystery	800-638-3389	15500 Highway 101 N.
La Jolla CA	San Diego Pet Driver	619-252-5244	7514 Girard Avenue
Lake Arrowhead CA	Arrowhead Queen Boat Tours	909-336-6992	28200 H 189 Building C100
Lake Arrowhead CA	Lake Arrowhead Village	909-337-2533	28200 Highway 189
Lake Shasta CA	Self Guided Audio Cassette Tour	530-926-4511	204 West Alma St
Lee Vining CA	Mono Basin National Forest Scenic Area	760-647-3044	Hwy 395, 1/2 mile North of Lee Vining
Leggett CA	Leggett Drive Thru Tree		Hwy 1 and Hwy 101
Lewiston CA	Trinity Alps Marina	530-286-2282	Fairview Marina Rd.
Livermore CA	Marina Boat Rentals	925-373-0332	Del Valle Park
Lodi CA	Jessie's Grove Winery	209-368-0880	1973 W Turner Road
Lodi CA	Phillips Farm/ Michael-David Vineyards	209-368-7384	4580 H 12
Lompoc CA	La Purisima Mission State Historic Park	805-733-3713	2295 Purisima Road
Lone Pine CA	Alabama Hills	760-876-6222	Movie Road
Long Beach CA	Catalina Explorer Ferry	877-432-6276	100 Aquarium Way, Pine Avenue Pier
Long Beach CA	Catalina Express	800-360-1212	320 Golden Shore
Long Beach CA	Haute Dog Easter Parade and Pet Adoption Fair	562-439-3316	4900 E Livingston Drive
Long Beach CA	Haute Dog Howl'oween Parade	562-439-3316	4900 E Livingston Drive
Los Angeles CA	Century City Shopping Center	310-277-3898	10250 Santa Monica Blvd
Los Angeles CA	Griffith Observatory	323-664-1181	2800 East Observatory Road
Los Angeles CA	Hollywood Walk of Fame	323-469-8311	6100-6900 Hollywood Blvd.
Los Angeles CA	SkyBark	213-891-1722	1026 S Santa Fe Avenue
Los Angeles CA	The Grove Shopping Center	323-900-8080	189 The Grove Drive
Los Angeles CA	Travel Town Museum	323-662-5874	5200 Zoo Drive
Madera CA	Mariposa Wine Company	559-673-6372	20146 Road 21
Mammoth Lakes CA	Hot Creek Geologic Site	760-924-5500	Hot Creek Hatchery Road
Mammoth Lakes CA	Mammoth Mountain-Gondola	760-934-0745	#1 Minaret Road
Marina del Rey CA	Catalina Ferries	310-305-7250	13763 Fiji Way , C2 Terminal Building
Mariposa CA	Mount Bullion Vineyard	209-377-8450	6947 H 49N
Mendocino CA	Catch a Canoe Rentals	707-937-5615	44850 Comptche-Ukiah Rd
Mendocino CA	Mendocino Village		Main Street at Lansing Street
Mokelumne Hill CA	French Hill Winery	209-728-0638	8032 S Main Street
Monterey CA	La Mirada House and Gardens	831-372-3689	720 Via Mirada
Monterey CA	Monterey Bay Whale Watch Boat Tours	831-375-4658	Fisherman's Wharf
Monterey CA	Princess Monterey Whale Watch	800-200-2203	96 Fishermans Wharf
Monterey CA	Randy's Fishing Trips	800-251-7440	66 Old Fisherman's Wharf #1
Monterey CA	Sea Life Tours	831-372-7150	90 Fishermans Wharf
Monterey CA	Ventana Vineyards	831-372-7415	2999 Monterey-Salinas Highway, #10
Mount Aukum CA	Latcham Vineyards	530-620-6642	2860 Omo Ranch Road
Murphys CA	Black Sheep Winery	209-728-2157	West end of Main Street
Murphys CA	Rocco's Com'e Bella Winery	209-728-9030	457-C Algiers
Murphys CA	Stevenot Winery	209-728-0638	2690 San Domingo Road
Murphys CA	Twisted Oak Winery	209-736-9080	350 Main Street
Napa CA	Clos Du Val Winery	800-993-9463	5330 Silverado Trail
Napa CA	Darioush Winery	707-257-2345	4240 Silverado Trail
Napa CA	Hess Collection Winery	707-255-1144	4411 Redwood Road
Napa CA	Pine Ridge Winery	707-252-9777	5901 Silverado Trail
Nevada City CA	Nevada City Horse & Carriage	530-265-9646	downtown Nevada City
Newport Beach CA	Boat Rentals of America	949-673-7200	510 E Edgewater
Newport Beach CA	Fashion Island Mall	800-495-4753	1133 Newport Center Dr
Newport Beach CA	Fun Zone Boat Tours-Harbor Tours	949-673-0240	6000 Edgewater Place
Newport Beach CA	Fun Zone Boat-Whale Watching Tours	949-673-0240	600 Edgewater Place
Newport Beach CA	Marina Water Sports-Boat Rentals	949-673-3372	600 E Bay Ave
Oak View CA	Casitas Boat Rentals	805-649-2043	11311 Santa Ana Road
Oakland CA	Jack London Square	510-814-6000	Broadway & Embarcadero
Oakland CA	Juan Bautista de Anza National Historic Trail	510-817-1438	1111 Jackson Street #700
Oakland CA	Oakland A's Dog Day at the Park	510-638-4900	7000 Coliseum Way
Oceanside CA	California Surf Museum	760-721-6876	223 N Coast H
Ojai CA	Downtown Ojai	805-646-8126	E Ojai Ave at S Montgomery St
Olympic Valley CA	Ann Poole Weddings, Nature's Chapel	530-412-5436	P.O. Box 3768
Olympic Valley CA	Squaw Valley Chapel	530-525-4714	440 Squaw Peak Road
Olympic Valley CA	Squaw Valley USA-Gondola	530-583-5585	1910 Squaw Valley Rd
Olympic Valley CA	The Bark Festival	530-583-WAGS (9247)	The Village at Squaw Valley
Olympic Valley CA	The Village At Squaw Valley	530-584-6267	Squaw Valley
Orleans CA	Coates Family Vineyards	530-627-3369	3255 Red Cap Road
Oxnard CA	Hopper Boat Rentals	805-382-1100	3600 Harbor Blvd # 368
Pacific Palisades CA	Will Rogers State Hist. Park	310-454-8212	1501 Will Rogers State Park Rd.
Palm Desert CA	El Paseo Shopping District		El Paseo Drive
Palm Springs CA	Moorten Botanical Garden	760-327-6555	1701 S Palm Drive
Palm Springs CA	Palm Canyon Drive/Star Walk		Palm Canyon Drive
Palm Springs CA	Palm Canyon Shopping District		Palm Canyon Drive/H 111
Palo Alto CA	Downtown Palo Alto		University Ave
Palo Alto CA	Hewlett-Packard Garage		367 Addison Ave
Palo Alto CA	Stanford Shopping Center	650-617-8585	680 Stanford Shopping Center
Palomar Mountain CA	Palomar Observatory	760-742-2100	County Road S-6
Pasadena CA	Frisbee Golf Course		Oak Grove Drive

Dog-Friendly Attractions - Please always call ahead to make sure an establishment is still dog-friendly.

Pasadena CA	Old Town Pasadena		100W-100E Colorado Blvd.
Paso Robles CA	Chumeia Vineyards	888-343-9445	8331 H 46E
Paso Robles CA	Tablas Creek Vineyard	805-237-1231	9339 Adelaida Rd
Perris CA	Orange Empire Railway Museum	951-657-2605	2201 South A Street
Petaluma CA	Petaluma Adobe State Historic Park	707-762-4871	3325 Adobe Road
Petaluma CA	Petaluma Self-Guided Film Walking Tour	707-769-0429	Keller St. and Western Ave.
Petaluma CA	Petaluma Village Premium Outlets	707-778-9300	2200 Petaluma Blvd N.
Petaluma CA	River Walk	707-769-0429	Near D St. bridge and Washington St.
Phillipsville CA	Avenue of the Giants	707-722-4291	Highway 101
Philo CA	Christine Woods Vineyards	707-895-2115	3155 H 128
Philo CA	Esterlina Vineyards	707-895-2920	1200 Holmes Ranch Road
Philo CA	Handley Cellars	707-895-3876	3151 H 128
Philo CA	Husch Vineyards	1-800-55-HUSCH (555-8724)	4400 H 128
Philo CA	Navarro Vineyards	800-537-9463	5601 H 128
Philo CA	Toulouse Vineyards	707-895-2828	800 H 128
Pine Grove CA	Indian Grinding Rock State Historic Park	209-296-7488	14881 Pine Grove - Volcano Road
Pioneertown CA	Pioneertown	760-964-6549	Pioneertown Road
Piru CA	Lake Piru Marina	805-521-1231	4780 Piru Canyon Road
Placerville CA	Abel's Apple Acres	530-626-0138	2345 Carson Rd.
Placerville CA	Apple Creek Ranch	530-644-5073	2979 Carson Rd.
Placerville CA	Boa Vista Orchards	530-622-5522	2952 Carson Rd.
Placerville CA	Boeger Winery	530-622-8094	1709 Carson Road
Placerville CA	Gold Hill Vineyard	530-626-6522	5660 Vineyard Lane
Placerville CA	High Hill Ranch	530-644-1973	2901 High Hill Rd.
Placerville CA	Hooverville Orchards	530-622-2155	1100 Wallace Rd.
Placerville CA	Lava Cap Winery	530-621-0175	2221 Fruitridge Road
Placerville CA	Placerville Downtown Area		Main Street & Hwy 49
Placerville CA	Sierra Vista Winery & Vineyard	530-622-7841	4560 Cabernet Way
Plymouth CA	Convergence Vineyards	209-245-3600	14650 H 124
Plymouth CA	Deaver Vineyards	209-245-4099	12455 Steiner Road
Plymouth CA	Montevina Wines	209-245-6942	20680 Shenandoah School Road
Plymouth CA	Nine Gables Vineyard & Winery	209-245-3949	10778 Shenandoah Road
Plymouth CA	Renwood Winery	209-245-6979	12225 Steiner Road
Plymouth CA	Sobon Winery	209-245-6554	14430 Shenandoah Rd
Pollock Pines CA	Harris Tree Farm	530-644-2194	2640 Blair Road
Quartz Hill CA	Rattlesnake Avoidance Clinic		P. O. Box 3174
Rancho Bernardo CA	Bernardo Winery	858-487-1866	13330 Easeo Del Verano
Rancho Cordova CA	Nimbus Fish Hatchery	916-358-2884	2001 Nimbus Rd
Rancho Cucamonga CA	Victoria Gardens	909-463-2830	12505 North Mainstreet
Redwood Valley CA	Elizabeth Vineyards	707-485-9009	8591 Colony Drive
Redwood Valley CA	Gabrielli Winery	707-485-1221	10950 West Road
Riverside CA	Citrus State Historic Park	909-780-6222	Van Buren Blvd.
Rutherford CA	Frogs Leap Winery	707-963-4704	8815 Conn Creek Road
Rutherford CA	Mumm Napa Winery	800-686-6272	8445 Silverado Trail
Rutherford CA	Sullivan Vineyards	707-963-9646	1090 Galleron Rd
Sacramento CA	Capitol Park-Self-Guided Walk	916-324-0333	10th and L Streets
Sacramento CA	Doggy Dash	916-383-7387	915 I St
Sacramento CA	Downtown Plaza	915-442-4000	547 L Street
Sacramento CA	Old Sacramento Historic Area	916-442-7644	between I and L Streets
Sacramento CA	Scribner Bend Vineyards	916-744-1803	9051 River Road
Sacramento CA	Top Hand Ranch Carriage Rides	916-655-3444	Old Sacramento
San Diego CA	Action Sport Rentals	619-275-8945	1775 Mission Bay
San Diego CA	Cinderella Carriage Rides	619-239-8080	
San Diego CA	Family Kayak Adventure Center	619-282-3520	4217 Swift Avenue
San Diego CA	Gaslamp Quarter Guided Walking Tour	619-233-4692	410 Island Avenue
San Diego CA	Horton Plaza Shopping Center	619-239-8180	324 Horton Plaza
San Diego CA	Old Town State Historic Park	619-220-5422	San Diego Ave & Twiggs St
San Diego CA	SD Padres Dog Days of Summer at Petco Park	619-795-5000	100 Park Blvd
San Diego CA	San Diego Kayaking Tours	866 HB KAYAK (425-2925)	2246 Avenida de la Playa
San Diego CA	San Pasqual Winery	858-270-7550	5151 Santa Fe Street
San Diego CA	SeaWorld of California-Kennels	619-226-3901	1720 South Shore Rd.
San Diego CA	Seaforth Boat Rentals	619-223-1681	1641 Quivira Road
San Dimas CA	Inland Valley Humane Society Dog Walk	909-623977	120 Via Verde, Bonelli Park
San Francisco CA	Barbary Coast Trail	415-775-1111	
San Francisco CA	Coit Tower	415-362-0808	1 Telegraph Hill Blvd
San Francisco CA	Extranominal Tours	866-231-3752	690 Fifth Street (cross street Townsend)
San Francisco CA	Fisherman's Wharf Shopping		Jefferson Street
San Francisco CA	Fort Point National Historic Site	415-556-1693	Fort Mason, Building 201
San Francisco CA	Ghirardelli Square Shopping Center	415-775-5500	900 North Point Street
San Francisco CA	Golden Gate Bridge	415-921-5858	P.O. Box 9000, Presidio Station
San Francisco CA	Pac Bell Park	415-972-2000	24 Willie Mays Plaza
San Francisco CA	SF Giants Dog Days of Summer at AT&T Park	415-972-2361	24 Willie Mays Plaza
San Francisco CA	The Bark and Wine Ball	415-522-3535	888 Brannan Street
San Francisco CA	Vampire Tour of San Francisco	866-4-BITTEN (424-8836)	Nob Hill, Corner of California and Tayor Streets

Dog-Friendly Attractions - Please always call ahead to make sure an establishment is still dog-friendly.

San Francisco CA	Waterfront Carriage Rides	415-771-8687	Jefferson Street
San Jose CA	Bark in the Park	408-793-5125	William and South 16th Streets
San Jose CA	Ron's Tours / Pedicab Service	408-859-8961	Call to Arrange.
San Jose CA	Santana Row	408-551-4611	368 Santana Row
San Luis Obispo CA	San Luis Obispo Botanical Garden	805-546-3501	Post Office Box 4957
San Pedro CA	Catalina Classic Cruises	800-641-1004	Berth 95
Santa Barbara CA	Big Dog Parade and Canine Festival	805-963-8727, Ext:1398	121 Gray Ave
Santa Barbara CA	La Cumbre Plaza	805-687-3500	120 South Hope Avenue
Santa Barbara CA	Santa Barbara Botanical Garden	805-682-4726	1212 Mission Canyon Road
Santa Barbara CA	Santa Barbara Electric Car Rental	805-962-2585	101 State Street
Santa Barbara CA	State Street Shopping Area	805-963-2202	100-700 State Street
Santa Barbara CA	Stearns Wharf	805-897-1961	Cabrillo Blvd
Santa Barbara CA	Stearns Wharf Vinters	805-966-6624	217-G Stearns Wharf
Santa Barbara CA	TJ Paws Pet Wash	805-687-8772	2601 De La Vina Street
Santa Barbara CA	The French Festival Poodle Parade	805-564-PARIS (7274)	Junipero and Alamar Streets at Oak Park
Santa Cruz CA	De Laveaga Park Disc Golf		Branciforte
Santa Cruz CA	Harbor Water Taxis	831-475-6161	Lake Avenue
Santa Cruz CA	Lighthouse Point Surfer's Museum	831-420-6289	W. Cliff Dr
Santa Cruz CA	Santa Cruz Harley Davidson Motorcyles	831-421-9600	1148 Soquel Ave
Santa Rosa CA	Deloach Vineyards	707-526-9111	1791 Olivet Road
Santa Rosa CA	Hanna Winery	707-575-3371	5353 Occidental Road
Santa Rosa CA	Martini and Prati Wines	707-823-2404	2191 Laguna Road
Santa Rosa CA	Matanzas Creek Winery	707-528-6464	6097 Bennet Valley Road
Santa Rosa CA	Pacific Coast Air Museum	707-575-7900	2330 Airport Blvd
Santa Ynez CA	LinCourt Vineyards	805-688-8381	343 North Refugio Rd
Sebastopol CA	Taft Street Winery	707-823-2404	2030 Barlow Lane
Shasta CA	Shasta State Historic Park	530-243-8194	15312 H 299 W
Simi Valley CA	Simi Valley Town Center Mall	805-581-1430	1555 Simi Town Center Way
Sky Forest CA	Children's Forest	909-338-5156	Keller Peak Road
Solvang CA	Buttonwood Farm Winery	805-688-3032	1500 Alamo Pintado Rd
Solvang CA	Lucas and Lewellen Winery	805-686-9336	1645 Copenhagen Drive
Solvang CA	Mandolina Wines	888-777-6663	1665 Copenhagen Drive
Solvang CA	Solvang Horsedrawn Streetcars	805-686-0022	P.O. Box 531
Solvang CA	Solvang Village	800-468-6765	1500-2000 Mission Drive
Sonoma CA	Sebastiani Vineyards and Winery	800-888-5532	389 Fourth Street East
South Lake Tahoe CA	Tahoe Keys Boat Rentals	530-544-8888	2435 Venice Drive E.
South Lake Tahoe CA	Tahoe Sport Fishing	530-541-5448	900 Ski Run Boulevard
South Lake Tahoe CA	Tallac Historic Site		Highway 89
St Helena CA	Beringer Vineyards	707-963-4812	2000 Main Street
St Helena CA	Casa Nuestra Winery	866-844-WINE	3451 Silverado Trail North
St Helena CA	Rustridge	707-965-2871	2910 Lower Chiles Valley Rd
St Helena CA	V. Sattui Winery	707-963-7774	1111 White Lane
St Helena CA	V. Sattui Winery	707-963-7774	1111 White Lane
Stateline NV	Borges Sleigh and Carriage Rides	775-588-2953	P.O. Box 5905
Sutter Creek CA	Sutter Creek	209-267-5647	Highway 49
Sutter Creek CA	Sutter Creek Wine Tasting	209-267-5838	85 Main Street
Tahoe City CA	Reel Deal Sport Fishing & Lake Tours	530-318-6272	P.O. Box 1173
Tahoe City CA	Truckee River Raft Rentals	530-581-0123	185 River Road
Temecula CA	Baily Vineyard	951-676-WINE (9463)	33440 La Serena Way
Temecula CA	Falkner Winery	951-676-8231	40620 Calle Contento
Temecula CA	Filsinger Vineyards and Winery	909-302-6363	39050 De Portola Rd
Temecula CA	Keyways Vineyard and Winery	909-302-7888	37338 De Portola Rd
Temecula CA	Maurice Carrie Vineyard	951-676-1711	34225 Rancho California Road
Temecula CA	Miramonte Winery	951-506-5500	33410 Rancho California Road
Temecula CA	Mount Palomar Winery	951-676-5047	33820 Rancho California Road
Temecula CA	Oak Mountain Winery	951-699-9102	36522 Via Verde
Temecula CA	Old Town Temecula		Front Street
Temecula CA	Stuart Cellars	888-260-0870	33515 Rancho California Road
Temecula CA	Temecula Hills Winery	951-767-3450	47200 De Portola Road
Temecula CA	Tesoro Winery	951-308-0000	28475 Old Town Front Street
Temecula CA	Van Roekel Winery	909-699-6961	34567 Rancho California Rd
Trinity Center CA	Estrellita Marina	530-286-2215	49160 State Highway 3
Tulelake CA	Medicine Lake Highlands	530-233-5811	Forest Road 49
Tulelake CA	Volcanic Historic Loop	530-233-5811	State Route 139
Tuttletown CA	Mark Twain Cabin		Jackass Hill Rd.
Universal City CA	Universal Studios Kennel	818-508-9600	Hollywood Frwy (Hwy 101)
Vacaville CA	The Nut Tree	707-447-6000	1681 East Monte Vista Avenue
Valencia CA	Six Flags Magic Mountain	661-255-4100	26101 Magic Mountain Parkway
Ventura CA	Albinger Archaeological Museum	805-648-5823	113 East Main Street
Ventura CA	Pooch Parade Dog Walk and Pet Expo	805-488-7533	10 West Harbor Blvd
Ventura CA	Ventura Harbor Village	805-644-0169	1559 Spinnaker Drive
Ventura CA	Ventura Pier		668 Harbor Blvd
West Hollywood CA	Sunset Plaza	310-652-2622	8600 - 8700 Sunset Boulevard (at Sunset Plaza Drive).
Westlake Village CA	The Dogs Gallery	818-707-8070	31139 Via Colinas, Suite 204
Windsor CA	Martinell Vineyards	707-525-0570	3360 River Road
Wishon CA	Millers Landing Resort - Bass Lake	559-642-3633	37976 Road 222

Yermo CA	Calico Ghost Town	760-254-2122	PO Box 638
Yorkville CA	Meyer Family Cellars	707-895-2341	19750 H 128
Yorkville CA	Yorkville Cellars	707-894-9177	25701 H 128
Yountville CA	Domain Chandon	707-944-2280	One California Drive
Yountville CA	Hill Family Estate	707-944-9580	6512 Washington Street
Yreka CA	Blue Goose Steam Excursion Train	530-842-4146	300 East Miner Street

Colorado

Aurora CO	Cherry Creek Marina Boat Rentals	303-779-6144	Cherry Creek State Park
Bond CO	Colorado River Runs	800-826-1081	Star Route, Box 32
Boulder CO	Boulder Creek Winery	303-516-9031	6440 Odell Place
Boulder CO	Bus Transport	303-441-3266	1739 Broadway Street/H 7
Boulder CO	Twenty Ninth Street Mall	303-449-1189	1710 29th Street
Burlington CO	Kit Carson Carousel		Kit Carson County Fairgrounds
Canon City CO	Buckskin Joe Frontier Town and Railway	719-275-5149	1193 Fremont County Road 3A
Canon City CO	Royal Gorge Bridge & Park	719-275-7507	4218 Fremont County Road 3A
Castle Rock CO	Outlets at Castle Rock	303-688-4495	5050 Factory Shops Blvd
Clark CO	Steamboat Lake Marina	970-879-7019	P. O. Box 867/County Road 62
Colorado Springs CO	Pikes Peak Toll Road	719-385-PEAK	P.O. Box 1575-MC060
Colorado Springs CO	Prominade Shops at Briargate	719-265-6264	1885 Briargate Parkway
Cripple Creek CO	The Pikes Peak Heritage Center at Cripple Creek	719-689-3315	9283 S H 67
Denver CO	Denver Pavilions	303-260-6000	15th Street and Tremont
Denver CO	Larimer Square		Larimer Street
Denver CO	MaxFund Lucky Mutt Strut	720-482-1578	S Downing Street and E Louisianna Avenue
Denver CO	Rocky Mountain Audio Guides, LLC	303-898-7073	P.O. Box 22963
Denver CO	State Capitol Grounds	303-866-2604	200 E Colfax
Denver CO	Wag and Train Canine Carnival	720-312-5499	370 Kalamath Street
Durango CO	Horse Gulch Trail	800-463-8726	off 3rd Street and 8th/9th Avenue
Durango CO	Outlaw River and Jeep Tours	970-259-1800	555 Main Avenue
Durango CO	Rent A Wreck of Durango	970-259-5858	21760 Highway 160 West
Fort Collins CO	Grave of Annie the Railroad Dog		201 Peterson St
Golden CO	Buffalo Bills Gravesite and Museum	303-526-0744	987 1/2 Look-Out Mountain Road
Golden CO	Lookout Mountain Park	303-964-2589	Lookout Mountain Road
Golden CO	The Colorado Trail	303-384-3729	710 10th Street, Room 210 (Foundation Office)
Gunnison CO	Elk Creek Marina	970-641-0707	24830 H 50
Gunnison CO	Lake Fork Marina	970-641-3048	Lake Fork
Gunnison CO	Monarch Crest Tram	719-539-4091	H 50 between Salida and Gunnison
Idaho Springs CO	Argo Gold Mill and Museum	303-567-2421	2350 Riverside Drive
La Junta CO	Bent's Old Fort National Historic Site	719-383-5010	35110 Highway 194 East
Littleton CO	Aspen Grove Shopping Center	303-794-0640	7301 S Santa Fe Drive
Loveland CO	Promenade Shops at Centerra	970-461-1285	Centerra Parkway at Sky Pond Drive
Loveland CO	Promenade Shops at Centerra	970-461-1285	Centerra Parkway at Sky Pond Drive
Manitou Springs CO	Manitou Cliff Dwellings Museum	719-685-5242	Cliff Dwelling Road
Morrison CO	Dinosaur Ridge	303-697-3466	16831 West Alameda Parkway
Ouray CO	Colorado West Jeep Tours	800-648-JEEP (5337)	701 Main Street/H 550
Ouray CO	San Juan Scenic Jeep Tours	970-325-0089	210 7th Avenue
Ouray CO	Switzerland of America Jeep Tours & Rentals	970-325-4484	226 7th Avenue
Palisade CO	Colorado Cellars Winery	970-464-7921	3553 E Road
Red Feather Lakes CO	Dude Ranch	800-357-4930	17931 Red Feather Lakes Rd
Salida CO	Monarch Crest Tram	719-539-4091	H 50 between Salida and Gunnison
Silverton CO	Triangle Jeep Rentals	877-522-2354	864 Greene Street
Snowmass Village CO	Blazing Adventures	800-282-7238	P. O. Box 5068
Steamboat Springs CO	Amaze'n Steamboat	970-870-8682	1255 S Lincoln Avenue
Steamboat Springs CO	Silver Bullet Gondola Rides	970-879-0740	Gondola Square
Telluride CO	Dave's Mountain Tours	970-728-9749	P.O. Box 2736
Telluride CO	Telluride Fur Ball	970-626-CARE (2273)	113 Lost Creek Ln # A
Vallecito Lake CO	Vallecito Lake Trails	970-247-1573	

Connecticut

Brookfield CT	DeGrazia Vineyards	203-775-1616	131 Tower Road
Clinton CT	Chamard Vineyards	860-664-0299	115 Cow Hill Road
Hartford CT	State Historic Preservation Museum	860-566-3005	59 S Prospect Street
Litchfield CT	Haight-Brown Vineyard	860-567-4045	29 Chestnut Hill Road
Mystic CT	Downtown Mystic	866-572-9578	14 Holmes Street
Mystic CT	Mystic Seaport - The Museum of America and the Sea	860-572-0711	75 Greenmanville Ave
Mystic CT	Olde Mistic Village	860-536-4941	27 Coogan Blvd
New Milford CT	The Silo at Hunt Hill Farm	860-355-0300	44 Upland Road
New Preston CT	Hopkins Vineyard and Winery	860-868-7954	25 Hopkins Road
Norfolk CT	Norfolk Chamber Music Festival	203-432-1966	Routes 44 and 272
Old Lyme CT	Florence Griswold Museum	860-434-5542	96 Lyme Street

Dog-Friendly Attractions - Please always call ahead to make sure an establishment is still dog-friendly.

Pomfret Center CT	Connecticut Audubon Center	860-928-4948	189 Pomfret Street
Sharon CT	Sharon Audubon Center	860-364-0520	325 Cornwall Bridge/H 4
South Windsor CT	The Promenade Shops At Evergreen Walk	860-432-3398	503 Evergreen Way
Stonington CT	Stonington Vineyards	860-535-1222	523 Taugwonk Road
Weathersfield CT	Webb-Deane-Stevens Museum	860-529-0612	211 Main Street
West Cornwall CT	Clarke Outdoors Canoe Rental	860-672-6365	163 H 7
Woodbury CT	The Glebe House Museum and Gertrude Jekyll Garden	203-263-2855	49 Hollow Road

D.C.

Washington DC	Capitol River Cruises	301-460-7447	31st and K St, NW
Washington DC	Doggie Happy Hour at Cantina Marina	202-554-8396	600 Water Street SW
Washington DC	Doggie Happy Hour at the Helix	202-462-9001	1430 Rhode Island Avenue NW
Washington DC	FDR Memorial		National Mall
Washington DC	Fletcher's Boat House	202-244-0461	4940 Canal Rd NW
Washington DC	Gangplank on the Potomac	202-554-5000 Ext. 11	600 Water Street SW
Washington DC	Jefferson Memorial		National Mall
Washington DC	Lincoln Memorial		National Mall
Washington DC	National Mall		Independence Ave and 14th St.

Delaware

Dewey Beach DE	Greyhounds Reach the Beach	617-527-8843	The beach
Dover DE	Air Mobility Command Museum	302-677-5938	1301 Heritage Road
Lewes DE	Fisherman's Wharf by the Drawbridge	302-645-8862	Anglers Road
Lewes DE	Lil Angler Charters	302-645-8688	Angler Road
Rehoboth Beach DE	Tanger Outlets	302-226-9223	36470 Seaside Outlet Drive
Smyrna DE	Bombay Hook National Wildlife Refuge	302) 653-6872	2591 Whitehall Neck Road
Wilmington DE	Christina River Boat Company Inc.	302-530-5069	201 A Street
Wilmington DE	Rockwood Museum	302-761-4340	Washington Street Extension
Wilmington DE	The Shipyard Shops	302-425-5000	900 South Madison Street
Wilmington DE	Trolley Square Shopping Center	302-428-1040	21A Trolley Square

Florida

Belleview FL	The Land Bridge Trailhead	352-236-7143	H 475 A
Big Pine Key FL	Blue Hole - Big Pine	305-872-2239	Watson Blvd
Big Pine Key FL	Jack Watson's Nature Trail	305-872-2239	MM 30.5 H 1
Big Pine Key FL	National Key Deer Refuge	305-872-0774	175-179 Key Deer Blvd
Bradenton FL	De Soto National Memorial	941-792-0458	P. O. Box 15390
Bradenton FL	Hunsader U-Pick Farms	941-322-2168	5500 C.R. 675
Cape Canaveral FL	Kennedy Space Center Tours - Kennels	407-452-2121	S.R. 405
Celebration FL	Celebration		US 192 and I-4
Clermont FL	Lakeride Winery	352-394-8627	19239 H 27N
Coopertown FL	Coopertown Airboat Tours	305-226-6048	US-41
Coral Gables FL	Village of Merrick Park Shopping Plaza	305-529-0200	358 Avenue San Lorenzo
Crystal River FL	Crystal River State Archeological Site	352-795-3817	3400 N. Museum Point
Delray Beach FL	Carnival Flea Market	561-499-9935	5283 W Atlantic Avenue/H 806
Delray Beach FL	Easter Bonnet Dog Parade	561-276-8640	Pineapple Grove Way (NE 2nd Avenue) and Atlantic Avenue
Destin FL	HarborWalk Village	850-0269-0235	Harbor Blvd
Fernandina Beach FL	Amelia River Cruises/Charters and the Cumberland Ferry	904-261-9972	1 North Front Street
Fort Lauderdale FL	Club Nautico	954-467-6000	801 Seabreeze Blvd
Fort Lauderdale FL	Fort Lauderdale Riverwalk	954-761-5784	2nd St and 4th Ave
Fort Lauderdale FL	Las Olas District		Las Olas Blvd and Federal Hwy
Fort Myers FL	Manatee World Boat Tours	239-693-1434	5605 Palm Beach Blvd
Fort Myers Beach FL	Key West Express Ferry	888-539-2628	2200 Main Street
Gainesville FL	Kanapaha Botanical Gardens	352-372-4981	4700 SW 58th Drive
Gulf County FL	St.Vincent Island - Shuttle Services	850-229-1065	Indian Pass Boat Launch, Hwy C-30B
High Springs FL	Mutts and Pups Dog Show	386-454-3346	NW 1st Avenue and NW 1st Street
Homestead FL	Coral Castle	305-248-6345	28655 S Dixie H/H 1/5
Islamorada FL	Theatre of the Sea	305-664-2431	84721 H 1, MM 84.5 H 1
Jacksonville FL	Fort Caroline National Memorial	904-641-7155	12713 Ft. Caroline Road
Jacksonville FL	Kingsley Plantation	904-251-3537	11676 Palmetto Avenue
Jacksonville FL	Marjorie Harris Carr Cross Florida Greenway	850-245-2052	
Jacksonville FL	Playtime Drive-In Theater Flea Market	904-771-9939	6300 Blanding Blvd
Jupiter FL	Manatee Queen	561-744-2191	1065 N Ocean Blvd/H A1A
Key Biscayne FL	Club Nautica	305-361-9217	4000 Crandon Blvd
Key Largo FL	Dirty Waters Charters	305-304-2212	322 Bay View Avenue
Key West FL	Duval Street Shopping District		Duval Street
Key West FL	Fish Monster	305-432-0047	PO Box 2580
Key West FL	Key West Aquarium	305-296-2051	1 Whitehead St
Key West FL	Key West Tropical Forest & Garden	305-296-1504	5210 College Road
Key West FL	Lazy Dog Outfitters, Kayaks and Boat Charters	305-293-9550	5114 Overseas Highway

Dog-Friendly Attractions - Please always call ahead to make sure an establishment is still dog-friendly.

Key West FL	Mallory Square	305-296-4557	1 Whitehead St
Key West FL	No Worries Charters	305-393-2402	Eisenhower Drive, Garrison Bight Marina
Key West FL	Southernmost Point Monument		Whitehead St and South Street
Key West FL	Stephen Huneck Art Gallery	305-295-7616	218 Whitehead St
Kissimmee FL	Big Toho Airboat Rides	888-937-6843	100 Lakeshore Blvd
Kissimmee FL	Kissimmee Air Museum	407-870-7366	233 N Hoagland Blvd
Kissimmee FL	Old Town	407-396-4888	5570 W Irlo Bronson Memorial H/H 192
Lake Buena Vista FL	Walt Disney's Animal Kingdom - Kennels	407-842-4321	Walt Disney World Exit
Lake Buena Vista FL	Walt Disney's Epcot Center - Kennels	407-842-4321	Walt Disney World Exit
Lake Buena Vista FL	Walt Disney's MGM Studios - Kennels	407-842-4321	Walt Disney World Exit
Lake Buena Vista FL	Walt Disney's Magic Kingdom - Kennels	407-842-4321	Walt Disney World Exit
Lake Worth FL	Hoffman Chocolate Shop and Gardens	561-433-GIFT	5190 Lake Worth Rd
Land O Lakes FL	Florida Estates Winery	813-996-2113	25241 State Rd 52
Largo FL	Florida Botanical Gardens	727-582-2100	12175 125th Street N
Largo FL	Heritage Village	727-582-2123	11909 125th Street N
Miami FL	Bal Harbour Shopping Center	305-866-0311	9700 Collins Ave
Miami FL	Fruit and Spice Park	305-247-5727	24801 SW 187th Avenue
Miami FL	Monty's Marina	305-854-7997	2560 S Bayshore Dr
Miami Beach FL	Art Deco Self-Guided Walking Tour	305-672-2014	1001 Ocean Drive
Miami Beach FL	Club Nautico Power Boat Rentals	305-858-6258	300 Alton Rd Ste 112
Miami Beach FL	Lincoln Road Shops	305-531-3442	Lincoln Road
N Fort Myers FL	The Shell Factory and Nature Park	239-995-2141	2787 North Tamiami Trail/H 41
Naples FL	Collier-Seminole State Park Boat Tours	941-642-8898	20200 E. Tamiami Trail
Orlando FL	Sea World - Kennel	888-800-5447	7007 Sea World Drive
Orlando FL	Spring Fiesta in the Park	407-649-3152	195 N Rosalind Avenue
Palm Beach FL	Worth Avenue Shopping District		Worth Avenue
Pensacola FL	Fort Barrancas	850-455-5167	Pensacola Navel Air Station
Plant City FL	Dinosaur World	813-717-9865	5145 Harvey Tew Road
Pompano Beach FL	Festival Flea Market Mall	800-353-2627	2900 W Sample Road/H 834
Port St Joe FL	Constitution Convention Museum State Park	850-229-8029	200 Allen Memorial Way
Port St Joe FL	Port St Joe Marina	850-227-9393	340 Marina Drive
Port St Joe FL	Seahorse Water Safaris	850-227-1099	340 Marina Drive
Silver Springs FL	Silver Springs Nature Park	352-236-2121	5656 E Silver Springs Blvd/H 40
Singer Island FL	Palm Beach Water Taxi	561-683-TAXI (8294)	98 Lake Drive
St Augustine FL	Fountain of Youth	904-829-3168	11 Magnolia Ave.
St Augustine FL	Ghost Walk - Spirits of St. Augustine	904-829-2391	St. George Street
St Augustine FL	Ghostly Encounters Walking Tour	800-404-2531	3 Aviles Street
St Augustine FL	St Augustine Lighthouse	904-829-0745	81 Lighthouse Avenue
St Augustine FL	St Augustine Scenic Cruise	904-824-1806	St Augustine Municipal Marina
St Augustine FL	St. Augustine Historic Downtown		St. George St
St Augustine FL	St. Augustine Transfer Co. Carriages	904-829-2391	Avenida Menendez and Hypolita St.
St Petersburg FL	Florida Orange Groves Inc and Winery	800-338-7923	1500 Pasadena Ave South
St Petersburg FL	Saturday Morning Farmers' Market	727-455-4921	First Avenue South and First Street.
Stuart FL	B and A Flea Market	772-288-4915	2885 SE H 1
Tallahassee FL	Downtown MarketPlace	850-224-3252	Park Avenue and Monroe Street
Tamiami FL	Wings Over Miami Air Museum	305-233-5197	14710 128th Street SW
Tampa FL	Adventure Island - Kennel	888-800-5447	4500 Bougainvillea Avenue
Tampa FL	Busch Gardens - Kennel	888-800-5447	3605 Bougainvillea Avenue
Tarpon Springs FL	St Nicholas Boat Line	727-942-6225	693 Dodecanese Blvd
Titusville FL	Space Shuttle and Rocket Launches	321-867-4636	Kennedy Space Center
West Palm Beach FL	City Place	561-366-1000	700 S Rosemary Avenue
Winter Park FL	Hip Dog Canine Aquatic Rehabilitation and Fitness Ctr.	407-628-1476	P. O. Box 793/4965 N Palmetto Avenue
Winter Park FL	Winter Park Shopping District		Park Avenue and Osceola Ave

Georgia

Atlanta GA	Atlanta Preservation Center	404-876-2041	327 Saint Paul Ave Se
Atlanta GA	Bark at the Park at Turner Field	800-745-3000	755 Hank Aaron Drive
Atlanta GA	Bark in the Park	404-733-5000	Piedmont Park
Atlanta GA	Centennial Olympic Park	404-222-PARK	265 Park Avenue West
Dahlonega GA	Wolf Mountain Vineyards	706-867-9862	180 Wolf Mountain Trail
Darien GA	Preferred Outlets at Darien	912-437-8360	1111 Magnolia Bluff Way SW
Dawsonville GA	North Georgia Premium Outlets	706-216-3609	800 H 400 South
Fort Pulaski GA	Fort Pulaski National Monument	912-786-5787	On H 80E
Helen GA	Charlemagne's Kingdom	706-878-2200	8808 N Main Street/H 17/75
Helen GA	Charlemagne's Kingdom	706-878-2200	8808 North Main St
Jekyll Island GA	Amazing Spaces Tour	912-635-4036	History Center
Jekyll Island GA	Mini Golf	912-635-2648	Beachview Drive
Jekyll Island GA	Victoria's Carriages	912-635-9500	Stable Road
Kennesaw GA	Kennesaw Mountain National Battlefield Park	770-427-4686	900 Kennesaw Mountain Drive
Pine Mountain GA	Pine Mountain Wild Animal Safari Kennels	706-663-8744	1300 Oak Grove Road
Plains GA	Jimmy Carter National Historic Site	229-824-4104	300 North Bond Street
Savannah GA	Ghost Talk	912-233-3896	On Abercorn between Congress and Bryan
Savannah GA	Old Fort Jackson	912-232-3945	1 Fort Jackson Road
Savannah GA	Savannah Riverfront Area	912-644-6400	River Street
St Marys GA	Crooked River State Park	912- 882--5256	6222 Charlie Smith Sr. Highway

Dog-Friendly Attractions - Please always call ahead to make sure an establishment is still dog-friendly.

St Simons GA	Fort Frederica National Monument	912-638-3639	6515 Frederica Road
Stone Mountain GA	Stone Mountain Park	770-498-5600	Highway 78
Stone Mountain GA	Stone Mountain Village	770-879-4971	Main Street
Warner-Robins GA	Museum of Aviation	478-923-6600	247 Russell Parkway
Washington GA	Callaway Plantation	706-678-7060	2160 Lexington Road
Young Harris GA	Crane Creek Vineyards	706-379-1236	Crane Creek Road

Hawaii

Honolulu HI	The Ward Center	808-591-8411	Ala Moana Blvd/H 92
Ulupalkua HI	Tedeschi Vineyards (Maui's Winery)	877-878-6058	P.O. Box 953

Idaho

Bonners Ferry ID	Copper Falls Self-Guided Nature Trail	208-267-5561	Forest Road 2517
Caldwell ID	Ste Chapelle Winery	877-783-2427	19348 Lowell Rd
Challis ID	Custer Motorway	208-756-5100	West end of Main Street/H 93
Eagle ID	The Winery at Eagle Knoll	208-286-9463	3705 North Hwy 16
Elk City ID	Elk City Wagon Road/Nez Perce National Forest	208-842-2245	HC01, Box 416
Horseshoe Bend ID	Cascade Raft Company	208-793-2221	7050 H 55
Kellogg ID	Silver Mountain Gondola	208-783-1111	610 Bunker Avenue
Kune ID	Indian Creek (Stowe) Winery	208-922-4791	1000 North McDermott Rd
Lewiston ID	Kirkwood Historic Ranch	208-628-3916	Kirkwood Road
Riggins ID	Heavens Gate Observation Site/Hells Canyon	208-628-3916	Forest Road 517
Salmon ID	Sacajawea Interpretive Cultural and Education Center	208-756-1188	60 H 28
Sandpoint ID	Pend d'Oreille Winery	877-452-9011	220 Cedar St
Spencer ID	Spencer Opal Mine	208-374-5476	Main Street

Illinois

Albany IL	Albany Indian Mounds State Historic Site	309-788-0177	S Cherry Street and 12th Avenue
Alto Pass IL	Alto Vineyards	618-893-4898	Hwy 127
Arthur IL	Great Pumpkin Patch	217-543-2394	RR1 Box 100
Aurora IL	Chicago Premium Outlets	630-585-2200	1650 Premium Outlets Blvd
Batavia IL	Fermi National Accelerator Lab	630-840-3351	P.O. Box 500/Pine Street or Batavia Road
Belknap IL	Cache River Basin Vineyards and Winery	618-658-2274	315 Forman Lane
Belleville IL	Eckert's Orchards	618-233-0513	951 S Greenmount Road
Bourbonnais IL	Perry Farm Park	815-933-9905	459 N Kennedy Drive/H 45-H 52
Carbondale IL	Grammer Orchards	618-684-2471	4140 Dutch Ridge Road
Carbondale IL	Kite Hill Winery	618-684-5072	83 Kite Hill Road
Champaign IL	Alto Vineyards	217-356-4784	4210 N Duncan Rd
Chicago IL	Antique Coach and Carriage Company	773-735-9400	700 North Michigan
Chicago IL	Buckingham Fountain	312-742-7529	In Grant Park
Chicago IL	Chicago Horse and Carriage Rides	312-953-9530	Michigan Avenue
Chicago IL	Chicago White Sox Dog Day	866-769-4263	333 W. 35th Street
Chicago IL	Chicagoland Canoe Base	773-777-1489	4019 N Narragansett Avenue
Chicago IL	Mercury Canine Cruises	312-332-1353	Michigan Ave. & Wacker Dr.
Chicago IL	Navy Pier	312-595-7437	600 East Grand Avenue
Chicago IL	Of Mutts and Men	773-477-7171	2149 W. Belmont
Chicago IL	Retail Stores		See comments for details.
Chicago IL	Riverwalk Gateway/Riverwalk	312-744-6630	Lake Shore Drive
Chicago IL	Seadog Cruises at Navy Pier	888-840-6317	600 E. Grand (Entrance on Illinois)
Chicago IL	Shoreline Sightseeing Boat Tours	312-222-9328	Illinois Street
Chicago IL	Step in Time Carriages	773-501-7011	830 N Michigan Avenue
Cobden IL	Inheritance Valley Vineyards	618-893-6141	5490 Street Rte 127 North
Cobden IL	Owl Creek Vineyard	618-893-2557	2655 Water Valley Road
Collinsville IL	Cahokia Mounds State Historic Site	618-346-5160	30 Ramey Street
Dixon IL	John Deere Historic Site	815-652-4551	8393 S Main
Dixon IL	Ronald Reagan Boyhood Home	815-288-5176	810 S Hennepin Avenue
El Paso IL	Furrow Vineyards and Winery	866-880-9463	1131 State Route 251
Elizabeth IL	Long Hollow Scenic Overlook	800-747-9377	H 20
Evanston IL	Ladd Arboretum	847-448-8256	2024 Mc Cormick Blvd
Evanston IL	Shakespeare Garden at Northwestern University	847-491-3741	633 Clark Street
Galena IL	Fever River Outfitters	815-776-9425	525 Main Street
Galena IL	Galena Cellars Winery	800-397-9463	4746 N Ford Road
Galena IL	Galena Cellars Winery and Vineyard	800-397-9463	515 South Main St
Galena IL	Galena Trolley Tours	815-777-1248	314 S Main
Galena IL	President Ulysses S. Grant Home State Historic Park	815-777-3310	500 Bouphillier Street
Galena IL	Wooded Wonderland Country Store and Sawmill	815-777-3426	610 S Devil's Ladder Road
Galesburg IL	Carl Sandburg State Historic Site	309-342-2361	313 E Third Street
Galesburg IL	Seminary Street Shopping District	309-342-1000	Seminary Street
Geneva IL	Geneva Commons Outdoor Shopping Mall	630-262-0044	602 Commons Drive

Dog-Friendly Attractions - Please always call ahead to make sure an establishment is still dog-friendly.

Geneva IL	Kane County Cougars	630-232-8811	34W002 Cherry Lane
Geneva IL	The Fabyan Villa Museum	630-232-4811	1511 S Batavia Avenue/H 31
Grafton IL	Aeries Riverview Winery	618-786-VIEW (8439)	600 Mulberry Street
Grafton IL	Piasa Winery	618-786-9463	211 W Main Street /H 100
Greenup IL	Cameo Vineyards	217-923-9963	400 Mill Rd
Greenup IL	Cumberland County Covered Bridge	217-923-3401	Embarras River
Gurnee IL	Six Flags Great America Kennel	847-249-4636	542 N H 21
Hartford IL	The Lewis and Clark State Historic Site	618-251-5811	1 Lewis and Clark Trail/H 3
Huntley IL	Prime Outlets	847-669-9100	11800 Factory Shops Blvd
Joliet IL	Joliet Iron Works Historic Site	815-724-3760	E Columbia Street
Lake Forest IL	Lake Forest Open Lands Association Dog Day	847-234-3880 x10	155 W Deerpath Road/Deerpath Middle School
Long Grove IL	Historic Long Grove Shopping District	847-634-9440	Old McHenry Road
Makanda IL	Makanda Boardwalk	800-526-1500	Makanda Road
Moline IL	Channel Cat Water Taxi	309-788-3360	13th Street
Monticello IL	Monticello Railway Museum	217-762-9011	993 Iron Horse Road
Mount Vernon IL	GenKota Winery	618-246-WINE	301 North 44th Street
Niles IL	The Leaning Tower of Niles	847-647-8222	6300 W Touhy Avenue
Oak Brook IL	Graue Mill and Museum	630-655-2090	3800 S. York Road
Oak Park IL	Hemingways Birthplace	708-848-2222	339 N Oak Park
Oak Park IL	Oak Park Conservatory	708-725-2450	615 Garfield Street
Oak Park IL	Oak Park Self-Guided Walking Tours	708-848-1500	158 N Forest Avenue
Olney IL	Fox Creek Vineyards	618-392-0418	5502 North Fox Rd
Ottawa IL	Starved Rock Adventures	815-434-9200	1 Dee Bennett Road/H 34
Pana IL	Coal Creek Pioneer Village	217-562-4240	Fairgrounds Road
Peoria IL	Carriage Classics	309-579-2833	Main Street and Water Streets
Pomona IL	Pomona Winery	618-893-2623	2865 Hickory Ridge Rd
Pomona IL	Von Jakob Vineyard	618-893-4500	1309 Sadler Rd
Red Bud IL	Lau-Nae Winery, Inc.	618-282-WINE (9463)	1522 H 3
Rockford IL	Klehm Arboretum and Botanic Garden	815-965-8146	2715 S Main Street/H 2
Roselle IL	Lynfred Winery	630-529-9463	15 S Roselle Road
Sandwich IL	Fox Valley Winery	815-786-3124	120 South Main St
Springfield IL	Lincoln's Tomb State Historic Site	217-782-2717	1500 Monument Avenue/Oak Ridge Cemetary
Springfield IL	Pampered Pet Center	217-483-9106	3401 Gateway Drive
St Charles IL	Concerts in the Park at Lincoln Park	630-513-6200	W Main Street/H 64
St Charles IL	Pride of the Fox Riverfest	630-377-6161	Main Street/H 64
St Charles IL	Sculptures in the Park in Mt. St. Mary Park	630-513-4316	H 31/Geneva Road
St Charles IL	St Charles Holiday Homecoming and Electric Christmas Parade	630-516-5386	Main Street/H 64
St Charles IL	St Charles Paddlewheel Riverboats	630-584-2334	2 North Avenue
Stewardson IL	Vahling Vineyards	217-682-5409	Mode Road/400 N
Tuscola IL	Tanger Outlet	217-253-2282	4045 Tuscola Blvd
Union IL	Illinois Railway Museum	815-923-4000	7000 Olson Road
Urbana IL	University of Illinois Arboretum	217-333-7579	Lincoln Avenue, Urbana Champaign Campus
Urbana IL	University of Illinois Campus	217-333-4666	1401 W Green Street
Vienna IL	Shawnee Winery	618-658-8400	200 Commercial Street
Whittington IL	Pheasant Hollow Winery	618-629-2302	14931 State Hwy 37

Indiana

Bloomington IN	Indiana University Campus	812-856-4648	300 N Jordan Avenue
Bloomington IN	Lake Monroe Boat Rental	812-837-9909	4855 H 446
Bloomington IN	Oliver Winery	812-876-5800	8024 H 37N
Borden IN	Huber Orchard and Winery	812-923-9813	19816 Huber Road
Columbus IN	Irwin Gardens	812-378-2622	5th Street and Layfette Avenue
Elkhart IN	Amish Heritage Driving Tour	574-262-8161	219 Caravan Drive
Elkhart IN	National New York Central Railroad Museum	574-294-3001	721 S Main Street
French Lick IN	Indiana Railway Museum and Train Ride	800-74-TRAIN	8594 H 56W
Hagerstown IN	Wilbur Wright Birthplace	765-332-2495	1525 N 750 E
Indianapolis IN	Blue Ribbon Carriage Company	317-631-4169	1311 S. Drover St
Indianapolis IN	Crown Hill Cemetery	317-925-3800	700 W. 38th St.
Indianapolis IN	Fountain Square	317-686-6010	1105 Prospect Street
Indianapolis IN	Garfield Park Conservatory	317-327-7184	2450 S. Shelby St
Indianapolis IN	Indiana World War Memorial	317-232-7615	5 Block Memorial Plaza
Indianapolis IN	Medal of Honor Memorial in White River State Park	317-233-2434	801 W. Washington St
Indianapolis IN	President Benjamin Harrison Home	317-631-1888	1230 N Delaware Street
Indianapolis IN	Soldiers and Sailors Monument	317-232-7615	Monument Circle
Kendallville IN	Mid-America Windmill Museum	260-347-5273	732 S Allen Chapel Road
Lincoln City IN	Lincoln Boyhood National Memorial	812-937-4541	3027 E South Street
Linn Grove IN	Swiss Heritage Village and Museum	260-589-8007	1200 Swiss Way
Mauckport IN	Squire Boone Caverns and Village	812-732-4381	100 Squire Boone Road SW
Nashville IN	T.C. Steele's State Historic Site	812-988-2785	4220 T.C. Steele Rd.
Peru IN	Grissom Air Museum	765-689-8011	1000 W Hoosier Blvd

Dog-Friendly Attractions - Please always call ahead to make sure an establishment is still dog-friendly.

Plainfield IN	Chateau Thomas Winery	317-837-WINE (9463)	6291 Cambridge Way
Santa Claus IN	Holiday World Theme Park Kennel	877-463-2645	452 E Christmas Blvd
South Bend IN	University of Notre Dame Campus	574-631-5726	S Dixie Way/H 31/933
Valparaiso IN	Taltree Arboretum & Gardens	219-462-0025	71 N 500 W
Vincennes IN	George Rogers Clark National Historical Park	812-882-1776, ext 210	401 S 2nd Street

Iowa

Amana IA	Amana Colonies	319-622-7622	622 46th Avenue (Visitor's Bureau)
Bedford IA	Taylor County Historical Museum and Round Barn	712-523-2041	1001 W Pollock Avenue/H 2 W
Bloomfield IA	Pioneer Ridge Nature Area and Nature Center	641-682-3091	1339 H 63
Burlington IA	Starr's Cave Park and Preserve	319-753-5808	11627 Starr's Cave Road
Cedar Falls IA	Hartman Reserve Nature Center	319-277-2187	657 Reserve Drive
Cedar Rapids IA	Czech Village	319-364-0001	16th Ave SW
Cedar Rapids IA	Indian Creek Nature Center	319-362-0664	6665 Otis Road SE
Clear Lake IA	Iowa Trolley Park	641-357-7433	3429 Main Avenue
Clive IA	Clive Greenbelt Trail	515-223-5246	156th Street
Creston IA	Union County Historical Village & Museum	515-782-4247	McKinley Street
Decorah IA	Seed Savers Exchange/Heritage Farm	563-382-5990	3074 N Winn Road
Des Moines IA	Des Moines Botanical Center	515-323-6290	909 Robert D Ray Drive
Des Moines IA	Des Moines Farmers Market	515-286-4919	4th and Court Streets
Des Moines IA	Fort Des Moines	888-828-FORT (3678)	75 E Army Post Road
Des Moines IA	Four-Mile Greenway Trail	515-266-1563	Copper Creek Drive
Des Moines IA	Salisbury House and Gardens	515-274-1777	4025 Tonawanda Drive
Des Moines IA	The Great Western Trail	515-323-5300	Valley Drive
Dubuque IA	Mines of Spain	563-556-0620	8991 Bellevue Heights
Dyersville IA	Field of Dreams Movie Site	888-875-8404	28995 Lansing Road
Fort Dodge IA	Fort Museum and Frontier Village	515-573-4231	South Kenyon and Museum Road
Fredericksburg IA	Hawkeye Buffalo Ranch	563-237-5318	3034 Pembroke Avenue
Greenfield IA	Iowa Aviation Museum	641-343-7184	2251 Airport Road
Harpers Ferry IA	Effigy Mounds National Monument	563-873-3491	151 H 76
Hawarden IA	Calliope Village	712-551-2403	19th Street and Avenue E
Indianola IA	Buxton Park Arboretum	515-961-9420	N Buxton Street and W Girard Avenue
Knoxville IA	Marion County Historical Village	641-842-5526	Willetts Drive
Leighton IA	Tassel Ridge Winery	641-672-WINE (9463)	1681 220th Street
Lime Springs IA	Lidtke Mill Historical Site	563-566-2893	Mill Street
Long Grove IA	Dan Nagle Walnut Grove Pioneer Village	563-328-3283	18817 290th Street
Lorimor IA	Mount Pisgah/Mormon Trail	641-782-7021	H 169
Maharishi Vedic City IA	Maharishi Vedic City Self-Guided Walking	641-472-9580	1734 Jasmine Avenue (The Raj Hotel)
Maharishi Vedic City IA	Vedic Observatory	641-472-9580	1734 Jasmine Avenue (Visitors Center at The Raj)
Mason City IA	Kinney Pioneer Museum	641-423-1258	H 122 W at airport entrance
Mason City IA	Lime Creek Nature Center	641-423-5309	3501 Lime Creek Road
Moline IL	Channel Cat Water Taxi	309-788-3360	13th Street
Monticello IA	Riverside Gardens	319-465-6384	441 E 3rd Street
Mount Pleasant IA	Old Threshers Park and Campground	319-385-8937	405 E Threshers Road
Nashua IA	The Old Bradford Pioneer Village	641-435-2567	H 346 East
Odebolt IA	Prairie Pedlar	712-668-4840	1609 270th Street
Oelwein IA	Hub City Heritage Railway Museum	319-283-1939	26 Second Avenue SW
Pella IA	Pella Historical Village	641-628-4311	507 Franklin Street
Pella IA	The Molengracht Plaza	877-954-8400	Main Street
Polk City IA	Big Creek Boat Rental	515-984-6083	8550 NW 142nd Avenue
Princeton IA	Buffalo Bill Cody Homestead	563-225-2981	28050 230th Avenue
Red Oak IA	Heritage Hill Tour	712-623-4821	First and Coolbaugh Streets
Rockford IA	Fossil and Prairie Park Preserve and Center	641-756-3490	1227 215th Street
Ruthven IA	Lost Island Prairie Wetland Nature Center	712-837-4866	3259 355th Avenue
Shenandoah IA	Iowa Walk of Fame	712-246-3455	Sheridan Avenue
Sioux City IA	Dorothy Pecaut Nature Center	712-258-0838	4500 Sioux River Road/H 12
Sioux City IA	Milwaukee Railroad Shops Historic District	712-276-6432	3400 Sioux River Road/H12
Sioux City IA	Sergeant Floyd Monument	712-279-0198	2601 S Lewis Blvd
South Amana IA	Ackerman Winery	319-622-3379	4406 220th Trail/H 220
South Amana IA	The Barn Museum	South Amana	413 P Street
St Ansgar IA	Bel-Aire Estates Winery	641-420-7092	4351 Dancer Avenue
Storm Lake IA	Buena Vista County Wind Farm	712-732-3780	119 W 6th Street
Urbandale IA	Living History Farms	515-278-5286	2600 111th Street
Wapello IA	Toolesboro Mound Group	319-523-8381	6568 Toolesboro Road
West Bend IA	Grotto of the Redemption	515-887-2371	300 N Broadway
West Branch IA	Herbert Hoover Presidential Library, Museum and Birthplace Cottage	319-643-5301	210 Parkside Drive
West Des Moines IA	Historic Valley Junction	515-222-3642	5th Street
West Des Moines IA	Jordan Creek Trail	515-222-3444	Off the E. P. True Parkway
Williamsburg IA	Tanger Outlet Center	319-668-2885	150 Tanger Drive

Kansas

Abilene KS	Heritage Center of Dickinson County	785-263-2681	412 S Campbell
Antiock KS	Overland Park Arboretum and Botanical Gardens	913-685-3604	8909 W 179th Street
Atchison KS	Amelia Earhart Birthplace Museum	913-367-4217	223 NTerrace Street
Atchison KS	Forest of Friendship	913-367-1419	17862 274th Rd
Bonner Springs KS	National Agricultural Hall of Fame	913-721-1075	630 Hall of Fame Drive
Dodge City KS	Fort Dodge Kansas State Soldier's Home	620-227-2121	714 Sheridan
Dodge City KS	The Dodge City Trail of Fame	620-561-1925	P. O. Box 1243
Fort Scott KS	Fort Scott National Historic Site	620-223-0310	2 S Main Street
Hays KS	Stone Gallery and Scupture Tour	785-625-7619	107 ½ West 6th
Hiawatha KS	Brown County Agriculture Museum	785-742-3702	301 E Iowa
Kansas City KS	Grinter Place State Historic Site	913-299-0373	1400 S 78th Street
Kansas City KS	The Boulevard Drive-In	913-262-2414	1051 Merriam Lane/H 12
Kansas City KS	The Legends at Village West	913-788-3700	1843 Village West Parkway
Larned KS	Fort Larned National Historic Site	620-285-6911	H 156
Lawrence KS	University of Kansas	785-864-2700	Jayhawk Boulevard
Lenexa KS	Legler Barn Museum	913-492-0038	14907 W 87th Street Parkway
Liberal KS	Dorothy's House/Land of Oz	316-624-7624	567 East Cedar
Olathe KS	Mahaffie Stagecoach Stop and Farm	913-971-8600	1200 Kansas City Road
Olathe KS	The Prairie Center	913-856-7669	26325 W 135th
Somerset KS	Sumerset Ridge Winery	913-491-0038	29725 Somerset Road
Stafford KS	Quivira National Wildlife Refuge	620-486-2393	1434 NE 80th Street
Topeka KS	Old Prairie Town at Ward Meade Park	785-368-3888	124 NW Fillmore
Wichita KS	Bradley Fair	316-630-9990	2000 N Rock Road
Wichita KS	Lake Afton Public Observatory	316-978-7827	MacArthur Road and 247th St W
Wichita KS	Old Town Wichita	316-262-3555	E 2nd Street N

Kentucky

Barbourville KY	Dr. Thomas Walker State Historic Site	606-546-4400	4929 H 459
Bardstown KY	Central Kentucky Canoe and Kayak	502-507-9364	
Bowling Green KY	Civil War Discovery Trail	800-326-7465	352 Three Springs Road (Visitor Center)
Bowling Green KY	Lost River Cave and Valley	270-393-0077	2818 Nashville Road/H 31W
Cadiz KY	Elk and Bison Prairie	270-924-2000	The Trace Road
Cave City KY	Dinosaur World	270-773-4345	711 Mammoth Cave Rd
Clermont KY	Bernheim Arboretum	502-955-8512	2499 H 245
Frankfort KY	Kentucky State Capitol Grounds	502-564-3449	700 Capitol Avenue
Frankfort KY	Kentucky Vietnam Veterans Memorial	800-960-7200	Coffee Tree Road
Georgetown KY	Factory Stores of America	502-868-0682	401 Outlet Center Drive
Georgetown KY	The Official Kentucky-Japan Friendship Garden	502-316-4554	N Broadway Street/H 25
Harrodsburg KY	Shaker Village of Pleasant Hill	800-734-5611	3501 Lexington Road/H 68
Hodgenville KY	Abe Lincoln Birthplace National Historic Site	270-358-3137	2995 Lincoln Farm Road/H 31E
Lexington KY	American Saddlebred Museum	859-259-2746	4093 Iron Works Pkwy
Lexington KY	Aviation Museum of Kentucky	859-231-1219	4316 Hanger Drive, # 13
Lexington KY	Chrisman Mill Winery	859-264-WINE (9463)	2300 Sir Barton Way, Suite #175
Lexington KY	Kentucky Horse Park	800-678-8813	4089 Ironworks Parkway
Lexington KY	Talon Winery and Vineyards	859-971-3214	7086 Tates Creek Road/H 1974
Lexington KY	University of Kentucky Campus	859-323-6371	410 Administration Drive
Louisville KY	Riverside - The Farnsley-Moremen Landing	502-935-6809	7410 Moorman Street
Louisville KY	The Old Louisville Walking Tour	502-635-5244	218 W Oak Street (Visitor Center)
Midway KY	Equus Run Vineyards	859-846-9463	1280 Moores Mill Road
Perryville KY	Perryville Battlefield State Historic Site	859-332-8631	1825 Battlefield Road
Renfro Valley KY	Bittersweet Cabin Museum	606-256-0715	H 25
Springfield KY	Lincoln Homestead State Park	859-336-7461	5079 Lincoln Park RoadH 528
Stearns KY	Barthell Coal Mining Camp	606-376-8749	552 Barthell Road
Whitesburg KY	Little Shepherd Trail	606-573-4156	H 119
Wickliffe KY	Wickliffe Mounds State Historic Site	270-335-3681	94 Green Street/H 60

Louisiana

Alexandria LA	Kent Plantation	318-487-5998	3601 Vayou RapidesH 496
Baton Rouge LA	BREC's Bluebonnet Swamp	225-757-8905	10503 North Oak Hills Parkway
Baton Rouge LA	BREC's Magnolia Mound Plantation	225-343-4955	2161 Nicholson Drive
Baton Rouge LA	Louisiana State Capitol	225-342-7317	900 North Third Street on State Capital Drive
Baton Rouge LA	Perkins Rowe Shopping District	225-761-6905	10107 Park Row Avenue
Calcasieu and Cameron parishes LA	Creole Nature Trail	800-456-7952	H 27
Clinton LA	Casa De Sue Winery	225-405-4692	12324 St Helena
Darrow LA	Houmas House Plantation and Gardens	225-473-9380	40136 H 942
DeQuincy LA	DeQuincy Railroad Museum Park	337-786-2823	400 Lake Charles Avenue
Folsom LA	Landry Vineyards	985-294-7790	11650 Tantela Ranch Rd
Frogmore LA	Frogmore Cotton Plantation	318-757-2453	11054 H 84
Jackson LA	Feliciana Cellars	225-634-7982	1848 Charter St

Kraemer LA	Torres Cajun Swamp Tours	985-633-7739	105 Torres Road
Lafayette LA	Acadian Village	337-981-2364	200 Greenleaf Drive
Lafayette LA	Atchafalaya Experience	337-261-5150	338 N Sterling Street
Layfayette LA	The Real French Destination Scenic Byway	800-4BYWAYS option 3	H 93
Marksville LA	Marksville State Historic Site	318-253-8954	837 Martin Luther King Drive
Napoleonville LA	Madewood Plantation	800-375-7151	4250 H 308
New Orleans LA	Algiers Ferry	504-376-8100	Canal Street
New Orleans LA	Bloody Mary's Tours	504-523-7684	4905 Canal Street (meet outside)
New Orleans LA	Buggy Rides		Decatur Street at Jackson Square
New Orleans LA	French Quarter District	504-522-7226	Canal Street to Esplanade Avenue up to Rampart Street
New Orleans LA	Good Old Days Buggies Inc	504-523-0804	1229 Saint Thomas Street
New Orleans LA	Haunted History Tours	504-861-2727	97 Fontainebleau Dr.
New Orleans LA	Historic New Orleans Walking Tours, Inc	504-947-2120	2727 Prytania St. Suite 8
New Orleans LA	Jazz Walk of Fame	504-589-4841	Algiers Point
Shreveport LA	Gardens of the American Rose Center	318-938-5402	8877 Jefferson Paige Road
Shreveport LA	Just Pets Gourmet	318-798-5858	7030 Youree Drive
Slidell LA	Pearl River Eco-Tours	866-59-SWAMP (597-9267)	55050 H 90
St Francisville LA	Audubon State Historic Site and Oakley House	225-635-3739	11788 H 965
St Francisville LA	Rosedown Plantation State Historic Site	225-635-3332	12501 H 10
Vacherie LA	Laura Plantation	225-265-7690	2247 H 18

Maine

Bar Harbor ME	Acadia Outfitters	207-288-8118	106 Cottage Street
Bar Harbor ME	Bar Harbor Downtown Shopping District	800-345-4617	Downtown Bar Harbor
Bar Harbor ME	Downeast Windjammer Cruises	207-288-4585	Bar Harbor Pier
Bar Harbor ME	Wildwood Stables Carriage Tours	207-276-3622	Route 3
Belfast ME	Water Walker Sea Kayaks	207-338-6424	152 Lincolnville Avenue
Boothbay ME	Boothbay Railway Village	207-633-4727	586 Wiscasset Road /H 29
Boothbay Harbor ME	Balmy Day Cruises	207-633-2284	42 Commercial Street/Pier 8
Boothbay Harbor ME	Cap'n Fish Boat Tours	207-633-3244	65 Atlantic Avenue
Boothbay Harbor ME	Tidal Transit Kayak Company	207-633-7140	18 Granary Way
Camden ME	Lively Lady Too Boat Tours	207-236-6672	Bay View Landing Wharf
Camden ME	Merryspring Nature Park	207-236-2239	30 Conway Road
Camden ME	Schooner Olad	207-236-2323	Camden Harbor/Camden Public Landing
Greenville ME	Northwoods Outfitters	207-695-3288	5 Lily Bay Road
Kennebunkport ME	Gallery on Chase Hill	207-967-0049	10 Chase Hill Road
Kittery ME	Kittery Premium Outlets	207-439-6548	375 H 1
Milbridge ME	Robertson Sea Tours and Adventures	207-546-3883	Milbridge Marina
New Harbor ME	Hardy Boat Cruises	207-677-2026	132 H 32
Northeast Harbor ME	Beal and Bunker Mail Boat Ferry	207-244-3575	Harbor Drive
Phippsburg ME	Fort Popham State Historic Site	207-389-1335	10 Perkins Farm Lane
Portland ME	Bay View Cruises	207-761-0486	184 Commercial Street
Portland ME	Casco Bay Lines Boats	207-74-7871	56 Commercial Street
Portland ME	Eagle Island Tours	207-774-6498	170 Commercial Street
Portland ME	Greater Portland Landmarks Walking Tours	207-774-5561	165 State Street/H 77
Portland ME	Maine Narrow Gauge Railroad Co. and Museum	207-828-0814	58 Fore Street
Portland ME	Old Port Waterfront District	207-772-6828	Congress Street
Portland ME	The Maine Narrow Gauge Railroad	207-828-0814	58 Fore Street
Round Pond ME	Salt Water Charters	207-677-6229	Town Landing Road/Round Pond Dock
South Freeport ME	Atlantic Seal Cruises	207-865-6112	25 Main Street
Southwest Harbor ME	Masako Queen Fishing Company	207-244-5385	Beal's Wharf
Stonington ME	Old Quarry Ocean Adventures	207-367-8977	130 Settlement Road
Wells ME	World Within Sea Kayaking	207-646-0455	746 Ocean Avenue
Winterport ME	Winterport Winery	207-223-4500	279 South Main St

Maryland

Annapolis MD	Animal Tales Walking Tour	410-263-0033	64 State Circle
Annapolis MD	Annapolis Digital Walking Tours	410-267665	99 Main Street
Annapolis MD	Annapolis Harbor Center	410-266-5857	2472 Solomon's Island Road/H2
Annapolis MD	Annapolis Maritime Museum	410-295-0104	723 2nd Street
Annapolis MD	Annapolis Small Boat Rentals	410-268-2628	808 Boucher Avenue
Annapolis MD	Annapolis Trolley Tours	410-626-6000	99 Main Street
Annapolis MD	Canines and Cocktails		126 West Street/H 436
Annapolis MD	Watermark Cruises	800-569-9622	1 Dock Street
Baltimore MD	Baltimore Adventures	410-342-2004	1001 Fell Street
Baltimore MD	Cylburn Arboretum	410-367-2217	4915 Greenspring Avenue
Baltimore MD	Henderson's Wharf Marina	410-342-2004	1001 Fell Street
Baltimore MD	Heritage Walk Self-Guided Walking Tour	877-BALTIMORE(225-8466)	401 Light Street/H2
Baltimore MD	Horse and Carriage Rides		Inner Harbor
Baltimore MD	Maryland Sled Dog Adventures LLC	443-562-5736	

Dog-Friendly Attractions - Please always call ahead to make sure an establishment is still dog-friendly.

Baltimore MD	The Original Fell's Point Ghost Walk Tour	410-522-7400	P. O. Box 38140
Baltimore MD	Westminster Cemetery	410-706-2072	509 W. Fayette Street
Berlin MD	Victorian Christmas	410-641-1554	Main Street/H 818
Cambridge MD	Dorchester Arts Center Walking Tours	410-228-7782	120 High Street
Catonsville MD	Benjamin Banneker Historical Park and Museum	410-887-1081	300 Oella Avenue
Chestertown MD	Virginia Gent Decker Arboretum	800-422-1782 ext/7726	300 Washington Avenue/H 213
Crisfield MD	Tangier Island Cruises	410-968-2338	1001 West Main Street/H 413
Cumberland MD	George Washington's Headquarters	301-777-5132	Greene Street
Easton MD	Historical Society of Talbot County	410-822-0773	25 S Washington Street
Ellicott City MD	Ghost Tours	410-313-8141	8267 Main Street
Frederick MD	The Monocacy National Battlefield	301-662-3515	5201 Urbana Pike/H 355
Grantsville MD	Spruce Forest Artisan Village	301-895-3332	177 Casselman Road
Hagerstown MD	Prime Outlets	888-883-6288	495 Prime Outlets Boulevard
Havre de Grace MD	The Skipjack Martha Lewis	410-939-4078	South end of Union Avenue/Tidings Park
Knoxville MD	River and Trail Outfitters	301-695-5177	604 Valley Road
Oakland MD	Bill's Marine Service Boat Rentals	410-387-5536	20721 Garrett H/H 219
Red House MD	Red House School Country Mall	301-334-2800	3039 Garrett Highway/H 219
Scotland MD	Point Lookout Confererate Monument	301-872-5688	11175 Point Lookout Road
Sharpesburg MD	Antietam National Battlefield	301-432-5124	5831 Dunker Church Road
Solomons MD	Bunky's Charter Boats	410-326-3241	14448 Solomons Island Road S
St Michaels MD	St. Michaels Harbor Shuttle	410-924-2198	101 N Harbor Road
Tilghman MD	Dockside Express Cruises	888-312-7847	Phillips Wharf
Tilghman Island MD	Tilghman Island Marina	410-886-2500	6140 Mariners Court

Massachusetts

Boston MA	Bay State Cruise Company	617-748-1428	The Pier at the World Trade Center
Boston MA	Black Heritage Trail	617-725-0022	46 Joy Street
Boston MA	Boston African American National Historic Site	617-742-5415	14 Beacon Street Ste 503
Boston MA	Boston Harbor Cruises	617-227-4320	1 Long Wharf
Boston MA	Downtown Crossing Shopping Center	617-482-2139	59 Temple Place
Boston MA	Faneuil Hall Marketplace		North St and Merchants Row
Boston MA	Freedom Trail		Tremont and Temple
Boston MA	Horse and Carriage (Bridal Carriage)	781-871-9224	Faneuil Hall Marketplace
Boston MA	Secret Tour of Boston's North End	617-720-2283	Four Battery Street
Boston MA	The Cheers Building-Outside View		84 Beacon St
Brookline MA	John F Kennedy National Historic Site	617-566-7937	83 Beals Street
Cambridge MA	Harvard Square Shopping Center	617-491-3434	JFK Street at Massachusetts Avenue
Cambridge MA	Harvard University Campus	617-495-1000	1350 Massachusetts Avenue/Harvard Square
Cambridge MA	Longfellow National Historic Site	617-876-4491	105 Brattle Street
Chester MA	Chester Hill Winery	413-354-2340	47 Lyon Hill Road
Chestnut Hill MA	Boston College Campus	617-552-8000	140 Commonwealth Avenue
Concord MA	Concord Guides & Press Walking Tours	978-287-0897	P.O. Box 1335
Concord MA	Minute Man National Historical Park		Rt 2A and I-95
Deerfield MA	Historic Deerfield Village	413-775-7214	Old Main Street
East Boston MA	City Water Taxi's Island Romp for Dogs	617-633-9240	Long Wharf/Columbus Park
East Sandwich MA	Green Briar Nature Center	508-888-6870	6 Discovery Hill
Gloucester MA	Cape Ann Whale Watch	978-283-5110	415 Main Street
Gloucester MA	Dogtown Common		Dogtown Road at Cherry
Hyannis MA	Hy-Line Harbor Cruises	508-790-0696	Ocean Street Docks
Hyannis MA	Hyannisport Harbor Cruises	508-778-2600	Ocean Street Dock
Lee MA	Windy Knoll Farm	413-243-0989	40 Stringer Avenue
Nantucket MA	Nantucket Adventures	508-228-6365	34 Washington St #77
Nantucket MA	Nantucket Regional Transit Authority (NRTA)	508-228-7025	22 Federal Street
New Marlborough MA	Les Trois Emme Winery and Vineyard	413-528-1015	8 Knight Road
Newton MA	Charles River Canoe Center	617-965-5110	2401 Common Wealth Avenue
North Adams MA	The Mohawk Trail	413-743-8127	P. O. Box 1044
North Weymouth MA	Pilgrim Congregational Church	781-337-2075	24 Athens Street
Onset MA	Cape Cod Canal Cruise	508-295-3883	Town Pier
Orleans MA	Goose Hummock Outdoor Center	508-255-2620	13 Old County Road
Provincetown MA	Bay State Cruise Company	617-748-1428	MacMillan Pier
Provincetown MA	Dolphin Fleet of Provincetown Whale Watch	508-349-1900	307 Commercial Street
Provincetown MA	Flyer's Boat Rentals	508-487-0898	131 Commercial Street
Salem MA	Haunted Foot Steps Ghost Tour	978-645-0666	8 Central Street
Salem MA	Salem Trolley	978-744-5469	2 New Liberty Street
Salem MA	Salem Walking Tour		
Salem MA	Salem Willows Amusement Park	978-745-0251	171-185 Fort Avenue
Shelburne Falls MA	Bridge of Flowers	413-625-2526	16-22 Water Street
Wellfleet MA	Wellfleet Drive-in Movie Theater	508-349-7176	51 H 6
West Tisbury MA	West Tisbury Farmer's Markets	508-693-0085	State Road
Worcester MA	Blackstone River Bikeway	401-762-0250	Worcester Square

Michigan

Dog-Friendly Attractions - Please always call ahead to make sure an establishment is still dog-friendly.

Ann Arbor MI	Ann Arbor Street Art Fair	800-888-9487	PO Box 1352
Ann Arbor MI	Argo Canoe Livery	734-794-6000 X 42530	1055 Longshore Drive
Ann Arbor MI	Border to Border Trail	734-971-6337	P.O. Box 8645
Ann Arbor MI	Cobblestone Farm Museum	734-994-2928	2781 Packard Road
Ann Arbor MI	Domino's Petting Farm	734-998-0182	24 Frank Lloyd Wright Drive
Ann Arbor MI	Gallup Park Livery	734-662-9319	3000 Fuller Road
Ann Arbor MI	Nichols Arboretum	734-647-7600	1600 Washington Heights
Ann Arbor MI	Skip's Huron River Canoe Livery	734-769-8686	3780 Delhi Court
Ann Arbor MI	Yellow Cab	734-663-3355	2050 Commerce Ann Arbor
Ann Arbor/Ypsilanti MI	Blue Cab	734-547-2222	
Augusta MI	W.K. Kellogg Experiment Station	269-731-4597	7060 N. 42nd Street
Bad Axe MI	Pioneer Log Cabin Village	989-269-8325	210 S Hanselman Street
Baldwin MI	Shrine of the Pines	231-745-7892	8962 S H 37
Baroda MI	Round Barn Winery	269-422-1617	10981 Hills Road
Bay City MI	Appledore Tall Ships	989-895-5193	901 Saginaw Street
Birch Run MI	Prime Outlets at Birch Run	989-624-4868	12240 S Berey Road
Birmingham MI	Birmingham Principal Shopping District	248-530-1200	Woodward Avenue/H 1
Bridgeport MI	Price Nature Center	989-790-5280	6685 Sheridan Road
Buchanan MI	Tabor Hill Winery	800-283-3363	185 Mt Tabor Road
Capac MI	Blueridge Blueberry Farm	810-395-2245	16276 Donald Road
Caspian MI	Iron County Historical Museum	906-265-2617	Brady at Museum Drive
Cedar MI	Bel Lago Vineyards and Winery	231-228-4800	6530 S Lake Shore Drive/H 643
Cedar MI	Longview Winery	231-228-2880	8697 Good Harbor Trail
Chelsea MI	Chelsea Farmers' Market	734-475-1145	Park Street
Clinton Township MI	The Mall at Partridge Creek	586-416-3839	17420 Hall Road/H 59
Copper Harbor MI	Delaware Mine	906-289-4688	H 41
Copper Harbor MI	Sunset Cruises	906-289-4437	5th Street at Waterfront Landing
Davison MI	Johnny Panther Quests	810-653-3859	8065 E Coldwater Rd
Dearborn MI	University of Michigan - Dearborn Campus	734 764-1817	4901 Evergreen Road
Detroit MI	Bray's Charter Boat Service	313-273-9183	14767 Riverside Blvd
Detroit MI	Rivard Plaza	313-566-8200	1340 E Atwater Street
Detroit MI	The Detroit RiverFront Conservancy	313-566-8200	Renaissance Center
Drummond Island MI	Drummond Island Yacht Haven	800-543-4743	33185 S Water Street
East Lansing MI	Michigan State University Campus	517-355-1855	South Harrison Road
Eau Claire MI	Tree-Mendus Fruit Farm	269-782-7101	9351 E Eureka Road
Flint MI	Crossroads Village and Huckleberry Railroad	801-736-7100	6140 Bray Road
Flushing MI	Almar Orchard	810-659-6568	1431 Duffield Road
Grand Rapids MI	Downtown Center	616-459-8287	Monroe Center St NW at Ionia Ave NW
Grand Rapids MI	Grand River Sculpture and Fish Ladder	616-459-8287	Grand River at Front and Fourth NW
Hancock MI	The Quincy Mine/A Keweenaw Heritage Site	906-482-3101	49750 H 41
Harrison Township MI	Eddie's Drive-in	586-469-2345	36111 Jefferson Avenue
Hickory Corners MI	Gilmore Car Club Museum	269-671-5089	6865 W Hickory Road
Holland MI	Holland Town Center	616-396-1808	12330 James Street
Holland MI	Nelis Dutch Village	616 396-1475	12350 Jane Street
Holly MI	Michigan Renaissance Festival	800-601-4848	12600 Dixie Highway
Howell MI	Tanger Outlets	517-545-0500	1475 N Burkhart
Kalamazoo MI	Husted Farm	269-372-1237	9191 W Main
Kalamazoo MI	Kalamazoo Mall and Arcadia Creek Festival Place	269-344-0795	S Kalamazoo Mall
Kalamazoo MI	Peterson and Sons Natural Wines	269-626-9755	9375 E P Avenue
Lansing MI	Frandor Shopping Center	517-351-8300	416 Frandor Avenue, Suite 103
Lansing MI	J & K Steamboat Line Paddleboat Tours	517-627-2154	At Grand River Park
Lansing MI	Planet Walk	517-702-6730	On the Riverwalk between Michigan Avenue & Potters Park
Leland MI	Good Harbor Vineyards	231-256-7165	34 S Manitou Trail/H 22
Ludington MI	White Pine Village	231-843-4808	1687 S Lakeshore Drive
Mackinac Island MI	Mackinac Island	800-454-5227	Accessible by ferry
Mackinac Island MI	Mackinac Island Carriage Tours	906-847-3307	Main Street
Mackinaw City MI	Colonial Michilimackinac	231-436-4100	Nicolet Street
Mackinaw City MI	Historic Mill Creek	231-436-4100	Huron Avenue H 23
Midland MI	Bark in the Park	989-837-6930	Ann and Ashman Streets
Midland MI	Midland Public Dog Park	989-837-6930	Ann and Ashman Streets
Milford MI	Heavner Canoe Rental	248-685-2379	2775 Garden Road
Monroe MI	River Raisin Battlefield	734-243-7136	1403 E Elm Avenue
Montaque MI	Happy Mohawk Canoe Livery	231-894-4209	735 Fruitvale Road
Munising MI	Pictured Rock Cruises Kennels	906-387-2379	City Dock (P. O. Box 355)
Munising MI	Seaberg Pontoon Rentals LLC	906-387-2685	1330 Commercial Street
Munising MI	Shipwreck Boat Tours Kennels	906-387-4477	1204 Commercial Street
Muskegon MI	Dog Star Ranch	231-766-0444	4200 Whitehall Road
Newberry MI	Two Hearted Canoe Trips	906 658-3357	9706 County Road 423/Mouth of Two Heart Road
Paradise MI	Great Lakes Shipwreck Museum	888-492-3747	18335 Whitefish Point Road
Paw Paw MI	St Julian Winery	269-657-5568	716 S Kalamazoo Street/H 40
Paw Paw MI	Warner Vineyards	800-756-5357	706 S Kalamazoo Street/H 40
Port Austin MI	Tip-A-Thum Canoe Rental	989-738-7656	2475 Port Austin Road/H 25
Richland MI	Braelock Farm	269-629-9884	9124 N 35th Street

Rochester MI	Spectacular Strolls	248-608-8352	
Rochester Hills MI	Meadow Brook Hall and Gardens	248-370-3140	480 S Adams Road/Oakland University Campus
Rockford MI	AAA Rogue River Canoe Rental	616-866-9264	49 E Bridge Street
Rockford MI	Rockford and Squires Street Square	616-866-2000	12 Squires Street Square
Saline MI	Saline Farmers Market	734-429-3518	South Ann Arbor Street
Sault Ste. Marie MI	Soo Locks Boat Tours Kennels	800-432-6301	Dock 1, 1157 E Portage Ave/Dock 2, 515 E Portage Ave
Soo Junction MI	Toonerville Trolley and Riverboat	888-778-7246	
St Johns MI	Andy T's Farms	989-224-7674	3131 S Bus H 27
St Johns MI	Uncle John's Cider Mill	989-224-3686	8614 N H 127
Suttons Bay MI	Mawby Vineyards	231-271-3522	4519 S Elm Valley Road
Thompsonville MI	Michigan Legacy Art Park at Crystal Mountain	800-9687686	12500 Crystal Mountain Drive
Tipton MI	Hidden Lake Gardens	517-431-2060	6214 Monroe Road/H 50
Traverse City MI	Brys Estate Vineyard and Winery	231-223-9303	3309 Blue Water Road
Traverse City MI	Chateau Grand Traverse Winery	231-938-2291	4176 E Traverse H/H 72
Traverse City MI	Peninsula Cellars	231-223-4050	11480 Center Road/H 37
Traverse City MI	Preferred Outlets	231-941-9211	3639 Market Place Circle
Traverse City MI	Sail and Power Boat Rental	231-922-9336	615 Front Street
Waterford MI	Drayton Plains Nature Center	248-674-2119	2125 Denby Drive
Wellston MI	Pine River Paddlesport Center	231-862-3471	9590 S Grandview H/H 37S
West Branch MI	Tanger Outlet Center	989-345-2594	2990 Cook Road #28
White Cloud MI	Loda Lake Wildflower Sanctuary	231-745-4631	Fletch Avenue

Minnesota

Baxter MN	Northland Arboretum	218-829-8770	14250 Conservation Drive
Duluth MN	Fitger's Brewery Complex	218-279-2739	600 East Superior Street
Ely MN	Dorothy Molter Museum	218-365-4451	2002 E Sheridan Street
Excelsior MN	Excel Boat Club Boat Rentals	952-401-3880	141 Minnetonka Blvd
Grand Marais MN	Anderson Aero	218-387-1687	80 Skyport Lane
International Falls MN	Rainy Lake Houseboats	218-286-5391	2031 Town Road 488
Lanesboro MN	Scenic Valley Winery	507-467-2958	101 Copy Street E
Medford MN	Medford Outlet Center	507-455-2042	6750 W Frontage Road
Minneapolis MN	Chain of Lakes Byway	612 230-6400	2117 West River Road (MN Park and Recreation)
Minneapolis MN	Midwest Mountaineering	612-339-3433	309 Cedar Avenue
Minneapolis MN	Minneapolis Sculpture Garden	612-375-7600	1750 Hennepin
Minneapolis MN	Nicollet Mall	888-676-6757	Between Washinton Avenue S and 13th Street S
Minneapolis MN	St Anthony Falls Heritage Trail	612-661-4800	Plymouth/8th Avenue Bridge to Franklin Avenue Bridge
Minneapolis MN	The Hitching Company	612-338-7777	925 N 5th Street
Minneapolis MN	Upper St Anthony Falls Lock and Dam	877-552-1416	1 Portland Avenue S
Montevideo MN	Historic Chippewa City	320-269-7636	151 Arnie Anderson Drive
Montevideo MN	Olof Swensson Farm	320-269-7636	115 H 15 SE
Morton MN	Birch Coulee Battlefield	507-697-6321	32469 H 2
Orr MN	Ebels Voyageur Houseboats	218-374-3571	10326 Ash River Trail
Park Rapids MN	Summerhill Farm	218-732-3865	24013 H 71
Pipestone MN	Pipestone National Monument	507-825-5464	36 Reservation Avenue
Plummer MN	Two Fools Vineyard and Winery	218-465-4655	12501 240th Avenue SE
Rochester MN	Miracle Mile Shopping Center	507-288-2455	115 16th Avenue NW
Rochester MN	Quarry Hill Nature Center	507-281-6114	701 Silver Creek Road NE
Rochester MN	Silver Lake Boat and Bike Rentals	507-261-9049	700 W Silver Lake Drive NE
Shakopee MN	The Minnesota Renaissance Festival and Pet Fest	952-445-7361	H 169
St Paul MN	Jackson Street Roundhouse Railway Museum and Other Sites	651-228-0263	193 Pennsylvania Ave E
Tower MN	Vermilion Houseboats	218-753-3548	9482 Angus Road/H 77
Worthington MN	Pioneer Village	507-376-3125	501 Stower Drive
Zimmerman MN	Sherburne National Wildlife Refuge	763-389-3323	17076 293rd Avenue/H 9

Mississippi

Bay St Louis MS	Old Town Bay St Louis	800-466-9048	1928 Depot Way
Belzoni MS	Wister Gardens	662-247-3025	1440 H 7
Biloxi MS	The Biloxi Shrimping Trip	228-385-1182	693 Beach Blvd
Cleveland MS	Historic Downtown Cotton Row	800-295-7473	Cotton Row
Grenada MS	Historic Walking Tours	662-226-2571	95 SW Frontage Road
Gulfport MS	Prime Outlets at Gulfport	228-867-6100	10000 Factory Shop Blvd
Hattiesburg MS	All American Rose Garden	601-266-4491	118 College Drive
Holly Springs MS	Holly Springs Driving Tour	662-252-2515	104 East Gholson Avenue
Jackson MS	Civil Rights Driving Tour	601-960-1891	111 E Capitol Street
Long Beach MS	Wolf River Canoe and Kayak	228-452-7666	21652 Tucker Road
Madison MS	Cypress Swamp	800-305-7417	MP 122 Natchez Trace Parkway
Natchez MS	Emerald Mound Broken Arrows	601-43-2111	66 Emerald Mound Road
Natchez MS	Forks of the Road Slave Market Site	800-647-6724	Intersection of D'Evereux Drive, Saint Catherine Street and Liberty Road

Dog-Friendly Attractions - Please always call ahead to make sure an establishment is still dog-friendly.

Natchez MS	Grand Village of the Natchez Indians	601-446-6502	400 Jefferson Davis Blvd
Natchez MS	Southern Carriage Tours	800-647-6724	200 State Street
Pascagoula MS	Scranton Nature Center	228-938-6612	3928 Nathan Hale Avenue
Port Gibson MS	Grand Gulf Military Park	601-437-5911	12006 Grand Gulf Road
Tupelo MS	Brices Cross Roads National Battlefield Site	800-305-7417	2680 Natchez Trace Parkway
Tupelo MS	Chickasaw Village	662-680-4027	Natchez Trace Parkway
Tupelo MS	Elvis Presley Birthplace	662-841-1245	306 Elvis Presley Drive
Tupelo MS	Tupelo National Battlefield	800-305-7417	2680 Natchez Trace Parkway
Vicksburg MS	Mississippi River Boat Tours	866-807-2628	1208 Levee Street
Vicksburg MS	Vicksburg Factory Outlets	601-636-7434	4000 S Frontage Road
Vicksburg MS	Vicksburg National Cemetery	601-636-0583	3201 Clay Street
Vicksburg MS	Vicksburg National Military Park	601-636-0583	3201 Clay Street

Missouri

Altenburg MO	Tower Rock Winery	573-824-5479	10769 Highway A
Ash Grove MO	Nathan Boone's Homestead	417-751-3266	7850 N State Hwy V
Augusta MO	Mount Pleasant Winery	636-482-4419	5634 High St
Berger MO	Bias Vineyards and Winery	800-905-2427	3166 Highway B
Boonville MO	Boone's Lick State Historic Site	660-837-3330	H 187
Branson MO	Factory Merchants Outlet Center	417-335-6686	1000 Pat Nash Drive
Branson MO	Stone Hill Winery	888-926-WINE	601 State Hwy 165
Branson MO	The Shoppes at Branson Meadows	417-339-2580	2651 Shepard of the Hills
Branson West MO	Talking Rocks Cavern	417-272-3366	423 Ferry Cave Lane
Brazeau MO	Hemman Winery	573-824-6040	13022 Hwy C
Burfordville MO	Bollinger Mill State Historic Site	573-243-4591	113 Bollinger Mill Rd
Camdenton MO	Bridal Cave and Thunder Mountain Park	573-346-2676	526 Bridal Cave Rd
Camdenton MO	Lake of the Ozarks Marina	573-873-3705	H 5 N, Niangua Arm
Commerce MO	River Ridge Winery	573-264-3712	850 County Rd 321
Eureka MO	Six Flags St Louis	636-938-4800	I-44 & Six Flag Rd
Florida MO	Mark Twain Birthplace State Historical Site	573-565-3449	37352 Shrine Road
Fulton MO	Auto World Museum	573-642-2080	200 Peacock Drive
Grafton IL	Piasa Winery	618-786-WINE	211 West Main St
Hannibal MO	Mark Twain Riverboat	573-221-3222	Center Street Landing
Hermann MO	Adam Puchta Winery	573-486-5596	1947 Frene Creek Road
Hermann MO	Hermannhof Vineyards	800-393-0100	330 E First Street/H 100
Hermann MO	Stone Hill Winery	800-909-WINE	1110 Stone Hill Highway
Holts Summit MO	Summit Lake Winery	573-896-9966	1707 South Summit Dr
Independence MO	Harry S. Truman Farm Home	816-254-2720	223 North Main Street
Jefferson City MO	Missouri Veterinary Museum	573-636-8737	2500 Country Club Drive
Jefferson City MO	Native Stone Vineyard and Bull Rock Brewery	573-584-8600	4301 Native Stone Rd
Kansas City MO	Country Club Plaza	816-561-3456	310 Ward Pkwy
Kansas City MO	Walk and Tour Wesport	816-561-1821	4000 Baltimore
Lebanon MO	Factory Stores of America	417-588-4142	2020 Evergreen Parkway
Lees Summit MO	Stonehaus Farm Winery	816-554-8800	24607 NE Colburn Rd
Lone Jack MO	Bynum Winery	816-566-2240	13520 South Sam Moore Rd
Mound City MO	Squaw Creek National Wildlife Refuge	660-442-3187	H 159S
Osage Beach MO	Blue Moon Marina, Inc	573-348-3178	5395 Bruce Lane
Osage Beach MO	Osage Premium Outlets	573-348-2065	4540 H 54
Park Hills MO	Missouri Mines State Historic Site	573-431-6226	75 H 32
Puxico MO	Mingo National Wildlife Refuge	573-222-3589	24279 H 51
Red Bud IL	Lau-Nae Winery	618-282-9463	1522 State Route 3
Republic MO	Wilson's Creek National Battlefield	417-732-2662 ext. 227	6424 W Farm Road 182/Elm Street
Springfield MO	Annual Dog Swim	417-564-1049	1300 S Campbell Ave
Springfield MO	Bark in the Park	417-564-1049	South Lone Pine Avenue
Springfield MO	Dog Fest at Chesterfield Family Center Park	417-564-1049	2511 W Republic Road
Springfield MO	Fantastic Caverns	417-833-2010	4872 N Farm Rd 125
Springfield MO	Japanese Stroll Garden	417-864-1049	2400 S Scenic Avenue
St Charles MO	Lewis and Clark Boat House and Nature Center	636-947-3199	1050 Riverside Drive
St James MO	Ferrigno Winery	573-265-7742	17301 State Route B
St James MO	Heinrichhaus Vineyards and Winery	573-265-5000	18500 State Route U
St James MO	Meremec Vineyards	877-216-WINE	600 State Road Rte B
St Joseph MO	Pony Express National Memorial	816-279-5059	914 Penn Street
St Louis MO	Gateway Riverboat Cruises	314-621-4040	800 N. First St.
St Louis MO	Laclede's Landing Self Guided Walking tour	314-241-5875	Laclede's Landing Blvd
St Louis MO	Laumeier Sculpture Park	314-821-1209	12580 Rott Road
St Louis MO	Museum of Transportation	314-965-7998	3015 Barrett Station Rd
St Louis MO	The American Kennel Club Museum of the Dog	314-821-3647	1721 S Mason Road
St Louis MO	The Boathouse in Forest Park	314-367-2224	6101 Government Dr
St Louis MO	Ulysses S. Grant National Historical Site	314-842-3298	7400 Grant Rd
Ste Genevieve MO	Cave Vineyard	573-543-5284	21124 Cave Rd
Ste Genevieve MO	Chaumette Vineyards and Winery	573-747-1000	24345 State Route WW
Steelville MO	Peaceful Bend Vineyard	573-775-3000	1942 Hwy T
Stover MO	Grey Bear Vineyards	573-377-4313	25992 Hwy T
Sumner MO	Swan Lake National Wildlife Refuge	660-856-3323	16194 Swan Lake Avenue
University City MO	St. Louis Walk of Fame	314-727-7827	Delmar Boulevard

Washington MO	La Dolce Vita Vineyard and Winery	636-239-0399	72 Forest Hills Drive
Waterloo IL	Schorr Lake Vineyards	618-939-3174	1032 S Library St
Wellington MO	New Oak Vineyards	816-240-2311	11644 Flourney School Rd

Montana

Anaconda MT	Cable Mine Ghost Town	406-563-3357	H 10A/H 1
Big Sky MT	The Historic Crail Ranch	406-995-2160	2110 Spotted Elk Road
Bigfork MT	Pointer Scenic Cruises	406-837-5617	452 Grand Drive
Billings MT	Billings Trolley and Bus Company	406-252-1778	1509 Rosebud Lane
Bozeman MT	Bohart Ranch Cross Country Ski Center	406-586-9070	16620 Bridger Canyon Road/H 86
Browning MT	Camp Disappointment	406-338-4015	H 2
Helena MT	Rimini Ghost Town	406-442-4120	Rimini Road
Livingston MT	Bark in the Park	406-222-2111	3 Business Park Road
Nevada City MT	Nevada City Ghost Town	406-843-5247	H 287
Virginia City MT	Historic Tour Company	406-843-5421	Wallace Street/H 287
Virginia City MT	Virginia City Ghost Town	406-843-5247	H 287
Virginia City MT	Virginia City Overland Stagecoach	406-843-5200	Wallace Street/H 287

Nebraska

Alliance NE	Dobby's Frontier Town	308-762-4321	320 E 25th Street
Blair NE	Black Elk/Neihardt Park	402-533-4455	College Drive
Comstock NE	Second Wind Ranch	800-658-4443	H 21C
Elm Creek NE	Chevyland U.S.A. Auto Museum	308-856-4208	7245 Buffalo Creek Road
Fairbury NE	McDowell's Tomb "Magic Etched in Stone"	402-729-3000	566th Avenue
Fremont NE	Fremont and Elkhorn Valley Railroad and Nebraska Railroad Museum	402-727-0615	1835 N Somers Avenue
Gering NE	Farm and Ranch Museum	308-436-1989	H 92
Gering NE	Robidoux Pass and Robidoux Trading Post	308-436-6886	Carter Canyon Road
Grand Island NE	Stolley Park	308-385-5444	Stolley Park Road
Grand Island NE	Stuhr Museum of the Prairie Pioneer	308-385-5316	3133 W H 34
Gretna NE	Nebraska Crossings Outlet Stores	402-332-4940	14333 S H 31
Kearney NE	Apple Acres	308-893-2845	7460 W 100th Street
Kearney NE	Great Platte River Road Archway	877-511-ARCH (2724)	3060 E 1st Street
Lexington NE	Heartland Museum of Military Vehicles	308-324-6329	606 Heartland Road
Lexington NE	Mac's Creek Vineyards and Winery	308-324-0440	43315 Road 757
Lincoln NE	Deer Springs Winery	402-327-8738	16255 Adams Street
Lincoln NE	Lester F Larsen Tractor Test and Power Museum	402-472-8389	35th and Fair Streets
Lincoln NE	Veterans Memorial Garden	402-441-7847	3200 Veterans Memorial Drive
Lynch NE	Old Baldy - The Tower	402-569-3143	Off H 12
Macy NE	Blackbird Scenic Overlook	402-837-5391	H 75
Mitchell NE	Prairie Vine Vineyard & Winery	308-623-2955	1463 17th Avenue
Nebraska City NE	Arbor Day Farm	402-873-8733	2700 Sylvan Road
Nebraska City NE	Arbor Lodge State Historical Park and Arboretum	402-873-7222	2600 Arbor Avenue
Nebraska City NE	Factory Stores of America	402-873-7727	1001 H 2
Nebraska City NE	Kimmel Orchard and Vineyard	402-873-5293	5995 G Road
Neligh NE	Antelope County Pioneer Jail Museum	402-887-5046	509 L Street
North Platte NE	Bailey Railroad Yard and Golden Spike Tower and Visitor Center	308-660-3776	1249 N Homestead Road
Omaha NE	Gerald R Ford Birthsite and Gardens	402-444-5955	3202 Woolworth Avenue
Omaha NE	Heartland of America Park and Fountain	402-444-5900	8th and Douglas Streets
Omaha NE	Joslyn Castle	402-595-2199	3902 Davenport Street
Omaha NE	Lewis and Clark National Historic Trail	402-661-1804	601 Riverfront Drive
Omaha NE	Mormon Trail Center at Historic Winter Quarters	402-453-9372	3215 State Street
Omaha NE	Old Market Shopping District	402-346-4445	Farnam to Jackson Streets/10th to 13th Streets
Omaha NE	One Pacific Place	402-399-8049	103rd and Pacific Street
Pawnee City NE	SchillingBridge Winery and Microbrewery	402-852-2400	62193 710th Road
Raymond NE	James Arthur Vineyards	402-783-5255	2001 W Raymond Rd
Scotia NE	Happy Jack Peak and Chalk Mine	308-245-3276	NE H 11
Springfield NE	Soaring Wings Vineyard	402-253-2479	17111 S 138th Street
Trenton NE	Massacre Canyon Monument and Visitor Center	308-539-1736	H 34
Winnebago NE	Honoring-the-Clans Sculpture Garden and Cultural Plaza	402-846-5353	Ho-Chunk Plaza

Nevada

Beatty NV	Rhyolite Ghost Town	760-786-3200	off Highway 374
Henderson NV	District at Green Valley Ranch	702-564-8595	2240 Village Walk Drive
Las Vegas NV	Camp Bow Wow	702-255-2267	5175 S Valley View Blvd
Las Vegas NV	Historic Spring Mountain Ranch	702-875-4141	State Route 159
Las Vegas NV	Las Vegas Strip Walking Tour		3300-3900 Las Vegas Blvd.
Las Vegas NV	Old Las Vegas Mormon Fort	702-486-3511	500 E Washington Ave

Las Vegas NV	Strut Your Mutt	702-455-8264	5800 E Flamingo/H 592
Tonopah NV	Tonopah Historic Mining Park	775-482-9274	520 McCulloch Avenue
Virginia City NV	Virginia & Truckee Railroad Co.	775-847-0380	565 S. K Street
Virginia City NV	Virginia City	775-847-0311	Hwy 341

New Hampshire

Center Conway NH	Saco Bound Canoe Rental	603-356-5251	2561 E Main Street
Concord NH	Concord Downtown Shopping District	603-226-2150	Main Streets and surrounding streets
Cornish NH	Saint-Gaudens National Historic Site	603-675-2175	139 Saint-Gaudens Road
Gorham NH	Mount Washinton Auto Road	603-466-3988	Mount Washinton Auto Road
Intervale NH	Hartmann Model Railroad Museum	603-356-9922	15 Town Hall Road/H 16
Portsmouth NH	Portsmouth Guided Walking Tours	603-436-3988	500 Market Street
Rye NH	Granite State Whale Watch	603-964-5545	PO Box 768
St-Lunaire-Griquet NH	L'Anse aux Meadows National Historic Site	709-623-5229	Viking Trail/H 436
Wolfeboro NH	Wet Wolfe Watercraft Rentals	603-271-3254	17 Bay Street

New Jersey

Atco NJ	Amalthea Cellars	856-768-8585	209 Vineyard Road
Atlantic City NJ	The Civil Rights Garden	609-347-0500	Martin Luther King Blvd.
Bayville NJ	Blackbeards Cave Entertainment Center	732-286-4414	136 H 9
Belvidere NJ	Four Sisters Winery	908-475-3671	783 H 519
Blairstown NJ	Double D Guest Ranch	908-459-9044	81 Mount Hermon Road
Bridgeton NJ	Dutch Neck Village	856-451-2188	97 Trench Road
Brielle NJ	Salt Water Safari-Treasure Island	732-528-9248	201 Union Lane
Cape May NJ	Cape May Whale Watcher	609-884-5445	2nd Avenue & Wilson Drive
Cape May NJ	Cape May Winery and Vineyard	609-884-1169	711 Town Bank Road
Cape May NJ	Historic Cold Spring Village	609-898-2300	720 H 9S
Cape May NJ	Miss Chris Marina	609-884-3351	1218 Wilson Drive
Chatsworth NJ	Mick's Canoe and Kayak Rental	609-726-1380	3107 H 563
Chatsworth NJ	Pine Barrens Canoe Rental	609-726-1515	3260 H 563
Chester NJ	Alstede Farms	908-879-7189	84 H 513 (Old Route 24),
Cream Ridge NJ	Cream Ridge Winery	609-259-9797	145 H 539
Eatontown NJ	Bliss Price Arboretum and Wildlife Sanctuary	732-389-7621	North side of Wykcoff Road/H 537
Farmingdale NJ	Allaire Village	732-919-3500	4265 Atlantic Avenue
Flemington NJ	Liberty Village Premium Outlets	908-782-8550	One Church Street
Hamilton NJ	Sayen House and Gardens	609-890-3543	155 Hughes Drive
Hammonton NJ	Tomasello Winery	800-MMM-WINE (666-9463)	225 N White Horse Pike/H 30
Holmdel NJ	A. Casola Farms	732-332-1533	178 Hwy 34
Jackson NJ	Jackson Premium Outlets	732-833-0503	537 Monmouth Road
Jackson NJ	Rova Farm Resort	732-928-0928	120 Cassville Road
Lafayette NJ	Olde LaFayette Village Shopping Center	973-383-8323	75 H 15q
Lake Hopatcong NJ	Dow's Boat Rental	973-663 3820	145 Nolan's Point Rd
Landing NJ	Lakes End Marina	973-398-5707	91 Mount Arlington Blvd
Landisville NJ	Bellview Winery	856-697-7172	150 Atlantic Street
Manalapan NJ	Monmouth Battlefield State Park	732-462-9616	347 Freehold Road
Medford NJ	Lewis W Barton Arboretum at Medford Leas	609-654-3000	One Medford Leas Way
Millville NJ	Glasstown Arts District	800-887-4957	22 N High Street
Montague NJ	Westfall Winery	973-293-3428	141 Clove Road
Mount Laurel NJ	Rancocas Woods Village of Shops	856-235-0758	114 Creek Road
New Brunswick NJ	The Rutgers Gardens at Rutgers University	732-932-8451	112 Ryders Lane
Newark NJ	New Jersey Transit	973-491-7000	1 Penn Plaza E
North Cape May NJ	Turdo Vineyards and Winery	609-898-3424	3911 Bayshore Road
Ocean City NJ	Bay Cats	609-391-7960	316 Bay Avenue
Ogdensburg NJ	Sterling Hill Mining Museum	973-209-7212	30 Plant Street
Piscataway NJ	East Jersey Olde Towne Village	732-745-3030	1050 River Road
Princeton NJ	Morven Museum and Gardens	609-683-4495	55 Stockton Street
Princeton NJ	Princeton Canoe and Kayak Rental	609-452-2403	483 Alexander Street
Princeton NJ	Princeton University Campus	609-258-1766	Nassau Street
Richwood NJ	Heritage Vineyards of Richmond	856-589-4474	480 Mullica Hill Road
Ringoes NJ	Unionville Vineyards	908-788-0400	9 Rocktown Road
Ringwood NJ	Long Pond Ironworks Historic District	973-962-7031	1304 Sloatsburg Road, c/o Ringwood State Park
Robbinsville NJ	Silver Decoy Winery	609-371-6000	610 Perrineville Road
Rosenhayn NJ	Bisconte Farms	856-455-3405	350 Morton Avenue
Shamong NJ	Valenzano Winery	609-268-6731	1320 Old Indian Mills Road
Stone Harbor NJ	The Wetlands Institute	609-368-1211	1075 Stone Harbor Blvd
Trenton NJ	Trenton Battle Monument	609-737-0623	N Broad Street/H 206
West Orange NJ	Edison National Historic Site	973-736-0551	Main Street and Lakeside Avenue

New Mexico

Albuquerque NM	Albuquerque Museum's Historic Old Town Walking Tours	505-243-7255	2000 Mountain Road NW
Albuquerque NM	Doggie Dash and Dawdle	505-255-5523, ext. 105	1801 4th St NW # A

Albuquerque NM	New Mexico Ghost Tours	505-249-7827	303 Romero Street NW
Albuquerque NM	Petroglyph National Monument	505-899-0205	6001 Unser Boulevard NW
Aztec NM	Aztec Museum and Pioneer Village	505-334-9829	125 N Main Avenue
Belen NM	The Harvey House Museum	505-861-0581	104 North First Street
Cerrillos NM	Old Coal Mine Museum	505-438-3780	2846 H 14
Chimayo NM	High Road Market Place	505-351-1078	HC 64 Box 12/Santuario Drive
Espanola NM	Santa Fe Vineyards	505-753-8100	Route 1 Box 216A
Farmington NM	Four Corners Monument	928-871-6647	Navajo Reservation
Fort Sumner NM	Fort Sumner State Monument	505-355-2573	3647 Billy the Kid Road
Gallup NM	Gallup Cultural Center	505-863-4131	201 E H 66
Holloman AFB NM	White Sands National Monuments	505-679-2599	PO Box 1086
La Mesa NM	Stahmann Pecan Farms	505-526-8974	22505 H 28
La Union NM	LaVina Winery	505-882-7632	4201 South Highway 28
Las Cruces NM	Blue Teal Tasting Room	866-336-7360	1720 Avenida de Mesilla
Lincoln NM	Lincoln Historic Town		Highway 380
Madrid NM	Old Coal Mine Museum	505-473-0743	2846 Highway 14
Mesilla NM	The Shops at Mesilla	575-523-5561	Calle del Norte and various side streets
Mountainair NM	Salinas Pueblo Missions National Monument	505-847-2585	PO Box 517
Placitas NM	Anasazi Fields	505-867-3062	26 Camino de los Pueblos
Placitas NM	Sandia Man Cave	505-281-3304	Cibola National Forest
Roseburg NM	Shakespeare Ghost Town	505-542-9034	Ghost Town Road
Roswell NM	International UFO Museum & Research Center	505-625-9495	114 N. Main Street
Santa Fe NM	El Camino Real de Tierra Adentro National Historic Trail	505-988-6888	1100 Old Santa Fe Trail
Santa Fe NM	Galloping Galleries	505-988-7016	22B Stacy Rd
Santa Fe NM	Historic Walking Tour of Santa Fe	505-986-8388	San Francisco Street
Santa Fe NM	Old Spanish National Historic Trail	505-988-6888	1100 Old Santa Fe Trail
Santa Fe NM	Santa Fe National Historic Trail	505-988-6888	1100 Old Santa Fe Trail
Santa Fe NM	Santa Fe Premium Outlets	505-474-4000	8380 Cerrillos Rd Ste 412
Santa Fe NM	State Capitol Grounds	505-986-4589	491 Old Santa Fe Trail
Santa Fe NM	Trail of Tears National Historic Park	505-988-6888	1100 Old Santa Fe Trail
Socorro NM	Very Large Array (VLA) Radio Telescope	505-835-7000	U.S. Hwy 60
Steins NM	Steins Railroad Ghost Town	505-542-9791	Interstate 10, Exit 3
Tularosa NM	Tularosa Vineyards	505-585-2260	23 Coyote Canyon Rd
Velarde NM	Black Mesa Winery	800-852-6372	1502 State Hwy 68
Watrous NM	Fort Union National Monument	505-425-8025	Po Box 127

New York

Albany NY	Hudson River Way Pedestrian Bridge	518-434-2032	Broadway
Albany NY	Stuyvesant Plaza	518-482-8986	1475 Western Avenue
Alexandria Bay NY	Uncle Sam Boat Tours	315-482-2611	47 James Street
Aquebogue NY	Paumanok Vineyards	631-722-8800	1074 Main Road/H 25
Ballston Spa NY	Bliss Glad Farm	518-885-9314	129 Hop City Road
Barryville NY	Indian Head Canoes	800-874-2628	3883 H 97
Bellport NY	Outlets at Bellport	631-286-3872	Farber Drive
Bolton Landing NY	Lake George Kayak Company	518-644-9366	3 Boathouse Ln
Branchport NY	Hunt Country Vineyards	315-595-2812	4021 4021 Italy Hill Road
Bridgehampton NY	Hampton Classic Horse Show	631-537-3177	240 Snake Hollow Road
Brooklyn NY	New York City Boardwalks	212-NEW-YORK	Various
Buffalo NY	Theodore Roosevelt Inaugural National Historic Site	716-884-0095	641 Delaware Avenue
Central Valley NY	Woodbury Common Premium Outlets	845-928-4000	498 Red Apple Court
Clinton Corners NY	Clinton Vineyards	845-266-5372	450 Schultzville Road
Cutchogue NY	Bedell Cellars	631-734-7537	36225 Main Road/H 25
Cutchogue NY	Castello di Borghese Vineyard & Winery	631-734-5111	17150 H 48
Cutchogue NY	Peconic Bay Winery	631-734-7361	31320 Main Rd
Dundee NY	Woodbury Vineyards-Senaca Lake	866-331-9463	4141 State Route 14
Elmira NY	Walking Tour of Elmira	607-733-4924	353 Davis Street
Elmira NY	Woodlawn Cemetery - Mark Twain's Burial Site	607-732-0151	1200 Walnut Street
Flushing NY	New York Mets Dog Day at Shea		Shea Stadium
Fly Creek NY	Fly Creek Cider Mill and Orchard	607-547-9692	288 Goose Street
Forestville NY	Merritt Estate Winery	888-965-4800	2264 King Rd
Fort Montgomery NY	Fort Montgomery State Historical Site	845-446-2134 (Summer)	690 H 9W
Fredonia NY	Woodbury Vineyards	716-679-9463	3215 S Roberts Road
Gardiner NY	Whitecliff Vineyard	845-255-4613	331 McKinstry Road
Gardiner NY	Wright's Apple Farm	845-255-5300	699 H 208
Geneva NY	Roy's Marina	315-789-3094	4398 Clark's Point/H 14
Germantown NY	Clermont State Historic Site	518-537-4240	One Clermont Avenue
Hammondsport NY	North Country Kayak and Canoe Rentals	607-868-7456	16878 West Lake Road/H 54A
Herkimer NY	Herkimer Diamond Mine	800-562-0897	4601 H 28N
Howes Cave NY	Howe Caverns	518-296-8900	255 Discovery Drive
Hyde Park NY	Vanderbilt Mansion - FDR Homesite	800-337-8474	4079 Albany Post Road
Inlet NY	Mountainman Outdoor Supply Company	315-357-6672	221 H 28
Ithaca NY	Cornell Plantations	607-255-3020	1 Plantations Road

Dog-Friendly Attractions - Please always call ahead to make sure an establishment is still dog-friendly.

Ithaca NY	Tiohero Tours Boat Cruises	866-846-4376	435 Old Taughannock Blvd
Jamesport NY	Jamesport Vineyards	631-722-5256	1216 Main Road /H 25
Kinderhook NY	Martin Van Buren National Historic Site	518-758-9589	1013 Old Post Road
Kingston NY	Hudson River Maritime Museum	845-338-0071	50 Rondout Landing
Lake George NY	Lake George Plaza Factory Outlets Center	518-798-7234	H 9
Lockport NY	Lockport Cave & Underground Boat Ride	716-438-0174	2 Pine Street
Manhasset NY	Americana Manhasset	516-627-2277	2060 Northern Boulevard at Searingtown Road
Marlboro-on-Hudson NY	Benmarl Vineyards and Winery at Slate Hill	845-236-4265	156 Highland Avenue
Mattituck NY	Sherwood House Vineyards	631-298-1396	2600 Oregon Road
Montgomery NY	Pooch A Palooza		86 Grove Street
New York NY	Brooklyn Bridge Self-Guided Walk		Park Row
New York NY	Federal Hall National Memorial	212-825-6888	26 Wall Street
New York NY	General Grant National Monument	212-666-1640	Riverside Drive and 122nd St
New York NY	Horse & Carriage Rides		59th Street and Fifth Avenue
New York NY	NY's Long Island Rail Road	212-867-6149	Throughout Region
New York NY	NYC Dog Walking Tour	914-633-7397	various (see below)
New York NY	New York City Boardwalks	212-NEW-YORK	Various
New York NY	South Street Seaport	212-732-8257	South Street
New York NY	Statue of Liberty National Monument	212-363-3200	Liberty Island
New York NY	TV Broadcasts		various (see below)
New York NY	Theodore Roosevelt Birthplace National Historic Site	212-260-1616	28 East 20th Street
New York NY	Time Warner Center	212-823-6000	10 Columbus Circle
New York NY	Times Square Walking Tour	212-768-1560	1560 Broadway
New York NY	William Secord Gallery	212-249-0075	52 East 76th Street
Niagara Falls NY	Niagara Falls State Park	716-278-1796	Robert Moses Parkway
Old Chatham NY	Old Chatham Sheepherding Company	888-SHEEP-60 (743-3760)	155 Shaker Museum Road
Old Forge NY	Water Safari Enchanted Forest	315-369-6145	3138 H 28
Oyster Bay NY	Sagamore Hill Estate	516-922-4447	20 Sagamore Hill Road
Penn Yan NY	Prejean Winery	315-536-7524	2634 Route 14
Phoenicia NY	Phoenicia Library	845-688-7811	48 Main Street/H 214
Prattsville NY	Pratt Rock Park	518-299-3395	H 23
Red Hook NY	Alison Wines	845-758-6335	231 Pitcher Lane
Rhinebeck NY	Old Rhinebeck Aerodrome	845-752-3200	42 Old Stone Church Road
Riverhead NY	Tanger Outlet Center	631-369-2732	1770 W Main Street
Rochester NY	VRA Imperial Limousine, Inc.	800-303-6100	
Rome NY	Erie Canal Village	315-337-3999	5789 New London Road /H 46 & 49
Rome NY	Fort Stanwix National Monument	315-338-7730	112 E Park Street
Romulus NY	Buttonwoodgrove Winery	607-869-9760	5986 State Route 89
Sagaponack NY	Wolffer Estate Vineyard	631-537-5106	139 Sagg Road
Saranac NY	Adirondack Lakes and Trails Outfitters	518-891-7450	541 Lake Flower AvenueH 86
Saranac Lake NY	St Regis Canoe Outfitters	518-891-1838	73 Dorsey Street
Saratoga Springs NY	Downtown Saratoga Springs		Broadway Avenue/H 9/29/50 (and surrounding streets)
Saratoga Springs NY	Point Breeze Marina	518-587-3397	1459 H 9P
Saratoga Springs NY	Saratoga Boatworks	518-584-2628	549 Union Avenue
Saratoga Springs NY	Saratoga Horse and Carriage	518-584-8820	P. O. Box 5184
Saratoga Springs NY	The Inn at Saratoga Dog Days of Summer	518-583-1890	231 Broadway
Saratoga Springs NY	Yaddo Gardens	518-584-0746	H 9P/P. O. Box 395
Schuylerville NY	Saratoga Apple, Inc.	518-695-3131	1174 H 29
Seneca Falls NY	Montezuma National Wildlife Refuge	315-568-5987	3395 Route 5 and 20 East
Sheridan NY	Willow Creek Winery	716-934-9463	2627 Chapin Rd Box 54
Skaneateles NY	Skaneateles Historical Walking Tour	315-685-1360	The Creamery, 28 Hannum Street
Sleepy Hollow NY	Sleepy Hollow Cemetery	914-631-0081	540 N Broadway
Southold NY	Eagle's Neck Paddling Company	631-765-3502	49295 Main Road/ H25
Stamford NY	Catskill Scenic Trial	607-652-2821	Railroad Avenue and South Street
Tannersville NY	The Mountain Top Arboretum	518-589-3903	H 23C and Maude Adams Road
Tappan NY	The De Wint House, George Washington Historical Site	845-359-1359	20 Livingston Street
Victor NY	Ganondagan State Historic Site	585-742-1690	1488 H 444
Washingtonville NY	Brotherhood America's Oldest Winery	845-496-3661	100 Brotherhood Plaza Drive
Water Mill NY	Duck Walk Vineyards	631-726-7555	231 Montauk H
Waterloo NY	Waterloo Premium Outlets	315-539-1100	655 H 318
Westfield NY	Johnson Estate Winery	716-326-2191	8419 W Main Road
Westport NY	Westport Marina	800-626-0342	20 Washington Street
Williamsville NY	The Canine Rehabilitation Center of Western New York	716-634-0000	6551 Main St. Williamsville
Wilmington NY	Whiteface Mountain Veterans Memorial Highway	518-523-1655	5021 RT 86
Woodstock NY	Woodstock Byrdcliffe	845-679-2079	Upper Byrdcliffe Road
Youngstown NY	Old Fort Niagara	716-745-7611	Robert Moses Parkway North

North Carolina

Asheville NC	Asheville Historic Trolley Tour	888-667-3600	151 Haywood Street/Asheville Visitor Center
Asheville NC	Asheville Urban Trail	828-258-0710	2 South Pack Square (Pack Place)
Asheville NC	Biltmore Estate	800-624-1575	1 Approach Road

Dog-Friendly Attractions - Please always call ahead to make sure an establishment is still dog-friendly.

Asheville NC	Biltmore Village	888-561-5437	Biltmore Plaza
Asheville NC	Craggy Gardens	828-298-0398	Milepost 364 Blue Ridge Parkway
Asheville NC	Ghost Hunters of Asheville Tours	828-779-HUNT (4868)	1 Battery Park Avenue (Haywood Park Hotel)
Asheville NC	Grove Arcade Public Market	828-252-7799, ext.302	1 Page Avenue
Asheville NC	North Carolina Arboretum	828-665-2492	100 Fredrick
Atlantic Beach NC	Sea Water Marina	252-726-1637	400 Atlantic Beach Causeway
Beaufort NC	Beaufort Historic Site	252-728-5225	150 Turner Street
Beaufort NC	Good Fortune Sail Charters	252-241-6866	600 Front Street
Blowing Rock NC	Blowing Rock	828-295-7111	H 321 S
Blowing Rock NC	Tanger Shoppes on the Parkway	828-295-4444	H 321
Blowing Rock NC	Tweetsie Railroad	828-264-9061	300 Tweetsie Railroad Lane
Boone NC	Wahoo's Adventures	828-262-5774	H 321S
Boonville NC	RagApple Lassie Vineyards	336-367-6000	3724 RagApple Lassie Lane
Burlington NC	Burlington Outlet Village	336-227-2872	2839 Corporation Parkway
Canton NC	Old Pressley Sapphire Mine	828-648-6320	240 Pressley Mine Road
Chapel Hill NC	Historic Chapel Hill	919-942-7818	610 E Rosemary Street
Chapel Hill NC	The North Carolina Botanical Garden	919-962-0522	Old Mason Farm Road
Charlotte NC	Carolinas Aviation Museum	704-359-8442	Carolinas Aviation Museum
Charlotte NC	Carowinds Amusement Park	704-588-2600	14523 Carowinds
Charlotte NC	Carowinds Theme Park	803-548-5300	14523 Carowinds Park Road
Cherokee NC	Smoky Mountain Gold and Ruby Mine	828-497-6574	H 441 North
Corolla NC	Corolla Wild Horses	252-453-8002	1126 Old Schoolhouse Lane
Corolla NC	Currituck Beach Lighthouse	252-453-4939	H 12
Corolla NC	Rick's Jeep Adventures	252-489-4878	610 Currituck Clubhouse Drive
Corolla NC	Wild Horse Days	252-453-8002	Highway 12
Creswell NC	Somerset Place	252-797-4560	2572 Lake Shore Road
Creswell NC	The Davenport Homestead	252-793-3248	2637 Mt Tabor Road
Currie NC	Moores Creek Bridge	910-283-5591	40 Patriots Hall Drive
Dobson NC	Black Wolf Vineyards	336-374-2532	283 Vineyard Lane
Durham NC	Duke Homestead	919-477-5498	2828 Duke Homestead Road
Durham NC	Duke University	919-684-3701	Duke University Road
Durham NC	Durham Downtown Walking Tour	919-687-0288	101 East Morgan Street
Fayetteville NC	Fayetteville Technical Community College Campus	910-678-8400	2201 Hull Road
Flat Rock NC	Carl Sandburg Historical Park	828-693-4178	81 Carl Sandburg Lane
Fort Mill SC	Charlotte Knights-Dog Day Game	704-357-8071	Gold Hill Road (Exit 88 off I-77)
Four Oaks NC	Bentonville Battlefield State Historic Site	910-594-0789	5466 Harper House Road
Franklin NC	Gold City Gem Mine	828-369-3905	9410 Sylva Road
Graham NC	Benjamin Vineyards and Winery	336-376-1080	6516 Whitney Raod
Hatteras Island NC	Pea Island National Wildlife Refuge	252-987-2394	14500 H 12 @ MM #31
Hendersonville NC	Historic Johnson Farm	828-891-6585	3346 Hayward Road
High Point NC	Piedmont Environmental Center	336-883-8531	1220 Penny Road
Highlands NC	Highlands Botanical Garden	828-526-2602	930 Horse Cove Road
Highlands NC	Highlands Nature Center and Botanical Gardens	828-526-2623	930 Horse Cove Road
Jamestown NC	Mendenhall Plantation	33-454-3819	603 W Main Street
Jarvisburg NC	Sanctuary Vineyards:	252-491-2387	7005 Caratoke H/H 158
Jarvisburg NC	Weeping Radish Farm Brewery	252-491-5205	6810 Caratoke H/H 158
Kannapolis NC	Cannon Village	704-938-3200	200 West Avenue (Visitor Center)
Kannapolis NC	Dale Earnhardt Plaza and Statue	704-938-3200	Dale Earnhardt Blvd/H 3
Knotts Island NC	Moonrise Bay Vineyard	252-429-9463	134 Moonrise Bay Landing
Lake Toxaway NC	Lake Toxaway Marine	828-877-3155	15885 Rosman H/H 64/281
Linville NC	Grandfather Mountain	828-733-4337	near Blue Ridge Parkway
Little Switzerland NC	Emerald Village Mining Museum	828-ROK-MINE (765-6463)	331 McKinney Mine Road
Manteo NC	Fort Raleigh National Historic Site	252-473-5772	1401 National Park Drive
Manteo NC	Manteo Beaches	252-441-5508	N Virginia Dare Trail/H 12
Manteo NC	Outer Banks Air Charters	252-256-2322	400 Airport Road
Manteo NC	The Roanoke Marshes Lighthouse	252-475-1750	207 Queen Elizabeth Avenue
Manteo NC	Wright Brothers National Memorial	252-441-7430	1401 National Park Drive
Mebane NC	Winery at Iron Gate Farm	919-304-9463	2540 Lynch Store Road
Midland NC	Reed Gold Mine State Historic Site	704-721-4653	9621 Reed Mine Road
Mount Gilead NC	Town Creek Indian Mound	910-439-6802	509 Town Creek Mound Road
Nags Head NC	Tanger Outlet	252-441-5634	7100 S Croatan H/H 158
New Bern NC	Barnacle Bob's Boat and Jet Ski Rentals	252-634-4100	Sheraton Marina
New Bern NC	Heritage Walking Tours	800-437-5767	203 S Front Street
New Bern NC	On the Wind Sailing Cruises	252-322-5804	104 Marina Drive
Ocracoke NC	Cottage Ghost Tales and Murder Mysteries	252-928-6300	170 Howard Street
Ocracoke NC	Ghost Tours and Walking Tours	252-928-5541	170 Howard Street
Ocracoke NC	Ocracoke Pony Pen	252-473-2111	Hwy 12
Ocracoke NC	Ocracoke Sports Fishing Charters	252-928-4841	PO Box 429
Ocracoke NC	Restless Native Boat Rentals	252-928-1421	109 Lighthouse Road
Ocracoke Village NC	The Anchorage Inn Marina	252-928-6661	180 Irvin Garrish H/H 12
Pittsboro NC	Fearrington Village	919-542-2121	2000 Fearrington Village Center
Raleigh NC	Art Space	919-821-2723	201 E Davie Street
Raleigh NC	Cameron Village Shopping Center	919-821-1350	1900 Cameron Street
Raleigh NC	City Market	919-821-1350	Person and Martin Streets
Raleigh NC	Raleigh Little Theatre Rose Garden	919-821-4579	301 Pogue Street

Raleigh NC	The Raleigh Flea Market	919-899-FLEA (3532)	1025 Blue Ridge Road
Salem NC	Old Salem	336-721-7350	601 Old Salem Road
Sanford NC	House in the Horseshoe	910-947-2051	288 Alston House Road
Smithfield NC	Carolina Premium Outlets	919-989-8757	1025 Industrial Park Drive
Southern Pines NC	Weymouth Woods-Sandhills Nature Preserve	910-692-2167	1024 Ft. Bragg Road
Waynesboro VA	Blue Ridge Parkway Auto Tour	828-271-4779	Blue Ridge Parkway, Milepost 0
Weaverville NC	Vance Birthplace	828-645-6706	911 Reems Creek Rd.
Westfield NC	Hanging Rock River Trips	336-593-8283	3466 Moores Spring Road
Winnabow NC	Orton Plantation Gardens	910-371-6851	9149 Orton Road SE

North Dakota

Bismarck ND	Chief Lookings Earthlodge Village Interpretive Trail	701-222-6455	Burnt Boat Drive
Bismarck ND	George Bird Rotary Park Arboretum Trail	701-222-6455	Divide Avenue and College Drive
Churchs Ferry ND	Garden Dwellers Farm	701-351-2520	7th and Summit Streets
Dickinson ND	Crooked Crane Trail	701-456-2074	8th Street SW
Dickinson ND	Prairie Outpost Park	701-456-6225	200 Museum Drive
Dunseith ND	International Peace Garden	701-263-4390	RR 1, Box 116/H 3
Fargo ND	Celebrity Walk of Fame	701-282-3653	2001 44th Street S
Fargo ND	Fargo Air Museum	701-293-8043	1609 19th Avenue N/H 81
Fort Yates ND	Fort Yates Historical Site	701-222-4308	Standing Rock Avenue
Grand Forks ND	Japanese Gardens	701-746-2750	3300 11th Avenue South
Grand Forks ND	The Greenway/ Grand Forks Park District	701-746-2750	1210 7th Avenue S
Minot ND	Riverwalk of Minot	701-857-8206	1020 South Broadway
New Town ND	Crow Flies High Butte Overlook	701-627-4812	H 23
Riverdale ND	Misty the Mermaid	701-654-7636	300 2nd Street
Stanton ND	Knife River Indian Villages	701-745-3300	564 H 37
Valley City ND	Medicine Wheel Park	800-532-8541	Winter Show Drive
Valley City ND	Scenic Bridges Tour	701-845-1891	250 W Main Street/H 52
Williston ND	Missouri-Yellowstone Confluence Interpretive Center	701-572-9034	15349 39th Lane NW

Ohio

Canal Winchester OH	Blacklick Creek Greenways Trail	614-891-0700	7680 Wright Road
Chagrin Falls OH	Chagrin Falls Main Street	440-247-4470	Main Street
Chillicothe OH	Disc Golf Course - Great Seal State Park	740-663-2125	635 Rocky Road
Columbus OH	Polaris Fashion Place	614-846-1500	1500 Polaris Parkway
Coshocton OH	Historic Roscoe Village	740-622-9310	Hill Street
Groveport OH	Loop Trails	614-891-0700	3860 Bixby Road
Hilliard OH	Heritage Park, Multi-Use Trail	614-891-0700	7262 Hayden Run Road
Jeffersonville OH	Jeffersonville Outlet Mall	740-948-9090	8000 Factory Shops Blvd
Kirtland OH	Holden Arboretum	440-946-4400	9500 Sperry Road
Lancaster OH	Farmers Flea Market	740-974-7991	Route 33, 10 mi. s. of Lancaster
Lancaster OH	Historic Lancaster	740-653-8251	1 North Broad Street
Logan OH	Hocking Hills Canoe Livery	740-385-0523	12789 St. Rt. 664 South
Logan OH	Hocking Valley Canoe Livery	740-385-8685	31251 Chieftain Drive
Logan OH	Lake Logan Boat Rentals	740-380-9233	30443 Lake Logan Road
Nelsonville OH	Robbins Crossing at Hocking College	740-753-3591	3301 Hocking Parkway
Port Clinton OH	African Safari Wildlife Park	800-521-2660	267 Lightner Road
Put-in-Bay OH	Put-in-Bay Tour Train	419-285-4855	Box 190
Rockbridge OH	Barnebey Pet Trail	614-891-0700	185 Clear Creek Road
Rockbridge OH	Old Man River Canoe Livery	866-380-0510	10653 Jackson Street
Sandusky OH	Cedar Point Amusement Park Kennels	419-627-2350	One Cedar Point Drive
Westerville OH	Goldenrod Pet Trail	614-891-0700	4265 E Dublin-Granville Road
Worthington OH	Olde Worthington		High Street (near SR 161)
Worthington OH	Pooch Parade	614-473-9244	High St and SR 161
Worthington OH	Worthington Farmers Market	614-891-6293	High Street
Xenia OH	Doggie Dash ?N Splash Fest	937-562-7440	Fairground Recreation Center, 210 Fairground Road

Oklahoma

Anadarko OK	Woods and Water Winery	580-588-2515	Route 3 Box 160 C
Bartlesville OK	Woolaroc Museum and Wildlife Preserve	918-336-0307	H 123
Beggs OK	Natura Vineyards and Winery	918-756-9463	8500 North 245 Rd
Big Cabin OK	Cabin Creek Vineyards and Winery	918-783-5218	32153 South 4360 Rd
Bristow OK	Nuyaka Creek Winery	918-756-8485	35230 South 177th West Ave
Caney OK	Cimarron Cellars Winery	580-889-5997	1280 S. US Highway 69/75
Cheyenne OK	Washita Battlefield National Historic Site	580-497-2742	RR 1 Box 55A/On H 47A
Claremore OK	Claremore Lake Park	918-341-1238	E Blue Starr Drive
Claremore OK	The Rogers State University Conservation Education Reserve	918-341-4147	1701 W Will Rogers Blvd/H 88
Davis OK	Arbuckle Wilderness	580-369-3383	Route 1 Box 63
Elk City OK	Old Town Museum Complex	580-225-6266	2717 W 3rd Street
Enid OK	Railroad Museum of Oklahoma	580-233-3051	702 N Washington Street

Fort Gibson OK	Fort Gibson Historic Site	918-478-4088	907 N Garrison/H 80
Fort Sill OK	Fort Sill National Historic Landmark & Missile Park	580-442-5123	437 Quanah Road
Grove OK	Har-Ber Village	918-786-6446	4404 W 20th Street
Grove OK	Lendonwood Gardens	918-786-2938	Harbor Road
Heavener OK	Heavener Runestone State Park	918-653-2241	18365 Runestone Road
Jet OK	Salt Plains National Wildlife Refuge	580-626-4794	Route 1 Box 76
Lexington OK	Canadian River Vineyards and Winery	405-872-5565	7050 Slaughterville Rd
Luther OK	Tres Suenos Vineyards and Winery	405-277-7089	19691 East Charter Oak Rd
Norman OK	The University of Oklahoma Campus	405-325-2151	1000 Asp Avenue
Oklahoma City OK	Bricktown Canal and Entertainment District	405-236-8666	West Reno and N Hudson Avenues
Oklahoma City OK	Casady Square Shopping Center	405-843-7474	W Britton Road and N Pennsylvania Avenue
Oklahoma City OK	Stockyard City	405-235-8675	1305 S Agnew Avenue
Oklahoma City OK	Water Taxi on the Canal	405-234-8294	115 E California Avenue, Suite 300
Oologah OK	Will Rogers Birthplace Ranch	918-275-4201	9501 E 380 Road
Pawnee OK	Pawnee Bill's Wild West Show	918-762-2513	1141 Pawnee Bill Road
Perry OK	Cherokee Strip Museum	580-336-2405	2617 W Fir Avenue
Ringwood OK	Indian Creek Village Winery	580-883-4919	RR 2 Box 174
Tulsa OK	Gardens at Gilcrease Museum	918-596-2700	1400 Gilcrease Museum Road
Tulsa OK	Tulsa Garden Center	918-746-5125	2435 S Peoria Avenue
Tulsa OK	Utica Square Shopping Center	918-742-5531	1579 E 21st Street S

Oregon

Astoria OR	Fort Astoria	503-325-6311	15th and Exchange Streets
Beaverton OR	Cooper Mountain Vineyards	503-649-0027	9480 SW Grabhorn Road
Carlton OR	Anne Amie Vineyards	503-864-2991	6580 NE Mineral Springs Road
Carson OR	Wind River Experimental Forest/Arboretum	509-427-3200	1262 Hemlock Road
Coos Bay OR	Cape Arago Lighthouse		Chief's Island
Coos Bay OR	New Carissa Shipwreck	800-547-7842	North Spit Beach
Depoe Bay OR	Dockside Charters Whale Watching	541-765-2445	PO Box 1308/ Coast Guard Place
Dundee OR	Erath Winery	503-538-3318	9409 NE Worden Hill Road
Dundee OR	Sokol Blosser Winery	503-864-2282	5000 Sokol Blosser Lane
Eugene OR	King Estate Winery	541-942-9874	80854 Territorial Road
Gaston OR	Elk Cove Vineyards	503-985-7760	27751 NW Olson Road
Haines OR	Eastern Oregon Museum	541-856-3380	610 3rd Street
Hillsboro OR	Oak Knoll Winery	530-648-8198	29700 SW Burkhalter Rd.
Hood River OR	Pheasant Valley Vineyard and Winery	541-387-3040	3890 Acree Drive
Monmouth OR	Airlie Winery	503-838-6013	15305 Dunn Forest Road
Newberg OR	Rex Hill Vineyards	800-739-4455	30835 N H 99W
Newport OR	Agate Beach Golf Course	541-265-7331	4100 N Coast H/H 101
Port Orford OR	Prehistoric Gardens	541-332-4463	36848 H 101S
Portland OR	Crystal Springs Rhododendron Garden	503-771-8386	SE 28th Avenue and Woodstock
Portland OR	Dogtoberfest	503-228-7281	915 SE Hawthorne Blvd
Portland OR	Hoyt Arboretum	503-865-8733	4000 SW Fairview Blvd
Portland OR	Oaks Park Amusement Park	503-233-5777	7100 SE Oaks Parkway
Portland OR	Peninsula Rose Garden	503-823-7529	700 N Portland Blvd
Portland OR	Portland Farmers' Markets	503-241-0032	240 N Broadway, Suite 129
Portland OR	Portland Saturday Market	503-222-6072	108 West Burnside
Portland OR	Portland Walking Tours	503-774-4522	SW Broadway and Salmon
Portland OR	The Grotto	503-254-7371	NE 85th and Sandy Blvd.
Redmond OR	Peterson Rock Gardens	541-382-5574	7930 SW 77th Street
Roseburg OR	Hillcrest Vineyards	541-673-3709	240 Vineyard Lane
Roseburg OR	Spangle Vineyards	541-679-9654	491 Winery Lane
Rouge River OR	Rouge River Palmerton Arboretum	541-582-4401	W Evans Creek Road
Salem OR	Ankeny Vineyard Winery	503-378-1498	2565 Riverside Road S
Salem OR	Reed Opera House	503-391-4481	189 Liberty Street NE
Silverton OR	The Oregon Garden	877-674-2733	879 W Main Street
Sunriver OR	Sunriver Nature Center	541-593-4394	57245 River Road
The Dalles OR	Dalles Farmer Market	541-490-6420	City Park, Union and E 5th Street
Winston OR	Wildlife Safari Kennels	541-679-6761	1790 Safari Road

Puerto Rico

Jayuya PR	Enscribed Rock	800-866-7827	H 144, Km 7.8 (dept. of tourism)
Mayaguez PR	USDA-ARS Tropical Agriculture Research Station	787-831-3435	2200 Pedro Albizu Campos Avenue
San Juan PR	Castillo de San Cristobal	787-729-6777	Calle Norzagaray
San Juan PR	Castillo de San Felipe del Morro	787-729-6777	Calle del Morro
San Juan PR	Old San Juan Walking Tour	787-750-0000	
San Juan PR	Walking Tour of Old San Juan	787-605-9060	P.O. Box 9021692
Utado PR	Caguana Indian Ceremonial Park	787-894-7325	H 11 at km 12.3

Pennsylvania

Allenwood PA	Reptiland	570-538-1869	18628 H 15
Annville PA	Union Canal Canoe Rental	717-838-9580	1929 Blacks Bridge Road
Apollo PA	Roaring Run Natural Area	724-238-1200	end of Canal Road

Dog-Friendly Attractions - Please always call ahead to make sure an establishment is still dog-friendly.

Ashland PA	Ashland Coal Mine and Steam Train	570-325-3850	19th and Oak Streets
Beaver Falls PA	Air Heritage Museum	724-843-2820	35 Piper Street
Bedford PA	Old Bedford Village	800-238-4347	220 Sawblade Road
Bethlehem PA	Burnside Plantation	610-868-5044	1461 Schoenersville Road
Bethlehem PA	Colonial Industrial Quarter	610-691-6055	459 Old York Road
Bird-in-hand PA	Aaron and Jessica's Buggy Rides	717-768-8828	3121A Old Philadelphia Pike/H 340
Bird-in-hand PA	Abe's Buggy Rides	717-392-1794	2596 Old Philadelphia Pike
Birdsboro PA	Daniel Boone Homestead	610-582-4900	400 Daniel Boone Road
Breinigsville PA	Clover Hill Winery	610-395-2468	9850 Newtown Road
Chadds Ford PA	Brandywine Battlefield Historic Site	610-459-3342	H 1
Chadds Ford PA	Glen Eagle Square	610-558-8000	H 202 at Springhill Road
Chalkhill PA	Christian W. Klay Winery	724-439-3424	412 Fayette Spring Road
Dingmans Ferry PA	Kittatinny Canoes	800-356-2852	2130 H 739
Easton PA	Moyer Aviation	610-258-0473	3800 Sullivan Trail
Elverson PA	Hopewell Furnace National Historic Site	610-582-8773	2 Mark Bird Lane
Elysburg PA	Knoebel's Amusement Park	800-ITS-4FUN	Route 487
Farmington PA	Fort Necessity National Battlefield	724-329-5805	1 Washington Parkway
Gallitzin PA	Allegheny Portage Railroad National Heritage Site	814-886-6150	110 Federal Park Road/H 22
Gettysburg PA	Eisenhower National Historic Site	717-338-9114	97 Taneytown Road
Gettysburg PA	Gettysburg National Military Park	717-334-1124	
Gettysburg PA	Gettysburg Village	717-337-9705	1863 Gettysburg Village Drive
Glen Mills PA	Newlin Grist Mill	610-459-2359	219 S Cheyney Road
Grove City PA	Prime Outlets at Grove City	724-748-4770	1911 Leesburg Grove City Road/H 208
Harrisburg PA	Pennsylvania State Capitol Complex	717-787-6810	N 3rd and State Streets
Hermitage PA	Avenue of the Flags, Hillcrest Memorial Park	724-346-3818	2619 East State Street
Hershey PA	Hersheypark Amusement Park Kennels	800-HERSHEY (437-7439)	100 W Hershey Park Drive
Hershey PA	The Outlets at Hershey	717-520-1236	150 Hershey Park Drive
Intercourse PA	Carriage Rides at Kitchen Kettle Village	717-768-8261	Route 340
Intercourse PA	Kitchen Kettle Village	717-768-8261	3529 Old Philadelphia Pike
Jeannette PA	Bushy Run Battlefield	724-527-5584	151 Bushy Field Road
Jim Thorpe PA	The Switch Back Trail	570-325-8255	Railroad Station
King of Prussia PA	Valley Forge National Historical Park	610-783-1077	1400 North Outer Line Drive
Kutztown PA	Dutch Hex Tour	800-HEX-TOUR (439-8687)	Old Route 22
Lahaska PA	Peddler's Village	215-794-4000	81 Peddler Village Road
Lahaska PA	Penn's Purchase Factory Outlet Village	215-794-2232	H 202
Lancaster PA	Tanger Outlet	717-392-7260	311 Stanley K. Tanger Blvd
Lancaster PA	The Amish Farm and House	717-394-6185	2395 Covered Bridge Drive (for GPS: 2395 Lincoln H E)
Lancaster PA	Wheatland - The Estate of President James Buchanan	717-392-8721	1120 Marietta Avenue
New Castle PA	Harlansburg Station Transportation Museum	724-652-9002	424 Old Route 19
North East PA	Penn Shore Vineyards	814-725-8688	10225 E Lake Road
North East PA	Winery at Mazza	814-725-0695	11510 E Lake Road
Philadelphia PA	Ben Franklin Bridge		5th St and Vine St
Philadelphia PA	Ben Franklin's Grave		5th St and Arch St
Philadelphia PA	Edgar Allan Poe National Historic Site	215-597-8780	532 N Seventh Street
Philadelphia PA	Gloria Dei Church National Historic Site	215-389-1513	Columbus Blvd and Christian Street
Philadelphia PA	Horse and Carriage Rides at Independence Mall		At the Liberty Bell Pavilion
Philadelphia PA	Independence National Historic Park		Market St and 5th St
Philadelphia PA	South Street District		South St and 2nd Ave
Philadelphia PA	Thaddeus Kosciuszko National Memorial	215-597-9618	301 Pine Street
Pittsburgh PA	Station Square	412-261-2811	100 W Station Square Drive
Point Marion PA	Friendship Hill National Historic Site	724-725-9190	223 New Geneva Road
Scranton PA	Steamtown National Historic Site	570-340-5206	150 South Washington Avenue
Smicksburg PA	Windgate Vineyards	814-257-8797	1998 Hemlock Acres Road
Somerset PA	Georgian Place	814-443-3818	317 Georgian Place
Somerset PA	Glades Pike Winery	814-445-3753	2208 Glades Pike/H 31
Tannersville PA	The Crossing Premium Outlets	570-629-4650	1000 H 611
Titusville PA	Oil Creek and Titusville Railroad	814-676-1733	409 S Perry Street
Upper Black Eddy PA	Bucks County Trolley Company	610-982-5200	1469 River Road/H 32
Washington Crossing PA	Washington Crossing Historical Park	215-493-4076	1112 River Road
Weatherly PA	Eckleys Miners Village	570-636-2070	2 Eckley Main Street
Wellsboro PA	Pine Creek Outfitters and Rentals	570-724-3003	5142 H 6
West Chester PA	Northbrook Canoe Company	610-793-2279	1810 Beagle Road
Wrightstown PA	Carousel Village at Indian Walk	215-598-0707	591 Durham Road/H 413
Wyomissing PA	VF Outlets Village	610-378-0408	801 Hill Avenue

Rhode Island

Little Compton RI	Sakonnet Vineyards	401-635-8486	162 W Main Road
Newport RI	Cliff Walk	401-421-5055	Memorial Blvd/H 138A
Newport RI	Gansett Cruises	401-787-4438	Private Dock at the Inn on Long Wharf, 142 Long Wharf,
Newport RI	Newport Historical Society	401-846-0813	82 Touro Street
Newport RI	Ten-Mile Drive		Ocean Avenue
Newport RI	Touro Synagogue National Historic Site	401-847-4794	85 Touro Street

Portsmouth RI	Greenvale Vineyard	401-847-3777	582 Wapping Road
Providence RI	New England Fast Ferry	617-748-1428	8 Point Street
Providence RI	Providence Preservation Society Walking Tours	401-831-7440	21 Meeting Street
Providence RI	Roger Williams National Memorial	401-521-7266	282 North Main Street
Providence RI	Walking Tours of Providence	401-331-8575	52 Power Street
Woonsocket RI	Blackstone River Valley National Heritage Corridor	401-762-0250	One Depot Square

South Carolina

Aiken SC	Hopeland Gardens	803-642-7630	135 Dupree Place
Beech Island SC	Redcliffe Plantation State Historic Site	803-827-1473	181 Redcliffe Road
Blacksburg SC	Overmountain Victory National Historic Trail	864-936-3477	2635 Park Road
Bluffton SC	Tanger Factory Outlet Center	843-689-6767	1414 Fording Island Rd # B9
Cayce SC	Adventure Carolina	803-796-4505	1107 State Street/H 2
Charleston SC	Battery and White Point Gardens	843-853-8000	East Battery Street and Murray Blvd.
Charleston SC	Carolina Polo and Carriage Company	843-577-6767	181 Church St (In lobby of Doubletree Hotel) and 16 Hayne St
Charleston SC	Charleston Strolls	843-766-2080	115 Meeting Street
Charleston SC	Magnolia Plantation and Gardens	843-571-1266	3550 Ashley River Road
Charleston SC	Palmetto Carriage Works	843-723-8145	40 N Market Street
Charleston SC	Taylored Tours	888-449-TOUR (8687)	375 Meeting Street/H 52
Charleston SC	The Original Charleston Walks and Ghost Tours	843-577-3800	58 1/2 Broad Street
Clemson SC	South Carolina Botanical Garden	864-656-3405	Perimeter Road
Clinton SC	Musgrove Mill State Historic Site	864-938-0100	398 State Park Road
Columbia SC	African-American Historical Museum	803-734-2430	1100 Gervais Street
Columbia SC	Historic Columbia Foundation Tours	803-252-1770, ext. 24	Main Street
Columbia SC	River Runner Outdoor Center	803-771-0353	905 Gervais Street/H 1/378
Dillon SC	South of the Border	843-774-2411	H 301 N
Gaffney SC	Cowpens National Battlefield	864-461-2828	4001 Chesnee H/H 11
Gaffney SC	Prime Outlets	864-902-9900	1 Factory Shops Blvd
Georgetown SC	Captain Sandy's Tours	843-527-4106	343 Ida Drive
Georgetown SC	Swamp Fox Tours	843-527-1112	600 Front Street
Greenwood SC	Emerald Farm	864-223-2247	409 Emerald Farm Road
Hartsville SC	Kalmia Gardens	843-383-8145	1624 W Carolina Avenue/H 151
Hilton Head SC	Calibogue Cruises to Daufuskie Island	843-342-8687	Broad Creek Marina, Mathews Dr.
Hilton Head SC	The Mall at Shelter Cove	843-686-3090	24 Shelter Cove Lane
Hilton Head Island SC	Adventure Cruises Inc	843-785-4558	1 Shelter Cove Lane
Hilton Head Island SC	Runaway Charters	843-689-2628 or cell # 843-384-6511	Hudson Road (Charley's Crab Restaurant Docks)
Hilton Head Island SC	Vagabond Cruise	843-342-2345	149 Lighthouse Road
Hopkins SC	Congaree Swamp Canoe Tours	803-776-4396	100 National Park Road
Isle of Palms SC	Barrier Island Ecotours	843-886-5000	50 41st Avenue
Little River SC	La Belle Amie Vineyard	843-399-9463	1120 St. Joseph Road
Moncks Corner SC	Cypress Gardens	843-553-0515	3030 Cypress Gardens Road/H 9
Mount Pleasant SC	Boone Hall Plantation and Gardens	843-571-1266	1235 Long Point Road
Mount Pleasant SC	Cap'n Richards ACE Basin Kayak Rentals	843-884-7684	514B Mill Street
Myrtle Beach SC	Hammock Shop Complex	843-237-9122	9600 N Kings H/H 17
North Myrtle Beach SC	Barefoot Landing	843-272-8349	4898 H 17S
Orangeburg SC	Edisto Memorial Gardens	803-533-6020	250 Riverside Drive SW
Pinopolis SC	Blackwater Adventures	843-761-1850	1944 Pinopolis Road/H 5
Rock Hill SC	Glencairn Garden	803-329-5620	725 Crest St
Sheldon SC	Oyotunji Village	843-846-8900	56 Bryant Lane
Sullivan Island SC	Fort Moultrie National Historic Site	843-883-3123	1214 Middle Street
Union SC	Rose Hill Plantation State Historic Site	864-427-5966	2677 Sardis Road
Wadmalaw Island SC	Bohicket Boat - Adventure and Tour Co.	843-559-3525	2789 Cherry Point Road
York SC	Windy Hill Orchard and Cider Mill	803-684-0690	1860 Black H/H 5

South Dakota

Aberdeen SD	Kuhnert Arboretum	605-626-7015	E Melgaard Road/H 19W
Columbia SD	Sand Lake National Wildlife Refuge	605-885-6320	39650 Sand Lake Drive
Crazy Horse SD	Crazy Horse Mountain Memorial	605-673-4681	12151 Avenue Of The Chiefs
Custer SD	The Flintstones Bedrock City Theme Park	605-673-4079	US Highways 16 and 385
Deadwood SD	Boondocks	605-578-1186	21559 H 385
Deadwood SD	Historic Downtown Deadwood	605-578-1876	Main Street
Edgemont SD	Centennial Trail	605-255-4515	Off H 385/Wind Cave National Park
Hill City SD	Black Hills Central Railroad	605-574-2222	222 Railroad Avenue
Hill City SD	Prairie Berry Winery	605-574-3898	23837 H 385, PO Box 8
Kadoka SD	Badlands Petrified Gardens	605-837-2448	23104 H 248
Keystone SD	Mt. Rushmore National Memorial	605-574-2523	13000 Highway 244
Kimball SD	SD Tractor Museum	605-778-6421	201 W Cemetery Road
Lead SD	Homestake Mining Company	605-584-3110	160 West Main Street/H 85
Lead SD	President's Park	605-584-9925	104 Galena Street

Mitchell SD	Corn Palace (Outside View Only)	605-995-8427	612 North Main Street
Mitchell SD	Mitchell Prehistoric Indian Village	605-996-5473	3200 Indian Village Road
Mitchell SD	Prehistoric Indian Village	605-995-1017	3200 Indian Village Road
Mobridge SD	Ft Leavenworth Monument	605-845-2387	W H 12
Mobridge SD	Sitting Bull Monument	605-845-2387	H 1806
Montrose SD	Porter Sculpture Park	605-853-2266	25700 451st Avenue
Murdo SD	1880 Town	605-344-2259	I-90 at exit 170
Murdo SD	Pioneer Auto Show	605-669-2691	I 90 & US 83
Piedmont SD	Petrified Forest of the Black Hills	605-787-4884	8220 Elk Creek Road
Pierre SD	Lewis and Clark National Historic Trail	605-773-3458	900 Governor's Drive (SD Cultural Heritage Center)
Pierre SD	Pierre Historic Homes Driving Tour	605-224-7361	800 W Dakota
Pierre SD	Pierre Loop Trail	605-773-7445	http://ci.pierre.sd.us/parks/trailmaps.shtm
Pierre SD	State Capitol Grounds	605-773-3765	500 E Capitol Avenue
Rapid City SD	Bear Country U.S.A.	605-343-2290	13820 South Highway 16
Rapid City SD	Berlin Wall	605-394-4175	In Memorial Park
Rapid City SD	Reptile Gardens	605-342-5873	Highway 16
Rapid City SD	South Dakota Air and Space Museum	605-385-5188	off I-90
Rapid City SD	Thunderhead Underground Falls	605-343-0081	10940 W. Highway 44
Sioux Falls SD	Gone to the Dogs Swim	605-367-8222	various sites
Sioux Falls SD	Great Bear Recreation Park	605-367-4309	2401 W 49th Street
Sioux Falls SD	Historic Downtown Sioux Falls	605-338-4009	Phillips Avenue
Sioux Falls SD	Self-Guided Historic Walking Tours	605-367-4210	200 W 6th Street and N Main (Old Court House)
Spearfish SD	Spearfish Canyon Scenic Byway	605-673-9200	MP 10.5 at Colorado Boulevard and Scenic Byway/H 14A
Yankton SD	Lewis and Clark Marina	605-665-3111	43527 Shore Drive

Tennessee

Antioch TN	4 Corners Boat Rentals	651-641-9523	4027 LaVergne Couchville Pike
Blountville TN	Tri-Cities Factory Stores of America	423-323-6866	354 Shadowtown Road
Chattanooga TN	Ruby Falls at Lookout Mountain	423-821-2544	1720 S Scenic H/H 148
Clarksville TN	Beachaven Vineyards & Winery	931-645-8867	1100 Dunlop Lane
Clarksville TN	DoggiePalooza	931-645-7476	1190 Cumberland Drive (H 48/13)
Crossville TN	Stonehaus Winery Inc	931-484-9463	2444 Genesis Rd # 103
Dover TN	Fort Donelson National Battlefield	931-232-5348	120 National Park Road
Dover TN	Fort Donelson National Cemetery	931-232-5706	PO Box 434
Fort Oglethorpe GA	Chickamauga and Chattanooga National Military Park	706-866-9241	3370 Lafayette Road
Franklin TN	Factory At Franklin	615-791-1777	230 Franklin Road/H 6/31
Franklin TN	Historic Carnton Plantation	615-794-0903	1345 Carnton Lane
Gatlinburg TN	Smoky Mountain Winery	865-436-7551	450 Cherry Street, Ste. #2
Gatlinburg TN	The Salt and Pepper Shaker Museum	888-778-1802	461 Brookside Village Way
Goodlettsville TN	Long Hollow Winery and Vineyards	615-859-5559	665 Long Hollow Pike/H 174
Grand Junction TN	National Bird Dog Museum	731-764-2058	505 H 57W
Greeneville TN	Andrew Johnson National Historic Site	423-638-3551	121 Monument Ave
Hampshire TN	Amber Falls Winery & Cellars	931-285-0088	794 Ridgetop Road
Jackson TN	Casey Jones Village	931-296-7700	56 Casey Jones Lane
Kingsport TN	Bays Mountain Nature Preserve	423-229-9447	853 Bays Mountain Park Road
Knoxville TN	Ijams Nature Center	865-577-4717	2915 Island Home Avenue
Knoxville TN	Marble Springs Historic Farmstead	865-573-5508	1220 W Governor John Sevier H/H 168
Lafayette TN	Red Barn Winery and Vineyard	615-688-6012	1805 Tanyard Road
Lakeland TN	Lakeland Factory Outlet Mall	901-386-3180	3536 Canada Road
Lebanon TN	Prime Outlets	615-444-0433	One Outlet Village Boulevard
Lebanon TN	Prime Outlets of Lebanon	615-444-0433	One Outlet Village Blvd
Lookout Mountain TN	Rock City Gardens	706-820-2531	I-24, Exit 174 or 178
Manchester TN	Beachaven Vineyards and Winery	931-645-8867	426 Ragsdale Road
Memphis TN	Carriage Tours of Memphis	901-527-7542	393 North Main Street
Memphis TN	Memphis Riverboats Inc.	901-527-BOAT (2628)	45 Riverside Drive
Memphis TN	National Ornamental Metal Museum	901-774-6380	374 Metal Museum Drive
Memphis TN	University of Memphis: Chucalissa Archaeological Museum	901-785-3160	1987 Indian Village Drive
Morristown TN	David Crockett Tavern and Museum	423-587-9900	2106 Morningside Drive
Mount Juliet TN	Providence MarketPlace	615-773-2298	401 S Mt Juliet Road/H 171
Murfreesboro TN	Cannonsburgh Village	615-890-0355	312 S Front Street
Murfreesboro TN	Discovery Center At Murfree Spring	615-890-2300	502 SE Broad Street
Murfreesboro TN	Stones River National Battlefield	615-893-9501	3501 Old Nashville H
Murfreesboro TN	Stones River National Battlesite	615-893-9501	3501 Old Nashville Highway
Murfreesboro TN	Stones River National Cemetery	615-893-9501	3501 Old Nashville Highway
Murfreesboro TN	The Avenue Murfreesboro	615-893-4207	2615 Medical Center Parkway
Nashville TN	BiCentennial Mall State Park	615-741-5800	598 James Robertson Pkwy
Nashville TN	CityWalk	615-862-7970	
Nashville TN	Fort Nashborough	615-862-8400	100 1st Avenue N
Nashville TN	Fort Negley	615-862-8470	1100 Fort Negley Blvd
Nashville TN	Horse and Carriages		Broadway and 1st St
Nashville TN	Legends Corner	615-248-6334	428 Broadway
Nashville TN	Nashville City Cemetery	615-862-8400	1001 Fourth Avenue S
Nashville TN	Nashville Downtown Partnership	615-743-3090	150 Fourth Avenue North, Suite G-150

Nashville TN	Nashville Ghost Tours	615-884-3999	600 Union Square
Pigeon Forge TN	Alabama Touring Bus	865-908-8777	2050 Parkway
Pigeon Forge TN	Dollywood Amusement Park Kennels	865-428-9488	1020 Dollywood Lane
Pigeon Forge TN	Mountain Valley Vineyards	865-453-6334	2174 Parkway/H 441
Pigeon Forge TN	Pigeon Forge Factory Outlet Mall	865-428-2828	2850 Parkway/H 321/441
Pigeon Forge TN	Tanger Factory Outlet	865-428-7002	161 E Wears Valley Road/H 321
Portland TN	Sumner Crest Winery	615-325-4086	5306 Old H 52
Sevierville TN	Tanger Outlets at Five Oaks	865-453-1053	1645 Parkway
Shiloh TN	Shiloh National Cemetery	731-689-5696	1055 Pittsburg Landing
Shiloh TN	Shiloh National Military Park	731-689-5696	1055 Pittsburg Landing Road
Springfield TN	Chateau Ross Winery	615-654-9463	5823 Fulton Road
Townsend TN	Little River Railroad and Lumber Company	865-428-0099	H 321
Winchester TN	Franklin County Old Jail	931-967-0524	400 Dinah Shore Blvd/H 41

Texas

Abilene TX	Fort Phantom Hill	325-677-1309	H 600 N
Adrian TX	Adrian Lions Farm & Ranch Museum	806-267-2828	H 66
Amarillo TX	Amarillo Botanical Gardens	806-352-6513	1400 Streit Street
Amarillo TX	Cadillac Ranch		Old Route 66
Amarillo TX	River Breaks Ranch	806-355-7838	612 S Van Buren Street
Amarillo TX	Route 66 Historic District	806-374-8474	401 S Buchanan Street
Arlington TX	Six Flags Over Texas - Kennel	817-530-6000	2201 Road to Six Flags
Athens TX	East Texas Arboretum and Botanical Society	903-675-5630	1601 Patterson
Austin TX	Austin Carriage Service	512-243-0044	various downtown locations
Austin TX	Austin Guided Walking Tours	512-478-0098	11th and Congress Avenue
Austin TX	Congress Avenue Bridge Bats	512-416-5700	305 South Congress Avenue
Austin TX	Zilker Botanical Gardens	512-477-8672	2220 Barton Springs Drive
Austin TX	Zilker Park Boat Rentals	512-327-1388	2201 Barton Springs Road
Big Spring TX	Hangar 25 Air Museum	432-264-1999	1911 Apron Drive
Brackettville TX	Alamo Village Out Door Movie Set	830-563-2580	7 Miles North on H 674
Brenham TX	Pleasant Hill Winery	979-830-VINE	1441 Salem Rd
Brownsville TX	Brownsville Heritage Trail	9565463721	650 FM 802/E Rueben M Torres Sr Blvd
Brownsville TX	Palo Alto Battlefield	956-541-2785	Paredes Line Road and H 511
Buffalo Gap TX	Buffalo Gap Historic Village	325-572-3365	133 N William
Burnet TX	Highland Lakes CAF Air Museum	512-756-2226	H 281 at Burnet Municiple Airport
Canutillo TX	Zin Valle Vineyards	915-877-4544	7315 H 28
Canyon TX	Elkins Ranch Cowboy Morning	806-488-2100	RR2 Box 289
Canyon Lake TX	Fawn Crest Vineyards	830-935-2407	1370 Westside Circle
Cedar Hill TX	Penn Farm Agricultural History Center	972-291-3900	1570 W H 82
Clarendon TX	Bar H Working Dude Ranch	806-874-2634	12064 Bar H Ranch Road
Concordia TX	Concordia Cemetery	915-562-7062	3700 W Yandell Street
Corpus Christi TX	Captain Clark's Flagship	361-884-8306	Peoples Street T-Head Marina
Corpus Christi TX	Corpus Christi Botanical Gardens		8545 South Staples Street
Corpus Christi TX	South Texas Botanical Gardens	361-852-2100	8545 S Staples/H 2444
Corsicana TX	Corsicana Pioneer Village	903-654-4846	912 W Park Avenue
Dallas TX	Dallas Foundation Self-Guided Walking Tours	214-741-9898	900 Jackson St, Suite 150
Dallas TX	McKinney Avenue Trolley	214-855-5267	McKinney Avenue
Dallas TX	Old City Park	214-428-5448	1717 Gano St.
Dallas TX	Party Animals Carriage Rides	214-441-9996	Market Street-West End Area
Dallas TX	Pioneer Plaza	214-953-1184	Young Street and Griffin Street
Del Rio TX	Val Verde Winery	830-775-9714	100 Qualia Drive
Devine TX	Shooting Star Museum	830-931-3837	5445 CR 5710
El Paso TX	Chamizal National Memorial	915-532-7273	800 S San Marcial Street
El Paso TX	Las Palmas Marketplace	915-633-8841	1317 George Dieter
El Paso TX	Railroad and Transportation Museum	915-422-3240	400 W San Antonio Avenue
Fort Davis TX	Fort Davis National Historic Site	432-426-3224	101 Lieutenant Henry Flipper Drive
Fort Worth TX	Stockyards Station	817-624-4741	
Fort Worth TX	Vintage Flying Museum	817-624-1935	505 NW 38th Street Hangar 33 S
Fredericksburg TX	Chisholm Trail Winery	830-990-2675	2367 Usener Road
Galveston TX	Caribbean Breeze Boat Rental	409-740-0400	1723 61st Street
Galveston TX	Island Carriages	409-765-6951	Pier 21 or 22
Gonzales TX	Gonzales Pioneer Village	210-672-2157	2122 N St Joseph Street/H 183
Houston TX	Houston Arboretum and Nature Center	713-681-8433	4501 Woodway Drive
Houston TX	Miller Outdoor Theater	713-533-3285	100 Concert Drive
Houston TX	My Dog and Me - A Unique Dog Club	713-864-3436	2215 Lawrence
Humble TX	Mercer Arboretum and Botanic Gardens	281-443-8731	22306 Aldine Westfield Road
Huntsville TX	Sam Houston's Grave-Oakwood Cemetery	936-291-9726	7600 H 76S
Idalou TX	Apple Country-Hi Plains Orchards	806-892-2961	12206 E H 62
Ingleside TX	Dolphin Connection	361-882-4126	off 1069
Iowa Park TX	Wichita Falls Vineyards and Wine	940-855-2093	3399 B Peterson Rd South
Jacksonville TX	Lookout Mountain Camping	903-586-2217	43822 H 69N
Johnson City TX	Lyndon B. Johnson National Historical Park	830-868-7128	Lady Bird Lane
La Grange TX	Monument Hill and Kreische Brewery State Historic Sites	979-968-5658	414 H Loop 92
LaPorte TX	San Jacinto Battleground State Historic Site	281-479-2431	3523 Battleground Road NH 134
Lubbock TX	American Museum of Agriculture	806-744-3786	1501 Canyon Lake Drive
Lubbock TX	American Wind Power Center	806-747-8734	1701 Canyon Lake Drive

Lubbock TX	Llano Estacado Winery	806-745-2258	3426 E H 85
McKinney TX	Chestnut Square Historical Park	972-562-8790	315 S Chestnut Street
McKinney TX	Happy Trails Horse-Drawn Carriage Service	214-662-6705	
Midland TX	George W Bush Childhood Home	432-685-1112	1412 W Ohio Avenue
Midland TX	The Permian Basin Petroleum Museum	432-683-4403	1500 I 20 W
Nacogdoches TX	Millard's Crossing Historic Village	936-564-6631	6020 North Street (B H 59 N)
Nacogdoches TX	Stephen F. Austin Mast Arboretum	936-468-1832	Wilson Drive
Needville TX	George Observatory	281-242-3055	21901 H 762
New Braunfels TX	Dry Comal Creek Vineyards	830-885-4076	1741 Herbelin Road
Oak Island TX	Frascone Winery	800-920-2248	311 Bayside Dr
Odessa TX	Odessa Meteor Crater	432-381-0946	3100 Meteor Crater Road
Orange TX	Piney Woods Country Wines	409-883-5408	3408 Willow Street
Paint Rock TX	Pictographs of Painted Rocks	325-732-4376	Box 186/On H 83
Parker TX	Southfork Ranch	972-442-7800	3700 Hogge Road
Plano TX	Heritage Farmstead Museum	972-881-0140	1900 W 15th Street
Rusk TX	Maydelle Country Wines	903-795-3915	RR4 Box 19102
San Angelo TX	Fort Concho Museum	325-481-2646	630 S Oakes St
San Antonio TX	La Villita		King Phillip Walk
San Antonio TX	Market Square - El Mercado	210-207-8600	W. Commerce Street
San Antonio TX	Natural Bridge Wildlife Ranch African Safari	830-438-7400	726515 Natural Bridge Caverns Road
San Antonio TX	Pearl Farmers Market	210-212-7260	300 E Grayson Street
San Antonio TX	Riverwalk	210-207-3000	South Alamo
San Antonio TX	San Antonio Missions National Historical Park	210-932-1001	6701 San Jose Drive
San Antonio TX	Sea World	210-523-3000	10500 Sea World Drive
San Antonio TX	Six Flags Fiesta Texas - Kennels	210-697-5050	17000 I 10W
San Antonio TX	Texas Transportation Museum	210-490-3554	11731 Wetmore Road
San Antonio TX	The Alamo		300 Alamo Plaza
San Antonio TX	Veterans Memorial Plaza	800-447-3372	100 Auditorium Circle
San Antonio TX	Westover Marketplace	210-494-3338	At Intersection H Loop 410 & H 151
San Antonio TX	Yellow Rose Carriage Co.	210-337-6495	Crockett Street
San Elizario TX	The Mission Trail Art Market	915-594-8424	1500 Main Street/Veteran's Memorial Plaza
Santa Fe TX	Haak Vineyards	409-925-1401	6310 Ave T
Sisterdale TX	Sister Creek Vineyards	830-324-6704	1142 Sisterdale Road/H 473
Spicewood TX	Spicewood Vineyards	830-693-5328	1419 Burnet County Rd
Stonewall TX	Becker Vineyards	830-644-2681	464 Becker Farms Road
Stonewall TX	Woodrose Winery	830-644-2111	662 Woodrose Lane
Tarrant TX	Lightcatcher Winery	817-237-2626	6435A Nine Mile Bridge Rd
Tow TX	Fall Creek Vineyards	325-379-5361	1820 County Rd 222
Umbarger TX	Buffalo Lake National Wildlife Refuge	806-499-3382	H 168
Uncertain TX	Caddo Lake Steamboat Company	903-789-3978	328 Bois D'Arc Lane
Vega TX	Oldham County Farm and Ranch Heritage Museum	806-267-2828	H 66
Washington TX	Washington-on-the-Brazos State Historic Site	936-878-2214	12300 Park Road 12
Weatherford TX	Chandor Gardens	817-613-1700	711 West Lee Avenue
Weatherford TX	Clark Gardens Botanical Park	940-682-4856	567 Maddux Road
Woodville TX	Heritage Village Museum	409-283-2272	157 Private Road 6000/H 190W

Utah

Brigham City UT	Transcontinental Railroad National Back Country Byway	801-471-2209	P. O. Box 897
Eureka UT	Tintic Mining Museum	435-433-6842	241 W Main Street
Farmington UT	Lagoon Amusement Park and Pioneer Village	801-451-8000	375 N Lagoon Drive
Kanab UT	Frontier Movie Town		297 W Center Street
Kaysville UT	Utah Botanical Center	801-593-8969	725 South Sego Lily Drive
Moab UT	Red River Canoe Company	800-753-8216	1371 Main Street/N H 191
Monument Valley UT	Goulding's Tours	435-727-3231	1000 Main Street
Promontory UT	Golden Spike National Historical Site	435-471-2209	6200 N 22300 W
Salt Lake City UT	California National Historic Trail	801-741-1012	324 South State Street Ste 200
Salt Lake City UT	Carriage for Hire	801-363-8687	across from Crossroads Mall
Salt Lake City UT	KUTV2 Main Street News Studio	801-973-3000	299 South Main Street
Salt Lake City UT	Olympic Cauldron Park	801-972-7800	451 South 1400 East
Salt Lake City UT	Oregon National Historic Trail	801-741-1012	324 South State Street Ste 200
Salt Lake City UT	Pony Express National Historic Trail	801-741-1012	324 South State Street Ste 200
Salt Lake City UT	Strut Your Mutt	801-364-0370	2100 South 1300 East
Salt Lake City UT	The Gateway Shopping District	801-456-0000	400 W 100 S
Salt Lake City UT	Wheeler Historic Farm	801-264-2241	6351 S 900 E
Stansbury Park UI	Benson Grist Mlll	435-882-7678	325 H 138
West Jordan UT	Gardner Village Shopping Center	801-566-8903	1100 W 7800 S

Vermont

Bennington VT	Apple Barn and Country Bake Shop	802-447-7780	604 H 7S
Bennington VT	Bennington Battle Monument	802-447-0550	15 Monument Circle
Brattleboro VT	Vermont Canoe Touring Center	802-257-5008	451 Putney Road

Dog-Friendly Attractions - Please always call ahead to make sure an establishment is still dog-friendly.

Burlington VT	Church Street Marketplace	802-863-1648	2 Church Street
Burlington VT	Ethan Allen Homestead Park Area	802-865-4556	1 Ethan Allen Homestead, Suite 1
Burlington VT	Lake Champlain Ferries	802-864-9804	King Street Dock
Cambridge VT	Boyden Valley Winery	802-644-8151	64 H 104
Essex VT	Essex Shoppes and Cinema	802-657-2777	21 Essex Way
Middlebury VT	Robert Frost Interpretive Trail	802-388-4362	H 125
Putney VT	Harlow's Sugar House	802-387-5852	563 Bellows Falls Road
South Hero VT	Allenholm Farm	802-372-5566	150 South Street
South Hero VT	Apple Island Marina	802-372-3922	H 2
St Johnsbury VT	Stephen Huneck Gallery Summer Party and Fall Dog Fest	800-449-2580	143 Parks Road
St Johnsbury VT	Stephen Huneck Gallery at Dog Mountain	800-449-2580	143 Parks Road
Wilmington VT	Green Mountain Flagship Company	802-464-2975	389 H 9 West
Woodstock VT	Sugarbush Farm	802-457-1757	591 Sugarbush Farm Road

Virginia

Abingdon VA	Historic Main Street	276-676-2282	Main Street
Abingdon VA	The Cave House	276-628-7721 (store)	279 E Main Street/H 11
Abingdon VA	White's Mill	276-628-2960	White's Mill Road
Alexandria VA	Alexandria's Footsteps to the Past Walking Tours	703-683-3451	221 King Street
Alexandria VA	Doggie Happy Hour	703-549-6080	480 King Street
Alexandria VA	Fort Ward Museum and Historic Site	703-838-4848	4301 W Braddock Road
Alexandria VA	George Washington's Grist Mill and Distillery	703-780-2000	Mt Vernon Memorial H/H 235
Alexandria VA	Old Town Horse and Carriage	703-765-8976	Duke St
Alexandria VA	Potomac Riverboat Co. Canine Cruises	703-548-9000	Cameron and Union Streets
Alexandria VA	Woodlawn Plantation	703-780-4000	9000 Richmond H/H 1
Amherst VA	Rebec Vineyards	434-946-5168	2229 North Amherst Highway
Amissville VA	Unicorn Winery	540-349-5885	489 Old Bridge Rd
Appomattox VA	Appomattox Court House NHP	434-352-8987	Hwy 24, PO Box 218
Arlington VA	Arlington National Cemetery		Memorial Drive
Arlington VA	Iwo Jima Memorial		
Bentonville VA	Downriver Canoe Company	540-635-5526	884 Indian Hollow Road
Brookneal VA	Red Hill - The Patrick Henry National Memorial	434-376-2044	1250 Red Hill Road
Chantilly VA	Sully Historic Site	703-437-1794	3601 Sully Road
Charles City VA	Berkeley Plantation	804-829-6018	12602 Harrison Landing Road
Charlottesville VA	Charlottesville Historic Downtown Mall	434-977-1783	Downtown Charlottesville
Charlottesville VA	Jefferson Vineyards	434-977-3042	1353 Thomas Jefferson Parkway
Charlottesville VA	Kluge Estate Winery and Vineyard	434-984-4855	3550 Blenheim Road
Charlottesville VA	Thomas Jefferson's Monticello Estate	434-984-9822	931 Thomas Jefferson Parkway
Chesapeake VA	Dismal Swamp Canal Trail	757-382-CITY (2489)	Dominion Blvd and Old Route 17 (North Trailhead)
Chincoteague VA	Chincoteague Ponies at the Carnival Grounds		Carnival Grounds
Chincoteague Island VA	Barnacle Bill's Boat Tours	757-336-5920	3691 Main Street
Colonial Beach VA	Ingleside Vineyards	804-224-8687	5872 Leedstown Road
Delaplane VA	Barrel Oak Winery	703-798-8308	3623 Grove Lane/H 55
Delaplane VA	Three Fox Vineyards	540-364-6073	10100 Three Fox Lane
Doswell VA	Kings Dominion Amusement Park Kennels	804-876-5400	16000 Theme Park Way
Fincastle VA	Fincastle Vineyard and Winery	540-591-9000	203 Maple Ridge Lane
Floyd VA	Chateau Morrisette Winery	540-593-2865	287 Winery Road SW
Floyd VA	Villa Appalaccia	540-593-3100	752 Rock Castle Gorge
Forest VA	Thomas Jefferson's Poplar Forest Estate	434-525-1806	1008 Poplar Forest Drive
Fredericksburg VA	Chancellorsville Battlefield	540-786-2880	9001 Plank Road
Fredericksburg VA	Fredericksburg Battlefield Park	540-373-6122	1013 Lafayette Blvd
Fredericksburg VA	Gari Melchers Home and Studio	540-654-1015	Belmont, 224 Washington Street
Fredericksburg VA	George Washington's Ferry Farm	540-373-3381	268 Kings Hwy/H 3
Fredericksburg VA	Kenmore Plantation and Gardens	540-373-3381	1201 Washington Ave
Glen Allen VA	James River Cellars	804-550-7516	11008 Washington Highway
Gordonsville VA	Horton Vineyards	540-832-7440	6399 Spotwood Trial
Hardy VA	Booker T. Washington National Monument	540-721-2094	12130 Booker T. Washington H
Huntly VA	Rappahannock Cellars Vineyard	540-635-9398	14437 Hume Road
Irvington VA	White Fences Vineyard	804-761-4866	170 White Fence Drive
Jamestown VA	Historic Jamestown	757-898-2410	Colonial Parkway
Keswick VA	Keswick Vineyards	434-244-3341	1575 Keswick Winery Drive
Leesburg VA	Leesburg Corner Premium Outlets	703-737-3071	241 Fort Evans Road NE
Leesburg VA	Tarara Winery	703-443-9836	13648 Tarara Lane
Lexington VA	Hull's Drive-In	540-463-2621	Rr 5
Lexington VA	Lexington Antique and Craft Mall	540-463-9511	1495 N Lee Hwy/H 11
Lexington VA	Lexington Carriage Company	540-463-5647	106 E Washington Street
Manassas VA	Manassas National Battlefield	703-361-1339	6511 Sudley Road
Max Meadows VA	Fort Chiswell Outlets	276-637-6214	Factory Outlet Drive
Middleburg VA	Chrysalis Vineyards	800-235-8804	23876 Champe Ford Rd
Mount Vernon VA	Mount Vernon	703-780-2000	George Washington Pkwy
Natural Bridge VA	Natural Bridge	540-291-2121	15 Appledore Lane
Newport News VA	Endview Plantation	757-887-1862	362 Yorktown Road

Newport News VA	Mariner's Museum	757-596-2222	100 Museum Drive
Norfolk VA	Kayak Adventure Rentals	757-480-1999	110 W Randall Avenue
Petersburg VA	Petersburg National Battlefield	804-732-3531	1539 Hickory Hill Drive
Pocahontas VA	Pocahontas Exhibition Coal Mine and Museum	276-945-9522	Centre Street
Portsmouth VA	Portsmouth Olde Towne Walking Tour	757-393-5111	6 Crawford Parkway
Purcellville VA	Breaux Vineyards	540-668-6299	36888 Breaux Vineyards Lane
Raphine VA	Rockbridge Vineyard	540-377-6204	35 Hillview Lane
Reston VA	Reston Town Center	703-689-4699	11900 Market Street
Richmond VA	Hollywood Cemetery	804-648-8501	412 S Cherry Street
Richmond VA	Richmond National Battlefield	804-226-1981	470 Tredegar Street
Richmond VA	Riverfront District and Canal Walk	804-788-6466	N 14th and E Cary Street
Richmond VA	Stony Point Fashion Park	804-560-SHOP	9200 Stony Point Parkway
Richmond VA	Virginia State Capitol	804-698-1788	Bank Street
Stafford VA	Potomac Point Winery	540-446-2266	275 Decatur Road
Staunton VA	Historic Staunton Guided and Self-Guided Walking Tours	540-332-3971	35 S New Street/H 250
Staunton VA	Woodrow Wilson Library and Birthplace	540-885-0897	18-24 N Coalter Street
Tangier Island VA	Tangier Island Buggy Tours		Tangier Pier
Waterford VA	Waterford Village	540-882-3018	Main Street
Waynesboro VA	Blue Ridge Parkway Auto Tour	828-271-4779	Blue Ridge Parkway, Milepost 0
Williamsburg VA	Busch Gardens Kennels	800-343-7946	1 Busch Garden Blvd
Williamsburg VA	Colonial Williamsburg		
Williamsburg VA	Mini-Golf America	757-229-7200	1901 Richmond Rd
Williamsburg VA	Prime Outlets	757-565-0702	5715 Richmond Road/H 60
Williamsburg VA	The College of William and Mary	757-221-4000	Grigsby Drive
Winchester VA	African-American Heritage Driving Tour	540-542-1326	1360 S Pleasant Valley Road
Winchester VA	Battle of Third Winchester Driving Tour	540-542-1326	1360 S Pleasant Valley Road
Winchester VA	Deer Meadow Wines	800-653-6632	199 Vintage Lane
Winchester VA	Follow the Apple Trail Auto Tour	540-542-1326	1360 S Pleasant Valley Road
Winchester VA	Old Town Mall	877-871-1326	Loudoun Street
Winchester VA	Pirates of the Shenandoah Treasure Hunt	877-871-1326	1360 S Pleasant Valley Road
Winchester VA	Stonewall Jackson's Headquarters Museum	540-667-3242	415 N Braddock Street/H 522/11
Winchester VA	Washington's Office Museum	540-662-4412	32 W Cork Street
Woodford VA	Stonewall Jackson Shrine	804-633-6076	12019 Stonewall Jackson Road/H 606
Yorktown VA	Historic Yorktown	757-898-2410	Historical Tour Drive
Yorktown VA	Yorktown Riverwalk Landing	757-890-3300	Water Street

Washington

Bainbridge Island WA	Bainbridge Island Vineyards	206-842-9463	8989 Day Road East
Ballard WA	Carl English Jr Botanical Garden	206-783-7059	3015 NW 54th Street
Bellingham WA	Sehome Hill Arboretum	360-676-6985	25th Street and McDonald Parkway
Bellingham WA	Victoria San Juan Cruises	800-443-4552	355 Harris Avenue, Ste 104
Blaine WA	M.V. Plover Ferry	360-332-5742	Marine Drive / Blaine Moorage Dock at Gate II
Chehalis WA	Chehalis-Centralia Railroad	360-748-9593	1101 Sylvenus Street
Chelan WA	Chelan Airways	509-682-5555	1328 West Woodin Ave/H Alt 97
Chelan WA	Lady of the Lake Boat Ride	888-682-4584	1418 W Wooden Avenue/H 97A
Chelan WA	The Tour Boat	509-682-8287	Lake Chelan Marina
Chewelah WA	49 Degrees North Mountain Resort	509-935-6049	3311 Flowery Trail Road
Clarkston WA	Snake Dancer Excursions	509-758-8927	1550 Port Drive, Suite B (Below Roosters Landing)
Everson WA	Mt Baker Vineyards	360-592-2300	4298 Mt Baker H
Federal Way WA	Marlene's	253-839-0933	2565 S Gateway Center Place
Friday Harbor WA	San Juan Island National Historic Park	360-378-2902	125 Spring Street
Greenbank WA	Wag n' Walk Festival	360-321-WAIF (9243)	760 E Wonn Road
Hoodsport WA	Hoodsport Winery	360-877-9894	23522 N H 101
Kenmore WA	Kenmore Air Seaplanes	800-543-9595	6321 Northeast 175th
Kennewick WA	Badger Mountain Vineyard and Winery	800-643-WINE	1106 N Jurupa Street
Leavenworth WA	Tube Leavenworth	509-548-TUBE	220 9th St. #104
Ocean Park WA	Willapa Bay Oyster House Interpretive Center	360-665-4547	3311 275th Street
Paterson WA	Columbia Crest Winery	509-875-2061	Columbia Crest Drive
Port Angeles WA	Black Diamond Winery	360-457-0748	2976 Black Diamond Road
Port Angeles WA	Harbinger Winery	360-452-4262	2358 H 101W
Port Angeles WA	Olympic National Park	360-565-3130	600 East Park Avenue
Port Angeles WA	Rite Bros Aviation	360-452-6226	1406 Fairchild International Airport
Port Townsend WA	Puget Sound Express/Point Hudson Marina	360-385-5288	227 Jackson Street
Port Townsend WA	Sidewalk Tours	360-385-1967	Old City Hall
Ruston WA	Fort Nisqually	253-591-5339	5400 N Pearl Street
Seattle WA	Argoys Cruises Water Taxi	206-623-1445	1101 Alaskan Way, Pier 55/H 99
Seattle WA	Blake Island Adventure Cruise/Tillicum Village	206-933-8600	2992 SW Avalon Way
Seattle WA	Broadway Sunday Farmers Market	206-547-2278	10th Avenue E and E Thomas Street
Seattle WA	Columbia City Farmers Market	206-547-2278	4801 Rainier Avenue S
Seattle WA	Dog Gone Taxi	888-761-8626	Throughout City
Seattle WA	Emerald Country Carriages	425-868-0621	Piers 55-56
Seattle WA	Fun Forest Amusement Park	206-728-1586	305 Harrison Street

Dog-Friendly Attractions - Please always call ahead to make sure an establishment is still dog-friendly.

Seattle WA	Kubota Garden	206-684-4584	9817 55th Avenue S
Seattle WA	Lake Washington Ship Canal and Ballard Locks	206-783-7059	3015 NW 54th St.
Seattle WA	Magnolia Farmers Market	206-547-2278	2550 34th Avenue W
Seattle WA	Paws Walk	425-787-2500	7400 Sand Point Way NE
Seattle WA	Pioneer Square		First Street and Yesler Way
Seattle WA	Seattle Center	206-684-7200	Mercer Street and Broad St.
Seattle WA	Seattle Ferry Service	206-713-8446	Valley Street and Terry Avenue N
Seattle WA	The Center for Wooden Boats	206-382-2628	1010 Valley Street
Seattle WA	University Village	206-523-0622	2623 NE University Village
Seattle WA	Vancouver Farmers Market	206-547-2278	505 W 8th Street
Seattle WA	Washington Park Arboretum	206-543-8800	4300 Arboretum Drive E
Seattle WA	Woodland Park Rose Garden	206-684-4863	700 N 50th Street
Sequim WA	The Water Limousine	360-457-4491	W Sequim Bay Road
Snoqualmie WA	Northwest Railway Museum	425-888-3030	38625 SE King Street
Union Gap WA	Central Washington Agricultural Museum	509-457-8735	4508 Main Street
Vancouver WA	Fort Vancouver National Historic Site	800-832-3599	612 E Reserve St
Vancouver WA	Fort Vancouver National Historical Reserve	360-696-7655	1501 E Evergreen Blvd
Vancouver WA	McLoughlin House National Historic Site	800-832-3599	612 E Reserve St
Vancouver WA	Vancouver Farmers Market	360-737-8298	8th and Ester Streets
Walla Walla WA	Whitman Mission National Historic Site	509-522-6357	328 Whitman Mission Road
Yakima WA	McAllister Museum of Aviation	509-457-4933	2008 S 16th Avenue

West Virginia

Arthurdale WV	Arthurdale Heritage	304-864-3959	H 92
Berkeley Springs WV	Berkeley Springs Walking Tour	800-447-8797	127 Fairfax Street
Berkeley Springs WV	Washington Heritage Trail	800-447-8797	127 Fairfax Street (Visitor Center)
Crab Orchard WV	Daniel Vineyards	304-252-9750	200 Twin Oaks Road
Fayetteville WV	New River Gorge National River Bridge Day	800-927-0263	H 19 (Box 202)
Harpers Ferry WV	Appalachian National Scenic Trail	304-535-6278	Harpers Ferry Center
Harpers Ferry WV	Appalachian Trail in West Virginia	304-535-6331	Off Sandy Hook Road
Harpers Ferry WV	Ghost Tours of Harpers Ferry	304-725-8019	175 High Street
Harpers Ferry WV	Harpers Ferry National Historical Park	304-535-6029	P.O. Box 65
Lewisburg WV	Historic Downtown Lewisburg	304-645-4333	209 W Washington Street
Summersville WV	The Kirkwood Winery	888-4WV-WINE (498-9463)	45 Winery Lane/Phillips Run Road

Wisconsin

Alma WI	Fun'N the Sun Houseboat Rentals	888-343-5670	S2221 H 35
Baileys Harbor WI	Lynn's Fishing Charter	920-854-5109	Ridges Road
Baraboo WI	Mirror Lake Rentals	608-254-4104	E10320 Fern Dell Road
Baraboo WI	Tanger Outlet Center	608-253-5380	210 Gasser Road
Beloit WI	Beloit River Walk	608-364-2929	Riverside Drive
Bristol WI	Pringle Nature Center	262-857-8008	9800 160th Avenue/H MB
Chetek WI	Stardust Drive-In Theater	715-458-4587	995 22nd St
Cochrane WI	Prairie Moon Garden and Museum	608-687-9511	S2727 Prairie Mood Road
Deerfield WI	Schuster's Playtime Farm	608-764-8488	1326 H 12 and 18
Door County WI	The Salmon Depot Charter Fishing	800-345-6701	Box 141, Billy's Harbor
Ephraim WI	Stiletto Sailing Cruises	920-854-7245	9993 H 42
Fish Creek WI	Classic Boat Tours of Door County	920-421-2080	9145 Spring Road
Fish Creek WI	Lautenbachs Orchard Country	920-868-3479	9197 H 42
Gillsrock WI	Island Clipper	920-854-2972	12731 H 42
Green Bay WI	Fox River Trail	920-448-4466	Porlier and Adams Streets
Jacksonport WI	Simon Creek Vineyard and Winery	920-746-9307	5896 Bochek Road
La Pointe WI	Bog Lake Outfitters	715-747-2685	2848 School House Road
La Pointe WI	Madeline Island Ferry	715-747-2051	100 Main Street
Lac du Flambeau WI	Waswagoning Indian Village	715-588-3560	H 47
Lake Delton WI	Lost Canyon Horse Carriage Tours	608-254-8757	720 Canyon Road
Lake Delton WI	Shipwreck Lagoon Mini Golf	608-253-7772	1450 Parkway
Madison WI	State Street Shopping Area	800-373-6376	State Street
Madison WI	University of Wisconsin Botanical Garden	608-263-2400	University Avenue
Madison WI	University of Wisconsin Campus	608-263-2400	21 N Park Street
Madison WI	Wiconsin State Capitol Grounds	608-266-0382	2 E Main Street
Marshfield WI	Jusrustic park	http://www.jurustic.com/	M222 Sugar Bush Lane
Milwaukee WI	Blue Max Charters	414-828-1094	740 N Plankinton
Milwaukee WI	Henry Aaron State Trail	414-263-8559	2300 N Martin Luthur King Jr Drive (Dept.of Natural Resources)
Milwaukee WI	Historic Third Ward District	414-287-4100	North Milwaukee Street/H 32
Milwaukee WI	Milwaukee Boat Line	414-294-9450	505 N RiverWalk Way
Milwaukee WI	Movies Under the Stars	414-276-6696	North Old World 3rd Street
Milwaukee WI	Riverwalk	414-287-4100	Riverwalk Row (several connecting streets)
New Glarus WI	Swiss Village Museum	608-527-2317	612 7th Avenue
New Munster WI	New Munster Wildlife Area	888-WDNRINFo (1-888-936-7463)	34315 Geneva Road
North Freedom WI	Mid-Continent Railway Museum	608-522-4261	E8948 Diamond Hill Road

690

Pleasant Prairie WI	Prime Outlets	262-857-2101	11211 120th Avenue
Prairie Du Sac WI	Wollersheim Winery	800-VIP-WINE (847-9463)	7876 H 188
Racine WI	River Bend Nature Center	262-639-0930	3600 N Green Bay Road
Sister Bay WI	Shoreline Charters at Sister Bay Village Marina	920-854-4707	12747 H 42
Sturgeon Bay WI	Boat Door County	920-743-2337	3662 N Duluth Avenue
Sturgeon Bay WI	Door Peninsula Winery	920-743-7431	5608 H 42
Sturgeon Bay WI	Snug Harbor Inn and Marina	920-743-2337	1627 Memorial Drive
Washington Island WI	Rock Island Ferry	920-847-3322	Jackson Harbor Road
Washington Island WI	Washington Island Ferry	800-223-2094	Northport Pier
Wisconsin Dells WI	Dells Army Ducks	608-254-6080	1550 Wisconsin Dells Parkway
Wisconsin Dells WI	Dells Boat Tours	608-254-8555	1890 Wisconsin Dells Parkway
Wisconsin Dells WI	Dells Duck Tours	608-254-8751	1890 Wisconsin Dells Parkway
Wisconsin Dells WI	Dells Mining Company	608-253-7002	1480 Wisconsin Dells Parkway/H 12/23
Wisconsin Dells WI	Pirate's Cove Mini-Golf	608-254-8336	Intersection of Highways 12-13-16-23

Wyoming

Banner WY	Fort Phil Kearny State Historic Site	307-684-7629	528 Wagon Box Road
Casper WY	Casper Downtown Shopping District	800-852-1889	992 N Poplar Street (Visitor Bureau)
Casper WY	Casper Walking Tours and Ghost Tours	307-267-7243	330 S Center Suite 414
Casper WY	Fort Caspar Museum	307-235-8462	4001 Fort Caspar Road
Casper WY	Platte River Parkway	307-577-7162	P.O Box 1228
Casper WY	The Casper Mountain Sled Dog Race	307-577-7162	Casper Mountain Road
Cheyenne WY	Capitol City Cab	307-632-8294	2504 E 7th Street
Cheyenne WY	Cheyenne Botanic Gardens	307-637-6458	710 S Lions Park Drive
Cheyenne WY	Cheyenne Street Railway Trolley	800-426-5009	121 W 15th Street
Cheyenne WY	Cheyenne Taxi Service	307-638-4530	2504 E 8th Street
Cheyenne WY	Historic Downtown Walking Tour	307-778-3133	121 W 15th Street
Cody WY	Cody Trolley Tours	307-527-7043	Corner of 12th Street and Sheridan Ave
Cody WY	Paul Stock Nature Trail	307-587-0400	801 Spruce Drive
Cody WY	River Runners of Wyoming	307-527-7238	1491 Sheridan Avenue/H 14/16/20
Evansville WY	Independence Rock State Historic Site	307-577-5150	Milepost 63 H 220
Fort Bridger WY	Fort Bridger State Historic Site	307-782-3842	37000 Business Loop I 80
Fort Laramie WY	Fort Laramie National Historic Site	307-837-2221	965 Gray Rocks Road
Glendo WY	Hall's Glendo Marina	307-735-4216	383 Glendo Park Road
Green River WY	Buckboard Marina	307-875-6927	H 530/Flaming Gorge Lake (HCR 65, Box 100)
Guernsey WY	Oregon Trail Ruts and Register Cliff	307-777-6323	S Wyoming Avenue
Jackson WY	Amaze'n Jackson Hole	307-734-0455	85 Snow King Ave
Jackson WY	Gaper Guide	307-733-4626	145 W Gill Avenue
Jackson WY	National Elk Refuge	307-733-9212	532 N Cache Street (Visitor Center)/H 26/89/191
Jackson Hole WY	Wild West Jeep Tours	307-733-9036	P.O. Box 7506
Kemmerer WY	Fossil Butte National Monument	307-877-4455	864 Chicken Creek Road
Laramie WY	Ames Monument	307-777-6323	Monument Road
Laramie WY	Snowy Range Scenic Byway	307-745-2300	H 130
Laramie WY	University Of Wyoming Campus	307-766-1121	1000 E University Avenue
Laramie WY	Wyoming Territorial Prison	307-745-6161	975 Snowy Range Road
Lovell WY	Medicine Wheel National Historic Landmark	307-548-6541	Forest Road
Lovell WY	Yellowtail Wildlife Habitat Management Area	307-527-7125	H 14/16/20
Lusk WY	Historic Hat Creek Stage Station	307-334-2950	H 85
Pine Bluffs WY	University of Wyoming Archaeological Dig Site	307-245-3695	Muddy Creek Drive
Pinedale WY	Museum of the Mountain Man	307-367-4101	700 E Hennick Street
Rawlins WY	Wyoming Frontier Prison Museum	307-324-4422	500 W Walnut Street
Rock Springs WY	Pilot Butte Wild Horse Scenic Loop	307-352-0256	County Road 53 north of Rock Springs
Sheridan WY	Trail End State Historic Site	307-674-4589	400 Clarendon Avenue
South Pass WY	South Pass City State Historic Site	307-332-3684	125 South Pass Main

Canada

Alberta

Calgary AB	Calaway Amusement Park Kennel	403-290-1875	245033 Range Road 33
Calgary AB	Calgary Downtown Walking Tour (including Stephen Ave)	403-215-1570	320 8th Avenue SE, Suite 720 (Calgary Downtown Association)
Calgary AB	Eau Claire Festival Market	403-264-6450	200 Barclay Parade SW
Calgary AB	Fort Calgary Historic Park	403-290-1875	750 9th Avenue SE
Calgary AB	Kensington Village	403-215-1570	10th Street NW
Calgary AB	Uptown 17th Shopping Center	403-245-1703	17th Avenue SW
Edmonton AB	Downtown Walking Tours	780-424-4085	9990 Jasper Avenue (World Trade Centre street front office)
Edmonton AB	South Edmonton Common	780-466-2221	10180 111th Street

Jasper AB	Jasper Carriage Company	780-852-RIDE (7433)	P.O. Box 1200
Lethbridge AB	Fort Whoop-up Interpretive Centre	403-329-0444	P. O. Box 1074
Longview AB	Bar U Ranch National Historic Site	403-395-2212	H 22, Foothills # 31
Nanton AB	Big Sky Garden Railway	403-646-1190	2121 18th Street
Nanton AB	The Nanton Lancaster Society Air Museum	403-646-2270	H 2 Southbound at 17th Street
Wetaskiwin AB	Reynolds-Alberta Museum	780-361-1351	H 13W (P.O. Box 6360)

British Columbia

108 Mile House BC	108 Mile House Heritage Site	250-791-5288	4690 Telqua Drive
9851 H 93/95 BC	Fort Steele Heritage Town	250-417-6000	Fort Steele
Abbotsford BC	Trethewey House Heritage Museum	604-853-0313	2313 Ware Street
Boston Bar BC	Hell's Gate Airtram	604-867-9277	43111 Trans Canada Highway
Campbell River BC	Northwest Seaplanes	800-690-0086	3050 Spit Road
Clinton BC	South Cariboo Historical Museum	250-459-2442	1419 Cariboo H
Dawson Creek BC	Alaska Highway Mile Zero Sign	250-782-9595	900 Alaska Hwy
Fort Nelson BC	Fort Nelson Heritage Museum	250-774-3536	Mile 300 Alaska H
Fort St John BC	Heritage Kiosk Walking Tour	250-785-3033	9523 100th Street (Ft St John Visitor Center)
Mount Washington BC	Mount Washington Alpine Resort	250-338-1515	1 Strathcona Parkway
North Vancouver BC	Capilano Suspension Bridge and Park	604-985-7474	3735 Capilano Road
Osoyoos BC	Nk'Mip Cellars	250-495-2985	1400 Rancher Creek Road
Port Hardy BC	Pacific Coastal Airlines	250-949-6353	3675 Byng Road
Port Hardy BC	Sea Legend Water Taxi Services	250-949-6541	Hardy Bay Road
Prince George BC	Railway and Forestry Museum	250-563-7351	850 River Road
Prince Rupert BC	Skeena Kayaking Rentals and Tours	250-624-4393	1534 11th Ave East
Rosedale BC	Minter Gardens	604-794-7191	52892 Bunker Road
Sidney BC	The British Columbia Aviation Museum	250-655-3300	1910 Norseman Road
Tofino BC	Tofino Sea-Kayaking Co	250-725-4222	320 Main Street
Vancouver BC	AquaBus Ferries	604-689-5858	230-1333 Johnston Street/Granville Island
Vancouver BC	Granville Island	604-666-6655	
Vancouver BC	Historic Gastown	604-683-5650	Water Street
Vancouver BC	Historic Gastown Guided Walking Tours	604-683-5650	Water and Carrall Streets
Vancouver BC	Sam Kee Building		Pender Street
Vancouver Island BC	The Butchart Gardens		
Victoria BC	Adam's Fishing Charters	250-370-2326	Wharf Street
Victoria BC	Alcheringa Gallery	250-383-8224	665 Fort Street
Victoria BC	Discover the Past Walking Tours	250-384-6698	812 Wharf Street
Victoria BC	Grandpas Antique Photo Studio	250-920-3800	1252 Wharf Street
Victoria BC	Great Pacific Adventures	250-386-2277	450 Swift Street
Victoria BC	Kabuki Kabs	250-385-4243	526 Discovery Street
Victoria BC	Ocean River Sports	250-381-4233	1824 Store Street
Victoria BC	Tally Ho Horse and Carriage	866-383-5067	Belleville and Menzies Streets
Victoria BC	Victoria Carriage Tours	250-383-2207	Menzies and Belleville Street
Victoria BC	Victoria Harbour Ferry and Tours	250-708-0201	1234-N Wharf Street
Whistler BC	Whistler Village	800-WHISTLER	Village Stroll

Manitoba

Brandon MB	Assiniboine Riverbank Trail System	204-729-2141	#1-545 Conservation Drive/Riverbank Discovery Center
Brandon MB	Eleanor Kidd Gardens	204-729-2141	18th Street N/H 10 and John Avenue
Brandon MB	Manitoba Agricultural Hall Of Fame	204-728-3736	1129 Queens Avenue
Steinbeck MB	Mennonite Heritage Village	204-326-9661	H 12N
Winnipeg MB	Assiniboine Park and the Leo Mol Sculpture Garden	204-986-5717	460 Assiniboine Park Drive
Winnipeg MB	Cityplace	204 989-1817	333 St Mary Avenue at Hargrave Street
Winnipeg MB	Exchange District	204-942-6716	Main Street
Winnipeg MB	Exchange District Guided Walking Tours	204-942-6716	King Street and Bannatyne Avenue
Winnipeg MB	Historic District of St Boniface	866-808-8338	Provencher Blvd/H 57 and surrounding streets
Winnipeg MB	Splash Dash Boats	204-783-6633	1 Forks Market Road

New Brunswick

Fredericton NB	Guided Heritage Walking Tours	506-460-2129	397 Queen Street
Fredericton NB	Haunted Hike	506-457-1975	745 George Street
Fredericton NB	Historic Garrison District	506-460-2041	457 Queen Street
Fredericton NB	Time Travel Tours	506-460-2129	397 Queen Street
Hampton NB	Osprey Adventures	506-832-6025	1075 Main Street/Lighthouse Park River Center
Hampton NB	Zelda's River Adventures	506-653-0726	55 Randall Drive
Hartland NB	Hartland Covered Bridge	506-375-4357	H 2 between H 105 and H 103
Hopewell Cape NB	Hopewell Rocks	877-734-3429	131 Discovery Road
Moncton NB	Wharf Village Shoppes and Restaurant	506-858-8841	50 Magic Blvd
Richmond Corner NB	Maliseet Trail	800-526-7070	109 Tourist Bureau Road
St Edouard de Kent NB	Irving Eco-Centre - La Dune de Bouctouche	506-743-2600	1932 H 475

St John NB	Carleton Martello Tower National Historic Site of Canada	506-636-4011	454 Whipple Street
St John NB	Gibson Creek Canoeing	506-672-8964	821 Anderson Drive
St John NB	Irving Nature Park	506-653-7367	Sand Cove Road
St John NB	Reversing Falls Visitor Information Centre	506-658-2937	200 Bridge Road/H 100 (Visitor Information Centre)
St John NB	Rockwood Park Stables	506-633-7659	PO Box 686 Stn Main
St John NB	Turn of the Century Trolley Tours	506-633-7659	
St John NB	Walking Tour of Old Saint John	866-463-8639	15 Market Square
Woodstock NB	Woodstock Walking Tour	506-328-9706	679 Main Street

Newfoundland

Bishop's Falls NF	Bishop's Falls Trestle	709-258-2228	
Bishop's Falls NF	Jiggs' Fun Farm	709-258-5229	H 350
Fleur de Lys NF	Dorset Soapstone Quarry National Historic Site	709-253-2126	H 410/Baie Verte Peninsula
Fleur de Lys NF	Fleur de Lys Trails	709-253-2126	H 410/Baie Verte Peninsula
Gander NF	North Atlantic Aviation Museum	709-256-2923	H 135
St Johns NF	Bowring Park	709-576-8601	305 Waterford Bridge Road
St Johns NF	Dee Jay Charters	709-753-8687 (in season) 709-726-2141 (all year)	Harbour Drive

Nova Scotia

Bear River NS	Bear River Vineyards	902-467-4156	133 Chute Road
Canning NS	Blomidon Estate Winery	902-582-7565	10318 H 221
Dartmouth NS	Dartmouth Heritage Walk	902-490-4000	Alderney Drive
Halifax NS	Halifax Citadel National Historic Site	902-426-5080	5425 Sackeille
Halifax NS	Tall Ship Silva	902-429-9463	Lower Water Street/H 102
Hubbards NS	Peers' Fancy Sailing Charters	902-476-4437	St Margaret's Bay Rd
Lower West Pubnico NS	Nova Scotia Historic Acadian Village	902-762-2530	Old Church Road
Port Maitland NS	Port Maitland Provincial Beach Park	800-565-0000	3297 Main Shore Road
Port Maitland NS	Tight Lines Guide Service	902-649-2428	Box 44
Sydney NS	Smart Shop Place	902-564-5777	314 Charles Street
Yarmouth NS	Deep Sea Fishing Charters	902-742-2713	R.R.#5, Box 2003

Ontario

Amherstburg ON	Fort Malden National Historic Site	519-736-5416	100 Laird Avenue
Belle River ON	Captain Dan Charters	519-982-8934	Lake Street
Bracebridge ON	Muskoka Rails Museum	705-646-9711	14 Gray Road
Burlington ON	Royal Botanical Gardens	905-527-1158	680 Plains Road W
Gananoque ON	1000 Islands Kayaking Company	613-329-6265	P. O. Box 166
Gananoque ON	Houseboat Holidays Ltd.	613-382-2842	11 Clark Drive
Gravenhurst ON	Swift Canoe and Kayak	800-661-1429	2394 H 11N
Hamilton ON	Dundurn Castle	905-546-2872	610 York Blvd
Hamilton ON	Hamilton Museum of Steam and Technology	905-546-4797	900 Woodward Avenue
Kingston ON	Kingston Public Market and Craft Fair	613-546-49291	216 Ontario Street
Kingston ON	Kingston's Waterfront Pathway	613-546-0000	E King Street
Kingston ON	Portsmouth Village	613-546-0000	King Street and surrounding streets
Kingston ON	Wolfe Island Ferry Service	613-548-7227	Ontario and Barrack Streets
Kingsville ON	Mastronardi Estate Winery	519-733-9463	1193 Concession 3 E
Kingsville ON	Pelee Island Winery	519-724-2469	455 Seacliff Drive/ H 20
LaSalle ON	Windsor Crossing Premium Outlets	519-972-7111	1555 Talbot Road/H 3
Landsdowne ON	1000 Islands Boat Tours	613-659-3350	574 1000 Islands Parkway
Leamington ON	Pelee Island Ferry	800-661-2220	500 Erie Street
London ON	Fanshawe Pioneer Village	519-457-1296	1424 Clarke Road
London ON	Springbank Park	519-661-5575	929 Springbank Drive
Morrisburg ON	Upper Canada Village	613-543-4328	13740 H 2
Niagara Falls ON	Niagara Falls	800-563-2557	off Queen Elizabeth Way
Niagara on the Lake ON	Konzelmann Estate Winery	905-935-2866	1096 Lakeshore Road, RR#3
Ottawa ON	Parliament Hill	613-992-4793	Parliament Hill
Ottawa ON	Rideau Canal and Trail	613-239-5234	90 Wellington Street
Ottawa ON	Stony Swamp Conservation Area	613-239-5000	Hunt Club Road
Parry Sound ON	Georgian Nordic Ski and Canoe Club	705-746-5067	9 Mile Bay Road
Portland ON	Bayview Yacht Harbour	613-272-2787	2785 H 15
Portland ON	Big Rideau Lake Boat Rentals	613-880-9288	15 Water Street
Portland ON	Len's Cove Marina	613-272-2581	1 Water Street
Renfrew ON	Storyland	613-432-2222	793 Storyland Road
Sault Ste. Marie ON	Sault Ste. Marie Canal National Historic Site	705-941-6262	1 Canal Drive
Tobermory ON	Chi-Cheemaun Ferry/Tobermory Terminal	519 596 2510	8 Eliza Street
Toronto ON	Black Creek Pioneer Village	416-736-1733	1000 Murray Ross Parkway
Toronto ON	Centreville Amusement Park	416-203-0405	Centre Island
Toronto ON	City Walks Guided Tours	416-966-1550	Call to arrange.
Toronto ON	Great Lakes Schooner Company	416-203-2322	Queen's Quay

Dog-Friendly Attractions - Please always call ahead to make sure an establishment is still dog-friendly.

Toronto ON	Harbourfront Centre	416-973-3000	York and John Quays
Toronto ON	Toronto Islands Park	416-392-8186	
Vineland ON	Vineland Estates Winery	888-VINELAND (846-3526)	3996 Moyer Road
Virgil ON	Hillebrand Estates Winery	905-468-7123	1249 Niagara Stone Road/H 55

Prince Edward Island

Cavendish PE	Green Gables Heritage Site	902-963-7874	8619 H 6
Charlottetown PE	Northumberland Ferries Ltd.	877-635-SAIL (7245)	94 Water Street, Box 634
Charlottetown PE	Prince Edward Air Ltd.	902-566-4488	250 Brackley Point Road

Quebec

Beauport PQ	Parc de la Chute-Montmorency	418-663-3330	2490, avenue Royale
Mont-Tremblant PQ	Mont-Tremblant Dog Sled Tours	819-681-4848	Le Johannsen
Montreal PQ	Caleche Andre Boisrt	450-653-0751	St Lawrence Blvd at De La Commune
Montreal PQ	Caleche Lucky Luc	514-934-6105	
Montreal PQ	Circuit des Fantoms du Vieux Ghost Tours	514-868-0303	469 Francis Xavier
Montreal PQ	Guidatour Walking Tours of Montreal	514-844-4021	Sulpice at Notre Dame Street
Montreal PQ	Lachine Canal National Historic Site	514-283-6054	East to West across Montreal
Montreal PQ	Place Jacques Cartier and Vieux Montreal		Rue St-Paul E at Place Jacques Cartier
Montreal PQ	Tours Kaleidoscope	514-990-1872	6592, Chateaubriand
Pointe-Claire PQ	Geordie Charters	514-695-2552	20 Westwood Drive Pointe-Claire
Quebec PQ	Association des guides touristiques de Quebec	418-624-2851	
Quebec PQ	CSA Historical Walking Tour	418-692-3033	4, rue Toussaint
Quebec PQ	Fortifications of Québec National Historic Site	418-648-7016	100 Saint-Louis St.
Quebec PQ	Horse and Carriage Tours	418-683-9222	Place d'Armes or rue d'Auteuil
Quebec PQ	Le Promenade des Ecrivains (Writer's Walking Tour)	418-264-2772	1588, avenue Bergemont
Quebec PQ	Le Promenades du Vieux-Quebec	418-692-6000	43, rue De Buade
Quebec PQ	Parc Nautique de Cap-Rouge Boat Rentals	418-641-6148	4155, chemin de la Plage-Jacques-Cartier
Quebec PQ	Quebec - Levis Ferry	418-644-3704	Rue Dalhousie, Lower Town
Quebec PQ	Rue du Tresor Open Air Artist District	418-259-7453	Rue du Tresor
Quebec PQ	Voir Quebec Walking Tours	418-694-2001	12, rue Ste-Anne
Quebec City PQ	Ghost Tours of Quebec	418-692-9770	85, rue St-Louis
St-Joseph-du-Lac PQ	La Roche des brises Vineyard	450-472-2722	2007, rue Principale
Val-David PQ	Santa Claus Village	819-322-2146	987 Marin

Saskatchewan

Battleford SK	Fort Battleford National Historic Site	306-937-2621	13th Street and Central Avenue
Lumsden SK	Corn Maiden Market at Lincoln Gardens	306-731-3133	On H 20 between Lumsden and Craven
Maple Creek SK	Fort Walsh National Historic Site	306-662-2645	H 271 (PO Box 278)
Regina SK	Silver Springs Trout Ranch	306-543-5575	H 11
Rosthern SK	Batoche National Historic Site	306-423-6227	H 225
Rosthern SK	Seager Wheeler National Historic Site	306-232-5959	Seager Wheeler Road
Saskatoon SK	Berry Barn	306-978-9797	830 Valley Rd
Saskatoon SK	Wanuskewin Heritage Park	306-931-6767	RR4 Penner Road

Yukon

Watson Lake YU	Signpost Forest		
Whitehorse YU	Whitehorse Fishway	867-633-5965	Nisutlin Drive

Chapter 6

Dog-Friendly Outdoor Dining

United States

Alabama

Birmingham AL	Café Ciao	205-871-2423	2031 Cahaba Road
Birmingham AL	Organic Harvest Market and Cafe	205-978-0318	1580 Montgomery Hwy/H 31
Birmingham AL	The Cantina	205-323-6980	2901 Second Avenue S
Fairhope AL	Fairhope Restaurant	251-928-6226	62 S Church Street
Fairhope AL	Original Ben's Jr.	251-928-1211	552 N Section Street/H 98
Fairhope AL	Panini Pete's Cafe and Bakeshoppe	251-929-0122	42 1/2 South Section Street, Suite 2/H 3
Fairhope AL	Sandra's Place	251-990-3344	218 Fairhope Avenue/H 48
Fayetteville AL	Ozark Natural Foods and Deli	479-521-7558	1554 N College Avenue/H 71/180
Gulf Shores AL	Big O's Seafood Grill	251-948-6969	1209 Gulf Shores Parkway
Hoover AL	Cajun Steamer	205-985-7785	180 Main Street
Huntsville AL	Bandito Burrito	256-534-0866	3017 Governors Drive SW
Huntsville AL	Jamo's Cafe	256-837-7880	413 Jordan Lane NW
Huntsville AL	Stanlieo's Sub Villa	256-837-7220	605 Jordan Lane
Huntsville AL	Stanlieo's Sub Villa	256-536-6585	602 Governors Drive
Mobile AL	Bakery Cafe	251-433-2253	1104 Dauphin Street
Mobile AL	Café 615	251-432-8434	615 Dauphin Street
Mobile AL	Callaghan's Irish Social Club	251-433-9374	916 Charleston Street
Mobile AL	Panera Bread	251-342-5101	3691 Airport Blvd # D
Mobile AL	Panera Bread	251-634-9604	750 Schillinger Road S
Mobile AL	Trolleys Neighborhood Pub	251-479-7778	2101 Airport Blvd
Northport AL	The Globe	205-391-0949	430 Main Ave
Orange Beach AL	Angler's Oyster Bar and Grill	251-981-1864	26619 Perdido Beach Blvd/H 182
Orange Beach AL	Cosmos Restaurant and Bar	251-948-WOOF (9663)	25753 Canal Road/H 180
Troy AL	Sonic	334-807-0011	1140 Hwy 231 South

Alaska

Anchorage AK	Alaska Salmon Chowder House	907-278-6901	443 W Fourth Avenue
Anchorage AK	Artic Roadrunner	907-561-1245	5300 Old Sewar H
Anchorage AK	L'Aroma Bakery and Deli	907-274-9797	900 W 13th Avenue
Anchorage AK	New Sagayaas City Market	907-274-6173	900 W 13th Avenue
Anchorage AK	Snow City Cafe	907-272-2489	1034 W 4th Avenue
Delta Junction AK	Rika's Roadhouse and Landing	907-895-4201	Mile 275 Richardson H
Douglas AK	The Island Pub	907-364-1595	1102 2nd Street
Fairbanks AK	C and J Drive In	907-452-3159	2233 S Cushman Street
Fairbanks AK	Gambardella's Pasta Bella	907-456-3417	706 2nd Avenue
Gustavus AK	Glacier Bay Lodge Restaurant	907-697-2225	Park Road/Bartlett Cove Station
Haines AK	Mountain Market & Cafe	907-766-3340	151 3rd Ave Haines Hwy
Haines AK	Top Frog	907-766-2423	2nd Avenue
Homer AK	Boardwalk Fish and Chips	907-235-7749	Homer Spit Road
Homer AK	Fresh Sourdough Express Bakery and Cafe	907-235-7571	1316 Ocean Drive
Homer AK	Panarelli's Cafe and Deli	907-235-1555	106 W Brunell Homer
Homer AK	The Homer Spit	907-235-7148	3789 Homer Spit Road #B
Juneau AK	Silverbow Inn and Bakery	907-586-4146	120 2nd Street
Juneau AK	Twisted Fish Company	907-463-5033	550 S Franklin Street
Ketchikan AK	Burger Queen	907-225-6060	518 Water Street/H7
Ketchikan AK	Dave's Red Anchor Cafe	907-247-5287	1935 Tongass Avenue #A/H7
Ketchikan AK	Ocean View Restaurant	907-225-7566	3159 Tongass Avenue/H 7
Metlakatla AK	Mini-Mart and Deli	907-886-3000	Milton Street
Valdez AK	Fish Central	888-835-5002	217 N Harbor Drive (office)
Whittier AK	Cafe Orca	520-531-1833	Whittier Harbor Loop

Arizona

Bisbee AZ	Alley Cafe	520-432-3733	15 Main Street
Bisbee AZ	Jimmy's Hot Dog Company	520-432-5911	938 W H 92
Cave Creek AZ	Big Earl's Greasy Eats	480-575-7889	6135 E Cave Creek Road
Cave Creek AZ	Cave Creek Coffee Company & Wine Bar	480-488-0603	6033 Cave Creek Road
Chandler AZ	Iguana Mack's	480-899-6735	1371 N Alma School Rd
Gilbert AZ	Uncle Bear's Grill and Bar	480-792-1945	825 S Cooper Road
Glendale AZ	Starbucks	623-362-9288	20249 North 67th Ave #B
Glendale AZ	Starbucks	623-878-1717	7410 W Bell Rd #310
Grand Canyon AZ	Grand Canyon Snack Bars		Grand Canyon National Park
Lake Havasu City AZ	Javelina Cantina	928-855-8226	1420 McCulloch Drive
Mesa AZ	Dos Gringos Mexigrill	480-633-5525	1958 S Greenfield
Mesa AZ	Honey Baked Ham and Co and Cafe	480-854-3300	6736 E Baseline Rd
Mesa AZ	Salty Senorita	480-632-TACO (8226)	1860 S Stapley Drive

Dog-Friendly Outdoor Dining - Please always call ahead to make sure an establishment is still dog-friendly.

Mesa AZ	The Mesa Monastery	480-474-4477	4810 East McKillips
Peoria AZ	Salty Senorita	623-979-GUAC (4822)	8011 W Paradise Lane
Phoenix AZ	Aunt Chiladas	602-944-1286	7330 North Dreamy Draw Drive
Phoenix AZ	Baja Fresh Mexican Grill	602-263-0110	1615 E Camelback Rd Ste F
Phoenix AZ	Baja Fresh Mexican Grill	602-843-6770	430 East Bell Rd.
Phoenix AZ	Baja Fresh Mexican Grill	602-256-9200	50 N. Central Ave
Phoenix AZ	Beans Books and Barks	602-788-0332	4030 E Bell Road, Ste 112
Phoenix AZ	Duck and Decanter	602-274-5429	1651 East Camelback Road
Phoenix AZ	Honey Baked Ham and Co and Cafe	602-996-0600	4635 E Cactus Road
Phoenix AZ	NYPD Pizza	602-294-6969	1949 E Camelback Rd
Phoenix AZ	Pita Jungle	602-955-PITA (7482)	4340 E Indian School Road
Phoenix AZ	Red Brick Pizza	602-305-8883	2170 E Baseline Road
Phoenix AZ	Red Robin	623-581-8635	2501 W Happy Valley Road
Phoenix AZ	Rock Bottom Brewery and Restaurant	480-598-1300	14205 S 50th St
Phoenix AZ	Rubio's Fresh Mexican Grill	602-508-1732	4340 E. Indian School Rd., Ste. 1
Phoenix AZ	Rubio's Fresh Mexican Grill	602-867-1454	4747 East Bell Road #17
Phoenix AZ	Sam's Cafe	602-954-7100	2566 E. Camelback Rd.
Phoenix AZ	The Capital Grille	602-952-8900	2502 E. Camelback Rd.
Phoenix AZ	The Farm at South Mountain	602-276-6360	6106 South 32nd Street
Phoenix AZ	Z Pizza	602-997-4992	2815 W Peoria Avenue
Phoenix AZ	Z Pizza	602-254-4145	111 W Monroe Street
Phoenix AZ	Z Pizza	602-234-3289	53 W Thomas Road
Phoenix AZ	Z Pizza	602-765-0511	13637 N Tatum Blvd
Scottsdale AZ	Baja Fresh Mexican Grill	480-429-8270	4032 N. Scottsdale Rd, Ste 1
Scottsdale AZ	Dos Gringos Scottsdale Cantina	480-423-3800	4209 N Craftsman Court
Scottsdale AZ	Kashman's Deli	480-585-6221	23425 N Scottsdale Road
Scottsdale AZ	Kashman's Deli	480-488-5274	32531 N Scottsdale Road
Scottsdale AZ	Muze Bistro	480-222-3366	15680 N Pima Rd
Scottsdale AZ	Rubio's Fresh Mexican Grill	480-575-7280	32415 N. Scottsdale Road, Ste. C
Scottsdale AZ	Salty Senorita	480-946-SALTY (7258)	3636 N Scottsdale Road
Scottsdale AZ	Salty Senorita	480-922-MARG (6274)	14950 N Northsight Blvd
Scottsdale AZ	Veneto Trattoria	480-948-9928	6137 N Scottsdale Road #B115
Scottsdale AZ	Veneto Trattoria	480-948-9928	6137 N Scottsdale Road # B115
Scottsdale AZ	Z Pizza	480-515-9792	20511 N. Hayden Road, , AZ - (480) 515-9792
Sedona AZ	Cucina Rustica	928-284-3010	7000 H 179
Sedona AZ	Open Range Grill and Tavern	928-282-0002	320 N H 89A
Sedona AZ	Red Planet Diner	928-282-6070	1655 W Highway 89A
Sedona AZ	The Grille at ShadowRock at the Hilton Sedona	928-284-4040	90 Ridge Trail Dr
Sedona AZ	Troia's Pizza Pasta Amore	928-282-0123	1885 W H 89A
Sierra Vista AZ	Sonic Drive-In	520-458-4530	3640 E Fry Blvd
Surprise AZ	Big Buddha Chinese Restaurant	623-266-3328	16572 W Greenway Road #115
Tempe AZ	Baja Fresh Mexican Grlll	480-446-3116	414 W. University Drive
Tempe AZ	Green Vegetarian Restaurant	480-941-9003	2240 N Scottsdale Road
Tempe AZ	Pier 54	480-820-0660	5394 S Lakeshore Drive
Tempe AZ	Pita Jungle	480-804-0234	1250 E Apache Blvd
Tempe AZ	Rubio's Fresh Mexican Grill	480-897-3884	1712 East Guadalupe Rd., Ste. 109
Tombstone AZ	Nellie Cashman Restaurant	520-457-2212	131 S 5th Street
Tombstone AZ	O.K. Cafe	520-457-3980	220 E. Allen Street
Tucson AZ	Baggin's Gourmet Sandwiches	520-327-4342	2741 E Speedway Blvd
Tucson AZ	Buck and Lil's BBQ	520-325-5185	5121 East Grant Rd
Tucson AZ	Cafe Jasper	520-577-0326	6370 N Campbell Avenue
Tucson AZ	Cafe Jasper	520-577-0326	6370 N Campbell Avenue
Tucson AZ	Chopped	520-319-CHOP (2467)	4205 N. Campbell Avenue
Tucson AZ	Cup Cafe	520-622-8848	311 E Congress Street
Tucson AZ	Dakota Cafe and Catering Company	520-298-7188	6541 E Tanque Verde Rd
Tucson AZ	Eegee's	520-881-3280	4510 E Speedway
Tucson AZ	Famous Sam's Restaurant and Bar	520-531-9464	8058 North Oracle Rd
Tucson AZ	Ghini's	520-326-9095	1803 E Prince Rd
Tucson AZ	Honey Baked Ham	520-544-2121	7090 N Oracle/H 77
Tucson AZ	Honey Baked Ham	520-745-0700	5350 E Broadway
Tucson AZ	Li'l Abner's Steakhouse	520-744-2800	8500 North Silverbell Rd
Tucson AZ	Mama's Famous Pizza and Heros	520-297-3993	7965 North Oracle Rd
Tucson AZ	Ric's Cafe	520-577-7272	5605 East River Rd
Tucson AZ	Saga Restaurant and Sushi Bar	520-320-0535	2955 E Speedway Blvd
Tucson AZ	Schlotzsky's Deli	520-741-2333	3270 East Valencia
Tucson AZ	The Cereal Boxx	520-622-BOXX (2699)	943 E University Blvd
Tucson AZ	The Cup Cafe (in Hotel Congress)	520-798-1618	311 E Congress St
Williams AZ	Cruiser's Cafe	928-635-2445	233 West Route 66
Williams AZ	The Route 66 Place	928-635-0266	417 East Route 66

Arkansas

Dog-Friendly Outdoor Dining - Please always call ahead to make sure an establishment is still dog-friendly.

Eureka Springs AR	New Delhi Cafe	479-253-2525	2 N Main Street/H 23
Hot Springs AR	Angel's Italian Restaurant	501-609-9323	600 Central Avenue/H 7
Hot Springs AR	El Patio	501-620-4428	1301 Albert Pike Road/H 270
Little Rock AR	Arkansas Burger Company	501-663-0600	7410 Cantrell Road
Little Rock AR	Leo's Greek Castle	501-666-7414	2925 Kavanaugh Blvd

California

Alameda CA	Pappo Restaurant	510-337-9100	2320 Central Avenue
Alameda CA	Tucker's Super-Creamed Ice Cream	510-522-4960	1349 Park Street
Albany CA	Cugini Restaurant	510-558-9000	1556 Solano Ave
Albany CA	Schmidts Pub	510-525-1900	1492 Solano Avenue
Alhambra CA	Diner on Main	626-281-3488	201 W Main Street
Aliso Viejo CA	Z Pizza	949-425-0102	26921 Aliso Creek Road
Anaheim CA	Rubios Baja Grill	714-999-1525	520 N Euclid St
Anaheim CA	Subway Sandwiches	714-535-3444	514 N Euclid Street
Anaheim Hills CA	Z Pizza	714-998-4171	5745 E Santa Ana Canyon Road
Aptos CA	Britannia Arms Restaurant	831-688-1233	8017 Soquel Drive
Aptos CA	Cole's Bar-B-Q	831-662-1721	8059 Aptos Street
Aptos CA	Ma Maison Restaurant	831-688-5566	9051 Soquel Drive
Arcadia CA	Matt Denny's Ale House	626-462-0250	145 E Huntington Dr
Arnold CA	Giant Burger	209-795-1594	846 Highway 4
Arnold CA	Pablito's of the Mother Lode	209-795-3303	925 Highway 4 # J
Arroyo Grande CA	Branch Street Deli	805-489-9099	203 E. Branch St
Arroyo Grande CA	Old Village Grill	805-489-4915	101 E. Branch St
Auburn CA	Bootleggers Tavern and Grill	530-889-2229	210 Washington St
Auburn CA	Ikeda's	530-885-4243	13500 Lincoln Way
Auburn CA	La Bou	530-823-2303	2150 Grass Valley Hwy
Auburn CA	Lou La Bonte's	530-885-9193	13460 Lincoln Way
Auburn CA	Max's	530-823-6297	11960 Heritage Oak Place
Auburn CA	Tio Pepe's	530-888-6445	216 Washington Street
Bakersfield CA	Black Angus	661-324-0814	3601 Rosedale Highway
Bakersfield CA	Cafe Med	661-834-4433	4809 Stockdale Hwy
Bakersfield CA	Filling Station	661-323-5120	1830 24th Street
Bakersfield CA	Jamba Juice	661-322-6722	5180 Stockdale Hwy #AB
Bakersfield CA	Los Hermanos	661-328-1678	3501 Union Ave
Bakersfield CA	Los Hermanos	661-835-7294	8200 Stockdale Hwy #N
Bakersfield CA	Mimi's Cafe	661-326-1722	4025 California Ave
Bakersfield CA	Patio Mexican Grill	661-587-6280	13001 Stockdale Hwy
Bakersfield CA	Plumberry's	661-589-8889	13001 Stockdale Hwy
Bakersfield CA	Rosemary's Family Creamery	661-395-0555	2733 F Street
Bakersfield CA	Sequoia Sandwich Company	661-323-2500	1231 18th Street
Bakersfield CA	Sonic Drive In	661-324-9100	1402 23rd Street
Bakersfield CA	Sonic Drive-In	661-587-9400	13015 Stockdale Hwy
Bakersfield CA	Sub Station	661-323-2400	5464 California Ave
Bakersfield CA	Subway	661-366-3300	8346 East Brundage Lane
Bakersfield CA	The Gourmet Shoppe	661-834-5522	4801 Stockdale Hwy
Bakersfield CA	Village Grill	661-325-1219	2809 F Street
Barstow CA	El Pollo Loco	760-253-5222	2820 Lenwood Road
Belmont CA	Coyote Cafe	650-595-1422	1003 Alameda de las Pulgas
Ben Lomond CA	Spanky's	831-336-8949	9520 H 9
Berkeley CA	Bel Forno	510-644-1601	1400 Shattuck Ave
Berkeley CA	Cafe Gratitude	510-725-4418	1730 Shattuck Avenue
Berkeley CA	Cafe Trieste	510-548-5198	2500 San Pablo Ave
Berkeley CA	French Hotel Cafe	510-548-9930	1538 Shattuck Ave
Berkeley CA	Homemade Cafe	510-845-1940	2454 Sacramento St
Berkeley CA	La Mediterranee	510-540-7773	2936 College Avenue
Berkeley CA	Pasta Shop	510-528-1786	1786 4th Street
Berkeley CA	Tacubaya	510-525-5160	1788 4th Street
Berkeley CA	Whole Foods Market	510-649-1333	3000 Telegraph Ave.
Beverly Hills CA	Joan's on 3rd	323-655-2285	8350 W Third Street
Beverly Hills CA	Kings Road Expresso Cafe	323-655-9044	8361 Beverly Blvd
Beverly Hills CA	The Lazy Daisy	310-859-1111	9010 Wilshire Blvd
Beverly Hills CA	Urth Cafe	310-205-9311	267 S Beverly Dr
Big Bear Lake CA	Alpine High Country Cafe	909-866-1959	41546 Big Bear Blvd
Big Bear Lake CA	Big Bear Mountain Brewery	909-866-2337	40260 Big Bear Blvd
Big Bear Lake CA	Jasper's Smokehouse and Steaks	909-866-2434	607 Pine Knot Avenue
Big Bear Lake CA	Log Cabin Restaurant and Bar	909-866-3667	39976 Big Bear Blvd/H 18
Big Bear Lake CA	Nottingham's Restaurant and Tavern	909-866-4644	40797 Lakeview Drive
Big Bear Lake CA	Village Pizza	909-866-8505	40568 Village Dr
Bishop CA	Pizza Factory	760-872-8888	970 N Main Street/H 6/395
Bishop CA	Raymond's Deli	760-873-7275	206 N Main Street/H 6/395
Bolinas CA	Coast Cafe	415-868-2298	46 Wharf Road
Bolinas CA	Coast Cafe	415-868-2298	46 Wharf Rd
Bolinas CA	Smiley's Schooner Saloon	415-868-1311	41 Wharf Road
Boonville CA	Boonville Hotel	707-895-2210	14050 H 128
Boonville CA	Mosswood Market Cafe	707-895-2210	14111 H 128 Suite A
Boonville CA	Redwood Cafe	707-895-3441	13980 H 128
Borrego Springs CA	The Red Ocotillo	760-767-7400	818 Palm Canyon Drive
Brea CA	La Cucina	714-529-0138	975 Birch Street

Dog-Friendly Outdoor Dining - Please always call ahead to make sure an establishment is still dog-friendly.

Brea CA	Schlotzsky's Deli	714-256-1100	2500 E. Imperial Hwy #196
Brentwood CA	Baja Fresh Mexican Grill	925-634-7373	5601 Lone Tree Way
Brentwood CA	San Gennaro Cafe	310-476-9696	140 Barrington Place
Burbank CA	La Bamba	818-846-3358	2600 North Glenoaks Blvd.
Burbank CA	Priscilla's Coffee and Tea	818-843-5707	4150 W Riverside Street, Suite A
Burbank CA	The Riverside Cafe	818-563-3567	1221 Riverside Dr
Burbank CA	Z Pizza	818-840-8300	116 E Palm Avenue
Burlingame CA	Copenhagen Bakery and Cafe	650-342-1357	1216 Burlingame Ave
Burlingame CA	La Scala	650-347-3035	1219 Burlingame Ave
Calistoga CA	Buster's BBQ	707-942-5605	1207 Foothills Blvd
Calistoga CA	Home Plate Cafe	707-942-5646	Hwy 128 & Petrified Forest Rd.
Camarillo CA	Essential Wine Company	805-445-4424	2390 Las Posas Rd
Camarillo CA	Panda Express	805-987-3368	199 W Ventura Blvd
Cambria CA	Las Cambritas	805-927-0175	2336 Main Street
Cambria CA	Madeline's	805-927-4175	788 Main St
Cambria CA	Mustache Pete's	805-927-8589	4090 Burton Drive
Camino CA	Forrester Restaurant	530-644-1818	4110 Carson Road
Camino CA	Mountain Mike's Pizza	530-644-6000	3600 Carson Rd #C
Campbell CA	Camille's Sidewalk Cafe	408-559-0310	1700 S Bascom Avenue
Campbell CA	Le Boulanger Bakery	408-369-1820	1875 S Bascom Ave
Campbell CA	Rock Bottom Restaurant & Brewery	408-377-0707	1875 S Bascom Ave
Campbell CA	Stacks	408-376-3516	139 E Campbell Ave
Campbell CA	Yiassoo	408-559-0312	2180 S Bascom Ave
Canyon Country CA	Telly's Diner	661-250-0444	27125 Sierra Hwy
Canyon Country CA	Telly's Drive In and Diner	661-250-0444	27125 Sierra Hwy
Capitola CA	Cafe Misk at Capitola Village	831-464-3400	201 Monterey
Capitola CA	Gayle's Bakery and Rosticceria	831-462-1200	504 Bay Avenue
Carlsbad CA	Cafe Elysa	760-434-4100	3076 Carlsbad Blvd
Carlsbad CA	Grand Deli	760-729-4015	595 Grand Ave
Carlsbad CA	Gregorio's Restaurant	760-720-1132	300 Carlsbad Village Dr #208
Carlsbad CA	Mas Fina Cantina	760-434-3497	2780 State Street
Carlsbad CA	Pizza Port	760-720-7007	571 Carlsbad Village Dr
Carlsbad CA	Tom Giblin's Irish Pub	760-729-7234	640 Grand Ave
Carlsbad CA	Vigilucci's Cucina Italiana	760-434-2500	2943 State Street
Carlsbad CA	Village Grille	760-729-3601	2833 State Street
Carlsbad CA	Vinaka Cafe	760-720-7890	300 Carlsbad Village Dr #211
Carlsbad Village CA	Tom Giblin's Irish Pub	760-729-7234	640 Grand Avenue
Carmel CA	Allegro Gourmet Pizzeria	831-626-5454	3770 The Barnyard
Carmel CA	Anton and Michel	831-624-2406	Mission Street and 7th Avenue
Carmel CA	Casanova Restaurant	831-625-0501	Mission & 5th
Carmel CA	Forge in the Forest	831-624-2233	5th and Junipero, SW Corner
Carmel CA	Hog's Breath Inn	831-625-1044	San Carlos St and 5th Ave
Carmel CA	Le Coq D'Or	831-626-9319	Mission between 4th & 5th
Carmel CA	Nico's	831-624-6545	San Carlos St and Ocean Ave
Carmel CA	PortaBella	831-624-4395	Ocean Ave
Carmel CA	R. G. Burgers	831-626-8054	201 Crossroads Shopping Village
Carmel CA	The Forge In the Forest	831-624-2233	Fifth and Junipero Avenues
Carmel Valley CA	Cafe Stravaganza	831-625-3733	241 The Crossroads
Carmel Valley CA	Carmen's Place	831-625-3030	211 The Crossroads
Carmel Valley CA	Plaza Linda	831-659-4229	9 Del Fino Pl
Carmel Valley CA	The Corkscrew Cafe	831-659-8888	55 W Carmel Valley Rd
Carmel-by-the-Sea CA	Jack London's Grill and Taproom	831-624-2336	Delores Street between 5th & 6th Streets
Carmel-by-the-Sea CA	Village Corner Mediterranean Bistro	831-624-3588	Dolores & 6th Avenue
Carmichael CA	Bella Bru Coffee Co	916-485-2883	5038 Fair Oaks Blvd
Carmichael CA	Java Central	916-972-7800	7429 Fair Oaks Blvd
Carnelian Bay CA	Old Post Office Coffee Shop	530-546-3205	5245 North Lake Blvd
Carpinteria CA	Tony's Italian Dinners and BBQ Ribs	805-684-3413	699 Linden Ave
Cathedral City CA	Michael's Cafe	760-321-7197	35955 Date Palm Drive
Chico CA	Bellachinos	530-892-2244	800 Bruce Road
Chico CA	Cafe Flo	530-892-0356	365 E 6th Street
Chico CA	Cal Java	530-893-2662	2485 Notre Dame Blvd.
Chico CA	Celestino's Pasta and Pizza	530-345-7700	1354 East Ave
Chico CA	Dog House	530-894-3641	1008 W Sacramento Avenue
Chico CA	Grilla Bites	530-343-4876	196 Cohasset Road
Chico CA	Leftcoast Pizza Co	530-892-9000	800 Bruce Road
Chico CA	S & S Organic Produce and Natural Foods	530-343-4930	1924 Mangrove Avenue
Chico CA	Shubert's Ice Cream	530-342-7163	178 E 7th Street
Chico CA	Spiteri's Delicatessen	530-891-4797	971 East Avenue
Chino Hills CA	Z Pizza	909-631-2224	3090 Chino Avenue
Clairemont CA	Cucina Italiana	858-274-9732	4705-A Clairemont Drive
Claremont CA	Aruffo's Italian Cuisine	909-624-9624	126 Yale Ave
Claremont CA	Danson's Restaurant	909-621-1818	109 Yale Ave
Claremont CA	Some Crust Bakery	909-621-9772	119 Yale Avenue
Claremont CA	Village Grill	909-626-8813	148 Yale Ave
Clayton CA	Skipolini's Pizza	925-672-1111	1033 Diablo St
Colfax CA	Drooling Dog Bar BBQ	530-346-8883	212 N Canyon Way
Coloma CA	Argonaut Cafe		Hwy 49
Coloma CA	Sutter Center Market	530-626-0849	378 Highway 49
Columbia CA	Columbia Frosty	209-532-9949	22652 Parrotts Ferry Rd
Concord CA	Guadalajara Grill Mexican	925-672-4430	5446 Ygnacio Valley Road # B6

Dog-Friendly Outdoor Dining - Please always call ahead to make sure an establishment is still dog-friendly.

Concord CA	Memo's Mexican Cuisine	925-691-6200	2118 Mount Diablo Street
Corona Del Mar CA	Caffe Panini	949-675-8101	2333 E Pacific Coast Hwy
Coronado CA	Cafe 1134	619-437-1134	1134 Orange Ave
Coronado CA	McP's Irish Pub and Grill	619-435-5280	1107 Orange Avenue
Coronado CA	Spiro's Gyros	619-435-1225	1201 First Street
Coronado CA	Tartine	619-435-4323	1106 1st Street
Corte Madera CA	A.G. Ferrari Foods	415-927-4347	107 Corte Madera Town Ctr
Corte Madera CA	Book Passage Bookstore and Cafe	415-927-1503	51 Tamal Vista
Corte Madera CA	World Wrapps	415-927-3663	208 Corte Madera Town Center
Costa Mesa CA	Avanti Cafe	949-548-2224	259 E 17th Street
Costa Mesa CA	Rainbow Bridge Store and Deli	949-631-4741	225 East 17th Street
Costa Mesa CA	Side Street Cafe	949-650-1986	1799 Newport Blvd Ste A105
Costa Mesa CA	Terra Nova Restaurant at the Wyndham OC	714-751-5100	3350 Avenue of the Arts
Cotati CA	Mi Pueblito Restaurant	707-795-7600	7600 Commerce Blvd
Cotati CA	Redwood Cafe	707-795-7868	8240 Old Redwood Highway
Crescent City CA	Beacon Burger	707-464-6565	160 Anchor Way
Crescent City CA	Betterbean Espresso	707-465-1248	315 M Street
Crescent City CA	Bistro Gardens	707-464-5627	110 Anchor Way
Crescent City CA	Good Harvest Cafe	707-465-6028	700 Northcrest Drive
Crescent City CA	Los Compadres Mexican Food	707-464-7871	457 Highway 101
Cupertino CA	Cafe Society	408-725-8091	21265 Stevens Creek Blvd #202
Cupertino CA	Whole Foods Market	408-257-7000	20830 Stevens Creek Blvd.
Danville CA	Z Pizza	925-362-4010	95 Railroad Avenue
Davenport CA	Whale City Bakery	831-423-9803	490 Hwy 1
Davis CA	Ali Baba Middle Eastern Restaurant	530-758-2251	220 3rd Street
Davis CA	Ben & Jerry's	530-756-5964	500 1st St #9
Davis CA	Davis Food Co-op	530-758-2667	620 G Street
Davis CA	Jamba Juice	530-757-8499	500 1st Street #3
Davis CA	Mishka's	530-759-0811	514 2nd Street
Davis CA	Posh Bagels	530-753-6770	206 F Street
Davis CA	Redrum Burger	530-756-2142	978 Olive Drive
Davis CA	Steve's Place Pizza, Pasta & Grill	530-758-2800	314 F Street
Davis CA	Subway	530-753-2141	4748 Chiles Rd
Davis CA	Sudwerk	530-758-8700	2001 2nd Street
Death Valley CA	Panamint Springs Resort	775-482-7680	Hwy 190
Del Mar CA	Americana	858-794-6838	1454 Camino Del Mar
Del Mar CA	Del Mar French Pastry Cafe	858-481-8622	1140 Camino Del Mar
Del Mar CA	En Fuego Cantina & Grill	858-792-6551	1342 Camino del Mar
Del Mar CA	Pacifica Breeze Cafe	858-509-9147	1555 Camino Del Mar #209
Del Mar CA	Stratford Court Cafe	858-792-7433	1307 Stratford Court
Duncans Mills CA	Cape Fear Cafe	707-865-9246	25191 Main Street/H 116
Dunsmuir CA	Cafe Maddalena	530-235-2725	5801 Sacramento Avenue
Dunsmuir CA	Cornerstone Bakery & Cafe	530-235-4677	5759 Dunsmuir Avenue
El Dorado Hills CA	Bella Bru Coffee Company	916-933-5454	3941 Park Drive #50
El Dorado Hills CA	Juice It Up	916-941-7140	4355 Town Center Blvd, #113
El Dorado Hills CA	Mama Ann's Deli & Bakery	916-939-1700	4359 Town Center Blvd #111
El Dorado Hills CA	Steve's Place Pizza & Pasta	916-939-2100	3941 Park Drive, #100
El Segundo CA	Mandy's Family Restaurant	310-322-7272	241 Main Street
Encinitas CA	Beachside Bar and Grill	760-942-0738	806 N Coast H 101
Encinitas CA	Encinitas Cafe	760-632-0919	531 S Coast Hwy 101
Encinitas CA	Firenze Trattoria	760-944-9000	162 S Rancho Santa Fe Road
Encinitas CA	St Germain's Cafe	858-509-9293	1010 S Coast H 101
Encino CA	More Than Waffles	818-789-5937	17200 Ventura Blvd.
Escondido CA	Centre City Cafe	760-489-6011	2680 S Escondido Blvd
Escondido CA	Charlie's Family Restaurant	760-738-1545	210 N Ivy Street
Etiwanda CA	Johnny Rockets	909-463-2800	7800 Kew Avenue
Eureka CA	Hana Sushi Restaurant	707-444-3318	2120 4th Street
Eureka CA	Los Bagels	707-442-8525	403 Second Street
Eureka CA	Starbucks Coffee	707-445-2672	1117 Myrtle Avenue
Fair Oaks CA	Steve's Place Pizza	916-961-1800	11711 Fair Oaks Blvd
Fairfax CA	Fairfax Scoop	415-453-3130	63 Broadway Blvd
Fairfax CA	Iron Springs Pub and Brewery	415-485-1005	765 Center Blvd
Fallbrook CA	Firehouse Broiler	760-728-8008	1019 S. Main Ave
Fallbrook CA	Greek Style Chicken	760-723-8050	904 S. Main Ave
Fallbrook CA	J.J. Landers Irish Pub Sports Bar and Restaurant	760-731-0839	125 S Main Street
Felton CA	Rocky's Cafe	831-335-4637	6560 H 9
Felton CA	The Trout Farm	831-335-4317	7701 E Zayante Road
Folsom CA	Coffee Republic	916-987-8001	6610 Folsom Auburn Rd
Folsom CA	Pizzeria Classico	916-351-1430	702 Sutter St
Folsom CA	Rubio's Baja Grill	916-983-0645	2776 E Bidwell Street
Folsom CA	Snook's Candies and Ice Cream	916-985-0620	731 Sutter Street
Folsom CA	Thai Ginger and Satay Bar	916-983-4003	1115 E Bidwell St #126
Forestville CA	Russian River Pub	707-887-7932	11829 River Road
Fort Bragg CA	Home Style Cafe	707-964-6106	790 S. Main Street
Fort Bragg CA	Laurel Deli	707-964-7812	401 N Main Street
Fort Bragg CA	Piaci Pub and Pizzeria	707-961-1133	120 W. Redwood Avenue
Fort Bragg CA	Rendezvous Inn and Restaurant	707-964-8142	647 North Main Street
Fortuna CA	Shotz Coffee	707-725-8000	1665 Main Street
Foster City CA	El Torito Mexican Restaurant and Cantina	650-574-6844	388 Vintage Park Drive

Dog-Friendly Outdoor Dining - Please always call ahead to make sure an establishment is still dog-friendly.

Fountain Valley CA	Z Pizza	714-444-4260	18011 Newhope Street
Fresno CA	Dai Bai Dang Restaurant	559-448-8894	7736 N Blackstone Ave
Fresno CA	Revue News	559-499-1844	620 E. Olive Avenue
Fresno CA	TGI Fridays	559-435-8443	1077 E. Herndon Avenue
Fresno CA	Whole Foods Market	559-241-0300	650 West Shaw Avenue
Fresno CA	Z Pizza	559-433-9995	1512 E Champlain Drive
Fullerton CA	Table Ten	714-526-3210	124 W Commonwealth Avenue
Fullerton CA	Z Pizza	714-738-4249	1981 Sunnycrest Drive, Fullerton, Ca
Glen Ellen CA	Garden Court Cafe & Bakery	707-935-1565	13875 Sonoma Highway 12
Glendora CA	Z Pizza	909-599-4500	1365 E Gladstone Street
Goleta CA	Mc Master's Steak and Hoagie Restaurant	805-685-7010	910 Embarcadero Del Norte
Goleta CA	New Baja Grill	805-571-6000	7024 Camino Real Marketplace
Goleta CA	The Natural Cafe	805-692-2363	5892 Hollister Avenue
Granite Bay CA	La Bou	916-791-2142	4110 Douglas Blvd
Grass Valley CA	Bubba's Bagels	530-272-8590	11943 Nevada City Hwy
Grass Valley CA	Cousin Jack Pastries	530-272-9230	100 S Auburn St
Guerneville CA	Main Street Station Ristorante, Cabaret & Pizzeria,	707-869-0501	16280 Main Street
Guerneville CA	Roadhouse Restaurant at Dawn Ranch Lodge	707-869-0656	16467 River Road
Guerneville CA	Sea Horse Restaurant at Russian River Resort	707-869-3333	16390 4th Street
Half Moon Bay CA	Casey's Cafe	650-560-4880	328 Main Street
Half Moon Bay CA	Half Moon Bay Brewery	650-728-2739	390 Capistrano Road
Half Moon Bay CA	Half Moon Bay Coffee Company	650-726-3664	20 Stone Pine Rd #A
Half Moon Bay CA	It's Italia Pizzeria	650-726-4444	401 Main Street
Half Moon Bay CA	Pasta Moon	650-726-5125	315 Main Street
Half Moon Bay CA	Three-Zero Cafe	650-728-1411	9850 Cabrillo Hwy N
Healdsburg CA	Dry Creek General Store	707-433-4171	3495 Dry Creek Rd
Healdsburg CA	Giorgio's Pizzeria	707-433-1106	25 Grant Avenue
Hermosa Beach CA	Martha's Corner	310-379-0070	25 22nd St
Hillcrest CA	Babbo Grande	619-269-8038	1731 University Avenue
Hollywood CA	Birds Cafe-Bar	323-465-0175	5925 Franklin Avenue
Hollywood CA	In-N-Out Burgers	800-786-1000	7009 Sunset Blvd.
Hollywood CA	La Poubelle Bistro and Bar	323-465-0807	5907 Franklin Avenue
Hollywood CA	The Cat and Fiddle	323-468-3800	6530 Sunset Blvd
Huntington Beach CA	Alice's Breakfast in the Park	714-848-0690	Huntington Central Park
Huntington Beach CA	Java City Bakery Cafe	714-842-5020	18685 Main St #G
Huntington Beach CA	Smokin' Mo's BBQ	714-374-3033	301 Main Street
Huntington Beach CA	Spark Woodfire Grill	714-960-0996	300 Pacific Coast H
Huntington Beach CA	Taste of France	714-895-5305	7304 Center Ave
Huntington Beach CA	The Park Bench Cafe	714-842-0775	17732 Golden West Dr
Huntington Beach CA	Z Pizza	714-968-8844	10035 Adams Avenue
Huntington Beach CA	Z Pizza	714-536-3444	19035 Golden West Avenue, Huntington Beach, CA - (
Huntington Beach CA	Zimzala	714-861-4470	500 Pacific Coast H/H 1
Idyllwild CA	Cafe Aroma	951-659-5212	54750 North Circle Drive
Idyllwild CA	El Diablo Cafe	951-659-2560	54225 N Circle Dr. #13
Idyllwild CA	Joanne's Restaurant and Bar	951-659-0295	25875 N Village Drive
Imperial Beach CA	Katy's Cafe	619-863-5524	704 Seacoast Drive
Incline Village NV	Grog & Grist Market & Deli	775-831-1123	800 Tahoe Blvd
Incline Village NV	T's Rotisserie	775-831-2832	901 Tahoe Blvd
Inverness CA	Priscilla's Pizza	415-669-1244	12781 Sir Francis Drake Blvd.
Inverness CA	Vladimir's Czechoslovakian Restaurant	415-669-1021	12785 Sir Francis Drake Blvd.
Irvine CA	Britta's Cafe	949-509-1211	4237 Campus Drive
Irvine CA	Corner Bakery Cafe	714-734-8270	13786 Jamboree Rd
Irvine CA	Mother's Market & Kitchen	949-752-6667	2963 Michelson Drive
Irvine CA	Philly's Best	949-857-2448	4250 Barranca Parkway #R
Irwindale CA	Picasso?s Cafe Bakery and Catering Co	626-969-6100	6070 N. Irwindale Ave.
Jackson CA	Mel & Faye's Drive In	209-223-0853	205 N. State Hwy 49
Jamestown CA	Historic National Hotel	209-984-3446	18187 Main St
Jamestown CA	Pizza Plus	209-984-3700	18251 Main St
Julian CA	Apple Alley Bakery	760-765-2532	2122 Main Street
Julian CA	Buffalo Bills	760-765-1560	2603 B Street
Julian CA	Julian Pie Company	760-765-2449	2225 Main Street
Julian CA	The Bailey Wood Pit Barbecue	760-765-3757	Main and A Streets
Julian CA	The Julian Grille	760-765-0173	2224 Main Street
Julian CA	Wynola Pizza Express	760-765-1004	4355 H 78/79
Kings Beach CA	Brockway Bakery	530-546-2431	8710 North Lake Blvd
Kings Beach CA	Char-Pit	530-546-3171	8732 N Lake Blvd
Kings Beach CA	Straddles	530-546-3774	9980 N Lake Blvd
La Habra CA	Z Pizza	714-870-4743	1202 S Idaho Street
La Jolla CA	Cass Street Café and Bakery	858-454-9094	5550 La Jolla Blvd
La Jolla CA	Cups	858-459-CUPS (2877)	7857 Girard Avenue
La Jolla CA	Elijah's	858-455-1461	8861 Villa La Jolla Drive
La Jolla CA	Girard Gourmet	858-454-3321	7837 Girard Avenue
La Jolla CA	Harry's Coffee Shop	858-454-7381	7545 Girard Avenue
La Jolla CA	The 910 Restaurant and Bar	858-454-2181	910 Prospect St
La Jolla CA	Whole Foods Market	858-642-6700	8825 Villa La Jolla Drive

Dog-Friendly Outdoor Dining - Please always call ahead to make sure an establishment is still dog-friendly.

La Jolla CA	Yummy Maki Yummy Box	858-587-9848	3211 Holiday Ct # 101A
La Jolla CA	Z Pizza	858-450-0660	8657 Villa La Jolla Drive
La Jolla CA	Zenbu Sushi Bar & Restaurant	858-454-4540	7660 Fay Avenue
La Verne CA	Aoki Japanese Restaurant	909-593-2239	2307 D Street
La Verne CA	Cafe Allegro	909-593-0788	2124 3rd Street
La Verne CA	Casa Garcia's Grill	909-593-9092	2124 Bonita Ave
La Verne CA	Phoenix Garden	909-392-2244	2232 D Street #101
Ladera Ranch CA	Z Pizza	949-347-8999	25672 Crown Valley Parkway
Lafayette CA	Chow Restaurant	925-962-2469	53 Lafayette Circle
Lafayette CA	Uncle Yu's Szechuan	925-283-1688	999 Oak Hill Rd
Laguna Beach CA	Cottage Restaurant	949-494-3023	308 N Coast H/H 1
Laguna Beach CA	Food Village	949-464-0060	211-217 Broadway St
Laguna Beach CA	Madison Squar and Garden Cafe	949-494-0137	320 North Coast Hwy
Laguna Beach CA	Z Pizza	949-499-4949	30902 S Coast H/H 1
Laguna Beach CA	Zinc Cafe and Market	949-494-6302	350 Ocean Avenue
Laguna Niguel CA	Z Pizza	949-481-3948	32371 Golden Lantern Street
Lake Forest CA	Fresca's Mexican Grill	949-837-8397	22681 Lake Forest Dr
Lakewood CA	Z Pizza	562-425-5558	3221 Carson Street
Lancaster CA	Camille's Sidewalk Cafe	661-940-5878	43901 15th Street W
Larkspur CA	Left Bank	415-927-3331	507 Magnolia Avenue
Livermore CA	Bella Roma Pizza	925-447-4992	853 E Stanley Blvd
Livermore CA	Chevys Fresh Mex	925-960-0071	4685 First Street
Livermore CA	First Street Ale House	925-371-6588	2086 1st Street
Livermore CA	Manpuku	925-371-9038	4363 First Street
Livermore CA	Olive Tree Café and Catering	925-960-0636	7633 Southfront Road
Livermore CA	Panama Bay Coffee Co.	925-245-1700	2115 First Street
Lone Pine CA	Pizza Factory	760-876-4707	301 S Main Street/H 395
Long Beach CA	Eggs Etc.	562-433-9588	550 Redondo Avenue
Long Beach CA	Rubio's Fresh Mexican Grill	562-496-1892	7547 Carson Blvd
Long Beach CA	The Library A Coffee House	562-433-2393	3418 E Broadway
Long Beach CA	Wild Oats Natural Marketplace	562-598-8687	6550 E. Pacific Coast Highway
Long Beach CA	Z Pizza	562-987-4500	4612 E 2nd Street
Long Beach CA	Z Pizza	562-498-0778	5718 E 7th Street
Los Angeles CA	Alcove	323-644-0100	1929 Hillhurst Avenue
Los Angeles CA	Delilah Bakery	213-975-9400	1665 Echo Park Avenue
Los Angeles CA	Fred's 62	323-667-0062	1850 N Vermont Ave
Los Angeles CA	Good Microbrew and Grill	323-660-3645	3725 Sunset Blvd
Los Angeles CA	Good Microbrew and Grill	323-660-3645	922 Lucille Avenue
Los Angeles CA	Griffith Park snack stand		Vermont Ave
Los Angeles CA	Hollywood Blvd restaurants		Hollywood Blvd.
Los Angeles CA	Home	323-669-0211	1760 Hillhurst Avenue
Los Angeles CA	Il Capriccio on Vermont	323-662-5900	1757 N Vermont Avenue
Los Angeles CA	Johnnie's New York Pizza	310-553-1188	10251 Santa Monica Blvd
Los Angeles CA	Lala's Argentine Grill	323-934-6838	7229 Melrose Avenue
Los Angeles CA	Le Figaro Bistro	323-662-1587	1802 N Vermont Avenue
Los Angeles CA	Leaf Organic	310-390-6005	11938 W Washington Blvd
Los Angeles CA	Mel's Drive-In	310-854-7200	8585 Sunset Blvd.
Los Angeles CA	Millie's Restaurant	323-664-0404	3524 W Sunset Blvd
Los Angeles CA	Sante La Brea	323-857-0412	345 N La Brea
Los Angeles CA	Sonora Cafe	323-857-1800	180 S La Brea
Los Angeles CA	Tiago Café	323-466-5600	7080 Hollywood
Los Angeles CA	Toast Bakery Cafe Inc	323-655-5018	8221 W 3rd St
Los Angeles CA	Whole Foods Market	310-826-4433	11737 San Vicente Blvd.
Los Angeles CA	Whole Foods Market	323-964-6800	6350 West 3rd Street
Los Angeles CA	Whole Foods Market	323-848-4200	7871 West Santa Monica Blvd.
Los Angeles CA	Whole Foods Market	310-996-8840	11666 National Boulevard
Los Angeles CA	Whole Foods Market	310-824-0858	1050 S. Gayley
Los Angeles CA	Z Pizza	323-466-6969	123 N Larchmont
Los Feliz CA	Home	323-665-HOME (4663)	1760 Hillhurst Avenue
Los Gatos CA	Whole Foods Market	408-358-4434	15980 Los Gatos Blvd.
Los Gatos CA	Willow Street Pizza	408-354-5566	20 S. Santa Cruz Ave
Los Olivos CA	Los Olivos Cafe	805-688-7265	2879 Grand Ave
Los Olivos CA	Patrick's Side Street Cafe	805-686-4004	2375 Alamo Pintado Ave
Madera CA	IHOP Restaurant	559-675-5179	2201 W Cleveland Avenue
Mammoth Lakes CA	Base Camp Cafe	760-934-3900	3325 Main Street
Manhattan Beach CA	Johnny Rockets	310-536-9464	1550 Rosecrans Ave.
Martinez CA	La Beau's Louisiana kitchen	925-229-9232	436 Fairy Street
Mendocino CA	Mendo Burgers	707-937-1111	10483 Lansing Street
Mendocino CA	The Moosse Cafe	707-937-4323	390 Kasten
Menlo Park CA	Cafe Borrone	650-327-0830	1010 El Camino Real
Menlo Park CA	Left Bank	650-473-6543	635 Santa Cruz Avenue
Mill Valley CA	Round Table Pizza	415-383-5100	50 Belvedere Drive
Milpitas CA	Bento Xpress	408-262-7544	23 N. Milpitas Blvd
Milpitas CA	Erik's Deli Cafe	408-262-7878	148 N. Milpitas Blvd
Mission Valley CA	Seau's	619-291-7328	1640 Camino del Rio North
Mission Viejo CA	Skimmer's Panini Cafe	949-276-6300	25290 Marguerite Parkway
Mission Viejo CA	Skimmer's Panini Grill	949-855-8500	25290 Marguerite Pkwy
Mission Viejo CA	Taco Mesa	949-364-1957	27702 Crown Valley Parkway
Modesto CA	Harvest Moon	209-523-9723	1213 I Street

Monrovia CA	Peach Cafe	626-599-9092	141 E Colorado Blvd
Montecito CA	Pierre Lafond Montecito Deli	805-565-1502	516 San Ysidro Road
Monterey CA	Ambrosia India Bistro	831-641-0610	565 Abrego Street
Monterey CA	Archie's Hamburgers & Breakfast	831-375-6939	125 Ocean View Blvd.
Monterey CA	Bubba Gump Shrimp Co.	831-373-1884	720 Cannery Row
Monterey CA	East Village Coffee Lounge	831-373-5601	498 Washington St
Monterey CA	El Palomar Mexican Restaurant	831-372-1032	724 Abrego St
Monterey CA	Ghiradelli Ice Cream	831-373-0997	660 Cannery Row
Monterey CA	Grill and Ryan Ranch	831-647-0390	1 Harris Court
Monterey CA	Indian Summer	831-372-4744	220 Olivier Street
Monterey CA	Jose's Restaurant	831-655-4419	638 Wave St
Monterey CA	Louie Linguini's	831-648-8500	660 Cannery Road
Monterey CA	Paluca Trattoria	831-373-5559	6 Fishermans Wharf #1
Monterey CA	Parker-Lusseau Pastries	831-641-9188	539 Hartnell Street
Monterey CA	Peter B's Brewery & Restaurant	831-649-4511	2 Portola Plaza
Monterey CA	Pino's Italian Cafe & Ice Cream	831-649-1930	211 Alvarado St
Monterey CA	Tarpy's Road House	831-647-1444	2999 Monterey Salinas Hwy #1
Monterey CA	Trailside Cafe	831-649-8600	550 Wave Street
Monterey CA	Turtle Bay Taqueria	831-333-1500	431 Tyler St
Monterey CA	Whole Foods Market	831-333-1600	800 Del Monte Center
Montgomery CA	Bubba Gump Shrimp Company Restaurant	831-373-1884	720 Cannery Row
Montrose CA	Zeke's Smokehouse Restaurant	818-957-7045	2209 Honolulu Avenue
Moorpark CA	The Natural Cafe	805-523-2016	840 New Los Angeles Avenue #A-2/H 23/118
Morro Bay CA	Dorn's Original Breakers Cafe	805-772-4415	801 Market Ave
Morro Bay CA	Tognazzini's Dockside Too	805-772-8100	1245 Embarcadero
Moss Beach CA	Moss Beach Distillery	650-728-5595	140 Beach Way @ Ocean Blvd
Mount Shasta CA	Lalo's Mexican Restaurant	530-926-5123	520 N Mount Shasta Blvd
Mountain View CA	Amici's East Coast Pizza	650-961-6666	790 Castro Street
Mountain View CA	Cafe Baklava	650-969-3835	341 Castro Street
Mountain View CA	Clarkes Charcoal Broiler	650-967-0851	615 W El Camino Real
Mountain View CA	Hobee's	650-968-6050	2312 Central Expressway
Mountain View CA	La Salsa Restaurant	650-917-8290	660 San Antonio Rd
Mountain View CA	Le Boulanger	650-961-1787	650 Castro St #160
Mountain View CA	Posh Bagel	650-968-5308	444 Castro Street #120
Mountain View CA	Z Pizza	650-314-0088	146 Castro Street
Napa CA	Angele	707-252-8115	540 Main Street
Napa CA	Angele	707-252-8115	540 Main Street
Napa CA	Bistro Don Giovanni	707-224-3300	4110 Howard Street
Napa CA	Napa General Store Restaurant	707-259-0762	540 Main Street
Napa CA	Sweetie Pies	707-252-8115	520 Main Street
Nevada City CA	Broad Street Bistro	530-265-4204	426 Broad St
Nevada City CA	California Organics	530-265-9392	135 Argall Way
Nevada City CA	Ike's Quarter Cafe	530-265-6138	401 Commercial Street
Nevada City CA	New Moon Cafe	530-265-6399	203 York Street
Nevada City CA	Posh Nosh	530-265-6064	318 Broad St
Newark CA	JEBZ Restaurant and Bar	510-661-0355	39742 Cedar Blvd
Newbury Park CA	The Natural Cafe	805-523-2016	1714 Newbury Road, Suite R
Newport Beach CA	Champagne French Bakery Cafe	949-646-0520	1120 Irvine Avenue
Newport Beach CA	Charlie's Chili	949-675-7991	102 McFadden Place
Newport Beach CA	Park Avenue Cafe	949-673-3830	501 Park Avenue
Newport Beach CA	Wilma's Patio	949-675-5542	203 Marine Avenue
Newport Beach CA	Z Pizza	949-715-1117	7956 E Pacific Coast H/H 1
Newport Beach CA	Z Pizza	949-760-3100	2549 Eastbluff Drive
Newport Beach CA	Z Pizza	949-219-9939	1616 San Miguel Drive-
Newport Beach CA	Z Pizza	949-723-0707	3423 Via Lido
Norco CA	Rubio's Baja Grill	951-898-3591	110 Hidden Valley Pkwy
North Hollywood CA	Chez Nous	818-760-0288	10550 Riverside Drive
Northridge CA	Whole Foods Market	818-363-3933	19340 Rinaldi
Novato CA	El Encanto Restaurant and Cantina	415-892-1471	940 7th Street
Novato CA	Maya Palenque Restaurant	415-883-6292	349 Enfrente Rd
Oak View CA	Oak Pit Restaurant	805-649-9903	820 Ventura Ave
Oakhurst CA	Pizza Factory	559-683-2700	40120 Highway 41 #B
Oakland CA	Filippo's	510-601-8646	5400 College
Oakland CA	Heinolds First & Last Chance	510-839-6761	56 Jack London Sq
Oakland CA	Italian Colors Ristorante	510-482-8094	2220 Mountain Boulevard
Oakland CA	Posh Bagel	510-597-0381	4037 Piedmont Avenue
Ocean Beach CA	Bar-B-Que House	619-222-4311	5025 Newport Avenue
Ocean Beach CA	Tower Two Beach Cafe	619-223-4059	5083 Santa Monica Avenue # 1B
Oceanside CA	Don's Country Kitchen	760-722-7337	1938 Coast Highway
Oceanside CA	Hill Street Coffee House	760-966-0985	524 S Coast Hwy
Oceanside CA	Rice Garden	760-721-4330	401 Mission Ave #B110
Oceanside CA	Robins Nest Cafe	760-722-7837	280 S Harbor
Ojai CA	Antonio's Breakfast Coffee	805-646-6353	106 S Montgomery St
Ojai CA	Deer Lodge Tavern	805-646-4256	2261 Maricopa Hwy
Ojai CA	Full of Beans	805-640-8500	11534 N Ventura Avenue/H 33
Ojai CA	Jim & Rob's Fresh Grill	805-640-1301	535 E Ojai Ave
Ojai CA	Rainbow Bridge Natural Foods Market	805-646-4017	211 East Matilija Street
Ojai CA	Rainbow Bridge Natural Store and Deli	805-646-6623	211 E Matilija St
Ojai CA	Vesta Home and Hearth	805-646-2339	242 E. Ojai Avenue

Dog-Friendly Outdoor Dining - Please always call ahead to make sure an establishment is still dog-friendly.

Olympic Valley CA	Auld Dubliner	530-584-6041	The Village at Squaw Valley
Olympic Valley CA	Mamasake Sushi	530-584-0110	The Village at Squaw Valley
Olympic Valley CA	Starbucks Coffee	530-584-6120	The Village at Squaw Valley
Ontario CA	In-N-Out Burger	800-786-1000	1891 E. G Street
Ontario CA	Joey's Pizza	909-944-6701	790 N. Archibald Ave.
Orange CA	Byblos Mediterranean Cafe	714-538-7180	129 W Chapman Ave
Orange CA	Francoli	949-721-1289	100 S. Glassell Street
Orange CA	Krispy Kreme Doughnuts	714-769-4330	330 The City Dr S
Orange CA	The Filling Station	714-289-9714	201 N Glassell St
Orange CA	Two's Company	714-771-7633	22 Plaza Square
Orinda CA	Shelby's	925-254-9687	2 Theater Square
Pacific Grove CA	Bagel Bakery	831-649-6272	1132 Forest Ave
Pacific Grove CA	First Awakenings	831-372-1125	125 Ocean View Blvd #105
Pacific Grove CA	Seventeenth Street Grill	831-373-5474	617 Lighthouse Ave
Pacific Grove CA	Toasties Cafe	831-373-7543	702 Lighthouse Ave
Palm Desert CA	Native Foods	760-836-9396	73-890 El Paseo
Palm Desert CA	Z Pizza	760-568-5405	73607 H 111
Palm Springs CA	Hair of the Dog English Pub	760-323-9890	238 N Palm Canyon Dr
Palm Springs CA	Native Foods	760-416-0070	1775 E. Palm Canyon Drive
Palm Springs CA	Nature's Health Food and Café	760-323-9487	555 South Sunrise Way
Palm Springs CA	New York Pizza Delivery	760-778-6973	260 N. Palm Canyon Drive
Palm Springs CA	Peabody's Coffee Bar	760-322-1877	134 S Palm Canyon Dr
Palm Springs CA	Pomme Frite	760-778-3727	256 S. Palm Canyon Drive
Palm Springs CA	Rock Garden Cafe	760-327-8840	777 S Palm Canyon Drive
Palm Springs CA	Shermans Deli and Bakery	760-325-1199	401 Tahquitz Canyon Way
Palm Springs CA	Spencer's Restaurant	760-327-3446	701 West Baristo Road
Palm Springs CA	Starbucks	760-323-8023	682 S. Palm Canyon Drive
Palo Alto CA	Abbey's	650-322-8294	403 University Ave
Palo Alto CA	Izzy's Brooklyn Bagels	650-329-0700	477 S California Ave
Palo Alto CA	Joanie's Cafe	650-326-6505	447 S California Ave
Palo Alto CA	Spalti Ristorante	650-327-9390	417 S California Ave
Palo Alto CA	St. Michael's Alley	650-326-2530	806 Emerson St.
Palo Alto CA	Whole Foods Market	650-326-8676	774 Emerson Street
Pasadena CA	All India Cafe	626-440-0309	39 S Fair Oaks Ave
Pasadena CA	Barney's Ltd	626-577-2739	93 W. Colorado Blvd.
Pasadena CA	Camille's Sidewalk Cafe	626-440-1212	285 E Green Street
Pasadena CA	Il Fornaio	626-683-9797	24 W Union
Pasadena CA	Jake's Diner & Billiards	626-568-1602	38 W. Colorado Blvd.
Pasadena CA	Jones Coffee Roasters	626-564-9291	537 S Raymond Ave
Pasadena CA	Kabuki Japanese Restaurant	626-568-9310	88 W. Colorado Blvd.
Pasadena CA	Malagueta	626-564-8696	43 E. Colorado Blvd.
Pasadena CA	Mi Piace	626-795-3131	25 E Colorado Blvd
Pasadena CA	Niko and Friends Cafe	626- 510-6151	900 Valley View Avenue
Pasadena CA	Sorriso Ristorante	626-793-2233	168 W Colorado Blvd
Paso Robles CA	Big Bubba's BBQ	805-238-6272	1125 24th Street
Paso Robles CA	Chubby Chandler's	805-239-2141	1304 Railroad St.
Paso Robles CA	Good Ol' Burgers	805-238-0655	1145 24th Street
Petaluma CA	Apple Box	707-762-5222	224 B Street
Petaluma CA	Lombardi's Downtown Deli and BBQ	707-763-6959	139 Petaluma Blvd N.
Pine Grove CA	88 Burgers	209-296-7277	19845 State Highway 88
Pismo Beach CA	Mo's Smokehouse BBQ	805-773-6193	221 Pomeroy Ave
Pismo Beach CA	Seaside Cafe and Bakery	805-773-4360	1327 Shell Beach Road
Placerville CA	Creekside Cantina	530-626-7966	451 Main Street #10
Placerville CA	Noah's Ark	530-621-3663	535 Placerville Drive
Placerville CA	Pizza Factory	530-644-6043	4570 Pleasant Valley Road
Placerville CA	Quiznos Sub	530-622-7878	3967 Missouri Flat Road
Placerville CA	Straw Hat Pizza	530-626-8511	3970 Missouri Flat Rd
Placerville CA	Sweetie Pie's	530-642-0128	577 Main Street
Placerville CA	Teriyaki Junction	530-295-1413	1216 Broadway
Pleasant Hill CA	Left Bank	925-288-1222	60 Crescent Drive
Pleasanton CA	Baci Restaurant	925-600-0600	500 Main Street
Pleasanton CA	Erik's Deli	925-847-9755	4247 Rosewood Drive
Pleasanton CA	High Tech Burrito	925-462-2323	349 Main Street
Pleasanton CA	New York Pizza	925-484-4757	690 Main Street
Pleasanton CA	New York Pizza and Deli	925-847-1700	5321 Hopyard Road
Pleasanton CA	TGI Fridays	925-225-1995	3999 Santa Rita Road
Pleasanton CA	Tomo Sushi Bar & Grill	925-600-9136	724 Main Street
Plymouth CA	Cafe at the Park	209-245-6981	18265 Hwy 49
Plymouth CA	Gold Country Cafe	209-245-6218	17830 State Highway 49
Plymouth CA	Marlene and Glen's Diner	209-245-5778	18726 Highway 49
Point Reyes Station CA	Cowgirl Creamery	415-663-9335	80 Fourth Street
Point Reyes Station CA	Pine Cone Diner	415-663-1536	60 4th Street
Port Hueneme CA	Chinese Dumpling House	805-985-4849	575 W. Channel Islands Blvd.
Port Hueneme CA	Manhattan Bagel	805-984-3550	585 W Channel Islands Blvd.
Porter Ranch CA	Z Pizza	818-363-2600	19300 Rinaldi Street
Poway CA	A Whole Lotta Yogurt	858-668-2996	12222 Poway Road # 3
Poway CA	Chicken Pie Shop	858-748-2445	14727 Pomerado Road
Princeton CA	Half Moon Bay Brewing Company	650-728-BREW	390 Capistrano Rd
Quincy CA	Stoney's Country Burgers	530-283-3911	11 Lindan Avenue
Quincy CA	Sweet Lorraine's	530-283-5300	384 W Main Street/H 70

Dog-Friendly Outdoor Dining - Please always call ahead to make sure an establishment is still dog-friendly.

Rancho Cucamonga CA	Corner Bakery Cafe	909-803-2600	12375 N Main Street
Rancho Cucamonga CA	Panera Bread	909-919-7999	8055 Haven Avenue
Rancho Penasquitos CA	Cafe 56	858-484-5789	13211 Black Mountain Rd
Rancho Santa Margarita CA	Wing Star Pizza	949-459-6199	22307 El Paseo, Suite C
Redding CA	Burrito Bandito	530-222-6640	8938 Airport Road
Redding CA	Coffee Creek Juice and Java	530-229-7500	2380 Athens Avenue
Redding CA	In-n-Out	800-786-1000	1275 Dana Dr
Redding CA	La Palomar Mexican Dining	530-222-1208	2586 Churn Creek Road
Redding CA	Manhattan Bagel	530-222-2221	913 Dana Drive
Redding CA	Sandwichery	530-246-2020	1341 Tehama Street
Redding CA	Togos	530-222-9212	1030 East Cypress Avenue Ste B
Redlands CA	Z Pizza	909-307-2921	27512 Lugonia Avenue
Redondo Beach CA	Kool Dog Diner	310-944-3232	1666 South Pacific Coast Highway
Redondo Beach CA	Whole Foods Market	310-376-6931	405 N. Pacific Coast Hwy.
Redwood City CA	City Pub	650-363-2620	2620 Broadway
Redwood City CA	Diving Pelican Cafe	650-368-3668	650 Bair Island Rd #102
Redwood City CA	Talk of Broadway	650-368-3295	2096 Broadway Street
Redwood City CA	Whole Foods Market	650-367-1400	1250 Jefferson Avenue
Riverside CA	Antonious Pizza	951-682-9100	3737 Main Street
Riverside CA	Jazz-n-Java	951-780-1990	497 E Alessandro Blvd Suit A
Rohnert Park CA	Golden B Cafe	707-585-6185	101 Golf Course Drive
Roseville CA	Bravo! Pastaria Market and Eatery Restaurant	916-772-8777	1465 Eureka Road
Roseville CA	Cafe Elletti	916-774-6704	2240 Douglas Blvd
Roseville CA	Dos Coyotes Border Cafe	916-772-0775	2030 Douglas Blvd #4
Roseville CA	Mas Mexican Food	916-773-3778	1563 Eureka Roa
Roseville CA	Nugget Market	916-746-7799	771 Pleasant Grove Blvd
Roseville CA	Quizno's Classic Subs	916-787-1940	1228 Galleria Blvd #130
Roseville CA	Togo's Eatery	916-782-4546	1825 Douglas Blvd
Roseville CA	Z Pizza	916-786-9797	3984 Douglas Blvd
Rutherford CA	Rutherford Grill	707-963-1792	1180 Rutherford Road
S Lake Tahoe CA	Murphy's Irish Pub and Rockwater Restaurant	530-544-8004	787 Emerald Bay Road/H 89
Sacramento CA	Annabelle's Pizza-Pasta	916-448-6239	200 J Street
Sacramento CA	Bella Bru Cafe and Catering	916-928-1770	4680 Natomas Blvd
Sacramento CA	Broiler Steakhouse	916-444-3444	1201 K Street, Suite #100
Sacramento CA	Cafe Bernardo	916-443-1180	2726 Capitol Avenue
Sacramento CA	Danielle's Creperie	916-972-1911	3535 B Fair Oaks Blvd
Sacramento CA	Gonuls J Street Cafe	916-457-1155	3839 J Street
Sacramento CA	Hangar 17 Bar and Grill	916-447-1717	1630 S Street
Sacramento CA	Hot Rods Burgers	916-443-7637	2007 K Street
Sacramento CA	La Bou	916-369-7824	10395 Rockingham Dr
Sacramento CA	Original Pete's Pizza, Pasta and Grill	916-442-6770	2001 J Street
Sacramento CA	River City Brewing Company	916-447-2739	545 Downtown Plaza Ste 1115
Sacramento CA	Rubicon Brewing Company	916-448-7032	2004 Capitol Avenue
Sacramento CA	Sacramento Natural Foods Cooperative	916-455-2667	1900 Alhambra Blvd.
Sacramento CA	Streets of London Pub	916-498-1388	1804 J Street
Sacramento CA	The Bread Store	916-557-1600	1716 J Street
Sacramento CA	Whole Foods Market	916-488-2800	4315 Arden Way
San Anselmo CA	Easy Street Cafe	415-453-1984	882 Sir Francis Drake Blvd
San Anselmo CA	Java Hub Cafe	415-451-4928	60 Greenfield Avenue
San Carlos CA	Laurel Street Cafe	650-598-7613	741 Laurel Street
San Carlos CA	Ristorante Piacere	650-592-3536	727 Laurel Street
San Carlos CA	Santorini	650-637-8283	753 Laurel Street
San Clemente CA	Z Pizza	949-498-3505	1021 Avenida Pico
San Diego CA		858-689-9449	10006 Scripps Ranch Blvd
San Diego CA	Bareback Grill	858-274-7117	4640 Mission Blvd
San Diego CA	Bread Bites and Moore	858-780-2501	7845 Highland Village Place
San Diego CA	Brick Alley	619-523-1480	3577 Midway Drive
San Diego CA	Bull's Smokin' BBQ	619-276-2855	1127 W Morena Blvd
San Diego CA	Cafe 222	619-236-9902	222 Island Street
San Diego CA	Champagne French Bakery Cafe	858-792-2222	12955 El Camino Real
San Diego CA	City Delicatessen	619-295-2747	535 University Ave
San Diego CA	El Indio	619-299-0333	3695 India Street
San Diego CA	Gulf Coast Grill	619-295-2244	4130 Park Blvd
San Diego CA	Hudson Bay Seafood	619-222-8787	1403 Scott Street
San Diego CA	Kemo Sabe	619-220-6802	3958 Fifth Ave.
San Diego CA	King's Fish House	619-574-1230	825 Camino de la Reina
San Diego CA	Korky's Ice Cream and Coffee	619-297-3080	2371 San Diego Avenue
San Diego CA	Oggi's Pizza	619-640-1072	2245 Fenton Parkway
San Diego CA	Pampas Argentine Grill	858-278-5971	8690 Aero Drive Suite 105
San Diego CA	Saffron Thai Grilled Chicken	619-574-0177	3137 India Street
San Diego CA	Sally's Seafood on the Water	619-358-6740	1 Market Place
San Diego CA	Terra Bar and Restaurant	619-293-7088	3900 Vermont Street
San Diego CA	The Alamo	619-296-1112	2502 San Diego Ave
San Diego CA	Trattoria Fantastica	619-234-1735	1735 India Street
San Diego CA	Whole Foods Market	619-294-2800	711 University Avenue
San Diego CA	Z Pizza	858-675-9300	11975 Carmel Mountain Road
San Diego CA	Z Pizza	619-272-0022	5175 Linda Vista Road
San Diego CA	Zia's	619-234-1344	1845 India Street

Dog-Friendly Outdoor Dining - Please always call ahead to make sure an establishment is still dog-friendly.

San Dimas CA	Roady's Restaurant	909-592-0980	160 W. Bonita Ave
San Francisco CA	24th Street Cafe and Grill	415-282-1213	3853 24th Street
San Francisco CA	Alaturca Restaurant	415-345-1011	869 Geary Street
San Francisco CA	Alive!	415-923-1052	1972 Lombard Street/H 101
San Francisco CA	B44 Bistro	415-986-6287	44 Belden Place
San Francisco CA	Beach Chalet Brewery & Restaurant	415-386-8439	1000 Great Highway @ Ocean Beach
San Francisco CA	Blissful Bites	415-750-9460	397 Arguello Blvd
San Francisco CA	Blue Danube Coffee House	415-221-9041	306 Clement St
San Francisco CA	Cafe De La Presse	415-398-2680	352 Grant Ave
San Francisco CA	Cafe Divine	415-986-3414	1600 Stockton Street
San Francisco CA	Cafe Gratitude	415-824-4652	2400 Harrison Street (@20th Street)
San Francisco CA	Cafe Niebaum-Coppola	415-291-1700	916 Kearny Street
San Francisco CA	Calzone's	415-397-3600	430 Columbus Ave
San Francisco CA	Camille's Sidewalk Cafe	415-348-1514	One Market Plaza, 30 Mission Street
San Francisco CA	Chez Spencer Restaurant	415-864-2191	82 14th St
San Francisco CA	Cioppino's	415-775-9311	400 Jefferson Street
San Francisco CA	Coffee Bean and Tea Leaf	415-447-9733	2201 Fillmore St
San Francisco CA	Coffee Roastery	415-922-9559	2191 Union Street
San Francisco CA	Crepes a Go Go	415-928-1919	2165 Union St
San Francisco CA	Dolores Park Cafe	415-621-2936	18th and Dolores
San Francisco CA	Farley's	415-648-1545	1315-18th Street
San Francisco CA	Flippers	415-552-8880	482 Hayes Street
San Francisco CA	Ghirardelli Ice Cream Fountain	415-771-4903	Ghirardelli Square
San Francisco CA	Judy's Cafe	415-922-4588	2268 Chestnut St #248
San Francisco CA	La Mediterranee	415-431-7210	288 Noe Street
San Francisco CA	Lou's Pier 47 Restaurant	415-771-5687	300 Jefferson St
San Francisco CA	Martha & Brothers Coffee Company	415-648-1166	1551 Church Street
San Francisco CA	Mona Lisa	415-989-4917	353 Columbus Ave
San Francisco CA	Noe's Bar	415-282-4007	1199 Church Street
San Francisco CA	Panta Rei	415-591-0900	431 Columbus
San Francisco CA	Park Chow	415-665-9912	12 49th Avenue
San Francisco CA	Peet's Coffee and Tea	415-563-9930	2197 Fillmore St
San Francisco CA	Plouf	415-986-6491	40 Belden Place
San Francisco CA	Pluto's Fresh Food	415-775-8867	3258 Scott St
San Francisco CA	Polly Ann Ice Cream	415-664-2472	3142 Noriega St
San Francisco CA	Pompei's Grotto	415-776-9265	340 Jefferson St
San Francisco CA	Rogue Ales Public House	415-362-7880	673 Union
San Francisco CA	Royal Ground Coffee	415-567-8822	2060 Fillmore St
San Francisco CA	The Curbside Cafe	415-929-9030	2417 California St
San Francisco CA	Ti Couz	415-252-7373	3108 16th St
San Francisco CA	Zazie Cafe	415-564-5332	941 Cole Street
San Jose CA	Amato Pizzeria	408-997-7727	6081 Meridian Avenue #A
San Jose CA	Ben and Jerry's	408-423-8115	377 Santana Row #1120
San Jose CA	Bill's Cafe	408-294-1125	1115 Willow Street
San Jose CA	Britannia Arms	408-278-1400	173 W Santa Clara Street
San Jose CA	Camille's Sidewalk Cafe	408-436-5333	90 Skyport Drive
San Jose CA	Casa Vicky's Catering and Cafe	408-995-5488	792 E Julian St
San Jose CA	Consuelo Mexican Bistro	408-260-7082	377 Santana Row #1125
San Jose CA	Fu Kee Chinese Restaurant	408-225-3218	121 Bernal Road
San Jose CA	Left Bank	408-984-3500	377 Santana Row, Suite 1100
San Jose CA	Noah's Bagels	408-371-8321	1578 S Bascom Ave
San Jose CA	Pamela's East Side Cafe	408-254-4000	2122 McKee Road
San Jose CA	Pasta Pomodoro	408-241-2200	378 Santana Row #1130
San Jose CA	Pizza Antica	408-557-8373	334 Santana Row #1065
San Jose CA	Poor House Bistro	408-292-5837	91 S Autumn Street/H 82
San Jose CA	Siena Bistro	408-271-0837	1359 Lincoln Avenue
San Jose CA	Sonoma Chicken Coop	408-997-1272	5925 Almaden Expressway
San Jose CA	Sonoma Chicken Coop	408-287-4098	31 North Market Street
San Jose CA	Straits	408-246-6320	333 Santana Row
San Jose CA	Tanglewood	408-244-0464	334 Santana Row, Suite 1000
San Jose CA	The Loft Bar and Bistro	408-291-0677	90 S Second Street
San Jose CA	Willow Street Wood Fired Pizza	408-971-7080	1072 Willow St
San Jose CA	Yankee Pier	408-244-1244	378 Santana Row #1100
San Juan Bautista CA	JJ's Homemade Burgers	831-623-1748	100 The Alameda
San Juan Bautista CA	Joan and Peter's German Restaurant	831-623-4521	322 Third Street
San Juan Bautista CA	La Casa Rosa	831-623-4563	107 Third Street
San Juan Capistrano CA	Skimmer's Panini Cafe	949-276-6300	31451 Rancho Viejo Road
San Juan Capistrano CA	Z Pizza	949-429-8888	32341 Camino Capistrano
San Luis Obispo CA	Novo Restaurant	805-543-3986	726 Higuera Street
San Luis Obispo CA	Pizza Solo	805-544-8786	891 Higuera Street
San Luis Obispo CA	Splash Cafe	805-544-7567	1491 Monterey Street
San Marcos CA	Old California Coffee House	760-744-2112	1080 W. San Marcos Blvd #176
San Mateo CA	Left Bank	650-345-2250	1100 Park Place
San Mateo CA	Whole Foods Market	650-358-6900	1010 Park Place
San Rafael CA	Cafe Gratitude	415-578-4928	2200 Fourth Street
San Rafael CA	Planet Juice	415-457-8115	343 3rd Street
San Rafael CA	Ristorante La Toscana	415-492-9100	3751 Redwood Hwy.
San Rafael CA	The Lighthouse Diner	415-721-7700	1016 Court Street
San Rafael CA	Whole Foods Market	415-451-6333	340 Third Street
San Ramon CA	Whole Foods Market	925-355-9000	100 Sunset Drive

Dog-Friendly Outdoor Dining - Please always call ahead to make sure an establishment is still dog-friendly.

San Ramon CA	Z Pizza	925-328-0525	3141-D Crow Canyon Place
San Simeon CA	San Simeon Restaurant	805-927-4604	9520 Castillo Dr.
Sand City CA	Ol Factory Cafe	831-394-7336	1725 Contra Costa Street #D
Santa Ana CA	Z Pizza	714-437-1111	3941 South Bristol
Santa Barbara CA	City Barbeque	805-892-4483	901 North Milpas
Santa Barbara CA	Dargan's Irish Pub	805-568-0702	18 E. Ortega Street
Santa Barbara CA	Emilio's Restaurant	805-966-4426	324 W Cabrillo Blvd
Santa Barbara CA	Intermezzo	805-966-9463	813 Anacapa Street
Santa Barbara CA	Jeannine's Bakery and Cafe	805-687-8701	3607 State St
Santa Barbara CA	Pascucci's Restaurant	805-963-8123	729 State Street
Santa Barbara CA	Pierre Lafond Wine Bistro	805-962-1455	516 State Street
Santa Barbara CA	Pizza Mizza	805-564-3900	140 S Hope Avenue, Suite 102A
Santa Barbara CA	The Natural Cafe	805-962-9494	508 State Street
Santa Barbara CA	The Natural Cafe	805-563-1163	361 Hitchcock Way
Santa Clara CA	Pizz'a Chicago	408-244-2246	1576 Halford Ave
Santa Clara CA	Red Robin Gourmet Burgers	408-855-0630	3906 Rivermark Plaza
Santa Clara CA	Tony & Alba's Pizza & Pasta	408-246-4605	3137 Stevens Creek Blvd
Santa Clarita CA	Cavi at The Big Oaks	661-296-5656	33101 Bouquet Canyon Road
Santa Cruz CA	Aldo's Harbor Restaurant	831-426-3736	616 Atlantic Avenue
Santa Cruz CA	Black China Cafe and Bakery	831-460-1600	1121 Soquel Avenue
Santa Cruz CA	Cafe Limelight	831-425-7873	1016 Cedar Street
Santa Cruz CA	Cole's Bar-B-Q	831-476-4424	2590 Portola Drive
Santa Cruz CA	Engfer Pizza Works	831-429-1856	537 Seabright Ave
Santa Cruz CA	Firefly Coffee House	801-598-3937	131 A Front Street
Santa Cruz CA	Harbor Bay	831-475-4948	535 7th Avenue
Santa Cruz CA	Kelly's French Bakery,	831-423-9059	402 Ingalls Street, Santa Cruz, Ca 95060:
Santa Cruz CA	Las Palmas Taco Bar	831-429-1220	55 Front Street
Santa Cruz CA	Pleasure Pizza	831-475-4999	4000 Portola Drive
Santa Maria CA	The Cravings Deli	805-937-5170	2880 Santa Maria Way
Santa Maria CA	The Natural Cafe	805-937-2735	2407 S Broadway/H 135
Santa Monica CA	Babalu	310-395-2500	1002 Montana Avenue
Santa Monica CA	Bay Cities Italian Deli and Bakery	310-359-8279	1517 Lincoln Blvd
Santa Monica CA	Blue Plate	310-260-8877	1415 Montana Avenue
Santa Monica CA	Cezanne	310-395-9700	1740 Ocean Avenue
Santa Monica CA	Interim Cafe	310-319-9100	530 Wilshire Blvd
Santa Monica CA	Jinky's	310-917-3311	1447 2nd Street
Santa Monica CA	News Room Cafe	310-319-9100	530 Wilshire Street
Santa Monica CA	Pourtal Wine Tasting Bar	310-393-7693	104 Santa Monica Blvd/H 2
Santa Rosa CA	Chevy's Fresh Mex	707-571-1082	24 4th Street
Santa Rosa CA	Flying Goat Coffee	707-575-1202	10 4th Street
Santa Rosa CA	Sonoma Valley Bagel	707-579-5484	2194 Santa Rosa Ave
Santa Rosa CA	Sunnyside Tokyo	707-526-2652	3800 Sebastopol Road
Santa Rosa CA	Whole Foods Market	707-575-7915	1181 Yulupa Ave.
Santa Ysabel CA	Dudley's Bakery	760-765-0488	30218 H 78
Santa Ysabel CA	Jeremy's on The Hill	760-765-1587	4354 H 78
Saratoga CA	La Fondue	408-867-3332	14550 Big Basin Way
Saratoga CA	Lupretta's Delicatessen	408-484-0004	14480 Big Basin Way
Sausalito CA	Anchorage 5	415-331-8329	475 Gate 5 Road
Sausalito CA	Cafe Trieste	415-332-7660	1000 Bridgeway
Sausalito CA	Poggio Trattoria	415-332-7771	777 Bridgeway
Sausalito CA	Scoma's	415-332-9551	588 Bridgeway
Seal Beach CA	River's End Cafe	562-431-5558	15 1st Street
Seal Beach CA	Z Pizza	562-596-9300	148 Main Street
Seal Beach CA	Z Pizza	562-493-3440	12430 Seal Beach Blvd
Seaside CA	Jamba Juice	831-583-9696	2160 California Ave
Sebastopol CA	Pasta Bella	707-824-8191	796 Gravenstein Highway
Sebastopol CA	Whole Foods Market	707-829-9801	6910 McKinley St.
Shell Beach CA	Zorro's Cafe and Cantina	805-773-ZORO (9676)	927 Shell Beach Road
Sherman Oaks CA	Whole Foods Market	818-762-5548	12905 Riverside Drive
Sherman Oaks CA	Whole Foods Market	818-382-3700	4520 Sepulveda Boulevard
Shingle Springs CA	Shingle Springs Coffee Company	530-676-2623	4056 Mother Lode Dr
Simi Valley CA	The Natural Cafe	805-527-2272	2667 Tapo Canyon Road, Unit G
Solana Beach CA	Beach Grass Cafe	858-509-0632	159 S H 101
Solana Beach CA	Pacific Coast Grill	858-794-4632	437 S Highway 101 #112
Solana Beach CA	Zinc Cafe and Market	858-793-5436	132 S Cedros
Solano Beach CA	Pacific Coast Grill	858-794-4632	437 S H 101
Solvang CA	Bit O'Denmark	805-688-5426	473 Alisal Rd.
Solvang CA	Giovanni's Italian Restaurant	805-688-1888	1988 Old Mission Drive
Solvang CA	Greenhouse Cafe	805-688-8408	487 Atterdag Road
Solvang CA	Heidleberg Inn	805-688-6213	1618 Copenhagen Drive
Solvang CA	Olsen's Danish Village Bakery	805-688-6314	1529 Mission Drive
Solvang CA	Panino	805-688-0608	475 First Street
Solvang CA	River Grill at The Alisal	805-688-7784	150 Alisal Rd
Solvang CA	Subway	805-688-7650	1641 Mission Dr
Solvang CA	The Belgian Cafe	805-688-6630	1671 Copenhagen Drive
Solvang CA	The Big Bopper	805-688-6018	1510 Mission Drive
Solvang CA	The Bulldog Cafe	805-686-9770	1680 Mission Drive
Solvang CA	The Touch	805-686-0222	475 First Street

Dog-Friendly Outdoor Dining - Please always call ahead to make sure an establishment is still dog-friendly.

Solvang CA	Tower Pizza	805-688-3036	436 Alisal Rd, Units C + D
Solvang CA	Viking Garden Restaurant	805-688-1250	446C Alisal Rd
Solvang CA	Wandering Dog Wine Bar	805-686-9126	1539 Mission Drive 'C'/H 246
Sonoma CA	Harmony Club	707-996-9779	480 First Street East
Sonoma CA	La Casa	707-996-3406	121 E Spain Street
Sonora CA	Pine Tree Restaurant	209-536-6065	19601 Hess Ave
Soquel CA	Michael's on Main	831-479-9777	2591 Main Street
South Lake Tahoe CA	Big Daddy's Burgers	530-541-3465	3490 Lake Tahoe Blvd/H 50
South Lake Tahoe CA	Colombo's Burgers A-Go-Go	530-541-4646	841 US Hwy 89 Emerald Bay Rd
South Lake Tahoe CA	Izzy's Burger Spa	530-544-5030	2591 Highway 50
South Lake Tahoe CA	Meyer's Downtown Cafe	530-573-0228	3200 Highway 50
South Lake Tahoe CA	Nikkis Restaurant	530-541-3354	3469 Lake Tahoe Blvd
South Lake Tahoe CA	Quiznos Sub	530-544-9600	1001 Heavenly Village
South Lake Tahoe CA	Rude Brothers Bakery and Coffee House	530-541-8195	3117 Harrison Ave #B
South Lake Tahoe CA	Shoreline Cafe	530-541-7858	3310 Lake Tahoe Blvd/H 50
South Lake Tahoe CA	Sno-Flake Drive In	530-544-6377	3059 Harrison
South Lake Tahoe CA	Sprouts Health Foods	530-541-6969	3125 Harrison Avenue
South Lake Tahoe CA	The Burger Lounge	530-542-4060	717 Emerald Bay Rd
South Pasadena CA	Fair Oaks Pharmacy and Soda Fountain	626-799-1414	1526 Mission St
St Helena CA	Cindy's Backstreet Kitchen	707-963-1200	1327 Railroad Ave
St Helena CA	Ristorante Tra Vigne	707-963-4444	1050 Charter Oak Avenue
St Helena CA	Silverado Brewing Company	707-967-9876	3020 St Helena H N/H 29
St Helena CA	Tra Vigne Cantinetta	707-963-4444	1050 Charter Oak Avenue
Stinson Beach CA	Parkside Cafe	415-868-1272	43 Arenal Avenue
Stinson Beach CA	Sand Dollar Restaurant	415-868-0434	3458 Shoreline Highway
Studio City CA	Killer Shrimp	818-508-1570	4000 Colfax Avenue
Studio City CA	Le Pain Quotidien	818-986-1929	13045 Ventura Blvd
Studio City CA	Louise's Trattoria	818-762-2662	12050 Ventura Blvd.
Studio City CA	Studio Yogurt	818-508-7811	12050 Ventura Blvd
Sun Valley CA	Big Jim's	818-768-0213	8950 Laurel Canyon Blvd
Sunnyvale CA	Fibbar Magees Irish Pub	408-749-8373	156 Murphy Avenue
Tahoe City CA	Bridgetender Tavern and Grill	530-583-3342	65 West Lake Blvd
Tahoe City CA	Front Street Station Pizza	530-583-3770	205 River Road
Tahoe City CA	Rosie's Cafe	530-583-8504	571 North Lake Blvd
Tahoe City CA	Syd's Bagelery & Expresso	530-583-2666	550 N Lake Blvd
Tahoe City CA	Tahoe House Bakery and Gourmet Store	530-583-1377	625 W Lake Blvd
Tahoe City CA	The Blue Agave	530-583-8113	425 N Lake Blvd
Temecula CA	5th Avenue Dog House	951-695-3136	41958 5th Street
Temecula CA	Aloha J's	951-506-9889	27497 Ynez Rd
Temecula CA	Cafe Daniel	951-676-8408	28601 Old Town Front Street
Temecula CA	California Tea and Coffee Brewery	951-693-5727	40315-A Winchester Road/H 79
Temecula CA	Carol's Restaurant	951-676-9243	33440 La Serena Way
Temecula CA	Front Street Bar and Grill	951-676-9567	28699 Old Town Front Street
Temecula CA	Mad Madeline's Grill	877-805-6653	28495 Front Street Suite A
Temecula CA	Mad Madeline's Grill	951-699-3776	28495 Front Street
Temecula CA	Marie Callender's	951-699-9339	29363 Rancho California Rd
Temecula CA	Milanos Delicatessen	951-491-0600	32240 H 79S
Temecula CA	Scarcella's Italian Grille	951-676-5450	27525 Ynez Rd
Temecula CA	Temecula Pizza Company	951-694-9463	44535 Bedford Ct # D
Temecula CA	Texas Lil's Mesquite Grill	951-699-LILS (5457)	28495 Old Town Front Street
Thousand Oaks CA	Lazy Dog Cafe	805-449-5206	172 W Hillcrest Drive
Thousand Oaks CA	Thousand Oaks Meat Locker	805-495-3211	2684 E Thousand Oaks Blvd
Thousand Oaks CA	Z Pizza	818-991-4999	5776 Lindero Canyon Road
Tiburon CA	Shark's Deli	415-435-9130	1600 Tiburon Blvd
Tiburon CA	Three Degrees Restaurant at The Lodge at Tiburon	415-435-3133	1651 Tiburon Blvd/H 131
Toluca Lake CA	Priscilla's Gourmet Cafe	818-843-5707	4150 Riverside Dr
Tomales CA	Tomales Bakery	707-878-2429	27000 Highway One
Topanga CA	Abuelitas Restaurant	310-455-8788	137 South Topanga Canyon Blvd
Torrance CA	The Lazy Dog Cafe	310-921-6080	3525 Carson Street
Torrance CA	Whole Foods Market	310-257-8700	2655 Pacific Coast Highway
Tustin CA	Whole Foods Market	714-731-3400	14945 Holt Ave.
Tustin CA	Z Pizza	714-734-9749	12932 Newport Avenue
Ukiah CA	Porter Street BBQ	707-468-9222	225 E Perkins Street
Upland CA	Molly's Souper	909-982-1114	388 N 1st Avenue
Upland CA	Z Pizza	909-949-1939	1943-C N Campus Avenue
Upper Lake CA	Blue Wing Saloon and Cafe	707-275-2233	9520 Main Street
Valencia CA	Wahoo's Fish Taco	661-255-5138	24230 Valencia Blvd
Valencia CA	Z Pizza	661-259-5000	27015 McBean Parkway
Valley Ford CA	Route 1 Diner	707-876-9600	14450 Highway 1
Van Nuys CA	Springbok Bar and Grill	818-988-9786	16153 Victory Blvd
Venice CA	Brick House Cafe	310-581-1639	826 Hampton Dr
Venice CA	French Market Cafe	310-577-9775	2321 Abbot Kinney
Venice CA	The Terrace	310-578-1530	7 Washington Blvd
Ventura CA	Anacapa Brewing Company	805-643-BEER (2337)	472 E Main Street
Ventura CA	Cafe Nouveau	805-648-1422	1497 E Thompson Blvd
Ventura CA	Full of Beans	805-648-5645	1124 S Seaward Ave # A
Ventura CA	Lassen Ventura Market and Deli	805-644-6990	4071 E Main Street

Ventura CA	Nature's Grill	805-643-7855	566 E Main Street
Ventura CA	Spinnaker Seafood	805-658-6220	1583 Spinnaker Dr.
Ventura CA	Tony's Pizzeria	805-643-8425	186 E Thompson Blvd
Walnut Creek CA	Pacific Bay Coffee Co and Micro-Roastry	925-935-1709	1495 Newell Ave
Watsonville CA	El Alteno	831-768-9876	323 Main Street
West Hollywood CA	Basix Cafe	323-848-2460	8333 Santa Monica Blvd.
West Hollywood CA	Champagne Cafe	310-657-4051	8917 Santa Monica Blvd
West Hollywood CA	Joey's Cafe	323-822-0671	8301 Santa Monica Blvd/H 2
West Hollywood CA	Le Pain Quotidien	310-854-3700	8607 Melrose Avenue
West Hollywood CA	Marix West Hollywood	323-656-8800	1108 N. Flores Street
West Hollywood CA	Miyagi's Sushi Restaurant	323-650-3524	8225 Sunset Blvd
West Hollywood CA	Urth Cafe	310-659-0628	8565 Melrose Ave
West Hollywood CA	Z Pizza	310-360-1414	8869 Santa Monica Blvd/H 2
West Hollywood CA	Zeke's Smokehouse	323-850-9353	7100 Santa Monica Blvd
Westlake Village CA	Jack's Restaurant and Deli	805-495-8181	966 South Westlake Blvd
Westminster CA	Lazy Dog Cafe	714-848-4300	16310 Beach Blvd
Winter Park CA	Carver's Restaurant	970-726-8202	93 Cooper Creek Way
Woodland CA	Morrison's Upstairs Restaurant	530-666-6176	428 1/2 1st Street
Woodland CA	Steve's Place Pizza Pasta	530-666-2100	714 Main Street
Woodland Hills CA	My Brother's BBQ	818-348-2020	21150 Ventura Blvd
Woodland Hills CA	Pickwick's Pub	818-340-9673	21010 Ventura Blvd
Yountville CA	Bistro Jeanty	707-944-0103	6510 Washington Street
Yountville CA	Bouchon	707-944-8037	6534 Washington Street
Yountville CA	Hurley's Restaurant	707-944-2345	6518 Washington Street
Yountville CA	Napa Valley Grille	707-944-8686	6795 Washington Street
Yountville CA	Pacific Blues Cafe	707-994-4455	6525 Washington Street
Yuba City CA	Sonic Drive-in	530-671-3736	981 Grey Avenue
Yuba City CA	The City Cafe	530-671-1501	667 Plumas Street

Colorado

Aspen CO	Ajax Tavern	970-920-9333	685 E Durant
Aspen CO	Grateful Deli	970-925-6647	233 E Main Street
Aurora CO	Baja Fresh	303-367-9700	14301 E Cedar Avenue, Suite A
Boulder CO	Boulder Beer	303-444-8448	2880 Wilderness Place
Boulder CO	Half Fast Subs	303-449-0404	1215 13th Street
Boulder CO	Old Chicago	303-443-5031	1102 Pearl Street
Colorado Springs CO	Caspian Cafe	719-528-1155	4375 Sinton Road
Colorado Springs CO	Nosh	719-635-6674	121 South Tejon Street
Colorado Springs CO	Pizzeria Rustica	719-632-8121	2527 W Colorado Avenue
Colorado Springs CO	Poor Richard's	719-632-7721	324 North Tejon
Denver CO	Baja Fresh	303-296-1800	99918th Street, #107
Denver CO	Corner Bakery Cafe	303-572-0170	500 16th Street
Denver CO	Croc's Cafe	303-436-1144	1630 Market Street
Denver CO	Dixons Downtown Grill	303-573-6100	1610 16th Street
Denver CO	Paris Coffee Roasting	303-455-2451	1553 Platte Street
Denver CO	Rubios Baja Grille	303-765-0036	703 S Colorado Blvd
Denver CO	St Mark's Coffeehouse	303-322-8384	2019 E 17th Ave
Denver CO	Strings	303-831-7310	1700 Humboldt St
Denver CO	The Market	303-534-5140	1445 Larimer Street
Denver CO	Wall Street Deli	303-296-6277	1801 California Street
Durango CO	Cocina Linda	970-259-6729	309 W College Drive
Durango CO	Cyprus Cafe	970-385-6884	725 East Second Avenue
Durango CO	Durango Natural Foods Deli	970-247-8129	575 East 8th Avenue
Durango CO	Guido's Favorite Foods	970-259-5028	1201 Main Avenue
Durango CO	Homeslice Pizza	970-259-5551	441 E College Drive
Durango CO	Ike's Coffee House	970-247-2883	100 Jenkins Ranch Road, Suite A
Durango CO	Just Bo's Pizza and Rib Company	970-259-0010	1301 Florida Road
Durango CO	Magpie's Newsstand Cafe	970-259-1159	707 Main Street
Durango CO	Serious Texas BBQ	970-247-2240	3535 N Main Avenue/H 550
Durango CO	Serious Texas Bar-B-Q II	970-259-9507	650 S Camino Del Rio/H 550
Estes Park CO	Grumpy Gringo	970-586-7705	1560 BigThompson Avenue
Estes Park CO	Molly B's	970-586-2766	200 Moraine Avenue
Estes Park CO	Notchtop Bakery & Cafe	970-586-0272	459 E Wonderview Avenue
Golden CO	Old Capitol Grill	303-279-6390	1122 Washington Avenue
Greenwood Village CO	Yia Yia's Eurocafe	303-741-1110	8310 East Belleview Avenue
Greenwood Village CO	Z Pizza	303-221-0015	4940 S Yosemite Street
Highlands Ranch CO	Rubios Baja Grille	303-471-6222	3620 Highlands Ranch Parkway
Littleton CO	Baja Fresh	303-730-1466	5350 S Santa Fe Drive, Suite F
Lone Tree CO	Leo's Cafe	303-649-9200	9234 Park Meadows Drive, Suite 100
Lone Tree CO	Rio Grande Mexican Restaurant	303-799-4999	9535 Park Meadows Drive
Loveland CO	Serious Texas Bar-B-Q III	970-667-1415	201 W 71st Street
Manitou Springs CO	The Garden of the God Trading Post and Cafe	719-685-9045	324 Beckers Lane
Ouray CO	Billy Goat Gruff's Beer Garden	970-325-4370	Corner of 4th and Main
Pueblo CO	Giacomo's	719-546-0949	910 W H 50W
Redstone CO	Crystal Club Cafe	970-963-9515	467 Redstone Blvd
Steamboat Springs CO	Geeks Garage	970-879-2976	730 Lincoln Ave
Steamboat Springs CO	Rio Grande Restaurant	970-871-6277	628 Lincoln Avenue/H 40

Dog-Friendly Outdoor Dining - Please always call ahead to make sure an establishment is still dog-friendly.

Connecticut

Bethel CT	Molten Java	203-739-0313	102 Greenwood Ave
Guilford CT	The Place	203-453-9276	901 Boston Post Road
Hartford CT	Hot Tomato's Restaurant	860-249-5100	1 Union Place
Stonington CT	Nonis Deli	860-535-0797	142 Water Street

D.C.

Washington DC	Bangkok Bistro	202-337-2424	3251 Prospect Street NW
Washington DC	Furin's of Georgetown	202-965-1000	2805 M St NW
Washington DC	Logan at the Heights	202-797-7227	3115 14th Street NW
Washington DC	Paper Moon	202-965-6666	1073 31st St NW
Washington DC	Park Place Gourmet	202-783-4496	1634 I St NW
Washington DC	Pasha Bistro	202-588-7477	1523 17th St NW
Washington DC	The Sacraficial Lamb	202-797-2736	1704 R Street NW

Delaware

Dewey Beach DE	Arena's Deli & Bar	302-227-1272	149 Rehoboth Avenue/H 15
Dewey Beach DE	Eden	302-227-3330	23 Baltimore Avenue
Dewey Beach DE	Sharky's Grill	302-226-3116	Hwy 1 and Read Street
Lewes DE	Arena's Cafe	302-644-0370	17314 N Village Main Blvd
Lewes DE	Gilligan's Waterfront Restaurant and Bar	302-644-7230	134 Market Street
Newark DE	Iron Hill Brewery	302-266-9000	147 E Main Street/H 2/273
Newark DE	Santa Fe Mexican Grill	302-369-2500	190 East Main Street/H 2
Rehoboth DE	The Gallery Espresso	302-231-2113	62 A Rehoboth Avenue
Rehoboth Beach DE	Arena's Deli & Bar	302-227-1272	149 Rehoboth Avenue/H 15
Rehoboth Beach DE	Arena's Deli & Bar	302-226-CAFE (2233)	4113 H 1
Rehoboth Beach DE	Big Fish Grill	302-227-FISH (3474)	4117 H 1
Rehoboth Beach DE	Dogfish Head Brewings & Eats	302-226-2739	320 Rehoboth AvenueH 1/15
Rehoboth Beach DE	Hobo's Restaurant and Bar	302-226-2226	56 Baltimore Avenue
Rehoboth Beach DE	Rigby's Bar & Grill	302-227-6080	404 Rehoboth Avenue/H 1/15
Wilmington DE	Catherine Rooney's	302-654-9700	1616 Delaware Avenue, Trolley Square

Florida

Altamonte Springs FL	QDOBA Mexican Grill	407-628-9217	380 H 434, Suite 1005
Altamonte Springs FL	Smoothie King	407-786-5464	931 N H 434
Altamonte Springs FL	TooJay's Gourmet Deli	407-830-1770	515 E Altamonte Drive
Atlantic Beach FL	Al's Pizza	904-249-0002	303 Atlantic Blvd
Atlantic Beach FL	Joseph's Pizza	904-270-1122	30 Ocean Blvd
Belleview FL	B.D. Beans Coffee Company	352-245-3077	5148 SE Abshier Blvd/H 25/27/441
Belleview FL	The Land Bridge Trailhead	352-236-7143	H 475 A
Boca Raton FL	Bangkok in Boca	561-394-6912	500 Via De Palmas
Boca Raton FL	Brasserie Mon Ami	561-394-2428	1400 Glades Road
Boca Raton FL	Courtyard Cafe	561-994-5210	2650 North Military Trail
Boca Raton FL	Einstein Bros Bagels	561-477-0667	9795 Glades Rd
Boca Raton FL	Ichiban Japanese Restaurant	561-451-0420	8841 Glades Rd
Boca Raton FL	Jamba Juice	561-620-8895	1400 Glades Rd
Boca Raton FL	Lion and Eagle English Pub	561-447-7707	2401 N Federal Hwy
Boca Raton FL	Smoothie King	561-981-9922	7401 N Federal H
Boca Raton FL	TooJay's Gourmet Deli	561-241-5903	5030 Champion Blvd
Boca Raton FL	TooJay's Gourmet Deli	561-997-9911	3013 Yamato Road
Boca Raton FL	Truluck's	561-391-0755	351 Plaza Real
Bonita Springs FL	Chato's	949-366-5203	27160 Bay Landing Drive
Boynton Beach FL	Pei Wei Asian Diner	561-364-1830	1750 N Congress Avenue/H 807
Boynton Beach FL	TooJay's Gourmet Deli	561-740-7420	801 N Congress Avenue/H 807
Boyton Beach FL	Hurricane Alley	561-364-4008	529 E Ocean Avenue
Bradenton FL	Mattison's Riverside	941-748-8087	1200 First Avenue W
Bradenton FL	Smoothie King	941-758-1000	3543 53rd Avenue W
Bradenton FL	Smoothie King	941-747-5464	3816 Manatee Avenue W/H 64
Cape Coral FL	Longboards at Cape Harbour	239-542-0123	5785 Cape Harbour Drive
Cape Coral FL	Pete's Philly Steaks	239-542-3611	1239 Cape Coral Parkway E
Cape Coral FL	Subway	239-540-0444	1616 Cape Coral Parkway W
Clearwater FL	Clearwater Wine Co	727-446-8805	483 Mandalay Ave # 113
Clearwater FL	Fish Tail Willy's	727-791-4270	2543 Countryside Blvd
Cocoa FL	Sonic Drive-in	321-631-4121	1112 Clearlake Road/H 501
Cooper City FL	Beverly Hills Cafe	954-434-2220	5544 S. Flamingo Road
Coral Springs FL	TooJay's Gourmet Deli	954-346-0006	2880 North University Drive
Dania Beach FL	The Field Irish Pub and Eatery	954-964-5979	3281 Griffin Road
Davie FL	San Francisco Burrito Co.	954-680-4040	5187 S University Drive/H 817
Deerfield Beach FL	Bru's Room Sports Grill	954-420-5959	123 NE 20th Avenue
Deerfield Beach FL	Pizza Fusion	954-427-5353	196 N Federal H
Delray Beach FL	Bru's Room Sports Grill	561-276-3663	35 NE 2nd Avenue
Delray Beach FL	City Oyster	561-272-0220	213 E Atlantic Ave

Dog-Friendly Outdoor Dining - Please always call ahead to make sure an establishment is still dog-friendly.

Delray Beach FL	Nature's Way Cafe	561-272-6200	20 W Atlantic Avenue #103/H 806
Delray Beach FL	Nutrition Cottage and the Natural Juice Bar and Cafe	561-272-8571	407 E Atlantic Avenue
Destin FL	Harry T's	850-654-4800	46 Harbor Blvd
Destin FL	Jim N Nicks	850-351-1991	9300 Emerald Coast Parkway/H 30/98
Dunedin FL	Dunedin Brewery	727-736-0606	937 Douglas Avenue
Fort Lauderdale FL	33rd and Dine French Cafe	954-630-0235	3330 NE 33rd Street
Fort Lauderdale FL	Briny Riverfront Pub	954-376-4742	305 S Andrews Avenue
Fort Lauderdale FL	Coconuts	954-525-2421	429 Seabreeze Blvd/H 1A
Fort Lauderdale FL	Dogma Grill	954-525-1319	900 S Federal H/H 1/5
Fort Lauderdale FL	Einstein's Bros Bagels	954-462-1132	19 N Federal H/H 1/5
Fort Lauderdale FL	Einstein's Bros Bagels	954-463-1717	1499 SE 17th Street Causeway/H 1A
Fort Lauderdale FL	Einsteins Bagel	954-565-2155	3200 N Federal Hwy
Fort Lauderdale FL	Georgie's Alibi	954-565-2526	2266 Wilton Drive/NE 4th AvenueH 811
Fort Lauderdale FL	Grill Room On Las Olas	954-467-2555	620 E Las Olas Blvd
Fort Lauderdale FL	Indigo Restaurant	954-467-0045	620 E Las Olas Blvd
Fort Lauderdale FL	Japanese Steak House	954-525-8386	350 E. Las Olas Blvd
Fort Lauderdale FL	Johnny V Restaurant	954-761-7920	625 E Las Olas Blvd
Fort Lauderdale FL	Kitchenetta	954-567-3333	2850 N Federal H/H 1/5
Fort Lauderdale FL	Panera Bread	954-567-5925	1762 North Federal H/H 1/5
Fort Lauderdale FL	Pizza Fusion	954-358-5353	1013 N Federal H/H 1/838
Fort Lauderdale FL	Rino's Tuscan Grill	954-766-8700	1105 E Las Olas Blvd
Fort Lauderdale FL	Samba Room	954-468-2000	350 E Las Olas Blvd
Fort Lauderdale FL	Simply Natural Cafe	954-742-8384	8267 Sunset Strip
Fort Lauderdale FL	Starbucks	954-791-7265	6781 W Broward Blvd
Fort Lauderdale FL	Stromboli Pizza	954-472-2167	801 S University Dr
Fort Lauderdale FL	Tokyo Sushi	954-767-9922	1499 SE 17th Street/H 1A
Fort Lauderdale FL	Zona Fresca	954-566-1777	1635 N Federal Hwy
Fort Myers Beach FL	Parrot Key Caribbean Grill	239-463-3257	2500 Main Street
Fort Myers Beach FL	The Fish House and Restaurant	239-765-6766	7225 Estero Blvd
Fort Worth FL	Dave's Last Resort and Raw Bar	561-588-5208	632 Lake Ave
Gainesville FL	Books Inc. and Book Lover's Cafe	352-384-0090	505 NW 13th Street/H 20/25/441
Gotha FL	Yellow Dog Eats Cafe	407-296-0609	1236 Hempel Ave
Grayton Beach FL	Shorty's	850-468-0417	Defuniak Street & Hotz Avenue
Gulf Breeze FL	Smoothie King	850-932-3749	880 Gulf Breeze Blvd
Harbour Island FL	Café Dufrain	813-275-9701	707 Harbour Post Drive
Harmony FL	Harmony Town Tavern/Greensides Restaurant	407-891-2630	7251 Five Oaks Drive/H 192
Hobe Sound FL	Nature's Way Cafe	772-546-4881	8767 Bridge Road
Hollywood FL	Einstein's Bros Bagels	954-989-4500	5341 Sheridan Street/H 822
Hollywood FL	Einstein's Bros Bagels	954-893-8701	340 N Park Road
Hollywood FL	Lola's on Harrison	954-927-9851	2032 Harrison Street
Hollywood FL	Nakorn Japanese and Thai Restaurant	954-921-1200	2039 Hollywood Blvd
Hollywood FL	Smoothie King	954-364-7093	250 Federal H
Hudson FL	Sam's Hudson Beach Restaurant	727-868-1971	6325 Clark Street
Hurst FL	R.J. Gator's Hometown Grill and Bar	817-595-0182	1101 Melbourne Road, #6600
Indian Shores FL	The Pub Waterfront Restaurant	727-595-3172	20025 Gulf Blvd/H 689
Islamorada FL	Village Gourmet of Islamorada	305-664-4030	H 1/5 MM 82.7
Jacksonville FL	Brick Restaurant	904-387-0606	3585 Saint Johns Avenue/H 211
Jacksonville FL	QDOBA Mexican Grill	904-807-9161	4624 Town Crossing Drive
Jacksonville FL	Smoothie King	904-996-2889	4624 Town Crossing Drive, Suite 119
Jacksonville FL	The Brick Restaurant	904-387-0606	3585 St Johns Avenue/H 211
Jupiter FL	Nature's Way Cafe	561-743-0401	103 S H 1
Jupiter FL	Nature's Way Cafe	561-799-9972	1203 Town Center Drive
Jupiter FL	TooJay's Gourmet Deli	561-627-5555	4050 H 1
Key Largo FL	Key Largo Conch House	305-453-4844	100211 Overseas Hwy
Key Largo FL	Snooks Bayside Restaurant and Grand Tiki Bar	305-453-3799	99470 Overseas H/MM 99.9/H 1/5
Key West FL	Blue Heaven	305-296-8666	729 Thomas St
Key West FL	Bo's Fish Wagon	305-294-9272	801 Caroline St
Key West FL	Casablanca Bogart	305-296-0815	904 Duval St
Key West FL	Conch Republic Seafood Company	305-294-4403	631 Greene St
Key West FL	Cowboy Bills Honky Tonk Saloon	305-295-8219	610 1/2 Duval Street
Key West FL	El Meson de Pepe on Mallory Square,	305-295-2620	410 Wall Street
Key West FL	Fat Tuesday's	305-296-9373	305 Duval Street
Key West FL	Grand Cafe Key West	305-292-4740	314 Duval Street
Key West FL	Half Shell Raw Bar	305-294-7496	231 Margaret Street
Key West FL	Harpoon Harry's	305-294-8744	832 Caroline Street
Key West FL	Hogs Breath Saloon	305-296-4222	400 Front Street
Key West FL	Hurricane Joe's Seafood Bar and Grill	305-294-0200	Hurricane Hole Marina Mile Marker 4
Key West FL	Iguana Cafe	305 296-6420	425 Greene Street
Key West FL	Kelly's Restaurant	305-293-8484	301 Whitehead Street
Key West FL	New York Pizza Cafe	305-292-1991	1075 Duval St
Key West FL	Old Town Mexican Cafe	305-296-7500	609 Duval St
Key West FL	Outback Steakhouse	305-292-0667	3230 N Roosevelt Blvd/H1
Key West FL	Pepe's Cafe and Steakhouse	305-294-7192	806 Caroline Street
Key West FL	Salsa Loca	305-292-1865	623-625 Duval Street
Key West FL	Schooner Wharf Bar	305-292-9520	202 William Street
Key West FL	Turtle Kraals Restaurant and Bar	305-294-2640	231 Margaret Street
Kissimmee FL	Pei Wei Asian Diner	407-846-0829	2501 W Osceola Parkway

Dog-Friendly Outdoor Dining - Please always call ahead to make sure an establishment is still dog-friendly.

Lady Lake FL	TooJay's Gourmet Deli	352-753-3510	990 Delmar Drive
Lake Mary FL	Dexter's of Lake Mary	407-805-3090	950 Promenade Avenue
Lake Mary FL	TooJay's Gourmet Deli	407-833-0848	3577 Lake Emma Road
Lake Sumter Landing FL	TooJay's Gourmet Deli	352-430-0410	1129 Canal Street
Lake Worth FL	Nature's Way Cafe	561-721-0232	517 N Lake Avenue/H 802
Lake Worth FL	The Soma Center Organic, Vegetarian and Raw Cafe	561-296-9949	609 Lake Avenue
Lake Worth FL	TooJay's Gourmet Deli	561-582-8684	419 Lake Avenue/H 802
Lakeland FL	Smoothie King	863-647-9602	3423 S Florida Avenue
Lantana FL	Nature's Way Cafe	561-642-0800	5897 S Congress Avenue/H 807
Largo FL	Einstein's Bros Bagels	727-533-0800	5395 E Bay Drive, Suite 104 (H 686)
Longboat Key FL	The Dry Dock	941-383-0102	412 Gulf of Mexico Dr
Maitland FL	QDOBA Mexican Grill	407-644-1247	400 S Orlando Avenue/H 17/92
Matlacha FL	Bert's Bar and Grill	239-282-3232	4271 Pine Island Road/H 78
Melbourne FL	TooJay's Gourmet Deli	321-369-0450	1700 W New Haven Avenue
Miami FL	Catalina Hotel and Beach Club	305-674-1160	1732-1756 Collins Avenue
Miami FL	Groovy's Pizza	305-476-6018	3030 Grand Ave
Miami FL	Johnny Rockets	305-444-1000	3036 Grand Ave
Miami FL	Smoothie King	305-377-0085	1010 S Miami Avenue
Miami FL	Smoothie King	305-661-5464	6637 S Dixie Hwy
Miami FL	The Last Carrot	305-445-0805	3133 Grand Avenue
Miami FL	Tutto Pasta	305-857-0709	1751 SW 3rd Ave
Miami Beach FL	Fratelli la Bufala	305-532-0700	437 Washington Avenue
Miami Beach FL	Les Deux Fontaines	305-672-7878	1230 Ocean Drive
Miami Beach FL	Nexxt Cafe	305-532-6643	700 Lincoln Road
Miami Beach FL	Sushi Rock Cafe	305-532-4639	1351 Collins Ave
Miami Beach FL	Taste Bakery Cafe	305-695-9930	900 Alton Road
Miami Beach FL	Van Dyke Cafe	305-534-3600	1641 Jefferson Ave
Miami Beach FL	World Resources Cafe	305-535-8987	719 Lincoln Rd
Miami Lakes FL	Beverly Hills Cafe	305-558-8201	7321 Miami Lakes Drive
Mount Dora FL	5th Avenue Cafe	352-383-0090	116 E 5th Avenue/H 46
Naples FL	Smoothie King	239-261-1322	2338 Pine Ridge Road, The Crossings
Naples FL	Sunsplash Market and Deli	239-434-7221	850 Neapolitan Way
Neptune Beach FL	Caribbee Key Island Grille and Cruzan Rum Bar	904-270-8940	100 First Street
North Miami Beach FL	Pizza Fusion	305-405-6700	14815 Biscayne Blvd/H 1/5
Ocala FL	Harry's Seafood and Grille	352-840-0900	24 SE 1st Avenue
Ocala FL	Ker's WingHouse	352-671-7880	2145 E Silver Springs Blvd/H 40
Ocala FL	Panera Bread	352-732-0099	2370 SW College Road/H 200
Ocala FL	Panera Bread	352-509-9123	4414 SW College Road/H 200
Ocoee FL	TooJay's Gourmet Deli	407-798-2000	10185 W Colonial Drive/H 50
Orlando FL	Cafe Bravissimo	407-898-7333	337 N Shine Avenue
Orlando FL	Casey's on Central	407-648-4218	50 East Central Blvd
Orlando FL	Dexter's of Thornton Park	407-629-1150	808 Washington Street
Orlando FL	K Restaurant Wine Bar	407-872-2332	2401 Edgewater Drive
Orlando FL	NYPD Pizza	407-293-8880	2589 S Hiawassee Road
Orlando FL	Panera Bread	407-481-1060	227 N Eola Dr
Orlando FL	Pei Wei Asian Diner	407-563-8777	3011 E Colonial Drive/H 50
Orlando FL	QDOBA Mexican Grill	407-238-4787	12376 Apopka Vineland Road/H 535
Orlando FL	QDOBA Mexican Grill	407-275-3820	4000 Central Florida Blvd, UCF Student Union Bldg, #52
Orlando FL	QDOBA Mexican Grill	407-273-2396	423 Alafaya Trail/H 434
Orlando FL	Quiznos	407-827-1110	12515 H 535
Orlando FL	Sanctuary Diner	407-481-2250	100 S Eola Drive
Orlando FL	Smoothie King	407-381-2900	12140 Collegiate Way, #100
Orlando FL	Smoothie King	407-380-3333	UCF, Student Union, Pegasus Circle, Bldg 52
Orlando FL	The Beacon	407-841-5444	100 S Eola Drive
Orlando FL	TooJay's Gourmet Deli	407-894-1718	2400 E Colonial Drive
Orlando FL	TooJay's Gourmet Deli	407-355-0340	7600 Dr Phillips Blvd
Orlando FL	TooJay's Gourmet Deli	407-249-9475	715 N Alafaya Trail
Orlando FL	Venezia Bakery & Cafe	407-851-1141	13586 Village Park Drive #302
Orlando FL	White Wolf Cafe	407-895-5590	1829 N Orange Avenue
Orlando FL	Wildside BBQ	407-872-8665	700 E Washington Street
Orlando FL	Wildside BBQ and Grill	407-872-8665	700 E Washington Street
Palm Beach Gardens FL	Pizza Fusion	561-721-0123	4783 PGA Blvd/H 786
Palm Beach Gardens FL	TooJay's Gourmet Deli	561-622-8131	11701 Lake Victoria Gardens
Palm Harbor FL	Consciousness Blossoms	727-789-1931	3390 Tampa Road/H 584
Palm Harbor FL	Einstein's Bros Bagels	727-771-9448	33119 H 19N
Palm Harbor FL	Smoothie King	727-232-1299	4956 Ridgemoor Blvd
Pembroke Pines FL	Juice It Up!	954-437-5299	532 SW 145th Terrace
Pembroke Pines FL	Lime Fresh Mexican Grill	954-436-4700	601 SW 145th Terrace
Pensacola FL	Sunset Grille	850-492-1063	14050 Canal A Way
Pensacola FL	Tuscan Oven Pizzeria	850-484-6836	4801 N 9th Avenue/H 289
Plantation FL	Einstein's Bros Bagels	954-370-3105	8500 W Broward Blvd/H 842
Plantation FL	Einstein's Bros Bagels	954-423-3030	989 Nob Hill Road
Plantation FL	TooJay's Gourmet Deli	954-423-1993	801 S University Drive/H 817
Pompano Beach FL	Bru's Room Sports Grill	954-785-2227	235 S Federal H
Pompano Beach FL	Galuppi's	954-785-0226	1103 N Federal H/H 1
Ponce Inlet FL	Lighthouse Landing	386-761-9271	4940 S Peninsula

Dog-Friendly Outdoor Dining - Please always call ahead to make sure an establishment is still dog-friendly.

Port Charlotte FL	Patera's Bistro	941-743-0626	24150 Tiseo Blvd #4
Port St Joe FL	Dockside Cafe	850-229-5200	342 Marina Drive
Riverview FL	Acropolis	813-654-2255	6108 Winthrop Town Center Avenue
Riverview FL	Green Iguanna	813-643-7800	6264 Winthrop Town Center Avenue
Royal Palm Beach FL	Friendly's	561-333-5757	1001 H 7
Safety Harbor FL	Einstein's Bros Bagels	727-791-3909	2519 N McMullen Booth Road
Safety Harbor FL	Taste Safety Harbor	727-723-1116	500 Main Street/H 590
Sanford FL	Angelo's Pizzaria	407-320-0799	107 W 1st St
Sanford FL	Dalli's Riverwalk Pizzeria	407-328-0018	350 E. Seminole Blvd
Sanford FL	Hollerbach's Willow Tree Cafe	407-321-2204	205 E First Street
Sanford FL	QDOBA Mexican Grill	407-330-3039	202 W Lake Mary Blvd
Sanford FL	Tin Lizzie Tavern	407-321-1908	111 W 1st St
Sanford FL	Two Blondes and a Shrimp	407-688-4745	112 E First Street
Sarasota FL	Barnacle Bill's Seafood	941-365-6800	1526 Main Street
Sarasota FL	Columbia Restaurant	941-388-3987	411 St Armands Circle
Sarasota FL	O'leary's Tiki Bar and Grill	941-953-7505	5 Bayfront Drive/H 41/45
Sarasota FL	Old Salty Dog	941-349-0158	5023 Ocean Blvd
Sarasota FL	Smoothie King	941-924-3339	1629 Rinehart Road
Sarasota FL	Smoothie King	941-942-3339	1880 Stickney Point Road
Sarasota FL	Smoothie King	941-365-2244	3800 S Tamiami Trail, Suite 108/H 41/45
Sebring FL	Hammock Inn Restaurant	863-385-7025	5931 Hammock Road
Seminole FL	Einstein's Bros Bagels	727-392-8515	11234 Park Blvd
Seminole FL	The Purple Onion	727-394-0064	10525 Park Blvd/H 694
Siesta Key FL	Old Salty Dog	941-388-4311	1601 Ken Thompson Pkwy
South Miami FL	QDOBA Mexican Grill	305-668-3770	5748 Sunset Drive
St Augustine FL	American Graffiti Restaurant and Bar	904-825-0900	410 Anastasia Blvd/H 1A
St Augustine FL	Cafe Cordova	904-827-1888	95 Cordova Street
St Augustine FL	Carrabba's Italian Grill	904-819-9093	155 H 312 W
St Augustine FL	Casa Maya 17	904-217-3039	17 Hypolita Street
St Augustine FL	Crispers	904) 825-9901	200 CBL Drive FL
St Augustine FL	Firehouse Subs	904-819-1808	200 Cobblestone Drive
St Augustine FL	Fish Tales Market and Grill	904-824-0900	121 Yacht Club Drive
St Augustine FL	Florida Cracker Cafe	904-829-0397	81 St. George Street
St Augustine FL	Grabbers Seafood Grill	904-829-5410	21 Hypolita Street
St Augustine FL	Harry's Seafood Bar Grille	904-824-7765	46 Avenida Menendez
St Augustine FL	La Pentola	904-824-3282	58 Charlotte Street
St Augustine FL	Love Tree Cafe	904-823-1818	6 Cordova Street
St Augustine FL	Milltop Tavern	904-829-2329	19 1/2 Saint George Street
St Augustine FL	Old City House Inn and Restaurant	904-826-0184	115 Cordova Street
St Augustine FL	Present Moment Cafe	904-827-4499	224 W King Street
St Augustine FL	Scarlett O'Hara's Bar and Restaurant	904-824-6535	70 Hypolita Street
St Augustine FL	Sonic Drive Inn	904) 808-4788	704 E Geoffrey Street
St Augustine FL	The Reef	904-824-8008	4100 Coastal H/H 1A
St Augustine FL	Tony's Pizza	904-461-0002	1935 H A1A
St George Island FL	Ocean Front Cafe	850-927-2987	68 W Gorrie Dr #A
St Petersburg FL	Buffy's Southern Pit Bar-b-que	727-522-0088	3911 49th North
St Petersburg Fl	Captain Al's Waterfront Grill and Bar	727-890-5000	000 2nd Avenue NE
St Petersburg FL	Corned Beef Corner	727-347-3921	4040 Park St North
St Petersburg FL	Einstein's Bros Bagels	727-578-9800	9346 4th Street N/H 92/687
St Petersburg FL	Foxy's Cafe	727-363-3699	160 107th Ave
St Petersburg FL	Pei Wei Asian Diner	727-347-1351	1402 66th Street
Stuart FL	Nature's Way Cafe	772-220-7306	25 SW Osceola Street
Stuart FL	Pei Wei Asian Diner	772-219-0466	2101 SE Federal H/H 1/5
Stuart FL	TooJay's Gourmet Deli	772-287-6514	2504 SE Federal H/H 1/5
Sunrise FL	Simply Natural Cafe	954-742-8384	8267 Sunset Strip
Tallahassee FL	Andrew's Capital Grill & Bar	850-222-3444	228 S Adams Street
Tallahassee FL	Food,Glorious Food	850-224-9974	1950 Thomasville Rd
Tallahassee FL	New Leaf Market	850-942-2557	1235 Apalachee Parkway
Tallahassee FL	QDOBA Mexican Grill	850-671-3334	1594 Governor's Square Blvd #2
Tamarac FL	Einstein's Bros Bagels	954-718-6088	5705 N University Drive/H 817
Tampa FL	Bagels Plus	813-971-9335	2706 E Fletcher Ave
Tampa FL	Bernini Restaurant	813-248-0099	1702 E 7th Ave
Tampa FL	Einstein's Bros Bagels	813-968-8868	10802 N Dale Mabry H/H 597
Tampa FL	Einstein's Bros Bagels	813-871-1074	619 S Dale Mabry H/H 92
Tampa FL	Gaspar's Grotto	813-248-5900	1805 E 7th Avenue
Tampa FL	Grassroot Organic Restaurant	813-221-7668	2702 N Florida Avenue/H 41/685
Tampa FL	GrillSmith	813-250-3850	1108-D S Dale Mabry H
Tampa FL	Java & Cream	813-254-8162	225 E Davis Blvd
Tampa FL	Mad Dogs and Englishmen	813-832-3037	4115 S Macdill Ave
Tampa FL	Pei Wei Asian Diner	813-207-1190	217 S Dale Mabry/H 92
Tampa FL	Pei Wei Asian Diner	813-960-2031	12927 N Dale Mabry H/H 597
Tampa FL	QDOBA Mexican Grill	813-984-4650	5001A E Fowler Avenue/H 582
Tampa FL	Rick's Italian Cafe	813-253-3310	214 E Davis Blvd
Tampa FL	Rolling Oats Market and Cafe	813-873-7428	1021 N MacDill Avenue
Tampa FL	Sail Pavilion	813-274-8511	333 S Franklin Street
Tampa FL	Smoothie King	813-963-6480	13106 N Dale Mabry H/H 597
Tampa FL	Smoothie King	813-963-5581	15788 N Dale Mabry H/H 597
Tampa FL	Smoothie King	813-866-4847	17521 Preserve Walk Lane
Tampa FL	Smoothie King	813-250-3888	2205 W Swann Avenue
Tampa FL	The Bungalow	813-253-3663	2202 W Kennedy Blvd/H 60

Tampa FL	TooJay's Gourmet Deli	813-348-4101	2223 NW Shore Blvd
Tarpon Springs FL	Costa's	727-938-6890	521 Athens Street
Tarpon Springs FL	Mama's Greek Cuisine	727-944-2888	735 Dodecanese Blvd # 40
Tarpon Springs FL	Tarpon Turtle	727-722-9030	1513 Lake Tarpon Avenue
Titusville FL	Bruster's Ice Cream	321-385-0400	855 Cheney Hwy
Venice FL	TJ Carney's	941-480-9244	231 W Venice Avenue
Wellington FL	Pei Wei Asian Diner	561-753-6260	10610, Bay 10, Forest Hill Blvd
Wellington FL	Pizza Fusion	561-721-9020	10160 Forest Hill Blvd,Unit G130/H 882
West Palm Beach FL	Nature's Way Cafe	561-659-1993	105 Narcissus Avenue
West Palm Beach FL	Nature's Way Cafe	561-622-0440	9920 H A1A
West Palm Beach FL	Outback Steakhouse	561-683-1011	871 Village Blvd
West Palm Beach FL	Rooney's Public House	561-833-7802	213 Clematis St
Weston FL	Pizza Fusion	954-641-5353	2378 Weston Road
Winter Park FL	Bosphorous	407-644-8609	108 Park Avenue S
Winter Park FL	Dexter's of Winter Park	407-629-1150	558 W New England Avenue
Winter Park FL	Hot Olives	407-629-1030	463 W New England Avenue
Winter Park FL	Hot Olives Restaurant	407-629-1030	463 W New England Avenue
Winter Park FL	Luma on Park	407-599-4111	290 Park Avenue
Winter Park FL	Luma on Park	407-599-4111	290 S Park Avenue
Winter Park FL	Luma on Park	407-599-4111	290 S Park Avenue
Winter Park FL	Park Plaza Gardens	407-645-2475	319 Park Ave South
Winter Park FL	Park Plaza Gardens	407-645-2475	319 S Park Avenue
Winter Park FL	Three Ten Park South	407-647-7277	310 S Park Ave
Winter Park FL	Wazzabi Sushi	407-647-8744	1408 Gay Road
Winter Springs FL	Smoothie King	407-774-5464	5220 Red Bug Lake Road

Georgia

Alpharetta GA	Z Pizza	678-205-4471	5315 Windward Parkway
Athens GA	Five Star Day Cafe	706-543-8552	229 W Broad Street/H 10/78
Atlanta GA	Anis Cafe and Bistro	404-233-9889	2974 Grandview Avenue
Atlanta GA	Brewhouse Cafe	404-525-7799	401 Moreland Avenue NE
Atlanta GA	Bruster's Real Ice Cream	404-320-7166	2095 LaVista Rd NE/H 236
Atlanta GA	Corner Bakery Cafe	404-816-5100	3368 Peachtree Rd. NE
Atlanta GA	Dakota Blue	404-589-8002	454 Cherokee Ave SE
Atlanta GA	Nancy G's Cafe	404-705-8444	4920 Roswell Road, Suite 55/H 19/9
Atlanta GA	Park Tavern	404-249-0001	500 10th St NE
Atlanta GA	Park Tavern	404-249-0001	500 10th Street NE
Atlanta GA	Quattro	404-881-0000	1071 Piedmont Road
Atlanta GA	Vermont Mustard Company	770-333-9119	2355 Cumberland Parkway, Suite 110
Atlanta GA	Waterhaven	404-214-6740	75 Fifth St NW
Atlanta GA	Z Pizza	404-745-9911	860 Peachtree Street
Augusta GA	The Pizza Joint	706-774-0037	1245 Broad Street/H 25
Darien GA	Skipper's Fish Camp	912-437-FISH (3474)	85 Screven Street
Decatur GA	Matador Mexican Restaurant	404-377-0808	350 Mead Road
Decatur GA	Mo Jo Pizza	404-373-1999	659 East Lake Drive
Decatur GA	Mojo Pizza	404-373-0399	657 E Lake Drive
Decatur GA	Steinbecks Restaurant	404-373-0399	659 E Lake Drive
Decatur GA	Universal Joint	404-373-6260	906 Oakview Road
Duluth GA	Z Pizza	770-817-0526	11720 Medlock Bridge Road/H 141
Evans GA	Dino's Chicago Express	706-434-0002	4446 Washington Road, Suite 20/H 104
Jekyll Island GA	Latitude 31	912-635-3800	1 Pier Road
Jekyll Island GA	SeaJays Waterfront Cafe and Pub	912-635-3200	1 Harbor Rd
Jekyll Island GA	Zach's Eats and Treats	912-635-2040	44 Beachview Drive
Kingsland GA	Starters	912-729-7010	1301 E King Avenue/H40
Marietta GA	Marietta Pizza Company	770-419-0900	3 Whitlock Avenue SW/H 120
Martinez GA	Dino's Chicago Express	706-228-4476	500 Fury's Ferry Road, Suite 101/H 28
Sandy Springs GA	Teela Taqueria	404-459-0477	227 Sandy Springs Place, Suite 506
Savannah GA	Bonna Bella Yacht Club	912-352-3134	2740 Livingston Avenue
Savannah GA	Vinnie VanGoGo's	912-233-6394	317 W Bryan Street
Savannah GA	Wild Wing Cafe	912-790-9464	27 Barnard Street
Savannah GA	Wild Wing Cafe	912-790-WING (9464)	27 Barnard Street
Vinings GA	Meehan's Public House	770-433-1920	2810 Paces Ferry Road
Woodstock GA	Props 'N Hops	678-919-7802	1001 Victoria Landing Drive

Hawaii

Honolulu HI	Bluwater Grill	803-395-6224	377 Keahole Street, Unit D1A
Honolulu HI	The Wedding Cafe	808-591-1005	1240 Ala Moana Blvd/H 92
Honolulu HI	Z Pizza	808-596-0066	1200 Ala Moana Blvd/H 92

Idaho

Boise ID	Baja Fresh	208-327-0099	992 N Milwaukee
Boise ID	Baja Fresh	208-331-1100	980 Broadway Avenue
Boise ID	Quiznos	208-389-1177	2237 University Drive

Dog-Friendly Outdoor Dining - Please always call ahead to make sure an establishment is still dog-friendly.

Creekside ID	Muley's Mountain Coffee	208-412-7528	H 21, Creekside, Just upstream of mile marker 24
Driggs ID	Tony's Pizza and Pasta	208-354-8829	634 N Main Street/H 33
Ketchum ID	Rico's Pizza	208-726-RICO (7426)	200 N Main
Meridian ID	Baja Fresh	208-855-2468	1440 N Eagle Road
Sandpoint ID	Ivano's Italian Ristoranté	208-263-0211	102 S First Street

Illinois

Berwyn IL	Wishbone Restaurant	708-749-1295	6611 W Roosevelt
Braidwood IL	Polka Dot Drive-in	815-458-3377	222 N Front St/H 53
Carbondale IL	Neighborhood Co-op Grocery	618-529-3533	1815 W Main Street/H 13
Champaign IL	Mike and Molly's	217-355-1236	105 N Market St
Chicago IL	Amarit	312-649-0500	1 E Delaware Pl
Chicago IL	Bistrot Margot	312-587-3660	1437 N Wells Street
Chicago IL	Bordo's Eatery and Sauce	773-529-6900	2476 N Lincoln Ave
Chicago IL	Brasserie Jo	312-595-0800	59 West Hubbard St.
Chicago IL	Brasserie Ruhlmann	312-494-1900	500 West Superior Street
Chicago IL	Brownstone Tavern	773-528-3700	3937 N Lincoln Avenue
Chicago IL	Charmers	773-743-2233	1500 W Jarvis Avenue
Chicago IL	Cody's Public House	773-528-4050	1658 W Barry Ave
Chicago IL	Corner Bakery	312-787-1969	1121 N. State Street
Chicago IL	Corner Bakery	312-266-AJ70	676 North St. Clair
Chicago IL	Corner Bakery	312-263-4258	188 W. Washington Street
Chicago IL	Costello Sandwich and Sides	773-989-7788	4647 North Lincoln
Chicago IL	Crust	773-235-5511	2056 W. Division Street
Chicago IL	Cyrano's Bistro and Wine Bar	312-467-0546	546 North Wells St.
Chicago IL	Dream Boutique Lounge	312-932-1750	1750 North Clark St.
Chicago IL	Dunlay's on Clark	773-883-6000	2600 North Clark Street
Chicago IL	For Dog's Sake	773-278-4355	2257 W North Ave
Chicago IL	Four Farthings Tavern and Grill	773-935-2060	2060 N Cleveland Ave
Chicago IL	Four Moon Tavern	773-929-6666	1847 W Roscoe Street
Chicago IL	Jake Melnicks Corner Tap	312-266-0400	41 E Superior St
Chicago IL	Joe's Bar	312-337-3486	940 W Weed Street
Chicago IL	Kitsch'n on Roscoe	773-248-SERA	2005 W. Roscoe Street
Chicago IL	Morgan Street Cafe	312-850-0292	111 S Morgan
Chicago IL	O'Donavan's Restaurant	773-478-2100	2100 West Irving Park Road
Chicago IL	Orange Restaurant	773-248-0999	2011 West Roscoe
Chicago IL	Parline's	773-561-8573	1754 W Balmoral Ave
Chicago IL	Scoozi	312-943-5900	410 W Huron Street
Chicago IL	Swim Cafe	312-492-8600	1357 W. Chicago Ave
Chicago IL	The Beachstro at Oak Street Beach	312-915-4100	End of Oak Street Beach
Chicago IL	The Daily Bar and Grill	773-561-6198	4560 N Lincoln Avenue
Chicago IL	Uncommon Ground	773-929-3680	1214 W Grace
Chicago IL	Via Veneto Ristorante	773-267-0888	6340 N Lincoln Ave
Chicago IL	Wishbone	312-850-2663	1001 W Washington Blvd
Decatur IL	Panera Bread	217-872-6435	255 E Ash Avenue
Downers Grove IL	Borrowed Earth Cafe	630-795-1RAW (630-795-1729)	970 Warren Avenue
Evanston IL	Hartigan's Ice Cream Shoppe	847-491-1232	2909 Central Street
Evanston IL	Oceanique	847-864-3435	505 Main Street
Galena IL	Kaladi's 925 Coffee Bar	815-776-0723	309 S Main Street
Glencoe IL	Foodstuffs	847-835-5105	338 Park Avenue
Glencoe IL	Little Red Hen	847-835-4900	653 Vernon Avenue
Glenview IL	Mitchell's Fish Market	847-729-3663	2601 Navy Blvd
Highland Park IL	Cafe Central	847-266-7878	455 Central Avenue
Highland Park IL	Hot Tamales	847-433-4070	493 Central Avenue
Highland Park IL	Little Szechwan	847-433-7007	1900 First Street
Highwood IL	Hoagie Hut	847-432-3262	17 Bank Lane
Jacksonville IL	CR's Drive-in	217-243-2421	403 E Morton Avenue/H 104
Moline IL	Dead Poets Espresso	309-736-7606	1525 3rd Avenue A
Oak Park IL	Buzz Cafe	708-524-2899	905 S. Lombard Avenue
Oak Park IL	Philander's Oak Park	708-848-4250	1120 Pleasant Street
Oglesby IL	Moore's Root Beer Stand	815-883-9254	225 Columbia Avenue
Oregon IL	Jay's Drive In	815-732-2396	107 N Washington Street/H 64
Peoria IL	Camille's Sidewalk Cafe	309-692-9727	5201 W War Memorial Drive/H 150
Peoria IL	Coldstone Creamery	309-691-5630	7728 N Grand Prairie Drive
Peoria IL	Jalapeno's Bar, Grill, and Patio	309-691-3599	4620 N University Street
Peoria IL	Panera Bread	309-682-3300	2601 W Lake Avenue
Peoria IL	Panera Bread	309-692-8400	1101 W Bird Blvd
Rockford IL	Franchesco's	815-332-4992	2404 S Perryville Road/H 11
Springfield IL	Maldaner's Restaurant	217-522-4313	222 S 6th Street
Springfield IL	Panera Bread	217-726-5070	3101 W White Oaks Drive
Springfield IL	Panera Bread	217-529-6200	3019 S Dirksen Parkway
Springfield IL	Sammy's Sports Bar	217-789-9803	217 S Fifth Street
Springfield IL	Tuscany Italian Restaurant	217-726-5343	3123 Robbins Road
St Charles IL	Ray's Evergreen Tavern	630-584-3535	1400 W Main Street/H 64
Wilmette IL	The Noodle Cafe	847-251-2228	708 12th Street

Indiana

Fort Wayne IN	Three Rivers Food Co-op	260-424-8812	1612 Sherman Street
Goshen IN	Maple City Market	574-534-2355	314 S Main Street/H 15
Indianapolis IN	Aesop's Tables	317-631-0055	600 Massachusetts Avenue
Indianapolis IN	Front Page Tavern	317-631-6682	310 Massachusetts Avenue
Indianapolis IN	Mikado Japanese Restaurant	317-972-4180	148 S Illinois Street
Indianapolis IN	Panera Bread	317-542-7450	9145 E 56th Street
Indianapolis IN	Panera Bread	317-334-7800	2902 W 86th Street
Indianapolis IN	Plump's Last Shot	317-257-5867	6416 Cornell Avenue
Indianapolis IN	Whole Foods Market	317-706-0900	1300 E 86th Street
Indianapolis IN	Yats	317-253-8817	5363 N College Avenue
Mooresville IN	Zedeco Grill	317-834-3900	11 E Main

Iowa

Amana IA	Millstream Brewing Company	319-622-3672	835 48th Avenue
Coralville IA	New Pioneer Food Co-op and Bakehouse	319-358-5513	1101 2nd Street/H 6
Council Bluffs IA	Panera Bread	712-366-3033	1751 Madison Avenue # 226
Davenport IA	Thunder Bay Grille	563-386-2722	6511 N Brady Street
Decorah IA	Oneota Community Co-op	563-382-4666	312 W Water Street
Des Moines IA	9th Street Deli & Catering	515-246-6592	1111 9th Street
Des Moines IA	Ritual Cafe	515-288-4872	1301 Locust Street # D
Iowa City IA	Buffalo Wild Wing	319-887-9464	201 S Clinton Street, Suite 120
Iowa City IA	New Pioneer Food Co-op	319-338-9441	22 S Van Buren Street
Sioux City IA	Panera Bread	712-202-0580	1909 Hamilton Blvd
Urbandale IA	Mama Lacona's Italian Ristorante	515-270-0022	2743 86th Street
Urbandale IA	Panera Bread	515-253-9223	2839 86th Street

Kansas

Kansas City KS	Grinders	816-472-5454	417 E 18th Street
Kansas City KS	MeMa's Old-Fashioned Bakery	913-299-9121	1829 Village W Parkway
Lawrence KS	Community Mercantile Co-Op	785-843-8544	901 Iowa Street/H 59
Lawrence KS	Local Burger	785-856-7827	714 Vermont Street
Prairie Village KS	Cafe Provence	913-384-5998	3936 W 69th Terrace
Prairie Village KS	The Blue Moose Bar and Grill	913-722-9463	4160 W 71st Street
Shawnee Mission KS	Sonic Drive-In	913-901-8511	8905 Santa Fe Dr
Wichita KS	Bella Donna	316-315-0000	2121 Webb Road
Wichita KS	Buffalo Wild Wings Grill and Bar	316-636-9464	3236 N Rock Road

Kentucky

Bowling Green KY	440 Main Restaurant and Bar	270-793-0450	440 E Main Avenue
Bowling Green KY	Motor City Bar and Grill	270-846-1125	191 Cumberland Trace Road
Lexington KY	Azur Restaurant and Patio	859-296-1007	3070 Lakecrest Circle, Suite 550
Lexington KY	Good Foods Market & Cafe	859-278-1813	455 Southland Dr # D
Louisville KY	Moe's	502-245-6250	12001 Shelbyville Road
Louisville KY	Moe's Southwest Grill	502-491-1800	2001 S Hurstbourne Parkway

Louisiana

Baton Rouge LA	Bistro Byronz	225-218-1433	5412 Government Street
Baton Rouge LA	La Madeleine French Bakery and Cafe	225-927-6001	7615 Jefferson H/H 73
Lake Charles LA	Pujo Street Cafe	337-439-2054	901 Ryan Street
New Orleans LA	Asian Pacific Cafe	504-945-1919	3125 Esplanade Avenue
New Orleans LA	Broussard's Restaurant & Patio	504-581-3866	819 Conti Street
New Orleans LA	CC's Community Coffee House	504-482-9865	2800 Esplanade Avenue
New Orleans LA	Cafe Amelie	504-412-8965	912 Royal Street
New Orleans LA	Cafe Du Monde Coffee Stand	504-525-4544	800 Decatur Street
New Orleans LA	Cafe Envie	504-524-3689	1241 Decatur St
New Orleans LA	Cafe Freret	504-861-7890	7329 Freret Street
New Orleans LA	Cafe Lafitte in Exile	504-522-8397	901 Bourbon St
New Orleans LA	Chartres House Cafe	504-586-8383	601 Chartres
New Orleans LA	Chi-WA-WA-GA-GA LLC	504-581-4242	37 French Market Place
New Orleans LA	Evan's Creole Candy Factory	504-522-7111	848 Decatur St
New Orleans LA	Fellini's Cafe	504-488-2155	900 N Carrollton Avenue
New Orleans LA	Gazebo Cafe	504-525-8899	1018 Decatur St
New Orleans LA	Rue De La Course	504-899-0240	3121 Magazine St, New Orleans
New Orleans LA	Seminola's Bistro Italia	504-895-4260	3226 Magazine Street
New Orleans LA	The Bulldog	504-891-1516	3236 Magazine Street
New Orleans LA	The Louisiana Pizza Kitchen	504-522-9500	95 French Market Place
New Orleans LA	The Market Cafe	504-527-5000	1000 Decatur St
New Orleans LA	Tomatillo's Mexican Restaurant	504-945-9997	437 Esplanade Avenue

Maine

Dog-Friendly Outdoor Dining - Please always call ahead to make sure an establishment is still dog-friendly.

Ba Harbor ME	Siam Orchid	207-288-1586	30 Rodick Street
Bar Harbor ME	Cafe Milagro	207-288-9592	37 Cottage Street
Bar Harbor ME	Cafe This Way	207-288-4483	14 1/2 Mt Desert Street/H 3
Bar Harbor ME	China Joy Restaurant	207-288-8666	195 Main Street
Bar Harbor ME	Chowdah's	207-288-3040	297 Main Street/H 3
Bar Harbor ME	Cottage Street Bakery & Deli	207-288-3010	59 Cottage St
Bar Harbor ME	Fish House Grill	207-288-3070	1 West Street
Bar Harbor ME	Jack Russell Pub	207-288-5214	102 Eden Street/H 3
Bar Harbor ME	Jordon Pond House Restaurant	207-276-3316	Route 3
Bar Harbor ME	Mainly Meat Barbeque	207-288-1100	369 H 3
Bar Harbor ME	Mama DiMatteo's	207-288-3666	34 Kennebec Place
Bar Harbor ME	McKays Public House	207-288-2002	231 Main Street/H 3
Bar Harbor ME	Parkside Restaurant	207-288-3700	185 Main Street/H 3
Bar Harbor ME	Rupununi	207-288-2886	119 Main St
Bar Harbor ME	Stewman's Lobster Pound	207-288-0346	35 West Street
Bar Harbor ME	Stewman's Lobster Pound at the Bar Harbor Regency	207-288-9723	123 Eden Street/H 3
Boothbay ME	Boothbay Lobster Wharf	207-633-4900	97 Atlantic Avenue
Boothbay Harbor ME	The Lobster Dock	207-633-7120	49 Atlantic Avenue
Brunswick ME	Fat Boy Drive-in	207-729-9431	111 Bath Road/H 24
Cape Porpoise ME	Cape Pier Chowder House	207-967-0123	84 Pier Road
Cape Porpoise Harbor ME	Cape Pier Chowder House	207-967-0123	79 Pier Road
Falmouth ME	O'Naturals	207-781-8889	240 US Route 1
Kennebunkport ME	Bartley's Restaurant	207-967-5050	Dockside by the Bridge
Oquossoc ME	The Gingerbread House	207-864-3602	55 Carry Road, Rangeley Lk
Portland ME	Beals Old Fashioned Ice Cream	207-820-1335	12 Moulton St
Portland ME	Gritty McDuffs	207-772-BREW (2739)	396 Fore Street
Portland ME	Portland Lobster Company	207-775-2112	180 Commercial Street/H 1
Portland ME	Sebago Brewpub	207-775-2337	164 Middle Street
Portland ME	The Flatbread Company	207-772-8777	72 Commercial Street/H 1
Southwest Harbor ME	Moorings Restaurant & Pier	207-244-7070	131 Shore Road

Maryland

Annapolis MD	Buddy's Crabs and Ribs	410-626-1100	100 Main Street
Annapolis MD	Grump's Cafe	410-267-0229	Bay Ridge Plaza 117 Hillsmere Drive
Annapolis MD	Rams Head Tavern	410-268-4545	33 West Street
Annapolis MD	Sly Fox Pub	443-482-9000	7 Church Circle
Annapolis MD	Stan and Joe's Saloon	410-263-1993	37 West Street/H 450
Baltimore MD	Bonjour	410-372-0238	6070 Falls Rd
Baltimore MD	Dangerously Delicious Pies	410-522-PIES (7437)	1036 Light Street
Baltimore MD	Ethel and Ramone's	410-664-2971	1615 Sulgrave Ave
Baltimore MD	Germano's Trattoria	410-752-4515	300 S High Street
Baltimore MD	Greene Turtle	410-342-4222	722 S Broadway
Baltimore MD	Iqgies Pizza	410 528 0818	010 N Calvert Street
Baltimore MD	Max's Taphouse	888-675-6297	737 S Broadway
Baltimore MD	Metropolitan	410-234-0235	904 S Charles St
Baltimore MD	Patterson Perk	410-534-1286	2501 Eastern Avenue
Baltimore MD	Shuckers	410-522-6300	1629 Thames Street
Baltimore MD	Taste Restaurant	443-278-9001	510 E Belvedere Ave
Burtonsville MD	Pepino's Trattoria Italiano	301-384-1655	15721 Columbia Pike
Callaway MD	Bear Creek Open Pit BBQ	301-994-1030	21030 Point Lookout Road/H 5
Cambridge MD	Snappers Waterfront Cafe	410-228-0112	112 Commerce Street
Chesapeake City MD	Bayard House	410-885-5040	11 Bohemia Avenue
Crisfield MD	The Waterman Inn	410-968-1565	901 W Main Street/H 413
Cumberland MD	City Lights	301-722-9800	59 Baltimore St
Deep Creek Lake MD	Lakeside Creamery	301-387-2580	20282 Garrett H/H 219
Frederick MD	La Paz	301-694-8980	51 South Market Street
McHenry MD	Canoe on the Run	301-387-5933	2622 Deep Creek Drive
Mechanicsville MD	Bert's 50's Diner	301-884-3837	28760 Three Notch Road/H 5/235
Ocean City MD	Macky's Bayside Bar and Grill	410-723-5565	54th Street on the Bay
Rock Hall MD	Miss Virginia's Crabcakes	410-639-7871	5793 Kent Avenue
Rockville MD	Chicken Out Rotisserie	301-230-2020	1560 Rockville Pike
Rockville MD	Z Pizza	240-403-1163	807-H Rockville Pike/H 355
S Chesapeake City MD	Chesapeake Inn	410-885-2040	605 Second Street/H 286
Silver Spring MD	Eggspectation	301-585-1700	923 Ellsworth Drive
Silver Spring MD	Red Dog Cafe	301-588-6300	8301 Grubb Road
St Michaels MD	St Michaels Crab House	410-745-3737	305 Mulberry Street

Massachusetts

Amesbury MA	The Flatbread Company	978-834-9800	5 Market Square
Amherst MA	Rao's Coffee Roasting Company	413-253-9441	17 Kellogg Avenue
Beverly MA	Rawbert's Organic Cafe	978-922-0004	294 Cabot Street/H 22
Beverly MA	Tapas Corner	978-927-9983	284 Cabot Street (Route 62)
Boston MA	Hamersley's Bistro	617-423-2700	553 Tremont St
Boston MA	Joe's American Bar and Grill	617-536-4200	279 Dartmouth St

Dog-Friendly Outdoor Dining - Please always call ahead to make sure an establishment is still dog-friendly.

Boston MA	Kinsale Irish Pub	617-742-5577	2 Center Plz
Boston MA	Salty Dog Seafood Grille	617-742-2094	206 Faneuil Hall Market P1
Boston MA	Sel De La Terre	617-720-1300	255 State St
Boston MA	Whole Foods Market	617-375-1010	15 Westland Avenue
Brewster MA	Cobie's Outdoor restaurant	508-896-7021	3260 Main St
Brookline MA	Taberna de Haro	617-277-8272	999 Beacon Street
Cambridge MA	Au Bon Pain	617-497-9797	1360 Massachusetts Avenue, Harvard Square
Cambridge MA	Cambridge Brewing Company	617-494-1994	One Kendall Square
Cambridge MA	Henrietta's Table	617-661-5005	1 Bennett Street
Concord MA	Country Kitchen	978-371-0181	181 Sudbury Road
Edgartown MA	Espresso Love	508-627-9211	17 Church Street
Fiskdale MA	Pioneer Brewing Company	508-347-7500	195 Arnold Road
Gloucester MA	Virgilios Italian Bakery	978-283-5295	29 Main Street
Lexington MA	Dabin Restaurant	781-860-0171	10 Muzzey St #1
Lexington MA	Khushboo Restaurant	781-863-2900	1709 Massachusetts Avenue
Mashpee MA	Starbuck's Coffee House	508-477-5806	38 Nanthan Ellis Hwy
Mashpee MA	The Tea Shoppe	508-477-7261	13 Steeple Street
Nantucket MA	Espresso To Go	508-228-6930	1 Toombs Court
Nantucket MA	Henry's Sandwich Shop	508-228-0123	2 Broad Street
Nantucket MA	Something Natural	508-228-0504	50 Cliff Road
New Bedford MA	Candleworks Restaurant	508-997-1294	72 N Water Street
Oak Bluffs MA	Carousel Ice Cream Factory	508-693-7582	15 Circuit Avenue
Plymouth MA	Lobster Hut	508-746-2270	25 Town Wharf
Provincetown MA	Frappo66	508-487-9066	214 Commercial Street
Rockport MA	Helmut's Strudel Shop	978-546-2824	69 Bearskin Neck
Rockport MA	Roy Moore Lobster Company	978-546-6696	39 Bearskin Neck
Southbridge MA	Vienna Restaurant (and Historic Inn)	508-764-0700	14 South Street
Swampscott MA	Red Rock Bistro and Bar	781-595-1414	141 Humphrey Street
Vineyard Haven MA	Daily Grind	508-693-5200	79 Beach Road
Vineyard Haven MA	Louis' Tisbury Cafe	508-693-3255	350 State Road
Wellfleet MA	P.J.'s Family Restaurant	508-349-2126	H 6 and School Street

Michigan

Ann Arbor MI	Amadeus Cafe	734-665-8767	122 E Washington Street
Ann Arbor MI	Arbor Brewing Company	734-213-1393	114 E Washington Street
Ann Arbor MI	Aut Bar	734-994-3677	315 Braun Court
Ann Arbor MI	Cafe Felix	734-662-8650	204 S Main Street
Ann Arbor MI	Connor O'Neill's Irish Pub and Restaurant	734-665-2968	318 S Main Street
Ann Arbor MI	Full Moon Restaurant & Saloon	734-994-8484	207 S Main Street
Ann Arbor MI	Gratzi	734-663-5555	326 S Main Street
Ann Arbor MI	Monahan's Seafood	734-662-5118	415 N Fifth Ave - 1st Floor
Ann Arbor MI	Palio	734-930-6100	347 S Main Street
Ann Arbor MI	Panera Bread	734-677-0400	3205 Washtenaw Avenue
Ann Arbor MI	Panera Bread	734-213-5800	5340 Jackson Road
Ann Arbor MI	Panera Bread	734-222-4944	903 W Eisenhower Parkway
Ann Arbor MI	People's Food Co-op and Cafe Verde	734-994-9174	216 N 4th Avenue
Ann Arbor MI	Quiznos	734-222-9383	108 S Main Street
Ann Arbor MI	Real Seafood Company	734-769-7738	341 S Main
Ann Arbor MI	The Rendez Vous Cafe	734-761-8600	1110 S University Avenue
Ann Arbor MI	Zanzibar	734-994-7777	216 S State Street
Ann Arbor MI	Zingerman's Deli	734-663-3354	422 Detroit St
Ann Arbor MI	Zingerman's Roadhouse	734-663-3663	2501 Jackson Ave
Ann Arbor MI	aut BAR	734-994-3677	315 Braun Court
Birmingham MI	Brooklyn Pizza	248-258-6690	111 Henrietta
Birmingham MI	Schakolad Chocolate Factory	248-723-8008	167 N Old Woodward Avenue
Chelsea MI	Mike's Deli	734-475-5980	114 W Middle Street
Chelsea MI	Zou Zou's Cafe	734-433-4226	101 Main Street/H 52
Chesterfield MI	Panera Bread	586-598-5728	51490 Gratiot Avenue
Clarkston MI	Outback Steakhouse	248-620-4329	6435 Dixie Hwy
Dearborn MI	A & W Family Restaurant	313-271-1676	210 Town Center Dr
Detroit MI	Chelis Chili Bar and Restaurant	313-961-1700	47 E Adams Avenue
East Lansing MI	Crunchy's Bar and Grill	517-351-2506	254 W Grand Avenue
Farmington Hills MI	Baja Fresh	248-848-9700	37660 W. 12th Mile
Grand Rapids MI	Noto's Old World Restaurant	616-493-6686	6600 28th Street SE
Grand Rapids MI	Panera Bread	619-949-1200	6080 28th Street SE
Grand Rapids MI	Panera Bread	616-363-9100	2044 Celebration Drive NE
Jackson MI	Bella Notte Ristorante	517-782-5727	137 W Michigan Avenue
Lansing MI	Cones and Bones	517-321-1520	412 Elmwood Road
Lansing MI	Panera Bread	517-332-9183	310 N Clippert Street
Lansing MI	Panera Bread	517-703-9340	5330 W Saginaw H/H 43
Mackinac Island MI	Bistro on the Greens	906-847-3312	One Lakeshore Drive
Mackinac Island MI	Cannonball Drive In	906-847-3549	Historic British Landing
Mackinac Island MI	Feedbag	906-847-3593	Surrey Hills
Mackinac Island MI	Lakeside Marketplace/Freighters Deli	906-847-3312	One Lakeshore Drive
Mackinac Island MI	Murray's Cafe and Deli	800-462-2546	100 Main Street
Mackinac Island MI	Verandah at Carriage House	906-847-3321	7485 Main Street
Manistee MI	Boathouse Grill	231-723-2300	440 River Street
Manistee MI	Goody's Juice and Java	231-398-9580	343 River Street

Dog-Friendly Outdoor Dining - Please always call ahead to make sure an establishment is still dog-friendly.

Marquette MI	Border Grill	906-228-5228	180 S McClellan Avenue
Milan MI	The Dairy Barn	734-439-7677	805 Dexter Street
Northville MI	Northville Baja Fresh	248-347-3500	17933 Haggerty
Novi MI	Baja Fresh	248-735-7000	43271 Crescent Blvd
Okemos MI	Stillwater Grill	517-349-1500	3544 Meridian Crossing Drive
Oxford MI	Red Knapps American Grill	248-628-1200	2 N Washington Street/H 24
Petoskey MI	Chandler's	231-347-2981	215 1/2 Howard Street
Port Huron MI	The Quay Street Brewing Company	810-982-4100	330 Quay Street
Rochester Hills MI	Baja Fresh	248-375-1900	176 N. Adams #E176
Rochester Hills MI	Chipotle Mexican Grill	248-853-2850	2611 S Rochester Road/H 150
Saline MI	Mickey's Dairy Twist Ice Cream	734-429-4450	751 W Michigan Avenue
Saugatuck MI	Pumpernickel's Eatery	269-857-1196	202 Butler Street
Sault Ste. Marie MI	Clyde's Drive-in	906-623-2581	1425 Riverside Drive
Sault Ste. Marie MI	Cup of the Day	906-635-7272	406 Ashmun Street
Shelby Township MI	Panera Bread	586-532-1520	14121 Hall Road
Southfield MI	Chipotle Mexican Grill	248-353-3448	26147 Evergreen Rd.
St Joseph MI	Caffe Tosi	269-983-3354	516 Pleasant Street
Sterling Heights MI	Baja Fresh	586-698-0313	35720 Van Dyke Avenue/H 53
Sterling Heights MI	Chipotle Mexican Grill	586-532-1139	13975 Lakeside Circle
Traverse City MI	Oryana Natural Foods Market	231-947-0191	260 E 10th Street
West Bloomfield MI	Chipotle Mexican Grill	248-539-9014	6753 Orchard Lake Road
Ypsilanti MI	Harvest Moon Cafe	734-434-8100	5484 W Michigan/H 12

Minnesota

Albuquerque MN	La Montanita Co-op	505-265-4631	3500 Central SE/H 66
Albuquerque MN	La Montanita Co-op	505-242-8800	2400 Rio Grande Blvd NW
Anoka MN	Lakewinds Natural Foods	763-427-4340	1917 2nd Avenue S
Bemidji MN	Harmony Natural Foods	218-751-2009	117 3rd Street NW
Blaine MN	Neptune Cafe Italiana	763-754-5628	2330 Cloud Drive NE
Chanhassen MN	Lakewinds Natural Foods	952-697-3366	435 Pond Promenade
Duluth MN	Chester Creek Cafe	218-724-6811	1902 East 8th Street
Ely MN	The Front Porch Coffee and Tea Company	218-365-2326	343 E Sheridan Street/H 1/169
Grand Marais MN	Angry Trout Cafe	218-387-1265	416 H 61W
Grand Marais MN	The Angry Trout	218-387-1265	416 W Highway 61
Minneapoli MN	Linden Hills Co-op	612-922-1159	2813 W 43rd Street
Minneapolis MN	331 Bar	612-331-1746	331 13th Avenue NE/H 47
Minneapolis MN	Chipotle Mexican Grill	612-659-7955	1040 Nicollet Avenue
Minneapolis MN	Chipotle Mexican Grill	612-331-6330	225 Hennepin Avenue E
Minneapolis MN	Corner Coffee	612-338-2002	514 N 3rd St Suite 102
Minneapolis MN	Eastside Food Co-op	612-788-0950	2551 Central Avenue NE/H 65
Minneapolis MN	Joe's Garage	612-904-1163	1610 Harmon Place
Minneapolis MN	Lucia's Restaurant	612-825-1572	1432 W 31st Street
Minneapolis MN	Picosa	612-746-3970	65 Main Street SE
Minneapolis MN	Town Hall Brewery	612-339-8696	1430 Washington Avenue SE
Minneapolis MN	Urban Bean	612-824-6611	3255 Bryant Ave South
Minneapolis MN	View Calhoun	612-920-5000	2730 West Lake Street
Minnetonka MN	Lakewinds Natural Foods	952-473-0292	17501 Minnetonka Blvd
Rochester MN	Beetles Bar and Grill	507-529-9599	230 20th Avenue SW
Rochester MN	Good Food Store Co-op -- and The Back Room Deli	507-289-9061	1001 6th Street NW
Roseville MN	Joe Senser's Sports Grill and Bar	651-631-1781	2350 Cleveland Avenue
Roseville MN	Z Pizza	651-633-3131	1607 County Road C
St Peter MN	St Peter Food Co-op and Deli	507-934-4880	119 W Broadway
St Paul MN	Eagle Street Grill and Pub	651-225-1382	174 W 7th Street/H 5
St Paul MN	The Happy Gnome	651-287-2018	498 Selby Avenue
St Paul MN	W.A. Frost and Company	651-224-5715	374 Selby Avenue
Stillwater MN	River Market Community Co-op	651-439-0366	221 N Main Street, Suite 1/H 95
Tofte MN	Bluefin Grill	800-258-3346	7192 H 61W
Tofte MN	Coho Cafe	218-663-8032	7126 H 61W
Winona MN	Winona Island Cafe	507-454-1133	2 Johnson Street

Mississippi

Biloxi MS	Mary Mahoney's	228-374-0163	110 Rue Magnolia Blvd
Jackson MS	Broad Street Baking Company	601-362-2900	4465 I-55 North Banner Hall
Vicksburg MS	Cedar Grove Inn Restaurant	601-636-1000	2200 Oak Street

Missouri

Columbia MO	International Cafe	573-449-4560	209 Hitt Street
Hannibal MO	Mark Twain Dinette	800-786-5193	400 N 3rd Street (H 36/61)
Kansas City MO	Aixois	816-333-3305	301 E 55th Street
Kansas City MO	B.B.'s Lawnside Barbecue	816-822-7427	1205 E 85th Street
Kansas City MO	Blue Bird Bistro	816-221-7559	1700 Summit St
Kansas City MO	M and S Grill	816-531-7799	4646 JC Nichols Parkway
Kansas City MO	Panera Bread Company	816-931-8181	4700 Pennsylvania Avenue
Kansas City MO	Reverse on the Plaza	816-931-7811	616 Ward Parkway
Kansas City MO	Shields Manor Bistro	816-858-5557	121 Main Street

Kirkwood MO	Graham's Grill and Bayou Bar	505-751-1350	612 W Woodbine Avenue
Osage Beach MO	Backwater Jack's	573-348-6639	4341 Beach Drive
Osage Beach MO	Miller's Landing	573-348-5268	MM 28 1/2 Runabout Drive
Overland MO	Woofie's Hot Dogs	314-426-6291	1919 Woodson Rd
Springfield MO	Springfield Brewing Co	417-832-TAPS (8277)	301 S Market Avenue
St Charles MO	Garden Cafe ala Fleur	636-946-2020	524 S Main Street
St Louis MO	Atlas Restaurant	314-367-6800	5513 Pershing Avenue
St Louis MO	Boathouse Restaurant in Forest Park	314-367-2224	6101 Government Dr.
St Louis MO	Coffee Cartel	314-454-0000	2 Maryland Plaza
St Louis MO	Downtown Cantina And Brick Oven Cafe	314-231-5620	901 Pine Street
St Louis MO	Duff's Restaurant	314-361-0522	392 North Euclid Avenue
St Louis MO	Quiznos	314-842-6654	12676 Lamplighter Square
St Louis MO	Whole Foods Market	314-968-7744	1601 S Brentwood Blvd

Montana

Billings MT	George Henry's Restaurant	406-245-4570	404 N 30th Street
Billings MT	The Rex	406-245-7477	2401 Montana Avenue
Billings MT	The Windmill Restaurant	406-252-8100	3429 TransTech Way
Billings MT	Z Pizza	406-839-9333	1430 Country Manor Blvd
West Yellowstone MT	Petes Rocky Mountain Pizza and Pasta	406-646-7820	Canyon Street and Madison Ave.

Nebraska

Las Vegas NE	Create	702-586-0430	7290 W Lake Mead Blvd #2
Lincoln NE	Buzzard Billy's Armadillo Bar-N-Grillo	402-475-8822	247 N 8th Street Suite 101
Lincoln NE	Open Harvest Natural Foods Cooperative Grocery	402-475-9069	1618 South Street
Lincoln NE	Parthenon Restaurant	402-423-2222	5500 S 56th Street #100
Omaha NE	Chipotle Mexican Grill	402-391-9979	201 S 72nd Street
Omaha NE	Chipotle Mexican Grill	402-498-3633	3605 N 147th Street, # 111
Omaha NE	Chipotle Mexican Grill	402-697-4903	13203 W Center Road/H 38
Omaha NE	Goldberg's II Dundee	402-556-2006	2936 S 132nd Street
Omaha NE	La Buvette	402-344-8627	511 S 11th Street
Omaha NE	Mc Foster's Natural Kind Cafe	402-345-7477	302 S 38th Street
Omaha NE	Trovato's Italian Restaurant	402-556-9505	5013 Underwood Avenue
Omaha NE	Upstream Brewing Company	402-344-0200	514 South 11th Street

Nevada

Boulder City NV	Milo's Best Cellars	702-293-9540	538 Nevada Way
Carson City NV	Comma Coffee	775-883-2662	312 S. Carson Street
Carson City NV	Mom and Pops Diner	775-884-4411	224 S. Carson St.
Henderson NV	The Brooklyn Bagel	702-260-9511	1500 N. Green Valley Parkway
Las Vegas NV	Baja Fresh Mexican Grill	702-699-8920	1380 E Flamingo Rd
Las Vegas NV	Baja Fresh Mexican Grill	702-948-4043	8780 W Charleston Blvd # 100
Las Vegas NV	Baja Fresh Mexican Grill	702-838-4100	7501 W Lake Mead Blvd # 100
Las Vegas NV	Baja Fresh Mexican Grill	702-563-2800	9310 S Eastern Ave
Las Vegas NV	Einstein Brothers Bagels	702-254-0919	9031 W. Sahara Ave
Las Vegas NV	In-N-Out Burger	800-786-1000	2900 W. Sahara Ave.
Las Vegas NV	It's A Grind	702-360-4232	8470 W Desert Inn Rd
Las Vegas NV	Mountain Springs Saloon	702-875-4266	Highway 160
Las Vegas NV	ReJAVAnate	702-253-7721	3300 E Flamingo Rd
Las Vegas NV	Starbucks	702-369-5537	395 Hughes Center Drive
Las Vegas NV	TGI Fridays	702-889-1866	4570 W Sahara Avenue/H 589
Las Vegas NV	Whole Foods Market	702-254-8655	8855 West Charleston Blvd.
Las Vegas NV	Wild Oats Natural Marketplace	702-942-1500	7250 W. Lake Mead Blvd
Minden NV	Barone and Reed Food Company	775-783-1988	1599 Esmeralda Avenue
Reno NV	Archie's Grill	775-322-9595	2195 N. Virginia St.
Reno NV	Java Jungle	775-329-4484	246 W. 1st Street
Reno NV	My Favorite Muffin & Bagel Cafe	775-333-1025	340 California Ave.
Reno NV	Peg's Glorified Ham & Eggs	775-329-2600	420 S. Sierra St.
Reno NV	Quiznos	775-828-5252	4965 S. Virginia Street
Reno NV	The Wild River Grille	775-284-7455	17 S Virginia Street/BH 395
Reno NV	Walden's Coffee Co.	775-787-3307	3940 Mayberry Drive
Reno NV	Wild Oats Natural Marketplace	775-829-8666	5695 S. Virginia St.
Reno NV	Wild River Grille	775-284-7455	17 S Virginia Street, # 180/H 395
Reno NV	Z Pizza	775-828-6565	4796 Caughlin Parkway

New Hampshire

Concord NH	Concord Cooperative Market Celery Stick Cafe	603-225-6840	24 S Main Street
Jackson Village NH	Wildcat Inn & Tavern	603-356-8700	H 16A/Village Road
Keene NH	Luca's Mediterranean Café	603-358-3335	10 Central Square
Lebanon NH	The Co-op Food Store	603-643-2667	12 Centerra Parkway
New London NH	Jack's of New London	603-526-8003	207 Main Street
North Conway NH	The Flatbread Company	603-356-4470	2760 White Mountain H/H 16/302

Dog-Friendly Outdoor Dining - Please always call ahead to make sure an establishment is still dog-friendly.

Northwood NH	Susty's	603-942-5862	159 1st New Hampshire Turnpike
Portsmouth NH	Annabelle's Natural Ice Cream	603-436-3400	49 Ceres Street
Portsmouth NH	Portsmouth (Redhook) Brewery and Cataqua	603-430-8600	35 Corporate Drive
West Ossipee NH	Yankee Smokehouse	603-539-7427	H 16 and H 25W

New Jersey

Barnegat NJ	Sweet Jenny's Ice Cream Parlor	609-698-2228	107 S Main Street/H 9
Belmar NJ	Circus Drive-In	732-449-2650	State Hwy 35 North
Belmar NJ	Federico's Pizza and Restaurant	732-774-8448	700 Main St
Belmar NJ	Windmill Hot Dogs	732-870-6098	1201 River Road
Bradley Beach NJ	Bagel International	732-775-7447	48 Main St
Bradley Beach NJ	Giamano's Restaurant	732-775-4275	301 Main St
Bradley Beach NJ	Piancone's Deli and Bakery	732-775-0846	804 Main St
Cape May NJ	Jackson Mountain Cafe	609-884-5648	400 Washington Street
East Hanover NJ	Baja Fresh	973-952-0080	136 H 10
East Rutherford NJ	Panera Bread	201-531-1480	51 State Route 17
Exton NJ	Appetites on Main	610-594-2030	286 Main Street
Frenchtown NJ	Buck's Ice Cream and Espresso Bar,	908-996-7258	52 Bridge Street
Frenchtown NJ	The Frenchtown Inn	908-996-3300	7 Bridge Street
High Bridge NJ	Circa Restaurant	908-638-5560	37 Main Street
Hoboken NJ	Arthur's Steak House	201-656-5009	237 Washington Street
Hoboken NJ	Helmer's Restaurant	201-963-3333	1306 Washington Street
Hoboken NJ	Margherita's Pizza and Cafe	201-222-2400	740 Washington St
Hoboken NJ	Panera Bread	201-876-3233	308 Washington St
Hoboken NJ	Sinatra Park Cafe	201-420-9900	525 Sinatra Drive
Hoboken NJ	Sushi Lounge	201-386-1117	200 Hudson Street
Hoboken NJ	Texas-Arizona's	201-420-0304	76 River Street
Hoboken NJ	Tutta Pasta Restaurant	201-792-9102	200 Washington St
Jersey City NJ	Bertucci's Brick Oven Pizzeria	201-222-8160	560 Washington Blvd
Lambertville NJ	De Anna's Restaurant	609-397-8957	54 N Franklin Street
Lambertville NJ	Hamilton's Grill Room at the Porkyard	609-397-4343	8 Coryell Street
Morristown NJ	Camille's Sidewalk Cafe	973-540-9727	161 South Street
Mount Holly NJ	Olde World Bakery	609-265-1270	1000 Smithville Road
Mount Holly NJ	Robin's Nest Restaurant and the Crow Bar	609-261-6149	2 Washington Street
Normandy Beach NJ	Labrador Lounge	732-830-5770	3581 H 35 N
North Long Branch NJ	Windmill Hot Dogs	732-870-6098	200 Ocean Avenue
Ocean City NJ	Bashful Banana Cafe and Bakery	609-398-9677	944 Ocean City Boardwalk
Red Bank NJ	Zebu Forno Inc	732-936-9330	20 Broad St
Sea Isle City NJ	Mike's Seafood and Raw Bar	609-263-1136	4222 Park Road
Shrewsbury NJ	Cypress Cafe	732-219-8646	555 Shrewsbury Ave
Spring Lake Heights NJ	Susan Murphy's Ice Cream	732-449-1130	601 Warren Avenue
Springfield NJ	Cathay 22	973-467-8688	124 Route 22 West
Stockton NJ	Cravings	609-397-2911	10 Risler Street
Stockton NJ	Stockton Inn Restaurant and Tavern	609-397-1250	1 Main Street
Tenafly NJ	Café Angelique	201-541-1010	1 Piermont Road
Voorhees NJ	Baja Fresh	856-784-5955	1120 White Horse Road, Suite 138
Wayne NJ	Baja Fresh	973-872-2555	1600 H 23N

New Mexico

Albuquerque NM	Flying Star Cafe	505-255-6633	3416 Central AVe SE
Albuquerque NM	Geckos Bar and Tapas	505-262-1848	3500 Central Avenue SE/H 66
Albuquerque NM	Geckos Bar and Tapas	505-821-8291	5801 Academy Rd NE
Albuquerque NM	Kelly's Brew Pub	505-262-2739	3222 Central Avenue SE/H 66
Albuquerque NM	Sonic Drive-In	505-243-7880	531 Bridge Blvd SW
Albuquerque NM	Sonic Drive-In	505-897-7538	220 Alameda Blvd NW
Albuquerque NM	Sonic Drive-In	505-292-6979	11715 Central Avenue NE/Historic H 66
Albuquerque NM	Whole Foods Market	505-856-0474	5815 Wyoming Blvd NE
Jemez Springs NM	The Laughing Lizard Inn and Cafe	505-753-3211	17526 H 4
Las Cruces NM	Caliche's Frozen Custard	505-521-1161	131 Roadrunner Parkway
Las Cruces NM	International Delights	505-647-5956	1245 El Paseo Road
Las Cruces NM	Spirit Winds Coffee Bar	575-521-1222	2260 S Locust Street
Santa Fe NM	Atomic Grill	505-820-2866	103 E Water Street
Santa Fe NM	Bobcat Bite	505-983-5319	420 Old Las Vegas H
Santa Fe NM	Counter Culture	505-995-1105	930 Baca Street
Santa Fe NM	Downtown Subscription	505-983-3085	376 Garcia Street
Santa Fe NM	La Montanita Co-op	505-984-2853	913 W Alameda Street
Santa Fe NM	The Gate House	505-992-0957	150 E DeVargas
Santa Fe NM	Whole Foods Market	505-992-1700	753 Cerrillos Road
Silver City NM	Vicki's Eatery	505-388-5430	107 W Yankie Street
Taos NM	Alley Cantina	505-758-2121	121 Teresina Lane
Taos NM	BRAVO! Fine Wine Food & Spirits	505-758-8100	1353A Paseo del Pueblo Sur
Taos NM	Dragonfly Cafe	505-737-5859	402 Paseo Del Pueblo Norte/H 64
Taos Ski Valley NM	Tim's Stray Dog Cantina	505-776-2894	105 Sutton Place

New York

Dog-Friendly Outdoor Dining - Please always call ahead to make sure an establishment is still dog-friendly.

Albany NY	Londonberry Cafe	518-489-4288	1475 Western Avenue, Suite 30
Albany NY	Nicole's Bistro	518-467-1111	25 Quackenbush Square
Amityville NY	The Bulldog Grill	631-691-1947	292 Merrick Road
Amityville NY	Toomey's Tavern on the Crik	631-264-0564	251 S Ketcham Avenue
Beacon NY	The Piggy Bank Restaurant	845-838-0028	448 Main Street
Brooklyn NY	Brooklyn Ice Cream Factory	718-246-3963	1 Water Street
Brooklyn NY	El Greco Diner	718-934-1288	1821 Emmons Avenue
Brooklyn NY	Maria's Mexican Bistro	718-638-2344	669 Union St
Brooklyn NY	The Gate	718-768-4329	321 5th Avenue
Buffalo NY	Lexington Co-operative Market	716-886-COOP (2667)	807 Elmwood Avenue
Buffalo NY	Spot Coffee	716-332-2299	227 Delaware Avenue
Buffalo NY	The Saigon Cafe	716-883-1252	1098 Elmwood Avenue
Callicoon NY	Matthews on Main	845-887-5636	19 Lower Main Street
East Hampton NY	Rowdy Hall	631-324-8555	10 Main Street
Elmira NY	The Green Star Natural Foods Market	607-273-8213	215 N Cayuga Street
Freeport NY	Bracco's Clam and Oyster Bar	516-378-6575	319 Woodcleft Avenue
Garden City NY	Grimaldi's Restaurant	516-294-6565	980 Franklin Avenue
Glens Falls NY	Davidson Brothers Restaurant and Brewery	518-743-9026	184 Glen St/H 9
High Falls NY	DePuy Canal House Restaurant	845-687-7700	1315 H 213
Ithaca NY	Blue Stone Bar and Grill	607-272-2371	110 N Aurora Street
Ithaca NY	Madeline's Restaurant	607-277-2253	215 East State Street, The Commons
Lake George NY	Christie's on the Lake	518-668-2515	6 Christie Lane
Lake George NY	Frank's Pizzeria	518-793-7909	1483 State Rt 9
Lake George NY	King Neptune's Pub and Night Club	518-668-2017	4 Kurosaka Lane
Lake George NY	Lake George Barnsider Restaurant	518-668-5268	Route 9 South Lake George
Lake George NY	Sicilian Spaghetti House	518-668-2582	371 Canada Street
Lake Luzerne NY	Waterhouse Restaurant	518-696-3115	Route 9 North
Lake Placid NY	Bazzi's Pizza	518-523-9056	138 Main St
Lake Placid NY	The Downhill Grill	518-523-9510	434 Main Street
Long Island City NY	The Creek and the Cave	718-706-8783	1093 Jackson Ave
New Paltz NY	The Bakery	845-255-8840	13-A North Front Street
New York NY	Amish Market	212-871-6300	17 Battery Place
New York NY	Bangkok House	212-541-5943	360 W 46th Street
New York NY	Barking Dog Luncheonette	212-861-3600	1453 York Ave
New York NY	Cascina	212-633-2941	281 Bleecker St
New York NY	Da Rosina Ristorante	212-977-7373	342 W 46th St
New York NY	Fetch	212-289-2700	1649 Third Avenue
New York NY	Firehouse	212-787-FIRE (3473)	522 Columbus Avenue
New York NY	Flex Mussels	212-717-7772	174 E 82nd Street
New York NY	Fratelli Ristorante	212-226-5555	115 Mulberry St
New York NY	Gavroche	212-647-8553	212 West 14th Street
New York NY	Il Porto	212-791-2181	11 Fulton Street
New York NY	Kaijou	212-786-9888	21 S End Ave
New York NY	P J Clarke's on the Hudson	212-285-1500	250 Vesey Street
New York NY	Phillip Marie Restaurant	212-242-6200	569 Hudson
New York NY	San Martin Restaurant	212-832-0888	143 E 49th Street
New York NY	Sidewalks	212-473-7373	94 Avenue A
New York NY	Sorrento Restaurant	212-219-8634	132 Mulberry St
New York NY	The Old Homestead Steakhouse	212-242-9040	56 9th Avenue
New York NY	The Park	212-352-3313	118 10th Avenue
New York NY	Tre	212-353-3313	173 Ludlow Street
New York NY	Yum Yum 3	212-956-0176	658 9th Avenue Corner of W 46th Street
Newburgh NY	Cena 2000 Restorante and Bar	845-561-7676	50 Front Street
Niagara Falls NY	Papa Leo's Pizzeria	716-731-5911	2265 Niagara Falls Blvd.
Nyack NY	Lanterna Tuscan Bistro	845-353-8361	3 S Broadway
Oswego NY	Rudy's Lakeside	315-343-2671	Washington Blvd
Plainview NY	Quiznos	516-942-5188	1161 Old Country Road
Potsdam NY	Potsdam Food Co-op	315-265-4630	24 Elm Street
Rochester NY	Open Face	585-232-3050	651 South Avenue
Seneca Falls NY	Downtown Deli	315-568-9943	53 Falls Street/H 5
South Glens Falls NY	Jake's Round- Up	518-761-0015	23 Main Street
Syracuse NY	Dinosaur Barbecue	315-476-4937	246 W Willow Street
Syracuse NY	Pastabilities	315-474-1153	311 S Franklin Street
Tarrytown NY	Horsefeathers	914-631-6606	94 N Broadway/H 9

North Carolina

Asheville NC	Asheville Pizza and Brewing Company	828-254-1281	675 Merrimon Avenue
Asheville NC	Carmel's Restaurant and Bar	828-252-8730	Corner of Page Avenue and Battery Park
Asheville NC	Cats and Dawgs	828-281-8100	1 Page Avenue, Suite 132
Asheville NC	Earth Fare Natural Food Market	828-253-7656	66 Westgate Parkway
Asheville NC	French Broad Food Coop	828-255-7650	90 Biltmore Avenue/H 25
Asheville NC	KAMM'S Frozen Custard Shop	828-225-7200	111 O'Henry Avenue
Asheville NC	Little Venice	828-299-8911	800 Fairview Road, Suite 9
Asheville NC	Posana Cafe	828-505-3969	One Biltmore Avenue
Asheville NC	Sunny Point Cafe and Bakery	828-252-0055	626 Haywood Road
Asheville NC	The Laughing Seed Cafe	828-252-3445	40 Wall Street
Asheville NC	Urban Burrito	828-251-1921	640 Merrimon Avenue

Dog-Friendly Outdoor Dining - Please always call ahead to make sure an establishment is still dog-friendly.

Barco NC	Currituck BBQ Company	252-453-6618	4467 Caratoke H/H 158
Carrboro NC	Panzanella	919-929-6626	200 Greensboro Street
Carrboro NC	The Cafe at Weaver Street Market	919-929-0010	101 E Weaver Street
Cary NC	Ruckus Pizza	919-851-3999	8111-208 Tryon Woods Drive
Cary NC	Z Pizza	919-465-9009	96 Cornerstone Drive
Charlotte NC	Burgers & Bagels	704-525-5295	4327 Park Road Bldg 25
Charlotte NC	Burgers on East Blvd	704-332-5991	1531 East Blvd
Charlotte NC	Fuel Pizza	704-350-1680	214 N Tryon
Charlotte NC	Fuel Pizza	704-376-3835	1501 Central Avenue
Charlotte NC	Fuel on the Green	704-370-2755	500 S College Street
Charlotte NC	Moe's Southwest Grill	704-377-6344	1500 East Blvd.
Charlotte NC	Rudino's Pizza and Grinders	704-333-3124	2000 South Blvd
Charlotte NC	Smelly Cat Coffee House	704-374-9656	514 E 36th Street
Charlotte NC	Starbucks	704-338-9911	1401 East Blvd
Charlotte NC	Thomas Street Tavern	704-376-1622	1218 Thomas Ave.
Charlotte NC	Wolfman Pizza	704-552-4979	8418 Park Rd
Clayton NC	The Coffee Mill and Flipside Restaurant	919-550-0174	105 S Lombard Street
Coinjock NC	Coinjock Marina Restaurant	252-453-3271	321 Waterlily Road
Coinjock NC	Corolla Village Barbecue	252-457-0076	1129 Corolla Village Rd
Coinjock NC	Crabbie's Restaurant	252-453-6225	159 Coinjock Development Road
Corolla NC	Bacchus Wine and Cheese	252-453-4333	891 Albacore Street
Corolla NC	Donkey Hotay's	252-453-8877	1159 C Austin Street
Corolla NC	Mr Munchies	252-453-6607	799 Sunset Blvd
Corolla NC	Pizza Guy	252-453-9976	501 Old Stoney Road
Corolla NC	Steamer's Shellfish To Go	252-453-3305	798 Sunset Blvd # B
Davidson NC	Fuel Pizza	704-655-3835	402 S Main Street
Duck NC	Aqua S Restaurant	252-261-9700	1174 Duck Road/H 12
Duck NC	Baldy's Burgers and Ice Cream	252-261-2660	1213 Duck Road/H 12
Duck NC	Duck's Cottage Coffee and Books	252-261-5510	1240 Duck Road/H-12
Durham NC	Cosmic Cantina	919-286-1875	1920 Perry Street
Durham NC	Grayson's Cafe	919-403-9220	2300 Chapel Hill Road
Durham NC	The Original Q Shack	919-402-4227	2510 University Drive
Grandy NC	Mels Diner	252-457-1010	6684 Caratoke H/H 158
Harbinger NC	Sauls Bar-B-Que	252-491-5000	8627 Caratoke H/H 158
Hatteras NC	Harbor Deli	252-986-2500	58058 H 12
Hendersonville NC	Henderson Community Co-op	828-693-0505	715 Old Spartanburg H
Huntersville NC	Fox and Hound Pub and Grill	704-895-4504	8711 Lindholm Drive
Kill Devil Hills NC	Kill Devil's Frozen Custard and Beach Fries	252-441-5900	1002 S Croatan H/H 158
Kitty Hawk NC	Jimmy's Buffet	252-261-4973	4117 N Croatan H/H 158
Kitty Hawk NC	John's Drive In	252-261-6227	3716 Virginia Dare Trail N/H 12/158
Kitty Hawk NC	Sooey's BBQ & Rib Shack	252-255-5394	Kitty Hawk Road
Kitty Hawk NC	The Run Down Cafe	252-255-0026	5218 N Virginia Dare Trail/H 12/158
Nags Head NC	Fatboyz Ice Cream and Grill	252-441-6514	7208 S Virginia Dare Trail
Nags Head NC	Sonic Drive-in	252-441-9030	5205 S Croatan H/H 158
Nags Head NC	Sooey's BBQ At Jockey's Ridge	252-449-6465	3919 S Croatan H/H 158
Nags Head NC	Tropical Smoothie Cafe	252-441-3500	2236 S Croatan H/H 158
New Bern NC	Cow Cafe	252-636-7900	319 Middle Street
New Bern NC	Morgan's Tavern & Grill	252-636-2430	235 Craven Street
New Bern NC	Port City Java	252-633-7900	323 Middle Street
Ocracoke NC	Jolly Roger Pub and Marina	252-928-3703	396 Irvin Garrish H/H 12
Ocracoke NC	Pelican Restaurant and Patio Bar	252-928-7431	H 12
Point Harbor NC	PDX Grille	252-491-2474	9175 Caratoke H/H 158
Poplar Branch NC	Diggers Diner	252-453-0971	5658 Caratoke H/H 158
Raleigh NC	Armadillo Grill	919-546-0555	439 Glenwood Avenue
Raleigh NC	Bella Monica Restaurant	919-881-9778	3121 Edwards Mill Road
Raleigh NC	Ben's Place	919-782-5900	8511-105 Cantilever Way
Raleigh NC	Cloos' Coney Island	919-834-3354	2233 Avent Ferry Road #102
Raleigh NC	Flying Saucer Draught Emporium	919-821-7468	328 W Morgan St
Raleigh NC	Helios	919-838-5177	413 Glenwood Avenue
Raleigh NC	Lilly's Pizza	919-833-0226	1813 Glenwood Avenue
Raleigh NC	MoJoe's Burger Joint	919-832-6799	620 Glenwood Avenue
Raleigh NC	New World Coffee House	919-782-5900	4112 Pleasant Valley Road #124
Raleigh NC	Porter's Tavern	919-821-2133	2412 Hillsborough Street/H 54
Raleigh NC	Ruckus Pizza	919-835-2002	2233-112 Avent Ferry Road
Raleigh NC	Sosta Cafe	919-833-1006	130 E Davie Street
Raleigh NC	The Players Retreat	919-755-9589	105 Oberlin Road
Raleigh NC	The Third Place	919-834-6566	1811 Glenwood Avenue
Raleigh NC	The Village Draft House	919-833-1373	428 Daniels Street
Raleigh NC	Z Pizza	919-844-0065	9630 Falls of the Neuse Road
Salisbury NC	Outback Steakhouse	704-637-1980	1020 E Innes St
Southern Shores NC	Tropical Smoothie Cafe	252-441-9996	5381 Virginia Dare Trail N/H 12/158
Southport NC	Trolley Stop	910-457-7017	111A S Howe Street/H 211
Wilmington NC	Airlie Seafood Company	910-256-3693	1410 Airlie Road
Wilmington NC	Fat Tony's Italian Pizza	910-343-8881	131 N Front Street
Wilmington NC	Firebelly Lounge	910-763-0141	265 N Front Street
Wilmington NC	Flaming Amy's Burrito Barn	910-799-2919	4002 Oleander Drive/H 76
Wilmington NC	The Caffe Phoenix	910-343-1395	9 S Front Street
Wilmington NC	Tidal Creek Cooperative Market	910-799-2667	5329 Oleander Drive/H 76
Winston-Salem NC	Celtic Cafe	336-703-0641	201 S Stratford/H 158
Winston-Salem NC	Foothills Brewing	336-777-3348	638 W 4th Street

Wrightsville Beach NC	South Beach Grill	910-256-4646	100 S Lumina Avenue

North Dakota

Dickinson ND	Serendipity Coffee House	701-483-1946	789 State Avenue

Ohio

Bellefontaine OH	Subway Sandwiches & Salads	937-592-3000	800 S. Main Street
Berea OH	The Station Restaurant	440-234-1144	30 Depot Street
Berlin OH	Java Jo Coffee Bar	330-893-9211	4860 East Main Street
Cincinnati OH	ALREDDY Coffee & Cafe	513-563-4550	11083 Reading Road
Cincinnati OH	Indigo Restaurant	513-321-9952	2637 Erie Avenue
Cincinnati OH	Molly Malone's	513-531-0700	6111 Montgomery Road/H 3/22
Cleveland OH	Great Lake Brewing Company	216-771-4404	2516 Market Avenue
Cleveland OH	LaBodega	216-621-7075	869 Jefferson
Cleveland OH	Market Avenue Wine Bar	216-696-WINE (9463)	2526 Market Avenue
Columbus OH	Bodega	614-299-9399	1044 N High Street
Columbus OH	City Barbecue	614-538-8890	2111 West Henderson Road
Columbus OH	La Chatelaine French Bakery	614-488-1911	1550 West Lane Avenue
Columbus OH	Max and Ermas	614-840-9466	1515 Polaris Parkway
Columbus OH	Northstar Cafe	614-298-9999	951 N High Street
Columbus OH	Spagio Restaurant	614-486-1114	1295 Grandview Avenue
Columbus OH	Z Pizza	614-299-3289	945 N High Street
Fremont OH	DaVinci's Gallery and Coffee House	419-334-4816 ext. 2	115 S Front Street
Lancaster OH	Fatcat Pizza	740-687-1966	323 Washington Avenue
Lancaster OH	Four Reasons Bakery & Deli	740-654-2253	135 W Main Street
Lancaster OH	Panera Bread	740-654-8902	1374 Ety Road NW
Logan OH	Great Expectations Bookstore-Cafe	740-380-9177	179 South Market Street
Norwood OH	Wild Oat Natural Marketplace	513-531-8015	2693 Edmonson Road
Port Clinton OH	Rudder's	419-797-3260	3260 N.E. Catawba Road
Portland OH	Food Front Cooperative Grocery	503-546-6559	6344 SW Capitol H/H 10
Put-in-Bay OH	Book's Seafood	419-285-3695	Bay View Avenue
Put-in-Bay OH	Chicken Patio	419-285-3581	Delaware Avenue
Put-in-Bay OH	Fish Shack	419-285-3695	Bay View Avenue
Put-in-Bay OH	Little Galley	419-285-3695	Bay View Avenue
Sandusky OH	DeMore's Fish Den	419-626-8861	302 West Perkins
Toledo OH	Subway Sandwiches & Salads	419-473-0836	4030 Monroe Street
Upper Arlington OH	Wild Oats Natural Marketplace	614-481-3400	1555 West Lane Avenue
Worthington OH	La Chatelaine French Bakery	614-848-6711	627 N. High Street
Worthington OH	P.K. O'Ryans Irish Pub	614-781-0770	666 High Street
Zanesfield OH	Firehouse Pizza	937-592-9375	2793 Sandusky Street

Oklahoma

Oklahoma City OK	Earl's Barbecue	405-272-9898	216 Johnny Bench Drive
Oklahoma City OK	Musashi's	405-602-5574	4315 N Western Avenue
Oklahoma City OK	Museum Cafe	405-235-6262	415 Couch Drive
Oklahoma City OK	Tom and Jerry's Steak and Fish Grill	405-524-9100	1501 NW 23rd Street
Oklahoma City OK	Vito's Ristorante	405-848-4867	7521 N May Avenue
Tulsa OK	BruHouse	918-743-7200	3421 S Peoria Avenue
Tulsa OK	Ti Amo	918-499-1919	6024-A S Sheridan
Tulsa OK	Tucci's	918-582-3456	1344 E 15th Street

Oregon

Astoria OR	Astoria Cooperative	503-325-0027	1355 Exchange Street
Beaverton OR	Iron Mutt Coffee Company	503-645-9746	530 SW 205th Avenue
Beaverton OR	Monteaux's Public House	503-439-9942	16165 SW Regatta Lane
Corvallis OR	First Alternative	541-753-3115	1007 SE 3rd Street/H 99W
Corvallis OR	First Alternative	541-452-3115	2855 NW Grant Avenue
Medford OR	Grilla Bites	541-245-9802	226 E Main Street
Newport OR	Rogue Ale Public House	541-265-3188	748 SW Bay Blvd
Portland OR	Baja Fresh Mexican Grill	503-595-2252	1121 W. Burnside St.
Portland OR	Baja Fresh Mexican Grill	503-331-1000	1505 NE 40th Ave
Portland OR	Berlin Inn German Restaurant and Bakery	503-236-6761	3131 SE 12th and Powell
Portland OR	Casa Colima	503-892-9944	6319 SW Capitol H/H 10
Portland OR	City Thai	503-293-7335	6341 S.W. Capitol Highway
Portland OR	Crackerjacks	503-222-9069	2788 NW Thurman @ 28th Avenue
Portland OR	Equinox Restaurant	503-460-3333	830 N Shaver Street
Portland OR	Food Front Cooperative Grocery	503-222-5658	2375 NW Thurman Street
Portland OR	Goose Hollow at the Cove	503-228-7010	1927 SW Jefferson
Portland OR	Jake's Famous Crawfish	503-226-1419	401 SW 12th Ave.
Portland OR	La Costita Restaurant II	503-293-1899	7405 SE Barbur Blvd, Suite 110
Portland OR	Lucky Labrador Public House	503-244-2537	7675 SW Capitol Highway
Portland OR	MacTarnahan's Taproom	503-228-5269	2730 NW 31st Avenue
Portland OR	Old Market Pub & Brewery	503-244-0450	6959 SW Multnomah Blvd

Dog-Friendly Outdoor Dining - Please always call ahead to make sure an establishment is still dog-friendly.

Portland OR	Pizzicato Northwest	503-873-1333	505 NW 23rd Avenue
Portland OR	The Blue Moon Tavern and Grill	503-223-3184	432 NW 21st Ave
Portland OR	The Three Degrees Restaurant at RiverPlace Hotel	503-295-6166	1510 SW Harbor Way
Portland OR	Thirst Wine Bar and Bistro	503-295-2747	0315 SW Montgomery Street
Portland OR	Tin Shed Garden Cafe	503-288-6966	1438 NE Alberta St
Portland OR	Wild Oats Natural Marketplace	503-288-3414	3535 15th Ave.
Portland OR	Wild Oats Natural Marketplace	503-232-6601	2825 East Burnside Street
Seaside OR	Goose Hollow at the Cove	503-717-1940	220 Avenue U
The Dalles OR	Holstein's	541-298-2326	3rd and Taylor

Pennsylvania

Abington PA	Baja Fresh	215-885-4296	1437 Old York Road
Bethel Park PA	Panera Bread	412-854-2007	5243 Library Road
Bethlehem PA	The Brew Works	610-882-1300	569 Main Street
Bethlehem Townplace PA	Geakers Drive In	610-419-4869	6th Street and Freemansburg Avenue
Clarks Summit PA	State Street Grill	570-585-5590	114 S State Street/H 6/11
Conshohocken PA	Spring Mill Cafe	610-828-2550	164 Barren Hill Road
Exton PA	The Brickside Grill	610-321-1600	540 Wellington Square
Gettysburg PA	Friendly's Restaurant	717-337-1426	445 Steinwehr Avenue/H 15
Gettysburg PA	Hunt's Fresh Cut Fries	717-334-4787	61 Steinwehr Avenue
Gettysburg PA	O'Rorkes	717-334-2333	44 Steinwehr Ave
Glenshaw PA	The Hartwood Restaurant	412-767-3500	3400 Harts Run Road
Intercourse PA	Kettle House Cafe	717-768-8261	Route 340
Intercourse PA	Lapp Valley Farm Ice Cream		Route 340
Kennett Square PA	Kennett Square Inn	610-444-5687	201 E State Street
King of Prussia PA	Baja Fresh	610-337-2050	340 W DeKalb Pike
King of Prussia PA	Starbucks	610-768-5130	140 West DeKalb Pike
Lancaster PA	Isaac's Restaurant and Deli	717-394-5544	25 N Queen Street/H 72
Mechanicsburg PA	Z Pizza	717-691-1112	6416 Carlisle Pike/H 11
Milford PA	Muir House Inn and Restaurant	570-296-6373	102 H 2001
Mount Lebanon PA	Il Pizzaiolo	412-344-4123	703 Washington Rd
New Hope PA	Triumph Brewing Company	215-862-8300	400 Union Square
New Hope PA	Wildflowers Garden Cafe	215-862-2241	8 W Mechanic Street
Philadelphia PA	Bucks County Coffee Co.	215-487-3927	4311 Main Street
Philadelphia PA	Cafe Zesty	215-483-6226	4382 Main St
Philadelphia PA	Cantina Dos Segundos	215-629-0500	931 N Second Street
Philadelphia PA	Caribou Cafe	215-625-9535	1126 Walnut St
Philadelphia PA	Cebu Restaurant and Bar	215-629-1100	123 Chestnut Street
Philadelphia PA	Crescent City Restaruant	215-627-6780	600-602 S 9th Street
Philadelphia PA	Devon's Seafood	215-546-5940	225 18th St F1 1
Philadelphia PA	Fork Restaurant	215-625-9425	306 Market Street
Philadelphia PA	Le Bus	215-487-2663	4266 Main St
Philadelphia PA	Pat's King of Steaks	215-468-1546	1237 E Passyunk Ave
Philadelphia PA	Philadelphia Java Company	215-928-1811	518 4th St
Philadelphia PA	Positano Coast by Aldo Lamberti	215-238-0499	212 Walnut Street, 2nd Floor
Philadelphia PA	Q BBQ & Tequila	215-625-8605	207 Chestnut Street
Philadelphia PA	Tavern 17	215-790-1799	220 S 17th Street
Philadelphia PA	The Abbaye	215-627-6711	637 N 3rd Street
Philadelphia PA	The Continental	215-923-6069	134 Market Street
Philadelphia PA	Valley Green Inn	215-247-1730	Springfield Ave and Wissahickon
Philadelphia PA	White Dog Cafe	215-386-9224	3420 Sansom St
Phoenixville PA	Franco's Italian Restaurant	610-933-0880	226 Bridge Street
Pittsburgh PA	Cafe Zinho	412-363-1500	238 Spahr St
Pittsburgh PA	Crazy Mocha Café	412-281-7940	420 Fort Duquesne
Pittsburgh PA	Del's Bar and Ristorante	412-683-1448	4428 Liberty Ave
Pittsburgh PA	East End Food Co-op and Cafe	412-242-3598	7516 Meade Street
Pittsburgh PA	Lot 17 Bar and Grill	412-687-8117	4617 Liberty Ave
Pittsburgh PA	Panera Bread	412-799-0210	942 Freeport Road #114
Pittsburgh PA	Roland's Seafood Grill	412-261-3401	1904 Penn Ave
Pittsburgh PA	Whole Foods Market	412-441-3040	5880 Centre Ave
Stroudsburg PA	Everybody's Cafe	570-424-0896	905 Main Street
Swarthmore PA	Swarthmore CO-OP	610-543-9805	341 Dartmouth Avenue
University Park PA	Berkey Creamery at PSU	814-865-7535	119 Food Science Building
W Chester PA	Iron Hill Brewery	610-738-9600	3 W Gay Street/H 3
West Chester PA	Four Dogs Tavern	610-692-5702	1300 W Strasburg Road/H 162

Rhode Island

Block Island RI	Old Post Office Bagel Shop	401-466-5959	Corner of Corn Neck Road & Ocean Avenue
East Greenwich RI	Chianti's Italian Cuisine	401-884-3810	195 Old Forge Road
Jamestown RI	East Ferry Market and Deli	401-423-1592	47 Conanicus Avenue
Jamestown RI	Slice of Heaven	401-423-9866	32 Narragansett Avenue
Jamestown RI	Trattoria Simpatico	401-423-3731	13 Narragansett Avenue
Jamestown RI	Tricias	401-423-1490	14 Narragansett Ave
Middletown RI	Frosty Freeze	401-846-1697	496 East Main Road/H 138
Newport RI	Canfield House Restaurant and Pub	401-847-0416	5 Memorial Blvd

Newport RI	H2O	401-849-4466	359 Thames Street
Newport RI	Loca	401-843-8300	109 Long Wharf
Newport RI	Nikolas Pizza Newport	401-849-6611	38 Memorial Blvd W
Newport RI	O'Brien's Pub	401-849-6623	501 Thames Street
Newport RI	Salvation Army Cafe	401-847-2620	140 Broadway
Newport RI	Sardella's Restaurant	401-849-6312	30 Memorial Blvd
Newport RI	The Canfield House Restaurant	401-847-0416	5 Memorial Blvd
Providence RI	Amy's Place	401-274-9966	214 Wickenden Street
Providence RI	Cable Car Cinema	401-272-3970	204 S Main
Providence RI	Hemenway's	401-351-8570	121 S Main Street
Providence RI	India Restaurant	401-421-2600	1060 Hope Street
Providence RI	Joe's American Bar and Grill	401-270-4737	148 Providence Place
Tiverton RI	Gray's Ice Cream	401-624-45000	16 East Street

South Carolina

Beaufort SC	Hemmingway's Bistro	843-521-4480	920 Bay St
Charleston SC	39 Rue de Jean	843-722-8881	39 John Street
Charleston SC	Jaunita Greenburg's	843-723-6224	439 King Street
Charleston SC	Juanita Greenberg's	843-723-NACHO(6224)	439 King Street
Charleston SC	The Bubba Gump Shrimp Co. Restaurant & Market	843-723-5665	99 S Market St
Columbia SC	Rosewood Market & Deli	803-765-1083	2803 Rosewood Drive
Columbia SC	Saluda's	803-799-9500	751 Saluda Avenue
Columbia SC	Z Pizza	803-708-4703	1004 Gervais Street/H 1/378
Greenville SC	Overlook Grill	864-271-9700	601 S Main Street/H 124
Greenville SC	Smoke on the Water	864-232-9091	1 Augusta Street
Greenville SC	Strossner's Bakery and Cafe	864-233-3996	21 Roper Mountain Road
Hilton Head SC	Crazy Crab	843-681-5021	104 N H 278
Hilton Head Island SC	Bistro 17 at Shelter Cove Marina	843-785-5517	17D Harborside Lane
Hilton Head Island SC	Hinchey's Chicago Bar and Grill	843-686-5959	2 N Forest Beach Drive
Hilton Head Island SC	Skillet's	843-785-3131	1 N Forest Beach Drive #J 11
Mount Pleasant SC	Dog and Duck Food and Spirits	843-881-3056	624 A Longpoint Road
Mount Pleasant SC	Red's Ice House	843-388-0003	98 Church St
Sullivan's Island SC	Poe's Tavern	843-883-0083	2210 Middle Street

South Dakota

Custer SD	Bavarian Inn Motel	605-673-2802	907 N 5th Street/H 16/385
Custer SD	Cattlemans Steakhouse and Fish	605-673-4402	140 Mount Rushmore Road/H 16/385
Custer SD	Flintstones Drive-In	605-673-4079	US Highways 16 and 385
Custer SD	Pizza Works	605-673-2020	429 Mt Rushmore Road
Custer SD	Reetz's Old Fashion Ice Cream and Pie Shop	605-673-4070	19 Mt Rushmore Road/H 16/385
Custer SD	Wrangler Cafe	605-673-4271	302 Mt. Rushmore Rd.
Deadwood SD	Big Al's Buffalo Steakhouse	605-578-1300	658 Main Street
Hot Springs SD	FlatIron Coffee Bar, Grill and Guest Suites	605-745-6439	745 North River Street/H 385
Keystone SD	Big Time Pizza	605-666-4443	206 Old Cemetery Road
Keystone SD	Executive Order Grill	605-666-5142	609 Highway 16A
Keystone SD	Ruby House Restaurant	605-666-4404	126 Winter Street
Lead SD	Cheyenne Crossing General Store and Café	605-584-3510	21415 H/14A/85
Rapid City SD	Flying T Chuckwagon	605-342-1905	8971 S H 16
Rapid City SD	Mostly Chocolates	605-341-2264	1919 Mount Rushmore Rd # 1/H 16
Rapid City SD	Sonic Drive-In	605-716-3663	2316 Mount Rushmore Road/H 16
Rapid City SD	Stonewalls Espresso Cafe	605-342-6100	5955 S H 16
Rapid City SD	Subway	605-341-0387	2415 Mount Rushmore Rd # 2/H 16

Tennessee

Chattanooga TN	212 Market Restaurant	423-265-1212	212 Market Street/H 8
Chattanooga TN	Aretha Frankensteins	423-285-SOUL (7685)	518 Tremont Street, Chattanooga, TN
Chattanooga TN	Big River Grille	423-267-2739	222 Broad Street
Chattanooga TN	Clumpies Ice Cream	423-267-5425	26 Frazier Avenue # B
Chattanooga TN	Food Works	423-752-7487	205 Manufacturers Road
Chattanooga TN	Greenlife Grocery and Deli	423-702-7300	301 Manufacturer's Road
Chattanooga TN	Hair of the Dog Pub	423-265-4615	334 Market Street/H 8
Chattanooga TN	MudPie	423-267-9043	12 Frazier Avenue
Chattanooga TN	Pisa Pizza	423-756-PIZA (7492)	551 River Street
Chattanooga TN	Quiznos	423-648-1125	330 Frazier Avenue, Suite G
Chattanooga TN	Stone Cup Cafe	888-698-4404	330 Frazier Avenue
Chattanooga TN	Terra Nostra Tapas and Wine	423-634-0238	105 Frazier Avenue
Chattanooga TN	The Blue Plate	423-648-6767	191 Chestnut Street, unit B
Chattanooga TN	The Bluewater Grille	423-266-4200	224 Broad Street
Fort Worth TN	Fuzzy's Taco Shop	817-831-TACO (8226)	2719 Race Street
Fort Worth TN	Love Shack So7	817-740-8812	817 Matisse Lane

Dog-Friendly Outdoor Dining - Please always call ahead to make sure an establishment is still dog-friendly.

Fort Worth TN	The Gingerman Pub	817-886-2327	3716 Camp Bowie Blvd
Gatlinburg TN	Heidelburg Restaurant	865-430-3094	148 Parkway
Gatlinburg TN	Howards Restaurant	865-436-3600	976 Parkway/H71/73/441
Gatlinburg TN	Subway	865-436-6792	223 Airport Rd
Germantown TN	Swanky's Taco Shoppe	901-737-2088	6641 Poplar Avenue/H 57/72
Johnson City TN	Russo's Restaurant	423-928-4441	300 E Main Street, Ste 101
Knoxville TN	Barley's Taproom and Pizzeria	865-521-0092	200 E Jackson Avenue
Memphis TN	Cafe Society	901-722-2177	208 N Evergreen Street
Memphis TN	Central BBQ	901-272-9377	2249 Central Avenue
Memphis TN	Harry's Detour	901-276-7623	532 S Cooper Street
Memphis TN	Napa Cafe	901-683-0441	5101 Sanderlin Avenue
Memphis TN	Stella Restaurant	901-526-4950	39 S Main Street
Memphis TN	Tsunami	901-274-2556	928 S Cooper Street
Nashville TN	Baja Fresh	615-341-0100	1720 W End Avenue
Nashville TN	Baja Fresh	615-279-1620	2116 Green Hills Village Drive
Nashville TN	Blackstone Restaurant and Brewery	615-327-9969	1918 West End Avenue
Nashville TN	Bongo Java	615-385-5282	2007 Belmont Blvd
Nashville TN	Bruegger's Bagel Bakery	615-327-0055	422 21st Avenue S
Nashville TN	Bruegger's Bagel Bakery	615-352-1128	5305 Harding Rd
Nashville TN	Cantina Laredo	615-259-9282	592 12th Avenue S
Nashville TN	Chipotle Mexican Grill	615-320-1693	2825 West End Avenue/H 1/70S
Nashville TN	Fido's	615-777-3436	1812 21st Avenue S/H 106/431
Nashville TN	Jack's Barbecue	615-254-5715	416 Broadway
Nashville TN	Jackson's Bar and Bistro	615-385-9968	1800 21st Avenue
Nashville TN	Mambu	615-329-1293	1806 Hayes Street
Nashville TN	Pizza Perfect	615-329-2757	1602 21st Avenue S
Nashville TN	Quiznos	615-313-7842	315 Deadrick Street, Suite 140
Nashville TN	The Frothy Monkey Coffeehouse	615-292-1808	2509 12th Avenue South
Pigeon Forge TN	Baskin Robbins Ice Cream	865-453-3337	3668 Parkway
Sevierville TN	Connors Steak and Seafood	865-428-1991	1641 Parkway Drive/H 71/441
Townsend TN	Subway	865-448-6909	8213 State Highway 73

Texas

Amarillo TX	Big Texan Steakhouse	806-372-6000	7701 I-40 East
Amarillo TX	Macaroni Joe's	806-463-7829	1619 S Kentucky
Arlington TX	Chipotle Mexican Grill	817-860-0010	1390 South Cooper Street, Ste. #100/H 157
Arlington TX	Fuzzy's Taco Shop	817-265-TACO (8226)	510 E Abram
Austin TX	Artz Rib House	512-442-8283	2330 South Lamar Blvd.
Austin TX	Austin Java Company	512-476-1829	1206 Parkway
Austin TX	BB Rover's Cafe and Pub	512-335-9504	12636 Research Blvd.
Austin TX	Billy's on Burnet	512-407-9305	2105 Hancock Street
Austin TX	Boomerang's	512-380-0032	3110 Guadalupe
Austin TX	Bouldin Creek Coffee House	512-416-1601	1501 S 1st Street
Austin TX	Carmelo's Italian Restaurant	512-477-7497	504 East 5th St.
Austin TX	Carrabba's Italian Grill	512-345-8232	11590 Research Blvd.
Austin TX	Cipollina	512-477-5211	1213 West Lynn St.
Austin TX	Crown and Anchor Pub	512-322-9168	2911 San Jacinto Blvd
Austin TX	Dog & Duck Pub	512-479-0598	406 West 17th Street
Austin TX	Freddie's Place	512-445-9197	1703 South 1st Street
Austin TX	Ginger Man Pub	512-473-8801	304 W. Fourth Street
Austin TX	Green Man Mesquite BBQ & More	512-479-0485	1400 Barton Springs Road
Austin TX	Jo's Coffee	512-444-3800	1300 S. Congress Avenue
Austin TX	Judges Hill Restaurant and Bar	512-495-1857	1900 Rio Grande Street
Austin TX	Mangia Chicago Stuffed Pizza	512-478-6600	2401 Lake Austin Blvd.
Austin TX	Mangia Chicago Stuffed Pizza	512-302-5200	3500 Guadalupe
Austin TX	Max's Wine Dive	512-904-0111	207 San Jacinto Blvd
Austin TX	Moonshine Patio Bar & Grill	512-236-9599	303 Red River Street
Austin TX	North by North West Restaurant and Brewery	512-467-6969	10010 N. Capitol of Texas Hwy.
Austin TX	Opal Divines	512-477-3308	700 West 6th Street
Austin TX	Opal Divines	512-707-0237	3601 S Congres Avenue, Suite K
Austin TX	Opal Divines	512-733-5353	12709 Mopac and Parmer Lane
Austin TX	P Terry's Burger Stand	512-473-2217	404 S Lamar Blvd
Austin TX	Portabela	512-481-8646	1200 W. 6th Street
Austin TX	Red River Cafe	512-472-0385	2912 Medical Arts
Austin TX	Rio Grande Restaurant	512-476-8300	301 San Jacinto Blvd
Austin TX	Ross' Old Austin Cafe	512-835-2414	11800 N Lamar Blvd/H 275
Austin TX	Scholz Beer Garden	512-474-1958	1607 San Jacinto Blvd.
Austin TX	Snack Bar	512-445-2626	1224 S Congress
Austin TX	Spider House	512-480-9562	2908 Fruth St.
Austin TX	Texas Land and Cattle Steakhouse	512-451-6555	6007 North IH 35
Austin TX	The Gingerman Pub	512-473-8801	301 Lavaca
Austin TX	The One2One Bar	512-473-0121	121 E. 5th Street
Austin TX	Third Base Sports Bar and Restaurant	512-476-BASE (2273)	1717 West 6th Street, Building 2, Suite 210R
Austin TX	Whole Foods Market	512-345-5003	9607 Research Blvd. #300
Austin TX	Z Pizza	512-472-9800	452 W 2nd Street

Dog-Friendly Outdoor Dining - Please always call ahead to make sure an establishment is still dog-friendly.

Corpus Christi TX	Dotz Dawgs and Drafts	361-904-0630	2825 N Shoreline Blvd
Corpus Christi TX	Sonic Drive-In	361-949-7886	14401 South Padre Island Drive
Dallas TX	Big Shucks Oyster Bar	214-887-6353	6232 E Mockingbird Lane
Dallas TX	Breadwinner Cafe and Bakery	214-351-3339	5560 W Lovers Lane #260
Dallas TX	Cafe Brazil	214-461-8762	3847 Cedar Springs Rd
Dallas TX	Cafe Brazil	214-747-2730	2815 Elm Street
Dallas TX	Cafe Italia	214-357-4200	4615 West Lovers Lane
Dallas TX	Café Toulouse	214-520-8999	3314 Knox Street
Dallas TX	Campisi's	214-752-0141	1520 Elm Street, Suite 111
Dallas TX	Chipotle Mexican Grill	214-691-7755	8301 Westchester Drive
Dallas TX	Chipotle Mexican Grill	214-871-3100	2705 McKinney Ave
Dallas TX	Corner Bakery Cafe	972-407-9131	7615 Campbell Rd
Dallas TX	Dali Wine Bar & Cellar	214-646-1947	1722 Routh Street
Dallas TX	Dream Cafe	214-954-0486	2800 Routh Street
Dallas TX	Dubliner	214-818-0911	2818 Greenville Avenue
Dallas TX	Gloria's Restaurant	214-874-0088	3715 Greenville Avenue
Dallas TX	Hunky's	214-522-1212	4000 Cedar Springs Rd
Dallas TX	La Calle Doce	214-941-4304	415 W 12th Street
Dallas TX	La Calle Doce	214-824-9900	1925 Skillman St.
Dallas TX	Lee Harvey's	214-428-1555	1807 Gould Street
Dallas TX	Pappasito's Cantina	214-350-1970	10433 Lombardy Ln.
Dallas TX	Parigi's Restaurant	214-521-0295	3311 Oak Lawn Avenue, Suite 102
Dallas TX	Ristorante Bugatti	214-350-2470	3802 West Northwest Hwy
Dallas TX	San Francisco Rose	214-826-2020	3024 Greenville Ave
Dallas TX	State and Allen Lounge	214-239-1990	2400 Allen Street
Dallas TX	TCBY Frozen Yogurt	214-821-5757	6402 E. Mockingbird Lane
Dallas TX	Texas Land and Cattle Steakhouse	214-526-4664	3130 Lemmon Avenue
Dallas TX	The Bronx	214-521-5821	3835 Cedar Springs Rd
Dallas TX	The Ginger Man Pub	214-754-8771	2718 Boll Street
Dallas TX	Twisted Root Burger Company	214-741-ROOT (7668)	2615 Commerce Street
Denton TX	Fuzzy's Taco Shop	940-380-TACO (8226)	115 Industrial Street
El Paso TX	Cafe Central	915-545-2233	109 N Oregon Street # 1
El Paso TX	Mango's at Nash Gardens	915-587-6000	150 E Sunset Road
Flower Mound TX	Z Pizza	972-355-8585	2911 Cross Timbers Road
Fort Worth TX	Chadra Mezza	817-9CHADRA (817-924-2372)	1622 Park Place Avenue
Fort Worth TX	Chipotle Mexican Grill	817-348-8530	3000 W 7th Street
Fort Worth TX	Chipotle Mexican Grill	817-735-8355	3050 S. Hulen Street, Unit C
Fort Worth TX	Fuzzy's Taco Shop	817-924-7943	2917 W Berry Street
Fort Worth TX	Love Shack	817-740-8812	110 E Exchange Avenue
Fort Worth TX	Mimi's Cafe	817-731-9644	5858 SW Loop 820
Fort Worth TX	Ye Olde Bull and Bush Pub	817-731-9206	2300 Montgomery Street
Fredericksburg TX	Hondo's	830-997-1633	312 W Main Street/H 87/290
Galveston TX	Charlie's Burgers and Mexican Food	409-765-7065	1110 Tremont (23rd St.)
Galveston TX	Mosquito Cafe	409-763-1010	628 14th Street
Galveston TX	Sonic Drive-In	409-740-9009	6502 Seawall Boulevard
Galveston TX	The Spot	409-621-5237	3204 Seawall Blvd
Galveston TX	Yaga's Cafe and Bar	409-762-6676	2314 Strand
Houston TX	Becks Prime	713-266-9901	2615 Augusta Drive
Houston TX	Boondoggle's Pub and Pizzeria	281-326-BREW	4106 Nasa Rd
Houston TX	Chatter's Cafe and Bistro	713-864-8080	140 S Heights Blvd
Houston TX	Fox and Hound English Pub and Grille	281-589-2122	11470 Westheimer Road
Houston TX	Gingerman's	713-526-2770	5607 Morningside Dr
Houston TX	Hickory Hollow BBQ	713-869-6300	101 Heights Blvd
Houston TX	Jason's Deli	713-522-2660	23530 University Blvd
Houston TX	Jason's Deli	713-975-7878	5860 Westheimer Road
Houston TX	McCormick and Schmick's Seafood Restaurant	713-840-7900	1151 Uptown Park Blvd.
Houston TX	Mission Burritos	713-529-0535	2245 West Alabama St.
Houston TX	Panera Bread Bakery and Cafe	281-469-5623	12220 Farm Road 1960
Houston TX	Paulie's	713-660-7057	1834 Westheimer Road
Houston TX	The Ginger Man Pub	713-526-2770	5607 Morningside
Houston TX	The Red Lion	713-782-3030	2316 S Shephard Drive
Houston TX	The Tasting Room Lounge	713-528-6402	114 Gray Street
Houston TX	Tila's Restaurant and Bar	713-522-7654	1111 S Shepard Dr
Houston TX	West Alabama Icehouse	713-528-6874	1919 West Alamaba
Houston TX	Z Pizza	713-432-7219	4010 Bissonnet St
Hurst TX	Danny D's BBQ	817-280-9741	565 W Bedford-Euless Road
Leon Springs TX	Fralo's Art of Pizza	210-698-6616	23651 H WW
Live Oak TX	The Lion and the Rose	210-547-3000	8211 Agora Parkway #112
Lubbock TX	Fuzzy's Taco Shop	806-740-TACO (8226)	2102 Broadway Street
Lubbock TX	Well Body Natural Foods	806-793-1015	3708 34th Street
Pflugerville TX	Hanover's Draft Haus	512-670-9617	108 E Main St
Plano TX	It's A Grind Coffee House	972-985-2704	4152 W Spring Creek Parkway
Round Rock TX	Third Base Sports Bar and Restaurant	512-388-BASE (2273)	3107 S IH 35 Suite 810
Round Rock TX	Z Pizza	512-863-8118	200 University Blvd

Dog-Friendly Outdoor Dining - Please always call ahead to make sure an establishment is still dog-friendly.

San Angelo TX	Chilangos City	325-655-3553	1911 S Bryant Blvd/H 277/87
San Antonio TX	Cappy's	210-828-9669	5011 Broadway Ave
San Antonio TX	Chipotle Mexican Grill	210-832-9812	3928 Broadway Street
San Antonio TX	Chipotle Mexican Grill	210-340-0571	438 NW Loop 410, Suite 101
San Antonio TX	Chipotle Mexican Grill	210-521-0672	8227 H 151, Suite 105
San Antonio TX	Crumpets Restaurant and Bakery	210-821-5600	3920 Harry Wurzback Rd
San Antonio TX	Dolores Del Rio	210-223-0609	106 E. River Walk
San Antonio TX	Flower Power Cafe	210-694-9288	11703 Huebner Road, Suite 200
San Antonio TX	Flying Saucer	210-696-5080	11255 Huebner Road
San Antonio TX	Fralo's Art of Pizza	210-698-6616	23651 IH 10 West
San Antonio TX	Guadalajara Grill	210-222-1992	301 S. Alamo Street
San Antonio TX	La Tuna Icehouse	210-224-8862	100 Probandt/H 536
San Antonio TX	Luther's Cafe	210-223-7727	1425 N Main Avenue
San Antonio TX	Madhatters Tea House and Cafe	210-212-4832	320 Beauregard
San Antonio TX	Quarry Cantina	210-290-8066	7310 Jones Maltsberger Road
San Antonio TX	Rita's On The River	210-227-7482	245 E Commerce Street
San Antonio TX	Taco Garage	210-826-4405	8403 Broadway Street
San Antonio TX	The Cove	210-227-2683	606 W Cypress
San Antonio TX	The Landing	210-223-7266	123 Losoya St
San Antonio TX	The Lion and the Rose	210-798-4145	700 E Sonterra Blvd #318
San Antonio TX	The Original Mexican Restaurant	210-224-9951	102 W Crockett Street
San Antonio TX	Tito's Mexican Restaurant	210-212-TACO (8226)	955 S Alamo Street
San Antonio TX	Tycoon Flats	210-320-0819	2926 N St. Mary's Street
San Antonio TX	Zuni Grill	210-227-0864	223 Losoya St.
South Padre Island TX	Naturally's Veggie Cafe	956-761-5332	5712 Padre Blvd.
South Padre Island TX	Yummies Coffee Shack	956-761-2526	708 Padre Blvd
Sunland Park NM	Ardovino's Desert Crossing	505-589-0653	One Ardovino Drive
West Lake Hills TX	The Lion and the Rose	512-335-5466	701 S Capital of Texas H (Inside the Village at Westlake)/H 360

Utah

Kanab UT	Escobar's Mexican Restaurant	435-644-3739	373 E 300 S/H 89
Kanab UT	Grandma Tina's	435-644-8295	198 S 100 E/H 89
Ogden UT	Great Harvest Bread Co	801-394-6800	272 25th Street
Ogden UT	Two Bit Street - Club Cafe & Antiques	801-393-1225	126 Historic 25th Street
Park City UT	Wild Oats Natural Marketplace	435-575-0200	1748 W Redstone Center Drive
Salt Lake City UT	Atlantic Cafe & Market	801-524-9900	325 S Main St.
Salt Lake City UT	Blue Plate Dinner	801-463-1151	2041 S 2100 E
Salt Lake City UT	Citris Grill	801-466-1202	2991 E 3300 S/H 171
Salt Lake City UT	Log Haven Restaurant	801-272-8255	6451 E Mill Creek Canyon Road
Salt Lake City UT	Noodle and Company	801-466-8880	1152 E 2100 S
Salt Lake City UT	Rubios Baja Grille	801-363-0563	358 S 700 E, Suite F
Salt Lake City UT	Rubios Baja Grille	801-466-1220	1160 E 2100 S
Salt Lake City UT	Toaster's	801-328-2928	151 W 200 S
Salt Lake City UT	Wild Oats Natural Marketplace	801-355-7401	645 E 400 South

Vermont

Brandon VT	Cafe Provence	802-247-9997	11 Center Street
Brattleboro VT	Top of the Hill Grill	802-258-9178	632 Putney Road
Burlington VT	City Market, Onion River Co-op	802-861-9700	82 S Winooski Avenue/H 7
Burlington VT	Lake Champlain Chocolates	802-864-1807	750 Pine Street
Burlington VT	Sweetwaters	802-864-9800	120 Church Street
Burlington VT	Vermont Pub & Brewery	802-865-0500	144 College Street
Powhatan VT	The Home Team Grill	804-897-9425	1795 S Creek One/H 60
Putney VT	Putney Food Co-op	802-387-5866	8 Carol Brown Way
S Burlington VT	Quiznos Sub	802-864-0800	1335 Shelburne Road
Stowe VT	Gracie's Gourmutt Shop	802-253-8741	1652 Mountain Road/H 108

Virginia

Alexandria VA	Baja Fresh	703-823-2888	3231 Duke Street
Alexandria VA	Caboose Cafe & Bakery	703-566-1283	2419 Mount Vernon Avenue
Alexandria VA	Five Guys Burgers and Fries	703-549-7991	107 N Fayette Street
Alexandria VA	Gadsby's Tavern	703-548-1288	138 N Royal Street
Alexandria VA	Overwood Restaurant and Bar	703-535-3340	220 N Lee Street
Alexandria VA	Pat Troy's Irish Pub	703-549-4535	111 N Pitt Street
Alexandria VA	Taqueria Poblano	703-548-8226	2400-B Mount Vernon Ave
Alexandria VA	Z Pizza	703-660-8443	6328-C Richmond H /H 1
Alexandria VA	Z Pizza	703-600-1193	3217 Duke Street
Alexandria VA	Z Pizza	703-660-8443	6328-C Richmond H /H 1
Arlington VA	Faccia Luna	703-276-3099	2909 Wilson Blvd
Arlington VA	Il Raddiccio	703-276-2627	1801 Clarendon Blvd
Arlington VA	Mexicali Blues	703-812-9352	2933 Wilson Blvd
Arlington VA	Quiznos	703-248-8888	2201 Wilson Blvd
Arlington VA	Quiznos	703-248-9585	1555 Wilson Blvd
Arlington VA	The Boulevard Wood Grille	703-875-9663	2901 Wilson Blvd

Arlington VA	Withlows	703-276-9693	2854 Wilson Blvd
Chantilly VA	Baja Fresh	703-378-3804	13940 Lee-Jackson Memorial Highway
Chantilly VA	Quiznos	703-817-1244	13661 Lee Jackson Memorial H
Charlottesville VA	Baja Bean Company	434-293-4507	1327 W Main Street
Charlottesville VA	Bang!	434-984-2264	213 Second Street SW
Charlottesville VA	Blue Light Grill and Raw Bar	434-295-1223	120 E Main Street
Charlottesville VA	Downtown Grille	434-817-7080	201 W Main Street
Charlottesville VA	Oxo Restaurant	434-977-8111	215 W Water Street
Charlottesville VA	The Biltmore Grill	434-293-6700	16 Elliewood Avenue
Charlottesville VA	The Mudhouse	434-984-6833	213 W Main Street
Charlottesville VA	Zocalo Restaurant	434-977-4944	201 E Main Street
Clarendon VA	Baja Fresh	703-528-7010	2815 Clarendon Blvd
Clarendon VA	Hard Times Cafe	703-528-2233	3028 Wilson Blvd
Fairfax VA	Baja Fresh	703-352-1792	12150 Fairfax Town Center
Fairfax VA	Coyote Grill Cantina	703-591-0006	10266 Main Street/H 236
Falls Church VA	Z Pizza	703-536-6969	1051 W Broad Street/H 7
Fredericksburg VA	TruLuv's	540-373-6500	1101 Sophia Street
Haymarket VA	Z Pizza	703-753-7492	5471 Merchants View Square
Herndon VA	Bagel Cafe	703-318-7555	300 Elder St
Herndon VA	Baja Fresh	703-793-0878	2405 Centerville Road
Herndon VA	Z Pizza		2320-C Woodland Crossing Drive
Irvington VA	The Local	804-438-9356	4337 Irvington Road/H 200
Irvington VA	Trick Dog Cafe	804-438-1055	4357 Irvington Road/H 200
Leesburg VA	Eiffel Tower Cafe	703-777-5142	107 Loudoun Street SE
Leesburg VA	South Street Under	703-771-9610	203 Harrison St SE
Leesburg VA	Z Pizza	703-669-4020	659 Potomac Station Drive
Lexington VA	Joyful Spirit Cafe	540-463-4191	26 Main Street/H 11
Lorton VA	Z Pizza	703-372-1538	9451 Lorton Market Street
Manassas VA	Baja Fresh	703-365-2077	8099 Sudley Road
Manassas VA	Z Pizza	703-580-8100	12817 Galveston Court
Midlothian VA	McAlister's Deli	804-897-9686	11400 West Huguenot Road
Norfolk VA	Carrot Tree	757-246-9559	411 Reed Street
Norfolk VA	Kincaid's Fish, Chop, and Steak House	757-622-8000	300 Monticello Avenue, Suite 147 (MacArthur Center)
Reston VA	Clyde's of Reston	703-787-6601	11905 Market Street
Richmond VA	Acacia Restaurant	804-354-6060	3325 E Cary Street/H 147
Richmond VA	Chipotle Mexican Grill	804-272-6322	9200 Stony Point Parkway
Richmond VA	Millies Diner	804-643-5512	2603 E Main Street/H 5
Richmond VA	Panera Bread	804-560-9700	9200 Stony Point Parkway, Suite 158D
Richmond VA	Poe's Pub	804-648-2120	2706 E Main Street/H 60/5
Richmond VA	The Home Team Grill	804-254-7360	1630 W Main/H 147
Roanoke VA	Awful Arthur's	540-344-2997	2229 Colonial Avenue SW
Springfield VA	Z Pizza	703-313-8181	6699-B Frontier Drive
Staunton VA	Wright's Dairy-Rite	540-886-0435	346 Greenville AvenueH 250
Sterling VA	Z Pizza	703-433-1313	22000 Dulles Retail Plaza, Sterling, VA - (703) 433-1313
Virginia Beach VA	Abby Road Restaurant and Pub	757-425-6330	203 22nd Street
Virginia Beach VA	Z Pizza	757-368-9090	3376 Princess Anne Road/H 165
Williamsburg VA	Aroma's	757-221-6676	431 Prince George St
Williamsburg VA	Blue Talon Bistro	757-476-BLUE (2583)	420 Prince George Street
Williamsburg VA	Pierce's Bar-B-Que	757-565-2955	447 Rochambeau Dr

Washington

Anacortes WA	Brown Lantern	360-293-2544	412 Commercial Avenue
Bainbridge Island WA	Bainbridge Thai Cuisine	206-780-2403	330 Madison Avenue S
Bainbridge Island WA	Emmy's VegeHouse	206-855-2996	100 Winslow Way W
Bainbridge Island WA	Pegasus Coffee House	206-842-6725	131 Parfitt Way
Bainbridge Island WA	Subway	206-780-5354	278 E Winslow Way
Bellingham WA	Community Food Coop	360-734-8158	315 Westerly Road
Edmonds WA	The Dining Dog	425-314-4612	9635 Firdale Avenue N
Federal Way WA	Great Harvest Bread Co.	253-529-2177	31889 Gateway Center Blvd S
Friday Harbor WA	Friday's Crabhouse	360-378-8801	65 Front Street
Friday Harbor WA	SJ Coffee Roasting Company	360-378-4443	18 Cannery Landing
Friday Harbor WA	Vic's Driftwood Drive In	360-378-VICS (8427)	25 2nd Street
Okremos WA	Gilbert and Blake's	517-349-1300	3554 Okemos Road
Port Angeles WA	Olympic Bagel Company	360-452-9100	802 E 1st Street/H 101
Redmond WA	Taste the Moment	425-556-9838	8110 164th Avenue NE
Redmond WA	Victors Celtic Coffee Company	425-881-6451	7993 Gilman Street
Richland WA	Shilo Inn	509-946-9006	50 Comstock Road
Seattle WA	Essential Baking Company and Cafe	206-545-3804	1604 N 34th Street
Seattle WA	Essential Baking Company and Cafe	206-328-0078	2719 E Madison Street
Seattle WA	Great Harvest Bread	206-365-4778	17171 Bothell Way NE # A121/H 522
Seattle WA	Great Harvest Bread Co.	206-706-3434	2218 NW Market Street
Seattle WA	India Bistro Ballard	206-783-5080	2301 NW Market Street
Seattle WA	Lombardi's Cucina	206-783-0055	2200 N.W. Market Street
Seattle WA	Lottie's Lounge	206-725-0519	4900 Rainier Avenue S/H 167
Seattle WA	Madison Park Cafe	206-324-2626	1807 42nd Ave E

Dog-Friendly Outdoor Dining - Please always call ahead to make sure an establishment is still dog-friendly.

Seattle WA	Maggie Bluff's Marina Grill	206-283-8322	2601 W. Marina Place
Seattle WA	Mulleadys Irish Pub and Restaurant	206-283-8843	3055 21st Avenue W
Seattle WA	Norm's Eatery and Ale House	206-547-1417	460 N 36th Street
Seattle WA	Norm's Eatery and Ale House	206-547-1417	460 N 36th Street
Seattle WA	Pink Door	206-443-3241	1919 Post Aly
Seattle WA	Portage Bay Cafe	206-547-8230	4130 Roosevelt Way NE
Seattle WA	Stumbling Goat	206-784-3535	6722 Greenwood Avenue N
Seattle WA	The Luna Park Cafe	206-935-7250	2918 SW Avalon Way
Seattle WA	Tutta Bella	206-624-4422	2200 Westlake, Suite 112
Settle WA	Great Harvest Bread Co.	206-524-4873	5408 Sand Point Way NE/H 513
Silverdale WA	Kataluma Chai Cafe	360-613-2832	Byron and McConnell
Snohomish WA	Grilla Bites	360-568-7333	1020 1st Street, Suite 104
Vancouver WA	Burgerville	360-892-9781	10903 NE Fourth Plain Blvd

West Virginia

Beckley WV	Pasquale Mira Restaurant	304-255-5253	224 Harper Park Drive
Berkeley Springs WV	Maria's Garden and Inn	304-258-2021	42 Independence Street
Charleston WV	Cozumel Mexican Restaurant	304-342-0113	1120 Fledderjohn Road

Wisconsin

Appleton WI	Brewed Awakenings	920-882-9336	107 E College Avenue/H 125
Baileys Harbor WI	Harbor Fish Market and Grille	920-839-9999	8080 H 57
Eau Claire WI	Mike's Smokehouse BBQ	715-834-8153	2235 N Clairemont Avenue/H 12
Egg Harbor WI	Blue Horse Bistro	920-868-1471	4158 Main Street
Egg Harbor WI	The Bistro at Liberty Square	920-868-4800	7755 H 42
Ellison Bay WI	The Viking Grill	920-854-2998	12029 H 42
Elm Grove WI	The Grove Restaurant	262-814-1890	890 Elm Grove Road
Fish Creek WI	Pelletier's	920-868-3313	4199 Main Street
Fish Creek WI	Sweetie Pie's	920-868-2743	9106 H 42
Glendale WI	Panera Bread	414-962-4775	5595 Port Washington Road
Green Bay WI	The Wellington	920-499-2000	2850 Humboldt Road
La Crosse WI	Rudy's Drive In Restaurant	608-782-2200	1004 La Crosse Street/H 16
Lake Delton WI	Buffalo Phil's Pizza and Grille	608-254-7300	150 Gasser Road
Lake Delton WI	Uno Chicago Grill	608-253-2111	1000 S Wisconsin Dells Parkway/H 12/23
Madison WI	Bandung Indonesian Restaurant	608-255-6910	600 Williamson Street
Madison WI	Come Back In	608-258-8619	508 E Wilson Street
Madison WI	Hawk's Bar and Grill	608-256-4296	425 State Street
Madison WI	Kabul Restaurant	608-256-6322	541 State Street
Madison WI	Marigold Kitchen	608-661-5559	118 S Pinckney Street
Madison WI	Panera Bread	608-826-0808	601 Junction Road
Madison WI	Tutto Pasta	608-250-9000	107 King Street
Middleton WI	Capital Brewery	608-836-7100	7734 Terrace Avenue
Middleton WI	Chipotle Mexican Grill	608-826-0919	8422 Old Sauk Road
Milwaukee WI	Alterra Cafe At the Lake	414-223-4551	1701 N Lincoln Memorial Drive
Milwaukee WI	Apollo Cafe	414-272-2233	1310 E Brady Street
Milwaukee WI	Beer Belly's	414-481-5520	512 W Layton Avenue
Milwaukee WI	Broadway Bakery	414-431-2880	241 N Broadway
Milwaukee WI	Coast	414-727-5555	931 E Wisconsin Avenue
Milwaukee WI	Crazy Water	414-645-2606	839 S 2nd Street
Milwaukee WI	Eagan's	414-271-6900	1030 N Water Street
Milwaukee WI	Milwaukee Waterfront Deli	414-220-9300	761 N Water Street
Milwaukee WI	Mimma's	414-271-7337	1307 E Brady Street
Milwaukee WI	Nomad World Pub	414-224-8111	1401 E Brady Street
Milwaukee WI	Rock Bottom Restaurant and Brewery	414-276-3030	740 N Plankinton Ave, #1
Milwaukee WI	The Wicked Hop	414-223-0345	345 N Broadway
Oshkosh WI	Ardy and Ed's Drive In	920-231-5455	2413 S Main Street/H 45
Oshkosh WI	Leon's Frozen Custard	920-231-7755	121 W Murdock
Racine WI	Freddie's Friki Tiki	262-635-0533	207 Gas Light Drive
Shorewood Hills WI	Panera Bread	608-442-9994	3416 University Avenue
Sister Bay WI	Patio Restaurant	920-854-1978	10440 Orchard Drive
Sturgeon Bay WI	Gilmo's	920-824-5440	3600 H CC
Sturgeon Bay WI	Stone Harbor Restaurant and Pub	920-746-9004	107 N 1st Avenue
Sturgeon Bay WI	Waterfront Mary's	920-743-3191	3662 N Duluth Avenue
Washington Island WI	Deer Run Pub and Grill	920-847-2017	1885 Michigan Road
Waupaca WI	Clear Water Harbor	715-258-2866	N2757 H QQ
Wisconsin Dells WI	Brat House Grill	608-254-8505	49 Wisconsin Dells Parkway S/H 12/23
Wisconsin Dells WI	Cheesecake Heaven Cafe and Bakery	608-253-3073	17 Broadway/H 13/16/23
Wisconsin Dells WI	Culver's Restaurant	608-253-9080	312 Broadway
Wisconsin Dells WI	Culvers of Lake Delton	608-253-3195	1070 Wisconsin Dells Parkway/H 12/23
Wisconsin Dells WI	Sand Bar	608-253-3073	130 Washington Ave
Wisconsin Dells WI	Syno's Pizza	608-253-6200	560 Wisconsin Dells Parkway/H 12/23

Wyoming

Casper WY	Bosco's Italian Restaurant	307-265-9658	847 E A Street
Cheyenne WY	Chipotle Mexican Grill	307-632-6200	1508 Dell Range Blvd

Dog-Friendly Outdoor Dining - Please always call ahead to make sure an establishment is still dog-friendly.

Cheyenne WY	Shadows Pub & Grill	307-634-7625	115 W 15th Street
Cody WY	Clark's Fork and Spoon	307-527-5510	4 Van Dyke Road
Cody WY	Grizzly Creek Coffee Co	307-527-7238	1491 Sheridan Avenue/H 14/16/20
Cody WY	Silver Dollar Bar	307-527-7666	1313 Sheridan Avenue/H 14/16
Jackson WY	Betty Rock Coffee House & Cafe	307-733-0747	325 Pearl Avenue
Jackson WY	Bon Appe Thai	307-734-0245	245 W Pearl Street
Laramie WY	Bailey's Restaurant and Patio	307-742-6411	2410 E Grand Avenue/H 30
Sheridan WY	Sidewalk Cafe	307-673-3195	1333 W 5th Street/H 330
Wilson WY	Pearl Street Bagels	307-739-1261	Fish Creek Center

Canada

Alberta

Calgary AB	La Chaumière Restaurant	403-228-5690	139 17th Avenue SW
Red Deer AB	East Side Mario's	403-342-2279	2004 50th Avenue, Suite 193/H 2A
Whitecourt AB	A & W	780-778-6611	3811 Caxen Street

British Columbia

Boston Bar BC	Salmon House Restaurant	604-867-9277	43111 Trans Canada H
Chilliwack BC	La Mansione	604-792-8910	46290 Yale Road
Coquitlam BC	Bread Garden Bakery Cafe	604-945-9494	2991 Lougheed Highway
Coquitlam BC	Bread Garden Bakery Cafe	604-515-0295	100 Schoolhouse Street
Fort Nelson BC	Pizzarama Pizzaria	250-774-7100	4916 50th Avenue N # 12
Kelowna BC	The Rotten Grape	250-717-8466	231 Bernard Avenue
Nanaimo BC	Modern Cafe	250-754-5022	221 Commercial Street
Port Hardy BC	A&W Restaurant	250-949-2345	8950 Granville Street
Port Hardy BC	Captain Hardy's	250-949-7133	7145 Market Street
Prince Rupert BC	Cowpuccino's Coffee House	250-627-1395	25 Cow Bay Road
Prince Rupert BC	Javadotcup	250-622-2822	516 Third Avenue W
Prince Rupert BC	Lewis Fishing Adventures	250-624-5361	618 11th Avenue E
Toad River BC	Toad River Lodge Restaurant	250-774-7270	Mile 422 Alaska H
Tofino BC	Caffe Vincente	250-725-2599	441 Campbell Street/H 4
Tofino BC	SOBO Good Food To Go	250-725-2341	311 Neill
Vancouver BC	Andale's Mexican Restaurant	604-738-9782	3211 Broadway West
Vancouver BC	Bread Garden Bakery Cafe	604-638-3982	889 West Pender Street
Vancouver BC	Cafe Dolcino	604-801-5118	12 Powell Street
Vancouver BC	Cafe Il Nido	604-685-6436	780 Thurlow Street
Vancouver BC	Dockside Patio Restaurant	604-683-7373	1253 Johnston Street
Vancouver BC	Don Francesco Ristorante	604-685-7770	860 Burrard Street
Vancouver BC	Le Gavroche Restaurant	604-685-3924	1616 Alberni Street
Vancouver BC	Quattro on Fourth	604-734-4444	2611 West 4th Avenue
Victoria BC	Cafe Brio	250-383-0009	944 Fort Street
Victoria BC	Canoe Brew Pub, Marina, and Restaurant	250-361-1940	450 Swift Street
Victoria BC	Golden Saigon Vietnamese Restaurant	250-361-0015	1002 Johnson Street
Victoria BC	Noodle Box	250-360-1312	626 Fisgard St
Victoria BC	Pagliacci's	250-386-1662	1011 Broad Street
Victoria BC	Red Dragon Bistro	250-361-1736	1480 Government Street
Victoria BC	Saigon Harbor Vietnamese Restaurant	250-386-3354	1012 Blanshard St
Victoria BC	Sauce Bar and Restaurant	250-382-8662	1245 Wharf St
West Vancouver BC	Bread Garden Bakery Cafe	604-925-0181	550 Park Royal North
Whistler BC	Brew House	604-905-2739	4355 Blackcomb Way RR 4
Whistler BC	Rim Rock Café	604-932-5565	2117 Whistler Road
Whistler BC	The Dubh Linn Gate Irish Pub & Restaurant	604-905-4047	170-4320 Sundial Crescent
Williams Lake BC	Joey's Grill	250-398-8727	177 Yorston Street

Manitoba

| Portage la Prairie MB | Boston Pizza | 204-239-8200 | 2180 Saskatchewan Avenue/H 1A |
| Winnipeg MB | Deen's Caribbean Restaurant and Patio | 204-233-2208 | 205 Marion Street/H 115 |

New Brunswick

| St John NB | Infusion Tea Room | 506-693-8327 | 41 Charlotte Street |

Nova Scotia

| Yarmouth NS | Old Mill Seafood and Dairy Bar | 902-742-2686 | 785 Hardscratch Road |
| Yarmouth NS | Old World Bakery And Deli | 902-742-6566 | 232 Main Street/H 1 |

Ontario

Dog-Friendly Outdoor Dining - Please always call ahead to make sure an establishment is still dog-friendly.

Kingston ON	Pan Chanco	613-544-7790	44 Princess Street/H 2
Markham ON	Carmelina	905-477-7744	7501 Woodbine Avenue
Ottawa ON	Carmello's	613-563-4349	300 Sparks Street
Toronto ON	Charlotte Room Restaurant	416-598-2882	19 Charlotte Street
Toronto ON	Linux Caffe	416-534-2116	326 Harbord Street
Toronto ON	McSorley's Saloon and Grill	416-932-0655	1544 Bayview Avenue
Toronto ON	Mitzi's Cafe and Gallery	416-588-1234	100 Sorauren Avenue
Toronto ON	Sassafraz Restaurant	416-964-2222	100 Cumberland Street
Toronto ON	The Longest Yard Restaurant and Bar	416-480-9273	535 Mount Pleasant Road
Toronto ON	Whistler's Grille and Cafe Bar	416-421-1344	995 Broadview Avenue

Prince Edward Island

Charlottetown PE	Fishbone's	902-628-6569	136 Richmond Street
Charlottetown PE	Just Us Girls Fashion Café	902-566-1285	100 Queen Street
Charlottetown PE	Peake's Quay Restaurant and Bar	902-368-1330	Corner of Water and Great George Streets
Charlottetown PE	Water Prince Corner Shop	902-368-3212	141 Water Street

Quebec

Gatineau PQ	Le Tartuffe	819-776-6424	Notre-Dame-de-Ille Street
Montreal PQ	Bistro Cote Soleil	514-282-8037	3979, rue Saint-Denis
Montreal PQ	Brioche Lyonnaise	514-842-7017	1593 St. Denis Street
Montreal PQ	Guy and Dodo Morali	514-842-3636	1445, Peel Street
Montreal PQ	Jardin Asean Garden	514-487-8868	5828 Sherbrooke West
Montreal PQ	La Iguana	514-844-0893	51 Roy Est at St-Dominique
Quebec PQ	Bistrot Le Pape Georges	418-692-1320	8, rue Cul-de-Sac
Quebec PQ	Chez Rabelais	418-694-9460	2, rue du Petit-Champlain
Quebec PQ	L'Ardoise	418-694-0213	71, rue St-Paul
Quebec PQ	Le Buffet de l'Antiquaire	418-692-2661	95 rue Saint-Paul

Saskatchewan

Regina SK	Copper Kettle Restaurant	306-525-3545	1953 Scarth Street

Yukon

Haines Junction YU	The Village Bakery	867-634-BUNS (2867)	Corner of Logan and Kluane Streets

Chapter 7

Off-Leash Dog Parks

United States

Alabama

Daphne AL	Daphne Dog Park	251-621-3703	Whispering Pines Road
Prattville AL	Cooter's Dog Park	334-365-9997	1844 Cooters Pond Road

Alaska

Anchorage AK	Conners Lake Park	907-343-8118	Jewel Lake Road
Anchorage AK	Far North Bicentennial Park	907-343-4355	Campbell Airstrip Road
Anchorage AK	Russian Jack Springs Park	907-343-8118	6th Avenue and Boniface Parkway
Anchorage AK	University Lake Park	907-343-8118	Bragaw Street and University Lake Drive

Arizona

Avondale AZ	Dog Park	623-333-2400	12325 W McDowell Road
Casa Grande AZ	Casa Grande Dog Park	520-421-8600	Pinal Ave at Rodeo Rd
Chandler AZ	Shawnee Bark Park	480-782-2727	1400 W. Mesquite
Chandler AZ	Snedigar Bark Park	480-782-2727	4500 S. Basha Rd
Chandler AZ	West Chandler Bark Park	480-782-2727	250 S. Kyrene Rd
Flagstaff AZ	Bushmaster Dog Park		3150 N. Alta Vista
Flagstaff AZ	Thorpe Park Bark Park	928-779-7690	191 N. Thorpe Road
Fountain Hills AZ	Desert Vista Off-Leash Dog Park	480-816-5152	11800 North Desert Vista
Gilbert AZ	Cosmo Dog Park	480-503-6200	2502 E. Ray Road
Gilbert AZ	Dog Park at Crossroads	480-503-6200	2155 E. Knox Rd
Glendale AZ	Foothills Park Dog Park	623-930-2820	57th Avenue and Union Hills Drive
Glendale AZ	Northern Horizon Dog Park	623-930-2820	63rd and Northern Avenue
Glendale AZ	Saguaro Ranch Dog Park		63rd Avenue
Goodyear AZ	Goodyear Dog Park	623-882-7537	15600 W Roeser
Lake Havasu City AZ	Lions Dog Park	928-453-8686	1340 McCulloch Blvd.
Mesa AZ	Quail Run Park Dog Park	480-644-2352	4155 E. Virginia
Oro Valley AZ	James D. Kreigh Dog Park	520-229-5050	23 W Calle Concordia
Phoenix AZ	Grovers Basin Dog Park	602-262-6696	20th Street at Grovers Ave
Phoenix AZ	Mofford Sports Complex Dog Park	602-261-8011	9833 N. 25th Avenue
Phoenix AZ	Pecos Park Dog Park	602-262-6862	48th Street
Phoenix AZ	PetsMart Dog Park	602-262-6971	21st Avenue
Phoenix AZ	Steele Indian School Dog Park	602-495-0739	7th Street at Indian School Road
Prescott AZ	Willow Creek Dog Park	928-777-1100	Willow Creek Road
Sahuarita AZ	Anamax Off-Leash Dog Park	520-625-2731	17501 S. Camino de las Quintas
Scottsdale AZ	Chaparral Park Dog Park	480-312-2353	5401 N. Hayden Road
Scottsdale AZ	Horizon Park Dog Park	480-312-2650	15444 N. 100th Street
Scottsdale AZ	Vista del Camino Park Dog Park	480-312-2330	7700 E. Roosevelt Street
Sedona AZ	Sedona Dog Park	928-301-0226	NW Corner of Carruth and Soldiers Pass Roads
Surprise AZ	Surprise Dog Park	623-266-4500	15930 N. Bullard Avenue
Tempe AZ	Creamery Park	480-350-5200	8th Street and Una Avenue
Tempe AZ	Jaycee Park	480-350-5200	5th Street and Hardy Drive
Tempe AZ	Mitchell Park	480-350-5200	Mitchell Drive and 9th Street
Tempe AZ	Papago Park	480-350-5200	Curry Road and College Avenue
Tempe AZ	Tempe Sports Complex Dog Park	480-350-5200	Warner Rd & Hardy Dr
Tucson AZ	Christopher Columbus Dog Park	520-791-4873x0	4600 N. Silverbell
Tucson AZ	Gene C. Reid Park Off-Leash Area	520-791-3204	900 S. Randolph Way
Tucson AZ	Jacobs Dog Park	520-791-4873x0	3300 N. Fairview Ave.
Tucson AZ	McDonald District Park Off-Leash Area	520-877-6000	4100 N. Harrison Road
Tucson AZ	Northwest Center Off-Leash Dog Park	520-791-4873x0	2075 N. 6th Ave
Tucson AZ	Palo Verde Park Off-Leash Area	520-791-4873	300 S. Mann Avenue
Tucson AZ	Udall Dog Park	520-791-5930	7290 E. Tanque Verde

California

Aptos CA	Polo Grounds Dog Park	831-454-7900	2255 Huntington Avenue
Arcadia CA	Arcadia Dog Park	626-574-5400	Second Avenue and Colorado Blvd
Atascadero CA	Heilmann Dog Park		
Auburn CA	Ashley Memorial Dog Park	530-887-9993	Auburn Ravine Road (back of Ashford Park)
Bakersfield CA	Centennial Park Off-Leash Dog Park	661-326-3866	On Montclair north of Stockdale Hwy
Bakersfield CA	Kroll Park Off-Leash Dog Park	661-326-3866	Kroll Way and Montalvo Dr
Bakersfield CA	University Park Off-Leash Dog Park	661-326-3866	University Ave east of Columbus
Bakersfield CA	Wilson Park Off-Leash Dog Park	661-326-3866	Wilson Road and Hughes Lane
Belmont CA	City of Belmont Dog Park	650-365-3524	2525 Buena Vista Avenue
Berkeley CA	Cesar Chavez Park Off-Leash Dog Area	510-981-6700	11 Spinnaker Way
Berkeley CA	Ohlone Dog Park		Hearst Avenue

Off-Leash Dog Parks - Please always call ahead to verify rules, policies and hours.

Buena Park CA	Bellis Park Dog Park	714-236-3860	7171 8th Street
Burlingame CA	Bayside Park Dog Park	650-558-7300	1125 South Airport Blvd
Calabasas CA	Calabasas Bark Park		Las Virgines Road
Cambria CA	Cambria Dog Park		Main Street and Santa Rosa Creek Rd
Campbell CA	Los Gatos Creek County Dog Park	408-866-2105	1250 Dell Avenue
Carlsbad CA	Ann D. L'Heureaux Memorial Dog Park	760-434-2825	Carlsbad Village Drive
Carmichael CA	Carmichael Park and Dog Park	916-485-5322	Fair Oaks Blvd & Grant Ave
Castro Valley CA	Castro Valley Dog Park	510-881-6700	4660 Crow Canyon
Chula Vista CA	Dog Park at Otay Ranch Town Center	619-656-9100	Eastlake Pkwy At Olympic Pkwy
Chula Vista CA	Montevalle Park Dog Park	619-691-5269	840 Duncan Ranch Road
Citrus Heights CA	P.O.O.C.H. Park of Citrus Heights	916-725-1585	Oak Avenue east of Fair Oaks
Claremont CA	Pooch Park		100 S. College Avenue
Concord CA	Newhall Community Park Dog Park	925-671-3329	Turtle Creek Road
Concord CA	Paw Patch in Newall Community Park	925-671-3329	Clayton Rd & Newhall Pkwy
Corona CA	Butterfield Park Dog Park	909-736-2241	1886 Butterfield Drive
Corona CA	Corona Dog Park	888-636-7387	Butterfield Drive and Smith Avenue
Corona CA	Harada Heritage Dogs Park	888-636-7387	13100 65th Street
Costa Mesa CA	Bark Park Dog Park	949-73-4101	Arlington Dr
Culver City CA	Culver City Off-Leash Dog Park	310-390-9114	Duquesne Ave near Jefferson Blvd
Davis CA	Toad Hollow Dog Park	530-757-5656	1919 Second Street
Dublin CA	Dougherty Hills Dog Park	925-833-6600	Stagecoach Road and Amador Valley Blvd
East Camarillo CA	Camarillo Grove Dog Park	805-482-1996	off Camarillo Springs Road
El Cajon CA	Wells Park & Off-Leash Dog Park	619-441-1680	1153 E. Madison Ave
Elk Grove CA	Elk Grove Dog Park	916-405-5600	9950 Elk Grove Florin Rd
Elk Grove CA	Laguna Dog Park	916-405-5600	9014 Bruceville Rd
Encinitas CA	Encinitas Park		D Street
Encinitas CA	Rancho Coastal Humane Society Dog Park	760-753-6413	389 Requeza Street
Encino CA	Sepulveda Basin Dog Park	818-756-7667	17550 Victory Blvd.
Escondido CA	Mayflower Dog Park		3420 Valley Center Road
Fair Oaks CA	Phoenix Dog Park	916-966-1036	9050 Sunset Ave
Foster City CA	Foster City Dog Run		Foster City Blvd at Bounty
Fremont CA	Central Park Dog Park	510-494-4800	1110 Stevenson Blvd
Fresno CA	Basin AH1 Dog Park and Pond	559-621-2900	4257 W. Alamos
Fresno CA	Woodward Park Dog Park	559-621-2900	E. Audubon Drive
Fullerton CA	Fullerton Pooch Park	714-738-6575	S Basque Avenue
Glen Ellen CA	Elizabeth Anne Perrone Dog Park	707-565-2041	13630 Sonoma H/H 12
Half Moon Bay CA	Coastside Dog Park	650-726-8297	Wavecrest Road
Highland CA	Aurantia Dog Park	909-864-6861	Greenspot Road
Huntington Beach CA	Huntington Beach Dog Park	949-536-5672	Edwards Street
Irvine CA	Central Bark	949-724-7740	6405 Oak Canyon
La Mesa CA	Harry Griffen Park	619-667-1307	9550 Milden Street
Laguna Beach CA	Laguna Beach Dog Park		Laguna Canyon Rd at El Toro Rd
Laguna Niguel CA	Laguna Niguel Pooch Park		Golden Latern
Larkspur CA	Canine Commons	415-927-5110	Doherty, East of Magnolia
Lincoln CA	Lincoln Dog Park	916-624-6808	Third Street
Livermore CA	Del Valle Dog Run	510-562-PARK	Del Valle Road
Livermore CA	Livermore Canine Park		Murdell Lane
Loma Linda CA	Loma Linda Dog Park		Beaumont Ave and Mountain View Ave.
Long Beach CA	Recreation Park Dog Park	562-570-3100	7th St & Federation Dr
Los Angeles CA	Barrington Dog Park	310-476-4866	333 South Barrington Avenue
Los Angeles CA	Griffith Park Dog Park	323-913-4688	North Zoo Drive
Los Angeles CA	Herman Park Dog Park	323-255-0370	5566 Via Marisol
Los Angeles CA	Laurel Canyon Park		8260 Mulholland Dr.
Los Angeles CA	Runyon Canyon Park	323-666-5046	Mulholland Hwy
Los Angeles CA	Silverlake Dog Park		2000 West Silverlake Blvd.
Mill Valley CA	Mill Valley Dog Run		Sycamore Ave At Camino Alto
Milpitas CA	City of Milpitas Dog Park	408-262-6980	3100 Calveras Blvd.
Milpitas CA	Humane Society Silicon Valley	408-262-2133 x164	901 Ames Avenue
Moraga CA	Rancho Laguna Park	925-888-7045	2101 Camino Pablo
Morgan Hill CA	Morgan Hill Off-Leash Dog Park	408-779-3451	Edumundson Avenue
Mountain View CA	Mountain View Dog Park		Shoreline Blvd at North Rd
Napa CA	Canine Commons Dog Park	707-257-9529	Dry Creek Rd at Redwood Rd
Napa CA	Shurtleff Park Dog Park	707-257-9529	Shetler Avenue
North Hollywood CA	Whitnall Off-Leash Dog Park	818-756-8190	5801 1/2 Whitnall Highway
Novato CA	Ohair Park Dog Park		Novato Blvd at Sutro
Oakland CA	Hardy Dog Park	510-238-PARK	491 Hardy Street
Ocean Beach CA	Dusty Rhodes Dog Park	619-236-5555	Sunset Cliffs Blvd.
Oceanside CA	Oceanside Dog Park	760-757-4357	2905 San Luis Rey Rd
Ojai CA	Soule Dog Park	805-654-3951	310 Soule Park Drive
Orange CA	Yorba Dog Park	714-633-2980	190 S Yorba Street
Oxnard CA	Oxnard Park Dog Park	805-385-7950	3250 S Rose Avenue
Palm Desert CA	Civic Center Dog Park	760-346-0611	73-510 Fred Waring Dr
Palm Desert CA	Joe Mann Dog Park	888-636-7387	California Drive
Palm Desert CA	Palm Desert Civic Center Park	888-636-7387	Fred Waring
Palm Springs CA	Palm Springs Dog Park	888-636-7387	222 Civic Drive N
Palo Alto CA	Greer Dog Park	650-329-2261	1098 Amarillo Avenue
Palo Alto CA	Hoover Park	650-329-2261	2901 Cowper St
Palo Alto CA	Mitchell Park/Dog Run	650-329-2261	3800 Middlefield Rd

Pasadena CA	Alice Frost Kennedy Off-Leash Dog Area	626-744-4321	3026 East Orange Grove Blvd
Petaluma CA	Rocky Memorial Dog Park	707-778-4380	W. Casa Grande Road
Pinole CA	Pinole Dog Park	510-741-2999	3790 Pinole Valley Road
Pleasanton CA	Muirwood Dog Exercise Area	925-931-5340	4701 Muirwood Drive
Poway CA	Poway Dog Park		13094 Civic Center Drive
Poway CA	The Poway Dog Park	858-668-4673	13094 Civic Center Drive
Rancho Cucamonga CA	Etiwanda Dog Park		5939 East Avenue
Redding CA	Benton Dog Park	530-941-8200	1700 Airpark Drive
Redondo Beach CA	Redondo Beach Dog Park	310-376-9263	Flagler Lane and 190th
Redwood City CA	Shores Dog Park		Radio Road
Richmond CA	Point Isabel Regional Shoreline	510-562-PARK	Isabel Street
Rio Linda CA	West Side Dog Park	916) 991-5929	810 Oak Lane
Riverside CA	Carlson Dog Park	888-636-7387	At the foot of Mt. Rubidoux
Riverside CA	Pat Merritt Dog Park	888-636-7387	Limonite Frontage Road
Riverside CA	Riverwalk Dog Park	951-358- 7387	Pierce Street and Collett Avenue
Roseville CA	Marco Dog Park	916-774-5950	1800 Sierra Gardens Drive
S Lake Tahoe CA	Bijou Dog Park		1201 Al Tahoe Blvd
Sacramento CA	Bannon Creek Dog Park	916-264-5200	Bannon Creek Drive near West El Camino
Sacramento CA	Granite Park Dog Park	916-264-5200	Ramona Avenue near Power Inn Rd
Sacramento CA	Howe Dog Park	916-927-3802	2201 Cottage Way
Sacramento CA	Partner Park Dog Park	916-264-5200	5699 South Land Park Drive
Sacramento CA	Tanzanite Community Park Dog Park	916-808-5200	Tanzanite Dr at Innovator Dr
San Bernardino CA	Wildwood Dog Park		536 E. 40th St
San Bruno CA	San Bruno Dog Park	650-877-8868	Commodore Lane and Cherry Ave
San Carlos CA	Heather Dog Exercise Area	650-802-4382	2757 Melendy Drive
San Carlos CA	Pulgas Ridge Off-Leash Dog Area	650-691-1200	Edmonds Road and Crestview Drive
San Clemente CA	San Clemente Dog Park		310 Avenida La Pata
San Diego CA	Balboa Park Dog Run	619-235-1100	Balboa Dr
San Diego CA	Capehart Dog Park	619-525-8212	Felspar at Soledad Mountain Rd
San Diego CA	Doyle Community Park	619-525-8212	8175 Regents Road
San Diego CA	Grape Street Park Off-Leash Area	619-525-8212	Grape Street at Granada Ave
San Diego CA	Kearny Mesa Dog Park	619-525-8212	3170 Armstrong Street
San Diego CA	Maddox Dog Park	619-525-8212	7815 Flanders Dr
San Diego CA	Rancho Bernardo Off-Leash Park	858-538-8129	18448 West Bernardo Drive
San Diego CA	Rancho Peasquitos Park	619-221-8901	Salmon River Road at Fairgrove Lane
San Diego CA	Torrey Highlands Park	619-525-8212	Landsdale Drive at Del Mar Heights Road
San Dimas CA	San Dimas Dog Park	909-394-6230	301 Horsethief Canyon Rd
San Francisco CA	Alamo Square Off Leash Dog Park	415-831-2084	Scott Street, between Hayes and Fulton Streets
San Francisco CA	Alta Plaza Off Leash Dog Park	415-831-2084	Steiner and Clay Street
San Francisco CA	Bernal Heights Off Leash Dog Park	415-831-2084	Bernal Heights and Esmerelda
San Francisco CA	Brotherhood Mini Off Leash Dog Park	415-831-2084	Brotherhood Way
San Francisco CA	Buena Vista Off Lead Dog Park	415-831-2084	Buena Vista West at Central Avenue
San Francisco CA	Corona Heights	415-831-2084	16th and Roosevelt
San Francisco CA	Crocker Amazon Off Leash Dog Park	415-831-2084	At Geneva Avenue and Moscow Street
San Francisco CA	Delores Off Lead Dog Park	415-831-2084	19th Street and Delores Street
San Francisco CA	Douglass Park, Upper Field Off Leash Dog Area	415-831	27th and Douglass Streets
San Francisco CA	Eureka Valley Off Leash Dog Park	415-695-5012	100 Collingwood Street
San Francisco CA	Fort Miley Off Lead Dog Area	415-561-4700	Point Lobos and 48th Avenues
San Francisco CA	Glen Park Off Leash Dog Area	415-337-4705	400 O'Shaughnessy Blvd
San Francisco CA	Golden Gate Park Off Leash Dog Areas	415-751-8987	Sloat & Great Highway
San Francisco CA	Jefferson Square Off Lead Dog Park	415-831-2084	Eddy and Laguna Streets
San Francisco CA	Lafayette Park	415-831-2084	Washington/Clay/Laguna
San Francisco CA	McKinley Off Leash Dog Park	415-666-7005	20th Street and Vermont
San Francisco CA	McLaren Park Off Leash Dog Areas	415-831-2084	1600 Geneva Avenue
San Francisco CA	Mountain Lake Off Leash Dog Park	415-666-7005	12th Avenue and Lake Street
San Francisco CA	Pine Lake Off Leash Dog Park	415-831-2700	Sloat Boulevard & Vale Street
San Francisco CA	Pine Lake/Stern Grove Trail	415-252-6252	Between H 1(Stern Grove) and Wawona (Pine Lake)
San Francisco CA	Portrero Hill Mini Off Leash Dog Park	415-695-5009	22nd Street and Arkansas
San Francisco CA	St Mary's Off Leash Dog Park	415-695-5006	95 Justin Drive
San Francisco CA	Stern Grove Off Leash Dog Park	415-252-6252	19th Avenue and Wawona Avenue
San Francisco CA	Upper Noe Off Lead Dog Park	415-831-2084	30th and Church Street
San Francisco CA	Walter Haas Playground and Dog Park	415-831-2084	Diamond Heights and Addison Street
San Francisco CA	West Pacific Avenue Park	415-831-2084	Pacific Avenue and Lyon Street
San Jose CA	Butcher Dog Park	408-277-2757	Camden Avenue at Lancaster Drive
San Jose CA	Delmas Dog Park	408-535-3570	Park Avenue and Delmas Avenue
San Jose CA	Fontana Dog Park	408-535-3570	Golden Oak Way at Castello Drive
San Jose CA	Hellyer Park/Dog Run	408-225-0225	Hellyer Ave
San Jose CA	Miyuki Dog Park	408-277-4573	Santa Teresa Boulevard
San Jose CA	Ryland Dog Park	408-535-3570	First Street at Bassett Street
San Luis Obispo CA	El Chorro Regional Park and Dog Park	805-781-5930	Hwy 1
San Luis Obispo CA	Nipomo Park Off-Leash Area	805-781-5930	W. Tefft St and Pomery Rd
San Marcos CA	San Elijo Hills Community Bark Park	760-798-1765	Elfin Forest Road
San Pedro CA	Knoll Hill Off-Leash Dog Park	310-514-0338	200 Knoll Drive
San Rafael CA	Field of Dogs		Civic Center Drive behind the Marin County Civic Center

San Ramon CA	Del Mar Dog Park	925-973-3200	Del Mar and Pine Valley
San Ramon CA	Memorial Park Dog Run	925-973-3200	Bollinger Canyon Road at San Ramon Valley Blvd
Santa Barbara CA	Douglas Family Preserve	805-564-5418	Linda Street
Santa Barbara CA	Santa Barbara Off-Leash Areas	805-564-5418	Various
Santa Clara CA	Santa Clara Dog Park	408-615-3140	888 Reed Street
Santa Cruz CA	University Terrace Dog Run	831-420-5270	Meder Street and Nobel Drive
Santa Maria CA	Woof-Pac Park	805-896-2344	300 Goodwin Rd
Santa Monica CA	Airport Dog Park	310-458-8411	3201 Airport Avenue
Santa Monica CA	Joslyn Park Dog Park	310-458-8974	633 Kensington Road
Santa Monica CA	Memorial Park	310-450-1121	1401 Olympic Blvd
Santa Monica CA	Pacific Street Park	310-450-6179	Main and Pacific Street
Santa Rosa CA	Dog Park-Deturk Park	707-543-3292	819 Donahue Street
Santa Rosa CA	Dolye Community Park Dog Park	707-543-3292	700 Doyle Park Drive
Santa Rosa CA	Galvin Community Park Dog Park	707-543-3292	3330 Yulupa Avenue
Santa Rosa CA	Northwest Community Dog Park	707-543-3292	2620 W. Steele Lane
Santa Rosa CA	Rincon Valley Community Park Dog Park	707-543-3292	5108 Badger Road
Sausalito CA	Sausalito Dog Park		Bridgeway and Ebbtide Avenues
Scotts Valley CA	Scotts Valley Dog Park	831-438-3251	Bluebonnet Road
Seal Beach CA	Arbor Dog Park	562-799-9660	Lampson Avenue at Heather St.
Sebastopol CA	Sebastopol Dog Park	707-823-7262	500 Ragle Rd
Sonoma CA	Ernie Smith Community Park Dog Park	707-539-8092	18776 Gilman Drive
Stockton CA	BarkleyVille Dog Park	209-937-8206	5505 Feather River Drive
Sunnyvale CA	Las Palmas Park/Dog Park	408-730-7506	850 Russett Drive
Temecula CA	Temecula Dog Exercise Area	951-694-6444	44747 Redhawk Parkway
Thousand Oaks CA	Thousand Oaks Dog Park	805-495-6471	Avenida de las Flores
Union City CA	Drigon Dog Park	510-471-3232x702	Mission Blvd at 7th Street
Upland CA	Baldy View Dog Park	909-931-4280	11th Street at Mountain Ave.
Vallejo CA	Wardlaw Dog Park		Redwood Pkwy at Ascot Pkwy
Venice CA	Westminster Dog Park	310-392-5566	1234 Pacific Ave
Ventura CA	Arroyo Verde Park, Parks and Recreation	805-658-4740	Foothill and Day Road
Ventura CA	Camino Real Park	805-658-4740	At Dean Drive and Varsity Street
Walnut Creek CA	Walnut Creek Dog Park	925-671-3329	301 N San Carlos Drive
Watsonville CA	Watsonville Dog Park	831-454-7900	757 Green Valley Road
West Sacramento CA	Sam Combs Dog Park	916-617-4620	205 Stone Blvd
Yuba City CA	Yuba Sutter Off-Leash Dog Park	530-329-1997	2050 Wild River Drive

Colorado

Arvada CO	Arvada Dog Park	303-421-3487	17975 West 64th Parkway
Aurora CO	Grandview Park Dog Park	303-739-7160	17500 E. Salida Street
Boulder CO	East Boulder Park	303-413-7258	5660 Sioux Drive
Boulder CO	Foothills Park Dog Park	303-413-7258	Cherry Ave at 7th St
Boulder CO	Howard Hueston Dog Park	303-413-7258	34th Street
Boulder CO	Valmont Dog Park	303-413-7258	5275 Valmont Road
Brighton CO	Happy Tails Dog Park	303-655-2049	1111 Judicial Center Drive
Broomfield CO	Broomfield County Commons Dog Park	303-464-5509	13th and Sheridan Blvd
Castle Rock CO	Glendale Open Space Dog Park	303-660-7495	100 Third Street
Colorado Springs CO	Cheyenne Meadows Dog Park	719-385-2489	Charmwood Dr. and Canoe Creek Dr.
Colorado Springs CO	Garden of the Gods Park Off-Leash Area	719-385-2489	Gateway Road
Colorado Springs CO	Palmer Park Dog Park	719-385-2489	3650 Maizeland Road
Colorado Springs CO	Rampart Park Dog Park	719-385-2489	8270 Lexington Drive
Colorado Springs CO	Red Rock Canyon Off-Leash Dog Loops	719-385-2489	31st Street at Highway 24
Conifer CO	Beaver Ranch Bark Park	303-829-1917	11369 Foxton Rd
Denver CO	Barnum Park Off-Leash Area	720-913-0696	Hooker and West 5th
Denver CO	Berkeley Park Dog Park	720-913-0696	Sheridan and West 46th
Denver CO	Denver's Off Leash Dog Park	303-698-0076	666 South Jason Street
Denver CO	Fuller Park Dog Park	720-913-0696	Franklin and East 29th
Denver CO	Green Valley Ranch East Off-Leash Area	720-913-0696	Jebel and East 45th
Denver CO	Kennedy Soccer Complex Off-Leash Area	720-913-0696	Hampden and South Dayton
Durango CO	Durango Dog Park	970-385-2950	Highway 160 at Highway 550
Eagle CO	Eagle Dog Park	970-328-6354	Sylvan Lake Rd at Lime Park Dr
Englewood CO	Centennial Park Off-Leash Area	303-762-2300	4630 S. Decatur
Englewood CO	Duncan Park Off-Leash Area	303-762-2300	4800 S. Pennsylvania
Englewood CO	Englewood Canine Corral	303-762-2300	4848 S. Windermere
Englewood CO	Jason Park Off-Leash Area	303-762-2300	4200 S. Jason
Englewood CO	Northwest Greenbelt Off-Leash Area	303-762-2300	Tejon at W Baltic Pl
Estes Park CO	Estes Valley Dog Park	970-586-8191	off Highway 36
Fort Collins CO	Fossil Creek Dog Park	970-221-6618	5821 South Lemay Avenue
Fort Collins CO	Soft Gold Dog Park	970-221-6618	520 Hickory Street
Fort Collins CO	Spring Canyon Dog Park	970-221-6618	Horsetooth Road
Grand Junction CO	Canyon View Dog Park	970-254-3846	Interstate 70 at 24 Road
Longmont CO	Longmont Dog Park #1	303-651-8447	21st and Francis
Longmont CO	Longmont Dog Park #2	303-651-8447	Airport Road at St Vrain Rd
Louisville CO	Louisville Community Park Dog Park	303-335-4735	955 Bella Vista Drive
Morrison CO	Lakewood Dog Park		15900 W Alameda Parkway/H 26
Windsor CO	Poudre Pooch Park	970-674-3500	Eastman Park Dr at 7th Street

Connecticut

Granby CT	Granby D.O.G.G.S. Park	860-653-0173	215 Salmon Brook Street/H 202
Hamden CT	The Hamden Dog Park at Bassett		On Waite Street at Ridge Road
Milford CT	Eisenhower Park Dog Run	203-783-3280	North Street
Norwich CT	Pawsitive Park Dog Park, Estelle Cohn Memorial Dog Park	860-367-7271	261 Asylum Street
Ridgefield CT	Bark Park		Governor Street
Southbury CT	Bark Park		Main Street N
Wethersfield CT	Mill Woods Park Dog Park	860-721-2890	154 Prospect St

Delaware

Bear DE	Lums Pond Dog Area	302-368-698	
Wilmington DE	Brandywine Dog Park	302-577-7020	North Park Drive at North Adams
Wilmington DE	Carousel Park Off-Leash Area	302-995-7670	3700 Limestone Rd
Wilmington DE	Rockford Dog Park	302-577-7020	Rockford Rd at Tower Road
Wilmington DE	Talley Day Bark Park	302-395-5654	1300 Foulk Road

Florida

Boca Raton FL	Boca Raton Dog Park	561-393-7821	751 Banyan Trail
Bonita Beach FL	Dog Beach	239-461-7400	County Road 865
Bradenton FL	Happy Trails Canine Park	941-742-5923	5502 33rd Avenue Drive W
Cape Coral FL	Waggin Tails Dog Park	239-549-4606	5505 Rose Garden Road
Clearwater FL	Sand Key Park Paw Playground	727-588-4852	1060 Gulf Blvd.
Coconut Grove FL	Dog Chow Dog Park	954-570-9507	2400 S Bayshore Drive
Coral Springs FL	Dr. Paul's Pet Care Center Dog Park	954-346-4428	2575 Sportsplex Drive
Coral Springs FL	Sportsplex Dog Park	954-346-4428	2575 Sportsplex Drive
Debary FL	Gemini Springs Dog Park	386-736-5953	37 Dirksen Drive
Deland FL	Barkley Square Dog Park	386-736-5953	1010 N Ridgewood Avenue
Delray Beach FL	Lake Ida Dog Park	561-966-6600	2929 Lake Ida Road
Estero FL	Estero Community Dog Park	239-498-0415	9200 Corkscrew Palms Blvd
Estero FL	K-9 Corral at Estero Park	239-498-0415	9200 Corkscrew Palms Blvd
Fort Lauderdale FL	Bark Park At Snyder Park	954-828-3647	3299 S.W. 4th Avenue
Fort Myers FL	Barkingham Park	239-338-3288	9800 Buckingham Road
Hialeah FL	Bark Park	305-769-2693	401 E. 65th Street
Hollywood FL	Poinciana Dog Park	954-921-3404	1301 S 21st Avenue
Jacksonville FL	Dogwood Park	904-296-3636	7407 Salisbury Rd South
Jacksonville Beach FL	Paws Park	904-513-9240	Penman Road S
Key West FL	Higgs Beach Dog Park	305-809-3765	White Street and Atlantic Blvd
Largo FL	Walsingham Park Paw Playground	727-549-6142	12615 102nd Avenue North
Miami FL	Amelia Earhart Park Bark Park	305-755-7800	401 East 65th Street
Miami FL	East Greynolds Park	305-945-3425	16700 Biscayne BlvdH 1/5
Miami FL	Tropical Dog Park	305 226 8316	7900 SW 40 Street
Miami Beach FL	Flamingo Bark Park	305-673-7224	13th Street and Michigan Avenue
Miami Beach FL	Pinetree Bark Park	305-673-7730	4400 Pinetree Drive
Miami Beach FL	Washington Avenue Bark Park	305-673-7766	201 2nd Street
Mount Dora FL	Mount D.o.r.a. Dog Park	352-735-7183	East end of 11th Avenue
Naples FL	Rover Run Dog Park	239-566-2367	1895 Veterans Park Drive
North Fort Myers FL	Pooch Park	239-656-7748	1297 Driftwood Drive
North Miami Beach FL	Northeast Dog Park	305-673-7730	16700 Biscayne Blvd/H 1/5
Ocala FL	Millennium Dog Park		2513 SE 32nd Avenue
Orlando FL	Downey Dog Park	407-249-6195	10107 Flowers Avenue
Orlando FL	Dr. Phillips Dog Park	407-254-9037	8249 Buenavista Woods Blvd
Palm Harbor FL	Chestnut Park Paw Playground	727-669-1951	2200 East Lake Road
Pembroke Pines FL	Pembroke Pines Dog Park	954-435-6525	9751 Johnson Street
Pensacola FL	Scott Complex Dog Park	850-436-5511	Summit Blvd
Plantation FL	Happy Tails Dog Park at Seminole Park	954-452-2510	6600 SW 16th Street
Sanford FL	Paw Park of Historic Sanford	407-330-5688	427 S. French Avenue
Satellite Beach FL	Satellite Beach Off-leash Dog Park	321-777-8004	Satellite Beach Sports & Rec Park
Seffner FL	Mango Dog Park	813-975-2160	11717 Claypit Road
Seminole FL	Boca Ciega Park Paw Playground	727-588-4882	12410 74th Ave. N
Spring Hill FL	Rotary Centennial Park Dog Park	352-754-4027	10375 Sandlor Street
Sunrise FL	Barkham at Markham Park	954-389-2000	16001 W H 84
Tampa FL	Al Lopez Dog Park	813-274-8615	4810 North Himes
Tampa FL	Davis Islands Dog Park	813-274-8615	1002 Severn
Tampa FL	Palma Ceia	813-274-8615	San Miguel & Marti
Tarpon Springs FL	Anderson Park Paw Playground	727-943-4085	39699 U.S. Highway 19 North
Tierra Verde FL	Fort DeSoto Park Paw Playground	727-582-2267	3500 Pinellas Bayway South
Wellington FL	Dog Park	561-791-4005	2975 Greenbriar Blvd
West Palm Beach FL	Pooch Park	561-966-6600	7715 Forest Hill Blvd/H 882
Winter Garden FL	West Orange Dog Park	407-656-3299	12400 Marshall Farms Road
Winter Park FL	Fleet Peeples Park Dog Park	407-740-8897	South Lakemont Avenue

Georgia

Alpharetta GA	Waggy World Dog Park	678-297-6100	175 Roswell Street

739

Athens GA	Memorial Park Dog Park	706-613-3580	293 Gran Ellen Drive
Athens GA	Sandy Creek Park Dog Parks	706-613-3800	400 Bob Holman Rd
Athens GA	Southeast Clarke Park Dog Park	706-613-3871	4440 Lexington Road
Atlanta GA	Piedmont Park Off Leash Dog Park	404-875-7275	Park Drive
Cumming GA	Windermere Dog Park	770-781-2215	3355 Windermere Parkway
Dunwoody GA	Brook Run Dog Park	404-371-2631	4770 N. Peachtree Rd
Gainesville GA	Laurel Park Dog Park	770-535-8280	3100 Old Cleveland Hwy
Lawrenceville GA	Ronald Reagan Dog Park		2777 Five Forks Trickum Rd
Macon GA	Macon Dog Park	478-742-5084	Chestnut and Adams
Marietta GA	Sweat Mountain Dog Park	770-591-3160	4346 Steinhauer Road
Milton GA	Wolf Brook Private Dog Park and Club	770-772-0440	13665 New Providence Rd
Norcross GA	Graves Dog Park	770-822-8840	1540 Graves Rd
Norcross GA	Pinckneyville Dog Park	770-822-8840	4758 S Old Peachtree Road
Roswell GA	Leila Thompson Dog Park	770-641-3760	1355 Woodstock Rd
Savannah GA	Savannah Dog Park		41st and Drayton St
Smyrna GA	Burger Dog Park	770-431-2842	680 Glendale Pl
Stone Mountain GA	Red Dog Park	770-879-4971	3rd and 4th Streets
Tybee GA	City of Tybee Dog Park	912-786-4573	Van Horne and Fort Streets

Hawaii

Honolulu HI	McInerny Dog Park	808-946-2187	2700 Waialae Avenue
Honolulu HI	Mililani Dog Park	808-946-2187	95-1069 Ukuwai St
Honolulu HI	Moanalua Dog Park		Moanalua Park Rd and Hahiole St
Honolulu HI	Oahu Dog-Friendly Parks (Leashes Required)	808-946-2187	Various
Honolulu HI	The Bark Park		Diamond Head Rd at 18th Avenue
Hui 'Ilio HI	Hawai'i Kai Dog Park		Keahole Street
Waikiki HI	Ala Wai K9 Playground		Ala Wai Blvd

Idaho

Boise ID	Military Reserve Flood Basin Dog Off-Leash Area	208-384-4060 ext. 333	750 Mountain Cove Road
Boise ID	Military Reserve Off-Leash Park	208-384-4240	Mountain Cove Road and Reserve St
Boise ID	Morris Hill Park	208-384-4060 ext 338	10 Roosevelt Street
Boise ID	Ridge to Rivers Trails	208-384-4060 ext. 333	Boise Foothills

Illinois

Aurora IL	Aurora West Forest Preserve	630-232-5980	Hankes Road
Chicago IL	Challenger Playlot Park	312-742-PLAY	1100 W. Irving Park Rd
Chicago IL	Churchill Field Park Dog Park	312-742-PLAY	1825 N. Damen Ave.
Chicago IL	Coliseum Park Dog Park	312-742-PLAY	1466 S. Wabash Ave.
Chicago IL	Grant Park Bark Park	312-742-PLAY	9th and Columbus
Chicago IL	Hamlin Park Dog Park	312-742-PLAY	3035 N. Hoyne Ave.
Chicago IL	Margate Park Dog Park	312-742-PLAY	4921 N. Marine Drive
Chicago IL	Noethling (Grace) Park Dog Park	312-742-PLAY	2645 N. Sheffield Ave.
Chicago IL	River Park Dog Park	312-742-PLAY	5100 N. Francisco Ave
Chicago IL	Walsh Park Dog Park	312-742-PLAY	1722 N. Ashland Ave.
Chicago IL	Wicker Park Dog Park	312-742-PLAY	1425 N. Damen Ave.
Dundee IL	Schweitzer Woods	630-232-5980	16N690 Sleepy Hollow Road
Naperville IL	Whalon Lake Dog Park	815-727-8700	Royce Road
Peoria IL	Bradley Dog Park		1314 Park Road
Peoria IL	Vicary Bottoms Dog Exercise Area	309-682-6684	Kickapoo Creek Road
Shorewood IL	Hammel Woods Dog Park	815-727-8700	DuPage River Access on E Black Road
St Charles IL	Fox River Bluff & Fox River Bluff West Forest Preserve	630-232-5980	H 25 and H 31
Urbana IL	Urbana Park District Dog Park	217-344-9583	1501 E. Perkins Rd.

Indiana

Crown Point IN	Dogwood Run at Lemon Lake County Park	219-945-0543	6322 W. 133rd Avenue
Fort Wayne IN	Pawster Park Pooch Playground	260-427-6000	Winchester Road and Bluffton Road
Goshen IN	Robert Nelson Dog Park		60376 C.R. 13
Highland IN	Wicker Memorial Park	219-838-3420	8554 Indianapolis Boulevard
Indianapolis IN	Bark Park	317-327-7076	11300 E Prospect Street
Indianapolis IN	Broad Ripple Park Bark Park	317-327-7161	1550 Broad Ripple Avenue
Indianapolis IN	Eagle Creek Park Bark Park	317-327-7110	7840 W 56th St
Lafayette IN	Shamrock Park Dog Park	765-225-8388	Wabash Avenue
Michigan City IN	Creek Ridge County Park Dog Park	219-325-8315	7943 W 400 North
Muncie IN	ARF (Animal Rescue Fund) Park	765-282-2733 (ARFF)	1209 W Riggin Road
Valparaiso IN	Canine Country Club	219-548-3604	3556 Sturdy Road
Westville IN	Bluhm County Park Dog Park	219-325-8315	3855 South 1100 W

Iowa

Bettendorf IA	Crow Creek Dog Park	563-344-4113	4800 N Devils Glen Road
Cedar Falls IA	Cedar Falls Paw Park	319-273-8624	S Main and Hwy 58 Overpass
Cedar Rapids IA	Cheyenne Park Off-Leash Area	319-286-5760	1500 Cedar Bend Lane SW
Clinton IA	Prairie Pastures Dog Park	563-242-9088	3923 N 3rd Street
Clinton IA	Prairie Pastures Dog Park at Soaring Eagle Nature Center	563-243-3022	3923 North 3rd Street
Indianola IA	Indianola Off-Leash Dog Playground	515-480-9746	S K Street and W 17th Avenue
Iowa City IA	Thornberry Off-Leash Dog Park	319-356-5107	Foster Road
Runnells IA	Rover's Ranch Dog Park	515-967-6768	200 SE 108th Street
Sioux City IA	Lewis and Clark Dog Park	712-279-6311	5015 Correctionville Road
Washington IA	Sunset Park Dog Park	319-653-6584	S H Avenue
Washington IA	Washington Sunset Dog Park	319-653-6584	915 W Main Street
West Des Moines IA	Racoon River Dog Park	515-222-3444	2500 Grand Avenue
West Des Moines IA	West Des Moines Dog	515-222-3444	2500 Grand Avenue

Kansas

De Soto KS	Kill Creek Streamway Park	913-831-3355	33460 West 95th St
Hutchinson KS	Hutchinson Dog Park		1501 S Severance
Lawrence KS	Mutt Run	785-832-3405	1330 East 902 Road
Manhattan KS	Stretch Dog Park	785-539-7941	5800 A River Pond Road
Olathe KS	Heritage Park	913-831-3355	16050 Pflumm
Overland Park KS	Thomas S. Stoll Memorial Dog Park	913-831-3355	12500 W. 119th Street
Shawnee KS	Shawnee Mission Park	913-831-3355	7900 Renner Rd/87th St
Topeka KS	Bark Park (Gage Park)	785-368-3838	10th and Gage St

Kentucky

Ashland KY	Ashland Boyd County Dog Park		Fraley Field
Lexington KY	Coldstream Dog Park		1875 Newtown Pike
Lexington KY	Jacobson Dog Park		4001 Athens-Boonesboro Road
Lexington KY	Masterson Station Dog Park		Leestown Road/H 421
Lexington KY	Wellington Dog Park		New Circle Road
Louisville KY	Cochran Hill Dog Run	502-291-6873	Cochran Hill Road
Louisville KY	Sawyer Dog Park	502-291-6873	Freys Hill Road
Louisville KY	Vettiner Dog Run	502-291-6873	Mary Dell Road
Milford KY	Kennel Resorts		5825 Meadowview Drive

Louisiana

Baton Rouge LA	Forest Park Dog Park	225-752-1853	13950 Harrell's Ferry Road
Baton Rouge LA	Raising Cane's Dog Park	225-272-9200	1442 City Park Avenue
Lake Charles LA	Calcasieu Parish Animal Control Public Dog Park	337-439-8879	5500-A Swift Plant Rd.

Maine

Belfast ME	Belfast Dog Park		Lincolnville Avenue
Kennebunk ME	Kennebunk Dog Park	207-985-3244	36 Sea Road
Old Orchard Park ME	Old Orchard Beach Dog Park	207-934-0860	Memorial Park at 1st St.
Portland ME	Capisic Pond Park	207-874-8793	Capisic Street
Portland ME	Eastern Promenade Park Off-Leash Area	207-874-8793	Cutter Street
Portland ME	Hall School Woods	207-874-8793	23 Orono Road
Portland ME	Jack School Dog Run	207-874-8793	North St. and Washington Ave.
Portland ME	Pine Grove Park	207-874-8793	Harpswell Road
Portland ME	Portland Arts & Technology School Dog Run	207-874-8793	196 Allen Avenue
Portland ME	Riverton Park	207-874-8793	Riverside Street
Portland ME	University Park	207-874-8793	Harvard Street
Portland ME	Valley Street Park	207-874-8793	Valley St.
Seal Harbor ME	Little Long Pond Leash-Free Area	207-288-3338	Peabody Drive

Maryland

Annapolis MD	Broadneck Park	410-222-7317	618 Broadneck Road
Annapolis MD	Quiet Waters Dog Park	410-222-1777	600 Quiet Waters Park Rd
Baltimore MD	Canton Dog Park	410-396-7900	Clinton & Toone Streets
Bowie MD	Bowie Dog Park		Northview Drive and Enfield Drive
Boyds MD	Black Hills Regional Park Dog Park	301-972-9396	20930 Lake Ridge Rd
Ellicott City MD	Worthington Park	410-313-PARK (7275)	8170 Hillsborough Road
Gaithersburg MD	Green Run Dog Park		Bickerstaff Rd and I-370
Germantown MD	Ridge Road Recreational Dog Park	301-972-9396	21155 Frederick Road
Laurel MD	Laurel Dog Park	410-222-7317	Brock Bridge Road
Ocean City MD	Ocean City Dog Park		94th Street

Owings Mills MD	BARC (Baltimore Animal Recreation Center) Park	410-887-3630	Reisterstown Road
Pasadena MD	Downs Park	410-222-7000	8311 John Downs Loop
Rockville MD	Cabin John Dog Park	301-495-2525	7400 Tuckerman Lane
Silver Spring MD	Wheaton Regional Park Dog Exercise Area	301-680-3803	11717 Orebaugh Ave

Massachusetts

Boston MA	Boston Common Off-Leash Dog Hours	617-635-4505	Beacon Street/H 2
Boston MA	Peters Park Dog Run		E. Berkeley and Washington St.
Cambridge MA	Cambridge Dog Park	617-349-4800	Mt. Auburn and Hawthorne
Cambridge MA	Danehy Park	617-349-4800	99 Sherman Street
Cambridge MA	Fort Washington Park		Waverly Street
Egremont MA	French Park Dog Park	413-528-0182	Baldwin Hill Road
Hingham MA	Stoddard's Neck Dog Run		Route 3A
Medway MA	Henry Garnsey Canine Recreation Park		Cottage Street and Village Street
Oak Bluffs MA	Trade Winds Preserve	508-693-0072	County Road
Provincetown MA	Pilgrim Bark Park	508-487-1325	Corner of Shank Painter Road and H 6
Saugus MA	Breakheart Reservation	781-233-0834	177 Forest Street
Sharon MA	Sharon Dog Park		East Foxboro Street
Somerville MA	Nunziato Field		22 Vinal Avenue

Michigan

Ada MI	Shaggy Pines Dog Park	616-676-9464	3895 Cherry Lane SE
Bay City MI	Bay County Dog Park		800 Livingston Street
Clinton Township MI	Clinton Township Dog Park	586-286-9336	Romeo Plank Rd
Frankenmuth MI	Frankenmuth Hund Platz	989-652-3440	624 E Tuscola
Holland MI	Ottawa County Dog Park	800-506-1299	1286 Ottawa Beach Road
Howell MI	E-Z Dog Park and Training Center	810-229-7353	230 Norlynn Dr
Lake Orion MI	Orion Oaks Dog Park	248-858-0906	2301 Clarkston Road
Lansing MI	Soldan Dog Park		1601 East Cavanaugh Road
Mount Clemens MI	Behnke Memorial Dog Park		300 N Groesbeck Highway
Royal Oak MI	Cummingston Park Dog Run	248-246-3300	Torquay & Leafdale
Royal Oak MI	Mark Twain Park Dog Run	248-246-3300	4600 North Campbell
Royal Oak MI	Quickstad Park Dog Run	248-246-3300	Marais between Normandy & Lexington
Royal Oak MI	Wagner Park Dog Run	248-246-3300	Detroit Ave, between Rochester and Main
Saline MI	Saline Dog Park		W. Bennett St
Saugatuck MI	Tails 'N Trails Park	269-857-7721	134th Avenue
Westland MI	Hines Park Dog Park		Hawthorne Ridge west of Merriman
Wixom MI	Lyon Oaks Dog Park	248-437-7345	52221 Pontiac Trail

Minnesota

Bloomington MN	Bloomington Off-leash Recreation Area	952-563-8892	111th Street
Burnsville MN	Alimagnet Dog Park		1200 Alimagnet Parkway
Coates MN	Dakota Woods Dog Park	651-437-3191	16470 Blaine Ave.
Coon Rapids MN	Trackside Park	763-767-6462	10425 Hummingbird Street
Eden Prairie MN	Bryant Lake Regional Park Dog Park	763-694-7764	6800 Rowland Road
Hanover MN	Crow-Hassan Park Reserve Off-Leash Area	763-694-7860	11629 Crow-Hassan Park Road
Maplewood MN	Battle Creek Dog Park	651-748-2500	Lower Afton Rd E at McKnight Rd S
Minneapolis MN	Franklin Terrace Off-Leash Rec Area	612-230-6400	Franklin Terrace at SE Franklin Ave
Minneapolis MN	Lake of the Isles Off-Leash Rec Area	612-230-6400	Lake of the Isles Pkwy at W. 28th St
Minneapolis MN	Loring Park Off-Leash Dog Park		Maple St at Harmon Place
Minneapolis MN	Minnehaha Off-Leash Rec Area	612-230-6400	54th St and Hiawatha Ave
Minneapolis MN	St. Anthony Parkway Off-Leash Rec Area	612-230-6400	St. Anthony Parkway
Osseo MN	Elm Creek Park Reserve Off-Leash Area	763-559-9000	Elm Creek Rd at Zachary Lane N
Prior Lake MN	Cleary Lake Regional Park Dog Park	763-559-9000	Eagle Creek Ave SE at Texas Ave
Rockford MN	Lake Sarah Regional Park Off-Leash Area	763-559-9000	S Lake Sarah Dr at W Lake Sarah Drive
Roseville MN	Woodview Off-Leash Area	651-748-2500	Kent St at Larpenteur Ave W
Shoreview MN	Rice Creek North Trail Corridor Off-Leash Area	651-748-2500	Lexington Avenue at County Road J
St Paul MN	Arlington Arkwright Off-Leash Dog Area	651-266-8989	Arlington Ave E at Arkwright St
St Paul MN	Trackside Park	763-767-6462	10425 Hummingbird Street
Victoria MN	Carver Park Reserve Off-Leash Dog Park	763-694-7650	7025 Victoria Drive
White Bear MN	Otter Lake Regional Park Dog Park	651-748-2500	County Rd H2 E at Otter Lake Rd

Mississippi

Petal MS	Petal Dog Park	601-554-5440	Dawson Cut Off

Missouri

Arnold MO	Arnold Dog Park	636-282-2380	Bradley Beach Road and Jeffco Blvd
Columbia MO	Twin Lakes Recreation Area	573-445-8839	2500 Chapel Hill Road
Defiance MO	Broemmelsiek Park	636-949-7535	Schwede and Wilson Roads
Kansas City MO	Penn Valley Off-Leash Park	816-784-5030	W. 28th St. and Wyandotte St.

Kansas City MO	Penn Valley Off-Leash Park	816-513-7500	Pershing Road and Main Street
Kansas City MO	Wayside Waifs Bark Park	816-761-8151	3901 Martha Truman Rd
Springfield MO	Cruse Dog Park	417-864-1049	2100 W Catalpa Street
St Charles MO	DuSable Dog Park	636-949-3372	2598 N Main Street
St Louis MO	Frenchtown Dog Park		S 10th and Emmet Streets
St Louis MO	Lister Dog Park		Taylor Rd and Olive St
St Louis MO	Shaw Neighborhood Dog Park		Thurman and Cleveland Ave
St Louis MO	Taylor Dog Park		Taylor Rd
St Louis MO	Water Tower Dog Park	314-552-9000	S Grand and Russel Blvds
Wentzville MO	Quail Ridge Park		Quail Ridge Rd

Montana

Bozeman MT	Bozeman Dog Park	406-582-3200	Highland Blvd at Haggerty Lane
Bozeman MT	Burke Park	406-582-3200	S. Church and E. Story
Livingston MT	Moja Campbell Dog Park	406-222-2111	View Vista Drive
Missoula MT	Jacob's Island Park Dog Park	406-721-7275	off VanBuren Street

Nebraska

Hastings NE	Hastings Dog Park	402-461-2324	E South Street/H 6
Kearney NE	Meadowlark North Dog Park	308-237-4644	30th Avenue at 39th Street
Las Vegas NE	Winding Trails Park	702-633-1171	S Buffalo Drive and Oakey Boulevard
Lincoln NE	Holmes Lake Dog Run	402-441-7847	70th Street
Norfolk NE	Off-Leash Dog Recreation Area	402-844-2000	2201 South 13th Street
North Platte NE	Waggin' Tails Dog Park	308-535-6772	S McDonald Street
Omaha NE	Hefelinger Park Dog Park	402-444-5900	112th Street and West Maple Road
Scottsbluff NE	Dog Park	308-630-6238	Off S Beltline Road
Scottsbluff NE	Scottsbluff Dog Park	308-630-6238	S Beltline Road

Nevada

Henderson NV	Acacia Park Dog Park	702-267-4000	S Gibson Road and Las Palmas Entrada
Henderson NV	Dos Escuelas Park Dog Park	702-267-4000	1 Golden View Street
Las Vegas NV	All American Park	702-317-7777	121 E Sunset Road
Las Vegas NV	Barkin' Basin Park	702-229-6297	Alexander Road and Tenaya Way
Las Vegas NV	Centennial Hills	702-229-6297	Buffalo Drive and Elkhorn Road
Las Vegas NV	Charlie Kellogg and Joe Zaher Sports Complex	702-229-6297	7901 W Washington Avenue
Las Vegas NV	Childrens Memorial Park	702-229-6718	6601 W Gowan Road
Las Vegas NV	Desert Breeze Dog Run		8425 W. Spring Mtn. Road
Las Vegas NV	Desert Inn Dog Park	702-455-8200	3570 Vista del Monte
Las Vegas NV	Dog Fancier's Park	702-455-8200	5800 E. Flamingo Rd.
Las Vegas NV	Justice Myron E. Leavitt Family Park (formerly known as Jaycee Park)	702-229-6718	E St Louis Avenue and Eastern Avenue
Las Vegas NV	Lorenzi Park	702-229-4867	3075 W Washington Avenue
Las Vegas NV	Molasky Park Dog Run	702-455-8200	1065 E. Twain Ave
Las Vegas NV	Police Memorial Park	702-229-6297	Cheyenne Avenue and Metro Academy Way
Las Vegas NV	Shadow Rock Dog Run	702-455-8200	2650 Los Feliz on Sunrise Mountain
Las Vegas NV	Silverado Ranch Park Dog Park	702-455-8200	9855 S. Gillespie
Las Vegas NV	Sunset Park Dog Run	702-455-8200	2601 E. Sunset Rd
Las Vegas NV	Woofter Park	702-633-1171	Rock Springs and Vegas Drive
Reno NV	Link Piazzo Dog Park	775-823-6501	4740 Parkway Drive
Reno NV	Rancho San Rafael Regional Park	775-785-4512	1595 North Sierra Street
Reno NV	Sparks Marina Park	775-353-2376	300 Howard Drive
Reno NV	Virginia Lake Dog Park	775-334-2099	Lakeside Drive
Reno NV	Whitaker Dog Park	775-334-2099	550 University Terrace

New Hampshire

Conway NH	Dog Park	603-447-3811	E Main Street
Derry NH	Town of Derry Dog Park	603-432-6100	45 Fordway
Portsmouth NH	Portsmouth Dog Park	603-431-2000	South Mill Pond

New Jersey

Barnegat Light NJ	Barnegat Light Dog Park/Beach	609-494-9196	W 10th Street
Bayonne NJ	Bayonne Dog Park	201-858-7181	1st Street at Kennedy Blvd
Bedminster NJ	Bedminster Dog Park	908-212-7014	River Road at Rt 206
Berkeley Township NJ	RJ Miller Airpark Dog Park	732-506-9090	Route 530
Cherry Hill NJ	Cooper River Dog Park	856-795-PARK	North Park Drive at Cuthbert Blvd
Cherry Hill NJ	Pooch Park (Cooper River Park)	856-225-5431	North Park Drive
Flemington NJ	The Hunterdon County Off-Leash Dog Area	908-782-1158	1020 State Route 31
Hamilton NJ	Veteran's Park Dog Park		Kuser Road
Hoboken NJ	Church Square Dog Run		4th and 5th, between Garden and Willow
Hoboken NJ	Elysian Park Dog Run		Hudson between 10th and 11th
Hoboken NJ	Stevens Park Dog Run		Hudson between 4th and 5th

Jersey City NJ	Van Vorst Dog Park	201-433-5127	Jersrey Avenue and Montgomery Street
Lakewood NJ	Ocean County Park Dog Park	732-506-9090	Route 88
Leonia NJ	Overpeck County Park Dog Run	201-336-7275	Fort Lee Road
Lincroft NJ	Thompson Park Dog Park	732-842-4000x4256	805 Newman Springs Road
Lyndhurst NJ	Riverside County Park Dog Run	201-336-7275	Riverside Ave
Medford NJ	Freedom Park Dog Park	609-654-2512	Union Street at Main Street
Millburn NJ	Essex County South Mountain Dog Park	973-268-3500	Crest Drive
North Bergen NJ	Hudson County Park Dog Park	201-915-1386	Bergenline Ave at 81st
Ocean City NJ	Cape May County Dog Park		45th Street and Haven Avenue
Oceanport NJ	Wolf Hill Off Leash Dog Park	732-229-7025	3 Crescent Place
Princeton NJ	Rocky Top Private Dog Park	732-297-6527	4106 Route 27
West Windsor NJ	Mercer County Park	609-448-1947	Old Trenton Road at Robbinsville Rd
Westfield NJ	Echo Lake Dog Park	908-527-4900	Rt 22
Woodcliff Lake NJ	Wood Dale County Park Dog Run	201-336-7275	Prospect Avenue

New Mexico

Albuquerque NM	Coronado Dog Park	505-768-1975	301 McKnight Ave. NW
Albuquerque NM	Los Altos Dog Park	505-768-1975	821 Eubank Blvd. NE
Albuquerque NM	Montessa Park Off-Leash Area	505-768-1975	3615 Los Picaros Rd SE
Albuquerque NM	Rio Grande Park Dog Park	505-873-6620	Iron Avenue
Albuquerque NM	Roosevelt Park Dog Park	505-873-6620	Hazeldine Avenue
Albuquerque NM	Santa Fe Village Dog Park	505-768-1975	5700 Bogart St. NW
Albuquerque NM	Tom Bolack Urban Forest Dog Park	505-873-6620	Haines Avenue
Albuquerque NM	USS Bullhead Dog Park	505-768-1975	1606 San Pedro SE
Rio Rancho NM	Rainbow Dog Park		Southern Blvd at Atlantic
Santa Fe NM	Frank Ortiz Park Off-Leash Area	505-955-2100	Camino Las Crucitas

New York

Albany NY	Department of General Services Off Lead Area	518-434-CITY	Erie Blvd
Albany NY	Hartman Road Dog Park	518-434-CITY	Hartman Road
Albany NY	Normanskill Farm Dog Park	518-434-CITY	Mill Road/Delaware Avenue
Albany NY	Westland Hills Dog Park	518-434-CITY	Anthony Street
Ballston Spa NY	Kelly Park Dog Run	518-885-9220	Ralph Street
Bronx NY	Ewen Park Dog Run	212-NEWYORK	Riverdale to Johnson Aves., South of West 232nd St.
Bronx NY	Frank S. Hackett Park Dog Run	212-NEWYORK	Riverdale Ave. and W. 254th Street
Bronx NY	Pelham Bay Park Dog Run	212-NEWYORK	Middletown Rd. & Stadium Ave., Northwest of Parking Lot
Bronx NY	Seton Park Dog Run	212-NEWYORK	West 232nd St. & Independence Ave.
Bronx NY	Van Cortlandt Park Dog Run	212-NEWYORK	West 251st Street & Broadway
Bronx NY	Williamsbridge Oval Dog Run	212-NEWYORK	3225 Reservoir Oval East
Brooklyn NY	Brooklyn Bridge Park Dog Run	212-NEWYORK	Adams Street and N/S Plymouth St
Brooklyn NY	Cooper Park Dog Run	212-NEWYORK	Olive St at Maspeth Ave
Brooklyn NY	DiMattina Park Dog Run	212-NEWYORK	Hicks, Coles and Woodhull Streets
Brooklyn NY	Dyker Beach Park Dog Run	212-NEWYORK	86th Street from 7th Ave to 14th Ave
Brooklyn NY	Hillside Park Dog Run	212-NEWYORK	Columbia Heights & Vine Street
Brooklyn NY	J J Byrne Memorial Park Dog Run	212-NEWYORK	3rd to 4th Streets between 4th & 5th Ave
Brooklyn NY	Manhattan Beach Dog Run	212-NEWYORK	East of Ocean Avenue, North Shore Rockaway inlet
Brooklyn NY	McCarren Park Dog Run	212-NEWYORK	Nassau Ave, Bayard,Leonard & N. 12th
Brooklyn NY	McGolrick Park Dog Run	212-NEWYORK	North Henry Street at Driggs Ave
Brooklyn NY	Owls Head Park Dog Run	212-NEWYORK	Shore Pkwy, Shore Rd, Colonial Rd, 68th Street
Brooklyn NY	Palmetto Playground Dog Run	212-NEWYORK	Atlantic Ave, Furman, Columbia, State St
Brooklyn NY	Prospect Park	212-NEWYORK	
Brooklyn NY	Seth Low Playground Dog Run	212-NEWYORK	Avenue P, Bay Parkway, W. 12th Street
Elmsford NY	Elmsford Dog Park		North Everts at Winthrop Avenue
Forest Park NY	Forest Park Dog Run	212-NEWYORK	Park Lane South & 85th Street
Huntington NY	West Hills County Park Dog Run	631-854-4423	Sweet Hollow Rd at Old Country Road
Jamesville NY	Jamesville Beach Park Off-Leash Area		South Street at Coye Rd
Lido Beach NY	Nickerson Beach Park Dog Run	516-571-7700	Merrick Road at Wantagh Avenue
Liverpool NY	Wegmans Good Dog Park		Route 370
Montebello NY	Kakiat Park Dog Park	845-364-2670	668 Haverstraw Road
Montgomery NY	The Dog Park	845-457-4900	Grove Street
New City NY	Kennedy Dells Dog Park	845-364-2670	355 North Main Street
New Rochelle NY	Ward Acres Park		Broadfield Rd at Quaker Ridge Road
New York NY	Carl Schurz Park Dog Run	212-NEWYORK	East End Ave.between 84th and 89th Street
New York NY	Central Park Off-Leash Hours and Areas	212-NEWYORK	
New York NY	Chelsea Waterside Park Dog Run	212-627-2020	22nd St and 11th Avenue
New York NY	Coleman Oval Park Dog Run	212-NEWYORK	Pike St at Monroe St
New York NY	DeWitt Clinton Park Dog Run	212-NEWYORK	Between 10th and 11th Ave at 52nd and 54th
New York NY	East River Esplanade Dog Run	212-NEWYORK	East River at East 60th Street
New York NY	Fish Bridge Park Dog Run	212-NEWYORK	Dover St., between Pearl & Water St.

New York NY	Fort Tryon Park Dog Run	212-NEWYORK	Margaret Corbin Drive, Washington Heights
New York NY	Highbridge Park Dog Run	212-NEWYORK	Amsterdam at Fort George Avenue
New York NY	Hudson River Park - Greenwich Village Dog Run	212-NEWYORK	Leroy Street at Pier 40
New York NY	Hudson River Park - North Chelsea Dog Run	212-NEWYORK	W 44th Street at Pier 84
New York NY	Inwood Hill Park Dog Run	212-NEWYORK	Dyckman St and Payson Ave
New York NY	J. Hood Wright Dog Run	212-NEWYORK	Fort Washington & Haven Aves., West 173rd St.
New York NY	Madison Square Park Dog Run	212-NEWYORK	Madison Ave. To 5th Ave. between East 23rd St. & East 26th St.
New York NY	Marcus Garvey Park Dog Run	212-NEWYORK	Madison Ave at East 120th Street
New York NY	Morningside Park Dog Run	212-NEWYORK	Morningside Avenue between 114th and 119th Streets
New York NY	Peter Detmold Park Dog Run	212-NEWYORK	West Side of FDR Drive between 49th and 51st
New York NY	Riverside Park Dog Runs	212-NEWYORK	Riverside Dr at W 72nd,87th, and 105th
New York NY	Robert Moses Park Dog Run	212-NEWYORK	41st Street and 1st Ave.
New York NY	Sirius Dog Run		Liberty St and South End Avenue
New York NY	St Nicholas Park Dog Run	212-NEWYORK	St Nicholas Ave at 135th Street
Central New York	Theodore Roosevelt Park Dog Run	212-NEWYORK	Central West and W 81st St.
New York NY	Thomas Jefferson Park Dog Run	212-NEWYORK	East 112th Street at FDR Drive
New York NY	Tompkins Square Park Dog Run	212-NEWYORK	1st Ave and Ave B between 7th and 10th
New York NY	Union Square Dog Run	212-NEWYORK	Union Square
New York NY	Washington Sq. Park Dog Run		Washington Sq. South
Ossining NY	Cedar Lane Dog Park	914-941-3189	235 Cedar Lane
Queens NY	Alley Pond Park Dog Run	212-NEWYORK	Alley Picnic Field Number 12
Queens NY	Cunningham Park Dog Run	212-NEWYORK	193rd Street between Aberdeen Road and Radnor Road
Queens NY	K-9 Dog Run in Forest Park	212-NEWYORK	Park Lane South at 85th Street
Queens NY	Little Bay Dog Run	212-NEWYORK	Cross Island Parkway between Clearview Expwy and Utopia Parkway
Queens NY	Murray Playground Dog Run	212-NEWYORK	21st Street & 45th Road on the SE side of park
Queens NY	Sherry Park Dog Run	212-NEWYORK	Queens Boulevard, 65 Place and the BQE
Queens NY	Underbridge Playground Dog Run	212-NEWYORK	64th Ave and 64th Road on Grand Central Parkway service road
Queens NY	Veteran's Grove Dog Run	212-NEWYORK	Judge & Whitney on the south side of the park
Queens NY	Windmuller Park Dog Run	212-NEWYORK	Woodside Ave., 54-56 Sts.
Rome NY	Bark Park	315-339-7656	500 Chestnut Street
Roslyn NY	Christopher Morley Park Dog Run	516-571-8113	Searingtown Road
Seaford NY	Cedar Creek Dog Run	516-571-7470	Merrick Road at Wantagh Avenue
Sleepy Hollow NY	Kingsland Point Park Dog Park	914-366-5104	Palmer Ave at Munroe Ave
Smithtown NY	Blydenburgh County Park Dog Park	631-854-4949	Veterans Memorial Highway
Staten Island NY	Silver Lake Park Dog Run	212-NEWYORK	Victory Blvd just within Silver Lake Park
Staten Island NY	Wolfe's Pond Park Dog Run	212-NEWYORK	End of Huguenot & Chester Avenues
Wantagh NY	Wantagh Park Dog Run	516-571-7460	Kings Road at Canal Place
White Plains NY	White Plains Bark Park	914-422-1336	Brockway Place at South Kensico Road

North Carolina

Charlotte NC	Barkingham Park Dog Park - Reedy Creek	704-336-3854	2900 Rocky River Rd.
Charlotte NC	Fetching Meadows Dog Park	704-336-3854	McAlpine Park
Gastonia NC	George Poston Park Dog Park	704-922-2162	1101 Lowell Spencer Mountain Road
Greensboro NC	Bark Park	336-545-5343	3905 Nathaneal Greene Drive
Raleigh NC	Carolina Pines	919-831-8113	2305 Lake Wheeler Road/H 1375
Raleigh NC	Millbrook Exchange Off Leash Dog Park	919-872-4156	1905 Spring Forest Road
Raleigh NC	Oakwood Dog Park		910 Brookside Drive
Southern Pines NC	Martin Off-Leash Dog Park	910-692-2463	350 Commerce Avenue
Wilmington NC	Wilmington Dog Park at Empie	910-341-3237	Independence Blvd at Park Avenue

North Dakota

Fargo ND	Village West Dog Park		45th Street
Grand Forks ND	Roaming Paws	218-779-5037	Lincoln Drive

Ohio

Cincinnati OH	Kellogg Park Dog Field	513-357-6629 ext. 1	6701 Kellogg Avenue/H 52
Cincinnati OH	Mt. Airy Forest Dog Park	513-352-4080	Westwood Northern Blvd.
Columbus OH	Big Walnut Dog Park	614-645-3300	5000 E Livingston Avenue
Delaware OH	Companion Club Dog Park	740-881-2000	6306 Home Road
Dublin OH	Nando's Dog Park		Cosgray and Shier Rings Road
Gahanna OH	Alum Creek Dog Park	614-342-4250	Hollenback Road
Gahanna OH	Pooch Playground	614-342-4250.	6547 Clark State Road

Grove City OH	Wagtail Trail	614-891-0700	Off Georgesville Wrightsville Road
Lewis Center OH	Alum Creek Dog Park		3992 Hollenback Road
Mason OH	Schappacher Park Dog Run	513-701-6958	4686 Old Irwin Simpson Road
West Chester OH	Wiggly Field	513-759-7304	8070 Tylersville Road
Weterville OH	Brooksedge Park Bark Park		708 Park Meadow Road
Xenia OH	Scout Burnell-Garbrecht Dog Park	937-562-7440	210 Fairground Road

Oklahoma

Del City OK	Wiggly Field		E Reno Avenue
Norman OK	Norman Community Dog Park		Robinson and 12th St NE
Oklahoma City OK	Paw Park	405-782-4311	Grand Blvd. and Lake Hefner Parkway
Tulsa OK	Biscuit Acres at Hunter Park	918-596-7275	5804 E 91 Street
Tulsa OK	Joe Station Bark Park		2279 Charles Page Blvd
Yukon OK	Pets and People Dog Park		701 Inla

Oregon

Ashland OR	The Dog Park	541-488-6002	Nevada and Helman Streets
Beaverton OR	Hazeldale Park Dog Park		Off 196th, N of Farmington
Bend OR	Awbrey Resevoir	541-388-5435	NW 10th and Trenton
Bend OR	Big Sky Dog Park	541-389-7275	21690 NE Neff Road
Bend OR	Hollinshead Community Park	541-388-5435	1235 NE Jones Road
Bend OR	Overturf Butte Reservoir	541-388-5435	Skyliner Summit Loop
Bend OR	Pine Nursery Community Park	541-388-5435	Yeoman Road
Bend OR	Ponderosa Community Park	541-388-5435	225 SE 15th Street
Bend OR	Riverbend Beach	541-388-5435	799 SW Columbia Street
Canby OR	Molalla River State Park Off-Leash Area	800-551-6949	Canby Ferry Road
Corvallis OR	Bald Hill Park Dog Park	541-766-6918	Oak Creek Drive
Corvallis OR	Chip Ross Park Dog Park	541-766-6918	Lester Avenue
Corvallis OR	Crystal Lake Sports Field Dog Park	541-766-6918	Crystal Lake Drive
Corvallis OR	Martin Luther King Jr Park Dog Park	541-766-6918	Walnut Boulevard
Corvallis OR	Williamette Park Dog Park	541-766-6918	SE Goodnight Avenue
Corvallis OR	Woodland Meadow Park Dog Park	541-766-6918	Circle and Witham Hill Drive
Estacada OR	Milo McIver State Park Off-Leash Area	503-630-7150	Springwater Road
Eugene OR	Alton Baker Park Off-Leash Area	541-682-4800	Leo Harris Parkway
Eugene OR	Amazon Park Off-Leash Area	541-682-4800	Amazon Parkway
Eugene OR	Candlelight Park Off-Leash Area	541-682-4800	Royal Avenue
Eugene OR	Morse Ranch Park Off-Leash Area	541-682-4800	595 Crest Drive
Medford OR	Bear Creek Park Dog Park	541-774-2400	Highland Drive
Milwaukie OR	North Clackamas Park	503-794-8002	5440 SE Kellog Ck Drive
Portland OR	Brentwood Park Dog Park	503-823-PLAY	60th Street and Duke
Portland OR	Chimney Dog Park	503-823-7529	9360 N. Columbia Blvd
Portland OR	East Delta Park Off-Leash Area	503-823-7529	N. Union Court
Portland OR	Gabriel Park and Off-Leash Area	503-823-7529	SW 45 Ave and Vermont
Portland OR	Normandale Off-Leash Dog Park	503-823-7529	NE 57th Ave at Halsey St
Portland OR	Portland's Unfenced Off-Leash Dog Areas	503-823-PLAY	Various
Portland OR	Rooster Rock State Park Off-Leash Area	503-695-2261	I-84
Portland OR	West Delta Park Off-Leash Area	503-823-7529	N. Expo Road & Broadacre
Salem OR	Minto-Brown Island Park	503-588-6336	2200 Minto Island Road
Salem OR	Orchard Heights Park	503-588-6336	1165 Orchard Heights Road NW
Tigard OR	Ash Street Dog Park	503-639-4171	12770 SW Ash Avenue
Tigard OR	Potso Dog Park	503-639-4171	Wall Street at Hunziker Street
Tigard OR	Summerlake Park Dog Park	503-639-4171	11450 SW Winterlake Drive
West Linn OR	Mary S. Young Dog Park	503-557-4700	Hwy 43
Wilsonville OR	Memorial Park Off-Leash Dog Park	503-682-3727	8100 SW Wilsonville Road

Pennsylvania

Conneaut Lake PA	Conneaut Lake Bark Park	814-382-2267	12810 Foust Road
Fort Washington PA	Mondaug Bark Park		1130 Camphill Road
Harrisburg PA	Lower Paxton Dog Park		Dowhower and Union Deposit Roads
Lancaster PA	Buchanon Park Dog Park		Buchanan Avenue and Race Avenue
Levittown PA	Falls Township Community Dog Park	215-949-9000 ext. 220 or 221	9125 Millcreek Road
Library PA	South Park Dog Park	412-350-7275	Corrigan Drive at South Park
McKeesport PA	White Oak Dog Park	412-350-7275	Route 48
Mechanicsburg PA	Lower Allen Dog Park	717-975-7575	4075 Lisburn Road
Monroeville PA	Heritage Dog Park	412-350-7275	2364 Saunders Station Road
Philadelphia PA	Chester Avenue Dog Park	215-748-3440	Chester Ave and 48th
Philadelphia PA	Eastern State Dog Pen		Corinthian Ave & Brown St
Philadelphia PA	Orianna Hill Dog Park	215-423-4516	North Orianna St, between Poplar and Wildey
Philadelphia PA	Pretzel Park Dog Run		Cresson St
Philadelphia PA	Schuylkill River Park Dog Run		25th St between Pine and Locust
Philadelphia PA	Segar Dog Park		11th Street between Lombard and South St.
Pittsburgh PA	Frick Park	412-255-2539	6750 Forbes Avenue
Pittsburgh PA	Hartwood Acres Off-Leash Park	412-767-9200	Middle Road

Pittsburgh PA	Upper Frick Dog Park		Beechwood and Nicholson
Washington Township PA	Howlabaloo Dog Park	814-734-1161	Lay Road
Wyncote PA	Curtis Dog Park		Church Road (H 73) and Greenwood Avenue
York PA	Canine Meadows		Mundis Race Road

Rhode Island

Barrington RI	Haines Park Dog Park	401-253-7482	Rt 103
Newport RI	Newport Dog Park	401-845-5800	Connell Highway
Providence RI	Gano Street Dog Park	401-785-9450	Gano Street and Power
Warwick RI	Warwick Dog Park	401-738-2000	Buttonwoods Avenue and Asylum Road

South Carolina

Charleston SC	Hampton Park Off-Leash Dog Park		corner of Rutledge and Grove
Charleston SC	James Island County Park Dog Park	843-795-PARK (7275)	871 Riverland Drive
Columbia SC	Sesqui Dog Park	803-788-2706	9564 Two Notch Rd
Greenville SC	Cleveland Park Dog Park	864-271-5333	Woodland Way
Greer SC	Six Wags of Greer K-9 Fun Park		3669 North Highway 14
Hilton Head SC	Best Friends Dog Park	843-785-7616	William Hilton Parkway/H 278
Hilton Head SC	Best Friends Dog Park		Off Hwy 40
Isle of Palms SC	Isle of Palms Dog Park	843-886-8294	29th Ave behind Rec Center
Mount Pleasant SC	Palmetto Islands County Park Dog Park	843-572- PARK (7275)	444 Needlerush Parkway
Myrtle Beach SC	Myrtle Beach Barc Parc	843-918-1000	Kings Hwy at Mallard Lake Drive
North Charleston SC	Wannamaker County Park Dog Park	843-572- PARK (7275)	8888 University Blvd

South Dakota

Sioux Falls SD	Lien Park Off-Leash Area	605-367-6076	North Cliff Avenue
Sioux Falls SD	Spencer Park Off-Leash Area		3501 South Cliff Avenue

Tennessee

Chattanooga TN	Ross's Landing and South Riverfront	423-643-6081	Ross's Landing Near the Pier
Knoxville TN	Dogwood Park @ Victor Ashe Park	865-215-1413	4901 Bradshaw Road
Knoxville TN	PetSafe Village Dog Park	865-777-DOGS (3647)	10427 Electric Avenue
Nashville TN	Centennial Dog Park	615-862-8400	31st Avenue and Park Plaza
Nashville TN	Edwin Warner Dog Park	615-862-8400	Vaughn Gap Road at Old Hickory Blvd
Nashville TN	Shelby Park	615-862-8400	South 20th and Shelby

Texas

Austin TX	Auditorium Shores Off-Leash Area	512-974-6700	920 W. Riverside Drive
Austin TX	Bull Creek District Off-Leash Area	512-974-6700	6701 Lakewood Drive
Austin TX	Emma Long Metro Park Off-Leash Area	512-974-6700	1600 City Park Rd.
Austin TX	Far West Off-Leash Area	512-974-6700	Far West at Great Northern Blvd
Austin TX	Northeast District Park Off-Leash Area	512-974-6700	5909 Crystalbrook Drive
Austin TX	Norwood Estate Off-Leash Area	512-974-6700	I-35 and Riverside Drive
Austin TX	Onion Creek District Park Off-Leash Area	512-974-6700	6900 Onion Creek Drive
Austin TX	Red Bud Isle Off-Leash Area	512-974-6700	3401 Red Bud Trail Unit Circle
Austin TX	Shoal Creek Greenbelt Off-Leash Area	512-974-6700	2600-2799 Lamar Blvd.
Austin TX	Walnut Creek District Off-Leash Area	512-974-6700	12138 North Lamar Blvd.
Austin TX	West Austin Park Off-Leash Area	512-974-6700	1317 W 10th Street
Austin TX	Zilker Off-Leash Area	512-974-6700	2100 Barton Springs Rd.
Baytown TX	Baytown Bark Park	713-865-4500	4334 Crosby Cedar Bayou Road
Dallas TX	Wagging Tail Dog Park.	214-670-4100	5841 Keller Springs Road
Dallas TX	White Rock Lake Dog Park	214-670-8895	8000 Mockingbird Lane
Denton TX	Wiggly Field at Lake Forest Park	940-349-8731	1400 E Ryan Road
Fort Worth TX	Fort Woof Off-Leash Dog Park	817-871-7638	3500 Gateway Park Drive
Grand Prairie TX	Central Bark		2222 W Warrior Trail
Grand Prairie TX	Paw Pals of Grand Prairie Dog Park		2222 W Warrior Trl
Houston TX	Ervan Chew Dog Park	713-845-1000	4502 Dunlavy
Houston TX	Maxey Park Dog Park		601 Maxey Road
Houston TX	Millie Bush Dog Park	713-755-6306	Westheimer Parkway
Houston TX	TC Jester Dog Park	713-865-4500	4201 TC Jester W
Houston TX	Tanglewood Bark Park	713-865-4500	Bering and Woodway
Leander TX	Devine Lake Off Lead Area	512-528-9909	1000 Maple Creek
Midland TX	Hogans Run Dog Park	432-685-7424	1201 E Wadley
N Richland Hills TX	Tipps Canine Hollow	817-427-6620	7804 Davis Boulevard
Pasadena TX	Bay Area Dog Park	713-865-4500	7500 Bay Area Blvd
Plano TX	Jack Carter Park Dog Park	972-941-7250	Pleasant Valley Drive
Round Rock TX	Round Rock Dog Depot (Dog Park)	512-218-5540	800 Deerfoot Drive
San Antonio TX	McAllister Dog Park	210-207-3000	13102 Jones-Maltsberger

San Antonio TX	Pearsall Park Dog Park	210-207-3000	4700 Old Pearsall Road

Utah

Salt Lake City UT	Herman Frank's Park		700 E 1300 S
Salt Lake City UT	Jordan Park	801-972-7800	1060 South 900 West
Salt Lake City UT	Lindsey Gardens	801-972-7800	9th Avenue and M Street
Salt Lake City UT	Memory Grove Park Off-Leash Park	801-972-7800	485 N. Canyon Road
Salt Lake City UT	Parley's Gulch	801-269-7499	2700 East Salt Lake City
Sandy UT	Sandy City Dog Park	801-568-2900	9980 South 300 East
South Ogden UT	South Ogden Dog Park		4150 South Palmer Drive
St George UT	J.C. Snow Park	435-627-4500	900 S 400 E
Taylorsville UT	Millrace Off-Leash Dog Park	801-963-5400	5400 South at 1100 West

Vermont

Burlington VT	Starr Farm Dog Park	802-864-0123	Starr Farm Rd
Burlington VT	Waterfront Dog Park	802-865-7247	near Moran Building
Hartford VT	Watson Upper Valley Dog Park	802-295-5036	H 14 W
Martinsville VT	SPCA of Henry County	276-638-PAWS (7297)	132 Joseph Martin H

Virginia

Alexandria VA	Ben Brenman Dog Park	703-838-4343	at Backlick Creek
Alexandria VA	Braddock Road Dog Run Area	703-838-4343	SE Corner of Braddock Rd and Commonwealth
Alexandria VA	Chambliss Street Dog Run Area	703-838-4343	Chambliss St
Alexandria VA	Chinquapin Park Dog Run Area	703-838-4343	Chinquapin Park East of Loop
Alexandria VA	Duke Street Dog Park	703-838-4343	5000 block of Duke Street
Alexandria VA	Fort Ward Park Offleash Dog Run	703-838-4343	East of Park Road
Alexandria VA	Fort Williams Dog Run Area	703-838-4343	Between Ft Wiliams and Ft Williams Parkway
Alexandria VA	Founders Park Dog Run Area	703-838-4343	Oronoco St and Union St
Alexandria VA	Hooff's Run Dog Run Area	703-838-4343	Commonwealth between Oak and Chapman St
Alexandria VA	Montgomery Park Dog Park	703-838-4343	Fairfax and 1st Streets
Alexandria VA	Monticello Park Dog Run Area	703-838-4343	Monticello Park
Alexandria VA	Simpson Stadium Dog Park	703-838-4343	Monroe Avenue
Alexandria VA	Tarleton Park Dog Run Area	703-838-4343	Old Mill Run west of Gordon St
Alexandria VA	W&OD Railroad Dog Run Area	703-838-4343	Raymond Avenue
Alexandria VA	Windmill Hill Park Dog Run Area	703-838-4343	Gibbon and Union Streets
Annandale VA	Mason District		6621 Columbia Pike
Arlington VA	Benjamin Banneker Park Dog Run		1600 Block North Sycamore
Arlington VA	Fort Barnard Dog Run		Corner of South Pollard St and South Walter Reed Drive
Arlington VA	Glencarlyn Park Dog Run		301 South Harrison St
Arlington VA	Madison Community Center Dog Park		3829 North Stafford St
Arlington VA	Shirlington Park Dog Run		2601 South Arlington Mill Drive
Arlington VA	Towers Park Dog Park		801 South Scott St
Charlottesville VA	Darden Towe Park	434-296-5844	1445 Darden Towe Park Road
Chesapeake VA	Chesapeake City Dog Park	757-382-6411	900 Greenbrier Parkway
Chesapeake VA	Western Branch Park	757-382-6411	4437 Portsmouth Blvd
Herndon VA	Chandon Dog Park		900 Palmer Drive
Norfolk VA	Brambleton Dog Park	757-441-2400	Booth Street and Malloy Ave
Norfolk VA	Cambridge Dog Park	757-441-2400	Cambridge Place and Cambridge Place
Norfolk VA	Dune Street Dog Park	757-441-2400	Dune St & Meadow Brook Lane
Oakton VA	Blake Lane Dog Park		10033 Blake Lane
Reston VA	Baron Cameron Dog Park		11300 Baron Cameron Avenue
Richmond VA	Barker Field	804-646-5733	South Boulevard
Richmond VA	Church Hill Dog Park	804-646-0954	2900 E Grace Street
Springfield VA	South Run Dog Park		7550 Reservation Drive
Virginia Beach VA	Red Wing Park Dog Park	757-437-2038	1398 General Booth Blvd.
Virginia Beach VA	Woodstock Park Dog Park	757-366-4538	5709 Providence Rd.

Washington

Bainbridge Island WA	Eagledale Park Off-Leash Dog Park	206-842-2306	5055 Rose Avenue NE
Ballard WA	Golden Gardens Park Dog Park	206-684-4075	8498 Seaview Place NW
Bellevue WA	Robinswood Off Leash Dog Corral	425-452-6881	2430 148th Ave SE
Bremerton WA	Bremerton Bark Park	360-473-5305	1199 Union Avenue
Burley WA	Bandix Dog Park		Bandix Road SE at Burley-Olalla Rd
Coupeville WA	Patmore Pit Off-Leash Area	360-321-4049	Patmore Rd At Keystone Hill Rd
Everett WA	Loganberry Lane Off-Leash Area	425-257-8300	18th Ave. W.
Everett WA	Lowell Park Off-Leash Area	425-257-8300	46th St at S 3rd Ave.
Federal Way WA	French Lake Dog Park	253-835-6901	31531 1st Ave S
Freeland WA	Marguerite Brons Dog Park	360-321-4049	WA 525 at Bayview Rd
Friday Harbor WA	Eddie and Friends Dog Park	360-378-4953	Mullis Street
Issaquah WA	Bark Park	425-507-1107	2702 Magnolia Street

Lakewood WA	Fort Steilacoom Park Off-Leash Area		8714 87th Avenue SW
Marysville WA	Strawberry Fields for Rover	360-651-0633	6102 152nd Street NE
Mercer Island WA	Luther Burbank Dog Park	206-236-3545	2040 84th Avenue SE
Oak Harbor WA	Clover Valley Dog Park	360-321-4049	Oak Harbor at Ault Field Rd
Oak Harbor WA	Oak Harbor Dog Park	360-321-4049	Technical Park at Goldie Rd
Port Orchard WA	Howe Farm Historic Park and Off-Leash Dog Area	360-337-5350	Long Lake Rd at Sedgwick Rd
Poulsbo WA	Raab Dog Park	360-779-9898	18349 Caldart Ave
Redmond WA	Marymoor Park Off-Leash Area	206-205-3661	6046 West Lake
Sammamish WA	Beaver Lake Park Off-Leash Area	425-295-0500	SE 24th Street at 244th Avenue SE
Seatac WA	Grandview Park Dog Park	425-881-0148	
Seattle WA	Genesee Park Dog Park	206-684-4075	46th Avenue S & S Genesee Street
Seattle WA	I-5 Colonnade Dog Park	206-684-4075	E. Howe Street at Lakeview Blvd
Seattle WA	I-90 "Blue Dog Pond" Off-Leash Area	206-684-4075	S Massachusetts
Seattle WA	Jose Rizal Park Off-Leash Area	206-684-4075	1008 12th Avenue S
Seattle WA	Northacres Park Off-Leash Area	206-684-4075	North 130th Street
Seattle WA	Plymouth Pillars Dog Park	206-684-4075	Boren Avenue at Pike Street
Seattle WA	Regrade Park Off-Leash Area	206-684-4075	2251 3rd Avenue
Seattle WA	Sand Point Magnuson Park Dog Off-Leash Area	206-684-4946	7400 Sand Point Way NE
Seattle WA	Westcrest Park	206-684-4075	8806 8th Avenue SW
Seattle WA	Woodland Park Off-Leash Area	206-684-4075	W Green Lake Way N
Spokane WA	SCRAPS Dog Park	509-477-2532	26715 E Spokane Bridge Rd
Tacoma WA	Rogers Park Off-Leash Dog Park	253-305-1060	E L St At E Wright Ave
Vancouver WA	Pacific Community Park Dog Park	360-619-1123	NE 18th Street between NE 164th and 172nd Avenues
Vancouver WA	Ross Off-Leash Rec Area	360-619-1111	NE Ross St at NE 18th St

Wisconsin

Brookfield WI	Brookfield Dog Park		River Rd
Cross Plains WI	Indian Lake Pet Exercise Area	608-266-4711	Hwy 19
Eau Claire WI	Eau Claire Dog Park	715-839-4923	4503 House Rd
Grafton WI	Muttland Meadows Dog Park		789 Green Bay Road
Green Bay WI	Brown County Park Pet Exercise Area	920-448-4466	Highway 54
Janesville WI	Palmer Park Pet Exercise Area		Palmer Park
Janesville WI	Rock River Parkway Pet Exercise Area		Rock River Parkway
Johnson Creek WI	Jefferson County Dog Park		Hwy 26
Madison WI	Brittingham Park Dog Park	608-266-4711	401 West Shore Dr
Madison WI	Quann Park Dog Park	608-266-4711	1802 Expo Drive
Madison WI	Sycamore Park Dog Park	608-266-4711	4517 Sycamore Park
Madison WI	Token Creek Park Pet Exercise Area	608-266-4711	Hwy 51
Madison WI	Warner Park Dog Park	608-266-4711	Sheridan Drive
Madison WI	Yahara Heights Pet Exercise Area	608-266-4711	5428 State Highway 113
Mequon WI	Katherin Kearny Carpenter Dog Run		N Katherine Dr
Middleton WI	Middleton Pet Exercise Area	608-266-4711	County Highway Q S of Hwy K
Milton WI	Milton Dog Park	608-868-6900	Elm and West High Streets
Milwaukee WI	Runway Dog Exercise Area		1214 E Rawson Ave
Oshkosh WI	Winnebago County Community Park Dog Park	920-232-1960	501 East County Road Y
Portage WI	Standings Rock Park Dog Exercise Area	715-346-1433	Standing Rocks Road
Stoughton WI	Viking Park Pet Exercise Area	608-266-4711	Highway N
Sun Prairie WI	Sun Praire Pet Exercise Area	608-266-4711	S. Bird Street
Tomahawk WI	Tomahawk Dog Park		SARA Park
Verona WI	Praire Moraine Parkway Pet Exercise Area	608-266-4711	County Hwy PB
Waupaca WI	Waupaca County Dog Park	715-258-6243	Hwy K
Wausau WI	Dog Exercise Area	715-261-1550	Stewart Avenue (H 52) and 17th Avenue
Weston WI	The Village of Weston Dog Park	715-359-9988	6100 Rogan Lane

Canada

Alberta

Acadia AB	Acadia Off-Leash Areas	403-268-2489	Various
Altadore AB	Altadore Off-Leash Areas	403-268-2489	Various
Bankview AB	Bankview Off-Leash Areas	403-268-2489	Various
Beaverdam AB	Beaverdam Off-Leash Areas	403-268-2489	Various
Beddington Heights AB	Beddington Heights Off-Leash Areas	403-268-2489	Various
Belgravia AB	Belgravia Off-Leash Area	780-496-1475	Saskatchewan Dr at University Ave
Bowness AB	Bowness Off-Leash Areas	403-268-2489	Various
Braeside AB	Braeside Off-Leash Areas	403-268-2489	Various
Brentwood AB	Brentwood Off-Leash Areas	403-268-2489	Various
Briar Hill AB	Briar Hill Off-Leash Areas	403-268-2489	Various
Bridgeland AB	Bridgeland Off-Leash Areas	403-268-2489	Various
Britannia AB	Britannia Off-Leash Areas	403-268-2489	Various

Calgary AB	Bowmont Park Home Road Off-Leash Area	403-268-2489	Home Road at 52 St NW
Calgary AB	Bowmont Park Silver Springs Gate Area	403-268-2489	SilverView Dr and SilverView Way NW
Callingwood North AB	West Jasper Place Park Off-Leash Area	780-496-1475	69 Ave at 172 St
Cambrian Heights AB	Cambrian Heights Off-Leash Areas	403-268-2489	Various
Coach Hill AB	Coach Hill Off-Leash Areas	403-268-2489	Various
Collingwood AB	Collingwood Off-Leash Areas	403-268-2489	Various
Crescent Heights AB	Crescent Heights Off-Leash Areas	403-268-2489	Various
Cromdale AB	Cromdale Off-Leash Area	780-496-1475	Kinnard Ravine at 78 St.
Deer Ridge AB	Deer Ridge Off-Leash Areas	403-268-2489	Various
Diamond Cove AB	Diamond Cove Off-Leash Areas	403-268-2489	Various
Dunluce AB	Orval Allen Park Off-Leash Area	780-496-1475	127 St South of 162 Ave
Eagleridge AB	Eagleridge Off-Leash Areas	403-268-2489	Various
East Village AB	East Village Off-Leash Areas	403-268-2489	Various
Edgemont AB	Edgemont Off-Leash Areas	403-268-2489	Various
Edmonton AB	Buena Vista Great Meadow Off-Leash Area	780-496-1475	Buena Vista Dr and Valleyview Cres NW
Edmonton AB	Jackie Parker Park Off-Leash Area	780-496-1475	Whitemud Dr and 50 St.
Elbow Park AB	Elbow Park Off-Leash Areas	403-268-2489	Various
Elboya AB	Elboya Off-Leash Areas	403-268-2489	Various
Fairview AB	Fairview Off-Leash Areas	403-268-2489	Various
Falconridge AB	Falconridge Off-Leash Areas	403-268-2489	Various
Forest Lawn Industrial AB	Forest Lawn Off-Leash Areas	403-268-2489	Various
Glenbrook AB	Glenbrook Off-Leash Areas	403-268-2489	Various
Greenview AB	Greenview Off-Leash Areas	403-268-2489	Various
Hawkwood AB	Hawkwood Off-Leash Areas	403-268-2489	Various
Haysboro AB	Haysboro Off-Leash Areas	403-268-2489	Various
Hidden Valley AB	Hidden Valley Off-Leash Areas	403-268-2489	Various
Huntington Hills AB	Huntington Hills Off-Leash Areas	403-268-2489	Various
Inglewood AB	Inglewood Off-Leash Areas	403-268-2489	Various
Lake Bonavista AB	Lake Bonavista Off-Leash Areas	403-268-2489	Various
Lakeview AB	Lakeview Off-Leash Areas	403-268-2489	Various
Lauderdale AB	Grand Trunk Park Off-Leash Area	780-496-1475	127 Ave at 109 St
Lynnwood Ridge AB	Lynnwood Ridge Off-Leash Areas	403-268-2489	Various
Mapleridge AB	Mapleridge Off-Leash Areas	403-268-2489	Various
Marlborough AB	Marlborough Off-Leash Areas	403-268-2489	Various
Martindale AB	Martindale Off-Leash Areas	403-268-2489	Various
Mayland Heights AB	Mayland Heights Off-Leash Areas	403-268-2489	Various
North Haven AB	North Haven Off-Leash Areas	403-268-2489	Various
Ogden AB	Ogden Off-Leash Areas	403-268-2489	Various
Parkland AB	Parkland Off-Leash Areas	403-268-2489	Various
Pineridge AB	Pineridge Off-Leash Areas	403-268-2489	Various
Pumphill AB	Pumphill Off-Leash Areas	403-268-2489	Various
Queensland AB	Queensland Off-Leash Areas	403-268-2489	Various
Ramsay AB	Ramsay Off-Leash Areas	403-268-2489	Various
Ranchlands AB	Ranchlands Off-Leash Areas	403-268-2489	Various
Renfrew AB	Renfrew Off-Leash Areas	403-268-2489	Various
Riverbend AB	Riverbend Off-Leash Areas	403-268-2489	Various
Riverdale AB	Riverdale Off-Leash Areas	403-268-2489	Various
Rosedale AB	Rosedale Off-Leash Areas	403-268-2489	Various
Roxboro AB	Roxboro Off-Leash Areas	403-268-2489	Various
Rundle AB	Rundle Off-Leash Areas	403-268-2489	Various
Sandstone AB	Sandstone Off-Leash Areas	403-268-2489	Various
Scarboro AB	Scarboro Off-Leash Areas	403-268-2489	Various
Scenic Acres AB	Scenic Acres Off-Leash Areas	403-268-2489	Various
Shaganappi AB	Shaganappi Off-Leash Areas	403-268-2489	Various
Southwood AB	Southwood Off-Leash Areas	403-268-2489	Various
Spruce Cliff AB	Spruce Cliff Off-Leash Areas	403-268-2489	Various
Strathcona AB	Strathcona Off-Leash Areas	403-268-2489	Various
Sunalta AB	Sunalta Off-Leash Areas	403-268-2489	Various
Thorncliffe AB	Thorncliffe Off-Leash Areas	403-268-2489	Various
Varsity AB	Varsity Off-Leash Areas	403-268-2489	Various
Wellington AB	Wellington Off-Leash Area	780-496-1475	West of 141 St from 137 Ave to 132 Ave
Willowpark AB	Willowpark Off-Leash Areas	403-268-2489	Various
Woodbine AB	Woodbine Off-Leash Areas	403-268-2489	Various

British Columbia

Burnaby BC	Confederation Park Off-Leash Area	604-294-7450	Willingdon Avenue
South Burnaby BC	Burnaby Fraser Foreshore Park Off-Leash Area	604-294-7450	Byrne Road
Vancouver BC	37th and Oak Park Off-Leash Dog Park	604-257-8689	West 37th Avenue at Oak Street
Vancouver BC	Balaclava Park Off-Leash Dog Park	604-257-8689	4594 Balaclava Street
Vancouver BC	Charleston Park Off-Leash Dog Park	604-257-8400	999 Charleson Street
Vancouver BC	Cooper's Park Off-Leash Dog Park	604-257-8400	1020 Marinaside Crescent
Vancouver BC	Dusty Greenwell Park Off-Leash Dog Park	604-257-8613	2799 Wall Street
Vancouver BC	Falaise Park Off-Leash Dog Park	604-257-8613	3434 Falaise Avenue
Vancouver BC	Fraserview Golf Course Off-Leash Dog Park	604-257-8613	8101 Kerr Street
Vancouver BC	George Park Off-Leash Dog Park	604-257-8689	500 E 63rd Avenue
Vancouver BC	Jones Park Off-Leash Dog Park	604-257-8613	5350 Commercial Street
Vancouver BC	Killarney Park Off-Leash Dog Park	604-257-8613	6205 Kerr Street
Vancouver BC	Kingcrest Park Off-Leash Dog Park	604-257-8613	4150 Knight Street

Off-Leash Dog Parks - Please always call ahead to verify rules, policies and hours.

Vancouver BC	Locarno Park Off-Leash Dog Park	604-257-8689	NW Marine Drive and Trimble Street
Vancouver BC	Musqueam Park Off-Leash Dog Park	604-257-8689	4000 SW Marine Drive
Vancouver BC	Nat Bailey Stadium Off-Leash Dog Park	604-257-8689	4601 Ontario Street
Vancouver BC	Nelson Park Off-Leash Dog Park	604-257-8400	1030 Bute Street
Vancouver BC	Queen Elizabeth Park Off-Leash Dog Park	604-257-8689	4600 Cambie Street
Vancouver BC	Quilchena Park Off-Leash Dog Park	604-257-8689	4590 Magnolia Street
Vancouver BC	Sparwood Park Off-Leash Dog Park	604-257-8613	6998 Arlington Street
Vancouver BC	Stanley Park Dog Park for Small Dogs Only	604-257-8400	Stanley Park Shuffleboard Court Area
Vancouver BC	Strathcona Park Off-Leash Dog Park	604-257-8613	857 Malkin Avenue
Vancouver BC	Sunrise Park Off-Leash Dog Park	604-257-8613	1950 Windermere Street
Vancouver BC	Sunset Park Off-Leash Dog Park	604-257-8689	300 E 53rd Avenue
Vancouver BC	Tecumseh Park Off-Leash Dog Park	604-257-8613	1751 E 45th Avenue
Vancouver BC	Valdez Park	604-257-8689	3210 W 22nd Avenue
Victoria BC	Alexander Park Off-Leash Area	250-361-0600	
Victoria BC	Arbutus Park Off-Leash Area	250-361-0600	Washington Street
Victoria BC	Oswald Park Off-Leash Area	250-361-0600	Stroud Rd at Gosworth Rd
Victoria BC	Redfern Park Off-Leash Area	250-361-0600	Redfern St at Leighton Ave
Victoria BC	Topaz Park Off-Leash Area	250-361-0600	Topaz at Blanshard
Victoria BC	Victoria West Park Off-Leash Area	250-361-0600	Wilson St at Bay St

Manitoba

Brandon MB	Paw Park	204-729-2150	Van Horne Avenue E and 11th Street E
Brandon MB	Pooch Park	204-729-2150	John Avenue, West of 18th Street N/H 10
Winnipeg MB	Bourkevale Park Off-Leash Area	204-986-7623	100 Ferry Rd
Winnipeg MB	Juba Park Off-Leash Area	204-986-7623	Bannatyne Ave at Ship St.
Winnipeg MB	Kilcona Park Off-Leash Area	204-986-7623	Lagimodiere Blvd at Springfield Road
Winnipeg MB	King's Bark Park Off-Leash Area	204-986-7623	King's Drive at Kilkenny Drive
Winnipeg MB	Little Mountain Park Off-Leash Area	204-986-7623	Klimpke Road at Farmers Rd
Winnipeg MB	Maple Grove Park Off-Leash Area	204-986-7623	190 Frobisher Road
Winnipeg MB	St. Boniface Industrial Park Off-Leash Area	204-986-7623	Mazenod Rd at Camile Sys
Winnipeg MB	Sturgeon Road Off-Leash Area	204-986-7623	Sturgeon Rd at Silver Avenue
Winnipeg MB	Westview Park Off-Leash Area	204-986-7623	Midland Street and Saskatchewan Avenue
Winnipeg MB	Woodsworth Park Off-Leash Area	204-986-7623	King Edward Ave at Park Lane

Nova Scotia

Halifax NS	Point Pleasant Park Off-Leash Area		Point Pleasant Dr at Tower Rd
Halifax NS	Seaview Park Off-Leash Area		North end of Barrington Street below the A.Murray MacKay Bridge

Ontario

Ancaster ON	Cinema Park	905-546-2424 ext. 2045	Golf Links Road
Dundas ON	Chegwin Park	905-546-2424 ext. 2045	Chegwin Road
Dundas ON	Little John Park	905-546-2424 ext. 2045	Lynden Avenue (behind Wentworth Lodge)
Dundas ON	Warren Park	905-546-2424 ext. 2045	Tally Ho Drive
Hamilton ON	Hamilton Dog Park	905-546-2424 ext. 2045	245 Dartnall Road
London ON	Greenway Off-Leash Dog Park		Springbank Dr at Greenside Ave
London ON	Pottersburg Dog Park		Hamilton Rd at Gore Rd
London ON	Stoney Creek Off-Leash Dog Park		Adelaide St N. at Windermere
Mississauga ON	Totoredaca Leash Free Park		2715 Meadowvale Blvd
Orillia ON	Clayt French Dog Park	705-325-1311	Atlantis Drive
Toronto ON	Dog Park - High Park	416-397-8186	1873 Bloor Street

Quebec

Lachine Borough PQ	Autoroute 20 at 55e Avenue Off-Leash Area	514-637-7587	Autoroute 20 at 55e Avenue
Lachine Borough PQ	Promendade du rail Off-Leash Area	514-637-7587	rue Victoria between 10e and 15e
Lachine Borough PQ	Rue Victoria and 28e Avenue Off-Leash Area	514-637-7587	Rue Victoria and 28e Avenue
Lachine Borough PQ	Rue Victoria and 40e Avenue Off-Leash Area	514-637-7587	Rue Victoria and 40e Avenue
Lachine Borough PQ	Rue des Erables Off-Leash Area	514-637-7587	Rue des Erables at Rue Emile-Pominville
Lachine Borough PQ	Stoney Point River Park Off-Leash Area	514-637-7587	Between 54e and 56e Avenues
Montreal PQ	Notre-Dame-de-Grace Park	514-637-7587	Girouard and Sherbrooke West
Westmount PQ	King George Park Off-Leash Area	514-989-5200	Cote St. Antoine and Murray

Saskatchewan

Saskatoon SK	Off Leash Dog Parks	306-975-2611	Various sites

Chapter 8

Emergency Veterinarians

Emergency Veterinarians - Please always call ahead to make sure an establishment is still open.

United States

Alabama

Auburn AL	Auburn University Critical Care Program	334-844-4690	College of Veterinary Medicine
Birmingham AL	Emergency and Specialty Animal Clinic	205-967-7389	2864 Acton Rd
Birmingham AL	Red Mountain Animal Clinic	205-326-8080	2148 Green Springs Highway
Huntsville AL	Animal Emergency Clinic of North Alabama	256-533-7600	2112 Memorial Pkwy SW
Mobile AL	Animal Emergency Clinic	251-476-2020	2811 Airport Blvd
Montgomery AL	Animal Emergency Clinic	334-264-5555	1231 Perry Hill Rd # C
Tuscaloosa AL	Indian Hills Animal Clinic	205-345-1231	200 Mcfarland Circle North

Alaska

Anchorage AK	Diamond Animal Hospital	907-562-8384	2545 E. Tudor Road
Anchorage AK	Pet Emergency Treatment	907-274-5636	2320 E. Dowling Rd
Cantwell AK	Cantwell Veterinary Services	907-768-2228	Denali Hy
Fairbanks AK	After Hours Veterinary Emergency Clinic	907-479-2700	8 Bonnie Ave
Homer AK	Homer Veterinary Clinic	907-235-8960	326 Woodside Avenue
Juneau AK	Southeast Alaska Animal Medical Center	907-789-7551	8231 Glacier Highway
Kenai AK	Kenai Veterinary Hospital	907-283-4148	10976 Kenai Spur Hwy
Seward AK	Seward Animal Clinic	907-224-5500	Mile 3 1/2 Seward Hwy
Sitka AK	Sitka Animal Hospital	907-747-7387	209 Jarvis St
Wasilla AK	All Creatures Veterinary Clinic	907-376-7930	4360 Snider Drive
Wasilla AK	Wasilla Veterinary Clinic	907-376-3993	

Arizona

Bullhead City AZ	Spirit Mountain Animal Hospital	928-758-3979	1670 E Lakeside Dr
Flagstaff AZ	Flagstaff Animal Hospital	928-779-4565	2308 E. Route 66
Flagstaff AZ	Westside Veterinary Clinic	928-779-0148	963 West Route 66 Suite 230
Gilbert AZ	Emergency Animal Clinic	480-497-0222	86 West Juniper Ave.
Kingman AZ	Kingman Animal Hospital	928-757-4011	1650 Northern Ave.
Kingman AZ	Stockton Hill Animal Hospital	928-757-7979	4335 Stockton Hill Rd
Page AZ	Page Animal Hospital	928-645-2816	87th South 7th Avenue
Peoria AZ	Emergency Animal Clinic	623-974-1520	9875 W. Peoria Ave.
Phoenix AZ	Emergency Animal Clinic	602-995-3757	2260 W. Glendale Ave.
Scottsdale AZ	Emergency Animal Clinic	480-949-8001	14202 N. Scottsdale Rd. #163
Sedona AZ	Oak Creek Small Animal Clinic	928-282-1195	3130 West Highway 89A
Sierra Vista AZ	New Frontier Animal Medical Center	520-459-0433	2045 Paseo San Luis
Tucson AZ	Southern Arizona Veterinary Specialty and Emergency Center	520-888-3177	141 East Fort Lowell Road
Tucson AZ	Southern Arizona Veterinary Specialty and Emergency Center	520-888-3177	7474 E Broadway Blvd
Willcox AZ	Willcox Veterinary Clinic	520-384-2761	889 N Taylor Rd
Window Rock AZ	Navajo Nation Veterinary Clinics		P.O. Box 4889
Yuma AZ	Desert Veterinary Clinic		995 South 5th Avenue

Arkansas

El Dorado AR	Ralson Animal Hospital	870-863-4194	3500 North Jefferson
Fort Smith AR	Fort Smith Animal Emergency Clinic	479-649-3100	4301 Regions Park Dr # 3
Hot Springs AR	Hot Springs Animal Hospital	501-623-2411	1533 Malvern Avenue
Hot Springs AR	Lake Hamilton Animal Hospital	501-767-8503	1525 Airport Road
Jonesboro AR	Vetcare	870-972-5320	619 W Parker Rd
Little Rock AR	Animal Emergency Clinic	501-224-3784	801 John Barrow Rd
Mountain Home AR	Spring Park Animal Hospital	870-425-6201	404 Highway 201 North
North Little Rock AR	Animal Emergency & Specialty Clinic	501-224-3784	8735 Sheltie Dr, Ste G
Springdale AR	Animal Emergency Clinic of Northwest Arkansas	479-927-0007	1110 Mathias Drive Suite E

California

Anaheim CA	Yorba Regional Animal Hospital	714-921-8700	8290 E. Crystal Drive
Arroyo Grande CA	Central Coast Pet Emergency Clinic	805-489-6573	1558 W Branch St
Bakersfield CA	Kern Animal Emergency Clinic	661-322-6019	4300 Easton Dr #1
Berkeley CA	Pet Emergency Treatment Service	510-548-6684	1048 University Ave
Big Bear City CA	Bear City Animal Hospital	909-585-7808	214 Big Bear Blvd W
Big Bear City CA	VCA Lakeside Animal Hospital	909-866-2021	42160 N Shore Dr
Bishop CA	Bishop Veterinary Hospital	760-873-5801	1650 N. Sierra Highway
Buellton CA	Valley Pet Emergency Clinic	805-688-2334	914 W Highway 246
Cameron Park CA	Mother Lode Pet Emergency Clinic	530-676-9044	4050 Durock Rd
Campbell CA	United Emergency Animal Clinic	408-371-6252	911 Dell Avenue

Carson City NV	Carson Tahoe Veterinary Hospital	775-883-8238	3389 S. Carson Street
Concord CA	Veterinary Emergency Clinic	925-798-2900	1410 Monument Blvd
Culver City CA	Affordable Emergency Clinic	310-397-4883	5558 Sepulveda Blvd
Davis CA	UC Davis Medical Teaching Hospital	530-752-1393	One Shields Avenue
Diamond Bar CA	East Valley Emergency Pet Clinic	909-861-5737	938 N Diamond Bar Blvd
El Monte CA	Emergency Pet Clinic	626-579-4550	3254 Santa Anita Ave
Escondido CA	Animal Urgent Care	760-738-9600	2430-A S. Escondido Blvd
Fair Oaks CA	Greenback Veterinary Hospital	916-725-1541	8311 Greenback Lane
Fremont CA	Ohlone Veterinary Emergency	510-657-6620	1618 Washington Blvd
Fresno CA	Veterinary Emergency Services	559-486-0520	1639 N Fresno St
Garden Grove CA	Orange County Emergency Pet Hospital	714-537-3032	12750 Garden Grove Blvd
Glendale CA	Animal Emergency Clinic	818-247-3973	831 Milford St
Granada Hills CA	Affordable Animal Emergency Clinic	818-363-8143	16907 San Fernando Mission
Grand Terrace CA	Animal Emergency Clinic	909-783-1300	12022 La Crosse Ave
Lancaster CA	Animal Emergency Clinic	661-723-3959	1055 W Avenue M #101
Long Beach CA	Evening Pet Clinic	562-422-1223	6803 Cherry Ave
Los Angeles CA	Animal Emergency Clinic	310-473-1561	1736 S Sepulveda Blvd #A
Los Angeles CA	Eagle Rock Emergency Pet Clinic	323-254-7382	4252 Eagle Rock Blvd
Mammoth Lakes CA	Alpen Veterinary Hospital	760-934-2291	217 Sierra Manor Rd
Mammoth Lakes CA	High Country Veterinary Hospital	760-934-3775	148 Mountain Blvd
Mission Viejo CA	Animal Urgent Care Clinic	949-364-6228	28085 Hillcrest
Modesto CA	Veterinary Medical Clinic	209-527-8844	1800 Prescott Rd
Montclair CA	Emergency Pet Clinic of Pomona	909-981-1051	8980 Benson Ave
Monterey CA	Monterey Peninsula - Salinas Emer. Vet	831-373-7374	2 Harris Court Suite A1
Norwalk CA	Crossroads Animal Emergency Hospital	562-863-2522	11057 Rosecrans Ave
Oakhurst CA	Hoof and Paw Veterinary Hospital	559-683-3313	41149 Highway 41
Oakhurst CA	Oakhurst Veterinary Hospital	559-683-2135	40799 Highway 41
Palo Alto CA	Emergency Veterinary Clinic	650-494-1461	3045 Middlefield Rd
Pasadena CA	Animal Emergency Clinic	626-564-0704	2121 E Foothill Blvd
Roseville CA	Pet Emergency Center	916-783-4655	1100 Atlantic St
Sacramento CA	Emergency Animal Clinic	916-362-3146	9700 Business Park Dr #404
Sacramento CA	Sacramento Emergency Vet Clinic	916-922-3425	2201 El Camino Ave
San Diego CA	Animal ER of San Diego	858-569-0600	5610 Kearny Mesa Rd
San Diego CA	Animal Emergency Clinic	858-748-7387	13240 Evening Creek Dr S
San Diego CA	Emergency Animal Clinic	619-299-2400	2317 Hotel Cir S # A
San Francisco CA	All Animals Emergency Hospital	415-566-0531	1333 9th Ave
San Jose CA	Emergency Animal Clinic	408-578-5622	5440 Thornwood Dr.
San Leandro CA	Alameda County Emergency Pet Hospital	510-352-6080	14790 Washington Ave
San Rafael CA	Pet Emergency & Specialty	415-456-7372	901 Francisco Blvd E
Santa Barbara CA	CARE Hospital	805-899-2273	301 E. Haley St.
Santa Cruz CA	Santa Cruz Veterinary	831-475-5400	2585 Soquel Dr
Sherman Oaks CA	Emergency Animal Clinic	818-788-7860	14302 Ventura Blvd
South Lake Tahoe CA	Avalanche Natural Health Office for Pets and Kennel	530-541-3551	964 Rubicon Trail
Stockton CA	Associated Veterinary Emergency Hospital	209-952-8387	3008 E Hammer Lane #115
Studio City CA	Animal Emergency Center	818-760-3882	11730 Ventura Blvd
Sun City CA	Menifee Valley Animal Clinic	951-672-8077	26900 Newport Rd # 105
Sun City CA	Sun City Veterinary Clinic	951-672-1802	27994 Bradley Rd # J
Temecula CA	Emergency Pet Clinic	909-695-5044	27443 Jefferson Ave
Thousand Oaks CA	Pet Emergency Clinic	805-492-2436	2967 N Moorpark Rd
Thousand Palms CA	Animal Emergency Clinic	760-343-3438	72374 Ramon Rd
Ventura CA	Pet Emergency Clinic	805-642-8562	2301 S Victoria Ave
Ventura CA	Veterinary Medical and Surgical Group	805-339-2290	2199 Sperry Avenue

Colorado

Arvada CO	Animal Urgent Care	303-420-7387	7851 Indiana St
Aspen CO	Aspen Animal Hospital	970-925-2611	301 Aabc
Boulder CO	Boulder Emergency Pet Clinic	303-440-7722	1658 30th Street
Colorado Springs CO	Animal Emergency Care Center	719-578-9300	3775 Airport Rd. and Academy Blvd.
Colorado Springs CO	Animal Emergency Care Center North	719-260-7141	5520 North Nevada Avenue #150
Durango CO	Durango Animal Hospital	970-247-3174	2461 Main Ave
Fort Collins CO	Fort Collins Veterinary Emergency Hospital	970-484-8080	816 S. Lemay Ave.
Grand Junction CO	Veterinary Emergency Center	970-255-1911	1660 North Ave
Lakewood CO	Access Animal Critical Care	303-239-1200	1597 Wadsworth Blvd
Pueblo CO	Animal Emergency Room	719-595-9495	225 E 4th St
Westminster CO	Northside Emergency Pet Clinic	303-252-7722	945 West 124th Avenue

Connecticut

Avon CT	Farmington Valley Veterinary Emergency Hospital	860-674-1886	9 Avonwood Rd
Bolton CT	East of the River Veterinary Emergency Clinic	860-646-6134	222 Boston Turnpike
Bridgeport CT	A-1 Emergency Animal Hospital	203-334-5548	2727 Main St
Danbury CT	Animal Emergency Clinic of Danbury	203-790-6383	22 Newtown Rd
New Haven CT	New Haven Central Hospital for Veterinary Medicine	203-865-0878	843 State Street
Oakdale CT	Veterinary Emergency Treatment Services	860-444-8870	8 Enterprise Lane

D.C.

Washington DC	Friendship Hospital for Animals	202-363-7300	4105 Brandywine St NW

Delaware

Dover DE	Delmarva Animal Emergency Center	302-697-0850	1482 E Lebanon Rd
Wilmington DE	Veterinary Emergency Center of Delaware	302-691-3647	1212 East Newport Pike

Florida

Boca Raton FL	Calusa Veterinary Center	561-999-3000	6900 Congress Avenue
Boynton Beach FL	PetPB Animal Emergency Center	561-752-3232	2246 North Congress Ave
Brandon FL	Animal Emergency Clinic of Brandon	813-684-3013	693 W. Lumsden Rd.
Casselberry FL	Veterinary Emergency Clinic	407-644-4449	195 Concord Drive
Cooper City FL	Animal Medical Center at Cooper City	954-432-5611	9410 Stirling Road
Delray Beach FL	Atlantic Animal Hospital Emergency Clinic	561-272-1552	10160 La Reina Dr.
Doral FL	Animal Emergency Clinic of Doral	305-598-1234	9589 NW 41st St
Fort Myers FL	Emergency Veterinary Clinic	239-939-5542	2045 Collier Avenue
Fort Pierce FL	Animal Emergency & Referral Center	772-466-3441	3984 SO. US 1
Gainesville FL	University of Florida Veterinary Medical Center	352-392-2235	2015 SW 16th Ave
Jacksonville FL	Animal ER	904-642-4357	3444 Southside Blvd, Suite 101
Jacksonville Beach FL	Emergency Pet Clinic	904-223-8000	14185 Beach Blvd
Key West FL	Animal Hospital - Olde Key West	305-296-5227	6150 2nd Street
Lakeland FL	Veterinary Emergency Clinic	863-665-3199	3609 Highway 98 South
Leesburg FL	Veterinary Emergency Clinic	352-728-4440	33040 Professional Drive
Melbourne FL	Animal Emergency & Critical Care Center	321-725-5365	2281 W Eau Gallie Blvd
Miami FL	Animal Emergency Clinic South	305-251-2096	8429 SW 132nd St
Miami FL	Emergency Animal Clinic	305-754-7000	570 NW 103RD St
Miami FL	Jonicer Emergency Animal Clinic	305-757-3030	570 NW 103rd St
Miami FL	Miami Emergency and Critical Center	305-598-0157	8601 SW 72nd St
Miami FL	Miami Pet Emergency	305-273-8100	114 NE 108th St
Naples FL	Emergency Pet Hospital of Collier County	239-263-8010	6530 Dudley Drive
Niceville FL	Emergency Veterinary Clinic	850-729-3335	212 Government Ave
Oakland Park FL	Animal Emergency Trauma Center	954-670-8823	2200 W Oakland Park Blvd
Ocala FL	Ocala Animal Emergency Hospital	352-840-0044	1815 NE Jacksonville Rd
Orange Park FL	Clay-Duval Pet Emergency Clinic	904-264-8281	275 Corporate Way
Orlando FL	Animal Emergency Center	407-273-3336	7313 Lake Underhill Rd
Orlando FL	Veterinary Emergency Clinic	407-438-4449	2080 Principal Row
Palm Harbor FL	Animal Emergency Hospital of Countryside	727-786-5755	30606 Us Highway 19 N
Pensacola FL	Veterinary Emergency Referral Center	850-477-3914	4800 N. Davis Highway
Sarasota FL	Sarasota Veterinary Emergency	941-923-7260	7519 S Tamiami Trl
St Augustine FL	Animal Emergency Hospital of St. Johns		2505 Old Moultrie Rd
St Augustine FL	Veterinary Emergency Service of St Johns County	904-824-1414	195 San Marco Ave
St Petersburg FL	Animal Emergency Clinic	727-323-1311	3165 22nd Ave N
Stuart FL	Pet Emergency & Critical Care	772-781-3302	2239 S Kanner Hwy
Tallahassee FL	Allied Veterinarians Emergency Hospital	850-222-0123	401 E 9th Ave
Tallahassee FL	Northwood Animal Hospital	850-385-8181	1818-B North Martin Luther King Blvd.
Tampa FL	Tampa Bay Veterinary Emergency Clinic		238 E Bears Ave
West Palm Beach FL	Pet Emergency of Palm Beach County	561-691-9999	3816 Northlake Blvd
Winter Haven FL	Veterinary Healthcare Associates	863-324-3340	3025 Dundee Rd

Georgia

Athens GA	University of Georgia Vet Teaching Hospital	706-542-3221	Carlton St at DW Brooks Dr
Atlanta GA	Georgia Veterinary Specialists	404-459-0903	455 Abernathy Rd NE
Augusta GA	Augusta Animal Emergency	706-733-7458	208 Hudson Trace
Columbus GA	Animal Emergency Center	706-324-6659	2507 Manchester Expressway
Decatur GA	Animal Emergency Center of Decatur	404-371-9774	217 N. McDonough Street
Gainesville GA	An-Emerg	770-534-2911	275 #3 Pearl Nix Pkwy
Macon GA	Animal Emergency Care	478-750-0911	2009 Mercer University Dr
Marietta GA	Cobb Emergency Veterinary Clinics	770-424-9157	http://www.decaturanimaler.com
Sandy Springs GA	Animal Emergency Center of Sandy Springs	404-252-7881	228 Sandy Springs Place, NE
Savannah GA	Savannah Regional Veterinary Emergency and Critical Care	912-355-6113	317 Eisenhower Dr
Savannah GA	Savannah Veterinary Emergency Clinic	912-355-6113	5509 Waters Ave
St Simons Island GA	Tyler Animal Hospital	912-342-4108	132 Airport Rd
Tucker GA	DeKalb Gwinnett Animal Emergency Clinic	770-491-0661	6430 Lawrenceville Hwy
Woodstock GA	Cherokee Emergency Veterinary Clinic	770-924-3720	7800 Highway 92

Hawaii

Hilo HI	East Hawaii Veterinary Center	808-959-2273	111 E.Puainako St. A-109

Emergency Veterinarians - Please always call ahead to make sure an establishment is still open.

Idaho

Idaho Falls ID	Idaho Falls Emergency Vet Clinic	208-552-0662	3120 S Woodruff Ave
Ketchum ID	Sun Valley Animal Center	208-726-7777	P.O. Box 177
Meridian ID	WestVet Emergency & Specialty Center		3085 E. Magic View Drive, Suite 110
Post Falls ID	North Idaho Pet Emergency Clinic	208-777-2707	2700 E Seltice Way
Twin Falls ID	Twin Falls Veterinary Clinic & Hospital	208-736-1727	2148 4th Avenue East

Illinois

Bloomington IL	Animal Emergency Clinic	309-665-5020	2505 E Oakland Avenue
Carbondale IL	Lakeside Veterinary Hospital	618-529-2236	2001 Sweets Dr.
Chicago IL	Chicago Veterinary Emergency Services	773-281-7110	3123 North Clybourn
Dolton IL	Dolton Veterinary Emergency Service	708-849-2608	15022 Lincoln Ave
Galena IL	Galena Square Veterinary Clinic	815-777-2592	984 James St
Lisle IL	Emergency Veterinary Service	630-960-2900	820 Ogden Ave
Mokena IL	Animal Emergency of Mokena	708-326-4800	19110 S. 88th Ave
Northbrook IL	Animal Emergency Referral Center	847-564-5775	1810 Skokie Blvd
Peoria IL	Tri-County Animal Emergency		1800 North Sterling
Rockford IL	Animal Emergency Clinic of Rockford	815-229-7791	4236 Maray Drive
Schaumburg IL	Animal Emergency Services	847-885-3344	1375 N. Roselle Road
Springfield IL	Animal Emergency Clinic	217-698-0870	1333 Wabash Ave

Indiana

Evansville IN	All Pet Emergency Clinic	812-422-3300	104 S Heidelbach Ave
Fort Wayne IN	Northeast Indiana Veterinary Emergency and Specialty Hospital	260-426-1062	5818 Maplecrest Road
Indianapolis IN	Animal Emergency Center	317-849-4925	8250 Bash St
Indianapolis IN	Indianapolis Veterinary Emergency Center	317-782-4418	5425 Victory Drive
Lafayette IN	Animal Emergency Clinic	765-449-2001	1343 Sagamore Pkwy N
Mishawaka IN	Animal Emergency Clinic	574-259-8387	2324 Grape Rd
Schererville IN	Calumet Emergency Vet Clinic	219-865-0970	216 W Lincoln Hwy
South Bend IN	Animal Emergency Clinic	574-272-9611	17903 State Rd 23
South Bend IN	Western Veterinary Clinic	574-234-3098	25190 SR 2
Terre Haute IN	Animal Emergency Clinic	812-242-2273	1238 S 3rd St

Iowa

Ames IA	Iowa State University Veterinary Teaching Hospital	515-294-1500	1600 S 16th St
Bettendorf IA	Animal Emergency Center	563-344-9599	1510 State Street
Cedar Rapids IA	Eastern Iowa Veterinary Specialty Center	319-841-5160	755 Capital Dr SW
Des Moines IA	Iowa Veterinary Specialties	515-280-3051	6110 Creston Avenue
Iowa City IA	Bright Eyes & Bushy Tails Veterinary Hospital	319-351-4256	3030 Northgate Dr

Kansas

Dodge City KS	Dodge City Veterinary Clinic		1920 E Trail Street
Goodland KS	Prairieland Animal Clinic		204 N Caldwell St
Lawrence KS	Clinton Parkway Animal Hospital	785-841-3131	4340 Clinton Parkway
Manhattan KS	Kansas State University Veterinary Hospital	785-532-5690	Kimball Ave at Denison Ave
Meriden KS	Meriden Animal Hospital	785-484-3358	7146 K-4 Hwy
Mission KS	Mission MedVet	913-722-5566	5914 Johnson Drive
Overland Park KS	Emergency Veterinary Clinic of Greater KC	913-649-5314	10333 Metcalf Ave
Overland Park KS	Veterinary Specialty and Emergency Center	913-642-9563	11950 West 110th Street
Russell KS	Town and Country Animal Hospital	785-483-2435	655 S Van Houten St
Salina KS	Animalcare ER		645 S Ohio St
Topeka KS	Emergency Animal Clinic	785-272-2926	839 SW Fairlawn Rd
Wichita KS	Emergency Veterinary Clinic	316-262-5321	727 S Washington St

Kentucky

Bowling Green KY	Snodgrass Veterinary Medical Center	270-781-5041	6000 Scottsville Road
Lexington KY	AA Small Animal Emergency Service	859-276-2505	200 Southland Drive
Louisville KY	Jefferson Animal Hospital	866-689-0233	4504 Outer Loop
Louisville KY	Louisville Veterinary	502-244-3036	12905 Shelbyville Rd Suite 3
Taylor Mill KY	OKI Veterinary Emergency and Critical Care	606-261-9900	5052 Old Taylor Mill Rd

Louisiana

Alexandria LA	Crossroads Animal Emergency	318-427-1292	5405 North Blvd
Baton Rouge LA	Animal Emergency Clinic	225-927-8800	7353 Jefferson Hwy
Baton Rouge LA	Baton Rouge Pet Emergency Hospital	225-925-5566	1514 Cottondale Dr
Baton Rouge LA	LSU Veterinary Teaching Hospital	225-578-9600	Skip Bertman Drive
Lafayette LA	Lafayette Animal Emergency Clinic	337-989-0992	206 Winchester Dr

Emergency Veterinarians - Please always call ahead to make sure an establishment is still open.

Lake Charles LA	Pet Emergency Clinic	337-562-0400	1501 W Mcneese St
Metairie LA	Animal Emergency Clinic	504-835-8508	1955 Veterans Memorial Blvd
Metairie LA	Southeast Veterinary Emergency Clinic	504-219-0444	400 N. Causeway Blvd
Shreveport LA	Animal Emergency Clinic	318-227-2345	2421 Line Ave
Terrytown LA	Westbank Pet Emergency Clinic	504-392-1932	1152 Terry Pkwy
West Monroe LA	Animal Emergency Clinic of NE Louisiana	318-410-0555	102 Downing Pines Rd

Maine

Arundel ME	York County Veterinary Emergency & Referral Center	207-284-9911	20 Hill Rd
Bar Harbor ME	Acadia Veterinary Hospital	207-288-5733	21 Federal St
Brewer ME	Eastern Maine Emergency Veterinary Clinic	207-989-6267	15 Dirigo Dr
Ellsworth ME	Ellsworth Veterinary Hospital	207-667-3437	381 State St
Lewiston ME	Animal Emergency Clinic-Mid Maine	207-777-1110	37 Strawberry Ave
Portland ME	Animal Emergency Clinic	207-878-3121	739 Warren Ave
South Thomaston ME	Harbor Road Veterinary Hospital	207-354-0266	626 Saint George Road

Maryland

Annapolis MD	Anne Arundel Veterinary Emergency Clinic	410-224-0331	808 Bestgate Rd
Baltimore MD	Eastern Animal Hospital	410-633-8808	6404 Eastern Ave
Baltimore MD	Falls Road Animal Hospital	410-825-9100	6314 Falls Road
Easton MD	Midshore Veterinary Service	410-820-9229	602 Dutchmans Lane
Frederick MD	Frederick Emergency Vet		434 Prospect Blvd
Glendale MD	Beltway Emergency Animal Hospital	301-464-3737	11660 Annapolis Rd
Hollywood MD	Three Notch Veterinary Hospital	301-373-8633	44215 Airport View Drive
Huntington MD	Allied Partners Veterinary Emer. Service	301-420-5240	4135 Old Town Road
LaVale MD	LaVale Veterinary Hospital	301-729-6084	913 National Highway
Ocean City MD	Ocean City Animal Hospital	410-213-1170	11843 Ocean Gateway
Rockville MD	Metropolitan Emergency Animal Clinic	301-770-5225	12106 Nebel St
Urbana MD	Greenbriar Veterinary Hospital	301-874-8880	3051 Thurston Road
Waldorf MD	Southern Maryland Veterinary Referral Service	301-638-0988	3485 Rockefeller Court

Massachusetts

Boston MA	Angell Animal Medical Center - Boston	617-522-7282	350 South Huntington Avenue
Edgartown MA	Vineyard Veterinary Clinic	508-627-5292	276 Edgartown Vineyard Hvn Rd
Nantucket MA	Angell Animal Medical Center - Nantucket	508-228-1491	21 Crooked Lane
North Andover MA	Essex County Veterinary Referral Hospital	978-725-5544	247 Chickering Road
Orleans MA	Animal Hospital of Orleans	508-255-1194	65 Finlay Road
Pittsfield MA	Animal ER (Pittsfield Veterinary Hospital)	413-997-3425	1634 West Housatonic St
South Deerfield MA	Veterinary Emergency & Specialty Hospital	413-665-4911	141 Greenfield Road
South Dennis MA	Cape Animal Referral and Emergency Center	508-398-7575	79 Theophilus Smith Rd
Springfield MA	Western Massachusetts Veterinary Emergency Service	413-783-0603	1235 Boston Rd
Swansea MA	Bay State Vet Emergency Services	508-379-1233	76 Baptist St
Walpole MA	Tufts Veterinary Emergency Treatment	508-668-5454	525 South Street
Waltham MA	Veterinary Specialty Center of New England	781-684-8387	180 Bear Hill Rd
West Bridgewater MA	New England Animal Medical Center	508-580-2515	595 West Center Street
Woburn MA	Massachusetts Veterinary Referral Hospital	781-932-5802	20 Cabot Road

Michigan

Ann Arbor MI	Animal Emergency Clinic	734-971-8774	4126 Packard Road
Carrollton Township MI	Great Lakes Pet Emergency Hospital	989-752-1960	1220 Tittabawassee Road
Detroit MI	Animal Emergency Room	313-255-2404	24429 Grand River Ave
East Lansing MI	Michigan State University Veterinary Teaching Hospital	517-353-5420	Wilson Rd at Bogue St
Flint MI	Animal Emergency Hospital of Flint	810-238-7557	1007 S. Ballenger Hwy.
Grand Rapids MI	Animal Emergency Hospital	616-361-9911	3260 Plainfield Av NE
Harbor Springs MI	Bay Pines Veterinary Clinic	231-347-1383	8769 M 119
Kalamazoo MI	Southwest Michigan Veterinary Referral Center	269-381-5228	3301 S. Burdick St.
Mackinac Island MI	Mackinac Island Veterinary Clinic	906-847-3737	1st MCKNC Is
Madison Heights MI	Veterinary Emergency Service East	248-547-4677	28223 John R
Marquette MI	Animal Medical Center of Marquette	906-226-7400	3145 Wright Street
Milford MI	Veterinary Care Specialists	248-684-0468	205 Rowe Road
Plymouth MI	Veterinary Emergency Service West	734-207-8500	40850 Ann Arbor Rd
Sault Ste Marie MI	Animal Kingdom Veterinary Clinic	906-635-1200	305 West 3 Mile Road
Sault Ste Marie MI	Sault Animal Hospital	906-635-5910	2067 Ashmun Street
Southgate MI	Affiliated Veterinary Emergency	734-284-1700	14085 Northline Rd
Traverse City MI	Companion Animal Hospital	231-935-1511	1885 Chartwell Drive

Minnesota

Albert Lea MN	Albert Lea Veterinary Clinic	507-373-8161	401 Saint Thomas Ave
Blaine MN	Midwest Veterinary Specialty Group	763-754-5000	11850 Aberdeen Street NE
Coon Rapids MN	Affiliated Emergency Veterinary Service	763-754-9434	1615 Coon Rapids Blvd
Duluth MN	Affiliated Emergency Veterinary Service	218-302-8000	2314 W. Michigan St.
Eden Prairie MN	Affiliated Emergency Veterinary Service	952-942-8272	7717 Flying Cloud Drive
Fergus Falls MN	Fergus Falls Animal Care Clinic	218-736-6961	112 N Cascade St
Golden Valley MN	Affiliated Emergency Veterinary Service	763-529-6560	4708 Highway 55
Jackson MN	Jackson Veterinary Clinic	507-847-2010	210 1st St
Kasson MN	K-M Regional Veterinary Hospital	507-634-8000	200 5TH ST SE
Luverne MN	Rock Veterinary Clinic	507-283-9524	1295 101st Street
Rochester MN	Affiliated Emergency Veterinary Service	507-424-3976	121 23rd Ave SW
St Cloud MN	Affiliated Emergency Veterinary Service	320-258-3481	4180 Thielman Ln

Mississippi

Biloxi MS	Gulf Coast Veterinary Emergency Hospital	228-392-7474	13095 Hwy 67
Gulfport MS	Gulfport Veterinary Hospital	228-865-0575	204 Pass Rd
Hattiesburg MS	Emergency Vets	601-450-3838	6335 US Highway 49 #40
Jackson MS	Animal Emergency Clinic	601-352-8383	607 Monroe Street
Meridian MS	Till-Newell Animal Hospital	601-485-8049	200 Highway 45 North
Tupelo MS	Tupelo Small Animal Hospital	662-840-0210	2096 South Thomas St

Missouri

Bridgeton MO	Animal Emergency Clinic	314-739-1500	12501 Natural Bridge Rd
Columbia MO	University of Missouri Veterinary Teaching Hospital	573-882-7821	379 East Campus Drive
Kansas City MO	Animal Emergency Center	816-455-5430	8141 N Oak Trfy
Lees Summit MO	Animal ER and Refer	816-554-4990	3495 NE Ralph Powell Rd
Springfield MO	Emergency Veterinary Clinic of Southwest Missouri	417-890-1600	400 S. Glenstone Ave.
St Louis MO	Animal Emergency Clinic	314-822-7600	9937 Big Bend Blvd
Wildwood MO	Veterinary Emergency Referral Center		16457 Village Plaza View Dr

Montana

Billings MT	Animal Clinic of Billings	406-252-9499	10th St.West & Ave. B
Billings MT	Granite Peak Veterinary Hospital	406-655-1122	Shilo at Grand Avenue
Bozeman MT	Animal Medical Center	406-587-2946	216 N. 8th Ave
Bozeman MT	Montana Veterinary Hospital	406-586-2019	6588 Tawny Brown Lane
Glendive MT	Dawson County Veterinary Clinic	406-377-6554	2210 W Towne St
Great Falls MT	Big Sky Animal Medical Center	406-761-8387	5101 North Star Boulevard
Missoula MT	Missoula Veterinary Clinic	406-251-2400	3701 Old US Highway 93
West Yellowstone MT	High West Veterinary Services	406-646-4410	201 S Canyon St

Nebraska

Alliance NE	Alliance Animal Clinic	308-762-4140	903 Flack Ave
Chadron NE	Panhandle Veterinary Clinic	308-432-2020	985 So. Hwy385
Grand Island NE	Stolley Park Veterinary Hospital	308-384-6272	3020 W. Stolley Park Road
Kearney NE	Cottonwood Veterinary Clinic	308-234-8118	5912 2nd Ave West
Lincoln NE	Belmont Veterinary Center	402-435-4947	2200 Cornhusker Hwy
Lincoln NE	Veterinary Emergency Services of Lincoln	402-489-6800	3700 South 9th Street
Norfolk NE	Companion Animal Veterinary Clinic	402-379-1200	1113 Riverside Boulevard
North Platte NE	America's Heartland Animal Center	308-532-4880	220 West Fremont Drive
Ogallala NE	Animal Clinic & Pharmacy	308-284-2182	105 W O St
Ogallala NE	Baltzell Veterinary Hospital	308-284-4313	1710 W 4th St
Omaha NE	Animal Emergency Clinic	402-504-1731	15791 W Dodge Rd
Omaha NE	Emergency Animal Clinic	402-339-6232	9664 Mockingbird Dr
Pine Bluffs WY	Bluffs Veterinary Clinic	307-245-9263	722 West 7th Street
Scottsbluff NE	Animal Health Center	308-635-0116	190624 Highway 26
Scottsbluff NE	Pioneer Animal Clinic	308-635-3188	1905 East 20th St
South Sioux City NE	South Sioux Animal Hospital	402-494-3844	301 West 29th St.
Valentine NE	Cherry County Veterinary Clinic	402-376-3750	604 E C St

Nevada

Bullhead City AZ	Spirit Mountain Animal Hospital	928-758-3979	1670 E Lakeside Dr
Carson City NV	Carson Tahoe Veterinary Hospital	775-883-8238	3389 S. Carson Street
Elko NV	Elko Veterinary Clinic	775-738-6116	1850 Lamoille Hwy
Ely NV	White Pine Veterinary Clinic	775-289-3459	159 MC Gill Hwy
Las Vegas NV	Animal Emergency Service	702-457-8050	1914 E Sahara Ave
Las Vegas NV	Las Vegas Animal Emergency Hospital	702-822-1045	5231 W. Charleston Boulevard
Mesquite NV	Virgin Valley Veterinary Hospital	702-346-4401	660 Hardy Way Suite #44
Reno NV	Animal Emergency Center	775-851-3600	6425 S Virginia St
Winnemucca NV	Keystone Veterinary Hospital	775-623-5100	1050 Grass Valley Rd

Emergency Veterinarians - Please always call ahead to make sure an establishment is still open.

New Hampshire

Brentwood NH	Veterinary Emergency & Surgery Hospital	603-642-9111	168 Crawley Falls Rd
Concord NH	Capital Area Veterinary Emergency Service	603-227-1199	22 Bridge Street
Littleton NH	Littleton Veterinary Clinic	603-444-0132	59 W Main St
Manchester NH	Veterinary Emergency Center of Manchester	603-666-6677	55 Carl Drive
Meredith NH	Winnipesaukee Veterinary Emergency Center	603-279-1117	8 Maple Street, Suite 2
North Conway NH	North Country Animal Hospital	603-356-5538	2237 West Side Road
Portsmouth NH	The Veterinary Emergency Center of NH	603-431-3600	15 Piscataqua Drive

New Jersey

Cape May NJ	Cape May Veterinary Hospital	609-884-1729	694 Petticoat Creek Lane
Fairfield NJ	Animal Emergency & Referral Associates	973-788-0500	1237 Bloomfield Ave
Forked River NJ	Veterinary Emergency Services	609-693-6900	720 Lacey Rd
Freehold NJ	Emergency Veterinary Care	732-845-0200	44 Thoreau Dr
Iselin NJ	Central Jersey Veterinary Emergency Services	732-283-3535	643 Lincoln Hwy
Linwood NJ	Red Bank Veterinary Hospital	609-926-5300	535 Maple Avenue
Lyndhurst NJ	New Jersey Veterinary Emergency Services	201-438-7122	724 Ridge Road
Mount Laurel NJ	Animal Emergency Service of South Jersey	856-727-1332	220 Moorestown - Mount Laurel Road
Newton NJ	Newton Veterinary Hospital	973-383-4321	116 Hampton House Road
Princeton NJ	Princeton Animal Hospital	609-951-0400	726 Alexander Rd
Tinton Falls NJ	Garden State Veterinary Specialists	732-922-0011	One Pine Street

New Mexico

Albuquerque NM	Veterinary Emergency & Specialty Center	505-884-3433	4000 Montgomery Blvd NE
Angel Fire NM	Angel Fire Small Animal Hospital	575-377-3165	3382 Mountain View Blvd
Carlsbad NM	Carlsbad Animal Clinic	575-887-3653	103 E Blodgett St
Deming NM	Deming Animal Clinic	505-546-2621	2117 Columbus Rd SE
Gallup NM	Red Rock Animal Hospital	505-722-2251	816 South Boardman
Las Cruces NM	Veterinary Emergency Services	505-527-8100	162 Wyatt Drive
Las Cruces NM	Veterinary Emergency Services	575-527-8100	1700 E Lohman Ave
Roswell NM	Country Club Animal Hospital	575-623-9191	301 W Country Club Rd
Santa Fe NM	Emergency Veterinary Clinic	505-984-0625	2001 Vivigen Way
Santa Fe NM	Emergency Veterinary Clinic of Santa Fe	505-984-0625	1311 Calle Nava
Socorro NM	Animal Haven Veterinary Clinic of Socorro		1433 Frontage Rd NW
Taos NM	Salazar Road Veterinary Clinic	575-758-9115	1025 Salazar Rd
Tucumcari NM	Tucumcari Animal Hospital	575-461-3900	101 N 10th St
Window Rock AZ	Navajo Nation Veterinary Clinics		P.O. Box 4889

New York

Amherst NY	Greater Buffalo Veterinary Emergency Clinic	716-839-4043	4949 Main St
Baldwinsville NY	Veterinary Emergency Center	315-638-3500	2115 Downer Street Rd
Briarcliff Manor NY	Animal Health Center		438 North state Rd.
Brooklyn NY	Veterinary Emergency & Referral Group	718-522-9400	318 Warren St
Commack NY	Animal Emergency Services	631-462-6044	6230 Jericho Tpke # C
East Syracuse NY	Veterinary Medical Center of Central NY	315-446-7933	5841 Bridge Street, Suite 200
Elmhurst NY	Elmhurst Animal Emergency Hospital	718-426-4444	8706 Queens Blvd
Farmingdale NY	Veterinary Emergency Service	631-249-2899	2233 Broadhollow Rd
Forest Hills NY	NYC Veterinary Specialists - Queens	718-263-0099	107-28 71st Road
Gansevoort NY	Northway Animal Emergency Clinic	518-761-2602	35 Fawn Road
Grand Island NY	Grand Island Small Animal Hospital	716-773-7646	2323 Whitehaven Rd
Ithaca NY	Cornell University Hospital for Animals	607-253-3060	Cornell Campus
Kingston NY	Animal Emergency Clinic of the Hudson Valley	845-336-0713	1112 Morton Blvd
Latham NY	Capital District Animal Emergency Clinic	518-785-1094	Rt. 2, 222 Troy-Schenectady Rd
Middletown NY	Orange County Animal Emergency Service	845-692-0260	517 Route 211 East
New York NY	Animal Medical Center - 24 hours	212-838-8100	510 East 62nd Street
New York NY	At Home Veterinary	646-688-3087	At Your Location
New York NY	NYC Veterinary Specialists	212-767-0099	410 West 55th Street
Orchard Park NY	Orchard Park Veterinary Medical Center	716-662-6660	3930 North Buffalo Road
Plainview NY	Long Island Veterinary Specialists	516-501-1700	163 South Service Rd
Poughkeepsie NY	Animal Emergency Clinic of the Hudson Valley	845-471-8242	84 Patrick Ln
Ray Brook NY	High Peaks Animal Hospital	518-891-4410	1087 Route 86
Rochester NY	Animal Emergency Service		825 White Spruce Blvd
Saranac Lake NY	Adirondack Park Pet Hospital	518-891-3260	25 Brandy Brook Avenue
Selden NY	Animal Emergency Services	631-698-2225	280-L Middle Country Rd.
Staten Island NY	Veterinary Emergency Center	718-720-4211	1293 Clove Road
Vestal NY	Vestal Veterinary Hospital	607-754-3933	2316 Vestal Parkway East
Westbury NY	Nassau Animal Emergency Group	516-333-6262	740 Old Country Road
Westmoreland NY	Rome Area Veterinary Emergency	315-853-2408	4769 State Route 233
Yonkers NY	Animal Specialty Center	914-457-4000	9 Odell Plaza

North Carolina

Asheville NC	Regional Emergency Animal Care Hospital	828-665-4399	677 Brevard Rd
Durham NC	Triangle Veterinary Emergency Clinic	919-489-0615	3319 Durham Chapel Hill Blvd
Fayetteville NC	Animal Urgent Care	910-864-2844	3635 Sycamore Dairy Rd
Greensboro NC	Happy Tails Emergency Veterinary Clinic	336-288-2688	2936 Battleground Avenue
Greenville NC	Pet Emergency Clinic of Pitt County	252-321-1521	2207-A Evans Street
Huntersville NC	Carolina Veterinary Specialists	704-932-1182	12117 Statesville Road
Jacksonville NC	Jacksonville Veterinary Hospital	910-455-3838	1200 Hargett St
Kannapolis NC	Cabarrus Emergency Veterinary Clinic	704-932-1182	1317 South Cannon Blvd
Kitty Hawk NC	Coastal Animal Hospital	252-261-3960	3616 N. Croatan Hwy
Matthews NC	Emergency Veterinary Clinic	704-844-6440	2440 Plantation Center Drive
Raleigh NC	After Hours Emergency Clinic	919-781-5145	409 Vick Ave
Raleigh NC	Quail Corners Animal Hospital	919-876-0739	1613 E Millbrook Rd
Wilmington NC	Animal Emergency Hospital of Wilmington	910-791-7387	5333 Oleander Dr
Wilson NC	East Carolina Veterinary Emergency Treatment Services	252-265-9920	4909-D Expressway Dr

North Dakota

Bismarck ND	Bismarck Animal Clinic & Hospital	701-222-8255	1414 E Calgary Ave
Bismarck ND	Pinehurst Veterinary Hospital	701-222-0551	755 Interstate Ave
Devils Lake ND	Lake Region Veterinary Service	701-662-3321	Highway 2 E
Dickinson ND	West Dakota Veterinary Clinic	701-483-0240	93 21st St E
Dickinson ND	Yost Veterinary Clinic	701-483-4863	1171 E Villard St
Fargo ND	Animal Health Clinic	701-237-9310	1441 South University Drive
Fargo ND	Red River Animal Emergency	701-478-9299	1401 Oak Manor Ave S # 2
Grand Forks ND	Kindness Animal Hospital	701-772-7289	4400 32nd Avenue
Jamestown ND	Prairie Veterinary Hospital	701-252-9470	1305 Business Loop E
Jamestown ND	Southwood Veterinary Clinic	701-252-3430	833 18th St SW
Minot ND	Minot Veterinary Clinic	701-852-4831	3010 Burdick Expy E
Williston ND	Kitterz Total Pet Veterinary	701-774-7979	308 26th St W
Williston ND	Western Veterinary Clinic	701-572-7878	# 85W, Highway 2

Ohio

Akron OH	Akron Veterinary Referral & Emergency Center	330-665-4996	1321 Centerview Circle
Bedford OH	Veterinary Referral Clinic & Emergency Center	216-831-6789	5035 Richmond Rd
Canton OH	Stark County Veterinary Emergency Clinic		2705 Fulton Dr NW
Cincinnati OH	CARE Center Emergency Vet	513-530-0911	6995 East Kemper Rd.
Cincinnati OH	Emergency Veterinary Clinic	513-561-0069	4779 Red Bank Rd
Cincinnati OH	Grady Veterinary Hospital	513-931-8675	9255 Winton Rd
Cleveland OH	Animal Emergency Clinic West	216-362-6000	5320 W 140th St
Columbus OH	Capital Veterinary Referral & Emergency Center	614-870-0480	5230 Renner Road
Columbus OH	Capital Veterinary Referral and Emergency Center	614-351-5290	3578 W Broad St
Columbus OH	Ohio State University Veterinary Hospital	614-292-3551	601 Vernon L. Tharp Street
Dayton OH	Centerville Veterinary Emergency Hospital	937-434-0260	6880 Loop Rd
Dayton OH	Dayton Emergency Veterinary Hospital	937-293-2714	2714 Springboro Rd West
Findlay OH	Findlay Animal Hospital	419-423-7232	2141 Bright Rd
Girard OH	After Hours Animal Emergency Clinic	330-530-8387	Placement on map is approximate
Logan OH	Hocking Hills Animal Clinic	740-380-7387	1978 E Front St
Lorain OH	Animal Emergency Center	440-240-1400	5152 Grove Ave
Mentor OH	Animal Emergency Clinic Northeast	440-255-0770	8250 Tyler Boulevard
Parkersburg WV	Animal Veterinary Emergency	304-428-8387	3602 E 7th St # B
Toledo OH	Animal Emergency & Critical	419-473-0328	2785 W Central Avenue
Westerville OH	Animal Care Clinic of Central Ohio	614-882-4728	25 Collegeview Rd
Worthington OH	Columbus Veterinary Emergency Service	614-846-5800	300 E. Wilson Bridge Rd

Oklahoma

Elk City OK	Circle M Animal Hospital	580-225-4321	1420 E Highway 66
Lawton OK	Midtown Animal Hospital	580-353-3438	1101 SW Park Ave
Moore OK	After Hours Emergency Pet Hospital	405-703-1741	9225 S Interstate 35 St
Norman OK	Animal Emergency Center of Norman	405-360-7828	2121 McKown Drive
Oklahoma City OK	Animal Emergency Center	405-631-7828	931 SW 74th Street
Oklahoma City OK	Neel Veterinary Hospital	405-947-8387	2700 N. MacArthur Blvd
Stillwater OK	Oklahoma State University Vet	405-744-8468	1 Bvmth
Tulsa OK	Animal Emergency Center	918-665-0508	7220 E 41st Street

Oregon

Albany OR	River's Edge Pet Medical Center	541-924-1700	202 NW Hickory Street

Emergency Veterinarians - Please always call ahead to make sure an establishment is still open.

Bend OR	Animal Emergency Center of Central Oregon	541-385-9110	1245 SE 3rd Street #C3
Clackamas OR	Northwest Veterinary Specialists	503-656-3999	16756 SE 82nd Drive
Corvallis OR	Williamette Veterinary Clinic	541-753-2223	1562 SW 3rd Street
Medford OR	Southern Oregon Veterinary Specialists	541-282-7711	3265 Biddle Road
Portland OR	Northwest Hospital	503-228-7281	1945 NW Pettygrove
Portland OR	Southeast Hospital	503-262-7194	10564 SE Washington Street #205
Portland OR	VCA Southeast Portland Animal Hospital	503-255-8139	13830 SE Stark Street
Salem OR	Salem Veterinary Emergency Clinic	503-588-8082	3215 Market Street NE
Springfield OR	Emergency Veterinary Hospital	541-746-0112	103 W. Q Street
Tualatin OR	Emergency Veterinary Clinic	503-691-7922	19314 SW Mohave Court

Pennsylvania

Erie PA	Northwest PA Pet Emergency Center	814-866-5920	429 West 38th Street
Lancaster PA	Pet Emergency Treatment Services	717-295-7387	930 North Queen Street
Langhorne PA	Veterinary Specialty and Emergency Center	215-750-7884	1900 W. Old Lincoln Hwy
Malvern PA	Veterinary Referral Center	610-647-2950	340 Lancaster Ave
Malvern PA	Veterinary Referral Center & Emergency Service	610-647-2950	340 Lancaster Ave
Mechanicsburg PA	Animal Emergency Medical Center	717-796-2334	11 Willow Mill Park Rd
Monroeville PA	Avets	412-373-4200	4224 Northern Pike
Philadelphia PA	Penn Veterinary Hospital (Ryan Veterinary Hospital)	215-746-8387	3800 Spruce St
Pittsburgh PA	Pittsburgh Veterinary Specialists	412-366-3400	807 Camp Horne Road
Pittston PA	Animal Emergency & Referral Hospital	570-655-3600	755 South Township Blvd.
Scotrun PA	Pocono Veterinary Emergency & Critical Care	570-620-1800	19 Scotrun Ave
Springfield PA	AAA Veterinary Emergency Hospital	610-328-1301	820 W Springfield Rd
State College PA	Mt Nittany Veterinary Hospital	814-237-4272	200 Elmwood St
Warrington PA	Bucks County Veterinary Emergency Trauma Services	215-918-2200	968 Easton Road
Watsontown PA	Animal Emergency Center	570-742-7400	395 Susquehanna Trl
Wexford PA	Bradford Hills Veterinary Hospital	724-935-5827	13055 Perry Highway
Whitehall PA	Valley Central Veterinary Referral Center		210 Fullerton Avenue
York PA	Animal Emergency Clinic	717-767-5355	1640 S Queen St

Rhode Island

Block Island RI	Block Island Veterinary Service	401-466-8500	Cooneymus Rd
East Greenwich RI	Ocean State Veterinary Specialists	401-886-6787	1480 South Country Trail
Middletown RI	Newport Animal Hospital	401-849-3400	333 Valley Rd
Warwick RI	Emergency Veterinary Service of Rhode Island	401-732-1811	205 Hallene Road

South Carolina

Columbia SC	South Carolina Veterinary Emergency Care	803-798-3837	3924 Fernandina Rd
Florence SC	VCA Pee Dee Animal Hospital	843-662-9223	815 2nd Loop Road
Greenville SC	Animal Emergency Clinic	864-232-1878	393 Woods Lake Road
Mount Pleasant SC	Veterinary Emergency Care	843-216-7554	930 Pine Hollow Rd
Myrtle Beach SC	Animal Emergency Hospital of The Strand	843-445-9797	303 Highway 15 Suite 1
North Charleston SC	Greater Charleston Emergency Veterinary Clinic	843-744-3372	3163 W Montague Ave
North Charleston SC	Veterinary Specialists of the Southeast	843-566-0023	3169 West Montague Avenue

South Dakota

Aberdeen SD	Animal Health Clinic	605-229-1691	704 S Melgaard Rd
Chamberlain SD	Mid River Veterinary Clinic	605-234-6562	1950 E King Ave
Fort Pierre SD	Oahe Veterinary Clinic	605-223-2562	118 E Missouri Ave #1
Hot Springs SD	Fall River Veterinary Clinic	605-745-3786	Fall River Road
Huron SD	Huron Veterinary Hospital	605-352-6063	340 4th St NW
Kadoka SD	Kadoka Veterinary Clinic	605-837-2436	1004 Main Street
Mitchell SD	Lakeview Veterinary Clinic	605-996-3242	2020 W Havens Ave
Mobridge SD	Oahe Veterinary Hospital	605-845-3634	721 20th St E
Pierre SD	Animal Clinic of Pierre	605-224-1075	118 E Missouri Ave #1
Rapid City SD	Dakota Hills Veterinary Clinic	605-342-7498	1571 Hwy 44
Rapid City SD	Emergency Veterinary Hospital	605-342-1368	1655 E 27th St
Rapid City SD	Noahs Ark Animal Hospital	605-343-3225	1315 Mount Rushmore
Sioux Falls SD	Dale Animal Hospital	605-371-3791	3642 Southeastern Ave
Sioux Falls SD	Veterinary Emergency Hospital	605-977-6200	3508 South Minnesota Avenue Suite 104
Sturgis SD	Sturgis Veterinary Hospital	605-347-4436	2421 Vanocker Canyon Rd
Wall SD	Golden Veterinary Service	605-279-2077	308 James Ave
Watertown SD	Howard Veterinary Clinic	605-882-4188	1400 N Highway 20

Tennessee

Alcoa TN	Midland Pet Emergency Center	865-982-1007	235 Calderwood St.
Blountville TN	Airport Pet Emergency Clinic	423-279-0574	2436 Highway 75
Brentwood TN	Pet Emergency Treatment Service	615-333-1212	1668 Mallory Lane
Chattanooga TN	River Vet Emergency Clinic		2132 Amnicola Hwy
Cordova TN	PetMed Emergency Center	901-624-9002	830 N. Germantown Parkway Suite 105
Jackson TN	Jackson Pet Emergency Center	731-660-4343	8 Yorkshire Cv
Knoxville TN	Pet Emergency Clinic	865-637-0114	1819 Ailor Ave
Livingston TN	Ragland and Riley Veterinary Hospital	931-498-3153	3207 Cookeville Hwy
Memphis TN	Animal Emergency Center	901-323-4563	3767 Summer Avenue
Murfreesboro TN	Animal Medical Center	615-867-757	234 River Rock Blvd
Nashville TN	Nashville Pet Emergency Clinic	615-383-2600	2000 12th Ave S
Talbott TN	Five Rivers Pet Emergency	423-581-9492	6057 W Andrew Johnson Hwy # 1

Texas

Amarillo TX	Small Animal Emergency Clinic	806-352-2277	4119 Business Park Dr
Arlington TX	I-20 Emergency Animal Clinic	817-478-9238	5820 W. Interstate 20
Austin TX	Austin Vet - Emergency	512-459-4336	4106 North Lamar Blvd
Austin TX	Emergency Animal Hospital - North	512-331-6121	12034 Research Blvd - Suite 8
Austin TX	Emergency Animal Hospital - South	512-899-0955	4434 Frontier Trail
Beaumont TX	Southeast Texas Animal Emergency Clinic	409-842-3239	3420 W Cardinal Dr
Carrollton TX	Emergency Pet Clinic of North Texas	972-323-1310	1712 W. Frankford Road Suite #108
Corpus Christi TX	Northwest Animal Emergency Center	361-242-3337	11027 Leopard St
El Paso TX	Animal Emergency Center	915-545-1148	2101 Texas Ave
El Paso TX	El Paso Animal Emergency Center	915-545-1148	1220 Airway Blvd
Euless TX	Animal Freeway Animal Emergency Clinic	817-571-2088	411 N Main St
Fort Stockton TX	Southwest Vet Clinic	432-336-7048	3010 W Dickinson Blvd
Fort Worth TX	Metro West Emergency Veterinary Center	817-731-3734	3201 Hulen Street
Grapevine TX	Animal Emergency Hospital		2340 W Southlake Blvd
Houston TX	Animal Emergency Center of West Houston	832-593-8387	4823 Highway 6 North
Houston TX	Animal Emergency Clinic	713-693-1100	1111 West Loop South Suite 200
Houston TX	Animal Emergency Clinic SH 249	281-890-8875	19311 SH 249
Houston TX	Veterinary Emergency Referral Group	713-932-9589	8921 Katy Freeway
Longview TX	East Texas Pet Emergency Clinic	903-759-8545	812 Gilmer Road
Lubbock TX	Small Animal Emergency Clinic	806-797-6483	5103 34th St # A
Odessa TX	Permian Basin Emergency Veterinary Clinic	432-561-8301	13528 W Highway 80 E
Richardson TX	Emergency Animal Clinic	972-479-9110	401 W. Pres Bush Tpke, Ste 113
Round Rock TX	Animal Emergency Clinic of Central Texas	512-671-6252	2000 N Mays St # 112
San Angelo TX	Animal Emergency Hospital	325-653-8781	59 E Avenue L
San Antonio TX	Animal Emergency Room	210-737-7380	4315 Fredericksburg Road #2
San Antonio TX	Emergency Pet Clinic	210-822-2873	8503 Broadway, Suite 105
San Antonio TX	I-10 Pet Emergency	210-691-0900	10822 Fredericksburg Road
Sonora TX	Sonora Animal Hospital	325-387-2481	300 N Service Rd
Vernon TX	Vernon Veterinary Clinic	940-552-5548	
Waco TX	Animal Emergency Clinic - Waco	254-753-0905	4900 Steinbeck Bend Dr
Wichita Falls TX	Colonial Park Veterinary Hospital	940-691-0261	4713 Taft Blvd

Utah

Cedar City UT	Color Country Animal Hospital	435-865-7264	390 N 4050 W
Cedar City UT	Southern Utah Animal Hospital	435-586-6216	1203 N Main St
Clearfield UT	Animal Emergency Center	801-776-8118	2465 N Main St # 5
Kanab UT	Kanab Veterinary Hospital	435-644-2400	484 S 100 E
Moab UT	Moab Veterinary Clinic	435-259-8710	4575 Spanish Valley Drive
Orem UT	Veterinary Emergency Services	801-426-8727	525 S State St
Park City UT	White Pine Veterinary Clinic	435-649-7182	2100 West Rasmussen Road
Salt Lake City UT	Central Valley Veterinary Hospital	801-487-1321	55 East Miller Avenue
Salt Lake City UT	Cottonwood Animal Hospital	801-278-3367	6360 Highland Dr
Sandy UT	Animal Emergency South	801-572-4357	10572 S 700 E
St George UT	Southwest Animal Emergency Clinic	435-627-2522	435 N 1680 E
Wendover UT	A Visiting Veterinarian	435-665-7704	479 E Wendover Blvd

Vermont

Middlesex VT	Onion River Animal Hospital	802-223-7765	36 Three Mile Bridge Road
Newbury VT	River Valley Veterinary Hospital	802-866-5922	3890 Route 5 North
Rutland VT	Rutland Veterinary Clinic	802-773-2779	90 E. Pittsford Road
Williston VT	Burlington Emergency Veterinary Service	802-863-2387	200 Commerce St

Virginia

Alexandria VA	Alexandria Animal Hospital and Veterinary Emergency Service	703-751-2022	2660 Duke Street
Ashburn VA	Emergency Vet	571-223-0811	20207 Birdsnest Pl
Charlottesville VA	Veterinary Emergency Treatment Service	434-973-3519	370 Greenbrier Drive Suite A-2
Chesapeake VA	Greenbrier Veterinary Emergency Clinic	757-366-9000	1100 Eden Way North, Suite 101B
Fairfax VA	Pender Veterinary Centre and Emergency Clinic	703-591-3304	4001 Legato Road
Fairfax VA	SouthPaws Veterinary Center	703-752-9100	8500 Arlington Blvd

Lawrenceville VA	Greensville Veterinary Clinic Emergency	434-848-2876	2024 Lawrenceville Plank Rd
Leesburg VA	Animal Emergency Hospital Leesburg	703-777-5755	165 Fort Evens Rd NE
Lynchburg VA	Animal Emergency & Critical Care	434-846-1504	3432 Odd Fellows Road
Manakin-Sabot VA	Veterinary Referral & Critical Care	804-784-8722	1596 Hockett Road
Manassas VA	Prince William Emergency Veterinary Clinic	703-361-8287	8610 Centreville Road
Midlothian VA	Veterinary Emergency Center South	804-353-9000	2460 Colony Crossing Place
Roanoke VA	Emergency Veterinary Service of Roanoke	540-563-8575	4902 Frontage Rd NW
Springfield VA	Springfield Emergency Pet Hospital	703-451-8900	6651 Backlick Rd
Vienna VA	Hope Center	703-281-5121	140 Park Street SE
Virginia Beach VA	Beach Veterinary Emergency Center	757-468-4900	1124 Lynnhaven Parkway, Suite C
Virginia Beach VA	Tidewater Animal Emergency & Referral Center	757-499-5463	364 South Independence Blvd
Williamsburg VA	James City Veterinary Clinic	757-220-0226	95 Brookwood Drive
Winchester VA	Valley Emergency Veterinary Clinic	540-662-7811	164 Garber Ln
Yorktown VA	Emergency Veterinary Clinic	757-874-8115	1120 George Wash Mem Hwy

Washington

Auburn WA	After Hours Animal Emergency Clinic	253-939-6272	718 Auburn Way N
Bellevue WA	After Hours Animal Emergency Clinic	425-641-8414	2975 156th Ave SE
Bellingham WA	Bellingham Animal Emergency Care	360-758-2200	317 Telegraph Road
Lacey WA	Olympia Pet Emergency	360-455-5155	4242 Pacific Ave SE
Mount Vernon WA	Pet Emergency Center	360-848-5911	14434 Avon Allen Road
Pasco WA	Pet Emergency Service	509-547-3577	8913 Sandifur Pkwy
Pullman WA	Washington State University Veterinary Hospital	509-335-0711	Washington State University
Seattle WA	Animal Critical Care and Emergency Services	206-364-1660	11536 Lake City Way NE
Seattle WA	Emerald City Emergency Clinic	206-634-9000	4102 Stone Way N
Seattle WA	Five Corners Animal Hospital	206-243-2982	15707 1st Ave S
Spokane WA	Pet Emergency Clinic	509-326-6670	21 E Mission Ave
Tacoma WA	Animal Emergency Clinic	253-474-0791	5608 South Durango St
Vancouver WA	Clark County Emergency Veterinary Service	360-694-3007	6818 NE Fourth Plain Blvd
Vancouver WA	St Francis 24 Hour Pet Hospital	360-253-5446	12010 NE 65th St
Yakima WA	Pet Emergency Service of Yakima	509-452-4138	510 W Chestnut Ave

West Virginia

Fairmont WV	North Central WV Veterinary Emergency Clinic	304-363-2227	Ih 79 # 139
Morgantown WV	After Hours Veterinary Clinic	304-599-3111	149 N Main St
Parkersburg WV	Animal Veterinary Emergency	304-428-8387	3602 E 7th St # B
South Charleston WV	Animal Emergency Clinic	304-768-2911	5304 MacCorkle Av SW

Wisconsin

Ashland WI	Ashland Area Veterinary Clinic	715-682-4199	2700 Farm Rd
Eau Claire WI	Oakwood Hills Animal Hospital	715-835-0112	4616 Commerce Valley Road
Glendale WI	Animal Emergency Center	414-540-6710	2100 W. Silver Spring Drive
Grafton WI	Wisconsin Veterinary Referral Center	262-546-0249	1381 Port Washington Road
Green Bay WI	Green Bay Animal Emergency Center	920-494-9400	933 Anderson Drive, Suite F
Madison WI	Veterinary Emergency Service - East	608-222-2455	4902 East Broadway
Madison WI	Veterinary Specialty & Emergency Care	608-845-0002	1848 Waldorf Boulevard
Middleton WI	Veterinary Emergency Service - Middleton	606-831-1101	1612 N. High Point Road, Suite 100
Mosinee WI	Emergency Vet of Central Wisconsin	715-693-6934	1420 Kronenwetter Dr
Port Washington WI	Lakeshore Veterinary Specialists	262-268-7800	207 W. Seven Hills Rd.
Sheboygan WI	Animal Clinic & Emergency Hospital	920-565-2125	2734 Calumet Dr
Waukesha WI	Wisconsin Veterinary Referral Center	866-542-3241	360 Bluemound Road

Wyoming

Casper WY	Animal Hospital of Casper	307-266-1660	2060 Fairgrounds Road
Cheyenne WY	Cheyenne Pet Clinic	307-635-4121	3740 E. Lincolnway
Cody WY	Advanced Veterinary Care Center	307-527-6828	1901 Demaris Dr
Cody WY	Lifetime Small Animal Hospital	307-587-4324	2627 Big Horn Ave
Evanston WY	Bear River Veterinary Clinic	307-789-5230	619 Almy Road 107
Evanston WY	MJB Animal Clinic	307-789-4289	2301 Wasatch Rd
Green River WY	Animal Clinic of Green River	307-875-9827	Animal Clinic of Green River
Jackson WY	Jackson Hole Veterinary Clinic	307-733-4279	2950 W Big Trail Dr
Jackson WY	Spring Creek Animal Hospital	307-733-1606	1035 West Broadway
Jackson WY	Teton Veterinary Clinic	307-733-2633	1225 Gregory Ln
Laramie WY	Alpine Animal Hospital	307 745 7341	610 Skyline Rd
Pine Bluffs WY	Bluffs Veterinary Clinic	307-245-9263	722 West 7th Street
Rawlins WY	Hones Veterinary Services	307-324-9999	519 W Spruce St
Rock Springs WY	Mountainaire Animal Clinic	307-362-1440	1801 Yellowstone Road
Sheridan WY	Bischoff Veterinary Services	307-674-4500	241 Centennial Ln
Sheridan WY	Crook County Veterinary Services	307-283-2115	Stock Tank Highway 14
Sheridan WY	Moxey Veterinary Hospital	307-672-5533	1650 Commercial Ave
Thermopolis WY	Hot Springs Veterinary Clinic	307-864-5553	827 S 6th St

Emergency Veterinarians - Please always call ahead to make sure an establishment is still open.

Canada

Alberta

Calgary AB	Care Center Animal Hospital	403-541-0815	7140 - 12th Street S.E.
Edmonton AB	Edmonton Veterinarian's Emergency Clinic	780-433-9505	11104 102 Ave NW

British Columbia

Coquitlam BC	Central Animal Emergency Clinic	604-931-1911	812 Roderick Avenue
Dawson Creek BC	Dawson Creek Veterinary Clinic	250-782-1080	238 116 Avenue
Langley BC	Animal Emergency Clinic of the Fraser Valley	604-514-1711	#306-6325 204th St
Vancouver BC	Vancouver Animal Emergency Clinic	604-734-5104	1590 West 4th Ave
Victoria BC	Central Victoria Veterinary Hospital	250-475-2495	760 Roderick Street

Manitoba

Winnipeg MB	Pembina Veterinary Hospital	204-452-9427	400 Pembina Highway

New Brunswick

Moncton NB	The Oaks Veterinary Medical & Emergency Referral Center	506-854-6257	565 Mapleton Road

Newfoundland

St Johns NF	St John's Veterinary Hospital	709-722-7766	335 Freshwater Road

Nova Scotia

Dartmouth NS	Metro Animal Emergency Clinic	902-468-0674	201 Brownlow Avenue

Ontario

Oakville ON	Veterinary Emergency Hospital	905-829-9444	2285 Bristol Circle
Toronto ON	Veterinary Emergency Clinic - North	416-226-3663	280 Sheppard Ave
Toronto ON	Veterinary Emergency Clinic - South	416-920-2002	920 Yonge St

Quebec

Montreal PQ	Veterinary Clinic - Villeray - Papineau	514-593-6777	7655 Papineau Avenue

Saskatchewan

Martensville SK	Martensville Veterinary Hospital	306-933-2677	Hwy 12

Yukon

Whitehorse YU	Alpine Veterinary Medical Center	867-633-5700	107 Copper Road
Whitehorse YU	Copper Road Veterinary Clinic	867-633-5184	128B Copper Road